PRONUNCIATION KEY

The symbol (ˊ), as in **moth·er** (muth′ər) and **Grand′ Can′yon**, is used to show primary, or heavy, stress; the syllable preceding it is pronounced with greater emphasis than the other syllables in the word or phrase. The symbol (ˊ), as in **grand·moth·er** (grand′muth′ər) and **Marine′ Corps′**, is used to show secondary, or lighter, stress. A syllable marked for secondary stress is pronounced with less emphasis than one marked for primary stress, but with more emphasis than those having no stress mark at all.

a	act, bat	**m**	my, simmer, him	**w**	west, away
ā	aid, cape, way			**y**	yes, lawyer
â(r)	air, dare	**n**	now, sinner, on		
ä	alms, art, calm	**n͡g**	sing, Washington	**z**	zeal, lazy, those
				zh	vision, pleasure
b	back, cabin, cab	**o**	ox, box, wasp		
		ō	over, boat, no	**ə**	occurs only in unaccented syllables and indicates the sound of
ch	chief, butcher, beach	**ô**	ought, ball, before		a *in* alone
		oi	oil, joint, joy		e *in* system
d	do, rudder, bed	**o͞o**	book, poor		i *in* easily
		o͞o	ooze, fool, too		o *in* gallop
e	ebb, set	**ou**	out, loud, prow		u *in* circus
ē	equal, seat, bee				
ēr	ear, mere	**p**	pot, supper, stop	**ə**	occurs in unaccented syllables before l preceded by t, d, or n, or before n preceded by t or d, as in
f	fit, differ, puff	**r**	read, hurry, near		**cra·dle** (krād′əl)
					red·den (red′ən)
g	give, trigger, beg	**s**	see, passing, miss		**met·al** (met′əl)
		sh	shoe, fashion, push		**men·tal** (men′təl)
h	hit, behave, hear				and in accented syllables
hw	white, nowhere	**t**	ten, butter, bit		between ī and r, as in
		th	thin, ether, path		**fire** (fīər)
i	if, big, mirror	**th**	that, either, smooth		**hire** (hīər)
ī	ice, pirate, deny				
		u	up, love		
j	just, badger, fudge	**û(r)**	urge, burn, cur		
		yo͞o	use, fuse		
k	kept, token, make				
		v	voice, river, live		
l	low, mellow, all				

ABBREVIATIONS USED IN THIS DICTIONARY

ab.	about	**esp.**	especially	**NW**	northwest
abbr.	abbreviation	**etc.**	et cetera (and so on)	**pl.**	plural
adj.	adjective	**fol.**	followed or following	**prep.**	preposition
adv.	adverb	**ft.**	foot or feet	**pron.**	pronoun
c	circa (about)	**illus.**	illustration	**S**	south or southern
cap(s).	capital letter(s)	**interj.**	interjection	**SE**	southeast
Cap.	capital city	**l.c.**	lower case (small letter)	**sing.**	singular
Chem.	chemistry	**mi.**	mile or miles	**sq.**	square
conj.	conjunction	**N**	north or northern	**SW**	southwest
def(s).	definition(s)	**n.**	noun	**v.**	verb
E	east or eastern	**NE**	northeast	**W**	west or western

THE RANDOM HOUSE SCHOOL DICTIONARY

RANDOM HOUSE DICTIONARIES

A widely acclaimed series of modern
authoritative dictionaries suitable for
many different needs and levels

Editorial Director: **Jess Stein**

Associate Director: **Leonore C. Hauck**

Senior Editor: **P.Y. Su**

Based on

THE RANDOM HOUSE DICTIONARY
OF THE ENGLISH LANGUAGE

The Unabridged Edition

JESS STEIN Editor in Chief

and

THE RANDOM HOUSE
COLLEGE DICTIONARY, Revised Edition

THE
RANDOM
HOUSE
DICTIONARY
OF
THE
ENGLISH
LANGUAGE

SCHOOL
EDITION

THE RANDOM HOUSE SCHOOL DICTIONARY

Stuart Berg Flexner EDITOR IN CHIEF

Eugene F. Shewmaker MANAGING EDITOR

RANDOM HOUSE/NEW YORK

Library of Congress Cataloging in Publication Data

Main entry under title:

The Random House school dictionary.
   "Based on the Random House dictionary of the
English language: the unabridged edition...and
the Random House college dictionary."
   Published in 1970 under title: The Random
House dictionary of the English language, school edition.
   SUMMARY: A dictionary for intermediate and junior-high
students reflecting current American usage.
   1. English language—Dictionaries, Juvenile.
[1. English language—Dictionaries] I. Flexner,
Stuart Berg.
PE1628.5.R3   423   77-29053
ISBN 0-394-00044-7

a.aa./hs.

PREFACE

This entirely new school dictionary was created to fill the need for a fresh, up-to-date, and authoritative dictionary for today's students and teachers. We have tried to make it both easier to use and more complete than any other school dictionary. It contains more entries and definitions than any other dictionary of its kind and more sample sentences and phrases, more idioms, more usage notes, more pronunciations, and more etymologies.

Although this book is based on the Random House Dictionary of the English Language—the Unabridged Edition, and on the Random House College Dictionary, it is not merely an abridgment of these dictionaries. It does make full use of the word frequency studies, citation files, and other scholarly resources that formed the foundations of the well-received Random House unabridged and college dictionaries and does follow their principles of sound lexicography and linguistics.

The greatest care and professional judgment were used in building the word list and in adjusting the language used to the vocabulary level and needs of the student. The word list was specially compiled with the assistance of many teachers, principals, linguists, textbook editors, and consultants from every region of the country. It is based on the occurrence of words in (1) a wide variety of textbooks now in use in schools throughout the United States, (2) traditional and classic works of children's literature, (3) modern stories and popular magazines and newspapers recommended for students, and (4) everyday, conversational English that the student is likely to encounter.

Because today's students are encountering greatly increased vocabularies in their textbooks, outside reading, television and radio programs, conversations, etc., a large number of new words and meanings not found in other school dictionaries are included. Special attention has been given to the many new terms that the student is expected to know in today's mathematics, language arts and grammar, life sciences, geography and current events, history, music, art, etc.

All the entries are given in one A-to-Z listing, including all biographical and geographical entries, abbreviations, and contractions. Definitions are written in clear, concise language, and the parts of speech and meanings are given in order of frequency, with the more common uses appearing first. The part of speech of each meaning is specified. Each of the many thousands of synonyms is given immediately after the definition to which it applies.

We have attempted to give full coverage to every aspect of the language that would be useful to students. Thus there are no long lists of undefined words, such as those prefixed with *un-*, *non-*, or *re-*, and no large number of entries that serve only as cross references to other entries.

However, run-ons have been appended to basic or root words so that they can be used for simple vocabulary building, as in the case of *hastiness* and *clarinetist.* A large number of prefix and suffix entries are also included as a teaching aid for use in vocabulary building.

The thousands of example sentences and phrases used throughout this dictionary have been specially chosen to show words in their proper context and to be relevant to the student's experience. These sample sentences and phrases can help students gain a feeling for words and develop an ear for the structures and patterns of effective English.

Well over a thousand idioms have also been included in this book. They are placed in alphabetical order as the last group of definitions in an entry, and most are accompanied by example sentences or phrases to show their customary context.

There are also more complete pronunciations given in this book than in any other school dictionary at this level. These are presented in a combination of letters and symbols that is easy to learn and use, yet is closely related to those used in adult dictionaries. This pronunciation system is also designed to enable a student to pronounce unfamiliar words as they are pronounced by the educated people in his own region of the country.

A guide to good usage is presented in the many usage notes appearing throughout the book. The purpose of these notes is to correct and explain the common mistakes made by students in English usage, such as the use of *lay* for *lie,* *effect* for *affect,* and *infer* for *imply.* In addition, all purely British uses, archaic words, informal uses, and the very small number of slang words included are clearly labeled.

The many etymologies in this dictionary can be used to introduce the student to the fascinating history of the English language, as well as to give the student explanations of where words come from, how they were formed, and how they have changed. These etymologies are in plain language and use no symbols or special notations.

The Student's Guide, immediately following this preface, can be used to teach the student how to use a dictionary efficiently. It has a wide variety of Suggested Activities that the teacher can adapt to oral or written exercises to fit the needs of any class or individual student.

Our clear goal in developing this modern dictionary has been to help all students and teachers by making available a sound, useful, authoritative school dictionary for classroom and reference use. Now, in presenting the dictionary to you, we feel a sense of pride and accomplishment. We believe it is a book that you will be proud to use.

STUART B. FLEXNER
Editor in Chief

The Random House School Dictionary

Stuart Berg Flexner, *Editor in Chief*

Eugene F. Shewmaker, *Managing Editor*

SENIOR EDITORS

Thomas Hill Long
Salvatore Ramondino
Edwin M. Ripin
P. Y. Su

EDITORS

Hazel G. Kahn
Richard McDougall
Margaret Miner

ASSISTANT EDITORS

Janet R. Goldstein
Daniel L. Heiple
Alice Kovac
June Rephan

EDITORIAL ASSISTANTS

Pauline G. Demetri
James Gartenlaub
Kevin Gleason
Jean Henrickson
Paul Merrill
Patricia J. Napolin
Lynn St. C. Strong

RESEARCH ASSISTANTS

Elizabeth G. Christensen
David S. Disenhouse
Carolyn R. Herzog
Brian Phillpotts

ADMINISTRATIVE STAFF

Rona S. Goodman
Gunilla Kronvall
Marianne G. Thomas

ARTISTS

BEN FEDER, INC.: George Buctel
Albert J. Carreno
Don Spaulding

CARTOGRAPHER (Spot Maps)

Clare O. Ford

Guide Words. The two words at the top of each page, which indicate the first and last entry words on that page.

Entry Word. The word being defined, which appears in boldface type and is separated into syllables by dots when it consists of more than one syllable.

Homograph. A main entry word that is spelled exactly the same as another main entry word but has a completely different meaning and origin.

Pronunciation. The phonetic transcription of a word, showing how it is pronounced.

Part of Speech Label. An abbreviation, in italics, for the part of speech of an entry or a group of definitions within an entry.

Illustration. A drawing or diagram that illustrates an entry word.

Definition. The meaning of a particular word or group of words.

Definition Number. All definitions within an entry are numbered consecutively.

Noun Inflection. The plural of a noun entry is shown when it is irregularly formed.

Sentence or Phrase Example. A sample sentence or phrase in italics that follows a definition and shows its correct use in context.

Biographical Entry. An entry that is the name of a real or legendary person.

Variant Pronunciation. Another pronunciation of the main entry word that is also widely used.

Usage Note. A note giving precise information about the way certain words should be used.

Cross Reference. A note that directs the reader to another entry for additional information.

Short Pronunciation Key. A shorter version of the full pronunciation key, located at the bottom of each right-hand page.

---

effort

ef·fort (ef′ərt), *n.* **1.** the use of physical or mental power: *Studying for exams requires effort.* **2.** an attempt; try: *He made an effort to finish the job.*

egg¹ (eg), *n.* **1.** the rounded body produced by the female of many kinds of animals from which the young later develop. Birds, most reptiles, and fish lay eggs. **2.** such a body produced by a domestic bird, esp. the hen. [from a Scandinavian word]

egg² (eg), *v.* to urge or encourage (usually fol. by *on*): *They egged me on to try the high diving board.* [from a Scandinavian word related to Icelandic *eggja* "to incite"]

egg·nog (eg′nog′), *n.* a drink made of eggs, milk or cream, sugar, and sometimes liquor.

egg·shell (eg′shel′), *n.* **1.** the hard, brittle shell of a bird's egg. **2.** a pale yellowish tan. —*adj.* **3.** thin and delicate. **4.** of a pale yellowish tan.

ei′der duck′ (ī′dər), any of several large sea ducks, the females of which yield eiderdown. Also, **ei′der.**

eight (āt), *n.* **1.** a number that is seven plus one. **2.** a set of this many persons or things: *Only eight will be there.* —*adj.* **3.** amounting to eight in number: *eight persons.*

eight·een (ā′tēn′), *n.* **1.** a number that is ten plus eight. **2.** a set of this many persons or things: *Eighteen of them will be there.*

Eider duck (length 2 ft.)

eight·y (ā′tē), *n., pl.* **eight·ies.** **1.** a number that is eight times ten. **2.** a set of this many persons or things: *Eighty of them will be there.* **3. eighties,** the numbers, years, degrees, etc., between 80 and 89: *He was a man in his early eighties. The temperature was in the lower eighties.* —*adj.* **4.** amounting to eighty in number: *eighty persons.*

Ei·sen·how·er (ī′zən hou′ər), *n.* Dwight David, 1890–1969, U.S. general and statesman: 34th President of the U.S. 1953–1961.

ei·ther (ē′ᵺər, ī′ᵺər), *adj.* **1.** one or the other of two: *You may sit at either end of the table.* **2.** each of two: *There are trees on either side of the river.* —*pron.* **3.** one or the other: *Either will be fine.* —*conj.* **4.** (used before a word or statement that is followed by *or* to show the possibility of choice): *Either come or write.* **5.** also; too; as well: *He doesn't like it, and I don't either.*

—**Usage.** When used as an adjective or pronoun, *either* is generally followed by a singular verb: *Either book is satisfactory. Either is good enough.* When used to connect two subjects, *either* is always followed by *or* and may be used with a singular or plural verb, depending on the second subject: *Either milk or ginger ale is available. Either Bill or I am going. Either food or dishes are in this box.* See also **neither.**

---

act, āble, dâre, ärt; ebb, ēqual; if, īce; hot, ōver, ôrder; ə as in *button* (but′ən), *fire* (fīᵊr); chief; shoe; thin; ᵺat;

Everglades

e·lim·i·nate (i lim′ə nāt′), v., **e·lim·i·nat·ed, e·lim·i·nat·ing.** to remove or get rid of: *to eliminate smudges.* [from the Latin *ēliminātus* "turned out of doors," which comes from *ē-* "out" + *līmen* "threshold"]

El Sal·va·dor (el sal′və dôr′), a republic in NW Central America. 13,176 sq. mi. *Cap.:* San Salvador.

E·ly·si·um (i lizh′ē əm, i liz′ē əm), n. 1. Also, **Ely′sian Fields′.** (in Greek and Roman mythology) a place where the spirits of good people dwelt after death. 2. any place or state of perfect happiness.

e·ma·ci·ate (i mā′shē āt′), v., **e·ma·ci·at·ed, e·ma·ci·at·ing.** to make very thin by a gradual wasting away of flesh. —**e·ma′ci·at′ed,** adj. —**e·ma′ci·a′tion,** n.

em·er·y (em′ə rē), n. a mineral used in powdered form for grinding and polishing.

emp·ty (emp′tē), adj., **emp·ti·er, emp·ti·est.** 1. containing nothing: *an empty bottle.* 2. vacant; unoccupied: *an empty house.* 3. without force or significance; meaningless: *empty compliments.* —v., **emp·tied, emp·ty·ing.** 4. to make empty: *to empty a bottle.* 5. to discharge (contents): *to empty the water out of a bucket.* 6. to flow out; drain: *The river empties into a lake at the foot of the mountain.* —**emp′ti·ly,** adv. —**emp′ti·ness,** n.

en-, a prefix meaning 1. to put in or into: *encase; enclose.* 2. to put on or upon: *enroll; enthrone.* 3. to make or cause to be: *enlarge; endear; enable.* 4. to provide with: *encourage.*

-en, a suffix used to form 1. verbs with the meaning **a.** to make or become: *harden; sweeten.* **b.** to provide with or acquire: *strengthen; lengthen.*

encl., 1. enclosed. 2. enclosure.

en·close (en klōz′), v., **en·closed, en·clos·ing.** 1. to shut or hem in; close in on all sides; surround: *to enclose the yard with a fence.* 2. to put in the same package or envelope with whatever is being sent: *She enclosed a check with the letter.* Also, **inclose.**

e·ven (ē′vən), n. *Archaic.* evening or eve: *as even falls.* [from the Old English word *æfen*]

eve·ning (ēv′niñg), n. the latter part of the day and early part of the night, or the time from sunset to bedtime.

eve′ning star′, a bright planet, usually Venus, seen in the west directly after sunset.

e·vent (i vent′), n. 1. anything that happens; an occurrence, esp. an important one: *the events leading up to the American Revolution.* 2. a contest in a sports program: *We hope to win the figure-skating events.* 3. **in the event of,** if there should be; in case of: *In the event of rain, the game will be postponed.*

Ev·er·glades (ev′ər glādz′), n. (used as pl.) a swampy and partly forested region in S Florida, the S part forming a national park (**Ev′erglades Na′tional Park′**). about 5000 sq. mi.

Etymology. Information about the origin of a word, given at the end of an entry in brackets.

Geographical Entry. An entry that is the name of a country, city, river, etc.

Variant Name. Another name by which something is often known.

Context Clue. Information in parentheses before or after a definition, indicating that a word is usually used in a certain way.

Adjective Inflection. The comparative and superlative of an adjective are shown when they are irregularly formed.

Verb Inflection. The past tense, past participle, and present participle of a verb are shown when these tenses are irregularly formed.

Direct Object. A word or words placed in parentheses within the definition to indicate the usual direct object of a verb.

Run-on Entry. A word that is formed from the main entry word by adding a suffix and is not listed or defined separately.

Affix Entry. An entry that is a common prefix or suffix and may be added to a word to change its meaning.

Abbreviation Entry. An entry showing the abbreviation of a particular word.

Variant Spelling. Another spelling of the entry word that is sometimes used.

Restrictive Label. A word in italics indicating that a definition or an entry is used in a limited or special way.

Multiple Word Entry. A main entry consisting of a group of words that have a special meaning when used together.

Idiomatic Expression (Idiom). A phrase having a special meaning that cannot be determined merely by knowing the meanings of the individual words.

Hidden Entry. A word or phrase that is closely related to the main entry word and whose definition is obvious from the definition of the main entry word.

---

oil; bŏŏk; ōōze; out; up, ûrge; ə = *a* as in *alone;* zh as in *measure* (mezh′ər). See full key inside cover.

CONTENTS

Student's Guide to the Dictionary

by Edward B. Jenkinson

Director, English Curriculum Study Center
Indiana University

WORDS AND DICTIONARIES

What Is a Dictionary? A dictionary is the most important book you will use to learn about the language you speak and write. It is a record of the meanings, spellings, and pronunciations of words you already know or will need to know. As you read this introductory section and work the exercises, you will also discover that a dictionary gives you a great deal of additional information about the words in your language and how they are used.

How Is a Dictionary Prepared? The people who prepare dictionaries by recording the definitions, spellings, pronunciations, and other information about words are called *lexicographers.* One of the first jobs of a team of lexicographers is to collect as many samples as possible of the different ways people have used a word. They get these samples by reading hundreds of books, magazines, and newspapers and by listening to radio and television programs, records, and movie sound tracks. Then they record the uses of new words or of familiar words used in a new way on *citation slips* that look something like this:

voiceprint

The new method of identifying a person by the sound of his voice is called the <u>voiceprint.</u> It is a picture of his speech patterns that is very similar to a fingerprint.

— *Newsquest Magazine*
p. 19, col. 1
July, 1970

When a lexicographer makes a citation slip, he first writes the word that he is recording. Then he copies the sentence in which the word appears and any other sentences that can help him define the word. Finally, he records the source of the word, noting the title of the book, movie, or record, or the name of the magazine or newspaper and the page number on which he found the word. He also records the date of publication of the newspaper, magazine, or book, and the name of the author, if possible.

Where and when a word is used is extremely important to a lexicographer. A single word can have one meaning on a sports page of a newspaper and another on the financial page. Before he can define a word, therefore, a lexicographer needs to know where it was used. He also needs to know when it was used, because people sometimes change the meaning of a word or add meanings to a word from one century to the next—or sometimes from one decade to the next.

Study these citation slips for the past tense of the verb *mushroom*. What definition would you give to *mushroom?*

mushroom

Phil Jones recently borrowed 40,000 dollars and mush-roomed the amount into half a million by shrewd investments.

—*Modern Day News*
p. 47, Col. 2
June, 1970

mushroom

As for the town itself, five years of boom have mushroomed population figures to five times their pre-1952 level. Moab business men, who have filled hundreds of acres with new three-bedroom, two-bath houses, confidently predict they will live to see the total reach 10,000.

—*New York Times*
Sec. 1/p. 39/Col. 2
April 6, 1958

If you were a lexicographer, you would try to define *mushroom* from its uses in these sentences and any others that you might find. Often, you would have hundreds of citations for just one word. You would not decide by yourself what the word *mushroom* means; instead, you would base your definition on the actual meaning people have given to the word as shown by your citation file. Your definition would be a *lexical definition*.

What lexical definitions would you write for the words *ambassador* and *besiege* if you were a lexicographer who had made citation slips like these?

ambassador

There's a letter for you, Sir: It comes from the <u>ambassadors</u> that were bound for England . . .

— Shakespeare, <u>Hamlet</u>
Act IV, Scene 6
1602

ambassador

The Guatemalan <u>ambassador</u> here, Antonio Gandara, was politely told that it would be desirable for him to leave Bonn.

— New York Times
p.1, Col. 2
April 7, 1970

besiege

pious souls . . . who daily and nightly <u>besieged</u> Heaven with supplications.

—Parkman, <u>Jesuits</u>
1867

besiege

Policemen <u>besieged</u> the house for nearly 14 hours. Two of the gunmen were found shot to death when the battle ended.

— Midwest Daily News
p.1, Col. 8
July 6, 1970

Look up the definitions of *ambassador* and *besiege,* and see how your definitions compare with the definitions of professional lexicographers.

What Is a Word? A word is a sound or group of sounds that people use to stand for some person, place, action, idea, object, or quality. A sound or group of sounds is not a word until people give it meaning. People can give many meanings to the same sound or group of sounds so that any word may refer to many people, places, actions, ideas, objects, or qualities. When you discover all of the things that a single word refers to, you have found its *denotations* or *denotative meanings.*

English-speaking people use the word *ameba* to refer to a tiny, one-celled water animal that constantly changes shape as it moves and takes in food. Since that is its only meaning, you can say that *ameba* has only one *denotative meaning.*

Some words have many denotative meanings. A familiar word like *brand,* for example, has at least five denotative meanings:

1. a particular kind of product
2. a trademark
3. a mark made by burning, as on the hide of an animal
4. an iron used for branding
5. a burning or partly burned piece of wood

Before he writes the definitions of a word, a lexicographer studies all the different ways people use the word to discover all its denotations. He tries to find out all the things the word refers to or has referred to, collecting citation slips for each denotative meaning in order to define the word accurately. To define the word *fare,* for example, a lexicographer needs to consider all of these denotative meanings:

1. the cost of riding a bus, taxi, train, plane, or ship: *The round-trip airplane fare from Indianapolis to New York is $90.*
2. a person who pays to ride on a bus, taxi, train, plane, or ship: *The taxi driver wanted to pick up another fare before he went home for the evening.*
3. food and drink: *The restaurant on the corner serves good fare.*
4. to do something in a particular way or to get along in a certain manner: *Margaret fares quite well in homemaking class.*
5. to happen or to turn out: *Mother's cake didn't fare too well.*
6. to travel: *He fared to England last summer.*

What are the lexical definitions of *fare* in this dictionary?

People no longer give *fare* the meaning of *to travel,* so lexicographers mark that definition as *Archaic.* An archaic definition is one that is no longer commonly used. It is included in the dictionary because you might find it in a book or song written many years ago.

A word, then, is a sound or group of sounds that people use to represent a person, place, action, idea, object, quality, or expression of feeling. It can also be a group of sounds used to show relationships between other words, such as *at, to, and, on,* and so forth. People can give many meanings to any group of sounds, and a major job of lexicographers is to record the meanings in dictionaries such as this one.

---

1. Write the following words in a column on a sheet of paper, skipping three lines between each word. After each word place a dash, and then list as many meanings of the word as you can think of.

> **Example:** dog—(1) a four-legged animal that is usually kept as a pet; (2) a four-legged animal that is usually related to these dogs, such as a fox or wolf; (3) a mechanical device used for gripping and holding; (4) a person who does something mean—a dirty dog; (5) a kind of meat—hot dog.

| glass | circus | orchid |
| airplane | school | cat |

The meanings you have listed for each word above are denotations. Now compare your denotations with the definitions in this dictionary. What other definitions does this dictionary give?

2. Make up four meanings for the nonsense word *glidl.* Write four sentences, one for each meaning, using *glidl.* Make certain that you have given your reader enough clues in each sentence so that he can decide what *glidl* refers to in each one.

> **Example:** I got a nail in my front glidl, and I couldn't ride my bike until I got a new inner tube.

After you have written your four sentences, exchange papers with a classmate. As he examines your uses of the word, you examine his. Ask each other what *glidl* refers to in each sentence, then write definitions based on your partner's sentences. Discuss the accuracy of these definitions with your partner.

3. Study these citation slips for the nonsense word *zizz.* Then write a definition for *zizz.* Why is it important to know where the word was used?

SUGGESTED ACTIVITIES 1–4

zizz

The quarterback threw a perfect spiral <u>zizz</u> to the tight end for the winning touchdown.

— *The Midvale Daily Banner*
p. 21/Col. 6 *(Sports Corner)*
January 27, 1970

zizz

Captain Vollmer watched nervously as the ground crew put the 5,000-pound atomic <u>zizz</u> in the B-52. He knew that he could blow up a whole city with it.

— *Roscoe Barnett*
Skyways Magazine
p. 47
March, 1970

4. (a) Study these citation slips for *freestanding,* and then write a lexical definition for that word. Compare your definition with the definition recorded in this dictionary.

freestanding

freestanding

Standing thoughtfully among these images, the goat, with its painted face and its encircling tire, looks oddly at home. Since it is a <u>freestanding</u> object and cannot be hung on a wall, it can hardly be called a painting, even under the most elastic definition. Nor is it sculpture, since painting figures importantly in it. As a result of this ambiguity, Rauschenberg decided to call it a "combine." It is probably his most famous single work.

— *New Yorker Magazine*
p. 84/Col. 2
February 29, 1964

Now, at last, your own decorator fireplace and at a price you can afford! The new 1970 <u>freestanding</u> model can easily be installed in the center of your living room or den. It harmonizes with any decor and will provide years of cozy comfort.

— *Superstore Catalog 1970*
p. 642

(b) Now write a short paragraph explaining how words get their meanings and how lexicographers know what words mean.

FINDING ENTRY WORDS

The words that are defined in a dictionary are called *entry words*. The information given for each main entry word includes spelling, syllabification, pronunciation, part of speech, and definitions.

Guide Words

All entry words in a dictionary are arranged in alphabetical order. To help you find words easily and quickly, lexicographers put *guide words* at the top of each page. Printed in boldface type, the guide words and the page numbers look like this:

blacksnake	83	**blaze**
blaze	84	**blindfold**

The guide word on the top left of each page is the first entry on that page. The guide word on the top right of each page is the last entry on that page. By looking at the guide words *blacksnake* and *blaze*, you know that all the entry words on page 83 come between *blacksnake* and *blaze* in the alphabet. You also know that the word *black*, for example, will not be on page 83 since the first word on that page comes after the word *black* in alphabetical order.

As you turn the pages of your dictionary, looking for a particular entry word, the guide words will help you find the page on which it is defined. Look at the sample guide words above, and tell which page will contain the definition of *bleak*. How do you know?

Dividing the Dictionary into Four Parts

Knowing the main alphabetical groups into which English words fall will help you locate words quickly. Think of the dictionary as being divided into four equal parts. These parts are not made up by dividing the twenty-six letters of the alphabet into four equal groups, because each letter does not contain the same number of entries. For example, more words begin with the letters *c, p,* and *s* than with the letters *j, q,* and *x.* If you examine your dictionary, you will see that the entries for *a* alone consist of 56 pages, and that the number of pages for words beginning with only the first four letters of the alphabet (a, b, c, d) is greater than the number of pages needed for words beginning with the next eight letters, *e* through *l.* English words seem to fall equally into these four main alphabetical groups:

a to **d**   **e** to **l**   **m** to **r**   **s** to **z**

Thinking of the dictionary as having these four main parts, you can train yourself to open it at approximately the right place to find any particular word. If you wanted to find the word *wigwam,* you wouldn't start looking near the front of the dictionary. Instead, you would open the book to the last part and look for guide words that start with the letters *wi.*

SUGGESTED ACTIVITY 5

What guide words in this dictionary show you the page on which each of the following entries is located?

jump	stewardess	diamond	FBI
gridiron	hostess	block	wax

If you divide the dictionary into the four parts listed above, in which part will you find each of these words?

Arrangement of Entries

To help you look up a word easily, lexicographers put entry words in alphabetical order and have them printed in boldface type like this:

Mo·ab	**moat**	**mo·bile**	**mo·bi·lize**
moan	**mob**	**Mo·bile**	

By examining these entry words, you can learn three things about how entry words appear in a dictionary:

First, you should note that an entry word is printed in boldface type: **mob.**

Second, you can see that entry words are divided into syllables by dots: **mo·bi·lize.**

Third, you can see that a proper noun, like **Mo·bile,** follows a word that is spelled the same but is not capitalized.

On page 57, you will find the first entries in the **B** section listed like this:

B, b	**Ba·al**	**ba·by**
B	**bab·ble**	**Bab·y·lon**
Ba	**babe**	**Bab·y·lo·ni·a**
B.A.	**Ba·bel**	**ba·by·sit**
baa	**ba·boon**	**bac·ca·lau·re·ate**

By turning to page 57 and examining the first column of entry words on that page, you can learn these additional things about the alphabetical arrangement of entry words:

First, there are two entries for the capital letter **B.** The first entry of each letter contains only those meanings that relate to that particular letter of the alphabet. The second entry for **B** shows how that letter is used as a symbol for a grade, a chemical element, and a blood type. When a letter is used as an abbreviation, those meanings are placed together in an entry that comes just before the entry for symbols.

Second, lexicographers do not stop with the first letter in a word to arrange it alphabetically; they frequently have to go to the third, fourth, or even fifth letter, as they did to arrange *baa, Baal* and *babe, Babel.*

Third, when a word is spelled with a hyphen, lexicographers include the hyphen in the entry word, as in **baby-sit,** shown above. In this way, you will know which words have to be spelled with hyphens.

When a word begins with a capital letter and there is an entry for the same word beginning with a lower-case letter, the capitalized word always follows the lower-case word. (See the entries **providence** and **Providence.**) For abbreviations and symbols, this order is reversed, so that upper-case entries precede lower-case entries. (See the entries **L.** and **l., RA** and **Ra.**)

---

6. On a sheet of paper, put the following entry words in alphabetical order.

SUGGESTED ACTIVITIES 6–7

experimental	fasten	experienced
moor	MacArthur	music box
musical instrument	musician	Moor
machine gun	FBI	facial
fascinate	facile	music
FCC	machine	experiment
macaroni	fast	

7. On a sheet of paper, put the following entry words in alphabetical order.

ameba	amen	ameliorate
amble	ambrosia	amenable
ambidextrous	ambush	ambiguity
ambition	ambulance	
ambulatory	ambiguous	

Now compare your list of the above words with the alphabetical arrangement of the same words in this dictionary. On what pages do you find
these words listed? What are the guide words on those pages?

Homographs

It is not unusual to find two completely different words in our language that are actually spelled alike, but whose meanings and histories
have little, if anything, in common. These words, which are spelled alike
but are different in meaning and origin, are called homographs. They are
arranged like this:

> **mole¹** (mōl), *n.* a small spot on the skin ....
> **mole²** (mōl), *n.* any of various small furry animals ....

Homographs are arranged according to frequency of use: **mole¹** is
listed first in the dictionary because research shows that it is more
frequently used than **mole²**. The raised numbers merely indicate that,
in this case, there are at least two words spelled exactly the same way
but with entirely different meanings and word histories.

Homographs sometimes come into the language from completely
different sources. For example, **mole¹** comes from an Old English word
that was spelled *māl;* **mole²** comes from a Middle English word that
was spelled *molle.* Although they are spelled alike in Modern English,
these two words have such different meanings and have come into the
language from such different sources that lexicographers recognize them
as completely separate words and list them as different entries.

If one of two homographs is capitalized, the capitalized homograph
appears last, regardless of its frequency of use, and neither is followed
by a raised number. The capital letter is enough to distinguish it from
the lower-case entry.

> **fed·er·al** (fed′ər əl), *adj.* **1.** of or referring to a com-
> pact ....
> **Fed·er·al** (fed′ər əl), *adj.* **1.** (in U.S. history) of or re-
> ferring to the Federalists ....

**SUGGESTED
ACTIVITIES
8–9**

8. Find the word **fawn** on page 282. Why are there two entry words
for *fawn?* Which definition of *fawn* appears first? Why? What do you
call the two entries for *fawn?*

9. Look up the word **batter** on page 67. How many homographs are
listed? Look at the last item of information for *batter¹*. What Middle
English word is the basis of *batter¹*? From what word do we get *batter²*?
Why, then, do you think that the lexicographers gave you three separate
entries for *batter¹*, *batter²*, and *batter³*?

PARTS OF AN ENTRY

Arrangement within Entries

As you have already seen, a dictionary contains a great deal of different kinds of information about words. To help you use a dictionary easily, lexicographers arrange the information within each entry in a definite order.

Examine these entries for **root**[1] and **supply.**

root[1] (rōōt, rŏŏt), *n.* **1.** the part of a plant that develops and spreads under the ground, anchoring the plant and providing it with water and nourishment from the soil. **2.** any underground part of a plant, such as a bulb. **3.** the hidden base of a hair, tooth, fingernail, etc. **4.** a quantity that, when multiplied by itself a specified number of times, yields a certain number: *The square root of 9 is 3, since 3 x 3 = 9. The cube root of 8 is 2, since 2 x 2 x 2 = 8.* **5.** the basic or most important part: *the root of the matter.* **6.** the source or origin of a thing: *the root of all evil.* **7.** (in grammar) a basic word or stem from which other words are derived. *Cover* is the root of such words as *covering, coverage, coverall, uncover,* and *discover.* —*v.* **8.** to grow roots. **9.** to become fixed or established: *She was rooted to the spot.* **10.** to pull, tear, or dig up by the roots. **11. take root,** to send out roots; begin to grow: *Transplant the bush as soon as it takes root.* [from the Old English word *rōt,* which comes from Scandinavian] —**root′like′,** *adj.*

sup·ply (sə plī′), *v.,* **sup·plied, sup·ply·ing. 1.** to provide or furnish: *to supply someone with clothing; to supply information.* **2.** to make up for or fill: *to supply a need.* —*n., pl.* **sup·plies. 3.** the act of providing or furnishing: *He is generous in his supply of money.* **4.** an amount on hand or available for use: *a large supply of fuel.* **5.** Usually, **supplies.** a stock or store of food or necessary items: *to buy supplies for a camping trip.* [from the Old French word *souplier,* which comes from Latin *supplēre* "to fill up"] —**sup·pli′er,** *n.*

The major kinds of information found in an entry are included in the examples above. They are as follows:

1. Spelling. The boldface entry word gives the correct spelling of that word. If more than one spelling is acceptable, the entry will give all the acceptable spellings.

2. Syllabification. When a word has more than one syllable, as *supply* does, the syllables of the boldface entry word are separated by dots or stress marks.

3. Pronunciation. Following the entry word is the pronunciation. When a word has more than one pronunciation, as *root*[1] does, all of the common, acceptable ones are shown. The pronunciation is surrounded by parentheses and contains a simple phonetic transcription and stress marks to show you exactly how the word is pronounced.

4. Part of Speech Label. The first part of speech label follows the pronunciation of the entry. This label is an abbreviation for a part of speech and shows the ways the word can be used in sentences. If a word is commonly used as more than one part of speech, other part of speech labels occur throughout the entry. Both *root*[1] and *supply* show noun and verb definitions.

5. Inflected Forms. When a noun, verb, adjective, or adverb changes its form irregularly, the form is given. Thus, irregular plurals of nouns are shown, as are irregular past tenses and past and present participles of verbs and irregular comparative and superlative forms of modifiers. Note the inflected forms preceding definitions 1 and 3 of *supply.*

6. Definition. The meaning of the word is given. When there is more than one meaning, each one is numbered. In this dictionary, the most common meaning of a word is usually given first and the other meanings are given in decreasing order of use. A definition may begin with a usage label, such as *Slang* or *Archaic,* which shows you how the word is generally used. It may also begin with words in parentheses, such as "in baseball" or "in Greek mythology", which give you information on the way the word is used. Following the definition, there may be other information in parentheses, telling you that the word is often followed or preceded by other words, that it is not to be confused with a similar word, or that it is the opposite of some other word. All of this is information to help you learn the word and be able to use it correctly and quickly.

7. Sentence and Phrase Examples. Example sentences and phrases are often included after definitions to show how the word is actually used in writing and speaking.

8. Illustration. Many entries are accompanied by an illustration to give you a better understanding of the word. There are more than 1250 illustrations in this dictionary. Note the illustration in the sample entry of **root**[1].

9. Idioms. When certain words are used only in combination, they are called *idiomatic expressions,* or *idioms.* These expressions must be understood as a whole, since their meanings cannot be found simply by knowing the meaning of each individual word. Idioms are printed in boldface type and are grouped together in alphabetical order as the last definitions in an entry. This dictionary defines more than 1500 such idiomatic expressions.

10. Etymology (Word History). The history or origin of a word is given for most homographs and many words of unusual interest. There are more than 1800 etymologies in this dictionary. They appear in brackets at the end of an entry.

11. Run-on Entries. A main entry may have derived forms that are not defined because they can be easily understood from the definition of the main entry word. These forms are called run-on entries and appear in boldface type at the very end of the entry. The syllabification is also given for these run-on entries, as well as the pronunciation if needed. The part of speech is also given for each run-on. Note that **root**[1] and **supply** each have one run-on entry.

12. Usage Note. An entry often includes information on how a word is used in standard speech as well as on certain forms or uses of the word that should be avoided. There are many usage notes in this dictionary, for example at the entries **affect, Asiatic, bad, compliment,** and **good.**

Additional information may often be given in an entry, depending on the word being defined. On the following pages of the Student's Guide, you will learn about the many kinds of information this dictionary includes.

Spelling

The boldface main entry word always appears in its most common form. This shows you how the word is usually spelled and whether it begins with a capital or lower-case letter. You will also see if it contains a hyphen, such as *baby-sit,* or ends with a period, as in the case of the abbreviation *adj.*

Sometimes you will note that a certain entry is another spelling or another form of a word that appears in boldface type. This indicates that this form is an acceptable spelling of the word, but you are being referred back to the more common spelling of the word for the definition. For example, there are two common spellings for *brier:* **brier** and **briar.** If you look under the entry **briar,** you will find that it is "another spelling of **brier**[1]." Therefore, you should look under **brier**[1] for the definition and know that *brier* is the more common, or preferred, spelling. You will note, too, that the entry for **A-bomb** refers you back to **atomic bomb,** which is the more common name.

These variants, or less common spellings, are listed at the principal entry following the definitions. Note the variant **air′mail′** at the end of the entry for **air-mail;** also, the variant **af′ter·wards** at the end of the entry for **afterward.**

SUGGESTED ACTIVITY 10

On a sheet of paper, write the appropriate second spelling for each of the following words. Also write out the information that this dictionary gives you about the second or third spelling. Which spelling is preferred as being the most common?

anesthetic	bogy	counselor
marvelous	adviser	labeled

Syllabification

The dots separating the letters of the boldface entry words are called *syllable dots.* The words are divided like this:

back·ward	ba·con
back·wa·ter	bac·te·ri·a
back·woods	bac·te·ri·ol·o·gist
back·woods·man	bac·te·ri·ol·o·gy
back·yard	Bac′tri·an cam′el

If there are no syllable dots, then the word has only one syllable. All words of two or more syllables are divided by syllable dots. This division is particularly helpful in writing. When you need to divide a word at the end of a line and put part of it on a second line, the syllable dots in the entry word show you where the word can be divided. However, you must remember not to divide words at the end of a line, even when there is a syllable dot, if that leaves only one letter by itself on a line. For example, you should not separate the final *a* in **bac·te·ri·a** from the rest of the word, even though the final *a* has a dot before it and is a separate syllable. Instead, you would either write out the word completely on the first line or separate it between *bac-* and *teria* or *bacte-* and *ria*. As a general rule, no fewer than three letters should be carried over to the next line. In a word like **bac·te·ri·ol·o·gy,** you would not put *gy* on a second line. Instead, you would probably divide the word like this: *bacteri—ology.*

Some main entries, like **Bactrian camel** above, contain more than one word. These are called multiple word entries and are printed with a space between the words to show you that they are two words instead of one. Typical of such entries are **fighting fish, French Revolution,** and **guided missile.**

On a sheet of paper, write out the following words and divide them into syllables with dots. Compare your divisions with those in this dictionary. On which page do you find these words listed? What are the guide words for this page?

SUGGESTED
ACTIVITY 11

altar	alteration	alternate	alternating current
altar boy	altercation	alternately	alternative

Pronunciation

Immediately after a boldface entry word, a phonetic transcription in parentheses shows you how the word is pronounced. For example:

bal·lis·tic (bə lis′tik)

Sometimes a main entry will be followed by two or even three pronunciations. This does not mean that one pronunciation is better than the other or others. It merely shows you that educated people in different parts of the country often pronounce the word in different ways. Note the different pronunciations for **garage, status, February,** and **lever.** Each is widely used and is entirely acceptable.

If you were a lexicographer, what could you do to show someone how to pronounce a printed word? Obviously, it would be far too expensive and awkward to give him a set of records containing the pronunciation of all the words in the dictionary. And obviously, it would take him too much time to listen to a great number of words, waiting to hear the one that he wants to learn how to pronounce. Therefore, the quickest and easiest way to show him the correct pronunciation is in writing, right after the entry word itself. This is exactly what lexicographers do. But how can this be done? Could you use the twenty-six letters of the alphabet only? Or would you need additional letters or symbols to show exactly how words are pronounced?

Before you answer these questions, say these three words aloud several times, listening carefully to the first sound you make as you say each word:

> *apple*   *able*   *area*   *argue*

Although these three words begin with exactly the same letter, *a*, when written, they do not all begin with the same sound when spoken.

Next, say these two words aloud, listening carefully to the first sound you make as you say each word:

> *thin*   *that*

Now say the words again and notice the position of your tongue as you say each initial sound. Then say the words again several times, placing your fingers lightly on your throat so that you can feel the different vibrations of your throat when you say each word. Although these two words, *thin* and *that*, begin with exactly the same letters, *th*, when written, they do not begin with the same sound when spoken.

When you write English words, you use the twenty-six letters of the alphabet. But when you say English words, you make forty-five distinct sounds plus variations of these sounds. Thus, you can see that there are more sounds in English than there are letters of the alphabet.

If you were a lexicographer and wanted to show someone how to pronounce a word, you would need more symbols than just the twenty-six letters of the alphabet. You would have to design some system to indicate to a person using your dictionary that he does not make the same initial sound when he says such words as *apple, able, area,* and *argue.* The lexicographers who created and prepared this dictionary give you four symbols for the initial sounds in these words—a, ā, â, and ä.

The first symbol, **a,** is used to indicate the sound that is commonly called the "short" *a*. It is the sound you hear in words such as *apple, act, ant, bat, map,* and *cat*.

The second symbol, **ā,** indicates the sound that is often called the "long" *a*. It is the sound you hear in words such as *able, aid, cape, tape,* and *way*.

The third symbol, **â,** which is shown with an **r** in the pronunciation key inside the front cover and facing page 1, represents the sound you hear in words such as *area, air, care, dare,* and *vary*.

The fourth symbol, **ä,** indicates the relatively long sound of *a* that you hear in words such as *argue, alms, art, calm,* and *farm*.

When you look up the words *apple, able, area,* and *argue* in this dictionary, the key to their pronunciation will appear in parentheses immediately after the entry words:

ap·ple (ap′əl)   **ar·e·a** (âr′ē ə)
a·ble (ā′bəl)   **ar·gue** (är′gyo͞o)

When you say these words, you make four different initial sounds—a, ā, â, and ä—which are represented in writing by the letter *a.* Thus, to help you pronounce a word that is new to you, lexicographers use more symbols than the twenty-six letters of the alphabet because speakers of English make more than twenty-six distinct sounds in speech.

Consonants

Whenever possible, of course, lexicographers do use the letters of the alphabet to represent sounds. This is usually possible with consonants because consonants usually have only one sound, though some, such as *c, g,* and *s,* have more. Look at the pronunciation key inside the front cover. It contains these consonants to represent certain sounds:

b	as in back, cabin, cab	**n**	as in now, sinner, on
d	as in do, rudder, bed	**p**	as in pot, supper, stop
f	as in fit, differ, puff	**r**	as in read, hurry, near
g	as in give, trigger, beg	**s**	as in see, passing, miss
h	as in hit, behave, hear	**t**	as in ten, butter, bit
j	as in just, badger, fudge	**v**	as in voice, river, live
k	as in kept, token, make	**w**	as in west, away
l	as in low, mellow, all	**y**	as in yes, lawyer
m	as in my, simmer, him	**z**	as in zeal, lazy, those

The letter *c* is not used in the phonetic transcriptions except for *ch* sounds. The letter *s* is used to indicate the sound of a soft *c,* as in *cellar.* The letter *k* is used to indicate the sound of a hard *c,* as in *cat.* Other letters that do not appear are *q* and *x.*

Combinations

To represent other sounds, a combination of two consonants is used, like this:

ch	as in chief, butcher, beach
hw	as in white, nowhere
ng	as in sing, Washington
sh	as in shoe, fashion, push
th	as in thin, ether, path
th	as in that, either, smooth
zh	as in vision, pleasure

Vowels

Because vowels tend to represent more than one sound, other symbols are often needed to represent all the vowel sounds.

a	as in <u>a</u>ct, b<u>a</u>t	ō	as in <u>o</u>ver, b<u>oa</u>t, n<u>o</u>
ā	as in <u>ai</u>d, c<u>a</u>pe, w<u>ay</u>	ô	as in <u>ou</u>ght, b<u>a</u>ll, <u>o</u>rder
â	as in <u>ai</u>r, d<u>a</u>re	oi	as in <u>oi</u>l, j<u>oi</u>nt, joy
ä	as in <u>a</u>lms, <u>a</u>rt, c<u>a</u>lm	o͝o	as in b<u>oo</u>k, h<u>oo</u>d
e	as in <u>e</u>bb, s<u>e</u>t	o͞o	as in <u>oo</u>ze, f<u>oo</u>l, t<u>oo</u>
ē	as in <u>e</u>qual, s<u>ea</u>t, b<u>ee</u>	ou	as in <u>ou</u>t, l<u>ou</u>d, pr<u>ow</u>
ēr	as in h<u>ear</u>, m<u>ere</u>	u	as in <u>u</u>p, l<u>o</u>ve
i	as in <u>i</u>f, b<u>i</u>g, m<u>i</u>rror	û	as in <u>ur</u>ge, b<u>ur</u>n, c<u>ur</u>
ī	as in <u>i</u>ce, p<u>i</u>rate, den<u>y</u>	yo͞o	as in <u>u</u>se, f<u>u</u>se
o	as in <u>o</u>x, b<u>o</u>x, w<u>a</u>sp		

The Schwa

The most common sound in English words is identified in phonetic transcription by the symbol ə . The schwa, as it is called, occurs only in unaccented syllables. It is a sound something like "uh" and is used to indicate the sound you make in the following words:

the sound of the letter **a** in *alone* (ə lōn′)
the sound of the letter **e** in *system* (sis′təm)
the sound of the letter **i** in *easily* (ē′zə lē)
the sound of the letter **o** in *gallop* (gal′əp)
the sound of the letter **u** in *circus* (sûr′kəs)
the sound of the letter **y** in *martyr* (mär′tər)

As you can see, any vowel—*a, e, i, o, u,* or *y*—may at times have the schwa sound.

The small superscript schwa (ᵊ) is used to indicate the weaker sounds made in unaccented syllables ending in *l* preceded by *t, d,* or *n,* as in:

bottle (bot′ᵊl)
cradle (krād′ᵊl)
cardinal (kär′dᵊnᵊl)

The superscript schwa(ᵊ)is also used in unaccented syllables ending in *n* preceded by *t* or *d,* as in:

kitten (kit′ᵊn)
redden (red′ᵊn)

The superscript schwa(ᵊ)also occurs in accented syllables between *ī* and *r,* as in:

fire (fīᵊr)
hire (hīᵊr)

A complete list of the pronunciation symbols and the sounds they represent is given on the inside of the front cover and facing page 1. To help you pronounce words without having to refer to this complete Pronunciation Key every time, a shorter version of the key appears at the bottom of every right-hand page in this dictionary. The short version contains only the vowel sounds and a few symbols that are different from the letters of the alphabet. Here is the shorter version as it appears at the bottom of each right-hand page:

act, āble, dâre, ärt; ebb, ēqual; if, īce; hot, ōver, ôrder; oil; bo͝ok; o͞oze; out; up, ûrge; ə = *a* as in *alone*; ᵊ as in *button* (but′ᵊn), *fire* (fiᵊr); c͡hief; s͡hoe; thin; ᵗhat; z͟h as in *measure* (mez͟h′ər). See full key inside cover.

---

12. Here are the phonetic transcriptions of twenty words. Say the words aloud. Then, on a sheet of paper, write the correctly spelled words which they represent:

SUGGESTED
ACTIVITIES
12–14

ab′sənt	är′mər	ûr′lē	jep′ər dē
an͡g′grē	dā′zē	kem′i strē	hev′ē
ā′kôrn	ev′ə lo͞o′s͡hən	ig zakt′	ō′s͡hən
ā′tēn′	ə dis͡h′ən	get′ō	fiz′i kəl
âr′ē ə	uth′ər	ī′ə wə	kic͟h′ən

13. What symbol is used in this dictionary to represent the initial sound of each of the following words? Write the symbol on a separate sheet of paper.

through	work	phony
theater	list	of
their	utensil	operator
this	urgent	open
shoot	quarter	island

14. Look up the phonetic transcriptions of the following words. Note that each word has more than one acceptable pronunciation. Say each word aloud according to the two or more pronunciations given. Which of these pronunciations do you usually use in your speech? Is this the same one that your family uses? Do all of your friends pronounce these words the way you do?

juvenile	falcon	persist	whoop
kindergarten	status	finance	economical

Stress Marks

When you say a word that has two or more syllables, you usually say one syllable slightly louder than the other. The emphasis that you give to a particular syllable by saying it slightly louder is called *stress*. To be able to detect this emphasis, ask someone to say the following words aloud three times as you listen carefully to them:

finger	result	Lincoln	lunar	appetite
mirror	apple	Egypt	ocean	pleasing
window	Henry	Ohio	entirely	mountain
hospital	fantastic	Alabama	ridiculous	population

As you listened to these words, you probably noted that the first syllable in *finger* and *mirror* was emphasized more than the final one. The *win-* in *window* was emphasized more than the *-dow*, the syllable *hos-* in *hospital* was emphasized more than the other two syllables, and so on.

Now say all of these words aloud, giving equal emphasis to each syllable. As you do so, you will find that you are not speaking naturally. As you say any word with two or more syllables, you automatically emphasize at least one of the syllables. To show you which syllable is normally emphasized in speech, the lexicographers who prepared this dictionary placed this mark ′ after the stressed syllable of the phonetic transcription that appears in parentheses following the entry word.

This symbol ′ means that the syllable receives primary stress, as the *ap* in *apple* (ap′əl). The ′ is called a primary, or main, stress mark. Primary stress means that you say the syllable that is marked with this symbol ′ slightly louder than the other syllables in a word. In some multiple word entries, like *family tree,* two elements of the entry receive primary stress. In this dictionary, such an entry will be marked like this: **fam′ily tree′.** Note also the entries for **ice′ cream′, fair′y tale′,** and **beast′ of bur′den.** The stress mark also may indicate a syllable division, as in the above words *fair·y* and *bur·den* where it replaces the syllable dot.

This symbol ′ indicates that a syllable receives secondary stress. Secondary stress means that you say the syllable preceding the mark ′ with less emphasis than you give a syllable having a primary stress mark ′. But a syllable marked with ′ receives more emphasis and is said slightly louder than a syllable that has no stress mark at all. **Bacteriology** (bak tēr′ē ol′ə jē) is an example of a word containing syllables that have primary stress (ol′), secondary stress (tēr′), and no noticeable stress (bak, ē, ə, and jē).

As some words shift in use from verb to noun, their stress changes. For example, **record** (ri kôrd′) is a verb that means to set down in writing, to put on tape or a disk, or to tell something. **Record** (rek′ərd) is a noun that means a disk to be played on a phonograph, an account of something in writing, or information or knowledge preserved in writing. The stress marks indicate that when the word *record* is used as a verb in a sentence, you stress the second syllable. When the same word is used as a noun, you stress the first syllable.

Note that the divisions of words in the phonetic transcriptions are not always the same as the division by syllable dots in the entry words. The division by syllables indicates how words are normally divided at the end of lines when written. The division in a phonetic transcription shows how certain sounds are linked together when spoken and how certain groups of sounds are stressed. Note, for example, the difference between the written syllabification of *everlasting*—**ev·er·last·ing**—and the division of the sounds in the phonetic transcription (ev′ ər las′tiñg). As you can see, syllable divisions are not always the same in writing as they are in speaking.

---

15. Say aloud each word below. As you say each word, listen carefully to determine which syllables you stress. Then, on a sheet of paper, write the phonetic transcription of the word. Put in the primary and secondary stress marks where you think they belong, and then compare your transcriptions with those in this dictionary.

eventual	everglade	everlasting
ever	evergreen	evermore

16. Look up the following words on page 273. Pronounce the words according to the phonetic transcriptions given. Which syllables receive primary stress? Which words contain secondary stresses? Do any of the words have more than one pronunciation?

extradite	extrasensory	extravagantly	extremist
extraneous	extravagance	extreme	extremity
extraordinary	extravagant	extremely	extricate

17. Before you look up the pronunciation of the words in the two columns below, write two sentences for each word on a sheet of paper. In the first sentence, use the word as a verb; in the second sentence, use the word as a noun.

Example: *record*
1. Mother said she will *record* my little sister's voice on her second birthday. (*record* as a verb)
2. The disk jockey played my favorite *record* on his radio show. (*record* as a noun)

present	combat	object	contract
conflict	content	permit	subject

SUGGESTED
ACTIVITIES
15–17

After you have written the two sentences for each word on the list, compare the way the word is pronounced in each sentence. Note the changes in stress that you make as the function of the word changes from verb to noun. Underneath each sentence, write the word, placing a stress mark on the syllable that receives primary stress when the word is used in that sentence. After you have completed this procedure for all the words on the list, compare your stress marks with those given in the dictionary.

Dialects

As a speaker of English, you do not pronounce all words in exactly the same way as all other speakers of English do. For example, if you live in the eastern United States, you do not say every word the same way as a person who lives in the South, nor do you say every word the same way as a person who lives in the Midwest or West. The different pronunciations and speech habits that people from various regions use are a natural part of language and are called *dialects*.

English is, of course, a single language, but within it you will find a number of dialects. A dialect is the way a language is spoken by people living in a particular geographical region. Each dialect of a country contains its own variations in word pronunciation, vocabulary, and even sentence structure. Within the United States, different dialects of American English are spoken in New England and in the South, Midwest, and West.

Everybody speaks a dialect. You do, too. You pronounce most words in much the same way as do other people who were born in or who live in your part of the United States. You also use the same words as they do to refer to familiar things. For example, if you live in the South, you might refer to peanuts as *goobers*. And, depending on where you live in the United States, you probably use one of these words to refer to pancakes: *battercakes, flannel cakes, griddlecakes, flapjacks, wheat cakes, slapjacks,* or *hotcakes*.

No dialect is better than another. Just because you speak a Midwestern dialect, or a Southern dialect, or a New England dialect does not mean that your dialect is superior to anyone else's. The differences in pronunciation merely indicate where you were born or where you spent most of your life.

Fortunately, most dialectal differences are so minor that they do not hamper communication between people born in different parts of the United States. You would notice the "Southern drawl" and the so-called broad *a* sound of the New Englander if you were born in the Midwest. But these differences in pronunciation do not prevent you from understanding the person who is born in the South or in New England.

Nor does the Hoosier's nasal twang prevent your understanding him if you were not born in Indiana.

When lexicographers try to show how words are pronounced, they cannot record a separate pronunciation for each dialect. Instead, they use symbols that will guide *any* speaker to the pronunciation that is appropriate for *his* dialect. This is possible because the speaker of any dialect is fairly consistent in the way he pronounces a particular sound. For example, while a speaker in the South may pronounce the vowel sound in *house* quite differently from a speaker in the North, he is likely to pronounce the vowel sounds in *town, out,* and *mouse* the same way he does in *house.* In this instance, the symbol *ou* of the pronunciation key stands for the sounds made by a speaker of any dialect. Each speaker discovers what that symbol stands for in his own dialect from the pronunciation key, which gives a common word in which that sound appears. Thus, when he sees *ball* as an example of the sound *ô,* he will know that he should use the same sound as he uses in such words as *awful, law,* and *taught.*

For some words, of course, lexicographers must record several different phonetic transcriptions to show how pronunciation varies in different dialects. Look up the phonetic transcriptions for *greasy* and *amateur* in this dictionary. How many phonetic transcriptions are given? Why is more than one given?

SUGGESTED ACTIVITY 18

Because pronunciations vary, lexicographers frequently record two pronunciations of a word, just as they sometimes record two spellings. The first pronunciation is the one most frequently heard in the United States.

al·ien (āl′yən, ā′lē ən)

Which way do you pronounce *alien?* Which sound or group of sounds do you emphasize when you say it? Is one of the two pronunciations shown better than the other?

How many pronunciations are given for each of the words below? Why is more than one pronunciation given? How do you pronounce each of these words?

ideal	creek	roof
forehead	route	wash

Parts of Speech

You have already seen how your dictionary can help you spell words, divide them into syllables, and pronounce them correctly. To speak and write more effectively, you will also want to know how words are used.

Many words can change their function. Some words that came into the language as nouns now function as both nouns and verbs. Some even function as nouns, verbs, and adjectives. Still others function as nouns, adjectives, and adverbs. In the following sentences, *fast* functions as a noun, verb, adjective, and adverb:

1. The baby is fast asleep. (In this sentence, *fast* functions as an adverb.)
2. The tape sticks fast. (Again, *fast* functions as an adverb.)
3. Your clock is fast. (*Fast* functions as an adjective.)
4. He is a fast runner. (Here, *fast* also functions as an adjective.)
5. During Lent some people fast. (*Fast* functions as a verb.)
6. The man was very weak from his long fast. (Here, *fast* functions as a noun. Under which homograph do you find this meaning of *fast* defined in this dictionary?)

As you know, when you look up an entry word in this dictionary, you find the entry word divided into syllables and printed in boldface type. The pronunciation of the word immediately follows the entry word and appears in parentheses. Thus, the first part of the entry for the word *minister* looks like this:

min·is·ter (min′i stər),

The next item in the entry is the part of speech label:

min·is·ter (min′i stər), *n.*

The *n.* indicates that the definitions following it are for *minister* when it is used as a noun. The three noun definitions are listed like this:

> **min·is·ter** (min′i stər), *n.* **1.** a clergyman, esp. of a Protestant denomination; pastor. **2.** (in some countries) the head of a government department: *a minister of education.* **3.** a person, ranking below an ambassador, who represents his country abroad.

In each of the three sentences below, *minister* is used according to one of its noun definitions listed above:

1. We helped our *minister* raise money for a new church. (definition 1)
2. The *Minister* of Finance told the government officials that they were spending too much money. (definition 2)
3. The king sent his *minister* to meet with the President of the United States. (definition 3)

Definitions for *minister* when it is used as a verb appear in the dictionary entry following the part of speech label *v.:*

—*v.*
4. to perform the functions of a clergyman or pastor.
5. to give service, care, or aid: *to minister to the sick and needy.*

Here are two sentences in which *minister* is used as a verb:

1. The Reverend Mr. Smith *ministers* to the needs of his parish-ioners. (definition 4)
2. A nurse *ministers* to the sick. (definition 5)

In this dictionary, definitions for each word are grouped together after a specific part of speech label. If a word functions most frequently as a noun, the noun definitions will be given first. If it functions most frequently as a verb, the verb definitions will be given first. And likewise for adjectives, adverbs, and the other parts of speech.

Muddy, for example, can be used as both an adjective and a verb. Since *muddy* functions more frequently as an adjective than as a verb, the definitions for *muddy* as an adjective are given first in this dictionary, with the single definition for *muddy* as a verb coming last:

mud·dy (mud′ē), *adj.,* **mud·di·er, mud·di·est. 1.** cov-ered with mud: *muddy boots.* **2.** not clear or pure: *a muddy stream.* **3.** not clear in meaning; obscure: *muddy writing.* —*v.,* **mud·died, mud·dy·ing. 4.** to make or become muddy: *to muddy one's shoes.* —**mud′di·ness,** *n.*

The abbreviations used in this dictionary for the eight parts of speech are:

n. for *noun*	*pron.* for *pronoun*
v. for *verb*	*prep.* for *preposition*
adj. for *adjective*	*conj.* for *conjunction*
adv. for *adverb*	*interj.* for *interjection*

---

19. On a sheet of paper, write the part of speech labels given in the dictionary for these words:

far	room	nor	each
favor	turn	fear	to
fancy	small	whip	but
myself	slow	between	ouch

20. Words change meaning according to their function. Therefore, it is important in locating the right definition to know whether a word used in a sentence is a noun, a verb, or another part of speech.

SUGGESTED
ACTIVITIES
19–20

For each of the following sentences, write the part of speech for the italicized word. Then look up the word and write the number of the definition that applies to that part of speech.

Example: The tree will bear fruit when it is *mature.*
adj.—definition 1

a. Red is her *favorite* color.
b. That boxer always *feints* twice with his left before trying to hit his opponent with his right.
c. The aircraft carrier was protected by a destroyer *escort.*
d. His sister said she wanted to exchange the present for something of *equivalent* value.
e. Their new house is *extremely* large.
f. The building superintendent told us not to *monkey* around.
g. Jack made a *mobile* for his room.
h. *Who* knows where Bill is?
i. It is easy to make a wrong *move* in chess.
j. Uncle Ralph said that he will not *run* for governor.
k. Mother has a *set* time for doing everything.
l. He bought a new leash *for* his dog.

Inflected Forms

You know that the verb *run* has several different forms. And you know how to use those forms. For example, you do not say, "He run yesterday"; instead, you say, "He ran yesterday." Since you know the different forms of a verb like *run,* you are not likely to look them up in a dictionary. But you might use a dictionary to find the more difficult past tense of a verb like *beat.*

In a dictionary, lexicographers usually list the plural forms of nouns, the past tense and past and present participial forms of verbs, and the comparative and superlative forms of adjectives and adverbs when these forms are not made in a regular manner.

Look up the adjective *muddy* in the dictionary. You will note that two additional forms are given for it: *muddier* and *muddiest.* You use *muddier* when you compare two things: *This creek is muddier than Buck Creek.* You use *muddiest* when you compare more than two things: *Those are the muddiest shoes I have ever seen.* These two forms of *muddy,* as well as the two forms *muddied* and *muddying* which appear after the *v.,* are called *inflected forms.* If you do not find such forms listed, you will know that they follow the simple, standard patterns.

Noun Inflections.   You form the plurals of most nouns by adding the letter *s* to the basic singular form. Thus, the inflected forms of *street,* *boy,* and *song* are *streets, boys,* and *songs.* When a noun ends with the letters *s, ch, sh, x,* or *z,* you form the plural by adding the letters *es.* Thus, the inflected forms of *glass, church, bush, box,* and *buzz* are *glasses, churches, bushes, boxes,* and *buzzes.*

When the plural of a noun is formed regularly, by simply adding *-s* or *-es,* lexicographers usually do not list its inflected form. But if a noun does *not* form its plural by adding *-s* or *-es,* or if there might be some confusion as to how the plural is formed, this dictionary lists the plural form immediately after the part of speech label. Here are some examples:

a·lum·nus (ə lum′nəs), *n., pl.* **a·lum·ni** (ə lum′nī).
mad·ame (mad′əm, ma dam′, mə däm′), *n., pl.* **mes·dames** (mā dam′, mā däm′).
en·e·my (en′ə mē), *n., pl.* **en·e·mies.**
Min·ute·man (min′it man′), *n., pl.* **Min·ute·men.**
moth·er·in·law (muŧħ′ər in lô′), *n., pl.* **moth·ers·in·law** (muŧħ′ərz in lô′).
mouse (mous), *n., pl.* **mice** (mīs).
phe·nom·e·non (fi nom′ə non′), *n., pl.* for def. 1 **phe·nom·e·na** (fi nom′ə nə);

Verb Inflections. You form the past tense and past participial forms of many verbs by adding *-ed* to the basic present tense form. *Walked,* for example, is both the past tense and past participle of *walk.*

I *walked* home yesterday.

I have *walked* five miles today.

You form the present participle of most verbs by adding *-ing* to the basic present tense form: *walk, walking.*

This dictionary does not give the inflected forms of regular verbs whose past tense and past participles are made by adding *-ed* to the basic present tense form, nor does it show the inflected *-ing* form unless there might be some confusion about the spelling.

This dictionary does list the inflected verb forms that are not formed in a regular manner or whose spellings differ slightly from the basic present tense form. Here are some examples:

ride (rīd), *v.,* **rode** (rōd), **rid·den** (rid′ᵊn), **rid·ing.**
see (sē), *v.,* **saw** (sô), **seen** (sēn), **see·ing.**
stead·y (sted′ē), *v.,* **stead·ied, stead·y·ing.**
fine (fīn), *v.,* **fined, fin·ing.**

If the past tense and past participial forms of a verb are exactly the same, this dictionary lists only the one form that is used for both, as is done above for *steadied* and *fined.*

Adjective and Adverb Inflections. The comparative and superlative forms of most adjectives and adverbs are formed by adding *-er* and *-est* to the basic form. Thus, the two inflected forms of the adjective *tall* are *taller* and *tallest;* the inflected forms of the adverb *slow* are *slower* and *slowest.*

Dorothy is *taller* than Jane.

Sherry is the *tallest* girl in the class.

The sign says to drive *slow*.

Which boy walks *slowest?*

This dictionary lists only the inflected forms of those adjectives and adverbs that do not form their comparative and superlative forms by adding *-er* and *-est*.

good (good), *adj.*, **bet·ter** (bet′ər), **best** (best).
far (fär), *adv.*, **far·ther** *or* **fur·ther; far·thest** *or* **fur·thest**.

Inflected forms are also listed if you must change the basic form before adding *-er* and *-est:*

stead·y (sted′ē), *adj.*, **stead·i·er, stead·i·est.**
fine (fīn), *adj.*, **fin·er, fin·est.**
big (big), *adj.*, **big·ger, big·gest.**
well (wel), *adv.*, **bet·ter** (bet′ər), **best** (best).
bad·ly (bad′lē), *adv.*, **worse** (wûrs), **worst** (wûrst).

SUGGESTED ACTIVITIES 21–25

21. Select any six nouns from the list below. For each word you choose, write a sentence in which you use the plural form of that word.

Example: *cupful*—Mother put three cupfuls of flour in the mixing bowl.

leaf	calf	mother superior
goose	library	Siamese
father-in-law	memorandum	buffalo
handful	fish	census

Compare the plural forms of the nouns you used with the forms listed in this dictionary.

22. On a sheet of paper, write the inflected forms of each of the verbs listed below. Then compare your forms with those listed in this dictionary.

cut	transmit	lay	go
speak	hurry	analyze	come
hurt	ride	judge	travel

23. What are the inflected forms of the following verbs? Why aren't the inflected forms listed in this dictionary?

talk	pick	jump
listen	detach	scream

24. Write a sentence in which you use the comparative form of each of the following adjectives. Check your comparative forms with those listed in this dictionary.

> ruddy   bad   sleepy   lively

Now write a sentence in which you use the comparative form of each of the following adverbs. Then check your comparative forms with those listed in this dictionary.

> well   little   badly   far

25. Sometimes an adjective or adverb has no comparative or superlative form of its own. Such a word must form its comparative and superlative with the help of *more* and *most*. Because these are not true inflected forms, you will not find them listed in the dictionary.

> **beautiful:** more beautiful, most beautiful
> **nearly:** more nearly, most nearly

A few adjectives, such as *unique* and *supreme*, have no comparative and superlative forms.

On a sheet of paper, write the comparative and superlative forms of the following adjectives and adverbs. Which do not have comparative and superlative forms? Compare your answers with the dictionary entries.

good	friendly	completely	few
responsible	marshy	sly	much
enough	spacious	secret	bad

Labels and Context Clues

In addition to the part of speech labels, lexicographers often use other labels to help you better understand what certain words mean in specific contexts. For example, if people no longer give a certain meaning to a word, the definition of that word will be labeled *Archaic*. *Archaic* meanings of words are included in dictionaries because these words are found in books, plays, and songs written more than a hundred years ago. They are also used in stories that take place many years ago, such as those about King Arthur or Robin Hood. If you use words labeled *Archaic*, people may not understand you, since these words, or certain of their meanings, are no longer used.

In the entry for *anon*, you find the label *Archaic*.

> **a·non** (ə non′), *adv. Archaic.* 1. soon; in a short time.
> 2. at another time.

In addition to *Archaic*, there are other labels such as *Slang*, *Chem.*, and *British*. The label *Slang* indicates that you are more likely to use the word in casual conversation than in the classroom or in writing.

Chem. indicates that the meaning of a word refers to its use in chemistry. The label *British* indicates that the following is the British spelling or use, which differs from the American. For example, you will find that Americans write *armor* and the British write *armour.*

In some entries in this dictionary, you will find a definition or definitions preceded by information in parentheses. This is to show that the word has a special meaning when used in a particular context. For example, there are three context clues in parentheses in the entry for *bunt:*

> **bunt** (bunt), *v.* **1.** (of a goat or calf) to push with the horns or head. **2.** (in baseball) to bat (a pitched ball) very gently so that it does not roll far into the infield. —*n.* **3.** a push with the horns or head. **4.** (in baseball) **a.** the act of bunting. **b.** a bunted ball.

After reading the information in parentheses, you know that definition 1 of *bunt* refers to the action of a goat or calf, and, therefore, the verb *bunt* is used when talking about animals pushing one another with their heads or horns. Definitions 2 and 4 refer to the use of *bunt* in the context of baseball.

As you look up the definition of a word, you need to consider the context in which it is used to find the appropriate meaning.

SUGGESTED ACTIVITY 26

On a sheet of paper, write a definition for each italicized word below. Base your definition on the use of the word in the sentence. Indicate in parentheses the context in which the word has that specific meaning. Compare your labels or context clues with those in this dictionary.

> **Example:** The tree *bled.* Definition of *bleed:* (of a plant) to have sap, resin, or the like, ooze out from a cut spot.

> a. The conductor said to play that passage *andante.*
> b. The admiral called the sailor a daring young *blood.*
> c. What's a *body* to do?
> d. Ellen told us to go talk to the top *brass.*
> e. Right in the middle of the song, his voice began to *break.*

Definitions

You already know a great deal about lexical definitions since you have written several as you worked through the activities in this introduction. Before you can use any dictionary intelligently, you need to know how lexicographers arrange their definitions in a dictionary. This brief entry for *beard* will give you some clues to the arrangement of definitions in this dictionary:

> **beard** (bērd), *n.* **1.** the growth of hair on a man's face. **2.** any tuft or growth resembling a man's beard, as the tuft of long hair on a goat's jaw or the bristly growths on stalks of grain. —*v.* **3.** to oppose or defy boldly. —**beard·ed** (bēr′did), *adj.*

According to this entry, *beard* is used most frequently as a noun. And people use the noun most often to refer to the growth of hair on a man's face. The second definition, which refers both to the growth of hair on a goat and the hairlike growth of bristle on stalks of grain, is not used as frequently as the first definition. The third definition is for *beard* when it is used as a verb, as in "Mark *bearded* the boss in his office."

Definitions are grouped first according to the part of speech that is most often used. Within the grouping of definitions by part of speech, the most common meaning is listed first. Thus, the definitions for *minus*, which can function as three different parts of speech, appear in this order:

> **mi·nus** (mī′nəs), *prep.* **1.** less by the subtraction of; decreased by: *Nine minus three is six.* **2.** lacking; without: *a silver teapot minus a lid.* —*adj.* **3.** indicating or used in subtraction: *a minus sign.* **4.** less than or lower than zero: *a temperature of minus ten degrees.* **5.** less than or lower than a fixed point: *a grade of B minus.* —*n.* **6.** a minus sign. **7.** a quantity subtracted: *You get a minus for each wrong answer.*

When you look up a word that you do not know, you should not stop after reading the first definition. The best way to find a specific meaning of a word is to read all the definitions, or at least all the definitions for the particular part of speech that functions in the same way as your unfamiliar word. Then you should be able to tell by the way the word is used in that particular sentence whether or not you have selected the most appropriate definition. The illustrative sentences and phrases in the entry should also help you find the most appropriate definition.

Not all definitions are arranged on the basis of frequency or familiarity. Abbreviation entries, for example, have the definitions, which are usually one word, arranged in alphabetical order. (Look up **L.**, **g.**, **c.**) Biographical entries are also arranged in alphabetical order by first name. (Look up **Adams, Roosevelt.**) Geographical entries are arranged so that the most important or the largest, longest, or highest appears first. (Look up **Georgia, Geneva.**) Sometimes biographical and geo-graphical definitions are included in the same entry, as at **Lincoln** and **Washington.** In these instances, persons are placed first, followed by places.

SUGGESTED ACTIVITIES 27–32

27. Read each of the following sentences in which *mute* is used, and then look up the entry for **mute.** On a sheet of paper, write the number of the definition that seems most appropriate to the way *mute* is used in each sentence. Then write your own sentence using that particular definition of *mute.*

> **Example:** Donald *muted* the roar of the old car's engine by putting a new muffler on it—definition 6
> The neighbors were happy when Jerry *muted* his trombone.
>
> a. The musician put a *mute* in his trumpet.
> b. The poor old man could not speak because he was a *mute.*
> c. Whenever we asked the man about his work, he was *mute.*

28. Which definition of *spring* best applies to the words used in each of these five sentences?
   a. He has a distinct *spring* in his walk.
   b. That book is a *spring* of inspiration.
   c. Paul was afraid that the car radiator would *spring* a leak as we drove through the desert.
   d. The mushrooms seemed to *spring* up overnight.
   e. We found a cool *spring* in the mountains.

29. Give the number of the definition that best suits the words as they are used in these sentences.
   a. The professor gave his *talk* without notes.
   b. That private detective likes to *dog* his suspects.
   c. Uncle Bruce *runs* a machine in a factory that makes toys.
   d. The jeweler *set* the diamond in the ring.
   e. George built a ham radio *set.*
   f. The teacher *named* Ronna chairman of the committee.

30. Find the entries for the following words in this dictionary. On a sheet of paper, write a sentence for each word according to the definition indicated.

fashion—definition 3	execute—definition 3
exude—definition 2	talk—definition 10
expression—definition 4	run—definition 23

31. In an earlier section, you learned that two or more words which are spelled alike but which have different meanings and origins are called homographs. Because of their different origins, homographs are given separate entries. For example, *bank* has three separate entries.

Find the following homographs in the dictionary. On a sheet of paper, write a sentence for each of the entries according to the definition indicated.

bank^2—definition 4   fair^1—definition 2

fawn^2—definition 1   fast^2—definition 2

32. A. What does each of these abbreviations or symbols mean?
   (a) A.W.O.L.   (b) e.g.   (c) Pfc.   (d) Cf   (e) cf.
B. How much are you told about the following persons?
   (a) Lee, Robert E. (b) Twain, Mark (c) Gandhi, Mohandas (d) Addams, Jane
C. Where are the following located?
   (a) Río de la Plata   (b) K2   (c) Falkland Islands   (d) Cape of Good Hope

Sentence and Phrase Examples

This dictionary also gives you many example sentences and phrases to help you better understand the different ways a word is used in speaking or writing. These examples always come immediately after the definition and are printed in italic type. For example, with the first definition of *exponent,* you find this illustrative sentence: *He was an exponent of Darwin's theory.* For the second definition of the same word, there is this illustrative sentence: *Lincoln is an exponent of American democracy.* For the third definition of *explosive,* there is this illustrative phrase: *an explosive situation.* For the fourth definition of *export,* there is this illustrative phrase: *an export business.* Such illustrative sentences and phrases appear frequently in this dictionary. They help you use a word more precisely in your own writing and speaking by showing you how it is used in a particular context for a specific meaning.

Synonyms

A synonym is a word that has the same, or nearly the same, meaning as another word. In many definitions in this dictionary, you will find a single word that can be substituted for the entry word. However, synonyms cannot always be substituted without changing the meaning of a sentence. Here is a portion of the entry for *great,* an adjective that is often used with little concern for its true meanings. The single-word synonyms are placed after the main definitions and are always separated by semicolons.

great (grāt), *adj.* **1.** unusually large in size; <u>big</u>; vast: *a great oak tree.* **2.** large in number; very <u>numerous</u>: *a great flock of birds.* **3.** unusual in strength, degree, or the like: *to feel great pain.* **4.** outstanding or remarkable; <u>excellent</u>: *a great book.* **5.** having important consequences; very <u>important</u>: *The president was faced with a great decision.* **6.** of notable length or duration; <u>long</u>: *to wait a great while.*

By examining the definitions of *great,* you can find several words that you can substitute for *great* according to the meaning that you intend to give to that word. For example:

1. Inside the building was a *great* ballroom.
   Inside the building was a *vast* ballroom.
2. The movie was *great.*
   The movie was *excellent.*
3. We haven't seen her in a *great* while.
   We haven't seen her in a *long* while.

For definition 1, you could also make this substitution:

1. We sat beneath a *great* oak tree.
2. We sat beneath a *big* oak tree.

As you write and speak, you should sometimes search for synonyms to avoid repeating the same words. But you need to be careful when choosing substitute words. For example, although *excellent* is a substitute for *great* in definition 4 of the entry, these two sentences do not have exactly the same meaning:

1. Most people agree that *Grapes of Wrath* is a *great* book.
2. Most people agree that *Grapes of Wrath* is an *excellent* book.

As you read the first sentence, you get the impression that *Grapes of Wrath* is probably one of the best books ever written. But the use of the word *excellent* in the second sentence indicates that, although the book is first-rate, there are probably any number of books that are just as good. You can see from these examples how important it is to choose the right words in order to express your thoughts clearly and accurately.

SUGGESTED ACTIVITIES 33–34

33. Study the entry for **low**[1] on page 455 of this dictionary. On a sheet of **paper,** write the single-word synonyms given in the various definitions of *low*[1].

Example: unhappy—definition 6

Also look for those definitions that consist of one or more synonyms. For example, in definition 10 you find the words *mean* and *base* as definitions of *low*[1]. These definitions should also be listed on your sheet of paper.

Now write two sentences for each definition of *low*[1] in which you found a synonym. In the first sentence, use the word *low*. In the second sentence, use an appropriate synonym in place of *low*.

> **Example:** 1. He made a *low* bow when he was introduced.
> 2. He made a *deep* bow when he was introduced.

34. What words can you substitute for the italicized words in the sentences below? After you find a synonym for an italicized word, read the sentence aloud with your synonym instead of with the italicized word. Then see whether or not your sentences have the same meanings as the ones below.

    a. Joan carried a *bucket* of water to the barn.
    b. The teacher told her class that reading is a *basic* course in all elementary schools.
    c. Earl refused to *bicker* over the price of the used car.
    d. Marjorie is very *depressed* today.
    e. Arthur was *happy* when he heard the good news.

Illustrations

Some objects cannot be described in detail in the few lines that lexicographers have space for. For example, if you look up *devilfish*, you will find this definition: "a large ray found in tropical waters, having a pair of horns on its head." Those few words describe the fish accurately, but you may not be able to picture the fish completely. Therefore, this illustration of *devilfish* accompanies the entry word.

The many drawings in this dictionary give you a better idea of what certain objects look like, and often supply additional information. Just by looking at the drawing of a *yak* below, you can tell that the animal lives in a mountainous country because of the background the artist drew. Underneath the drawing, you will find the animal's approximate size.

Yak
(6 ft. high at shoulder)

SUGGESTED ACTIVITIES 35–41

35. What is the exact size of a *basketball court?* How big is the center circle?

36. What is an *ocarina?* What do you learn about an *ocarina* from the drawing in this dictionary?

37. What is the size of a *spider monkey?* Why do you think the lexicographers decided to illustrate this entry?

38. Where is *Asia Minor?* How does the map help you to determine its location?

39. How are *cymbals* played? How does this dictionary show you how *cymbals* are played?

40. What is a *bighorn?* In what kind of country will you usually find a *bighorn?* What information about the size of a *bighorn* are you given in the illustration?

41. On a sheet of paper, write as complete a description of a *saxophone* as you can. How many words did you use to describe the instrument? How many words did the lexicographers for this dictionary use to describe a *saxophone?* Why do you think the lexicographers decided to include a drawing of a *saxophone* in this dictionary?

Idioms

If you were not born in the United States and if you were trying to learn American English, you might have this picture flash through your mind when you read this sentence: *He had to pull strings to get the job.*

You would undoubtedly be confused, because you could not understand why it would be necessary to tug at strings in order to obtain employment. Such expressions as *pull strings* are called *idioms.*

An idiom is a phrase that is peculiar to a specific language. It is a phrase whose meaning cannot be decided by knowing the meaning of each of the words in the phrase. For example, in the idiom *pull strings,* the words do not literally mean to tug at a bunch of strings. The individual words in that phrase have nothing to do with its idiomatic meaning: "to use influence to get special favors."

But where in the dictionary will you find the definition of an expression like *pull strings?* The key word, that is the word in the idiom that seems least clear, is *strings*. You should look up the entry for **string.** For the idiom *hit the road,* look up the entry for **road.** To find the definitions of an idiom, you must look up the key word of the idiom.

Before you look up the meanings of the idioms given below, write a definition for each of them on a sheet of paper. Which of the idioms do you think has more than one meaning? If you think an idiom has more than one meaning, write all of its meanings on your sheet of paper. Then compare the definitions you wrote with those given in this dictionary.

SUGGESTED
ACTIVITY 42

back out	fall back on	at full blast
run over	go to bat for	give way to
up to the minute	break down	stand pat

Affixes (Prefixes and Suffixes)

One type of entry in the dictionary with which you should familiarize yourself is the affix. Though they cannot have meanings by themselves, as words do, affixes are used to form words or to add to or change the meanings of words. An *affix* may be only a letter, or it may be a syllable or several syllables. Its characteristic is that, as an affix, it cannot stand alone as a word itself but is always added to the main part of the word in which it occurs.

An affix added to the beginning of a word is called a *prefix.* For example, *un-* may be used to form a new word opposite in meaning to the word to which it is added: compare *happy* and *unhappy.* *Pre-* adds the meaning "before" to a word: for example, *preschool.* *Re-* has the meaning "back," as in *recall,* or "again," as in *readjust.*

An affix added to the end of a word is called a *suffix.* Suffixes are used for many purposes. For example, under the heading Inflected Forms, you have seen that adding *-s* or *-es* to most nouns will form their plurals; that *-ed* forms the past tense of many verbs; and that *-er* and *-est* form the comparative and superlative degrees of many adjectives and adverbs.

Not all suffixes, however, are used in inflected forms. For example, *-ly* can be added to adjectives to make adverbs, such as *honestly, sweetly,* and *loudly.* Adding the suffix *-y* to some nouns changes them to adjectives, such as *cloudy, milky,* and *soapy.* These are only a few examples of the many prefixes and suffixes defined in this dictionary, with examples of their use. You will be able to figure out the meanings of a great many words that you have not seen before if you learn the meanings and uses of prefixes and suffixes.

Etymologies

Etymologies are word histories. They will show you how words change and develop in spelling and meaning and where they came from. Many Modern English words are native and have come down to us from the earlier stages of our language (Old English and Middle English). Thousands of other Modern English words were borrowed from other languages at some time during the history of English. These loan words, as they are called, often retain the same meanings they had in other languages. Some of them, however, have developed totally different meanings.

To show you the interesting sources of words and to give you an idea of how the English vocabulary has been created, the lexicographers who prepared this dictionary give you the etymologies at the end of many entries:

> **mob** (mob), *n.* **1.** a disorderly crowd that may easily be moved to riot and violence. **2.** any group of persons or things: *There was a mob at the sale.* **3.** the common people: *Her style of folk singing pleases the mob.* **4.** a gang of criminals. —*v.,* **mobbed, mob·bing. 5.** to crowd around noisily: *The stars were mobbed by fans.* **6.** to attack violently: *If you say that in this town, they'll mob you.* [short for the Latin phrase *mobile vulgus* "the fickle crowd"]

The information in brackets [ ] at the end of the entry word is the etymology.

This dictionary gives you the etymologies of words that have interesting origins, and histories that help clarify the meaning. For example, at the end of the entry for the word **alphabet,** you learn that this word comes from the Greek word *alphabētos,* which comes from the names of the first two letters of the Greek alphabet, *alpha* and *bēta.*

If you look up the word **marathon,** you will find at the end of the entry that it comes from the name of a plain in Greece, the place from which the messenger Pheidippides ran to Athens, 26 miles away, with the news that the Greeks had defeated the Persians in 490 B.C.

This dictionary also lists the etymologies for most homographs to show you the source of each homograph and the differences in their meanings. For example, if you look up the three homographs for **bank** on page 62, you will find that *bank*[1] comes from a Danish word. *Bank*[2] comes from the Italian word *banca,* which means "moneychanger's table." The Italians borrowed the word *banca* from a Germanic word meaning "bench." *Bank*[3] comes from the Old English word *banc.*

What are the etymologies of these words?

SUGGESTED
ACTIVITY 43

academy	potter's field
bunk²	tantalize
travel	torch
muscle	zany
sandwich	

Run-on Entries

To give you as much information about words in as little space as possible, lexicographers list different forms of a word at the end of a dictionary entry in this way:

> **am·a·teur·ish** (am/ə chŏŏr/ish, am/ə tyŏŏr/ish, am/-
> ə tûr/ish), *adj.* of or like an amateur, esp. in having
> faults; not expert or skillful: *an amateurish perfor-
> mance of a concerto.* —**am/a·teur/ish·ly,** *adv.* —**am/
> a·teur/ish·ness,** *n.*

Amateurishly and *amateurishness* are examples of run-on entries. By carefully studying the definition for **amateurish,** and by learning the meanings of the separate suffix entries -*ly* and -*ness,* you can decide that *amateurishly* means "in an amateurish manner" and that *amateurishness* means "the quality of being amateurish." You also learn from the run-on entries that *amateurishly* is an adverb and *amateurishness* is a noun, as well as how they are syllabified and pronounced.

Run-on entries, then, are additional words that can be formed from a main entry word. They appear at the end of the entry in boldface type and are not defined because their meanings are clear from the definition of the main entry word.

Some words that have been formed by adding a suffix are not treated as run-on entries because they have inflected forms or because they have more than one meaning or a meaning not easily derived from the suffix. They are therefore defined separately as main entry words. *Antiquity,* for example, has three different meanings and will be found as a main entry rather than as a run-on entry under *antique.*

> **an·tiq·ui·ty** (an tik/wi tē), *n., pl.* **an·tiq·ui·ties. 1.** the
> quality or condition of being ancient; oldness: *a vase
> of great antiquity.* **2.** ancient times; former ages: *the
> Greek philosophers of antiquity.* **3. antiquities,**
> monuments, relics, customs, etc., of ancient times: *a
> student of antiquities.*

SUGGESTED
ACTIVITY 44

On a sheet of paper, list the run-on entries for each of these words:

annual	astonish	back[1]	brawl
anonymous	meddle	ball[1]	kidnap
apologetic	forceful	bashful	evaluate

After studying the definitions for the above main entry words, write definitions for any four of the run-on entries. Now write sentences using the four run-on entries that you defined.

Usage Notes

Language is the product of people; therefore, people ultimately decide what words mean and how they should be put together for more effective communication. However, people sometimes limit the ways in which certain words are used. When these limits are ignored, some people might consider the usage incorrect.

In this dictionary, you are given *usage notes* that show how certain words are to be used, or that show the appropriate use of certain other words. Usage notes appear at the end of entries, as in the example below:

> **al·to·geth·er** (ôl′tə geth′ər, ôl′tə geth′ər), *adv.* **1.** completely; entirely: *I am altogether certain that I mailed the letter this morning.* **2.** with everything or everyone included; in all: *The bill came to ten dollars altogether.* **3.** with everything considered; on the whole: *Altogether, I'm glad it's over.*
> —**Usage.** *Altogether* is an adverb meaning "wholly, completely, entirely": *an altogether delightful afternoon.* It should not be confused with *all together,* which means "in a group": *They were all together in the kitchen.*

In this usage note, the difference between *altogether* and *all together* is explained. In the usage note at the end of the entry for **among,** you find this information about *among* and *between:*

> —**Usage.** In careful English, the difference between *among* and *between* is important. *Among* is used when three or more things or persons are involved, *between* when only two are mentioned: *The apple pie was divided among the four of us. He stepped between John and me.*

In the usage notes for *altogether* and *among,* the correct usage of *altogether, all together, among,* and *between* is explained. If you look up the word **between,** the usage note for *between* will refer you to **among.** Such referral is called a *cross reference.* To save space in dictionaries, information related to several words may be given under only one of them rather than repeated at each. When this is done, a cross reference will refer you to the entry where the information may be found.

Not all usage notes explain how two different words, such as *altogether* and *all together,* should be used. Nor do all of them contain cross references. In some usage notes, such as the one for *Asiatic,* you are told that some people consider the use of *Asiatic* offensive when applied to themselves:

> **—Usage.** Although *Asiatic* is often used as a variant of *Asian,* it is sometimes regarded as offensive when used in referring to the people of that continent. Careful speakers and writers, therefore, refer to them as *Asians* rather than *Asiatics.*

Each italicized word below is used incorrectly. Write each sentence on a sheet of paper, inserting the correct word for the italicized word. Then check your corrections with the usage notes in this dictionary.

SUGGESTED ACTIVITY 45

a. She is an *alumnus* of the University of Texas.
b. Be careful that you don't *bust* the vase.
c. There is no one but *myself* who can do it.
d. These apples taste good *like* apples should.
e. Myra felt *badly* about being late for the party.
f. Miss Roberts, *can* I go to the library?

PRONUNCIATION KEY

The symbol (′), as in **moth·er** (muth′ər) and **Grand′ Can′yon,** is used to show primary, or heavy, stress; the syllable preceding it is pronounced with greater emphasis than the other syllables in the word or phrase. The symbol (′), as in **grand·moth·er** (grand′muth′ər) and **Marine′ Corps′,** is used to show secondary, or lighter, stress. A syllable marked for secondary stress is pronounced with less emphasis than one marked for primary stress, but with more emphasis than those having no stress mark at all.

a	act, bat	**m**	my, simmer, him	**w**	west, away	
ā	aid, cape, way			**y**	yes, lawyer	
â(r)	air, dare	**n**	now, sinner, on			
ä	alms, art, calm	**n̅g**	sing, Washington	**z**	zeal, lazy, those	
				zh	vision, pleasure	
b	back, cabin, cab	**o**	ox, box, wasp			
		ō	over, boat, no	**ə**	occurs only in unac-	
ch	chief, butcher, beach	**ô**	ought, ball, before		cented syllables and in-	
		oi	oil, joint, joy		dicates the sound of	
d	do, rudder, bed	**o̅o̅**	book, poor		a *in* alone	
		o̅o̅	ooze, fool, too		e *in* system	
e	ebb, set	**ou**	out, loud, prow		i *in* easily	
ē	equal, seat, bee				o *in* gallop	
ēr	ear, mere				u *in* circus	
		p	pot, supper, stop			
f	fit, differ, puff			**ə**	occurs in unaccented	
		r	read, hurry, near		syllables before **l** pre-	
g	give, trigger, beg				ceded by **t, d,** or **n,** or	
		s	see, passing, miss		before **n** preceded by **t**	
h	hit, behave, hear	**sh**	shoe, fashion, push		or **d,** as in	
hw	white, nowhere				**cra·dle** (krād′əl)	
		t	ten, butter, bit		**red·den** (red′ən)	
i	if, big, mirror	**th**	thin, ether, path		**met·al** (met′əl)	
ī	ice, pirate, deny	**th**	that, either, smooth		**men·tal** (men′təl)	
					and in accented syllables	
j	just, badger, fudge	**u**	up, love		between **ī** and **r,** as in	
		û(r)	urge, burn, cur		**fire** (fīər)	
k	kept, token, make	**yo̅o̅**	use, fuse		**hire** (hīər)	
l	low, mellow, all	**v**	voice, river, live			

ABBREVIATIONS USED IN THIS DICTIONARY

ab.	about	**esp.**	especially	**NW**	northwest
abbr.	abbreviation	**etc.**	et cetera (and so on)	**pl.**	plural
adj.	adjective	**fol.**	followed or following	**prep.**	preposition
adv.	adverb	**ft.**	foot or feet	**pron.**	pronoun
c	circa (about)	**illus.**	illustration	**S**	south or southern
cap(s).	capital letter(s)	**interj.**	interjection	**SE**	southeast
Cap.	capital city	**l.c.**	lower case (small letter)	**sing.**	singular
Chem.	chemistry	**mi.**	mile or miles	**sq.**	square
conj.	conjunction	**N**	north or northern	**SW**	southwest
def(s).	definition(s)	**n.**	noun	**v.**	verb
E	east or eastern	**NE**	northeast	**W**	west or western

A

A, a (ā), *n., pl.* **A's** *or* **As, a's** *or* **as.** 1. the first letter of the English alphabet. 2. **from A to Z,** from beginning to end; thoroughly: *He knows chemistry from A to Z.*

a (ə; *when stressed* ā), *indefinite article.* 1. one or a particular one of a group or kind: *A man is at the door. Socrates was a Greek.* 2. any: *A horse could jump that fence.* —*prep.* 3. every; each; for each: *three times a day; 50 cents a ride.* See also **an.**

A, 1. ampere; amperes. 2. area.

A, 1. (in some grading systems) a grade or mark indicating scholastic work of the highest quality. 2. *Chem.* a symbol for **argon.** 3. a major blood group or type.

a-, a prefix 1. meaning on: *afire; afoot;* in: *abed;* to: *ashore;* at: *aside.* 2. meaning of or from: *anew; akin; afresh.* 3. meaning not: *atypical;* without: *amoral.* 4. used to form verbs **a.** from nouns: *amass.* **b.** from adjectives: *abase.*

A., answer.

a., acre; acres.

A.A., antiaircraft artillery.

A.A.A., Automobile Association of America.

AAF, Army Air Force. Also, **A.A.F.**

AAM, air-to-air missile.

aard·vark (ärd/värk/), *n.* an African anteater having a long snout and tongue and feeding on ants and termites. [from an Afrikaans word meaning "earth pig"]

Aar·on (âr/ən, ar/ən), *n.* (in the Bible) the brother of Moses, and the first high priest of the Hebrews.

Aardvark
(total length 5½ ft.)

AB, a major blood group or type.

ab., about.

a·back (ə bak/), *adv.* **taken aback,** surprised or confused; upset: *I was taken aback by his rude answer.* [from a Middle English word, which comes from the Old English phrase *on bæc* "to the back"]

ab·a·cus (ab/ə kəs), *n.* a simple calculating device in which beads on rods or in grooves are used as counters. It has been in use since ancient times, esp. in the Orient.

Abacus

a·baft (ə baft/), *prep.* 1. (on a ship) nearer the stern than; aft of or to the rear of: *abaft the mainmast.* —*adv.* 2. toward the stern; astern; aft.

ab·a·lo·ne (ab/ə lō/nē), *n.* a shellfish of the snail family, having a flat, round shell that is lined with mother-of-pearl. Its flesh is used for food.

a·ban·don (ə ban/dən), *v.* 1. to leave completely; desert; forsake: *to abandon a sinking ship; to abandon a friend in need.* 2. to give up or discontinue: *to abandon hope; to abandon a plan.* —*n.* 3. a complete giving over of oneself to a feeling or impulse: *He fought with abandon.* —**a·ban/don·ment,** *n.*

a·ban·doned (ə ban/dənd), *adj.* 1. left alone or behind; deserted; forsaken: *an abandoned cat; an abandoned building.* 2. having no shame or self-control; wicked; immoral: *an evil, abandoned man.* —**a·ban/doned·ly,** *adv.*

a·base (ə bās/), *v.,* **a·based, a·bas·ing.** to lower in rank or reputation; make less important or powerful; degrade; humble: *He abased himself by begging for food.* —**a·base/ment,** *n.*

a·bash (ə bash/), *v.* to make ashamed, embarrassed, or confused: *She was abashed when we all laughed at her.* —**a·bash·ed·ly** (ə bash/id lē), *adv.* —**a·bash/ed·ness,** *n.* —**a·bash/ment,** *n.*

a·bate (ə bāt/), *v.,* **a·bat·ed, a·bat·ing.** to make or become less in amount, force, or intensity; decrease; diminish: *The tax was abated. The storm abated.* —**a·bate/ment,** *n.*

ab·bé (a bā/, ab/ā), *n.* 1. an abbot. 2. a title of a priest or clergyman.

ab·bess (ab/is), *n.* a woman who is head of a convent of nuns; mother superior.

ab·bey (ab/ē), *n., pl.* **ab·beys.** 1. a group of monks or nuns living in a monastery or convent. 2. the building or buildings of a monastery or convent. 3. a church that is or was once part of a monastery or convent: *Westminster Abbey.*

ab·bot (ab/ət), *n.* the head of a monastery. —**ab/bot·cy, ab/bot·ship/,** *n.*

abbr., abbrev., abbreviation. Also, **abbrev.**

ab·bre·vi·ate (ə brē/vē āt/), *v.,* **ab·bre·vi·at·ed, ab·bre·vi·at·ing.** 1. to shorten (a word or phrase) by omitting letters: *Rhode Island is abbreviated "R.I."* 2. to make shorter; condense: *to abbreviate a speech.* —**ab·bre/vi·a/tor,** *n.*

ab·bre·vi·a·tion (ə brē/vē ā/shən), *n.* 1. a shortened form, esp. of a word or phrase. In this book "esp." is the abbreviation for "especially." 2. a shortening or condensing of something.

ABC (ā/bē/sē/), *n., pl.* **ABC's** or **ABCs.** 1. the basic facts and rules: *the ABC of electricity.* 2. **ABC's,** the alphabet.

ab·di·cate (ab/di kāt/), *v.,* **ab·di·cat·ed, ab·di·cat·ing.** 1. to resign from (a throne or being king): *Edward VIII abdicated the throne to marry a commoner.* 2. to give up or resign from (any high position or responsibility): *He abdicated his leadership of the group.* —**ab/di·ca/tion,** *n.* —**ab/di·ca/tor,** *n.*

ab·do·men (ab/də mən, ab dō/mən), *n.* 1. (in man and in animals with backbones) the part of the body between the chest and the hips, containing the stomach and other organs of digestion; belly. 2. (in insects and related animals) the rear section of the body. —**ab·dom·i·nal** (ab dom/ə nəl), *adj.* —**ab·dom/i·nal·ly,** *adv.*

ab·duct (ab dukt/), *v.* to kidnap or carry off by force or trickery. —**ab·duc/tion,** *n.* —**ab·duc/tor,** *n.*

a·beam (ə bēm/), *adv., adj.* at or perpendicular to the side of a ship: *We saw the enemy ship sailing abeam. The wind is directly abeam.*

a·bed (ə bed/), *adv.* in bed: *to lie abed till noon.*

A·bel (ā/bəl), *n.* (in the Bible) the second son of Adam and Eve, slain by his older brother, Cain.

ab·er·ra·tion (ab/ə rā/shən), *n.* 1. a departure or deviation from what is right, normal, or usual: *Aberrations in climate can ruin crops.* 2. a minor mental disorder. 3. the failure of a lens or mirror to focus light rays sharply. —**ab·er·rant** (ə ber/ənt), *adj.*

a·bet (ə bet/), *v.,* **a·bet·ted, a·bet·ting.** to help or encourage (someone), esp. in doing something wrong: *to abet a criminal.* —**a·bet/tor, a·bet/ter,** *n.*

a·bey·ance (ə bā/əns), *n.* the state of being postponed or set aside for future action: *Plans for the class trip are in abeyance until after exams.*

ab·hor (ab hôr/), *v.,* **ab·horred, ab·hor·ring.** to feel disgust or hate for; loathe: *Elephants abhor mice.*

ab·hor·rence (ab hôr/əns), *n.* a feeling of disgust, loathing, or hate: *an abhorrence of dirt.*

ab·hor·rent (ab hôr/ənt), *adj.* disgusting or loathsome; hateful: *Snakes are abhorrent to Eloise.* —**ab·hor/rent·ly,** *adv.*

a·bide (ə bīd/), *v.,* **a·bode** (ə bōd/) or **a·bid·ed; a·bid·ing.** 1. to remain; stay: *Abide with me.* 2. to have one's home; dwell: *animals abiding in the forest.* 3. to be able to last or continue for a long time. 4. to put up with; endure; stand: *She can't abide noise.* 5. **abide by,** to accept and follow: *to abide by the rules.*

a·bid·ing (ə bī/ding), *adj.* continuing without lessening; lasting: *an abiding faith.* —**a·bid/ing·ly,** *adv.*

a·bil·i·ty (ə bil/i tē), *n., pl.* **a·bil·i·ties.** 1. the power or capacity to do something: *the ability to make yourself understood.* 2. natural skill; talent: *Music is only one of her abilities.*

-ability, a suffix used to form nouns meaning 1. ability; capability: *readability.* 2. tendency: *changeability.*

ab·ject (ab/jekt, ab jekt/), *adj.* 1. utterly hopeless; wretched: *abject poverty.* 2. lacking spirit or courage; contemptible; base: *an abject coward.* —**ab·ject·ly** (ab jekt/lē, ab/jekt lē), *adv.* —**ab·ject/ness,** *n.*

ab·jure (ab jŏŏr/), *v.,* **ab·jured, ab·jur·ing.** to swear to renounce or give up (something): *to abjure falsehoods.* —**ab/ju·ra/tion,** *n.* —**ab·jur/er,** *n.*

a·blaze (ə blāz/), *adj.* 1. on fire; in flames: *The house was ablaze.* 2. shining brightly; gleaming with light or color: *a room ablaze with candlelight.* 3. excited; burning with emotion: *ablaze with enthusiasm.*

a·ble (ā/bəl), *adj.,* **a·bler, a·blest.** 1. having the power, skill, means, or right to do something: *He is able to build a house. We are able to buy a car.* 2. competent; talented or skilled: *an able lawyer.* 3. showing talent or skill: *an able performance.*

-able, a suffix used to form adjectives meaning 1. able to be: *readable.* 2. tending to: *changeable.*

a·ble-bod·ied (ā/bəl bod/ēd), *adj.* having a strong, healthy body; physically fit: *We need three more able-bodied men for the job.*

a/ble-bod/ied sea/man, a sailor in the merchant marine who has passed an examination on his ability.

ab·lu·tion (ə bloo/shən), *n.* 1. a washing of the body, hands, feet, etc., as part of a religious ceremony. 2. **ablutions,** a washing of the body or of any part of the body.

a·bly (ā/blē), *adv.* in an able way; with skill or ability: *She skated ably.*

ab·ne·ga·tion (ab/nə gā/shən), *n.* a giving up of a privilege, convenience, or comfort; self-denial.

ab·nor·mal (ab nôr/məl), *adj.* different from what is usual or normal; not typical: *He drinks an abnormal amount of coffee. Cold weather is abnormal in San Juan.* —**ab·nor/mal·ly,** *adv.*

ab·nor·mal·i·ty (ab/nôr mal/i tē), *n., pl.* **ab·nor·mal·i·ties.** 1. an abnormal condition. 2. something that is abnormal: *surgery to correct an abnormality.*

a·board (ə bôrd/), *adv.* 1. on, in, or into a ship, train, airplane, etc.: *All aboard!* —*prep.* 2. on board of: *We slept aboard the ship.*

a·bode (ə bōd/), *n.* 1. a person's home; the place where one lives: *a small but cozy abode.* —*v.* 2. a past tense and past participle of **abide.**

a·bol·ish (ə bol/ish), *v.* to eliminate completely; put an end to: *to abolish slavery.*

ab·o·li·tion (ab/ə lish/ən), *n.* 1. the elimination, destruction, or ending of something: *the abolition of* *unjust laws.* 2. the passing of laws to end Negro slavery in the U.S. before the Civil War.

ab·o·li·tion·ist (ab/ə lish/ə nist), *n. (sometimes cap.)* a person who wants to abolish something, esp. one who favored the abolition of slavery in the U.S. before the Civil War.

A-bomb (ā/bom/), *n.* another word for **atomic bomb.**

a·bom·i·na·ble (ə bom/ə nə bəl), *adj.* 1. arousing hate or loathing; detestable: *an abominable war.* 2. very unpleasant; disagreeable: *abominable weather.* 3. very bad; very poor: *Your work has been abominable.* [from the Latin word *abōminābilis* "hateful," which comes from *ab-* "away from" + *ōmen* "omen." The original meaning was "to be avoided as an evil omen"] —**a·bom/i·na·bly,** *adv.*

Abom/inable Snow/man, a large, hairy, manlike creature that is reported to live in the Himalayas. [from the translation of the Tibetan word *metoh-kangmi,* which comes from *metoh* "foul" + *kangmi* "snowman"]

a·bom·i·nate (ə bom/ə nāt/), *v.,* **a·bom·i·nat·ed, a·bom·i·nat·ing.** to feel hate and loathing for; think of with disgust: *to abominate cruelty to animals.*

a·bom·i·na·tion (ə bom/ə nā/shən), *n.* 1. something abominable, hateful, or very bad: *I think snakes are an abomination.* 2. a strong feeling of hate, loathing, or disgust.

ab·o·rig·i·ne (ab/ə rij/ə nē), *n.* a member of the first or earliest-known people of a country or region: *The Australian aborigines still live in the Stone Age.* [from the Latin phrase *ab orīgine* "from the beginning"] —**ab·o·rig·i·nal** (ab/ə rij/ə nəl), *adj.*

a·bor·tion (ə bôr/shən), *n.* 1. the birth of a fetus or embryo before it is able to live; miscarriage. 2. an idea, project, etc., that has failed to develop fully. —**a·bor/tive,** *adj.*

a·bound (ə bound/), *v.* 1. to exist in great numbers; be plentiful: *Fish abound along these shores.* 2. **abound in** (or **with**), to have much of; be filled with: *The hills abound in rich minerals.*

a·bout (ə bout/), *prep.* 1. of or concerning: *a movie about the Civil War.* 2. in the nature of; connected with: *There is something frightening about this place.* 3. in, on, or somewhere near: *He is about the house.* 4. on the verge of; just ready: *We are about to leave.* 5. around: *a fence about the playground.* —*adv.* 6. close to; approximately: *to walk about a mile.* 7. here and there; all around: *to run about; to look about.* 8. in the opposite direction; halfway around: *Turn the car about.* —*adj.* 9. moving around; doing things: *He was up and about very early.*

a·bout-face (ə bout/fās/), *n.* 1. a quick turn in the opposite direction. 2. a complete, sudden change in behavior, ideas, etc.: *He did an about-face after promising to go.* —*v.,* **a·bout-faced, a·bout-fac·ing.** 3. to turn in the opposite direction. 4. to change one's behavior, opinions, etc., esp. suddenly or without warning.

a·bove (ə buv/), *adv.* 1. in or to a higher place; overhead or farther up: *the sky above; the floor above.* 2. before or earlier, esp. in a book or other piece of writing: *the quotation given above.* —*prep.* 3. in or to a higher place than; over: *to fly above the earth; the floor above ours.* 4. more than; over: *all boys above 12; loads above a ton.* 5. higher in rank or power than: *A captain is above a lieutenant.* 6. incapable of by nature; superior to: *He is above lying.* 7. north of; beyond: *above the border; above the bend in the river.* —*adj.* 8. written or mentioned before: *Look at the above questions.* —*n.* 9. heaven: *a gift from above.* 10. **above all,** most important of all: *Above all, don't be late for dinner.*

a·bove·board (ə buv/bôrd/), *adv., adj.* in an open way; without tricks; straightforward: *He is both honest and aboveboard.*

ab·ra·ca·dab·ra (ab/rə kə dab/rə), *n.* 1. a word that supposedly has magical powers. 2. any sort of nonsense or gibberish: *a speech full of abracadabra.*

a·brade (ə brād/), *v.,* **a·brad·ed, a·brad·ing.** to wear down or away by friction; scrape; rub: *Sand abrades the sea shells. A soft material abrades easily.*

A·bra·ham (ā/brə ham/), *n.* (in the Bible) the father of Isaac and founder of the Hebrew nation.

a·bra·sion (ə brā/zhən), *n.* 1. a scraped spot or area, as on the skin: *an abrasion on the elbow.* 2. the act or process of scraping, rubbing, or wearing away.

a·bra·sive (ə brā/siv), *n.* 1. a material or substance, such as sandpaper, that is used for grinding or smoothing. —*adj.* 2. causing or able to cause abrasion: *the abrasive effect of wind on rocks.* —**a·bra/sive·ly,** *adv.* —**a·bra/sive·ness,** *n.*

a·breast (ə brest/), *adv., adj.* 1. side by side in a line: *They walked three abreast.* 2. **abreast of** (or **with**), up-to-date on; equal to in achievement: *to keep abreast of current events.*

a·bridge (ə brij/), *v.,* **a·bridged, a·bridg·ing.** 1. to reduce in size, length, etc., by shortening; cut: *to abridge a novel.* 2. to make less; reduce or take away completely: *to abridge all privileges.* [from the Old French word *abregier,* which comes from Latin *abbreviāre* "to abbreviate"] —**a·bridg/a·ble,** *adj.*

a·bridg·ment (ə brij/mənt), *n.* 1. a shortened form of a book, speech, etc. 2. the act or process of abridging something.

a·broad (ə brôd/), *adv.* 1. in or to a foreign country or countries: *a trip abroad; to study abroad.* 2. out of doors: *I never go abroad at this time of night.* 3. all around; in wide circulation: *Rumors are abroad.*

ab·ro·gate (ab/rə gāt/), *v.,* **ab·ro·gat·ed, ab·ro·gat·ing.** to cancel; put an end to; abolish: *to abrogate a law.* —**ab/ro·ga/tion,** *n.*

ab·rupt (ə brupt/), *adj.* 1. sudden or unexpected: *an abrupt turn in the road.* 2. curt in speech or manner; blunt: *an abrupt good-by.* 3. steep: *an abrupt descent.* —**ab·rupt/ly,** *adv.* —**ab·rupt/ness,** *n.*

ab·scess (ab/ses), *n.* a pocket of pus in any part of the body, usually causing a painful sore.

---

act, āble, dâre, ärt; ebb, ēqual; if, īce; hot, ōver, ôrder; oil; boŏk; ooze; out; up, ûrge; ə = *a* as in *alone;* ˀ as in *button* (but/ˀn), *fire* (fiˀr); ᴄhief; ѕhoe; thin; ŧħat; zh as in *measure* (mezh/ər). See full key inside cover.

ab·scessed (ab′sest), *adj.* having an abscess: *an abscessed tooth.*

ab·scis·sa (ab sis′ə), *n.* the distance of a point measured horizontally from the vertical axis of a graph.

ab·scond (ab skond′), *v.* to leave suddenly and secretly, esp. to avoid being found out or captured: *The butler absconded with the jewels.*

ab·sence (ab′səns), *n.* 1. the state of being away or not being present: *His absence was noted by his teacher.* 2. a period of being away: *an absence of several days.* 3. a lack; state of being without something: *an absence of proof.*

ab·sent (ab′sənt), *adj.* 1. not in a certain place at a given time; missing: *Was she absent from assembly?* 2. lacking; nonexistent: *His proof was absent.* —*v.* (ab sent′). 3. to take or keep (oneself) away: *to absent oneself from school.*

ab·sen·tee (ab′sən tē′), *n.* a person who is absent or away, as from school, a job, etc. —**ab′sen·tee′ism,** *n.*

ab·sent·ly (ab′sənt lē), *adv.* in an absent-minded way; inattentively.

ab·sent-mind·ed (ab′sənt mīn′did), *adj.* so lost in thought that one does not realize what one is doing, what is happening, etc. —**ab′sent-mind′ed·ly,** *adv.* —**ab′sent-mind′ed·ness,** *n.*

ab·so·lute (ab′sə lo͞ot′), *adj.* 1. free from restrictions or limitation; unconditional: *absolute authority; an absolute monarch.* 2. not mixed; pure; perfect: *absolute alcohol.* 3. complete; outright: *an absolute lie.* 4. positive; certain: *absolute proof.*

ab·so·lute·ly (ab′sə lo͞ot′lē, ab′sə lo͞ot′lē), *adv.* 1. entirely; completely: *absolutely wrong.* 2. positively; certainly: *absolutely essential.* —*interj.* 3. certainly; without a doubt: *Will you be there? Absolutely!*

ab′solute ze′ro, the lowest temperature that any matter can have, equal to −273.16°C or −459.7°F: in theory, the temperature at which all molecular motion stops.

ab·so·lu·tion (ab′sə lo͞o′shən), *n.* a pardon from punishment; forgiveness for sins.

ab·solve (ab zolv′, ab solv′), *v.*, **ab·solved, ab·solv·ing.** 1. to pardon or forgive (sin, wrongdoing, etc.): *to absolve a person's sins.* 2. to find (a person) not guilty: *to absolve a man of a crime.* 3. to free (a person) from a duty, promise, etc.: *to be absolved from one's oath.* —**ab·solv′er,** *n.*

ab·sorb (ab sôrb′, ab zôrb′), *v.* 1. to soak up (liquid): *A blotter absorbs ink.* 2. to take in completely; make a part of oneself or itself: *He absorbed the entire lesson. The empire absorbed the smaller nations.* 3. to take all the attention of: *The movie completely absorbed him.* 4. to take up (sound, light, etc.) without reflection: *A cork wall absorbs sounds.* —**ab·sorb′a·ble,** *adj.*

ab·sorb·ent (ab sôr′bənt, ab zôr′bənt), *adj.* 1. capable of absorbing: *absorbent cotton.* —*n.* 2. a material or substance that can absorb something.

ab·sorb·ing (ab sôr′biṅg, ab zôr′biṅg), *adj.* extremely interesting: *an absorbing book.*

ab·sorp·tion (ab sôrp′shən, ab zôrp′shən), *n.* 1. the act or process of absorbing: *The water was taken up*

by absorption. 2. complete attention; the state of being completely occupied: *Because of his absorption in the game, he forgot to feed the dog.*

ab·stain (ab stān′), *v.* 1. to deny oneself; refrain (usually fol. by *from*): *to abstain from fattening foods.* 2. to refrain from voting: *Ten members voted "yes," and two abstained.* —**ab·stain′er,** *n.*

ab·ste·mi·ous (ab stē′mē əs), *adj.* moderate or sparing in one's eating and drinking: *an abstemious life.* —**ab·ste′mi·ous·ly,** *adv.*

ab·sten·tion (ab sten′shən), *n.* 1. the act of abstaining or denying oneself something: *abstention from smoking.* 2. the act or an instance of withholding one's vote: *three ayes, two noes, and one abstention.*

ab·sti·nence (ab′stə nəns), *n.* the restraining of one's appetites, esp. for rich food, alcoholic liquors, pleasures, etc.: *to practice abstinence during Lent.*

ab·stract (ab′strakt, ab strakt′), *adj.* 1. general rather than specific: *Goodness is an abstract idea, but good deeds are concrete examples of it.* 2. theoretical; not for practical purposes: *abstract science.* 3. of or referring to a style of art that emphasizes design, color, etc., rather than portraying actual objects: *an abstract painting.* —*n.* (ab′strakt). 4. a summary: *an abstract of a long article.* —*v.* (ab strakt′ for def. 5, ab′strakt for def. 6). 5. to separate; take out or away: *to abstract gold from ore.* 6. to make a summary of; summarize: *to abstract a long article.* —**ab·stract′er,** *n.* —**ab′stract·ly,** *adv.* —**ab′stract·ness,** *n.*

ab·strac·tion (ab strak′shən), *n.* 1. an abstract or general idea or term, as "redness" or "beauty." 2. the act or process of forming an abstract idea. 3. the act or process of taking away or separating: *The feeling of cold is due to the abstraction of heat from our bodies.*

ab·struse (ab stro͞os′), *adj.* hard to understand; obscure. —**ab·struse′ly,** *adv.* —**ab·struse′ness,** *n.*

ab·surd (ab sûrd′, ab zûrd′), *adj.* ridiculously senseless; contrary to reason or common sense: *an absurd explanation.* —**ab·surd′ly,** *adv.*

ab·surd·i·ty (ab sûr′di tē, ab zûr′di tē), *n., pl.* **ab·surd·i·ties.** 1. the state or quality of being absurd; foolishness; ridiculousness: *The absurdity of his dance made us laugh.* 2. something absurd, senseless, ridiculous, etc.: *Her story was full of absurdities.*

A·bu Dha·bi (ä′bo͞o dä′bē), the capital city of the United Arab Emirates, in the SE part.

a·bun·dance (ə bun′dəns), *n.* an amount that is ample or more than enough; an extremely plentiful supply: *an abundance of fish in the sea.*

a·bun·dant (ə bun′dənt), *adj.* 1. present in great quantity; plentiful; more than enough: *an abundant supply of water.* 2. having in great quantity; abounding (usually fol. by *in*): *a city abundant in museums.* —**a·bun′dant·ly,** *adv.*

a·buse (ə byo͞oz′), *v.*, **a·bused, a·bus·ing.** 1. to use in a wrong, improper, or unfair way; misuse: *The foreman abused his authority by giving his friends special favors.* 2. to treat in a way that is harmful, hurtful, or cruel: *to abuse one's eyes by reading in a bad light; to abuse a dog by kicking it.* 3. to insult (a person);

speak meanly or harshly to or about. —*n.* (ə byōōs′).
4. wrong, improper, or unfair use; misuse: *an abuse of
authority.* **5.** harmful or cruel treatment. **6.** insulting
or harsh language. **7.** an improper or unjust custom
or practice: *the abuses of bad government.*

a·bu·sive (ə byōō′siv), *adj.* **1.** using or containing insulting or harsh language: *an abusive person; abusive
remarks.* **2.** causing harm; hurtful or cruel: *abusive
punishment.* **3.** wrongly used; improper, unjust, or
corrupt: *an abusive use of one's authority.* —**a·bu′
sive·ly,** *adv.* —**a·bu′sive·ness,** *n.*

a·but (ə but′), *v.,* **a·but·ted, a·but·ting. 1.** to touch or
join at the edge or border (often fol. by *on*): *The
field abuts on a highway.* **2.** to be
next to; border on; end at: *a wall
abutting the church.*

a·but·ment (ə but′mənt), *n.* a supporting structure for an arch, wall,
road, etc., esp. a structure that

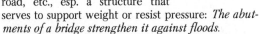

A, Abutment

serves to support weight or resist pressure: *The abut-
ments of a bridge strengthen it against floods.*

a·bys·mal (ə biz′məl), *adj.* of or like an abyss; too
great to be measured: *abysmal poverty; abysmal ignorance.* —**a·bys′mal·ly,** *adv.*

a·byss (ə bis′), *n.* a deep, bottomless space or gulf; a
vast chasm.

Ab·ys·sin·i·a (ab′i sin′ē ə), *n.* former name of **Ethiopia.** —**Ab′ys·sin′i·an,** *n., adj.*

AC, alternating current. Also, **A.C., ac, a.c.**

Ac, *Chem.* the symbol for **actinium.**

a·ca·cia (ə kā′shə), *n.* **1.** a tree or shrub with feathery
leaves, small yellow or white flowers, and thorny
stems. **2.** the locust tree.

ac·a·dem·ic (ak′ə dem′ik), *adj.* **1.** of or referring to a
school or academy. **2.** scholarly; of or referring to
studies or scholarship. **3.** of or referring to a general
or liberal education rather than to a technical or specialized education: *The town has two academic high
schools and a trade school.* **4.** not useful or practical;
theoretical: *to raise academic questions.* —**ac′a·dem′
i·cal·ly,** *adv.*

a·cad·e·my (ə kad′ə mē), *n., pl.* **a·cad·e·mies. 1.** a
high school, esp. a private one. **2.** a school or college
for special instruction or
training: *a military academy.* **3.** an association for
the advancement of art,
literature, or science.
[from the Greek word
Akadēmia, the name of a
grove near Athens, where
the philosopher Plato
gathered with his stu-
dents]

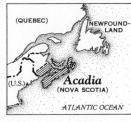

(QUEBEC)   NEWFOUND-
LAND

(U.S.)   **Acadia**
(NOVA SCOTIA)

ATLANTIC OCEAN

A·ca·di·a (ə kā′dē ə), *n.* a former French colony in
SE Canada, ceded to Great Britain in 1713: now
Nova Scotia. —**A·ca′di·an,** *n., adj.*

ac·cede (ak sēd′), *v.,* **ac·ced·ed, ac·ced·ing. 1.** to give
consent or approval; agree: *to accede to a request.* **2.**

to attain a position, title, etc. (usually fol. by *to*): *to
accede to the throne.*

ac·cel·er·ate (ak sel′ə rāt′), *v.,* **ac·cel·er·at·ed, ac·cel·
er·at·ing. 1.** to cause to move, develop, or happen
more quickly: *to accelerate an automobile; to accelerate the growth of plants.* **2.** to move faster: *The train
suddenly accelerated.* —**ac·cel′er·a′tion,** *n.*

ac·cel·er·a·tor (ak sel′ə rā′tər), *n.* **1.** a device, substance, etc., that increases the speed of something. **2.**
the gas pedal of an automobile, used to control the
speed of the engine.

ac·cent (ak′sent), *n.* **1.** the emphasis or stress put on
a syllable, word, or note of music: *In "baboon" the
accent is on the second syllable.* **2.** a mark (′) usually
placed following a syllable to show where a word
should be emphasized, as in *Mar′y, Mar′y, quite′
contrar′y.* **3.** a mark (′) showing how certain vowels
are to be pronounced in foreign words. In French,
"é" is pronounced "ā." **4.** a particular or special way
of pronouncing: *a foreign accent; a Southern accent.*
—*v.* (ak′sent, ak sent′). **5.** to pronounce with emphasis or stress: *to accent the first word of "White
House"; to accent one's words carefully.* **6.** to emphasize or stress; accentuate: *to accent the importance of
reading instructions.*

ac·cen·tu·ate (ak sen′chōō āt′), *v.,* **ac·cen·tu·at·ed, ac·
cen·tu·at·ing.** to emphasize; stress; point up: *The
President's speech accentuated the need for peace.*
—**ac·cen′tu·a′tion,** *n.*

ac·cept (ak sept′), *v.* **1.** to take or receive (something
offered): *to accept gifts.* **2.** to agree or consent to; receive with approval: *to accept an apology.* **3.** to assume (a duty, obligation, etc.); undertake: *She
accepted the responsibility for the job.*

—**Usage.** *Accept* and *except* are sometimes confused
because of their similarity in sound. *Accept* means
"to take or receive": *I accept this gift. Except* means
"to omit or exclude": *Bill and Fred were excepted
from punishment.*

ac·cept·a·ble (ak sep′tə bəl), *adj.* **1.** capable or
worthy of being accepted; satisfactory; agreeable: *an
acceptable suggestion.* **2.** barely satisfactory: *Your
work should be outstanding instead of just acceptable.* —**ac·cept′a·bly,** *adv.* —**ac·cept′a·bil′i·ty, ac·
cept′a·ble·ness,** *n.*

ac·cept·ance (ak sep′təns), *n.* **1.** the act of taking or
receiving something offered: *His acceptance of bribes
got him into trouble.* **2.** approval; favorable reception: *Her suggestions met with acceptance.* **3.** the act
of believing something; assent to the truth of something: *the acceptance of a theory.*

ac·cess (ak′ses), *n.* **1.** the ability or permission to
speak with someone, use something, enter a place,
etc.: *We have access to the top-secret files.* **2.** a means
of reaching or entering something; approach: *The
country needs access to the sea.*

ac·ces·si·ble (ak ses′ə bəl), *adj.* **1.** possible to approach, enter, speak with, or use: *The new principal
was accessible to all the students.* **2.** able to be used,

obtained, entered, etc.: *accessible information.* —**ac·ces′si·bil′i·ty,** *n.* —**ac·ces′si·bly,** *adv.*

ac·ces·sion (ak sesh′ən), *n.* **1.** the act of taking possession of a right, title, office, etc.: *accession to the throne.* **2.** the act of adding or acquiring something: *The nation grew larger by the accession of new territories.* **3.** something added; addition: *New accessions to the library include 50 novels.*

ac·ces·so·ry (ak ses′ə rē), *n., pl.* **ac·ces·so·ries. 1.** something that is added to increase usefulness or improve appearance: *The car's accessories include a spotlight.* **2.** an article of dress, such as gloves, a scarf, purse, or the like, that is not a part of one's basic outfit: *accessories for a new dress.* **3.** a person who knowingly helps or encourages another in a criminal act. —*adj.* **4.** being an addition or supplement; additional: *accessory touches of color.*

ac·ci·dent (ak′si dənt), *n.* **1.** an incident or event that happens unexpectedly or by chance: *The discovery was an accident.* **2.** a collision, injury, or other damaging or harmful event due to chance or carelessness: *There was an automobile accident on our street.* **3.** chance or luck: *I was there by accident.*

ac·ci·den·tal (ak′si den′t³l), *adj.* happening by chance or accident; unexpected; unplanned: *an accidental meeting.* —**ac′ci·den′tal·ly,** *adv.*

ac·claim (ə klām′), *v.* **1.** to greet with a show of approval or praise: *to acclaim the nation's heroes; to acclaim a new book.* **2.** to announce or proclaim with great approval: *They acclaimed him president.* —*n.* **3.** a show or expression of approval, such as shouts, praise, or applause: *an act that met with acclaim.*

ac·cla·ma·tion (ak′lə mā′shən), *n.* **1.** a loud shout, burst of applause, or other show of welcome and enthusiasm: *a great acclamation for the speaker.* **2.** an instance of praise or approval: *an acclamation in the daily press.* **3.** a voice vote indicating a decisive majority: *He was elected by acclamation.*

ac·cli·mate (ə klī′mit, ak′lə māt′), *v.,* **ac·cli·mat·ed, ac·cli·mat·ing.** to get used to or adapt to a new climate or new surroundings; acclimatize: *It took the new students a few days to become acclimated.* —**ac·cli·ma·tion** (ak′lə mā′shən), *n.*

ac·cli·ma·tize (ə klī′mə tīz′), *v.,* **ac·cli·ma·tized, ac·cli·ma·tiz·ing.** to acclimate.

ac·co·lade (ak′ə lād′), *n.* **1.** an award, honor, or great compliment: *The new play received accolades from the critics.* **2.** a ceremony by which a man was made a knight, usually a light tap on the shoulder with the flat side of a sword.

ac·com·mo·date (ə kom′ə dāt′), *v.,* **ac·com·mo·dat·ed, ac·com·mo·dat·ing. 1.** to do a kindness or a favor for; oblige; help: *to accommodate a friend with a loan.* **2.** to supply or provide (usually fol. by *with*): *to accommodate a friend with money.* **3.** to provide with a room, food, or other necessity: *The village couldn't accommodate all the refugees.* **4.** to adapt or adjust: *to accommodate oneself to having less money.* **5.** to have or make room for; hold: *Will this elevator accommodate ten people?*

ac·com·mo·dat·ing (ə kom′ə dā′tiṅg), *adj.* easy to deal with; helpful: *an accommodating salesman.* —**ac·com′mo·dat′ing·ly,** *adv.*

ac·com·mo·da·tion (ə kom′ə dā′shən), *n.* **1.** an agreement despite differences; adjustment; compromise: *If the two sides reach an accommodation, war can be avoided.* **2.** a change to fit new circumstances: *accommodation to life in a foreign country.* **3.** a favor, such as a loan; something that is needed or helpful. **4. accommodations,** lodging, or a seat, berth, etc., sometimes with food available: *We wrote for accommodations at the hotel.*

ac·com·pa·ni·ment (ə kum′pə ni mənt), *n.* **1.** something that goes along with something else: *The accompaniments of war are misery and sorrow.* **2.** a musical background for a voice, instrument, etc.: *a song with piano accompaniment.*

ac·com·pa·nist (ə kum′pə nist), *n.* a person who plays a musical accompaniment.

ac·com·pa·ny (ə kum′pə nē), *v.,* **ac·com·pa·nied, ac·com·pa·ny·ing. 1.** to go along or in company with: *to accompany a friend on a walk.* **2.** to happen or exist in connection with: *Thunder accompanies lightning.* **3.** to put together with something else: *to accompany a speech with gestures.* **4.** to play or sing an accompaniment for: *The pianist accompanied the singers.*

ac·com·plice (ə kom′plis), *n.* a person who knowingly helps another in a crime or other wrongdoing.

ac·com·plish (ə kom′plish), *v.* **1.** to bring to a successful conclusion; carry out: *The spy accomplished his mission.* **2.** to do; finish: *You would accomplish more if you didn't look out the window all day.*

ac·com·plished (ə kom′plisht), *adj.* **1.** completed or established: *Space flights are now an accomplished fact.* **2.** expert or skilled: *an accomplished pianist.*

ac·com·plish·ment (ə kom′plish mənt), *n.* **1.** the act or an instance of accomplishing or carrying out something: *We must work for the accomplishment of our plans.* **2.** something accomplished or done; achievement: *the accomplishments of scientists.* **3.** a special skill or knowledge: *A good game of tennis is just one of his many accomplishments.*

ac·cord (ə kôrd′), *v.* **1.** to be in agreement or harmony; agree: *Our views accord in this matter.* **2.** to grant; give as earned or due: *to accord praise for honesty.* —*n.* **3.** the state of being in agreement; harmony: *We are not in accord on the subject of new taxes.* **4. of one's own accord,** voluntarily: *I offered to help of my own accord.*

ac·cord·ance (ə kôr′d³ns), *n.* **1.** the state of conforming or being in agreement: *We must act in accordance with the rules.* **2.** the act of according or granting: *the accordance of praise where it is due.*

ac·cord·ing (ə kôr′diṅg), *adj.* **1.** agreeing: *The two reporters gave according accounts of the game.* **2. according to, a.** as said by or written in: *According to her the temperature is 68.* **b.** in accord or agreement with: *Play according to the rules.* **c.** in proportion to: *You'll be taxed according to your income.*

ac·cord·ing·ly (ə kôr′diṅg lē), *adv.* **1.** in a corresponding or suitable manner: *If he speaks to you po-*

litely, do answer him accordingly. **2.** thus; therefore.

ac·cor·di·on (ə kôr′dē ən), *n.* **1.** a musical instrument having a large bellows at the center: opening and closing the bellows forces wind past metal reeds, which are sounded by means of a keyboard. —*adj.* **2.** having folds like those in the bellows of an accordion: *a skirt with accordion pleats.*

Accordion

ac·cost (ə kôst′, ə kost′), *v.* to approach boldly and force to halt, esp. with a request or greeting: *The rioters accosted the prime minister and presented him with a list of their demands.* —**ac·cost′er,** *n.*

ac·count (ə kount′), *n.* **1.** a description or explanation: *Give us your account of what happened.* **2.** a cause for action; reason: *On this account, I'm refusing to give you permission.* **3.** importance or worth; value: *questions of no account.* **4.** an amount of money deposited with a bank. **5.** a charge account. **6.** a financial statement or record showing money received, paid out, and owed. —*v.* **7.** to consider or regard as: *He accounts himself lucky.* **8. account for, a.** to give an explanation for; explain: *How do you account for her change in attitude?* **b.** to be responsible for: *You will have to account for any shortage.* **c.** to cause; be the reason for: *Carelessness accounts for most accidents.* **9. on account,** as part payment of a debt: *I gave him $10 on account.* **10. on account of, a.** because of: *I can't go on account of the weather.* **b.** for the sake of: *He promised on account of our friendship.* **11. on no account,** not for any reason whatever: *On no account are you to leave without permission.* **12. on someone's account,** for the sake of someone: *Don't promise on my account.* **13. take into account,** to make allowance for; consider: *Also take into account the wind speed.*

ac·count·a·ble (ə koun′tə bəl), *adj.* responsible or answerable; in a position where one must give an explanation if required to: *They held him accountable for the mischief.* —**ac·count′a·bly,** *adv.*

ac·count·ant (ə koun′t°nt), *n.* a person whose job is to make or inspect financial reports of money that is spent, received, owed, etc.

ac·count·ing (ə koun′tiṅg), *n.* the method of setting up, keeping, and inspecting financial records, esp. the financial records of a business.

ac·cou·ter·ments (ə kōō′tər mənts), *n.pl.* **1.** equipment or accessories. **2.** the equipment of a soldier, excluding arms or clothing: *They brought few accouterments on the long march.* Also, *esp.* British, **ac·cou·tre·ments** (ə kōō′tər mənts, ə kōō′trə mənts).

Ac·cra (ak′rə, ə krä′), *n.* a seaport and the capital city of Ghana.

ac·cred·it (ə kred′it), *v.* **1.** to attribute to; consider as belonging to: *a discovery accredited to Einstein.* **2.** to provide with credentials of authority, official position, etc.: *to accredit a representative.* **3.** to accept as true; believe: *to accredit a newspaper story.*

ac·cre·tion (ə krē′shən), *n.* **1.** an increase in size by natural growth or by one thing being added to another: *Coral reefs grow by accretion.* **2.** an addition; something added: *This boulder was formed by accretions of many kinds of rock.*

ac·crue (ə krōō′), *v.,* **ac·crued, ac·cru·ing. 1.** to happen as a result of natural growth; follow automatically: *The benefits of good work accrue rapidly.* **2.** to be added regularly at a certain period of time: *Interest on savings accrues every three months.*

ac·cu·mu·late (ə kyōō′myə lāt′), *v.,* **ac·cu·mu·lat·ed, ac·cu·mu·lat·ing.** to heap up; gather together; collect: *Dust is accumulating under the bed.*

ac·cu·mu·la·tion (ə kyōō′myə lā′shən), *n.* **1.** the act or process of accumulating, piling up, or collecting: *His hobby was the accumulation of baseball cards.* **2.** something that is accumulated or piled up; heap; collection: *an accumulation of toys in the closet.*

ac·cu·ra·cy (ak′yər ə sē), *n.* the quality of being true, correct, or exact; correctness; exactness: *the accuracy of a watch; the accuracy of a story.*

ac·cu·rate (ak′yər it), *adj.* **1.** truthful; free from error: *What she says is accurate.* **2.** agreeing exactly with an original standard or model; exact: *an accurate copy of a picture.* **3.** very careful; not making mistakes: *an accurate speller.* —**ac′cu·rate·ly,** *adv.*

ac·curs·ed (ə kûr′sid, ə kûrst′), *adj.* **1.** under a curse; ruined: *The people fled from the accursed city.* **2.** deserving of curses; hateful; miserable: *Get that accursed dog out of the living room!* —**ac·curs·ed·ly** (ə kûr′sid lē), *adv.* —**ac·curs′ed·ness,** *n.*

ac·cu·sa·tion (ak′yōō zā′shən), *n.* **1.** the act of accusing a person of wrongdoing; a statement charging someone with blame or guilt: *Don't make accusations without proof!* **2.** a crime or offense with which a person is charged: *The accusation was murder.*

ac·cu·sa·tive (ə kyōō′zə tiv), *adj.* **1.** indicating or used as the direct object of a verb or the object of a preposition; objective. —*n.* **2.** the accusative case.

ac·cuse (ə kyōōz′), *v.,* **ac·cused, ac·cus·ing. 1.** to bring a charge against; charge with a fault, offense, or crime (usually fol. by *of*): *He accused her of treason. They were accused of kidnapping.* **2.** to blame: *You have no reason to accuse her.* —**ac·cus′ing·ly,** *adv.*

ac·cused (ə kyōōzd′), *adj.* **1.** charged with or blamed for a crime, fault, offense, etc.: *the accused boy.* —*n.* **2.** the person or persons on trial for a crime, offense, etc.: *Will the accused take the stand?*

ac·cus·tom (ə kus′təm), *v.* to make or get used to by custom or habit; habituate: *to accustom oneself to cold weather.*

ac·cus·tomed (ə kus′təmd), *adj.* **1.** customary; usual; habitual: *In their accustomed manner, they left early.* **2.** in the habit of; used to (usually fol. by *to* or an infinitive): *He is accustomed to staying up late.* —**ac·cus′tomed·ly,** *adv.* —**ac·cus′tomed·ness,** *n.*

AC/DC, usable on both alternating and direct current: *an AC/DC radio.* Also, **A.C./D.C., ac/dc, a.c./d.c.**

ace (ās), *n.* **1.** a playing card having a single mark in the center. **2.** a fighter pilot who has destroyed five enemy aircraft in flight. **3.** a very skilled person; expert: *an ace at tap-dancing.* —*adj.* **4.** of outstanding quality or skill; excellent: *an ace basketball player.*

ac·e·tate (as′i tāt′), *n.* **1.** a man-made fiber, or the cloth woven from it. **2.** a clear plastic sheet or film.

a·ce′tic ac′id (ə sē′tik, ə set′ik), a sharp-smelling acid found in vinegar and composed of carbon, oxygen, and hydrogen.

a·cet·y·lene (ə set′ªlēn′, ə set′ªlin), *n.* a gas that burns with a very hot flame: used in cutting and welding metals.

ache (āk), *v.,* **ached, ach·ing. 1.** to have or feel a continuous, dull pain: *His whole body ached with fever.* **2.** to feel pity, sympathy, or the like: *Her heart ached for the starving animals.* **3.** *Slang.* to be eager; yearn; long: *He's aching to go to summer camp.* —*n.* **4.** a continuous, dull pain. —**ach′ing·ly,** *adv.*

a·chieve (ə chēv′), *v.,* **a·chieved, a·chiev·ing. 1.** to bring to a successful result; accomplish: *They achieved the purpose of their journey.* **2.** to get or attain by effort; gain; obtain: *to achieve victory.* [from the Old French word *achever,* literally "to bring to a head," from *a* "to" + *chef* "head." See *chef*] —**a·chiev′er,** *n.*

a·chieve·ment (ə chēv′mənt), *n.* **1.** something done or accomplished, esp. by special effort, ability, or courage: *The first heart transplant was a great achievement.* **2.** the act or an instance of achieving or attaining something; accomplishment.

A·chil·les (ə kil′ēz), *n.* (in Greek mythology) the greatest Greek warrior of the Trojan War, killed by an arrow wound in his right heel, the only place where he could be injured.

ac·id (as′id), *n.* **1.** a substance that combines with a base to yield water and a salt. Acids corrode most metals and turn litmus red. —*adj.* **2.** referring to or containing an acid. **3.** sharp or biting to the taste; sour: *acid fruits.* **4.** sharp, biting, or bad-tempered: *an acid remark.* —**ac′id·ly,** *adv.* —**ac′id·ness,** *n.*

a·cid·i·ty (ə sid′i tē), *n.* **1.** the quality or state of being acid. **2.** sourness or tartness: *the acidity of lemons; the acidity of his remarks.* **3.** a condition of discomfort, esp. in the stomach, caused by too much acid in the gastric juice.

ac·knowl·edge (ak nol′ij), *v.,* **ac·knowl·edged, ac·knowl·edg·ing. 1.** to admit to be real or true; recognize the fact or truth of: *to acknowledge that the earth is round.* **2.** to show or express recognition of (someone): *to acknowledge a friend by waving.* **3.** to recognize and admit the authority, rights, or status of: *The states acknowledge the powers of the president.* **4.** to indicate or make some sign that one has noticed or is grateful for (something): *to acknowledge a favor.* **5.** to indicate or make known that one has received (something): *to acknowledge a letter.*

ac·knowl·edg·ment (ak nol′ij mənt), *n.* **1.** the act or an instance of acknowledging or admitting that something is real or true. **2.** an expression of thanks: *the acknowledgment of a gift.* **3.** something done or

given in appreciation: *The banquet was an acknowledgment of his services to the city.*

ac·me (ak′mē), *n.* the highest point; peak; summit: *the acme of a career.*

ac·ne (ak′nē), *n.* an inflammation of small glands in the skin that results in pimples and blackheads.

ac·o·lyte (ak′ə līt′), *n.* **1.** a person who assists a priest during a religious service; altar boy. **2.** any other assistant, attendant, or follower: *a great man and his acolytes.*

A·con·ca·gua (ä′kông kä′gwə), *n.* a mountain in W Argentina, in the Andes: highest peak in the Western Hemisphere. 22,834 ft.

a·corn (ā′kôrn), *n.* the nut of the oak tree.

a·cous·tic (ə kōō′stik), *adj.* **1.** referring to sound or hearing. **2.** used for absorbing or reflecting sound waves: *acoustic tiles.* Also, **a·cous′ti·cal.**

Acorn

a·cous·tics (ə kōō′stiks), *n.* **1.** *(used as sing.)* the branch of physics or engineering that deals with sound and sound waves: *Acoustics is a fascinating subject.* **2.** *(used as pl.)* the qualities of a room, auditorium, etc., that influence the ease or clarity with which speech or music can be heard in it: *The acoustics of the concert hall are superb.*

ac·quaint (ə kwānt′), *v.* **1.** to make known to; make more or less familiar (usually fol. by *with*): *to acquaint the mayor with our plan.* **2.** to introduce; bring together socially: *I acquainted my roommate with my cousin.*

ac·quaint·ance (ə kwān′t³ns), *n.* **1.** a person that one knows slightly but does not regard as a close friend. **2.** the state or period of being acquainted with someone: *I had a brief acquaintance with them years ago.* **3.** personal knowledge; understanding; familiarity: *a good acquaintance with the public school system.* **4. make someone's acquaintance,** to meet or get to know someone: *We made his acquaintance on the trip to Bermuda.* Also, **ac·quaint′ance·ship′** (for defs. 2, 3).

ac·quaint·ed (ə kwān′tid), *adj.* **1.** having personal knowledge; informed (usually fol. by *with*): *She is acquainted with life in Africa.* **2.** known to one or to each other: *We became acquainted last year.*

ac·qui·esce (ak′wē es′), *v.,* **ac·qui·esced, ac·qui·esc·ing.** to agree or submit quietly; consent (often fol. by *in* or *to*): *to acquiesce to another's authority.* —**ac′qui·es′cence,** *n.* —**ac′qui·es′cent,** *adj.*

ac·quire (ə kwīªr′), *v.,* **ac·quired, ac·quir·ing. 1.** to get as one's own; come into possession of: *He acquired a baseball glove from his brother.* **2.** to gain for oneself through one's actions or efforts: *to acquire learning.* —**ac·quir′a·ble,** *adj.* —**ac·quir′er,** *n.*

ac·quire·ment (ə kwīªr′mənt), *n.* **1.** the act of acquiring: *the acquirement of new equipment.* **2.** something acquired or attained: *One of his acquirements is a knowledge of American history.*

ac·qui·si·tion (ak′wi zish′ən), *n.* **1.** the act of acquiring or getting something: *the acquisition of books for the library.* **2.** something acquired or owned: *The* *museum will display its new acquisitions from India.*

ac·quis·i·tive (ə kwiz′i tiv), *adj.* inclined to acquire things; greedy: *The pack rat is an acquisitive animal.* —**ac·quis′i·tive·ly,** *adv.*

ac·quit (ə kwit′), *v.,* **ac·quit·ted, ac·quit·ting. 1.** to free (someone) from a criminal charge; declare not guilty: *The jury acquitted her.* **2.** to conduct (oneself); behave: *He acquitted himself well in battle.*

ac·quit·tal (ə kwit′əl), *n.* the act of acquitting someone of a criminal charge or freeing someone of blame for a crime or fault: *The defense lawyer was sure she would win an acquittal for her client.*

a·cre (ā′kər), *n.* a unit of measure equal to 43,560 square feet, or ¹⁄₆₄₀ square mile (4047 square meters): used for measuring areas of land. [from the Old English word *æcer* "field"; related to Latin *ager* "field"]

a·cre·age (ā′kər ij), *n.* **1.** the area of land reckoned in acres: *How much acreage do you have here?* **2.** a plot of land amounting to about one acre.

ac·rid (ak′rid), *adj.* **1.** sharp or biting to the taste or smell; bitter; irritating: *the acrid smoke of burning rubber.* **2.** extremely sharp or sarcastic: *The sergeant's acrid remarks kept the men working hard.* —**ac′rid·ly,** *adv.* —**ac′rid·ness,** *n.*

ac·ri·mo·ni·ous (ak′rə mō′nē əs), *adj.* stinging or bitter; sarcastic: *His remarks were so acrimonious, I just got up and left.* —**ac′ri·mo′ni·ous·ly,** *adv.*

ac·ri·mo·ny (ak′rə mō′nē), *n.* a sharpness, harshness, or bitterness of speech or disposition; hard feeling: *an angry man, full of hate and acrimony.*

ac·ro·bat (ak′rə bat′), *n.* a skilled performer of gymnastic feats, such as walking on a tightrope, swinging on a trapeze, etc.

ac·ro·bat·ic (ak′rə bat′ik), *adj.* of or concerning an acrobat or acrobatics: *an acrobatic show at the circus.* —**ac′ro·bat′i·cal·ly,** *adv.*

ac·ro·bat·ics (ak′rə bat′iks), *n.* **1.** *(used as pl.)* feats of agility or physical dexterity performed by an acrobat: *Acrobatics are dizzying to watch.* **2.** *(used as sing.)* the art or skill of doing acrobatic feats or tricks: *Acrobatics is a difficult sport.*

a·crop·o·lis (ə krop′ə lis), *n.* **1.** the high, fortified part of an ancient Greek city; an ancient Greek citadel. **2. the Acropolis,** the citadel of ancient Athens: site of the Parthenon. [from a Greek word, which comes from *akros* "high" + *polis* "city"]

a·cross (ə krôs′), *prep.* **1.** from one side to the other of: *a bridge across a river.* **2.** on the other side of: *He lives across the street.* **3.** into contact with; into the presence of, usually by accident: *to come across an old friend.* **4.** crosswise of; athwart: *He fell across the bed.* —*adv.* **5.** from one side to another: *We swam all the way across.* **6.** on the other side: *We'll soon be across.* **7.** so as to be understood or learned: *He finally got the idea across to the class.*

act (akt), *n.* **1.** anything done or performed; deed: *the act of washing one's hands.* **2.** the process of doing: *to be caught in the act.* **3.** a formal decision, law, or the like, passed by Congress, a ruler, or other authority: *a civil-rights act.* **4.** one of the main divisions of a play or opera: *a comedy in three acts.* **5.** a short performance by one or more entertainers: *His magic act is very popular.* **6.** insincere behavior; pretense: *Her surprise was just an act.* —*v.* **7.** to do something; perform: *His mind acts quickly. They had to act at once to catch the runaway lion.* **8.** to behave, work, or operate in a particular way: *to act as chairman; to act well at all times.* **9.** to produce an effect: *The medicine didn't act.* **10.** to pretend something that is false: *Try to act interested.* **11.** to perform as an actor. **12.** to behave as: *Don't act the fool with me.* **13. act for,** to substitute for; take the place of: *The teacher appointed me to act for you.* **14. act on** (or **upon**), to behave according to; follow: *She acted on my advice.* **15. act up,** to behave badly; misbehave: *If you act up, you're going home.*

act·ing (ak′ting), *adj.* **1.** serving in someone's place for a time; being a temporary substitute: *You'll be acting chairman today.* **2.** being in action; working. —*n.* **3.** the art or profession of those who perform in stage plays, motion pictures, etc.

ac·tin·i·um (ak tin′ē əm), *n. Chem.* a highly radioactive element resembling the rare earths in chemical behavior. *Symbol:* Ac

ac·tion (ak′shən), *n.* **1.** the process or state of acting or being active: *The pump is not now in action.* **2.** something done; act; deed. **3.** physical or mental activity directed to a particular purpose: *Now is the time for action.* **4.** the power or force working on something: *The action of wind against the sails moves the boat.* **5.** effect or influence: *the action of acid on litmus.* **6.** a way or manner of moving: *the smooth action of a gear shift.* **7.** military combat: *troops that haven't seen action.* **8. actions,** conduct; behavior: *A baby is not responsible for its actions.* **9. take action,** to begin an action; start dealing with a particular matter: *When will the committee take action on our plan?* —**ac′tion·less,** *adj.*

ac·ti·vate (ak′tə vāt′), *v.,* **ac·ti·vat·ed, ac·ti·vat·ing.** to make active; put into action: *This switch will activate the fire alarm.* —**ac′ti·va′tion,** *n.*

ac·tive (ak′tiv), *adj.* **1.** full of action or activity; busy; strenuous: *an active life; active sports.* **2.** actually functioning, existing, or happening: *active warfare; active members.* **3.** full of vigor or energy; lively; energetic: *an active boy.* **4.** erupting or capable of erupting: *an active volcano.* **5.** noting the active voice. —**ac′tive·ly,** *adv.*

ac′tive voice′, the inflected form of a verb that shows that the subject of the clause or sentence performs the action of the verb. In the sentence *Jack hit the ball,* the verb *hit* is in the active voice.

ac·tiv·ist (ak′tə vist), *n.* a person who supports a cause energetically or militantly.

ac·tiv·i·ty (ak tiv′i tē), *n., pl.* **ac·tiv·i·ties. 1.** the state or quality of being active; doing; action: *activity on the playgrounds; mental activity.* **2.** a particular deed, action, or kind of action: *classroom activities.*

ac·tor (ak′tər), *n.* 1. a person, esp. a man or boy, who acts in stage plays, motion pictures, etc. 2. a person who performs an activity; doer.

ac·tress (ak′tris), *n.* a woman or girl who acts in stage plays, motion pictures, television shows, etc.

Acts′ of the Apos′tles, a book of the New Testament. Also, **Acts.**

ac·tu·al (ak′chōō əl), *adj.* 1. existing in fact; real: *an actual train robbery.* 2. existing now; present: *the actual position of the moon.* —**ac′tu·al′i·ty,** *n.*

ac·tu·al·ly (ak′chōō ə lē), *adv.* as an actual or existing fact; really: *I was actually there when you came.*

ac·tu·ate (ak′chōō āt′), *v.,* **ac·tu·at·ed, ac·tu·at·ing.** 1. to incite to action; motivate; impel: *She was actuated by selfish motives.* 2. to put into action; turn on: *to actuate a machine.*

a·cu·men (ə kyōō′mən), *n.* keen mental insight; superior ability to understand matters: *She showed remarkable acumen in managing the family business.*

a·cute (ə kyōōt′), *adj.* 1. sharp at the end; ending in a point; not blunt. 2. sharp or severe; very great; intense: *an acute pain; an acute shortage.* 3. sharp or keen: *acute eyesight; an acute observer.* —**a·cute′ly,** *adv.* —**a·cute′ness,** *n.*

acute′ an′gle, an angle smaller than 90°.

A.D., in the year of Our Lord; since Christ was born (used in reckoning dates): *From 20 B.C. to A.D. 50 is 70 years.* [from the Latin phrase *annō Dominī*]

ad·age (ad′ij), *n.* an old saying that expresses a common experience or observation; proverb: *Mother quoted the adage, "A stitch in time saves nine."*

a·da·gio (ə dä′jō, ə dä′zhē ō′), *adj., adv.* 1. (in music) slow; slowly. —*n., pl.* **a·da·gios.** 2. a slow piece or section. [from the Italian phrase *ad agio* "at ease"]

Ad·am (ad′əm), *n.* (in the Bible) the first man: the father of the human race.

ad·a·mant (ad′ə mənt), *adj.* completely set and unyielding in attitude, opinion, etc.: *He's absolutely adamant about not going.*

Ad·ams (ad′əmz), *n.* 1. **John,** 1735–1826, 1st Vice President of the U.S. 1789–1797; 2nd President of the U.S. 1797–1801: a leader in the American Revolution. 2. his son, **John Quincy,** 1767–1848, 6th President of the U.S. 1825–1829. 3. **Samuel,** 1722–1803, American patriot: a leader in the American Revolution.

Ad′am's ap′ple, the bulge at the front of the neck, esp. in men, formed by the cartilage that surrounds the larynx.

a·dapt (ə dapt′), *v.* 1. to make suitable to special requirements or new conditions; adjust or modify: *to adapt a car for use in races; to adapt a novel for the stage.* 2. to adjust oneself to different conditions, new surroundings, etc.: *He didn't adapt easily to the new school.* —**a·dapt′er,** *n.* —**a·dap′tive,** *adj.*

a·dapt·a·ble (ə dap′tə bəl), *adj.* 1. capable of being adapted, adjusted, or modified: *a sports stadium adaptable for different events.* 2. able to adapt or adjust oneself easily to different conditions or surroundings: *an adaptable child.* —**a·dapt′a·bil′i·ty,** *n.*

ad·ap·ta·tion (ad′əp tā′shən), *n.* 1. the act of adapting, adjusting, or modifying something: *the adaptation of a car for racing.* 2. something produced by adapting: *an adaptation of an opera for television.*

add (ad), *v.* 1. to join or unite so as to increase the number, size, or importance of something: *to add another stone to the pile.* 2. to find the sum or amount of (often fol. by *up*): *to add up a score.* 3. to perform addition in arithmetic: *children learning to add and subtract.* 4. to say or write further: *I would like to add a suggestion.* 5. to include (usually fol. by *in*): *Don't forget to add in Jimmy.* 6. **add to,** to make greater; enlarge or increase: *Her illness has added to the family's troubles.* 7. **add up,** to seem reasonable or plausible: *There were parts of her story that didn't add up.* 8. **add up to,** to amount to; indicate: *Her symptoms add up to a case of flu.*

Ad·ams (ad′əmz), *n.* **Jane,** 1860–1935, U.S. social worker and writer.

ad·dend (ad′end, ə dend′), *n.* a number that is added to another in forming a sum. For example, in $6 + 3 = 9$, 6 and 3 are the addends.

ad·der (ad′ər), *n.* 1. a small, poisonous European snake; viper. 2. any of several other small snakes, some of them harmless. [from the Middle English word *nadder.* When *nadder* was used with the indefinite article *a,* the phrase *a nadder* was incorrectly pronounced *an adder,* thus causing the *n* of *nadder* to be lost. See *apron* for a similar development]

ad·dict (ad′ikt), *n.* 1. a person who is so accustomed to or dependent upon something that he feels he cannot live without it: *a drug addict.* —*v.* (ə dikt′). 2. to give (oneself) over completely to a habit, practice, etc.: *to addict oneself to cigarettes.* —**ad·dict′ed,** *adj.* —**ad·dic′tion,** *n.*

Ad·dis A·ba·ba (ad′is ab′ə bə, ä′dis ä′bə bä′), the capital city of Ethiopia, in the central part.

ad·di·tion (ə dish′ən), *n.* 1. the act or process of adding or joining: *the addition of two new members to the club.* 2. the process or technique of adding two or more numbers together to yield a sum: represented by a plus sign (+). 3. anything added; the result of adding: *a new addition to a house.* 4. **in addition to,** as well as; besides: *In addition to editing the class newspaper, she wrote the class play.*

ad·di·tion·al (ə dish′ə nəl), *adj.* added; extra or supplementary: *You can have additional time if you need it.* —**ad·di′tion·al·ly,** *adv.*

ad·di·tive (ad′i tiv), *adj.* 1. of, referring to, or produced by addition. —*n.* 2. something that is added, as one substance that is added to another for change or improvement: *Additives are put into food to keep it from spoiling.*

ad·dle (ad′əl), *v.,* **ad·dled, ad·dling.** to make muddled or confused: *All those questions addled her, and she forgot what she meant to say.*

ad·dress (ə dres′, ad′res), *n.* 1. a formal speech or written statement: *the President's address to the nation.* 2. an indication of where a letter, package, or the like, is to be delivered: *Is there an address on the* envelope? **3.** the place where a person, business, government office, etc., is located or may be reached: *What is your address? —v.* (ə dres′). **4.** to direct a speech or written statement to: *to address an assembly.* **5.** to use a particular title when speaking or writing to: *How does one address the Governor?* **6.** to cause (oneself) to speak: *I am addressing myself to you.* **7.** to write directions for delivery on: *You didn't address this letter.* **8.** to direct to the attention of a person or group: *to address a warning to someone.* **9.** address oneself to, to direct one's energy, thoughts, or attention to; deal with or attend to: *He addressed himself to the task.* **—ad·dress′er**, *n.*

ad·dress·ee (ad′re sē′, ə dres′ē), *n.* a person, company, or the like, to whom mail is addressed.

Ad·e·laide (ad′ᵊlād′), *n.* a city in S Australia: capital of South Australia.

A·den (äd′ᵊn, ād′ᵊn), *n.* a port city in the People's Democratic Republic of Yemen.

ad·e·noids (ad′ᵊnoidz′), *n.pl.* growths of tissue between the nose and the throat: when infected, the adenoids become enlarged and interfere with normal breathing. See illus. at **tonsil.**

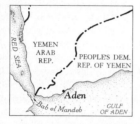

a·dept (ə dept′), *adj.* **1.** very skilled; expert: *to be adept at playing the guitar. —n.* (ad′ept, ə dept′). **2.** a person who is adept. **—a·dept′ly**, *adv.*

ad·e·qua·cy (ad′ə kwə sē), *n.* the state of being sufficient for a particular purpose; the quality of being adequate: *to attain adequacy in speaking Spanish.*

ad·e·quate (ad′ə kwit), *adj.* **1.** equal to what is needed; sufficient; suitable or fit (often fol. by *to* or *for*): *adequate time to finish one's homework.* **2.** barely good enough; just sufficient: *It was an adequate performance, but we expected more.* [from the Latin word *adaequātus* "made equal"] **—ad′e·quate·ly**, *adv.* **—ad′e·quate·ness**, *n.*

ad·here (ad hēr′), *v.*, **ad·hered, ad·her·ing. 1.** to stick fast; cling: *The mud adhered to his shoes.* **2.** to be devoted; hold closely; give support: *to adhere to a political party; to adhere to a plan.*

ad·her·ence (ad hēr′əns), *n.* **1.** the quality of adhering or remaining closely attached to a person, cause, etc; faithfulness: *adherence to the rules.* **2.** the act or state of adhering physically; adhesion: *the adherence of iron filings to a magnet.*

ad·her·ent (ad hēr′ənt), *n.* **1.** a person who follows or upholds a cause, leader, or the like; follower; supporter: *an adherent of the United Nations. —adj.* **2.** sticking or clinging; holding fast; adhering: *Putty is an adherent substance.*

ad·he·sion (ad hē′zhən), *n.* **1.** the act or state of adhering or sticking fast: *the adhesion of a stamp to an envelope.* **2.** steady attachment of the mind or feelings; loyalty: *adhesion to one's friends.*

ad·he·sive (ad hē′siv), *adj.* **1.** adhering; clinging or sticking fast: *Chewing gum is adhesive.* **2.** gummed; sticky: *an adhesive surface on which one can stick things. —n.* **3.** an adhesive material or substance, such as adhesive tape or glue. **—ad·he′sive·ly**, *adv.* **—ad·he′sive·ness**, *n.*

adhe′sive tape′, cotton or other fabric coated with a sticky substance, used esp. for holding bandages in place.

a·dieu (ə dōo′, ə dyōo′), *interj.* **1.** good-by; farewell. **—n., pl. a·dieus or a·dieux** (ə dōoz′, ə dyōoz′). **2.** the act of leaving or departing and saying good-by; farewell. [from the French word *adieu*, which comes from *à* "to" + *Dieu* "God"]

ad·i·os (ad′ē ōs′, ä′dē ōs′), *interj.* good-by; farewell. [from a Spanish word meaning literally "to God"]

ad·i·pose (ad′ə pōs′), *adj.* fatty; of or resembling fat: *An excess of adipose tissue is what makes people look fat.* **—ad′i·pose′ness**, *n.*

Ad′i·ron′dack Moun′tains (ad′ə ron′dak), a mountain range in NE New York. Also, **the Adirondacks.**

adj., **1.** adjective. **2.** adjourned.

ad·ja·cent (ə jā′sənt), *adj.* being near or connected; neighboring; adjoining: *a field adjacent to the highway.* **—ad·ja′cen·cy**, *n.* **—ad·ja′cent·ly**, *adv.*

ad·jec·ti·val (aj′ik tī′vəl), *adj.* **1.** of or referring to an adjective: *Give two adjectival meanings of this word.* **2.** used as or in place of an adjective: *an adjectival phrase.* **—ad′jec·ti′val·ly**, *adv.*

ad·jec·tive (aj′ik tiv), *n.* **1.** a word used to describe or limit a noun or pronoun, as *good, bad, red, tall,* or *sick. —adj.* **2.** another word for **adjectival.**

ad·join (ə join′), *v.* **1.** to be close to or in contact with: *The park adjoins the school.* **2.** to be joined or touching: *a border where two countries adjoin.*

ad·journ (ə jûrn′), *v.* **1.** to postpone (the meeting of a club, legislature, committee, etc.): *We adjourned the meeting until next week. Congress adjourned for the holidays.* **2.** to go to another place: *Let us adjourn to the living room.* **—ad·journ′ment**, *n.*

ad·judge (ə juj′), *v.*, **ad·judged, ad·judg·ing. 1.** to decree or decide formally, esp. by judicial proceedings: *The law was adjudged unconstitutional.* **2.** to consider or think: *We adjudged it best to follow the other suggestion.*

ad·junct (aj′ungkt), *n.* something added to another thing but not essential: *The stop at Yellowstone Park was an adjunct to our trip.*

ad·jure (ə jōor′), *v.*, **ad·jured, ad·jur·ing. 1.** to command earnestly and solemnly, often under oath: *We adjure you to forsake rebellion and piracy.* **2.** to request or entreat earnestly. **—ad′ju·ra′tion**, *n.*

ad·just (ə just′), *v.* **1.** to arrange or change (one thing) to suit another: *to adjust a camera to the light indoors.* **2.** to put in working order; regulate; fix to suit what is needed: *to adjust a television set.* **3.** to adapt oneself; become accustomed to new conditions or surroundings: *The children adjusted quickly to the* *new school.* **4.** to settle; work out so that both sides are satisfied: *to adjust differences between two warring countries.* —**ad·just′er,** *n.*

ad·just·a·ble (ə jus′tə bəl), *adj.* capable of being adjusted: *Is this chair adjustable?* —**ad·just′a·bly,** *adv.*

ad·just·ment (ə just′mənt), *n.* **1.** the act of adjusting something or making a suitable change; state of being adjusted or regulated: *the adjustment of a pair of binoculars.* **2.** a means of adjusting something, such as a knob or lever. **3.** an agreement or settlement.

ad·ju·tant (aj′ə tənt), *n.* a military officer who assists the commanding officer. —**ad′ju·tan·cy,** *n.*

ad lib (ad lib′), something that is ad-libbed or made up: *I know the joke wasn't very funny, but it was an ad lib.* [from the Latin phrase *ad libitum* "at (one's) pleasure"]

ad-lib (ad lib′, ad′-), *v.,* **ad-libbed, ad-lib·bing.** to improvise or make up (a speech, joke, etc.); perform without using prepared material: *He ad-libbed the entire introduction.*

ad·min·is·ter (ad min′i stər), *v.* **1.** to manage; have charge of: *to administer a school.* **2.** to put into use; dispense; apply: *to administer medicine; to administer justice.* **3.** to give assistance, aid, or supplies (usually fol. by *to*): *to administer to the poor.*

ad·min·is·trate (ad min′i strāt′), *v.,* **ad·min·is·trat·ed, ad·min·is·trat·ing.** to administer.

ad·min·is·tra·tion (ad min′i strā′shən), *n.* **1.** the process of managing or directing an organization, government, office, etc. **2.** the act of administering: *the administration of medicine to a sick person.* **3.** a group of persons officially in charge of a government, organization, office, or the like: *There will be a meeting of the administration at 5:00.* **4. the Administration,** the President of the United States and his cabinet. **5.** the period of service of a body of administrators or a Presidential administration: *the events of the last administration.*

ad·min·is·tra·tive (ad min′i strā′tiv, ad min′i strə-tiv), *adj.* of or concerning administration; executive; managerial: *a man with administrative ability.*

ad·min·is·tra·tor (ad min′i strā′tər), *n.* a person who directs or manages business affairs, financial matters, government programs, etc.

ad·mi·ra·ble (ad′mər ə bəl), *adj.* deserving admiration or approval; excellent: *an admirable effort; an admirable proposal.* —**ad′mi·ra·bly,** *adv.*

ad·mi·ral (ad′mər əl), *n.* **1.** the commander in chief of a fleet. **2.** a high-ranking U.S. naval officer. The grades of admiral are fleet admiral, admiral, vice admiral, and rear admiral. **3.** an officer in the U.S. Navy, ranking above a vice admiral and below a fleet admiral.

ad·mi·ral·ty (ad′mər əl tē), *n.* **1.** the officials or government department in charge of naval matters, esp. in Great Britain. **2.** the position or authority of an admiral. —*adj.* **3.** of or referring to maritime affairs: *admiralty law.*

ad·mi·ra·tion (ad′mə rā′shən), *n.* **1.** a feeling of wonder, pleasure, and approval: *We were filled with admiration for the courage of Christopher Columbus*

and his men. **2.** the act of regarding with pleasure and approval: *He spent the day in admiration of the paintings in the museum.* **3.** something or someone that is regarded with wonder and approval.

ad·mire (ad mīᵊr′), *v.,* **ad·mired, ad·mir·ing.** to regard with wonder, pleasure, and approval: *to admire a great man; to admire the workings of nature.* —**ad·mir′ing·ly,** *adv.*

ad·mir·er (ad mīᵊr′ər), *n.* someone who regards something or someone else with approval and pleasure: *The poet has many admirers.*

ad·mis·si·ble (ad mis′ə bəl), *adj.* **1.** permitted or allowed: *Talking is admissible before class.* **2.** capable or worthy of being admitted: *admissible evidence.* —**ad·mis′si·bil′i·ty,** *n.* —**ad·mis′si·bly,** *adv.*

ad·mis·sion (ad mish′ən), *n.* **1.** the act of admitting or granting permission to enter: *The admission of customers is not permitted after 5:00.* **2.** the right or permission to enter: *to grant someone admission.* **3.** the price paid for admission to a theater, ball park, etc.: *Admission to the game is one dollar.* **4.** a confession or acknowledgment of something: *His admission of the theft solved the mystery.*

ad·mit (ad mit′), *v.,* **ad·mit·ted, ad·mit·ting.** **1.** to allow to enter; grant entrance to: *to admit a student to college.* **2.** to give the right or means of entrance to: *This ticket admits two people.* **3.** to confess or acknowledge: *She admitted her guilt. I must admit you have a point.* **4.** to allow or give opportunity or permission (usually fol. by *of*): *The rules of this game do not admit of shoving your opponent.* —**ad·mit′ter,** *n.*

ad·mit·tance (ad mit′ᵊns), *n.* **1.** permission to enter; the power or right to enter: *I could not gain admittance to the movie.* **2.** the act or fact of entering.

ad·mit·ted·ly (ad mit′id lē), *adv.* by one's own admission: *He was admittedly at fault.*

ad·mix·ture (ad miks′chər), *n.* **1.** an ingredient added to a substance. **2.** a mixture or compound.

ad·mon·ish (ad mon′ish), *v.* **1.** to caution or advise against something; warn: *The scouts were admonished not to enter the cave.* **2.** to scold in a mild way: *The teacher admonished him about running in the halls.* **3.** to remind of a duty: *to admonish someone about his obligations.* —**ad·mon′ish·ing·ly,** *adv.*

ad·mo·ni·tion (ad′mə nish′ən), *n.* **1.** the act of admonishing, warning, or scolding: *The admonition of jaywalkers is part of a policeman's job.* **2.** a warning, scolding, or advice: *an admonition concerning the need for exercise.*

a·do (ə dōō′), *n.* busy activity; fuss; bustle: *There was much ado at our house over the holidays.*

a·do·be (ə dō′bē), *n.* **1.** sun-dried brick made from silt or clay: commonly used in dry regions. **2.** a building made of adobe. —*adj.* **3.** made of adobe: *Adobe houses are common in the southwest U.S. and Mexico.* [from an Arabic phrase meaning "the brick"]

ad·o·les·cence (ad′ᵊles′əns), *n.* the period between childhood and adulthood, esp. the teen years.

ad·o·les·cent (ad′ᵊles′ənt), *adj.* **1.** growing to adulthood or maturity; youthful: *an energetic, adolescent boy.* —*n.* **2.** a youthful, adolescent person; teen-ager:

a discussion group for adolescents. —**ad′o·les′cent·ly**, *adv.*

a·dopt (ə dopt′), *v.* **1.** to choose or take as one's own: *to adopt a new name.* **2.** to become the legal parent or parents of: *My aunt and uncle just adopted a baby.* **3.** to accept or formally approve: *to adopt a plan.* —**a·dopt′a·ble,** *adj.* —**a·dopt′er,** *n.*

a·dop·tion (ə dop′shən), *n.* **1.** the act of adopting or taking as one's own: *the adoption of a child.* **2.** acceptance; approval: *the adoption of a plan.* —**a·dop′ tive,** *adj.*

a·dor·a·ble (ə dôr′ə bəl), *adj.* delightful and charming: *an adorable child.* —**a·dor′a·bly,** *adv.*

ad·o·ra·tion (ad′ə rā′shən), *n.* **1.** the act of worshiping or paying the greatest honor, as to a deity: *This painting shows the angels kneeling in adoration of God.* **2.** strong and devoted love; devotion.

a·dore (ə dôr′), *v.,* **a·dored, a·dor·ing. 1.** to worship; pay divine honor to: *to adore God.* **2.** to feel deep love and respect for: *to adore one's grandparents.* **3.** to like very much: *She adores swimming.* —**a·dor′ ing·ly,** *adv.*

a·dorn (ə dôrn′), *v.* to decorate or add ornaments to; make more beautiful: *Roses adorned her hair.*

a·dorn·ment (ə dôrn′mənt), *n.* **1.** the act of adorning or decorating: *to watch the adornment of a Christmas tree.* **2.** an ornament or decoration: *They dressed the prince with rich adornments.*

ad·re′nal gland′ (ə drēn′əl), a ductless gland located on the top of each kidney. The adrenal glands secrete adrenalin. See illus. at **kidney.**

a·dren·a·lin (ə dren′- əlin), *n.* the hormone secreted by the adrenal glands, which stimulates the heart, causes a rise in blood pressure, and quickens the rate of breathing. Adrenalin is secreted in times of anger, fear, or the like.

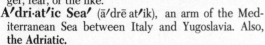

A′dri·at′ic Sea′ (ā′drē at′ik), an arm of the Mediterranean Sea between Italy and Yugoslavia. Also, **the Adriatic.**

a·drift (ə drift′), *adj., adv.* not anchored or fastened by a mooring; drifting freely: *They were adrift on the open sea.*

a·droit (ə droit′), *adj.* **1.** expert or nimble in the use of one's hands: *an adroit carpenter.* **2.** cleverly skillful: *an adroit politician.* —**a·droit′ly,** *adv.* —**a·droit′ ness,** *n.*

ad·u·la·tion (aj′ə lā′shən), *n.* excessive admiration, flattery, or fawning devotion: *children's adulation of a movie star.*

a·dult (ə dult′, ad′ult), *n.* **1.** a mature, full-grown person, animal, or plant. —*adj.* **2.** mature or grown-up: *an adult person.* **3.** of or for adults: *adult behavior; adult education.* —**a·dult′hood,** *n.*

a·dul·ter·ate (ə dul′tə rāt′), *v.,* **a·dul·ter·at·ed, a·dul· ter·at·ing.** to make less good by adding something inferior: *to adulterate hamburger by mixing it with bread crumbs.* —**a·dul′ter·a′tion,** *n.*

a·dul·ter·er (ə dul′tər ər), *n.* a person, esp. a man, who commits adultery. Also, *referring to a woman,* **a·dul·ter·ess** (ə dul′tər is).

a·dul·ter·y (ə dul′tə rē), *n., pl.* **a·dul·ter·ies.** the act of being physically unfaithful to one's wife or husband.

adv., adverb.

ad·vance (ad vans′), *v.,* **ad·vanced, ad·vanc·ing. 1.** to bring or send forward: *The general advanced his men to the front lines.* **2.** to come or go forward. **3.** to make progress or show improvement. **4.** to further the progress of; promote: *to advance a student to the next grade.* **5.** to put forward for consideration: *to advance an idea.* **6.** to give or supply on credit: *He advanced me the money for a new guitar.* —*n.* **7.** a forward movement: *a stealthy advance through the woods.* **8.** progress or improvement: *the advance of science.* **9.** something supplied on credit: *an advance of $10 on next week's salary.* **10. advances,** an attempt to make friends: *The kitten made shy advances to its new owners.* —*adj.* **11.** before all others; forward: *an advance section of the train.* **12.** done or ready beforehand: *an advance sale of tickets.* **13. in advance,** prior to a particular time: *I wish I'd known in advance what it was like.* **14. in advance of,** ahead of in time or position: *The band marched in advance of the first float.*

ad·vanced (ad vanst′), *adj.* **1.** placed ahead or forward: *with one foot advanced.* **2.** beyond some beginning stage; further along than another in progress, development, etc.: *an advanced understanding of mathematics; to be advanced for one's age.* **3.** rather old or very old: *advanced in years.*

ad·vance·ment (ad vans′mənt), *n.* **1.** the act of moving forward. **2.** progress or promotion: *His advancement from colonel to general was well-deserved.*

ad·van·tage (ad van′tij), *n.* **1.** anything that is of benefit or gain; something that is helpful or especially useful: *His knowledge of how to fix automobiles was a great advantage to us on our trip.* **2.** a superior or dominating position (often fol. by *of* or *over*): *He's so tall he has an advantage over the others.* **3. take advantage of, a.** to make use of; utilize: *to take advantage of an opportunity.* **b.** to use selfishly: *He takes advantage of my generosity.* **4. to advantage,** with benefit or profit: *It's an idea I can use to advantage.* **5. to one's advantage,** to one's benefit or profit: *Will the plan work to our advantage?*

ad·van·ta·geous (ad′vən tā′jəs), *adj.* providing an advantage or benefit; profitable; useful: *His long run with the ball gave us an advantageous position on the field.* —**ad′van·ta′geous·ly,** *adv.*

ad·vent (ad′vent), *n.* the arrival or coming into being of something: *the advent of spring.*

Ad·vent (ad′vent), *n.* (in Christian churches) **1.** the birth of Christ. **2.** the period that begins on the

---

act, āble, dâre, ärt; ebb, ēqual; if, īce; hot, ōver, ôrder; oil; bŏŏk; ōōze; out; up, ûrge; ə = *a* as in *alone*; ə as in *button* (but′ən), *fire* (fiər); chief; shoe; thin; ᵺhat; zh as in *measure* (mezh′ər). See full key inside cover.

fourth Sunday before Christmas and ends on Christmas Eve.

ad·ven·ture (ad ven′chər), *n.* 1. an undertaking that involves risk and danger, often something that has never been done before: *the adventure of flights to the moon.* 2. an exciting or remarkable experience: *Being on television was an adventure for me.* 3. dangerous and daring activity: *to live a life of adventure.* —*v.,* **ad·ven·tured, ad·ven·tur·ing.** 4. to take part in an adventure. [from the Latin word *adventura,* in the phrase *res adventura* "a thing about to happen"]

ad·ven·tur·er (ad ven′chər ər), *n.* 1. a person who takes part in adventures or dangerous and bold undertakings. 2. a person who seeks wealth or power by illegal or underhand means. Also, *referring to a woman,* **ad·ven·tur·ess** (ad ven′chər is).

ad·ven·ture·some (ad ven′chər səm), *adj.* adventurous; daring: *an adventuresome child; an adventuresome life.* —**ad·ven′ture·some·ly,** *adv.* —**ad·ven′ture·some·ness,** *n.*

ad·ven·tur·ous (ad ven′chər əs), *adj.* 1. seeking or taking part in adventures: *an adventurous explorer.* 2. full of adventure; exciting or risky: *an adventurous expedition.* —**ad·ven′tur·ous·ly,** *adv.* —**ad·ven′tur·ous·ness,** *n.*

ad·verb (ad′vûrb), *n.* a word used to modify a verb, an adjective, or another adverb. Adverbs may ask or tell how, when, where, or why. Typical adverbs are *well, now, inside,* and *therefore.*

ad·ver·bi·al (ad vûr′bē əl), *adj.* 1. of or referring to an adverb: *This word has an adverbial form.* 2. used as or in place of an adverb: *an adverbial clause.* —**ad·ver′bi·al·ly,** *adv.*

ad·ver·sar·y (ad′vər ser′ē), *n., pl.* **ad·ver·sar·ies.** a person who opposes another; opponent; foe: *They were bitter political adversaries.*

ad·verse (ad vûrs′, ad′vûrs), *adj.* 1. negative or unfriendly: *He was discouraged by the adverse criticism.* 2. opposing what one needs or desires: *Adverse circumstances prevented him from escaping.* 3. being or acting in a contrary direction: *Adverse winds blew them off course.* —**ad·verse′ly,** *adv.* —Usage. See **averse.**

ad·ver·si·ty (ad vûr′si tē), *n., pl.* **ad·ver·si·ties.** 1. misfortune; an adverse or unfavorable set of circumstances: *All her life she struggled against adversity.* 2. an adverse or unfortunate event or circumstance: *The pioneers faced many adversities.*

ad·ver·tise (ad′vər tīz′), *v.,* **ad·ver·tised, ad·ver·tis·ing.** 1. to attract public attention or support for (a product, cause, etc.) by radio and television announcements, posters, notices in newspapers, etc.: *They advertised the book so as to increase sales.* 2. to make known by some sort of public announcement: *to advertise a reward.* 3. to seek to acquire something by placing an advertisement (often fol. by *for*): *to advertise for a used car.* —**ad′ver·tis′er,** *n.*

ad·ver·tise·ment (ad′vər tīz′mənt, ad vûr′tis mənt), *n.* 1. a public announcement or description of something, such as goods for sale: *We plan to place advertisements in the newspapers and on radio.* 2. the act

of making something generally known: *to begin the advertisement of a new product.*

ad·ver·tis·ing (ad′vər ti′ziñg), *n.* 1. the act or practice of placing advertisements: *You'll get more customers by advertising.* 2. advertisements; paid announcements: *That station carries a lot of advertising.* 3. the business or profession of making and placing advertisements: *to work in advertising.*

ad·vice (ad vīs′), *n.* 1. an opinion or suggestion offered as a guide to action, conduct, etc.: *I shall act on your advice.* 2. a message or information: *advice from abroad that the government had fallen.*

ad·vis·a·ble (ad vī′zə bəl), *adj.* desirable or wise, as a course of action; proper to be advised or recommended: *Is it advisable for me to write him?* —**ad·vis′a·bil′i·ty,** *n.* —**ad·vis′a·bly,** *adv.*

ad·vise (ad vīz′), *v.,* **ad·vised, ad·vis·ing.** 1. to offer an opinion or suggestion for action or conduct; give counsel or advice: *I advise you to be careful.* 2. to recommend as wise: *I advise secrecy.* 3. to give (someone) information (often fol. by *of*): *We advised him of the risks, but he decided to go anyway.*

ad·vise·ment (ad vīz′mənt), *n.* careful consideration; deliberation or consultation: *The matter has been taken under advisement.*

ad·vis·er (ad vī′zər), *n.* 1. a person who gives advice. 2. a teacher who helps students choose studies, deal with personal problems, etc. Also, **ad·vi′sor.**

ad·vi·so·ry (ad vī′zə rē), *adj.* 1. giving or containing advice: *an advisory letter.* 2. having the power or duty to advise: *the mayor's advisory council.*

ad·vo·ca·cy (ad′və kə sē), *n.* the act of pleading for or supporting a cause: *He was famous for his advocacy of democracy.*

ad·vo·cate (ad′və kāt′), *v.,* **ad·vo·cat·ed, ad·vo·cat·ing.** 1. to plead in favor of; urge by argument; recommend publicly: *to advocate laws to control air pollution.* —*n.* (ad′və kit, ad′və kāt′). 2. a person who publicly supports and argues in favor of a cause (usually fol. by *of*): *an advocate of prohibition.* 3. a person who argues the case for someone in court; lawyer; attorney. [from the Latin word *advocātus* "legal counselor"]

adz (adz), *n., pl.* **adz·es.** a heavy, curved tool with a broad, chisellike steel end mounted on a wooden handle: used for cutting rough timbers or planks. Also, **adze.**

Ae·ge′an Sea′ (i jē′ən), an arm of the Mediterranean Sea located between Greece and Turkey. Also, **the Aegean.**

ae·gis (ē′jis), *n.* protection or sponsorship: *The picnic was under the aegis of the Chamber of Commerce.*

Ae·ne·as (i nē′əs), *n.* (in Roman mythology) a famous Trojan warrior whose descendants founded Rome: hero of Virgil's *Aeneid.*

Ae·o·lus (ē′ə ləs), *n.* (in Greek mythology) the god who controlled the winds.

ae·on (ē′on, ē′ən), *n.* another spelling of **eon.**

aer·ate (âr′āt), *v.,* **aer·at·ed, aer·at·ing. 1.** to expose to the air: *Water is aerated to help purify it.* **2.** to pass air through: *A small pump is used to aerate the water in a fish tank.* **3.** to supply (the blood) with oxygen, as in respiration. —**aer·a′tion,** *n.*

aer·i·al (âr′ē əl), *n.* **1.** a radio or television antenna. —*adj.* **2.** of, in, or produced by the air: *Aerial currents carried our kite out over the water.* **3.** being, living, or taking place in the air: *butterflies and other aerial creatures; an aerial ski lift.* **4.** of or referring to aircraft: *aerial maneuvers; aerial support for troops.* [from the Greek word *aërios* "of the air"]

aer·i·al·ist (âr′ē ə list), *n.* a person who performs on a trapeze.

aer·ie (âr′ē, ēr′ē), *n.* **1.** the nest of an eagle or a hawk, located high above the ground. **2.** the young of such a bird. **3.** any very high place. Also, **eyrie.**

aer·o·naut (âr′ə nôt′), *n.* the pilot of a dirigible or balloon.

aer·o·naut·ics (âr′ə nô′tiks), *n. (used as sing.)* the science or techniques of flight. —**aer′o·nau′ti·cal,** *adj.*

aer·o·plane (âr′ə plān′), *n.* the British spelling of **airplane.**

aer·o·sol (âr′ə sôl′), *n.* **1.** a mass of fine particles in a gas, such as a cloud of smoke, fog, etc. **2.** a liquid sealed in a container with a compressed gas that can be released in a fine spray.

aer·o·space (âr′ə spās′), *n.* the earth's atmosphere and the space beyond it.

Ae·sop (ē′səp, ē′sop), *n.* c620–c560 B.C., Greek writer of fables.

aes·thet·ic (es thet′ik), *adj.* **1.** referring to what is beautiful or to an appreciation of beauty: *to develop one's aesthetic sense.* **2.** having an appreciation of beauty: *an aesthetic person.* **3.** of or referring to aesthetics: *a book that outlines aesthetic theories.* Also, **esthetic.** —**aes·thet′i·cal·ly,** *adv.*

aes·thet·ics (es thet′iks), *n. (used as sing.)* the study of the nature of beauty and other qualities that make up a work of art. Also, **esthetics.**

AF, Air Force. Also, **A.F.**

a·far (ə fär′), *adv.* **1.** from a distance; at or to a distance; far away (sometimes fol. by *off*): *The dog ran afar into the fields. He heard them afar off.* —*n.* **2.** **from afar,** from a long way off: *She saw him riding toward her from afar.*

A·fars′ and Is′sas Ter′ritory (ə färz′ ənd ē′säz), an overseas territory of France in E Africa, on the Gulf of Aden. 8492 sq. mi. Formerly, **French Somaliland.**

AFB, Air Force Base. Also, **A.F.B.**

af·fa·ble (af′ə bəl), *adj.* **1.** pleasantly easy to talk to; friendly; cordial: *an affable and generous host.* **2.** showing warmth and friendliness; pleasant: *an affable, open manner.* —**af′fa·bil′i·ty,** *n.* —**af′fa·bly,** *adv.*

af·fair (ə fâr′), *n.* **1.** anything done or to be done; anything requiring action or effort; business: *This election is an affair of the greatest importance.* **2.** an object, process, or the like, that is not described; thing: *This machine is a complicated affair.* **3.** a private or personal matter: *That's my affair, not yours.* **4.** a party or social gathering: *a very grand affair.* **5. affairs,** matters of public interest or concern; public or private business matters: *affairs of state; to put one's affairs in order.* [from the Old French phrase *a faire* "to do"]

af·fect¹ (ə fekt′), *v.* **1.** to act on; produce a change or effect in: *Cold affects the body.* **2.** to impress the mind or move the feelings of (a person); move; touch: *The music affected him deeply.* [from the Latin word *affectus* "acted upon"]

—**Usage.** *Affect* is often confused with *effect. Affect* means to cause a change in a person or thing: *Dampness may affect a person's health. Dirt had affected the machine's operation. Effect* means to accomplish or complete some action or plan: *I could not effect a reconciliation between my friends. Our move to Denver was effected smoothly.*

af·fect² (ə fekt′), *v.* **1.** to give the appearance of; pretend; feign: *She affected surprise, but she knew we were coming.* **2.** to show a fondness for; choose for oneself; use or adopt as one's own: *He wears cowboy clothes and affects a Western accent.* [from the Latin word *affectāre* "to strive after"]

af·fec·ta·tion (af′ek tā′shən), *n.* **1.** behavior or appearance that is artificial and is meant to attract attention or give a false impression; pretense: *Despite his affectation of respectability, we always thought he was a swindler.* **2.** an instance of such behavior or appearance: *Her eyesight is perfect, so those glasses are just an affectation.*

af·fect·ed¹ (ə fek′tid), *adj.* **1.** acted upon; influenced; changed: *Was the clock affected by being dropped?* **2.** upset, harmed, or injured: *Her mind was affected by her husband's death.* **3.** moved or touched in mind or feelings: *I was deeply affected by your performance in the play.* [affect¹ + -ed]

af·fect·ed² (ə fek′tid), *adj.* artificial or unnatural; feigned: *an affected, prissy way of speaking.* [affect² + -ed] —**af·fect′ed·ly,** *adv.*

af·fect·ing (ə fek′ting), *adj.* moving or exciting the emotions; touching: *an affecting movie about a lost child.* —**af·fect′ing·ly,** *adv.*

af·fec·tion (ə fek′shən), *n.* **1.** fond attachment, devotion, or love: *the affection of a parent for a child.* **2.** a disease or disorder; state of being affected by a disorder: *an affection of the lungs; an affection of the mind.*

af·fec·tion·ate (ə fek′shə nit), *adj.* showing or characterized by affection; loving; tender: *an affectionate greeting.* —**af·fec′tion·ate·ly,** *adv.*

af·fi·ance (ə fī′əns), *v.,* **af·fi·anced, af·fi·anc·ing.** to promise (someone) in marriage; betroth: *to affiance a daughter.*

af·fi·da·vit (af′i dā′vit), *n.* a written declaration or statement, made under oath: *The judge will want an affidavit from anyone who saw the accident.* [from a Latin word meaning "he has sworn"]

af·fil·i·ate (ə fil′ē āt′), *v.*, **af·fil·i·at·ed, af·fil·i·at·ing. 1.** to bring into close connection or association: *Both schools are affiliated with the university.* **2.** to associate oneself; join; unite: *Our club members want to affiliate with your club.* —*n.* (ə fil′ē it, ə fil′ē āt′). **3.** a branch of an organization: *That office is one of our affiliates.* —**af·fil′i·a′tion,** *n.*

af·fin·i·ty (ə fin′i tē), *n., pl.* **af·fin·i·ties. 1.** a natural liking for or attraction to a person or thing: *She has an affinity for chocolate.* **2.** a natural similarity; close resemblance or connection: *an affinity between dogs and wolves.*

af·firm (ə fûrm′), *v.* **1.** to state or assert positively; maintain as true: *He affirmed the truth of his statement.* **2.** to confirm or ratify: *The higher court affirmed the judgment of the lower court.*

af·fir·ma·tion (af′ər mā′shən), *n.* **1.** an assertion that something exists or is true: *an affirmation of one's innocence.* **2.** a confirmation or ratification: *an affirmation of the decision of the lower court.*

af·firm·a·tive (ə fûr′mə tiv), *adj.* **1.** stating that something is true or permissible; being in agreement; giving a "yes" answer: *Her reply was affirmative.* —*n.* **2.** an affirmative answer or response, such as "yes" or "I do": *Her reply was an affirmative.* **3.** the side that is in favor of the question in a debate: *He gave the arguments for the affirmative.* —**af·firm′a·tive·ly,** *adv.*

af·fix (ə fiks′), *v.* **1.** to attach; put or add on (usually fol. by *to*): *to affix a stamp to a letter; to affix a signature to a document.* —*n.* (af′iks). **2.** a part added to a word or stem in order to form a new word with a different meaning; prefix or suffix.

af·flict (ə flikt′), *v.* to cause to suffer mental or bodily pain; trouble greatly: *Heart disease afflicts many older people.* —**af·flict′er,** *n.*

af·flic·tion (ə flik′shən), *n.* **1.** a feeling of pain, distress, or sorrow. **2.** a cause of pain or grief, such as sickness or hardship: *Job endured many afflictions in his lifetime.*

af·flu·ence (af′lo̅o̅ əns), *n.* **1.** a great amount of money, property, material goods, etc.; wealth: *to envy the affluence of one's neighbors.* **2.** abundance of anything: *an affluence of ideas.*

af·flu·ent (af′lo̅o̅ ənt), *adj.* wealthy or rich; prosperous: *Ancient Rome was an affluent city.* [from the Latin word *affluēns* "rich"] —**af′flu·ent·ly,** *adv.*

af·ford (ə fôrd′), *v.* **1.** to be able to do or bear without suffering any bad effects: *They can afford to take chances, because they're winning by a big score.* **2.** to be able to meet the expense of; have the price of: *Can you afford two tickets?* **3.** to give or supply: *The rainy weather afforded us a chance to work on our puppet show.*

af·fray (ə frā′), *n.* a public fight; noisy quarrel; brawl: *a wild affray after the soccer match.*

af·front (ə frunt′), *n.* **1.** an offensive or insulting act or speech; insult: *His comments were an affront to the guests.* —*v.* **2.** to offend by an open show of disrespect; insult: *Your rudeness affronted us all.*

af·ghan (af′gan, af′gən), *n.* a knitted, crocheted, or woven woolen blanket.

Af·ghan (af′gan, af′gən), *n.* a hunting dog with a narrow head and a long, silky coat. Also, **Af′ghan hound′.**

Af·ghan·i·stan (af gan′i stan′), *n.* a republic in S Asia. 250,000 sq. mi.

a·fi·ci·o·na·do (ə fish′yə nä′dō), *n., pl.* **a·fi·ci·o·na·dos.** an enthusiastic follower or supporter; fan: *an aficionado of baseball.* [from a Spanish word meaning "devoted, fond (of)," which comes from *afición* "affection, fondness"]

a·field (ə fēld′), *adv.* **1.** far away; abroad; away from home: *The knight traveled far afield.* **2.** off the beaten track; far and wide; beyond what is usual: *He went far afield in his reading.*

a·fire (ə fi°r′), *adj.* burning; on fire: *to set a house afire.*

a·flame (ə flām′), *adj.* **1.** on fire; ablaze. **2.** glowing or burning, as with excitement: *aflame with anger.*

AFL-CIO, American Federation of Labor and Congress of Industrial Organizations.

a·float (ə flōt′), *adv., adj.* **1.** borne on the water; floating: *The model ship was set afloat.* **2.** on board ship; at sea: *We have cargo afloat and on land.* **3.** covered with water; flooded; awash: *The main deck was afloat.* **4.** passing from place to place; in circulation: *The story is afloat that you visited the President.*

a·flut·ter (ə flut′ər), *adj.* in a flutter: *She was all aflutter before her birthday party.*

a·foot (ə fo̅o̅t′), *adv., adj.* **1.** on foot; walking: *I came afoot because my car broke down.* **2.** astir; in progress: *There is mischief afoot here.*

a·fore·men·tioned (ə fôr′men′shənd), *adj.* mentioned before or earlier: *the aforementioned persons.*

a·fore·said (ə fôr′sed′), *adj.* said or mentioned earlier or before: *The aforesaid rules are still in effect.*

a·fore·thought (ə fôr′thôt′), *adj.* deliberately planned; premeditated: *He committed the crime with malice aforethought.*

a·foul (ə foul′), *adv., adj.* **1.** in a state of confusion; entangled: *The ropes were all afoul.* **2. run afoul of,** to come into conflict with: *to run afoul of the law.*

a·fraid (ə frād′), *adj.* **1.** feeling fear; worried that something bad will happen; frightened: *I am afraid to jump from this height.* **2.** feeling unhappiness, regret, or the like: *I'm afraid I can't visit you this afternoon.* [from an older form of the past participle of the verb *affray* "to disturb, frighten"]

a·fresh (ə fresh′), *adv.* anew or again: *Let's start afresh.*

Af·ri·ca (af′ri kə), *n.* a continent S of Europe and between the Atlantic and Indian oceans. It covers about 11,700,000 sq. mi. —**Af′ri·can,** *n., adj.*

Af·ri·kaans (af′ri käns′, af′ri känz′), *n.* a language of South Africa, developed from Dutch.

Af·ro-A·mer·i·can (af′rō ə mer′i kən), *adj.* 1. referring to black Americans of African descent. — *n.* 2. a black American of African descent.

aft (aft), *adv.* 1. at, near, or toward the stern or rear of a boat: *The captain is walking aft.* —*adj.* 2. located near or at the stern: *the aft sail.*

af·ter (af′tər), *prep.* 1. behind in place or position: *The ducklings walked after their mother.* 2. later in time than; following in time: *Let's see a movie after dinner.* 3. as a conclusion to; as the ending of: *After all that work we still lost the game.* 4. as a result of: *After what happened, I can never go there again.* 5. in imitation of or as a copy of: *This dress is after the French fashion.* 6. in search or pursuit of: *Sooner or later he'll be coming after you.* 7. concerning; about: *She asked after your health.* 8. with the name of: *He was named after his father.* 9. in agreement or sympathy with: *a man after my own heart.* —*adv.* 10. behind; in the rear: *Jill came tumbling after.* 11. later in time; afterward. —*adj.* 12. later in time; subsequent: *In after years we never heard of her again.* —*conj.* 13. following the time that: *After the boys left we had a good visit.*

af·ter·ef·fect (af′tər i fekt′), *n.* a delayed effect or result, esp. one that follows some time after its cause: *The aftereffects of the shock were severe.*

af·ter·math (af′tər math′), *n.* something that results from or follows from an event, esp. the consequence of a violent event: *The aftermath of war was starvation.* [*after* + the earlier English word *math* "a mowing." The original meaning was "a new growth of grass after a mowing"]

af·ter·noon (af′tər nōōn′), *n.* 1. the time from noon until evening; the latter part of the day. —*adj.* 2. referring to or happening in the latter part of the day: *an afternoon nap.*

af·ter·thought (af′tər thôt′), *n.* a second or later thought; reconsideration: *As an afterthought, I think I'll follow your advice.*

af·ter·ward (af′tər wərd), *adv.* in later time; subsequently: *We'll go to the beach first and to the amusement park afterward.* Also, **af′ter·wards.**

Ag, *Chem.* the symbol for silver. [from the Latin word *argentum*]

a·gain (ə gen′), *adv.* 1. once more; anew; another time: *Please spell your name again.* 2. on the other hand; as another possibility: *It might happen and again it might not.* 3. to the same situation, place, or person: *We shall return again.*

a·gainst (ə genst′), *prep.* 1. in opposition to; contrary to: *It was one man against five. Talking is against the rules.* 2. in contact with or close to: *a chair against the wall.* 3. in an opposite direction to; toward: *to swim against the current.* 4. into contact or

collision with: *The rain beat against the window.* 5. in preparation for; as a protection from: *money saved against a rainy day.* 6. with a background of: *a design of flowers against a dark wall.*

Ag·a·mem·non (ag′ə mem′non), *n.* (in Greek mythology) a leader of the Greeks in the Trojan War.

a·gape (ə gāp′), *adv., adj.* 1. with the mouth wide open; in an attitude of amazement or eagerness: *He stood agape when it was announced that he had won.* 2. wide open: *The window was left agape.*

ag·ate (ag′it), *n.* 1. a mineral that is a kind of quartz, usually having curved, colored bands. 2. a playing marble made of this stone or of glass resembling it.

a·ga·ve (ə gā′vē, ə gä′vē), *n.* any of several tall plants of the southern U.S. or Mexico, having long, stiff leaves.

age (āj), *n.* 1. the length of time during which a living thing or object has existed: *His age is 20 years.* 2. a stage of human life: *the age to vote; middle age.* 3. a particular period of history; historical epoch: *the age of atomic science.* 4. a great length of time: *Ages passed before his works were discovered.* 5. advanced years; old age: *a face wrinkled by age.* —*v.,* **aged, ag·ing.** 6. to grow old: *to age rapidly.* 7. to cause to grow old; make old: *Fear aged him overnight.* 8. to mature or ripen, as wine, cheese, wood, etc.: *to age Cheddar.* 9. **of age,** being old enough for certain legal rights, as voting, marrying, etc.: *You are of age when you reach 21.*

-age, a suffix used to form nouns meaning 1. an action or process: *truckage.* 2. a state or condition: *bondage.* 3. the number of: *mileage.* 4. a group: *assemblage.* 5. the cost of: *postage.*

a·ged (ā′jid *for defs. 1, 4;* ājd *for defs. 2, 3*), *adj.* 1. of advanced age; old: *an aged tree.* 2. of the age of: *a man aged 40.* 3. brought to maturity or mellowness, as wine, cheese, wood, etc.: *aged whiskey.* —*n.* 4. **the aged,** old persons collectively: *medical care for the aged.* —**a′ged·ness,** *n.*

age·less (āj′lis), *adj.* never growing old or out of date: *the ageless beauty of a great painting.*

a·gen·cy (ā′jən sē), *n., pl.* **a·gen·cies.** 1. an organization or business that provides some service: *An employment agency helps people find jobs.* 2. a means of getting something done; power; action: *He was released from prison through the agency of the governor.*

a·gen·da (ə jen′də), *n.* a list or plan of things to be done: *What is on your agenda for this afternoon?*

a·gent (ā′jənt), *n.* 1. a person who acts on behalf of another: *You must speak to my agent about the contract.* 2. a person or thing that acts or produces an effect: *Ammonia is a bleaching agent.*

ag·gran·dize (ə gran′dīz), *v.,* **ag·gran·dized, ag·gran·diz·ing.** 1. to make wider, larger, or more intense; enlarge; extend: *to aggrandize one's business.* 2. to increase in power, wealth, or honor; exalt: *The king aggrandized the loyal knights.* —**ag·gran·dize·ment** (ə gran′diz mənt), *n.*

---

act, āble, dâre, ärt; ebb, ēqual; if, īce; hot, ōver, ôrder; oil; bŏŏk; ōōze; out; up, ûrge; ə = *a* as in *alone*; ᵊ as in *button* (but′ᵊn), *fire* (fiᵊr); ᴄhief; ѕhoe; thin; ŧhat; zh as in *measure* (mezh′ər). See full key inside cover.

ag·gra·vate (ag′rə vāt′), v., **ag·gra·vat·ed, ag·gra·vat·ing. 1.** to make worse or more severe: *to aggravate misfortune; to aggravate an illness.* **2.** to annoy or irritate. [from the Latin word *aggravātus* "made heavier"] —**ag′gra·vat′ing·ly,** adv.

ag·gra·va·tion (ag′rə vā′shən), n. **1.** an increase in seriousness or severity; the condition of becoming worse: *the aggravation of a headache by noise.* **2.** the state of being made worse: *Cruel measures only led to an aggravation of the rebellion.* **3.** a cause of irritation or annoyance.

ag·gre·gate (ag′rə git, ag′rə gāt′), adj. **1.** formed by the collection of separate items into one mass or whole; total; combined: *What is your aggregate score?* —n. **2.** a mass or collection of separate items; total: *an aggregate of everyone's suggestions.* —v. (ag′rə gāt′), **ag·gre·gat·ed, ag·gre·gat·ing. 3.** to collect into one sum or mass: *to aggregate all one's savings.* **4.** to amount to a specific number: *The fish we caught aggregated to 30.* —**ag′gre·gate·ly,** adv.

ag·gre·ga·tion (ag′rə gā′shən), n. **1.** a group or mass of things or persons: *an aggregation of plants.* **2.** the act of collecting into one whole or mass: *the aggregation of funds.*

ag·gres·sion (ə gresh′ən), n. **1.** any hostile act or procedure carried out against another; attack or assault: *wartime aggressions; an aggression upon one's rights.* **2.** the action of one nation that first uses force against another; an unprovoked attack: *The seizure of the ship was a serious aggression.*

ag·gres·sive (ə gres′iv), adj. **1.** marked by aggression or the tendency to attack: *an aggressive, warlike people.* **2.** energetic and forceful; bold: *an aggressive leader.* —**ag·gres′sive·ly,** adv. —**ag·gres′sive·ness,** n.

ag·gres·sor (ə gres′ər), n. a person, nation, or group that attacks first or begins fighting; attacker.

ag·grieved (ə grēvd′), adj. wronged, offended, or injured: *The aggrieved people asked for protection.*

a·ghast (ə gast′), adj. struck with shock or amazement; filled with sudden fright or horror: *The elves were aghast at the sight of the giant.*

ag·ile (aj′əl), adj. **1.** quick and graceful in movement; lithe: *an agile acrobat; an agile leap.* **2.** able to think quickly: *an agile debater.* —**ag′ile·ly,** adv.

a·gil·i·ty (ə jil′i tē), n. the ability to move or think quickly and easily: *agility of mind and body.*

ag·i·tate (aj′i tāt′), v., **ag·i·tat·ed, ag·i·tat·ing. 1.** to move, stir up, or shake: *The wind agitates the sea.* **2.** to disturb or excite: *The sight of the soldiers agitated the angry crowd.* **3.** to arouse public interest in a cause: *to agitate for better highways.* —**ag′i·tat′ed·ly,** adv.

ag·i·ta·tion (aj′i tā′shən), n. **1.** the act of agitating or stirring up: *The agitation of milk yields butter.* **2.** the state of being agitated or excited: *She left in great agitation.* **3.** the act of constantly urging a public issue: *agitation for higher wages.*

ag·i·ta·tor (aj′i tā′tər), n. **1.** a person who stirs up others in support of a cause: *a labor agitator.* **2.** a machine or device that stirs or shakes and mixes.

a·glow (ə glō′), adj. glowing or shining: *a house aglow with lights; a face aglow with happiness.*

Ag·new (ag′nōō, ag′nyōō), n. **Spiro T.,** born 1918, 39th Vice President of the U.S. 1969–73.

ag·nos·tic (ag nos′tik), n. a person who believes that the existence of God cannot be proved. —**ag·nos·ti·cism** (ag nos′ti siz′əm), n.

a·go (ə gō′), adj. **1.** gone; gone by; past: *five days ago.* —adv. **2.** in past time: *It happened long ago.*

a·gog (ə gog′), adj. very excited by eagerness, curiosity, or the like: *The audience was agog when the curtain went up.*

ag·o·nize (ag′ə nīz′), v., **ag·o·nized, ag·o·niz·ing. 1.** to suffer extreme pain or anguish; be in agony: *to agonize and weep for sorrow.* **2.** to distress with extreme pain; cause agony; torture: *The terrible news agonized him.*

ag·o·nized (ag′ə nīzd′), adj. involving or showing a severe struggle or agony: *an agonized effort; an agonized look.* —**ag·o·niz·ed·ly** (ag′ə nī′zid lē), adv.

ag·o·ny (ag′ə nē), n., pl. **ag·o·nies. 1.** extreme pain; terrible suffering. **2.** a violent struggle, as against death: *the agonies of her last illness.*

a·gou·ti (ə gōō′tē), n., pl. **a·gou·tis** or **a·gou·ties.** any of several short-haired, short-eared, rabbitlike rodents of South and Central America, destructive to sugar cane.

A·gra (ä′grə), n. a city in N India: site of the Taj Mahal.

a·grar·i·an (ə grâr′ē ən), adj. **1.** of or related to land, esp. farmland: *Agrarian reform will give each peasant a farm of his own.* **2.** of or relating to farmers or agricultural groups: *an agrarian organization.* —n. **3.** a person who favors an equal or fairer division of land.

Agouti
(length 20 in.)

a·gree (ə grē′), v., **a·greed, a·gree·ing. 1.** to have the same opinion or feeling; be of one mind: *I don't agree with you.* **2.** to concede or grant: *I agree that he is the best singer we have.* **3.** to give consent (usually fol. by *to*): *She agreed to my plan.* **4.** to come to an agreement; arrive at a settlement: *The two sides couldn't agree.* **5.** to be consistent or in harmony: *Your book and mine don't agree.* **6.** (in grammar) to be in agreement. **7. agree with, a.** to be consistent with; conform to: *Your story doesn't agree with hers.* **b.** to be digestible or healthful for: *Peppers don't agree with me. A warm climate agrees with him.*

a·gree·a·ble (ə grē′ə bəl), adj. **1.** to one's liking; pleasing: *an agreeable smile.* **2.** willing or ready to agree: *Are you agreeable to my plan?* —**a·gree′a·ble·ness,** n. —**a·gree′a·bly,** adv.

a·gree·ment (ə grē′mənt), n. **1.** the act of agreeing or of coming to an arrangement: *friendly agreement.* **2.** the state of agreeing or being in harmony: *There had better be an agreement between your story and Bill's.* **3.** something that is agreed to or arranged: *Describe the agreement you made.* **4.** (in grammar) a rule that one word must agree with another, as in gender, number, person, or case. In *The boy runs,* the verb *runs* is in agreement with the singular subject *boy.*

ag·ri·cul·tur·al (ag′rə kul′chər əl), *adj.* of or referring to agriculture, farming, or crops: *to buy agricultural machinery.* —**ag′ri·cul′tur·al·ly,** *adv.*

ag·ri·cul·ture (ag′rə kul′chər), *n.* the science or art of cultivating land and raising crops; farming: *The new country is advancing in both agriculture and industry.*

ag·ri·cul·tur·ist (ag′rə kul′chər ist), *n.* an expert in agriculture. Also, **ag′ri·cul′tur·al·ist.**

a·gron·o·my (ə gron′ə mē), *n.* the science of soil conservation, crop rotation and production, etc. —**a·gron′o·mist,** *n.*

a·ground (ə ground′), *adv., adj.* on or into the ground or bottom; in a stranded state: *The ship ran aground on a sand bar. Our boat was aground after the storm.*

agt., agent.

a·gue (ā′gyōō), *n.* 1. a malarial fever that produces regularly recurring hot, cold, and sweating periods. 2. a fit of shaking or shivering.

ah (ä), *interj.* (used as an exclamation of pain, surprise, joy, etc.)

a·ha (ä hä′), *interj.* (used as an exclamation of triumph, mockery, surprise, etc.)

a·head (ə hed′), *adv.* 1. in front of or in advance of a person or thing: *The pavement is icy ahead. We'll go on ahead and say that you'll be late.* 2. in a forward direction; onward: *We are moving ahead slowly.* 3. in or for the future: *There are good days ahead. Plan ahead.* 4. into a better state or situation: *She's sure to get ahead.* 5. **ahead of,** **a.** in front of: *The drum major marched ahead of the band.* **b.** earlier than: *I arrived ahead of the others.* **c.** more advanced or up-to-date than: *This car is ahead of all competitors.*

a·hoy (ə hoi′), *interj.* (used as a call by seamen for hailing, attracting attention, or the like.)

aid (ād), *v.* 1. to help or support; assist: *to aid the snowbound travelers; to aid in a business venture.* —*n.* 2. help or assistance; support: *aid given to another country.* 3. a person or thing that helps, assists, or makes easier: *Pictures are used as an aid to learning.* [from the Old French word *aidier* "to help," which comes from Latin *adjūtāre*]

aide (ād), *n.* 1. an aide-de-camp. 2. any official assistant or helper: *the ambassador's aides; a hospital aide.* [from a French word meaning "helper," which comes from *aider* "to help, aid"]

aide-de-camp (ād′də kamp′), *n., pl.* **aides-de-camp.** an assistant to a high military or naval officer.

ail (āl), *v.* 1. to cause pain, discomfort, trouble, or worry to: *What on earth is ailing you?* 2. to be ill: *That old parrot is ailing again.*

ai·ler·on (ā′lə ron′), *n.* a movable section of the back edge of an airplane wing. Turning the ailerons up and down in opposite directions tilts the plane to one side or the other.

ail·ment (āl′mənt), *n.* a physical disorder or illness: *Nervousness is just one of his ailments.*

aim (ām), *v.* 1. to point or position (a weapon or missile, such as a ball, dart, or rocket) so as to hit a target: *to aim a rifle.* 2. to direct or intend for a particular object or purpose: *a lecture aimed at stopping lateness.* 3. to try or strive; have the intention: *We aim to please.* —*n.* 4. the act of aiming or directing at a point or target: *His aim is bad.* 5. something desired or intended; purpose: *Her aim is to go to London.* 6. **take aim,** to aim a gun, missile, etc., at a target: *to take aim and fire.*

aim·less (ām′lis), *adj.* without aim or purpose: *aimless talk; aimless wandering.* —**aim′less·ly,** *adv.* —**aim′less·ness,** *n.*

air (âr), *n.* 1. the mixture of oxygen, nitrogen, carbon dioxide, water vapor, and other gases that surrounds the earth and forms its atmosphere. 2. the area around the earth; sky: *a balloon high in the air.* 3. a light breeze or stir in the atmosphere. 4. the general feeling or atmosphere of something; peculiar appearance: *an abandoned house with an air of mystery.* 5. a tune or melody: *They played a familiar air.* 6. **airs,** affected or haughty conduct or behavior. —*v.* 7. to expose to the air; ventilate: *to air the blankets.* 8. to bring to general or public notice; display; expose: *to air one's views.* —*adj.* 9. operated by compressed air: *air rifle; air brakes.* 10. containing air: *air cushion.* 11. of, referring to, or by means of aircraft: *air travel.* 12. **on the air,** broadcasting on radio or television: *We will be on the air at 10 o'clock.* —**air′less,** *adj.*

air′ bag′, a large plastic bag that inflates automatically inside an automobile upon impact in a collision, to protect riders from injury.

air′ base′, a center from which a military air force can operate, including a landing field and buildings.

air-con·di·tion (âr′kən dish′ən), *v.* 1. to furnish with an air-conditioning unit or system. 2. to treat (air) with such a unit or system.

air′ condi′tioner, an air-conditioning unit.

air′ condi′tioning, a system that cools, dries, and filters the air in a room, building, automobile, etc.

air·craft (âr′kraft′), *n., pl.* **air·craft.** any machine that can sustain itself above the ground by its motion through the air, as an airplane or glider, or by being lighter than the air it displaces, as a dirigible.

air′craft car′rier, a warship having a deck for the taking off and landing of fighters and other aircraft.

air·drome (âr′drōm′), *n.* a landing field for airplanes.

air·drop (âr′drop′), *v.,* **air·dropped,** **air·dropping.** 1. to drop (persons, equipment, etc.) by parachute from an aircraft in flight: *to airdrop food to starving cattle.* —*n.* 2. the act of dropping persons, equipment, etc., from an aircraft by parachute: *to make an airdrop of food and ammunition to troops in enemy territory.*

Aircraft carrier

Aire·dale (âr′dāl′), *n.* a large terrier having a wiry, black-and-tan coat, and usually a very short tail.

air·field (âr′fēld′), *n.* a level area, usually having runways, where airplanes can take off and land.

air′ force′, a military department that is in charge of all operations involving aircraft.

Air′ Force′, the U.S. military department in charge of aviation forces and air warfare.

air′ gun′, a gun operated by compressed air.

Airedale
(23 in. high
at shoulder)

air·i·ly (âr′ə lē), *adv.* 1. in a gay or breezy manner: *He left airily as if nothing were wrong.*

air·lift (âr′lift′), *n.* 1. a system for transporting passengers or cargo by air, esp. in an emergency: *an airlift to a blockaded city.* —*v.* 2. to transport (passengers or cargo) by airlift.

air·line (âr′līn′), *n.* 1. a system of scheduled air transport for passengers or cargo. 2. Often, **airlines.** a company that owns and runs a system of air transport.

air·lin·er (âr′lī′nər), *n.* a passenger airplane that is owned and operated by an airline.

air′ mail′, 1. the system of sending mail by airplane. 2. mail sent by airplane: *a bag full of air mail.*

air-mail (âr′māl′), *adj.* 1. of or concerning air mail: *an air-mail letter.* —*adv.* 2. by air mail: *Send all the letters air-mail.* —*v.* 3. to send by air mail: *to air-mail a package.* Also, **air′mail′.**

air·man (âr′mən), *n., pl.* **air·men.** 1. a man who flies an aircraft, or a member of the crew. 2. an enlisted man in the U.S. Air Force.

air′ mile′. See **mile** (def. 2).

air·plane (âr′plān′), *n.* 1. an aircraft that has one or more rigid wings and is powered by propellers or by jet engines. 2. a glider. Also, *esp. British,* **aeroplane.**

air′ pock′et, a downward air current that can cause an airplane to drop suddenly.

air·port (âr′pôrt′), *n.* an area of land or water used for the landing and takeoff of aircraft and equipped to receive and discharge passengers and cargo, make repairs, etc.

air′ pow′er, the military strength of a nation for operations involving aircraft.

air′ pres′sure, 1. the pressure exerted in all directions by the atmosphere: 14.7 pounds per square inch at sea level. 2. the pressure of a mass of compressed air.

air′ raid′, an attack by enemy aircraft, esp. for bombing a particular area.

air·ship (âr′ship′), *n.* an aircraft that is lighter than air, is kept aloft by a large gas-filled container, and can be steered.

air·sick (âr′sik′), *adj.* sick at the stomach while traveling in an airplane because of the airplane's motion. —**air′sick′ness,** *n.*

air·strip (âr′strip′), *n.* See **runway** (def. 2).

air·tight (âr′tīt′), *adj.* 1. preventing the entrance or escape of air: *Tennis balls usually come in airtight cans.* 2. having no weak points: *an airtight alibi.*

air-to-air (âr′tōō âr′), *adj., adv.* between aircraft in flight: *air-to-air missiles; to refuel air-to-air.*

air·way (âr′wā′), *n.* 1. a route for airplanes. 2. a passage in a mine for a current of air.

air·y (âr′ē), *adj.,* **air·i·er, air·i·est.** 1. of or in the air. 2. open to a current of air; breezy: *an airy room.* 3. light in manner; sprightly: *an airy tune.* 4. without substance; imaginary: *airy dreams.* —**air′i·ness,** *n.*

aisle (īl), *n.* 1. a passage between seats, esp. in a church or theater. 2. a narrow passage: *We walked in the aisle between the trees.* 3. a part of a church separated from the main part by arches or columns. [from the Latin word *āla* "wing"; the spelling *aisle* is due to confusion with the word *isle*]

a·jar[1] (ə jär′), *adj., adv.* partly open: *He left the door ajar.* [from the Middle English phrase *on char* "on the turn," that is, "easily turned"]

a·jar[2] (ə jär′), *adv., adj.* not in agreement; at variance: *That story is ajar with the facts.* [from the earlier phrase *at jar* "at discord"]

a·kim·bo (ə kim′bō), *adj., adv.* with hands on hips and elbows bent outward: *to stand with arms akimbo.* [from the Middle English phrase *in kene bowe* "in a sharp bend"]

a·kin (ə kin′), *adj.* 1. being members of the same family; related by blood. 2. very much alike: *We are akin in our love of fine music.* 3. having a resemblance; similar: *something akin to whooping cough.*

Ak·ron (ak′rən), *n.* a city in NE Ohio.

Al, *Chem.* the symbol for **aluminum.**

-al, a suffix used to form 1. adjectives meaning of, like, or relating to: *personal; national.* Some of these adjectives are used also as nouns: *a formal.* 2. nouns meaning **a.** the act of: *refusal; denial.* **b.** the amount or cost of: *rental.*

Ala., Alabama.

Al·a·bam·a (al′ə bam′ə), *n.* a state in the SE United States. 51,609 sq. mi. *Cap.:* Montgomery. —**Al·a·bam·i·an** (al′ə bam′ē ən), **Al′a·bam′an,** *n., adj.*

al·a·bas·ter (al′ə bas′-ter), *n.* 1. a fine-grained mineral, often white and translucent, that is used to make vases, statues, etc. —*adj.* 2. smooth and white as alabaster: *alabaster skin.*

a·lack (ə lak′), *interj. Archaic.* (used as an exclamation of sorrow, regret, or dismay.)

a·lac·ri·ty (ə lak′ri tē), *n.* 1. cheerful readiness, willingness, or promptness: *He always replies with alacrity.* 2. liveliness; briskness: *The old man can still move around with a great deal of alacrity.*

Al·a·mo (al′ə mō′), *n.* a mission in San Antonio, Texas: taken by Mexicans on March 6, 1836, during the Texan war for independence.

à la mode (ä′ lə mōd′), 1. according to fashion; stylish. 2. (of pie or other dessert) served with a topping of ice cream.

a·larm (ə lärm′), *n.* 1. a warning of danger. 2. a call to arms: *A soldier gave the alarm to the men.* 3. a device that warns or signals people by its sound: *a fire alarm; a burglar alarm.* 4. a sudden fear of danger: *We reacted with alarm to the news of the flood.* —*v.* 5. to make fearful; cause to worry: *It really alarmed me when I saw the ambulance in front of his house.* 6. to warn of danger. [from the Italian word *allarme* "to arms," which comes from *alle* "to the" + *arme* "arms"] —**a·larm′ing·ly,** *adv.*

alarm′ clock′, a clock with a bell or buzzer that can be set to sound at a certain time to awaken people.

a·larm·ist (ə lär′mist), *n.* a person who is alarmed or alarms others without good reason, usually by exaggerating or predicting dangers: *The alarmists say the country is heading for war.*

a·las (ə las′), *interj.* (used as an exclamation of grief, self-pity, or concern.)

Alas., Alaska.

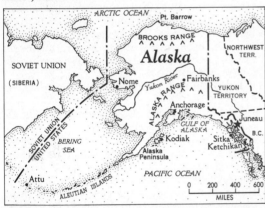

A·las·ka (ə las′kə), *n.* a state of the United States in NW North America. 586,400 sq. mi. *Cap.:* Juneau. —**A·las′kan,** *n., adj.*

alb (alb), *n.* a white linen robe with close-fitting sleeves, worn in church by priests.

Al·ba·ni·a (al bā′nē ə), *n.* a republic in S Europe, on the Balkan Peninsula. 10,632 sq. mi. *Cap.:* Tirana. —**Al·ba′ni·an,** *n., adj.*

Al·ba·ny (ôl′bə nē), *n.* the capital city of New York, in the E part.

al·ba·tross (al′bə trôs′), *n.* any of several large, web-footed sea birds: noted for their ability to remain aloft for long periods.

Albatross
(length 4 ft.;
wingspread to 12 ft.)

al·be·it (ôl bē′it), *conj.* although; even if: *It was a successful albeit costly expedition.*

Al·ber·ta (al bûr′tə), *n.* a province in W Canada. 255,288 sq. mi. *Cap.:* Edmonton.

al·bi·no (al bī′nō), *n., pl.* **al·bi·nos.** 1. a person or animal having pale skin, light hair, and pink eyes, owing to a lack of pigmentation. 2. a plant that has no pigmentation.

Al·bi·on (al′bē ən), *n. Archaic.* another name for England.

al·bum (al′bəm), *n.* 1. a book with blank pages for holding photographs, autographs, etc. 2. a long-playing phonograph record, or set of such records. 3. the package for such a record or records.

al·bu·men (al byōō′mən), *n.* the white of an egg.

al·bu·min (al byōō′mən), *n.* a protein that dissolves in water and is contained in egg white, animal tissues, and plant juices.

Al·bu·quer·que (al′bə kûr′kē), *n.* a city in central New Mexico.

al·che·mist (al′kə mist), *n.* (in former times) a person who practiced alchemy.

al·che·my (al′kə mē), *n.* the medieval form of chemistry, concerned with magic and aimed chiefly at turning ordinary metals into gold. [from the Arabic phrase *al kimiyā′* "the changing (of metals into gold)," which comes from the Greek word *chymeia* "the method of alloying metals, alchemy"]

al·co·hol (al′kə hôl′), *n.* 1. Also, **grain alcohol.** a colorless, flammable liquid, produced by distilling fermented solutions of molasses or grain, and used as a disinfectant and solvent. The alcohol in whiskey, gin, wine, beer, etc., makes them intoxicating. 2. any of several similar liquids, such as wood alcohol. [from the Arabic phrase *al kuhul* "the powdered antimony." The word acquired its modern meaning because this powder, used as a cosmetic in the East, was obtained by a process similar to distillation]

al·co·hol·ic (al′kə hô′lik), *adj.* 1. of, referring to, or caused by alcohol: *an alcoholic beverage.* —*n.* 2. a person suffering from alcoholism.

al·co·hol·ism (al′kə hô liz′əm), *n.* 1. addiction to alcoholic drinks. 2. a diseased condition resulting from excessive use of alcohol.

Al·cott (ôl′kət, ôl′kot), *n.* **Louisa May,** 1832–1888, U.S. writer.

al·cove (al′kōv), *n.* 1. a recess next to or opening out of a room: *a dining alcove.* 2. an opening in the wall of a room for a bed, bookcases, etc.

Al·den (ôl′dən), *n.* **John,** 1599?–1687, Pilgrim settler in Plymouth, Massachusetts, 1620.

al·der (ôl′dər), *n.* a tree or shrub resembling the birch and growing in wet places.

al·der·man (ôl′dər mən), *n., pl.* **al·der·men.** a person who is elected to represent a certain district on a municipal board or council.

ale (āl), *n.* an alcoholic drink made from malt and hops: darker, heavier, and more bitter than beer.

a·lee (ə lē′), *adv., adj.* on or toward the lee side of a ship; away from the wind.

a·lert (ə lûrt′), *adj.* 1. wide-awake; fully aware: *an*

alert mind. **2.** very quick; nimble. —*n.* **3.** a warning signal: *to sound an alert.* **4.** the period during which such a warning signal is in effect. **5.** a period of watchfulness and readiness, as before an attack. —*v.* **6.** to warn: *The lifeguard alerted us to the dangers of swimming in deep water.* **7. on the alert,** on guard against danger; watchful: *Be on the alert for an escaped criminal.* [from the Italian phrase *all'erta* "on the lookout," which comes from *alla* "to the" + *erta* "high place"] —**a·lert′ly,** *adv.* —**a·lert′ness,** *n.*

A·leu′tian Is′lands (ə lōō′shən), a group of islands extending SW from Alaska: part of Alaska. Also, **the Aleutians.** See illus. at **Alaska.**

Al·ex·an′der the Great′ (al′ig zan′dər), 356–323 B.C., king of Macedonia 336–323: conquered Greece and Persia.

Al·ex·an·dri·a (al′ig-zan′drē ə), *n.* a port city in N Egypt, on the delta of the Nile. —**Al′ex·an′dri·an,** *n., adj.*

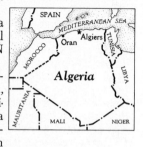
Fourth Century B.C.

al·fal·fa (al fal′fə), *n.* a plant that has long roots, leaves resembling clover, and bluish-purple flowers, grown as fodder for cattle and sometimes as an enrichment for soil.

Al′fred the Great′ (al′fred, al′frid), A.D. 849–899, English king 871–899.

al·ga (al′gə), *n., pl.* **al·gae** (al′jē). any of numerous kinds of water plants containing chlorophyll and ranging in size from one-celled forms to the largest kelps.

al·ge·bra (al′jə brə), *n.* a branch of mathematics in which quantities are represented by letters or symbols and problems are solved by using equations. [from an Arabic phrase meaning "the setting" (of broken bones), later applied to the putting together of equations]

al·ge·bra·ic (al′jə brā′ik), *adj.* of or involving algebra.

Al·ge·ri·a (al jēr′ē ə), *n.* a republic in NW Africa: gained independence from France in 1962. 919,595 sq. mi. *Cap.:* Algiers. —**Al·ge′ri·an,** *n., adj.*

Al·giers (al jērz′), *n.* a seaport and the capital city of Algeria, in the N part.

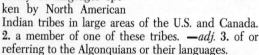
Algeria

Al·gon·qui·an (al gong′-kē ən, al gong′kwē ən), *n., pl.* for def. 2 **Al·gon·qui·ans** *or* **Al·gon·qui·an. 1.** a family of languages spoken by North American Indian tribes in large areas of the U.S. and Canada. **2.** a member of one of these tribes. —*adj.* **3.** of or referring to the Algonquians or their languages.

Al·gon·quin (al gong′kin, al gong′kwin), *n., pl.* for def. 1 **Al·gon·quins** *or* **Al·gon·quin. 1.** a member of a group of North American Indian tribes formerly living along the Ottawa River and the northern tribu-

taries of the St. Lawrence. **2.** the language spoken by the members of these Indian tribes.

a·li·as (ā′lē əs), *n., pl.* **a·li·as·es. 1.** an assumed name; another name that a person is known by. —*adv.* **2.** at another time or place; in other circumstances. *"Simpson alias Smith"* means that Simpson is otherwise known as Smith. [from a Latin word meaning "otherwise"]

al·i·bi (al′ə bī′), *n., pl.* **al·i·bis. 1.** the defense by an accused person that he was elsewhere when the crime of which he is accused was committed. **2.** an excuse: *He had no alibi for arriving late.* [from a Latin word meaning "elsewhere"]

al·ien (āl′yən, ā′lē ən), *n.* **1.** a person who is not a citizen of the country in which he is living. —*adj.* **2.** of or referring to an alien or aliens: *alien property.* **3.** coming from another country; foreign: *alien speech.* **4.** very different; opposed: *His ideas are alien to ours.*

al·ien·ate (āl′yə nāt′, ā′lē ə nāt′), *v.,* **al·ien·at·ed, al·ien·at·ing.** to make indifferent or unfriendly where friendship and attachment once existed: *His strange behavior alienated his old friends.* —**al′ien·a′tion,** *n.*

a·light¹ (ə līt′), *v.,* **a·light·ed** *or* **a·lit** (ə līt′); **a·light·ing. 1.** to get off a horse, get out of a vehicle, etc. **2.** to settle or stay after descending: *A bird alights on a tree.* **3.** to find by chance: *He somehow alighted on the correct answer.* [from the Old English word *ālīhtan* "to relieve of weight"]

a·light² (ə līt′), *adv., adj.* lighted up; burning: *The room was alight with torches. Her face was alight with enthusiasm.* [from the Old English word *onlihtan* "to light up"]

a·lign (ə līn′), *v.* **1.** to arrange in a straight line: *He neatly aligned the numbers in columns.* **2.** to join with others in a cause: *He aligned himself with the people who wanted a new school.*

a·lign·ment (ə līn′mənt), *n.* **1.** an arrangement of things in a straight line; adjustment to a straight line. **2.** the adjustment of parts, as in a machine, for more efficient operation: *My brakes are out of alignment.*

a·like (ə līk′), *adv.* **1.** in the same manner or way; equally: *The salesman treats all his customers alike.* —*adj.* **2.** showing similarity: *They are very much alike in their love of good food.*

al·i·men′ta·ry canal′ (al′ə men′tə rē), the tubular passage, consisting of the mouth, esophagus, stomach, and intestines, in which the digestion and absorption of food take place.

al·i·mo·ny (al′ə mō′nē), *n.* a sum of money paid regularly to a woman by her husband or former husband after legal separation or divorce.

a·live (ə līv′), *adj.* **1.** having life; not dead or lifeless: *The plant we watered every day is alive.* **2.** full of life; lively: *She is more alive than most of her friends.* **3. alive to,** aware of; sensitive to: *to be alive to the dangers of taking drugs.* **4. alive with,** full of; swarming with: *The swamp was alive with poisonous snakes.* **5. look alive!** pay attention! move quickly!: *Look alive or we'll never get finished on time!*

al·ka·li (al′kə lī′), *n., pl.* **al·ka·lis** *or* **al·ka·lies.** any of numerous caustic substances, as lye, some of which

occur in nature as minerals: used in manufacturing soaps. Alkalis neutralize acids to form salts. See also **base**[1] (def. 8). [from an Arabic phrase meaning "the burnt ashes" (of certain sea plants)]

al·ka·line (al′kə līn′, al′kə lin), *adj.* 1. of, containing, or like an alkali. 2. containing excess alkali.

al·ka·loid (al′kə loid′), *n.* any of numerous substances found in plants and useful in medicine. Many are highly poisonous.

all (ôl), *adj.* 1. the whole of: *We ate all the cake.* 2. the whole number of; every one of: *All classes attended the assembly.* 3. the greatest possible: *He told us the story in all seriousness.* —*pron.* 4. the whole quantity, number, or amount: *All of us went home early.* 5. everything: *Is that all you want to say?* —*adv.* 6. entirely; completely: *all alone; all worn out.* 7. each; apiece: *The score after two innings was one all.* 8. **after all,** regardless of any other circumstances: *After all, your parents' wishes have to be respected.* 9. **all at once,** suddenly; without warning: *All at once we heard an explosion.* 10. **all in,** exhausted; fatigued: *I'm all in after that long climb.* 11. **all in all,** everything considered; in general: *All in all, he's making progress.* 12. **at all,** in the slightest degree: *It's not my business at all.* 13. **in all,** taken or considered altogether: *There were 40 guests in all.*

Al·lah (al′ə, ä′lə), *n.* the Supreme Being, or God, in the Muslim religion.

all-a·round (ôl′ə round′), *adj.* skilled, accomplished, or useful in many different ways: *an all-around athlete; an all-around education.* Also, **all-round.**

al·lay (ə lā′), *v.*, **al·layed, al·lay·ing.** 1. to make calm or quiet; put to rest: *to allay one's fears.* 2. to lessen or relieve: *to allay pain with medicine.*

all-day (ôl′dā′), *adj.* lasting or taking place throughout a day: *an all-day meeting; an all-day sucker.*

al·le·ga·tion (al′ə gā′shən), *n.* 1. a statement made as a plea, excuse, or justification. 2. a statement or declaration made without proof.

al·lege (ə lej′), *v.*, **al·leged, al·leg·ing.** 1. to declare without proof: *He alleged that he saw the burglar escape.* 2. to declare with certainty: *He alleged that the statistics were correct.* 3. to give as a reason or an excuse: *He alleges that illness kept him home.*

al·leged (ə lejd′), *adj.* 1. declared to be as described: *The police are searching for the alleged thief.* 2. doubtful or supposed: *an alleged cure for cancer.*

al·leg·ed·ly (ə lej′id lē), *adv.* according to what has been stated or believed; supposedly: *He allegedly was there at the time of the robbery.*

Al′le·ghe′ny Moun′tains (al′ə gā′nē), a mountain range in Pennsylvania, Maryland, West Virginia, and Virginia: a part of the Appalachian Mountains. Also, **the Al′le·ghe′nies.**

al·le·giance (ə lē′jəns), *n.* 1. a citizen's loyalty to his country. 2. loyalty to any person, group, or cause.

al·le·go·ry (al′ə gôr′ē), *n., pl.* **al·le·go·ries.** a story whose characters and events have a meaning that is deeper than it appears and that teaches a lesson or moral: *Many of the Bible stories are allegories.* —**al′le·gor′i·cal,** *adj.*

al·le·gro (ə leg′rō), *adj., adv.* 1. (in music) quick; quickly. —*n., pl.* **al·le·gros.** 2. a lively, quick piece or section of music. [from an Italian word meaning "merry, gay"]

al·le·lu·ia (al′ə lōō′yə), *interj.* 1. praise ye the Lord; hallelujah! —*n.* 2. a song of praise to God.

Al·len·town (al′ən toun′), *n.* a city in E Pennsylvania.

al·ler·gic (ə lûr′jik), *adj.* of, referring to, or having an allergy: *to be allergic to fur.*

al·ler·gy (al′ər jē), *n., pl.* **al·ler·gies.** 1. an abnormal sensitivity to a substance, such as a food, pollen, dust, etc. 2. a condition, such as asthma, hayfever, or the like, caused by such a sensitivity.

al·le·vi·ate (ə lē′vē āt′), *v.*, **al·le·vi·at·ed, al·le·vi·at·ing.** to make easier to endure; lessen: *The medicine will alleviate the pain.* —**al·le′vi·a′tion,** *n.*

al·ley[1] (al′ē), *n., pl.* **al·leys.** 1. a narrow back street or passage between buildings, properties, etc. 2. a path in a park or garden that is enclosed with hedges. 3. a long wooden lane or floor along which a bowling ball is rolled. [from the Old French word *allee* "path," which comes from *aller* "to go"]

al·ley[2] (al′ē), *n., pl.* **al·leys.** a large playing marble for shooting at other marbles. [short for *alabaster*]

All·hal·lows (ôl′hal′ōz), *n.* another name for **All Saints' Day.**

al·li·ance (ə lī′əns), *n.* 1. a formal agreement or treaty between two or more nations to cooperate for specific purposes. 2. an agreement or joining of interests of two or more persons or groups: *Three civic groups formed an alliance to support the candidate.* 3. the nations, persons, or groups in an alliance.

al·lied (ə līd′, al′īd), *adj.* 1. joined by treaty: *The allied nations met in Rome to discuss military questions.* 2. related or connected in some way: *Geography and history are allied subjects.*

al·lies (al′īz, ə līz′), *n.* 1. the plural of **ally.** —*v.* (ə līz′). 2. the third person singular, present tense of **ally.**

Al·lies (al′īz, ə līz′), *n.pl.* the 26 nations, including the United States, that fought against the Axis in World War II and, with some additions, signed the United Nations Charter in 1945.

al·li·ga·tor (al′ə gā′tər), *n.* a large reptile of the southern U.S., having a thick hide, a long tail, and a long, broad snout. [from the Spanish phrase *el lagarto* "the alligator," which comes from Latin *lacertus* "lizard"]

al′ligator pear′. See **avocado** (def. 1).

al·lit·er·a·tion (ə lit′ə rā′shən), *n.* the repetition of an initial letter or sound in a group of

Alligator
(length to 12 ft.)

words, as in *big brown bear* or *many more marbles.*

al·lo·cate (al′ə kāt′), *v.,* **al·lo·cat·ed, al·lo·cat·ing.** to set aside for a particular purpose: *We allocated five hours for work on the project.* —**al′lo·ca′tion,** *n.*

al·lot (ə lot′), *v.,* **al·lot·ted, al·lot·ting. 1.** to divide or distribute in shares or portions; assign: *Tasks were allotted to everyone in the family.* **2.** to give or grant as a portion or share of something: *They allotted me five dollars to buy the teacher a present.*

al·lot·ment (ə lot′mənt), *n.* **1.** the act of allotting: *the allotment of tasks to class members.* **2.** a portion or thing allotted; share: *My allotment for the concert is five tickets.*

all-out (ôl′out′), *adj.* using all one's strength or abilities; complete: *an all-out effort to win the game.*

al·low (ə lou′), *v.* **1.** to give permission to or for: *Father allowed us to stay up late to watch television.* **2.** to take into consideration by adding or subtracting: *to allow an hour for changing trains.* **3.** to give or assign as one's portion or share: *I'm allowed a dollar for school supplies.* **4.** to agree to; concede: *to allow a claim.* **5.** to make possible; permit: *more than my budget allows.* **6. allow for,** to take into consideration: *Add more water to allow for evaporation.*

al·low·a·ble (ə lou′ə bəl), *adj.* permitted by certain rules; not forbidden: *Parking is allowable here.*

al·low·ance (ə lou′əns), *n.* **1.** an amount of money given regularly for a particular purpose: *a weekly allowance for lunches and spending money.* **2.** an addition or subtraction made to take something into consideration: *an allowance of ten percent for depreciation.* **3. make allowance** (or **allowances**) **for, a.** to take into consideration: *You have to make allowance for her ill health.* **b.** to pardon or excuse: *We made allowances for Helen because she'd been ill.*

al·loy (al′oi, ə loi′), *n.* **1.** a mixture of two or more different metals: *Brass is an alloy of copper and zinc.* —*v.* (ə loi′). **2.** to mix (metals). [from the Old French word *aleier* "to combine," which comes from Latin *alligāre* "to bind up"]

all-pur·pose (ôl′pûr′pəs), *adj.* suitable for every purpose: *all-purpose flour.*

all′ right′, 1. safe or unharmed: *The doctor said my leg was all right.* **2.** yes; very well: *All right, I'll go with you.* **3.** acceptable; satisfactory: *His report card is all right, but it could be better.* **4.** properly; correctly: *Is the car running all right?* **5.** without fail; certainly; absolutely: *I'll tell him, all right!*
—**Usage.** *Alright* is sometimes used as a variant of *all right,* but it is not considered acceptable English.

all-round (ôl′round′), *adj.* another form of **all-around.**

All′ Saints′′ Day′, a church festival celebrated November 1, in honor of all the saints; Allhallows.

all·spice (ôl′spīs′), *n.* **1.** a spice made from the brown berry of a tree that grows esp. in the West Indies. It smells and tastes like a mixture of cloves, cinnamon, and nutmeg. **2.** the berry itself, or the tree producing it.

all-time (ôl′tīm′), *adj.* greater or less than at any previous time: *Sales are at an all-time high.*

al·lude (ə lo̅o̅d′), *v.,* **al·lud·ed, al·lud·ing.** to mention briefly or indirectly; speak of in passing: *He often alluded to his visit to New York.*

al·lure (ə lo̅o̅r′), *v.,* **al·lured, al·lur·ing. 1.** to attract with something flattering or desirable: *to allure fish with bait.* **2.** to fascinate; charm: *Travel allures him.* —*n.* **3.** charm or fascination: *the allure of the Orient.* —**al·lur′ing·ly,** *adv.*

al·lure·ment (ə lo̅o̅r′mənt), *n.* **1.** the power of alluring; charm. **2.** the means of alluring; enticement: *They used flattery and other allurements to get him on their team.*

al·lu·sion (ə lo̅o̅′zhən), *n.* a casual reference or mention: *an allusion to the Bible in a story we read.*

al·lu·vi·al (ə lo̅o̅′vē əl), *adj.* formed of sand, gravel, etc., deposited by flowing water.

al·ly (ə lī′), *v.,* **al·lied, al·ly·ing. 1.** to unite or join together for a common purpose: *One nation often allies itself with other nations in time of war.* —*n.* (al′ī, ə lī′), *pl.* **al·lies. 2.** a person or country united or joined with another for a common purpose: *The United States was an ally of France in World War II.*

al·ma ma·ter (äl′mə mä′tər, al′mə mā′tər), a school or college at which a person has studied and, usually, one from which he has graduated. [from a Latin phrase meaning "nourishing mother"]

al·ma·nac (ôl′mə nak′), *n.* an annual publication that contains a calendar, information about the weather, tides, planets and stars, and usually other interesting facts about countries, famous people, sports, etc. [from a medieval Latin word, which comes from Arabic *al 'manākh* "the calendar"]

al·might·y (ôl mī′tē), *adj.* **1.** having unlimited power. **2. the Almighty,** another name for **God.**

al·mond (ä′mənd, am′ənd), *n.* **1.** the nutlike seed of a tree that grows in warm climates. **2.** the tree itself. —*adj.* **3.** made or flavored with almonds: *almond cookies.*

Almond
A, Closed nut
B, Open nut

al·most (ôl′mōst, ôl mōst′), *adv.* very nearly: *He almost won the race.*

alms (ämz), *n.* money or other gifts given to the poor: *to beg alms.*

alms·house (ämz′hous′), *n., pl.* **alms·hous·es** (ämz′hou′ziz). *British.* a home for persons dependent on charity for support.

a·loft (ə lôft′), *adv.* **1.** high up; in or into the air: *He held the trophy aloft.* **2.** on the masts or in the rigging of a ship: *Go aloft and mend the sail.*

a·lo·ha (ə lō′ə, ä lō′hä), *interj.* (in Hawaiian) hello, welcome, or good-by.

a·lone (ə lōn′), *adj.* **1.** apart from any other: *The second volume alone is of no value.* **2.** with none else besides; excluding all others or all else: *She alone is to blame for all our troubles.* **3.** having no equal; unique: *The Grand Canyon is alone in splendor.* —*adv.* **4.** without anyone else: *He works alone.* **5. let alone, a.** to keep from bothering or interfering with: *Let the baby alone!* **b.** without even considering: *I* *can't even do one push-up, let alone thirty-seven.*

a·long (ə lông⁄), *prep.* 1. through, on, beside, or over: *to walk along the side of the road.* —*adv.* 2. onward; forward: *The line moved right along.* 3. as a companion: *He brought his sister along.* 4. **all along,** all the time; throughout: *He knew all along he wasn't going to go.* 5. **along with, a.** in the company of: *Is she going along with you?* **b.** in addition to: *Sweep the porch along with the sidewalk.* 6. **be along,** to arrive at a place: *Sid will be along in 15 minutes.* 7. **get along, a.** to leave; depart: *We'd better be getting along.* **b.** to be friendly or congenial: *It's hard to get along with somebody you don't trust.* **c.** to carry on one's affairs; manage: *She can't get along without her sister's help.*

a·long·side (ə lông⁄sīd⁄), *adv.* 1. along, at, or to the side of something: *We brought the boat alongside.* —*prep.* 2. beside; by the side of: *The car pulled up alongside the house.*

a·loof (ə lōōf⁄), *adv.* 1. at a distance in feeling or interest: *to remain aloof from an argument.* —*adj.* 2. reserved or indifferent: *an aloof manner.* —**a·loof⁄ness,** *n.*

a·loud (ə loud⁄), *adv.* 1. with the normal speaking voice: *to read aloud.* 2. with a loud voice; loudly: *to cry aloud.*

al·pac·a (al pak⁄ə), *n.* 1. a domesticated South American animal, related to the llama, having long, silky hair, or wool. 2. cloth woven from this wool.

Alpaca
(3½ ft. high at shoulder)

al·pha (al⁄fə), *n.* 1. the first letter of the Greek alphabet. 2. the first or the beginning of something.

al·pha·bet (al⁄fə bet⁄), *n.* 1. the letters of a language in their usual order. 2. any system of letters or signs with which a language is written. [from the Greek word *alphabētos,* which comes from the names of the first two letters of the Greek alphabet, *alpha* and *bēta*]

al·pha·bet·i·cal (al⁄fə bet⁄i kəl), *adj.* in the order of the letters in the alphabet: *an alphabetical list of names.* —**al⁄pha·bet⁄i·cal·ly,** *adv.*

al·pha·bet·ize (al⁄fə bi tīz⁄), *v.,* **al·pha·bet·ized, al·pha·bet·iz·ing.** to put or arrange in alphabetical order. —**al⁄pha·bet·iz⁄er,** *n.*

al⁄pha par⁄ticle, a positively charged particle, consisting of two protons and two neutrons, that is given off in some radioactive processes: identical to the nucleus of a helium atom.

al·pine (al⁄pīn, al⁄pin), *adj.* of or referring to very high mountains.

Al·pine (al⁄pīn, al⁄pin), *adj.* of, referring to, or situated in the Alps: *an Alpine vacation.*

Alps (alps), *n. (used as pl.)* a mountain range in S Europe, extending from France through Switzerland and Italy into Austria and Yugoslavia. Highest peak, Mont Blanc, 15,781 ft.

al·read·y (ôl red⁄ē), *adv.* 1. before a given time or event: *The airplane had already landed when we arrived.* 2. so soon; so early: *Is it time to leave already?* —**Usage.** *Already,* which means "previously," should not be confused with *all ready,* which means "completely prepared or ready": *The train had already gone. The children are all ready to go.*

Al·sace-Lor·raine (al⁄sas lô rān⁄, al⁄sās-), *n.* a region in NE France: part of Germany 1871–1919, 1940–1945. 5607 sq. mi.

al·so (ôl⁄sō), *adv.* in addition; too: *He swims and also plays tennis.*

Alta., Alberta (Canada).

al·tar (ôl⁄tər), *n.* 1. a raised table, esp. in a church, at which religious rites are performed. 2. a platform, mound, or other raised structure on which sacrifices are offered to gods, spirits, etc.

al⁄tar boy⁄, a person who assists a priest during a religious service; acolyte.

al·ter (ôl⁄tər), *v.* to change; make or become different in some way: *The tailor altered my dress. My attitude has not altered.* —**al⁄ter·a·ble,** *adj.*

al·ter·a·tion (ôl⁄tə rā⁄shən), *n.* 1. the act of changing, or the state of being changed: *The store will be closed during alteration.* 2. a change or modification: *The tailor made some alterations in the suit.*

al·ter·ca·tion (ôl⁄tər kā⁄shən), *n.* an angry dispute; heated argument; quarrel.

al·ter·nate (ôl⁄tər nāt⁄), *v.,* **al·ter·nat·ed, al·ter·nat·ing.** 1. to change repeatedly and regularly with one another; take turns: *My sister and I alternate doing the dishes.* 2. to occur repeatedly one after another: *Black and white stripes alternate on a zebra.* —*adj.* (ôl⁄tər nit). 3. occurring or arranged one next to the other: *alternate snow and rain; alternate black and white stripes.* 4. every second; every other: *I wash the dishes on alternate days of the week.* 5. in place of another; substitute: *an alternate date for a picnic.* —*n.* (ôl⁄tər nit). 6. a person who substitutes for another when necessary; standby: *An alternate went to the meeting when I was ill.* —**al⁄ter·na⁄tion,** *n.*

al·ter·nate·ly (ôl⁄tər nit lē), *adv.* in alternate order or position: *Chairs and tables were placed alternately around the room.*

al⁄ternating cur⁄rent, an electric current that reverses its direction many times per second. *Abbr.:* AC, A.C., ac, a.c. See also **direct current.**

al·ter·na·tive (ôl tûr⁄nə tiv), *n.* 1. a choice of one from among two or more things that are available: *You have the alternative of skiing or skating.* 2. one of these choices: *The alternative to skiing is skating.* —*adj.* 3. offering or requiring a choice: *alternative designs for a new flag.* —**al·ter⁄na·tive·ly,** *adv.*

al·though (ôl thō⁄), *conj.* in spite of the fact that; even though: *Although he knew the song, he refused to sing it.* Also, **al·tho⁄.**

al·tim·e·ter (al tim⁄ə tər, al⁄tə mē⁄tər), *n.* a device for measuring altitude, such as that used in an airplane to indicate its height above sea level.

---

act, āble, dâre, ärt; ebb, ēqual; if, īce; hot, ōver, ôrder; oil; bŏŏk; ōōze; out; up, ûrge; ə = *a* as in *alone;* ᵊ as in *button* (but⁄ᵊn), *fire* (fīᵊr); **ch**ief; **sh**oe; **th**in; **th**at; **zh** as in *measure* (mezh⁄ər). See full key inside cover.

al·ti·tude (al'ti tōōd', -tyōōd'), *n.* **1.** height above sea level. **2.** height above the ground. **3.** the height of a geometrical figure. **4.** a region or place high above sea level.

al·to (al'tō), *n., pl.* **al·tos. 1.** a low female voice or, sometimes, a very high male voice. **2.** a singer with such a voice. **3.** a musical part for such a voice. —*adj.* **4.** of a pitch between soprano and tenor: *an alto saxophone; an alto voice.*

al·to·geth·er (ôl'tə geŧh'ər, ôl'tə geŧh'ər), *adv.* **1.** completely; entirely: *I am altogether certain that I mailed the letter this morning.* **2.** with everything or everyone included; in all: *The bill came to ten dollars altogether.* **3.** with everything considered; on the whole: *Altogether, I'm glad it's over.*
—**Usage.** *Altogether* is an adverb meaning "wholly, completely, entirely": *an altogether delightful afternoon.* It should not be confused with *all together,* which means "in a group": *They were all together in the kitchen.*

al·tru·ism (al'trōō iz'əm), *n.* unselfish concern for the welfare of others. —**al'tru·is'tic,** *adj.*

al·tru·ist (al'trōō ist), *n.* a person who practices altruism.

al·um (al'əm), *n.* a mineral salt used in dyeing, tanning, and to stop the bleeding of small cuts.

a·lu·mi·num (ə lōō'mə nəm), *n.* a light, silvery metal that does not easily corrode: a chemical element. It is used in making airplanes, kitchen utensils, automobile engines, etc. *Symbol:* Al

a·lum·na (ə lum'nə), *n., pl.* **a·lum·nae** (ə lum'nē). a female graduate or former student of a certain school or college.
—**Usage.** See **alumnus.**

a·lum·nus (ə lum'nəs), *n., pl.* **a·lum·ni** (ə lum'nī). a male graduate or former student of a certain school or college.
—**Usage.** A male graduate is an *alumnus* (plural *alumni*) and a female graduate is an *alumna* (plural *alumnae*). The masculine form *alumni* is used in referring to male and female graduates together.

al·ways (ôl'wāz, ôl'wēz), *adv.* **1.** every time; without exception: *He always walks home from school.* **2.** forever; for all time: *Will you love me always?*

am (am), *v.* the first person singular of **be** in the present tense: *I am a friend of his.*

AM, amplitude modulation.

Am, *Chem.* the symbol for **americium.**

Am., **1.** America. **2.** American. Also, **Amer.**

a.m., **1.** between midnight and noon: *Come at 9 a.m.* **2.** the period from midnight to noon, esp. the period between dawn and noon. Also, **A.M.** See also **p.m.** [from the Latin phrase *ante meridiem*]

a·mal·gam (ə mal'gəm), *n.* **1.** a mixture of mercury with one or more other metals, esp. powdered gold or silver. **2.** any kind of a mixture or combination: *the amalgam of cultures in New York City.*

a·mal·gam·ate (ə mal'gə māt'), *v.,* **a·mal·gam·at·ed, a·mal·gam·at·ing.** to combine, unite, or blend: *to amalgamate two companies into one.* —**a·mal'gam·a'tion,** *n.* —**a·mal'gam·a·tor,** *n.*

Am·a·ril·lo (am'ə ril'ō), *n.* a city in NW Texas.

am·a·ryl·lis (am'ə ril'is), *n.* a plant having large, reddish lilylike flowers on a single stem.

a·mass (ə mas'), *v.* **1.** to gather or collect; make a pile of: *He amassed all the old newspapers that could be burned.* **2.** to gather for oneself; collect as one's own: *He amassed a large fortune.*

Amaryllis

am·a·teur (am'ə chŏōr', am'ə tyŏōr', am'ə tûr'), *n.* **1.** a person who engages in an activity for pleasure instead of for profit. **2.** a person who has little experience or skill in a particular field or activity: *When it comes to skiing, I'm only an amateur.* —*adj.* **3.** by or like an amateur; not professional: *an amateur photographer; an amateur performance.*

am·a·teur·ish (am'ə chŏōr'ish, am'ə tyŏōr'ish, am'ə tûr'ish), *adj.* of or like an amateur, esp. in having faults; not expert or skillful: *an amateurish performance of a concerto.* —**am'a·teur'ish·ly,** *adv.* —**am'a·teur'ish·ness,** *n.*

a·maze (ə māz'), *v.,* **a·mazed, a·maz·ing.** to surprise very much; astonish: *The boy's expert knowledge of chemistry amazed us all.*

a·maze·ment (ə māz'mənt), *n.* overwhelming surprise or astonishment.

a·maz·ing (ə mā'zing), *adj.* causing great surprise or astonishment: *an amazing story of adventure.* —**a·maz'ing·ly,** *adv.*

Am·a·zon (am'ə zon'), *n.* **1.** a river in N South America, flowing E from the Peruvian Andes through N Brazil to the Atlantic Ocean: the largest river in the world in volume of water carried. about 3900 mi. long. **2.** (in classical mythology) a member of a race of female warriors that were believed to live near the Black Sea. **3.** (*often l.c.*) a large, manlike woman who is exceptionally powerful.

am·bas·sa·dor (am bas'ə dər), *n.* **1.** a diplomat of the highest rank who is sent by his own country as its official representative to another country. **2.** any authorized representative or messenger.

am·ber (am'bər), *n.* **1.** a pale-yellow, sometimes reddish or brownish, substance that is hard and translucent, often used as jewelry. Amber is the fossil resin of pine trees that decayed millions of years ago. **2.** a yellowish brown. —*adj.* **3.** of a light golden brown.

am·ber·gris (am'bər grēs', -gris), *n.* a grayish, waxlike substance secreted from the intestines of the sperm whale, used in making perfume.

am·bi·dex·trous (am'bi dek'strəs), *adj.* able to use both hands equally well: *Although John is ambidextrous, he usually writes with his left hand.* —**am'bi·dex'trous·ly,** *adv.*

am·bi·gu·i·ty (am'bə gyōō'i tē), *n., pl.* **am·bi·gu·i·ties.**

1. lack of clarity in meaning; the possibility of having more than one meaning: *The man spoke with such ambiguity that no one could tell which side he favored.* 2. an unclear expression or word: *That story is too full of ambiguities.*

am·big·u·ous (am big′yoo əs), *adj.* 1. having several possible meanings or interpretations: *His statement about America was ambiguous, because it could have meant North America, South America, or both.* 2. unclear; not definite or distinct: *an ambiguous shape.* —**am·big′u·ous·ly,** *adv.*

am·bi·tion (am bish′ən), *n.* 1. a strong desire for success in achieving power, fame, or wealth: *Good students often have a lot of ambition.* 2. the goal or object for which one has a strong desire: *Her ambition is to become a doctor.*

am·bi·tious (am bish′əs), *adj.* 1. having ambition: *Ambitious athletes spend a lot of time training.* 2. showing or caused by ambition: *an ambitious attempt.* 3. requiring great effort, ability, etc.: *an ambitious plan to reorganize the Student Council.* —**am·bi′tious·ly,** *adv.*

am·ble (am′bəl), *v.,* **am·bled, am·bling.** 1. to walk at a slow, leisurely pace: *I ambled down the street looking in the shop windows.* 2. (of a horse) to move by lifting and putting down the two legs on each side in turn. —*n.* 3. an ambling pace or gait.

am·bro·sia (am brō′zhə), *n.* 1. the food or drink of the Greek and Roman gods. 2. something very delicious to eat or drink. [from a Greek word meaning "immortal"]

am·bu·lance (am′byə ləns), *n.* a vehicle equipped for transporting sick or injured people.

am·bu·la·to·ry (am′byə lə tôr′ē), *adj.* capable of walking; not confined to bed: *an ambulatory patient.*

am·bush (am′boosh), *n.* 1. a surprise attack from a concealed position. 2. the concealed position itself. 3. the act or an instance of concealing oneself so as to attack by surprise. —*v.* 4. to attack from a concealed position: *The highwaymen ambushed the stagecoach.*

Ameba
A, Nucleus
B, Food intake

a·me·ba (ə mē′bə), *n., pl.* **a·me·bae** (ə mē′bē) *or* **a·me·bas.** a tiny, one-celled water animal that constantly changes shape as it moves and takes in food. It can be seen only through a microscope. Also, **amoeba.**

a·mel·io·rate (ə mēl′yə rāt′), *v.,* **a·mel·io·rat·ed, a·mel·io·rat·ing.** to make or become better; improve: *Twenty new buses will ameliorate the transportation shortage.* —**a·mel′io·ra·ble** (ə mēl′yə rə bəl), *adj.* —**a·mel′io·ra′tion,** *n.* —**a·mel′io·ra′tor,** *n.*

a·men (ā′men′, ä′men′), *interj.* may it be so (used after a prayer, creed, or other formal religious statement to express solemn agreement). [from Hebrew]

a·me·na·ble (ə mē′nə bəl, ə men′ə bəl), *adj.* 1. ready or willing to listen or agree; agreeable: *The teacher is often amenable to suggestions.* 2. ready or willing to yield or submit: *amenable to discipline.* 3. accountable or answerable, as in law: *A citizen is amenable to the laws of his country.* —**a·me′na·bly,** *adv.*

a·mend (ə mend′), *v.* 1. to change or revise, esp. by formal procedure: *The committee plans to amend the constitution at the next meeting.* 2. to change for the better; improve: *to amend bad habits.* —**a·mend′a·ble,** *adj.* —**a·mend′er,** *n.*

a·mend·ment (ə mend′mənt), *n.* 1. a change of or an addition to a law, bill, constitution, etc. 2. a change for the better; improvement.

a·mends (ə mendz′), *n. (used as sing. or pl.)* something done, given, or paid to make up for a loss, injury, etc.: *to make amends for property damage.*

a·men·i·ty (ə men′i tē), *n., pl.* **a·men·i·ties.** 1. the quality of being pleasant and agreeable. 2. amenities, agreeable and pleasant manners: *Observing social amenities always makes a good impression.*

Amer., 1. America. 2. American. Also, **Am.**

A·mer·i·ca (ə mer′i kə), *n.* 1. the United States. 2. the continent of North America. 3. the continent of South America. 4. **the Americas,** North and South America, considered together; the Western Hemisphere.

A·mer·i·can (ə mer′i kən), *adj.* 1. of or referring to the United States of America or its people. 2. of or referring to North or South America. —*n.* 3. a citizen of the United States of America. 4. a native or inhabitant of the Western Hemisphere.

A·mer·i·can·ism (ə mer′i kə niz′əm), *n.* 1. devotion to or preference for the United States of America and its way of life. 2. a custom or trait peculiar to the people of the United States. 3. a word or phrase originated or chiefly used in the United States, such as "rodeo" or "hot dog."

A·mer·i·can·ize (ə mer′i kə nīz′), *v.,* **A·mer·i·can·ized, A·mer·i·can·iz·ing.** to make or become American in customs, manners, or character: *Immigrants often become Americanized very quickly.* —**A·mer′i·can·i·za′tion,** *n.*

Amer′ican Revolu′tion, the war between Great Britain and the 13 American colonies, 1775–1783, by which the colonies won their independence and formed the United States of America. Also, **Revolutionary War.**

Amer′ican Samo′a, the E islands of Samoa, belonging to the U.S. 76 sq. mi. *Cap.:* Pago Pago. See also **Western Samoa.**

am·er·i·ci·um (am′ə rish′ē əm), *n. Chem.* a man-made, radioactive, metallic element. *Symbol:* Am

A·mer·i·go Ves·puc·ci (ə mer′ə gō′ ve spōō′chē). See Vespucci, Amerigo.

am·e·thyst (am′i thist), *n.* 1. a purple or violet quartz, used as a gem. 2. a purplish violet. —*adj.* 3. of a purplish violet color. [from the Greek word *amethystos* "not intoxicating." It was believed that the stone prevented drunkenness]

a·mi·a·ble (ā′mē ə bəl), *adj.* friendly and agreeable:

an amiable girl; an amiable personality. —a'mi·a·bil'i·ty, a'mi·a·ble·ness, *n.* —a'mi·a·bly, *adv.*

am·i·ca·ble (am'i kə bəl), *adj.* showing good will and friendliness; peaceable: *The nations settled their dispute in an amicable manner.* —am'i·ca·bil'i·ty, am'i·ca·ble·ness, *n.* —am'i·ca·bly, *adv.*

a·mid (ə mid'), *prep.* in the middle of or surrounded by; among: *The moon was clearly visible amid the stars.* Also, *esp. British,* **a·midst** (ə midst').

a·mid·ships (ə mid'ships), *adv.* in or toward the middle part of a vessel or aircraft.

a·mi·no ac·id (ə mē'nō, am'ə nō'), any of a large and important group of compounds containing carbon, oxygen, hydrogen, and nitrogen that are the basic units that make up proteins.

a·miss (ə mis'), *adv.* 1. wrongly; improperly: *Did I speak amiss?* —*adj.* 2. not in the correct order or condition: *When I walked in the house I knew something was amiss.*

am·i·ty (am'i tē), *n.* a relationship of peace and understanding; friendship: *amity between nations.*

Am·man (äm män'), *n.* the capital city of Jordan, in the N central part.

am·me·ter (am'mē'tər), *n.* an instrument for measuring the strength of electric currents in amperes.

am·mo·nia (ə mōn'yə, ə mō'nē ə), *n.* 1. a colorless gas with a suffocating odor, a compound of nitrogen and hydrogen. 2. a solution of this gas in water, used for household cleaning.

am·mo·nite (am'ə nīt'), *n.* a coiled fossil shell of certain extinct mollusks.

am·mu·ni·tion (am'yə nish'ən), *n.* 1. the material used for firing a firearm, as shells, bullets, fuzes, etc. 2. information used to support or fortify one side in a debate or argument.

am·ne·sia (am nē'zhə), *n.* the complete or partial loss of memory due to injury, illness, shock, etc.

Ammonite

am·nes·ty (am'ni stē), *n., pl.* **am·nes·ties.** a general pardon, esp. one given by a government to people who have committed certain crimes against it.

a·moe·ba (ə mē'bə), *n., pl.* **a·moe·bae** (ə mē'bē) *or* **a·moe·bas.** another spelling of **ameba.**

a·mok (ə muk', ə mok'), *adv.* another spelling of **amuck.**

a·mong (ə mung'), *prep.* 1. in or into the midst of: *a path among the trees.* 2. with a share for each of: *The work was divided among us.* 3. in the group or class of: *a choice among possibilities.* 4. in, with, or throughout: *a man popular among the people.* 5. with each other: *They often quarrel among themselves.* Also, *esp. British,* **a·mongst** (ə mungst').

—**Usage.** In careful English, the difference between *among* and *between* is important. *Among* is used when three or more things or persons are involved, *between* when only two are mentioned: *The apple pie was divided among the four of us. He stepped between John and me.*

a·mor·al (ā môr'əl), *adj.* neither moral nor immoral; without interest or concern in moral standards.

—a·mor·al·i·ty (ā'mə ral'i tē), *n.* —a·mor'al·ly, *adv.*

am·o·rous (am'ər əs), *adj.* 1. showing or expressing love: *an amorous sigh.* 2. inclined or disposed to love: *an amorous disposition.* —am'o·rous·ly, *adv.*

a·mor·phous (ə môr'fəs), *adj.* 1. having no definite form; shapeless: *amorphous clouds.* 2. of no particular kind or character: *an amorphous group of buildings.* 3. *Chem.* (of a solid) not crystalline in form. *Lampblack is amorphous carbon, whereas diamond is crystalline carbon.* —a·mor'phous·ly, *adv.*

A·mos (ā'məs), *n.* 1. (in the Bible) a Hebrew prophet. 2. a book of the Old Testament.

a·mount (ə mount'), *n.* 1. the sum of two or more quantities; sum total: *What is the amount of the bill?* 2. a measure or quantity: *a large amount of energy.* —*v.* 3. to combine to give a sum: *His savings amount to $100.* 4. to be the same as; become: *His good intentions amount to nothing if he doesn't change his ways.*

amp., ampere; amperes. Also, **A, amp**

am·pere (am'pēr), *n.* a unit for expressing the strength of an electric current. A current of one ampere is a flow of one coulomb of charge per second in an electric circuit. *Abbr.:* A, amp., amp

am·per·sand (am'pər sand'), *n.* a symbol (&) for *and: In the name "Smith & Company," the words "Smith" and "Company" are joined by an ampersand.*

am·phib·i·an (am fib'ē ən), *n.* 1. any of a group of related cold-blooded animals, including frogs and salamanders, that can live both on land and in water. The young breathe by means of gills, whereas the adults have lungs. 2. any other amphibious animal, such as a seal. 3. an airplane equipped for taking off and landing on land and on water. —*adj.* 4. of or referring to amphibians. 5. another word for **amphibious.**

am·phib·i·ous (am fib'ē əs), *adj.* 1. living or able to live both on land and in water. 2. equipped to operate on both land and water: *amphibious vehicles.* 3. referring to a military operation that involves both land and naval forces. Also, **amphibian.**

am·phi·the·a·ter (am'fə thē'ə tər), *n.* 1. a large building, usually round or oval in shape, having rows of seats rising around a central area; arena or stadium. 2. a level area surrounded by rising ground, esp. one that may be used for outdoor performances or meetings.

am·ple (am'pəl), *adj.,* **am·pler, am·plest.** 1. of adequate size or amount; enough: *The teacher gave us ample time to finish the test.* 2. of greater size or amount than required: *We packed an ample supply of food for the picnic.* —am'ple·ness, *n.*

am·pli·fi·ca·tion (am'plə fə kā'shən), *n.* 1. the act or process of amplifying; enlargement; expansion: *The report needs amplification.* 2. the matter or substance used to amplify or enlarge. 3. the process of increasing the strength of an electrical signal.

am·pli·fi·er (am'plə fī'ər), *n.* 1. a person or device that amplifies. 2. an electronic device that strengthens an electrical signal, as in a phonograph.

am·pli·fy (am'plə fī'), v., **am·pli·fied, am·pli·fy·ing. 1.** to make larger or greater; enlarge; extend. **2.** to make more complete by adding details or examples: *He amplified his remarks by quoting statistics.* **3.** to strengthen (an electrical signal).

am·pli·tude (am'pli tōōd', -tyōōd'), n. **1.** the state or quality of being ample, esp. in breadth or width; largeness. **2.** large or full measure or quantity; abundance. **3.** the distance from the center or average to a point of maximum displacement of a pendulum, wave, or the like.

am'plitude modula'tion, a method of radio broadcasting in which the desired signal varies the amplitude of the radio wave being broadcast. *Abbr.:* AM See also **frequency modulation.**

am·ply (am'plē), adv. **1.** in an ample way; sufficiently. **2.** to a greater extent than required: *We were amply supplied with food.*

amps., amperes. Also, **A, amps**

am·pu·tate (am'pyōō tāt'), v., **am·pu·tat·ed, am·pu·tat·ing.** to cut off (all or part of an arm or leg), usually by surgery. —**am'pu·ta'tion,** n.

Am·ster·dam (am'stər dam'), n. a port city and the official capital of the Netherlands. Government offices are located at The Hague.

amt., amount.

a·muck (ə muk'), adv. **run amuck,** to rush about wildly, esp. in a murderous rage: *The maniac ran amuck on the crowded street.* Also, **amok.** [from the Malay word *amok* "a violent assault, frenzied attack"]

am·u·let (am'yə lit), n. a charm worn to ward off evil or harm.

A·mund·sen (ä'mənd sən), n. **Roald,** 1872–1928, Norwegian explorer: discovered South Pole 1911.

a·muse (ə myōōz'), v., **a·mused, a·mus·ing. 1.** to hold the attention of by entertaining pleasantly: *He amused the whole family with the game.* **2.** to cause to smile or laugh: *The speaker's joke amused us all.* —**a·mus'a·ble,** adj.

a·muse·ment (ə myōōz'mənt), n. **1.** something that amuses; entertainment: *Going to the movies is her favorite form of amusement.* **2.** the state of being amused; enjoyment: *We watched her amusement when she opened the gift.*

amuse'ment park', a park having rides, such as a Ferris wheel, roller coaster, etc., and stalls where refreshments, souvenirs, etc., may be purchased.

a·mus·ing (ə myōō'zing), adj. causing laughter or amusement; entertaining: *an amusing story; an amusing person.* —**a·mus'ing·ly,** adv.

an (an), *indefinite article.* the form of a before an initial vowel sound and sometimes before an *h,* esp. when the first syllable of such a word is not stressed: *an event; an honor; an historian.*

-an, a suffix used to form **1.** adjectives meaning of, like, or referring to: *republican; suburban.* Some of these adjectives are used also as nouns: *an American; an Elizabethan.* **2.** nouns meaning **a.** a person who

comes from or belongs to: *a Chicagoan; a Rotarian.* **b.** a person who is connected with: *librarian.*

a·nach·ro·nism (ə nak'rə niz'əm), n. **1.** a person, object, or event that is out of place in time. **2.** an error made by placing a person, object, or event in the wrong time: *Christopher Columbus traveling by airplane is an anachronism.* —**a·nach'ro·nis'tic,** adj.

an·a·con·da (an'ə kon'də), n. a South American snake, often growing to more than 20 feet in length, that crushes its prey.

an·aes·the·sia (an'is thē'zhə), n. another spelling of **anesthesia.**

an·aes·thet·ic (an'is thet'ik), n. another spelling of **anesthetic.**

an·a·gram (an'ə gram'), n. **1.** a word or phrase formed by transposing the letters of another word or phrase: *"Angel" is an anagram of "glean."* **2.** ana-grams, *(used as sing.)* a game in which the players build words by adding letters or switching them around.

An·a·heim (an'ə hīm'), n. a city in SW California, SE of Los Angeles.

a·nal·o·gous (ə nal'ə gəs), adj. alike or similar in some way or ways: *The heart is analogous to a pump.*

a·nal·o·gy (ə nal'ə jē), n., pl. **a·nal·o·gies.** a partial similarity between two things not otherwise alike: *the analogy between a bird and an airplane.*

a·nal·y·sis (ə nal'i sis), n., pl. **a·nal·y·ses** (ə nal'i sēz'). **1.** the separation of something into its various parts to identify its components or to study their relationship, function, etc.: *the analysis of water into hydrogen and oxygen; the analysis of a problem.* **2.** short for **psychoanalysis.**

an·a·lyst (an'əlist), n. **1.** a person who is skilled in analysis. **2.** a psychoanalyst.

an·a·lyt·ic (an'əlit'ik), adj. **1.** referring to or obtained by analysis. **2.** skilled in analysis: *You need an analytic mind for solving math problems.* Also, **an'a·lyt'i·cal.** —**an'a·lyt'i·cal·ly,** adv.

an·a·lyze (an'əlīz'), v., **an·a·lyzed, an·a·lyz·ing. 1.** to separate (something) into parts, ingredients, etc.: *to analyze blood for anemia.* **2.** to study carefully in order to discover the essentials: *to analyze a poem to discover its meaning.*

an·ar·chist (an'ər kist), n. **1.** a person who believes men should rule themselves and that governments and laws should be abolished. **2.** a person who revolts against any established rule, law, or custom.

an·ar·chy (an'ər kē), n. **1.** political and social disorder due to the absence of government or law. **2.** any disorder, confusion, or chaos.

a·nath·e·ma (ə nath'ə mə), n. **1.** a person or thing that is cursed or hated. **2.** a solemn curse, esp. one pronounced by a church.

a·nath·e·ma·tize (ə nath'ə mə tīz'), v., **a·nath·e·ma·tized, a·nath·e·ma·tiz·ing.** to pronounce a solemn curse against (a person, belief, practice, etc.): *to be anathematized by one's church.*

a·nat·o·my (ə nat'ə mē), n. **1.** the science dealing

with the relationship and organization of tissues, parts, or organs of humans, animals, and plants. **2.** the structure of a human, animal, or plant, or of any part of one: *the anatomy of the lobster; the anatomy of the hand.* **3.** *Informal.* the human body. —**an·a·tom·i·cal** (an/ə tom/i kəl), *adj.*

-ance, a suffix used to form nouns meaning **1.** an action or process: *resistance.* **2.** a quality or condition: *appearance.* **3.** a means or instrument: *hindrance.*

an·ces·tor (an/ses tər), *n.* **1.** a person from whom others are descended; forefather: *My ancestors came from England.* **2.** something from which another thing is descended, derived, or developed; forerunner: *the ancestor of the modern locomotive.*

an·ces·tral (an ses/trəl), *adj.* **1.** of or concerning ancestors: *our ancestral history.* **2.** descending or inherited from ancestors: *He returned to Ireland to visit his ancestral home.*

an·ces·try (an/ses trē), *n., pl.* **an·ces·tries. 1.** descent from ancestors; lineage: *Many Americans are of European ancestry.* **2.** a person's ancestors.

an·chor (ang/kər), *n.* **1.** a metal device that is lowered from a ship or boat by a chain, cable, or rope to hold the vessel in place by hooking into the bottom of a body of water. **2.** any device or thing that supports or holds something in place. **3.** a source of stability or hope: *the anchor of faith when one is troubled.* —*v.* **4.** to hold by an anchor. **5.** to drop an anchor from a vessel: *We anchored off Newport.* **6.** to fasten firmly: *to anchor a post in the ground.*

Anchor

an·chor·age (ang/kər ij), *n.* **1.** a place for anchoring a ship. **2.** a charge for occupying such a place. **3.** the act of anchoring, or the state of being anchored. **4.** a source of stability or support: *The tent pegs will provide anchorage.*

an·cho·rite (ang/kə rīt/), *n.* a person who lives alone and away from society, esp. for a life of religious meditation.

an·cho·vy (an/chō vē, an chō/vē), *n., pl.* **an·cho·vies.** a small herringlike fish, usually salted or pickled and used as food.

an·cient (ān/shənt), *adj.* **1.** of or in time long past, esp. before the end of the western Roman Empire in A.D. 476. **2.** very old; aged: *ancient rocks.* —*n.* **3.** a person who lived in ancient times, esp. a Greek, Roman, or Hebrew. **4.** a very old person.

an/cient his/tory, the history of civilization from its beginnings to the fall of the Roman Empire in A.D. 476.

and (and), *conj.* **1.** together with; in addition to: *pens and pencils.* **2.** as well as: *tasty and filling.* **3.** to: *Try and do it.*

—**Usage.** Since *etc.* is an abbreviation for *et cetera,* which means "and others," the use of *and* with *etc.* is unnecessary: *A student needs books, pencils, etc.* (not *books, pencils, and etc.*).

an·dan·te (än dän/tā), *adj., adv.* (in music) **1.** moder-

ately slow. —*n.* **2.** a moderately slow piece or section.

An·der·sen (an/dər sən), *n.* **Hans Christian,** 1805–1875, Danish author of fairy tales.

An·des (an/dēz), *n. (used as pl.)* a mountain range in W South America, extending about 4500 mi. from N Colombia and Venezuela S to Cape Horn. Highest peak, Aconcagua, 22,834 ft.

and·i·ron (and/ī ərn), *n.* one of a pair of metal supports for logs in a fireplace.

Andirons

An·dor·ra (an dôr/ə), *n.* a small republic in the Pyrenees, between France and Spain. 191 sq. mi. *Cap.:* Andorra. —**An·dor/ran,** *n., adj.*

An·drew (an/drōō), *n.* (in the Bible) one of Christ's 12 apostles.

an·ec·dote (an/ik dōt/), *n.* a brief story about an interesting incident or event: *The speaker entertained the audience with many anecdotes.* —**an·ec·do·tal** (an/ik dōt/ə l, an/ik dōt/ə l), *adj.*

a·ne·mi·a (ə nē/mē ə), *n.* a condition in which there is too little hemoglobin in the blood. —**a·ne/mic,** *adj.*

an·e·mom·e·ter (an/ə mom/i tər), *n.* an instrument for measuring the speed of the wind.

a·nem·o·ne (ə nem/ə nē/), *n.* **1.** a plant bearing white or colored flowers that bloom in the spring; windflower. **2.** the sea anemone.

an·es·the·sia (an/is thē/zhə), *n.* the inability to feel pain, heat, cold, etc., produced by an anesthetic. Also, **anaesthesia.**

an·es·thet·ic (an/is thet/ik), *n.* a substance that produces the inability to feel pain either by inducing loss of consciousness (**general anesthetic**) or by causing a loss of feeling in a particular area or part (**local anesthetic**). Also, **anaesthetic.**

a·new (ə nōō/, ə nyōō/), *adv.* **1.** over again; once more: *to play the tune anew.* **2.** over again in a new form or way: *He wrote the story anew.*

an·gel (ān/jəl), *n.* **1.** a spiritual being who serves God as a messenger or attendant. **2.** a picture, statue, etc., of such a being as a human with wings. **3.** a person who resembles an angel in being kind, good, beautiful, etc. —**an·gel·ic** (an jel/ik), *adj.* —**an·gel/i·cal·ly,** *adv.*

an·ger (ang/gər), *n.* **1.** a very strong feeling of displeasure and annoyance, usually hostile or violent: *My anger increased when he insulted my friend.* —*v.* **2.** to make or become angry: *His behavior angered everyone.*

an·gle[1] (ang/gəl), *n.* **1.** the space between two lines that meet at a point or between two planes that meet along a line. **2.** the difference in the direction of two such lines or planes: *The sides of a picture frame form a right angle.* —*v.,* **an·gled, an·gling. 3.** to turn sharply in a different direction (sometimes fol. by *off*): *The road*

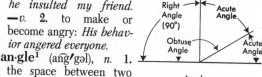

Angles

angles to the right near the lake. [from the Latin word *angulus*]

an·gle² (aṅg'gəl), *v.,* **an·gled, an·gling.** 1. to fish with hook and line. 2. to try to get something by clever means: *to angle for a favor.* [from the Old English word *angul* "hook"]

an·gler (aṅg'glər), *n.* a person who fishes with hook and line as a sport or hobby.

an·gle·worm (aṅg'gəl wûrm'), *n.* an earthworm, esp. one used for bait in angling.

An·gli·can (aṅg'glə kən), *adj.* 1. of or referring to the Church of England or to related churches. —*n.* 2. a member of the Church of England or a related church.

An·gli·cize (aṅg'gli sīz'), *v.,* **An·gli·cized, An·gli·ciz·ing.** to make or become English in customs, manners, or usage. "Bulletin" is a French word that has been Anglicized. —**An'gli·ci·za'tion,** *n.*

an·gling (aṅg'gliṅg), *n.* the act or method of fishing with a hook and line attached to a rod.

Anglo-, a prefix meaning English or England: *Anglo-American.*

An·glo-Sax·on (aṅg'glō sak'sən), *n.* 1. a person whose native language is English. 2. an Englishman who lived before the Norman Conquest. 3. a person of English descent. 4. another term for **Old English.** —*adj.* 5. of or referring to the Anglo-Saxons or the Anglo-Saxon language.

An·go·la (aṅg gō'lə), *n.* a country in SW Africa: a former Portuguese province. 481,226 sq. mi. *Cap.:* Luanda. Former name, **Portuguese West Africa.**

An·go·ra (aṅg gôr'ə), *n.* 1. Also, **Ango'ra wool'.** the hair of the Angora goat or the Angora rabbit. 2. *(often l.c.)* yarn, fabric, or a garment made from this hair. 3. Also, **Ango'ra cat'.** a kind of domestic cat having long, silky hair. 4. Also, **Ango'ra goat'.** a kind of goat having long, silky hair called mohair. 5. Also, **Ango'ra rab'bit.** a kind of rabbit, raised for its long, silky hair.

an·gry (aṅg'grē), *adj.,* **an·gri·er, an·gri·est.** 1. feeling anger; furious; enraged; infuriated: *I was very angry at him for coming so late.* 2. showing anger or a quality that suggests anger: *angry words; an angry sea.* 3. inflamed, as a sore. —**an'gri·ly,** *adv.*

an·guish (aṅg'gwish), *n.* very sharp pain, suffering, or distress: *The wounded animal was in anguish.*

an·guished (aṅg'gwisht), *adj.* feeling or showing anguish; greatly distressed: *an anguished scream.*

an·gu·lar (aṅg'gyə lər), *adj.* 1. having an angle or angles: *an angular drawing of the ship.* 2. forming an angle; sharp-cornered: *angular rocks.* 3. bony and thin: *an angular face.*

an·gu·lar·i·ty (aṅg'gyə lar'i tē), *n., pl.* for def. 2 **an·gu·lar·i·ties.** 1. the quality of being angular. 2. a sharp corner: *This new furniture is full of angularities.*

an·i·line (an'ᵊlin), *n.* a colorless liquid derived from coal tar and used in making dyes.

an·i·mal (an'ə məl), *n.* 1. any of the large group of living things that differ from plants in having the ability to move voluntarily, having a nervous system, and requiring plants or other animals as food. 2. any such living thing other than man. 3. a mammal, as distinguished from a bird, fish, insect, etc.

an·i·mate (an'ə māt'), *v.,* **an·i·mat·ed, an·i·mat·ing.** 1. to give life to; make alive. 2. to make lively; give spirit to: *Her presence animated the party.* 3. to cause to act; inspire: *An interest in science animated his work.* —*adj.* (an'ə mit). 4. alive; having life.

an·i·mat·ed (an'ə mā'tid), *adj.* 1. full of life and spirit; lively: *animated discussion.* 2. made to seem alive and active: *an animated puppet.* —**an'i·mat'ed·ly,** *adv.*

an'imated cartoon', a motion picture made from a sequence of drawings, each so slightly different that when filmed and projected onto a screen the figures seem to move.

an·i·ma·tion (an'ə mā'shən), *n.* 1. liveliness and spirit: *to talk with animation.* 2. the process of preparing animated cartoons.

an·i·mos·i·ty (an'ə mos'i tē), *n., pl.* **an·i·mos·i·ties.** a feeling of ill will and strong dislike; hostility: *There is such strong animosity between the two sisters that they refuse to speak to each other.*

an·i·mus (an'ə məs), *n.* an intense dislike; hostility; animosity: *an animus against snobs.*

An·ka·ra (aṅg'kər ə), *n.* the capital city of Turkey, in the central part.

an·kle (aṅg'kəl), *n.* 1. the joint between the foot and the leg. 2. the slender part of the leg above the foot.

an·klet (aṅg'klit), *n.* 1. a sock that reaches just above the ankle. 2. a piece of jewelry, similar to a bracelet, that is worn around the ankle.

ann., 1. annual. 2. annuity.

an·nals (an'ᵊlz), *n. (used as pl.)* 1. a year-by-year record of events. 2. historical records in general; history: *the annals of crime.*

An·nap·o·lis (ə nap'ə lis), *n.* the capital city of Maryland, in the central part: U.S. Naval Academy.

an·neal (ə nēl'), *v.* to make (glass, metals, etc.) stronger and less brittle by heating and gradually cooling.

an·nex (ə neks'), *v.* 1. to attach or add, esp. to something larger or more important: *Germany annexed part of Poland.* —*n.* (an'eks). 2. something that is annexed or added: *A new annex to the hospital is being built.* —**an·nex·a·tion** (an'ek sā'shən), *n.*

an·ni·hi·late (ə nī'ə lāt'), *v.,* **an·ni·hi·lat·ed, an·ni·hi·lat·ing.** to destroy entirely: *The bombing annihilated the city.* —**an·ni'hi·la'tion,** *n.* —**an·ni'hi·la'tor,** *n.*

an·ni·ver·sa·ry (an'ə vûr'sə rē), *n., pl.* **an·ni·ver·sa·ries.** 1. the yearly occurrence of the date of a past event: *a wedding anniversary.* 2. the celebration of such an event. —*adj.* 3. referring to an anniversary: *an anniversary party.*

an·no Dom·i·ni (an'ō dom'ə nī', dom'ə nē'). See **A.D.**

an·no·tate (an'ō tāt'), *v.,* **an·no·tat·ed, an·no·tat·ing.** to add explanatory notes to (a book, article, or other piece of writing). —**an′no·ta′tive,** *adj.*

an·no·ta·tion (an′ō tā′shən), *n.* **1.** the act of adding notes. **2.** a critical or explanatory note added to a text.

an·nounce (ə nouns′), *v.,* **an·nounced, an·nounc·ing. 1.** to make known publicly or officially: *The teacher announced a test for tomorrow.* **2.** to make known to the mind or senses: *The first robin announces the arrival of spring.* **3.** to declare orally the approach or presence of: *The butler announced the dinner guests.* **4.** to work as an announcer: *He announces for WQXR.*

an·nounce·ment (ə nouns′mənt), *n.* **1.** a written or oral notice or message: *a special announcement about the fire; an announcement of the club's activities.* **2.** the act of announcing. **3.** a card or piece of stationery containing a formal declaration of a special event: *The wedding announcements were mailed.*

an·nounc·er (ə noun′sər), *n.* a person who announces or makes known, esp. one who introduces programs or reads advertisements on radio and television.

an·noy (ə noi′), *v.* to disturb or bother in a troublesome and irritating way: *His habit of being late annoys all his friends.* —**an·noy′ing·ly,** *adv.*

an·noy·ance (ə noi′əns), *n.* **1.** the act or an instance of annoying or bothering. **2.** a person or thing that annoys or bothers; nuisance: *Breaking a shoelace is an annoyance.* **3.** the feeling of being annoyed or bothered.

an·nu·al (an′yoō əl), *adj.* **1.** of, referring to, or lasting a year; yearly: *the annual enrollment in grade schools.* **2.** taking place once a year: *Birthdays are an annual event.* **3.** done or performed during a year: *the annual course of the sun.* —*n.* **4.** a plant that lives for only one year or season. **5.** a book, report, etc., published once a year. —**an′nu·al·ly,** *adv.*

an·nu·i·ty (ə noō′i tē, ə nyoō′-), *n., pl.* **an·nu·i·ties. 1.** a contract providing regular payments of money to a person over a specific period of time or for life. **2.** the income received under such an agreement.

an·nul (ə nul′), *v.,* **an·nulled, an·nul·ling.** to deprive of legal force; abolish; cancel: *to annul a marriage.* —**an·nul′ment,** *n.*

an·num (an′əm), *n.* **1.** the Latin word for **year. 2. per annum,** by the year; yearly: *The membership costs them $50 per annum.*

an·nun·ci·a·tion (ə nun′sē ā′shən), *n.* **1.** the announcement by the angel Gabriel to the Virgin Mary that she would be the mother of Christ. **2.** the church festival on March 25 in memory of this.

a·noint (ə noint′), *v.* **1.** to put oil on; smear with an ointment or liquid. **2.** to make holy or sacred by applying oil: *He anointed the new high priest.* —**a·noint′ment,** *n.*

a·nom·a·lous (ə nom′ə ləs), *adj.* different from the usual or accepted rule or type; abnormal; inconsistent: *A professor is an anomalous figure in politics.*

a·nom·a·ly (ə nom′ə lē), *n., pl.* **a·nom·a·lies.** something different from the usual rule or type; a strange

situation, condition, etc.: *His rude remark was an anomaly, since he's always so polite.*

a·non (ə non′), *adv. Archaic.* **1.** soon; in a short time. **2.** at another time.

anon., anonymous.

a·non·y·mous (ə non′ə məs), *adj.* **1.** without any name acknowledged, as that of author, contributor, etc.: *to receive an anonymous letter.* **2.** of unknown name: *an anonymous author.* —**an·o·nym·i·ty** (an′ə nim′i tē), *n.* —**a·non′y·mous·ly,** *adv.*

an·oth·er (ə nuth′ər), *adj.* **1.** one more of the same; additional: *May I have another piece of cake?* **2.** of a different kind: *The saleslady showed me another style, which I liked better.* —*pron.* **3.** an additional one: *Since you enjoyed that first piece of pie so much, have another.* **4.** someone or something different: *He went from one house to another looking for his lost dog. He told her he loved another.*

an·swer (an′sər), *n.* **1.** a spoken or written reply or response to a question, request, communication, etc.: *I received an answer to my letter.* **2.** an action serving as a reply or response: *The answer to our demand to surrender was a volley of fire.* **3.** a solution to a problem: *He worked out all the answers to the arithmetic problems.* —*v.* **4.** to reply or respond to by words or action: *to answer with a nod; to answer the telephone.* **5.** to be responsible (usually fol. by *for*): *I will answer for his safety.* **6.** to conform or correspond to: *That man answers the description.* **7. answer back,** to reply rudely or impertinently: *Don't answer back when I tell you to do something!*

an·swer·a·ble (an′sər ə bəl), *adj.* **1.** responsible; liable: *He is answerable for his conduct.* **2.** capable of being answered: *an answerable problem.*

ant (ant), *n.* any of numerous small, crawling insects that live together in colonies in the ground or in tunnels bored in wood.

ant., antonym.

an·tag·o·nism (an tag′ə niz′əm), *n.* active hostility or opposition: *Antagonism between the two countries has existed for years.*

Ant

A, Male
B, Female
(length to ¼ in.)

an·tag·o·nist (an tag′ə nist), *n.* a person who is opposed to another; opponent; adversary: *His antagonist in the battle was a giant nearly seven feet tall.*

an·tag·o·nis·tic (an tag′ə nis′tik), *adj.* acting in opposition; unfriendly; hostile: *an antagonistic remark.* —**an·tag′o·nis′ti·cal·ly,** *adv.*

an·tag·o·nize (an tag′ə nīz′), *v.,* **an·tag·o·nized, an·tag·o·niz·ing.** to make an enemy or antagonist of; arouse dislike in: *His speech antagonized many voters. His insults antagonized me.* —**an·tag′o·niz′er,** *n.* —**an·tag′o·niz′ing·ly,** *adv.*

ant·arc·tic (ant ärk′tik), *adj.* **1.** of, at, or near the South Pole. —*n.* **2. the Antarctic,** another name for **Antarctica.**

Ant·arc·ti·ca (ant ärk′ti kə), *n.* the continent surrounding the South Pole. about 5,000,000 sq. mi.

Antarc′tic Cir′cle, an imaginary line that is parallel to the equator and is located below the tropic of

Capricorn, 23°28′ north of the South Pole.

Antarc′tic O′cean, the waters surrounding Antarctica, comprising the southernmost parts of the Pacific, Atlantic, and Indian oceans.

ante-, a prefix meaning before: *anteroom; antedate.*

ant·eat·er (ant′ē′tər), *n.* any of several large, toothless mammals that have a long, sticky tongue and feed chiefly on ants and termites.

an·te·ced·ent (an′ti-sēd′[ə]nt), *adj.* 1. existing or taking place before: *an antecedent event.* —*n.* 2. a preceding event, circumstance, object, etc.: *What was the antecedent of his decision?* 3. a

Anteater
(total length to 7 ft.)

word, phrase, or clause, usually a noun, that is replaced by a pronoun. In *I called John and spoke to him, John* is the antecedent of *him.* 4. **antecedents,** ancestors.

an·te·cham·ber (an′tē chām′bər), *n.* an anteroom.

an·te·date (an′ti dāt′, an′ti dāt′), *v.,* **an·te·dat·ed, an·te·dat·ing.** 1. to precede in time; happen before: *The Stone Age antedates the Bronze Age.* 2. to assign to an earlier date; give too early a date to: *to antedate an historical event.*

an·te·di·lu·vi·an (an′tē di loo′vē ən), *adj.* 1. belonging to the period before the Flood. 2. very old-fashioned: *antediluvian ideas.*

an·te·lope (an′t[ə]lōp′), *n.* any of several cud-chewing animals of Africa and Asia, having large permanent horns and noted for their ability to run swiftly.

an·ten·na (an ten′ə), *n., pl.* for def. 1 **an·ten·nas,** for def. 2 **an·ten·nae** (an ten′ē). 1. an assembly of wires or rods for broadcasting or receiving radio or television signals; aerial. 2. one of the two or more jointed feelers on the head of an insect, lobster, etc.

an·te·ri·or (an tēr′ē ər), *adj.* 1. located in or toward the front (opposite of *posterior*): *The anterior part of many insects contains antennae.* 2. going before in time; earlier: *an anterior event.*

an·te·room (an′tē room′, -room′), *n.* a room used as a waiting room or an entrance to a larger room, as in a palace; antechamber.

an·them (an′thəm), *n.* 1. a hymn of praise, devotion, or patriotism: *the national anthem of Spain.* 2. a piece of sacred music with words from the Bible, usually sung by a church choir.

an·ther (an′thər), *n.* the part of the stamen of a flower that carries the pollen. See illus. at **flower.**

ant′ hill′, a mound of dirt, mud, leaves, etc., formed by a colony of ants in making their nest.

an·thol·o·gy (an thol′ə jē), *n., pl.* **an·thol·o·gies.** a book or other collection of stories, poems, articles, etc., either by several authors or by one author: *an anthology of Shakespeare's poems.*

an·thra·cite (an′thrə sīt′), *n.* a kind of coal that produces very little smoke and flame when it burns;

hard coal. Also, **an′thracite coal′.** See also **bituminous coal.**

an·thrax (an′thraks), *n.* an infectious, often fatal disease of cattle, sheep, and other mammals, including man.

an·thro·poid (an′thrə poid′), *adj.* 1. resembling man: *an anthropoid ape.* —*n.* 2. any of the apes that resemble man, including the gorilla and chimpanzee.

an·thro·pol·o·gist (an′thrə pol′ə jist), *n.* a person who specializes in anthropology.

an·thro·pol·o·gy (an′thrə pol′ə jē), *n.* the science that deals with the origins, development, physical characteristics, beliefs, and customs of mankind.

anti-, a prefix meaning 1. against: *antifreeze; antidote.* 2. opposite: *anticlimax.*

an·ti·air·craft (an′tē âr′kraft′), *adj.* 1. designed for or used in defense against enemy aircraft. —*n.* 2. artillery used against enemy aircraft.

an·ti·bi·ot·ic (an′ti bī ot′ik), *n.* a substance, produced by bacteria or fungi, that kills or stops the growth of harmful organisms, such as germs: *Penicillin is a well-known antibiotic.*

an·ti·bod·y (an′ti bod′ē), *n., pl.* **an·ti·bod·ies.** a substance in the blood that acts to overcome the effects of a particular kind of germ.

an·tic (an′tik), *n.* Usually, **antics.** playful and funny tricks, pranks, etc.: *His silly antics amused everyone at the party.*

An·ti·christ (an′ti krīst′), *n.* the enemy or opponent of Christ.

an·tic·i·pate (an tis′ə pāt′), *v.,* **an·tic·i·pat·ed, an·tic·i·pat·ing.** 1. to look forward to; expect: *We are anticipating an early vacation.* 2. to foresee and act in advance of: *to anticipate a request.* 3. to be ahead of in doing or accomplishing: *The ancient Phoenicians anticipated certain modern inventions.*

an·tic·i·pa·tion (an tis′ə pā′shən), *n.* 1. the act of anticipating or looking forward to something; expectation: *We were full of anticipation for the party.* 2. an action that prevents or prepares for a future action: *We studied hard in anticipation of the exam.* 3. an instance of imagining or knowing ahead of time that something will happen; intuition.

an·ti·cli·max (an′ti klī′maks), *n.* an event, statement, or the like, that is less important or interesting than expected: *The last act of the play was an anticlimax.* —**an·ti·cli·mac·tic** (an′ti klī mak′tik), *adj.*

an·ti·dote (an′ti dōt′), *n.* a medicine or other substance that counteracts the effects of a poison.

An·tie·tam (an tē′təm), *n.* a creek flowing from S Pennsylvania through NW Maryland into the Potomac: Civil War battle fought near here at Sharpsburg, Maryland, in 1862.

an·ti·freeze (an′ti frēz′), *n.* a liquid added to the water in the cooling system of an engine to prevent the water from freezing in winter.

An·til·les (an til′ēz), *n. (used as pl.)* a chain of islands in the West Indies divided into two parts: the one including Cuba, Hispaniola, Jamaica, and Puerto

Rico (**Greater Antilles**), the other a group of islands to the SE (**Lesser Antilles**).

an·ti·mis·sile (an/tē mis/əl), *adj.* designed for use against enemy missiles: *an antimissile device.*

an·ti·mo·ny (an/tə mō/nē), *n. Chem.* a metallic element used chiefly to harden lead alloys. Its compounds are used in medicines and paints. *Symbol:* Sb

an·ti·pas·to (an/ti pä/stō), *n.* (in Italian cooking) a course of assorted appetizers, such as olives, anchovies, salami, celery, etc.

an·tip·a·thy (an tip/ə thē), *n., pl.* **an·tip·a·thies. 1.** strong dislike; aversion: *to show antipathy toward a person.* **2.** a person or thing that arouses strong dislike: *Liver is one of my antipathies.* —**an·ti·pa·thet·ic** (an/ti pə thet/ik, an tip/ə thet/ik), *adj.*

an·tip·o·des (an tip/ə dēz/), *n.pl.* two places that are exactly opposite each other on the globe, such as the North and South poles.

an·ti·quar·i·an (an/tə kwâr/ē ən), *adj.* referring to antiquaries or to the study of antiquities.

an·ti·quar·y (an/tə kwer/ē), *n., pl.* **an·ti·quar·ies.** a person who studies or collects antique things.

an·ti·quat·ed (an/tə kwā/tid), *adj.* very old; out of date; old-fashioned: *antiquated ideas about the way a person should behave.*

an·tique (an tēk/), *adj.* **1.** belonging to the past; not modern: *He collects antique cars.* **2.** dating from or in the style of an earlier time: *That antique chair is only an imitation.* —*n.* **3.** a work of art, piece of furniture, etc., that was produced or created at least 100 years ago.

an·tiq·ui·ty (an tik/wi tē), *n., pl.* **an·tiq·ui·ties. 1.** the quality or condition of being ancient; oldness: *a vase of great antiquity.* **2.** ancient times; former ages: *the Greek philosophers of antiquity.* **3. antiquities,** monuments, relics, customs, etc., of ancient times: *a student of antiquities.*

an·ti·Sem·ite (an/tē sem/īt, an/tī-), *n.* a person who is prejudiced against Jews. —**an·ti·Se·mit·ic** (an/tē sə·mit/ik, an/tī-), *adj.* —**an·ti·Sem·i·tism** (an/tē sem/i·tiz/əm, an/tī-), *n.*

an·ti·sep·tic (an/ti sep/tik), *n.* **1.** a substance that kills germs; disinfectant. —*adj.* **2.** free of germs.

an·ti·slav·er·y (an/tē slā/və rē), *n.* **1.** opposition to slavery, esp. Negro slavery. —*adj.* **2.** done, written, etc., in opposition to slavery.

an·ti·so·cial (an/tē sō/shəl), *adj.* **1.** unwilling or unable to associate with other people; unfriendly: *He seems antisocial, but he is only shy.* **2.** hostile toward society; opposed to social order and principles.

an·tith·e·sis (an tith/i sis), *n., pl.* **an·tith·e·ses** (an·tith/i sēz/). **1.** the direct opposite; contrast: *He is the antithesis of his brother. Right is the antithesis of wrong.* **2.** the opposition or contrast of ideas in a sentence, as in "Give me liberty or give me death."

an·ti·tox·in (an/ti tok/sin), *n.* **1.** a substance, formed in the body, that counteracts the poison produced by a germ. **2.** a substance used to treat certain diseases that is made from the blood of an animal injected with the poison produced by the disease germ.

ant·ler (ant/lər), *n.* one of the branched horns of an animal of the deer family.

ant·li·on (ant/lī/ən), *n.* any of several insects the larva of which digs a pit in sand, where it lies in wait for ants or other insects on which it feeds.

an·to·nym (an/tə nim), *n.* a word that is opposite in meaning to another: *"Fast" is an antonym of "slow."*

Antlers on a stag

Ant·werp (an/twərp), *n.* a port city in N Belgium.

an·vil (an/vil), *n.* **1.** a heavy iron block on which metals are hammered into shapes, usually after being heated. **2.** one of three small bones in the middle ear.

Anvil (def. 1)

anx·i·e·ty (ang zī/i tē), *n., pl.* **anx·i·e·ties. 1.** distress or uneasiness caused by danger, doubt, or misfortune: *He felt anxiety when he heard she was in an accident.* **2.** eagerness; earnest interest and desire.

anx·ious (angk/shəs), *adj.* **1.** full of anxiety or worry due to fear of danger or misfortune: *Her parents were anxious about her poor health.* **2.** full of eagerness; wanting very much: *The clerk was anxious to help.* —**anx/ious·ly,** *adv.*

an·y (en/ē), *adj.* **1.** one, a, an, or some; one or more without naming someone or something definite: *Pick out any hat you like.* **2.** whatever or whichever it may be: *We have no more at any price.* **3.** in whatever quantity or number; some: *Have you any butter?* **4.** every; all: *Read any books you can find on the subject.* **5.** even the smallest amount of: *She doesn't like any help.* —*pron.* **6.** a single one or ones: *Are any of you coming?* **7.** one or another, regardless of which: *Any of these books is worth reading.* —*adv.* **8.** to some extent; at all: *Do you feel any better after your nap?*

an·y·bod·y (en/ē bod/ē, -bud/ē), *pron.* **1.** any person: *Is anybody home?* —*n.* **2.** a person of some importance: *Is she anybody?*

—**Usage.** Because *anybody* and *anyone* refer to one person only, they are followed by the singular form of a verb, pronoun, etc.: *Anybody is welcome to come. Anyone who wants to may bring his* (or *her,* but not *their*) *own lunch.*

an·y·how (en/ē hou/), *adv.* **1.** in any way whatever. **2.** in any case; under any circumstances: *Anyhow, I won't be able to come.* **3.** carelessly; haphazardly.

an·y·one (en/ē wun/), *pron.* any person at all; anybody: *Don't tell anyone where I am.*

—**Usage.** See **anybody.**

an·y·place (en/ē plās/), *adv.* in any place; anywhere.

an·y·thing (en/ē thing/), *pron.* **1.** any thing whatever. —*n.* **2.** a thing of any kind: *Is there anything to eat?* —*adv.* **3.** in any degree; at all: *The movie wasn't anything like the book.*

an·y·time (en/ē tīm/), *adv.* **1.** at any hour, date, etc.; whenever: *Call me anytime.* **2.** without doubt or exception; always: *I can do better than that anytime.*

an·y·way (en′ē wā′), *adv.* 1. in any way or manner. 2. in any case; anyhow: *Anyway, I'll call before I come.* 3. carelessly; haphazardly: *Don't do the job just anyway.* 4. in spite of this; nevertheless: *I haven't any money, but I'm going anyway.*

an·y·where (en′ē hwâr′, -wâr′), *adv.* 1. in, at, or to any place: *That book could be anywhere in the house.* 2. to any extent; to some degree: *Does my answer come anywhere near the correct one?*

A-O.K. (ā′ō kā′) *adj.* perfect; great; A one: *an A-O.K. rocket launching.* Also, **A-OK, A-O·kay′.**

A one (ā′ wun′), first-class; excellent.

a·or·ta (ā ôr′tə), *n.* the large artery that carries blood from the heart to all parts of the body except the lungs. See illus. at **heart.**

a·pace (ə pās′), *adv.* with speed; very fast.

A·pach·e (ə pach′ē), *n.* a member of an Indian tribe living in the southwestern U.S.

a·part (ə pärt′), *adv.* 1. into pieces or parts: *The old car is falling apart.* 2. separately in place, time, etc.: *Boston and New York are over 200 miles apart.* 3. to or at one side; separately: *to keep apart from the group.* 4. **apart from,** in addition to; besides: *Apart from swimming, what would you like to do?*

a·part·heid (ə pärt′hīt, -hāt), *n.* (in the Republic of South Africa) racial segregation and discrimination against blacks.

a·part·ment (ə pärt′mənt), *n.* 1. a room or a set of rooms in one building, designed for use as a dwelling. 2. a building containing such rooms.

ap·a·thet·ic (ap′ə thet′ik), *adj.* having or showing little or no emotion, interest, etc.; indifferent: *an apathetic audience.* —**ap′a·thet′i·cal·ly,** *adv.*

ap·a·thy (ap′ə thē), *n.* the absence of emotion, interest, or concern; indifference: *The class listened with apathy to the speaker.*

ape (āp), *n.* 1. a monkey having either no tail or a very short one. —*v.,* **aped, ap·ing.** 2. to imitate; mimic: *He apes his little brother's way of speaking.*

Ap·en·nines (ap′ə nīnz′), *n. (used as pl.)* a mountain range extending along the length of the Italian peninsula. Also, **Ap′ennine Moun′tains.**

ap·er·ture (ap′ər chər), *n.* an opening, as a hole, slit, gap, etc.

a·pex (ā′peks), *n., pl.* **a·pex·es** *or* **ap·i·ces** (ap′i sēz′, ā′pi sēz′). the highest part or point; summit; tip: *the apex of a triangle; the apex of his career.*

a·phe·li·on (ə fē′lē ən, ə fēl′yən), *n., pl.* **a·phe·li·a** (ə fē′lē ə, ə fēl′yə). the point in the orbit of a planet or a comet that is farthest from the sun. See also **perihelion.**

a·phid (ā′fid, af′id), *n.* any of numerous small insects that suck the sap from the stems and leaves of plants.

aph·o·rism (af′ə riz′əm), *n.* a short saying that expresses a general truth, as "Art is long, and life is short."

Aphid
A, Male
B, Female
(length ⅛ in.)

Aph·ro·di·te (af′rə dī′tē), *n.* (in Greek mythology) the goddess of love and beauty: identified with the Roman goddess Venus.

a·piece (ə pēs′), *adv.* of, by, or for each one: *Oranges are 10 cents apiece. We ate one apiece.*

a·plomb (ə plom′, ə plum′), *n.* complete self-confidence and composure; poise: *She introduced the speaker with her usual aplomb.*

a·poc·a·lypse (ə pok′ə lips), *n.* a revelation; discovery.

A·poc·a·lypse (ə pok′ə lips), *n.* the book of Revelation; the last book of the New Testament.

A·poc·ry·pha (ə pok′rə fə), *n.* a group of books included in certain translations of the Old Testament but not accepted by everyone as authentic.

a·poc·ry·phal (ə pok′rə fəl), *adj.* probably not true; of doubtful authority: *The story about her great-grandfather's being a pirate is apocryphal.*

ap·o·gee (ap′ə jē′), *n.* the point in the orbit of the moon or an artificial satellite that is farthest from the earth. See also **perigee.**

A·pol·lo (ə pol′ō), *n.* (in Greek and Roman mythology) the god of the sun and of healing, music, poetry, and prophecy, usually pictured as a young and handsome man, driving the chariot of the sun across the heavens.

Apollo XI, a U.S. spacecraft, the first manned vehicle to land on the moon July 20, 1969.

a·pol·o·get·ic (ə pol′ə jet′ik), *adj.* 1. containing or making an apology: *an apologetic letter.* 2. offering excuses, esp. for faults or failures: *an apologetic person.* —**a·pol′o·get′i·cal·ly,** *adv.*

Apollo

a·pol·o·gist (ə pol′ə jist), *n.* a person who makes an apology or defense of an argument, idea, etc., in speech or writing.

a·pol·o·gize (ə pol′ə jīz′), *v.,* **a·pol·o·gized, a·pol·o·giz·ing.** 1. to offer an apology; express regret: *He apologized for coming late.* 2. to make a formal defense in speech or writing.

a·pol·o·gy (ə pol′ə jē), *n., pl.* **a·pol·o·gies.** 1. an expression of regret for having insulted, injured, or wronged someone: *I made an apology to the teacher for misbehaving.* 2. a defense or justification in speech or writing for a cause, doctrine, etc.: *an apology for his change of belief.* 3. a substitute of poor quality: *He wore an apology for a necktie.*

ap·o·plex·y (ap′ə plek′sē), *n.* a sudden paralysis due to the breaking of a blood vessel in the brain. —**ap·o·plec·tic** (ap′ə plek′tik), *adj.*

a·pos·tle (ə pos′əl), *n.* 1. *(sometimes cap.)* one of the 12 disciples sent forth by Christ to preach the gospel. 2. the first or the best-known Christian missionary in any region or country. 3. a pioneer of any reform movement: *an apostle of free speech.*

ap·os·tol·ic (ap′ə stol′ik), *adj.* 1. of or referring to the apostles or their teachings. **2.** of or referring to the pope; papal.

a·pos·tro·phe[1] (ə pos′trə fē), *n.* the sign (′), as used to show that one or more letters have been left out of a word, as in *o'er* for *over;* to show possession, as in *my friend's dog;* or to show plurals of abbreviations and symbols, as in *several M.D.'s.* [from the Greek word *apostrophos* "turning away"]

a·pos·tro·phe[2] (ə pos′trə fē), *n.* a speech addressed to someone not present or to an object: *"Sun, shine down on the trees!" is an apostrophe to the sun.* [from the Greek word *apostrophē* "a turning away"]

a·poth·e·car·y (ə poth′ə ker′ē), *n., pl.* **a·poth·e·car·ies.** a person who prepares, fills, and sells prescriptions; pharmacist; druggist.

a·poth·e·o·sis (ə poth′ē ō′sis, ap′ə thē′ə sis), *n., pl.* **a·poth·e·o·ses** (ə poth′ē ō′sēz, ap′ə thē′ə sēz′). **1.** the exaltation, or raising, of a person to the rank of a god: *the apotheosis of the king.* **2.** the glorification of a person, act, principle, etc., as an ideal: *The movie star was the apotheosis of courage to his fans.*

Ap·pa·la·chi·an Moun·tains (ap′ə lā′chē ən, ap′ə lā′chən), a mountain range in E North America, extending from S Quebec province to N Alabama. Highest elevation 6684 ft. Also, **the Appalachians.**

ap·pall (ə pôl′), *v.* to fill with horror or dismay; terrify: *The damage from the fire appalled him.*

ap·pal·ling (ə pô′ling), *adj.* causing great horror, dismay, or shock: *the appalling conditions in slums.* —**ap·pal′ling·ly,** *adv.*

ap·pa·rat·us (ap′ə rat′əs, ap′ə rā′təs), *n., pl.* **ap·pa·rat·us·es** *or* **ap·pa·rat·us.** **1.** instruments, tools, machinery, materials, etc., used for a specific purpose; equipment: *skin-diving apparatus; laboratory apparatus.* **2.** any system of activities directed toward a certain goal: *the apparatus of government.*

ap·par·el (ə par′əl), *n.* **1.** clothing; garments: *Only women's apparel is sold in the shop.* —*v.,* **ap·par·eled** *or* **ap·par·elled; ap·par·el·ing** *or* **ap·par·el·ling.** **2.** to dress or clothe: *to be appareled like gypsies.* **3.** to adorn or decorate: *a book cover appareled in gold.*

ap·par·ent (ə par′ənt), *adj.* **1.** exposed to sight; visible: *The shore was apparent through the trees.* **2.** easily understood; obvious: *The answer was apparent.* **3.** according to appearances; probable but not certain: *He was the apparent winner of the election.*

ap·par·ent·ly (ə par′ənt lē), *adv.* in an apparent manner; evidently: *The dog is apparently lost.*

ap·pa·ri·tion (ap′ə rish′ən), *n.* **1.** a ghostly image; ghost; phantom. **2.** anything surprising or out of place: *an apparition of cowboys in New York City.*

ap·peal (ə pēl′), *n.* **1.** an earnest request; entreaty; plea: *an appeal for money; an appeal for understanding.* **2.** the power to attract, interest, or amuse: *The game has appeal for children and adults.* **3.** a request to have a case tried again by a higher court or judge: *The lawyer said he would make an appeal.* —*v.* **4.** to request earnestly: *The teacher appealed for quiet.* **5.** to ask for help: *When I have a problem I appeal to my family* **6.** to attract, be of interest, etc.: *The blue dress appeals to me.* **7.** to ask to have a case

reviewed before a higher court or judge. —**ap·peal′ing·ly,** *adv.*

ap·pear (ə pēr′), *v.* **1.** to come into sight; become visible: *A man appeared in the doorway.* **2.** to give an impression; seem: *He appeared shy.* **3.** to be obvious: *It appears to me that we were wrong.* **4.** to come or be placed before the public; be published: *The book will appear next month.* **5.** to perform publicly: *She has appeared in several plays.* **6.** to come formally before a court, authority, etc.: *The witness was asked to appear at the trial.*

ap·pear·ance (ə pēr′əns), *n.* **1.** the act or fact of appearing, as to the eye or mind or before the public: *the appearance of a car; a television appearance.* **2.** the way a person or thing looks: *a neat appearance.* **3.** outward show or effect of something, esp. when different from its true nature; impression: *to give the appearance of being unselfish; rapidly flashed pictures that gave the appearance of continuous motion.*

ap·pease (ə pēz′), *v.,* **ap·peased, ap·peas·ing. 1.** to make calm; pacify: *His explanation appeased me.* **2.** to satisfy: *to appease hunger.* **3.** to give in to demands, often at the expense of principles: *to appease an enemy.* —**ap·pease′ment,** *n.* —**ap·peas′er,** *n.*

ap·pel·late (ə pel′it), *adj.* referring to or dealing with appeals: *an appellate court.*

ap·pel·la·tion (ap′ə lā′shən), *n.* a name, title, or descriptive phrase. In *Alexander the Great,* the appellation of *Alexander* is *the Great.*

ap·pend (ə pend′), *v.* to add or attach: *to append a supplement to a book.*

ap·pend·age (ə pen′dij), *n.* **1.** something attached to a larger thing; addition. **2.** a limb or tail.

ap·pen·di·ci·tis (ə pen′di sī′tis), *n.* a dangerous inflammation of the appendix.

ap·pen·dix (ə pen′diks), *n., pl.* **ap·pen·dix·es** *or* **ap·pen·di·ces** (ə pen′di sēz′). **1.** material added at the end of a book or article. **2.** a small, closed tube growing out from the large intestine. In man, the appendix serves no useful function. See illus. at **intestine.**

ap·per·tain (ap′ər tān′), *v.* to belong as a part, right, possession, etc.; relate; be appropriate: *privileges that appertain to royalty.*

ap·pe·tite (ap′i tīt′), *n.* **1.** a desire for food or drink. **2.** an eagerness for something: *an appetite for adventure.*

ap·pe·tiz·er (ap′i tī′zər), *n.* a portion of food or drink served before a meal to stimulate the appetite.

ap·pe·tiz·ing (ap′i tī′zing), *adj.* appealing to the appetite; attractive: *an appetizing bowl of fruit.*

Ap′pi·an Way′ (ap′ē ən), an ancient Roman road extending SE from Rome to the Adriatic Sea. about 350 mi. long.

ap·plaud (ə plôd′), *v.* to express approval of (a person or thing), esp. by clapping the hands together: *The audience applauded loudly. The voters applauded the mayor's new programs by reelecting him.*

ap·plause (ə plôz′), *n.* a demonstration of approval, appreciation, etc., by or as if by clapping the hands together: *The book review gave the author the applause he expected.*

ap·ple (ap′əl), *n.* **1.** a firm, fleshy, round fruit, having a red, yellow, or green skin. **2.** the usually large, spreading tree that bears this fruit.

ap·ple·sauce (ap′əl sôs′), *n.* apples stewed to a soft pulp and sweetened.

ap·pli·ance (ə plī′əns), *n.* **1.** an apparatus or device for a particular purpose or use: *A corkscrew is an appliance for opening wine bottles.* **2.** a piece of equipment, usually electrical, for use in the home: *Toasters and vacuum cleaners are electrical appliances.*

ap·pli·ca·ble (ap′lə kə bəl), *adj.* applying or capable of being applied or used; suitable: *a solution that is applicable to the problem.*

ap·pli·cant (ap′lə kənt), *n.* a person who applies for or requests something: *an applicant for a job.*

ap·pli·ca·tion (ap′lə kā′shən), *n.* **1.** the act of applying or spreading on: *the application of a coat of paint.* **2.** the quality of being usable for a particular purpose or in a special way: *His solution had no application to the problem.* **3.** something applied to heal or for comfort, as an ointment. **4.** a written or spoken request or appeal: *a job application.* **5.** close attention; hard work: *application to one's studies.*

ap·pli·ca·tor (ap′lə kā′tər), *n.* a simple device for applying a substance not usually touched with the fingers: *an applicator for shoe polish.*

ap·plied (ə plīd′), *adj.* having a practical purpose, said esp. of fields of study that are to some degree theoretical: *Applied mathematics is used in business.*

ap·ply (ə plī′), *v.,* **ap·plied, ap·ply·ing. 1.** to make practical or active use of; use for a particular purpose: *to apply knowledge to a problem; to apply pressure to open a door.* **2.** to bring into action; use: *You must apply the brakes to come to a stop.* **3.** to lay or spread on: *to apply paint to a wall.* **4.** to devote (oneself) intently: *If you apply yourself, your grades will improve.* **5.** to be suitable or related: *The rule does not apply to the case.* **6.** to make a request or application: *My brother applied for a summer job.*

ap·point (ə point′), *v.* **1.** to name or assign to a position or office: *We appointed John chairman of the committee.* **2.** to fix or set officially: *to appoint a time for the meeting.* **3.** to equip; furnish (usually used in combination): *a well-appointed house.*

ap·point·ee (ə poin tē′), *n.* a person who is appointed, rather than elected, to an office or position.

ap·poin·tive (ə poin′tiv), *adj.* of, concerning, or filled by appointment: *an appointive office.*

ap·point·ment (ə point′mənt), *n.* **1.** the act of naming or selecting someone to fill an office or position: *to make a political appointment.* **2.** an office, position, or the like, to which a person is named: *He received an appointment to West Point.* **3.** an agreement to meet at a certain place and time: *We made an appointment for Friday morning.* **4.** the meeting itself: *a dental appointment.* **5.** appointments, furnishings or equipment: *All the appointments of their new home are Colonial.*

Ap·po·mat·tox (ap′ə mat′əks), *n.* a town in central Virginia where Lee surrendered to Grant, ending the Civil War.

ap·por·tion (ə pôr′shən), *v.* to distribute or divide proportionately: *to apportion expenses among three people.* —**ap·por′tion·a·ble,** *adj.*

ap·por·tion·ment (ə pôr′shən mənt), *n.* **1.** the act of distributing or dividing proportionately. **2.** the calculation of the number of representatives in a legislative body according to the population of the area from which they come.

ap·po·si·tion (ap′ə zish′ən), *n.* **1.** the act of placing together. **2.** a placing together of two words or phrases so that each explains the other and both have the same function in the sentence. In *Washington, our first President,* the phrase *our first President* is in apposition to *Washington.*

ap·pos·i·tive (ə poz′i tiv), *n.* **1.** a word or phrase used in apposition. In *Washington, our first President,* the phrase *our first President* is an appositive. —*adj.* **2.** placed or used in apposition.

ap·prais·al (ə prā′zəl), *n.* an estimate or judgment of the nature or value of someone or something: *an appraisal of the car.*

ap·praise (ə prāz′), *v.,* **ap·praised, ap·prais·ing.** to estimate the nature or the value of: *He appraised the car at $1200.* —**ap·prais′er,** *n.* —**ap·prais′ing·ly,** *adv.*

ap·pre·ci·a·ble (ə prē′shē ə bəl, ə prē′shə bəl), *adj.* large enough or important enough to be easily noticed: *appreciable damage; an appreciable improvement.* —**ap·pre′ci·a·bly,** *adv.*

ap·pre·ci·ate (ə prē′shē āt′), *v.,* **ap·pre·ci·at·ed, ap·pre·ci·at·ing. 1.** to be grateful for. **2.** to value highly; place a high estimate on: *Her friends appreciate her talent as an artist.* **3.** to be aware of: *to appreciate the problems involved.* **4.** to raise or increase in value: *Property values appreciated last year.*

ap·pre·ci·a·tion (ə prē′shē ā′shən), *n.* **1.** gratitude or thankfulness: *The class showed its appreciation by giving the teacher a gift.* **2.** clear understanding and recognition of quality or value: *appreciation of music.* **3.** an increase in the value of property, goods, etc. **4.** a written evaluation or opinion.

ap·pre·ci·a·tive (ə prē′shə tiv), *adj.* feeling or showing appreciation; grateful.

ap·pre·hend (ap′ri hend′), *v.* **1.** to arrest by legal authority: *to apprehend a criminal.* **2.** to grasp the meaning of; understand: *to apprehend a statement.* **3.** to look ahead to with fear: *to apprehend danger.*

ap·pre·hen·sion (ap′ri hen′shən), *n.* **1.** a suspicion or fear of future trouble or evil: *to feel apprehension before opening a telegram.* **2.** the act of arresting: *the apprehension of a thief.* **3.** clear understanding.

ap·pre·hen·sive (ap′ri hen′siv), *adj.* uneasy or afraid of something that might happen: *Why do you look so apprehensive?* —**ap′pre·hen′sive·ly,** *adv.*

ap·pren·tice (ə pren′tis), *n.* **1.** a person who works for another in order to learn a trade. In the trade guilds of the Middle Ages an apprentice belonged to the lowest rank, being below a journeyman: *an ap-*

prentice to a plumber. **2.** a learner or beginner. **—v., ap·pren·ticed, ap·pren·tic·ing. 3.** to bind to or place with an employer for instruction in a trade: *to be apprenticed to a carpenter.*

ap·prise (ə prīz′), *v.,* **ap·prised, ap·pris·ing.** to give notice to; inform; advise (often fol. by *of*): *The doctor apprised her of her condition.*

ap·proach (ə prōch′), *v.* **1.** to come near or nearer to: *The car approached the curb.* **2.** to draw near or nearer: *Christmas is approaching.* **3.** to come near to in amount, character, condition, etc.; come within range of for comparison: *Few poets approach Shakespeare in greatness.* **4.** to go to with a request, plan, etc.: *He approached his friends with the idea of starting a club.* **5.** to begin work on; set about: *He approached the problem boldly.* **—n. 6.** the act of drawing near: *The deer were startled by our approach.* **7.** any means of getting to a place, as a road, ramp, etc. **8.** a method of doing something: *His whole approach to the problem is wrong.* **9.** Sometimes, **approaches.** an offer or proposal: *A hostile person rejects all approaches for friendship.*

ap·proach·a·ble (ə prō′chə bəl), *adj.* **1.** capable of being approached; accessible: *The mountain slopes are not approachable in the winter.* **2.** easy to talk with or know: *The boss is very approachable.*

ap·pro·ba·tion (ap′rə bā′shən), *n.* wholehearted approval, acceptance, or praise.

ap·pro·pri·ate (ə prō′prē it), *adj.* **1.** suitable or proper: *Shorts are not appropriate for church.* **2.** characteristic of or belonging exclusively to a certain person: *Each played his appropriate part.* **—v.** (ə prō′prē āt′), **ap·pro·pri·at·ed, ap·pro·pri·at·ing. 3.** to set apart for a special purpose or use: *The legislature appropriated money for education.* **4.** to take to or for oneself: *The settlers appropriated vast, uninhabited regions.* **5.** to take without permission: *She appropriated her sister's best dresses.* **—ap·pro′pri·ate·ly,** *adv.* **—ap·pro′pri·ate·ness,** *n.*

ap·pro·pri·a·tion (ə prō′prē ā′shən), *n.* **1.** the act of appropriating. **2.** anything appropriated for a special purpose, esp. money: *Congress voted an appropriation for the arts center.*

ap·prov·al (ə prōō′vəl), *n.* **1.** the act of approving; approbation: *Applause indicates approval.* **2.** consent or permission: *You acted without my approval.* **3. on approval,** without obligation to buy unless satisfactory: *The books were sent to him on approval.*

ap·prove (ə prōōv′), *v.,* **ap·proved, ap·prov·ing. 1.** to consider or judge favorably: *to approve the policies of the government.* **2.** to consent to: *I won't approve your swimming alone.* **3.** to speak or consider favorably (often fol. by *of*): *Mother doesn't approve of my friends.* **—ap·prov′a·ble,** *adj.* **—ap·prov′ing·ly,** *adv.*

ap·prox·i·mate (ə prok′sə mit), *adj.* **1.** nearly exact; more or less correct or precise: *The approximate time is 10 o'clock.* **—v.** (ə prok′sə māt′), **ap·prox·i·mat·ed, ap·prox·i·mat·ing. 2.** to come near to; approach closely: *Her paper flowers approximate real roses.* **3.** to estimate: *We approximated the distance at three miles.* **—ap·prox′i·mate·ly,** *adv.*

ap·prox·i·ma·tion (ə prok′sə mā′shən), *n.* **1.** the act of coming near to or approaching closely. **2.** an estimate: *to make an approximation of distance.* **3.** something that is nearly true, correct, exact, etc.: *His story was an approximation of the actual event.*

ap·pur·te·nance (ə pûr′tᵊnəns), *n.* something that is a minor part of another, more important thing; accessory: *The old house has a bathroom, garage, and other modern appurtenances.*

Apr., April.

ap·ri·cot (ap′rə kot′, ā′prə kot′), *n.* **1.** a downy fruit of a light orange color, resembling a small peach. **2.** the tree that produces this fruit. **3.** a light orange. [from the Arabic phrase *al birqūq,* which comes from the Latin word *praecox* "early," in the phrase *persicum praecox* "early peach"]

A·pril (ā′prəl), *n.* the fourth month of the year, having 30 days.

A′pril Fools′′ Day′, April 1, a day when jokes are played on unsuspecting people.

a·pron (ā′prən), *n.* **1.** an article of apparel covering part of the front of the body. **2.** a paved or hard-packed area near an airfield's buildings and hangars, where planes are parked, loaded, or the like. **3.** the part of the floor of a stage in front of the curtain.

ap·ro·pos (ap′rə pō′), *adj.* **1.** suitable to or fitting the occasion; appropriate; apt: *I find your remarks extremely apropos.* **—adv. 2.** suitably or appropriately as to a subject or occasion: *to speak apropos.* **3. apropos of,** with reference to; in regard to: *Apropos of my plan, what do you think?*

apse (aps), *n.* a vaulted, usually semicircular recess in a church, esp. at the east end behind the altar.

apt (apt), *adj.* **1.** having a natural tendency or inclination; prone: *Angry cats are apt to scratch.* **2.** likely: *Am I apt to find him at home?* **3.** extremely intelligent: *apt students.* **4.** suited to the purpose or occasion: *an apt remark.* **—apt′ly,** *adv.* **—apt′ness,** *n.*

apt., apartment.

ap·ti·tude (ap′ti tōōd′, -tyōōd′), *n.* **1.** a natural talent or ability; capability: *an aptitude for mathematics.* **2.** quickness in learning; intelligence.

aq·ua·lung (ak′wə luŋ′), *n.* a device used by a person for breathing underwater, usually consisting of a tank of compressed air that is strapped to the back and supplies air to a mouthpiece.

aq·ua·ma·rine (ak′wə mə rēn′), *n.* **1.** a transparent, light-blue or greenish-blue type of beryl, used as a gem. **2.** a light blue-green. **—adj. 3.** of a light blue-green or greenish-blue color.

aq·ua·plane (ak′wə plān′), *n.* a board that skims over water when towed at high speed by a motorboat, used to carry a rider in water sports.

a·quar·i·um (ə kwâr′ē əm), *n.* **1.** a tank, pool, bowl, etc., in which live fish, water plants, and water animals are kept and exhibited. **2.** a building in which fish and such plants and animals are kept for exhibition, study, etc.

A·quar·i·us (ə kwâr′ē əs), *n.* the Water Bearer: a constellation and sign of the zodiac.

a·quat·ic (ə kwat′ik, ə kwot′ik), *adj.* **1.** living or growing in water: *Whales are aquatic animals.* **2.** taking place in or on water: *aquatic sports.*

aq·ue·duct (ak/wi dukt/), *n.* **1.** a pipe or channel for transporting water over a distance: *Aqueducts ran from the mountains to the cities.* **2.** a bridgelike structure for carrying such a pipe or channel.

a·que·ous (ā/kwē əs, ak/wē əs), *adj.* of, like, or containing water; watery: *the aqueous fluid of the eye.*

a/queous hu/mor, the clear, watery fluid that fills the space between the cornea and lens of the eye.

aq·ui·line (ak/wə līn/, ak/wə lin), *adj.* **1.** of or like an eagle. **2.** (of a person's nose) shaped like an eagle's beak; curved or hooked.

A·qui·nas (ə kwī/nəs), *n.* **Saint Thomas,** 1225?–1274, Italian philosopher: a major theologian of the Roman Catholic Church.

Ar, *Chem.* a symbol for **argon.**

-ar, a suffix used to form adjectives meaning of, like, or referring to: *molecular; polar.*

Ar·ab (ar/əb), *n.* **1.** a member of a people inhabiting Arabia, Iraq, Jordan, Syria, Lebanon, and parts of northern Africa; an Arabian. —*adj.* **2.** Arabian.

ar·a·besque (ar/ə besk/), *n.* **1.** a fanciful, elaborate design of flowers, leaves, fruits, etc. **2.** a pose in ballet dancing. —*adj.* **3.** decorated with or like arabesques: *a rug with an arabesque design.*

A·ra·bi·a (ə rā/bē ə), *n.* a peninsula in SW Asia: mostly desert. about 1,000,000 sq. mi.

A·ra·bi·an (ə rā/bē ən), *adj.* **1.** of or concerning Arabia or the Arabs. —*n.* **2.** an Arab.

Ara/bian horse/, one of a breed of rather small, highly spirited horses, raised originally in Arabia and nearby countries, and noted for their speed, beauty, and intelligence.

Ara/bian Sea/, the NW arm of the Indian Ocean between India and Arabia.

Ar·a·bic (ar/ə bik), *n.* **1.** the Semitic language spoken chiefly in Arabia, Egypt, Jordan, Syria, Iraq, Lebanon, and North Africa. —*adj.* **2.** of or concerning Arabia, the Arabs, or the Arabic language.

Ar/abic nu/meral, any of the number symbols 1, 2, 3, 4, 5, 6, 7, 8, 9, and 0, or a combination of them. Also, **Ar/abic num/ber.** See also **Roman numerals.**

ar·a·ble (ar/ə bəl), *adj.* suitable for farming; fit to be plowed and tilled. — **ar/a·bil/i·ty,** *n.*

Ar/ab Repub/lic of E/gypt, a republic in NE Africa, between the Red Sea and the Mediterranean. 386,198 sq. mi. *Cap.:* Cairo. Former name (1958–1971), **United Arab Republic.**

MEDITERRANEAN SEA
ISRAEL
Alexandria
Cairo
JORDAN
SAUDI ARABIA
LIBYA
Arab Republic of Egypt
RED SEA
Administrative Boundary
SUDAN

a·rach·nid (ə rak/nid), *n.* a member of the group of animals that includes spiders, scorpions, and ticks.

Ar/al Sea/ (ar/əl), an inland sea in the SW Soviet Union in Asia, E of the Caspian Sea. 26,166 sq. mi.

Ar·a·rat (ar/ə rat/), *n.* a mountain in E Turkey: said to be the landing place of Noah's Ark. 16,945 ft.

ar·bit·er (är/bi tər), *n.* a person having the power to decide matters, as in a dispute or game.

ar·bi·trar·y (är/bi trer/ē), *adj.* **1.** depending on choice or will rather than on law or rule. **2.** marked by or based on whim or caprice, without regard for what is right or just: *a selfish, arbitrary change of plans.* **3.** having unlimited power: *an arbitrary ruler.* —**ar/bi·trar/i·ly,** *adv.* —**ar/bi·trar/i·ness,** *n.*

ar·bi·trate (är/bi trāt/), *v.,* **ar·bi·trat·ed, ar·bi·trat·ing.** **1.** to decide (a matter) as arbiter or arbitrator. **2.** to submit to or settle by arbitration: *to arbitrate a dispute.* **3.** to act as arbiter or arbitrator.

ar·bi·tra·tion (är/bi trā/shən), *n.* the settling of a dispute between two sides by a person, group, state, etc., chosen or agreed upon by both.

ar·bi·tra·tor (är/bi trā/tər), *n.* a person who has the power to decide a dispute.

ar·bor (är/bər), *n.* a shaded, sheltered place formed by trees or bushes or by a trellis covered with vines; bower. Also, *esp. British,* **ar/bour.**

ar·bo·re·al (är bôr/ē əl), *adj.* **1.** referring to or resembling trees. **2.** living in or among trees.

ar·bo·re·tum (är/bə rē/təm), *n.* a place where trees or shrubs are grown for study or display.

ar·bor·vi·tae (är/bər vī/tē), *n.* an evergreen tree having broad, fanlike branches and small, fine leaves.

ar·bu·tus (är byoo/təs), *n.* **1.** any of several evergreen trees or shrubs that bear red berries. **2.** a creeping North American plant that bears fragrant white or pink flowers.

arc (ärk), *n.* **1.** a curve, esp. part of a circle. **2.** the spark created when an electric current passes across a gap between two conductors. **3.** anything bowshaped. —*v.,* **arced** (ärkt) *or* **arcked; arc·ing** (är k/ing) *or* **arck·ing. 4.** to form an electric arc. **5.** to move in an arclike curve: *The arrow arced through the air.*

ar·cade (är kād/), *n.* **1.** a series of arches supported by columns. **2.** a roofed or arched passageway, esp. one with shops on each side.

Ar·ca·di·a (är kā/dē ə), *n.* a mountainous region of ancient Greece, famous in legend as the home of innocent and happy shepherds. —**Ar·ca/di·an,** *n., adj.*

arch¹ (ärch), *n.* **1.** a curved structure that bears the weight of what is above it, used for spanning a doorway, supporting a bridge, etc. **2.** a doorway, gateway, etc., having an arch. **3.** a monument having an arched opening in the center: *a triumphal arch.* **4.** anything that resembles or is thought to resemble an arch: *the arch of a rainbow; the arch of the foot.* —*v.* **5.** to cover or span with an arch: *A bridge arched the river.* **6.** to make into the shape of an arch: *The angry cat arched its back.* **7.** to form an arch. [from an Old French word, which comes from Latin *arcus* "bow"]

Arch

arch² (ärch), *adj.* **1.** chief; most important: *the arch*

rebel. **2.** sly or roguish; mischievous: *an arch smile.*
[from the prefix *arch-*, which comes from Greek
archē "head, chief"] —**arch′ly,** *adv.* —**arch′ness,** *n.*

arch-, a prefix meaning chief or principal: *archangel; archbishop.*

Arch., Archbishop. Also, **Archbp.**

ar·chae·o·log·i·cal (är′kē ə loj′i kəl), *adj.* of or referring to archaeology. Also, **ar′che·o·log′i·cal.**

ar·chae·ol·o·gist (är′kē ol′ə jist), *n.* a person who
specializes in archaeology. Also, **ar′che·ol′o·gist.**

ar·chae·ol·o·gy (är′kē ol′ə jē), *n.* the scientific study
of ancient peoples and their cultures by examining
remains of their skeletons and things made by them,
such as buildings, pottery, inscriptions, etc., esp.
those found by excavation. Also, **ar′che·ol′o·gy.**

ar·chae·op·ter·yx (är′kē op′tə riks), *n.* the earliest
known bird. The archaeopteryx had several reptilian
characteristics and lived
about 150 million years
ago.

ar·cha·ic (är kā′ik), *adj.* **1.**
having the characteristics
of an earlier time; old-
fashioned or out-of-date;
antiquated: *Stagecoaches
are an archaic means of
transportation.* **2.** noting

Archaeopteryx
(total length about 2 ft.)

a word or phrase no longer used in ordinary speech
or writing, as the pronouns *thee, thou, thy* and the
verb forms *hast* and *doth.* **3.** ancient or primitive:
archaic civilizations. —**ar·cha′i·cal·ly,** *adv.*

arch·an·gel (ärk′ān′jəl), *n.* a chief or principal angel: *Gabriel is an archangel.*

arch·bish·op (ärch′bish′əp), *n.* a bishop of the
highest rank.

arch·duch·ess (ärch′duch′is), *n.* **1.** the wife of an
archduke. **2.** a royal Austrian princess by birth.

arch·duke (ärch′dook′, -dyook′), *n.* a prince of the
former royal family of Austria.

Ar′che·o·zo′ic e′ra (är′kē ə zō′ik), the earliest
geological period, extending from about 5 billion to
about 1½ billion years ago, from the formation of
the earth's crust to the appearance of the first living
things: followed by the Proterozoic era.

arch·er (är′chər), *n.* **1.** a person who shoots with a
bow and arrow; bowman. **2.** **the Archer,** another
name for **Sagittarius.**

ar·cher·y (är′chə rē), *n.* **1.** the art, practice, or skill
of an archer. **2.** a group of archers.

Ar·chi·me·des (är′kə mē′dēz), *n.* 287?–212 B.C.,
Greek mathematician, physicist, and inventor: discoverer of the principles of buoyancy and the lever.

ar·chi·pel·a·go (är′ki pel′ə gō′), *n., pl.* **ar·chi·pel·a·
gos** *or* **ar·chi·pel·a·goes.** **1.** a group of many islands in
a large expanse of water. **2.** any large expanse of water having many islands.

ar·chi·tect (är′ki tekt′), *n.* **1.** a person whose profession is architecture. **2.** a person whose profession is
to design large constructions other than buildings:
naval architect. **3.** the maker or creator of anything:
the architects of the Constitution.

ar·chi·tec·ture (är′ki tek′chər), *n.* **1.** the science or
art of designing buildings and similar constructions,
such as bridges, monuments, etc. **2.** a style of building: *the architecture of Paris.* **3.** the design or form of
anything: *the architecture of a novel.* —**ar′chi·tec′
tur·al,** *adj.* —**ar′chi·tec′tur·al·ly,** *adv.*

ar·chive (är′kīv), *n.* **1.** Usually, **archives.** a place for
keeping historical records or documents, such as
those having to do with a country, family, etc. **2.** **archives,** the records or documents themselves.

arch·way (ärch′wā′), *n.* an entrance or passage under an arch.

arc·tic (ärk′tik), *adj.* **1.** of, at, or near the North Pole.
2. like the weather at or near the North Pole: *arctic
temperatures.* **3.** cold in manner: *An arctic glance
was all the welcome she gave us.* —*n.* **4.** *(often cap.)*
the region lying north of the Arctic Circle. [from the
Greek word *arktikos* "northern," which comes from
arktos "bear." The constellation of the Bear is found
in the northern sky]

Arc′tic Cir′cle, an imaginary line parallel to the
equator and located above the tropic of Cancer, 23°
28′ south of the North Pole.

Arc′tic O′cean, an ocean in the northern polar regions, mostly glacial.

ar·dent (är′dənt), *adj.* **1.** showing great eagerness or
enthusiasm: *an ardent patriot.* **2.** intensely hot; burning; fiery: *the ardent sun.* —**ar′dent·ly,** *adv.*

ar·dor (är′dər), *n.* great strength of feeling; fervor;
zeal; passion: *He spoke with ardor in favor of his
friend.* Also, *esp. British,* **ar′dour.**

ar·du·ous (är′jōō əs), *adj.* **1.** demanding great effort;
difficult; hard: *an arduous undertaking.* **2.** energetic;
vigorous; strenuous: *an arduous effort.* **3.** hard to
climb; steep. **4.** hard to bear; full of hardships;
severe: *an arduous winter.* —**ar′du·ous·ly,** *adv.* —**ar′
du·ous·ness,** *n.*

are (är), *v.* the present tense of **be,** used with *you,
we,* and *they.*

ar·e·a (âr′ē ə), *n.* **1.** size or amount of surface or flat
space: *a country having a great area; an area of 400
square feet.* **2.** any region or section: *tropical areas; a
swampy area.* **3.** any section set aside for a particular
purpose: *the dining area of a house.* **4.** scope or field:
to choose a career in the area of science.

ar′ea code′, a series of three numbers representing
one of the large areas of a country for communication
by telephone.

a·re·na (ə rē′nə), *n.* **1.** an oval space in a Roman am-
phitheater for combats or other performances. **2.** a
platform, ring, or the like, used for sports and other
entertainments, surrounded by seats for the audience: *a boxing arena.* **3.** a building that houses an
arena. **4.** a field of activity: *the arena of politics.*

aren't (ärnt, är′ənt), *v.* contraction of *are not.*

Ar·es (âr′ēz), *n.* (in Greek mythology) the god of war:
identified with the Roman god Mars.

Ar·gen·ti·na (är′jən tē′nə), *n.* a republic in S South
America. 1,084,120 sq. mi. *Cap.:* Buenos Aires.

Ar·gen·tine (är′jən tēn′), *n.* **1.** a native or inhabitant
of Argentina. **2.** **the Argentine,** Argentina: *They va-*

cationed in the Argentine. —*adj.* **3.** of or referring to Argentina or its people.

ar·gon (är′gon), *n. Chem.* an inert gaseous element used for filling electric light bulbs. *Symbol:* Ar, A

Ar·go·naut (är′gə nôt′), *n.* (in Greek mythology) any one of Jason's followers who sailed with him on the *Argo* in search of the Golden Fleece.

ar·go·sy (är′gə sē), *n., pl.* **ar·go·sies. 1.** a large merchant ship, esp. one with a rich cargo. **2.** a fleet of such ships.

ar·gue (är′gyo͞o), *v.,* **ar·gued, ar·gu·ing. 1.** to present reasons for or against a thing: *He argued for a larger allowance.* **2.** to dispute or quarrel: *They argued about who would drive the car.* **3.** to state the reasons for or against; debate: *The lawyers argued the case.* **4.** to maintain by reason: *He argued that crime does not pay.* **5.** to persuade, drive, etc., by reasoning: *He argued me out of going.* **6.** to show or indicate: *His clothes argued his poverty.* —**ar′gu·a·ble,** *adj.* —**ar′gu·er,** *n.*

ar·gu·ment (är′gyə mənt), *n.* **1.** a discussion involving different points of view. **2.** a disagreement or dispute: *a violent argument.* **3.** a series of reasons; line of reasoning: *to follow the argument of a speaker.* **4.** a speech, essay, or the like, intended to convince or persuade: *an argument against war.* **5.** subject matter or theme; central idea: *the argument of an essay.* **6.** a summary or statement of what a book, poem, etc., is about.

ar·gu·men·ta·tive (är′gyə men′tə tiv), *adj.* quarrelsome; given to argument and dispute. —**ar′gu·men′ta·tive·ly,** *adv.* —**ar′gu·men′ta·tive·ness,** *n.*

a·ri·a (är′ē ə), *n.* a song in an opera that is sung by one person accompanied by musical instruments.

ar·id (ar′id), *adj.* **1.** without moisture; dry; parched: *an arid plain.* **2.** not having enough rainfall for things to grow: *arid farmland.* **3.** providing no interest; dull; boring: *an arid novel.*

Ar·ies (ar′ēz, âr′ē ēz′), *n.* the Ram: a constellation and sign of the zodiac.

a·right (ə rīt′), *adv.* rightly; correctly: *Do I understand you aright?*

a·rise (ə rīz′), *v.,* **a·rose** (ə rōz′), **a·ris·en** (ə riz′ən), **a·ris·ing. 1.** to get up from sitting, lying, or kneeling; rise. **2.** to move upward; climb; mount; rise: *Smoke arose from the chimney.* **3.** to come into being; appear; spring up: *New problems arise daily.* **4.** to result or proceed (sometimes fol. by *from*): *Quarrels arise from misunderstandings.*

ar·is·toc·ra·cy (ar′i stok′rə sē), *n., pl.* **ar·is·toc·ra·cies. 1.** a class of persons having the highest rank in a society, esp. the nobility. **2.** a government or state ruled by such a class. **3.** a government conducted by the best or most able men. **4.** any class or group considered to be superior: *an aristocracy of artists and scientists.*

a·ris·to·crat (ə ris′tə krat′), *n.* **1.** a person who belongs to an aristocracy, esp. a nobleman. **2.** a person who has the tastes, manners, etc., of someone who belongs to an aristocracy. **3.** a person who is in favor of an aristocratic form of government. —**a·ris′to·crat′ic,** *adj.* —**a·ris′to·crat′i·cal·ly,** *adv.*

Ar·is·tot·le (ar′i stot′əl), *n.* 384–322 B.C., Greek philosopher: pupil of Plato; tutor of Alexander the Great.

a·rith·me·tic (ə rith′mə tik), *n.* **1.** the science or process of computing with numbers, esp. in adding, subtracting, multiplying, and dividing. —*adj.* (ar′ith met′ik). **2.** Also, **ar′ith·met′i·cal.** of or referring to arithmetic. —**ar′ith·met′i·cal·ly,** *adv.*

a·rith·me·ti·cian (ə rith′mə tish′ən), *n.* an expert in arithmetic.

Ariz., Arizona.

Ar·i·zo·na (ar′i zō′nə), *n.* a state in the SW United States. 113,909 sq. mi. *Cap.:* Phoenix. —**Ar′i·zo′nan, Ar·i·zo·ni·an** (ar′i zō′nē ən), *n., adj.*

ark (ärk), *n.* **1.** (in the Bible) the large boat in which Noah saved himself, his family, and a pair of every kind of animal during the Flood. **2.** Also, **ark′ of the cov′enant.** the chest or box representing the presence of God and containing the Ten Commandments, carried by the Israelites after the Exodus. **3.** the Holy Ark.

Ark., Arkansas.

Ar·kan·sas (är′kən sô′), *n.* a state in the S central United States. 53,103 sq. mi. *Cap.:* Little Rock. —**Ar·kan·san** (är kan′zən), **Ar·kan·si·an** (är kan′zē ən), *n., adj.*

arm[1] (ärm), *n.* **1.** the upper limb of the human body, esp. the part between the shoulder and the wrist. **2.** the front limb of certain animals. **3.** a part of various other animals that resembles an arm in some way: *The octopus has eight arms.* **4.** anything that resembles an arm: *an arm of the sea; an arm of a chair.* **5.** a sleeve of a coat, shirt, dress, etc. **6.** a branch of an organization: *a special arm of the government.* **7.** the power or authority of an organization, government, etc.: *the long arm of the law.* **8. arm in arm,** with arms linked or intertwined: *They walked along arm in arm.* **9. at arm's length,** at a distance, as from dislike, fear, etc.: *to keep one's enemies at arm's length.* **10. with open arms,** with a warm welcome; cordially: *He greeted his guests with open arms.* [from the Old English word *earm*] —**arm′less,** *adj.* —**arm′like′,** *adj.*

arm[2] (ärm), *n.* **1.** Usually, **arms.** weapons, esp. firearms. **2. arms,** a coat of arms. —*v.* **3.** to prepare for war or battle; take up arms. **4.** to equip with weapons: *to arm the troops.* **5.** to provide with protection: *A warm coat will arm you against the cold.* **6.** to equip or prepare: *to go to class armed with facts.* **7. bear arms,** to carry weapons or serve as a member of a military force: *a conscientious objector who refused to bear arms.* **8. To arms!** Prepare to fight! **9. up in arms,** indignant or outraged; extremely angry: *She was up in arms because I was 15 minutes late.* [from the Latin word *arma* "weapons"] —**arm′less,** *adj.*

ar·ma·da (är mä′də, är mā′də), *n.* **1.** a fleet of warships. **2.** any large group or force of vehicles, airplanes, etc. **3. the Armada,** another name for **Spanish Armada.**

ar·ma·dil·lo (är′mə dil′ō), *n., pl.* **ar·ma·dil·los.** a small, toothless, burrowing mammal of the southern U.S. and South America, having strong claws and a jointed, bony covering on its body and head.

Armadillo
(total length 2½ ft.)

ar·ma·ment (är′mə mənt), *n.* **1.** the total number of weapons with which a combat airplane, warship, tank, etc., is equipped. **2.** a land, sea, or air force equipped for war. **3.** See **armor** (def. 3). **4.** Usually, **armaments.** military strength as a whole; all weapons and other means for waging war: *a drastic reduction in world armaments.*

ar·ma·ture (är′mə chər), *n.* **1.** the rotating part of an electric generator or motor. **2.** a piece of iron or steel placed across the poles of a magnet or one that is attracted by the electromagnet in devices like electric buzzers.

arm·chair (ärm′châr′), *n.* a chair having arms.

armed (ärmd), *adj.* **1.** carrying or bearing arms, esp. firearms. **2.** kept or maintained by arms: *an armed peace.* **3.** involving the use of weapons: *armed conflict.* **4.** equipped or prepared for a particular purpose: *The students came armed with pencils and notebooks.* **5.** (esp. of an animal) covered protectively, as by a shell.

armed′ forc′es, the total military, naval, and air forces of a country or a number of countries. Also, **armed′ serv′ices.**

Ar·me·ni·a (är mē′nē ə), *n.* **1.** an ancient country in W Asia: now part of the Soviet Union, E Turkey, and NW Iran. **2.** Official name, **Arme′nian So′viet So′cialist Repub′lic.** a republic of the Soviet Union, in S Caucasia, bordering on Turkey and Iran. about 11,-500 sq. mi. —**Ar·me′ni·an,** *n., adj.*

arm·ful (ärm′fŏŏl), *n., pl.* **arm·fuls.** the amount that can be held by one or both arms; a large quantity: *Bring an armful of wood for the fire.* Also, **arm·load** (ärm′lōd′).

arm·hole (ärm′hōl′), *n.* an opening at the shoulder of a garment for the arm to pass through into a sleeve.

ar·mi·stice (är′mi stis), *n.* a temporary halt in a war

by agreement of each of the opposing sides; truce.

Ar′mistice Day′, former name of **Veterans Day.**

ar·mor (är′mər), *n.* **1.** any covering used as a defense against weapons: *the armor of a battleship.* **2.** a suit of armor. **3.** any protective covering, as on certain animals; armament. —*v.* **4.** to equip or cover with armor or armor plate. Also, *esp. British,* **ar′mour.**

ar·mored (är′mord), *adj.* **1.** protected by armor or armored plate. **2.** provided with or using armored equipment: *an armored patrol.* Also, *esp. British,* **ar′moured.**

ar·mor·er (är′mər ər), *n.* **1.** a person who makes or repairs arms or armor. **2.** a manufacturer of firearms. **3.** an enlisted man responsible for the upkeep of small arms. Also, *esp. British,* **ar′mour·er.**

ar·mo·ri·al (är môr′ē əl), *adj.* of or referring to heraldry or to a coat of arms.

Armor

ar·mor·y (är′mə rē), *n., pl.* **ar·mor·ies. 1.** a storage place for weapons and other war equipment. **2.** a building in which a National Guard or Army reserve unit has its headquarters and an area for drilling. **3.** a place where arms are manufactured; arsenal.

arm·pit (ärm′pit′), *n.* the hollow under the arm where it joins the body.

Arm·strong (ärm′strông′), *n.* **Neil A.,** born 1930, U.S. astronaut: first man to set foot on the moon July 20, 1969.

ar·my (är′mē), *n., pl.* **ar·mies. 1.** a large group of soldiers trained and armed for war, esp. on land: *An army was sent to recapture the lost province.* **2.** a military force made up of all the soldiers of a country: *Their army was larger than their navy.* **3.** any body of persons organized for any purpose: *an army of workers.* **4.** any very large number or group; multitude: *an army of bathers on the beach.*

Ar·nold (är′nəld), *n.* **Benedict,** 1741–1801, American general in the Revolutionary War who became a traitor.

a·ro·ma (ə rō′mə), *n.* any pleasant, agreeable odor, as one given off by spices, flowers, food cooking, etc.

ar·o·mat·ic (ar′ə mat′ik), *adj.* having an aroma; fragrant; sweet-scented. —**ar′o·mat′i·cal·ly,** *adv.*

a·rose (ə rōz′), *v.* the past tense of **arise.**

a·round (ə round′), *adv.* **1.** in a circle, ring, or the like, so as to surround: *The crowd gathered around.* **2.** in all directions: *He owns the land for miles around.* **3.** in circumference: *The tree was 40 inches around.*

4. in a circular or rounded course: *The birds flew around and around.* **5.** back to the present time again: *When spring rolls around, we can take a trip.* **6.** through or throughout a place: *Let me show you around.* **7.** in or to another direction, point of view, etc.: *Sit still and don't look around.* **8.** back into consciousness: *She fainted, but we were able to bring her around.* **9.** into action, circulation, etc.: *to be up and around after an illness.* **10.** nearby: *I'll be around if you need me.* —*prep.* **11.** about; on all sides; encircling: *a halo around his head.* **12.** throughout or about: *The news quickly got around town.* **13.** within the area that surrounds; in the vicinity of: *I like the country around Boston. Look around you.* **14.** approximately; about: *around five o'clock.* **15.** beyond the turn of: *the church around the corner.* **16.** so as to turn about an axis or center: *The earth revolves around the sun.*

a·rouse (ə rouz′), *v.,* **a·roused, a·rous·ing.** **1.** to awaken, as from sleep, inaction, etc.; rouse: *The alarm clock aroused him.* **2.** to excite or provoke: *to arouse anger.*

ar·que·bus (är′kwə bəs), *n., pl.* **ar·que·bus·es.** another form of **harquebus.**

ar·raign (ə rān′), *v.* **1.** to call or bring before a court to answer a charge. **2.** to accuse of a fault; criticize. —**ar·raign′ment,** *n.*

ar·range (ə rānj′), *v.,* **ar·ranged, ar·rang·ing.** **1.** to place in proper or desired order: *to arrange books on the shelves; to arrange flowers in a vase.* **2.** to plan or schedule; make preparations for: *to arrange a meeting.* **3.** to make preparations: *to arrange for a meeting.* **4.** to come to an agreement or understanding regarding; settle: *to arrange a truce.* **5.** to make a settlement; come to an agreement (usually fol. by *for*). **6.** to adapt (a musical composition) for a particular style of performance: *to arrange an orchestral piece for piano.* —**ar·rang′er,** *n.*

ar·range·ment (ə rānj′mənt), *n.* **1.** the act of arranging, or the state of being arranged. **2.** the order or way in which things are placed: *I like this arrangement of the furniture best.* **3.** a final settlement: *an arrangement of a dispute.* **4.** Usually, **arrangements.** preparations or plans: *They made arrangements for their vacation.* **5.** something ordered or placed in a particular way: *a floral arrangement.* **6.** the adaptation of a musical composition for a certain style of performance: *an arrangement for piano.*

ar·rant (ar′ənt), *adj.* downright; thorough; out-and-out: *arrant nonsense; an arrant lie.*

ar·ray (ə rā′), *v.* **1.** to place in proper or desired order: *to array books on a shelf.* **2.** to clothe, esp. richly: *The queen was arrayed for her coronation.* —*n.* **3.** a regular order or arrangement: *an array of troops.* **4.** a large and impressive arrangement or display. **5.** rich dress or attire.

ar·rears (ə rērz′), *n.pl.* **1.** the state of being behind or late in paying a bill, keeping a promise, or the like. **2.** something that is behind in being paid: *ar-*

rears in rent. **3. in arrears,** behind in paying off a debt: *They are in arrears with their monthly payments.*

ar·rest (ə rest′), *v.* **1.** to seize by legal authority: *The policeman arrested him for speeding.* **2.** to attract and hold: *The beauty of the song arrested the attention of the audience.* **3.** to check the course of; stop or slow down: *to arrest progress.* —*n.* **4.** the act of arresting, as by a policeman. **5. under arrest,** in a state of arrest; in legal custody.

ar·ri·val (ə rī′vəl), *n.* **1.** the act or instance of arriving. **2.** a person or thing that has arrived: *New arrivals filled the bus depot.*

ar·rive (ə rīv′), *v.,* **ar·rived, ar·riv·ing.** **1.** to come to a certain point; reach one's destination: *He finally arrived in Rome.* **2.** to come to be present: *The time has finally arrived.* **3.** to become successful or reach one's goal in life: *Some musicians arrive at an early age.* —**ar·riv′er,** *n.*

ar·ro·gance (ar′ə gəns), *n.* an excess of pride that shows itself in rudeness and disrespect; haughtiness.

ar·ro·gant (ar′ə gənt), *adj.* characterized by or showing arrogance: *It is arrogant to boast of one's wealth.* —**ar′ro·gant·ly,** *adv.*

ar·row (ar′ō), *n.* **1.** a straight, slender shaft usually having a point at one end and feathers at the other, made to be shot from a bow. **2.** anything resembling an arrow in form, use, etc., esp. a figure having a pointed end, used on signs, maps, or the like, to show a direction, place, etc.

ar·row·head (ar′ō hed′), *n.* the pointed head or tip of an arrow, esp. one that is wedge-shaped and can be separated from the shaft.

ar·row·root (ar′ō rōōt′, -rŏŏt′), *n.* **1.** a tropical American plant whose root yields a nutritious starch. **2.** this or similar starches, used in puddings, cookies, etc. [so called because its root was used to treat wounds made by poisoned arrows]

ar·se·nal (är′sə nəl), *n.* a place for manufacturing or storing guns and ammunition.

ar·se·nic (är′sə nik), *n. Chem.* an element many of whose compounds are highly poisonous. *Symbol:* As

ar·son (är′sən), *n.* the crime of deliberately setting fire to a building or other property. —**ar′son·ist,** *n.*

art¹ (ärt), *n.* **1.** the realm of things that have beauty and form: *Music, poetry, and painting are forms of art.* **2.** a particular field of this realm; any one of the fine arts: *Singing is an art.* **3.** the works or objects belonging to this realm, as paintings, musical compositions, etc. **4.** the skill, talent, or genius necessary to produce such works or objects: *Rembrandt's paintings reveal his great art.* **5.** the fine arts, as distinguished from the sciences. **6.** the methods and principles necessary for mastering any craft or skill: *the art of sailing.* **7.** any artful device: *the innumerable arts and wiles of politics.* [from the Latin word *ars*]

art² (ärt), *v.* an old form of **are,** found now chiefly in Biblical and poetic writing (used with *thou*): *Thou* *art the son of Abraham.* [from the Old English word *eart*]

Ar·te·mis (är′tə mis), *n.* (in Greek mythology) the goddess of hunting and the moon: identified with the Roman goddess Diana.

ar·ter·y (är′tə rē), *n., pl.* **ar·ter·ies.** 1. any of the blood vessels that carry blood from the heart to the rest of the body. See also **vein.** 2. a major highway or channel. —**ar·te·ri·al** (är tēr′ē əl), *adj.*

ar·te′sian well′ (är tē′zhən), a deep well in which water is forced upward through a man-made shaft by natural underground pressure.

art·ful (ärt′fəl), *adj.* 1. crafty or cunning; tricky: *artful flattery.* 2. skillful or clever: *an artful speaker.* —**art′ful·ly,** *adv.* —**art′ful·ness,** *n.*

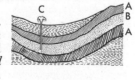

Artesian well (cross section) A, Rock layer through which water cannot seep; B, Rock layer through which water flows; C, Artesian well

ar·thri·tis (är thrī′tis), *n.* a painful inflammation and stiffening of the joints. —**ar·thrit·ic** (är thrit′ik), *adj.*

ar·thro·pod (är′thrə pod′), *n.* a member of the important group of related animals, including the insects, arachnids, and crustaceans, that have jointed legs and segmented bodies without backbones.

Ar·thur (är′thər), *n.* 1. **Chester A(lan),** 1830–1886, 20th Vice President of the U.S. 1881; 21st President of the U.S. 1881-1885. 2. a legendary king in ancient Britain: leader of the Knights of the Round Table.

ar·ti·choke (är′ti chōk′), *n.* 1. a plant resembling the thistle and having a flowerlike head eaten as a vegetable. 2. the vegetable itself.

ar·ti·cle (är′ti kəl), *n.* 1. a factual piece of writing on a single topic, forming part of a magazine, newspaper, or book. 2. an item or particular thing: *an article of clothing.* 3. a clause, item, or point in a con-

Artichoke

tract, treaty, or other formal agreement: *the articles of a constitution.* 4. a word placed before a noun in order to point out or limit the person or thing named. In English, *the* is the definite article; *a* and *an* are the two forms of the indefinite article.

Ar′ticles of Confedera′tion, the constitution of the 13 American colonies, adopted in 1781 and replaced in 1789 by the Constitution of the United States.

ar·tic·u·late (är tik′yə lit), *adj.* 1. spoken clearly in distinct syllables: *an articulate sentence.* 2. capable of speech: *Dogs and cats are not articulate creatures.* 3. using language easily and fluently: *an articulate teacher.* 4. organized and expressed with clarity: *an articulate argument.* —*v.* (är tik′yə lāt′), **ar·tic·u·lat·ed, ar·tic·u·lat·ing.** 5. to pronounce clearly and distinctly. 6. to express clearly: *to articulate an idea.* 7. to connect by a joint or joints: *articulated bones.* —**ar·tic′u·late·ly,** *adv.* —**ar·tic′u·late·ness,** *n.*

ar·tic·u·la·tion (är tik′yə lā′shən), *n.* 1. a manner of

pronouncing and speaking; enunciation. 2. a joining part; joint. 3. the manner of joining things together.

ar·ti·fice (är′tə fis), *n.* 1. a clever trick or stratagem. 2. craftiness or cunning: *He is a master of artifice.* 3. skill or cleverness; ingenuity: *Dressing on a small budget demands considerable artifice.*

ar·ti·fi·cial (är′tə fish′əl), *adj.* 1. made by man rather than by nature: *an artificial waterfall.* 2. made in imitation or as a substitute: *artificial flowers; artificial teeth.* 3. lacking naturalness or sincerity: *an artificial smile.* —**ar·ti·fi·ci·al·i·ty** (är′tə fish′ē al′i tē), *n.* —**ar′ti·fi′cial·ly,** *adv.*

artifi′cial respira′tion, the act of forcing air into and out of the lungs of a person who has stopped breathing, used to revive victims of drowning, smoke poisoning, etc.

ar·til·ler·y (är til′ə rē), *n.* 1. mounted guns, such as cannon. 2. the troops or the branch of an army concerned with such weapons.

ar·til·ler·y·man (är til′ə rē mən), *n., pl.* **ar·til·ler·y·men.** a soldier in an army artillery unit.

ar·ti·san (är′ti zən), *n.* a person skilled in a trade; craftsman.

art·ist (är′tist), *n.* 1. a person who practices one of the fine arts, esp. a painter or sculptor. 2. a person who shows great skill, cleverness, or the like, in some craft or occupation.

ar·tis·tic (är tis′tik), *adj.* 1. fulfilling the standards and requirements of art; having good form, color, etc. 2. showing skill or excellence in performance: *an artistic rendering of a symphony.* 3. having or showing good taste, sensitivity, etc.: *an artistic dress designer.* 4. of or referring to art or artists: *artistic interests; artistic careers.* —**ar·tis′ti·cal·ly,** *adv.*

art·ist·ry (är′ti strē), *n.* 1. artistic ability. 2. artistic quality or workmanship: *a painting that lacks artistry.*

art·less (ärt′lis), *adj.* 1. free from deceit or cunning; open, frank, or candid: *to be artless in one's dealings with other people.* 2. not artificial; natural: *the artless beauty of wild flowers.* 3. lacking art, knowledge, or skill. —**art′less·ly,** *adv.* —**art′less·ness,** *n.*

-ary, a suffix used to form 1. adjectives meaning of or belonging to: *honorary; secondary.* 2. nouns meaning **a.** a person or thing connected with: *functionary; boundary.* **b.** a place where persons or things are kept: *infirmary; dispensary.*

as (az), *adv.* 1. to such a degree or extent; similarly; equally: *It's not as cold today.* 2. for example: *spring flowers, as the tulip.* 3. regarded or considered: *the square as distinct from the rectangle.* 4. in the manner indicated: *She sang as promised.* —*conj.* 5. to such a degree that: *He doesn't work so hard as he says he does.* 6. in the degree, manner, etc., of or that: *Do as we do.* 7. at the same time that; when: *Pay as you enter.* 8. since; because: *As you are leaving last, lock up.* 9. though: *Strange as it seems, it is so.* 10. that the result or effect was: *Her song was so beautiful as to move her audience to tears.* —*pron.* 11. that; who; which: *I have the same trouble as you had.* 12. a fact that: *She spoke the truth, as can be*

proved. **—prep. 13.** in the role or function of: *to act as chairman of the club.* **14. as for,** in regard to: *As for Helen, she can do the work without help.* **15. as good as,** the same as; equivalent to: *This old coat looks as good as new.* **16. as if** (or **as though**), as it would be if: *It looks as if it were raining.* **17. as is,** in the present condition: *The chair will be sold as is.* **18. as long as,** considering that; since: *As long as you feel that way I won't go either.* **19. as of,** at or on a particular time: *As of 9 o'clock he hadn't arrived.* **20. as well,** in addition; besides: *Take this book to her as well.* **21. as yet,** up to now; as of the present time: *As yet we've had no word from him.*
—Usage. See **like**[1].

As, *Chem.* the symbol for **arsenic.**

as·bes·tos (as bes′təs, az bes′təs), *n.* a fibrous, gray mineral that can be pressed into sheets or woven into fabrics that are fireproof and resist the passage of heat.

as·cend (ə send′), *v.* **1.** to move, climb, or go upward: *The road ascended steeply.* **2.** to rise in rank, importance, etc.: *to ascend in the world.* **3.** to go or move upward along or upon: *The cat ascended the tree.* **4.** to succeed to: *The prince ascended the throne when the king died.* **—as·cend′er,** *n.*

as·cend·an·cy (ə sen′dən sē), *n.* the state of being in a position to dominate, rule, command, etc.: *to have ascendancy over an enemy.* Also, **as·cend′en·cy,** *n.*

as·cend·ant (ə sen′dənt), *n.* **1.** a position of dominance, influence, superiority, etc. **—adj. 2.** ascending; rising. **3.** superior or dominant. Also, **as·cend′ent.**

as·cen·sion (ə sen′shən), *n.* **1.** the act of ascending; ascent. **2. the Ascension,** the bodily ascending of Christ from earth to heaven, celebrated 40 days after Easter.

as·cent (ə sent′), *n.* **1.** the act or movement of a person or thing that ascends. **2.** a movement upward in rank, importance, etc.: *ascent in the world of business.* **3.** a way or means of ascent: *This road offers an easy ascent to the top of the mountain.*

as·cer·tain (as′ər tān′), *v.* to find out definitely; make sure: *He looked at the calendar to ascertain what day of the week it was.* **—as′cer·tain′a·ble,** *adj.* **—as′cer·tain′ment,** *n.*

as·cet·ic (ə set′ik), *n.* **1.** a person who leads a meager existence for religious reasons: *Many of the saints were ascetics.* **2.** any person who refrains from the usual pleasures and satisfactions of life: *As an ascetic, he was in favor of hard work and simple living.* **—adj. 3.** extremely strict or severe for religious reasons. **4.** refraining from pleasure. **5.** referring to asceticism: *to cultivate ascetic habits.* **—as·cet′i·cal·ly,** *adv.* **—as·cet·i·cism** (ə set′i siz′əm), *n.*

as·cribe (ə skrīb′), *v.,* **as·cribed, as·crib·ing. 1.** to place the responsibility for (something) on a particular person or source: *He ascribed his success to hard work.* **2.** to think of as belonging to a particular person or source: *We are likely to ascribe only good*

qualities to people that we love. **—as·crib′a·ble,** *adj.*

as·crip·tion (ə skrip′shən), *n.* **1.** the act of ascribing. **2.** a statement that ascribes something.

ash[1] (ash), *n.* **1.** the powdery, gray material that remains after something has been burned: *the ash on the tip of a cigarette.* **2. ashes, a.** a mass, heap, or other collection of such matter: *the ashes of a city that has been ravaged by fire.* **b.** the remains of a body that has been cremated. [from the Old English word *æsce*] **—ash′less,** *adj.*

ash[2] (ash), *n.* a shade tree whose hard wood is used for ax handles, bats, etc. [from the Old English word *æsc*]

a·shamed (ə shāmd′), *adj.* **1.** feeling shame; distressed or embarrassed by feelings of guilt, foolishness, or disgrace. **2.** unwilling because of the fear of ridicule, disapproval, etc.: *He was ashamed to play the piano in front of strangers.* **—a·sham·ed·ly** (ə shā′mid lē), *adv.*

ash·can (ash′kan′), *n.* a metal can for holding ashes, garbage, or refuse.

ash·en[1] (ash′ən), *adj.* **1.** ash-colored; gray: *ashen winter skies.* **2.** very pale, as the complexion: *an ashen face.* **3.** consisting of ashes: *the ashen remains of an ancient city.* [from *ash*[1] + *-en*]

ash·en[2] (ash′ən), *adj.* **1.** concerning the ash tree or its timber. **2.** made of wood from the ash tree. [from *ash*[2] + *-en*]

a·shore (ə shôr′), *adv.* **1.** to the shore; onto the shore: *The boat ran ashore in the storm.* **2.** on the shore; on land rather than at sea or on the water.

Ash′ Wednes′day, the first day of Lent.

ash·y (ash′ē), *adj.,* **ash·i·er, ash·i·est. 1.** very pale, as the complexion; ashen. **2.** of or resembling ashes: *an ashy deposit.* **3.** sprinkled or covered with ashes.

A·sia (ā′zhə), *n.* a continent bounded by Europe and by the Arctic, Pacific, and Indian oceans. It covers an area of about 16,000,000 sq. mi.

A′sia Mi′nor, a peninsula in W Asia between the Black and Mediterranean seas, including most of Asiatic Turkey.

A·sian (ā′zhən), *adj.* **1.** of, belonging to, or characteristic of Asia or its inhabitants. **—n. 2.** a native or inhabitant of Asia.

Asia Minor

A·si·at·ic (ā′zhē at′ik), *adj., n.* another word for **Asian:** *a ship in Asiatic waters.*

—Usage. Although *Asiatic* is often used as a variant of *Asian,* it is sometimes regarded as offensive when used in referring to the people of that continent. Careful speakers and writers, therefore, refer to them as *Asians* rather than *Asiatics.*

a·side (ə sīd′), *adv.* **1.** on or to one side; away from some place or direction: *to turn a car aside to let another pass.* **2.** away from one's thoughts: *to put one's cares aside.* **3.** in a separate place or in reserve: *to* put money aside for an emergency. **4.** away from a group of people, as for privacy: *He took his friend aside and told him a secret.* **5.** out of the way; notwithstanding: *Politeness aside, tell me what you really think.* —*n.* **6.** a comment spoken directly to the audience by an actor, supposedly not heard by others on the stage. **7.** a comment spoken so as not to be heard by others who are present: *He made witty asides at the dinner table.* **8. aside from,** except for; apart from: *I have no money aside from my allowance.*

as·i·nine (as′ə nīn′), *adj.* stupid or foolish; silly; unintelligent: *It is asinine to discuss a book one hasn't read.* —**as′i·nine′ly,** *adv.*

ask (ask), *v.* **1.** to put a question to; inquire of: *Ask him for directions.* **2.** to request information about or an answer to: *to ask the way; to ask a question.* **3.** to try to get by using words: *to ask a favor; to ask advice.* **4.** to request of: *I ask you a great favor.* **5.** to demand, expect, or desire: *What price are they asking?* **6.** to invite: *to ask guests to dinner.* **7.** to make inquiry; inquire: *to ask about a person.* **8.** to request or petition (usually fol. by *for*): *The prisoner asked the court for leniency.*

a·skance (ə skans′), *adv.* **1.** with suspicion, mistrust, or disapproval: *He looked askance at strangers who were too friendly.* **2.** with a side glance; sidewise.

a·skew (ə skyōō′), *adv.* **1.** to one side; out of line: *to wear one's hat askew.* —*adj.* **2.** crooked; awry: *His hat was askew.*

a·slant (ə slant′), *adv.* **1.** at a slant; slantingly: *The willows grow aslant along the stream.* —*adj.* **2.** slanting; oblique: *He read with his head aslant over the desk.* —*prep.* **3.** slantingly across; athwart: *The shadows fell aslant the lawn.*

a·sleep (ə slēp′), *adv.* **1.** into a state of sleep: *to fall asleep.* —*adj.* **2.** being in a state of sleep; sleeping: *I was asleep when you called.* **3.** (of the foot, hand, etc.) numb, as from lack of circulation.

asp (asp), *n.* any of several small poisonous snakes, esp. a small Egyptian cobra.

as·par·a·gus (ə spar′ə gəs), *n.* **1.** a plant whose slim, green, pointed shoots are eaten as a vegetable. **2.** the vegetable itself.

as·pect (as′pekt), *n.* **1.** the appearance that something has to the eye or mind: *The countryside has a pleasant aspect.* **2.** a particular way in which something may be looked at: *the good and bad aspects of a situation.* **3.** a feature or part of something under consideration: *the geographical aspects of a country.* **4.** a view in a certain direction, as from a building: *a house with a southern aspect.*

as·pen (as′pən), *n.* a tree related to the poplar, having leaves that tremble in the slightest breeze.

as·per·i·ty (ə sper′i tē), *n.* **1.** roughness or harshness of manner or temper. **2.** hardship or difficulty: *the asperity of winter.* **3.** roughness of surface: *the asperity of sandpaper.*

as·per·sion (ə spûr′zhən), *n.* a false or damaging remark: *to cast aspersions on someone's honesty.*

as·phalt (as′fôlt), *n.* **1.** a substance, resembling tar, found in natural deposits. **2.** a similar substance made from petroleum. **3.** a mixture of this substance, often with gravel, used for paving roads. **4.** a pavement made of this substance.

as·phyx·i·ate (as fik′sē āt′), *v.,* **as·phyx·i·at·ed, as·phyx·i·at·ing. 1.** to cause to die or become unconscious by reducing the amount of oxygen in the blood through interference with breathing; suffocate; smother. **2.** to die or become unconscious in such a way. —**as′phyx·i·a′tion,** *n.* —**as·phyx′i·a′tor,** *n.*

as·pic (as′pik), *n.* a jelly made with juice from meat or fish, tomatoes, etc.: chilled and used as a salad.

as·pir·ant (ə spī′r′ənt, as′pər ənt), *n.* a person who aspires, esp. toward a career, a better position, etc.

as·pi·rate (as′pə rāt′), *v.,* **as·pi·rat·ed, as·pi·rat·ing. 1.** to pronounce (a consonant) with aspiration. —*n.* (as′pər it). **2.** a consonant pronounced with aspiration. —*adj.* (as′pər it). **3.** pronounced with aspiration; aspirated.

as·pi·ra·tion (as′pə rā′shən), *n.* **1.** a strong desire, longing, or aim; ambition. **2.** a goal or objective desired: *His aspiration is success.* **3.** pronunciation of a consonant with a strong puff of breath following it, as the *t* in *time,* or the *wh* in *which.*

as·pire (ə spī′r′), *v.,* **as·pired, as·pir·ing.** to be extremely ambitious to obtain something great or of high value (often fol. by *to*): *to aspire to a career in medicine; to aspire to a better job.*

as·pi·rin (as′pə rin), *n.* a drug used to relieve pain and reduce fever.

ass (as), *n.* **1.** a small donkey. **2.** a fool; blockhead.

as·sail (ə sāl′), *v.* **1.** to attack with physical violence; strike; assault: *Ruffians assailed him in the street.* **2.** to attack with criticism, ridicule, etc.: *They assailed the president for his foreign policy.* **3.** to worry or harass: *His mind was assailed by fear and doubt.* —**as·sail′a·ble,** *adj.*

Ass
(3¹/₂ ft. high at shoulder)

as·sail·ant (ə sā′lənt), *n.* a person who attacks: *His assailant fled before the police arrived.*

as·sas·sin (ə sas′in), *n.* a murderer or killer, esp. a fanatic or someone acting for or hired by a group, who murders a prominent person, as a government leader. [from the Arabic word *hashshāshin* "eaters of hashish," the name given to a fanatical Muslim sect formed for the purpose of killing Crusaders]

as·sas·si·nate (ə sas′ə nāt′), *v.,* **as·sas·si·nat·ed, as·sas·si·nat·ing.** to murder treacherously, esp. a government leader or other prominent person. —**as·sas′si·na′tion,** *n.* —**as·sas′si·na′tor,** *n.*

as·sault (ə sôlt′), *n.* **1.** a violent attack; onslaught: *The town could not resist the assault of the besiegers.* **2.** an attempt or threat to do violence to another, with or without actually striking him. —*v.* **3.** to make an assault upon; attack.

assault′ and bat′tery, a threat to another person that is followed by a physical attack upon him.

as·say (ə sā′), *v.* **1.** to try or test; put to trial: *to assay one's strength.* **2.** to analyze (an ore, alloy, etc.) to determine the quantity of gold, silver, or other metal in it. **3.** to analyze (a drug) to determine the presence of an ingredient or ingredients. **4.** to analyze (a situation, event, etc.): *to assay the present world situation.* —*n.* (ə sā′, as′ā). **5.** an analysis, as of an ore or a drug. —**as·say′er,** *n.*

as·sem·blage (ə sem′blij), *n.* **1.** a number of persons or things assembled; assembly or collection. **2.** the act of coming together or assembling.

as·sem·ble (ə sem′bəl), *v.,* **as·sem·bled, as·sem·bling. 1.** to bring together; gather into one place or group. **2.** to put or fit together: *to assemble information; to assemble a machine.* **3.** to come together; gather; meet: *The members of the club assemble every Tuesday.* —**as·sem′bler,** *n.*

as·sem·bly (ə sem′blē), *n., pl.* **as·sem·blies. 1.** a body of persons gathered together, usually for a particular purpose. **2.** *(often cap.)* a legislative body, esp. a lower house in a legislature. **3.** a signal, as by a drum or bugle, for troops to fall into ranks or otherwise assemble. **4.** the putting together of a machine, as an engine, from parts of a standard size. **5.** a group of machine parts of a standard size.

as·sent (ə sent′), *v.* **1.** to agree or concur: *The club assented to his proposal.* —*n.* **2.** agreement, as to a proposal; concurrence. —**as·sent′ing·ly,** *adv.*

as·sert (ə sûrt′), *v.* **1.** to state with assurance, confidence, or force: *The minister asserted the existence of God.* **2.** to defend or maintain, as rights, claims, etc.: *to assert freedom of speech.* **3.** to put (oneself) forward boldly and insistently.

as·ser·tion (ə sûr′shən), *n.* **1.** a positive statement or declaration. **2.** the act of asserting.

as·ser·tive (ə sûr′tiv), *adj.* asserting one's opinions boldly and insistently; positive; confident. —**as·ser′tive·ly,** *adv.* —**as·ser′tive·ness,** *n.*

as·sess (ə ses′), *v.* **1.** to estimate officially the value of (property, income, etc.) for the purpose of taxation. **2.** to fix or determine the amount of (damages, a tax, a fine, etc.). **3.** to tax, fine, or impose another charge on. **4.** to judge or estimate: *to assess a situation.* —**as·sess′a·ble,** *adj.*

as·sess·ment (ə ses′mənt), *n.* **1.** the act of assessing; appraisal. **2.** an amount of money due as a tax, damages, a fine, etc.

as·ses·sor (ə ses′ər), *n.* a person who makes assessments for the purposes of taxation.

as·set (as′et), *n.* **1.** a useful thing or quality: *Intelligence is one of the greatest of all assets.* **2. assets,** items owned by a person, such as property, that can be converted into cash, esp. for the payment of debts (opposite of *liabilities*).

as·si·du·i·ty (as′i dōō′i tē, -dyōō′-), *n.* constant application; diligence or industry: *He pursued his task with assiduity.*

as·sid·u·ous (ə sij′ōō əs), *adj.* **1.** constant or diligent: *assiduous reading.* **2.** persevering or industrious: *assiduous students.* —**as·sid′u·ous·ly,** *adv.* —**as·sid′u·ous·ness,** *n.*

as·sign (ə sīn′), *v.* **1.** to give or allot (something) for a certain person or purpose: *to assign hotel rooms to guests; to assign homework to students.* **2.** to appoint, as to a post or duty: *Assign him to guard duty.* **3.** to name or mention definitely; fix; appoint: *to assign a day for a meeting.* **4.** to hand over or transfer to another legally, as rights, property, etc. —**as·sign′a·ble,** *adj.* —**as·sign′er,** *n.*

as·sign·ment (ə sīn′mənt), *n.* **1.** something assigned, as a particular task or duty: *a homework assignment.* **2.** a position to which one is appointed: *an important assignment in the government.* **3.** the act of assigning. **4.** the legal transfer of property, rights, etc., to another person.

as·sim·i·late (ə sim′ə lāt′), *v.,* **as·sim·i·lat·ed, as·sim·i·lat·ing. 1.** to take in and absorb: *The body assimilates food. He assimilated new experiences while traveling.* **2.** to take in and make a part of a country, community, etc.: *America has assimilated many foreign-born people.* **3.** to be or become absorbed: *Some foods assimilate more easily than others.* **4.** to become adjusted, esp. to new or different surroundings.

as·sim·i·la·tion (ə sim′ə lā′shən), *n.* **1.** the act or process of assimilating: *The assimilation of some foods may take hours. The assimilation of the immigrants was accomplished quickly.* **2.** the state of being assimilated.

as·sist (ə sist′), *v.* **1.** to give support or aid to; help: *He assisted his friends when they were in need.* —*n.* **2.** a helpful act; aid: *She finished her homework without an assist from her father.*

as·sis·tance (ə sis′təns), *n.* the act of assisting; help; aid.

as·sis·tant (ə sis′tənt), *n.* **1.** a person who assists or gives aid and support; helper. **2.** a person whose rank is beneath that of another whom he serves in an office or post: *He was assistant to the manager.* —*adj.* **3.** assisting; helpful. **4.** serving in the next lower position: *an assistant manager.*

as·siz·es (ə sī′ziz), *n.pl.* court sessions held at regular intervals in each county in England.

assn., association. Also, **assoc.**

assoc., 1. associate. **2.** associated. **3.** association.

as·so·ci·ate (ə sō′shē āt′, ə sō′sē āt′), *v.,* **as·so·ci·at·ed, as·so·ci·at·ing. 1.** to connect or bring together in the mind, as thought, feeling, memory, etc.: *to associate red with heat.* **2.** to join as a companion, partner, or ally: *to associate oneself with a cause.* **3.** to keep company: *to associate with a bad crowd.* **4.** to come together; unite: *They associated in a common cause.* —*n.* (ə sō′shē it, ə sō′sē it). **5.** a person who shares in a business or other enterprise; partner; colleague. **6.** a comrade or companion. —*adj.* (ə sō′shē it, ə sō′sē-it). **7.** connected or related, esp. as a companion or colleague, but without certain rights or full rank: *an associate judge; an associate professor.*

as·so·ci·a·tion (ə sō'sē ā'shən, ə sō'shē ā'shən), *n.* **1.** an organization of people with a purpose in common. **2.** the act of associating, or the state of being associated. **3.** friendship or companionship. **4.** the connection or relation of thoughts, feelings, etc.: *The color green has an association with freshness and coolness.*

as·so·ci·a·tive (ə sō'shē ā'tiv, ə sō'sē ā'tiv), *adj.* **1.** concerning or resulting from association. **2.** (of a mathematical operation on a set of elements) giving an equivalent expression when elements are grouped without change of order, such as $(1 + 2) + 3 = 1 + (2 + 3)$, or $(1 \times 2) \times 5 = 1 \times (2 \times 5)$.

as·sort (ə sôrt'), *v.* to arrange according to kind; classify; sort: *to assort a heap of nickels, dimes, and quarters.* —**as·sort'er,** *n.*

as·sort·ed (ə sôr'tid), *adj.* **1.** arranged in sorts or varieties: *rows of assorted vegetables.* **2.** selected so as to consist of various kinds: *assorted candies.*

as·sort·ment (ə sôrt'mənt), *n.* **1.** the act of assorting. **2.** a collection of various kinds of things.

asst., assistant.

as·suage (ə swāj'), *v.,* **as·suaged, as·suag·ing. 1.** to make milder or less severe: *Weeping assuaged her grief.* **2.** to satisfy or appease: *A good meal assuaged his hunger.* **3.** to calm or make peaceful; pacify: *to be assuaged by music.* —**as·suage'ment,** *n.*

as·sume (ə sōōm'), *v.,* **as·sumed, as·sum·ing. 1.** to take for granted without proof; suppose: *May I assume that what you say is true?* **2.** to attempt to fulfill or complete: *to assume an obligation.* **3.** to take over the duties or responsibilities of: *to assume office.* **4.** to take on, as an appearance, form, manner, etc.: *The weather assumed a threatening character.* **5.** to pretend to have; feign: *He assumed interest in order to seem polite.* **6.** to take without right or permission; appropriate: *The dictator assumed complete power.*

as·sumed (ə sōōmd'), *adj.* **1.** taken in order to deceive; pretended; feigned: *Her assumed kindness hid a heart full of spite.* **2.** taken for granted; supposed: *The assumed reason for his absence was sickness.* **3.** usurped or appropriated: *The dictator ruled with assumed power.* —**as·sum·ed·ly** (ə sōō'mid lē), *adv.*

as·sump·tion (ə sump'shən), *n.* **1.** the act of taking for granted or supposing. **2.** something taken for granted: *Our assumption proved to be correct.* **3.** the act of agreeing to fulfill or comply with: *the assumption of an obligation.* **4.** the act of taking possession of something: *the assumption of public office.* **5.** the act of usurping or appropriating: *the assumption of absolute power.* **6.** arrogance or presumption. **7. the Assumption,** (in Roman Catholic belief) the bodily taking up into heaven of the Virgin Mary, or the feast commemorating this, celebrated on August 15.

as·sur·ance (ə shōōr'əns), *n.* **1.** something that is said or done in order to give confidence: *His parents gave him assurances that they were on his side.* **2.** a pledge or promise: *He gave his assurance that the job*

would be done. **3.** full confidence; freedom from timidity or doubt: *He acted with assurance that he would succeed.* **4.** extreme or excessive boldness; impudence. **5.** *Chiefly British.* another word for **insurance.**

as·sure (ə shōōr'), *v.,* **as·sured, as·sur·ing. 1.** to declare earnestly to; inform or tell positively: *He assured them that he was telling the truth.* **2.** to cause to know surely; reassure: *They checked his story to assure themselves that it was true.* **3.** to pledge or promise; guarantee: *I'm assured a job in the spring.* **4.** to make sure to happen or come to be: *Send the letter by messenger to assure a speedy delivery.* **5.** to insure, as against loss. —**as·sur'er, as·sur'or,** *n.* —**as·sur'ing·ly,** *adv.*

as·sured (ə shōōrd'), *adj.* **1.** guaranteed or certain; secure: *an assured income.* **2.** bold or confident: *in an assured manner.* **3.** impudent or presumptuous: *a brazen, assured young man who always got his way.* —**as·sur·ed·ly** (ə shōōr'id lē), *adv.*

As·syr·i·a (ə sir'ē ə), *n.* an ancient empire in SW Asia. —**As·syr'i·an,** *n., adj.*

as·ta·tine (as'tə tēn'), *n. Chem.* a rare, nonmetallic element of the halogen family. *Symbol:* At

as·ter (as'tər), *n.* any of various flowering plants related to the daisy, usually blooming in the fall.

as·ter·isk (as'tə risk), *n.* the figure of a star (*), used in writing or printing to call attention to a footnote or to indicate an omission in the text.

Aster

a·stern (ə stûrn'), *adv.* **1.** in a position behind a ship or aircraft: *The cutter was close astern.* **2.** at or toward the stern. **3.** in a backward direction; with stern foremost.

as·ter·oid (as'tə roid'), *n.* any of thousands of celestial bodies ranging in size from less than one mile to 480 miles in diameter, most of which move around the sun in orbits lying between those of Mars and Jupiter.

asth·ma (az'mə), *n.* a condition that causes wheezing and shortness of breath. —**asth·mat·ic** (az mat'ik), *adj.*

a·stig·ma·tism (ə stig'mə tiz'əm), *n.* a defect of the eye that causes blurred vision because lines in some directions can be less clearly focused than lines in other directions. —**as·tig·mat·ic** (as'tig mat'ik), *adj.*

a·stir (ə stûr'), *adj.* **1.** moving or active; full of life or movement: *The boulevards were astir with people.* **2.** up and about; out of bed: *It was dawn and no one was astir in the house.*

as·ton·ish (ə ston'ish), *v.* to strike with sudden and overpowering wonder; amaze: *The progress we have made will astonish you.* —**as·ton'ish·ment,** *n.*

as·ton·ish·ing (ə ston'ish ing), *adj.* surprising; amazing: *an astonishing dive.* —**as·ton'ish·ing·ly,** *adv.*

as·tound (ə stound'), *v.* to overwhelm with amazement; shock with wonder: *The invention of the atom bomb astounded the world.* —**as·tound'ing·ly,** *adv.*

a·strad·dle (ə strad'əl), *prep.* **1.** with a leg on each

side of; astride: *He sat there astraddle the fence.*
—*adv., adj.* **2.** with one leg on each side; astride: *to sit astraddle on a horse.*

as·tra·khan (as'trə kan'), *n.* **1.** a fur of young lambs, with glossy, closely curled wool. **2.** a cloth made in imitation of this.

a·stray (ə strā'), *adv., adj.* **1.** out of the right way; off the correct or known path or course: *This letter had the wrong address and went astray.* **2.** away from what is right; in or into error: *Bad acquaintances led him astray when he was a child.*

a·stride (ə strīd'), *prep.* **1.** with a leg on each side of; straddling: *She sat astride the horse.* **2.** on both sides of: *The town lay astride the main road.* —*adv., adj.* **3.** in a posture of straddling; with one leg on each side: *to sit astride on a fence.*

as·trin·gent (ə strin'jənt), *n.* **1.** a substance that shrinks living tissue and slows the flow of mucus or blood where it is applied. —*adj.* **2.** acting as an astringent. **3.** stern or severe; austere.

as·trol·o·ger (ə strol'ə jər), *n.* an expert in astrology. Also, **as·trol'o·gist.**

as·trol·o·gy (ə strol'ə jē), *n.* a supposed science that is founded on a belief that the planets, stars, and moon have an influence upon human affairs, and that claims to interpret this influence. —**as·tro·log·i·cal** (a'strə loj'i kəl), *adj.* —**as'tro·log'i·cal·ly,** *adv.*

astron., **1.** astronomer. **2.** astronomical. **3.** astronomy.

as·tro·naut (as'trə nôt'), *n.* a person engaged in or trained for space flight. —**as'tro·naut'i·cal,** *adj.*

as·tro·nau·tics (as'trə nô'tiks), *n. (used as sing.)* the science of travel beyond the earth's atmosphere, including flights to stars and other planets.

as·tron·o·mer (ə stron'ə mər), *n.* a person who is learned in astronomy.

as·tro·nom·i·cal (as'trə nom'i kəl), *adj.* **1.** of, related to, or used in astronomy: *an astronomical observatory.* **2.** extremely large; enormous: *an astronomical sum of money.* —**as'tro·nom'i·cal·ly,** *adv.*

as·tron·o·my (ə stron'ə mē), *n.* the science that deals with stars, planets, and the rest of the universe beyond the earth's atmosphere.

as·tute (ə stōōt', ə styōōt'), *adj.* having or showing a keen mind or judgment; shrewd; clever: *an astute businessman.* —**as·tute'ly,** *adv.* —**as·tute'ness,** *n.*

A·sun·ci·ón (ə sōōn'sē ōn'), *n.* the capital city of Paraguay, in the S part.

a·sun·der (ə sun'dər), *adv., adj.* **1.** into separate parts; in or into pieces: *to break a coconut shell asunder.* **2.** apart or widely separated: *two people who are asunder in their beliefs.*

As·wan (as'wän), *n.* a dam in the SE Arab Republic of Egypt, on the Nile. See map at **Nile.**

a·sy·lum (ə sī'ləm), *n.* **1.** an institution for the housing and care of people who are homeless or who need special attention, as orphans, the insane, etc. **2.** a refuge or place of safety, as in former times for criminals and debtors: *In the Middle Ages churches*

were asylums for those who were hunted by the law. **3.** the protection given by a nation to political offenders in exile from another nation.

at (at), *prep.* **1.** in, on, or near in space: *Stand at the door.* **2.** in, on, or near a certain time: *We left at dawn. He died at the age of 85.* **3.** in a certain place or attending: *He is not at home.* **4.** to the amount or degree of: *to drive at a great speed.* **5.** toward: *Shoot at the target.* **6.** busy or involved with: *He was happy at his work.* **7.** in a state or condition of: *The United States was at war with Japan.* **8.** (used to show a cause): *to be annoyed at bad manners.*

At, *Chem.* the symbol for **astatine.**

ate (āt), *v.* the past tense of **eat.**

-ate, a suffix used to form **1.** adjectives meaning of, like, or having the quality of: *affectionate.* **2.** verbs meaning **a.** to make or cause to be: *activate.* **b.** to perform the act or process of: *amalgamate; formulate.* **c.** to become like or take the form of: *ulcerate.* **3.** nouns meaning **a.** something resulting from an action: *distillate.* **b.** an office or function: *directorate.* **c.** a group: *electorate.*

a·the·ism (ā'thē iz'əm), *n.* the state or fact of not believing in the existence of God.

a·the·ist (ā'thē ist), *n.* a person who denies or disbelieves the existence of God. —**a'the·is'tic,** *adj.*

A·the·na (ə thē'nə), *n.* (in Greek mythology) the goddess of wisdom: identified with the Roman goddess Minerva. Also, **A·the·ne** (ə-thē'nē), **Pallas, Pallas Athena.**

Ath·ens (ath'inz), *n.* the capital city of Greece, in the SE part. —**A·the·ni·an** (ə thē'nē ən), *n., adj.*

a·thirst (ə thûrst'), *adj.* **1.** having thirst; thirsty. **2.** having a keen desire; eager (often fol. by *for*): *He was athirst for adventure.*

ath·lete (ath'lēt), *n.* a person trained to compete in contests involving physical skill, endurance, or strength: *Both swimmers and ballplayers are athletes.*

Athena

ath'lete's foot', an infection caused by a fungus and producing itching and cracking of the skin, esp. between the toes.

ath·let·ic (ath let'ik), *adj.* **1.** physically active and strong: *an athletic build.* **2.** of, like, or befitting an athlete. **3.** of or referring to athletics. —**ath·let'i·cal·ly,** *adv.*

ath·let·ics (ath let'iks), *n.* **1.** *(usually used as pl.)* athletic sports, as running, rowing, boxing, etc. **2.** *(usually used as sing.)* the practice of athletic exercises; the principles of athletic training.

a·thwart (ə thwôrt'), *adv.* **1.** from side to side; crosswise: *Roads ran athwart to the main highway.* **2.** across or at right angles to a course, as of a ship: *The tide was running athwart.* —*prep.* **3.** from side to side of. **4.** in opposition or contrary to: *to act athwart the wishes of another.*

---

act, āble, dâre, ärt; ebb, ēqual; if, īce; hot, ōver, ôrder; oil; bŏŏk; ōōze; out; up, ûrge; ə = *a* as in *alone*; ə as in *button* (but'ən), *fire* (fiªr); chief; shoe; thin; ŧħat; zh as in *measure* (mezh'ər). See full key inside cover.

-ation, a suffix used to form nouns meaning 1. a state or condition: *deprivation; starvation.* 2. an action or process: *consolation; perspiration.* 3. the result of an action: *civilization; combination.*

-ative, a suffix used to form adjectives meaning 1. doing or connected with: *administrative; qualitative.* 2. having a tendency to: *talkative; argumentative.*

At·lan·ta (at lan′tə), *n.* the capital city of Georgia, in the N part.

At·lan′tic O′cean (at lan′tik), an ocean bounded by North America and South America in the Western Hemisphere and by Europe and Africa in the Eastern Hemisphere. about 31,530,000 sq. mi. Greatest known depth, 30,246 ft. Also, **the Atlantic.**

at·las (at′ləs), *n., pl.* **at·las·es.** a bound collection of maps.

At·las (at′ləs), *n.* (in Greek mythology) a Titan or giant who was forced to carry the sky on his shoulders.

At′las Moun′tains, a mountain range in NW Africa, extending through Morocco, Algeria, and Tunisia.

at·mos·phere (at′məs fēr′), *n.* 1. the gas that surrounds the earth; air. 2. the gas surrounding any planet or star. 3. a unit of pressure, the normal pressure of the air at sea level, equal to 14.7 pounds per square inch. 4. the spirit or mood of a place: *Their house in the country has a peaceful atmosphere.*

at·mos·pher·ic (at′məs fer′ik), *adj.* 1. of, referring to, or existing in the atmosphere: *atmospheric vapors.* 2. caused or affected by the atmosphere: *atmospheric pressure.* 3. having or producing an appropriate atmosphere: *atmospheric lighting for a chapel.*

at·oll (at′ôl, ə tôl′), *n.* a coral reef or group of small coral islands in the shape of a ring, enclosing or nearly enclosing a shallow lagoon.

at·om (at′əm), *n.* 1. the smallest possible piece of any chemical element that can have the characteristics of the element. Atoms are composed of still smaller particles, including protons, neutrons, and electrons. 2. anything extremely small; a minute quantity; particle: *There is not an atom of food in the house.* —**a·tom·ic** (ə tom′ik), *adj.*

atom′ic bomb′, a bomb in which the explosive power is produced by the splitting of uranium or plutonium atoms. Also, **A-bomb, at′om bomb′.**

atom′ic en′ergy, the energy that can be obtained by the splitting of heavy atoms or the fusion of light atoms. Also, **nuclear energy.**

atom′ic num′ber, the number of protons in the nucleus of an atom.

atom′ic weight′, the average weight of an atom of an element compared to that of one kind of carbon atom assigned a weight of 12 units.

at·om·iz·er (at′ə mī′zər), *n.* an apparatus for turning liquids, such as medicines and perfumes, to a fine spray for application.

a·tone (ə tōn′), *v.,* **a·toned, a·ton·ing.** to make amends or make up, as for doing something that is wrong, harmful, sinful, etc. (usually fol. by *for*): *He atoned for his rudeness by apologizing.*

a·tone·ment (ə tōn′mənt), *n.* 1. the act of atoning. 2. something that makes up for a wrong or harmful act: *His apology was an atonement for his mistake.*

a·top (ə top′), *adj., adv.* 1. on or at the top: *a large cake with candles atop.* —*prep.* 2. on the top of: *The flag waved atop the pole.*

a·tro·cious (ə trō′shəs), *adj.* 1. extremely or shockingly wicked, cruel, or brutal: *atrocious crimes against a conquered people.* 2. very bad; completely unacceptable: *atrocious manners.* —**a·tro′cious·ly,** *adv.* —**a·tro′cious·ness,** *n.*

a·troc·i·ty (ə tros′i tē), *n., pl.* for def. 2 **a·troc·i·ties.** 1. the quality or state of being wicked, cruel, or brutal: *the atrocity of Hitler's regime.* 2. an atrocious thing, act, or circumstance: *to commit atrocities on innocent people during a war.*

at·ro·phy (a′trə fē), *n.* 1. a wasting away of the body or an organ, as from disease. 2. any wasting away, as from neglect and disuse: *an atrophy of talent.* —*v.,* **at·ro·phied, at·ro·phy·ing.** 3. to affect with or undergo atrophy.

at·tach (ə tach′), *v.* 1. to fasten or join; connect: *to attach a door to a hinge.* 2. to join in an action or function: *to attach oneself to a group.* 3. to place on temporary duty with a military unit: *He was attached to the infantry.* 4. to bind by ties of affection, love, or esteem: *to be attached to one's friends.* 5. to take (persons or property) by legal authority: *His creditors attached his house when he could not pay his debts.* 6. to belong or pertain (usually fol. by *to* or *upon*): *No blame attaches to you for his mistake.* —**at·tach′a·ble,** *adj.*

at·ta·ché (at′ə shā′), *n.* a diplomat who is a staff member of an embassy or ministry in a foreign country.

at·tach·ment (ə tach′mənt), *n.* 1. the act of attaching, or the state of being attached. 2. love, devotion, esteem, etc., that binds one to a person, thing, cause, etc.: *He had a deep attachment to his father.* 3. something that attaches; fastening or tie: *an attachment for a door.* 4. a device that is attached, as to a machine, for performing a certain function: *an electric mixer with all attachments.* 5. the seizure of property or a person by legal authority: *An attachment was put on his house.*

at·tack (ə tak′), *v.* 1. to set upon violently in order to hurt or destroy; assault: *The dog attacked the intruder.* 2. to blame, abuse, or criticize severely: *The government was attacked for its foreign policy.* 3. to begin (a task) vigorously: *to attack house cleaning.* 4. to begin hostilities; make an attack. —*n.* 5. the act of attacking or beginning hostilities: *an attack upon the enemy.* 6. the beginning of any action; onset, such as a seizure by a disease or illness: *an attack of indigestion.* —**at·tack′er,** *n.*

at·tain (ə tān′), *v.* 1. to achieve or accomplish: *He attained success through hard work.* 2. to come to or arrive at; reach: *He attained a ripe old age.*

at·tain·der (ə tān′dər), *n.* the loss of all civil rights as a result of a sentence of death or outlawry.

at·tain·ment (ə tān′mənt), *n.* 1. the act of attaining

a desired state, position, etc. **2.** something attained; achievement: *Fame is considered an attainment.*

at·tar (at′ər), *n.* a perfume obtained from flower petals: *attar of roses.*

at·tempt (ə tempt′), *v.* **1.** to make an effort at; try: *He attempted an almost impossible task.* **2.** to attack; make an effort against: *He attempted the life of his enemy.* —*n.* **3.** an effort made to accomplish something: *All his attempts failed.* **4.** an attack or assault: *an attempt upon someone's life.*

at·tend (ə tend′), *v.* **1.** to be present at (a meeting, gathering, etc.): *to attend church.* **2.** to go with; accompany: *A fever attended his cold.* **3.** to care for or wait upon: *A nurse attended the patient.* **4.** to listen to; give heed to: *Attend my words!* **5.** to pay attention: *The audience attended as he spoke.* **6. attend to,** to take care or charge of: *to attend to a sick person; to attend to one's own business.*

at·tend·ance (ə ten′dəns), *n.* **1.** the act or fact of attending: *His attendance was perfect for the school year.* **2.** the persons or the number of persons attending: *There was a large attendance at the opera.*

at·tend·ant (ə ten′dənt), *n.* **1.** a person who attends another, as for service or company: *an attendant for an ill person.* **2.** a person who is present, as at a meeting. —*adj.* **3.** being present or in attendance. **4.** associated or related: *war and its attendant evils.*

at·ten·tion (ə ten′shən), *n.* **1.** the act or power of giving thought to something, esp. by concentration: *to fix one's attention on a picture.* **2.** watchful care; consideration or notice: *Individual attention is given each patient.* **3.** courtesy or politeness: *to show attention to a stranger.* **4.** an act of courtesy or politeness: *The attentions of the host pleased the guests.* **5.** a military command to stand or sit in a straight position. **6.** the act or state of so standing or sitting: *The soldiers stood at attention awaiting orders.*

at·ten·tive (ə ten′tiv), *adj.* **1.** giving attention; observant: *He was attentive to all his studies.* **2.** thoughtful of others; polite; courteous: *He was attentive to the needs of others.* —**at·ten′tive·ly,** *adv.*

at·ten·u·ate (ə ten′yōō āt′), *v.,* **at·ten·u·at·ed, at·ten·u·at·ing. 1.** to make or become thin, slender, or fine: *to attenuate gold by beating it into fine sheets.* **2.** to make or become weaker or less: *to attenuate a fever with drugs.* —**at·ten′u·a′tion,** *n.*

at·test (ə test′), *v.* **1.** to testify or bear witness, esp. that something is correct or genuine (usually fol. by *to*): *to attest to the truth of a statement.* **2.** to give proof or evidence of: *His work attests his industry.*

at·tic (at′ik), *n.* the part of a building, esp. of a house, directly under the roof; garret.

At·ti·ca (at′ə kə), *n.* an ancient region in SE Greece, surrounding Athens.

At·ti·la (at′ᵊlə, ə til′ə), *n.* (*"Scourge of God"*) A.D. 406?–453, king of the Huns who invaded Europe.

at·tire (ə tīr′), *v.,* **at·tired, at·tir·ing. 1.** to dress, esp. in rich clothing; array: *She was attired in a white silk gown.* —*n.* **2.** clothes or apparel, esp. of a rich and

splendid kind: *The guests were all in formal attire.*

at·ti·tude (at′i tōōd′, -tyōōd′), *n.* **1.** a manner of behaving that expresses how one feels or thinks about something or someone: *His attitude toward life is cheerful.* **2.** a position or posture of the body expressing an emotion, action, etc.: *a relaxed attitude.*

at·tor·ney (ə tûr′nē), *n., pl.* **at·tor·neys. 1.** a person who is legally entitled to act on behalf of another. **2.** a lawyer.

attor′ney gen′eral, *pl.* **attorneys general** *or* **attorney generals.** the chief law officer of a country or state and head of its legal department.

at·tract (ə trakt′), *v.* **1.** to cause to approach or come together: *A bar of iron is attracted by a magnet.* **2.** to draw by making an appeal to the emotions, sense of beauty, interest, etc.: *Her loveliness attracted us.*

at·trac·tion (ə trak′shən), *n.* **1.** the act, power, or property of attracting: *Movies have a great attraction for me.* **2.** a person or thing that attracts: *The elephant was the main attraction for the children.*

at·trac·tive (ə trak′tiv), *adj.* having the power to attract, esp. by a pleasing, friendly, charming appearance or manner: *an attractive girl; an attractive flower.* —**at·trac′tive·ly,** *adv.* —**at·trac′tive·ness,** *n.*

at·trib·ute (ə trib′yōōt), *v.,* **at·trib·ut·ed, at·trib·ut·ing. 1.** to consider as caused by, belonging to, or produced by: *to attribute success to hard work; to attribute an unsigned painting to Picasso.* —*n.* (a′trə byōōt′). **2.** something regarded as belonging to someone or something, as a trait, character, etc.: *Intelligence is one of his attributes.* **3.** an object that is associated with some person, character, position, etc.: *The owl is an attribute of Athena.* —**at′tri·bu′tion,** *n.*

at·tri·tion (ə trish′ən), *n.* **1.** a wearing down or away by friction. **2.** a wearing down or weakening of resistance, as by continuous annoyance or persecution: *the attrition of cold and hunger.*

at·tune (ə tōōn′, ə tyōōn′), *v.,* **at·tuned, at·tun·ing.** to bring into harmony or a sympathetic relationship; adjust: *He was attuned to living in the mountains.*

Au, *Chem.* the symbol for **gold.** [from the Latin word *aurum*]

au·burn (ô′bərn), *n.* **1.** a reddish or golden brown. —*adj.* **2.** of the color auburn: *auburn hair.*

Auck·land (ôk′lənd), *n.* a port city on N North Island, in New Zealand.

auc·tion (ôk′shən), *n.* **1.** a public sale in which property or goods are sold item by item to the highest bidder. —*v.* **2.** to sell (something) by auction (often fol. by *off*): *He auctioned off his furniture.*

auc·tion·eer (ôk′shə nēr′), *n.* **1.** a person who conducts sales by auction. —*v.* **2.** to auction (something).

au·da·cious (ô dā′shəs), *adj.* **1.** extremely bold or daring; recklessly brave; fearless: *an audacious warrior.* **2.** extremely original or inventive: *an audacious artist.* **3.** without respect for persons, customs, etc.; impudent: *an audacious remark.* —**au·da′cious·ly,** *adv.*

au·dac·i·ty (ô das′i tē), *n.* **1.** boldness or courage: *the*

act, āble, dâre, ärt; ebb, ēqual; if, īce; hot, ōver, ôrder; oil; bŏŏk; ōōze; out; up, ûrge; ə = *a* as in *alone;* ᵊ as in *button* (but′ᵊn), *fire* (fīᵊr); **ch**ief; **sh**oe; **th**in; **t͟h**at; **zh** as in *measure* (mezh′ər). See full key inside cover.

audacity of the pioneers to move westward. **2.** objectionable boldness; insolence or effrontery: *He had the audacity to cheat and then lie about it.*

au·di·ble (ô′də bəl), *adj.* actually heard or capable of being heard: *an audible cough.* **—au′di·bly,** *adv.*

au·di·ence (ô′dē əns), *n.* **1.** a group of persons gathered to witness a public event, as the spectators at a theater, concert, etc. **2.** the persons reached by a book, radio or television broadcast, etc.; public. **3.** a regular public that follows a sport, form of art, etc.: *Baseball has a large audience.* **4.** an opportunity to be heard; hearing: *He sought an audience with the council.* **5.** an interview or meeting with an eminent or powerful person: *He was granted an audience with the queen.*

au·di·o (ô′dē ō′), *adj.* **1.** referring to sound or sound waves. **—n. 2.** the sound portion of a television program or signal, as distinguished from the picture portion or video.

au·di·o·vis·u·al (ô′dē ō vizh′ōō əl), *adj.* **1.** of or using films, tape recordings, television, and pictures for education. **2.** of both hearing and sight.

au·dit (ô′dit), *n.* **1.** an examination of financial accounts and records. **2.** a statement concerning the result of such an examination. **—v. 3.** to examine (financial accounts and records). **4.** to make an audit.

au·di·tion (ô dish′ən), *n.* **1.** the act or power of hearing. **2.** a hearing given to an actor, musician, etc., in order to test ability or suitability. **— v. 3.** to try (someone) in an audition: *to audition actors for a play.*

au·di·tor (ô′di tər), *n.* **1.** a person who has the authority to audit accounts. **2.** a listener or hearer.

au·di·to·ri·um (ô′di tôr′ē əm), *n.* **1.** a large room in which an audience gathers, as in a theater, school, etc. **2.** a building for public gatherings.

au·di·to·ry (ô′di tôr′ē), *adj.* **1.** of or referring to hearing or the organs of hearing: *an auditory defect; the auditory nerve.* **—n., pl. au·di·to·ries. 2.** an auditorium, esp. in the nave of a church.

Au·du·bon (ô′də bon′), *n.* **John James,** 1785–1851, U.S. naturalist who painted and wrote about the birds of North America.

Aug., August.

au·ger (ô′gər), *n.* a tool used to bore holes, as in wood or the earth.

aught[1] (ôt), *n.* **1.** anything whatever; any part: *For aught I know, it may be too late.* **—adv. 2.** in any degree; at all; in any respect: *I do not care aught for what you say.* [from the Old English word *āht*]

aught[2] (ôt), *n.* a cipher (0); zero. [from the Middle English word *naught.* When *naught* was used with the indefinite article *a,* the phrase *a naught* was incorrectly pronounced *an aught.* This caused the *n* of *naught* to be lost, leaving *aught* as the present form of the word]

aug·ment (ôg ment′), *v.* to make or become larger or greater; increase: *He augmented his income by doing odd jobs.* **—aug·men·ta·tion** (ôg′men tā′shən), *n.*

au·gur (ô′gər), *n.* **1.** an ancient Roman priest whose duty was to observe and interpret omens. **2.** any soothsayer; prophet. **—v. 3.** to predict, as from

omens. **4.** to be an omen or sign of: *This weather augurs an early spring.* **5.** to be a sign; bode (usually fol. by *well* or *ill*): *The present unrest in the world augurs ill for peace.*

au·gu·ry (ô′gyə rē), *n., pl.* **au·gu·ries. 1.** the practice of an augur; foretelling of the future. **2.** an omen or indication; sign.

au·gust (ô gust′), *adj.* inspiring awe and reverence; of great dignity or majesty: *the august works of Michelangelo.* **—au·gust′ly,** *adv.*

Au·gust (ô′gəst), *n.* the eighth month of the year, having 31 days.

Au·gus·ta (ô gus′tə), *n.* the capital city of Maine, in the S part.

Au·gus·tine (ô′gə stēn′, ô gus′tin), *n.* **Saint,** A.D. 354–430, one of the Latin fathers of the early Christian church, author, and bishop in N Africa.

Au·gus·tus (ô gus′təs), *n.* (*Augustus Caesar*) 63 B.C.–A.D. 14, first Roman emperor 27 B.C.–A.D. 14.

auk (ôk), *n.* any of several northern sea birds having webbed feet, short wings, and usually black and white plumage.

aunt (ant), *n.* **1.** the sister of one's father or mother. **2.** the wife of one's uncle.

au·ra (ôr′ə), *n.* a distinctive quality or atmosphere that surrounds and seems to come from a person, place, or thing, and that produces a certain feeling: *The old house had an aura of peace and dignity.*

Auk
(length 1½ ft.)

au·ral (ôr′əl), *adj.* of or referring to the ear or the sense of hearing. **—au′ral·ly,** *adv.*

au·ri·cle (ôr′i kəl), *n.* **1.** one of the two upper chambers of the heart into which blood flows from the veins. See illus. at **heart. 2.** the part of the ear that grows from the head. **—au·ric·u·lar** (ô rik′yə lər), *adj.*

Au·ro·ra (ə rôr′ə), *n.* (in Roman mythology) the goddess of the dawn.

au·ro·ra bo·re·al·is (ə rôr′ə bôr′ē al′is), another term for **northern lights.** Also, **au·ro′ra.**

aus·pice (ô′spis), *n., pl.* **aus·pic·es** (ô′spi siz). **1.** Often, **auspices.** an omen or sign of a future event. **2.** Usually, **auspices.** support or sponsorship: *a concert under the auspices of the city council.*

aus·pi·cious (ô spish′əs), *adj.* promising success; favorable: *to begin a career under auspicious circumstances.* **—aus·pi′cious·ly,** *adv.*

aus·tere (ô stēr′), *adj.* **1.** stern, solemn, or severe in manner or appearance: *The judge was a strict, austere man.* **2.** without luxury, ease, or comfort: *an austere life in the wilderness.* **3.** plain and unadorned: *an austere style of architecture.* **—aus·tere′ly,** *adv.*

aus·ter·i·ty (ô ster′i tē), *n., pl.* **aus·ter·i·ties. 1.** austere quality; severity of manner, life, etc.: *the austerity of pioneer life.* **2.** Usually, **austerities.** practices that require self-discipline and doing without comfort, luxury, etc., esp. for religious reasons.

Aus·tin (ô′stən), *n.* **1. Stephen Fuller,** 1793–1836, American pioneer in Texas. **2.** the capital city of Texas, in the central part.

Aus·tral·a·sia (ô′strə lā′zhə), *n.* Australia, New Zealand, and nearby islands in the S Pacific Ocean. —**Aus′tral·a′sian,** *n., adj.*

Aus·tral·ia (ô strāl′yə), *n.* **1.** a continent SE of Asia, between the Indian and Pacific oceans. 2,948,366 sq. mi. **2.** the nation occupying this continent and Tasmania: a member of the British Commonwealth of Nations. 2,974,581 sq. mi. *Cap.:* Canberra.

Aus·tral·ian (ô strāl′yən), *n.* **1.** a native or inhabitant of Australia. **2.** any of a number of languages spoken by the original natives of Australia. —*adj.* **3.** of or referring to Australia or its people. **4.** of or referring to the languages of the Australian aborigines.

Aus·tri·a (ô′strē ə), *n.* a republic in central Europe. 32,381 sq. mi. *Cap.:* Vienna. —**Aus′tri·an,** *n., adj.*

Aus·tri·a-Hun·ga·ry (ô′strē ə hung′gə rē), *n.* a monarchy in central Europe from 1867 to 1918: composed of Austria, Hungary, and nearby lands.

au·then·tic (ô then′tik), *adj.* **1.** deserving to be accepted as true or reliable; trustworthy: *an authentic history of early American life.* **2.** not false or copied; genuine; real: *an authentic antique.* —**au·then′ti·cal·ly,** *adv.*

au·then·ti·cate (ô then′tə kāt′), *v.,* **au·then·ti·cat·ed, au·then·ti·cat·ing.** to establish as genuine or valid; show to be authentic. —**au·then′ti·ca′tion,** *n.*

au·then·tic·i·ty (ô′then tis′i tē), *n.* the quality of being authentic; reliability or genuineness: *They questioned the authenticity of the news report.*

au·thor (ô′thər), *n.* **1.** a person who writes a novel, poem, etc. **2.** the maker of anything; creator: *God is regarded as the author of the universe.* Also, *referring to a woman,* **au′thor·ess.**

au·thor·i·ta·tive (ə thôr′i tā′tiv), *adj.* **1.** having authority or the power to command obedience, respect, etc.: *an authoritative decree of the king.* **2.** showing or marked by the possession of authority or command: *The policeman conducted the traffic with authoritative gestures.* **3.** worthy of being accepted and trusted: *an authoritative report written by scientific experts.* —**au·thor′i·ta·tive·ly,** *adv.*

au·thor·i·ty (ə thôr′i tē), *n., pl.* **au·thor·i·ties. 1.** the power to judge, act, or command: *A judge has authority to sentence offenders.* **2.** a person or group having authority: *to appeal to the authorities for fair treatment.* **3.** an accepted and trustworthy source of information, advice, etc.: *a leading authority on etiquette.*

au·thor·ize (ô′thə rīz′), *v.,* **au·thor·ized, au·thor·iz·ing. 1.** to give authority or power to: *to authorize a detective to make arrests.* **2.** to give authority for: *The doctors authorized a new treatment for the disease.* —**au·thor′i·za′tion,** *n.*

au·thor·ship (ô′thər ship′), *n.* **1.** the occupation or career of writing books, articles, etc. **2.** the origin of a work, esp. a book, poem, play, etc.: *Many of the most beautiful poems are of unknown authorship.*

au·to (ô′tō), *n., pl.* **au·tos.** an automobile.

auto-, a prefix meaning **1.** self: *autobiography.* **2.** of or by oneself or itself: *automotive.*

au·to·bi·og·ra·phy (ô′tə bī og′rə fē), *n., pl.* **au·to·bi·og·ra·phies.** an account of a person's life written by himself. —**au′to·bi·og′ra·pher,** *n.* —**au·to·bi·o·graph·i·cal** (ô′tə bī′ə graf′i kəl), *adj.*

au·toc·ra·cy (ô tok′rə sē), *n., pl.* **au·toc·ra·cies. 1.** absolute power over others, possessed by one person, such as a king or dictator. **2.** a country or state ruled by a person having this power.

au·to·crat (ô′tə krat′), *n.* **1.** a ruler who holds absolute power: *Charlemagne was an autocrat.* **2.** a domineering person.

au·to·crat·ic (ô′tə krat′ik), *adj.* **1.** of or like an autocrat ·or an autocracy; having absolute power. **2.** tyrannical or despotic: *an autocratic father; autocratic behavior.* —**au′to·crat′i·cal·ly,** *adv.*

au·to·graph (ô′tə graf′), *n.* **1.** a person's signature, esp. a signature of a famous person for keeping as a memento. **2.** anything written in a person's own hand. —*v.* **3.** to write one's name on or in; sign: *autograph a book.*

au·to·mate (ô′tə māt′), *v.,* **au·to·mat·ed, au·to·mat·ing.** to apply automation to (a process, factory, etc.).

au·to·mat·ic (ô′tə mat′ik), *adj.* **1.** operating or moving by itself: *an automatic device.* **2.** done or occurring without thought or consciousness: *Breathing can be entirely automatic.* —*n.* **3.** a rifle or other firearm that fires repeatedly while the trigger is squeezed. —**au′to·mat′i·cal·ly,** *adv.*

au·to·ma·tion (ô′tə mā′shən), *n.* the use of automatic machinery to perform complicated jobs or to operate other machines so that people are not required except for maintenance.

au·tom·a·ton (ô tom′ə ton′), *n.* **1.** a mechanical contrivance that operates by itself; robot. **2.** a person who acts or behaves mechanically.

au·to·mo·bile (ô′tə mə bēl′, ô′tə mə bēl′), *n.* a passenger vehicle that is moved by its own engine and is operated by a single person.

au·to·mo·tive (ô′tə mō′tiv), *adj.* **1.** referring to automobiles: *automotive manufacturing.* **2.** moved by a self-contained motor, engine, or the like.

au·ton·o·mous (ô ton′ə məs), *adj.* self-governing or independent, such as a country or organization. —**au·ton′o·mous·ly,** *adv.*

au·ton·o·my (ô ton′ə mē), *n.* the condition of being autonomous; the right of self-government; independence: *England granted autonomy to India in 1947.*

au·top·sy (ô′top sē), *n., pl.* **au·top·sies.** the medical examination of a person's body after death to find the cause of death or to examine the damage done by a disease or injury; post-mortem.

au·tumn (ô′təm), *n.* the season between summer

and winter, usually from September 21 to December 21; fall.

au·tum·nal (ô tum′n^əl), *adj.* belonging to, coming in, or suggesting autumn: *autumnal skies.*

aux·il·ia·ry (ôg zil′yə rē, ôg zil′ə rē), *adj.* **1.** providing help or assistance, as someone or something held for later or supplementary use: *an auxiliary motor; auxiliary troops.* **2.** of or referring to an auxiliary verb; used as an auxiliary verb. —*n., pl.* **aux·il·ia·ries.** **3.** a person, thing, or group that is auxiliary: *He served as the president's auxiliary.* **4.** short for **auxiliary verb.**

auxil′iary verb′, a verb used with an infinitive or participle of another verb to express differences of tense, mood, and voice. In the sentences *I do think, I am going, We have spoken,* and *You may go,* the verbs *do, am, have,* and *may* are auxiliary verbs.

a·vail (ə vāl′), *n.* **1.** use or advantage: *Our efforts were of no avail.* —*v.* **2.** to be of use or advantage to (a person): *All our efforts availed us little. No amount of intelligence will avail if ambition is lacking.* **3. avail oneself of,** to use (something) to one's advantage: *Why don't you avail yourself of the new library?*

a·vail·a·bil·i·ty (ə vā′lə bil′i tē), *n.* the state of being available: *the availability of seats for a movie.*

a·vail·a·ble (ə vā′lə bəl), *adj.* **1.** suitable or ready for use or service: *I am always available if you should need me.* **2.** obtainable or accessible: *There is no money available for the project.*

av·a·lanche (av′ə lanch′), *n.* **1.** a large mass of snow, ice, etc., sliding or falling suddenly from the slope of a mountain. **2.** anything like an avalanche in force or abundance: *an avalanche of letters.*

av·a·rice (av′ə ris), *n.* the extreme desire to gain and hoard wealth; greed for riches: *Because of his avarice, he never spent a penny on luxuries.*

av·a·ri·cious (av′ə rish′əs), *adj.* marked by avarice; greedy for riches: *The avaricious landlord preyed on the poor.* —**av′a·ri′cious·ly,** *adv.*

a·vast (ə vast′), *interj.* stop! cease! (a term used by sailors): *"Avast!" cried the captain of the ship.*

Ave., Avenue.

A·ve Ma·ri·a (ä′vā mə rē′ə), the Latin name for **Hail Mary.**

a·venge (ə venj′), *v.,* **a·venged, a·veng·ing.** to get revenge for (an insult, crime, etc.): *to avenge the death of a brother.* —**a·veng′er,** *n.*

av·e·nue (av′ə nōō′, -nyōō′), *n.* **1.** a street, esp. a wide one of some importance: *Paris has many famous avenues.* **2.** a way of reaching or attaining: *an avenue of escape.*

a·ver (ə vûr′), *v.,* **a·verred, a·ver·ring.** to declare or state positively: *He averred that he could do it.*

av·er·age (av′ə rij, av′rij), *n.* **1.** a number obtained by adding two or more quantities together and dividing the sum by the number of quantities added: *The average of 5, 6, and 10 is 7.* **2.** the typical or normal size or amount: *He is taller than average.* —*adj.* **3.** of or referring to an average: *The average score was 90.* **4.** typical; common; ordinary: *people of average in-*

come. —*v.,* **av·er·aged, av·er·ag·ing. 5.** to find an average for: *to average a sum.* **6.** to reach, do, be, etc., on an average: *The car has been averaging 20 miles per gallon.* **7. on the average,** usually; typically: *On the average I practice an hour a day.*

a·verse (ə vûrs′), *adj.* having a strong feeling of opposition, dislike, etc.: *Cats are averse to getting wet.* —**a·verse′ly,** *adj.*
—**Usage.** *Averse,* which means opposed or unwilling, should not be confused with *adverse,* which means unfavorable or unfriendly: *I am not averse to the change in plans. The ship sailed under adverse conditions.*

a·ver·sion (ə vûr′zhən), *n.* **1.** a strong desire to avoid something or someone because of dislike (usually fol. by *to*): *She has an aversion to talkative people.* **2.** a person or thing that causes dislike: *Borrowers are my aversion.*

a·vert (ə vûrt′), *v.* **1.** to turn away or aside: *to avert one's eyes.* **2.** to ward off or prevent: *Quick thinking on the part of the pilot averted disaster.* —**a·vert′i·ble, a·vert′a·ble,** *adj.*

a·vi·ar·y (ā′vē er′ē), *n., pl.* **a·vi·ar·ies.** a place for keeping birds, as a building or large cage.

a·vi·a·tion (ā′vē ā′shən), *n.* the act or science of flying aircraft, esp. airplanes.

a·vi·a·tor (ā′vē ā′tər), *n.* the pilot of an airplane.

av·id (av′id), *adj.* **1.** extremely eager; greedy: *The hungry dog is avid for his food.* **2.** devoted or enthusiastic: *an avid stamp collector.* —**a·vid·i·ty** (ə vid′i tē), *n.* —**av′id·ly,** *adv.*

av·o·ca·do (av′ə kä′dō), *n., pl.* **av·o·ca·dos. 1.** Also, **alligator pear.** a green, pear-shaped fruit of tropical America, containing a large pit and rich, yellow flesh that is used in salads. **2.** the tree on which it grows.

Avocado

av·o·ca·tion (av′ə kā′shən), *n.* an occupation or activity that a person takes up apart from his regular work; hobby: *Raising tropical fish is her avocation.*

a·void (ə void′), *v.* to keep away from; shun: *to avoid danger.* —**a·void′a·ble,** *adj.* —**a·void′a·bly,** *adv.*

a·void·ance (ə void′^əns), *n.* the act of avoiding or keeping away from something: *avoidance of danger.*

avoir., avoirdupois (weight).

av·oir·du·pois (av′ər də poiz′), *adj.* referring to the system of weights used in the U.S. and Britain, which is based on a pound that contains 16 ounces. The avoirdupois system is not used for most scientific work or for weighing drugs, gems, or precious metals.

a·vow (ə vou′), *v.* to declare frankly or openly; confess; admit: *He avowed that he did not understand.*

a·vow·al (ə vou′əl), *n.* an open statement or affirmation; frank admission: *His quick avowal of his mistake won him forgiveness.*

a·vowed (ə voud′), *adj.* acknowledged; declared: *That man is my avowed enemy.*

a·wait (ə wāt′), *v.* **1.** to wait for; expect; look for: *to await the arrival of guests.* **2.** to be in store for; be ready for: *A pleasant surprise awaited him.*

a·wake (ə wāk′), *v.,* **a·woke** (ə wōk′) *or* **a·waked;**

a·wak·ing. 1. to wake up; rouse from sleep: *The noise in the street awoke him.* **2.** to make or become active; arouse: *The story awoke his imagination.* **3.** to become aware (often fol. by *to*): *Faced by poverty, he awoke to the difficulties of life.* —*adj.* **4.** not sleeping: *He lay awake for hours.* **5.** alert; aware: *He was awake to the danger ahead.*

a·wak·en (ə wā′kən), *v.* **1.** to awake; waken. **2.** to make or become aware or active: *to awaken someone's interest.*

a·wak·en·ing (ə wā′kə niñg), *adj.* **1.** rousing; quickening: *an awakening interest.* —*n.* **2.** the act of awaking from sleep. **3.** an instance of becoming aware, interested, or aroused: *a rude awakening to the facts of a situation.*

a·ward (ə wôrd′), *v.* **1.** to give after careful consideration, as something that is merited or due: *to award prizes to the winners.* **2.** to give as a result of a decree: *The judge awarded $500 to the plaintiff.* —*n.* **3.** something that is given as a prize: *an award for writing.*

a·ware (ə wâr′), *adj.* having knowledge; conscious: *He was aware of his mistake.* —**a·ware′ness,** *n.*

a·wash (ə wosh′, ə wôsh′), *adj., adv.* covered with water; flooded: *During the storm the decks of the ship were awash.*

a·way (ə wā′), *adv.* **1.** from this or that place; off: *to go away from the city.* **2.** far; apart: *away back in time and place; to talk away from the main subject.* **3.** in another direction; aside: *Turn your eyes away.* **4.** out of one's possession or use: *to give money away; to give away a secret.* **5.** out of notice, sight, hearing, or existence: *to fade away.* **6.** continuously; repeatedly: *He kept hammering away.* **7.** without hesitation or delay: *Fire away.* —*adj.* **8.** absent: *He is away from home.* **9.** distant: *six miles away.* **10. do away with,** to get rid of; stop; abolish: *Let's do away with some of these rules and regulations.*

awe (ô), *n.* **1.** an overwhelming feeling of wonder and fear, caused by something that is great, majestic, etc.: *to look with awe at a cathedral.* —*v.,* **awed, aw·ing. 2.** to fill with awe: *awed by the thought of God.*

awe·some (ô′səm), *adj.* inspiring awe: *an awesome task.* —**awe′some·ly,** *adv.* —**awe′some·ness,** *n.*

awe-struck (ô′struk′), *adj.* filled with awe: *He was awe-struck by the great beauty of the Alps.* Also, **awe′struck′, awe-strick·en, awe·strick·en** (ô′strik′-ən).

aw·ful (ô′fəl), *adj.* **1.** very bad, unpleasant, or ugly: *an awful meal.* **2.** inspiring dread or fear: *The war caused awful destruction.* **3.** inspiring awe or great wonder: *the awful expanse of the universe.*
—**Usage.** The use of *awful* in place of *awfully* to mean "very" or "extremely" should be avoided: *It was awfully* (not *awful*) *warm in the house.*

aw·ful·ly (ô′fə lē, ôf′lē), *adv.* **1.** very; extremely: *awfully kind.* **2.** in a way that calls forth or causes blame or disapproval: *The dog behaved awfully.*

a·while (ə hwīl′, ə wīl′), *adv.* for a short time or

period: *Let's relax and talk awhile until he comes.*
—**Usage.** *Awhile* is an adverb meaning "for a short time" and should not be confused with the article and noun *a while: Please stay awhile. Let's walk for a while longer.*

awk·ward (ôk′wərd), *adj.* **1.** lacking skill or grace; clumsy: *an awkward dancer.* **2.** not easy to use or handle; unwieldy: *an awkward type of hammer.* **3.** requiring caution; troublesome or difficult: *an awkward corner to turn in the dark.* **4.** embarrassing or inconvenient: *an awkward moment.* —**awk′ward·ly,** *adv.* —**awk′ward·ness,** *n.*

awl (ôl), *n.* a pointed instrument for piercing small holes in leather, wood, etc.

awn·ing (ô′niñg), *n.* a rooflike shade of canvas or other material extending over a doorway, from the top of a window, over a deck, etc., in order to provide protection from the sun and rain.

Awls
A, For making holes
B, For sewing

a·woke (ə wōk′), *v.* a past tense and past participle of **awake.**

A.W.O.L., absent without leave: away from military duties without permission, but without the intention of deserting.

a·wry (ə rī′), *adv., adj.* **1.** with a turn or twist to one side; askew: *His hat is awry.* **2.** away from the intended direction or goal; amiss: *Our plans went awry.*

ax (aks), *n., pl.* **ax·es** (ak′siz). a tool for chopping wood, consisting of a flat, sharp blade attached to a wooden handle. Also, **axe.**

ax·es[1] (ak′sēz), *n.* the plural of **axis.**

ax·es[2] (ak′siz), *n.* the plural of **ax.**

ax·i·om (ak′sē əm), *n.* a basic statement or principle that is accepted without proof, either because its truth is obvious or because it is widely accepted as true: *It is an axiom that a straight line is the shortest distance between two points.* —**ax·i·o·mat·ic** (ak′sē ə-mat′ik), *adj.*

Axes
A, Ax
B, Hatchet

ax·is (ak′sis), *n., pl.* for defs. 1–3 **ax·es** (ak′sēz). **1.** a line around which a rotating body turns or may be imagined to turn: *The axis of the earth is an imaginary line that runs between the North Pole and the South Pole.* **2.** either of the lines on a graph from which the coordinates of a point are measured. **3.** a central line that divides a body, form, or the like, into two equal and symmetrical parts: *the axis of a cone.* **4. the Axis,** the military alliance of Germany, Italy, and Japan in World War II. —**ax·i·al** (ak′sē əl), *adj.*

ax·le (ak′səl), *n.* a bar on which or with which a wheel or a pair of wheels turns.

ay[1] (ā), *adv.* ever; always. Also, **aye.** [from the Middle English word *ai,* which comes from Scandinavian]

---

act, āble, dâre, ärt; ebb, ēqual; if, īce; hot, ōver, ôrder; oil; book; ooze; out; up, ûrge; ə = *a* as in *alone;* ə as in *button* (but′ᵊn), *fire* (fīᵊr); chief; shoe; thin; ᴛʜat; zh as in *measure* (mezh′ər). See full key inside cover.

ay² (ī), *adv., n.* another spelling of **aye¹.**

aye¹ (ī), *adv.* 1. yes. —*n.* 2. an affirmative vote or voter: *The ayes were in the majority.* Also, **ay.** [from the Middle English word *ye,* which comes from Old English *gī* "yea"]

aye² (ā), *adv.* another spelling of **ay¹.**

aye-aye (ī´ī´), *n.* a small animal that is active at night and feeds on insects and fruit, having large cutting teeth and long fingers.

a·zal·ea (ə zāl´yə), *n.* a usually small garden bush that bears white, pink, or red flowers. [from a Greek word meaning "dry." The plant grows in dry soil]

Az·er·bai·jan (ä´zər bī jän´), *n.* a republic of the Soviet Union, bordering on Iran and the Caspian Sea.

A·zores (ə zôrz´, ā´zôrz), *n.pl.* a group of islands in the N Atlantic, W of Portugal: an overseas province of Portugal. 890 sq. mi.

Az·tec (az´tek), *n.* 1. a member of an Indian people in central Mexico whose empire was conquered by Cortés in 1519. 2. the language of the Aztecs. —**Az´tec·an,** *adj.*

az·ure (azh´ər), *n.* 1. the blue of a clear or unclouded sky. —*adj.* 2. of the color azure: *white clouds against an azure sky.*

	Semitic	Greek	Etruscan	Latin	Gothic	Modern Roman
DEVELOPMENT OF UPPER-CASE LETTERS	𝟫	𝔞	B	𝟪	B	𝕭	B

	Greek		Medieval		Gothic	Modern Roman
DEVELOPMENT OF LOWER-CASE LETTERS	β	λ	B	b	b	b

B

B, b (bē), *n., pl.* **B's** *or* **Bs, b's** *or* **bs.** the second letter of the English alphabet.

B, 1. (in some grading systems) a grade or mark indicating scholastic work of good but not the highest quality. 2. *Chem.* the symbol for **boron.** 3. a major blood group or type.

Ba, *Chem.* the symbol for **barium.**

B.A., Bachelor of Arts. [from the Latin phrase *Baccalaureus Artium*]

baa (ba, bä), *v.,* **baaed, baa·ing.** 1. to make the sound of a sheep; bleat. —*n.* 2. the sound a sheep makes.

Ba·al (bā′əl, bāl, bäl), *n.* 1. a god of the ancient Semitic peoples, representing the reproductive powers of nature. 2. *(often l.c.)* any idol or false god.

bab·ble (bab′əl), *v.,* **bab·bled, bab·bling.** 1. to make meaningless sounds. 2. to talk nonsense; speak foolishly. 3. to murmur: *The brook babbled along.* 4. *Slang.* to tell secrets. —*n.* 5. meaningless sounds or talk. 6. the murmur of a brook or stream. —**bab′bler,** *n.* —**bab′bling·ly,** *adv.*

babe (bāb), *n.* a baby or child.

Ba·bel (bā′bəl, bab′əl), *n.* 1. (in the Bible) a Babylonian city, now identified with Babylon, whose people tried to build a tower **(Tower of Babel)** that would reach heaven, but failed because they could not understand each other's language. 2. *(often l.c.)* confusion and noise.

ba·boon (ba bo͞on′), *n.* a large monkey of Africa and Arabia having a dog-like face and living on the ground.

Baboon
(2½ ft. high at shoulder)

ba·by (bā′bē), *n., pl.* **ba·bies.** 1. a very young child. 2. the youngest of a group. 3. a childish person. —*adj.* 4. small; very young: *a baby pig.* —*v.,* **ba·bied, ba·by·ing.** 5. to treat like a baby: *Her older brother still ba-*bies her. —**ba′by·hood′,** *n.* —**ba′by·ish,** *adj.* —**ba′by·like′,** *adj.*

Bab·y·lon (bab′ə lən, bab′ə lon′), *n.* 1. an ancient city in SW Asia on the Euphrates River: capital of Babylonia. 2. (in the Bible) the city of Babel.

Bab·y·lo·ni·a (bab′ə lō′nē ə), *n.* an ancient empire in SW Asia, in the lower Euphrates valley: flourished 2800–1750 B.C. *Cap.:* Babylon. —**Bab′y·lo′ni·an,** *n., adj.*

ba·by-sit (bā′bē sit′), *v.,* **ba·by-sat** (bā′bē sat′), **ba·by-sit·ting.** to take care of a child or children while the parents are temporarily away. —**ba′by-sit′ter,** *n.*

bac·ca·lau·re·ate (bak′ə lôr′ē it), *n.* 1. another term for **bachelor's degree.** 2. a religious service held at a school, usually on the Sunday before graduation. 3. a farewell sermon given to a graduating class.

Bac·chus (bak′əs), *n.* (in Greek and Roman mythology) the god of wine; Dionysus.

Bach (bäk), *n.* **Johann Sebastian,** 1685–1750, German composer and organist.

bach·e·lor (bach′ə lər, bach′lər), *n.* 1. an unmarried man. 2. a person who has a bachelor's degree. —**bach′e·lor·hood′,** *n.*

bach·e·lor's-but·ton (bach′ə lərz but′ʰn, bach′-lərz-), *n.* any of various plants, esp. the cornflower, having round flower heads that look like buttons.

bach′elor's degree′, a degree, such as Bachelor of Arts, given by a college or university to a person who has completed undergraduate studies. Also, **baccalaureate.**

ba·cil·lus (bə sil′əs), *n., pl.* **ba·cil·li** (bə sil′ī). 1. a rod-shaped or cylindrical bacterium. See also **coccus.** 2. (loosely) any bacterium.

back[1] (bak), *n.* 1. the rear part of the human body, from the neck to the end of the spine. 2. a similar part of an animal's body. 3. the rear side or part of any structure or object: *the back of a chair; the back of the classroom.* 4. (esp. in football) a player whose regular position is behind the players on his line. —*v.* 5. to support by approval or assistance: *He*

act, āble, dâre, ärt; ebb, ēqual; if, īce; hot, ōver, ôrder; oil; bo͝ok; o͞oze; out; up, ûrge; ə = *a* as in *alone;* ə as in *button* (but′ʰn), *fire* (fī′ər); chief; shoe; thin; that; zh as in *measure* (mezh′ər). See full key inside cover.

backed the plan. **6.** to move backward. *—adj.* **7.** located at the rear: *the back door.* **8.** not paid; overdue: *back rent.* **9.** belonging to the past: *a back issue of a magazine.* **10. back down,** to abandon an argument or opinion, esp. under pressure: *He backed down when we proved he was mistaken.* **11. back out** (or **out of**), to fail to keep (a promise, engagement, etc.): *She backed out of the trip at the last minute.* **12. back up, a.** to support with approval, assistance, etc.: *to back up a friend.* **b.** to move backward: *I backed up to the parking place.* **13. in back of,** on the other side of; behind: *He hid in back of the sofa.* Also, **back of.** [from the Old English word *bæc*] —**back′er,** *n.* —**back′less,** *adj.*

back² (bak), *adv.* **1.** at, to, or toward the rear: *to step back.* **2.** in or toward the past. **3.** at or toward a starting point or place. **4.** in return: *to pay back; to talk back.* **5.** under control: *He kept back his tears.* **6. back and forth,** in one direction and then in the other; to and fro: *He swam back and forth from the boat to the raft.* **7. go back on,** to fail to keep; not live up to: *to go back on one's promise.* [short for *aback*]

back-and-forth (bak′ən fôrth′), *adj.* backward and forward; side to side: *A clock's pendulum has a back-and-forth movement.*

back·bone (bak′bōn′), *n.* **1.** the column of bones in the back of man and many animals, such as fish, amphibians, reptiles, birds, and mammals; spine; spinal column. **2.** strength of character. **3.** the strongest or most important part of something: *He's the backbone of our organization.* See illus. at **skeleton.**

back·break·ing (bak′brā′king), *adj.* requiring much effort or physical strength; exhausting: *a backbreaking job.* —**back′break′er,** *n.*

back·field (bak′fēld′), *n.* **1.** the members of a football team stationed behind the linemen or the linebackers. **2.** the positions played by these members.

back·fire (bak′fīər′), *n.* **1.** a loud combustion of fuel in an engine occurring either at the wrong time in the engine's cycle or outside the engine's cylinders. **2.** a controlled fire started on purpose to check a forest fire by burning trees and brush ahead of it. —*v.*, **back·fired, back·fir·ing. 3.** to have or cause a backfire. **4.** to result in the opposite of what was expected: *His plan backfired.*

back·gam·mon (bak′gam′ən), *n.* a board game for two persons, with pieces or men moved according to throws of dice.

back·ground (bak′ground′), *n.* **1.** the part of a picture or scene that is behind the main person or thing (opposite of *foreground*). **2.** a place, part, or position that attracts little attention. **3.** a person's previous experience and education.

back·hand (bak′hand′), *n.* **1.** a stroke in any game played with a racket, such as tennis, squash, or badminton, made from the side of the body opposite the side holding the racket. **2.** handwriting that slants toward the left.

back·hand·ed (bak′han′did), *adj.* **1.** done with the back of the hand turned in the direction of forward movement: *a backhanded stroke in tennis.* **2.** slanting

toward the left: *backhanded writing.* **3.** not wholehearted or sincere: *"You're not a bad swimmer for a kid" is a backhanded compliment.* —**back′hand′ed·ly,** *adv.* —**back′hand′ed·ness,** *n.*

back·ing (bak′ing), *n.* **1.** help or support; aid. **2.** those who help or support; helpers. **3.** something that forms the back of an object and supports or protects it: *The belt has a leather backing.*

back·log (bak′lôg′, -log′), *n.* **1.** unfinished work or business: *a large backlog of orders.* **2.** a large log at the back of a hearth to keep a fire going.

back·pack (bak′pak′), *n.* **1.** a pack or bundle of supplies carried on one's back. —*v.* **2.** to go on an outing, using a backpack. —**back′pack′er,** *n.*

back·slide (bak′slīd′), *v.*, **back·slid** (bak′slid′); **back·slid** *or* **back·slid·den** (bak′slid′ᵊn); **back·slid·ing.** to go back to bad habits or improper conduct. —**back′slid′er,** *n.*

back·stage (bak′stāj′), *adv.* behind the curtain in a theater; on the stage, in the dressing rooms, etc.

back·stroke (bak′strōk′), *n.* a swimming stroke made while swimming on one's back.

back·swim·mer (bak′swim′ər), *n.* any of various bugs that live in water and swim on their backs.

back′ talk′, rude or impertinent replies.

back·ward (bak′wərd), *adv.* Also, **back′wards. 1.** toward the back or rear: *to jump backward.* **2.** toward the past or toward a starting point: *to count backward from 50 to 1.* **3.** with the back first: *He fell over backward.* **4.** toward a worse condition: *Instead of improving, he is going backward.* —*adj.* **5.** turned away from the front: *a backward glance.* **6.** slow in learning or development: *a backward student.* **7.** shy; bashful: *She becomes backward when meeting strangers.* **8. backward and forward,** completely; thoroughly: *She knew the lesson backward and forward.* Also, **backwards and forwards.** —**back′ward·ly,** *adv.* —**back′ward·ness,** *n.*

back·wa·ter (bak′wô′tər), *n.* **1.** water held back by a dam or other force. **2.** a place or condition of backwardness or stagnation.

back·woods (bak′woodz′), *n.pl.* areas that are remote, unpopulated, or without cultural advantages.

back·woods·man (bak′woodz′mən), *n., pl.* **back·woods·men.** a person who lives in or comes from the backwoods.

back·yard (bak′yärd′), *n.* the section of land that is behind a house and is sometimes fenced in.

ba·con (bā′kən), *n.* meat from the back and sides of a hog, usually salted and smoked.

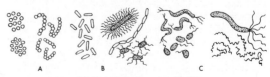

Bacteria (greatly magnified)
A, Spherical; B, Rod; C, Spiral

bac·te·ri·a (bak tēr′ē ə), *n.pl., sing.* **bac·te·ri·um** (bak-tēr′ē əm). tiny one-celled plants, many of which are

beneficial but some of which cause diseases. —**bac·
te′ri·al,** *adj.*

bac·te·ri·ol·o·gy (bak tēr′ē ol′ə jē), *n.* the science
that deals with bacteria. —**bac·te′ri·ol′o·gist,** *n.*

Bac′tri·an cam′el (bak′trē ən), an Asian camel
having two humps. See illus. at **camel.** [named after
Bactria, an ancient country in W Asia]

bad (bad), *adj.,* **worse** (wûrs), **worst** (wûrst). **1.** not
good; poor: *bad weather; bad marks.* **2.** morally
wrong: *a bad way to behave.* **3.** dangerous; unhealthy: *Eating too much candy is bad for your teeth.*
4. not correct: *bad spelling.* **5.** severe; very harsh: *a
bad storm.* **6.** unpleasant: *a bad smell.* **7.** rotten or
spoiled: *bad fish.* **8.** cross or disagreeable: *He is in a
bad mood today.* **9.** not well; sick or ill: *The flu
makes you feel bad.* **10.** sorry or dejected: *to feel bad
about missing school.* **11.** unfavorable or inconvenient: *The gift arrived at a bad time.* —*n.* **12.** anything that is bad: *to go from bad to worse.* **13. in
bad,** in disfavor; having someone's disapproval: *He's
in bad with the teacher for being late.*
—**Usage.** In spoken English, either *bad* or *badly* is
used after *feel.* In formal writing, however, *bad* is
usually preferred: *She felt bad about being late.* It is
also preferred after *look, sound, smell,* etc., in either
spoken or written English: *It looks bad for our team.*

bad′ blood′, unfriendly feeling; hostility or hatred:
There is bad blood between the neighbors.

bade (bad), *v.* a past tense of **bid:** *She bade him
leave.*

badge (baj), *n.* an emblem, mark, or device worn by
a person to show that he belongs to a certain profession, group, or organization: *a policeman's badge.*

badg·er (baj′ər), *n.* **1.** a furry, flesh-eating, burrowing mammal of North America, Europe, and Asia.
—*v.* **2.** to tease or annoy:
*He's badgering me to go
to the ball game.* —**badg′
er·ing·ly,** *adv.*

bad·lands (bad′landz′),
n.pl. an area of barren
land marked by erosion of
the soil and rocks.

bad·ly (bad′lē), *adv.,*
worse (wûrs), worst (wûrst). **1.** in a bad manner; incorrectly, dangerously, or offensively: *The furnace
works badly. The boy behaved badly.* **2.** to a great
degree; very much: *They are badly in need of help.*
—**Usage.** See **bad.**

bad·man (bad′man′), *n., pl.* **bad·men.** a bandit or
outlaw, esp. in the early history of the western U.S.

bad·min·ton (bad′min t°n), *n.* a game similar to tennis in which the players use light rackets to hit a
shuttlecock over a high net.

bad-tem·pered (bad′tem′pərd), *adj.* having a bad
temper; cross or irritable.

Baf′fin Bay′ (baf′in), a part of the Arctic Ocean
between Greenland and Baffin Island.

Baf′fin Is′land, a Canadian island in the Arctic

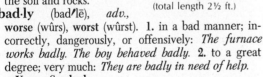
Badger
(total length 2½ ft.)

Ocean, between Greenland and N Canada. It covers
an area of 190,000 sq. mi. Also, **Baf′fin Land′.**

baf·fle (baf′əl), *v.,* **baf·fled, baf·fling.** to confuse,
bewilder, or perplex: *The math problem baffled the
whole class.*

bag (bag), *n.* **1.** a container or sack capable of being
closed at the top: *a paper bag.* **2.** a suitcase or valise.
3. a woman's purse or pocketbook. —*v.,* **bagged, bag·
ging.** **4.** to swell or bulge. **5.** to hang loosely like an
empty bag: *His coat bagged at the elbows.* **6.** to put
into a bag: *to bag groceries.* **7.** to kill or catch while
hunting: *to bag a deer.* **8. hold the bag,** to bear the
entire blame or responsibility: *He was never caught,
so I was left holding the bag.* **9. in the bag,** certain to
have the desired result: *The game is in the bag.*

ba·gel (bā′gəl), *n.* a doughnut-shaped hard roll.

bag·gage (bag′ij), *n.* **1.** trunks, suitcases, etc., used in
traveling; luggage. **2.** the portable equipment of an
army.

bag·gy (bag′ē), *adj.,* **bag·gi·er, bag·gi·est.** hanging
loosely; loose: *baggy slacks.* —**bag′gi·ness,** *n.*

Bagh·dad (bag′dad), *n.* the capital city of Iraq, in
the central part, on the Tigris. Also, **Bag′dad.**

bag·pipe (bag′pīp′), *n.* a musical instrument having
several reed pipes that are fed air from a leather bag
filled either by blowing
or by pumping a bellows.
—**bag′pip′er,** *n.*

bah (bä, ba), *interj.* (used
as an exclamation of
strong dislike.)

Ba·ha·mas (bə hä′məz),
n. an independent coun-
try consisting of a group of
islands in the British West
Indies, SE of Florida: formerly British. 5380 sq. mi.
Cap.: Nassau.

Bagpipe

Bai·kal (bī käl′), *n.* **Lake,**
a lake in the S Soviet Union in Asia: deepest lake in
the world. 13,200 sq. mi.; 5714 ft. deep.

bail¹ (bāl), *n.* **1.** money given as a guarantee that a
person released from jail will return for trial at an appointed time. —*v.* **2.** to obtain the release of (an arrested person) by providing bail. [from the Old
French word *baillier* "to hand over," which comes
from Latin *bāiulāre* "to serve as a porter"]

bail² (bāl), *v.* **1.** to clear of water by dipping (usually
fol. by *out*): *to bail out a boat.* **2. bail out, a.** to
make a parachute jump from an airplane: *We had to
bail out at 3000 feet.* **b.** to assist (someone) in an
emergency or crisis: *I bailed him out when he was in
debt.* [from the French word *baille* "bucket"]

bail·iff (bā′lif), *n.* **1.** an officer similar to a sheriff or
his deputy, employed to make arrests, keep order in
the court, etc. **2.** an overseer of a farm or estate.

bairn (bârn), *n.* (esp. in Scotland) a child.

bait (bāt), *n.* **1.** food or the like used to attract and
trap animals: *Worms are often used as bait for fish.* **2.**

anything that attracts or lures. —*v.* **3.** to prepare with bait: *to bait a hook.* **4.** to torment or annoy with unkind remarks; tease. **5.** to set dogs upon (an animal) for sport.

Ba′ja Califor′nia (bä′hä), Spanish name of **Lower California.**

bake (bāk), *v.,* **baked, bak·ing. 1.** to cook or become cooked by dry heat in an oven, under coals, or on heated metal or stones: *to bake cookies.* **2.** to harden by heat, as pottery.

bak·er (bā′kər), *n.* a person who bakes and sells bread, cakes, etc.

bak′er's doz′en, a group of 13; a dozen plus one extra: from the former practice among bakers of giving 13 items to the dozen.

bak·er·y (bā′kə rē), *n., pl.* **bak·er·ies.** a place where baked goods are made or sold. Also, **bake·shop** (bāk′-shop′).

bak·ing (bā′king), *n.* **1.** the act of a person or thing that bakes. **2.** the amount baked at one time; batch. **3.** the food baked: *Her baking is always delicious.*

bak′ing pow′der, a mixture of bicarbonate of soda and an acid, used in baking to make dough rise.

bak′ing so′da, another name for **bicarbonate of soda.**

Ba·laam (bā′ləm), *n.* (in the Bible) a Mesopotamian prophet who blessed the Israelites after being rebuked by his donkey.

Balalaika

bal·a·lai·ka (bal′ə lī′kə), *n.* a Russian musical instrument having a triangular body, a neck like that of a guitar, and usually three strings.

bal·ance (bal′əns), *n.* **1.** a device for weighing, esp. one used in a laboratory. **2.** a state of steadiness or equilibrium among weights or forces. **3.** stability or steadiness of the body or emotions: *He lost his balance and fell on the ice.* **4.** equality between the total debits and the total credits of an account. **5.** the difference between the total of debits and the total of credits. **6.** the amount still owed on a partly paid bill. **7.** the remainder or rest: *The balance of the class was absent.* **8.** a wheel that regulates the beats of a watch or clock. **9. the Balance,** another name for **Libra.** —*v.,* **bal·anced, bal·anc·ing. 10.** to estimate the weight or importance of; compare: *to balance several possibilities.* **11.** to bring to or hold in equilibrium; keep or remain steady: *Trained seals can balance balls on their noses.* **12.** to adjust or make equal the total of debits and the total of credits (of an account). **13.** to be or make equal in quantity, number, or amount: *Cash on hand balances expenses.* **14.** to serve as a counterbalance to; offset: *The good balances the bad.* **15. in the balance,** not

Balance (def. 1)

settled or definite; undecided: *The criminal's fate is still in the balance.*

Bal·bo·a (bal bō′ə), *n.* **Vas·co Nú·ñez de** (väs′kō nōōn′yez dā), 1475?–1517, Spanish adventurer and explorer who discovered the Pacific Ocean in 1513 by crossing the Isthmus of Panama.

bal·co·ny (bal′kə nē), *n., pl.* **bal·co·nies. 1.** a railed platform projecting from the side of a building. **2.** an upper floor in a theater or hall with seats; gallery.

bald (bôld), *adj.* **1.** having little or no hair on the scalp. **2.** without some natural growth or covering: *a bald mountain.* **3.** open or straightforward; not disguised: *a bald lie.* —**bald′ness,** *n.*

bald′ ea′gle, a large eagle of the U.S. and Canada having a white head and neck: emblem of the United States.

Bald eagle
(length 2½ ft.;
wingspread to 7½ ft.)

bal·der·dash (bôl′dər-dash′), *n.* a senseless jumble of words; nonsense.

bale (bāl), *n.* **1.** a large bundle of something, usually packed tightly and secured by wires or cords: *a bale of cotton; a bale of hay.* —*v.,* **baled, bal·ing. 2.** to make or form into bales: *to bale hay.*

Bal·e·ar′ic Is′lands (bal′ē ar′ik), a group of Spanish Islands near the E coast of Spain.

bale·ful (bāl′fəl), *adj.* very dangerous or threatening; evil: *His baleful predictions upset everyone.* —**bale′ful·ly,** *adv.*

Ba·li (bä′lē), *n.* an island in Indonesia, E of Java. 2147 sq. mi. —**Ba·li·nese** (bä′lə nēz′), *n., adj.*

balk (bôk), *v.* **1.** to stop, as at an obstacle, and refuse to continue: *The horse balked at jumping the fence.* **2.** to place an obstacle in the way of; hinder: *The weather balked our plans for a picnic.* —*n.* **3.** a check or hindrance; defeat; disappointment.

Bal·kan (bôl′kən), *adj.* **1.** of or referring to the Balkan States or their inhabitants. —*n.* **2. the Balkans,** the Balkan States.

Bal′kan Penin′sula, a peninsula in S Europe, S of the Danube River and bordering on the Adriatic, Ionian, Aegean, and Black seas.

Bal′kan States′, the countries on the Balkan Peninsula.

balk·y (bô′kē), *adj.,* **balk·i·er, balk·i·est.** tending to balk; stubborn: *a balky mule.* —**balk′i·ly,** *adv.* —**balk′i·ness,** *n.*

ball¹ (bôl), *n.* **1.** a round mass or body; sphere: *a ball of string.* **2.** a round or roundish body, of any of various sizes and materials, either hollow or solid, for use in games: *a tennis ball.* **3.** a game played with a ball, esp. baseball: *The boys play ball in the park.* **4.** (in baseball) a pitched ball, not swung at by the batter, that does not pass over the home plate between the batter's shoulders and knees. **5.** a solid, usually round, projectile for a cannon, rifle, pistol, etc. —*v.* **6.** to gather or form into a ball or balls. **7.** **on the ball,** alert, capable, or efficient: *You've got to be on the ball if you want to make the team.* [from Scandinavian] —**ball′-like′,** *adj.*

ball² (bôl), *n.* **1.** a large, elaborate party with dancing. **2.** *Slang.* a very good time. [from the French word *bal,* which comes from Greek *ballizein* "to dance"]

bal·lad (bal′əd), *n.* **1.** a simple poem that tells a story and can be sung. **2.** any simple song having two or more stanzas, all sung to the same melody.

ball′-and-sock′et joint′ (bôl′ən sok′it), a joint between rods, links, pipes, etc., consisting of a ball-like part held within a round socket.

bal·last (bal′əst), *n.* **1.** any heavy material carried in a ship to provide stability. **2.** any heavy material, such as sandbags, carried in the car of a passenger balloon for control of altitude and stability. **3.** gravel, broken stone, etc., used in making the foundation for a railroad track. —*v.* **4.** to supply with ballast.

Ball-and-socket joint

ball′ bear′ing, **1.** a group of rings holding small metal balls in which a shaft turns. **2.** any small metal ball.

bal·le·ri·na (bal′ə rē′nə), *n.* a female ballet dancer.

bal·let (ba lā′, bal′ā), *n.* **1.** a dance form demanding grace and using formal steps and gestures. **2.** a performance of such dancing with music, often telling a story: *a ballet about Cinderella.* **3.** Also, **ballet′ com′pany.** a group of dancers who perform ballets.

bal·lis·tic (bə lis′tik), *adj.* of or concerning missiles, projectiles, or ballistics.

ballis′tic mis′sile, a missile, as a rocket, that is guided only during takeoff and while powered, after which it travels unguided like a falling bomb.

bal·lis·tics (bə lis′tiks), *n. (used as sing.)* the science that deals with projectiles, their firing, and their motion.

bal·loon (bə lōōn′), *n.* **1.** a bag, usually round, filled with a gas lighter than air so that it will float above the ground: used for flying and for carrying scientific instruments. **2.** a thin rubber bag that can be inflated, used as a toy. —*v.* **3.** to swell or puff out like a balloon.

bal·lot (bal′ət), *n.* **1.** a sheet of paper on which a voter marks his choice or choices. **2.** the total number of votes cast or recorded: *a large ballot.* **3.** the method of secret voting by printed or written ballots or by voting machines. **4.** voting in general, or a round of voting: *He won on the second ballot.* **5.** the list of candidates to be voted on: *There were three*

names on the ballot. —*v.,* **bal·lot·ed, bal·lot·ing. 6.** to vote by ballot. —**bal′lot·er,** *n.*

ball·play·er (bôl′plā′ər), *n.* a person who plays ball professionally, esp. baseball.

ball′-point pen′ (bôl′point′), a pen whose point is a fine ball bearing that transfers ink from a cartridge to a writing surface.

ball·room (bôl′rōōm′, -rŏŏm′), *n.* a large room with a polished floor for dancing.

balm (bäm), *n.* **1.** any of various oily, fragrant substances obtained from certain plants and often used as a soothing or healing ointment. **2.** a plant or tree yielding such a substance. **3.** anything that heals, cures, or lessens pain: *the balm of kind words.*

balm·y (bä′mē), *adj.,* **balm·i·er, balm·i·est. 1.** mild and refreshing: *balmy weather.* **2.** like balm; fragrant. —**balm′i·ness,** *n.*

bal·sa (bôl′sə), *n.* **1.** the very light, soft wood of a South American tree, used for making life preservers. **2.** the tree itself.

bal·sam (bôl′səm), *n.* **1.** an evergreen tree, often used as a Christmas tree, that yields a fragrant oil. **2.** any plant yielding a similar oil. **3.** the oil itself.

Bal·tic (bôl′tik), *adj.* **1.** of, near, or on the Baltic Sea. **2.** of or referring to the Baltic States.

Bal′tic Sea′, a sea in N Europe, bounded by Sweden, Finland, the Soviet Union, Poland, Germany, and Denmark. It covers an area of about 160,000 sq. mi. Also, **the Baltic.**

Bal′tic States′, the formerly independent republics of Estonia, Latvia, and Lithuania, and sometimes including Finland.

Bal·ti·more (bôl′tə môr′), *n.* a port city in N Maryland, near Chesapeake Bay.

bal·us·ter (bal′ə stər), *n.* any of a number of closely spaced supports for a railing.

bal·us·trade (bal′ə strād′, bal′ə strād′), *n.* a railing consisting of supporting balusters.

bam·boo (bam bōō′), *n., pl.* **bam·boos.** a tall tropical plant whose hollow, jointed stem is used for building and for making fishing poles, furniture, etc.

bam·boo·zle (bam bōō′zəl), *v.,* **bam·boo·zled, bam·boo·zling.** to trick (a person) into doing something, esp. by coaxing or flattering: *You let him bamboozle you into playing hooky.*

Bamboo

ban (ban), *v.,* **banned, ban·ning. 1.** to prohibit or forbid officially; bar: *to ban parking on one side of the street.* —*n.* **2.** the act of forbidding by law.

---

act, āble, dâre, ärt; ebb, ēqual; if, īce; hot, ōver, ôrder; oil; bŏŏk; ōōze; out; up, ûrge; ə = a as in *alone*; ᵊ as in *button* (but′ᵊn), *fire* (fīᵊr); chief; shoe; thin; that; zh as in *measure* (mezh′ər). See full key inside cover.

ba·nal (bə nal′, bān′əl), *adj.* trite or stale; common-place: *banal remarks about an important subject.* —**ba·nal·i·ty** (bə nal′i tē), *n.* —**ba·nal′ly**, *adv.*

ba·nan·a (bə nan′ə), *n.* 1. a long fruit, usually having a tough, yellow rind, that grows in bunches on a tropical plant. 2. the plant itself.

band¹ (band), *n.* 1. a company of persons, or sometimes animals or things, acting together: *a band of thieves.* 2. a group of musicians: *a jazz band.* —*v.* 3. to unite in a group; join together: *We banded together to support the mayor.* [from the Old French word *bande,* which comes from Gothic *bandwa* "standard"]

Banana plant

band² (band), *n.* 1. a thin, flat strip of some material for tying, trimming, etc. 2. a stripe, usually for decoration: *a blue band around the collar.* 3. a range of frequencies, as of light or radio waves. —*v.* 4. to furnish with a band or bands. [from the Old French word *bande,* which comes from Germanic]

band·age (ban′dij), *n.* 1. a strip of cloth or other material used to bind up a wound, sore, sprain, etc. —*v.,* **band·aged, band·ag·ing.** 2. to bind or cover with a bandage: *to bandage a cut thumb.*

ban·dan·na (ban dan′ə), *n.* a large, colored handkerchief or scarf, usually with white figures on a red or blue background. [from the Hindi word *bāndhnū,* a way of dyeing cloth by knotting it tightly, thus keeping the dye from reaching some parts]

band·box (band′boks′), *n.* a round box for holding a hat, collars, etc.

ban·di·coot (ban′də koot′), *n.* 1. any of several large, East Indian rats destructive to rice fields and gardens. 2. any of several small mammals, having a pouch for their young, that feed on insects and plants: found in Australia and New Guinea.

Bandicoot (def. 2) (total length 2 ft.)

ban·dit (ban′dit), *n.* a robber or outlaw. [from the Italian word *bandito* "outlaw, one who has been banned"]

band·mas·ter (band′mas′tər), *n.* the conductor of a military band, circus band, etc.

band·stand (band′stand′), *n.* a platform where members of a band or orchestra sit while performing.

band·wag·on (band′wag′ən), *n.* 1. a large, decorated wagon for carrying a musical band. 2. **jump on the bandwagon,** to support a candidate, cause, etc., that seems assured of success: *He jumped on the bandwagon two days before the election.*

ban·dy (ban′dē), *v.,* **ban·died, ban·dy·ing.** 1. to throw or pass from one to another; give and take: *to bandy a tennis ball; to bandy insults.* —*adj.* 2. (of a person's legs) having a bend outward; bowed.

ban·dy-leg·ged (ban′dē leg′id, -legd′), *adj.* another word for **bowlegged.**

bane (bān), *n.* a person or thing that ruins, destroys, or spoils: *Gambling was the bane of his existence.*

bang¹ (bang), *n.* 1. a loud, sudden noise: *the bang of an explosion.* 2. a hard blow or stroke: *a bang on the head.* 3. *Slang.* strong pleasure or enjoyment; excitement: *We got a big bang out of going to the circus.* —*v.* 4. to strike or beat noisily: *to bang a drum.* 5. to close noisily: *to bang the door shut.* —*adv.* 6. suddenly and loudly; violently: *He fell bang against the wall.* [probably from a Scandinavian word, such as Icelandic *banga* "to beat, hammer"]

bang² (bang), *n.* Usually, **bangs.** a fringe of hair combed or brushed forward over the forehead. [a shortened form of the word *bangtail* "a short tail, a horse with a short tail"]

Bang·kok (bang′kok), *n.* the capital city of Thailand, in the S central part.

Ban·gla·desh (bäng′glə desh′), *n.* an independent country E of India, on the Bay of Bengal. 54,501 sq. mi. *Cap.:* Dacca. Former name, **East Pakistan.**

ban·gle (bang′gəl), *n.* a bracelet or anklet in the form of a ring.

ban·ish (ban′ish), *v.* 1. to expel or send away from a country; exile: *The prince banished him from France.* 2. to send or put away: *to banish sadness.* —**ban′ish·ment,** *n.*

ban·is·ter (ban′i stər), *n.* 1. a slender supporting post at the edge of a staircase; baluster. 2. Sometimes, **banisters.** a railing and the supporting posts of a staircase; balustrade.

ban·jo (ban′jō), *n., pl.* **ban·jos** or **ban·joes.** a musical instrument having strings stretched over a shallow frame covered with skin. It is played with fingers or with a pick.

bank¹ (bangk), *n.* 1. a long pile or heap; mass: *a bank of earth; a bank of clouds.* 2. the slope or higher ground bordering a stream or river. 3. an elevation or rise in the sea floor around which the water is quite shallow. —*v.* 4. to border with a bank: *to bank a river with sandbags.* 5. to form into a bank or heap: *to bank snow.* 6. to slope the bed of (a road or railroad). 7. to tip (an airplane) so that one wing is higher than the other. 8. to cover (a fire) with ashes or fuel to make it burn long and slowly. [from Danish]

Banjo

bank² (bangk), *n.* 1. a place for receiving, lending, exchanging, and guarding money. 2. a storage place: *a blood bank.* —*v.* 3. to have an account with a bank. 4. to deposit (money) in a bank. 5. **bank on,** to depend on; have confidence in: *She may agree, but I wouldn't bank on it.* [from the Italian word *banca* "moneychanger's table"]

bank³ (bangk), *n.* 1. an arrangement of objects in a line: *a bank of seats; a bank of lights.* 2. a row of keys on a pipe organ. 3. a bench for rowers in a galley. 4. a row of oars. [from Old English]

bank·book (bangk′book′), *n.* a book held by a depositor in which a bank enters a record of his deposits and withdrawals.

bank·er (bang′kər), *n.* a person who works in a bank, esp. an executive.

bank·ing (bang′king), *n.* the business carried on by a bank or banker.

bank·rupt (bangk′rupt), *n.* **1.** a person who has been declared unable to pay his debts by a court and· whose property is divided among the people to whom he owes money. —*adj.* **2.** unable to pay one's debts. —*v.* **3.** to make bankrupt: *He was warned that gambling would bankrupt him.* [from the medieval Latin phrase *banca rupta* "broken bank"]

bank·rupt·cy (bangk′rupt sē), *n.* the state of being or becoming bankrupt.

ban·ner (ban′ər), *n.* **1.** the flag of a country, army, etc. **2.** a piece of cloth with a motto, slogan, or message painted or printed on it. **3.** a newspaper headline extending across the top of a page. —*adj.* **4.** leading; outstanding: *a banner year for crops.*

banns (banz), *n.pl.* the announcement of an intended marriage, given three times in the church of both the man and the woman who are to be married.

ban·quet (bang′kwit), *n.* **1.** a large and elaborate meal; feast. **2.** a public dinner, often with speeches following the meal. —*v.*, **ban·quet·ed, ban·quet·ing.** **3.** to entertain at a banquet. **4.** to have or attend a banquet; feast.

ban·shee (ban′shē), *n.* (in Irish folklore) a spirit in the form of a woman whose appearance or wailing is a sign that a loved one will soon die.

ban·tam (ban′təm), *n.* **1.** *(often cap.)* a small chicken known for its fighting ability. **2.** a small, quarrelsome person. —*adj.* **3.** very small; tiny: *bantam editions of the classics.* [the chicken is named after *Bantam*, a village in Indonesia where it was bred]

ban·tam·weight (ban′təm wāt′), *n.* a professional boxer weighing up to 118 pounds.

ban·ter (ban′tər), *n.* **1.** an exchange of light, playful, teasing remarks: *good-natured banter among friends.* —*v.* **2.** to tease or make fun of in a joking way.

Ban·tu (ban′tōō), *n.*, *pl.* **Ban·tus** or **Ban·tu.** **1.** a member of any of several Negro groups of central or southern Africa. **2.** a large group of about 500 languages spoken by Bantus. —*adj.* **3.** of or referring to the Bantus or their languages.

ban·yan (ban′yən), *n.* an East Indian tree whose branches send roots to the ground, causing the tree to spread over a wide area.

bap·tism (bap′tiz əm), *n.* **1.** a sacrament or rite of the Christian church in which new members are immersed in or sprinkled with water. **2.** a first experience or new start. —**bap·tis·mal** (bap tiz′məl), *adj.*

bap·tist (bap′tist), *n.* a person who baptizes: *John the Baptist.*

Banyan
(height 70 to 100 ft.)

Bap·tist (bap′tist), *n.* a member of a Protestant denomination that baptizes believers by immersing them in water.

bap·tis·ter·y (bap′ti strē), *n.*, *pl.* **bap·tis·ter·ies.** a building or place in which people are baptized.

bap·tist·ry (bap′ti strē), *n.*, *pl.* **bap·tist·ries.** another spelling of **baptistery.**

bap·tize (bap tīz′, bap′tīz), *v.*, **bap·tized, bap·tiz·ing.** **1.** to immerse in water, sprinkle, or pour water on, in the Christian rite of baptism. **2.** to give a name to; christen: *My brother was baptized Charles.* **3.** to cleanse or purify spiritually. —**bap·tiz′er,** *n.*

bar (bär), *n.* **1.** a long, evenly shaped piece of some solid substance, usually metal or wood, used as a guard or obstruction: *the bars of a cage.* **2.** an oblong piece of anything: *a bar of soap.* **3.** a long ridge of sand or gravel near or slightly above the surface of a body of water: *It is difficult to swim at that beach because of the sand bars.* **4.** anything that hinders or causes difficulty; obstacle: *a bar to success.* **5.** a counter or place where drinks and food are served: *a snack bar.* **6.** the legal profession: *to be admitted to the bar.* **7.** any court: *the bar of public opinion.* **8.** a band or strip: *a bar of light.* **9.** (in music) one of the vertical lines crossing the staff and dividing it into measures. **10.** a unit of time in music; measure. —*v.*, **barred, bar·ring.** **11.** to equip or fasten with a bar or bars; lock: *I barred the door before going to bed.* **12.** to shut in or out; block; prevent: *The police barred the exits. He was barred from membership.* **13. bar none,** without exceptions: *It was the worst exam I ever took, bar none.*

barb (bärb), *n.* **1.** a point or pointed part that sticks out backward from a main point: *a barb on the end of a fishhook.* **2.** an unpleasant remark; insult: *He kept making barbs about my pitching ability.* —*v.* **3.** to furnish with a barb or barbs.

Bar·ba·dos (bär bā′dōs), *n.* an independent island republic in the E West Indies, part of the British Commonwealth. 161 sq. mi. *Cap.:* Bridgetown.

bar·bar·i·an (bär bâr′ē ən), *n.* **1.** a person belonging to a group whose ways and customs are savage and uncivilized. **2.** a person who does not appreciate or is completely uninterested in culture. —*adj.* **3.** uncivilized or savage; primitive. **4.** foreign or alien.

bar·bar·ic (bär bar′ik), *adj.* **1.** primitive; not civilized: *barbaric invaders.* **2.** of or like barbarians: *barbaric customs.* —**bar·bar′i·cal·ly,** *adv.*

bar·ba·rism (bär′bə riz′əm), *n.* **1.** an uncivilized state or condition. **2.** an uncivilized or savage act. **3.** an incorrect use of a word.

bar·bar·i·ty (bär bar′i tē), *n.*, *pl.* **bar·bar·i·ties.** **1.** brutal or inhuman behavior; cruelty. **2.** an act of cruelty. **3.** something that is crude or coarse, as in style, taste, or expression.

bar·ba·rous (bär′bər əs), *adj.* **1.** uncivilized or savage; wild: *the barbarous tribes that invaded ancient Rome.* **2.** extremely cruel or harsh; brutal; inhuman: *barbarous treatment of prisoners.* —**bar′ba·rous·ly,** *adv.* —**bar′ba·rous·ness,** *n.*

Bar′ba·ry Coast′ (bär′bə rē), the Mediterranean coastline of N Africa: a former pirate refuge.

bar·be·cue (bär′bə-kyoo′), *n.* **1.** a picnic or party at which meats are roasted over an open hearth or pit. **2.** a grill or spit on which food is cooked over an open fire. **3.** pieces of meat or fish roasted over an open fire. —*v.,* **bar·be·cued, bar·be·cu·ing. 4.** to broil or roast over an open fire: *to barbecue a chicken.* **5.** to cook (meat or fish) in a highly seasoned sauce.

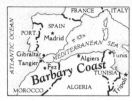

barbed′ wire′, a type of wire having barbs, or small pieces of sharply pointed wire, twisted around it at short intervals, used mostly to fence in livestock.

bar·ber (bär′bər), *n.* **1.** a person whose job is cutting hair and shaving and trimming beards. —*v.* **2.** to cut or trim the hair of; shave or trim the beard of.

bar·but (bär′bət), *n.* a steel helmet worn in the 15th century, completely enclosing the head and having a T-shaped face slit.

Bar·ce·lo·na (bär′sə lō′nə), *n.* a port city in NE Spain, on the Mediterranean Sea.

bard (bärd), *n.* **1.** a person who wrote or sang narrative poems long ago. **2.** any poet. **3. the Bard,** William Shakespeare.

bare (bâr), *adj.,* **bar·er, bar·est. 1.** without clothing or covering; naked: *bare legs.* **2.** without the usual furnishings; empty: *bare walls.* **3.** plain and undisguised: *the bare facts.* **4.** just enough: *a family with only the bare necessities.* —*v.,* **bared, bar·ing. 5.** to remove the clothes or covering from. **6.** to open to view: *to bare the truth.* —**bare′ness,** *n.*

Barbut

bare·back (bâr′bak′), *adv., adj.* without a saddle on the back of a horse: *to ride bareback; a bareback rider.*

bare·faced (bâr′fāst′), *adj.* without concealment or disguise; open; bold: *a barefaced lie.*

bare·foot (bâr′foot′), *adj., adv.* with the feet bare: *a barefoot boy; to run barefoot.* Also, **bare·foot·ed** (bâr′foot′id).

bare·head·ed (bâr′hed′id), *adj., adv.* with the head uncovered. —**bare′head′ed·ness,** *n.*

bare·leg·ged (bâr′leg′id, -legd′), *adj., adv.* with bare legs. —**bare′leg′ged·ness,** *n.*

bare·ly (bâr′lē), *adv.* **1.** no more than; only; just: *She is barely 12.* **2.** without disguise; openly.

bar·gain (bär′gin), *n.* **1.** an agreement between persons settling what will be given or performed and what will be received. **2.** something worth more than the price asked or paid: *We found a few bargains at the dress sale.* —*v.* **3.** to discuss the terms of an agreement or purchase: *She bargained with him until he lowered the price.* **4. bargain for,** to be prepared for; expect: *Inviting all her friends was more than we bargained for.* **5. in** (or **into**) **the bargain, in**

addition to what was expected; besides: *She dropped the dish and cut her toe in the bargain.*

barge (bärj), *n.* **1.** a flat-bottomed boat, usually pushed or towed, used to transport freight or passengers. —*v.,* **barged, barg·ing. 2.** to carry or transport by barge. **3.** to move clumsily; bump into things: *to barge through a crowd.* **4. barge in** (or **into**), to intrude or interrupt, esp. in a rude or clumsy manner: *She always barges in without an invitation.*

bar·i·tone (bar′i tōn′), *n.* **1.** a male voice with a range between tenor and bass. **2.** a singer with such a voice. —*adj.* **3.** of a size and pitch between tenor and bass: *a baritone saxophone.*

bar·i·um (bâr′ē əm, bar′ē am), *n. Chem.* a heavy metallic element. It is used in alloys, and its compounds are used in medicine and in manufacturing paints. *Symbol:* Ba

bark¹ (bärk), *n.* **1.** the abrupt, harsh cry of a dog. **2.** a sharp, explosive noise. **3.** a sharp order or reply. —*v.* **4.** to utter a bark. **5.** to speak or cry out sharply: *The sergeant barked the orders to his men.* **6. bark up the wrong tree,** to waste one's efforts: *If she expects me to help her, she's barking up the wrong tree.* [from the Old English word *beorcan* "to bark"]

bark² (bärk), *n.* **1.** the outermost covering of the woody parts of a tree. —*v.* **2.** to strip or remove the bark from. **3.** to rub off the skin of: *to bark one's shins.* [from Scandinavian]

bark³ (bärk), *n.* **1.** a kind of sailing vessel having three or more masts. **2.** (esp. in poetry and literature)

Bark

any boat or sailing vessel. Also, **barque.** [from the Latin word *barca*]

bark·er (bär′kər), *n.* **1.** an animal or person that barks. **2.** a person who stands outside a theater, side show of a carnival, etc., calling out to people who are passing by to come in.

Bark·ley (bärk′lē), *n.* **Alben W.,** 1877–1956, 35th Vice President of the U.S. 1949–1953.

bar·ley (bär′lē), *n.* **1.** a kind of grain used as a food and in making beer, whiskey, etc. **2.** the plant bearing this grain.

bar′ mag′net, a magnet made from a straight metal bar. See also **horseshoe magnet.**

bar mitz·vah (bär mits′və), *(often caps.)* a solemn ceremony for admitting a Jewish boy of 13 as an adult member of the Jewish community.

barn (bärn), *n.* a large building on a farm for storing hay and grain and often for housing livestock.

bar·na·cle (bär′nə kəl), *n.* a small shellfish that attaches itself to underwater objects, esp. to the bottoms of ships.

Bar·nard (bär′närd), *n.* **Chris·ti·aan N(eeth·ling)** (kris′tyän nit′-liṅg), born 1923, South African surgeon: performed first successful heart transplant 1968.

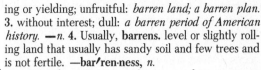

Barnacles

barn·storm (bärn′stôrm′), *v.* to tour rural areas giving political campaign speeches, presenting theatrical performances, playing exhibition baseball games, etc.: *The presidential candidate barnstormed across the country.* —**barn′storm′er,** *n.*

barn·yard (bärn′yärd′), *n.* a yard next to or near a barn, esp. a fenced area where animals are kept.

ba·rom·e·ter (bə rom′i tər), *n.* **1.** a device for measuring air pressure: used in weather forecasting and as an altimeter. **2.** anything that shows changes.

bar·o·met·ric (bar′ə me′trik), *adj.* referring to or measured by a barometer: *barometric pressure.*

bar·on (bar′ən), *n.* **1.** a member of the lowest grade of nobility. **2.** a very important financier or industrialist.

bar·on·ess (bar′ə nis), *n.* **1.** the wife of a baron. **2.** a lady holding a baronial title in her own right.

bar·on·et (bar′ə nit), *n.* a member of a British hereditary order of honor, ranking below the barons and above the knights.

ba·ro·ni·al (bə rō′nē əl), *adj.* **1.** referring to a baron. **2.** suitable for or befitting a baron.

ba·roque (bə rōk′), *adj.* of or referring to a European style of art, architecture, furniture, etc., of the 17th and early 18th centuries, that is very ornate.

barque (bärk), *n.* another spelling of **bark³.**

bar·racks (bar′əks), *n.* **1.** a building or group of buildings for housing soldiers. **2.** any large, plain building where many people are housed.

bar·ra·cu·da (bar′ə kōō′-də), *n., pl.* **bar·ra·cu·das** *or* **bar·ra·cu·da.** any of several large, slim, ferocious ocean fishes.

Barracuda
(length to 6 ft.)

bar·rage (bə räzh′), *n.* **1.** a barrier of artillery fire. **2.** a very large, overwhelming quantity: *a barrage of questions.*

bar·rel (bar′əl), *n.* **1.** a round container, usually of wood, with slightly bulging sides. **2.** the amount a barrel can hold: in the U.S., 31½ gallons (119.24 liters) of liquid or 105 dry quarts (115.62 liters) of fruits or vegetables. **3.** any large quantity: *a barrel of fun.* **4.** the tube of a gun. — *v.,* **bar·reled** *or* **bar·relled; bar·rel·ing** *or* **bar·rel·ling. 5.** to put or pack in a barrel or barrels. **6. over a barrel,** in a position where one cannot refuse a demand: *After promising to go, I was really over a barrel.*

bar·ren (bar′ən), *adj.* **1.** not producing or unable to produce offspring: *a barren woman.* **2.** not produc-

ing or yielding; unfruitful: *barren land; a barren plan.* **3.** without interest; dull: *a barren period of American history.* —*n.* **4.** Usually, **barrens.** level or slightly rolling land that usually has sandy soil and few trees and is not fertile. —**bar′ren·ness,** *n.*

bar·rette (bə ret′), *n.* a clasp worn by women or girls to hold hair in place.

bar·ri·cade (bar′ə kād′, bar′ə kād′), *n.* **1.** a hastily constructed barrier for defense. **2.** any barrier that blocks or prevents passage. —*v.,* **bar·ri·cad·ed, bar·ri·cad·ing. 3.** to block or shut in with a barricade: *to barricade oneself behind a stack of books.*

bar·ri·er (bar′ē ər), *n.* **1.** anything that blocks or prevents passage, as a fence or railing or some natural obstacle: *a mountain barrier.* **2.** anything that blocks or limits: *an age barrier; a trade barrier.*

bar·ring (bär′iṅg), *prep.* except for; excepting: *Barring delays, I'll be there before dark.*

bar·ris·ter (bar′i stər), *n.* *Chiefly British.* a lawyer who pleads cases in the higher courts.

bar·row (bar′ō), *n.* **1.** a flat, rectangular frame for carrying a load, usually with shafts or handles at each end. **2.** a wheelbarrow.

bar·tend·er (bär′ten′dər), *n.* a person who mixes and serves drinks at a bar.

bar·ter (bär′tər), *v.* **1.** to trade one thing for another without the use of money: *Before people used money, they bartered. The trapper bartered skins for weapons.* —*n.* **2.** the act or practice of bartering: *They got food and supplies by barter.*

Bar·thol·di (bär thol′dē), *n.* **Frédéric Auguste,** 1834–1904, French sculptor: designed the Statue of Liberty.

Bar·thol·o·mew (bär thol′ə myōō′), *n.* (in the Bible) one of Christ's 12 apostles.

Bar·ton (bär′t°n), *n.* **Clara,** 1821–1912, U.S. philanthropist: organized American Red Cross in 1881.

ba·sal (bā′zəl), *adj.* **1.** of, at, or forming the base of something. **2.** forming a basis; basic; fundamental.

ba·salt (bə sôlt′, bas′ôlt), *n.* a dark, heavy, volcanic rock.

base¹ (bās), *n.* **1.** the bottom part or support of anything: *the base of a lamp.* **2.** an underlying principle; foundation; basis: *What's at the base of the problem?* **3.** the main ingredient of a mixture or combination: *chowder with a fish base.* **4.** the bottom layer or coating, as of make-up or paint. **5.** a starting line or point for a race or game. **6.** one of the four corners of a baseball diamond. **7.** a place where military supplies are kept or from which military operations begin. **8.** *Chem.* a substance that combines with an acid to yield a salt. Bases turn litmus blue. See also **alkali.** —*v.,* **based, bas·ing. 9.** to place or establish on a base or foundation: *a skit based on Snow White.* **10.** to establish or locate: *a business based in New York.* **11. off base, a.** (in baseball) not touching a base. **b.** badly mistaken. [from the Greek word *basis*]

base² (bās), *adj.,* **bas·er, bas·est. 1.** morally low; of poor character; mean: *a base person.* **2.** poor quality;

inferior: *a base metal.* [from the Latin word *bassus* "short, low"] —**base′ly,** *adv.* —**base′ness,** *n.*

base·ball (bās′bôl′), *n.* **1.** a game of ball played by two nine-man teams on a square space, called a diamond, formed by lines connecting four bases, all of which must be touched by a base runner in order to score a run. **2.** the ball used in this game.

base·board (bās′bôrd′), *n.* a strip of wood close to the floor along the wall of a room.

base′ hit′, (in baseball) a batted ball that allows the batter to reach base safely.

base·less (bās′lis), *adj.* having no base in reason or fact: *a baseless rumor.* —**base′less·ly,** *adv.*

base·ment (bās′mənt), *n.* the bottom story of a building, partly or completely underground.

ba·ses¹ (bā′sēz), *n.* the plural of **basis.**

bas·es² (bā′siz), *n.* the plural of **base¹.**

bash·ful (bash′fəl), *adj.* very shy and easily embarrassed; timid: *to be bashful with strangers.* —**bash′ful·ly,** *adv.* —**bash′ful·ness,** *n.*

ba·sic (bā′sik), *adj.* **1.** of or forming a base or basis; fundamental: *the basic ingredient; the basic idea.* **2.** *Chem.* referring to or containing a base.

ba′sic sen′tence, another term for **kernel sentence.**

bas·il (baz′əl, bā′zəl), *n.* a sweet-smelling plant whose leaves are used in cooking.

ba·sil·i·ca (bə sil′i kə), *n.* **1.** a large oblong building with a semicircular section at one end and rows of columns along each side, used in ancient Rome as a hall of justice and public meeting place. **2.** an early Christian church built in this style. [from the Greek word *basilikē,* in the phrase *basilikē oikia* "royal house," which comes from *basileus* "king"]

bas·i·lisk (bas′ə lisk, baz′ə lisk), *n.* **1.** any of several tropical American lizards, noted for their ability to run over the surface of water on their hind legs. **2.** (in classical mythology) a lizard, serpent, or the like, that could kill by its breath or its stare.

Basilisk
(length to 3 ft.)

ba·sin (bā′sən), *n.* **1.** a shallow, round container used esp. for holding water. **2.** the quantity held by such a container. **3.** a partly sheltered area along a shore where boats may be moored: *a yacht basin.* **4.** an area of land drained by a river and its tributaries.

ba·sis (bā′sis), *n., pl.* **ba·ses** (bā′sēz). **1.** the bottom or base of anything. **2.** anything upon which something is based; fundamental: *The article he read about Mexico was the basis for his report.*

bask (bask), *v.* **1.** to lie in or be exposed to a pleasant warmth: *to bask in the sunshine.* **2.** to enjoy something: *to bask in compliments.*

bas·ket (bas′kit), *n.* **1.** a container made of straw, string, strands of wire, etc., woven, sewn, or looped together. **2.** the quantity held by such a container. **3.** an open net suspended from a backboard through which a basketball must pass for a player to score points. **4.** a score in basketball.

bas·ket·ball (bas′kit bôl′), *n.* **1.** a game played by two five-man teams on a rectangular court having a raised basket at each end, points being scored by tossing a ball through the opponent's basket. **2.** the large, round ball used in this game.

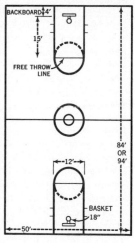

Basketball court

Basque (bask), *n.* **1.** a member of a people living in the western Pyrenees region of Spain and France. **2.** the language of the Basques, not known to be related to any other language. —*adj.* **3.** of or concerning the Basques or their language.

bas-re·lief (bä′ri lēf′), *n.* sculpture in which the figures stand out slightly from the background.

bass¹ (bās), *n.* **1.** the lowest male voice. **2.** a singer with such a voice. **3.** a double bass. **4.** the lowest part in a piece of music. —*adj.* **5.** low in pitch or range: *a bass note; a bass clarinet.* [from the Italian word *basso,* which comes from Latin *bassus* "low"]

bass² (bas), *n., pl.* **bass·es** *or* **bass.** any of various freshwater and ocean food fishes. [from the Old English word *bærs*]

bass′ clef′ (bās), the sign indicating that the fourth line of the staff is F below middle C. Also, **F clef.** See illus. at **clef.**

bass′ drum′ (bās), a large, round drum with two heads that gives a powerful low-pitched sound.

bas·set (bas′it), *n.* a short-haired dog with long ears and very short legs. Also, **bas′set hound′.**

bass′ horn′ (bās), another name for **tuba.**

bas·si·net (bas′ə net′), *n.* a basket with a hood over one end, for use as a baby's cradle.

bas·soon (bə sōōn′, ba sōōn′), *n.* a large double-reed musical instrument, the bass member of the oboe family of woodwinds. —**bas·soon′ist,** *n.*

bass′ vi′ol (bās), another name for **double bass.**

bass·wood (bas′wŏŏd′), *n.* **1.** the light, soft wood of the American linden tree. **2.** the tree itself.

bas·tard (bas′tərd), *n.* a person born of unmarried parents.

baste¹ (bāst), *v.,* **bast·ed, bast·ing.** to sew with long, loose stitches to hold a garment together temporarily in the early stages of making it. [from a French word, which comes from Germanic]

Bassoon

baste² (bāst), *v.,* **bast·ed, bast·ing.** to moisten (meat or other food) with fat or other liquid while cooking.

Bas·tille (ba stēl′), *n.* a fortress and prison in Paris, attacked and captured by French Revolutionaries on

July 14, 1789. July 14 (**Bastille′ Day′**) is a French
national holiday.

bas·tion (bas′chən), *n.* **1.** a part of a rampart or fortification that projects from the main part in the form
of an irregular pentagon.
2. a fortified place.

Ba·su·to·land (bə so͞o′tō-
land′), *n.* the former
name of **Lesotho.**

bat[1] (bat), *n.* **1.** a wooden
stick or club, esp. one
used in certain games to
strike the ball: *a baseball
bat.* —*v.,* **bat·ted, bat·ting.**
2. to strike or hit with a

Bastion

bat or club. **3.** (in baseball) to have a batting average
of: *He batted .325 in spring training.* **4. at bat,** (in
baseball) taking one's turn to bat in a game. **5. go to
bat for,** to defend (a person), esp. against harsh criticism: *They wanted to expel her, but we all went to
bat for her.* **6. right off the bat,** immediately; at
once: *He agreed right off the bat.* [from Old English]

bat[2] (bat), *n.* a usually small, furry mammal whose
front limbs are covered with skin, forming wings.
Bats are the only mammals capable
of true flight. [from Scandinavian]

bat[3] (bat), *v.,* **bat·ted, bat·ting. 1.** to
blink or wink. **2. not bat an eye,** to
show no emotion or surprise; remain calm: *We knew she was lying,
but she didn't bat an eye.* [from an
Old French word, which comes
from Latin *battuere* "to beat"]

batch (bach), *n.* **1.** a number of
things of the same kind made at
one time or considered as one
group: *a batch of Christmas cards.*
2. the amount of something baked at one time: *a
batch of brownies.*

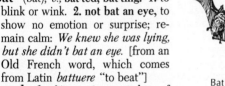

Bat
(length 3 ½ in.;
wingspread
14 in.)

bate (bāt), *v.,* **bat·ed, bat·ing. 1.** to restrain, lessen, or
hold back. **2. with bated breath,** with or as if with
the breath held in because of suspense, fear, or excitement: *I listened to the tale with bated breath.*

bath (bath), *n., pl.* **baths** (bathz, baths). **1.** a washing
or immersion of the body in water for cleansing or
therapy. **2.** the amount of water used for this purpose: *to run a bath.* **3.** a bathroom, or any room
equipped for bathing. **4.** a liquid in which something
is dipped, soaked, or washed: *Film is placed in a
bath when it is being developed.*

bathe (bāth), *v.,* **bathed, bath·ing. 1.** to immerse in
water or some other liquid for cleaning or treating;
wash: *to bathe a dog.* **2.** to apply water or some
other liquid to: *to bathe a wound.* **3.** to cover or surround as water does: *The room was bathed in sunlight.* **4.** to take a bath or sun bath. **5.** to swim for
pleasure. —**bath′er,** *n.*

bath·house (bath′hous′), *n., pl.* **bath·hous·es** (bath′-
hou′ziz). **1.** a building at a beach or near a swimming

pool containing dressing rooms for bathers. **2.** a
building with facilities for bathing.

bath·robe (bath′rōb′), *n.* a long, loose, coatlike garment worn before or after a bath or for leisure.

bath·room (bath′ro͞om′, -ro͝om′), *n.* a room containing a bathtub or shower and usually a washbowl and
toilet.

bath·tub (bath′tub′), *n.* a tub to bathe in, usually
found as a permanent fixture in a bathroom.

ba·tiste (bə tēst′), *n.* a fine, sheer linen or cotton
fabric.

ba·ton (bə ton′), *n.* **1.** a staff or club used as a mark
of office or authority. **2.** the slender stick with which
a conductor directs an orchestra. **3.** a staff carried
and twirled by a drum major or drum majorette.

Bat·on Rouge (bat′ən ro͞ozh′), a river port and the
capital city of Louisiana, in the SE part, on the Mississippi River.

bat·tal·ion (bə tal′yən), *n.* **1.** a military unit smaller
than a regiment and made up of a headquarters and
two or more companies. **2.** Often, **battalions.** a large
number of persons or things: *battalions of workers.*
[from the Italian word *battaglione* "large troop of
soldiers," which comes from *battaglia* "battle"]

bat·ten[1] (bat′°n), *v.* **1.** to grow fat. **2.** to make fat.
[from Scandinavian]

bat·ten[2] (bat′°n), *n.* **1.** a small board or strip of wood
used for various building purposes. —*v.* **2.** to cover
or furnish with small boards or strips of wood: *to bat-
ten down the hatches.* [from the French word *bâton*
"stick"]

bat·ter[1] (bat′ər), *v.* **1.** to beat or pound repeatedly
and very hard. **2.** to damage by beating very hard: *to
batter down a door.* [from the Middle English word
bateren]

bat·ter[2] (bat′ər), *n.* a thick mixture of flour, milk or
water, eggs, etc., beaten together for use in cooking
or baking. [from the Middle English word *bater*]

bat·ter[3] (bat′ər), *n.* a person who bats or whose turn
it is to bat, in baseball or cricket.

bat′tering ram′, an ancient military device consisting of a long, thick wooden post used to break
down walls, doors, gates, etc.

bat·ter·y (bat′ə rē), *n., pl.* **bat·ter·ies. 1.** a group of
electric cells connected together to yield a higher
voltage or current than a single cell. **2.** any group or
series of similar or related events, persons, or things:
a battery of tests; a battery of reporters. **3.** a group of
guns used for combined action by a military or naval
unit. **4.** (in baseball) a team's pitcher and catcher
considered as a unit. **5.** an unlawful attack upon another person by beating or touching.

bat·ting (bat′iŋ), *n.* **1.** the act or manner of using a
bat in a game: *His batting has improved.* **2.** sheets of
cotton or wool used to fill quilts or bedcovers.

bat·tle (bat′əl), *n.* **1.** a fight between opposing military forces. **2.** any fight or conflict between two persons, groups, teams, etc. —*v.,* **bat·tled, bat·tling. 3.** to
fight or struggle; engage in battle: *The teams battled*

for first place. **4.** to accomplish by battling: *We battled our way through the crowd.* —**bat′tler,** *n.*

bat·tle-ax (bat′ᵊl aks′), *n., pl.* **bat·tle-ax·es.** a large ax used long ago as a weapon of war. Also, **bat′tle-axe′.**

bat·tle-field (bat′ᵊl fēld′), *n.* the field or ground on which a battle is fought. Also, **bat·tle-ground** (bat′ᵊl-ground′).

bat·tle·ment (bat′ᵊl mənt), *n.* **1.** Often, **battlements.** a wall built at the top of a castle or building with holes through which soldiers can shoot. **2.** a wall similar to this built for decoration.

Battlement

bat·tle-ship (bat′ᵊl ship′), *n.* any of a class of warships that have the heaviest armor and are equipped with the largest and most powerful weapons.

bat·ty (bat′ē), *adj.,* **bat·tier, bat·ti·est.** *Slang.* insane; crazy; silly: *a batty person; batty remarks.*

bau·ble (bô′bəl), *n.* a worthless piece of jewelry or ornamentation; trinket.

Bau·douin I (bō dwan′), born 1930, king of Belgium since 1951.

baux·ite (bôk′sīt), *n.* a mixture of minerals resembling clay. Bauxite is the principal ore of aluminum.

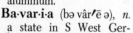

Ba·var·i·a (bə vâr′ē ə), *n.* a state in S West Germany: formerly a kingdom. 27,239 sq. mi. *Cap:* Munich. —**Ba·var′i·an,** *n., adj.*

bawd·y (bô′dē), *adj.,* **bawd·i·er, bawd·i·est.** indecent or improper. —**bawd′i·ness,** *n.*

bawl (bôl), *v.* **1.** to utter or shout out loudly. **2.** to cry or weep loudly. —*n.* **3.** a loud shout; outcry. **4. bawl out,** *Slang.* to scold (a person) loudly and severely: *If I'm late again, they'll really bawl me out.*

bay¹ (bā), *n.* a body of water forming an indentation of the shoreline. [from a French word, which comes from Latin *baia*]

bay² (bā), *n.* **1.** a division or compartment of a large room set off by columns, screens, walls, etc.; alcove; nook. **2.** a bay window. [from the Old French word *baee* "opening in a wall," which comes from Latin *batāre* "to stand open"]

bay³ (bā), *n.* **1.** a long, deep howl of a dog. **2.** the position or situation of an animal or person no longer able to escape and forced to face pursuers: *a stag at bay.* —*v.* **3.** to howl with a deep, long sound: *The hound bayed at the moon.* [from the Old French word *abai* "barking"]

bay⁴ (bā), *n.* See **laurel** (defs. 1, 2). [from the French word *baie,* which comes from Latin *bāca* "berry"]

bay⁵ (bā), *n.* **1.** a reddish brown. **2.** a horse or other animal that is reddish brown. —*adj.* **3.** of a reddish brown. [from an Old English word, which comes from Latin *badius*]

bay·ber·ry (bā′ber′ē), *n., pl.* **bay·ber·ries. 1.** a shrub that bears berries containing a wax used for candles. **2.** the berry of this shrub.

bay·o·net (bā′ə net′, bā′ə net′), *n.* **1.** a daggerlike steel weapon for attaching to the end of a gun and used in hand-to-hand combat. —*v.,* **bay·o·net·ed** *or* **bay·o·net·ted; bay·o·net·ing** *or* **bay·o·net·ting. 2.** to kill or wound with a bayonet. [from the French word *baïonnette,* which comes from *Bayonne,* the name of a city in France where the weapon was first made or used]

bay·ou (bī′ōō, bī′ō), *n., pl.* **bay·ous.** (in the southern U.S.) **1.** an arm, outlet, or tributary of a lake or river. **2.** any marshy creek, lake, etc., that flows slowly.

bay′ win′dow, a window or a set of windows projecting from the wall of a building, thus forming an alcove in the room inside the building.

ba·zaar (bə zär′), *n.* **1.** a marketplace or shopping quarter, esp. in the Middle East. **2.** a place where many kinds of goods are sold. **3.** a place where many kinds of items are sold to benefit a charity: *a church bazaar.* Also, **ba·zar′.**

ba·zoo·ka (bə zōō′kə), *n.* a tube-shaped weapon that fires a rocket able to pierce armor.

BB (bē′bē′), *n.* a size of shot for firing from an air rifle (**BB gun**).

B.C., before Christ (used in reckoning dates): *Plato was born in 427 B.C.*

bd., **1.** board. **2.** bond. **3.** bundle.

bd. ft., board foot; board feet.

bds., **1.** boards. **2.** bonds. **3.** bundles.

be (bē), *v.,* **was** (wuz, woz) *and* **were** (wûr); **been** (bin); **being. 1.** to exist or live: *There were three cats on the farm.* **2.** to take place; occur: *The party is on Saturday.* **3.** to occupy a place or position: *The book is on the table.* **4.** to continue or remain as before: *Let it be.* **5.** (used to connect the subject of a sentence with another word that describes it): *He is very tall. I was late this morning.* **6.** (used to introduce or form a question or command): *Is that right? Be quiet!* **7.** (used as an auxiliary verb to form the future tense and certain forms of the present and past tenses): *I am working hard in school. He was walking down the street when I saw him.* **8.** (used as an auxiliary verb to form the passive voice): *He was called on three times in class today.*

Be, *Chem.* the symbol for **beryllium.**

be-, a prefix used to form **1.** verbs meaning **a.** about or around: *beset; besiege.* **b.** upon or over: *becloud; bespatter.* **c.** completely or greatly: *berate; belabor.* **d.** to make or cause to be: *befriend; belie.* **e.** to provide with or cover with: *bemire; bespangle.* **2.** adjectives meaning provided with or covered with: *beribboned.*

beach (bēch), *n.* **1.** an area of sand or pebbles along a seashore. —*v.* **2.** to run (a boat) onto a beach.

beach·head (bēch′hed′), *n.* the area first attacked and held by a military force landing on an enemy shore.

bea·con (bē′kən), *n.* **1.** a guiding or warning signal, such as a light or fire. **2.** a tower or hill from which guiding or warning signals are given: *A lighthouse is a beacon for ships.* —*v.* **3.** to guide or warn.

bead (bēd), *n.* **1.** a small, round object of glass, wood, or stone with a hole through it, often strung with other objects of its kind. **2.** any small round body, as a drop of liquid, a bubble of gas in a liquid, or the like: *beads of sweat.* **3.** the front sight of a gun. —*v.* **4.** to decorate with beads. **5.** to form in beads or drops. **6. beads, a.** a necklace made of strung beads. **b.** a rosary. **7. draw** (or **get**) **a bead on,** to take careful aim at: *He drew a bead on the target.*

bead·ing (bē′diṅg), *n.* **1.** material made of or decorated with beads. **2.** a narrow, lacelike trimming.

bea·dle (bēd′ºl), *n.* a church officer who keeps order during services, assists the clergyman, and acts as an usher.

bead·y (bē′dē), *adj.,* **bead·i·er, bead·i·est.** small and round like a bead: *beady eyes.* —**bead′i·ness,** *n.*

bea·gle (bē′gəl), *n.* a small, short-haired hunting dog.

beak (bēk), *n.* **1.** the bill of a bird. **2.** anything that resembles a beak.

beak·er (bē′kər), *n.* **1.** a large drinking cup with a wide mouth. **2.** a cylindrical cup with a lip for pouring, used in laboratories.

Beagle
(15 in. high
at shoulder)

beam (bēm), *n.* **1.** a long piece of metal, wood, stone, etc., used in building. **2.** a horizontal supporting part as in a building or ship. **3.** the widest part of a ship's hull. **4.** a ray of light or other radiation. **5.** a radio signal used to guide aircraft. —*v.* **6.** to send out beams of light. **7.** to send a radio signal in a certain direction. **8.** to smile happily. **9. off the beam, a.** not on the course indicated by a radio beam. **b.** *Slang.* wrong or mistaken: *His guess was really off the beam.* **10. on the beam, a.** on the course indicated by a radio beam. **b.** *Slang.* proceeding correctly or exactly: *You were really on the beam in that last race.*

bean (bēn), *n.* **1.** the slightly flattened seed or the seed pod of various plants, used for food. **2.** a plant bearing such a seed or pod. **3. spill the beans,** to tell a secret and spoil a surprise or plan: *It was supposed to be a surprise, but Marvin spilled the beans.*

bear[1] (bâr), *v.,* **bore** (bôr); **borne** or **born** (bôrn); **bear·ing. 1.** to give birth to: *to bear a child.* **2.** to produce by natural growth: *a tree that bears fruit.* **3.** to support or remain firm under: *The columns bear the weight of the building.* **4.** to carry or bring: *to bear gifts.* **5.** to carry in the mind or heart: *to bear love.* **6.** to endure or tolerate: *He can't bear teasing.* **7.** to have or show; exhibit: *My sister bears a strong resemblance to my mother. The book bears an inscription.* **8.** to apply to; relate: *The discussion did not bear on the problem.* **9.** to press or push against: *The crowd was borne back by the police.* **10.** to manage or conduct (oneself): *to bear oneself with pride.* **11.** to tend in a course or direction: *to bear west.* **12. bear down, a.** to press or weigh down: *Bear down harder so I can close this suitcase.* **b.** to try harder; increase one's efforts: *Bear down if you want to pass history.* **c.** to ap-

proach rapidly, as a boat, enemy, etc.: *The torpedo boat was bearing down on us at 40 knots.* **13. bear out,** to support or confirm: *The facts will bear me out.* **14. bear up,** to face hardship bravely; endure: *to bear up despite a bad cold.* **15. bear with,** to be patient with: *Bear with me while I make a quick phone call.* [from the Old English word *beran*]

bear[2] (bâr), *n.* **1.** a large mammal having coarse fur and a short tail, as the grizzly bear or polar bear. **2.** any of various animals resembling the bear, as the koala. **3.** a gruff, clumsy, or rude person. [from the Old English word *bera*]

Bear
(3 ft. high at shoulder)

bear·a·ble (bâr′ə bəl), *adj.* capable of being borne; endurable: *The pain of the toothache was hardly bearable.* —**bear′a·bly,** *adv.*

beard (bērd), *n.* **1.** the growth of hair on a man's face. **2.** any tuft or growth resembling a man's beard, as the tuft of long hair on a goat's jaw or the bristly growths on stalks of grain. —*v.* **3.** to oppose or defy boldly. —**beard·ed** (bēr′did), *adj.*

bear·er (bâr′ər), *n.* **1.** a person or thing that carries, supports, or brings. **2.** the person who presents an order for money or goods: *Pay to the bearer.*

bear·ing (bâr′iṅg), *n.* **1.** the manner in which a person conducts or carries himself: *a man of dignified bearing.* **2.** the act, capability, or period of producing or bringing forth: *The tree is past bearing.* **3.** reference or relation: *The joke had no bearing on the story he was telling.* **4.** the direction to or from a given point. **5.** Often, **bearings.** understanding of one's position or situation: *I lost my bearings in the tunnel.* **6.** a support or guide for a moving part of a machine, esp. one that reduces friction for a rotating part.

beast (bēst), *n.* **1.** any animal other than man, esp. a large, four-footed mammal. **2.** a cruel, coarse person.

beast·ly (bēst′lē), *adj.,* **beast·li·er, beast·li·est. 1.** of or like a beast. **2.** *British Informal.* nasty; disagreeable: *beastly weather.* —**beast′li·ness,** *n.*

beast′ of bur′den, an animal used to carry heavy loads or pull heavy equipment, as a mule or ox.

beat (bēt), *v.,* **beat; beat·en** or **beat; beat·ing. 1.** to give a series of blows to; strike again and again: *to beat a piece of metal; to beat a drum.* **2.** to thrash very hard as punishment. **3.** to flutter or flap in or against: *The bird beat the air with its wings.* **4.** to stir vigorously: *to beat eggs.* **5.** to make (a path) by repeated walking. **6.** to overcome in a contest; defeat: *Our basketball team beat last year's champions.* **7.** to be better than: *Making reservations beats standing in line.* **8.** to throb or pulsate: *His heart beat quickly.* **9.** to mark (musical time or accent) with or as if with a baton. —*n.* **10.** a stroke or blow. **11.** the sound made by one or more such blows: *the beat of drums.* **12.** a throb or pulsation: *a pulse of 60 beats per minute.* **13.**

act, āble, dâre, ärt; ebb, ēqual; if, īce; hot, ōver, ôrder; oil; book; ooze; out; up, ûrge; ə = *a* as in *alone*; ə as in *button* (but′ºn), *fire* (fiºr); chief; shoe; thin; that; zh as in *measure* (mezh′ər). See full key inside cover.

the ticking sound a clock or watch makes. **14.** an assigned or regular route: *The policeman's beat included 20 blocks.* **15.** meter, pulse, or accent in music. **16.** a unit of time in music. —*adj. Informal.* **17.** very tired; exhausted: *I was beat after the hike.* **18.** of or concerning beatniks. **19. beat around the bush.** See bush (def. 3). **20. beat back** (or **off**), to force to withdraw; drive back: *to beat back an enemy attack; to beat off mosquitoes.* **21. beat it,** *Slang.* to leave without delay: *We'd better beat it before the storm begins.* **22. beat time,** to mark the rhythm of a musical composition with strokes of the hand, a metronome, etc.: *We took turns beating time to the record.* —**beat′a·ble,** *adj.*

beat·en (bēt′ən), *adj.* **1.** formed or shaped by blows; hammered: *a pin made of beaten silver.* **2.** used often: *a beaten path.* **3.** defeated or overcome: *the beaten team.* **4.** (of food) whipped up or pounded: *beaten egg whites.*

beat·er (bē′tər), *n.* **1.** a person or thing that beats. **2.** a utensil for beating food: *an egg beater.* **3.** (in hunting) a person who drives game out from hiding.

be·a·tif·ic (bē′ə tif′ik), *adj.* giving or showing bliss, saintliness, or happiness; blissful: *a beatific smile.*

be·at·i·fy (bē at′ə fī′), *v.,* **be·at·i·fied, be·at·i·fy·ing. 1.** to make blissfully happy. **2.** (in the Roman Catholic Church) to declare (a dead person) to be among the blessed in heaven. —**be·at·i·fi·ca·tion** (bē at′ə fə kā′-shən), *n.*

beat·ing (bē′tiṅ), *n.* **1.** the act of a person or thing that beats; whipping: *Give the rug a good beating.* **2.** a defeat: *The enemy suffered a beating.*

be·at·i·tude (bē at′ə tood′, -tyood′), *n.* **1.** supreme blessedness or happiness. **2. the Beatitudes,** the declarations of blessedness pronounced by Jesus in the Sermon on the Mount.

beat·nik (bēt′nik), *n.* a person who avoids conventional behavior, dress, etc.

beau (bō), *n., pl.* **beaus** *or* **beaux** (bōz). **1.** a man who is courting a woman. **2.** a man who pays a great deal of attention to the way he dresses; dandy. [from a French word meaning "handsome, beautiful," which comes from Latin *bellus* "beautiful"]

Beau·mont (bō′mont), *n.* a city in SE Texas.

beau·te·ous (byoo′tē əs), *adj.* beautiful: used esp. in literature. —**beau′te·ous·ly,** *adv.*

beau·ti·cian (byoo tish′ən), *n.* a person who manages or who works in a beauty parlor.

beau·ti·ful (byoo′tə fəl), *adj.* **1.** very pleasing to the senses or mind; pretty: *beautiful weather; a beautiful story.* **2.** excellent of its kind: *The basketball player made a beautiful shot.* —**beau′ti·ful·ly,** *adv.*

beau·ti·fy (byoo′tə fī′), *v.,* **beau·ti·fied, beau·ti·fy·ing.** to make or become beautiful: *a plan to beautify the park.* —**beau·ti·fi·ca·tion** (byoo′tə fə kā′shən), *n.*

beau·ty (byoo′tē), *n., pl.* for defs. 2, 3 **beau·ties. 1.** a quality in a person or thing that pleases the senses or mind. **2.** a beautiful person or thing, esp. an attractive girl or woman. **3.** a certain advantage: *the beauties of living in the country.*

beau′ty par′lor, a place where women can go for hairdressing, manicuring, and other beauty treatments. Also, **beau′ty shop′.**

bea·ver (bē′vər), *n., pl.* **bea·vers** *or* for def. 1 **beaver. 1.** a furry mammal that has a broad, flat tail and builds dams across streams using trees it has cut down with its teeth. **2.** the fur of this animal.

be·calm (bi käm′), *v.* to deprive (a sailing vessel) of the wind necessary to move it: *The schooner was becalmed.*

Beaver
(total length
3½ ft.)

be·came (bi kām′), *v.* the past tense of **become.**

be·cause (bi kôz′), *conj.* **1.** for the reason that; due to the fact that: *I did not go to school yesterday because I was sick.* **2. because of,** due to; on account of: *The game was postponed because of rain.*

Bech·u·a·na·land (bech′oo ä′nə land′), *n.* the former name of **Botswana.**

beck (bek), *n.* **1.** a gesture motioning someone to come closer. **2. at someone's beck and call,** ready to carry out another person's wishes: *He kept me at his beck and call all afternoon.*

beck·on (bek′ən), *v.* **1.** to signal or summon (someone) with a gesture of the head or hand. **2.** to lure or entice.

be·cloud (bi kloud′), *v.* **1.** to darken or hide with clouds: *The top of the skyscraper was beclouded.* **2.** to make confused: *He beclouded the problem by discussing unrelated matters.*

be·come (bi kum′), *v.,* **be·came** (bi kām′), **be·come, be·com·ing. 1.** to come, change, or grow to be: *I became tired.* **2.** to be attractive or look nice on: *Your new coat becomes you.* **3.** to be suitable and proper for the position or responsibility of: *behavior that becomes a gentleman.* **4. become of,** to happen to: *Whatever became of your friend Joe?*

be·com·ing (bi kum′iṅg), *adj.* tending to suit or look well on: *a becoming dress.* —**be·com′ing·ly,** *adv.*

bed (bed), *n.* **1.** a piece of furniture upon which or within which a person sleeps. **2.** the act of or time for sleeping: *a cup of cocoa and then bed.* **3.** the use of a bed for a night; lodging: *five dollars for bed and breakfast.* **4.** any resting place: *a bed in the grass.* **5.** a part of a lawn or garden in which plants or flowers are grown. **6.** the bottom of a lake, river, etc. **7.** an area on the bottom of a body of water where plant or animal life grows: *an oyster bed.* **8.** a foundation surface of earth or rock supporting a track, pavement, or the like: *a road bed.* —*v.,* **bed·ded, bed·ding. 9.** to put to bed. **10.** to go to bed. **11.** to place in a bed or layer: *to bed oysters.*

be·daz·zle (bi daz′əl), *v.,* **be·daz·zled, be·daz·zling. 1.** to dazzle so as to blind or confuse: *The bright lights bedazzled us.* **2.** to impress very much: *The new folk singer bedazzled the audience.*

bed·bug (bed′bug′), *n.* a flat, biting insect that infests bedding.

bed·cham·ber (bed′chām′bər), *n.* a bedroom.

bed·clothes (bed′klōz′), *n.pl.* coverings for a bed, as sheets, blankets, pillowcases, etc.; bedding.

bed·ding (bed′ing), *n.* 1. another word for **bed-clothes.** 2. material used to make beds for animals, as litter, straw, etc.

be·deck (bi dek′), *v.* to decorate, esp. in a showy manner: *to bedeck the auditorium for the party.*

bed·fel·low (bed′fel′ō), *n.* 1. a person who shares one's bed. 2. a person who associates with another in order to gain an advantage for himself.

be·di·zen (bi dī′zən), *v.* to dress in a showy or gaudy way: *The horse was bedizened with feathers and spangles.*

bed·lam (bed′ləm), *n.* a scene of wild uproar and confusion. [from the Middle English word *Bethlehem,* which comes from *St. Mary of Bethlehem,* the name of a lunatic asylum in London]

Bed′ling·ton ter′rier (bed′ling tən), one of an English breed of terriers, having a thick, fleecy coat, and groomed to resemble a lamb.

Bed·ou·in (bed′oo in) *n., pl.* **Bed·ou·ins** or **Bed·ou·in.** 1. an Arab who lives in the deserts of Asia or Africa. 2. a nomad or wanderer.

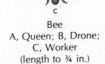

Bedlington
terrier

(15 in. high
at shoulder)

be·drag·gle (bi drag′əl), *v.,* **be·drag·gled, be·drag·gling.** to make limp and soiled, as with rain or dirt.

bed·rid·den (bed′rid′ʻn), *adj.* forced to remain in bed: *She was bedridden for a month after the operation.*

bed·rock (bed′rok′), *n.* the solid rock that exists underneath soil and loose rock fragments.

bed·roll (bed′rōl′), *n.* bedding that can be rolled up and carried, used for sleeping outdoors.

bed·room (bed′room′, -room′), *n.* a room furnished and used for sleeping.

bed·side (bed′sīd′), *n.* 1. the side of a bed, esp. as the place of one attending the sick. —*adj.* 2. at or for a bedside: *a bedside table.*

bed·spread (bed′spred′), *n.* an outer covering for a bed.

bed·stead (bed′sted′), *n.* the framework of a bed supporting the springs and mattress.

bed·time (bed′tīm′), *n.* the time to go to bed: *Her bedtime is ten o'clock.*

bee (bē), *n.* 1. an insect with four wings and, usually, a sting. Some kinds of bees live in hives and make honey. 2. a community social gathering in order to perform some task, engage in a contest, etc.: *a sewing bee; a spelling bee.* 3. **have a bee in one's bonnet,** to insist on talking about one subject; dwell on one idea repeatedly: *She's had a bee in her bonnet all year about building a new hospital.*

Bee
A, Queen; B, Drone;
C, Worker
(length to ¾ in.)

bee·bread (bē′bred′), *n.* a mixture of pollen and honey stored by bees to feed their young.

beech (bēch), *n.* 1. a tree having a smooth, gray bark and bearing small, sweet nuts. 2. the hard wood of this tree.

beech·nut (bēch′nut′), *n.* the sweet, triangular nut of the beech tree.

beef (bēf), *n., pl.* for def. 2 **beeves** (bēvz), for def. 3 **beefs.** 1. the flesh of a cow, steer, or bull for use as meat. 2. an adult cow, steer, or bull raised for its meat. 3. *Slang.* a complaint. —*v.* 4. to complain; grumble. 5. **beef up,** *Slang.* to give added strength or interest to: *to beef up a report with more facts.*

beef·steak (bēf′stāk′), *n.* a steak of beef for broiling or pan-frying.

beef·y (bē′fē), *adj.,* **beef·i·er, beef·i·est.** thickset or heavy: *He's too beefy to be a good athlete.*

bee·hive (bē′hīv′), *n.* 1. a hive for bees. 2. a crowded, busy place.

bee·line (bē′līn′), *n.* a direct course or route: *He made a beeline for the kitchen.*

been (bin), *v.* the past participle of **be.**

beep (bēp), *n.* 1. a short, usually high-pitched tone. —*v.* 2. to make a beeping sound. 3. to sound (a horn, warning signal, etc.).

beer (bēr), *n.* 1. an alcoholic drink made from malt and flavored with hops. 2. a soft drink made from roots, molasses or sugar, yeast, etc.: *root beer.*

bees·wax (bēz′waks′), *n.* 1. the yellow wax used by bees to make their honeycombs. 2. a similar wax made from paraffin.

beet (bēt), *n.* any of various plants, some having a red root used as a vegetable, others having a white root from which sugar is made.

Bee·tho·ven (bā′tō vən), *n.* **Lud·wig van** (lud′wig van, lood′wig), 1770–1827, German composer.

bee·tle¹ (bēt′ʻl), *n.* any of numerous kinds of insects whose wings are protected by hard cases when folded. [from the Old English word *bitela* "beetle," which is related to *bitan* "to bite"]

bee·tle² (bēt′ʻl), *n.* 1. a heavy wooden instrument used to hammer, beat, or mash: *Beetles are used to force down paving stones.* —*v.,* **bee·tled, bee·tling.** 2. to use a beetle on: *to beetle stakes into the ground.* [from the Old English word *bētl* "hammer"]

bee·tle³ (bēt′ʻl), *adj.* 1. projecting or overhanging: *beetle brows.* —*v.,* **bee·tled, bee·tling.** 2. to project or overhang; jut out: *a cliff that beetles over the sea.* [from the Middle English word *bitelbrowed* "having projecting brows, like a beetle's." See *beetle¹*]

Beetle
(length
⅓ in.)

beeves (bēvz), *n.* a plural of **beef.**

be·fall (bi fôl′), *v.,* **be·fell** (bi fel′), **be·fall·en, be·fall·ing.** 1. to happen or occur. 2. to happen or occur to: *An accident befell us.*

be·fit (bi fit′), *v.,* **be·fit·ted, be·fit·ting.** to be fitting or appropriate for; suit: *Her new dress befits the occasion.*

be·fog (bi fog′, bi fôg′), v., **be·fogged, be·fog·ging.** 1. to cover with or enclose in fog: *The airport was befogged for several days.* 2. to make unclear; confuse with unrelated or unimportant matters: *Personal differences befogged the campaign issues.*

be·fore (bi fôr′), adv. 1. in front; ahead: *He entered the room with guards walking before.* 2. in time preceding; previously: *I saw the movie once before.* 3. earlier or sooner: *I would have called before, but I couldn't find your number.* —prep. 4. in front of; ahead of: *He was before you in line.* 5. earlier than; previous to: *before the movie.* 6. in the future of: *The summer vacation is before us.* 7. in the presence or sight of: *to appear before an audience.* —conj. 8. previously to the time when: *He fed the dog before he left for school.* 9. rather than: *We will do it ourselves before accepting a favor from them.*

be·fore·hand (bi fôr′hand′), adv., adj. in advance; ahead of time: *I wish you had told me beforehand.*

be·friend (bi frend′), v. to make friends with or act as a friend to: *to befriend new neighbors.*

be·fud·dle (bi fud′əl), v., **be·fud·dled, be·fud·dling.** 1. to make drunk. 2. to confuse.

beg (beg), v., **begged, beg·ging.** 1. to ask for as a gift, as charity, or as a favor: *to beg forgiveness; to beg money.* 2. to ask earnestly or politely; implore: *He begged for a new bicycle. Sit down, I beg you.* 3. **beg off,** to ask to be excused from a promise or obligation: *He begged off taking me to the party. I'd like to go, but I have to beg off.*

be·gan (bi gan′), v. the past tense of **begin.**

be·gat (bi gat′), v. an old form of **begot,** used esp. in poetic and Biblical writings: *Abraham begat Isaac.*

be·get (bi get′), v., **be·got** (bi got′); **be·got·ten** or **be·got; be·get·ting.** 1. to be the father of; procreate: *to beget children.* 2. to cause; produce as an effect: *Hard work begets success.* —**be·get′ter,** n.

beg·gar (beg′ər), n. 1. a person who lives by begging. 2. an extremely poor person. —v. 3. to make very poor; impoverish. 4. to cause to seem very poor or inadequate: *The costume beggars description.*

beg·gar·ly (beg′ər lē), adj. like or befitting a beggar; inadequate: *a beggarly suit of clothes.*

be·gin (bi gin′), v., **be·gan** (bi gan′), **be·gun** (bi gun′), **be·gin·ning.** 1. to do the first or earliest part of some action; start: *I began the book yesterday.* 2. to come or cause to come into existence; originate: *The custom began a long time ago.*

be·gin·ner (bi gin′ər), n. a person who has very little experience or who is doing something for the first time: *She's a beginner at skiing.*

be·gin·ning (bi gin′iñg), n. 1. the earliest part; start. 2. the point of time when something begins: *the beginning of the war.* 3. the first cause; source: *the beginning of a disagreement.*

be·gone (bi gôn′), v. Archaic. go away!: *Begone with you!*

be·gon·ia (bi gōn′yə), n. a tropical plant having smooth leaves and small waxy flowers. [named after Michel *Bégon,* a 17th-century French patron of science]

be·got (bi got′), v. the past tense and a past participle of **beget.**

be·got·ten (bi got′ᵊn), v. a past participle of **beget.**

be·grime (bi grīm′), v., **be·grimed, be·grim·ing.** to make grimy or dirty.

be·grudge (bi gruj′), v., **be·grudged, be·grudg·ing.** 1. to envy the pleasure or good fortune of (someone): *She begrudged her the prize.* 2. to hesitate or be reluctant to give or grant: *We did not begrudge the time spent on the party.* —**be·grudg′ing·ly,** adv.

be·guile (bi gīl′), v., **be·guiled, be·guil·ing.** 1. to influence or take away by trickery: *to be beguiled of money.* 2. to distract pleasantly; charm: *The circus beguiled the whole family.* 3. to pass (time) pleasantly: *to beguile an evening with a good book.*

be·gun (bi gun′), v. the past participle of **begin.**

be·half (bi haf′), n. 1. **in** (or **on**) **behalf of,** as a representative for (another person, organization, etc.): *On behalf of my family, I thank you.* 2. **in** (or **on**) **someone's behalf,** in aid or support of (another person): *He spoke to the principal on my behalf.*

be·have (bi hāv′), v., **be·haved, be·hav·ing.** 1. to act in a particular way: *to behave badly.* 2. to conduct (oneself) properly; act correctly: *Behave yourself. He didn't behave, so he was taken home.*

be·hav·ior (bi hāv′yər), n. 1. a person's manner of behaving or acting: *His behavior has improved.* 2. the action or reaction of any material under certain circumstances: *the behavior of tin under intense heat.*

be·head (bi hed′), v. to cut off the head of.

be·held (bi held′), v. the past tense and past participle of **behold.**

be·hind (bi hīnd′), prep. 1. in back of: *The pen fell behind the sofa.* 2. late as compared with: *The train is behind schedule.* 3. in the state of making less progress than: *to fall behind one's class.* 4. supporting or promoting: *There were several people behind the plan.* —adv. 5. at or toward the rear: *to lag behind.* 6. in a place or time that is past: *We left one suitcase behind.* 7. not meeting a certain deadline or certain standards: *to be behind in rent; to be behind in one's school work.*

be·hold (bi hōld′), v., **be·held** (bi held′), **be·hold·ing.** to observe; look at; see: *They beheld the breathtaking sight. Behold, the king is approaching!*

be·hold·en (bi hōl′dᵊn), adj. obligated or indebted: *I feel beholden to you for your help.*

be·hoove (bi hōōv′), v., **be·hooved, be·hoov·ing.** to be necessary or proper for: *It behooves you to work hard if you want better grades.*

beige (bāzh), n. 1. a light grayish brown. —adj. 2. of the color beige: *a beige sweater.*

be·ing (bē′iñg), n. 1. the fact of existing; existence. 2. something that exists or lives; a living thing: *a human being.*

—**Usage.** *Being, being as,* or *being that* should never be used as a substitute for *since* or *because: Since* (not *Being*) *he's your friend, you call him.*

Bei·rut (bā rōōt′, bā′rōōt), n. a seaport and the capital city of Lebanon.

be·jew·el (bi jōō′əl), v., **be·jew·eled** or **be·jew·elled;**

be·jew·el·ing *or* **be·jew·el·ling.** to decorate with or as if with jewels: *The street was bejeweled with lights.*

be·la·bor (bi lā/bər), *v.* **1.** to discuss, work at, or worry about for an unreasonable amount of time: *He belabored the point for hours after we reached a decision.* **2.** to make fun of; ridicule: *to belabor a person's prejudices.* **3.** *Archaic.* to beat very hard.

be·lat·ed (bi lā/tid), *adj.* coming after the usual time: *belated birthday greetings.* —**be·lat/ed·ly,** *adv.*

be·lay (bi lā/), *v.,* **be·layed, be·lay·ing. 1.** to fasten (a rope) by winding around a pin or cleat or by attaching to an object offering stable support. **2.** to secure (a person) at one end of a rope. **3.** (used by sailors as a command) Stop!

belay/ing pin/, (on a sailing ship) a short, round bar of metal or wood to which a rope is fastened.

belch (belch), *v.* **1.** to eject gas from the stomach through the mouth. **2.** to gush forth violently: *The geyser belched water and steam.* —*n.* **3.** the act of belching.

Belaying pins

be·lea·guer (bi lē/gər), *v.* **1.** to surround with an army: *to beleaguer a city.* **2.** to surround with annoyances: *We beleaguered him with phone calls.*

Bel·fast (bel/fast), *n.* a seaport and the capital city of Northern Ireland, on the E coast.

bel·fry (bel/frē), *n., pl.* **bel·fries. 1.** a tower containing a bell, either attached to a building or standing apart. **2.** the part of a steeple or other structure in which a bell is hung.

Bel·gian (bel/jən), *n.* **1.** a native or inhabitant of Belgium. —*adj.* **2.** of or referring to Belgium or its people.

Bel·gium (bel/jəm), *n.* a kingdom in W Europe, bordering on the North Sea, N of France. 11,779 sq. mi. *Cap.:* Brussels.

Bel·grade (bel/grād), *n.* the capital city of Yugoslavia, in the E part, on the Danube River.

be·lie (bi lī/), *v.,* **be·lied, be·ly·ing. 1.** to show to be false; contradict: *His smile belied his rage.* **2.** to present falsely; misrepresent: *The article belied the facts.*

be·lief (bi lēf/), *n.* **1.** something believed; opinion: *It is my belief that we should accept the proposal.* **2.** confidence in the truth or existence of something without absolute proof. **3.** confidence, faith, or trust: *belief in one's friends.* **4.** a religious faith: *the Christian belief.*

be·lieve (bi lēv/), *v.,* **be·lieved, be·liev·ing. 1.** to have confidence in the truth of (something): *to believe a story.* **2.** to have confidence in the statement of (a person): *He jokes so much I don't know when to believe him.* **3.** to be more or less confident; suppose: *I believe he went to the movies.* **4. believe in, a.** to be convinced of the truth or existence of: *to believe in ghosts.* **b.** to have faith in the honesty or ability of: *I can help you only if you believe in me.* —**be·liev/a·ble,** *adj.* —**be·liev/a·bly,** *adv.* —**be·liev/er,** *n.*

be·lit·tle (bi lit/ʾl), *v.,* **be·lit·tled, be·lit·tling.** to con-

sider or make seem less important: *He belittled her good marks because he was jealous.*

Be·lize (be lēz/), *n.* a British crown colony in N Central America. 8867 sq. mi. *Cap.:* Belmopan. Former name, **British Honduras.** —**Be·liz/e·an,** *adj.; n.*

bell (bel), *n.* **1.** a hollow cup, usually of metal, that produces a ringing sound when its rim is struck. **2.** the stroke or sound of such an instrument. **3.** the expanding, open end of a woodwind or brass instrument. **4.** anything in the form of a bell. **5.** any of the half-hour units of time rung on the bell of a ship. —*v.* **6.** to put a bell on: *The cat was belled to warn birds.* **7.** to take or have the form of a bell. **8. ring a bell,** to cause a person to remember something: *Does that name ring a bell?* —**bell/-like,** *adj.*

Bell (bel), *n.* **Alexander Graham,** 1847–1922, U.S. scientist, born in Scotland: inventor of the telephone.

bel·la·don·na (bel/ə don/ə), *n.* **1.** a poisonous herb having purplish-red flowers and black berries. **2.** a drug from this herb, used to ease stomach spasms.

bell·boy (bel/boi/), *n.* a man who is employed to carry luggage, run errands, etc., at a hotel or club. Also, **bell·hop** (bel/hop/).

belle (bel), *n.* a woman or girl admired for her beauty and charm, esp. the most admired in a group.

bel·lig·er·ent (bə lij/ər ənt), *adj.* **1.** eager to fight; warlike: *a belligerent attitude.* **2.** engaged in war; fighting: *a battle between belligerent countries.* —*n.* **3.** a person or nation at war. —**bel·lig/er·ence,** *n.* —**bel·lig/er·ent·ly,** *adv.*

bel·low (bel/ō), *v.* **1.** to utter a hollow, loud animal cry: *The bull bellowed with rage.* **2.** to utter in a loud deep voice; roar: *He bellowed his answer across the room.* —*n.* **3.** the act or sound of bellowing.

bel·lows (bel/ōz), *n.* *(used as sing. or pl.)* an instrument for producing a strong current of air, as for fanning a fire or sounding a musical instrument, consisting of an air chamber that can be expanded to draw in air through a valve and contracted to expel the air through a tube or tubes.

bel·ly (bel/ē), *n., pl.* **bel·lies. 1.** the front or underside of an animal's body. **2.** the stomach. **3.** the abdomen. **4.** the inside of anything. **5.** a bulging surface: *the belly of a sail.* —*v.,* **bel·lied, bel·ly·ing. 6.** to swell out.

bel·ly·ache (bel/ē āk/), *Informal.* —*n.* **1.** a stomach ache. —*v.,* **bel·ly·ached, bel·ly·ach·ing. 2.** to complain or grumble: *to bellyache about too much work.* —**bel/ly·ach/er,** *n.*

be·long (bi lông/), *v.* **1.** to be in the correct or proper place: *The book belongs on the shelf.* **2. belong to, a.** to be a member or inhabitant of: *He belongs to the Boy Scouts.* **b.** to be the property of: *The blue coat belongs to her.* **c.** to be a part of: *The red blouse belongs to the plaid suit.*

be·long·ings (bi lông/ingz), *n.pl.* the things a person owns; possessions.

be·lov·ed (bi luv/id, bi luvd/), *adj.* **1.** greatly loved: *a beloved friend.* —*n.* **2.** a person who is greatly loved.

be·low (bi lō′), *adv.* **1.** in or toward a lower place or level: *From the mountain top we could see the valley below.* —*prep.* **2.** lower than in place, rank, degree, amount, etc: *below the knee; below 10 dollars.*
belt (belt), *n.* **1.** a band of leather, cloth, or other material for encircling the waist. **2.** any encircling band, strip, or stripe. **3.** a long area or region characterized by certain products or activities: *the cotton belt; the farm belt.* **4.** an endless flexible band passing around two or more pulleys, used to transmit motion or carry materials. —*v.* **5.** to furnish with a belt. **6.** to fasten by means of a belt: *He belted his trousers.* **7.** *Slang.* to give a hard blow to; hit.
be·moan (bi mōn′), *v.* to moan over; bewail or lament: *He bemoaned his loss.*
bench (bench), *n.* **1.** a long, often backless seat for several persons: *a park bench.* **2.** a long table for work with tools or machinery; workbench: *a carpenter's bench.* **3.** a seat occupied by judges. **4.** the office and dignity of a judge or of judges as a group. **5.** (in sports) the players usually used as substitutes on a team. —*v.* **6.** (in sports) to remove (a player) from a game: *to bench the pitcher.*
bend (bend), *v.,* **bent** (bent), **bend·ing. 1.** to force (an object, esp. a long or thin one) from a straight shape into a curved or angular shape or from a curved shape into some other shape: *to bend a piece of wire to make an arch.* **2.** to become curved or crooked: *The road bends just ahead.* **3.** to take a bent posture; stoop: *to bend down and touch one's toes.* **4.** to cause to submit or follow: *He bent us to his will, and we did what he said.* **5.** to submit or follow; yield: *to bend in the face of strong opposition.* **6.** to turn in a particular direction: *to bend one's steps toward home.* —*n.* **7.** a bent thing or part; curve or crook: *a bend in the road.* **8. the bends,** Also, **caisson disease.** an acutely painful, paralyzing condition resulting from bubbles of nitrogen in the blood. It is caused by too rapid reduction in the pressure of the air being breathed, as when a skin diver comes to the surface too rapidly. **9. bend over backward** (or **backwards**), to make every effort; do the utmost: *I've bent over backward trying to please her.* —**bend′a·ble,** *adj.*
bend·ed (ben′did), *v.* **1.** an old form of **bent,** used esp. in poetic writing. —*adj.* **2. on bended knee,** on one's knees, or on one knee; kneeling.
be·neath (bi nēth′), *adv.* **1.** below; in or to a lower place or position: *We could hear the trains rumbling beneath.* —*prep.* **2.** below or under: *two families living beneath the same roof.* **3.** further down or lower than: *A captain is beneath a major.* **4.** below the dignity of: *Cheating is beneath her.*
Ben·e·dict (ben′i dikt), *n.* Saint, A.D. 480?–543?, Italian monk: founded the Benedictine order.
Ben·e·dic·tine (ben′i dik′tēn), *n.* **1.** a member of an order of monks or nuns leading a religious life according to the rules of St. Benedict. —*adj.* **2.** of or referring to St. Benedict or the Benedictines.
ben·e·dic·tion (ben′i dik′shən), *n.* **1.** the act of saying a blessing, esp. at the close of a religious service. **2.** the blessing itself: *The bishop gave a benediction.*

ben·e·fac·tion (ben′ə fak′shən), *n.* **1.** the act of doing good or giving a benefit. **2.** charitable donation: *to provide benefactions for earthquake victims.*
ben·e·fac·tor (ben′ə fak′tər), *n.* a person who gives a benefit or money; kindly helper: *A generous benefactor gave him his start in the world.* Also, *referring to a woman,* **ben·e·fac·tress** (ben′ə fak′tris).
be·nef·i·cent (bə nef′i sənt), *adj.* doing good or resulting in good; showing kindness in action or purpose: *a beneficent act.* —**be·nef′i·cence,** *n.*
ben·e·fi·cial (ben′ə fish′əl), *adj.* giving benefit; helpful; advantageous: *Sunshine is beneficial to living things.* —**ben′e·fi′cial·ly,** *adv.*
ben·e·fi·ci·ar·y (ben′ə fish′ē er′ē, -ə rē), *n., pl.* **ben·e·fi·ci·ar·ies.** a person who receives a benefit, advantage, or money: *His wife is the beneficiary of his life insurance.*
ben·e·fit (ben′ə fit), *n.* **1.** anything that is helpful or for the good of a person or thing: *She explained the benefits of the new library. Did you do that for my benefit?* **2.** a performance in a theater, or some other entertainment given to raise money for charity. —*v.,* **ben·e·fit·ed** *or* **ben·e·fit·ted; ben·e·fit·ing** *or* **ben·e·fit·ting. 3.** to do good to; be of help to: *a discovery that will benefit all mankind.* **4.** to get a benefit or advantage; profit: *to benefit from new information.*
be·nev·o·lence (bə nev′ə ləns), *n.* **1.** the desire to do good to others; good will; charitableness: *to be filled with benevolence toward others.* **2.** an act of kindness; charitable gift.
be·nev·o·lent (bə nev′ə lənt), *adj.* **1.** desiring to do good to others; kind: *a benevolent old man.* **2.** marked by or showing good will and kindly feelings: *a benevolent smile.* —**be·nev′o·lent·ly,** *adv.*
Ben·gal (ben gôl′, ben′gəl), *n.* **1.** a former province in NE India: now divided between India and Bangladesh. **2. Bay of,** a part of the Indian Ocean between India and Burma. about 1000 mi. wide.
Ben·ga·li (ben gä′lē), *n.* **1.** a native or inhabitant of Bengal. **2.** the modern language of Bengal, belonging to the Indic branch of the Indo-European family. —*adj.* **3.** of or concerning Bengal, its people, or their language: *a Bengali custom.*

be·night·ed (bi nī′tid), *adj.* **1.** mentally or morally ignorant; not enlightened: *a benighted time of fear and superstition.* **2.** overtaken by darkness of night.
be·nign (bi nīn′), *adj.* **1.** having a kindly personality; gentle and gracious: *a benign uncle.* **2.** showing or caused by gentleness or kindness: *a benign smile.* **3.** favorable or lucky: *benign omens.* **4.** pleasant and mild; healthful: *a benign climate.* —**be·nign′ly,** *adv.*
Be·nin (be nēn′), *n.* a republic in W Africa. 43,483 sq. mi. *Cap.:* Porto Novo. Former name, **Dahomey.** —**Be·ni·nese** (be′ni nēz′), *n., adj.*
Ben·ja·min (ben′jə mən), *n.* (in the Bible) the

youngest son of Jacob and Rachel: founder of one of the 12 tribes of ancient Israel.

bent (bent), *v.* **1.** the past tense and past participle of **bend.** —*adj.* **2.** curved or crooked: *a bent stick.* **3.** determined or resolved; set (usually fol. by *on*): *a boy bent on going to sea.* —*n.* **4.** a natural interest or inclination: *to have a bent for art.*

bent·wood (bent′wŏŏd′), *n.* **1.** wood that has been steamed and bent for use in furniture. —*adj.* **2.** noting furniture made mostly of pieces of wood steamed, bent, and screwed together.

be·numb (bi num′), *v.* **1.** to make numb; cause to be without feeling: *fingers benumbed by cold.* **2.** to make incapable of action: *The sight of the tiger benumbed her.*

ben·zene (ben′zēn, ben zēn′), *n.* a flammable liquid obtained from coal tar and used in making chemicals and as a solvent.

ben·zine (ben′zēn, ben zēn′), *n.* a flammable liquid obtained by distilling petroleum and used chiefly in dry cleaning.

be·queath (bi kwēth′, bi kwēth′), *v.* **1.** to give (property) in one's will: *He bequeathed his house to his daughter.* **2.** to hand down; pass on: *The senior class bequeathed us their mascot.* —**be·queath′al,** *n.*

be·quest (bi kwest′), *n.* **1.** the act of leaving or giving property in one's will: *I have a bequest to make to my nephew.* **2.** the property that is given in a will; legacy: *This necklace was a bequest from my aunt.*

be·rate (bi rāt′), *v.*, **be·rat·ed, be·rat·ing.** to scold or rebuke.

be·reave (bi rēv′), *v.*, **be·reaved** *or* **be·reft** (bi reft′); **be·reav·ing.** to take away from by death or violence: *Illness bereaved them of their mother. The war bereaved them of their home.* —**be·reave′ment,** *n.*

be·reft (bi reft′), *v.* **1.** a past tense and past participle of **bereave.** —*adj.* **2.** deprived: *You must be bereft of your senses to act that way.*

be·ret (bə rā′, ber′ā), *n.* a soft, round cap that has no brim or visor, and fits snugly on the head.

berg (bûrg), *n.* an iceberg.

ber·i·ber·i (ber′ē ber′ē), *n.* a severe disease that causes paralysis of the limbs and either swelling or wasting away of the body. It is caused by a lack of the proper foods.

Ber′ing Sea′, a part of the N Pacific Ocean, N of the Aleutian Islands. 878,000 sq. mi.

Ber′ing Strait′, a strait between Alaska and the Soviet Union in Asia, connecting the Bering Sea and the Arctic Ocean. 36 mi. wide.

Berke·ley (bûrk′lē), *n.* a city in W California, on San Francisco Bay.

ber·ke·li·um (bər kē′lē əm), *n. Chem.* a man-made, radioactive, metallic element. *Symbol:* Bk

Ber·lin (bər lin′), *n.* a city in E East Germany and former capital of Germany: now divided into a western zone (**West Berlin**), a state of West Germany, and an eastern zone (**East Berlin**), the capital of East Germany.

Ber·mu·da (bər myŏŏ′də), *n.* a group of islands in the Atlantic Ocean, 580 miles east of North Carolina: a British colony. 19 sq. mi. *Cap:* Hamilton. —**Ber·mu′dan, Ber·mu·di·an** (bər myŏŏ′dē ən), *n., adj.*

Bern (bûrn), *n.* the capital city of Switzerland, in the W part. Also, **Berne.**

ber·ry (ber′ē), *n., pl.* **ber·ries. 1.** any of numerous kinds of small, juicy fruits, as the blueberry, strawberry, or gooseberry. **2.** the dry seed of certain plants: *coffee berries.* —*v.,* **ber·ried, ber·ry·ing. 3.** to gather or pick berries: *Do you want to go berrying?* —**ber′ry·like′,** *adj.*

ber·serk (bər sûrk′, bər zûrk′), *adj.* **1.** being in a violent frenzy; out of control; completely enraged: *The berserk horse kicked down his stall and escaped.* **2. go berserk,** to give way to a sudden, violent rage: *The sergeant went berserk and attacked his own men.*

berth (bûrth), *n.* **1.** a shelflike sleeping place for one person on a ship, train, plane, etc. **2.** a place for a ship to stay either at anchor or at a wharf. **3.** a job or position. **4. give a wide berth to,** to go out of one's way to avoid; shun: *He gives a wide berth to that laundry since they lost his shirts.*

ber·yl (ber′əl), *n.* a mineral having some varieties that are valued as gems.

be·ryl·li·um (bi ril′ē əm), *n. Chem.* a light, metallic element used chiefly in copper alloys to make springs. *Symbol:* Be

be·seech (bi sēch′), *v.,* **be·sought** (bi sôt′) *or* **be·seeched; be·seech·ing. 1.** to ask, beg, or implore urgently; entreat: *We beseech you to send aid before it is too late.* **2.** to beg eagerly for: *to beseech help.* —**be·seech′er,** *n.* —**be·seech′ing·ly,** *adv.*

be·seem (bi sēm′), *v. Archaic.* to be worthy of; be fitting or proper for: *It does not beseem a young lady to repeat gossip.*

be·set (bi set′), *v.,* **be·set, be·set·ting. 1.** to attack on all sides; assail; harass: *Angry complaints beset him wherever he went.* **2.** to surround; hem in: *We found ourselves beset by bramble bushes.* **3.** to set or place upon: *a crown beset with jewels.*

be·set·ting (bi set′ing), *adj.* constantly attacking or undermining with temptation: *His besetting sin is greed.*

be·side (bi sīd′), *prep.* **1.** by or at the side of; near: *Stand beside me.* **2.** compared with: *Beside the snow they're having up north this is nothing.* **3.** apart or away from; not connected with: *Your comments are beside the point.* **4. beside oneself,** almost out of

---

act, āble, dâre, ärt; ebb, ēqual; if, īce; hot, ōver, ôrder; oil; bŏŏk; ōōze; out; up, ûrge; ə = *a* as in *alone;* ə as in *button* (but′ən), *fire* (fīər); chief; shoe; thin; ᴛʜat; zh as in *measure* (mezh′ər). See full key inside cover.

one's senses, as from fear, anxiety, etc.: *He was beside himself with rage after that argument.*
—**Usage.** *Beside* usually indicates physical closeness or similarity: *She walked beside me. Beside my snowman his was nothing.* It should not be used in place of *besides* to mean "in addition to": *Besides roses there were hyacinths and daisies.*

be·sides (bi sīdz/), *adv.* 1. moreover; furthermore: *I don't really want to go out, and besides I promised to wait here.* 2. in addition: *There's plenty of cake and some cookies besides.* 3. otherwise; else: *They had a roof over their heads but not much besides.* —*prep.* 4. over and above; in addition to: *Besides my homework I have to do the dishes.* 5. other than; except: *There's no one here besides Bill and me.*
—**Usage.** See **beside.**

be·siege (bi sēj/), *v.*, **be·sieged, be·sieg·ing.** 1. to lay siege to; surround and attack: *For a whole summer their armies besieged the city.* 2. to bother or annoy with requests, problems, or the like: *The reporters besieged the mayor with questions.* —**be·sieg/er,** *n.*

be·smear (bi smēr/), *v.* 1. to smear all over: *to besmear the wall with jam.* 2. to soil or sully: *to besmear someone's good reputation.*

be·smirch (bi smûrch/), *v.* 1. to soil or discolor: *Mud besmirched his new suit.* 2. to harm or sully: *Gossip had besmirched his reputation.*

be·som (bē/zəm), *n.* a broom, esp. one made of brush or twigs.

be·sot (bi sot/), *v.*, **be·sot·ted, be·sot·ting.** 1. to make drunk; stupefy with drink: *The wine besotted him.* 2. to make stupid or foolish: *a mind besotted with superstition.* —**be·sot/ted·ly,** *adv.*

be·sought (bi sôt/), *v.* a past tense and past participle of **beseech.**

be·span·gle (bi spang/gəl), *v.*, **be·span·gled, be·span·gling.** to cover with spangles or something that sparkles like a spangle: *Dewdrops bespangled the grass.*

be·spat·ter (bi spat/ər), *v.* to soil by spattering; splash with water, dirt, etc.: *The taxi bespattered his trousers.*

be·speak (bi spēk/), *v.*, **be·spoke** (bi spōk/); **be·spo·ken** (bi spō/kən) *or* **be·spoke; be·speak·ing.** 1. to ask for in advance: *to bespeak the audience's patience.* 2. to reserve beforehand: *to bespeak a seat in the theater.* 3. to show or indicate: *This gift bespeaks love.*

be·spoke (bi spōk/), *v.* 1. the past tense and a past participle of **bespeak.** —*adj.* 2. spoken for; engaged to be married.

be·spo·ken (bi spō/kən), *v.* 1. a past participle of **bespeak.** —*adj.* 2. engaged to be married; bespoke.

Bes/se·mer proc/ess (bes/ə mər), a process for making steel in which impurities are removed by forcing a blast of air through molten iron. [named after Sir Henry *Bessemer* (1813–1898), English engineer, its inventor]

best (best), *adj.*, *superlative of* **good** *with* **better** *as comparative.* 1. of the highest quality; excellent: *The best papers will be put up on the bulletin board.* 2. most desirable or helpful: *the best way.* 3. largest or most: *We spent the best part of the day fishing.*
—*adv.*, *superlative of* **well** *with* **better** *as comparative.* 4. most excellently; with most advantage or success: *Which sled coasts best?* 5. most fully; in or to the highest degree (usually used in combination): *best-known; best-loved.* —*n.* 6. a person or thing that is the best, finest, highest, etc.: *The best of us can make mistakes.* 7. the best or hardest effort: *We did our best.* 8. a person's most pleasant personality, greatest competence, etc.; best side: *She's at her best in the morning.* 9. best wishes or kindest regards: *Give my best to your father.* 10. **at best,** under the most favorable conditions or circumstances: *At best the paint job will take a week.* 11. **get the best of,** to defeat or subdue: *He got the best of me in every match.* 12. **had best,** ought to: *You had best wear your raincoat.* 13. **make the best of,** to manage as well as one can under the circumstances: *to make the best of a bad bargain.*

bes·tial (bes/chəl, best/yəl), *adj.* brutal or beastly; inhuman: *bestial treatment of prisoners.* —**bes·ti·al·i·ty** (bes/chē al/i tē, bes/tē al/i tē), *n.* —**bes/tial·ly,** *adv.*

be·stir (bi stûr/), *v.*, **be·stirred, be·stir·ring.** to stir up; rouse to action; get going (often used reflexively): *to bestir oneself in the morning.*

be·stow (bi stō/), *v.* 1. to present as a gift or prize; give or confer: *The trophy was bestowed on the winner.* 2. to put to some use; apply: *the time that one bestows on study.*

be·strew (bi strōo/), *v.*, **be·strewed; be·strewed** *or* **be·strewn** (bi strōon/); **be·strew·ing.** 1. to strew or cover (a surface): *sidewalks bestrewed with paper.* 2. to scatter or strew about: *The children bestrewed flowers in front of the bride.*

be·stride (bi strīd/), *v.*, **be·strode** (bi strōd/) *or* **be·strid** (bi strid/); **be·strid·den** (bi strid/ʰn) *or* **be·strid; be·strid·ing.** 1. to get or be astride of; straddle: *to bestride a horse.* 2. to step over or across with long strides: *to bestride puddles in the street.*

bet (bet), *v.*, **bet** *or* **bet·ted; bet·ting.** 1. to wager or risk (something) on the chance that one has correctly guessed some future event, usually in return for a similar wager by someone who makes an opposite guess: *I'll bet a dollar they miss their train.* 2. to place a wager: *Do you want to bet?* —*n.* 3. an act or instance of betting: *We made a bet.* 4. something that is risked in betting: *My bet is two dollars.* 5. someone or something that looks likely to win, happen, or turn out well: *He's our best bet in the spelling contest.*

be·take (bi tāk/), *v.*, **be·took** (bi took/), **be·tak·en** (bi tā/kən), **be·tak·ing.** to cause to go (usually used reflexively): *I must betake myself to the market.*

be/ta par/ticle (bā/tə), an electron ejected from the nucleus of an atom.

be·think (bi thingk/), *v.*, **be·thought** (bi thôt/), **be·think·ing.** 1. to cause (oneself) to think or consider: *He bethought himself a moment.* 2. to cause (oneself) to remember or recall: *He bethought himself of his needy family.*

Beth·le·hem (beth/lē əm, beth/li hem/), *n.* a town

in Israeli-occupied Jordan, near Jerusalem: birthplace of David and Jesus.

be·tide (bi tīd′), v., **be·tid·ed, be·tid·ing. 1.** to happen or befall; come to: *May woe betide him!* **2.** to come to pass; happen: *Whatever betides, stay well.*

be·times (bi tīmz′), adv. **1.** early; at a good hour: *He was up betimes and out milking the cows.* **2.** within a short time; soon: *We shall visit you again betimes.*

be·to·ken (bi tō′kən), v. **1.** to show or indicate; give a sign or evidence of: *His cold look betokened anger.* **2.** to show (something) to be likely; promise or threaten: *This cold weather betokens snow.*

be·took (bi tŏŏk′), v. the past tense of **betake.**

be·tray (bi trā′), v. **1.** to give over or expose to the enemy by disloyalty or treachery: *to betray one's country.* **2.** to be unfaithful or disloyal in guarding or keeping; reveal disloyally: *to betray a secret.* **3.** to reveal by accident; show: *That laugh betrayed her real feelings.* **4.** to fail to fulfill or live up to: *He betrayed our faith in him.* **5.** to mislead or deceive: *to be betrayed by overconfidence.* —**be·tray′er,** n.

be·tray·al (bi trā′əl), n. **1.** the act of betraying: *We were shocked by his betrayal of our plans.* **2.** the state of being betrayed: *The betrayal of our fortress forced us to retreat.*

be·troth (bi trōth′, bi trôth′), v. to promise in marriage; arrange for the engagement of (usually used passively): *His daughter is betrothed to a young man from the next town.*

be·troth·al (bi trō′thəl, bi trô′thəl), n. the act or state of being betrothed: *We celebrated their betrothal.*

be·trothed (bi trōthd′, bi trôtht′), adj. **1.** engaged to be married. —n. **2.** the person one is engaged to.

bet·ted (bet′id), v. a past tense and past participle of **bet.**

bet·ter (bet′ər), adj., *comparative of* **good** *with* **best** *as superlative.* **1.** of superior or higher quality: *This coat is better than that one.* **2.** of greater value, use, suitability, etc.: *Tomorrow the ice will be better for skating.* **3.** larger or greater: *She spent the better part of her lifetime fighting for women's rights.* **4.** stronger or healthier: *You'll feel better soon.* —adv., *comparative of* **well** *with* **best** *as superlative.* **5.** in a superior way or manner: *Try to behave better.* **6.** more completely or thoroughly: *He knows the way better than I do.* **7.** more, greater, or farther: *She walked better than a mile.* —v. **8.** to make better; improve: *to better one's grades.* —n. **9.** something that has greater excellence, value, usefulness, or the like: *the better of two choices.* **10. better off,** happier or in better circumstances: *You'd be better off admitting your mistake.* **11. for the better,** in an improved way: *His health has changed for the better.* **12. get the better of,** get the advantage over; defeat: *to get the better of a rival.* **13. had better,** would be wiser or more sensible; should: *You had better get out of those wet clothes.* **14. think better of,** to reconsider: *I started to object, but thought better of it.*

bet·ter·ment (bet′ər mənt), n. **1.** the act or state of getting better; improvement: *We are hoping for some betterment in the situation.* **2.** something that improves; improvement: *The addition of the gymnasium is a betterment to the school.*

bet·tor (bet′ər), n. a person who bets or makes a wager.

be·tween (bi twēn′), prep. **1.** in or into the space separating (two places, objects, persons, etc.): *The cat ran between the buildings.* **2.** linking or connecting: *a highway between two cities.* **3.** within the range separating (two times, amounts, degrees, etc.); intermediate to: *between 5 and 6 o'clock.* **4.** by joint action or sharing of: *Between them they ate up the cake.* **5.** distinguishing one from another: *What is the difference between them?* **6.** indicating one or the other of: *to make a choice between two desserts.* —adv. **7.** in the space or time separating: *two doors with a window between.* **8. between you and me,** in confidence; confidentially: *Between you and me, he's sure to win.* **9. in between,** in the space or time between two things: *You'll see two buildings and a parking lot in between.* [from the Old English word *betwēonan,* which comes from *be* "by" + *twēon* "two each"]

—**Usage.** See **among.**

be·twixt (bi twikst′), prep., adv. **1.** *Archaic.* between. **2. betwixt and between,** neither the one nor the other; in an unsettled or undecided condition: *The starting time is still betwixt and between.*

bev·el (bev′əl), n. **1.** the slant or slope of an inclined or tilted surface; a slanting edge, as on a ruler. **2.** a tool, resembling a try square, with a movable blade for checking that bevels are at the correct angle. —v., **bev·eled** *or* **bev·elled; bev·el·ing** *or* **bev·el·ling. 3.** to cut or slant at a bevel: *to bevel an edge to prevent splintering.*

Bevel (def. 2)

bev·er·age (bev′ər ij, bev′rij), n. a drink of some kind, esp. other than water: *As beverages we serve coffee, tea, and milk.* [from the Old French word *bevrage,* which comes from Latin *bibere* "to drink"; see *-age*]

bev·y (bev′ē), n., pl. **bev·ies. 1.** a flock of birds, esp. of quail or larks. **2.** a group, esp. of girls or women: *A bevy of relatives was waiting for him at the station.*

be·wail (bi wāl′), v. to express or show deep sorrow for; lament; mourn: *to bewail the loss of a friend.*

be·ware (bi wâr′), v., **be·wared, be·war·ing. 1.** to be careful, cautious, or wary of: *Beware the dog.* **2.** to be wary, careful, or on guard: *Beware of thieves.*

be·wil·der (bi wil′dər), v. to confuse or puzzle completely; perplex: *It bewildered her when all of us shouted different instructions.* —**be·wil′der·ing,** adj.

be·wil·der·ment (bi wil′dər mənt), n. a state of confusion or puzzlement: *The small girl just stood there in bewilderment, wondering which way to go.*

be·witch (bi wich′), v. **1.** to use witchcraft or magic on; cast a spell over: *The princess was bewitched and turned into a deer.* 2. to delight or enchant; charm; fascinate: *His sense of humor bewitches people.* —be·witch′ing·ly, *adv.*

be·yond (bē yond′), *prep.* 1. on or to the farther side of: *Beyond those trees you'll find his house.* 2. farther on than; more distant than: *They went beyond the last human settlements.* 3. outside the understanding, limits, or reach of: *Algebra is still beyond me.* 4. superior to; above: *wise beyond all others.* 5. more than; over and above: *He talked beyond the time allowed.* —*adv.* 6. farther on or away: *We walked to the drugstore and beyond.* —*n.* 7. **the beyond,** the afterlife: *Man cannot see into the beyond.*

Bhu·tan (bōō tän′), *n.* a kingdom in the Himalayas, NE of India: foreign affairs guided by India. about 18,000 sq. mi. *Cap.:* Thimbu. —Bhu·tan·ese (bōōt′ə nēz′), *n., adj.*

Bi, *Chem.* the symbol for bismuth.

bi-, a prefix meaning 1. two: *bicycle; biplane.* 2. twice or doubly: *biannual.* 3. every two: *biweekly.*

Bi·a·fra (bē ä′frə), *n.* a former secessionist state (1967–1970) in SE Nigeria, in W Africa. 29,484 sq. mi. *Cap.:* Enugu. —Bi·a′fran, *n., adj.*

bi·an·nu·al (bī an′yōō əl), *adj.* occurring twice each year; semiannual: *a biannual meeting.* —bi·an′nu·al·ly, *adv.*

—Usage. Because *biannual* is often confused with *biennial,* it is better replaced by *semiannual* or the phrase "twice each year."

bi·as (bī′əs), *n.* 1. a slanting or diagonal line, esp. across a woven fabric. 2. a prejudice or limited point of view: *He has a bias in favor of people from his own state.* —*adj.* 3. drawn, cut, folded, etc., on a diagonal across the weave of a fabric: *I want a bias cut for the pocket.* —*v.,* bi·ased *or* bi·assed; bi·as·ing *or* bi·as·sing. 4. to cause prejudice in a person: *Her lies biased me against her neighbors.* 5. **on the bias,** in a diagonal direction across a piece of material: *This cloth must be cut on the bias.*

bi·ased (bī′əst), *adj.* having or showing prejudice or bias: *Everyone knows that is a biased newspaper.*

bib (bib), *n.* 1. a cloth tied under the chin of a baby to keep it from soiling its clothes when it eats. 2. the upper part of an apron, covering the chest. [from the Middle English word *bibben* "to drink," which comes from Latin *bibere*]

Bi·ble (bī′bəl), *n.* 1. the collection of sacred writings of the Christian religion, comprising the Old and New Testaments. 2. the collection of sacred writings of the Jewish religion, comprising the Old Testament only. 3. the sacred writings of any other religion. [from the Greek word *biblia* "books," which comes from *byblos* "paper," from *Byblos,* the name of a city in Phoenicia noted for its trade in paper]

Bib·li·cal (bib′li kəl), *adj. (sometimes l.c.)* of or in the Bible: *Biblical studies; Biblical heroes.*

bib·li·og·ra·phy (bib′lē og′rə fē), *n., pl.* bib·li·og·ra·phies. 1. a list of readings on a particular subject: *a bibliography of articles on the care of tropical fish.* 2. a list of works by a particular author. 3. the study of the history of books and how they have been printed, published, etc. —bib′li·og′ra·pher, *n.*

bi·cam·er·al (bī kam′ər əl), *adj.* (of a legislative body) having two branches, chambers, or houses: *The U.S. Congress is bicameral.* [from *bi-* + the Latin word *camera* "chamber" + *-al*]

bi·car′bo·nate of so′da (bī kär′bə nit), a white, mildly alkaline powder used in cooking and in medicine. Also, **baking soda.**

bi·ceps (bī′seps), *n., pl.* bi·ceps *or* bi·ceps·es (bī′sepsiz). the muscle of the upper arm that bends the elbow. [from the Latin prefix *bi-* "two" + *caput* "head"]

bick·er (bik′ər), *v.* 1. to take part in a peevish argument; quarrel. —*n.* 2. peevish argument.

bi·cus·pid (bī kus′pid), *n.* a tooth having two points. The bicuspids are located on the sides of the jaws between the canines and the molars.

bi·cy·cle (bī′sik′əl), *n.* 1. a vehicle, usually for one person to ride upon, having two wheels, one in front and one in back, that turn together, a light metal frame, a saddlelike seat, pedals for turning the wheels, and handlebars for steering. —*v.,* bi·cy·cled, bi·cy·cling. 2. to ride a bicycle: *to bicycle in the park.* —bi′cy·clist, bi′cy·cler, *n.*

bid (bid), *v.,* bade (bad) *or* bad (bad) for defs. 1, 2, 5 *or* bid for defs. 3, 4; bid·den (bid′ᵊn) *or* bid for defs. 1, 2, 5 *or* bid for defs. 3, 4; bid·ding. 1. to command or order; direct: *The king bids you depart.* 2. to say as a greeting, farewell, or good wish: *We bade him good-by.* 3. to make an offer of (a price) to buy something or as the cost of doing a job: *She bid $30 for the china at the auction.* 4. to make an offer to buy something or do a job: *to bid for a painting.* 5. to invite; summon or direct by invitation: *We bade the strangers enter.* —*n.* 6. a price offered: *That's my final bid.* 7. an invitation: *a bid to join a club.* 8. an attempt to get something: *a bid for attention.* —bid′der, *n.*

bid·da·ble (bid′ə bəl), *adj.* willing to do what is asked; obedient; docile: *a gentle, biddable horse.*

bid·ding (bid′ing), *n.* 1. a command or summons: *I went there at his bidding.* 2. the act or process of making bids: *The bidding was fast and furious.*

bide (bīd), *v.,* bid·ed *or* bode (bōd); bid·ed; bid·ing. 1. *Archaic.* to wait or endure; abide. 2. **bide one's time,** to wait for a favorable opportunity or moment: *He's biding his time until he can escape.*

bi·en·ni·al (bī en′ē əl), *adj.* 1. happening every two years: *a biennial exhibition of paintings.* 2. lasting for two years, as the life cycle of some plants. —*n.* 3. any event occurring once in two years. 4. a biennial plant. —bi·en′ni·al·ly, *adv.*

bier (bēr), *n.* a frame or stand on which a corpse, or coffin containing a corpse, is laid before burial.

bi·fo·cal (bī fō′kəl), *adj.* 1. (of an eyeglass lens) having two portions, one for seeing things that are close and one for seeing things at a distance. —*n.* 2. **bifocals,** eyeglasses with bifocal lenses.

big (big), *adj.,* **big·ger, big·gest.** 1. large, as in size, height, width, amount, etc.; huge; immense: *a big office building.* 2. important; of major importance: *a big problem.* 3. boastful or conceited; haughty: *a big talker.* 4. generous and kind: *a big heart.* 5. grown-up or mature: *a big girl.* —**big′ness,** *n.*

big·a·my (big′ə mē), *n., pl.* **big·a·mies.** the act of remarrying when one already has a legal spouse: *He was arrested for bigamy.* See also **monogamy, polygamy.** —**big′a·mist,** *n.* —**big′a·mous,** *adj.*

Big′ Dip′per. See under **dipper** (def. 2).

big·horn (big′hôrn′), *n., pl.* **big·horns** or **big·horn.** a large wild sheep of the Rocky Mountains having massive, curling horns.

bight (bīt), *n.* 1. the middle, loop, or bent part of a rope, as distinguished from the ends. 2. a curve or indentation in the shoreline of a sea or river. 3. a body of water, as a bay, bounded by a curve in the shoreline.

Bighorn
(3½ ft. high at shoulder; horns to 3½ ft.)

big·ot (big′ət), *n.* a person who is completely prejudiced against any religion, belief, or race that is not his own. [from an Old French name applied by the French to the Normans, which comes from the Old English phrase *bi God* "by God"]

big·ot·ed (big′ə tid), *adj.* intolerant of another person's beliefs, race, religion, etc.: *a bigoted writer.*

big·ot·ry (big′ə trē), *n., pl.* **big·ot·ries.** 1. complete prejudice against any religion, belief, or race that is not one's own. 2. an instance of such prejudice.

big′ tree′, a large sequoia tree of California.

bike (bīk), *Informal.* —*n.* 1. a bicycle. —*v.,* **biked, bik·ing.** 2. to ride a bicycle.

bike·way (bīk′wā′), *n.* a road esp. suitable for bicycle riding.

bi·lat·er·al (bī lat′ər əl), *adj.* 1. indicating or affecting both the right and left sides of a structure, plant, animal, etc. 2. having two sides; two-sided. 3. indicating or affecting both sides in an agreement, contract, or the like: *bilateral truce arrangements.* —**bi·lat′er·al·ly,** *adv.*

bile (bīl), *n.* 1. a bitter yellow or greenish liquid produced by the liver that aids in digesting fats; gall. 2. bad temper or peevishness: *full of spite and bile.*

bilge (bilj), *n.* 1. the curved, bottom part of a ship. 2. Also, **bilge′ wa′ter.** the water that seeps into the bottom of a ship. 3. *Slang.* utter nonsense; rubbish.

bil·ious (bil′yəs), *adj.* 1. of or like bile. 2. caused by an excess of bile. 3. peevish or irritable: *a bilious mood.* —**bil′ious·ly,** *adv.* —**bil′ious·ness,** *n.*

bill¹ (bil), *n.* 1. a statement of money owed: *The store sends out bills on the first of the month.* 2. a piece of paper money worth a specified amount: *a ten-dollar bill.* 3. a proposal for a new law that has been presented to a legislature but not yet passed: *The President just sent a new tax bill to Congress.* 4. a written or printed public notice or advertisement: *to post a bill on a wall.* 5. any written list: *a bill of expenses.* 6. scheduled entertainment; program: *a good bill at the movies.* —*v.* 7. to send a bill to: *We'll bill you later.* 8. to list in a bill. 9. to advertise in a bill. 10. **fill the bill,** to be exactly what a person wants or needs: *This new floor wax really fills the bill.* [from the Latin word *bulla* "notice"] —**bill′a·ble,** *adj.* —**bill′er,** *n.*

bill² (bil), *n.* the horny mouth parts of a bird. [from the Old English word *bille*]

bill·board (bil′bôrd′), *n.* a board, usually outdoors, on which large advertisements or notices are posted: *The new billboards have spoiled the view along the highway.*

Bill

bil·let¹ (bil′it), *n.* 1. lodging for soldiers in nonmilitary buildings. —*v.,* **bil·let·ed, bil·let·ing.** 2. to lodge or quarter: *to billet troops in a house.* [from the medieval Latin word *billetta* "notice." See *bill¹*]

bil·let² (bil′it), *n.* 1. a small chunk of wood, esp. one cut for fuel. 2. a narrow, generally square bar of steel. [from the French word *billette* "small log"]

bill·fold (bil′fōld′), *n.* a folding leather case for carrying money; wallet.

bil·liards (bil′yərdz), *n. (used as sing.)* a game played with hard balls that are driven with a long stick called a cue on a cloth-covered table.

bil·lion (bil′yən), *n., pl.* **bil·lions** or (after a numeral) **bil·lion.** 1. (in the United States and France) a number that is one thousand times one million (1,000,000,000). 2. (in Great Britain and Germany) a number that is one million times one million (1,000,000,000,000). 3. this many or about this many persons or things: *A billion will be spent on construction next year.* —*adj.* 4. amounting to one billion in number: *a billion dollars.*

bil·lionth (bil′yənth), *adj.* 1. being number one billion in a series: *the billionth revolution of the engine.* —*n.* 2. one of a billion equal parts. 3. a person or thing that is number one billion.

bill′ of fare′, a list of foods that are served; menu.

Bill′ of Rights′, the first ten amendments to the Constitution of the United States, which guarantee the fundamental rights of the people, freedom of speech, the right to assemble and bear arms, etc.

bil·low (bil′ō), *n.* 1. a great wave or surge of the sea: *The small boat was tossed on the billows.* 2. anything that surges or moves like a wave: *billows of smoke.* —*v.* 3. to puff up, swell, or roll in or like billows: *The flags were billowing in the breeze.*

bil·low·y (bil′ō ē), *adj.*, **bil·low·i·er, bil·low·i·est.** of, like, or full of billows: *a rough, billowy sea.*

bil·ly (bil′ē), *n., pl.* **bil·lies.** a police officer's club or stick, usually made of wood.

bil′ly goat′, a male goat.

bi·month·ly (bī munth′lē), *adj.* **1.** occurring every two months: *bimonthly examinations.* —*n., pl.* **bi·month·lies. 2.** a publication that comes out once every two months: *Our class paper is a bimonthly.* —*adv.* **3.** every two months: *published bimonthly.* —**Usage.** Because *bimonthly* is sometimes used to mean "twice a month," it is generally less confusing to use *semimonthly* for this meaning and the phrase "every two months" in place of *bimonthly.*

bin (bin), *n.* a box or enclosed place for storing coal, grain, wood, or the like.

bi·na·ry (bī′ne rē), *adj.* **1.** consisting of or involving two components: *a binary star.* **2.** based upon the number 2: *binary numbers.*

bind (bīnd), *v.,* **bound** (bound), **bind·ing. 1.** to fasten, hold tight, or tie up with something, as a band or bond: *to bind sticks of wood together.* **2.** to cause to hold together firmly: *Ice bound the soil.* **3.** to bandage (often fol. by *up*): *to bind up a wound.* **4.** to obligate or compel by law, good sense, etc. (often used passively): *to be bound to tell the truth.* **5.** to be obligatory: *a promise that binds.* **6.** to fasten or hold together in a cover: *to bind a book in leather.* **7.** to cover the edge of with ribbon, tape, or the like: *to bind a hem.* **8.** (of clothes) to chafe or be too tight.

bind·er (bīn′dər), *n.* **1.** a person or thing that binds, such as a machine for tying together grain when it is mowed. **2.** a removable cover for loose papers.

bind·ing (bīn′diñg), *n.* **1.** something that binds or fastens. **2.** the outer covering for the leaves of a book: *My name is stamped on the binding.* **3.** a strip of material for edging a tablecloth, rug, etc. —*adj.* **4.** being an obligation: *a binding agreement.*

bin·na·cle (bin′ə kəl), *n.* a stand or case for holding or enclosing a ship's compass.

bin·oc·u·lar (bə nok′yə lər), *adj.* **1.** of, referring to, or for use by both eyes. —*n.* **2.** Usually, **binoculars.** a pair of small telescopes fitted side by side for use by both eyes; field glasses. [from *bi-* + the Latin word *oculus* "eye" + the suffix *-ar*]

bio-, a prefix meaning life or living: *biography; biology.*

bi·o·de·grad·a·ble (bī′ō di grā′də bəl), *adj.* that can decay by bacterial action and be absorbed by the environment.

Binnacle

bi·og·ra·pher (bī og′rə fər), *n.* a person who writes the story of someone else's life.

bi·o·graph·i·cal (bī′ə graf′i kəl), *adj.* **1.** of or about a person's life: *biographical facts for a book on Lincoln.* **2.** of or about biography: *biographical writing.* Also, **bi′o·graph′ic.** —**bi′o·graph′i·cal·ly,** *adv.*

bi·og·ra·phy (bī og′rə fē), *n., pl.* **bi·og·ra·phies. 1.** a

written account of another person's life: *a biography of Washington.* **2.** such writings taken together. **3.** the writing of people's life stories as an occupation: *a specialist in biography.* See also **autobiography.**

bi·o·log·i·cal (bī′ə loj′i kəl), *adj.* of or concerning biology: *biological studies; biological processes.* —**bi′o·log′i·cal·ly,** *adv.*

bi·ol·o·gy (bī ol′ə jē), *n.* the science that deals with living matter and all forms of plants and animals. —**bi·ol′o·gist,** *n.*

bi·on·ics (bī on′iks), *n.* *(used as sing.)* the study of how man and animals perform certain tasks and solve certain problems, and of the application of these findings to the design of computers and other electronic equipment. —**bi·on′ic,** *adj.*

bi·par·ti·san (bī pär′ti zən), *adj.* representing or supported by two opposing parties, esp. the Democratic and Republican parties.

bi·ped (bī′ped), *n.* **1.** a two-footed animal: *Chickens and geese are bipeds.* — *adj.* **2.** having two feet.

bi·plane (bī′plān′), *n.* an airplane with two sets of wings, one above the other.

birch (bûrch), *n.* **1.** a tree with smooth, white, paperlike bark. **2.** the hard, light-colored wood of this tree, used for making furniture.

bird (bûrd), *n.* any of numerous kinds of warmblooded, egg-laying animals having bodies covered with feathers and front limbs formed into wings.

bird·bath (bûrd′bath′), *n., pl.* **bird·baths** (bûrd′-baz̤z′, -baz̤hs′). a shallow basin, often on a stand, that is placed out of doors for birds to drink from or bathe in.

Bird (Pigeon)

A, Bill; B, Ear opening; C, Tail; D, Wing; E, Breast

bird′ dog′, any of various kinds of dogs trained to hunt or retrieve birds, such as pointers, setters, retrievers, etc.

bird·house (bûrd′hous′), *n., pl.* **bird·hous·es** (bûrd′-hou′ziz). **1.** a box for birds to live in, usually made of wood and resembling a small house. **2.** an aviary.

bird′ of par′adise, any of several kinds of birds of New Guinea, the males of which have colorful, elaborate plumage.

bird′ of prey′, any of various flesh-eating birds, such as eagles, hawks, vultures, etc.

bird·seed (bûrd′sēd′), *n.* a small seed or mixture of small seeds used for feeding caged birds.

bird's-eye (bûrdz′ī′), *adj.* **1.** seen from above, as by a bird in flight; sweeping; panoramic: *a bird's-eye view of the city.* **2.** having spots or markings that resemble birds' eyes; dotted: *bird's-eye tweed.*

bird′ watch′er, a person who observes and studies the habits, movements, etc., of wild birds.

Bir·ming·ham (bûr′miñg əm *for def. 1;* bûr′miñg-ham′ *for def. 2*), *n.* **1.** a city in central England: manufacturing center. **2.** a city in central Alabama.

birth (bûrth), *n.* **1.** the act or fact of being born or coming into being. **2.** the act of bearing or bringing forth offspring; childbirth. **3.** descent or family background: *of Italian birth; of noble birth.* **4.** any beginning or coming into being: *the birth of a new era.* **5.** **give birth to, a.** to bear (a child or other offspring): *Mrs. Jones gave birth to a little girl.* **b.** to start or begin: *The doctor's research gave birth to a new vaccine.*

birth·day (bûrth′dā′), *n.* **1.** the day on which someone was born. **2.** the day on which something began: *July 14, 1789, was the birthday of the French Revolution.* **3.** the anniversary of the day someone was born or something began.

birth·mark (bûrth′märk′), *n.* a mark on a person's skin since birth: *a strawberry birthmark on his neck.*

birth·place (bûrth′plās′), *n.* the place where someone was born or something began: *Greece was the birthplace of democracy.*

birth′ rate′, the relationship of the number of births to the total population of a given place. See also **death rate.**

birth·right (bûrth′rīt′), *n.* any right or privilege that a person has by birth: *Freedom is a birthright.*

birth·stone (bûrth′stōn′), *n.* a precious or semiprecious stone associated with a particular sign of the zodiac or month of the year, considered suitable for someone born under that sign or in that month.

Bis·cay (bis′kā, bis′kē), *n.* **Bay of,** a bay of the Atlantic Ocean between W France and N Spain.

bis·cuit (bis′kit), *n.* **1.** a kind of bread baked in small, soft cakes. **2.** a cookie or cracker. [from a French word meaning "twice cooked," which comes from *bis* "twice" + *cuire* "to cook"]

bi·sect (bī sekt′, bī′sekt), *v.* **1.** to cut or divide into two equal parts: *to bisect an orange.* **2.** to cross or intersect: *The railroad tracks bisect the highway.* —**bi·sec′tor,** *n.*

bish·op (bish′əp), *n.* **1.** a high clergyman who supervises a number of local churches or a sizable church district. **2.** a chess piece that is moved diagonally. See illus. at **chess.** [from Old English *bisceop,* which comes from Greek *episkopos* "overseer"]

bish·op·ric (bish′əp rik), *n.* the office of bishop, or the area in which a bishop has authority.

Bis·marck (biz′märk), *n.* **1. Otto von,** 1815–1898, German statesman: united the German states; first chancellor of Germany 1871–1890. **2.** the capital city of North Dakota, in the central part.

bis·muth (biz′məth), *n. Chem.* a heavy, metallic element. It is used in making alloys that melt at low temperatures, and its compounds are used in medicine. *Symbol:* Bi

bi·son (bī′sən, bī′zən), *n.,* *pl.* **bi·son.** a North American mammal resembling an ox but having shorter horns and a shaggy head, shoulders, and front legs. Also, **buffalo.**

Bison
(7 ft. high at shoulder)

bit¹ (bit), *n.* **1.** the part of a bridle, usually a bar of metal or hard rubber, that goes into the horse's mouth and is attached to the reins. **2.** the removable metal head of a drilling tool, such as a brace, that is used for boring holes. **3.** the cutting part of an ax or hatchet. [from the Old English word *bīte* "act of biting," which comes from *bītan* "to bite"]

bit² (bit), *n.* **1.** a small piece or amount of anything: *The pigeon ate up bits of bread.* **2.** a short time: *Wait a bit longer.* **3.** *Slang.* an amount equal to 12½ cents (used only in multiples of two): *Two bits is twenty-five cents.* **4.** a bit, rather; just a little: *a bit frightened.* **5. bit by bit,** by degrees; gradually: *Add the milk bit by bit.* [from the Old English word *bita* "bit, morsel," which comes from *bītan* "to bite"]

bit³ (bit), *v.* the past tense and a past participle of **bite.**

bitch (bich), *n.* a female dog.

bite (bīt), *v.,* **bit** (bit); **bit·ten** (bit′ᵊn) *or* **bit; bit·ing. 1.** to attack, grip, cut, or tear with the teeth: *The dog bit my arm.* **2.** to sting, as an insect does. **3.** to cause to smart or sting: *The icy wind bit their ears and noses.* **4.** (of fish) to take bait: *The fish aren't biting today.* **5.** to take a firm hold or dig into: *The drill bit into the wood.* —*n.* **6.** the act of biting. **7.** a wound made by a bite or sting: *a mosquito bite.* **8.** a cutting, stinging, or nipping effect: *the bite of an icy wind.* **9.** a piece bitten off. **10.** a small amount of food: *All I want is a bite.*

bit·ing (bī′ting), *adj.* **1.** nipping or smarting: *biting cold.* **2.** cutting or sarcastic: *a biting remark.* —**bit′ing·ly,** *adv.*

bit·ter (bit′ər), *adj.* **1.** having a harsh, rather biting taste; not sweet: *Unsweetened chocolate is bitter.* **2.** hard to bear; painfully sharp: *a bitter sorrow.* **3.** stinging or biting: *a bitter wind.* **4.** full of anger or resentment: *His suffering has made him bitter.* **5.** marked by or showing anger or resentment: *a bitter argument.* —**bit′ter·ly,** *adv.* —**bit′ter·ness,** *n.*

bit·tern (bit′ərn), *n.* a large marsh bird, related to the heron, noted for its loud, deep cry.

bit·ter·sweet (bit′ər swēt′), *n.* **1.** a climbing plant bearing orange capsules that open to reveal bright-red seeds. —*adj.* (bit′ər swēt′). **2.** both bitter and sweet to the taste: *bittersweet chocolate.* **3.** both pleasant and painful: *a bittersweet memory.*

bi·tu′mi·nous coal′ (bi tōō′mə nəs, -tyōō′-), a kind of coal that produces a yellow, smoky flame; soft coal. See also **anthracite.**

bi·valve (bī′valv′), *n.* a mollusk having two shells that are hinged together, such as the oyster or clam.

biv·ou·ac (biv′ōō ak′, biv′wak), *n.* **1.** a temporary military camp made with tents or improvised shelters. —*v.,* **biv·ou·acked, biv·ou·ack·ing. 2.** to make or

Bits¹
A, For wood
B, For metal

rest in such a camp: *Let's bivouac here for the night.*

bi·week·ly (bī wēk′lē), *adj.* 1. occurring every two weeks. —*n.* 2. a magazine or other periodical that is issued every two weeks. —*adv.* 3. every two weeks: *Our club will meet biweekly.*
—**Usage.** Because *biweekly* is sometimes used to mean "twice a week," it is generally less confusing to use *semiweekly* for this meaning and the phrase "every two weeks" in place of *biweekly.*

bi·zarre (bi zär′), *adj.* fantastically strange; odd: *a bizarre sense of humor; a large, bizarre hat.*

Bk, *Chem.* the symbol for berkelium.

bl., 1. bale; bales. 2. barrel; barrels.

blab (blab), *v.*, **blabbed, blab·bing.** 1. to reveal (secrets) by thoughtless talking: *He blabbed everything I told him.* 2. to talk or chatter constantly and thoughtlessly. —**blab′ber,** *n.*

black (blak), *adj.* 1. without color and not reflecting light, as the print on this page or coal: *a black dress.* 2. *(sometimes cap.)* of or concerning a people having dark skin and other Negroid characteristics, or their culture: *black literature.* 3. marked by an absence of light; full of darkness: *a black night.* 4. gloomy or dismal: *a black view of the world.* 5. angry or threatening: *a black look.* 6. evil or wicked: *a black deed.* — *n.* 7. the color opposite to white that does not reflect any light; the color of the print on this page or of coal. 8. *(sometimes cap.)* a member of a dark-skinned people, esp. a person of black African ancestry. 9. something that is black, such as black clothes or the black pieces in a checkers game. — *v.* 10. to blacken. 11. to put black polish on (shoes, boots, etc.): *to black boots.* 12. **black out, a.** to put out or conceal (lights) in defense against air raids. **b.** to become unconscious: *to black out at high altitudes from lack of oxygen.* [from the Old English word *blæc,* which is related to *blāc* "pale, colorless." See *bleach*] —**black′ness,** *n.*
—**Usage.** The term *black* is now preferred instead of *Negro* by many people.

black-and-blue (blak′ən blōō′), *adj.* bruised and discolored: *His shins were black-and-blue.*

black·ball (blak′bôl′), *n.* 1. a vote against a person, sometimes in the form of a black circle drawn on a piece of paper and dropped in a ballot box. —*v.* 2. to vote against (a person).

black·ber·ry (blak′ber′ē), *n., pl.* **black·ber·ries.** 1. the black or dark-purple fruit of several kinds of thorny bushes or vines. 2. a plant bearing this fruit.

black·bird (blak′bûrd′), *n.* any of numerous species of birds, the males of which have black feathers.

black·board (blak′bôrd′), *n.* a panel of smooth, hard material, usually of dark slate, used esp. in schools for writing or drawing on with chalk. Also, **chalkboard.**

black·en (blak′ən), *v.* 1. to make or become black; darken: *The sky suddenly blackened.* 2. to speak evil of; defame: *to blacken someone's reputation.*

black′ eye′, a dark bruise on the skin around the eye, caused by a blow, fall, or the like.

black′-eyed Su′san (blak′īd′), a kind of daisy, having a dark center and yellow petals.

black′ flag′, another name for Jolly Roger.

Black′ For′est, a wooded mountain region in SW West Germany.

black·guard (blag′ərd, blag′ärd), *n.* a low, mean person; scoundrel; rogue; villain.

black·head (blak′hed′), *n.* a dark-colored bit of hardened fatty matter in a pore of the skin.

Black′ Hills′, a group of mountains in W South Dakota and NE Wyoming. Highest point, Harney Peak, 7242 ft.

black·ing (blak′ing), *n.* black polish: *He put blacking on his shoes.*

black·jack (blak′jak′), *n.* 1. a small club having a flexible handle and a heavy, weighted head. 2. a large drinking mug, originally made of leather and coated with tar. 3. the game of twenty-one. —*v.* 4. to hit (someone) with a blackjack.

black·list (blak′list′), *n.* 1. a list of persons under suspicion, in disfavor, etc., often used to prevent such persons from getting certain

Blackjack (def. 2)

kinds of work: *For a while he was on the government's blacklist.* —*v.* 2. to put (someone) on a blacklist: *to blacklist a man for not paying his bills.*

black·mail (blak′māl′), *n.* 1. payment made or something done under force of threats, esp. a threat to reveal a secret: *The crook collected thousands of dollars in blackmail.* 2. an attempt to get money or special treatment or advantage by force of threats: *I wouldn't submit to his blackmail.* —*v.* 3. to threaten (someone) in order to get money or favorable treatment. [from *black* + the Scottish word *mail* "tribute, rent," which comes from Old English *māl* "agreement"] —**black′mail′er,** *n.*

black′ mar′ket, illegal trade in goods, as the selling of food secretly at high prices during wartime.

black·out (blak′out′), *n.* 1. complete darkness in an area as a result of all light being turned off or concealed, either because of a power failure or in order to deceive enemy planes in time of war. 2. the loss of consciousness, esp. temporarily.

black′ pow′der, an explosive made from saltpeter, sulfur, and charcoal: formerly used in gunnery, now principally used in fireworks.

Black′ Sea′, a sea between Europe and Asia, bordered by the Soviet Union, Turkey, Rumania, and Bulgaria. 164,000 sq. mi.

black·smith (blak′smith′), *n.* 1. a person who shoes horses or makes horseshoes. 2. a person who forges objects in iron.

black·snake (blak′snāk′), *n.* a large, harmless, dark-colored North American snake.

black′ stud′ies, a program of studies in black culture offered by a school or college, often including Afro-American history, black literature, jazz, and sometimes Swahili.

black·thorn (blak′thôrn′), *n.* 1. a European shrub whose thorny branches are used to make walking sticks. 2. a walking stick made of this.

black′ wid′ow, a small, black, poisonous spider having a red hourglass-shaped mark on the underside of its body.

blad·der (blad′ər), *n.* 1. the bag or sac into which urine passes from the kidneys before being excreted. 2. any similar thin-walled bag, such as the inflatable lining of a football or the air-filled sac in the body of a fish.

blade (blād), *n.* 1. the flat cutting part of a sword, knife, etc. 2. a leaf of grass or other similar plant. 3. a metal runner on an ice skate. 4. a thin, flat part of something, such as an oar or bone: *the shoulder blade.* 5. a thin piece of metal with one or two very sharp edges, used in a razor. —**blade′like′,** *adj.*

blame (blām), *v.,* **blamed, blam·ing.** 1. to place the responsibility for (a fault, wrong, error, etc.) on someone: *I blame the accident on her.* 2. to find fault with: *I don't blame you for getting angry.* —*n.* 3. the responsibility for a fault, wrong, error, etc.: *I'll take the blame.* 4. **to blame,** at fault; in the wrong: *Who is to blame for the defeat?* —**blam′a·ble,** *adj.*

blame·less (blām′lis), *adj.* free from blame; guiltless. —**blame′less·ly,** *adv.* —**blame′less·ness,** *n.*

blame·wor·thy (blām′wûr′thē), *adj.* deserving blame: *blameworthy behavior.*

Blanc (blängk), *n.* **Mont.** See **Mont Blanc.**

blanch (blanch), *v.* 1. to whiten by removing color; bleach: *to blanch linen in the sun.* 2. to make pale, as with sickness or fear: *The long illness had blanched her cheeks.* 3. to become white; turn pale: *She blanched at the very thought of diving from the high board.* 4. to dip (food) briefly into boiling water: *If you blanch peaches, they're easier to peel.*

bland (bland), *adj.* 1. mild and agreeable: *bland weather; a bland manner.* 2. uninteresting; dull: *a bland movie.* —**bland′ly,** *adv.* —**bland′ness,** *n.*

blan·dish (blan′dish), *v.* to use gentle flattery to coax (someone); cajole: *We blandished the guard into opening the gate.*

blan·dish·ment (blan′dish mənt), *n.* Often, **blandishments.** a flattering action, speech, etc.: *Despite his blandishments, Dad won't let him go to the dance.*

blank (blängk), *adj.* 1. having no writing, marks, or decoration; unmarked; empty: *a blank piece of paper; a blank wall.* 2. not completed or filled in: *a blank check.* 3. meaningless; empty: *long, blank days in prison.* 4. showing no interest or understanding: *a blank stare.* —*n.* 5. a place where something is lacking: *a blank in someone's memory.* 6. a space where something is to be filled in: *Write your answers in the blanks.* 7. a printed form having spaces to be filled in: *an application blank.* 8. a cartridge filled with gunpowder but with no bullet. —*v.* 9. to cross out or delete (usually fol. by *out*): *to blank out a question.* 10. **blank out,** to become unconscious: *I blanked out after my fall.* 11. **draw a blank,** to fail to remember or recognize something: *I should have known the answer, but I drew a blank.* —**blank′ly,** *adv.* —**blank′ness,** *n.*

blan·ket (blang′kit), *n.* 1. a large, usually rectangular piece of soft, warm cloth, used as a covering. 2. any deep covering: *a blanket of snow.* —*v.* 3. to cover with or as if with a blanket: *flowers blanketing the hillside.* [from an Old French word, which comes from *blanc* "white." See *blank*]

blare (blâr), *v.,* **blared, blar·ing.** 1. to give out a loud, harsh sound: *The trumpets blared.* 2. to sound loudly; proclaim noisily: *The radio blared the news.* —*n.* 3. a loud, harsh noise. —**blar′ing·ly,** *adv.*

blar·ney (blär′nē), *n.* 1. flattering or coaxing talk; flattery: *He's a master of the blarney.* —*v.,* **blarneyed, blar·ney·ing.** 2. to use blarney or achieve by blarney: *He'll blarney his way out of trouble.*

Blar′ney stone′, a stone in Blarney Castle in Ireland, said to give skill in flattery to those who kiss it.

blas·pheme (blas fēm′, blas′fēm), *v.,* **blas·phemed, blas·phem·ing.** 1. to speak of (God or sacred things) without respect or reverence. 2. to say impious things; curse. —**blas·phe·mous** (blas′fə məs), *adj.* —**blas′phe·mous·ly,** *adv.*

blas·phe·my (blas′fə mē), *n., pl.* **blas·phe·mies.** an irreverent act or statement concerning God or sacred things; profanity.

blast (blast), *n.* 1. a sudden and strong gust of wind. 2. a loud, sudden sound or noise: *the blast of a siren.* 3. a forceful stream of air, as one produced by a pump. 4. the act of exploding; explosion. —*v.* 5. to make a loud noise (on a trumpet, siren, etc.): *to blast the horn of one's car.* 6. to produce a loud, blaring sound: *The jukebox blasted.* 7. to cause to wither and die; ruin; destroy: *Frost blasted the farm's crops.* 8. to make, open up, break up, etc., by explosion: *to blast a tunnel through a mountain.* 9. **at full blast,** at the greatest speed or capacity: *The factory is operating at full blast.* 10. **blast off,** (of a rocket) to take off from a launch pad.

blast′ fur′nace, a large furnace for smelting iron that uses a blast of heated air to produce the high temperatures required.

bla·tant (blāt′ᵊnt), *adj.* 1. flagrantly obvious; impossible to miss: *a blatant lie.* 2. loud, noisy, or lacking in taste: *blatant colors.* —**bla′tant·ly,** *adv.*

blaze¹ (blāz), *n.* 1. a bright flame or fire: *a welcome blaze in the fireplace.* 2. a bright, hot gleam or glow: *a noonday blaze of sunlight.* 3. a sparkling brightness: *a blaze of diamonds.* 4. a sudden outburst, as of emotions: *a blaze of anger.* —*v.,* **blazed, blaz·ing.** 5. to burn brightly (often fol. by *away, up,* or *forth*): *The bonfire blazed away for hours.* 6. to shine like a flame or fire: *His face blazed with excitement.* **7.** to burn with or express a strong feeling (often fol. by *up*): *She blazed up at the insult.* **8.** to shoot steadily or continuously (often fol. by *away*): *The desperadoes blazed away at the sheriff.* [from the Old English word *blase* "torch"] —**blaz′ing·ly,** *adv.*

blaze² (blāz), *n.* **1.** a mark made on a tree to show a path or boundary in a forest. —*v.,* **blazed, blaz·ing. 2.** to mark or show with blazes: *to blaze a trail through the jungle.* **3.** to lead in forming or finding: *Columbus blazed the way for later explorers.* [related to the German word *blass* "pale"]

blaze³ (blāz), *v.,* **blazed, blaz·ing.** to make known; proclaim: *Headlines blazed the news.* [from an early Dutch word *blasen* "to blow"]

blaz·er (blā′zər), *n.* a lightweight sports jacket, usually having metal buttons.

bla·zon (blā′zən), *v.* **1.** to proclaim with a great show: *The posters blazoned the arrival of the circus.* **2.** to depict (a coat of arms). —*n.* **3.** a coat of arms.

bldg., building.

bleach (blēch), *v.* **1.** to make or become white by the action of chemicals or the sun: *to bleach shirts.* —*n.* **2.** a substance that makes things white, such as ammonia: *Add some bleach to the wash.* **3.** the act of bleaching. —**bleach′a·ble,** *adj.*

bleach·er (blē′chər), *n.* **1.** a person or thing that bleaches or whitens something. **2.** Usually, **bleachers.** a structure consisting of rows of benches, each row being set higher than the one in front: used esp. for viewing athletic events.

bleak (blēk), *adj.* **1.** bare and windswept: *a bleak and lonely plain.* **2.** cold and piercing; raw: *a bleak wind.* **3.** offering little or no hope; grim: *The outlook is bleak.* —**bleak′ly,** *adv.* —**bleak′ness,** *n.*

blear (blēr), *v.* **1.** to make (the eyes or sight) dim, as with tears or soreness: *The cold wind bleared his eyes.* —*adj.* **2.** (of the eyes) dim, as from tears.

blear·y (blēr′ē), *adj.,* **blear·i·er, blear·i·est. 1.** (of the eyes or sight) blurred or dimmed, as from sleep or tiredness: *He worked so long his eyes were bleary.* **2.** unclear or dim. —**blear′i·ly,** *adv.* —**blear′i·ness,** *n.*

bleat (blēt), *v.* **1.** to give out the cry of a sheep, goat, or calf, or a sound like such a cry: *to bleat from fright.* —*n.* **2.** the cry of a sheep, goat, or calf, or a sound like such a cry: *the bleat of auto horns.*

bleed (blēd), *v.,* **bled** (bled), **bleed·ing. 1.** to lose blood, as from a cut. **2.** to be wounded or die, as in battle. **3.** (of a plant) to have sap, resin, or the like, ooze out from a cut spot. **4.** (of dye or paint) to run: *The colors bled when I washed my dress.* **5.** to cause to bleed: *Doctors used to think that bleeding a patient would cure a disease.* **6.** to feel pity or sorrow: *Her heart bleeds at the sight of a lost animal.*

blem·ish (blem′ish), *n.* **1.** a defect or flaw: *a blemish on the skin; a blemish on one's record.* —*v.* **2.** to harm or spoil: *That lie will blemish his reputation.*

blench¹ (blench), *v.* to flinch or quail; shrink away: *He blenched at the sight of blood.* [from the Old English word *blencan*]

blench² (blench), *v.* to make or become pale or white: *Fear blenched his cheeks.* [another form of the word *blanch*]

blend (blend), *v.* **1.** to mix smoothly together: *First blend the sugar and butter.* **2.** to prepare by such a mixture: *This tea is blended by mixing two different kinds.* **3.** to fit harmoniously; go well: *This red rug doesn't blend with the walls.* —*n.* **4.** a mixture or kind produced by blending: *our own blend of coffee.* **5.** a word formed by putting together parts of other words. *Motel* is a blend of *motor* and *hotel.*

blend·er (blen′dər), *n.* **1.** a person or thing that blends. **2.** a kitchen appliance for mixing foods.

bless (bles), *v.,* **blessed** *or* **blest** (blest); **bless·ing. 1.** to make holy or consecrate by a religious ceremony or ritual: *The priest blessed the new church.* **2.** to favor or give benefit to: *Fortune blessed him with a long life.* **3.** to guard from harm or evil (usually used as an interjection): *Bless you!*

bless·ed (bles′id *for defs. 1, 2, 4;* blest *for def. 3*), *adj.* **1.** sacred or holy: *a blessed shrine.* **2.** worthy of reverence: *the blessed Trinity.* **3.** Also, **blest** (blest). divinely or supremely fortunate: *He is blessed with health.* **4.** bringing happiness or joy: *blessed peace.* —**bless′ed·ly,** *adv.* —**bless′ed·ness,** *n.*

bless·ing (bles′ing), *n.* **1.** the act of making a place or thing holy or consecrating it in a religious ceremony. **2.** a prayer of thanks or asking for God's favor, as grace said before a meal. **3.** a special benefit or advantage: *the blessings of liberty.* **4.** a benefit or advantage given by God. **5.** approval or backing: *This plan has the blessing of our teacher.*

blew (blōō), *v.* the past tense of **blow².**

blight (blīt), *n.* **1.** any disease of plants that causes them to wilt and often to die. **2.** any cause of harm or ruin: *Hunger was a blight on the land.* —*v.* **3.** to cause (plants) to wither and decay: *Frost blighted the orange grove.* **4.** to destroy or ruin: *Illness blighted his hopes.*

blimp (blimp), *n.* a dirigible balloon that has no supporting framework to make it rigid.

blind (blīnd), *adj.* **1.** unable to see; lacking the sense of sight. **2.** unwilling or unable to understand: *blind to someone else's point of view.* **3.** without reason or control: *a blind rage.* **4.** hidden from view: *a blind driveway that cannot be seen from the road.* **5.** having no outlets; closed at one end: *a blind alley.* **6.** done without seeing; using instruments alone: *blind flying in a fog.* —*v.* **7.** to make unable to see permanently or temporarily: *The bright light blinded me.* **8.** to take away reason or judgment: *Jealousy blinded her to the true facts.* **9.** to make shaded or dark. —*n.* **10.** something that limits vision or keeps out light: *Pull down the blinds.* **11.** something that hides or covers something else: *The hunters hid in a blind made of brush.* —*adv.* **12.** without the ability to see or to know what will happen: *They were driving blind in a snowstorm.*

blind·er (blīn′dər), *n.* a blinker for a horse that keeps him from seeing to the side.

blind·fold (blīnd′fōld′), *v.* **1.** to cover the eyes so that one cannot see: *You have to blindfold the player* *in the center of the circle.* —*n.* **2.** a cloth or the like used to cover the eyes: *to wear a blindfold.* —*adj.* **3.** with the eyes covered: *a blindfold game of tag.*

blind·ly (blīnd′lē), *adv.* **1.** in a blind manner: *We felt our way blindly in the dark.* **2.** without questioning or understanding: *to obey blindly.*

blind·man's buff (blīnd′manz′ buf′), a children's game in which a blindfolded player tries to catch and identify one of the other players. Also, **blind′man's bluff′.**

blind·ness (blīnd′nis), *n.* **1.** the state or fact of being unable to see. **2.** the state or fact of being unable to understand: *blindness to the needs of others.*

blink (blingk), *v.* **1.** to wink rapidly, esp. without meaning to: *The bright light made him blink.* **2.** to shine off and on: *The light blinked in the distance.* **3.** to cause something to blink: *We blinked our lights twice.* **4.** to ignore or overlook (often fol. by *at*): *to blink at small mistakes.* —*n.* **5.** the act of blinking. **6. on the blink,** *Slang.* not working properly; out of order: *The steam iron is on the blink again.*

blink·er (bling′kər), *n.* **1.** a person or thing that blinks, such as a light that flashes on and off. **2.** (on a bridle) either of two leather flaps that prevent a horse from seeing sideways.

bliss (blis), *n.* supreme happiness; perfect joy.

bliss·ful (blis′fəl), *adj.* full of or enjoying great happiness: *a blissful vacation; a blissful young woman.* —**bliss′ful·ly,** *adv.* —**bliss′ful·ness,** *n.*

blis·ter (blis′tər), *n.* **1.** a small pouch under the skin that contains a watery liquid. It is caused by a burn or by rubbing. **2.** any similar swelling, such as an air bubble or loose spot in a coat of paint. —*v.* **3.** to cause blisters on: *The sun blistered his nose.* **4.** to become blistered: *The paint is blistering.*

blithe (blīth, blĭth), *adj.* **1.** having a joyous, merry, or happy nature. **2.** thoughtless; heedless: *a blithe indifference to others' feelings.* —**blithe′ly,** *adv.*

blitz (blits), *n.* **1.** a sudden, all-out military attack. **2.** an all-out attack or rush of any sort: *a blitz of news stories on corruption in government.* [from a German word meaning "lightning war"]

bliz·zard (bliz′ərd), *n.* a heavy snowstorm, usually with a powerful wind and extreme cold.

bloat (blōt), *v.* to expand or swell; puff up: *Overeating bloated the horse's stomach.*

blob (blob), *n.* a small lump, drop, or spot of something, esp. a sticky lump: *a blob of paint.*

bloc (blok), *n.* a group having similar political needs and interests: *The farmers voted as a bloc.*

Blocks (def. 6)

block (blok), *n.* **1.** a solid mass of wood, stone, or the like, usually having at least one flat side: *a wall made of concrete blocks; toy blocks.* **2.** a mold or support on which something is shaped or kept in shape:

a hat block. **3.** an obstacle; something in the way; hindrance: *a traffic block.* **4.** a small section of a city or town that is bounded by streets on all sides: *a walk around the block.* **5.** one side of such a section: *I live on this block.* **6.** an assembly of one or more pulleys in a supporting frame. **7.** a collection of things treated as a unit: *This block of seats is reserved.* —*v.* **8.** to slow or stop (someone or something) by putting one or more obstacles in the way: *to block someone's path.* **9.** to shape or prepare something on or with a block: *to block hats.* **10. block out,** to cover or hide from view: *In a solar eclipse, the moon blocks out the light of the sun.*

block·ade (blo kād′), *n.* **1.** military control of all passage into or out of a city, island, area, or the like, esp. the use of ships to close off an enemy port. **2.** anything that obstructs passage or progress: *A blockade of bodyguards surrounded the President.* —*v.,* **block·ad·ed, block·ad·ing.** **3.** to set up a blockade of something: *to blockade an island.*

block·head (blok′hed′), *n.* a stupid person; dolt; dunce. —**block′head′ed,** *adj.*

block·house (blok′hous′), *n., pl.* **block·hous·es** (blok′hou′ziz). **1.** a small, fortified structure with ports or loopholes through which the defenders may fire weapons. **2.** (formerly) a building, usually made of timbers, having an upper story built out over the lower one and loopholes for firing muskets.

bloke (blōk), *n. British Slang.* fellow or guy; man: *Who is the bloke in the yellow hat?*

blond (blond), *adj.* **1.** light-colored; yellowish or pale: *blond hair; blond wood.* **2.** having light-colored hair and skin: *a blond man.* —*n.* **3.** a person having light-colored hair and skin. Also, *esp. referring to a woman or girl,* **blonde.**

blood (blud), *n.* **1.** the red liquid that circulates in the arteries, veins, and capillaries, carrying nutrients and oxygen throughout the body and transporting wastes from all parts of the body. **2.** the basis or source of life and energy. **3.** a person's state of mind; temperament: *a person of hot blood.* **4.** family background; descent: *royal blood.* **5.** *Chiefly British.* a high-spirited man; adventurer: *a dashing young blood.* **6. in cold blood,** deliberately and without feeling: *to kill someone in cold blood.*

blood′ bank′, a place where human blood is collected, stored, or distributed for use in blood transfusions.

blood·hound (blud′hound′), *n.* a large dog having long ears, loose skin, and an acute sense of smell.

Bloodhound
(26 in. high at
shoulder)

blood·less (blud′lis), *adj.* **1.** without blood or bloodshed: *bloodless surgery.* **2.** wan or pale: *bloodless cheeks.* **3.** having no spirit, zest, or energy: *a bloodless young man.* —**blood′less·ly,** *adv.*

blood′ pres′sure, the pressure exerted by the blood against the walls of the blood vessels.

---

act, āble, dâre, ärt; ebb, ēqual; if, īce; hot, ōver, ôrder; oil; bŏŏk; ōōze; out; up, ûrge; ə = *a* as in *alone*; ə as in *button* (but′ᵊn), *fire* (fīᵊr); chief; shoe; thin; ŧħat; zh as in *measure* (mezh′ər). See full key inside cover.

blood·shed (blud′shed′), *n.* 1. killing, as in war; slaughter: *The troops conquered the city without bloodshed.* 2. a loss of blood through an injury, wound, or the like.

blood·shot (blud′shot′), *adj.* (of the eyes) reddish, as a result of the widening of small blood vessels.

blood·suck·er (blud′suk′ər), *n.* any animal that feeds on blood, esp. a leech.

blood·thirst·y (blud′thûr′stē), *adj.* eager to shed blood or see blood shed; murderous: *a bloodthirsty criminal.* —**blood′thirst′i·ness,** *n.*

blood′ ves′sel, a vessel, as an artery, capillary, or vein, through which the blood passes.

blood·y (blud′ē), *adj.,* **blood·i·er, blood·i·est.** 1. stained with blood or bleeding: *Your knee is bloody.* 2. marked by bloodshed: *a bloody battle.* —*v.,* **blood·ied, blood·y·ing.** 3. to stain or smear with blood: *to bloody a handkerchief.* —**blood′i·ness,** *n.*

bloom (bloom), *n.* 1. the flower of a plant. 2. flowers, taken together: *the bloom of a cherry tree.* 3. the condition of having the buds open: *The roses are in bloom.* 4. a time of vigor and beauty: *the bloom of youth.* 5. a glow or flush showing health and vigor. 6. a whitish, powdery coating on the surface of certain fruits and leaves: *the bloom of a grape.* —*v.* 7. to produce flowers. 8. to flourish; do well: *a talent that has bloomed.*

bloom·ers (bloo′mərz), *n.* *(used as pl.)* 1. loose trousers gathered at the knee, formerly worn by women engaged in sports. 2. an undergarment for women, of similar design but gathered around the upper leg.

blos·som (blos′əm), *n.* 1. the flower of a plant. 2. the condition of being in flower: *The apple tree is in blossom.* —*v.* 3. to produce flowers: *The lilac is blossoming.* 4. to flourish or develop (often fol. by *into* or *out*): *She blossomed into a great beauty.*

blot (blot), *n.* 1. a spot or stain, esp. of ink. 2. a mark against oneself: *a blot on one's reputation.* —*v.,* **blot·ted, blot·ting.** 3. to spot or stain with a blot or blots: *to blot a page with ink.* 4. to cause a spot or stain: *The ink has blotted.* 5. to dry or remove with a blotter, cloth, etc.: *to blot spilled ink.* 6. **blot out, a.** to darken or cover over: *The moon blotted out the sun during the eclipse.* **b.** to erase, wipe out, or destroy: *Bombs blotted out the city.*

blotch (bloch), *n.* 1. a large spot or blot: *a blotch of paint on the floor.* 2. a skin blemish. —*v.* 3. to mark with blotches: *I blotched the tablecloth with gravy.*

blotch·y (bloch′ē), *adj.,* **blotch·i·er, blotch·i·est.** having blotches or blemishes: *blotchy skin.* —**blotch′i·ness,** *n.*

blot·ter (blot′ər), *n.* 1. a piece of blotting paper, used to blot ink, protect a desk top, or the like. 2. a book for recording events as they happen: *the police blotter.*

blouse (blous, blouz), *n.* 1. a garment for women or children, covering the neck or shoulders and extending to the waist. 2. a jacket, formerly part of the uniform of the U.S. Army. 3. a loose shirt, reaching to the hip or knees, and often belted.

blow¹ (blō), *n.* 1. a sudden, hard hit with a hand or weapon: *A blow to the head knocked him out.* 2. a sudden shock or disaster: *It was a terrible blow when he lost his property.* 3. **come to blows,** to begin to fight: *We separated them before they could come to blows.* [from the Middle English word *blaw*]

blow² (blō), *v.,* **blew** (bloo), **blown** (blōn), **blow·ing.** 1. (of wind or air) to move swiftly or forcefully: *It's blowing hard today.* 2. to carry by means of a current of air: *The breeze blew the smoke away.* 3. to be moved along by or as if by wind: *Dust blew across the field.* 4. to produce or give forth a current of air: *Blow on your hands to warm them.* 5. to clear or empty by forcing air through: *Blow your nose.* 6. to cause a horn to sound. 7. to give out sound: *The siren blew at noon.* 8. to burst, explode, burn out, or the like: *We blew a tire.* 9. to destroy by exploding: *Dynamite blew the bridge to bits.* 10. to shape by a current of air: *to blow bubbles.* —*n.* 11. a rush of air. 12. a windstorm or gale. 13. **blow out, a.** to put out (a flame) by blowing; extinguish: *to blow out a candle.* **b.** to burn out because of overloading: *A fuse blew out.* **c.** to burst by exploding: *The front right tire blew out.* 14. **blow over,** to pass away: *His anger soon blew over.* 15. **blow up, a.** to destroy by exploding: *to blow up a bridge.* **b.** to expand or enlarge: *to blow up a snapshot.* **c.** to lose one's temper: *He blew up because I was late.* **d.** to fill with air: *to blow up a tire.* [from the Old English word *blāwan* "to blow"]

blow·er (blō′ər), *n.* 1. a person or thing that blows. 2. a machine for supplying air, such as the fan in an air conditioner.

blow·gun (blō′gun′), *n.* a pipe or tube through which missiles, as poison darts, are blown by the breath. Also, **blowpipe.**

blown (blōn), *v.* 1. the past participle of **blow².** —*adj.* 2. swollen or expanded: *blown stomachs.* 3. out of breath; exhausted: *The horses were blown after that long run.*

blow·out (blō′out′), *n.* a sudden bursting, esp. of a tire.

blow·pipe (blō′pīp′), *n.* 1. a small tube through which air is blown to concentrate a flame or to make it hotter. 2. a long, metal tube used to gather and blow molten glass. 3. another word for **blowgun.**

blow·torch (blō′tôrch′), *n.* a device that produces a very hot flame from gasoline and air compressed by a built-in pump.

bls., 1. bales. 2. barrels.

blub·ber (blub′ər), *n.* 1. the thick layer of fat found under the skin of whales and other sea mammals. —*v.* 2. to weep noisily and openly.

Blowtorch

bludg·eon (bluj′ən), *n.* 1. a short, heavy club with one end weighted or thicker and heavier than the other. —*v.* 2. to strike with a bludgeon. 3. to force (someone) into something; bully: *They bludgeoned him into going.*

blue (bloo), *n.* 1. the pure color of a clear sky, usually between green and violet in the spectrum. 2. something having a blue color: *Put the blue next to the red.* 3. a person wearing or identified with blue: *The* *blues will play the grays.* —*adj.* **4.** of a blue color: *a blue dress.* **5.** (of the skin) discolored by cold, a bruise, or the like. **6.** depressed in spirits; dejected: *I'm lonely and blue.* **7. out of the blue,** suddenly; without warning: *They dropped in out of the blue.* —**blue′ness,** *n.* —**blu′ish, blue′ish,** *adj.*

blue·bell (blŌō′bel′), *n.* a plant with blue, bell-shaped flowers.

blue·ber·ry (blōō′ber′ē), *n., pl.* **blue·ber·ries. 1.** the small, round, bluish fruit of several kinds of low shrubs. **2.** a plant bearing this fruit.

blue·bird (blōō′bûrd′), *n.* a small North American songbird with mostly blue feathers.

blue·bot·tle (blōō′bot′ʾl), *n.* **1.** a large fly with an iridescent blue body. **2.** another word for **corn·flower.**

blue·fish (blōō′fish′), *n., pl.* **blue·fish·es** *or* **blue·fish.** a bluish or greenish food fish of the Atlantic coast.

Bluebird
(length 7 in.)

blue·grass (blōō′gras′), *n.* a grass having bluish-green stems.

blue-green (blōō′grēn′), *n.* **1.** a color about midway between blue and green. —*adj.* **2.** of the color blue-green.

blue·ing (blōō′ing), *n.* another spelling of **bluing.**

blue·jack·et (blōō′jak′it), *n.* a sailor.

blue′ jay′, a North American bird with a crested head and a blue back: noted for its raucous cry.

blue′ laws′, puritanical laws, originating in colonial New England, that forbid certain practices, esp. working or dancing on Sunday.

blue·print (blōō′print′), *n.* **1.** a photographic print, esp. of an architectural drawing, having white lines on a blue background. **2.** any plan: *a blueprint for victory.*

blue′ rib′bon, the highest award or prize: *The calf he raised won a blue ribbon at the state fair.*

Blue′ Ridge′, a mountain range extending SW from N Virginia to N Georgia: part of the Appalachian Mountains. Also, **Blue′ Ridge′ Moun′tains.**

blues (blōōz), *n.* **1.** *(used as pl.)* downheartedness; depression; low spirits. **2.** *(usually used as sing.)* a melancholy style of folk music that originated among American Negroes.

blue′ whale′, a bluish-gray whale: largest animal now living.

bluff¹ (bluf), *adj.* **1.** good-naturedly frank; hearty and outspoken: *a big, bluff, generous man.* **2.** having a large, rough, steep front, as a cliff. —*n.* **3.** a cliff, promontory extending into the sea, or hill with a broad, steep front. [perhaps from an early Dutch word *blaf* "broad, flat"]

bluff² (bluf), *v.* **1.** to mislead by a very good pretense, esp. a show of confidence: *He bluffed me into believing that I couldn't beat him.* **2.** to gain by bluffing or fooling someone with a show of confidence: *She bluffed her way into the job.* —*n.* **3.** the

act, instance, or practice of bluffing: *Her story was just a bluff.* **4.** someone who bluffs. **5. call someone's bluff,** to challenge a person to make good on a boast: *Next time I'm going to call his bluff and just see if he can do it.* [perhaps from the German dialect word *bluffen* "to bluster, frighten"]

blu·ing (blōō′ing), *n.* a chemical substance, as indigo, used to whiten clothes or give them a bluish tinge. Also, **blueing.**

blun·der (blun′dər), *n.* **1.** a large, stupid, or careless mistake: *What a blunder to arrive on the wrong day all dressed for a party!* —*v.* **2.** to act or move blindly or stupidly: *Without my glasses I blundered into the wrong room.* **3.** to bungle or botch: *Pray that she doesn't blunder this chance.* **4.** to make a stupid mistake.

blun·der·buss (blun′dər bus′), *n.* a gun of the 17th and 18th centuries with a funnel-shaped muzzle that scattered shot at close range.

blunt (blunt), *adj.* **1.** having a thick or dull edge or point; not sharp: *a blunt knife.* **2.** frank and to the point; abrupt: *a blunt, outspoken man; a blunt remark.* —*v.* **3.** to make blunt or dull: *You blunted the scissors by using them to cut rope.* **4.** to make insensitive or dull: *Exhaustion blunted his mind.* —**blunt′ly,** *adv.* —**blunt′ness,** *n.*

blur (blûr), *v.,* **blurred, blur·ring. 1.** to make dark or indistinct: *Fog blurred the outline of the buildings.* **2.** to make dull or insensitive; dim: *A hard fall blurred his vision for a few minutes.* **3.** to become confused, dark, or indistinct: *Everything blurred as the merry-go-round went faster and faster.* —*n.* **4.** a smudge or smear that dims or darkens: *a blur of smoke.* **5.** a dimmed, fuzzy, or darkened condition: *Everything was just a blur.* **6.** something that appears as an indistinct smudge: *The building was just a blur in the distance.* —**blur′ry,** *adj.*

blurt (blûrt), *v.* to say suddenly, often without thinking (often fol. by *out*): *to blurt out a secret.*

blush (blush), *v.* **1.** to redden, esp. in the face, from embarrassment: *She blushes when someone compliments her.* **2.** to feel shame or embarrassment: *I couldn't help but blush for him when he tried to sing.* —*n.* **3.** a reddening, esp. of the face, as a result of embarrassment. **4.** a rosy or pinkish tinge: *the first blush of morning light.* —**blush′ing·ly,** *adv.*

blus·ter (blus′tər), *v.* **1.** to be loud, noisy, or swaggering; make loud threats or protests: *He blusters a lot, but you mustn't take him seriously.* **2.** to force or get (something) by behaving in a loud, threatening manner: *He blustered his way into the meeting.* **3.** to roar and gust, as the wind: *The wind blustered through the old house.* —*n.* **4.** boisterous noise or noisy talk: *He's full of boasts and bluster.* —**blus′ter·y, blus′ter·ous,** *adj.*

blvd., boulevard.

bo·a (bō′ə), *n., pl.* **bo·as.** any of several species of snakes that kill their prey by squeezing with their coils, such as the python.

act, āble, dâre, ärt; ebb, ēqual; if, īce; hot, ōver, ôrder; oil; bŏŏk; ōōze; out; up, ûrge; ə = *a* as in *alone;* ʾ as in *button* (but′ʾn), *fire* (fīʾr); chief; shoe; thin; ŧħat; zh as in *measure* (mezh′ər). See full key inside cover.

bo′a constric′tor, a large boa of tropical America.

boar (bôr), *n.* **1.** a male hog or pig. **2.** a wild hog.

board (bôrd), *n.* **1.** a piece of wood sawed thin, and of greater length and breadth than thickness. **2.** a piece or sheet of wood, cardboard, paper, or the like, for some special use (sometimes used in combination): *a cutting board; a checkerboard.* **3.** a table, esp. to serve food on: *a board laden with ham and turkey.* **4.** daily meals, esp. when provided for pay: *You can find room and board downtown.* **5.** a flat surface or piece of material on which something may be posted: *a bulletin board.* **6.** an official group of persons who direct some activity or business: *a board of directors.* —*v.* **7.** to cover or close up with or as if with boards (often fol. by *up* or *over*): *to board up a house.* **8.** to furnish with meals or with meals and lodging, esp. for pay: *to board tourists.* **9.** to take one's meals, or be supplied with food and lodging, esp. at a fixed price. **10.** to go onto (a ship, train, airplane, etc.). **11. on board,** on or in a ship, train, or other vehicle: *We have to be on board by ten o'clock.*

Boa constrictor (length 10 ft.)

board·er (bôr′dər), *n.* a person, esp. a lodger, who is supplied with regular meals.

board·ing·house (bôr′diṅg hous′), *n., pl.* **board·ing·hous·es** (bôr′diṅg hou′ziz). a house at which one may obtain meals or meals and lodging, for payment: *a homey boardinghouse.* Also, **board′ing house′.**

board′ing ramp′. See **ramp** (def. 2).

board′ing school′, a school at which meals and lodging are provided for the pupils.

board·walk (bôrd′wôk′), *n.* a long area for walking, as along a beach, made of wooden boards.

boast (bōst), *v.* **1.** to speak with exaggeration and pride, esp. about oneself or someone or something connected with oneself; brag. **2.** to be proud of having or owning: *Our school boasts a new library.* —*n.* **3.** exaggerated speech; bragging: *empty boasts and threats.* **4.** something boasted or bragged about: *His boast is that he can fight better than anyone else on the block.* —**boast′er,** *n.* —**boast′ing·ly,** *adv.*

boast′ful (bōst′fəl), *adj.* **1.** tending to boast or brag: *a boastful person.* **2.** marked by boasting or exaggeration: *a boastful speech.* —**boast′ful·ly,** *adv.* —**boast′ful·ness,** *n.*

boat (bōt), *n.* **1.** a small vessel, used for traveling on water, that is moved by a pole, oars, sails, or a motor: *We want to get a boat to go fishing on the lake.* **2.** a ship, esp. a small one. **3.** a serving dish shaped somewhat like a boat: *a gravy boat.* —*v.* **4.** to go in a boat: *We boated down the river.* **5.** to transport in a boat. **6. in the same boat,** in the same situation or predicament: *None of us knew the way, so we were all in the same boat.* **7. miss the boat,** to miss an opportunity: *You missed the boat by not mailing your entry before the contest closed.*

boat·man (bōt′mən), *n., pl.* **boat·men. 1.** a person who is skilled in the use of boats. **2.** one who sells, rents, or works on boats.

boats·man (bōts′mən), *n., pl.* **boats·men.** another form of **boatman.**

boat·swain (bō′sən), *n.* an officer on a ship in charge of rigging, anchors, cables, etc. Also, **bosun.**

bob¹ (bob), *n.* **1.** a short, jerky motion: *a bob of the head.* —*v.,* **bobbed, bob·bing. 2.** to move quickly down and up: *He bobbed his head in agreement. The cork bobbed on the waves.* [from the Middle English word *bobben* "to move back and forth in the wind"]

bob² (bob), *n.* **1.** a style of short haircut for women and children. **2.** a horse's tail when cut short. **3.** a weight at the end of something, as on a pendulum or plumb line. **4.** a float on a fishing line. —*v.,* **bobbed, bob·bing. 5.** to cut short: *She bobbed her hair.* **6.** to try to snatch floating or dangling objects with the teeth: *to bob for apples.* [from the Middle English word *bobbe* "spray, cluster, bunch"]

bob·bin (bob′in), *n.* a reel or spool upon which yarn or thread is wound for use in spinning, machine sewing, lacemaking, etc.

bob·by (bob′ē), *n., pl.* **bob·bies.** *British.* a policeman. [named after Sir Robert *(Bobby)* Peel, who organized the London police force in 1828]

bob′by pin′, a flat, metal hairpin having the prongs close together.

bob·cat (bob′kat′), *n.* an American wildcat having brownish fur with black spots.

bob·o·link (bob′ə liṅgk′), *n.* a common North American songbird: named for the sound of its call.

Bobolink (length 7 in.)

bob·sled (bob′sled′), *n.* **1.** a sled having two pairs of runners, a brake, and a steering wheel. **2.** a sled made up of two short sleds, one behind the other. —*v.,* **bob·sled·ded, bob·sled·ding. 3.** to ride on a bobsled. —**bob′sled′der,** *n.*

bob·tail (bob′tāl′), *n.* **1.** a short tail, or a tail that has been cut short. **2.** a cat or other animal with such a tail. —*adj.* **3.** having a short tail: *a bobtail cat.*

bob·white (bob′hwīt′, -wīt′), *n.* a small North American quail named in imitation of its call. See illus. at **quail.**

bode¹ (bōd), *v.,* **bod·ed, bod·ing. 1.** to be a sign or omen of; foretell; portend: *The outbreak of war bodes evil times.* **2. bode ill,** to threaten something bad: *That stormy sky bodes ill.* **3. bode well,** to give a sign or promise of something good: *Your fever is down, and that bodes well.* [from the Old English word *bodian* "to announce"]

bode² (bōd), *v.* a past tense of **bide.**

bod·ice (bod′is), *n.* **1.** the part of a woman's dress that covers the body from the neck or shoulders to

Bodice

the waist. **2.** a woman's vest, tied with cross laces in the front.

bod·i·less (bod′ē lis), *adj.* having no body or material form: *bodiless phantoms.*

bod·i·ly (bod′ᵊlē), *adj.* **1.** of or referring to the body: *bodily aches and pains.* —*adv.* **2.** as a complete physical unit: *The tornado picked him up bodily and threw him across the road.*

bod·y (bod′ē), *n., pl.* **bod·ies. 1.** the physical structure of man or an animal, not including the head, limbs, or tail. **2.** a corpse or carcass: *Those buzzards are circling the body of some animal.* **3.** the main or central mass or part of a thing, such as the enclosed portion of an automobile or airplane. **4.** any solid object. **5.** the major portion of a group of people, such as an army or nation: *The body of the American people favors equal rights for all.* **6.** a group of people taken together: *the student body.* **7.** a separate physical being, mass, or quantity: *heavenly bodies.* **8.** richness or thickness: *a soup with body; a wine with body.* **9.** *Informal.* a person: *What's a body to do?*

bod·y·guard (bod′ē gärd′), *n.* a person or group of persons hired to accompany someone and protect him from physical harm: *The President must always have a bodyguard.*

Boer (bôr), *n.* **1.** a South African of Dutch descent. —*adj.* **2.** of or concerning the Boers.

Boer′ War′, a war in South Africa between Great Britain and the Dutch colonists, 1899–1902.

bog (bog, bôg), *n.* **1.** an area of wet, spongy ground, as a marsh, having soil that is made up largely of decayed plants. —*v.,* **bogged, bog·ging. 2.** to sink in or as if in a bog (usually fol. by *down*): *We were bogged down in work.* —**bog′gy,** *adj.*

bo·gey (bō′gē), *n., pl.* **bo·geys.** another spelling of **bogy.**

bo·gie (bō′gē), *n.* another spelling of **bogy.**

Bo·go·tá (bō′gə tä′), *n.* the capital city of Colombia, in the W central part.

bo·gus (bō′gəs), *adj.* counterfeit or false; sham; made-up; not real: *bogus money; bogus excuses.*

bo·gy (bō′gē), *n., pl.* **bo·gies. 1.** a hobgoblin or evil spirit. **2.** anything that haunts, frightens, or annoys: *the bogy of final exams.* Also, **bogey, bogie.**

Bo·he·mi·a (bō hē′mē ə), *n.* **1.** a region in W Czechoslovakia. 20,101 sq. mi. **2.** an area where unconventional people live, or the life led by such people, often artists and writers.

Bo·he·mi·an (bō hē′mē ən), *n.* **1.** a native or inhabitant of Bohemia. **2.** *(often l.c.)* a person who leads an unconventional life, esp. an artist or writer. **3.** a gypsy. **4.** *Archaic.* the Czech language. —*adj.* **5.** of or referring to Bohemia or its people. **6.** *(often l.c.)* referring to or characteristic of a Bohemian or a wandering, unconventional way of life. [the gypsies were called Bohemians by the French, who believed they came from Bohemia. This name was later applied to artists, writers, etc., because of their carefree way of life]

boil¹ (boil), *v.* **1.** to change from a liquid to a gaseous state, typically as a result of heating, with bubbles of gas rising to the surface of the liquid. **2.** to reach or bring to the boiling point: *When the water boils, turn off the kettle.* **3.** to cook (something) in boiling water: *to boil eggs.* **4.** to contain a boiling liquid or be surrounded by a boiling liquid: *The kettle is boiling. The vegetables are boiling.* **5.** to move or toss about like boiling water: *boiling surf.* **6.** to be very angry: *She was boiling because I was so late.* **7. boil down, a.** to reduce the quantity of (something) by boiling. **b.** to reduce the length of (something); shorten: *Boil down this article to two pages.* **8. boil over,** to overflow while boiling: *Turn down the fire before the soup boils over.* [from an Old French word, which comes from Latin *bullīre* "to bubble"]

boil² (boil), *n.* a painful, swollen sore caused by an infection. [from the Old English word *bȳle*]

boil·er (boi′lər), *n.* a closed vessel in which steam is generated by heat from a furnace or burner.

Boi·se (boi′zē, boi′sē), *n.* the capital city of Idaho, in the SW part.

bois·ter·ous (boi′stər əs), *adj.* of noisy or rowdy good spirits: *a boisterous child; a boisterous party.* —**bois′ter·ous·ly,** *adv.* —**bois′ter·ous·ness,** *n.*

bold (bōld), *adj.* **1.** courageous and daring: *a bold explorer; a bold attack.* **2.** rude or fresh; forward: *That child is too bold.* **3.** highly imaginative: *a bold scientist.* **4.** flashy or showy: *bold colors.* **5.** steep or abrupt: *a bold cliff.* —**bold′ly,** *adv.* —**bold′ness,** *n.*

bold·face (bōld′fās′), *n.* type that has thick, heavy lines, used for emphasis, headings, or the like.

This is a sample of boldface

bo·le·ro (bə lâr′ō), *n., pl.* **bo·le·ros. 1.** a lively Spanish dance in triple meter. **2.** music for this dance. **3.** a waist-length jacket, worn open in the front.

Bo·lí·var (bō lē′vär), *n.* **Si·món** (sē mōn′), ("*The Liberator*"), 1783–1830, South American statesman and revolutionary leader.

Bo·liv·i·a (bə liv′ē ə), *n.* a republic in W South America. 404,388 sq. mi. *Capitals:* La Paz and Sucre. —**Bo·liv′i·an,** *n., adj.*

boll (bōl), *n.* a rounded seed pod, esp. that of cotton or flax.

boll′ wee′vil, a small, gray beetle that attacks the bolls of cotton.

bo·lo·gna (bə lō′nē), *n.* a large, seasoned sausage made of finely ground beef and pork that has been cooked and smoked. [from *Bologna*, the name of a city in Italy where it was first made]

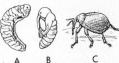

Boll weevil
A, Larva; B, Pupa; C, Adult
(length ¼ in.)

Bol·she·vik (bōl′shə vik), *n., pl.* **Bol·she·viks** *or* **Bol·she·vik·i** (bōl′shə vik′ē). **1.** (between 1903 and 1917) a member of the more extreme, radical majority of the Socialist party in Russia that gained complete control of the government in 1917. **2.** (since 1918) any member of the Russian Communist party. **3.** any member of a communist party. **4.** *(sometimes l.c.)* a political extremist; revolutionary; anarchist.

Bol·she·vism (bōl′shə viz′əm), *n.* **1.** the doctrines or methods of the Bolsheviks. **2.** *(sometimes l.c.)* the ideas or methods of an extreme or violent political position associated with socialism.

Bol·she·vist (bōl′shə vist), *n.* **1.** a follower of the doctrines or methods of the Bolsheviks. **2.** *(sometimes l.c.)* an anarchist. —**Bol′she·vis′tic,** *adj.*

bol·ster (bōl′stər), *n.* **1.** a long cushion or pillow for a bed, sofa, or the like. **2.** any cushion or pad. —*v.* **3.** to support with or as if with a pillow or cushion: *to bolster a stack of wood.* **4.** to add to, support, or uphold (a theory, belief, story, or the like): *to bolster an argument with facts.*

bolt (bōlt), *n.* **1.** a movable bar or rod that slides into a socket to fasten a door, gate, etc. **2.** the part of a lock that is extended or drawn back by the action of the key. **3.** a fastening rod or pin with a head at one end and the other end threaded to receive a nut. **4.** a sliding bar that closes the breech of a rifle. **5.** a sudden dash, run, flight, or escape: *The horse made an unexpected bolt and threw his rider.* **6.** a length of woven cloth, esp. on a roll: *a bolt of wool.* **7.** an

Bolts with nuts

arrow, esp. a short, heavy one for a crossbow. **8.** a thunderbolt. —*v.* **9.** to fasten with or as if with a bolt or bolts: *to bolt a gate.* **10.** to make a sudden, swift dash, run, flight, or escape: *The rabbit bolted into its burrow.* **11.** to desert, esp. from a political movement or party: *If he is nominated, many will bolt the party.* **12.** to eat or swallow hurriedly: *Don't bolt your food.*

bomb (bom), *n.* **1.** a hollow case filled with explosives for dropping from an airplane. **2.** a similar device for use as a weapon, for dispersing crowds, etc.: *a time bomb; a tear-gas bomb.* —*v.* **3.** to attack with bombs; drop bombs on; bombard: *to bomb a city.*

bom·bard (bom bärd′), *v.* **1.** to attack or batter with artillery fire: *to bombard an enemy position.* **2.** to assail or attack vigorously: *to bombard someone with snowballs; to bombard someone with questions.* —**bom·bard′er,** *n.* —**bom·bard′ment,** *n.*

bom·bar·dier (bom′bər dēr′), *n.* the member of a bomber crew who works the bombsight and releases the bombs.

bom·bast (bom′bast), *n.* pompous speech or writing; words that are more impressive in sound than meaning: *a lecture full of bombast.* —**bom·bas′tic,** *adj.* —**bom·bas′ti·cal·ly,** *adv.*

Bom·bay (bom bā′), *n.* a seaport and city in W India.

bomb·er (bom′ər), *n.* a plane for carrying and dropping bombs.

bomb·shell (bom′shel′), *n.* **1.** a bomb. **2.** something

or someone that has a sudden or sensational effect: *His arrest for murder was a bombshell in the community.*

bomb·sight (bom′sīt′), *n.* an instrument for aiming bombs at a target, often one that automatically guides the plane and aims and releases the bombs.

bo·na fide (bō′nə fīd′, fī′dē), in good faith; without fraud: *a bona fide agreement.*

bo·nan·za (bə nan′zə), *n.* **1.** a rich mass of metal ore, as found in mining. **2.** a source of great and sudden wealth or luck; an unusually large windfall: *His new store turned out to be a bonanza.*

Bo·na·parte (bō′nə pärt′), family name of **Napoleon.**

bon·bon (bon′bon′), *n.* a small candy, usually having a filling of fruit jam.

bond[1] (bond), *n.* **1.** something that binds, fastens, or holds, as a rope: *The prisoner struggled to escape from his bonds.* **2.** something that binds or unites people, nations, or the like: *the bonds of matrimony.* **3.** a written guaranty or promise, esp. to pay a stated amount of money as insurance against loss or failure to fulfill an obligation: *The prisoner was released under bond until the trial.* **4.** a certificate issued by a government or company to raise money by promising to repay the sum at a later date with interest. —*v.* **5.** to give a bond or bonds for: *a bonded messenger.* **6.** to connect or bind. [from the Middle English word *bond* "fetter," which comes from Scandinavian]

bond[2] (bond), *adj. Archaic.* in serfdom or slavery; forced to work for someone without pay: *a bond servant.* [from the Middle English word *bonde* "peasant, serf," which comes from Old English *bōnda* "householder"]

bond·age (bon′dij), *n.* slavery or enforced servitude: *The nation was held in bondage by its conquerors.*

bond·man (bond′mən), *n., pl.* **bond·men.** a male slave or servant forced to work without pay; serf.

bonds·man[1] (bondz′mən), *n., pl.* **bonds·men.** another form of **bondman.**

bonds·man[2] (bondz′mən), *n., pl.* **bonds·men.** a person who puts up money to guarantee that another person will meet certain obligations, esp. a man whose business is furnishing bail for prisoners. [from the phrase *bond's man* "man of the bond," that is, signer of the bond. See *bond*[1]]

bonds·wom·an (bondz′wŏŏm′ən), *n., pl.* **bonds·wom·en.** another form of **bondwoman.**

bond·wom·an (bond′wŏŏm′ən), *n., pl.* **bond·wom·en.** a female slave or servant forced to work without pay.

bone (bōn), *n.* **1.** the white, hard material of which the skeleton is composed. **2.** a piece of the skeleton: *a bone in the foot.* **3.** any similar material or piece of material taken from an animal, such as ivory or whalebone. —*v.,* **boned, bon·ing. 4.** to remove the bones from: *to bone a fish.* **5. have a bone to pick with someone,** to have reason to quarrel with another person: *After the way you behaved, young man, I have a bone to pick with you.* **6. make no bones about,** to speak or act frankly and without hesitation

about: *She made no bones about her dislike of cats.*
—**bone′less,** *adj.*

bone′ meal′, bones that have been ground to a coarse powder: used as fertilizer or feed.

bon·fire (bon′fi³r′), *n.* a large fire in the open air: *They built a bonfire to celebrate their victory.*

bon·go (boñg′gō), *n., pl.* **bon·gos** or **bon·go.** a large reddish-brown antelope of the forests of tropical Africa, having white stripes and large, twisted horns.

bon′go drums′ (boñg′gō), a pair of small drums played with the fingers. Also, **bon′gos, bon′goes.**

Bonn (bon), *n.* the capital city of West Germany, on the Rhine River.

Bongo
(4 ft. high
at shoulder)

bon·net (bon′it), *n.* 1. a hat for wearing out of doors, usually having a wide brim and tying under the chin: formerly worn by women, but now worn chiefly by children. 2. a Scottish cap for a man or boy, having a large crown and without a visor. 3. a bonnetlike headdress, esp. an Indian feathered headdress: *a war bonnet.*

bon·ny (bon′ē), (esp. in Scotland) —*adj.,* **bon·ni·er, bon·ni·est.** 1. pleasing to look at; handsome; pretty: *a bonny lad.* 2. sweet and lively; agreeable; good: *a generous, bonny girl.* —*n., pl.* **bon·nies.** 3. *Archaic.* a pretty girl or young woman: *My bonny sailed over the ocean.* Also, **bon′nie.**

bo·nus (bō′nəs), *n., pl.* **bo·nus·es.** something given or paid over and above what is due: *Everyone will get a $10 bonus on payday.*

bon vo·yage (bon′ voi äzh′), (have a) pleasant trip: a French expression used in farewell.

bon·y (bō′nē), *adj.,* **bon·i·er, bon·i·est.** 1. of or like bone: *a hard, bony material.* 2. filled with bones: *a bony piece of meat.* 3. big-boned; having bones that are large or prominent: *a bony finger.*

boo (boo), *interj.* 1. (used as an exclamation of disapproval.) 2. (used as an exclamation to frighten or startle someone.) —*n., pl.* **boos.** 3. an exclamation of disapproval or contempt: *a loud boo from the audience.* —*v.,* **booed, boo·ing.** 4. to shout "boo": *First they cheered, and then they booed.* 5. to shout "boo" at: *to boo the villain.*

boo·by (boo′bē), *n., pl.* **boo·bies.** a stupid person; dunce.

boo′by trap′, 1. a bomb or mine hidden in some ordinary place in such a way that it will be set off by an unsuspecting person. 2. any trap set for a person.

book (book), *n.* 1. a written or printed work of some length, as a novel, history, or the like, esp. on sheets of paper that are bound together in one volume: *a book on the Civil War.* 2. a number of sheets of blank or ruled paper bound together for writing, figuring, or the like. 3. a division of a written work: *the books of the Bible.* 4. a set or pack of tickets,

stamps, matches, etc., bound together like a book. —*v.* 5. to enter in a book or list; record. 6. to arrange for beforehand; engage ahead of time: *to book a seat on an airplane.* 7. to enter official charges against in a police register: *to book someone for robbery.* 8. **by the book,** in the correct or approved way: *She has to do everything by the book.* 9. **throw the book at,** *Slang.* to punish or criticize (someone) severely: *The boss threw the book at the office boy for being late.*

book·case (book′kās′), *n.* a set of shelves for books.

book·keep·er (book′kē′pər), *n.* a person who keeps financial accounts or records, as for a business.

book·keep·ing (book′kē′piñg), *n.* the business or skill of keeping financial accounts or records: *to study bookkeeping.*

book·let (book′lit), *n.* a little book, esp. one with a paper cover; pamphlet: *a booklet on first aid.*

book·mark (book′märk′), *n.* a ribbon, slip of paper, or the like, placed between the pages of a book to mark a place.

book·mo·bile (book′mō bēl′), *n.* an automobile or truck that serves as a traveling library.

book·store (book′stôr′), *n.* a store where books are sold. Also, **book·shop** (book′shop′).

book·worm (book′wûrm′), *n.* 1. a person devoted to reading or studying. 2. any of various insects that feed on books.

boom¹ (boom), *v.* 1. to make a deep rumbling or droning sound: *The ocean surf boomed in the distance.* 2. to give forth with a booming sound (often fol. by *out*): *The tower clock boomed out the hour.* 3. to grow or flourish rapidly: *The frontier towns were booming.* —*n.* 4. a deep, long, full sound: *the boom of cannons.* 5. a rapid increase in growth, prosperity, or popularity: *a boom in business; a boom for a presidential candidate.* [from the Middle English word *bombon* "to buzz"]

boom² (boom), *n.* 1. any or various more or less horizontal poles or spars for extending the bottom of sails on a boat, loading and unloading cargo, pushing a boat away from a wharf, or the like. 2. a chain, cable, or structure of floating timbers, used to shut off navigation, confine floating logs, or the like. 3. a spar or beam used for any of various purposes, as the spar on a derrick that supports or guides a load being lifted, or the long beam on which a microphone is extended, as in a television studio. [from a Dutch word meaning "tree, pole, beam"]

boom·er·ang (boo′mə rañg′), *n.* 1. a curved piece of wood that can be thrown in such a way that it returns to the thrower. 2. something, as a trap, that catches or affects the very person who tried to use it on somebody else: *My judo throw was a boomerang, and I landed on the ground.* —*v.* 3. to return, as a

Boomerangs

boomerang does, esp. in such a way that it unexpectedly harms the user: *Our sneak attack boomeranged when the enemy learned of our plan.*

---

act, āble, dâre, ärt; ebb, ēqual; if, īce; hot, ōver, ôrder; oil; book; ooze; out; up, ûrge; ə = *a* as in *alone;* ³ as in *button* (but′³n), *fire* (fi³r); chief; shoe; thin; ŧħat; zh as in *measure* (mezh′ər). See full key inside cover.

boom′ town′, a town that has grown rapidly as the result of the sudden development of one or more sources of wealth in the neighborhood: *The discovery of gold turned the settlement into a boom town.*

boon¹ (bo͞on), *n.* **1.** a benefit to be enjoyed; a thing to be thankful for: *Your help was a great boon to me.* **2.** *Archaic.* a favor asked; request. [from Scandinavian]

boon² (bo͞on), *adj.* jolly or jovial; friendly: *a boon companion.* [from the Latin word *bonus* "good"]

boon·docks (bo͞on′doks′), *n.* **the boondocks,** *Slang.* a marsh, backwoods, or remote rural area.

Boone (bo͞on), *n.* **Daniel,** 1734–1820, American pioneer, mainly in Kentucky.

boor (bo͞or), *n.* a rude, unmannerly person. **—boor′ish,** *adj.*

boost (bo͞ost), *v.* **1.** to lift or raise by pushing from behind or below: *Boost me up to the first branch of the tree.* **2.** to help by speaking well of; promote: *He's always boosting his brother's restaurant.* **3.** to increase or raise: *to boost prices.* **—n. 4.** an upward shove or raise; lift: *Give me a boost onto the horse.* **5.** an increase or rise: *a boost in food prices.* **6.** an act, remark, or the like, that helps, encourages, or promotes: *The team got a boost in the town paper.*

boost·er (bo͞o′stər), *n.* **1.** a person or thing that boosts, esp. a person who enthusiastically or energetically supports something: *He's a great booster of the symphony orchestra.* **2.** something that adds to or strengthens the action of something else: *I'll give you one shot today and a booster next week.* **3.** the first stage of a rocket, which provides thrust for takeoff and the first part of the flight.

boot¹ (bo͞ot), *n.* **1.** a covering of leather, rubber, etc., for the foot and all or part of the leg. **2.** any of various protective coverings, such as a guard worn on a horse's leg, or a patch on the inside of an automobile tire. **—v. 3.** *Slang.* to move by kicking; kick: *The boy booted a tin can down the street.* **4.** to provide with boots. [from the Old French word *bote*]

boot² (bo͞ot), *v.* **1.** *Archaic.* to be of advantage: *It boots not to complain.* **2. to boot,** besides; also: *I got three dollars and a jackknife to boot.* [from the Old English word *bōt* "advantage"] **—boot′less,** *adj.*

boot·black (bo͞ot′blak′), *n.* a person whose work is shining shoes, boots, etc.

boot·ee (bo͞o′tē), *n.* a baby's socklike shoe, usually knitted or crocheted. Also, **boot′ie.**

booth (bo͞oth), *n., pl.* **booths** (bo͞othz, bo͞oths). **1.** a stand or covered area where goods are displayed or sold, as at a market or fair. **2.** a small compartment or boxlike room, having a specific use: *a telephone booth; a voting booth.* **3.** an area that is partly enclosed or set off by partitions, as in a restaurant.

Booth (bo͞oth), *n.* **1. Edwin (Thomas),** 1833–1893, U.S. actor. **2.** his brother, **John Wilkes,** 1838–1865, U.S. actor: assassin of Abraham Lincoln.

boot·leg (bo͞ot′leg′), *n.* **1.** alcoholic liquor that has been illegally made, sold, or transported. **—v.,** **bootlegged, boot·leg·ging. 2.** to make, deal in, or transport (goods, esp. liquor) illegally: *to bootleg whiskey; to be*

arrested for bootlegging. [from *boot*¹ + *leg,* referring to the practice of hiding a liquor bottle in the leg of one's boot] **—boot′leg′ger,** *n.*

boo·ty (bo͞o′tē), *n., pl.* **boo·ties. 1.** loot or plunder seized in war or by robbery: *pirate's booty.* **2.** any prize or gain.

booze (bo͞oz), *Slang.* **—n. 1.** any alcoholic beverage. **—v.,** boozed, booz·ing. **2.** to drink heavily.

bo·rax (bôr′aks), *n.* a white substance occurring naturally as a mineral, used as a cleaning agent and in making glass.

Bor·deaux (bôr dō′), *n.* **1.** a port city in SW France. **2.** any of various wines produced in this region.

bor·der (bôr′dər), *n.* **1.** the part or edge of something that forms its outer boundary. **2.** the line that separates one country, state, province, etc., from another; frontier: *He crossed the border into Canada.* **3.** brink or verge: *on the border of real success.* **4.** a decorative strip, design, or fringe on the edge of something: *a tablecloth with a flowered border.* **—v. 5.** to decorate with a border: *Why not border the curtains in blue?* **6.** to form a boundary with; adjoin: *Mexico borders Texas.* **7. border on** (or **upon**), **a.** to be next to: *The market borders on the park.* **b.** verge on; be very much like: *That plan borders on madness.*

bore¹ (bôr), *v.,* **bored, bor·ing. 1.** to drill or make a hole in: *Worms bore into the earth. Bore this piece of metal.* **2.** to make (a hole, tunnel, well, or the like) by hollowing out or cutting through: *The woodpecker bored a hole in the maple tree.* **—n. 3.** the inside diameter of a tube, gun barrel, or the like; caliber. [from the Old English word *borian*]

bore² (bôr), *v.,* **bored, bor·ing. 1.** to tire by dullness or repetition: *That game bores me.* **—n. 2.** a dull or tiresome person or thing: *His jokes are a bore.* [perhaps from a special use of *bore*¹] **—bore′dom,** *n.* **—bor′ing·ly,** *adv.*

bore³ (bôr), *v.* the past tense of **bear**¹.

bor·er (bôr′ər), *n.* **1.** a person or thing that bores. **2.** a tool for boring; auger. **3.** an insect or other animal that bores into wood, plants, etc.

bo′ric ac′id (bôr′ik), a substance diluted with water and used as a mild antiseptic, esp. for the eyes.

born (bôrn), *v.* **1.** a past participle of **bear**¹. **—adj. 2.** brought forth by birth: *I was born in St. Paul, Minnesota.* **3.** having from birth a certain quality or character: *a born musician.*

borne (bôrn), *v.* a past participle of **bear**¹.

Bor·ne·o (bôr′nē ō′), *n.* a large island in the East Indies, SW of the Philippines. about 290,000 sq. mi.

bo·ron (bôr′on), *n. Chem.* a nonmetallic element occurring in borax, boric acid, etc. *Symbol:* B

bor·ough (bûr′ō, bur′ō), *n.* **1.** (in certain states in the U.S.) a town having its own local government. **2.** one of the five divisions of New York City: *the borough of Manhattan.* **3.** (in England) an area or town that has its own local government or is represented by a member of Parliament.

bor·row (bor′ō), *v.* **1.** to take or get (something) with the promise to return it: *May I borrow your pencil?* **2.** to take and use a word, idea, or the like, from another source; adapt: *Many English words are borrowed from French.* —**bor′row·er,** *n.*

borscht (bôrsht), *n.* a soup often made of beets, served hot or chilled, usually with sour cream. Also, **borsch** (bôrsh), **borsht.**

bor·zoi (bôr′zoi), *n.* one of a breed of tall, slender dogs having long, silky hair, raised originally in Russia for hunting wolves.

bos·om (boōz′əm), *n.* **1.** the breast or chest of a human being, esp. the breasts of a woman. **2.** the part of a garment that covers the breast or chest. **3.** the breast as the center of human thought or emotion: *Rage stormed in his bosom.* **4.** something that is likened to a bosom as a center of life or comfort: *the bosom of the family.*

TURKEY (IN EUROPE)
BLACK SEA
Istanbul
Bosporus
SEA OF MARMARA
TURKEY (IN ASIA)

Bos·po·rus (bos′pər əs), *n.* a strait connecting the Black Sea and the Sea of Marmara. 18 mi. long.

boss[1] (bôs), *n.* **1.** a person who employs or supervises others; foreman or manager. **2.** a politician who controls an organization in his party: *The county boss controlled the votes.* **3.** any person who controls or manages a group, family, etc.: *He is the boss in his house.* —*v.* **4.** to act as boss to; command or control. [from the Dutch word *baas* "master"]

boss[2] (bôs), *n.* **1.** a knob or stud of metal, ivory, etc., used to ornament a surface: *a leather case covered with bosses.* —*v.* **2.** to ornament with bosses. [from the Old French word *boce*]

boss·y (bô′sē), *adj.*, **boss·i·er, boss·i·est.** having a domineering manner; fond of ordering and controlling others. —**boss′i·ness,** *n.*

Bos·ton (bô′stən), *n.* a seaport and the capital city of Massachusetts, in the E part. —**Bos·to·ni·an** (bô-stō′nē ən), *n., adj.*

Bos′ton Tea′ Par′ty, a raid on three British ships in Boston Harbor (December 16, 1773) by Boston colonists, disguised as Indians, who threw the contents of several hundred chests of tea into the harbor in protest against British taxes on tea.

Boston terrier (14 in. high at shoulder)

Bos′ton ter′rier, one of an American breed of small, pug-faced, short-haired dogs having erect ears, a short tail, and a brindled or black coat with white markings. Also, **Bos′ton bull′.**

bo·sun (bō′sən), *n.* another spelling of **boatswain.**

bo·tan·i·cal (bə tan′i kəl), *adj.* of, referring to, or containing plants: *botanical gardens.*

bot·a·ny (bot′ə nē), *n.* the branch of biology that deals with plant life. —**bot′a·nist,** *n.*

botch (boch), *v.* **1.** to spoil by poor work or clumsiness; bungle: *He botched the job and had to start over.* —*n.* **2.** a clumsy or poor piece of work; bungle.

both (bōth), *adj.* **1.** one and the other; the two together: *Both girls are beautiful.* —*pron.* **2.** the one as well as the other: *Both of us agree.* —*conj.* **3.** alike; equally: *He is both ready and willing.*

both·er (both′ər), *v.* **1.** to give trouble to; annoy; worry: *The children bothered the neighbors.* **2.** to take the trouble or make the effort: *Don't bother to answer the phone.* —*n.* **3.** a cause of trouble, annoyance, or worry: *The dog can be a terrible bother.*

both·er·some (both′ər səm), *adj.* troublesome; annoying.

Bot·swa·na (bot swä′nä), *n.* a republic in S Africa, independent since 1966: a member of the British Commonwealth. 275,000 sq. mi. *Cap.:* Gaborone. Former name, **Bechuanaland.**

bot·tle (bot′əl), *n.* **1.** a container for liquids, usually having a neck and a mouth and made of glass: *a milk bottle.* **2.** the amount held by such a container: *They drank a bottle of milk.* —*v.,* **bot·tled, bot·tling. 3.** to put into or seal in a bottle: *to bottle grape juice.*

bot·tle·neck (bot′əl nek′), *n.* something that delays movement or progress, as a narrow passage, difficulty, etc.: *The old road is full of bottlenecks.*

bot·tom (bot′əm), *n.* **1.** the lowest or deepest part: *the bottom of a well.* **2.** the under or lower side: *the bottom of a saucer.* **3.** the ground under a body of water, as an ocean. **4.** Usually, **bottoms.** low land that extends along the sides of a river. **5.** the seat of a chair. **6.** the buttocks; rump. **7.** the most important or basic part: *to get to the bottom of a problem.* —*adj.* **8.** located on or at the bottom: *the bottom step.*

bot·tom·less (bot′əm lis), *adj.* **1.** lacking a bottom: *a bottomless box.* **2.** very deep: *a bottomless well.* **3.** very mysterious or profound: *a bottomless secret; bottomless learning.*

bou·doir (boō′dwär), *n.* a lady's bedroom or private sitting room.

bough (bou), *n.* a branch of a tree, esp. one of the larger or main branches.

bought (bôt), *v.* the past tense and past participle of **buy.**

bouil·lon (boōl′yon), *n.* a clear, seasoned broth made from beef, chicken, etc.

boul·der (bōl′dər), *n.* a large rock that has been worn or made round by the action of water or the weather.

NEVADA — UTAH
Las Vegas
River
CALIFORNIA — Boulder Dam
Los Angeles — Colorado — ARIZONA
Phoenix
MEXICO

Boul′der Dam′ (bōl′dər), a dam on the Colorado River, on the boundary between SE Nevada and NW

Arizona: the highest dam in the world. 727 ft. high; 1180 ft. long. Official name, **Hoover Dam.**

boul·e·vard (bŏŏl′ə värd′), *n.* a broad avenue in a city, often lined with trees.

bounce (bouns), *v.,* **bounced, bounc·ing. 1.** to strike a surface and spring back or rebound, as a ball. **2.** to cause to strike and rebound: *She bounced the ball on the sidewalk.* **3.** to move or walk in a quick, lively way: *She was happily bouncing down the street.* —*n.* **4.** a bound or rebound: *With one bounce the ball went over the fence.* **5.** the ability to rebound: *The old football was losing its bounce.* **6.** energy; vitality; liveliness: *She wakes up full of bounce.*

bounc·ing (boun′sing), *adj.* strong, sturdy, or active: *a bouncing baby boy.*

bound¹ (bound), *adj.* **1.** tied; in bonds: *a bound prisoner.* **2.** having a cover, as a book. **3.** obliged or required, as by law, duty, etc.: *You are bound by the rules.* **4.** certain; sure: *In winter it is bound to snow.* **5.** determined; resolved: *If you are bound to win, go ahead and try.* [from the past participle of *bind*]

bound² (bound), *v.* **1.** to move by leaps: *The deer bounded through the forest.* **2.** to bounce; rebound: *The ball bounded over the wall.* —*n.* **3.** a leap onward or upward; jump: *With a bound he was over the hedge.* **4.** a bounce; rebound. [from the French word *bond* "leap"]

bound³ (bound), *n.* **1.** a limit or boundary: *the bounds of a province.* **2.** something that limits, confines, or restrains: *to go beyond the normal bounds of duty.* **3.** land within boundary lines: *the vast bounds of a nation.* —*v.* **4.** to serve as a boundary for: *A river bounds the state on one side.* **5. out of bounds, a.** outside the boundary lines or limits, as on a playing field: *The runner was tackled out of bounds.* **b.** forbidden; prohibited: *The building is out of bounds to military personnel.* [from the Old French word *bonde*] —**bound′a·ble,** *adj.*

bound⁴ (bound), *adj.* going or intending to go; destined (usually fol. by *for*): *The train is bound for Denver.* [from a Scandinavian word meaning "ready"]

bound·a·ry (boun′də rē), *n., pl.* **bound·a·ries.** something that shows bounds or limits; a limiting or bounding line: *The Mississippi River is one of the boundaries of Iowa.*

bound·less (bound′lis), *adj.* without bounds; limitless; immense: *the boundless prairies; boundless happiness.* —**bound′less·ly,** *adv.*

boun·te·ous (boun′tē əs), *adj.* **1.** giving freely and generously: *bounteous patrons.* **2.** abundant, plentiful, or freely given: *bounteous support; a bounteous harvest.* —**boun′te·ous·ly,** *adv.*

boun·ti·ful (boun′tə fəl), *adj.* **1.** generous in bestowing gifts, favors, etc. **2.** abundant or plentiful: *a bountiful supply.* —**boun′ti·ful·ly,** *adv.* —**boun′ti·ful·ness,** *n.*

boun·ty (boun′tē), *n., pl.* **boun·ties. 1.** generosity in giving: *The bounty of the good king was endless.* **2.** a generous gift: *Land and wealth were the hero's bounty.* **3.** a reward, esp. one offered by a govern-

ment for capturing or killing an animal or criminal.

bou·quet (bō kā′, bŏŏ kā′ *for def.1;* bŏŏ kā′ *for def. 2*), *n.* **1.** a bunch of flowers. **2.** an aroma, esp. that of a wine.

bour·bon (bûr′bən), *n.* a whiskey that is distilled largely from corn. Also, **bour′bon whis′key.**

bour·geois (bŏŏr zhwä′, bŏŏr′zhwä), *n., pl.* **bour·geois. 1.** a member of the middle class. **2.** a person whose outlook on life is limited and smug. —*adj.* **3.** belonging to, characteristic of, or composed of the middle class: *a bourgeois custom; bourgeois society.*

bour·geoi·sie (bŏŏr′zhwä zē′), *n.* the bourgeois or middle class.

bout (bout), *n.* **1.** a contest, as of boxing. **2.** a spell, term, or session: *a bout of pneumonia; a bout of work.*

bo·vine (bō′vīn), *adj.* **1.** of the ox family. **2.** oxlike or cowlike. —*n.* **3.** an ox or related animal.

bow¹ (bou), *v.* **1.** to bend the head, knee, or body in respect, submission, greeting, etc.: *He bowed to his audience.* **2.** to give in; yield; submit: *He bowed to the decisions of his elders.* **3.** to cause to stoop, bend, or incline: *The old woman was bowed by years.* —*n.* **4.** a motion of bending the head, knee, or body in respect, submission, greeting, etc. **5. bow out,** to leave or resign: *The president will bow out when his term of office is finished.* [from the Old English word *būgan* "to bend"]

bow² (bō), *n.* **1.** a pliant strip of wood or other material, bent by a string stretched between its ends, used for shooting arrows. **2.** a knot having a loop or loops: *to tie a package with a bow.* **3.** a slightly curved rod bearing a stretched band of horsehair for playing musical instruments of the violin family. **4.** anything curved or in the shape of an arc, as a rainbow. —*v.* **5.** to bend into the form of a bow; curve. **6.** to play a stringed instrument by means of a bow. [from the Old English word *boga*]

bow³ (bou), *n.* the forward end of a vessel or airship. [from the Dutch word *boeg*]

bow·el (bou′əl), *n.* **1.** a part of the intestines. **2.** Usually, **bowels. a.** the intestines. **b.** the deepest inward parts: *the bowels of the earth.* —*adj.* **3.** of or concerning the bowels of the human body: *bowel movement.*

bow·er (bou′ər), *n.* a sheltered place shaded by trees, shrubbery, or vines on a trellis; arbor.

bow′ie knife′ (bō′ē, bŏŏ′ē), a knife having a long, pointed blade with a single edge. [named after James Bowie (1799–1836), U.S. soldier and pioneer]

Bowie knife

bowl¹ (bōl), *n.* **1.** a deep, round dish used for holding liquid, food, etc. **2.** the contents of such a dish: *a bowl of milk.* **3.** a rounded, hollow part: *the bowl of a sink.* **4.** an oval or round stadium: *They played football in the college bowl.* [from the Old English word *bolla*] —**bowl′like′,** *adj.*

bowl² (bōl), *n.* **1.** a ball used in playing bowls. **2.** a cast of the ball in bowling. —*v.* **3.** to play at bowling or bowls. **4.** to roll a bowl or ball. **5.** to move along smoothly or rapidly: *The car bowled down the highway.* [from a French word, which comes from Latin *bulla* "bubble"]

bow·leg·ged (bō′leg′id, -legd′), *adj.* having legs that curve outward; bandy-legged. —**bow·leg·ged·ness** (bō′leg′id nis), *n.*

bowl·er (bō′lər), *n. Chiefly British.* a derby hat.

bowl·ing (bō′ling), *n.* **1.** a game in which players roll balls along a wooden alley to knock down wooden pins at the far end. **2.** the act or an instance of playing this game.

bowls (bōlz), *n. (used as sing.)* a game similar to bowling, played on a level lawn with a heavy ball of wood, the object being to come as near as possible to a stationary ball at the far end of the court.

Bowling (arrangement of pins)

bow·man (bō′mən), *n., pl.* **bow·men.** an archer.

bow·sprit (bou′sprit, bō′sprit), *n.* a spar that sticks out from the bow of a sailing vessel, used for holding ropes from the front sails and mast.

bow·string (bō′string′), *n.* the string of an archer's bow.

box[1] (boks), *n.* **1.** a container or receptacle, usually rectangular and having a lid. **2.** the contents of a box: *a box of marshmallows.* **3.** a compartment for holding one or more persons: *a theater box; a jury box.* **4.** a space on a baseball diamond marking the position of a player, such as the catcher or batter. —*v.* **5.** to put into a box: *to box a gift.* **6.** to confine as in a box: *His car was boxed in by the traffic.* [from an Old English word originally meaning "boxwood," which was used for making boxes. See *box*[3]] —**box′like′,** *adj.*

box[2] (boks), *n.* **1.** a blow, as with the hand or fist. —*v.* **2.** to strike with the hand or fist: *to box someone's ears.* **3.** to fight in a boxing match: *The challenger boxed the champion for three rounds.* [from a Middle English word meaning "buffet"]

box[3] (boks), *n.* a boxwood tree. [from an Old English word, which comes from Latin *buxus,* the name of the tree, from Greek *pyxos*]

box·car (boks′kär′), *n.* a completely enclosed freight car.

box·er (bok′sər), *n.* **1.** a person who fights with his fists, esp. as a sport; prize fighter. **2.** a medium-sized, stocky, short-haired dog having a brindled or tan coat, sometimes with white markings.

box·ing (bok′sing), *n.* the act, sport, or profession of fighting with the fists.

box′ of′fice, the office of a theater, stadium, or the like, at which tickets are sold.

box·wood (boks′wŏŏd′), *n.* **1.** a yellow, hard, close-grained wood of an evergreen shrub or tree, used for wood engravings. **2.** Also, **box.** the shrub or tree itself.

boy (boi), *n.* **1.** a male child, from birth to full growth. **2.** a grown man, esp. when referred to with familiarity: *Dad is playing poker with the boys.* **3.** a servant, waiter, or the like. —*interj.* **4.** an exclamation of wonder, pleasure, etc.: *Boy, did we have fun!*

boy·cott (boi′kot), *v.* **1.** to combine in refusing to have dealings with (a person or organization): *The housewives boycotted the neighborhood grocery.* **2.** to act together in refusing to buy or use: *They boycotted all of the company's products.* —*n.* **3.** the act or practice of boycotting: *a boycott of the city's buses.*

boy·hood (boi′hŏŏd), *n.* the state or period of being a boy.

boy·ish (boi′ish), *adj.* of, like, or befitting a boy: *a boyish smile; boyish enthusiasm.* —**boy′ish·ly,** *adv.* —**boy′ish·ness,** *n.*

boy′ scout′, a member of an organization (**Boy′ Scouts′**), consisting of boys and having as its purpose the development of character and self-reliance.

bp., **1.** birthplace. **2.** (in chess) bishop.

Br, *Chem.* the symbol for **bromine.**

brace (brās), *n.* **1.** something that strengthens, stiffens, or holds parts together. **2.** a device for holding and turning a wood-boring bit. **3.** Usually, **braces.** a device for straightening crooked teeth. **4.** an appliance, as on an arm or leg, for supporting a weak joint or joints. **5.** **braces,** *Chiefly British.* another word for **suspenders. 6.** a pair; couple: *a brace of partridges.* **7.** one of two characters ({) or (}) used to enclose words, lines, or staves of music. —*v.,* **braced, brac·ing. 8.** to supply, fasten, or strengthen with or as if with a brace: *They braced the shed with boards to keep it from falling.* **9.** to steady (oneself), as against a shock. **10.** to stimulate, arouse, refresh, etc.: *The cold shower braced him.* **11. brace up,** to gather one's courage; become resolute or determined: *Brace up, it will soon be over.* [from an Old French word meaning "an arm's length," which comes from Latin *bracchium* "arm"]

Brace and bit

brace·let (brās′lit), *n.* an ornamental band or chain worn on the wrist or arm.

brack·en (brak′ən), *n.* **1.** a large fern or brake. **2.** a thicket of such ferns. [from the Middle English word *braken,* which comes from Scandinavian]

brack·et (brak′it), *n.* **1.** a support projecting from a wall to hold the weight of a shelf, a roof, etc. **2.** a shelf so supported. **3.** one of two marks, ([) or (]), used in writing or printing to enclose words that explain or comment on the text. **4.** a class or grouping, esp. a grouping of tax-

Brackets supporting a roof

payers based on the amount of their income: *the highest economic bracket.* —*v.,* **brack·et·ed, brack·et· ing.** 5. to supply with or support by a bracket or brackets: *to bracket a shelf.* 6. to place within brackets: *to bracket a remark.* 7. to group or class together: *to bracket problems into groups.*

brack·ish (brak′ish), *adj.* 1. salty or briny, as the water of ponds, bays, or marshes near the sea. 2. unpleasant to the taste; unpalatable: *a bowl of thin, brackish soup.* —**brack′ish·ness,** *n.*

brad (brad), *n.* a thin wire nail having a small head. See illus. at **nail.**

brae (brā, brē), *n.* (in Scotland) a slope or hillside.

brag (brag), *v.,* **bragged, brag·ging.** 1. to speak boastfully; boast. —*n.* 2. a boast, or boastful talk. —**brag′ ging·ly,** *adv.*

brag·gart (brag′ərt), *n.* 1. a person who brags, esp. habitually: *A braggart always speaks well of himself.* —*adj.* 2. bragging; boastful: *braggart talk.*

Brah·ma (brä′mə), *n.* (in the Hindu religion) the god who made the world.

Brah·man (brä′mən), *n., pl.* **Brah·mans.** a Hindu of the priestly caste, the highest social class. Also, **Brahmin.**

Brah·man·ism (brä′mə niz′əm), *n.* the social and religious system of the Brahmans.

Brah·min (brä′min), *n., pl.* **Brah·min** *or* **Brah·mins.** another spelling of **Brahman.**

Brahms (brämz), *n.* **Jo·han·nes** (yō hä′nəs), 1833–1897, German composer.

braid (brād), *v.* 1. to weave together strips or strands of; plait: *to braid hair.* 2. to form by such weaving: *to braid a rope.* —*n.* 3. a braided length or plait, esp. of hair. 4. a band of plaited or woven strands of silk, cotton, etc., used as trimming.

Braille (brāl), *n. (sometimes l.c.)* a system of lettering for use by the blind, in which each character is a combination of raised dots that are read by touch. [named after its inventor, Louis *Braille* (1809–1852), French teacher of the blind]

brain (brān), *n.* 1. the mass of gray and white nerve tissue enclosed in the skull that controls mental and physical actions. 2. *Informal.* a very smart person.

brain·child (brān′-child′), *n., pl.* **brain·chil·dren.** something invented, imagined, or created by oneself: *The electric light was Edison's brainchild.*

brain·less (brān′lis), *adj.* stupid, silly, or foolish.

brain·storm (brān′- stôrm′), *n.* a sudden, clever idea.

brain·y (brā′nē), *adj.,* **brain·i·er, brain·i·est.** intelligent; smart. —**brain′i·ness,** *n.*

braise (brāz), *v.,* **braised, brais·ing.** to brown (meat or vegetables) in fat and then cook slowly in very little liquid in a covered pot.

Brain (Human)

A, Cerebrum;
B, Cerebellum; C, Spinal cord;
D, Medulla oblongata;
E, Pituitary gland

brake¹ (brāk), *n.* 1. a device for slowing or stopping the motion of a vehicle or other machine, esp. by friction. —*v.,* **braked, brak·ing.** 2. to slow or stop by means of a brake: *He braked the car at the intersection. The car braked to a stop.* [from Dutch]

brake² (brāk), *n.* a place that is thickly grown with bushes, shrubs, brambles, or cane; thicket. [from a medieval German word meaning "thicket"]

brake³ (brāk), *n.* a large, coarse fern; bracken. [another form of the word *bracken*]

brake·man (brāk′mən), *n., pl.* **brake·men.** a trainman who assists the conductor in the operation of a train.

bram·ble (bram′bəl), *n.* any of numerous kinds of prickly shrubs.

bran (bran), *n.* the partly ground husks of grain separated by sifting from the flour or meal.

branch (branch), *n.* 1. a division or offshoot of the stem or trunk of a tree, shrub, or other plant. 2. a limb, offshoot, or member of any main part: *branches of a deer's antlers; the branches of a river.* 3. a section or part: *Poetry is a branch of literature.* 4. a division of an organization: *the executive branch of government.* —*v.* 5. to put forth branches or branchlike parts: *The old oak branches in all directions.* 6. **branch out,** to expand, as a business organization: *The company has branched out into 13 states.*

brand (brand), *n.* 1. a kind, grade, or make, as indicated by a stamp, trademark, or the like: *the best brand of coffee.* 2. a trademark. 3. a mark made by burning, as on the hide of an animal, to indicate ownership: *the brand of the Smith ranch.* 4. an iron used for branding. 5. a burning or partly burned piece of wood. 6. a mark of shame or disgrace: *the brand of thief.* —*v.* 7. to mark with a brand: *to brand cattle.* 8. to point out as shameful, criminal, or the like: *His accusers branded him a thief.*

bran·dish (bran′dish), *v.* to shake or wave, as a weapon; flourish: *The sentry brandished his sword at the intruder.*

brand-new (brand′nōō′, -nyōō′), *adj.* completely new; unworn or unused: *a brand-new suit for Easter.*

bran·dy (bran′dē), *n., pl.* **bran·dies.** 1. an alcoholic beverage made by distilling wine or fermented fruit juice. —*v.,* **bran·died, bran·dy·ing.** 2. to mix, flavor, or preserve with brandy: *to brandy fruit.* [from the word *brandywine,* which comes from Dutch *brandewijn* "burnt (that is, distilled) wine"]

brash (brash), *adj.* 1. too quick to act; rash: *a brash decision to be regretted.* 2. unpleasantly bold: *a brash, rude person.* —**brash′ly,** *adv.* —**brash′ ness,** *n.*

Bra·síl·ia (brä zēl′yə), *n.* the capital city of Brazil, on the central plateau.

brass (bras), *n.* 1. a yellow metal, an alloy of copper and zinc. 2. a musical instrument of the trumpet or horn families.

ATLANTIC OCEAN
Amazon River
Recife
BRAZIL
Brasília
São Paulo
Rio de Janeiro
PACIFIC OCEAN

3. such instruments as a group. **4.** boldness or rudeness. **5.** *Slang.* high-ranking officers or officials in any organization.

brass·y (bras′ē), *adj.*, **brass·i·er, brass·i·est. 1.** made of brass or like brass in color. **2.** loud or noisy, like the sound made by a brass musical instrument: *a brassy tone of voice.* **3.** rude or impudent. —**brass′i·ness,** *n.*

brat (brat), *n.* a spoiled or rude child.

bra·va·do (brə vä′dō), *n., pl.* **bra·va·does** *or* **bra·va·dos.** a showy, swaggering display of courage, esp. to hide fear or uncertainty.

brave (brāv), *adj.*, **brav·er, brav·est. 1.** having or displaying courage; fearless: *brave soldiers.* **2.** splendid or fine: *She made a brave appearance in all her finery.* —*n.* **3.** a North American Indian warrior. —*v.*, **braved, brav·ing. 4.** to meet or face courageously: *He braved the winter weather.* —**brave′ly,** *adv.*

brav·er·y (brā′və rē), *n.* **1.** brave spirit or conduct; courage; valor. **2.** showiness; splendor; magnificence: *The king appeared in the bravery of royal attire.*

bra·vo (brä′vō), *interj.* **1.** well done! good! —*n., pl.* **bra·vos. 2.** a shout of bravo: *the bravos of an audience.*

brawl (brôl), *n.* **1.** a noisy quarrel, squabble, or fight; row. —*v.* **2.** to quarrel angrily or noisily; fight; squabble. —**brawl′er,** *n.*

brawn (brôn), *n.* **1.** well-developed muscles, esp. of the arms or legs. **2.** muscular strength: *You need plenty of brawn to lift that piano.*

brawn·y (brô′nē), *adj.*, **brawn·i·er, brawn·i·est.** muscular; strong. —**brawn′i·ness,** *n.*

bray (brā), *n.* **1.** the loud, harsh cry of a donkey. **2.** any sound resembling this: *the brays of the jeering mob.* —*v.* **3.** to utter the loud, harsh cry of a donkey. **4.** to utter with a loud, harsh sound: *to bray one's disapproval.*

bra·zen (brā′zən), *adj.* **1.** made of brass, or like brass in color. **2.** shameless or impudent: *a brazen falsehood.* —*v.* **3. brazen it out,** to face a situation boldly or without shame: *We hated to go, but decided to brazen it out.* —**bra′zen·ly,** *adv.* —**bra′zen·ness,** *n.*

bra·zier (brā′zhər), *n.* an open container for live coals or charcoal, used for heating purposes.

Bra·zil (brə zil′), *n.* a republic in E South America. 3,286,170 sq. mi. *Cap.:* Brasília. Official name, **United States of Brazil.** —**Bra·zil·ian** (brə zil′yən), *n., adj.*

Brazil′ nut′, a large, oily nut, the seed of a South American tree, having a very hard shell.

breach (brēch), *n.* **1.** a gap made in a wall, fortification, line of soldiers, etc.: *The attack made a breach in the enemy's ranks.* **2.** a violation or breaking, as of a law, trust, or promise: *a breach of the peace.* **3.** a breaking of friendly relations. —*v.* **4.** to make a breach or opening in. **5.** to break (a law, promise, etc.).

bread (bred), *n.* **1.** food made of baked dough or batter. **2.** food regarded as a symbol of one's livelihood: *to earn one's bread.* —*v.* **3.** to coat with bread crumbs or meal: *Bread the veal before cooking.* **4. know which side one's bread is buttered on,** to know what is most advantageous to one: *If you know which side your bread is buttered on, you'll take the job.*

bread·fruit (bred′frōōt′), *n., pl.* **bread·fruits** *or* **bread·fruit. 1.** a large, round, starchy fruit used for food, esp. in Pacific islands. **2.** the tree that bears this fruit.

breadth (bredth), *n.* **1.** the side-to-side measure of a thing; width. **2.** a piece of fabric in full width as made: *a breadth of silk.* **3.** wideness of viewpoint or interests: *a mind of great breadth.* **4.** size or extent: *the breadth of the prairies.*

Breadfruit
(fruit 5 inches
in diameter)

bread·win·ner (bred′win′ər), *n.* a person who earns a livelihood for himself and his family or other dependents.

break (brāk), *v.*, **broke** (brōk), **bro·ken** (brō′kən), **break·ing. 1.** to crack or divide or become cracked or divided through injury: *to break a bone; a dish that breaks when dropped.* **2.** to twist or wrench away from something (often fol. by *off*): *to break off a piece of bread.* **3.** to become detached or separated (usually fol. by *away* or *off*): *The balcony broke away from the wall of the house.* **4.** to injure so as to make useless: *He broke the radio beyond repair.* **5.** to become useless through injury: *The radio broke when he played it too loud.* **6.** to end or interrupt (often fol. by *off*): *to break off negotiations.* **7.** to divide (money) into lesser units: *He broke a large bill at the bank.* **8.** to reveal or make public, as news. **9.** to appear, happen, or become public or known: *Day broke. The news broke.* **10.** to tame or train, as an animal: *to break wild horses.* **11.** to train away from a habit (often fol. by *of*): *to break someone of speaking out of turn.* **12.** to overcome or master: *He broke the smoking habit.* **13.** to bankrupt or deprive of money. **14.** to weaken the impact of: *The awning broke his fall and saved his life.* **15.** to outdo or surpass: *He broke all the records for swimming.* **16.** to escape from: *to break jail.* **17.** to escape (usually fol. by *away*): *He broke away from his captors.* **18.** to make a sudden dash: *He broke and ran.* **19.** to violate or disregard: *to break the law.* **20.** to intrude (usually fol. by *in, into,* or *through*): *The thieves broke into the house.* **21.** to give forth a sound, expression of feeling, etc. (usually fol. by *into*): *to break into tears.* **22.** to come forth suddenly; erupt: *Laughter broke out.* **23.** to overwhelm (the heart) with grief or compassion: *His heart was broken by the tragedy.* **24.** to fail, as one's health, courage, etc. **25.** (of the voice) to change pitch or become interrupted suddenly: *His voice broke as he told his sad story.* —*n.* **26.** the act of breaking, or an instance of being broken. **27.** a crack or opening made by breaking: *a break in the plaster.* **28.** the act or an instance of separating from a person, thing, tradition, etc.: *a break with the past.* **29.** an interruption in an action: *a break in the con-*

versation. **30.** a brief rest or pause: *a coffee break.* **31.** a sudden dash, as in making an escape. **32.** a stroke of luck or a chance to improve one's lot: *The job was quite a break for him.* **33. break down, a.** to cease to function or be effective: *The car broke down on the highway.* **b.** to lose control of one's emotions: *She broke down and sobbed.* **c.** to separate into parts so as to study or analyze: *to break down a math problem.* **34. break up, a.** to separate or scatter: *to break up an angry mob.* **b.** to put an end to: *to break up a quarrel.* —**break′a·ble,** *adj.*

break·age (brā′kij), *n.* **1.** the act of breaking, or the state of being broken. **2.** the amount or value of things broken: *The breakage was $10.*

break·down (brāk′doun′), *n.* **1.** a collapse, as of a machine or of physical and mental health: *a nervous breakdown.* **2.** a division into parts: *a breakdown of the steps necessary for performing a task.*

break·er (brā′kər), *n.* **1.** a person or thing that breaks. **2.** a wave that breaks into foam on the shore.

break·fast (brek′fəst), *n.* **1.** the first meal of the day; morning meal. —*v.* **2.** to eat breakfast.

break·neck (brāk′nek′), *adj.* dangerously or recklessly swift: *breakneck speed.*

break·up (brāk′up′), *n.* **1.** a disintegration, separation, or dispersal: *the breakup of ice on northern lakes in the spring.* **2.** the end of a relationship, as between friends, a husband and wife, etc.

break·wa·ter (brāk′wô′tər, -wot′ər), *n.* a barrier, as a wall or jetty, built in a harbor to break the force of waves.

bream (brēm), *n., pl.* **breams** *or* **bream. 1.** any of several European freshwater fishes. **2.** any of several saltwater fishes.

breast (brest), *n.* **1.** the front part of the upper body. **2.** one of the milk glands located on the chest of a woman and certain other female mammals. **3.** the chest or bosom regarded as the center of emotions: *Love filled his breast.* **4. make a clean breast of,** to confess: *to make a clean breast of all one's misdeeds.*

breast·bone (brest′bōn′), *n.* the flat bone running down the center of the chest and connected to the ribs.

breast·plate (brest′plāt′), *n.* a piece of armor to cover the chest.

breast·work (brest′wûrk′), *n.* a wall, about as high as the chest, put up quickly for defense in battle.

breath (breth), *n.* **1.** the air taken into and then forced out of the lungs. **2.** the ability to breathe easily and normally: *She stopped on the landing and got her breath.* **3.** life or spirit: *We will fight while breath remains.* **4. in the same breath,** at once; immediately: *She said she'd go, then in the same breath she decided not to.* **5. save one's breath,** to avoid useless discussion: *I can't lend you any money, so save your breath.* **6. under one's breath,** in a low voice or whisper: *He said under his breath that he would never agree to that.*

breathe (brēth), *v.,* **breathed, breath·ing. 1.** to inhale and exhale: *He breathed the fresh mountain air.* **2.** to inhale and exhale air: *He breathed more freely now*

that the window was open. **3.** to be alive; live; exist: *I will hope as long as I breathe.* **4.** to whisper: *I wouldn't breathe a word of that to anyone.*

breath·er (brē′thər), *n.* a pause, as for breath: *After walking for an hour, they decided to take a breather.*

breath·less (breth′lis), *adj.* **1.** deprived of breath: *They were breathless after the long swim.* **2.** with the breath held, as in suspense or excitement: *Breathless, they watched the acrobats perform.* **3.** without life; dead. —**breath′less·ly,** *adv.* —**breath′less·ness,** *n.*

breath·tak·ing (breth′tā′king), *adj.* causing extreme pleasure, awe, or excitement: *a breath-taking drive through the mountains.* Also, **breath′tak·ing.**

breath·y (breth′ē), *adj.,* **breath·i·er, breath·i·est.** (of the voice) marked by too much outgoing breath: *to be breathy with excitement.* —**breath′i·ness,** *n.*

Breck·in·ridge (brek′ən rij′), *n.* **John C.,** 1821–1875, 14th Vice President of the U.S. 1857–1861: Confederate general in the U.S. Civil War.

bred (bred), *v.* the past tense and past participle of **breed.**

breech (brēch), *n.* **1.** the lower, rear part of the body; buttocks. **2.** the lower or hind part of anything. **3.** the rear part of a gun, behind the barrel.

breech·cloth (brēch′klôth′), *n., pl.* **breech·cloths** (brēch′klôthz′, -klôths′). a loincloth. Also, **breech·clout** (brēch′klout′).

breech·es (brich′iz), *n. (used as pl.)* **1.** men's or boys' knee-length trousers. **2.** any trousers. Also, **britches.**

breed (brēd), *v.,* **bred** (bred), **breed·ing. 1.** to produce offspring: *Rabbits breed in large numbers.* **2.** to raise for use and cause to reproduce, as a plant or animal: *to breed livestock; to breed flowers.* **3.** to mate (an animal). **4.** to educate or develop: *School breeds a love of learning.* **5.** to arise or develop: *Disease breeds in the slums.* —*n.* **6.** a kind of animal or plant that can be distinguished from other, similar kinds, esp. one developed by man. —**breed′er,** *n.*

breed·ing (brē′ding), *n.* **1.** the raising of plants and animals, esp. to produce improved kinds. **2.** upbringing or training, as shown by one's manners.

breeze (brēz), *n.* **1.** a light wind or current of air. —*v.,* **breezed, breez·ing. 2.** to move quickly or in a carefree manner: *She breezed gaily into the room.*

breez·y (brē′zē), *adj.,* **breez·i·er, breez·i·est. 1.** swept by or abounding in breezes: *a breezy deck; a breezy day.* **2.** fresh or lively: *a long, breezy conversation.* —**breez′i·ness,** *n.*

Bren′ner Pass′ (bren′-ər), a mountain pass in the Alps, between Italy and Austria.

breth·ren (breth′rin), *n.pl.* **1.** fellow members, esp. of a church. **2.** *Archaic.* brothers.

Bret·on (bret′ⁿn), *n.* **1.** a native or inhabitant of Brittany. **2.** the Celtic language of Brittany. —*adj.* **3.** referring to Brittany, the Bretons, or their language.

brev·i·ty (brev′i tē), *n.* a shortness of time or length: *We liked the brevity of his speech.*

brew (broō), *v.* 1. to make (beer, ale, etc.) by steeping, boiling, and fermenting malt and hops. 2. to prepare as a beverage by steeping or soaking: *to brew tea.* 3. to contrive or bring about: *to brew mischief.* 4. to gather or form: *A storm was brewing.* —*n.* 5. any beverage that has been brewed, esp. beer or ale. —**brew′er,** *n.*

brew·er·y (broō′ə rē), *n., pl.* **brew·er·ies.** a building or establishment for brewing beer and ale.

Brezh·nev (brezh′nef), *n.* Le·o·nid I. (le o nēt′), born 1906, Soviet communist leader.

bri·ar (brī′ər), *n.* another spelling of **brier¹**.

bribe (brīb), *n.* 1. anything given or promised to a person to persuade him to act against his wishes or to behave wrongly: *A public official should not accept bribes.* —*v.,* **bribed, brib·ing.** 2. to give or promise a bribe to: *They tried to bribe him to betray his country.* —**brib′a·ble,** *adj.*

brib·er·y (brī′bə rē), *n., pl.* **brib·er·ies.** the act or practice of giving or accepting a bribe.

brick (brik), *n.* 1. an oblong block of clay hardened by drying in the sun or baking in a kiln, used for building, paving, etc. 2. such blocks as a building material. 3. anything shaped like a brick: *a brick of gold.* —*v.* 4. to build, pave, or fill with brick. —*adj.* 5. made with bricks: *a brick fireplace.*

brick·bat (brik′bat′), *n.* 1. a piece of broken brick used as a weapon. 2. an unkind remark or harsh criticism.

brick·lay·ing (brik′lā′ing), *n.* the process or occupation of building with bricks. —**brick′lay′er,** *n.*

brick·work (brik′wûrk′), *n.* brick construction, or something made of brick: *a tower of brickwork.*

brid·al (brīd′əl), *adj.* of or concerning a bride or a wedding.

bride (brīd), *n.* a newly married woman, or a woman about to be married.

bride·groom (brīd′groōm′), *n.* a newly married man, or a man about to be married.

brides·maid (brīdz′mād′), *n.* a young woman who attends the bride at a wedding ceremony.

bridge¹ (brij), *n.* 1. a structure spanning and permitting passage over a river, chasm, road, or the like. 2. any connection between two nearby or related things, ideas, etc.: *The added paragraph is a bridge to connect the two topics.* 3. a raised platform, usually on the forward part of a ship, used by the captain and the navigators. 4. the ridge of the nose. 5. an artificial tooth or teeth set in a frame and attached to adjacent natural teeth. 6. a thin wedge for raising the strings of a musical instrument, such as a violin or cello, over the sounding board. —*v.,* **bridged, bridg·ing.** 7. to make a bridge or passage over; span: *The road bridged the river.* [from the Old English word *brycg*]

bridge² (brij), *n.* a card game for two pairs of players, each pair playing against the other. [another

form of the earlier word *biritch,* which is of unknown origin]

bridge·head (brij′hed′), *n.* a military position taken on the enemy side of a river or other obstacle.

Bridge·port (brij′pôrt′), *n.* a port city in SW Connecticut, on Long Island Sound.

bri·dle (brīd′əl), *n.* 1. a part of the harness of a horse, including the bit and the reins. —*v.,* **bri·dled, bri·dling.** 2. to put a bridle on (a horse). 3. to control as with a bridle; check; curb: *Bridle your anger.* 4. to draw up the head and draw in the chin, as in anger.

brief (brēf), *adj.* 1. short in time: *a brief wait at the station.* 2. using few words; concise: *His instructions were brief and to the point.* —*n.* 3. a summary of the major facts and points of a law case. 4. **briefs,** close-fitting, legless underpants. —*v.* 5. to provide with major facts and points: *to be briefed by one's advisers.* 6. **in brief,** in a few words; in short: *In brief, I forbid you to go.* —**brief′ly,** *adv.* —**brief′ness,** *n.*

brief·case (brēf′kās′), *n.* a flat, oblong leather case for carrying books, papers, etc.

bri·er¹ (brī′ər), *n.* a prickly plant or shrub. Also, **briar.** [from the Old English word *brǣr*]

bri·er² (brī′ər), *n.* 1. a shrub that grows near the Mediterranean Sea, having a hard, woody root used for making tobacco pipes. 2. a pipe made from the root of this plant. [from the French word *bruyère,* which comes from Latin *brūcus* "heather"]

brig (brig), *n.* 1. a two-masted vessel with square sails. 2. a prison on a ship.

Brig

bri·gade (bri gād′), *n.* 1. a military unit smaller than a division and made up of several regiments, squadrons, groups, or battalions. 2. any group of people organized for a specific purpose: *a fire brigade.*

brig′a·dier′ gen′eral (brig′ə dēr′), *pl.* **brigadier generals.** an officer in the U.S. Army, ranking above a colonel and below a major general.

brig·and (brig′ənd), *n.* a bandit, esp. a member of a roving and plundering gang.

brig·an·tine (brig′ən tēn′), *n.* a two-masted vessel

resembling a brig, but having square sails only on the foremast.

bright (brīt), *adj.* **1.** giving or reflecting much light; shining: *the bright stars.* **2.** filled with light: *bright rooms.* **3.** vivid or brilliant: *the bright plumage of a parrot.* **4.** having or showing quick wit or intelligence: *bright students; bright answers.* **5.** lively or cheerful: *bright, pleasant talk.* **6.** hopeful or favorable: *bright prospects.* —*adv.* **7.** in a bright manner; brightly. —**bright′ly**, *adv.* —**bright′ness**, *n.*

bright·en (brīt′ən), *v.* to make or become bright or brighter: *The new drapes brighten the room. Our spirits brightened at the news.*

bril·liance (bril′yəns), *n.* **1.** great brightness; splendor: *the brilliance of the sun at noon.* **2.** excellence or outstanding quality: *a pianist of brilliance.*

bril·liant (bril′yənt), *adj.* **1.** shining brightly; sparkling. **2.** distinguished or illustrious: *a time of brilliant achievements.* **3.** having or showing great talent or intelligence: *a brilliant artist.* —**bril′liant·ly**, *adv.*

brim (brim), *n.* **1.** the upper edge of anything hollow; rim: *the brim of a bowl.* **2.** a rim or edge that projects: *the brim of a hat.* —*v.*, **brimmed, brimming. 3.** to fill or be full to the brim: *Her eyes brimmed with tears.*

brim·ful (brim′fōol′), *adj.* full to the brim.

brim·stone (brim′stōn′), *n.* another word for **sulfur.**

brin·dle (brin′dəl), *n.* **1.** a brindled coloring. **2.** a brindled animal. —*adj.* **3.** another form of **brindled.**

brin·dled (brin′dəld), *adj.* having a coat that is gray or tawny with darker streaks or spots.

brine (brīn), *n.* **1.** heavily salted water: *Brine is used for pickling.* **2.** the sea, or sea water.

bring (bring), *v.*, **brought** (brôt), **bring·ing. 1.** to cause to come to the speaker or to accompany the speaker to another person or place: *Bring me more coffee. I have brought the book you wanted.* **2.** to cause to appear or happen: *Her screams brought the police. Sadness brings tears.* **3.** to persuade, convince, or compel: *He couldn't bring himself to do it.* **4.** to sell for; fetch: *Good violins bring high prices.* **5.** to begin (a legal action): *to bring an action for damages.* **6. bring about,** to cause (something) to happen: *What brought about this sudden change?* **7. bring forth,** to produce; give birth to: *She brought forth a male child. He brought forth a new proposal.* **8. bring out, a.** to expose or reveal: *The crisis brought out the weakness in his character.* **b.** to introduce to the public: *to bring out a new book.* **9. bring up, a.** to care for during childhood; rear: *They brought up six children.* **b.** to mention for consideration: *He brought up a point we had overlooked.*

brink (bringk), *n.* **1.** the edge or margin of a steep place or of land bordering water: *the brink of an abyss; the brink of the sea.* **2.** the extreme point beyond which something dangerous or momentous is bound to occur: *on the brink of ruin.*

brin·y (brī′nē), *adj.*, **brin·i·er, brin·i·est. 1.** of or like brine; salty: *a briny taste.* **2. the briny deep,** the ocean, esp. the depths of the ocean.

bri·quette (bri ket′), *n.* a small brick of compressed

coal dust or charcoal used for fuel.

Bris·bane (briz′bān, briz′bən), *n.* a seaport and the capital city of Queensland, in E Australia.

brisk (brisk), *adj.* **1.** quick and active; lively: *to walk at a brisk pace.* **2.** sharp and rousing: *brisk autumn weather.* —**brisk′ly**, *adv.* —**brisk′ness**, *n.*

bris·ket (bris′kit), *n.* the breast of an animal used for meat: *brisket of beef.*

bris·tle (bris′əl), *n.* **1.** a stiff hair, esp. from a hog. **2.** one of the hairs of a brush. —*v.*, **bris·tled, bris·tling. 3.** to stand or rise stiffly, like bristles: *The dog's coat bristled at the approach of danger.* **4.** to raise the bristles, as an angry or disturbed animal: *The dog bristled.* **5.** to become stiff with anger: *to bristle at an unkind remark.* **6.** to be thickly set or filled with something resembling bristles: *The skyline of New York bristles with tall buildings.* —**bris′tly**, *adj.*

Bris·tol (bris′təl), *n.* a port city in SW England.

Brit., British.

Brit·ain (brit′ən), *n.* another name for **Great Britain.**

Bri·tan·ni·a (bri tan′ē ə), *n.* the ancient Roman name for **Great Britain.**

britch·es (brich′iz), *n. (used as pl.)* another spelling of **breeches.**

Brit·ish (brit′ish), *adj.* **1.** of or concerning Great Britain, the British Commonwealth, or its inhabitants. —*n.* **2.** the people native to or inhabiting Great Britain or the British Commonwealth.

Brit′ish Colum′bia, a province in W Canada on the Pacific coast. 366,255 sq. mi. *Cap.:* Victoria.

Brit′ish Com′monwealth, a group of nations and dependent territories united by a common allegiance to Great Britain.

Brit′ish Em′pire, (formerly) the territories under the control of Great Britain.

Brit·ish·er (brit′i shər), *n.* a native or inhabitant of Great Britain, esp. of England.

Brit′ish Guia′na, former name of **Guyana.**

Brit′ish Hondu′ras, former name of **Belize.**

Brit′ish Isles′, a group of islands in W Europe: Great Britain, Ireland, and adjacent small islands. 120,592 sq. mi.

Brit′ish Soma′liland, a former British protectorate in E Africa, now part of Somalia.

Brit′ish ther′mal u′nit. See **Btu.**

Brit′ish West′ In′dies, the members of the British Commonwealth on the Caribbean Sea, including the Bahamas, Barbados, Jamaica, Trinidad and Tobago, and other small islands. about 12,500 sq. mi.

Brit·on (brit′ən), *n.* **1.** a native or inhabitant of Great Britain or the British Commonwealth, esp. of England. **2.** a member of a Celtic people occupying the southern part of Great Britain in ancient times.

Brit·ta·ny (brit′ə nē), *n.* a region in NW France, on a peninsula between the English Channel and the Bay of Biscay.

brit·tle (brit′ʼl), *adj.* 1. breaking easily and sharply; fragile: *Glass is a very brittle substance.* —*n.* 2. a brittle candy: *peanut brittle.* —**brit′tle·ness**, *n.*

broach (brōch), *v.* 1. to mention or suggest for the first time: *to broach a subject.* 2. to tap or pierce: *to broach a barrel of beer.* 3. to draw (beer, wine, etc.) by tapping.

broad (brôd), *adj.* 1. measured from side to side; wide: *The desk was three feet broad.* 2. of great breadth or area: *a broad expanse of desert.* 3. open and full: *in broad daylight.* 4. not limited; of wide range or scope: *a broad treatment of a subject.* 5. plain or clear: *a broad hint.* 6. main or general: *the broad outlines of a subject.* —**broad′ly**, *adv.*

broad·cast (brôd′kast′), *v.*, **broad·cast** *or* **broad·cast·ed; broad·cast·ing.** 1. to send out or transmit by radio or television: *to broadcast a program.* 2. to send out or transmit a program by radio or television. 3. to cast or scatter over an area, as seed. —*n.* 4. an instance of broadcasting. 5. a single radio or television program. —*adj.* 6. transmitted from a radio or television station. 7. cast or scattered over an area, as seed. —**broad′cast′er**, *n.*

broad·cloth (brôd′klôth′), *n.* 1. a woolen or worsted fabric having a fine weave and a smooth finish. 2. a fine fabric of cotton, silk, or rayon.

broad·en (brôd′ʼn), *v.* to make or become broad: *to broaden a road; an expanse of land that broadens.*

broad′ jump′, a track event in which a contestant jumps for distance, either from a standing position or with a running start. —**broad′ jump′er.**

broad·loom (brôd′lōōm′), *adj.* 1. of or referring to rugs or carpets woven on a wide loom and having no seams. —*n.* 2. a rug or carpet woven in this way.

broad·mind·ed (brôd′mīn′did), *adj.* having one's mind open to different ways, beliefs, etc.; tolerant. —**broad′·mind′ed·ly**, *adv.* —**broad′·mind′ed·ness**, *n.*

broad·side (brôd′sīd′), *n.* 1. the whole side of a ship above the water line. 2. a firing of all the guns on one side of a warship at the same time. 3. any strong attack, as by criticism: *a broadside against prejudice.* 4. Also, **broad·sheet** (brôd′shēt′). a sheet of paper printed on one side, as with a notice or advertisement. —*adv.* 5. with the broader side toward a given object: *The car hit the fence broadside.*

broad·sword (brôd′sôrd′), *n.* a sword having a straight, broad, flat blade.

Broad·way (brôd′wā′), *n.* 1. a major avenue in New York City. 2. the theater district on or near this avenue: center of the U.S. professional theater.

bro·cade (brō kād′), *n.* 1. a fabric woven with a raised design. —*v.*, **bro·cad·ed, bro·cad·ing.** 2. to weave with such a design.

broc·co·li (brok′ə lē), *n.* a kind of cauliflower with green stalks and flowerlike heads used as a vegetable.

bro·chure (brō shōōr′), *n.* a booklet or pamphlet.

bro·gan (brō′gən), *n.* a coarse, heavy shoe, esp. an ankle-high work shoe.

brogue[1] (brōg), *n.* an Irish accent in the speaking of English: *to speak with a heavy brogue.* [perhaps from a special use of *brogue*[2]]

brogue[2] (brōg), *n.* a long-wearing oxford shoe, often decorated with a pattern of small holes. [from the Irish word *brōg* "shoe"]

broil (broil), *v.* 1. to cook by direct heat, as with burning charcoal or a gas flame. 2. to make or become very hot: *a broiling July afternoon.*

broil·er (broi′lər), *n.* 1. a grate, pan, or part of a stove for broiling meat or fish. 2. a young chicken suitable for broiling.

broke (brōk), *v.* 1. the past tense of **break.** —*adj.* 2. *Informal.* without money; penniless.

bro·ken (brō′kən), *v.* 1. the past participle of **break.** —*adj.* 2. in fragments: *a broken bowl.* 3. out of operation or working condition: *a broken elevator.* 4. incomplete, or lacking parts: *a broken set of books.* 5. violated or not kept: *broken promises.* 6. interrupted; not continuous: *broken sleep; broken lines.* 7. weakened in strength, spirit, etc.: *broken health.* 8. tamed or trained: *a horse broken to the saddle.* 9. imperfectly spoken: *broken English.* —**bro′ken·ly**, *adv.*

bro·ken-heart·ed (brō′kən här′tid), *adj.* full of great sorrow, grief, or disappointment: *He's brokenhearted because his plans came to nothing.* —**bro′ken-heart′ed·ly**, *adv.*

bro·ker (brō′kər), *n.* a person who acts as an agent for another in business matters, as in buying or selling stock or real estate.

bro·ker·age (brō′kər ij), *n.* 1. the business of a broker. 2. the fee or commission paid to a broker.

bro·mide (brō′mīd), *n.* 1. a chemical compound containing bromine. 2. any of various bromine compounds used to calm the nerves or induce sleep. 3. an overly familiar saying; platitude.

bro·mine (brō′mēn), *n. Chem.* a nonmetallic element, a reddish-brown fuming liquid: member of the halogen group. *Symbol:* Br

bron·chi (brong′kī), *n.pl., sing.* **bron·chus** (brong′kəs). the two main branches of the windpipe, each of which conducts air to one of the lungs. See illus at **lung.**

bron·chi·al (brong′kē əl), *adj.* referring to or affecting the bronchi or the smaller tubes branching from them: *a bronchial infection.*

bron·chi·tis (brong kī′tis), *n.* an inflammation of the lining of the bronchi or of the smaller tubes leading from them, causing a severe cough.

bron·co (brong′kō), *n.* a pony or other small horse of the western U.S., esp. one that has not been tamed. Also, **bron′cho.**

Brontosaurus
(height 12 ft.;
length 60 ft.)

bron·to·saur·us (bron′tə sôr′əs), *n.* a large, plant-eating dinosaur of North America. [from the Greek words *brontē* "thunder" + *sauros* "lizard"]

act, āble, dâre, ärt; ebb, ēqual; if, īce; hot, ōver, ôrder; oil; book; ōōze; out; up, ûrge; ə = *a* as in *alone;* ʼ as in *button* (but′ʼn), *fire* (fīʼr); chief; shoe; thin; ŧħat; zh as in *measure* (mezh′ər). See full key inside cover.

Bronx (broñgks), *n.* **the,** a borough of New York City, N of Manhattan. 43 sq. mi. —**Bronx′ite,** *n.*

bronze (bronz), *n.* **1.** a brownish or reddish metal, an alloy of copper and tin. **2.** a metallic brown. **3.** a work of art, as a statue, made of bronze. —*v.,* **bronzed, bronz·ing. 4.** to make or become bronze in color, as by exposure to the sun.

Bronze′ Age′, the period in the history of mankind, following the Stone Age and preceding the Iron Age, marked by the use of bronze tools and weapons.

brooch (brōch, brōōch), *n.* a clasp or ornament having a pin at the back for fastening to clothing.

brood (brōōd), *n.* **1.** all the birds hatched by a mother bird at one time. **2.** the children of one mother. —*v.* **3.** to sit upon eggs in order to hatch them. **4.** to dwell moodily on something; worry: *He brooded over the loss of his dog.* —**brood′ing·ly,** *adv.*

brook¹ (brōōk), *n.* a small, natural stream of fresh water. [from the Old English word *brōc*]

brook² (brōōk), *v.* to bear, allow, or tolerate: *I will brook no more of his interference.* [from the Old English word *brūcan* "to bear"]

brook·let (brōōk′lit), *n.* a small brook.

Brook·lyn (brōōk′lin), *n.* a borough of New York City, on W Long Island. 76.4 sq. mi. —**Brook·lyn·ite** (brōōk′lə nīt′), *n.*

broom (brōōm), *n.* **1.** a device for sweeping, consisting of a brush, usually of straw, bound to a long handle. **2.** a plant with long, slender branches bearing numerous yellow flowers.

broom·stick (brōōm′stik′), *n.* the long, sticklike handle of a broom.

bros., brothers. Also, **Bros.**

broth (brôth), *n.* a thin soup made from boiling meat, fish, or vegetables in water.

broth·er (bruħ′ər), *n.* **1.** a boy or man who has the same mother and father as another person. **2.** Also, **half brother.** a brother who is the son of either one's mother or one's father; a brother by one parent only. **3.** a male person who is a member of the same group, profession, trade, etc., as another. **4.** a member of a religious order who is not a priest.

broth·er·hood (bruħ′ər hōōd′), *n.* **1.** the tie that unites brothers or members of the same group, profession, race, etc.: *to believe in the brotherhood of man.* **2.** all those who share the same trade, profession, interest, etc.: *the brotherhood of architects.*

broth·er-in-law (bruħ′ər in lô′), *n., pl.* **broth·ers-in-law** (bruħ′ərz in lô′). **1.** the brother of one's husband or wife. **2.** the husband of one's sister.

broth·er·ly (bruħ′ər lē), *adj.* of, like, or befitting a brother or brothers, as in being affectionate or loyal: *brotherly love.* —**broth′er·li·ness,** *n.*

Brougham

brough·am (brōō′əm, brōōm), *n.* a four-wheeled, closed carriage for two or four persons, having the driver's seat outside.

brought (brôt), *v.* the past tense and past participle of **bring.**

brow (brou), *n.* **1.** the bony arch over the eye, or the hair growing upon it. **2.** the forehead: *He wrinkled his brow in amazement.* **3.** the edge of a steep place: *the brow of a cliff.*

brow·beat (brou′bēt′), *v.,* **brow·beat, brow·beat·en, brow·beat·ing.** to frighten by fierce looks or harsh words; bully: *The soldiers browbeat their captives.*

brown (broun), *n.* **1.** a dark color with a yellowish or reddish hue; the color of chocolate, soil, or coffee. —*adj.* **2.** of the color brown: *a brown horse.* —*v.* **3.** to make or become brown, as by cooking, frying, etc.: *to brown a steak.* —**brown′ish,** *adj.*

Brown (broun), *n.* **John,** 1800–1859, U.S. abolitionist leader.

brown·ie (brou′nē), *n.* **1.** (in folklore) a little brown fairy or goblin, esp. one who helps secretly in household work. **2.** a small, flat, chewy chocolate cake, usually containing nuts.

Brown·ie (brou′nē), *n.* a member of the junior division (ages 8–11) of the Girl Scouts.

brown′ rice′, rice that has not been polished.

brown·stone (broun′stōn′), *n.* **1.** a reddish-brown sandstone, used esp. as a building material. **2.** a building, esp. a dwelling, fronted with this stone.

brown′ sug′ar, sugar that has not been refined.

browse (brouz), *v.,* **browsed, brows·ing. 1.** to eat or nibble at grass, shoots, etc., as cattle or deer; graze. **2.** to look through or over something without hurry: *to browse in a bookstore.*

bru·in (brōō′in), *n.* a bear.

bruise (brōōz), *v.,* **bruised, bruis·ing. 1.** to injure or become injured by means of a blow and without breaking the skin. **2.** to offend or hurt, as with an insult. **3.** to damage, as by handling: *Be careful not to bruise the tomatoes.* —*n.* **4.** the injury resulting from a blow, usually a discolored area caused by bleeding beneath the skin.

brunch (brunch), *n.* a meal eaten in the late morning that serves as both breakfast and lunch.

bru·net (brōō net′), *adj.* **1.** (of a boy or man) having dark hair and eyes. —*n.* **2.** a boy or man with dark hair and eyes.

bru·nette (brōō net′), *adj.* **1.** (of a girl or woman) having dark hair and eyes. —*n.* **2.** a girl or woman with dark hair and eyes.

brunt (brunt), *n.* the main shock, force, or impact, as of an attack or blow: *the brunt of the hurricane.*

brush¹ (brush), *n.* **1.** a tool consisting of bristles, hair, or the like, set in or attached to a handle, used for grooming, painting, polishing, etc. **2.** the act of brushing. **3.** a light, grazing stroke: *He felt the brush of cobwebs across his face.* **4.** the bushy tail of an animal, esp. a fox. **5.** a part of an electric motor or generator that makes contact with the rotating armature. **6.** a brief, hostile meeting: *a brush with the law.* —*v.* **7.** to paint, clean, etc., with a brush: *to brush one's teeth.* **8.** to touch lightly in passing over: *The leaves brushed his face.* **9.** to remove with or as if with a brush: *to brush lint from one's lapel.* **10.**

brush aside, to ignore or disregard: *to brush aside criticism.* **11. brush off,** to dismiss rudely or abruptly: *He brushed us off as though he didn't know us.* [from the Old French word *broce,* which comes from Germanic]

brush² (bru̱sh), *n.* **1.** a dense growth of bushes, shrubs, etc.; brushwood. **2.** See **brushwood** (def. 1). **3.** land covered with a dense growth of trees, shrubs, etc. [from the Middle English word *brusshe*] —**brush′y,** *adj.*

brush·wood (bru̱sh′wŏŏd′), *n.* **1.** branches that have been cut or broken off a tree or shrub; brush. **2.** See **brush²** (def. 1).

brusque (brusk), *adj.* abrupt in manner or speech; blunt: *to receive a brusque reply.* —**brusque′ly,** *adv.* —**brusque′ness,** *n.*

Brus·sels (brus′əlz), *n.* the capital city of Belgium, in the central part.

Brus′sels sprouts′, 1. the small, cabbagelike heads that grow along the stalk of a plant related to the cabbage and cauliflower, used as a vegetable. **2.** the plant itself.

bru·tal (brōōt′ᵊl), *adj.* **1.** savage or cruel; inhuman: *a brutal dictator.* **2.** crude or coarse; harsh: *brutal manners.* —**bru′tal·ly,** *adv.*

bru·tal·i·ty (brōō tal′i tē), *n., pl.* **bru·tal·i·ties. 1.** the fact of being brutal or cruel. **2.** a brutal act: *the brutalities of war.*

brute (brōōt), *n.* **1.** an animal: *The brutes cannot speak or think.* **2.** a brutal, insensitive, or crude person: *War makes brutes of men.* —*adj.* **3.** like an animal; not human: *brute nature.* **4.** savage; cruel: *brute indifference to the suffering of others.* —**brut′ish,** *adj.*

Brussels sprouts

B.S.A., Boy Scouts of America.

Btu, British thermal unit: the amount of heat required to raise the temperature of one pound of water one Fahrenheit degree. Also, **BTU, B.t.u., B.T.U.**

bu., **1.** bureau. **2.** bushel; bushels.

bub·ble (bub′əl), *n.* **1.** a thin′film of liquid forming a ball and containing gas or air: *to blow soap bubbles.* **2.** a small ball of air or gas in a liquid or solid: *bubbles in a glass of soda; bubbles in a cake of ice.* **3.** anything that is not real or practical. —*v.,* **bub·bled, bub·bling. 4.** to make or release bubbles: *Water bubbles when it boils.* **5.** to flow or spout with a gurgling noise: *The stream bubbled among the rocks.* **6.** to behave or exist in a happy, lively manner: *He bubbled with enthusiasm.* —**bub′bly,** *adj.*

bu·bon′ic plague′ (byōō bon′ik, bōō-), a highly contagious, usually fatal disease spread by fleas.

buc·ca·neer (buk′ə nēr′), *n.* a pirate. [from the French word *boucanier* "a person who barbecues (meat)." The word was applied to seafaring adventurers who, on their visits ashore, adopted the South American Indian device for smoking or drying their meat]

Bu·chan·an (byōō kan′ən), *n.* **James,** 1791–1868, 15th President of the U.S. 1857–1861.

Bu·cha·rest (bōō′kə rest′), *n.* the capital city of Rumania, in the S part.

buck¹ (buk), *n.* **1.** the male of certain animals, as the deer, antelope, or goat. **2.** *Slang.* a dollar. **3. pass the buck,** to avoid responsibility or blame by shifting it to someone else: *He always passed the buck to his younger brother.* [from the Old English word *bucca* "he goat" or *bucc* "male deer"]

buck² (buk), *v.* **1.** to leap with arched back and come down with head low and forelegs stiff, as a horse does in order to throw a rider. **2.** to resist stubbornly; object strongly: *He bucked at every attempt to make him work.* **3.** to force a way through or against: *The car had to buck heavy traffic.* **4. buck up,** to become more cheerful, vigorous, etc.: *Maybe he'll buck up now that he has a new hobby.* [from *buck¹.* The original sense is "to leap like a buck"]

buck·board (buk′bôrd′), *n.* a light, four-wheeled carriage in which a long board frame is used in the place of a body and springs.

buck·et (buk′it), *n.* **1.** a round vessel having a flat bottom and a semicircular handle, used for holding or carrying water, sand, etc.; pail. **2.** a scoop on a steam shovel. **3.** a bucketful: *a bucket of sand.*

Buckboard

buck·et·ful (buk′it fŏŏl′), *n., pl.* **buck·et·fuls.** the amount a bucket can hold.

buck·eye (buk′ī′), *n.* **1.** any of various trees or shrubs related to the horse chestnut. **2.** the smooth, brown seed of this tree.

buck·le (buk′əl), *n.* **1.** a clasp for fastening two loose ends, as of a strap or belt. **2.** an ornament resembling this: *shoes with large silver buckles.* **3.** a bend, warp, or kink. —*v.,* **buck·led, buck·ling. 4.** to fasten or be fastened with a buckle or buckles: *He buckled his belt.* **5.** to bend, warp, or collapse: *The bridge buckled in the storm.* **6. buckle down,** to settle down to work; concentrate on one's job, responsibility, etc.: *If he doesn't buckle down, he's never going to graduate.*

buck·ler (buk′lər), *n.* a round shield carried on the arm.

buck·ram (buk′rəm), *n.* a stiff cotton fabric used for binding books, lining clothes, etc.

buck·saw (buk′sô′), *n.* a two-handled saw having a blade set in a frame, used for sawing wood.

buck·shot (buk′shot′), *n.* heavy lead shot used for hunting game.

Bucksaw

buck·skin (buk′skin′), *n.* **1.** a strong, soft, yellowish or grayish leather made from the skin of deer or sheep. **2. buckskins,** clothes, esp. breeches, or shoes made of buckskin.

---

act, āble, dâre, ärt; ebb, ēqual; if, īce; hot, ōver, ôrder; oil; bŏŏk; ōōze; out; up, ûrge; ə = *a* as in *alone;* ᵊ as in *button* (but′ᵊn), *fire* (fīᵊr); chief; shoe; thin; ᵗhat; zh as in *measure* (mezh′ər). See full key inside cover.

buck·tooth (buk′tooth′), *n., pl.* **buck·teeth** (buk′-tēth′). a tooth, esp. an upper front tooth, that sticks out. —**buck′toothed′**, *adj.*

buck·wheat (buk′hwēt′, -wēt′), *n.* a plant whose dark triangular seeds are used as a feed for animals or are ground into flour.

bu·col·ic (byoo kol′ik), *adj.* 1. of or concerning shepherds; pastoral. 2. of, concerning, or suggesting a peaceful country life: *a pleasant, bucolic scene of cows grazing in deep grass.*

bud (bud), *n.* 1. a small growth that develops into a flower, leaf, or branch. 2. an unopened flower. —*v.,* **bud·ded, bud·ding.** 3. to put forth or produce buds: *The trees budded in the early spring.* 4. to begin to grow or develop: *His talent budded when he was very young.* 5. **nip in the bud,** to stop (something) in the beginning of its development: *Our plans were nipped in the bud.*

Bu·da·pest (boo′də pest′), *n.* the capital city of Hungary, in the central part, on the Danube River.

Bud·dha (boo′də), *n.* 1. 566?–c480 B.C., Indian religious leader: founded Buddhism. 2. a statue or picture of Buddha.

Bud·dhism (boo′diz-əm), *n.* an Asian religion founded by Buddha, which teaches that suffering is caused by desire, and that freedom from this suffering can be found through certain practices based on right living and right thinking. —**Bud′dhist,** *n., adj.*

bud·dy (bud′ē), *n., pl.* **bud·dies.** a comrade or chum; pal.

budge (buj), *v.,* **budged, budg·ing.** to move slightly in position, opinion, etc.: *Strong as they were, they could not budge the car. She would not budge in her decision.*

Buddha

budg·et (buj′it), *n.* 1. a plan for spending an available sum of money, which lists the amounts to be spent for different purposes: *Their budget included the cost of their vacation.* —*v.,* **budg·et·ed, budg·et·ing.** 2. to plan how to spend or use: *to budget time to allow for study and recreation.*

Bue·nos Ai·res (bwā′nəs ī°r′iz, âr′ez), a seaport and the capital city of Argentina, in the E part, on the Río de la Plata.

buff (buf), *n.* 1. a thick, light-yellow leather, originally made of buffalo skin. 2. a wheel or small stick covered with leather or the like, used in polishing. 3. a medium or dark tan; yellowish brown. —*adj.* 4. made of buff: *a buff jacket.* 5. of a medium or dark tan: *a buff complexion.* —*v.* 6. to clean or polish with buff or the like: *to buff one's shoes.*

buf·fa·lo (buf′ə lō′), *n., pl.* **buf·fa·loes** *or* **buf·fa·lo.** 1. any of a number of species of large oxlike animals, as

the water buffalo, Cape buffalo, etc. 2. another word for **bison.**

Buf·fa·lo (buf′ə lō′), *n.* a port city in W New York, on Lake Erie.

Buf′falo Bill′. See **Cody, William Frederick.**

buff·er¹ (buf′ər), *n.* 1. any device, material, or apparatus used as a shield, cushion, or bumper, esp. on machinery: *A buffer on a railroad car absorbs shock.* 2. a person who protects another against annoyance, danger, etc.: *His wife was his buffer, keeping the outside world away while he worked.* —*v.* 3. to cushion, shield, or protect: *to buffer someone against bad news.* 4. to lessen the bad effect of: *to buffer bad news with words of hope.* [from the Scottish word *buff* "to strike, beat," which comes from Old French *buffe* "a blow" (see *buffet¹*) + the suffix *-er*]

buff·er² (buf′ər), *n.* 1. a device for buffing. 2. a worker who uses such a device. [from *buff* + *-er*]

buf·fet¹ (buf′it), *n.* 1. a blow, as with the hand or fist. 2. any shock or concussion: *to suffer from the buffets of misfortune.* —*v.,* **buf·fet·ed, buf·fet·ing.** 3. to strike, as with the hand or fist. 4. to strike against or push repeatedly: *The wind buffeted the house.* [from the Old French word *buffe* "a blow"]

buf·fet² (bə fā′, boo fā′), *n.* 1. a cabinet or sideboard, used in a dining room, for holding china, table linen, etc. 2. a meal laid out on a table or sideboard so that guests may serve themselves. [from French]

buf·foon (bə foon′), *n.* 1. a clown. 2. a person who habitually makes jokes, plays tricks, etc. —**buf·foon·er·y** (bə foo′nə rē), *n.*

bug (bug), *n.* 1. any of a group of insects that have sucking or biting mouth parts and sometimes lack wings. 2. any insect or insectlike crawling thing. 3. any germ that causes a disease: *a flu bug.* 4. *Informal.* a defect, as in a machine. 5. *Slang.* an electronic spying device. 6. *Slang.* a person who is devoted to a hobby or other pursuit: *a film bug.* —*v.,* **bugged, bug·ging.** 7. *Slang.* to install a secret listening device in (a room, building, etc.) or on (a telephone). 8. *Slang.* to annoy; pester.

bug·a·boo (bug′ə boo′), *n.* another word for **bugbear.**

bug·bear (bug′bâr′), *n.* 1. a cause of groundless fears: *Riding in an elevator is his greatest bugbear.* 2. (in folklore) a goblin or monster supposed to eat naughty children.

bug·gy (bug′ē), *n., pl.* **bug·gies.** 1. a light, four-wheeled carriage with a single seat for two people. 2. a carriage for a baby.

bu·gle (byoo′gəl), *n.* a brass instrument resembling the trumpet but usually lacking valves. Bugles are used esp. for playing military signals and calls. —**bu′gler,** *n.*

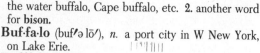

Bugle

build (bild), *v.,* **built** (bilt), **build·ing.** 1. to construct by putting together materials or parts: *to build a bridge; to build a wall.* 2. to increase or strengthen (often fol. by *up*): *to build a business; to build up one's hopes.* 3. to mold, form, or create: *to build boys into men.* 4. to form or construct something (often fol. by *on* or *upon*): *They built on firm ground.* —*n.* **5.** the manner or form of construction, physique, etc.: *The athlete had a strong build.* —**build′er,** *n.*

build·ing (bil′diñg), *n.* **1.** any more or less permanent structure having walls and a roof, used as a dwelling, place of business, etc. **2.** the act, business, or practice of constructing houses, office buildings, etc.

built-in (bilt′in′), *adj.* built as a permanent part of a larger construction: *a built-in bookcase.*

bulb (bulb), *n.* **1.** the rounded underground bud from which certain plants, such as onions, tulips, or lilies, grow. **2.** anything having such a shape: *the bulb of a thermometer; an electric light bulb.*

bulb·ous (bul′bəs), *adj.* **1.** shaped like a bulb: *a bulbous ornament.* **2.** having or growing from bulbs.

Bul·gar·i·a (bŏŏl gâr′ē ə), *n.* a republic in SE Europe. 42,800 sq. mi. *Cap.:* Sofia. —**Bul·gar′i·an,** *n., adj.*

bulge (bulj), *n.* **1.** a part that bends or swells out: *a bulge in a wall.* —*v.,* **bulged, bulg·ing. 2.** to bend or swell outward: *The bag bulged with groceries.*

bulk (bulk), *n.* **1.** largeness of size; mass: *The whale is an animal of great bulk.* **2.** the greater part: *The bulk of the debt was paid.* —*v.* **3.** to be or seem large or important: *The problem bulks in his mind.* **4. in bulk, a.** unpackaged; loose: *to buy potatoes in bulk.* **b.** in large quantities: *Sugar can be had by the pound or in bulk.*

bulk·head (bulk′hed′), *n.* **1.** any of a number of upright partitions in a ship forming watertight compartments. **2.** a wall built along a waterfront for protection against damage by water.

bulk·y (bul′kē), *adj.,* **bulk·i·er, bulk·i·est.** large and cumbersome: *a bulky package.* —**bulk′i·ness,** *n.*

bull[1] (bŏŏl), *n.* **1.** the male of animals in the ox family. **2.** the male of several other large animals, such as elephants or whales. **3. the Bull,** another name for Taurus. [from the Old English word *bula*]

bull[2] (bŏŏl), *n.* an official document or decree sent by the pope. [from the medieval Latin word *bulla* "seal"]

bull·dog (bŏŏl′dôg′), *n.* a medium-sized, short-haired, muscular dog with powerful jaws.

bull·doze (bŏŏl′dōz′), *v.,* **bull·dozed, bull·doz·ing. 1.** to level or clear away by using a bulldozer. **2.** to bully: *They tried to bulldoze him into changing his mind.*

bull·doz·er (bŏŏl′dō′-zər), *n.* a large powerful tractor having a vertical blade at the front end for moving dirt, rocks, etc.

Bulldozer

bul·let (bŏŏl′it), *n.* a shaped piece of metal, forming the front part of a cartridge, for shooting from small arms. See also **cartridge** (def. 1).

bul·le·tin (bŏŏl′i t°n), *n.* **1.** a short statement or announcement issued to inform the public: *a news bulletin.* **2.** a newspaper, magazine, or catalog published by a group for its members or other interested persons: *a college bulletin; a club bulletin.*

bull·fight (bŏŏl′fīt′), *n.* a traditional Spanish and Latin American spectacle in which a bull is fought and killed by a matador using only a cape and a sword. —**bull′fight′er,** *n.* —**bull′fight′ing,** *n.*

bull·finch (bŏŏl′finch′), *n.* a brightly colored European songbird.

bull·frog (bŏŏl′frôg′, -frog′), *n.* a large frog with a loud, deep croak.

bull·head (bŏŏl′hed′), *n.* any of a number of American freshwater fishes with broad heads, as certain catfishes.

bull·head·ed (bŏŏl′hed′id), *adj.* very stubborn; obstinate. —**bull′head′ed·ness,** *n.*

bul·lion (bŏŏl′yən), *n.* gold or silver in the form of bars or ingots.

bull·ock (bŏŏl′ək), *n.* **1.** a young bull. **2.** an ox or steer.

Bull′ Run′, a creek in NE Virginia: site of Civil War battles 1861 and 1862.

bull's-eye (bŏŏlz′ī′), *n.* **1.** the round spot, usually black or outlined in black, at the center of a target. **2.** a shot that strikes the center of a target. **3.** a small, round opening or window.

bull·ter·ri·er (bŏŏl′ter′ē ər), *n.* one of an English breed of medium-sized, short-haired dogs, usually having a white or brindled coat.

bul·ly (bŏŏl′ē), *n., pl.* **bul·lies. 1.** a person who habitually teases and annoys smaller or weaker people. —*v.,* **bul·lied, bul·ly·ing. 2.** to tease and annoy smaller and weaker people. —*adj.* **3.** very good; fine: *We had a bully time.* —*interj.* **4.** good! well done! hurrah!: *Bully for you!*

Bullterrier
(18 in. high
at shoulder)

bul·rush (bŏŏl′rush′), *n.* a tall plant with thin stems that grows in wet places.

bul·wark (bŏŏl′wərk), *n.* **1.** a wall of earth or other material built for defense. **2.** any protection against injury or annoyance: *The new dam is a bulwark against floods.* **3.** any source of support or comfort: *Religion is his bulwark.*

bum (bum), *n.* **1.** *Informal.* a person who loafs, esp. a tramp or hobo. —*v.,* **bummed, bum·ming.** *Informal.* **2.** to get (something) for nothing: *He's always bumming candy from me.* **3.** to spend time doing nothing; loaf: *He spent the summer bumming around.* —*adj.* **4.** *Slang.* bad or wrong: *bum directions.*

Bumblebee
(Queen)
(length ¾ in.)

bum·ble·bee (bum′bəl bē′), *n.* a large bee that makes a humming sound.

bump (bump), *v.* **1.** to come in contact or collide

with (often fol. by *into*): *The car bumped into a telephone pole.* 2. to cause to strike or collide: *The boy bumped the stick against every fence post.* 3. to displace by force of collision; knock: *The cat bumped the vase off the shelf.* 4. to bounce along; move with jerks: *The old car bumped down the road.* —n. 5. the act or an instance of bumping; collision. 6. the shock of a blow or collision. 7. a small area raised above the level of the surrounding surface: *a bump in the road.* 8. **bump into,** to meet accidentally: *We bumped into an old friend.*

bump·er (bum′pər), *n.* 1. a person or thing that bumps. 2. a metal guard for protecting the front or rear of an automobile, truck, etc. 3. a cup or glass filled to the brim, esp. when drunk as a toast. —*adj.* 4. unusually large or abundant: *a bumper crop.*

bump·kin (bump′kin), *n.* an awkward, clumsy person from the country; yokel.

bump·y (bum′pē), *adj.,* **bump·i·er, bump·i·est.** 1. having a rough, uneven surface: *a bumpy road.* 2. full of bumps and jolts: *a bumpy ride on a country road.* —**bump′i·ness,** *n.*

bun (bun), *n.* 1. a bread roll, either plain or slightly sweetened, sometimes containing spices, raisins, etc. 2. hair gathered into a round coil or knot at the nape of the neck or on top of the head.

bunch (bunch), *n.* 1. a connected group; cluster: *a bunch of grapes.* 2. a group of people or things. —*v.* 3. to gather together in a group or cluster.

bun·dle (bun′dəl), *n.* 1. several objects bound or wrapped together: *a bundle of sticks.* 2. an item wrapped for carrying; package. —*v.,* **bun·dled, bun·dling.** 3. to tie together or wrap in a bundle. 4. to send away hurriedly: *The children were bundled off to school.* 5. **bundle up,** to dress warmly or snugly: *It's snowing, so bundle up.*

bung (bung), *n.* 1. a stopper for the opening of a cask. 2. Also, **bunghole.** a hole for filling or tapping a cask. —*v.* 3. to fill or stop with a bung; cork; plug.

bun·ga·low (bung′gə lō′), *n.* a small, one-storied house; cottage.

bung·hole (bung′hōl′), *n.* See **bung** (def. 2).

bun·gle (bung′gəl), *v.,* **bun·gled, bun·gling.** 1. to do clumsily and awkwardly: *to bungle a job.* —*n.* 2. something that has been done clumsily or awkwardly. —**bun′gler,** *n.*

bun·ion (bun′yən), *n.* a painful swelling on the foot, esp. at the base of the big toe.

bunk¹ (bungk), *n.* 1. a built-in platform bed. —*v.* 2. to sleep in or occupy a bunk. [short for *bunker*]

bunk² (bungk), *n. Slang.* nonsense; humbug: *Your story is a lot of bunk.* [short for *bunkum,* which comes from *Buncombe,* a county in North Carolina. The meaning arose because a 19th-century congressman from that district repeatedly said that he was speaking for Buncombe]

bunk·er (bung′kər), *n.* 1. a large bin or receptacle; a fixed chest or box: *a coal bunker.* 2. a mound of sand or dirt serving as an obstacle on a golf course. 3. a fortification set mostly below the surface of the ground, fitted with openings through which to fire,

and having overhead protection. —*v.* 4. to hit (a ball) into a bunker on a golf course.

Bunk′er Hill′, a hill near Boston, Massachusetts. The first major battle of the American Revolution, called the Battle of Bunker Hill, was fought on a nearby hill on June 17, 1775.

bun·ny (bun′ē), *n., pl.* **bun·nies.** a rabbit, esp. a young one.

Bun′sen burn′er (bun′sən), a gas burner used in laboratories. [named after R. W. *Bunsen* (1811–1899), German chemist]

bunt (bunt), *v.* 1. (of a goat or calf) to push with the horns or head. 2. (in baseball) to bat (a pitched ball) very gently so that it does not roll far into the infield. —*n.* 3. a push with the horns or head. 4. (in baseball) **a.** the act of bunting. **b.** a bunted ball.

Bunsen burner

bun·ting¹ (bun′ting), *n.* 1. a coarse open fabric used for flags and patriotic decorations. 2. patriotic and festive decorations made from such cloth or from paper, esp. in the colors of the national flag. [from the Middle English word *bonten* "to sift." The cloth was originally used for sifting grain or powders]

bun·ting² (bun′ting), *n.* a hooded sleeping garment for infants. [from a special use of *bunting*¹]

Bun·yan (bun′yən), *n.* **Paul,** a legendary giant lumberjack: an American folk hero.

bu·oy (boo′ē, boi), *n.* 1. a distinctively shaped and colored floating object, anchored to mark a channel or dangerous area. 2. a life preserver; life buoy. —*v.* 3. to prevent from sinking; keep afloat: *The life jacket buoyed her up until help arrived.* 4. to raise the spirits; encourage: *The teacher's compliment buoyed him up.*

buoy·an·cy (boi′ən sē, boo′yən sē), *n.* 1. the tendency to float or rise when immersed in a liquid or gas: *the buoyancy of a ship; the buoyancy of a balloon.* 2. the ability of a liquid or gas to float an object immersed in it. 3. cheerfulness of spirit; light-heartedness.

A, Anchor; B, Buoy

buoy·ant (boi′ənt, boo′yənt), *adj.* 1. tending to rise or float when immersed in a liquid or gas. 2. capable of keeping an object afloat. 3. cheerful and light-hearted. —**buoy′ant·ly,** *adv.*

bur (bûr), *n.* 1. the rough, prickly case around the seeds of certain plants. 2. a plant bearing burs.

bur·den¹ (bûr′dən), *n.* 1. something that is carried; load. 2. something that is borne or carried with difficulty: *the burden of responsibility.* —*v.* 3. to load heavily: *to burden a donkey; to burden someone with problems.* [from the Old English word *byrthen*]

bur·den² (bûr′d³n), *n.* **1.** the principal idea of a statement, message, or the like. **2.** the refrain or chorus of a song. [from the French word *bourdon* "droning sound"]

bur·den·some (bûr′d³n səm), *adj.* **1.** very heavy. **2.** very distressing or troublesome.

bur·dock (bûr′dok), *n.* a broad-leaved weed bearing burs.

bu·reau (byŏŏr′ō), *n.* **1.** a chest of drawers, often with a mirror at the top. **2.** a division of a government department: *the Housing Bureau.* **3.** an agency or office that collects or distributes news or information: *a travel bureau.*

bu·reauc·ra·cy (byŏŏ rok′rə sē), *n., pl.* **bu·reauc·ra·cies.** **1.** government with many bureaus, offices, and minor officials. **2.** a group of officials and administrators. **3.** administration characterized by confusion and delays because of too many employees and complicated work procedures.

bu·reau·crat (byŏŏr′ə krat′), *n.* **1.** an official of a bureaucracy. **2.** an official who works by a set routine without thinking things out independently. **—bu′reau·crat′ic,** *adj.* **—bu′reau·crat′i·cal·ly,** *adv.*

bur·gess (bûr′jis), *n.* **1.** an inhabitant or representative of an English borough. **2.** a representative in the colonial legislature of Virginia or Maryland.

burgh·er (bûr′gər), *n.* an inhabitant of a borough or town; citizen.

bur·glar (bûr′glər), *n.* a person who commits burglary.

bur·glar·ize (bûr′glə rīz′), *v.,* **bur·glar·ized, bur·glar·iz·ing.** to break into and steal from (a place): *Thieves burglarized the warehouse.*

bur·gla·ry (bûr′glə rē), *n., pl.* **bur·gla·ries.** the act of breaking into and entering the building of another with intent to steal: *a series of burglaries in our neighborhood.*

bur·go·mas·ter (bûr′gə mas′tər), *n.* the mayor of a town in Holland, Flanders, Germany, or Austria.

Bur·gun·dy (bûr′gən dē), *n., pl.* for def. 2 **Bur·gun·dies.** **1.** a region in central France. **2.** *(often l.c.)* any of various table wines produced in this region.

bur·i·al (ber′ē əl), *n.* the act or ceremony of burying a dead body.

bur·lap (bûr′lap), *n.* a coarse fabric of jute or hemp used to make sacks and wrappings; gunny.

bur·lesque (bər lesk′), *n.* **1.** a sarcastic or mocking comic imitation of a serious subject. **2.** a stage show featuring slapstick and vulgar humor. **—adj. 3.** treating a serious subject in a mocking way. **4.** of or referring to stage-show burlesque. **—v.,** **bur·lesqued, bur·les·quing. 5.** to make ridiculous by a mocking imitation.

bur·ly (bûr′lē), *adj.,* **bur·li·er, bur·li·est.** big and sturdy; strong: *a burly man.* **—bur′li·ness,** *n.*

Bur·ma (bûr′mə), *n.* an independent republic in SE Asia. 261,789 sq. mi. *Cap.:* Rangoon.

Bur·mese (bər mēz′), *n., pl.* **Bur·mese. 1.** a native or inhabitant of Burma. **2.** the language of Burma, related to Chinese and Tibetan. **—adj. 3.** of or concerning Burma, its people, or their language.

burn (bûrn), *v.,* **burned** *or* **burnt** (bûrnt); **burn·ing. 1.** to be or cause to be on fire. **2.** to destroy or cause to be destroyed by fire: *I burned the trash. The cabin burned.* **3.** to give off light or glow brightly: *The candles burned all night.* **4.** to feel heat or pain from or as if from a fire: *His face burned in the wind.* **5.** to use as a fuel or a source of light: *The furnace burns coal.* **6.** to give off heat or be hot: *He burned with fever.* **7.** to injure or harm with fire or heat: *to burn one's hand.* **8.** to produce with or as if with fire: *He burned the image of a horse into the wood panel.* **9.** to cause sharp pain or a stinging feeling: *The iodine burned his cut.* **10.** to feel strong emotion: *to burn with anger.* **—n. 11.** an injury caused by heat, abnormal cold, chemicals, etc., and characterized by reddening (**first-degree burn**), blistering (**second-degree burn**), or charring (**third-degree burn**). **12.** the process or an instance of burning. **13.** damage caused by burning: *a burn in the tablecloth.* **14. burn down,** to burn to the ground; be destroyed by fire. **15. burn up, a.** to burn completely; be consumed by fire: *The letter fell into the fire and burned up.* **b.** to make angry: *That kind of meanness really burns me up.*

burn·er (bûr′nər), *n.* **1.** the part of an appliance, as a stove or oven, from which the flame or heat issues: *Put the teakettle on the front burner.* **2.** a device for burning a fuel, as gas or oil.

bur·nish (bûr′nish), *v.* **1.** to polish by friction: *to burnish gold.* **—n. 2.** gloss or brightness; luster.

bur·noose (bər nōōs′, bûr′nōōs), *n.* a hooded cloak worn by Arabs.

burn·out (bûrn′out′), *n.* the end of the powered portion of a rocket in flight when the fuel is used up.

Burns (bûrnz), *n.* **Robert,** 1759–1796, Scottish poet.

burnt (bûrnt), *v.* a past tense and past participle of **burn.**

burp (bûrp), *n.* **1.** a belch. **—v. 2.** to belch. **3.** to cause (a baby) to belch by patting or rubbing its back.

burr¹ (bûr), *n.* **1.** a small tool for deepening, widening, or undercutting small holes. **2.** a similar tool used by dentists to remove decayed material from teeth. **3.** a ragged metal edge raised on a surface in drilling. [from Scandinavian]

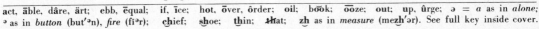

Burnoose

burr² (bûr), *n.* **1.** a harsh pronunciation of the *r*-sound. **2.** a whirring noise or sound. **—v. 3.** to speak with a burr. **4.** to make a whirring noise or sound.

Burr (bûr), *n.* **Aaron,** 1756–1836, 3rd Vice President of the U.S. 1801–1805.

bur·ro (bûr′ō, bur′ō), *n.* a small donkey used as a pack animal in the southwestern U.S. and Mexico.

bur·row (bûr′ō, bur′ō), *n.* **1.** a hole or tunnel in the ground made by a small animal. **—v. 2.** to make a hole or passage: *to burrow into the ground.* **3.** to make by or as if by burrowing: *to burrow a hole in the ground.*

burst (bûrst), *v.,* **burst, burst·ing. 1.** to break, break open, or fly apart with sudden violence: *The balloon burst when the pin touched it.* **2.** to come forth suddenly: *He burst through the doorway.* **3.** to give sudden expression to emotion: *to burst into tears.* **4.** to be very full, as if ready to break open: *The house was bursting with people.* —*n.* **5.** a sudden display of intense activity, energy, or emotion: *a burst of speed.*

bur·then (bûr′thən), *n., v.* an old spelling of **burden**[1].

Bu·run·di (bə run′dē, bə roon′dē), *n.* a republic in central Africa. 10,747 sq. mi. *Cap.:* Bujumbura. Former name, **Urundi.** See map at **Rwanda.**

bur·y (ber′ē), *v.,* **bur·ied, bur·y·ing. 1.** to put in the ground and cover with earth: *The pirates buried the treasure chest.* **2.** to put (a dead body) in the ground or into the sea. **3.** to cover from sight; hide. **4.** to involve (oneself) deeply: *He buried himself in his work.* **5. bury one's head in the sand,** to ignore unpleasant facts: *Burying your head in the sand doesn't solve the problem.*

bus (bus), *n., pl.* **bus·ses** *or* **bus·es. 1.** a large motor vehicle with seats for passengers. —*v.,* **bussed** *or* **bused; bus·sing** *or* **bus·ing. 2.** to transport or travel by bus: *to bus children to school.* [short for *omnibus*]

bus., **1.** bushels. **2.** business.

bush (boosh), *n.* **1.** a plant that grows near the ground and has a thick growth of branches. **2.** a large, uncleared area that is sparsely populated, such as parts of Australia. **3. beat around the bush,** to avoid coming to the point: *Stop beating around the bush and give me an answer!*

bush·el (boosh′əl), *n.* **1.** a unit of measure containing 4 pecks and equal to 1.24 cubic feet (35.239 liters), used for fruit, vegetables, grain, etc. **2.** a basket holding this quantity.

bush·man (boosh′mən), *n., pl.* **bush·men. 1.** a woodsman. **2.** a person who lives in the bush of Australia.

bush·y (boosh′ē), *adj.,* **bush·i·er, bush·i·est. 1.** resembling a bush: *bushy hair.* **2.** full of or overgrown with bushes: *bushy land.* —**bush′i·ness,** *n.*

busi·ness (biz′nis), *n.* **1.** an occupation, profession, or trade: *His business is poultry farming.* **2.** the purchase and sale of goods in an attempt to make a profit. **3.** volume or amount of buying and selling. **4.** a person's rightful concern: *I don't think my plans are your business.* **5.** affair; situation: *The whole business bothered me.* —*adj.* **6.** of or referring to business: *a business office; business school.* **7. mean business,** to be serious about taking action: *When he says not to do that, he means business.*

busi·ness·like (biz′nis līk′), *adj.* characteristic of business; efficient; serious: *a businesslike manner.*

busi·ness·man (biz′nis man′), *n., pl.* **busi·ness·men.** a man who engages in business or commerce.

busi·ness·wom·an (biz′nis woom′ən), *n., pl.* **busi·ness·wom·en.** a woman who engages in business or commerce.

bus·kin (bus′kin), *n.* a thick-soled, laced boot worn by ancient Greek and Roman actors.

buss (bus), *n., v. Informal.* kiss.

bust[1] (bust), *n.* **1.** a sculpture of the head and shoulders of a human being: *a bust of John Adams.* **2.** the chest or breast of a woman; bosom. [from the medieval Latin word *bustum* "torso"]

bust[2] (bust), *v. Slang.* **1.** to burst or break: *The balloon busted. I busted two dishes accidentally.* **2.** to ruin financially: *That last bill busted me.* **3.** to demote in military rank or grade: *They busted him to private.* **4.** to break or tame: *to bust a bronco.* **5.** to hit or strike: *He threatened to bust me in the mouth.* **6.** to arrest (a person).

Buskins

—**Usage.** Educated speakers and writers of English avoid the use of *bust* in all of the above senses.

bus·tle[1] (bus′əl), *v.,* **bus·tled, bus·tling. 1.** to move or act with a great show of energy: *We bustled about getting ready for the trip.* —*n.* **2.** activity with a great show of energy: *the hustle and bustle of Christmas shopping.* [from the Middle English word *bustelen* "to hurry about"]

bus·tle[2] (bus′əl), *n.* a pad or framework formerly worn by women to expand the back of a skirt.

bus·y (biz′ē), *adj.,* **bus·i·er, bus·i·est. 1.** actively engaged; occupied; not at leisure: *Janet is always busy at the office.* **2.** full of activity: *a busy week.* **3.** (of a telephone line) not immediately available for use; engaged. —*v.,* **bus·ied, bus·y·ing. 4.** to keep occupied: *She busies herself with sewing.* —**bus′i·ly,** *adv.*

bus·y·bod·y (biz′ē bod′ē), *n., pl.* **bus·y·bod·ies.** a person who meddles in the affairs of others.

but (but), *conj.* **1.** on the contrary; yet: *My brother went, but I did not.* **2.** except; other than: *We could do nothing but laugh at his funny costume.* **3.** without the circumstance that: *It never rains but it pours.* **4.** that: *I don't doubt but he will do it.* —*prep.* **5.** with the exception of: *Everyone but Jane came to the party.* —*adv.* **6.** only; just: *There is but one seat left.*

bu·tane (byoo′tān, byoo tān′), *n.* a colorless, flammable gas that is easily compressed to a liquid. Butane is used in cigarette lighters.

butch·er (booch′ər), *n.* **1.** a person who sells meat. **2.** a person who slaughters animals for food or market. **3.** a person guilty of brutal murder. —*v.* **4.** to slaughter (animals) for food or market. **5.** to kill cruelly or brutally. **6.** to mess up; botch; bungle: *to butcher a job.*

butch·er·y (booch′ə rē), *n., pl.* **butch·er·ies. 1.** a slaughterhouse. **2.** the trade or business of a butcher. **3.** brutal or cruel slaughter.

but·ler (but′lər), *n.* the head male servant of a household. [from the Old French word *bouteillier* "servant in charge of the wines," which comes from *bouteille* "bottle"]

butt[1] (but), *n.* **1.** the end of anything, esp. the thicker, larger, or blunt end: *a rifle butt.* **2.** an end that is not used or consumed; remnant: *a cigar butt.*

[from an Old English word meaning "tree stump"]

butt² (but), *n.* a person or thing that is made fun of: *to be the butt of someone's joke.* [from the Old French word *but* "end, goal"]

butt³ (but), *v.* 1. to strike or push with the head or horns: *The goat butted the can.* —*n.* 2. a push or blow with the head or horns. 3. **butt in,** *Slang.* to intrude into someone else's affairs, conversation, etc.: *When we're talking, don't butt in.* [from the Old French word *bouter* "to thrust"]

butt⁴ (but), *n.* a large cask or barrel, esp. for wine, beer, or ale. [from the earlier French word *botte,* which comes from Latin *butta*]

butte (byōōt), *n.* a steep, isolated hill or mountain, having a flat top and standing alone.

but·ter (but′ər), *n.* 1. the fatty portion of milk, which separates as a soft whitish or yellowish solid when milk or cream is churned and is used for cooking, as a spread for bread, etc. 2. any of various other soft spreads for bread: *apple butter; peanut butter.* —*v.* 3. to spread or grease with butter: *to butter bread.* 4. **butter up,** to flatter (someone) so as to gain a favor: *If you butter her up, maybe she'll let you go.*

but·ter·cup (but′ər kup′), *n.* a common plant having small, cup-shaped, yellow flowers.

but·ter·fat (but′ər fat′), *n.* the fat that becomes butter when milk or cream is churned.

but·ter·fly (but′ər flī′), *n., pl.* **but·ter·flies.** any of numerous insects having slender bodies and broad, often brightly marked wings.

but·ter·milk (but′ər milk′), *n.* the sour liquid remaining after the butter has been separated from milk or cream.

but·ter·nut (but′ər nut′), *n.* 1. the oily nut of an American walnut tree. 2. the tree itself.

but·ter·scotch (but′ər skoch′), *n.* 1. a hard, brittle candy made with butter and brown sugar. 2. a flavor made esp. with butter and brown sugar. —*adj.* 3. having the flavor of butterscotch.

but·tock (but′ək), *n.* either of the two fleshy parts on the back of the human body between the waist and the thigh.

but·ton (but′ən), *n.* 1. a small disk or knob for attaching to an article of clothing, serving as a fastening when passed through a buttonhole or loop. 2. anything small and round that resembles a button, as any of various candies, tags, badges, markers, etc. 3. a small knob or disk that, when pressed, operates an electric circuit: *Push the button for the elevator.* —*v.* 4. to fasten by means of a button or buttons: *Button your coat.* 5. to be capable of being buttoned: *The dress buttons in the back.*

but·ton·hole (but′ən hōl′), *n.* 1. the hole, slit, or loop through which a button is passed and by which it is secured. —*v.,* **but·ton·holed, but·ton·hol·ing.** 2. to make buttonholes in. 3. to hold (someone) in conversation: *The reporter buttonholed the mayor for a statement on the elections.*

but·ton·wood (but′ən wŏŏd′), *n.* See **sycamore** (def. 1).

but·tress (bu′tris), *n.* 1. a prop or support built into or against the outside of a wall to steady the structure. —*v.* 2. to support by a buttress; prop up. 3. to give encouragement or support to: *to buttress a plan.*

Buttress

bux·om (buk′səm), *adj.* (of a woman) healthy, plump, cheerful, and lively. —**bux′om·ness,** *n.*

buy (bī), *v.,* **bought** (bôt), **buy·ing.** 1. to obtain by paying or promising to pay; purchase: *I bought a new dress.* 2. to bribe: *Most public officials cannot be bought.* 3. to be the buying equivalent of: *Twenty dollars will buy a lot of groceries.* —*n.* 4. something bought at a fair or reasonable price; bargain. 5. **buy out,** to purchase the share of a business owned by (another person): *We bought out the chief stockholder.* 6. **buy up,** to buy as much as possible of (something): *to buy up milk before a dairy strike.*

buy·er (bī′ər), *n.* 1. a person who buys; purchaser. 2. a person who buys merchandise for a retail store.

buzz (buz), *n.* 1. a low, humming sound, as of bees, machinery, or people talking. —*v.* 2. to make a low, humming sound. 3. to speak or whisper with such a sound. 4. to signal or summon with a buzzer. 5. to fly an airplane very low over: *to buzz a field.*

buz·zard (buz′ərd), *n.* 1. a North American vulture. 2. a large European hawk.

buzz·er (buz′ər), *n.* an electric device that produces a buzzing sound, esp. one used as a doorbell.

B.W.I., British West Indies.

by (bī), *prep.* 1. near to or next to: *a home by a lake.* 2. over the surface of, by way of, or using as a route: *She travels by air.* 3. on, as a means of transportation: *They arrived by ship.* 4. to and beyond; past: *We walked by the store.* 5. within the time of; during: *by night.* 6. not later than; at or before: *I'm usually home by three o'clock.* 7. to the amount of: *taller by two inches.* 8. according to: *The club meetings are run by the rules. Apples are sold by the pound.* 9. through the agency or authority of: *The papers were passed out by the teacher.* 10. from the hand, mind, or invention of: *a poem by Robert Frost.* 11. on behalf of: *He did well by his children.* 12. using as a multiplier: *Multiply 5 by 7.* —*adv.* 13. near; at hand: *The school is close by.* 14. to and beyond a point near something; past: *The car drove by.* —*adj.* 15. located to one side: *a by passage.* 16. **by and by,** before long; presently: *We'll go for a walk by and by.* 17. **by and large,** in general; on the whole: *By and large, this is the best way to do it.*

by-, a prefix meaning 1. near or close by: *bystander.* 2. out of the way: *by-path.* 3. of less importance: *by-product.*

act, āble, dâre, ärt; ebb, ēqual; if, īce; hot, ōver, ôrder; oil; bŏŏk; ōōze; out; up, ûrge; ə = a as in alone; ə as in *button* (but′ən), *fire* (fīᵊr); chief; shoe; thin; ᵗħat; zh as in *measure* (mezh′ər). See full key inside cover.

Bye·lo·rus·sia (byel′ō ru͟sh′ə), *n.* a republic that forms part of the Soviet Union, in the W part. 80,154 sq. mi. *Cap.:* Minsk. Also, **White Russia.** —**Bye′lo·rus′sian,** *n., adj.*

by·gone (bī′gôn′, bī′gon′), *adj.* **1.** past; gone by; out of date: *memories of bygone days.* —*n.* **2. bygones,** that which happened in the past. **3. let bygones be bygones,** to forget past differences; become friends again.

by·law (bī′lô′), *n.* **1.** a rule made by an organization to govern its own business. **2.** a secondary law.

by-line (bī′līn′), *n.* a printed line accompanying a news story or article, giving the author's name.

by-pass (bī′pas′), *n.* **1.** a road around a city or other heavy traffic area. —*v.* **2.** to avoid by following a by-pass: *to by-pass traffic.* **3.** to neglect or ignore the opinion or position of; avoid: *He by-passed the manager and took his complaint straight to the owner.* Also, **by′pass′.**

by-path (bī′path′), *n., pl.* **by-paths** (bī′pathz′, -paths′). a side path or road. Also, **by′path′.**

by-prod·uct (bī′prod′əkt), *n.* a product made or resulting from the manufacture of another product: *Asphalt is a by-product of coke manufacture.*

Byrd (bûrd), *n.* **Richard E(velyn),** 1888–1957, rear admiral of U.S. Navy and polar explorer.

by-road (bī′rōd′), *n.* a side road. Also, **by′road′.**

By·ron (bī′rən), *n.* **George Gordon, Lord,** 1788–1824, English poet.

by·stand·er (bī′stan′dər), *n.* a person who is present at but not involved in some event.

by·way (bī′wā′), *n.* a secluded or private road.

by·word (bī′wûrd′), *n.* **1.** a common saying; proverb. **2.** an object of dislike and scorn: *His mean disposition has made him a byword all over town.*

Byz·an·tine (biz′ən tēn′), *adj.* **1.** of or concerning Byzantium or the Byzantine Empire. **2.** noting or referring to the architecture of the Byzantine Empire and later architecture influenced by it: characterized by round arches, low domes, and rich colors. —*n.* **3.** a native or inhabitant of Byzantium.

Byz′antine Em′pire, the Eastern Roman Empire, founded after the fall of the Western Roman Empire

in A.D. 476, and lasting until conquered by the Turks in 1453. *Cap.:* Constantinople.

By·zan·ti·um (bi zan′shē əm, bi zan′tē əm), *n.* an ancient Greek city on the Bosporus strait and the Sea of Marmara. See also **Istanbul.**

C, c (sē), *n., pl.* **C's** *or* **Cs, c's** *or* **cs.** the third letter of the English alphabet.

C, 1. Celsius. 2. Centigrade. 3. coulomb.

C, 1. (in some grading systems) a grade or mark indicating work of fair or average quality. 2. the Roman numeral for 100. 3. *Chem.* the symbol for **carbon.**

c, (used with a year) about: *c1775.* Also, **c.**

C., 1. Catholic. 2. Celsius. 3. Centigrade. 4. College.

c., 1. carat. 2. case. 3. cent; cents. 4. centimeter; centimeters. 5. chapter. 6. chief. 7. church. 8. (used with a year) about: *c. 1775.* 9. copy.

Ca, *Chem.* the symbol for **calcium.**

cab (kab), *n.* 1. a taxicab. 2. the covered or enclosed part of a truck, locomotive, derrick, etc., where the driver sits. 3. (formerly) any of various horse-drawn carriages, esp. one for hire.

ca·bal (kə bal′), *n.* 1. a small group of plotters, esp. against the government: *A cabal of generals planned a revolt.* 2. the plottings of such a group.

ca·ban·a (kə ban′ə), *n.* 1. a cabin or cottage. 2. a small cabin or tentlike shelter for use as a bathhouse at a beach, swimming pool, etc.

cab·a·ret (kab′ə rā′), *n.* a large restaurant that provides music for dancing and often a floor show.

cab·bage (kab′ij), *n.* a vegetable with large, thick leaves formed into a compact, round head.

cab·in (kab′in), *n.* 1. a small, usually simple house or cottage: *a cabin in the woods for hunters.* 2. an apartment or room in a ship: *The captain has the best cabin.* 3. an enclosed space for travelers to occupy, as the seating area in an airplane.

cab·i·net (kab′ə nit), *n.* 1. (*often cap.*) an official group of advisers for a president, king, or other head of state: *The Secretary of State is a member of the cabinet.* 2. a piece of furniture with shelves, drawers, etc., for holding or showing objects: *a kitchen cabinet; a cabinet for one's trophies.* 3. any boxlike case for holding something, such as a case for a television

set or a case for jewelry. 4. a closet or small room.

cab·i·net·mak·er (kab′ə nit mā′kər), *n.* a person who makes fine furniture, esp. cabinets, chests, etc.

ca·ble (kā′bəl), *n.* 1. a group of electric wires assembled into a single ropelike bundle, used for power lines and for transmitting messages, as by telephone or telegraph. 2. a heavy, strong rope. 3. a cablegram. —*v.,* **ca·bled, ca·bling.** 4. to send (a message) by underwater cable: *You had better cable the news.* 5. to send a message to (a person, place, etc.) by underwater cable.

ca′ble car′, a vehicle that is pulled along the ground by a cable or is carried through the air on a cable, often up and down hills or mountains.

ca·ble·gram (kā′bəl gram′), *n.* a telegram sent by underwater cable.

ca·boose (kə bōōs′), *n.* a car on a freight train, usually attached to the rear, for the use of the crew.

Cab·ot (kab′ət), *n.* **John,** c1450–1498?, Italian navigator in the service of England: discovered the North American mainland.

cab·ri·o·let (kab′rē ə lā′), *n.* a light, two-wheeled, one-horse carriage with a folding top, capable of seating two persons.

ca·ca·o (kə kā′ō, kə kä′ō), *n., pl.* **ca·ca·os.** a small South American tree whose seeds are the source of cocoa and chocolate.

Cabriolet

cache (kash), *n.* 1. a hiding place, esp. one in the ground, for provisions or treasure. 2. anything hidden or stored: *a rich cache of jewels.* —*v.,* **cached, cach·ing.** 3. to put in a cache or hiding place; conceal; hide: *to cache jewels after a robbery.*

cack·le (kak′əl), *v.,* **cack·led, cack·ling.** 1. to give the shrill, broken sound or cry of a hen: *chickens cackling in the yard.* 2. to laugh in a shrill, broken manner: *to cackle with amusement.* 3. to chatter noisily:

old men cackling over a card game. **4.** to say in a shrill, broken voice like that of a hen: *She cackled her complaints to the butcher.* —*n.* **5.** the act or sound of cackling: *a noisy cackle.* —**cack′ling·ly,** *adv.*

cac·tus (kak′təs), *n., pl.* **cac·tus·es** *or* **cac·ti** (kak′tī). any of numerous plants having fleshy stems and usually spines instead of leaves: chiefly native to the hot, dry regions of America.

cad (kad), *n.* a man who behaves in a rude, selfish, or dishonorable manner.

ca·dav·er (kə dav′ər), *n.* a dead body; corpse.

ca·dav·er·ous (kə dav′ər əs), *adj.* haggard, pale, or very thin in a way that resembles a corpse.

Cactus
(height to 50 ft.)

cad·die (kad′ē), *n., pl.* **cad·dies. 1.** a person hired to help a golf player by carrying clubs, finding the ball, giving advice concerning the course, or the like. —*v.,* **cad·died, cad·dy·ing. 2.** to work as a caddie. Also, **caddy.** [a variant of *cadet*]

cad·dis·fly (kad′is flī′), *n., pl.* **cad·dis·flies.** any of various insects having two pairs of often hairy wings.

cad·dy[1] (kad′ē), *n., pl.* **cad·dies.** *British.* a small box, can, or chest for holding small objects: *a pencil caddy.* [from the Malay word *kati,* a unit of weight equal to about 1½ pounds, used in the Orient]

cad·dy[2] (kad′ē), *n., pl.* **cad·dies;** *v.,* **cad·died, cad·dy·ing.** another spelling of **caddie.**

ca·dence (kād′ns), *n.* **1.** a rhythmic pattern, as that of marching. **2.** the notes or chords at the end of a phrase, section, or piece of music.

ca·det (kə det′), *n.* **1.** a student in a military school. **2.** a young man in training to be an officer in the U.S. Army, Air Force, or Coast Guard. See also **midshipman.**

cad·mi·um (kad′mē əm), *n.* a white metal used chiefly to plate other metals: a chemical element. *Symbol:* Cd

ca·du·ce·us (kə dōō′sē əs, -dyōō′-), *n.* **1.** (in Roman mythology) the staff of Mercury, the messenger of the gods. **2.** a representation of this staff used as an emblem of the medical profession.

Cae·sar (sē′zər), *n.* **1. Gaius Julius,** c100–44 B.C., Roman general, statesman, and historian. **2.** a title of the Roman emperors. **3.** any emperor.

Caduceus

ca·fé (ka fā′), *n.* **1.** a restaurant, usually a small, simple one. **2.** a barroom or nightclub. Also, **ca·fe′.** [from the French word *café* "coffee, coffeehouse"]

caf·e·te·ri·a (kaf′i tēr′ē ə), *n.* a restaurant in which the customers wait on themselves, buying their food at counters and carrying it to their tables.

caf·feine (ka fēn′, kaf′ēn), *n.* the stimulating substance found in coffee and tea.

cage (kāj), *n.* **1.** a boxlike container or enclosure having wire, bars, or the like, for holding and displaying birds or other animals. **2.** any place that confines or imprisons. **3.** something that looks like a cage, such as an enclosure for a cashier or the goal in hockey. —*v.,* **caged, cag·ing. 4.** to shut up in or as if in a cage: *to cage a prisoner.* —**cage′like′,** *adj.*

cag·ey (kā′jē), *adj.,* **cag·i·er, cag·i·est.** careful, wary, or shrewd: *He gave such a cagey answer, I don't know whether he agreed with me or not.* —**cag′i·ly,** *adv.* —**cag′i·ness,** *n.*

Cain (kān), *n.* (in the Bible) the eldest son of Adam and Eve: the murderer of his brother Abel.

Cai·ro (kī′rō), *n.* the capital city of the Arab Republic of Egypt, in the N part on the E bank of the Nile.

cais·son (kā′sən, kā′son), *n.* **1.** a watertight structure in which men can do underwater construction work. **2.** a two-wheeled ammunition wagon.

cais′son disease′. See **bend** (def. 8).

cai·tiff (kā′tif), *Archaic.* —*n.* **1.** a low, mean, dishonest, or cowardly person. —*adj.* **2.** base or low; dishonest or cowardly. [from a Middle English word, which comes from Latin *captivus* "captive"]

ca·jole (kə jōl′), *v.,* **ca·joled, ca·jol·ing.** to use flattery and promises to get something from (someone); wheedle: *The small boy cajoled his grandfather into taking him to the circus.* —**ca·jol′ing·ly,** *adv.*

ca·jol·er·y (kə jō′lə rē), *n.* the use of flattery and promises to get something; coaxing; wheedling.

cake (kāk), *n.* **1.** a baked food like bread but sweeter, made of flour, eggs, sugar, baking powder or soda, flavoring, and often shortening: *a chocolate cake.* **2.** any cooked mass of dough or batter, such as a pancake. **3.** a shaped mass of some other kind of food: *a fish cake.* **4.** a shaped mass of some other material: *a cake of soap.* —*v.,* **caked, cak·ing. 5.** to harden, as into a crust: *The mud caked and cracked in the hot sun.* **6. take the cake,** to exceed or surpass anything of a similar kind: *I always knew she was rude, but this takes the cake.*

Cal., 1. California. **2.** (large) calorie.

cal., 1. caliber. **2.** (small) calorie.

cal·a·bash (kal′ə bash′), *n.* **1.** a kind of gourd that is dried and used to make bowls, cups, rattles, tobacco pipes, etc. **2.** a rattle, bowl, pipe, or the like, made from such a gourd.

cal·a·mine (kal′ə mīn′), *n.* a pink powder used to make a soothing lotion for the skin.

ca·lam·i·tous (kə lam′i təs), *adj.* causing or concerned with disaster or calamity; disastrous: *a calamitous defeat.* —**ca·lam′i·tous·ly,** *adv.*

ca·lam·i·ty (kə lam′i tē), *n., pl.* **ca·lam·i·ties. 1.** an event that is a great misfortune; disaster: *That earthquake was a calamity.* **2.** terrible suffering; misery.

Calash

ca·lash (kə lash′), *n.* a light, two-wheeled, horse-drawn carriage having inside seats for two passengers, an outside seat for the driver, and usually a folding top.

cal·ci·fy (kal′sə fī′), *v.,* **cal·ci·fied, cal·ci·fy·ing.** to become hardened or stiffened by the deposit of calcium compounds. —**cal·ci·fi·ca·tion** (kal′sə fə kā′shən), *n.*

cal·ci·mine (kal′sə mīn′), *n.* **1.** a thin white or tinted paint for walls and ceilings. —*v.,* **cal·ci·mined, cal·ci·min·ing. 2.** to paint or cover with calcimine.

cal·ci·um (kal′sē əm), *n. Chem.* a metallic chemical element found in chalk and limestone. Calcium is important in a person's diet because it helps to make bones, teeth, etc. *Symbol:* Ca

cal·cu·late (kal′kyə lāt′), *v.,* **cal·cu·lat·ed, cal·cu·lat·ing. 1.** to figure by using mathematics: *to calculate the speed of light.* **2.** to figure or estimate by using common sense or reason: *I calculate we'll win by 10 points.* **3.** to intend to have a particular effect or result (usually used passively and with an infinitive): *a remark calculated to inspire confidence.* [from the Latin word *calculātus* "counted," which comes from *calculus* "pebble." Pebbles were used as counters] —**cal′cu·lat′ed·ly,** *adv.*

cal·cu·lat·ing (kal′kyə lā′tiñg), *adj.* **1.** able to perform mathematical calculations: *a calculating machine.* **2.** shrewd, careful, or inclined to scheme for selfish reasons: *He's a cold, calculating man who is very ambitious.* —**cal′cu·lat′ing·ly,** *adv.*

cal·cu·la·tion (kal′kyə lā′shən), *n.* **1.** the act or process of calculating or figuring by the use of mathematics: *Simple calculation will give you the answer.* **2.** the result or answer obtained by calculation or by figuring mathematically: *His calculation agrees with mine.* **3.** an estimate or rough idea obtained by using reason or common sense: *By their calculation it will take us only two hours to reach the border.* **4.** careful planning; forethought: *calculation of the best way to beat the other team.* **5.** selfish scheming; plotting: *She got her way by lies and calculation.*

cal·cu·la·tor (kal′kyə lā′tər), *n.* **1.** a person who calculates or does figuring by mathematics. **2.** Also, **cal′ culating machine′.** a machine, such as an adding machine, that does mathematical calculations. **3.** a person who runs such a machine.

cal·cu·lus (kal′kyə ləs), *n.* an advanced branch of mathematics useful for solving problems involving things that are changing in complicated ways and for finding areas and volumes of things that have complicated shapes.

Cal·cut·ta (kal kut′ə), *n.* a port city in E India: former capital of British India.

cal·dron (kôl′drən), *n.* another spelling of **cauldron.**

cal·en·dar (kal′ən dər), *n.* **1.** any of various ways of dividing the year into months, weeks, and days: *The Gregorian calendar has been used in America since 1752.* **2.** a chart that shows the arrangement of months, weeks, and days. **3.** a list or schedule of things to be done: *The nurse wrote in my appointment on the doctor's calendar.*

cal·en·der (kal′ən dər), *n.* **1.** a machine for smoothing or giving a glaze to cloth or paper by running it between rollers. —*v.* **2.** to press (cloth or paper) in such a manner.

calf[1] (kaf), *n., pl.* **calves** (kavz). **1.** the young of cows, oxen, etc. **2.** the young of certain other large mammals, as the elephant, seal, or whale. **3.** calfskin leather. [from the Old English word *cealf*]

calf[2] (kaf), *n., pl.* **calves** (kavz). the fleshy part of the back of the human leg below the knee. [from Scandinavian]

calf·skin (kaf′skin′), *n.* **1.** the skin or hide of a calf. **2.** leather made from this skin: *shoes made of calfskin.*

Cal·ga·ry (kal′gə rē), *n.* a city in S Alberta, in SW Canada.

Cal·houn (kal hōōn′), *n.* **John C.,** 1782–1850, 7th Vice President of the U.S. 1825–1832.

cal·i·ber (kal′ə bər), *n.* **1.** the inside diameter of a tube, esp. that of a gun barrel; bore. **2.** degree of worth, merit, or importance: *a scientist of high caliber.* Also, *esp. British,* **cal′i·bre.**

cal·i·brate (kal′ə brāt′), *v.,* **cal·i·brat·ed, cal·i·brat·ing.** to mark graduations on (a measuring instrument): *a ruler calibrated in inches.* —**cal′i·bra′tion,** *n.*

cal·i·co (kal′ə kō′), *n., pl.* **cal·i·cos** *or* **cal·i·coes. 1.** a cotton cloth with a black-and-white or colored pattern printed on it. —*adj.* **2.** made of calico: *calico curtains.* **3.** looking like a calico print; spotted or having several colors: *a calico cat.*

cal·if (kal′if, kā′lif), *n.* another spelling of **caliph.**

Calif., California. Also, **Cal.**

Cal·i·for·nia (kal′ə fôr′nyə), *n.* a state in the W United States, on the Pacific coast. 158,693 sq. mi. *Cap.:* Sacramento. —**Cal′i·for′nian,** *n., adj.*

cal·i·for·ni·um (kal′ə-fôr′nē əm), *n. Chem.* a man-made, radioactive, metallic element. *Symbol:* Cf

cal·i·pers (kal′ə pərz), *n.pl.* an instrument for measuring thickness and internal and external diameters, consisting of a pair of legs pivoted so as to be adjustable.

cal·iph (kal′if, kā′lif), *n.* **1.** a Muslim leader, descended from Muhammad or claiming descent from him. **2.** (formerly) a ruler of a Muslim state. Also, **calif.**

cal·is·then·ics (kal′is then′iks), *n.* **1.** *(used as sing.)* the performance of exercises for health and strength: *Calisthenics is scheduled for Tuesday and Thursday afternoons.* **2.** *(used as pl.)* any such exercises: *Those calisthenics were really tiring.*

calk[1] (kôk), *v.* another spelling of **caulk.**

calk[2] (kôk), *n.* **1.** Also, **cal·kin** (kô′kin, kal′kin). a part of a horseshoe that sticks out like a cleat on a football shoe and helps to keep the horse from slipping on ice, wet pavement, or the like. **2.** Also, **calk·er** (kô**′**kər). a similar device on the heel or sole of a shoe. —*v.* **3.** to put calks on: *to calk a horseshoe.* [from the Latin word *calx* "spur, heel"]

call (kôl), *v.* **1.** to speak or cry out in a loud voice: *to call the roll; to call to someone.* **2.** to ask or invite to come; summon or invite: *to call the family to dinner.* **3.** to wake from sleep or summon from one activity to another: *Call me at 8:30.* **4.** to command or request to come: *to call a dog; to call a cab.* **5.** to telephone (a person or place): *I called you twice, but nobody answered.* **6.** to make a short visit: *to come to call.* **7.** to announce or proclaim; order: *to call a strike.* **8.** to cause to begin officially, as a meeting or court proceedings: *to call a case in court.* **9.** to give a name or label to: *The boys call him Tex.* **10.** to demand payment of (a loan). —*n.* **11.** a cry or shout: *a call for help.* **12.** the cry of a bird or other animal. **13.** a signal or summons sounded by a bugle, bell, or the like: *a trumpet call.* **14.** a short visit: *to make a call on someone.* **15.** a summons, command, or invitation: *He got a call for jury duty.* **16.** the act or an instance of telephoning: *I didn't make any calls today.* **17.** an inner feeling that one's life should be devoted to a particular vocation: *a call to the ministry.* **18.** need or right: *He didn't have any call to say that.* **19.** a demand or claim: *We do sell tricycles, but there isn't much call for them except at Christmas.* **20.** a demand for payment. **21. call for, a.** to go or come to get; pick up: *I'll call for you about 8 o'clock.* **b.** to require or need: *The recipe calls for three eggs.* **22. call off, a.** to summon away; distract: *Please call off your dog.* **b.** to cancel: *She called off the party because of rain.* **23. call on, a.** to make an appeal to: *They called on Mother for a donation.* **b.** to visit briefly: *May I call on you this afternoon?* **24. call up, a.** to telephone: *Call me up if you can't come.* **b.** to summon for action or service: *to call up the reserves in wartime.*

call·er (kô**′**lər), *n.* **1.** a person or animal that calls, such as a person that calls out names or instructions. **2.** a person who comes for a short visit: *I had many callers when I was in the hospital.*

call·ing (kô**′**ling), *n.* **1.** the act of a person or thing that calls: *a loud calling at the door.* **2.** a vocation, profession, or trade. **3.** a summons or invitation.

cal·li·o·pe (kə lī**′**ə pē, kal**′**ē ōp**′**), *n.* a kind of organ using steam instead of air to make the pipes sound. It is used esp. for circus music.

cal·lous (kal**′**əs), *adj.* **1.** made hard; hardened: *The palms of his hands were callous from digging.* **2.** unsympathetic; cold, hard, and insensitive. —**cal′lous·ly,** *adv.* —**cal′lous·ness,** *n.*

cal·lus (kal**′**əs), *n., pl.* **cal·lus·es.** a hardened or thickened part of the skin. —**cal′lused,** *adj.*

calm (käm), *adj.* **1.** still or nearly still; without wind or rough motion: *a calm day; a calm sea.* **2.** free from excitement or strong emotion; peaceful: *to remain calm.* —*n.* **3.** a stillness without wind or motion: *the* *calm before the storm.* **4.** peacefulness; freedom from excitement or strong emotion. —*v.* **5.** to make calm or quiet: *He calmed the barking dog.* **6.** to become calm or peaceful (often fol. by *down*): *Things will calm down after the holidays.* —**calm′ly,** *adv.* —**calm′ness,** *n.*

cal·o·rie (kal**′**ə rē), *n., pl.* **cal·o·ries.** **1.** Also, **small calorie, gram calorie.** a unit of energy: the amount of heat required to raise the temperature of one gram of water by one degree Celsius (centigrade). *Abbr.:* cal. **2.** *(sometimes cap.)* Also, **great caloric, kilogram calorie, kilocalorie.** a unit of energy 1000 times as large, used esp. in discussing the energy content of foods. *Abbr.:* Cal. —**ca·lor·ic** (kə lôr**′**ik), *adj.*

cal·o·ry (kal**′**ə rē), *n., pl.* **cal·o·ries.** another spelling of **calorie.**

cal·u·met (kal**′**yə met**′**), *n.* another name for **peace pipe.**

ca·lum·ni·ate (kə lum**′**nē āt**′**), *v.,* **ca·lum·ni·at·ed, ca·lum·ni·at·ing.** to make false or harmful statements about; slander. —**ca·lum′ni·a′tion,** *n.*

cal·um·ny (kal**′**əm nē), *n., pl.* **cal·um·nies.** a false and harmful statement intended to injure someone or something: *a speech full of calumnies.* —**ca·lum·ni·ous** (kə lum**′**nē əs), *adj.*

Cal·va·ry (kal**′**və rē), *n.* (in the Bible) a place near Jerusalem where Jesus was crucified.

calve (kav), *v.,* **calved, calv·ing.** to give birth to a calf.

calves (kavz), *n.* the plural of **calf.**

Cal·vin (kal**′**vin), *n.* **John,** 1509–1564, French theologian and reformer in Geneva, Switzerland: leader in the Protestant Reformation.

Cal·vin·ism (kal**′**və niz**′**əm), *n.* the Protestant teachings of John Calvin and his followers, esp. that salvation comes only to those whom God has chosen. —**Cal′vin·ist,** *n.*

ca·lyp·so (kə lip**′**sō), *n., pl.* **ca·lyp·sos.** a West Indian song, usually about a particular person or event, having words that are often made up by the singer as he goes along.

ca·lyx (kā**′**liks, kal**′**iks), *n.* the outermost, usually green, part of a flower: composed of the sepals and surrounding the petals.

C, Calyx

cam (kam), *n.* an irregular disk or a projection on a rotary shaft that gives an up-and-down motion to a part resting on it.

cam·bi·um (kam**′**bē əm), *n.* the growing layer of a tree just underneath the bark, which develops into new wood and bark and which produces the annual rings in the wood.

C, Cam

Cam·bo·di·a (kam bō**′**dē ə), *n.* a country in SE Asia: formerly part of French Indochina. 69,866 sq. mi. *Cap.:* Phnom Penh. —**Cam·bo′di·an,** *n., adj.*

cam·bric (kām**′**brik), *n.* a thin, plain cotton or linen fabric of fine close weave, usually white.

Cam·bridge (kām**′**brij), *n.* **1.** a city in E England:

site of a university founded in the 12th century. **2.** a city in E Massachusetts, near Boston.

Cam·den (kam′dən), *n.* a port city in SW New Jersey, opposite Philadelphia.

came (kām), *v.* the past tense of **come.**

cam·el (kam′əl), *n.* either of two large, cud-chewing mammals, the Bactrian camel with two humps or the

Camel (Bactrian)
(length 9 ft.)

Camel (Dromedary)
(length 9½ ft.)

dromedary with one hump, used as pack animals and for riding in the desert.

ca·mel·lia (kə mēl′yə), *n.* **1.** an Asian plant having glossy evergreen leaves and bearing large white, pink, or red flowers. **2.** the flower of this plant.

Cam·e·lot (kam′ə lot′), *n.* the legendary site of King Arthur's palace and court, near Exeter, England.

cam·e·o (kam′ē ō′), *n., pl.* **cam·e·os.** a gem or other stone having a small, raised sculpture on it.

cam·er·a (kam′ər ə), *n.* a device for taking photographs, usually consisting of a box that holds the film to be exposed, a lens that focuses an image on the film, and a shutter that controls the length of time that light strikes the film. [from a Latin word meaning "chamber," which comes from Greek *kamara*]

cam·er·a·man (kam′ər ə man′, -mən), *n., pl.* **cam·er·a·men.** a person trained to operate a camera, esp. a television or motion-picture camera.

Cam·e·roon (kam′ə rōon′), *n.* an independent republic in W Africa. 183,350 sq. mi.

cam·i·sole (kam′i sōl′), *n.* **1.** a short, sliplike garment for women, usually worn under a thin blouse. **2.** a woman's dressing gown or bed jacket.

cam·o·mile (kam′ə mīl′), *n.* a plant having strong-smelling leaves and flowers used in medicine.

cam·ou·flage (kam′ə fläzh′), *n.* **1.** the act or technique of disguising military equipment or clothing so that it cannot easily be seen by the enemy. **2.** any disguise that blends into the background or looks like something else: *The coloring of most animals serves as a camouflage.* **3.** something used or done to hide something else: *His grumpy manner is just a camouflage for shyness.* —*v.,* **cam·ou·flaged, cam·ou·flag·ing. 4.** to disguise or cover up (something).

camp (kamp), *n.* **1.** a place having tents or other temporary shelter for soldiers, hunters, hikers, or the like: *a camp in the woods.* **2.** the equipment used in setting up such a temporary shelter: *It's time to pack up the camp.* **3.** a place in the country where people go for a vacation and to enjoy sports and other activities: *a summer camp for children.* **4.** the people stay-

ing in a camp: *The whole camp gathered around the fire.* —*v.* **5.** to make or pitch a camp: *The army camped in the valley.* **6.** to stay in a temporary shelter, esp. in tents. [from an Old English word meaning "battlefield," which comes from Latin *campus* "field"] —**camp′er,** *n.*

cam·paign (kam pān′), *n.* **1.** general military action aimed at a particular goal: *a campaign to drive back the enemy on the western front.* **2.** any organized, energetic action aimed at a specific goal: *a sales campaign.* **3.** the competition to win votes for public office: *a hard-fought campaign for the presidency.* —*v.* **4.** to work in or go on a campaign: *to campaign for a candidate.* —**cam·paign′er,** *n.*

cam·pa·ni·le (kam′pə nē′lē), *n.* a bell tower, esp. one that is connected to a church but not a part of the main building.

camp·fire (kamp′fīªr′), *n.* **1.** an outdoor fire for warmth or cooking. **2.** a reunion or social gathering of soldiers, scouts, campers, etc.

Camp′fire Girls′, an organization for girls of ages 7 to 18, designed to promote health and good citizenship.

Campanile

cam·phor (kam′fər), *n.* a white aromatic substance obtained from an Asiatic tree, used in medicines and, formerly, in mothballs.

cam·pus (kam′pəs), *n.* the grounds of a college or other school. [from a Latin word meaning "field"]

can¹ (kan, kən), *auxiliary verb, past tense* **could** (kŏŏd). **1.** to be able to; have the ability, power, or skill to: *She can solve that problem easily.* **2.** to know how to: *He can play chess.* **3.** to have the right to: *The governor can pardon prisoners.* **4.** *Informal.* may; have permission to: *Can I leave now?* [from the Old English word *cunnan* "to know how"]

—**Usage.** Although both *can* and *may* are used informally in requesting or granting permission, *may* is the preferred usage: *May* (not *Can*) *I go? Yes, you may* (not *can*) *go. Can* should be used for statements expressing skill or ability: *I can do 100 push-ups. Can she speak Dutch?*

can² (kan), *n.* **1.** a metal container for food or beverages: *a can of soup.* **2.** any of various large containers, often made of metal: *a garbage can.* —*v.,* **canned, can·ning. 3.** to preserve (food) by sealing it in an airtight can or jar: *We canned tomatoes from our garden.* [from the Old English word *canne* "cup"] —**can′ner,** *n.*

Can., Canada.

Ca·naan (kā′nən), *n.* **1.** an ancient region lying

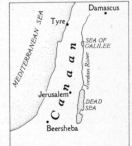

between the Jordan River and the Mediterranean Sea. **2.** the Biblical name of **Palestine.**

Ca·naan·ite (kā′nə nīt′), *n.* a member of the group of people who lived in Canaan and were conquered by the Israelites after the Exodus.

Can·a·da (kan′ə də), *n.* a nation in N North America: a member of the British Commonwealth of Nations. 3,690,410 sq. mi. *Cap.:* Ottawa. **—Ca·na·di·an** (kə nā′dē ən), *n., adj.*

Can′ada goose′, a large North American wild goose having a grayish-brown body and a black head and neck.

ca·nal (kə nal′), *n.* **1.** a man-made waterway, esp. for boats or irrigation: *a canal connecting two rivers.* **2.** a tubelike passage for food, liquid, air, or the like, esp. in a plant or the body of an animal; duct. [from the Latin word *canālis* "waterpipe"]

Canal′ Zone′, a zone in central Panama on both sides of the Panama Canal: governed by the U.S. 10 mi. wide; 553 sq. mi. See map at **Central America.**

ca·nard (kə närd′), *n.* a false story or report, usually one that causes harm; false rumor or hoax: *There was a canard that the town's only bank had failed.* [from a French word meaning literally "duck." The meaning arose from the practice of swindlers who sold half a duck, pretending it was a whole one]

ca·nar·y (kə nâr′ē), *n., pl.* **ca·nar·ies.** a small, usually yellow songbird native to the Canary Islands.

Ca·nar′y Is′lands (kə nâr′ē), a group of mountainous islands in the Atlantic Ocean near the NW coast of Africa: making up two provinces of Spain. 2894 sq. mi. Also, **the Canaries.**

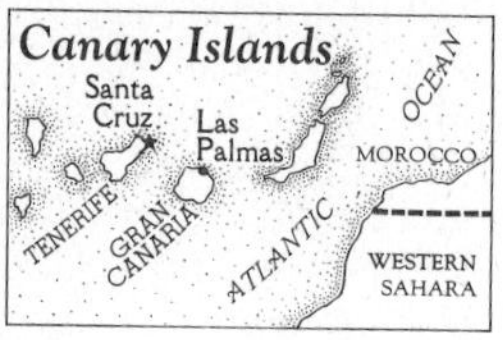

ca·nas·ta (kə nas′tə), *n.* a card game similar to the game of rummy. [from a Spanish word meaning literally "basket," which comes from Greek *kanastron*]

Can·ber·ra (kan′ber ə, kan′bər ə), *n.* the capital city of Australia, in the SE part.

can·cel (kan′sel), *v.,* **can·celed** *or* **can·celled; can·cel·ing** *or* **can·cel·ling. 1.** to call back or call off, as an order for tickets or plans for a trip; abolish; annul: *to cancel a football game.* **2.** to mark (something) so that it cannot be used again: *to cancel a stamp.* **3.** to cross out (a word, letter, sum, or the like). **4.** to make up for: *His apology cancels his rudeness.* **5.** to cross out a factor present in both the numerator and denominator of a fraction or on both sides of an equation.

can·cel·la·tion (kan′sə lā′s͟hən), *n.* **1.** the act of canceling, abolishing, or calling off something: *the cancellation of an order.* **2.** something canceled: *At first I couldn't get a ticket, but then I got a cancellation.* **3.** the marks made when something is canceled, as the marks on a used stamp.

can·cer (kan′sər), *n.* **1.** a growth of abnormal cells that can spread throughout the body and cause death. **2.** the disease characterized by such a growth. [from a Latin word meaning "crab"]

Can·cer (kan′sər), *n.* **1.** the Crab: a constellation and sign of the zodiac. **2. tropic of.** See **tropic of Cancer.**

can·de·la (kan dē′lə), *n.* a unit for measuring the brightness of a source of light.

can·de·la·bra (kan′d^{ə}lä′brə), *n., pl.* for def. 2 **can·de·la·bras. 1.** a plural of **candelabrum. 2.** another form of the word **candelabrum.**

can·de·la·brum (kan′d^{ə}lä′brəm), *n., pl.* **can·de·la·bra** (kan′d^{ə}lä′brə) *or* **can·de·la·brums.** a candlestick with arms or branches for holding more than one candle.

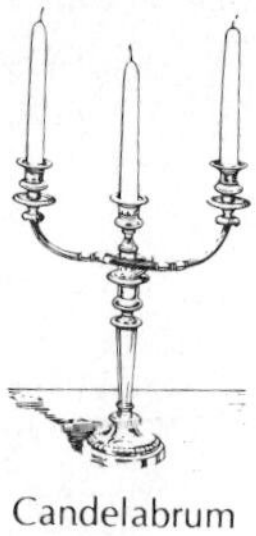
Candelabrum

can·did (kan′did), *adj.* **1.** open and sincere; frank; straightforward: *a candid person; a candid answer.* **2.** informal; done without posing: *a candid photograph.* **—can′did·ly,** *adv.* **—can′did·ness,** *n.*

can·di·da·cy (kan′di də sē), *n.* the state or fact of being a candidate or running for office: *He announced his candidacy for mayor.*

can·di·date (kan′di dāt′), *n.* a person who seeks or could be chosen for an office, honor, or the like: *Two outstanding men are candidates for mayor.* [from the Latin word *candidatus* "clothed in white," which comes from *candidus* "white." In Rome the candidates for office wore a white toga]

can·died (kan′dēd), *adj.* **1.** crusted with or full of sugar: *candied orange peel.* **2.** cooked in sugar or syrup: *candied sweet potatoes.*

can·dle (kan′d^{ə}l), *n.* **1.** a long piece of wax, tallow, or the like, that has a wick running through the middle and is burned to give light. **2.** (formerly) a unit for measuring brightness: now replaced by the candela. **—***v.,* **can·dled, can·dling. 3.** to test the freshness of (an egg) by holding it up to a light that is bright enough so that one can see through the shell.

can·dle·light (kan′d^{ə}līt′), *n.* **1.** the light of a candle: *to eat by candlelight.* **2.** dim artificial light.

can·dle·pow·er (kan′d^{ə}l pou′ər), *n.* **1.** brightness or brilliance. **2.** a unit for measuring the brightness of a source of light, now replaced by the candela.

can·dle·stick (kan′d^{ə}l stik′), *n.* a holder for one candle.

can·dor (kan′dər), *n.* **1.** frankness, openness, and sincerity. **2.** freedom from prejudice; fairness.

can·dy (kan′dē), *n., pl.* **can·dies. 1.** a very sweet food made with sugar or syrup, combined with other ingredients, such as chocolate and nuts. **2.** a single piece of this: *May I have a candy?* **—***v.,* **can·died, can·dy·ing. 3.** to make (something) very sweet, as by cooking or covering it with sugar or syrup: *to candy apples.* [from the French phrase *sucre candi* "candied sugar," which comes from Arabic *qand* "sugared"]

cane (kān), *n.* **1.** a stick to help one walk; walking stick. **2.** any rod or stick used for flogging or whipping. **3.** the hollow, jointed stem of certain plants, such as bamboo or sugar cane. **4.** the plant itself. **5.** rattan, esp. the stems as split for wickerwork for caning furniture. **—***v.,* **caned, can·ing. 6.** to beat or flog with a cane: *He caned his dog for biting the postman.* 7. to provide (furniture) with wickerwork: *to cane a chair.*

ca·nine (kā′nīn), *adj.* 1. of or referring to dogs. —*n.* 2. a dog. 3. one of the pointed teeth next to the incisors. See also **eyetooth.**

can·is·ter (kan′i stər), *n.* a container, usually of metal, for holding a household supply of tea, flour, sugar, etc.

can·ker (kang′kər), *n.* 1. a small sore in the mouth. 2. anything that causes weakness, pain, or destruction: *Greed was the canker in his character.*

canned (kand), *adj.* 1. preserved in a can or jar: *canned peas.* 2. *Slang.* recorded or taped: *a program of canned music.*

can·ner·y (kan′ə rē), *n., pl.* **can·ner·ies.** a place where food, such as fish or fruit, is packed in cans.

can·ni·bal (kan′ə bəl), *n.* 1. a person who eats human flesh. 2. an animal that eats other animals of its own kind: *Rats are sometimes cannibals.* [from the Spanish word *caníbal,* another form of *Caríbal,* which comes from *Carib,* the name of a West Indian people thought to eat human flesh]

can·ni·bal·ism (kan′ə bə liz′əm), *n.* the practice of eating the flesh of others of one's own kind. —**can′ni·bal·is′tic,** *adj.*

can·non (kan′ən), *n., pl.* **can·nons** or **can·non.** a big gun set on a base or movable stand: *a warship with 40 cannons.*

can·non·ade (kan′ə nād′), *n.* 1. a continued shooting or firing of cannons, esp. during an attack: *When the cannonade began, the soldiers started to advance.* —*v.,* **can·non·ad·ed, can·non·ad·ing.** 2. to shoot or attack with cannons.

can·non·ball (kan′ən bôl′), *n.* a large, heavy ball of iron or steel, made to be fired from an old-fashioned cannon.

can·not (kan′ot, ka not′), *v.* another form of *can not.*

can·ny (kan′ē), *adj.,* **can·ni·er, can·ni·est.** careful or wary; foxy; shrewd. —**can′ni·ness,** *n.*

ca·noe (kə nōō′), *n.* 1. a small, narrow, open boat that is moved with paddles. —*v.,* **ca·noed, ca·noe·ing.** 2. to go or travel in a canoe: *Let's canoe across the lake.* [from the Spanish word *canoa,* which comes from a word in a West Indian language]

can·on¹ (kan′ən), *n.* 1. a rule or law of a church, esp. the Roman Catholic Church. 2. a general rule; standard: *the canons of good manners.* 3. a collection of rules or standards; code. 4. the books of the Bible, or any other group of sacred books. 5. an official list, as of saints or sacred books. [from a Latin word meaning "rule, law," which comes from Greek *kanōn* "measuring rod, rule"]

can·on² (kan′ən), *n.* 1. a clergyman assigned to a cathedral or other large church. 2. a clergyman who is a member of a special religious order. [from the Latin word *canōnicus* "a person who lives according to a (religious) rule." See *canon¹*]

ca·ñon (kan′yən), *n.* another spelling of **canyon.**

ca·non·i·cal (kə non′i kəl), *adj.* 1. referring to or according to a canon or established law, esp. church law: *a canonical judgment.* 2. included in the canon or official books of the Bible.

can·on·ize (kan′ə nīz′), *v.,* **can·on·ized, can·on·iz·ing.** to declare (someone) to be a saint; place in the canon of saints: *St. Francis of Assisi was canonized two years after he died.*

can·o·py (kan′ə pē), *n., pl.* **can·o·pies.** 1. a covering that is set over an entranceway, a bed, a throne, etc., or set on poles and carried over an honored person or object, as in a procession. 2. something that resembles a canopy or covering, esp. the sky: *a canopy of stars.* —*v.,* **can·o·pied, can·o·py·ing.** 3. to cover with or as if with a canopy: *Branches canopied the country road.*

canst (kanst), *v.* an old form of **can,** found now chiefly in Biblical and poetic writing and used with *thou: Thou canst not sail all the seas of the world.*

cant¹ (kant), *n.* 1. insincere statements, esp. pious or righteous remarks said without thought. 2. the words or expressions used by a particular group of people; jargon: *gypsy cant.* [from the Old English word *cantic* "song," which comes from Latin *cantus*]

cant² (kant), *n.* 1. a tilt or slant. —*v.* 2. to tilt, turn, or slant. [from Middle English]

can't (kant), contraction of *cannot.*

can·ta·loupe (kan′t³lōp′), *n.* a melon with a rough skin and sweet, orange meat. Also, **can′ta·loup′.**

can·tan·ker·ous (kan tang′kər əs), *adj.* grouchy and quarrelsome; peevish: *to be in a cantankerous mood.* —**can·tan′ker·ous·ly,** *adv.* —**can·tan′ker·ous·ness,** *n.*

can·ta·ta (kən tä′tə), *n.* a musical composition usually for chorus, but sometimes for one or more solo singers, with instrumental accompaniment.

can·teen (kan tēn′), *n.* 1. a small container for water or other liquid, used by soldiers, campers, hikers, etc. 2. a building, usually on a military post, where soldiers can buy food and drinks, personal supplies, etc.

can·ter (kan′tər), *n.* 1. an easy, slow gallop. —*v.* 2. to go or ride at an easy gallop.

Can·ter·bur·y (kan′tər ber′ē), *n.* a city in SE England: cathedral; early religious center of England.

can·ti·cle (kan′ti kəl), *n.* a hymn or chant, usually from the Bible.

can·ti·lev·er (kan′t³lev′ər, kan′t³lē′vər), *n.* a structure extending horizontally from a vertical support, as a beam projecting from a wall.

can·to (kan′tō), *n., pl.* **can·tos.** one of the larger divisions of a long poem.

can·ton (kan′t³n, kan′ton), *n.* a small district within a country, esp. one of the states of Switzerland.

Can·ton (kan ton′, kan′ton *for def. 1;* kan′t³n *for def. 2*), *n.* 1. a port city in SE China. 2. a city in NE Ohio.

Can·ton·ese (kan′t³nēz′), *n., pl.* **Can·ton·ese.** 1. a native or inhabitant of Canton, China. 2. a dialect of Chinese spoken in Canton. —*adj.* 3. of or concerning Canton, its inhabitants, or their language.

---

act, āble, dâre, ärt; ebb, ēqual; if, īce; hot, ōver, ôrder; oil; book; ōoze; out; up, ûrge; ə = a as in alone; ³ as in button (but′³n), fire (fī³r); chief; shoe; thin; ŧħat; zh as in measure (mezh′ər). See full key inside cover.

can·tor (kan'tər), *n.* the head singer in a synagogue who leads the prayers that are to be sung and sings the solo parts himself.

can·vas (kan'vəs), *n.* **1.** a heavy, strong cloth that is used for tents, sails, oil paintings, etc. **2.** a piece of this on which an oil painting is made: *He has 12 canvases in the exhibition.* **3.** something made of canvas, as sails. [from the Latin word *cannabis* "hemp"]

can·vas·back (kan'vəs bak'), *n.* a North American wild duck, the male of which has a gray-white back and a reddish-brown head and neck.

can·vass (kan'vəs), *v.* **1.** to try to get votes, opinions, etc., from (a district, group of people, etc.), often by going from door to door: *The Democrats have canvassed this neighborhood.* **2.** to examine or investigate; discuss or debate: *to canvass a difficult problem.* —*n.* **3.** an attempt to get votes, support, etc., usually by going into a neighborhood and talking to people: *a canvass of Elm Street.* **4.** a general examination of a situation, issue, or the like: *a canvass of the latest election returns.* —**can'vass·er,** *n.*

can·yon (kan'yən), *n.* a deep valley with steep sides, often with a stream flowing through it: common in the western U.S. Also, **cañon.**

cap (kap), *n.* **1.** a covering for the head, usually close-fitting and having a small visor but no brim. **2.** any similar head covering, esp. one that shows occupation, rank, or the like: *a nurse's cap.* **3.** any sort of small covering or top: *a bottle cap.* **4.** a small amount of explosive powder wrapped in paper, for use in toy pistols. —*v.,* **capped, cap·ping. 5.** to cover with or as if with a cap or top. **6.** to equal or better something: *to cap one joke with another.*

Cap., Capital.

cap., **1.** capitalize. **2.** capitalized. **3.** capital letter.

ca·pa·bil·i·ty (kā'pə bil'i tē), *n., pl.* for def. 2 **ca·pa·bil·i·ties. 1.** the quality of being capable or able; ability; capacity: *He had the capability to succeed.* **2. capabilities,** qualities or abilities that can be developed: *a person of many capabilities.*

ca·pa·ble (kā'pə bəl), *adj.* **1.** having intelligence and ability; competent: *a capable student.* **2. capable of, a.** having the ability, skill or experience for: *capable of being captain of a ship.* **b.** able to be changed in a particular way: *This house is capable of improvement.* **c.** having the personality or being in the mood for: *capable of murder.* —**ca'pa·bly,** *adv.*

ca·pa·cious (kə pā'shəs), *adj.* capable of holding a large amount; roomy; spacious: *a capacious handbag.*

ca·pac·i·ty (kə pas'i tē), *n., pl.* **ca·pac·i·ties. 1.** ability to contain, hold, or receive; amount of space; volume: *That oil tank has a capacity of 20 gallons.* **2.** ability to do or withstand something; strength; power: *a capacity for hard work.* **3.** mental or physical ability; power; intelligence: *a student of outstanding capacity.* **4.** position or job: *She's working in the capacity of assistant principal.*

ca·par·i·son (kə par'i sən), *n.* **1.** a decorative covering for a horse, esp. in medieval times for the horses of knights. **2.** rich clothing. —*v.* **3.** to cover with a caparison. **4.** to dress in rich clothing.

cape[1] (kāp), *n.* a sleeveless garment, worn over other clothes, that fastens at the neck and lies over the shoulders, sometimes extending to the ground. [from an Old English word, which comes from Latin *cappa* "cloak with a hood"]

cape[2] (kāp), *n.* a piece of land jutting into the ocean, sea, or other large body of water: *The people living out on the cape suffered the most from the hurricane.* [from the French word *cap,* which comes from Latin *caput* "head"]

Cape' Ca·nav'er·al (kə nav'ər əl), site in Florida of U.S. center for space explorations.

Cape' Cod', a sandy peninsula in SE Massachusetts.

Cape' Horn', a headland on a small Chilean island at the S extremity of South America.

Cape' Ken'ne·dy, former name (1963–1973) of **Cape Canaveral.**

Cape' of Good' Hope', a cape in S Africa, in the SW part of the Republic of South Africa.

ca·per (kā'pər), *v.* **1.** to leap or skip about in a lively manner; prance; gambol. —*n.* **2.** a playful leap. **3.** a happy, carefree event or activity.

Cape' Town', a seaport and the legislative capital of the Republic of South Africa, in the SW part. See also **Pretoria.**

Cape' Verde' (vûrd), a republic consisting of a group of islands in the Atlantic Ocean, W of Senegal: formerly Portuguese. 1557 sq. mi.

cap·il·lar·y (kap'ə ler'ē), *n., pl.* **cap·il·lar·ies. 1.** one of the tiny blood vessels between the arteries and the veins. **2.** a tube with a very small bore, as that used in making thermometers.

cap·i·tal[1] (kap'i t°l), *n.* **1.** the city or town that is the official center of government of a nation, state, county, or the like: *Paris is the capital of France.* **2.** a letter that is written or printed large in a form that is used to begin a sentence, show a proper name, etc., as A, B, Q, and R. **3.** wealth in money or property that can produce more wealth: *A company in business must have capital.* —*adj.* **4.** chief or principal; most important: *a capital city; the capital question in a debate.* **5.** written or printed as a capital letter, as distinguished from lower-case. **6.** excellent or first-rate: *a capital fellow.* **7.** of or referring to capital or wealth: *Capital gains are earnings a person makes from money he has invested.* **8.** involving the loss of life: *capital punishment.* **9.** punishable by death: *a capital crime.* **10. make capital of,** to use to one's advantage: *He made capital of other people's weaknesses.* [partly from the Latin word *capitālis* "of the head, principal, chief," and partly from medieval Latin *capitāle* "wealth," both of which come from Latin *caput* "head"]

cap·i·tal² (kap'i t^əl), *n.* the uppermost part of a column, pillar, or the like, often having an ornamental design. [from the Latin word *capitellum*, which comes from *caput* "head"]

Capital²

cap·i·tal·ism (kap'i t^əliz'əm), *n.* an economic system in which land and means of production, as factories, are owned mainly by private individuals or companies rather than by the government, and there is competition among businesses: *The economic system of the U.S. is based on capitalism.* —**cap'i·tal·is' tic,** *adj.*

cap·i·tal·ist (kap'i t^əlist), *n.* **1.** a wealthy person, esp. one who has invested his wealth in business. **2.** a person who believes that capitalism is the best economic system.

cap·i·tal·i·za·tion (kap'i t^əli zā'shən), *n.* **1.** the act or an instance of using a capital letter or capital letters: *Capitalization is used for proper names.* **2.** the act or process of supplying or raising money or capital, esp. for a business project.

cap·i·tal·ize (kap'i t^əlīz'), *v.,* **cap·i·tal·ized, cap·i·tal·iz· ing. 1.** to write or print in capital letters or with a capital letter at the beginning of a word: *Always capitalize "Mary."* **2.** to supply or raise (money or capital), esp. for a project: *to capitalize a new chain of filling stations.* **3.** to take advantage of (often fol. by *on*): *He capitalized on my slowness by getting an early start.*

Cap·i·tol (kap'i t^əl), *n.* **1.** the building in Washington, D.C., in which the U.S. Congress holds its sessions. **2.** *(often l.c.)* a building occupied by a state legislature; statehouse. [from the Latin word *Capitōlium,* the temple of Jupiter on the Capitoline hill in Rome]

ca·pit·u·late (kə pich'ə lāt'), *v.,* **ca·pit·u·lat·ed, ca·pit· u·lat·ing.** to surrender, sometimes on specified terms: *The rebels capitulated when their ammunition ran out.* —**ca·pit'u·la'tion,** *n.*

ca·pon (kā'pon), *n.* a castrated rooster, raised for its meat.

ca·price (kə prēs'), *n.* a sudden, unexpected, and usually odd change in someone's behavior, the weather, etc.: *Her decision to take up motorcycling was nothing more than a caprice.* [from the Italian word *capriccio*]

ca·pri·cious (kə prish'əs), *adj.* **1.** apt to change suddenly and unexpectedly; governed by whims; eccentric: *a capricious young man who went to five colleges before he graduated.* **2.** based on or showing caprice or changeableness: *a capricious decision to play hooky.* —**ca·pri'cious·ly,** *adv.*

Cap·ri·corn (kap'rə kôrn), *n.* **1.** the Goat: a constellation and sign of the zodiac. **2. tropic of.** See **tropic of Capricorn.**

caps., capital letters.

cap·size (kap'sīz, kap sīz'), *v.,* **cap·sized, cap·siz·ing.** to overturn or tip over: *The boat capsized in the sudden storm.*

cap·stan (kap'stən), *n.* a device on a ship for winding in cables, pulling up anchors, etc. It usually stands upright and is turned by hand or by machinery.

Capstan

cap·sule (kap'səl), *n.* **1.** a small case, as that holding the seeds of certain plants or the gelatine case holding a dose of medicine. **2.** a small, sealed cabin for space flights, as that mounted on top of a large rocket.

cap·tain (kap'tən), *n.* **1.** a person in charge of others; chief; leader: *the captain of a team.* **2.** an officer in the U.S. Army, ranking above a first lieutenant and below a major. **3.** an officer in the U.S. Navy, ranking above a commander and below a rear admiral. **4.** the person in charge of a ship. **5.** the pilot of a plane. —*v.* **6.** to lead or command as a captain: *to captain a ship.* [from the Old French word *capitaine,* which comes from Latin *capitāneus* "chief," from *caput* "head"]

cap·tion (kap'shən), *n.* **1.** a title, brief description, or the like, esp. for a picture or illustration: *Read the caption underneath the photograph.* —*v.* **2.** to supply a caption or captions for; entitle: *to caption a picture.*

cap·tious (kap'shəs), *adj.* **1.** apt to complain or find fault: *a peevish, captious person.* **2.** likely or meant to trap or confuse someone: *captious questions.* —**cap' tious·ly,** *adv.* —**cap'tious·ness,** *n.*

cap·ti·vate (kap'tə vāt'), *v.,* **cap·ti·vat·ed, cap·ti·vat· ing.** to charm or fascinate by beauty, intelligence, or the like: *Her singing captivated the audience.* —**cap' ti·vat'ing·ly,** *adv.* —**cap'ti·va'tor,** *n.*

cap·tive (kap'tiv), *n.* **1.** someone who is captured and held; prisoner: *Captives taken in war were sold as slaves.* —*adj.* **2.** made or held prisoner; locked up; confined: *captive soldiers; captive animals.*

cap·tiv·i·ty (kap tiv'i tē), *n.* the state of being held captive, or the period of time one is held captive: *This is the largest tiger in captivity.*

cap·tor (kap'tər), *n.* a person who takes a prisoner or who captures something: *The captors of the city were merciful to the inhabitants.*

cap·ture (kap'chər), *v.,* **cap·tured, cap·tur·ing. 1.** to take by force or trickery; seize; take prisoner: *to capture a castle.* —*n.* **2.** the act or process of capturing or seizing: *The capture of the enemy general was carefully planned.* **3.** the person or thing captured.

cap·u·chin (kap'yə chin, kap'yə shin), *n.* a monkey found in Central and South America, having a tail that can be wrapped around objects and hair on the head resembling a hood.

cap·y·ba·ra (kap'ə bär'ə), *n.* a South American rodent, living along the banks of rivers and lakes, having no tail and partly webbed feet. It is the largest living rodent.

Capuchin (total length 2½ ft.)

car (kär), *n.* **1.** an automobile. **2.** a

streetcar or other wheeled vehicle run by a motor, electricity, or the like. 3. an elevator, cable car, or other enclosed compartment for transporting passengers or freight. 4. the gondola of a balloon. [from the Latin word *carrus,* which comes from Celtic]

Ca·ra·cas (kə rä′kəs), *n.* the capital city of Venezuela, in the N part.

car·a·cul (kar′ə kəl), *n.* the pelt of the karakul lamb: *She has a new coat of caracul.*

car·a·mel (kar′ə məl, kar′ə mel′), *n.* 1. liquid flavoring made by cooking sugar until it becomes brown. 2. a kind of candy, usually in small blocks, made from sugar, butter, and milk.

car·at (kar′ət), *n.* a unit of weight used in weighing gems: equal to ¹/₅ of a gram.

car·a·van (kar′ə van′), *n.* 1. a group of travelers, such as merchants or pilgrims, who are banded together for safety during a long journey. 2. any similar group using a particular type of transportation: *a camel caravan.* 3. a large covered truck; van. 4. *British.* a trailer; house on wheels.

car·a·vel (kar′ə vel′), *n.* a small Spanish or Portuguese sailing ship of the 15th and 16th centuries. Also, **carvel.**

Caravel

car·a·way (kar′ə wā′), *n.* a plant having seeds that are used as a flavoring and in medicine.

car·bine (kär′bīn, kär′bēn), *n.* 1. a short rifle. 2. (formerly) a musket.

car·bo·hy·drate (kär′bō hī′drāt), *n.* any of a class of substances, including sugar, starch, and cellulose, that are made up of carbon, hydrogen, and oxygen.

car·bol′ic ac′id (kär bol′ik), a very powerful disinfectant and antiseptic extracted from coal tar.

car·bon (kär′bən), *n.* 1. *Chem.* a nonmetallic element existing as lampblack, graphite, and diamond and found in all living things. *Symbol:* C 2. a sheet of carbon paper, or a copy of something made by using it. [from the French word *carbone,* which comes from Latin *carbō* "charcoal"]

car·bon·ate (kär′bə nāt′), *v.,* **car·bon·at·ed, car·bon·at·ing.** to treat (water, wine, etc.) with carbon dioxide so as to make it fizzy: *a carbonated beverage.*

car·bon·a·tion (kär′bə nā′shən), *n.* the fizziness resulting from treatment with carbon dioxide.

car′bon diox′ide, a gas in which each molecule contains one atom of carbon and two atoms of oxygen: a waste product of respiration that is used by plants in photosynthesis.

car′bon monox′ide, a highly poisonous gas in which each molecule contains one atom of carbon and one atom of oxygen: formed by the incomplete burning of fuel, as in automobile engines.

car′bon pa′per, paper coated on one side with a preparation of carbon, used between two sheets of plain paper to transfer to the lower sheet whatever one writes or draws on the top sheet.

car·bun·cle (kär′bung kəl), *n.* 1. a painful swelling under the skin, resembling a boil but more serious in its effects. 2. a rounded red jewel.

car·bu·re·tor (kär′bə rā′tər), *n.* the part of a gasoline engine in which the fuel and air are mixed.

car·cass (kär′kəs), *n., pl.* **car·cass·es.** 1. the dead body of an animal. 2. *Slang.* a person's body: *I can't lift my old carcass out of this chair.*

card¹ (kärd), *n.* 1. a piece of stiff paper or thin cardboard, usually rectangular, for various uses, such as filing information or identifying the owner: *He kept his class notes on cards. Show your membership card at the door.* 2. *Informal.* an amusing person: *The announcer was a real card.* 3. a postcard. 4. one of a set of small, glazed cardboards having special marks and pictures, used in playing various games. 5. **cards,** *(usually used as sing.)* any of various games played with such a set: *I don't know how to play cards.* [from a Middle English word meaning "letter, writing paper," which comes from Greek *chartēs* "leaf of paper"]

card² (kärd), *n.* 1. a machine or tool for combing out fibers of cotton, flax, etc., before spinning. —*v.* 2. to prepare (wool or the like) with a card for spinning: *to card flax.* [from the Latin word *carduus* "thistle"]

card·board (kärd′bôrd′), *n.* a thin, stiff, boardlike material made of sheets or layers of paper stuck or pressed together, used for boxes, signs, etc.

car·di·ac (kär′dē ak′), *adj.* of or referring to the heart.

Car·diff (kär′dif), *n.* a port city in SE Wales.

car·di·gan (kär′də gən), *n.* a knitted jacket or sweater that opens in front and has no collar. [named after the 7th Earl of *Cardigan* (1797–1868), a British cavalryman in the Crimean War]

car·di·nal (kär′d³n³l), *n.* 1. an American songbird, the male of which has bright red plumage. 2. a deep, rich red. 3. any of a group of high-ranking churchmen in the Roman Catholic Church that are appointed by the pope. —*adj.* 4. of first or basic importance: *a cardinal rule of behavior.* 5. of the color cardinal: *a cardinal coat.* [from the Latin word *cardinālis* "something on which other things hinge," which comes from *cardō* "hinge"]

Cardinal (length 9½ in.)

car′dinal num′ber, a number that expresses amount, as 1, 2, 3, 100, etc. See also **ordinal number.**

car′dinal point′, any of the four principal points of the compass; north, south, east, or west.

care (kâr), *n.* 1. worry, distress, or concern: *Care had aged him.* 2. a cause or object of worry or concern: *His greatest care right now is whether he can pass his exams.* 3. serious attention: *to work with great care.* 4. protection; keeping or charge: *He's under the care of a doctor. Send my mail in care of my father.*

—*v.*, **cared, car·ing. 5.** to be concerned or worried: *Do you really care?* **6.** to wish or be interested in (usually fol. by an infinitive): *Would you care to dance?* **7. care for, a.** to attend to the needs of: *She cares for her sick father.* **b.** to have a liking or affection for: *I never did care for liver. She was the first girl he ever cared for.* **8. take care,** be alert; be careful: *The walk is icy, so take care!* **9. take care of, a.** to watch over: *Take care of your little brother.* **b.** to deal with; attend to: *We'd better take care of these bills.*

CARE (kâr), *n.* an organization that collects funds, food, goods, etc., for distribution to the needy in foreign countries. Also, **Care** [from the words *C(ooperative for) A(merican) R(elief) E(verywhere)*]

ca·reen (kə rēn′), *v.* **1.** to lean, sway, or tip from side to side while in motion: *The speeding car careened through the empty streets.* **2.** to cause (a boat) to lie on its side to permit cleaning or repair of the hull.

ca·reer (kə rēr′), *n.* **1.** a person's chief business or general course of action in a particular phase of his life: *He had a brief career as a soldier.* **2.** a profession or occupation followed as one's life work: *to prepare for a career in law.* **3.** speed, esp. full speed: *The horse stumbled in full career.* —*v.* **4.** to run or move rapidly along; go at full speed: *The police car careered down the highway.* —*adj.* **5.** having or following a career or occupation: *a career girl.*

care·free (kâr′frē′), *adj.* without worry or concern; free of care; happy-go-lucky: *a carefree boy; a carefree afternoon.*

care·ful (kâr′fəl), *adj.* **1.** cautious, alert, and watchful so as to avoid harm, trouble, mistakes, or the like: *Always be careful when lighting a fire in the woods.* **2.** done or said with accuracy or caution: *careful work; a careful answer.* **3.** thoughtful or considerate (usually fol. by *of, about,* or *in*): *to be careful of other people's feelings.* —**care′ful·ly,** *adv.*

care·less (kâr′lis), *adj.* **1.** not paying enough attention to what one does so as to avoid mistakes, harm, etc. **2.** done or said without thought, attention, or consideration: *careless work; a careless remark.* **3.** resulting from lack of attention: *a careless mistake.* **4.** not caring or troubling; unconcerned (usually fol. by *of*): *careless of other people's feelings.* **5.** carefree or untroubled: *the careless days of childhood.* **6.** done or achieved without′ effort: *careless beauty.* —**care′less·ly,** *adv.* —**care′less·ness,** *n.*

ca·ress (kə res′), *n.* **1.** an act or gesture showing affection, as a gentle stroking, a hug, or a kiss. —*v.* **2.** to touch or stroke gently: *The boy caressed the lost dog. The breeze caressed the trees.* —**ca·ress′ing·ly,** *adv.*

car·et (kar′it), *n.* a mark (∧) made in written or printed work to show where something should be added or inserted. [from a Latin word meaning "(there) is lacking," which comes from *carēre* "to lack"]

care·tak·er (kâr′tā′kər), *n.* a person who is in charge

of keeping up or caring for a building, country home, or the like.

care·worn (kâr′wôrn′), *adj.* showing signs of care or worry; haggard: *a careworn look in her eyes.*

car·fare (kär′fâr′), *n.* the amount charged for a ride on a streetcar, bus, or the like.

car·go (kär′gō), *n., pl.* **car·goes** *or* **car·gos.** the load or freight transported by a ship, airplane, etc.: *a valuable cargo of wheat.*

Car·ib·be·an Sea′ (kar′ə bē′ən, kə rib′ē ən), a part of the Atlantic Ocean bounded by Central America,

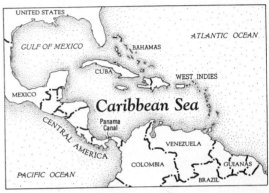

the West Indies, and South America. about 750,000 sq. mi.; greatest known depth 22,788 ft. Also, **the Caribbean.**

car·i·bou (kar′ə bōō′), *n., pl.* **car·i·bous** *or* **car·i·bou.** a large North American deer related to the reindeer. [from the Algonquian word *khalibu* "animal that paws (at the earth in search of food)"]

car·i·ca·ture (kar′ə kə chŏŏr′), *n.* **1.** a picture or description of a person or thing that exaggerates certain points, esp. faults, in a comic way; cartoon. **2.** the art of producing caricatures or cartoons: *He's good at caricature.* —*v.,* **car·i·ca·tured, car·i·ca·tur·ing. 3.** to make a caricature of; show or describe in an exaggerated, absurd way: *to caricature political leaders.* —**car′i·ca·tur·ist,** *n.*

car·ies (kâr′ēz), *n., pl.* **car·ies.** decay, as of a bone, tooth, or plant tissue.

car·il·lon (kar′ə lon′), *n.* a set of bells on which melodies can be played.

car·load (kär′lōd′), *n.* the amount that will fill a freight car, an automobile, or the like: *a carload of coal; a carload of people.*

Car·mel (kär mel′), *n.* **Mount,** a mountain in NW Israel near the Mediterranean coast. Highest point, 1818 ft.; about 14 mi. long.

car·mine (kär′min, kär′mīn), *n.* **1.** a crimson or purplish red. **2.** a crimson pigment.

car·nage (kär′nij), *n.* the slaughter of many people, as in battle: *a scene of terrible carnage.*

car·nal (kär′nəl), *adj.* **1.** not spiritual; human or worldly. **2.** of the body or bodily senses.

car·na·tion (kär nā′shən), *n.* a flower with frilly petals and a spicy smell, usually red, pink, or white.

---

act, āble, dâre, ärt; ebb, ēqual; if, īce; hot, ōver, ôrder; oil; bŏŏk; ōōze; out; up, ûrge; ə = *a* as in *alone*; ᵊ as in *button* (but′ᵊn), *fire* (fīᵊr); chief; shoe; thin; ŧħat; zh as in *measure* (mezh′ər). See full key inside cover.

car·ni·val (kär′nə vəl), *n.* **1.** a traveling amusement show, usually having side shows, a Ferris wheel, merry-go-rounds, shooting galleries, etc. **2.** any festival, such as a program of sports, parades, and entertainment: *a winter sports carnival.* **3.** a time of merrymaking, parades, dances, etc., just before Lent: *In Brazil no one works during carnival.* [from the Italian word *carnevale* "taking meat away," which comes from *carne* "flesh" + *levare* "to lift, take away"]

car·niv·o·rous (kär niv′ər əs), *adj.* meat-eating or flesh-eating: *Wolves are carnivorous, but sheep are not.* See also **herbivorous, omnivorous** (def. 1).

car·ol (kar′əl), *n.* **1.** a song of joy, esp. a Christmas song or hymn. —*v.,* **car·oled** *or* **car·olled; car·ol·ing** *or* **car·ol·ling. 2.** to sing, esp. to sing Christmas songs. **3.** to sing in praise of: *The birds caroled the coming of spring.* —**car′ol·er, car′ol·ler,** *n.*

Car·o·li·na (kar′ə li′nə), *n.* **1.** North Carolina or South Carolina. **2. the Carolinas,** North Carolina and South Carolina. —**Car·o·lin·i·an** (kar′ə lin′ē ən), *n., adj.*

Car′o·line Is′lands (kar′ə lin′, kar′ə lin), a group of over 500 islands in the Pacific Ocean, E of the Philippines: under U.S. administration. 525 sq. mi.

ca·rous·al (kə rou′zəl), *n.* a noisy, lively feast or party, esp. one with a great deal of drinking.

ca·rouse (kə rouz′), *v.,* **ca·roused, ca·rous·ing.** to take part in a feast or drinking party: *to carouse with one's friends.* —**ca·rous′er,** *n.*

car·ou·sel (kar′ə sel′), *n.* another spelling of **carrousel.**

carp¹ (kärp), *v.* to find fault; complain unreasonably. [from Scandinavian] —**carp′er,** *n.*

carp² (kärp), *n., pl.* **carps** *or* **carp.** a large freshwater fish used for food. [from Dutch]

car·pel (kär′pəl), *n.* a seed-bearing organ of a flower; a single pistil.

car·pen·ter (kär′pən tər), *n.* a person who builds or repairs wooden structures, such as houses and other buildings, boats, bleachers, shelving, and the like.

car·pen·try (kär′pən trē), *n.* **1.** the trade of a carpenter: *He plans to buy some tools and learn carpentry.* **2.** the work produced by a carpenter: *This chest of drawers is a good example of his carpentry.*

C, Carpels

car·pet (kär′pit), *n.* **1.** a heavy fabric, usually of wool or nylon, for covering floors. **2.** any covering like a carpet: *a carpet of grass.* —*v.* **3.** to cover with or as if with a carpet: *Mother wants to carpet the living room. Flowers carpeted the hillside.* **4. on the carpet,** reprimanded by a person or persons in authority: *We were on the carpet for playing hooky.*

car·pet·bag (kär′pit bag′), *n.* a bag for traveling, esp. one made of carpeting.

car·pet·bag·ger (kär′pit bag′ər), *n.* a Northerner who went to the South after the U.S. Civil War to seek political office or to take financial advantage of the confused social and political situation. [so called

because he traveled to the South carrying his belongings in a carpetbag]

car·pet·ing (kär′pi tiṅg), *n.* **1.** material for carpets. **2.** carpets in general.

car′ pool′, an arrangement among automobile owners by which each owner in turn drives the others to and from a certain place.

car·port (kär′pôrt′), *n.* a roofed shed without walls, jutting out from the side of a building, used as a shelter for an automobile.

car·riage (kar′ij), *n.* **1.** a wheeled vehicle for transporting persons, sometimes drawn by horses and designed for comfort and elegance. **2.** the act of transporting: *an additional charge for carriage.* **3.** the price or cost of transportation. **4.** the manner of carrying the head and body; bearing: *the erect carriage of a soldier.* **5.** a wheeled support, as for a cannon or gun. **6.** a movable part of a machine designed for carrying something: *a typewriter carriage.*

car·ri·er (kar′ē ər), *n.* **1.** a person or thing that carries. **2.** any person or organization in the business of transporting persons or goods. **3.** a person, animal, or thing that harbors and transmits disease.

car·ri·on (kar′ē ən), *n.* **1.** dead and decaying flesh. —*adj.* **2.** feeding on carrion. **3.** of or like carrion.

Car·roll (kar′əl), *n.* Lewis, (pen name of *Charles Lutwidge Dodgson*) 1832–1898, English writer of children's books.

car·rot (kar′ət), *n.* **1.** a plant having a long, tapering, yellow-orange root. **2.** the root of this plant, used as a vegetable.

car·rou·sel (kar′ə sel′), *n.* See **merry-go-round** (def. 1). Also, **carousel.**

car·ry (kar′ē), *v.,* **car·ried, car·ry·ing. 1.** to move while supporting; transport: *I carried the groceries home.* **2.** to wear, hold, or have around one: *He carries change in his pocket.* **3.** to hold or be capable of holding; contain: *The suitcase will carry enough clothes for a week.* **4.** to behave or conduct (oneself): *She carries herself with dignity.* **5.** to hold (the body, head, etc.) in a certain manner: *She carries her head high.* **6.** to bring, hear, transmit, or communicate, as news or a message: *The newspapers carried a special article on the elections.* **7.** to win a majority of votes in (a district, state, etc.). **8.** to lead or conduct: *The pipe carries the water five miles.* **9.** to support: *Our grain supply will carry the cattle through the winter.* **10.** to sing (a tune) accurately. **11.** to transfer (one or more digits) to the next column when adding numbers. **12.** to keep in stock or on hand: *Does that store carry sweat shirts?* **13. carry away,** to excite or influence greatly: *She always gets carried away by ballet music.* **14. carry on, a.** to continue or persevere: *to carry on rescue operations.* **b.** to behave foolishly or excitedly: *There's no need to carry on just because you lost a dime.* **15. carry out,** to put into operation; complete or accomplish: *Can you carry out my instructions?*

car·ry·all¹ (kar′ē ôl′), *n.* a light, four-wheeled, covered carriage having seats for four persons, usually drawn by one horse. [from the French word *carriole,* "a kind of carriage," from Latin *carrus* "car"]

car·ry·all² (kar′ē ôl′), *n.* a large basket, bag, or case. [from *carry* + *all*]

Car·son (kär′sən), *n.* Christopher *("Kit")*, 1809–1868, U.S. frontiersman and scout.

Car′son Cit′y, the capital city of Nevada, in the W part.

cart (kärt), *n.* 1. a heavy, two-wheeled vehicle, usually drawn by mules or oxen, and used for transporting heavy goods. 2. a light, two-wheeled vehicle drawn by a horse or pony. 3. any small vehicle moved by hand: *a shopping cart.* —*v.* 4. to carry in or as if in a cart: *to cart groceries.*

car·tel (kär tel′), *n.* 1. an international group formed to regulate prices and output in some field of business. 2. a written agreement between nations at war for the exchange of prisoners.

Car·ter (kär′tər), *n.* Jimmy *(James Earl, Jr.)*, born 1924, 39th President of the U.S. since 1977.

Car·thage (kär′thij), *n.* an ancient city in North Africa, near modern Tunis: founded by the Phoenicians in the 9th century B.C.; destroyed by the Romans 146 B.C. —**Car·tha·gin·i·an** (kär′thə jin′ē ən), *n., adj.*

Car·tier (kär′tē ā′), *n.* Jacques, 1491–1557, French navigator and explorer of Canada: discovered the St. Lawrence River.

car·ti·lage (kär′t³lij), *n.* tough, springy tissue that forms part of the skeleton; gristle.

car·ton (kär′t³n), *n.* 1. a cardboard box or container. 2. the contents of a carton: *a carton of milk.* [from the Italian word *cartone* "pasteboard," which comes from *carta* "paper"]

car·toon (kär tōōn′), *n.* 1. a sketch or drawing in a magazine or newspaper that represents, often humorously and satirically, a person, action, or event. 2. an animated cartoon. [from the Italian word *cartone* "pasteboard." See *carton*] —**car·toon′ist**, *n.*

car·tridge (kär′trij), *n.* 1. a case for holding a complete charge of powder, and often also the bullet or the shot for a rifle, machine gun, or other small arm. 2. any container for powder, liquid, etc., made for use in a larger instrument: *a cartridge of ink for a fountain pen; a film cartridge.*

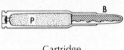

Cartridge
P, Powder; B, Bullet

cart·wheel (kärt′hwēl′, -wēl′), *n.* 1. the wheel of a cart. 2. an acrobatic feat in which a person starts from a standing position and revolves the body sideways, landing first on the hands and then on the feet.

Ca·ru·so (kə rōō′sō), *n.* **En·ri·co** (en rē′kō), 1873–1921, Italian operatic tenor.

carve (kärv), *v.,* **carved, carv·ing.** 1. to cut (a solid material) so as to form something: *to carve stone for a statue.* 2. to form from a solid material by cutting: *to carve a statue out of stone.* 3. to cut into slices or pieces: *to carve a turkey.* —**carv′er**, *n.*

car·vel (kär′vəl), *n.* another form of **caravel.**

Car·ver (kär′vər), *n.* **George Washington**, 1864?–1943, U.S. botanist and chemist.

carv·ing (kär′viñg), *n.* 1. the act of fashioning or producing by cutting. 2. a carved work or design: *a wood carving.*

car·y·at·id (kar′ē at′id), *n.* a sculptured female figure used as a column.

Ca·sa·blan·ca (kä′sə bläñg′kə), *n.* a port city in NW Morocco.

cas·cade (kas kād′), *n.* 1. a waterfall or series of waterfalls descending over a steep, rocky surface. —*v.,* **cas·cad·ed, cas·cad·ing.** 2. to fall in or like a cascade.

cas·car·a (kas kâr′ə), *n.* a laxative made from the bark of a shrub or tree growing on the Pacific coast of the U.S.

case¹ (kās), *n.* 1. an instance of the occurrence or existence of something: *a case of poor judgment.* 2. the actual state of things: *That is not the case.* 3. a situation requiring discussion, decision, or investigation: *the case of the missing jewels; a case brought before a court.* 4. an instance of disease or injury requiring medical or surgical attention: *a case of measles.* 5. a medical or surgical patient. 6. the grammatical relation of a noun, pronoun, or adjective to the other words in a sentence. The case of a word may be shown either by its form or by its position in the sentence. See also **nominative** (def. 1), **objective** (def. 3), **possessive** (def. 3). 7. **in any case**, regardless of the situation or circumstances: *In any case, you are never to do that again.* 8. **in case**, if it should happen that; if: *In case I'm late, go on without me.* 9. **in case of**, in the event of: *In case of rain, we'll postpone the game.* [from the Latin word *cāsus*]

case² (kās), *n.* 1. a container for holding something: *a jewel case.* 2. an outer covering: *a knife case.* 3. a box with its contents: *a case of ginger ale.* 4. a frame or framework, as of a door or window. [from the Latin word *capsa*]

ca·sein (kā′sēn), *n.* a protein extracted from milk and used in manufacturing paints, plastics, and glues.

case·ment (kās′mənt), *n.* 1. a window sash opening on hinges. 2. Also, **case′ment win′dow.** a window with such a sash or sashes.

cash (kash), *n.* 1. money in the form of coins or paper. 2. money or an equivalent, such as a check, paid at the time of making a purchase: *If you can't charge it, you'll have to pay cash.* —*v.* 3. to give or obtain cash for: *to cash a check.*

cash·ew (kash′ōō), *n.* the small, soft, kidney-shaped nut of a tropical American tree.

cash·ier¹ (ka shēr′), *n.* an employee of a store, restaurant, bank, etc., who has charge of money. [from a

Dutch word, which comes from French *caissier*]

cash·ier² (ka shēr′), *v.* to dismiss from a position of command or trust, esp. with disgrace. [from a French word, which comes from Latin *quassāre* "to break"]

cash·mere (kazh′mēr, kash′mēr), *n.* **1.** the fine, downy wool obtained from the Kashmir goats of India. **2.** a garment or yarn made from this wool.

Cash′mere goat′. See Kashmir goat.

cas·ing (kā′sing), *n.* **1.** a case or covering, esp. the outermost covering of an automobile tire. **2.** a frame or framework, esp. of a door or window. **3.** the thin membrane of the intestines of sheep, cattle, or hogs, used for encasing sausages, salamis, etc.

ca·si·no (kə sē′nō), *n., pl.* for def. 1 **ca·si·nos.** **1.** a building or large room used for meetings, entertainment, dancing, or gambling. **2.** a card game.

cask (kask), *n.* **1.** a container made and shaped like a barrel for holding liquids. **2.** the quantity it holds.

cas·ket (kas′kit), *n.* **1.** a coffin. **2.** a small chest or box, as for jewels.

Cas′pi·an Sea′ (kas′pē-ən), a salt lake between SE Europe and Asia: the largest inland body of water in the world. about 169,000 sq. mi.; 85 ft. below sea level.

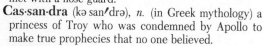

casque (kask), *n.* an open, cone-shaped helmet with a nose guard.

Cas·san·dra (kə san′drə), *n.* (in Greek mythology) a princess of Troy who was condemned by Apollo to make true prophecies that no one believed.

cas·sa·va (kə sä′və), *n.* a tropical plant, whose root yields the starch from which tapioca is made.

cas·se·role (kas′ə rōl), *n.* **1.** a baking dish of glass, pottery, etc., usually with a cover. **2.** any food, usually a mixture, served in such a dish.

cas·sette (ka set′, kə set′), *n.* a compact case containing magnetic tape for quick insertion into a tape recorder or player.

cas·sock (kas′ək), *n.* a long, close-fitting garment worn by clergymen.

cas·so·war·y (kas′ə wer′ē), *n., pl.* **cas·so·war·ies.** any of several large flightless birds of Australia and New Guinea. [from the Malay word *kasuāri*]

cast (kast), *v.,* cast, cast·ing. **1.** to throw or hurl; fling: *to cast dice; to cast a pebble.* **2.** to direct or cause to fall upon something: *to cast a glance down the page; to cast a soft light on the room.* **3.** to deposit or give: *to cast a vote.* **4.** to assign a role in a play. **5.** to form (an object) by pouring metal, plaster, etc., into a mold and letting it harden: *to cast a statue of a horse.* **6.** to form (a substance) by this process: *to cast metal.* —*n.* **7.** the act of casting or throwing. **8.** the distance a thing may be thrown. **9.** the performers in a play, story, etc. **10.** something formed from a material poured into a mold. **11.** a stiff surgical bandage, usually made of plaster of Paris: *to set a broken leg in a cast.* **12.** outward form or appearance. **13.** a permanent twist or turn: *to have a cast in one's eye.* **14.**

cast about, to search for something: *We cast about for something to do during vacation.*

cas·ta·net (kas′tə net′), *n.* either of a pair of shell-shaped pieces of wood clicked together by the fingers of one hand and used as a rhythm instrument, esp. to accompany Spanish dancing. [from the Spanish word *cas·tañeta* "chestnut"]

Castanets

cast·a·way (kast′ə wā′), *n.* **1.** a ship-wrecked person. **2.** an outcast. —*adj.* **3.** cast adrift. **4.** thrown away.

caste (kast), *n* **1.** a distinctive social group of persons of the same rank, occupation, etc. **2.** any of the four social divisions of Hindu society.

cast·er (kas′tər), *n.* **1.** a person or thing that casts. **2.** a small wheel on a swivel, set under a piece of furniture, a machine, etc., to make it easier to move. **3.** a small bottle or container for spices or seasonings. Also, **castor** (for defs. 2, 3).

cas·ti·gate (kas′tə gāt′), *v.,* cas·ti·gat·ed, cas·ti·gat·ing. to punish or criticize harshly. —**cas′ti·ga′tion,** *n.*

Cas·tile (ka stēl′), *n.* **1.** a former kingdom in central Spain. **2.** Also, **Castile′ soap′.** a mild soap made from olive oil.

Cas·til·ian (kə stil′yən), *n.* **1.** the standard form of the Spanish language as spoken in Spain. **2.** a native or inhabitant of Castile. —*adj.* **3.** of or referring to Castile or its people.

cast·ing (kas′ting), *n.* **1.** any article that has been cast in a mold: *to make a casting of a statue.* **2.** the act or process of a person or thing that casts: *The fisherman worked to perfect his casting.*

cast′ i′ron, a form of iron, usually hard and brittle, produced by pouring molten iron into a mold.

cast-i·ron (kast′ī′ərn), *adj.* **1.** made of cast iron. **2.** very strong; unyielding: *a cast-iron will; a cast-iron stomach.*

cas·tle (kas′əl), *n.* **1.** a fortified residence, as of a prince or noble in feudal times. **2.** a large, stately, elegant residence. **3.** another word for **rook².**

cast·off (kast′ôf′, -of′), *adj.* **1.** thrown away; discarded: *castoff clothing.* —*n.* **2.** a person or thing that has been cast off.

cas·tor (kas′tər), *n.* See **caster** (defs. 2, 3).

cas′tor oil′, a clear, yellowish oil pressed from the seeds of a tropical tree. Castor oil is used as a laxative and as a high-quality engine lubricant.

cas·trate (kas′trāt), *v.,* cas·trat·ed, cas·trat·ing. to remove the testicles of; emasculate. —**cas·tra′tion,** *n.*

cas·u·al (kazh′ōō əl), *adj.* **1.** happening by chance: *a casual meeting.* **2.** without serious intention; offhand; indifferent: *a casual remark.* **3.** (of clothes) suitable for informal wear. **4.** occasional or irregular: *a casual visitor.* —*n.* **5.** a person employed only irregularly. —**cas′u·al·ly,** *adv.* —**cas′u·al·ness,** *n.*

cas·u·al·ty (kazh′oo̅ əl tē), *n.*, *pl.* **cas·u·al·ties.** 1. a member of the armed forces lost to his unit by being killed, wounded, sick, captured, or missing. 2. a person who is injured or killed in an accident: *There were no casualties in the automobile accident.*

cat (kat), *n.* 1. a small, furry mammal kept as a pet and for catching rats and mice. 2. any of the larger animals of the same family, as the lion, tiger, leopard, cougar, etc. 3. **let the cat out of the bag,** to tell a secret: *The party was to be a surprise, but Selma let the cat out of the bag.* —**cat′like′,** *adj.*

cat·a·clysm (kat′ə kliz′əm), *n.* 1. any violent change, esp. one of a social or political nature. 2. a sudden and violent physical action, such as a flood or earthquake. —**cat′a·clys′mic,** *adj.*

cat·a·comb (kat′ə kōm′), *n.* Usually, **catacombs.** an underground cemetery with tunnels and small rooms for tombs.

cat·a·falque (kat′ə falk′, kat′ə fôk′), *n.* a raised structure on which the body of a dead person lies in state.

Cat·a·lan (kat′ᵊlan′), *n.* 1. a native or inhabitant of Catalonia. 2. the Romance language of Catalonia, Valencia, and the Balearic Islands. —*adj.* 3. of or referring to Catalonia, its people, or their language.

Catafalque

cat·a·log (kat′ᵊlôg′), *n.* 1. a list, usually in alphabetical order, with short notes on the names, articles, books, or subjects listed. 2. a book, leaflet, or file containing such a list or record: *The university publishes a catalog of courses offered.* —*v.,* **cat·a·loged, cat·a·log·ing.** 3. to enter in a catalog; make a catalog of: *The librarian cataloged the new books.* Also, **cat′a·logue.**

Cat·a·lo·ni·a (kat′ᵊlō′nē ə), *n.* a region in NE Spain, formerly a province.

ca·tal·pa (kə tal′pə), *n.* an Asian or American tree having large, heart-shaped leaves, white flowers, and long seed pods.

cat·a·pult (kat′ə pult′), *n.* 1. an ancient military engine for hurling stones, arrows, etc. 2. a device for launching an airplane from the deck of a ship. —*v.* 3. to hurl, as from a catapult or slingshot.

Catapult (def. 1)

cat·a·ract (kat′ə rakt′), *n.* 1. a large waterfall. 2. a downpour, rush, or flood. 3. a cloudy or completely opaque area on the lens of the eye that can cause a total loss of sight.

ca·tarrh (kə tär′), *n.* an inflammation of the throat and nose membranes that causes an excessive secretion of mucus.

ca·tas·tro·phe (kə tas′trə fē), *n.* 1. a sudden and widespread disaster: *the catastrophe of war.* 2. any misfortune or failure. —**cat·a·stroph·ic** (kat′ə strof′ik), *adj.*

cat·bird (kat′bûrd′), *n.* a small, gray American songbird having a call resembling the mewing of a cat.

cat·boat (kat′bōt′), *n.* a boat having one mast set well forward and one large sail.

cat·call (kat′kôl′), *n.* 1. a cry like that of a cat, made by the human voice and used for expressing disapproval. —*v.* 2. to make catcalls.

catch (kach), *v.,* **caught** (kôt), **catch·ing.** 1. to capture in a trap or after pursuit: *to catch a deer.* 2. to deceive: *I was caught by his lies.* 3. to reach or arrive at in time: *to catch a train; to catch a late movie.* 4. to come upon suddenly: *to catch a thief stealing.* 5. to strike or hit: *The blow caught him on the head.* 6. to capture and hold: *to catch a ball; to catch rain in a pail.* 7. to check or hold back suddenly: *She caught her breath in surprise.* 8. to receive or contract: *to catch the flu.* 9. to grasp or grip: *He caught her arm. The hook caught his sleeve.* 10. to become or allow to become gripped or entangled: *His sleeve caught in the door.* 11. to attract or captivate: *The play caught my attention.* 12. to grasp with the mind; understand: *I didn't catch the meaning.* 13. to fasten or become fastened: *The lock doesn't catch.* —*n.* 14. the act of catching. 15. a device that catches or fastens: *a catch on a bracelet.* 16. a tricky or hidden drawback or disadvantage: *It seems so easy that there must be a catch somewhere.* 17. an amount caught at one time: *a catch of fish.* 18. a slight break or crack in the voice. 19. **catch on, a.** to grasp something with the mind; understand: *I didn't catch on until I saw the answer.* **b.** to become popular: *His newest record has really caught on.* 20. **catch up, a.** to come up to or overtake a person or thing: *We'll have to run to catch up.* **b.** to pick up and carry along: *The leaves were caught up in the wind.* [from the Old French word *cachier* "to chase, capture," which is a northern dialect word related to *chacier* "to hunt, chase." See *chase*]

catch·er (kach′ər), *n.* 1. a person or thing that catches. 2. (in baseball) the player behind home plate whose duty is to catch pitches and foul tips.

catch·ing (kach′ing), *adj.* 1. contagious or infectious: *a catching disease; an enthusiasm that was catching.* 2. very attractive or fascinating.

catch·up (kach′əp, kech′əp), *n.* another spelling of ketchup.

catch·y (kach′ē), *adj.,* **catch·i·er, catch·i·est.** 1. pleasing and easily remembered: *a catchy tune.* 2. tricky or deceptive: *a catchy question.* —**catch′i·ness,** *n.*

cat·e·chism (kat′ə kiz′əm), *n.* 1. a book containing a summary of the principles of the Christian religion, in the form of questions and answers. 2. a series of questions and answers used for teaching.

cat·e·chize (kat′ə kīz′), *v.,* **cat·e·chized, cat·e·chiz·ing.** 1. to instruct or teach by use of the catechism. 2. to question closely and at length.

cat·e·gor·i·cal (kat′ə gôr′i kəl), *adj.* absolute and unconditional: *a categorical refusal.* —**cat′e·gor′i·cal·ly,** *adv.*

cat·e·go·ry (kat′ə gôr′ē), *n., pl.* **cat·e·go·ries.** a class, group, or division within a system: *The paintings at the museum are divided into several categories.*

ca·ter (kā′tər), *v.* 1. to provide food and service for: *to cater a banquet.* 2. to supply or give something desired or demanded: *The store caters to skiers.* —**ca′ter·er,** *n.*

cat·er·pil·lar (kat′ər pil′ər), *n.* 1. the larva of a butterfly or moth that hatches from an egg: usually resembling a furry worm. 2. a machine, such as a tank or power shovel, that moves on endless treads (**cat′erpillar treads′**) that permit it to travel over rough or soft ground.

cat·fish (kat′fish′), *n., pl.* **cat·fish·es** *or* **cat·fish.** any of numerous fishes having a scaleless skin and feelers around the mouth that resemble a cat's whiskers.

Catfish
(length to 4 ft.)

cat·gut (kat′gut′), *n.* cord made from the intestines of sheep and other animals, used for stringing musical instruments and, formerly, tennis rackets.

ca·thar·tic (kə thär′tik), *n.* a strong laxative.

Ca·thay (ka thā′), *n.* a literary and poetic word for **China.**

ca·the·dral (kə thē′drəl), *n.* the principal church of a diocese, containing the bishop's throne.

cath·o·lic (kath′ə lik), *adj.* 1. referring to the whole Christian church. 2. very broad in scope; universal: *She has a catholic taste in books.*

Cath·o·lic (kath′ə lik), *adj.* 1. of or concerning the Roman Catholic Church. —*n.* 2. a Roman Catholic.

Ca·thol·i·cism (kə thol′i siz′əm), *n.* the faith, system, and practices of the Roman Catholic Church. Also, **Roman Catholicism.**

cat·kin (kat′kin), *n.* a soft, spike-shaped, drooping flower cluster, as that of the willow or birch trees.

cat·nip (kat′nip), *n.* a plant related to mint, having fragrant leaves of which cats are fond.

cat-o'-nine-tails (kat′ə nīn′tālz′), *n., pl.* **cat-o'-nine-tails.** a whip usually having nine knotted lines or cords fastened to a handle, used for flogging.

Cats′kill Moun′tains (kat′skil), a range of low mountains in E New York. Also, **the Catskills.**

cat's-paw (kats′pô′), *n.* a person used by another for doing something unpleasant, dangerous, or wrong. Also, **cats′paw′.**

cat·sup (kech′əp, kat′səp), *n.* another spelling of **ketchup.**

cat·tail (kat′tāl′), *n.* a tall, reedlike marsh plant having flowers in long, cylindrical, furry spikes.

Cattails

cat·tle (kat′əl), *n. (used as pl.)* 1. animals of the ox family, as cows, bulls, and steers. 2. farm animals; livestock. [from the Middle English word *catel,* which comes from Old French *catel,* a northern dialect word related to *chatel* "personal property." See *chattel*]

cat·tle·man (kat′əl mən, -man′), *n., pl.* **cat·tle·men.** a man who breeds and raises cattle.

cat·ty (kat′ē), *adj.,* **cat·ti·er, cat·ti·est.** 1. resembling a cat; catlike. 2. spiteful; mean: *catty remarks.* —**cat′ti·ness,** *n.*

cat·walk (kat′wôk′), *n.* any narrow walkway, esp. one high above a surrounding area.

Cau·ca·sia (kô kā′zhə), *n.* a region in the Soviet Union between the Black and Caspian seas.

Cau·ca·sian (kô kā′zhən), *n.* 1. a member of a racial group, or its descendants, originally living in Europe and parts of North Africa, Asia, and India: complexion may be fair or very dark. 2. a native of Caucasia. —*adj.* 3. of the Caucasian racial group. 4. of or referring to the Caucasus. Also, **Cau·ca·soid** (kô′kə soid′) (for defs. 1, 3).

Cau·ca·sus (kô′kə səs), *n.* a mountain range in Caucasia, in the SW Soviet Union: divides Europe from Asia. Also, **Cau′casus Moun′tains.**

cau·cus (kô′kəs), *n., pl.* **cau·cus·es.** 1. a meeting of the local members of a U.S. political party to nominate candidates, determine policy, etc. —*v.* 2. to hold or meet in a caucus: *The politicians caucused for three hours this morning.*

caught (kôt), *v.* the past tense and past participle of **catch.**

caul·dron (kôl′drən), *n.* a very large kettle or pot for boiling things. Also, **caldron.**

cau·li·flow·er (kô′lə flou′ər, kô′lē flou′ər), *n.* a plant related to cabbage, having a firm white head that is eaten as a vegetable.

caulk (kôk), *v.* 1. to fill or close (a seam, joint, etc.) so as to make watertight or airtight. 2. to make watertight or airtight by filling the seams: *to caulk a boat.* Also, **calk.**

cause (kôz), *n.* 1. a person or thing that acts, happens, or exists so that something happens as a result: *What was the cause of the accident?* 2. the reason for some human action: *a cause for celebrating; to complain without cause.* 3. a goal or a set of goals to which a person or group is dedicated: *the cause of freedom.* —*v.,* **caused, caus·ing.** 4. to be the cause of; bring about: *The storm caused a lot of damage.*

cause·way (kôz′wā′), *n.* 1. a raised road or path across low or wet ground: *They're building a causeway from the mainland over to the island.* 2. a highway. [from the Old French word *caucie,* which comes from the Latin phrase *(via) calciāta* "(way) paved with limestone" + English *way*]

caus·tic (kô′stik), *n.* 1. a substance capable of burning or destroying living tissue, such as lye. —*adj.* 2. able to burn or destroy living tissue: *a caustic substance.* 3. severely critical or sarcastic: *a caustic remark.* —**caus′ti·cal·ly,** *adv.*

cau·ter·ize (kô′tə rīz′), *v.,* **cau·ter·ized, cau·ter·iz·ing.** to burn with a hot iron or a caustic substance, esp. in disinfecting wounds. —**cau′ter·i·za′tion,** *n.*

cau·tion (kô′shən), *n.* 1. alertness and care in a dangerous situation: *We drove with caution down the icy street.* 2. a warning against danger or evil. —*v.* 3. to warn or advise: *He cautioned us to be careful.*

cau·tious (kô′shəs), *adj.* showing or using caution; careful: *a cautious person.* —**cau′tious·ly,** *adv.*

cav·al·cade (kav′əl kād′, kav′əl kād′), *n.* **1.** a procession, esp. of persons riding horseback or on floats. **2.** a pageant: *a cavalcade of movie stars.*

cav·a·lier (kav′ə lēr′, kav′ə lēr′), *n.* **1.** a mounted soldier. **2.** a man having a courtly and chivalrous manner: —*adj.* **3.** haughty and disdainful: *a cavalier attitude toward work.* **4.** offhand and easygoing.

cav·al·ry (kav′əl rē), *n., pl.* **cav·al·ries. 1.** the part of the military force composed of troops that ride on horseback. **2.** mounted soldiers. **3.** the motorized armored units of a military force.

cav·al·ry·man (kav′əl rē mən, -man′), *n., pl.* **cav·al·ry·men.** a member of the cavalry.

cave (kāv), *n.* **1.** a hollow in the earth or in the side of a hill or mountain. **2.** a storage cellar, esp. for wine. —*v.,* **caved, cav·ing. 3.** to hollow out. **4. cave in,** to collapse or cause to collapse: *The tunnel caved in. Heavy rains caved in the basement.*

cave-in (kāv′in′), *n.* a collapse, esp. of a mine or tunnel: *They're calling it the worst cave-in in history.*

cave′ man′, 1. a human being who lived in caves, esp. during the Stone Age. **2.** a rough, brutish man.

cav·ern (kav′ərn), *n.* a large cave that is mostly underground.

cav·ern·ous (kav′ər nəs), *adj.* **1.** containing caverns. **2.** deep-set: *cavernous eyes.* **3.** hollow and deep-sounding: *a cavernous voice.* **4.** resembling a cavern: *a cavernous room.* —**cav′ern·ous·ly,** *adv.*

cav·i·ar (kav′ē är′), *n.* the eggs or roe of sturgeon, usually served as an appetizer.

cav·il (kav′il), *v.,* **cav·iled** *or* **cav·illed; cav·il·ing** *or* **cav·il·ling. 1.** to bring up unnecessary objections; find fault needlessly. —*n.* **2.** an objection about an unimportant matter.

cav·i·ty (kav′i tē), *n., pl.* **cav·i·ties. 1.** any hollow place: *a cavity in the earth.* **2.** a hollow place in a tooth, commonly caused by decay: *I had two cavities in one tooth.*

ca·vort (kə vôrt′), *v.* to caper or prance about: *The frisky horse cavorted in the pasture.*

caw (kô), *n.* **1.** the cry of the crow, raven, etc. —*v.* **2.** to utter this cry or a similar sound.

cay·enne (kī en′, kā en′), *n.* a hot spice made from the ground pods and seeds of a red-pepper plant. Also, **cayenne′ pep′per.**

cay·use (kī yōōs′, ki′ōōs), *n.* (in the western U.S.) an Indian pony.

CB, citizens band.

cc, cubic centimeter; cubic centimeters.

Cd, *Chem.* the symbol for **cadmium.**

cd, 1. candela; candelas. **2.** cord; cords.

cd., cord; cords.

cds, 1. candelas. **2.** cords.

cds., cords.

Ce, *Chem.* the symbol for **cerium.**

cease (sēs), *v.,* **ceased, ceas·ing.** to stop or discontinue; end: *The war has ceased. Cease that noise!*

cease·less (sēs′lis), *adj.* without stop or pause; unending: *the ceaseless noise of the engine room.* —**cease′less·ly,** *adv.*

ce·dar (sē′dər), *n.* **1.** any of several kinds of evergreen trees having reddish to pale-yellow wood. **2.** the wood of any of these trees, esp. the reddish wood, which is hard and fragrant: formerly used for cigar boxes, pencils, and storage chests.

cede (sēd), *v.,* **ced·ed, ced·ing.** to yield or formally surrender to another: *to cede a territory.*

ceil·ing (sē′ling), *n.* **1.** the overhead interior lining of a room. **2.** the top limit: *a ceiling on prices.* **3.** the height of the lowest layer of clouds above the ground. **4.** the cloud layer itself.

cel·e·brate (sel′ə brāt′), *v.,* **cel·e·brat·ed, cel·e·brat·ing. 1.** to observe or commemorate with ceremonies and festivities: *to celebrate a birthday.* **2.** to make known and praise publicly; proclaim: *The newspapers celebrated the visiting star.* **3.** to perform in a solemn manner: *to celebrate a mass.* —**cel′e·bra′tor,** *n.*

cel·e·brat·ed (sel′ə brā′tid), *adj.* famous or well-known: *a celebrated opera star.*

cel·e·bra·tion (sel′ə brā′shən), *n.* **1.** the act of celebrating. **2.** the activities for celebrating an event or special day: *a birthday celebration.*

ce·leb·ri·ty (sə leb′ri tē), *n., pl.* for def. 1 **ce·leb·ri·ties. 1.** a famous or well-known person: *to interview a celebrity.* **2.** fame and renown.

ce·ler·i·ty (sə ler′i tē), *n.* swiftness and speed: *He completed the job with celerity.*

cel·er·y (sel′ə rē), *n.* a vegetable related to parsley, the crisp stalks of which are kept white by covering them with earth as the plant grows.

ce·les·ta (sə les′tə), *n.* a keyboard instrument in which hammers strike tuned metal bars.

Celesta

ce·les·tial (sə les′chəl), *adj.* **1.** referring to the spiritual heaven; heavenly; divine: *celestial happiness.* **2.** referring to the sky: *Stars are celestial bodies.*

cel·i·ba·cy (sel′ə bə sē), *n.* the state of being unmarried, esp. for religious reasons.

cel·i·bate (sel′ə bit), *n.* **1.** a person who remains unmarried, esp. for religious reasons. —*adj.* **2.** not married.

cell (sel), *n.* **1.** a small room, as in a convent or prison. **2.** a small compartment forming part of a whole: *Honeycombs have many cells.* **3.** a small group acting as a unit within a large organization: *a local cell of the Communist party.* **4.** a tiny plant or animal structure that is the fundamental unit of any living thing. **5.** a container that holds two unlike materials and a conducting medium, used to generate electricity; a unit in an electric battery: *a dry cell.*

Cell
(greatly magnified)
A, Nucleus
B, Cell wall

cel·lar (sel′ər), *n.* a room or set of rooms completely or partly underground and usually beneath a building. [from the Latin word *cellārium* "pantry"]

cel·lo (chel′ō), *n., pl.* **cel·los.** a large instrument of the violin family, between a viola and double bass in size and range: held between the knees when played. Also, **'cel′lo, violoncello.** —**cel′list,** *n.*

Cello

cel·lo·phane (sel′ə fān′), *n.* a transparent film of plastic, used for wrapping, as a backing for transparent tape, etc.

cel·lu·lar (sel′yə lər), *adj.* referring to or made up of cells: *cellular plant tissue.*

Cel·lu·loid (sel′yə loid′), *n. Trademark.* a highly flammable plastic formerly used for making detachable collars, photographic film, combs, etc.

cel·lu·lose (sel′yə lōs′), *n.* a substance of which all the woody and fibrous parts of plants are composed.

Cel·si·us (sel′sē əs), *adj.* referring to the scale of temperature (**Cel′sius scale′**) in which the freezing point of water is 0° and the boiling point 100°. It is now replacing centigrade in both general and scientific use. *Symbol:* C See also **Fahrenheit.** See illus. at **thermometer.** [named after Anders *Celsius* (1701–1744), Swedish astronomer who devised the scale]

Celt (selt, kelt), *n.* a member of an Indo-European people, now represented mainly by the Irish, Gaels, Welsh, and Bretons.

Celt·ic (sel′tik, kel′tik), *n.* 1. a branch of the Indo-European family of languages, including the languages of the ancient Britons and Gauls, as well as modern Irish, Scots Gaelic, Welsh, Cornish, and Breton. —*adj.* 2. of or referring to the Celts, their language, or their culture.

ce·ment (si ment′), *n.* 1. any of numerous kinds of glues. 2. a material made by burning limestone and clay, usually mixed with sand and water to make concrete. —*v.* 3. to unite by or as if by cement: *to cement a broken dish; to cement a friendship with trust and understanding.* 4. to cover or coat with cement: *to cement a sidewalk.*

cem·e·ter·y (sem′i ter′ē), *n., pl.* **cem·e·ter·ies.** an area containing graves or tombs; graveyard.

Ce′no·zo′ic e′ra (sē′nə zō′ik), the geologic period following the Mesozoic era and extending from about 70 million years ago to the present.

cen·ser (sen′sər), *n.* a container in which incense is burned, esp. as part of a religious service.

cen·sor (sen′sər), *n.* 1. an official who examines books, plays, etc., for the purpose of keeping out parts considered improper or harmful. 2. a person who supervises the manners and behavior of others.

Censer

3. (in ancient Rome) an official who kept the census and supervised manners and behavior. —*v.* 4. to examine and take action against as censor: *to censor an objectionable new book.*

cen·so·ri·ous (sen sōr′ē əs), *adj.* very critical; ready to find fault: *to be censorious of someone's behavior.* —**cen·so′ri·ous·ly,** *adv.*

cen·sor·ship (sen′sər ship′), *n.* 1. the act of censoring: *Some states have strict laws of censorshtp.* 2. the office or power of a censor.

cen·sur·a·ble (sen′shər ə bəl), *adj.* deserving censure: *censurable conduct.*

cen·sure (sen′shər), *n.* 1. a very strong and harsh expression of disapproval. —*v.*, **cen·sured, cen·sur·ing.** 2. to express very harsh disapproval: *to censure improper behavior.*

cen·sus (sen′səs), *n., pl.* **cen·sus·es.** an official count of the population with details regarding age, sex, occupation, etc. In the U.S. the census is taken every 10 years, as in 1960, 1970, etc.

cent (sent), *n.* a bronze coin of the U.S., the 100th part of a U.S. dollar. [short for the Latin word *centēsimus* "hundredth," from *centum* "hundred"]

cent., 1. central. 2. century.

cen·taur (sen′tôr), *n.* (in Greek mythology) one of a race of creatures having the head, trunk, and arms of a man, and the body and legs of a horse.

cen·ten·ni·al (sen ten′ē-əl), *adj.* 1. referring to a 100th anniversary: *a centennial celebration.* —*n.* 2. a 100th anniversary: *This year is the centennial of the town.*

cen·ter (sen′tər), *n.* 1. the middle point of a circle or sphere equally distant from all points of the circumference or surface. 2. a point, pivot, or axis around which anything rotates or revolves: *The sun is the center of the solar system.* 3. the source of interest, action, or force: *the center of attention.* 4. a main point or place: *a shipping center.* 5. the middle area or part: *the center of the skating rink; candies with fruit centers.* 6. a player who occupies a middle position in many team sports. —*v.* 7. to place in or on a center: *to center a picture on the wall.* 8. to concentrate or focus: *Center your attention on the blackboard.* Also, *esp. British,* **centre.**

Centaur

cen′ter of grav′ity, the point in a body around which its weight is equally distributed and at which it would balance.

centi-, a prefix meaning a hundredth: *centimeter.*

cen·ti·grade (sen′tə grād′), *adj.* another term for **Celsius.** *Symbol:* C

cen·ti·gram (sen′tə gram′), *n.* a unit of mass or weight in the metric system, equal to ¹/₁₀₀ gram. *Symbol:* cg

cen·ti·li·ter (sen′tə lē′tər), *n.* a unit of volume or capacity in the metric system, equal to ¹/₁₀₀ liter. *Symbol:* cl

cen·time (sän′tēm), *n.* the 100th part of the francs of various countries, including France and Belgium.

cen·ti·me·ter (sen′tə mē′tər), *n.* a unit of length in the metric system: equal to ¹/₁₀₀ meter (0.3937 inch); 1 inch is equivalent to 2.54 centimeters. *Symbol:* cm

cen·ti·pede (sen′tə pēd′), *n.* a small, flat, wormlike animal related to the insects, which has many legs and is able to inflict a painful bite.

cen·tral (sen′trəl), *adj.* **1.** of or forming the center. **2.** in, at, or near the center: *a central position.* **3.** being that from which other things come or upon which other things depend: *central air conditioning; a central agency.* **4.** most important; main; chief: *the central character.* —*n.* **5.** the office of a telephone system. —**cen′tral·ly,** *adv.*

Cen′tral Af′rican Repub′lic, a republic in central Africa. 238,000 sq. mi.

Cen′tral Amer′ica, continental North America S of Mexico. 227,933 sq. mi. —**Cen′tral Amer′ican.**

Centipede (body length about 1 in.)

cen·tral·ize (sen′trə līz′), *v.,* **cen·tral·ized, cen·tral·iz·ing. 1.** to gather about a center or central point. **2.** to bring under one control: *to centralize the clothing industry.* —**cen′tral·i·za′tion,** *n.*

cen′tral nerv′ous sys′tem, the part of the nervous system consisting of the brain and the spinal cord.

cen·tre (sen′tər), *n., v.,* **cen·tred, cen·tring.** a British spelling of **center.**

cen·trif′u·gal force′ (sen trif′yə gəl, -ə gəl), a force on a body traveling on a curved path that acts to make the body travel in a straight line away from the center of the curve. [*centrifugal* comes from the modern Latin word *centrifugus* "fleeing the center," from Latin *centrum* "center" + *fugere* "to flee"]

cen·trip′e·tal force′ (sen trip′i t²l), a force acting toward the center of a curve that makes a body

travel in a curved path rather than in a straight line. [*centripetal* comes from the modern Latin word *centripetus* "seeking the center," which comes from Latin *centrum* "center" + *petere* "to seek"]

cen·tu·ri·on (sen tŏŏr′ē ən, -tyŏŏr′), *n.* (in the ancient Roman army) the commander of a century.

cen·tu·ry (sen′chə rē), *n., pl.* **cen·tu·ries. 1.** a period of 100 years. **2.** such a period when counted forward or backward from a certain time, esp. from the date of the birth of Jesus. **3.** (in the ancient Roman army) a company of approximately 100 men.

cen′tury plant′, a tall Mexican plant that grows in the desert and has long, spiky leaves. It blooms only once, after many years of growth.

ce·ram·ic (sə ram′ik), *adj.* **1.** of or referring to products made from clay. —*n.* **2.** a ceramic product.

ce·ram·ics (sə ram′iks), *n.* *(used as sing.)* the art or process of making objects of clay.

Century plant (height to 30 ft.)

Cer·ber·us (sûr′bər əs), *n.* (in Greek and Roman mythology) the three-headed dog that guarded the entrance to Hades.

ce·re·al (sēr′ē əl), *n.* **1.** any of several grasslike plants, such as rye, wheat, oats, etc., that yield an edible grain. **2.** the grain itself. **3.** a food made from the grain, esp. a breakfast food. —*adj.* **4.** of or referring to grain or the plants producing it. [from the Latin word *Cereālis,* which comes from the name of the goddess *Ceres*]

cer·e·bel·lum (ser′ə bel′əm), *n.* a part of the brain, in back of and below the cerebrum, that controls the coordination of voluntary actions and balance. See illus. at **brain.**

cer·e·brum (ser′ə brəm, sə rē′brəm), *n., pl.* **cere·brums** *or* **cer·e·bra** (ser′ə brə, sə rē′brə). the largest and uppermost part of the brain, which controls thought and voluntary movements. See illus. at **brain.** —**cer′e·bral,** *adj.*

cer·e·mo·ni·al (ser′ə mō′nē əl), *adj.* **1.** requiring or showing ceremony or ritual; formal: *a ceremonial manner.* **2.** used in ceremonies: *ceremonial robes.* —*n.* **3.** a system of rituals for a particular occasion.

cer·e·mo·ni·ous (ser′ə mō′nē əs), *adj.* very careful about ceremony; formal and very polite: *a ceremonious welcome.* —**cer′e·mo′ni·ous·ly,** *adv.*

cer·e·mo·ny (ser′ə mō′nē), *n., pl.* **cer·e·mo·nies. 1.** a formal act or actions for observing a solemn or important occasion: *a marriage ceremony.* **2.** formal and very polite behavior: *He left without ceremony.* **3. stand on ceremony,** to behave in a formal and very polite way: *No need to stand on ceremony with us.*

Ce·res (sēr′ēz), *n.* (in Roman mythology) the goddess of agriculture: identified with the Greek Demeter.

ce·rise (sə rēs′, sə rēz′), *adj., n.* moderate to deep red. [from a French word meaning "cherry"]

ce·ri·um (sēr′ē əm), *n. Chem.* a metallic element of the rare-earth group. *Symbol:* Ce

act, āble, dâre, ärt; ebb, ēqual; if, īce; hot, ōver, ôrder; oil; bŏŏk; ōoze; out; up, ûrge; ə = a as in *alone;* ª as in *button* (but′ªn), *fire* (fīªr); chief; shoe; thin; ŧħat; zh as in *measure* (mezh′ər). See full key inside cover.

cer·tain (sûr′t³n), *adj.* 1. free from doubt; sure: *I am certain that I mailed the letter.* 2. bound to happen; inevitable: *War was certain.* 3. definite but not named: *a certain person.* 4. some though not much: *a certain hesitation.* 5. fixed; agreed upon: *a certain amount.* 6. **for certain,** without any doubt; surely: *Do you know for certain?*

cer·tain·ly (sûr′t³n lē), *adv.* 1. without doubt; surely: *She certainly is smart.* 2. yes, of course: *Will you be there? Certainly.*

cer·tain·ty (sûr′t³n tē), *n., pl.* for def. 2 **cer·tain·ties.** 1. the state or quality of being certain or sure: *He spoke with certainty.* 2. something certain; an assured fact: *It is a certainty that the sun will rise.*

cer·tif·i·cate (sûr tif′ə kit), *n.* a document that proves something is true or has taken place: *a baptism certificate; a certificate of ownership.*

cer·ti·fy (sûr′tə fī′), *v.,* **cer·ti·fied, cer·ti·fy·ing.** 1. to confirm as true, usually in writing. 2. to guarantee the worth, quality, or value of: *to certify a check.*

ce·ru·le·an (sə rōō′lē ən), *adj., n.* sky blue.

Cer·van·tes (sər van′tēz), *n.* **Mi·guel de** (mi gel′ dā), 1547–1616, Spanish novelist.

ce·si·um (sē′zē əm), *n. Chem.* a rare metallic element that gives off electrons when struck by light: used in photoelectric cells. *Symbol:* Cs

ces·sa·tion (se sā′shən), *n.* a temporary or complete stopping: *a cessation of bombing.*

cess·pool (ses′pōōl′), *n.* a well or pit for retaining the sewage from the toilets, sinks, etc., of a house.

Cey·lon (si lon′, sā lon′), *n.* former name of **Sri Lanka.** —**Cey·lon·ese** (sē′lə nēz′, sā′lə nēz′), *adj., n.*

Cf, *Chem.* the symbol for **californium.**

cf., (in scholarly writing) compare. Also, **Cf.** [from the Latin word *confer*]

cg, centigram; centigrams.

chac·ma (chak′mə), *n.* a large, brownish-gray baboon of southern Africa. [from Hottentot]

Chad (chad), *n.* a republic in W central Africa. 510,000 sq. mi.

chafe (chāf), *v.,* **chafed, chaf·ing.** 1. to warm by rubbing: *to chafe cold hands.* 2. to wear or make sore by rubbing: *This collar chafes my neck.* 3. to be irritated or annoyed: *He chafed at their silly questions.*

chaff[1] (chaf), *n.* 1. the husks of grains and grasses that are usually separated during threshing. 2. straw cut up for fodder. 3. worthless matter; rubbish. [from the Old English word *ceaf*]

chaff[2] (chaf), *v.* 1. to make fun of or tease in a good-natured way: *His friends chaffed him about his freckles.* —*n.* 2. good-natured teasing. [perhaps from a special use of *chaff*[1]]

chaf′ing dish′ (chā′fing), a metal dish with a lamp or heating appliance beneath it, for cooking or keeping food hot at the table.

cha·grin (shə grin′), *n.* 1. a feeling of shame and distress caused by disappointment or failure. —*v.,* **cha·grined** *or* **cha·grinned; cha·grin·ing** *or* **cha·grin·ning.** 2. to cause to feel chagrin.

chain (chān), *n.* 1. a series of metal rings passing through one another. 2. something that binds or restrains. 3. a series of things that are connected: *a chain of events.* 4. a range of mountains. 5. a number of similar establishments under one ownership: *a chain of restaurants.* —*v.* 6. to fasten or confine with or as if with a chain.

chain′ reac′tion, 1. a nuclear reaction in which the neutrons produced by the fission of one nucleus cause the fission of other nuclei, thereby permitting the reaction to continue once it has begun. 2. any closely related series of events.

chain′ store′, one of a group of retail stores under the same ownership.

chair (châr), *n.* 1. a seat, usually having four legs for support and a rest for the back. 2. a seat or position of authority, or the person occupying it: *The speaker addressed the chair.* —*v.* 3. to preside over or act as chairperson of.

chair·man (châr′mən), *n., pl.* **chair·men.** an officer who presides over a meeting or heads a committee, board, etc. —**chair′man·ship′,** *n.* —**chair′wom′an,** *n. fem.*

chair·per·son (châr′pur′sən), *n.* another term for **chairman** or **chairwoman:** now often used in preference to *chairman* or *chairwoman.*

chaise (shāz), *n.* a light, open carriage, usually with a hood.

chaise longue (shāz′ lông′, chāz′), a couch in the form of a reclining chair. Also, **chaise lounge** (shāz′ lounj′, chāz′).

Chal·de·a (kal dē′ə), *n.* an ancient region in the lower Tigris and Euphrates valley. —**Chal·de′an,** *n., adj.*

cha·let (sha lā′, shal′ā), *n.* 1. a herdsman's hut in the Swiss mountains. 2. a low farmhouse with wide eaves in the Swiss mountains. 3. any house of this style.

chal·ice (chal′is), *n.* 1. a drinking cup. 2. a cup for the wine of the Communion service.

chalk (chôk), *n.* 1. a soft, usually white, form of limestone chiefly composed of the shells of tiny sea animals. 2. a piece of this substance or something like it used for marking, as on a blackboard. —*v.* 3. to mark, rub, or write with chalk. 4. **chalk up, a.** to score: *We chalked up two runs in the first inning.* **b.** to consider as caused by: *You can chalk up his remark to bad manners.* [from the Old English word *cealc,* which comes from Latin *calx* "lime"]

chalk·board (chôk′bôrd′), *n.* another word for **blackboard.**

Chalet

chalk·y (chô′kē), *adj.,* **chalk·i·er, chalk·i·est. 1.** of or like chalk: *a chalky white.* **2.** containing chalk: *chalky soil.* —**chalk′i·ness,** *n.*

chal·lenge (chal′inj), *n.* **1.** a call to engage in any contest, battle, etc.: *a challenge from the rival team.* **2.** something that serves to test one's strength, intelligence, etc.: *Exploring outer space is a challenge.* **3.** a demand to explain or justify: *a challenge to support a statement.* **4.** the demand of a sentry for a person to identify himself. —*v.,* **chal·lenged, chal·leng·ing. 5.** to summon to a contest of skill, strength, etc.: *to challenge a rival.* **6.** to express doubt about; question: *to challenge a statement.* **7.** to stop and demand identification of: *The guard challenged the soldier.* **8.** to arouse and interest by being somewhat difficult: *to be challenged by a problem.* —**chal′leng·er,** *n.*

chal·lis (shal′ē), *n.* a soft fabric of plain weave in wool, cotton, or rayon, usually in a small print.

cham·ber (chām′bər), *n.* **1.** a room in a house or apartment, esp. a bedroom. **2.** a room in a palace or official residence. **3.** the meeting hall of a legislative or other assembly. **4.** a legislative or judicial body. **5.** an enclosed space; cavity: *a chamber of the heart.* **6.** the part of a gun for the cartridge or shell. **7. chambers,** a place where a judge hears matters not requiring action in court. [from the Old French word *chambre,* which comes from Latin *camera.* See *camera*]

cham·ber·lain (chām′bər lin), *n.* **1.** a person who manages a king's or nobleman's household. **2.** a person who receives rents and taxes; treasurer.

cham·ber·maid (chām′bər mād′), *n.* a maid who cleans and tidies bedrooms.

cham·bray (sham′brā), *n.* a fine cloth, usually woven from white and colored threads.

cha·me·le·on (kə mē′lē ən, kə mēl′yən), *n.* **1.** a kind of lizard that can change the color of its skin to match that of its surroundings. **2.** a person who often changes his mind or behavior. [from the Greek word *chamaileōn,* which comes from *chamai* "dwarf" + *leōn* "lion"]

Chameleon
(length 8 in.)

cham·ois (sham′ē), *n., pl.* **cham·ois** (sham′ē, sham′-ēz). **1.** an agile, goatlike antelope of the high mountains of Europe and southwestern Russia. **2.** a soft, yellow leather made from the skins of various animals.

champ[1] (champ), *v.* **1.** to bite or grind impatiently. **2.** to chew forcefully or noisily; munch. [perhaps another form of the word *chap*[1]]

Chamois
(2½ ft. high at shoulder)

champ[2] (champ), *n. Informal.* champion.

cham·pagne (sham pān′), *n.* a sparkling, dry, white table wine. [from *Champagne,* a region in NE France, where it is produced]

cham·pi·on (cham′pē ən), *n.* **1.** a person who has defeated all opponents in a competition and holds first place: *a tennis champion.* **2.** a person who fights for or defends any person or cause: *a champion of civil rights.* —*v.* **3.** to act as a champion of; defend; support: *to champion the cause of freedom.* —*adj.* **4.** first among all contestants or competitors: *a champion football player.*

cham·pi·on·ship (cham′pē ən ship′), *n.* **1.** the distinction, condition, or position of being a champion: *to win a championship.* **2.** defense or support: *championship of the underprivileged.*

Cham·plain (sham plān′), *n.* **Samuel de,** 1567–1635, French explorer in the Americas.

chance (chans), *n.* **1.** the unpredictable way in which things take place; fortune: *to leave the future to chance.* **2.** a possibility or probability of anything happening: *There's no chance our team will win.* **3.** an opportunity: *another chance to take a test.* **4.** a risk or danger: *He took a chance by riding his bicycle at night without lights.* —*v.,* **chanced, chanc·ing. 5.** to happen or occur by chance: *It chanced to rain that day.* **6.** to take the chances or risks of: *I'll have to chance it.* —*adj.* **7.** taking place or occurring by chance: *a chance meeting.*

chan·cel (chan′səl), *n.* the space around the altar of a church, for the clergy and other officials.

chan·cel·lor (chan′sə lər), *n.* **1.** the chief minister of state in some countries. **2.** the chief administrative officer in certain American universities. **3.** the judge in certain U.S. courts.

chan·de·lier (shan′də lēr′), *n.* a light fixture, often of elaborate design, that is suspended from a ceiling.

change (chānj), *v.,* **changed, chang·ing. 1.** to make or become different in some way: *We changed our plans. Styles change quickly.* **2.** to exchange or substitute (another or others) for: *I changed the sweater for a blouse.* **3.** to give or receive money in smaller denominations in exchange for: *to change a quarter for five nickels.* **4.** to remove and replace: *to change shoes.* —*n.* **5.** the act, fact, or result of changing: *a change of plans.* **6.** the passing from one state or form to another: *a change of seasons.* **7.** something different: *We took a different road for a change.* **8.** a fresh set of clothing: *I packed three changes for the trip.* **9.** money given in exchange for the same amount of higher denomination: *change for a dollar.* **10.** the amount of money received when the amount paid is more than what is owed: *The cashier gave me three dollars change.* **11.** coins: *a pocket full of change.* —**chang′er,** *n.*

change·a·ble (chān′jə bəl), *adj.* **1.** likely to change; variable: *a month of changeable weather.* **2.** of changing color: *a necktie of changeable silk.* —**change′a·bly,** *adv.*

change·less (chānj′lis), *adj.* not changing; constant.

chan·nel (chan′əl), *n.* 1. the bed of a stream or waterway. 2. the deepest part of a river, stream, or other waterway. 3. a wide strait or passage between two bodies of land: *the English Channel.* 4. a route through which anything passes or progresses: *channels of trade and commerce.* 5. a tube-like passage for liquids. 6. a groove. 7. a band of frequencies used by a single television station. —*v.*, **chan·neled** *or* **chan·nelled; chan·nel·ing** *or* **chan·nel·ling.** 8. to direct or convey through or as if through a channel: *to channel information.* 9. to form or cut a channel in; groove: *The river channeled its course through the valley.* [from the Old French word *chanel*, which comes from Latin *canālis* "waterpipe." See *canal*]

Chan′nel Is′lands, a group of British Islands in the English Channel, near the coast of France.

chant (chant), *n.* 1. a kind of music, melody, or way of singing in which many syllables are sung to the same note: used esp. in religious services. 2. a monotonous way of speaking. —*v.* 3. to sing to a chant: *to chant prayers.*

chant·ey (shan′tē, chan′tē), *n.*, *pl.* **chant·eys.** a rhythmic song sung by seamen when hoisting, hauling, etc. Also, **chanty.**

chan·ti·cleer (chan′tə klēr′), *n.* another name for **rooster:** used esp. in literature.

chant·y (shan′tē, chan′tē), *n.*, *pl.* **chant·ies.** another spelling of **chantey.**

Cha·nu·kah (hä′nə kə, hä′noo kä′), *n.* another spelling of **Hanukkah.**

cha·os (kā′os), *n.* a state of utter confusion or disorder: *The room was in chaos after the party.*

cha·ot·ic (kā ot′ik), *adj.* in utter confusion or disorder: *a chaotic situation.* —**cha·ot′i·cal·ly,** *adv.*

chap¹ (chap), *v.*, **chapped, chap·ping.** 1. to crack, roughen, or redden: *His face was chapped by the winds.* —*n.* 2. a crack in the skin. [from the Middle English word *chappen*]

chap² (chap), *n.* a fellow; man or boy: *There's a chap here to see you.* [from the Middle English word *chapman* "trader"]

chap·el (chap′əl), *n.* 1. a small church. 2. a section of a church having its own altar. 3. a room or building for religious services, as in a school.

chap·er·on (shap′ə rōn′), *n.* 1. a person, usually an elderly or married woman, who accompanies an unmarried young woman in public or attends a social gathering of young, unmarried couples in order to ensure proper behavior. —*v.*, **chap·er·oned, chap·er·on·ing.** 2. to act as a chaperon to. Also, **chap′er·one′.**

chap·lain (chap′lin), *n.* a clergyman who provides for the religious needs of a special group, as in the armed forces, a hospital, or a school.

chaps (chaps, shaps), *n.pl.* strong, leather coverings worn for protection over the front of the trousers, esp. by cowboys. [shortened from the Mexican Spanish word *chaparajos*, which is a blend of *chaparral* "a dense thicket" + *aparejos* "gear, equipment"]

chap·ter (chap′tər), *n.* 1. a main division of a book. 2. an important portion or division of anything: *The Renaissance is an important chapter in the history of civilization.* 3. a branch of a society, club, organization, etc.

char (chär), *v.*, **charred, char·ring.** 1. to turn into charcoal by burning. 2. to burn slightly or scorch.

char·ac·ter (kar′ik tər), *n.* 1. the total of traits and qualities that make up the individual nature of a person or thing: *His character was formed early in life.* 2. moral nature or quality: *a man of weak character.* 3. honesty or moral strength; integrity: *The professor was a man of character.* 4. a person considered according to his behavior or personality: *A suspicious character was spotted by the police.* 5. an odd or eccentric person. 6. a person in a play, story, etc.: *a novel with many characters.* 7. a symbol used in writing, such as a letter of the alphabet.

char·ac·ter·is·tic (kar′ik tə ris′tik), *adj.* 1. showing the character or peculiar quality of a person or thing; typical: *Red and gold are the characteristic colors of autumn.* —*n.* 2. a distinguishing or special quality: *Generosity is his chief characteristic.* —**char′ac·ter·is′ti·cal·ly,** *adv.*

char·ac·ter·ize (kar′ik tə rīz′), *v.*, **char·ac·ter·ized, char·ac·ter·iz·ing.** 1. to be characteristic of: *Rich carving characterizes the furniture.* 2. to portray as having a certain character: *He characterized the situation as dangerous.* —**char′ac·ter·i·za′tion,** *n.*

cha·rades (shə rādz′), *n. (used as sing.)* a game in which players try to guess a word that another player acts out in pantomime, often syllable by syllable.

char·coal (chär′kōl′), *n.* a black, soft substance composed largely of carbon, made by heating wood in a place where there is no air: used as a fuel, drawing material, etc.

charge (chärj), *v.*, **charged, charg·ing.** 1. to demand as a price: *How much do you charge for that bicycle?* 2. to make a demand of for payment: *They charged him a good deal of money.* 3. to put off payment for until a certain time, as for goods received: *The store allowed her to charge the coat.* 4. to require payment: *Do you charge for this service?* 5. to fill or load: *air charged with dust and pollen.* 6. to command or order: *His father charged him to be careful.* 7. to lay the blame for: *They charged the accident to his carelessness.* 8. to blame (usually fol. by *with*): *They charged him with theft.* 9. to attack by rushing violently against: *The cavalry charged the enemy.* 10. to rush, as to an attack: *The cavalry charged.* —*n.* 11. payment required for something. 12. a sudden onslaught or attack: *a charge of cavalry.* 13. care or custody: *Two children are in the nurse's charge.* 14. a person who is in the care of someone: *Her two little charges worried her.* 15. an accusation in court: *a charge of murder.* 16. advice given by a judge to a jury before its deliberations. **17.** the amount necessary to load something: *a charge of gunpowder.* **18.** the amount of electricity in or on an object, such as a battery or nonconducting object that has been rubbed. **19. in charge,** in command: *Who is in charge here?* **20. in charge of, a.** having command or supervision of: *The manager is in charge of the business.* **b.** under the command or supervision of: *The children were left in charge of a sitter.*

charge·a·ble (chär′jə bəl), *adj.* **1.** that may or should be charged: *chargeable duty on imported goods.* **2.** liable to be accused or held responsible.

charg·er[1] (chär′jər), *n.* **1.** a horse that is used in battle. **2.** a device for charging batteries.

charg·er[2] (chär′jər), *n.* a large platter. [from the Middle English word *chargeour* "load-bearer," which comes from Old French *chargier* "to carry"]

char·i·ot (char′ē ət), *n.* a light, two-wheeled vehicle for one person, usually drawn by two horses, used in ancient times in warfare, racing, hunting, etc.

char·i·ot·eer (char′ē ə tēr′), *n.* the driver of a chariot.

char·i·ta·ble (char′i tə-bəl), *adj.* **1.** generous in gifts to help the needy. **2.** kindly or forgiving in one's judgment of others: *A charitable person overlooks the shortcomings of his friends.* **3.** concerned

Chariot

with assisting those in need: *a charitable institution for the poor.* —**char′i·ta·ble·ness,** *n.* —**char′i·ta·bly,** *adv.*

char·i·ty (char′i tē), *n., pl.* **char·i·ties. 1.** the giving of money or other assistance to a person or persons in need. **2.** something given to such a person or persons: *She asked for work, not charity.* **3.** a charitable fund, foundation, or institution: *He left his money to a number of charities.* **4.** goodwill or love.

char·la·tan (shär′lə tən), *n.* a person who claims to have more knowledge or skill than he really possesses; quack. [from the Italian word *ciarlatano*]

Char·le·magne (shär′lə mān′), *n.* A.D. 742–814, king of the Franks and emperor of the Holy Roman Empire.

Charles·ton (chärlz′-tən), *n.* the capital city of West Virginia, in the W part.

char′ley horse′ (chär′-lē), pain and stiffness in a muscle, esp. of the leg.

Char·lotte (shär′lət), *n.* a city in S North Carolina.

Char·lot·te A·ma·li·e (shär lot′ə ä mä′lē ə), *n.* a seaport and the capital city of the Virgin Islands of the United States.

Char·lotte·town (shär′lət toun′), *n.* a seaport and

the capital city of Prince Edward Island, in SE Canada.

charm (chärm), *n.* **1.** the power of pleasing or attracting, as through beauty, personality, etc.: *a woman of great charm.* **2.** a trait or feature that has this power: *One of her charms is her voice.* **3.** an action, word, or speech supposed to have magical power: *The witch recited a charm.* **4.** a trinket to be worn on a chain, bracelet, etc. —*v.* **5.** to delight or please greatly: *She charmed us all with her kindness.* **6.** to act on (someone or something) with or as if with magic: *He charmed us into going.* [from the Old French word *charme,* which comes from Latin *carmen* "song, magical formula"] —**charm′er,** *n.*

charm·ing (chär′miñg), *adj.* pleasing or delightful: *a charming girl.* —**charm′ing·ly,** *adv.*

Char·on (kâr′ən, kar′ən), *n.* (in Greek mythology) the ferryman who carried the souls of the dead across the Styx to Hades.

chart (chärt), *n.* **1.** a map, esp. one used by mariners that shows depths of water, landmarks, currents, etc. **2.** a sheet showing information in the form of a graph or diagram: *a chart showing the rise of prices.* —*v.* **3.** to make a chart of or show on a chart. **4.** to plan: *to chart a course of action.* —**chart′a·ble,** *adj.*

char·ter (chär′tər), *n.* **1.** a document granting certain rights and privileges, as one issued by a country, king, etc., to a person or group intending to establish a business, colony, or other organization. **2.** a document setting forth the purposes and principles of an organization. —*v.* **3.** to grant a charter to or establish by charter: *English kings chartered new colonies in North America.* **4.** to lease or hire: *They chartered a bus for a tour of the city.*

char·wom·an (chär′wŏŏm′ən), *n., pl.* **char·wom·en.** a woman hired to do household work, esp. heavy cleaning, usually by the day.

char·y (châr′ē), *adj.,* **char·i·er, char·i·est. 1.** careful; wary: *He was chary of his reputation.* **2.** shy; timid. **3.** choosy; finicky: *to be chary about one's food.* —**char′i·ly,** *adv.* —**char′i·ness,** *n.*

Cha·ryb·dis (kə rib′dis), *n.* a whirlpool off the coast of Sicily opposite the rock Scylla.

chase (chās), *v.,* **chased, chas·ing. 1.** to pursue in order to seize, overtake, etc.: *The police chased the robbers down the street.* **2.** to hunt: *to chase game through the woods.* **3.** to follow in pursuit: *to chase after someone.* **4.** to drive or put to flight by pursuing or attacking: *She chased the children from her garden.* —*n.* **5.** the act of chasing or hunting. **6. give chase,** to pursue a person, animal, etc.: *When the criminal escaped, the police gave chase.* [from the Old French word *chacier,* which comes from Latin *captāre* "to hunt, seize." See *catch*]

chasm (kaz′əm), *n.* **1.** a yawning gap in the earth; gorge. **2.** any gap, breach, or division: *a chasm in time; a chasm of misunderstandings.*

chas·sis (shas′ē, chas′ē), *n., pl.* **chas·sis** (shas′ēz, chas′ēz). **1.** the main frame of an automobile, tele-

Map labels: NORTH SEA; ANGLO-SAXONS; London; SLAVIC PEOPLES; Paris; BAY OF BISCAY; Empire of Charlemagne; Rome; MEDIT. SEA; 771-814

vision set, etc., to which all other parts are attached. **2.** the frame, engine, wheels, etc., of an automobile, contrasted to the body.

chaste (chāst), *adj.,* **chast·er, chast·est. 1.** virtuous, moral, or pure. **2.** pure in style; simple. —**chaste′ly,** *adv.* —**chaste′ness,** *n.*

chas·ten (chā′sən), *v.* **1.** to punish or discipline, esp. in order to improve or correct. **2.** to subdue or restrain: *He tried to chasten his anger before he spoke.*

chas·tise (chas tīz′, chas′tīz), *v.,* **chas·tised, chas·tis·ing. 1.** to punish, esp. by beating. **2.** to scold severely; reprimand. —**chas·tise·ment** (chas′tiz mənt, chas tīz′mənt), *n.* —**chas·tis′er,** *n.*

chas·ti·ty (chas′ti tē), *n.* the state or quality of being chaste; moral purity.

chas·u·ble (chaz′yə bəl), *n.* a sleeveless outer garment worn by a priest while celebrating a Mass.

chat (chat), *v.,* **chat·ted, chat·ting. 1.** to talk in a friendly, informal way: *The neighbors chatted over their coffee.* —*n.* **2.** friendly, informal conversation: *They stopped work to have a chat.*

C, Chasuble

cha·teau (sha tō′), *n., pl.* **cha·teaus** *or* **cha·teaux** (sha tōz′). **1.** a castle in France. **2.** a large country house in France, or a house built in the style of a French castle.

Chat·ta·noo·ga (chat′⁹nōō′gə), *n.* a city in SE Tennessee.

chat·tel (chat′⁹l), *n.* (in law) a movable article of personal property, such as household furniture or equipment.

chat·ter (chat′ər), *v.* **1.** to make quick, sharp sounds that resemble speech: *The monkeys chattered in the trees.* **2.** to talk foolishly and rapidly. **3.** to make a quick, clicking noise, as teeth that strike together from cold. —*n.* **4.** foolish, aimless talk. **5.** the sound of chattering. —**chat′ter·er,** *n.*

chat·ty (chat′ē), *adj.,* **chat·ti·er, chat·ti·est. 1.** fond of or having the habit of chatting: *a chatty neighbor.* **2.** full of chat, or having a friendly, informal style: *a chatty letter.* —**chat′ti·ness,** *n.*

Chau·cer (chô′sər), *n.* **Geoffrey,** 1340?–1400, English poet: first poet laureate of England.

chauf·feur (shō′fər, shō fûr′), *n.* **1.** a person employed to drive another's automobile. —*v.* **2.** to drive or work as a chauffeur: *to chauffeur a limousine.* [from the French word *chauffer* "to heat." The original meaning was "stoker, fireman"]

chau·vin·ism (shō′və niz′əm), *n.* **1.** zealous and blind patriotism. **2.** prejudiced devotion to any cause: *male chauvinism.* [from a French word based on the name of a soldier, N. *Chauvin,* in Napoleon's army, noted for excessive patriotism] —**chau′vin·ist,** *n.* —**chau′vin·is′tic,** *adj.* —**chau′vin·is′ti·cal·ly,** *adv.*

cheap (chēp), *adj.* **1.** low in price: *Eggs are cheap this month.* **2.** costing little work or effort: *Words are cheap.* **3.** charging low prices: *to shop at a cheap store.* **4.** of little worth; poor or shoddy: *a cheap pair*

of shoes that quickly wore out. **5.** vulgar, common, or immoral: *cheap behavior.* **6.** stingy; miserly. —*adv.* **7.** at a low price; at small cost: *She is willing to sell the house cheap.* —**cheap′ly,** *adv.*

cheap·en (chē′pən), *v.* to make or become cheap or cheaper; lower in price, value, etc.: *to cheapen the cost of goods; to cheapen an automobile with wear.*

cheap·skate (chēp′skāt′), *n.* a stingy person; miser.

cheat (chēt), *v.* **1.** to trick or deceive: *to cheat someone out of money.* **2.** to practice trickery or act unfairly: *He cheated on the exam.* **3.** to escape a danger, penalty, or the like, through good luck or cleverness: *The aviator cheated death many times.* —*n.* **4.** a person who cheats. —**cheat′er,** *n.*

check (chek), *v.* **1.** to stop the motion of (something) suddenly or with force: *He checked the horse at the edge of the cliff.* **2.** to hold back or limit: *Bad health checked his progress.* **3.** to test for correctness, good conditions, etc.: *to check answers; to check an automobile engine.* **4.** to prove to be right or in agreement: *Your story of what happened checks with his in every detail.* **5.** to look into or search through: *We checked the files but could not find the letter.* **6.** to make a search or investigation: *We will check on the matter.* **7.** to mark (something) with a check: *Please check the correct answers.* **8.** to leave (clothes, baggage, etc.) at a checkroom. **9.** to mark with a pattern of squares: *to check fabric.* **10.** (in chess) to place (the king of an opponent) in check. —*n.* **11.** a person or thing that stops, limits, slows, or holds back: *His bad health was a check on his progress.* **12.** a test or other means of finding out whether something is correct, in good condition, etc. **13.** a mark (√) placed next to something to show that it has been checked. **14.** a written order, as on a printed form, directing a bank to pay money: *to write a check for a large amount.* **15.** a slip of paper showing an amount owed, esp. a bill for food or beverages in a restaurant. **16.** a ticket given to a person who checks something in a checkroom to show that he is the owner. **17.** a pattern of squares, as on a fabric. **18.** one of these squares. **19.** (in chess) the position of a king when it is threatened by direct attack. **20. in check,** under control: *to hold one's anger in check.*

check·er[1] (chek′ər), *n.* **1.** a small, round, flat piece of wood or plastic used in playing checkers. **2.** a pattern of squares or checks, as on fabric or a checkerboard; check. **3.** one of these squares; check. —*v.* **4.** to mark like a checkerboard. **5.** to fill with changes, as from one extreme to another: *Joy and sorrow checkered his life.* [from the Old French word *eschiquier* "checkered pattern, chessboard," which comes from *eschec* "a check (in chess)"]

check·er[2] (chek′ər), *n.* **1.** a person who checks, esp. one who inspects, tests, or investigates. **2.** a person who checks coats, bags, baggage, etc.

check·er·board (chek′ər bôrd′), *n.* a board marked into 64 two-color squares, used for checkers and chess.

check·ered (chek′ərd), *adj.* **1.** having a pattern of squares. **2.** full of changes, as from one extreme to another: *a checkered life of wealth and poverty, joy* *and sorrow.* **3.** having a varied pattern, as of dark and light: *the checkered shade underneath trees.*

check·ers (chek′ərz), *n. (used as sing.)* a game played by two people, each having 12 pieces, on a checkerboard.

check·mate (chek′māt′), *n.* **1.** a move in chess in which an opponent's king is put in a position from which it cannot escape. **2.** a complete check or defeat. —*v.*, **check·mat·ed, check·mat·ing. 3.** (in chess) to put (an opponent's king) into a position from which it cannot escape. **4.** to check completely; defeat: *Napoleon was checkmated at Waterloo.* [from the Arabic phrase *shāh māt,* which comes from a Persian phrase meaning "the king is dead"]

check·room (chek′rōōm′, -rŏŏm′), *n.* a room in a public building, station, etc., where coats, packages, and other possessions may be checked.

check·up (chek′up′), *n.* an examination to find out whether someone is in good condition.

Ched·dar (ched′ər), *n.* a hard, smooth cheese. Also, **Ched′dar cheese′.** [named after *Cheddar,* a village in England where it was first made]

cheek (chēk), *n.* **1.** either side of the face below the eye and above the jaw. **2.** impudence or insolence.

cheek·y (chē′kē), *adj.*, **cheek·i·er, cheek·i·est.** impudent or insolent. —**cheek′i·ness,** *n.*

cheep (chēp), *v.* **1.** to chirp. —*n.* **2.** a chirp.

cheer (chēr), *n.* **1.** a shout of approval, encouragement, etc.: *The team was welcomed home with cheers.* **2.** anything that gives joy, comfort, or encouragement: *to speak words of cheer.* **3.** gladness or gaiety: *Their Christmas was full of cheer.* —*v.* **4.** to utter or salute with shouts of approval, encouragement, etc.: *They cheered when the team scored. They cheered the winning team.* **5.** to make or become more cheerful (often fol. by *up*): *The party cheered her up.* **6. be of good cheer,** be cheerful; cheer up. **7. with good cheer,** cheerfully; willingly: *He accepted the duty with good cheer.*

cheer·ful (chēr′fəl), *adj.* **1.** full of cheer; in good spirits. **2.** giving cheer; pleasant: *a colorful, cheerful house.* **3.** eager to give or help; willing: *a cheerful giver.* —**cheer′ful·ly,** *adv.* —**cheer′ful·ness,** *n.*

cheer·lead·er (chēr′lē′dər), *n.* a person who leads the spectators at a game in cheering the team they back. —**cheer′lead′ing,** *n.*

cheer·less (chēr′lis), *adj.* without cheer; joyless; gloomy: *cheerless winter days.* —**cheer′less·ly,** *adv.*

cheer·y (chēr′ē), *adj.*, **cheer·i·er, cheer·i·est. 1.** in good spirits; happy or gay; cheerful: *a smiling, cheery person.* **2.** giving cheer; cheerful: *a bright, cheery room.* —**cheer′i·ly,** *adv.* —**cheer′i·ness,** *n.*

cheese (chēz), *n.* a food made of the curds of milk, usually pressed together to form a cake.

cheese·cloth (chēz′klôth′), *n.* thin, lightly woven cotton cloth.

chees·y (chē′zē), *adj.*, **chees·i·er, chees·i·est. 1.** *Slang.* of poor or inferior quality. **2.** resembling cheese: *a cheesy aroma.* —**chees′i·ness,** *n.*

chee·tah (chē′tə), *n.* a long-legged cat of southwestern Asia and Africa that resembles a leopard and can run very fast.

chef (shef), *n.* a cook, usually a man, in charge of other cooks in a kitchen.

chem., **1.** chemical. **2.** chemist. **3.** chemistry.

chem·i·cal (kem′i kəl), *n.* **1.** a substance used in chemistry. —*adj.* **2.** of,

Cheetah
(2½ ft. high at shoulder)

used in, or produced by chemistry: *chemical substances; chemical processes.* —**chem′i·cal·ly,** *adv.*

che·mise (shə mēz′), *n.* **1.** a loose-fitting, shirtlike undergarment worn by women. **2.** a dress that hangs straight from the shoulders, fitting loosely at the waist.

chem·ist (kem′ist), *n.* **1.** a person who is skilled in or who works in chemistry. **2.** *British.* a druggist.

chem·is·try (kem′i strē), *n.* the science that deals with the composition and properties of substances and the changes that take place when they combine to form new substances.

cher·ish (cher′ish), *v.* **1.** to hold dear: *to cherish one's native land.* **2.** to take tender care of: *to cherish a child.* **3.** to cling to fondly or stubbornly: *to cherish hopes.*

Cher·o·kee (cher′ə kē′), *n., pl.* for def. 1 **Cher·o·kees** or **Cher·o·kee. 1.** a member of an Indian tribe formerly located in North and South Carolina, Georgia, Alabama, and Tennessee, now mostly in E Oklahoma. **2.** the language of the Cherokee. —*adj.* **3.** of or referring to the Cherokee or their language.

cher·ry (cher′ē), *n., pl.* **cher·ries. 1.** a berrylike red fruit that contains one round pit. **2.** the tree bearing this fruit. **3.** the hard, reddish wood of this tree, sometimes used for furniture. **4.** a bright red. —*adj.* **5.** made with or containing cherries: *cherry pie; cherry marmalade.* **6.** of the color cherry: *a cherry scarf.*

cher·ub (cher′əb), *n., pl.* for def. 1 **cher·u·bim** (cher′ə bim, cher′yə bim), for def. 2 **cher·ubs. 1.** a kind of angel pictured as a beautiful child with wings. **2.** an innocent, beautiful child. —**che·ru·bic** (chə rōō′bik), *adj.*

Ches′a·peake Bay′ (ches′ə pēk′), an inlet of the Atlantic Ocean, in Maryland and Virginia. 200 mi. long; 4 to 40 mi. wide.

chess (ches), *n.* a game played by two persons, each with 16 chessmen, on a chessboard.

chess·board (ches′bôrd′), *n.* the board, the same as a checkerboard, used in playing chess.

chess·man (ches′man′, -mən), *n., pl.*

Chessmen
A, Kings
B, Queens
C, Rooks
D, Bishops
E, Knights
F, Pawns

chess·men. one of the pieces used in playing chess.

chest (chest), *n.* **1.** the front, upper part of the body. **2.** a box, usually a large, strong one with a lid, used for storage, safekeeping, etc.: *a toy chest; a silver chest.* **3.** a chest of drawers.

chest·nut (ches'nut), *n.* **1.** the dark reddish-brown nut of a tree related to the beech. **2.** the tree itself. **3.** the wood of this tree. **4.** a dark reddish brown. **5.** an old or stale joke. —*adj.* **6.** of or containing chestnuts: *chestnut stuffing.* **7.** of a dark reddish brown: *chestnut hair.*

chest′ of drawers′, a piece of furniture having drawers; bureau.

chev·a·lier (shev'ə lēr′, shə val′yā), *n.* **1.** a member of a French order of merit: *a chevalier of the Legion of Honor.* **2.** *Archaic.* a knight.

chev·ron (shev'rən), *n.* a badge consisting of stripes meeting at an angle, worn on the sleeve of a military or police uniform to show rank or length of service.

chew (chōō), *v.* **1.** to crush or grind with the teeth, as food, gum, tobacco, etc. —*n.* **2.** something that is chewed, such as a piece of gum or a bite of tobacco.

chew′ing gum′, sweetened and flavored chicle for chewing.

chew·y (chōō'ē), *adj.,* **chew·i·er, chew·i·est.** requiring much chewing, esp. because of toughness: *chewy steak* —**chew′i·ness,** *n.*

Chevrons
(U.S. military)

Chey·enne (shī an′, shī en′), *n., pl.* for def. 1 **Chey·ennes** *or* **Chey·enne. 1.** a member of an Indian tribe originally located in Minnesota and on the Great Plains, now mostly in Oklahoma and Montana. **2.** the language of the Cheyenne. **3.** the capital city of Wyoming, in the S part.

chic (shēk), *adj.* **1.** stylish or elegant: *a chic dress.* —*n.* **2.** style or elegance: *Her clothes have chic.*

Chi·ca·go (shi kä′gō, shi kô′gō), *n.* a city in NE Illinois, on Lake Michigan: second largest city in the United States. —**Chi·ca′go·an,** *n.*

chi·can·er·y (shi kā′nə rē), *n.* the use of deception or cunning to get one's way: *The politician practiced chicanery to get elected.*

Chi·ca·no (chi kä′nō, chi kä′nō), *n.* a U.S. citizen or resident of Mexican descent.

chic·co·ry (chik′ə rē), *n., pl.* **chic·co·ries.** another spelling of **chicory.**

chick (chik), *n.* a young chicken or other bird.

chick·a·dee (chik′ə dē′), *n.* a small North American bird having black feathers at the throat and on the top of the head.

chick·en (chik′ən), *n.* **1.** a hen or rooster, esp. a young one. **2.** the flesh of a chicken, used as food.

Chickadee
(length 5½ in.)

chick·en-heart·ed (chik′ən här′tid), *adj.* timid or cowardly.

chick′en pox′, a mild disease, esp. of children, in which the skin breaks out in red spots that may scar.

chick·weed (chik′wēd′), *n.* a common weed having seeds and leaves that are eaten by birds.

chic·le (chik′əl), *n.* the dried sap of a South American tree: the principal ingredient of chewing gum.

chic·o·ry (chik′ə rē), *n., pl.* **chic·o·ries.** a plant having leaves that are used as a salad and a root that is ground and roasted and often added to coffee. Also, **chiccory.**

chide (chīd), *v.,* **chid·ed** *or* **chid** (chid); **chid·ed** *or* **chid** (chid) *or* **chid·den** (chid′ᵊn); **chid·ing.** to scold or find fault: *Their mother chided them for being rude.* —**chid′ing·ly,** *adv.*

chief (chēf), *n.* **1.** the head or leader of a group: *the chief of a company; an Indian chief.* —*adj.* **2.** highest in rank: *the chief officer.* **3.** most important; principal; main: *the chief difficulty.*

Chief′ Exec′utive, the President of the United States.

chief·ly (chēf′lē), *adv.* mainly; mostly: *He went along chiefly for the ride.*

chief·tain (chēf′tən), *n.* the leader of a band, clan, tribe, etc.: *a native chieftain; a bandit chieftain.*

chif·fon (shi fon′, shif′on), *n.* **1.** a thin, light fabric made of silk, rayon, or nylon, used in women's clothing. —*adj.* **2.** having a light, frothy texture, as some pies and cake: *lime chiffon pie.*

chif·fo·nier (shif′ə nēr′), *n.* a high chest of drawers or bureau, often having a mirror on top.

chig·ger (chig′ər), *n.* the bloodsucking larva of several species of mites whose bite causes intense itching and spreads certain diseases.

Chi·hua·hua (chi wä′wä), *n.* a very little dog, originally from Mexico, having a delicate body and large, pointed ears.

chil·blain (chil′blān′), *n.* a painful reddening, swelling, and itching of the hands or feet caused by exposure to cold.

Chiffonier

child (chīld), *n., pl.* **chil·dren** (chil′drən). **1.** a boy or girl. **2.** a son or daughter. **3.** a baby or infant. —**child′less,** *adj.*

child·birth (chīld′bûrth′), *n.* the act or instance of bringing forth a child: *an easy childbirth.*

child·hood (chīld′hŏŏd), *n.* the state or time of being a child: *a happy childhood.*

child·ish (chīl′dish), *adj.* **1.** of, like, or befitting a child: *a childish liking for candy.* **2.** weak or silly: *childish fear of the dark.* —**child′ish·ly,** *adv.* —**child′ish·ness,** *n.*

child·like (chīld′līk′), *adj.* like or befitting a child in frankness, innocence, etc.: *a childlike pleasure.*

chil·dren (chil′drən), *n.* the plural form of **child.**

Chil·e (chil′ē), *n.* a country in SW South America, on the Pacific coast. 286,396 sq. mi. *Cap.:* Santiago. —**Chil′e·an,** *n., adj.*

chil·i (chil′ē), *n., pl.* **chil·ies. 1.** the pod of certain pepper plants: usually dried and ground for use as a seasoning. **2.** short for **chili con carne.** Also, **chil′e.**

chil·i con car·ne (chil′ē kon kär′nē), a Mexican dish of meat, beans, onion, peppers, etc., seasoned with chili. Also, **chil′e con car′ne.**

chill (chil), *n.* **1.** mild coldness: *the chill of early spring.* **2.** a sudden coldness of the body, often accompanied by shivering: a symptom of certain fevers. —*adj.* **3.** chilly. —*v.* **4.** to make or become cold.

chil·ly (chil′ē), *adj.,* **chil·li·er, chil·li·est. 1.** mildly cold; cool: *Fall air is chilly.* **2.** feeling cold: *Please shut the window, I'm chilly.* **3.** without friendliness: *We were given a chilly welcome.* —**chil′li·ness,** *n.*

chime (chīm), *n.* **1.** Often, **chimes.** a set of tuned bells or metal tubes that sound like bells. **2.** the sound of such bells or tubes. —*v.,* **chimed, chim·ing. 3.** to produce a chime or chimes: *The bells are chiming in the tower.* **4.** to give forth (music, sound, etc.), as a bell or bells. **5.** to announce by chiming: *The bells chimed the hour.* **6. chime in,** to intrude into a conversation or the like: *Every time we start talking, he chimes in.*

chi·me·ra (ki mēr′ə, kī mēr′ə), *n.* a wild or fantastic idea or illusion: *His dream of wealth is only a chimera.* —**chi·mer·i·cal** (ki mer′i kəl, kī mer′i kəl), *adj.*

Chi·me·ra (ki mēr′ə, kī mēr′ə), *n.* (in Greek mythology) a fire-breathing monster with a lion's head, a goat's body, and a serpent's tail.

chim·ney (chim′nē), *n., pl.* **chim·neys. 1.** a pipe or shaft passing from a fireplace, furnace, or stove, to a roof, used to carry off smoke from a fire. **2.** a tube of glass surrounding the flame of a lamp.

chim′ney sweep′, a person, esp. a boy or man, whose business is to clean out chimneys.

chim′ney swift′, a small, gray North American bird that often builds its nest in an unused chimney.

chim·pan·zee (chim′pan zē′, chim pan′zē), *n.* a highly intelligent African ape that is easily trained to do tricks.

chin (chin), *n.* **1.** the part of the face below the mouth. **2.** the point of the lower jaw. —*v.,* **chinned, chin·ning. 3.** to pull (oneself) up by the hands while hanging from a level bar until the chin can be passed over the top of the bar.

chi·na (chī′nə), *n.* **1.** a fine porcelain, originally made in China. **2.** cups, saucers, plates, ornaments, etc., made of this: *The cabinet is full of china.* **3.** any porcelain dishes.

Chimpanzee
(height 4 ft.)

Chi·na (chī′nə), *n.* **1. People's Republic of.** Also, **Communist China, Red China.** a large country in E Asia: under Communist control since 1949. It covers an area of 3,691,502 sq. mi. *Cap.:* Peking. **2. Republic of.** Also, **Nationalist China.** a republic consisting mainly of the island of Taiwan off the SE coast of mainland China. Its area is 13,885 sq. mi. *Cap.:* Taipei.

chinch′ bug′ (chinch), a small bug that feeds on corn, wheat, and other grains.

chin·chil·la (chin chil′ə), *n.* **1.** a small South American rodent having a soft, silver-gray fur. **2.** the fur of this animal, which is extremely valuable.

Chinchilla
(total length
to 20 in.)

Chi·nese (chī nēz′), *n.* **1.** the standard spoken language of China; Mandarin. **2.** any of the related languages spoken in China. **3.** a system of writing based on symbols that represent ideas rather than sounds. It is used and understood by all the Chinese people, even though their spoken languages may differ greatly. **4.** a native or inhabitant of China. —*adj.* **5.** of or referring to China, its people, or one of their languages.

chink[1] (chingk), *n.* **1.** a crack or narrow opening: *a chink in a wall.* —*v.* **2.** to fill up chinks in: *to chink a wall with plaster.* [from Old English *cinu* "crevice"]

chink[2] (chingk), *v.* **1.** to make a short, sharp, ringing sound, as of coins or glasses striking together. —*n.* **2.** a chinking sound: *the chink of ice in a glass.* [imitative of the sound]

chi·nook (shi nŏŏk′, chi nŏŏk′), *n.* **1.** a warm, dry wind that blows down the eastern slopes of the Rocky Mountains. **2.** a warm, moist, southwest wind on the coast of Oregon and Washington.

chintz (chints), *n.* a printed cotton fabric, used esp. for draperies and slipcovers.

chip (chip), *n.* **1.** a small piece of wood, stone, ice, etc., broken or cut off a larger piece. **2.** a very thin or small piece of food, candy, etc.: *potato chips.* **3.** a mark or flaw left by a piece that has been broken or cut off: *The cup has a chip.* **4.** a small disk used in place of money in a gambling game. —*v.,* **chipped, chip·ping. 5.** to break or cut off a chip or chips from: *I chipped the glass on the sink.* **6.** to become chipped: *China chips easily.* **7.** to make or shape by chipping: *to chip a hole in ice; to chip a statue from wood.* **8. chip in,** to give money along with others: *We all chipped in to buy Dorothy a birthday present.*

chip·munk (chip′mungk), *n.* a small, striped, North American squirrel. [from the Algonquian word *atchitamon,* literally "head first," referring to its way of coming down a tree trunk]

chip·per (chip′ər), *adj.* lively; cheerful.

chirp (chûrp), *v.* **1.** to make a short, sharp sound, as small birds and some insects do. —*n.* **2.** a chirping sound: *the chirps of the sparrows.*

chir·rup (chēr′əp, chûr′-), *v.,* **chir·ruped, chir·rup·ing. 1.** to chirp again and again: *Crickets chirrup at night.* —*n.* **2.** the act or sound of chirruping.

chis·el (chiz′əl), *n.* **1.** a tool with a sharp edge in the shape of a wedge, used for cutting wood, stone, etc. —*v.,* **chis·eled** *or* **chis·elled; chis·el·ing** *or* **chis·el·ling. 2.** to cut or form with a chisel. **3.** to

A   B   C
Chisels
A, Wood chisel;
B, Bricklayer's
chisel; C, Cold
chisel

work with a chisel. **4.** *Slang.* to cheat or trick (someone): *He chiseled me out of $20.* **5.** *Slang.* to get (something) by trickery or cheating: *He chisels money from his friends.* —**chis·el·er, chis·el·ler,** *n.*

chit·chat (chit′chat′), *n.* **1.** light talk about things of little importance; gossip: *chitchat at a party.* —*v.,* **chit·chat·ted, chit·chat·ting. 2.** to make chitchat; gossip.

chiv·al·rous (shiv′əl rəs), *adj.* **1.** like a knight of old in bravery, courtesy, and loyalty. **2.** having to do with chivalry. —**chiv′al·rous·ly,** *adv.*

chiv·al·ry (shiv′əl rē), *n.* **1.** the qualities that were expected of knights of old, including bravery, courtesy, and loyalty. **2.** the way of life followed by these knights: *to live according to the strict rules of chivalry.*

chive (chīv), *n.* a plant related to the onion and having thin leaves resembling grass that are used in salads and cooking.

chlo·ride (klôr′īd), *n.* a chemical compound containing chlorine, esp. with only one other element, as sodium chloride.

chlo·rin·ate (klôr′ə nāt′), *v.,* **chlo·rin·at·ed, chlo·rin·at·ing.** to treat (water) with chlorine in order to kill any germs it may contain. —**chlo′rin·a′tion,** *n.*

chlo·rine (klôr′ēn), *n.* a greenish, highly poisonous gas, used in purifying water and in making bleaches: a chemical element. *Symbol:* Cl

chlo·ro·form (klôr′ə fôrm′), *n.* a volatile liquid used as an anesthetic and as a solvent.

chlo·ro·phyll (klôr′ə fil), *n.* the green coloring matter in leaves and plants necessary for photosynthesis, the process by which plants manufacture food from carbon dioxide and water, using the energy from sunlight. Also, **chlo′ro·phyl.**

chm., chairman. Also, **chmn.**

chock (chok), *n.* **1.** a wedge or block used to hold something in place. —*v.* **2.** to hold in place with a chock or chocks.

chock-full (chok′fool′), *adj.* completely full; crammed: *a Christmas stocking chock-full of candies.*

choc·o·late (chô′kə lit, chô′-), *n.* **1.** ground and roasted cacao seeds. **2.** a drink made of chocolate mixed with sugar and milk or water. **3.** a candy made of chocolate. **4.** a dark brown. —*adj.* **5.** made, flavored, or covered with chocolate: *chocolate ice cream.* **6.** having the color of chocolate: *chocolate walls with white drapes.* —**choc′o·lat·y,** *adj.*

choice (chois), *n.* **1.** the act of choosing: *Her choice was the last to be made.* **2.** the right to choose; alternative: *You must go, for you have no choice.* **3.** a person or thing that is chosen or may be chosen: *He is my choice for class president.* **4.** a number of persons or things from which to choose: *There is a wide choice of movies.* —*adj.,* **choic·er, choic·est. 5.** very good or well chosen: *choice vegetables; a choice remark.*

choir (kwīˀr), *n.* **1.** a group of singers, as in a church. **2.** the part of a church in which the choir sings.

choke (chōk), *v.,* **choked, chok·ing. 1.** to stop or hinder the breathing of: *The dense smoke choked us.*

2. to have difficulty breathing: *We were choking in the smoky room.* **3.** to make or become clogged or stopped up: *Gravel choked the pipe. The drain choked.* **4.** to stop or hinder the growth of: *Weeds were choking the lawns.* —*n.* **5.** the act or sound of choking: *He spoke with a choke in his voice.* **6.** a device that regulates the amount of air taken into a gasoline engine. **7. choke back,** to hold back, as a strong feeling or tears. **8. choke down,** to swallow in spite of choking: *He choked down the medicine.* **9. choke off,** to stop with force: *to choke off discussion.* **10. choke up,** to become speechless as a result of emotion, nervousness, or the like: *He tried to thank us, but he choked up.*

choke·cher·ry (chōk′cher′ē), *n., pl.* **choke·cher·ries. 1.** a wild cherry tree bearing a bitter fruit that puckers the mouth. **2.** the fruit of this tree.

chok·er (chō′kər), *n.* **1.** a person or thing that chokes. **2.** a necklace that fits closely around the neck.

chol·er·a (kol′ə rə), *n.* an acute, often fatal, infectious disease of the intestines that causes diarrhea, cramps, and vomiting.

cho·les·ter·ol (kə les′tə rōl′, kə les′tə rôl′), *n.* a fatty substance occurring naturally in the body, accumulations of which are believed to cause serious diseases, esp. in older people.

choose (chooz), *v.,* **chose** (chōz), **cho·sen** (chō′zən), **choos·ing. 1.** to pick out from a number; select: *She chose the green dress.* **2.** to make a choice: *With all those desserts, he found he could not choose.* **3.** to prefer or decide: *He does not choose to go with us to the game.*

choos·y (choo′zē), *adj.,* **choos·i·er, choos·i·est.** hard to please; fussy: *She is very choosy about what she eats.* —**choos′i·ness,** *n.*

chop¹ (chop), *v.,* **chopped, chop·ping. 1.** to cut with a quick, heavy blow or blows: *to chop down a tree.* **2.** to cut in small pieces; mince: *to chop an onion.* —*n.* **3.** a quick cutting stroke. **4.** a slice of lamb, veal, etc., usually containing a rib. **5.** a short, broken movement of waves. [from the Middle English word *choppen* "to crack"] —**chop′per,** *n.*

chop² (chop), *v.,* **chopped, chop·ping.** to shift or change suddenly: *The wind chopped to the west.* [from the Old English word *cēapian* "to bargain, trade." The modern meaning developed from the idea of bartering or making frequent changes as in bargaining for something]

Cho·pin (shō′pan), *n.* **Frédéric François** (fred′ə-rik fran swä′), 1810-1849, Polish composer and pianist, in Paris after 1831.

chop·py (chop′ē), *adj.,* **chop·pi·er, chop·pi·est.** (of the sea, a lake, etc.) covered with broken, rough waves: *The bay is too choppy for us to row today.* —**chop′pi·ly,** *adv.* —**chop′pi·ness,** *n.*

chops (chops), *n.pl.* **1.** the jaws. **2.** the mouth and the flesh around it: *The dog licked his chops.*

chop·stick (chop′stik′), *n.* one of a pair of thin sticks used by Chinese, Japanese, and other Oriental peoples to carry food from a dish to the mouth.

chop su·ey (chop′ sōō′ē), a Chinese-American dish made with meat, onions, green peppers, mushrooms, etc., often served with rice.

cho·ral (kôr′əl), *adj.* 1. written for or performed by a chorus or choir. —*n.* (kə ral′, kô ral′). 2. another spelling of **chorale.**

cho·rale (kə ral′, kô ral′), *n.* 1. a hymn or hymn tune. 2. a chorus.

Chords on a circle (AB, AC)

chord[1] (kôrd), *n.* the straight line between two points on a curve. [from the Greek word *chordē* "gut, string"]

chord[2] (kôrd), *n.* the combination of several musical tones sounded at once, esp. one that produces a harmonious blending. [from the Middle English word *cord*, which is short for *accord*]

chore (chôr), *n.* 1. a household task. 2. a difficult or unpleasant task: *Typing for him is a chore.*

cho·re·og·ra·pher (kôr′ē og′rə fər), *n.* a person who composes ballets and other dances for the stage.

cho·re·og·ra·phy (kôr′ē og′rə fē), *n.* the composing of ballets and other dances for the stage: *Who did the choreography for the show?*

chor·is·ter (kôr′i stər), *n.* a singer in a choir.

chor·tle (chôr′t'l), *v.,* **chor·tled, chor·tling.** 1. to chuckle or utter with glee: *We chortled at the joke.* —*n.* 2. a gleeful chuckle: *a chortle of delight.* [a blend of *chuckle* + *snort.* The word was coined by Lewis Carroll in *Through the Looking Glass* (1871)]

cho·rus (kôr′əs), *n., pl.* **cho·rus·es.** 1. a part of a song that is repeated after each verse. 2. a group of singers. 3. the music sung by such a group. 4. a number of voices speaking together, or a number of things said at once: *The class answered the question in a chorus.* 5. a group of people who act, sing, or dance together in a play, opera, etc. —*v.,* **cho·rused, cho·rus·ing.** 6. to sing or speak in chorus.

chose (chōz), *v.* the past tense of **choose.**

cho·sen (chō′zən), *v.* 1. the past participle of **choose.** —*adj.* 2. carefully selected: *Only the chosen few were told.*

chow[1] (chou), *n. Slang.* food. [short for the pidgin English word *chow-chow* "food, relish"]

chow[2] (chou), *n.* a Chinese breed of dog having a thick, usually red coat and a black tongue. Also, **chow′ chow′.** [from a word in a Chinese dialect related to Cantonese *kau* "dog"]

chow·der (chou′dər), *n.* a thick soup made with clams or fish and vegetables.

chow mein (chou′ mān′), a Chinese-American dish made of mushrooms, celery, and other vegetables, topped with shrimp, chicken, etc., and usually served with fried noodles.

Chow (20 in. high at shoulder)

Christ (krīst), *n.* a name for Jesus considered as the Messiah whose coming was prophesied by the Hebrews in the Old Testament. [from the Greek word *christos* "anointed," which is a translation of the Hebrew word *māshīah* "anointed, messiah"] —**Christ′like′,** *adj.*

Christ·church (krīst′church′), *n.* a city on E South Island, in New Zealand.

chris·ten (kris′ən), *v.* 1. to baptize or name at baptism: *He was christened Paul.* 2. to give a name to: *A ship is often christened at the time it is launched.* —**chris′ten·er,** *n.*

Chris·ten·dom (kris′ən dəm), *n.* 1. all Christians. 2. the Christian world: *all the saints of Christendom.*

chris·ten·ing (kris′ə ning), *n.* 1. the ceremony of naming and baptizing a baby. 2. the ceremony of naming and launching a ship.

Chris·tian (kris′chən), *n.* 1. a person who believes in Jesus Christ. —*adj.* 2. having to do with Jesus Christ and His teachings: *Christian belief; Christian worship.* 3. belonging to the religion founded by Jesus Christ: *Italy is a Christian country.* 4. showing the spirit proper to a believer in Christ: *Christian love.*

Chris·ti·an·i·ty (kris′chē an′i tē), *n.* 1. the Christian religion. 2. all Christians: *Christianity celebrates Christmas in many different ways.*

Chris′tian Sci′ence, a religion founded about 1866 by Mary Baker Eddy. —**Chris′tian Sci′entist.**

Christ·mas (kris′məs), *n.* the yearly celebration, on December 25, of the birth of Christ.

Chris·to·pher (kris′tə fər), *n.* **Saint,** died A.D. c250, Christian martyr: patron saint of travelers.

chro·mat·ic (krō mat′ik), *adj.* 1. referring to color or colors. 2. (in music) progressing by half steps: *the chromatic scale.* —**chro·mat′i·cal·ly,** *adv.*

chrome (krōm), *n.* chromium-plated trim, as on a bicycle or automobile: *Our new car has lots of chrome.*

chro·mi·um (krō′mē əm), *n.* a hard metal that resists corrosion and is used in plating and in making alloys: a chemical element having several bright-colored compounds that are used in paints. *Symbol:* Cr

chro·mo·some (krō′mə sōm′), *n.* any of several threadlike bodies in the nucleus of all plant and animal cells. Chromosomes carry the genes that determine hereditary characteristics.

chron·ic (kron′ik), *adj.* 1. continuing over a long time or recurring frequently, as a disease. 2. habitual or of long standing: *He is a chronic liar.* —**chron′i·cal·ly,** *adv.*

chron·i·cle (kron′i kəl), *n.* 1. a record of events in the order of their happening; history: *a chronicle of colonial days.* —*v.,* **chron·i·cled, chron·i·cling.** 2. to record: *to chronicle the lives of England's kings and queens.* —**chron′i·cler,** *n.*

Chron·i·cles (kron′i kəlz), *n. (used as sing.)* either of two books of the Old Testament, I Chronicles or II Chronicles.

chron·o·log·i·cal (kron′ᵊloj′i kəl), *adj.* arranged in the order of occurrence: *Put these dates in chronological order.* —**chron′o·log′i·cal·ly,** *adv.*

chro·nol·o·gy (krə nol′ə jē), *n., pl.* for def. 2 **chro·nol·o·gies.** 1. an order of events from earliest to latest: *a chronology of the main battles of a war.* 2. a book, list, etc., containing a chronology. 3. the science of dating events and arranging them in the order in which they happened.

chrys·a·lis (kris′ə lis), *n.* 1. the hard-shelled pupa of a moth or butterfly. 2. the shell or case of such a pupa.

chry·san·the·mum (kri san′thə məm), *n.* a plant, originally from China, that bears many-petaled, round flowers that bloom in the fall.

Chrysalis of a butterfly

chub·by (chub′ē), *adj.,* **chub·bi·er, chub·bi·est.** round and plump: *a chubby baby.* —**chub′bi·ness,** *n.*

chuck¹ (chuk), *v.* 1. to pat or tap lightly, as under the chin. 2. to toss quickly: *He chucked the paper into the wastebasket.*

chuck² (chuk), *n.* a cut of beef between the neck and the shoulder blade. [probably another form of *chock*]

chuck·le (chuk′əl), *v.,* **chuck·led, chuck·ling.** 1. to laugh softly or to oneself: *We chuckled at the comic strips.* —*n.* 2. a soft laugh: *chuckles of satisfaction.*

chuck′ wag′on, a wagon carrying equipment for cooking and food for men working out of doors, such as cowboys used in the western U.S.

chug (chug), *n.* 1. a short, dull, explosive sound: *the chug of a steam engine.* —*v.,* **chugged, chug·ging.** 2. to move with this sound: *The locomotive chugged along the track.*

chum (chum), *n.* 1. a close friend; pal: *They were chums at school.* —*v.,* **chummed, chum·ming.** 2. to be very friendly: *They chummed together at school.*

chum·my (chum′ē), *adj.,* **chum·mi·er, chum·mi·est.** friendly; intimate. —**chum′mi·ness,** *n.*

Chung·king (choong′king′), *n.* a city in SW China, on the Yangtze River.

chunk (chungk), *n.* a thick, solid lump or piece: *a chunk of coal; a chunk of ice.*

chunk·y (chung′kē), *adj.,* **chunk·i·er, chunk·i·est.** thick or solid; solidly built: *a chunky steak; a chunky dog.* —**chunk′i·ness,** *n.*

church (chûrch), *n.* 1. a building used for religious worship, esp. by Christians. 2. a religious service in such a place: *to go to church on Sunday.* 3. all Christians, or a particular group or sect of Christians: *the Catholic Church.*

Church·ill (chûr′chil), *n.* **Sir Winston (Leonard Spencer),** 1874–1965, British statesman and author: prime minister 1940–1945, 1951–1955.

church·man (chûrch′mən), *n., pl.* **church·men.** 1. a clergyman, as a minister or priest. 2. a member of a church.

Church′ of Eng′land, the national English church, having the reigning monarch as its head.

church·yard (chûrch′yärd′), *n.* the yard or ground around a church, often used as a burial place.

churl (chûrl), *n.* a rude, boorish, or surly person. —**churl′ish,** *adj.* —**churl′ish·ly,** *adv.*

churn (chûrn), *n.* 1. a container or machine in which milk or cream is beaten or shaken to make butter. —*v.* 2. to beat or shake in order to make butter: *to churn cream.* 3. to make (butter) by beating or shaking cream. —**churn′er,** *n.*

chute¹ (shoot), *n.* 1. a sloping shaft, tube, trough, etc., for moving things downward: *a laundry chute; a mail chute.* 2. a waterfall or steep slope in a river. 3. a toboggan slide. [from a French word meaning "a fall, a falling"]

chute² (shoot), *n.* short for **parachute.**

CIA, the Central Intelligence Agency: a U.S. federal agency that coordinates governmental intelligence activities.

ci·ca·da (si kā′də, si kä′də), *n.* a kind of locust the male of which produces a shrill sound by means of vibrating membranes on the underside of its abdomen.

Cicada (length 1 in.)

-cide, a suffix used to form nouns meaning 1. the act of killing: *infanticide.* 2. a killer or destroyer: *insecticide.*

ci·der (sī′dər), *n.* the juice of apples, drunk as a beverage: often made alcoholic by fermentation.

ci·gar (si gär′), *n.* a tight roll of cured tobacco leaves for smoking. [from the Spanish word *cigarro*]

cig·a·rette (sig′ə ret′, sig′ə ret′), *n.* a narrow, short roll of finely cut tobacco for smoking, usually wrapped in thin white paper.

cil·i·a (sil′ē ə), *n.pl., sing.* **cil·i·um** (sil′ē əm). 1. short, hairlike projections, or outgrowths, on the surface of certain animal and plant cells. 2. the eyelashes.

cinch (sinch), *n.* 1. a strap for holding a pack or saddle to a horse or other animal. 2. *Slang.* something that is easy: *This problem is a cinch.* —*v.* 3. to tie or bind with a cinch; gird. 4. *Slang.* to make certain; guarantee: *Hard work cinched his success.*

cin·cho·na (sin kō′nə), *n.* a South American tree whose bark yields quinine.

Cin·cin·nat·i (sin′sə nat′ē), *n.* a city in SW Ohio, on the Ohio River.

cin·der (sin′dər), *n.* 1. a partly burned small piece of wood, coal, etc. 2. the ashes of wood, coal, etc.

Cin·der·el·la (sin′də rel′ə), *n.* a girl in a fairy tale who is saved from a life of hard work in the house of a wicked stepmother by her fairy godmother, who makes it possible for her to go to a ball, where she meets a prince whom she eventually marries.

cin·e·ma (sin′ə mə), *n.* 1. motion pictures as a form of art: *a lecture on the cinema.* 2. *Chiefly British.* a movie theater. —**cin·e·mat·ic** (sin′ə mat′ik), *adj.*

cin·na·mon (sin′ə mən), *n.* the aromatic inner bark of an East Indian tree, used as a spice.

ci·pher (sī′fər), *n.* 1. a zero; nothing; naught. 2. a person or thing of little or no importance. 3. a message in code. 4. the key to a code. —*v.* 5. to use figures in arithmetic. 6. to write in code. [from the medieval Latin word *ciphra*, which comes from Arabic *çifr* "empty, zero"]

cir·ca (sûr′kə), *prep., adv.* about. It is used esp. in giving approximate dates: *The artist did most of his* *best work circa 1900. Abbr.:* c, c. [from Latin]

Cir·ce (sûr′sē), *n.* (in Greek mythology) an enchantress who changed the companions of Odysseus into swine by means of a magic drink.

cir·cle (sûr′kəl), *n.* **1.** a closed curve, all points on which are the same distance from a given point inside it. **2.** the round area enclosed by such a curve. **3.** any ringlike object or circular arrangement: *a circle of children.* **4.** a group of people having interests in common or brought together by friendship or family ties. **5.** a series that ends where it began, esp. one that keeps repeating: *the circle of the years.* —*v.,* **cir·cled, cir·cling. 6.** to enclose in a circle; surround: *Circle the right answer.* **7.** to move or revolve around: *The earth circles the sun.*

Circle
BC, Radius
AD, Diameter

cir·cuit (sûr′kit), *n.* **1.** the act of going or moving around: *The circuit of the earth around the sun takes a full year.* **2.** a journey around a certain area taken by judges, ministers, salesmen, etc. **3.** the line bounding any area. **4.** the distance around an area: *The circuit of the field is one mile.* **5.** the complete path traveled by an electric current. **6.** an assembly of parts, such as tubes, transistors, resistors, wires, etc.

cir·cu·i·tous (sər kyōo′i təs), *adj.* roundabout; not direct: *a slow and circuitous route to the city.* —**cir·cu′i·tous·ly,** *adv.* —**cir·cu′i·tous·ness,** *n.*

cir·cu·lar (sûr′kyə lər), *adj.* **1.** in the shape of a circle; round. **2.** moving in a circle: *a circular dance.* —*n.* **3.** a letter, advertisement, etc., of which many copies are made for sending to many people. —**cir·cu·lar·i·ty** (sûr′kyə lar′i tē), *n.*

cir′cular saw′, 1. a power-operated saw having a flat, circular blade. **2.** a blade for such a saw. See illus. at **saw.**

cir·cu·late (sûr′kyə lāt′), *v.,* **cir·cu·lat·ed, cir·cu·lat·ing. 1.** to move in a circle or circuit, as blood through the body. **2.** to move or send about from place to place or person to person: *The counterfeit money was circulated throughout the country.*

cir·cu·la·tion (sûr′kyə lā′shən), *n.* **1.** the continuous movement of blood in the body. **2.** the movement of anything from place to place or person to person: *the circulation of money; the circulation of air.* **3.** the number of copies of a magazine, newspaper, etc., that are distributed with each issue: *New York newspapers have a large circulation.*

cir·cu·la·to·ry (sûr′kyə lə tôr′ē), *adj.* having to do with circulation, esp. of the blood: *The circulatory system carries blood throughout the body.*

circum-, a prefix meaning around or about: *circumpolar; circumnavigate.*

cir·cum·cise (sûr′kəm sīz′), *v.,* **cir·cum·cised, cir·cum·cis·ing.** to cut off the foreskin of. —**cir·cum·ci·sion** (sûr′kəm sizh′ən), *n.*

cir·cum·fer·ence (sər kum′fər əns), *n.* **1.** the dis-

tance around a circle: always equal to 3.1416 times the diameter of the circle. **2.** the boundary of a polygon or any closed curve. **3.** the distance around anything having a more or less circular form: *the circumference of a tree; the circumference of the earth.*

cir·cum·lo·cu·tion (sûr′kəm lō kyōo′shən), *n.* **1.** a roundabout way of speaking. **2.** a roundabout expression: *"A craft for water travel" is a circumlocution for "boat."*

cir·cum·nav·i·gate (sûr′kəm nav′ə gāt′), *v.,* **cir·cum·nav·i·gat·ed, cir·cum·nav·i·gat·ing.** to sail around: *The Portuguese were the first to circumnavigate the earth.* —**cir′cum·nav·i·ga′tion,** *n.*

cir·cum·scribe (sûr′kəm skrīb′, sûr′kəm skrīb′), *v.,* **cir·cum·scribed, cir·cum·scrib·ing. 1.** to draw a line around; encircle; surround: *to circumscribe a city on a map.* **2.** to limit or confine; restrict: *His shyness caused him to lead a very circumscribed life.*

cir·cum·spect (sûr′kəm spekt′), *adj.* watchful and careful; discreet: *He was circumspect about making important decisions.* —**cir′cum·spec′tion,** *n.*

cir·cum·stance (sûr′kəm stans′), *n.* **1.** a detail or fact, esp. one forming a part of a total situation or event: *Do not judge me until you know all the circumstances.* **2. circumstances,** a condition or state of affairs, esp. in regard to money: *During the war they lived in very poor circumstances.* **3.** ceremony and splendor: *The king was crowned with great pomp and circumstance.* **4. under the circumstances,** because of such conditions; as the case stands: *Under the circumstances a strike seems inevitable.*

cir·cum·stan·tial (sûr′kəm stan′shəl), *adj.* connected with or based on a set of circumstances: *His possession of the gun was regarded as circumstantial evidence that he was the murderer.*

cir·cum·vent (sûr′kəm vent′, sûr′kəm vent′), *v.* to outwit, avoid, or get the better of: *He was able to circumvent every plan of the enemy to capture him.*

cir·cus (sûr′kəs), *n., pl.* **cir·cus·es. 1.** a large, traveling entertainment, consisting esp. of clowns, acrobats, and performing animals. **2.** a single show put on by such a group: *Hurry, or we'll be late for the circus.* **3.** a large tent containing rows of seats, used for such a show. **4.** (in ancient Roman times) a large, oblong stadium used for games and chariot races.

cir·rus (sir′əs), *n., pl.* **cir·rus.** a kind of cloud made up of thin streamers of ice crystals and formed at high altitudes.

cis·tern (sis′tərn), *n.* a reservoir or tank for storing water or other liquid.

cit·a·del (sit′ə dᵊl, sit′ə del′), *n.* **1.** a fortress built above a city for defense. **2.** any stronghold or fortified place: *The university is a citadel of learning.*

ci·ta·tion (sī tā′shən), *n.* **1.** the act of citing or quoting a passage from a book, a spoken statement, etc. **2.** the passage that is cited; quotation: *His book report contained many citations from the book.* **3.** an official statement praising a person or a group for some action, esp. an honorable mention of a soldier or military unit for bravery.

cite (sīt), *v.*, **cit·ed, cit·ing.** 1. to quote, esp. in order to prove something: *As proof of his argument, he cited the Bible.* 2. to mention with praise officially: *He was cited by the President for heroism in combat.*

cit·i·zen (sit′i zən), *n.* 1. a member of a nation, either by birth or by law, from whom certain duties are expected and to whom certain privileges, such as political rights, are granted. 2. an inhabitant of a city or town: *the citizens of New York and Paris.*

cit·i·zen·ry (sit′i zən rē), *n., pl.* **cit·i·zen·ries.** the citizens of a city, nation, or the like: *The citizenry protested against high taxes.*

cit′izens band′, a two-way radio channel set aside for short-distance use by private citizens.

cit·i·zen·ship (sit′i zən ship′), *n.* the state of being a citizen, with its rights and duties.

cit′ric ac′id (si′trik), a sour-tasting substance found in citrus fruits.

cit·ron (si′trən), *n.* 1. a pale-yellow fruit, larger than a lemon. 2. its candied rind, used in cakes.

cit·rus (si′trəs), *n.* 1. any of a group of trees or shrubs that grow in warm climates and bear such fruits as the lemon, lime, orange, and grapefruit. —*adj.* 2. Also, **cit′rous.** of or referring to such trees or shrubs: *citrus fruits.*

cit·tern (sit′ərn), *n.* an old musical instrument, related to the guitar, having a flat, pear-shaped soundbox and wire strings.

cit·y (sit′ē), *n., pl.* **cit·ies.** 1. a very large or important town. 2. a town and its surrounding area having its own local government, usually headed by a mayor. 3. all the people that live in a city: *The whole city will celebrate the holiday.*

Cittern

cit′y hall′, the main government building of a city, where the mayor has his office.

cit′y man′ager, an official appointed by a city council to act as mayor of the city.

cit′y slick′er. See **slicker** (def. 2).

civ·et (siv′it), *n.* 1. Also, **civ′et cat′.** a catlike, carnivorous mammal of southern Asia and Africa, which secretes a yellowish, oily substance with a strong, musklike odor. 2. this substance, used in making perfume.

Civet
(total length 4 ft.)

civ·ic (siv′ik), *adj.* 1. of or referring to a city or cities: *a speech on civic problems.* 2. of or referring to citizenship or citizens; civil: *Voting is a civic duty.*

civ·ics (siv′iks), *n. (used as sing.)* the study of government and the rights and duties of citizens.

civ·il (siv′əl), *adj.* 1. of or referring to citizens: *civil liberties.* 2. of or referring to a country as a whole and its government: *a discussion of civil affairs.* 3. of or referring to the ordinary life and rights of citizens,

esp. as distinguished from military or religious matters: *In our country the civil government is more powerful than the army.* 4. polite or courteous: *a civil manner of speaking.*

ci·vil·ian (si vil′yən), *n.* 1. a person who is not in any of the armed services: *Civilians are not permitted to enter this part of the camp.* —*adj.* 2. of or concerning civilians; nonmilitary: *civilian clothes.*

ci·vil·i·ty (si vil′i tē), *n., pl.* for def. 2 **ci·vil·i·ties.** 1. politeness or courtesy: *He always treats strangers with civility.* 2. a polite act or speech: *After a round of civilities the ambassador was escorted in to dinner.*

civ·i·li·za·tion (siv′ə li zā′shən), *n.* 1. an advanced stage of human society and culture in which there is a well-developed knowledge of agriculture, writing, architecture, government, and trade. Modern civilization also includes very large cities, heavy industry, and many achievements in science. 2. civilized peoples and nations: *Civilization has brought modern medicine into all parts of the world.* 3. a particular advanced culture or society: *ancient Roman civilization.* 4. the act of civilizing, or the process of becoming civilized: *The civilization of the mountain tribes will still take many years.*

civ·i·lize (siv′ə līz′), *v.*, **civ·i·lized, civ·i·liz·ing.** to bring civilization to; teach a more advanced way of life to: *The Romans civilized many peoples.*

civ′il lib′erties, those liberties to which a citizen is legally entitled and guaranteed.

civ′il rights′, *(often caps.)* the rights of citizens to personal liberty, esp. the rights established in the 13th and 14th Amendments to the U.S. Constitution.

civ′il serv′ice, those branches of government work or service that are not a part of the military, legislative, or judicial systems: *Mail carriers work in the civil service.*

civ′il war′, a war between regions or political groups within the same country.

Civ′il War′, the war between the North and South in the United States 1861–1865.

ck., check.

Cl, *Chem.* the symbol for **chlorine.**

cl, centiliter; centiliters.

cl., 1. carload. 2. claim. 3. class. 4. classification. 5. clause. 6. clearance. 7. clerk. 8. cloth.

clack (klak), *v.* 1. to make a quick, sharp sound or a number of such sounds: *The typewriter clacked busily in the next room.* 2. to cause to make a quick, sharp sound: *to clack a cup against a saucer.* —*n.* 3. a quick, sharp sound; clacking sound.

clad (klad), *v.* a past tense and past participle of **clothe.**

claim (klām), *v.* 1. to say or maintain as a fact; declare to be true: *He claimed that he saw a bear.* 2. to demand or ask as one's right: *She went home to claim her inheritance.* 3. to collect or pick up (something) that belongs to one: *to claim luggage at the airport.* —*n.* 4. a statement or assertion: *His claim is that he was home all evening.* 5. a demand for something as one's right or due: *The doctor's patients made claims on his time.* 6. a right to claim or demand: *a claim to* *the throne.* **7.** something that is claimed, esp. land for mining: *The old prospector finally got a rich claim.* **8. claim to,** to make the claim or assertion that: *I don't claim to be an expert.* —**claim′a·ble,** *adj.*

claim·ant (klā′mənt), *n.* a person who makes a claim: *There were two claimants for the lost wallet.*

clair·voy·ant (klâr voi′ənt), *adj.* **1.** having the supposed power of seeing objects or events that one could not see by natural means: *Ever since he forecast the flood, they say he is clairvoyant.* —*n.* **2.** a person who is supposed to have such a power. —**clair·voy′ance,** *n.*

clam (klam), *n.* **1.** a shellfish having a soft body and a hinged, two-part shell. Its flesh is used for food. —*v.,* **clammed, clam·ming. 2.** to gather or dig for clams: *Let's go clamming.*

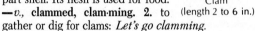

Clam
(length 2 to 6 in.)

clam·bake (klam′bāk′), *n.* a seashore picnic at which clams and often other foods are baked, usually on hot stones under seaweed.

clam·ber (klam′bər, klam′ər), *v.* to climb, using both feet and hands, usually with difficulty: *to clamber up a steep cliff.*

clam·my (klam′ē), *adj.,* **clam·mi·er, clam·mi·est.** cold and damp: *clammy hands.* —**clam′mi·ness,** *n.*

clam·or (klam′ər), *n.* **1.** a loud, continuous noise; uproar: *the clamor of traffic.* **2.** a public outcry; popular demand: *a clamor for lower taxes.* —*v.* **3.** to make a clamor; raise an outcry (often fol. by *for*): *The audience clamored for the show to begin.*

clam·or·ous (klam′ər əs), *adj.* noisy or loudly demanding: *Clamorous shouts of protest broke up the meeting.* —**clam′or·ous·ly,** *adv.*

clamp (klamp), *n.* **1.** a device for holding or squeezing, esp. one for holding parts in position that are being glued together. —*v.* **2.** to hold with or in a clamp: *to clamp two pieces of wood together.*

clan (klan), *n.* **1.** a group of families all claiming descent from the same ancestor. In the Scottish

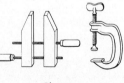

Clamps

Highlands the clan chiefs used to be powerful warriors and leaders. **2.** any group of people united by some common interest: *a clan of dog fanciers.*

clan·des·tine (klan des′tin), *adj.* secret or concealed, and usually involving danger and deception: *a clandestine plot to overthrow the government.* —**clan·des′tine·ly,** *adv.*

clang (klang), *v.* **1.** to give out a loud, resounding sound like that of a large bell or two pieces of metal striking together: *The fire engine clanged noisily.* **2.** to cause to make a loud, resounding noise: *to clang sword against shield.* —*n.* **3.** a clanging sound: *There was a clang when the pail hit the floor.*

clank (klangk), *n.* **1.** a sharp, hard, flat sound like that made by pieces of heavy metal rattling against

each other: *the clank of chains.* —*v.* **2.** to make or cause to make such a sound: *The boy clanked his wagon down the steps.*

clan·nish (klan′ish), *adj.* **1.** friendly only with people in one's own group: *Rich people are usually very clannish.* **2.** of or referring to clans: *clannish customs.* —**clan′nish·ly,** *adv.* —**clan′nish·ness,** *n.*

clans·man (klanz′mən), *n.,* *pl.* **clans·men.** a member of a clan.

clap (klap), *v.,* **clapped, clap·ping. 1.** to hit the palms of (one's hands) together, making a short, sharp sound, often as a sign of pleasure: *The audience clapped loudly.* **2.** to hit with a quick, light slap of the hand: *He clapped his friend on the back.* **3.** to hit or make a sharp, sudden sound: *The loose shutter clapped against the side of the house.* **4.** to put or place quickly or forcefully: *They clapped him into jail.* —*n.* **5.** a slap: *a clap on the back.* **6.** a short, sharp clapping sound: *She closed the book with a clap.* **7.** a loud, sudden noise: *a clap of thunder.*

clap·board (klab′ərd, klap′bôrd′), *n.* **1.** a long, thin board, thinner on one edge than the other, used for covering the outside of buildings. The boards are set horizontally one over another, with the thick edge of each board overlapping the thin edge of the one below it. —*adj.* **2.** of or built with such boards: *a clapboard house.*

clap·per (klap′ər), *n.* **1.** the part of a bell that strikes the rim from the inside, causing the bell to ring. **2.** a person or thing that claps.

clar·et (klar′it), *n.* **1.** a type of red wine. **2.** a deep purplish red.

clar·i·fy (klar′ə fī′), *v.,* **clar·i·fied, clar·i·fy·ing. 1.** to make (an idea, statement, etc.) clear or easily understandable: *Can you clarify that statement?* **2.** to make (a substance) clear or pure; remove impurities from: *to clarify butter.* **3.** to become clear or easily understandable: *The political situation will probably clarify in time.* **4.** to become clear or pure. —**clar′i·fi·ca′tion,** *n.*

clar·i·net (klar′ə net′), *n.* a musical instrument of the woodwind family having a single reed and a cylindrical bore.

clar·i·on (klar′ē ən), *adj.* **1.** shrill and clear: *The clarion call of the bugle roused the soldiers.* —*n.* **2.** an obsolete trumpet with a high, clear, and penetrating sound. **3.** the sound of this trumpet, or a sound that closely resembles it.

Clarinet

clar·i·ty (klar′i tē), *n.* **1.** the quality of being clear or understandable; clearness: *He stated his plan with clarity.* **2.** the quality of being clear or transparent to the eye; clearness: *the clarity of pure water.*

Clark (klärk), *n.* **William,** 1770–1838, U.S. soldier and explorer: made expedition with Meriwether Lewis 1804–1806.

clash (klash), *v.* **1.** to make a loud, harsh noise: *The cymbals clashed.* **2.** to disagree or conflict: *His ideas clash with mine. Those colors clash.* **3.** to engage in a rough or violent conflict or contest: *The German armies clashed with the French near the border.* —*n.* **4.** a loud, harsh noise: *a clash of pots and pans.* **5.** a conflict or disagreement: *a clash of ideas.* **6.** a battle or contest: *a clash between troops.*

clasp (klasp), *n.* **1.** a device, usually of metal, for fastening together two or more things or parts of the same thing; clip: *a clasp on a necklace.* **2.** a firm grip or embrace: *They parted with a clasp of hands. She held the baby in a loving clasp.* —*v.* **3.** to fasten with a clasp. **4.** to hold or embrace: *to clasp a baby.*

class (klas), *n.* **1.** a group of persons or things of the same kind or having something in common: *the class of precious metals.* **2.** any division of persons or things according to rank or grade: *a second-class hotel.* **3.** a number of students following the same studies or graduating in the same year: *the class of '60.* **4.** a period during which students meet for instruction: *a morning class.* **5.** a division of society by wealth, education, occupation, etc. **6.** a major subdivision of the plant or animal kingdom, such as the mosses or the mammals. —*v.* **7.** to place in a class; classify: *I class that statement as a plain lie.*

class., **1.** classic. **2.** classical. **3.** classification. **4.** classified.

clas·sic (klas'ik), *adj.* **1.** of the highest rank or class; serving as a standard or model: *a classic work on European history.* **2.** of or referring to ancient Greece and Rome, esp. their art or literature: *the classic style of architecture.* **3.** following or based on a traditional or widely accepted standard, style, method, etc.: *the classic positions in ballet; a classic example of early American furniture.* —*n.* **4.** a book or other work of art of the highest rank: *He has read all the classics.* **5.** an author of such a work: *Homer is among the classics.* **6.** something that is a first-class example of its kind: *His comedy act is a classic.* **7.** **the classics,** the literature of ancient Greece and Rome.

clas·si·cal (klas'i kəl), *adj.* **1.** of or referring to ancient Greece and Rome: *We are studying the classical period. The museum has a collection of classical sculpture.* **2.** of the highest rank; traditionally held to be outstanding; classic: *classical works of literature.* —**clas'si·cal·ly,** *adv.*

clas·si·cism (klas'i siz'əm), *n.* a style of literature and art that observes traditional standards of taste and emphasizes simplicity, balance, proportion, and the control of emotions. See also **Romanticism.**

clas·si·fi·ca·tion (klas'ə fə kā'shən), *n.* **1.** the act of classifying or placing something in a group or class: *The classification of plants is not always easy.* **2.** the result of classifying: *His classification of American birds is famous.*

clas·si·fied (klas'ə fīd'), *adj.* **1.** arranged or placed in groups or classes. **2.** secret; only available to certain people: *The government document contained classified information.* **3.** containing advertisements

for jobs, apartments, etc.: *I need the classified section of Sunday's paper.*

clas·si·fy (klas'ə fī'), *v.,* **clas·si·fied, clas·si·fy·ing.** to arrange or put in order by classes or groups: *to classify books according to subject.* —**clas'si·fi'a·ble,** *adj.*

class·mate (klas'māt'), *n.* a member of the same class at school or college.

class·room (klas'room', -room'), *n.* a room in a school or college in which classes meet.

clat·ter (klat'ər), *v.* **1.** to make or cause to make a loud, rattling sound, like the sound of two hard objects hitting rapidly together: *The rickety bridge clattered as we drove across it.* **2.** to move with a loud, rattling noise: *The old cart clattered up the street.* —*n.* **3.** a loud, rattling noise; racket.

clause (klôz), *n.* **1.** a grammatical construction that contains a subject and a verb. See also **dependent clause, independent clause, main clause.** **2.** a part of a law, contract, treaty, or the like.

claus·tro·pho·bi·a (klô'strə fō'bē ə), *n.* an unusually strong fear or terror of enclosed, narrow, or crowded places.

clav·i·chord (klav'ə kôrd'), *n.* an early keyboard instrument whose strings are struck by small metal blades.

clav·i·cle (klav'ə kəl), *n.* another term for **collarbone.**

claw (klô), *n.* **1.** a sharp, usually curved nail on an animal's foot. **2.** a foot having such nails, as that on a bird of prey. **3.** a pincerlike organ of a lobster, crab, etc. **4.** something that resembles a claw, such as the curved, divided part of a hammer head, used to pull out nails. —*v.* **5.** to scratch, tear, or pull with or as if with claws: *The kitten clawed my sweater.* **6.** to make by scratching, digging, etc., with claws or hands: *to claw a hole in the ground.*

Claw of a bird

clay (klā), *n.* a kind of earth that is easily shaped when wet, hardens when dry, and can be baked to make bricks and pottery.

Clay (klā), *n.* Henry, 1777–1852, U.S. statesman and orator.

Claw of a lobster

clean (klēn), *adj.* **1.** free from dirt, dust, spots, stains, or the like: *clean clothes.* **2.** free from any fault or defect: *a clean piece of work.* **3.** having the habit of staying free of dirt: *Cats are clean animals.* **4.** upright, honorable, or fair: *a clean life.* **5.** neatly or evenly made or done: *a clean cut with a razor.* **6.** neat or regular; fine; shapely: *clean, handsome features.* **7.** complete or thorough: *to make a clean break with bad habits.* —*adv.* **8.** completely; entirely: *The beavers chewed clean through that tree.* —*v.* **9.** to make clean; remove dirt from: *to clean the windows.* **10.** to do or undergo a process of cleaning: *That dress cleans easily.* **11. clean out, a.** to empty so as to straighten or clean: *to clean out the garage.* **b.**

to use up; exhaust: *I had to clean out my savings to pay that bill.* **12. clean up, a.** to wash or tidy up: *We'll eat as soon as you clean up.* **b.** to finish or complete: *I have a few chores to clean up before dinner.* **c.** to make a large profit: *to clean up in the stock market.* **—clean′ness,** *n.*

clean-cut (klēn′kut′), *adj.* **1.** having a neat, clear, regular shape: *He has a clean-cut face.* **2.** clear or unmistakable: *a clean-cut argument.* **3.** neat and well-behaved: *a clean-cut boy.*

clean·er (klē′nər), *n.* **1.** a person or thing that cleans, such as a powder or liquid for cleaning: *Sprinkle some cleaner over here.* **2.** a person who runs a dry-cleaning business. **3. cleaners,** a place where clothes are dry-cleaned: *Take this suit to the cleaners.*

clean·li·ness (klen′lē nis), *n.* **1.** the state of being clean or neat; cleanness. **2.** the habit of keeping clean and neat: *She's famous for her cleanliness.*

clean·ly (klen′lē), *adj.* **1.** personally neat and clean; clean by habit. **—adv.** (klēn′lē). **2.** in a clean, neat, or thorough manner: *The surgeon worked cleanly.*

cleanse (klenz), *v.,* **cleansed, cleans·ing. 1.** to make clean: *The rain cleansed the gutters.* **2.** to free of something impure, evil, or unwanted: *to cleanse one's soul of anger.*

cleans·er (klen′zər), *n.* **1.** a liquid or powder for cleaning or scouring: *You'll have to use cleanser on that pot.* **2.** any person or thing that cleanses.

clear (klēr), *adj.* **1.** free from darkness or cloudiness; bright; pure: *a clear day; clear colors.* **2.** able to be seen through easily; transparent: *clear water; a clear pane of glass.* **3.** easily heard or seen: *a clear voice; a clear picture.* **4.** easy to understand; plain: *This lesson isn't clear to me yet.* **5.** free from doubt or confusion: *a clear mind; clear thinking.* **6.** having nothing in the way; free of obstructions or obstacles: *a clear view; a clear road.* **7.** complete or absolute: *a clear victory.* **—adv. 8.** in a clear or distinct manner; clearly: *He said it loud and clear.* **9.** entirely or completely: *We ran clear off the road.* **—v. 10.** to become clear: *The weather should clear today.* **11.** to make clear by removing any cloudiness, doubt, barriers, or the like: *to clear a path.* **12.** to remove (people, objects, etc.) (usually fol. by *from*): *to clear people from a room.* **13.** to pass by or over without touching or becoming entangled: *The horse cleared the fence easily.* **14. clear up, a.** to make clear; explain or solve: *to clear up a mystery.* **b.** to return to a normal condition: *It soon cleared up after the rain.* **15. in the clear, a.** free of blame or guilt: *His alibi has put him in the clear.* **b.** out of debt: *We're finally in the clear for the first time since the business started.* **—clear′ly,** *adv.*

clear·ance (klēr′əns), *n.* **1.** the amount of clear, free space between two things, for example between a road and a bridge overhead: *Trucks can't pass here because there isn't enough clearance.* **2.** the act of clearing.

clear-cut (klēr′kut′), *adj.* **1.** having clear, sharp outlines: *a face with clear-cut features.* **2.** obvious or unmistakable; plain: *That is a clear-cut case of treason.*

clear·ing (klēr′ing), *n.* **1.** a piece of land in a forest or wooded area that has no trees or bushes: *Let's have our picnic in this little clearing.* **2.** the act of a person or thing that clears, or the process of being cleared: *The clearing of the trail took a month.*

clear·ness (klēr′nis), *n.* the state of being clear; clarity: *the clearness of water; the clearness of an explanation.*

cleat (klēt), *n.* **1.** one of several small, cone-shaped or rectangular pieces of metal, hard rubber, or the like, attached to the sole of a shoe to keep one from slipping: used esp. in sports. **2.** any small piece of wood or metal used to prevent slipping or provide a support. **3.** a strip of wood, hard rubber, or the

Cleat (def. 4)

like, fixed across a ramp or gangplank to prevent people or things from slipping. **4.** an object of wood or metal, usually shaped like the top of a T, that is fixed to a boat or pier and used to hold ropes securely, for example when tying up a boat to a dock.

cleav·age (klē′vij), *n.* **1.** the act of splitting or cleaving. **2.** the state of being split or cleft; a split: *the cleavage in a rock formation.* **3.** the tendency of such materials as crystals to break in specific directions when struck.

cleave[1] (klēv), *v.,* **cleaved, cleav·ing. 1.** to hold or cling; stick firmly (usually fol. by *to*): *The ivy cleaved to the old wall.* **2.** to remain loyal or faithful (usually fol. by *to*): *to cleave to one's friends.* [from the Old English word *cleofian*]

cleave[2] (klēv), *v.,* **cleaved** *or* **cleft** (kleft) *or* **clove** (klōv); **cleaved** *or* **cleft** *or* **clo·ven** (klō′vən); **cleav·ing. 1.** to split or divide, esp. along a natural line, such as the grain of wood: *He cleaved the log with a sharp ax.* **2.** to make by or as if by cutting: *to cleave a path through the wilderness.* **3.** to cut off; sever: *to cleave a branch from a tree.* **4.** to advance by or as if by cutting (usually fol. by *through*): *The ship cleaved through the water.* [from the Old English word *cleofan*]

cleav·er (klē′vər), *n.* a heavy knife or long-bladed hatchet, used by butchers to cut large pieces of meat.

clef (klef), *n.* a symbol placed on a musical staff that indicates which notes are meant by the lines and spaces. See also **bass clef, treble clef.** [from an Old French word meaning "key"]

A   B

Clefs
A, Treble clef
B, Bass clef

cleft (kleft), *v.* **1.** a past tense and past participle of **cleave**[2]. **—n. 2.** a space or opening made by or as if by cleavage; split or crack: *We climbed down into the cleft in the cliff.* **—adj. 3.** split by or as if by cleavage; divided: *a cleft branch.*

clem·en·cy (klem′ən sē), *n., pl.* for def. 2 **clem·en·cies. 1.** willingness to forgive or treat gently; mercy;

mercifulness: *His sense of justice is softened by clemency.* **2.** an act of mercy or forgiveness: *We were grateful for her many clemencies.* **3.** mildness or pleasantness: *the clemency of the weather in spring.*

Clem·ens (klem′ənz), *n.* **Samuel Lang·horne** (laṅg′-hôrn). See **Twain, Mark.**

clem·ent (klem′ənt), *adj.* **1.** mild or merciful in character; lenient; compassionate: *a clement judge.* **2.** pleasant or mild: *clement weather.*

clench (klench), *v.* **1.** to close (the hands, teeth, etc.) tightly: *He clenched his teeth to hold his temper.* **2.** to grasp firmly; grip: *to clench a sword.* **3.** See **clinch** (defs. 1–3). —*n.* **4.** a tight hold; grip: *She held my arm in a firm clench.* **5.** See **clinch** (defs. 5, 6).

Cle·o·pat·ra (klē′ə pa′trə, klē′ə pā′trə), *n.* 69–30 B.C., queen of Egypt 51–49, 48–30.

cler·gy (klûr′jē), *n., pl.* **cler·gies.** all persons officially given the right to perform religious services; all ordained persons.

cler·gy·man (klûr′jē mən), *n., pl.* **cler·gy·men.** a member of the clergy, such as a priest, minister, or rabbi.

cler·ic (kler′ik), *n.* **1.** a clergyman. —*adj.* **2.** of or referring to the clergy; clerical.

cler·i·cal (kler′i kəl), *adj.* **1.** of or referring to clerks: *They have a large clerical staff.* **2.** of or referring to the sort of office work done by clerks: *a clerical job.* **3.** of, characteristic of, or referring to the clergy or clergymen: *clerical garments.*

clerk (klûrk), *n.* **1.** a person employed in an office to keep records and accounts, take care of correspondence, do typing and filing, etc. **2.** a salesclerk in a store or shop. —*v.* **3.** to act or work as a clerk: *He clerked for five years while he went to school.*

Cleve·land (klēv′lənd), *n.* **1.** (Stephen) Grover, 1837–1908, 22nd and 24th President of the U.S. 1885–1889, 1893–1897. **2.** a port city in NE Ohio, on Lake Erie.

clev·er (klev′ər), *adj.* **1.** mentally bright; smart; quick: *a lively, clever girl.* **2.** showing quickness of mind or cleverness; inventive: *a clever trick; a clever idea.* —**clev′er·ly,** *adv.* —**clev′er·ness,** *n.*

clew (klōō), *n.* **1.** a ball or skein of thread, yarn, or the like. **2.** *British.* See **clue** (def. 1).

cli·ché (klē shā′), *n.* a trite expression or phrase that has been used so often that it has little meaning or effect. Examples of clichés are *as strong as an ox* and *to cry one's eyes out.*

click (klik), *n.* **1.** a quick, sharp sound: *the click of a lock snapping shut.* —*v.* **2.** to make or give such a sound: *The switch clicked on.* **3.** to cause to make such a sound: *She clicked her tongue.*

cli·ent (klī′ənt), *n.* **1.** a person who consults or is helped by a lawyer or other professional person: *He always does his best for his clients.* **2.** a customer.

cli·en·tele (klī′ən tel′), *n.* clients or customers as a group; all the clients of a lawyer or a store: *That shop has a wealthy clientele.*

cliff (klif), *n.* the high, steep front of a rocky mass or hill overlooking a lower area, such as a valley.

cliff′ dwell′er, a member of an Indian people located in Colorado, New Mexico, Arizona, and Utah, from c1100 to c1400, who built houses in caves or under cliff ledges. The cliff dwellers are the ancestors of the Pueblo Indians. —**cliff′ dwell′ing.**

cli·mac·tic (klī mak′tik), *adj.* indicating or approaching a climax: *the climactic scene in a movie.* —**Usage.** See **climatic.**

cli·mate (klī′mit), *n.* **1.** the general weather conditions of a place or region, including temperature, rainfall, sunshine, winds, etc. **2.** a place or region having a particular kind of weather: *to live in a hot climate.* **3.** general opinion or feeling among many people; trend: *a climate of political unrest.*

cli·mat·ic (klī mat′ik), *adj.* of or referring to general weather patterns or climate: *good climatic conditions; climatic studies.* —**cli·mat′i·cal·ly,** *adv.* —**Usage.** The adjectives *climatic* and *climactic* are often confused. *Climatic* refers to climate, the weather, etc.: *sudden and violent climatic changes.* *Climactic* refers to a climax, high point of interest, etc.: *the climactic moment of a story or drama.*

cli·max (klī′maks), *n.* **1.** the highest point of interest or most exciting moment in a series of events; peak: *The climax of his career came when he was elected president.* **2.** a decisive point or moment of highest interest in a story, play, or the like: *The climax comes when the hero is arrested for murder.*

climb (klīm), *v.* **1.** to move to the top of or up, down, or around by using the hands and feet: *The monkey climbed the bars. The boys climbed down from the roof.* **2.** to move upward or toward the top of (something): *The ivy climbed the wall. The airplane climbed steadily.* —*n.* **3.** the act of moving upward; a climbing. **4.** a place to be climbed: *That mountain is quite a climb.* —**climb′er,** *n.*

clime (klīm), *n.* **1.** an area or region of the earth: *They sailed to western climes.* **2.** climate: *a sunny clime.*

clinch (klinch), *v.* **1.** to settle (a matter) so that there is no doubt: *Your second goal clinched the victory.* **2.** to hammer down (the point of a nail or screw) so that it will not work loose from its position: *He drove the nails through the board and clinched the points flat with a hammer.* **3.** to fasten (objects) together with nails or screws that are secured in this way: *to clinch two boards.* **4.** (in boxing) to hold one's opponent around the arms and body. —*n.* **5.** the act of clinching. **6.** the bent part of a clinched nail or screw. Also, **clench** (for defs. 1–3, 5, 6).

cling (kliṅg), *v.,* **clung** (kluṅg), **cling·ing.** **1.** to stick or hold closely: *Mud clings to your shoes. The children clung to each other in the dark.* **2.** to hold fast; be loyal: *to cling to a belief.* —**cling′ing·ly,** *adv.*

clin·ic (klin′ik), *n.* **1.** a place in a medical school, hospital, or the like, where patients come in for treatment, often at a low cost or without charge: *a clinic for eye diseases.* **2.** a group of doctors working together or sharing the same offices, equipment, etc. **3.** any place where people come for special instruction, advice, or help: *a clinic to help people stop smoking.*

clin·i·cal (klin/i kəl), *adj.* **1.** referring to or used in a clinic, infirmary, sickroom, or the like: *a clinical bandage.* **2.** based on or concerned with the actual treatment of patients rather than research or theory. **3.** unemotional or impersonal: *He talked about his problems in a clinical way.* —**clin/i·cal·ly,** *adv.*

clink¹ (klingk), *v.* **1.** to make a light, sharp, ringing sound: *The coins clinked in her purse.* **2.** to cause to make such a sound: *to clink glasses together.* —*n.* **3.** a clinking sound: *the clink of ice cubes in a glass.* [from the Middle English word *clinken*]

clink² (klingk), *n. Slang.* a jail: *They threw him in the clink.* [from *Clink,* the name of a prison in London, perhaps from Dutch *klink* "doorlatch"]

clink·er (kling/kər), *n.* a hardened mass of ash.

Clin·ton (klin/t³n), *n.* George, 1739–1812, 4th Vice President of the U.S. 1805–1812.

clip¹ (klip), *v.,* **clipped; clipped** *or* **clipt; clip·ping. 1.** to cut, cut off, or trim with scissors, shears, or the like: *to clip dead branches from a rosebush; to clip hair.* **2.** to cut off, trim, or cut out something: *to clip a story from the newspaper.* **3.** to cut or trim the hair or fleece of: *to clip a poodle.* **4.** to pronounce in a short, sharp way: *to clip one's words.* **5.** to move swiftly: *The horse clipped along.* **6.** *Informal.* to hit with a quick, sharp blow: *to clip someone on the chin.* —*n.* **7.** a trim or clipping. **8.** something clipped off, esp. the wool from a sheep. **9.** *Informal.* a quick, sharp blow or punch: *a clip on the nose.* **10.** *Informal.* rate of speed or pace: *traveling at a terrific clip.* [from Scandinavian]

clip² (klip), *n.* **1.** a device, usually of metal, that grips and holds tightly, esp. one used to hold things together: *a money clip; a clip for the hair.* **2.** a paper clip. —*v.,* **clipped, clip·ping. 3.** to fasten or hold with a clip: *to clip papers together.* [from the Old English word *clyppan* "to embrace"]

clip·per (klip/ər), *n.* **1.** a person or thing that clips or cuts. **2.** a sailing ship built for speed, esp. a type of

Clipper

three-masted ship built in the U.S. 1845 to 1870. **3. clippers,** a tool for cutting or clipping: *hedge clippers; nail clippers.*

clip·ping (klip/ing), *n.* **1.** the act of a person or thing that clips: *Give the hedge a clipping.* **2.** something that is cut off or out: *hair clippings; a clipping from a magazine.*

clipt (klipt), *v.* a past participle of **clip¹.**

clique (klēk, klik), *n.* a small group of people who are very friendly with each other and usually do not let outsiders join their activities.

cloak (klōk), *n.* **1.** a loose outer garment, such as a cape or a long, full coat. **2.** something that covers or hides; disguise or cover: *The smugglers worked under the cloak of night.* —*v.* **3.** to cover with or as if with a cloak: *She was cloaked in furs.* **4.** to cover or conceal: *a trip cloaked in mystery.*

cloak·room (klōk/rōōm/, -rŏŏm/), *n.* a room in a club, restaurant, or the like, where hats, coats, and packages, etc., may be left temporarily.

clob·ber (klob/ər), *v. Slang.* **1.** to hit or batter severely; strike heavily. **2.** to defeat thoroughly; trounce: *Our team clobbered them.*

clock (klok), *n.* **1.** an instrument for measuring and showing time, esp. by mechanical means, usually having hands that move to show the hour and minute. —*v.* **2.** to time or test by using a clock or watch: *The race horse was clocked at two minutes and thirty-three seconds.* **3. around the clock,** all day and all night: *He has to have a nurse around the clock.*

clock·wise (klok/wiz/), *adj.* in the direction that the hands of a clock move; in a circle to the right: *Tighten the lid by turning it clockwise.*

clock·work (klok/wûrk/), *n.* **1.** the mechanism of a clock or any similar mechanism, esp. one run by a spring. **2. like clockwork,** regularly; without fail: *He stops by here every day like clockwork.*

clod (klod), *n.* **1.** a lump or mass, esp. of earth or clay. **2.** a stupid person; blockhead.

clog (klog), *v.,* **clogged, clog·ging. 1.** to stop up or choke up: *Fallen branches clogged the brook.* **2.** to become stopped or choked up: *The sink clogs easily.* **3.** to crowd or overfill: *Traffic clogged the road.* —*n.* **4.** anything that gets in the way of motion or action. **5.** a shoe with a thick sole of wood or cork.

clois·ter (kloi/stər), *n.* **1.** a monastery, convent, or other place where one may follow a quiet, undisturbed, religious way of life. **2.** any quiet place where one will not be disturbed: *The library is his cloister.* **3.** a covered walk, esp. in a monastery or convent, having an open arcade or colonnade, and often enclosing a courtyard.

Cloister (def. 3)

close (klōz), *v.,* **closed, clos·ing. 1.** to put (a door, window, or the like) in a position to shut off a passage, opening, etc.; shut:

to close a gate. **2.** to shut off or stop up (an entrance, space, gap, or the like): *to close a hole in the wall with plaster.* **3.** to become closed or shut: *The door closed with a bang.* **4.** to block or hinder passage across; shut off approaches to: *to close a border to tourists.* **5.** to bring together; join the parts of; unite (sometimes fol. by *up*): *to close the lips firmly; to close up ranks in a parade.* **6.** to come together: *The tiger's jaws closed with a snap.* **7.** to bring to an end or conclude: *to close a show; to close a sale on a car.* **8.** to shut down or stop temporarily: *He closed the store at night.* **9.** to set (the mind) against: *to close one's mind to reason.* **10.** to draw near; come close: *His pursuers closed rapidly.* —*adj.* (klōs), **clos·er, clos·est. 11.** being near or next to in place or time: *The barn is close to the house.* **12.** having the parts near to one another; dense; tight: *a close formation of battleships; a close weave.* **13.** similar, alike, or near: *Pink is close to red. He is a close relative.* **14.** based on a feeling of love, warmth, or respect: *a close friendship.* **15.** sharing such a feeling; familiar: *close friends.* **16.** very short, neat, or smooth: *a close haircut; a close shave.* **17.** nearly even or equal: *a close contest.* **18.** lacking fresh air; heavy: *a hot, close room; a muggy, close day.* **19.** narrow; cramped: *close quarters.* **20.** thorough or searching; strict: *close questioning.* **21.** held tightly, or closed in: *a close prisoner.* **22.** not inclined to talk; secretive: *a close, mysterious man.* **23.** stingy with money: *a close, miserly woman.* —*adv.* (klōs). **24.** in a close manner; closely: *He cut the lawn close.* **25.** near; close by: *Walk close to your brother.* —*n.* (klōz *for def. 26;* klōs *for def. 27*). **26.** the end or conclusion: *the close of day.* **27.** an enclosed place, esp. one beside a cathedral. **28. close down,** to stop the operation of (a business, trade, etc.) temporarily or permanently: *They closed down the air base after the war. We usually close down about 6 o'clock.* **29. close in,** to approach and surround someone or something: *If the fog closes in, our flight will be canceled.* **30. close out,** to offer (merchandise) for sale at greatly reduced prices: *The store is closing out fur coats.* **31. close up,** to cease business operations; shut down: *In the Depression many small businesses closed up.* —**close·ly** (klōs′lē), *adv.* —**close·ness** (klōs′nis), *n.*

close′ hel′met (klōz), a completely closed helmet of the late 15th century and after.

clos·et (kloz′it), *n.* **1.** a small room or enclosed space for storing clothes, household items, tools, or the like. **2.** a small private room, esp. one used for prayer or study. —*v.,* **clos·et·ed, clos·et·ing. 3.** to shut up in a private room for a conference, interview, or the like (usually used in passive constructions): *The Secretary of State was closeted with the Senator for two hours.*

Close helmet

close-up (klōs′up′), *n.* a picture or camera shot giving a close and detailed view: *The movie opened with a close-up of the hero's face.*

clo·sure (klō′zhər), *n.* **1.** the act of closing, or the state of being closed. **2.** a method of closing debate in Congress or other legislative body so that a vote will be taken immediately. —*v.,* **clo·sured, clo·sur·ing. 3.** to end (debate) by such a method. Also, **clo·ture** (for defs. 2, 3).

clot (klot), *n.* **1.** a lump, esp. of partially coagulated blood. —*v.,* **clot·ted, clot·ting. 2.** to form into a clot: *When you are cut, the blood should clot quickly.* **3.** to cause to form a clot: *Exposure to air clots the blood.*

cloth (klôth), *n., pl.* **cloths** (klôthz, klôths). **1.** fabric made from wool, silk, cotton, or other fiber, and used for clothing, furniture covering, drapery, and the like: *I want this chair covered in cloth, not leather.* **2.** a piece of such a fabric for a particular purpose: *a cloth for polishing silver.* **3. the cloth,** the profession of clergymen; the clergy: *a man of the cloth.*

clothe (klōth), *v.,* **clothed** *or* **clad** (klad); **cloth·ing. 1.** to dress; put clothing on: *I'll bathe the baby and clothe him.* **2.** to provide clothing for: *He needs money to feed and clothe his family.* **3.** to cover with or as if with clothing: *Snow clothed the hills.*

clothes (klōz, klōthz), *n.pl.* coverings for the body; clothing, including pants, dresses, shirts, etc.: *He always wears clean clothes.*

clothes·line (klōz′līn′, klōthz′-), *n.* a strong rope, cord, or the like, on which wet laundry is hung to dry.

clothes′ moth′, any of several small moths whose larvae feed on wool, fur, etc.

clothes·pin (klōz′pin′, klōthz′-), *n.* a small device, such as a forked piece of wood, used to fasten laundry to a clothesline.

Clothes moth
A, Adult;
B, Larva
(length ¾ in.)

cloth·ier (klōth′yər, klōth′ē ər), *n.* **1.** a person who sells clothing, esp. for men. **2.** a person who makes or sells cloth.

cloth·ing (klō′thiñg), *n.* coverings for the body; garments or articles of dress of any kind; clothes: *You need warm clothing for winter.*

clo·ture (klō′chər), *n.* **1.** See **closure** (def. 2). —*v.,* **clo·tured, clo·tur·ing. 2.** See **closure** (def. 3).

cloud (kloud), *n.* **1.** a mass of small drops of water or particles of ice floating in the air. **2.** any similar mass, as of dust or smoke particles. **3.** anything that darkens something or causes gloom, sorrow, etc.: *a cloud of grief.* **4.** something that resembles a cloud, such as a great number of insects or birds flying together: *a cloud of mosquitoes.* —*v.* **5.** to cover with or as if with a cloud: *Smoke from the fire clouded the valley.* **6.** to darken; make sad or troubled: *Fear clouded his mind.* **7.** to make confused or vague: *Say exactly what you mean and don't cloud the issue.* **8.** to grow cloudy; become clouded: *The sky clouded at sunset.* —**cloud′less,** *adj.*

cloud·burst (kloud′bûrst′), *n.* a sudden and very heavy rainfall.

cloud·y (klou′dē), *adj.,* **cloud·i·er, cloud·i·est. 1.** full of or covered by clouds: *a cloudy sky.* **2.** having little or no sunshine: *a cloudy day.* **3.** of or like a cloud:

Cloudy shapes blew across the night sky. **4.** not clear or easily seen through; murky; muddy: *cloudy water.* **5.** not clear or distinct; confused; vague: *a cloudy photograph; cloudy thinking.* **—cloud′i·ness,** *n.*

clout (klout), *n.* **1.** *Informal.* a blow or hit, esp. with the hand; cuff. **2.** *Slang.* a long, hard hit in baseball. **3.** *Archaic.* a patch or piece of cloth. *—v.* **4.** *Informal.* to hit hard, esp. with the hand; cuff.

clove¹ (klōv), *n.* the dried flower bud of a tropical tree used as a spice. [from the French word *clou* "nail." Cloves are so named because of their shape]

clove² (klōv), *n.* one of the small bulbs or sections of a larger bulb of certain plants: *a clove of garlic.* [from the Old English word *clufu* "bulb"]

clove³ (klōv), *v.* a past tense of **cleave².**

clo·ven (klō′vən), *v.* **1.** a past participle of **cleave².** *—adj.* **2.** split or divided; cleft: *the cloven hoof of a goat or cow.*

clo·ver (klō′vər), *n.* a low plant having three-part leaves and rounded white or purple flowers: sometimes grown for hay.

clo·ver·leaf (klō′vər lēf′), *n., pl.* **clo·ver·leaves** (klō′vər lēvz′).** a highway intersection, shaped like a four-leaf clover, in which one highway passes over another and a system of curved, ramplike roads permits cars to enter and leave the highways without crossing the traffic.

Cloverleaf

clown (kloun), *n.* **1.** a person in a circus, show, parade, or the like, who wears odd, funny clothes and make-up, does tricks, and attempts to make people laugh. **2.** any person who tells jokes or plays tricks. *—v.* **3.** to act like a clown. **—clown′ish,** *adj.*

cloy (kloi), *v.* **1.** to tire or wear out by too much food, sweetness, fun, pleasure, etc.: *My appetite was cloyed by too much Christmas candy.* **2.** to become dull or distasteful through excess or overabundance: *A diet of sweets can soon cloy.*

club (klub), *n.* **1.** a heavy stick, usually thicker at one end than the other, that can be used as a weapon. **2.** a stick or bat used to drive a ball, as in golf. **3.** a group of persons who meet from time to time for fun or for a particular purpose: *a social club; an athletic club.* **4.** the building or room where such a group meets. **5.** a design, similar to a clover leaf, on a playing card. **6.** a playing card having such a design on it. **7.** clubs, *(used as sing. or pl.)* the suit in cards having such a design. *—v.,* **clubbed, club·bing. 8.** to beat with or as if with a club: *to club a burglar.* **9.** to combine or join together: *They clubbed their dollars to buy the present.*

club·by (klub′ē), *adj.,* **club·bi·er, club·bi·est.** sociable and warm: *a friendly, clubby man; a room with a clubby atmosphere.* **—club′bi·ness,** *n.*

club·foot (klub′foot′), *n.* a deformed or twisted foot. **—club′foot′ed,** *adj.*

club′ sand′wich, a sandwich made with three pieces of toast and having two layers of sliced meat, tomato, bacon, lettuce, etc.

cluck (kluk), *v.* **1.** to make the sound that a hen makes when sitting on eggs or calling its chicks. **2.** to make a similar sound: *The father clucked over the new baby.* *— n.* **3.** a clucking sound.

clue (kloo), *n.* **1.** any sign, bit of evidence, or hint that can be used in solving a mystery or problem: *Those footprints may be an important clue to the burglar's identity.* **2.** See **clew** (def. 1).

clump (klump), *n.* **1.** a close group or cluster, esp. of trees or other plants; mass: *a clump of violets; a clump of grass.* **2.** a lump or mass: *a clump of dirt.* **3.** a heavy, thumping sound: *He landed with a clump.* *—v.* **4.** to walk with a heavy, thumping step or sound: *She clumped up the stairs.* **5.** to gather or form into a clump, lump, or mass.

clum·sy (klum′zē), *adj.,* **clum·si·er, clum·si·est. 1.** awkward in movement; not graceful or skilled. **2.** awkwardly or carelessly done or made: *That essay you wrote was a clumsy piece of work.* **—clum′si·ly,** *adv.* **—clum′si·ness,** *n.*

clung (klung), *v.* the past tense and past participle of **cling.**

clus·ter (klus′tər), *n.* **1.** a number of things of the same kind growing or held together; bunch: *a cluster of daisies.* **2.** a close group of things or persons: *a cluster of people in the doorway.* *—v.* **3.** to gather or form into a cluster: *The people clustered to watch the fight.*

clutch¹ (kluch), *v.* **1.** to grasp or hold tightly or firmly: *She clutched her baby as she crossed the street.* **2.** to try to seize or grasp (often fol. by *at*): *The cowboy clutched at the runaway horse.* *—n.* **3.** the act of clutching; a grasp or grip. **4.** a mechanism for engaging or disengaging two gears or other rotating parts: *Step on the clutch before you shift gears.* [from the Middle English word *clucchen,* which comes from Old English *clyccan* "to clench"]

clutch² (kluch), *n.* **1.** a number of eggs hatched at one time. **2.** a group of chickens. *—v.* **3.** to hatch (chickens). [from the English dialect word *cletch,* related to a Scandinavian word meaning "to hatch"]

clut·ter (klut′ər), *v.* **1.** to fill or litter with things in a messy way: *He cluttered the room with books and newspapers.* *—n.* **2.** a disorderly heap; litter; mess: *She threw her clothes down in a clutter.* **3.** a state of disorder or confusion.

Cm, *Chem.* the symbol for **curium.**

cm, centimeter; centimeters.

Cmdr., Commander.

cms, centimeters.

CO, Commanding Officer. Also, **C.O.**

Co, *Chem.* the symbol for **cobalt.**

c/o, care of. Also, **c.o.**

Co., **1.** Company. **2.** County. Also, **co.**

co-, a prefix meaning with or together: *cooperate; copilot; codiscoverer.*

coach (kōch), *n.* **1.** a large, horse-drawn, four-wheeled carriage, usually enclosed: *The king and queen rode in a golden coach.* **2.** a public passenger bus or railway car. **3.** an inexpensive type of passenger accommodation on a train, bus, or plane: *Do you want first class or coach on this trip?* **4.** a person who

Coach

trains or instructs athletes: *a baseball coach.* **5.** a tutor or instructor: *a singing coach.* —*v.* **6.** to act as a coach to; give instruction or advice to: *to coach a basketball team.* **7.** to act or work as a coach. **8.** to study or work with a coach: *I'm coaching with the mathematics teacher.*

coach·man (kōch'mən), *n., pl.* **coach·men.** a man employed to drive a horse-drawn coach or carriage.

co·ag·u·late (kō ag'yə lāt'), *v.,* **co·ag·u·lat·ed, co·ag·u·lat·ing. 1.** to change from a liquid to a nearly solid mass: *Blood coagulates in air.* **2.** to cause such a change: *a special drug to coagulate blood.* —**co·ag'u·la'tion,** *n.*

coal (kōl), *n.* **1.** a black mineral formed of buried plants and mined for use as a fuel. **2.** a piece of glowing or burned coal, wood, or other kind of material used as fuel: *Take the coals out of the fireplace.* —*v.* **3.** to provide with coal: *to coal a ship.* **4.** to take in coal for fuel. **5. drag** (or **rake**) **over the coals,** to scold (someone) severely: *He was really dragged over the coals for cheating.*

co·a·lesce (kō'ə les'), *v.,* **co·a·lesced, co·a·lesc·ing.** to grow together or unite to form one thing or mass: *The two lakes coalesced into one. The groups coalesced to form a crowd.* —**co'a·les'cence,** *n.* —**co'a·les'cent,** *adj.*

co·a·li·tion (kō'ə lish'ən), *n.* a union or alliance, esp. a temporary alliance between political parties: *A conservative coalition won the election.*

coal' tar', a thick, black, sticky liquid formed when coal is heated in the absence of air. It is the source of many important chemicals, dyes, and drugs.

coarse (kôrs), *adj.,* **coars·er, coars·est. 1.** having rather large particles or parts: *to cover a path with rough, coarse sand.* **2.** lacking fineness or delicacy; rough; crude; harsh: *The coarse fabric irritated her skin.* **3.** lacking good taste; rough and crude; vulgar: *coarse manners; coarse language.* **4.** of low quality; common; ordinary: *coarse, plain food.* —**coarse'ly,** *adv.* —**coarse'ness,** *n.*

coars·en (kôr'sən), *v.* to make or become coarse, rough, or crude.

coast (kōst), *n.* **1.** land next to or near the sea; seashore: *We have a cabin on the coast, a mile from the ocean.* —*v.* **2.** to move or advance without effort or power: *The car coasted to the bottom of the hill.* **3.** to slide or sled down a snowy or icy slope: *to coast down a hill on a sled.*

coast·al (kōs'təl), *adj.* of or referring to a coast; bordering on or located near a coast: *a coastal town; coastal waters.*

coast·er (kō'stər), *n.* **1.** a person or thing that coasts, such as a sled for coasting. **2.** a small dish or mat, esp. for placing under a glass to protect it from moisture. **3.** a roller coaster.

coast' guard', any organization like the U.S. Coast Guard that patrols the coast, saves lives at sea, etc.

Coast' Guard', a military service in the U.S. that in peacetime enforces laws having to do with ships and shipping, saves lives at sea, and aids navigation. In wartime it usually is placed under the command of the U.S. Navy.

coast·line (kōst'līn'), *n.* the outline of a coast; shoreline: *a jagged coastline.*

coat (kōt), *n.* **1.** an outer garment with sleeves, covering at least the upper half of the body. **2.** the hair, fur, or wool of an animal. **3.** the skin of a fruit. **4.** a layer of anything that covers a surface: *a coat of paint.* —*v.* **5.** to cover with a layer or coating: *He coated the wall with paint.*

co·a·ti (kō ä'tē), *n., pl.* **co·a·tis.** a tropical American animal, related to the raccoon, having a long body, a long, ringed tail, and a slender snout.

coat·ing (kō'tiṅg), *n.* **1.** a layer of any substance spread over a surface; covering: *a coating of wax on the floor.* **2.** fabric for making coats.

coat' of arms', *pl.* **coats of arms.** an emblem in the shape of a shield having designs and pictures. Noble families and certain organizations, such as fraternities, often have their own distinctive coats of arms.

coat' of mail', *pl.* **coats of mail.** a long garment made of links of metal, worn esp. by medieval knights for protection in battle.

Coat of arms

coax (kōks), *v.* **1.** to try to persuade or influence (someone) by the use of gentle words, flattery, encouragement, etc.: *to coax a small boy to try to swim by himself.* **2.** to get or obtain by coaxing: *See if you can coax the secret out of him.*

cob (kob), *n.* **1.** a corncob. **2.** a short-legged, stocky horse.

co·balt (kō'bôlt), *n. Chem.* a metallic element used in magnetic alloys. Some of its compounds are used in blue dyes and paints. *Symbol:* Co

co'balt blue', **1.** a pigment containing cobalt. **2.** a deep blue or a strong greenish blue.

cob·ble¹ (kob'əl), *n.* a cobblestone. [from *cob* + *-le*]

cob·ble² (kob'əl), *v.,* **cob·bled, cob·bling.** to mend (shoes, boots, etc.); patch. [formed from *cobbler,* which comes from Middle English *cobelere*]

cob·bler (kob'lər), *n.* **1.** a person who mends shoes. **2.** a deep-dish fruit pie, usually having a crust only on the top.

cob·ble·stone (kob'əl stōn'), *n.* a naturally rounded stone, formerly used as a rough form of paving for streets.

co·bra (kō′brə), *n.* any of several large poisonous snakes of Asia and Africa that flatten the neck when disturbed, forming a hood. [from the Portuguese word *cobra,* in the phrase *cobra de capello* "snake with a hood"]

Cobra
(length to 6 ft.)

cob·web (kob′web′), *n.* **1.** a web spun by a spider to catch flies and other kinds of prey. **2.** something that resembles a cobweb in being very fine, delicate, or flimsy.

co·caine (kō kān′, kō′kān), *n.* a strong, dangerous drug formerly used as a local anesthetic.

coc·cus (kok′əs), *n., pl.* **coc·ci** (kok′sī). a sphere-shaped bacterium. See also **bacillus** (def. 1).

Co·chise (kō chēs′, kō chēz′), *n.* c1815–1874, a chief of the Apaches.

cock[1] (kok), *n.* **1.** a rooster. **2.** the male of many other kinds of birds. **3.** a valve or faucet that is turned by hand. **4.** the hammer of a firearm. **5.** the position of the hammer of a firearm when it is drawn back in preparation for shooting: *a rifle at half cock.* —*v.* **6.** to draw back the hammer of (a firearm): *to cock a pistol.* [from a Middle English word, which comes from Old English *cocc*]

cock[2] (kok), *v.* **1.** to turn to one side or raise, esp. in a bold, jaunty, or questioning way: *The dog cocked his head when I called his name. The boy cocked his fists at the bully.* —*n.* **2.** the act of doing this: *a cock of the head.* [probably from *cock*[1]]

cock[3] (kok), *n.* **1.** a cone-shaped pile of hay, straw, or the like. —*v.* **2.** to stack (hay, straw, etc.) into such piles. [from a Middle English word, which is related to Norwegian *kok* "lump, heap"]

cock·ade (ko kād′), *n.* a knot of ribbon worn as a badge, often on a hat or as part of a uniform.

Cockatoo
(length 1½ ft.)

cock·a·too (kok′ə tōō′, kok′ə tōō′), *n., pl.* **cock·a·toos.** any of numerous kinds of large parrots having a crest of feathers on top of the head.

cock·a·trice (kok′ə tris), *n.* an imaginary monster in legends or folk tales, having the body of a serpent and the head, legs, and wings of a cock. It was supposed to be able to kill with a single look.

cocked′ hat′, a man's wide-brimmed hat of the 18th century, turned up on three sides toward a peaked crown.

Cocked hat

cock·er·el (kok′ər əl), *n.* a young rooster.

cock′er span′iel (kok′ər), a small dog having a long, silky coat and long ears.

cock-eyed (kok′īd′), *adj.* **1.** cross-eyed or squinting: *a cockeyed look.* **2.** *Slang.* crooked or twisted: *Your hat is cockeyed.* **3.** *Slang.* foolish or absolutely wrong: *a cockeyed idea.*

cock·le (kok′əl), *n.* **1.** a shellfish having a two-part, heart-shaped shell resembling that of the scallop. Its flesh is used for food. **2.** a shell of a cockle; cockleshell. **3.** a wrinkle or pucker: *a cockle in fabric.* **4.** a small, shallow, light boat. —*v.,* **cock·led, cock·ling. 5.** to wrinkle or ripple: *Dampness cockled the pages of the book.* **6. warm the cockles of one's heart,** to make a person extremely happy, grateful, or the like: *Your kindness warmed the cockles of my heart.*

cock·le·shell (kok′əl shel′), *n.* **1.** a shell of a cockle; shellfish. **2.** a small, light boat; cockle.

cock·ney (kok′nē), *n., pl.* **cock·neys. 1.** a native of the East End district of London. **2.** the form of English spoken by cockneys. —*adj.* **3.** of or referring to cockneys or their speech.

cock·pit (kok′pit′), *n.* **1.** a separate area in an airplane for the pilot and copilot. **2.** an open area in a boat, lower than the deck, for the helmsman and members of the crew or passengers. **3.** a pit or enclosed place where gamecocks are set to fighting.

cock·roach (kok′rōch′), *n.* any of numerous common insects having a flattened body, several of which are household pests.

cocks·comb (koks′kōm′), *n.* **1.** the comb of a rooster. **2.** a cap resembling a rooster's comb, formerly worn by jesters. **3.** any of several plants that bear red or purple flowers shaped somewhat like a rooster's comb. **4.** another spelling of **coxcomb.**

Cockroach
(length ½ in.)

cock·sure (kok′shoor′), *adj.* **1.** perfectly sure or certain: *He is cocksure he can win.* **2.** too sure; overconfident: *a reckless, cocksure attitude.*

cock·tail (kok′tāl′), *n.* **1.** a chilled drink made of liquor and juice or other flavorings. **2.** an appetizer of juice, fruit, or seafood: *a shrimp cocktail.*

cock·y (kok′ē), *adj.,* **cock·i·er, cock·i·est. 1.** bold or high-spirited; scrappy: *a cocky little terrier.* **2.** conceited or fresh: *a rude, cocky boy.* —**cock′i·ness,** *n.*

co·co (kō′kō), *n., pl.* **co·cos.** another name for the **coconut palm.**

co·coa (kō′kō), *n.* **1.** the ground, powdered seeds of the cacao plant. **2.** a sweet, chocolate drink made from this powder.

co·co·nut (kō′kə nut′), *n.* **1.** the large, hard-shelled seed of the coconut palm, which is lined with sweet, white meat and filled with a sweet liquid (**co′conut milk′**). **2.** the meat of the coconut, often shredded for use in pies, cakes, and the like.

Coconut
A, Coconut husk; B, Half-open husk; C, Fruit

act, āble, dâre, ärt; ebb, ēqual; if, īce; hot, ōver, ôrder; oil; book; ōoze; out; up, ûrge; ə = a as in *alone;* ə as in *button* (but′ə n), *fire* (fī r); *chief;* shoe; thin; that; zh as in *measure* (mezh′ər). See full key inside cover.

co'conut palm', the tall, tropical palm tree that bears coconuts. Also, **co'co palm'**.

co·coon (kə kōon′), *n.* the silky case that a caterpillar spins around itself, which serves as a covering for the insect while it is in the pupal stage. See illus. at **silkworm.**

cod (kod), *n., pl.* **cods** or **cod.** any of various large food fishes found in the colder waters of the North Atlantic Ocean. Also, **codfish.**

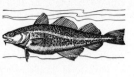
Cod
(length to 6 ft.)

Cod (kod), *n.* **Cape.** See **Cape Cod.**

C.O.D., cash (or collect) on delivery: payment to be made when goods are delivered to the buyer. Also, **c.o.d.**

cod·dle (kod′ᵊl), *v.*, **cod·dled, cod·dling. 1.** to treat tenderly or pamper: *to coddle a sick kitten.* **2.** to cook in simmering water: *to coddle eggs.*

code (kōd), *n.* **1.** a system of signs or signals for sending messages, based on long and short sounds, flashing lights, colored flags, or the like: *Morse code.* **2.** any system for keeping messages brief or secret, in which words, letters, numbers, etc., are given special meanings of their own. **3.** anything written in code. **4.** a collection of laws set forth in an organized arrangement. **5.** any collection or set of rules, regulations, principles, etc.: *a code of behavior.* —*v.*, **cod·ed, cod·ing. 6.** to put (a message) into code.

co·deine (kō′dēn), *n.* a drug obtained from opium and used to relieve pain and to inhibit coughing.

cod·fish (kod′fish′), *n., pl.* **cod·fish·es** or **cod·fish.** another name for **cod.**

codg·er (koj′ər), *n. Informal.* a man who seems odd or has peculiar ways: *He's a lovable old codger.*

cod·i·fy (kod′ə fī′, kō′də fī′), *v.*, **cod·i·fied, cod·i·fy·ing.** to collect and organize (laws, rules, etc.): *to codify the laws of a nation.* —**cod′i·fi·ca′tion,** *n.*

Co·dy (kō′dē), *n.* **William Frederick** *("Buffalo Bill"),* 1846–1917, U.S. Army scout and showman.

co·ed (kō′ed′), *n. Informal.* a female student, esp. at a college or university. Also, **co′-ed′.**

co·ed·u·ca·tion (kō′ej ə kā′shən), *n.* the education of both male and female students in the same classes in a school or college. —**co′ed·u·ca′tion·al,** *adj.* —**co′ed·u·ca′tion·al·ly,** *adv.*

co·erce (kō ûrs′), *v.*, **co·erced, co·erc·ing.** to force (someone) to do something by using threats or violence: *They coerced him into opening the safe.* —**co·er·cion** (kō ûr′shən), *n.* —**co·er′cive,** *adj.*

co·ex·ist (kō′ig zist′), *v.* **1.** to exist together or at the same time: *Many different kinds of animals coexist in this forest.* **2.** to live together peacefully: *They are two nations that have learned to coexist.* —**co′ex·ist′ence,** *n.* —**co′ex·ist′ent,** *adj.*

cof·fee (kô′fē), *n.* **1.** a drink prepared from the seeds (**cof′fee beans′**) of a tropical tree. **2.** a darkish brown. —*adj.* **3.** of a darkish brown.

cof·fee·cake (kô′fē kāk′), *n.* a sweet cake or bread, usually containing nuts and raisins.

cof·fer (kô′fər), *n.* **1.** a box or chest, esp. one for valuables such as gold or jewelry. **2. coffers,** a treasury; money stored away.

cof·fin (kô′fin), *n.* a box or case in which a dead body is placed for burial; casket.

cog (kog), *n.* **1.** a cogwheel or gear. **2.** a tooth on a cogwheel or gear.

co·gent (kō′jənt), *adj.* convincing because of being clear and forceful: *a cogent argument.* —**co′gen·cy,** *n.* —**co′gent·ly,** *adv.*

cog·i·tate (koj′i tāt′), *v.*, **cog·i·tat·ed, cog·i·tat·ing. 1.** to think hard; ponder; meditate. **2.** to think about; consider: *to cogitate a problem.* —**cog′i·ta′tion,** *n.*

co·gnac (kōn′yak, kon′yak), *n.* *(often cap.)* a kind of brandy made in France.

cog·nate (kog′nāt), *adj.* **1.** related by birth or by being of the same kind or quality: *cognate families; cognate ideas.* **2.** related by descent from the same source, as words or languages: *English and German are cognate languages.* —*n.* **3.** a cognate word: *English "cold" is a cognate of German "kalt."* **4.** any person or thing related to another.

cog·ni·zance (kog′ni zəns), *n.* **1.** notice or recognition: *The guests took no cognizance of her rudeness.* **2.** knowledge, or the extent of one's knowledge.

cog·ni·zant (kog′ni zənt), *adj.* having knowledge; aware (usually fol. by *of*): *I am cognizant of that fact.*

cog·wheel (kog′hwēl′, -wēl′), *n.* a toothed wheel that drives or is driven by one or more similar wheels; gear.

co·here (kō hēr′), *v.*, **co·hered, co·her·ing. 1.** to stick together; be united into one mass or group: *Magnetized iron filings cohere.* **2.** to be naturally or logically connected or in agreement: *The facts in your story don't cohere.* —**co·her′ence,** *n.*

Cogwheels

co·her·ent (kō hēr′ənt), *adj.* **1.** logical or consistent; having the parts connected or in harmony: *The detective wrote a coherent report of the crime.* **2.** cohering or sticking together: *a coherent mass of sticky candies.* —**co·her′ent·ly,** *adv.*

co·he·sion (kō hē′zhən), *n.* a sticking together or cohering. —**co·he·sive** (kō hē′siv), *adj.* —**co·he′sive·ly,** *adv.* —**co·he′sive·ness,** *n.*

co·hort (kō′hôrt), *n.* **1.** a friend, companion, or accomplice: *He hangs out at the drugstore with his cohorts.* **2.** a group, esp. a group of warriors. **3.** one of the 10 divisions of an ancient Roman legion, numbering 300 to 600 men.

coif (koif *for def. 1;* kwäf *for def. 2*), *n.* **1.** a hoodlike cap worn by men or women, esp. the white head covering worn by a nun. **2.** *Informal.* See **coiffure** (def. 1). —*v.* (koif *for def. 3;* kwäf *for def. 4*). **3.** to cover (the head or hair) with a coif or similar head covering. **4.** to comb and arrange (hair).

coif·fure (kwä fyŏor′), *n.* **1.** a style of arranging the hair, esp. a lady's hair. —*v.*, **coif·fured, coif·fur·ing. 2.** to style and arrange (the hair).

coil (koil), *v.* **1.** to wind into a spiral or series of circles, one next to the other: *to coil wire around a pencil.* **2.** to gather rope, wire, etc., into loops: *She coiled the clothesline and hung it on a hook.* **3.** to form spirals or circles: *The snake coiled, ready to strike.* **4.** to move in a winding course; wind. —*n.* **5.** a spiral of wire, tubing, or the like: *an electric heating coil.* **6.** a single ring of such a spiral: *a coil in the rope.* **7.** a conductor wound in a spiral or other form for use in electric and electronic circuits.

coin (koin), *n.* **1.** a piece of metal stamped by the government for use as money: *a gold coin.* **2.** this kind of money, esp. as distinguished from paper money: *Please don't pay in coin.* —*v.* **3.** to make (metal money): *to coin pennies.* **4.** to make (metal) into money. **5.** to invent, make, or create: *to coin a new word.*

coin·age (koi′nij), *n.* **1.** the act or right of making coins. **2.** coins as a group; kinds of coin: *The coinage of England is different from that of the U.S.* **3.** anything that is invented or made; invention: *That word is his own coinage.*

co·in·cide (kō′in sīd′), *v.*, **co·in·cid·ed, co·in·cid·ing. 1.** to occupy or come to occupy the same place or point in space: *The two lines in an x coincide at the point where they cross.* **2.** to occupy the same point or period in time: *Our vacations coincide this year.* **3.** to agree or correspond exactly: *They never argue because their views coincide.*

co·in·ci·dence (kō in′si dəns), *n.* **1.** a chance occurrence of events that seems remarkable or unusually lucky: *It was just a coincidence that we arrived at the same time.* **2.** a coinciding of things in the same place in space or in the same period of time: *the coincidence of two holidays.* —**co·in·ci·den·tal** (kō in′si den′t³l), *adj.* —**co·in′ci·den′tal·ly,** *adv.*

coke (kōk), *n.* a solid fuel made by heating coal in the absence of air.

Col., **1.** Colonel. **2.** Colorado.

col., **1.** collected. **2.** collector. **3.** college. **4.** colonial. **5.** colony. **6.** color. **7.** colored. **8.** column.

col·an·der (kul′ən dər, kol′ən dər), *n.* a metal or plastic bowl-shaped container with holes in the bottom and sides for draining or straining food.

cold (kōld), *adj.* **1.** having little or no warmth; having a low temperature, esp. one that is very much lower than body temperature: *cold water; a cold day.* **2.** feeling an uncomfortable lack of warmth; chilled. **3.** lacking in feeling; unfriendly; distant: *a cold person; a cold greeting.* **4.** not new; faint or faded, esp. from the passing of time: *The dogs couldn't follow the cold scent.* **5.** *Informal.* unconscious; in a faint. —*n.* **6.** a lack of warmth or heat. **7.** a sickness marked by coughing, sneezing, a sore throat, etc. **8. catch cold,** to get or suffer from a cold: *Wear your hat and you won't catch cold.* —**cold′ly,** *adv.* —**cold′ness,** *n.*

cold-blood·ed (kōld′blud′id), *adj.* **1.** referring to animals, such as reptiles and amphibians, whose body temperature varies with the temperature of their surroundings. See also **warm-blooded** (def. 1). **2.** with-

out feeling or sympathy; cruel: *a cold-blooded murder.* —**cold′blood′ed·ly,** *adv.* —**cold′blood′ed·ness,** *n.*

cold′ chis′el, a steel chisel used on cold metal. See illus. at **chisel.**

cold′ cream′, a thick, oily lotion used to soften and clean the skin.

cold′ war′, economic and political rivalry between nations that stops short of military conflict.

cole·slaw (kōl′slô′), *n.* a salad of finely sliced or chopped raw cabbage. [from the Dutch word *kool-sla,* which comes from *kool* "cabbage" + *sla,* short for *salade* "salad"]

Col·fax (kol′faks), *n.* Schuyler, 1823–1885, 17th Vice President of the U.S. 1869–1873.

col·ic (kol′ik), *n.* acute pain in the abdomen or bowels. —**col·ick·y** (kol′ə kē), *adj.*

col·i·se·um (kol′i sē′əm), *n.* a stadium, large theater, or large building for sports events, exhibitions, public meetings, etc.

coll., **1.** collect. **2.** collection. **3.** collective. **4.** collector. **5.** college. **6.** collegiate. **7.** colloquial.

collab., **1.** collaboration. **2.** collaborator.

col·lab·o·rate (kə lab′ə rāt′), *v.*, **col·lab·o·rat·ed, col·lab·o·rat·ing. 1.** to work with another or others, esp. in composing a written work: *Three authors collaborated on that play.* **2.** to aid the enemy, esp. enemy forces that have occupied one's country. —**col·lab′o·ra′tion,** *n.* —**col·lab′o·ra′tor,** *n.*

col·lapse (kə laps′), *v.*, **col·lapsed, col·laps·ing. 1.** to fall or cave in; crumble suddenly: *The roof collapsed.* **2.** to cause to fall in or fold up: *to collapse an abandoned mine shaft; to collapse a folding table.* **3.** to break down completely; fail: *Despite our efforts the project collapsed.* **4.** to become unconscious or very ill: *She collapsed from tiredness.* —*n.* **5.** a falling in; cave-in: *The collapse of the tunnel trapped three workers.* **6.** a sudden and complete breakdown or failure of health, plans, efforts, etc.

col·laps·i·ble (kə lap′sə bəl), *adj.* capable of folding up or being folded up: *a collapsible chair.*

col·lar (kol′ər), *n.* **1.** the part of a shirt, coat, or other garment that goes around the neck. Often the fabric is folded over to form the collar. **2.** anything worn around the neck: *a collar of flowers.* **3.** a band of leather or metal for fastening around the neck of an animal: *a dog collar.* **4.** a band of material for wearing around the neck; neckband. **5.** a ring on a shaft, esp. one for holding or positioning the shaft or a part mounted on it. —*v.* **6.** to put a collar on: *to collar a dog.* **7.** to grab or hold by the collar or neck. **8.** to stop and hold (a person) in conversation: *The reporters collared the mayor after the meeting.*

col·lar·bone (kol′ər bōn′), *n.* a bone that runs horizontally from the breastbone to the shoulder blade.

col·lat·er·al (kə lat′ər əl), *adj.* **1.** additional, extra, or auxiliary: *He was awarded a scholarship and collateral aid.* **2.** being placed to the side: *a collateral wing of a house.* **3.** being or running side by side;

parallel: *collateral mountain ranges.* **4.** aside from the main subject, primary goal, etc.; secondary: *a collateral point in an argument.* **5.** descended from the same family but in a different line: *A cousin is a collateral relative.* —*n.* **6.** security for a loan, such as jewelry, stocks, etc. —**col·lat′er·al·ly,** *adv.*

col·league (kol′ēg), *n.* a co-worker or associate.

col·lect (kə lekt′), *v.* **1.** to gather together; assemble: *The teacher collected the students' papers. A crowd collected on the street.* **2.** to accumulate or pile up: *Leaves collect in the yard in autumn.* **3.** to make a collection of; bring together many examples of: *to collect old coins.* **4.** to pick up; call for: *to collect a package.* **5.** to receive payment: *to collect on a bill.* **6.** to get control of (oneself, one's thoughts, feelings, etc.): *Calm down and try to collect yourself!* —*adj., adv.* **7.** having to be paid by the receiver: *a collect telephone call; a telegram sent collect.* —**col·lect′i·ble, col·lect′a·ble,** *adj.* —**col·lec′tor,** *n.*

col·lect·ed (kə lek′tid), *adj.* **1.** in control of oneself; calm: *He remained collected while saving his neighbors from the flood.* **2.** brought together in one place: *the collected works of Shakespeare.*

col·lec·tion (kə lek′shən), *n.* **1.** the act of collecting or gathering together. **2.** something that is collected or gathered into one place: *a collection of stamps.* **3.** a sum of money collected, esp. for charity or a church: *I put a dollar in the collection.*

col·lec·tive (kə lek′tiv), *adj.* **1.** combined; forming a whole: *collective profits.* **2.** of or characteristic of a group of people considered as a whole: *collective action in a strike.* **3.** (of a word or phrase) singular in form but referring to a group, such as *herd, jury,* or *company.* —*n.* **4.** a collective word or phrase. **5.** a collective farm. —**col·lec′tive·ly,** *adv.*

collec′tive farm′, a large farm worked by an entire community of people under the supervision of the state, esp. in the U.S.S.R.

collec′tive noun′, a noun that is singular in form but refers to a group. A collective noun may take a singular or plural verb, depending upon whether it stands for a group as a unit, as in *My family lives in the city,* or the members of the group as individuals, as in *My family are all away.*

col·leen (kol′ēn, ko lēn′), *n.* a young Irish girl.

col·lege (kol′ij), *n.* **1.** a school for higher learning, esp. one that gives a general education rather than technical or professional training in a particular subject. **2.** a school for a particular field of study, often a part of a university: *an agricultural college; a business college.* **3.** all the persons attending, teaching, or working in a college: *The entire college turned out for the football game.* **4.** any organized group of persons having certain powers, rights, and duties: *the electoral college.*

col·le·giate (kə lē′jit), *adj.* **1.** of or referring to a college: *collegiate life.* **2.** of, typical of, or intended for college students: *collegiate clothes.*

col·lide (kə līd′), *v.,* **col·lid·ed, col·lid·ing. 1.** to hit or run into one another suddenly and with great impact; crash: *Two cars collided at the corner.* **2.** to

clash, conflict, or disagree: *Our views often collide.*

col·lie (kol′ē), *n.* a large dog having a long black, tan, and white coat, raised originally in Scotland for herding sheep.

col·li·sion (kə lizh′ən), *n.* **1.** the act of colliding; a crash: *a collision of speedboats.* **2.** a clash or conflict: *a collision of troops; a collision of ideas.*

Collie
(2 ft. high
at shoulder)

col·lo·qui·al (kə lō′kwē əl), *adj.* used in or typical of ordinary conversation rather than formal speech or writing. The expression *He hasn't got any* is colloquial, whereas *He has none* is formal. —**col·lo′qui·al·ly,** *adv.*

col·lo·qui·al·ism (kə lō′kwē ə liz′əm), *n.* a word or expression used in ordinary, informal conversation but not correct in formal speech or writing.

col·lu·sion (kə lōō′zhən), *n.* a secret agreement for purposes of treachery or fraud; conspiracy.

Colo., Colorado. Also, **Col.**

co·logne (kə lōn′), *n.* a light perfume.

Co·lom·bi·a (kə lum′bē ə), *n.* a republic in NW South America. 439,828 sq. mi. *Cap.:* Bogotá. —**Co·lom′bi·an,** *n., adj.*

co·lon[1] (kō′lən), *n.* a punctuation sign (:) used as a division of a sentence, indicating that what follows is a further explanation, an example, a list of items, etc. It is also used to separate numbers: *There were four kinds of fruit: apples, pears, grapes, and oranges. The time is 5:10.* [from a Greek word meaning "limb, clause"]

co·lon[2] (kō′lən), *n.* the principal part of the large intestine. See illus. at **intestine.** [from Greek]

colo·nel (kûr′nəl), *n.* an officer in the U.S. Army, ranking above a lieutenant colonel and below a brigadier general.

co·lo·ni·al (kə lō′nē əl), *adj.* **1.** of or referring to a colony or colonies: *colonial government.* **2.** referring to the 13 British colonies that became the United States of America: *a book on colonial history.* **3.** *(usually cap.)* noting a style of architecture and furniture of the British colonies in America in the 17th and 18th centuries: *a Colonial house.* —*n.* **4.** a person who lives in a colony.

col·o·nist (kol′ə nist), *n.* a person who lives in a colony, esp. a settler.

col·o·nize (kol′ə nīz′), *v.,* **col·o·nized, col·o·niz·ing. 1.** to create or found a colony or colonies in: *to colonize the New World.* **2.** to form a colony or colonies: *They went to Australia to colonize.* —**col′o·ni·za′tion,** *n.*

col·on·nade (kol′ə nād′), *n.* a series or row of columns, as at the entrance of a Greek temple.

col·o·ny (kol′ə nē), *n., pl.* **col·o·nies. 1.** a group of settlers in a new land, who live under the general rule of the nation from which they came. **2.** any people or territory separate from but ruled by a nation. **3.** a group of people having similar interests and living near to each other: *an artists' colony.* **4.** a group of animals or plants of the same kind living closely together. **5. the Colonies,** the British colonies that formed the original 13 states of the United States:

New Hampshire, Massachusetts, Rhode Island, Connecticut, New York, New Jersey, Pennsylvania, Delaware, Maryland, Virginia, North Carolina, South Carolina, and Georgia.

col·or (kul′ər), *n.* **1.** the quality of the appearance of something that results from the way it reflects light. Different wavelengths of light show different colors. The basic colors are red, blue, and yellow, and all other colors are a combination of these. **2.** the natural appearance of the skin: *She has good color.* **3.** a reddish complexion, or a blush: *color in the cheeks.* **4.** something used for coloring, such as a pigment, dye, or paint. **5.** general tone or feeling: *It was the color of his remarks that upset me.* —*v.* **6.** to give color to; paint; dye: *to color a table.* **7.** to cause to seem different from reality; give a particular appearance or sound to (something): *Her prejudices color her writing.* **8.** to take on or change color; blush: *She colors easily when we tease her.* **9. the colors,** the nation's flag: *to salute the colors.* **10. call to the colors,** to summon (a person) for service in the armed forces: *He hopes to finish school before being called to the colors.* **11. show one's true colors,** to reveal one's true nature: *He showed his true colors when he let John take the blame.*

Col·o·ra·do (kol′ə rad′ō, kol′ə rä′dō), *n.* **1.** a state in the W United States. 104,247 sq. mi. *Cap.:* Denver. **2.** a river flowing SW from N Colorado through Utah, Arizona, and California: Grand Canyon; Boulder Dam. 1450 mi. long. —**Col′o·rad′an, Col′o·rad′o·an,** *n., adj.*

col·or·a·tion (kul′ə rā′shən), *n.* the appearance of something with regard to color; coloring: *the bright coloration of tropical birds.*

col′or blind′ness, the inability to tell certain colors apart, often red and green. —**col·or-blind** (kul′ər blīnd′), *adj.*

col·ored (kul′ərd), *adj.* **1.** having color. **2.** *(Now Often Offensive)* belonging either partly or entirely to a race other than the white, esp. to the black race. **3.** influenced or prejudiced: *His opinion is colored too much by his unhappy experiences.*

col·or·ful (kul′ər fəl), *adj.* **1.** full of bright color: *a colorful dress.* **2.** very lively and interesting; vivid; picturesque: *a colorful era.* —**col′or·ful·ly,** *adv.*

col·or·ing (kul′ər ing), *n.* **1.** the act or method of applying color. **2.** the appearance of something with regard to color: *healthy coloring.* **3.** a substance used to color something: *food coloring.*

col·or·less (kul′ər lis), *adj.* **1.** without color. **2.** dull in color; pale; pallid: *a colorless complexion.* **3.** dull and uninteresting: *a colorless description.*

co·los·sal (kə los′əl), *adj.* extremely large; huge; vast.

Col·os·se·um (kol′ə sē′əm), *n.* an ancient amphithe-

ater in Rome, begun about A.D. 70.

Co·los·sians (kə losh′ənz), *n. (used as sing.)* a book of the New Testament, written by Paul.

co·los·sus (kə los′əs), *n., pl.* **co·los·sus·es** *or* **co·los·si** (kə los′ī). **1.** any statue of gigantic size. **2.** anything gigantic or very powerful.

Colos′sus of Rhodes′, the legendary bronze statue of Apollo at Rhodes: one of the Seven Wonders of the World.

colt (kōlt), *n.* a young male animal of the horse family, esp. a male horse less than four years old. See also **filly.**

Co·lum·bi·a (kə lum′bē ə), *n.* **1.** a river in SW Canada and NW United States. 1214 mi. long. **2.** the capital city of South Carolina, in the central part.

col·um·bine (kol′əm bīn′), *n.* a plant having bluish-purple flowers with petals ending in spurs.

Co·lum·bus (kə lum′bəs), *n.* **1. Christopher,** 1446?–1506, Italian navigator in Spanish service: discovered America 1492. **2.** the capital city of Ohio, in the central part. **3.** a city in W Georgia.

Colum′bus Day′, October 12, a legal holiday in various states of the U.S. in commemoration of the discovery of America by Columbus in 1492: now officially observed on the second Monday in October.

col·umn (kol′əm), *n.* **1.** a slender, upright support or pillar: *Many ancient buildings have columns.* **2.** anything resembling a column: *a column of smoke; the spinal column.* **3.** a vertical arrangement on a page: *There are two columns on each page.* **4.** a vertical row or list: *Add up this column of numbers.* **5.** a regular article or feature in a newspaper or magazine: *a sports column.* **6.** a long, narrow formation of troops or ships.

Column

col·um·nist (kol′əm nist), *n.* the writer of a newspaper or magazine column.

com-, a prefix meaning with or together: *commingle; compose.*

Com., **1.** Commander. **2.** Commission. **3.** Commissioner. **4.** Commodore.

com., **1.** commerce. **2.** committee. **3.** common.

co·ma (kō′mə), *n.* a state of prolonged unconsciousness due to serious illness.

Co·man·che (kə man′chē), *n., pl.* **Co·man·ches** *or* **Co·man·che.** a member of an Indian tribe that ranged from Wyoming to Texas, now mostly in Oklahoma.

comb (kōm), *n.* **1.** a toothed strip of bone, metal, or plastic, for arranging the hair or holding it in place. **2.** a machine for separating fibers. **3.** the usually red, fleshy growth on the head of a chicken or other fowl. **4.** a honeycomb. —*v.* **5.** to arrange (the hair) with a

---

comb. **6.** to remove with a comb: *to comb burs from the dog's fur.* **7.** to look or search everywhere: *We combed the house for the tickets.*

com·bat (kəm bat′, kom′bat), *v.,* **com·bat·ed** *or* **com·bat·ted; com·bat·ing** *or* **com·bat·ting.** **1.** to fight or oppose strongly: *to combat disease.* —*n.* (kom′bat). **2.** a fight or controversy between two ideals, people, etc. **3.** active fighting between enemy forces.

com·bat·ant (kəm bat′ᵊnt, kom′bə tᵊnt), *n.* **1.** a person or group that fights. —*adj.* **2.** engaged in fighting: *combatant armies.*

com·bat·ive (kəm bat′iv, kom′bə tiv), *adj.* ready or inclined to fight: *a combative spirit.*

com·bi·na·tion (kom′bə nā′shən), *n.* **1.** several things joined together or combined: *a combination of ideas.* **2.** something formed by combining: *A chord is a combination of notes.* **3.** a group of persons or parties joined together for a common purpose; union. **4.** the set or series of letters used in setting the mechanism on locks: *the combination of a safe.* **5.** the act of combining, or the state of being combined.

com·bine (kəm bīn′), *v.,* **com·bined, com·bin·ing.** **1.** to bring or join together; unite; mix: *She combined the ingredients to make the dough.* —*n.* (kom′bīn). **2.** a combination of persons or groups for the advancement of their interests. **3.** a machine for cutting and threshing grain in the field.

com·bus·ti·ble (kəm bus′tə bəl), *adj.* **1.** able to catch fire and burn: *Paper is combustible.* —*n.* **2.** a combustible material. —**com·bus′ti·bil′i·ty,** *n.*

com·bus·tion (kəm bus′chən), *n.* rapid oxidation with the release of light and heat; burning: *the combustion of fuel in an engine.*

come (kum), *v.,* **came** (kām), **come, com·ing.** **1.** to move toward a certain person or place; approach: *Come here!* **2.** to arrive: *The train is coming now.* **3.** to take place; occur; happen: *Christmas comes once a year. The idea just came to me.* **4.** to reach; extend: *The dress comes to her knees.* **5.** to be available or produced: *Toothpaste comes in a tube.* **6.** to be a native, resident, or descendant; originate: *She comes from Ohio.* **7.** to do or manage: *He is coming along well with his project.* **8.** to be or become: *His shoes came untied. Her wish came true.* **9. come about,** to happen; take place: *I heard she was leaving, but how did it come about?* **10. come across,** to meet (someone) by chance: *I came across an old friend last week.* **11. come around, a.** to change an opinion, decision, etc., so as to agree with another person: *He's against the plan, but I think he'll come around.* **b.** to regain consciousness: *That was a nasty fall, but I think she's coming around.* **12. come back, a.** to return to a place: *Come back after class.* **b.** to return to one's memory: *It all comes back to me now.* **c.** to return to a position, esp. of superiority or excellence: *The team came back with three wins in a row.* **13. come down with,** to become afflicted with (an illness): *She suddenly came down with a cold.* **14. come forward,** to offer one's services; volunteer: *When we asked for volunteers, several came forward.* **15. come into,** to get, esp. by inheritance: *When he's*

21 *he will come into a lot of money.* **16. come off, a.** to happen or occur: *When does the meeting come off?* **b.** to be completed; result: *If his speech comes off well he'll go to the state contest.* **17. come out, a.** to become known; be revealed: *It came out that he was the son of a nobleman.* **b.** to end or result: *How did your films come out?* **c.** to make a social debut: *My sister is coming out next spring.* **18. come to, a.** to regain consciousness: *When I came to, I was in the hospital.* **b.** to amount to; total: *That comes to $3.29.* **19. come up,** to be referred to or presented: *The subject comes up often. The question will come up for a vote Wednesday.*

co·me·di·an (kə mē′dē ən), *n.* **1.** an entertainer who amuses an audience by telling jokes, acting out funny situations, etc. **2.** an actor in comedy. Also, *referring to a woman,* **co·me·di·enne** (kə mē′dē en′).

com·e·dy (kom′i dē), *n., pl.* **com·e·dies. 1.** a play, movie, etc., that is humorous or that has a happy or cheerful ending. **2.** any funny or comic incident.

come·ly (kum′lē), *adj.,* **come·li·er, come·li·est. 1.** pleasing in appearance; fair; pretty. **2.** proper or becoming: *comely behavior.* —**come′li·ness,** *n.*

com·et (kom′it), *n.* a heavenly body consisting of a mass of ice and dust particles and a long, misty tail. A comet moves in a path around the sun. [from the Greek word *komētēs* "long-haired"]

com·fort (kum′fərt), *v.* **1.** to cheer up; console; soothe: *to comfort someone who is sad.* —*n.* **2.** the providing of relief or consolation; solace: *He needs comfort at a time like this.* **3.** a person or thing that gives consolation or comfort: *She was a comfort to him when he was sick.* **4.** a state of ease and satisfaction with freedom from pain, displeasure, anxiety, etc.: *a life of comfort.* —**com′fort·ing·ly,** *adv.*

com·fort·a·ble (kumf′tə bəl, kum′fər tə bəl), *adj.* **1.** allowing physical comfort and ease: *a comfortable chair.* **2.** being in a state of physical or mental comfort; contented; at ease: *I'm comfortable in soft chairs. I feel very comfortable at my aunt's house.* —**com′fort·a·bly,** *adv.*

com·fort·er (kum′fər tər), *n.* **1.** a person or thing that comforts. **2.** a long, woolen scarf. **3.** a thick, quilted bedcover.

com·ic (kom′ik), *adj.* **1.** of, referring to, or providing comedy: *a comic situation.* **2.** acting in or writing comedies: *a comic actor.* —*n.* **3.** a comic actor or comedian.

com·i·cal (kom′i kəl), *adj.* producing laughter; amusing; funny. —**com′i·cal·ly,** *adv.*

com′ic book′, a booklet of comic strips.

com′ic strip′, a series of drawings or cartoons that tells a funny or adventurous story.

com·ing (kum′ing), *n.* **1.** arrival or approach: *His coming home was a good idea.* —*adj.* **2.** arriving next or soon; approaching: *The meeting is this coming Friday.*

comm., 1. commander. **2.** commerce. **3.** commission. **4.** committee. Also, **Comm.**

com·ma (kom′ə), *n.* a punctuation sign (,) that is used esp. to show a division or break in a sentence, to separate items in a list, or to mark off thousands in numerals.

com·mand (kə mand′), *v.* **1.** to direct or require with authority; order: *He commanded the men to stand up.* **2.** to have control over; be in charge of: *The captain commands his ship.* **3.** to deserve and receive: *He commands our respect.* **4.** to appear to dominate because of position; overlook: *The hill commands the sea.* —*n.* **5.** an order given by a person in authority. **6.** a group of troops or a station or ship under a commander. **7.** the possession and carrying out of control: *a lieutenant in command of a platoon; to be in command of a situation.* **8.** control or mastery: *He has a good command of German.*

com·man·dant (kom′ən dant′, kom′ən dänt′), *n.* the commanding officer of a place, group, etc.

com·man·deer (kom′ən dēr′), *v.* **1.** to order or force a civilian into fighting or working for a military unit. **2.** to seize (private property) for military or other public use.

com·mand·er (kə man′dər), *n.* **1.** a person who commands. **2.** an officer in command of a military unit. **3.** an officer in the U.S. Navy, ranking below a captain and above a lieutenant commander.

command′er in chief′, 1. Also, **Command′er in Chief′.** the supreme commander of the armed forces of a nation: *In the United States the President is Commander in Chief.* **2.** an officer in command of a particular portion of an armed force.

com·mand·ing (kə man′ding), *adj.* **1.** having the manner or air of authority; imposing: *a commanding voice.* **2.** being in command. **3.** dominating by position or location: *a commanding view of the river.* —**com·mand′ing·ly,** *adv.*

com·mand·ment (kə mand′mənt), *n.* **1.** a command or law. **2.** any of the Ten Commandments.

com·man·do (kə man′dō), *n., pl.* **com·man·dos** *or* **com·man·does. 1.** a specially trained military unit used for surprise raids. **2.** a member of such a unit.

com·mem·o·rate (kə mem′ə rāt′), *v.,* **com·mem·o·rat·ed, com·mem·o·rat·ing. 1.** to serve as a reminder of: *The statue commemorates a Civil War battle.* **2.** to honor by celebrating or observing: *to commemorate an anniversary.* —**com·mem′o·ra′tion,** *n.*

com·mence (kə mens′), *v.,* **com·menced, com·menc·ing.** to begin; start: *The graduation ceremonies will commence at 9 a.m.*

com·mence·ment (kə mens′mənt), *n.* **1.** the act or an instance of commencing; beginning. **2.** the ceremony held at schools, universities, colleges, etc., at the end of the academic year at which degrees and diplomas are given.

com·mend (kə mend′), *v.* **1.** to present or mention as worthy of confidence, notice, kindness, etc.; recommend: *to commend a new book.* **2.** to entrust; give in charge; deliver with confidence: *I commend my child to your care.* **3.** to name or mention with approval; praise: *to commend a soldier for bravery.* —**com·mend′a·ble,** *adj.*

com·men·da·tion (kom′ən dā′shən), *n.* the act of praising or approving; recommendation; recognition.

com·men·su·rate (kə men′sər it, kə men′shər it), *adj.* **1.** having the same measure; of equal extent or duration. **2.** proportionate; adequate: *His wages are commensurate with the amount of work he does.*

com·ment (kom′ent), *n.* **1.** a note or remark that explains or criticizes: *The author added comments in footnotes.* **2.** a remark, observation, or criticism; talk; conversation: *The new play caused much comment.* —*v.* **3.** to make a comment or remark.

com·men·tar·y (kom′ən ter′ē), *n., pl.* **com·men·tar·ies. 1.** a series of comments or explanations. **2.** anything that illustrates a point; comment.

com·men·ta·tor (kom′ən tā′tər), *n.* **1.** a person who makes commentaries. **2.** a person who discusses news, sports, or the like, on radio or television.

com·merce (kom′ərs), *n.* the buying and selling of goods, esp. on a large scale; trade; business.

com·mer·cial (kə mûr′shəl), *adj.* **1.** of, referring to, or engaged in commerce: *commercial problems.* **2.** prepared, done, or acting with emphasis on profit, success, or ability to be sold: *a commercial product.* —*n.* **3.** a radio or television announcement that advertises a product. —**com·mer′cial·ly,** *adv.*

com·mer·cial·ize (kə mûr′shə līz′), *v.,* **com·mer·cial·ized, com·mer·cial·iz·ing.** to make commercial in character or method; emphasize the profitable aspects of: *to commercialize Christmas.*

com·mis·er·ate (kə miz′ə rāt′), *v.,* **com·mis·er·at·ed, com·mis·er·at·ing.** to express sorrow or sympathy; sympathize: *They commiserated with him over the bad news.* —**com·mis′er·a′tion,** *n.*

com·mis·sar (kom′i sär′), *n.* (formerly) the head of a major governmental division in the U.S.S.R.

com·mis·sar·y (kom′i ser′ē), *n., pl.* **com·mis·sar·ies.** a store that sells food and supplies, esp. at a military post.

com·mis·sion (kə mish′ən), *n.* **1.** the act of committing or performing: *the commission of a crime.* **2.** authority granted for a particular action or purpose. **3.** a document that grants such authority. **4.** the position or rank of an officer in any of the armed forces: *He received a commission in the Air Force.* **5.** a group of persons in charge of certain functions: *a commission to study the problems of education.* **6.** a sum or percentage given to an agent or salesman for his services.* —*v.* **7.** to give a commission to: *to commission a graduate of a military academy.* **8.** to give an order for: *to commission a painting.* **9.** to order (a ship) to active duty. **10. out of commission,** not in working order: *The stove is out of commission again.*

com·mis·sion·er (kə mish′ə nər), *n.* **1.** a member of a commission. **2.** an official in charge of a department: *a police commissioner.*

com·mit (kə mit′), *v.,* **com·mit·ted, com·mit·ting. 1.** to do; perform: *to commit a crime.* **2.** to give over for safekeeping or custody: *to commit a juvenile delinquent to a reform school; to commit a poem to mem-*

ory. **3.** to place in a mental institution or hospital: *to commit a patient.* **4.** to pledge or devote (oneself) to a position on an issue or question; promise: *He has committed himself to support the candidate.* —com·mit′ment, *n.*

com·mit·tee (kə mit′ē), *n.* a group of persons elected or appointed to perform certain services or functions: *a committee to study slum conditions.*

com·mode (kə mōd′), *n.* **1.** a low cabinet containing drawers or shelves behind doors. **2.** a stand or cupboard, often containing a washbasin.

com·mo·di·ous (kə mō′dē əs), *adj.* spacious and convenient; roomy: *a commodious apartment.*

Commode

com·mod·i·ty (kə mod′i-tē), *n., pl.* **com·mod·i·ties.** **1.** something of use, advantage, or value. **2.** an article of trade or commerce: *a farm commodity.*

com·mo·dore (kom′ə dôr′), *n.* **1.** an officer in the U.S. Navy, ranking above a captain and below a rear admiral: a rank not used in peacetime. **2.** the senior captain of a line of merchant vessels. **3.** the president or head of a yacht club.

com·mon (kom′ən), *adj.* **1.** belonging equally to or shared by two or more persons or groups: *common property; a common language.* **2.** widespread; general: *common knowledge.* **3.** happening often; usual; familiar: *a common mistake.* **4.** of poor quality: *a common fabric.* **5.** coarse or vulgar: *common manners.* **6.** having no rank, station, or distinction: *a common soldier.* —*n.* **7.** Often, **commons.** a tract of land owned or used jointly by the members of a community. **8. in common,** shared or enjoyed by both alike: *Our mothers have many interests in common.*

com′mon denom′inator, a number for which the denominators of a group of fractions are all divisors: *12 is a common denominator for* $^1/_2$, $^1/_3$, $^1/_4$, *and* $^1/_6$.

com·mon·er (kom′ə nər), *n.* a member of the common people; a person without a title of nobility.

com·mon·ly (kom′ən lē), *adv.* usually or generally; ordinarily: *We commonly agree about clothes.*

Com′mon Mar′ket, **1.** an association established in 1958 by Belgium, France, Italy, Luxembourg, the Netherlands, and West Germany, to lower tariffs and cooperate on other matters of trade. **2.** *(usually l.c.)* such an agreement among any group of nations.

com′mon mul′tiple, a number that is a multiple of each of a group of numbers: *20 is a common multiple of 2, 4, 5, and 10.*

com′mon noun′, a noun used as the name of any of a class of similar things, such as *boy, garden,* or *truck.* See also **proper noun.**

com·mon·place (kom′ən plās′), *adj.* **1.** ordinary or uninteresting; dull. —*n.* **2.** a well-known or obvious comment or remark; an uninteresting saying. **3.** any-

thing that is common, ordinary, or uninteresting.

com′mon sense′, sound practical judgment; normal, basic intelligence.

com·mon·wealth (kom′ən welth′), *n.* **1.** any group of persons united by some common interest. **2.** the people of a nation or state.

Com·mon·wealth (kom′ən welth′), *n.* **1.** a group of states or nations associated by their own choice and linked with common interests: *the British Commonwealth of Nations.* **2.** the official name (rather than "State") of Kentucky, Massachusetts, Pennsylvania, and Virginia.

com·mo·tion (kə mō′shən), *n.* noisy disturbance; agitation, confusion, or excitement.

com·mu·nal (kə myōōn′əl, kom′yə nəl), *adj.* of, by, or belonging to the people of a community: *communal land.*

com·mune[1] (kə myōōn′), *v.,* **com·muned, com·mun·ing.** to talk or communicate intimately. [from the earlier French word *comuner* "to share," which comes from Latin *commūnis* "common"]

com·mune[2] (kə myōōn′), *v.,* **com·muned, com·mun·ing.** to receive communion. [from *communion*]

com·mune[3] (kom′yōōn), *n.* the smallest administrative division in France, Italy, Switzerland, and several other European countries, governed by a mayor. [from a French word, which comes from Latin *commūne* "community," from *commūnis* "common"]

com·mu·ni·ca·ble (kə myōō′nə kə bəl), *adj.* capable of being easily communicated or transmitted: *a communicable disease.*

com·mu·ni·cate (kə myōō′nə kāt′), *v.,* **com·mu·ni·cat·ed, com·mu·ni·cat·ing.** **1.** to make known; impart knowledge of: *to communicate news.* **2.** to give to another; transmit: *to communicate a disease.* **3.** to interchange or give thoughts, information, or the like, by writing, speaking, etc. **4.** to have or form a connecting passage: *The living room communicates with the dining room.* **5.** to receive Holy Communion.

com·mu·ni·ca·tion (kə myōō′nə kā′shən), *n.* **1.** the imparting or interchange of thoughts, opinions, or information by speech, writing, etc.: *communication by mail.* **2.** a document or message giving information. **3.** a passage or means of passage between two places: *communication between rooms.* **4. communications, a.** the means of sending messages, orders, etc., including telephone, telegraph, radio, and couriers. **b.** routes and transportation for moving troops and supplies from a base to an area of operations.

com·mun·ion (kə myōōn′yən), *n.* **1.** an act of participating, sharing, or holding in common: *a communion of thoughts and ideas.* **2.** association or fellowship: *a communion of scholars.* **3.** a period of concentrating on intellectual or spiritual matters: *communion with nature.* **4.** a group of persons having a common religious faith; a religious denomination: *Anglican communion.* **5.** Also, **Holy Communion, Eucharist.** (in Christian churches) **a.** the religious ceremony or sacrament commemorating the Last Supper of Jesus with bread and wine. **b.** the blessed bread and wine used in this ceremony. **c.** the act of taking part in this ceremony. [from a Middle English word, which comes from Latin *commūniō* "a sharing," from *commūnis* "common"]

Com·mun·ism (kom**′**yə niz**′**əm), *n.* **1.** the practices and beliefs of the Communist party. **2.** *(usually l.c.)* a theory or system of social organization based on the holding of all property in common. **3.** a system of social organization in which all economic and social activity is controlled by a totalitarian state dominated by a single political party.

Com·mun·ist (kom**′**yə nist), *n.* **1.** a member of the Communist party. **2.** *(usually l.c.)* a person who believes in communism. *—adj.* **3.** of or referring to Communism or the Communist party. **4.** *(usually l.c.)* of or referring to communism. [from the Latin word *commūnis* "common"] *—com′mu·nis′tic, adj.*

Com′munist Chi′na. See China, People's Republic of.

Com′munist par′ty, a political party advocating Communism.

com·mu·ni·ty (kə myōō**′**ni tē), *n., pl.* **com·mu·ni·ties.** **1.** a social group whose members live in a certain place, share government, and have a common background: *We live in a small community near Boston.* **2.** a group of people sharing common interests: *the business community.* **3.** similar character; agreement; likeness: *community of interest.* **4.** the community, the public; society.

com·mu·ta·tive (kə myōō**′**tə tiv, kom**′**yə tā**′**tiv), *adj.* **1.** of or concerning commutation, exchange, substitution, or interchange. **2.** (in mathematics) having the property that one term operating on a second is equal to the second operating on the first, such as $2+1=1+2$ or $3\times5=5\times3$.

com·mute (kə myōōt**′**), *v.,* **com·mut·ed, com·mut·ing.** **1.** to exchange for another or for something else: *to commute foreign money into dollars.* **2.** to change; transform: *to commute iron into silver.* **3.** to change to something less severe: *to commute a prison sentence.* **4.** to travel regularly over a fairly long distance, usually between home and work: *He commutes daily from New York to Washington.* *—com·mut′er, n.* *—com·mu·ta·tion* (kom**′**yə tā**′**shən), *n.*

comp., **1.** comparative. **2.** compare. **3.** compensation. **4.** compiled. **5.** complimentary. **6.** composition. **7.** compound.

com·pact[1] (kəm pakt**′**; *for def. 3* kom**′**pakt), *adj.* **1.** joined or packed together; arranged within a fairly small space: *compact soil; a compact shopping center.* **2.** designed to be small in size and economical in operation: *a compact car.* **3.** expressed in a few words; brief. *—v.* (kəm pakt**′**). **4.** to join or pack closely together. *—n.* (kom**′**pakt). **5.** a small case containing a mirror, face powder, and a puff. **6.** a compact automobile. [from the Latin word *compactus* "compact, firm," from *compingere* "to join, fasten"]

com·pact[2] (kom**′**pakt), *n.* a formal agreement; contract. [from the Latin word *compactum* "agree-

ment," which comes from *compacisci* "to agree"]

com·pac·tor (kəm pak**′**tər), *n.* an electric appliance for grinding and compressing kitchen refuse.

com·pan·ion (kəm pan**′**yən), *n.* **1.** a person who often associates with another person or other persons; comrade; friend. **2.** a person employed to live with another person as a helpful friend. **3.** a mate or match for something: *There is a companion to that chair.*

com·pan·ion·a·ble (kəm pan**′**yə nə bəl), *adj.* possessing the qualities of a good companion; agreeable.

com·pan·ion·ship (kəm pan**′**yən ship**′**), *n.* association as companions; fellowship.

com·pan·ion·way (kəm pan**′**yən wā**′**), *n.* **1.** a stair or ladder within the hull of a vessel. **2.** the space occupied by this stair or ladder.

com·pa·ny (kum**′**pə nē), *n., pl.* **com·pa·nies.** **1.** a group of people gathered or associated together, esp. for business purposes: *an investment company; a company of actors.* **2.** companionship or fellowship: *They invited two people along for company.* **3.** a guest or guests. **4.** a military unit smaller than a battalion and made up of two or more squads commanded by a captain. **5.** a ship's officers and crew. **6. keep company, a.** to associate with or visit: *Mind if I keep you company while you're waiting?* **b.** to go steady: *Mary and Joe have been keeping company for two years.* **7. part company,** to stop associating or being friends: *We parted company after our argument.*

com·pa·ra·ble (kom**′**pər ə bəl), *adj.* **1.** capable of being compared; similar enough to be compared: *The shop is comparable to a country store.* **2.** worthy of or fit for comparison: *a restaurant comparable to the best in the world.* *—com′pa·ra·bly, adv.*

com·par·a·tive (kəm par**′**ə tiv), *adj.* **1.** of, referring to, or using comparison as a method of study: *comparative literature.* **2.** estimated or judged by comparison; relative: *a comparative newcomer in politics.* **3.** of or referring to the intermediate degree of comparison of adjectives and adverbs. *Better* and *more beautiful* are comparative forms of the adjectives *good* and *beautiful. Sooner* and *more carefully* are comparative forms of the adverbs *soon* and *carefully.* *—n.* **4.** the comparative degree. **5.** a comparative form. *—com·par′a·tive·ly, adv.*

com·pare (kəm pâr**′**), *v.,* **com·pared, com·par·ing.** **1.** to study (two or more things) for the purpose of finding similarities and differences: *to compare two versions of a story.* **2.** to consider or describe as similar; liken: *He compared the mountains to the Swiss Alps.* **3.** to be worthy of or fit for comparison: *His work does not compare to yours.* **4.** (in grammar) to list or recite the positive, comparative, and superlative degrees of (an adjective or adverb). **5. beyond compare,** above any kind of comparison; without an equal: *Bach's music is beyond compare.*

—Usage. Things of the same kind or quality are compared *with* each other: *They compared my jacket with his.* Things of different kinds or quality are

---

act, āble, dâre, ärt; ebb, ēqual; if, īce; hot, ōver, ôrder; oil; bŏŏk; ōōze; out; up, ûrge; ə = *a* as in *alone;* ᵊ as in *button* (but**′**ᵊn), *fire* (fī**ᵊ**r); chief; shoe; thin; ŧħat; zh as in *measure* (mezh**′**ər). See full key inside cover.

compared *to* each other: *We compared the music to a thunderstorm.*

com·par·i·son (kəm par′i sən), *n.* 1. the act of comparing; a likening: *to make a comparison of two movies.* 2. capability of being compared or likened: *There is no comparison between the two books.* 3. the changes in form of adjectives and adverbs to show different degrees of a quality or quantity. *Mild, milder,* and *mildest* are the positive, comparative, and superlative degrees of the adjective *mild.*

com·part·ment (kəm pärt′mənt), *n.* an area or space marked or partitioned off.

com·pass (kum′pəs), *n.* 1. a device for determining direction, such as a pivoted magnetized needle that points north. 2. an instrument for drawing circles, usually consisting of a pair of pivoted arms, one bearing a point and the other holding a pencil or pen. 3. the enclosing line or limits of any area; boundary: *within the compass of 10 square blocks.* 4. space within limits; area; extent; scope: *the broad compass of the ranch.* 5. the total range of tones of a voice or of a musical instrument. —*v.* 6. to go or move around; make the circuit of: *to compass the yard.* 7. to surround or encircle. 8. to achieve or accomplish: *to compass success.* 9. to grasp mentally; understand: *to compass a situation.*

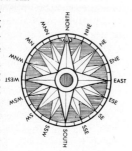

Points of the compass

com·pas·sion (kəm pash′ən), *n.* a feeling of deep sympathy and sorrow for another's suffering or unhappiness, accompanied by a desire to help.

com·pas·sion·ate (kəm pash′ə nit), *adj.* having or showing compassion. —**com·pas′sion·ate·ly,** *adv.*

com·pat·i·ble (kəm pat′ə bəl), *adj.* capable of existing together in harmony: *She and her brother just aren't compatible.* —**com·pat′i·bil′i·ty,** *n.*

com·pa·tri·ot (kəm pā′trē ət), *n.* a native or inhabitant of a person's own country; fellow countryman.

com·pel (kəm pel′), *v.,* **com·pelled, com·pel·ling.** 1. to force or drive: *His poor behavior compelled the teacher to send him out of the room.* 2. to bring about by force: *to compel proper behavior.*

com·pen·sate (kom′pən sāt′), *v.,* **com·pen·sat·ed, com·pen·sat·ing.** 1. to recompense for something; pay: *They gave him $10 to compensate him for his trouble.* 2. to provide an equivalent; make amends; make up (usually fol. by *for*): *His good behavior today does not compensate for his usual rudeness.*

com·pen·sa·tion (kom′pən sā′shən), *n.* 1. something given or received to make up for something else: *The insurance company paid him $2000 as compensation.* 2. pay or salary: *Are you entitled to compensation when you're sick?*

com·pete (kəm pēt′), *v.,* **com·pet·ed, com·pet·ing.** to try to do better than someone else; engage in a contest of any kind: *to compete for a prize.*

com·pe·tence (kom′pi t∂ns), *n.* 1. the quality of being able to do something adequately; ability: *He has competence in French.* 2. enough money to supply the necessities of life and a few of the comforts.

com·pe·ten·cy (kom′pi t∂n sē), *n., pl.* **com·pe·ten·cies.** another form of **competence.**

com·pe·tent (kom′pi t∂nt), *adj.* having enough skill, knowledge, experience, etc., for some purpose; properly qualified: *a competent mechanic.* —**com′pe·tent·ly,** *adv.*

com·pe·ti·tion (kom′pi tish′ən), *n.* 1. the act of competing; struggle or rivalry: *There is very little competition for grades in my class.* 2. a contest for some prize, honor, or advantage.

com·pet·i·tive (kəm pet′i tiv), *adj.* of or referring to competition: *competitive sports.* —**com·pet′i·tive·ly,** *adv.*

com·pet·i·tor (kəm pet′i tər), *n.* a person, team, company, etc., that competes; rival.

com·pile (kəm pīl′), *v.,* **com·piled, com·pil·ing.** 1. to put or gather in one list, book, etc.: *to compile information.* 2. to make (a book) of materials from various sources: *to compile a collection of short stories.*

com·pla·cen·cy (kəm plā′sən sē), *n.* a feeling of quiet pleasure or security, often while unaware of some danger; smugness; self-satisfaction. Also, **com·pla′cence.**

com·pla·cent (kəm plā′sənt), *adj.* pleased with oneself or one's situation; smug; self-satisfied. —**com·pla′cent·ly,** *adv.*

com·plain (kəm plān′), *v.* 1. to find fault; express dissatisfaction: *to complain about poor service.* 2. to make a formal accusation, as in court.

com·plaint (kəm plānt′), *n.* 1. an expression of discontent, pain, etc. 2. a cause of discontent, pain, etc.: *The flu is a common complaint in winter.*

com·plai·sant (kəm plā′sənt, kəm plā′zənt), *adj.* inclined or tending to please; agreeable; obliging. —**com·plai′sant·ly,** *adv.*

com·ple·ment (kom′plə mənt), *n.* 1. something that completes or makes perfect: *A good dessert is a complement to a good meal.* 2. the amount required to complete or fill: *a full complement of men on a ship.* 3. a word or phrase used to complete a grammatical construction, usually in the predicate. In the sentence *The house is large, large* is a predicate adjective complement. In *He is a lawyer, lawyer* is a predicate noun complement. —*v.* (kom′plə ment′). 4. to complete: *The scarf complemented her new Easter outfit.*

—**Usage.** See **compliment.**

com·ple·men·ta·ry (kom′plə men′tə rē), *adj.* forming a complement; completing: *to choose complementary accessories for a new outfit.*

com·plete (kəm plēt′), *adj.* 1. having all its parts; whole; entire: *a complete set of dishes.* 2. finished; concluded; ended: *a complete month.* 3. thorough; entire; absolute: *a complete victory.* —*v.,* **com·plet·ed, com·plet·ing.** 4. to make whole, entire, or perfect: *to complete a puzzle.* 5. to bring to an end; finish. —**com·plete′ly,** *adv.* —**com·plete′ness,** *n.*

com·ple·tion (kəm plē′shən), *n.* **1.** the act of completing or finishing: *The completion of the project will be difficult.* **2.** the state of being completed; finish; end: *the completion of the present school year.*

com·plex (kəm pleks′, kom′pleks), *adj.* **1.** made up of many connected and related parts: *a complex highway system.* **2.** very complicated; difficult to understand: *a complex problem.* —*n.* (kom′pleks). **3.** a complicated association or grouping of related things, parts, units, etc.: *a complex of roads.* **4.** a set of ideas, feelings, prejudices, etc., that affect a person's behavior in ways that he himself may not understand: *He has a complex about small dogs.*

com·plex·ion (kəm plek′shən), *n.* **1.** the natural color and appearance of a person's skin, esp. of the face: *a clear complexion.* **2.** general appearance or character; aspect: *Her sudden departure put a different complexion on the situation.*

com·plex·i·ty (kəm plek′si tē), *n., pl.* for def. 2 com·plex·i·ties. **1.** the state or quality of being complex or complicated: *the complexity of city living.* **2.** something complicated: *the complexities of politics.*

com′plex sen′tence, a sentence that contains a principal clause and one or more dependent clauses.

com·pli·ance (kəm plī′əns), *n.* **1.** the act of conforming or yielding; giving in: *We expect your compliance with the rules.* **2.** a tendency to conform, yield, or give in. **3.** conformity or accordance: *in compliance with the law.* —**com·pli′ant,** *adj.*

com·pli·cate (kom′plə kāt′), *v.,* com·pli·cat·ed, com·pli·cat·ing. to make difficult or involved: *The diagram complicated the instructions instead of making them easier to understand.*

com·pli·cat·ed (kom′plə kā′tid), *adj.* **1.** made up of many interconnected parts; complex: *complicated machinery.* **2.** difficult to understand, analyze, or explain: *a complicated situation.*

com·pli·ca·tion (kom′plə kā′shən), *n.* **1.** something that causes some difficulty, problem, or change: *His early arrival was a complication.* **2.** a complicated or involved state or condition: *The complication of this game makes it hard to play.*

com·plic·i·ty (kəm plis′i tē), *n., pl.* com·plic·i·ties. the state of being an accomplice; partnership or involvement in wrongdoing: *He was accused of complicity in the crime.*

com·pli·ment (kom′plə mənt), *n.* **1.** an expression of admiration, praise, or approval. **2. compliments,** greetings; good wishes; regards. —*v.* (kom′plə ment′). **3.** to pay compliments to: *We all complimented her on her recitation.*
—**Usage.** The verbs *compliment* and *complement* are often confused. *Compliment* means to praise or admire: *I complimented him on his home run. Complement* means to complete or make perfect: *I need a new hat to complement my spring outfit.*

com·pli·men·ta·ry (kom′plə men′tə rē), *adj.* **1.** expressing a compliment or compliments: *a complimentary remark.* **2.** free: *a complimentary ticket.*

com·ply (kəm plī′), *v.,* com·plied, com·ply·ing. to act according to wishes, requests, demands, etc.: *You must comply with the rules of the game.*

com·po·nent (kəm pō′nənt), *adj.* **1.** being or serving as an element (in something larger); composing: *component parts.* —*n.* **2.** a part that belongs to a whole: *hi-fi components.*

com·pose (kəm pōz′), *v.,* com·posed, com·pos·ing. **1.** to make or form by combining things, parts, or elements: *to compose a song.* **2.** to be a part or element of: *a sauce composed of many ingredients.* **3.** to end or settle: *to compose a dispute.* **4.** to calm or quiet; settle: *I composed myself before the show even though I was very nervous.*

com·posed (kəm pōzd′), *adj.* calm or serene.

com·pos·er (kəm pō′zər), *n.* a person who composes, esp. one who writes music.

com·pos·ite (kəm poz′it), *adj.* made up of separate parts or elements: *A composite photograph is made up of several different photographs.*

compos′ite num′ber, a number that is a multiple of at least two other numbers, none of which is equal to 1.

com·po·si·tion (kom′pə zish′ən), *n.* **1.** the act of combining parts to form a whole: *The composition of the letter was hard work.* **2.** the product resulting from combining parts: *a musical composition.* **3.** the manner of being composed; structure: *The painting has an orderly composition.* **4.** the make-up or constitution of something: *The composition of a chemical compound includes two or more elements.* **5.** a short essay written as a school exercise.

com·post (kom′pōst), *n.* **1.** a mixture of dead leaves, manure, etc., for fertilizing land. **2.** a mixture or compound.

com·po·sure (kəm pō′zhər), *n.* a calm state of mind; tranquillity.

com·pound¹ (kom′pound, kom pound′), *adj.* **1.** made up of two or more parts, elements, or ingredients: *a compound flower; a compound word.* —*n.* (kom′pound). **2.** something formed by combining parts. **3.** *Chem.* a substance formed by the chemical combination of two or more elements. **4.** a word formed by adding to a word or stem one or more other words or stems, or prefixes or suffixes. *Inhalation, exclamatory,* and *concertmaster* are compounds. —*v.* (kəm pound′). **5.** to put together into a whole; combine: *to compound several drugs to form a medicine.* **6.** to make or form by combining parts: *to compound a medicine from drugs.* **7.** to settle or adjust by agreement: *to compound an argument.* **8.** to increase or add to: *His laziness is compounded by his indifference.* [from the Latin word *compōnere* "to put together"]

com·pound² (kom′pound), *n.* **1.** an enclosure containing houses, stores, hospitals, etc., esp. for Europeans in the Far East. **2.** any enclosed area, as for housing prisoners of war. [from the Malay word *kampong*]

act, āble, dâre, ärt; ebb, ēqual; if, īce; hot, ōver, ôrder; oil; book; ooze; out; up, ûrge; ə = a as in *alone*; ³ as in *button* (but′³n), *fire* (fi³r); chief; shoe; thin; ᴛнat; zh as in *measure* (mezh′ər). See full key inside cover.

com'pound leaf', a leaf made up of a number of leaflets on a single stalk.

com'pound sen'tence, a sentence that contains two or more independent clauses that are usually joined by conjunctions, but does not contain a dependent clause.

Compound leaf

com·pre·hend (kom/pri hend/), *v.* 1. to understand the nature or meaning of: *to comprehend a math problem.* 2. to take in or include: *The list comprehends the entire class.* —**com'pre·hend'ing·ly,** *adv.*

com·pre·hen·si·ble (kom/pri hen/sə bəl), *adj.* capable of being comprehended or understood; understandable: *The problem became comprehensible only after the teacher explained it.*

com·pre·hen·sion (kom/pri hen/shən), *n.* the capacity or power to understand or comprehend; understanding: *comprehension of physics.*

com·pre·hen·sive (kom/pri hen/siv), *adj.* 1. of large scope; including a great deal: *a comprehensive study of housing problems.* 2. having a very broad understanding: *a comprehensive mind.* —**com'pre·hen'sive·ly,** *adv.*

com·press (kəm pres/), *v.* 1. to press together; force into less space: *to compress gas; to compress cotton into bales.* —*n.* (kom/pres). 2. a soft cloth or pad held in place by a bandage and used to provide pressure or supply moisture, heat, or medication.

compressed' air', air under pressure, such as that used for powering drills, spraying paint, etc.

com·pres·sion (kəm presh/ən), *n.* 1. the act of compressing: *After compression the gas is stored in steel cylinders.* 2. the state of being compressed: *air compression.*

com·pres·sor (kəm pres/ər), *n.* a device for compressing, esp. a motor- or engine-driven pump for compressing gases.

com·prise (kəm prīz/), *v.,* **com·prised, com·pris·ing.** to include or contain; consist of: *The Soviet Union comprises several socialist republics.*

com·pro·mise (kom/prə mīz/), *n.* 1. a settlement of differences or disagreements by the giving in of each side to some demands of the other side. —*v.,* **com·pro·mised, com·pro·mis·ing.** 2. to make a compromise: *We compromised by taking turns.* 3. to expose to suspicion, danger, or risk: *to compromise a person's reputation.* —**com'pro·mis'ing·ly,** *adv.*

comp·trol·ler (kən trō/lər), *n.* See **controller** (def. 1).

com·pul·sion (kəm pul/shən), *n.* 1. the act of compelling or forcing: *The compulsion of his parents drove him to succeed.* 2. the state or condition of being compelled or forced: *Under compulsion he agreed.*

com·pul·so·ry (kəm pul/sə rē), *adj.* 1. using compulsion or force: *a compulsory action.* 2. required; obligatory: *compulsory education.*

com·pu·ta·tion (kom/pyə tā/shən), *n.* 1. an act or method of computing; calculation. 2. a result of computing: *My computation is off three cents.*

com·pute (kəm pyoot/), *v.,* **com·put·ed, com·put·ing.** to determine by calculation; calculate; reckon: *to compute the cost of building a house.* [from the Latin word *computāre* "to reckon, consider"]

com·put·er (kəm pyoo/tər), *n.* 1. a person or thing that computes. 2. a complex electronic device for making calculations at very high speeds.

com·rade (kom/rad), *n.* a person who shares closely in the activities, occupation, or interests of another; companion; friend. —**com'rade·ship',** *n.*

con¹ (kon), *adv.* 1. in opposition; against. —*n.* 2. the argument, position, arguer, or voter against something: *the pros and cons of an issue.* See also **pro¹.** [from the Latin word *contrā* "against"]

con² (kon), *v.,* **conned, con·ning.** to learn or study very thoroughly; learn by heart. [another form of *can¹,* used in its earlier meaning "to learn"]

con³ (kon), *v.,* **conned, con·ning.** to steer, guide, or maneuver: *to con a ship through rough seas.* [from the Middle English word *condue,* which comes from Old French *conduire* "to lead, conduct"]

con-, a prefix meaning with or together: *confirm; conjoin.*

con., 1. connection. 2. consolidated. 3. consul. 4. continued. 5. against. [from the Latin word *contrā*]

Concave lenses

con·cave (kon kāv/, kon/kāv), *adj.* curved like the inside of a bowl: *a concave mirror.* —**con·cav·i·ty** (kon kav/i tē), *n.*

con·ceal (kən sēl/), *v.* to hide; cover or keep from sight: *He concealed the pictures in a stack of papers.* —**con·ceal'a·ble,** *adj.*

con·ceal·ment (kən sēl/mənt), *n.* 1. the act of concealing; a hiding: *the concealment of evidence.* 2. a means or place of hiding: *He remained in concealment until danger passed.*

con·cede (kən sēd/), *v.,* **con·ced·ed, con·ced·ing.** 1. to grant as true, just, or proper; admit: *to concede that an argument is reasonable.* 2. to admit (another person's victory, success, etc.) before it has been officially determined: *to concede an election.*

con·ceit (kən sēt/), *n.* an exaggerated estimate of one's own ability, importance, etc.; vanity.

con·ceit·ed (kən sē/tid), *adj.* having an exaggerated opinion of one's own abilities or importance; vain. —**con·ceit'ed·ly,** *adv.*

con·ceiv·a·ble (kən sē/və bəl), *adj.* capable of being conceived or imagined; imaginable: *We tried every conceivable way to get in.* —**con·ceiv'a·bly,** *adv.*

con·ceive (kən sēv/), *v.,* **con·ceived, con·ceiv·ing.** 1. to form (a notion, opinion, plan, etc.): *He conceived the project while on vacation.* 2. to form an idea; imagine; think (usually fol. by *of*): *I cannot conceive of what living at the North Pole would be like.* 3. to become pregnant.

con·cen·trate (kon/sən trāt/), *v.,* **con·cen·trat·ed, con·cen·trat·ing.** 1. to bring or draw to a common center or point; focus: *to concentrate one's attention on a problem.* 2. to put or bring to a single place, group, etc.: *The nation's population has been concentrated* *in a few cities.* **3.** to make thicker, stronger, or denser: *to concentrate a fruit juice.* **4.** to fix all thoughts, attention, etc., on one thing (often fol. by *on* or *upon*): *to concentrate on solving a problem.* —*n.* **5.** a concentrated form of something, esp. a fruit juice.

con·cen·tra·tion (kon'sən trā'shən), *n.* **1.** the act of concentrating: *Concentration is difficult in a noisy room.* **2.** something that is concentrated: *a concentration of stars.* **3.** close attention to one subject: *He shifted his concentration to the swinging pendulum.*

concentra'tion camp', a guarded compound for the imprisonment of prisoners of war, aliens, and political enemies, esp. any of the camps established by the Nazis in World War II.

con·cen·tric (kən sen'trik), *adj.* having a common center, as circles or spheres.

con·cept (kon'sept), *n.* a general notion or idea: *the concept of freedom.*

con·cep·tion (kən sep'shən), *n.* **1.** the act of conceiving or forming an idea. **2.** a notion, idea, or concept: *He has no conception of what I mean.* **3.** the beginning of pregnancy.

con·cern (kən sûrn'), *v.* **1.** to relate to; be connected with; be of interest or importance to; affect: *The problem concerns all of us.* **2.** to interest, engage, or involve: *He concerns himself too much with trifles.* **3.** to worry or trouble: *I am concerned about his health.* —*n.* **4.** something that relates to a person; business; affair: *What he does with his spare time is his own concern.* **5.** worry or anxiety: *to show concern for someone in trouble.* **6.** a commercial or manufacturing company or establishment; firm: *an insurance concern.*

con·cerned (kən sûrnd'), *adj.* **1.** interested or participating: *to be concerned in politics.* **2.** troubled or worried: *a concerned look.*

con·cern·ing (kən sûr'ning), *prep.* relating to; regarding; about: *a story concerning two cats.*

con·cert (kon'sûrt), *n.* **1.** a public musical performance, esp. one in which a number of musicians participate. **2.** an agreement of two or more individuals; harmony; combined action. **3. in concert,** together: *The suspects were accused of acting in concert.*

con·cert·ed (kən sûr'tid), *adj.* arranged or done by agreement; planned or carried out together: *a concerted effort.*

con·cer·ti·na (kon'sər tē'nə), *n.* an instrument that looks like a small accordion and works in a similar way.

con·cer·to (kən cher'tō), *n., pl.* **con·cer·tos.** a musical composition for one or more solo instruments with orchestral accompaniment: *a piano concerto.*

Concertina

con·ces·sion (kən sesh'ən), *n.* **1.** the act of conceding or yielding: *He made a concession on one point.* **2.** the thing or point that is yielded. **3.** a

space, right, or privilege conceded by an authority: *a hot-dog concession at the park.*

conch (kongk, konch), *n., pl.* **conchs** (kongks) *or* **conches** (kon'chiz). a shellfish, related to the snail, whose large, spiral shell is often made into a horn for signaling. [from a Middle English word, which comes from Latin *concha,* from Greek *konchē* "mussel, shell"]

Conch (length 3 to 4 in.)

con·cil·i·ate (kən sil'ē āt'), *v.,* **con·cil·i·at·ed, con·cil·i·at·ing.** **1.** to overcome the distrust of; win over: *He conciliated the enemy.* **2.** to make compatible; reconcile: *to conciliate two versions of a story.* —**con·cil'i·a'tion,** *n.*

con·cise (kən sīs'), *adj.* expressing or covering much in a few words: *a concise explanation.* —**con·cise'ly,** *adv.* —**con·cise'ness,** *n.*

con·clude (kən klood'), *v.,* **con·clud·ed, con·clud·ing.** **1.** to bring or come to an end; finish: *He concluded his speech with a summary.* **2.** to bring to a decision or settlement: *to conclude a treaty.* **3.** to form or arrive at an opinion; decide: *We concluded that it would be best to stay home.*

con·clu·sion (kən kloo'zhən), *n.* **1.** the end or close; final part: *the conclusion of a story.* **2.** a result, issue, or outcome: *One conclusion of the meeting was a decision to cut expenses.* **3.** a final settlement or arrangement: *the conclusion of a trade pact.* **4.** a final decision reached by careful thinking: *He promised to tell us his conclusion.*

con·clu·sive (kən kloo'siv), *adj.* serving to settle or decide a question; decisive: *conclusive evidence.*

con·coct (kon kokt', kən kokt'), *v.* **1.** to prepare or make by combining ingredients: *to concoct a meal from leftovers.* **2.** to make up; devise; contrive: *to concoct an excuse.*

con·coc·tion (kon kok'shən, kən kok'shən), *n.* **1.** the act or process of concocting. **2.** something concocted: *She fixed us a concoction of milk, egg, and prune juice.*

con·cord (kon'kôrd, kong'kôrd), *n.* agreement between persons or things; peace or harmony: *a long period of concord between the two countries.*

Con·cord (kong'kərd), *n.* **1.** the capital city of New Hampshire, in the S part. **2.** a town in E Massachusetts, NW of Boston: second battle of the American Revolution fought here April 19, 1775.

con·course (kon'kôrs, kong'kôrs), *n.* **1.** a coming, flowing, or moving together; gathering: *a concourse of streams.* **2.** a large gathering; crowd; assemblage; throng. **3.** a large open space where crowds gather or roads meet: *a concourse in a railway station.*

con·crete (kon'krēt, kon krēt'), *n.* **1.** a mixture of cement, sand, and water that hardens until it resembles stone. Concrete is used as a building and paving material. —*adj.* (kon krēt', kon'krēt). **2.** made of concrete: *a concrete sidewalk.* **3.** actual; real: *to furnish concrete proof.* **4.** specific; definite: *This is a concrete* *example of her ingratitude.* —con·crete**′**ly, *adv.* —con·crete**′**ness, *n.*

con·cur (kən kûr**′**), *v.,* **con·curred, con·cur·ring. 1.** to agree: *We concurred that he was right.* **2.** to cooperate; work together: *Both classes concurred in presenting the play.* **3.** to occur or happen at the same time; coincide: *His graduation day concurred with his birthday.*

con·cur·rence (kən kûr**′**əns), *n.* **1.** accordance in opinion; agreement. **2.** a combined action or effort; cooperation. **3.** a happening together; coincidence: *The concurrence of several unusual events created a good news story.*

con·cur·rent (kən kûr**′**ənt), *adj.* **1.** happening, occurring, or existing at the same time or side by side: *concurrent events.* **2.** consistent; agreeing: *concurrent ideas.* —con·cur**′**rent·ly, *adv.*

con·cus·sion (kən kush**′**ən), *n.* **1.** a shock or violent shaking caused by the impact of a collision, blow, etc. **2.** injury to the brain, spinal cord, etc., from a blow, fall, or the like.

cond., 1. condition. **2.** conditional. **3.** conduct.

con·demn (kən dem**′**), *v.* **1.** to express strong disapproval of; pronounce as wrong: *to condemn someone's behavior.* **2.** to pronounce guilty or sentence to punishment: *to condemn a murderer to life imprisonment.* **3.** to judge or pronounce to be unfit for use or service: *The ship was condemned and sold for scrap.* **4.** to acquire ownership of for a public purpose: *The city condemned the property.* —con·dem·na·tion (kon**′**dem nā**′**shən), *n.*

con·den·sa·tion (kon**′**den sā**′**shən), *n.* **1.** the act of condensing, or the state of being condensed. **2.** a condensed form of something: *The condensation of the novel sold well.* **3.** the process of changing from a vapor to a liquid. **4.** the drops of liquid resulting from this process.

con·dense (kən dens**′**), *v.,* **con·densed, con·dens·ing. 1.** to make more dense or compact; reduce the size of. **2.** to shorten: *to condense a book from 300 pages to 200 pages.* **3.** to change from a gas or vapor to a liquid: *Steam condenses to water when it strikes a cold surface.* —con·den**′**sa·ble, *adj.*

con·dens·er (kən den**′**sər), *n.* **1.** a person or thing that condenses. **2.** a device for condensing a vapor to a liquid. **3.** (not in technical use) a capacitor.

con·de·scend (kon**′**di send**′**), *v.* **1.** to put oneself willingly on a level with one's inferiors: *The president of the firm condescended to have lunch with the secretaries.* **2.** to behave as if superior: *She condescended to do the job she considered beneath her.* —con**′**de·scend**′**ing·ly, *adv.*

con·de·scen·sion (kon**′**di sen**′**shən), *n.* **1.** voluntary assumption of equality with an inferior person. **2.** proud, condescending, or patronizing behavior: *He has few friends because he treats everyone with condescension.*

con·di·ment (kon**′**də mənt), *n.* something used to give additional flavor to food, such as mustard, salt, or spices.

con·di·tion (kən dish**′**ən), *n.* **1.** a particular state of being of a person or thing; situation with respect to circumstances: *The old car is in poor condition.* **2.** state of health: *He was in serious condition after the accident.* **3.** an abnormal state of part of the body; disorder: *Her father suffers from a heart condition.* **4.** social position or standing. **5.** a circumstance that limits or restricts; provision; stipulation: *He agreed to come with us on the condition that his brother be included.* —*v.* **6.** to put in a fit or proper state: *He conditions his muscles by exercise.* **7.** to make used to certain circumstances; accustom: *Three winters in the north have conditioned her to the cold.* **8.** to determine, limit, or restrict: *Her attitude will condition her success.*

con·di·tion·al (kən dish**′**ə nᵊl), *adj.* **1.** depending on a condition or conditions; not absolute: *a conditional acceptance.* **2.** of or referring to a clause, tense, or mood that expresses or contains a condition. In the sentence *If I see him, I'll tell him, If I see him* is a conditional clause. —*n.* **3.** the conditional tense. —con·di**′**tion·al·ly, *adv.*

con·do·lence (kən dō**′**ləns), *n.* an expression of sympathy with a person who is suffering sorrow, misfortune, or grief.

con·done (kən dōn**′**), *v.,* **con·doned, con·don·ing.** to pardon, forgive, or overlook: *People often condone the mistakes of their friends.*

Condor

(length 4 ft.; wingspread 10 ft.)

con·dor (kon**′**dər), *n.* either of two very large vultures of the Western Hemisphere. [from a Spanish word, which comes from South American Indian *kuntur*]

con·duce (kən dōōs**′**, -dyōōs**′**), *v.,* **con·duced, con·duc·ing.** to lead to or help to bring about: *Understanding among men conduces to peace.*

con·du·cive (kən dōō**′**siv, -dyōō**′**-), *adj.* helpful in bringing about: *Eating the proper food is conducive to good health.*

con·duct (kon**′**dukt), *n.* **1.** a way of behaving or acting; behavior: *He was praised for his good conduct.* **2.** a way of directing or managing something: *the conduct of a business.* —*v.* (kən dukt**′**). **3.** to guide or lead: *The usher conducted us to our seats.* **4.** to behave (oneself): *He conducted himself badly at the party.* **5.** to direct or manage: *to conduct a business.* **6.** to direct (an orchestra or band) or act as a conductor. **7.** to transmit (heat, electricity, etc.): *Wires conduct electric current.*

con·duc·tion (kən duk**′**shən), *n.* the transmission of heat, electricity, sound, etc.

con·duc·tor (kən duk**′**tər), *n.* **1.** a person on a train, bus, etc., who collects fares and is in charge. **2.** the director of an orchestra or band. **3.** a material through which heat, electricity, etc., can be transmitted.

con·duit (kon**′**dwit, kon**′**dōō it), *n.* **1.** a pipe or passage for carrying water, gas, etc. **2.** a tube for covering electric wires and cables.

cone (kōn), *n.* **1.** a solid that tapers to a point from a circular base. **2.** a piece of material rolled into this shape: *an ice-cream cone.* **3.** the scaly, cone-shaped fruit of such evergreen trees as the pine, fir, spruce, etc.

Cone

con·fec·tion (kən fek′shən), *n.* any sweet food, as candy, preserves, etc.: *Chocolate is a popular confection.*

con·fec·tion·ar·y (kən fek′shə ner′ē), *n., pl.* **con·fec·tion·ar·ies.** **1.** a place where confections are made or sold. **2.** candies, sweets, or other confections.

con·fec·tion·er (kən fek′shə nər), *n.* a person who makes or sells confections, esp. candies.

con·fec·tion·er·y (kən fek′shə ner′ē), *n., pl.* **con·fec·tion·er·ies.** another spelling of **confectionary.**

con·fed·er·a·cy (kən fed′ər ə sē), *n., pl.* **con·fed·er·a·cies.** **1.** an alliance of persons, states, etc., for some joint purpose. **2.** the Confederacy, another name for **Confederate States of America.**

Pine cone

con·fed·er·ate (kən fed′ər it), *adj.* **1.** being united in a confederacy. —*n.* **2.** an ally or accomplice: *a confederate in crime.* —*v.* (kən fed′ə rāt′), **con·fed·er·at·ed, con·fed·er·at·ing.** **3.** to join in a league, alliance, or conspiracy.

Con·fed·er·ate (kən fed′ər it), *adj.* **1.** of or having to do with the Confederacy. —*n.* **2.** a person who belonged to or aided the Confederacy.

Confed′erate States′ of Amer′ica, the group of 11 Southern states that seceded from the United States in 1860–1861. Also, **the Confederacy.**

con·fed·er·a·tion (kən fed′ə rā′shən), *n.* **1.** the act of confederating, or the state of being confederated. **2.** a confederated group; confederacy; alliance: *The 13 original colonies formed a confederation.*

con·fer (kən fûr′), *v.,* **con·ferred, con·fer·ring.** **1.** to bestow or give, as a favor, honor, etc.: *to confer an award on a winner.* **2.** to consult together; carry on a discussion: *We conferred for over an hour about the problem.* —**con·fer′ment,** *n.*

con·fer·ence (kon′fər əns), *n.* a meeting for the purpose of discussion.

con·fess (kən fes′), *v.* **1.** to admit or reveal (a secret, fault, etc.): *He confessed that he was the thief.* **2.** to admit that one is guilty of a crime or wrongdoing: *They questioned him for an hour before he confessed.* **3.** to admit one's sins to a priest.

con·fes·sion (kən fesh′ən), *n.* **1.** an admission or acknowledgment of a secret, fault, etc. **2.** the admission of sin to a priest. **3.** something that is confessed, esp. a statement by a criminal admitting his guilt.

con·fes·sion·al (kən fesh′ə nəl), *n.* a stall or booth in a church where a priest hears confessions.

con·fes·sor (kən fes′ər), *n.* **1.** a person who confesses. **2.** a priest who hears confessions.

con·fet·ti (kən fet′ē), *n.pl. (used as sing.)* bits of colored paper thrown for fun at a party, parade, etc.

con·fi·dant (kon′fi dant′), *n.* a person to whom secrets are confided: *His friend became his confidant.* Also, *referring to a woman,* **con′fi·dante′.**

con·fide (kən fīd′), *v.,* **con·fid·ed, con·fid·ing.** **1.** to tell secrets to (usually fol. by *in*): *She confides in no one.* **2.** to tell in secrecy and with trust: *She confided her problems to her older sister.* **3.** to entrust or commit to the good care or safekeeping of another.

con·fi·dence (kon′fi dəns), *n.* **1.** full trust or belief in a person or thing: *I have confidence that you will win.* **2.** self-reliance; trust in oneself: *He is talented, but lacks confidence.* **3.** a secret: *to exchange confidences.* **4. in confidence,** as a secret; privately: *I told him our plans in confidence.*

con·fi·dent (kon′fi dənt), *adj.* **1.** having strong belief; sure: *We are confident that we will win the game.* **2.** sure of oneself; bold: *He is a confident speaker.* —**con′fi·dent·ly,** *adv.*

con·fi·den·tial (kon′fi den′shəl), *adj.* **1.** told in confidence; secret: *a confidential remark.* **2.** having the confidence of another: *a confidential secretary.* —**con′fi·den′tial·ly,** *adv.*

con·fig·u·ra·tion (kən fig′yə rā′shən), *n.* the form, shape, or arrangement of parts of a thing: *land with a hilly configuration.*

con·fine (kən fīn′), *v.,* **con·fined, con·fin·ing.** **1.** to limit or restrict: *Let us confine our remarks to the matter at hand.* **2.** to shut or keep in; prevent from leaving a place: *to confine an ill person to his bed.* —*n.* (kon′fīn). **3.** Usually, **confines.** the land within a boundary or limits: *Stay within the confines of the park.*

con·fine·ment (kən fīn′mənt), *n.* **1.** the act of confining, or the state of being confined: *confinement in bed.* **2.** imprisonment: *He was sentenced to 20 years of confinement.*

con·firm (kən fûrm′), *v.* **1.** to prove to be right or true: *He confirmed the report that he was leaving.* **2.** to agree to or approve of in a way that is binding: *The board confirmed his appointment.* **3.** to make a full member of a church.

con·fir·ma·tion (kon′fər mā′shən), *n.* **1.** the act of confirming, or the state of being confirmed. **2.** something that confirms; proof: *We have no confirmation that what you say is true.* **3.** a ritual that admits a person to full membership in a church.

con·firmed (kən fûrmd′), *adj.* **1.** proved to be correct or true: *a confirmed report.* **2.** firmly established; habitual or chronic: *a confirmed liar.*

con·fis·cate (kon′fi skāt′), *v.,* **con·fis·cat·ed, con·fis·cat·ing.** to seize by authority: *The government confiscated the smuggled goods.* —**con′fis·ca′tion,** *n.*

con·fla·gra·tion (kon′flə grā′shən), *n.* a large and destructive fire: *Chicago was nearly destroyed by the conflagration of 1871.*

con·flict (kən flikt′), *v.* **1.** to come into disagreement; be in opposition; clash: *Our ideas often con-*

flict. —*n.* (kon'flikt). **2.** a battle or fight; struggle: *armed conflict.* **3.** a violent opposition or clash, as between ideas, principles, etc.: *There is a conflict between what you think is right and what I think is right.* —**con·flict'ing·ly,** *adv.*

con·flu·ence (kon'flōō əns), *n.* **1.** a flowing together of two or more streams or rivers: *Cairo, Illinois, is at the confluence of the Ohio and Mississippi rivers.* **2.** a coming together of people; assembly: *a confluence in the town square.* —**con'flu·ent,** *adj.*

con·form (kən fôrm'), *v.* **1.** to act in agreement with some model, rule, or pattern: *to conform to local customs.* **2.** to make or become similar: *Their ideas conform to ours.* —**con·form'a·ble,** *adj.*

con·for·ma·tion (kon'fər mā'shən), *n.* **1.** the act or process of conforming. **2.** the general shape or arrangement of something: *The conformation of the valley was gradually changed as the river shifted its course.*

con·form·ist (kən fôr'mist), *n.* a person who readily accepts and follows the customs of a group or class.

con·form·i·ty (kən fôr'mi tē), *n.* **1.** agreement or harmony: *to live in conformity with one's beliefs.* **2.** the act or practice of conforming: *Too much conformity can destroy the ability to think for oneself.*

con·found (kən found'), *v.* to perplex or amaze; confuse: *His strange illness confounded his doctors.* —**con·found'er,** *n.* —**con·found'ing·ly,** *adv.*

con·front (kən frunt'), *v.* **1.** to stand or come in front of, esp. with boldness or defiance: *He bravely confronted the enemy.* **2.** to bring face to face: *He was confronted with the most difficult problem of his life.* —**con·fron·ta·tion** (kon'frən tā'shən), *n.*

Con·fu·cius (kən fyōō'shəs), *n.* 6th–5th century B.C., Chinese philosopher and teacher.

con·fuse (kən fyōōz'), *v.,* **con·fused, con·fus·ing. 1.** to bewilder or perplex: *He was confused about which road to take.* **2.** to fail to see the difference between; mix up: *You are confusing the date of his birth and the date of his death.* **3.** to make unclear: *By bringing up unimportant details you are confusing the issue.* —**con·fus·ed·ly** (kən fyōō'zid lē), *adv.* —**con·fus'ing·ly,** *adv.*

con·fu·sion (kən fyōō'zhən), *n.* **1.** the act of confusing, or the state of being confused. **2.** disorder or upheaval: *His early arrival threw everything into confusion.* **3.** embarrassment: *The unexpected question made him stammer in confusion.*

con·fute (kən fyōōt'), *v.,* **con·fut·ed, con·fut·ing. 1.** to prove to be false: *to confute an argument.* **2.** to prove to be wrong: *to confute an opponent.* —**con·fu·ta·tion** (kon'fyōō tā'shən), *n.*

Cong., 1. Congregational. **2.** Congressional.

con·geal (kən jēl'), *v.* to change from a liquid state to a solid state, esp. by freezing: *The surface of the pond congeals in winter.* —**con·geal'ment,** *n.*

con·gen·ial (kən jēn'yəl), *adj.* **1.** similar in likings and disposition: *a congenial classmate.* **2.** agreeable and pleasing: *a congenial pastime.* —**con·ge·ni·al·i·ty** (kən jē'nē al'i tē), *n.* —**con·gen'ial·ly,** *adv.*

con·gen·i·tal (kən jen'i təl), *adj.* existing at or from

one's birth: *congenital deafness.* —**con·gen'i·tal·ly,** *adv.*

con·ger (kong'gər), *n.* a large marine eel.

con·gest (kən jest'), *v.* to fill up or crowd: *All the roads were congested with traffic.* —**con·ges'tion,** *n.*

con·glom·er·ate (kən glom'ər it), *n.* **1.** anything composed of various parts or materials that do not properly belong together: *a conglomerate of old and new buildings.* —*adj.* **2.** made of parts gathered into a mass: *Conglomerate rock is gravel that has become cemented together.* —*v.* (kən glom'ə rāt'), **con·glom·er·at·ed, con·glom·er·at·ing. 3.** to bring or cluster together in a mass. —**con·glom·er·a'tion,** *n.*

Con·go (kong'gō), *n.* **1. People's Republic of the,** a republic in central Africa, W of Zaïre: a former French colony. 132,046 sq. mi. *Cap.:* Brazzaville. **2.** former name (1960–1971) of **Zaïre** (def. 1): formerly Belgian. **3.** former name of the Zaïre River.

Con·go·lese (kong'gə lēz'), *adj.* **1.** of or concerning either of the two Congos or their inhabitants. —*n., pl.* **Con·go·lese. 2.** a native or inhabitant of either of the two Congos.

con·grat·u·late (kən grach'ə lāt'), *v.,* **con·grat·u·lat·ed, con·grat·u·lat·ing.** to give one's best wishes to (a person) on some happy occasion: *They congratulated him on his marriage.*

con·grat·u·la·tion (kən grach'ə lā'shən), *n.* **1.** the act of congratulating. **2. congratulations,** words that congratulate: *We sent congratulations to the winners.*

con·gre·gate (kong'grə gāt'), *v.,* **con·gre·gat·ed, con·gre·gat·ing.** to come or bring together; gather; assemble: *A large crowd congregated to watch the fire.*

con·gre·ga·tion (kong'grə gā'shən), *n.* **1.** the act of congregating. **2.** a group of people brought together for some purpose, esp. for religious worship.

Con·gre·ga·tion·al (kong'grə gā'shə nəl), *adj.* of or belonging to a Protestant denomination of churches in which each congregation is independent and self-governing. —**Con'gre·ga'tion·al·ism,** *n.* —**Con'gre·ga'tion·al·ist,** *n.*

con·gress (kong'gris), *n.* **1.** a group brought together for the purpose of discussing something of common interest, often composed of delegates or representatives of different branches of an organization: *a business congress.* **2.** the body of lawmakers of a country. —**con·gres·sion·al** (kən gresh'ə nəl), *adj.*

Con·gress (kong'gris), *n.* the body of officials having the power to make the laws of the U.S., consisting of the Senate and the House of Representatives. —**Con·gres·sion·al** (kən gresh'ə nəl), *adj.*

con·gress·man (kong'gris mən), *n., pl.* **con·gress·men.** a male member of Congress, esp. of the House of Representatives.

con·gress·wom·an (kong'gris wōōm'ən), *n., pl.* **con·gress·wom·en.** a female member of Congress, esp. of the House of Representatives.

con·gru·ent (kong′grōō ənt), *adj.* **1.** having the same size and shape, such as two identical triangles. **2.** in agreement or harmony: *Your actions are not congruent with what you preach.*

con·i·cal (kon′i kəl), *adj.* shaped like a cone. **—con′i·cal·ly,** *adv.*

con·i·fer (kon′ə fər, kō′nə fər), *n.* a cone-bearing tree, such as the pine, fir, or spruce. **—co·nif·er·ous** (kō nif′ər əs), *adj.*

con·jec·ture (kən jek′chər), *n.* **1.** an opinion formed without full knowledge of the facts; guess: *It is our conjecture that it will rain tomorrow.* **—v.,** **con·jec·tured, con·jec·tur·ing. 2.** to form an opinion without full knowledge of the facts; guess: *Can you conjecture what life in China is like?*

con·join (kən join′), *v.* to join together; unite; combine: *We conjoined our strength to complete the task.*

con·ju·gate (kon′jə gāt′), *v.,* **con·ju·gat·ed, con·ju·gat·ing.** to list or recite the inflected forms of a verb, showing the differences of number, tense, mood, voice, etc. The verb *to be* is conjugated as follows in the present tense indicative: *I am, you are, he is, we are, you are, they are.*

con·ju·ga·tion (kon′jə gā′shən), *n.* **1.** a listing or reciting of the inflected forms of a verb or class of verbs. **2.** a class of verbs having similar conjugation. In English, verbs of the type *I sing, I sang, I have sung* belong to the *strong* conjugation. Verbs of the type *I talk, I talked, I have talked* belong to the *weak* conjugation.

con·junc·tion (kən jungk′shən), *n.* **1.** a combination or union: *The snow in conjunction with high winds produced a blizzard.* **2.** a word used to connect words, phrases, clauses, or sentences, such as *and, or, but,* or *for.*

con·jure (kon′jər *for defs. 1, 3;* kən jŏŏr′ *for def. 2*), *v.,* **con·jured, con·jur·ing. 1.** to make appear or disappear by magic: *The witch conjured evil spirits.* **2.** to plead with or beg: *We conjured him to free the prisoner.* **3. conjure up,** to bring to mind or recall as if by magic: *That song conjured up happy memories.*

con·jur·er (kon′jər ər), *n.* a magician. Also, **con′jur·or.**

Conn., Connecticut.

con·nect (kə nekt′), *v.* **1.** to join or become joined together: *to connect two ends of a rope; rooms that connect.* **2.** to bring or come together in the mind: *to connect two ideas.* **—con·nect′i·ble,** *adj.*

Con·nect·i·cut (kə net′ə kət), *n.* a state in the NE United States. 5009 sq. mi. *Cap.:* Hartford.

con·nec·tion (kə nek′shən), *n.* **1.** the act of connecting, or the state of being connected. **2.** anything that connects: *a connection between two pipes.* **3.** an association or relation: *the connection between crime and pov-*

erty. **4.** a relative: *She is a connection on my father's side of the family.* **5.** a person with whom one shares something in common: *a business connection.* **6.** a meeting of trains, planes, etc., for transfer of passengers: *He missed his connection for Boston.*

con·nec·tive (kə nek′tiv), *adj.* serving or tending to connect: *connective tissue between bones.*

con·nive (kə nīv′), *v.,* **con·nived, con·niv·ing. 1.** to pretend not to notice something that is wrong and that one ought to condemn (usually fol. by *at*): *to connive at a friend's stealing.* **2.** to conspire (usually fol. by *with*): *He connived with the plotters against the king.* **—con·niv′ance,** *n.* **—con·niv′ing·ly,** *adv.* **—con·niv′er,** *n.*

con·nois·seur (kon′ə sûr′), *n.* a person who knows a great deal about one of the arts or some matter requiring good taste and experience: *a connoisseur of painting; a connoisseur of wines.* [from the Old French word *conoiseor* "knower"]

con·no·ta·tion (kon′ə tā′shən), *n.* the associated or suggested meaning of a word or expression: *One connotation of "home" is "a place of warmth, comfort, and affection."* See also **denotation** (def. 1).

con·note (kə nōt′), *v.,* **con·not·ed, con·not·ing.** to signify or suggest (certain meanings, ideas, etc.) in addition to the primary or basic meaning: *The word "fireplace" often connotes hospitality and warm comfort.* See also **denote.**

con·quer (kong′kər), *n.* **1.** to defeat in war: *to conquer an enemy.* **2.** to overcome by effort of the will: *to conquer a bad habit.* **—con′quer·a·ble,** *adj.*

con·quer·or (kong′kər ər), *n.* a person who conquers; victor.

con·quest (kon′kwest, kong′kwest), *n.* **1.** the act of conquering, or the state of being conquered. **2.** anything won by conquering: *Gaul was one of Caesar's conquests.*

con·quis·ta·dor (kən kwis′tə dôr′), *n.* one of the early Spanish conquerors of Mexico, Peru, and other parts of North and South America.

con·science (kon′shəns), *n.* the sense of right and wrong that a person has of his actions: *His conscience would not let him steal the money.*

con·sci·en·tious (kon′shē en′shəs), *adj.* **1.** acting with a sense of what is right or correct: *He was a careful, conscientious worker.* **2.** done with a sense of what is right or correct: *a conscientious piece of work.* **—con′sci·en′tious·ly,** *adv.*

con·scious (kon′shəs), *adj.* **1.** having awareness; able to feel and think: *After the accident he was not conscious for three days.* **2.** fully aware of something: *I was not conscious that someone had come in.* **3.** done or doing with awareness; deliberate: *a conscious effort to improve one's work.* **—con′scious·ly,** *adv.*

con·scious·ness (kon′shəs nis), *n.* **1.** the state of being conscious; awareness: *to regain consciousness.* **2.** all the thoughts and feelings of a person: *A new thought entered his consciousness.*

con·script (kən skript′), v. 1. to draft for military service: *to conscript troops.* —n. (kon′skript). 2. a person drafted for military service: *new conscripts.* —adj. (kon′skript). 3. drafted or formed by drafting: *a conscript army.* —**con·scrip′tion,** n.

con·se·crate (kon′sə krāt′), v., **con·se·crat·ed, con·se·crat·ing.** 1. to make or declare sacred: *to consecrate a church.* 2. to devote entirely: *He consecrated his life to helping the poor.* —**con′se·cra′tion,** n.

con·sec·u·tive (kən sek′yə tiv), adj. following one another in an unbroken order: *May, June, and July are consecutive months.* —**con·sec′u·tive·ly,** adv.

con·sen·sus (kən sen′səs), n., pl. **con·sen·sus·es.** a general agreement about something; opinion of the majority: *It was the consensus of the voters that a new bridge should be constructed.*

con·sent (kən sent′), v. 1. to agree, permit, or approve: *They will not consent to do what I say.* —n. 2. agreement, permission, or approval: *They took my suitcase without my consent.*

con·se·quence (kon′sə kwens′), n. 1. something that follows from an event; outcome; result: *Failure is often the consequence of laziness.* 2. importance: *events of great consequence.*

con·se·quent (kon′sə kwent′), adj. following as an effect or result: *The heavy rains and consequent flood damaged the little town.*

con·se·quen·tial (kon′sə kwen′shəl), adj. 1. following as an effect or result; consequent. 2. of consequence or importance. 3. self-important; snobbish or pretentious. —**con′se·quen′tial·ly,** adv.

con·se·quent·ly (kon′sə kwent′lē), adv. as a result or effect; therefore: *I have a cold, and consequently do not feel too well.*

con·ser·va·tion (kon′sər vā′shən), n. care for or careful use of something; preservation from loss, waste, decay, etc.: *conservation of our forests.*

con·serv·a·tism (kən sûr′və tiz′əm), n. unwillingness to change; desire to preserve things as they are: *We favor conservatism in government.*

con·serv·a·tive (kən sûr′və tiv), adj. 1. wishing to keep things as they are; cautious about changing: *a conservative voter.* 2. cautious or moderate; not extreme: *to be conservative in one's promises.* —n. 3. a person who is conservative, esp. in political matters. —**con·serv′a·tive·ly,** adv. —**con·serv′a·tive·ness,** n.

con·serv·a·to·ry (kən sûr′və tôr′ē), n., pl. **con·serv·a·to·ries.** 1. a greenhouse. 2. a music school.

con·serve (kən sûrv′), v., **con·served, con·serv·ing.** 1. to keep from loss, decay, waste, or injury; preserve: *Conserve your strength for the race.* 2. to preserve (fruit). —n. (kon′sûrv, kən sûrv′). 3. Often, **conserves.** preserves made of fruit; jam.

con·sid·er (kən sid′ər), v. 1. to think carefully about, esp. in order to make a decision: *He considered all the possibilities before he acted.* 2. to regard, think, believe, or suppose: *The teacher considered him the best student in the class.* 3. to bear in mind; make allowances for: *His dismissal was hardly justified if you consider his past record.* 4. to be aware of; respect: *We must always consider the feelings of others.*

con·sid·er·a·ble (kən sid′ər ə bəl), adj. rather large or great; of some size or importance: *a considerable achievement.* —**con·sid′er·a·bly,** adv.

con·sid·er·ate (kən sid′ər it), adj. having respect for another's feelings, wishes, etc.; thoughtful: *It was very considerate of you to lend me the money.* —**con·sid′er·ate·ly,** adv. —**con·sid′er·ate·ness,** n.

con·sid·er·a·tion (kən sid′ə rā′shən), n. 1. the act of considering; deliberation. 2. thoughtfulness for others: *to act with consideration for another person's feelings.* 3. something that should be kept in mind in making a decision or in acting: *My own safety is an important consideration.* 4. **take into consideration,** to allow for: *We should take into consideration the fact that he is very young.*

con·sid·er·ing (kən sid′ər ing), prep. 1. taking into account; in view of: *Considering your delay, you did very well.* —conj. 2. taking into consideration that: *Considering you got a late start, you did very well.*

con·sign (kən sīn′), v. 1. to hand over or commit: *The criminal was consigned to prison.* 2. to send or ship (goods to be sold).

con·sign·ment (kən sīn′mənt), n. 1. the act of consigning. 2. something that is consigned: *The store received a new consignment of shoes.*

con·sist (kən sist′), n. 1. to be made up or composed: *Bread consists largely of flour.* 2. to exist or be found in: *Our strength consists in unity.*

con·sist·en·cy (kən sis′tən sē), n., pl. **con·sist·en·cies.** 1. degree of thickness, firmness, etc.: *The soup has the consistency of cream.* 2. a steadfast or faithful way of acting, behaving, etc.: *He is a person of great consistency and always keeps his promises.* 3. harmony or agreement: *The colors of this painting have no consistency with one another.*

con·sist·ent (kən sis′tənt), adj. 1. constant and unchanging: *He is consistent in arriving on time.* 2. in agreement or harmony: *Words should be consistent with actions.* 3. having unity and wholeness: *a well-organized, consistent report.* —**con·sist′ent·ly,** adv.

con·so·la·tion (kon′sə lā′shən), n. 1. the act of consoling, or the state of being consoled; comfort; solace. 2. a person or thing that consoles: *Cheerful friends are a consolation in times of trouble.*

con·sole¹ (kən sōl′), v., **con·soled, con·sol·ing.** to comfort or cheer up: *Her mother consoled her for the loss of her ring.* [from the Latin word *consolāri*] —**con·sol′a·ble,** adj. —**con·sol′ing·ly,** adv.

con·sole² (kon′sōl), n. 1. the desk-shaped part of an organ containing the keyboards, pedals, etc. 2. a radio, phonograph, or television cabinet that stands on the floor. [from French]

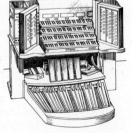

Console of a pipe organ

con·sol·i·date (kən sol′i·dāt′), v., **con·sol·i·dat·ed, con·sol·i·dat·ing.** 1. to bring or come together into a single whole; unite; combine:

The two classes were consolidated and taught by one teacher. **2.** to strengthen or make sure: *Winning the race consolidated his position on the team.* —**con·sol′i·da′tion,** *n.*

con·som·mé (kon′sə mā′, kon′sə mā′), *n.* a clear soup made by boiling meat, bones, and sometimes vegetables.

con·so·nance (kon′sə nəns), *n.* a pleasing or harmonious combination of musical tones. See also **dissonance.**

con·so·nant (kon′sə nənt), *n.* **1.** a speech sound produced with partial or complete stoppage of the breath stream by the tongue, teeth, or lips, as English *t, d, g, m, p, l, r.* **2.** a letter or group of letters representing a consonant sound, as *b, c, d, sh, ph.* —*adj.* **3.** consonantal. **4.** harmonious in sound. **5.** in agreement or harmony: *The chewing of gum is not consonant with refined behavior.*

con·so·nan·tal (kon′sə nan′t³l), *adj.* of, like, or consisting of a consonant or consonants.

con·sort (kon′sôrt), *n.* **1.** a husband or wife. **2.** a ship that accompanies another. —*v.* (kən sôrt′). **3.** to keep company or associate: *to consort with thieves.*

con·spic·u·ous (kən spik′yo͞o əs), *adj.* **1.** standing out; easily noticed or seen: *a conspicuous mistake in spelling.* **2.** outstanding or remarkable: *a woman of conspicuous beauty.* —**con·spic′u·ous·ly,** *adv.* —**con·spic′u·ous·ness,** *n.*

con·spir·a·cy (kən spir′ə sē), *n., pl.* **con·spir·a·cies.** a secret plan by two or more persons to do something evil or against the law; plot.

con·spire (kən spi̇̄r′), *v.,* **con·spired, con·spir·ing. 1.** to agree or plan together in secret to do something evil or against the law: *The outlaws conspired against the life of the dictator.* **2.** to act or work together toward the same result or goal: *Weather conditions conspired to make it a beautiful day.* —**con·spir·a·tor** (kən spir′ə tər), *n.*

con·sta·ble (kon′stə bəl), *n.* a policeman. [from the Latin phrase *comes stabuli* "keeper of the stables"]

con·stan·cy (kon′stən sē), *n.* **1.** faithfulness or firmness of mind: *We admire the constancy of those who keep their promises.* **2.** freedom from change: *the constancy of climate near the equator.*

con·stant (kon′stənt), *adj.* **1.** not changing or varying; uniform: *a constant temperature.* **2.** continuing without pause; unceasing: *a constant noise.* **3.** faithful or loyal: *a constant friend.* —**con′stant·ly,** *adv.*

Con·stan·ti·no·ple (kon′stan t³nō′pəl), *n.* a former name of Istanbul.

con·stel·la·tion (kon′stə lā′shən), *n.* a group of stars whose arrangement suggests the shape of a person, animal, or thing.

con·ster·na·tion (kon′stər nā′shən), *n.* great and sudden fear that makes one helpless; dismay: *To our consternation the boat sprang a leak.*

con·sti·pate (kon′stə pāt′), *v.,* **con·sti·pat·ed, con·sti·pat·ing.** to cause constipation in (a person).

con·sti·pa·tion (kon′stə pā′shən), *n.* a condition in

which bowel movements are infrequent or difficult.

con·stit·u·en·cy (kən stich′o͞o ən sē), *n., pl.* **con·stit·u·en·cies. 1.** all of the voters of a district: *The congressman had the approval of his constituency.* **2.** the district itself.

con·stit·u·ent (kən stich′o͞o ənt), *adj.* **1.** necessary to make up a whole thing: *Wheels are constituent parts of a vehicle.* —*n.* **2.** a necessary part: *Water is a constituent of mud.* **3.** a voter represented by an elected official: *the constituents of a congressman.*

con·sti·tute (kon′sti to͞ot′, -tyo͞ot′), *v.,* **con·sti·tut·ed, con·sti·tut·ing. 1.** to form or compose: *a beverage constituted of fruit juice, sugar, and water.* **2.** to set up or establish: *A committee was constituted to handle the work.* **3.** to appoint: *He was constituted chairman of the group.*

con·sti·tu·tion (kon′sti to͞o′shən, -tyo͞o′-), *n.* **1.** the way in which a thing is composed or made up; composition: *the constitution of concrete.* **2.** the condition of the body as to strength, health, etc.: *Plenty of exercise had given him a strong constitution.* **3.** the principles upon which a country, state, or the like, is founded. **4.** the act of constituting, or the state of being constituted.

con·sti·tu·tion·al (kon′sti to͞o′shə n³l, -tyo͞o′-), *adj.* **1.** belonging to or having to do with a person's constitution: *a constitutional ailment.* **2.** of or concerning the constitution of a state, country, etc.: *constitutional guarantees of freedom of speech.* —*n.* **3.** a walk or other exercise taken for the benefit of one's health. —**con′sti·tu′tion·al·ly,** *adv.*

con·sti·tu·tion·al·i·ty (kon′sti to͞o′shə nal′i tē, -tyo͞o′-), *n.* agreement with the constitution of a state or nation: *the constitutionality of a law.*

Constitu′tion of the Unit′ed States′, the fundamental law upon which the government of the U.S. is based, drawn up in 1787 and put into effect in 1789. Also, **the Constitution.**

con·strain (kən strān′), *v.* to force or oblige: *He was constrained to apologize for his insult.*

con·straint (kən strānt′), *n.* **1.** the act of constraining, or the state of being constrained. **2.** the holding back of one's feelings: *She spoke with constraint about her grief.*

con·strict (kən strikt′), *v.* to draw or press in so as to make smaller or narrower; compress: *The tight belt constricted his waist.* —**con·stric′tion,** *n.*

con·struct (kən strukt′), *v.* to form by putting together parts; build: *to construct a house.*

con·struc·tion (kən struk′shən), *n.* **1.** the act of putting together or building: *The construction of the new skyscraper took several months.* **2.** something that is constructed; a building or structure. **3.** the way in which a thing is constructed: *a house of sound construction.* **4.** an explanation or interpretation: *Suspicious people are likely to put a wrong construction even on compliments.* **5.** an arrangement of words in a meaningful sentence or part of a sentence. **6.** the grammatical relation of a word or phrase to others in a sentence or part of a sentence.

con·struc·tive (kən struk′tiv), *adj.* helping to improve or create: *constructive criticism.* —**con·struc′tive·ly,** *adv.* —**con·struc′tive·ness,** *n.*

con·strue (kən strōō′), *v.,* **con·strued, con·stru·ing.** 1. to show the meaning of; explain or interpret: *I don't know how to construe that strange remark.* 2. to explain the grammatical construction of (a word, phrase, or sentence). —**con·stru′a·ble,** *adj.*

con·sul (kon′səl), *n.* 1. an officer appointed by a government to live in a foreign country in order to further the interests of his own country, help fellow citizens, etc. 2. either of two head officials of the ancient Roman republic. —**con′su·lar,** *adj.*

con·su·late (kon′sə lit), *n.* 1. the building or offices in which a consul works. 2. the position, work, or term of office of a consul.

con·sult (kən sult′), *v.* 1. to seek advice or information from: *to consult a doctor; to consult an encyclopedia.* 2. to consider or have regard for (the interests of another person) in making plans: *Nobody consulted me about the trip.* 3. to deliberate together; confer: *We consulted before deciding.*

con·sult·ant (kən sul′t°nt), *n.* a person who gives expert advice: *a business consultant.*

con·sul·ta·tion (kon′səl tā′shən), *n.* 1. the act of consulting. 2. a meeting for the purpose of deliberating or of reaching a decision.

con·sume (kən sōōm′), *v.,* **con·sumed, con·sum·ing.** 1. to use up or spend: *This job will consume a lot of our time.* 2. to eat up or devour: *Fire consumed the building.* 4. to absorb or engross the interest of: *She was consumed with curiosity.*

con·sum·er (kən sōō′mər), *n.* 1. a person who buys and uses anything for sale on the market, as food, clothing, services, etc. 2. a person or thing that uses up or wastes something: *Worry is a consumer of time.*

con·sum·mate (kon′sə māt′), *v.,* **con·sum·mat·ed, con·sum·mat·ing.** 1. to complete, fulfill, or make perfect: *He consummated his ambition to go to college.* —*adj.* (kən sum′it, kon′sə mit). 2. complete or perfect: *a consummate musician.* —**con′sum·ma′tion,** *n.*

con·sump·tion (kən sump′shən), *n.* 1. the act of consuming, as by use or waste. 2. an amount consumed: *the daily consumption of electricity.* 3. a former name for **tuberculosis.**

con·sump·tive (kən sump′tiv), *adj.* 1. having tuberculosis. —*n.* 2. a person suffering from tuberculosis.

cont., 1. containing. 2. contents. 3. continued.

con·tact (kon′takt), *n.* 1. the act or state of touching: *The cup is in contact with the saucer.* 2. connection: *We could not make contact with you by telephone.* —*v.* 3. to touch. 4. to reach or get in touch with: *We will contact you by mail.*

con′tact lens′, a thin lens of plastic placed directly over the cornea to correct faulty vision.

con·ta·gion (kən tā′jən), *n.* 1. the transmitting of disease by direct or indirect contact. 2. a contagious disease. 3. the quick and easy spread of an idea, feeling, etc., from one person to another: *the contagion of laughter.*

con·ta·gious (kən tā′jəs), *adj.* 1. capable of being spread from person to person, as a disease: *Measles are contagious.* 2. easily spread: *contagious laughter.* —**con·ta′gious·ly,** *adv.* —**con·ta′gious·ness,** *n.*

con·tain (kən tān′), *v.* 1. to hold or include: *This folder contains all my reports.* 2. to be capable of holding: *This bottle contains one quart.* 3. to have as a part or parts: *A cake contains flour and other ingredients.* 4. to control or hold back: *He could not contain his amusement.* —**con·tain′ment,** *n.*

con·tain·er (kən tā′nər), *n.* anything that contains or can contain something, such as a carton, box, or can.

con·tam·i·nate (kən tam′ə nāt′), *v.,* **con·tam·i·nat·ed, con·tam·i·nat·ing.** to make dirty or spoil by mixing with or touching something unclean, bad, etc.; pollute: *Waste matter from the factories contaminates the rivers.* —**con·tam′i·na′tion,** *n.* —**con·tam′i·na′tor,** *n.*

contd., continued. Also, **cont'd.**

contemp., contemporary.

con·tem·plate (kon′təm plāt′), *v.,* **con·tem·plat·ed, con·tem·plat·ing.** 1. to look at carefully and for a long time: *We contemplated the beautiful scenery.* 2. to think deeply about: *to contemplate a problem.* 3. to have as a purpose; plan: *to contemplate traveling.* 4. to expect or look forward to: *to contemplate trouble.* —**con′tem·pla′tion,** *n.*

con·tem·pla·tive (kən tem′plə tiv, kon′təm plā′tiv), *adj.* given to contemplation; thoughtful: *Often a contemplative person would rather think than act.*

con·tem·po·ra·ne·ous (kən tem′pə rā′nē əs), *adj.* contemporary; simultaneous: *Growth of sea power was contemporaneous with exploration of the New World.* —**con·tem′po·ra·ne·ous·ly,** *adv.*

con·tem·po·rar·y (kən tem′pə rer′ē), *adj.* 1. living, happening, or existing at the same period of time, past or present: *Newspapers report contemporary events.* —*n., pl.* **con·tem·po·rar·ies.** 2. a person who lives at the same time as another: *General Lee and General Grant were contemporaries.*

con·tempt (kən tempt′), *n.* 1. the feeling with which a person thinks of anyone or anything that he considers low, bad, or worthless; scorn: *We have only contempt for people who betray their friends.* 2. the state of being despised; disgrace; dishonor: *We hold traitors in contempt.*

con·tempt·i·ble (kən temp′tə bəl), *adj.* deserving to be held in contempt; mean; low: *It is contemptible to hurt animals.* —**con·tempt′i·bly,** *adv.*

—**Usage.** *Contemptible,* which means "deserving contempt," should not be confused with *contemptuous,* which means "showing or expressing contempt": *That is a contemptible crime, and we should be contemptuous of anyone who commits it.*

con·temp·tu·ous (kən temp′chōō əs), *adj.* showing contempt or disdain; scornful: *He was contemptuous of foreigners.* —**con·temp′tu·ous·ly,** *adv.*

—**Usage.** See **contemptible.**

con·tend (kən tend′), *v.* 1. to struggle or fight: *to contend with difficulties.* 2. to compete: *to contend for a prize.* 3. to argue or declare: *He contended that there was life on other planets.*

con·tent[1] (kon'tent), *n.* **1.** Usually, **contents.** something that is contained: *the contents of a box; the contents of a book.* **2.** the thoughts, ideas, information, etc., contained in a speech or piece of writing: *He spoke for hours, but what he said had little content.* **3.** the amount that is or can be contained: *The jar has a content of three pints.* [from the Latin word *contentum* "what is contained"]

con·tent[2] (kən tent'), *adj.* **1.** satisfied with what one has; not wanting more or anything else: *I am content with very little.* —*v.* **2.** to make content; satisfy: *He was contented by the good food and a rest.* —*n.* **3.** contentment; satisfaction: *We sang and played to our heart's content.* [from the Latin word *contentus* "satisfied"]

con·tent·ed (kən ten'tid), *adj.* satisfied; content: *I am contented with my life as it is.* —**con·tent'ed·ly,** *adv.*

con·ten·tion (kən ten'shən), *n.* **1.** a struggle, quarrel, or dispute. **2.** something that is argued over, as an idea or point: *to dispute a contention.*

con·ten·tious (kən ten'shəs), *adj.* tending to or causing quarrels: *a stubborn, contentious person.* —**con·ten'tious·ly,** *adv.*

con·tent·ment (kən tent'mənt), *n.* the state of being contented; satisfaction: *to live in contentment.*

con·test (kon'test), *n.* **1.** a struggle, conflict, or competition: *After a long contest we won the game.* —*v.* (kən test'). **2.** to struggle or fight for, as in battle or a competition: *They bravely contested the victory.* **3.** to dispute or call in question: *They contested my right to speak.*

con·test·ant (kən tes'tənt), *n.* a person who takes part in a contest or competition.

con·text (kon'tekst), *n.* the parts of something written or spoken that come before or follow a word or passage, usually influencing its meaning: *In this context "passage" means "a group of words."*

con·tig·u·ous (kən tig'yoo əs), *adj.* **1.** touching or in contact: *The house and the garage are contiguous.* **2.** near or close: *The town is contiguous to the ocean.* —**con·tig'u·ous·ly,** *adv.*

con·ti·nence (kon't³nəns), *n.* self-restraint; temperance; moderation. Also, **con'ti·nen·cy.**

con·ti·nent (kon't³nənt), *n.* one of the seven main bodies of land of the globe, including Europe, Asia, Africa, North America, South America, Australia, and Antarctica.

Con·ti·nent (kon't³nənt), *n.* **the,** the mainland of Europe; Europe without the British Isles.

con·ti·nen·tal (kon't³nen't³l), *adj.* of or referring to a continent: *continental distances.* —**con'ti·nen'tal·ly,** *adv.*

Con·ti·nen·tal (kon't³nen't³l), *adj.* **1.** of or referring to the mainland of Europe, to Europeans, or to European customs, manners, etc.: *a Continental tour; Continental politeness.* **2.** of or referring to the 13 American colonies at or around the time of the American Revolution.

Continen'tal Divide', the summits of the Rocky Mountains, separating the streams flowing east and west. Also, **Great Divide.**

con·tin·gen·cy (kən tin'jən sē), *n., pl.* for def. 2 **con·tin·gen·cies.** **1.** the condition of being dependent on chance or accident: *the contingency of future events over which we have no control.* **2.** something that happens by chance or accident: *We must be prepared for every contingency.*

con·tin·gent (kən tin'jənt), *adj.* **1.** happening by chance or accident: *contingent events.* **2.** depending for existence, occurrence, etc., on something not yet certain (often fol. by *on* or *upon*): *Our plans are contingent on the weather.* —*n.* **3.** a number of troops to be provided. **4.** a group that is a part of a larger organization.

con·tin·u·al (kən tin'yoo əl), *adj.* **1.** proceeding without interruption or stoppage: *her continual dread of serious illness.* **2.** happening again and again: *continual visits to the doctor.* —**con·tin'u·al·ly,** *adv.*

—**Usage.** See **continuous.**

con·tin·u·ance (kən tin'yoo əns), *n.* **1.** an act or instance of continuing: *We hope for a continuance of the fine weather.* **2.** a remaining in the same place, circumstances, etc.: *a continuance on a job.*

con·tin·u·a·tion (kən tin'yoo ā'shən), *n.* **1.** the act or state of continuing or going on, after or without an interruption: *continuation of study after an illness.* **2.** anything that continues an event or procedure that has already appeared, taken place, etc.: *Today's weather will be a continuation of yesterday's.*

con·tin·ue (kən tin'yoo), *v.,* **con·tin·ued, con·tin·u·ing.** **1.** to go on or keep on: *We continued with our game all morning.* **2.** to go on with: *to continue an action.* **3.** to go on after a break or interruption: *The program continued after an intermission.* **4.** to carry on or take up again after an interruption: *We continued the program after an intermission.* **5.** to remain or stay, as in a place, position, state, etc.: *The mayor will continue in office.*

con·ti·nu·i·ty (kon'ti noo'i tē, -nyoo'-), *n.* the state or quality of being continuous; continuation without a break: *No rainy days broke the continuity of the warm, sunny weather.*

con·tin·u·ous (kən tin'yoo əs), *adj.* **1.** having its parts in close or unbroken order: *a continuous row of trees.* **2.** uninterrupted in time from beginning to end: *continuous interest.* —**con·tin'u·ous·ly,** *adv.*

—**Usage.** *Continuous* means "without stop or interruption." It should not be confused with *continual,* which means "happening at regular intervals; frequent or repeated": *a continuous flow of water; continual demands for payment.*

con·tort (kən tôrt'), *v.* to twist; bend out of shape; distort: *A look of hatred contorted his face.*

con·tor·tion (kən tôr'shən), *n.* **1.** the act or process of contorting. **2.** the state of being contorted; twisted condition. **3.** a contorted shape or position:

We were amazed by the contortions of the acrobats.

con·tour (kon'tŏŏr), *n.* the outline of a figure or body, or a line that represents it in a map or drawing. [from a French word, which is formed on the model of Italian *contorno* "outline"]

con·tra·band (kon'trə band'), *n.* **1.** anything forbidden by law to be brought into or carried out of a country; smuggled goods. —*adj.* **2.** forbidden by law to be brought into or carried out of a country: *a truckload of contraband goods.*

con·tra·bass (kon'trə bās'), *n.* another name for **double bass.**

con·tract (kon'trakt), *n.* **1.** an agreement between two or more persons, groups, etc., for doing or not doing something, esp. one that is enforceable by law. **2.** the written form of such an agreement. —*v.* (kən-trakt'). **3.** to draw or come closer together: *to contract a muscle.* **4.** to get or acquire: *to contract a disease.* **5.** to make a contract: *He contracted to build a house for his neighbors.* **6.** to shorten (a word or phrase) by combining or omitting some of its letters: *"Do not" may be contracted to "don't."*

con·trac·tion (kən trak'shən), *n.* **1.** an act or instance of contracting: *the contraction of a muscle.* **2.** the state of being contracted: *Metal is in contraction when cold.* **3.** a shorter form of a word or group of words, as *e'er* for *ever,* or *don't* for *do not.*

con·trac·tor (kon'trak tər, kən trak'tər), *n.* a person who contracts to furnish supplies or perform work at a certain rate or price.

con·tra·dict (kon'trə dikt'), *v.* **1.** to deny or state the opposite of: *He contradicted the statement I made.* **2.** to speak contrary to (another person): *He contradicts me, no matter what I say.* **3.** to be contrary to: *His behavior contradicts his fine words.*

con·tra·dic·tion (kon'trə dik'shən), *n.* **1.** the act of contradicting; denial. **2.** a statement or fact that contradicts: *His report is full of contradictions.* **3.** an instance of disagreement: *There is a contradiction between his behavior and his words.*

con·tra·dic·to·ry (kon'trə dik'tə rē), *adj.* **1.** stating the opposite or contrary: *a contradictory report.* **2.** tending to contradict: *a contradictory person.*

con·tral·to (kən tral'tō), *n., pl.* **con·tral·tos.** (in music) **1.** the lowest female voice. **2.** a singer with such a voice.

con·trap·tion (kən trap'shən), *n.* a contrivance, gadget, or device: *What do you call that contraption with the long handle?*

con·tra·ry (kon'trer ē; *for def. 4 also* kən trâr'ē), *adj.* **1.** opposite in nature; opposed: *Your likes are contrary to mine.* **2.** opposite in direction or position: *contrary currents.* **3.** unfavorable: *contrary weather conditions.* **4.** tending always to disagree or contradict: *Contrary people love to deny what we believe true.* —*n.* **5.** something that is contrary or opposite: *to prove the contrary of a statement.* —*adv.* **6.** in opposition: *He acts contrary to his desires.* **7.** **on the contrary,** in opposition to what is said: *Is it snowing? On the contrary, the sun is shining.* —**con'tra·ri·ness,** *n.*

con·trast (kən trast'), *v.* **1.** to compare in order to show unlikeness or differences: *to contrast the present with the past.* **2.** to show unlikeness or differences when compared: *The green blouse will contrast with the red skirt.* —*n.* (kon'trast). **3.** the act of contrasting, or the state of being contrasted: *In contrast to yesterday, today is quite warm.* **4.** a difference shown by making a comparison: *There is a remarkable contrast between them although they are brothers.* **5.** a person or thing that is strikingly unlike in comparison: *He is quite a contrast to his brother.*

contrib., **1.** contribution. **2.** contributor.

con·trib·ute (kən trib'yŏŏt), *v.,* **con·trib·ut·ed, con·trib·ut·ing.** **1.** to give (money, help, time, etc.) along with others: *He contributed a large sum to our charity.* **2.** to help bring about or cause something (usually fol. by *to*): *Exercise contributes to health.* —**con·trib'u·tor,** *n.* —**con·trib'u·to'ry,** *adj.*

con·tri·bu·tion (kon'tri byŏŏ'shən), *n.* **1.** the act of contributing. **2.** something contributed: *a generous contribution to charity.*

con·trite (kən trīt'), *adj.* feeling or showing guilt and regret; repentant: *She was contrite about her unkind remarks. He offered a contrite apology.* —**con·trite'ly,** *adv.*

con·tri·tion (kən trish'ən), *n.* sorrow and regret for a fault, sin, etc.; repentance: *She remembered her unkindness with contrition.*

con·triv·ance (kən trī'vəns), *n.* **1.** something contrived or invented, such as a device, machine, etc.: *a contrivance for opening cans.* **2.** the act or manner of contriving: *a plan that shows painstaking contrivance.* **3.** a plan or scheme: *No contrivance could get him to come with us.*

con·trive (kən trīv'), *v.,* **con·trived, con·triv·ing.** **1.** to invent or devise: *to contrive a machine.* **2.** to plot or plan with cleverness: *to contrive a murder.* **3.** to bring about: *to contrive an escape.* **4.** to manage, as by a plan or scheme: *We contrived to go with them even though we were not invited.* —**con·triv'er,** *n.*

con·trol (kən trōl'), *v.,* **con·trolled, con·trol·ling.** **1.** to direct or command: *The captain controls the ship.* **2.** to hold back or in check; curb: *to control a horse; to control one's anger.* —*n.* **3.** the act or power of control: *He lost control of the plane. She lost control of her temper.* **4.** the state of being controlled: *The car is out of control.* **5.** something that serves to check, limit, etc.; a means of controlling: *a price control.* **6.** a device for regulating or guiding a vehicle, machine, etc.: *the controls of an airplane.* —**con·trol'la·ble,** *adj.*

con·trol·ler (kən trō'lər), *n.* **1.** Also, **comptroller.** a person in charge of spending, as for a government or company. **2.** a person who controls or restrains.

con·tro·ver·sial (kon'trə vûr'shəl), *adj.* causing or likely to cause an argument, quarrel, etc.: *Politics is a very controversial subject.* —**con'tro·ver'sial·ly,** *adv.*

con·tro·ver·sy (kon'trə vûr'sē), *n., pl.* **con·tro·ver·sies.** a dispute, debate, argument, or quarrel: *The plans for the building caused a controversy.*

con·tu·sion (kən tŏŏ'zhən, -tyŏŏ'-), *n.* an injury to

the flesh in which the skin is not broken; bruise: *He suffered cuts and contusions in the accident.*

co·nun·drum (kə nun′drəm), *n.* a riddle whose answer is in the form of a pun, as "Why is a man with a sore throat like a colt? Because he's a little hoarse."

con·va·lesce (kon′və les′), *v.,* **con·va·lesced, con·va·lesc·ing.** to regain one's health, esp. slowly, after an illness.

con·va·les·cence (kon′və les′əns), *n.* **1.** the gradual return to health and strength after an illness. **2.** the period in which this takes place: *His convalescence was shorter than the doctors had expected.*

con·va·les·cent (kon′və les′ənt), *adj.* **1.** returning to health and strength again after an illness; convalescing. **2.** of or referring to convalescence: *a convalescent hospital.* —*n.* **3.** a convalescent person.

con·vec·tion (kən vek′shən), *n.* a process by which heat is transmitted in liquids and gases and that involves movement of the liquid or gas from a warm region to a cooler one.

con·vene (kən vēn′), *v.,* **con·vened, con·ven·ing. 1.** to come together; gather; assemble: *The committee will convene at noon.* **2.** to cause to come together: *The chairman convened the members of the club.*

con·ven·ience (kən vēn′yəns), *n.* **1.** the quality of being convenient; suitability: *the convenience of a large kitchen.* **2.** use, enjoyment, or assistance: *Timetables are issued for the convenience of travelers.* **3.** anything that saves or simplifies work, adds to comfort, etc.: *Their new house is equipped with all the modern conveniences.*

con·ven·ient (kən vēn′yənt), *adj.* **1.** easy to use, reach, etc.; handy or suitable: *a convenient arrangement of utensils.* **2.** at hand or nearby: *My house is convenient to the park.* —**con·ven′ient·ly,** *adv.*

con·vent (kon′vent), *n.* **1.** a group of women who live together for the purpose of devoting their lives to religion: *a convent of nuns.* **2.** the building or buildings in which such a group lives.

con·ven·tion (kən ven′shən), *n.* **1.** a meeting held for the purpose of discussing or acting on matters of concern for all: *a convention of lawyers; a political convention.* **2.** the accepted customs of a society or a social class: *He defied convention and lived as he pleased.* **3.** an accepted way of behaving or doing something; custom: *It is a convention for a man to rise when a woman enters the room.* **4.** *(often cap.)* an agreement between countries: *The Geneva Convention set rules for the treatment of war prisoners.*

con·ven·tion·al (kən ven′shə nəl), *adj.* **1.** following a custom or customs: *"Hello" is a conventional greeting.* **2.** living or acting in the accepted or customary way: *Conventional people are often suspicious of artists.* **3.** usual or ordinary: *conventional cooking.* —**con·ven′tion·al·ly,** *adv.*

con·ven·tion·al·i·ty (kən ven′shə nal′i tē), *n., pl.* for def. 2 **con·ven·tion·al·i·ties. 1.** acceptance of or devotion to convention: *the conventionality of life in a small town.* **2.** a conventional way of acting, doing

something, etc.: *He was extremely polite and followed all the conventionalities.*

con·verge (kən vûrj′), *v.,* **con·verged, con·verg·ing.** to come together at a point: *Traffic converged from all directions.*

con·ver·gence (kən vûr′jəns), *n.* **1.** an act or instance of converging. **2.** a point of converging: *We met at the convergence of the two streets.* —**con·ver′gent,** *adj.*

con·ver·sant (kən vûr′sənt), *adj.* familiar or acquainted (usually fol. by *with*): *to be conversant with French history.*

con·ver·sa·tion (kon′vər sā′shən), *n.* talk between two or more persons. —**con′ver·sa′tion·al,** *adj.*

con·verse¹ (kən vûrs′), *v.,* **con·versed, con·vers·ing.** to talk together; have a conversation: *We conversed about the weather.* [from the Latin word *conversāri* "to associate with"]

con·verse² (kən vûrs′, kon′vûrs), *adj.* **1.** opposite or contrary; turned around: *the converse direction.* —*n.* (kon′vûrs). **2.** something that is the opposite or contrary of another: *"Hot" is the converse of "cold."* [from the Latin word *conversus* "turned around"] —**con·verse·ly** (kən vûrs′lē, kon′vûrs lē), *adv.*

con·ver·sion (kən vûr′zhən), *n.* **1.** a change into another form or use: *the conversion of water into ice.* **2.** a change in a person's beliefs or opinions: *conversion to Christianity.*

con·vert (kən vûrt′), *v.* **1.** to change into a different form or alter for a different use: *to convert a barn into a house.* **2.** to cause a change of belief or opinion in: *We converted him to our point of view.* —*n.* (kon′vûrt). **3.** a person who has been converted.

con·vert·i·ble (kən vûr′tə bəl), *adj.* **1.** capable of being converted. —*n.* **2.** an automobile having a folding top. —**con·vert′i·bil′i·ty,** *n.*

con·vex (kon veks′, kon′veks), *adj.* curved or rounded outward, as the surface of a ball: *a convex mirror.* —**con·vex′ly,** *adv.*

con·vey (kən vā′), *v.* **1.** to carry, bring, or take from one place to another; conduct: *Pipes convey water.* **2.** to make known: *I will convey your message to him.* **3.** to put into the possession of another person, such as land.

Convex lenses

con·vey·ance (kən vā′əns), *n.* **1.** the act of conveying: *to charge for the conveyance of goods.* **2.** a means of transporting, such as a truck, bus, or other vehicle.

con·vey·or (kən vā′ər), *n.* a device used to transport materials, such as a set of rollers or an endless belt (**convey′or belt′**) or chain.

con·vict (kən vikt′), *v.* **1.** to prove or declare guilty, esp. after a trial: *He was convicted for the murder.* —*n.* (kon′vikt). **2.** a person proved or declared guilty, esp. one serving his sentence in prison.

con·vic·tion (kən vik′shən), *n.* **1.** the act of convicting, or the state of being convicted. **2.** a strong or fixed belief: *a religious conviction.* **3.** steadfastness in belief or purpose: *He argued with great conviction.*

con·vince (kən vins´), *v.*, **con·vinced, con·vinc·ing.** to persuade or cause to believe: *I convinced him that he was wrong.* —**con·vinc´ing·ly,** *adv.*

con·viv·i·al (kən viv´ē əl), *adj.* 1. fond of parties and good times; sociable. 2. merry and festive: *a convivial dinner.* —**con·viv´i·al·ly,** *adv.*

con·vo·ca·tion (kon´və kā´shən), *n.* 1. the act of convoking. 2. a group of people convoked; assembly: *A large convocation filled the auditorium.*

con·voke (kən vōk´), *v.*, **con·voked, con·vok·ing.** to call together; summon to meet: *The club members were convoked for the annual election.*

con·voy (kon´voi, kən voi´), *v.* 1. to accompany or escort, usually for protection. —*n.* (kon´voi). 2. the act of convoying, or the state of being convoyed: *the convoy of ships in time of war.* 3. an escort for protection: *The warships were a convoy for the freighters.* 4. a ship, fleet, group of vehicles, etc., together with their escort.

con·vulse (kən vuls´), *v.*, **con·vulsed, con·vuls·ing.** 1. to cause to respond with or show violent emotion, pain, etc.: *Laughter convulsed the audience.* 2. to throw into convulsions: *The fit convulsed his body.* 3. to shake or disturb violently: *The earthquake convulsed the town.*

con·vul·sion (kən vul´shən), *n.* 1. a violent, involuntary contortion of the body; fit. 2. a violent disturbance: *the convulsions of war.* 3. an outburst of laughter: *the audience was in convulsions.*

con·vul·sive (kən vul´siv), *adj.* 1. like a convulsion: *a convulsive earthquake.* 2. having or showing convulsions: *convulsive behavior.* —**con·vul´sive·ly,** *adv.*

coo (ko͞o), *n.* 1. the murmuring sound of a pigeon or dove. —*v.*, **cooed, coo·ing.** 2. to make this sound. 3. to speak softly and lovingly.

cook (ko͝ok), *v.* 1. to prepare (food) by using heat, as by boiling, baking, roasting, etc. 2. to undergo cooking: *The chicken has been cooking for an hour.* 3. to prepare food by cooking: *She cooks for us on weekends.* 4. **cook up,** *Informal.* to invent or think up: *to cook up an excuse.*

cook·book (ko͝ok´bo͝ok´), *n.* a book containing recipes and instructions for cooking.

cook·er (ko͝ok´ər), *n.* a utensil for cooking: *a pressure cooker.*

cook·er·y (ko͝ok´ə rē), *n.* the craft or skill of cooking.

cook·ie (ko͝ok´ē), *n., pl.* **cook·ies.** a small, thin, sweet cake. Also, **cooky.**

cook·y (ko͝ok´ē), *n., pl.* **cook·ies.** another spelling of **cookie.**

cool (ko͞ol), *adj.* 1. slightly cold; not warm: *a cool evening.* 2. feeling free of uncomfortable warmth: *We were much cooler after our swim.* 3. allowing one to feel cool: *light, cool clothing.* 4. calm; unexcited: *He remained cool in spite of the danger.* 5. lacking in friendliness: *a cool greeting.* 6. (of colors) not bright or rich, as blue and green. 7. *Informal.* (of a number or sum) full or entire: *He made a cool million in the stock market.* —*n.* 8. a cool part or portion: *the cool of the evening.* —*v.* 9. to make or become cool: *Let*

your tea cool a bit before you drink it. —**cool´ly,** *adv.* —**cool´ness,** *n.*

cool·er (ko͞o´lər), *n.* 1. a container or device in which something may be cooled or kept cool: *to take a cooler along on a picnic.* 2. something that cools, such as a cold beverage. 3. *Slang.* a jail.

Cool·idge (ko͞o´lij), *n.* Calvin, 1872–1933, 29th Vice President of the U.S. 1921–1923; 30th President of the U.S. 1923–1929.

coo·lie (ko͞o´lē), *n., pl.* **coo·lies.** a cheaply paid, unskilled laborer in the Orient, esp. China and India.

coon (ko͞on), *n.* short for **raccoon.**

co-op (kō´op, kō op´), *n.* a cooperative.

coop (ko͞op), *n.* 1. a cage or pen for fowls and other small animals, such as rabbits. —*v.* 2. to shut up in or as if in a coop (often fol. by *up*): *to be cooped up in one's house because of illness.*

coop·er (ko͞o´pər, ko͝op´er), *n.* a person who makes or mends casks, barrels, etc.

co·op·er·ate (kō op´ə rāt´), *v.*, **co·op·er·at·ed, co·op·er·at·ing.** to work together willingly for a common purpose: *If we all cooperate, we can finish the job in about an hour.*

co·op·er·a·tion (kō op´ə rā´shən), *n.* an act or instance of cooperating; a working together for a common purpose: *A clean city requires the cooperation of all citizens.*

co·op·er·a·tive (kō op´ə rā´tiv, kō op´ər ə tiv), *adj.* 1. working or acting together willingly for a common purpose. 2. of or referring to cooperation: *a cooperative effort.* 3. of or referring to a cooperative. —*n.* (kō op´ər ə tiv) 4. a store, apartment house, etc., owned by the group of people who use it. —**co·op´er·a·tive·ly,** *adv.*

co·or·di·nate (kō ôr´dᵊnāt´), *v.*, **co·or·di·nat·ed, co·or·di·nat·ing.** 1. to place in or assume proper order or relation; harmonize: *to coordinate facts before making a report; to coordinate colors in decorating a room.* —*adj.* (kō ôr´dᵊnit, kō ôr´dᵊnāt´). 2. of the same importance; equal: *the coordinate branches of government.* —*n.* (kō ôr´dᵊnit, kôr´dᵊnāt´). 3. one of a group of numbers that give the position of a point, line, or the like.

co·or·di·na·tion (kō ôr´dᵊnā´shən), *n.* 1. the act of coordinating, or the state of being coordinated. 2. proper or harmonious order or relationship: *The coordination of the dancers was perfect.*

coot (ko͞ot), *n.* 1. a North American water bird having short wings and a very short tail. 2. a foolish or crotchety old man.

Coot
(length 16 in.)

cop¹ (kop), *v.*, **copped, cop·ping.** *Slang.* to steal; filch. [from an Old English word such as *copian* "to plunder, steal"]

cop² (kop), *n.* *Informal.* a policeman. [short for *copper,* which comes from *cop¹ + -er*]

cope (kōp), *v.*, **coped, cop·ing.** to struggle or contend successfully or with hope of success: *to cope with a problem.*

Co·pen·ha·gen (kō/pən hā/gən), *n.* a seaport and the capital city of Denmark, in the E part.

Co·per·ni·cus (kə pûr/nə kəs), *n.* **Nic·o·la·us** (nik/ə-lā/əs), 1473–1543, Polish astronomer: proposed the theory that the earth rotated around the sun. —**Co·per/ni·can,** *adj.*

co·pi·lot (kō/pī/lət), *n.* a pilot who is second in command in an aircraft.

cop·ing (kō/pĭng), *n.* the top layer of a wall of brick or stone, usually sloped so as to shed rain water.

cop/ing saw/, a saw having a light, ribbonlike blade held in a U-shaped frame: used for cutting small curves in wood.

co·pi·ous (kō/pē əs), *adj.* in great supply; plentiful; abundant: *a copious harvest.* —**co/pi·ous·ly,** *adv.*

Coping saw

cop·per (kop/ər), *n.* a soft reddish metal that is an excellent conductor of heat and electricity: a chemical element. *Symbol:* Cu [from the Old English word *coper,* which comes from the Latin phrase *aes Cyprium* "Cyprian bronze"]

cop·per·head (kop/ər hed/), *n.* a poisonous snake of the eastern U.S. having a brown or copper-colored body marked with darker bands.

cop·per·smith (kop/ər smith/), *n.* a person who works in copper, for example making kitchenware or jewelry.

cop·ra (kop/rə), *n.* the dried meat of the coconut, a source of coconut oil.

copse (kops), *n.* a thicket of bushes or small trees. Also, **cop·pice** (kop/is).

Copperhead
(length to 3 ft.)

cop·y (kop/ē), *n., pl.* **cop·ies.** **1.** an imitation, reproduction, or likeness of something: *a copy of a letter.* **2.** written material or pictures to be reproduced in printed form in books, magazines, etc. **3.** a single one of a number of books, magazines, etc., made alike: *I lost my copy of the geography book.* —*v.,* **cop·ied, cop·y·ing.** **4.** to make a copy of. **5.** to follow as a model or pattern: *to copy the behavior of others.* —**cop/i·er,** *n.*

cop·y·right (kop/ē rīt/), *n.* **1.** the exclusive right granted by law for a certain amount of time to make and sell copies of a book, piece of music, etc. —*v.* **2.** to protect by such a right: *to copyright a book.*

co·quette (kō ket/), *n.* a girl or woman who has the habit of flirting with men in order to gain their attentions. —**co·quet/tish,** *adj.*

Coral

cor·al (kôr/əl, kor/əl), *n.* **1.** a hard substance, usually reddish, pink, or white, made up of the skeletons of tiny sea animals. **2.** the animal itself. **3.** a light yellowish red or pink. —*adj.* **4.** made of coral: *a coral reef.* **5.** of a yellowish red.

Cor/al Sea/, a part of the S Pacific Ocean, between Australia and New Guinea.

cor/al snake/, a small, poisonous snake of the southeastern U.S., marked with brilliant bands of red, yellow, and black.

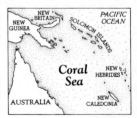
Coral Sea

cord (kôrd), *n.* **1.** a heavy string or thin rope made of several strands braided, twisted, or woven together. **2.** a cordlike structure in the body: *the spinal cord.* **3.** anything resembling a cord, esp. a small, insulated electric wire: *to attach a cord to a lamp.* **4.** a unit of volume equal to 128 cubic feet. It is used esp. for measuring firewood and is usually considered as a pile 4 feet high, 4 feet deep, and 8 feet long. —*v.* **5.** to bind or fasten with a cord or cords: *to cord a bundle.* **6.** to pile or stack up (wood) in cords.

cord·age (kôr/dij), *n.* ropes, lines, etc., esp. the ropes that form the rigging of a ship.

cor·dial (kôr/jəl), *adj.* **1.** courteous and gracious: *We received a very cordial welcome from the host and hostess.* —*n.* **2.** a strong, sweet alcoholic liquor. —**cor/dial·ly,** *adv.*

cor·dial·i·ty (kôr/jē al/i tē), *n.* cordial quality or feeling.

cor·don (kôr/dən), *n.* **1.** a line of policemen, sentinels, soldiers, etc., surrounding an area for protection. **2.** a braid or ribbon worn as a decoration or as a badge of honor.

cor·do·van (kôr/də vən), *n.* **1.** a soft, smooth leather made of horsehide, pigskin, etc. —*adj.* **2.** made of this leather: *a new pair of cordovan shoes.* [from *Cordova,* a city in Spain where the leather was originally made]

cor·du·roy (kôr/də roi/), *n.* **1.** a thick cotton cloth with lengthwise ridges, used esp. in clothing. —*adj.* **2.** made of this cloth: *corduroy trousers.*

cord·wood (kôrd/wŏŏd/), *n.* wood for fuel that is stacked in cords or sold by the cord.

core (kôr), *n.* **1.** the central part of such fruits as apples and pears, which contains the seeds. **2.** the central or innermost part of anything: *the core of the earth.* —*v.,* **cored, cor·ing.** **3.** to remove the core of: *She cored the apples before she baked them.*

CORE (kôr), *n.* Congress of Racial Equality. Also, **C.O.R.E.**

Cor·inth (kôr/inth), *n.* an ancient city in central Greece.

Co·rin·thi·an (kə rin/thē ən), *adj.* **1.** of, referring to, or characteristic of Corinth. **2.** noting a very ornate style, or order, of ancient Greek architecture. See also **Doric, Ionic.** See illus. at **order.** —*n.* **3.** a native or inhabitant of Corinth.

Co·rin·thi·ans (kə rin'thē ənz), *n. (used as sing.)* either of two books of the New Testament, believed to have been written by Paul to the people of Corinth.

cork (kôrk), *n.* **1.** the bark of a kind of oak tree that grows in southern Europe. It is soft and light in weight and is used for making bottle stoppers, floats, and floor coverings. **2.** a piece of cork that has been shaped, esp. to make a bottle stopper. **3.** any stopper made of other material, as rubber or glass. —*v.* **4.** to stop with a cork: *to cork a bottle.* [from the Arabic word *qurq,* which comes from Latin *quercus* "oak"]

cork·screw (kôrk'skrōō'), *n.* **1.** a tool consisting of a spiral of metal with a sharp point and a handle, used for piercing and drawing out corks from bottles. —*adj.* **2.** like a corkscrew in shape; spiral.

corm (kôrm), *n.* a fleshy bulblike base of a stem.

cor·mo·rant (kôr'mər ənt), *n.* a sea bird with a long neck, used esp. in the Orient for catching fish.

corn[1] (kôrn), *n.* **1.** a tall cereal plant native to America that bears kernels on large ears. **2.** the grain of this plant. **3.** the grain borne by certain other cereal plants, esp. wheat in England and oats in Scotland. —*v.* **4.** to preserve and season with heavily salted water or dry salt: *to corn beef.* Also, **Indian corn, maize** (for defs. 1, 2). [from an Old English word meaning "grain, seed," related to Latin *grānum* "grain"]

Cormorant
(length 3 ft.)

corn[2] (kôrn), *n.* a small, usually painful callus on the toes or feet, sometimes caused by shoes that do not fit properly. [from an Old French word, which comes from Latin *cornū* "horn"]

corn' bread', a bread made from corn meal.

corn·cob (kôrn'kob'), *n.* the woody core of an ear of corn.

cor·ne·a (kôr'nē ə), *n.* the transparent outer covering of the front of the eyeball. See illus. at **eye.** [from the Latin word *corneus* "hard as horn," which comes from *cornū* "horn"] —**cor'ne·al,** *adj.*

corned (kôrnd), *adj.* preserved and seasoned with salt: *corned beef.*

cor·ner (kôr'nər), *n.* **1.** the place where two lines or surfaces meet. **2.** the space between these lines or surfaces: *the corner of a room.* **3.** the point where two streets meet: *to wait on the corner.* **4.** a secret, hidden, or narrow place; nook. **5.** a faraway region or place: *People come here from all corners of the earth.* —*adj.* **6.** on or at a corner: *the corner store.* —*v.* **7.** to place in or drive into a corner. **8.** to force into a difficult or dangerous position or one from which it is impossible to escape: *The thief was cornered by the police.* **9. cut corners, a.** to go by a shorter route. **b.** to reduce costs or use less care: *He cut corners by using old lumber.*

cor·ner·stone (kôr'nər stōn'), *n.* a stone built into the corner of a building, esp. such a stone laid during a ceremony at the time the building is begun.

cor·net (kôr net'), *n.* a valved musical instrument similar to a trumpet, usually made of brass.

corn·flow·er (kôrn'flou'er), *n.* a field plant having small blue, pink, or white flowers. Also, **bluebottle.**

cor·nice (kôr'nis), *n.* a molding that runs along the side of a wall at the very top, used outside of buildings or in rooms, where it appears just below the ceiling.

Cornet

Cor·nish (kôr'nish), *adj.* **1.** of or referring to Cornwall, its people, or the Cornish language. —*n.* **2.** a Celtic language formerly spoken in Cornwall.

corn' meal', meal made of ground corn.

corn·starch (kôrn'stärch'), *n.* a starchy flour made from corn, used to thicken sauces, puddings, etc.

cor·nu·co·pi·a (kôr'nə kō'pē ə), *n.* **1.** (in Greek mythology) a horn filled with an endless supply of whatever its owner desired. **2.** an ornament or container in the shape of a horn or cone, esp. one used to decorate Christmas trees. Also, **horn of plenty.** [from the Latin words *cornū* "horn" + *copiae* "of plenty"]

Corn·wall (kôrn'wôl), *n.* a county in SW England. 1357 sq. mi.

Cornucopia

corn·y (kôr'nē), *adj.,* **corn·i·er, corn·i·est.** *Informal.* trite, silly, or stale: *corny jokes.* —**corn'i·ness,** *n.*

co·rol·la (kə rol'ə), *n.* the petals of a flower considered as a group.

co·ro·na (kə rō'nə), *n.* **1.** the faintly glowing gas surrounding the sun. **2.** a ring of light seen around the sun or moon caused by mist or dust in the air.

cor·o·nar·y (kôr'ə ner'ē), *adj.* of or referring to the heart: *coronary arteries.*

cor·o·na·tion (kôr'ə nā'shən), *n.* the act or ceremony of crowning a king, queen, or other sovereign.

cor·o·ner (kôr'ə nər), *n.* a public official who investigates any death not due to natural causes.

cor·o·net (kôr'ə net'), *n.* a small crown worn by royalty below the rank of king or queen and by the nobility.

corp., **1.** corporal. **2.** corporation. Also, **Corp.**

corpl., corporal. Also, **Corpl.**

cor·po·ral[1] (kôr'pər əl), *adj.* of or referring to the body: *corporal punishment.* [from the Latin word *corporālis,* which comes from *corpus* "body"] —**cor'po·ral·ly,** *adv.*

cor·po·ral[2] (kôr'pər əl), *n.* a noncommissioned officer of lowest rank in the U.S. Army, ranking below a sergeant and above a private. [from the Italian word *caporale,* which comes from *capo* "head, chief," from Latin *caput* "head"]

cor·po·rate (kôr'pər it), *adj.* **1.** forming a corporation: *a corporate business.* **2.** of or belonging to a corporation: *corporate debts.*

cor·po·ra·tion (kôr'pə rā'shən), *n.* a group of persons permitted by law to act like a single individual, as in owning and operating a business, college, or other establishment.

cor·po·re·al (kôr pôr′ē əl), *adj.* of the nature of the body; bodily or material.

corps (kôr), *n., pl.* **corps** (kôrz). **1.** a large military unit made up of two or more divisions. **2.** a special branch in the armed forces: *a medical corps.* **3.** any group of persons working together for some purpose: *a corps of engineers.* [from a French word, which comes from Latin *corpus* "body"]

corpse (kôrps), *n.* a dead body, usually of a human being. [from the Old French word *cors,* which comes from Latin *corpus* "body"]

cor·pu·lent (kôr′pyə lənt), *adj.* stout; fat. —**cor′pu·lence,** *n.*

Cor·pus Chris·ti (kôr′pəs kris′tē), a port city in S Texas, on the Gulf of Mexico.

cor·pus·cle (kôr′pus əl), *n.* a red or white blood cell. See also **red corpuscle, white corpuscle.**

cor·ral (kə ral′), *n.* **1.** a fenced-in place or pen for horses, cattle, etc. **2.** a circle of wagons drawn together for defense during an encampment. —*v.,* **cor·ralled, cor·ral·ling. 3.** to drive into or shut up in a corral. **4.** to arrange (wagons) in a corral.

cor·rect (kə rekt′), *v.* **1.** to set or make right; remove the errors or faults from: *The new glasses corrected his eyesight.* **2.** to point out or mark the errors in: *The teacher corrected the exam papers.* **3.** to scold or punish in order to improve: *A mother should correct her children when they behave badly.* —*adj.* **4.** free from error: *a correct answer.* **5.** proper or fitting: *correct behavior.* —**cor·rect′ly,** *adv.* —**cor·rect′ness,** *n.*

cor·rec·tion (kə rek′shən), *n.* **1.** the act of correcting. **2.** something put in the place of a mistake or error: *He erased the mistake and put in a correction.* **3.** punishment; discipline.

cor·rec·tive (kə rek′tiv), *adj.* **1.** tending to correct; remedial: *Braces are a corrective device for the teeth.* —*n.* **2.** something that corrects or remedies.

cor·re·late (kôr′ə lāt′), *v.,* **cor·re·lat·ed, cor·re·lat·ing.** to bring into or have a meaningful relation; connect or come together in an orderly fashion: *to correlate two versions of a story.* —**cor′re·la′tion,** *n.*

cor·re·spond (kôr′i spond′), *v.* **1.** to send letters back and forth: *We correspond regularly.* **2.** to be in agreement: *His actions do not correspond with his words.* **3.** to be like or similar: *His views correspond to mine.*

cor·re·spond·ence (kôr′i spon′dəns), *n.* **1.** the letters or other mail that one receives or sends: *Today's correspondence was very large.* **2.** agreement, likeness, or similarity: *There is no correspondence of age between them.* **3.** the sending of letters back and forth: *Our correspondence continued for months.*

cor·re·spond·ent (kôr′i spon′dənt), *n.* **1.** a person with whom one exchanges letters: *I have correspondents all over the country.* **2.** a person employed by a newspaper, magazine, etc., to write and send news from a distant place.

cor·re·spond·ing (kôr′i spon′ding), *adj.* identical or in agreement: *corresponding fingerprints.* —**cor′re·spond′ing·ly,** *adv.*

cor·ri·dor (kôr′i dər), *n.* a long passage or hallway into which several rooms or apartments open.

cor·rob·o·rate (kə rob′ə rāt′), *v.,* **cor·rob·o·rat·ed, cor·rob·o·rat·ing.** to confirm or make more certain: *His facts corroborate my story of what happened.* —**cor·rob′o·ra′tion,** *n.*

cor·rode (kə rōd′), *v.,* **cor·rod·ed, cor·rod·ing.** to become eaten away or to eat away, esp. by chemical action. —**cor·rod′i·ble,** *adj.*

cor·ro·sion (kə rō′zhən), *n.* the process or result of corroding. —**cor·ro′sive,** *adj.*

cor·ru·gate (kôr′ə gāt′), *v.,* **cor·ru·gat·ed, cor·ru·gat·ing.** to draw or bend into folds or ridges: *to corrugate paper.* —**cor′ru·ga′tion,** *n.*

cor·rupt (kə rupt′), *adj.* **1.** dishonest or dishonorable: *a corrupt official.* **2.** wicked or depraved. **3.** spoiled or rotten: *corrupt meat.* —*v.* **4.** to make or become corrupt: *to corrupt public officials with bribes.* —**cor·rupt′i·ble,** *adj.* —**cor·rupt′ly,** *adv.*

cor·rup·tion (kə rup′shən), *n.* **1.** the act of corrupting, or the state of being corrupted. **2.** evil ways; depravity. **3.** dishonest practices, such as bribery: *corruption in public office.* **4.** decay or rottenness: *the smell of corruption.*

cor·sage (kôr säzh′), *n.* a small bunch of flowers worn by a woman, usually at the shoulder.

cor·sair (kôr′sâr), *n.* **1.** a pirate. **2.** a pirate ship. **3.** a privateer.

corse·let (kôrs′lit), *n.* a suit of light armor formerly worn by knights. Also, **cors′let.**

C, Corselet

cor·set (kôr′sit), *n.* a close-fitting undergarment worn by women over the waist and hips to shape them and give support. [from the Old French word *cors* "body, bodice," which comes from Latin *corpus* "body"]

Cor·si·ca (kôr′si kə), *n.* an island in the Mediterranean Sea, SE of France: a French department. 3367 sq. mi. —**Cor′si·can,** *n., adj.*

cor·tege (kôr tezh′), *n.* **1.** a group of attendants; retinue: *the king and his cortege.* **2.** a procession: *a funeral cortege.* Also, **cor·tège′.**

Cor·tés (kôr tez′), *n.* **Her·nan·do** (hûr nan′dō) *or* **Her·nán** (hûr nan′), 1485–1547, Spanish conqueror of Mexico. Also, **Cor·tez′.**

cor·tex (kôr′teks), *n., pl.* **cor·ti·ces** (kôr′ti sēz′). **1.** the outer covering of a body organ: *the cortex of the brain.* **2.** the bark of a stem or tree. —**cor′ti·cal,** *adj.*

Corsica

cos·met·ic (koz met**/**ik), *n.* a powder, lotion, or other preparation for beautifying the skin, nails, etc.

cos·mic (koz**/**mik), *adj.* **1.** of or referring to the entire universe. **2.** vast in size; immense: *an explosion of cosmic proportions.* —**cos/mi·cal·ly,** *adv.*

cos/mic rays/, radiation that enters the earth's atmosphere from outer space. It consists partly of subatomic particles of very high energy.

cos·mo·naut (koz**/**mə nôt**/**), *n.* a Russian astronaut.

cos·mo·pol·i·tan (koz**/**mə pol**/**i t°n), *adj.* **1.** belonging to or having contact with all the world: *New York and London are cosmopolitan cities.* **2.** familiar with or at home in many places in the world: *cosmopolitan travelers.* —*n.* **3.** a person who is at home in many places in the world and who has a wide understanding of different customs and ways of living.

cos·mos (koz**/**məs), *n.* **1.** the universe considered as an orderly system. **2.** a tall plant that bears white or pink flowers that resemble daisies. [from the Greek word *kosmos* "order, arrangement, universe"]

Cos·sack (kos**/**ak), *n.* a member of a people in czarist Russia famous for their skill as warriors and horsemen.

cost (kôst), *n.* **1.** the price paid or charged for something. **2.** a sacrifice or loss: *He continued to work at the cost of his health.* **3. costs,** legal expenses: *the costs of a law suit.* —*v.,* **cost, cost·ing. 4.** to be priced at; sell for: *The camera costs $40.* **5.** to cause the loss or sacrifice of: *Carelessness in driving may cost lives.* **6.** to demand or require: *Courtesy costs little effort.*

Cos·ta Ri·ca (kôs**/**tə rē**/**kə), a republic in Central America, between Panama and Nicaragua. 19,238 sq. mi. *Cap.:* San José. —**Cos/ta Ri/can.**

cost·ly (kôst**/**lē), *adj.,* **cost·li·er, cost·li·est. 1.** costing much; high-priced; expensive. **2.** resulting in much loss or harm: *a costly mistake.* —**cost/li·ness,** *n.*

cos·tume (kos**/**tōōm, -tyōōm), *n.* **1.** a style of dress worn at a certain time in history or in a certain country: *ancient Roman costume.* **2.** an imitation of a style of dress, as worn on the stage, at a party, etc. **3.** a way of dressing for a particular occasion: *a dancing costume.* —*v.,* **cos·tumed, cos·tum·ing. 4.** to dress in a costume.

co·sy (kō**/**zē), *adj.,* **co·si·er, co·si·est;** *n., pl.* **co·sies.** another spelling of **cozy.** —**co/si·ly,** *adv.* —**co/si·ness,** *n.*

cot[1] (kot), *n.* a light bed that can usually be folded, often made of canvas stretched over a frame. [from the Hindi word *khāt*]

cot[2] (kot), *n.* **1.** a small house; cottage. **2.** a small shelter for birds or animals; cote. [from the Old English word *cote*]

cote (kōt), *n.* a shelter for sheep, pigs, pigeons, etc.

co·til·lion (kō til**/**yən), *n.* a formal dance; ball.

cot·tage (kot**/**ij), *n.* a small house.

cot/tage cheese/, a loose, white, mild-flavored cheese made from skim-milk curds.

cot/ter pin/ (kot**/**ər), a split pin whose ends are spread after driving it through a hole. Cotter pins are sometimes used to keep wheels from coming off shafts.

cot·ton (kot**/**°n), *n.* **1.** a soft, white, downy substance consisting of the fibers attached to the seeds of a plant grown in warm climates. **2.** the plant bearing this substance. **3.** cloth woven from this substance.

cot/ton gin/, a machine for separating the fibers of cotton from the seeds, invented by Eli Whitney in 1793. [short for *cotton engine.* Formerly the word *engine* meant any kind of machine]

Cotton boll

cot·ton·mouth (kot**/**°n mouth**/**), *n., pl.* **cot·ton·mouths** (kot**/**°n mou*th*z**/**). a large, poisonous snake found in the swamps of the southeastern U.S. Also, **water moccasin.**

cot·ton·seed (kot**/**°n sēd**/**), *n.* the seed of the cotton plant. It yields an oil used in cooking and in making soaps, cosmetics, etc.

cot·ton·tail (kot**/**°n tāl**/**), *n.* any of several North American rabbits having a fluffy, white tail.

cot·ton·wood (kot**/**°n wood**/**), *n.* any of several poplar trees whose seeds bear tufts that resemble cotton.

couch (kouch), *n.* **1.** a piece of furniture for seating two or more persons, usually upholstered and having a back; sofa. —*v.* **2.** to put into words; express: *He couched his request in polite language.*

cou·gar (kōō**/**gər), *n.* a large, tawny animal of the cat family found in North and South America. Also, **mountain lion, panther, puma.**

Cougar
(total length 8 ft.)

cough (kôf), *v.* **1.** to force air from the lungs suddenly and usually involuntarily, producing a harsh noise. **2.** to get rid of by coughing (usually fol. by *up* or *out*): *to cough up a fish bone.* —*n.* **3.** a sickness that is marked by coughing. **4.** the sound or act of coughing: *a loud cough.*

cough/ drop/, a small piece of candy, often medicated, for relieving a cough, sore throat, etc.

could (kood), *v.* the past tense of **can**[1].

could·n't (kood**/**°nt), contraction of *could not: We couldn't go away for the weekend.*

couldst (koodst), *v.* an old form of **could,** found now chiefly in Biblical and poetic writing and used with *thou: Thou couldst marry the king's daughter.*

cou·lomb (kōō**/**lom, kōō**/**lōm), *n.* a unit of electric charge: the amount of charge transferred by a current of one ampere flowing for one second. *Abbr.:* C [named after Charles A. de *Coulomb* (1736–1806), French physicist and inventor]

coun·cil (koun**/**səl), *n.* **1.** a group of persons called together to decide on or discuss something of importance: *a council of clergymen.* **2.** a group of persons having the power to make laws or govern: *a city council.*

coun·cil·or (koun**/**sə lər, koun**/**slər), *n.* a member of a council. Also, **coun/ci·lor.**

coun·cil·man (koun**/**səl mən), *n., pl.* **coun·cil·men.** a member of a council, esp. of the lawmaking or governing body of a city or town.

coun·sel (koun'səl), *n.* **1.** advice or opinion: *to seek good counsel.* **2.** the act of advising or interchanging opinion: *to take counsel with friends.* **3.** a lawyer or group of lawyers in court: *the counsel for the defense.* —*v.,* **coun·seled** *or* **coun·selled; coun·sel·ing** *or* **coun·sel·ling.** **4.** to give advice to; advise: *He was counseled not to go.* **5.** to call for or recommend: *to counsel patience.*

coun·se·lor (koun'sə lər), *n.* **1.** a person who counsels; adviser. **2.** a lawyer. **3.** a person who supervises activities at a summer camp. Also, *esp. British,* **coun'sel·lor.**

count[1] (kount), *v.* **1.** to check over one by one to find the total number: *to count the apples in a bowl.* **2.** to say numbers in order: *to count up to 100.* **3.** to list the numbers up to: *When angry, count ten.* **4.** to include or take into account: *There will be five of us going if you count me.* **5.** to consider or judge: *I count myself lucky to be your friend.* **6.** to be worth something: *Every little bit counts.* —*n.* **7.** the act of counting. **8.** the number arrived at by counting. **9.** **count on,** to depend or rely on: *Can I count on you to be there?* [from the Old French word *conter,* which comes from Latin *computāre* "to compute"]

count[2] (kount), *n.* (in some European countries) a nobleman equal in rank to an English earl. [from the Old French word *conte,* which comes from Latin *comes* "companion"]

count·down (kount'doun'), *n.* **1.** the backward counting, usually by seconds, from the start of a process, such as a rocket launching, with the completion of the process occurring when zero is reached. **2.** the process taking place during such backward counting.

coun·te·nance (koun't³nəns), *n.* **1.** the appearance or expression of the face: *a gloomy countenance.* **2.** the face: *A troubled look crossed his countenance.* **3.** approval or encouragement: *He would not give his countenance to the plan.* —*v.,* **coun·te·nanced, coun·te·nanc·ing.** **4.** to permit, support, or approve: *The teacher did not countenance talking in class.*

count·er[1] (koun'tər), *n.* **1.** a long, narrow table in a store or bank at which business is carried on, such as the sale of goods and the handling of money. **2.** a small disk of metal or wood used in some games, such as checkers, as a playing piece, or as a means of keeping score. [from the medieval Latin word *computātōrium* "a place for computing or counting"]

count·er[2] (koun'tər), *n.* a person or thing that counts. [from the Latin word *computātor* "computer, counter"]

coun·ter[3] (koun'tər), *adv.* **1.** in the wrong or opposite way: *He acted counter to my wishes.* —*adj.* **2.** opposite or contrary: *Your wishes are counter to my own.* —*v.* **3.** to oppose: *He countered my suggestion with one that was completely different.* **4.** to answer (a move, blow, etc.) by another in return: *The boxer*

countered his opponent's punch. [from an early French word *countre* "against," which comes from Latin *contrā*]

counter-, a prefix meaning **1.** opposite or against: *counteract.* **2.** contrary: *counterclockwise.* **3.** corresponding: *counterfoil.* **4.** responding or returning: *counteroffer; counterattack.*

coun·ter·act (koun'tər akt'), *v.* to act against so as to hinder or remove: *Aspirin counteracts colds.*

coun·ter·at·tack (koun'tər a tak'), *n.* **1.** an attack made in return for another attack: *Wrongly accused, he was quick to make a counterattack.* —*v.* (koun'tər ə tak'). **2.** to make a counterattack; attack in return. —**coun'ter·at·tack'er,** *n.*

coun·ter·bal·ance (koun'tər bal'əns), *n.* **1.** a weight that balances another weight. **2.** a force that opposes or offsets another: *Knowledge is a counterbalance to superstition.* —*v.* (koun'tər bal'əns), **coun·ter·bal·anced, coun·ter·bal·anc·ing.** **3.** to offset or oppose with equal weight or force: *Love counterbalances fear.*

coun·ter·claim (koun'tər klām'), *n.* a claim made to offset another claim, esp. in law.

coun·ter·clock·wise (koun'tər klok'wīz'), *adj., adv.* in a direction opposite to that in which the hands of a clock turn.

coun·ter·feit (koun'tər fit'), *adj.* **1.** made in imitation with intent to fool or cheat; forged: *counterfeit money.* —*n.* **2.** an imitation intended to be passed off as genuine; forgery: *The painting proved to be a counterfeit.* —*v.* **3.** to make a counterfeit of: *to counterfeit money.* **4.** to pretend: *to counterfeit happiness.* —**coun'ter·feit'er,** *n.*

coun·ter·pane (koun'tər pān'), *n.* a quilt or cover for a bed; bedspread.

coun·ter·part (koun'tər pärt'), *n.* **1.** a person or thing that closely resembles or can be compared with another in some way: *The Alps are Europe's counterpart of the Rocky Mountains.* **2.** something that goes with or fits together with something else: *The right shoe is the counterpart of the left.* **3.** a copy or duplicate: *Your dress is the exact counterpart of mine.*

coun·ter·point (koun'tər point'), *n.* **1.** the technique of composing two or more melodies that combine harmoniously. **2.** a melody composed to be played or sung with another melody.

coun·ter·poise (koun'tər poiz'), *n.* **1.** a counterbalancing weight, power, or force. **2.** the state of being in balance. —*v.,* **coun·ter·poised, coun·ter·pois·ing.** **3.** to balance with an equal weight, power, or force; counterbalance.

coun·ter·rev·o·lu·tion (koun'tər rev'ə lōō'shən), *n.* a revolution that attempts to overcome a government established by a revolution.

coun·ter·sign (koun'tər sīn'), *n.* **1.** a secret signal or password that one must give in order to pass into a guarded place: *He gave the sentry the countersign.* **2.** a signature added to another signature, esp. to show that it is genuine. —*v.* **3.** to sign (a piece of writing having a signature), esp. as a guarantee of genuineness.

coun·ter·sink (koun′tər sĭngk′), *v.*, **coun·ter·sank** (koun′tər săngk′), **coun·ter·sunk** (koun′tər sŭngk′), **coun·ter·sink·ing.** 1. to enlarge the upper part of (a hole) to fit the head of a screw, bolt, etc. 2. to fit (the head of a screw, bolt, etc.) into such a hole so as to be even with the surface.

coun·tess (koun′tĭs), *n.* 1. the wife or widow of a count or earl. 2. a woman having the rank of a count or earl in her own right.

count·less (kount′lĭs), *adj.* too many to count; numberless; innumerable: *The sea is full of countless fish.*

coun·tri·fied (kŭn′trĭ fĭd′), *adj.* having a rustic or rural appearance, way of acting, style of dress, etc.: *a simple, countrified house; plain, countrified people.* Also, **coun′try·fied′.**

coun·try (kŭn′trē), *n., pl.* **coun·tries.** 1. a region, area, or territory: *heavily wooded, hilly country.* 2. all the land of a nation: *The country of Australia is an island.* 3. a nation: *France is a country in Europe.* 4. the people of a country: *The whole country mourned the death of the king.* 5. the country one belongs to: *loyalty to one's country.* 6. land used for farming; rural areas: *a drive in the country.* —*adj.* 7. of the country; rural: *country people; country roads.*

coun·try·man (kŭn′trē mən), *n., pl.* **coun·try·men.** 1. a native or inhabitant of one's own country. 2. a person who lives in the country, such as a farmer.

coun·try·side (kŭn′trē sĭd′), *n.* 1. a rural region; country. 2. the people of such a region: *The whole countryside came to the wedding.*

coun·try·wom·an (kŭn′trē wŏŏm′ən), *n., pl.* **coun·try·wom·en.** 1. a woman who is a native or inhabitant of one's own country. 2. a woman who lives in the country.

coun·ty (koun′tē), *n., pl.* **coun·ties.** 1. (in the U.S.) one of the sections into which a state is divided, having its own local laws, government, etc. 2. one of the districts into which a country is divided, as in Great Britain. 3. the people of a county.

coun′ty seat′, a town in which the administrative offices of a county are located.

coup (kŏŏ), *n., pl.* **coups** (kŏŏz). a highly successful action or accomplishment.

coupe (kŏŏp), *n.* 1. a closed, two-door automobile with a body shorter than that of a sedan of the same model. 2. a four-wheeled closed carriage having an outside seat for the driver. Also, **cou·pé** (kŏŏ pā′).

cou·ple (kŭp′əl), *n.* 1. two of a kind; pair. 2. a man and a woman who are together, esp. a married or engaged pair. 3. any two persons together, as in playing a game. —*v.,* **cou·pled, cou·pling.** 4. to join together: *to couple freight cars.* 5. **a couple of,** *Informal.* a small number of; a few: *I'll be with you in a couple of minutes.*

cou·plet (kŭp′lĭt), *n.* two lines of verse that go together, esp. a pair that rhyme.

cou·pling (kŭp′lĭng), *n.* 1. a device that joins two parts, lengths of pipe, shafts, etc., together. 2. a device for joining two railroad cars.

cou·pon (kŏŏ′pŏn, kyŏŏ′-), *n.* 1. a ticket or a part of a ticket that can be exchanged for a gift or a discount on the price of something: *Each box of soap had a coupon good for a free spoon.* 2. a section of a bond to be clipped off and presented for a payment of interest.

cour·age (kûr′ĭj), *n.* the ability to face dangers and difficulties without fear; bravery: *It takes courage to be a mountain climber.*

cou·ra·geous (kə rā′jəs), *adj.* having courage; brave or fearless. —**cou·ra′geous·ly,** *adv.*

cou·ri·er (kûr′ē ər), *n.* a messenger, usually traveling in haste, who carries diplomatic messages, important reports, etc.

course (kôrs), *n.* 1. forward or onward movement: *in the course of time.* 2. a direction or route taken or to be taken: *The ship's course was northward.* 3. a way of proceeding or acting: *Our best course would be to leave as soon as possible.* 4. a group of things in order; series: *a course of sports events.* 5. a number of classes or lessons in a certain subject, as at college: *a course in chemistry.* 6. a part of a meal: *the dessert course.* 7. the ground, water, etc., on which a race or a game takes place: *a golf course.* —*v.,* **coursed, cours·ing.** 8. to run, flow, or race through or after: *The river coursed through the valleys.* 9. **of course,** certainly; to be sure: *Of course I'll be there.*

court (kôrt), *n.* 1. an open space mostly or entirely surrounded by a building or buildings: *the court of an apartment house.* 2. a space laid out for playing tennis, handball, etc. 3. a short street. 4. the home of a king, queen, etc.; palace. 5. the family, friends, advisers, etc., of a ruler at a palace: *Some of the kings of France had large courts.* 6. a meeting or assembly held by a ruler: *The king held court in the morning.* 7. the wooing of a woman by a man; courtship. 8. a judge or judges who hold trials, make legal decisions, etc. 9. a place for holding trials: *The jury assembled at court.* 10. a session attended by all the persons involved in a case of law: *The court will convene tomorrow afternoon.* —*v.* 11. to try to win the favor of: *to court people in important positions.* 12. to seek the affections of; woo: *He courted her for a year before she agreed to marry him.* 13. to behave in such a way as to invite or provoke: *to court trouble.*

cour·te·ous (kûr′tē əs), *adj.* having or showing good manners; polite: *courteous behavior.* —**cour′te·ous·ly,** *adv.* —**cour′te·ous·ness,** *n.*

cour·te·sy (kûr′tĭ sē), *n., pl.* for def. 2 **cour·te·sies.** 1. fineness of manners; good behavior. 2. a courteous or considerate act: *Thank you for your courtesies.*

court·house (kôrt′hous′), *n., pl.* **court·hous·es** (kôrt′hou′zĭz). 1. a building in which courts of law are held. 2. a building in a county seat housing the offices of the county government.

cour·ti·er (kôr′tē ər), *n.* 1. a person who is part of the court of a ruler: *The king was surrounded by flattering courtiers.* 2. a person who tries to win the favor of another, esp. by flattery.

court·ly (kôrt′lē), *adj.,* **court·li·er, court·li·est.** 1. polite, refined, or elegant. 2. flattering, or too eager to please: *The rich woman was surrounded by courtly admirers.* —**court′li·ness,** *n.*

court-mar·tial (kôrt′mär′shəl), *n., pl.* **courts-mar·tial** *or* **court-mar·tials.** 1. a court made up of military officers to try members of the armed forces for offenses against military law. 2. a trial by such a court. —*v.,* **court-mar·tialed** *or* **court-mar·tialled; court-mar·tial·ing** *or* **court-mar·tial·ling.** 3. to try (a person) by court-martial.

court·room (kôrt′rōōm′, -rŏŏm′), *n.* a room in which the sessions of a law court are held.

court·ship (kôrt′ship), *n.* the wooing of a woman by a man, or the time during which this takes place.

court·yard (kôrt′yärd′), *n.* an enclosed court that is open to the sky, esp. one attached to a building.

cous·in (kuz′ən), *n.* a daughter or son of one's uncle or aunt.

cove (kōv), *n.* a small bay.

cov·e·nant (kuv′ə nənt), *n.* 1. a solemn, formal agreement between two or more persons or groups: *a covenant to advance the cause of peace.* —*v.* 2. to make a covenant.

Cov·en·try (kuv′ən trē), *n.* a city in central England.

cov·er (kuv′ər), *v.* 1. to place something over or upon: *to cover the floor with a carpet.* 2. to lie or extend over: *Snow covered the fields.* 3. to hide or conceal: *to cover a mistake.* 4. to include or deal with: *This book covers the subject well.* 5. to gather news or publish reports of: *Her column covers the local scene.* 6. to protect against mishap: *He is covered by insurance.* 7. to go or pass over: *We covered a lot of territory during our trip.* —*n.* 8. anything that covers, protects, shelters, hides, etc.: *the cover of a book; a lie that is a cover for mistakes.*

cov·er·age (kuv′ər ij), *n.* 1. the amount of protection provided by an insurance policy. 2. the gathering and reporting or publishing of news: *He was famous for his coverage of the war.*

cov·er·all (kuv′ər ôl′), *n.* a work garment in one piece that covers and protects one's regular clothes.

cov′ered wag′on, a large wagon having a rounded canvas top, much used by early settlers in the western U.S.

cov·er·ing (kuv′ər iñg), *n.* 1. something laid over or wrapped around something else; a cover or wrapping: *a covering of wax paper for food.* —*adj.* 2. serving as a cover: *a covering layer of snow.*

cov·er·let (kuv′ər lit), *n.* the top covering of a bed; bedspread.

cov·ert (kuv′ərt, kō′vərt), *adj.* 1. concealed or secret: *a covert look of dislike.* —*n.* 2. a shelter or hiding place. 3. a thicket for wild animals or game. —**cov′ert·ly,** *adv.*

cov·et (kuv′it), *v.,* **cov·et·ed, cov·et·ing.** to desire eagerly or wrongfully, esp. another's property: *He coveted his neighbor's wealth.*

cov·et·ous (kuv′i təs), *adj.* full of greedy or envious desire: *The wealth of others made him covetous.* —**cov′et·ous·ly,** *adv.* —**cov′et·ous·ness,** *n.*

cov·ey (kuv′ē), *n., pl.* **cov·eys.** 1. a brood or small flock of partridges or similar birds. 2. a small group of people: *A covey of friends met us at the airport.*

cow[1] (kou), *n.* 1. the female of any animal of the ox family, esp. a dairy animal that provides milk. 2. the female of certain other mammals, as the elephant, seal, or whale. [from the Old English word *cū*]

cow[2] (kou), *v.* to frighten with threats, blows, etc.: *He was cowed by the neighborhood bully.* [from Scandinavian]

cow·ard (kou′ərd), *n.* a person who lacks courage.

cow·ard·ice (kou′ər dis), *n.* lack of courage to face danger, difficulty, etc.

cow·ard·ly (kou′ərd lē), *adj.* 1. lacking courage; timid: *a cowardly person.* 2. like or befitting a coward: *a cowardly retreat.* —**cow′ard·li·ness,** *n.*

cow·bell (kou′bel′), *n.* a bell that is usually rectangular rather than round, and has a dull, clanking tone. It is hung around a cow's neck to indicate where the animal is.

cow·bird (kou′bûrd′), *n.* any of several black American birds that follow herds of cattle and are noted for laying their eggs in the nests of other birds.

cow·boy (kou′boi′), *n.* a man, usually on horseback, who herds or tends cattle on a ranch.

cow·er (kou′ər), *v.* to crouch in fear.

cow·girl (kou′gûrl′), *n.* a woman who herds or tends cattle on a ranch.

cow·hand (kou′hand′), *n.* a person, as a cowboy or cowgirl, employed on a cattle ranch.

cow·herd (kou′hûrd′), *n.* a person who tends cows.

cow·hide (kou′hīd′), *n.* 1. the hide of a cow. 2. the leather made from it. 3. a whip made of rawhide or flexible leather. —*v.,* **cow·hid·ed, cow·hid·ing.** 4. to whip with a cowhide.

cowl (koul), *n.* 1. a hooded cloak worn by monks. 2. the hood of this garment. 3. the part of an automobile body that supports the instrument panel and the windshield. 4. the metal covering of an aircraft engine.

cow·lick (kou′lik′), *n.* an unruly tuft of hair.

co-work·er (kō′wûr′kər), *n.* a person who works with one; fellow worker; colleague.

cow·pox (kou′poks′), *n.* a contagious disease of cattle, marked by the formation of small blisters containing material used for making smallpox vaccine.

cow·punch·er (kou′pun′chər), *n. Informal.* a cowboy.

Cowl

cow·slip (kou′slip′), *n.* 1. an English plant having flowers resembling primroses. 2. a plant that grows in marshy places and has yellow flowers resembling buttercups.

cox·comb (koks′kōm′), *n.* a conceited, foolish fellow; fop; dandy. Also, **cockscomb.**

cox·swain (kok′sən, kok′swān′), *n.* a person who steers a boat, as a racing shell.

coy (koi), *adj.* **1.** shy; bashful. **2.** pretending to be shy or bashful. —**coy′ly**, *adv.* —**coy′ness,** *n.*

coy·ote (kī′ōt, kī ō′tē), *n., pl.* **coy·otes** *or* **coy·ote.** an animal of western North America that resembles a small wolf. [from a Spanish word, which comes from Nahuatl *coyotl*]

coy·pu (koi′pōō), *n., pl.* **coy·pus** *or* **coy·pu.** a large South American rodent that can live in water. [from the Spanish word *coipú,* which comes from a word in a South American Indian language]

co·zy (kō′zē), *adj.,* **co·zi·er, co·zi·est. 1.** snugly warm and comfortable: *a cozy room; a cozy little chat.* —*n., pl.* **co·zies. 2.** a padded covering for a teapot to aid in retaining heat. Also, **cosy.** —**co′zi·ly,** *adv.* —**co′zi·ness,** *n.*

cpl., corporal. Also, **Cpl.**

C.P.O., chief petty officer. Also, **c.p.o.**

cps, cycles per second. Also, **c.p.s.**

Cr, *Chem.* the symbol for chromium.

crab¹ (krab), *n.* **1.** any of numerous shellfish having a broad, flattened body, eight legs, and two claws. Its flesh is used for food. **2. the Crab.** See **Cancer** (def. 1). —*v.,* **crabbed, crab·bing. 3.** to catch or try to catch crabs. [from the Old English word *crabba*]

crab² (krab), *Informal.* —*n.* **1.** a grouchy person. —*v.,* **crabbed, crab·bing. 2.** to find fault; complain. [shortened from *crabbed*]

Crab
(length 3 in.)

crab′ ap′ple, 1. any of various small, sour apples used for making jelly. **2.** the tree bearing this fruit.

crab·bed (krab′id), *adj.* hard to read or make out, as handwriting.

crab·by (krab′ē), *adj.,* **crab·bi·er, crab·bi·est.** *Informal.* grouchy; bad-tempered. —**crab′bi·ness,** *n.*

crab′ grass′, a spreading weed with broad, flat leaves that infests lawns.

crack (krak), *v.* **1.** to make a sudden, sharp sound: *He cracked the whip.* **2.** to break or cause to break without complete separation into parts; split: *The ball cracked the window.* **3.** to strike with a sharp sound: *He cracked his head against the wall.* **4.** to change pitch suddenly; become harsh: *Her voice cracked in the middle of the song.* **5.** to give way under severe emotional strain. **6.** *Informal.* to break into (a safe, vault, etc.). **7.** *Informal.* to solve, as a code. **8.** to say in a flippant or humorous way: *to crack jokes.* —*n.* **9.** a sudden, sharp sound, as of something breaking: *the crack of falling dishes.* **10.** the snap of a whip. **11.** a loud blow. **12.** a split or break without complete separation into parts: *a crack in a dish.* **13.** a narrow opening: *a crack between two boards.* **14.** *Informal.* a chance or try: *Let me have a crack at fixing that.* **15.** *Informal.* a joke or wisecrack. —*adj.* **16.** *Informal.* first-rate; excellent: *a crack athlete.* **17. crack down,** to become stricter, as in enforcing rules or regulations: *They're cracking down on illegal parking.*

cracked (krakt), *adj.* **1.** broken without separation into parts; split. **2.** *Informal.* mad; insane.

crack·er (krak′ər), *n.* **1.** a thin, crisp biscuit; saltine. **2.** a firecracker.

Crack′er Jack′, *Trademark.* caramel-coated popcorn.

crack·er·jack (krak′ər jak′), *Slang.* —*n.* **1.** a person or thing that is unusually excellent or skilled: *The new salesman is a crackerjack.* —*adj.* **2.** first-rate; exceptionally good: *a crackerjack show.*

crack·le (krak′əl), *v.,* **crack·led, crack·ling. 1.** to make slight, sudden, sharp noises: *The papers crackled in his hands.* —*n.* **2.** a crackling noise: *the crackle of burning wood.*

crack-up (krak′up′), *n.* **1.** a crash; collision: *an automobile crack-up.* **2.** a breakdown in health of one's body or mind.

-cracy, a suffix used to form nouns meaning **1.** rule or government: *democracy; autocracy; bureaucracy.* **2.** social class: *aristocracy; plutocracy.*

cra·dle (krād′əl), *n.* **1.** a little bed or cot for a baby, usually having rockers. **2.** a place where something begins or exists for the first time: *Greece was the cradle of democracy.* **3.** (in farming) a frame attached to a scythe, for laying grain in bunches as it is cut. **4.** a framework supporting a ship in construction or repair. —*v.,* **cra·dled, cra·dling. 5.** to place and rock in or as if in a cradle: *She cradled the baby in her arms.* **6.** to cut (grain) with a cradle. **7.** to place (a ship) on a cradle.

craft (kraft), *n.* **1.** skill or ability: *Handwriting is a craft.* **2.** skill in tricking others; cunning: *a thief with great craft.* **3.** a trade requiring skill: *to learn the craft of carpentry.* **4.** the members of a trade. **5.** a ship or ships. **6.** an aircraft, or aircraft as a group.

crafts·man (krafts′mən), *n., pl.* **crafts·men.** a person skilled in a craft.

craft·y (kraf′tē), *adj.,* **craft·i·er, craft·i·est.** cunning; deceitful; sly: *a crafty pickpocket; a crafty way to do business.* —**craft′i·ly,** *adv.* —**craft′i·ness,** *n.*

crag (krag), *n.* a steep, rugged rock.

crag·gy (krag′ē), *adj.,* **crag·gi·er, crag·gi·est.** full of crags: *a craggy mountain.* —**crag′gi·ness,** *n.*

cram (kram), *v.,* **crammed, cram·ming. 1.** to fill completely or with more than can be easily held: *to cram a suitcase with clothes.* **2.** to force or stuff: *to cram clothes into a suitcase.* **3.** *Informal.* to study for a test hurriedly at the last minute: *He crammed for his arithmetic exam.*

cramp¹ (kramp), *n.* **1.** a sudden, painful, involuntary tightening of a muscle. **2.** a sudden, sharp pain in the stomach or abdomen. [from the Old French word *crampe,* which comes from a Germanic word meaning "hook"]

cramp² (kramp), *n.* **1.** a bar bent at both ends, used to hold things together, as blocks of stone or wood; clamp. —*v.* **2.** to hamper or hold back: *He was cramped by lack of money.* [from a Middle English word, which comes from the earlier Dutch word *crampe* "hook"]

cran·ber·ry (kran′ber′ē), *n., pl.* **cran·ber·ries. 1.** a red berry that grows on a swamp plant and is used for making sauces and jelly. **2.** the plant itself.

crane (krān), *n.* **1.** any of several large birds with long legs and a long neck that live in swamps and marshes. **2.** a large machine with a long boom for lifting heavy weights. —*v.,* **craned, cran·ing. 3.** to stretch (the neck) in order to see better.

Whooping crane
(height about 5 ft.;
wingspread 7½ ft.)

cra·ni·um (krā′nē əm), *n.* **1.** another term for **skull. 2.** the part of the skull that encloses the brain. —**cra′ni·al,** *adj.*

crank (krangk), *n.* **1.** a bent handle for turning something, such as the drum of a winch or the cutters of a pencil sharpener. **2.** *Informal.* a nasty, bad-tempered person. —*v.* **3.** to turn or work by means of a crank. **4.** to start (an engine) with a crank.

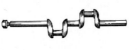

Crankshaft

crank·shaft (krangk′shaft′), *n.* a shaft having one or more cranks, such as that in an automobile engine, which converts the up-and-down motion of the pistons to rotary motion.

crank·y (krang′kē), *adj.,* **crank·i·er, crank·i·est.** *Informal.* grouchy; cross: *a cranky old man.* —**crank′i·ness,** *n.*

cran·ny (kran′ē), *n., pl.* **cran·nies.** a small, narrow opening in a wall, rock, etc.; chink or crack.

crape (krāp), *n.* another spelling of **crepe.**

crash (krash), *v.* **1.** to break, strike, or fall with a loud noise: *The tower crashed to the ground. He crashed the vase on the floor.* **2.** to collide: *The cars crashed into each other.* **3.** to fail, as a business. **4.** to gain admittance to (a game, party, etc.) without a ticket or invitation. —*n.* **5.** a breaking or falling to pieces with a loud noise. **6.** a collision or crashing, as of automobiles, an airplane, etc. **7.** a failure of a business. **8.** a sudden, loud noise: *the crash of thunder.*

crass (kras), *adj.* coarse, stupid, vulgar, or gross: *crass rudeness and lack of concern for others.* —**crass′ly,** *adv.* —**crass′ness,** *n.*

-crat, a suffix used to form nouns meaning **1.** a person who rules or governs: *autocrat; bureaucrat.* **2.** a member of a social class: *aristocrat; plutocrat.* **3.** a person who belongs to or favors a certain form of government: *democrat.*

crate (krāt), *n.* **1.** a box, usually made of wooden slats, used for packing and shipping fruit, dishes, furniture, etc. —*v.,* **crat·ed, crat·ing. 2.** to put in a crate: *to crate oranges.*

cra·ter (krā′tər), *n.* **1.** the mouth of a volcano. **2.** a bowl-shaped hollow in the surface of the earth made by a meteor, cannonball, etc. **3.** a circular, hollowed area on the surface of the moon, usually surrounded by a high ridge.

cra·vat (krə vat′), *n.* a necktie.

crave (krāv), *v.,* **craved, crav·ing. 1.** to long for or desire eagerly. **2.** to ask for earnestly; beg: *to crave forgiveness.*

cra·ven (krā′vən), *adj.* **1.** cowardly. —*n.* **2.** a coward.

crav·ing (krā′ving), *n.* deep longing; great or eager desire: *a craving for food and rest.*

craw (krô), *n.* **1.** the crop of a bird or insect. **2.** the stomach of an animal.

craw·fish (krô′fish′), *n., pl.* **craw·fish·es** *or* **craw·fish.** another name for **crayfish.**

crawl (krôl), *v.* **1.** to move slowly with the body resting on the ground, as a worm, or on the hands and knees, as a young child. **2.** to put out tendrils, as plants or vines; creep. **3.** to move slowly: *Cars were crawling along the crowded road.* **4.** to be overrun or covered with crawling things: *The cellar is crawling with spiders.* —*n.* **5.** the act of crawling; a slow, crawling motion. **6.** a stroke in swimming in which the face is kept down and the arms are lifted one after the other from the water.

Crayfish
(length 3½ in.)

cray·fish (krā′fish′), *n., pl.* **cray·fish·es** *or* **cray·fish. 1.** a small freshwater shellfish that looks like a tiny lobster. **2.** a larger saltwater shellfish resembling a lobster but having a spiny shell and lacking the lobster's large claws. Also, **crawfish.**

cray·on (krā′on, krā′ən), *n.* **1.** a pointed stick or pencil of colored chalk, wax, etc., used for drawing. —*v.,* **cray·oned, cray·on·ing. 2.** to draw or color with crayons.

craze (krāz), *v.,* **crazed, craz·ing. 1.** to drive mad: *to be crazed by hunger and thirst.* —*n.* **2.** a widespread, highly popular fad.

cra·zy (krā′zē), *adj.,* **cra·zi·er, cra·zi·est. 1.** mad; insane. **2.** very silly or foolish: *a crazy notion.* **3.** very enthusiastic: *She's crazy about movies.* **4.** very fond: *She's crazy about him.* **5.** odd or unusual: *a crazy necktie.* —**cra′zi·ly,** *adv.* —**cra′zi·ness,** *n.*

creak (krēk), *v.* **1.** to make a harsh grating or squeaking sound: *The door creaked on its hinges.* —*n.* **2.** a creaking sound.

creak·y (krē′kē), *adj.,* **creak·i·er, creak·i·est.** creaking or likely to creak: *creaky steps; a creaky old chair.* —**creak′i·ness,** *n.*

cream (krēm), *n.* **1.** the part of whole milk that is rich in butterfat. **2.** a soft solid or thick liquid used as a cosmetic. **3.** Usually, **creams.** a soft-centered candy coated with chocolate. **4.** a soup containing cream or milk. **5.** a yellowish white. **6.** the best part of anything: *the cream of society.* —*v.* **7.** to work (butter and sugar, or the like) to a smooth, creamy mass. **8.** to prepare with cream, milk, or a cream sauce. **9.** to take the cream from: *to cream whole milk.*

cream·er·y (krē′mə rē), *n., pl.* **cream·er·ies. 1.** a place where milk and cream are processed and where butter and cheese are produced. **2.** a place for the sale of milk and its products.

cream·y (krē′mē), *adj.*, **cream·i·er, cream·i·est.** resembling cream in appearance, consistency, or taste: *a creamy frosting; a creamy complexion.* —**cream′i·ness,** *n.*

crease (krēs), *n.* **1.** a mark or line produced by folding, heat, pressure, etc.; fold. —*v.,* **creased, creas·ing. 2.** to make a crease or creases in or on; wrinkle: *He creased his suit by packing it too tightly.*

cre·ate (krē āt′), *v.,* **cre·at·ed, cre·at·ing. 1.** to cause to come into being; produce: *God created Eve from Adam's rib. The author created a masterpiece.* **2.** to be the cause of; cause to happen: *to create a fuss.*

cre·a·tion (krē ā′shən), *n.* **1.** the act of creating, producing, or causing to exist. **2.** anything that is or has been created. **3.** all things that have been created; world; universe. **4.** an original product of the mind, esp. an imaginative artistic work. **5. the Creation,** (in the Bible) the bringing into existence of the universe by God.

cre·a·tive (krē ā′tiv), *adj.* **1.** having the quality, power, or ability to create: *a creative writer.* **2.** showing originality: *creative writing.* —**cre·a′tive·ly,** *adv.*

cre·a·tor (krē ā′tər), *n.* **1.** a person or thing that creates. **2. the Creator,** God.

crea·ture (krē′chər), *n.* **1.** any living being: *all God's creatures.* **2.** an animal: *creatures of the sea.* **3.** a person; human being: *The poor creature has had bad luck lately.*

cre·den·tial (kri den′shəl), *n.* **1.** anything that provides the basis for confidence, belief, credit, etc. **2.** Usually, **credentials.** the evidence of a persons's authority, status, rights, etc., usually in written form: *The French ambassador presented his credentials to the President of the United States.*

cred·i·ble (kred′ə bəl), *adj.* **1.** capable of being believed; believable: *That is not a very credible story.* **2.** worthy of being believed: *a credible witness.* —**cred′i·bil′i·ty,** *n.*

cred·it (kred′it), *n.* **1.** honor given for some action, quality, etc.: *Give credit where it is due.* **2.** a source of honor: *You are a credit to your school.* **3.** belief in the truth of a person, his word, etc.: *a witness worthy of credit.* **4.** official acceptance and recording of a student's work in a particular course of study: *He received credit for the music course.* **5.** time allowed for payment for goods or services: *90 days' credit.* **6.** the privilege of borrowing or of buying goods for payment at a later time: *I have credit at several banks and stores.* **7.** a sum of money allowed a person, as against a debt or bill: *He has a credit of $50.* —*v.* **8.** to believe; put confidence in; trust: *Do you credit his version of the story?* **9.** to make or enter a record in favor of: *The salesman credited me with ten dollars.*

cred·it·a·ble (kred′i tə bəl), *adj.* bringing or deserving credit, honor, reputation, or esteem: *He did a very creditable job.* —**cred′i·ta·bly,** *adv.*

cred·i·tor (kred′i tər), *n.* a person to whom money is due.

cre·du·li·ty (kri dōō′li tē, -dyōō′-), *n.* a willingness to believe or trust too easily, esp. without proper evidence: *His ridiculous story strained my credulity.*

cred·u·lous (krej′ə ləs), *adj.* too willing to believe or trust; gullible: *She was so credulous you could make her believe anything.* —**cred′u·lous·ly,** *adv.*

creed (krēd), *n.* **1.** a formal statement of religious beliefs. **2.** any system of belief or of opinion. [from the Old English word *crēda,* which comes from Latin *crēdō* "I believe"]

creek (krēk, krik), *n.* **1.** a stream of fresh water, smaller than a river. **2.** *British.* an inlet in the shore of the sea.

creel (krēl), *n.* a basket made of wicker or other material, for holding fish, lobster, etc.

creep (krēp), *v.,* **crept** (krept), **creep·ing. 1.** to move with the body on or close to the ground; crawl. **2.** to move slowly and quietly so as to be unnoticed: *We crept up and peeked over the wall.* **3.** to move or slip slowly along: *The automobile crept through the heavy traffic.* **4.** to grow along the ground, a wall, etc., as a plant. —*n.* **5.** the act of creeping. **6. the creeps,** *Slang.* a feeling of horror, fear, disgust, etc.: *Big bugs give me the creeps.*

creep·er (krē′pər), *n.* **1.** a person or thing that creeps. **2.** a creeping plant, such as ivy.

creep·y (krē′pē), *adj.,* **creep·i·er, creep·i·est. 1.** that creeps, as an insect. **2.** having or causing a creeping sensation of the skin, as from horror or fear: *a creepy ghost story.*

cre·mate (krē′māt), *v.,* **cre·mat·ed, cre·mat·ing.** to burn and reduce (a dead body) to ashes, esp. as a funeral rite. —**cre·ma·tion** (kri mā′shən), *n.*

Cre·ole (krē′ōl), *n.* **1.** a person born in the West Indies or Latin America but of European, esp. Spanish, ancestry. **2.** a person of French ancestry born in Louisiana. **3.** the French language as spoken in Louisiana, Haiti, and some other areas originally settled by French-speaking peoples. —*adj.* **4.** *(sometimes l.c.)* of or referring to the Creoles or their language. [from the Portuguese word *crioulo* "native"]

crepe (krāp), *n.* a thin, light fabric of silk, cotton, or other fiber, with a finely crinkled or ridged surface. Also, **crape.**

crepe′ pa′per, thin paper densely wrinkled to resemble crepe, used for decorating, wrapping, etc.

crept (krept), *v.* the past tense and past participle of **creep.**

cre·scen·do (kri shen′dō), *n., pl.* **cre·scen·dos. 1.** a gradual increase in loudness: *The speaker was greeted with a crescendo of applause.* **2.** a musical passage of gradually increasing loudness. —*adj.* **3.** (in music) gradually becoming louder. —*v.* **4.** to become louder. See also **decrescendo.**

cres·cent (kres′ənt), *n.* **1.** the figure of the moon in its first or last quarter. **2.** a shape resembling this: *The flag of Turkey has a crescent and a star.* —*adj.* **3.** having such a shape.

cress (kres), *n.* any of several plants related to mustard and having leaves that are used in salads and as a garnish.

cres·set (kres′it), *n.* a metal cup or basket, usually mounted on a pole or suspended from above, in which oil, pitch, or the like, is burned as a light or beacon.

crest (krest), *n.* **1.** a tuft of feathers or other natural growth on the head of a bird or other animal. **2.** anything resembling or suggesting such a tuft. **3.** the head, top, or highest part of anything: *the crest of a hill; the crest of a wave.* **4.** a decoration at the top of a helmet. **5.** a design at the top of a coat of arms. —**crest′ed,** *adj.*

Cresset

crest·fall·en (krest′fô′lən), *adj.* low in spirits; dejected; depressed: *He was crestfallen at his defeat.*

Crete (krēt), *n.* a Greek island in the Mediterranean Sea, SE of Greece. 3235 sq. mi. —**Cre·tan** (krēt′ʰn), *n., adj.*

cre·tonne (kri ton′, krē′ton), *n.* a heavy cotton material in printed designs, used esp. for drapery and slipcovers.

cre·vasse (krə vas′), *n.* **1.** a fissure or deep crack in glacial ice or the earth's surface. **2.** a crack or hole in an embankment, dike, or levee.

crev·ice (krev′is), *n.* a crack forming an opening; cleft; fissure: *a crevice in the wall.*

crew[1] (kroo), *n.* **1.** a group of persons working together: *the crew of a train; a wrecking crew.* **2.** the company of men who operate a ship or boat. **3.** *Informal.* a company; crowd: *What a strange crew at the party!* [from a Middle English word, which comes from Old French *creue* "increase." The word meant originally "increase," hence "reinforcements"]

crew[2] (kroo), *v.* a past tense of **crow**[2]: used esp. in British English.

crib (krib), *n.* **1.** a child's bed with enclosed sides. **2.** a stall or pen for cattle. **3.** a rack or manger for fodder, as in a stable or barn. **4.** a bin for storing grain. **5.** a framework used in the construction of foundations, dams, retaining walls, etc.

crib·bage (krib′ij), *n.* a card game in which players make certain combinations of numbers from the cards used in order to earn points that are scored with pegs on a small board (**crib′bage board′**).

crick·et[1] (krik′it), *n.* a small insect related to the grasshopper. The male cricket makes a chirping sound by rubbing its front wings together. [from the French word *criquet* "creak"]

crick·et[2] (krik′it), *n.* **1.** a game for two teams of 11 members each, played with balls, bats, and wickets. **2.** fair play; gentlemanly conduct: *It wouldn't be cricket to give away his secret.* [from a French word, which comes from Flemish *krick* "a stick"]

Cricket (length ¾ in.)

cried (krīd), *v.* the past tense of **cry.**

cri·er (krī′ər), *n.* **1.** a person who cries. **2.** a court or town official who makes public announcements.

crime (krīm), *n.* **1.** an act that is considered dangerous to the public welfare or morals or to the interests of the state and that is legally forbidden. **2.** any serious offense or wrongdoing; sin. **3.** *Informal.* a foolish or senseless act: *It's a crime to waste food.*

Cri·me·a (krī mē′ə), *n.* a peninsula in the SW Soviet Union, between the Black Sea and the Sea of Azov. —**Cri·me′an,** *adj.*

crim·i·nal (krim′ə nʰl), *adj.* **1.** of or referring to crime or its punishment. **2.** guilty of crime. —*n.* **3.** a person guilty or convicted of a crime. —**crim′i·nal·ly,** *adv.*

crimp (krimp), *v.* **1.** to press into small, regular folds; make wavy: *to crimp paper.* —*n.* **2.** a wavy surface produced by crimping.

crim·son (krim′zən), *adj.* **1.** of a deep, purplish red. —*n.* **2.** a crimson color, pigment, or dye. —*v.* **3.** to make or become crimson.

cringe (krinj), *v.,* **cringed, cring·ing. 1.** to bend or crouch, esp. from fear; cower. **2.** to act very humbly; fawn. —**cring′ing·ly,** *adv.*

crin·kle (kriŋ′kəl), *v.,* **crin·kled, crin·kling. 1.** to turn or wind in many little bends and twists; wrinkle; ripple: *to crinkle paper.* **2.** to make slight, sharp sounds; rustle: *The leaves crinkled under our feet.*

crin·kly (kriŋ′klē), *adj.,* **crin·kli·er, crin·kli·est. 1.** having crinkles. **2.** making a rustling sound. —**crin′kli·ness,** *n.*

crin·o·line (krin′ʰlin), *n.* **1.** a stiff, coarse cotton material for interlining. **2.** a petticoat of stiff material worn to bell out a skirt.

crip·ple (krip′əl), *n.* **1.** a lame person or animal. —*v.,* **crip·pled, crip·pling. 2.** to make a cripple of; lame: *The accident crippled him.* **3.** to disable in any way: *The snowstorm crippled transportation.* —**crip′pler,** *n.* —**crip′pling·ly,** *adv.*

cri·sis (krī′sis), *n., pl.* **cri·ses** (krī′sēz). **1.** a stage in a sequence of events that determines the trend of all future events; turning point: *the crisis in the story.* **2.** the point in the course of a serious disease at which a change takes place, leading either to recovery or to death. **3.** an unstable, tense political, social, or economic condition: *the gold crisis.*

crisp (krisp), *adj.* **1.** hard but easily breakable; brittle: *crisp toast.* **2.** firm and fresh; not soft or wilted: *a crisp leaf of lettuce.* **3.** brisk; sharp; decided: *a crisp manner.* **4.** lively; sparkling: *crisp conversation.* **5.** clean and neat; well-groomed: *a crisp appearance.* **6.** snappy; invigorating: *a crisp breeze.* **7.** in small, stiff curls; curly. —*v.* **8.** to make or become crisp.

crisp·y (kris′pē), *adj.,* **crisp·i·er, crisp·i·est.** easily crushed or broken; brittle. —**crisp′i·ness,** *n.*

criss·cross (kris′krôs′), *adj.* **1.** having many crossing lines, paths, etc. —*n.* **2.** a crisscross mark, pattern, etc. —*v.* **3.** to mark with or form crossing lines: *The* *highway crisscrosses the countryside.* **4.** to move or cause to move in a crisscross manner.

cri·te·ri·on (krī tēr′ē ən), *n., pl.* **cri·te·ri·a** (krī tēr′ē-ə). a standard of judgment or criticism; an established rule for testing anything: *There are many criteria to consider when buying a car.*

crit·ic (krit′ik), *n.* **1.** a person who judges, evaluates, or criticizes. **2.** a person whose occupation is judging literary or artistic works, dramatic or musical performances, etc. **3.** a person who tends to make hasty, harsh judgments and finds fault easily.

crit·i·cal (krit′i kəl), *adj.* **1.** inclined to find fault easily: *He's too critical of his friends.* **2.** involving skillful judgment: *a critical analysis.* **3.** of or referring to critics or criticism: *critical writings.* **4.** referring to or of the nature of a crisis: *a critical moment.* **5.** involving danger or uncertainty: *a critical wound.* —**crit′i·cal·ly,** *adv.*

crit·i·cism (krit′i siz′əm), *n.* **1.** the act or art of analyzing and judging the quality of something, esp. a literary or artistic work, musical performance, dramatic production, etc. **2.** the act of judging harshly; faultfinding. **3.** a critical comment, article, or essay.

crit·i·cize (krit′i sīz′), *v.,* **crit·i·cized, crit·i·ciz·ing. 1.** to make judgments on the good and bad points of (something): *to criticize a new play.* **2.** to find fault with: *He's always criticizing his little brother.*

croak (krōk), *v.* **1.** to utter a low, hoarse cry: *Frogs croak.* **2.** to speak with a low, hoarse cry. —*n.* **3.** the act or sound of croaking.

Cro·at (krō′at), *n.* **1.** a native or inhabitant of Croatia; Croatian. **2.** See **Croatian** (def. 3).

Cro·a·tia (krō ā′shə), *n.* a region in NW Yugoslavia, formerly a kingdom.

Cro·a·tian (krō ā′shən), *adj.* **1.** of or referring to Croatia, its people, or their language. —*n.* **2.** a Croat. **3.** Also, **Croat.** the Serbo-Croatian language, esp. as written in Croatia, in the Roman alphabet.

cro·chet (krō shā′), *n.* **1.** needlework done with a needle having a small hook at one end for drawing the thread or yarn to form intertwined loops. —*v.,* **cro·cheted** (krō shād′), **cro·chet·ing** (krō shā′ing). **2.** to make by crochet: *to crochet a dress.*

crock (krok), *n.* an earthen pot or jar.

crock·er·y (krok′ə rē), *n.* crocks collectively; earthenware.

croc·o·dile (krok′ə dīl′), *n.* a large tropical reptile with a thick skin, a long tail, and a long, pointed snout. [from the Latin word *crocodilus,* which comes from Greek *krokodeilos* "lizard"]

Crocodile (length 20 ft.)

cro·cus (krō′kəs), *n., pl.* **cro·cus·es.** a small flowering plant that blooms in the early spring.

crone (krōn), *n.* a mean, ugly, withered old woman.

cro·ny (krō′nē), *n., pl.* **cro·nies.** a close friend or companion; chum.

crook (krŏŏk), *n.* **1.** an instrument having a bent or curved part, as a shepherd's staff. **2.** the hooked part of anything: *the crook of a cane.* **3.** any bend, turn, or curve: *a crook in the road.* **4.** *Informal.* a dishonest person, esp. a thief or a cheat. —*v.* **5.** to bend or curve: *to crook one's finger.*

crook·ed (krŏŏk′id; *also for def. 1* krŏŏkt), *adj.* **1.** bent or twisted; not straight. **2.** dishonest: *a crooked deal.* —**crook′ed·ly,** *adv.* —**crook′ed·ness,** *n.*

croon (krōōn), *v.* to sing or hum in a soft, low voice: *to croon a lullaby.*

crop (krop), *n.* **1.** the produce of the ground, while growing or when gathered. **2.** the yield of such produce for a particular season: *We had a large wheat crop last year.* **3.** a group of persons or things appearing or occurring together: *a crop of lies.* **4.** the stock or handle of a whip. **5.** a pouch in the gullet of many birds, in which food is held and prepared for digestion. **6.** a similar organ in an insect. —*v.,* **cropped, crop·ping. 7.** to cut very closely; clip; trim. **8. crop out,** to rise to the surface; become visible: *a vein of gold that cropped out of the ore; a bad trait that cropped out in his character.* **9. crop up,** to appear, esp. suddenly or unexpectedly: *A new problem has cropped up.*

crop·per (krop′ər), *n.* **1.** a person who raises a crop, esp. one who works on a farm and receives a share of the crop. **2.** a machine that crops or trims. **3. come a cropper, a.** to fall headfirst, esp. from a horse. **b.** to have a sudden and complete failure or defeat: *Our team came a cropper in the state finals.*

cro·quet (krō kā′), *n.* an outdoor game played by knocking wooden balls through a series of wire wickets by means of mallets.

cro·quette (krō ket′), *n.* a small mass of minced meat, fish, etc., usually coated with bread crumbs and fried in deep fat.

cross (krôs), *n.* **1.** a structure consisting of an upright piece and a crossing piece, upon which persons were formerly put to death. **2.** the **Cross,** the cross upon which Jesus died. **3.** a figure of the Cross as a Christian symbol, emblem, badge, etc. **4.** any figure, mark, or object resembling a cross, as two intersecting lines. **5.** any misfortune or trouble; burden. **6.** a crossbreed. —*v.* **7.** to cancel by marking with a cross or with a line or lines (usually fol. by *off* or *out*): *Cross out the wrong answers.* **8.** to move or pass from one side to the other side: *to cross the street.* **9.** to meet and pass: *We crossed each other on the highway.* **10.** to make the sign of the cross upon or over. **11.** to crossbreed: *to cross a spaniel and a terrier.* —*adj.* **12.** lying or passing across each other: *cross timbers.* **13.** angry and annoyed. —**cross′ly,** *adv.*

Crosses
A, Latin cross;
B, Maltese cross;
C, St. Andrew's cross;
D, Greek cross

cross·bar (krôs′bär′), *n.* a crosswise bar, line, or stripe.

cross·bones (krôs′bōnz′), *n.pl.* two bones placed crosswise, usually below a skull, symbolizing death.

cross·bow (krôs′bō′), *n.* a weapon consisting of a bow placed across a stock, the string of which is released by a trigger.

Crossbow

cross·breed (krôs′brēd′), *n.* 1. a plant or animal produced from parents of different but related breeds. —*v.,* **cross·bred** (krôs′bred′), **cross·breed·ing.** 2. to breed (such a plant or animal). —**cross′breed′er,** *n.*

cross·coun·try (krôs′kun′trē), *adj.* 1. directed or going over fields, through woods, etc., rather than on a road or path: *a cross-country race.* 2. from one end of the country to the other: *a cross-country flight.*

cross·cut (krôs′kut′), *adj.* 1. made or used for cutting crosswise: *a crosscut saw.* —*n.* 2. a crosswise cut or course. 3. a shortcut. —*v.,* **cross·cut, cross·cut·ting.** 4. to cut or go across.

cross′cut saw′, a saw or saw blade for cutting wood across the grain. See also **ripsaw.**

cross·ex·am·ine (krôs′ig zam′in), *v.,* **cross·ex·am·ined, cross·ex·am·in·ing.** 1. to examine very closely, esp. as a check on a previous examination. 2. to examine (a witness called by the opposing side) for the purpose of discrediting his testimony. —**cross′-ex·am′in·er,** *n.* —**cross′-ex·am′i·na′tion,** *n.*

cross-eyed (krôs′īd′), *adj.* having eyes turned toward the nose.

cross·ing (krô′sing), *n.* 1. the act of a person or thing that crosses: *We had a smooth crossing on our trip to Europe.* 2. a place at which a road, river, etc., may be crossed: *We waited at the crossing for the light to change.* 3. a place where lines, streets, railroad tracks, etc., cross.

cross·piece (krôs′pēs′), *n.* a piece of any material placed across something.

cross·pur·pose (krôs′pûr′pəs), *n.* 1. a purpose in opposition or contrary to another purpose. 2. **at cross-purposes,** in a way that produces mutual misunderstanding, usually unintentionally: *We were working at cross-purposes and didn't even realize it.*

cross′ ref′erence, a reference from one part of a book, index, or the like, to another, usually to provide the reader with information on a related subject.

cross·road (krôs′rōd′), *n.* 1. a road that crosses another road or connects main roads. 2. Often, **crossroads.** *(used as sing. or pl.)* **a.** the place where roads meet. **b.** a point at which an important decision must be made. **c.** a main center of activity.

cross′ sec′tion, 1. a slice cut at right angles to the longest direction of anything. 2. a pictorial representation of such a slice. 3. a typical selection or sample: *a cross section of American opinion.*

cross·tree (krôs′trē′), *n.* either of a pair of timbers or metal bars placed either across the top of a ship's mast to spread the shrouds leading to the mast above, or on the head of a lower mast to support the platform or top.

cross·walk (krôs′wôk′), *n.* a lane, usually marked, for pedestrians crossing a street or highway.

cross·wise (krôs′wīz′), *adv.* 1. across. 2. in the form of a cross: *to place logs crosswise.* Also, **cross·ways** (krôs′wāz′).

cross′word puz′zle (krôs′wûrd′), a puzzle in which words corresponding to numbered clues or definitions are fitted into a pattern of horizontal and vertical squares so that most letters form part of two words.

crotch (kroch), *n.* 1. a forked piece, part, support, etc.: *the crotch of a tree.* 2. a branching off or place of branching off, as of the human body between the legs. 3. the part of a pair of trousers, panties, etc., formed by the joining of the two legs.

crotch·et (kroch′it), *n.* 1. a small hook. 2. an odd or whimsical idea.

crouch (krouch), *v.* 1. to stoop or bend low: *The cat crouched before springing at the mouse.* —*n.* 2. the act or position of crouching.

croup[1] (krōōp), *n.* a children's disease marked by severe coughing and difficult breathing. [from an English dialect word meaning "to cry hoarsely"]

croup[2] (krōōp), *n.* the highest part of the rump of a horse. [from an Old French word, which comes from Germanic]

crow[1] (krō), *n.* 1. any of several large, black birds noted for their intelligence and their harsh cry. 2. **eat crow,** to be embarrassed or humiliated, esp. in having to admit a mistake or apologize: *He couldn't carry out his threat, so he had to eat crow.* [from the Old English word *crāwe*]

Crow
(length 19 in; wingspread 3 ft.)

crow[2] (krō), *v.,* **crowed** *or,* for def. 1, **crew** (krōō); **crowed; crow·ing.** 1. to utter the cry of a rooster. 2. to utter a cry of pleasure or delight. 3. to boast loudly: *Stop crowing about your good luck.* —*n.* 4. the cry of a rooster. 5. a cry of pleasure or delight. [from the Old English word *crāwan*]

crow·bar (krō′bär′), *n.* a steel bar, usually flattened and slightly bent at one or both ends, used as a lever.

crowd (kroud), *n.* 1. a large number of persons gathered closely together. 2. common or ordinary people; the masses. 3. a group or class of persons; set: *an interesting crowd at a party.* —*v.* 4. to gather in large numbers. 5. to press forward; advance by pushing. 6. to push; shove: *to crowd someone into a corner.* 7. to press closely together; force into a small space; cram: *to crowd clothes into a suitcase.*

crowd·ed (krou′did), *adj.* filled with a crowd; packed: *crowded streets; a crowded store.*

crown (kroun), *n.* 1. any of various types of symbolic headgear worn by a king, queen, emperor, etc., representing royal power. 2. an ornamental wreath for the head, given in ancient times as a mark of victory. 3. **the crown,** the ruler of a monarchy, or the supreme power of a monarch. 4. any of various coins having the figure of a crown or a crowned head. 5. a former coin of the United Kingdom, equal to five shillings. 6. the top or highest part of anything: *the crown of a hat.* 7. the top of the head. 8. the part of a tooth that is covered by enamel. 9. a gold or porcelain cover for the crown of a tooth. —*v.* 10. to place a crown or garland on the head of: *to crown the winner.* 11. to give royal power to: *He was crowned king.* 12. to complete; bring to a successful conclusion: *The Nobel prize crowned his career as an author.* 13. to cap (a tooth) with an artificial crown. 14. (in checkers) to change a checker into a king by putting another checker of the same color on top of it.

Crown

crown′ col′ony, a colony in which the crown controls the government, different from one that has a constitution and a representative government.

crown′ prince′, the son of a monarch who is first in line for the throne.

crown′ prin′cess, 1. the wife of a crown prince. 2. a woman or girl who is first in line for the throne.

crow's-nest (krōz′nest′), *n.* a platform or shelter for a lookout at or near the top of a mast of a ship.

cru·cial (krōō′shəl), *adj.* involving a final decision; decisive; critical: *a crucial test.* —**cru′cial·ly,** *adv.*

cru·ci·ble (krōō′sə bəl), *n.* a pot or vessel made of some material that can withstand very high temperatures, used esp. for melting and purifying metals.

cru·ci·fix (krōō′sə fiks), *n.* a cross with the figure of the crucified Jesus on it.

cru·ci·fix·ion (krōō′sə fik′shən), *n.* 1. the act of crucifying. 2. **the Crucifixion,** the death of Jesus by being nailed upon a cross.

cru·ci·fy (krōō′sə fī′), *v.,* **cru·ci·fied, cru·ci·fy·ing.** 1. to put to death by nailing or binding a person to a cross. 2. to treat with great injustice; persecute.

crude (krōōd), *adj.,* **crud·er, crud·est.** 1. in a raw or unrefined state: *crude oil.* 2. lacking finish; uncompleted: *a crude summary; a crude shack.* 3. lacking good taste, refinement, etc.; vulgar: *a crude sense of humor.* —**crude′ly,** *adv.* —**crude′ness,** *n.*

cru·el (krōō′əl), *adj.* 1. willfully causing pain or distress to others: *She is cruel to her dog.* 2. enjoying the pain or distress of others: *a cruel audience.* 3. causing great pain or distress: *a cruel remark; a cruel war.* —**cru′el·ly,** *adv.*

cru·el·ty (krōō′əl tē), *n., pl.* for def. 2 **cru·el·ties.** 1. cruel disposition, conduct, or behavior: *No one could understand his cruelty toward animals.* 2. a cruel act: *the cruelties of the enemy.*

cru·et (krōō′it), *n.* a glass bottle for holding vinegar or oil for the table.

cruise (krōōz), *v.,* **cruised, cruis·ing.** 1. to sail about without going directly from one point to another, as a yacht on a pleasure trip or a warship in search of enemy ships. 2. to travel about without a particular purpose or destination. 3. to travel at a moderate speed that permits the greatest operating efficiency: *The airplane cruised at 350 miles per hour.* —*n.* 4. a pleasure trip made by cruising: *an ocean cruise.*

cruis·er (krōō′zər), *n.* 1. a person or thing that cruises. 2. a warship designed for high speed. 3. a power-driven pleasure vessel equipped for living aboard and intended for cruising.

crul·ler (krul′ər), *n.* a light, sweet cake fried in deep fat, often having a ring-shaped or twisted form.

crumb (krum), *n.* 1. a small particle of bread, cake, etc., such as breaks or falls off. 2. a small portion of anything: *crumbs of information.* —*v.* 3. to prepare or coat with crumbs: *to crumb chicken before frying.* 4. to break into crumbs.

crum·ble (krum′bəl), *v.,* **crum·bled, crum·bling.** 1. to break into small fragments or crumbs: *to crumble crackers.* 2. to decay or fall apart gradually: *The garden wall is crumbling.* —**crum′bly,** *adj.*

crum·ple (krum′pəl), *v.,* **crum·pled, crum·pling.** 1. to press into irregular folds; rumple; wrinkle: *to crumple a piece of paper.* 2. to become wrinkled: *My dress crumpled in the suitcase.* 3. to give way suddenly; collapse: *The boxer crumpled to the floor.*

crunch (krunch), *v.* 1. to crush with the teeth; chew with a crushing sound: *to crunch a carrot.* 2. to crush or grind noisily. 3. to make a crunching sound: *The leaves crunched under our feet.* —*n.* 4. the act or sound of crunching.

crunch·y (krun′chē), *adj.,* **crunch·i·er, crunch·i·est.** very crisp or brittle. —**crunch′i·ness,** *n.*

cru·sade (krōō sād′), *n.* 1. *(often cap.)* any of the military expeditions undertaken by the Christians of Europe in the 11th, 12th, and 13th centuries for the recovery of the Holy Land from the Muslims. 2. any strong movement in support of an idea, cause, etc.: *crusade against crime.* —*v.,* **cru·sad·ed, cru·sad·ing.** 3. to go on or participate in a crusade. —**cru·sad′er,** *n.*

crush (krush), *v.* 1. to press with a force that destroys or deforms: *to crush a hat.* 2. to squeeze or pound into small fragments or pieces: *to crush stone.* 3. to hug or embrace strongly. 4. to destroy, subdue, or oppress: *to crush a revolt.* 5. to press or crowd: *The people crushed into the subway.* —*n.* 6. the act of crushing. 7. a great crowd. 8. *Informal.* a strong feeling of love or admiration: *She has a crush on the boy next door.* —**crush′er,** *n.* —**crush′ing·ly,** *adv.*

Cru·soe (krōō′sō), *n.* **Robinson,** the hero of the book *Robinson Crusoe,* written by Daniel Defoe.

crust (krust), *n.* 1. the hard outer portion of a loaf of bread. 2. a piece of this. 3. the baked shell of a pie. 4. any fairly hard covering or coating: *a crust of snow.* 5. the outer portion of the earth, about 22 miles deep under the continents and 6 miles deep under the oceans. —*v.* 6. to cover or become covered with or as if with crust: *The path is crusted with ice.*

crus·ta·cean (kru stā′shən), *n.* any of a class of animals having hard shells and jointed legs, including lobsters, crabs, barnacles, etc.

crust·y (krus′tē), *adj.*, **crust·i·er, crust·i·est. 1.** resembling or having a crust. **2.** harsh; rude; surly: *a crusty remark.* —**crust′i·ness,** *n.*

crutch (kruch), *n.* **1.** a staff or support to help a lame person in walking, usually with a crosspiece fitting under the armpit. **2.** anything that supports or helps: *to use a translation as a crutch.*

crux (kruks), *n.* the basic or main point: *What is the crux of the matter?*

cry (krī), *v.*, **cried, cry·ing. 1.** to utter sounds of grief or suffering, usually with tears. **2.** to weep; shed tears. **3.** to shout or yell; call out. **4.** to beg or plead: *to cry for mercy.* **5.** to announce publicly as being for sale: *to cry one's wares.* **6.** to make characteristic sounds or calls, as animals; yelp; bark. —*n., pl.* **cries. 7.** the act or sound of crying; a shout, scream, or wail. **8.** clamor or outcry: *the cry of the crowd.* **9.** an appeal or plea: *a cry for freedom.* **10.** the call of an animal. **11. a far cry,** far removed; quite different: *This is a far cry from the goal we set.*

cry·o·gen·ics (krī′ō jen′iks), *n. (used as sing.)* the branch of physics that deals with the effects of very low temperatures.

crypt (kript), *n.* an underground chamber or vault, usually beneath a church, used as a burial place. [from the Greek word *kryptē* "hidden place"]

cryp·tic (krip′tik), *adj.* hidden; secret; puzzling: *No one understood his cryptic reply.* —**cryp′ti·cal·ly,** *adv.*

crys·tal (kris′t³l), *n.* **1.** a very clear transparent mineral resembling ice. **2.** a solid having an orderly internal structure and a definite outer form composed of flat surfaces meeting at regular angles. **3.** very fine, clear glass, used to make bowls, goblets, etc. **4.** the glass or plastic cover over the face of a watch. —*adj.* **5.** made of crystal: *a crystal chandelier.* **6.** resembling crystal; clear or transparent: *a crystal lake.*

crys·tal·line (kris′t³lin), *adj.* **1.** of or resembling a crystal. **2.** composed of crystals. **3.** formed by crystallization.

crys·tal·lize (kris′t³līz′), *v.*, **crys·tal·lized, crys·tal·liz·ing. 1.** to become a crystal or something resembling one. **2.** to acquire definite form: *His plans have crystallized.* —**crys·tal·li·za·tion** (kris′t³li zā′shən), *n.*

Cs, *Chem.* the symbol for cesium.

ct., **1.** carat. **2.** cent. **3.** county. **4.** court.

Ctr., Center. Also, **ctr.**

cts., **1.** cents. **2.** certificates.

Cu, *Chem.* the symbol for **copper.** [from the Latin word *cuprum*]

cu., cubic.

cub (kub), *n.* the young of certain animals, such as the fox, bear, etc.

Cu·ba (kyōō′bə), *n.* an island republic in the Caribbean Sea, S of Florida. 44,218 sq. mi. *Cap.:* Havana. —**Cu′ban,** *n., adj.*

cub·by·hole (kub′ē hōl′), *n.* a small, snug place, room, or cabin.

cube (kyōōb), *n.* **1.** a solid having six identical square faces meeting at right angles. **2.** a piece of anything shaped like a cube: *a cube of cheese.* **3.** the number obtained by multiplying a given number by itself twice: *64 is the cube of 4, since* $4 \times 4 \times 4 = 64.$ —*v.*, **cubed, cub·ing. 4.** to make into a cube or cubes: *to cube potatoes.* **5.** to multiply a number by itself twice.

Cube

cu·bic (kyōō′bik), *adj.* **1.** shaped like a cube. **2.** referring to volume or the measurement of volume.

cu·bi·cle (kyōō′bi kəl), *n.* any small space or compartment formed by making partitions: *The big office was divided into cubicles.*

cu·bit (kyōō′bit), *n.* an obsolete unit of length, equivalent to about 20 inches: the length of the forearm from the elbow to the tip of the middle finger.

cub′ scout′, a member of the junior division (ages 8–11) of the Boy Scouts.

cuck·oo (kōō′kōō), *n., pl.* **cuck·oos. 1.** a European bird noted for its two-note call and the habit of laying its eggs in the nests of other birds. **2.** the call of the cuckoo. —*adj.* **3.** *Slang.* silly or foolish.

cu·cum·ber (kyōō′kum bər), *n.* **1.** a long, cylindrical vegetable with a green skin, used in salads and often pickled. **2.** the vine that bears this vegetable.

cud (kud), *n.* the portion of food that a cow returns from the first stomach to the mouth to chew again.

cud·dle (kud′³l), *v.*, **cud·dled, cud·dling. 1.** to hold close in an affectionate manner; hug tenderly: *to cuddle a kitten.* **2.** to lie close and snug: *to cuddle up under a blanket.* —**cud′dly,** *adj.*

cudg·el (kuj′əl), *n.* **1.** a short, thick stick used as a weapon; club. —*v.*, **cudg·eled** *or* **cudg·elled; cudg·el·ing** *or* **cudg·el·ling. 2.** to strike with a cudgel; beat.

cue¹ (kyōō), *n.* **1.** anything said or done in a play that is used as a signal for something to follow. **2.** any hint or signal: *He gave me a cue that it was time for us to go.* —*v.*, **cued, cu·ing. 3.** to provide or give a cue to: *to cue an actor.* [In ancient Roman plays the director would call the actors on stage by using the word *quando* "when." In the script the word was abbreviated by the letter *q.* In the English theater it became the custom for the director to call the actors with the sound of the letter *q,* which came to be written *cue*]

cue² (kyōō), *n.* a long, tapering rod, tipped with leather, used to strike the ball in billiards or pool. [from the Old French word *coue,* which comes from Latin *cauda* "tail"]

cuff¹ (kuf), *n.* **1.** a fold or band used as a trimming or finish for the bottom of a sleeve. **2.** a turned-up fold at the bottom of a trouser leg. **3. off the cuff,** without planning one's words in advance; on the spur of the moment: *to speak off the cuff.* **4. on the cuff,** with the promise of later payment; on credit: *That restaurant lets him eat on the cuff.* [from the Old

English word *cuffie* "cap," which comes from medieval Latin *cuphia*]

cuff² (kuf), *v.* 1. to strike or hit with the fist or the open hand. —*n.* 2. a blow with the fist or open hand. [perhaps from Scandinavian]

cu. ft., cubic foot; cubic feet.

cu. in., cubic inch; cubic inches.

cui·rass (kwi ras′), *n.* armor for the upper part of the body, including a breastplate and backplate.

cui·sine (kwi zēn′), *n.* a style or quality of cooking; cookery: *French cuisine.*

cu·li·nar·y (kul′ə ner′ē, kyōo′lə ner′ē), *adj.* referring to or used in the kitchen or in cookery: *to develop one's culinary skills.*

cull (kul), *v.* 1. to choose or select; pick the best things or parts from: *We culled the best pears for market.* 2. to remove the inferior parts of: *to cull a flock of sheep.* —*n.* 3. anything put aside as inferior: *We saved the best beans and discarded the culls.*

cul·mi·nate (kul′mə nāt′), *v.*, **cul·mi·nat·ed, cul·mi·nat·ing.** 1. to end at the highest point or development (usually fol. by *in*): *The campaign culminated in a huge rally.* 2. to end or conclude; arrive at a final stage (usually fol. by *in*): *The argument culminated in a fistfight.* —**cul′mi·na′tion,** *n.*

cul·pa·ble (kul′pə bəl), *adj.* deserving blame; guilty: *to determine who is culpable.*

cul·prit (kul′prit), *n.* 1. a person charged with a crime or offense. 2. a person guilty of an offense.

cult (kult), *n.* 1. a system of religious worship, esp. with reference to its rites and ceremonies. 2. a great admiration of and devotion to a person or thing: *a movie cult.* 3. the people who share such an admiration and devotion: *a cult of bird watchers.*

cul·ti·vate (kul′tə vāt′), *v.*, **cul·ti·vat·ed, cul·ti·vat·ing.** 1. to prepare and work on (land) in order to raise crops. 2. to improve the growth of (a plant, crop, etc.) by labor and attention. 3. to loosen the earth and destroy weeds around (growing plants). 4. to develop or improve by education or training: *to cultivate an interest in music; to cultivate one's mind.* 5. to seek the acquaintance and friendship of: *He cultivated people who would do him favors.*

cul·ti·va·tion (kul′tə vā′shən), *n.* 1. the act or skill of cultivating: *cultivation of the soil.* 2. culture; refinement.

cul·ti·va·tor (kul′tə vā′tər), *n.* 1. a person or thing that cultivates. 2. a tool drawn between rows of growing plants to loosen the earth and destroy weeds.

cul·tur·al (kul′chər əl), *adj.* of or referring to culture or cultivation. —**cul′tur·al·ly,** *adv.*

cul·ture (kul′chər), *n.* 1. the quality in a person or society that comes from an interest in and knowledge of what is usually considered excellence in art, music, literature, etc. 2. a particular form or stage of civilization: *Greek culture.* 3. a special growth of bacteria, yeast, mold, etc., esp. one cultivated in a laboratory. 4. the act or practice of cultivating the soil. 5. the raising of plants or animals, esp. with a view to their improvement. 6. development or im-

provement of the mind by education or training.

cul·tured (kul′chərd), *adj.* 1. cultivated or refined: *cultured tastes.* 2. artificially grown.

cul·vert (kul′vərt), *n.* a drain or channel crossing under a road, sidewalk, etc.; sewer.

cum·ber·some (kum′bər səm), *adj.* hard to manage; clumsy; unwieldy: *a cumbersome package.*

cu·mu·la·tive (kyōo′myə lā′tiv, kyōo′myə lə tiv), *adj.* growing by additions: *cumulative evidence.*

cu·mu·lus (kyōo′myə ləs), *n., pl.* **cu·mu·lus.** a kind of cloud having a flat base and a domed, fluffy top.

cu·ne·i·form (kyōo nē′ə fôrm′), *adj.* 1. having the form of a wedge; wedge-shaped. 2. made up of slim triangular parts, as the characters used in writing by the ancient Assyrians, Babylonians, and others. —*n.* 3. cuneiform writing.

Cuneiform writing

cun·ning (kun′iŋ), *n.* 1. skill used in a crafty, sly way; craftiness. 2. dexterity; cleverness. —*adj.* 3. showing cleverness; cleverly made. 4. very subtle or shrewd; sly. 5. *Informal.* charmingly cute: *a cunning little baby.* —**cun′ning·ly,** *adv.* —**cun′ning·ness,** *n.*

cup (kup), *n.* 1. a small, open container of china, glass, metal, etc., usually having a handle and used for drinking coffee, tea, etc. 2. an ornamental cup or vessel often made of a precious metal and offered as a prize in a contest. 3. the quantity contained in a cup; cupful. 4. anything shaped like a cup: *the cup of a flower.* —*v.*, **cupped, cup·ping.** 5. to take or place in or as if in a cup. 6. to form into a cuplike shape: *He cupped his hands to drink from the stream.*

cup·board (kub′ərd), *n.* a closet with shelves for dishes, cups, etc.

cup·cake (kup′kāk′), *n.* a small cake baked in a cup-shaped pan.

cup·ful (kup′fŏol), *n., pl.* **cup·fuls.** 1. the amount that a cup can hold. 2. (in cooking) a half pint; eight fluid ounces (about ¼ liter).

Cu·pid (kyōo′pid), *n.* (in Roman mythology) the god of love, usually pictured as a small, winged boy with a bow and arrow: identified with the Greek god Eros.

cu·pid·i·ty (kyōo pid′i tē), *n.* eager desire for wealth; greed.

cu·po·la (kyōo′pə lə), *n.* 1. a small, round tower on a dome or roof. 2. a dome-shaped roof or ceiling.

cur (kûr), *n.* 1. a worthless, unfriendly mongrel dog. 2. a low, mean person.

cur·a·ble (kyōor′ə bəl), *adj.* that can be cured: *a curable disease.*

Cu·ra·çao (kŏor′ə sou′, kyōor′ə sō′), *n.* a Dutch island off the NW coast of Venezuela. 173 sq. mi.

cu·rate (kyōor′it), *n.* a clergyman who is employed as an assistant to a rector or vicar.

cu·ra·tor (kyōo rā′tər, kyōor′ā tər), *n.* the person in charge of a museum, zoo, etc.

curb (kûrb), *n.* **1.** a rim of concrete or joined stones, forming an edge for a sidewalk. **2.** Also, **curb′ bit′.** a chain or strap attached to a horse's bit, used for controlling or restraining a horse. **3.** anything that controls or restrains; check: *to put a curb on one's spending.* —*v.* **4.** to restrain or check; control: *to curb one's excitement.*

curd (kûrd), *n.* a thick substance obtained from milk and used as food or made into cheese.

cur·dle (kûr′dªl), *v.,* **cur·dled, cur·dling. 1.** to change into curd; thicken; coagulate. **2. curdle the** (or **one's**) **blood,** to fill a person with horror or fear; terrify: *The ghost story curdled my blood.*

cure (kyŏŏr), *v.,* **cured, cur·ing. 1.** to restore or bring back good health; make well: *to cure a patient.* **2.** to rid of something troublesome or dangerous: *to cure a cold.* **3.** to prepare (meat, fish, etc.) for preservation by salting and drying. —*n.* **4.** a method or course of medical treatment. **5.** successful medical treatment; restoration to health. **6.** a method or process of preserving meat, fish, etc., by salting or smoking.

cur·few (kûr′fyŏŏ), *n.* **1.** an order establishing a period of time, usually at night, when unauthorized persons must be indoors and public places are closed. **2.** the time at which such restrictions begin: *an 11 o'clock curfew.* **3.** (in medieval Europe) the ringing of a bell at a fixed hour in the evening as a signal for extinguishing fires. [from the Old French phrase *cuevre feu* "cover (the) fire," that is, "lights out"]

cu·ri·o (kyŏŏr′ē ō′), *n., pl.* **cu·ri·os.** any unusual or rare object of art.

cu·ri·os·i·ty (kyŏŏr′ē os′i tē), *n., pl.* for def. 3 **cu·ri·os·i·ties. 1.** the desire to learn or know: *Curiosity made her read the postcard.* **2.** a strange, curious, or interesting quality. **3.** a rare or unusual thing.

cu·ri·ous (kyŏŏr′ē əs), *adj.* **1.** eager to learn or know: *Most people are curious about space travel.* **2.** causing interest by being unusual; odd; strange: *a curious way to dress.* —**cu′ri·ous·ly,** *adv.*

cu·ri·um (kyŏŏr′ē əm), *n. Chem.* a man-made, radioactive, metallic element. *Symbol:* Cm

curl (kûrl), *v.* **1.** to form into tight waves or ringlets: *I curled my hair.* **2.** to form into a curved shape; coil: *He curled up in the chair.* **3.** to move in a curving direction or path: *Smoke curled from the bonfire.* —*n.* **4.** a coil or ringlet of hair. **5.** anything having a curved shape, as a lettuce leaf, wood shaving, etc.

cur·lew (kûr′lŏŏ), *n.* any of several shore birds, having a long, slender, downward curved bill.

Curlew
(length 23 in.;
wingspread 3¼ ft.)

curl·ing (kûr′liñg), *n.* a game played on ice in which two teams of four players each compete in sliding a large, heavy stone or similar object made of iron (**curl′ing stone′**) toward a mark in the center of a circle.

curl·y (kûr′lē), *adj.,* **curl·i·er, curl·i·est. 1.** curling or tending to curl: *curly hair.* **2.** having curls (usually used in combination): *curlyheaded.* —**curl′i·ness,** *n.*

cur·rant (kûr′ənt), *n.* **1.** a small, seedless raisin used in cooking and baking. **2.** a small, round, sour berry used in making preserves and jellies.

cur·ren·cy (kûr′ən sē), *n., pl.* for def. 1 **cur·ren·cies. 1.** something that is used as a medium of exchange; money. **2.** general acceptance: *an idea that has currency.* **3.** circulation; spreading from one person to another: *the currency of a rumor.*

cur·rent (kûr′ənt), *adj.* **1.** belonging to the time actually passing: *the current month.* **2.** publicly reported or known: *a rumor that is current.* **3.** customary; usual: *the current practice.* **4.** popular; in style: *the current fashions.* —*n.* **5.** flow in a certain direction: *the current of a stream; an air current.* **6.** the movement or flow of electric charge. **7.** the general tendency; trend: *a current of discontent.*

cur·rent·ly (kûr′ənt lē), *adv.* now; at present.

cur·ric·u·lum (kə rik′yə ləm), *n.* the courses of study given in a school, college, etc.

cur·ry¹ (kûr′ē), *n., pl.* **cur·ries. 1.** Also, **cur′ry pow′der.** a yellowish powder made of several different spices, used esp. in the cookery of India. **2.** a highly spiced dish of meat, fish, vegetables, etc., flavored with this powder: *a shrimp curry.* —*v.,* **cur·ried, cur·ry·ing. 3.** to prepare food as a curry: *to curry chicken.* [from an Indian word *kari* "sauce"]

cur·ry² (kûr′ē), *v.,* **cur·ried, cur·ry·ing. 1.** to rub and clean (a horse) with a currycomb. **2.** to dress (tanned hides) by soaking, scraping, etc. **3. curry favor,** to try to win favor by insincere flattery: *He curried favor with her by telling her she was his favorite teacher.* [from a Middle English word, which comes from Old French *correer* "to make ready"]

cur·ry·comb (kûr′ē kōm′), *n.* **1.** a comb, usually with rows of metal teeth, for currying horses. —*v.* **2.** to rub or clean with such a comb; curry.

curse (kûrs), *n.* **1.** the expression of a wish that misfortune, harm, evil, etc., befall a person. **2.** an evil that has been wished for. **3.** the cause of evil, misfortune, or trouble. **4.** a word used in swearing; profane oath. —*v.,* **cursed** *or* **curst; curs·ing. 5.** to wish evil or destruction upon: *to curse an enemy.* **6.** to afflict with great evil: *to be cursed with poor health.* **7.** to utter curses; swear profanely.

curs·ed (kûr′sid, kûrst), *adj.* **1.** under a curse; damned. **2.** deserving a curse; hateful.

cur·so·ry (kûr′sə rē), *adj.* performed or done quickly without noticing details; hasty; superficial: *a cursory look at the book.*

curt (kûrt), *adj.* short, abrupt, or rudely brief: *a curt answer.* —**curt′ly,** *adv.* —**curt′ness,** *n.*

cur·tail (kər tāl′), *v.* to cut short; reduce or lessen: *to curtail a speech; to curtail shipments of wheat.*

cur·tain (kûr′t²n), *n.* **1.** a hanging piece of fabric used to shut out the light from a window, decorate a room, etc. **2.** a drapery hanging in front of and concealing the stage in a theater. **3.** anything that shuts

off, covers, or conceals: *a curtain of artillery fire.*
—*v.* **4.** to decorate, shut off, or conceal with or as if
with a curtain: *to curtain a wall.*

Cur·tis (kûr′tis), *n.* **Charles,** 1860–1936, 31st Vice
President of the U.S. 1929–1933.

curt·sey (kûrt′sē), *n., pl.* **curt·seys;** *v.,* **curt·seyed,**
curt·sey·ing. another spelling of **curtsy.**

curt·sy (kûrt′sē), *n., pl.* **curt·sies.** **1.** a bow made by
women in recognition or respect, consisting of bend-
ing the knees and lowering the body. —*v.,* **curt·sied,**
curt·sy·ing. 2. to make a curtsy.

cur·va·ture (kûr′və chər), *n.* a curved condition or
state; curving: *the curvature of a lens.*

curve (kûrv), *n.* **1.** a continuously bending line, without angles. **2.** any outline, form, or thing shaped like
a curve: *a curve in the road.* **3.** Also, **curve′ ball′.** a
pitched baseball that veers to the left or the right.
—*v.,* **curved, curv·ing. 4.** to bend or cause to bend in
a curve: *The path curves to the right.*

cush·ion (koʊsh′ən), *n.* **1.** a soft pad or bag of cloth,
leather, or rubber filled with feathers, air, etc., on
which to sit, kneel, or lie. **2.** anything used for absorbing shocks or jolts. —*v.* **3.** to place on or support
by a cushion. **4.** to furnish with a cushion or cushions. **5.** to suppress or soften the effects of: *to cushion the blow to his pride.* —**cush′ion·like′,** *adj.*

cus·pid (kus′pid), *n.* See **canine** (def. 3).

cus·tard (kus′tərd), *n.* a dessert made of eggs and
milk, sweetened, and baked, boiled, or frozen.

Cus·ter (kus′tər), *n.* **George Armstrong,** 1839–1876,
U.S. general and Indian fighter.

cus·to·di·an (ku stō′dē ən), *n.* a person who has custody; keeper; guardian: *the custodian of the school
building.*

cus·to·dy (kus′tə dē), *n.* **1.** guardianship or care: *in
the custody of her father.* **2.** confinement or imprisonment: *The criminal was taken into custody.*

cus·tom (kus′təm), *n.* **1.** a habitual practice; the
usual way of acting: *It is their custom to take a vacation in spring.* **2.** a practice so long established that
it is accepted by almost all people and has the force
of law: *the social and religious customs of Indian
tribes.* **3. customs, a.** *(used as sing. or pl.)* taxes imposed by law on imported and sometimes on exported goods. **b.** *(used as sing.)* the government
department that collects these taxes. —*adj.* **4.** made
especially for individual customers: *custom shoes.* **5.**
dealing in such items, or doing work to order: *a custom tailor.*

cus·tom·ar·y (kus′tə mer′ē), *adj.* according to or depending on custom; usual; habitual: *We met at the
customary time and place.*

cus·tom·er (kus′tə mər), *n.* **1.** a patron, buyer, or
shopper. **2.** *Informal.* a person one has to deal with:
a tough customer; a cool customer.

cus′tom house′, a government office, often at a
seaport, for collecting customs, clearing vessels, etc.
Also, **cus′toms house′.**

cus·tom-made (kus′təm mād′), *adj.* made to individual order: *custom-made shoes.*

cut (kut), *v.,* **cut, cut·ting. 1.** to penetrate or divide

with or as if with a sharp-edged instrument: *to cut a
loaf of bread.* **2.** to hurt the feelings of severely: *His
remark cut me badly.* **3.** to refuse to recognize socially; snub: *She cut Jim at the dance.* **4.** to trim by
clipping, shearing, paring, or pruning: *to cut hair.* **5.**
to shorten or leave out: *to cut a speech.* **6.** to lower,
reduce, or diminish: *to cut prices.* **7.** to make or fashion by cutting: *to cut a statue.* **8.** to grow (a tooth or
teeth) through the gum. **9.** to allow to be cut: *Warm
butter cuts easily.* **10.** to make a sudden or sharp
change in direction: *The driver cut to the right.* **11.**
to record a selection on: *to cut a record.* **12.** to cross,
esp. in the most direct way (usually fol. by *across,
through, in,* etc.): *to cut across an empty lot.* **13.** *Informal.* to stop or discontinue: *Cut that nonsense!*
—*n.* **14.** a stroke or blow, as with a knife, whip, etc.
15. the result of cutting, as an incision, wound, passage, channel, etc. **16.** a piece cut off: *a cut of pie.*
17. the manner or fashion in which anything is cut:
the cut of a dress. **18.** a passage or course straight
across or through: *a cut through the woods.* **19.** a reduction in price, salary, etc. **20.** an act, speech, etc.,
that hurts the feelings: *His mean remark was an unnecessary cut.* **21.** an engraved plate or block used
for printing. **22.** *Informal.* share: *His cut of the profits was $10.* **23. cut and dried,** fixed or settled in ad-
vance: *It was cut and dried that John would be class
president.* **24. cut down,** to make less; decrease:
You'll have to cut down those between-meal snacks.
25. cut down on, to lessen the amount of; use less of:
The dentist told her to cut down on candy. **26. cut
in, a.** to come in between, esp. abruptly: *The other
car cut in and nearly caused an accident.* **b.** to interrupt: *He cut in with a very funny remark.* **27. cut
off, a.** to stop suddenly: *Dad cut off my allowance.* **b.**
to disinherit: *to be cut off without a cent.* **28. cut
out, a.** to stop; refrain from: *My brother had to cut
out smoking.* **b.** to delete or omit: *They had cut out
the best parts of the movie.* **29. cut out for,** to be fitted or suited for: *He was not cut out for the ministry.*
30. cut up, to play pranks; misbehave: *He got
spanked for cutting up in church.*

cut′a·way coat′, (kut′ə wā′), a coat that is worn by
a man for formal daytime dress, tapering from the
front waist downward toward tails at
the back.

cute (kyoot), *adj.,* **cut·er, cut·est.** *Informal.* **1.** pleasingly pretty or dainty: *a
cute hat.* **2.** mentally keen; clever;
shrewd.

cu·ti·cle (kyoo′ti kəl), *n.* **1.** the hardened skin surrounding the edges of the
fingernails and toenails. **2.** the outermost layer of skin.

cut·lass (kut′ləs), *n.* a short, heavy,
slightly curved sword. Also, **cut′las.**

Cutaway coat

cut·ler·y (kut′lə rē), *n.* **1.** cutting instruments, esp. those used for serving or eating food.
2. the business of making and selling cutting instruments, such as knives, scissors, etc.

cut·let (kut′lit), *n.* **1.** a slice of meat, esp. of veal or mutton, for broiling or frying. **2.** a flat cake or croquette of minced chicken, lobster, etc.

cut·ter (kut′ər), *n.* **1.** a person or thing that cuts: *a paper cutter.* **2.** a single-masted sailing vessel. **3.** a boat carried aboard large ships for transporting passengers and supplies to and from the shore. **4.** a lightly armed vessel, used by a government to prevent smuggling. **5.** a small, light sleigh.

cut·throat (kut′thrōt′), *n.* **1.** a person who cuts throats; murderer. —*adj.* **2.** without mercy; ruthless: *cutthroat competition.*

cut·ting (kut′iṅg), *n.* **1.** the act of a person or thing that cuts. **2.** a root, stem, or leaf, cut from a plant and used to form a new plant. —*adj.* **3.** able to cut: *a good cutting edge.* **4.** wounding the feelings severely: *a cutting remark.* **5.** piercing; sharp: *a cutting wind.*

cut·tle·fish (kut′əl fish), *n., pl.* **cut·tle·fish·es** *or* **cut·tle·fish.** any of several ten-armed sea animals related to the octopus and squid.

cut·worm (kut′wûrm′), *n.* any of several caterpillars that feed on the stems of young plants.

CWO, chief warrant officer.

-cy, a suffix used to form nouns meaning **1.** a state or condition: *bankruptcy; accuracy.* **2.** rank, office, or position: *captaincy; presidency.*

cy·a·nide (sī′ə nīd′), *n.* any of a number of compounds containing carbon and nitrogen, many of which are highly poisonous.

cy·ber·net·ics (sī′bər net′iks), *n. (used as sing.)* the study of human functions and of mechanical and electric systems, such as computers, designed to imitate or replace them.

cy·cle (sī′kəl), *n.* **1.** a period of time in which certain events repeat themselves in the same order and at the same intervals: *the annual cycle of the seasons.* **2.** any complete series of occurrences that repeats or is repeated: *the gasoline-engine cycle.* **3.** any long period of years; age. **4.** a group of poems or stories about a central theme or person. **5.** a bicycle, tricycle, or similar vehicle. —*v.,* **cy·cled, cy·cling. 6.** to ride or travel by bicycle, tricycle, or similar vehicle: *to cycle through the park.*

cy·clist (sī′klist), *n.* a person who travels by or rides a bicycle, tricycle, etc.

cy·clone (sī′klōn), *n.* **1.** a weather system in which an area of low barometric pressure is surrounded by a circular flow of wind. **2.** a tornado. [from the Greek word *kyklōn* "revolving," which comes from *kyklos* "circle"]

cy·clo·pe·di·a (sī′klə pē′dē ə), *n.* an encyclopedia. Also **cy′clo·pae′di·a.**

Cy·clops (sī′klops), *n., pl.* **Cy·clo·pes** (sī klō′pēz). (in Greek mythology) a member of a race of giants having a large, round eye in the center of the forehead.

cy·clo·tron (sī′klə tron′), *n.* a machine in which subatomic particles are accelerated to high speeds. It is used for research in atomic structure.

cyg·net (sig′nit), *n.* a young swan.

cyl·in·der (sil′ən dər), *n.* **1.** a solid or hollow body with straight sides and a circular cross section, similar to a tree trunk or a length of pipe. **2.** the cylindrical space in which the piston of an engine moves. —**cy·lin·dri·cal** (si lin′dri-kəl), *adj.*

cym·bal (sim′bəl), *n.* a circular, concave piece of brass or bronze that produces a ringing sound when struck.

Cymbals

cyn·ic (sin′ik), *n.* a person who distrusts the sincerity and honesty of others and believes that most human actions are the result of selfishness. —**cyn′i·cal,** *adj.*

cyn·i·cism (sin′i siz′əm), *n.* **1.** the disposition, character, or belief of a cynic. **2.** a cynical remark.

cy·press (sī′prəs), *n.* any of several evergreen trees having scalelike, dark-green, overlapping leaves.

Cy·prus (sī′prəs), *n.* an island republic in the Mediterranean Sea, S of Turkey: formerly a British colony. 3572 sq. mi. —**Cyp·ri·ot** (sip′rē ət), *n., adj.*

Cy·ril·lic (si ril′ik), *adj.* **1.** of or referring to the alphabet, derived from Greek, used in writing Russian, Bulgarian, Serbian, and some other Slavic languages. —*n.* **2.** the Cyrillic alphabet or writing.

Cy·rus (sī′rəs), *n.* *("the Great")* c600–529 B.C., king of Persia 558?–529: founder of the Persian empire.

cyst (sist), *n.* an abnormal, baglike growth in the body, usually containing liquid matter.

C.Z., Canal Zone.

czar (zär), *n.* **1.** *(often cap.)* the former emperor of Russia. **2.** any person in a position of power: *an industrial czar.* Also, **tsar.** [from the Russian word *tsar',* which comes from Gothic *kaisar* "emperor," from Latin *Caesar* "Caesar"]

cza·ri·na (zä rē′nə), *n.* the wife of a czar; Russian empress. Also, **tsarina.**

Czech (chek), *n.* **1.** a member of the branch of the Slavic race including the Bohemians and sometimes the Moravians. **2.** the Slavic language of the western part of Czechoslovakia. —*adj.* **3.** of or referring to Czechoslovakia, its people, or their language: *a program of Czech music.*

Czech·o·slo·vak (chek′ə slō′väk), *n.* **1.** a member of the branch of the Slavic race including the Bohemians, Moravians, and Slovaks. **2.** a native or inhabitant of Czechoslovakia. —*adj.* **3.** of or concerning Czechoslovakia, its people, or their language.

Czech·o·slo·va·ki·a (chek′ə slə vä′kē ə), *n.* a republic in central Europe: formed after World War I. It covers an area of 49,379 sq. mi. *Cap.:* Prague.

D
Semitic	Greek	Etruscan	Latin	Gothic	Modern Roman
△	△	◁	◁	D	𝕯	D

DEVELOPMENT OF UPPER-CASE LETTERS

Greek	Medieval	Gothic	Modern Roman
δ	∂	∂	ɒ	ɖ	d

DEVELOPMENT OF LOWER-CASE LETTERS

D, d (dē), *n., pl.* **D's** *or* **Ds, d's** *or* **ds.** the fourth letter of the English alphabet.

D, 1. (in some grading systems) a grade or mark indicating scholastic work of poor or barely acceptable quality. 2. the Roman numeral for 500. 3. *Chem.* the symbol for **deuterium.**

d, (in the United Kingdom) pence. [from the Latin word *denarius,* a Roman coin]

D., 1. day. 2. Democrat. 3. Democratic. 4. density.

d., 1. date. 2. daughter. 3. degree. 4. density. 5. diameter. 6. died. 7. dollar. 8. dose.

D.A., District Attorney. Also, **DA**

dab (dab), *v.,* **dabbed, dab·bing.** 1. to pat or tap gently, esp. with something soft: *to dab one's eyes with a handkerchief.* 2. to apply or put on by dabbing: *to dab lotion on a sunburn.* —*n.* 3. a small amount; bit: *a dab of mustard.* 4. a quick, light touch; pat.

dab·ble (dab′əl), *v.,* **dab·bled, dab·bling.** 1. to play or splash in or as if in water, esp. with the hands or feet: *The baby dabbled in the rain puddle.* 2. to wet slightly by splashing or splattering: *to dabble water on laundry before ironing.* 3. to study or work at something without a serious purpose or interest: *to dabble in art.* —**dab′bler,** *n.*

dachs·hund (däks′hŏŏnt′), *n.* a small dog having a long body, long ears, and very short legs. It was originally bred in Germany for hunting badgers. [from a German word which comes from *Dachs* "badger" + *Hund* "dog"]

Dachshund
(8 in. high
at shoulder)

Da·cron (dā′kron, dak′ron), *n. Trademark.* a strong, man-made fiber, used esp. in making a cloth that does not wrinkle easily.

dad (dad), *n. Informal.* father.

dad·dy (dad′ē), *n., pl.* **dad·dies.** *Informal.* father; dad.

dad·dy-long·legs (dad′ē lông′legz′), *n. (used as sing. or pl.)* a small animal resembling a spider and having very long, thin legs and a small round body.

Daed·a·lus (ded′ələs), *n.* (in Greek mythology) an architect who built a labyrinth in Crete and, after being imprisoned there, made wings for himself and his son in order to escape.

daf·fo·dil (daf′ə dil), *n.* a yellow flower that blooms in the spring and is grown from a bulb.

daff·y (daf′ē), *adj.,* **daff·i·er, daff·i·est.** *Informal.* silly or crazy: *a daffy idea.*

daft (daft), *adj. Chiefly British.* crazy or foolish: *You're daft to take such chances.* —**daft′ly,** *adv.* —**daft′ness,** *n.*

dag, dekagram; dekagrams.

dag·ger (dag′ər), *n.* 1. a weapon resembling a knife or short sword, used for stabbing. 2. **look daggers at,** to look at (someone) angrily: *She looked daggers at me when I shushed her.*

Daffodil

da·guerre·o·type (də ger′ə tīp′), *n.* one of the earliest types of photographs, made with a silver-coated plate and requiring a long exposure time. [named after Louis *Daguerre* (1789–1851), French painter, inventor of the process]

dahl·ia (dal′yə), *n.* any of numerous tall plants that grow from a tuber and bear brightly colored flowers in the fall.

Da·ho·mey (də hō′mē), *n.* former name of **Benin.** — **Da·ho·me·an** (də hō′mē ən), *n., adj.*

dai·ly (dā′lē), *adj.* 1. done or happening each day: *daily chores.* 2. issued or coming out each day or each weekday: *a daily newspaper.* 3. figured by the day: *a daily wage.* —*n., pl.* **dai·lies.** 4. a newspaper published each day.

dain·ty (dān′tē), *adj.,* **dain·ti·er, dain·ti·est.** 1. fine and delicate; delicately pretty: *a dainty flower; a dainty girl.* 2. very particular or delicate; fussy: *a dainty eater; dainty manners.* 3. sweet or delicious to eat: *a dainty morsel of food.* —*n., pl.* **dain·ties.** 4. something sweet or delicious; delicacy: *a platter of dainties.* —**dain′ti·ly,** *adv.* —**dain′ti·ness,** *n.*

dair·y (dâr′ē), *n., pl.* **dair·ies.** 1. a building or room where milk and cream are kept fresh and where butter and cheese are made. 2. Also, **dair′y farm′.** a farm that has cows and sells milk, cream, and often also butter and cheese. **3.** a shop or company that sells milk, butter, cheese, etc. —*adj.* **4.** of or concerning milk, cheese, butter, etc., or their production and sale: *the dairy business.*

dair·y·maid (dâr′ē mād′), *n.* a girl or woman who works in a dairy or on a dairy farm; milkmaid.

dair·y·man (dâr′ē mən), *n., pl.* **dair·y·men.** a man who owns or works in a dairy or dairy farm.

da·is (dā′is, dī′is), *n.* a raised platform for a throne, a lecturer's desk, etc.

dai·sy (dā′zē), *n., pl.* **dai·sies.** any of a large family of plants the flowers of which have white or yellow petals surrounding a darker center. [from the Old English phrase *dæges eage* "day's eye"]

Da·ko·ta (də kō′tə), *n.* a former U.S. territory divided into the states of North Dakota and South Dakota. —**Da·ko′tan,** *n., adj.*

dal, dekaliter; dekaliters.

dale (dāl), *n.* a valley: *They walked up hill and down dale.*

Dal·las (dal′əs), *n.* **1.** George M., 1792–1864, 11th Vice President of the U.S. 1845–1849. **2.** a city in NE Texas.

dal·ly (dal′ē), *v.,* **dal·lied, dal·ly·ing. 1.** to hang back; loiter: *He dallied at the corner while we went on ahead.* **2.** to play, toy, or fool: *to dally with danger.*

Dal·ma·tia (dal mā′shə), *n.* a region in W Yugoslavia, along the Adriatic Sea.

Dal·ma·tian (dal mā′shən), *adj.* **1.** of or concerning Dalmatia or its people. —*n.* **2.** a native or inhabitant of Dalmatia. **3.** Also, **Dalma′tian dog′.** a medium-sized dog having a short, white coat with black spots.

Dalmatian
(21 in. high at shoulder)

dam¹ (dam), *n.* **1.** a wall or other barrier built across a stream or river to hold back the flow of water: *Beavers build dams of logs, branches, and mud.* — *v.,* **dammed, dam·ming. 2.** to block or hold back with a dam: *to dam a river.* [from Middle English]

dam² (dam), *n.* a female parent (used of horses, cattle, and other four-footed animals): *a colt and his dam.* [from a Middle English word, which is another form of *dame*]

dam, dekameter; dekameters.

dam·age (dam′ij), *n.* **1.** injury or harm to the appearance, value, or usefulness of something: *The hurricane caused much damage to property.* **2. damages,** money that is legally awarded to someone to make up for damage, hurt, harm, etc.: *to collect damages for an injury.* —*v.,* **dam·aged, dam·ag·ing. 3.** to cause damage to; spoil, injure, or harm: *Fire damaged our furniture.*

dam·ag·ing (dam′i jing), *adj.* causing or capable of causing damage; harmful, esp. to someone's reputation: *a damaging rumor.* —**dam′ag·ing·ly,** *adv.*

Da·mas·cus (də mas′kəs), *n.* the capital city of Syria, in the SW part: perhaps the world's oldest city.

dam·ask (dam′əsk), *n.* **1.** a rich cloth of linen, silk, cotton, or wool, woven with patterns. It is reversible and is often used for tablecloths, napkins, etc. **2.** a pinkish red or rose. —*adj.* **3.** made of damask.

dame (dām), *n.* **1.** a woman of rank, or one having a position of authority, such as the wife of a knight or baronet. **2.** an elderly woman; matron.

damn (dam), *v.* **1.** to declare to be bad; condemn as evil or a failure: *The critics damned the new play.* **2.** to ruin; bring condemnation on: *The outbreak of war damned his chances of becoming president.* **3.** to doom to eternal punishment; condemn to hell: *God had damned the angel Lucifer.* **4.** to swear at or curse, using the word "damn": *Damn the torpedoes! Full speed ahead!* —*n.* **5.** the saying of the word "damn" as a curse or for emphasis.

dam·na·ble (dam′nə bəl), *adj.* **1.** detestable; awful; outrageous: *a damnable crime.* **2.** worthy of damnation. —**dam′na·bly,** *adv.*

dam·na·tion (dam nā′shən), *n.* **1.** the act of damning or condemning. **2.** the state of being damned: *eternal damnation.* **3.** an oath or curse expressing anger, hurt, disappointment, etc.

Dam·o·cles (dam′ə klēz′), *n.* (in Greek mythology) a member of the court of the king of Syracuse, invited by the king to a banquet at which he was seated under a sword that hung from a single hair to remind him of the dangers that go with the good fortune for which he had praised the king.

damp (damp), *adj.* **1.** rather wet; moist: *The grass is damp.* —*n.* **2.** moist, humid air: *Stay out of the damp when you have a cold.* **3.** poisonous or stifling vapor or gas, esp. in a mine. **4.** something that holds back or depresses: *The bad news was a damp on our spirits.* —*v.* **5.** to make damp; moisten; dampen. **6.** to depress or hold back: *The loss did not damp the team's hopes.* —**damp′ly,** *adv.* —**damp′ness,** *n.*

damp·en (dam′pən), *v.* **1.** to make damp; moisten: *to dampen a shirt for ironing.* **2.** to dull or deaden; depress: *His stern warning dampened our enthusiasm.*

damp·er (dam′pər), *n.* **1.** any person or thing that depresses, holds back, or discourages: *Her bad mood put a damper on the party.* **2.** a movable plate for controlling the draft in a furnace, stove, etc.

dam·sel (dam′zəl), *n.* a maiden, esp. in olden times one of a noble or aristocratic family.

dance (dans), *v.,* **danced, danc·ing. 1.** to move the feet and body in time to music. **2.** to leap, skip, or bob up and down: *The children danced with joy. The toy boat danced on the pond.* **3.** to do or take part in a dance: *to dance a jig.* **4.** to cause to skip or bob up and down: *He danced the puppet across the stage.* —*n.* **5.** a pattern of steps or movements used in dancing: *I haven't learned that dance yet.* **6.** a round of dancing: *Tom is your partner for the next dance.* **7.** a piece of music for dancing. **8.** a party or social event for dancing; ball: *Are you going to the dance?*

danc·er (dan′sər), *n.* a person who dances, esp. for pay.

dan·de·li·on (dan′d³lī′ən), *n.* a common weed that has bright yellow flowers that bloom in the spring. Its leaves are eaten in salads or cooked as a vegetable. [from the French word *dent-de-lion,* literally "lion's tooth" (referring to the shape of its leaves)]

dan·dle (dan′d³l), *v.,* **dan·dled, dan·dling.** to move (a baby, child, etc.) lightly up and down in one's arms, on one's knee, or the like.

dan·druff (dan′drəf), *n.* **1.** a condition that produces small, loose scales of dead skin on the scalp. **2.** the scales themselves.

Dandelion

dan·dy (dan′dē), *n., pl.* **dan·dies. 1.** a man who gives too much attention to his clothing and appearance; fop. **2.** *Informal.* a person or thing that is first-rate: *That little racing car is a dandy.* —*adj.,* **dan·di·er, dan·di·est. 3.** *Informal.* fine or very good; first-rate: *a dandy idea.*

Dane (dān), *n.* a native of Denmark, or a person of Danish descent.

dan·ger (dān′jər), *n.* **1.** risk or chance of injury or harm; peril: *The life of the pioneers was full of danger.* **2.** the state of being open or exposed to injury or harm: *We stayed under cover until the danger was past.* **3.** something that may cause injury or harm: *That broken step is a danger to everyone.*

dan·ger·ous (dān′jər əs), *adj.* full of danger or peril; apt to cause injury or harm; unsafe: *It's dangerous to swim too far out.* —**dan′ger·ous·ly,** *adv.*

dan·gle (dang′gəl), *v.,* **dan·gled, dan·gling.** to hang loosely, esp. with a jerking or swaying motion; swing: *His arm was dangling over the side of the boat.*

Dan·iel (dan′yəl), *n.* **1.** (in the Bible) a Hebrew prophet whose faith in God saved him from a den of lions. **2.** a book of the Old Testament bearing his name.

Dan·ish (dā′nish), *adj.* **1.** of or referring to Denmark, Danes, or their language: *a Danish custom.* —*n.* **2.** the Germanic language of the Danes.

dank (dangk), *adj.* unpleasantly damp or humid: *a dank, dark cellar.*

Dan·te (dän′tā, dan′tē), *n.* 1265–1321, Italian poet: author of the *Divine Comedy.*

Dan·ube (dan′yo͞ob), *n.* a river in central and SE Europe. 1725 mi. long.

Dan·zig (dan′sig), *n.* a port city in N Poland, formerly part of Germany.

dap·per (dap′ər), *adj.* **1.** neat and trim; smartly dressed and groomed: *a handsome, dapper man.* **2.** lively or brisk: *He walked with a dapper step.* **3.** small and active.

dap·ple (dap′əl), *n.* **1.** a spot or roundish marking, usually one of many: *There were dark gray dapples*

on the horse's coat. —*adj.* **2.** dappled or spotted. —*v.,* **dap·pled, dap·pling. 3.** to mark with spots or mottles; cover with small patches of a different color: *Floating leaves dappled the pond.*

dap·pled (dap′əld), *adj.* having spots or dapples; mottled: *Gray horses are often dappled.*

Dar·da·nelles (där′d³nelz′), *n. (used as pl.)* the strait between European and Asian Turkey, connecting the Aegean Sea with the Sea of Marmara. 40 mi. long; 1–5 mi. wide. Ancient name, **Hellespont.**

dare (dâr), *v.,* **dared, dar·ing. 1.** to have the necessary courage or boldness; be bold enough: *She dared to swim the English Channel.* **2.** to challenge (a person) to do something: *to dare someone to fight.* **3.** to meet or face with courage: *The explorers dared the dangers of the jungle.* —*n.* **4.** a challenge; act of defiance: *Pay no attention to his dares.*

dare·dev·il (dâr′dev′əl), *n.* **1.** a reckless, daring person. —*adj.* **2.** reckless or daring: *a daredevil acrobat.*

dar·ing (dâr′ing), *n.* **1.** boldness or bravery; courage: *He was famous for his daring and love of adventure.* —*adj.* **2.** bold or courageous; adventurous: *a daring pirate; a daring call for freedom.* —**dar′ing·ly,** *adv.*

dark (därk), *adj.* **1.** having very little or no light: *a dark room.* **2.** not bright, pale, or light; close to or relatively close to black: *dark hair; a dark color.* **3.** evil or wicked: *a dark crime.* **4.** gloomy or very sad: *That was a dark day for us.* **5.** angry or sullen; frowning: *He gave me a dark look.* **6.** hidden or concealed; secret: *He kept his plan dark.* —*n.* **7.** the absence of light; darkness. **8. in the dark,** having no knowledge; not being informed: *He kept me in the dark about his summer plans.* —**dark′ness,** *n.*

dark·en (där′kən), *v.* **1.** to make dark or darker. **2.** to become dark or darker: *The sky darkened before the storm.*

dark′ horse′, a race horse, candidate for political office, or other competitor about whom little is known or who wins unexpectedly: *Senator X, a dark horse, won the Democratic nomination for President.*

dark·ly (därk′lē), *adv.* **1.** in a dark way. **2.** in a mysterious or threatening way: *He hinted darkly at revenge.* **3.** imperfectly or faintly: *to see only darkly.*

dark·room (därk′ro͞om′, -ro͝om′), *n.* a room in which film or the like is developed and from which all light that might affect the film can be shut out.

dar·ling (där′ling), *n.* **1.** a person very dear to another (often used as a term of address). **2.** a person who is loved or is held in great favor: *a darling of the stage.* —*adj.* **3.** much loved; very dear: *my darling son.* **4.** *Informal.* lovable or cute: *a darling puppy.*

darn (därn), *v.* **1.** to mend, esp. by weaving stitches over each other until the hole is filled up: *to darn the heel of a sock.* —*n.* **2.** a darned place on cloth or clothing: *There's a darn in the elbow of this jacket.*

dart (därt), *n.* **1.** a small, slender missile, resembling a little arrow with a needlelike point, that can be thrown by hand or shot from a blowgun, rifle, etc. **2. darts,** *(used as sing.)* a game in which darts are thrown at a target: *Darts is a popular game in England.* **3.** a sudden, quick movement. **4.** a tapered seam in fabric for giving a blouse or other garment a better fit. —*v.* **5.** to move quickly; jump and run suddenly and quickly: *The chipmunk darted up the tree.* **6.** to throw or cause to move quickly or suddenly: *to dart one's eyes back and forth.* —**dart'ing·ly,** *adv.*

Dar·win (där'win), *n.* Charles (Robert), 1809–1882, English naturalist. —**Dar·win'i·an,** *adj., n.*

dash (dash), *v.* **1.** to throw or hit violently, esp. so as to break to pieces. **2.** to hit or strike with force or violence: *The waves dashed against the rocks.* **3.** to move with a rush: *to dash from the room.* **4.** to splash roughly; spatter: *to dash paint onto a canvas.* **5.** to ruin or destroy: *to dash someone's hopes.* —*n.* **6.** the act of dashing; a throwing or splashing. **7.** a sudden rush: *a dash for the finish line.* **8.** a small amount of something added to something else: *a dash of salt.* **9.** a short race: *a 100-yard dash.* **10.** the punctuation sign (—) used to show a break in a sentence, for example, to allow a word of explanation to be added. **11.** a long sound in Morse code (distinguished from *dot*): *Three dashes stand for the letter "O."* **12. dash off, a.** to leave quickly; go hurriedly: *I had to dash off to a meeting.* **b.** to write hurriedly: *You'd better dash off a note to your grandmother.*

dash·board (dash'bôrd'), *n.* **1.** an instrument panel beneath the front window of an automobile or other vehicle, having dials for showing speed, amount of fuel, etc., and controls. **2.** a board or panel in front of an open carriage or the like for protecting the passengers from mud, dust, etc.

dash·ing (dash'ing), *adj.* **1.** lively or high-spirited: *a dashing young man.* **2.** showy or stylish: *a dashing suit.* —**dash'ing·ly,** *adv.*

das·tard (das'tərd), *n.* **1.** a mean, sneaking coward. —*adj.* **2.** mean and cowardly; dastardly.

das·tard·ly (das'tərd lē), *adj.* cowardly or mean; sneaking: *a dastardly habit of cheating at cards.*

da·ta (dā'tə, dat'ə), *n. (used as sing. or pl.)* facts, figures, or any kind of information: *to gather data for a report.* [from the plural of Latin *datum* "something given, a piece of information"]

date¹ (dāt), *n.* **1.** a particular point of time at which some event has happened or is scheduled to happen, often stated in terms of the day, month, and year: *July 4, 1776, is the date of the signing of the Declaration of Independence.* **2.** a piece of writing, group of figures or symbols, or the like, showing the point in time that something was made, done, is to be done, etc.: *The date has worn off this old penny.* **3.** the time or period to which an event or thing belongs: *This Roman statue is of a later date than the Greek one.* **4.** an appointment or agreement to meet: *I have a date with some friends this afternoon.* **5.** the person with whom one has such an agreement; partner for a social event: *Who is going to be your date?* —*v.,* **dat·ed, dat·ing. 6.** to belong to a particular point or period of time; have a particular date: *This church dates from the 16th century.* **7.** to show age; become old-fashioned: *This fine silverware hasn't dated.* **8.** to put a date on: *Please date your homework papers.* **9.** give a date to; establish as belonging to a particular period of time: *The museum dates this painting as a late 18th-century work.* **10.** to make a date with; go out with (someone) socially: *She dates my cousin.* **11.** to go out on dates: *I'm not allowed to date yet.* **12. out of date,** no longer in style; old-fashioned: *Baggy pants have been out of date for years.* **13. to date,** to the present time: *To date I haven't heard a thing from him.* **14. up to date,** in agreement with the latest information, methods, fashions, etc.: *Get the book that's more up to date.* [from the Latin word *data* "given," in a phrase such as *data Romæ* "written at Rome" in the heading of a letter]

date² (dāt), *n.* **1.** the sweet, oblong, fleshy fruit of a tall palm tree. **2.** Also, **date' palm'.** the tree itself. [from an Old French word, which comes from Greek *daktylos* "finger" (referring to its shape)]

dat·ed (dā'tid), *adj.* **1.** out-of-date; old-fashioned: *a dated hat.* **2.** having or showing a date: *a dated painting.*

date·less (dāt'lis), *adj.* **1.** of permanent interest or value regardless of age: *a dateless work of art.* **2.** without a date; undated.

date' line', another name for **international date line.**

da·tive (dā'tiv), *adj.* **1.** (in some languages) noting or used as the indirect object of a verb, or the object of some prepositions. —*n.* **2.** the dative case. **3.** a word in the dative case.

da·tum (dā'təm, dat'əm), *n., pl.* **da·ta** (dā'tə, da'tə). a single fact, figure, or item of information: now used chiefly in the plural.

daub (dôb), *v.* **1.** to cover or coat with a soft and sticky stuff, such as plaster or mud: *to daub a wasp sting with mud.* **2.** to spread (plaster, mud, paint, etc.) on something: *to daub plaster on a wall.* **3.** to smear or soil. —*n.* **4.** the act of daubing. **5.** something that is daubed on: *a daub of paint.* **6.** an unskillful painting.

daugh·ter (dô'tər), *n.* **1.** a female child, or a girl or woman thought of in her relation to her parents: *They have three grown daughters and a teen-age son.* **2.** any female descendant. **3.** any girl or woman who is connected with or related to a country, church, etc., in a close or devoted way: *a daughter of France; a daughter of the church.*

daugh·ter-in-law (dô'tər in lô'), *n., pl.* **daugh·ters-in-law** (dô'tərz in lô'). the wife of one's son.

daugh·ter·ly (dô'tər lē), *adj.* **1.** referring to or proper for a daughter: *daughterly obedience.* **2.** like that of a daughter: *She treated her old uncle with daughterly affection.*

daunt (dônt, dänt), *v.* to defeat by frightening; discourage; dishearten: *The roaring of the dragon did not daunt the gallant knight.*

daunt·less (dônt′lis, dänt′lis), *adj.* fearless; bold; not to be daunted. —**daunt′less·ly,** *adv.* —**daunt′less·ness,** *n.*

dau·phin (dô′fin), *n.* the oldest son of a king of France, used as a title from 1349 to 1830: *Joan of Arc fought with the dauphin.*

dav·en·port (dav′ən pôrt′), *n.* a large sofa, often one that can be converted to a bed.

Da·vid (dā′vid), *n.* died c970 B.C., the second king of Israel c1010–c970.

da Vin·ci (də vin′chē), **Le·o·nar·do** (lē′ə när′dō), 1452–1519, Italian painter.

Da·vis (dā′vis), *n.* **Jefferson,** 1808–1889, U.S. statesman: president of the Confederate States of America 1861–1865.

dav·it (dav′it, dā′vit), *n.* a cranelike device on a ship, often one of a pair, used for raising and lowering lifeboats, anchors, etc., over the side.

Da′vy Jones′ (jōnz), the spirit of the sea; the sailors' devil.

Da′vy Jones′'s lock′er, the ocean's bottom; the grave of those who die at sea.

daw·dle (dôd′∂l), *v.,* **daw·dled, daw·dling.** to waste (time); idle: *to dawdle away a morning; to dawdle on the way to school.*

D, Davit

Dawes (dôz), *n.* **Charles G.,** 1865–1951, 30th Vice President of the U.S. 1925–1929.

dawn (dôn), *n.* **1.** the first appearance of daylight in the morning. **2.** the beginning or rise of anything: *the dawn of modern science.* —*v.* **3.** to begin to grow light in the morning. **4.** to begin or begin to develop: *A new hope dawned slowly.* **5.** to begin to be seen, recognized, or understood (usually fol. by *on*): *Later it dawned on me that he was right.*

day (dā), *n.* **1.** the time between sunrise and sunset. **2.** a period of 24 hours, equal to the average length of the period during which the earth rotates once on its axis. **3.** the light of day; daylight. **4.** the portion of the day given to work or labor: *an eight-hour day.* **5.** *(often cap.)* a day set aside for some particular purpose or celebration: *New Year's Day.* **6.** Often, **days,** a particular time or period: *the present day; in the days of old.* **7.** a day of contest, or the contest itself: *to win the day.* **8. day in, day out,** every day without fail; continuously: *Day in, day out we work.*

day·break (dā′brāk′), *n.* the first appearance of light in the morning; dawn: *The rooster crows at daybreak.*

day·dream (dā′drēm′), *v.* **1.** to imagine events and scenes in a dreamlike way, often events in which one behaves heroically; lose oneself in imaginings. —*n.* **2.** a made-up, dreamlike happening imagined while one is awake. —**day′dream′er,** *n.*

day·light (dā′līt′), *n.* **1.** the light of day: *to read by daylight.* **2.** daytime; the period between dawn and

sunset. **3.** daybreak or dawn. **4.** the state of being open, in full view, or publicly known: *The newspapers brought the whole story into the daylight.* **5. scare** (or **frighten**) **the daylights out of** (someone), to cause extreme fright to (a person): *That thunderstorm scared the daylights out of her.*

day′light-sav′ing time′ (dā′līt′sā′ving), time that is an hour ahead of standard time, often used in the summer to give more hours of daylight in the afternoon and evening. When daylight-saving time begins, one sets the clock ahead, usually one hour. This remains in effect generally from the last Sunday in April until the last Sunday in October.

day·time (dā′tīm′), *n.* the time between sunrise and sunset; day.

day-to-day (dā′tə dā′), *adj.* **1.** happening each day; daily: *day-to-day chores.* **2.** of or concerning ordinary, daily needs and happenings: *day-to-day worries about paying one's bills.*

Day·ton (dāt′∂n), *n.* a city in SW Ohio.

daze (dāz), *v.,* **dazed, daz·ing. 1.** to stun or make dizzy with a blow, shock, or the like: *The fall dazed her.* **2.** to bewilder or dazzle: *The splendor of the palace dazed him.* —*n.* **3.** a dazed condition; state of shock, dizziness, or bewilderment: *to wander in a daze.* —**daz·ed·ly** (dā′zid lē), *adv.*

daz·zle (daz′∂l), *v.,* **daz·zled, daz·zling. 1.** to overpower or daze by a very strong light; dim the vision of: *The spotlights dazzled him.* **2.** to impress or bewilder by brilliance, magnificence, or the like: *They were dazzled by the queen's beauty.* —*n.* **3.** a dazzling light or brilliance: *the dazzle of city lights.* —**daz′zling·ly,** *adv.*

DC, direct current. Also, **D.C., dc, d.c.**

D.C., District of Columbia.

DDT, a highly poisonous chemical used as an insecticide. [abbreviated from the chemical name *d(i-chloro)d(iphenyl)t(richloroethane)*]

de-, a prefix meaning **1.** down: *demerit; degrade.* **2.** away: *deport; decamp.* **3.** reversal of an action: *decentralize.* **4.** removal: *defrost.*

dea·con (dē′kən), *n.* **1.** a member of the clergy ranking just below a priest. **2.** an appointed or elected official of a church who helps the minister.

dead (ded), *adj.* **1.** no longer living; having no life. **2.** not given or having life; inanimate: *wastes and other dead matter.* **3.** no longer in use: *a dead language.* **4.** not working: *The engine is dead.* **5.** having no force, motion, liveliness, etc.; inactive: *a dead tennis ball.* **6.** accurate or sure: *a dead shot.* **7.** exact or precise: *the dead center of a circle.* **8.** complete or absolute: *a dead loss.* —*n.* **9.** the period of greatest darkness, coldness, or the like: *the dead of night; the dead of winter.* **10. the dead,** *(used as pl.)* all dead persons. —*adv.* **11.** absolutely or completely: *He stopped dead.* **12.** directly or exactly: *dead ahead.*

dead·en (ded′∂n), *v.* **1.** to make less sensitive or active; dull: *A local anesthetic will deaden the nerve so you won't feel pain.* **2.** to make less forceful, loud, etc.: *to deaden sound.*

dead′ end′, 1. a street, passage, water pipe, etc.,

that is closed at one end. **2.** any situation in which progress is impossible.

dead′ heat′, a race ending in a tie.

dead′ let′ter, a letter that can be neither delivered nor returned to the sender, because the addresses are missing, incomplete, or wrong.

dead·line (ded′līn′), *n.* the latest time for finishing something: *the deadline for paying a bill.*

dead·lock (ded′lok′), *n.* **1.** a complete standstill in a conflict or the like, when both sides are equally strong: *The debate ended in a deadlock.* —*v.* **2.** to come or bring to a deadlock or standstill: *They deadlocked over the question of an increase in wages.*

dead·ly (ded′lē), *adj.,* **dead·li·er, dead·li·est. 1.** causing or able to cause death; fatal: *a deadly poison.* **2.** seeking to kill or destroy; mortal: *a deadly enemy.* **3.** like death: *a deadly paleness.* **4.** too great; excessive: *a deadly hurry.* **5.** very accurate: *a deadly aim.* **6.** terribly boring; dull: *a deadly party.* —*adv.* **7.** in a way that resembles death: *a deadly pale face.* **8.** completely or very: *a deadly dull book.*

Dead′ Sea′, a salt lake between Israel and Jordan: lowest point in the world. 46 mi. long; 10 mi. wide; 1293 ft. below sea level.

deaf (def), *adj.* **1.** unable to hear, or partially unable to hear. **2.** refusing to listen (often fol. by *to*): *deaf to advice.* —**deaf′ly,** *adv.* —**deaf′ness,** *n.*

deaf·en (def′ən), *v.* **1.** to make deaf. **2.** to stun with noise: *The roar of traffic deafened us.* —**deaf′en·ing·ly,** *adv.*

deaf-mute (def′myo͞ot′), *n.* a person who is deaf and dumb; one who is unable to hear or to speak.

deal (dēl), *v.,* **dealt** (delt), **deal·ing. 1.** to take care of; consider; handle (usually fol. by *with*): *to deal with a problem.* **2.** to have to do with; consider; treat (usually fol. by *with*): *Botany deals with the study of plants.* **3.** to behave in a particular way: *to deal fairly with people.* **4.** to trade or do business; buy and sell (usually fol. by *in*): *to deal in cars.* **5.** to pass out or distribute (cards or the like): *You deal five cards to each player.* **6.** to give or administer (often fol. by *out*): *to deal out punishment.* —*n.* **7.** the act of dealing cards, or a person's turn at dealing: *It's your deal.* **8.** *Informal.* a business affair; transaction: *We'll sign a contract on that deal.* **9.** *Informal.* a bargain. **10.** *Informal.* an agreement by which two people profit or gain something, sometimes secretly or illegally. **11. a good** (or **great**) **deal,** a large amount; very much: *We talked a great deal.*

deal·er (dē′lər), *n.* **1.** a person who behaves toward others in a particular way: *a fair dealer.* **2.** a person whose business is buying and selling; trader; merchant: *a used-car dealer.* **3.** the person dealing the cards in a card game.

deal·ing (dē′liNG), *n.* Usually, **dealings.** personal or

business relations; transactions: *to have dealings with several companies.*

dealt (delt), *v.* the past tense and past participle of **deal.**

dean (dēn), *n.* **1.** an official in a university or college in charge of the admission of students, guiding them in their studies, enforcing rules, and the like. **2.** the head of a faculty in a university or college: *a dean of music.* **3.** an official in the clergy who is in charge of a cathedral or assists a bishop. **4.** the most experienced or respected member of a group, profession, or the like: *the dean of American sportswriters.*

dear (dēr), *adj.* **1.** beloved or loved; favorite; regarded as precious: *a dear friend.* **2.** (in the greeting or opening phrase of a letter) respected or esteemed: *Dear Mr. Smith.* **3.** earnest or sincere; close to one's heart: *My dearest wish is that you will arrive home safely.* **4.** expensive or costly: *These gloves were very dear.* —*n.* **5.** a person who is good, kind, or generous: *She's a dear.* **6.** beloved one (often used in direct address): *Thank you, my dear.* —*adv.* **7.** dearly, or at a high price: *That painting cost me dear.* —*interj.* **8.** (used as an exclamation of surprise, dismay, etc.): *Oh dear, that's terrible!*

Dear·born (dēr′bərn, dēr′bôrn), *n.* a city in SE Michigan, near Detroit.

dear·ly (dēr′lē), *adv.* **1.** fondly, or with great affection: *He loved his uncle dearly.* **2.** very much: *I would dearly love to see her.* **3.** at a high price; highly: *to pay dearly for a mistake.*

dearth (dûrth), *n.* a scarcity or lack; inadequate supply: *Because of the bad harvest, there is a dearth of wheat.*

death (deth), *n.* **1.** the end of life in a living thing; a dying. **2.** the state of being dead: *to lie peacefully in death.* **3.** an ending that is like death: *the death of a newspaper; the death of a great hope.* **4.** a cause of death: *Your complaints are going to be the death of me.* **5. put to death,** to execute; kill: *The assassin was put to death by the mob.* **6. to death,** to an extreme degree; thoroughly: *I'm sick to death of your excuses.*

death·less (deth′lis), *adj.* immortal or enduring; never to die, or never to be forgotten: *the deathless words of a poet; a deathless love of freedom.*

death·ly (deth′lē), *adj.* **1.** like death: *A deathly quiet fell on the room.* **2.** causing death; deadly; fatal: *A deathly cold settled over the valley.* —*adv.* **3.** in the manner of death; as in death: *a deathly white skin.* **4.** very or utterly: *deathly afraid.*

death′ rate′, the relationship of the number of deaths to the total population of a given place, usually expressed in deaths per thousand of population per year. See also **birth rate.**

death's-head (deths′hed′), *n.* a human skull, esp. as a symbol of death.

Death′ Val′ley, a very dry basin in SE California and S Nevada: lowest point in the Western Hemisphere. about 1500 sq. mi.; 280 ft. below sea level.

de·bar (di bär′), *v.,* **de·barred, de·bar·ring.** to prevent, prohibit, or exclude: *to debar someone from practicing medicine.* —**de·bar′ment**, *n.*

de·bark (di bärk′), *v.* to disembark; land. —**de·bar·ka·tion** (dē′bär kā′shən), *n.*

de·base (di bās′), *v.*, **de·based, de·bas·ing.** 1. to make less in value or rank: *When money is debased it buys less.* 2. to lower in dignity: *Don't debase yourself by answering him.* —**de·base′ment**, *n.*

de·bat·a·ble (di bā′tə bəl), *adj.* 1. in dispute; open to question; doubtful: *Whether our team can win is debatable.* 2. capable of being debated.

de·bate (di bāt′), *n.* 1. a discussion, esp. of a public question: *a debate in Congress.* 2. a contest in which two speakers or teams of speakers present opposing arguments. —*v.*, **de·bat·ed, de·bat·ing.** 3. to engage in a discussion or debating contest: *to debate for an hour.* 4. to argue (a question); discuss: *to debate how the tax money should be spent.* 5. to consider; think about: *I debated voting for him.* —**de·bat′er**, *n.*

de·bauch (di bôch′), *v.* 1. to corrupt or ruin the character of (a person). 2. to indulge in too much drinking, revelry, etc. —*n.* 3. a time or occasion of debauchery. —**de·bauch′er**, *n.*

de·bauch·er·y (di bô′chə rē), *n.*, *pl.* **de·bauch·er·ies.** excessive indulgence in pleasure; intemperance.

de·bil·i·tate (di bil′i tāt′), *v.*, **de·bil·i·tat·ed, de·bil·i·tat·ing.** to make physically weak or feeble: *Lack of food debilitated him.*

de·bil·i·ty (di bil′i tē), *n.* physical weakness; extreme feebleness.

deb·it (deb′it), *n.* 1. an entry in an account book for a sum of money that is owed or has been paid out: *Debits and credits must balance.* —*v.* 2. to charge (a person, account, etc.) with a debit: *We'll debit your account $17.50 for this purchase.* 3. to charge as a debt: *to debit a purchase to someone's account.*

deb·o·nair (deb′ə nâr′), *adj.* having pleasant manners; charming and carefree in manner: *a debonair young man.* Also, **deb′o·naire′.**

de·bris (də brē′, dā′brē), *n.* the remains of anything broken down or destroyed; ruins; fragments; rubbish: *the debris left by a fire.* Also, **dé·bris′.**

debt (det), *n.* 1. something that is owed, such as money, a favor, or the like: *a $5 debt.* 2. the obligation to pay or do something: *I wish I could get out of that debt.* 3. the condition of owing something: *He's in debt for his new car.*

debt·or (det′ər), *n.* a person who owes money, a favor, or the like.

de·but (dā byōō′, dā′byōō), *n.* 1. a first public appearance: *the debut of a pianist.* 2. a formal introduction to society, esp. of a young girl. Also, **dé·but′.**

deb·u·tante (deb′yə tänt′), *n.* 1. a girl making a debut or formal entrance into society. 2. a girl who has made a formal debut. Also, **déb′u·tante′.**

Dec., December.

dec., 1. deceased. 2. declaration. 3. decrease.

deca-, a prefix meaning ten: *decagon.*

dec·ade (dek′ād), *n.* a period of ten years: *the three decades from 1921 to 1951.*

dec·a·dence (dek′ə dəns), *n.* 1. moral decay or cor-

ruption: *an era of decadence.* 2. the process of falling or declining into an inferior condition; a decaying or declining.

dec·a·dent (dek′ə dənt), *adj.* 1. corrupt or immoral; characterized by decadence. —*n.* 2. a decadent person.

dec·a·gon (dek′ə gon′), *n.* a plane figure having ten sides and ten angles.

Dec·a·logue (dek′ə lôg′, dek′ə log′), *n.* the Ten Commandments.

Decagon (regular)

de·camp (di kamp′), *v.* 1. to leave a camp; pack up equipment and leave a camping ground. 2. to leave quickly or secretly.

de·cant (di kant′), *v.* 1. to pour (wine or other liquid) gently so as not to disturb the sediment at the bottom. 2. to pour (a liquid) from one container to another.

de·cant·er (di kan′tər), *n.* an ornamental glass bottle for holding wine, brandy, or other alcoholic beverage.

de·cap·i·tate (di kap′i tāt′), *v.*, **de·cap·i·tat·ed, de·cap·i·tat·ing.** to cut off the head of. —**de·cap′i·ta′tion**, *n.*

de·cath·lon (di kath′lon), *n.* a contest made up of 10 different track-and-field events and won by the contestant having the highest total score. See also **pentathlon.**

Decanter

de·cay (di kā′), *v.* 1. to rot; become decomposed: *decaying tree stumps.* 2. to cause to rot: *Sweet foods can decay your teeth.* 3. to decline in health, strength, wealth, etc.; deteriorate: *Skills decay from lack of use.* 4. to cause to decline or deteriorate in this way. —*n.* 5. a rotting place; rot: *decay in a tooth.* 6. a decline in strength, wealth, health, etc.: *the decay of a nation's morals.*

decd., deceased.

de·cease (di sēs′), *n.* 1. death; departure from life. —*v.*, **de·ceased, de·ceas·ing.** 2. to die.

de·ceased (di sēst′), *adj.* 1. no longer living; dead: *a deceased person.* —*n.* 2. **the deceased, a.** a particular dead person: *The deceased requested that his money be given to charity.* **b.** those persons who have died: *Among the deceased were three American soldiers.*

de·ceit (di sēt′), *n.* 1. the act or practice of deceiving, as by lying or cheating. 2. something intended to deceive, such as a trick, forged letter, etc. 3. the quality of being deceitful; falseness; trickiness; sneakiness: *a man full of deceit.*

de·ceit·ful (di sēt′fəl), *adj.* 1. having the habit of deceiving, tricking, cheating, etc.; insincere; tricky: *a deceitful person.* 2. intended to deceive, mislead, or cheat: *a deceitful trick.* —**de·ceit′ful·ly**, *adv.*

de·ceive (di sēv′), *v.*, **de·ceived, de·ceiv·ing.** 1. to mislead by a false appearance or by false words; trick; cheat. 2. to practice deceit, dishonesty, or trickery. —**de·ceiv′er**, *n.*

de·cel·er·ate (dē sel′ə rāt′), *v.*, **de·cel·er·at·ed, de·cel·er·at·ing.** to slow down. —**de·cel′er·a′tion**, *n.*

De·cem·ber (di sem′bər), *n.* the 12th and last

month of the year, having 31 days. [from a Latin word, which comes from *decem* "ten." In the early Roman calendar, December was the tenth month]

de·cen·cy (dē′sən sē), *n., pl.* for def. 2 **de·cen·cies. 1.** the quality of being decent; a proper degree of kindness, courtesy, etc.: *I hope you had the decency to thank her for the gift.* **2. decencies,** the things that are necessary in order to be decent or proper: *the common decencies of behavior.*

de·cent (dē′sənt), *adj.* **1.** correct or modest; in good taste: *He promised to stop swearing and use decent language.* **2.** suitable or proper: *I couldn't find a decent gift for her.* **3.** good enough; fair; passable: *a decent wage.* **4.** kind or generous: *It was decent of him to help.* —**de′cent·ly,** *adv.*

de·cen·tral·ize (dē sen′trə līz′), *v.,* **de·cen·tral·ized, de·cen·tral·iz·ing. 1.** to lessen the central control of (a government, corporation, etc.) by spreading out authority and responsibilities among a number of groups, such as local governments. **2.** to undertake to do this within a government, corporation, etc. —**de·cen′tral·i·za′tion,** *n.*

de·cep·tion (di sep′shən), *n.* **1.** the act of deceiving or misleading. **2.** the state of being deceived. **3.** something that deceives or is intended to deceive; trick; fraud: *They escaped by a clever deception.*

de·cep·tive (di sep′tiv), *adj.* likely or tending to deceive or mislead: *The test looked easy, but it was deceptive.* —**de·cep′tive·ly,** *adv.*

deci-, a prefix meaning a tenth part of: *decigram.*

de·cide (di sīd′), *v.,* **de·cid·ed, de·cid·ing. 1.** to settle (a question, dispute, etc.), often by giving the victory to one side: *The judge decided the case in our favor.* **2.** to make up one's mind; come to a conclusion: *They decided to leave early.* **3.** to cause (a person) to make up his mind: *What finally decided him?*

de·cid·ed (di sī′did), *adj.* **1.** unmistakable or unquestionable: *a decided victory.* **2.** free from wavering or hesitation; determined: *He dealt with the mutineers in a decided manner.* —**de·cid′ed·ly,** *adv.*

de·cid·u·ous (di sij′ōō əs), *adj.* **1.** referring to plants that shed their leaves every year. **2.** falling off at the end of a period of growth: *deciduous antlers.* [from the Latin word *dēciduus* "falling down," which comes from *de-* "down" + *cadere* "to fall"]

dec·i·gram (des′ə gram′), *n.* a unit of mass or weight in the metric system, equal to ¹⁄₁₀ gram. *Symbol:* dg

dec·i·li·ter (des′ə lē′tər), *n.* a unit of volume or capacity in the metric system, equal to ¹⁄₁₀ liter. *Symbol:* dl

dec·i·mal (des′ə məl), *adj.* **1.** referring to tenths or the number 10. **2.** based on 10: *the decimal monetary system of the U.S.* —*n.* **3.** a mixed number or a fraction written with a decimal point: *7.5 and 0.125 are decimals.*

dec′imal point′, a period or dot placed before the fraction in writing a decimal.

dec·i·mate (des′ə māt′), *v.,* **dec·i·mat·ed, dec·i·mat·ing. 1.** to kill or destroy a great number of or a large part of: *Disease decimated the herds of cattle.* **2.** to

kill or destroy a tenth of. —**dec′i·ma′tion,** *n.*

dec·i·me·ter (des′ə mē′tər), *n.* a unit of length in the metric system, equal to ¹⁄₁₀ meter. *Symbol:* dm

de·ci·pher (di sī′fər), *v.* **1.** to make out the meaning of (something difficult to read, etc.): *I can't decipher your handwriting.* **2.** to translate (a coded message) into ordinary language. —**de·ci′pher·a·ble,** *adj.*

de·ci·sion (di sizh′ən), *n.* **1.** the act of deciding or making up one's mind: *a time of decision.* **2.** something that is decided; judgment; conclusion: *He will announce his decision.* **3.** the quality of being decided or determined; firmness: *She spoke with decision.*

de·ci·sive (di sī′siv), *adj.* **1.** having the power or quality of deciding something once and for all: *a decisive test.* **2.** showing decision or determination; resolute; firm: *The senator has always been famous for his decisive manner.* —**de·ci′sive·ly,** *adv.* —**de·ci′sive·ness,** *n.*

deck (dek), *n.* **1.** a floorlike surface on a boat or ship. **2.** any open platform or raised surface, such as a flat roof, resembling the deck of a ship: *a sun deck.* **3.** a pack of playing cards. — *v.* **4.** to dress or attire (often fol. by *out*): *She was all decked out for the ball.*

de·claim (di klām′), *v.* **1.** to say (a speech, words, etc.) aloud and in a formal manner: *He declaimed the prologue to the play.* **2.** to criticize loudly or strongly (usually fol. by *against*): *to declaim against war.*

dec·la·ma·tion (dek′lə mā′shən), *n.* **1.** the act of declaiming or making speeches. **2.** speech or writing intended as a public, formal statement: *a declamation favoring changes in the government.* —**de·clam·a·to·ry** (di klam′ə tôr′ē), *adj.*

dec·la·ra·tion (dek′lə rā′shən), *n.* **1.** a statement or announcement, esp. a positive or formal statement; proclamation: *a declaration of war.* **2.** something that is declared or announced. **3.** a document containing a formal proclamation. **4.** an official list or statement of items: *a tax declaration.*

Declara′tion of Indepen′dence, the document by Thomas Jefferson declaring the American colonies to be free from England.

de·clar·a·tive (di klar′ə tiv), *adj.* making a statement. "I like ice cream" is a declarative sentence.

de·clare (di klâr′), *v.,* **de·clared, de·clar·ing. 1.** to announce clearly, esp. in a positive or formal way: *He declared that he was against the plan.* **2.** to announce officially; proclaim: *to declare war.* **3.** to make an official statement or list, such as a list of items that one has bought in a foreign country.

de·clen·sion (di klen′shən), *n.* **1.** a listing or reciting of the inflected forms of a noun, pronoun, or adjective, showing the differences of case, number, gender, etc. **2.** a class of nouns, pronouns, or adjectives having similar declension.

de·cline (di klīn′), *v.,* **de·clined, de·clin·ing. 1.** to refuse or turn down politely: *to decline an offer.* **2.** to bend or slant down; slope or move downward: *The hill declined to the lake.* **3.** to become less strong, valuable, etc.; deteriorate: *to decline in health.* **4.** to become less in amount: *Sales are declining.* **5.** (in grammar) to give the declension of. —*n.* **6.** a downward slope. **7.** a failing or gradual loss, as in strength, morals, etc.: *a decline in health.* **8.** a downward movement or dropping off in number, size, degree, etc.: *a decline in prices.* —**de·clin′a·ble,** *adj.* —**dec·li·na·tion** (dek′lə nā′shən), *n.*

de·cliv·i·ty (di kliv′i tē), *n., pl.* **de·cliv·i·ties.** a downward slope; descent.

de·code (di kōd′), *v.,* **de·cod·ed, de·cod·ing.** to translate (a message) in code into ordinary language.

de·com·pose (dē′kəm pōz′), *v.,* **de·com·posed, de·com·pos·ing.** to rot, decay, disintegrate, or break down into separate parts: *Fallen leaves decompose. Some chemical compounds decompose explosively.* —**de·com·po·si·tion** (dē′kom pə zish′ən), *n.*

de·com·pres·sion (dē′kəm presh′ən), *n.* the gradual return of a diver to conditions of normal air pressure after breathing compressed air.

dec·o·rate (dek′ə rāt′), *v.,* **dec·o·rat·ed, dec·o·rat·ing. 1.** to adorn or make more attractive, beautiful, pleasing, etc., by the addition of ornaments, paintings, furnishings, or the like: *to decorate a Christmas tree.* **2.** to honor with a decoration: *to decorate a hero.*

dec·o·ra·tion (dek′ə rā′shən), *n.* **1.** the act of decorating or making more attractive. **2.** an ornament or anything used for decorating. **3.** a badge, medal, ribbon, etc., awarded as a mark of honor.

Decora′tion Day′, another name for **Memorial Day.**

dec·o·ra·tive (dek′ər ə tiv, dek′ə rā′tiv), *adj.* used to decorate or make more pleasing in appearance; ornamental: *decorative carving on woodwork; a decorative hat.* —**dec′o·ra·tive·ly,** *adv.*

dec·o·ra·tor (dek′ə rā′tər), *n.* a person who decorates, esp. an interior decorator.

dec·o·rous (dek′ər əs, di kôr′əs), *adj.* proper or correct in manners, dress, speech, etc.; sedate; dignified. —**dec′o·rous·ly,** *adv.*

de·co·rum (di kôr′əm), *n.* correctness of behavior, speech, dress, etc.; good manners; dignity: *to behave with decorum.*

de·coy (di koi′, dē′koi), *n.* **1.** a person or thing that is used as a lure to set a trap, to distract attention, or the like: *The accident was a decoy to draw the guards away from the bank during the robbery.* **2.** a likeness of a bird, esp. a carved likeness of a duck, used by hunters to attract other birds. **3.** a trained bird used as a lure to attract other birds. —*v.* (di koi′). **4.** to trap or distract by the use of a decoy: *One unit of soldiers decoyed the enemy troops away from the town while the other units were attacking.* [from the Dutch phrase *de kooi* "the cage"]

de·crease (di krēs′), *v.,* **de·creased, de·creas·ing. 1.** to lessen in amount, size, strength, etc.: *Daylight decreases in the wintertime.* **2.** to make less: *to decrease a debt.* —*n.* (dē′krēs, di krēs′). **3.** a lessening; gradual reduction: *a decrease in accidents.* **4.** the amount by which something decreases: *a decrease of 10%.* —**de·creas′ing·ly,** *adv.*

de·cree (di krē′), *n.* **1.** an official ruling or order, for

example by the president; edict; law. —*v.,* **de·creed, de·cree·ing. 2.** to order or decide by decree: *to decree a national holiday.*

de·crep·it (di krep′it), *adj.* **1.** weakened by old age; feeble; infirm: *an old, decrepit horse.* **2.** broken down; dilapidated: *a weather-beaten, decrepit house.*

de·cre·scen·do (dē′kri shen′dō), *n., pl.* **de·cre·scen·dos. 1.** a gradual decrease in loudness. **2.** a part of a musical work in which a gradual decrease in loudness takes place. —*adj., adv.* **3.** (in music) gradually becoming softer. —*v.,* **de·cre·scen·doed, de·cre·scen·do·ing. 4.** to become softer. See also **crescendo.**

de·cry (di krī′), *v.,* **de·cried, de·cry·ing.** to speak against; criticize the faults of; denounce: *to decry the pollution of our rivers.*

ded·i·cate (ded′ə kāt′), *v.,* **ded·i·cat·ed, ded·i·cat·ing. 1.** to devote or give completely to a cause, care of a person, etc.: *He dedicated his life to his country.* **2.** to set apart in honor of God, a respected person, a cause, or the like, often by a special ceremony: *to dedicate a library to the memory of the founders of the town.* **3.** to inscribe (a book, piece of music, or the like) to a loved or respected person or to a cause: *He dedicated his last book to his children.*

ded·i·ca·tion (ded′ə kā′shən), *n.* **1.** the act of dedicating: *the dedication of a new building.* **2.** the state of being dedicated: *His dedication to music inspired all his students.* **3.** an inscription or writing on a book, piece of music, or the like, dedicating it to a particular person or cause.

de·duce (di dōōs′, -dyōōs′), *v.,* **de·duced, de·duc·ing.** to reach (a conclusion) by using reasoning; figure out logically: *to deduce the answer to a problem in arithmetic.* —**de·duc′i·ble,** *adj.*

de·duct (di dukt′), *v.* to take away, or subtract, from a sum, amount, or the like: *to deduct expenses from one's income.* —**de·duct′i·ble,** *adj.*

de·duc·tion (di duk′shən), *n.* **1.** the act or process of deducing; the reaching of a conclusion by reasoning: *I figured it out by deduction.* **2.** the act or process of deducting or subtracting: *The next step is the deduction of expenses.* **3.** something that is deduced; conclusion: *a clever deduction.* **4.** an amount that is deducted or subtracted, such as an amount that one is allowed to deduct from one's tax.

de·duc·tive (di duk′tiv), *adj.* based on logical deduction: *a deductive method for solving problems.*

deed (dēd), *n.* **1.** something that is done, performed, or accomplished; an act: *His brave deeds will always be remembered.* **2.** a legal document showing who is the owner of a certain property, such as a piece of land. —*v.* **3.** to give or transfer (property) by a deed: *to deed an estate to one's son.*

deem (dēm), *v.* to think or regard; have as an opinion: *He deemed it wise to postpone his visit.*

deep (dēp), *adj.* **1.** going far down from the top or surface: *a deep well; a deep scratch.* **2.** going far in or far back from the front or edge: *a deep shelf; a deep cave.* **3.** ranging far from the earth and sun: *a deep space probe.* **4.** having a specified depth: *a pool eight feet deep.* **5.** located far down, far in, or far back:

deep below the surface; deep in the woods. **6.** reaching or going far down or very low: *a deep dive; a deep bow.* **7.** difficult to understand or figure out: *a deep question; a deep book.* **8.** felt very strongly: *deep love.* **9.** involving all one's attention or consciousness; profound; heavy: *a deep sleep; deep study.* **10.** (of colors) dark and strong: *a deep red.* **11.** low in pitch: *a deep voice.* **12.** involved, absorbed, or immersed: *He's deep in a book.* **13.** thorough or profound; going far into a subject: *a deep understanding.* —*n.* **14.** the deep part of the sea, a river, etc.; a deep place: *The ship was lost in the briny deep.* **15.** the part or time that is coldest, darkest, etc.: *the deep of winter.* —*adv.* **16.** to or at a considerable depth; far: *to sink deep in the water; to go deep into the woods.* **17.** thoroughly or profoundly: *He went deep into the study of art.* **18. in deep water,** in a difficult or serious situation; in trouble: *If you hadn't lied you wouldn't be in such deep water.* —**deep′ly,** *adv.* —**deep′ness,** *n.*

deep·en (dē′pən), *v.* **1.** to make deeper: *to deepen a ditch.* **2.** to become deeper: *The river deepens here.*

deep-seat·ed (dēp′sē′tid), *adj.* firmly implanted; very strong: *a deep-seated prejudice; a deep-seated fear.*

deer (dēr), *n., pl.* **deer.** any of numerous swift-running, hoofed, cud-chewing mammals, the males of which have antlers.

deer·hound (dēr′-hound′), *n.* one of a Scottish breed of large dogs, having a shaggy, gray or brindled coat.

deer·skin (dēr′skin′), *n.* **1.** the skin of a deer. **2.** leather made from this. —*adj.* **3.** made of deerskin: *a deerskin jacket.*

Virginia deer
(3½ ft. high at shoulder)

def., **1.** deferred. **2.** defined. **3.** definition.

de·face (di fās′), *v.,* **de·faced, de·fac·ing.** to mar or damage the front or face of; disfigure: *to deface a picture by scratching it.* —**de·fac′er,** *n.* —**de·face′ment,** *n.*

de fac·to (dē fak′tō), in fact; in reality; actually existing although not authorized by law: *The frontiersmen formed de facto courts to try criminals.*

def·a·ma·tion (def′ə mā′shən), *n.* the act of defaming someone; false or unjustified injury of someone's good reputation by libel, slander, or the like.

de·fame (di fām′), *v.,* **de·famed, de·fam·ing.** to attack or injure the good name or reputation of (someone); slander or libel: *That magazine article defamed the senator.*

de·fault (di fôlt′), *n.* **1.** failure to meet an obligation, such as an obligation to appear in court or play a sports match. —*v.* **2.** to fail to fulfill an obligation. **3.** (in sports) to lose by default.

de·feat (di fēt′), *v.* **1.** to overcome in a contest, battle, or the like. **2.** to block, frustrate, or destroy: *to*

defeat someone's hopes. —*n.* **3.** a defeating or being defeated: *That game was our worst defeat so far.*

de·feat·ist (di fē′tist), *n.* **1.** a person who feels sure that he, his party, a cause, or the like, is bound to be defeated. —*adj.* **2.** characteristic of a defeatist or his beliefs: *a defeatist attitude.* —**de·feat′ism,** *n.*

de·fect (dē′fekt, di fekt′), *n.* **1.** a fault or imperfection; flaw: *There are several defects in this automobile.* **2.** a want or lack, esp. of something essential: *a defect in hearing.* —*v.* (di fekt′). **3.** to desert a country, cause, or the like, esp. in order to go over to the other side: *He defected to the enemy.* —**de·fec·tor** (di fek′tər), *n.*

de·fec·tion (di fek′shən), *n.* desertion from allegiance, loyalty, or duty: *The soldier was accused of defection from his company.*

de·fec·tive (di fek′tiv), *adj.* having a defect; faulty: *a defective machine.* —**de·fec′tive·ness,** *n.*

de·fend (di fend′), *v.* **1.** to guard against attack, assault, or injury; protect (usually fol. by *from* or *against*): *She defended her children from the mad dog.* **2.** to support or uphold by argument: *to defend one's statement.* **3.** to act as lawyer for (a defendant). —**de·fend′er,** *n.*

de·fend·ant (di fen′dənt), *n.* a person against whom a claim or charge is brought in a court (opposite of *plaintiff*).

de·fense (di fens′), *n.* **1.** resistance against attack; protection: *defense against the enemy.* **2.** something that defends: *to build defenses around a city.* **3.** the defending or support of a cause or point of view: *The teacher spoke in defense of student government.* **4.** the denial or pleading of the defendant in answer to the claim or charge against him. **5.** a defendant and his lawyers, or the case presented by them. —**de·fense′less,** *adj.*

de·fen·sive (di fen′siv), *adj.* **1.** serving to defend; protective: *defensive armament; a defensive attitude.* —*n.* **2.** a position or attitude of defense: *to be on the defensive about one's mistakes.* —**de·fen′sive·ly,** *adv.*

de·fer[1] (di fûr′), *v.,* **de·ferred, de·fer·ring.** to put off to a future time; delay: *He asked for permission to defer his decision.* [from the Middle English word *deferren,* which comes from Latin *differre* "to put off, delay," from *dis-* "apart, away" + *ferre* "to bear"]

de·fer[2] (di fûr′), *v.,* **de·ferred, de·fer·ring.** to yield in judgment or opinion: *We all defer to him in these matters since he is the best informed.* [from the Middle English word *deferren,* which comes from Latin *dēferre* "to carry down," from *dē-* "down" + *ferre* "to bear"]

def·er·ence (def′ər əns), *n.* **1.** submission or yielding to the judgment, opinion, will, etc., of another. **2.** respectful regard: *in deference to his wishes.*

de·fer·ment (di fûr′mənt), *n.* **1.** the act of putting off; postponement. **2.** a postponement from induction into military service: *a student deferment.*

de·fi·ance (di fī′əns), *n.* bold resistance to or disregard of authority or any opposing force: *The boys* *stayed out late in defiance of their mothers' orders.*

de·fi·ant (di fī′ənt), *adj.* marked by defiance or bold opposition: *a defiant look.* —**de·fi′ant·ly,** *adv.*

de·fi·cien·cy (di fish′ən sē), *n., pl.* **de·fi·cien·cies.** 1. the condition of being deficient; incompleteness; shortage: *a deficiency of vitamins and minerals.* 2. the amount lacked; deficit: *a deficiency of five dollars.*

de·fi·cient (di fish′ənt), *adj.* lacking some essential part or quality; insufficient: *This town is deficient in parks and playgrounds.* —**de·fi′cient·ly,** *adv.*

def·i·cit (def′i sit), *n.* the amount by which a sum falls short of the required amount: *The club's deficit is $50, since we have $100 in the treasury and owe $150 in bills.*

de·file¹ (di fīl′), *v.,* **de·filed, de·fil·ing.** 1. to make dirty or unclean. 2. to make impure; destroy the sacredness or pureness of: *The vandals defiled the church.* [from the Old French word *defouler* "to trample on"] —**de·file′ment,** *n.*

de·file² (di fīl′, dē′fīl), *n.* 1. any narrow passage, esp. between mountains. —*v.,* **de·filed, de·fil·ing.** 2. to march in a line or by files. [from the French word *défiler* "to march in file"]

de·fine (di fīn′), *v.,* **de·fined, de·fin·ing.** 1. to state or set forth the meaning of (a word, phrase, etc.): *A dictionary defines words.* 2. to explain clearly: *The captain defined the duties of each soldier.* 3. to make clear the outline or form of: *The tower was boldly defined against the sky.* —**de·fin′a·ble,** *adj.*

def·i·nite (def′ə nit), *adj.* 1. clearly defined or determined; exact: *definite directions.* 2. having fixed limits: *a definite area.* 3. positive; certain; sure: *It is definite that he will take the job.*

def′inite ar′ticle, (in grammar) the article used to point out one or more particular persons or things. In English, the definite article is *the.*

def·i·nite·ly (def′ə nit lē), *adv.* 1. in a definite manner. 2. positively: *I'm definitely coming.* —*interj.* 3. certainly; to be sure.

def·i·ni·tion (def′ə nish′ən), *n.* 1. the act of defining or making definite or clear: *His definition of the situation cleared up the misunderstandings.* 2. the formal statement of the meaning or significance of a word, phrase, etc.

de·fin·i·tive (di fin′i tiv), *adj.* 1. most reliable or complete: *a definitive biography.* 2. providing a solution or final answer: *a definitive method of solving the problem.* —**de·fin′i·tive·ly,** *adv.*

de·flate (di flāt′), *v.,* **de·flat·ed, de·flat·ing.** 1. to remove the air or gas from: *to deflate a balloon.* 2. to reduce from an unusually high level: *to deflate prices.* —**de·fla′tion,** *n.*

de·flect (di flekt′), *v.* to bend or turn aside; swerve: *The tree deflected the tennis ball.* —**de·flec′tion,** *n.*

De·foe (di fō′), *n.* Daniel, 1659–1731, English novelist and satirist.

de·form (di fôrm′), *v.* to mar the natural form or shape of; put out of shape: *Years of violent storms had deformed the tree.*

de·form·i·ty (di fôr′mi tē), *n., pl.* for def. 2 **de·for·mi·**

ties. 1. the quality or state of being deformed, disfigured, or misshapen. 2. an abnormally formed part of the body.

de·fraud (di frôd′), *v.* to deprive of a right or property by fraud; cheat.

de·fray (di frā′), *v.* to bear or pay (the costs, expenses, etc.): *The award money helped defray his tuition.*

de·frost (di frôst′), *v.* to remove the frost or ice from: *to defrost a refrigerator.*

defs., definitions.

deft (deft), *adj.* skillful or clever; quick: *The seamstress has deft hands.* —**deft′ly,** *adv.* —**deft′ness,** *n.*

de·funct (di fungkt′), *adj.* no longer in existence or operation; dead; extinct: *a defunct machine.*

de·fy (di fī′), *v.,* **de·fied, de·fy·ing.** 1. to challenge the power of; resist boldly: *He defied the school rules.* 2. to offer successful resistance to: *The fort defies attack.* 3. to challenge (a person) to do something difficult; dare: *We defied him to dive off the high board.*

deg., degree.

de Gaulle (də gôl′), **Charles,** 1890–1970, French general and statesman: president 1959–1969.

de·gen·er·ate (di jen′ə rāt′), *v.,* **de·gen·er·at·ed, de·gen·er·at·ing.** 1. to decline in physical, mental, or moral qualities. —*adj.* (di jen′ər it). 2. having declined in physical or moral qualities; deteriorated. —*n.* (di jen′ər it). 3. a person whose character or moral standards have declined. —**de·gen·er·a·cy** (di jen′ər ə sē), *n.* —**de·gen′er·a′tion,** *n.*

deg·ra·da·tion (deg′rə dā′shən), *n.* 1. the act of degrading. 2. a decline or deterioration, as of character, wealth, livelihood, etc.

de·grade (di grād′), *v.,* **de·grad·ed, de·grad·ing.** 1. to reduce to a lower rank or title: *They degraded him to assistant.* 2. to lower in character, quality, or dignity: *He felt degraded by having to wash the dishes.*

de·gree (di grē′), *n.* 1. a step or stage in a series of steps or stages: *He grew weaker by degrees.* 2. rank or social standing: *a lady of high degree.* 3. extent, amount, measure, scope, or the like: *To what degree will he cooperate?* 4. a unit of measure of temperature. On the Fahrenheit scale, water freezes at 32 degrees and boils at 212 degrees; on the Centigrade (Celsius) scale, water freezes at 0 degrees and boils at 100 degrees. 5. a unit

Degrees
of a circle

of measure for angles, equivalent to $1/360$ of a circle. A complete circle contains 360 degrees, a half-circle or a straight angle 180 degrees, and a right angle 90 degrees. *Symbol:* ° 6. the classification of a crime according to its seriousness: *murder in the first degree.* 7. a title given by universities and colleges to show the completion of a course of study or as an honor: *a law degree.* 8. (in grammar) one of the inflected forms showing comparison of adjectives and adverbs. The three degrees of comparison are the positive, the comparative, and the superlative.

de·hu·mid·i·fy (dē′hyōō mid′ə fī′), *v.,* **de·hu·mid·i·fied, de·hu·mid·i·fy·ing.** to take moisture out of (the air). —**de′hu·mid′i·fi′er,** *n.*

de·hy·drate (dē hī′drāt), *v.,* **de·hy·drat·ed, de·hy·drat·ing.** 1. to remove the water from (fruits, vegetables, or other foods). 2. to lose water from (body tissues). —**de′hy·dra′tion,** *n.*

de·ice (dē īs′), *v.,* **de·iced, de·ic·ing.** to free or keep free of ice. —**de·ic′er,** *n.*

de·i·fy (dē′ə fī′), *v.,* **de·i·fied, de·i·fy·ing.** to make a god of: *to deify a king.* —**de·i·fi·ca·tion** (dē′ə fə kā′shən), *n.*

deign (dān), *v.* to think fit; condescend: *He would not deign to discuss the matter with us.*

de·i·ty (dē′i tē), *n., pl.* **de·i·ties.** 1. a god or goddess. 2. divine character or nature: *to believe in the deity of an emperor.* 3. **the Deity,** God.

de·ject·ed (di jek′tid), *adj.* depressed in spirits; disheartened; unhappy: *The team was dejected after losing the game.* —**de·ject′ed·ly,** *adv.*

de·jec·tion (di jek′shən), *n.* depression; sadness.

deka-, a prefix meaning ten: *dekagram.*

dek·a·gram (dek′ə gram′), *n.* a unit of mass or weight in the metric system, equal to 10 grams. *Symbol:* dag

dek·a·li·ter (dek′ə lē′tər), *n.* a unit of volume or capacity in the metric system, equal to 10 liters. *Symbol:* dal

dek·a·me·ter (dek′ə mē′tər), *n.* a unit of length in the metric system, equal to 10 meters. *Symbol:* dam

Del., Delaware.

del., delegate.

Del·a·ware (del′ə wâr′), *n.* a state in the E United States, on the Atlantic coast. 2057 sq. mi. *Cap.:* Dover.

de·lay (di lā′), *v.* 1. to put off to a later time; postpone: *The pilot delayed the flight until the weather cleared.* 2. to make late; retard; hinder: *The dense fog delayed the plane's landing.* 3. to put off action; linger: *He delayed because he could not make up his mind.* —*n.* 4. the act of delaying; loitering: *Too much delay will ruin the plan.* 5. an instance of being delayed: *There were five delays during the train trip.*

de·lec·ta·ble (di lek′tə bəl), *adj.* delightful; highly pleasing. —**de·lec′ta·bly,** *adv.*

del·e·gate (del′ə gāt′, del′ə git), *n.* 1. a person chosen to act for another person or other persons; representative: *Joan was elected a delegate to the conference.* —*v.* (del′ə gāt′), **del·e·gat·ed, del·e·gat·ing.** 2. to send or appoint (a person) as deputy or representative. 3. to give (powers, functions, etc.) to another as agent or deputy: *to delegate responsibility.*

del·e·ga·tion (del′ə gā′shən), *n.* 1. the act of delegating, or the state of being delegated. 2. a group of delegates.

de·lete (di lēt′), *v.,* **de·let·ed, de·let·ing.** to strike out or remove (something written or printed); erase: *to delete unnecessary words in a sentence.*

de·le·tion (di lē′shən), *n.* 1. the act of deleting. 2. a word, part, etc., that has been deleted.

Del·hi (del′ē), *n.* a city in N India. Also, **Old Delhi.**

de·lib·er·ate (di lib′ər it), *adj.* 1. carefully considered; studied; intentional: *a deliberate lie.* 2. careful or slow in deciding or being decided: *a deliberate critic; a deliberate judgment.* 3. leisurely and steady; slow and even: *He took deliberate aim and fired.* —*v.* (di lib′ə rāt′), **de·lib·er·at·ed, de·lib·er·at·ing.** 4. to think over carefully; consider: *to deliberate a question.* 5. to consult formally: *The jury deliberated for hours.* —**de·lib′er·ate·ly,** *adv.* —**de·lib′er·ate·ness,** *n.*

de·lib·er·a·tion (di lib′ə rā′shən), *n.* 1. careful consideration before decision. 2. formal consultation or discussion: *The committee's deliberations lasted several hours.* 3. slowness and care of movement or action: *She paced the floor with great deliberation.*

de·lib·er·a·tive (di lib′ə rā′tiv, di lib′ər ə tiv), *adj.* of or referring to deliberation or careful consideration: *The legislature is a deliberative body.*

del·i·ca·cy (del′ə kə sē), *n., pl.* **del·i·ca·cies.** 1. fineness of texture, quality, etc.: *the delicacy of lace.* 2. a choice food that is often rare and expensive: *Caviar is a delicacy.* 3. fineness of feeling; sensitiveness: *She criticized him with such delicacy that he was not offended.* 4. the quality of being easily broken or damaged: *the delicacy of glass.* 5. the quality of requiring or involving great care or tact: *negotiations of great delicacy.* 6. extreme accuracy and precision: *the delicacy of a skillful surgeon's touch.* 7. bodily weakness; liability to sickness: *the delicacy of his health.*

del·i·cate (del′ə kit), *adj.* 1. fine in texture, quality, construction, etc. 2. fragile; easily damaged or injured: *delicate porcelain.* 3. weak of body; liable to sickness: *a delicate child.* 4. pleasingly fine and soft; subtle: *a delicate flavor; a delicate shade of pink.* 5. able to distinguish fine or subtle differences: *a delicate sense of smell.* 6. fine or exact: *a delicate instrument.* 7. requiring great care, caution, or tact: *It's a delicate situation when one country threatens another.* —**del′i·cate·ly,** *adv.*

del·i·ca·tes·sen (del′ə kə tes′ən), *n.* 1. a store selling foods already prepared, such as cooked meats, cheese, relishes, salads, etc. 2. *Informal.* the food products sold in such a store.

de·li·cious (di lish′əs), *adj.* very pleasing to the senses, esp. to taste or smell: *a delicious dinner.* —**de·li′cious·ly,** *adv.* —**de·li′cious·ness,** *n.*

de·light (di līt′), *n.* 1. a high degree of pleasure or enjoyment; joy: *The children's faces showed their delight.* 2. something that gives great pleasure: *The concert was a delight.* —*v.* 3. to give great pleasure or joy to: *The good news delighted us.* 4. to have great pleasure (often fol. by *in*): *She delights in camping.*

de·light·ful (di līt′fəl), *adj.* very pleasing: *Seeing her was a delightful surprise.* —**de·light′ful·ly,** *adv.*

de·lin·e·ate (di lin′ē āt′), *v.,* **de·lin·e·at·ed, de·lin·e·at·ing.** 1. to trace the outline of: *He delineated the house to show us what it looked like.* 2. to describe in words: *In his speech he carefully delineated the plot of the play.* —**de·lin′e·a′tion,** *n.*

de·lin·quen·cy (di liṅ′kwən sē), *n., pl.* **de·lin·quen·cies.** 1. failure in or neglect of a duty or obligation; fault; guilt. 2. a misdeed or offense. See also **juvenile delinquency.**

de·lin·quent (di liṅ′kwənt), *adj.* 1. neglectful of a duty or obligation; guilty of a misdeed or offense. 2. past due: *a delinquent bill.* —*n.* 3. a person who is delinquent, esp. a juvenile delinquent.

de·lir·i·ous (di lēr′ē əs), *adj.* 1. suffering from delirium: *delirious with fever.* 2. wildly excited: *delirious with joy.* —**de·lir′i·ous·ly,** *adv.*

de·lir·i·um (di lēr′ē əm), *n.* 1. a mental condition producing excitement, rambling talk, illusions, etc., often caused by a severe fever or other illness. 2. violent excitement or emotion.

de·liv·er (di liv′ər), *v.* 1. to carry and turn over: *to deliver a package.* 2. to give into another person's keeping: *to deliver a prisoner to the police.* 3. to utter or pronounce: *to deliver a speech.* 4. to direct or throw: *to deliver a blow.* 5. to set free, liberate, or save: *to deliver slaves.* 6. to assist at the birth of: *The doctor delivered triplets.* —**de·liv′er·er,** *n.*

de·liv·er·ance (di liv′ər əns), *n.* 1. an act or instance of delivering. 2. the state of being delivered; liberation.

de·liv·er·y (di liv′ə rē), *n., pl.* **de·liv·er·ies.** 1. a handing over: *mail delivery.* 2. the way in which a speech is presented: *His speech was ruined by poor delivery.* 3. the act or manner of giving or sending forth: *the pitcher's fine delivery of the ball.* 4. release or rescue; liberation; deliverance. 5. the act of giving birth to a child.

dell (del), *n.* a small valley; vale: *the farmer in the dell.*

Del·phi (del′fī), *n.* an ancient city in central Greece: site of the oracle (**Del′phic or′acle**) of Apollo. —**Del′phic,** *adj.*

del·ta (del′tə), *n.* a nearly flat and often triangular plain of sandy deposit formed between diverging branches of the mouth of a river.

de·lude (di lood′), *v.,* **de·lud·ed, de·lud·ing.** to mislead the mind or judgment of (a person); deceive: *No one was deluded by his ridiculous promises of sudden wealth.*

del·uge (del′yooj), *n.* 1. a great flood of water; flood. 2. a drenching rain; downpour. 3. anything that overwhelms like a flood: *a deluge of mail.* —*v.,* **del·uged, del·ug·ing.** 4. to flood. 5. to overrun; overwhelm: *She was deluged with job offers.*

de·lu·sion (di loo′zhən), *n.* a false belief or opinion: *He had a delusion that he was a king.*

de·luxe (də looks′, də luks′), *adj.* of the best quality; elegant; luxurious: *a deluxe restaurant.*

delve (delv), *v.,* **delved, delv·ing.** 1. to carry on thorough research for information: *He delved in the library for data for his project.* 2. *Archaic.* to dig.

de·mag·net·ize (dē mag′ni tīz′), *v.,* **de·mag·net·ized, de·mag·net·iz·ing.** to remove the magnetization from.

dem·a·gogue (dem′ə gog′), *n.* a speaker or political leader who gains power and popularity by arousing the emotions and the prejudices of the people.

de·mand (di mand′), *v.* 1. to ask for with authority: *He demanded payment.* 2. to ask for urgently: *She demanded that we let her in.* 3. to call for or require: *The job demands patience.* —*n.* 4. the act of demanding: *He made a demand for more pay.* 5. something that is demanded: *His demands are reasonable.* 6. an urgent or pressing requirement: *These meetings make too many demands on my time.* 7. **in demand,** desired by many persons; very popular: *His new recording is much in demand.*

de·mar·ca·tion (dē′mär kā′shən), *n.* 1. the determining and marking off of the boundaries of something: *demarcation of public lands.* 2. separation by distinct boundaries: *a demarcation by age.*

de·mean¹ (di mēn′), *v.* to lower in dignity or standing: *He would not demean himself by asking for pity.* [from *de-* + *mean²*]

de·mean² (di mēn′), *v.* to conduct or behave (oneself) in a certain way: *He demeans himself like a gentleman.* [from the Old French word *demener*]

de·mean·or (di mē′nər), *n.* conduct; behavior; bearing: *a shy demeanor.*

de·ment·ed (di men′tid), *adj.* insane; out of one's mind. —**de·ment′ed·ly,** *adv.* —**de·ment′ed·ness,** *n.*

de·mer·it (dē mer′it), *n.* 1. a mark against a person for misconduct: *I got another demerit for being tardy.* 2. a fault or weakness.

De·me·ter (di mē′tər), *n.* (in Greek mythology) the goddess of agriculture: identified with the Roman goddess Ceres.

dem·i·god (dem′ē god′), *n.* a being who is partly divine and partly human.

de·mil·i·ta·rize (dē mil′i tə rīz′), *v.,* **de·mil·i·ta·rized, de·mil·i·ta·riz·ing.** to remove military power from: *to demilitarize an area.* —**de·mil′i·ta·ri·za′tion,** *n.*

de·mise (di mīz′), *n.* death; the ending of life.

dem·i·tasse (dem′i tas′), *n.* 1. a small cup for serving black coffee after dinner. 2. the coffee contained in such a cup.

de·mo·bi·lize (dē mō′bə līz′), *v.,* **de·mo·bi·lized, de·mo·bi·liz·ing.** 1. to disband (an army, troop unit, etc.). 2. to discharge (a person) from military service. —**de·mo′bi·li·za′tion,** *n.*

de·moc·ra·cy (di mok′rə sē), *n., pl.* **de·moc·ra·cies.** 1. government by the people; a form of government in which the supreme power is vested in the people and is exercised directly or through elected representatives. 2. a state having such a form of government. 3. political or social equality; democratic spirit.

[map illustration labeled: AETOLIA, Delphi, BOEOTIA, PELOPONNESUS, Athens, IONIAN SEA, AEGEAN SEA]

dem·o·crat (dem′ə krat′), *n.* **1.** a person who believes in democracy. **2.** a person who believes in the social equality of all people.

Dem·o·crat (dem′ə krat′), *n.* a member of the Democratic party.

dem·o·crat·ic (dem′ə krat′ik), *adj.* **1.** referring to or of the nature of democracy: *a democratic government.* **2.** characterized by social equality: *democratic treatment of all people.* —**dem′o·crat′i·cal·ly,** *adv.*

Dem·o·crat·ic (dem′ə krat′ik), *adj.* of, concerning, or belonging to the Democratic party.

Dem′ocrat′ic par′ty, one of the two major political parties in the U.S., founded in 1828. See also **Republican party.**

de·mol·ish (di mol′ish), *v.* to tear down; destroy; ruin: *to demolish a building.*

dem·o·li·tion (dem′ə lish′ən), *n.* **1.** the act or an instance of demolishing. **2.** the state of being demolished; destruction.

de·mon (dē′mən), *n.* **1.** an evil spirit; devil. **2.** a very wicked, evil, or cruel person. **3.** a person with great energy, drive, etc.: *He's a demon for work.* —**de·mon·ic** (di mon′ik), *adj.*

de·mo·ni·ac (di mō′nē ak′), *adj.* Also, **demoniacal. 1.** of, referring to, or like a demon. **2.** possessed by or as if by an evil spirit; raging. —*n.* **3.** a person who seems to be possessed by a demon or evil spirit.

de·mo·ni·a·cal (dē′mə nī′ə kəl), *adj.* another form of **demoniac.**

de·mon·stra·ble (di mon′strə bəl), *adj.* capable of being demonstrated. —**de·mon′stra·bly,** *adv.*

dem·on·strate (dem′ən strāt′), *v.,* **dem·on·strat·ed, dem·on·strat·ing. 1.** to describe, explain, or illustrate by examples, experiments, etc.: *The teacher demonstrated two ways to solve the problem.* **2.** to exhibit or show: *The salesman demonstrated the vacuum cleaner to my mother.* **3.** to make clear by arguments or reasoning; prove: *The speaker demonstrated his point of view.* **4.** to show feelings openly by marching, meeting, or picketing: *The workers demonstrated for higher wages.*

dem·on·stra·tion (dem′ən strā′shən), *n.* **1.** a description or explanation illustrated by examples. **2.** the act of exhibiting the operation or use of a device or machine: *a demonstration of a sewing machine.* **3.** an exhibition or expression of feeling or emotion: *a demonstration of grief.* **4.** a public exhibition of the attitude of a group of persons concerning a controversial issue, usually· involving parading and picketing: *a civil-rights demonstration.*

de·mon·stra·tive (də mon′strə tiv), *adj.* **1.** given to open expression of one's emotions, attitudes, feelings, etc.: *a very demonstrative person.* **2.** (in grammar) pointing out a person or thing. *This, that, these,* and *those* are demonstrative adjectives or pronouns. —*n.* **3.** (in grammar) a demonstrative word.

dem·on·stra·tor (dem′ən strā′tər), *n.* **1.** a person or thing that demonstrates. **2.** a person who takes part in a public demonstration.

de·mor·al·ize (di môr′ə līz), *v.,* **de·mor·al·ized, de·mor·al·iz·ing. 1.** to deprive (a person or persons) of spirit, courage, etc.: *The constant criticism demoralized him.* **2.** to corrupt the morals of. —**de·mor′al·i·za′tion,** *n.*

de·mote (di mōt′), *v.,* **de·mot·ed, de·mot·ing.** to reduce to a lower grade, class, or rank: *The soldier was demoted from sergeant to corporal.* —**de·mo′tion,** *n.*

de·mur (di mûr′), *v.,* **de·murred, de·mur·ring. 1.** to make an objection: *to demur at being asked to lend money.* —*n.* **2.** an objection raised.

de·mure (di myŏŏr′), *adj.,* **de·mur·er, de·mur·est. 1.** shy and modest; reserved. **2.** seeming to be shy and modest; coy. —**de·mure′ly,** *adv.*

den (den), *n.* **1.** a secluded place, as a cave, used by animals for shelter or hiding. **2.** any hiding place: *a thieves' den.* **3.** a dirty, vile place. **4.** a quiet, secluded room in a house, used for reading, writing, etc. **5.** one of the units of a cub-scout pack, equivalent to a patrol in the Boy Scouts.

de·na·ture (dē nā′chər), *v.,* **de·na·tured, de·na·tur·ing. 1.** to deprive (something) of its natural character, properties, etc. **2.** to add a substance to (alcohol) that makes it undrinkable but does not affect its usefulness as a solvent, fuel, etc.

de·ni·al (di nī′əl), *n.* **1.** an assertion that a statement is false. **2.** the refusal to satisfy a claim or request. **3.** refusal to recognize or acknowledge: *Peter's denial of Christ.*

den·im (den′əm), *n.* a heavy, twill cotton for work and leisure clothes. [from the French words *de Nîmes,* in the phrase *serge de Nîmes* "serge of Nîmes (a city in France)"]

den·i·zen (den′i zən), *n.* **1.** an inhabitant; resident: *denizens of the sea.* **2.** an animal, plant, etc., adapted to a new place, condition, etc.

Den·mark (den′märk), *n.* a kingdom in N Europe. 16,576 sq. mi. *Cap:* Copenhagen.

de·nom·i·na·tion (di nom′ə nā′shən), *n.* **1.** a name for a class of things. **2.** a religious group, usually including many churches. **3.** one of the grades in a series of values, measures, weights, etc.: *bills of small denomination.* —**de·nom′i·na′tion·al,** *adj.*

de·nom·i·na·tor (di nom′ə nā′tər), *n.* the number in a fraction that is written below the line or after the slash and indicates the number of equal parts into which the whole is divided: *In the fractions* $\frac{1}{4}$ *and* $\frac{3}{4}$, *the denominator is 4.* See also **numerator.**

de·no·ta·tion (dē′nō tā′shən), *n.* **1.** the meaning of a word or expression. See also **connotation. 2.** the act or fact of denoting; indication.

de·note (di nōt′), *v.,* **de·not·ed, de·not·ing. 1.** to be a mark or sign of; indicate: *A quick pulse often denotes fever.* **2.** to be a name for; mean: *The word "demeanor" denotes behavior.* See also **connote.**

de·nounce (di nouns′), *v.,* **de·nounced, de·nounc·ing. 1.** to speak against or condemn publicly: *The teacher denounced cheating as being dishonest.* **2.** to make a formal accusation against: *to denounce a thief.*

dense (dens), *adj.,* **dens·er, dens·est. 1.** closely packed together; crowded; compact: *a dense forest.* **2.** stupid; dull. —**dense′ly,** *adv.* —**dense′ness,** *n.*

den·si·ty (den′si tē), *n., pl.* for def. 2 **den·si·ties. 1.** the state or quality of being dense; compactness. **2.** relative heaviness; weight per unit of volume: *The density of lead is greater than that of cork.* **3.** stupidity; slow-wittedness.

dent (dent), *n.* **1.** a hollow or depression in a surface made by a blow or pressure. —*v.* **2.** to make or become dented: *He dented the fender of his car.*

den·tal (den′t∍l), *adj.* of or referring to the teeth or to dentistry.

den′tal floss′. See **floss** (def. 3).

den·ti·frice (den′t∍ fris), *n.* a powder, paste, or other preparation for cleaning the teeth.

den·tin (den′t∍n, den′tin), *n.* the hard bonelike material of which teeth are formed. Also, **den·tine** (den′tēn). See illus. at **tooth.**

den·tist (den′tist), *n.* a doctor who treats and prevents diseases of the teeth, gums, and mouth.

den·tist·ry (den′ti strē), *n.* the occupation or work of a dentist.

den·ture (den′ch∍r), *n.* an artificial replacement for one or more missing teeth.

de·nude (di nōōd′, -nyōōd′), *v.,* **de·nud·ed, de·nud·ing.** to make naked or bare; strip the covering from: *The storm completely denuded the trees.*

de·nun·ci·a·tion (di nun′sē ā′sh∍n), *n.* **1.** an act or instance of denouncing. **2.** an accusation of crime before a public prosecutor or tribunal.

Den·ver (den′v∍r), *n.* the capital city of Colorado, in the central part.

de·ny (di nī′), *v.,* **de·nied, de·ny·ing. 1.** to declare (something) to be untrue: *to deny an accusation.* **2.** to refuse to agree to: *to deny a petition.* **3.** to withhold something from; refuse: *to deny a beggar.* **4.** to refuse to acknowledge: *to deny one's religion.*

de·o·dor·ant (dē ō′d∍r ∍nt), *n.* a substance that covers up or destroys unpleasant odors.

de·o·dor·ize (dē o′d∍ rīz′), *v.,* **de·o·dor·ized, de·o·dor·iz·ing.** to rid of odor, esp. of unpleasant odor.

de·ox·y·ri′bo·nu·cle′ic a′cid (dē ok′si ri′bō nōō-klē′ik, -nyōō-). See **DNA.**

de·part (di pärt′), *v.* **1.** to go away; leave: *The train departs at three o'clock.* **2.** to differ or deviate; change (usually fol. by *from*): *The new method departs from the old in several ways.* **3.** to die.

de·part·ment (di pärt′m∍nt), *n.* **1.** a distinct part of anything arranged in divisions; a part of an organized system. **2.** one of the principal administrative districts in France.

depart′ment store′, a large store organized into various departments for selling different kinds of merchandise.

de·par·ture (di pär′ch∍r), *n.* **1.** an act or instance of departing: *the departure of a boat.* **2.** deviation; a turning away: *a departure from the usual routine.*

de·pend (di pend′), *v.* **1.** to rely; place trust (usually fol. by *on* or *upon*): *to depend on the accuracy of a*

report. **2.** to rely for support, help, etc. (usually fol. by *on* or *upon*): *Children depend on their parents.* **3.** to be determined or conditioned (usually fol. by *on* or *upon*): *His success depends upon effort and ability.* **4.** to hang down (usually fol. by *from*): *The chandelier depended from the ceiling.* **5.** to be undecided: *I may go or I may not—it all depends.*

de·pend·a·ble (di pen′d∍ b∍l), *adj.* worthy of trust; reliable: *a dependable worker.* —**de·pend′a·bil′i·ty,** —**de·pend′a·bly,** *adv.*

de·pend·ence (di pen′d∍ns), *n.* **1.** the state of depending on or needing someone or something. **2.** reliance, confidence, or trust. **3.** the state of being determined by something: *the dependence of good health upon proper food.*

de·pend·en·cy (di pen′d∍n sē), *n., pl.* **de·pend·en·cies. 1.** the state of being dependent; dependence. **2.** a subject territory that is not part of the ruling country.

de·pend·ent (di pen′d∍nt), *adj.* **1.** depending on someone or something else for help, support, etc.: *The dog is dependent on us for food and shelter.* **2.** conditioned or determined by something else: *My decision is dependent on yours.* **3.** subject to the control of another: *dependent territories.* —*n.* **4.** a person who is dependent on another: *Does he have any dependents?* —**de·pend′ent·ly,** *adv.*

depend′ent clause′, a clause that cannot form a complete sentence by itself, used together with a main clause to form a complex sentence. In the sentence *When the whistle blows, everybody will stop, When the whistle blows* is a dependent clause. Also, **subordinate clause.**

de·pict (di pikt′), *v.* **1.** to represent by or as if by painting. **2.** to represent or characterize in words; describe. —**de·pic′tion,** *n.*

de·plete (di plēt′), *v.,* **de·plet·ed, de·plet·ing.** to decrease or exhaust the supply of: *The funds were depleted before we could buy a gift.* —**de·ple′tion,** *n.*

de·plor·a·ble (di plôr′∍ b∍l), *adj.* **1.** causing grief or regret. **2.** deserving disapproval; wretched; bad: *This dirty floor is deplorable.* —**de·plor′a·bly,** *adv.*

de·plore (di plôr′), *v.,* **de·plored, de·plor·ing. 1.** to regret deeply or strongly; lament: *to deplore the death of a friend.* **2.** to disapprove of: *to deplore the increase of crime.*

de·pop·u·late (dē pop′y∍ lāt′), *v.,* **de·pop·u·lat·ed, de·pop·u·lat·ing.** to reduce or remove the number of inhabitants of: *The famine depopulated the small country.* —**de·pop′u·la′tion,** *n.*

de·port (di pôrt′), *v.* **1.** to expel (a foreigner) from a country. **2.** to conduct or behave (oneself) in a particular manner: *She deports herself like a lady.*

de·por·ta·tion (dē′pôr tā′sh∍n), *n.* the expulsion of a foreigner from a country: *the deportation of enemy aliens.*

de·port·ment (di pôrt′m∍nt), *n.* conduct or behavior: *The teacher gave him a low grade in deportment.*

de·pose (di pōz′), *v.,* **de·posed, de·pos·ing. 1.** to remove from a high office or position: *to depose a ruler.* **2.** to declare or testify under oath.

de·pos·it (di poz′it), *v.* **1.** to put, place, or set down: *He deposited his burden. The river deposited soil at its mouth.* **2.** to deliver and leave: *Please deposit your books with the librarian.* **3.** to place for safekeeping: *to deposit money in the bank.* **4.** to give as security or in part payment: *I deposited ten dollars on the bicycle.* —*n.* **5.** a natural accumulation or occurrence: *rich deposits of gold.* **6.** money placed in a bank account: *a deposit of five dollars.* **7.** anything given as security or in part payment: *a two-cent deposit on a pop bottle.*

dep·o·si·tion (dep′ə zish′ən), *n.* **1.** removal from an office or position. **2.** the act or process of depositing. **3.** something that is deposited. **4.** a statement under oath, taken down in writing, to be used in court in place of the spoken testimony of the witness.

de·pos·i·tor (di poz′i tər), *n.* a person or thing that deposits, esp. a person who deposits money in a bank.

de·pos·i·to·ry (di poz′i tôr′ē), *n., pl.* **de·pos·i·to·ries.** a place where anything is deposited or stored for safekeeping or future shipment.

de·pot (dē′pō; *also for def. 2* dep′ō), *n.* **1.** a railroad or bus station. **2.** a place to which military supplies and materials are shipped and are stored for distribution. **3.** a storehouse or warehouse.

de·prave (di prāv′), *v.,* **de·praved, de·prav·ing.** to make bad or worse; corrupt.

de·praved (di prāvd′), *adj.* corrupt or wicked.

de·prav·i·ty (di prav′i tē), *n., pl.* **de·prav·i·ties.** a depraved condition, act, or practice; wickedness; sin.

dep·re·cate (dep′rə kāt′), *v.,* **dep·re·cat·ed, dep·re·cat·ing.** to express strong disapproval of: *He deprecates any changes in the old system.* —**dep′re·ca′tion,** *n.*

de·pre·ci·ate (di prē′shē āt′), *v.,* **de·pre·ci·at·ed, de·pre·ci·at·ing.** **1.** to reduce the purchasing value of (money). **2.** to lessen the price or value of. **3.** to make seem unimportant or of little value; belittle: *He depreciated our efforts.* **4.** to decline in value: *Our property depreciated rapidly.* —**de·pre′ci·a′tion,** *n.*

de·press (di pres′), *v.* **1.** to lower in spirits; make sad or gloomy. **2.** to lower in force, activity, amount, etc.; weaken; lessen: *The new shopping center has depressed business in the older shops.* **3.** to put in a lower position; press down: *to depress a key on a piano.* —**de·press′ing·ly,** *adv.*

de·pres·sion (di presh′ən), *n.* **1.** the act of depressing, or the state of being depressed. **2.** a sunken place or part. **3.** sadness; gloom. **4.** a period during which business, employment, and stock-market values decline or remain at a low level: *During a depression it is difficult to find work.*

de·prive (di prīv′), *v.,* **de·prived, de·priv·ing.** to take away or withhold something from: *to deprive a ruler of power.* —**dep·ri·va·tion** (dep′rə vā′shən), *n.*

dept., department.

depth (depth), *n.* **1.** a measurement taken through an object from top to bottom or from front to back. **2.**

Often, **depths.** a deep part or place: *the depths of the ocean.* **3.** Sometimes, **depths.** the farthest, innermost, or extreme part or state: *the depths of the forest.* **4.** deepness of thought or feeling: *depth of understanding.* **5.** lowness of tonal pitch: *the depth of a voice.* **6.** **beyond one's depth,** beyond a person's knowledge or ability: *Algebra is beyond my depth.*

dep·u·ta·tion (dep′yə tā′shən), *n.* **1.** the act of appointing a person or persons to represent or act for another or others. **2.** the person or group of persons appointed: *The mayor met with a deputation of property owners.*

dep·u·tize (dep′yə tīz′), *v.,* **dep·u·tized, dep·u·tiz·ing.** **1.** to appoint as deputy. **2.** to act as deputy; substitute.

dep·u·ty (dep′yə tē), *n., pl.* **dep·u·ties.** a person appointed or authorized to act as a substitute for another or others.

de·rail (dē rāl′), *v.* to run or cause to run off the rails of a track: *to derail a streetcar.* —**de·rail′ment,** *n.*

de·range (di rānj′), *v.,* **de·ranged, de·rang·ing.** **1.** to disturb the condition, arrangement, or order of: *The storm deranged our vacation plans.* **2.** to make insane. —**de·range′ment,** *n.*

der·by (dûr′bē), *n., pl.* **der·bies.** **1.** a man's stiff felt hat with a rounded crown and a narrow brim. **2.** a race or contest open to anyone who wishes to enter.

Der·by (dûr′bē), *n., pl.* **Der·bies.** **1.** a race for three-year-old horses run annually near London, England. **2.** any of other certain important annual horse races, usually for three-year-old horses, esp. the one held in Louisville, Kentucky.

der·e·lict (der′ə likt), *adj.* **1.** left or abandoned: *a derelict ship.* **2.** neglectful of duty; negligent: *a derelict guard.* —*n.* **3.** personal property abandoned by the owner. **4.** a person abandoned by society; a homeless person; bum.

der·e·lic·tion (der′ə lik′shən), *n.* **1.** deliberate neglect; carelessness; negligence: *dereliction of duty.* **2.** the act of abandoning something.

de·ride (di rīd′), *v.,* **de·rid·ed, de·rid·ing.** to make fun of; mock; jeer at: *They derided him for being a snob.*

de·ri·sion (di rizh′ən), *n.* ridicule; mockery: *The derision of his classmates upset him very much.*

de·ri·sive (di rī′siv), *adj.* showing derision; ridiculing; mocking: *a derisive sneer.* —**de·ri′sive·ly,** *adv.*

der·i·va·tion (der′ə vā′shən), *n.* **1.** the act or fact of deriving. **2.** the source from which something comes; origin: *His family is of French derivation.* **3.** the tracing of a word or phrase from its earlier sources; etymology. **4.** a word or phrase that is the source or origin of another word or phrase. **5.** the forming of new words by adding suffixes to existing words or stems, as *coolness* from *cool* or *starvation* from *starve.*

de·riv·a·tive (də riv′ə tiv), *adj.* **1.** derived from something else. **2.** formed by derivation. —*n.* **3.** something derived from something else. **4.** a word formed by derivation from another word or stem.

de·rive (di rīv′), *v.*, **de·rived, de·riv·ing. 1.** to obtain (something) from a particular source (usually fol. by *from*): *He derives pleasure from reading.* **2.** to trace (a word or phrase) from its earlier sources, giving its derivation or etymology. **3.** to form (a word) from another word or a stem by derivation.

der·mis (dûr′mis), *n.* the lower, inner layer of the skin. See also **epidermis.** See illus. at **hair.**

de·rog·a·to·ry (di rog′ə tôr′ē), *adj.* belittling or disparaging: *a derogatory remark.*

der·rick (der′ik), *n.* **1.** a machine for lifting heavy weights, having a boom hinged to the bottom of a tall mast. **2.** the structure over an oil well that supports the drilling machinery. [named after *Derrick*, a 17th-century hangman in London. It is so called from its resemblance to a gallows]

der·rin·ger (der′in jər), *n.* a short-barreled pocket pistol.

de·scend (di send′), *v.* **1.** to move or pass from a higher to a lower place; climb or come down: *He descended the hill.* **2.** to slope downward: *The hill descends into the valley.*

Derringer

3. to be inherited: *The title descends through eldest sons.* **4.** to have a specific person or family among one's ancestors (usually fol. by *from*): *He is descended from Lincoln.* **5.** to come from something past: *The custom descends from an old Indian ceremony.* **6.** to attack violently and suddenly (usually fol. by *on* or *upon*): *to descend upon enemy soldiers.*

de·scend·ant (di sen′dənt), *n.* a person who is descended from a specific ancestor; offspring.

de·scent (di sent′), *n.* **1.** the act or process of descending: *the descent of a kite.* **2.** a downward slope: *a steep descent.* **3.** ancestry or lineage: *She is of Indian descent.* **4.** a sudden raid or attack: *a descent on the enemy.*

de·scribe (di skrīb′), *v.*, **de·scribed, de·scrib·ing. 1.** to tell in written or spoken words; give an account of: *to describe a problem.* **2.** to draw or trace the outline of: *to describe an arc.* **—de·scrib′a·ble,** *adj.*

de·scrip·tion (di skrip′shən), *n.* **1.** a statement, account, or picture in words that describe: *A good description of the thief helped the police.* **2.** sort, kind, or variety: *The store sells every description of cheese.*

de·scrip·tive (di skrip′tiv), *adj.* having the quality of describing: *He wrote a descriptive paragraph about engines.* **—de·scrip′tive·ly,** *adv.*

des·e·crate (des′ə krāt′), *v.*, **des·e·crat·ed, des·e·crat·ing.** to treat something sacred with disrespect and dishonor: *to desecrate a church.* **—des′e·cra′tion,** *n.*

de·seg·re·gate (dē seg′rə gāt′), *v.*, **de·seg·re·gat·ed, de·seg·re·gat·ing.** to eliminate racial segregation in: *to desegregate all schools.* **—de′seg·re·ga′tion,** *n.*

des·ert¹ (dez′ərt), *n.* **1.** a very dry region with little or no vegetation. **—adj. 2.** of or like a desert; barren. [from the Latin word *dēsertum* "abandoned place"]

de·sert² (di zûrt′), *v.* **1.** to leave (a person, place,

etc.) without intending to return, esp. in violation of a duty, promise, etc.; abandon: *The man deserted his family.* **2.** to fail (someone) at a time of need: *All his friends had deserted him.* [from the Latin word *dēsertāre* "to abandon"] **—de·sert′er,** *n.*

de·sert³ (di zûrt′), *n.* Often, **deserts.** reward or punishment that is deserved: *to get one's just deserts.* [from the Old French word *deserte* "deserved," which comes from *deservir* "to deserve"]

de·ser·tion (di zûr′shən), *n.* **1.** the act of deserting, or the state of being deserted. **2.** an intentional abandonment of a person or thing to which one has a responsibility: *desertion from the army.*

de·serve (di zûrv′), *v.*, **de·served, de·serv·ing.** to be worthy of; merit: *She deserved the prize.*

de·serv·ed·ly (di zûr′vid lē), *adv.* justly; rightly: *He was deservedly punished.*

de·serv·ing (di zûr′ving), *adj.* worthy of reward, praise, or help: *a deserving student.*

de·sign (di zīn′), *v.* **1.** to prepare drawings, sketches, or plans for: *to design a dress.* **2.** to intend for a definite purpose: *a scholarship designed for medical students.* **3.** to form or conceive in the mind; plan: *to design a scheme.* **—n. 4.** an outline, sketch, or plan: *a design for the new office building.* **5.** the organization, arrangement, or structure of parts or features: *a new design for an engine.* **6.** a decorative pattern or motif: *a flowered design.* **7.** a plan or project: *a design for becoming successful.* **8.** a plot or scheme: *a design to ruin an enemy.* **9.** the art of making designs: *to study design.* **—de·sign′er,** *n.*

des·ig·nate (dez′ig nāt′), *v.*, **des·ig·nat·ed, des·ig·nat·ing. 1.** to mark or point out; show: *He designated a parking space for the car.* **2.** to choose for some office or duty; appoint: *He was designated to be treasurer of the club.* **3.** to name or call: *A proper noun designates a person or place.* **—des′ig·na′tion,** *n.*

de·sign·ing (di zī′ning), *adj.* **1.** scheming; crafty: *Envious people are often designing.* **—n. 2.** the act or art of making designs: *to study designing.*

de·sir·a·ble (di zīˀr′ə bəl), *adj.* worth desiring or having, as something that is pleasant, good, right, etc.: *We know a desirable spot for a picnic.* **—de·sir′a·bil′i·ty,** *n.*

de·sire (di zīˀr′), *v.*, **de·sired, de·sir·ing. 1.** to wish or long for; crave; want: *to desire a room of one's own.* **2.** to ask for; request: *They desired a prompt answer.* **—n. 3.** a longing or craving; want: *a desire for food.* **4.** something longed for: *A room of his own is his chief desire.*

de·sir·ous (di zīˀr′əs), *adj.* having desire; desiring; eager: *to be desirous of new clothes.*

de·sist (di zist′, di sist′), *v.* to cease doing something; stop: *to desist from fighting.*

desk (desk), *n.* a piece of furniture having a broad, usually level writing surface, and often drawers for keeping papers, pencils, etc.

Des Moines (də moin′), the capital city of Iowa, in the central part.

des·o·late (des′ə lit), *adj.* **1.** barren, ruined, or neglected: *desolate wasteland.* **2.** having no inhabitants: *a desolate seacoast.* **3.** set apart; lonely: *a desolate lighthouse.* **4.** feeling neglected or lonely: *He was desolate without his family.* **5.** dreary; dismal: *a desolate future.* —*v.* (des′ə lāt′), **des·o·lat·ed, des·o·lat·ing. 6.** to lay waste; ruin: *The flood desolated several towns.* **7.** to abandon or leave alone. **8.** to make sad or miserable: *The cold winter nights desolated him.* —**des′o·la′tion,** *n.*

De So·to (də sō′tō), **Hernando,** c1500–1542, Spanish explorer and soldier in America.

de·spair (di spâr′), *n.* **1.** loss of hope; hopelessness: *to face the future with despair.* **2.** something that causes hopelessness: *He was the despair of his family.* —*v.* **3.** to be without hope (often fol. by *of*): *He despaired of success.* —**de·spair′ing·ly,** *adv.*

des·patch (di spach′), *v., n.* another spelling of **dispatch.**

des·per·a·do (des′pə rä′dō, des′pə rā′dō), *n., pl.* **des·per·a·does** *or* **des·per·a·dos.** a bold, reckless criminal.

des·per·ate (des′pər it), *adj.* **1.** reckless or dangerous because of despair or great need: *a desperate thief.* **2.** done out of despair or great need: *a desperate effort to reach safety.* **3.** very bad or grave: *a desperate illness.* **4.** giving in to despair: *After a week of being lost he became desperate.* —**des′per·ate·ly,** *adv.*

des·per·a·tion (des′pə rā′shən), *n.* **1.** the state of being desperate or despairing: *The good news brought an end to his desperation.* **2.** a reckless urge to act when faced by despair: *In desperation, he leaped from the window to escape his pursuers.*

des·pi·ca·ble (des′pi kə bəl, di spik′ə bəl), *adj.* deserving to be despised or held in contempt: *a despicable liar.* —**des′pi·ca·bly,** *adv.*

de·spise (di spīz′), *v.,* **de·spised, de·spis·ing.** to dislike very much; scorn; loathe: *I despise cruel people.*

de·spite (di spīt′), *prep.* **1.** in spite of: *I will go despite the cold weather.* —*n.* **2.** insulting, scornful treatment: *His bad behavior won the despite of his family.*

de·spoil (di spoil′), *v.* to rob, plunder, or pillage: *The enemy troops despoiled the countryside.*

de·spond·ent (di spon′dənt), *adj.* discouraged; feeling hopeless: *Poverty can make one despondent.* —**de·spond′en·cy,** *n.*

des·pot (des′pət, des′pot), *n.* a ruler having absolute power; tyrant; dictator.

des·pot·ic (di spot′ik), *adj.* of or like a despot or despotism. —**des·pot′i·cal·ly,** *adv.*

des·pot·ism (des′pə tiz′əm), *n.* the rule of a despot; absolute power; tyranny.

des·sert (di zûrt′), *n.* pie, ice cream, cake, etc., served as the last course of a meal. [from the French verb *desservir* "to clear the table," which comes from *des-* "from, away" + *servir* "to serve"]

des·ti·na·tion (des′tə nā′shən), *n.* the place to which a person or thing travels or is sent: *I hope that my letter reaches its destination.*

des·tine (des′tin), *v.,* **des·tined, des·tin·ing. 1.** to set apart for some purpose; intend: *He was destined by*

his family to become a doctor. **2.** to cause by fate or destiny: *He was destined to become great.*

des·tined (des′tind), *adj.* **1.** bound for a certain destination: *a ship destined for France.* **2.** caused by destiny: *a destined end.*

des·ti·ny (des′tə nē), *n., pl.* **des·ti·nies. 1.** something that is to happen or has happened to a person or thing: *It was his destiny to be a hero.* **2.** the power that decrees what is to happen; fate: *Some say that destiny rules our lives.*

des·ti·tute (des′ti tōōt′, -tyōōt′), *adj.* **1.** too poor to afford the things necessary to live, as food, clothing, etc. **2.** deprived or lacking: *a barren land, destitute of growing things.* —**des′ti·tu′tion,** *n.*

de·stroy (di stroi′), *v.* to harm or damage beyond repair; ruin; kill: *The enemy destroyed the city.*

de·stroy·er (di stroi′ər), *n.* **1.** a person or thing that destroys. **2.** a swift, small warship, used to escort convoys, hunt enemy submarines, etc.

de·struc·tion (di struk′shən), *n.* **1.** the act of destroying: *The destruction of the old building took months.* **2.** the fact or state of being destroyed; ruin: *The storm caused widespread destruction.*

de·struc·tive (di struk′tiv), *adj.* tending to destroy; causing much damage: *a destructive earthquake.* —**de·struc′tive·ly,** *adv.* —**de·struc′tive·ness,** *n.*

des·ul·to·ry (des′əl tôr′ē), *adj.* lacking in order or purpose; fitful; random: *desultory study habits.*

de·tach (di tach′), *v.* **1.** to unfasten or separate: *to detach a belt.* **2.** to send away on a special mission or duty: *to detach troops.* —**de·tach′a·ble,** *adj.*

de·tached (di tacht′), *adj.* **1.** separated; not attached: *a detached ticket stub.* **2.** not taking sides; impartial: *A judge must be detached.* **3.** aloof or cold: *a detached, unfeeling person.*

de·tach·ment (di tach′mənt), *n.* **1.** the act of detaching, or the state of being detached; separation. **2.** aloofness; indifference. **3.** freedom from taking sides; impartiality. **4.** a force sent on a special mission or duty: *a detachment of troops.*

de·tail (di tāl′, dē′tāl), *n.* **1.** an individual item or small part that goes to make up a whole: *He did every detail of the job by himself.* **2.** all such parts considered together: *He liked the detail of the portrait.* **3.** an item-by-item or fact-by-fact approach to or treatment of something: *He told us the story, but without going into detail.* **4.** an assignment to a special task in the army, navy, etc. **5.** the task so assigned. **6.** the persons doing the task: *A detail was assigned to clean the barracks.* —*v.* (di tāl′). **7.** to report completely or thoroughly: *He detailed all the necessary information.* **8.** to appoint or assign (a soldier, sailor, etc.) to some duty.

de·tain (di tān′), *v.* to keep from going or going on; keep waiting; delay: *We were detained by the blizzard.* —**de·tain′ment,** *n.*

de·tect (di tekt′), *v.* to discover or find out; uncover or bring to light: *to detect a thief; to detect a mistake in grammar.* —**de·tect′a·ble,** *adj.* —**de·tec′tor,** *n.*

de·tec·tion (di tek'shən), *n.* the act of detecting, or the fact of being detected; discovery: *the detection of a leak in a water pipe; the detection of a crime.*

de·tec·tive (di tek'tiv), *n.* a person who searches out hidden information or evidence, such as a police officer or private investigator.

de·ten·tion (di ten'shən), *n.* 1. the act of detaining, or the state of being detained. 2. confinement in a jail.

de·ter (di tûr'), *v.,* **de·terred, de·ter·ring.** to prevent or keep back, as through fear or doubt; discourage; hinder: *The snow deterred us from taking the trip.*

de·ter·gent (di tûr'jənt), *n.* any of numerous synthetic cleaning agents resembling soap.

de·te·ri·o·rate (di tēr'ē ə rāt'), *v.,* **de·te·ri·o·rat·ed, de·te·ri·o·rat·ing.** to make or become worse; lessen in value, strength, etc.: *His health deteriorated for lack of sleep.* —**de·te'ri·o·ra'tion,** *n.*

de·ter·mi·na·tion (di tûr'mə nā'shən), *n.* 1. the act of deciding or settling some matter: *the determination of a name for the baby.* 2. a finding out by observation or investigation; ascertainment: *the determination of one's position.* 3. the fixing or settling of amount, limit, character, etc.: *the determination of how much to spend for new clothes.* 4. strong resolve or firmness of purpose: *a leader of great determination.*

de·ter·mine (di tûr'min), *v.,* **de·ter·mined, de·ter·min·ing.** 1. to settle or decide: *They determined the time they would meet.* 2. to come to a decision; resolve; decide: *He determined that he would live in the city.* 3. to find out by observation or investigation: *We determined our direction by studying the compass.* 4. to cause, affect, or control: *Ambition determined his actions.* —**de·ter'mi·na·ble,** *adj.*

de·ter·mined (di tûr'mind), *adj.* full of resolve; resolute; unwaveringly decided: *a determined defender of freedom.* —**de·ter'mined·ly,** *adv.*

de·ter·min·er (di tûr'mə nər), *n.* 1. a person or thing that determines. 2. (in grammar) an adjective that may be used with a noun to form a noun phrase, such as *a, the, my, this, each,* etc.

de·ter·rent (di tûr'ənt), *adj.* 1. serving or tending to deter: *a deterrent police force.* —*n.* 2. something that deters: *The threat of punishment is a deterrent to mischief-makers.*

de·test (di test'), *v.* to feel hatred or great dislike for: *I detest rudeness.* —**de·test'a·ble,** *adj.*

de·throne (dē thrōn'), *v.,* **de·throned, de·thron·ing.** to remove from a throne or prominent position; depose: *to dethrone a king.* —**de·throne'ment,** *n.*

det·o·nate (det'ᵊnāt'), *v.,* **det·o·nat·ed, det·o·nat·ing.** to explode or cause to explode suddenly and violently: *to detonate dynamite.* —**det'o·na'tion,** *n.*

det·o·na·tor (det'ᵊnā'tər), *n.* a device for setting off an explosive charge.

de·tour (dē'tŏŏr, di tŏŏr'), *n.* 1. a roundabout way or route, esp. one that is temporary: *As the main highway was closed for repairs, we had to make a detour.* —*v.* 2. to make or cause to make a detour: *We had to detour near Omaha.*

de·tract (di trakt'), *v.* to take away a part, esp. of something that is of value (usually fol. by *from*): *Her way of dressing detracts from her beauty.* —**de·trac'tion,** *n.* —**de·trac'tor,** *n.*

det·ri·ment (det'rə mənt), *n.* 1. an injury, loss, or damage: *the detriment of poor eyesight.* 2. a cause of injury, loss, or damage: *The lack of food is a detriment to health.* —**det·ri·men·tal** (det'rə men't²l), *adj.*

De·troit (di troit'), *n.* a city in SE Michigan.

deuce¹ (dōōs, dyōōs), *n.* 1. a card, domino, etc., marked with two spots. 2. (in tennis) a tie score of 40 each or five games each. [from the Old French word *deus* "two," which comes from Latin *duo*]

deuce² (dōōs, dyōōs), *n. Informal.* devil; dickens; mischief (used as a mild oath to express annoyance): *Where the deuce did I put my glasses?* [from the Middle English word *deus,* which is the same word as *deuce¹,* used in a special sense]

deu·te·ri·um (dōō tēr'ē əm, dyōō-), *n.* a kind of hydrogen in which the nucleus of each atom contains one neutron in addition to the proton present in the nucleus of the ordinary hydrogen atom. *Symbol:* D

Deu·ter·on·o·my (dōō'tə ron'ə mē, dyōō'-), *n.* the fifth book of the Old Testament.

dev·as·tate (dev'ə stāt'), *v.,* **dev·as·tat·ed, dev·as·tat·ing.** to lay waste; destroy; overwhelm: *An earthquake devastated the town.* —**dev'as·ta'tion,** *n.*

de·vel·op (di vel'əp), *v.* 1. to grow or expand: *His muscles developed with exercise.* 2. to cause to grow or expand: *Warm weather developed the flowers.* 3. to improve or advance: *Careful farming developed the soil.* 4. to come about or cause to come about gradually and surely: *to develop a plan of action.* 5. to be revealed: *It developed that he had been lying.* 6. to treat (an exposed photographic negative) with chemicals in order to bring out the picture. —**de·vel'op·er,** *n.*

de·vel·op·ment (di vel'əp mənt), *n.* 1. the act or process of developing; progress: *the development of scientific knowledge.* 2. something that has developed: *a new development in science.*

de·vi·ate (dē'vē āt'), *v.,* **de·vi·at·ed, de·vi·at·ing.** to turn aside, as from a way, route, or course: *to deviate from the main highway.* —**de'vi·a'tion,** *n.*

de·vice (di vīs'), *n.* 1. an invention or contrivance: *a new device for opening cans.* 2. a plan, scheme, or trick: *a clever device for getting attention.* 3. **leave to one's own devices,** to allow (a person) to do as he pleases; leave alone: *I'll be gone all day, so I'm leaving you to your own devices.*

dev·il (dev'əl), *n.* 1. any evil spirit at war with God. 2. a wicked or cruel person: *The invaders were a band of devils.* 3. a very clever, reckless, or mischievous person: *a smart little devil.* 4. an unlucky, pitiful person: *The poor devil lost his wallet.* 5. a printer's errand boy or helper. —*v.,* **dev·iled** *or* **dev·illed; dev·il·ing** *or* **dev·il·ling.** 6. to annoy; harass; pester: *He deviled us with silly questions.* 7. to chop up and highly season (food). [from the Old English word *dēofol,* which comes from Greek *diabolos* "slanderer, enemy"]

Dev·il (dev/əl), *n.* the spirit of evil and chief enemy of God; Satan.

dev·iled (dev/əld), *adj.* (of food) chopped up and highly seasoned: *deviled ham.*

dev·il·fish (dev/əl fish/), *n., pl.* **dev·il·fish·es** *or* **dev·il·fish.** 1. a large ray found in tropical waters, having a pair of horns on its head. 2. an octopus.

dev·il·ish (dev/ə lish), *adj.* of, like, or suitable to a devil; wicked; mischievous: *We discovered his devilish scheme.* —**dev/il·ish·ly,** *adv.* —**dev/il·ish·ness,** *n.*

Devilfish
(total length
to 20 ft.)

dev·il·ment (dev/əl mənt), *n.* devilish action or conduct; mischief: *children who are capable of any devilment.*

dev·il·try (dev/əl trē), *n.* 1. mischievous behavior; mischief. 2. extreme wickedness.

de·vi·ous (dē/vē əs), *adj.* 1. roundabout or indirect: *a devious road among the mountains.* 2. not direct or open; dishonest: *a devious way of winning an election.* —**de/vi·ous·ly,** *adv.* —**de/vi·ous·ness,** *n.*

de·vise (di vīz/), *v.,* **de·vised, de·vis·ing.** 1. to contrive or plan: *to devise a method.* 2. to leave (property) to someone by a will: *to devise farmlands to one's relatives.*

de·void (di void/), *adj.* not having; without; empty (usually fol. by *of*): *a man devoid of humor.*

de·volve (di volv/), *v.,* **de·volved, de·volv·ing.** 1. to pass on or transfer (a duty, responsibility, etc.) to or upon another: *to devolve authority.* 2. to be passed on or transferred (usually fol. by *upon*): *When the king died, his power devolved upon his son.*

Dev·on (dev/ən), *n.* a county in SW England. 2612 sq. mi. Also, **Dev·on·shire** (dev/ən shēr/).

de·vote (di vōt/), *v.,* **de·vot·ed, de·vot·ing.** to give up to some purpose, pursuit, person, etc.: *He devoted his life to science.*

de·vot·ed (di vō/tid), *adj.* completely attached to or involved with some purpose, pursuit, person, etc.: *a devoted mother.* —**de·vot/ed·ly,** *adv.*

dev·o·tee (dev/ə tē/), *n.* a person devoted to or enthusiastic over something: *a devotee of jazz.*

de·vo·tion (di vō/shən), *n.* 1. deep dedication or attachment to a purpose, pursuit, person, etc. 2. a giving up of oneself, time, etc., to something or someone: *the devotion of a lifetime to science.* 3. love for God. 4. Often, **devotions.** religious worship.

de·vo·tion·al (di vō/shə nəl), *adj.* of or having to do with religious devotion: *devotional writings.*

de·vour (di vour/), *v.* 1. to swallow or eat up greedily: *The tiger devoured its prey.* 2. to destroy; ruin; ravage. 3. to take in greedily with the mind or senses: *His eyes devoured the beautiful scene.* 4. to absorb or engross: *He was devoured by fear.*

de·vout (di vout/), *adj.* 1. very religious: *a devout worshiper.* 2. earnest or sincere: *a devout lover of nature.* —**de·vout/ly,** *adv.*

dew (dōō, dyōō), *n.* 1. moisture from the air that condenses upon cool surfaces at night. 2. something like dew in freshness or purity: *the dew of youth.* 3. moisture in small drops, such as tears or sweat. —*v.* 4. to wet with or as if with dew.

dew·drop (dōō/drop/, dyōō/-), *n.* a drop of dew.

dew·lap (dōō/lap/, dyōō/-), *n.* a hanging fold of skin under the throat of cattle and certain other animals.

dew/ point/, the temperature to which air must be cooled in order for dew to form. Finding the dew point is one means of measuring the relative humidity of the air.

dew·y (dōō/ē, dyōō/ē), *adj.,* **dew·i·er, dew·i·est.** 1. moist with or as if with dew: *a dewy lawn; a face dewy with sweat.* 2. like dew in appearance or freshness: *dewy tears; dewy skin.* —**dew/i·ness,** *n.*

dex·ter·i·ty (dek ster/i tē), *n.* skill and ease in using the hands, mind, or body: *the dexterity of a surgeon.*

dex·ter·ous (dek/stər əs), *adj.* skillful in the use of the hands, mind, or body. [from the Latin word *dexter* "skillful," literally "right, right hand"] —**dex/ter·ous·ly,** *adv.*

dex·trous (dek/strəs), *adj.* another spelling of **dexterous.** —**dex/trous·ly,** *adv.*

D.F.C., Distinguished Flying Cross.

dg, decigram; decigrams.

dhow (dou), *n.* any of various types of two- or three-masted sailing vessels, used by Arabs on the coasts of Africa, Arabia, and India. [from the Arabic word *dāwā*]

di-, a prefix meaning two: *dioxide.*

di·a·be·tes (dī/ə bē/tis, dī/ə bē/tēz), *n.* a disease that affects the body's ability to use sugar and is caused by a lack of insulin.

Dhow

di·a·bet·ic (dī/ə bet/ik), *adj.* 1. referring to diabetes or to persons having it. 2. having diabetes. —*n.* 3. a person who has diabetes.

di·a·bol·ic (dī/ə bol/ik), *adj.* like a devil; fiendish; wicked: *a diabolic plot.* Also, **di/a·bol/i·cal.** —**di/a·bol/i·cal·ly,** *adv.*

di·a·crit/i·cal mark/ (dī/ə krit/i kəl), a mark added to a letter or group of letters to show a difference in pronunciation, accent, length of vowels, etc.

di·a·dem (dī/ə dem/), *n.* 1. a crown. 2. an ornamental headband worn by kings and queens.

di·ag·nose (dī/əg nōs/, dī/əg nōs/), *v.,* **di·ag·nosed, di·ag·nos·ing.** 1. to identify (an illness) by examination. 2. to examine (a problem, situation, etc.) in detail.

di·ag·no·sis (dī/əg nō/sis), *n., pl.* **di·ag·no·ses** (dī/əg nō/sēz). 1. the act or process of identifying a disease by means of a medical examination. 2. a detailed examination of a problem, situation, etc.: *a diagnosis of the causes of unemployment.* —**di·ag·nos·tic** (dī/əg nos/tik), *adj.*

di·ag·o·nal (dī ag/ə nəl), *n.* 1. a straight line running

---

act, āble, dâre, ärt; ebb, ēqual; if, īce; hot, ōver, ôrder; oil; bŏŏk; ōōze; out; up, ûrge; ə = a as in alone; ᵊ as in button (but/ᵊn), fire (fī°r); chief; shoe; thin; ŧħat; zh as in measure (mezh/ər). See full key inside cover.

across or through something on a slant, esp. one running from corner to corner. —*adj.* 2. on a slant, or from corner to corner; slanting: *a diagonal line; a diagonal direction.* —di·ag′o·nal·ly, *adv.*

di·a·gram (dī′ə gram′), *n.* 1. a drawing or plan that shows the parts of something as an aid to understanding how it is put together, arranged, operated, etc.: *the diagram of a building; the diagram of a motor.* —*v.*, di·a·gramed *or* di·a·grammed; di·a·gram·ing *or* di·a·gram·ming. 2. to show by a diagram; make a diagram of: *to diagram the parts of an engine.*

di·al (dī′əl, dīl), *n.* 1. the face of a clock or sundial. 2. the face of other instruments used to measure or indicate, as a compass or meter, having marks to show amount, direction, etc., and a moving pointer. 3. a disk on a telephone that is rotated in making a phone call. —*v.*, di·aled *or* di·alled; di·al·ing *or* di·al·ling. 4. to select or tune to by means of a dial: *Try dialing another station.* 5. to place a call to (another telephone) by working the dial.

di·a·lect (dī′ə lekt′), *n.* a variety of a language used in a particular locality or region or by the members of a group or social class. —di′a·lec′tal, *adj.*

di·a·logue (dī′ə lôg′, dī′ə log′), *n.* 1. a conversation between two or more persons. 2. conversation in a play, story, etc.

di·am·e·ter (dī am′ə tər), *n.* 1. a straight line passing from one side of a circle or sphere to the other that goes through the center. See illus. at circle. 2. the length of such a line. 3. the width of a circular, spherical, or cylindrical object.

di·a·met·ri·cal (dī′ə me′tri kəl), *adj.* 1. of or along a diameter: *a diametrical measurement.* 2. direct; complete; absolute: *diametrical opposites.* Also, di′a·met′ric. —di′a·met′ri·cal·ly, *adv.*

dia·mond (dī′mənd, dī′ə mənd), *n.* 1. a brilliant, usually colorless gem composed of pure carbon and noted for its extreme hardness. 2. a geometrical figure formed by four straight lines of equal length with its diagonals running vertically and horizontally. 3. a playing card of a suit marked with such a figure in red. 4. the space on a baseball field enclosed by lines connecting home plate and the three bases; infield.

Di·an·a (dī an′ə), *n.* (in Roman mythology) the goddess of hunting and the moon: identified with the Greek goddess Artemis.

di·a·per (dī′pər, dī′ə pər), *n.* 1. a piece of cloth that forms part of a baby's underclothing. 2. a cloth of linen or cotton with a woven pattern of small, constantly repeated figures, as diamonds. —*v.* 3. to put a diaper on (a baby).

di·a·phragm (dī′a fram′), *n.* 1. a sheet of muscle that divides the chest from the abdomen. Its motion inflates and deflates the lungs. 2. a springy steel disk in a telephone receiver whose vibrations produce the sound one hears. 3. a similar disk in a microphone that is

Diana

vibrated by sound waves. 4. a ring, plate, or other system for controlling the amount of light entering a camera.

di·ar·rhe·a (dī′ə rē′ə), *n.* a disease of the intestines that causes frequent, fluid bowel movements. Also, di′ar·rhoe′a.

di·a·ry (dī′ə rē), *n., pl.* di·a·ries. 1. a daily record, esp. of the writer's own experiences, thoughts, etc. 2. a book for keeping such a record.

di·a·tom (dī′ə tom′), *n.* any of numerous tiny water plants having a hard, two-piece outer covering.

di·a·tribe (dī′ə trīb′), *n.* a speech or piece of writing that bitterly and abusively attacks a person or thing: *a diatribe by the congressman against the rising cost of living.*

dice (dīs), *n.pl., sing.* die (dī). 1. small cubes, marked on each side with one to six spots, usually used in pairs in games or gambling. —*v.*, diced, dic·ing. 2. to cut into small cubes: *to dice carrots.* 3. no dice, *Slang.* without agreement, success, etc.: *He wanted to trade kites, but I said it was no dice.*

Dick·ens (dik′inz), *n.* **Charles,** 1812–1870, English novelist.

dick·er (dik′ər), *v.* to trade with petty bargaining; haggle: *We dickered over the price of the vegetables.*

dic·tate (dik′tāt), *v.*, dic·tat·ed, dic·tat·ing. 1. to say or read aloud (something) for another to write down or for a machine to record: *to dictate a letter.* 2. to rule with authority; command or order: *The king dictated the lives of his people.* —*n.* 3. a rule, order, requirement, etc.: *The subjects had to obey the dictates of the king.*

dic·ta·tion (dik tā′shən), *n.* 1. the act of dictating words to be written down or recorded by machine. 2. words that are dictated. 3. the act of ordering or commanding: *the dictation of terms for a surrender.*

dic·ta·tor (dik′tā tər), *n.* 1. a person having absolute power in governing a country, esp. one who takes control without the consent of the people. 2. any person who has great authority in some matter: *a dictator of etiquette.* 3. a person who gives dictation.

dic·ta·to·ri·al (dik′tə tôr′ē əl), *adj.* 1. of or concerning a dictator or dictatorship: *a dictatorial command.* 2. inclined to dictate or command; tyrannical: *a dictatorial boss.* —dic′ta·to′ri·al·ly, *adv.*

dic·ta·tor·ship (dik tā′tər ship′), *n.* 1. a country or government in which all power is in the hands of a dictator. 2. absolute or overbearing power. 3. the office or position held by a dictator.

dic·tion (dik′shən), *n.* 1. manner of speaking or writing, involving choice of words, grammar, etc.; the way in which one expresses oneself: *to admire a speaker's excellent diction.* 2. one's manner of pronouncing words; enunciation: *We couldn't understand him because of his careless diction.*

dic·tion·ar·y (dik′shə ner′ē), *n., pl.* dic·tion·ar·ies. 1. a book containing a selection of the words of a language or words of a special subject, usually in alphabetical order, giving their meanings, pronunciations, etc. 2. a book giving words of one language and their meanings in another: *I bought a*

French-English dictionary for my French class.

did (did), *v.* the past tense of **do**[1].

did·n't (did/³nt), contraction of *did not.*

didst (didst), *v.* an old form of **did,** found chiefly in Biblical and poetic writing and used with *thou.*

die[1] (dī), *v.*, **died, dy·ing. 1.** to stop living or existing. **2.** to pass slowly away (usually fol. by *away, out,* or *down*): *The storm died down before evening.* **3.** to break down or stop: *The motor died halfway up the hill.* **4.** to suffer as if dying: *I'm dying of the heat.* **5.** to desire or want keenly or greatly: *I'm dying to find out what happens next.* [from the Old English word *dīegan,* which comes from Scandinavian]

die[2] (dī), *n., pl.* for def. 1 **dies,** for def. 2 **dice. 1.** any of various devices for cutting or forming including those for cutting screw threads, stamping designs on coins, and forming wires. **2.** the singular form of **dice. 3. the die is cast,** a decision has been made that cannot be changed: *The die was cast as soon as they declared war.* [from the Latin word *datum* "something given." This meaning refers to what is given by fortune. In ancient times fortunes were told by casting dice]

A

B

Die²

A, Greek coin
B, Die for coin

die·sel (dē/zəl), *n.* **1.** another name for **diesel engine. 2.** a truck or locomotive powered by a diesel engine. [named after Rudolph *Diesel* (1858–1913), German automotive engineer, its inventor]

die'sel en'gine, an engine that burns fuel oil, which is ignited by heat produced by the compression of air in the engine's cylinders.

di·et[1] (dī/it), *n.* **1.** a special selection of food prescribed for losing weight, curing disease, etc. **2.** a person's usual foods: *to exist on a diet of rice.* —*v.,* **di·et·ed, di·et·ing. 3.** to select or limit the food one eats to improve one's health or lose weight. [from an Old French word, which comes from Greek *diaita* "way of living"] —**di·e·tar·y** (dī/i ter/ē), *adj.*

di·et[2] (dī/it), *n.* the lawmaking body of certain countries, such as Japan. [from the medieval Latin word *dīēta* "public assembly," which in form comes from Greek *diaita* "diet[1]," but in sense is influenced by Latin *diēs* "day"]

di·e·tet·ic (dī/i tet/ik), *adj.* **1.** referring to diet. **2.** prepared for special diets, esp. for those requiring low sugar intake. —*n.* **3. dietetics,** *(used as sing.)* the science dealing with nutritional planning and the preparation of food. —**di/e·tet/i·cal·ly,** *adv.*

di·e·ti·tian (dī/i tish/ən), *n.* an expert in nutrition or dietetics. Also, **di/e·ti/cian.**

dif·fer (dif/ər), *v.* **1.** to be unlike: *His story differs from yours.* **2.** to disagree in opinion, belief, etc.: *We differ about many things.*
—**Usage.** See **different.**

dif·fer·ence (dif/ər əns), *n.* **1.** the state of being different: *There is a difference between saying something and meaning it.* **2.** a particular way of being different: *One of the differences between them is their age.* **3.** the degree in which one person or thing differs from another: *a great difference in weight.* **4.** the amount by which one quantity is greater or less than another: *The difference between 100 and 40 is 60.* **5.** a disagreement in opinion, belief, etc.

dif·fer·ent (dif/ər ənt), *adj.* **1.** not alike; unlike: *to be different from others.* **2.** separate or distinct: *different times of the year.* **3.** various; several: *Different people told me the same story.* —**dif/fer·ent·ly,** *adv.*
—**Usage.** When expressing a comparison, both *differ* and *different* should be followed by *from,* not *than*: *His necktie differs from mine. Why is his story different from yours?*

dif·fer·en·tial (dif/ə ren/shəl), *n.* **1.** a set of gears between the halves of the rear axle of a car that enables the wheels to be driven at two different speeds when the car travels along a curved path. —*adj.* **2.** indicating or based on a difference; making a distinction: *differential rates for services.*

dif·fer·en·ti·ate (dif/ə ren/shē āt/), *v.,* **dif·fer·en·ti·at·ed, dif·fer·en·ti·at·ing. 1.** to see the difference in or between: *to differentiate various kinds of rock.* **2.** to make a distinction: *to differentiate between colors.* **3.** to mark off as different; distinguish: *It is care that differentiates good workmanship from bad workmanship.* —**dif/fer·en/ti·a/tion,** *n.*

dif·fi·cult (dif/ə kult/), *adj.* **1.** hard to do or understand: *a difficult job; a difficult problem.* **2.** hard to deal with, satisfy, persuade, etc.: *a difficult pupil; a difficult customer.* **3.** full of hardship or danger: *a difficult situation.* —**dif/fi·cult/ly,** *adv.*

dif·fi·cul·ty (dif/ə kul/tē), *n., pl.* **dif·fi·cul·ties. 1.** the fact or condition of being difficult. **2.** something that is hard to do, understand, or surmount: *the difficulties of arithmetic.* **3.** trouble, or a cause of trouble: *to get into difficulty with the authorities.*

dif·fi·dence (dif/i dəns), *n.* distrust of oneself; shyness; timidity: *Diffidence prevented him from doing his best.* —**dif/fi·dent,** *adj.* —**dif/fi·dent·ly,** *adv.*

dif·fuse (di fyōoz/), *v.,* **dif·fused, dif·fus·ing. 1.** to spread as a liquid does when poured. **2.** to spread throughout another substance by an intermingling of molecules. —*adj.* (di fyōos/). **3.** spread out rather than concentrated: *diffuse illumination.* **4.** having more words than necessary, such as a speech or a piece of writing; wordy. —**dif·fuse·ly** (di fyōos/lē), *adv.* —**dif·fu/sion,** *n.*

dig (dig), *v.,* **dug** (dug), **dig·ging. 1.** to break up, turn over, or remove (earth, sand, etc.) with a spade, the hands, etc. **2.** to make (a hole) in such a way. **3.** to make one's way by or as if by removing or turning material: *to dig through a stack of papers.* **4.** to unearth, obtain, or remove by digging: *to dig clams.* **5.** to find or discover by searching (usually fol. by *out*): *to open a book and dig out facts.* **6.** to poke, thrust, or force: *He dug his heel into the ground.* **7. dig into,** to begin (something) with enthusiasm or vigor: *to dig into one's work.* **8. dig up, a.** to uncover by digging: *The dog dug up one of his old bones.* **b.** to obtain, search out, or find: *to dig up facts.*

di·gest (di jest′, dī jest′), *v.* **1.** to convert (food) to a form that can be absorbed by the body. Digestion takes place in the alimentary canal. **2.** to undergo digestion: *foods that are slow to digest.* **3.** to take in mentally; think over thoroughly so as to understand: *to digest the ideas in a book.* —*n.* (dī′jest). **4.** a summary or condensation of a piece of writing.

di·gest·i·ble (di jes′tə bəl, dī jes′tə bəl), *adj.* **1.** capable of being digested. **2.** easy to digest. —**di·gest′i·bil′i·ty,** *n.*

di·ges·tion (di jes′chən, dī jes′chən), *n.* **1.** the process of digesting food. **2.** the ability to digest food.

di·ges·tive (di jes′tiv, dī jes′tiv), *adj.* of, referring to, or active in digestion: *a person's digestive system.*

dig·ger (dig′ər), *n.* **1.** a person or animal that digs. **2.** a tool, part of a machine, etc., for digging.

dig·it (dij′it), *n.* **1.** any of the Arabic numerals 1, 2, 3, 4, 5, 6, 7, 8, 9, and 0. **2.** a finger or toe.

dig·it·al (dij′i t°l), *adj.* **1.** having digits or numerals. **2.** concerning or representing data in the form of numerals: *a digital computer.* **3.** that tells time in numerals rather than by the conventional hands of a timepiece: *a digital watch.* **4.** of or resembling a digit or finger.

dig·ni·fied (dig′nə fīd′), *adj.* having dignity; noble.

dig·ni·fy (dig′nə fī′), *v.,* **dig·ni·fied, dig·ni·fy·ing. 1.** to give dignity to; honor or make stately, noble, etc.: *a house dignified by a magnificent garden.* **2.** to give a high-sounding name or title to: *to dignify the dog-catcher by calling him the collector of canines.*

dig·ni·tar·y (dig′ni ter′ē), *n., pl.* **dig·ni·tar·ies.** a person who holds a high rank or office, as in the government: *the mayor and other dignitaries.*

dig·ni·ty (dig′ni tē), *n., pl.* **dig·ni·ties. 1.** proud, noble, or honorable conduct, character, speech, etc.: *Self-respecting people have dignity no matter what their position in life.* **2.** the quality of being noble, worthy, honorable, etc.: *There is no dignity in begging.* **3.** high rank or office: *the dignity of a king.*

di·gress (di gres′, dī gres′), *v.* to wander away from the main topic: *The speaker digressed frequently.* —**di·gres·sion** (di gresh′ən, dī gresh′ən), *n.*

dike (dīk), *n.* **1.** a bank of earth, stone, etc., for keeping back the waters of the sea or a river: *Holland is protected by dikes.* —*v.,* **diked, dik·ing. 2.** to enclose or protect with dikes. Also, **dyke.**

di·lap·i·dat·ed (di lap′i dā′tid), *adj.* broken down or falling apart: *a dilapidated wooden fence.*

di·lap·i·da·tion (di lap′i dā′shən), *n.* the condition of being dilapidated; decay or ruin.

di·late (dī lāt′), *v.,* **di·lat·ed, di·lat·ing.** to make larger or wider; cause to expand: *Special eye drops are used to dilate the pupils.* —**di·la′tion,** *n.*

dil·a·to·ry (dil′ə tôr′ē), *adj.* tending to delay or be neglectful of what should be done; slow; tardy: *to be dilatory about one's homework.*

di·lem·ma (di lem′ə), *n.* a situation that demands a choice between two things that seem equally unpleasant: *His dilemma was whether to borrow some money or miss the movie.*

dil·et·tante (dil′i tänt′), *n.* a person who loves painting, music, poetry, etc., but does not study any of them seriously.

dil·i·gence¹ (dil′i jəns), *n.* hard and painstaking effort to do something that one has undertaken: *It took diligence to complete the task.* [from a French word, which comes from Latin *dīligentia*]

dil·i·gence² (dil′i jəns), *n.* a public stagecoach formerly used in France. [short for the French phrase *carosse de diligence* "speed coach"]

dil·i·gent (dil′i jənt), *adj.* **1.** hard-working and painstaking: *a diligent student.* **2.** done with care and hard work; thorough; painstaking: *a diligent search.* —**dil′i·gent·ly,** *adv.*

Diligence

dill (dil), *n.* an herb with feathery leaves, the seeds of which are used to flavor pickles.

dil·ly-dal·ly (dil′ē dal′ē), *v.,* **dil·ly-dal·lied, dil·ly-dal·ly·ing.** to waste time, esp. by hesitating; loiter: *to dilly-dally over the choice of a dress.*

di·lute (di l$\overline{oo}$t′, dī l$\overline{oo}$t′), *v.,* **di·lut·ed, di·lut·ing. 1.** to make (a liquid) thinner by the addition of water or the like: *to dilute paint with turpentine.* **2.** to reduce in strength, force, etc., by mixing with something else: *He diluted his speech with too many jokes.* —*adj.* (di l$\overline{oo}$t′, dī l$\overline{oo}$t′, dī′l$\overline{oo}$t). **3.** weakened by the addition of water or another liquid: *a dilute solution of a chemical.* —**di·lu′tion,** *n.*

dim (dim), *adj.,* **dim·mer, dim·mest. 1.** not bright; having or giving only a small amount of light: *a dim hallway.* **2.** not seen clearly or distinctly: *a dim figure in the distance.* **3.** not clear to the mind; vague; remote: *a dim idea.* **4.** not seeing clearly: *eyes dim with tears.* — *v.,* **dimmed, dim·ming. 5.** to make or become dim or dimmer: *The stars dimmed as day approached.* **6.** take **a dim view of,** to regard with distaste or disapproval: *Mother takes a dim view of that kind of talk.* —**dim′ly,** *adv.* —**dim′ness,** *n.*

dime (dīm), *n.* a silver coin of the U.S., the 10th part of a dollar, equal to 10 cents. [from an earlier French word meaning "tenth"]

di·men·sion (di men′shən), *n.* **1.** a measurement in width, length, or thickness: *the dimensions of a box.* **2. dimensions,** size, scope, or importance: *a problem of great dimensions.* —**di·men′sion·al,** *adj.*

di·min·ish (di min′ish), *v.* to make or become smaller in size, importance, etc.: *The length of the day diminishes as winter approaches.*

dim·i·nu·tion (dim′ə n$\overline{oo}$′shən, -ny$\overline{oo}$′-), *n.* the act, fact, or process of diminishing.

di·min·u·tive (di min′yə tiv), *adj.* **1.** small; tiny: *a diminutive tree.* **2.** having a form that expresses smallness or affection, such as "doggy" for "dog." —*n.* **3.** a word having a diminutive meaning.

dim·i·ty (dim′i tē), *n., pl.* **dim·i·ties.** a thin, cotton cloth woven with a stripe or check of heavier yarn.

dim·mer (dim′ər), *n.* **1.** a device for dimming lights, esp. on a stage. **2. dimmers,** the low-beam headlights on a car or truck.

dim·ple (dim′pəl), *n.* **1.** a small hollow in the flesh, usually in the cheek or chin. **2.** any small hollow: *The tide left dimples in the sand.* —*v.,* **dim·pled, dim·pling. 3.** to mark with or as if with a dimple or dimples: *His chin is dimpled.* **4.** to show a dimple or dimples: *Her cheek dimpled in a smile.*

din (din), *n.* **1.** a loud, continued, confused noise: *the din of traffic.* —*v.,* **dinned, din·ning. 2.** to say over and over: *He was forever dinning into our ears the need to be careful.* **3.** to sound loudly: *The surf dinned along the shore.*

dine (dīn), *v.,* **dined, din·ing. 1.** to eat dinner. **2.** to entertain at dinner; give a dinner to: *They like to dine their friends.*

din·er (dī′nər), *n.* **1.** a person who dines. **2.** a railroad car in which meals are served. **3.** a small restaurant built to resemble this.

di·nette (dī net′), *n.* a small space in a home, usually near the kitchen, that is used for dining.

ding (diñg), *v.* **1.** to sound, as a bell; ring. —*n.* **2.** the sound of a bell.

ding-dong (diñg′dông′), *n.* the sound of a bell struck repeatedly.

din·ghy (diñg′ē, diñg′gē), *n., pl.* **din·ghies. 1.** a small boat used as a tender by a larger craft. **2.** a small sailboat or rowboat. Also, **din′gey.** [from the Bengali word *dingi* "boat"]

Dingo
(21 in. high at shoulder)

din·go (diñg′gō), *n., pl.* **din·goes.** a wolflike, wild dog of Australia, having a reddish-brown coat.

din·gy (din′jē), *adj.,* **din·gi·er, din·gi·est.** dark, dull, or dirty in color; lacking brightness or freshness: *dingy, unpainted walls; dingy, unwashed sheets.* —**din′gi·ness,** *n.*

din′ing room′, a room in which meals are eaten, as in a home or hotel.

dink·y (diñg′kē), *adj.,* **dink·i·er, dink·i·est.** *Informal.* very small and unimportant. —**dink′i·ness,** *n.*

din·ner (din′ər), *n.* **1.** the main meal of the day, eaten in the evening or at midday. **2.** a meal in honor of some person or event; banquet.

di·no·saur (dī′nə sôr′), *n.* any of a large group of extinct reptiles that lived 100 million to 200 million years ago, some of which were the largest known land animals. [from the Greek words *deinos* "fearful" + *sauros* "lizard"]

Dinosaur
(height 20 ft.; length 50 ft.)

dint (dint), *n.* **1.** force; power: *He got his way by dint of argument.* **2.** a dent. —*v.* **3.** to make a dent or dents in: *The tin roof was dinted by hail.*

di·o·cese (dī′ə sēs′, dī′ə sis), *n.* a church district under the authority of a bishop. —**di·oc·e·san** (dī os′i-sən), *adj.*

Di·og·e·nes (dī oj′ə nēz′), *n.* 412?–323 B.C., Greek philosopher.

Di·o·ny·sus (dī′ə nī′səs), *n.* (in Greek mythology) the god of fertility, wine, and the drama.

di·ox·ide (dī ok′sīd), *n. Chem.* a compound containing two atoms of oxygen in each molecule: *carbon dioxide.*

dip (dip), *v.,* **dipped, dip·ping. 1.** to put briefly into a liquid, as water, paint, dye, a beverage, etc.: *to dip a roll in coffee; to dip a brush in varnish.* **2.** to plunge or go briefly into water or other liquid: *The boat dipped into the waves.* **3.** to lower and raise: *to dip a flag in salute.* **4.** to raise or take up by bailing, scooping, or ladling: *to dip water from a well.* **5.** to put the hand, a dipper, etc., down into a liquid or container, esp. to remove something: *He dipped into the jar for an olive.* **6.** to sink or drop down: *The sun dipped below the horizon.* **7.** to slope downward: *The road dipped into the valley.* **8.** to make (a candle) by plunging a wick again and again into melted wax. **9.** to study a subject slightly: *to dip into mathematics.* —*n.* **10.** the act of dipping or plunging into or as if into a liquid. **11.** a brief swim: *a dip in the pond.* **12.** something taken up by dipping, such as a scoop of ice cream. **13.** a soft mixture of food into which crackers, potato chips, etc., are dipped: *The dip was made of sour cream and minced clams.* **14.** a brief sinking down or lowering: *the dip of a flag.* **15.** a sloping downward: *a dip in the road.*

diph·the·ri·a (dif thēr′ē ə, dip thēr′ē ə), *n.* an infectious disease of the throat, formerly a major cause of death in children. It has now been largely conquered by the use of vaccine.

diph·thong (dif′thoñg), *n.* a speech sound consisting of two different vowel sounds pronounced together in the same syllable. In *loud, boil,* and *pain,* the vowel sounds *ou, oi,* and *ai* are pronounced as diphthongs.

dipl., 1. diplomat. **2.** diplomatic.

di·plo·ma (di plō′mə), *n.* a document given by a school or college showing that a person has completed a course of study or has received a degree.

di·plo·ma·cy (di plō′mə sē), *n.* **1.** the management of negotiations and other business between nations. **2.** skill in handling people or difficult situations so as to avoid ill will, trouble, or the like; tact: *With a little diplomacy, you could get permission to go.*

dip·lo·mat (dip′lə mat′), *n.* **1.** a government official who manages negotiations and other business with foreign countries, such as ambassadors or consuls. **2.** a person who is tactful and skillful in dealing with people, difficult situations, etc.: *You really have to be a diplomat to get along with Marvin.*

dip·lo·mat·ic (dip/lə mat/ik), *adj.* **1.** of, referring to, or engaged in diplomacy: *a diplomatic official.* **2.** skilled in diplomacy; tactful; adroit: *a diplomatic person; a diplomatic answer.* —**dip/lo·mat/i·cal·ly,** *adv.*

dip·per (dip/ər), *n.* **1.** a cuplike container with a long, straight handle. **2.** either of two groups of seven stars in the northern sky, whose arrangement suggests the shape of a dipper. One (**Little Dipper**) includes the North Star; the other (**Big Dipper**) contains two stars that are in a line with the North Star.

dire (dīər), *adj.*, **dir·er, dir·est. 1.** causing great fear or suffering; dreadful: *a dire calamity.* **2.** indicating or foretelling misfortune or disaster: *a dire prophecy.*

di·rect (di rekt/, dī rekt/), *v.* **1.** to guide or supervise; manage: *to direct traffic.* **2.** to give instructions or commands to; order: *to direct someone to leave.* **3.** to serve as a director for (a play, movie, or the like): *Who directed that television show?* **4.** to tell or show (a person) the way; guide: *Could you direct me to the nearest exit?* **5.** to aim or send toward a place or in a particular direction: *to direct radio waves around the globe.* **6.** to cause to move or work toward a particular goal (often fol. by *to* or *toward*): *He directed all his energy toward solving the mystery.* **7.** to address (words, a remark, etc.) to someone: *That lecture was directed at you.* **8.** to mark (a letter, package, etc.) with the name and address of the person who is to receive it. —*adj.* **9.** going in a straight line or by the shortest route; going straight to some point without a stop: *a direct flight to Rome.* **10.** proceeding in an unbroken line of descent traced through the parents, grandparents, etc.: *a direct descendant of John Adams.* **11.** personal or immediate: *direct contact with the voters.* **12.** straightforward or frank; open; honest: *a direct answer.* **13.** absolute or exact: *the direct opposite; a direct hit.* —*adv.* **14.** in a direct manner; directly; straight: *Answer me direct.* —**di·rect/ness,** *n.*

direct/ cur/rent, an electric current that flows continuously in one direction, like that from a battery. *Abbr.:* DC, D.C., dc, d.c. See also **alternating current.**

di·rec·tion (di rek/shən, dī rek/shən), *n.* **1.** management or guidance; supervision: *The entire trip will be under the direction of Mr. Allen.* **2.** the line along which anything lies, faces, moves, etc.: *We were walking in the direction of the house.* **3.** the point or area toward which something faces or is moving: *That direction is north.* **4.** a tendency or inclination; line of thought or action: *Keep thinking in that direction and you'll get the answer.* **5.** a command, order, or instruction: *directions for making a kite.* **6.** a name and address written on a letter, package, etc., showing where it should be delivered. **7.** the job of guiding actors and supervising other elements in the presentation of a stage play, movie, etc. —**di·rec/tion·al,** *adj.*

di·rec·tive (di rek/tiv, dī rek/tiv), *n.* an official instruction or direction: *a directive to evacuate all villages in the area of flooding.*

di·rect·ly (di rekt/lē, dī rekt/lē), *adv.* **1.** in a direct line, way, or manner; straight: *Go directly home.* **2.** at once; immediately: *Stop that directly!* **3.** soon or shortly; presently: *They'll be here directly.* **4.** absolutely or exactly; precisely: *It's directly opposite the store.* **5.** next in line or order; just; immediately: *Your car is parked directly behind mine.*

direct/ ob/ject, a word, phrase, or clause expressing the person or thing that receives the action of a verb. In the sentence *John hit the ball, ball* is the direct object of the verb.

di·rec·tor (di rek/tər, dī rek/tər), *n.* **1.** a person who directs, manages, supervises, etc., such as one who is in charge of the direction of a movie, or someone who helps to control and manage a company or corporation. **2.** anything that directs or guides, such as a device that figures distance, direction, etc., of an enemy airplane or missile.

di·rec·to·ry (di rek/tə rē, dī rek/tə rē), *n., pl.* **di·rec·to·ries.** a listing of names and addresses or other information: *a telephone directory.*

dire·ful (dīər/fəl), *adj.* **1.** dreadful or terrible: *a direful day of battle.* **2.** indicating or foretelling misfortune or disaster: *a direful omen.*

dirge (dûrj), *n.* **1.** a somber musical composition to be performed at a funeral. **2.** a musical composition that resembles a dirge in being slow, mournful, etc.

dir·i·gi·ble (dir/ə jə bəl), *n.* a usually cigar-shaped balloon having rudders and engines so that its flight can be directed.

dirk (dûrk), *n.* a dagger.

dirt (dûrt), *n.* **1.** anything, such as mud, grime, dust, etc., that can soil something or make it unclean; filth. **2.** earth or soil: *to dig in the dirt.* **3.** something that is vile, mean, or worthless: *This book is just dirt.* **4.** gossip, esp. harmful or cruel gossip: *That magazine prints a lot of dirt.*

dirt·y (dûr/tē), *adj.*, **dirt·i·er, dirt·i·est. 1.** soiled with dirt; unclean: *dirty clothes.* **2.** spreading dirt or soiling; full of dirt: *dirty smoke.* **3.** mean or nasty: *a dirty trick.* **4.** in bad taste; vulgar: *a dirty joke.* **5.** hard or unpleasant: *He left the dirty work to me.* **6.** not fair or sportsmanlike: *a dirty fighter.* **7.** insulting or rude; full of or showing anger or contempt: *a dirty look.* **8.** dingy or murky; not clear or bright; darkish: *a dirty yellow.* **9.** (of the weather) stormy; rainy and windy. —*v.*, **dirt·ied, dirt·y·ing. 10.** to make or become dirty: *to dirty one's shirt; curtains that dirty too easily.* —**dirt/i·ness,** *n.*

dis-, a prefix meaning **1.** away or out: *dislodge; discharge.* **2.** opposite of: *dishonor; disloyal.* **3.** reverse of: *disorganize; disarrange.*

dis·a·bil·i·ty (dis/ə bil/i tē), *n., pl.* for defs. 2, 3 **dis·a·bil·i·ties. 1.** a lack of adequate physical or mental strength or ability; incapacity; inability: *Some soldiers were left behind because of disability.* **2.** a physical or mental handicap or flaw: *Despite his disability he plays a good game of golf.* **3.** anything that is likely to cause disability or put one at a disadvantage: *His temper is a serious disability.*

dis·a·ble (dis ā/bəl), *v.*, **dis·a·bled, dis·a·bling.** to make incapable or less capable; cripple; incapacitate:

He was disabled by a bad fall on the icy sidewalk.

dis·a·buse (dis'ə byōoz'), *v.*, **dis·a·bused, dis·a·bus·ing.** to free (a person) from a mistaken idea or error; set right: *His friends disabused him of his belief in Santa Claus.*

dis·ad·van·tage (dis'əd van'tij), *n.* 1. an unfavorable position or condition. 2. something that puts one into an unfavorable position or state: *Missing school can be a real disadvantage.* 3. injury or harm to someone's reputation, well-being, etc.; loss: *The change of plans worked to my disadvantage.*

dis·ad·van·ta·geous (dis ad'vən tā'jəs), *adj.* causing or involving disadvantage; unfavorable: *It is disadvantageous to be the visiting team rather than the home team.*

dis·af·fect·ed (dis'ə fek'tid), *adj.* not contented or loyal; hostile; embittered: *As the war dragged on, the number of disaffected citizens increased.*

dis·a·gree (dis'ə grē'), *v.*, **dis·a·greed, dis·a·gree·ing.** 1. to fail to agree; be different; differ: *Your story disagrees with hers.* 2. to differ in opinion: *I disagree with your political views.* 3. to quarrel; argue: *They disagreed violently before class.* 4. to cause physical discomfort or illness: *Eggs disagree with me.*

dis·a·gree·a·ble (dis'ə grē'ə bəl), *adj.* 1. unpleasant or offensive: *a disagreeable experience.* 2. unpleasant in manner; ill-tempered: *a cold, disagreeable person.* —**dis'a·gree'a·ble·ness,** *n.* —**dis'a·gree'a·bly,** *adv.*

dis·a·gree·ment (dis'ə grē'mənt), *n.* 1. difference in opinion: *I expressed my disagreement with his statement.* 2. a quarrel or argument: *We had a terrible disagreement.* 3. lack of agreement; difference: *disagreement among the witnesses' testimonies.*

dis·al·low (dis'ə lou'), *v.* 1. to refuse to allow; reject; veto: *to disallow a claim for damages.* 2. to refuse to accept as true or valid: *to disallow an explanation.* —**dis'al·low'a·ble,** *adj.*

dis·ap·pear (dis'ə pēr'), *v.* 1. to vanish from sight: *The submarine disappeared under the water.* 2. to cease to exist or be known; pass away; end: *Once he started to talk, his shyness disappeared.*

dis·ap·pear·ance (dis'ə pēr'əns), *n.* the act of disappearing; a passing out of sight or out of existence: *His disappearance is a mystery.*

dis·ap·point (dis'ə point'), *v.* to fail to live up to the hopes or expectations of (someone): *Rather than disappoint you I'd better not promise to come.* —**dis'ap·point'ing·ly,** *adv.*

dis·ap·point·ed (dis'ə poin'tid), *adj.* depressed or discouraged because what one expected or hoped for did not happen: *She was disappointed she didn't get a part in the play.* —**dis'ap·point'ed·ly,** *adv.*

dis·ap·point·ment (dis'ə point'mənt), *n.* 1. a person or thing that disappoints: *That horse was a real disappointment, and he never did win a race.* 2. the act of disappointing: *I can't stand another disappointment like that.* 3. the state or feeling of being disappointed: *to suffer from disappointment.*

dis·ap·prov·al (dis'ə prōo'vəl), *n.* the act of disap-

proving; a feeling or judgment that is unfavorable to something or condemns it: *Mother showed her disapproval of the movie by turning off the TV.*

dis·ap·prove (dis'ə prōov'), *v.*, **dis·ap·proved, dis·ap·prov·ing.** to regard (something) as wrong or bad; condemn: *to disapprove of war.* —**dis'ap·prov'ing·ly,** *adv.*

dis·arm (dis ärm'), *v.* 1. to take away a weapon or weapons from: *to disarm a prisoner.* 2. to lay down one's weapons: *The knights disarmed before approaching the king.* 3. to take away the hostility or suspicions of; make friendly: *His frank and honest explanations disarmed us.* 4. (of a nation) to limit or reduce the armed forces. —**dis·arm'ing·ly,** *adv.*

dis·ar·ma·ment (dis är'mə mənt), *n.* 1. the cutting down of or limitation of the size, equipment, and armament of a nation's armed forces. 2. the act of disarming: *the disarmament of soldiers.*

dis·ar·range (dis'ə rānj'), *v.*, **dis·ar·ranged, dis·ar·rang·ing.** to disturb the arrangement of something; disorder; unsettle: *The living room furniture was disarranged by the children's game.* —**dis'ar·range'ment,** *n.*

dis·ar·ray (dis'ə rā'), *v.* 1. to throw into a state of disorder; unsettle; confuse: *The storm disarrayed the party decorations in the garden.* —*n.* 2. disorder or confusion: *The army retreated in disarray.* 3. a disorderly or careless state of dress.

dis·as·ter (di zas'tər), *n.* a terrible event that causes great damage or suffering. [from the Italian word *disastro,* which comes from *dis-* "bad, ill" + *astro* "star." It was superstitiously believed that the stars brought good or bad luck]

dis·as·trous (di zas'trəs), *adj.* causing great damage or harm; ruinous; calamitous: *a disastrous forest fire.* —**dis·as'trous·ly,** *adv.* —**dis·as'trous·ness,** *n.*

dis·a·vow (dis'ə vou'), *v.* to deny knowledge of or responsibility for (something): *He disavowed the reports that he would resign.* —**dis'a·vow'al,** *n.*

dis·band (dis band'), *v.* to break up or dissolve (an organization, military group, or the like); disperse: *The soldiers disbanded after the armistice.*

dis·bar (dis bär'), *v.*, **dis·barred, dis·bar·ring.** to remove (a lawyer) officially from the legal profession and prevent him from practicing law: *He was disbarred for trying to bribe a juror.*

dis·be·lief (dis'bi lēf'), *n.* refusal to believe or accept as true: *His face showed his disbelief.*

dis·be·lieve (dis'bi lēv'), *v.*, **dis·be·lieved, dis·be·liev·ing.** to refuse to believe or to reject belief in: *to disbelieve all magical and superstitious practices.*

dis·bur·den (dis bûr'dᵊn), *v.* to remove a burden, worry, responsibility, etc., from (someone or something); unburden: *to disburden a mule; to disburden one's mind of doubt.*

dis·burse (dis bûrs'), *v.*, **dis·bursed, dis·burs·ing.** to pay out (money); spend; expend: *to disburse profits from a rummage sale.*

dis·burse·ment (dis bûrs'mənt), *n.* 1. a disbursing

or paying out of money. **2.** money paid out or spent.

disc (disk), *n.* another spelling of **disk.**

dis·card (di skärd′), *v.* **1.** to cast aside or get rid of (something) that one no longer wants or that is useless: *to discard old shoes.* **2.** to throw out (a card) from one's hand when one is playing cards. —*n.* (dis′kärd). **3.** a thing or person that has been discarded.

dis·cern (di sûrn′, di zûrn′), *v.* to see or perceive with the senses or the mind; recognize; apprehend: *to discern a sail on the horizon; to discern right from wrong.* —**dis·cern′i·ble, dis·cern′a·ble,** *adj.*

dis·cern·ing (di sûr′ning, di zûr′ning), *adj.* showing good judgment and understanding: *a discerning review of a concert.* —**dis·cern′ing·ly,** *adv.*

dis·cern·ment (di sûrn′mənt, di zûrn′mənt), *n.* **1.** sharpness of judgment; good understanding: *He showed discernment in the way he handled the problem.* **2.** the act of discerning; perception.

dis·charge (dis chärj′), *v.,* **dis·charged, dis·charg·ing.** **1.** to fire or shoot (a weapon or missile): *to discharge a gun.* **2.** to unload or release: *The ship is discharging its cargo.* **3.** to pour forth or give off (something): *That engine is discharging oil.* **4.** to do, perform, or fulfill (a responsibility, job, etc.): *The soldier discharged his duties efficiently.* **5.** to dismiss or fire: *He was discharged from his job.* **6.** to release or dismiss (usually fol. by *from*): *to discharge children early from school.* **7.** to lose electrical charge; give off electrical energy. —*n.* (dis′chärj, dis chärj′). **8.** the act or process of discharging, for example a giving off of electrical energy. **9.** a document showing that one has been officially released from the army, prison, etc. **10.** something that is discharged, such as an electric spark or flash. **11.** a flow from some part of the body: *a discharge of mucus from the nose.*

dis·ci·ple (di sī′pəl), *n.* **1.** a follower or pupil: *a disciple of Einstein.* **2.** one of the followers of Jesus Christ.

dis·ci·pli·nar·i·an (dis′ə plə nâr′ē ən), *n.* a person who enforces discipline or who believes that discipline should be enforced strictly: *My grandfather was a stern disciplinarian.*

dis·ci·pli·nar·y (dis′ə plə ner′ē), *adj.* consisting of or used as discipline: *disciplinary action.*

dis·ci·pline (dis′ə plin), *n.* **1.** the training of a person or animal to act according to rules or in a proper manner: *military discipline.* **2.** punishment used to correct or train: *Those who are guilty will be subject to discipline.* **3.** training or learning that is a part of life itself: *the discipline of growing up.* **4.** behavior that is according to the rules; self-control: *The discipline of a fireman helps to save lives.* —*v.,* **dis·ci·plined, dis·ci·plin·ing.** **5.** to train to behave in an orderly or obedient way: *to discipline new troops.* **6.** to punish or correct: *to discipline a runaway boy.*

dis·claim (dis klām′), *v.* **1.** to deny knowledge of (something); disavow; disown: *to disclaim any part in the plot.* **2.** to renounce or set aside a right or claim to (something). —**dis·claim′er,** *n.*

dis·close (di sklōz′), *v.,* **dis·closed, dis·clos·ing. 1.** to

make known; reveal: *He was accused of disclosing government secrets.* **2.** to reveal to view; cause to be seen: *The fog lifted and disclosed a nearby island.*

dis·clo·sure (di sklō′zhər), *n.* **1.** the act of disclosing or making known; revelation. **2.** something that is disclosed; a revelation: *a startling disclosure.*

dis·col·or (dis kul′ər), *v.* **1.** to change or spoil the color of; fade or stain: *The sunlight discolored the curtains.* **2.** to change color; become faded or stained: *This fabric discolors too easily.*

dis·col·or·a·tion (dis kul′ə rā′shən), *n.* **1.** the act or process of discoloring. **2.** the state of being discolored. **3.** a discolored mark or place; stain; bruise.

dis·com·fit (dis kum′fit), *v.* **1.** to thwart or block the plans of (someone): *His quick thinking discomfited the bandits.* **2.** to embarrass or confuse: *to be discomfited by a difficult question.* —**dis·com·fi·ture** (dis-kum′fi chər), *n.*

dis·com·fort (dis kum′fərt), *n.* **1.** hardship; annoyance, or mild pain: *The dentist doesn't really hurt, but you may feel some discomfort.* **2.** anything that causes hardship, annoyance, or mild pain: *Walking the whole distance will be a discomfort.* —*v.* **3.** to make uncomfortable, uneasy, or mildly unhappy.

dis·com·pose (dis′kəm pōz′), *v.,* **dis·com·posed, dis·com·pos·ing.** to disturb the calm or composure of (someone); upset; perturb: *Her rudeness discomposed me.* —**dis·com·po·sure** (dis′kəm pō′zhər), *n.*

dis·con·cert (dis′kən sûrt′), *v.* to upset, confuse, or annoy; ruffle: *The pitcher was disconcerted by the heckling.* —**dis′con·cert′ing·ly,** *adv.*

dis·con·nect (dis′kə nekt′), *v.* to cut or break off the connection of or between: *to disconnect a telephone; to disconnect two wires.*

dis·con·nect·ed (dis′kə nek′tid), *adj.* **1.** not connected. **2.** not developed in a logical or reasonable way; jumbled; mixed up: *We were confused by his disconnected speech.* —**dis′con·nect′ed·ly,** *adv.*

dis·con·so·late (dis kon′sə lit), *adj.* sad or heartbroken; inconsolable: *Homesickness made him disconsolate.* —**dis′con·so·late·ly,** *adv.*

dis·con·tent (dis′kən tent′), *n.* **1.** Also, **dis′con·tent′ment.** dissatisfaction or resentment; a restless desire for a change, improvement, or the like: *He was full of discontent because he couldn't find a job.* —*v.* **2.** to make (someone) discontented.

dis·con·tent·ed (dis′kən ten′tid), *adj.* uneasy in mind; dissatisfied; restlessly unhappy: *My sister has been sulky and discontented for a week now.* —**dis′con·tent′ed·ly,** *adv.*

dis·con·tin·ue (dis′kən tin′yoo), *v.,* **dis·con·tin·ued, dis·con·tin·u·ing. 1.** to put an end to; stop: *to discontinue a subscription.* **2.** to come to an end; stop; cease.

dis·con·tin·u·ous (dis′kən tin′yoo əs), *adj.* not continuous; interrupted; broken off at times: *discontinuous broadcasting from a radio station.*

dis·cord (dis′kôrd), *n.* **1.** disagreement or conflict; strife: *discord between father and son; discord among nations.* **2.** any confused, harsh noise. **3.** an unpleasant combination of musical sounds; dissonance.

dis·cord·ant (dis kôr′d^ənt), *adj.* **1.** disagreeing or opposing: *discordant opinions.* **2.** inharmonious or harsh; dissonant: *the discordant sounds of traffic.*

dis·co·theque (dis′kə tek′), *n.* a cabaret that provides dancing to recorded music.

dis·count (dis′kount, dis kount′), *v.* **1.** to deduct or subtract (a sum of money) from a price or charge: *to discount $25 from the price of a car.* **2.** to offer for sale or sell at a reduced price: *The store has discounted all its winter coats.* **3.** to consider as exaggerated or less than true: *to discount someone's boasts.* —*n.* (dis′kount). **4.** an amount of money deducted or taken off: *a $5 discount on a dress.*

dis·coun·te·nance (dis koun′t^ənəns), *v.*, **dis·coun·te·nanced, dis·coun·te·nanc·ing. 1.** to embarrass or disconcert; abash: *to be discountenanced by teasing.* **2.** to show disapproval of; treat with disfavor: *to discountenance practical jokes.*

dis·cour·age (di skûr′ij), *v.*, **dis·cour·aged, dis·cour·ag·ing. 1.** to take away away the courage, hope, or confidence of: *Bad roads discouraged the travelers. He was discouraged by my criticism.* **2.** to persuade (someone) not to do something; deter (usually fol. by *from*): *The weather reports discouraged us from going.* **3.** to hinder or obstruct: *The steep, rocky land discouraged settlement.* —**dis·cour′ag·ing·ly,** *adv.*

dis·cour·age·ment (di skûr′ij mənt), *n.* **1.** the act of discouraging. **2.** the state being discouraged; depression: *Her discouragement is interfering with her work.* **3.** something that discourages: *His poor health was a discouragement.*

dis·course (dis′kôrs), *n.* **1.** talk or conversation, esp. on serious subjects: *The Greeks were masters of discourse.* **2.** a formal discussion of a subject in speech or writing, for example a sermon, essay, or treatise. —*v.* (dis kôrs′), **dis·coursed, dis·cours·ing. 3.** to converse or talk, esp. on a serious subject.

dis·cour·te·ous (dis kûr′tē əs), *adj.* not courteous; impolite or rude: *It's discourteous to keep interrupting someone.* —**dis·cour′te·ous·ly,** *adv.*

dis·cour·te·sy (dis kûr′tə sē), *n., pl.* for def. 2 **dis·cour·te·sies. 1.** lack of courtesy; rudeness. **2.** a discourteous or rude act.

dis·cov·er (di skuv′ər), *v.* **1.** to gain sight or knowledge of something for the first time: *to discover a cave; to discover a new medicine.* **2.** to notice or realize: *We were halfway there when we discovered we'd forgotten Tim.* —**dis·cov′er·er,** *n.*

dis·cov·er·y (di skuv′ə rē), *n., pl.* **dis·cov·er·ies. 1.** the act of discovering something: *the discovery of America.* **2.** something that is discovered: *Electricity was an important discovery.*

dis·cred·it (dis kred′it), *v.* **1.** to harm the reputation or good name of: *He tried to discredit his opponent in the election.* **2.** to show to be untrue; destroy confidence in: *Modern science has discredited magical practices.* **3.** to disbelieve; put no faith in: *We had good reason to discredit that witness.* —*n.* **4.** loss or lack of good reputation; disrepute. **5.** something that

damages someone's reputation or good name: *His arrest was a discredit to his family.* **6.** disbelief or distrust: *His ideas have fallen into discredit.*

dis·cred·it·a·ble (dis kred′i tə bəl), *adj.* bringing discredit; disgraceful: *discreditable behavior.*

dis·creet (di skrēt′), *adj.* careful in behavior and speech, esp. with regard to matters that might cause embarrassment; prudent: *a tactful, discreet person.* —**dis·creet′ly,** *adv.* —**dis·creet′ness,** *n.*

dis·crep·an·cy (di skrep′ən sē), *n., pl.* **dis·crep·an·cies.** inconsistency, difference, or disagreement: *There is a discrepancy between your story and his.*

dis·cre·tion (di skresh′ən), *n.* **1.** the power or right to decide or act according to one's own judgment: *The choice of colors was left to my discretion.* **2.** the quality of being discreet or careful of what one says; prudence: *He threw discretion to the winds and blurted out the secret.* —**dis·cre′tion·ar·y,** *adj.*

dis·crim·i·nate (di skrim′ə nāt′), *v.*, **dis·crim·i·nat·ed, dis·crim·i·nat·ing. 1.** to treat (a person) in an unfavorable or favorable way because of his race, religion, wealth, etc.: *That company discriminates against foreigners in its hiring.* **2.** to notice or see a difference; distinguish accurately: *He has trouble discriminating between green and blue.*

dis·crim·i·nat·ing (di skrim′ə nā′tiñ), *adj.* able to distinguish fine differences in an intelligent way; having or showing good judgment and taste: *a discriminating critic.* —**dis·crim′i·nat′ing·ly,** *adv.*

dis·crim·i·na·tion (di skrim′ə nā′shən), *n.* **1.** prejudice, or prejudiced treatment of a person, group, etc.: *Discrimination still exists in many organizations.* **2.** the act of distinguishing or seeing differences. **3.** the power of making fine distinctions; accurate judgment.

dis·crim·i·na·to·ry (di skrim′ə nə tôr′ē), *adj.* showing prejudice, or used to discriminate: *That law is discriminatory.*

dis·cur·sive (di skûr′siv), *adj.* **1.** lengthy or rambling. **2.** proceeding by reasoning or logical argument. —**dis·cur′sive·ness,** *n.*

dis·cus (dis′kəs), *n., pl.* **dis·cus·es.** a circular disk, usually of wood with a metal rim, for throwing in a sports competition. [from the Greek word *diskos*, which comes from *dikein* "to throw"]

Discus

dis·cuss (di skus′), *v.* to consider (a matter) by talking it over or writing about it: *The newspapers are all discussing the coming elections.*

dis·cus·sion (di skush′ən), *n.* argument, talk, or debate; the act of considering something by talking it over or writing about it: *a discussion of current problems; new rules that caused a lot of discussion.*

dis·dain (dis dān′), *v.* **1.** to look upon or treat as beneath oneself: *to disdain manual labor.* **2.** to consider unworthy of notice: *He disdained to answer our invitation.* —*n.* **3.** a feeling of contempt; scorn: *I* *have nothing but disdain for cruel people.* —**dis·dain′ful,** *adj.* —**dis·dain′ful·ly,** *adv.*

dis·ease (di zēz′), *n.* **1.** a condition of the body or some part of it in which there is improper function, pain, or other abnormality; sickness; illness; ailment. **2.** any similar condition in an animal or plant. —**dis·eased′,** *adj.*

dis·em·bark (dis′em bärk′), *v.* to put or go on shore from a ship; land: *The passengers are disembarking.* —**dis·em·bar·ka·tion** (dis em′bär kā′shən), *n.*

dis·em·bod·ied (dis′em bod′ēd), *adj.* separated from or existing without a body: *disembodied spirits.*

dis·en·chant (dis′en chant′), *v.* to take away the illusions of; disillusion: *I was disenchanted by my trip to South America.* —**dis′en·chant′ment,** *n.*

dis·en·gage (dis′en gāj′), *v.,* **dis·en·gaged, dis·en·gag·ing. 1.** to unfasten or become unfastened; separate: *to disengage a horse from a carriage.* **2.** to free (oneself) from an obligation or entanglement; withdraw. —**dis′en·gage′ment,** *n.*

dis·en·tan·gle (dis′en tang′gəl), *v.,* **dis·en·tan·gled, dis·en·tan·gling. 1.** to free from entanglement; untangle (often fol. by *from*): *You'd better disentangle the cat from the yarn.* **2.** to become untangled or free of entanglement.

dis·fa·vor (dis fā′vər), *n.* **1.** displeasure or dislike: *He feared the king's disfavor.* **2.** the state of being out of favor: *to be in disfavor with one's employer.* **3.** an unkind or harmful act: *You did her a disfavor by tattling.*

dis·fig·ure (dis fig′yər), *v.,* **dis·fig·ured, dis·fig·ur·ing.** to spoil or mar the appearance of; deface: *A scar disfigured her face.*

dis·fran·chise (dis fran′chīz), *v.,* **dis·fran·chised, dis·fran·chis·ing.** to take away a right from (a citizen), esp. the right to vote.

dis·gorge (dis gôrj′), *v.,* **dis·gorged, dis·gorg·ing.** to vomit forth; throw out or eject: *The whale disgorged Jonah on the beach.*

dis·grace (dis grās′), *n.* **1.** shame or dishonor: *the disgrace of being known as a liar.* **2.** something that causes shame or dishonor: *That book is a disgrace.* **3.** a state of being out of favor; disfavor: *The dog is in disgrace and has to stay outside.* —*v.,* **dis·graced, dis·grac·ing. 4.** to bring shame or dishonor on: *He disgraced his family by his cowardice.*

dis·grace·ful (dis grās′fəl), *adj.* shameful or dishonorable; bringing disgrace or deserving disgrace: *disgraceful behavior; a disgraceful, sneaky crime.* —**dis·grace′ful·ly,** *adv.* —**dis·grace′ful·ness,** *n.*

dis·grun·tled (dis grun′t°ld), *adj.* dissatisfied or discontented; sulky: *She's moody and disgruntled this morning.*

dis·guise (dis gīz′), *v.,* **dis·guised, dis·guis·ing. 1.** to change the appearance of (someone or something) so as to hide who or what it really is, esp. in order to fool or mislead people: *The spy disguised the camera as a matchbox.* **2.** to hide or cover up: *He disguised his anger with a smile.* —*n.* **3.** something that serves to disguise or change the appearance, such as makeup or a costume: *A wig and a false mustache will be*

my disguise. **4.** the state of being disguised: *He went to the party in disguise.* **5.** the art of using disguises: *a master of disguise.* —**dis·guis′a·ble,** *adj.*

dis·gust (dis gust′), *v.* **1.** to fill with a feeling of strong dislike; sicken: *It disgusted me when I saw that bully hit a little boy.* —*n.* **2.** a strong feeling of dislike; loathing; distaste: *The princess looked at the frog with disgust.* —**dis·gust′ed·ly,** *adv.*

dis·gust·ing (dis gus′ting), *adj.* causing disgust; loathsome; sickening; revolting: *That's a disgusting way to behave.* —**dis·gust′ing·ly,** *adv.*

dish (dish), *n.* **1.** a plate, shallow bowl, or other container for holding or serving food. **2.** a particular kind of food or way of preparing food: *Rice is an inexpensive dish.* **3.** the amount held in a dish; dishful: *She ate a dish of applesauce.* —*v.* **4.** to put into or on a dish (often fol. by *up* or *out*): *to dish food onto a plate; to dish up the stew.* [from the Old English word *disc,* which comes from Latin *discus* "disk"]

dis·heart·en (dis här′t°n), *v.* to discourage or depress: *Don't let one bad mark dishearten you.*

di·shev·eled (di shev′əld), *adj.* hanging loosely or in disorder; untidy; unkempt: *uncombed, disheveled hair; rumpled, disheveled clothes.*

dis·hon·est (dis on′ist), *adj.* **1.** not honest or trustworthy; likely to lie, cheat, or steal: *We don't want any dishonest men on this police force.* **2.** showing a lack of honesty; done in order to cheat or deceive: *a dishonest way to do business.* —**dis·hon′est·ly,** *adv.*

dis·hon·es·ty (dis on′i stē), *n.* lack of honesty; a tendency to lie, cheat, or steal: *No one trusts her because she has a reputation for dishonesty.*

dis·hon·or (dis on′ər), *n.* **1.** lack or loss of honor; disgrace; shame: *The traitor brought dishonor upon his family.* **2.** a cause of shame or disgrace: *His unsportsmanlike behavior was a dishonor to our team.* **3.** an insult or slight: *You do him a dishonor by keeping him waiting.* —*v.* **4.** to bring shame or disgrace on; take away the honor of: *to dishonor one's name.*

dis·hon·or·a·ble (dis on′ər ə bəl), *adj.* showing a lack of honor or honesty; low and petty; disgraceful; shameful: *It is dishonorable to make promises you do not mean to keep.* —**dis·hon′or·a·bly,** *adv.*

dish·wash·er (dish′wosh′ər, -wô′shər), *n.* **1.** a machine for washing dishes, silverware, etc. **2.** a person who washes dishes, esp. for pay.

dis·il·lu·sion (dis′i loō′zhən), *v.* **1.** to take away an illusion or false belief from: *My little brother thought he could dig a hole to China until we disillusioned him.* —*n.* **2.** the loss of one's illusions, or the state of being disillusioned: *I remember my disillusion when I learned there was no pot of gold at the end of the rainbow.* —**dis′il·lu′sion·ment,** *n.*

dis·in·clined (dis′in klīnd′), *adj.* not inclined to do something; unwilling: *He was disinclined to listen to excuses.* —**dis·in·cli·na·tion** (dis in′klə nā′shən), *n.*

dis·in·fect (dis′in fekt′), *v.* to clean (clothing, surgical instruments, a wound, etc.) in order to destroy germs that may be present; free from infection: *Disinfect the cut with iodine before you bandage it.*

dis·in·fect·ant (dis'in fek'tənt), *n.* a substance that kills germs; antiseptic.

dis·in·her·it (dis'in her'it), *v.* to take away the inheritance of; keep (someone) from inheriting money, an estate, or the like: *to disinherit a child.*

dis·in·te·grate (di sin'tə grāt'), *v.,* **dis·in·te·grat·ed, dis·in·te·grat·ing.** 1. to separate into parts; break up; crumble: *This old house is slowly disintegrating.* 2. to break down into fragments, bits, or particles: *Rain and frost disintegrate rocks.* —**dis·in'te·gra'tion,** *n.*

dis·in·ter (dis'in tûr'), *v.,* **dis·in·terred, dis·in·ter·ring.** to take out from the earth or a grave: *to disinter a corpse.* —**dis'in·ter'ment,** *n.*

dis·in·ter·est·ed (dis in'tə res'tid), *adj.* not influenced by selfish motives or personal interest; fair; unbiased: *a judge's disinterested decision.* —**dis·in' ter·est'ed·ly,** *adv.* —**dis·in'ter·est'ed·ness,** *n.*
—**Usage.** *Disinterested* should not be used as a synonym for *uninterested. Disinterested* means impartial or without prejudice: *The committee gave a disinterested report. Uninterested* means indifferent or without interest: *Some liked the story, but others remained uninterested.*

dis·joint (dis joint'), *v.* 1. to separate the joints or joinings of; take apart at the joints: *to disjoint a roast duck.* 2. to disturb the order of; make jumbled or disconnected: *My thoughts were disjointed by the interruption.*

dis·joint·ed (dis join'tid), *adj.* 1. having the joints or connections separated: *a disjointed chicken.* 2. not connected or presented in an order that is easy to understand; rambling; mixed up: *a disjointed story.* —**dis·joint'ed·ly,** *adv.*

disk (disk), *n.* 1. any thin, flat, circular object, such as a phonograph record. 2. any surface that is flat and round, or appears to be so: *the disk of the sun.* Also, **disc.**

dis·like (dis līk'), *v.,* **dis·liked, dis·lik·ing.** 1. to have a feeling of not liking or being set against (something or someone); regard with some annoyance, disgust, or fear: *Cats dislike dogs. John dislikes rainy weather.* —*n.* 2. a feeling of annoyance, displeasure, or the like: *Most people have a dislike of criticism.*

dis·lo·cate (dis'lō kāt'), *v.,* **dis·lo·cat·ed, dis·lo·cat·ing.** to force one part of a joint out of place: *That fall dislocated his knee.* —**dis'lo·ca'tion,** *n.*

dis·lodge (dis loj'), *v.,* **dis·lodged, dis·lodg·ing.** to move or force out of a place: *to dislodge a brick from a wall; to dislodge enemy troops from a hill.*

dis·loy·al (dis loi'əl), *adj.* not loyal; unfaithful to one's promises, obligations, etc.: *It was disloyal of you to blame your friend.* —**dis·loy'al·ty,** *n.*

dis·mal (diz'məl), *adj.* 1. causing gloom or depression; sad; dreary: *dismal, rainy weather; dismal, unhappy news.* 2. very bad; clumsy; poor: *We played a dismal game.* —**dis'mal·ly,** *adv.* —**dis'mal·ness,** *n.*

dis·man·tle (dis man't³l), *v.,* **dis·man·tled, dis·man·tling.** 1. to take apart; take to pieces: *We dismantled the engine and then put it together again.* 2. to pull

down; tear down: *We had to dismantle our tree house.* 3. to remove all equipment, furnishings, etc.: *to dismantle a ship and leave it bare.*

dis·may (dis mā'), *v.* 1. to take away the courage of; frighten; distress: *The news of defeat dismayed the soldiers.* 2. to surprise in a way that disappoints or disillusions: *I was dismayed that you couldn't come.* —*n.* 3. a sudden loss of courage; alarm; fright. 4. a feeling of disappointment or disillusionment: *the dismay of learning that a friend can't be trusted.*

dis·mem·ber (dis mem'bər), *v.* 1. to divide limb from limb: *The lion dismembered its prey.* 2. to divide into parts; destroy the unity of: *Revolution dismembered the country.*

dis·miss (dis mis'), *v.* 1. to order or allow to leave: *to dismiss a class.* 2. to discharge from a job: *to dismiss an employee.* 3. to refuse to consider or believe; reject as false or worthless: *to dismiss a rumor.*

dis·miss·al (dis mis'əl), *n.* 1. the act of dismissing, or the state of being dismissed: *My dismissal forced me to look for another job.* 2. a discharge or notification that one has been released from a job, military service, or the like: *He handed me my dismissal this morning.*

dis·mount (dis mount'), *v.* 1. to get off or down from a horse, bicycle, etc. 2. to bring down from a horse or the like; unhorse: *The knight fought to dismount his opponent.* 3. to remove (something) from its mounting or setting: *to dismount a cannon.*

dis·o·be·di·ence (dis'ə bē'dē əns), *n.* lack of obedience; failure or refusal to follow an order, rule, or the like: *He was punished for disobedience.*

dis·o·be·di·ent (dis'ə bē'dē ənt), *adj.* failing or refusing to obey an order, rule, or the like; not obedient; rebellious. —**dis'o·be'di·ent·ly,** *adv.*

dis·o·bey (dis'ə bā'), *v.* to fail or refuse to obey; refuse to follow an order, rule, or the like: *She disobeyed the teacher. He's always disobeying.*

dis·or·der (dis ôr'dər), *n.* 1. lack of order, neatness, or proper arrangement; confusion: *The whole house was thrown into disorder by the wedding.* 2. an illness or disturbance of health: *Indigestion is a stomach disorder.* 3. a public disturbance: *The police rushed to the scene of the disorder.* —*v.* 4. to disturb the order or arrangement of: *His unexpected arrival disordered our plans.*

dis·or·der·ly (dis ôr'dər lē), *adj.* 1. marked by disorder; untidy: *a disorderly desk.* 2. causing trouble or a public disturbance; unruly; unlawful: *to be arrested for disorderly behavior.* —**dis·or'der·li·ness,** *n.*

dis·or·gan·ize (dis ôr'gə nīz'), *v.,* **dis·or·gan·ized, dis·or·gan·iz·ing.** to destroy the organization or order of (something); throw into confusion or disorder: *Constant interruptions disorganized the meeting.* —**dis·or'gan·i·za'tion,** *n.*

dis·own (dis ōn'), *v.* to refuse to treat or recognize as one's own; deny any connection with or responsibility for: *to disown one's son.*

dis·par·age (di spar'ij), *v.,* **dis·par·aged, dis·par·ag·**

ing. to speak of or treat as having little importance, value, interest, etc.; belittle: *She's always disparaging her sister's boyfriends.* [from the Old French word *desparagier* "to match unequally," which comes from *des-* "away, from" + *parage* "equality"] —**dis·par′age·ment,** *n.* —**dis·par′ag·ing·ly,** *adv.*

dis·par·i·ty (di spar′i tē), *n., pl.* **dis·par·i·ties.** lack of similarity or equality; difference: *There's such a disparity between the two boys it's hard to compare them.*

dis·pas·sion·ate (dis pash′ə nit), *adj.* free from strong emotion; impartial: *I made my argument as dispassionate as possible.* —**dis·pas′sion·ate·ly,** *adv.*

dis·patch (di spach′), *v.* **1.** to send off or away with speed: *to dispatch a telegram; to dispatch a messenger.* **2.** to carry out or finish (a business matter or the like) promptly and speedily. **3.** to put to death; kill: *to dispatch a wounded animal.* —*n.* **4.** the act of dispatching or sending off something: *the dispatch of a letter.* **5.** a message or report sent in haste: *a dispatch from the battlefront.* **6.** prompt or speedy action: *to work with dispatch.* Also, **despatch.**

dis·patch·er (di spach′ər), *n.* **1.** an official who oversees the departure of trains, trucks, buses, etc. **2.** any person who dispatches.

dis·pel (di spel′), *v.,* **dis·pelled, dis·pel·ling.** to drive off in different directions; scatter; cause to disappear: *to dispel fumes; to dispel fears.*

dis·pen·sa·ble (di spen′sə bəl), *adj.* capable of being dispensed with or done without; not essential: *Movies are dispensable if you want to save money.*

dis·pen·sa·ry (di spen′sə rē), *n., pl.* **dis·pen·sa·ries.** a place where medicines and medical advice are available without charge or for a low fee.

dis·pen·sa·tion (dis′pen sā′shən), *n.* **1.** a dispensing or dealing out of something; distribution: *the dispensation of medicine.* **2.** something that is given out or distributed. **3.** a particular order, system, or arrangement; administration or management. **4.** the ordering of the world under God; divine order. **5.** (in the Roman Catholic Church) permission not to follow a particular rule.

dis·pense (di spens′), *v.,* **dis·pensed, dis·pens·ing. 1.** to give out; distribute: *to dispense food to hungry people.* **2.** to carry out or administer: *to dispense the law fairly.* **3.** to prepare and give out (medicine), esp. on a prescription. **4. dispense with,** to do without; give up: *Let's dispense with roll call today.*

dis·pens·er (di spen′sər), *n.* **1.** a person or thing that dispenses. **2.** a vending machine, special container, or the like, that dispenses or releases items in small amounts: *a paper cup dispenser.*

dis·perse (di spûrs′), *v.,* **dis·persed, dis·pers·ing. 1.** to drive off or send off in various directions; scatter; cause to disappear: *The police dispersed the crowd.* **2.** to move apart or become scattered; vanish; disappear: *The audience dispersed after the show.* —**dis·per·sion** (di spûr′zhən, di spûr′shən), **dis·per′sal,** *n.*

dis·pir·it (di spir′it), *v.* to take away the spirit, hope, enthusiasm, etc., of (someone); discourage; depress: *The small catch dispirited the fishermen.*

dis·place (dis plās′), *v.,* **dis·placed, dis·plac·ing. 1.** to take the place of; take a position occupied by (something or someone else); replace: *Modern medicine has displaced magical cures.* **2.** to force (a person, group, etc.) to leave home or country: *The war displaced thousands of families.* **3.** to move or put out of the usual or proper place: *How much water does the ship displace?* **4.** to remove from a position or office; oust: *to displace a sheriff.*

displaced′ per′son, a person driven from his homeland by war or tyranny.

dis·place·ment (dis plās′mənt), *n.* **1.** a displacing of something: *the displacement of the horse and carriage by the automobile.* **2.** the state of being displaced. **3.** the weight or volume of fluid displaced by a floating or submerged body, such as a ship.

dis·play (di splā′), *v.* **1.** to show or put on view; exhibit: *to display a sign.* **2.** reveal or show; give signs of: *to display fear.* —*n.* **3.** the act of displaying something; a show or exhibition: *a display of rare coins.* **4.** a show or exhibition of something, done to impress people: *a display of wealth.*

dis·please (dis plēz′), *v.,* **dis·pleased, dis·pleas·ing.** to fail to please; annoy, bother, or offend: *Did my jokes displease him?* —**dis·pleas′ing·ly,** *adv.*

dis·pleas·ure (dis plezh′ər), *n.* annoyance or dislike; dissatisfaction; disapproval: *The courtiers feared the king's displeasure.*

dis·port (di spôrt′), *v.* to amuse (oneself); play: *The children disported themselves around the maypole.*

dis·pos·a·ble (di spō′zə bəl), *adj.* capable of being thrown away after use: *a disposable paper plate.*

dis·pos·al (di spō′zəl), *n.* **1.** a disposing of or getting rid of something: *the disposal of garbage.* **2.** a disposing or arranging of something in a particular order or position; arrangement: *a disposal of troops.* **3.** a disposing of something by gift, sale, or the like: *the disposal of surplus goods.* **4. at one's disposal,** available for one's use or enjoyment: *We had a car at our disposal during our visit.*

dis·pose (di spōz′), *v.,* **dis·posed, dis·pos·ing. 1.** to give a tendency to; incline: *Her impatience disposes her to fight with people.* **2.** to put or set in a particular order or way; arrange; adjust: *The toy soldiers were disposed in a row.* **3.** to arrange or decide matters: *Man proposes, God disposes.* **4. dispose of, a.** to get rid of; discard: *Empty the wastebaskets and dispose of the trash.* **b.** to bring to a conclusion; finish or settle: *to dispose of a problem.* —**dis·pos′er,** *n.*

dis·posed (di spōzd′), *adj.* inclined or prepared: *I am not disposed to follow his advice.*

dis·po·si·tion (dis′pə zish′ən), *n.* **1.** the general quality or nature of someone's personality; mental outlook or mood; temperament: *He has a pleasant, agreeable disposition.* **2.** a tendency or inclination: *a disposition to gamble.* **3.** arrangement or placing: *the disposition of buildings around a park.* **4.** the final settlement of a matter. **5.** disposal or bestowal by gift or sale: *the disposition of an estate in a will.*

dis·pos·sess (dis′pə zes′), *v.* **1.** to take away the property of: *When they couldn't keep up the pay-*

ments on their farm the bank dispossessed them. **2.** to deprive of the possession of anything; take away: *Illness dispossessed him of his strength.*

dis·proof (dis proŏf′), *n.* **1.** the act of disproving or showing to be false: *the disproof of a theory.* **2.** proof against something; refutation.

dis·pro·por·tion (dis′prə pôr′shən), *n.* a lack of proportion; lack of a proper relationship or balance in size, number, etc.: *a disproportion between one side of a house and the other.*

dis·pro·por·tion·ate (dis′prə pôr′shə nit), *adj.* out of proportion or not balanced with something in terms of size, number, amount, etc.: *a disproportionate share of the expenses.* —**dis′pro·por′tion·ate·ly,** *adv.*

dis·prove (dis proŏv′), *v.,* **dis·proved, dis·prov·ing.** to prove (a theory, claim, etc.) to be false or wrong; refute: *to disprove someone's statement.*

dis·put·a·ble (di spyōō′tə bəl), *adj.* capable of being disputed or argued; not completely settled; questionable; debatable: *He might make a good senator, but it's disputable.* —**dis·put′a·bly,** *adv.*

dis·pu·tant (di spyōōt′ᵊnt), *n.* a person who disputes; debater.

dis·pu·ta·tion (dis′pyōō tā′shən), *n.* the act of disputing or debating; a discussion or debate.

dis·pute (di spyōōt′), *v.,* **dis·put·ed, dis·put·ing. 1.** to argue or debate; discuss: *They were disputing the question of a 30-hour work week.* **2.** to argue against; call into question; doubt: *to dispute the wisdom of climbing a tree.* **3.** to strive or fight against; oppose: *The cattlemen disputed the presence of sheepmen on the grazing lands.* —*n.* **4.** a debate or controversy. **5.** a quarrel or argument: *a bitter family dispute.*

dis·qual·i·fy (dis kwol′ə fī′), *v.,* **dis·qual·i·fied, dis·qual·i·fy·ing. 1.** to make unqualified or unsuitable; cause to be unfit or unable to do a job or the like: *His poor eyesight disqualified him from being a pilot.* **2.** to declare ineligible to enter a contest, win a prize, etc.: *The winning horse was disqualified for bumping another horse.* —**dis·qual′i·fi·ca′tion,** *n.*

dis·qui·et (dis kwī′it), *n.* **1.** lack of calm or peacefulness; uneasiness: *There's an atmosphere of fear and disquiet in this town.* —*v.* **2.** to make uneasy or upset; trouble: *Thunderstorms disquiet our dog and make him hide.*

dis·re·gard (dis′ri gärd′), *v.* **1.** to pay no attention to; ignore: *to disregard a scolding; to disregard a warning.* —*n.* **2.** neglect or inattention; lack of regard or concern: *the lion tamer's disregard of danger.*

dis·re·pair (dis′ri pâr′), *n.* the condition of needing repair or mending; a run-down or broken-down state: *an old house in disrepair.*

dis·rep·u·ta·ble (dis rep′yə tə bəl), *adj.* **1.** having or causing a bad reputation; corrupt, dishonest, or unreliable: *disreputable business dealings.* **2.** shabby, worn-out, or broken-down: *a disreputable, noisy jalopy.* —**dis·rep′u·ta·bly,** *adv.*

dis·re·pute (dis′ri pyōōt′), *n.* the state of being in low regard; bad repute or reputation (usually preceded by *in* or *into*): *His ideas have fallen into disrepute.*

dis·re·spect (dis′ri spekt′), *n.* a lack of respect; rudeness: *You showed disrespect when you ignored her question.*

dis·re·spect·ful (dis′ri spekt′fəl), *adj.* showing disrespect; rude; impolite: *It was disrespectful to make noise during his lecture.* —**dis′re·spect′ful·ly,** *adv.* —**dis′re·spect′ful·ness,** *n.*

dis·robe (dis rōb′), *v.,* **dis·robed, dis·rob·ing.** to undress.

dis·rupt (dis rupt′), *v.* **1.** to cause disorder or confusion in; upset; interrupt: *The fire drill disrupted the morning classes.* **2.** to break apart. —**dis·rup′tion,** *n.*

dis·rup·tive (dis rup′tiv), *adj.* causing or tending to cause disorder or confusion; disrupting: *loud, disruptive remarks.* —**dis·rup′tive·ly,** *adv.* —**dis·rup′tive·ness,** *n.*

dis·sat·is·fac·tion (dis′sat is fak′shən), *n.* a feeling of not being satisfied; lack of contentment; disappointment.

dis·sat·is·fied (dis sat′is fīd′), *adj.* not satisfied or pleased: *to wear a dissatisfied expression.*

dis·sat·is·fy (dis sat′is fī′), *v.,* **dis·sat·is·fied, dis·sat·is·fy·ing.** to cause to be displeased or disappointed: *My spelling grade really dissatisfied me.*

dis·sect (di sekt′, dī sekt′), *v.* **1.** to cut (an animal body, a plant, etc.) apart in order to study its structure or its parts. **2.** to examine and study part by part; analyze: *to dissect a story.* —**dis·sec′tion,** *n.*

dis·sem·ble (di sem′bəl), *v.,* **dis·sem·bled, dis·sem·bling. 1.** to hide or give a false appearance to: *to dissemble fear by boasting.* **2.** to hide one's true motives, thoughts, etc., by pretense; speak or act hypocritically: *to lie and dissemble so that no one trusts you.* —**dis·sem′bler,** *n.*

dis·sem·i·nate (di sem′ə nāt′), *v.,* **dis·sem·i·nat·ed, dis·sem·i·nat·ing.** to scatter or spread widely: *to disseminate new ideas.* —**dis·sem′i·na′tion,** *n.*

dis·sen·sion (di sen′shən), *n.* strong disagreement; discord or conflict: *dissension among members of a political party.*

dis·sent (di sent′), *v.* **1.** to differ in opinion; disagree (often fol. by *from*): *One judge dissented from the majority opinion.* **2.** to reject the doctrines of an established church. —*n.* **3.** a difference of opinion; disagreement: *dissent among the members of a jury.* **4.** separation from an established church, esp. the Church of England. —**dis·sent′er,** *n.*

dis·ser·ta·tion (dis′ər tā′shən), *n.* an essay or thesis, esp. one written for a college degree.

dis·serv·ice (dis sûr′vis), *n.* harm or injury; a bad turn: *He did himself a disservice by taking the test when he was sick.*

dis·si·dent (dis′i dᵊnt), *adj.* **1.** disagreeing or differing in opinion, attitude, or the like: *A dissident newspaper makes people think.* —*n.* **2.** a person who disagrees or dissents. —**dis′si·dence,** *n.*

dis·sim·i·lar (di sim′ə lər), *adj.* not similar; unlike; different: *dissimilar sisters.*

dis·sim·i·lar·i·ty (di sim′ə lar′i tē), *n., pl.* **dis·sim·i·lar·i·ties.** 1. unlikeness or difference: *the dissimilarity of people.* 2. a point of difference.

dis·sim·u·late (di sim′yə lāt′), *v.,* **dis·sim·u·lat·ed, dis·sim·u·lat·ing.** to hide or disguise (one's thoughts, motives, etc.); dissemble. —**dis·sim′u·la′tion,** *n.*

dis·si·pate (dis′ə pāt′), *v.,* **dis·si·pat·ed, dis·si·pat·ing.** 1. to waste or squander: *to dissipate a fortune.* 2. to scatter in various directions; disperse: *The fan dissipated the smoke.* 3. to indulge in excessive drinking or the like; be intemperate. —**dis′si·pa′tion,** *n.*

dis·si·pat·ed (dis′ə pā′tid), *adj.* unhealthy or corrupt as a result of too much indulgence in drinking, gambling, or the like; dissolute.

dis·so·ci·ate (di sō′shē āt′, di sō′sē āt′), *v.,* **dis·so·ci·at·ed, dis·so·ci·at·ing.** to break off the association of (oneself) with something; separate: *She dissociated herself from that organization.*

dis·so·lute (dis′ə lo͞ot′), *adj.* immoral and corrupt; dissipated.

dis·so·lu·tion (dis′ə lo͞o′shən), *n.* 1. the breaking up or ending of something: *the dissolution of the feudal system.* 2. a dissolving or dispersing of a substance, such as a gas. 3. destruction, decay, or death.

dis·solve (di zolv′), *v.,* **dis·solved, dis·solv·ing.** 1. to mix (a substance) completely into another substance, esp. so that it disappears from sight: *to dissolve sugar in coffee.* 2. to cause to mix in this way: *Cleaning fluid dissolves grease spots.* 3. to break up or end: *They dissolved their partnership.* 4. to fade or fade away. —**dis·solv′a·ble,** *adj.*

dis·so·nance (dis′ə nəns), *n.* a harsh or inharmonious combination of musical tones; discord. See also **consonance.**

dis·so·nant (dis′ə nənt), *adj.* 1. out of harmony; harsh; discordant: *a dissonant chord.* 2. not in agreement or harmony with the general views, opinions, feelings, etc., of others; at variance: *There was one dissonant voice at the meeting.* —**dis′so·nant·ly,** *adv.*

dis·suade (di swād′), *v.,* **dis·suad·ed, dis·suad·ing.** to stop or prevent by advice or persuasion; persuade not to do something (usually fol. by *from*): *She dissuaded him from running away from home.* —**dis·sua·sive** (di swā′siv), *adj.*

dist., 1. distance. 2. district.

dis·taff (dis′taf), *n.* a staff or stick for holding wool and flax so that the fibers can be spun out into thread either by a spinning wheel or by hand. [from the Old English word *distæf,* which comes from *dis-* "flax" + *stæf* "staff"]

dis′taff side′, the female or maternal side of a family.

dis·tance (dis′təns), *n.* 1. the amount or extent of space between two things, points, lines, or the like: *The distance from one end of a football field to the other is 100 yards.* 2. the state of being apart or far from: *He stood off at a distance from the group.* 3. an expanse or extent of space: *to walk a great distance.* 4. a distant or far part or place: *We saw a ship*

in the distance. 5. any separation or difference in time, viewpoint, nature, etc. —*v.,* **dis·tanced, dis·tanc·ing.** 6. to leave behind at a distance, as in a race. 7. **keep one's distance,** to remain cool or aloof; not be on friendly terms: *We've both been keeping our distance since the argument.*

dis·tant (dis′tənt), *adj.* 1. far off or apart in space; not near; remote or removed (often fol. by *from*): *a town three miles distant from here.* 2. apart or far off in time: *the distant past.* 3. far apart or remote in any sense: *a distant relative.* 4. not friendly; cool: *a vague, distant smile.* —**dis′tant·ly,** *adv.*

dis·taste (dis tāst′), *n.* dislike or aversion: *a distaste for dull work.*

dis·taste·ful (dis tāst′fəl), *adj.* causing dislike or disgust; unpleasant: *I find scrubbing floors distasteful.* —**dis·taste′ful·ly,** *adv.* —**dis·taste′ful·ness,** *n.*

dis·tem·per (dis tem′pər), *n.* 1. an infectious, often fatal disease of dogs, causing sluggishness, fever, vomiting, and loss of appetite. 2. a similar disease of cats.

dis·tend (di stend′), *v.* to swell or expand: *to distend a balloon with a pump.*

dis·till (di stil′), *v.* 1. to purify (a liquid) by vaporizing it and condensing the vapor. 2. to extract or get by this process: *to distill whiskey; to distill gasoline.* 3. to extract or get (the truth, main idea, or the like) by separating it from what is not necessary or useful: *to distill the most important points from a chapter.* 4. to give off or form into drops. —**dis·till′er,** *n.*

dis·til·la·tion (dis′t^əlā′shən), *n.* 1. the process of distilling. 2. the state of being distilled. 3. something that is produced by distillation.

dis·till·er·y (di stil′ə rē), *n., pl.* **dis·till·er·ies.** a place where the distilling of alcoholic liquors is done.

dis·tinct (di stingkt′), *adj.* 1. not the same; separate or different: *three distinct kinds of turtles.* 2. clear to the mind or senses; plain; unmistakable: *a distinct shout for help.* 3. unusual or rare; notable: *a distinct honor.* —**dis·tinct′ly,** *adv.* —**dis·tinct′ness,** *n.*

dis·tinc·tion (di stingk′shən), *n.* 1. the making of a difference, or a recognition of a difference: *She must learn to make distinctions between right and wrong.* 2. a difference, or the points of difference: *to show the distinction between monkeys and apes.* 3. a quality or characteristic that separates or marks off something: *the distinction of being the oldest house in town.* 4. a mark of honor or favor: *He was awarded many distinctions for his work in science.* 5. marked superiority; first-rate quality or character: *a violinist of distinction.*

dis·tinc·tive (di stingk′tiv), *adj.* serving to distinguish or mark off something or someone: *You can't miss him because of his distinctive red hair.* —**dis·tinc′tive·ly,** *adv.* —**dis·tinc′tive·ness,** *n.*

dis·tin·guish (di sting′gwish), *v.* 1. to mark off as different; be characteristic of (often fol. by *from*): *His height distinguished him from the other boys.* 2. to recognize as distinct or different: *I can't distinguish their voices on the telephone.* 3. to perceive or make out clearly by the sight or other senses; recognize: *I can't distinguish anything in this fog.* **4.** to set apart from others; make noticeable or famous: *She distinguished herself by getting the highest score.* —**dis·tin′guish·a·ble,** *adj.*

dis·tin·guished (di sting′gwisht), *adj.* **1.** excellent, honored, or famous: *a distinguished work; a distinguished historian.* **2.** elegant; having the appearance of being or belonging to someone famous: *a distinguished, elderly man; distinguished manners.*

dis·tort (di stôrt′), *v.* **1.** to give a false or one-sided appearance or meaning to: *The newspapers distorted the facts of the crime.* **2.** to twist out of shape; make crooked or deformed: *The explosion distorted the iron gate.* —**dis·tor′tion,** *n.*

dis·tract (di strakt′), *v.* **1.** to draw the mind or attention away from something: *The baseball game distracted him from his work.* **2.** to disturb or trouble greatly: *Worry distracted her so that she couldn't think.* **3.** to amuse; provide entertainment for: *The television show distracted the hospital patients.*

dis·trac·tion (di strak′shən), *n.* **1.** the act of distracting or drawing away the mind or attention: *the distraction of a crying baby with a toy.* **2.** the state of being distracted: *Distraction interfered with his work.* **3.** mental distress or upset: *to drive someone to distraction.* **4.** something that distracts. **5.** something that amuses: *Fishing is my favorite distraction.*

dis·traught (di strôt′), *adj.* extremely troubled or upset; distracted; crazed: *She was distraught when her dog was lost.*

dis·tress (di stres′), *n.* **1.** extreme suffering, pain, or sorrow; agony. **2.** anything that causes suffering, trouble, or sorrow. **3.** a state of misfortune, danger, or of needing help immediately: *a ship in distress.* —*v.* **4.** to cause someone suffering, trouble, or sorrow: *The news of your accident distressed us.* —**dis·tress′ful,** *adj.* —**dis·tress′ing·ly,** *adv.*

dis·trib·ute (di strib′yoot), *v.,* **dis·trib·ut·ed, dis·trib·ut·ing.** **1.** to divide or give out in shares: *to distribute prizes.* **2.** to spread through a space or over an area: *Try to distribute the grass seed evenly.* **3.** to divide into groups or categories: *to distribute mail.*

dis·tri·bu·tion (dis′trə byoo′shən), *n.* **1.** the act of distributing: *the distribution of exam papers.* **2.** the manner or way in which something is distributed; arrangement: *an uneven distribution of snow on the ground.* **3.** the total number of items distributed or sold: *The distribution of our school paper is now 800.*

dis·trib·u·tive (di strib′yə tiv), *adj.* **1.** of or concerning distribution; serving to distribute, divide, or classify. **2.** (of a mathematical operation) producing the same result when acting on a whole set as when acting on each member of the set separately. Multiplication is distributive with regard to addition. An example is $5(3+8) = (5 \times 3) + (5 \times 8)$

dis·trib·u·tor (di strib′yə tər), *n.* **1.** a person or thing that distributes. **2.** a device on internal-combustion engines for distributing the voltage in the proper order to the spark plugs.

dis·trict (dis′trikt), *n.* **1.** a division of territory, such as a country or state, marked off for a special purpose: *an election district.* **2.** a region or locality: *the theater district.* —*v.* **3.** to divide into districts.

dis′trict attor′ney, an officer who acts as attorney for the people or government of a district.

Dis′trict of Colum′bia, a federal area in the E United States on the Potomac, established for the capital, Washington: governed by Congress. 69 sq. mi.

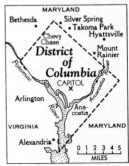

dis·trust (dis trust′), *v.* **1.** to regard with doubt or suspicion; have no trust in; suspect: *I distrusted his version of the story because it was so different from the others.* —*n.* **2.** a lack of trust or confidence; suspicion; doubt. —**dis·trust′ful,** *adj.*

dis·turb (di stûrb′), *v.* **1.** to interrupt the quiet, rest, or peace of: *The telephone disturbed me while I was napping.* **2.** to interfere with; hinder: *The rain disturbed our plans for a picnic.* **3.** to throw into disorder; unsettle: *The pebble disturbed the smooth surface of the water.* **4.** to trouble or worry; perplex: *His strange behavior disturbed us.* —**dis·turb′ing·ly,** *adv.*

dis·turb·ance (di stûr′bəns), *n.* **1.** the act of disturbing, or an instance of being disturbed: *to study without any disturbance.* **2.** something that disturbs: *The phone call was a disturbance.* **3.** an outbreak of disorder: *Political disturbances shook the city.*

dis·un·ion (dis yoon′yən), *n.* **1.** separation; division. **2.** lack of unity; disagreement.

dis·u·nite (dis′yoo nit′), *v.,* **dis·u·nit·ed, dis·u·nit·ing.** to destroy the union of; separate; divide.

dis·use (dis yoos′), *n.* the condition or state of not being used: *Some customs are falling into disuse.*

ditch (dich), *n.* **1.** a long, narrow hole dug in the ground for draining or irrigating land; trench. —*v.* **2.** to dig a ditch or ditches in or around. **3.** to derail (a train) or force (a car, bus, etc.) off the road. **4.** to crash-land (an airplane) on water. **5.** *Slang.* to get rid of; escape from: *Let's ditch him at the corner.*

dith·er (dith′ər), *n. Informal.* a state of flustered excitement or fear: *He was in a dither over the test.*

dit·to (dit′ō), *n., pl.* **dit·tos. 1.** the same. **2.** a mark (〃) showing the repetition of something, usually placed beneath the thing repeated, as

He walked to school yesterday.

　　〃 walks 〃 〃 today.　　[from an Italian word, which is another form of *detto* "said, aforesaid"]

dit·ty (dit′ē), *n., pl.* **dit·ties. 1.** a poem intended to be sung. **2.** a short, simple song.

di·van (di van′, dī′van), *n.* a long couch, often without arms or back.

dive (dīv), *v.*, **dived** *or* **dove** (dōv); **dived; div·ing.** 1. to plunge headfirst into water. 2. to submerge, as a submarine. 3. to plunge, fall, or descend through the air: *The acrobats dived into nets.* 4. to enter deeply into something: *to dive into one's work.* 5. to dart: *to dive into a doorway.* —*n.* 6. a jump or plunge into water. 7. a sharp descent or decline. 8. a dash, plunge, or lunge: *He made a dive for the football.* 9. *Informal.* a dingy, cheap bar or nightclub.

div·er (dī'vər), *n.* 1. a person or thing that dives. 2. a person who makes a business of diving in water, searching for pearl oysters, sunken vessels, etc.

di·verge (di vûrj', dī vûrj'), *v.*, **di·verged, di·verg·ing.** 1. to move, lie, or extend in different directions from a common point; branch off: *Two roads diverge near the river.* 2. to differ in opinion, character, form, etc.: *Our feelings about him diverge quite sharply.*

di·ver·gence (di vûr'jəns, dī vûr'jəns), *n.* the act or an instance of diverging: *a divergence in opinion.*

di·vers (dī'vərz), *adj.* several; various: *He has written divers articles about monkeys.*

di·verse (di vûrs', dī vûrs'), *adj.* of a different kind, form, character, etc.; unlike: *diverse opinions.*

di·ver·si·fy (di vûr'sə fī'), *v.*, **di·ver·si·fied, di·ver·si·fy·ing.** to make diverse; give variety to: *to diversify a diet.* —**di·ver·si·fi·ca·tion** (di vûr'sə fə kā'shən), *n.*

di·ver·sion (di vûr'zhən, dī vûr'zhən), *n.* 1. the act of diverting or turning aside: *a diversion of attention.* 2. entertainment; amusement; distraction: *Summer camp offers many diversions.* —**di·ver'sion·ar'y,** *adj.*

di·ver·si·ty (di vûr'si tē, dī vûr'si tē), *n.* the state or fact of being diverse; variety: *a diversity of ideas.*

di·vert (di vûrt', dī vûrt'), *v.* 1. to turn aside or from a path or course: *The detour diverted traffic.* 2. to distract; amuse: *to be diverted by a television show.* —**di·vert'ing·ly,** *adv.*

di·vest (di vest', dī vest'), *v.* 1. to strip of clothing, ornament, etc.: *The wind divested the trees of their leaves.* 2. to strip or deprive of anything.

di·vide (di vīd'), *v.*, **di·vid·ed, di·vid·ing.** 1. to separate into parts, groups, sections, etc. 2. to separate or part from something else: *The fence divided their land from ours.* 3. to deal out in parts; distribute in shares: *Divide the orange between us.* 4. to separate in opinion; cause to disagree: *The issue divided the senators.* 5. to distinguish the kinds of; classify: *He divided the songs according to subject.* 6. to perform division. —*n.* 7. the line or zone of higher ground between two streams: *the Continental Divide.*

div·i·dend (div'i dend'), *n.* 1. a sum of money paid out of a corporation's earnings to people who own stock or shares in the corporation. 2. (in arithmetic) the number that is divided: *In dividing 72 by 3, 72 is the dividend.* See also **divisor, quotient.**

di·vid·er (di vī'dər), *n.* 1. a person or thing that divides. 2. **dividers,** a compass having two legs, both equipped with points, used by draftsmen for transferring measurements, dividing lengths, etc.

div·i·na·tion (div'ə nā'shən), *n.* the attempt, esp. by supernatural means, to foretell future events or discover hidden knowledge.

di·vine (di vīn'), *adj.* 1. of or concerning God or a god: *divine mercy.* 2. devoted to God or a god; religious; sacred: *divine worship.* 3. godlike; heavenly: *the divine kingdom.* 4. of superhuman excellence: *a divine talent.* —*n.* 5. a scholar in religion; theologian. —*v.*, **di·vined, di·vin·ing.** 6. to discover or declare by divination; prophesy. 7. to know by intuition or insight; guess. [from the Latin word *divīnus,* which comes from *divus* "god"]

div'ing bell', an open-bottomed chamber in which persons can go underwater. Water is kept from the upper part of the chamber by the pressure of the air trapped inside.

di·vin·i·ty (di vin'i tē), *n., pl.* **di·vin·i·ties.** 1. the quality of being divine. 2. the study of religion; theology. 3. (often cap.) a divine being; God.

di·vis·i·ble (di viz'ə bəl), *adj.* 1. capable of being divided or split. 2. capable of being evenly divided, without remainder: *Nine is divisible by three.*

di·vi·sion (di vizh'ən), *n.* 1. the act of dividing, or the state of being divided: *the division of a book into chapters.* 2. (in arithmetic) the process or method of determining the number of times a certain number is contained in another number. 3. something that divides or marks a division; partition. 4. one of the parts into which a thing is divided; section. 5. separation by difference of opinion or feeling. 6. a military unit smaller than a corps and larger than a brigade or regiment.

di·vi·sor (di vī'zər), *n.* (in arithmetic) the number by which another number is divided: *In dividing 72 by 3, 3 is the divisor.* See also **dividend** (def. 2), **quotient.**

di·vorce (di vôrs'), *n.* 1. the ending of a marriage contract by legal means. 2. total separation: *a divorce between thought and action.* —*v.*, **di·vorced, di·vorc·ing.** 3. to end the marriage of by divorce: *The judge divorced the couple.* 4. to break the marriage contract with (one's spouse) by divorce. 5. to separate or isolate: *to divorce fact from fiction.*

di·vor·cee (di vôr sē', di vôr sā'), *n.* a divorced woman. Also, **di·vor·cée'.**

di·vulge (di vulj', dī vulj'), *v.*, **di·vulged, di·vulg·ing.** to disclose or reveal: *to divulge the secret.* [from the Latin word *dīvulgāre* "to make common," which comes from *vulgus* "the common people"]

Dix·ie (dik'sē), *n.* the southern states of the U.S., esp. those that were part of the Confederacy.

diz·zy (diz'ē), *adj.*, **diz·zi·er, diz·zi·est.** 1. having a feeling of whirling and a tendency to fall. 2. bewildered; confused. 3. causing a feeling of unsteadiness: *dizzy heights.* —*v.*, **diz·zied, diz·zy·ing.** 4. to make dizzy. —**diz'zi·ly,** *adv.* —**diz'zi·ness,** *n.*

Dja·kar·ta (jə kär'tə), *n.* a seaport and the capital city of Indonesia, on the NW coast of Java. Also, **Jakarta.**

dl, deciliter; deciliters.

dm, decimeter; decimeters.

DMZ, demilitarized zone.

DNA, deoxyribonucleic acid: a complex chemical compound found in the nuclei of cells that controls heredity and makes it possible for living things to produce offspring like themselves. See also **RNA.**

Dnie·per (nē′pər), *n.* a river in the W Soviet Union, flowing S to the Black Sea. 1400 mi. long.

do¹ (dōō), *v.,* **did** (did), **done** (dun), **do·ing. 1.** to perform or carry out: *to do a job.* **2.** to accomplish; finish: *He has already done it.* **3.** to be the cause of: *to do harm.* **4.** to deal with, fix, arrange, etc.: *She did her hair.* **5.** to make or prepare: *I'll do the salad.* **6.** to study or work at: *What does he do for a living?* **7.** to act or conduct oneself; behave: *Do as you're told!* **8.** to get along; manage: *He does very well on skis.* **9.** to be enough or satisfactory: *Will this do?* **10.** to render or give: *She doesn't do him justice.* —*auxiliary verb.* **11.** (used without special meaning in interrogative and negative constructions): *Do you like to swim? I don't think so.* **12.** (used to emphasize a main verb): *Do come back soon!* **13.** (used to avoid repetition of a verb): *I'll go if you do.* **14. do away with, a.** to put an end to; abolish: *This machine will do away with all that paperwork.* **b.** to kill: *He was suspected of doing away with his neighbor.* **15. do over,** to refurnish or redecorate: *We did the house over in Early American.* **16. do up, a.** to wrap and tie: *to do up a Christmas package.* **b.** to set or arrange (the hair). **c.** to dress: *Why did they do the waiters up in such funny costumes?* **17. do well by,** to behave kindly or generously toward: *He has always done well by his family.* **18. do without,** to dispense with or give up (something): *I did without candy to buy the book.* **19. have to do with, a.** be connected or associated with: *Does this have anything to do with our work yesterday?* **b.** be on friendly terms with: *I won't have anything to do with her now.* **20. make do,** to get along as well as possible: *I can't afford a new bicycle, so you'll just have to make do with the old one.* [from the Old English word *dōn*]

do² (dō), *n., pl.* **dos.** the first note of a musical scale: *C is do in the C scale.* [from Italian]

dob·bin (dob′in), *n.* a quiet, plodding horse, esp. one used for farm work.

Do·ber·man pin·scher (dō′bər mən pin′shər), one of a German breed of medium-sized, short-haired dogs having a black, brown, or blue coat with rusty brown markings.

doc·ile (dos′əl), *adj.* easily managed, trained, or taught. —**doc′ile·ly,** *adv.* —**do·cil·i·ty** (do-sil′i tē), *n.*

dock¹ (dok), *n.* **1.** a wharf. **2.** the space or waterway between two piers or wharves for receiving a ship while in port. **3.** short for **dry dock.** —*v.* **4.** to come or go into a dock or dry dock: *to dock a ship.* **5.** to join one space vehicle with another in outer space. [from Dutch]

Doberman pinscher

(27 in. high at shoulder)

dock² (dok), *n.* **1.** the solid or fleshy part of an animal's tail, as distinguished from the hair. —*v.* **2.** to cut short the tail of: *to dock a horse.* **3.** to deduct a part from: *to dock one's wages for habitual lateness.* [from Old English]

dock³ (dok), *n.* the place in a courtroom where a prisoner is placed during trial. [from the Flemish word *dok* "cage"]

dock·er (dok′ər), *n.* a laborer on shipping docks; longshoreman.

dock·et (dok′it), *n.* **1.** a list of cases in court for trial. **2.** the list of business to be taken care of by a board, council, legislative assembly, or the like. **3.** *British.* writing on a letter or document that states its contents; a label or ticket. —*v.,* **dock·et·ed, dock·et·ing. 4.** to list (a case) in the docket of a court.

dock·yard (dok′yärd′), *n.* a waterside area having docks, workshops, warehouses, etc., for building and repairing ships, storing naval vessels, etc.

doc·tor (dok′tər), *n.* **1.** a person who is licensed to practice medicine; physician, dentist, or the like. **2.** a person who has been awarded a doctor's degree. —*v.* **3.** to give medical treatment to: *to doctor a scratch.* **4.** to tamper with; falsify: *to doctor a passport.* [from a Latin word meaning "teacher," which comes from *docēre* "to teach"]

doc′tor's degree′, any of various academic degrees of the highest rank awarded by universities and some colleges for completing advanced work in a graduate or professional school, as the Doctor of Medicine (M.D.) or Doctor of Philosophy (Ph. D.).

doc·trine (dok′trin), *n.* **1.** a particular principle, position, or policy taught or advocated, usually by a church, government, etc.: *Catholic doctrines.* **2.** something taught; teachings: *religious doctrine.* —**doc·tri·nal** (dok′trə nəl), *adj.*

doc·u·ment (dok′yə mənt), *n.* **1.** a written or printed paper giving information or evidence, such as a passport or deed. —*v.* (dok′yə ment′). **2.** to furnish with documents, evidence, etc.: *He wrote a carefully documented biography of George Washington.* —**doc′u·men·ta′tion,** *n.*

doc·u·men·ta·ry (dok′yə men′tə rē), *adj.* **1.** based on documents: *a documentary history of France.* —*n., pl.* **doc·u·men·ta·ries. 2.** a film or program about an actual event, life of a real person, period of history, etc.

dod·der (dod′ər), *v.* to shake or tremble, as from old age or weakness.

Do·dec·a·nese (dō dek′ə nēz′), *n.* a group of 12 Greek Islands in the Aegean Sea, off the coast of Turkey, occupied by Italy 1911–1945.

dodge (doj), *v.,* **dodged, dodg·ing. 1.** to move aside or change position suddenly to avoid a blow or get behind something. **2.** to avoid by a sudden shift of position: *to dodge a ball.* **3.** to avoid by cunning or trickery: *to dodge a question.* —*n.* **4.** a quick, sudden jump aside or away. **5.** *Informal.* a shifty trick. —**dodg′er,** *n.*

Dodg·son (doj′sən), *n.* **Charles Lut·widge** (lut′wij). See **Carroll, Lewis.**

do·do (dō′dō), *n., pl.* **do·dos** *or* **do·does.** any of several large, clumsy, extinct birds that formerly inhabited two islands in the Indian Ocean near Madagascar. [from the Portuguese word *doudo* "silly, dodo"]

doe (dō), *n., pl.* **does** *or* **doe.** the female of deer, antelope, rabbits, and certain other animals.

do·er (dōō′ər), *n.* a person or thing that does something, esp. a person who gets things done efficiently.

does (duz), *v.* the third person singular, present tense of **do**[1]: *He does his homework every evening.*

doe·skin (dō′skin′), *n.* **1.** the skin of a doe. **2.** a soft, smooth leather made from this. **3.** a closely woven woolen cloth.

Doe of Virginia deer
(3½ ft. high at shoulder)

does·n't (duz′ənt), contraction of *does not.*

doff (dof), *v.* **1.** to remove or take off, as clothing. **2.** to remove or tip (the hat) as in greeting. [from a Middle English word, which is a contraction of the phrase *do off* "to take off." See *don*[2]]

dog (dôg), *n.* **1.** a domesticated, flesh-eating mammal kept as a pet and for protection, hunting, herding sheep, etc. **2.** any of various animals belonging to the same family, including wolves and foxes. **3.** a mechanical device for gripping or holding something. **4.** a mean person. —*v.*, **dogged, dog·ging. 5.** to follow or track like a dog. **6. go to the dogs,** to become ruined, either morally or physically: *Because of water pollution, the lake has just gone to the dogs.* **7. let sleeping dogs lie,** to keep oneself from stirring up a situation that could become more unpleasant. **8. put on the dog,** to put on airs; be affected: *It's silly to put on the dog when you haven't a dollar to your name.*

Dog

dog′ days′, a hot, uncomfortable part of the summer, often reckoned from July 3rd to August 11th.

dog-ear (dôg′ēr′), *n.* (in a book) the corner of a page folded over like a dog's ear. —**dog′-eared′,** *adj.*

dog·fish (dôg′fish′), *n., pl.* **dog·fish·es** *or* **dog·fish.** any of several small sharks that prey on food fish.

dog·ged (dô′gid), *adj.* stubbornly persistent: *a dogged scholar.* —**dog′ged·ly,** *adv.*

dog·house (dôg′hous′), *n., pl.* **dog·hous·es** (dôg′hou′ziz). **1.** a small shelter for a dog. **2. in the doghouse,** *Slang.* in disfavor or disgrace: *I'm in the doghouse for losing his book.*

do·gie (dō′gē), *n.* a motherless calf in a cattle herd.

dog·ma (dôg′mə), *n.* **1.** a system of principles or beliefs set forth by a church. **2.** any doctrine or opinion that is considered true beyond question.

dog·mat·ic (dôg mat′ik), *adj.* **1.** of or concerning a

dogma or dogmas. **2.** stating opinions in a positive manner as if one were the best informed and the highest authority. —**dog·mat′i·cal·ly,** *adv.*

dog·trot (dôg′trot′), *n.* **1.** a gentle trot, like that of a dog. —*v.*, **dog·trot·ted, dog·trot·ting. 2.** to go or move at a dogtrot: *We dogtrotted all the way home.*

dog·wood (dôg′wŏŏd′), *n.* a tree whose true flowers are surrounded by pink or white leaves resembling petals.

doi·ly (doi′lē), *n., pl.* **doi·lies.** a small embroidered or lace mat.

do·ing (dōō′ing), *n.* **1.** action; performance: *Your bad luck is your own doing.* **2. doings,** happenings; deeds; events.

dol·drums (dōl′drəmz, dol′drəmz), *n. (used as pl.)* **1.** a band of latitudes near the equator where the winds are light and unpredictable. **2.** a dull, depressed mood or state of mind.

Dogwood flower

dole (dōl), *n.* **1.** a portion of money, food, etc., given as charity. **2.** a dealing out or distribution of charity. **3.** a payment by a government to an unemployed person. —*v.*, **doled, dol·ing. 4.** to distribute as charity. **5.** to distribute in small quantities (usually fol. by *out*): *The last of the water was doled out to the thirsty crew.*

dole·ful (dōl′fəl), *adj.* full of sadness; sorrowful. —**dole′ful·ly,** *adv.*

doll (dol), *n.* **1.** a toy representing a baby or other human being. **2. doll up,** *Slang.* to dress in elegant or stylish clothes: *Let's get dolled up and go out.*

dol·lar (dol′ər), *n.* **1.** a currency bill and monetary unit of the U.S., equal to 100 cents. **2.** a monetary unit of various other nations and territories, equal to 100 cents. [from the Dutch word *daler,* which comes from German *-thaler* in *Joachimsthaler,* a coin minted in Joachimsthal in Bohemia]

dol·ly (dol′ē), *n., pl.* **doll·ies. 1.** a doll. **2.** a low truck or cart with small wheels for moving heavy loads.

do·lor·ous (dō′lər əs, dol′ər əs), *adj.* full of, expressing, or causing pain or sorrow; mournful: *a dolorous melody; dolorous news.*

dol·phin (dol′fin), *n.* **1.** any of several sea-dwelling mammals resembling small whales and having a beaklike, toothed snout. Dolphins are noted for their keen intelligence and their ability to be trained. **2.** either of two large, slender food fishes found in warm or temperate seas.

Dolphin
(length 8½ ft.)

dolt (dōlt), *n.* a dull, stupid person. —**dolt′ish,** *adj.*

-dom, a suffix used to form nouns meaning **1.** state or condition: *freedom.* **2.** rank or position: *dukedom.* **3.** realm or jurisdiction: *kingdom.* **4.** group or class: *officialdom.*

do·main (dō mān′), *n.* **1.** complete ownership and control over the use of land. **2.** the territory governed by a single ruler or government; realm. **3.** a field of action, knowledge, influence, etc.: *the domain of science.*

dome (dōm), *n.* **1.** a roof or ceiling having the shape of an upside-down bowl or cup. **2.** something shaped like a dome: *the dome of the sky.*

do·mes·tic (də mes′tik), *adj.* **1.** of or referring to the home, the household, or the family: *domestic problems.* **2.** devoted to home life or household affairs: *a domestic woman.* **3.** tame; domesticated: *a domestic animal.* **4.** of, referring to, or produced in one's own or a particular country: *domestic news; domestic products.* —*n.* **5.** a hired household servant. —**do·mes′ti·cal·ly,** *adv.*

do·mes·ti·cate (də mes′tə kāt′), *v.,* **do·mes·ti·cat·ed, do·mes·ti·cat·ing. 1.** to convert to domestic uses; tame: *to domesticate an animal.* **2.** to accustom to household life and affairs. —**do·mes′ti·ca′tion,** *n.*

do·mes·tic·i·ty (dō′me stis′i tē), *n.* the state or quality of being domestic; devotion to home life.

dom·i·cile (dom′i sīl′), *n.* **1.** a place of residence; house; home. **2.** a permanent legal residence. —*v.,* **dom·i·ciled, dom·i·cil·ing. 3.** to establish in a domicile: *to domicile troops in barracks.*

dom·i·nance (dom′ə nəns), *n.* rule; control; authority: *The party members were under the dominance of the leader.*

dom·i·nant (dom′ə nənt), *adj.* **1.** ruling; controlling; most powerful or influential: *a dominant country.* **2.** occupying a commanding position: *a dominant hill.* —**dom′i·nant·ly,** *adv.*

dom·i·nate (dom′ə nāt′), *v.,* **dom·i·nat·ed, dom·i·nat·ing. 1.** to rule over; govern; control: *He dominates his group of friends.* **2.** to tower above; overlook: *High mountains dominate the town.* —**dom′i·na′tion,** *n.*

dom·i·neer (dom′ə nēr′), *v.* to rule in an arrogant, tyrannical way. —**dom′i·neer′ing,** *adj.*

Dom·i·nic (dom′ə nik), *n.* **Saint,** 1170–1221, Spanish priest: founder of the Dominican order.

Do·min·i·can (də min′ə kən), *n.* **1.** a member of one of the religious orders founded by St. Dominic. —*adj.* **2.** of or referring to St. Dominic or the Dominicans.

Do·min·i·can (də min′ə kən), *adj.* **1.** of or referring to the Dominican Republic. —*n.* **2.** a native or inhabitant of the Dominican Republic.

Domin′ican Repub′lic, a republic in the West Indies, occupying the E part of the island of Hispaniola. 19,129 sq. mi. *Cap.:* Santo Domingo.

do·min·ion (də min′yən), *n.* **1.** the power or right to govern and control; rule; domination. **2.** a territory under a single rule. **3.** one of the self-governing member nations of the British Commonwealth.

dom·i·no¹ (dom′ə nō′), *n., pl.* **dom·i·noes** or **dom·i·nos. 1.** a large, loose cloak, usually hooded, worn with a small mask by persons in masquerade. **2.** the mask itself. [from an Italian word meaning originally "a black hood worn by priests," which comes from Latin *dominus* "lord," a word often used by priests]

dom·i·no² (dom′ə nō′), *n., pl.* **dom·i·noes. 1.** a flat, rectangular piece of ivory, bone, wood, or plastic, the face of which is divided into two parts, each left blank or bearing from one to six dots. **2. dominoes,** *(used as sing.)* any of various games, usually played with 28 such pieces. [from *domino¹,* probably because of its black color]

don¹ (don), *n.* (in the English universities) a head, fellow, or tutor of a college. [from an Italian word, which comes from Latin *dominus* "lord, master"]

don² (don), *v.,* **donned, don·ning.** to put on or dress in: *to don one's clothes.* [a contraction of the phrase *do on* "to put on." See *doff*]

Don (don), *n.* Mr.; Sir: a Spanish title put before a man's Christian name.

Don (don), *n.* a river in the central Soviet Union, flowing S to the Sea of Azov. about 1200 mi. long.

do·nate (dō′nāt, dō nāt′), *v.,* **do·nat·ed, do·nat·ing.** to contribute or give: *to donate money to charity.*

do·na·tion (dō nā′shən), *n.* **1.** the act of presenting something as a gift, grant, or contribution: *the donation of clothing to the poor.* **2.** a gift; contribution.

done (dun), *v.* **1.** the past participle of **do¹:** *We have done the dishes.* —*adj.* **2.** finished; completed: *The project is done.* **3.** cooked enough: *Is the cake done?* **4. done for, a.** tired; exhausted: *After those stairs I'm done for.* **b.** dead, or close to death: *A week in the desert and you'd be done for.* **5. done in,** extremely tired; exhausted: *We were done in after the race.*

don·key (dong′kē), *n., pl.* **don·keys. 1.** an animal related to but smaller than the horse, having long ears and a tufted tail; ass. **2.** a stupid, silly, or stubborn person.

do·nor (dō′nər), *n.* a person who gives or donates.

don't (dōnt), contraction of *do not.*

doo·dle (dood′l), *v.,* **doo·dled, doo·dling. 1.** to draw or scribble. —*n.* **2.** a design, figure, etc., made by scribbling. —**doo′dler,** *n.*

doom (doom), *n.* **1.** fate or destiny, esp. a bad or terrible fate. **2.** ruin; death: *to have a feeling of doom.* **3.** a judgment or decision, esp. an unfavorable one. —*v.* **4.** to condemn to a terrible fate: *doomed to death by hanging.*

dooms·day (doomz′dā′), *n.* the day of the Last Judgment, at the end of the world.

door (dôr), *n.* **1.** a movable, usually solid barrier for opening and closing an entranceway, cupboard, cabinet, etc. **2.** a doorway. **3.** the building, house, etc., to which a door belongs: *The Jenkinsons now live two doors down the street.* **4. out of doors,** in the open air; outside: *Let's have a picnic out of doors.* **5. show (someone) the door,** to ask or order (someone) to leave; dismiss: *If they don't behave, I'll show them the door.*

door·man (dôr′man′, -mən), *n., pl.* **door·men.** a man at the entrance of an apartment house, night club, etc., who helps people coming in or going out.

door·step (dôr′step′), *n.* a step or one of a series of steps leading to a door from the ground outside.

---

door·way (dôr′wā′), *n.* the passage or opening into a building, room, etc., usually containing a door.

door·yard (dôr′yärd′), *n.* a yard in front of the door of a house.

dope (dōp), *n.* 1. a lacquer or varnish used esp. for strengthening and waterproofing the fabric on aircraft. 2. any narcotic drug. 3. *Slang.* information, data, or news: *What's the latest dope on the weather?* 4. *Slang.* a stupid person. —*v.*, **doped, dop·ing. 5.** to apply or treat with dope.

Dor·ic (dôr′ik), *adj.* noting the oldest and simplest style or order of ancient Greek architecture. See also **Corinthian** (def. 2), **Ionic.** See illus. at **order.**

dorm (dôrm), *n. Informal.* a dormitory.

dor·mant (dôr′mənt), *adj.* 1. lying asleep or as if asleep: *Tulip bulbs are dormant in winter.* 2. inactive: *The volcano has been dormant for many years.*

dor·mer (dôr′mər), *n.* 1. Also, **dor′mer win′dow.** a vertical window in a projection built out from a sloping roof. 2. the entire projecting structure.

dor·mi·to·ry (dôr′mi tôr′ē), *n., pl.* **dor·mi·to·ries.** 1. a building at a college or university used for housing and recreational activities. 2. a room containing a number of beds and serving as sleeping quarters for many people.

Dormer

dor·mouse (dôr′mous′), *n., pl.* **dor·mice** (dôr′mīs′). a small, furry animal of Europe, Asia, and Africa that resembles a squirrel but hibernates in winter.

dor·sal (dôr′səl), *adj.* referring to or located on the back: *Many kinds of sharks have prominent dorsal fins.*

do·ry (dôr′ē), *n., pl.* **do·ries.** a boat with a narrow, flat bottom, high bow, and flaring sides.

Dormouse
(length 6 in.)

dos·age (dō′sij), *n.* 1. the giving of medicine in doses. 2. the amount of medicine to be given: *a dosage of two teaspoons every four hours.*

dose (dōs), *n.* 1. a quantity of medicine prescribed to be taken at one time. —*v.*, **dosed, dos·ing. 2.** to give a dose of medicine to. [from the Greek word *dosis* "a giving, something given"]

dost (dust), *v.* an old form of **do**[1], found now chiefly in Biblical and poetic writing and used with *thou*: *Thou dost appear tired.*

dot (dot), *n.* 1. a small, roundish mark. 2. a short sound in Morse code (distinguished from *dash*): *You signal S with three dots.* —*v.*, **dot·ted, dot·ting. 3.** to mark with or as if with a dot or dots: *He forgets to dot his i's. Trees dotted the landscape.* **4. on the dot,** exactly at the time agreed on; prompt: *Be here at 9 o'clock on the dot.*

dot·age (dō′tij), *n.* 1. feebleness of mind, esp. because of old age; senility: *to be in one's dotage.* 2. foolish or excessive fondness, affection, or the like.

dote (dōt), *v.*, **dot·ed, dot·ing. 1.** to show too much love or fondness (usually fol. by *on* or *upon*): *She*

dotes on her youngest son. **2.** to be weak-minded, esp. from old age. —**dot′ing·ly,** *adv.*

doth (duth), *v.* an old form of **does,** found now chiefly in Biblical and poetic writing: *He doth talk of wondrous things.*

dou·ble (dub′əl), *adj.* 1. twice as large, heavy, strong, etc.: *double pay.* 2. made up of two like parts; paired: *double doors.* 3. made up of two unlike parts: *a double meaning.* 4. folded in two; having one half folded over the other. 5. (of flowers) having many more than the normal number of petals: *double petunias.* —*n.* 6. something that is twice the usual size, amount, strength, etc. 7. a duplicate; something exactly or closely resembling another: *He is the double of his cousin.* 8. a sudden backward turn; reversal. 9. (in baseball) a base hit that enables a batter to reach second base safely. 10. **doubles,** *(used as sing.)* a tennis game with two players on each side. —*v.*, **dou·bled, dou·bling. 11.** to make or become twice as great: *to double one's weight; to double in value.* 12. to bend or fold: *Double over the edge before sewing.* 13. to clench (the fist). 14. to sail around: *to double Cape Horn.* 15. to serve in two capacities: *The girl doubles as secretary and receptionist.* 16. to turn back or change direction (often fol. by *back*): *We doubled back to look for the lost package.* —*adv.* 17. doubly; twice as much: *You pay double at that store.* 18. two at a time; two together: *to walk double.* 19. **double up, a.** to share living quarters intended for one person or family: *We'll be glad to double up if you want to stay all night.* **b.** to bend over, esp. with intense pain: *He doubled up in agony after eating those green apples.* 20. **on the double,** without delay; rapidly: *Get down here on the double!*

dou′ble bass′ (bās), the largest and lowest-pitched member of the violin family, played either with a bow or by plucking. Also, **contrabass, bass, bass viol.**

dou·ble-breast·ed (dub′əl bres′tid), *adj.* 1. (of a coat or jacket) overlapping in front so as to allow for two rows of buttons. 2. (of a suit) having such a coat or jacket. See also **single-breasted.**

dou′ble cross′, *Informal.* a betrayal or swindle of a friend or associate.

dou·ble-cross (dub′əl krôs′), *v. Informal.* to betray or cheat by treachery. —**dou′ble-cross′er,** *n.*

dou·ble-deal·ing (dub′əl dē′ling), *n.* 1. a dishonest way of dealing with someone; deception. —*adj.* 2. using dishonesty in dealing with people; dishonest; treacherous.

dou·ble-head·er (dub′əl hed′ər), *n.* (in sports) two games between the same teams or two different pairs of teams, one immediately following the other.

dou·ble-joint·ed (dub′əl join′tid), *adj.* having very flexible joints that can bend in unusual ways.

dou′ble play′, (in baseball) a play in which two runners are put out.

dou·ble-quick (dub′əl kwik′), *adj.* 1. very quick or rapid. —*adv.* 2. in a very quick or rapid manner: *Come here double-quick!* —*n.* (dub′əl kwik′). 3. another word for **double time.** —*v.* 4. (dub′əl kwik′). to double-time.

dou·blet (dub′lit), *n.* a close-fitting jacket, some-times with a short skirt, worn by men from about 1400 to 1650.

dou′ble time′, a very fast marching step.

dou·ble-time (dub′əl-tīm′), *v.,* **dou·ble-timed, dou·ble-tim·ing.** to move or cause to move in dou-ble time: *We double-timed to the store and got there just before it closed.*

Doublets

dou·bloon (du bloon′), *n.* a former gold coin of Spain and Spanish America.

dou·bly (dub′lē), *adv.* to a double measure or de-gree: *to be doubly careful.*

doubt (dout), *v.* 1. to be uncertain about: *I doubt that I will be able to come.* 2. to distrust: *She doubts his word.* —*n.* 3. a feeling of uncertainty about the truth, reality, or nature of something: *There was doubt concerning the genuineness of the painting.* 4. distrust. 5. **beyond** (or **without**) **doubt,** certainly; definitely: *You did the right thing beyond doubt. He is without doubt the best player in the league.* 6. **in doubt,** having doubt; being uncertain: *If you're in doubt, you'd better not go.* 7. **no doubt,** without any question; certainly: *No doubt there's a reason why you were late.*

doubt·ful (dout′fəl), *adj.* 1. uncertain; full of doubt: *It is doubtful that he will come.* 2. of questionable honesty: *He won by doubtful methods.* —**doubt′ful·ly,** *adv.*

doubt·less (dout′lis), *adv.* Also, **doubt′less·ly.** 1. without doubt: *He was doubtless an excellent student.* 2. probably: *She will doubtless be on time.* —*adj.* 3. free from doubt or uncertainty: *a doubtless genius.*

dough (dō), *n.* 1. flour or meal combined with water, milk, etc., in a pasty mass for baking into bread, cake, etc. 2. *Slang.* money.

dough·nut (dō′nut), *n.* a small, usually round pastry, often with a hole in the center, fried in deep fat.

dough·ty (dou′tē), *adj.,* **dough·ti·er, dough·ti·est.** very courageous and determined: *doughty soldiers.*

dough·y (dō′ē), *adj.,* **dough·i·er, dough·i·est.** of or like dough; soft and heavy; pasty.

dour (door, dour), *adj.* 1. sullen; gloomy; sad. 2. strict; severe; stern. —**dour′ly,** *adv.*

douse (dous), *v.,* **doused, dous·ing.** 1. to plunge into water or other liquid; drench. 2. to splash or throw water or other liquid on: *She doused the thirsty plants with water.* 3. *Informal.* to extinguish; put out: *Douse the lights, please.*

dove[1] (duv), *n.* 1. any of several birds resembling small pigeons. 2. a symbol of peace. [from Old English]

dove[2] (dōv), *v.* a past tense of **dive.**

Do·ver (dō′vər), *n.* 1. the capital city of Delaware, in the central part. 2. a port city in SE England: point nearest France.

dove·tail (duv′tāl′), *n.* 1. a projection on a board. 2. a joint formed by fitting the projections or dovetails of one board into the correspond-ing openings of another board. —*v.* 3. to join or fit (two boards) together by means of dovetails. 4. to join or fit together exactly: *Our travel plans dovetailed and we met in Chicago.*

Dovetail joint

dow·a·ger (dou′ə jər), *n.* 1. a woman who holds some title or property from her dead husband. 2. an elderly, dignified woman.

dow·dy (dou′dē), *adj.,* **dow·di·er, dow·di·est.** not neat or stylish; frumpy; old-fashioned: *dowdy clothes.* —**dow′di·ness,** *n.*

dow·el (dou′əl), *n.* 1. a round wooden rod of small diameter. 2. a wooden or metal pin that is fitted into holes in two pieces to fasten them together.

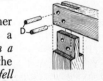
D, Dowels

down[1] (doun), *adv.* 1. from higher to lower; toward, into, or in a lower position: *He pulled down a book from the shelf.* 2. on or to the ground, floor, or bottom: *He fell down.* 3. to or at a lower value, volume, amount, strength, etc.: *Prices went down. Turn down the TV.* 4. seriously; earnestly: *Let's get down to work.* 5. on paper or in a book: *Write down the address.* 6. in cash at the time of purchase: *We paid $10 down.* 7. from an earlier to a later time: *down to the present.* —*prep.* 8. in a de-scending or more remote direction in or on: *They ran down the hill.* —*adj.* 9. going or directed downward: *the down trail.* 10. being at a lower position or level: *Prices are down.* 11. downcast; sad; dejected: *We're all a bit down today because our team lost.* 12. con-fined to bed because of illness: *I'm down with a cold.* —*n.* 13. a downward movement or turn; descent or reverse. —*v.* 14. to cause to fall; knock, throw, or shoot down: *The boxer downed his opponent in the third round. The guns downed three bombers.* 15. to swallow quickly: *to down a glass of milk.* 16. **down and out,** without money or resources; reduced to poverty: *Many people were down and out when they came to this country.* 17. **down in the mouth,** sad; discouraged; glum: *He's been down in the mouth since our team lost.* 18. **down on,** angry at; provoked with: *She's been down on me ever since our misun-derstanding.* [from the Old English word *dūne,* which comes from *adūne* "off the hill"]

down[2] (doun), *n.* 1. the soft, under feathers of a bird. 2. soft hair; fluff. [from Scandinavian]

down·cast (doun′kast′), *adj.* 1. low in spirit; sad; de-pressed. 2. directed downward: *downcast eyes.*

down·fall (doun′fôl′), *n.* 1. descent to a lower posi-tion or standing; overthrow; ruin: *His enemies caused his downfall.* 2. a sudden, heavy fall of rain or snow.

down·grade (doun′grād′), *n.* 1. a downward slope, esp. of a road. —*v.,* **down·grad·ed, down·grad·ing.** 2.

to reduce in rank, income, importance, etc.: *The sergeant was downgraded to corporal.*

down·heart·ed (doun′här′tid), *adj.* sad; depressed; discouraged: *He's downhearted about his grades.*

down·hill (doun′hil′), *adv.* 1. down the slope of a hill; downward: *to walk downhill.* 2. into a worse condition: *Her health has gone downhill this year.*

down·pour (doun′pôr′), *n.* a heavy rain.

down·right (doun′rīt′), *adj.* 1. thorough; absolute: *a downright lie.* 2. frankly direct; blunt: *a downright reply; a downright person.* —*adv.* 3. completely; thoroughly: *a downright confusing problem.*

downs (dounz), *n.pl.* a region of low, rolling hills that have smooth, grass-covered slopes: a term used esp. in southern England. [plural of the earlier word *down*, which comes from Old English *dūn* "hill"]

down·stairs (doun′stârz′), *adv.* 1. down the stairs: *to fall downstairs.* 2. to or on a lower floor: *I'll be downstairs if you want me.* —*adj.* (doun′stârz′). 3. located on a lower floor: *a downstairs office.* —*n.* (doun′stârz′). 4. *(used as sing.)* the lower floor or floors of a building.

down·stream (doun′strēm′), *adv.* in the direction of the current of a stream: *to swim downstream.*

down·town (doun′toun′), *adv.* 1. to or in the central business section of a city: *to walk downtown.* —*adj.* 2. of, referring to, or located in the central business section of a city: *downtown stores.*

down·trod·den (doun′trod′ən), *adj.* ruled harshly by a superior power; oppressed.

down·ward (doun′wərd), *adv.* 1. Also, **down′wards.** from a higher to a lower place or condition: *to climb downward.* 2. from a past or earlier time: *to come downward through history.* —*adj.* 3. moving to a lower place or condition: *a downward trend.*

down·wind (doun′wind′), *adv.* in the same direction that the wind is blowing.

down·y (dou′nē), *adj.*, **down·i·er, down·i·est.** 1. of or resembling down; fluffy; soft. 2. made of or covered with down.

dow·ry (dou′rē), *n., pl.* **dow·ries.** the money, goods, or property that a bride brings to her husband.

dox·ol·o·gy (dok sol′ə jē), *n., pl.* **dox·ol·o·gies.** 1. a hymn praising God. 2. **the Doxology,** the hymn beginning "Praise God from whom all blessings flow."

doz., dozen; dozens.

doze (dōz), *v.*, **dozed, doz·ing.** 1. to sleep lightly; nap. —*n.* 2. a light sleep; nap.

doz·en (duz′ən), *n., pl.* **doz·ens** *or* (after a numeral) **doz·en.** a group of 12.

drab (drab), *n.* 1. a dull brownish gray. —*adj.* 2. having a drab color. 3. dull; cheerless: *a drab room.* —**drab′ly,** *adv.* —**drab′ness,** *n.*

draft (draft), *n.* 1. a drawing, sketch, or design. 2. a first or preliminary form of something written: *He made three drafts of the report before he was satisfied.* 3. a current of air in any enclosed space. 4. a device for regulating the current of air in a stove, fireplace, etc. 5. a selection or drawing of persons for military service. 6. the act of drawing or pulling loads. 7. a written order drawn by one person upon

another for payment of money: *a draft for $50.* 8. the drawing of a liquid from its container: *ale on draft.* 9. the act of drinking or inhaling. 10. something that is taken in by drinking or inhaling; a drink. 11. a quantity of fish caught. 12. the depth to which the hull of a vessel is immersed when carrying a certain load: *The freighter has a draft of 16 feet.* —*v.* 13. to draw the outlines or plan of; sketch. 14. to put in written form: *to draft a treaty.* 15. to take or select for military service. —*adj.* 16. used for pulling loads: *a draft ox.* 17. available to be drawn from a cask or keg: *draft beer.* 18. being a rough or preliminary outline, version, etc.: *a draft resolution.* Also, *esp. British,* **draught.** —**draft′er,** *n.*

draft′ an′imal, an animal that pulls loads. Horses, mules, camels, etc., are often used as draft animals. See also **pack animal.**

draft·ee (draf tē′), *n.* a person who is drafted into military service.

draft·ing (draf′tiṅg), *n.* the technique of making engineers' or architects' plans and blueprints.

drafts·man (drafts′mən), *n., pl.* **drafts·men.** 1. a person who draws plans and blueprints. 2. a person skilled in drawing.

drafts·man·ship (drafts′mən ship′), *n.* skill in drawing: *to be trained in draftsmanship.*

draft·y (draf′tē), *adj.*, **draft·i·er, draft·i·est.** exposed to or having drafts or currents of air: *a drafty room.*

drag (drag), *v.*, **dragged, drag·ging.** 1. to pull heavily or slowly along: *The mule dragged the cart.* 2. to search or catch with a seine, net, or the like: *to drag the lake for fish.* 3. to be drawn or pulled along: *His coat dragged in the mud.* 4. to pass very slowly: *The discussion dragged on for hours.* 5. to lag or trail behind: *The dog dragged along after us.* —*n.* 6. any device for searching a body of water, such as a seine or net. 7. *Informal.* anything that slows down progress: *He is a drag on the job because he's so lazy.*

drag·gle (drag′əl), *v.*, **drag·gled, drag·gling.** to soil or become soiled by dragging over damp ground or in mud.

drag·net (drag′net′), *n.* 1. a net to be drawn along the bottom of a river, pond, etc., or along the ground to catch fish, small game, etc. 2. a system or network of police officers for finding or catching criminals.

drag·on (drag′ən), *n.* an imaginary monster, usually represented as a huge winged snake spouting fire.

drag·on·fly (drag′ən flī′), *n., pl.* **drag·on·flies.** an insect having a long, straight body and four wings that preys on other insects but is harmless to humans.

dra·goon (drə gōōn′), *n.* 1. a cavalryman of a heavily armed troop. —*v.* 2. to force by oppression; coerce: *They dragooned the enemy into building shelters.*

Dragonfly
(length 1½ in.;
wingspread 2½ in.)

drain (drān), *v.* 1. to draw off (a liquid) gradually: *to drain water from a pool.* 2. to empty of a liquid: *to drain a swamp.* 3. to flow off: *The water drained slowly.* **4.** to deplete by gradual withdrawal or exhaustion: *The long hike drained his strength.* **5.** to become empty or dry by the gradual flowing off of liquid or moisture: *The swimming pool drains in a day.* —*n.* **6.** a device, such as a pipe, by which anything is drained. **7.** a gradual using up: *The trip was a drain on our savings.*

drain·age (drā′nij), *n.* **1.** the act or process of draining. **2.** channels, pipes, etc., forming a system for draining something. **3.** that which is drained off: *a drainage of five gallons.*

drake (drāk), *n.* a male duck.

Drake (drāk), *n.* **Sir Francis,** 1540–1596, English admiral and explorer: sailed around the world 1577–1580.

dram (dram), *n.* **1.** a unit of weight used by druggists, equal to ⅛ ounce (3.887 grams). **2.** a weight of 1/16 ounce (1.771 grams). **3.** a unit of volume equal to ⅛ fluid ounce (3.696 milliliters).

dra·ma (drä′mə, dram′ə), *n.* **1.** a piece of writing that is acted out on a stage; a play. **2.** the art of writing and producing plays. **3.** any series of vivid, exciting, suspenseful events: *the drama of a murder trial.* [from a Greek word meaning "action (of a play)," which comes from *dran* "to do"]

dra·mat·ic (drə mat′ik), *adj.* **1.** of or concerning drama or the theater: *a dramatic program.* **2.** like a drama or play in excitement, interest, etc.: *the dramatic years of the war.* —**dra·mat′i·cal·ly,** *adv.*

dra·mat·ics (drə mat′iks), *n.* *(used as sing. or pl.)* the art of producing or acting in plays.

dram·a·tist (dram′ə tist, drä′mə tist), *n.* a writer of plays; playwright.

dram·a·tize (dram′ə tīz′, drä′mə tīz′), *v.,* **dram·a·tized, dram·a·tiz·ing. 1.** to put into the form of a play. **2.** to express vividly and excitingly: *He dramatized the battle for us.* —**dram′a·ti·za′tion,** *n.*

drank (drangk), *v.* the past tense of **drink.**

drape (drāp), *v.,* **draped, drap·ing. 1.** to cover or hang with cloth or other fabric: *The front of the building was draped with flags.* **2.** to arrange in folds: *to drape a gown so that it hangs properly.* **3.** to hang, fall, or become arranged in folds. —*n.* **4.** a draped curtain or hanging: *to buy new drapes.*

dra·per·y (drā′pə rē), *n., pl.* **dra·per·ies. 1.** clothing, curtains, etc., arranged in loose, graceful folds. **2.** the draping or arranging of cloth in folds.

dras·tic (dras′tik), *adj.* **1.** acting with force, severity, or violence: *drastic measures to control crime.* **2.** very severe or extensive: *a drastic reduction in price.* —**dras′ti·cal·ly,** *adv.*

draught (draft), *n., v., adj.* a British spelling of **draft.**

draw (drô), *v.,* **drew** (drōō), **drawn** (drôn), **draw·ing. 1.** to pull or drag: *The horses drew the wagon.* **2.** to pull or take out: *to draw names from a hat; to draw water from a well.* **3.** to approach: *The day draws near.* **4.** to attract: *The accident drew a crowd.* **5.** to make appear; bring forth: *The cut drew blood.* **6.** to sketch: *to draw a picture.* **7.** to write out: *to draw a*

check. **8.** to write out formally or legally: *to draw a will.* **9.** to get, take, or receive: *to draw a salary; to draw interest.* **10.** to arrive at by thought: *to draw a conclusion.* **11.** to inhale: *to draw breath.* **12.** to need (a certain depth of water) in order to float or move: *This boat draws five feet.* **13.** to lengthen or stretch: *to draw glass into fine threads.* —*n.* **14.** the act or an instance of drawing: *a draw for first prize.* **15.** a game that ends in a tie, neither side winning. **16. beat to the draw,** to outdo (someone) by taking advantage of an opportunity before he can: *I beat him to the draw in applying for the job.* **17. draw out, a.** to prolong or lengthen: *The lecture was drawn out for an hour.* **b.** to persuade (someone) to talk freely with one: *I tried to be friendly, but I couldn't draw him out.* **18. draw up, a.** to write out according to a plan, legal form, etc.: *to draw up a will.* **b.** to stop or halt: *His car drew up at the curb.*

draw·back (drô′bak′), *n.* a hindrance or disadvantage: *The lack of education is a drawback when seeking a job.*

draw·bridge (drô′brij′), *n.* a bridge that can be turned or raised, wholly or in part, to prevent passage or to open a way for boats, barges, etc.

Drawbridge

draw·er (drô′ər *for def. 1;* drôr *for defs. 2, 3*), *n.* **1.** a person or thing that draws. **2.** a box with handles and no lid, which fits into the side of a piece of furniture so as to be easily pulled out and pushed in. **3. drawers,** an undergarment, with legs, for the lower part of the body.

draw·ing (drô′ing), *n.* **1.** the act of a person or thing that draws. **2.** a picture made with pencil, pen, crayon, or the like; sketch. **3.** the art of making such a picture: *to study drawing.*

draw′ing board′, a rectangular board on which paper is placed or mounted for drawing.

draw′ing room′, a room for entertaining guests, esp. with some formality; parlor.

draw·knife (drô′nīf′), *n., pl.* **draw·knives** (drô′nīvz′). a knife with a handle at each end, used by drawing over a surface.

drawl (drôl), *v.* **1.** to say or speak in a slow manner, usually by drawing out the vowels. —*n.* **2.** the speech of someone who drawls.

Drawknife

drawn (drôn), *v.* **1.** the past participle of **draw.** —*adj.* **2.** gaunt; haggard.

dray (drā), *n.* a low, strong cart with removable sides, used for carrying heavy loads.

dray·man (drā′mən), *n., pl.* **dray·men.** a man who drives a dray.

dread (dred), *v.* **1.** to fear greatly: *I dread the coming of winter.* —*n.* **2.** terror or fear, as of something in the future: *He has a dread of failure.* —*adj.* **3.** greatly feared; frightful: *a dread disease.*

dread·ful (dred′fəl), *adj.* **1.** causing great fear; frightful; terrible: *a dreadful noise.* **2.** very bad, unpleasant, etc.: *a dreadful scene.* —**dread′ful·ly,** *adv.*

dread·nought (dred′nôt′), *n.* a large, heavily armored battleship with powerful guns.

dream (drēm), *n.* **1.** a number of thoughts, pictures, or feelings passing through the mind during sleep. **2.** something imagined while awake; daydream; reverie: *a dream of being a famous singer.* **3.** a goal or ambition: *It is his dream to be an athlete.* **4.** something of great beauty and loveliness: *Yesterday the weather was a dream.* —*v.,* **dreamed** *or* **dreamt** (dremt); **dream·ing. 5.** to have a dream or dreams. **6.** to see or imagine in a dream: *He dreamed that he was an Arabian prince.* **7.** to have daydreams or reveries: *He stood dreaming by the window.* **8.** to think vaguely or remotely (usually fol. by *of*): *I wouldn't dream of hurting your feelings.* **9. dream up,** to form (an idea, plan, etc.) in the imagination: *Let's try to dream up something original for the party.* —**dream′er,** *n.*

dreamt (dremt), *v.* a past tense and past participle of **dream.**

dream·y (drē′mē), *adj.,* **dream·i·er, dream·i·est. 1.** full of dreams: *dreamy sleep.* **2.** vague or dim: *a distant, dreamy sound.* **3.** tending to daydream: *a dreamy pupil.* —**dream′i·ly,** *adv.* —**dream′i·ness,** *n.*

drear (drēr), *adj.* another form of **dreary,** used esp. in poetic writing.

drear·y (drēr′ē), *adj.,* **drear·i·er, drear·i·est.** joyless or cheerless; sad; dull; gloomy: *a dreary, rainy day.* —**drear′i·ly,** *adv.* —**drear′i·ness,** *n.*

dredge¹ (drej), *n.* **1.** a boat or barge equipped with machinery for removing earth from the bottom of a river, bay, etc. **2.** a net or scoop for gathering objects, esp. shellfish, from the bottom of a river, bay, etc. —*v.,* **dredged, dredg·ing. 3.** to clear out or deepen with a dredge: *to dredge a river.* **4.** to gather or remove with a dredge: *to dredge oysters; to dredge mud.* [from Middle English]

dredge² (drej), *v.,* **dredged, dredg·ing.** to sprinkle or coat (food) with flour, sugar, etc.: *to dredge cookies with powdered sugar.* [from the Old French word *dragie* "sweetmeat," from Greek *tragēma*]

dregs (dregz), *n.pl.* **1.** bits of matter that settle to the bottom of a liquid, such as a beverage; lees; grounds. **2.** the lowest and worst part of something: *Criminals are the dregs of society.*

drench (drench), *v.* **1.** to soak or wet thoroughly: *The rain drenched us to the skin.* —*n.* **2.** something that drenches: *a drench of rain.*

Dres·den (drez′dən), *n.* a city in SE East Germany.

dress (dres), *n.* **1.** the most common outer garment of women and girls, consisting of blouse and skirt in one piece. **2.** clothing; apparel: *The party requires formal dress.* —*adj.* **3.** of or for a dress or dresses: *a dress pattern.* **4.** meant for wear on a formal occasion: *a dress suit.* **5.** requiring formal dress: *a dress occasion.* —*v.* **6.** to clothe or put on clothes: *to dress oneself; to dress for school.* **7.** to put on formal or fancy clothes

(often fol. by *up*): *It's just a small party, so don't dress up.* **8.** to trim, ornament, or adorn: *to dress a window with Christmas decorations.* **9.** to comb out and arrange (hair). **10.** to prepare (meat) for cooking. **11.** to apply a dressing to (a wound or sore). **12.** to bring or come into line, as troops: *to dress ranks.* **13. dress down,** to scold or reprimand: *He was dressed down for whistling in the hall.*

dress·er¹ (dres′ər), *n.* **1.** a person whose work is to dress others, such as actors in a theater. **2.** a person who dresses wounds. **3.** a person who prepares meat, decorates windows, etc.

dress·er² (dres′ər), *n.* **1.** a bureau or similar piece of furniture having drawers. **2.** a cupboard or set of shelves for dishes and utensils. [from the French word *dressoir* "sideboard," which comes from *dresser* "to set upright" (referring to the manner of displaying the dishes)]

dress·ing (dres′ing), *n.* **1.** the act of a person who dresses. **2.** a sauce for food: *salad dressing.* **3.** stuffing for a fowl: *turkey dressing.* **4.** a bandage, medicine, etc., used to treat a wound.

dress′ing gown′, a robe worn while one dresses or rests.

dress′ing ta′ble, a table with a mirror at which a person sits while dressing, putting on make-up, etc.

dress·mak·er (dres′mā′kər), *n.* a person whose work is to make women's dresses, coats, and the like.

dress·mak·ing (dres′mā′king), *n.* the act or process of making women's clothes, esp. as an occupation.

dress·y (dres′ē), *adj.,* **dress·i·er, dress·i·est. 1.** wearing or fond of stylish clothes: *a dressy young woman.* **2.** stylish in appearance or requiring stylish clothes: *a dressy coat; a dressy party.*

drew (drōō), *v.* the past tense of **draw.**

drib·ble (drib′əl), *v.,* **drib·bled, drib·bling. 1.** to fall or let fall drop by drop; trickle: *Water dribbled over the side of the cup.* **2.** to let saliva flow from the mouth. **3.** to bounce or kick a ball while moving forward, as in basketball or soccer. **4.** to move (a ball) in this way: *He dribbled the basketball close to the net.* —*n.* **5.** a small trickling stream. **6.** a small quantity of anything: *a dribble of money.* **7.** the act of dribbling a ball. —**drib′bler,** *n.*

drib·let (drib′lit), *n.* a small portion, part, or amount: *a driblet of money.*

dried (drīd), *v.* the past tense and past participle of **dry.**

dri·er¹ (drī′ər), *n.* **1.** a person or thing that dries. **2.** a substance added to paints, varnishes, etc., to make them dry more quickly. **3.** See **dryer** (def. 1). Also, **dryer** (for defs. 1, 2).

dri·er² (drī′ər), *adj.* the comparative of **dry.**

dri·est (drī′ist), *adj.* the superlative of **dry.**

drift (drift), *v.* **1.** to be carried along by currents of water or air: *a leaf drifting on the stream.* **2.** to wander aimlessly or be carried along by the force of circumstances: *to drift from town to town; to drift through life without plans.* **3.** to be driven into heaps by the wind: *drifting snow.* **4.** to drive into heaps: *The wind drifted the sand against the tree.*

—*n.* **5.** a drifting. **6.** a course or direction of movement: *a southward drift of ice.* **7.** a meaning or intent: *the drift of a remark.* **8.** a heap formed by drifting: *a drift of snow.*

drift·er (drif′tər), *n.* a person who goes from place to place or changes jobs frequently.

drift·wood (drift′wŏŏd′), *n.* wood floating on or cast ashore by the water.

drill[1] (dril), *n.* **1.** any of various devices for boring holes in firm materials, esp. by rotating a cutting tool. **2.** the cutting tool itself. **3.** training or exercises in marching, as in the army. **4.** any strict training or exercise that teaches by repeating something over and over again: *a fire drill.* —*v.* **5.** to pierce with or as if with a drill: *to drill wood.* **6.** to exercise or go through exercise in marching or other training: *to drill troops; to drill for an exam.* [from Dutch]

drill[2] (dril), *n.* **1.** a small furrow made in the soil in which to sow seeds. **2.** a machine for sowing and covering seeds. —*v.* **3.** to sow in drills. [from the earlier word *rill* "furrow"]

dri·ly (drī′lē), *adv.* another spelling of **dryly.**

drink (drĭngk), *v.*, **drank** (drăngk), **drunk** (drŭngk), **drink·ing.** **1.** to take (water or other liquid) into the mouth and swallow it: *He drank a cup of tea.* **2.** to indulge in alcoholic liquors. **3.** to absorb or draw in: *The thirsty plants drank the rain.* **4.** to take in with the mind or the senses (often fol. by *in*): *to drink in knowledge; to drink in a beautiful scene.* —*n.* **5.** any liquid that one swallows as nourishment, to quench thirst, etc.; beverage. **6.** alcoholic liquor. —**drink′a·ble,** *adj.*

drink·er (drĭng′kər), *n.* a person who drinks alcoholic liquors habitually or to excess.

drink·ing (drĭng′kĭng), *adj.* **1.** good or safe to drink: *drinking water.* **2.** used in drinking: *a drinking glass.* **3.** indulging in alcoholic liquor: *a drinking man.*

drip (drip), *v.*, **dripped** *or* **dript** (dript); **drip·ping.** **1.** to fall or let fall in drops: *Rain dripped from the eaves. The eaves dripped rain.* **2.** to let drops fall; shed drops: *The gas tank is dripping.* —*n.* **3.** the act or sound of dripping: *the drip of rain outside the window.* **4.** a liquid that drips: *the drip from a faucet.*

drip·pings (drip′ĭngz), *n.pl.* fat and juices that drip from meat while it is cooking.

drive (drīv), *v.*, **drove** (drōv), **driv·en** (driv′ən), **driv·ing.** **1.** to cause and control the movement of (a vehicle, animal, etc.): *to drive a car; to drive a mule.* **2.** to set and keep in operation: *Steam drives some machines.* **3.** to go or travel in a driven vehicle: *Shall we drive to Florida?* **4.** to carry or transport in a driven vehicle: *He drove his wife to the station.* **5.** to cause to move by force (often fol. by *away, off,* etc.): *to drive away flies.* **6.** to cause to move by hitting: *to drive a golf ball.* **7.** to force to work or act: *Ambition drove him night and day.* **8.** to carry through with force: *to drive a hard bargain.* **9.** to sink or dig (a shaft, hole, etc.) down into the ground: *to drive a*

well. —*n.* **10.** the act of driving. **11.** a short trip in an automobile, carriage, etc.: *a drive around the park.* **12.** a forceful effort toward a goal: *a drive to finish in time.* **13.** energy or forcefulness: *a man of terrific drive.* **14.** a campaign to raise money, get something done, etc.: *a drive for charity.* **15.** a road: *A long drive led to the house.* **16.** the part of a vehicle, machine, etc., that transmits power from the source to the operating parts: *automatic drive.* **17. drive at,** to suggest something that one fails to make clear or is reluctant to say: *Do you know what he's driving at?*

drive-in (drīv′ĭn′), *n.* **1.** a movie theater, bank, etc., built to accommodate customers in their automobiles. —*adj.* **2.** of or relating to such a business: *a chain of drive-in restaurants.*

driv·el (driv′əl), *v.*, **driv·eled** *or* **driv·elled; driv·el·ing** *or* **driv·el·ling.** **1.** to let saliva flow from the mouth or mucus from the nose. **2.** to talk childishly or idiotically: *He driveled on and on about how smart he was.* —*n.* **3.** childish or foolish talk; nonsense.

driv·en (driv′ən), *v.* the past participle of **drive.**

driv·er (drī′vər), *n.* **1.** a person who drives an automobile, carriage, or other vehicle. **2.** a person, esp. a cowboy, who drives an animal or animals.

drive·way (drīv′wā′), *n.* a road leading from a street to a house, garage, etc.

driz·zle (driz′əl), *v.*, **driz·zled, driz·zling.** **1.** to rain steadily in fine drops; sprinkle: *It drizzled all night.* —*n.* **2.** a very light rain. —**driz′zly,** *adj.*

droll (drōl), *adj.* amusing or funny in an odd way: *a droll little clown.* —**droll′ness,** *n.*

droll·er·y (drō′lə rē), *n., pl.* **droll·er·ies.** **1.** something droll, as a joke, trick, etc. **2.** a droll manner: *The clown's drollery set everyone to laughing.*

drom·e·dar·y (drom′i der′ē), *n., pl.* **drom·e·dar·ies.** the one-humped camel of Arabia and northern Africa. See illus. at **camel.** [from the Latin phrase *dromedārius camēlus* "running camel"]

drone[1] (drōn), *n.* **1.** a male bee. Drones have no stings and do not make honey. See illus. at **bee.** **2.** a person who lives on the labor of others; loafer; idler. [from the Old English word *dran*]

drone[2] (drōn), *v.*, **droned, dron·ing.** **1.** to make a dull, low, humming or buzzing sound: *The motors droned in the factory.* **2.** to speak in a monotonous tone. —*n.* **3.** a humming or buzzing sound: *the drone of bees.* **4.** a monotonous tone: *a drone of voices.* [from *drone*[1], with reference to the humming of a bee]

drool (drŏŏl), *v.* to water at the mouth, esp. in anticipation of food. —**drool′er,** *n.*

droop (drŏŏp), *v.* **1.** to sag, sink, bend, or hang down: *Vines drooped over the fence.* **2.** to become weak or lose courage: *He was drooping from lack of sleep.* —*n.* **3.** a sagging, sinking, bending, or hanging down. —**droop′y,** *adj.*

drop (drop), *n.* **1.** a small quantity of liquid having a rounded shape: *a drop of rain on the window.* **2.** a very small quantity of liquid: *a drop of tea.* 3. a small quantity of anything: *a drop of kindness.* 4. something in the form of a rounded drop of liquid, such as a piece of jewelry, candy, etc. 5. the act of dropping; fall: *a drop to the bottom of a well.* 6. the distance or depth to which anything drops: *a drop of 50 feet.* 7. a container for depositing something: *a mail drop.* 8. a decline in amount, value, etc.: *a drop in prices.* —*v.,* **dropped** *or* **dropt** (dropt); **drop·ping.** 9. to fall or let fall in drops: *Rain was dropping over the sea. He dropped lemon juice into his tea.* 10. to fall, let fall, or cause to fall: *The glass dropped to the floor. He dropped the pencil.* 11. to go or make lower in position, value, etc.: *Prices dropped. He dropped his voice.* 12. to withdraw, quit, vanish, etc. (often fol. by *out* or *from*): *He dropped out of the game. They dropped from sight.* 13. to visit or stop at a place (usually fol. by *in, by,* or *over*): *Let's drop in at Tim's.* 14. to send or mail (a message, letter, etc.): *Drop me a note.* 15. to cease to employ, have as a friend, etc.: *He was dropped by all his friends.* 16. to set down or unload, as from a car, ship, etc.: *Drop me at the corner.* 17. **drop behind,** to fail to keep up one's pace or progress: *to drop behind in a race; to drop behind in one's schoolwork.* 18. **drop off, a.** to fall asleep: *Dad always drops off right after dinner.* **b.** to decrease or decline: *Sales have dropped off.*

drop′ leaf′, an extension attached to a table (**drop′-leaf′ ta′ble**) and folded downward when not needed.

drop·let (drop′lit), *n.* a very small drop.

drop·per (drop′ər), *n.* 1. a person or thing that drops. 2. a glass tube with a rubber bulb at one end, used for drawing in a liquid, such as a medicine, and measuring it out by drops.

Drop-leaf table

drop·sy (drop′sē), *n.* a disease in which a liquid gathers in cavities and tissues of the body.

dross (drôs), *n.* 1. waste matter taken off the surface of molten metal during the process of smelting. 2. any waste matter; refuse.

drought (drout), *n.* a period of dry weather, esp. one that lasts a long time and is harmful to crops. Also, **drouth** (drouth).

drove¹ (drōv), *v.* the past tense of **drive.**

drove² (drōv), *n.* 1. a number of oxen, sheep, etc., driven in a group; herd; flock. 2. Usually, **droves.** a large crowd of people, esp. in motion: *The vacationers arrived in droves.* [from the Old English word *drāf,* which is related to *drīfan* "to drive"]

dro·ver (drō′vər), *n.* a person who drives oxen, sheep, etc., to market.

drown (droun), *v.* 1. to die or cause to die from lack of air as a result of being under water or some other liquid. 2. to overpower (often fol. by *out*): *Our voices were drowned out by the cheering crowd.*

drowse (drouz), *v.,* **drowsed, drows·ing.** 1. to be sleepy or half asleep. 2. to pass or spend in drowsing (usually fol. by *away*): *He drowsed away the morning.* —*n.* 3. a light sleep: *a long drowse in the sun.*

drow·sy (drou′zē), *adj.,* **drow·si·er, drow·si·est.** 1. half asleep; sleepy: *a drowsy cat.* 2. causing sleepiness: *drowsy spring weather.* —**drow′si·ly,** *adv.* —**drow′si·ness,** *n.*

drub (drub), *v.,* **drubbed, drub·bing.** 1. to beat with a stick; thrash. 2. to defeat, as in a game or contest: *The team was thoroughly drubbed.*

drudge (druj), *n.* 1. a person who does dull or hard work. —*v.,* **drudged, drudg·ing.** 2. to do dull or hard work: *He had to drudge to support his family.*

drudg·er·y (druj′ə rē), *n., pl.* **drudg·er·ies.** dull or hard work.

drug (drug), *n.* 1. a substance taken to cure disease or improve health; medicine. 2. a dangerous, habit-forming substance; narcotic. —*v.,* **drugged, drug·ging.** 3. to mix (food or drink) with a drug, esp. one that is harmful or numbs the senses. 4. to poison or numb the senses of with a drug. 5. to give a drug to as a medicine. [from the French word *drogue,* which comes from a Germanic word related to English *dry.* The original meaning was "dry merchandise"]

drug·gist (drug′ist), *n.* 1. a person who sells drugs, medicines, etc., esp. one who fills prescriptions; pharmacist. 2. the owner or operator of a drugstore.

drug·store (drug′stôr′), *n.* a store that sells drugs, medicines, and often stationery, cigarettes, etc.

Dru·id (drōō′id), *n.* a priest of an ancient Celtic religion in France, Britain, and Ireland.

drum (drum), *n.* 1. any of numerous kinds of musical instruments consisting of a hollow body usually covered at one or both ends with a stretched skin and sounded by being struck or tapped with the hand, a stick, or a pair of sticks. 2. a round and deep container, esp. one used for shipping oil. 3. anything having a round shape and flat ends. —*v.,* **drummed, drum·ming.** 4. to play on a drum or drums. 5. to tap with the fingers: *He drummed nervously on the table.* 6. **drum up,** to increase or create (interest, customers, etc.) through intense efforts: *to drum up business with television commercials.*

drum′ ma′jor, the leader of a marching band or drum corps. Also, *referring to a girl,* **drum′ majorette′.**

drum·mer (drum′ər), *n.* 1. a person who plays on a drum or drums. 2. a traveling salesman.

drum·stick (drum′stik′), *n.* 1. any of various specially shaped sticks, used for beating drums. 2. the meaty lower joint of the leg of a fowl.

drunk (drungk), *adj.* 1. overpowered by alcohol; intoxicated. 2. overpowered or dominated by great emotion: *drunk with joy; drunk with power.* —*n.* 3. a drunken person. —*v.* 4. the past participle of **drink.**

drunk·ard (drung′kərd), *n.* a person who is frequently drunk.

drunk·en (drung′kən), *adj.* 1. intoxicated; drunk. 2. caused by being drunk: *a drunken quarrel; drunken anger.* —**drunk′en·ly,** *adv.* —**drunk′en·ness,** *n.*

dry (drī), *adj.,* **dri·er, dri·est. 1.** free from moisture; not wet or damp: *a dry towel; dry air.* **2.** having little or no rain; arid: *a dry climate.* **3.** not under, in, or on water: *It was good to be on dry land after the ocean voyage.* **4.** having all its water or other liquid used up, drained away, etc.: *a dry well; a dry fountain pen.* **5.** wanting to drink; thirsty: *Salty food makes me dry.* **6.** dull or uninteresting; boring: *a dry book.* **7.** funny in a straight-faced, matter-of-fact way: *dry humor.* **8.** not sweet: *dry wine.* **9.** not allowing the sale of alcoholic liquors: *a dry state.* —*v.,* **dried, dry·ing. 10.** to make or become dry or free from moisture (often fol. by *up*): *He dried his hands. The well dried up.* **11.** to evaporate or cause to evaporate (often fol. by *up* or *away*): *The sun dried up the dew.* —**dry′ly,** *adv.* —**dry′ness,** *n.*

dry·ad (drī′əd), *n.* (in Greek mythology) a nymph of a kind that lived in the woods.

dry′ cell′, a portable device for producing a steady electric current by chemical action that consists of two different materials separated by a conducting paste rather than by a liquid.

dry-clean (drī′klēn′), *v.* to clean clothes with a liquid other than water, such as benzine or gasoline.

dry′ clean′er, a person who owns or operates a dry-cleaning business. —**dry′ clean′ing.**

dry′ dock′, a dock that can be emptied of water, allowing for the repair, painting, etc., of ships.

dry·er (drī′ər), *n.* **1.** Also, **drier.** a machine for removing moisture by heat or blowing air: *a clothes dryer; a hair dryer.* **2.** See **drier**[1] (defs. 1, 2).

dry′ goods′, cloth, clothing, ribbon, and the like.

dry′ meas′ure, a system of units of volume, used esp. for fruits and grain, in which 2 pints equal 1 quart, 8 quarts equal 1 peck, and 4 pecks equal 1 bushel, the pints and quarts representing different volumes than those of liquid measure.

D.S.C., Distinguished Service Cross.

du·al (dōō′əl, dyōō′-), *adj.* composed or consisting of two persons, items, parts, etc., together; double; twofold: *dual ownership; dual controls.*

dub[1] (dub), *v.,* **dubbed, dub·bing. 1.** to make (someone) a knight by striking his shoulder lightly with a sword: *He was dubbed a knight by the queen.* **2.** to give a name, nickname, or title to; name or call: *The dog was dubbed "Blackie."* [from the Middle English word *dubben* "to strike"]

dub[2] (dub), *v.,* **dubbed, dub·bing. 1.** to furnish (a film) with a different sound track, as in another language. **2.** to add (music, speech, etc.) to a film or tape (usually fol. by *in*): *They had to dub in the singing for the star of the picture.* [short for *double*]

du·bi·ous (dōō′bē əs, dyōō′-), *adj.* **1.** causing doubt; not definite or clear in meaning: *a dubious reply.* **2.** being in doubt; not sure: *She was dubious about going.* **3.** of doubtful goodness, reliability, etc.: *dubious acquaintances.* —**du′bi·ous·ly,** *adv.*

Dub·lin (dub′lin), *n.* a seaport and the capital city of the Republic of Ireland, in the E part.

du·cal (dōō′kəl, dyōō′-), *adj.* of or referring to a duke: *a ducal title.*

duc·at (duk′ət), *n.* any of several kinds of gold coins once used in various parts of Europe. [from the Italian word *ducato,* which comes from *duca* "duke." The coin was originally so named from the portrait of a duke of Venice stamped on it]

duch·ess (duch′is), *n.* **1.** the wife or widow of a duke. **2.** a woman who has the rank of a duke in her own right.

duch·y (duch′ē), *n., pl.* **duch·ies.** the territory ruled by a duke or duchess.

duck[1] (duk), *n., pl.* **ducks** *or* **duck.** any of numerous webfooted, swimming fowls having broad, flat bills, some species of which are raised for their meat. [from the Old English word *dūce,* which is related to *duck*[2]]

Wild duck
(length 1½ ft.)

duck[2] (duk), *v.* **1.** to plunge underwater briefly: *He ducked into the pool.* **2.** to stoop or bend suddenly; bob: *When he saw the ball coming he ducked.* **3.** to avoid or evade (a blow, unpleasant task, etc.): *to duck an embarrassing question.* —*n.* **4.** a brief plunge underwater. **5.** the act of stooping or bending suddenly. [from the Middle English word *duken*]

duck[3] (duk), *n.* a heavy cotton fabric resembling canvas but lighter, used for tents, small sails, clothing, etc. [from the Dutch word *doek* "cloth"]

duck·bill (duk′bil′), *n.* **1.** a bill resembling that of a duck. **2.** Also, **duck′billed′ plat′ypus.** another name for **platypus.** —**duck′billed′,** *adj.*

duck′ing stool′, a former instrument of punishment consisting of a chair, attached to a long pole or board, in which offenders were tied before being plunged into water.

duck·ling (duk′ling), *n.* a young duck.

duck·weed (duk′wēd′), *n.* any of several small green plants that float on still water.

Ducking stool

duct (dukt), *n.* **1.** a tube for carrying a fluid or air. **2.** a tube that carries a body fluid, esp. the secretion of a gland. —**duct′less,** *adj.*

duc·tile (duk′t°l), *adj.* **1.** (of a metal) capable of being hammered out thin or drawn into thin wires. See also **malleable** (def. 1). **2.** able to undergo change of shape without breaking: *Wax is ductile.* **3.** easily led or managed; tractable: *a ductile child.*

duct′less gland′, any of a group of important glands in the body that secrete hormones directly into the bloodstream. Also, **endocrine gland.**

dud (dud), *n. Informal.* **1.** a bomb or shell that fails to explode after being fired. **2.** a person or thing that proves to be useless or a failure: *This car is a dud.*

dude (dood, dyood), *n*. **1.** a man who is very much concerned with his clothes and general appearance. **2.** (in the western U.S.) a city-bred person, esp. an Easterner, who is vacationing on a ranch.

dude′ ranch′, a ranch operated as a vacation resort.

dudg·eon (duj′ən), *n*. a feeling of offense or resentment; anger: *After being insulted, he left in high dudgeon.*

duds (dudz), *n.pl. Informal*. **1.** clothes. **2.** personal belongings in general: *Let's pack our duds and go.*

due (doo, dyoo), *adj*. **1.** owed as a debt or bill. **2.** owing as a right: *the respect that is due to a lady.* **3.** rightful; proper; fitting: *Take due care of the books.* **4.** expected to be ready, be present, or arrive: *The plane is due at noon.* —*n*. **5.** something due, owed, or naturally belonging to someone: *Freedom is our due.* **6.** Usually, **dues.** a regular fee or charge, esp. one that is paid for membership in a club. **7. due to,** caused or produced by: *The delay in the game was due to rain.*

du·el (doo′əl, dyoo′-), *n*. **1.** a combat between two persons to settle a quarrel, fought with deadly weapons and watched by witnesses, according to set rules. **2.** any contest between two groups, persons, animals, etc.: *a duel between Germany and England; a duel of debating teams.* —*v.*, **du·eled** *or* **du·elled; du·el·ing** *or* **du·el·ling. 3.** to fight in a duel.

du·el·ist (doo′ə list, dyoo′-), *n*. a person who fights in a duel. Also, **du′el·list, du′el·er, du′el·ler.**

du·et (doo et′, dyoo-), *n*. a musical composition for two voices or instruments.

dug (dug), *v*. the past tense and past participle of **dig.**

du·gong (doo′gong), *n*. a plant-eating mammal that lives in water, having a fishlike body, flipperlike forelimbs, and a paddlelike tail. [from the Malay word *duyong*]

Dugong (length 9 ft.)

dug·out (dug′out′), *n*. **1.** a rough shelter or dwelling formed by making a hollow in the earth. **2.** a boat made by hollowing out a log. **3.** a small shelter at the side of a baseball field, used by players who are not on the field.

duke (dook, dyook), *n*. **1.** the ruler of a duchy. **2.** (in England) a nobleman ranking immediately below a prince. **3.** a male member of the British royal family, other than a king or prince. [from the Old French word *duc,* which comes from Latin *dux* "leader"]

duke·dom (dook′dəm, dyook′-), *n*. **1.** a duchy. **2.** the office or rank of a duke.

dul·cet (dul′sit), *adj*. pleasant to the ear; melodious: *The dulcet tones of a lute.* —**dul′cet·ly,** *adv.*

Dulcimer

dul·ci·mer (dul′sə mər), *n*. **1.** a musical instrument having strings struck with light hammers held in the hands. **2.** a modern folk instrument related to the guitar, played by plucking the strings with the fingers.

dull (dul), *adj*. **1.** not sharp; blunt: *a dull blade.* **2.** not felt keenly: *a dull pain.* **3.** lacking sharpness in feeling or perceiving: *dull eyesight.* **4.** slow in thinking, learning, or understanding: *a very dull student.* **5.** slow in motion or action; not brisk; sluggish: *a dull day in business.* **6.** not interesting; boring: *a dull, endless speech.* **7.** lacking richness or brightness in color: *dull, sunless rooms; a dull painting.* —*v*. **8.** to make or become dull: *Whittling dulls a knife.* —**dull′ness,** *n*. —**dul′ly,** *adv.*

dull·ard (dul′ərd), *n*. a stupid person.

Du·luth (də looth′), *n*. a port city in E Minnesota, on Lake Superior.

du·ly (doo′lē, dyoo′-), *adv*. in a proper or fitting manner; as due: *He duly thanked them for the gift.*

dumb (dum), *adj*. **1.** lacking the power of speech: *dumb animals.* **2.** unable to speak for a time; speechless: *dumb with amazement.* **3.** *Informal.* stupid. —**dumb′ly,** *adv*. —**dumb′ness,** *n*.

dumb·bell (dum′bel′), *n*. **1.** a bar of wood or metal having heavy, ball-shaped ends, used for exercise. **2.** *Informal.* a stupid person.

dumb·wait·er (dum′wā′tər), *n*. a small elevator used for moving food, garbage, etc., from floor to floor in apartment houses, restaurants, etc.

dum·found (dum found′), *v*. to make speechless with amazement; astonish: *They were dumfounded by the sight of the comet.* Also, **dumb·found′.**

dum·my (dum′ē), *n., pl.* **dum·mies. 1.** a figure resembling a person, used to display clothing, esp. in a store window; mannequin. **2.** a person who carries out the will of others while seeming to act for himself. **3.** a player in bridge whose cards are laid face up and played by his partner. **4.** any imitation or copy of something: *The guns used by the actors were all dummies.* **5.** *Informal.* a stupid person. —*adj*. **6.** made or done in imitation; sham: *dummy guns.* **7.** carrying out the will of others while seeming to act for oneself: *a dummy king.*

dump (dump), *v*. **1.** to drop or let fall in a mass or heap: *He dumped his books on the table.* **2.** to unload or empty out: *to dump garbage.* —*n*. **3.** a place where garbage, refuse, etc., is left: *the city dump.* **4.** a place for storing ammunition and other military supplies. **5.** the act of dumping or unloading. **6.** *Slang.* a place, house, town, etc., that is dirty, disreputable, or broken-down.

dump·ling (dump′ling), *n*. **1.** a ball of boiled or steamed dough that is served in soup, with meat, etc. **2.** a pastry made of fruit, such as apples or berries, coated with thin dough and boiled or baked.

dumps (dumps), *n.pl. Informal.* a gloomy state of mind: *He's in the dumps because of the bad weather.*

dump·y (dum′pē), *adj.*, **dump·i·er, dump·i·est.** short and stout: *a dumpy little person.* —**dump′i·ness,** *n*.

dun[1] (dun), *v.*, **dunned, dun·ning. 1.** to demand payment of repeatedly, esp. for a debt: *He was dunned by the store, but never paid his bills.* —*n*. **2.** a person who duns another. **3.** a demand for payment, esp. one in writing. [from the Middle English word *donen* "to make a noise"]

dun² (dun), *n.* **1.** a dull, grayish brown. —*adj.* **2.** of the color dun. [from the Old English word *dunn*]

dunce (duns), *n.* an ignorant or stupid person.

dune (dōōn, dyōōn), *n.* a sand hill or sand ridge formed by the wind.

dung (dung), *n.* waste matter left by animals; manure.

dun·ga·ree (dung′gə rē′), *n.* **1. dungarees,** work clothes, overalls, etc., made usually of blue denim. **2.** blue denim.

dun·geon (dun′jən), *n.* a strong, underground prison or cell: *the dungeon of a castle.*

dunk (dungk), *v.* to dip (a doughnut, cake, etc.) into coffee, milk, or the like, before eating.

du·o (dōō′ō, dyōō′ō), *n., pl.* **du·os. 1.** (in music) a duet. **2.** two persons who associate with each other and are usually thought of as a couple; pair.

dup., duplicate.

dupe (dōōp, dyōōp), *n.* **1.** a person who is easily deceived or fooled: *Swindlers are always on the lookout for dupes.* —*v.,* **duped, dup·ing. 2.** to make a dupe of; deceive; trick; fool: *He was duped into buying things he did not really need.*

du·plex (dōō′pleks, dyōō′-), *adj.* **1.** having two parts; double; twofold. —*n.* **2.** a house for two families, or an apartment having two floors.

du·pli·cate (dōō′plə kit, dyōō′-), *n.* **1.** anything exactly like something else, such as a copy: *She made a duplicate of the letter.* —*v.* (dōō′plə kāt′, dyōō′-), **du·pli·cat·ed, du·pli·cat·ing. 2.** to make a copy of (something): *He duplicated the letter by using carbon paper.* —*adj.* (dōō′plə kit, dyōō′-). **3.** exactly like something else: *a duplicate key.* **4.** double; twofold: *the duplicate pattern of a butterfly's wings.* **5. in duplicate,** in two copies; with an additional copy: *Fill out the application in duplicate.*

du·pli·ca·tion (dōō′plə kā′shən, dyōō′-), *n.* **1.** the act of duplicating, or the state of being duplicated. **2.** a duplicate.

du·pli·ca·tor (dōō′plə kā′tər, dyōō′-), *n.* a machine for making copies of printed or written matter.

du·plic·i·ty (dōō plis′i tē, dyōō-), *n., pl.* **du·plic·i·ties.** deceitfulness in speech or behavior: *the duplicity of false friends.*

du·ra·ble (dōōr′ə bəl, dyōōr′-), *adj.* lasting or enduring in spite of much use, wear, age, etc.: *shoes with durable soles; durable beliefs.* —**du′ra·bil′i·ty,** *n.*

dur·ance (dōōr′əns, dyōōr′-), *n.* imprisonment, or long confinement.

du·ra·tion (dōō rā′shən, dyōō-), *n.* the length of time during which something lasts or continues: *a friendship of long duration.*

du·ress (dōō res′, dyōō-), *n.* the use of force or threats to make a person do something: *He made the confession under duress.*

dur·ing (dōōr′ing, dyōōr′-), *prep.* **1.** throughout the duration of: *During the summer they live in the country.* **2.** at some time or point in the course of: *They left the house sometime during the night.*

durst (dûrst), *v.* an old form of **dared,** found now chiefly in Biblical and poetic writing.

dusk (dusk), *n.* **1.** the part of twilight just before dark. **2.** shade or gloom: *the dusk of a deep forest.*

dusk·y (dus′kē), *adj.,* **dusk·i·er, dusk·i·est. 1.** somewhat dark; dim; gloomy. **2.** having a dark skin or complexion. **3.** of a dark color. —**dusk′i·ness,** *n.*

dust (dust), *n.* **1.** earth or other substance in fine, dry particles. **2.** what is left of anything after death or destruction: *the dust of ancient cities.* **3.** earth or ground, esp. as a place of burial: *to return to the dust.* —*v.* **4.** to wipe the dust from (an object): *to dust furniture.* **5.** to sprinkle with powder or dust: *to dust a cake with sugar.* **6. bite the dust, a.** to die; be killed: *a cowboy movie in which many Indians bit the dust.* **b.** to fail; be defeated: *Many small companies bit the dust during the Depression.* **7. dust off,** to make (something) ready to use again: *Mother is dusting off her French before her trip to Canada.*

dust·er (dus′tər), *n.* **1.** a person who removes dust or applies a dustlike substance. **2.** a cloth, rag, brush, or the like, for removing dust. **3.** a machine or device for sprinkling a powdery substance, such as an insecticide. **4.** a garment worn to protect the clothes from dust.

dust·pan (dust′pan′), *n.* a shovellike utensil with a short handle, used to collect dust that is swept up.

dust′ storm′, a storm of dust-filled wind occurring in regions stricken with drought.

dust·y (dus′tē), *adj.,* **dust·i·er, dust·i·est. 1.** filled or covered with dust: *a dusty table; dusty wind.* **2.** like dust; powdery; dry: *dusty pollen.* **3.** of the color of dust; grayish: *dusty pink.* —**dust′i·ness,** *n.*

Dutch (duch), *adj.* **1.** of, referring to, or characteristic of Holland, its people, or their language. **2.** of, referring to, or characteristic of the Pennsylvania Dutch. **3.** *Slang.* German. —*n.* **4.** the people of Holland. **5.** the Germanic language of Holland. **6. go Dutch,** to divide expenses evenly: *If you want to stop for a hamburger, we can go Dutch.* **7. in Dutch,** in trouble or disfavor: *After tattling that way, he's in Dutch with the whole class.*

Dutch′ door′, a door made of two units divided so that the upper part can be opened while the lower remains closed.

Dutch′ East′ In′dies, a former name of Indonesia.

Dutch′ Guian′a, former name of Surinam.

Dutch·man (duch′mən), *n., pl.* **Dutch·men.** a native or inhabitant of the Netherlands.

Dutch door

Dutch′ treat′, a meal or entertainment for which each person pays his own share of the expense.

du·ti·ful (dōō′ti fəl, dyōō′-), *adj.* performing the duties expected or required of one: *a dutiful child; a dutiful citizen.* —**du′ti·ful·ly,** *adv.*

du·ty (dōō′tē, dyōō′-), *n., pl.* **du·ties. 1.** something that one is expected or required to do: *It is one's duty to obey the law.* **2.** the force that binds one to do what is considered right: *the call of duty.* **3.** the tasks demanded by one's position: *the duties of a clergyman.* **4.** the respect and obedience owed to a parent, elder, etc. **5.** a tax to be paid on goods brought into or taken out of a country.

dwarf (dwôrf), *n.* **1.** a person, plant, or animal that is much smaller than is usual for most others of his or its kind. **2.** (in fairy tales and legends) a small, ugly old man with magic powers. —*adj.* **3.** unusually small; diminutive: *dwarf roses.* —*v.* **4.** to cause (something) to seem small in size, amount, etc.: *In New York, the tall buildings dwarf the houses near them.* **5.** to stunt the growth of. —**dwarf′ish,** *adj.*

dwell (dwel), *v.,* **dwelt** (dwelt) *or* **dwelled; dwell·ing. 1.** to live or stay more or less permanently: *We dwell in the city.* **2.** to linger over in thought, speech, or writing (often fol. by *on*): *Don't dwell on unhappy memories.* —**dwell′er,** *n.*

dwell·ing (dwel′ing), *n.* a building or place to live in: *A house is a dwelling.*

dwelt (dwelt), *v.* a past tense and past participle of **dwell.**

dwin·dle (dwin′dᵊl), *v.,* **dwin·dled, dwin·dling.** to become smaller and smaller or less and less: *The water supply is dwindling.*

Dy, *Chem.* the symbol for **dysprosium.**

dye (dī), *n.* **1.** a coloring matter. **2.** a liquid containing coloring matter, in which paper, cloth, etc., is steeped. **3.** a color or hue, esp. one given by dyeing: *robes of rich dye.* —*v.,* **dyed, dye·ing. 4.** to color or stain with dye. —**dy′er,** *n.*

dyed-in-the-wool (dīd′ᵊn *th*ə wŏŏl′), *adj.* fixed in one's habits; confirmed: *a dyed-in-the-wool Republican.*

dye·stuff (dī′stuf′), *n.* a material that can be used for dyeing or from which dyes are made.

dy·ing (dī′ing), *adj.* **1.** approaching death. **2.** given, said, or shown just before death: *his dying wish.* **3.** coming to an end; drawing to a close: *the dying year.*

dyke (dīk), *n., v.,* **dyked, dyk·ing.** another spelling of **dike.**

dy·nam·ic (dī nam′ik), *adj.* **1.** of or concerning force or power in motion. **2.** active; vigorous; forceful: *a dynamic speaker.* —**dy·nam′i·cal·ly,** *adv.*

dy·nam·ics (dī nam′iks), *n.* **1.** *(used as sing.)* the branch of physics concerned with objects that are in motion and the ways in which forces affect this motion. **2.** *(used as pl.)* (in music) variation in loudness. **3.** *(used as pl.)* the forces in any field that drive or motivate.

dy·na·mite (dī′nə mīt′), *n.* **1.** an explosive made in the form of sticks and used for blasting rocks. —*v.,* **dy·na·mit·ed, dy·na·mit·ing. 2.** to blow up or destroy with dynamite: *to dynamite a bridge.*

dy·na·mo (dī′nə mō′), *n., pl.* **dy·na·mos. 1.** an electric generator, esp. one that produces direct current. **2.** *Informal.* a forceful, energetic person.

dy·nas·ty (dī′nə stē), *n., pl.* **dy·nas·ties. 1.** a series of rulers from the same family: *the dynasties of ancient Egypt.* **2.** the period of time during which a dynasty rules.

dys·en·ter·y (dis′ən ter′ē), *n.* a serious infectious disease of the intestines that causes severe diarrhea, including the discharge of mucus and blood.

dys·pro·si·um (dis prō′sē əm), *n. Chem.* a metallic element of the rare-earth group. *Symbol:* Dy

dys·tro·phy (dis′trə fē), *n.* any of several diseases that cause a wasting away of the muscles.

dz., dozen; dozens.

	Semitic	Greek	Latin	Gothic	Modern Roman	
DEVELOPMENT OF UPPER-CASE LETTERS	ⴺ	ⴺ E	ⴺ	E	𝔈	E
DEVELOPMENT OF LOWER-CASE LETTERS	ϵ	ϝ	ϵ	ℓ	ℓ	e
	Greek		Medieval		Gothic	Modern Roman

E

E, e (ē), *n., pl.* **E's** *or* **Es, e's** *or* **es.** the fifth letter of the English alphabet.

E, 1. east. 2. eastern.

E, 1. *(sometimes l.c.)* (in some grading systems) a grade or mark that indicates scholastic work that is unacceptable or that needs improvement in order to be passing. 2. *(sometimes l.c.)* (in some grading systems) a grade or mark that indicates scholastic work of high or excellent quality. 3. the symbol for **electromotive force.**

E., 1. east. 2. eastern. 3. English.

ea., each.

each (ēch), *adj.* 1. every one of two or more things considered separately: *each stone in a building.* —*pron.* 2. each person or thing: *Each went his way.* —*adv.* 3. to, from, or for each; apiece: *The apples cost ten cents each.* 4. **each other,** each the other; one another: *We write each other every week.* —**Usage.** *Each* is always used with a singular verb: *Each child has his own book. Each of the boys is a member of the team.*

ea·ger (ē′gər), *adj.* 1. desiring very much; impatient: *eager for news.* 2. enthusiastic or earnest: *an eager swimmer.* —**ea′ger·ly,** *adv.* —**ea′ger·ness,** *n.*

ea·gle (ē′gəl), *n.* any of several large birds of prey noted for their size, strength, and powers of flight and vision.

ea·glet (ē′glit), *n.* a young eagle.

ear[1] (ēr), *n.* 1. the organ of hearing in man and other animals. 2. the sense of hearing: *sounds pleasing to the ear.* 3. keen perception or awareness of the differences of sound: *an ear for music.* 4. **be all ears,** to pay close attention; listen: *Tell me, I'm all ears.* [from the Old English word *ēare*]

Ear (Human)
A, Outer ear; B, Middle ear; C, Inner ear; D, Eardrum; E, Eustachian tube

ear[2] (ēr), *n.* the part of a cereal plant that contains or holds the grain: *an ear of corn.* [from the Old English word *ēar*]

ear·ache (ēr′āk′), *n.* a pain in the ear.

ear·drum (ēr′drum′), *n.* a membrane between the outer and middle parts of the ear that vibrates when sound waves strike it. See illus. at **ear**[1].

earl (ûrl), *n.* a British nobleman of a rank below that of marquis and above that of viscount.

ear·ly (ûr′lē), *adv.*, **ear·li·er, ear·li·est.** 1. in or during the first part of a period of time, a course of action, a series of events, etc.: *early in the year; early in the game.* 2. before the usual time; ahead of time: *to come early.* —*adj.,* **ear·li·er, ear·li·est.** 3. occurring in the first part of a period of time, course of action, series of events, etc.: *an early hour of the day.* 4. occurring before the usual time: *an early dinner.* —**ear′li·ness,** *n.*

ear·muffs (ēr′mufs′), *n.pl.* a pair of adjustable coverings for protecting the ears in cold weather.

earn (ûrn), *v.* 1. to gain or get in return for one's work: *to earn a living.* 2. to deserve or merit: *to receive more than one has earned.* 3. to gain through effort or merit: *to earn a reputation for honesty.*

ear·nest (ûr′nist), *adj.* 1. serious in intention, purpose, or effort; eager: *an earnest worker.* 2. showing sincerity of feeling: *an earnest plea.* 3. **in earnest, a.** determined; sincere; serious: *He's in earnest when he says he won't come.* **b.** seriously; with determination: *He started studying in earnest the day before the test.* —**ear′nest·ly,** *adv.* —**ear′nest·ness,** *n.*

earn·ings (ûr′ningz), *n.pl.* money earned; wages; profits.

ear·phone (ēr′fōn′), *n.* a receiver for a telephone, radio, or the like, that is fitted over or into the ear.

ear·ring (ēr′ring′), *n.* an ornament worn on the lobe of the ear.

ear·shot (ēr′shot′), *n.* the range or distance within which a sound can be heard: *Stay within earshot in case I need you.*

---

act, āble, dâre, ärt; ebb, ēqual; if, īce; hot, ōver, ôrder; oil; bŏŏk; ōōze; out; up, ûrge; ə = *a* as in *alone;* ⁊ as in *button* (but′ᵊn), *fire* (fīᵊr); chief; shoe; thin; ŧħat; zh as in *measure* (mezh′ᵊr). See full key inside cover.

earth (ûrth), *n.* **1.** *(often cap.)* the planet, third in order of distance from the sun, on which we live. The earth has a diameter of 7926 miles at the equator; its average distance from the sun is 92,900,000 miles. **2.** soil and dirt, as distinguished from rock and sand.

earth·en (ûr'thən), *adj.* **1.** made of earth. **2.** made of baked clay.

earth·en·ware (ûr'thən wâr'), *n.* pottery made of baked or hardened clay.

earth·ly (ûrth'lē), *adj.,* **earth·li·er, earth·li·est. 1.** of or referring to the earth; worldly: *earthly belongings.* **2.** possible or imaginable: *of no earthly value.* —**earth'li·ness,** *n.*

earth·quake (ûrth'kwāk'), *n.* a shaking or trembling of the ground caused by sudden movement of underground rock layers. Earthquakes can be very destructive.

earth' sci'ence, a science, such as geography or geology, that deals with the earth and its composition.

earth·work (ûrth'wûrk'), *n.* a construction formed mostly of earth for protection from enemy fire.

earth·worm (ûrth'wûrm'), *n.* any of numerous worms that burrow in soil and are of value in loosening and fertilizing it.

earth·y (ûr'thē), *adj.,* **earth·i·er, earth·i·est. 1.** of or like earth or soil: *an earthy smell.* **2.** realistic; practical. **3.** coarse or unrefined: *an earthy sense of humor.* —**earth'i·ness,** *n.*

ease (ēz), *n.* **1.** freedom from pain or discomfort. **2.** freedom from concern or worry. **3.** freedom from difficulty or great effort: *It can be done with ease.* —*v.,* **eased, eas·ing. 4.** to lessen: *to ease pain.* **5.** to move with great care: *to ease a car into a narrow parking spot.* **6.** to lessen the pressure of; loosen: *to ease a belt that is too tight.* **7. at ease, a.** in a position of rest or relaxation: *The soldiers stood at ease during the rest period.* **b.** without discomfort or nervousness; normal or natural: *to be at ease with strangers.*

ea·sel (ē'zəl), *n.* a stand or frame for supporting an artist's canvas, a blackboard, etc.

eas·i·ly (ē'zə lē), *adv.* **1.** in an easy manner; with ease. **2.** beyond question; by far: *easily the best.*

east (ēst), *n.* **1.** one of the four principal compass points, the direction of the rising sun. *Abbr.:* E **2.** the eastern part of a region or country. **3. the East, a.** the Orient; Far East. **b.** the countries east of Europe. **c.** the part of the U.S. east of the Mississippi River. **d.** the part of the U.S. east of the Alleghenies. —*adj.* Also, **eastern. 4.** situated in the east: *the east part of the state.* **5.** coming from the east: *an east wind.* —*adv.* **6.** toward the east: *to sail east.*

East' Berlin'. See under **Berlin.**

east·bound (ēst'bound'), *adj.* going toward the east: *eastbound traffic.*

East' Chi'na Sea', a part of the N Pacific, bounded by China, Korea, and Japan. 480,000 sq. mi.

East·er (ē'stər), *n.* an annual Christian festival in commemoration of the resurrection of Jesus Christ, observed on the first Sunday after the first full moon that occurs on or after March 21.

East'er Is'land, an island in the S Pacific, W of and belonging to Chile. about 45 sq. mi.

east·er·ly (ē'stər lē), *adj.* **1.** directed toward the east: *in an easterly course.* **2.** coming from the east: *The wind is easterly.* —*adv.* **3.** toward the east: *sailing easterly.* **4.** from the east, as a wind.

east·ern (ē'stərn), *adj.* **1.** See **east** (defs. 4, 5). **2.** *(often cap.)* of or referring to the East. **3.** *(usually cap.)* of or referring to the Far East; Oriental.

East'ern Church', any of the churches originating in countries that formerly made up the Eastern Roman Empire; Byzantine Church.

east·ern·er (ē'stər nər), *n. (often cap.)* a native or inhabitant of an eastern area, esp. of the eastern U.S.

East'ern Hem'isphere, the eastern part of the earth, including Europe, Asia, Africa, and Australia.

east·ern·most (ē'stərn mōst'), *adj.* farthest east: *the easternmost city in the state.*

East'ern Or'thodox Church', another name for **Orthodox Church.**

East'ern Ro'man Em'pire, the E part of the Roman Empire, esp. after the division in A.D. 395, having its capital at Constantinople.

East' Ger'many, a country in central Europe: consists of the Soviet zone of occupied Germany. 41,535 sq. mi. *Cap.:* East Berlin. —**East' Ger'man.**

East' In'dies, the islands in the Indian Ocean between Asia and Australia. Also, **the Indies.** —**East' In'dian.**

east-north·east (ēst'nôrth'ēst'), *n.* **1.** the point on the compass halfway between east and northeast. *Abbr.:* ENE —*adj.* **2.** directed toward this point. **3.** coming from this point, as a wind. —*adv.* **4.** toward this point. **5.** from this point, as a wind.

East' Pak'istan, former name of **Bangladesh.**

East' Riv'er, a strait in SE New York separating the island of Manhattan from Long Island.

east-south·east (ēst'south'ēst'), *n.* **1.** the point on the compass halfway between east and southeast. *Abbr.:* ESE —*adj.* **2.** directed toward this point. **3.** coming from this point, as a wind. —*adv.* **4.** toward this point. **5.** from this point, as a wind.

east·ward (ēst'wərd), *adj.* **1.** directed toward the east. **2.** situated in the east. —*adv.* **3.** Also, **east'wards.** toward the east: *to sail eastward.* —*n.* **4.** an eastward direction or point: *to sail to the eastward.*

eas·y (ē'zē), *adj.,* **eas·i·er, eas·i·est. 1.** not difficult; demanding little effort or labor: *an easy book; an easy victory.* **2.** free from pain or worry: *an easy mind.* **3.** providing ease or comfort; comfortable: *an easy life.* **4.** given to ease; easygoing; relaxed: *an easy disposition.* **5.** not strict; lenient: *an easy teacher.* **6.** not hurried; relaxed; moderate: *an easy pace.* **7.** not tight or uncomfortable: *an easy fit.* —*adv.* **8.** *Informal.* in an easy manner; comfortably: *to go easy.* **9. take it easy, a.** to enjoy one's leisure; relax: *Dad is retired now and just takes it easy.* **b.** to avoid anger or emotional upset: *He didn't mean to insult you, so take it easy.* —**eas'i·ness,** *n.*

eas·y·go·ing (ē'zē gō'ing), *adj.* calm and unworried; relaxed.

eat (ēt), *v.*, **ate** (āt), **eat·en** (ēt/ᵊn), **eat·ing. 1.** to take into the mouth and swallow for nourishment; chew and swallow (food): *to eat a sandwich.* **2.** to consume food: *to eat three times a day.* **3.** to destroy gradually; wear away: *The patient was eaten by disease and pain.* **4.** to make a hole, passage, etc., such as by gnawing or corrosion: *Acid ate through the linoleum.* **5. eat one's words.** See word (def. 11). —**eat/er,** *n.*

eat·a·ble (ē/tə bəl), *adj.* **1.** fit to be eaten; edible. —*n.* **2.** Usually, **eatables.** food.

eaves (ēvz), *n.pl.* the overhanging lower edge of a roof.

eaves·drop (ēvz/drop/), *v.*, **eaves·dropped, eaves·drop·ping.** to listen secretly to a private conversation. —**eaves/drop/per,** *n.*

ebb (eb), *n.* **1.** the flowing back of the tide as the water returns to the sea (opposite of *flood*). **2.** a point of decline: *His fortunes were at a low ebb.* —*v.* **3.** to flow back or away, as the water of a tide (opposite of *flow*). **4.** to decline; fade away: *His life is ebbing.*

ebb/ tide/, the tide that flows away from the shore and back to sea (opposite of *flood tide*).

eb·on·y (eb/ə nē), *n., pl.* **eb·on·ies. 1.** the hard, heavy, black wood of several tropical trees, formerly used for the black keys of pianos. **2.** a deep, lustrous black. —*adj.* **3.** made of ebony. **4.** of the color ebony.

ec·cen·tric (ek sen/trik), *adj.* **1.** departing from the regular or usual character, practice, etc.; peculiar; odd: *a sweet but eccentric person.* **2.** not having the same center: said of two circles, one of which contains the centers of both. **3.** not circular: *The orbits of the planets are eccentric.* — *n.* **4.** an odd or peculiar person. **5.** a cam or crank. —**ec·cen/tri·cal·ly,** *adv.*

ec·cen·tric·i·ty (ek/sən tris/i tē), *n., pl.* **ec·cen·tric·i·ties. 1.** an odd or peculiar habit. **2.** the quality of being eccentric.

eccl., ecclesiastical. Also, **eccles.**

Ec·cle·si·as·tes (i klē/zē as/tēz), *n.* a book of the Old Testament.

ec·cle·si·as·tic (i klē/zē as/tik), *n.* **1.** a clergyman. —*adj.* **2.** ecclesiastical.

ec·cle·si·as·ti·cal (i klē/zē as/ti kəl), *adj.* of or referring to the church or the clergy; churchly: *ecclesiastical writings.* —**ec·cle/si·as/ti·cal·ly,** *adv.*

ech·e·lon (esh/ə lon/), *n.* **1.** a level of command, authority, or rank: *The decision was made in the highest echelon.* **2.** a formation of troops, airplanes, etc., in which a group of men or an individual craft or vehicle is placed to the right or left of the one in front. **3.** one of the groups of such a formation.

ech·o (ek/ō), *n., pl.* **ech·oes. 1.** the repetition of a sound produced by reflection of the sound waves from some obstacle. —*v.*, **ech·oed, ech·o·ing. 2.** to resound with an echo: *The room echoes.* **3.** to be re-

peated by an echo: *The sounds echo.* **4.** to repeat or imitate the words, sentiments, etc.: *He echoed everything I said.*

Ech·o (ek/ō), *n.* (in Greek mythology) a nymph who pined away for love of Narcissus until only her voice was left.

é·clair (ā klâr/), *n.* a long pastry, filled with whipped cream or custard and coated with icing.

e·clipse (i klips/), *n.* **1.** the darkening of the moon by the earth's passing between it and the sun (**lunar eclipse),** or the darkening of the sun by the moon's passing between it and the earth (**solar eclipse). 2.** a similar darkening of a satellite of one of the other planets. **3.** a reduction or loss of status, reputation, etc.: *an eclipse of power.* —*v.*, **e·clipsed, e·clips·ing. 4.** to cause (a body) to undergo eclipse: *The earth eclipses the moon.* **5.** to make dim by comparison; surpass; outshine: *His performance eclipsed all others.*

e·clip·tic (i klip/tik), *n.* the path along which the sun seems to travel throughout the year; the plane that contains the sun and the earth's orbit, which is tilted at an angle of 22½° to the plane of the equator.

e·col·o·gy (i kol/ə jē), *n.* the branch of biology that deals with the relations of living things with each other and with their surroundings. —**e·col/o·gist,** *n.*

econ., 1. economic. **2.** economical. **3.** economics. **4.** economy.

e·co·nom·ic (ē/kə nom/ik, ek/ə nom/ik), *adj.* **1.** referring to the production, distribution, and use of income, wealth, and goods: *a report on economic problems.* **2.** of or relating to the science of economics. **3.** referring to personal money matters.

e·co·nom·i·cal (ē/kə nom/i kəl, ek/ə nom/i kəl), *adj.* avoiding waste or extravagance; thrifty: *an economical car; an economical shopper.* —**e/co·nom/i·cal·ly,** *adv.*

e·co·nom·ics (ē/kə nom/iks, ek/ə nom/iks), *n. (used as sing.)* the science that deals with the production, distribution, and consumption of goods and services. —**e·con·o·mist** (i kon/ə mist), *n.*

e·con·o·mize (i kon/ə mīz/), *v.*, **e·con·o·mized, e·con·o·miz·ing. 1.** to practice economy; avoid waste: *She's economizing to buy a new car. We're economizing on oil.* **2.** to manage or use economically: *to economize water during a drought.* —**e·con/o·miz/er,** *n.*

e·con·o·my (i kon/ə mē), *n., pl.* **e·con·o·mies. 1.** thrifty management of money, resources, etc., to avoid waste. **2.** the management of the resources of a community or country: *the American economy.*

e·co·sys·tem (ek/ō sis/təm, ē/kō sis/təm), *n.* the system of biological relations between living things and their environment.

ec·sta·sy (ek/stə sē), *n., pl.* **ec·sta·sies.** an overpowering feeling of joy and delight; rapture; exaltation.

ec·stat·ic (ek stat/ik), *adj.* **1.** full of ecstasy; joyful; rapturous. **2.** causing ecstasy. —**ec·stat/i·cal·ly,** *adv.*

Ec·ua·dor (ek/wə dôr/), *n.* a republic in NW South America. 104,510 sq. mi. *Cap.:* Quito. —**Ec/ua·do/ran, Ec/ua·do/ri·an,** *n., adj.*

Eccentric circles

A, Center of small circle; B, Center of large circle

ec·u·men·i·cal (ek/yə men/i kəl), *adj.* 1. referring to the whole world; universal; worldwide. 2. of or referring to the whole Christian church or to Christian unity. 3. of or referring to a movement (**ec/umen/ical move/ment**) aimed at achieving worldwide Christian unity and cooperation.

ec·ze·ma (ek/sə mə, ig zē/mə), *n.* a disease of the skin that causes itching and the formation of red, scaly patches.

-ed, a suffix used to form 1. the past tense of regular verbs: *I talked.* 2. the past participle of regular verbs: *We have talked.* 3. adjectives meaning **a.** having or provided with: *bearded; tasseled.* **b.** like or of the nature of: *honeyed words.* **c.** having been acted on in a certain way: *inflated balloons.*

ed., 1. edited. 2. edition. 3. editor.

ed·dy (ed/ē), *n., pl.* **ed·dies.** 1. a current of water or air that runs against the main current, making a whirling or circular motion. —*v.,* **ed·died, ed·dy·ing.** 2. to move or whirl in eddies.

Ed·dy (ed/ē), *n.* **Mary Baker,** 1821–1910, U.S. founder of the Christian Science Church.

E·den (ēd/ʳn), *n.* 1. (in the Bible) the place where Adam and Eve lived. 2. any delightful region or place; paradise.

edge (ej), *n.* 1. a line at which a surface ends; border: *Grass grew along the edges of the road.* 2. the thin, sharp side of the blade of a cutting instrument. —*v.,* **edged, edg·ing.** 3. to put an edge on; sharpen: *to edge a knife.* 4. to provide with an edge or border: *to edge a skirt with lace.* 5. to move sideways gradually: *to edge through a crowd.* 6. **on edge,** nervous, irritable, anxious, or the like: *I've been on edge ever since she phoned me.*

edge·wise (ej/wīz/), *adv.* 1. with the edge forward; in the direction of the edge. 2. sideways. Also, **edge·ways** (ej/wāz/).

edg·ing (ej/iñg), *n.* something that is placed along an edge or border: *an edging of lace.*

edg·y (ej/ē), *adj.,* **edg·i·er, edg·i·est.** nervous and impatient. —**edg/i·ness,** *n.*

ed·i·ble (ed/ə bəl), *adj.* fit to be eaten; eatable: *Pick only the berries that are edible.* —**ed/i·ble·ness,** *n.*

e·dict (ē/dikt), *n.* a decree or proclamation issued by some authority.

ed·i·fice (ed/ə fis), *n.* a building, esp. a large and imposing one.

ed·i·fy (ed/ə fī/), *v.,* **ed·i·fied, ed·i·fy·ing.** to build up or increase the faith or morality of; instruct or benefit morally or spiritually: *religious paintings that edify the spirit.* —**ed·i·fi·ca·tion** (ed/ə fə kā/shən), *n.*

Ed·in·burgh (ed/ʳn bûr/ə), *n.* the capital city of Scotland, in the SE part.

Ed·i·son (ed/i sən), *n.* **Thomas Alva,** 1847–1931, U.S. inventor, esp. of the electric light, phonograph, etc.

ed·it (ed/it), *v.* 1. to supervise or direct the preparation of (a newspaper, magazine, book, etc.). 2. to collect, prepare, and arrange (materials) for publication.

edit., 1. edited. 2. edition. 3. editor.

e·di·tion (i dish/ən), *n.* 1. the form in which a literary work is published: *a new edition of Shakespeare.*

2. the total number of copies of a book, newspaper, etc., printed from one set of type at one time.

ed·i·tor (ed/i tər), *n.* 1. a person who is the head of a newspaper, magazine, or the like, or one of its departments. 2. a person who edits material for publication.

ed·i·to·ri·al (ed/i tôr/ē əl), *n.* 1. an article in a newspaper or magazine presenting the opinion of the publisher, editor, or editorial staff. —*adj.* 2. of or referring to an editor or to editing: *editorial policies; editorial offices.* —**ed/i·to/ri·al·ly,** *adv.*

Ed·mon·ton (ed/mən tən), *n.* the capital city of Alberta, in the central part, in SW Canada.

ed·u·cate (ej/ōō kāt/), *v.,* **ed·u·cat·ed, ed·u·cat·ing.** 1. to develop, train, or teach. 2. to provide education for; send to school: *to educate children.*

ed·u·ca·tion (ej/ōō kā/shən), *n.* 1. the act or process of gaining general knowledge and of developing the powers of reasoning and judgment. 2. the act or process of gaining particular knowledge or skills: *a medical education.* 3. a degree, level, or kind of schooling: *a university education.* 4. the science or art of teaching.

ed·u·ca·tion·al (ej/ōō kā/shə nʳl), *adj.* 1. referring to education: *the educational system.* 2. tending or intended to educate: *an educational TV show.*

ed·u·ca·tor (ej/ōō kā/tər), *n.* a teacher, principal, or other person who plans or directs education.

-ee, a suffix used to form 1. nouns meaning a person or thing that **a.** is the object of an action: *employee.* **b.** is the receiver of something: *grantee.* **c.** is or does something: *standee.* 2. diminutive nouns: *bootee.*

eel (ēl), *n., pl.* **eels** *or* **eel.** any of numerous long, slim fishes that resemble snakes and have smooth, often slimy skins.

e'en (ēn), *adv.* even[1]: used esp. in poetry.

e'er (âr), *adv.* ever: used esp. in poetry.

-eer, a suffix used to form nouns meaning a person who is employed in or connected with something: *auctioneer; profiteer.*

Eel
(length to 6 ft.)

ee·rie (ēr/ē), *adj.,* **ee·ri·er, ee·ri·est.** arousing or causing fear; weird: *eerie noises.* —**ee/ri·ly,** *adv.* —**ee/ri·ness,** *n.*

ef·face (i fās/), *v.,* **ef·faced, ef·fac·ing.** to wipe out; destroy; do away with: *to efface a memory; to efface an inscription.* —**ef·face/ment,** *n.*

ef·fect (i fekt/), *n.* 1. something that is produced by a cause; result; consequence: *the terrible effects of war.* 2. the power to produce results; influence: *His speech had no effect.* 3. the state of being effective; operation; accomplishment: *to bring a plan into effect.* 4. an impression produced: *the effect of music.* —*v.* 5. to produce as an effect; bring about; accomplish: *The medicine effected a cure.* 6. **take effect,** to begin to function or produce a result: *The new law takes effect at midnight. The medicine took effect immediately.*

—**Usage.** See **affect**[1].

ef·fec·tive (i fek′tiv), *adj.* **1.** producing the expected or desired result: *effective laws.* **2.** in operation or in force; operating: *The new rules will become effective at the next meeting.* **3.** producing a strong impression: *an effective photograph.* —**ef·fec′tive·ly,** *adv.* —**ef·fec′tive·ness,** *n.*

ef·fec·tu·al (i fek′chōō əl), *adj.* producing or capable of producing an intended effect; adequate. —**ef·fec′tu·al·ly,** *adv.*

ef·fem·i·nate (i fem′ə nit), *adj.* (of a man or boy) having traditionally feminine traits, such as softness, delicacy, or the like. —**ef·fem·i·na·cy** (i fem′ə nə sē), *n.* —**ef·fem′i·nate·ly,** *adv.*

ef·fer·vesce (ef′ər ves′), *v.,* **ef·fer·vesced, ef·fer·vesc·ing.** **1.** to give off bubbles of gas. **2.** to show enthusiasm, excitement, liveliness, etc. —**ef′fer·ves′cence,** *n.*

ef·fer·ves·cent (ef′ər ves′ənt), *adj.* **1.** bubbling. **2.** gay; lively: *an effervescent personality.*

ef·fete (i fēt′), *adj.* **1.** lacking in wholesome vigor; decadent or morally corrupt: *an effete society.* **2.** exhausted of energy; worn out.

ef·fi·ca·cious (ef′ə kā′shəs), *adj.* having or showing the desired result or effect: *efficacious medicine.*

ef·fi·ca·cy (ef′ə kə sē), *n.* capacity for producing a desired result or effect; effectiveness.

ef·fi·cien·cy (i fish′ən sē), *n.* **1.** the ability to accomplish a job well with a minimum of time and effort. **2.** the relationship between the work done by a machine and the amount of energy it requires, often expressed as a percentage.

ef·fi·cient (i fish′ənt), *adj.* performing or functioning in the best possible and least wasteful manner; capable: *an efficient worker; an efficient machine.* —**ef·fi′cient·ly,** *adv.*

ef·fi·gy (ef′i jē), *n., pl.* **ef·fi·gies.** **1.** a painted or sculptured representation of a person. **2.** a crude representation of someone who is disliked.

ef·fort (ef′ərt), *n.* **1.** the use of physical or mental power: *Studying for exams requires effort.* **2.** an attempt; try: *He made an effort to finish the job.*

ef·fort·less (ef′ərt lis), *adj.* requiring little or no effort; easy: *an effortless performance.* —**ef′fort·less·ly,** *adv.*

ef·fron·ter·y (i frun′tə rē), *n.* shameless audacity; boldness: *She had the effrontery to ask another favor.*

ef·ful·gence (i ful′jəns), *n.* extreme radiance or brilliance; splendor. —**ef·ful′gent,** *adj.*

ef·fu·sion (i fyōō′zhən), *n.* **1.** the act of pouring forth: *the effusion of blood from a wound.* **2.** an unrestrained expression of feelings: *sentimental effusions.*

ef·fu·sive (i fyōō′siv), *adj.* overly emotional; showing emotion openly: *an effusive note of thanks.* —**ef·fu′sive·ly,** *adv.*

e.g., for example; such as. [from the Latin phrase *exempli grātiā* "for the sake of example"]

egg¹ (eg), *n.* **1.** the rounded body produced by the female of many kinds of animals from which the young later develop. Birds, most reptiles, and fish lay eggs. **2.** such a body produced by a domestic bird, esp. the hen. [from a Scandinavian word]

egg² (eg), *v.* to urge or encourage (usually fol. by *on*): *They egged me on to try the high diving board.* [from a Scandinavian word related to Icelandic *eggja* "to incite"]

egg·nog (eg′nog′), *n.* a drink made of eggs, milk or cream, sugar, and sometimes liquor.

egg·plant (eg′plant′), *n.* **1.** a large, egg-shaped, usually purple vegetable related to the tomato. **2.** the vine on which it grows.

egg·shell (eg′shel′), *n.* **1.** the hard, brittle shell of a bird's egg. **2.** a pale yellowish tan. —*adj.* **3.** thin and delicate. **4.** of a pale yellowish tan.

e·go (ē′gō), *n., pl.* **e·gos. 1.** the inner self of any person; the thoughts and feelings of a person that distinguish him from others. **2.** conceit; self-importance.

e·go·tism (ē′gə tiz′əm), *n.* the habit of mentioning oneself constantly in speaking or writing; boastfulness. —**e′go·tist,** *n.*

e·go·tis·tic (ē′gə tis′tik), *adj.* given to talking about oneself; vain; boastful. Also, **e′go·tis′ti·cal.** —**e′go·tis′ti·cal·ly,** *adv.*

e·gre·gious (i grē′jəs), *adj.* remarkable in some bad way; glaring; notorious; flagrant: *an egregious blunder.* —**e·gre′gious·ly,** *adv.*

e·gress (ē′gres), *n.* **1.** the act or an instance of going out. **2.** a means or place of going out; exit.

e·gret (ē′grit), *n.* a large, white heron having long plumes formerly used for decorating hats.

E·gypt (ē′jipt), *n.* an ancient kingdom in NE Africa along the Nile River: now called the Arab Republic of Egypt.

E·gyp·tian (i jip′shən), *adj.* **1.** of or concerning Egypt or its people. **2.** of or concerning the language of the ancient Egyptians. —*n.* **3.** a native or inhabitant of Egypt. **4.** the language of the ancient Egyptians.

Egret
(length 3½ ft.)

eh (ā, e), *interj.* (used as an exclamation of surprise, doubt, etc.): *Eh? What did you say?*

ei·der·down (ī′dər doun′), *n.* **1.** the soft breast feathers of the female eider duck, used for stuffing quilts. **2.** a quilt stuffed with these feathers.

ei′der duck′ (ī′dər), any of several large sea ducks, the females of which yield eiderdown. Also, **ei′der.**

eight (āt), *n.* **1.** a number that is seven plus one. **2.** a set of this many persons or things: *Only eight will be there.* —*adj.* **3.** amounting to eight in number: *eight persons.*

eight·een (ā′tēn′), *n.* **1.** a number that is ten plus eight. **2.** a set of this many persons or things: *Eight-*

Eider duck
(length 2 ft.)

een of them will be there. —*adj.* **3.** amounting to eighteen in number: *eighteen persons.*

eight·eenth (ā/tēnth/), *adj.* **1.** being number eighteen in a series: *the eighteenth floor.* —*n.* **2.** one of eighteen equal parts. **3.** a person or thing that is eighteenth.

eighth (ātth), *adj.* **1.** being number eight in a series: *the eighth floor.* —*n.* **2.** one of eight equal parts. **3.** a person or thing that is eighth.

eighth′ note′, (in music) a note one eighth the time value of a whole note. See illus. at **note.**

eight·i·eth (ā/tē ith), *adj.* **1.** being number eighty in a series: *the eightieth floor.* —*n.* **2.** one of eighty equal parts. **3.** a person or thing that is eightieth.

eight·y (ā/tē), *n., pl.* **eight·ies.** **1.** a number that is eight times ten. **2.** a set of this many persons or things: *Eighty of them will be there.* **3. eighties,** the numbers, years, degrees, etc., between 80 and 89: *He was a man in his early eighties. The temperature was in the lower eighties.* —*adj.* **4.** amounting to eighty in number: *eighty persons.*

Ein·stein (īn/stīn), *n.* **Albert,** 1879–1955, U.S. physicist, born in Germany.

ein·stein·i·um (īn stī/nē əm), *n. Chem.* a man-made, radioactive, metallic element. *Symbol:* Es

Eir·e (âr/ə, ī/rə), *n.* Gaelic name of Ireland.

Ei·sen·how·er (ī/zən hou/ər), *n.* **Dwight David,** 1890–1969, U.S. general and statesman: 34th President of the U.S. 1953–1961.

ei·ther (ē/thər, ī/thər), *adj.* **1.** one or the other of two: *You may sit at either end of the table.* **2.** each of two: *There are trees on either side of the river.* —*pron.* **3.** one or the other: *Either will be fine.* —*conj.* **4.** (used before a word or statement that is followed by *or* to show the possibility of choice): *Either come or write.* **5.** also; too; as well: *He doesn't like it, and I don't either.*

—**Usage.** When used as an adjective or pronoun, *either* is generally followed by a singular verb: *Either book is satisfactory. Either is good enough.* When used to connect two subjects, *either* is always followed by *or* and may be used with a singular or plural verb, depending on the second subject: *Either milk or ginger ale is available. Either Bill or I am going. Either food or dishes are in this box.* See also **neither.**

e·jac·u·late (i jak/yə lāt/), *v.,* **e·jac·u·lat·ed, e·jac·u·lat·ing.** to utter suddenly and briefly; exclaim. —**e·jac/u·la/tion,** *n.*

e·ject (i jekt/), *v.* to drive or force out: *The pilot ejected himself from the airplane.* —**e·jec/tion,** *n.*

e·jec·tor (i jek/tər), *n.* **1.** a person or thing that ejects. **2.** the mechanism on a gun that throws out the empty cartridge or shell after firing.

eke (ēk), *v.,* **eked, ek·ing. eke out, 1.** to supply what is lacking in; add to: *He eked out his earnings by working at a second job.* **2.** to make (a living) or support (existence) by hard work.

EKG, See **electrocardiogram.**

el (el), *n.* short for **elevated railroad.**

e·lab·o·rate (i lab/ər it), *adj.* **1.** worked out with

great care and detail: *an elaborate scheme.* **2.** marked by much detail; fancy: *an elaborate dress.* —*v.* (i lab/ə rāt/), **e·lab·o·rat·ed, e·lab·o·rat·ing. 3.** to work out carefully: *to elaborate a plan.* **4.** to add details in writing or speaking (usually fol. by *on* or *upon*): *to elaborate on a theme.* —**e·lab/o·ra/tion,** *n.*

e·land (ē/lənd), *n., pl.* **e·lands** *or* **e·land.** a large African antelope having long, spirally twisted horns. [from Afrikaans]

e·lapse (i laps/), *v.,* **e·lapsed, e·laps·ing.** (of time) to slip by or pass away: *Two hours elapsed before he came.*

e·las·tic (i las/tik), *adj.* **1.** capable of returning to its original size or shape after being stretched: *Rubber is highly elastic.* **2.** able to recover or adapt easily; flexible: *an elastic spirit.* —*n.* **3.** any elastic fabric or material.

Eland
(5 ½ ft. high
at shoulder)

e·las·tic·i·ty (i la stis/i tē), *n.* the quality or property of being elastic.

e·late (i lāt/), *v.,* **e·lat·ed, e·lat·ing.** to make very happy or proud.

e·lat·ed (i lā/tid), *adj.* very happy or proud; in high spirits: *We're elated at the news.* —**e·lat/ed·ly,** *adv.*

e·la·tion (i lā/shən), *n.* a feeling of great joy or pride.

El·ba (el/bə), *n.* an Italian island in the Mediterranean Sea, between Corsica and Italy: the scene of Napoleon's first exile 1814–1815. It covers an area of 94 sq. mi.

El·be (el/bə, elb), *n.* a river in central Europe, flowing into the North Sea. 725 mi. long.

el·bow (el/bō), *n.* **1.** the joint between the upper arm and the forearm. **2.** something that is bent sharply, such as a piece of pipe bent to a right angle. —*v.* **3.** to push with or as if with the elbow: *He elbowed his way through the crowd.* **4. elbow grease,** hard work or strenuous effort: *Cleaning out the attic is going to take some elbow grease.*

eld·er[1] (el/dər), *adj.* **1.** a comparative of **old.** —*n.* **2.** a person who is older or higher in rank than oneself. **3.** one of the older and more important men of a tribe or community. **4.** a church official. [from the Old English word *eldra,* comparative of *eald* "old"] —**Usage.** See **older.**

eld·er[2] (el/dər), *n.* a tree or shrub that bears white flowers and berrylike fruit. [from the Old English word *ellærn*]

el·der·ber·ry (el/dər ber/ē), *n., pl.* **el·der·ber·ries.** the fruit of the elder, used esp. in making jellies.

eld·er·ly (el/dər lē), *adj.* rather old; between middle and old age.

eld·est (el/dist), *adj.* a superlative of **old.** —**Usage.** See **oldest.**

El Do·ra·do (el/ də rä/dō), a legendary city of South America, believed by the early Spanish explorers to contain immense treasure.

e·lect (i lekt/), *v.* **1.** to select by vote: *to elect a president.* **2.** to pick out; choose: *to elect a course in school.* —*adj.* **3.** selected for an office, but not yet serving (usually used in combination following a noun): *the governor-elect.*

elect., 1. electric. 2. electricity. Also, **elec.**

e·lec·tion (i lek′shən), *n.* 1. the selection of a person or persons for office by vote. 2. the act of electing; choice.

e·lec·tion·eer (i lek′shə nēr′), *v.* to work for the success of a candidate, ticket, etc., in an election.

e·lec·tive (i lek′tiv), *adj.* 1. appointed or chosen by election: *an elective official.* 2. settled or derived from election: *an elective office.* 3. open to choice; not required: *an elective course.* —*n.* 4. a course that a student may select from among several.

e·lec·tor (i lek′tər), *n.* a person who is qualified to vote in an election.

e·lec·tor·al (i lek′tər əl), *adj.* 1. referring to electors or an election. 2. consisting of electors.

elec′toral col′lege, a body of electors chosen by the voters in each state to elect the President and Vice President.

e·lec·tor·ate (i lek′tər it), *n.* the body of persons entitled to vote in an election.

e·lec·tric (i lek′trik), *adj.* 1. referring to or produced by electricity: *an electric wire; an electric shock.* 2. producing or operated by electricity: *an electric generator; an electric toaster.* 3. thrilling; exciting.

e·lec·tri·cal (i lek′tri kəl), *adj.* another form of **electric,** preferred in certain instances: *electrical engineer; electrical storm; electrical wiring.* —**e·lec′tri·cal·ly,** *adv.*

elec′tric eel′, a large South American fish, resembling an eel, that stuns its prey by releasing powerful charges of electricity.

elec′tric eye′, a device that operates switches, opens doors, activates counters, etc., in response to changes in the amount of light that strikes it.

e·lec·tri·cian (i lek trish′ən), *n.* a person who installs, repairs, or maintains electric devices or electrical wiring.

e·lec·tric·i·ty (i lek tris′i tē), *n.* 1. a property of matter that causes electrons to repel each other but to be attracted to protons, and causes the motion of electrons to produce magnetism. 2. electric current or electrical energy: *This clock runs on electricity.* 3. electric charge: *Metals conduct electricity.*

e·lec·tri·fy (i lek′tri fī), *v.,* **e·lec·tri·fied, e·lec·tri·fy·ing.** 1. to supply with electricity or equip so as to use electricity: *to electrify a cabin in the woods; to electrify a railroad.* 2. to charge with electricity: *to electrify a comb by running it through one's hair.* 3. to startle greatly; thrill: *The announcement electrified the crowd.* —**e·lec′tri·fi·ca′tion,** *n.*

electro-, a prefix meaning 1. electricity: *electrocute.* 2. electric: *electromagnet.*

e·lec·tro·car·di·o·gram (i lek′trō kär′dē ə gram′), *n.* a written record made by an electrocardiograph.

e·lec·tro·car·di·o·graph (i lek′trō kär′dē ə graf′), *n.* a machine that measures and records the action of a person's heart. It is used to detect heart disease.

e·lec·tro·cute (i lek′trə kyo͞ot′), *v.,* **e·lec·tro·cut·ed, e·lec·tro·cut·ing.** to kill by means of a severe electric shock. —**e·lec′tro·cu′tion,** *n.*

e·lec·trode (i lek′trōd), *n.* a conductor through which electric current enters or leaves a battery, electron tube, transistor, or the like.

e·lec·trol·y·sis (i lek trol′i sis), *n.* the separation of a solution or other liquid into its components by passing an electric current through it.

e·lec·tro·lyte (i lek′trə līt′), *n.* 1. a solution or other liquid that conducts electricity. 2. a substance that can be dissolved or melted and used to conduct electricity.

e·lec·tro·mag·net (i lek′trō mag′nit), *n.* a magnet made by passing an electric current through a coil of wire, esp. one wound on an iron core. —**e·lec·tro·mag·net·ic** (i lek′trō mag net′ik), *adj.*

e·lec·tro·mo′tive force′ (i lek′trə mō′tiv), (in physics) a difference in electric potential that causes an electric current to flow; voltage. *Abbr.:* emf, e.m.f., EMF, E.M.F. *Symbol:* E

Electromagnet

A, Battery; B, Core; C, Coil; D, Armature; E, Object picked up

e·lec·tron (i lek′tron), *n.* a tiny particle, one of the basic pieces of all matter. Electrons carry a negative charge and move in orbits around the positively charged nuclei of atoms. The motion of large groups of electrons constitutes an electric current.

e·lec·tron·ic (i lek tron′ik), *adj.* of, referring to, or employing electrons or electronics. —**e·lec·tron′i·cal·ly,** *adv.*

e·lec·tron·ics (i lek tron′iks), *n. (used as sing.)* the science that deals with the ways in which electrons move in a vacuum, in conductors, and in semiconductors, esp. the branches of engineering concerned with radio, television, and computers.

elec′tron mi′croscope, a device that uses a stream of electrons instead of a beam of light to produce very great magnifications.

elec′tron tube′, a glass or metal bulb containing one or more electrodes and used to generate, amplify, or rectify electrical signals or alternating currents. Electron tubes are used in radio and television transmitters and receivers, hi-fi sets, etc.

e·lec·tro·scope (i lek′trə skōp′), *n.* a device for detecting electric charges and determining whether they are positive or negative.

el·e·gance (el′ə gəns), *n.* fine taste and luxuriousness: *elegance of dress.*

el·e·gant (el′ə gənt), *adj.* 1. tastefully fine or luxurious in style, dress, design, etc.: *elegant furnishings.* 2. refined and dignified. —**el′e·gant·ly,** *adv.*

el·e·gy (el′i jē), *n., pl.* **el·e·gies.** a mournful or sad poem, esp. a lament for the dead.

elem., elementary.

el·e·ment (el′ə mənt), *n.* 1. one of the parts into

which a whole may be broken down: *Letters are the elements from which words are formed.* **2.** a necessary part; principle: *the elements of grammar.* **3.** the natural environment of someone or something: *He felt out of his element with so many strangers.* **4.** a substance that cannot be made into anything simpler by chemical means. There are 105 known chemical elements, which in various combinations form all substances. See also **compound**[1]. **5. the elements,** the forces of nature, such as wind, rain, cold, etc.: *The rocks were worn smooth by the elements.*

el·e·men·ta·ry (el/ə men/tə rē), *adj.* referring to or dealing with elements or basic principles: *elementary education; elementary mathematics.*

elemen'tary school', a school that has six or eight grades and teaches elementary subjects. Also, **grade school, grammar school.**

el·e·phant (el/ə fənt), *n., pl.* **el·e·phants** *or* **el·e·phant.** a large, gray animal having a long trunk, floppy ears,

Indian elephant   African elephant
(9 ft. high at shoulder)   (11 ft. high at shoulder)

and large tusks. Elephants are the largest land animals now living.

el·e·phan·tine (el/ə fan/tēn), *adj.* **1.** referring to or resembling an elephant. **2.** very large, heavy, and clumsy: *elephantine movements.*

el·e·vate (el/ə vāt/), *v.,* **el·e·vat·ed, el·e·vat·ing.** to raise to a higher place, rank, or level: *to elevate a platform; to elevate an archbishop to cardinal.*

el·e·vat·ed (el/ə vā/tid), *adj.* **1.** raised up above the ground: *an elevated platform.* **2.** exalted or noble; lofty; dignified: *the elevated language of the Bible.* —*n.* **3.** an elevated railroad.

el'evated rail'road, a railway system operating on a raised structure over the streets. Also, **el, elevated.**

el·e·va·tion (el/ə vā/shən), *n.* **1.** the height to which something is elevated or to which it rises. **2.** the altitude of a place above sea level or ground level. **3.** an elevated place, thing, or part: *an elevation overlooking the lake.* **4.** the act of elevating, or the state of being elevated: *an elevation of prices.*

el·e·va·tor (el/ə vā/tər), *n.* **1.** a cage that moves up and down in a shaft, for transporting people or goods from one level to another in a building, mine, etc. **2.** a grain elevator.

el·ev·en (i lev/ən), *n.* **1.** a cardinal number, ten plus one. —*adj.* **2.** amounting to eleven in number.

el·ev·enth (i lev/ənth), *adj.* **1.** next after the tenth; being the ordinal number for 11. **2. the eleventh hour,** the last possible moment: *to change plans at the eleventh hour.*

elf (elf), *n., pl.* **elves** (elvz). a small, imaginary being with magical powers, who interferes mischievously in human affairs.

elf·in (el/fin), *adj.* of or like elves; small and charmingly mischievous; prankish; impish.

El Grec·o (el grek/ō), 1541–1614, Spanish painter, born in Crete.

e·lic·it (i lis/it), *v.* to bring out; draw forth; evoke: *The teacher elicited an answer from the shy boy.* —**Usage.** *Elicit* is often confused with *illicit. Elicit* is a verb meaning to bring out: *His speech elicited a flood of protests. Illicit* is an adjective meaning forbidden or illegal: *the illicit use of narcotics.*

el·i·gi·ble (el/i jə bəl), *adj.* fit or proper to be chosen; qualified; desirable: *eligible to vote; an eligible bachelor.* —**el/i·gi·bil/i·ty,** *n.*

E·li·jah (i lī/jə), *n.* (in the Bible) a Hebrew prophet of the 9th century B.C.

e·lim·i·nate (i lim/ə nāt/), *v.,* **e·lim·i·nat·ed, e·lim·i·nat·ing.** to remove or get rid of: *to eliminate smudges.* [from the Latin *ēliminātus* "turned out of doors," which comes from *ē-* "out" + *līmen* "threshold"]

e·lim·i·na·tion (i lim/ə nā/shən), *n.* **1.** the act of eliminating, or the state of being eliminated. **2.** the process by which wastes are expelled from the body.

e·lite (i lēt/, ā lēt/), *n. (often used as pl.)* the choice or best of anything considered as a group: *the elite of the school athletes.* Also, **é·lite/.**

e·lix·ir (i lik/sər), *n.* **1.** a sweetened solution of alcohol and water containing herbs and used as a medicine. **2.** an alchemic preparation supposedly capable of changing base metals into gold and of prolonging life.

E·liz·a·beth (i liz/ə bəth), *n.* a city in NE New Jersey.

Elizabeth I, 1533–1603, queen of England 1558–1603.

Elizabeth II, born 1926, queen of Great Britain since 1952.

E·liz·a·be·than (i liz/ə bē/thən), *adj.* **1.** of or referring to Elizabeth I, queen of England, or her times. —*n.* **2.** a person who lived in England during the Elizabethan period.

Elk
(5 ft. high at shoulder)

elk (elk), *n., pl.* **elks** *or* **elk. 1.** a large North American deer that has spreading antlers. **2.** a large deer of Europe and Asia related to the North American moose.

ell[1] (el), *n.* an extension usually at right angles to one end of a building. [from the Middle English word *ele* "transept," literally "wing," which comes from Latin *āla* "wing"]

ell[2] (el), *n.* a measure of length, now seldom used, varying in different countries. In England it is equal to 45 inches. [from the Old English word *eln,* a measure of length equal to the distance from the elbow to the fingertips, or about 18 inches]

el·lipse (i lips′), *n.* a closed symmetrical curve resembling a flattened circle.

el·lip·ti·cal (i lip′ti kəl), *adj.* shaped like an ellipse: *The planets move in elliptical orbits.* Also, **el·lip′tic.** —**el·lip′ti·cal·ly,** *adv.*

Ellipse

elm (elm), *n.* 1. a tall shade tree with gradually spreading branches. 2. the hard wood of this tree.

el·o·cu·tion (el′ə kyoo′shən), *n.* 1. a person's manner of speaking or reading aloud. 2. the study of public speaking. —**el′o·cu′tion·ist,** *n.*

e·lon·gate (i lông′gāt′), *v.,* **e·lon·gat·ed, e·lon·gat·ing.** to draw out to greater length; lengthen; extend. —**e·lon·ga′tion,** *n.*

e·lope (i lōp′), *v.,* **e·loped, e·lop·ing.** to run off secretly to be married. —**e·lope′ment,** *n.*

el·o·quence (el′ə kwəns), *n.* 1. the action, art, or practice of using language with clearness, force, and fluency. 2. eloquent language.

el·o·quent (el′ə kwənt), *adj.* 1. having the power of fluent, forceful speech: *an eloquent debater.* 2. showing fluent, forceful expression; unusually expressive: *an eloquent letter.* —**el′o·quent·ly,** *adv.*

El Pas·o (el pas′ō), a city in W Texas, on the Rio Grande.

El Sal·va·dor (el sal′və dôr′), a republic in NW Central America. 13,176 sq. mi. *Cap.:* San Salvador.

else (els), *adj.* 1. other than the persons or things mentioned: *What else could I have done?* 2. in addition to the persons or things mentioned: *Who else is there?* —*adv.* 3. if not (usually preceded by *or*): *I'll come or else I'll call.* 4. in some other way; otherwise: *Where else can I find the book?*

else·where (els′hwâr′, -wâr′), *adv.* somewhere else; in or to some other place: *We will go elsewhere.*

e·lu·ci·date (i loo′si dāt′), *v.,* **e·lu·ci·dat·ed, e·lu·ci·dat·ing.** to make clear; explain; clarify: *The examples elucidated the problem.* —**e·lu′ci·da′tion,** *n.*

e·lude (i lood′), *v.,* **e·lud·ed, e·lud·ing.** 1. to avoid or escape by speed or cleverness: *The criminal's car eluded the police.* 2. to slip away from: *The answer eludes me.*

e·lu·sive (i loo′siv), *adj.* 1. difficult to understand, express, or define: *an elusive idea.* 2. difficult to catch: *an elusive fish.* —**e·lu′sive·ness,** *n.*

elves (elvz), *n.* the plural of elf.

E·ly·sian (i lizh′ən, i lē′zhən), *adj.* 1. of, referring to, or resembling Elysium. 2. delightful; peaceful.

E·ly·si·um (i lizh′ē əm, i liz′ē əm), *n.* 1. Also, **Ely′sian Fields′.** (in Greek and Roman mythology) a place where the spirits of good people dwelt after death. 2. any place or state of perfect happiness.

'em (əm), *pron. Informal.* them: *Put 'em down there.*

em-, a form of en- used before *b* or *p*: *emboss; empower.*

e·ma·ci·ate (i mā′shē āt′), *v.,* **e·ma·ci·at·ed, e·ma·ci·at·**

ing. to make very thin by a gradual wasting away of flesh. —**e·ma′ci·at′ed,** *adj.* —**e·ma′ci·a′tion,** *n.*

em·a·nate (em′ə nāt′), *v.,* **em·a·nat·ed, em·a·nat·ing.** to flow or be sent forth; proceed: *The news emanated from the capital.* —**em′a·na′tion,** *n.*

e·man·ci·pate (i man′sə pāt′), *v.,* **e·man·ci·pat·ed, e·man·ci·pat·ing.** to free from control or slavery; liberate; free. —**e·man′ci·pa′tion,** *n.* —**e·man′ci·pa′tor,** *n.*

Emancipa′tion Proclama′tion, the proclamation issued by President Lincoln on January 1, 1863, freeing the slaves in those territories still in rebellion against the Union.

e·mas·cu·late (i mas′kyə lāt′), *v.,* **e·mas·cu·lat·ed, e·mas·cu·lat·ing.** 1. to castrate. 2. to deprive of strength; weaken. —**e·mas′cu·la′tion,** *n.*

em·balm (em bäm′), *v.* to treat (a dead body) with chemicals and drugs to preserve it. —**em·balm′er,** *n.*

em·bank·ment (em bangk′mənt), *n.* a bank, mound, or dike, raised to hold back water, carry a roadway, etc.

em·bar·go (em bär′gō), *n., pl.* **em·bar·goes.** 1. an order of a government forbidding the movement of merchant vessels from or into its ports. 2. any legal restriction on commerce: *an embargo on the shipment of arms.* —*v.,* **em·bar·goed, em·bar·go·ing.** 3. to place an embargo on. [from a Spanish word, which comes from *embargar* "to hinder"]

em·bark (em bärk′), *v.* 1. to put or receive on board a ship. 2. to board a ship. 3. **embark on,** to commence or begin: *to embark on a new adventure.* —**em′bar·ka′tion,** *n.*

em·bar·rass (em bar′əs), *v.* 1. to make uncomfortably self-conscious: *His bad manners embarrassed her.* 2. to make difficult or complicated; hinder. —**em·bar′rass·ment,** *n.*

em·bas·sy (em′bə sē), *n., pl.* **em·bas·sies.** 1. an ambassador and his staff. 2. the official headquarters of an ambassador.

em·bat·tle (em bat′əl), *v.,* **em·bat·tled, em·bat·tling.** 1. to arrange in order of battle; prepare for battle; arm: *embattled troops; embattled strikers.* 2. to fortify (a town, camp, etc.) against attack.

em·bed (em bed′), *v.,* **em·bed·ded, em·bed·ding.** to fix or place in a surrounding mass: *to embed stones in cement.* Also, **imbed.**

em·bel·lish (em bel′ish), *v.* to beautify or enhance by adding something: *to embellish a story with a few jokes.* —**em·bel′lish·ment,** *n.*

em·ber (em′bər), *n.* 1. a small live coal in a dying fire. 2. embers, the smoldering remains of a fire.

em·bez·zle (em bez′əl), *v.,* **em·bez·zled, em·bez·zling.** to steal money or property entrusted to one's care. —**em·bez′zle·ment,** *n.* —**em·bez′zler,** *n.*

em·bit·ter (em bit′ər), *v.* to make bitter or resentful: *A life of hardship embittered the man.*

em·bla·zon (em blā′zən), *v.* 1. to decorate with brilliant colors. 2. to proclaim with praise; honor: *The good news was emblazoned throughout the land.*

em·blem (em′bləm), *n.* a sign, design, or figure that

identifies or represents something: *The caduceus is the emblem of the medical profession.*

em·blem·at·ic (em′blə mat′ik), *adj.* used as an emblem; symbolic.

em·bod·i·ment (em bod′ē mənt), *n.* 1. the act of embodying. 2. the state or fact of being embodied. 3. a person or thing that embodies a particular quality, principle, etc.: *She is the embodiment of grace.*

em·bod·y (em bod′ē), *v.,* **em·bod·ied, em·bod·y·ing.** 1. to give a concrete, visible form to: *The painting embodies the artist's feelings about nature.* 2. to collect into or include in a body; organize: *The facts are embodied in the report.*

em·bold·en (em bōl′d³n), *v.* to make bold or bolder; encourage.

em·boss (em bôs′), *v.* 1. to raise (a surface design) in relief: *to emboss a monogram on stationery.* 2. to decorate with raised designs: *to emboss metal.*

em·brace (em brās′), *v.,* **em·braced, em·brac·ing.** 1. to clasp in the arms; hug. 2. to take or receive gladly; accept willingly: *to embrace an opportunity.* 3. to encircle or surround: *A fence embraced the house.* 4. to include or contain: *The report embraces many topics.* —*n.* 5. the act or an instance of embracing; hug.

em·broi·der (em broi′dər), *v.* 1. to decorate with small, ornamental stitches: *to embroider a tablecloth.* 2. to produce or form by small ornamental stitches: *to embroider flowers on an apron.* 3. to add fictitious details to: *to embroider a story.*

em·broi·der·y (em broi′də rē), *n., pl.* **em·broi·der·ies.** 1. the art of working ornamental designs with a needle and thread. 2. embroidered work or decoration.

em·broil (em broil′), *v.* 1. to bring into or involve in a conflict: *to become embroiled in an argument.* 2. to throw into confusion; complicate.

em·bry·o (em′brē ō′), *n., pl.* **em·bry·os.** 1. a plant or animal in the early stages of its growth or development, before sprouting, emerging from an egg, or birth. 2. the beginning stage of anything.

em·bry·on·ic (em′brē on′ik), *adj.* 1. referring to an embryo or embryos: *the stages of embryonic development.* 2. lacking development; undeveloped.

e·mend (i mend′), *v.* to free from faults or errors; correct: *to emend a text.* —**e·men·da·tion** (ē′mən dā′shən), *n.*

em·er·ald (em′ər əld), *n.* 1. a transparent, green precious stone. 2. a clear, deep green.

e·merge (i mûrj′), *v.,* **e·merged, e·merg·ing.** 1. to come forth into view or notice: *The seal emerged from the water.* 2. to come up or arise; develop: *New problems emerge every day.* —**e·mer′gence,** *n.*

e·mer·gen·cy (i mûr′jən sē), *n., pl.* **e·mer·gen·cies.** a sudden, urgent, usually unforeseen occurrence or occasion requiring immediate action.

Em·er·son (em′ər sən), *n.* **Ralph Wal·do** (wôl′dō), 1803–1882, U.S. poet and essayist.

em·er·y (em′ə rē), *n.* a mineral used in powdered form for grinding and polishing.

e·met·ic (ə met′ik), *n.* a medicine or other substance that causes vomiting.

emf, electromotive force. Also, **e.m.f., EMF, E.M.F.**

em·i·grant (em′ə grənt), *n.* a person who leaves his native country to settle in another (distinguished from *immigrant*).

em·i·grate (em′ə grāt′), *v.,* **em·i·grat·ed, em·i·grat·ing.** to leave one country or region to settle in another (distinguished from *immigrate*): *to emigrate to Australia.* —**em′i·gra′tion,** *n.*

em·i·nence (em′ə nəns), *n.* 1. high station, rank, or reputation: *philosophers of eminence.* 2. a high place or part; hill or elevation.

Em·i·nence (em′ə nəns), *n.* a title of honor applied to cardinals (usually preceded by *His* or *Your*).

em·i·nent (em′ə nənt), *adj.* high in station, rank, or reputation; distinguished: *an eminent statesman.* —**em′i·nent·ly,** *adv.*

—**Usage.** *Eminent* is used to refer to persons or things that are famous or outstanding: *He was an eminent scientist.* It should not be confused with *imminent,* which refers to things that threaten to occur at any moment: *We all feared that war was imminent.*

e·mir (ə mēr′), *n.* 1. an Arab chieftain or prince. 2. a title of honor of the descendants of Muhammad.

em·is·sar·y (em′i ser′ē), *n., pl.* **em·is·sar·ies.** 1. an agent of a national government sent on a mission. 2. a spy or other agent sent on a secret mission.

e·mis·sion (i mish′ən), *n.* 1. the act or an instance of emitting. 2. something that is emitted.

e·mit (i mit′), *v.,* **e·mit·ted, e·mit·ting.** to send forth; give out: *to emit light; to emit a scream.*

e·mol·u·ment (i mol′yə mənt), *n.* profit from employment or compensation for services; salary or fees.

e·mo·tion (i mō′shən), *n.* 1. strong feeling: *He spoke with emotion.* 2. a strong feeling, such as love, hate, sorrow, or fear: *to control one's emotions.*

e·mo·tion·al (i mō′shə n³l), *adj.* 1. of or concerning emotion or the emotions: *an emotional outburst; an emotional problem.* 2. easily affected by emotion: *an emotional person.* 3. appealing to the emotions: *an emotional request.* —**e·mo′tion·al·ly,** *adv.*

Emp., 1. Emperor. 2. Empire. 3. Empress.

em·per·or (em′pər ər), *n.* the sovereign or supreme ruler of an empire. [from the Old French word *empereor,* which comes from Latin *imperātor* "leader"]

em·pha·sis (em′fə sis), *n., pl.* **em·pha·ses** (em′fə sēz′). 1. the stress placed upon something, or the importance or significance attached to it: *The president's statement gave emphasis to the crisis.* 2. stress placed upon particular words or syllables: *In the word "habit," the emphasis is on the first syllable.*

em·pha·size (em′fə sīz′), *v.,* **em·pha·sized, em·pha·siz·ing.** to give emphasis to; stress: *He emphasized the importance of exercise.*

em·phat·ic (em fat′ik), *adj.* 1. said or done with emphasis; strongly expressive: *an emphatic answer.* 2. striking; forceful; decisive: *an emphatic victory.* —**em·phat′i·cal·ly,** *adv.*

em·pire (em′pī³r), *n.* 1. a group of nations, tribes, clans, or peoples ruled over by one supreme sovereign: *the British Empire under Queen Victoria.* 2. a government under an emperor. [from an Old French word, which comes from Latin *imperium* "command, rule, empire"]

em·ploy (em ploi′), *v.* **1.** to hire or engage the services of; provide employment for: *We employ two maids.* **2.** to keep busy; engage the attentions of: *He employs himself by reading.* **3.** to make use of; use: *to employ a hammer to drive a nail.* —*n.* **4.** employment; service: *He's in the employ of his uncle.*

em·ploy·ee (em ploi′ē), *n.* a person working for another person or for a business firm for pay; worker.

em·ploy·er (em ploi′ər), *n.* a person who employs another or others.

em·ploy·ment (em ploi′mənt), *n.* **1.** the act or an instance of employing. **2.** the state of being employed; employ; service: *to begin employment.* **3.** an occupation by which a person earns a living.

em·po·ri·um (em pôr′ē əm), *n.* a large store, esp. one selling a great variety of articles.

em·pow·er (em pou′ər), *v.* to give power or authority to; authorize: *The chairman empowered his assistant to take over in his absence.*

em·press (em′pris), *n.* **1.** a female ruler of an empire. **2.** the wife of an emperor.

emp·ty (emp′tē), *adj.,* **emp·ti·er, emp·ti·est. 1.** containing nothing: *an empty bottle.* **2.** vacant; unoccupied: *an empty house.* **3.** without force or significance; meaningless: *empty compliments.* —*v.,* **emp·tied, emp·ty·ing. 4.** to make empty: *to empty a bottle.* **5.** to discharge (contents): *to empty the water out of a bucket.* **6.** to flow out; drain: *The river empties into a lake at the foot of the mountain.* —**emp′ti·ly,** *adv.* —**emp′ti·ness,** *n.*

e·mu (ē′myōō), *n., pl.* **e·mus** *or* **e·mu.** a large, flightless bird of Australia, resembling but smaller than the ostrich.

em·u·late (em′yə lāt′), *v.,* **em·u·lat·ed, em·u·lat·ing.** to try to equal or excel; imitate with effort to equal or surpass: *to emulate a famous man.* —**em′u·la′tion,** *n.*

Emu
(height 5 ft.)

e·mul·si·fy (i mul′sə fī′), *v.,* **e·mul·si·fied, e·mul·si·fy·ing.** to make or blend (two or more substances) into an emulsion.

e·mul·sion (i mul′shən), *n.* **1.** a combination of two liquids that do not ordinarily mix, such as oil and water, in which tiny drops of one liquid are evenly distributed in the other. **2.** a material that is sensitive to light, used for coating photographic film.

en-, a prefix meaning **1.** to put in or into: *encase; enclose.* **2.** to put on or upon: *enroll; enthrone.* **3.** to make or cause to be: *enlarge; endear; enable.* **4.** to provide with: *encourage.*

-en, a suffix used to form **1.** verbs with the meaning **a.** to make or become: *harden; sweeten.* **b.** to provide with or acquire: *strengthen; lengthen.* **2.** adjectives

with the meaning **a.** made of or consisting of: *woolen; oaken.* **b.** like or resembling: *ashen; golden.* **3.** the past participle of some verbs: *taken; fallen.* **4.** the plural of some nouns: *oxen; children.*

en·a·ble (en ā′bəl), *v.,* **en·a·bled, en·a·bling.** to make able; give power, means, or ability to: *The scholarship enabled him to go to college.*

en·act (en akt′), *v.* **1.** to make into an act, law, or statute. **2.** to act the part of: *to enact Hamlet.* —**en·act′ment,** *n.*

e·nam·el (i nam′əl), *n.* **1.** a glassy substance applied to the surface of metal, pottery, etc., as an ornament or for protection. **2.** any of various enamellike varnishes or paints. **3.** the hard, white, shiny covering of the teeth. See illus. at **tooth.** —*v.,* **e·nam·eled** *or* **e·nam·elled; e·nam·el·ing** *or* **e·nam·el·ling. 4.** to inlay or overlay with enamel: *to enamel a vase.*

en·am·or (en am′ər), *v.* to inflame with love; charm; captivate (usually used in the passive and followed by *of*): *John is enamored of Mary.*

enc., 1. enclosed. **2.** enclosure. **3.** encyclopedia.

en·camp (en kamp′), *v.* to set up, settle, or lodge in a camp: *We encamped for the night by the stream.*

en·camp·ment (en kamp′mənt), *n.* **1.** the act or an instance of encamping. **2.** the place occupied in camping; campsite.

en·case (en kās′), *v.,* **en·cased, en·cas·ing.** to enclose in or as if in a case. Also, **incase.** —**en·case′ment,** *n.*

-ence, a suffix used to form nouns meaning **1.** an action or process: *adherence.* **2.** a state or condition: *existence.*

en·chant (en chant′), *v.* **1.** to cast a spell over; charm: *In the story the witch enchanted the prince for 20 years.* **2.** to delight; charm: *The concert enchanted us all.* —**en·chant′er,** *n.* —**en·chant′ing,** *adj.*

en·chant·ment (en chant′mənt), *n.* **1.** the art, act, or an instance of enchanting; fascination. **2.** something that enchants; spell; charm.

en·chant·ress (en chan′tris), *n.* **1.** a woman who enchants; sorceress. **2.** a fascinating woman.

en·cir·cle (en sûr′kəl), *v.,* **en·cir·cled, en·cir·cling. 1.** to form a circle around: *They encircled the speaker.* **2.** to make a circling movement around: *The plane encircled the airport.* —**en·cir′cle·ment,** *n.*

encl., 1. enclosed. **2.** enclosure.

en·close (en klōz′), *v.,* **en·closed, en·clos·ing. 1.** to shut or hem in; close in on all sides; surround: *to enclose the yard with a fence.* **2.** to put in the same package or envelope with whatever is being sent: *She enclosed a check with the letter.* Also, **inclose.**

en·clo·sure (en klō′zhər), *n.* **1.** the act or an instance of enclosing. **2.** the state of being enclosed. **3.** an area of land surrounded by a fence. **4.** something that encloses, such as a fence or a wall. **5.** something enclosed with a letter. Also, **inclosure.**

en·code (en kōd′), *v.,* **en·cod·ed, en·cod·ing.** to convert (a message, information, etc.) into code. —**en·cod′er,** *n.*

en·com·pass (en kum′pəs), *v.* **1.** to form a circle

around; encircle; surround. **2.** to include: *His speech encompassed many topics.*

en·core (än′kôr), *interj.* **1.** again; once more (used by an audience in calling for a repetition of a song or act or for an additional number). —*n.* **2.** a demand, usually expressed by applause, for a repetition of a song or act or for an additional number. **3.** the performance or selection given in response to such a demand. —*v.,* **en·cored, en·cor·ing. 4.** to call for an encore from (a performer). [from a French word meaning "yet, still, more"]

en·coun·ter (en koun′tər), *v.* **1.** to come upon; meet with, esp. unexpectedly: *to encounter bad weather.* **2.** to meet in conflict: *to encounter the enemy.* —*n.* **3.** a casual or unexpected meeting. **4.** a violent meeting of persons or groups in conflict; combat; battle: *an encounter with enemy forces.*

en·cour·age (en kûr′ij, en kur′ij), *v.,* **en·cour·aged, en·cour·ag·ing. 1.** to inspire with courage, spirit, or confidence: *We encouraged her to enter the contest.* **2.** to stimulate by help or approval; advance; foster: *An interesting subject encourages discussion.*

en·cour·age·ment (en kûr′ij mənt, en kur′ij mənt), *n.* **1.** the act of encouraging, or the state of being encouraged. **2.** something that encourages.

en·croach (en krōch′), *v.* **1.** to advance beyond proper or normal limits: *to encroach upon someone's privacy.* **2.** to trespass on the property or rights of another; intrude: *Enemy troops encroached upon the neighboring country.* —**en·croach′ment,** *n.*

en·crust (en krust′), *v.* another spelling of **incrust.**

en·cum·ber (en kum′bər), *v.* **1.** to hinder or slow down; retard; hamper: *Adding amendments encumbered the passage of the bill.* **2.** to burden or weigh down: *She was encumbered with several packages.*

en·cum·brance (en kum′brəns), *n.* something that encumbers; burden; hindrance.

-ency, another form of the suffix **-ence,** used to form nouns meaning quality or condition: *emergency; consistency.*

en·cyc·li·cal (en sik′li kəl), *n.* a letter addressed by the pope to all the bishops of the church concerning important religious matters.

en·cy·clo·pe·di·a (en sī′klə pē′dē ə), *n.* a book or set of books containing articles on various topics, usually in alphabetical arrangement, covering all branches of knowledge or all aspects of one subject. [from the modern Latin word *encyclopaedia,* which comes from the Greek phrase *enkyklios paideia* "circular or well-rounded education"]

en·cy·clo·pe·dic (en sī′klə pē′dik), *adj.* **1.** referring to or of the nature of an encyclopedia. **2.** including a wide variety of information; comprehensive: *an encyclopedic memory.*

end (end), *n.* **1.** the part or place at which something begins or stops: *the end of a street.* **2.** the concluding part: *the end of the movie.* **3.** a purpose or aim: *What ends does he wish to gain?* **4.** termination of existence; death: *He met his end in the war.* **5.** a leftover part; remnant; fragment: *ends and trimmings.* **6.** (in football) either of the linemen stationed farthest from

the center. —*v.* **7.** to bring or come to an end; terminate; stop: *to end a meeting.* **8. make ends meet,** to live within one's means: *Unless you buy wisely, you can't make ends meet.* Also, **make both ends meet.**

en·dan·ger (en dān′jər), *v.* to expose to danger; risk: *He endangers his life by driving too fast.*

en·dear (en dēr′), *v.* to make dear or beloved: *He endears himself to people because of his kindness.*

en·dear·ment (en dēr′mənt), *n.* **1.** the act of endearing, or the state of being endeared. **2.** something done or said as a show of affection: *to whisper endearments.*

en·deav·or (en dev′ər), *v.* **1.** to make an effort; try; attempt. —*n.* **2.** a determined effort; attempt: *He made an endeavor to do well on the test.*

end·ing (en′diñg), *n.* **1.** the final or concluding part; conclusion: *The book has a sad ending.* **2.** a suffix used to mark an inflected form, as *-s* in *cuts* or *-ed* in *walked.*

en·dive (en′dīv, än′dēv), *n.* either of two plants with crisp leaves that are used in salads.

end·less (end′lis), *adj.* **1.** having or seeming to have no end or limit: *endless patience.* **2.** made continuous; without end: *an endless chain.* —**end′less·ly,** *adv.*

en′do·crine gland′ (en′də krin), another name for **ductless gland.**

en·dorse (en dôrs′), *v.,* **en·dorsed, en·dors·ing. 1.** to approve or support: *to endorse a statement; to endorse a candidate.* **2.** to sign one's name on the back of (a check). Also, **indorse.** —**en·dors′er,** *n.*

en·dorse·ment (en dôrs′mənt), *n.* **1.** approval or support: *The Senator gave the bill his endorsement.* **2.** the placing of one's signature, instructions, etc., on a document. Also, **indorsement.**

en·dow (en dou′), *v.* **1.** to provide with a permanent fund or source of income: *to endow a university.* **2.** to supply with some gift, talent, or quality: *Nature endowed her with beauty.*

en·dow·ment (en dou′mənt), *n.* **1.** the act of endowing. **2.** the property or funds with which a person or institution is endowed. **3.** Usually, **endowments.** an ability or talent: *He has many natural endowments in addition to his good looks.*

end′ point′, either of the two points that mark the ends of a line segment or a ray.

en·dur·ance (en dŏŏr′əns, -dyŏŏr′-), *n.* the fact or power of enduring or bearing anything: *The long hike required endurance.*

en·dure (en dŏŏr′, -dyŏŏr′), *v.,* **en·dured, en·dur·ing. 1.** to withstand or hold out against; bear: *to endure pain.* **2.** to continue to exist; last: *Certain customs have endured for centuries.* —**en·dur′a·ble,** *adj.*

end·ways (end′wāz′), *adv.* **1.** on end: *to stack packages endways.* **2.** with the end upward or forward. **3.** toward the ends or end; lengthwise. Also, **end·wise** (end′wīz′).

ENE, east-northeast. Also, **E.N.E.**

en·e·ma (en′ə mə), *n.* **1.** an injection of liquid into the rectum, esp. as an aid to elimination. **2.** the liquid injected.

en·e·my (en′ə mē), *n., pl.* **en·e·mies. 1.** a person who feels hatred for and opposes another; opponent. **2.** an opposing military force; armed foe. **3.** a hostile nation or state. **4.** something harmful or destructive: *His own selfishness is his worst enemy. —adj.* **5.** belonging to a hostile power: *enemy aircraft.*

en·er·get·ic (en′ər jet′ik), *adj.* full of energy; active; vigorous: *an energetic athlete.* **—en′er·get′i·cal·ly,** *adv.*

en·er·gize (en′ər jīz′), *v.,* **en·er·gized, en·er·giz·ing. 1.** to give energy to; rouse into activity: *The machine is energized by four batteries.* **2.** to be in operation; put forth energy. **—en′er·giz′er,** *n.*

en·er·gy (en′ər jē), *n., pl.* **en·er·gies. 1.** the capacity to do work: *electrical energy; atomic energy.* **2.** vigorous activity; force: *to work with energy.*

en·er·vate (en′ər vāt′), *v.,* **en·er·vat·ed, en·er·vat·ing.** to deprive of force or strength; weaken; exhaust: *The hot sun enervated the hikers.* **—en′er·va′tion,** *n.*

en·fee·ble (en fē′bəl), *v.,* **en·fee·bled, en·fee·bling.** to make feeble; weaken.

en·fold (en fōld′), *v.* **1.** to wrap up; envelop. **2.** to clasp; embrace; hug. Also, **infold.**

en·force (en fôrs′), *v.,* **en·forced, en·forc·ing. 1.** to put or keep in force; compel obedience to: *to enforce laws strictly.* **2.** to obtain by force: *to enforce obedience.* **—en·force′a·ble,** *adj.*

en·force·ment (en fôrs′mənt), *n.* the act or process of enforcing: *the enforcement of laws.*

en·fran·chise (en fran′chīz), *v.,* **en·fran·chised, en·fran·chis·ing. 1.** to grant the right to vote to: *to enfranchise women.* **2.** to set free; liberate: *to enfranchise slaves.* **—en·fran′chise·ment,** *n.*

Eng., **1.** England. **2.** English.

en·gage (en gāj′), *v.,* **en·gaged, en·gag·ing. 1.** to occupy the attention or efforts of (a person or persons): *He engaged her in conversation.* **2.** to secure for aid, employment, use, etc.: *to engage a workman; to engage a room.* **3.** to attract or please: *His good nature engages everyone.* **4.** to attract and hold fast: *The novel engaged his interest.* **5.** to pledge or promise: *to be engaged to be married.* **6.** to bring into conflict: *to engage troops in battle.* **7.** to interlock or interlock with: *Let the clutch out to engage the gears.*

en·gaged (en gājd′), *adj.* **1.** busy or occupied; involved. **2.** pledged to be married.

en·gage·ment (en gāj′mənt), *n.* **1.** the act of engaging, or the state of being engaged. **2.** a pledge or agreement. **3.** a promise or pledge to marry; betrothal. **4.** employment, or a period of employment. **5.** an appointment: *a two-o'clock engagement.* **6.** an encounter, conflict, or battle: *an engagement with the enemy.*

en·gag·ing (en gā′jiŋ), *adj.* winning; attractive; pleasing: *an engaging smile.* **—en·gag′ing·ly,** *adv.*

en·gen·der (en jen′dər), *v.* to produce, cause, or give rise to: *Hatred engenders violence.*

en·gine (en′jən), *n.* **1.** a machine that transforms heat energy into mechanical energy for propulsion or for driving other machines, esp. one that uses the expansion of a hot gas to move one or more pistons: *a steam engine.* **2.** a railroad locomotive. **3.** any machine or instrument used for a certain purpose: *engines of war.*

en·gi·neer (en′jə nēr′), *n.* **1.** a person who is trained in one of the branches of engineering. **2.** a person who drives a railroad train. **—v. 3.** to plan, construct, or manage as an engineer. **4.** to arrange, manage, or carry through skillfully: *She engineered the project from start to finish.*

en·gi·neer·ing (en′jə nēr′iŋ), *n.* **1.** the method of applying science to practical things, such as the building of bridges, the design of machines, or the improvement of chemical processes. **2.** the work or profession of an engineer.

Eng·land (iŋ′glənd), *n.* the largest division of the United Kingdom, occupying, with Scotland and Wales, the island of Great Britain. 50,327 sq. mi.

Eng·lish (iŋ′glish), *adj.* **1.** of, referring to, or characteristic of England or its inhabitants, institutions, customs, etc. **2.** of or referring to, or spoken or written in the English language. **—n. 3.** the people of England. **4.** the Germanic language of Britain, the U.S., and most of the British Commonwealth.

Eng′lish Chan′nel, an arm of the Atlantic Ocean between S England and N France. 350 mi. long; 20–100 mi. wide.

Eng′lish horn′, a double-reed musical instrument with a pear-shaped bell, the alto member of the oboe family of woodwinds.

Eng·lish·man (iŋ′glish mən), *n., pl.* **Eng·lish·men.** a native or citizen of England.

Eng′lish set′ter, one of a breed of medium-sized, long-haired bird dogs having a flat, usually black-and-white or tan-and-white coat.

Eng·lish·wom·an (iŋ′glish woom′ən), *n., pl.* **Eng·lish·wom·en.** a woman who is a native or citizen of England.

English horn

en·graft (en graft′), *v.* to insert (a bud or cutting of one kind of plant) into another in order to produce a graft: *to engraft a peach onto a plum.*

en·grave (en grāv′), *v.,* **en·graved, en·grav·ing. 1.** to carve (letters, designs, etc.) on a hard surface, such as metal or stone: *to engrave a monogram on a silver cup.* **2.** to mark or decorate with carved letters or designs: *to engrave a silver cup.* **3.** to impress or fix deeply: *The incident is engraved on his mind.* **—en·grav′er,** *n.*

en·grav·ing (en grā′viŋ), *n.* **1.** the act of a person or thing that engraves. **2.** the art of forming designs by cutting, corrosion by acids, a photographic process, etc., on the surface of metal plates, blocks of wood, or the like. **3.** the design engraved. **4.** an engraved plate or block. **5.** an impression or print made from an engraved plate or block.

en·gross (en grōs′), v. to occupy completely; take up the attention of: *She is engrossed in her studies.*

en·gulf (en gulf′), v. to swallow in or as if in a gulf: *The waves engulfed the small boats.*

en·hance (en hans′), v., **en·hanced, en·hanc·ing.** to raise to a higher degree; add to: *The flowers enhanced the beauty of the room.* —**en·hance′ment,** n.

e·nig·ma (ə nig′mə), n. 1. a puzzling occurrence or situation. 2. a saying, question, picture, etc., containing a hidden meaning; riddle. 3. a puzzling person.

en·ig·mat·ic (en′ig mat′ik), adj. resembling an enigma; puzzling; mysterious: *an enigmatic smile.* Also, **en′ig·mat′i·cal.** —**en′ig·mat′i·cal·ly,** adv.

en·join (en join′), v. 1. to direct or order: *The police enjoined the crowd to disperse.* 2. to prohibit or restrain; forbid: *The order enjoined him from trespassing.*

en·joy (en joi′), v. 1. to take pleasure in: *to enjoy a movie.* 2. to have and use with satisfaction; have the benefit of: *to enjoy health and prosperity.* 3. **enjoy oneself,** to have a good time; find pleasure: *Helen wanted to leave, but I was enjoying myself.*

en·joy·a·ble (en joi′ə bəl), adj. giving or capable of giving enjoyment: *a very enjoyable evening.* —**en·joy′a·bly,** adv.

en·joy·ment (en joi′mənt), n. 1. the act of enjoying. 2. the possession or use of anything with satisfaction or pleasure: *the enjoyment of a large income.* 3. a particular form or source of pleasure: *Hunting is his greatest enjoyment.*

en·large (en lärj′), v., **en·larged, en·larg·ing.** 1. to make or become larger: *They enlarged the house by adding more rooms.* 2. **enlarge on,** to write or tell more about: *to enlarge on one's adventures.*

en·large·ment (en lärj′mənt), n. 1. the act of enlarging; expansion. 2. anything, such as a photograph, that is an enlarged form of something else.

en·light·en (en līt′ᵊn), v. to impart knowledge to; instruct; inform: *The teacher enlightened the class about African customs.* —**en·light′en·ment,** n.

en·list (en list′), v. 1. to enroll in the armed forces: *to enlist in the Navy.* 2. to obtain for some cause: *He enlisted the help of his friends.*

enlist′ed man′, any male member of the U.S. armed services who is not a commissioned officer or a warrant officer.

en·list·ment (en list′mənt), n. 1. the period of time for which a person is committed to a military service. 2. the act of enlisting.

en·liv·en (en lī′vən), v. to make lively, active, or spirited; brighten: *to enliven a party with games.*

en·mi·ty (en′mi tē), n., pl. **en·mi·ties.** a feeling or condition of hostility; hatred; ill will: *There was enmity between the two partners.*

en·no·ble (en nō′bəl), v., **en·no·bled, en·no·bling.** 1. to raise in degree, excellence, or respect; dignify: *His life was ennobled by good deeds.* 2. to raise to the rank of nobleman.

en·nui (än wē′, än′wē), n. a feeling of weariness and discontent; boredom.

e·nor·mi·ty (i nôr′mi tē), n., pl. **e·nor·mi·ties.** 1. outrageous or wicked character; wickedness. 2. something outrageous or wicked, such as an offense.

e·nor·mous (i nôr′məs), adj. extremely large; immense: *an enormous building.* —**e·nor′mous·ly,** adv.

e·nough (i nuf′), adj. 1. adequate or sufficient. —n. 2. an adequate amount. —adv. 3. in a sufficient or adequate quantity or degree: *to eat enough.* 4. fully or quite: *I was happy enough to leave.*

en·quire (en kwīᵊr′), v., **en·quired, en·quir·ing.** another spelling of **inquire.**

en·quir·y (en kwīᵊr′ē, en′kwə rē), n., pl. **en·quir·ies.** another spelling of **inquiry.**

en·rage (en rāj′), v., **en·raged, en·rag·ing.** to put into a rage; make angry; infuriate: *His rudeness enraged all of us.*

en·rap·ture (en rap′chər), v., **en·rap·tured, en·rap·tur·ing.** to move to rapture; delight greatly: *The music enraptured us all.*

en·rich (en rich′), v. 1. to supply with riches: *The discovery of valuable minerals enriched the territory.* 2. to supply with something desirable: *to enrich the mind with knowledge.* 3. to make finer in quality: *to enrich the soil with manure.* —**en·rich′ment,** n.

en·roll (en rōl′), v. 1. to make (someone) a member: *The teacher enrolled him in the class.* 2. to enlist oneself: *to enroll in college.* 3. to write the name of (a person) on a list or roll.

en·roll·ment (en rōl′mənt), n. 1. the act or process of enrolling. 2. the state of being enrolled. 3. the number of persons enrolled: *What is the enrollment in the history course?*

en route (än rōōt′, en), on the way: *We stopped en route to buy some food.*

Ens., Ensign.

en·sconce (en skons′), v., **en·sconced, en·sconc·ing.** to settle securely or snugly: *He ensconced himself in an armchair.*

en·sem·ble (än säm′bəl), n. 1. all the parts of a thing taken together. 2. a person's entire costume or outfit. 3. a group of musical or theatrical performers.

en·shrine (en shrīn′), v., **en·shrined, en·shrin·ing.** 1. to place in or as if in a shrine. 2. to hold as sacred: *to enshrine the nation's ideals.*

en·sign (en′sən or, for defs. 1, 2, en′sīn), n. 1. a flag or banner, such as a military or naval standard used to show nationality. 2. a badge of office or authority. 3. a commissioned officer of the lowest rank in the U.S. Navy, ranking below a lieutenant junior grade and above a petty officer.

en·slave (en slāv′), v., **en·slaved, en·slav·ing.** to make a slave of. —**en·slave′ment,** n.

en·snare (en snâr′), v., **en·snared, en·snar·ing.** to capture or trap in or as if in a snare. Also, **insnare.**

en·sue (en sōō′), v., **en·sued, en·su·ing.** 1. to follow in order; come afterward. 2. to follow as a consequence; result: *Whenever they get together a fight ensues.*

en·sure (en shōōr′), v., **en·sured, en·sur·ing.** 1. to secure or guarantee: *This letter will ensure you a hearing.* 2. to make sure or certain: *Hard work will ensure the success of the project.* 3. to make secure or safe: *to ensure someone from harm.* Also, **insure.**

-ent, a suffix used to form **1.** adjectives meaning doing or being something: *insistent; different.* **2.** nouns meaning a person or thing that does or is something: *correspondent; constituent.*

en·tail (en tāl′), *v.* to cause or involve by necessity: *His project will entail a lot of work.*

en·tan·gle (en taṅg′gəl), *v.,* **en·tan·gled, en·tan·gling. 1.** to catch in a tangle: *The kitten entangled itself in the ball of string.* **2.** to involve in anything like a tangle: *to be entangled with problems.* —**en·tan′gle·ment,** *n.*

en·tente (än tänt′), *n.* **1.** an understanding between nations. **2.** an alliance of parties involved in such an understanding.

en·ter (en′tər), *v.* **1.** to come or go in or into: *to enter a room.* **2.** to penetrate or pierce: *The bullet entered the bone.* **3.** to become a member of; join: *to enter a club.* **4.** to become involved in: *to enter politics.* **5.** to cause to be admitted or join: *to enter a friend in a contest.* **6.** to share or become involved in: *to enter the spirit of the party.* **7.** to record or register: *to enter a name on a list.*

en·ter·prise (en′tər prīz′), *n.* **1.** a project, esp. an important or difficult one. **2.** willingness and energy to undertake projects.

en·ter·pris·ing (en′tər prī′zĭng), *adj.* full of initiative and energy; resourceful; adventurous: *an enterprising young man.* —**en′ter·pris′ing·ly,** *adv.*

en·ter·tain (en′tər tān′), *v.* **1.** to hold the attention of agreeably; amuse: *The comedian entertained the audience.* **2.** to treat as a guest: *to entertain friends.* **3.** to have guests: *They like to entertain.* **4.** to have in mind; consider: *to entertain an idea.* —**en′ter·tain′ing·ly,** *adv.*

en·ter·tain·er (en′tər tā′nər), *n.* a singer, comedian, musician, or the like, esp. one who entertains professionally.

en·ter·tain·ment (en′tər tān′mənt), *n.* **1.** the act of entertaining. **2.** a diversion or amusement. **3.** something that entertains, such as a performance.

en·thrall (en thrôl′), *v.* **1.** to captivate or charm: *The song enthralled us.* **2.** to put or hold in slavery.

en·throne (en thrōn′), *v.,* **en·throned, en·thron·ing.** to place on or as if on a throne. —**en·throne′ment,** *n.*

en·thuse (en thōōz′), *v.,* **en·thused, en·thus·ing. 1.** to show enthusiasm: *to enthuse over a new recording.* **2.** to move to enthusiasm.

en·thu·si·asm (en thōō′zē az′əm), *n.* a lively, absorbing, active interest; zeal: *We all are looking forward to the play with enthusiasm.*

en·thu·si·ast (en thōō′zē ast′), *n.* a person who is filled with enthusiasm for something: *a sports enthusiast.*

en·thu·si·as·tic (en thōō′zē as′tik), *adj.* full of enthusiasm; eager: *an enthusiastic swimmer.* —**en·thu′si·as′ti·cal·ly,** *adv.*

en·tice (en tīs′), *v.,* **en·ticed, en·tic·ing.** to lead on by arousing attention or desire; attract: *We enticed the*

kitten into the house with the toy mouse. —**en·tice′ment,** *n.* —**en·tic′ing·ly,** *adv.*

en·tire (en tī⁼r′), *adj.* **1.** having all its parts or elements; whole: *The entire class went to the picnic.* **2.** not broken; intact: *We found the old dishes entire and without scratches.* **3.** undiminished; full; total: *He devoted his entire energy to his job.* —**en·tire′ly,** *adv.*

en·tire·ty (en tī⁼r′tē), *n., pl.* for def. 2 **en·tire·ties. 1.** the state of being entire; completeness: *The play was presented in its entirety.* **2.** something that is whole or entire: *He devoted the entirety of his life to research.*

en·ti·tle (en tīt′⁼l), *v.,* **en·ti·tled, en·ti·tling. 1.** to give (a person or thing) a right or claim to something: *A good grade on the test entitles you to a prize.* **2.** to give a title to; call: *to entitle an article.*

en·ti·ty (en′ti tē), *n., pl.* **en·ti·ties.** something that has a real existence, such as a body, structure, etc.

en·tomb (en tōōm′), *v.* to place in a tomb; bury.

en·to·mol·o·gist (en′tə mol′ə jist), *n.* an expert in the science of entomology.

en·to·mol·o·gy (en′tə mol′ə jē), *n.* the branch of biology that deals with the study of insects.

en·trails (en′trālz), *n.pl.* the internal parts of an animal, esp. the intestines.

en·train (en trān′), *v.* **1.** to board a train. **2.** to put aboard a train.

en·trance¹ (en′trəns), *n.* **1.** the act of entering: *a quiet entrance.* **2.** a point or place of entering, such as a doorway. **3.** the power or liberty of entering: *He gained entrance to the best clubs.* [from an Old French word, which comes from *entrer* "to enter"]

en·trance² (en trans′), *v.,* **en·tranced, en·tranc·ing. 1.** to fill with delight or wonder: *The parade entranced us.* **2.** to put into a trance. [from *en-* + *trance*]

en·trant (en′trənt), *n.* **1.** a person who enters. **2.** a new member of an association, university, etc. **3.** a competitor in a contest.

en·trap (en trap′), *v.,* **en·trapped, en·trap·ping. 1.** to catch in or as if in a trap. **2.** to lure or bring into a difficult situation: *He entrapped her into agreeing with him.* —**en·trap′ment,** *n.*

en·treat (en trēt′), *v.* **1.** to ask (a person) earnestly; beseech; beg: *to entreat the king for mercy.* **2.** to ask earnestly for (something): *to entreat help.*

en·treat·y (en trē′tē), *n., pl.* **en·treat·ies.** an earnest request or petition.

en·trench (en trench′), *v.* **1.** to dig trenches around: *The soldiers entrenched themselves.* **2.** to place in a position of strength: *to be safely entrenched behind facts.* Also, **intrench.** —**en·trench′ment,** *n.*

en·trust (en trust′), *v.* **1.** to give a trust to: *We entrusted him with our lives.* **2.** to commit (something) in trust to: *to entrust a secret.* Also, **intrust.**

en·try (en′trē), *n., pl.* **en·tries. 1.** the act of entering; entrance. **2.** a place of entrance. **3.** the act of recording an item in a book, list, register, etc. **4.** the item recorded: *There were two entries in the diary for* *yesterday.* **5.** a person or thing entered in a contest or competition.

en·twine (en twīn′), *v.*, **en·twined, en·twin·ing.** to twine with, around, or together: *They walked along with their arms entwined.*

e·nu·mer·ate (i nōō′mə rāt′, -nyōō′-), *v.*, **e·nu·mer·at·ed, e·nu·mer·at·ing. 1.** to mention separately as if in counting: *He enumerated all possibilities.* **2.** to determine the number of; count. —**e·nu′mer·a′tion,** *n.*

e·nun·ci·ate (i nun′sē āt′), *v.*, **e·nun·ci·at·ed, e·nun·ci·at·ing. 1.** to pronounce words, sentences, etc.: *The speaker enunciated clearly.* **2.** to state or declare definitely; announce: *to enunciate a theory.* —**e·nun′ci·a′tion,** *n.*

en·vel·op (en vel′əp), *v.* **1.** to wrap or cover: *The long cloak enveloped her.* **2.** to surround entirely: *Clouds enveloped the hills.* —**en·vel′op·ment,** *n.*

en·ve·lope (en′və lōp′, än′və lōp′), *n.* **1.** a flat paper container, as for a letter, usually having a gummed flap. **2.** any outer wrapping or covering.

en·ven·om (en ven′əm), *v.* **1.** to make poisonous: *to envenom darts.* **2.** to embitter: *The untrue gossip envenomed our friendship.*

en·vi·a·ble (en′vē ə bəl), *adj.* to be envied; desirable: *an enviable report card.* —**en′vi·a·bly,** *adv.*

en·vi·ous (en′vē əs), *adj.* full of or expressing envy; jealous: *She is envious of her sister's new pony.* —**en′vi·ous·ly,** *adv.*

en·vi·ron·ment (en vī′rən mənt), *n.* the surrounding conditions that affect the existence of someone or something: *a home environment.*

en·vi·ron·men·tal·ist (en vī′rən men′tə list), *n.* **1.** a person who works to protect our environment from pollution. **2.** an expert on the environment.

en·vi·rons (en vī′rənz), *n.pl.* surrounding parts or districts; outskirts; suburbs.

en·voy (en′voi, än′voi), *n.* **1.** a diplomatic agent, esp. one next in rank to an ambassador. **2.** a messenger or representative.

en·vy (en′vē), *n., pl.* **en·vies. 1.** a feeling of discontent or jealousy with regard to another's advantages or possessions. **2.** a desire for the advantage possessed by another. **3.** an object of envious feeling: *He is the envy of all his friends.* —*v.,* **en·vied, en·vy·ing. 4.** to be envious of: *I envy her beauty.* —**en′vi·er,** *n.*

en·wrap (en rap′), *v.*, **en·wrapped, en·wrap·ping.** to wrap or surround completely; envelop: *She was enwrapped in a long fur cloak.*

en·zyme (en′zīm), *n.* a substance produced by the body that aids in vital chemical processes taking place in the body: *a digestive enzyme.*

e·o·hip·pus (ē′ō hip′əs), *n., pl.* **e·o·hip·pus·es.** the earliest fossil ancestor of the horse.

Eohippus
(9 in. high at shoulder)

e·on (ē′on, ē′ən), *n.* a very long period of time; age: *Eons passed before the fossil was discovered.* Also, **aeon.**

ep·au·let (ep′ə let′), *n.* an ornamental shoulder piece worn on uniforms.

e·phem·er·al (i fem′ər əl), *adj.* lasting a very short time: *ephemeral pleasures; an ephemeral flower.*

E·phe·sians (i fē′zhəns), *n.* *(used as sing.)* a book of the New Testament, believed to be written by Paul.

ep·ic (ep′ik), *n.* **1.** a long poem that tells about a hero and his adventures and achievements. —*adj.* **2.** impressively great; heroic; majestic: *the epic events of history.*

ep·i·cure (ep′ə kyōor′), *n.* a person who is interested in and knows a great deal about food and drink. [from *Epicurus* (342?–270 B.C.), a Greek philosopher who taught that pleasure is the highest aim of life]

ep·i·cu·re·an (ep′ə kyōō rē′ən, -kyōor′ē ən), *adj.* **1.** having luxurious tastes or habits in eating or drinking. **2.** fit for an epicure: *an epicurean banquet.* — *n.* **3.** a person devoted to the pursuit of pleasure.

ep·i·dem·ic (ep′i dem′ik), *n.* **1.** the rapid spread of a contagious disease to a large number of persons. **2.** a rapid spread of anything: *an epidemic of lateness.* —*adj.* **3.** affecting a large number of persons at the same time and in the same locality; widespread.

ep·i·der·mis (ep′i dûr′mis), *n.* the outer layer of the skin. See also **dermis.** See illus. at **hair.**

ep·i·glot·tis (ep′ə glot′is), *n.* a flap in the throat that blocks the windpipe when food or liquid is being swallowed. See illus. at **mouth.**

ep·i·gram (ep′ə gram′), *n.* a clever saying expressed in few words, such as "Experience is the name everyone gives to his mistakes." —**ep·i·gram·mat·ic** (ep′ə grə mat′ik), *adj.*

ep·i·lep·sy (ep′ə lep′sē), *n.* a disorder of the nervous system that often produces fainting and involuntary muscular contractions. —**ep′i·lep′tic,** *adj., n.*

ep·i·logue (ep′ə lôg′, ep′ə log′), *n.* **1.** a speech delivered by one of the actors at the end of a play. **2.** a concluding part added to a literary work.

E·piph·a·ny (i pif′ə nē), *n., pl.* **E·piph·a·nies.** a Christian festival held on January 6 to celebrate the visit of the Magi to the infant Jesus at Bethlehem.

Epis., 1. Episcopal. **2.** Episcopalian. Also, **Episc.**

e·pis·co·pal (i pis′kə pəl), *adj.* **1.** of or referring to a bishop. **2.** based on or recognizing a governing order of bishops.

E·pis·co·pal (i pis′kə pəl), *adj.* designating the Church of England or some branch of it, as the Protestant Episcopal Church.

E·pis·co·pa·lian (i pis′kə pāl′yən), *adj.* **1.** referring to the Protestant Episcopal Church: *an Episcopalian service.* —*n.* **2.** a member of an Episcopal church. —**E·pis′co·pa′lian·ism,** *n.*

ep·i·sode (ep′i sōd′), *n.* **1.** an incident in the course of a person's life or experience. **2.** an incident or scene in a story. **3.** any one of the separate installments that make up a serial.

e·pis·tle (i pis′əl), *n.* a formal letter.

E·pis·tle (i pis′əl), *n.* any of the books of the New Testament that were written by the apostles in the form of letters.

ep·i·taph (ep′i taf′), *n.* an inscription on a tomb commemorating the person buried there.

ep·i·thet (ep′ə thet′), *n.* any word or phrase replacing or added to the name of a person or thing to describe a characteristic, as "the Lion-Hearted" in "Richard the Lion-Hearted."

e·pit·o·me (i pit′ə mē), *n.* 1. a person or thing that has the ideal features of a whole class: *He is the epitome of goodness.* 2. a summary or condensed account: *the epitome of a speech.*

e·pit·o·mize (i pit′ə mīz′), *v.,* **e·pit·o·mized, e·pit·o·miz·ing.** 1. to represent ideally; typify: *He epitomizes generosity.* 2. to make a summary of.

e plu·ri·bus u·num (ē′ pl\overline{oo}r′ə bəs yoō′nəm), out of many, one: motto of the United States. [from a Latin phrase]

ep·och (ep′ək), *n.* 1. a period of time marked by definite features or events: *an epoch of prosperity.* 2. the beginning of a definite period in the history of anything: *a new epoch in communications.*

Ep′som salts′ (ep′səm), white crystals that dissolve in water and are used as a strong laxative or a soothing bath.

e·qual (ē′kwəl), *adj.* 1. of the same quantity, degree, merit, etc.: *two students of equal ability.* 2. evenly balanced: *an equal contest.* —*n.* 3. a person or thing that is equal: *She is his equal in most sports.* —*v.,* **e·qualed** *or* **e·qualled; e·qual·ing** *or* **e·qual·ling.** 4. to be or become equal to; match: *Ten times ten equals 100.* 5. to make or do something equal to: *The home run equaled the score.* 6. **be equal to,** to have sufficient means or ability for: *He was not equal to the task.* —**e′qual·ly,** *adv.*

e·qual·i·ty (i kwol′i tē), *n.* the state or condition of being equal: *the equality of all men.*

e·qual·ize (ē′kwə līz′), *v.,* **e·qual·ized, e·qual·iz·ing.** to make equal: *The teacher equalized the number of jobs among the class members.* —**e′qual·iz′er,** *n.*

e·qua·nim·i·ty (ē′kwə nim′i tē, ek′wə nim′i tē), *n.* composure, esp. under tension; calmness: *to receive bad news with equanimity.*

e·quate (i kwāt′), *v.,* **e·quat·ed, e·quat·ing.** 1. to state the equality of or between, such as in an equation. 2. to regard or treat as equal: *We cannot always equate poor marks with laziness.*

e·qua·tion (i kwā′zhən), *n.* a mathematical expression stating that two things are equal: $2+2=4$ *is a simple equation.*

e·qua·tor (i kwā′tər), *n.* an imaginary line around the earth midway between the North Pole and the South Pole.

e·qua·to·ri·al (ē′kwə tôr′ē əl, ek′wə tôr′ē əl), *adj.* 1. of, referring to, or near the equator. 2. of, like, or typical of the regions near the equator: *equatorial temperatures; equatorial vegetation.*

Equato′rial Guin′ea, a republic in W equatorial Africa, made up of the mainland province of Río Muni and the island province of Fernando Po, formerly a Spanish colony.

eq·uer·ry (ek′wə rē), *n., pl.* **eq·uer·ries.** 1. an officer in a royal or noble household who is in charge of the horses. 2. an officer serving in the household of the king or queen of England.

e·ques·tri·an (i kwes′trē ən), *adj.* 1. of or referring to horsemen or horsemanship: *He doesn't ride well enough to compete in the equestrian events.* 2. mounted on horseback: *equestrian knights.* 3. showing a person mounted on horseback: *an equestrian statue.* —*n.* 4. a person who rides horses.

e·qui·dis·tant (ē′kwi dis′tənt), *adj.* equally distant: *All points on the circumference of the circle are equidistant from the center.* —**e′qui·dis′tance,** *n.*

e·qui·lat·er·al (ē′kwə lat′ər əl), *adj.* having all sides of equal length: *to draw an equilateral triangle.*

e·qui·lib·ri·um (ē′kwə lib′rē əm), *n.* a state of balance: *It is difficult to maintain one's equilibrium on a slippery street. A scale with equal weights on both sides is in equilibrium.*

Equilateral triangle

e·quine (ē′kwīn), *adj.* of or resembling a horse; like that of a horse.

e·qui·nox (ē′kwə noks′), *n.* either of two times in the year when the sun is directly over the equator and the day and night at all points on the earth are equally long. The vernal equinox occurs about March 21st and the autumnal equinox about September 21st. See also **solstice.** —**e·qui·noc·tial** (ē′kwə nok′shəl), *adj.*

e·quip (i kwip′), *v.,* **e·quipped, e·quip·ping.** to provide or furnish with whatever is needed: *to equip a boat for a voyage; to equip a mountain climber.*

eq·ui·page (ek′wə pij), *n.* 1. a carriage, often including its horses, driver, and attendants. 2. equipment of a ship, army, soldier, etc.

e·quip·ment (i kwip′mənt), *n.* anything kept or provided for a particular purpose; apparatus; gear.

e·qui·poise (ē′kwə poiz′, ek′wə poiz′), *n.* 1. an equal distribution of weight; even balance. 2. something, such as a weight, that balances something else.

eq·ui·ta·ble (ek′wi tə bəl), *adj.* fair and just; reasonable: *an equitable law.* —**eq′ui·ta·bly,** *adv.*

eq·ui·ty (ek′wi tē), *n., pl.* for def. 2 **eq·ui·ties.** 1. the quality of being fair or impartial; fairness: *the equity of a judgment.* 2. something that is fair and just.

e·quiv·a·lent (i kwiv′ə lənt), *adj.* 1. equal in value, measure, force, meaning, etc.: *A dime is equivalent to 10 cents. An SOS is equivalent to a cry for help.* —*n.* 2. something that is equivalent or equal to something else. —**e·quiv′a·lence,** *n.*

e·quiv·o·cal (i kwiv′ə kəl), *adj.* 1. having a doubtful meaning or two possible meanings; ambiguous: *an equivocal answer.* 2. of doubtful character; questionable; dubious: *equivocal loyalty.* —**e·quiv′o·cal·ly,** *adv.*

e·quiv·o·cate (i kwiv′ə kāt′), *v.,* **e·quiv·o·cat·ed, e·quiv·o·cat·ing.** to use unclear or confusing expressions, usually to avoid giving a direct answer: *The*

---

governor equivocated when asked if he would run for president. —**e·quiv′o·ca′tion,** *n.*

Er, *Chem.* the symbol for **erbium.**

-er, a suffix used to form **1.** nouns meaning **a.** a person or thing that performs an action: *teacher; starter.* **b.** a person who makes or works at something: *hatter; tiler.* **c.** a person who lives in or comes from a certain place: *villager; westerner.* **2.** the comparative degree of **a.** adjectives: *harder; smaller.* **b.** adverbs: *faster.*

E.R., Queen Elizabeth. [from the Latin phrase *Elizabeth Rēgina*]

e·ra (ēr′ə, er′ə), *n.* **1.** a period in history marked by particular ways of doing things, special events, a particular quality, or the like: *the era of the horse and carriage; the era of space exploration.* **2.** an historical period figured as beginning with a particular event: *The birth of Christ marks the beginning of the Christian Era.* **3.** any of the major divisions of geological time, usually covering millions or billions of years.

ERA, Equal Rights Amendment (to the U.S. Constitution).

e·rad·i·cate (i rad′ə kāt′), *v.,* **e·rad·i·cat·ed, e·rad·i·cat·ing.** to destroy completely; wipe out: *to eradicate poverty.* —**e·rad′i·ca′tion,** *n.* —**e·rad′i·ca′tor,** *n.*

e·rase (i rās′), *v.,* **e·rased, e·ras·ing. 1.** to rub out (written letters or the like): *to erase a name from the blackboard.* **2.** to wipe out or remove (speech, music, etc.) recorded by a tape recorder. **3.** to remove or rub out written words, recorded sounds, etc., from (something): *to erase a blackboard.* **4.** to be capable of being erased. —**e·ras′a·ble,** *adj.*

e·ras·er (i rā′sər), *n.* a device used for erasing, such as a piece of rubber on the end of a pencil.

E·ras·mus (i raz′məs), *n.* **Des·i·de·ri·us** (dez′i dēr′ē-əs), 1466?–1536, Dutch scholar and theologian.

e·ras·ure (i rā′shər), *n.* **1.** the act of erasing or rubbing out something. **2.** a mark left after erasing.

er·bi·um (ûr′bē əm), *n. Chem.* a metallic element of the rare-earth group. *Symbol:* Er

ere (âr), *prep., conj.* before: used esp. in poetry.

e·rect (i rekt′), *adj.* **1.** upright; straight, rather than bending, stooping, or leaning: *to stand erect.* —*v.* **2.** to build or construct; raise: *to erect a house.* **3.** to raise and set in an upright position: *to erect a telephone pole.* —**e·rect′ly,** *adv.* —**e·rect′ness,** *n.*

e·rec·tion (i rek′shən), *n.* **1.** the act of erecting, raising, or building something: *the erection of a barn.* **2.** something erected, such as a building.

er·go (ûr′gō, er′gō), *conj., adv.* therefore; consequently; as a result of this.

Er·ic·son (er′ik sən), *n.* **Leif** (lēf), flourished c1000, Norse mariner: according to Icelandic saga, the discoverer of Vinland, or North America.

E·rie (ēr′ē), *n.* **1.** a lake between the U.S. and Canada, fourth largest of the Great Lakes. 9940 sq. mi. **2.** a port city in NW Pennsylvania, on Lake Erie.

E′rie Canal′, a canal in New York between Albany and Buffalo, part of New York State Barge Canal.

Er·in (er′in), *n.* Ireland: used esp. in literature.

er·mine (ûr′min), *n., pl.* **er·mines** *or* **er·mine. 1.** a kind of weasel whose fur is brown in summer and white in winter except for the tip of its tail, which is black. **2.** the white winter fur of this animal. [from the Old French word *hermine,* which comes from the Latin phrase *Armenius mūs* "Armenian rat"]

Ermine
(total length 1 ft.)

e·rode (i rōd′), *v.,* **e·rod·ed, e·rod·ing. 1.** to wear away; eat out or into: *Acid erodes metal. Heavy rains and wind eroded the farmland.* **2.** to become eroded. —**e·ro·sive** (i rō′siv), *adj.*

E·ros (ēr′os, er′os), *n.* (in Greek mythology) the god of love: identified with the Roman god Cupid.

e·ro·sion (i rō′zhən), *n.* **1.** the process by which glaciers, wind, water, etc., wear away earth and stone: *The Grand Canyon was formed by erosion.* **2.** the act of eroding, or the state of being eroded: *The erosion of the land made it impossible to farm.*

err (ûr, er), *v.* **1.** to be mistaken or incorrect: *I erred in my estimate.* **2.** to go astray from what is moral or right; sin: *a son who erred but was forgiven.*

er·rand (er′ənd), *n.* **1.** a trip to deliver a message, pick up something, arrange a matter of business, etc., often done for somebody else: *I have to go downtown on an errand for my mother.* **2.** the purpose of such a trip: *His errand was to deliver the groceries.*

er·rant (er′ənt), *adj.* **1.** journeying as medieval knights did in search of adventure: *a knight errant.* **2.** erring or mistaken: *errant behavior.*

er·rat·ic (i rat′ik), *adj.* **1.** not following any regular pattern or course of action; irregular or changeable: *an erratic wind.* **2.** unusual or changeable; odd or queer; eccentric: *moody, erratic behavior.* —**er·rat′i·cal·ly,** *adv.* —**er·rat′i·cism,** *n.*

er·ro·ne·ous (e rō′nē əs), *adj.* mistaken or incorrect: *an erroneous report of a crime.* —**er·ro′ne·ous·ly,** *adv.* —**er·ro′ne·ous·ness,** *n.*

er·ror (er′ər), *n.* **1.** a mistake; something that is not correct or right: *an error in spelling.* **2.** the condition of being mistaken: *You are in error when you say that.* **3.** (in baseball) a misplay in fielding the ball that allows a runner to advance or a batter to keep batting when there would otherwise have been an out.

erst·while (ûrst′hwīl′, -wīl′), *adj.* former; of past times: *my erstwhile enemy.*

er·u·dite (er′yŏŏ dīt′), *adj.* learned or scholarly: *an erudite critic; an erudite essay.* —**er′u·dite′ly,** *adv.*

er·u·di·tion (er′yŏŏ dish′ən), *n.* knowledge acquired by study, research, etc.; learning; scholarship: *a professor of great erudition.*

e·rupt (i rupt′), *v.* **1.** to burst forth or break out in an explosive manner: *Lava erupted from the volcano. His anger erupted suddenly.* **2.** to burst forth with lava, steam, etc.: *The geyser erupts every forty minutes.* **3.** to break out in a skin rash. **—e·rup′tive,** *adj.*

e·rup·tion (i rup′shən), *n.* **1.** a sudden, explosive giving forth of lava, steam, or the like: *the eruption of a volcano.* **2.** a bursting forth suddenly and violently; outburst or outbreak: *the eruption of hostilities.* **3.** the appearance of a rash or the like on one's skin.

-ery, a suffix used to form nouns meaning **1.** an occupation or business: *pottery; fishery.* **2.** a place where things are made, processed, or sold: *bakery; hatchery; bootery.* **3.** an action or process: *archery; cookery.* **4.** a collection of things: *cutlery; greenery.* **5.** a system or arrangement of things: *machinery; tracery.* **6.** a place where persons or things gather or dwell: *nunnery; rookery.* **7.** a trait or quality: *prudery; bravery.* **8.** a state or condition: *slavery; savagery.*

Es, *Chem.* the symbol for **einsteinium.**

-es, a suffix used to form **1.** the plural of nouns ending in *s (losses), z (fizzes), ch (ditches), sh (ashes), y* that changes to *i (bodies),* or *f* that changes to *v (leaves).* **2.** the third person singular of the present tense of verbs ending in *s (passes), z (buzzes), ch (pitches), sh (dashes),* or *y* that changes to *i (studies).* See also **-s.**

E·sau (ē′sô), *n.* (in the Bible) a son of Isaac and older brother of Jacob, to whom he sold his birthright.

es·ca·late (es′kə lāt′), *v.,* **es·ca·lat·ed, es·ca·lat·ing.** to increase in size, degree, amount, etc.: *to escalate a war; a time when prices escalate.* **—es′ca·la′tion,** *n.*

es·ca·la·tor (es′kə lā′tər), *n.* a continuously moving stairway for carrying passengers up and down.

es·ca·pade (es′kə pād′), *n.* a reckless adventure or wild prank: *On one of our escapades we stole the other team's mascot.*

es·cape (e skāp′), *v.,* **es·caped, es·cap·ing.** **1.** to get away or break away from (something that threatens or interferes with one's freedom); gain or regain freedom: *to escape the police; to break loose from prison and escape.* **2.** to avoid or slip away from (danger or harm): *We barely escaped death in the tornado.* **3.** to leak or flow out: *Gas is escaping from the stove.* **4.** to fail to be noticed by, or slip or fade away from (attention, memory, or the like): *Her name escaped my attention.* **5.** to slip out or be spoken by (a person, his lips, etc.): *Your secret shall never escape my lips.* **—n. 6.** a breaking away from imprisonment or from danger or harm: *a daring escape from the enemy.* **7.** a means of escape: *The tunnel was an escape.* **8.** a means of avoiding everyday worries: *Movies can be an escape.* **—es·cap·ee′,** *n.*

es·cape·ment (e skāp′mənt), *n.* **1.** the portion of a watch or clock that measures beats and controls the speed. **2.** a mechanism for regulating the motion of a typewriter carriage.

es·carp·ment (e skärp′mənt), *n.* **1.** a long, steep, clifflike ridge of land or rock. **2.** a steep slope at the base of a rampart surrounding a fortification.

es·chew (es chōō′), *v.* to abstain from or avoid; shun: *to eschew harmful habits.*

es·cort (es′kôrt), *n.* **1.** a person or group of persons accompanying another or others for protection, guidance, honor, courtesy, or the like: *The president was attended by a military escort.* **2.** a man or boy who accompanies a woman or girl to a dance, party, or the like. **3.** a group of airplanes, ships, cars, or the like, serving as a protection or sign of honor: *The admiral was met by an escort of five ships.* **—v.** (e-skôrt′). **4.** to attend or accompany as an escort.

es·cutch·eon (e skuch′ən), *n.* **1.** a shield, or surface shaped like a shield, on which there is a coat of arms. **2. blot on one's escutcheon,** a stain on one's honor or reputation; disgrace.

ESE, east-southeast. Also, **E.S.E.**

-ese, a suffix used to form nouns and adjectives referring to **1.** locality, nationality, or language: *Chinese; Japanese.* **2.** the style or jargon of a particular class or occupation: *journalese.*

Es·ki·mo (es′kə mō′), *n., pl.* **Es·ki·mos** *or* **Es·ki·mo. 1.** a member of a people related to the American Indian, who live on the arctic coasts of Greenland, northern Canada, Alaska, and northeastern Siberia. **2.** a group of languages spoken by Eskimos in various regions. **—adj. 3.** of or concerning the Eskimo people or their language.

Es′kimo dog′, a strong dog with a long, coarse coat, used in the arctic for pulling sleds. Also, **husky.**

e·soph·a·gus (i sof′ə gəs), *n.* the tube that connects the mouth with the stomach.

es·o·ter·ic (es′ə ter′ik), *adj.* **1.** understood by or meant for only a few people having a special knowledge or interest: *an esoteric book on 16th-century nautical terms.* **2.** private or secret.

Eskimo dog
(2 ft. high
at shoulder)

ESP, extrasensory perception: perception or knowledge that is not gained by the senses of seeing, hearing, etc. Mind reading would be an example of ESP.

esp., especially.

es·pe·cial (e spesh′əl), *adj.* another form of **special.**

es·pe·cial·ly (e spesh′ə lē), *adv.* **1.** for a special reason, or in a special way: *I came here especially to see you.* **2.** very; particularly: *Be especially careful.*

es·pi·o·nage (es′pē ə näzh′), *n.* the practice of spying, or the use of spies to get secret information.

es·pous·al (e spou′zəl), *n.* **1.** the adoption or backing of a cause, movement, or the like: *The senator's espousal of our cause will be a great help to us.* **2.** Sometimes, **espousals. a.** a marriage ceremony. **b.** an engagement or betrothal celebration.

es·pouse (e spouz′), *v.,* **es·poused, es·pous·ing. 1.** to adopt or support (a cause, movement, principle, etc.): *to espouse the principles of democracy.* **2.** to take in marriage; marry.

es·prit (e sprē′), *n.* spirit, character, or wit: *conversation full of esprit.*

es·prit de corps (e sprē′ də kôr′), a sense of unity, dedication, and loyalty within a group: *World*

War I pilots were famous for their esprit de corps.

es·py (e spī′), *v.,* **es·pied, es·py·ing.** to see at a distance; catch sight of: *Suddenly she espied smoke signals rising from the hilltop.*

Esq., Esquire.

es·quire (e skwī³r′, es′kwī³r), *n.* **1.** (in the Middle Ages) a squire who attended a knight. **2.** (in England) a man ranking below a knight.

Es·quire (es′kwī³r, e skwī³r′), *n.* an unofficial title of respect, used esp. in England. It is used instead of "Mr." when writing a man's name, being placed after the last name, and usually abbreviated, as *John Phillips, Esq.*

-ess, a suffix used to form feminine nouns: *countess; hostess; lioness.*

es·say (es′ā *for def. 1;* es′ā, e sā′ *for def. 2*), *n.* **1.** a short composition in writing on a particular theme or subject. **2.** an effort to do or gain something; attempt: *an essay at making friends.* —*v.* (e sā′). **3.** to try or attempt: *to essay a difficult task.*

es·say·ist (e′sā ist), *n.* a person who writes essays.

es·sence (es′əns), *n.* **1.** the basic quality or nature of something: *The essence of democracy is the principle that all citizens should have an equal voice in their government.* **2.** a concentrated substance having the qualities of the plant, drug, etc., from which it is made: *essence of cloves.* **3.** perfume or scent.

es·sen·tial (ə sen′shəl), *adj.* **1.** absolutely necessary; incapable of being done without: *A net is essential in tennis.* **2.** of or referring to the essence or nature of something; basic; fundamental: *the essential theme in a book.* —*n.* **3.** something that is basic or necessary; chief point: *to concentrate on essentials.*

es·sen·tial·ly (ə sen′shə lē), *adv.* in essence; basically: *He may seem gruff, but essentially he's a very kind person.*

EST, Eastern Standard Time. Also, **E.S.T., e.s.t.**

-est, a suffix used to form **1.** the superlative degree of **a.** adjectives: *greatest; warmest.* **b.** adverbs: *fastest; oftenest.* **2.** (in old use) the second person singular, present tense, of most verbs: *Thou doest.* See also **-st.**

est., **1.** established. **2.** estate. **3.** estimated.

es·tab·lish (e stab′lish), *v.* **1.** to bring into being on a firm or permanent basis; found: *to establish a university.* **2.** to set up or settle securely in a position, place, business, etc.: *He helped to establish his son in the grocery business.* **3.** to cause to be accepted or recognized; bring about permanently: *to establish a new way of doing something.* **4.** to show to be true; prove: *The trial established her innocence.*

estab′lished church′, a church that is recognized by law and often financially supported by the state as the official church of the nation: *The established church in England is the Anglican Church.*

es·tab·lish·ment (e stab′lish mənt), *n.* **1.** the act of establishing something: *to work toward the establishment of a hospital.* **2.** the state of being established: *His establishment here as a doctor has helped the town.* **3.** something that is established, such as a business or a household: *That hotel is a profitable establishment.*

es·tate (e stāt′), *n.* **1.** a piece of land owned by someone, esp. a large tract of land in the country with a fine house, stables, etc. **2.** property or possessions: *His children will inherit his estate.* **3.** a period or condition in life: *The boy looked forward to attaining a man's estate.* **4.** (formerly) a major political or social group or class, such as the nobles, clergy, and commons in France.

es·teem (e stēm′), *v.* **1.** to regard highly or favorably; admire: *I esteem her for her honesty.* **2.** to consider or regard in a special way: *I esteem it wise to forget the matter.* —*n.* **3.** favorable opinion or judgment; respect: *He stands high in my esteem.*

Es·ther (es′tər), *n.* **1.** the Jewish wife of a king of Persia, who saved her people from massacre. **2.** a book of the Old Testament in which her story is told.

es·thet·ic (es thet′ik), *adj.* another spelling of **aesthetic.** —**es·thet′i·cal·ly,** *adv.*

es·thet·ics (es thet′iks), *n.* another spelling of **aesthetics.**

es·ti·ma·ble (es′tə mə bəl), *adj.* worthy of esteem and admiration: *an estimable performance.*

es·ti·mate (es′tə māt′), *v.,* **es·ti·mat·ed, es·ti·mat·ing.** **1.** to figure approximately; make a judgment of the probable size, amount, value, weight, etc., of (something): *I estimate that our trip will cost $200.* —*n.* (es′tə mit). **2.** a calculation of the probable cost, value, size, etc., of something: *an estimate for the repair of a car.* **3.** a judgment or opinion: *In my estimate he hasn't got a chance.* —**es′ti·ma′tor,** *n.*

es·ti·ma·tion (es′tə mā′shən), *n.* **1.** judgment or opinion: *In her estimation the movie is bad.* **2.** esteem or respect. **3.** the act of estimating or figuring the approximate cost, size, etc., of something; estimate: *What was his estimation of the value?*

Es·to·ni·a (e stō′nē ə), *n.* a former country on the Baltic Sea, now part of the Soviet Union. —**Es·to′ni·an,** *n., adj.*

es·trange (e strānj′), *v.,* **es·tranged, es·trang·ing.** to turn away or spoil the feelings of friendship, liking, affection, etc., of (someone): *We used to be friendly, but the terrible argument we had estranged him.* —**es·trange′ment,** *n.*

es·tu·ar·y (es′chōō er′ē), *n., pl.* **es·tu·ar·ies. 1.** the part of a river where the river's current meets the sea's tide. **2.** an arm or inlet of the sea at the lower end of a river.

E.T.A., estimated time (of) arrival. Also, **ETA**

etc. (et set′ər ə, se′trə), and so forth. "Etc." is used to avoid having to name all of the items on a list. It shows that the list includes other things like the ones already mentioned: *A farm has chickens, ducks, goats, etc.* [short for the Latin phrase *et cetera* "and other things"]

—Usage. See **and.**

et cet·er·a (et set′ər ə, se′trə). See **etc.**

etch (ech), *v.* **1.** to make (a design, picture, or the like) by using acid to eat lines into a hard surface, such as a copper plate. When the lines are filled with ink, the plate can be used to print the picture on paper or other material. **2.** to practice the art of etching. —**etch′er**, *n.*

etch·ing (ech′ing), *n.* **1.** the act or process of making a design or picture by using acid to eat lines into a hard surface. **2.** a printed picture or design made from an etched plate.

e·ter·nal (i tûr′nəl), *adj.* **1.** without beginning or end; always existing; lasting forever: *to believe in one eternal God.* **2.** lasting or unchangeable: *eternal truths.* **3.** continual or endless: *eternal quarreling.* —**e·ter′nal·ly**, *adv.*

e·ter·ni·ty (i tûr′ni tē), *n., pl.* **e·ter·ni·ties. 1.** time without beginning or end; infinite time. **2.** everlasting life; the state into which the soul passes at death. **3.** a seemingly endless period of time: *We had to wait an eternity for the train.*

-eth, a suffix used to form **1.** ordinal numbers from cardinal numbers ending in *-y: twentieth; fortieth.* **2.** an old form of the third person singular of the present tense of most verbs: *He sitteth.* See also **-th.**

e·ther (ē′thər), *n.* a highly flammable liquid whose vapor is used as an anesthetic.

e·the·re·al (i thēr′ē əl), *adj.* **1.** light, airy, or delicate: *ethereal, fairylike beauty.* **2.** heavenly or celestial: *ethereal forces.* —**e·the′re·al·ly**, *adv.*

eth·i·cal (eth′i kəl), *adj.* **1.** referring to or dealing with ethics or the principles of morality: *a discussion of ethical questions, for example how a person determines whether an act is good or bad.* **2.** following certain rules or standards of right and wrong conduct, esp. within a profession: *It's not considered ethical for doctors to advertise.* —**eth′i·cal·ly**, *adv.*

eth·ics (eth′iks), *n.pl.* **1.** *(used as sing. or pl.)* rules of conduct, or a set of moral principles: *Christian ethics.* **2.** *(used as sing.)* the study of moral principles and of how one judges something to be good or bad.

E·thi·o·pi·a (ē′thē ō′pē ə), *n.* a country in E Africa. 472,000 sq. mi. *Cap.:* Addis Ababa. Formerly, **Abyssinia.** —**E′thi·o′pi·an**, *n., adj.*

eth·nic (eth′nik), *adj.* referring to or characteristic of a group of people, such as a racial or national group, who share a common language and culture. —**eth′ni·cal·ly**, *adv.*

Ethiopia

eth·nol·o·gy (eth nol′ə jē), *n.* the study of the different races and cultures of mankind in terms of origin, distribution, and characteristics.

et·i·quette (et′ə kit, et′ə ket′), *n.* rules of correct or courteous behavior, as at a party, wedding, christening, etc.: *According to etiquette, a gentleman should open the door for a lady.*

Et·na (et′nə), *n.* **Mount,** an active volcano in E Sicily. 10,758 ft.

E·tru·ri·a (i troor′ē ə), *n.* an ancient country N of the Tiber River in W Italy.

E·trus·can (i trus′kən), *adj.* **1.** concerning Etruria, its inhabitants, or their civilization: *Etruscan art.* —*n.* **2.** an inhabitant of ancient Etruria.

-ette, a suffix used to form **1.** diminutive nouns: *kitchenette.* **2.** feminine nouns: *usherette.* **3.** names of imitations or substitutes: *flannelette.*

é·tude (ā′tōod, ā′tyōod), *n.* a musical composition intended primarily for teaching or practice.

et·y·mol·o·gy (et′ə mol′ə jē), *n., pl.* **et·y·mol·o·gies. 1.** the study of the origin of words and how their form and meaning have developed. **2.** the origin and history of a given word. —**et·y·mo·log·i·cal** (et′ə mə loj′i kəl), *adj.*

Eu, *Chem.* the symbol for **europium.**

eu·ca·lyp·tus (yōo′kə lip′təs), *n., pl.* **eu·ca·lyp·ti** (yōo′kə lip′tī) *or* **eu·ca·lyp·tus·es.** a tall tree, native to Australia, that produces a valuable aromatic gum.

Eu·cha·rist (yōo′kə rist), *n.* See **communion** (def. 5).

Eu·clid (yōo′klid), *n.* flourished c300 B.C., Greek mathematician and teacher at Alexandria. —**Eu·clid′e·an**, *adj.*

eu·lo·gize (yōo′lə jīz′), *v.*, **eu·lo·gized, eu·lo·giz·ing.** to praise highly; speak or write a eulogy about: *The poet eulogized the king.* —**eu′lo·gist**, *n.*

eu·lo·gy (yōo′lə jē), *n., pl.* **eu·lo·gies.** a speech or writing in praise of someone or something, esp. a funeral speech in honor of a dead person. —**eu·lo·gis·tic** (yōo′lə jis′tik), *adj.*

eu·nuch (yōo′nək), *n.* a castrated man, esp. in former times one who was employed by an Oriental ruler to guard a harem.

eu·phe·mism (yōo′fə miz′əm), *n.* **1.** the substitution of a mild or vague expression for one that is thought to be too harsh or blunt. **2.** the expression so substituted: *"Pass away" is a euphemism for "die."* —**eu′phe·mis′tic**, *adj.* —**eu′phe·mis′ti·cal·ly**, *adv.*

eu·pho·ni·um (yōo fō′nē əm), *n.* a brass musical instrument like the tuba but with a mellower tone.

eu·pho·ny (yōo′fə nē), *n., pl.* **eu·pho·nies.** pleasantness of sound, or a harmonious combination of sounds: *the majestic euphony of great poetry.* —**eu·pho·ni·ous** (yōo-fō′nē əs), *adj.*

Eu·phra·tes (yōo frā′tēz), *n.* a river in SW Asia, flowing SW through Syria and Iraq to join the Tigris. 1700 mi. long.

Euphonium

Eur·a·sia (yōo rā′zhə), *n.* Europe and Asia as a whole.

Eur·a·sian (yōo rā′zhən), *adj.* **1.** of or concerning Eurasia: *Eurasian history.* —*n.* **2.** a person of mixed European and Asian descent.

eu·re·ka (yōo rē′kə), *interj.* (used as a shout of triumph upon making a discovery, solving a problem, or the like): *Eureka! There's gold in this stream!* [from the Greek word *heurēka* "I have discovered." This was supposedly uttered by Archimedes on discovering the principle of specific gravity]

Eu·rip·i·des (yōō rip′i dēz′), *n.* c480–406? B.C., Greek dramatist.

Eu·rope (yōōr′əp), *n.* a continent N of Africa and W of Asia: separated from Asia by the Ural and Caucasus mountains and the Black and Caspian seas. 3,-754,000 sq. mi.

Eu·ro·pe·an (yōōr′ə pē′ən), *adj.* 1. of or referring to Europe or its inhabitants: *European cities.* —*n.* 2. a native or inhabitant of Europe, or a person of European descent.

eu·ro·pi·um (yōō rō′pē əm), *n. Chem.* a metallic element of the rare-earth group. *Symbol:* Eu

Eu·ryd·i·ce (yōō rid′i sē′), *n.* (in Greek mythology) the wife of Orpheus.

Eu·sta′chian tube′ (yōō stā′shən, yōō stā′kē ən), a canal between the pharynx and the middle ear that helps to equalize air pressure on both sides of the eardrum. See illus. at **ear**[1]. [named after Bartolommeo *Eustachio* (1524?-1574), Italian anatomist]

e·vac·u·ate (i vak′yōō āt′), *v.,* **e·vac·u·at·ed, e·vac·u·at·ing.** 1. to leave empty; vacate; withdraw from (a place), esp. because of danger: *We evacuated the town as the hurricane approached.* 2. to remove (persons or things) from a place, esp. for reasons of safety: *to evacuate soldiers from a fort.* 3. to eliminate (wastes) from the body. 4. to produce a vacuum in (a vessel, electron tube, etc.). —**e·vac′u·a′tion**, *n.*

e·vac·u·ee (i vak′yōō ē′), *n.* a person who has been evacuated or removed from a place of danger.

e·vade (i vād′), *v.,* **e·vad·ed, e·vad·ing.** to escape or avoid, esp. by trickery or cleverness: *He evaded our questions by changing the subject.* —**e·vad′er,** *n.*

e·val·u·ate (i val′yōō āt′), *v.,* **e·val·u·at·ed, e·val·u·at·ing.** to figure the value or worth of; appraise: *to evaluate property at $1500; to evaluate an idea.* —**e·val′u·a′tion,** *n.*

ev·a·nes·cent (ev′ə nes′ənt), *adj.* vanishing or passing away quickly; fleeting: *the evanescent life of a butterfly.* —**ev′a·nes′cence,** *n.*

e·van·gel·i·cal (ē′van jel′i kəl), *adj.* 1. referring to or in keeping with the gospel and its teachings: *evangelical studies; evangelical faith.* 2. referring to or belonging to those Protestant churches that emphasize the authority of the Scriptures and salvation through faith: *an evangelical church.*

e·van·ge·lism (i van′jə liz′əm), *n.* the preaching and spreading of the gospel, esp. with enthusiasm and zeal; work of an evangelist.

e·van·ge·list (i van′jə list), *n.* a preacher of the gospel, esp. one who travels from place to place.

E·van·gel·ist (i van′jə list), *n.* any of the writers of the four gospels: Matthew, Mark, Luke, or John.

Ev·ans·ville (ev′ənz vil′), *n.* a city in SW Indiana, on the Ohio River.

e·vap·o·rate (i vap′ə rāt′), *v.,* **e·vap·o·rat·ed, e·vap·o·rat·ing.** 1. to turn from a liquid into a vapor: *Ether evaporates readily.* 2. to disappear: *Her hopes evap-*

orated when she heard the bad news. 3. to remove moisture from (food or other substances): *to evaporate milk.* —**e·vap′o·ra′tion,** *n.*

evap′orated milk′, thick, unsweetened milk made by removing some of the water from whole milk. It is packaged and sold in cans.

e·va·sion (i vā′zhən), *n.* the act of evading, escaping, or avoiding something, esp. by trickery or cleverness: *the evasion of one's duty.*

e·va·sive (i vā′siv), *adj.* seeking to evade or avoid something; not frank or straightforward: *an evasive answer.* —**e·va′sive·ly,** *adv.* —**e·va′sive·ness,** *n.*

eve (ēv), *n.* 1. *(often cap.)* the evening or the day before a holiday: *Christmas Eve.* 2. the period leading up to any event, crisis, or the like: *the eve of a revolution.* 3. the evening.

Eve (ēv), *n.* (in the Bible) the first woman and Adam's wife.

e·ven[1] (ē′vən), *adj.* 1. level, flat, or smooth: *an even floor.* 2. on the same level: *The cellar window is even with the ground.* 3. regular or steady: *an even speed.* 4. (of a number) divisible by 2 without having a remainder, such as 4, 6, 8, etc. (opposite of *odd*). 5. equal in amount, size, or the like: *two even portions.* 6. calm or placid; not easily excited or angered: *an even disposition.* 7. fair; having equal advantages or disadvantages on both sides: *an even contest; an even trade.* 8. exact; being neither larger nor smaller: *an even hundred.* 9. having no debt on either side; square: *I paid him, and now we're even.* —*adv.* 10. still or yet (used to emphasize the comparative form of an adjective): *That would be even better.* 11. (used to indicate that something mentioned is very unlikely or an unusual or extreme case): *Even if I come, I can't stay long.* 12. just; at the same time as: *Even as help was coming, the town surrendered.* 13. indeed (used for emphasis): *He was willing, even eager, to try it.* 14. *Archaic.* precisely or exactly: *He became king even as the old man had promised he would.* —*v.* 15. to make even, level, or smooth: *to even out the garden with a rake.* 16. to make equal; balance: *You should give him a head start to even the chances of winning.* 17. **break even,** to have one's profits equal one's losses: *On this venture you can at least break even.* 18. **get even,** to have revenge on someone; repay a wrong: *I finally got even with her for saying that.* [from the Old English word *efen*]

e·ven[2] (ē′vən), *n. Archaic.* evening or eve: *as even falls.* [from the Old English word *ǣfen*]

eve·ning (ēv′ning), *n.* the latter part of the day and early part of the night, or the time from sunset to bedtime.

eve′ning star′, a bright planet, usually Venus, seen in the west directly after sunset.

e·vent (i vent′), *n.* 1. anything that happens; an occurrence, esp. an important one: *the events leading up to the American Revolution.* 2. a contest in a sports program: *We hope to win the figure-skating events.* 3. **in the event of,** if there should be; in case of: *In the event of rain, the game will be postponed.*

e·vent·ful (i vent′fəl), *adj.* 1. full of important or

memorable events: *an eventful trip.* **2.** having important results; momentous: *an eventful decision.* —**e·vent′ful·ly,** *adv.*

e·ven·tide (ē′vən tīd′), *n.* evening: used chiefly in poetry.

e·ven·tu·al (i ven′chōō əl), *adj.* happening at some future time, esp. as a final result: *That cough may lead to an eventual illness.* —**e·ven′tu·al·ly,** *adv.*

e·ven·tu·al·i·ty (i ven′chōō al′i tē), *n., pl.* **e·ven·tu·al·i·ties.** a possible occurrence or circumstance; an event that may occur: *Rain is an eventuality that you should consider when planning your weekend.*

ev·er (ev′ər), *adv.* **1.** at any time: *Did you ever visit Mexico?* **2.** continuously; all the time: *They've been friends ever since college.* **3.** at all (used for emphasis): *How did you ever manage that?* **4.** at all times; always: *He is ever ready to help.*

Ev·er·est (ev′ər ist), *n.* **Mount,** a mountain in S Asia on the boundary between Nepal and Tibet, in the Himalayas: highest mountain in the world. 29,028 ft.

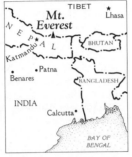

ev·er·glade (ev′ər glād′), *n.* an area of low, swampy land having tall grass and many waterways.

Ev·er·glades (ev′ər glādz′), *n.* *(used as pl.)* a swampy and partly forested region in S Florida, the S part forming a national park (**Ev′erglades Na′tional Park′**). about 5000 sq. mi.

ev·er·green (ev′ər grēn′), *adj.* **1.** having leaves that stay green throughout the year. —*n.* **2.** an evergreen plant, tree, or shrub.

ev·er·last·ing (ev′ər las′tiŋ), *adj.* **1.** lasting forever; eternal: *everlasting life.* **2.** lasting or going on for a very long time; continual: *the everlasting changes of season.* **3.** seeming to last forever; constant; tiresome: *her everlasting complaints.* —*n.* **4.** time without end; eternity. **5. the Everlasting,** God. —**ev′er·last′ing·ly,** *adv.*

ev·er·more (ev′ər môr′), *adv.* forever or always; henceforth: *He was evermore happy and content.*

eve·ry (ev′rē), *adj.* **1.** indicating each one of a group or series; each: *We visit every day.* **2.** all possible; the greatest possible: *You have every chance of winning.* **3. every bit,** *Informal.* in all respects; completely: *The cake is every bit as good as you promised.* **4. every other,** every second or alternate (person, thing, etc.): *We have milk delivered every other day.* **5. every which way,** *Informal.* in all directions; in a disorganized manner: *The books fell every which way.*

eve·ry·bod·y (ev′rē bod′ē), *pron.* every person: *Everybody is invited to the barbecue.*

eve·ry·day (ev′rē dā′), *adj.* **1.** daily; of or referring to every single day: *an everyday chore.* **2.** of or for

ordinary days rather than Sundays or holidays: *everyday clothes.* **3.** ordinary or commonplace: *a movie about everyday life.*

eve·ry·one (ev′rē wun′), *pron.* every person; everybody: *Everyone is required to have a notebook.*

eve·ry·thing (ev′rē thiŋ′), *pron.* **1.** every single thing; all: *Put away everything that's on the floor.* **2.** something very important: *His help meant everything.*

eve·ry·where (ev′rē hwâr′, -wâr′), *adv.* in every place: *We looked everywhere for the key.*

e·vict (i vikt′), *v.* to force (a person) to move out of his apartment, place of business, or the like, by legal means: *to evict someone for not paying the rent.* —**e·vic′tion,** *n.*

ev·i·dence (ev′i dəns), *n.* **1.** something that shows what has happened or can prove a statement to be true; proof: *We have evidence to prove his guilt.* **2.** a sign or indication: *Her blushing was evidence of her nervousness.* —*v.,* **ev·i·denced, ev·i·denc·ing.** **3.** to show or make evident: *Her grief was evidenced by her tears.* **4. in evidence,** plainly visible; conspicuous: *The signs of spring are in evidence.*

ev·i·dent (ev′i dənt), *adj.* plain or clear; easy to see; obvious: *It was evident that he was bored.*

ev·i·dent·ly (ev′i dənt lē), *adv.* obviously or apparently: *She's not here, so evidently she was delayed.*

e·vil (ē′vəl), *adj.* **1.** bad or wicked; morally wrong: *an evil deed.* **2.** causing misfortune and suffering; harmful: *Those were evil times.* —*n.* **3.** sin or moral wickedness: *to preach against evil.* **4.** something that is harmful or bad: *War is an evil.* —**e′vil·ly,** *adv.*

e·vil·do·er (ē′vəl dōō′ər), *n.* a person who does evil or wrong.

e·vil-mind·ed (ē′vəl mīn′did), *adj.* having a wicked or nasty character: *an evil-minded tyrant.*

e·vince (i vins′), *v.,* **e·vinced, e·vinc·ing.** to show clearly; make evident: *The dog evinced friendliness by wagging its tail.*

e·voke (i vōk′), *v.,* **e·voked, e·vok·ing.** to bring forth or call forth; suggest: *His speech evoked protests.*

ev·o·lu·tion (ev′ə lōō′shən), *n.* **1.** any process of growth or development: *the evolution of modern science.* **2.** the development of complex plants and animals from earlier simpler forms. **3.** a pattern formed by a series of movements: *the evolutions of a figure skater.* —**ev·o·lu′tion·ar′y,** *adj.*

ev·o·lu·tion·ist (ev′ə lōō′shə nist), *n.* a person who believes in the biological theory of evolution.

e·volve (i volv′), *v.,* **e·volved, e·volv·ing.** **1.** to develop gradually: *to evolve a plan.* **2.** to develop according to the biological theory of evolution: *Higher forms of life evolve from lower ones.*

ewe (yōō), *n.* a female sheep.

ew·er (yōō′ər), *n.* a tall, slender pitcher, often used for decorative purposes.

Ewer

ex-, a prefix meaning **1.** out or from: *ex-*

hale; expatriate. **2.** former: *ex-wife; ex-mayor.*

ex., **1.** examination. **2.** examined. **3.** example. **4.** except. **5.** exchange. **6.** executed. **7.** executive.

ex·act (ig zakt/), *adj.* **1.** accurate or correct: *an exact description.* **2.** precise rather than approximate: *What is the exact time?* —*v.* **3.** to call for or demand: *to exact obedience; to exact money from someone.* —**ex·act/ness,** *n.*

ex·act·ing (ig zak/tiñg), *adj.* **1.** strict or severe: *an exacting teacher.* **2.** requiring close attention or hard work: *an exacting task.* —**ex·act/ing·ly,** *adv.*

ex·ac·tion (ig zak/shən), *n.* **1.** the act of exacting or demanding something: *the exaction of strict discipline.* **2.** something exacted or demanded.

ex·act·i·tude (ig zak/ti tōōd/, -tyōōd/), *n.* exactness, preciseness, or accuracy: *I admire the exactitude of his work.*

ex·act·ly (ig zakt/lē), *adv.* **1.** in an exact manner; precisely; accurately: *to measure something exactly.* **2.** just or entirely: *He will do exactly what he wishes.* **3.** quite so; that's right.

ex·ag·ger·ate (ig zaj/ə rāt/), *v.,* **ex·ag·ger·at·ed, ex·ag·ger·at·ing.** **1.** to make (something) seem larger, more important, etc., than it really is; overstate: *to exaggerate a difficulty.* **2.** to use exaggeration in speech or writing: *He's exaggerating when he says we walked ten miles.* —**ex·ag/ger·at·ing·ly,** *adv.*

ex·ag·ger·a·tion (ig zaj/ə rā/shən), *n.* **1.** the act of exaggerating or overstating: *the exaggeration of a problem.* **2.** a statement that exaggerates; overstatement: *It's an exaggeration to say everyone was there.*

ex·alt (ig zôlt/), *v.* **1.** to raise in position, honor, power, etc.: *Fate exalted the soldier to the position of emperor.* **2.** to praise or honor: *a prayer exalting God.* **3.** to fill with feelings of joy, nobility, or the like: *The audience was exalted by the play.*

ex·al·ta·tion (eg/zôl tā/shən), *n.* **1.** the act of exalting, or the state of being exalted: *a man's exaltation to the position of governor.* **2.** the act of honoring; praise; worship: *to sing in exaltation.* **3.** a feeling of happiness, hope, or elation; rapture.

ex·alt·ed (ig zôl/tid), *adj.* **1.** high in rank, honor, power, etc.: *an aloof, exalted personage.* **2.** noble or elevated; lofty: *an exalted style of writing.* **3.** excited or happy: *an exalted mood.* —**ex·alt/ed·ly,** *adv.*

ex·am (ig zam/), *n.* *Informal.* an examination.

exam., **1.** examination. **2.** examined.

ex·am·i·na·tion (ig zam/ə nā/shən), *n.* **1.** the act of examining; an inspection or investigation: *a detective's thorough examination of the scene of a crime.* **2.** the process of testing students by asking them questions: *an examination in history.* **3.** the questions asked, or the answers given: *a hard examination.*

ex·am·ine (ig zam/in), *v.,* **ex·am·ined, ex·am·in·ing.** **1.** to look over carefully; inspect: *to examine a car before buying it.* **2.** to investigate or consider carefully: *to examine the reasons for losing a game.* **3.** to test the knowledge of (a student) by asking questions: *to examine the class in history.* —**ex·am/in·er,** *n.*

ex·am·ple (ig zam/pəl), *n.* **1.** one of a number of things that shows what the others are like; sample:

This test is an example of his work. **2.** a problem to be solved that illustrates how a rule or principle works: *an example in arithmetic.* **3. make an example of,** to punish (someone) as a warning to others: *to make an example of a tardy student.* **4. set an example,** to serve as a model or pattern, as something to be imitated or avoided: *His behavior sets a bad example for the class.*

ex·as·per·ate (ig zas/pə rāt/), *v.,* **ex·as·per·at·ed, ex·as·per·at·ing.** to annoy extremely: *The long wait exasperated her.* —**ex·as/per·at·ing·ly,** *adv.*

ex·as·per·a·tion (ig zas/pə rā/shən), *n.* extreme irritation or annoyance: *He was in a state of exasperation after waiting for two hours.*

ex·ca·vate (ek/skə vāt/), *v.,* **ex·ca·vat·ed, ex·ca·vat·ing.** **1.** to make a hole or tunnel in, esp. by digging: *to excavate a mountain.* **2.** to make (a hole, tunnel, etc.) by digging: *to excavate a tunnel.* **3.** to dig or scoop out (earth, sand, etc.): *to excavate rock.* **4.** to uncover by digging; unearth: *to excavate an ancient city.* —**ex/ca·va/tor,** *n.*

ex·ca·va·tion (ek/skə vā/shən), *n.* **1.** a hole or cavity made by digging: *a deep excavation for a foundation.* **2.** the act of excavating: *the excavation of an ancient Roman temple.*

ex·ceed (ik sēd/), *v.* **1.** to go beyond the bounds or limits of; go beyond (what is possible, permitted, etc.): *The job exceeded his strength. The driver exceeded the speed limit.* **2.** to excel.

ex·ceed·ing (ik sē/diñg), *adj.* **1.** unusual or extraordinary: *to run with exceeding swiftness.* —*adv.* **2.** exceedingly.

ex·ceed·ing·ly (ik sē/diñg lē), *adv.* very or extremely: *The children sang exceedingly well.*

ex·cel (ik sel/), *v.,* **ex·celled, ex·cel·ling.** to be better than (others) in some way: *He excels me at golf. She excels in singing.*

ex·cel·lence (ek/sə ləns), *n.* **1.** the quality of being outstanding or excelling; high quality; superiority: *to achieve excellence in ballet dancing.* **2.** (*usually cap.*) See **excellency** (def. 1).

ex·cel·len·cy (ek/sə lən sē), *n., pl.* **ex·cel·len·cies.** **1.** (*usually cap.*) Also, **Excellence.** a title of honor given to certain high officials, such as governors and ambassadors, and also to bishops and archbishops: *You should address the ambassador as "Your Excellency."* **2.** Usually, **excellencies.** excellent or outstanding qualities, characteristics, etc.

ex·cel·lent (ek/sə lənt), *adj.* very good; superior: *an excellent haircut.* —**ex/cel·lent·ly,** *adv.*

ex·cel·si·or (ik sel/sē ər), *n.* **1.** wood shavings, used esp. for packing breakable or fragile objects. —*adj.* (ik sel/sē ôr/). **2.** (*often cap.*) ever upward: used as a motto. [from a Latin word meaning "higher"; in def. 1, from a former trademark]

ex·cept (ik sept/), *prep.* **1.** leaving out; but; with the exception of: *They were all there except me.* —*conj.* **2.** only or but (often fol. by *that*): *They look alike except that the older one has blue eyes.* —*v.* **3.** to leave out or exclude: *You are excepted from taking the test.* —**Usage.** See **accept.**

ex·cept·ing (ik sep′ting), *prep.* except: *Excepting the Smiths, we're all going to the fair together.*

ex·cep·tion (ik sep′shən), *n.* **1.** a leaving out or exclusion of something or someone: *Everyone must stay after class with the exception of Jane.* **2.** something or someone that is different from others; something excepted: *Most of us have to study hard, but Bob is an exception.* **3. take exception, a.** to object: *We took exception to the new rule.* **b.** to take offense; become angry: *She took exception to my remarks about her hat.*

ex·cep·tion·al (ik sep′shə nəl), *adj.* **1.** unusual or extraordinary: *The warm weather was exceptional for January.* **2.** unusually excellent; superior: *an exceptional athlete.* —**ex·cep′tion·al·ly,** *adv.*

ex·cerpt (ek′sûrpt), *n.* **1.** a passage taken out of a book, play, film, or the like; extract: *She read an excerpt from the book we are studying.* —*v.* (ik sûrpt′). **2.** to take out as an excerpt: *to excerpt a poem from a story for reading in class.*

ex·cess (ik ses′, ek′ses), *n.* **1.** an amount that is more than enough; superabundance: *an excess of energy.* **2.** the amount by which one thing is more than another: *I spent an excess of two dollars over my allowance.* —*adj.* **3.** more than what is necessary, allowed, or the like; extra: *We had excess baggage on the trip.* **4. in excess of,** exceeding or surpassing; over: *He has debts in excess of $300.* **5. to excess,** beyond the proper amount: *to talk to excess.*

ex·ces·sive (ik ses′iv), *adj.* beyond the usual or proper limit or amount; extreme; extravagant: *a harsh, excessive punishment; an excessive amount of money.* —**ex·ces′sive·ly,** *adv.* —**ex·ces′sive·ness,** *n.*

ex·change (iks chānj′), *v.,* **ex·changed, ex·chang·ing.** **1.** to give up (something) and get something else in its place; trade: *He exchanged a toy car for a toy bulldozer.* **2.** to give back and forth; give and get in return; interchange: *to exchange presents; to exchange blows.* —*n.* **3.** the act of exchanging; a trade: *My ice-cream cone for your hot dog is a fair exchange.* **4.** a central place for buying and selling: *the stock exchange in New York.* **5.** a central office or station: *a telephone exchange.* —**ex·change′a·ble,** *adj.*

ex·cheq·uer (eks′chek ər, iks chek′ər), *n.* **1.** a treasury, esp. of a state or nation. **2. the Exchequer,** the department of the British government in charge of collecting taxes, import duties, and the like.

ex·cise[1] (ek′sīz, ek′sīs), *n.* a tax or duty within a country on the manufacture, sale, or use of certain goods: *an excise on tobacco.* [from the medieval Latin word *accisa* "tax"]

ex·cise[2] (ik sīz′), *v.,* **ex·cised, ex·cis·ing.** to cut out or remove: *to excise a wart.* [from the Latin word *excisus,* past participle of *excidere* "to cut out"]

ex·cit·a·ble (ik sī′tə bəl), *adj.* easily excited or aroused to action: *a very excitable horse.* —**ex·cit′a·bil′i·ty,** *n.* —**ex·cit′a·bly,** *adv.*

ex·cite (ik sīt′), *v.,* **ex·cit·ed, ex·cit·ing.** **1.** to stir up or arouse the emotions or feelings of: *Their insults excited him to anger.* **2.** to stir up or arouse (emotions or feelings): *to excite anger in a person.*

ex·cit·ed (ik sī′tid), *adj.* stirred up emotionally; not calm: *He was so excited about his camping trip that he could hardly sleep.* —**ex·cit′ed·ly,** *adv.*

ex·cite·ment (ik sīt′mənt), *n.* **1.** an excited or stirred-up state or condition: *She couldn't study because of her excitement over going to the theater.* **2.** something that excites.

ex·cit·ing (ik sī′ting), *adj.* causing excitement; thrilling; stirring: *an exciting adventure.* —**ex·cit′ing·ly,** *adv.*

ex·claim (ik sklām′), *v.* to cry out or speak suddenly and loudly, showing surprise, anger, or the like: *"That's not true!" he exclaimed.*

exclam., exclamation.

ex·cla·ma·tion (ek′sklə mā′shən), *n.* **1.** a word or phrase that expresses surprise, amazement, pain, triumph, or the like; interjection: *"Hurrah" and "ouch" are exclamations.* **2.** the act of exclaiming or crying out; outcry: *His speech was continually interrupted by exclamations from the crowd.*

exclama′tion point′, the sign (!) that is put after an exclamation in writing. Also, **exclama′tion mark′.**

ex·clam·a·to·ry (ik sklam′ə tôr′ē), *adj.* using, expressing, or referring to an exclamation: *"Watch out!" is an exclamatory phrase.*

ex·clude (ik sklood′), *v.,* **ex·clud·ed, ex·clud·ing.** **1.** to keep out or shut out; prevent from entering or joining: *to exclude someone from a club.* **2.** to keep out of consideration, discussion, or the like; fail to include: *to exclude a subject from discussion.*

ex·clu·sion (ik skloo′zhən), *n.* **1.** the act of excluding or keeping out someone or something: *the exclusion of someone from a conversation.* **2.** the state of being excluded or not permitted to enter: *His exclusion from the baseball game was unfair.*

ex·clu·sive (ik skloo′siv), *adj.* **1.** tending to exclude outsiders: *an exclusive circle of friends.* **2.** entire or complete: *I'll give that problem my exclusive attention.* **3.** single or sole: *an exclusive right.* **4. exclusive of,** not including: *It cost $30 exclusive of tax.* —**ex·clu′sive·ly,** *adv.* —**ex·clu′sive·ness,** *n.*

ex·com·mu·ni·cate (eks′kə myoo′nə kāt′), *v.,* **ex·com·mu·ni·cat·ed, ex·com·mu·ni·cat·ing.** to remove (someone) from membership in a church; exclude (someone) from taking part in the sacraments. —**ex′com·mu′ni·ca′tion,** *n.*

ex·cre·ment (ek′skrə mənt), *n.* waste matter discharged from the body.

ex·cres·cence (ik skres′əns), *n.* a growth, esp. an undesired one, on the outside of the body or an organ of the body: *A wart is an excrescence on the skin.*

ex·crete (ik skrēt′), *v.,* **ex·cret·ed, ex·cret·ing.** to separate and expel (wastes) from the body.

ex·cre·tion (ik skrē′shən), *n.* **1.** the act of excreting. **2.** the matter excreted: *Urine is an excretion.*

ex·cre·to·ry (ek′skri tôr′ē), *adj.* referring to or functioning in excretion.

---

act, āble, dâre, ärt; ebb, ēqual; if, īce; hot, ōver, ôrder; oil; bŏŏk; ōōze; out; up, ûrge; ə = a as in alone; ə as in button (but′ən), fire (fī°r); chief; shoe; thin; that; zh as in measure (mezh′ər). See full key inside cover.

ex·cru·ci·at·ing (ik skrōō′shē ā′tiŋ), *adj.* extremely painful; unbearable: *excruciating fear; excruciating pain.* —**ex·cru′ci·at′ing·ly,** *adv.*

ex·cur·sion (ik skûr′zhən), *n.* 1. a short journey or trip for a special purpose: *a pleasure excursion.* 2. a trip on a train, ship, etc., at a reduced fare: *That bus line runs weekend excursions to the beach.*

ex·cuse (ik skyōōz′), *v.,* **ex·cused, ex·cus·ing.** 1. to pardon or forgive; overlook: *to excuse bad manners.* 2. to give an apology or· explanation for: *He excused his rudeness by saying he was very tired.* 3. to serve as an apology or reason for forgiving: *Illness excuses children from missing school.* 4. to release from an obligation or duty: *She was excused from taking the test.* —*n.* (ik skyōōs′). 5. an explanation given as a reason for being excused or forgiven: *His excuse was that the bus was late.* 6. a statement that gives such an explanation: *You must bring a written excuse from home.* 7. **excuse oneself,** to offer an apology; apologize: *When you're rude, you should excuse yourself.* —**ex·cus′a·ble,** *adj.*

exec., executive.

ex·e·cra·ble (ek′sə krə bəl), *adj.* 1. completely detestable; abominable: *an execrable crime.* 2. very bad; dreadful: *an execrable report card.*

ex·e·crate (ek′sə krāt′), *v.,* **ex·e·crat·ed, ex·e·crat·ing.** 1. to hate or detest: *to execrate cruelty to animals.* 2. to curse or call down evil upon: *He execrated all who opposed him.*

ex·e·cra·tion (ek′sə krā′shən), *n.* 1. something detestable or very bad. 2. a curse. 3. the act of execrating.

ex·e·cute (ek′sə kyōōt′), *v.,* **ex·e·cut·ed, ex·e·cut·ing.** 1. to carry out; accomplish: *to execute a plan.* 2. to put to death according to law: *to execute a murderer.* 3. to perform or do: *to execute a high dive.*

ex·e·cu·tion (ek′sə kyōō′shən), *n.* 1. the act of executing or carrying out something: *the execution of a law.* 2. a putting to death according to law: *the execution of a prisoner.* 3. the manner in which something is performed: *The dancer's execution of his role was almost perfect.*

ex·e·cu·tion·er (ek′sə kyōō′shə nər), *n.* an official who puts legally condemned criminals to death.

ex·ec·u·tive (ig zek′yə tiv), *n.* 1. a person whose job is to carry out the goals or policies of an organization, esp. by the management and supervision of the work of other persons. 2. the person or branch of government responsible for carrying out laws: *The President is the Chief Executive of the United States.* —*adj.* 3. of or referring to management or the carrying out of plans, policies, etc.: *a young man with executive ability.* 4. of or concerning the carrying out of laws: *the executive branch of government.*

ex·ec·u·tor (ig zek′yə tər), *n.* a person who carries out some job, assignment, etc., esp. a person who is in charge of carrying out the provisions of a will.

ex·em·pla·ry (ig zem′plə rē), *adj.* 1. worthy of imitation: *exemplary behavior.* 2. serving as a warning: *exemplary punishment.* 3. serving as a model or example: *an exemplary type of Colonial house.*

ex·em·pli·fy (ig zem′plə fī′), *v.,* **ex·em·pli·fied, ex·em·pli·fy·ing.** to show or illustrate by example; be an example of: *This statue exemplifies the ancient Greek ideals of beauty.* —**ex·em′pli·fi·ca′tion,** *n.*

ex·empt (ig zempt′), *v.* 1. to free from an obligation or duty; release: *The army exempts people with very bad eyesight from military service.* —*adj.* 2. released from or not subject to an obligation, duty, etc.: *Charitable organizations are exempt from paying taxes.*

ex·emp·tion (ig zemp′shən), *n.* 1. the act of exempting or releasing from an obligation: *exemption from jury duty.* 2. the state of being exempt or not bound by an obligation or duty. 3. a person who can be listed on an income-tax form as a deduction, such as one's wife or child.

ex·er·cise (ek′sər sīz′), *n.* 1. physical or mental activity done to make one stronger or more skillful. 2. something to be done or performed as a means of practice or training: *piano exercises.* 3. a putting into action or use: *the exercise of caution.* 4. Often, **exercises.** a traditional ceremony: *graduation exercises.* —*v.,* **ex·er·cised, ex·er·cis·ing.** 5. to go through exercise; take bodily exercise: *to exercise by bicycling in the park.* 6. to put through exercises or practice to make stronger or more skillful: *to exercise a horse.* 7. to put (one's abilities, rights, etc.) into practice or use: *to exercise one's strength by chopping wood; to exercise one's rights by protesting.* 8. to use or show: *to exercise care in doing a job.*

ex·ert (ig zûrt′), *v.* 1. to put forth (strength, power, or the like); use in action: *He exerted all his strength in pushing the car.* 2. **exert oneself,** to put forth extreme or unusual effort: *I might help him a little, but I wouldn't exert myself.*

ex·er·tion (ig zûr′shən), *n.* 1. the use or exercise of one's powers or abilities: *the exertion of strength.* 2. vigorous action; effort: *By a great exertion the firemen rescued the people who were trapped.*

ex·hale (eks hāl′), *v.,* **ex·haled, ex·hal·ing.** to breathe out. —**ex·ha·la·tion** (eks′hə lā′shən), *n.*

ex·haust (ig zôst′), *v.* 1. to use up completely: *to exhaust a supply of water.* 2. to drain of strength or energy; make very tired: *Working all night exhausted him.* 3. to empty or make a vacuum in. —*n.* 4. the waste gases ejected by an engine. —**ex·haust′i·ble,** *adj.* —**ex·haust′ing·ly,** *adv.*

ex·haus·tion (ig zôs′chən), *n.* 1. extreme tiredness or weakness: *The soldiers suffered from exhaustion.* 2. the act of exhausting. 3. the state of being exhausted or used up: *the exhaustion of our food supply.*

ex·haus·tive (ig zôs′tiv), *adj.* dealing with every aspect of a subject, topic, issue, etc.; thorough: *an exhaustive study of a subject.* —**ex·haus′tive·ly,** *adv.*

ex·hib·it (ig zib′it), *v.* 1. to put on display: *to exhibit paintings.* 2. to show or give signs of: *to exhibit anger by shouting.* —*n.* 3. a public show; exhibition: *an exhibit of automobiles.* 4. an object or collection of objects shown in an exhibition, fair, or the like: *My favorite exhibit was the collection of antique swords.* —**ex·hib′i·tor,** *n.*

ex·hi·bi·tion (ek′sə bish′ən), *n.* **1.** a showing or exhibiting: *an exhibition of rage.* **2.** a public show or display of objects or skills: *an exhibition of stamps.*

ex·hil·a·rate (ig zil′ə rāt′), *v.*, **ex·hil·a·rat·ed, ex·hil·a·rat·ing.** to make very lively, full of high spirits, and cheerful: *The trip to the beach exhilarated all of us.* —**ex·hil′a·rat·ing·ly,** *adv.* —**ex·hil′a·ra′tion,** *n.*

ex·hort (ig zôrt′), *v.* to urge or advise urgently; warn strongly: *to exhort someone to be extremely careful.*

ex·hor·ta·tion (eg′zôr tā′shən, ek′sôr tā′shən), *n.* **1.** the act of exhorting, urging, or advising: *a minister's exhortation of his congregation.* **2.** speech or writing that gives strong advice or an urgent warning: *an exhortation on the dangers of reckless driving.*

ex·hume (ig zōōm′, -zyōōm′), *v.*, **ex·humed, ex·hum·ing.** to dig up from the earth; remove from a grave: *to exhume a corpse for an autopsy.*

ex·i·gen·cy (ek′si jən sē), *n.*, *pl.* **ex·i·gen·cies. 1.** an emergency or condition requiring prompt action: *He promised to help in any exigency.* **2.** **exigencies,** needs or requirements: *the exigencies of city life.*

ex·ile (eg′zīl, ek′sīl), *v.*, **ex·iled, ex·il·ing. 1.** to force a person to leave his country or home; banish: *The king exiled his enemies.* —*n.* **2.** a forced separation from home or country; banishment: *The punishment for traitors was either exile or death.* **3.** the state of being exiled: *to live in exile.* **4.** a period of exile or separation from home or country: *He wrote several books during his exile.* **5.** a person who is exiled: *a group of exiles living near the border.*

ex·ist (ig zist′), *v.* **1.** to have real being; be in existence: *How long has the earth existed?* **2.** to maintain life; live: *Can man exist under water?* **3.** to be found; occur: *Hunger exists in many parts of the world.*

ex·ist·ence (ig zis′təns), *n.* **1.** the state of existing, living, or being real: *Man did not come into existence until long after the dinosaurs.* **2.** the fact of existing or being real: *I don't believe in the existence of evil spirits.* **3.** a way of existing or living: *to work for a better existence.* —**ex·ist′ent,** *adj.*

ex·it (eg′zit, ek′sit), *n.* **1.** a way or passage out: *This building has ten different exits.* **2.** a going out or away: *I made a quick exit when the fight started.* —*v.* **3.** to go out or leave; depart: *We exited quietly from the theater.* [from the Latin word *exitus,* which comes from *exire* "to go out"]

ex·o·dus (ek′sə dəs), *n.* a going out or departure, esp. by a large number of people: *the exodus of a crowd from a sports stadium.*

Ex·o·dus (ek′sə dəs), *n.* **1.** the departure of the Israelites from Egypt under Moses. **2.** the second book of the Old Testament, containing the story of the Exodus.

ex of·fi·ci·o (eks ə fish′ē ō′), by reason of or because of one's office or official position: *The governor has the power ex officio to veto bills.* [from a Latin phrase] —**ex′-of·fi′ci·o′,** *adj.*

ex·on·er·ate (ig zon′ə rāt′), *v.*, **ex·on·er·at·ed, ex·on·er·at·ing.** to free from blame; clear of a charge or accu-

sation: *We have found evidence that exonerates the prisoner.* —**ex·on′er·a′tion,** *n.*

ex·or·bi·tant (ig zôr′bi t⁼nt), *adj.* beyond or higher than what is proper or usual: *to charge an exorbitant price.* —**ex·or′bi·tant·ly,** *adv.*

ex·or·cise (ek′sôr sīz′), *v.*, **ex·or·cised, ex·or·cis·ing. 1.** to drive out (a devil, evil spirit, or the like) by religious or magical rites: *to exorcise a demon from a castle.* **2.** to free (a person or place) of evil spirits, devils, etc.: *to exorcise a haunted house.*

ex·ot·ic (ig zot′ik), *adj.* **1.** foreign; not native: *exotic foods.* **2.** strikingly unusual or strange: *He wore an exotic cape.* —*n.* **3.** something foreign, such as an unusual kind of plant. —**ex·ot′i·cal·ly,** *adv.*

exp., 1. expenses. **2.** expired. **3.** export. **4.** express.

ex·pand (ik spand′), *v.* **1.** to grow or make larger; increase in size, extent, scope, etc.: *Heat expands metal.* **2.** to spread or stretch out; unfold: *The bird expanded its wings.* **3.** to make (a story, speech, etc.) longer or more detailed; develop: *to expand a short story into a novel.* —**ex·pand′a·ble,** *adj.*

ex·panse (ik spans′), *n.* a large, open space or area: *an expanse of desert.*

ex·pan·sion (ik span′shən), *n.* **1.** the act of expanding or increasing: *the expansion of metal when heated.* **2.** the state of being expanded: *The expansion of the town required us to build new roads.* **3.** something that is the result of expansion or development: *That play is an expansion of a television show.*

ex·pan·sive (ik span′siv), *adj.* **1.** unrestrained and open: *He has a generous, expansive personality.* **2.** having a wide range or scope; extensive: *an expansive view.* **3.** likely to expand or capable of expanding: *Gases are expansive.* —**ex·pan′sive·ly,** *adv.* —**ex·pan′sive·ness,** *n.*

ex·pa·ti·ate (ik spā′shē āt′), *v.*, **ex·pa·ti·at·ed, ex·pa·ti·at·ing.** to speak or write in great detail and at length; discuss lengthily: *She expatiated upon the need for a new school building.*

ex·pa·tri·ate (eks pā′trē āt′), *v.*, **ex·pa·tri·at·ed, ex·pa·tri·at·ing. 1.** to banish or drive (a person) from his native country; exile: *The war expatriated him.* **2.** to withdraw (oneself) from one's native country: *She expatriated herself and settled in France.* —*n.* (eks pā′trē it, eks pā′trē āt′). **3.** a person who lives in another country and cannot or does not plan to return to his native land. —**ex·pa′tri·a′tion,** *n.*

ex·pect (ik spekt′), *v.* **1.** to look forward to; believe likely or sure to happen or arrive: *to expect guests; to expect a thunderstorm.* **2.** to look for or demand with good reason: *to expect honesty.* **3.** *Informal.* to suppose or guess: *I expect you're tired from your trip.*

ex·pect·an·cy (ik spek′t⁼n sē), *n.*, *pl.* **ex·pect·an·cies. 1.** the state of expecting; expectation. **2.** something that is looked forward to.

ex·pect·ant (ik spek′t⁼nt), *adj.* having or showing expectation; looking forward to something: *an excited, expectant audience.* —**ex·pect′ant·ly,** *adv.*

ex·pec·ta·tion (ek′spek tā′shən), *n.* **1.** the act of expecting; a looking forward: *the expectation of a good time.* **2.** the state of expecting or looking forward to something; expectancy: *to wait in expectation.* **3.** something that is expected: *Our expectation is that he will arrive before sunset.* **4.** Often, **expectations.** a prospect or likelihood of future benefit or profit: *The young man has great expectations.*

ex·pec·to·rate (ik spek′tə rāt′), *v.,* **ex·pec·to·rat·ed, ex·pec·to·rat·ing.** to spit.

ex·pe·di·en·cy (ik spē′dē ən sē), *n.* **1.** the quality of being expedient or useful; advantageousness; advisability: *The officers discussed the expediency of a surprise attack.* **2.** a sense of self-interest or personal advantage; selfishness: *His policy wavered between justice and expediency.* Also, **ex·pe′di·ence.**

ex·pe·di·ent (ik spē′dē ənt), *adj.* **1.** helping to achieve some desired goal or end; useful; advantageous: *If you're in a hurry, it would be expedient to take a taxi.* **2.** advantageous to oneself rather than right or just; selfish: *to make an expedient decision.* —*n.* **3.** something that helps one to achieve a goal. —**ex·pe′di·ent·ly,** *adv.*

ex·pe·dite (ek′spi dīt′), *v.,* **ex·pe·dit·ed, ex·pe·dit·ing.** to speed up the progress or accomplishment of (something); hasten: *Sending the package by airmail will expedite its delivery.* [from the Latin word *expeditus* "set free"] —**ex′pe·dit′er,** *n.*

ex·pe·di·tion (ek′spi dish′ən), *n.* **1.** a journey or voyage made for some special purpose: *an expedition to explore the Arctic.* **2.** the people going on such a journey: *The expedition got back safely.*

ex·pe·di·tion·ar·y (ek′spi dish′ə ner′ē), *adj.* referring to or being an expedition: *an expeditionary force of specially trained soldiers.*

ex·pe·di·tious (ek′spi dish′əs), *adj.* prompt or quick: *to take expeditious action.* —**ex′pe·di′tious·ly,** *adv.*

ex·pel (ik spel′), *v.,* **ex·pelled, ex·pel·ling. 1.** to drive away or out; force out: *to expel air from the lungs.* **2.** to remove from membership in a school, club, or the like; dismiss: *to expel a student from college.*

ex·pend (ik spend′), *v.* **1.** to use up: *to expend energy doing a job.* **2.** to pay out; spend: *to expend funds from a treasury.*

ex·pend·a·ble (ik spen′də bəl), *adj.* **1.** able or available to be spent or used up: *expendable funds.* **2.** able to be given up or sacrificed in order to achieve some goal, esp. a military objective: *The bridge is expendable, but we must hold the fort.*

ex·pend·i·ture (ik spen′di chər), *n.* **1.** the act of expending or spending: *an expenditure of energy.* **2.** money that is spent; expense: *I kept a list of our expenditures on the trip.*

ex·pense (ik spens′), *n.* **1.** cost or charge: *the expense of a long trip.* **2.** a cause of spending; something that costs a great deal to keep up or do: *A car can be a great expense.* **3.** expenses, charges or costs that arise in the course of a trip, doing a job, or the like: *to pay one's own expenses on a trip.* **4. at the expense of,** at the sacrifice or neglect of: *He demanded quantity, but at the expense of quality.*

ex·pen·sive (ik spen′siv), *adj.* very high-priced; cost-

ing a great deal: *an expensive car.* —**ex·pen′sive·ly,** *adv.* —**ex·pen′sive·ness,** *n.*

ex·pe·ri·ence (ik spēr′ē əns), *n.* **1.** the act or process of personally doing, seeing, or living through something: *I know by experience that it's dangerous to try to swim here.* **2.** something that one does or that happens to one: *Our tour of the submarine was an interesting experience.* **3.** knowledge or skill gained by personally doing, seeing, or living through something: *He gained his mining experience in South America.* —*v.,* **ex·pe·ri·enced, ex·pe·ri·enc·ing. 4.** to feel or undergo something: *to experience fear.*

ex·pe·ri·enced (ik spēr′ē ənst), *adj.* wise or skillful through experience: *an experienced teacher.*

ex·per·i·ment (ik sper′ə mənt), *n.* **1.** a test or trial done in order to discover a reason for something or to find out if a theory is true: *experiments proving that blood circulates in the body.* —*v.* (ek sper′ə ment′). **2.** to make tests or try out something: *to experiment with a new medicine.*

ex·per·i·men·tal (ik sper′ə men′t°l), *adj.* **1.** referring to or based on experiments: *an experimental science.* **2.** like an experiment in being a beginning effort or trial; not yet secure; uncertain: *a baby's first, experimental steps.* —**ex·per′i·men′tal·ly,** *adv.*

ex·per·i·men·ta·tion (ik sper′ə men tā′shən), *n.* the act or practice of experimenting, trying out, or testing: *By experimentation they discovered the best woods for making bows and arrows.*

ex·pert (ek′spûrt), *n.* **1.** a person who has special skill or knowledge in some field; specialist; authority: *an expert on African history.* —*adj.* (ik spûrt′, ek′-spûrt). **2.** having special skill or knowledge; extremely skillful (often fol. by *in* or *at*): *to be expert at driving a car.* —**ex′pert·ly,** *adv.*

ex·pi·ate (ek′spē āt′), *v.,* **ex·pi·at·ed, ex·pi·at·ing.** to make up for (a crime, sin, etc.); atone for; make amends for: *to expiate a crime by going to prison.* —**ex′pi·a′tion,** *n.*

ex·pi·ra·tion (ek′spə rā′shən), *n.* **1.** a running out; close; ending: *the expiration of a driver's license.* **2.** a breathing out: *the expiration of air from the lungs.*

ex·pire (ik spī°r′), *v.,* **ex·pired, ex·pir·ing. 1.** to cease to be in effect; come to an end: *My driver's license expires in March.* **2.** to die or die out. **3.** to breathe out (air); exhale.

ex·plain (ik splān′), *v.* **1.** to make plain or clear; show or tell in detail: *to explain how to bake a cake.* **2.** to make clear the meaning of (something): *He asked us to explain the ending of the movie.* **3.** to give a reason for: *They demanded that he explain his absence.* **4.** to give an explanation: *There isn't time to explain.* **5. explain away,** to remove (doubts, difficulties, etc.) by explanation: *He explained away her fears by saying they were imaginary.* —**ex·plain′a·ble,** *adj.*

ex·pla·na·tion (ek′splə nā′shən), *n.* **1.** the act of explaining something; the process of making something clear or understandable: *The explanation of Einstein's theories is not an easy job.* **2.** a reason or meaning that explains something; statement or fact that makes something clear: *Her explanation for being late was that she was on an errand.*

ex·plan·a·tor·y (ik splan′ə tôr′ē), *adj.* serving to explain or make clear: *The explanatory remarks at the beginning help you to understand the book.*

ex·ple·tive (ek′spli tiv), *n.* 1. a word used to fill out a phrase or sentence, as *it* in *It is raining* or *there* in *There are three glasses on the shelf.* 2. an exclamation or interjection, such as "ugh" or "ouch."

ex·plic·it (ik splis′it), *adj.* fully and clearly expressed; plainly stated so that no misunderstanding will arise: *Dad gave me explicit instructions on how to mow the lawn.* —**ex·plic′it·ly,** *adv.*

ex·plode (ik splōd′), *v.,* **ex·plod·ed, ex·plod·ing.** 1. to burst with a loud noise: *They took cover when the dynamite exploded.* 2. to cause (something) to burst: *to explode a firecracker.* 3. to burst out noisily or violently: *to explode with laughter.* 4. to prove wrong; cause to be no longer believed: *His alibi was exploded by the evidence.*

ex·ploit¹ (ek′sploit), *n.* an heroic act; brave or noble deed, adventure, etc.: *He told of his exploits in the war.* [from the Old French word *esploit,* which comes from Latin *explicitum* "something set forth"]

ex·ploit² (ik sploit′), *v.* 1. to use to advantage; utilize in a practical way or for profit: *He exploited his talent for writing by working as a newspaper reporter.* 2. to use for selfish purposes; take unfair advantage of: *He exploited the miners by giving them low pay.* [from the French word *exploiter,* which comes from *exploit* "achievement." See *exploit¹*] —**ex·ploit′a·ble,** *adj.* —**ex·ploi·ta·tion** (ek′sploi tā′shən), *n.*

ex·plo·ra·tion (ek′splə rā′shən), *n.* 1. the act of exploring or traveling through new regions to discover what they are like: *exploration to discover the source of a river.* 2. an investigation or examination: *the exploration of different possibilities.*

ex·plor·a·to·ry (ik splôr′ə tôr′ē), *adj.* 1. referring to or concerned with exploration: *Lewis and Clark made an exploratory trip up the Missouri River.* 2. serving as a basis for further action; preliminary: *to hold exploratory talks about reduced tariffs.*

ex·plore (ik splôr′), *v.,* **ex·plored, ex·plor·ing.** 1. to travel through or over (an area, region, etc.) for the purpose of discovery: *to explore the bottom of the ocean.* 2. to look over or into closely; examine: *to explore a problem in science.* —**ex·plor′er,** *n.*

ex·plo·sion (ik splō′zhən), *n.* 1. a sudden, violent bursting or burning accompanied by a loud noise. 2. the noise of an explosion: *The explosion made us all jump.* 3. an outburst of laughter, anger, or the like.

ex·plo·sive (ik splō′siv), *n.* 1. a material, such as dynamite, used for blasting or in warfare. —*adj.* 2. likely to explode: *an explosive gas.* 3. likely to explode into anger, violence, revolution, etc.: *an explosive situation.* —**ex·plo′sive·ness,** *n.*

ex·po·nent (ik spō′nənt), *n.* 1. a person who explains or describes an idea, point of view, etc.: *He was an exponent of Darwin's theory.* 2. a person or thing that stands for or symbolizes something: *Lincoln is an exponent of American democracy.*

ex·port (ik spôrt′, ek′spôrt), *v.* 1. to send (food, raw materials, manufactured goods, etc.) to another country or region for sale: *Brazil exports coffee.* —*n.* (ek′spôrt). 2. the act of exporting; exportation: *the export of farm products.* 3. something that is exported: *Their major export is wheat.* —*adj.* (ek′spôrt). 4. of or referring to exporting or exports: *an export business.* —**ex·port′er,** *n.*

ex·por·ta·tion (ek′spôr tā′shən), *n.* 1. the act of exporting goods: *the exportation of copper.* 2. something that is exported: *an important exportation.*

ex·pose (ik spōz′), *v.,* **ex·posed, ex·pos·ing.** 1. to lay open to attack, danger, harm, etc.; put or leave in a position without protection from harm: *The soldiers' attack exposed them to enemy fire.* 2. to uncover or bare: *The wolf's snarl exposed his teeth.* 3. to make known; reveal: *to expose a secret.* 4. to make known to; put in contact with: *to expose a student to new ideas.* 5. to let light fall upon: *to expose a film.*

ex·po·si·tion (ek′spə zish′ən), *n.* 1. a public exhibition or show: *an automobile exposition.* 2. the act of explaining or setting forth: *a speaker's exposition of his views.* 3. a detailed discussion or explanation.

ex·pos·i·to·ry (ik spoz′i tôr′ē), *adj.* serving to set forth or explain; explanatory: *The first chapter is expository and outlines the main points in the book.*

ex·pos·tu·late (ik spos′chə lāt′), *v.,* **ex·pos·tu·lat·ed, ex·pos·tu·lat·ing.** to reason or argue with someone to try to persuade him not to do something; remonstrate: *The father expostulated with his son about borrowing money.* —**ex·pos′tu·la′tion,** *n.*

ex·po·sure (ik spō′zhər), *n.* 1. the act of exposing, laying open, or disclosing: *exposure to danger.* 2. the state of being exposed, esp. to cold, damp weather: *When rescued from the raft, he was suffering from exposure.* 3. location with regard to the direction from which sunlight, wind, etc., comes: *The room has a southern exposure.* 4. (in photography) **a.** the length of time that light strikes the film. **b.** the section of film exposed: *a roll of 36 exposures.*

ex·pound (ik spound′), *v.* to state in detail or explain: *to expound one's political views.*

ex·press (ik spres′), *v.* 1. to put (thought) into words: *She has trouble expressing her ideas.* 2. to show or reveal: *His smile expressed how pleased he was.* 3. to send (a package, freight, etc.) by a fast direct system. —*adj.* 4. clear or definite: *He gave express orders that no one was to enter.* 5. traveling very fast and skipping some stops: *an express train.* —*n.* 6. an express train, elevator, etc.: *The trip is shorter if you take the express.* 7. a system of sending freight, packages, money, etc., that is fast and direct: *Send it by express.* 8. a company that delivers packages or the like by express. 9. something sent by express. —*adv.* 10. by a direct, fast means; by express: *He sent the film express.* 11. **express oneself,** to express one's thoughts, feelings, etc., esp. in talking: *We* *weren't sure what he meant, because he doesn't express himself very well.*

ex·pres·sion (ik spresh′ən), *n.* **1.** the act of expressing ideas, feelings, etc., esp. in words: *The teacher encouraged them in the expression of their views.* **2.** the manner of expression; wording: *Notice the beauty of the author's expression.* **3.** a particular word or phrase: *"O.K." is an American expression.* **4.** a look on the face that shows what one is feeling: *He shook the package with a puzzled expression.* **5.** the quality of expressing emotion, meaning, etc., by the voice, gestures, or the like: *to read with expression.*

ex·pres·sive (ik spres′iv), *adj.* **1.** serving to express; showing what one feels or means: *a look expressive of sorrow.* **2.** full of expression, emotion, or meaning; meaningful: *He gave an expressive shrug.* —**ex·pres′sive·ly,** *adv.* —**ex·pres′sive·ness,** *n.*

ex·press·ly (ik spres′lē), *adv.* **1.** in a definite or clear way; plainly: *I expressly said to wait by the fountain.* **2.** for a particular purpose; specially: *I came here expressly to thank you.*

ex·press·way (ik spres′wā′), *n.* a highway, esp. one built for high-speed traffic.

ex·pul·sion (ik spul′shən), *n.* **1.** the act of driving out or expelling: *the expulsion of air from the lungs.* **2.** the state of being driven out or expelled: *His expulsion from school troubled his family.*

ex·punge (ik spunj′), *v.,* **ex·punged, ex·pung·ing.** to strike out or erase; remove: *The editor expunged the last paragraph from the reporter's story.*

ex·pur·gate (ek′spər gāt′), *v.,* **ex·pur·gat·ed, ex·pur·gat·ing.** **1.** to remove objectionable or offensive passages from: *to expurgate a book.* **2.** to remove (an objectionable part) from a book, speech, or the like: *to expurgate a scene from a movie.* —**ex′pur·ga′tion,** *n.*

ex·qui·site (ek′skwi zit, ik skwiz′it), *adj.* **1.** having an unusually fine or delicate beauty: *an exquisite flower.* **2.** extraordinarily excellent; superb: *exquisite workmanship.* **3.** keenly sensitive; highly refined: *She has exquisite taste in art.* —**ex′qui·site·ly,** *adv.*

ex·tem·po·ra·ne·ous (ik stem′pə rā′nē əs), *adj.* done or spoken without special preparation or practice: *She gave an extemporaneous speech.* —**ex·tem′po·ra′ne·ous·ly,** *adv.*

ex·tem·po·re (ik stem′pə rē), *adv.* **1.** on the spur of the moment; without special planning or preparation: *The professor lectured extempore.* —*adj.* **2.** done or spoken without special preparation; extemporaneous: *an extempore performance.* [from the Latin phrase *ex tempore* "out of the time"]

ex·tem·po·rize (ik stem′pə rīz′), *v.,* **ex·tem·po·rized, ex·tem·po·riz·ing.** to speak or perform without special forethought or preparation: *The speaker extemporized on the subject of his trip through India.* —**ex·tem′po·ri·za′tion,** *n.*

ex·tend (ik stend′), *v.* **1.** to stretch out or draw out: *He extended the measuring tape as far as it would go.* **2.** to reach or hold out: *to extend one's hand in welcome.* **3.** to make longer; lengthen: *to extend a visit for another week.* **4.** to make greater; improve or enlarge: *to extend one's knowledge of science.* **5.** to of-

fer or grant: *to extend an invitation.* **6.** to be or become extended; stretch or spread out; last: *Their discussion extended into the evening.*

ex·tend·ed (ik sten′did), *adj.* **1.** stretched out or spread out: *to stand with one's arms extended.* **2.** continued or prolonged; lasting a long time: *an extended argument.* **3.** widespread or extensive: *an extended investigation of ways to improve our schools.*

ex·ten·sion (ik sten′shən), *n.* **1.** the act of extending, or the state of being extended: *the extension of a visit for a few more days.* **2.** a part that extends something, making it longer, larger, etc.; addition: *He plans to build an extension onto his house.*

ex·ten·sive (ik sten′siv), *adj.* **1.** wide or broad; far-reaching: *an extensive jungle; an extensive knowledge.* **2.** lengthy or long: *an extensive discussion.* **3.** great in amount, number, strength, etc.: *an extensive fortune.* —**ex·ten′sive·ly,** *adv.*

ex·tent (ik stent′), *n.* **1.** the area over which something extends, spreads, or goes; the length, size, amount, or scope of something: *the extent of a farm; the extent of one's knowledge.* **2.** something extended: *an extent of water.*

ex·ten·u·ate (ik sten′yōō āt′), *v.,* **ex·ten·u·at·ed, ex·ten·u·at·ing.** to lessen the seriousness of (a fault, mistake, crime, etc.); partly explain, excuse, or justify: *Extenuating circumstances forced me to miss the skating party.* —**ex·ten′u·a′tion,** *n.*

ex·te·ri·or (ik stēr′ē ər), *adj.* **1.** outer or outside; being on the outside: *an exterior coat of paint for a house.* **2.** of, referring to, or from the outside; being on the outside; external: *American history has been influenced by exterior events in Europe and Asia.* —*n.* **3.** the outside; outer part or surface: *the exterior of a building.* **4.** outward appearance: *He has a pleasant exterior, but I don't know what he's really like.*

ex·ter·mi·nate (ik stûr′mə nāt′), *v.,* **ex·ter·mi·nat·ed, ex·ter·mi·nat·ing.** to get rid of by destroying; kill: *to exterminate rats with poison.* —**ex·ter′mi·na′tion,** *n.*

ex·ter·mi·na·tor (ik stûr′mə nā′tər), *n.* **1.** a person or thing that exterminates or kills vermin. **2.** a business that specializes in exterminating vermin.

ex·ter·nal (ik stûr′nəl), *adj.* **1.** of or referring to the outside or outer part: *Most fish have an external covering of scales.* **2.** (of a medicine) for the outside of the body; not to be swallowed or injected: *a salve for external use.* **3.** of or referring to outward appearance or behavior: *A smile is an external sign of friendliness.* **4.** of or from the outside: *external causes of trouble.* —*n.* **5.** something external; an outside part. **6. externals,** outward appearance: *Don't judge people by externals.* —**ex·ter′nal·ly,** *adv.*

ex·tinct (ik stingkt′), *adj.* **1.** having died out; not existing any more: *Dinosaurs are an extinct kind of animal.* **2.** no longer active: *an extinct volcano.*

ex·tinc·tion (ik stingk′shən), *n.* **1.** the act of wiping out or extinguishing something. **2.** the state or condition of being wiped out or destroyed: *Many kinds of wild animals are in danger of extinction.*

ex·tin·guish (ik sting′gwish), *v.* **1.** to put out (a fire, light, flame, etc.): *to extinguish a candle.* **2.** to put an end to; destroy: *to extinguish someone's hopes.*

ex·tin·guish·er (ik sting'gwi shər), *n.* a person or thing that extinguishes, esp. a fire extinguisher.

ex·tol (ik stōl'), *v.,* **ex·tolled, ex·tol·ling.** to praise highly: *a speech extolling a hero's courage.*

ex·tort (ik stôrt'), *v.* to force (money, information, etc.) from a person by the use of violence or threats: *to extort a confession from someone.*

ex·tor·tion (ik stôr'shən), *n.* **1.** the using of force or threats to get money or information from someone: *The gangster was sent to jail for extortion.* **2.** something extorted or forced from a person, such as an illegal charge or unfairly high price.

ex·tor·tion·ate (ik stôr'shə nit), *adj.* **1.** so high as to be illegal or very unfair: *extortionate prices.* **2.** characterized by extortion or practicing extortion: *extortionate moneylenders.*

ex·tor·tion·ist (ik stôr'shə nist), *n.* a person who practices extortion. Also, **ex·tor'tion·er.**

ex·tra (ek'strə), *adj.* **1.** beyond or more than what is expected or necessary; additional: *I made some extra sandwiches.* —*n.* **2.** something extra or additional: *The police chief's car has many extras, including a telephone.* **3.** a special edition of a newspaper. **4.** an actor or actress appearing in a very small part, esp. as part of a crowd scene. —*adv.* **5.** beyond what is usual; unusually: *These eggs are extra large.*

extra-, a prefix meaning outside or beyond: *extraordinary; extracurricular.*

ex·tract (ik strakt'), *v.* **1.** to pull or draw out; take out, esp. by the use of force or a special effort: *to extract a tooth.* **2.** to figure out or bring out: *to extract a moral from a story.* **3.** to get or derive: *to extract some amusement from an annoying situation.* **4.** to separate (a substance, ingredient, etc.) by pressing, distilling, or some other process: *to extract juice from lemons.* **5.** to copy out (a passage, verse, etc.) from a written work: *to extract some quotations from the Bible.* **6.** to force or extort: *to extract information by threats.* —*n.* (ek'strakt). **7.** something extracted or taken from something else: *lemon extract; extracts from a book.* —**ex·trac'tor,** *n.*

ex·trac·tion (ik strak'shən), *n.* **1.** the act or process of extracting: *the extraction of a tooth.* **2.** the state or fact of being extracted. **3.** descent or ancestry: *a person of Swedish extraction.* **4.** something extracted; an extract.

ex·tra·cur·ric·u·lar (ek'strə kə rik'yə lər), *adj.* not included in the regular curriculum or schedule of studies: *He's done a lot of extracurricular reading on the Civil War.*

ex·tra·dite (ek'strə dīt'), *v.,* **ex·tra·dit·ed, ex·tra·dit·ing.** **1.** to hand over (a prisoner, fugitive, etc.) to another state or authority: *New Mexico extradited the prisoner to Georgia to stand trial.* **2.** to obtain the extradition of (someone). —**ex·tra·di·tion** (ek'strə dish'ən), *n.*

ex·tra·ne·ous (ik strā'nē əs), *adj.* coming from outside; not related or pertinent; foreign: *an extraneous remark.* —**ex·tra'ne·ous·ly,** *adv.*

ex·traor·di·nar·y (ik strôr'dᵊner'ē), *adj.* **1.** exceptional or remarkable: *The whale is an animal of extraordinary size.* **2.** beyond what is usual or customary; special: *In an emergency the governor has extraordinary powers.* **3.** (of a government official, employee, etc.) having a special task or responsibility: *The president appointed him ambassador extraordinary.* —**ex·traor·di·nar·i·ly** (ik strôr'dᵊnâr'ə lē), *adv.*

ex·tra·sen·so·ry (ek'strə sen'sə rē), *adj.* outside of normal sense perception; experienced in some way other than through normal seeing, hearing, etc.

ex'tra·sen'sory percep'tion. See **ESP.**

ex·trav·a·gance (ik strav'ə gəns), *n.* **1.** too great or wasteful spending of money: *Because of our extravagance on our vacation we are short of money this month.* **2.** the quality of going to unreasonable or fantastic extremes in speech, behavior, manner of dressing, etc.: *The politician was famous for the extravagance of his promises to the voters.* **3.** anything that is extravagant, esp. something that costs more than one can afford.

ex·trav·a·gant (ik strav'ə gənt), *adj.* **1.** spending much more than is necessary or wise; wasteful: *She is very extravagant when she buys clothes.* **2.** very high; much too high: *These prices are extravagant.* **3.** beyond what is reasonable or justifiable; extreme; unrestrained: *extravagant praise.* —**ex·trav'a·gant·ly,** *adv.*

ex·treme (ik strēm'), *adj.* **1.** very far beyond what is usual or average; quite unusual or exaggerated: *extreme danger.* **2.** farthest or outermost: *There are woods at the extreme limits of the town.* —*n.* **3.** the highest or a very high degree: *You must be careful in the extreme when climbing a mountain.* **4.** something that is very far from what is usual or very different from something else: *the extremes of love and hate.* **5. to go to extremes,** to go beyond what is reasonable or proper: *The newspaper went to extremes in attacking the congressman.*

ex·treme·ly (ik strēm'lē), *adv.* very; much more than usual: *extremely cold; extremely generous.*

ex·trem·ist (ik strē'mist), *n.* a person who goes to extremes, esp. one who supports or demands radical changes in government.

ex·trem·i·ty (ik strem'i tē), *n., pl.* **ex·trem·i·ties.** **1.** the extreme or farthest point or part of something; end or top: *the northern extremities of the continent.* **2.** the quality of being extreme, exaggerated, or violent: *The extremity of his opinions got him into many arguments.* **3.** a condition of great need or danger: *In his extremity he appealed to his friends for help.* **4. the extremities,** a person's hands or feet.

ex·tri·cate (ek'strə kāt'), *v.,* **ex·tri·cat·ed, ex·tri·cat·ing.** to free or release from an entanglement or difficult or embarrassing situation: *to extricate a puppy from a tangled leash; to extricate oneself from a promise.* —**ex'tri·ca'tion,** *n.*

ex·tro·vert (ek′strə vûrt′), *n.* an outgoing person; one who enjoys the company of others and is very involved in things outside himself. See also **introvert.**

ex·u·ber·ant (ig zōō′bər ənt), *adj.* 1. full of energy and enthusiasm: *exuberant shouts.* 2. lavish and enthusiastic: *an exuberant welcome.* 3. growing richly or thickly; superabundant: *exuberant vegetation.* —**ex·u′ber·ance,** *n.* —**ex·u′ber·ant·ly,** *adv.*

ex·ude (ig zōōd′), *v.,* **ex·ud·ed, ex·ud·ing.** 1. to ooze out: *Sap exuded from the tree.* 2. to give off: *to exude sweat.* 3. to show or radiate: *He exudes confidence.*

ex·ult (ig zult′), *v.* to rejoice; be joyful or jubilant: *to exult in the coming of spring.* —**ex·ult′ing·ly,** *adv.*

ex·ult·ant (ig zul′t°nt), *adj.* joyful or jubilant: *an exultant hymn.* —**ex·ult′ant·ly,** *adv.*

ex·ul·ta·tion (eg′zul tā′shən), *n.* triumphant joy; jubilation: *to sing in exultation.*

eye (ī), *n.* 1. either of the two, round, hollow organs in the head by means of which one sees. 2. an organ of sight in an animal. 3. the iris or colored part of the eye: *blue eyes.* 4. the area surrounding the eye: *a black eye.* 5. sight or vision: *to have poor eyes.* 6. a look, glance, or gaze: *to cast an eye on something.* 7. close watch or observation: *to be under the eye of the teacher.* 8. regard, view, or attention: *an eye to one's own advantage.* 9. something resembling an eye in appearance,

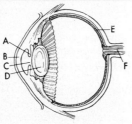

Eye (Human)
A, Iris; B, Cornea;
C, Pupil; D, Lens;
E, Retina; F, Optic nerve

shape, or the like, such as the bud of a potato or the hole in a needle. 10. Often, **eyes.** a way of looking at something; judgment; view: *In the eyes of the law, a man is innocent until proved guilty.* —*v.,* **eyed; eye·ing** *or* **eye·ing.** 11. to view or watch; look at: *The cat eyed the goldfish.* 12. **an eye for an eye,** revenge or punishment that is as severe as the injury. 13. **catch someone's eye,** to catch someone's attention: *That red sweater caught my eye.* 14. **have an eye for,** to have an interest in or appreciation for: *She has an eye for antique furniture.* 15. **keep an eye on,** to watch carefully, or guard: *Keep an eye on the baby.* 16. **lay** (or **set**) **eyes on,** *Informal.* to catch sight of;

see: *I never laid eyes on him before this morning.* 17. **see eye to eye,** to be in complete agreement: *We saw eye to eye on the whole plan.* 18. **with an eye to,** with the idea or plan in mind: *I bought the paint with an eye to redecorating my room.* —**eye′less,** *adj.* —**eye′like′,** *adj.* —**ey′er,** *n.*

eye·ball (ī′bôl′), *n.* the round body of the eye that is protected by the eyelids in front and held in a bony socket behind.

eye·brow (ī′brou′), *n.* 1. the fringe of hair growing above the eye. 2. the ridge on which it grows.

eye·drop·per (ī′drop′ər), *n.* a glass tube with a rubber bulb for applying a liquid drop by drop.

eye·glass (ī′glas′), *n.* 1. **eyeglasses.** Also, **glasses, spectacles.** a pair of lenses mounted in a frame, worn over the eyes as an aid to vision, protection from sunlight, etc. 2. a single lens for aiding vision.

eye·lash (ī′lash′), *n.* one of the hairs growing on the edge of the eyelids.

eye·let (ī′lit), *n.* a small hole for a shoelace, cord, or the like, to go through.

eye·lid (ī′lid′), *n.* the movable flap of skin that covers the front of the eyeball.

eye·piece (ī′pēs′), *n.* the part of a microscope, telescope, or the like, through which one looks. See illus. at **microscope.**

eye·sight (ī′sīt′), *n.* 1. the power of seeing; sight or vision: *to have good eyesight.* 2. the area as far as one can see: *There's no one within eyesight.*

eye·sore (ī′sôr′), *n.* something unpleasant to look at: *That junkyard is an eyesore.*

eye·strain (ī′strān′), *n.* discomfort or weakness of the eyes due to bad light, excessive use, or the like.

eye·tooth (ī′tōōth′), *n., pl.* **eye·teeth** (ī′tēth′). either of the upper canine teeth.

eye·wit·ness (ī′wit′nis), *n.* 1. a person who sees some act or event and can give a firsthand report of it: *Were you an eyewitness to the fire?* —*adj.* 2. given by an eyewitness: *an eyewitness account of the accident.*

ey·rie (âr′ē, ēr′ē), *n.* another spelling of **aerie.**

E·ze·ki·el (i zē′kē əl), *n.* 1. (in the Bible) a Hebrew prophet of the 6th century B.C. 2. a book of the Old Testament bearing his name.

Ez·ra (ez′rə), *n.* 1. (in the Bible) a Hebrew prophet of the 5th century B.C. 2. a book of the Old Testament bearing his name.

	Semitic	Greek	Etruscan	Latin	Gothic	Modern Roman	
DEVELOPMENT OF UPPER-CASE LETTERS	Y	ꓶ	ꓶ	ꓶ	F	ꟊ	F
DEVELOPMENT OF LOWER-CASE LETTERS	F	F	F	ſ	f	f	
			Medieval		Gothic	Modern Roman	

F

F, f (ef), *n., pl.* **F's** *or* **Fs, f's** *or* **fs.** the sixth letter of the English alphabet.

F, Fahrenheit. Also, **F.**

F, 1. *(sometimes l.c.)* (in some grading systems) a grade or mark that indicates scholastic work of the lowest or failing quality. 2. *Chem.* the symbol for **fluorine.** 3. the symbol for **force.**

f, 1. firm. 2. (in music) forte.

fa (fä), *n.* the fourth note of a musical scale.

fa·ble (fā′bəl), *n.* 1. a short story that teaches a moral or lesson, usually having animals, such as a hare and a tortoise, as the main characters. 2. a story that is made up or is untrue: *The story about George Washington and the cherry tree is probably a fable.* 3. any legend, myth, or fairy tale.

fa·bled (fā′bəld), *adj.* 1. not real; fictitious: *the unicorn and other fabled beasts.* 2. spoken of in fables or legends: *a fabled hero.*

fab·ric (fab′rik), *n.* 1. cloth made by weaving, knitting, or matting fibers. 2. a framework or structure: *the fabric of society.*

fab·ri·cate (fab′rə kāt′), *v.,* **fab·ri·cat·ed, fab·ri·cat·ing.** 1. to make or build; construct. 2. to invent or make up (a story, excuse, etc.): *to fabricate a reason for leaving early.* —**fab′ri·ca′tion,** *n.*

fab·u·lous (fab′yə ləs), *adj.* 1. almost unbelievable; incredible: *It was fabulous luck that she found the ring she had lost.* 2. unusually good; marvelous: *You played a fabulous game.* 3. told or known through fables, myths, or legends: *The roc is a fabulous bird.* —**fab′u·lous·ly,** *adv.*

fa·cade (fə säd′), *n.* 1. the front of a building, esp. when it is elaborately decorated with columns, arches, etc. 2. a false or superficial appearance or manner: *His politeness* seems nothing more than a facade. Also, **fa·çade′.**

Facade

face (fās), *n.* 1. the front part of the head from the forehead to the chin. 2. a look or expression: *a sad face.* 3. a special look or expression that shows dislike, annoyance, etc.: *The baby made a face when he saw spinach on his plate.* 4. outward appearance: *On the face of it, she seems to be telling the truth.* 5. good reputation or self-respect: *He felt he had lost face by not knowing the correct answer.* 6. the surface, front, or most important side of something: *the face of a building; the face of a watch.* 7. boldness or impudence: *She had the face to argue back.* —*v.,* **faced, fac·ing.** 8. to look toward or have the front turned in the direction of: *He stood facing the sea.* 9. to turn or be turned; be placed with the front in a certain direction (often fol. by *on, to,* or *toward*): *The house faces on the street.* 10. to cover or partly cover with a different material: *to face a house with brick.* 11. **face to face,** facing one another; opposite: *We sat face to face at the table.* 12. **face up to,** to admit, acknowledge, or deal with courageously: *You had better face up to the facts.* 13. **in the face of,** when meeting or confronting: *to be calm in the face of danger.* 14. **to one's face,** in one's presence; directly: *I told him to his face it was a lie.*

fac·et (fas′it), *n.* 1. one of the small, polished surfaces of a cut gem: *This emerald is cut with 16 facets.* 2. a side or aspect of something: *That question has several facets that could be discussed.*

fa·ce·tious (fə sē′shəs), *adj.* not meant to be serious; amusing; funny: *a facetious answer to a silly question.* —**fa·ce′tious·ly,** *adv.* —**fa·ce′tious·ness,** *n.*

fa·cial (fā′shəl), *adj.* 1. of or located on the face: *a facial expression; a facial scar.* 2. used on the face: *facial tissue.* —*n.* 3. a massage or other treatment to improve the appearance of the face.

fac·ile (fas′il), *adj.* 1. moving, acting, working, etc., quickly and with ease: *the facile fingers of a pianist.* 2. easily performed, used, etc.: *a facile method for finding the answer.* 3. glib or superficial; not show-

---

act, āble, dâre, ärt; ebb, ēqual; if, īce; hot, ōver, ôrder; oil; boŏk; ōoze; out; up, ûrge; ə = *a* as in *alone;* ə as in *button* (but′ən), *fire* (fīər); *chief;* shoe; thin; ŧħat; zh as in *measure* (mezh′ər). See full key inside cover.

ing thought or care: *a facile answer to a difficult problem.* —**fac′ile·ly,** *adv.*

fa·cil·i·tate (fə sil′i tāt′), *v.,* **fa·cil·i·tat·ed, fa·cil·i·tat·ing.** to make easier or help to advance: *Typewriters facilitate office work.*

fa·cil·i·ty (fə sil′i tē), *n., pl.* **fa·cil·i·ties.** 1. ease or readiness due to skill or practice: *to work with facility.* 2. ease or freedom from difficulty: *This tractor can be handled with facility.* 3. something designed or built for a particular purpose or to perform a special service: *trains, planes, and other transportation facilities.* 4. something to make a job or the like easier: *Our office will provide you with every facility.*

fac·ing (fā′sing), *n.* 1. a covering in front, such as a layer of stone on a brick wall. 2. a lining on the edge of a collar, cuff, or the like, often turned outward and used for strengthening or decoration.

fac·sim·i·le (fak sim′ə lē), *n.* an exact copy of something, such as a book, painting, or dress. [from the Latin phrase *fac simile* "make similar"]

fact (fakt), *n.* 1. something known to exist or to have happened. 2. something said to be true or to have happened: *The facts of her story don't make any sense.* 3. actuality or reality: *That theory has no basis in fact.* 4. **as a matter of fact,** really; actually: *As a matter of fact, it cost less than I thought it would.* Also, **in fact.**

fac·tion (fak′shən), *n.* 1. a group or clique within a larger group, political party, or the like: *One faction is definitely against the motion.* 2. dissension or strong disagreement, esp. within a political party: *The meeting was full of angry protest and faction.* —**fac′tion·al,** *adj.*

fac·tor (fak′tər), *n.* 1. something that contributes to a particular result or situation: *One factor in their losing the game was their pitcher's sore arm.* 2. one of two or more numbers that are multiplied together to yield a given product: *3 and 5 are factors of 15.*

fac·to·ry (fak′tə rē), *n., pl.* **fac·to·ries.** a building or group of buildings where goods are manufactured.

fac·to·tum (fak tō′təm), *n.* a person employed to do all kinds of work, esp. the chief servant in a household. [from the Latin phrase *fac tōtum* "do everything"]

fac·tu·al (fak′chōō əl), *adj.* of or concerning facts; based on facts: *a factual description.* —**fac′tu·al·ly,** *adv.*

fac·ul·ty (fak′əl tē), *n., pl.* **fac·ul·ties.** 1. the teachers working in a university, college, or school: *a meeting of the faculty.* 2. one of the departments of learning in a university or college: *He's a member of the history faculty.* 3. an ability for a particular kind of action or behavior: *She has a faculty for explaining things clearly.* 4. a power or capability of the mind: *the faculties of memory and reason.*

fad (fad), *n.* a fashion or kind of behavior that is followed enthusiastically for a brief time; craze: *Sitting on flagpoles used to be a fad.* —**fad′dish,** *adj.* —**fad′dist,** *n.*

fade (fād), *v.,* **fad·ed, fad·ing.** 1. to lose brightness of color; become pale: *Her blouse faded from red to pink.* 2. to become dim; lose brightness: *Daylight fades in the evening.* 3. to cause to lose brightness; make pale or dim: *Washing faded the drapes.* 4. to lose freshness, strength, or health: *The flower faded after it was picked.* 5. to lessen gradually; slowly disappear: *His anger faded when they apologized.* 6. to cause a scene or shot in a movie or television show to appear or disappear gradually (usually fol. by *in* or *out*): *to fade out on a picture of the hero riding away.* —**fad′ed·ness,** *n.*

fade-in (fād′in′), *n.* a camera shot at the beginning of a movie or television scene that is very dim at first and gradually becomes clearer and brighter.

fade-out (fād′out′), *n.* a camera shot at the end of a movie or television scene that slowly dims.

fag (fag), *v.,* **fagged, fag·ging.** 1. to tire or exhaust (often fol. by *out*): *The long climb fagged us out.* —*n.* 2. a boy in a British public school who is hazed by an older pupil and must do certain chores for him.

fag′ end′, 1. the last part or very end of something: *the fag end of the day.* 2. the end of a piece of cloth; remnant.

fag·ot (fag′ət), *n.* a bundle of sticks, twigs, or branches bound together and used as fuel. Also, **fag′got.**

Fahr·en·heit (far′ən hīt′), *adj.* referring to the scale of temperature (**Fahr′enheit scale′**) in which the freezing point of water is 32° and the boiling point 212° *Abbr.:* F, F. See illus. at **thermometer.** See also **centigrade.**

fail (fāl), *v.* 1. to be unsuccessful; fall short of obtaining or doing what one hopes or expects: *They failed to find the treasure.* 2. to get less than a passing grade in an exam, course of study, etc.: *to fail in geography.* 3. to give less than a passing grade to: *to fail three students.* 4. to fall short of completing; neglect: *to fail to do one's duty.* 5. to fall short; be less than enough; be lacking: *Our food supply failed, and we had to turn back.* 6. to become weaker; dwindle or die: *Her health failed. The crops failed for lack of rain.* 7. to lose money; be unable to bring in enough money to pay debts: *Their business failed.* 8. to stop working or operating: *His heart failed for five minutes before they revived him.* 9. **without fail,** with certainty; positively: *He said to be there without fail.*

fail·ing (fā′ling), *n.* 1. the act or condition of a person or thing that fails; failure. 2. a weakness or fault; shortcoming: *Her chief failing is laziness.*

fail·ure (fāl′yər), *n.* 1. the act of failing or proving unsuccessful; lack of success: *We were discouraged by our failure to find the right road.* 2. an instance of not doing something that is expected or required; neglect of what should be done: *failure to keep a promise.* 3. the condition of being less than what is needed or expected: *a failure of crops.* 4. a becoming bankrupt; the condition of being unable to pay what is owed. 5. a person or thing that fails: *This dog is a failure as a watchdog.*

fain (fān), *Archaic.* —*adv.* 1. gladly or willingly: *He fain would join us on our journey.* —*adj.* 2. willing or glad: *They were fain to obey the command.*

faint (fānt), *adj.* **1.** lacking brightness, clearness, loudness, etc.; weak or dim: *a faint light in the distance; a faint noise.* **2.** feeble or slight: *faint praise.* **3.** feeling weak, dizzy, or exhausted: *He was faint from hunger.* **4.** lacking courage; cowardly or timid: *a faint heart.* —*v.* **5.** to lose consciousness, esp. for a short time. —*n.* **6.** a temporary loss of consciousness. —**faint′ly,** *adv.* —**faint′ness,** *n.*

faint·heart·ed (fānt′här′tid), *adj.* lacking courage, or showing lack of courage; cowardly; timid: *a faint-hearted struggle.* —**faint′heart′ed·ly,** *adv.*

fair[1] (fâr), *adj.* **1.** free from dishonesty or prejudice; just: *The judge made a fair decision.* **2.** according to the rules: *a fair fight.* **3.** moderate or reasonable; average: *a fair amount of money; fair health.* **4.** sunny and fine; not stormy: *fair weather.* **5.** of a light color; not dark: *a fair complexion.* **6.** pleasing in appearance; attractive: *a fair young maiden.* **7.** without mistakes or faults: *to make a fair copy of one's homework to hand in.* **8.** polite or well-spoken: *a fair speech of welcome.* **9.** (in sports) not foul; within the foul lines: *a fair ball.* —*adv.* **10.** in a fair manner: *to play fair.* **11. fair and square,** honestly; justly: *She won the contest fair and square.* [from the Old English word *fæger*] —**fair′ness,** *n.*

fair[2] (fâr), *n.* **1.** an exhibition of farm products and farm animals, with contests to pick the best entries and various kinds of entertainment. **2.** any large exhibition of products: *a trade fair.* **3.** an exhibition and sale of articles to raise money, often for a charitable purpose: *a church fair.* **4.** *Chiefly British.* a gathering of buyers and sellers. [from an Old French word, which comes from Latin *fēria* "holiday"]

Fair·banks (fâr′baṅks′), *n.* **1. Charles W.,** 1852–1918, 26th Vice President of the U.S. 1905–1909. **2.** a town in central Alaska.

fair·ground (fâr′ground′), *n.* Often, **fairgrounds.** a place where fairs, horse races, carnivals, etc., are held.

fair·ly (fâr′lē), *adv.* **1.** in a fair manner; justly; honestly: *to settle a dispute fairly.* **2.** moderately; rather: *a fairly heavy rain.* **3.** positively or completely; actually: *The horse fairly flew over the fence.*

fair·way (fâr′wā′), *n.* a clear passage or area, esp. one of the mowed parts of a golf course between a tee and a green.

fair·y (fâr′ē), *n., pl.* **fair·ies. 1.** an imaginary being having magical powers, and usually thought of as very small. —*adj.* **2.** of or referring to fairies: *fairy magic.*

fair·y·land (fâr′ē land′), *n.* **1.** an imaginary land where fairies live. **2.** any beautiful and enchanting place.

fair′y tale′, 1. a story in which there are fairies, elves, or other imaginary creatures. **2.** an incredible or misleading story, statement, report, etc.

faith (fāth), *n.* **1.** trust or confidence in a person or thing: *I have faith that he will help us.* **2.** belief that is not based on proof: *to accept an explanation on*

faith. **3.** belief in God or in a particular religion: *to be firm in one's faith.* **4.** a religion: *the Jewish faith.* **5.** an obligation to be loyal: *He broke faith with his friends and betrayed them.* **6. in bad faith,** intending deceit or dishonesty: *to accept money in bad faith.* **7. in good faith,** in all honesty or sincerity: *I told her in good faith that I didn't agree.*

faith·ful (fāth′fəl), *adj.* **1.** loyal or true to one's promises, obligations, etc.; trustworthy: *a faithful friend; a faithful worker.* **2.** true to fact or to an original document, work of art, or the like: *a faithful report of what happened; a faithful copy of a painting.* —*n.* **3. the faithful,** those who believe in a religion or are loyal members of any group. —**faith′ful·ly,** *adv.* —**faith′ful·ness,** *n.*

faith·less (fāth′lis), *adj.* **1.** not loyal to one's promises, obligations, friends, etc.; untrustworthy: *a selfish, faithless man.* **2.** without religious faith or belief. —**faith′less·ness,** *n.*

fake (fāk), *v.,* **faked, fak·ing. 1.** to pretend or put on a false appearance of: *She faked illness in order to get out of going to class. You can't get away with faking this time.* **2.** to make or put together (something that is false or intended to deceive); counterfeit; forge: *to fake a photograph by putting two pictures together.* —*n. Informal.* **3.** something that is faked or false; a counterfeit or fraud. **4.** someone who fakes or pretends; impostor. —*adj.* **5.** not real; false or counterfeit: *fake money; a fake beard.*

fak·er (fā′kər), *n. Informal.* a person who fakes; phony; impostor.

fa·kir (fə kēr′, fā′kər), *n.* a Muslim or Hindu monk who lives by begging.

fal·con (fal′kən, fôl′kən), *n.* any of several small, swift birds of prey formerly used in hunting, esp. certain small hawks having long, pointed wings.

fal·con·er (fal′kə nər, fôl′kə nər), *n.* a person who trains or hunts with falcons or other birds of prey.

fal·con·ry (fal′kən rē, fôl′kən rē), *n.* **1.** the sport of hunting small game with falcons, hawks, or eagles; hawking. **2.** the method of training such birds for hunting.

Falcon
(length 18 in.)

Falk′land Is′lands (fôk′lənd), a group of more than a hundred islands in the S Atlantic Ocean, about 300 mi. E of the Strait of Magellan: a British crown colony. 4618 sq. mi.

fall (fôl), *v.,* **fell** (fel), **fall·en** (fô′lən), **fall·ing. 1.** to come down or drop down to a lower place or position: *Snow falls from the sky. The horse stumbled and fell to its knees.* **2.** to crash or tumble down: *to fall downstairs.* **3.** to move to a lower level, value, amount, etc.; become less or lower: *The price of gold is falling.* **4.** to hang down: *Her hair falls to her shoulders.* **5.** to surrender or be overthrown: *The city fell to the enemy.* **6.** to give in to temptation. **7.** to drop down wounded or dead: *to fall in battle.* **8.** to pass into a particular state or condition: *to fall asleep; to fall in love.* **9.** to come to by chance or be assigned to: *The chore of washing the dishes fell to Anne.* **10.** to happen or come to pass at a certain time: *Christmas falls on a Monday this year.* **11.** to have its proper place: *The accent falls on the last syllable.* **12.** to descend or drop: *The field falls gently to the stream. Night fell.* **13.** to appear disappointed; become sad: *Her face fell when she heard they were not coming.* **14.** to be naturally divisible (often fol. by *into*): *The story falls into three parts.* —*n.* **15.** a falling or dropping down to a lower place or position: *a fall from a ladder.* **16.** something that falls or drops: *a heavy fall of rain.* **17.** another word for **autumn. 18.** a decline or drop to a lower level: *a gradual fall in prices.* **19.** the distance through which something falls: *a long fall.* **20.** Usually, **falls.** a waterfall. **21.** a surrender or giving in to temptation; a lapse into sin: *a fall from virtue.* **22. the Fall,** the first sin of Adam and Eve; original sin. **23.** a throw in wrestling in which the fallen person's shoulders are pinned to the ground. **24. fall back,** to lose ground; retreat: *The army fell back during the enemy attack.* **25. fall back on,** to rely or depend on: *Thank heaven we had savings to fall back on!* **26. fall behind,** to fail to keep pace, meet an obligation, etc.: *I fell behind after the first mile. We fell behind in our payments on the car.* **27. fall down,** *Informal.* to disappoint or fail: *We all fell down in the final exam.* **28. fall for,** *Slang.* **a.** to be deceived by: *Did you fall for his story?* **b.** to fall in love with. **29. fall in,** to take one's place in ranks, as a soldier. **30. fall off,** to decline or decrease: *Business fell off last year.* **31. fall on** (or **upon**), **a.** to assault or attack: *The soldiers fell upon their attackers.* **b.** to experience or encounter: *His family has fallen on hard times. My warning fell on deaf ears.* **32. fall out, a.** to quarrel or disagree: *They fell out over whose turn it was.* **b.** to leave one's place in ranks, as a soldier. **33. fall short,** to fail to reach or attain something: *to fall short of one's goal.* **34. fall through,** to fail to be completed or fulfilled: *Our plans for the picnic fell through.*

fal·la·cious (fə lā′shəs), *adj.* **1.** not logical; containing a fallacy: *fallacious reasoning that led him to a wrong conclusion.* **2.** mistaken or misleading: *a fallacious account of what happened.* —**fal·la′cious·ly,** *adv.* —**fal·la′cious·ness,** *n.*

fal·la·cy (fal′ə sē), *n., pl.* **fal·la·cies. 1.** a false or misleading notion, belief, or the like: *It is a fallacy that people are poor because they don't want to work.* **2.** an error in reasoning or logic; false reasoning: *That argument contains a fallacy.*

fall·en (fô′lən), *v.* **1.** the past participle of **fall.** —*adj.* **2.** having dropped or come down from a higher or greater position, place, amount, value, etc.: *fallen prices.* **3.** down flat on the ground: *The exhausted runner lay fallen by the road.* **4.** immoral or sinful: *a fallen soul.* **5.** overthrown, destroyed, or conquered. **6.** dead: *fallen soldiers.*

fal·li·ble (fal′ə bəl), *adj.* liable to make a mistake or

be deceived: *We are all fallible.* —**fal′li·bil′i·ty,** *n.* —**fal′li·bly,** *adv.*

fall′ing star′, another name for **meteor.**

fall·out (fôl′out′), *n.* the often radioactive particles that fall to earth after a nuclear explosion.

fal·low (fal′ō), *adj.* **1.** (of land) plowed and left unseeded for a season or more; not cultivated: *fallow fields.* —*n.* **2.** farmland that has been plowed and left unseeded. —*v.* **3.** to make land fallow; plow and leave uncultivated so as to obtain a better crop: *to fallow twenty acres.* [from the Middle English word *falwe,* which comes from Old English *fealga* "fallow land"]

fal′low deer′, a small Eurasian deer with a

Fallow deer
(3 ft. high at shoulder)

pale, yellowish-brown coat that has white spots in summer. [fallow is from the Middle English word *falowe* "light brown," which comes from Old English *fealu*]

false (fôls), *adj.,* **fals·er, fals·est. 1.** not true or correct; mistaken: *the false belief that the earth is flat.* **2.** not faithful or loyal: *false friends.* **3.** untruthful or dishonest: *a false witness; a false report.* **4.** not real or genuine; artificial; fake: *a false mustache.* **5.** based on mistaken ideas: *false pride.* —*adv.* **6.** in a false manner; dishonestly; treacherously. **7. play someone false,** to deceive or betray someone. —**false′ly,** *adv.* —**false′ness,** *n.*

false·hood (fôls′hŏŏd), *n.* **1.** a false statement; lie. **2.** inaccuracy or untruthfulness. **3.** a mistaken or untrue idea, belief, or the like: *a superstitious falsehood.*

fal·set·to (fôl set′ō), *n., pl.* **fal·set·tos. 1.** an unnaturally or artificially high-pitched voice, esp. in a man. **2.** a person who sings or speaks with such a voice. —*adj.* **3.** of, referring to, or written for such a voice.

fal·si·fy (fôl′sə fī′), *v.,* **fal·si·fied, fal·si·fy·ing. 1.** to make false or incorrect; change so as to trick or deceive someone: *to falsify a record of profits and losses.* **2.** to show or prove to be false; disprove. **3.** to make false statements; tell lies. —**fal·si·fi·ca·tion** (fôl′sə fə kā′shən), *n.*

fal·si·ty (fôl′si tē), *n., pl.* for def. 2 **fal·si·ties. 1.** the quality of being false; incorrectness, untruthfulness, or unfaithfulness. **2.** something false, esp. a lie.

fal·ter (fôl′tər), *v.* **1.** to hesitate or waver in action or purpose; give way: *He never faltered in his fight for human rights.* **2.** to speak in a hesitating way; stammer. **3.** to stumble or sway; move unsteadily. —**fal′ter·ing·ly,** *adv.*

fame (fām), *n.* **1.** the condition or fact of being well-known; widespread renown: *He found fame as an explorer.* **2.** reputation; public opinion with regard to a person or thing: *a gangster of ill fame.*

famed (fāmd), *adj.* very well-known; famous.

fa·mil·iar (fə mil′yər), *adj.* **1.** well-known; seen or encountered frequently: *Jet planes are now a familiar* *sight.* **2.** well-acquainted or well-informed; skilled; learned: *He is familiar with Spanish history.* **3.** close or intimate: *familiar friends.* **4.** too friendly or informal; impertinent or forward. —*n.* **5.** a friend. **6.** a spirit, such as a black cat or other animal, used by a witch. —**fa·mil′iar·ly,** *adv.*

fa·mil·i·ar·i·ty (fə mil′ē ar′i tē), *n., pl.* for def. 5 **fa·mil·i·ar·i·ties. 1.** thorough knowledge of something: *a familiarity with classical music.* **2.** friendship; closeness between people. **3.** lack of ceremony; informality. **4.** too great informality; impertinence or forwardness. **5.** Often, **familiarities.** a forward or impertinent action or way of speaking.

fa·mil·iar·ize (fə mil′yə rīz′), *v.,* **fa·mil·iar·ized, fa·mil·iar·iz·ing. 1.** to make (a person) well-acquainted with something: *His travels familiarized him with many different customs.* **2.** to make (something) well-known; bring into common knowledge or use.

fam·i·ly (fam′ə lē), *n., pl.* **fam·i·lies. 1.** two parents and their children: *The apartment isn't large enough for a family.* **2.** the children of a parent or parents. **3.** a group of persons who are related to each other by birth or marriage; all one's relatives. **4.** a group of persons forming a household; all the persons living in the same house, on the same property, or the like. **5.** a group of people believed to be descended from one ancestor; clan; tribe. **6.** a major group of animals or plants, usually including several genera: *The wolf and the fox belong to the dog family.* **7.** any group of related languages that includes all languages known to have a common origin. —*adj.* **8.** of, referring to, or used by a family: *a family trait; a family automobile.*

fam·ine (fam′in), *n.* **1.** an extreme shortage or lack of food: *a country suffering from famine.* **2.** extreme hunger; starvation. **3.** an extreme shortage or lack of something: *a rice famine.*

fam·ished (fam′isht), *adj.* very hungry.

fa·mous (fā′məs), *adj.* **1.** widely known or of widespread reputation; renowned; celebrated. **2.** *Informal.* first-rate; excellent; wonderful: *We had a famous time at the beach.* —**fa′mous·ly,** *adv.*

fan[1] (fan), *n.* **1.** anything that is used to move or stir the air in order to make a breeze. **2.** a machine having wide blades that turn rapidly, causing a breeze. **3.** a device made of paper, feathers, or the like, that may be waved back and forth by hand to make a small breeze. **4.** anything that is wide and spread out like a fan, such as the tail of a bird. —*v.,* **fanned, fan·ning. 5.** to move or stir (the air) with or as if with a fan. **6.** to cause air to blow upon (someone or something) by or as if by using a fan: *to fan oneself; to fan a flame.* **7.** to stir up or excite: *Wild rumors fanned the fears of the people.* **8.** to spread out like a fan (often fol. by *out*): *The forest fire fanned out in all directions.* [from Old English]

fan[2] (fan), *n.* an enthusiastic follower: *a baseball fan.* [a shortened form of *fanatic*]

fa·nat·ic (fə nat′ik), *n.* **1.** a person with extreme and unreasonable enthusiasm for an idea, belief, cause, or the like: *a religious fanatic; a political fanatic.* —*adj.* **2.** another form of **fanatical.**

fa·nat·i·cal (fə nat′i kəl), *adj.* extremely and unreasonably enthusiastic or zealous: *to be fanatical about states' rights.* —**fa·nat′i·cal·ly,** *adv.*

fa·nat·i·cism (fə nat′i siz′əm), *n.* extreme enthusiasm or zeal in supporting an idea, belief, etc.

fan·cied (fan′sēd), *adj.* unreal or imaginary: *to be frightened by fancied dangers.*

fan·ci·er (fan′sē ər), *n.* a person who has a strong interest in something, esp. in breeding a particular kind of animal or plant: *a dog fancier.*

fan·ci·ful (fan′si fəl), *adj.* **1.** imaginative in an unusual, striking way; fantastic; odd or curious: *The jester wore a fanciful, multicolored costume.* **2.** imaginary or unreal; based on fancy or imagination: *the fanciful lands in fairy tales.* **3.** led by or full of fancy, imagination, or whims; whimsical; unpredictable. —**fan′ci·ful·ly,** *adv.*

fan·cy (fan′sē), *n., pl.* for def. 2 **fan·cies. 1.** imagination; the ability to invent unreal or unusual stories, images, designs, or the like. **2.** something imagined; illusion: *She had happy fancies of marrying a prince.* **3.** a liking or inclination: *to have a fancy for antique automobiles.* —*adj.,* **fan·ci·er, fan·ci·est. 4.** not plain or ordinary; unusual, showy, or very fine: *fancy clothes; fancy fruit.* **5.** extravagant or extremely high: *fancy prices.* —*v.,* **fan·cied, fan·cy·ing. 6.** to imagine; picture oneself: *Can you fancy that?* **7.** to believe without being absolutely sure: *I fancy they'll be here in time for dinner.* **8.** to take a liking to; like: *She rather fancies the idea of going west for her vacation.* —*interj.* **9.** (used as an exclamation of mild surprise) imagine.

fan·fare (fan′fâr), *n.* **1.** a short, brilliant tune for trumpets, bugles, etc.; flourish. **2.** any showy display, such as a parade, ovation, etc.

fang (fang), *n.* a long, pointed tooth like those of meat-eating animals or poisonous snakes.

fan·jet (fan′jet′), *n.* **1.** a jet engine having a large fan that takes in air, only part of which is used in the combustion of fuel, the remainder being mixed with the combustion products to form a low-speed jet. **2.** an airplane powered by one or more such engines. See also **prop-jet, turbojet.**

F, Fangs of a rattlesnake

fan·tail (fan′tāl′), *n.* **1.** a tail end or part shaped like a fan. **2.** a kind of pigeon having a fan-shaped tail. **3.** a kind of goldfish having large tail fins. **4.** (on a ship) the aftermost part of the main deck, directly over the rudder.

fan·tas·tic (fan tas′tik), *adj.* **1.** imaginative in a wild or strange way; amazing; weird: *a ghost story full of spooky, fantastic events.* **2.** great or extreme: *fantastic sums of money.* **3.** *Informal.* extremely good; marvelous: *a fantastic game.* Also, **fan·tas′ti·cal.** —**fan·tas′ti·cal·ly,** *adv.*

---

act, āble, dâre, ärt; ebb, ēqual; if, īce; hot, ōver, ôrder; oil; bŏŏk; ōōze; out; up, ûrge; ə = a as in *alone;* ə as in *button* (but′ən), *fire* (fīªr); chief; shoe; thin; ŧħat; zh as in *measure* (mezh′ər). See full key inside cover.

fan·ta·sy (fan′tə sē), *n., pl.* **fan·ta·sies. 1.** imagination, esp. very free or dreamlike imagination. **2.** something that is imagined or dreamed up, such as a story that is not like reality: *a fantasy about creatures living in the center of the earth.* Also, **phantasy.**

far (fär), *adv.,* **far·ther** *or* **fur·ther; far·thest** *or* **fur·thest. 1.** at or to a great distance or a distant point; a long way off: *We walked far ahead of the others.* **2.** at or to a distant or later time: *to look far into the future.* **3.** at or to a definite point of progress: *Having come this far, let's go on.* **4.** much; a great deal: *It's far better to keep trying.* —*adj.,* **far·ther** *or* **fur·ther; far·thest** *or* **fur·thest. 5.** being at a great distance; distant in place or time. **6.** more distant: *the far side of a river.* **7.** stretching or going to a great distance: *the far frontiers of the nation.* **8. a far cry from,** completely different from: *The new house is a far cry from the shanty he lived in before.* **9. as far as,** to the extent that: *It starts at 8:30 as far as I know.* **10. by far,** by a great deal; undoubtedly: *He is by far the best pitcher we have.* Also, **far and away. 11. far and wide,** over a large area; to a great extent: *He is known far and wide as a great storyteller.* Also, **far and near. 12. so far,** up to now: *So far I haven't heard a word from her.*

far·a·way (fär′ə wā′), *adj.* **1.** very distant or remote: *a faraway island.* **2.** dreamy or vague: *a faraway look.*

farce (färs), *n.* **1.** a comedy in which the humor is based on a complicated and exaggerated plot. **2.** the sort of humor found in such plays. **3.** a ridiculous pretense or absurd proceeding: *The supposedly free elections were a farce.*

far·ci·cal (fär′si kəl), *adj.* **1.** of or referring to a farce: *a farcical play.* **2.** like farce; ludicrous or absurd. —**far′ci·cal·ly,** *adv.*

fare (fâr), *n.* **1.** a price that a passenger must pay for a ride or trip on a bus, plane, train, ship, etc. **2.** a paying passenger: *The driver picked up six fares at the first stop.* **3.** food and drink: *They lived on simple fare.* —*v.,* **fared, far·ing. 4.** to do, manage, or get on in a particular way: *He fared well in school.* **5.** to happen or turn out: *It fared well with us on our trip.* **6.** *Archaic.* to go or travel: *to fare forth.*

Far′ East′, the countries of E Asia, usually including China, Japan, Korea, and nearby areas.

fare·well (fâr′wel′), *interj.* **1.** good-by or adieu; may you fare well. —*n.* **2.** a saying good-by; an expression of good wishes at parting: *They made their farewells at the train station.* —*adj.* **3.** parting or final: *The singer gave a farewell performance.*

far-fetched (fär′fecht′), *adj.* improbable or not natural: *a far-fetched excuse.*

far-flung (fär′fluñg′), *adj.* extending or spread over a great distance; distant: *the far-flung borders of the empire.*

farm (färm), *n.* **1.** an area of land, usually with a house, barn, etc., on which crops and often animals are raised. —*v.* **2.** to use (land) for raising crops; cultivate: *He is looking for new land to farm.* **3.** to run a farm. **4. farm out,** to lease or distribute; turn over to

someone: *to farm out work to people in the neighborhood.* [from a Middle English word meaning "lease, rented land"]

farm·er (fär′mər), *n.* a person who runs a farm.

farm·house (färm′hous′), *n., pl.* **farm·hous·es** (färm′hou′ziz). a house on a farm, esp. the main house.

farm·ing (fär′miñg), *n.* the business or occupation of running a farm.

farm·stead (färm′sted′), *n.* a farm with its buildings.

farm·yard (färm′yärd′), *n.* a yard or enclosure surrounded by or connected with farm buildings.

far-off (fär′ôf′), *adj.* distant in space or time: *a far-off land; at some far-off date.*

far-reach·ing (fär′rē′chiñg), *adj.* extending far in influence, effect, or the like; widespread: *This new law will have far-reaching effects.*

far·ri·er (far′ē ər), *n. Chiefly British.* **1.** a person who shoes horses; blacksmith. **2.** another name for **veterinarian.**

far·row (far′ō), *n.* **1.** a litter of pigs. —*v.* **2.** to give birth to pigs or hogs.

far·see·ing (fär′sē′iñg), *adj.* having foresight or vision into future events; wise.

far·sight·ed (fär′sī′tid), *adj.* **1.** seeing objects at a distance more clearly than those that are close by (opposite of *nearsighted*). **2.** wise or wisely planned: *a farsighted statesman; a farsighted plan.* —**far′sight′ed·ly,** *adv.* —**far′sight′ed·ness,** *n.*

far·ther (fär′thər), *adv., comparative of* **far** *with* **farthest** *as superlative.* **1.** at or to a greater distance: *I can run farther than you can.* **2.** at or to a more advanced point: *She wants to go farther in her studies.* **3.** to a greater degree or extent: *Prices dropped even farther.* —*adj., comparative of* **far** *with* **farthest** *as superlative.* **4.** more distant: *the farther side of the mountain.* **5.** going or reaching to a greater distance: *He made a still farther trip.*

—**Usage.** Although *farther* and *further* are often used as synonyms of each other, many writers and speakers prefer *farther* when speaking of physical distance: *I was too tired to walk farther. Let's not discuss the matter further.*

far·ther·most (fär′thər mōst′), *adj.* most distant; farthest: *We hung the picture in the farthermost corner of the room.*

far·thest (fär′thist), *adj., superlative of* **far** *with* **farther** *as comparative.* **1.** most distant or remote: *the farthest hill.* **2.** most extended; longest: *the farthest way home.* —*adv., superlative of* **far** *with* **farther** *as comparative.* **3.** at or to the greatest distance: *Who jumped farthest?* **4.** at or to the most advanced point: *She went farthest in school.*

far·thing (fär′thiñg), *n.* a British coin, equal to one fourth of a penny: not used after 1961.

Farthingale

far·thin·gale (fär′thiñ gāl′), *n.* a hoop or framework for expanding a woman's skirt, worn esp. in the 16th century.

Far′ West′, the area of the U.S. west of the Great Plains.

fas·ci·nate (fas′ə nāt′), *v.,* **fas·ci·nat·ed, fas·ci·nat·ing. 1.** to attract and hold attention or interest very strongly; charm. **2.** to hold as if spellbound; hold motionless.

fas·ci·na·tion (fas′ə nā′shən), *n.* **1.** the act of fascinating: *a snake's fascination of its prey.* **2.** the state of being fascinated: *The children watched the circus in fascination.* **3.** powerful attraction; charm or interest: *the fascination of foreign travel.*

fas·cism (fash′iz əm), *n.* a form of government led by a dictator in which there is strict governmental control of industry and labor, a strong emphasis on nationalism, and often racism.

Fas·cism (fash′iz əm), *n.* a fascist movement, esp. the one established by Mussolini in Italy 1922–1943.

fas·cist (fash′ist), *n.* **1.** a person who believes in fascism. —*adj.* **2.** Also, **fa·scis·tic** (fə shis′tik). of or like fascism or fascists.

fash·ion (fash′ən), *n.* **1.** a custom or style of dress or manners: *Short skirts are the fashion these days.* **2.** manner or way: *to run in a lopsided fashion.* —*v.* **3.** to give a particular shape or form to; make: *to fashion arrowheads from stone.* **4. after a fashion,** in a way that is careless or unsatisfactory: *He's a mechanic after a fashion.*

fash·ion·a·ble (fash′ə nə bəl), *adj.* **1.** following the fashion; in style: *fashionable clothes.* **2.** of, referring to, or popular with people who are stylish or wealthy: *a fashionable resort.* —**fash′ion·a·bly,** *adv.*

fast¹ (fast), *adj.* **1.** moving or able to move quickly; quick; rapid: *a fast horse.* **2.** done in or taking little time: *a fast race.* **3.** showing a time that is ahead of the correct time: *My watch is fast.* **4.** free and reckless in behavior, morals, etc.; wild or immoral: *to lead a fast life.* **5.** close and loyal: *fast friends.* **6.** secure or firm: *to keep a fast hold on something.* **7.** permanent, lasting, or unfading: *a fast color that won't fade.* —*adv.* **8.** tightly or firmly: *Hold fast!* **9.** soundly or completely: *fast asleep.* **10.** quickly, swiftly, or rapidly: *to run fast.* **11.** ahead of the correct time: *The clock is running fast.* **12. pull a fast one,** *Slang.* play an unfair or deceitful trick: *He tried to pull a fast one and keep my change.* [from the Old English word *fæst*]

fast² (fast), *v.* **1.** to go without food completely or partially, esp. as a religious practice. —*n.* **2.** the act of fasting or doing without food. **3.** a day or period of fasting: *to observe a fast.* [from the Old English word *fæstan* "to fast." The original meaning was "to stand fast," that is, to refrain from eating]

fas·ten (fas′ən), *v.* **1.** to attach; fix or tie securely to something else: *to fasten a leash on a dog.* **2.** to close; make or become secure or tightly shut: *The lock fastened when he slammed the door.* **3.** to seize or hold to (usually fol. by *on* or *upon*): *to fasten on a new idea.* **4.** to focus or fix: *His gaze was fastened on the toys in the store window.* —**fas′ten·er,** *n.*

fas·ten·ing (fas′ə ning), *n.* something that fastens, such as a lock or clasp: *the fastening on a bracelet.*

fas·tid·i·ous (fa stid′ē əs), *adj.* hard to please; very critical or particular: *a fastidious eater.* —**fas·tid′i·ous·ly,** *adv.* —**fas·tid′i·ous·ness,** *n.*

fast·ness (fast′nis), *n.* **1.** swiftness or speed. **2.** a fortified place; stronghold; fortress. **3.** the state of being fixed, firm, or secure: *the fastness of a knot.*

fat (fat), *n.* **1.** any of several greasy substances found in animals and plants, composed of carbon, hydrogen, and oxygen. Fats are important in nutrition and are used in making soaps, paints, and explosives. —*adj.,* **fat·ter, fat·test. 2.** chubby, heavy, or well-fed; having much flesh or fatty tissue. **3.** containing much fat; greasy; oily: *fat meat.* **4.** offering good chances for making money; profitable: *a fat job; a fat contract.* **5.** thick or bulging: *a fat briefcase.* —*v.,* **fat·ted, fat·ting. 6.** to make or become fat. **7. the fat is in the fire,** an action has been started that cannot be stopped: *Now that war has been declared, the fat is in the fire.* **8. the fat of the land,** the best or richest of anything: *With prices so cheap there, we can live on the fat of the land.* —**fat′ness,** *n.*

fa·tal (fāt′əl), *adj.* **1.** causing death: *a fatal accident.* **2.** causing misfortune or failure; ruinous: *a fatal mistake.* **3.** highly important; being a turning point: *a fatal decision.* —**fa′tal·ly,** *adv.*

fa·tal·ism (fāt′əliz′əm), *n.* the belief that all events are decided by fate or a power beyond one's control. —**fa′tal·is′tic,** *adj.* —**fa′tal·is′ti·cal·ly,** *adv.*

fa·tal·ist (fāt′əlist), *n.* a person who believes in fatalism.

fa·tal·i·ty (fā tal′i tē), *n., pl.* **fa·tal·i·ties. 1.** a death resulting from a disaster or accident: *The flood caused many fatalities.* **2.** the quality of causing death or disaster; deadliness: *the fatality of certain diseases.*

fate (fāt), *n.* **1.** the final power that is believed to control all things that happen; destiny: *Fate led him far from his homeland.* **2.** something that happens to a person; lot; fortune: *It was his fate to be chosen king.* **3.** something that is to happen; outcome: *The fate of this venture is now out of our hands.*

fat·ed (fā′tid), *adj.* controlled by fate; destined or doomed: *They were fated to fall in love.*

fate·ful (fāt′fəl), *adj.* **1.** extremely important; having important consequences; decisive: *a fateful choice.* **2.** fatal, deadly, or disastrous: *The cavalry made a fateful charge.* **3.** controlled by fate or destiny. **4.** prophetic or ominous; indicating what is fated to happen: *The three witches spoke fateful words to the prince.* —**fate′ful·ly,** *adv.* —**fate′ful·ness,** *n.*

Fates (fāts), *n.pl.* (in Greek and Roman mythology) three goddesses who controlled the destinies of men.

fa·ther (fä′thər), *n.* **1.** a male parent: *He is the father of two children.* **2.** a male ancestor; forefather. **3.** a man who begins or helps to establish something: *the fathers of our country.* **4.** one of the leading men in a city, town, etc.: *the city fathers.* **5.** *(often cap.)* a priest. **6. the Father,** God; the first person of the

Trinity. —*v.* **7.** to become the father of; beget: *to father a large family.* **8.** to begin or found; create: *to father a new invention.* **9.** to act as a father toward: *to father a homeless child.*

fa·ther·hood (fä′ᴕᴇhər hŏod′), *n.* the state of being a father.

fa·ther-in-law (fä′ᴕᴇhər in lô′), *n.*, *pl.* **fa·thers-in-law** (fä′ᴕᴇhərz in lô′). the father of one's husband or wife.

fa·ther·land (fä′ᴕᴇhər land′), *n.* the country where one was born.

fa·ther·less (fä′ᴕᴇhər lis), *adj.* **1.** without a living father. **2.** having no known father.

fa·ther·ly (fä′ᴕᴇhər lē), *adj.* of or like a father: *The old dog guarded the kittens with fatherly care.* —**fa′ther·li·ness,** *n.*

fath·om (fäᴕᴇh′əm), *n.*, *pl.* **fath·oms** or **fath·om.** **1.** a unit of length equivalent to 6 feet, used esp. by sailors. —*v.* **2.** to measure the depth of: *to fathom a river.* **3.** to understand thoroughly; get to the bottom of: *I can't fathom his reasons for doing that.* —**fath′om·a·ble,** *adj.*

fath·om·less (fäᴕᴇh′əm lis), *adj.* **1.** too deep to measure: *the fathomless seas.* **2.** impossible to understand.

fa·tigue (fə tēg′), *n.* **1.** tiredness or weariness. —*v.*, **fa·tigued, fa·ti·guing. 2.** to tire out; weary: *The long walk fatigued him.*

fat·ten (fat′ᵊn), *v.* **1.** to make fat: *to fatten cattle.* **2.** to grow fat. —**fat′ten·er,** *n.*

fat·ty (fat′ē), *adj.*, **fat·ti·er, fat·ti·est. 1.** made of or containing fat: *fatty meat.* **2.** resembling fat; like fat. —**fat′ti·ness,** *n.*

fat·u·ous (fach′ōō əs), *adj.* foolish or silly in a self-satisfied way; inane. —**fat′u·ous·ly,** *adv.*

fau·cet (fô′sit), *n.* a valve with a handle that is turned to control the flow of a liquid; tap.

fault (fôlt), *n.* **1.** something that spoils the perfection of a person or thing; defect, drawback, or failing: *His main fault is laziness.* **2.** a mistake or error. **3.** responsibility for failure or a wrongful act: *It wasn't his fault that we were late.* **4.** a break in the earth's crust along which masses of rock have shifted. **5. at fault,** deserving blame; guilty: *If you're at fault you'd better admit it.* **6. find fault,** to criticize or complain: *He always found fault with her cooking.*

fault·less (fôlt′lis), *adj.* without fault or defect; perfect: *a faultless performance.* —**fault′less·ly,** *adv.* —**fault′less·ness,** *n.*

fault·y (fôl′tē), *adj.*, **fault·i·er, fault·i·est.** having faults or defects; imperfect: *faulty machinery.* —**fault′i·ly,** *adv.* —**fault′i·ness,** *n.*

faun (fôn), *n.* (in Greek and Roman mythology) one of a group of country gods that were pictured as looking like men but with the ears, horns, tail, and often the hind legs of a goat.

fau·na (fô′nə), *n.* the animals of a particular place or time. See also **flora.**

fa·vor (fā′vər), *n.* **1.** a kind act: *He did me a favor by helping me with my homework.* **2.** goodwill or friendly regard; approval: *to win the favor of the king.* **3.** the state of being approved of or liked: *to be in favor with one's teacher.* **4.** a small gift given as a

sign of affection or for fun at a party. —*v.* **5.** to approve of; like or support: *I favor Michael's plan.* **6.** to prefer or treat with special attention: *to favor one child over another.* **7.** to oblige or do a kindness for: *The president favored him with an interview.* **8.** to make easier; be favorable to: *The wind favored their journey.* **9.** to use lightly or gently: *to favor a lame leg.* **10.** to look like; resemble: *He favors his father.* **11. in favor of,** on the side of; in support of: *I'm in favor of longer recesses.* **12. in one's favor,** to one's credit or advantage: *The score was 6 to 0 in our favor.* Also, *esp. British,* **fa′vour.**

fa·vor·a·ble (fā′vər ə bəl), *adj.* **1.** giving an advantage or help; advantageous: *a favorable position in a race.* **2.** showing approval or favor: *favorable remarks about someone's work.* **3.** helpful or promising well: *favorable weather for a trip.* —**fa′vor·a·bly,** *adv.*

fa·vor·ite (fā′vər it), *n.* **1.** a person or thing that is preferred or liked very much: *I like all desserts, but ice cream is my favorite.* **2.** the one that is favored to win in a contest: *The black horse is the favorite in this race.* —*adj.* **3.** preferred or liked the best: *What is your favorite color?*

fa·vor·it·ism (fā′vər i tiz′əm), *n.* the unfair favoring of one person or group over others: *Judges are not supposed to show favoritism in court.*

fawn[1] (fôn), *n.* a young deer. [from the French word *faune*]

Fawn

fawn[2] (fôn), *v.* **1.** to seek notice or favor through the use of flattery, slavish attention to someone's wishes, or the like: *The courtiers fawned on the king.* **2.** (of a dog) to show fondness by wagging the tail, licking one's hands, etc. [from the Old English word *fagnian* "to rejoice"]

fay (fā), *n.* a fairy.

faze (fāz), *v.*, **fazed, faz·ing.** *Informal.* to cause to be upset, confused, or embarrassed: *Our questions didn't faze him at all.*

FBI, Federal Bureau of Investigation: an agency of the federal government of the U.S. that is in charge of investigating federal crimes and threats to national security.

FCC, Federal Communications Commission.

F clef, (in music) another term for **bass clef.**

Fe, *Chem.* the symbol for **iron.** [from the Latin word *ferrum*]

fe·al·ty (fē′əl tē), *n.* **1.** loyalty to a feudal lord as sworn by a vassal. **2.** faithfulness or loyalty.

fear (fēr), *n.* **1.** a strong, dreadful feeling that one is in danger or going to be hurt; dread; terror: *The child has a fear of big dogs.* **2.** something that one is afraid of or that causes fright or worry: *My main fear is that we are lost.* **3.** deep respect or awe: *fear of God.* —*v.* **4.** to be frightened of: *to fear flying.* **5.** to be worried or frightened; feel fear or doubt: *to fear* *that one is going to fail a test.* **6.** to feel deep respect or awe for.

fear·ful (fēr'fəl), *adj.* **1.** causing fear; frightening: *The angry tiger was a fearful sight.* **2.** full of fear; afraid; scared: *to be fearful of lightning.* **3.** caused by or showing fear; frightened: *fearful behavior; a fearful answer.* —**fear'ful·ly,** *adv.* —**fear'ful·ness,** *n.*

fear·less (fēr'lis), *adj.* without fear; brave or bold: *a fearless mountain climber.* —**fear'less·ly,** *adv.* —**fear'less·ness,** *n.*

fear·some (fēr'səm), *adj.* **1.** causing fear; frightening: *a fearsome journey through the wilderness.* **2.** afraid or timid: *a tiny, fearsome mouse.*

fea·si·ble (fē'zə bəl), *adj.* capable of being carried out or used: *a feasible plan.* —**fea·si·bil·i·ty** (fē zə bil'i tē), *n.* —**fea'si·bly,** *adv.*

feast (fēst), *n.* **1.** a large, rich meal for many guests; banquet. **2.** a religious celebration or holiday in honor of a person or event: *a feast in honor of a saint.* —*v.* **3.** to have or take part in a feast. **4.** to entertain with a feast: *to feast guests.* **5.** to delight or please very much: *to feast one's eyes on a garden.*

feat (fēt), *n.* a brave or very difficult act; great deed.

feath·er (feth'ər), *n.* **1.** one of the light, horny outgrowths that cover the bodies and wings of birds. **2.** one's mood or state of health: *to be in fine feather.* **3.** kind or sort: *birds of the same feather.* **4.** something that resembles a feather, such as a fringe of hair. —*v.* **5.** to provide with feathers: *to feather an arrow.* **6.** to grow feathers. **7.** to turn (an oar) flat or edgewise while rowing. **8. a feather in one's cap,** an honor or accomplishment: *Completing school will be a feather in your cap.* **9. feather one's nest,** to acquire wealth, esp. selfishly or at someone else's expense: *He managed to feather his nest before the company went broke.* —**feath'er·less,** *adj.*

feath'er bed', a quilt or sack stuffed with feathers and used as a mattress.

feath·er·weight (feth'ər wāt'), *n.* a boxer or wrestler weighing between 118 and 126 pounds.

feath·er·y (feth'ə rē), *adj.* **1.** covered or clothed with feathers; feathered: *feathery creatures.* **2.** resembling feathers; light or airy; delicate: *feathery leaves.*

fea·ture (fē'chər), *n.* **1.** any part of the face, such as the nose, eyes, chin, etc.: *She has fine features.* **2.** any important, special, or very noticeable part or characteristic: *The most interesting feature of this house is the secret staircase.* **3.** something offered as a special attraction: *The feature of the show will be a comedy act.* **4.** the main motion picture in a movie program; a full-length motion picture. —*v.,* **fea·tured, fea·tur·ing. 5.** to present or have as a feature or special item: *The newspaper featured a story on the elections.* **6.** to be

Feather

a feature or distinctive part of. **7.** *Informal.* to imagine or picture to oneself: *Can you feature that?* [from the earlier French word *faiture,* which comes from Latin *factūra* "a creating"]

Feb., February.

Feb·ru·ar·y (feb'rōō er'ē, feb'yōō wer'ē), the second month of the year. Ordinarily it has 28 days, but in leap year it has 29 days.

fe·ces (fē'sēz), *n.pl.* waste matter discharged from the intestines; excrement.

fe·cund (fē'kund, fek'und), *adj.* fertile or fruitful: *fecund land.* —**fe·cun'di·ty,** *n.*

fed (fed), *v.* **1.** the past tense and past participle of **feed. 2. fed up,** *Informal.* disgusted, bored, or impatient: *I'm getting fed up with her complaints.*

Fed., Federal.

fed·er·al (fed'ər əl), *adj.* **1.** of or referring to a compact or union of states or nations: *a federal constitution.* **2.** of or referring to the central government, rather than state or local government: *a federal law; federal troops.*

Fed·er·al (fed'ər əl), *adj.* **1.** (in U.S. history) of or referring to the Federalists or the Federalist party. —*n.* **2.** a supporter of the Union government during the Civil War, esp. a soldier in the Union army.

Fed'eral Bu'reau of Investiga'tion. See FBI.

fed·er·al·ist (fed'ər ə list), *n.* **1.** a supporter of a federal form of government in which two or more states are joined in a union. —*adj.* **2.** Also, **fed'er·al·is'tic.** *(sometimes cap.)* of or concerning a federal form of government or the Federalists: *a federalist movement.*

Fed·er·al·ist (fed'ər ə list), *n.* (in U.S. history) a member or supporter of the Federalist party.

Fed'eralist par'ty, (in U.S. history) **1.** a political group that favored the adoption of the Constitution by the states following the Revolutionary War. **2.** a political party that was formed after the election of George Washington, and favored a strong central government.

fed·er·ate (fed'ə rāt'), *v.,* **fed·er·at·ed, fed·er·at·ing.** to unite in a league or federation: *to federate a number of states.*

fed·er·a·tion (fed'ə rā'shən), *n.* **1.** a union of separate states under a central government. **2.** any league or confederacy.

fe·do·ra (fi dôr'ə), *n.* a soft felt hat with a curled brim and a crown creased lengthwise.

fee (fē), *n.* **1.** a charge for services, a privilege, or the like: *a doctor's fee; an admission fee.* **2.** an estate consisting of land that has been inherited or may be passed on by inheritance.

fee·ble (fē'bəl), *adj.,* **fee·bler, fee·blest. 1.** physically weak; frail: *to be feeble after a long illness.* **2.** mentally or morally weak; lacking strength: *a feeble character.* **3.** lacking force or strength; not effective: *a feeble argument on behalf of states' rights.* —**fee'ble·ness,** *n.* —**fee'bly,** *adv.*

fee·ble-mind·ed (fē'bəl mīn'did), *adj.* lacking normal intelligence; mentally slow. **—fee′ble-mind′ed·ness,** *n.*

feed (fēd), *v.*, **fed** (fed), **feed·ing. 1.** to give food to: *Please feed the dog.* **2.** to provide food or serve as food for: *This roast will feed your whole family.* **3.** to give as food: *to feed bread crumbs to pigeons.* **4.** to take food; eat: *The horses are feeding now.* **5.** to provide or supply, esp. with something necessary: *to feed a fire with branches and logs.* **—***n.* **6.** food, esp. for farm animals.

feed·back (fēd′bak′), *n.* **1.** a howling or whistling sound that occurs when the microphone of a public address or other electronic system picks up sound from the loudspeaker. **2.** the use of information about the results of a process to influence or control the process itself. **3.** the information so used.

feed′ bag′, a bag for feeding horses, mules, etc., fastened to the head with straps.

feed·er (fē′dər), *n.* **1.** a person or thing that gives out food. **2.** a person or animal that takes food; eater: *That bull is a good feeder.* **3.** a bin or the like for holding food for animals. **4.** something that feeds, supplies, or leads into something else, for example a stream that runs into another stream or river.

feel (fēl), *v.*, **felt** (felt), **feel·ing. 1.** to touch; examine or sense by touching. **2.** to be aware of; have a sensation of; experience: *to feel a pain; to feel regret.* **3.** to sense (an emotional or physical condition); be aware of being: *to feel happy.* **4.** to seem to be; give a sensation of being: *This room feels warm.* **5.** to reach or grope: *She felt in her purse for a dime.* **6.** to find (one's way) by touching or groping: *We had to feel our way out of the tunnel.* **7.** to be sure or almost sure; believe: *I feel that you should try once more.* **8.** to have sympathy; share the feelings of (usually fol. by *with* or *for*): *to feel for someone who is unhappy.* **—***n.* **9.** a quality that is sensed by feeling or touching; feeling: *I like the feel of silk.* **10.** an impression or feeling: *a feel of winter in the air.* **11. feel like,** *Informal.* to have a desire for: *Do you feel like a movie tonight?* **12. feel like oneself,** to be in one's usual state of health or mind: *After a good rest you'll feel like yourself again.* Also, **feel oneself. 13. feel up to,** *Informal.* to feel able to; be capable of: *I don't feel up to playing tennis.*

feel·er (fē′lər), *n.* **1.** a part of an insect, fish, or other animal that serves as an organ of touch; antenna; tentacle. **2.** a proposal, remark, hint, or the like, that is made in order to find out what others are thinking or planning to do: *They put out a feeler about merging with our company.*

feel·ing (fē′ling), *n.* **1.** the sense of touch; the power to feel or sense heat, cold, roughness, smoothness, softness, hardness, lightness, heaviness, etc. **2.** a particular sensation: *a feeling of pain.* **3.** an emotion: *a feeling of sadness.* **4.** sympathy or emotional sensitivity; emotion: *to play the piano with great feeling.* **5.** sensation, awareness, or consciousness; capacity for physical or emotional sensation: *She lay in a faint without any feeling.* **6.** a vague sense or awareness; idea: *I have a feeling that we're going to win this*

game. **7.** belief or opinion. **8. feelings,** emotions with regard to oneself; the sensitive part of one's personality: *His rudeness hurt my feelings.* **—feel′ing·ly,** *adv.*

feet (fēt), *n.* **1.** the plural form of **foot. 2. on one's feet, a.** in a standing position: *The spectators were on their feet applauding.* **b.** in a restored or recovered state: *A week of rest and you'll be on your feet again.*

feign (fān), *v.* **1.** to pretend; put on an appearance of: *to feign sickness so that one can stay home.* **2.** to invent or make up (a story, excuse, or the like): *She feigned an excuse, but the teacher didn't believe her.* **3.** to imitate in order to deceive: *to feign someone else's voice.* **—feigned,** *adj.*

feint (fānt), *n.* **1.** an attack, blow, or the like, aimed at one point in order to distract attention from the real point of attack: *The cavalry made a feint to the left and then charged toward the center.* **2.** a pretense: *to make a feint at studying.* **—***v.* **3.** to make a feint or feints: *The boxer feinted with his left.*

feld·spar (feld′spär′), *n.* any of a group of minerals containing principally aluminum, silicon, and oxygen and forming an important part of volcanic rocks.

fe·lic·i·tate (fi lis′i tāt′), *v.*, **fe·lic·i·tat·ed, fe·lic·i·tat·ing.** to congratulate (someone) upon a happy event.

fe·lic·i·ta·tion (fi lis′i tā′shən), *n.* an expression of good wishes; congratulation: *He sent you his regards and felicitations.*

fe·lic·i·tous (fi lis′i təs), *adj.* well-suited for the occasion; apt; appropriate: *a felicitous speech of welcome.* **—fe·lic′i·tous·ly,** *adv.*

fe·lic·i·ty (fi lis′i tē), *n.* **1.** great happiness: *felicity in marriage.* **2.** skill in expressing oneself; effective use of words: *She writes with felicity.*

fe·line (fē′līn), *adj.* **1.** of or referring to cats or the cat family. **2.** resembling a cat; catlike: *a feline smile.* **—***n.* **3.** a cat or other member of the cat family.

fell[1] (fel), *v.* the past tense of **fall.**

fell[2] (fel), *v.* to cause to fall; bring down by striking, shooting, chopping, or the like: *to fell a tree with an ax.* [from the Old English word *fellan*]

fell[3] (fel), *adj.* **1.** fierce or cruel; dreadful: *a fell beast.* **2.** destructive or deadly: *a fell blow; fell disease.* [from Old French]

fel·low (fel′ō), *n.* **1.** a man or boy: *a handsome fellow.* **2.** a companion, comrade, or associate: *He and his fellows caused the trouble.* **3.** a person of the same class or level; equal; peer: *The doctor consulted with his fellows.* **4.** one of a pair; mate; match: *a shoe without its fellow.* **5.** a graduate student who has a fellowship. **6.** a member of a society of scholars. **7.** *Informal.* a person; one: *They don't treat a fellow very well around here.* **—***adj.* **8.** belonging to the same class or group; having the same occupation, interests, or the like: *fellow classmates.*

fel·low-man (fel′ō man′), *n., pl.* **fel·low-men.** a kindred member of the human race; fellow human being: *to respect one's fellow-men.* Also, **fel′low·man′.**

fel·low·ship (fel′ō ship′), *n.* **1.** friendliness or companionship: *the fellowship among old friends.* **2.** association or similarity as a result of sharing the same nature, needs, occupation, interests, etc.: *the fellow-*

ship of all human beings. **3.** a group or association formed on the basis of common occupation, religion, interests, etc.: *a fellowship of doctors.* **4.** a position or money awarded to a graduate student to help him go on with his studies.

fel·on (fel′ən), *n.* a person who has committed a serious crime.

fe·lo·ni·ous (fə lō′nē əs), *adj.* referring to or involving a felony; criminal: *felonious assault.*

fel·o·ny (fel′ə nē), *n., pl.* **fel·o·nies.** a serious crime, such as murder or burglary.

felt¹ (felt), *v.* the past tense and past participle of **feel.**

felt² (felt), *n.* **1.** a fabric of wool, fur, or hair that has been matted together by heat, moisture and great pressure. —*adj.* **2.** made of felt: *a felt hat.* —*v.* **3.** to cover with felt. [from Old English]

fe·luc·ca (fə luk′ə, fə lōō′kə), *n.* a sailing vessel, usually having two or three masts, used on the Mediterranean Sea and along the Spanish and Portuguese coasts.

Felucca

fe·male (fē′māl), *adj.* **1.** belonging to the sex that bears young or produces eggs. **2.** of or referring to this sex or to women; feminine: *the female birth rate; female charm.* —*n.* **3.** a woman or girl. **4.** a female animal.

fem·i·nine (fem′ə nin), *adj.* **1.** referring to women or girls: *feminine beauty.* **2.** of the female sex; female: *the feminine members of the teaching staff.* **3.** like a woman; gentle; womanish: *a feminine way of speaking.* **4.** (in grammar) having the gender of nouns and pronouns that refer to female persons or animals, or to things considered to be female. In the sentences *Mary lost her hat* and *Spain lost her colonies,* the words *Mary* and *Spain* are treated as feminine nouns.

fe·mur (fē′mər), *n., pl.* **fe·murs** *or* **fem·o·ra** (fem′ər ə). the thighbone of a man or animal.

fen (fen), *n.* low, marshy land; bog.

fence (fens), *n.* **1.** a barrier going around or along the border of a yard, field, lawn, or the like. Fences are usually made of wood or of posts and wire, and they are used to keep animals or people in or out and to mark boundaries. **2.** *Slang.* a person who receives and sells stolen goods. —*v.,* **fenced, fenc·ing. 3.** to enclose or separate by a barrier: *to fence a field.* **4.** to practice the art or sport of fencing with foils or swords. [from the Middle English word *fens,* which is short for *defens* "defense"]

fenc·er (fen′sər), *n.* a person who fences with foils or swords.

fenc·ing (fen′sing), *n.* **1.** the art or sport of using a sword or foil in attack and defense. **2.** a fence or fences. **3.** material for making fences: *wire fencing.*

fend (fend), *v.* **1.** to ward off or push away (often fol. by *off*): *to fend off blows.* **2.** to resist or make defense: *to fend against danger.* **3. fend for oneself,** to provide for oneself in any way possible: *When Father died we children had to fend for ourselves.*

fend·er (fen′dər), *n.* **1.** a metal part placed over the wheel of an automobile, bicycle, or the like, to lessen the splashing of mud and water. **2.** a metal part on the front of a locomotive, streetcar, or the like, to clear the track of objects that are in the way. **3.** a low, metal guard used in front of an open fireplace to keep back falling coals. **4.** any thing or person that wards off something.

fen·nel (fen′əl), *n.* a plant bearing yellow flowers whose seeds are used in cooking and in medicine.

Fer·di·nand V (fûr′d²nand′), *("the Catholic")* 1452–1516, king of Spain 1474–1516.

fer·ment (fər ment′), *v.* **1.** to undergo or cause to undergo fermentation. **2.** to inflame or excite: *His speeches fermented the crowd to violence.* **3.** to be full of excitement. —*n.* (fûr′ment). **4.** something that causes fermentation: *Yeast is a ferment.* **5.** unrest or excitement: *political ferment.*

fer·men·ta·tion (fûr′men tā′shən), *n.* a chemical process caused by yeasts, molds, or bacteria, esp. a souring process or one in which sugars are converted into alcohol, producing bubbles of carbon dioxide.

Fer·mi (fûr′mē), *n.* **En·ri·co** (en rē′kō), 1901–1954, Italian physicist, in the U.S. after 1939.

fer·mi·um (fûr′mē əm), *n. Chem.* a man-made, radioactive, metallic element. *Symbol:* Fm

fern (fûrn), *n.* any of a large number of nonflowering plants having feathery leaves that grow on opposite sides of tall stems.

Fer·nan·do Po (fər nan′dō pō′), an island near the W coast of Africa, forming a province of Equatorial Guinea.

Fern

fe·ro·cious (fə rō′shəs), *adj.* **1.** fierce or savage: *a ferocious mountain lion.* **2.** extreme or very strong; violent: *a ferocious headache.* —**fe·ro′cious·ly,** *adv.*

fe·roc·i·ty (fə ros′i tē), *n.* savage fierceness; the quality of being ferocious.

fer·ret (fer′it), *n.* **1.** a kind of European weasel, sometimes used for killing rats, mice, and rabbits. —*v.,* **fer·ret·ed, fer·ret·ing. 2.** to hunt with ferrets: *to ferret rabbits.* **3.** to drive out with or as if with ferrets (usually fol. by *out*): *to ferret out game; to ferret out a criminal.* **4.** to search out

Ferret
(total length 2 ft.)

or bring to light (usually fol. by *out*): *to ferret out the facts.*

Fer′ris wheel′ (fer′is), a very large, upright wheel that turns on a fixed stand. It has seats hanging around its rim in which passengers ride for amusement. [named after G. W. G. *Ferris* (died 1896), American engineer]

fer·rule (fer′əl, fer′ool), *n.* a metal ring or small cap put at the end of a cane, post, handle, etc., to prevent splitting. Also, **ferule.**

fer·ry (fer′ē), *n., pl.* **fer·ries. 1.** a boat for carrying passengers, automobiles, mail, etc., back and forth across a river, bay, or the like; ferryboat. **2.** a business that operates ferryboats. **3.** a dock or station for ferryboats. **4.** a service for flying airplanes over a particular route, esp. overseas. —*v.,* **fer·ried, fer·ry·ing. 5.** to carry over water in a boat or plane: *to ferry people across a river.* **6.** to travel over water in a ferryboat. **7.** to deliver (an airplane) to a particular place.

fer·ry·boat (fer′ē bōt′), *n.* a boat used for ferrying passengers, automobiles, etc., back and forth; ferry.

fer·tile (fûr′t’l), *adj.* **1.** producing or capable of producing abundant crops: *fertile soil.* **2.** bearing or capable of bearing offspring. **3.** capable of developing: *a fertile egg.* **4.** capable of producing or creating many new works or ideas; productive: *a fertile imagination; a fertile artist.* —**fer·til′i·ty,** *n.*

fer·ti·lize (fûr′t’l īz′), *v.,* **fer·ti·lized, fer·ti·liz·ing.** to make fertile, or to improve the fertility of. —**fer′ti·li·za′tion,** *n.*

fer·ti·liz·er (fûr′t’l ī′zər), *n.* a substance added to soil in order to make it more fertile, esp. manure or a mixture of nitrogen-containing chemicals.

fer·ule[1] (fer′əl, fer′ool), *n.* **1.** a rod, cane, or flat piece of wood for punishing children, esp. by striking them on the hand. —*v.,* **fer·uled, fer·ul·ing. 2.** to punish with a ferule. [from an Old English word, which comes from Latin *ferula*]

fer·ule[2] (fer′əl, fer′ool), *n.* another spelling of **ferrule.**

fer·vent (fûr′vənt), *adj.* **1.** having or showing great warmth and strength of feeling and enthusiasm; earnest; passionate: *a fervent plea for justice.* **2.** glowing or burning; hot. —**fer′vent·ly,** *adv.*

fer·vid (fûr′vid), *adj.* **1.** burning with enthusiasm, conviction, zeal, etc.; ardent; fervent: *a powerful, fervid preacher.* **2.** burning or glowing; hot. —**fer′vid·ly,** *adv.*

fer·vor (fûr′vər), *n.* **1.** strength and warmth of feeling and conviction; earnestness; ardor: *to speak with great fervor.* **2.** intense heat.

fes·tal (fes′t’l), *adj.* referring to or befitting a feast or celebration: *festal decorations.*

fes·ter (fes′tər), *v.* **1.** to form pus: *a wound that is festering.* **2.** to rankle or cause resentment, bitterness, hatred, etc.: *The desire for revenge festered in his mind.* —*n.* **3.** a sore or wound that has pus in it.

fes·ti·val (fes′tə vəl), *n.* **1.** a day or time of celebration: *the festival of Christmas.* **2.** a period or program of holiday activities, cultural events, or the like: *a music festival.*

fes·tive (fes′tiv), *adj.* **1.** referring to or suitable for a feast or festival: *festive decorations; a festive meal.* **2.** joyous or merry: *festive singing.* —**fes′tive·ly,** *adv.*

fes·tiv·i·ty (fe stiv′i tē), *n., pl.* **fes·tiv·i·ties. 1.** merrymaking and joyousness; gaiety: *Sounds of festivity filled the house.* **2.** a festive celebration or occasion. **3. festivities,** festive events or activities.

fes·toon (fe stoon′), *n.* **1.** a string or chain of flowers, leaves, ribbon, or the like, hung in a curve between two points. **2.** a sculptured or carved copy of this. —*v.* **3.** to decorate with festoons or garlands: *to festoon a room for a dance.* **4.** to make into a festoon: *to festoon flowers.*

Festoon

fetch (fech), *v.* **1.** to go for and bring back; get; bring: *to fetch a pail of water; to fetch a doctor.* **2.** to sell for or bring (a price, profit, etc.): *The horse fetched $50 more than it cost.*

fetch·ing (fech′ing), *adj.* charming or attractive: *She looked fetching in her new dress.* —**fetch′ing·ly,** *adv.*

fete (fāt, fet), *n.* **1.** a religious feast, or a festival; holiday. **2.** a large party or celebration, often with entertainment. —*v.,* **fet·ed, fet·ing. 3.** to entertain; give a party or parties for: *to fete a famous visitor.* Also, **fête.**

fet·id (fet′id), *adj.* having a bad smell as a result of being stale, rotten, or the like; stinking: *fetid air; a fetid swamp.*

fet·ish (fet′ish), *n.* **1.** an object believed to have magical power: *Many primitive people have sacred fetishes.* **2.** any object, idea, aim, etc., to which one is strongly and unreasonably devoted: *She makes a fetish of high grades.*

fet·lock (fet′lok′), *n.* **1.** the bump on the back of a horse's leg above the hoof. **2.** a tuft of hair growing on this bump.

fet·ter (fet′ər), *n.* **1.** a chain or shackle for fastening around a prisoner's ankles. **2.** Usually, **fetters.** anything that holds one back or lessens one's freedom. —*v.* **3.** to put fetters on; chain at the ankles. **4.** to confine or hold back: *His debts fettered him to a dull job.*

fet·tle (fet′’l), *n.* condition or state; spirits: *You seem to be in fine fettle this morning.*

fe·tus (fē′təs), *n., pl.* **fe·tus·es.** the young of a human or an animal while in the womb or egg, esp. in the later stages of development or shortly before birth.

feud (fyood), *n.* **1.** a bitter quarrel between two families, clans, or the like, often lasting many years and causing many deaths. **2.** a quarrel or strong disagreement or dislike between two persons or groups: *a feud between two senators.* —*v.* **3.** to engage in a feud.

feu·dal (fyood′’l), *adj.* of or referring to feudalism: *a feudal estate.*

feu·dal·ism (fyood′’liz′əm), *n.* the social and economic system in medieval Europe according to which a vassal held land from a lord and in return was obliged to perform military and other duties.

The lord also was responsible to his vassals, esp. to protect them from military attacks.

fe·ver (fē′vər), *n.* 1. an abnormally high body temperature: *The patient had a fever of 104°.* 2. a disease in which this condition is present. 3. a state of extreme excitement: *The family was in a fever of activity, getting ready for the holiday.*

fe·vered (fē′vərd), *adj.* 1. having a fever or affected by fever; hot: *a fevered brow.* 2. excited or restless: *fevered thoughts of escape.*

fe·ver·ish (fē′vər ish), *adj.* 1. having a fever, esp. a slight one. 2. affected by fever; hot, restless, or the like: *a feverish sleep.* 3. of or concerning fever: *a feverish disease.* 4. highly excited, nervous, or restless: *a feverish desire to get started.* —**fe′ver·ish·ly,** *adv.* —**fe′ver·ish·ness,** *n.*

few (fyoō), *adj.* 1. not many but more than one: *Few people live to be more than 100 years old.* —*n.* 2. *(used as pl.)* a small number or amount: *Send me a few.* 3. **quite a few,** many; a large number: *We ate several, but quite a few are left.* —**few′ness,** *n.*

few·er (fyoō′ər), *adj.* 1. the comparative of **few.** —*pron.* 2. *(used as pl.)* a smaller number: *Fewer were there than we had hoped.*

—**Usage.** When expressing a comparison with a larger number or amount, it is best to use *fewer* with plural nouns (and pronouns) and *less* with singular nouns (and pronouns): *I have fewer marbles than he has. You have fewer than either of us. We have less gasoline than I thought. It will be less than we need.*

fez (fez), *n., pl.* **fez·zes.** a brimless cap with a high, flat crown, usually of stiff red felt and having a black tassel, worn esp. by Turkish men.

ff., (and the) following (pages, verses, etc.).

FHA, Federal Housing Administration.

fi·an·cé (fē′än sā′, fē än′sā), *n.* a man engaged to be married.

fi·an·cée (fē′än sā′, fē än′sā), *n.* a woman engaged to be married.

fi·as·co (fē as′kō), *n., pl.* **fi·as·cos** *or* **fi·as·coes.** a complete failure: *The rain turned the picnic into a fiasco.*

fi·at (fī′ət, fī′at), *n.* an order or decree by a person with great authority, such as a king.

fib (fib), *n.* 1. a trivial or harmless lie. —*v.,* **fibbed, fib·bing.** 2. to tell a fib.

fi·ber (fī′bər), *n.* 1. a fine, threadlike piece, as of cotton, asbestos, etc. 2. a substance composed of such pieces: *muscle fiber.* 3. character or strength: *moral fiber.*

fi·ber·glass (fī′bər glas′), *n.* very fine filaments of glass twisted together into yarn for making fabrics, used in loose masses for heat and sound insulation, or embedded in plastics and used in making fishing poles, boat hulls, etc.

fi·brous (fī′brəs), *adj.* containing, made of, or like fibers: *fibrous paper; fibrous roots.*

Fez

fib·u·la (fib′yə lə), *n.* the outer and thinner of two bones that extend from the knee to the ankle.

-fication, a suffix used to form nouns corresponding to verbs ending in **-fy,** meaning action, process, or result: *glorification; edification.*

fick·le (fik′əl), *adj.* 1. changeable; unpredictable: *fickle weather.* 2. untrustworthy; without loyalty: *fickle friends.* —**fick′le·ness,** *n.*

fic·tion (fik′shən), *n.* 1. a type of prose writing made up of stories in which characters and events are completely or partly imaginary. 2. something made up or imagined, as a falsehood: *What he says is pure fiction.* —**fic′tion·al,** *adj.*

fic·ti·tious (fik tish′əs), *adj.* like fiction in being made up or false; not genuine: *He used a fictitious name.* —**fic·ti′tious·ly,** *adv.*

fid·dle (fid′ᵊl), *Informal.* —*n.* 1. a violin. —*v.,* **fid·dled, fid·dling.** 2. to play the fiddle. 3. to play on the fiddle: *to fiddle a tune.* 4. to waste or lose by trifling (usually fol. by *away*): *to fiddle away the afternoon.* 5. to fuss or toy (often fol. by *with*): *to fiddle with one's food.* —**fid′dler,** *n.*

fid′dler crab′, any of several crabs the males of which have one greatly enlarged claw.

fid·dle·sticks (fid′ᵊl-stiks′), *interj.* nonsense.

fi·del·i·ty (fi del′i tē), *n.* 1. loyalty; faithfulness: *the fidelity of close friends.* 2. exactness or accuracy: *to copy a letter with fidelity.*

fidg·et (fij′it), *v.,* **fidg·et·ed, fidg·et·ing.** 1. to move about nervously or restlessly: *He fidgeted in his chair.* —*n.* 2. Often, **fidgets.** the state of being restless or nervous: *Waiting for the dentist gives me the fidgets.* —**fidg′et·y,** *adj.*

Fiddler crab
(shell about 1 in. across)

fie (fī), *interj.* shame! for shame! (now usually said jokingly).

fief (fēf), *n.* (in the Middle Ages) a piece of land granted to a vassal by a feudal lord in return for loyal service.

field (fēld), *n.* 1. a piece of ground without trees, esp. one suitable for use as a pasture or for growing crops. 2. a piece of ground devoted to sports or contests: *a football field.* 3. all the contestants in a contest, for example all the horses running in a race. 4. (in baseball) **a.** position in the field rather than at bat: *Our team is in the field now.* **b.** the outfield. 5. a battlefield. 6. an expanse of anything: *a field of ice.* 7. any area where a natural product, such as a mineral, is found in abundance: *a coal field.* 8. the background against which something is shown, as on a flag, shield, etc.: *a blue field with a red cross.* 9. an area of study, interest, etc.: *the field of teaching.* 10. (in physics) an area in which a force operates: *a magnetic field.* 11. an area that is in view: *a person's field of vision.* —*v.* 12. (in baseball) to catch or pick up (the ball) in play. 13. to place (a player or players)

act, āble, dâre, ärt; ebb, ēqual; if, īce; hot, ōver, ôrder; oil; boŏk; oōze; out; up, ûrge; ə = *a* as in *alone;* ᵊ as in *button* (but′ᵊn), *fire* (fī³r); chief; shoe; thin; that; zh as in *measure* (mezh′ər). See full key inside cover.

in the field to play. —*adj.* **14.** (in sports) taking place on the field and not on the track: *field events.* **15.** working as a farm laborer in a field: *field hands.*

field′ day′, **1.** a day for outdoor sports events. **2.** a day for military exercises and display. **3.** any time for amusement or enjoyment: *The children had a field day with their new sleds.*

field·er (fēl′dər), *n.* (in baseball or cricket) a player in the field.

field′ glass′es. See **binocular** (def. 2).

field′ goal′, a three-point goal in football, scored by kicking the ball over the crossbar of the opponent's goal posts.

field′ mar′shal, an officer of the highest rank in the British army and certain other armies.

field′ trip′, a trip to gain firsthand knowledge away from a classroom, such as a visit to a museum, factory, farm, etc.

fiend (fēnd), *n.* **1.** a cruel or wicked person. **2.** an evil spirit; devil. **3.** *Informal.* a mischievous or annoying person: *My brother is a little fiend.* **4.** *Informal.* a person highly devoted to some sport, hobby, etc.: *a baseball fiend.*

fiend·ish (fēn′dish), *adj.* cruel and wicked: *a fiendish tyrant.* —**fiend′ish·ly,** *adv.* —**fiend′ish·ness,** *n.*

fierce (fērs), *adj.,* **fierc·er, fierc·est.** **1.** wild, savage, or hostile: *fierce lions and bears.* **2.** powerful or violent: *fierce winds.* **3.** very eager or intense: *fierce competition.* —**fierce′ly,** *adv.* —**fierce′ness,** *n.*

fier·y (fīr′ē, fī′ə rē), *adj.,* **fier·i·er, fier·i·est.** **1.** composed of or containing fire: *a fiery mass of fuel.* **2.** very hot: *a fiery summer day.* **3.** resembling fire in color. **4.** full of feeling; passionate: *a fiery speech.* **5.** easily angered: *a fiery temper.* —**fier′i·ness,** *n.*

fi·es·ta (fē es′tə), *n.* a festival, esp. a celebration held on a saint's day in Spain and Latin America.

fife (fīf), *n.* **1.** a small high-pitched flute used esp. in marching bands. —*v.,* **fifed, fif·ing. 2.** to play on this instrument.

fif·teen (fif′tēn′), *n.* **1.** a number that is ten plus five. **2.** a set of this many persons or things: *Fifteen of them will be there.* —*adj.* **3.** amounting to 15 in number: *fifteen persons.*

fif·teenth (fif′tēnth′), *adj.* **1.** being number fifteen in a series: *the fifteenth floor.* —*n.* **2.** one of fifteen equal parts. **3.** a person or thing that is fifteenth.

Fife

fifth (fifth), *adj.* **1.** being number five in a series: *the fifth floor.* —*n.* **2.** one of five equal parts. **3.** a person or thing that is fifth.

fif·ti·eth (fif′tē ith), *adj.* **1.** being number fifty in a series: *the fiftieth floor.* —*n.* **2.** one of fifty equal parts. **3.** a person or thing that is fiftieth.

fif·ty (fif′tē), *n., pl.* **fif·ties. 1.** a number that is five times ten. **2.** a set of this many persons or things: *Fifty of them will be there.* **3. fifties,** the numbers, years, degrees, etc., between 50 and 59: *The temperature was in the lower fifties.* —*adj.* **4.** amounting to fifty in number: *fifty persons.*

fif·ty-fif·ty (fif′tē fif′tē), *adv. Informal.* **1.** equally; with equal shares: *We shared the cost of the trip fifty-fifty.* —*adj.* **2.** shared equally: *a fifty-fifty expense.* **3.** half good and half bad: *He has a fifty-fifty chance of recovery.*

fig (fig), *n.* **1.** the small, sweet, pear-shaped fruit of a tree that grows in warm regions. **2.** the tree bearing this fruit.

fig., figure.

fight (fīt), *n.* **1.** a battle or combat: *a fight between two armies.* **2.** any contest or struggle: *a fight to recover one's health.* **3.** an angry argument; quarrel. **4.** the ability or desire to fight: *There was no fight left in him.* —*v.,* **fought** (fôt), **fight·ing. 5.** to contend or struggle: *to fight bravely in battle; to fight against bad habits.* **6.** to contend with or against: *to fight the enemy; to fight disappointment.* **7.** to carry on (a battle, duel, etc.): *to fight a long war.*

fight·er (fī′tər), *n.* **1.** a person who fights with his fists, esp. a boxer. **2.** an airplane used in warfare to attack enemy aircraft. **3.** a person who fights hard for a cause: *fighters for freedom.*

fight′ing fish′, any of several brightly colored, long-finned fishes found in SE Asia.

fig·ment (fig′mənt), *n.* a fantastic, purely imaginary notion, idea, etc.: *What you fear is only a figment of your imagination.*

Fighting fish (length 2½ in.)

fig·ur·a·tive (fig′yər ə tiv), *adj.* not to be taken literally or at face value; used as a figure of speech: *"To hurl insults" is a figurative statement.* —**fig′ur·a·tive·ly,** *adv.*

fig·ure (fig′yər), *n.* **1.** a symbol that stands for a number: *The figure for five is 5.* **2.** an amount or value expressed in numbers: *The expense reached a high figure.* **3. figures,** the use of numbers in adding, subtracting, etc.; arithmetic: *to be poor at figures.* **4.** the form of the body: *a dancer with a graceful figure.* **5.** a person as he appears to others: *His poverty made him a sorry figure in their eyes.* **6.** a character or personage: *an illustrious figure in history.* **7.** a symbol or emblem: *The dove is often used as a figure of peace.* **8.** a design or pattern: *a necktie with a bright figure.* **9.** a picture, drawing, diagram, outline, or the like: *a geometrical figure.* —*v.,* **fig·ured, fig·ur·ing. 10.** to compute or calculate, as by adding, subtracting, etc.: *to figure a sum.* **11.** to decorate with a design or pattern. **12.** *Informal.* to think, reason, or suppose: *He figured that it must be close to noon.* **13.** to appear or be present: *His name will figure in my report.* **14. figure on,** *Informal.* to take into consideration; plan on: *I hadn't figured on your leaving so early.* **15. figure out,** *Informal.* to understand or solve: *I can't figure out why you're angry.*

fig·ured (fig′yərd), *adj.* **1.** formed or shaped: *figured stones.* **2.** decorated with figures or a pattern: *a figured tablecloth.*

fig·ure·head (fig′yər hed′), *n.* **1.** a figure, usually of carved wood, formerly used to decorate the prow of a sailing ship. **2.** a person who is the head of a group, country, business, etc., but who has no real power.

fig′ure of speech′, an expression, such as a simile or metaphor, that is not to be taken literally but is used to give beauty or force to something said or written: *"The man stormed out of the room" is a figure of speech.*

Fi·ji (fē′jē), *n.* an independent nation E of Australia, made up of 800 islands in the S Pacific: formerly British.

fil·a·ment (fil′ə mənt), *n.* a very fine, thin thread of a substance, such as metal, or a threadlike part, esp. the fine piece of wire in an electric bulb that produces light when current passes through it.

fil·bert (fil′bərt), *n.* another name for **hazelnut.** [from the phrase *filbert nut,* so called because it ripens by August 22, St. *Philbert's* day]

filch (filch), *v.* to steal in a petty way: *He filched pennies from his brother.*

file[1] (fīl), *n.* **1.** a folder, cabinet, etc., in which papers, letters, etc., are arranged in order. **2.** an orderly collection of papers, letters, etc. **3.** a line of persons or things arranged one behind another: *a file of soldiers.* —*v.,* **filed, fil·ing. 4.** to arrange (papers, letters, etc.) in order. **5.** to submit (an application, request, etc.): *to file a claim.* **6.** to march in a file or line: *to file into a bus.* **7. on file,** arranged in a file for easy reference: *Names are on file in the office.* [from the French word *filer* "to string documents on a wire," which comes from *fil* "thread"]

file[2] (fīl), *n.* **1.** a long, narrow tool of metal having sharp ridges running crosswise, for shaping or smoothing surfaces. —*v.,* **filed, fil·ing. 2.** to smooth, cut, remove, etc., with or as if with a file: *to file rough edges.* [from the Old English word *fīl*]

fi·let (fi lā′, fil′ā), *n., v.,* **fi·leted, fi·let·ing.** See **fillet** (defs. 1, 3).

fil·i·al (fil′ē əl), *adj.* befitting a son or daughter: *filial love; filial obedience.*

fil·i·bus·ter (fil′i bus′tər), *n.* **1.** the use of long speeches and other tactics in a legislature in order to prevent the passage of a bill. — *v.* **2.** to attempt to prevent the passage of a bill by a filibuster.

fil·i·gree (fil′ə grē′), *n.* **1.** delicate ornamental work of fine wires shaped in graceful patterns. **2.** anything that has a delicate and fanciful design: *a filigree of frost on the window.* —*adj.* **3.** composed of or resembling filigree. —*v.,* **fil·i·greed, fil·i·gree·ing. 4.** to adorn with or form into filigree.

fil·ings (fī′lingz), *n.pl.* particles removed by a file.

Fil·i·pi·no (fil′ə pē′nō), *n., pl.* **Fil·i·pi·nos. 1.** an inhabitant of the Philippines. —*adj.* **2.** Philippine.

fill (fil), *v.* **1.** to make or become full: *Fill the jar with water.* **2.** to make or become completely occupied: *The audience filled the theater.* **3.** to feed fully: *They*

filled themselves with cake. **4.** to occupy or place someone in (an office, job, etc.): *to fill a vacancy in business.* **5.** to supply what is demanded in: *to fill an order.* **6.** to satisfy: *This book fills a great need.* **7.** to stop up or close: *to fill a hole.* —*n.* **8.** a full or satisfactory supply: *to eat one's fill.* **9. fill in, a.** to complete with the necessary information: *Fill in the blanks with your answers.* **b.** to be a substitute: *I filled in for the second baseman.* **10. fill out, a.** to complete (a questionnaire, application, etc.) with the necessary information: *Fill out this card and return it.* **b.** to become larger, fuller, plumper, etc.: *You've filled out since I last saw you.* **11. fill up,** to make or become full: *Please fill up my glass.*

fill·er (fil′ər), *n.* **1.** a person or thing that fills. **2.** a substance used to fill cracks, dents, etc., in a surface.

fil·let (fil′it; *usually* fi lā′, fil′ā *for defs. 1, 3*), *n.* **1.** a boneless cut or slice of meat or fish. **2.** a ribbon or the like for binding the hair. —*v.* **3.** to cut (meat or fish) into fillets. **4.** to bind with a fillet. Also, **filet** (for defs. 1, 3).

fill·ing (fil′ing), *n.* something that is used as a filler: *the filling of a pie; a filling for a tooth.*

fill′ing sta′tion, a roadside station for servicing motor vehicles with gasoline, etc. Also, **gas station.**

fil·lip (fil′əp), *v.* **1.** to strike with the nail of a finger snapped from the end of a thumb. —*n.* **2.** the act of filliping. **3.** anything that tends to excite, stir up, etc.: *His wit gave a fillip to the conversation.*

Fill·more (fil′môr), *n.* **Mil·lard** (mil′ərd), 1800–1874, 12th Vice President of the U.S. 1849–1850; 13th President of the U.S. 1850–1853.

fil·ly (fil′ē), *n., pl.* **fil·lies.** a young female horse. See also **colt.**

film (film), *n.* **1.** a thin layer or coating: *a film of dust.* **2.** thin sheets or a roll of a transparent material coated with a substance sensitive to light, used for taking photographs. **3.** a motion picture. —*v.* **4.** to cover with or become covered by a film. **5.** to photograph (something) with a motion-picture camera: *We watched them film a scene for the movie.* **6.** to make a motion picture of: *to film a novel.*

film·strip (film′strip′), *n.* a length of film for projection of one still picture or title on a screen at a time.

film·y (fil′mē), *adj.,* **film·i·er, film·i·est. 1.** covered with a film: *a filmy windowpane.* **2.** resembling film: *filmy silk cloth.* **—film′i·ness,** *n.*

fil·ter (fil′tər), *n.* **1.** a substance, such as cloth, paper, or charcoal, etc., through which water, air, smoke, etc., is passed to remove impurities. **2.** any device, such as a tank or tube, containing such a substance for filtering. **3.** a transparent screen placed over the lens of a camera to control color or light. —*v.* **4.** to remove by using a filter: *to filter dust from air.* **5.** to act as a filter for: *a tank that filters water.* **6.** to pass through or as if through a filter: *to filter water; light filtering through drawn blinds.* **—fil′ter·a·ble,** *adj.*

filth (filth), *n.* **1.** disgusting dirt or refuse: *the filth in* *gutters.* **2.** anything that is disgusting, dirty, etc.: *to speak filth.*

filth·y (fil'thē), *adj.,* **filth·i·er, filth·i·est. 1.** full of or covered with filth: *a filthy slum.* **2.** morally dirty; obscene: *filthy language.* —**filth'i·ness,** *n.*

fil·tra·tion (fil trā'shən), *n.* the act of filtering, or the state of being filtered.

fin (fin), *n.* **1.** an organ resembling a wing or a paddle and attached to the body of various water animals. Fins are used for steering, propelling, and balancing. **2.** the vertical tail surface of an airplane. **3.** Usually, **fins.** See **flipper** (def. 2).

fi·nal (fīn'əl), *adj.* **1.** coming at the end; last. **2.** allowing for no change; conclusive: *The decision of the judges shall be final.* —*n.* **3. finals,** the last games, tests, etc., in a series.

fi·nal·e (fi nal'ē, fi nä'lē), *n.* **1.** the last part of a piece of music, play, opera, etc. **2.** the last part of a course of action, career, etc.: *the finale of a reign.*

fi·nal·ist (fīn'əlist), *n.* a person who is entitled to take part in the final round or trial of an athletic event or other contest: *golf finalists.*

fi·nal·i·ty (fi nal'i tē), *n., pl.* **fi·nal·i·ties. 1.** the fact or quality of being final: *The judge spoke with finality.* **2.** something that is final; a final act, statement, etc.

fi·nal·ly (fīn'əlē), *adv.* **1.** at the final point or moment; at the end: *Finally, he thanked them and took leave.* **2.** eventually: *The rain finally washed away the lawn.* **3.** at last: *You've finally come!*

fi·nance (fi nans', fī'nans), *n.* **1.** the management of money matters: *an expert in finance.* **2. finances,** the amount of money had by a person, business, etc.; funds: *Their finances were dangerously low.* —*v.,* **fi·nanced, fi·nanc·ing. 3.** to supply money for; pay for: *He financed his children's education.*

fi·nan·cial (fi nan'shəl, fī nan'shəl), *adj.* having to do with money matters: *financial reports; financial troubles.* —**fi·nan'cial·ly,** *adv.*

fin·an·cier (fin'ən sēr'), *n.* a person, such as a stockbroker, who is skilled in financial matters.

Finback
(length 60 to 70 ft.)

fin·back (fin'bak'), *n.* any of various whales of the Atlantic and Pacific coasts having a prominent fin on its back. Also called **fin'back whale'.**

finch (finch), *n.* any of numerous small songbirds including the sparrows, canaries, and linnets.

find (find), *v.,* **found** (found), **find·ing. 1.** to come upon by chance; meet with: *to find a nickel in the street.* **2.** to learn, reach, or obtain by searching or trying: *He has been trying to find a job.* **3.** to discover: *Columbus found America.* **4.** to get back or recover (something lost): *Have you found your missing book?* **5.** to come to know by study, experience, etc.: *Let's try to find a solution to the problem.* **6.** to decide: *The jury found him*

Finch
(length 6 in.)

guilty. —*n.* **7.** something found, esp. a valuable or pleasing discovery: *Our new house was a find.* **8. find out,** to discover the truth about (something): *Try to find out where she's gone.*

find·er (fīn'dər), *n.* **1.** a person or thing that finds; discoverer. **2.** Also, **viewfinder.** a device on a camera that shows what will be included in the finished picture. **3.** a small telescope attached to a larger one to aid in pointing it toward the area to be observed.

find·ing (fīn'ding), *n.* **1.** the act of a person or thing that finds; discovery. **2.** something that is found: *important scientific findings.* **3.** the verdict of a jury or judge: *The finding was that he was guilty.*

fine¹ (fin), *adj.,* **fin·er, fin·est. 1.** very good; of the best quality or grade: *a fine student; fine foods.* **2.** made up of very small particles: *fine sand.* **3.** very thin or slender: *fine thread.* **4.** keen or sharp, as the blade of a knife. **5.** delicately made: *fine china.* **6.** polished or refined: *a fine lady.* **7.** without impurities; pure: *fine gold.* **8.** hard to define; subtle: *a fine distinction between the meanings of two words.* —*adv.* **9.** *Informal.* very well; excellently: *I'm doing fine, thanks.* [from the Latin word *finis* "end, limit"] —**fine'ly,** *adv.* —**fine'ness,** *n.*

fine² (fin), *n.* **1.** a sum of money paid as a penalty for breaking a rule or law: *a library fine for overdue books.* —*v.,* **fined, fin·ing. 2.** to demand the payment of a fine from: *They fined him for speeding.* [from the medieval Latin word *finis* "payment, settlement," which comes from Latin *finis* "end"]

fine' arts', the arts that appeal to one's sense of beauty, esp. painting, sculpture, drawing, etc., and sometimes music and poetry.

fin·er·y (fī'nə rē), *n.* fine or showy dress, ornaments, etc.: *She went to the party in all her finery.*

fi·nesse (fi nes'), *n.* **1.** skill in handling a situation: *to show finesse in settling a dispute.* **2.** skill in doing something: *to cook with finesse.*

fin·ger (fing'gər), *n.* **1.** any of the five separate parts forming the end of the hand, esp. one other than the thumb. **2.** part of a glove made to cover a finger. **3.** anything like a finger in shape or use: *the finger of a speedometer.* —*v.* **4.** to touch or handle with the fingers: *She nervously fingered her beads.*

Fin'ger Lakes', a group of long glacial lakes in central New York: resort region.

fin·ger·nail (fing'gər nāl'), *n.* the hard, horny covering at the end of a finger.

fin·ger·print (fing'gər print'), *n.* **1.** an impression of the marks on the tip of the finger, esp. when made with ink for the purpose of identifying a person. —*v.* **2.** to take the fingerprints of: *to fingerprint a criminal.*

fin·ick·y (fin'ə kē), *adj.* difficult to please; fussy: *He is very finicky about his clothes.*

fin·ish (fin'ish), *v.* **1.** to bring or come to an end: *Did you finish your work?* **2.** to come to the end of: *to finish school.* **3.** to use completely (often fol. by *up*): *to finish up a can of paint.* **4.** to destroy or kill (often fol. by *off*): *The spray finished off the flies.* **5.** to make complete: *to finish a painting.* **6.** to put a finish on (wood, metal, etc.): *to finish a table.* —*n.* **7.** the end or last stage: *the finish of a program.* **8.** polish in education, manners, etc. **9.** a paint, varnish, etc., used to coat a wood or metal surface. **10.** the coating of such a surface: *a table with an enamel finish.*

fin·ished (fin′isht), *adj.* **1.** ended or completed. **2.** perfect or polished: *a finished piece of writing.* **3.** highly skilled: *a finished musician.*

fi·nite (fi′nīt), *adj.* having limits in size, length, etc.; not infinite: *Man's life is finite.* —**fi′nite·ly,** *adv.*

Fin·land (fin′lənd), *n.* a republic in N Europe: formerly part of Russia. It covers an area of 130,119 sq. mi. *Cap.:* Helsinki.

Finn (fin), *n.* a native or inhabitant of Finland.

Fin·nish (fin′ish), *n.* **1.** the language of the Finns, related to Hungarian. —*adj.* **2.** of or concerning Finland, its people, or their language.

fiord (fyôrd), *n.* a long, narrow arm of the sea bordered by steep cliffs, esp. in Norway. Also, **fjord.**

fire (fīr), *n.* **1.** the light and heat given off in burning. **2.** a burning mass of fuel in a fireplace, furnace, or the like. **3.** the destructive burning of a building, forest, etc. **4.** heat used for cooking: *Put the kettle on the fire.* **5.** great enthusiasm, passion, etc.: *a speech full of fire.* **6.** the discharge of firearms: *to open fire on an enemy.* —*v.,* **fired, fir·ing. 7.** to discharge, as a gun or bullet: *to fire on an enemy.* **8.** to set on fire or take fire: *to fire wood.* **9.** to supply with fuel: *to fire a stove.* **10.** to fill with enthusiasm or inspire: *to be fired by courageous deeds.* **11.** *Informal.* to dismiss (someone) from a job. **12. catch fire,** to begin to burn: *Their barn caught fire during the storm.* **13. on fire,** burning or ignited; afire: *The house is on fire.* **14. under fire,** under attack, esp. by military forces: *The squadron was under fire for three days.*

fire·arm (fīr′ärm′), *n.* any weapon small enough to be carried, such as a rifle or pistol, from which shot, a bullet, etc., is fired by gunpowder.

fire·brand (fīr′brand′), *n.* **1.** a piece of burning wood or other material. **2.** a very active, energetic person, esp. one who stirs up trouble.

fire·bug (fīr′bug′), *n.* *Informal.* a person who deliberately starts destructive fires; arsonist.

fire·crack·er (fīr′krak′ər), *n.* a paper roll filled with gunpowder and having a fuse, used in celebrations because of the loud noise made when it is exploded.

fire·damp (fīr′damp′), *n.* a combustible gas, found in coal mines, that can cause dangerous explosions.

fire′ drill′, a practice drill of duties and procedures to be followed in case of fire.

fire′ en′gine, a motor truck equipped for fire fighting, usually having a pump for shooting water.

fire′ escape′, a metal stairway attached to the outside wall of a building, used for escape in case of fire.

fire′ extin′guisher, a portable device containing chemicals, water, etc., for putting out fires.

fire·fly (fīr′flī′), *n., pl.* **fire·flies.** any of several night-flying beetles having light-producing organs at the end of the abdomen. Also, **glowworm, light-ning bug.**

fire·house (fīr′hous′), *n., pl.* **fire·hous·es** (fīr′-hou′ziz). a fire station.

fire·light (fīr′līt′), *n.* the light from a fire, as in a fireplace.

fire·man (fīr′mən), *n., pl.* **fire·men. 1.** a man employed to put out or prevent fires. **2.** a man employed to tend fires, as on a locomotive; stoker.

Firefly
A, Adult; B, Larva
(length ½ in.)

fire·place (fīr′plās′), *n.* **1.** the part of a chimney which opens into a room and in which fires are burned. **2.** an outdoor structure of brick, stone, etc., used for fires, as at a campsite.

fire·plug (fīr′plug′), *n.* a hydrant.

fire·proof (fīr′proof′), *adj.* **1.** resistant to being burned: *a fireproof building.* —*v.* **2.** to treat so as to make fireproof.

fire·side (fīr′sīd′), *n.* **1.** the space around a fire or hearth. **2.** home or family life: *the joys of the fireside.*

fire′ sta′tion, a building in which fire engines and equipment for fighting fires are kept, and in which firemen are sometimes housed; firehouse.

fire·wood (fīr′wood′), *n.* wood for fuel.

fire·works (fīr′wûrks′), *n.pl.* **1.** devices that burn or explode, making loud noises or a display of colored, bright lights. **2.** a display of such devices.

firm¹ (fûrm), *adj.* **1.** not soft or yielding when pressed: *firm ground.* **2.** fixed in place: *firm foundations.* **3.** steady; not shaking: *a firm hand.* **4.** steadfast or unwavering: *a firm belief.* [from the Latin word *firmus*] —**firm′ly,** *adv.* —**firm′ness,** *n.*

firm² (fûrm), *n.* a business concern having two or more partners: *a law firm.* [from the Spanish word *firma* "signature," which comes from *firmar* "to sign," from Latin *firmāre* "to strengthen, confirm"]

fir·ma·ment (fûr′mə mənt), *n.* the heavens; the sky.

first (fûrst), *adj.* **1.** being number one in a series: *the first floor.* **2.** being before all others in grade, rank, or importance: *first mate.* **3.** (in music) being the chief among voices or instruments of the same class: *first violin.* —*n.* **4.** a person or thing that is first: *We were the first to arrive.* **5.** the beginning: *I liked him from the first.* —*adv.* **6.** before all others or anything else: *You go first.* **7.** for the first time: *I remember when I first met her.* **8.** rather; sooner; more willingly: *Steal? I'd die first.* **9. first thing,** before anything else: *I'll do it first thing tomorrow.*

first′ aid′, treatment or help given to someone who is sick or injured before regular medical treatment is available.

first-born (fûrst′bôrn′), *adj.* **1.** first to be born in a family; oldest. —*n.* **2.** a first-born child.

first′ class′, 1. the best or highest class, rank, etc., esp. the most expensive and luxurious class of travel on a ship, train, etc. 2. the class of mail consisting of postal cards, letters, and any mailable, sealed matter. —**first-class** (fûrst′klas′), *adj., adv.*

first′-de·gree′ burn′ (fûrst′di grē′). See under **burn** (def. 11).

first·hand (fûrst′hand′), *adv.* 1. from the first or the original source: *to learn about an event firsthand.* —*adj.* 2. direct from the original source: *firsthand information.* Also, **first′-hand′.**

first′ la′dy, 1. the wife of a U.S. president or governor. 2. the most prominent woman in any field: *the first lady of the theater.*

first′ lieuten′ant, an officer in the U.S. Army, ranking above a second lieutenant and below a captain.

first′ per′son, 1. the speaker or speakers of a word, phrase, or sentence. 2. the form of a pronoun or verb that refers to the speaker or speakers. In English, *I, me, my, we, us, our,* etc., are pronouns of the first person. *Am* is the first person singular, present tense of the verb *to be.*

first-rate (fûrst′rāt′), *adj.* of the best class; excellent; very good: *a first-rate performance.*

firth (fûrth), *n.* a long, narrow arm of the sea, esp. in Scotland: *Edinburgh is on the Firth of Forth.*

fis·cal (fis′kəl), *adj.* of or having to do with money matters; financial: *the city's fiscal program.* [from the Latin word *fiscālis,* which comes from *fiscus* "treasury," literally "basket, bag"] —**fis′cal·ly,** *adv.*

fish (fish), *n., pl.* **fish·es** *or* **fish.** 1. any of numerous kinds of cold-blooded water animals having backbones and fins but lacking legs. Fish breathe by means of gills and usually have scaly bodies. 2. the flesh of fishes used as food. 3. **the Fishes,** another name for **Pisces.**

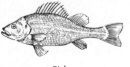

Fish

—*v.* 4. to catch or try to catch fish: *We fish for sport.* 5. to search for by groping: *He fished around in his pocket for a penny.* 6. to catch onto and draw as if by fishing: *He fished a piece of paper from his pocket.* 7. to try to get something in an indirect way: *to fish for compliments.*

fish·er (fish′ər), *n.* 1. a fisherman. 2. any animal that catches fish for food, esp. a kind of marten.

fish·er·man (fish′ər mən), *n., pl.* **fish·er·men.** a person who fishes for pleasure or for a living.

fish·er·y (fish′ə rē), *n., pl.* **fish·er·ies.** 1. the business or industry of catching fish. 2. a place for catching fish.

fish′ hawk′, another name for **osprey.**

fish·hook (fish′hook′), *n.* a hook used in fishing.

fish·ing (fish′ing), *n.* 1. the act of catching fish. 2. the work or sport of catching fish: *Fishing is one of his pleasures.*

fish·y (fish′ē), *adj.,* **fish·i·er, fish·i·est.** 1. like a fish in smell, taste, or the like. 2. *Informal.* doubtful; not likely: *There was something fishy about his explana-*

tion. 3. dull and without expression: *a fishy look.* —**fish′i·ness,** *n.*

fis·sion (fish′ən), *n.* 1. the act of splitting or dividing into parts. 2. a method of reproduction in which a one-celled organism divides in half to create two identical individuals. 3. the splitting of the nucleus of a heavy atom with the release of large amounts of energy. See also **fusion** (def. 4). —**fis′sion·a·ble,** *adj.*

fis·sure (fish′ər), *n.* 1. a long, narrow opening caused by splitting or dividing of parts: *a fissure in the ground caused by an earthquake.* —*v.,* **fis·sured, fis·sur·ing.** 2. to split open.

fist (fist), *n.* the hand closed tightly, with the fingers curled against the palm.

fist·i·cuffs (fis′tə kufs′), *n.pl.* a fighting between persons using the fists.

fit¹ (fit), *adj.,* **fit·ter, fit·test.** 1. adapted or suited: *Is this food fit to eat?* 2. proper or right: *fit behavior.* 3. qualified: *He is fit for the job.* 4. in good physical health or condition: *He exercises to keep fit.* —*v.,* **fit·ted** *or* **fit; fit·ting.** 5. to be adapted to or suitable for: *Your actions do not fit your words.* 6. to be of the right size or shape: *This shirt does not fit.* 7. to be right for in size and shape: *The suit fitted him perfectly.* 8. to adjust or try to make fit: *to fit a ring that is too large.* 9. to prepare or make qualified: *His experience fitted him for the job.* 10. to provide, furnish, or equip: *He fitted the windows with panes.* —*n.* 11. the manner in which a thing fits: *a perfect fit.* [from Old English] —**fit′ness,** *n.* —**fit′ter,** *n.*

fit² (fit), *n.* 1. a sudden, acute attack of a disease. 2. a sudden spasm: *a fit of sneezing.* 3. a violent outburst of feeling: *a fit of rage.* 4. **by fits and starts,** every now and then: *to work by fits and starts.* [from an Old English word meaning "a round of fighting"]

fit·ful (fit′fəl), *adj.* appearing or happening from time to time; not regular: *fitful gusts of wind; fitful attention.* —**fit′ful·ly,** *adv.*

fit·ting (fit′ing), *adj.* 1. suitable or proper: *behavior not fitting for a gentleman.* —*n.* 2. an act of trying on clothes that are being made or altered: *a fitting for a suit.* 3. **fittings,** furniture, fixtures, etc., as of an apartment, automobile, etc. —**fit′ting·ly,** *adv.*

five (fīv), *n.* 1. a number that is four plus one. 2. a set of this many persons or things: *Only five came.* —*adj.* 3. amounting to five in number: *five persons.*

five·fold (fīv′fōld′), *adj.* 1. made up of five parts: *a fivefold plan.* 2. five times as great or as much: *a fivefold increase.* —*adv.* 3. in fivefold measure: *The enrollment has increased fivefold.*

fix (fiks), *v.,* **fixed** *or* **fixt; fix·ing.** 1. to make fast or fix in place: *to fix a post in the ground.* 2. to settle or set definitely: *to fix a price.* 3. to direct (the eyes, mind, etc.) steadily: *He fixed his attention on the door.* 4. to make set or rigid: *He fixed his jaw in determination.* 5. to put or place (responsibility, blame, etc.) on a person. 6. to repair or mend: *to fix a broken plate with glue.* 7. to put in order; arrange: *to fix one's room.* 8. to prepare (a meal or food). 9. *Informal.* to bribe, arrange, or manage for dishonest purposes: *to fix a ball game.* 10. *Informal.* to get even with: *I'll fix you!* **11.** (in photography) to make (an image) permanent after it has been developed. —*n.* **12.** *Informal.* a bad position; predicament: *With so much work to do, he was in a fix.* **13. fix up,** *Informal.* **a.** to repair, mend, or cure: *Try to fix up that mistake.* **b.** to improve the appearance of; furnish or redecorate: *to fix up a house.*

fixed (fikst), *adj.* **1.** fastened or attached. **2.** set upon something: *a fixed stare.* **3.** not changing; definite: *a fixed price.* —**fix·ed·ly** (fik′sid lē), *adv.*

fix·ture (fiks′chər), *n.* **1.** something that is securely and usually permanently attached to a wall, ceiling, etc., as a household appliance: *a light fixture; kitchen fixtures.* **2.** a person or thing long established or located in the same position or place.

fizz (fiz), *v.* **1.** to make a hissing or sputtering sound, as soda water. —*n.* **2.** a hissing or sputtering sound.

fiz·zle (fiz′əl), *v.,* **fiz·zled, fiz·zling. 1.** to make a hissing or sputtering sound, esp. one that dies out weakly: *The wet match fizzled and went out.* **2.** *Informal.* to fail badly after a good beginning. —*n.* **3.** a hissing or sputtering sound. **4.** *Informal.* something that ends in failure: *The campaign was a fizzle.*

fizz·y (fiz′ē), *adj.,* **fizz·i·er, fizz·i·est.** having a bubbling or fizzing quality; carbonated: *a fizzy lemonade.* —**fizz′i·ness,** *n.*

fjord (fyôrd), *n.* another spelling of **fiord.**

fl., 1. flourished. **2.** fluid.

Fla., Florida.

flab·ber·gast (flab′ər gast′), *v.* *Informal.* to overcome with surprise; astound: *The amount of the bill flabbergasted her.*

flab·by (flab′ē), *adj.,* **flab·bi·er, flab·bi·est. 1.** limp and weak, as flesh or muscles: *muscles that are flabby from lack of exercise.* **2.** having such flesh. **3.** lacking will, courage, etc.: *flabby, lazy minds.* —**flab′bi·ness,** *n.*

flac·cid (flak′sid), *adj.* soft and limp; not firm; flabby: *flaccid muscles.*

flag[1] (flag), *n.* **1.** a piece of cloth having certain designs and colors, usually attached along one edge to a pole or staff: used to stand for a country, state, etc., or as a signal. —*v.,* **flagged, flag·ging. 2.** to signal or warn (a person, automobile, etc.) with or as if with a flag (sometimes fol. by *down*): *to flag down a passing car.* [perhaps a blend of *flap* (noun) + *fag,* used in an older meaning "flap, loose end"]

flag[2] (flag), *v.,* **flagged, flag·ging.** to lose strength; droop: *Our spirits flagged as the day grew hotter.* [perhaps a blend of *flap* (verb) + *fag,* used in an older meaning "to droop"]

fla·gel·lum (flə jel′əm), *n.* a long, thin appendage of certain one-celled organisms that serves as a means of propulsion.

Flageolet

flag·eo·let (flaj′ə let′, flaj′ə lā′), *n.* a small wind in-

strument resembling the recorder but sometimes having two pipes.

flag·on (flag′ən), *n.* **1.** a container for liquids to be drunk, esp. one having a handle, a spout, and usually a cover. **2.** a large bottle for holding wine, liquors, etc.

flag·pole (flag′pōl′), *n.* a staff or pole on which a flag is displayed; flagstaff.

fla·grant (flā′grənt), *adj.* shockingly wrong or bad in a highly noticeable way: *flagrant behavior; a flagrant crime.* —**fla′grant·ly,** *adv.*

flag·ship (flag′ship′), *n.* a ship bearing the commander of a fleet and displaying his flag.

flag·staff (flag′staf′), *n.* a flagpole.

flag·stone (flag′stōn′), *n.* a flat stone slab used esp. for paving.

flail (flāl), *n.* **1.** a tool for threshing grain by hand, having a handle with a freely swinging bar fastened to one end. —*v.* **2.** to strike with or as if with a flail: *to flail grain; to flail the water with one's arms.*

flair (flâr), *n.* talent or ability; bent; knack: *She has a flair for choosing the right clothes.*

flake (flāk), *n.* **1.** a small, flat, thin piece of something: *a flake of snow.* —*v.,* **flaked, flak·ing. 2.** to come off in flakes: *Paint was flaking from the wall.* **3.** to break into or remove in flakes: *to flake paint from a wall.*

flak·y (flā′kē), *adj.,* **flak·i·er, flak·i·est. 1.** of or like flakes: *a flaky crust.* **2.** peeling off in flakes: *flaky paint.* —**flak′i·ness,** *n.*

flam·boy·ant (flam boi′ənt), *adj.* **1.** strikingly brilliant or showy: *flamboyant colors.* **2.** ornate and elaborate: *a flamboyant speech.* —**flam·boy′ant·ly,** *adv.*

flame (flām), *n.* **1.** burning gas or vapor from wood, coal, etc., that has been set afire: *the flame of a candle.* **2.** Often, **flames.** the state of burning: *The whole house was in flames.* **3.** a color, light, etc., resembling flame. **4.** ardor or passion. —*v.,* **flamed, flam·ing. 5.** to burn with a flame or flames. **6.** to glow or shine brilliantly. **7.** to break into anger; rage.

Flamingo
(height 5 ft.)

fla·min·go (flə ming′gō), *n., pl.* **fla·min·gos** or **fla·min·goes.** any of several large pink or red water birds having very long legs and neck.

flam·ma·ble (flam′ə bəl), *adj.* easily set on fire; inflammable: *Some gases are highly flammable.* —**flam′ma·bil′i·ty,** *n.*

Flan·ders (flan′dərz), *n.* an area in W Europe: part of Belgium, France, and the Netherlands. In the Middle Ages it was a separate country.

flange (flanj), *n.* a projecting rim, collar, or

ridge on a shaft or pipe to give additional strength or stiffness or to permit other objects to be attached.

flank (flangk), *n.* **1.** the side of an animal or man between the ribs and the hip. **2.** the flesh of this part of an animal, used as food. **3.** the side of anything: *the flank of a hill.* —*v.* **4.** to stand or be placed at the side of: *Trees flank the avenue.*

flan·nel (flan′ǝl), *n.* **1.** a warm, soft, napped cloth, usually made of cotton or wool. **2.** flannels, outer garments or underclothes made of this cloth. —*adj.* **3.** made of flannel: *a flannel nightgown.*

flap (flap), *v.,* flapped, flap·ping. **1.** to swing or cause to swing about loosely, esp. with noise: *Curtains flapped in the wind.* **2.** to move up and down: *Birds flap their wings.* —*n.* **3.** a flapping motion or noise: *the flap of wings.* **4.** something broad and flat that hangs loosely over or covers an opening, attached at one side only: *the flap of a pocket.*

flap·jack (flap′jak′), *n.* a pancake; griddlecake: *a plate of flapjacks and bacon.*

flare (flâr), *v.,* flared, flar·ing. **1.** to burn with a swaying flame, as a torch in the wind. **2.** to blaze with a sudden burst of flame (often fol. by *up*): *The match flared up when struck.* **3.** to break out suddenly, as violence, anger, etc. (often fol. by *up*): *to flare up at an insult.* **4.** to spread gradually outward, as the end of a trumpet. —*n.* **5.** a flaring or swaying flame. **6.** a sudden burst of light. **7.** a blaze of fire or light used as a signal. **8.** a gradual spread outward in form: *the flare of a skirt.* **9. flare up,** to become angry suddenly: *He flares up when he is not obeyed.*

flash (flash), *n.* **1.** a brief, sudden burst of bright light. **2.** a brief, sudden outburst of joy, wit, etc.: *a play full of humorous flashes.* **3.** a very brief moment; instant: *I'll be back in a flash.* —*v.* **4.** to break forth into a sudden flame or light. **5.** to send forth (a flame or light). **6.** to move like a flash: *A new sports car just flashed by.* **7.** to send swiftly, as by radio, telegraph, etc.: *The news was flashed to all parts of the earth.*

flash·light (flash′līt′), *n.* a small, portable electric lamp, powered by dry batteries.

flash·y (flash′ē), *adj.,* flash·i·er, flash·i·est. **1.** showy or gaudy: *a closet full of flashy clothes.* **2.** bright and quick in a shallow way: *a flashy speaker.* —flash′i·ness, *n.*

flask (flask), *n.* a bottle, usually of glass, having a rounded body and a narrow neck, used to hold wine, oil, etc., or in laboratory experiments.

flat[1] (flat), *adj.* **1.** level and even: *The top of a table is flat.* **2.** spread out evenly: *to make a rug flat by smoothing it out.* **3.** not thick or deep: *flat dishes.* **4.** without air, as a tire or balloon; deflated. **5.** absolute, downright, or positive: *a flat refusal.* **6.** always the same; not changing: *a flat price for everyone.* **7.** without proper flavor or zest; tasteless: *flat food.* **8.** having lost its sparkle, as soda, beer, or the like. **9.** (in music) below the correct pitch, or lowered a half step from another note (distinguished from *sharp*). —*n.* **10.** a

Flask

flat part or surface: *the flat of his hand.* **11.** flat or level ground: *salt flats.* **12.** (in music) a tone a half step below another tone. **13.** the sign (♭) indicating the lowering of a tone by a half step. **14.** a deflated automobile tire. —*adv.* **15.** in a flat position: *to fall flat on one's face.* **16.** completely; utterly: *I've been flat broke all week.* [from Scandinavian] —flat′ly, *adv.* —flat′ness, *n.*

flat[2] (flat), *n.* an apartment or group of rooms on one floor. [from the Old English word *flet* "floor, hall"]

flat·boat (flat′bōt′), *n.* a large flat-bottomed boat for use in shallow water, esp. on rivers.

flat·car (flat′kär′), *n.* a railroad car without sides or top, used for carrying freight.

flat·fish (flat′fish′), *n., pl.* flat·fish·es *or* flat·fish. any of numerous kinds of fish including flounder, halibut, etc., that have flattened bodies and swim on their sides.

flat·foot·ed (flat′fŏŏt′id), *adj.* **1.** having a condition in which the bones in the foot are deformed in such a way that the entire sole rests on the ground. **2. catch someone flat-footed,** to catch (a person) off his guard: *The big dinner check caught us flat-footed.* —flat′-foot′ed·ly, *adv.* —flat′-foot′ed·ness, *n.*

flat·i·ron (flat′ī′ǝrn), *n.* a heavy iron for pressing clothes.

flat·ten (flat′ǝn), *v.* to make or become flat.

flat·ter (flat′ǝr), *v.* **1.** to praise too much or insincerely, esp. in order to win an advantage. **2.** to show as more attractive or better than is the case: *Her portrait flatters her.* **3.** to cause to feel pleased: *It flatters me to be asked for my opinion.* —flat′ter·er, *n.* —flat′ter·ing·ly, *adv.*

flat·ter·y (flat′ǝ rē), *n., pl.* flat·ter·ies. **1.** the act of flattering. **2.** a flattering compliment or speech.

flaunt (flônt), *v.* **1.** to show off proudly or boastfully: *to flaunt one's wealth.* **2.** to wave proudly in the air: *flags flaunting in the wind.* [from a Scandinavian word, related to Norwegian *flana* "to roam"] —flaunt′er, *n.* —flaunt′ing·ly, *adv.*

—**Usage.** *Flout* should never be mistaken as a synonym of *flaunt. Flout* means to treat with scorn or contempt, whereas *flaunt* means to show with great pride: *The cadets flouted* (not *flaunted*) *the regulations.*

fla·vor (flā′vǝr), *n.* **1.** the taste of something: *the flavor of tea; the flavor of bacon.* **2.** a substance that gives a certain taste: *cherry, strawberry, and other flavors.* **3.** the particular quality of something: *a book that captures the flavor of colonial days.* —*v.* **4.** to give flavor to: *to flavor cake with vanilla.* Also, *esp.* British, **fla′vour.**

fla·vor·ing (flā′vǝr ing), *n.* something that gives a particular flavor to food or drink, such as vanilla.

flaw (flô), *n.* **1.** a defect, such as a dent or crack, that mars the beauty, value, correctness, etc., of something; fault: *a flaw in the windowpane.* —*v.* **2.** to make or become defective, cracked, etc.: *A nasty temper flawed her personality.* —flaw′less, *adj.* —flaw′less·ly, *adv.*

flax (flaks), *n.* **1.** a plant bearing pale blue flowers and grown for its fibers and its seeds. **2.** the fiber of this plant, which is the source of linen.

flax·en (flak′ən), *adj.* **1.** of, referring to, or resembling flax. **2.** pale yellow in color, like flax.

flax·seed (flaks′sēd′), *n.* the seeds of the flax plant, the source of linseed oil. Also, **linseed.**

flay (flā), *v.* **1.** to strip off the skin of, as by whipping. **2.** to scold or criticize harshly: *The newspapers flayed the governor.*

flea (flē), *n.* any of numerous small, bloodsucking insects that live on animals and birds. Fleas have no wings, but are noted for their ability to leap.

fleck (flek), *n.* **1.** a spot or small patch of color, light, dirt, etc.: *flecks of soot on snow.* —*v.* **2.** to mark with a fleck or flecks: *a horse flecked with gray spots.*

Flea
(length ⅛ in.)

fled (fled), *v.* the past tense and past participle of **flee.**

fledg·ling (flej′ling), *n.* **1.** a young bird just able to fly. **2.** an inexperienced person.

flee (flē), *v.,* **fled** (fled), **flee·ing. 1.** to run away or run away from: *When he saw the tiger he fled. They fled the fire.* **2.** to pass quickly by; fly; speed.

fleece (flēs), *n.* **1.** the coat of wool that covers a sheep or similar animal. —*v.,* **fleeced, fleec·ing. 2.** to remove the fleece of: *to fleece sheep.* **3.** to take money or possessions from by fraud, trickery, etc.: *The swindlers fleeced him of his savings.*

fleec·y (flē′sē), *adj.,* **fleec·i·er, fleec·i·est.** covered with, made of, or resembling fleece: *fleecy snow; fleecy clouds.* —**fleec′i·ness,** *n.*

fleet[1] (flēt), *n.* **1.** a large group of ships under one command: *a fishing fleet; the Atlantic fleet.* **2.** the whole navy of a country: *the American fleet.* **3.** a large group of ships, trucks, buses, etc., owned and operated by a single company: *His father owns a fleet of taxis.* [from the Old English word *flēot* "flowing water"]

fleet[2] (flēt), *adj.* swift; rapid: *Gazelles are fleet of foot.* [from the Old English word *flēotan* "to float"] —**fleet′ness,** *n.*

fleet′ ad′miral, an officer of the highest rank in the U.S. Navy, ranking above an admiral.

fleet·ing (flē′ting), *adj.* passing swiftly; lasting only for a time: *Youth is fleeting.* —**fleet′ing·ly,** *adv.*

Flem·ing (flem′ing), *n.* Sir Alexander, 1881–1955, Scottish bacteriologist: codiscoverer of penicillin.

Flem·ish (flem′ish), *adj.* **1.** of or concerning Flanders, its people, or their language. —*n.* **2.** the people of Flanders. **3.** the Germanic language of Flanders, closely related to Dutch.

flesh (flesh), *n.* **1.** the soft parts of a human or animal body, consisting of muscle and fat. **2.** these parts of an animal, used as food. **3.** man's body, as apart from his spirit or soul. **4.** mankind: *to go the way of all flesh.* **5.** the soft part of a fruit or vegetable. **6. in the flesh,** in person: *She saw her movie hero in the*

flesh. **7. one's own flesh and blood,** a person's close relative or relatives: *To think he would do that to his own flesh and blood!*

flesh·ly (flesh′lē), *adj.* of or referring to the body, esp. to its weaknesses, desires, etc.: *fleshly ills.*

flesh·y (flesh′ē), *adj.,* **flesh·i·er, flesh·i·est. 1.** having much flesh; plump; fat: *fleshy arms.* **2.** made of or resembling flesh: *the fleshy part of a peach.* —**flesh′i·ness,** *n.*

fleur-de-lis (flŏŏr′dəlē′), *n., pl.* **fleurs-de-lis** (flŏŏr′dəlēz′). a design similar to an iris flower, formerly used as an emblem by the kings of France.

flew (flŏŏ), *v.* a past tense of **fly**[1].

flex (fleks), *v.* **1.** to bend, as a part of the body: *to flex one's legs and arms.* —*n.* **2.** the act of flexing: *a flex of the arm.*

flex·i·ble (flek′sə bəl), *adj.* **1.** capable of being bent; easily bent: *Rubber is a flexible material.* **2.** capable of being changed, rearranged, altered, etc.: *Our plans are quite flexible.* **3.** easily yielding or influenced: *a flexible personality.* —**flex′i·bil′i·ty,** *n.* —**flex′i·bly,** *adv.*

Fleur-de-lis
on French
coat of arms

flick (flik), *n.* **1.** a sudden, light blow or stroke, as with a whip or finger. **2.** the snapping sound made by such a blow or stroke. **3.** a light, quick movement: *a flick of the wrist.* —*v.* **4.** to strike lightly with a whip, finger, etc. **5.** to remove with such a stroke: *to flick dust from one's coat.*

flick·er[1] (flik′ər), *v.* **1.** to burn unsteadily; shine with a wavering light: *a candle flickering in the wind.* **2.** to move to and fro lightly and quickly: *flickering shadows of the leaves.* —*n.* **3.** an unsteady flame or light: *the flicker of a candle.* **4.** a flickering movement. **5.** a brief appearance: *a flicker of annoyance; a flicker of hope.* [from the Old English word *flicorian* "to flutter"] —**flick′er·ing·ly,** *adv.*

flick·er[2] (flik′ər), *n.* any of several large American woodpeckers whose wings and tail are brightly marked with yellow or red. [imitative of its cry]

flied (flīd), *v.* a past tense and past participle of **fly**[1], used in baseball.

fli·er (flī′ər), *n.* **1.** something that flies, as a bird or insect. **2.** an aviator. **3.** a person or thing that moves with great speed: *This train is a flier.* Also, **flyer.**

flies (flīz), *n.* **1.** the plural of **fly**[1] and **fly**[2]. —*v.* **2.** the third person singular, present tense of **fly**[1].

flight[1] (flīt), *n.* **1.** the act, manner, or power of flying: *birds in flight.* **2.** the distance covered by a bird, airplane, bullet, etc.: *a 500-mile flight.* **3.** a number of beings or things flying together: *a flight of ducks.* **4.** a trip by airplane, glider, etc. **5.** swift movement: *the flight of time.* **6.** a passing beyond ordinary limits: *a flight of the imagination.* **7.** a number of stairs between landings or floors: *to walk up three flights.* [from the Old English word *flyht,* which is related to *flēogan* "to fly"]

flight² (flīt), *n.* 1. the act of fleeing; a hasty departure. 2. **put to flight,** to make (someone) run away; cause to flee: *My shouts put the burglar to flight.* 3. **take flight,** to run away from something; retreat; flee: *The animals took flight when the forest fire broke out.* [from a Middle English word, which is related to Old English *flēon* "to flee"]

flight·less (flīt′lis), *adj.* incapable of flying: *The ostrich and the kiwi are flightless birds.*

flight·y (flī′tē), *adj.,* **flight·i·er, flight·i·est.** changing quickly from one mood, interest, etc., to another; frivolous; irresponsible. —**flight′i·ness,** *n.*

flim·sy (flim′zē), *adj.,* **flim·si·er, flim·si·est.** 1. without strength or soundness: *flimsy cloth.* 2. weak and inadequate: *a flimsy excuse.* —**flim′si·ness,** *n.*

flinch (flinch), *v.* 1. to draw back or shrink from what is difficult, dangerous, or unpleasant: *to flinch at the thought of a hard task.* 2. to wince. —*n.* 3. the act of flinching: *a flinch of pain.*

fling (fling), *v.,* **flung** (flung), **fling·ing.** 1. to throw, cast, or hurl with force or violence: *He flung the darts at the target.* 2. to move with haste or violence: *She flung herself angrily out of the house.* 3. to speak harshly and violently (usually fol. by *out*): *He flung out against his enemies.* —*n.* 4. the act of flinging. 5. a brief time during which one seeks unrestrained enjoyment: *to have a fling before school begins.* 6. Also, **Highland fling.** a lively Scottish dance calling for flinging movements of the arms and legs.

flint (flint), *n.* a hard stone chipped into arrowheads by the American Indians, struck against steel to make a spark for lighting fires, and ground to a powder for use as an abrasive. —**flint′like′,** *adj.*

Flint (flint), *n.* a city in SE Michigan.

flint·lock (flint′lok′), *n.* 1. a gunlock in which a piece of flint in the hammer strikes against a steel plate and sends off sparks that ignite the gunpowder. 2. an old-fashioned gun with such a lock.

flint·y (flin′tē), *adj.,* **flint·i·er, flint·i·est.** 1. made of, containing, or like flint. 2. cruel or unmerciful: *a flinty heart.* —**flint′i·ness,** *n.*

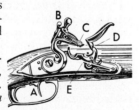

Flintlock
A, Trigger; B, Hammer;
C, Piece of flint;
D, Steel struck by flint;
E, Powder pan

flip (flip), *v.,* **flipped, flip·ping.** 1. to toss or flick, as with a snap of a finger and thumb: *to flip a coin.* 2. to make a flicking movement; snap: *He flipped at the dust on his lapel.* 3. to turn rapidly over: *to flip pages in a book; to flip in a somersault.* —*n.* 4. a flipping motion; tap; flick.

flip·pant (flip′ənt), *adj.* frivolous at a time when respectfulness or seriousness is called for. —**flip′pan·cy,** *n.* —**flip′pant·ly,** *adv.*

flip·per (flip′ər), *n.* 1. a broad, flat limb, esp. one adapted for swimming like those of a seal or whale. 2. Usually, **flippers.** Also, **fins.** a pair of rubber devices resembling the webbed feet of a duck, worn on one's feet to make swimming easier.

flirt (flûrt), *v.* 1. to make love lightly or playfully, esp. with looks: *He flirts with all the girls.* 2. to play or toy: *He flirted with the idea of buying a new bicycle.* —*n.* 3. a person who likes to flirt.

flir·ta·tion (flûr tā′shən), *n.* 1. the act of flirting. 2. a love affair that is not serious.

flir·ta·tious (flûr tā′shəs), *adj.* 1. having the habit of flirting. 2. characterized by flirting: *flirtatious behavior.* —**flir·ta′tious·ly,** *adv.*

flit (flit), *v.,* **flit·ted, flit·ting.** 1. to move lightly and swiftly; fly, dart, or skim along: *a bird flitting from tree to tree.* 2. to pass away quickly, as time. —*n.* 3. a light, quick movement; flutter.

float (flōt), *v.* 1. to rest on the surface of a liquid: *A cork will float.* 2. to cause to float: *to float a boat.* 3. to move gently on the surface of a liquid; drift along: *The boat floated downstream.* 4. to rest or move in a liquid, the air, etc.: *clouds floating in the sky.* 5. to move lightly or gracefully: *She floated downstairs.* 6. to get going or get started: *to float a new business.* —*n.* 7. something that floats, such as a raft. 8. a vehicle bearing a display, as in a parade.

flock (flok), *n.* 1. a number of animals of one kind keeping, feeding, or herded together, as sheep, goats, or birds. 2. a large number of people; crowd: *a flock of visitors.* —*v.* 3. to gather or go in a flock or crowd: *They flocked into the room.*

floe (flō), *n.* a large sheet of floating ice.

flog (flog, flôg), *v.,* **flogged, flog·ging.** to beat with a whip.

flood (flud), *n.* 1. a great flowing or overflowing of water. 2. **the Flood,** (in the Bible) the flood that covered the earth in the time of Noah. 3. any great outpouring or stream: *a flood of words.* 4. the flowing in of the tide (opposite of *ebb*). —*v.* 5. to fill to overflowing or cover with water or another liquid: *to flood a bathtub; a rain that flooded the fields.* 6. to fill completely or overwhelm: *to flood a road with cars; to flood someone with requests.*

flood·gate (flud′gāt′), *n.* 1. a gate designed to control the flow of water, as in a river, canal, etc. 2. anything that controls or regulates.

flood·light (flud′līt′), *n.* 1. a lamp that sends out a broad beam of light over a large area. 2. the beam of light from this lamp. —*v.,* **flood·light·ed** *or* **flood·lit** (flud′lit′); **flood·light·ing.** 3. to light with a floodlight: *to floodlight a stage.*

flood′ tide′, the tide that flows in from the sea toward the shore (opposite of *ebb tide*).

floor (flôr), *n.* 1. the part of a room that forms its lower surface and upon which one walks. 2. a story of a building: *We live on the second floor.* 3. the lower surface of anything: *the floor of the ocean.* 4. the part of an assembly hall where members sit and from which they speak: *the floor of a legislature.* 5. the right to speak, as at a club meeting: *He asked the chairman for the floor.* —*v.* 6. to cover or furnish with a floor: *to floor a room.* 7. to knock down: *The fighter floored his opponent.* 8. *Informal.* to confuse, bewilder, etc.: *The problem in division floored me.*

floor·ing (flôr′ing), *n.* 1. a floor or floors. 2. material for making floors: *oak flooring.*

floor·walk·er (flôr′wô′kər), *n.* a person employed, esp. in a department store, to direct customers, supervise employees, etc.

flop (flop), *v.,* **flopped, flop·ping.** 1. to move around in a heavy, clumsy manner: *The fish was flopping in the boat.* 2. to drop or fall heavily or noisily: *He flopped into a chair.* 3. to flap clumsily and heavily: *The buzzard flopped his wings.* 4. *Informal.* to fail; be unsuccessful: *The show flopped on Broadway.* —*n.* 5. the act or sound of flopping. 6. *Informal.* a failure: *The business was a flop.*

flop·py (flop′ē), *adj.,* **flop·pi·er, flop·pi·est.** tending to flop: *a dog with floppy ears.* —**flop′pi·ness,** *n.*

flo·ra (flôr′ə), *n.* the flowers, trees, and other plants of a particular place or time. See also **fauna.**

flo·ral (flôr′əl), *adj.* referring to or consisting of flowers: *a floral wreath; floral beauty.*

Flor·ence (flôr′əns, flor′əns), *n.* a city in central Italy: center of the Italian Renaissance.

flor·id (flôr′id, flor′id), *adj.* 1. reddish, ruddy, or rosy: *a florid complexion.* 2. too elaborate; showy; flowery: *a florid speech full of exaggerations.*

Flor·i·da (flôr′i də, flor′i də), *n.* a state in the SE United States. 58,560 sq. mi. *Cap.:* Tallahassee.

flor·in (flôr′in, flor′in), *n.* 1. any of various gold or silver coins used at different times in Europe. 2. a former British silver coin worth two shillings.

flo·rist (flôr′ist, flor′ist), *n.* a seller of flowers, plants, etc.

floss (flôs, flos), *n.* 1. the silky fibers of certain plants, such as the milkweed. 2. strands of untwisted silk used in embroidery. 3. Also, **dental floss.** a waxed thread used for cleaning the spaces between the teeth.

floss·y (flô′sē, flos′ē), *adj.,* **floss·i·er, floss·i·est.** 1. made of or resembling floss. 2. *Slang.* stylish or showy: *a flossy dress.*

flo·til·la (flō til′ə), *n.* 1. a small fleet. 2. a fleet of small ships: *a flotilla of yachts.*

flot·sam (flot′səm), *n.* the wreckage or cargo of a ship found floating on the water. See also **jetsam.**

flounce¹ (flouns), *v.,* **flounced, flounc·ing.** 1. to go with impatient or angry movements of the body: *She threw down the book and flounced from the room.* —*n.* 2. the act of flouncing. [from Scandinavian]

flounce² (flouns), *n.* 1. a strip of material wider than a ruffle, gathered and sewn at one edge to a woman's skirt, sleeve, etc.: *to lengthen a skirt with a flounce.* —*v.,* **flounced, flounc·ing.** 2. to trim with a flounce or flounces. [another form of the older word *frounce* "to pleat, curl," which comes from Old French *froncier* "to wrinkle, fold"]

floun·der¹ (floun′dər), *v.* 1. to struggle with stumbling, clumsy movements: *to flounder in mud.* 2. to struggle clumsily in embarrassment and confusion: *He floundered for an excuse.* —*n.* 3. the action of floundering; a floundering movement. [perhaps a blend of *flounce¹* + *founder²*] —**floun′der·ing·ly,** *adv.*

floun·der² (floun′dər), *n., pl.* **floun·ders** or **flounder.** any of many kinds of flatfishes used for food. [from an Old French word, which comes from Scandinavian]

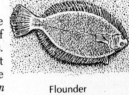

Flounder
(length 1½ ft.)

flour (flour), *n.* 1. the finely ground meal of wheat and other grains. —*v.* 2. to sprinkle or coat with flour, as food to be cooked: *to flour chicken before frying.* [from a Middle English word meaning literally "flower." Flour was so called because it was made from the finest part of the meal] —**flour′y,** *adj.*

flour·ish (flûr′ish, flur′ish), *v.* 1. to thrive or prosper: *a business that flourishes.* 2. to grow well, as plants: *Vegetables flourish in this soil.* 3. to wave about in the air: *to flourish swords and guns.* —*n.* 4. a waving about, as a sword, stick, etc. 5. a showy display in doing something. 6. a decoration in handwriting, as a curve, loop, or the like. 7. an elaborate passage in music: *a flourish of trumpets.*

flout (flout), *v.* to treat with scorn or contempt; mock; scoff at: *to flout rules.* —**flout′er,** *n.*

—**Usage.** See **flaunt.**

flow (flō), *v.* 1. to move along in a stream, as water or other liquid. 2. to come forth from a source: *Orders flowed from the office.* 3. to come or go smoothly or continuously: *The crowds flowed down the street.* 4. to fall or hang loosely, as hair. 5. to move with grace or ease: *flowing gestures.* 6. to abound in something: *a land flowing with plentiful harvests.* 7. to rise, as the tide (opposite of *ebb*). —*n.* 8. the act, rate, or amount of flowing. 9. any smooth, continuous movement: *a flow of words.* 10. anything that flows or pours out: *a flow of blood.*

act, āble, dâre, ärt; ebb, ēqual; if, īce; hot, ōver, ôrder; oil; bŏŏk; ōōze; out; up, ûrge; ə = a as in *alone;* ᵊ as in *button* (but′ᵊn), *fire* (fīᵊr); chief; shoe; thin; ŧħat; zh as in *measure* (mezh′ər). See full key inside cover.

flow·er (flou′ər), *n.* **1.** the part of a plant that blooms and produces seeds; blossom. Flowers are often brightly colored and sweet-smelling. **2.** a plant grown or admired for its blossoms: *They planted the garden with pansies and other flowers.* **3.** a state of bloom: *The roses were in flower.* **4.** the finest or best state or time: *when knighthood was in flower.* **5.** the best or finest part or group: *the flower of American youth.* —*v.* **6.** to produce flowers, as a plant; blossom; bloom. **7.** to develop fully; mature: *His talent flowered early.*

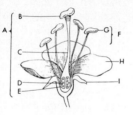

Flower

A, Pistil; B, Stigma;
C, Style; D, Ovule;
E, Ovary; F, Stamen;
G, Anther; H, Petal;
I, Sepal.

flow·ered (flou′ərd), *adj.* **1.** having flowers: *a flowered plant.* **2.** decorated with flowers or a design of flowers: *a flowered tablecloth.*

flow·er·pot (flou′ər pot′), *n.* a container, usually a clay pot, in which to grow plants.

flow·er·y (flou′ə rē), *adj.* **1.** covered with or having many flowers. **2.** decorated with a design of flowers. **3.** full of fancy or elaborate language: *a flowery speech.* —**flow′er·i·ness,** *n.*

flown (flōn), *v.* a past participle of **fly.**

fl. oz., fluid ounce.

flu (flōō), *n.* short for **influenza.**

fluc·tu·ate (fluk′chōō āt′), *v.,* **fluc·tu·at·ed, fluc·tu·at·ing.** to change or vary; rise and fall; move back and forth; waver: *fluctuating prices.* —**fluc′tu·a′tion,** *n.*

flue (flōō), *n.* a passage in a chimney for carrying off smoke.

flu·ent (flōō′ənt), *adj.* **1.** spoken or written with ease: *She speaks fluent French.* **2.** able to speak or write smoothly and easily. **3.** easy; graceful. —**flu′en·cy,** *n.* —**flu′ent·ly,** *adv.*

fluff (fluf), *n.* **1.** bits of light, downy material, as of cotton, feathers, etc. **2.** a soft mass of such material. —*v.* **3.** to make into fluff; shake or puff out into a fluffy mass: *to fluff a pillow.*

fluff·y (fluf′ē), *adj.,* **fluff·i·er, fluff·i·est. 1.** of, resembling, or covered with fluff: *a fluffy pillow.* **2.** light and airy: *a fluffy cake.* —**fluff′i·ness,** *n.*

flu·id (flōō′id), *n.* **1.** any substance, esp. a liquid or a gas, that is capable of flowing. —*adj.* **2.** capable of flowing: *Water is fluid.* **3.** easily changing; not fixed or stable: *Plans for the party are still fluid.* —**flu·id′i·ty,** *n.* —**flu′id·ly,** *adv.*

flu′id dram′, a unit of liquid measure, equal to ⅛ fluid ounce.

flu′id ounce′, a unit of liquid measure, equal to ¹/₁₆ pint, or 1.804 cubic inches (29.573 milliliters). *Abbr.:* fl. oz.

fluke¹ (flōōk), *n.* **1.** the part of an anchor that catches in ground, esp. the triangular point at the end of each arm. **2.** either half of the tail of a whale. [perhaps from a special use of *fluke³*, because of its flat shape]

fluke² (flōōk), *n.* a stroke of good luck: *By a fluke, he had the winning ticket.* [perhaps connected with the English dialect word *fluke* "a guess"]

fluke³ (flōōk), *n.* a large American flounder. [from a Middle English word, which comes from Old English *flōc,* probably from an earlier word meaning "flat"]

flung (flung), *v.* the past tense and past participle of **fling.**

flunk (flungk), *v. Informal.* **1.** to fail, as a student in an examination. **2.** to leave a school because of failing marks (usually fol. by *out*): *to flunk out of college.* **3.** to get a failing mark in: *to flunk arithmetic.* **4.** to give a failing mark to: *His teacher flunked him.*

flun·key (flung′kē), *n., pl.* **flun·keys.** another spelling of **flunky.**

flun·ky (flung′kē), *n., pl.* **flun·kies. 1.** a male servant, such as a footman; lackey. **2.** a meek and fawning follower; toady. Also, **flunkey.**

fluo·res·cence (flōō res′əns), *n.* **1.** the giving off of light when exposed to such invisible radiation as x-rays or ultraviolet rays. **2.** the light given off.

fluo·res·cent (flōō res′ənt), *adj.* capable of fluorescence: *fluorescent paint.*

fluores′cent lamp′, an electric lamp consisting of a gas-filled tube coated on the inside with a fluorescent powder that glows when an electric current passes through the gas.

fluor·i·date (flōōr′i dāt′), *v.,* **fluor·i·dat·ed, fluor·i·dat·ing.** to treat with fluorine or its compounds, esp. to treat water with fluorine compounds to help prevent tooth decay. —**fluor′i·da′tion,** *n.*

fluor·ide (flōōr′īd), *n.* a chemical compound containing fluorine and, usually, only one other element.

fluor·ine (flōōr′ēn), *n.* a pale-yellow, highly corrosive, poisonous gas: the most highly reactive of all nonmetallic chemical elements. *Symbol:* F

fluor·o·scope (flōōr′ə skōp′), *n.* a device for examining x-ray images on a fluorescent screen.

flur·ry (flûr′ē, flur′ē), *n., pl.* **flur·ries. 1.** a sudden, light snowfall. **2.** a sudden gust of wind. **3.** sudden excitement, commotion, or confusion: *His unexpected visit caused a flurry.*

flush¹ (flush), *n.* **1.** a blush: *a flush of pleasure.* **2.** a rushing flow, as of water. **3.** a sudden rise of feeling: *a flush of anger.* **4.** glowing freshness and strength: *the flush of youth.* —*v.* **5.** to blush or cause to blush. **6.** to flood or wash out with a sudden rush of water: *to flush a toilet.* **7.** to excite: *The players were flushed with victory.* [from a blend of *flash* + *gush,* and in some senses also blended with *blush*]

flush² (flush), *adj.* **1.** even or level, as with a surface: *a fireplace flush with the wall.* **2.** having direct contact; touching: *a table flush against the wall.* **3.** well supplied, as with money. — *adv.* **4.** on the same level; in a straight line: *The door shuts flush with the wall.* **5.** in direct contact; squarely: *set flush against the edge.* [perhaps from a special use of *flush¹*]

flus·ter (flus′tər), *v.* **1.** to make or become nervous or excited: *to be flustered by an unexpected visitor.* —*n.* **2.** nervous excitement; confusion; flutter.

flute (floot), *n.* **1.** a musical wind instrument consisting of a straight tube with finger holes and played by blowing across a hole near one end of the tube. **2.** a groove or furrow, as one running from the top to the bottom of a column. —*v.,* **flut·ed, flut·ing. 3.** to play on a flute. **4.** to make flutelike sounds. **5.** to make grooves or furrows in.

Flute

flut·ed (floo′tid), *adj.* decorated with flutes: *a fluted column.*

flut·ing (floo′ting), *n.* **1.** the act of playing on a flute. **2.** grooves or furrows, as on a column.

flut·ist (floo′tist), *n.* a person who plays the flute.

flut·ter (flut′ər), *v.* **1.** to wave or cause to wave in the air; toss about; flap: *flags fluttering in the breeze.* **2.** (of a bird) to flap the wings or fly: *sparrows fluttering in the trees.* **3.** to cause (the wings) to flap. **4.** to beat rapidly, as the heart. —*n.* **5.** a fluttering movement: *the flutter of wings.* **6.** a state of nervous excitement or confusion: *The proposal of marriage put her in a flutter.*

flux (fluks), *n.* **1.** a flowing or flow. **2.** continuous change or movement: *His feelings are always in a flux.* **3.** an abnormal discharge of fluid from the body. **4.** a substance, such as borax, used in the melting or soldering of metals.

fly[1] (flī), *v.,* **flew** (floo) *or,* for def. 9, **flied** (flīd); **flown** (flōn); **fly·ing. 1.** to move through the air on wings, as a bird. **2.** to move or cause to move through the air by any means or force: *to fly a kite; bullets flying to a target.* **3.** to float in the air: *flags flying in the breeze.* **4.** to hoist or display in the air, as a flag: *The ship was flying the Japanese flag.* **5.** to travel through the air in an airplane, rocket, etc. **6.** to operate (an aircraft). **7.** to move suddenly or quickly: *How time flies!* **8.** to flee: *to fly from an enemy.* **9.** (in baseball) to hit a fly ball: *He flied to left field.* —*n., pl.* **flies. 10.** a fold of material along one edge of a garment opening for hiding buttons, zippers, etc., esp. on a man's trousers. **11.** a flap forming the door of a tent. **12.** a fly ball. **13. fly at** (or **into**), to attack verbally or physically: *He flew at us for being late.* **14. fly out,** (in baseball) to be put out by hitting a fly ball that is caught by a player of the opposing team. **15. let fly,** to hurl (a weapon): *The soldiers let fly with a swarm of arrows.* **16. on the fly,** hurriedly; without pausing or stopping: *to eat lunch on the fly.* [from the Old English word *flēogan*]

fly[2] (flī), *n., pl.* **flies. 1.** any of a large number of insects having two wings, such as the common housefly. **2.** any of various other flying insects, such as the firefly. **3.** a fishhook adorned with feathers, hair, etc., so as to resemble a fly, used by fishermen as a lure or bait. **4. fly in the ointment,** something that detracts from one's complete enjoyment; drawback: *The only fly*

Fly used in fishing

in the ointment is that I have to be home early. [from the Old English word *flēoge*]

fly′ ball′, (in baseball) a ball that is batted high over the field.

fly·catch·er (flī′kach′ər), *n.* any of numerous small birds that feed on insects caught in flight.

fly·er (flī′ər), *n.* another spelling of **flier.**

fly·ing (flī′ing), *adj.* **1.** that flies; making flight or passing through the air: *a flying insect; a flying ball.* **2.** floating or fluttering in the air: *flying banners.* **3.** swift: *a flying express train.* **4.** brief: *a flying visit to a neighbor.* —*n.* **5.** the act of moving through the air on wings; flight: *Flying always makes her ill.*

fly′ing boat′, an aircraft whose main body consists of a single hull or boat.

fly′ing fish′, any of several fishes having very large, winglike fins that enable them to glide considerable distances after leaping out of the water.

fly′ing sau′cer, any of various disk-shaped objects said to have been seen flying at high speeds and thought by some to come from outer space.

fly′ing squir′rel, a small rodent resembling a squirrel but having webs of skin between its front and back legs that permit it to take long, gliding leaps.

Flying fish
(length 1½ ft.)

fly·leaf (flī′lēf′), *n., pl.* **fly·leaves** (flī′lēvz′). a blank leaf in the front or the back of a book.

fly·pa·per (flī′pā′pər), *n.* sticky, often poisonous paper, used to trap and kill flies.

fly·speck (flī′spek′), *n.* **1.** a tiny spot or stain left by a fly. **2.** any speck or tiny spot. —*v.* **3.** to mark with flyspecks.

fly′ swat′ter, a device for killing flies, usually a piece of wire mesh attached to a long handle.

fly·wheel (flī′hwēl′, -wēl′), *n.* a heavy wheel attached to a shaft to keep it turning, esp. at a nearly constant speed.

FM, frequency modulation.

Fm, *Chem.* the symbol for **fermium.**

foal (fōl), *n.* **1.** a young horse or related animal, esp. one less than a year old. —*v.* **2.** to give birth to a foal.

foam (fōm), *n.* **1.** a mass of tiny bubbles formed on the surface of a liquid by shaking, fermentation, etc.: *the foam on a glass of soda.* —*v.* **2.** to make foam; become foamy.

foam′ rub′ber, a light, spongy rubber, used for mattresses, cushions, etc.

foam·y (fō′mē), *adj.,* **foam·i·er, foam·i·est. 1.** covered with or full of foam: *foamy waves.* **2.** made of foam: *a foamy crest.* **3.** resembling foam: *a light, foamy dessert.* —**foam′i·ness,** *n.*

fob (fob), *n.* **1.** a short chain or ribbon attached to a watch and worn hanging from a pocket. **2.** a watch pocket just below the waistline in trousers.

act, āble, dâre, ärt; ebb, ēqual; if, īce; hot, ōver, ôrder; oil; boŏk; ōōze; out; up, ûrge; ə = a as in alone; ə as in button (but′ən), fire (fī′r); chief; shoe; thin; that; zh as in measure (mezh′ər). See full key inside cover.

fo·cal (fō′kəl), *adj.* of or concerning a focus. —**fo′cal·ly,** *adv.*

fo·ci (fō′sī), *n.* a plural of **focus.**

fo·cus (fō′kəs), *n., pl.* **fo·cus·es** or **fo·ci** (fō′sī). 1. a point where rays of light meet after being reflected by a curved mirror or refracted by a lens. 2. the position of an object or the adjustment of an optical device required to yield a clear image: *in focus; out of focus.* 3. any point of attraction, interest, etc.: *She was the focus of attention at the party.* —*v.,* **fo·cused** or **fo·cussed; fo·cus·ing** or **fo·cus·sing.** 4. to concentrate (rays of light, sound waves, etc.) at a single point. 5. to bring (a camera, telescope, etc.) into focus. [from a Latin word meaning "fireplace"]

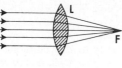

L, Lens; F, Focus

fod·der (fod′ər), *n.* coarse food for cattle, horses, etc.: *Hay is a common fodder.*

foe (fō), *n.* an enemy; adversary; opponent.

fog (fog, fôg), *n.* 1. a cloudlike layer of water droplets at the earth's surface; heavy mist. 2. a state of being bewildered, dazed, etc.: *His mind was in a fog from lack of sleep.* —*v.,* **fogged, fog·ging.** 3. to make or become covered with fog: *All day the harbor was fogged.* 4. to bewilder, daze, etc.: *to fog the mind.*

fog·gy (fog′ē, fô′gē), *adj.,* **fog·gi·er, fog·gi·est.** 1. thick with or having much fog: *a foggy day.* 2. confused or unclear; vague: *foggy thinking.* —**fog′gi·ness,** *n.*

fog·horn (fog′hôrn′, fôg′-), *n.* a deep, loud horn for sounding warning signals to ships in foggy weather.

fo·gy (fō′gē), *n., pl.* **fo·gies.** a dull, old-fashioned person: *an old fogy.*

foi·ble (foi′bəl), *n.* a minor fault or failing in one's character.

foil[1] (foil), *v.* to prevent the success of; frustrate; defeat: *Loyal troops foiled the revolt.* [from the Middle English word *foilen* "to trample," which comes from Old French *fouler.* The present meaning came from the habit of some game animals of trampling the earth to hide their tracks]

foil[2] (foil), *n.* 1. metal in the form of very thin sheets: *aluminum foil.* 2. a person or thing that makes another seem better, more beautiful, etc., by contrast: *The dark carpet is a perfect foil for the light furniture.* [from an Old French word, which comes from Latin *folium* "leaf"]

foil[3] (foil), *n.* a long, narrow, flexible sword having a blunt point to prevent injury, used in fencing. [perhaps from a special use of *foil*[1]]

foist (foist), *v.* to force upon, pass off, or sell, as something poor or worthless, by using trickery (usually fol. by *on* or *upon*): *He tried to foist the old chair on us by calling it an antique.*

fol., 1. followed. 2. following.

fold[1] (fōld), *v.* 1. to bend (cloth, paper, etc.) over upon itself: *to fold a letter.* 2. to be folded or be capable of folding: *Tissue paper folds easily.* 3. to cross or clasp together (the arms, hands, etc.). 4. to clasp

or embrace; enfold. 5. to bring (the wings) close to the body, as a bird. 6. to enclose or wrap: *to fold a sandwich in paper.* —*n.* 7. a part that is folded; pleat; layer: *to wrap something in folds of cloth.* 8. a crease made by folding: *Cut the paper along the fold.* [from the Old English word *faldan*]

fold[2] (fōld), *n.* 1. a pen for sheep. 2. a church, or its members. [from the Old English word *fald*]

-fold, a suffix used to form 1. adjectives meaning **a.** multiplied by: *a tenfold increase.* **b.** made up of so many parts: *a threefold plan.* 2. adverbs meaning a certain number of times: *He was rewarded tenfold.*

fold·er (fōl′dər), *n.* 1. a person or thing that folds. 2. a printed sheet, as a timetable, folded into a number of sections. 3. a folded sheet of light cardboard used to hold papers, letters, etc.

fo·li·age (fō′lē ij), *n.* the leaves of a plant or tree, considered all together.

folk (fōk), *n.* 1. Usually, **folks.** people in general: *Folks say there wasn't much rain last summer.* 2. Often, **folks.** people of a class or group: *poor folk; town folks.* 3. **folks,** *Informal.* one's family and close relations: *Give my best to your folks.* —*adj.* 4. having an unknown origin and reflecting the ways of a people: *folk art by unknown painters.*

folk′ dance′, 1. a dance originated and handed down by the people. 2. music for such a dance.

folk·lore (fōk′lôr′), *n.* the beliefs, legends, customs, etc., of a people.

folk′ mu′sic, 1. songs, ballads, or the like, whose composers are usually unknown, and which have been handed down for several generations without being written out. 2. music by a known composer that is written in this style.

folk′ song′, a song belonging to folk music.

folk·sy (fōk′sē), *adj.,* **folk·si·er, folk·si·est.** extremely sociable or neighborly: *People like the Senator's folksy manner.* —**folk′si·ness,** *n.*

folk′ tale′, a tale having no particular author, handed down by the people.

fol·li·cle (fol′i kəl), *n.* a small cavity, sac, or gland, for example the cavity surrounding the root of a hair. See illus. at **hair.**

fol·low (fol′ō), *v.* 1. to come after: *Spring follows winter.* 2. to come after as a result; result from: *peace that follows victory.* 3. to accept as a guide or leader: *The children followed the teacher.* 4. to obey; act according to: *Follow my advice.* 5. to go or come behind a person or thing in motion: *Go on ahead, and I'll follow.* 6. to move forward along: *to follow a path.* 7. to take as one's work: *He followed the law.* 8. to keep up with: *to follow the news.* 9. to keep the mind on and understand: *Do you follow what I am saying?* 10. **follow through,** to keep working at something until it is completed: *That was a great idea, but you never followed through on it.* 11. **follow up,** to strengthen the effect of (an action) with additional action: *The doctor followed up his treatment with regular visits.*

fol·low·er (fol′ō ər), *n.* 1. a person or thing that follows. 2. a person who follows another in his ideas, teachings, beliefs, etc.; disciple: *a writer with many followers.* **3.** a servant or attendant.

fol·low·ing (fol′ō ing), *n.* **1.** a group of followers. **2.** a group of admirers, fans, etc.: *That television show has a large following.* —*adj.* **3.** coming after or next: *the following day.* **4.** that follows or moves in the same direction: *the following wind.* **5. the following,** the one or ones that follow or come next: *The following have passed the final exam.*

fol·ly (fol′ē), *n., pl.* for def. 2 **fol·lies.** **1.** the state of being foolish; foolishness. **2.** a foolish action, practice, etc.: *the folly of skating on thin ice.*

fo·ment (fō ment′), *v.* to stir up or excite (trouble, a quarrel, etc.). —**fo·ment′er,** *n.*

fond (fond), *adj.* **1.** having a liking for (usually fol. by *of*): *to be fond of animals.* **2.** loving or affectionate: *a fond look.* **3.** doting; too tender: *to be spoiled by fond parents.* **4.** cherished without good reason: *fond hopes of becoming rich.* —**fond′ly,** *adv.*

fon·dle (fon′dəl), *v.,* **fon·dled, fon·dling.** to handle or touch lovingly; caress.

fond·ness (fond′nis), *n.* **1.** tenderness or affection. **2.** a liking or weakness for something: *a fondness for candy.*

font (font), *n.* **1.** a basin for the water used in baptism. **2.** a basin for holy water.

food (food), *n.* **1.** anything that is taken in by plants, animals, or human beings to provide nourishment: *Most plants draw food from the soil. Milk is a valuable food.* **2.** more or less solid nourishment: *to provide someone with food and drink.* **3.** anything that aids growth: *food for thought.*

Font (def. 1)

food·stuff (food′stuf′), *n.* any substance that can be used as food: *Hay is foodstuff for cattle.*

fool (fool), *n.* **1.** a silly or stupid person: *Only fools would argue that the earth is flat.* **2.** a person who has been made to appear silly and stupid: *He tried to make a fool of me in front of everyone.* **3.** a clown or jester once kept for amusement by a king or other high-ranking person. —*v.* **4.** to make a fool of; trick or deceive: *They thought he would give in, but he fooled them.* **5.** to act like a fool; play in a joking or silly way. **6.** to make believe; pretend: *I was only fooling when I said I didn't like you.* **7. fool around,** to waste time: *Stop fooling around and do your homework!* **8. fool with,** to handle or play with aimlessly or carelessly: *Never fool with a loaded gun.*

fool·har·dy (fool′här′dē), *adj.,* **fool·har·di·er, fool·har·di·est.** bold in a foolish way; rash; reckless: *a foolhardy attempt to drive a car without knowing how.* —**fool′har′di·ness,** *n.*

fool·ish (foo′lish), *adj.* lacking caution, good sense, etc.: *a foolish person; a foolish decision.* —**fool′ish·ly,** *adv.* —**fool′ish·ness,** *n.*

fool·proof (fool′proof′), *adj.* **1.** without risk or harm

even when tampered with: *a foolproof machine.* **2.** never-failing: *a foolproof method to get results.*

fools·cap (foolz′kap′), *n.* a size of drawing or printing paper measuring $13\frac{1}{2} \times 17$ inches.

fool's′ gold′, another name for **pyrite.**

foot (foot), *n., pl.* **feet** (fēt). **1.** the part at the end of the leg on which a man or animal walks. **2.** a unit of length originally based on the length of the human foot. There are 12 inches (30.48 centimeters) in a foot and 3 feet in a yard. *Abbr.:* f., ft. **3.** infantry soldiers. **4.** the part of a stocking, boot, etc., that covers the foot. **5.** any part that looks like or has the purpose of a foot: *the feet of a chair.* **6.** the bottom or lower part of anything: *the foot of a hill.* **7.** the bottom part of a bed, where the feet rest. **8.** (in poetry) one of the parts into which a line is divided metrically, consisting of accented and unaccented syllables: *"I wandered lonely as a cloud" has four feet.* —*v.* **9.** to walk; go on foot (usually fol. by *it*): *If the car breaks down, we'll have to foot it.* **10.** *Informal.* to pay: *to foot the bill.* **11. on foot,** by walking, rather than by riding: *We went into town on foot.* **12. put one's foot down,** to use one's authority, esp. to prevent an action: *We were all set to go, but Dad put his foot down.*

foot·ball (foot′bôl′), *n.* **1.** a game in which two teams play against each other, each attempting to carry a ball across a goal line at the opposite end of the opponent's part of the field. **2.** an oval ball used in playing this game. **3.** *British.* rugby or soccer.

-footed, a suffix used to form adjectives meaning **1.** having a certain number of feet: *a four-footed animal.* **2.** having a certain kind of feet: *a light-footed dancer.*

foot·fall (foot′fôl′), *n.* **1.** a footstep. **2.** the sound of a footstep.

foot·hill (foot′hil′), *n.* a low hill at the base of a mountain or mountain range: *the foothills of the Alps.*

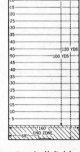

Football field

foot·hold (foot′hōld′), *n.* **1.** a place or support for the feet: *Though steep, the side of the mountain had many footholds.* **2.** a firm position that makes it possible for one to advance in doing something: *to gain a foothold in one's profession.*

foot·ing (foot′ing), *n.* **1.** a firm placing of the feet; stability: *He lost his footing and slipped in the mud.* **2.** a place or support for the feet; foothold. **3.** the way something is arranged, set up, etc.: *The new business is on a good footing.* **4.** the position one occupies in a group, society, etc.: *to be on a good footing with one's neighbors.*

foot·lights (foot′līts′), *n.pl.* a row of lights along the floor at the front of a stage.

foot·man (foot′mən), *n., pl.* **foot·men.** a servant, usually in uniform, who answers the door, waits on table, etc.

foot·note (foŏt′nōt′), *n.* a comment or explanatory note at the bottom of a page.

foot·path (foŏt′path′), *n., pl.* **foot·paths** (foŏt′pathz′, -paths′). a path for pedestrians.

foot·pound (foŏt′pound′), *n.* a unit of work or energy equal to the amount of work done in raising a one-pound weight a distance of one foot.

foot·print (foŏt′print′), *n.* a mark left by the foot, bare or shod, in sand, mud, snow, etc.

foot·sore (foŏt′sôr′), *adj.* having sore or tender feet, as from walking too much.

foot·step (foŏt′step′), *n.* 1. a step made in walking, or the sound of this; footfall; tread. 2. the distance covered by a step in walking; pace: *He stood a few footsteps away.* 3. a footprint.

foot·stool (foŏt′stool′), *n.* a low stool upon which to rest one's feet while seated.

foot·work (foŏt′wûrk′), *n.* a way of using the feet, as in tennis, boxing, dancing, etc.: *the expert footwork of a ballerina.*

fop (fop), *n.* a man who is very vain about the way he dresses and looks; dandy. —**fop′pish,** *adj.*

for (fôr), *prep.* 1. with the purpose of: *to run for exercise.* 2. meant to belong to or be used in connection with: *a closet for dishes.* 3. suiting the purpose or needs of: *food for babies.* 4. in order to gain or have: *to work for money.* 5. appreciating or responsive to: *an eye for beauty.* 6. fixed or centered upon: *a longing for freedom.* 7. in payment of: *to be rewarded for one's efforts.* 8. with regard or respect to: *It's warm for April.* 9. during or throughout: *to be away for the summer.* 10. in favor of: *Which team are you for?* 11. on behalf of: *to act for a friend.* 12. in place of; instead of: *a substitute for butter.* 13. in order to reach, find, or obtain: *to search for one's hat.* 14. in order to save: *to flee for one's life.* 15. as being: *Don't take me for a fool.* 16. because of: *a city famed for its beauty.* 17. in spite of: *For all his faults, I like him.* 18. to the distance or amount of: *to walk for a mile.* 19. to take place or happen in or on: *an appointment for the afternoon.* 20. assigned or appointed to: *time for work.* —*conj.* 21. since; because: *Eat, for you are hungry.* 22. O, for! if only I could have!: *O, for a place to rest my weary feet!*

for·age (fôr′ij, for′ij), *n.* 1. food for horses or cattle. —*v.,* **for·aged, for·ag·ing.** 2. to search for forage or any food. 3. to search about; rummage: *to forage in a desk for pennies.* 4. to strip of food, supplies, etc.; plunder: *soldiers foraging a town.* 5. to obtain by foraging: *to forage a dinner.* —**for′ag·er,** *n.*

for·ay (fôr′ā), *n.* 1. a quick raid or attack, esp. to plunder something. —*v.* 2. to make a foray: *to foray into enemy territory.*

for·bade (fôr bad′), *v.* the past tense of **forbid.**

for·bear¹ (fôr bâr′), *v.,* **for·bore** (fôr bôr′), **for·borne** (fôr bôrn′), **for·bear·ing.** 1. to hold oneself back: *to forbear from saying unkind things.* 2. to control or hold back one's feelings. 3. to refrain from: *He forbore laughing.* [from the Old English word *forberan,* which comes from *for-* "away, off, extremely" + *beran* "to bear, endure"]

for·bear² (fôr′bâr′), *n.* another spelling of **forebear.**

for·bear·ance (fôr bâr′əns), *n.* forbearing action or conduct; endurance; tolerance; indulgence: *to look with forbearance on the mistakes of others.*

for·bid (fôr bid′), *v.,* **for·bade** (fôr bad′), **for·bid·den** (fôr bid′ᵊn), **for·bid·ding.** 1. to order (a person) not to do something: *I forbid you to go without me.* 2. to prohibit; not allow: *to forbid the wearing of lipstick.*

for·bid·den (fôr bid′ᵊn), *v.* 1. the past participle of **forbid.** —*adj.* 2. not allowed: *forbidden words.*

for·bid·ding (fôr bid′ing), *adj.* 1. grim or unfriendly: *a forbidding look.* 2. threatening; dangerous: *forbidding weather.* —**for·bid′ding·ly,** *adv.*

for·bore (fôr bôr′), *v.* the past tense of **forbear¹.**

for·borne (fôr bôrn′), *v.* the past participle of **forbear¹.**

force (fôrs), *n.* 1. strength; energy; power: *a personality of great force.* 2. power to influence, affect, or control: *the force of law and order.* 3. physical strength of a living being: *He shoved with all his force.* 4. physical violence: *The soldiers used force to drive back the crowd.* 5. any group of people working together for the same cause or purpose: *a military force.* 6. a push or a pull that produces a change in the speed or direction of an object's motion. *Symbol:* F —*v.,* **forced, forc·ing.** 7. to drive or oblige (oneself or someone) to do something: *He was forced to admit his mistake.* 8. to drive or propel with strength: *They forced air into his lungs.* 9. to bring about by using force: *to force acceptance.* 10. to break open: *to force a lock.* 11. to impose upon: *He forced himself upon them.* 12. **in force,** in effect; in operation: *That rule is no longer in force.*

forced (fôrst), *adj.* 1. done because of necessity or without choice: *a forced landing; forced labor.* 2. not natural or easy; strained: *forced smiles; forced gaiety.*

force·ful (fôrs′fəl), *adj.* full of force; powerful: *a forceful push.* —**force′ful·ly,** *adv.* —**force′ful·ness,** *n.*

for·ceps (fôr′səps, fôr′seps), *n., pl.* **for·ceps.** a pair of tweezers, pincers, or tongs for seizing and holding something, esp. in surgical operations.

for·ci·ble (fôr′sə bəl), *adj.* 1. carried out by force: *a forcible entry into a house.* 2. having strength; forceful: *a forcible argument.* —**for′ci·bly,** *adv.*

ford (fôrd), *n.* 1. a place where a river or stream is shallow enough to be crossed by wading. —*v.* 2. to cross (a river or stream) by a ford.

Ford (fôrd), *n.* Gerald R., born 1913, 40th Vice President of the U.S. 1973–1974; 38th President of the U.S. 1974–1977.

fore¹ (fôr), *adj.* 1. at or toward the front or beginning: *the fore part of a ship; the fore part of a day.* —*adv.* 2. at or toward the bow of a ship: *to be placed fore of the mast.* — *n.* 3. the front part of anything. 4. **to the fore, a.** to the front or into view. **b.** into prominence: *She came to the fore as a doctor.* [special use of the prefix *fore-,* from Old English]

fore² (fôr), *interj.* (used as a shout of warning to persons on a golf course who are in danger of being hit by a ball.) [probably short for *before*]

fore-, a prefix meaning 1. before or earlier: *forenoon;*

forefather. **2.** beforehand or in advance: *foretell; forewarn.* **3.** superior in rank: *foreman.* **4.** at or near the front: *foremast; forelock.* **5.** the front part of: *forearm.*

fore-and-aft (fôr′ənd aft′), *adv.* lengthwise on a ship; from stem to stern.

fore-arm (fôr′ärm′), *n.* the part of the arm between the elbow and the wrist.

fore-bear (fôr′bâr′), *n.* an ancestor: *His forebears came here from Germany.* Also, **forbear.**

fore-bode (fôr bōd′), *v.,* **fore-bod-ed, fore-bod-ing.** to be an omen of; indicate beforehand: *clouds that forebode a storm.*

fore-bod-ing (fôr bō′ding), *n.* a feeling or sign of something evil, dangerous, etc., about to happen: *a foreboding of war; a foreboding of illness.*

fore-cast (fôr′kast′), *v.,* **fore-cast** or **fore-cast-ed; fore-cast-ing.** **1.** to try to tell ahead of time; predict: *to forecast the weather.* —*n.* **2.** a prediction: *a weather forecast.* —**fore′cast′er,** *n.*

fore-cas-tle (fōk′səl, fôr′kas′əl), *n.* **1.** the part of the upper deck of a ship before the forward mast. **2.** quarters for the crew in this part of a ship.

F, Forecastle

fore-close (fôr klōz′), *v.,* **fore-closed, fore-clos-ing.** to take away the right to redeem (a mortgage): *The bank foreclosed the mortgage on his house when he could no longer make the payments.* —**fore-clos-ure** (fôr klō′zhər), *n.*

fore-fa-ther (fôr′fä′thər), *n.* an ancestor.

fore-fin-ger (fôr′fing′ər), *n.* the finger next to the thumb. Also, **index finger.**

fore-foot (fôr′foot′), *n., pl.* **fore-feet** (fôr′fēt′). one of the front feet of a four-legged animal, an insect, etc.

fore-front (fôr′frunt′), *n.* the foremost part or place: *in the forefront of the news.*

fore-go[1] (fôr gō′), *v.,* **fore-went** (fôr went′), **fore-gone** (fôr gôn′, -gon′), **fore-go-ing.** to go before; precede.

fore-go[2] (fôr gō′), *v.,* **fore-went** (fôr went′), **fore-gone** (fôr gôn′, -gon′), **fore-go-ing.** another spelling of **forgo.**

fore-go-ing (fôr gō′ing), *adj.* going before; preceding; previous: *the foregoing remarks.*

fore-gone (fôr′gôn′, -gon′), *adj.* **1.** that has gone before. **2.** that could be known or told before: *His election was a foregone conclusion.*

fore-ground (fôr′ground′), *n.* the area or part of a landscape, picture, etc., that is or appears to be in front (opposite of *background*): *Trees stood in the foreground and mountains rose in the background.*

fore-hand (fôr′hand′), *n.* **1.** a stroke in tennis, squash, etc., made with the palm forward and on the same side of the body as that of the hand holding the racket, paddle, etc. —*adj.* **2.** made with such a stroke. —*adv.* **3.** with a forehand stroke: *He hit the ball forehand.*

fore-head (fôr′id, fôr′hed′), *n.* the part of the face above the eyes; brow.

for-eign (fôr′in, for′in), *adj.* **1.** from or belonging to a country that is not one's own: *To Frenchmen, English is a foreign language.* **2.** outside of one's own country: *foreign travel.* **3.** having to do with countries other than one's own: *foreign trade.* **4.** not belonging to the place or body where found: *a speck of foreign matter in the eye.* **5.** not characteristic or natural: *Cruelty is foreign to his nature.*

for-eign-er (fôr′ə nər, for′i nər), *n.* a person who is not native to or a citizen of a given country.

fore-knowl-edge (fôr′nol′ij), *n.* knowledge of a thing before it exists or happens: *He claims he had foreknowledge of the accident.*

fore-leg (fôr′leg′), *n.* one of the front legs of an animal.

fore-lock (fôr′lok′), *n.* a lock of hair growing from the front part of the head, esp. one that falls over the forehead.

fore-man (fôr′mən), *n., pl.* **fore-men.** **1.** a man in charge of a group or division of workers, as in a factory. **2.** the chairman or spokesman of a jury: *The foreman announced the verdict.*

fore-mast (fôr′məst, -mast′), *n.* the mast nearest the bow of a ship.

fore-most (fôr′mōst′), *adj.* first in place, order, rank, etc.: *our foremost statesman.*

fore-noon (fôr′nōon′), *n.* the part of day between sunrise and noon; morning.

fore-run-ner (fôr′run′ər), *n.* **1.** an ancestor; forebear: *our colonial forerunners.* **2.** a sign of something that is about to happen: *Gathering clouds were the forerunners of a storm.*

fore-see (fôr sē′), *v.,* **fore-saw** (fôr sô′), **fore-seen** (fôr sēn′), **fore-see-ing.** to see or know beforehand; expect: *They foresaw a shortage of food and water.* —**fore-see′a-ble,** *adj.*

fore-shad-ow (fôr shad′ō), *v.* to indicate beforehand; be an omen of: *events foreshadowing a war.*

fore-short-en (fôr shôr′t³n), *v.* to draw (lines or a figure) in such a way as to make some parts of a picture seem nearer to the eye than others, imitating the way one sees in real life.

fore-sight (fôr′sīt′), *n.* **1.** the act or power of foreseeing. **2.** careful planning and preparation for the future: *A leader must use foresight in governing.* —**fore′sight′ed,** *adj.* —**fore′sight′ed-ly,** *adv.* —**fore′sight′ed-ness,** *n.*

fore-skin (fôr′skin′), *n.* the fold of skin covering the end of the penis.

for-est (fôr′ist, for′ist), *n.* a large area covered with trees and undergrowth; large woods.

fore-stall (fôr stôl′), *v.* to prevent, hinder, or thwart by acting in advance: *The talks forestalled a war.*

for-est-er (fôr′i stər, for′i stər), *n.* a person who is expert in forestry.

for′est ran′ger, an officer who supervises the care of a forest, esp. a public forest.

for·est·ry (fôr′i strē, for′i strē), *n.* the science of planting and taking care of forests.

fore·taste (fôr′tāst′), *n.* a sample or brief experience of something to come: *The warm weather gave them a foretaste of summer.*

fore·tell (fôr tel′), *v.*, **fore·told** (fôr tōld′), **fore·tell·ing.** to tell of or indicate beforehand; predict or prophesy: *to foretell someone's future.*

fore·thought (fôr′thôt′), *n.* **1.** careful planning; foresight. **2.** a thinking of something beforehand: *He gave forethought to his answers.*

for·ev·er (fôr ev′ər, fər-), *adv.* **1.** eternally; for all time. **2.** continually: *We are forever making mistakes.*

for·ev·er·more (fôr ev′ər môr′, fər-), *adv.* from this moment onward and forever.

fore·went (fôr went′), *v.* the past tense of **forego.**

fore·word (fôr′wûrd′) *n.* a preface or introduction, esp. to a book.

for·feit (fôr′fit), *n.* **1.** a fine or penalty. **2.** the act of forfeiting; forfeiture. —*v.* **3.** to lose as a result of committing a crime, neglect, etc.: *He forfeited his freedom and went to jail.*

for·fei·ture (fôr′fi chər), *n.* **1.** the act of forfeiting. **2.** something that is forfeited.

for·gave (fər gāv′), *v.* the past tense of **forgive.**

forge[1] (fôrj), *n.* **1.** a fireplace, hearth, or furnace in which metal is heated before shaping. **2.** the workshop of a blacksmith; smithy. —*v.*, **forged, forg·ing. 3.** to form (metal) by heating and hammering; beat into shape. **4.** to make an imitation of (handwriting, a painting, etc.) with intent to deceive: *to forge another person's signature.* [from the Old French word *forgier,* which comes from Latin *fabricāre* "to fabricate"] —**forg′er,** *n.*

forge[2] (fôrj), *v.*, **forged, forg·ing.** to move forward slowly but steadily by overcoming difficulties (usually fol. by *ahead*): *to forge ahead with one's work.*

for·ger·y (fôr′jə rē), *n.*, *pl.* **for·ger·ies. 1.** the act of imitating another's handwriting, a painting, etc., with intent to deceive. **2.** something produced by forging: *The signature was a forgery.*

for·get (fər get′), *v.*, **for·got** (fər got′); **for·got·ten** (fər got′ᵊn) *or* **for·got; for·get·ting. 1.** to fail or cease to remember: *I forget phone numbers easily.* **2.** to neglect to do, think of, mention, etc.: *You forgot to bring the tickets.*

for·get·ful (fər get′fəl), *adj.* **1.** apt to forget; forgetting easily. **2.** heedless or neglectful (often fol. by *of*): *to be forgetful of others.* —**for·get′ful·ly,** *adv.* —**for·get′ful·ness,** *n.*

for·get-me-not (fər get′mē not′), *n.* a small plant that bears light-blue flowers often regarded as standing for faithful friendship.

for·give (fər giv′), *v.*, **for·gave** (fər gāv′), **for·giv·en** (fər giv′ən), **for·giv·ing. 1.** to grant pardon to; cease to blame or feel angry with: *I forgive you for your mistakes.* **2.** to pardon or excuse (a fault, mistake, etc.): *It's very hard to forgive cruelty.* **3.** to be forgiving or practice forgiveness: *We must learn to forgive.* —**for·giv′a·ble,** *adj.*

for·give·ness (fər giv′nis), *n.* **1.** the act of forgiving, or the state of being forgiven. **2.** willingness to forgive: *to show forgiveness to one's enemies.*

for·go (fôr gō′), *v.*, **for·went** (fôr went′), **for·gone** (fôr gôn′, -gon′), **for·go·ing.** to give up or do without: *to forgo dessert.* Also, **forego.**

for·got (fər got′), *v.* the past tense and a past participle of **forget.**

for·got·ten (fər got′ᵊn), *v.* a past participle of **forget.**

fork (fôrk), *n.* **1.** an instrument having two or more prongs or tines at the end of a handle, esp. such an instrument used for eating. **2.** a division into branches, as of a road or river. **3.** any of such branches. —*v.* **4.** to pierce, raise, dig, etc., with a fork: *to fork hay.* **5.** to divide into branches: *The town stands where the river forks.* —**fork′like′,** *adj.*

forked (fôrkt, fôr′kid), *adj.* having a fork or forklike branches: *a forked road; forked lightning.*

for·lorn (fôr lôrn′), *adj.* **1.** unhappy or wretched, as from being left alone: *He was forlorn when his friends left.* **2.** deserted or abandoned: *a forlorn little town far from the highway.* —**for·lorn′ly,** *adv.*

form (fôrm), *n.* **1.** shape or outline: *squares, circles, and other forms.* **2.** a body, esp. that of a human being: *a tall form.* **3.** something that gives shape; mold; frame: *a form for wet cement.* **4.** a particular state in which something appears: *water in the form of ice.* **5.** a kind or type: *A tree is a form of plant life.* **6.** order or arrangement in a work of art, piece of writing, musical composition, etc.: *a painting without form.* **7.** a set or customary way of doing something: *a form of religious worship.* **8.** social behavior; manners: *It is bad form to interrupt.* **9.** manner of performing; technique: *She is improving her swimming form.* **10.** fitness or condition: *I hope you are in good form today.* **11.** a sheet of paper having blank spaces to be filled in: *an order form.* **12.** (in grammar) the shape of a word, phrase, or sentence that shows its meaning or function. *Hats* is the plural form of *hat. Went* is the past-tense form of *go.* **13.** a grade or class in British and some American schools: *He is now in the fourth form.* **14.** *British.* a bench or long seat. —*v.* **15.** to make or shape: *to form a box from wood.* **16.** to take shape: *clouds forming in the sky.* **17.** to make up or compose: *The book is formed of ten chapters.*

for·mal (fôr′məl), *adj.* **1.** following usual requirements, customs, etc.: *formal behavior.* **2.** marked by form or ceremony: *The queen's garden parties are formal occasions.* **3.** made or done according to strict rules and regulations: *formal permission.* **4.** requiring the wearing of full dress: *a formal dance.* **5.** elaborately and exactly laid out or arranged: *formal gardens.* **6.** (in grammar) following strict rules of correct usage in speaking or writing, such as avoiding contractions, simplified spellings, slang expressions, etc. —*n.* **7.** a dance, party, etc., that requires full dress. **8.** a woman's gown worn for such a dance, party, etc. —**for′mal·ly,** *adv.*

form·al·de·hyde (fôr mal′də hīd′), *n.* a poisonous gas, which when dissolved in water is used as a preservative and in making plastics.

for·mal·i·ty (fôr mal′i tē), *n., pl.* **for·mal·i·ties.** 1. the condition or quality of being formal; observance of rules; conventionality. 2. a formal act or observance: *the formalities of a wedding.*

for·ma·tion (fôr mā′shən), *n.* 1. the act or process of forming: *the gradual formation of clouds.* 2. the way in which something is formed or arranged: *troops in battle formation.* 3. something formed in a particular way: *an interesting rock formation.*

form·a·tive (fôr′mə tiv), *adj.* 1. giving form or shape: *the formative influence of a teacher.* 2. referring to formation or development: *formative years.*

for·mer (fôr′mər), *adj.* 1. coming before in time; belonging to an earlier time; past: *former years; our former president.* 2. being the first mentioned of two (distinguished from *latter*): *The former statement is true, the latter is false.*

for·mer·ly (fôr′mər lē), *adv.* in time past; once.

for·mi·da·ble (fôr′mi də bəl), *adj.* 1. causing great fear or dread: *The lion is a formidable animal.* 2. extremely difficult or demanding: *a formidable task.* —**for′mi·da·bly,** *adv.*

form·less (fôrm′lis), *adj.* without a definite or clear form; shapeless. —**form′less·ly,** *adv.* —**form′less·ness,** *n.*

For·mo·sa (fôr mō′sə), *n.* another name for **Taiwan.**

for·mu·la (fôr′myə lə), *n.* 1. a mathematical rule or principle, usually expressed in the form of an equation. The formula for the area of a circle is $A = \pi r^2$. 2. the group of symbols that shows how many atoms of different elements make up one molecule of a chemical compound. The formula for water is H_2O, which means that each molecule of water contains two atoms of hydrogen and one atom of oxygen. 3. a recipe or prescription: *a formula for milk fed to babies.* 4. a set of words for use on formal occasions or in formal writing: *"Dear Sir" is a common formula for business letters.* 5. any statement, as of religious belief, to be accepted without question.

for·mu·late (fôr′myə lāt′), *v.,* **for·mu·lat·ed, for·mu·lat·ing.** to express clearly and exactly: *to formulate one's ideas.* —**for′mu·la′tion,** *n.*

for·sake (fôr sāk′), *v.,* **for·sook** (fôr sook′), **for·sak·en** (fôr sā′kən), **for·sak·ing.** to quit or leave completely.

for·sak·en (fôr sā′kən), *v.* 1. the past participle of **forsake.** —*adj.* 2. deserted; abandoned; forlorn: *an old, forsaken barn.*

for·sook (fôr sook′), *v.* the past tense of **forsake.**

for·sooth (fôr sooth′), *adv. Archaic.* in truth; in fact.

for·swear (fôr swâr′), *v.,* **for·swore** (fôr swôr′), **for·sworn** (fôr swôrn′), **for·swear·ing.** 1. to swear solemnly to give up something: *to forswear a bad habit.* 2. to swear falsely about something. 3. to perjure oneself.

for·syth·i·a (fôr sith′ē ə), *n.* a shrub grown for its yellow flowers that blossom in early spring.

fort (fôrt), *n.* a strong fortified place usually surrounded by walls, ditches, etc., used by troops for defense against an enemy.

forte¹ (fôrt), *n.* a strong point; something that one does very well: *Cooking is her forte.* [from the French word *fort* "strong, strong point," which comes from Latin *fortis* "strong"]

for·te² (fôr′tā), *adj., adv.* (in music) loud. *Abbr.:* f [from an Italian word, which comes from Latin *fortis* "strong"]

forth (fôrth), *adv.* 1. forward or onward: *to go forth into the world; from that day forth.* 2. into view or consideration: *to bring forth a reason.*

forth·com·ing (fôrth′kum′ing), *adj.* 1. about to appear or take place: *the forthcoming issue of a magazine.* 2. ready when wanted: *Money from his parents was always forthcoming.*

forth·right (fôrth′rīt′), *adj.* 1. going straight to the point; frank; open; direct: *forthright criticism.* —*adv.* Also, **forth′right′ly.** 2. in a direct or straightforward manner. 3. immediately; at once: *We left forthright.* —**forth′right′ness,** *n.*

forth·with (fôrth′with′), *adv.* immediately; without delay.

for·ti·eth (fôr′tē ith), *adj.* 1. being number forty in a series: *the fortieth floor.* —*n.* 2. one of forty equal parts. 3. a person or thing that is fortieth.

for·ti·fi·ca·tion (fôr′tə fə kā′shən), *n.* 1. the act of fortifying or strengthening. 2. a fortified place, such as a castle, fort, etc. 3. something used in fortifying a place, such as a tower, wall, etc.

for·ti·fy (fôr′tə fī′), *v.,* **for·ti·fied, for·ti·fy·ing.** 1. to strengthen against attack: *to fortify a besieged town.* 2. to strengthen against wear, strain, etc.: *to fortify concrete with steel.* 3. to build up; make strong: *Faith fortifies the mind.* 4. to add minerals or vitamins to: *to fortify flour.* —**for′ti·fi′a·ble,** *adj.*

for·tis·si·mo (fôr tis′ə mō′), *adj., adv.* (in music) very loud.

for·ti·tude (fôr′ti tood′, -tyood′), *n.* strength of mind to bear pain, misfortunes, etc.; courage; endurance.

Fort′ Knox′, a military reservation in N Kentucky: U.S. gold deposits stored here.

fort·night (fôrt′nīt′), *n.* the space of fourteen nights and days; two weeks. [from the Middle English word *fourtenight,* which is short for Old English *fēo·wertēne niht* "fourteen nights"] —**fort′night′ly,** *adj., adv.*

for·tress (fôr′tris), *n.* a large fortified place; fort.

Fort′ Sum′ter, a fort in SE South Carolina. The bombardment of this fort

SOUTH CAROLINA
Augusta
Charleston
GEORGIA
Fort Sumter
Savannah
ATLANTIC OCEAN

by the Confederates on April 12, 1861, opened the Civil War.

for·tu·nate (fôr′chə nit), *adj.* 1. lucky; having good fortune: *He is fortunate to have good health.* 2. bringing good luck; turning out successfully: *a fortunate undertaking.* —**for′tu·nate·ly,** *adv.*

for·tune (fôr'chən), *n.* **1.** a large amount of money; wealth: *He made a fortune in business.* **2.** chance or luck, whether good or bad. **3.** good luck; success. **4.** what is going to happen to a person; one's lot or destiny: *The gypsy told me my fortune.*

for·tune·tell·er (fôr'chən tel'ər), *n.* a person who represents himself as being able to predict what will happen to people, as by reading cards.

Fort' Wayne', a city in NE Indiana.

Fort' Worth', a city in N Texas.

for·ty (fôr'tē), *n., pl.* **for·ties. 1.** a number that is four times ten. **2.** a set of this many persons or things: *Forty of them will be there.* **3.** **forties,** the numbers, years, degrees, etc., between 40 and 49. —*adj.* **4.** amounting to forty in number: *forty persons.*

for·ty-nin·er (fôr'tē nīn'ər), *n.* a person who went to California in 1849 during the gold rush.

fo·rum (fôr'əm), *n.* **1.** the public square of an ancient Roman city, the center of legal and business affairs and a place of assembly for the people. **2.** a court or tribunal. **3.** a gathering of people to discuss matters of common interest.

for·ward (fôr'wərd), *adv.* **1.** Also, **for'wards.** toward or at a place, point, or time in advance or at the front; ahead: *The line moved slowly forward.* **2.** out; forth; into view: *to bring forward new ideas.* —*adj.* **3.** moving ahead; onward: *a forward motion.* **4.** too bold; impudent: *a forward, insulting remark.* **5.** placed or lying at or toward the front: *a forward seat in a plane.* —*n.* **6.** a player whose position is in front of others on his team, as in football or basketball. —*v.* **7.** to send forward, esp. to a new address: *to forward mail.* **8.** to help onward; advance: *to forward someone's career.*

for·ward·ness (fôr'wərd nis), *n.* **1.** overreadiness to push oneself forward; boldness; impudence. **2.** the condition of being forward or in advance.

for·went (fôr went'), *v.* the past tense of **forgo.**

fos·sil (fos'əl), *n.* **1.** any remains or trace of a prehistoric plant or animal, such as an impression in sand that has hardened to rock, a skeleton, shell, etc. **2.** *Informal.* an out-dated or old-fashioned person.

fos·ter (fô'stər), *v.* **1.** to promote the growth or development of; encourage: *to foster talent.* **2.** to bring up or rear: *to foster a child.* **3.** to cherish; hold lovingly in the mind: *to foster dreams of a happy future.* —*adj.* **4.** having a certain family relationship, but not by birth or adoption: *a foster child; a foster parent.*

Fos·ter (fô'stər, fos'tər), *n.* **Stephen,** 1826–1864, U.S. songwriter.

fought (fôt), *v.* the past tense and past participle of **fight.**

foul (foul), *adj.* **1.** disgusting or loathsome: *a foul odor.* **2.** filthy or dirty: *foul clothes.* **3.** stormy or bad, as weather. **4.** offensive or obscene: *foul language.* **5.** wicked; evil: *foul murder.* **6.** unfair according to rules or an accepted way of acting: *to use fair means or foul to get ahead.* **7.** of or referring to a ball in baseball that falls outside the base lines. **8.** tangled or caught: *a foul anchor.* —*adv.* **9.** in a foul manner; vilely. —*n.* **10.** something that is foul. **11.** a breaking of rules in a sport or game. **12.** a ball in baseball that is foul. —*v.* **13.** to make or become foul; dirty: *to foul a street with rubbish.* **14.** to make or become tangled or clogged. **15.** to make a foul play in a game. **16.** (in baseball) to hit a foul. —**foul'ness,** *n.*

found¹ (found), *v.* the past tense and past participle of **find.**

found² (found), *v.* **1.** to set up or establish: *to found a new nation.* **2.** to fix, set, or build upon a solid support or foundation: *to found an argument on facts.* [from the Old French word *fonder,* which comes from Latin *fundāre,* from *fundus* "foundation"]

found³ (found), *v.* **1.** to melt and pour (metal, glass, etc.) into a mold. **2.** to form or make from molten metal, glass, etc.: *to found a bell.* [from the Old French word *fondre,* which comes from Latin *fundere* "to pour, melt, cast"]

foun·da·tion (foun dā'shən), *n.* **1.** the lowest part of a wall, building, etc., that supports the rest of the structure. **2.** the basis of anything: *the foundation of an argument.* **3.** the act of founding, or the state of being founded: *the foundation of a new government.* **4.** an institution endowed with money.

found·er¹ (foun'dər), *n.* a person who founds or establishes: *the founders of our country.*

found·er² (foun'dər), *v.* **1.** to fill with water and sink, as a ship. **2.** to fall or sink down, as buildings, ground, etc. **3.** to fail completely: *The business foundered and went bankrupt.* **4.** to make or become sick from overeating. **5.** to stumble, break down, or go lame, as a horse. [from a Middle English word, which comes from Old French *fondrer* "to sink to the bottom"]

found·er³ (foun'dər), *n.* a person who founds or casts metal, glass, etc.

found·ling (found'ling), *n.* a baby found abandoned.

found·ry (foun'drē), *n., pl.* **found·ries. 1.** a place where molten metal is cast. **2.** the act or process of founding metal.

fount (fount), *n.* **1.** a spring of water; fountain. **2.** a source or origin: *a fount of goodness.*

foun·tain (foun't³n), *n.* **1.** a spring or source of water. **2.** the source or origin of anything: *a fountain of inspiration.* **3.** a jet of water made to flow or spout from an opening or structure, used for drinking, decoration, etc. **4.** a structure, as a basin, containing such a jet or jets: *marble fountains.* **5.** a soda fountain.

foun·tain·head (foun't³n hed'), *n.* **1.** the source or head of a stream. **2.** a chief source of anything.

foun'tain pen', a pen containing a supply of ink that is fed to the point.

four (fôr), *n.* **1.** a number that is three plus one. **2.** a set of this many persons or things: *Only four will be there.* —*adj.* **3.** amounting to four in number: *four persons.* **4.** **on all fours,** on one's hands and knees.

four·fold (fôr'fōld'), *adj.* **1.** made up of four parts: *a fourfold plan.* **2.** four times as great or as much: *a fourfold increase.* —*adv.* **3.** in fourfold measure: *Sales have increased fourfold.*

four-foot·ed (fôr′foot′id), *adj.* having four feet.

four-post·er (fôr′pō′stər), *n.* a bed with four posts, sometimes supporting curtains, a canopy, etc.

four·score (fôr′skôr′), *adj.* four times twenty; eighty.

four·square (fôr′skwâr′), *adj.* 1. having a square shape. 2. firm; steady: *a foursquare effort.* 3. forthright; frank: *a foursquare criticism.* —*adv.* 4. firmly: *to stand foursquare.* 5. forthrightly: *to come out foursquare in favor of something.*

four·teen (fôr′tēn′), *n.* 1. a number that is ten plus four. 2. a set of this many persons or things: *Fourteen will be there.* —*adj.* 3. amounting to 14 in number: *fourteen persons.*

four·teenth (fôr′tēnth′), *adj.* 1. being number fourteen in a series: *the fourteenth floor.* —*n.* 2. one of fourteen equal parts. 3. a person or thing that is fourteenth.

fourth (fôrth), *adj.* 1. being number four in a series: *the fourth floor.* —*n.* 2. one of four equal parts; a quarter. 3. a person or thing that is fourth.

fourth′ class′, the class of mail for merchandise over 16 ounces and all other matter 8 ounces or over that is not sealed. —**fourth′-class′,** *adj., adv.*

Fourth′ of July′, another name for **Independence Day.**

fowl (foul), *n., pl.* **fowls** *or* **fowl.** 1. a hen or rooster; chicken. 2. any of several other birds raised for their meat, such as ducks, turkeys, or pheasants.

fox (foks), *n., pl.* **fox·es** *or* **fox.** 1. a small furry animal related to the dog and having a reddish-brown coat and a bushy tail: noted for its cunning. 2. the fur of the fox. 3. a cunning or crafty person. —**fox′like′,** *adj.*

Fox
(16 in. high at shoulder)

fox·glove (foks′gluv′), *n.* a tall plant whose stalks bear bell-shaped flowers and whose leaves are used in making a medicine for heart disease.

fox·hole (foks′hōl′), *n.* a hole dug in the ground that is large enough to protect one or two soldiers from enemy fire.

fox·hound (foks′hound′), *n.* any of several breeds of medium-sized dogs having a keen sense of smell and often trained to hunt foxes.

Fox terrier
(15 in. high at shoulder)

fox′ ter′rier, either of two breeds of small dogs having either a long, wiry coat or a short, flat coat.

fox·y (fok′sē), *adj.,* **fox·i·er, fox·i·est.** foxlike; cunning or crafty; clever. —**fox′i·ness,** *n.*

foy·er (foi′ər), *n.* 1. the lobby of a theater or hotel. 2. the entrance hall of a house or apartment.

FPO, 1. (in the Armed Forces) field post office. 2. (in the Navy) fleet post office.

Fr, *Chem.* the symbol for **francium.**

fra·cas (frā′kəs), *n.* a noisy fight or quarrel.

frac·tion (frak′shən), *n.* 1. a number, such as $2/3$, $1/6$, $4/3$, etc., that represents either the quotient of two numbers or a number of equal parts of a whole. The upper number of a fraction is called the numerator and the lower number is called the denominator. See also **improper fraction, proper fraction.** 2. a part of a whole, esp. a very small part: *Only a fraction of the invited people came.*

frac·tion·al (frak′shə nəl), *adj.* 1. referring to fractions. 2. very small; insignificant: *Only a fractional amount of food was left.* —**frac′tion·al·ly,** *adv.*

frac·ture (frak′chər), *n.* 1. the breaking or cracking of a bone, cartilage, or the like. 2. the resulting condition: *a bad fracture of the arm.* 3. any break or crack: *a fracture in glass.* —*v.,* **frac·tured, frac·tur·ing.** 4. to suffer a fracture in (a bone). 5. to become fractured; break; crack.

frag·ile (fraj′əl), *adj.* delicate or easily broken; frail: *fragile glass.* —**fra·gil·i·ty** (frə jil′i tē), *n.*

Fractured bones

frag·ment (frag′mənt), *n.* 1. a broken-off part: *fragments of rock.* 2. an incomplete part: *a fragment of a poem.*

frag·men·tar·y (frag′mən ter′ē), *adj.* 1. made up of fragments. 2. not complete or connected: *a fragmentary account of the accident.*

fra·grance (frā′grəns), *n.* a sweet or pleasing smell.

fra·grant (frā′grənt), *adj.* having a sweet or pleasing smell. —**fra′grant·ly,** *adv.*

frail (frāl), *adj.* 1. easily broken or destroyed; fragile: *frail flowers.* 2. having a weak character; easily led astray. 3. physically weak; not robust.

frail·ty (frāl′tē), *n., pl.* **frail·ties.** 1. the quality of being frail: *flowers of great frailty.* 2. a weakness of character: *Boasting is one of his frailties.*

frame (frām), *n.* 1. an open border or case for enclosing a picture, mirror, window, etc. 2. the support or skeleton around which a house, piece of furniture, etc., is built; framework. 3. the build of a human body: *a man with a small frame.* 4. a particular mental state: *We found him in a good frame of mind.* —*v.,* **framed, fram·ing.** 5. to form, make, or construct: *to frame a law.* 6. to put into a frame, as a picture. 7. *Informal.* to cause to appear guilty; put the blame on falsely: *to frame an innocent man for a crime by giving false evidence.* —**fram′er,** *n.*

frame-up (frām′up′), *n.* a plot to put the blame for something on an innocent person.

frame·work (frām′wûrk′), *n.* a frame or structure made of parts fitted or joined together: *the framework of a house.*

franc (frangk), *n.* a unit of money that is used in

France, Belgium, Switzerland, and other countries.

France (frans), *n.* a republic in W Europe. 212,736 sq. mi. *Cap.:* Paris.

fran·chise (fran′chīz), *n.* **1.** a right granted to a person or group by a government: *a franchise to operate a taxi service.* **2.** the right to vote.

Fran·cis·can (fran sis′kən), *adj.* **1.** of or concerning Saint Francis of Assisi or the Franciscans. —*n.* **2.** a member of a religious order founded by Saint Francis in the 13th century.

Fran·cis of As·si·si (fran′sis əv ə sē′zē), **Saint,** 1182?–1226, Italian friar: founded Franciscan order.

fran·ci·um (fran′sē əm), *n. Chem.* a rare, radioactive, metallic element. *Symbol:* Fr

frank¹ (frangk), *adj.* **1.** open and forthright in speech; sincere. —*n.* **2.** a mark put on an envelope, package, etc., that allows it to be sent free of charge. —*v.* **3.** to mark (a letter, package, etc.) with a frank. [from the Old French word *franc,* which comes from Latin *francus* "free, freeman," originally "a Frank"] —**frank′ly,** *adv.* —**frank′ness,** *n.*

frank² (frangk), *n. Informal.* a frankfurter.

Frank (frangk), *n.* a member of a group of ancient Germanic tribes that lived along the Rhine and later conquered what is now France.

Frank·fort (frangk′fərt), *n.* the capital city of Kentucky, in the N part.

frank·furt·er (frangk′fər tər), *n.* a small, smoked sausage, usually of beef and pork.

frank·in·cense (frang′kin sens′), *n.* a fragrant resin from various trees of Asia and Africa, burned as incense and used in making perfumes.

Frank·ish (frang′kish), *n.* **1.** the Germanic language of the Franks. It was the source of many words borrowed by French, and in turn borrowed from French by English. —*adj.* **2.** of or concerning the Franks or their language.

Frank·lin (frangk′lin), *n.* **Benjamin,** 1706–1790, American statesman, scientist, and inventor.

Frank′lin stove′, a cast-iron stove having the general form of a fireplace with enclosed top, bottom, sides, and back.

fran·tic (fran′tik), *adj.* wild with excitement, fear, pain, etc. —**fran′ti·cal·ly,** *adv.*

fra·ter·nal (frə tûr′nᵊl), *adj.* brotherly: *fraternal affection.* —**fra·ter′nal·ly,** *adv.*

fra·ter·ni·ty (frə tûr′ni tē), *n., pl.* for defs. 2, 3 **fra·ter·ni·ties. 1.** friendliness and close ties among men; brotherhood. **2.** a

Franklin stove

social club for men or boys, esp. at a college. **3.** any group of persons having purposes or interests in common: *the medical fraternity.*

frat·er·nize (frat′ər nīz′), *v.,* frat·er·nized, frat·er·niz·

ing. to associate in a brotherly way; be friendly.

fraud (frôd), *n.* **1.** trickery; deceit; dishonesty: *He got all that money by using fraud.* **2.** a person or thing that is false.

frau·du·lent (frô′jə lənt), *adj.* **1.** using fraud; lying or cheating: *fraudulent advertisers.* **2.** involving or resulting from fraud: *fraudulent claims; fraudulent wealth.* —**frau′du·lent·ly,** *adv.*

fraught (frôt), *adj.* filled or laden: *a mission fraught with danger.*

fray¹ (frā), *n.* a noisy quarrel; fight, skirmish, or battle: *The soldiers rushed into the fray.* [from the Middle English word *frai,* which is short for *affrai* "affray"]

fray² (frā), *v.* to make or become worn out or raveled: *cuffs that are frayed.* [from the Old French word *frayer* "to rub," which comes from Latin *fricāre*]

fraz·zle (fraz′əl), *v.,* fraz·zled, fraz·zling. **1.** to fray; wear out. **2.** to weary or tire: *He was frazzled after the game.* —*n.* **3.** the state of being frazzled or worn-out: *The suit was worn to a frazzle.*

freak (frēk), *n.* **1.** a person, animal, or plant that is extremely abnormal. **2.** a strange or unexpected action, event, turn of mind, etc.: *a freak of the weather.* —*adj.* **3.** unusual; odd: *a freak snowfall in June.*

freck·le (frek′əl), *n.* **1.** a small, brownish spot on the skin. —*v.,* freck·led, freck·ling. **2.** to cover or become covered with freckles.

Fred·er·ic·ton (fred′ər ik tən), *n.* the capital city of New Brunswick, in SE Canada.

free (frē), *adj.,* fre·er, fre·est. **1.** independent; not under the control of another; not a slave or a prisoner. **2.** having political rights and liberties: *a land of free men.* **3.** unfettered; without restrictions: *a free spirit.* **4.** able to do as one pleases; at liberty. **5.** not bothered or worried by something: *to be free of debt.* **6.** without duties or taxes: *free trade.* **7.** without cost: *a free vacation.* **8.** loose; not held fast: *the free end of a rope.* **9.** easy and relaxed: *a free stride.* **10.** not following strict rules: *free verse.* **11.** generous: *He is free with his money.* **12.** frank and open: *a free manner of speaking.* **13.** unpleasantly bold or outspoken: *to be free with one's words.* **14.** not clogged up or obstructed, such as a road, hallway, etc. —*adv.* **15.** in a free manner; freely: *The door swung free.* **16.** without cost or charge: *Children will be admitted free.* —*v.,* freed, free·ing. **17.** to make free; set at liberty: *He was freed from prison.* —**free′ly,** *adv.*

free·boot·er (frē′boo̅′tər), *n.* a pirate or buccaneer.

freed·man (frēd′mən), *n., pl.* **freed·men.** a man who has been freed from slavery.

free·dom (frē′dəm), *n.* **1.** the state of being free: *to escape to freedom.* **2.** the power or right to act according to one's belief or choice: *We have freedom to worship as we please.* **3.** political independence: *This country won its freedom from England.* **4.** free use or enjoyment: *You have the freedom of my house.* **5.** ease in moving or acting: *This dress allows for freedom in walking.* **6.** frankness and openness: *to speak with freedom.* **7.** too much frankness; boldness.

free·hand (frē′hand′), *adj.*, *adv.* by hand without the help of instruments: *to draw a circle freehand.*

free·hand·ed (frē′han′did), *adj.* generous: *He was freehanded with his wealth.*

free·man (frē′mən), *n.*, *pl.* **free·men.** a man who is free, having political rights, the right to work, own property, etc.

Free·ma·son (frē′mā′sən), *n.* a member of a widespread secret society devoted to the ideals of charity and brotherly love.

free·stand·ing (frē′stan′ding), *adj.* unattached to a supporting unit or background: *They have a freestanding fireplace in the center of their living room.*

free·stone (frē′stōn′), *n.* 1. any stone, such as sandstone, that cuts without splitting. 2. a fruit, esp. a peach or plum, having a stone from which the pulp is easily separated. —*adj.* 3. referring to a freestone fruit.

free·think·er (frē′thing′kər), *n.* a person who forms his opinions independently of authority or tradition, esp. in religious matters.

free·way (frē′wā′), *n.* an express highway, usually having no toll charges.

free·will (frē′wil′), *adj.* made or done freely; voluntary: *a freewill contribution.*

freeze (frēz), *v.*, **froze** (frōz), **fro·zen** (frō′zən), **freez·ing.** 1. to harden into a solid by cooling: *Water freezes into ice when the temperature falls below 32° F.* 2. to become hard because of loss of heat: *The washing froze on the line.* 3. to become obstructed or clogged by the formation of ice: *The pipes froze during the cold spell.* 4. to have the sensation or suffer the effects of intense cold. 5. to die of frost or cold. 6. to stop or become motionless because of fear, shock, etc. 7. **freeze over,** to become covered with ice: *The pond froze over last night.*

freez·er (frē′zər), *n.* 1. a machine for making ice cream, sherbet, or the like. 2. a refrigerator or cabinet that holds its contents at or below 32° F.

freight (frāt), *n.* 1. the transportation of goods by ship, train, truck, or airplane. 2. the charges for such transportation. 3. the cargo carried for pay by either water, land, or air. —*v.* 4. to load with goods or merchandise for transportation. 5. to transport as freight; send by freight.

freight·er (frā′tər), *n.* a vessel used mainly for carrying cargo.

French (french), *adj.* 1. of, referring to, or characteristic of France, its inhabitants, or their language, customs, etc. —*n.* 2. the Romance language of France, parts of Belgium and Switzerland, Haiti, part of Canada, and of other areas that were colonized by France. 3. the French people.

French curve and line drawn through three points with a French curve

French′ curve′, a flat drafting instrument having several scroll-like curves enabling a draftsman to draw many curves of different shapes and sizes.

French′ door′, a door having panes of glass from top to bottom.

French′ dress′ing, salad dressing made of oil, vinegar, and seasonings.

French′ fried′ pota′toes, thin strips of potatoes, deep-fried. Also, **French′ fries′.**

French′ Guian′a, an overseas department of France, on the NE coast of South America. 35,135 sq. mi.

French′ horn′, a musical wind instrument of the brass family, consisting of a long, coiled tube having a conical bore and a wide bell.

French′ In′dochi′na, a former French colony in SE Asia made up of Vietnam, Cambodia, and Laos.

French·man (french′mən), *n.*, *pl.* **French·men.** a native or inhabitant of France.

French horn

French′ Revolu′tion, the revolution in France, beginning in 1789, that overthrew Louis XVI and ended with Napoleon's rise to power in 1799.

French′ Soma′liland, former name of **Afars and Issas Territory.**

French′ West′ In′dies, the French islands in the Caribbean Sea.

fren·zied (fren′zēd), *adj.* wildly excited; frantic: *A frenzied crowd attacked the palace.*

fren·zy (fren′zē), *n.*, *pl.* **fren·zies.** 1. wild excitement or enthusiasm: *The applause mounted to a frenzy.* 2. a spell of violent mental excitement; fury or rage.

fre·quen·cy (frē′kwən sē), *n.*, *pl.* **fre·quen·cies.** 1. the state or fact of occurring often; frequent occurrence: *the frequency of snowstorms in this area.* 2. the number of times something occurs in a given period of time: *House current alternates at a frequency of 60 cycles per second.*

fre′quency modula′tion, a method of radio broadcasting in which the desired signal varies the frequency of the radiowave being broadcast. *Abbr.:* FM. See also **amplitude modulation.**

fre·quent (frē′kwənt), *adj.* 1. happening at short intervals: *to take frequent trips.* 2. constant, habitual, or regular: *a frequent visitor.* —*v.* (fri kwent′, frē′kwənt). 3. to visit often; go often to: *to frequent museums.* —**fre′quent·ly,** *adv.*

fres·co (fres′kō), *n.*, *pl.* **fres·coes** *or* **fres·cos.** 1. the art or technique of painting on a moist plaster surface. 2. a picture or design so painted. —*v.*, **fres·coed, fres·co·ing.** 3. to paint in fresco.

fresh (fresh), *adj.* 1. newly made or obtained: *fresh lettuce; fresh tracks.* 2. new; not known or used before: *fresh experiences.* 3. newly arrived; just come: *fresh from school.* 4. not salt, such as water. 5. not spoiled or ruined; unimpaired: *Is the milk still fresh?* 6. not frozen or canned: *fresh fruit and vegetables.* 7. not tired; brisk; vigorous. 8. looking youthful and healthy. 9. pure, cool, or refreshing: *a fresh* breeze. **10.** *Informal.* impudent and rude: *a fresh answer.* —**fresh′ly,** *adv.* —**fresh′ness,** *n.*

fresh·en (fresh′ən), *v.* **1.** to make or become fresh: *Rain will freshen the flowers.* **2.** to wash oneself, change clothes, etc. (usually fol. by *up*): *to freshen up after a long trip.*

fresh·et (fresh′it), *n.* **1.** a sudden rise in the level of a stream due to heavy rains or the rapid melting of snow and ice. **2.** a freshwater stream flowing into the sea.

fresh·man (fresh′mən), *n., pl.* **fresh·men.** a student in the first year of the course at a school or college.

fresh·wa·ter (fresh′wô′tər, -wot′ər), *adj.* of or living in water that does not contain much salt: *Trout are freshwater fish.* Also, **fresh′-wa′ter.**

Fres·no (frez′nō), *n.* a city in central California, SE of San Francisco.

fret[1] (fret), *v.,* **fret·ted, fret·ting. 1.** to feel or express worry, annoyance, or discontent: *to fret over problems.* **2.** to gnaw into something; wear away: *acids that fret at the strongest metals.* —*n.* **3.** an irritated state of mind; vexation. [from the Old English word *fretan* "to eat up, consume"]

fret[2] (fret), *n.* an interlaced design consisting of short lines. Also, **fret·work** (fret′wûrk′). [from the Middle English word *frette,* which is probably related to Old English *frætwian* "to adorn"]

fret[3] (fret), *n.* any of the ridges running across the finger board of a guitar, ukulele, etc., which help the fingers to stop the strings at the correct points. [perhaps from the Old French word *frete* "ferrule," which is itself probably from Germanic]

fret·ful (fret′fəl), *adj.* tending to fret; irritable; peevish. —**fret′ful·ly,** *adv.*

fret′ saw′, a long, narrow-bladed saw, used to cut ornamental work from thin wood.

Frey·a (frā′ə), *n.* (in Scandinavian mythology) the goddess of love and beauty, and leader of the Valkyries.

Fri., Friday.

fri·ar (frī′ər), *n.* a man who is a member of any of certain orders in the Roman Catholic Church.

Fret saw

fric·as·see (frik′ə sē′), *n.* **1.** meat, esp. chicken or veal, browned lightly, stewed, and served in its own gravy. —*v.,* **fric·as·seed, fric·as·see·ing. 2.** to prepare as a fricassee.

fric·tion (frik′shən), *n.* **1.** the rubbing of one thing against another: *Friction with the air causes a meteor to glow when it enters the atmosphere.* **2.** the resistance to motion caused by such rubbing: *Much of the energy used by machines is wasted in overcoming friction.* **3.** conflict or disagreement between persons, nations, etc.

Fri·day (frī′dē, frī′dā), *n.* the sixth day of the week, following Thursday.

fried (frīd), *adj.* **1.** cooked in fat. —*v.* **2.** the past tense and past participle of **fry**[1].

friend (frend), *n.* **1.** a person attached to another by feelings of affection. **2.** a patron or supporter: *friends*

of the local symphony. **3.** a member of the same nation, group, etc.; ally. —**friend′less,** *adj.*

Friend (frend), *n.* a member of the Society of Friends; Quaker.

friend·ly (frend′lē), *adj.,* **friend·li·er, friend·li·est. 1.** like a friend; helpful; kind: *friendly advice.* **2.** showing a friendship, kindness, etc.: *a friendly neighborhood.* **3.** not hostile: *a friendly nation.* —**friend′li·ness,** *n.*

friend·ship (frend′ship), *n.* **1.** friendly feeling or disposition. **2.** the state of being a friend. **3.** a friendly relationship.

fries (frīz), *n.* **1.** the plural of **fry**[1]. —*v.* **2.** the third person singular, present tense of **fry**[1].

frieze (frēz), *n.* a decorative band around the walls of a room or below the cornice of a building.

frig·ate (frig′it), *n.* **1.** a fast naval vessel of the late 18th and early 19th centuries, having three masts and heavily armed on one or two decks. **2.** a modern warship.

fright (frīt), *n.* **1.** sudden and extreme fear; a sudden terror. **2.** a person or thing of shocking or ridiculous appearance: *That costume is a fright!* —*v.* **3.** to frighten.

fright·en (frīt′ən), *v.* **1.** to cause (someone) fright; make afraid; scare: *The loud noise frightened him.* **2.** to set in motion by scaring (usually fol. by *away, off,* etc.): *to frighten away pigeons.* **3.** to become afraid: *The little puppy frightens easily.* —**fright′en·ing·ly,** *adv.*

fright·ful (frīt′fəl), *adj.* **1.** causing fright; dreadful; terrible. **2.** horrible or shocking: *frightful damage.* **3.** *Informal.* unpleasant; disagreeable: *We had a frightful time.* —**fright′ful·ly,** *adv.*

frig·id (frij′id), *adj.* **1.** very cold in temperature: *a frigid climate.* **2.** without warmth of feeling or enthusiasm. —**fri·gid′i·ty, frig′id·ness,** *n.* —**frig′id·ly,** *adv.*

frill (fril), *n.* **1.** a trimming, such as a strip of cloth or lace, gathered at one edge and left loose at the other; ruffle. **2.** something that is unnecessary: *There's no money in the budget for frills.* —**frill′y,** *adj.*

fringe (frinj), *n.* **1.** a decorative border of short threads or cords. **2.** anything resembling or suggesting this: *a fringe of grass.* —*v.,* **fringed, fring·ing. 3.** to furnish with a fringe: *to fringe a tablecloth.* **4.** to serve as a fringe for: *Guards fringed the building.*

fringe′ ben′efit, a benefit, such as insurance, received by an employee in addition to his regular pay.

frisk (frisk), *v.* to dance, leap, or skip about playfully.

frisk·y (fris′kē), *adj.,* **frisk·i·er, frisk·i·est.** lively; frolicsome; playful. —**frisk′i·ness,** *n.*

frit·ter[1] (frit′ər), *v.* to waste little by little (usually fol. by *away*): *to fritter away an afternoon.* [another form of the earlier word *fitter* "a fragment," which comes from Old English *fitt* "a part"]

frit·ter[2] (frit′ər), *n.* a small, fried cake of batter, sometimes containing fruit, clams, etc. [from the Old French word *friture,* which comes from Latin *frictus* "fried"]

fri·vol·i·ty (fri vol′i tē), *n., pl.* for def. 2 **fri·vol·i·ties.**

1. the quality or state of being frivolous. 2. a frivolous act or thing.

friv·o·lous (friv′ə ləs), *adj.* 1. of little or no worth or importance: *a frivolous suggestion.* 2. characterized by lack of seriousness or common sense: *frivolous conduct.* —**friv′o·lous·ly,** *adv.*

friz·zle[1] (friz′əl), *v.,* **friz·zled, friz·zling.** 1. to form into small, crisp curls or little tufts. —*n.* 2. a short, crisp curl. [from the Old English word *frīs* "curled" + the suffix *-le*]

friz·zle[2] (friz′əl), *v.,* **friz·zled, friz·zling.** to make a sizzling or sputtering noise in frying. [a blend of *fry* and *frizzle*[1]]

friz·zy (friz′ē), *adj.,* **friz·zi·er, friz·zi·est.** formed into small, tight curls: *frizzy hair.* —**friz′zi·ness,** *n.*

fro (frō), *adv.* **to and fro,** back and forth.

frock (frok), *n.* 1. a dress or gown. 2. an outer garment with large sleeves, worn by monks.

frog[1] (frog, frôg), *n.* 1. any of numerous small, smooth-skinned, tailless animals that live in or near water and have long hind legs that enable them to swim rapidly and make long leaps. 2. **frog in one's throat,** a slight hoarseness: *I can't speak with this frog in my throat.* [from the Old English word *frogga*]

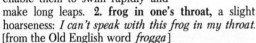

Frog[1]
(length to 8 in.)

frog[2] (frog, frôg), *n.* an ornamental fastening for the front of a coat, consisting of a button and a loop through which it passes. [probably from the Portuguese word *froco,* which comes from Latin *floccus* "a tuft"]

frog·man (frog′man′, -mən, frôg′-), *n., pl.* **frog·men.** a swimmer having special equipment that enables him to swim and explore underwater for long periods of time.

Frog[2]

frol·ic (frol′ik), *n.* 1. merry play; gaiety; fun. 2. a merrymaking or party. —*v.,* **frol·icked, frol·ick·ing.** 3. to play in a frisky, light-spirited manner; have fun.

frol·ic·some (frol′ik səm), *adj.* merrily playful; full of fun.

from (frum), *prep.* 1. (used to specify a starting point): *The train runs west from New York City.* 2. (used to express separation in space, time, order, etc.): *two miles from shore.* 3. (used to express discrimination or distinction): *She is very different from her sister.* 4. (used to indicate source or origin): *to come from Chicago.* 5. (used to indicate cause or reason): *From the evidence, he must be guilty.*

frond (frond), *n.* a large, finely divided leaf like that of a palm or a fern.

front (frunt), *n.* 1. the part or surface of anything that faces forward: *the front of the line.* 2. a place or position directly ahead: *He walked in front of me.* 3. the place where a war, battle, or the like, is carried on. 4. land facing a road, river, etc.: *a lake front.* 5. a

person's bearing or conduct in facing anything; appearance: *a calm front.* 6. the boundary between two moving masses of air having different temperatures. —*adj.* 7. situated in or at the front: *front seats.* —*v.* 8. to have the front toward; face: *The house fronts the lake.*

front·age (frun′tij), *n.* 1. the front of a building or lot. 2. the length of this front. 3. land facing and adjacent to a river, street, etc. 4. the space lying between a building and the street, a body of water, etc.

fron·tal (frun′t°l), *adj.* 1. of, in, or at the front: *a frontal attack.* 2. of, referring to, or situated near the forehead. —**fron′tal·ly,** *adv.*

fron·tier (frun tēr′), *n.* 1. the part of a country that borders another country; boundary; border. 2. land that forms the furthest extent of a country's settled or inhabited regions. 3. Often, **frontiers.** the limit of knowledge, or the most advanced achievement in a particular field: *the frontiers of chemistry.*

fron·tiers·man (frun tērz′mən), *n., pl.* **fron·tiers·men.** a man who lives on the frontier.

fron·tis·piece (frun′tis pēs′), *n.* an illustrated page preceding the title page of a book.

frost (frôst), *n.* 1. temperature low enough to freeze water; cold weather. 2. a white or sparkling covering of tiny ice crystals formed by dew that has frozen. —*v.* 3. to cover (a cake) with frosting; ice.

Frost (frôst), *n.* **Robert,** 1874–1963, U.S. poet.

frost·bite (frôst′bīt′), *n.* 1. a dangerous, painful condition of some part of the body that has been exposed to excessive cold. —*v.,* **frost·bit** (frôst′bit′), **frost·bit·ten** (frôst′bit′°n), **frost·bit·ing.** 2. to injure by frost or extreme cold.

frost·ed (frô′stid), *adj.* 1. covered with or having frost. 2. coated with frosting or icing: *frosted cookies.* 3. having a frostlike surface: *frosted glass.*

frost·ing (frô′stiñg), *n.* 1. a sweet mixture for coating or filling cakes, cookies, etc.; icing. 2. a dull finish on metal or glass.

frost·y (frô′stē), *adj.,* **frost·i·er, frost·i·est.** 1. freezing; very cold: *frosty weather.* 2. covered with frost. 3. lacking warmth of feeling: *a frosty stare.* —**frost′i·ness,** *n.*

froth (frôth), *n.* 1. a mass of bubbles; foam. 2. something light and unimportant; trivial ideas. —*v.* 3. to cover with or give out froth; foam.

froth·y (frô′thē), *adj.,* **froth·i·er, froth·i·est.** 1. of, like, or having froth; foamy. 2. unimportant; trifling. —**froth′i·ness,** *n.*

frown (froun), *v.* 1. to wrinkle the forehead, as in displeasure or deep thought; scowl. 2. to look disapprovingly; express disapproval (usually fol. by *on* or *upon*): *to frown upon someone's rudeness.* —*n.* 3. a frowning look; scowl.

frowz·y (frou′zē), *adj.,* **frowz·i·er, frowz·i·est.** dirty and untidy: *to have a frowzy appearance.* —**frowz′i·ness,** *n.*

froze (frōz), *v.* the past tense of **freeze.**

fro·zen (frō′zən), *v.* 1. the past participle of **freeze.**

—*adj.* **2.** covered with ice: *a frozen stream.* **3.** injured or killed by frost or cold. **4.** chilly or cold in manner; unfeeling: *a frozen stare.* **5.** (of food) chilled or refrigerated: *frozen custard.* **6.** unable to move because of fright, surprise, etc.: *to be frozen with fear.*

fru·gal (frōō′gəl), *adj.* **1.** economical in use; without waste; thrifty. **2.** costing little; meager; scanty: *a frugal meal.* —**fru·gal·i·ty** (frōō gal′i tē), *n.* —**fru′gal·ly,** *adv.*

fruit (frōōt), *n., pl.* **fruits** *or* **fruit.** **1.** the edible part of a plant that develops from the flower and encloses the seed. **2.** any useful part of a plant. **3.** anything produced; product; result: *the fruits of hard work.* —*v.* **4.** to bear or cause to bear fruit.

fruit·age (frōō′tij), *n.* **1.** the bearing of fruit. **2.** a crop of fruit.

fruit·cake (frōōt′kāk′), *n.* a rich cake containing raisins, nuts, and candied fruits.

fruit′ fly′, any of numerous small insects whose larvae feed on fruit.

fruit·ful (frōōt′fəl), *adj.* **1.** bearing much fruit. **2.** producing good results; profitable. —**fruit′ful·ly,** *adv.* —**fruit′ful·ness,** *n.*

fru·i·tion (frōō ish′ən), *n.* **1.** attainment of anything desired; fulfillment: *the fruition of one's labor.* **2.** enjoyment or pleasure, as from something attained. **3.** the state of bearing fruit.

fruit·less (frōōt′lis), *adj.* **1.** without results or success; useless; unproductive. **2.** without fruit; barren. —**fruit′less·ly,** *adv.*

fruit·y (frōō′tē), *adj.,* **fruit·i·er, fruit·i·est.** having the taste or flavor of fruit. —**fruit′i·ness,** *n.*

frus·trate (frus′trāt), *v.,* **frus·trat·ed, frus·trat·ing.** to make (plans, efforts, etc.) worthless; defeat; baffle; foil: *The bad weather frustrated our plans for a picnic.* —**frus·tra′tion,** *n.*

fry[1] (frī), *v.,* **fried, fry·ing. 1.** to cook (food) with fat, oil, etc., usually over direct heat. —*n.* **2.** a dish of something fried. **3.** an outing at which the chief food is fried: *a fish fry.* [from the Old French word *frire,* which comes from Latin *frigere*]

fry[2] (frī), *n., pl.* **fry. 1.** a fish's young. **2.** the young of other animals, such as frogs. [from a Middle English word meaning "seed"]

fry·er (frī′ər), *n.* **1.** a young chicken for frying. **2.** a person or thing that fries.

fry′ing pan′, a shallow, long-handled pan for frying food; skillet.

ft., 1. foot; feet. **2.** fort. **3.** fortification.

fuch·sia (fyōō′shə), *n.* **1.** a plant having bright-red, drooping flowers. **2.** a bright, purplish red. —*adj.* **3.** of the color fuchsia.

fud·dle (fud′³l), *v.,* **fud·dled, fud·dling.** to muddle or confuse with or as if with alcohol.

fudge (fuj), *n.* a candy made of sugar, butter, milk, chocolate, and sometimes nuts and other flavoring.

fu·el (fyōō′əl), *n.* **1.** something that is burned to give heat or to power an engine. **2.** something that stirs up or keeps alive an emotion: *The nasty remark added fuel to his anger.* —*v.,* **fueled** *or* **fuelled; fueling** *or* **fuel·ling. 3.** to supply with fuel.

fu·gi·tive (fyōō′ji tiv), *n.* **1.** a person who is fleeing; runaway. —*adj.* **2.** having run away: *a fugitive slave.* **3.** lasting a very short time; fleeting.

fugue (fyōōg), *n.* a piece of music in which the same theme is elaborated in various combinations by several parts entering in succession.

Füh·rer (fyōōr′ər), *n.* the German word for **leader.** In Nazi Germany it was the title of Adolf Hitler.

Fu·ji (fōō′jē), *n.* a dormant volcano in central Japan: highest mountain in Japan. 12,395 ft. Also, **Fu·ji·ya·ma** (fōō′jē yä′mə).

-ful, a suffix used to form **1.** adjectives meaning **a.** full of: *tearful eyes.* **b.** having the quality of: *mournful; careful.* **c.** having a tendency to: *forgetful.* **d.** having the ability or capacity of: *useful; harmful.* **2.** nouns meaning the amount contained in: *cupful; handful.*

ful·crum (fōōl′krəm, ful′krəm), *n.* the point on which a lever is balanced or around which it turns.

ful·fill (fōōl fil′), *v.* **1.** to carry out: *to fulfill a promise.* **2.** to perform or do; obey; follow: *to fulfill a duty.* **3.** to satisfy; meet: *to fulfill requirements.* —**ful·fill′ment,** *n.*

full (fōōl), *adj.* **1.** containing all that can be held: *a full cup.* **2.** complete; entire; maximum: *a full supply of food.* **3.** of the greatest possible size or amount: *a full load of five tons.* **4.** (of garments, drapery, etc.) wide, ample, or having wide folds: *a full skirt.* **5.** filled or rounded out: *a full face.* —*adv.* **6.** exactly or directly: *The blow struck him full in the face.* —*n.* **7.** the highest or fullest state, condition, or degree. **8.** **in full,** completely; fully: *to pay a bill in full.* —**full′ness,** *n.* —**ful′ly,** *adv.*

full·back (fōōl′bak′), *n.* (in football) a running back who lines up behind the quarterback and is farthest from the line of scrimmage.

full-fledged (fōōl′flejd′), *adj.* **1.** fully developed. **2.** of full rank or standing: *a full-fledged member.*

full-grown (fōōl′grōn′), *adj.* fully grown; mature.

full′ moon′, 1. the moon when the side facing the earth is completely illuminated by the sun. **2.** the time, roughly every 28 days, when the moon is full.

ful·mi·nate (ful′mə nāt′), *v.,* **ful·mi·nat·ed, ful·mi·nat·ing. 1.** to explode with a loud noise. **2.** to speak out, esp. in condemnation (usually fol. by *against*): *to fulminate against sin.* —**ful′mi·na′tion,** *n.*

ful·some (fōōl′səm), *adj.* offensive to good taste; disgusting; repulsive.

fum·ble (fum′bəl), *v.,* **fum·bled, fum·bling. 1.** to feel or grope about clumsily: *to fumble for the door.* **2.** to handle clumsily; drop instead of catch: *to fumble the ball.* —*n.* **3.** the act of fumbling.

fume (fyōōm), *n.* **1.** Usually, **fumes.** unpleasant, bad-smelling, or dangerous vapors: *automobile exhaust fumes.* —*v.,* **fumed, fum·ing. 2.** to give off such vapors. **3.** to show irritation or anger.

fu·mi·gate (fyōō′mə gāt′), *v.,* **fu·mi·gat·ed, fu·mi·gat·**

ing. to treat with smoke or vapors, esp. in order to disinfect or to kill vermin. **—fu′mi·ga′tion,** *n.*

fun (fun), *n.* **1.** something that provides amusement; enjoyment; playfulness. **2. for** (or **in**) **fun,** as a joke; not seriously: *The teasing was just for fun.* **3. make fun of,** to ridicule or mock: *They all made fun of my big feet.*

func·tion (fuñgk′shən), *n.* **1.** the kind of action or activity proper to any person or thing; role; use: *The function of eyeglasses is to improve vision.* **2.** any public or social gathering or occasion. **3.** (in grammar) the relation of a form to the others in a construction. In the sentence *I want two pencils, I* has the function of the subject, *want* has the function of the verb, *two* has the function of a modifier, and *pencils* has the function of the object. **—v. 4.** to perform a certain action or activity; serve; operate: *The battery doesn't function.* **—func′tion·al,** *adj.*

func·tion·ar·y (fuñgk′shə ner′ē), *n., pl.* **func·tion·ar·ies.** a person who functions in a certain capacity, esp. in government service; official.

fund (fund), *n.* **1.** an amount of money set aside for some purpose: *a retirement fund.* **2.** a store, stock, or supply of something: *a fund of information.* **3. funds,** money on hand; money available: *low funds.* **—v. 4.** to provide money for: *The new project will be funded by the Ford Foundation.*

fun·da·men·tal (fun′də men′t²l), *adj.* **1.** serving as or being an essential part of a foundation or basis; basic. **—n. 2.** a basic principle, rule, law, or the like, that serves as the groundwork of a system: *the fundamentals of physics.* **—fun′da·men′tal·ly,** *adv.*

Fun·dy (fun′dē), *n.* **Bay of,** an inlet of the Atlantic Ocean in SE Canada, between New Brunswick and Nova Scotia.

fu·ner·al (fyoo′nər əl), *n.* **1.** the ceremonies for a dead person before burial or cremation. **—adj. 2.** of or referring to a funeral: *a funeral march.*

fu·ne·re·al (fyoo nēr′ē əl), *adj.* **1.** of or referring to a funeral. **2.** mournful, gloomy, or dismal.

fun·gi (fun′jī), *n.* a plural of **fungus.**

fun·gous (fuñg′gəs), *adj.* **1.** of, referring to, or caused by fungi. **2.** resembling a fungus.

fun·gus (fuñg′gəs), *n., pl.* **fun·gi** (fun′jī) *or* **fun·gus·es.** any of a large group of plants, including mushrooms, molds, mildews, etc., that do not contain chlorophyll and live on decaying or living plant or animal matter.

funk (fuñgk), *Informal.* **—n. 1.** fright or terror; fear. **—v. 2.** to frighten. **3.** to shrink from; avoid; shirk.

fun·nel (fun′²l), *n.* **1.** a cone-shaped utensil with a tube at the narrow end, for conducting liquid or other substance through a small opening of a bottle, jar, etc. **2.** a smokestack, esp. of a steamship or a locomotive. **—v., fun·neled** *or* **fun·nelled; fun·nel·ing** *or* **fun·nel·ling. 3.** to pour through or as if through a funnel. **4.** to concentrate, channel, or focus: *to funnel attention.*

fun·ny (fun′ē), *adj.,* **fun·ni·er, fun·ni·est. 1.** providing fun; amusing; comical: *a funny remark.* **2.** *Informal.* strange; peculiar; odd: *a funny way of speaking.* **—n., pl.** **fun·nies. 3. funnies, a.** comic strips. **b.** Also, **fun′ny pa′per.** the section of a newspaper containing comic strips, word games, etc. **—fun′ni·ness,** *n.*

fun′ny bone′, a point on the elbow that, when struck, produces a tingling sensation in the arm and hand.

fur (fûr), *n.* **1.** the fine, soft, thick, hairy coat of a mammal. **2.** such a coat used for lining, trimming, or making garments. **—adj. 3.** made of fur: *a fur coat.* **—v., furred, fur·ring. 4.** to line, face, or trim with fur.

fur·bish (fûr′bish), *v.* to restore to freshness of appearance or condition: *to furbish an antique chair.*

Fu·ries (fyoor′ēz), *n.pl.* (in Greek and Roman mythology) goddesses who punished wrongdoers, esp. murderers.

fu·ri·ous (fyoor′ē əs), *adj.* **1.** full of fury, violent passion, or rage. **2.** very violent, such as wind, storms, etc. **3.** of unrestrained energy, speed, etc.: *a furious pace.* **—fu′ri·ous·ly,** *adv.*

furl (fûrl), *v.* to gather into a compact roll and bind tightly: *to furl a flag.*

fur·long (fûr′lông), *n.* a unit of distance equal to ⅛ mile.

fur·lough (fûr′lō), *n.* **1.** vacation granted to an enlisted man. **—v. 2.** to grant a furlough to.

fur·nace (fûr′nəs), *n.* a structure or device in which heat is produced for heating a house, melting metals, etc.

fur·nish (fûr′nish), *v.* **1.** to provide or supply: *The teacher furnished everyone with pencils and paper.* **2.** to fit out or supply with necessary appliances, esp. furniture: *to furnish a living room.*

fur·nish·ing (fûr′ni shing), *n.* **1.** that with which anything is furnished. **2. furnishings, a.** appliances, articles of furniture, etc., for a house or room. **b.** accessories of dress: *The store sells men's furnishings.*

fur·ni·ture (fûr′ni chər), *n.* the movable articles, such as tables, chairs, desks, etc., required for use or decoration in a house, office, or the like.

fu·ror (fyoor′ôr), *n.* **1.** a general outburst of enthusiasm, excitement, controversy, or the like: *The new movie caused quite a furor.* **2.** a mania or craze. **3.** fury; rage; madness.

fur·ri·er (fûr′ē ər), *n.* a fur dealer.

fur·row (fûr′ō, fur′ō), *n.* **1.** a narrow groove made in the ground, esp. by a plow. **2.** a narrow depression in any surface; wrinkle; crease: *the furrows of a wrinkled face.* **—v. 3.** to make a furrow or furrows in: *to furrow the soil.*

fur·ry (fûr′ē), *adj.,* **fur·ri·er, fur·ri·est. 1.** covered with fur: *a furry kitten.* **2.** made of or like fur. **—fur′ri·ness,** *n.*

fur·ther (fûr′ħər), *adv., comparative of* **far** with **furthest** *as superlative.* **1.** at or to a greater distance; farther: *The store is a few blocks further down the street.* **2.** at or to a more advanced point; to a greater extent: *He questioned the witness further.* **—adj.,**

comparative of **far** *with* **furthest** *as superlative.* **3.** more distant or remote; farther. **4.** additional; more: *further developments.* —*v.* **5.** to help or advance: *to further one's career.*
—Usage. See **farther.**

fur·ther·ance (fûr′ŧħər əns), *n.* the act of furthering; promotion; advancement: *furtherance of a cause.*

fur·ther·more (fûr′ŧħər môr′), *adv.* moreover; besides; in addition.

fur·ther·most (fûr′ŧħər mōst′), *adj.* most distant.

fur·thest (fûr′ŧħist), *adj., adv., superlative of* **far** *with* **further** *as comparative.* another form of **farthest.**

fur·tive (fûr′tiv), *adj.* **1.** taken, done, or used by stealth; secret: *a furtive glance.* **2.** sly; shifty: *a furtive manner.* —**fur′tive·ly,** *adv.*

fu·ry (fyŏŏr′ē), *n., pl.* **fu·ries. 1.** violent anger, rage, or passion. **2.** great force; violence; fierceness: *the fury of the hurricane.* **3.** a fierce and violent person.

furze (fûrz), *n.* a low, spiny shrub with yellow flowers that grows on wastelands in Europe. Also, **gorse.**

fuse[1] (fyŏŏz), *n.* **1.** Also, **fuze.** a tube, cord, or the like, filled or saturated with something that will burn, for igniting explosives. **2.** See **fuze** (def. 1). [from the Latin word *fūsus* "spindle"]

fuse[2] (fyŏŏz), *v.,* **fused, fus·ing. 1.** to melt, esp. to combine by melting together. **2.** to unite or blend into a whole. —*n.* **3.** a protective device in an electric circuit containing a piece of metal that melts if excessive current flows in the circuits, thereby stopping the flow of current. [from the Latin word *fūsus* "melted, poured"]

Furze

fu·se·lage (fyŏŏ′sə läzh′), *n.* the body of an airplane to which the wings and tail are attached.

fu·si·ble (fyŏŏ′zə bəl), *adj.* capable of being fused or melted. —**fu′si·bil′i·ty,** *n.*

fu·sil·lade (fyŏŏ′sə lād′, fyŏŏ′sə läd′), *n.* **1.** a continuous discharge of firearms. **2.** a general outpouring of anything: *a fusillade of questions.*

fu·sion (fyŏŏ′zhən), *n.* **1.** the act of joining two or more things together. **2.** the state of being fused. **3.** something that is fused; the result of fusing: *A circus is the fusion of many talents.* **4.** the union of two nuclei of light atoms with the release of large amounts of energy. See also **fission** (def. 3).

fuss (fus), *n.* **1.** a display of needless attention and activity: *She made such a fuss when the company came.* **2.** an argument or noisy dispute. **3.** a complaint or protest, esp. about something unimportant. —*v.* **4.** to make a fuss or commotion: *to fuss over dinner preparations.* **5.** to disturb or bother with unimportant things: *She fussed with the bow until it was just right.* **6.** to complain.

fuss·y (fus′ē), *adj.,* **fuss·i·er, fuss·i·est. 1.** difficult to please; too particular about unimportant matters: *a fussy eater; a fussy dresser.* **2.** elaborately made, trimmed, or decorated: *a fussy blouse with ruffles.* **3.** full of details: *a fussy job.* —**fuss′i·ness,** *n.*

fu·tile (fyŏŏt′[ə]l), *adj.* **1.** incapable of producing any result; useless: *futile attempts.* **2.** having no importance; trifling: *futile conversation.* —**fu′tile·ly,** *adv.*

fu·til·i·ty (fyŏŏ til′i tē), *n., pl.* for def. 3 **fu·til·i·ties. 1.** the quality of being futile; uselessness. **2.** unimportance or insignificance: *the futility of arguing over such small details.* **3.** a futile act or event.

fu·ture (fyŏŏ′chər), *n.* **1.** time that is to be. **2.** possibility for success; prospect: *The job has no future.* **3.** (in grammar) **a.** the future tense. **b.** a verb form in the future tense. —*adj.* **4.** that is to be or come: *future events.* **5.** (in grammar) referring to or expressed by the future tense.

fu′ture per′fect tense′, the form of verbs that expresses action or state that is expected to be completed at some future time. In English, the future perfect tense is formed by placing *shall have* or *will have* before the past participle: *By the time he gets back, we shall have finished.*

fu′ture tense′, the form of verbs that expresses action or state in future time. In English, the future tense is formed by placing *shall* or *will* before the verb: *I shall go. You will see it.*

fu·tu·ri·ty (fyŏŏ tŏŏr′i tē, -tyŏŏr′-, fyŏŏ chŏŏr′i tē), *n., pl.* **fu·tu·ri·ties. 1.** future time. **2.** a future state or condition; future event. **3.** the quality of being in the future.

fuze (fyŏŏz), *n.* **1.** Also, **fuse.** a device for setting off a shell or bomb. **2.** See **fuse**[1] (def. 1).

fuzz (fuz), *n.* **1.** loose, light, or fluffy matter. **2.** a mass or coating of such matter: *the fuzz on a peach.*

fuzz·y (fuz′ē), *adj.,* **fuzz·i·er, fuzz·i·est. 1.** of or resembling fuzz. **2.** covered with fuzz. **3.** not clear; blurred; indistinct: *a fuzzy picture.* —**fuzz′i·ness,** *n.*

-fy, a suffix used to form verbs meaning **1.** to make or cause to be: *beautify; simplify.* **2.** to become: *solidify.*

	Semitic	Greek	Etruscan	Latin	Gothic	Modern Roman	
DEVELOPMENT OF UPPER-CASE LETTERS		See the letter C		C	𝔊	G	**G**
DEVELOPMENT OF LOWER-CASE LETTERS	ς	ϛ	g	ℊ	g		
		Medieval			Gothic	Modern Roman	

G, g (jē), *n.*, *pl.* **G's** *or* **Gs, g's** *or* **gs.** the seventh letter of the English alphabet.

G, *pl.* **Gs** *or* **G's,** the sum of one thousand dollars. [abbreviation for *grand*]

G, 1. good. 2. a designation of a motion picture regarded as suitable for persons of all ages.

g, 1. good. 2. gram; grams. 3. gravity.

g, *pl.* **g's** *or* **gs,** gravitational acceleration: 32 feet per second per second: *The astronaut was subjected to an acceleration of 5 g's shortly after lift-off.*

G., 1. (specific) gravity. 2. Gulf.

g., 1. gauge. 2. grain; grains.

Ga, *Chem.* the symbol for **gallium.**

Ga., Georgia.

gab (gab), *Informal.* —*v.,* **gabbed, gab·bing.** 1. to talk idly; chatter. —*n.* 2. idle talk; chatter. —**gab′ber,** *n.*

gab·ar·dine (gab′ər dēn′), *n.* 1. a firm, woven fabric of worsted, cotton, or spun rayon, with a twill weave. 2. a long, loose coat or frock for men, worn in the Middle Ages. Also, **gab′er·dine′.**

gab·ble (gab′əl), *v.,* **gab·bled, gab·bling.** 1. to speak rapidly and without meaning; jabber. —*n.* 2. rapid, meaningless talk or sounds. —**gab′bler,** *n.*

ga·ble (gā′bəl), *n.* the portion of the front or side of a building enclosed by the end of a pitched roof. —**ga′bled,** *adj.*

Ga·bon (ga bon′), *n.* a republic in SW Africa. 102,-290 sq. mi. —**Gab·o·nese** (gab′ə nēz′), *n., adj.*

Ga·bri·el (gā′brē əl), *n.* (in the Bible) an archangel who is the messenger of God, bringing His tidings to men.

Gable

gad (gad), *v.,* **gad·ded, gad·ding.** to move restlessly or aimlessly about.

gad·a·bout (gad′ə bout′), *n.* a person who moves restlessly or aimlessly about.

gad·fly (gad′flī′), *n., pl.* **gad·flies.** 1. any of various flies that bite or annoy domestic animals. 2. a person who constantly annoys others; nuisance; pest.

gadg·et (gaj′it), *n.* a mechanical contrivance or device: *This gadget opens cans and sharpens knives.*

gad·o·lin·i·um (gad′ə lin′ē əm), *n. Chem.* a metallic element of the rare-earth group. *Symbol:* Gd

Gads′den Pur′chase (gadz′dən), a tract of land, now in southern Arizona and New Mexico, purchased from Mexico in 1853.

Gael·ic (gā′lik), *n.* 1. any of a group of Celtic languages including Irish and Scots Gaelic. —*adj.* 2. of or referring to, or written or spoken in, a Gaelic language.

gaff (gaf), *n.* 1. an iron hook with a handle for landing large fish. 2. a spar rising from a mast of a ship to support the head of a fore-and-aft sail. —*v.* 3. to hook or land (a fish) with a gaff.

gag¹ (gag), *v.,* **gagged, gag·ging.** 1. to stop up the mouth of (a person) by putting something in it, thus preventing speech or shouting. 2. to retch or choke: *He gagged on a bone.* —*n.* 3. something put into a person's mouth to prevent speech or shouting. [from the Middle English word *gaggen* "to suffocate"]

gag² (gag), *n. Informal.* a joke. [from *gag¹,* used in a special sense]

gage¹ (gāj), *n.* 1. something, such as a glove, thrown down to challenge a person to combat. 2. a challenge. 3. a pledge or pawn; security. —*v.,* **gaged, gag·ing.** 4. *Archaic.* to pledge, stake, or wager. [from a French word, which comes from Germanic]

gage² (gāj), *v.,* **gaged, gag·ing,** *n.* another spelling of **gauge:** used esp. in scientific work.

gai·e·ty (gā′i tē), *n., pl.* **gai·e·ties.** 1. the state of being gay or cheerful. 2. showiness; bright appearance: *gaiety of dress.* 3. Often, **gaieties.** merrymaking or festivity: *the gaieties of New Year's Eve.* Also, **gayety.**

gai·ly (gā'lē), *adv.* **1.** with merriment; merrily; cheerfully. **2.** with showiness; showily; brightly: *gaily dressed.* Also, **gayly.**

gain (gān), *v.* **1.** to get (something desired), esp. as a result of one's efforts; acquire; obtain: *to gain valuable experience.* **2.** to win: *to gain the prize.* **3.** to acquire as an increase or addition: *to gain weight.* **4.** to reach by effort: *to gain one's destination.* **5.** to improve; make progress; advance: *to gain in health.* —*n.* **6.** profit; advantage. **7.** an increase or advance. **8.** the act of gaining. **9. gains,** profits; winnings.

gain·ful (gān'fəl), *adj.* profitable; bringing gain: *gainful employment.* —**gain'ful·ly,** *adv.*

gain·say (gān'sā'), *v.,* **gain·said** (gān'sed'), **gain·say·ing.** **1.** to deny. **2.** to speak or act against; contradict.

'gainst (genst), *prep., conj.* against: used esp. in literature.

gait (gāt), *n.* a manner of walking or running.

gait·er (gā'tər), *n.* **1.** a covering of cloth or leather for the ankle and instep and sometimes also the lower leg. **2.** a cloth or leather shoe with elastic insertions at the sides.

gal., gallon; gallons.

ga·la (gā'lə, gal'ə), *adj.* **1.** festive; fancy; showy: *a gala party.* —*n.* **2.** a celebration or festive occasion.

Gal·a·had (gal'ə had'), *n.* the noblest and purest knight of the Round Table in King Arthur's court.

Ga·lá·pa·gos Is'lands (gə lä'pə gōs'), a chain of islands on the equator in the Pacific Ocean, W of and belonging to Ecuador. The islands have many unique animal species.

Ga·la·tians (gə lā'shənz), *n. (used as sing.)* a book of the New Testament, written by Paul.

gal·ax·y (gal'ək sē), *n., pl.* **gal·ax·ies.** **1.** a large group of stars, separated from any similar group by vast regions of space. **2.** any large and brilliant group of persons or things. **3. the Galaxy,** another name for the **Milky Way.** [from the Latin word *galaxias,* which comes from a Greek word meaning "milky"] —**ga·lac·tic** (gə lak'tik), *adj.*

gale (gāl), *n.* **1.** a very strong wind, esp. one with a speed between 32 and 63 miles per hour. **2.** a noisy outburst: *a gale of laughter.*

ga·le·na (gə lē'nə), *n.* a heavy, gray mineral, the principal ore of lead.

Gal·i·lee (gal'ə lē'), *n.* **1.** an ancient Roman province in N Israel. **2. Sea of,** a lake in NE Israel. 14 mi. long; 682 ft. below sea level. —**Gal·i·le·an** (gal'ə lē'ən), *n., adj.*

Gal·i·le·o (gal'ə lē'ō, gal'ə lā'ō), *n. (Galileo Galilei)* 1564–1642, Italian physicist and astronomer.

gall¹ (gôl), *n.* **1.** something bitter or severe. **2.** bitterness of spirit. **3.** See **bile** (def. 1). **4.** impudence; rudeness; effrontery: *She had the gall to invite herself to the party.* [from the Old English word *galla*]

gall² (gôl), *v.* **1.** to make or become sore by rubbing;

chafe. **2.** to irritate or annoy; vex: *Discourtesy galls me.* —*n.* **3.** a sore on the skin, esp. of a horse, caused by rubbing. [from the Latin word *galla* "tumor"]

gall³ (gôl), *n.* a round growth on the leaf or stem of a plant, caused by insects, fungi, chemicals, etc. [from a French word, which comes from Latin *galla*]

gal·lant (gal'ənt; *also, for defs. 2-4,* gə lant', gə länt'), *adj.* **1.** brave, high-spirited, or chivalrous: *a gallant knight.* **2.** polite and attentive to women. —*n.* **3.** a brave, chivalrous man. **4.** a man particularly polite and attentive to women. —**gal'lant·ly,** *adv.*

gal·lant·ry (gal'ən trē), *n., pl.* **gal·lan·tries.** **1.** dashing courage; heroic bravery. **2.** gallant or courtly attention to women. **3.** a gallant act, action, or speech.

gall' blad'der, a small sac on the underside of the liver in which bile is stored.

Galleon

gal·le·on (gal'ē ən, gal'yən), *n.* a large sailing vessel of the 15th to 19th centuries, used as a fighting or merchant ship.

gal·ler·y (gal'ə rē), *n., pl.* **gal·ler·ies.** **1.** a long, covered area, narrow and open at one or both sides, used esp. as a walk or corridor. **2.** a raised area or passageway in a theater, church, etc., to hold spectators. **3.** the highest of such areas in a theater. **4.** the people who sit in a theater gallery. **5.** a room, series of rooms, or building used for exhibiting works of art. **6.** a large room or building used for photography, target practice, etc.: *a shooting gallery.*

gal·ley (gal'ē), *n., pl.* **gal·leys.** **1.** a seagoing vessel propelled mainly by oars, sometimes with the aid of sails. **2.** a kitchen aboard a vessel or in an airplane. **3.** (in printing) a long, narrow tray, usually of metal, for holding type that has been set. **4.** Also, **gal'ley proof'.** a proof printed from type in a galley.

Gal·lic (gal'ik), *adj.* **1.** referring to the Gauls or Gaul. **2.** referring to the French or France.

gal·li·um (gal'ē əm), *n. Chem.* a rare metallic element, used instead of mercury in high-temperature thermometers. *Symbol:* Ga

gal·li·vant (gal'ə vant'), *v.* to gad about gaily.

gal·lon (gal'ən), *n.* a unit of liquid measure equal to four quarts, or 231 cubic inches (3.785 liters).

gal·lop (gal'əp), *n.* **1.** a fast gait of the horse or other

Buenaventura
COLOMBIA
ECUADOR
Guayaquil
Galápagos Islands
PERU
PACIFIC OCEAN

quadruped in which, in the course of each stride, all four feet are off the ground at once. —v. **2.** to ride a horse at a gallop; ride at full speed. **3.** to run rapidly by leaps. **4.** to go fast; race; hurry.

gal·lows (gal′ōz), *n.* a wooden frame on which criminals are executed by hanging.

gall·stone (gôl′stōn′), *n.* a hard mass, resembling a pebble, formed in the gall bladder.

ga·lore (gə lôr′), *adv.* in abundance; in plentiful amounts: *There was food galore at the picnic.*

ga·losh (gə losh′), *n.* Usually, **galoshes.** high overshoes, usually made of rubber.

gals., gallons.

gal·van·ic (gal van′ik), *adj.* **1.** referring to or produced by galvanism. **2.** affecting or affected as if by galvanism; startling; shocking.

gal·va·nism (gal′və niz′əm), *n.* electricity, esp. when produced by chemical action.

gal·va·nize (gal′və nīz′), *v.,* **gal·va·nized, gal·va·niz·ing. 1.** to stimulate by or as if by a galvanic current. **2.** to startle into sudden activity. **3.** to coat (a metal, esp. iron or steel) with zinc to prevent corrosion. —**gal′va·niz′er,** *n.*

gal′vanized i′ron, iron that has been coated with zinc to prevent its rusting.

gal·va·nom·e·ter (gal′və nom′i tər), *n.* a device for detecting and measuring small electric currents.

Gam·a (gam′ə), *n.* Vas·co da (vas′kō də), c1460–1524, Portuguese navigator.

Gam·bi·a, The (gam′bē ə), a republic in W Africa. 4003 sq. mi. —**Gam′bi·an,** *n., adj.*

gam·ble (gam′bəl), *v.,* **gam·bled, gam·bling. 1.** to play at any game of chance for stakes. **2.** to risk money, etc., on the outcome of something involving chance; bet; wager. **3.** to lose by betting (usually fol. by *away*): *He gambled away a fortune.* —*n.* **4.** anything involving risk. —**gam′bler,** *n.*

gam·bol (gam′bəl), *v.,* **gam·boled** *or* **gam·bolled; gam·bol·ing** *or* **gam·bol·ling. 1.** to skip about; frolic. —*n.* **2.** a skipping or frisking about; frolic.

game (gām), *n.* **1.** an amusement or pastime: *children's games.* **2.** the material or equipment used in playing certain games: *a store selling toys and games.* **3.** a competitive activity involving skill, chance, or endurance on the part of two or more persons who play according to a set of rules: *a football game.* **4.** the number of points required to win a game. **5.** anything resembling a game by requiring skill, endurance, etc.: *the game of politics.* **6.** sport of any kind; fun; joke. **7.** wild animals, including birds and fishes, that are hunted. **8.** the flesh of such wild animals, used as food. —*adj.,* **gam·er, gam·est. 9.** referring to animals hunted as game. **10.** having a fighting spirit; plucky: *a game sportsman.* —*v.,* **gamed, gam·ing. 11.** to play games of chance; gamble.

game·cock (gām′kok′), *n.* a rooster bred and trained for fighting.

gam·ete (gam′ēt, gə mēt′), *n.* a reproductive cell; sperm or egg.

gam·in (gam′in), *n.* a neglected boy who has been left to run about the streets. Also, *referring to a girl,* **ga·mine** (ga mēn′).

gam·ing (gā′ming), *n.* the act of gambling.

gam·ma glob·u·lin (gam′ə glob′yə lin), a protein in blood plasma that contains antibodies effective against many diseases.

gam′ma ray′, a highly penetrating radiation, similar to x-rays and emitted by the nuclei of atoms.

gam·ut (gam′ət), *n.* **1.** (in music) a scale or range of notes. **2.** the entire scale or range of anything.

gam·y (gā′mē), *adj.,* **gam·i·er, gam·i·est. 1.** having the flavor of game. **2.** plucky; spirited. —**gam′i·ness,** *n.*

gan·der (gan′dər), *n.* a male goose. See also **goose** (def. 2).

Gan·dhi (gän′dē, gan′dē), *n.* **Mo·han·das** (mō hän′dəs), *(Mahatma Gandhi),* 1869–1948, Hindu leader of independence movement in India.

gang (gang), *n.* **1.** a group or band of persons who work together or associate closely: *a gang of laborers; a neighborhood gang.* **2.** a group of criminals: *a gang of thieves.* **3.** a set of tools arranged to work together: *a gang of stapling machines.* **4. gang up on,** to attack (a person) in great numbers or as a group: *The class ganged up on Joe for tattling.*

Gan·ges (gan′jēz), *n.* a river in India flowing from the Himalayas to the Bay of Bengal: sacred to the Hindus. 1550 mi. long.

gan·gling (gang′gling), *adj.* awkwardly tall; lank and loosely built.

gan·gli·on (gang′glē ən), *n., pl.* **gan·gli·a** (gang′glē ə) *or* **gan·gli·ons.** a mass of nerve tissue outside the brain and spinal cord.

gang·plank (gang′plangk′), *n.* a flat plank for use by persons boarding or leaving a vessel at a pier. Also, **gangway.**

gan·grene (gang′grēn), *n.* the death of body tissue, caused by interrupted circulation of the blood in the tissue. Gangrene can result from injury, frostbite, etc., and may produce fatal blood poisoning.

gang·ster (gang′stər), *n.* a member of a gang of criminals.

gang·way (gang′wā′), *n.* **1.** a passageway. **2.** another word for **gangplank.** —*interj.* (gang′wā′). **3.** clear the way!

gan·net (gan′it), *n.* any of several large sea birds related to the pelican and usually found far from land.

Gan·y·mede (gan′ə mēd′), *n.* (in Greek mythology) a youth who served the gods on Mount Olympus.

gaol (jāl), *n., v.* a British spelling of **jail.** —**gaol′er,** *n.*

gap (gap), *n.* **1.** a break or opening: *a gap in a wall.* **2.** an empty space or period of time. **3.** a big difference: *a gap in ages.* **4.** a mountain pass.

gape (gāp, gap), *v.,* **gaped, gap·ing. 1.** to stare with open mouth: *He gaped in wonder at the comet.* **2.** to open the mouth wide, as the result of hunger, sleepiness, or close attention. **3.** to split or become open wide: *The dress gapes at the seams.* —*n.* **4.** a wide opening; gap. **5.** the act of gaping. **6.** a stare with the mouth wide open. **7.** a yawn. —**gap·ing·ly,** *adv.*

gar (gär), *n., pl.* **gars** or **gar.** any of several North American freshwater fishes that are covered with hard scales and have a long beak with large teeth.

Gar
(length to 5 ft.)

ga·rage (gə räzh′, gə räj′), *n.* **1.** a building or place for sheltering, cleaning, or repairing motor vehicles. —*v.,* **ga·raged, ga·rag·ing. 2.** to put or keep in a garage.

garb (gärb), *n.* **1.** wearing apparel or clothes, esp. a uniform: *a nurse's garb.* —*v.* **2.** to dress or clothe.

gar·bage (gär′bij), *n.* discarded waste from a kitchen, including scraps of food, cans, bottles, etc.

gar·ble (gär′bəl), *v.,* **gar·bled, gar·bling. 1.** to make unfair or misleading selections from or arrangement of (fact, statements, writings, etc.); distort: *to garble a quotation.* **2.** to confuse by mistake; jumble: *to garble instructions.* —**gar′bler,** *n.*

gar·den (gär′dən), *n.* **1.** a plot of ground, usually near a house, where flowers, vegetables, or herbs are grown. **2.** a piece of ground or other space used as a park or other public area: *a public garden.* —*v.* **3.** to work in or cultivate a garden. —**gar′den·er,** *n.*

gar·de·nia (gär dē′nyə, gär dē′nē ə), *n.* **1.** a white flower with waxy petals and a very sweet smell. **2.** the evergreen tree or shrub that bears this flower.

Gar·field (gär′fēld), *n.* **James A·bram** (ā′brəm), 1831–1881, 20th President of the U.S. 1881.

gar·gle (gär′gəl), *v.,* **gar·gled, gar·gling. 1.** to wash or rinse (the throat or mouth) with a liquid held in the throat and kept in motion by a stream of air from the lungs. —*n.* **2.** any liquid used for gargling.

gar·goyle (gär′goil), *n.* a spout, ending in a grotesque human or animal head with an open mouth, jutting out from the gutter of a building for throwing off rain water.

gar·ish (gâr′ish, gar′ish), *adj.* too colorful, showy, or elaborate; gaudy. —**gar′ish·ly,** *adv.*

gar·land (gär′lənd), *n.* **1.** a wreath of flowers or leaves, worn for ornament or hung on something as decoration. —*v.* **2.** to decorate with a garland or garlands.

Gargoyle

gar·lic (gär′lik), *n.* a plant, related to the lilies, whose strong-smelling bulb is used in cooking.

gar·ment (gär′mənt), *n.* any article of clothing.

gar·ner (gär′nər), *v.* **1.** to gather or deposit in a granary or other storage place. —*n.* **2.** a granary or grain bin.

Gar·ner (gär′nər), *n.* **John Nance** (nans), 1868–1967, 32nd Vice President of the U.S. 1933–1941.

gar·net (gär′nit), *n.* **1.** a deep-red transparent gem used in jewelry. **2.** a deep red.

gar·nish (gär′nish), *v.* **1.** to provide or supply with something ornamental; decorate: *to garnish a meat platter with parsley.* —*n.* **2.** something placed on or around food or in a beverage for flavor or decoration.

gar·ret (gar′it), *n.* another word for **attic.**

gar·ri·son (gar′i sən), *n.* **1.** a group of troops stationed in a fortified place. **2.** the place where such troops are stationed. —*v.* **3.** to provide (a fort, town, etc.) with a garrison. **4.** to occupy with troops.

gar·ru·lous (gar′ə ləs, gar′yo ləs), *adj.* very talkative. —**gar′ru·lous·ly,** *adv.*

gar·ter (gär′tər), *n.* an elastic band or strap for holding up a stocking or sock.

gar′ter snake′, any of numerous small, harmless snakes having striped backs.

Gar·y (gâr′ē, gar′ē), *n.* a port city in NW Indiana, on Lake Michigan.

gas (gas), *n., pl.* **gas·es. 1.** a substance that can expand to fit any container, as distinguished from a liquid or a solid. **2.** a mixture of such substances: *Air is a gas, consisting primarily of nitrogen and oxygen.* **3.** a gaseous substance used as a fuel or an anesthetic: *cooking with gas; using gas when extracting a tooth.* **4.** *Informal.* gasoline. **5.** an airborne substance that makes the air difficult or dangerous to breathe: *tear gas; poison gas.* —*v.,* **gassed, gas·sing. 6.** to overcome or poison with gas or fumes. **7. gas up,** to fill the gasoline tank of a car, truck, etc.: *We'd better gas up at the next filling station.* **8. step on the gas,** to increase one's speed; hurry: *If you don't step on the gas and fix dinner, we'll be late for the movie.*

gas·e·ous (gas′ē əs, gash′əs), *adj.* in the form of or resembling a gas.

gash (gash), *n.* **1.** a long, deep wound or cut; slash. —*v.* **2.** to make a long, deep cut in; slash.

gas·ket (gas′kit), *n.* a ring or sheet of some material for preventing leakage at a joint between two parts of a machine.

gas′ mask′, a device that covers the face and includes a filter containing charcoal or chemicals for protecting the wearer from fumes or poisonous gases.

gas·o·line (gas′ə lēn′, gas′ə lēn′), *n.* a highly flammable liquid distilled from petroleum and used as a solvent and esp. a fuel for internal-combustion engines.

Gas mask

gasp (gasp), *n.* **1.** a sudden, short breath. —*v.* **2.** to catch the breath or struggle for breath with one's mouth open: *to gasp with surprise.* **3.** to utter with gasps (often fol. by *out*): *She gasped out the words.*

gas′ sta′tion, another name for **filling station.**

gas·tric (gas′trik), *adj.* referring to the stomach.

gas′tric juice′, the fluid secreted by glands in the wall of the stomach. Gastric juice is important in the digestion of meats.

gate (gāt), *n.* **1.** a movable barrier closing an opening in a fence, wall, or other enclosure. **2.** an opening that permits passage through an enclosure. **3.** a sliding barrier for regulating the passage of water, steam, or the like, as in a dam or pipe; valve. **4. give (some-one) the gate, a.** to stop seeing a friend, sweetheart, or the like. **b.** to dismiss (a person) from a job: *They gave him the gate for stealing from the company.*

gate′-leg ta′ble (gāt′leg′), a table having drop leaves supported by legs attached to a hinged frame.

gate·way (gāt′wā′), *n.* **1.** a passage or entrance that may be closed by a gate. **2.** any passage by which a region may be entered: *New York became the gateway to America.*

Gate-leg table

gath·er (ga*th*′ər), *v.* **1.** to bring or come together into one group, collection, or place: *A crowd gathered on the corner.* **2.** to learn or conclude from observation: *I gather that he is an excellent student.* **3.** to pick or harvest: *to gather flowers.* **4.** to collect or accumulate: *Clouds gathered in the north.* **5.** to draw (cloth) up on a thread in fine folds or puckers. —*n.* **6.** Often, **gathers.** a fold or pucker in gathered cloth.

gath·er·ing (ga*th*′ər ing), *n.* **1.** an assembly or meeting: *There was a gathering at the church on Wednesday.* **2.** an inflamed swelling.

gau·cho (gou′chō), *n., pl.* **gau·chos.** a cowboy of the South American pampas.

gaud·y (gô′dē), *adj.,* **gaud·i·er, gaud·i·est.** showy without taste; flashy: *She wore a gaudy pink and orange dress.* —**gaud′i·ness,** *n.*

gauge (gāj), *v.,* **gauged, gaug·ing. 1.** to estimate or judge: *It is sometimes difficult to gauge driving speed.* **2.** to determine the exact dimensions, capacity, quantity, or force of; measure. —*n.* **3.** a standard of measurement, esp. one of diameter, width, or thickness. **4.** a device for measuring or indicating some quantity, such as thickness, pressure, or the like. See illus. at **water gauge. 5.** the distance between the inner edges of the heads of the rails in a track. Also, **gage.**

Gaul (gôl), *n.* **1.** an ancient region in W Europe: now France. **2.** an inhabitant of the ancient region of Gaul. **3.** an inhabitant of modern France.

gaunt (gônt), *adj.* **1.** very thin and bony: *a gaunt face.* **2.** bleak, desolate, or grim; barren: *a gaunt wilderness.*

gaunt·let (gônt′lit), *n.* **1.** a glove made of metal worn by knights as part of their armor. **2.** a glove with a long cuff.

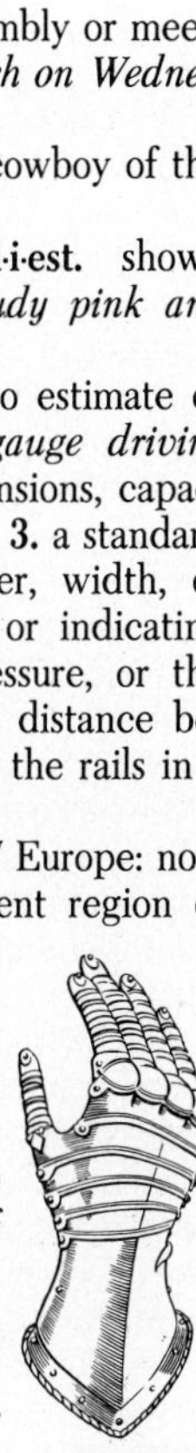

gauze (gôz), *n.* a thin, loosely woven, transparent fabric.

gauz·y (gô′zē), *adj.,* **gauz·i·er, gauz·i·est.** like gauze; very thin and light.

gave (gāv), *v.* the past tense of **give.**

Gauntlet

gav·el (gav′əl), *n.* a small mallet used by a judge, the presiding officer of a meeting, etc., for calling for attention or order.

Ga·wain (gä′win, ga wān′), *n.* one of the knights of the Round Table and a nephew of King Arthur.

gawk (gôk), *v.* **1.** to stare stupidly; gape. —*n.* **2.** an awkward, foolish person.

gawk·y (gô′kē), *adj.,* **gawk·i·er, gawk·i·est.** awkward or clumsy. Also, **gawk·ish** (gô′kish). —**gawk′i·ness,** *n.*

gay (gā), *adj.* **1.** having or showing a joyous mood. **2.** bright or showy: *gay colors.*

gay·e·ty (gā′i tē), *n., pl.* **gay·e·ties.** another spelling of **gaiety.**

gay·ly (gā′lē), *adv.* another spelling of **gaily.**

Ga′za Strip′ (gä′zə, gaz′ə), a small coastal area on the E Mediterranean Sea, between Israel and the Arab Republic of Egypt, formerly administered by the Arab Republic of Egypt, now occupied by Israel.

gaze (gāz), *v.,* **gazed, gaz·ing. 1.** to look steadily and intently. —*n.* **2.** a steady or intent look. —**gaz′er,** *n.*

ga·zelle (gə zel′), *n., pl.* **ga·zelles** *or* **ga·zelle.** any of various small antelopes noted for their graceful movement and large, beautiful eyes.

ga·zette (gə zet′), *n.* **1.** a newspaper (used chiefly in the names of newspapers): *The Phoenix Gazette.* **2.** a government journal containing official information.

gaz·et·teer (gaz′i tēr′), *n.* a geographical dictionary.

G.B., Great Britain.

G clef, (in music) another term for **treble clef.**

Gd, *Chem.* the symbol for **gadolinium.**

gds., goods.

Ge, *Chem.* the symbol for **germanium.**

gear (gēr), *n.* **1.** a wheel with a toothed edge for engaging the teeth of one or more similar wheels, esp. of different diameters. **2.** an assembly or arrangement of such wheels that provides a particular direction or speed of rotation: *reverse gear; low gear.* **3.** any of various mechanisms: *a steering gear.* **4.** tools or equipment: *fishing gear.* —*v.* **5.** to provide with or connect by gearing. **6.** to prepare, adjust, or adapt to a particular situation, person, etc.: *He geared the speech to his young audience.*

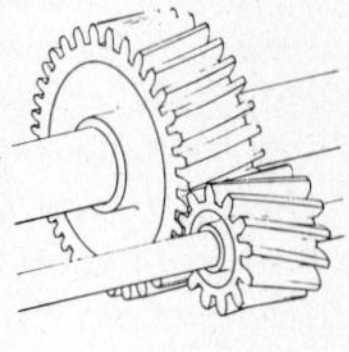

Gears

gear·shift (gēr′shift′), *n.* a lever or automatic device for engaging or disengaging gears, esp. in an automobile or other motor vehicle.

geck·o (gek′ō), *n., pl.* **geck·os** *or* **geck·oes.** any of numerous harmless tropical lizards that can walk on ceilings. [from the Malay word *gēkoq*]

gee¹ (jē), *interj.* (used as a word of command to an ox

Map labels: Tel Aviv; MEDITERRANEAN SEA; Jerusalem; JORDAN; Gaza Strip; Gaza; ISRAEL; EGYPT or horse directing it to turn to the right.) [of unknown origin]

gee² (jē), *interj. Informal.* (used to express surprise or enthusiasm): *Gee, I'm glad you could come to the party!* [a mild form of *Jesus*]

geese (gēs), *n.* a plural of **goose.**

Gei'ger count'er (gī'gər), an instrument for detecting and determining the intensity of radiation, esp. for detecting and counting subatomic particles.

gei·sha (gā'shə, gē'shə), *n., pl.* **gei·sha** *or* **gei·shas.** a Japanese girl trained as a professional singer, dancer, and companion for men.

gel·a·tin (jel'ə tin), *n.* a transparent substance obtained by boiling animal tissue that hardens to a jelly when mixed with water and chilled. Gelatin is used in foods, in making photographic film, and for medical capsules. [from the French word *gélatine,* which comes from Latin *gelatus* "frozen"] —**ge·lat·i·nous** (jə lat'ⁿəs), *adj.*

geld·ing (gel'diñg), *n.* a castrated horse.

gem (jem), *n.* **1.** a cut and polished precious stone fine enough for use in jewelry. **2.** something prized for its beauty or worth. **3.** a greatly respected and liked person. — *v.,* **gemmed, gem·ming. 4.** to decorate with or as if with gems. —**gem'like',** *adj.*

Gem·i·ni (jem'ə nī', jem'ə nē'), *n.pl.* the Twins; a constellation and sign of the zodiac.

gems·bok (gemz'bok'), *n., pl.* **gems·boks** *or* **gems·bok.** a large antelope of southern Africa, having long, straight horns and a long, tufted tail.

-gen, a suffix used to form nouns meaning producer of: *hydrogen; allergen.*

Gen., General.

gen·darme (zhän'därm), *n.* a policeman in any of several European countries, esp. a French policeman.

Gemsbok
(4½ ft. high
at shoulder)

gen·der (jen'dər), *n.* one of the classes, such as masculine, feminine, and neuter, into which nouns and pronouns (in some languages, also adjectives) are divided.

gene (jēn), *n.* one of the numerous tiny units in a cell that is responsible for the transmission of inherited characteristics. Genes are carried in the chromosomes in the nucleus of the cell.

ge·ne·al·o·gy (jē'nē ol'ə jē), *n., pl.* **ge·ne·al·o·gies. 1.** a record or account of the ancestry and descent of a person, family, group, etc. **2.** the study of family histories. **3.** descent from an original form; lineage; ancestry. —**ge'ne·al'o·gist,** *n.*

gen·er·a (jen'ər ə), *n.* a plural of **genus.**

gen·er·al (jen'ər əl), *adj.* **1.** of or referring to all persons or things belonging to a group or category: *a general meeting of the class.* **2.** referring to or true of most persons; widespread: *a general feeling of disappointment.* **3.** not limited to one class, field, group, etc.: *the general public.* **4.** not specific or definite: *I had a general idea about the book before I read it.* —*n.* **5.** a high-ranking U.S. Army officer. The highest

rank of general is general of the army, followed by general, lieutenant general, major general, and brigadier general. **6. in general,** as a rule; usually: *In general my sister and I get along well.*

gen'eral anesthet'ic. See under **anesthetic.**

Gen'eral Assem'bly, 1. the legislature in some states in the U.S. **2.** the main body of the United Nations, composed of delegations from member nations.

gen·er·al·i·ty (jen'ə ral'i tē), *n., pl.* **gen·er·al·i·ties. 1.** a statement that lacks details or is not definite: *He spoke in vague generalities about his plans.* **2.** the greater part or majority: *the generality of people.*

gen·er·al·i·za·tion (jen'ər ə li zā'shən), *n.* **1.** the act or process of generalizing. **2.** a general statement, idea, or principle: *It is a generalization to say that all children like ice cream.*

gen·er·al·ize (jen'ər ə līz'), *v.,* **gen·er·al·ized, gen·er·al·iz·ing. 1.** to infer or form a principle, opinion, conclusion, etc., from known facts: *Scientists generalize on the basis of careful observation.* **2.** to infer or form a principle, opinion, conclusion, etc., on the basis of too few facts. **3.** to deal, think, or speak in generalities. **4.** to make general; bring into general use or knowledge.

gen·er·al·ly (jen'ər ə lē), *adv.* **1.** for the most part; usually: *He's generally on time.* **2.** disregarding particular exceptions: *Generally speaking, men are taller than women.*

gen'eral of the air' force', the highest-ranking officer in the U.S. Air Force, just above a general.

gen'eral of the ar'my, the highest-ranking officer in the U.S. Army, ranking above a general.

gen·er·al·ship (jen'ər əl ship'), *n.* **1.** skill as commander of a large military force. **2.** management of tactics. **3.** the rank or functions of a general.

gen·er·ate (jen'ə rāt'), *v.,* **gen·er·at·ed, gen·er·at·ing. 1.** to bring into existence; cause to be. **2.** to produce by chemical means: *Hydrogen is generated by the action of hydrochloric acid on zinc.* **3.** to produce (electricity), esp. by the motion of something: *Static electricity can be generated by running a comb through the hair.* **4.** to produce (a geometrical figure): *A moving point generates a line.*

gen·er·a·tion (jen'ə rā'shən), *n.* **1.** the act or process of generating. **2.** the entire group of individuals born at about the same time. **3.** the average period of time between the birth of parents and the birth of their offspring: *A human generation is about 30 years.* **4.** the offspring of a particular group of parents considered as a step in natural descent.

genera'tion gap', the lack of communication between one generation and the next, brought about by differences of tastes, outlook, etc.

gen·er·a·tive (jen'ə rā'tiv), *adj.* **1.** referring to the production of offspring. **2.** capable of producing.

gen·er·a·tor (jen'ə rā'tər), *n.* **1.** a person or thing that generates. **2.** a device or machine for producing electricity, esp. from mechanical energy. **3.** an apparatus for producing a gas by chemical action.

ge·ner·ic (jə ner'ik), *adj.* **1.** of or referring to a genus, esp. in biology. **2.** referring to all the members of a genus, class, group, or kind; general: *"Metal" is a generic term.* **—ge·ner′i·cal·ly,** *adv.*

gen·er·os·i·ty (jen′ə ros′i tē), *n., pl.* for def. 3 **gen·er·os·i·ties.** 1. readiness to give. 2. freedom from meanness: *He praised his opponent with generosity.* 3. a generous act.

gen·er·ous (jen′ər əs), *adj.* 1. willing and ready to give; unselfish: *He is always generous to charities.* 2. free from meanness; noble. 3. large; abundant: *a generous helping of ice cream.* **—gen′er·ous·ly,** *adv.*

gen·e·sis (jen′i sis), *n.* an origin, creation, or beginning.

Gen·e·sis (jen′i sis), *n.* the first book of the Bible, dealing with the creation of the world by God.

gen·et (jen′it, ji net′), *n.* any of several small catlike animals, related to the civet but lacking a scent pouch.

ge·net·ic (jə net′ik), *adj.* 1. referring to or caused by the genes or heredity. 2. referring to genetics. 3. referring to origins or beginnings. **—ge·net′i·cal·ly,** *adv.*

ge·net·ics (jə net′iks), *n. (used as sing.)* the science dealing with heredity and the ways in which living things tend to change from one generation to another. **—ge·net′i·cist,** *n.*

Ge·ne·va (jə nē′və), *n.* 1. a city in SW Switzerland, on the Lake of Geneva. 2. **Lake of,** a lake between SW Switzerland and France. 225 sq. mi.

Genet
(total length
3 ft.; tail 18 in.)

Gen·ghis Khan (jeng′gis kän′), 1162–1227, Mongol conqueror of most of Asia and E Europe.

gen·ial (jēn′yəl, jē′nē əl), *adj.* 1. very cheerful and warm; cordial: *a genial host.* 2. favorable for life or comfort; pleasantly warm: *This is a genial climate for sufferers of hay fever.* **—ge·ni·al·i·ty** (jē′nē al′i tē), *n.* **—gen′ial·ly,** *adv.*

ge·nie (jē′nē), *n.* (in Arabian mythology) a spirit having great magical powers. Also, **jinn.**

gen·i·tal (jen′i t²l), *adj.* 1. referring to the production of offspring or to the sexual organs. **—n.** 2. **genitals,** the external sexual organs.

gen·i·tive (jen′i tiv), *adj.* 1. noting a case that in some languages, such as Latin, expresses possession or origin. **—n.** 2. the genitive case.

gen·ius (jēn′yəs), *n.* 1. an exceptional natural capacity of intellect or special talent. 2. a person having such capacity. 3. natural ability or capacity; strong inclination: *She has a genius for understanding.*

Genl., General.

Gen·o·a (jen′ō ə), *n.* a port city in NW Italy.

Gen·o·ese (jen′ō ēz′), *adj.* 1. of, concerning, or characteristic of Genoa or its inhabitants. **—n., pl. Gen·o·ese.** 2. a native or inhabitant of Genoa.

gen·teel (jen tēl′), *adj.* 1. well-bred or refined; polite. 2. pretending to be polite and elegant.

gen·tian (jen′shən), *n.* a tall plant that bears dark-blue flowers.

gen·tile (jen′tīl), *adj.* 1. of or referring to any person who is not Jewish, esp. a Christian. **—n.** 2. a person who is not Jewish.

gen·til·i·ty (jen til′i tē), *n.* 1. superior refinement or elegance. 2. the condition of belonging to the gentry. 3. the gentry; wellborn people as a group.

gen·tle (jen′t²l), *adj.,* **gen·tler, gen·tlest.** 1. kindly or tender. 2. not severe, rough, or violent; mild: *a gentle touch.* 3. not steep; gradual: *a gentle slope.* 4. of good birth; wellborn. 5. soft or low: *a gentle sound.* **—gen′tle·ness,** *n.* **—gen′tly,** *adv.*

gen·tle·folk (jen′t²l fōk′), *n. (used as pl.)* persons of good family and breeding.

gen·tle·man (jen′t²l mən), *n., pl.* **gen·tle·men.** 1. a civilized, educated, or well-mannered man. 2. a polite term for any man. 3. a man of good breeding and social standing.

gen·tle·man·ly (jen′t²l mən lē), *adj.* like or befitting a gentleman: *gentlemanly behavior.*

gen·tle·wom·an (jen′t²l wŏŏm′ən), *n., pl.* **gen·tle·wom·en.** 1. a woman of good family or breeding; lady. 2. a woman who attends a lady of rank.

gen·try (jen′trē), *n.* 1. wellborn and well-bred people. 2. (in England) the class under the nobility.

gen·u·flect (jen′yŏŏ flekt′), *v.* to bend the knee or knees in reverence or worship.

gen·u·ine (jen′yŏŏ in), *adj.* 1. possessing the claimed character, quality, or origin; authentic; real: *genuine leather.* 2. not affected; sincere: *genuine admiration.* **—gen′u·ine·ly,** *adv.* **—gen′u·ine·ness,** *n.*

ge·nus (jē′nəs), *n., pl.* **ge·nus·es** *or* **gen·e·ra** (jen′ər ə). 1. a kind; sort; class. 2. (in biology) a major subdivision of a family of plants or animals, usually containing several species. The two-part Latin name of a plant or animal is composed of its genus and its species. The genus of the common cat, *Felis domestica,* is *Felis.*

geo-, a prefix meaning earth: *geography; geocentric.*

ge·o·cen·tric (jē′ō sen′trik), *adj.* 1. viewed or measured as if from the center of the earth. 2. based on the idea that the earth is the center of the universe.

ge·o·des·ic (jē′ə des′ik, jē′ə dē′sik), *adj.* referring to the geometry of curved surfaces.

ge′odes′ic dome′, a light, domelike structure that is built on a rigid framework of triangles.

ge·og·ra·pher (jē og′rə-fər), *n.* a person who specializes in geographical research and the making of maps.

ge·o·graph·ic (jē′ə graf′-ik), *adj.* another form of **geographical,** preferred in certain instances: *a geographic survey.*

Geodesic dome

ge·o·graph·i·cal (jē′ə graf′i kəl), *adj.* of or concerned with geography: *geographical research.* **—ge′o·graph′i·cal·ly,** *adv.*

ge·og·ra·phy (jē og′rə fē), *n., pl.* for def. 2 **ge·og·ra·phies.** 1. the science that deals with the earth's surface, its climate, vegetation, population, land use, and industries. 2. a book, esp. a textbook, dealing with this subject. 3. the surface features of a region, usually of the earth, sometimes of the planets.

ge·o·log·ic (jē′ə loj′ik), *adj.* another form of **geological,** preferred in certain instances: *geologic time.*

ge·o·log·i·cal (jē′ə loj′i kəl), *adj.* referring to geology: *geological eras.* —**ge′o·log′i·cal·ly,** *adv.*

ge·ol·o·gy (jē ol′ə jē), *n., pl.* **ge·ol·o·gies.** 1. the science that deals with the history of the earth's development, the rocks that make up the earth's crust, and the changes the crust has undergone or is now undergoing. 2. the particular geological features or history of a given place: *the geology of the Grand Canyon.* —**ge·ol′o·gist,** *n.*

ge·o·mag·net·ism (jē′ō mag′ni tiz′əm), *n.* the earth's magnetic properties, esp. the magnetic field surrounding the earth. —**ge·o·mag·net·ic** (jē′ō magnet′ik), *adj.*

ge·o·met·ric (jē′ə me′trik), *adj.* 1. of or referring to geometry or its principles. 2. using straight lines or simple curves: *an Indian rug with a geometric pattern.*

ge·o·met·ri·cal (jē′ə me′tri kəl), *adj.* another form of **geometric,** preferred in certain instances: *geometrical construction.* —**ge′o·met′ri·cal·ly,** *adv.*

ge·om·e·try (jē om′i trē), *n.* the branch of mathematics that deals with points, lines, angles, surfaces, and solids, their interrelationships, and the properties and measurement of area space.

ge·o·phys·ics (jē′ō fiz′iks), *n. (used as sing.)* the physics of the earth and its atmosphere, including oceanography, seismology, volcanology, etc. —**ge′o·phys′i·cal,** *adj.* —**ge′o·phys′i·cist,** *n.*

George·town (jôrj′toun′), *n.* a seaport and the capital city of Guyana.

Geor·gia (jôr′jə), *n.* 1. a state in the SE United States. 58,876 sq. mi. *Cap.:* Atlanta. 2. Official name, **Geor′gian So′viet So′cialist Repub′lic.** a republic of the Soviet Union in Caucasia, bordering on the Black Sea. 26,872 sq. mi. —**Geor′gian,** *n., adj.*

ge·ra·ni·um (ji rā′nē əm), *n.* any of several hardy plants that bloom in the summer, esp. those that have bright red flowers.

ger·bil (jûr′bəl), *n.* any of numerous small Asian or African rodents having long hind legs. Gerbils are often kept as pets.

ger·fal·con (jûr′fal′kən, jûr′fôl′kən, jûr′fô′kən), *n.* another spelling of **gyrfalcon.**

germ (jûrm), *n.* 1. a tiny organism, esp. one that causes disease; microbe. 2. the first stage of something: *the germ of an idea.* 3. a bud or sprout.

Ger·man (jûr′mən), *adj.* 1. of or referring to Germany, its inhabitants, or their language. —*n.* 2. a native or inhabitant of Germany. 3. the Germanic language of Germany, Austria, and part of Switzerland.

ger·mane (jər mān′), *adj.* closely related; pertinent: *points that are germane to the subject.*

Ger·man·ic (jər man′ik), *n.* 1. a branch of the Indo-European family of languages, including English, German, Dutch, Afrikaans, Flemish, the Scandinavian languages, and Gothic. —*adj.* 2. of or referring to the Germanic languages, the peoples speaking them, or their cultures.

ger·ma·ni·um (jər mā′nē əm), *n. Chem.* a rare semiconducting element used in the manufacture of transistors. *Symbol:* Ge

Ger′man mea′sles, a contagious disease resembling but usually milder than measles.

Ger′man shep′herd, a large, highly intelligent dog having a gray or black-and-tan coat, often trained for use as a Seeing Eye dog. Also, **police dog.**

German shepherd (2 ft. high at shoulder)

Ger·ma·ny (jûr′mə nē), *n.* a former country in central Europe from 1871 to 1945, having Berlin as its capital. It is now divided into West Germany and East Germany.

germ′ cell′, a reproductive cell such as a pollen grain, sperm cell, or egg cell.

ger·mi·cide (jûr′mi sīd′), *n.* a substance that kills germs. —**ger′mi·cid′al,** *adj.*

ger·mi·nate (jûr′mə nāt′), *v.,* **ger·mi·nat·ed, ger·mi·nat·ing.** 1. to put out shoots; sprout. 2. to begin to grow or develop. —**ger′mi·na′tion,** *n.*

germ′ plasm′, the part of a germ cell that is vital to heredity and that contains the chromosomes and genes.

Ge·ron·i·mo (jə ron′ə mō′), *n.* 1829–1909, American Apache Indian chief.

Ger·ry (ger′ē), *n.* Elbridge, 1744–1814, 5th Vice President of the U.S. 1813–1814.

ger·und (jer′ənd), *n.* a verb form used as a noun. In English, the gerund is formed by adding *-ing* to the stem of the verb. In the sentence *Writing is easy, writing* is a gerund.

ges·ta·tion (je stā′shən), *n.* the carrying of offspring in the womb before their birth: *The period of gestation is 9 months for humans.*

ges·tic·u·late (je stik′yə lāt′), *v.,* **ges·tic·u·lat·ed, ges·tic·u·lat·ing.** to make or use gestures in an excited manner. —**ges·tic′u·la′tion,** *n.*

ges·ture (jes′chər), *n.* 1. a movement of the body, head, arms, hands, or face that expresses an idea, emotion, etc. 2. any action intended for effect or as a formality: *Since we're not really friends, his invitation was only a polite gesture.* —*v.,* **ges·tured, ges·tur·ing.** 3. to make or use a gesture or gestures.

get (get), *v.,* **got** (got); **got·ten** (got′ən) *or* **got; get·ting.** 1. to receive or obtain: *to get information.* 2. to go after; fetch: *Please get me my coat.* 3. to have

Georgia

done or cause to be done: *to get one's hair cut.* **4.** to communicate with over a distance; reach: *You can get me by telephone.* **5.** to hear: *I didn't get your last name.* **6.** to learn or understand; grasp: *to get a lesson.* **7.** to receive as punishment: *to get 20 years in jail.* **8.** to influence or persuade: *We'll get him to come with us.* **9.** to prepare; make ready: *to get dinner.* **10.** to suffer from: *He's got a bad cold.* **11.** to come to a certain place; arrive; reach: *The train gets to the city at 7 o'clock.* **12. get across,** to make (something) understandable: *to get across the need for fire prevention.* **13. get ahead,** to be successful: *to get ahead in the business world.* **14. get ahead of,** to surpass or outdo: *Nobody's going to get ahead of him in the poultry business.* **15. get along, a.** to leave or depart: *We must be getting along in a few minutes.* **b.** to be on good terms; agree: *She and her sister just can't get along.* **16. get around, a.** to move around; be active: *to get around again after a long illness.* **b.** to lead an active social life: *Since moving to the country, we don't get around much.* **c.** to avoid, bypass, or defeat: *I know a way to get around the entrance requirements.* **17. get at, a.** to reach or touch: *to get at something on the top shelf.* **b.** to hint or imply: *What are you getting at?* **18. get away,** to escape; flee: *The prisoners got away.* **19. get away with,** to avoid punishment for: *to lie and get away with it.* **20. get back, a.** to come back; return: *When will you get back?* **b.** to recover; regain: *to get back a lost watch.* **21. get back at,** be revenged on: *to get back at an enemy.* **22. get behind,** to give support to; back: *to get behind the president.* **23. get by, a.** to succeed in going past: *to get by a roadblock.* **b.** to manage to exist: *Can you get by on $50 a week?* **24. get down, a.** to climb down; descend: *Find a ladder so I can get down.* **b.** to swallow: *The pill was so large I couldn't get it down.* **c.** to depress; discourage: *Nothing gets me down like a rainy day.* **25. get even.** See **even**[1] (def. 18). **26. get going,** to hurry up and start: *Get going on your homework.* **27. get in, a.** to gain entrance; enter: *I forgot my key and couldn't get in.* **b.** to arrive: *Mother got in on the 5 o'clock bus.* **28. get it,** *Informal.* **a.** to be punished or scolded: *He really got it for breaking the window.* **b.** to understand something: *He thinks it's funny, but I don't get it.* **29. get off, a.** to alight or dismount: *I get off at the next corner.* **b.** to leave; depart: *She got off on the noon train.* **c.** to help (someone) escape punishment: *A good lawyer could get him off.* **30. get out, a.** to leave; go away: *Get out and stop bothering me!* **b.** to become publicly known: *He doesn't want the story to get out.* **31. get over,** to recover from: *to get over the measles.* **32. get through, a.** to complete; finish: *What time do you get through work?* **b.** to succeed in meeting or reaching: *I'm trying to get through to Oakland, but the line is busy.* **33. get together, a.** to meet or assemble: *Our family gets together every Sunday.* **b.** to reach an agreement: *to get together on a plan.* **34. get up, a.** stand up: *Get*

up and let Mother have your chair. **b.** to rise from bed: *to get up early.* **c.** to ascend or mount: *Get up those stairs and make your bed!* **d.** to dress (oneself) in a costume: *He got himself up as a pirate.*

get·a·way (get′ə wā′), *n.* **1.** a getting away; an escape. **2.** the start of a race: *a fast getaway.*

Geth·sem·a·ne (geth sem′ə nē), *n.* a garden near Jerusalem where Jesus suffered with the knowledge of His approaching death, and where He was betrayed and arrested.

Get·tys·burg (get′iz-bûrg′), *n.* a borough in S Pennsylvania: Civil War battle 1863; national cemetery.

gey·ser (gī′zər), *n.* a hot spring that sends jets of boiling water and steam into the air, often at regular intervals.

Gha·na (gä′nə), *n.* a republic in W Africa.

ghast·ly (gast′lē), *adj.,* **ghast·li·er, ghast·li·est. 1.** shockingly frightful or dreadful; horrible: *a ghastly accident.* **2.** resembling a ghost; very pale: *a ghastly complexion.* **3.** terrible; very bad: *a ghastly mistake.*

gher·kin (gûr′kin), *n.* a small cucumber used esp. for making pickles. [from the Dutch word *gurken,* which comes from Slavic]

ghet·to (get′ō), *n., pl.* **ghet·tos** *or* **ghet·toes. 1.** (formerly) a section of a city in most European countries in which all Jews were required to live. **2.** a thickly populated slum area of a city, inhabited mostly by a minority group.

ghost (gōst), *n.* **1.** the spirit of a dead person, imagined as wandering among or haunting living persons. **2.** a mere trace: *the ghost of a frown.* **3. give up the ghost,** to die. —**ghost′like′,** *adj.*

ghost·ly (gōst′lē), *adj.,* **ghost·li·er, ghost·li·est.** of or like a ghost: *ghostly shadows in the twilight.*

ghoul (gōōl), *n.* **1.** an evil demon, originally of Oriental legend, supposed to feed on human beings, rob graves, etc. **2.** a grave robber. **3.** a person who enjoys what is revolting and disgusting to most people. —**ghoul′ish,** *adj.* —**ghoul′ish·ly,** *adv.*

GI (jē′ī′), *n., pl.* **GI's** *or* **GIs. 1.** a member or former member of the U.S. Army, esp. an enlisted man. —*adj.* **2.** of, referring to, or characteristic of a GI. **3.** conforming to the regulations or practices of the U.S. Army: *a GI haircut.*

gi·ant (jī′ənt), *n.* **1.** an imaginary being of human form but superhuman size, strength, etc. **2.** a person or thing of unusually great size, power, etc. —*adj.* **3.** unusually large, great, or strong; gigantic.

gi′ant pan′da. See **panda** (def. 1).

gib·ber (jib′ər), *v.* **1.** to speak foolishly and without meaning; chatter. —*n.* **2.** a gibbering utterance.

gib·ber·ish (jib′ər ish), *n.* meaningless talk or writing.

gib·bet (jib′it), *n.* **1.** a gallows with a projecting arm at the top for suspending and displaying the bodies of criminals. —*v.*, **gib·bet·ed, gib·bet·ing. 2.** to put (someone) to death and display the body on a gibbet.

gib·bon (gib′ən), *n.* any of several small, long-armed apes that live in trees and are native to Asia and the East Indies.

gibe (jīb), *v.*, **gibed, gib·ing. 1.** to make fun of; mock; jeer. —*n.* **2.** a mocking, jeering, or sarcastic remark. Also, **jibe.**

gib·let (jib′lit), *n.* Usually, **giblets.** the heart, liver, gizzard, neck, wing, and leg ends of a fowl: *Chicken giblets are often used in making a gravy.*

Gi·bral·tar (ji brôl′tər), *n.* **1.** a tiny British crown colony near the S tip of Spain. 1⅞ sq. mi. **2. Rock of,** a long and very steep mountain in this colony. 1396 ft. high. **3. Strait of,** a strait between Europe and Africa at the Atlantic entrance to the Mediterranean Sea. 8½ to 23 miles wide.

Gibbon
(height 2 ft.)

Gib′son Des′ert (gib′sən), a desert in W central Australia.

gid·dy (gid′ē), *adj.*, **gid·di·er, gid·di·est. 1.** silly and light-hearted; flighty. **2.** affected with dizziness; dizzy. **3.** causing dizziness: *a giddy climb.* —**gid′di·ly,** *adv.* —**gid′di·ness,** *n.*

gift (gift), *n.* **1.** something given voluntarily and without charge; present. **2.** a special ability or capacity; talent: *a gift for music.*

gift·ed (gif′tid), *adj.* **1.** having a special talent or skill. **2.** having very high intelligence: *a gifted child.*

gig (gig), *n.* **1.** a long, light rowboat. **2.** a light, two-wheeled, one-horse carriage.

gi·gan·tic (jī gan′tik), *adj.* very large; huge; like a giant.

gig·gle (gig′əl), *v.*, **gig·gled, gig·gling. 1.** to laugh in a silly, nervous way. —*n.* **2.** a silly laugh; titter. —**gig′gler,** *n.*

Gi′la mon′ster (hē′lə), a large, poisonous lizard with a rough orange-and-black skin, native to the southwestern U.S. and northern Mexico. [named after the *Gila* River in Arizona]

Gila monster
(length to 20 in.)

gild (gild), *v.*, **gild·ed** *or* **gilt** (gilt); **gild·ing. 1.** to coat with gold, gold leaf, or a gold-colored substance. **2.** to make bright or pleasing.

gild·ed (gil′did), *adj.* **1.** covered with gold or something of a golden color. **2.** having a pleasing, fine, or showy appearance.

gill¹ (gil), *n.* the organ by means of which fish breathe. The gills extract dissolved oxygen from the water which then passes into the fish's bloodstream.

[from Scandinavian]

gill² (jil), *n.* a unit of liquid measure equal to ¼ pint, or 7.219 cubic inches (0.1183 liter). [from an Old French word meaning "vat," which comes from Latin *gillo* "wine vessel"]

gilt (gilt), *v.* **1.** a past tense and past participle of **gild.** —*adj.* **2.** gilded. **3.** gold in color; golden. —*n.* **4.** the gold or other material applied in gilding.

gim·let (gim′lit), *n.* a small tool for boring holes, consisting of a shaft with a pointed screw at one end and a cross handle at the other.

gin¹ (jin), *n.* an alcoholic liquor made by distilling grain mash with juniper berries. [shortened from Dutch *genever,* juniper]

gin² (jin), *n.* **1.** a cotton gin. —*v.*, **ginned, gin·ning. 2.** to clear (cotton) of seeds with a cotton gin. [short for Old French *engin* "engine"]

Gimlet

gin·ger (jin′jər), *n.* **1.** a spice made from the ground-up root of a tropical plant, used in cookery and medicine. **2.** the root of this plant. **3.** the plant itself.

gin′ger ale′, a carbonated soft drink flavored with ginger extract.

gin·ger·bread (jin′jər bred′), *n.* **1.** a type of cake or cookie flavored with ginger and molasses. **2.** elaborate or gaudy ornamentation, esp. on a building.

gin·ger·ly (jin′jər lē), *adv.* **1.** very carefully; warily: *He tiptoed gingerly so as not to disturb anyone.* —*adj.* **2.** cautious; wary: *gingerly steps.*

gin·ger·snap (jin′jər snap′), *n.* a small, thin, brittle cookie flavored with ginger and molasses.

ging·ham (gĭng′əm), *n.* yarn-dyed, plain-weave cotton fabric, usually striped or checked.

Gip·sy (jip′sē), *n., pl.* **Gip·sies.** another spelling of **Gypsy.**

gi·raffe (jə raf′), *n.* an African cud-chewing animal with a spotted hide and a very long neck that enables it to eat the leaves of tall trees. [from a French word, which comes from Arabic *zarāfah*]

gird (gûrd), *v.*, **gird·ed** *or* **girt** (gûrt); **gird·ing. 1.** to encircle or bind with a belt or band. **2.** to surround; hem in: *A high fence girded the cottage.* **3.** to prepare (oneself) for action: *He girded himself for the struggle.*

gird·er (gûr′dər), *n.* a large, heavy beam, usually of steel or wood, that acts as a horizontal support for the framework of a building or bridge.

Giraffe
(height 18 ft.)

gir·dle (gûr′d°l), *n.* **1.** a supporting undergarment for the abdomen and hips, usually elasticized. **2.** a belt, cord, or sash worn around the waist. **3.** anything that encircles, confines, or limits. —*v.*, **gir·dled, gir·dling. 4.** to encircle with a belt. **5.** to enclose or encircle: *Trees girdled the estate.*

girl (gûrl), *n.* **1.** a female child or young person. **2.** a young unmarried woman. **3.** a female servant or employee. **4.** a man's or boy's sweetheart. [from the Middle English word *girle* "child, young person"]

girl·hood (gûrl'hood), *n.* **1.** the state or time of being a girl. **2.** girls as a group: *the nation's girlhood.*

girl·ish (gûr'lish), *adj.* of, like, or befitting a girl or girlhood. —**girl'ish·ly,** *adv.* —**girl'ish·ness,** *n.*

girl' scout', a member of an organization of girls (**Girl' Scouts'**) founded in the U.S. in 1912 to develop health, character, and homemaking ability.

girt (gûrt), *v.* a past tense and past participle of **gird.**

girth (gûrth), *n.* **1.** the measure around anything; circumference. **2.** a band that passes underneath a horse, etc., to hold a saddle in place. —*v.* **3.** to bind or fasten with a girth. **4.** to girdle; encircle.

gist (jist), *n.* the main or essential point: *What was the gist of his speech?*

give (giv), *v.,* **gave** (gāv), **giv·en** (giv'ən), **giv·ing. 1.** to present willingly: *to give a birthday present.* **2.** to make a gift or gifts: *to give to charity.* **3.** to place in someone's care: *Give me your coat, and I'll hang it up.* **4.** to hand to someone: *Give me a glass of water, please.* **5.** to pay or transfer possession to another in exchange for something: *What will you give for my bicycle?* **6.** to set forth or show; present; provide: *to give a reason.* **7.** to put forth or utter: *to give a cry.* **8.** to yield under force or pressure: *The chair gave when he sat down heavily on it.* —*n.* **9.** the quality or state of being flexible or resilient; springiness: *The plastic has a lot of give.* **10. give away, a.** to give (something) as a present: *I didn't like the coat, so I gave it away.* **b.** to reveal (a secret, confidence, etc.): *We wanted to surprise you, but Herbie gave it away.* **11. give back,** to return (something), as to its owner: *She never gave back the book she borrowed.* **12. give in,** to admit defeat; yield: *Dad finally gave in and let me go.* **13. give out, a.** to distribute; hand out: *They were giving out handbills on the corner.* **b.** to become exhausted or used up: *I gave out after jogging twice around the block.* **14. give rise to.** See **rise** (def. 23). **15. give up, a.** to lose hope; despair: *Sure it's difficult, but don't give up.* **b.** to stop (something) voluntarily; renounce: *to give up candy during Lent.* **c.** to surrender, as to the authorities: *The thief gave up when he saw he was surrounded.* **16. give way.** See **way** (def. 21). —**giv'er,** *n.*

give·a·way (giv'ə wā'), *n.* **1.** the unintentional telling of a secret or of a clue to a secret. **2.** something given away free or sold for a very low price.

giv·en (giv'ən), *v.* **1.** the past participle of **give.** —*adj.* **2.** stated or fixed: *at a given time.* **3.** inclined or disposed (often fol. by *to*): *He is given to lying.*

giv'en name', the name given to a person, as contrasted with a family name; first name.

giz·zard (giz'ərd), *n.* the second, thick-walled stomach of a bird where food is ground.

gla·cial (glā'shəl), *adj.* **1.** of or referring to glaciers. **2.** produced by the action of glaciers. **3.** bitterly cold; icy.

gla·cier (glā'shər), *n.* a large, thick mass of ice that moves very slowly, carving deep valleys between mountains and smoothing the other terrain over which it passes.

glad (glad), *adj.,* **glad·der, glad·dest. 1.** feeling joy or pleasure; delighted; pleased: *I'm so glad to see you.* **2.** causing joy or pleasure: *a glad occasion; glad news.* —**glad'ly,** *adv.* —**glad'ness,** *n.*

glad·den (glad'ən), *v.* to make glad.

glade (glād), *n.* an open space in a forest.

glad·i·a·tor (glad'ē ā'tər), *n.* (in ancient Rome) an armed person, often a slave or captive, who was forced to fight as entertainment for spectators.

glad·i·o·lus (glad'ē ō'ləs), *n., pl.* **glad·i·o·lus·es** or **glad·i·o·li** (glad'ē ō'lī). a tall plant that bears brightly colored flowers spaced along its stalk. Also, **glad·i·o·la** (glad'ē ō'lə).

glam·or·ize (glam'ə rīz'), *v.,* **glam·or·ized, glam·or·iz·ing.** to make glamorous.

glam·or·ous (glam'ər əs), *adj.* full of glamour; fascinatingly attractive. —**glam'or·ous·ly,** *adv.*

glam·our (glam'ər), *n.* **1.** charm, fascination, and attractiveness. **2.** excitement and adventure: *the glamour of being an explorer.* Also, **glam'or.**

glance (glans), *v.,* **glanced, glanc·ing. 1.** to look quickly or briefly: *I glanced at the clock to see the time.* **2.** to strike a surface and bounce off at an angle (often fol. by *off*): *The arrow glanced off his shield.* —*n.* **3.** a quick or brief look. **4.** a bouncing off at an angle; deflected movement.

gland (gland), *n.* a group of cells, or an organ of the body, that produces a secretion: *the thyroid gland.*

glan·du·lar (glan'jə lər), *adj.* **1.** of, referring to, or resembling a gland. **2.** having or made up of glands.

glare (glâr), *n.* **1.** a very harsh, bright, dazzling light. **2.** an angry, piercing stare. —*v.,* **glared, glar·ing. 3.** to shine with a very harsh, dazzling light. **4.** to stare with an angry, piercing look: *She glared at him for making such a rude remark.*

glar·ing (glâr'ing), *adj.* **1.** dazzling or harshly bright: *glaring lights.* **2.** very showy or bright; gaudy: *glaring colors.* **3.** very obvious: *a glaring mistake.* **4.** staring angrily. —**glar'ing·ly,** *adv.*

Glas·gow (glas'gō, glaz'gō), *n.* a port city in SW Scotland.

glass (glas), *n.* **1.** a hard, brittle, usually transparent material produced by melting sand with other substances to improve its clarity, color, etc. **2.** any of several similar natural or man-made materials. **3.** something made of glass, such as a window. **4.** a tumbler or other drinking container. **5.** the amount a drinking glass can hold; glassful. **6.** a mirror. **7. glasses.** See **eyeglass** (def. 1). —*adj.* **8.** made of glass: *a glass tray.* —*v.* **9.** to cover, protect, or enclose with glass.

glass' blow'ing, the art or process of forming or shaping a mass of molten glass into ware by blowing air into it through a tube. —**glass' blow'er.**

glass·ful (glas'fool), *n.* the amount a glass will hold.

glass·ware (glas′wâr′), *n.* articles made of glass, esp. glasses for a table setting.

glass·y (glas′ē), *adj.,* **glass·i·er, glass·i·est. 1.** resembling glass: *a glassy sheet of water.* **2.** having an expressionless, dull stare: *glassy eyes.* —**glass′i·ness,** *n.*

glaze (glāz), *v.,* **glazed, glaz·ing. 1.** to furnish or fill with sheets of glass: *to glaze a window.* **2.** to coat (a ceramic or the like) with a hard transparent substance. **3.** to become glazed or glassy: *Her eyes glazed over with tears.* —*n.* **4.** a smooth, glossy surface or coating. **5.** the substance for producing such a coating.

gla·zier (glā′zhər), *n.* a person who fits windows, doors, etc., with panes of glass.

gleam (glēm), *n.* **1.** a flash or beam of light. **2.** a brief or slight occurrence; trace: *a gleam of hope.* —*v.* **3.** to send forth a gleam or gleams.

glean (glēn), *v.* **1.** to gather (grain or the like) after the reapers or regular gatherers. **2.** to gather, discover, or find out slowly: *to glean information.*

glee (glē), *n.* **1.** joy; exultation. **2.** a song for three or more voices, having no accompaniment.

glee′ club′, a chorus organized for singing choral music.

glee·ful (glē′fəl), *adj.* full of glee; merry; gay. —**glee′ful·ly,** *adv.*

glen (glen), *n.* a small, narrow, secluded valley.

Glen·dale (glen′dāl′), *n.* a city in SW California, near Los Angeles.

glen·gar·ry (glen gar′ē), *n., pl.* **glen·gar·ries.** a Scottish cap with straight sides, a crease along the top, and sometimes short ribbon streamers at the back. [named after *Glengarry,* a valley in Scotland]

glib (glib), *adj.* ready and fluent, often thoughtlessly or insincerely so: *a glib talker; a glib answer.* —**glib′ly,** *adv.* —**glib′ness,** *n.*

glide (glīd), *v.,* **glid·ed, glid·ing. 1.** to move smoothly and effortlessly. **2.** to pass gradually and unnoticed (often fol. by *along, away, by,* etc.): *Time glided by.* —*n.* **3.** a gliding movement.

Glengarry

glid·er (glī′dər), *n.* **1.** a person or thing that glides. **2.** a motorless airplane that can stay aloft for long periods with the help of rising air currents. **3.** a porch swing made of an upholstered seat suspended from a steel framework.

glim·mer (glim′ər), *n.* **1.** a faint or unsteady light; gleam. **2.** a hint or inkling; trace: *a glimmer of hope.* —*v.* **3.** to shine faintly or unsteadily.

glimpse (glimps), *n.* **1.** a very brief, passing look, sight, or view. —*v.,* **glimpsed, glimps·ing. 2.** to catch or take a glimpse of: *We glimpsed the movie star as she entered the restaurant.*

glint (glint), *n.* **1.** a gleam or glimmer; sparkle; flash. —*v.* **2.** to gleam or flash.

glis·ten (glis′ən), *v.* **1.** to reflect a sparkling light or a faint glow: *Snow glistens in the sunlight.* —*n.* **2.** a glistening; sparkle. —**glis′ten·ing·ly,** *adv.*

glit·ter (glit′ər), *v.* **1.** to reflect light with a brilliant luster; sparkle. **2.** to make a brilliant show. —*n.* **3.** a sparkling reflected light or luster. **4.** showy splendor; showiness. —**glit′ter·ing·ly,** *adv.* —**glit′ter·y,** *adj.*

gloam·ing (glō′miñ), *n.* twilight; dusk: used esp. in literature.

gloat (glōt), *v.* to look at or think about with great satisfaction: *to gloat over another's bad luck.*

glob (glob), *n.* a small drop or lump.

glob·al (glō′bəl), *adj.* **1.** referring to the whole world; world-wide. **2.** globular or globe-shaped.

globe (glōb), *n.* **1.** the planet earth. **2.** a spherical body; sphere. **3.** a sphere on which is depicted a map of the earth or of the heavens. **4.** anything more or less spherical: *Glass fishbowls are globes.*

glob·u·lar (glob′yə lər), *adj.* **1.** shaped like a globe; spherical. **2.** composed of or having globules.

glob·ule (glob′yool), *n.* a small, spherical body.

glock·en·spiel (glok′ən spēl′, glok′ən shpēl′), *n.* a musical instrument used esp. in marching bands and composed of a set of tuned steel bars mounted in a frame and struck with light hammers. [from a German word, which comes from *Glocke* "bell" + *Spiel* "play"]

Glockenspiel

gloom (gloom), *n.* **1.** darkness; dimness. **2.** a state of sadness or depression; low spirits. —*v.* **3.** to appear or become dark or dim.

gloom·y (gloo′mē), *adj.,* **gloom·i·er, gloom·i·est. 1.** dark or dim: *gloomy skies.* **2.** causing gloom; depressing: *a gloomy tale.* **3.** full of gloom; sad: *a gloomy mood.* —**gloom′i·ly,** *adv.* —**gloom′i·ness,** *n.*

glo·ri·fy (glôr′ə fī′), *v.,* **glo·ri·fied, glo·ri·fy·ing. 1.** to magnify with praise; worship; extol: *to glorify God.* **2.** to treat as more splendid, excellent, etc., than would normally be considered: *The book glorifies life in a fishing village.* **3.** to make glorious; give glory and honor to: *to glorify a hero.* —**glo′ri·fi·ca′tion,** *n.*

glo·ri·ous (glôr′ē əs), *adj.* **1.** delightful; wonderful: *a glorious day.* **2.** giving glory: *a glorious victory.* **3.** full of glory; worthy of fame: *a glorious musical composition.* **4.** brilliantly beautiful or magnificent; splendid: *the glorious heavens.* —**glo′ri·ous·ly,** *adv.*

glo·ry (glôr′ē), *n., pl.* **glo·ries. 1.** great praise, honor, or distinction given by common consent. **2.** something that brings honor, praise, or glory. **3.** adoring praise or worship: *Give glory to God.* **4.** great beauty or magnificence: *the glory of autumn.* **5.** a state of absolute happiness, contentment, etc.: *He's in his glory.* **6.** the splendor and bliss of heaven. —*v.,* **glo·ried, glo·ry·ing. 7.** to rejoice proudly (usually fol. by *in*): *He gloried in his success.*

gloss (glos, glôs), *n.* **1.** a luster or shine on the surface: *the gloss of satin.* **2.** a false appearance or show: *A gloss of politeness covered his angry mood.* —*v.* **3.** to put a gloss upon: *to gloss furniture.* **4.** to give a good appearance to by covering up something wrong: *He glossed over his mistakes by making excuses.* [from Scandinavian]

glos·sa·ry (glos′ə rē), *n., pl.* **glos·sa·ries.** a list of defined terms in a special subject, field, or area of usage: *Many technical books have glossaries of special terms.* [from the Latin word *glossārium,* which comes from *glōssa* "a difficult word needing explanation," from Greek *glōssa* "tongue, language"]

gloss·y (glos/ē), *adj., gloss·i·er, gloss·i·est.* having a luster or shine; smooth and shiny. —**gloss/i·ness,** *n.*

Glouces·ter (glos/tər, glô/stər), *n.* 1. a port city in SW England. 2. a port city in NE Massachusetts.

glove (gluv), *n.* 1. a covering for the hand made with a separate sheath for each finger. 2. a boxing glove. 3. a baseball glove. —*v.,* **gloved, glov·ing. 4.** to cover with or as if with a glove.

glow (glō), *n.* 1. a light given off by a heated substance: *the glow of a fire.* 2. brightness of color: *the glow of red cheeks.* 3. warmth of emotion. —*v.* 4. to give off bright light and heat without flame: *The coals glowed in the fireplace.* 5. to give off light: *The watch hands glow in the dark.* 6. to become filled with emotion: *to glow with pride.*

glow·er (glou/ər), *v.* 1. to look or stare with dislike or anger. —*n.* 2. a look of dislike or anger.

glow·worm (glō/wûrm/), *n.* 1. a larva that glows in the dark. 2. another name for **firefly.**

glu·cose (glōō/kōs), *n.* a sugar usually obtained from fruit. Glucose is only about half as sweet as ordinary sugar, but is far more readily absorbed by the body.

glue (glōō), *n.* 1. any of numerous substances used for sticking things together, esp. one that is made by boiling animal skins, hooves, etc. —*v.,* **glued, glu·ing. 2.** to join or attach firmly with or as if with glue: *to glue a label on a package; to glue one's eyes to TV.*

glum (glum), *adj.,* **glum·mer, glum·mest.** silently gloomy; sullen. —**glum/ly,** *adj.* —**glum/ness,** *n.*

glut (glut), *v.,* **glut·ted, glut·ting. 1.** to eat enough or too much; stuff: *He glutted himself with candy.* 2. to supply with too much; flood: *to glut the market with wheat.* —*n.* 3. a supply that is too large or great.

glu·ten (glōōt/³n), *n.* a tough, sticky substance contained in flour and remaining after the starch is removed. [from a Latin word meaning "glue"]

glu·ti·nous (glōōt/³nəs), *adj.* like glue; sticky.

glut·ton (glut/³n), *n.* 1. a person who eats too much. 2. a person with an unusually large capacity for something: *He's a glutton for work.* [from the Old French word *glouton,* which comes from Latin *glūttō*] —**glut/ton·ous,** *adj.* —**glut/ton·ous·ly,** *adv.*

glut·ton·y (glut/³nē), *n.* excessive eating and drinking.

glyc·er·in (glis/ər in), *n.* a clear, sweet, syrupy liquid obtained from fats and used in foods, medicines, and in making explosives.

glyp·to·dont (glip/tə dont/), *n.* an extinct mammal, related to the armadillos, having the body, the top of the head, and the tail covered by a horny and bony armor.

gm., gram; grams.

gms., grams.

gnarl (närl), *n.* a knot on a tree.

gnarled (närld), *adj.* 1. (of trees) full of or covered with gnarls. 2. having a rugged, weather-beaten, twisted appearance; knotted: *gnarled hands.*

gnash (nash), *v.* to grind or strike (the teeth) together, esp. in rage or pain.

gnat (nat), *n.* any of several very small flies that bite.

gnaw (nô), *v.,* **gnawed; gnawed** *or* **gnawn** (nôn); **gnaw·ing. 1.** to wear away by constant biting: *The kitten gnawed the slippers.* 2. to form or make by gnawing: *to gnaw a hole.* 3. to cause trouble or constant annoyance: *Her mistake gnawed at her conscience.*

gnome (nōm), *n.* (in fairy tales) one of a race of little old men who lived in the earth and guarded its treasures; dwarf; troll. —**gnom/ish,** *adj.*

Gnat
(length
¼ in.)

gnu (nōō, nyōō), *n., pl.* **gnus** *or* **gnu.** any of several large African antelopes having an oxlike head, long curved horns, and a long tail. Also, **wildebeest.** [from a Bantu name]

go (gō), *v.,* **went** (went), **gone** (gôn, gon), **go·ing. 1.** to move or proceed, esp. to or from something: *to go to the corner.* 2. to leave a place; depart: *Go away!* 3. to keep or be in motion; function: *The engine's going now.* 4. to be known: *to go by a false name.* 5. to lead or extend: *Where does the road go?* 6. to pass; elapse:

Gnu
(4 ft. high at shoulder)

Time went slowly today. 7. to be applied or used: *My allowance went for books.* 8. to be awarded or given: *The prize goes to our class.* 9. to result or end; turn out: *How did the game go?* 10. to belong; have a place: *The book goes on the top shelf.* 11. to be suited: *The colors go together.* 12. to fit or extend around or into: *The belt won't go around my waist.* 13. to make a certain sound: *The gun goes bang.* 14. to be about, intending, or destined (usually used in the present tense, fol. by an infinitive): *He is going to read.* —*n.* 15. energy, spirit, or animation: *a man with a lot of go.* 16. a try at something; attempt: *to have a go at winning the prize.* 17. **go after,** to try to obtain; strive for: *If you're sure that's what you want, then go after it.* 18. **go ahead,** to proceed without delay: *If you want to light the fire, go ahead.* 19. **go around, a.** to be sufficient for all: *Is there enough pie to go around?* **b.** to associate: *to go around with a bad crowd.* 20. **go back on.** See **back²** (def. 7). 21. **go by,** to rely on or be guided by: *You mustn't go by what she says.* 22. **go down,** to suffer defeat: *to go down fighting.* 23. **go in for,** to have an interest in; like: *Ted goes in for big cars and stylish clothes.* 24. **go in with,** to join (someone) in a partnership or other venture: *You want to go in with me on a new bicycle?* **25. go off, a.** to explode, fire, or begin to work without warning: *We held our ears when the dynamite went off. The alarm clock went off too early.* **b.** to happen as planned: *The meeting went off on schedule.* **26. go on, a.** to take place; happen: *What's going on here?* **b.** to continue: *Why do you go on talking when I told you to stop?* **c.** to have as a basis for a guess, suspicion, etc.: *I've nothing to go on, but I think he's moving to Seattle.* **27. go out, a.** to stop working: *When did the lights go out?* **b.** to engage in dating or other social activities: *He started going out with my sister last spring.* **28. go over, a.** to read or look over: *Go over your papers and see my corrections.* **b.** to repeat; review: *Let's go over the lesson very quickly.* **29. go through, a.** to experience or undergo: *She went through a lot during the war.* **b.** to examine or search carefully: *Go through your things and try to find that book.* **c.** to be approved or successful: *The plan is sure to go through.* **d.** to use up; spend completely: *She went through her allowance in one afternoon.* **30. go through with,** to complete or fulfill (a plan, obligation, etc.): *I only went through with it because I promised her I would.* **31. let go, a.** to release one's grasp or hold: *Please let go of my arm.* **b.** to free; release: *The suspect was let go for lack of evidence.* **c.** to dismiss from employment: *Three of the office staff were let go because business is so bad.* **32. on the go,** very busy; active: *Since moving here we've been on the go constantly.*

goad (gōd), *n.* **1.** a stick with a pointed or electrically charged end, for driving cattle, oxen, etc.; prod. **2.** anything that pricks, wounds, or urges in this way. —*v.* **3.** to drive with or as if with a goad; prod; incite: *His success goaded him on to new ventures.*

goal (gōl), *n.* **1.** the result or achievement toward which effort is directed; aim: *Her goal is to be a registered nurse.* **2.** the end point in a race. **3.** an area, basket, cage, etc., toward or into which players of various games try to throw, carry, kick, hit, or drive a ball, puck, etc., so as to score a point or points. **4.** the act of throwing, carrying, kicking, hitting, or driving a ball, puck, etc., into such an area or object. **5.** the score made by this action.

goal·keep·er (gōl'kē'pər), *n.* (in hockey, lacrosse, soccer, etc.) a player whose chief duty is to prevent the ball or puck from crossing or entering the goal.

goat (gōt), *n.* **1.** any of numerous cud-chewing animals having horns and noted for their liveliness and agility. **2. the Goat.** See **Capricorn** (def. 1).

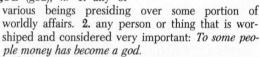

Goat
(2½ ft. high at shoulder)

goat·ee (gō tē'), *n.* a small, pointed beard on a man's chin.

goat·herd (gōt'hûrd'), *n.* a person who tends goats.

goat·skin (gōt'skin'), *n.* **1.** the skin or hide of a goat. **2.** leather made from it.

gob (gob), *n.* **1.** a mass or lump: *a gob of mashed potatoes.* **2. gobs,** *Informal.* a large amount: *She must have gobs of money.*

gob·ble[1] (gob'əl), *v.,* **gob·bled, gob·bling.** to swallow or eat quickly or hungrily in large pieces; gulp. [from *gob* + the suffix *-le,* indicating repeated action]

gob·ble[2] (gob'əl), *v.,* **gob·bled, gob·bling. 1.** to make the throaty cry of a male turkey. —*n.* **2.** this cry. [imitative of the sound]

gob·bler (gob'lər), *n.* a male turkey.

go-be·tween (gō'bi twēn'), *n.* a person who goes back and forth between persons or groups to settle differences, make arrangements, etc.

Go·bi (gō'bē), *n.* a desert in E Asia, mostly in Mongolia. It covers an area of about 450,000 sq. mi.

gob·let (gob'lit), *n.* a drinking glass with a flat base and a stem.

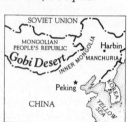

gob·lin (gob'lin), *n.* (in fairy tales) an ugly, mischievous, or wicked elf.

go-cart (gō'kärt'), *n.* a small carriage for children to ride in; stroller.

god (god), *n.* **1.** any of various beings presiding over some portion of worldly affairs. **2.** any person or thing that is worshiped and considered very important: *To some people money has become a god.*

God (god), *n.* the Supreme Being; the creator and ruler of the universe.

god·child (god'chīld'), *n., pl.* **god·chil·dren.** a child for whom a godparent serves as a sponsor at baptism.

god·daugh·ter (god'dô'tər), *n.* a female godchild.

god·dess (god'is), *n.* **1.** a female god or deity. **2.** a greatly admired or adored woman.

god·fa·ther (god'fä'thər), *n.* a man who serves as a sponsor for a child at baptism.

god·less (god'lis), *adj.* **1.** not believing in any god. **2.** wicked; evil. —**god'less·ness,** *n.*

god·like (god'līk'), *adj.* like or befitting God or a god; divine.

god·ly (god'lē), *adj.,* **god·li·er, god·li·est.** conforming to the laws and wishes of God. —**god'li·ness,** *n.*

god·moth·er (god'muth'ər), *n.* a woman who serves as a sponsor for a child at baptism.

god·par·ent (god'pâr'ənt, -par'ənt), *n.* a godfather or godmother.

god·send (god'send'), *n.* an unexpected thing or event that is greatly welcomed: *The rain was a godsend after the summer drought.*

god·son (god'sun'), *n.* a male godchild.

God·speed (god'spēd'), *n.* good fortune; success (used as a wish to a person starting on a journey, a new venture, etc.).

goes (gōz), *v.* the third person singular, present tense of **go:** *He usually goes to school by bus.*

go-get·ter (gō'get'ər), *n. Informal.* an ambitious, aggressive person.

gog·gle (gog'əl), *v.,* **gog·gled, gog·gling. 1.** to stare with bulging or wide-open eyes. —*adj.* **2.** (of the eyes) rolling, bulging, or staring. —*n.* **3. goggles,** large spectacles equipped with special lenses, protective rims, etc., to prevent injury to the eyes from strong wind, flying objects, blinding light, etc.

go·ing (gō'ing), *n.* **1.** the act of leaving or departing; departure. **2.** the condition of roads or other surfaces for walking or driving: *The going was bad.* —*adj.* **3.** continuing to operate or do business, esp. in a successful way: *a going company.* **4. going on,** nearly; almost: *It's going on ten o'clock.*

goi·ter (goi'tər), *n.* a swelling of the neck caused by enlargement of the thyroid gland.

gold (gōld), *n.* **1.** a soft, yellow metal used since ancient times for jewelry and coins. Gold is a chemical element and rarely combines with other elements to form compounds. *Symbol:* Au **2.** something compared to this metal in worth, goodness, superiority, etc.: *a heart of gold.* **3.** a bright metallic yellow. —*adj.* **4.** made of gold: *a gold bracelet.* **5.** of the color of gold; golden: *gold wallpaper.*

gold·en (gōl'dən), *adj.* **1.** of the color of gold; yellow: *golden hair.* **2.** made or consisting of gold: *golden earrings.* **3.** very valuable, advantageous, or fine: *a golden opportunity.*

Gold'en Fleece', (in Greek mythology) a fleece of pure gold captured by Jason and his Argonauts from a dragon that guarded it.

Gold'en Gate', the strait leading into San Francisco Bay in W California.

gold·en·rod (gōl'dən rod'), *n.* a tall weed that bears clusters of tiny yellow flowers.

gold'en rule', a rule of ethical conduct, usually phrased, "Do unto others as you would have them do unto you."

gold·finch (gōld'finch'), *n.* **1.** a European songbird having a scarlet face and wings marked with yellow. **2.** an American songbird the male of which has yellow plumage in the summer.

gold·fish (gōld'fish'), *n., pl.* **gold·fish·es** *or* **gold·fish.** a small yellow or orange fish of the carp family, many varieties of which are bred for aquariums and pools.

gold' leaf', gold in the form of very thin foil, used for gilding.

gold·smith (gōld'smith'), *n.* a person who makes or sells articles of gold.

Goldfish
(length 4 in.)

golf (golf), *n.* **1.** a game in which each player uses a number of golf clubs to hit a small, white ball into a succession of holes, the object being to get the ball into each hole in as few strokes as possible. —*v.* **2.** to play golf. —**golf'er,** *n.*

golf' course', the ground or course over which golf is played; links.

Go·li·ath (gə lī'əth), *n.* (in the Bible) a giant warrior whom David killed with a stone from a sling.

Go·mor·rah (gə môr'ə, gə mor'ə), *n.* (in the Bible) a city that was destroyed, with Sodom, because of its wickedness.

gon·do·la (gon'd⁰lə), *n.* **1.** a long, narrow, flat-bottomed boat, having a tall, ornamental stem and stern and sometimes a small cabin for passengers, rowed by a single oarsman, who stands at the stern, facing forward: used on the canals in Venice, Italy. **2.** a gondola car. **3.** an enclosure hanging from a balloon or dirigible for holding passengers or equipment.

Venetian gondola

gon'dola car', an open railroad freight car with low sides, for transporting freight in bulk.

gone (gôn, gon), *v.* **1.** the past participle of **go.** —*adj.* **2.** departed; left. **3.** lost or hopeless. **4.** dead. **5.** used up. **6.** weak and faint.

gong (gông, gong), *n.* a large bronze disk that produces a deep, vibrating sound when struck.

good (good), *adj.,* **bet·ter** (bet'ər), **best** (best). **1.** morally excellent; righteous: *a good man.* **2.** satisfactory in quality, quantity, or degree: *good food; good health.* **3.** right or proper; suited for a certain purpose: *It's a good day for swimming.* **4.** kind or friendly: *a good deed.* **5.** well-behaved: *a good child.* **6.** genuine; not false: *a good check; a good reason.* **7.** healthful: *Fresh fruit is good for you.* **8.** skillful; talented; clever: *a good golfer; a good student.* **9.** agreeable; pleasant: *Have a good time.* **10.** full; complete: *a good day's journey.* **11.** fairly great; considerable: *a good amount.* —*n.* **12.** profit; worth; benefit: *We shall work for the common good.* **13.** excellence or merit; kindness: *to do good.* **14. goods, a.** possessions; property. **b.** merchandise. **c.** cloth or textile material. **15. as good as.** See **as** (def. 15). **16. come to no good,** to end in failure, prove worthless, etc.: *Any boy who behaves like that will come to no good.* **17. for good,** finally; forever: *I've canceled my subscription for good.* **18. make good, a.** to become successful: *He made good in the shoe business.* **b.** to complete successfully; fulfill: *He made good his threat to sell the house.* **c.** to compensate for; repay: *It was a bad check, and his father had to make it good.*

—**Usage.** Except in very informal conversation, *good* should not replace *well* in adverbial constructions: *I can see well* (not *good*) *with these new glasses. You did well* (not *good*) *on the test. Well* is also an adjective, and in the sense of "healthy," is generally preferred after look, feel, etc.: *You're looking well* (not *good*). *I feel well* (not *good*).

good-by (good'bī'), *interj.* **1.** farewell (used at parting). —*n., pl.* **good-bys. 2.** a farewell: *He said his good-bys.* [short for *God be with you*]

good-bye (good'bī'), *interj., n., pl.* **good-byes.** another spelling of **good-by.**

Good' Fri'day, the Friday before Easter, commemorating the crucifixion of Jesus.

good-heart·ed (good'här'tid), *adj.* very kind and

considerate. Also, **good′heart′ed.** —**good′-heart′ed·ly,** *adv.* —**good′-heart′ed·ness,** *n.*

Good′ Hope′, Cape of. See Cape of Good Hope.

good-hu·mored (good′hyoo′mərd, -yoo′mərd), *adj.* having or showing a pleasant mood: *a good-humored man; a good-humored remark.* Also, *esp. British,* **good′-hu′moured.** —**good′-hu′mored·ly,** *adv.*

good-look·ing (good′look′ing), *adj.* of good or attractive appearance; handsome or beautiful.

good·ly (good′lē), *adj.,* **good·li·er, good·li·est. 1.** of a good quality: *a goodly gift.* **2.** of good or fine appearance. **3.** of fairly large size or amount; considerable: *a goodly sum of money.*

good-na·tured (good′nā′chərd), *adj.* cheerful or pleasant: *a good-natured boy; a good-natured answer.* —**good′-na′tured·ly,** *adv.*

good·ness (good′nis), *n.* **1.** the state or quality of being good; moral excellence: *the goodness of an honest deed.* **2.** kindness or generosity: *He was loved for his goodness toward people in trouble.* **3.** the best or most valuable part of anything: *If you boil the vegetables too long, they'll lose their goodness.* —*interj.* **4.** (used to express mild surprise, alarm, or the like): *Goodness, we never expected to see you here!*

goods (goodz), *n.pl.* See good (def. 14).

good′ Samar′itan, 1. (in the Bible) a traveler who came to the aid of another traveler who had been robbed and beaten by thieves. **2.** a person who unselfishly helps someone in trouble.

good-sized (good′sīzd′), *adj.* rather large; of large or ample size: *a strong, good-sized horse.*

good·wife (good′wīf′), *n., pl.* **good·wives** (good′wīvz′). **1.** *Chiefly Scottish.* the mistress of a household. **2.** *Archaic.* a title of respect for a woman, similar to "Mrs."

good·will (good′wil′), *n.* **1.** friendliness or kindness; a friendly attitude: *They prayed for goodwill among men.* **2.** the good reputation that a business has with its customers. —*adj.* **3.** expressing goodwill: *a goodwill mission.* Also, **good′ will′.**

good·y (good′ē), *Informal.* —*n., pl.* **good·ies. 1.** Usually, **goodies.** something very pleasing, esp. something sweet to eat: *They stuffed themselves with goodies.* —*interj.* **2.** good (used esp. by children to express pleasure): *Goody, we're going swimming!*

goose (goos), *n., pl.* **geese** (gēs). **1.** any of numerous swimming water birds, larger than ducks and having a longer neck and longer legs. **2.** a female goose, as, distinguished from a gander, or male goose.

goose·ber·ry (goos′ber′ē, gooz′-), *n., pl.* **goose·ber·ries. 1.** a small, smooth, sour berry used in making jams, pies, etc. **2.** the shrub bearing this berry.

goose′ flesh′, a rough condition of the skin, looking like that of a plucked goose, induced by cold or fear. Also, **goose′ pim′ples, goose′ bumps′.**

Wild goose
(length to 3½ ft.)

G.O.P., Grand Old Party: a name for the Republican party in the U.S.

go·pher (gō′fər), *n.* **1.** any of numerous small, ratlike, burrowing animals of western North America that have large cheek pouches. **2.** any of several ground squirrels of the North American prairies. [from American Indian]

Gopher
(total length
to 13 in.)

gore[1] (gôr), *n.* blood that is shed; clotted blood. [from the Old English word *gor* "dung, dirt"]

gore[2] (gôr), *v.,* **gored, gor·ing.** (of an animal) to wound or pierce with the horns or tusks. [from the Middle English word *goren,* which is related to Old English *gār* "spear"]

gore[3] (gôr), *n.* **1.** a triangular piece of material set into a garment, sail, or the like, to give it greater width or a desired shape. **2.** one of the panels of material making up a skirt or other garment. —*v.,* **gored, gor·ing. 3.** to make with gores or set a gore into (a garment, sail, etc.). [from the Old English word *gāra* "corner"]

gorge (gôrj), *n.* **1.** a narrow valley, canyon, or pass having steep, rocky walls. **2.** the throat or gullet. —*v.,* **gorged, gorg·ing. 3.** to stuff with food: *to gorge oneself.* **4.** to eat greedily.

gor·geous (gôr′jəs), *adj.* **1.** splendid or rich in appearance, esp. in coloring: *a gorgeous sunset.* **2.** extremely enjoyable: *to have a gorgeous time at a party.* —**gor′geous·ly,** *adv.*

Gor·gon (gôr′gən), *n.* (in Greek mythology) any of three monstrous sisters who had wings, claws, snakes for hair, and eyes that could turn men into stone.

go·ril·la (gə ril′ə), *n.* the largest of the manlike apes. Gorillas live in western equatorial Africa and feed on plants and fruits. [from a Greek word, which is probably of African origin]

gorse (gôrs), *n.* another name for **furze.**

gor·y (gôr′ē), *adj.,* **gor·i·er, gor·i·est. 1.** covered or stained with gore; bloody. **2.** involving much bloodshed: *a gory battle.* —**gor′i·ness,** *n.*

Gorilla
(standing height 6 ft.)

gosh (gosh), *interj.* (used as an exclamation or mild oath): *Gosh, how much longer are we supposed to wait?*

gos·hawk (gos′hôk′), *n.* any of several powerful hawks with short wings, formerly used in falconry.

Go·shen (gō′shən), *n.* **1.** a region in Egypt occupied by the Israelites before the Exodus. **2.** a land or place of comfort and plenty.

gos·ling (goz′ling), *n.* a young goose.

gos·pel (gos′pəl), *n.* **1.** something believed to be true and followed without question. **2.** the story of Christ's life and teachings in the Bible. —*adj.* **3.** referring to or proclaiming the gospel or its teachings: *a gospel hymn; a gospel preacher.*

Gos·pel (gos′pəl), *n.* (in the Bible) any of four books,

Matthew, Mark, Luke, or John, dealing with the life and teachings of Christ.

gos·sa·mer (gos′ə mər), *n.* **1.** a fine, filmy cobweb, or a thread or part of this. **2.** a very delicate, thin, light fabric. —*adj.* **3.** of gossamer: *a gossamer veil.* **4.** like gossamer; thin, light, or delicate.

gos·sip (gos′əp), *n.* **1.** idle talk or rumor, esp. about private or personal matters concerning others: *Don't believe all the silly gossip you hear.* **2.** Also, **gos′sip·er.** a person who makes a habit of discussing the private lives of others or of engaging in idle chatter. —*v.*, **gos·siped, gos·sip·ing. 3.** to talk idly; spread rumors: *They spend too much time gossiping about their classmates.* —**gos′sip·y,** *adj.*

got (got), *v.* a past tense and past participle of **get.**

Goth (goth), *n.* a member of a Germanic people who invaded and settled in parts of the Roman Empire during the 3rd to 5th centuries A.D.

Goth·am (goth′əm), *n.* a nickname for New York City.

Goth·ic (goth′ik), *adj.* **1.** referring to a style of architecture, painting, furniture, etc., developed in Europe from about 1150 to 1550, and characterized by the use of pointed arches and spires or towers. **2.** of or referring to the Goths or their language. —*n.* **3.** the extinct Germanic language of the Goths.

got·ten (got′ⁿn), *v.* a past participle of **get.**

gouge (gouj), *n.* **1.** a chisel that cuts a rounded or V-shaped groove. **2.** a groove, hole, cut, etc., made with or as if with a gouge. —*v.*, **gouged, goug·ing. 3.** to scoop out or force out with a gouge or as if with a gouge: *to gouge a hole in wood.* **4.** to make a gouge or cut in: *The horse gouged his leg when he fell.* **5.** to swindle or extort; cheat. —**goug′er,** *n.*

Gouges

gou·lash (gōō′läsh), *n.* a stew of beef, veal, vegetables, etc., with paprika or other seasonings. Also, **Hungarian goulash.** [from the Hungarian phrase *gulyas hus* "herdsman's meat"]

gourd (gôrd, gōōrd), *n.* **1.** any of numerous rounded vegetables of the melon family whose dried shell can be used for making bottles, rattles, cups, etc. **2.** a vine bearing such a vegetable.

gour·mand (gōōr′mänd), *n.* a person who loves to eat. [from the Old French word *gormant* "glutton"]

gour·met (gōōr mā′), *n.* a person who greatly enjoys and appreciates fine food and drink.

gout (gout), *n.* a disease that causes painful inflammation of the joints, esp. those of the big toe.

Gov., governor.

gov·ern (guv′ərn), *v.* **1.** to rule, manage, or direct: *to govern a nation.* **2.** to control or hold in check: *to govern one's temper.* **3.** to serve as a guide or rule for: *What governed your decision?* —**gov′ern·a·bil′i·ty,** *n.* —**gov′ern·a·ble,** *adj.*

gov·ern·ess (guv′ər nis), *n.* a woman who is employed in a private home to help take care of and educate a child or children.

gov·ern·ment (guv′ərn mənt, guv′ər mənt), *n.* **1.** political management or rule of a nation, state, city, etc. **2.** the form or system of rule of a nation, state, city, etc.: *We support democratic government.* **3.** the group of persons in charge of governing a place: *The government must deal with the crisis.* **4.** control or rule. —**gov·ern·men·tal** (guv′ərn men′təl), *adj.*

gov·er·nor (guv′ər nər), *n.* **1.** a person elected as the head or chief executive of a state in the U.S. **2.** a person who governs or rules: *the governor of a newly settled territory.* **3.** a device for regulating the speed of an engine or other machine.

gov·er·nor·ship (guv′ər nər ship′), *n.* the term in office, position, or duties of a governor.

Govt., government. Also, **govt.**

gown (goun), *n.* **1.** a woman's dress, esp. a dress for a party or dance. **2.** a loose, flowing outer garment or robe worn by graduates, judges, lawyers, etc. **3.** a nightgown or robe. —*v.* **4.** to dress in a gown.

G.P.O., general post office.

gr, **1.** grain; grains. **2.** gross.

gr., **1.** grade. **2.** grain; grains. **3.** gram; grams. **4.** grammar. **5.** great. **6.** gross. **7.** group.

grab (grab), *v.*, **grabbed, grab·bing. 1.** to take hold of suddenly and eagerly; seize; snatch: *He grabbed his hat and ran out the door.* **2.** to try to grasp or seize; reach out for (usually fol. by *at*): *He grabbed at the oar, but it drifted away.* —*n.* **3.** a sudden grasp or snatch: *to make a grab at a ball.*

grace (grās), *n.* **1.** beauty or elegance of movement or appearance: *In dancing class we're taught to walk with grace.* **2.** a pleasing or charming quality or skill: *Playing the piano used to be one of the graces taught to every young lady.* **3.** favor or goodwill: *to seek the king's grace.* **4.** mercy or pardon: *By the grace of His Majesty you are free to go.* **5.** extra time or an exemption given to someone who is under an obligation: *The teacher is giving me a week's grace to finish this paper.* **6.** the spirit of God in man; the love and favor of God: *to pray for grace.* **7.** *(usually cap.)* a formal title used in addressing or speaking of a duke, duchess, or archbishop (often preceded by *His, Your,* etc.): *You must ask His Grace for permission. Thank you, Your Grace.* —*v.*, **graced, grac·ing. 8.** to add grace or beauty to; adorn; beautify: *Many fine trees graced the country road.* **9.** to favor or honor: *The president graced their meeting with her presence.* **10. fall from grace, a.** (in religion) to fall back into sinful behavior. **b.** to lose favor with someone in power: *After falling from grace he never worked for the government again.* **11. have the grace to,** to have the good manners or kindness to: *At least you could have the grace to apologize.* **12. with good grace,** willingly; obligingly: *to assume responsibility with good grace.*

grace·ful (grās′fəl), *adj.* having or showing beauty or elegance of appearance, manner, motion, etc.; full of grace: *a graceful dancer; a graceful greeting.* —**grace′ful·ly,** *adv.* —**grace′ful·ness,** *n.*

grace·less (grās′lis), *adj.* 1. lacking grace, elegance, or charm: *a graceless performance.* 2. lacking any sense of what is right or proper: *graceless behavior.*

Grac·es (grā′siz), *n.pl.* (in Greek mythology) three sister goddesses, daughters of Zeus, who brought grace, charm, and beauty into life.

gra·cious (grā′shəs), *adj.* 1. kind and courteous; friendly: *They gave us a gracious welcome.* 2. marked by good taste, comfort, or luxury: *They enjoy gracious living.* —*interj.* 3. (used as an exclamation of surprise, relief, dismay, etc.): *Gracious, the lion is loose!* —**gra′cious·ly,** *adv.* —**gra′cious·ness,** *n.*

grack·le (grak′əl), *n.* any of several blackbirds having a harsh, grating cry.

gra·da·tion (grā dā′shən), *n.* 1. any process or change that takes place by degrees or stages: *As night falls, there is a gradation from light to darkness.* 2. any degree or stage in such a series: *the gradations of gray between white and black.*

grade (grād), *n.* 1. a class or level of advancement in school: *In American schools there are usually 12 grades before college.* 2. a degree or level in a scale of rank, quality, value, etc.: *This meat is of the highest grade.* 3. a number or letter showing the quality of a student's work; mark: *What was your grade on the spelling test?* 4. a slope or degree of slope: *There's a steep grade in the road ahead.* —*v.,* **grad·ed, grad·ing.** 5. to arrange in grades or classes; sort: *to grade eggs according to size.* 6. to give a grade to (a student's work); mark: *to grade essays.* 7. to change gradually; blend: *Blue grades into purple.* 8. to make level or even: *to grade a road.* 9. **make the grade,** to achieve one's goal; succeed: *to make the grade as a singer.*

grade′ cross′ing, a place where a railroad track crosses another track or a road on the same level.

grade′ school′, another name for **elementary school.**

grad·u·al (graj′ōō əl), *adj.* happening, moving, etc., little by little or by degrees; slow: *a gradual improvement in health.* —**grad′u·al·ly,** *adv.*

grad·u·ate (graj′ōō it), *n.* 1. a person who has received a degree or diploma upon finishing a course of study in a school, college, etc. —*adj.* 2. of, referring to, or engaged in studies beyond those of a college level: *graduate courses; a graduate student.* —*v.* (graj′ōō āt′), **grad·u·at·ed, grad·u·at·ing.** 3. to receive a degree or diploma upon completing a course of study (often fol. by *from*): *to graduate from high school.* 4. to award a degree or diploma to (a student) after completing a course of study: *Our school is graduating 90 students this spring.* 5. to mark degrees or gradations on (a ruler, tube, etc.).

grad·u·a·tion (graj′ōō ā′shən), *n.* 1. the act of graduating, or the state of being graduated: *He worked hard to reach graduation.* 2. a ceremony at which degrees or diplomas are given to students who have finished a course of study: *Are your parents coming to the graduation?* 3. marks or a mark on a ruler, thermometer, or the like, showing degree, length, etc.

graft¹ (graft), *n.* 1. a bud, shoot, or branch of a plant inserted into or spliced onto another plant that is rooted in the ground so that it will continue to grow. 2. the plant resulting from this operation. 3. a piece of living tissue transplanted from one part of the body to another or from one body to another: *a skin graft.* 4. the act of grafting. —*v.* 5. to insert or attach (part of one plant) into or onto another. 6. to transplant (tissue) from one part of the body to another or from one body to another. [from an Old French word meaning "hunting knife," which comes from Greek *grapheion* "stylus"] —**graft′er,** *n.*

Grafts

graft² (graft), *n.* 1. the gaining of money or advantage by dishonest or underhand means, esp. by unfair use of one's position or influence in politics or business: *The new mayor promises to wipe out graft.* 2. money gained in this way. —*v.* 3. to practice graft. 4. to get (money or advantage) by graft. [probably a special use of *graft¹*] —**graft′er,** *n.*

gra·ham (grā′əm), *adj.* made of unsifted whole-wheat flour: *graham crackers.* [named after S. *Graham* (1794–1851), U.S. dietitian]

Grail (grāl), *n.* (in medieval legend) a cup from which Jesus drank at the Last Supper, and which had supernatural powers. Also, **Holy Grail.**

grain (grān), *n.* 1. the small, hard seed of a food plant, such as wheat, corn, rye, oats, rice, etc. 2. the plants bearing such edible seeds: *a field of waving grain.* 3. any small hard particle: *a grain of sand.* 4. a unit of weight used in medicine, equivalent to about ¹/₅₀₀ ounce, or 0.0648 gram. 5. the pattern of fibers in wood, cloth, etc.: *Oak has a coarse, open grain.* 6. the smallest possible amount of anything: *There's not a grain of truth in his story.* 7. nature or natural temperament: *Lying goes against his grain.* 8. **with a grain of salt,** with caution; warily or suspiciously: *I take that excuse with a grain of salt.*

grain′ al′cohol. See **alcohol** (def. 1).

grain·y (grā′nē), *adj.,* **grain·i·er, grain·i·est.** 1. having many small particles or lumps; rough; coarse: *grainy soil; a grainy surface.* 2. full of grains or grain. 3. having a natural or artificial grain: *grainy wood.*

gram (gram), *n.* a unit of mass in the metric system, equal to ¹/₁₀₀₀ kilogram, or 0.0353 ounce. *Symbol:* g

-gram, a suffix used to form nouns meaning 1. something drawn: *diagram.* 2. something written: *monogram.* 3. a message: *cablegram.* 4. a weight of so many grams: *kilogram.*

gram′ cal′orie. See **calorie** (def. 1).

gram·mar (gram′ər), *n.* 1. the study of the forms and functions of language. 2. a book dealing with grammar. 3. grammatical rules: *He knows his grammar.* 4. correctness of speech or writing, according to these rules: *His grammar is poor.*

gram·mar·i·an (grə mâr′ē ən), *n.* a specialist in the study of grammar; an expert in grammar.

gram′mar school′, 1. another name for **elemen-**

tary school. **2.** (in Great Britain) a school on the same level as an American high school.

gram·mat·i·cal (grə mat′i kəl), *adj.* **1.** of or referring to grammar: *a grammatical construction.* **2.** conforming to the rules of grammar. "The boys were playing" is grammatical. "The boys was playing" is ungrammatical. —**grammat′i·cal·ly,** *adv.*

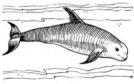

gram·pus (gram′pəs), *n.* a large ocean-dwelling animal related to the dolphin.

Grampus
(length 9 to 13 ft.)

Gra·na·da (grə nä′də), *n.* a city in S Spain: a Moorish stronghold in the Middle Ages.

gra·na·ry (grā′nə rē, gran′ə rē), *n., pl.* **gra·na·ries.** a storehouse for grain.

grand (grand), *adj.* **1.** very large and impressive; majestic; magnificent: *a grand castle.* **2.** stately or regal: *The prince greeted his guests in a grand manner.* **3.** very ambitious or lofty: *to be full of grand ideas.* **4.** noble or honored; of great distinction: *a grand old man.* **5.** highest or very high in rank: *a grand duke.* **6.** main or chief: *the grand prize.* **7.** complete or final: *the grand total.* **8.** very good or splendid: *We had a grand time at the circus.* —*n., pl.* **grand.** **9.** *Informal.* a thousand dollars. —**grand′ly,** *adv.*

grand·aunt (grand′ant′), *n.* another name for **great-aunt.**

Grand′ Can′yon, a gorge of the Colorado River in N Arizona: over 200 miles long; 1 mile deep.

grand·child (gran′-child′), *n., pl.* **grand·chil·dren.** a child of one's son or daughter.

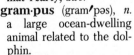

grand·dad (gran′dad′), *n. Informal.* grandfather.

grand·daugh·ter (gran′-dô′tər), *n.* a daughter of one's son or daughter.

gran·dee (gran dē′), *n.* a man of high rank or social position, esp. a Spanish or Portuguese nobleman.

gran·deur (gran′jər), *n.* the quality of being grand and impressive; majesty; splendor.

grand·fa·ther (gran′fä′thər, grand′-), *n.* the father of one's father or mother.

gran·dil·o·quent (gran dil′ə kwənt), *adj.* speaking or expressed in a lofty or pompous manner; too grand: *a long-winded, grandiloquent speaker; a grandiloquent sermon.* —**gran·dil′o·quence,** *n.*

gran·di·ose (gran′dē ōs′), *adj.* **1.** very grand; magnificent. **2.** grand in a false or artificial way; pompous; too lofty: *The guests were soon bored by their host's grandiose manners.* —**gran·di·ose′ly,** *adv.*

grand′ ju′ry, a jury, usually of 12 to 33 persons, appointed to inquire into alleged offenses to see if there is enough evidence to bring the matter to trial.

grand·ma (gran′mä, grand′-), *n. Informal.* one's grandmother.

grand·moth·er (gran′muth′ər, grand′-), *n.* the mother of one's father or mother.

grand·pa (gran′pä′, grand′-), *n. Informal.* grandfather.

grand·par·ent (gran′pâr′ənt, grand′-), *n.* a parent of either of one's parents.

grand′ pian′o, a harp-shaped piano whose case is horizontal. See also **upright piano.**

Grand′ Rap′ids, a city in SW Michigan.

grand′ slam′. See under **slam².**

grand·son (gran′sun′, grand′-), *n.* a son of one's son or daughter.

grand·stand (gran′stand′, grand′-), *n.* the main seating area of a sports stadium, racetrack, or the like, having raised rows of individual seats, and often covered by a roof.

grand·un·cle (grand′uñ′kəl), *n.* another name for **great-uncle.**

grange (grānj), *n.* **1.** *British.* a farm and its buildings. **2. the Grange,** an association of farmers in the U.S.

gran·ite (gran′it), *n.* a very hard volcanic rock used for buildings, tombstones, etc.

gran·ny (gran′ē), *n., pl.* **gran·nies.** **1.** *Informal.* a grandmother. **2.** an old woman. **3.** a fussy person.

gran′ny knot′, an incorrect square knot in which the second loop is pulled the wrong way so that the knot jams and is hard to untie. See illus. at **knot.**

gra·no·la (grə nō′lə), *n.* a dry mixture of cereals, nuts, dried fruit, etc., usually served in milk.

grant (grant), *v.* **1.** to give or allow, esp. in a formal way: *to grant a request.* **2.** to admit or accept for the sake of argument: *I grant that you were right, but why did you report us?* —*n.* **3.** something that is granted or bestowed: *a grant of land.* **4. take for granted,** to accept (something) as true, completed, permitted, etc.: *He took it for granted that you wouldn't mind.*

Grant (grant), *n.* **Ulysses S(imp·son)** (simp′-sən), 1822–1885, Union general in the Civil War: 18th President of the U.S. 1869–1877.

gran·u·lar (gran′yə lər), *adj.* having or made up of granules or little grains: *Sand is granular.*

gran·u·late (gran′yə lāt′), *v.*, **gran·u·lat·ed, gran·u·lat·ing.** to form into granules or grains; make or become granular. —**gran′u·la′tion,** *n.*

gran·ule (gran′yool), *n.* a little grain; small particle: *a granule of sugar.*

grape (grāp), *n.* **1.** a rounded, smooth-skinned fruit that grows in clusters or vines. Wine is made from the juice of grapes. **2.** short for **grapeshot.**

grape·fruit (grāp′froot′), *n., pl.* **grape·fruit** or **grape·fruits.** **1.** a large, rounded, pale-yellow citrus fruit. **2.** the tree that bears this fruit.

grape·shot (grāp′shot′), *n.* small iron balls formerly used as a charge for cannon. Also, **grape.**

grape·vine (grāp′vīn′), *n.* **1.** a vine that bears grapes. **2.** a person-to-person method of passing secret information: *The students learned through the grapevine that they were getting a new principal.*

graph (graf), *n.* a diagram that shows the way something changes with time, or the relationship between two or more things, by means of lines, dots, bars, portions of a circle, etc.

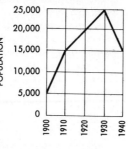

Line graph

-graph, a suffix used to form nouns meaning **1.** something written: *autograph.* **2.** something recorded: *photograph.* **3.** an instrument for making, reproducing, or transmitting any record or recording: *seismograph; phonograph; telegraph.*

graph·ic (graf′ik), *adj.* **1.** giving a clear picture; very descriptive; vivid: *a graphic story of adventure.* **2.** referring to the use of graphs or diagrams: *a graphic presentation of our findings.* **3.** referring to or expressed in writing: *The alphabet is made up of graphic symbols.* **4.** of or referring to drawing, painting, etching, lithography, etc.: *the graphic arts.* —**graph′i·cal·ly,** *adv.*

graph·ite (graf′īt), *n.* a soft black mineral, a form of carbon, used for making pencils and as a lubricant.

-graphy, a suffix used to form nouns meaning **1.** a written description: *geography.* **2.** a process of writing, drawing, or printing: *photography.*

grap·nel (grap′nəl), *n.* **1.** Also, **grap′pling i′ron, grap′pling hook′.** a device consisting of one or more large hooks on a single shaft, used for pulling or holding something; grapple: *The sailor used a grapnel to pull his boat alongside the ship.* **2.** a small anchor having three or more hooks.

Grapnel (def. 2)

grap·ple (grap′əl), *v.,* **grap·pled, grap·pling. 1.** to seize or hold with or as if with a grapnel; hold or fasten tightly: *The miser grappled his gold to his chest and fled.* **2.** to wrestle, struggle, or contend (usually fol. by *with*): *to grapple with an attacker; to grapple with a problem.* —*n.* **3.** a large hook; grapnel. —**grap′pler,** *n.*

grasp (grasp), *v.* **1.** to seize and hold firmly, esp. with a hand or hands. **2.** to understand; get hold of mentally: *I didn't grasp what she was trying to say.* **3.** to try to catch hold; grab (usually fol. by *at* or *for*): *He grasped at the railing to keep from falling.* —*n.* **4.** a hold or grip: *He had a firm grasp on the hammer.* **5.** one's arms or hands; an embrace or firm hold. **6.** power of reaching or attaining; reach: *Victory is within our grasp.* **7.** power to understand; understanding: *to have a good grasp of mathematics.* **8.** hold, control, or possession: *to wrest power from the grasp of a dictator.*

grasp·ing (gras′ping), *adj.* greedy; eager to acquire all one can: *a miserly, grasping person.*

grass (gras), *n.* **1.** any of numerous plants having slender leaves that wrap around jointed stems.

Grasses are used in lawns, and the family includes all the grains grown for food. **2.** ground or land on which there is grass.

grass·hop·per (gras′hop′ər), *n.* any of numerous plant-eating insects, having long, powerful hind legs that permit them to make large jumps.

grass·land (gras′land′), *n.* an area, such as a prairie, covered mainly with grass and having few trees.

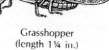

Grasshopper
(length 1¼ in.)

grass′ roots′, *(used as sing. or pl.)* the common or ordinary people, esp. those living in the country rather than in cities: *a candidate who has support among the grass roots.*

grass·y (gras′ē), *adj.,* **grass·i·er, grass·i·est. 1.** covered with grass: *a grassy hill.* **2.** of, like, or referring to grass: *a grassy green.* —**grass′i·ness,** *n.*

grate¹ (grāt), *n.* **1.** a frame of metal bars for holding fuel in a fireplace or furnace: *Stir the coals in the grate.* **2.** a framework of crossed bars or parallel bars, used to guard, cover, or the like; grating: *a grate over a drain.* **3.** a fireplace. —*v.,* **grat·ed, grat·ing. 4.** to furnish with a grate or grates. [from the medieval Latin word *grata* "grating"]

grate² (grāt), *v.,* **grat·ed, grat·ing. 1.** to irritate or annoy (usually fol. by *on*): *His practical jokes grate on me.* **2.** to rub (a vegetable, cheese, etc.) against a rough surface so that it is pared down to small bits or slivers: *to grate carrots.* **3.** to scrape or grind with a rough, harsh sound: *The car wheels grated against the curb.* [from the Old French word *grater* "to grate"]

grate·ful (grāt′fəl), *adj.* **1.** thankful or full of gratitude: *The shipwrecked men were grateful to be rescued.* **2.** showing or expressing thankfulness and gratitude: *a grateful letter; a grateful smile.* **3.** very welcome; pleasing: *the grateful sound of rain after a hot day.* —**grate′ful·ly,** *adv.* —**grate′ful·ness,** *n.*

grat·er (grā′tər), *n.* **1.** a metal device having a rough surface for grating vegetables, cheese, or the like. **2.** a person or thing that grates.

grat·i·fi·ca·tion (grat′ə fə kā′shən), *n.* **1.** satisfaction or pleasure. **2.** something that gives satisfaction or pleasure: *Your letters are a gratification to your family.* **3.** the act of gratifying or pleasing.

grat·i·fy (grat′ə fī′), *v.,* **grat·i·fied, grat·i·fy·ing. 1.** to give pleasure or satisfaction to: *Winning the ball game gratified the team.* **2.** to indulge or satisfy: *to gratify a taste for sweets by eating candy.*

grat·ing¹ (grā′ting), *n.* a framework of bars or the like set in or over an opening such as a window, or used as a divider for security; grate: *The hot-air register is covered by a grating.* [from *grate¹* + *-ing*]

grat·ing² (grā′ting), *adj.* **1.** annoying or irritating: *A whiny voice can be grating.* **2.** harsh or rasping: *a grating sound.* [from *grate²* + *-ing*]

grat·is (grat′is, grā′tis), *adv., adj.* without charge or payment; free: *He helped us change the tire gratis. The second cup of coffee was gratis.* [from Latin]

grat·i·tude (grat′i tood′, -tyood′), *n.* the quality or feeling of being grateful or thankful; gratefulness: *He is full of gratitude for your help.*

gra·tu·i·tous (grə tōō'i təs, -tyōō'-), *adj.* 1. given or obtained without charge or payment; free: *gratuitous help in an emergency.* 2. being without any apparent cause or reason: *a gratuitous insult.* —**gra·tu'i·tous·ly,** *adv.*

gra·tu·i·ty (grə tōō'i tē, -tyōō'-), *n., pl.* **gra·tu·i·ties.** a gift of money, or money given over and above what is due; tip: *to give a gratuity to a waiter.*

grave¹ (grāv), *n.* 1. a space dug in the earth to receive a dead body in burial. 2. any place where a body has been buried or has come to rest. 3. one's death: *He never feared danger or the grave.* [from the Old English word *græf*]

grave² (grāv), *adj.,* **grav·er, grav·est.** 1. serious or solemn; earnest: *a grave person.* 2. very important, serious, or demanding; critical: *a grave problem.* [from a French word, which comes from Latin *gravis*] —**grave'ly,** *adv.*

grave³ (grāv), *v.,* **graved; grav·en** (grā'vən) *or* **graved; grav·ing.** to engrave or shape with a chisel or other tool; sculpture. [from the Old English word *grafan* "to dig, engrave"]

grave' ac'cent (grāv, gräv), a mark (`) placed over certain letters, as in French words: *père* "father."

grav·el (grav'əl), *n.* small stones, pebbles, or pieces of stone. Gravel is used for walks, driveways, and under concrete in making roads.

grav·el·ly (grav'ə lē), *adj.* 1. of or like gravel: *a gravelly path.* 2. harsh and rough in sound: *a deep, gravelly voice.*

grav·en (grā'vən), *v.* 1. a past participle of **grave³.** —*adj.* 2. carved or sculptured: *a graven idol.*

grave·stone (grāv'stōn'), *n.* a stone marking a grave.

grave·yard (grāv'yärd'), *n.* a place for burying the dead; cemetery; burial ground.

grav·i·tate (grav'i tāt'), *v.,* **grav·i·tat·ed, grav·i·tat·ing.** 1. to move in response to the force of gravity; sink. 2. to tend or be attracted; move (usually fol. by *to* or *toward*): *to gravitate toward home.*

grav·i·ta·tion (grav'i tā'shən), *n.* 1. Also, **gravity.** the attraction that draws all the bodies in the universe toward one another. Gravitation draws things on the earth's surface toward the center of the earth and keeps the earth itself in its orbit around the sun. 2. a movement or tendency toward something or someone. —**grav'i·ta'tion·al,** *adj.*

grav'ita'tional accelera'tion. See g.

grav·i·ty (grav'i tē), *n.* 1. See **gravitation** (def. 1). 2. serious or dignified behavior; solemnity: *The gravity of the president's manner quieted the audience.* 3. serious or dangerous nature: *the gravity of an illness.*

gra·vy (grā'vē), *n., pl.* **gra·vies.** a sauce of the juices and fat from cooked meat.

gray (grā), *n.* 1. a color between black and white, and not including any red, yellow, or blue; a color

made by mixing black and white. 2. an object or material of this color: *You ride the black horse, and I'll ride the gray.* —*adj.* 3. of the color gray: *a gray sky.* 4. having hair that is gray: *My grandfather still isn't gray.* 5. gloomy or dismal: *We might succeed, but the outlook is very gray.* —*v.* 6. to make or become gray. Also, **grey.** —**gray'ish,** *adj.* —**gray'ness,** *n.*

gray·beard (grā'bērd'), *n.* an old man.

gray' mat'ter, 1. a kind of nerve tissue whose color is a reddish gray. 2. *Informal.* one's brains or intelligence.

graze¹ (grāz), *v.,* **grazed, graz·ing.** 1. to feed on growing grass, pasture land, etc.: *Buffalo herds grazed on the prairies.* 2. to put (cattle, sheep, or the like) out to graze: *Graze the cows in the lower pasture.* [from the Old English word *grasian,* which is related to English *grass*]

graze² (grāz), *v.,* **grazed, graz·ing.** 1. to touch, rub, or scrape (something) in passing: *He grazed me as he ran by. The car grazed against the wall.* 2. to scrape the skin from: *She grazed her elbow when she fell.* —*n.* 3. a scrape or scratch on the skin. 4. the act of grazing; a rubbing or scraping. [from a special use of *graze¹*]

Gr. Br., Great Britain. Also, **Gr. Brit.**

grease (grēs), *n.* 1. something that is fatty or oily, esp. a solid substance used as a lubricant: *axle grease.* —*v.* (grēs, grēz), **greased, greas·ing.** 2. to put grease on: *to grease a squeaky hinge.*

grease' paint', an oily make-up used by actors, clowns, etc.

greas·y (grē'sē, grē'zē), *adj.,* **greas·i·er, greas·i·est.** 1. smeared or soiled with grease: *greasy coveralls.* 2. made of or containing grease; oily: *greasy food.* 3. like grease in appearance; slippery. —**greas'i·ness,** *n.*

great (grāt), *adj.* 1. unusually large in size; big; vast: *a great oak tree.* 2. large in number; very numerous: *a great flock of birds.* 3. unusual in strength, degree, or the like: *to feel great pain.* 4. outstanding or remarkable; excellent: *a great book.* 5. having important consequences; very important: *The president was faced with a great decision.* 6. of notable length or duration; long: *to wait a great while.* 7. *Informal.* **a.** enthusiastic about or very good at something (usually fol. by *at, for,* or *on*): *to be great at playing basketball.* **b.** excellent or very good: *a great movie.* —*adv.* 8. *Informal.* very well: *Our team is going great.* —*n., pl.* **greats** *or* **great.** 9. an important or distinguished person, work of art, or the like: *Rembrandt is one of the greats.* —**great'ness,** *n.*

great-aunt (grāt'ant'), *n.* an aunt of one's father or mother; grandaunt.

Great' Bear', a constellation in the northern sky containing the seven stars of the Big Dipper.

Great' Bear' Lake', a lake in NW Canada. 1200 mi. long.

Great' Brit'ain, an island of NW Europe, made up of England, Scotland, and Wales. 88,139 sq. mi.

great' cal'orie. See **calorie** (def. 2).

great′ cir′cle, the circle formed by a plane passing through the center of a sphere, so called because planes that do not do so form circles of smaller diameter. Great circles are important in navigation because the shortest path between two points on the earth's surface is always part of a great circle.

great·coat (grāt′kōt′), *n.* a heavy overcoat.

Great′ Dane′, a very large, powerful, short-haired dog.

Great′ Divide′, another name for the Continental Divide.

Great′er Antil′les. See under Antilles.

great-grand·child (grāt′gran′child′), *n., pl.* **great-grand·chil·dren.** a grandchild of one's son or daughter.

Great Dane
(32 in. high
at shoulder)

great-grand·par·ent (grāt′gran′pâr′ənt, -grand′), *n.* a grandfather or grandmother of one's father or mother.

great-heart·ed (grāt′här′tid), *adj.* 1. having or showing a generous spirit; generous: *a great-hearted gift.* 2. high-spirited or courageous; fearless.

Great′ Lakes′, a series of five lakes between the U.S. and Canada: made up of Lakes Erie, Huron, Michigan, Ontario, and Superior.

great·ly (grāt′lē), *adv.* 1. in or to a great degree; very much: *greatly improved.* 2. in a great manner.

Great′ Plains′, a semiarid region in the central U.S. and Canada.

Great′ Salt′ Lake′, a shallow salt lake in NW Utah. 2300 sq. mi.; maximum depth 60 ft.

Great′ Slave′ Lake′, a lake in NW Canada. 11,-172 sq. mi.

great-un·cle (grāt′ung′kəl), *n.* an uncle of one's father or mother; granduncle.

Great′ Wall′ of Chi′na, a system of walls constructed as a defense for China against the nomads of the northern regions: completed in the 3rd century B.C. 2000 mi. long.

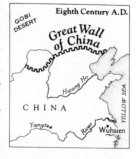

greave (grēv), *n.* a piece of armor for the leg between the knee and the ankle, usually made up of front and back parts.

grebe (grēb), *n.* any of several diving birds related to the loon.

Gre·cian (grē′shən), *adj.* 1. of Greece or the Greeks: *a Grecian vase.* —*n.* 2. a Greek person.

Greece (grēs), *n.* a republic in S Europe at the S end of the Balkan Peninsula. 50,944 sq. mi. *Cap.:* Athens. Ancient name, **Hellas.**

greed (grēd), *n.* a very great and selfish desire or hunger for something, esp. for money.

greed·y (grē′dē), *adj.,* **greed·i·er, greed·i·est.** 1. having a great and selfish desire for money. 2. having a strong desire or hunger for food or drink: *a greedy piglet.* 3. full of desire; eager (often fol. by *for*): *greedy for knowledge.* —**greed′i·ly,** *adv.* —**greed′i·ness,** *n.*

Greek (grēk), *adj.* 1. of or referring to Greece, the Greeks, or their language. —*n.* 2. a native or inhabitant of Greece, or a person of Greek descent. 3. a branch of the Indo-European family of languages, including the languages and dialects spoken in ancient and modern Greece.

Greek′ Or′thodox Church′, a branch of the Orthodox Church: the national church of Greece.

green (grēn), *n.* 1. the color of growing grass and leaves. 2. material or clothing of this color: *She wore green.* 3. an object of this color: *You play with the red marbles, and I'll take the green.* 4. grassy land or a plot covered by a lawn, for example an area of lawn surrounding a hole on a golf course. 5. **greens, a.** the leaves and stems of spinach, lettuce, cabbage, etc., used for food. **b.** fresh leaves and branches used for making wreaths or other decorations. —*adj.* 6. of the color green: *a green hat.* 7. covered with grass or leaves: *green fields.* 8. unripe; not grown enough: *These melons are still green.* 9. inexperienced or untrained: *green troops.* 10. not yet fully developed in age or judgment; young: *a green kid.* 11. made of green vegetables: *a green salad.* 12. not prepared for use; not dried or cured: *green lumber.* —**green′ish,** *adj.*

green·back (grēn′bak′), *n.* a piece of paper money issued by the U.S. government, and usually printed in green on the back.

green·er·y (grē′nə rē), *n.* green plants; leaves and grass: *to wander in the greenery of the countryside.*

green·gage (grēn′gāj′), *n.* any of several kinds of large, light-green plums.

green·horn (grēn′hôrn′), *n. Slang.* a person who is inexperienced or easily tricked; newcomer or beginner: *The cowboys played tricks on the greenhorns.*

green·house (grēn′hous′), *n., pl.* **green·hous·es** (grēn′hou′ziz). a building for growing plants and flowers, having a glass roof and walls.

Green·land (grēn′lənd, -land′), *n.* an island located NE of North America: the largest island in the world; an overseas territory of Denmark. ab. 840,000 sq. mi.

green·ness (grēn′nis), *n.* 1. the quality or state of being green: *the greenness of a lawn.* 2. growing plants; greenery. 3. the lack of maturity or experience; youthfulness; innocence.

Greens·bo·ro (grēnz′bûr′ō, grēnz′bur′ō), *n.* a city in N North Carolina.

green·sward (grēn′swôrd′), *n.* green, grassy turf; grassy ground.

Green·wich (gren′ich), *n.* a borough of London, England. The prime meridian, which passes through Greenwich, is used as a standard for reckoning longitude and time.

Green′wich Time′, a time standard used in international dealings, navigation, and much scientific work (formerly the time along the prime meridian, which passes through Greenwich, England). Also, **Green′wich Mean′ Time′**.

green·wood (grēn′wŏŏd′), *n.* a wood or forest when green, as it is in summer.

greet (grēt), *v.* 1. to speak words of welcome to (a person) or say "hello," "good morning," or the like; welcome: *He greeted us at the door.* 2. to meet or receive: *The audience greeted his suggestion with boos.* 3. to present itself to; appear before: *a horrible sight greeted our eyes.* —**greet′er,** *n.*

greet·ing (grē′tĭng), *n.* 1. the act or words of someone who greets another or others: *the greeting of guests; a kind greeting.* 2. Often, **greetings.** a friendly message from someone who is absent.

gre·gar·i·ous (grĭ gâr′ē əs), *adj.* 1. fond of the company of others; sociable: *a friendly, gregarious man.* 2. (of animals) living in flocks, herds, or groups: *Sheep are gregarious.* —**gre·gar′i·ous·ly,** *adv.*

Gre·go·ri·an (grĭ gôr′ē ən), *adj.* of or referring to any of the popes named Gregory, esp. Gregory I or Gregory XIII.

Grego′rian cal′endar, the calendar now in use. [named after Pope *Gregory* XIII]

Grego′rian chant′, a kind of music, consisting of unaccompanied melodies, sung during services in the Catholic Church.

Greg·o·ry I (greg′ə rē), A.D. c540–604, Italian pope A.D. 590–604: reformer of monastic life and thought to be the composer of Gregorian chant.

Gregory XIII, 1502–1585, Italian pope 1572–1585: devised modern calendar.

grem·lin (grem′lĭn), *n.* a mischievous invisible being.

gre·nade (grĭ nād′), *n.* a small bomb, esp. one designed to be thrown by hand. [from a French word, which comes from Spanish *granada* "pomegranate"]

gren·a·dier (gren′ə dēr′), *n.* 1. a member of a particular regiment (**Gren′adier Guards′**) in the British army. 2. (formerly) a soldier who threw grenades.

grew (grōō), *v.* the past tense of **grow**.

grey (grā), *n., adj., v.* another spelling of **gray**. —**grey′ish,** *adj.* —**grey′ness,** *n.*

grey·hound (grā′hound′), *n.* a tall, slender, graceful dog used for racing and hunting. [from the Old English word *grīghund,* which comes from Old Norse *greyhundr,* from *grey* "female dog, bitch" + *hundr* "hound"]

grid (grid), *n.* 1. a framework or grating of crossed or parallel bars; gridiron. 2. something resembling this, such as a system of vertical and horizontal lines on a map that divides the area into smaller squares. 3. a mesh of fine wires in an electron tube that is used to control the

Greyhound
(28 in. high
at shoulder)

flow of current through the tube. 4. a network of electric generating and distributing stations.

grid·dle (grid′əl), *n.* 1. a frying pan with a handle and a slightly raised edge, for cooking pancakes, bacon, etc. 2. any flat, heated surface, esp. on the top of a stove, for cooking food.

grid·dle·cake (grid′əl kāk′), *n.* a pancake.

grid·i·ron (grid′ī′ərn), *n.* 1. a rack or framework of metal bars on which meat or other food may be broiled; grill. 2. something resembling this, such as a framework of metal pipes; grid. 3. a football field.

grief (grēf), *n.* 1. deep sorrow or regret; great sadness. 2. a cause of deep sorrow or sadness. 3. **come to grief,** to suffer disappointment or misfortune; fail: *The show came to grief when the lights failed.*

griev·ance (grē′vəns), *n.* a real or imagined wrong or injustice that is considered a reason for complaint.

grieve (grēv), *v.,* **grieved, griev·ing.** 1. to feel grief or deep sadness; sorrow: *The captain grieved over the loss of his ship.* 2. to cause grief or great sorrow to (someone): *The death of the king grieved the nation.*

griev·ous (grē′vəs), *adj.* 1. causing grief or sorrow: *to suffer a grievous loss.* 2. full of or showing grief; sorrowful: *grievous tears.* 3. outrageous or atrocious; terrible: *a grievous crime.* 4. causing great pain; severe: *a grievous wound.* —**griev′ous·ly,** *adv.* —**griev′ous·ness,** *n.*

grif·fin (grif′in), *n.* an imaginary beast in legends and stories, having the head and wings of an eagle and the body of a lion.

grill[1] (gril), *n.* 1. a framework or rack of metal bars for broiling meat or other food over a fire; gridiron. 2. a dish of food that has been cooked on a grill. —*v.* 3. to broil; cook over or close to a fire: *to grill a steak.* 4. *Informal.* to question severely and thoroughly: *The police grilled the suspect about the crime.* [from the French word *gril* "gridiron," which comes from Latin *crāticula* "wickerwork, hurdle"]

Griffin

grill[2] (gril), *n.* another spelling of **grille**.

grille (gril), *n.* a grating serving as a barrier or screen, often decorative: *a wrought-iron grille over a window.* [from an Old French word, which comes from Latin *crāticula* "wickerwork"]

grill·work (gril′wûrk′), *n.* metal, wood, or the like, formed into a grille or to look like a grille.

grim (grim), *adj.,* **grim·mer, grim·mest.** 1. stern or harsh; deeply serious: *The general looked grim and angry when he heard the news.* 2. horrible or ghastly: *He made a grim joke about his own sickness.* 3. unyielding; not permitting change or compromise: *They fought with grim determination.* 4. fierce, savage, or cruel: *a grim battle.* —**grim′ly,** *adv.* —**grim′ness,** *n.*

grim·ace (grim′əs, grĭ mās′), *n.* 1. an expression of the face in which the features are twisted in a way that shows pain, disgust, or the like. —*v.,* **grim·aced,**

grim·ac·ing. 2. to make grimaces; make a face: *He grimaced when he was told to stay after school.*

grime (grīm), *n.* 1. dirt, soot, thick, oily grit, or the like, esp. when rubbed into a surface: *You'll have to scrub to get the grime out of these work clothes.* —*v.*, **grimed, grim·ing.** 2. to cover with dirt; soil.

Grimm (grim), *n.* **Jakob**, 1785–1863, and his brother **Wilhelm**, 1786–1859, German folklorists: noted for their collection of fairy tales.

Grim′ Reap′er. See reaper (def. 3).

grim·y (grī′mē), *adj.*, **grim·i·er, grim·i·est.** covered with grime or dirt: *grimy hands.* —**grim′i·ness,** *n.*

grin (grin), *v.*, **grinned, grin·ning.** 1. to smile broadly: *to grin at a joke.* 2. to draw back the lips and show the teeth in a snarl or grimace: *The watchdog grinned menacingly at the stranger.* —*n.* 3. a broad smile. 4. a snarling or grimacing expression.

grind (grīnd), *v.*, **ground** (ground), **grind·ing.** 1. to shape, smooth, or sharpen by rubbing against something rough: *to grind an ax on a grindstone.* 2. to break down into small bits or a powder by pounding or crushing: *to grind wheat into flour.* 3. to produce by crushing or rubbing roughly: *to grind flour.* 4. to rub harshly; grate together: *to grind one's teeth.* 5. to work by turning a crank: *to grind a hand organ.* 6. to wear down or make miserable; oppress: *Constant hunger can grind one's spirit.* 7. to produce with effort but not much imagination (usually fol. by *out*): *to grind out magazine articles.* 8. *Informal.* to work or study hard (usually fol. by *away*): *to grind away at one's homework.* —*n.* 9. the act of grinding; a grinding. 10. difficult, usually uninteresting, work: *Cleaning out the garage is a grind.* 11. *Informal.* a person who works or studies constantly, but without pleasure.

grind·er (grīn′dər), *n.* 1. a person or thing that grinds, esp. a person who sharpens axes, knives, scissors, etc. 2. a molar tooth.

grind·stone (grīnd′stōn′), *n.* a rotating stone disk used for sharpening knives, tools, etc.

grip (grip), *n.* 1. a grasping or holding tight; firm grasp. 2. power of gripping: *to have a strong grip.* 3. a grasp, hold, or control: *to be in the grip of fear.* 4. understanding; mental grasp: *to have a good grip on a problem.* 5. a special way of shaking or clasping hands: *Members of the club use a secret grip.* 6. a handle or hilt. 7. a small suitcase. —*v.*, **gripped** *or* **gript; grip·ping.** 8. to grasp or seize (something) firmly; hold fast: *to grip a child's hand while crossing the street.* 9. to hold the interest of; attract: *His stories grip the imagination.* 10. **come to grips with,** to deal with directly or firmly; face squarely: *The government came to grips with the problem of poverty.*

gripe (grīp), *v.*, **griped, grip·ing.** 1. to cause or suffer pain in the bowels. 2. to grip or clutch. 3. *Informal.* to complain naggingly or constantly; grumble: *He's always griping about the rules.* 4. *Informal.* to annoy or irritate: *Her tone of voice griped me.* —*n.* 5. a gripping or clutching. 6. Usually, **gripes.** a pain in the bowels; cramp. 7. *Informal.* a complaint.

grippe (grip), *n.* another name for **influenza.**

gris·ly (griz′lē), *adj.*, **gris·li·er, gris·li·est.** gruesome or horrible; causing one to shudder with fright or horror: *a grisly crime.*

grist (grist), *n.* 1. grain that is to be ground. 2. ground grain; meal produced by grinding in a mill or the like.

gris·tle (gris′əl), *n.* 1. tough, springy material sometimes found in cooked meat. 2. another name for **cartilage.**

gris·tly (gris′lē), *adj.*, **gris·tli·er, gris·tli·est.** of, resembling, or containing gristle: *tough, gristly meat.*

grist·mill (grist′mil′), *n.* a mill for grinding grain.

grit (grit), *n.* 1. fine, scratchy sand or dust. 2. toughness of character; courage and pluck. —*v.*, **grit·ted, grit·ting.** 3. to press together hard or grind together: *to grit one's teeth.*

grits (grits), *n. (used as sing. or pl.)* 1. grain that has been hulled and coarsely ground. 2. hominy or hominy grits.

grit·ty (grit′ē), *adj.*, **grit·ti·er, grit·ti·est.** 1. made of, containing, or like grit: *The salad was gritty.* 2. courageous and plucky: *a gritty little terrier.* —**grit′ti·ness,** *n.*

griz·zled (griz′əld), *adj.* gray or partly gray: *The old man had a grizzled beard.*

griz·zly (griz′lē), *adj.*, **griz·zli·er, griz·zli·est.** 1. somewhat gray; grayish: *grizzly hair.* —*n., pl.* **griz·zlies.** 2. a grizzly bear.

griz′zly bear′, a very large, ferocious bear of western North America having a grayish-brown coat.

groan (grōn), *n.* 1. a low, mournful sound like a moan, expressing pain, sorrow, disappointment, dislike, etc. 2. a deep, creaking sound made esp. by wood when too much weight is put on it. —*v.* 3. to give forth a groan of pain, disappointment, or the like. 4. to give forth a deep, creaking sound: *The rickety old stairs groaned as we climbed them.* —**groan′er,** *n.*

Grizzly bear
(length 6½ to 8 ft.)

gro·cer (grō′sər), *n.* a person who sells food supplies, such as flour, coffee, eggs, etc., and other household items, such as soap. [from the Old French word *grossier* "wholesale merchant"]

gro·cer·y (grō′sə rē), *n., pl.* **gro·cer·ies.** 1. a store selling food and other household supplies. 2. Usually, **groceries.** food and other items sold by a grocer.

grog (grog), *n.* 1. a mixture of alcoholic liquor, such as rum, and water: *The sailors were all given a cup of grog.* 2. strong drink; liquor. [named after Old *Grog*, nickname of Edward Vernon, 18th-century British admiral, who ordered the mixture for his men]

grog·gy (grog′ē), *adj.*, **grog·gi·er, grog·gi·est.** staggering or dazed from exhaustion, injury, etc.: *After the race, the runners were groggy.* —**grog′gi·ness,** *n.*

groin (groin), *n.* 1. the hollow on either side of the body where the thigh joins the abdomen. 2. (in architecture) the curved line or edge where two vaults on a ceiling meet.

groom (grōōm), *n.* **1.** a man in charge of horses or a stable. **2.** a bridegroom; a man who is about to be married or who has just been married. —*v.* **3.** to make clean, neat, and tidy; tend the appearance or clothes of: *She always grooms herself well.* **4.** to tend (a horse) by feeding it, brushing it, etc. **5.** to prepare (a person) for an official position, election, etc.: *He's being groomed for a career in politics.*

groove (grōōv), *n.* **1.** a long, narrow cut or dent in a surface; furrow: *the grooves on a phonograph record.* **2.** a fixed routine or way of doing things: *to get into a groove.* —*v.,* **grooved, groov·ing.** **3.** to cut a groove or grooves in; furrow: *to groove stone with a chisel.*

grope (grōp), *v.,* **groped, grop·ing.** **1.** to feel about with the hands; feel one's way: *to grope for a light switch in the dark.* **2.** to seek or find (one's way) by feeling with the hands: *to grope one's way out of a smoky room.* **3.** to search blindly or uncertainly: *to grope for the right answer.* —**grop′ing·ly,** *adv.*

gross (grōs), *adj.* **1.** having nothing deducted or subtracted (opposite of *net*): *Their gross profit was $10,-000, but they had to pay taxes out of that.* **2.** outrageous or flagrant; terrible: *a gross injustice.* **3.** vulgar and crude. **4.** large, bulky, or fat. —*n., pl.* **gross.** **5.** a group of 12 dozen, or 144, things: *a gross of pencils.* **6.** the entire amount or total, esp. the entire amount earned: *What was the store's gross today?* —*v.* **7.** to earn a total of; make a gross profit of: *The movie grossed two million dollars.* —**gross′ly,** *adv.* —**gross′ness,** *n.*

gro·tesque (grō tesk′), *adj.* odd or fantastic; distorted from what is or seems natural; weird: *carvings of grotesque demons.* —**gro·tesque′ly,** *adv.*

grot·to (grot′ō), *n., pl.* **grot·toes** *or* **grot·tos.** **1.** a cave or cavern. **2.** a man-made structure resembling a little cave, often used as a religious shrine.

grouch (grouch), *v.* **1.** to behave in a sulky, discontented way; complain: *to grouch about the weather.* —*n.* **2.** a sulky, discontented person; complainer.

grouch·y (grou′chē), *adj.,* **grouch·i·er, grouch·i·est.** sulky and discontented; full of complaints: *A toothache made him grouchy yesterday.* —**grouch′i·ly,** *adv.* —**grouch′i·ness,** *n.*

ground¹ (ground), *n.* **1.** the solid surface of the earth; firm or dry land. **2.** earth or soil. **3.** land, esp. of a particular kind: *The house is built on sloping ground.* **4.** Often, **grounds. a.** a tract of land used for a particular purpose: *picnic grounds.* **b.** a cause or reason for saying or doing something; the basis of a belief: *What grounds do you have for believing that he's guilty?* **5.** the main surface or background of a painting, decorative design, or the like: *silver stars on a ground of blue.* **6. grounds,** dregs or sediment: *coffee grounds.* **7.** the bottom of a lake, river, bay, ocean, etc.: *The boat hit ground.* **8.** a conducting path used by several circuits in common, often the earth itself. —*v.* **9.** to force to come down to, or re-

main, on the ground: *Bad weather grounded the planes.* **10.** to instruct in the basic rules or principles: *to ground a student in mathematics.* **11.** to run onto the bottom of a lake, river, bay, etc.: *We grounded our boat in the storm.* **12.** to establish on a base or foundation; base: *to ground an argument on facts.* **13.** to make an electric connection to the earth or to a conducting path that several circuits use in common. —*adj.* **14.** of, happening, or placed on or near the ground: *the ground floor of a building.* **15. break ground, a.** to plow. **b.** to begin excavation for a new building or other construction project: *to break ground for a new housing development.* **16. cover ground,** to make progress in dealing with a subject, topic, or the like: *We covered a lot of ground in our first discussion.* **17. from the ground up,** progressing upward from the most elementary level; gradually: *Dad learned the toy business from the ground up.* **18. give ground,** to yield or give way to force; retreat: *The enemy was forced to give ground during the assault.* **19. lose ground,** to lose one's advantage; begin to fail: *The candidate began to lose ground just before the election.* **20. off the ground,** into action or well under way: *My vacation plans never got off the ground.* **21. stand one's ground,** to maintain one's position; be firm or resolved: *I thought he would admit defeat, but he stood his ground.* [from the Old English word *grund* "bottom, ground"]

ground² (ground), *v.* **1.** the past tense and past participle of **grind.** —*adj.* **2.** broken down into small bits or dust by grinding: *ground steak.* **3.** having the surface roughened by grinding: *ground glass.*

ground′ ball′, (in baseball) a batted ball that rolls or bounces along the ground. Also, **ground·er** (groun′dər).

ground′ hog′, another name for **woodchuck.**

Ground′-hog Day′, February 2, the day on which the ground hog supposedly comes out of hibernation for the first time. According to legend, if he sees his shadow, there will be six more weeks of winter weather. Also, **Ground′hog's Day′.**

ground·less (ground′lis), *adj.* without reason or cause; not based on fact: *a groundless accusation.*

ground′ rules′, **1.** (in baseball) rules for dealing with situations relating to the playing area or to interference by spectators. **2.** the basic rules of conduct in any situation, profession, etc.

ground′ squir′rel, any of several members of the squirrel family that live on the ground, including the chipmunk.

ground′ swell′, a broad, deep swell or rolling of the sea, due to a distant storm or gale.

ground·work (ground′wûrk′), *n.* the foundation or basis of something; preparation: *Careful training is the groundwork for success in sports.*

group (grōōp), *n.* **1.** a collection or number of persons or things: *a group of students.* **2.** a number of persons or things considered as being alike or related in some way; class: *Your questions fall into two* groups. —v. **3.** to put into a group: *to group newcomers with beginners.* **4.** to form into a group: *The students grouped together in the hall.*

grouse[1] (grous), *n., pl.* **grouse** *or* **grous·es.** any of numerous game birds related to the domestic chicken.

grouse[2] (grous), *v.,* **groused, grous·ing.** *Informal.* to grumble or complain: *Stop grousing and get on with your work.* [perhaps another form of the word *grouch*]

grove (grōv), *n.* **1.** a cluster of trees, or a small wood: *to picnic in a shady grove.* **2.** a small orchard or group of fruit trees: *an orange grove.*

Grouse
(length 18 in.)

grov·el (gruv/əl, grov/əl), *v.,* **grov·eled** *or* **grov·elled; grov·el·ing** *or* **grov·el·ling.** **1.** to behave in an extremely humble manner; lower oneself out of fear or the like: *Fear made him grovel before the king.* **2.** to lie or crawl on the ground with the face downward.

grow (grō), *v.,* **grew** (grōō), **grown** (grōn), **grow·ing.** **1.** to become larger or more mature, as a living thing does: *Our plants grew very large.* **2.** to develop and live; exist: *Palm trees don't grow this far north.* **3.** to become larger, more numerous, stronger, or the like: *That city has grown tremendously in ten years.* **4.** to come to be; become: *to grow old; to grow angry.* **5.** to become gradually attached or united by or as if by growth: *to grow together.* **6.** to cause to grow; raise: *to grow corn.* **7.** to allow to grow: *to grow a beard.* **8. grow out of,** to become too large for; outgrow: *I've grown out of last year's clothes.* **9. grow up, a.** to become fully grown: *When I grow up I'm going around the world.* **b.** to come into existence: *Several cities grew up in the desert.* —**grow'er,** *n.*

growl (groul), *v.* **1.** to give forth a deep, rumbling sound in anger, as a warning, or the like: *The dog growled at the stranger.* **2.** to murmur or complain angrily; grumble. **3.** to make a rumbling noise; rumble: *His stomach growls when he's hungry.* **4.** to say in a deep, harsh voice: *to growl a good morning.* —*n.* **5.** the act or sound of growling.

grown (grōn), *v.* **1.** the past participle of **grow.** —*adj.* **2.** far along in growth: *a grown boy.* **3.** arrived at full growth or maturity; adult: *a grown man.*

grown-up (grōn/up/), *adj.* **1.** having reached full growth; mature; adult: *a grown-up person.* **2.** of, for, or proper for adults: *grown-up behavior.* —*n.* **3.** an adult person: *a party for grown-ups.*

growth (grōth), *n.* **1.** the act or process of growing; development: *the rapid growth of a city.* **2.** size or stage of development: *to reach full growth.* **3.** something that has grown or developed: *a growth of weeds.* **4.** amount grown: *one year's growth.*

grub (grub), *n.* **1.** a fat insect larva. **2.** a dull, plodding person; drudge. **3.** *Informal.* food; something to eat. —*v.,* **grubbed, grub·bing. 4.** to dig or dig up by the roots: *grubbing up tree stumps.* **5.** to lead a dull, hard life; drudge: *to grub for a living.*

grub·by (grub/ē), *adj.,* **grub·bi·er, grub·bi·est.** dirty or messy: *to be grubby after working in the garden.*

grudge (gruj), *n.* **1.** a feeling of ill will or resentment; spiteful, sullen feeling toward someone: *to bear a grudge against someone.* —*v.,* **grudged, grudg·ing. 2.** to give or permit with reluctance or bad temper; begrudge: *to grudge someone time off from work.* **3.** to resent the good fortune of (someone): *He grudges his sister her good marks in school.*

grudg·ing (gruj/ing), *adj.* showing reluctance or unwillingness; sullen: *a grudging agreement to cooperate.* —**grudg'ing·ly,** *adv.*

gru·el (grōō/əl), *n.* a thin cereal of oatmeal boiled in water or milk.

gru·el·ing (grōō/ə ling), *adj.* very tiring or exhausting; hard: *a grueling race.*

grue·some (grōō/səm), *adj.* horrible and disgusting: *the gruesome events of war.* —**grue'some·ly,** *adv.* —**grue'some·ness,** *n.*

gruff (gruf), *adj.* **1.** low and harsh; hoarse: *a gruff voice.* **2.** rough or surly: *a gruff way of talking to people.* —**gruff'ly,** *adv.* —**gruff'ness,** *n.*

grum·ble (grum/bəl), *v.,* **grum·bled, grum·bling. 1.** to murmur or mutter in discontent; mutter complaints: *Your father is grumbling because he can't find his pipe.* **2.** to make low murmuring or rumbling sounds; growl; rumble: *The plumbing in this house grumbles.* —*n.* **3.** a complaint or gripe. **4.** a rumble or growling sound. —**grum'bler,** *n.* —**grum'bling·ly,** *adv.*

grump·y (grum/pē), *adj.,* **grump·i·er, grump·i·est.** surly or ill-tempered; sulky: *a grumpy mood.*

grunt (grunt), *v.* **1.** to make a short, deep, hollow sound, as a pig does: *to grunt with the effort of lifting something heavy.* —*n.* **2.** a sound of grunting.

gr. wt., gross weight.

G.S.A., Girl Scouts of America.

Gt. Br., Great Britain. Also, **Gt. Brit.**

Gua·da·la·ja·ra (gwä/də lə här/ə), *n.* a city in W Mexico.

Guam (gwäm), *n.* an island belonging to the U.S. in the N Pacific: U.S. naval station. 206 sq. mi.

Guanaco
(3½ ft. high
at shoulder)

gua·na·co (gwä nä/kō), *n., pl.* **gua·na·cos.** a wild South American animal resembling the llama and alpaca and related to the camel. [from a Spanish word, which comes from Quechuan *huanacu*]

gua·no (gwä/nō), *n.* a natural manure, composed chiefly of the excrement of sea birds, found esp. on islands near the Peruvian coast. [from a Spanish word meaning "dung," which comes from South American Indian]

Guan·tá/na·mo Bay/ (gwän tä/nə mō/), a bay on the SE coast of Cuba.

guar., guaranteed.

guar·an·tee (gar/ən tē/), *n.* **1.** a promise or assurance, esp. one in writing, that something is of a certain quality, content, etc., or that it will continue to work for a certain length of time: *This radio comes with a one-year guarantee.* **2.** See **guaranty** (def. 1). **3.** any promise or assurance; something that has the same force as a written guarantee: *Wealth is no guarantee of happiness.* **4.** See **guaranty** (def. 2). **5.** a person who gives a guarantee or guaranty. *—v.,* **guar·an·teed, guar·an·tee·ing. 6.** to provide a guarantee for: *The company guarantees this camera.* **7.** to promise (usually fol. by a clause as object): *I guarantee that I'll be there.* **8.** to assure or make certain: *This ticket guarantees you a seat.* **9.** to protect (someone) from financial loss in the case of fire, theft, flood, or the like: *This contract guarantees you against damage by fire or flood.*

guar·an·tor (gar′ən tôr′, gar′ən tər), *n.* **1.** a person, group, system of government, or the like, that assures or guarantees something. **2.** a person who makes or gives a guaranty, warrant, or the like.

guar·an·ty (gar′ən tē′), *n., pl.* **guar·an·ties. 1.** a warrant, pledge, or formal promise that someone else's debt or obligation will be paid or fulfilled; guarantee. **2.** something that is taken or accepted as security for a loan or the like: *She left her jewels as a guaranty for the money she borrowed.* **3.** a guarantor.

guard (gärd), *v.* **1.** to keep safe from harm or danger; protect; watch over: *The dog guarded its puppies.* **2.** to keep under close watch in order to prevent escape, misbehavior, or the like: *to guard a prisoner.* **3.** to keep under control: *Guard your temper.* **4.** to provide with a safeguard or protection; shield: *He wore dark glasses to guard his eyes against the sun.* **5.** to take precautions or care (usually fol. by *against*): *to guard against mistakes. —n.* **6.** a person or group of persons that guards, watches over, protects, etc. **7.** the act of guarding; a close watch or control: *Keep a guard on the gate.* **8.** something that guards or protects: *a face guard for a football player.* **9.** a posture of defense or readiness in fencing, boxing, etc. **10.** (in football) either of the linemen stationed between a tackle and the center. **11.** (in basketball) either of the players stationed in the back court to defend the basket. **12. off guard,** not ready for an attack; unprepared: *The offensive caught the troops off guard.* **13. on guard,** on the alert for an attack; cautious: *to be on guard in enemy territory.* **14. stand guard over,** to watch over; protect: *The dog stood guard over his wounded master. —guard′er, n.*

guard·ed (gär′did), *adj.* **1.** careful or cautious: *a guarded answer.* **2.** protected, watched, or restrained; under guard. *—guard′ed·ly, adv. —guard′ed·ness, n.*

guard·house (gärd′hous′), *n., pl.* **guard·hous·es** (gärd′hou′ziz). a building used for housing soldiers on guard duty or as a temporary jail for prisoners.

guard·i·an (gär′dē ən), *n.* **1.** a person or thing that guards, protects, or preserves: *The courts should be the guardians of justice.* **2.** a person who is given legal charge of the care of another person or his property, or both: *His uncle is his guardian. —adj.* **3.**

guarding or protecting: *a guardian angel.* **—guard′i·an·ship′, n.**

guard·room (gärd′rōōm′, -rŏŏm′), *n.* a room used by soldiers on guard duty.

guards·man (gärdz′mən), *n., pl.* **guards·men. 1.** a man who acts as a guard. **2.** a member of the U.S. National Guard. **3.** a British soldier who is a member of one of the special bodies of troops that were traditionally formed to protect the king.

Gua·te·ma·la (gwä′tə mä′lə), *n.* **1.** a republic in N Central America. 42,042 sq. mi. **2.** Also, **Gua′tema′ la Cit′y.** the capital city of Guatemala, in the S part. **—Gua′te·ma′lan, n., adj.**

gua·va (gwä′və), *n.* a yellow fruit of a small tropical tree, used for making jelly.

gu·ber·na·to·ri·al (gōō′bər nə tôr′ē əl, gyōō′-), *adj.* of or referring to a state governor or the office of a state governor: *a gubernatorial election.*

gudg·eon (guj′ən), *n.* a small, easily caught, freshwater fish used as bait.

Guern·sey (gûrn′zē), *n., pl.* for def. 2 **Guern·seys. 1.** an island in the English Channel. **2.** a breed of tan and white cattle that produce very rich milk.

guer·ril·la (gə ril′ə), *n.* **1.** a member of a small independent band of soldiers that engages in quick, surprise attacks, sabotage, or other small-scale military actions. *—adj.* **2.** of or concerning such soldiers or their methods of fighting: *guerrilla warfare.* Also, **gue·ril′la.** [from a Spanish word meaning "guerrilla band," which comes from *guerra* "war"]

guess (ges), *v.* **1.** to judge or arrive at (an answer, opinion, etc.) without having enough facts to be sure: *to guess someone's weight; to guess at the height of a building.* **2.** to figure out or judge correctly: *to guess a riddle.* **3.** to suppose or think: *I guess you're right. —n.* **4.** an opinion arrived at by guessing or one that seems probable or at least as likely as any other. **—guess′er, n.**

guess·work (ges′wûrk′), *n.* **1.** the process of guessing. **2.** work done or opinions formed by this process: *What he told you may be true or merely guesswork.*

guest (gest), *n.* **1.** a person who is welcomed and entertained at another person's home; visitor: *We are having guests staying with us over the weekend.* **2.** a paying customer in a hotel, restaurant, or the like.

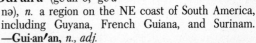

guf·faw (gə fô′), *n.* **1.** a burst of loud laughter. *—v.* **2.** to laugh suddenly and loudly: *They guffawed at the joke.*

Gui·an·a (gē an′ə, gē ä′nə), *n.* a region on the NE coast of South America, including Guyana, French Guiana, and Surinam. **—Gui·an′an, n., adj.**

guid·ance (gīd′[ə]ns), *n.* **1.** the act of guiding; leadership; direction: *Under the guidance of the science teacher, the children collected rocks.* **2.** advice or counseling in one's career or the like. **3.** something that guides.

guide (gīd), *v.,* **guid·ed, guid·ing. 1.** to help (a person) find his way in an area he does not know: *A scout guided the soldiers through the woods.* **2.** to force (a person, object, or animal) to move in a certain path: *to guide a sled around a tree.* **3.** to give (a person) advice or instruction. —*n.* **4.** a person who helps hunters, tourists, etc., find their way. **5.** something that helps one to find one's way, make a decision, or the like: *a guide to colleges.* **6.** a device for controlling direction, speed, etc.: *a sewing-machine guide.* **7.** a guidebook.

guide·book (gīd′book′), *n.* a book of directions and information for travelers, tourists, etc.

guid′ed mis′sile, a rocket or other flying weapon that is guided during flight instead of merely being aimed before launching.

guide·post (gīd′pōst′), *n.* a post beside a road or at a crossing that bears directions for travelers.

guild (gild), *n.* **1.** an organization of persons having similar interests, goals, etc.: *an actors' guild.* **2.** (in medieval times) any of various unions of merchants or tradesmen that maintained standards of work and protected the interests of its members. Sometimes such organizations served as the local government.

guil·der (gil′dər), *n., pl.* **guil·ders** *or* **guil·der.** another word for **gulden.**

guile (gīl), *n.* trickery and cunning used to deceive; slyness: *the guile of a fox.* —**guile′ful,** *adj.*

guile·less (gīl′lis), *adj.* being without guile or slyness; sincere; straightforward: *a guileless answer.* —**guile′less·ly,** *adv.* —**guile′less·ness,** *n.*

guil·lo·tine (gil′ə tēn′), *n.* **1.** a device for beheading persons by means of a heavy blade that is dropped between two posts. —*v.* (gil′ə tēn′), **guil·lo·tined, guil·lo·tin·ing. 2.** to behead by the guillotine: *Many noblemen were guillotined during the French Revolution.* [named after J. J. *Guillotin* (1738–1814), French physician who recommended its use]

Guillotine

guilt (gilt), *n.* **1.** the state or fact of having committed a crime, sin, or the like: *The thief confessed his guilt.* **2.** criminal or sinful behavior or acts. **3.** a feeling of responsibility or shame for some real or imagined wrongdoing: *to suffer from guilt.* —**guilt′less,** *adj.*

guilt·y (gil′tē), *adj.,* **guilt·i·er, guilt·i·est. 1.** responsible for a wrongdoing; having committed a crime or sin: *The jury will decide if he is guilty of the crime.* **2.** involving guilt: *a guilty act.* **3.** having or showing a sense of guilt: *a guilty conscience; a guilty look.* —**guilt′i·ly,** *adv.* —**guilt′i·ness,** *n.*

guin·ea (gin′ē), *n.* **1.** a gold coin of Great Britain issued from 1663 to 1813, equal to a pound or 20 shillings. **2.** (in Great Britain) an amount of money equal to 21 shillings: not used after February, 1971.

Guin·ea (gin′ē), *n.* **1.** a coastal region in W Africa. **2.** a country in W Africa: formerly French. 94,925 sq. mi. *Cap.:* Conakry. —**Guin′e·an,** *n., adj.*

Guin·ea-Bis·sau (gin′ē bi sou′), *n.* a republic on the W Coast of Africa, between Guinea and Senegal. 13,-948 sq. mi. Former name, **Portuguese Guinea.**

guin′ea fowl′, any of several African game birds having dark-gray feathers spotted with white, raised for their meat and eggs. Also, **guin′ea hen′.**

guin′ea pig′, a furry rodent having short ears and legs, used in experiments and often kept as a pet.

Guin·e·vere (gwin′ə vēr′), *n.* the wife of King Arthur.

guise (gīz), *n.* **1.** general outward appearance, manner, or the like, esp. when false or assumed in order to deceive: *an enemy in friendly guise; a speech that presents old ideas in a new guise.* **2.** style of dress; attire: *The princess escaped in the guise of a maid.*

Guinea pig (length 11 in.)

gui·tar (gi tär′), *n.* **1.** a musical instrument with a long fretted neck, a flat body, and six strings. It is played by plucking with the fingers or with a plectrum. **2.** a similar instrument, sometimes having a solid body, equipped with one or more electronic pickups connected to an amplifier and speaker system. [from the Spanish word *guitarra,* which comes from Greek *kithara*]

gui·tar·ist (gi tär′ist), *n.* a person who plays the guitar.

Guitar

gulch (gulch), *n.* a narrow, deep valley or ravine, esp. one marking the course of a forceful stream.

gul·den (gool′d^ən), *n., pl.* **gul·dens** *or* **gul·den.** a silver coin and unit of money of the Netherlands. Also, **guilder.**

gulf (gulf), *n.* **1.** a portion of an ocean or sea partly enclosed by land. **2.** a deep hollow or split in the earth; chasm; abyss. **3.** any wide separation, such as in wealth, point of view, or the like: *a gulf between the rich and the poor or the young and the old.*

Gulf′ Stream′, a warm ocean current flowing N along the Atlantic coast of North America.

gull[1] (gul), *n.* any of numerous birds found at sea and along the coast having long wings, webbed feet, and usually white body feathers with gray back and wings. [from the Middle English word *gulle,* which probably comes from Welsh *gŵylan*]

Gull (length 2 ft.; wingspread 4½ ft.)

gull[2] (gul), *v.* **1.** to trick, cheat, or fool: *to gull someone out of his money.* —*n.* **2.** a person who is easily deceived or cheated; dupe. [probably from the earlier word *gull* "to swallow"]

gul·let (gul′it), *n.* 1. the esophagus. 2. the throat, or the pharynx.

gul·li·ble (gul′ə bəl), *adj.* easily fooled or cheated: *My gullible little brother believes everything he's told.* [from *gull*² + -*ible*] —**gul′li·bil′i·ty,** *n.* —**gul′li·bly,** *adv.*

gul·ly (gul′ē), *n., pl.* **gul·lies.** 1. a small valley or ravine formed by running water. 2. a ditch or gutter. Also, **gul′ley.**

gulp (gulp), *v.* 1. to swallow eagerly or in large mouthfuls (often fol. by *down*): *to gulp down a sandwich.* 2. to choke or swallow hard: *He gulped with fright.* 3. to choke back: *to gulp down a sob.* —*n.* 4. the act of gulping; a hard swallowing: *He gave a gulp and swallowed his medicine.* 5. a mouthful: *She took a gulp of water.* —**gulp′ing·ly,** *adv.*

gum¹ (gum), *n.* 1. a sticky substance produced by certain trees and used in making glues, medicines, etc. 2. any of various other sticky substances, such as mucilage or glue. 3. short for **chewing gum.** 4. another word for **gum tree.** [from an Old French word, which comes from Greek *kommi*] —**gum′like′,** *adj.*

gum² (gum), *n.* Often, **gums.** the flesh surrounding the roots of the teeth. [from the Old English word *gōma* "palate"]

gum·bo (gum′bō), *n., pl.* **gum·bos.** 1. a stew or thick soup, usually made with chicken or seafood and okra and other vegetables. 2. the okra plant, or its pods.

gum·drop (gum′drop′), *n.* a small, soft or chewy candy.

gum·my (gum′ē), *adj.,* **gum·mi·er, gum·mi·est.** 1. of or resembling gum; sticky or chewy: *gummy candy.* 2. covered with or clogged with gum or something sticky. —**gum′mi·ness,** *n.*

gump·tion (gump′shən), *n. Informal.* 1. courage and initiative. 2. common sense; shrewdness.

gum′ tree′, any tree that yields gum, such as the eucalyptus.

gun (gun), *n.* 1. a weapon consisting basically of a metal tube through which shells, bullets, or the like, may be fired; a cannon, rifle, pistol, etc. 2. a device that resembles a gun in shooting out something under pressure: *a paint gun.* 3. a firing of a gun: *a twenty-one-gun salute.* —*v.,* **gunned, gun·ning.** 4. to shoot or hunt with a gun: *to gun an elephant; to go gunning for quail.* 5. **jump the gun, a.** to begin a race before the starting signal. **b.** to do something before the proper time: *I jumped the gun and left early.* 6. **stick to one's guns,** to stand firm in the face of opposition: *If you're right, stick to your guns.*

gun·boat (gun′bōt′), *n.* a small ship carrying mounted guns.

gun·cot·ton (gun′kot′ʰn), *n.* an explosive made from cotton and used in the manufacture of smokeless powder.

gun·fight (gun′fīt′), *n.* 1. a battle between people shooting guns. —*v.,* **gun·fought** (gun′fôt′), **gun·fight·ing.** 2. to fight with guns. —**gun′fight′er,** *n.*

gun·fire (gun′fīr′), *n.* the firing or shooting of a gun or guns: *the sound of gunfire.*

gun·lock (gun′lok′), *n.* the mechanism in a gun that fires the charge.

gun·man (gun′mən), *n., pl.* **gun·men.** a man armed with a gun or expert in using guns, esp. a criminal.

gun′ met′al, any of various alloys having a dark-gray or blackish color. —**gun′-met′al,** *adj.*

gun·ner (gun′ər), *n.* 1. a person who works a gun or cannon, esp in the armed forces. 2. a person who hunts with a rifle or shotgun; hunter.

gun·ner·y (gun′ə rē), *n.* 1. the process of making and managing guns, esp. large guns or cannon. 2. the act of firing guns. 3. guns collectively.

gun·ny (gun′ē), *n., pl.* **gun·nies.** a coarse fabric used for making sacks; burlap. [from the Hindi word *goṇi* "sack," which comes from Sanskrit]

gun·ny·sack (gun′ē sak′), *n.* a sack made of gunny or burlap.

gun·pow·der (gun′pou′dər), *n.* an explosive, esp. one used in firing bullets from guns. See also **black powder.**

gun·shot (gun′shot′), *n.* 1. a bullet, buckshot, or the like, fired from a gun. 2. the range of a gun. —*adj.* 3. made by a gunshot: *a gunshot wound.*

gun·smith (gun′smith′), *n.* a man who makes or repairs pistols, rifles, or other firearms.

gun·stock (gun′stok′), *n.* the wooden or metal piece to which the barrel and mechanism of a rifle or shotgun are attached.

gun·wale (gun′ʰl), *n.* the upper edge of the side of a rowboat, sailboat, or other vessel.

gup·py (gup′ē), *n., pl.* **gup·pies.** a very small freshwater fish often kept in aquariums. [named after R. J. L. *Guppy* of Trinidad, who presented specimens to the British Museum]

gur·gle (gûr′gəl), *v.,* **gur·gled, gur·gling.** 1. to flow in an irregular, noisy, or bubbling current: *Water gurgles from a bottle.* 2. to make a sound like gurgling water: *The baby gurgled in its crib.* —*n.* 3. the act of gurgling, or a gurgling noise. —**gur′gling·ly,** *adv.*

gu·ru (gōō′rōō, gōō rōō′), *n.* 1. a Hindu spiritual instructor. 2. any wise or respected leader.

gush (gush), *v.* 1. to flow out or pour forth suddenly and with force: *Water gushed from the faucet.* 2. to give forth suddenly and with force: *The well gushed water.* 3. to talk foolishly and emotionally: *They gush so about their grandchildren.* —*n.* 4. a sudden, rushing outflow: *a gush of oil.* 5. foolish, overly enthusiastic, or sentimental talk. —**gush′ing·ly,** *adv.*

gush·er (gush′ər), *n.* 1. a flowing oil well, usually of large capacity. 2. a person who gushes.

gush·y (gush′ē), *adj.,* **gush·i·er, gush·i·est.** 1. overly enthusiastic or sentimental: *gushy compliments.* 2. tending to talk in this way: *a gushy visitor.* —**gush′i·ness,** *n.*

gust (gust), *n.* 1. a sudden, strong rush of wind: *A gust carried away his hat.* 2. a sudden rush or burst of water, fire, or the like. 3. an outburst of anger, laughter, or the like. —*v.* 4. to blow or rush in gusts.

---

act, āble, dâre, ärt; ebb, ēqual; if, īce; hot, ōver, ôrder; oil; book; ōōze; out; up, ûrge; ə = a as in *alone*; ᵊ as in *button* (but′ᵊn), *fire* (fīᵊr); chief; shoe; thin; ŧħat; zh as in *measure* (mezh′ər). See full key inside cover.

gus·to (gus′tō), *n.* hearty enjoyment or enthusiasm: *to eat a good meal with gusto.*

gust·y (gus′tē), *adj.*, **gust·i·er, gust·i·est. 1.** blowing or coming in gusts or sudden rushes: *a gusty wind.* **2.** marked by gusts of wind, rain, etc.; windy; stormy: *a gusty day.* —**gust′i·ly,** *adv.* —**gust′i·ness,** *n.*

gut (gut), *n.* **1.** the alimentary canal, esp. the lower parts of it. **2.** the material of which the intestines are composed. Those of some animals are used for making strings for musical instruments. **3. guts, a.** the bowels or intestines. **b.** *Slang.* courage or nerve. —*v.*, **gut·ted, gut·ting. 4.** to take out the gut or intestines of. **5.** to destroy the interior or inner part of (a house, building, etc.).

gut·ter (gut′ər), *n.* **1.** a channel or ditch at the side of a road or street, for carrying off water. **2.** a channel or trough attached at the bottom edge of a roof, for carrying off rain water. **3.** a furrow or channel made by running water. **4.** (in bowling) a slightly sunken channel on each side of the alley. —*v.* **5.** (of a candle) to melt quickly with the wax flowing down the side in streams: *The candle guttered in the draft.* **6.** (of a flame, candle, oil lamp, etc.) to burn low or flicker so as almost to go out.

gut·ter·snipe (gut′ər snīp′), *n.* a low, vulgar person, esp. one living in the slums of a city.

gut·tur·al (gut′ər əl), *adj.* **1.** pronounced in the throat, as *g* in *good.* **2.** harsh or throaty: *a guttural voice.* —*n.* **3.** a guttural sound. —**gut′tur·al·ly,** *adv.*

guy[1] (gī), *n.* **1.** *Informal.* a fellow or person: *He's a nice guy.* **2.** *British Slang.* an oddly dressed person. —*v.*, **guyed, guy·ing. 3.** to tease or make fun of. [from the name of *Guy* Fawkes, who plotted to blow up the British Houses of Parliament in 1605]

guy[2] (gī), *n.* **1.** a rope or wire used to guide, steady, or brace an object, such as a mast. —*v.*, **guyed, guy·ing. 2.** to guide, steady, or hold fast with a guy or guys. [from the Old French word *guie* "guide"]

Guy·an·a (gī an′ə, gī ä′nə), *n.* a republic on the coast of NE South America. 82,978 sq. mi. *Cap.:* Georgetown. Formerly, **British Guiana.**

guz·zle (guz′əl), *v.*, **guz·zled, guz·zling.** to eat or drink greedily: *to guzzle one's food.* —**guz′zler,** *n.*

gym (jim), *n.* a gymnasium.

gym·na·si·um (jim nā′zē əm), *n.* **1.** a building or room designed and equipped for athletic activities, such as sports events or exercises. **2.** (in ancient Greece) a place where youths met for exercise and discussion. [from the Greek word *gymnasion,* which comes from *gymnazein* "to train"]

gym·nast (jim′nast), *n.* a person trained and skilled in gymnastics.

gym·nas·tic (jim nas′tik), *adj.* of or referring to gymnastics: *gymnastic exercises.*

gym·nas·tics (jim nas′tiks), *n.* **1.** *(used as pl.)* exercises designed to develop strength and agility: *Gymnastics are tiring.* **2.** *(used as sing.)* the practice of such exercises: *Gymnastics is a difficult subject.*

gyp (jip), *Informal.* —*v.*, **gypped, gyp·ping. 1.** to cheat or swindle; trick (someone) out of his money: *He gypped me out of my allowance.* —*n.* **2.** a swindle or cheat: *That movie was a real gyp.* **3.** Also, **gyp′per.** a swindler or cheat.

gyp·sum (jip′səm), *n.* a mineral used as a fertilizer and in making plaster of Paris. [from the Greek word *gypsos* "chalk, gypsum"]

Gyp·sy (jip′sē), *n.*, *pl.* **Gyp·sies. 1.** a member of a wandering people who came originally from India. **2.** *(usually l.c.)* a person who resembles the Gypsies in some way, as by leading a wandering life. **3.** the language of the Gypsies, belonging to the Indic branch of the Indo-European family. —*adj.* **4.** *(sometimes l.c.)* of or referring to the Gypsies or their language: *Gypsy music; gypsy dances.* Also, **Gipsy.**

gyp′sy moth′, a moth whose larvae damage trees by feeding on their leaves.

gy·rate (jī′rāt), *v.*, **gy·rat·ed, gy·rat·ing.** to move in a circle or spiral around a fixed point; whirl; rotate: *The top gyrated in the palm of his hand.* —**gy·ra′tion,** *n.*

gyr·fal·con (jûr′fal′kən, -fôl′kən, -fô′-), *n.* any of several large falcons native to arctic regions. Also, **gerfalcon.**

gy·ro·com·pass (jī′rō kum′pəs), *n.* a compass that contains a gyroscope rather than a magnet and always points true north.

gy·ro·scope (jī′rə skōp′), *n.* an apparatus consisting of a wheel mounted so that its axis can be tilted in various directions. When the wheel is spinning, its axis tends to point in the same direction even when the mounting is tilted. —**gy·ro·scop·ic** (jī′rə skop′ik), *adj.*

Gyroscope

H

H, h (āch), *n., pl.* **H's** *or* **Hs, h's** *or* **hs.** the eighth letter of the English alphabet.

H, *Chem.* the symbol for **hydrogen.**

H., **1.** height. **2.** high. **3.** (in baseball) hit; hits. **4.** hour; hours. **5.** hundred. Also, **h.**

ha (hä), *interj.* (used as an exclamation of surprise, triumph, suspicion, etc.): *Ha! I caught you!* Also, **hah.**

ha, hectare; hectares.

Ha·bak·kuk (hə bak′ək, hab′ə kuk′), *n.* **1.** (in the Bible) a Hebrew prophet of the 7th century B.C. **2.** a book of the Old Testament bearing his name.

ha·be·as cor·pus (hā′bē əs kôr′pəs), a legal order requiring that a prisoner be brought before a judge or court, esp. to find out whether he or she has been imprisoned illegally. [from a Latin phrase meaning "thou shalt have the body"]

hab·er·dash·er (hab′ər dash′ər), *n.* a dealer in accessories for men, such as hats, shirts, and gloves.

hab·er·dash·er·y (hab′ər dash′ə rē), *n., pl.* **hab·er·dash·er·ies. 1.** a haberdasher's shop. **2.** the goods that can be bought in such a shop.

hab·it (hab′it), *n.* **1.** customary practice; usual way of doing something: *It is his habit to rise early.* **2.** a particular custom or practice: *the habit of shaking hands.* **3.** an action or set of actions that one has done for so long that one repeats it without thinking: *Try to break the habit of biting your nails.* **4.** clothes or an outfit worn in a particular profession, for a particular activity, or the like: *a nun's habit; a riding habit.* **5.** typical way of growth or behavior of a plant or animal: *the twining habit of vines.*

hab·it·a·ble (hab′i tə bəl), *adj.* capable of being lived in: *That desert isn't habitable by human beings.*

hab·i·tat (hab′i tat′), *n.* **1.** the place or kind of place in which it is natural for an animal or plant to live or grow: *The ocean is the habitat of whales.* **2.** the place where one lives; dwelling; habitation. [from a Latin word meaning "it dwells"]

hab·i·ta·tion (hab′i tā′shən), *n.* **1.** the act of living in or inhabiting a place: *This building is not safe for habitation.* **2.** the place in which one lives; dwelling; abode. **3.** a settlement or community: *a few habitations on the frontier.*

ha·bit·u·al (hə bich′ōō əl), *adj.* **1.** of the nature of a habit; resulting from habit: *Chewing tobacco is habitual with him.* **2.** by habit; constant: *an habitual gossip.* **3.** usual, customary, or regular: *She took her habitual place at the table.* —**ha·bit′u·al·ly,** *adv.*

ha·bit·u·ate (hə bich′ōō āt′), *v.,* **ha·bit·u·at·ed, ha·bit·u·at·ing.** to make used to something; accustom: *Living at camp habituated her to getting up early.*

ha·ci·en·da (hä′sē en′də), *n.* (in Spanish America) **1.** an estate in the country, esp. one used for ranching or farming. **2.** the main house on such an estate.

hack[1] (hak), *v.* **1.** to cut, chop, break up, etc., with heavy, rough blows: *to hack the ground with a hoe; to hack away at underbrush.* **2.** to clear (a road, path, etc.) by cutting away vines, bushes, trees, or the like: *to hack a trail through the jungle.* **3.** to cough harshly. —*n.* **4.** a cut, gash, or notch: *a hack in a tree trunk made by an ax.* **5.** a cutting blow: *She gave the branch a hack with her hatchet.* **6.** a tool for hacking, such as an ax or pick. **7.** a short, rasping cough. [from the Old English word *haccian*]

hack[2] (hak), *n.* **1.** a person, such as an artist or writer, who does unimaginative, mediocre work simply to make money. **2.** an old or worn-out horse. **3.** a coach or carriage for hire; hackney. **4.** a horse for hire, or one used only for transportation rather than for hunting, show, or the like. **5.** *Informal.* **a.** a taxi. **b.** Also, **hack′ie.** a cabdriver. —*adj.* **6.** hired, or typical of a hired worker; dull; unimaginative: *a hack writer; hack writing.* [short for *hackney*]

hack·les (hak′əlz), *n.pl.* the hairs on the back of the neck of a dog or other animal, which stand up when the animal is angry or frightened.

hack·ney (hak′nē), *n., pl.* **hack·neys. 1.** a horse used for ordinary riding or driving. **2.** a trotting horse used for drawing a light carriage or the like. **3.** a carriage or automobile for hire; cab.

act, āble, dâre, ärt; ebb, ēqual; if, īce; hot, ōver, ôrder; oil; bŏŏk; ōōze; out; up, ûrge; ə = a as in *alone*;
ᵊ as in *button* (but′ᵊn), *fire* (fīᵊr); chief; shoe; thin; that; zh as in *measure* (mezh′ər). See full key inside cover.

hack·neyed (hak′nēd), *adj.* made commonplace or stale by too much use: *a story with a hackneyed plot.*

hack·saw (hak′sô′), *n.* a saw for cutting metal, consisting of a thin, fine-toothed blade held in a frame. See illus. at **saw.**

had (had), *v.* the past tense and past participle of **have.**

had·dock (had′ək), *n., pl.* **had·docks** *or* **had·dock.** a food fish of the North Atlantic, smaller than the cod but of the same family.

Ha·des (hā′dēz), *n.* 1. (in Greek mythology) the land in which the spirits of the dead live. 2. another word for **hell:** used in literature or as a polite synonym.

had·n't (had′³nt), contraction of *had not.*

hadst (hadst), *v.* an old form of **had,** found now chiefly in Biblical or poetic writing (used with *thou*).

haf·ni·um (haf′nē əm), *n.* *Chem.* a metallic element found in zirconium ores. *Symbol:* Hf

haft (haft), *n.* a handle, esp. of a knife, sword, dagger, etc.; hilt.

hag (hag), *n.* 1. an ugly old woman, esp. one who is mean or evil. 2. a witch.

hag·fish (hag′fish′), *n., pl.* **hag·fishes** *or* **hag·fish.** a small, saltwater fish, resembling an eel, having undeveloped eyes, a round mouth, and horny teeth for boring into the flesh of other fishes.

Hag·ga·i (hag′ē ī′, hag′ī), *n.* 1. (in the Bible) a Hebrew prophet of the 6th century B.C. 2. a book of the Old Testament bearing his name.

hag·gard (hag′ərd), *adj.* having an exhausted, worn-out appearance as a result of hunger, suffering, worry, or the like; gaunt; drawn: *a haggard soldier back from the war.* —**hag′gard·ness,** *n.*

hag·gle (hag′əl), *v.,* **hag·gled, hag·gling.** 1. to bargain in a petty, nagging way: *She haggled with the butcher to get a better price.* 2. to quarrel over a small matter in a tiresome way: *They're haggling over which movie to see.* —*n.* 3. the act of haggling; a quarrel or dispute. —**hag′gler,** *n.*

Hagfish (length 1½ ft.)

Hague, The (hāg), the actual capital city of the Netherlands, in the W part. See also **Amsterdam.**

hah (hä), *interj.* another spelling of **ha.**

ha-ha (hä′hä′), *interj.* (used as an exclamation expressing laughter.)

hah·ni·um (hä′nē əm), *n.* *Chem.* a man-made, radioactive, metallic element. *Symbol:* Ha

hail¹ (hāl), *v.* 1. to greet or welcome, esp. by calling out: *to hail an old friend on the street.* 2. to call out to (a cab, passer-by, etc.) in order to attract attention: *to hail a cab.* 3. to express enthusiastic approval of; acclaim: *The people hailed the new king.* —*n.* 4. the act of hailing; a shout, call, or enthusiastic greeting. —*interj.* 5. (used as a greeting, esp. one expressing honor and approval): *Hail to our captain!* 6. **hail from,** to have as one's home or birthplace: *Where in California do you hail from?* [from a Scandinavian word, related to Old English *hæl* "health"]

hail² (hāl), *n.* 1. rounded pieces of ice more than ⅓ inch in diameter that fall from the sky like rain. 2. a heavy fall; a shower of anything: *a hail of bullets.* —*v.* 3. to pour down hail (often used impersonally with *it*): *It hailed all afternoon.* 4. to drop or pour down like hail: *The plane hailed leaflets on the city.* [from the Old English word *hægl*]

Hail′ Mar′y, a prayer in the Roman Catholic Church to the Virgin Mary, named after its opening words. Also, **Ave Maria.**

hail·stone (hāl′stōn′), *n.* an individual piece of hail.

Hai·phong (hī′fong′), *n.* a port city near Hanoi in North Vietnam.

hair (hâr), *n.* 1. one of the threadlike growths on the skin of man and other mammals. 2. the covering on the head or body provided by such growths. 3. a very small distance, amount, etc.; hair's-breadth: *The arrow missed him by a hair.* 4. **get in someone's hair,** to annoy or bother someone: *Their constant bickering gets in my hair.* 5. **split hairs,** to be too concerned about details: *To argue whether it's bluish green or greenish blue is just splitting hairs.* 6. **tear one's hair,** to show extreme anxiety, anger, or grief: *When I thought she'd miss the train I was tearing my hair.*

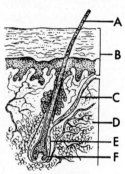

Hair (Human)
A, Hair
B, Epidermis
C, Muscle
D, Dermis
E, Follicle
F, Root

hair·brush (hâr′brush′), *n.* a brush for the hair.

hair·cloth (hâr′klôth′), *n.* stiff, wiry cloth made chiefly of hair from the manes and tails of horses and used in upholstery, to stiffen clothing, etc.

hair·cut (hâr′kut′), *n.* 1. a cutting of one's hair: *I need a haircut.* 2. the style in which one's hair is cut and worn: *I like your new haircut.* —**hair′cut·ter,** *n.*

hair·do (hâr′dōō′), *n., pl.* **hair·dos.** 1. the style in which a woman's hair is cut, arranged, and worn. 2. the hair itself when arranged in such a style: *Don't muss my hairdo!*

hair·dress·er (hâr′dres′ər), *n.* a person who cuts and arranges women's hair.

hair·dress·ing (hâr′dres′ing), *n.* 1. the act of cutting, styling, or arranging hair. 2. the profession of a hairdresser. 3. a style of arranging hair; hairdo. 4. a lotion or the like used on the hair.

hair·less (hâr′lis), *adj.* without hair; bald.

hair·line (hâr′līn′), *n.* 1. the edge of the hair growing on the head, esp. on the forehead. 2. a very thin line: *A hairline of light shone through the tiny crack.*

hair·pin (hâr′pin′), *n.* **1.** a slender, U-shaped piece of wire, plastic, etc., used by women to fasten up the hair or to hold a covering for the head. —*adj.* **2.** sharply curved; U-shaped: *a hairpin turn in a road.*

hair-rais·ing (hâr′rā′zing), *adj.* terrifying or scary: *a hair-raising escape.*

hair's-breadth (hârz′bredth′), *n.* a very small space or distance: *We missed the other car by a hair's-breadth.* Also, **hairs′breadth′.**

hair·spring (hâr′spring′), *n.* a very fine spiral spring in a watch or clock.

hair·y (hâr′ē), *adj.,* **hair·i·er, hair·i·est. 1.** covered with hair; having much hair: *a hairy dog.* **2.** made of or resembling hair: *a hairy rug.* —**hair′i·ness,** *n.*

Hai·ti (hā′tē), *n.* a republic in the West Indies, occupying the W part of the island of Hispaniola. 10,714 sq. mi. *Cap.:* Port-au-Prince.

Hai·tian (hā′shən), *adj.* **1.** of or referring to Haiti or its people. —*n.* **2.** a native or inhabitant of Haiti.

hake (hāk), *n., pl.* **hakes** or **hake.** any of several food fishes of the cod family.

hal·berd (hal′bərd, hôl′bərd), *n.* a weapon having a long handle, an axlike cutting blade on one side, a hook or beaklike point on the other side, and a spear point at the end. It was used esp. in the 15th and 16th centuries.

hal·cy·on (hal′sē ən), *adj.* **1.** calm, peaceful, or carefree: *halcyon weather; halcyon days of youth.* —*n.* **2.** a mythical bird, usually identified with the kingfisher, said to have the power of calming winds and waves at sea.

hale[1] (hāl), *adj.* in good health; healthy; robust. [from the Old English word *hāl* "whole, sound"]

hale[2] (hāl), *v.,* **haled, hal·ing. 1.** to haul, pull, or drag. **2.** to force (a person) to go: *The thief was haled into court.* [from the Middle English word *halen,* from Old French *haler,* which comes from Germanic]

Halberd

Hale (hāl), *n.* **Nathan,** 1755–1776, American soldier hanged as a spy by the British during the American Revolution.

half (haf), *n., pl.* **halves** (havz). **1.** either of the two equal or almost equal parts that make up the whole of something: *He ate one half of the sandwich and I ate the other.* —*adj.* **2.** being one of two equal or almost equal parts of something: *a half quart of milk.* —*adv.* **3.** not completely; partly: *half awake.* **4.** to the extent of half: *half full.* **5. in half,** in two equal parts: *The magician sawed the girl in half.*

half·back (haf′bak′), *n.* (in football) one of two players who usually line up on either side of the fullback, behind the line of scrimmage.

half-baked (haf′bākt′), *adj.* **1.** not completely baked: *half-baked bread.* **2.** not properly planned or prepared: *a half-baked plan for changing street numbers.*

half-breed (haf′brēd′), *n.* a person whose parents are of different races: usually an offensive term.

half′ broth′er. See **brother** (def. 2).

half-caste (haf′kast′), *n.* a person of mixed race.

half′ crown′, a coin of Great Britain equal to two shillings and sixpence: not used after February, 1971.

half′ dol′lar, a silver coin of the U.S., worth 50 cents.

half-heart·ed (haf′här′tid), *adj.* having or showing little enthusiasm or interest; unenthusiastic: *half-hearted applause.* —**half′-heart′ed·ly,** *adv.*

half′ hitch′, a simple knot used to secure a rope to an object, such as a pole or handle. See illus. at **knot.**

half-hour (haf′our′), *n.* **1.** a period of 30 minutes: *Wait a half-hour.* **2.** the midpoint between two hours, as 12:30, 1:30, etc.: *Buses leave on the half-hour.* —*adj.* **3.** of or lasting a half-hour: *a half-hour nap.*

half-mast (haf′mast′), *n.* a position halfway between the top of a mast, flagpole, etc., and its base. A flag is flown at half-mast as a sign of mourning for someone who has died or as a signal for help.

half-moon (haf′moon′), *n.* the moon when half the side facing the earth is illuminated by the sun.

half′ note′, (in music) a note having one half the time value of a whole note. See illus. at **note.**

half·pen·ny (hā′pə nē), *n., pl.* **half·pen·nies.** a bronze coin of Great Britain, equal to half a penny.

half′ sis′ter. See **sister** (def. 2).

half·way (haf′wā′), *adv.* **1.** to half the distance; to or at the middle of the way: *The rain caught me halfway between the store and my house.* **2.** somewhat or nearly; almost: *She halfway agrees with you.* —*adj.* **3.** midway between two places, points, or the like: *a halfway mark.* **4.** partial; not going far enough: *He took only halfway measures to improve his work.* **5. meet halfway,** to give in partially to (someone); make a compromise with: *I can't do everything he wants, but maybe I can meet him halfway.*

half-wit (haf′wit′), *n.* a person who lacks brains or good sense; fool; dunce. —**half′-wit′ted,** *adj.*

hal·i·but (hal′ə bət, hol′ə bət), *n., pl.* **hal·i·buts** or **hal·i·but.** either of two very large flatfishes used for food. [from the Middle English word *halybutte,* which comes from *haly* "holy" + *butte* "fish." The fish is so called because it was eaten on holy days]

Hal·i·fax (hal′ə faks′), *n.* a seaport and the capital city of Nova Scotia, in SE Canada.

hall (hôl), *n.* **1.** a passageway leading to an outside door or from room to room in a house or building; corridor. **2.** a large entrance room in a house or building; lobby. **3.** a large room or building for public gatherings or meetings. **4.** a large building at a college or university. **5.** (in Great Britain) a mansion or large home on a country estate.

hal·le·lu·jah (hal′ə loo′yə), *interj.* **1.** Praise ye the Lord! —*n.* **2.** a cry of "hallelujah!" **3.** a shout or song of joy, praise, or thanks.

hall·mark (hôl′märk′), *n.* **1.** (in England) an official mark stamped on gold or silver articles as an indication of their purity. **2.** any mark or indication of genuineness, good quality, etc.: *Correct speech is the hallmark of an educated person.*

hal·lo (hə lō′), *interj.* **1.** (used to call or answer someone or to drive dogs on in hunting.) —*n.*, *pl.* **hal·los.** **2.** the cry "hallo!" or any similar shout of excitement. —*v.*, **hal·loed, hal·lo·ing. 3.** to call with a loud voice; shout; cry: *to hallo after hounds.* Also, **halloo, hollo.**

hal·loo (hə lōō′), *interj.*; *n.*, *pl.* **hal·loos;** *v.*, **hal·looed, hal·loo·ing.** another form of **hallo.**

hal·low (hal′ō), *v.* to make holy or sacred; honor as holy: *to hallow the name of the Lord.*

hal·lowed (hal′ōd, hal′ō id), *adj.* holy or sacred: *He was buried in hallowed ground.*

Hal·low·een (hal′ō ēn′, hol′ō ēn′), *n.* the evening of October 31, the eve of All Saints' Day, celebrated by dressing up in costumes and playing pranks. [from the phrase *Allhallows Even* "All Saints' Eve"]

hal·lu·ci·na·tion (hə lōō′sə nā′shən), *n.* **1.** the experience of seeing or hearing something that is not really there. **2.** something that is seen or heard in such an experience: *Your ghost was an hallucination.*

hall·way (hôl′wā′), *n.* **1.** a passageway in a building or house; hall. **2.** an entrance hall.

ha·lo (hā′lō), *n.*, *pl.* **ha·los** *or* **ha·loes. 1.** (in art) a circle of light shown around or above the head of Christ, an angel, a saint, etc. **2.** a circle of light around the moon, sun, or other heavenly body. **3.** an atmosphere or quality of glory, majesty, holiness, etc.: *A halo of splendor surrounded the young prince.*

hal·o·gen (hal′ə jən), *n. Chem.* a member of the family of nonmetallic elements that includes fluorine, chlorine, bromine, iodine, and astatine.

halt¹ (hôlt), *v.* **1.** to stop or cause to stop: *The horse halted in front of the gate. The officer halted the marching troops.* —*n.* **2.** a stop: *to come to a halt.* —*interj.* **3.** (used as a command to stop and stand still): *"Halt!" shouted the guard.* [from the German word *Halt*, in the phrase *Halt machen* "make a halt"]

halt² (hôlt), *v.* **1.** to falter or waver; be hesitant: *He halted and stammered when asked to explain his behavior.* —*adj.* **2.** lame or limping: *an old, halt horse.* **3.** **the halt,** people who are lame: *the blind and the halt.* [from the Old English word *healt*]

hal·ter (hôl′tər), *n.* **1.** a rope or a strap used for leading horses, cattle, etc., usually attached around the top of the head with a loop going around the nose. **2.** a rope with a noose, for hanging criminals; hangman's noose. **3.** a woman's garment, worn above the waist and tied behind the neck and across the back, leaving the arms and back bare. —*v.* **4.** to put a halter on: *to halter a colt.*

halve (hav), *v.*, **halved, halv·ing. 1.** to divide into two equal parts: *to halve an apple.* **2.** to lessen by half: *The store halved its prices during the sale.*

halves (havz), *n.* **1.** the plural of **half. 2. by halves,** incompletely or half-heartedly: *He never does anything by halves.* **3. go halves,** to share expenses equally: *Let's go halves on a sweater for Dad.*

hal·yard (hal′yərd), *n.* any of various lines or tackles for hoisting a sail, flag, etc., into position.

ham (ham), *n.* **1.** the upper part of the hind leg. **2.** the meat of this part of a hog, esp. when salted and smoked for eating. **3.** *Informal.* an operator of an amateur radio station. **4.** *Informal.* an actor who overacts.

Ham·burg (ham′bûrg), *n.* a port city in N West Germany.

ham·burg·er (ham′bûr′gər), *n.* **1.** ground or chopped beef: *Buy a pound of hamburger.* **2.** a patty of this meat, usually broiled or fried and served as a sandwich in a roll or bun. [from the phrase *Hamburger steak*, after *Hamburg*, a city in Germany]

Ham·il·ton (ham′əl tən), *n.* **1.** Alexander, 1757–1804, American statesman. **2.** a port city in SE Canada, on Lake Ontario.

ham·let (ham′lit), *n.* a small village.

Ham·let (ham′lit), *n.* **1.** a play by Shakespeare. **2.** the hero of this play, a prince of Denmark.

Ham·lin (ham′lin), *n.* Hannibal, 1809–1891, 15th Vice President of the U. S. 1861–1865.

ham·mer (ham′ər), *n.* **1.** a tool having a metal head set on a handle, used for driving nails, shaping metals, etc. **2.** any of various other things resembling this tool either in appearance or use, such as the hammers in a piano, the striker of an electric bell, etc. **3.** the part of a gun that causes it to fire when the trigger is pulled. **4.**

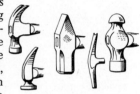

Hammers (def. 1)

one of three small bones in the middle ear. **5.** a metal ball attached to a steel wire, thrown for distance in athletic contests. —*v.* **6.** to pound or beat (something) with a hammer: *to hammer nails into wood.* **7.** to shape or make by using a hammer: *to hammer a shield out of a piece of copper.* **8.** to fasten by using a hammer and a nail or nails; nail: *to hammer up a shelf; to hammer down a lid.* **9.** to work hard at something (often fol. by *away*): *to hammer*

Hammer (def. 5)

away at one's studies. **10.** to impress (something) on someone by repeating it constantly. **11.** to form, accomplish, or reach by hard work and mental effort (usually fol. by *out*): *to hammer out an agreement.*

ham·mer·head (ham′ər hed′), *n.* a large shark whose head appears to be set crosswise like that of a double-headed hammer.

ham·mock (ham′ək), *n.* a kind of hanging bed or couch made of canvas, cord, or the like: *A hammock was hung between the two trees.*

Ham·mond (ham′ənd), *n.* a city in NW Indiana, near Chicago.

ham·per¹ (ham′pər), *v.* to hold back; interfere with: *Icy roads hampered our progress.* [from the Middle English word *hampren*, which is related to Old English *hamm* "enclosure"]

ham·per² (ham'pər), *n.* a large basket or container, usually having a top, used for holding laundry, carrying things, etc. [from the Middle English word *hampere,* which comes from medieval Latin *hanaperium*]

ham·ster (ham'stər), *n.* any of several furry rodents, somewhat larger than mice, having large cheek pouches and a short tail, often kept as pets.

ham·string (ham'string'), *v.,* **ham·strung** (ham'strung'), **ham·string·ing.** **1.** to disable (an animal) by cutting the tendons at the back of the rear legs. **2.** to make powerless or useless; block: *His plan was hamstrung by a series of delays.*

Hamster
(length 7 in.)

hand (hand), *n.* **1.** the part of the arm below the wrist, consisting of the palm, thumb, and fingers. **2.** one of the pointers on a watch or clock. **3.** a person employed as a laborer or worker: *a ranch hand.* **4.** a person who is skilled at a certain kind of work or action: *an old hand at police work.* **5.** an individual or characteristic touch; skill; workmanship: *You can see the hand of a fine carpenter in this woodwork.* **6.** one of a ship's crew; crewman: *All hands on deck!* **7.** Often, **hands.** possession, control, or care: *The decision is in your hands.* **8.** help or assistance: *Please give me a hand cleaning up.* **9.** style of handwriting; penmanship: *to write with a fine hand.* **10.** a side of a person, discussion, etc.: *A soldier stood at his right hand. On the other hand, you might find it easier to take the train.* **11.** a round or outburst of applause. **12.** a pledge or promise, such as a promise to marry someone. **13.** a measure equal to four inches, used esp. in figuring the height of horses: *The stallion stood 17 hands.* **14.** the cards dealt to a person in a card game: *She held a winning hand.* **15.** one round of a card game: *I haven't time to play another hand.* —*v.* **16.** to deliver or pass with the hand: *Hand me the saw.* **17.** to help, guide, etc., with the hand. —*adj.* **18.** of, for, or using the hand; made or done with the hands: *a page of hand lettering.* **19.** operated by hands; manual: *a hand drill.* **20. at hand,** nearby; ready for use: *Keep a bucket of water at hand in case of fire.* **21. change hands,** to pass from one owner to another: *That car has changed hands a dozen times.* **22. from hand to mouth,** with barely enough to survive: *They lived from hand to mouth.* **23. hand down, a.** to deliver (the decision of a court): *The Supreme Court handed down its opinion.* **b.** Also, **hand on.** to bequeath or pass on: *The farm has been handed down for six generations.* **24. hand out,** to distribute: *They were handing out leaflets on the corner.* **25. hand over,** to surrender possession of: *The landlord handed over the keys to the house.* **26. have a hand in,** to have a share in; participate in: *He had a hand in planning the shopping center.* **27. on hand,** in one's possession: *How much cash do we have on hand?*

hand·bag (hand'bag'), *n.* **1.** a woman's pocketbook

or purse. **2.** a small suitcase or bag for carrying clothes or the like when traveling.

hand·ball (hand'bôl'), *n.* **1.** a game for two or four players, in which a ball is batted by hand against a wall or walls. **2.** the small, hard, rubber ball used in this game.

hand·bill (hand'bil'), *n.* a small printed announcement, given out by hand.

hand·book (hand'book'), *n.* a book of instructions, information, directions, or the like, for use in traveling, doing a particular job, etc.; manual: *a handbook of European cathedrals; a handbook for nurses.*

hand·cart (hand'kärt'), *n.* a small cart drawn or pushed by hand: *He sold oranges from a handcart.*

hand·cuff (hand'kuf'), *n.* **1.** a metal ring or clasp that locks around the wrist, usually one of a pair joined by a short chain. Handcuffs are used to restrain a prisoner. —*v.* **2.** to put a handcuff or handcuffs on (a person).

hand·ful (hand'fool'), *n., pl.* **handfuls.** **1.** the amount that can be held in one hand: *a handful of beans.* **2.** a small amount; few: *a handful of people.* **3.** *Informal.* a person or thing that is almost more than one can manage or control: *That horse is a handful!*

hand·i·cap (han'dē kap'), *n.* **1.** a race or other contest in which those who are competing are given advantages or disadvantages in such a way that the contest is more equal. **2.** the advantage or disadvantage that is given, for example additional weight that must be carried by a race horse. **3.** anything that holds one back or makes one's life more difficult: *Blindness is a severe handicap.* —*v.,* **hand·i·capped, hand·i·cap·ping.** **4.** to place at a disadvantage; disable or burden: *Lack of education handicapped him when he was looking for work.* **5.** to assign handicaps to (contestants) in a race or other contest. [from the phrase *hand i' cap* "hand in the cap," which came from the custom of drawing the names of horses out of a cap before a race]

hand·i·craft (han'dē kraft'), *n.* **1.** skill in making things with one's hands: *Fine carpentry requires real handicraft.* **2.** an art, craft, or trade based on such skill: *weaving, leatherworking, and other handicrafts.* **3.** things made by hand: *a shop that sells handicraft.*

hand·i·work (han'dē wûrk'), *n.* **1.** work done by hand: *She does sewing and other handiwork.* **2.** the work of a particular person: *It was your handiwork that got us into this fix.*

hand·ker·chief (hang'kər chif, hang'kər chēf'), *n.* a small square of linen, cotton, or other fabric, used for wiping the eyes, face, nose, hands, etc.

han·dle (han'dəl), *n.* **1.** the part of a tool, container, or the like, that is made to be grasped by the hand: *Pick up your cup by the handle.* —*v.,* **han·dled, handling.** **2.** to touch, carry, or feel with the hands: *Please don't handle the kittens too much.* **3.** to manage, deal with, or take care of: *I'll handle the seating arrangements.* **4.** to use or work with: *You handled the colors well in that painting.* **5.** to run (an automobile, machine, etc.); work or operate: *He handles the tractor very well.* **6.** to deal or trade in; buy and sell: *He handles used cars.* **7. fly off the handle,** to become very angry: *She flew off the handle when I asked for a dog.*

han·dle·bar (han'dᵊl bär'), *n.* Usually, **handlebars.** the curved steering bar of a bicycle, motorcycle, etc.

han·dler (hand'lər), *n.* **1.** a person or thing that handles, manages, etc. **2.** a person who manages and shows a dog in a dog show.

hand·loom (hand'lōōm'), *n.* a loom for weaving fabric, operated by hand.

hand·made (hand'mād'), *adj.* made by hand, rather than by machine.

hand·maid (hand'mād'), *n.* a female servant or attendant. Also, **hand'maid'en.**

hand·out (hand'out'), *n.* **1.** food, clothing, money, or the like, given to a beggar or needy person. **2.** anything given away free, such as free samples of soap, toothpaste, etc.

hand·rail (hand'rāl'), *n.* a railing at the side of a staircase, ramp, or the like, that one may hold onto for support.

hand·saw (hand'sô'), *n.* a saw having a handle at one end and operated with one hand. See illus. at **saw.**

hands-down (handz'doun'), *adj.* **1.** done without effort; easy: *a hands-down victory.* **2.** certain or sure: *a hands-down winner.* —*adv.* **3.** easily; by a wide margin: *to win a race hands-down.*

hand·shake (hand'shāk'), *n.* the act of clasping and shaking the right hand of a person, done in greeting, parting, offering congratulations, etc.

hand·some (han'səm), *adj.,* **hand·som·er, hand·som·est. 1.** having a pleasing appearance, esp. in a strong or masculine way; good-looking: *a handsome boy.* **2.** generous; beyond what is required or usually expected: *He gave the driver a handsome tip.* [from the Middle English word *handsom* "easy to handle"] —**hand'some·ly,** *adv.* —**hand'some·ness,** *n.*

hand·spring (hand'spring'), *n.* a kind of somersault in which the person starts from a standing position and leaps forward or backward so that his hands touch the ground, his feet go completely over his head, and he lands on his feet again.

hand·stand (hand'stand'), *n.* the act of balancing oneself on one's hands with one's feet up in the air.

hand-to-hand (hand'tə hand'), *adj.* very near to, or in contact with, one's opponent; at close quarters: *The soldiers learned hand-to-hand combat.*

hand-to-mouth (hand'tə mouth'), *adj.* having barely enough to live on; impoverished: *a hand-to-mouth existence.*

hand·work (hand'wûrk'), *n.* work done by hand, rather than by machine.

hand·wo·ven (hand'wō'vən), *adj.* (of fabric) woven on a loom that is run by hand.

hand·writ·ing (hand'rī'ting), *n.* **1.** writing done with the hand, rather than typed or printed writing. **2.** a manner or style of handwriting: *She has very small handwriting.* **3. handwriting on the wall,** an

indication of something to come, esp. of disaster or calamity: *He should have seen the handwriting on the wall and not spent all his money.*

hand·y (han'dē), *adj.,* **hand·i·er, hand·i·est. 1.** within easy reach; easy to get hold of: *Always keep a fire extinguisher handy.* **2.** convenient or useful: *a handy pocketknife.* **3.** skillful with the hands: *a handy repairman; to be handy at fixing leaks.* —**hand'i·ly,** *adv.* —**hand'i·ness,** *n.*

hand·y·man (han'dē man'), *n., pl.* **hand·y·men.** a man hired to do various jobs, such as small repairs.

hang (hang), *v.,* **hung** (hung) *or* esp. for defs. 4, 5 **hanged; hang·ing. 1.** to fasten or place (a thing) so that it is held from a point at its top or near its top: *to hang curtains.* **2.** to be fastened in this way; be suspended; dangle: *The lamp hung from the ceiling.* **3.** to attach (something) so that it moves or swings freely: *to hang a gate on its hinges.* **4.** to die as a result of being suspended by a rope around the neck: *The murderer hanged for his crime.* **5.** to execute (a person) in this way. **6.** to attach or fix (something) to a wall or other upright surface: *to hang wallpaper.* **7.** to decorate with something that is suspended on a wall, from the ceiling, or the like: *to hang a room with pictures.* **8.** to lean over or forward; jut out: *The tree hung over the river.* **9.** to bow, bend down, or droop: *She hung her head. His head hung in shame.* **10.** to depend: *His future hangs on this election.* —*n.* **11.** the way in which a thing hangs: *the hang of a skirt.* **12.** *Informal.* the correct manner of doing or using something; knack: *to get the hang of skiing.* **13.** *Informal.* meaning or thought: *I didn't get the hang of what he was saying.* **14. hang around,** to spend time in a certain place; linger; loiter: *He hangs around the drugstore after school.* **15. hang back,** to hesitate to move forward: *to hang back out of fear.* **16. hang on, a.** to hold fast or cling to something: *The sled was going so fast I could hardly hang on.* **b.** to continue or persevere: *My cough hung on for a month.* **17. hang out, a.** to lean through (an opening): *We hung out the window to watch the parade.* **b.** to suspend in open view; display: *to hang out a flag.* **c.** *Slang.* to spend one's free time: *He sometimes hangs out at the swimming pool.* **18. hang up, a.** to suspend from a hook, peg, or the like: *Hang up your clothes.* **b.** to replace a telephone receiver on the hook: *They hung up as soon as I answered.*

hang·ar (hang'ər), *n.* a large shed used for housing airplanes or airships.

hang·dog (hang'dôg', -dog'), *adj.* showing feelings of shame, discouragement, embarrassment, etc.: *a hangdog look of defeat.*

hang·er (hang'ər), *n.* **1.** a shoulder-shaped device with a hook at the top, for hanging up a coat, dress, blouse, or the like: *Your coat is in the closet on a hanger.* **2.** a hook or other device for hanging something. **3.** a person who hangs something.

hang·er-on (hang'ər ôn', -on'), *n., pl.* **hang·ers-on.** a person who stays around another person or group in the hope of personal gain, rather than out of friendship: *The millionaire was surrounded by hangers-on.*

hang·ing (hang'ing), *n.* **1.** death or execution in which the person is suspended by a rope around his neck. **2.** Often, **hangings.** curtains, drapes, etc., that are hung as decoration. **3.** the act of a person who hangs something. —*adj.* **4.** attached from above; dangling; suspended: *a hanging lamp.* **5.** being on a steep slope or at a height: *hanging gardens.*

hang·man (hang'mən), *n., pl.* **hang·men.** a person who hangs criminals condemned to death.

hang·nail (hang'nāl'), *n.* a small piece of loose skin next to a fingernail.

hang·out (hang'out'), *n. Informal.* a place where a person lives or frequently visits: *The candy store is his favorite hangout.*

hang·o·ver (hang'ō'vər), *n.* the sick feeling that follows drunkenness, including headache, thirst, and nausea.

hank (hangk), *n.* **1.** a coil or loop of yarn, thread, or the like; skein. **2.** any coil or loop: *a hank of hair.*

han·ker (hang'kər), *v.* to have a restless longing; yearn (usually fol. by *after, for,* or an infinitive): *to hanker for a house in the country.*

han·ky (hang'kē), *n., pl.* **han·kies.** a handkerchief. Also, **han'kie.**

Han·ni·bal (han'ə bəl), *n.* 247–183 B.C., Carthaginian general who crossed the Alps and invaded Italy 218 B.C.

Ha·noi (ha noi'), *n.* the capital city of Vietnam: formerly of North Vietnam before reunification.

han·som (han'səm), *n.* a two-wheeled, covered, horse-drawn carriage, having seats for two passengers on the inside and a high seat for the driver outside, in back of the roof. Also, **han'som cab'.** [named after J. A. *Hansom* (1803–1882), English architect, its designer]

Hansom

Ha·nuk·kah (hä'nə kə), *n.* an eight-day Jewish festival celebrated in December or late November in memory of the rededication of the Temple in Jerusalem following the victory over the Syrians in 165 B.C. Also, **Chanukah.**

hap·haz·ard (hap haz'ərd), *adj.* showing no order; random: *to work in a careless, haphazard way.* —**hap·haz'ard·ly,** *adv.* —**hap·haz'ard·ness,** *n.*

hap·less (hap'lis), *adj.* unlucky or unfortunate: *a hapless occurrence.*

hap·pen (hap'ən), *v.* **1.** to take place; come about; occur: *Tell me how the accident happened.* **2.** to come about or occur by chance: *It happened that he was nearby.* **3.** to have the luck to do, be, or have what is mentioned: *He happens to have a rich uncle.* **4.** to befall or be done: *I wonder what will happen to me now?* **5.** to meet or discover by chance (usually fol. by *on* or *upon*): *He happened on the answer to the mystery.*

hap·pen·ing (hap'ə ning), *n.* an event or occur-

rence; something that happens.

hap·pi·ness (hap'ē nis), *n.* **1.** the state or quality of being happy; gladness; joy. **2.** good luck.

hap·py (hap'ē), *adj.,* **hap·pi·er, hap·pi·est. 1.** full of or showing feelings of pleasure, gladness, or joy; contented; joyful: *We were happy to see them. She wore a happy smile.* **2.** fortunate or lucky: *a happy coincidence.* **3.** fitting; highly suitable: *a happy choice of words.* —**hap'pi·ly,** *adv.*

hap·py-go-luck·y (hap'ē gō luk'ē), *adj.* carefree and cheerful; trusting to luck: *a happy-go-lucky wanderer.*

Haps·burg (haps'bûrg), *n.* a German princely family that furnished rulers for the Holy Roman Empire, Austria, Spain, and other countries of Europe.

ha·rangue (hə rang'), *n.* **1.** a long, ranting or pompous speech: *a harangue on the subject of higher taxes.* —*v.,* **ha·rangued, ha·rangu·ing. 2.** to speak in a ranting or pompous way. **3.** to deliver a harangue to. —**ha·rangu'er,** *n.*

har·ass (har'əs, hə ras'), *v.* **1.** to trouble or disturb by frequent attacks, raids, or the like: *Bands of armed farmers harassed the invading troops.* **2.** to pester or torment: *Stop harassing that poor dog!* —**har'ass·er,** *n.* —**har'ass·ing·ly,** *adv.* —**har'ass·ment,** *n.*

har·bin·ger (här'bin jər), *n.* **1.** a person who heralds the approach of another. **2.** a sign or omen: *The robin is a harbinger of spring.* —*v.* **3.** to make known the future; herald.

har·bor (här'bər), *n.* **1.** a place or port on a body of water where ships can anchor or dock and be protected against high winds, waves, etc. **2.** any shelter or refuge. —*v.* **3.** to give refuge to: *to harbor an escapee.* **4.** to hold in the mind: *to harbor suspicions.*

hard (härd), *adj.* **1.** not soft; solid and firm to the touch: *He banged his knee on the hard, stone pavement.* **2.** difficult to do, understand, answer, etc.: *a hard job; a hard question.* **3.** involving or using much effort or concentration: *hard study; a hard worker.* **4.** forceful or violent: *a hard fall; a hard rain.* **5.** harsh or severe: *a hard winter; hard luck.* **6.** stern, strict, or pitiless: *a hard teacher; a hard man.* **7.** unfriendly or full of anger, bitterness, etc.: *hard feelings between two people.* **8.** strong or intoxicating; containing a considerable amount of alcohol: *hard liquor.* **9.** (of water) containing minerals that interfere with the action of soap. **10.** describing the pronunciation of the consonant *c* as in *cat* and of *g* as in *go.* See also **soft** (def. 8). —*adv.* **11.** with great effort or concentration: *to work hard.* **12.** closely or earnestly: *to look hard at something.* **13.** so as to be solid, firm, or tight: *frozen hard.* **14.** with force; harshly or severely: *to rain hard; to fall down hard.* **15.** with strong feelings of sorrow or anger: *He took the news very hard.* **16.** with strain or difficulty; heavily: *to breathe hard.* **17.** close or near: *The dog stood hard by its master.* **18.** tightly or closely: *Bite down hard.* **19. hard of hearing,** slightly deaf. **20. hard up,** urgently in need of money or other resources: *He can't* *take care of his money, so he's always hard up. The company is hard up for workers.* —**hard'ness,** *n.*

hard-and-fast (härd'ᵊn fast'), *adj.* not able to be set aside, skipped, or overlooked: *hard-and-fast rules.*

hard-boiled (härd'boild'), *adj.* 1. (of an egg) boiled until it is hard inside. 2. tough and unsentimental.

hard' coal', another name for **anthracite.**

hard-core (härd'kôr'), *adj.* 1. firmly uncompromising or unyielding: *a hard-core segregationist.* 2. chronic and deep-seated: *hard-core unemployment.*

hard-en (här'dᵊn), *v.* 1. to make or become hard or harder: *Bread hardens when it gets stale.* 2. to make or become heartless or tough. —**hard'en-er,** *n.*

hard' hat', 1. a protective helmet worn by construction workers. 2. Also, **hard-hat** (härd'hat'). *Informal.* a construction worker.

hard-head-ed (härd'hed'id), *adj.* 1. not easily fooled; shrewd: *a hard-headed businessman.* 2. very stubborn; willful. —**hard'-head'ed-ness,** *n.*

hard-heart-ed (härd'här'tid), *adj.* without pity or mercy; unfeeling; cruel: *a hard-hearted tyrant.* —**hard'-heart'ed-ly,** *adv.* —**hard'-heart'ed-ness,** *n.*

har-di-hood (här'dē hŏod'), *n.* 1. hardiness or strength of character; courage: *The pioneers were noted for their hardihood.* 2. vigor or strength.

Har-ding (här'ding), *n.* **Warren G**(a-ma-li-el) (gə-mā'lē əl), 1865–1923, 29th President of the U.S. 1921–1923.

hard-ly (härd'lē), *adv.* 1. barely or scarcely: *There is hardly any food left.* 2. not quite: *This is hardly the time for joking.* 3. probably not: *It is hardly possible.* 4. *British.* harshly: *to treat someone hardly.*

hard' pal'ate, the front, bony part of the roof of the mouth. See also **soft palate.** See illus. at **mouth.**

hard-ship (härd'ship), *n.* something that is hard to bear; a condition that is difficult to endure: *Many families suffered great hardship during the war.*

hard-tack (härd'tak'), *n.* a hard, saltless biscuit, formerly fed to sailors and soldiers. Also, **ship biscuit.**

hard-ware (härd'wâr'), *n.* 1. things made from metal, esp. tools, nails, screws, etc. 2. the tools or machines required for a particular job or activity.

hard-wood (härd'wŏod'), *n.* the strong, heavy wood of various trees, including maple, oak, etc., used in making fine furniture. See also **softwood.**

har-dy (här'dē), *adj.,* **har-di-er, har-di-est.** 1. strong and sturdy; capable of bearing hardship, suffering, etc.: *hardy explorers.* 2. (of plants) able to survive the winter out of doors. 3. daring or courageous. —**har'di-ness,** *n.*

hare (hâr), *n., pl.* **hares** *or* **hare.** any of several animals related to the rodents, but having a split upper lip, long ears, and powerful back legs. Hares resemble rabbits but are larger and leap rather than run.

hare-brained (hâr'brānd'), *adj.* giddy, reckless, or silly: *a harebrained idea.*

hare-lip (hâr'lip'), *n.* a birth defect in which the upper lip is split like that of a hare.

har-em (hâr'əm, har'əm), *n.* 1. the part of a Muslim palace or house reserved for the residence of women. 2. the women of a Muslim household. [from the Arabic word *harim* "forbidden"]

hark (härk), *v.* to listen; harken (used chiefly in the imperative): *Hark! I hear them approaching.*

hark-en (här'kən), *v.* to listen; pay attention: *Harken to my words.* Also, **hearken.** —**hark'en-er,** *n.*

har-le-quin (här'lə kwin, här'lə kin), *n.* 1. *(often cap.)* a character in traditional pantomimes and comic plays, who usually appears wearing a multicolored costume and a mask and carrying a wooden sword or magic wand. 2. a clown or buffoon. —*adj.* 3. having many colors; multicolored.

Harlequin

har-lot (här'lət), *n.* a prostitute.

harm (härm), *n.* 1. damage or hurt; injury. 2. evil or wrong: *There's no harm in telling the truth now.* —*v.* 3. to do or cause harm to; injure; hurt: *to harm one's foot; to harm someone's chances.*

harm-ful (härm'fəl), *adj.* causing or capable of causing harm; dangerous. —**harm'ful-ly,** *adv.* —**harm'ful-ness,** *n.*

harm-less (härm'lis), *adj.* not causing or intending to cause harm: *a harmless joke; a harmless little bug.* —**harm'less-ly,** *adv.* —**harm'less-ness,** *n.*

har-mon-ic (här mon'ik), *adj.* 1. referring to harmony rather than to melody or rhythm: *a harmonic accompaniment.* —*n.* 2. any of the individual vibrations in a complex musical tone, usually the slowest vibration or a vibration at a speed that is an even multiple of the slowest one. See also **overtone.**

har-mon-i-ca (här mon'ə kə), *n.* a musical wind instrument consisting of a small case containing metal reeds that are sounded by blowing or sucking air through a row of holes over which the player places his mouth. Also, **mouth organ.**

Harmonica

har-mo-ni-ous (här mō'nē əs), *adj.* 1. forming an agreeable combination or blend: *harmonious colors.* 2. pleasant in sound: *harmonious chords.* 3. sharing the same feelings or goals; friendly: *a harmonious group of people.* —**har-mo'ni-ous-ly,** *adv.*

har-mo-nize (här'mə nīz'), *v.,* **har-mo-nized, har-mo-niz-ing.** 1. to bring into agreement: *to harmonize opposing ideas.* 2. to accompany with proper chords. 3. to sing in harmony. —**har'mo-niz'er,** *n.*

har-mo-ny (här'mə nē), *n., pl.* **har-mo-nies.** 1. the combination of musical tones that produces chords. 2. that part of music concerned with chords and the combinations of tones rather than with melody or rhythm. 3. agreement, peace, or friendship. [from the Latin word *harmonia,* which comes from a Greek word meaning "melody, a joining (of sounds)"]

har-ness (här'nis), *n.* 1. the combination of straps, bands, collar, etc., used to attach an animal, such as a work horse, to a plow, cart, or the like. —*v.* 2. to put a harness on: *to harness a pony.* 3. to gain control over and use: *to harness the energy of the sun.*

harp (härp), *n.* 1. a musical instrument having strings stretched across a triangular frame and played by plucking with the fingers of both hands. —*v.* 2. to play on the harp. 3. **harp on,** to talk or write about (something) without letup; dwell on: *to harp on one's achievements.* —**harp′ist,** *n.*

Harp

Har′pers Fer′ry (här′pərz), a small town in NE West Virginia: site of John Brown's raid 1859.

har·poon (här pōōn′), *n.* 1. a barbed, spearlike weapon attached to a rope and thrown by hand or shot from a gun. This weapon is used to kill and capture whales and large fish. —*v.* 2. to strike, catch, or kill with a harpoon: *to harpoon a whale.* —**har·poon′er,** *n.*

harp·si·chord (härp′si kôrd′), *n.* a keyboard instrument having the shape of a grand piano, whose strings are plucked by quills or leather points. —**harp′si·chord′ist,** *n.*

har·py (här′pē), *n., pl.* **har·pies.** 1. a nagging, bad-tempered woman; shrew. 2. a greedy, nasty person.

Har·py (här′pē), *n., pl.* **Har·pies.** (in Greek mythology) a filthy, greedy monster having the head of a woman and the body of a bird.

har·que·bus (här′kwə bəs) *n., pl.* **har·que·bus·es.** a long, portable gun, usually fired resting on an upright support, and first used about 1400. Also, **arquebus.**

Har·ris·burg (har′is bûrg′), *n.* the capital city of Pennsylvania, in the S part.

Har·ri·son (har′i sən), *n.* 1. Benjamin, 1833–1901, 23rd President of the U.S. 1889–1893. 2. William Henry, 1773–1841, 9th President of the U.S. 1841.

har·row (har′ō), *n.* 1. a piece of farm equipment having a set of toothlike spikes or upright disks fixed on a frame, used to break up chunks of earth in plowed land. —*v.* 2. to drag a harrow over (land): *to harrow a field.* 3. to distress or disturb painfully: *Grief and remorse harrowed her mind.* —**har′row·er,** *n.* —**har′row·ing·ly,** *adv.*

har·ry (har′ē), *v.,* **har·ried, har·ry·ing.** 1. to bother or annoy; torment. 2. to raid and plunder: *Pirates harried the coast.*

harsh (härsh), *adj.* 1. rough and unpleasant; unkind; cruel: *angry, harsh words.* 2. very stern or severe: *a harsh master.* 3. rough or grating to hear, touch, or the like; unpleasant to the senses: *He has a loud, harsh voice.* —**harsh′ly,** *adv.* —**harsh′ness,** *n.*

hart (härt), *n., pl.* **harts** or **hart.** a male deer.

har·te·beest (här′tə bēst′, härt′bēst′), *n., pl.* **har·te·beests** or **har·te·beest.** any of several large, African

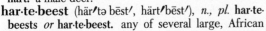

Hartebeest
(4½ ft. high at shoulder)

antelopes, having ringed horns that curve backward. [from Afrikaans]

Hart·ford (härt′fərd), *n.* the capital city of Connecticut, in the central part.

har·um-scar·um (hâr′əm skâr′əm, har′əm skar′əm), *adj.* 1. reckless or wild; irresponsible: *a harum-scarum young person.* —*adv.* 2. recklessly or wildly: *He rode harum-scarum across the fields.* —*n.* 3. a reckless, wild person.

har·vest (här′vist), *n.* 1. the gathering of crops, such as wheat, corn, fruit, etc.: *The farmers are working at the harvest.* 2. the season when ripened crops are gathered. 3. the supply or yield of a crop or crops grown in any one season: *a rich harvest of grain.* 4. the result of any act, process, or event; outcome: *He is enjoying the harvest of 20 years of hard work.* —*v.* 5. to gather (a crop); reap: *to harvest apples.* 6. to gather a crop from: *to harvest the fields.* 7. to gain, win, collect, etc.: *to harvest one's reward.*

har·ves·ter (här′vi stər), *n.* 1. a person who harvests crops. 2. a machine for harvesting field crops.

har′vest moon′, the full moon around the period of the fall equinox, when it appears to be especially bright.

has (haz), *v.* the third person singular, present tense of **have.**

hash (hash), *n.* 1. a dish of chopped meat, potatoes, and sometimes vegetables, usually cooked in a frying pan. 2. a mess, jumble, or muddle: *You certainly made a hash of that paint job.* —*v.* 3. to chop into small pieces; make into hash: *to hash leftovers.* 4. to muddle or mess up. 5. **hash over,** *Slang.* to bring up again for discussion or review: *He and Dad were hashing over their days in the navy.* [from the French word *hacher* "to cut up"]

hash·ish (hash′ēsh, hash′ish), *n.* a narcotic drug made from the flowers and leaves of an Indian hemp plant. [from Arabic]

has·n't (haz′ənt), contraction of *has not.*

hasp (hasp), *n.* a clasp or fastening for a door, lid, or the like, esp. one that is secured by a pin or padlock.

has·sle (has′əl), *n. Informal.* a squabble or fight; quarrel: *a hassle over the last piece of pie.*

has·sock (has′ək), *n.* 1. a big, thick cushion used for resting one's feet, sitting, etc. 2. a tuft of coarse grass.

hast (hast), *v.* an old form of **have,** found now chiefly in Biblical and poetic writing (used with *thou*).

haste (hāst), *n.* 1. swiftness of motion; speed; hurry: *to work with haste.* 2. careless speed or hurry in doing something: *Haste makes waste.*

has·ten (hā′sən), *v.* 1. to move or act quickly; hurry: *She hastened home.* 2. to cause to go or happen faster; quicken; speed: *They hastened their departure.*

hast·y (hā′stē), *adj.,* **hast·i·er, hast·i·est.** 1. done with haste or speed; quick; hurried: *a hasty visit to the doctor.* 2. too quick; rash: *a hasty decision.* 3. easily excited, esp. to anger: *a hasty temper.* —**hast′i·ly,** *adv.* —**hast′i·ness,** *n.*

hat (hat), *n.* **1.** a covering for the head, usually with a brim. —*v.,* **hat·ted, hat·ting. 2.** to put a hat on; provide with a hat. **3. pass the hat,** *Informal.* to take up a collection: *We passed the hat to get him a gift.* **4. under one's hat,** *Informal.* secret; confidential: *If I tell you, will you keep it under your hat?*

hatch¹ (hach), *v.* **1.** to bring forth (a young animal) from an egg: *to hatch chickens.* **2.** to cause a young animal to be born from (an egg) by keeping the egg warm. **3.** to bring forth or think up: *to hatch a plan of escape.* **4.** to be hatched: *Have the ducks hatched yet?* [from the Middle English word *hacchen*]

hatch² (hach), *n.* **1.** See **hatchway** (def. 1). **2.** an opening in the floor or roof of a building; hatchway. **3.** the covering for a hatch, such as a trap door. **4.** an opening or door in an aircraft. [from the Old English word *hæcc* "a grating"]

hatch·back (hach/bak/), *n.* an automobile with a back window and trunk opening combined into a wide door hinged at the top for easy loading.

Hatchback

hatch·er·y (hach/ə rē), *n., pl.* **hatch·er·ies.** a place for hatching eggs of hens, fish, or other animals.

hatch·et (hach/it), *n.* **1.** a small, short-handled ax, made to be used with one hand: *to chop off branches with a hatchet.* See illus. at **ax. 2.** a tomahawk. **3. bury the hatchet,** to agree on a truce; make peace: *Let's bury the hatchet and be friends again.*

hatch·way (hach/wā/), *n.* **1.** Also, **hatch.** a covered opening in the deck of a ship, used as a passage for cargo, people, etc. **2.** the opening of a trap door.

hate (hāt), *v.,* **hat·ed, hat·ing. 1.** to dislike (a person or thing) strongly or violently; detest: *to hate meanness.* **2.** to dislike; be unwilling: *I hate to break the news to her.* —*n.* **3.** strong dislike; loathing; hatred: *a man full of hate and bitterness.* —**hat/er,** *n.*

hate·ful (hāt/fəl), *adj.* **1.** causing or deserving hate: *a hateful crime.* **2.** full of or showing hate: *a hateful look.* **3.** unpleasant or distasteful: *a hateful duty.* —**hate/ful·ly,** *adv.* —**hate/ful·ness,** *n.*

hath (hath), *v.* an old form of **has,** found now chiefly in Biblical and poetic writing (used with *he, she,* or *it*): *He hath traveled in distant lands.*

ha·tred (hā/trid), *n.* the feeling of a person who hates; hate; loathing: *to be full of hatred and rage.*

hat·ter (hat/ər), *n.* a person who makes or sells hats.

Hat·ter·as (hat/ər əs), *n.* **Cape,** a point of land on an island off the E coast of North Carolina.

haugh·ty (hô/tē), *adj.,* **haugh·ti·er, haugh·ti·est.** too proud; scornful of others; arrogant: *a haughty aristocrat.* —**haugh/ti·ly,** *adv.* —**haugh/ti·ness,** *n.*

haul (hôl), *v.* **1.** to pull with force; drag: *The horse hauled the heavy wagon up the hill.* **2.** to carry, move, or transport in a truck, cart, or other vehicle: *to haul away garbage.* —*n.* **3.** the act of hauling; a strong pull or tug: *Give the rope a haul.* **4.** something that is hauled; load. **5.** an amount collected: *a large haul of fish.* **6.** the distance or route over which something is hauled: *It's a long haul up that hill.* **7. haul off,** *Informal.* to raise the arm for striking a blow: *He hauled off and socked the other fellow.* [another form of *hale²*] —**haul/er,** *n.*

haunch (hônch, hänch), *n.* **1.** the hip or the fleshy part of the body around the hip. **2.** a hindquarter of an animal. **3.** the loin or rear leg of an animal considered as meat: *a haunch of venison.*

haunt (hônt), *v.* **1.** to visit or appear frequently as a ghost or spirit: *to haunt a house; to haunt a person.* **2.** to visit frequently; go to often: *As a boy, he haunted the museums.* **3.** to return constantly to the mind of (a person), causing distress, longing, or the like: *Memories of her homeland haunted her.* —*n.* **4.** Often, **haunts.** a place or places frequently visited: *He's gone back to his old haunts in Denver.*

haunt·ed (hôn/tid), *adj.* **1.** lived in or visited by ghosts: *a haunted house.* **2.** distressed or absorbed by memories: *haunted by past crimes.*

haunt·ing (hôn/tiñg), *adj.* remaining in the mind; not easily forgotten: *a haunting beauty.* —**haunt/ing·ly,** *adv.*

Ha·van·a (hə van/ə), *n.* a seaport and the capital city of Cuba, on the NW coast.

have (hav), *v.,* **had** (had), **hav·ing. 1.** to possess, own, or hold: *He has red hair.* **2.** to contain or be made up of: *This book has 200 pages.* **3.** to get, receive, or take: *to have a rest.* **4.** to experience or undergo: *He had a good time at the party.* **5.** to be obliged or need (usually fol. by an infinitive): *I have to go out.* **6.** to engage in or carry on: *to have a fight.* **7.** to cause to do something specified: *Have them come to dinner.* **8.** to permit or allow: *I will not have any more complaining.* **9.** to be related to or have a certain relation to: *to have three cousins; to have a good boss.* **10.** to hold in the mind: *to have an idea.* **11.** to show or use: *Have some patience.* **12.** to give birth to: *to have a baby.* **13.** to eat or drink: *They had cookies and milk in the morning.* —*auxiliary verb.* **14.** (used with past participle to form perfect tenses): *She has gone. I have done the dusting.* **15. had better,** ought to: *You'd better ask permission first.* **16. had rather,** to prefer: *I'd rather go with you.* **17. have had it,** *Slang.* **a.** to become bored or disgusted with what one is doing: *I've helped him every day, but now I've had it.* **b.** to stop being popular: *Quiz shows have had it.* **18. have it in for,** to have a grudge against: *She has it in for anyone who gets better grades than she does.* **19. have it out,** to settle a problem by arguing or fighting: *They had it out with boxing gloves.*

ha·ven (hā/vən), *n.* **1.** a harbor or port. **2.** any place of shelter and safety; refuge: *the haven of faith.*

have·n't (hav/ənt), contraction of *have not.*

hav·er·sack (hav/ər sak/), *n.* a bag with a strap,

worn over the shoulder and used to carry food, supplies, and the like.

hav·oc (hav′ək), *n.* **1.** terrible damage or destruction; ruin; devastation: *The war brought havoc into the land.* **2. play havoc with,** to upset or ruin: *The rain played havoc with our vacation plans.*

haw¹ (hô), *n.* **1.** the hawthorn. **2.** the red berry of the hawthorn. [from the Old English word *haga*]

haw² (hô), *v.* **1.** to pause or falter in speaking: *He hemmed and hawed but finally agreed.* —*n.* **2.** a sound made by one who falters in speaking.

haw³ (hô), *interj.* (used as a word of command to a horse, ox, etc., to make the animal turn left.) [from the Middle English word *haw!* "look!"]

Ha·wai·i (hə wī′ē, hə wä′ē), *n.* **1.** a state of the United States consisting of a group of islands in the

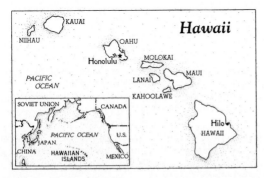

Hawaii

N Pacific Ocean. 6454 sq. mi. *Cap.:* Honolulu. **2.** the largest island of Hawaii.

Ha·wai·ian (hə wī′ən, hə wä′yən), *adj.* **1.** of or referring to Hawaii, the people of Hawaii, or their language. —*n.* **2.** a native or inhabitant of Hawaii. **3.** the language of the original inhabitants of Hawaii, a Polynesian language.

Hawai′ian Is′lands, a group of islands in the N Pacific Ocean, forming the state of Hawaii.

hawk¹ (hôk), *n.* **1.** any of numerous birds of prey, smaller than eagles, with a hooked beak and powerful claws. Many kinds of hawks were used in falconry. —*v.* **2.** to hunt with hawks. [from the Old English word *hafoc*] —**hawk′er,** *n.* —**hawk′like′,** *adj.*

hawk² (hôk), *v.* to peddle or offer for sale by calling aloud or by going from door to door: *He hawked his wares in the market.* [the verb *hawk* is formed from the noun *hawker,* which comes from an early German dialect word *haker* "retail dealer"] —**hawk′er,** *n.*

Hawk
(length 2 ft.)

hawk³ (hôk), *v.* **1.** to clear the throat noisily. **2.** to raise by hawking: *to hawk up phlegm.* [imitative of the sound]

haw·ser (hô′zər, hô′sər), *n.* a heavy rope for mooring or towing ships.

haw·thorn (hô′thôrn′), *n.* any of numerous thorny shrubs or trees some species of which bear white or pink blossoms and red berries.

Haw·thorne (hô′thôrn′), *n.* **Nathaniel,** 1804–1864, U.S. novelist.

hay (hā), *n.* **1.** grass, clover, etc., cut and dried for use as food for cattle. —*v.* **2.** to cut grass, clover, etc., for hay. **3.** to supply with hay: *to hay the horses.* **4. hit the hay,** to go to bed: *What time did you hit the hay?* **5. make hay while the sun shines,** to take advantage of an opportunity when it presents itself.

hay·cock (hā′kok′), *n.* a small stack of hay in a field.

Hay·dn (hīd′ən), *n.* **Franz Joseph,** 1732–1809, Austrian composer.

Hayes (hāz), *n.* **Ruth·er·ford B.** (ruth′ər fərd), 1822–1893, 19th President of the U.S. 1877–1881.

hay′ fe′ver, a condition that produces sneezing, itching eyes, wheezing, etc., and is caused by allergy to various plant pollens.

hay·field (hā′fēld′), *n.* a field of grass, clover, etc., grown for hay.

hay·loft (hā′lôft′), *n.* a loft in a stable or barn, used for storing hay.

hay·mow (hā′mou′), *n.* **1.** a place in a barn where hay is stored. **2.** a pile of hay stored in a barn.

hay·stack (hā′stak′), *n.* a large pile of hay outdoors.

hay·wire (hā′wī°r′), *n.* **1.** wire used to bind bales of hay. —*adj.* **2.** *Informal.* out of order; not working: *The car went haywire.*

haz·ard (haz′ərd), *n.* **1.** danger; risk; peril: *the hazards of mountain climbing.* **2.** any cause of danger: *Slippery floors are a hazard in the home.* **3.** chance; accident: *to meet by hazard.* **4.** (in golf) an obstacle, such as a water trap. —*v.* **5.** to venture or dare: *to hazard a guess.* **6.** to risk: *to hazard one's life.*

haz·ard·ous (haz′ər dəs), *adj.* full of risk; dangerous: *Icy roads are hazardous.* —**haz′ard·ous·ly,** *adv.*

haze¹ (hāz), *n.* **1.** a small amount of mist or smoke in the air, that makes things appear blurred. **2.** mild confusion in the mind: *He was in a haze about the cause of the accident.* [from the Old English word *hasu* "ashen, dusky"]

haze² (hāz), *v.,* **hazed, haz·ing.** to make (a newcomer) perform tricks, do unpleasant tasks, etc., as a part of becoming a member of a group, such as a fraternity or club. [from the Old French word *haser* "to irritate, annoy"] —**haz′er,** *n.*

ha·zel (hā′zəl), *n.* a shrub or small tree that bears hazelnuts.

ha·zel·nut (hā′zəl nut′), *n.* a small, round, sweet nut having a hard, thick shell. Also, **filbert.**

ha·zy (hā′zē), *adj.,* **ha·zi·er, ha·zi·est. 1.** full of haze: *a hazy day; a hazy sky.* **2.** confused; uncertain: *He had only a hazy notion of what was happening.* —**ha′zi·ly,** *adv.* —**ha′zi·ness,** *n.*

H-bomb (āch′bom′), *n.* another term for **hydrogen bomb.**

hdqrs., headquarters.

he (hē), *pron.* **1.** the man, boy, or male animal being spoken about or referred to. **2.** anyone; that person: *He who laughs last laughs best.* —*n.* **3.** a man, boy, or male animal: *The dog is a he.*

He, *Chem.* the symbol for **helium.**

head (hed), *n.* **1.** the upper part of the human body, containing the brain, eyes, nose, ears, and mouth. **2.** a similar part of an animal. **3.** intelligence or the mind: *I have a head for arithmetic.* **4.** the highest rank or position: *to be at the head of the class.* **5.** a leader, chief, director, or the like: *the head of a large company.* **6.** the top part or upper end of anything: *the head of a pin.* **7.** the front part or forward end of anything: *the head of a line.* **8.** the part of a weapon, tool, etc., used for striking. **9.** a person or animal considered merely as one of a number: *ten head of cattle; a dinner at so much a head.* **10.** a crisis or climax: *The event brought matters to a head.* **11.** froth or foam on the top of a liquid: *the head on a glass of beer.* **12.** the dense, clustered, rounded part of a plant: *flower heads; a head of lettuce.* **13. heads,** the main side of a coin, usually stamped with an image of a head (opposite of *tails*). **14.** a sculpture of the head: *a head of Lincoln.* **15.** the source of a river or stream. **16.** a stretched skin that covers the frame of a drum. —*adj.* **17.** first in rank; chief: *the head officer.* **18.** of or referring to the head: *a head injury.* **19.** at the top or in front: *the head person in a line.* —*v.* **20.** to go at the head of: *to head an attack.* **21.** to take the lead in or over: *to head the class.* **22.** to be the head or chief of: *to head a department.* **23.** to direct the course of: *to head a boat toward shore.* **24.** to move forward toward some point: *to head toward shore.* **25. go to one's head, a.** to make a person dizzy or drunk: *The champagne went to her head.* **b.** to make one conceited: *The beauty prize has certainly gone to her head.* **26. head off,** to catch up with and delay; intercept: *Try to head him off before he cashes that check.* **27. keep one's head,** to remain calm, esp. in a crisis: *Luckily, he kept his head and called the fire department.* **28. lose one's head,** to become wildly excited: *If you find yourself in deep water, don't lose your head.* **29. one's head off,** extremely or excessively: *She laughed her head off at the joke.* **30. out of one's head** (or **mind**), **a.** not rational; delirious: *to be out of one's head during a fever.* **b.** insane; crazy: *If you think I'm going, you're out of your head.* —**head′less,** *adj.*

head·ache (hed′āk′), *n.* a pain in the head.

head·dress (hed′dres′), *n.* a covering or decoration for the head: *an Indian headdress of bright feathers.*

-headed, a suffix used to form adjectives meaning **1.** having a certain kind of head: *red-headed; bare-headed.* **2.** having a certain kind of mentality, personality, or emotional state: *blockheaded; level-headed; light-headed.* **3.** having a certain number of heads: *two-headed.*

head·first (hed′fûrst′), *adv.* with the head in front or bent forward: *He dived headfirst into the sea.*

head·gear (hed′gēr′), *n.* any covering for the head, worn either as an ornament or for protection, such as a hat, bonnet, or helmet.

head·ing (hed′ing), *n.* **1.** something that is at the head, top, or front. **2.** a title of a page, chapter, etc. **3.** the compass direction in which a plane, ship, etc., is traveling: *The heading is north.*

head·land (hed′lənd), *n.* a piece of land jutting into a body of water; promontory.

head·light (hed′līt′), *n.* a light on the front of a car, locomotive, etc.

head·line (hed′līn′), *n.* **1.** a heading in large print at the top of a newspaper article. **2.** See **banner** (def. 3). —*v.,* **head·lined, head·lin·ing. 3.** to be the most important performer of (a show, nightclub, etc.).

head·long (hed′lông′), *adv., adj.* **1.** with the head foremost: *to plunge headlong into the water; a headlong plunge.* **2.** with haste or rashness: *to reply headlong; a headlong dash.*

head·mas·ter (hed′mas′tər), *n.* the principal of a private school in the U.S., or of any school for children in England.

head-on (hed′on′, -ôn′), *adj., adv.* with the head or front first: *a head-on crash; to crash head-on.*

head·piece (hed′pēs′), *n.* a covering for the head, such as a piece of armor, helmet, hat, etc.

head·quar·ters (hed′kwôr′tərz), *n.pl. (used as sing. or pl.)* a main office or center of a business, police force, etc., where orders are given.

head·set (hed′set′), *n.* a device consisting of one or two earphones with a band for holding them over the ears and sometimes with a mouthpiece attached.

head·stone (hed′stōn′), *n.* a stone marker set at the head of a grave; gravestone.

head·strong (hed′strông′), *adj.* **1.** determined to do what one pleases; willful: *a brash, headstrong young man.* **2.** done or said out of willfulness: *headstrong opinions.*

head·wa·ters (hed′wô′tərz, -wot′ərz), *n.pl.* the streams that come together to form a river; the source or upper waters of a river.

head·way (hed′wā′), *n.* **1.** movement forward or ahead: *to make headway through the snow.* **2.** progress or advancement: *to make headway in business.*

head′ wind′, a wind that blows in the opposite direction to the course of a ship or airplane.

head·y (hed′ē), *adj.,* **head·i·er, head·i·est. 1.** tending to make one dizzy or drunken: *heady wine.* **2.** reckless or headstrong: *heady, rash judgments.* **3.** exciting; rousing: *heady news of victory.* —**head′i·ness,** *n.*

heal (hēl), *v.* **1.** to make or become whole or healthy. **2.** to bring to an end, as a quarrel: *The explanation healed our differences.* [from the Old English word *hǣlan,* which comes from *hāl* "hale, whole"]

health (helth), *n.* **1.** the general condition of the body: *good health.* **2.** soundness of body; freedom from disease: *to lose one's health.* **3.** a toast to a person's health: *to drink a health to the queen.* **4.** vigor or strength: *a country's economic health.* [from the Old English word *hǣlth,* which comes from *hāl* "hale, whole" + the suffix *-th*]

health·ful (helth′fəl), *adj.* **1.** good for the health; wholesome: *a healthful diet.* **2.** healthy; well.

health·y (hel′thē), *adj.,* **health·i·er, health·i·est. 1.**

having good health: *a healthy person.* **2.** referring to or characteristic of good health: *a healthy appearance.* **3.** good for the health; healthful: *healthy exercise.* —**health′i·ness,** *n.*

heap (hēp), *n.* **1.** a group of things lying one on another; pile. **2.** *Informal.* a great quantity or number: *It costs a heap of money.* —*v.* **3.** to gather, put, or throw in a heap: *to heap stones.* **4.** to give, assign, etc., in large amounts; load: *to heap work on someone.* **5.** to load up or fill: *to heap a plate with food.*

hear (hēr), *v.,* **heard** (hûrd), **hear·ing. 1.** to receive or be able to receive sounds through the ear: *I hear you. I don't hear very well.* **2.** to learn by the ear or by being told: *to hear news.* **3.** to listen to: *to hear a concert.* **4.** to listen to legally or officially: *The judge heard the case.* **5.** to receive news, information, etc.: *to hear from a friend.* **6.** to listen to with mercy or favor: *Hear my plea!* —**hear′er,** *n.*

hear·ing (hēr′iŋ), *n.* **1.** the sense by which sounds are perceived. **2.** the act of perceiving sound: *At first hearing I didn't like the music.* **3.** an opportunity to be heard: *to grant a hearing.* **4.** a meeting or session at which something is investigated, discussed, etc.: *a special hearing of the city council.*

hear′ing aid′, a small amplifier and earphone that makes sounds louder and helps a person to hear.

heark·en (här′kən), *v.* another spelling of **harken.** —**heark′en·er,** *n.*

hear·say (hēr′sā′), *n.* something heard about but not necessarily true; rumor; gossip: *It is best not to trust hearsay.*

hearse (hûrs), *n.* a vehicle for carrying a dead person to the place of burial.

heart (härt), *n.* **1.** the organ of the body that pumps the blood. The heart is located in the chest between the lungs. **2.** the center of feeling or emotion: *In your heart you know I'm right.* **3.** spirit, courage, or enthusiasm: *He had no heart to fight.* **4.** the central part of anything: *the heart of the city.* **5.** the main part: *Get to the heart of the matter.* **6.** a design resembling a heart in shape. **7.** a playing card marked with this design. **8. hearts,** the suit of cards having this design. **9. break one's heart,** to cause a person disappointment or sorrow: *His defeat really broke his heart.* **10. by heart,** by memory; word for word: *I know my speech by heart.*

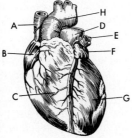

Heart (Human)

A, Blood from body
B, Right auricle
C, Right ventricle
D, Blood to lungs
E, Blood from lungs
F, Left auricle
G, Left ventricle
H, Aorta (blood to the body)

11. have a heart, to show pity or mercy: *Have a heart, that's my last cent!* **12. heart and soul,** completely; enthusiastically: *She worked at the problem heart and soul.* **13. with all one's heart,** with great zeal or feeling: *I wanted that prize with all my heart.*

heart′ attack′, a sudden inability of the heart to function properly.

heart·beat (härt′bēt′), *n.* **1.** the rhythmic sound of the heart. **2.** a single pulsation of the heart, including contraction and relaxation of the heart muscle.

heart·break·ing (härt′brā′kiŋ), *adj.* causing great sorrow or grief: *to receive heartbreaking news.*

heart·bro·ken (härt′brō′kən), *adj.* crushed with grief: *He was heartbroken when his dog died.*

heart·burn (härt′bûrn′), *n.* an unpleasant, burning sensation in the chest caused by an upset stomach.

-hearted, a suffix used to form adjectives meaning having a certain kind of heart: *light-hearted.*

heart·en (här′t³n), *v.* to give courage or confidence to; cheer: *He was heartened by the good news.*

heart′ fail′ure, a condition in which the heart fails to pump enough blood or even stops beating.

heart·felt (härt′felt′), *adj.* deeply or sincerely felt: *heartfelt joy; heartfelt sympathy.*

hearth (härth), *n.* **1.** the floor of a fireplace, usually of stone or brick, often extending a short distance into the room. **2.** home or family life. **3.** the lower part of a blast furnace, in which molten metal collects.

hearth·stone (härth′stōn′), *n.* **1.** a stone forming the hearth. **2.** one's fireside; home.

heart·i·ly (här′t³lē), *adv.* **1.** sincerely; genuinely: *I am heartily glad to see you.* **2.** cordially; warmly: *She greeted us heartily.* **3.** eagerly; with zest: *to laugh heartily.* **4.** with a hearty appetite: *They ate heartily.*

heart·less (härt′lis), *adj.* cruel; pitiless: *a heartless remark.* —**heart′less·ly,** *adv.* —**heart′less·ness,** *n.*

heart·rend·ing (härt′ren′diŋ), *adj.* causing great sorrow or distress: *a heartrending story of misery.*

heart·sick (härt′sik′), *adj.* sick at heart; very depressed or unhappy.

heart·y (här′tē), *adj.,* **heart·i·er, heart·i·est. 1.** warmhearted; friendly: *a hearty welcome.* **2.** heartfelt; genuine; sincere: *hearty approval.* **3.** vigorous; lively: *hearty laughter.* **4.** well and strong; healthy: *a hearty young man.* **5.** nourishing and satisfying: *a hearty meal.* **6.** enjoying and craving plenty of food: *a hearty appetite.* —**heart′i·ness,** *n.*

heat (hēt), *n.* **1.** the degree of hotness, or the state of being hot. **2.** the form of energy that an object has because of the vibration of its molecules, the transfer of which causes changes in temperature. **3.** hot weather. **4.** warmth of feeling; passion: *He spoke in the heat of anger.* **5.** a single course or division of a race or other contest: *She gained speed in the second heat.* —*v.* **6.** to make or become hot: *to heat water.* **7.** to make or become excited, angry, etc.

heat·er (hē′tər), *n.* a device for heating a room, automobile, etc.: *an electric heater.*

heath (hēth), *n.* **1.** a tract of open land overgrown with shrubs, mainly in Great Britain. **2.** any evergreen shrub that grows on wasteland, esp. heather.

hea·then (hē′thən), *n., pl.* **hea·thens** *or* **hea·then.** 1. a person who is thought to worship false gods. 2. a person who does not believe in the God of the Christians, Jews, or Muslims. 3. a coarse, uncultured person. —*adj.* 4. of heathens. —**hea′then·ish,** *adj.*

heath′er (heth′ər), *n.* a low evergreen shrub that bears purple flowers and grows wild, esp. in Scotland.

heat′ shield′, a coating or structure that protects a space vehicle from excessive heating while reentering the atmosphere.

heat′ wave′, a period of excessively hot weather.

heave (hēv), *v.,* **heaved** *or* (esp. for def. 3) **hove** (hōv); **heav·ing.** 1. to raise or lift with effort or force; hoist: *to heave a heavy ax.* 2. to lift and throw with effort: *He heaved a brick through the window.* 3. (of a ship) to move or cause to move in a certain direction or into a certain position: *The ship hove alongside.* 4. to utter with pain or difficulty: *to heave a sigh.* 5. to rise and fall, or cause to rise and fall: *waves that heave; to heave the chest in breathing.* 6. to vomit; retch. 7. to rise up: *The earth heaved during the quake.* 8. to pull or haul: *to heave a rope.* —*n.* 9. the act or effort of heaving. 10. a throw, toss, or cast: *a heave of the ball.* 11. **heave to,** (of a ship) to bring or be brought to a standstill: *We hove to off Long Island.*

Heather

heav·en (hev′ən), *n.* 1. the dwelling place of God, the angels, and the souls of good people who have died. 2. **heavens,** (used as an expression of surprise, protest, etc.): *Heavens, what a cold room!* 3. a place, state, time, etc., of great happiness: *The trip was heaven.* 4. **the heavens,** the sky. 5. **move heaven and earth,** to make a tremendous effort.

Heav·en (hev′ən), *n.* the Supreme Being; God.

heav·en·ly (hev′ən lē), *adj.* 1. of or referring to heaven or the heavens: *the heavenly bodies.* 2. resembling heaven; beautiful: *a heavenly spot.* 3. divine: *heavenly peace.* —**heav′en·li·ness,** *n.*

heav·en·ward (hev′ən wərd), *adv.* 1. Also, **heav′en·wards.** toward heaven: *Their prayers rose heavenward.* —*adj.* 2. turned or directed toward heaven.

heav·y (hev′ē), *adj.,* **heav·i·er, heav·i·est.** 1. of great weight; hard to lift or carry. 2. of great size or amount: *a heavy snowfall.* 3. rough or violent: *a heavy sea.* 4. of much more than usual or average weight: *a heavy person.* 5. deep; profound: *a heavy thinker.* 6. difficult to read or understand: *a heavy book.* 7. hard to bear or put up with: *heavy taxes.* 8. of great importance: *a heavy responsibility.* 9. using or taking in large amounts: *a heavy smoker.* 10. broad or thick: *heavy lines.* 11. clumsy or slow: *a heavy gait.* 12. overcast; cloudy: *heavy skies.* 13. hard to digest: *heavy, fatty foods.* 14. weighed down: *a tree heavy with fruit.* 15. deep or strong: *a heavy bass voice.* 16. sorrowful; sad: *a heavy heart.* —*adv.* 17. in a heavy manner: *Cares weighed heavy upon him.* —**heav′i·ly,** *adv.* —**heav′i·ness,** *n.*

heav·y·weight (hev′ē wāt′), *n.* 1. a person of more than average weight. 2. a boxer or wrestler weighing over 175 pounds. —*adj.* 3. of more than average weight or thickness: *a heavyweight cloth.*

He·brew (hē′brōō), *n.* 1. a member of the Semitic peoples living in ancient Palestine and claiming descent from Abraham; Jew. 2. a modern descendant of the ancient Hebrews. 3. the Semitic language of the Hebrews, including the modern national language of Israel. —*adj.* 4. of or referring to the Hebrews or their language.

He·brews (hē′brōōz), *n. (used as sing.)* a book of the New Testament.

Heb·ri·des (heb′ri dēz′), *n. (used as pl.)* a group of islands off the W coast of and belonging to Scotland.

Hec·a·te (hek′ə tē), *n.* (in Greek mythology) a goddess of ghosts and witchcraft.

heck·le (hek′əl), *v.,* **heck·led, heck·ling.** to harass or annoy with rude questions, insults, etc.: *The speaker was heckled by the audience.* —**heck′ler,** *n.*

hec·tare (hek′târ), *n.* a unit of land area in the metric system, equal to 10,000 square meters (2.471 acres). *Symbol:* ha

hec·tic (hek′tik), *adj.* 1. full of excitement, confusion, etc.: *the hectic life of a politician.* 2. flushed or feverish, as from an illness. —**hec′ti·cal·ly,** *adv.*

hecto-, a prefix meaning hundred: *hectogram.* Also, **hect-.**

hec·to·gram (hek′tə gram′), *n.* a unit of mass or weight in the metric system, equal to 100 grams. *Symbol:* hg

hec·to·li·ter (hek′tə lē′tər), *n.* a unit of capacity in the metric system, equal to 100 liters. *Symbol:* hl

hec·to·me·ter (hek′tə mē′tər), *n.* a unit of length in the metric system, equal to 100 meters. *Symbol:* hm

Hec·tor (hek′tər), *n.* (in Greek mythology) the greatest Trojan warrior in the Trojan War.

he'd (hēd), 1. contraction of *he had.* 2. contraction of *he would.*

hedge (hej), *n.* 1. a row of bushes or small trees planted close together to form a fence. 2. any barrier or boundary: *a hedge of stones.* 3. a protection against loss: *Money in the bank is a hedge against unforeseen expenses.* —*v.,* **hedged, hedg·ing.** 4. to surround with a hedge: *to hedge a garden.* 5. to surround or shut in (often fol. by *in, about,* etc.): *a country hedged about by water.* 6. to avoid being frank or straightforward: *to hedge when asked an embarrassing question.* —**hedg′er,** *n.*

hedge·hog (hej′hog′, -hôg′), *n.* 1. a small animal found in Europe, having spiny hairs on its back and sides. 2. (in the U.S.) another name for **porcupine.**

hedge·hop (hej′hop′), *v.,* **hedge·hopped, hedge·hop·ping.** to fly an airplane close to the ground, as for the purpose of spraying crops. —**hedge′hop′per,** *n.*

Hedgehog
(length 9 in.)

hedge·row (hej′rō′), *n.* a row of bushes or trees forming a hedge.

heed (hēd), *v.* 1. to give careful attention to; mind:

Heed my advice. **2.** to pay attention: *I warned them, but they did not heed.* —*n.* **3.** careful attention. —**heed′ful,** *adj.* —**heed′ful·ly,** *adv.*

heed·less (hēd′lis), *adj.* careless; thoughtless; unmindful. —**heed′less·ly,** *adv.* —**heed′less·ness,** *n.*

hee·haw (hē′hô′), *n.* **1.** the braying sound made by a donkey. **2.** a bray. Also, **hee′-haw′.**

heel¹ (hēl), *n.* **1.** the back part of the human foot, behind and below the ankle. **2.** the part of a stocking, shoe, etc., covering the back part of the foot. **3.** a solid, raised support attached under the back part of a shoe or boot. **4.** something resembling the back part of the foot in shape, position, etc.: *a heel of bread.* **5.** *Informal.* a rascal or villain. —*v.* **6.** to put a heel or heels on: *to heel a pair of shoes.* **7.** to follow at the heels; follow closely: *She taught her dog to heel.* **8. cool one's heels,** to be kept waiting, esp. because of deliberate discourtesy: *We let him cool his heels for an hour before talking with him.* **9. on the heels of,** immediately following: *There was an investigation on the heels of the election.* **10. take to one's heels,** to run away; flee: *We took to our heels when the bear appeared.* [from the Old English word *hēla*] —**heel′less,** *adj.*

heel² (hēl), *v.* to lean or cause to lean to one side: *The ship heeled in the storm.* [from the Old English word *hieldan* "to slope, lean"]

heft (heft), *n.* **1.** weight; heaviness. —*v.* **2.** to test or try to guess the weight of by lifting: *to heft an apple.* **3.** to heave or lift: *to heft an ax.*

heft·y (hef′tē), *adj.,* **heft·i·er, heft·i·est. 1.** heavy; weighty: *a hefty book.* **2.** big, strong, and muscular: *a hefty boxer.* —**hef′ti·ly,** *adv.* —**hef′ti·ness,** *n.*

Hei·del·berg (hīd′³l bûrg′), *n.* a city in SW West Germany: university founded in 1386.

heif·er (hef′ər), *n.* a young cow.

height (hīt), *n.* **1.** distance upward; measurement from top to bottom: *a height of 500 feet.* **2.** the stature of a human being: *a man of average height.* **3.** the highest point, or most extreme degree: *the height of rudeness.* **4.** a high place: *a view from a height.*

height·en (hīt′³n), *v.* **1.** to make or become higher: *to heighten a wall.* **2.** to increase: *to heighten one's efforts.* **3.** to make or become brighter or more intense: *to heighten a color.* —**height′en·er,** *n.*

hei·nous (hā′nəs), *adj.* wicked; atrocious: *a heinous crime.* —**hei′nous·ly,** *adv.* —**hei′nous·ness,** *n.*

heir (âr), *n.* a person who inherits or has the right to inherit the property, rank, position, etc., of a person who dies. —**heir′less,** *adj.*

heir′ appar′ent, *pl.* **heirs apparent.** a person who is bound to inherit the property, rank, position, etc., of another if he outlives him: *The king's eldest son is the heir apparent to the throne.*

heir·ess (âr′is), *n.* a female heir, esp. a woman or girl who has inherited or will inherit great wealth.

heir·loom (âr′lōōm′), *n.* a valued possession of a family handed down from generation to generation: *My most precious heirloom is this vase.*

held (held), *v.* the past tense and past participle of **hold.**

Hel·en (hel′ən), *n.* (in Greek mythology) a beautiful queen of Sparta who was taken by her lover, Paris, to Troy. To regain her, the Greeks destroyed the city in the Trojan War. Also, **Hel′en of Troy′.**

Hel·e·na (hel′ə nə), *n.* the capital city of Montana, in the W part.

hel·i·cal (hel′i kəl), *adj.* referring to or having the form of a helix or spiral. —**hel′i·cal·ly,** *adv.*

hel·i·con (hel′ə kon′), *n.* a coiled tuba carried over the shoulder and used esp. in military bands.

Helicon

hel·i·cop·ter (hel′ə kop′tər), *n.* an aircraft that is kept aloft by horizontally rotating blades or wings. Helicopters can take off and land vertically and can hover in addition to flying horizontally. [from the French word *hélicoptère,* which comes from Greek *helix* "helix" + *pteron* "wing"]

hel·i·o·trope (hē′lē ə trōp′), *n.* a garden plant that bears small, sweet-smelling, light-purple flowers.

hel·i·pad (hel′ə pad′), *n.* a small area for helicopters to land on or take off of.

hel·i·port (hel′ə pôrt′), *n.* a takeoff and landing place for helicopters.

he·li·um (hē′lē əm), *n.* *Chem.* a light, inert gas: a chemical element. Helium is used in balloons, blimps, etc., because it neither burns nor explodes as hydrogen does. *Symbol:* He [from a modern Latin word, which comes from Greek *hēlios* "sun." The gas was first discovered in the sun's atmosphere]

he·lix (hē′liks), *n., pl.* **he·lix·es** *or* **hel·i·ces** (hel′i sēz′). a spiral curve like the thread of a screw.

hell (hel), *n.* **1.** the place where the wicked are supposed to be punished after death. **2.** any place or state of torment or misery: *His life was hell on earth.* **3.** the abode of the dead; Hades.

Hel·las (hel′əs), *n.* ancient Greek name of **Greece.**

hell·bend·er (hel′ben′dər), *n.* a large salamander found in streams and rivers in the eastern U.S.

hel·le·bore (hel′ə bôr′), *n.* any of several plants whose roots are used in medicine and insecticides.

Hel·len·ic (he len′ik), *adj.* **1.** of or referring to the ancient Greeks or their language, culture, thought, etc. —*n.* **2.** the Greek branch of Indo-European languages. —**Hel·len′i·cal·ly,** *adv.*

Hel·les·pont (hel′i spont′), *n.* ancient name of the **Dardanelles.**

hell·ish (hel′ish), *adj.* **1.** like hell, or as if from hell: *a hellish war; a hellish crime.* **2.** very unpleasant, difficult, etc. —**hell′ish·ly,** *adv.* —**hell′ish·ness,** *n.*

hel·lo (he lō′, hə lō′), *interj.* **1.** (used to express a greeting, answer a telephone, etc.) **2.** (used to express surprise, attract attention, etc.) —*n., pl.* **hel·los. 3.** the call "hello": *She gave me a warm hello.* —*v.,* **hel·loed, hel·lo·ing. 4.** to call or say "hello."

---

act, āble, dâre, ärt; ebb, ēqual; if, īce; hot, ōver, ôrder; oil; bŏŏk; ōōze; out; up, ûrge; ə = *a* as in *alone;* ³ as in *button* (but′³n), *fire* (fī³r); chief; shoe; thin; ŧħat; zh as in *measure* (mezh′ər). See full key inside cover.

helm¹ (helm), *n.* 1. a wheel or tiller by which a ship is steered. 2. a place or position of control: *to be at the helm of a large business.* [from the Old English word *helma*]

helm² (helm), *n. Archaic.* a helmet. [from an Old English word, which is related to *helan* "to cover"]

hel·met (hel′mit), *n.* a hard, protective covering for the head, worn by soldiers, firemen, divers, cyclists, etc.

helms·man (helmz′-mən), *n., pl.* **helms·men.** a person who steers a ship; steersman.

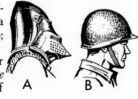

Helmets
A, Medieval; B, Modern

help (help), *v.* 1. to aid or assist: *to help someone with his work.* 2. to be of aid, assistance, use, etc.: *Every bit helps.* 3. to save; rescue: *Help me! I'm falling!* 4. to avoid, stop, or refrain from: *I couldn't help laughing.* 5. to make better or relieve: *This medicine will help your fever.* 6. to serve or provide with food, drink, etc.: *Please help yourself to the roast.* —*n.* 7. aid or assistance: *to give help where needed.* 8. a person or thing that helps: *She is a help in times of trouble.* 9. a person who is hired to help or work at something: *kitchen help.* 10. a means of stopping or changing something: *There's no help for it now.* 11. **help out,** to give assistance: *If you need someone, I'll be glad to help out.* 12. **so help me,** I swear it's the truth; on my honor: *That's exactly what happened, so help me.* —**help′er,** *n.*

help·ful (help′fəl), *adj.* giving aid or assistance; of service: *helpful advice.* —**help′ful·ly,** *adv.* —**help′ful·ness,** *n.*

help·ing (hel′ping), *n.* 1. the act of a person or thing that helps: *Your helping us is much appreciated.* 2. a portion of food served to a person at one time: *He asked for a second helping.* —*adj.* 3. giving help or support: *a helping hand.*

help′ing verb′, an auxiliary verb.

help·less (help′lis), *adj.* 1. unable to help oneself; weak: *a helpless invalid.* 2. without aid or help: *helpless miners trapped in a cave.* 3. bewildered; confused: *a helpless look.* —**help′less·ly,** *adv.* —**help′less·ness,** *n.*

help·mate (help′māt), *n.* a wife or husband. Also, **help·meet** (help′mēt).

Hel·sin·ki (hel′sing kē, hel sing′kē), *n.* a seaport and the capital city of Finland, on the S coast.

hel·ter-skel·ter (hel′tər skel′tər), *adv., adj.* 1. in wild haste and disorder: *They ran helter-skelter down the street.* 2. in a haphazard manner; having no regard for order: *Clothes lay helter-skelter all about the room.*

hem¹ (hem), *n.* 1. the border of a piece of cloth, garment, sleeve, etc., made by folding over the edge and sewing it down. —*v.,* **hemmed, hem·ming.** 2. to fold back and sew down the edge of (a piece of cloth, garment, etc.): *to hem a skirt.* 3. to shut in or confine: *to be hemmed in by a crowd.* [from an Old English word, probably related to *hamm* "enclosure"]

hem² (hem), *interj.* 1. a sound resembling a slight clearing of the throat, made in order to attract attention, express doubt, etc. —*v.,* **hemmed, hem·ming.** 2. to utter the sound of "hem," esp. when in doubt. 3. **hem and haw,** to speak without making a plain statement: *He hemmed and hawed about what he really felt.*

hem·a·tite (hem′ə tīt′), *n.* a common mineral, often reddish brown, that is the principal ore of iron.

hemi-, a prefix meaning half: *hemisphere.*

Hem·ing·way (hem′ing wā′), *n.* **Ernest,** 1899–1961, U.S. novelist and short-story writer.

hem·i·sphere (hem′i sfēr′), *n.* 1. half of a sphere. 2. *(usually cap.)* half of the earth's surface: *Eastern Hemisphere; Northern Hemisphere.* —**hem·i·spher·ic** (hem′i sfer′ik), *adj.*

hem·lock (hem′lok′), *n.* 1. any of several evergreen trees related to the pine tree and native to the U.S. 2. the light, soft wood of this tree. 3. a poisonous herb that bears small, white flowers.

he·mo·glo·bin (hē′mə glō′bin), *n.* the red pigment in blood that combines with and transports oxygen throughout the body.

he·mo·phil·i·a (hē′mə fil′ē ə, hē′mə fēl′yə), *n.* a disease of men and boys that prevents proper clotting of the blood and causes excessive bleeding from even small wounds.

he·mo·phil·i·ac (hē′mə fil′ē ak′), *n.* a person who suffers from hemophilia.

hem·or·rhage (hem′ər ij), *n.* 1. a flow of blood, esp. a heavy flow. —*v.,* **hem·or·rhaged, hem·or·rhag·ing.** 2. to bleed heavily.

hemp (hemp), *n.* a tall plant whose strong fibers are made into rope, fabrics, etc.

hem·stitch (hem′stich′), *n.* 1. a decorative stitch, made by tying together groups of threads that stick out from the edge of a piece of cloth after several threads along the edge have been removed. —*v.* 2. to make a hemstitch in: *to hemstitch a skirt.*

hen (hen), *n.* 1. a female chicken. 2. a female of any bird.

hence (hens), *adv.* 1. for this reason; therefore: *It is late, and hence we must hurry.* 2. from this time; from now: *A few years hence you will understand.* 3. from this place; away: *He lives a few miles hence.* —**Usage.** 3. Because "from" is contained in this meaning of *hence,* the two words should not be used together: *Get thee hence!* (not *from hence*).

hence·forth (hens′fôrth′), *adv.* from now on; from this point forward: *Henceforth I will try harder.* Also, **hence·for·ward** (hens′fôr′wərd).

hench·man (hench′mən), *n., pl.* **hench·men.** a loyal follower, esp. of a powerful person: *a gangster and his henchmen.* [from the Old English words *hengest* "horse" + *man* "man." A henchman was originally an attendant on horseback]

Hen·dricks (hen′driks), *n.* **Thomas A.,** 1819–1885, 21st Vice President of the U.S. 1885.

hen·na (hen′ə), *n.* 1. a plant whose leaves are used

to make a reddish-orange dye, used esp. to tint the hair. **2.** the dye itself. —*v.*, **hen·naed, hen·na·ing. 3.** to tint or dye with henna.

hen·peck (hen′pek′), *v.* to nag (one's husband).

Hen·ry (hen′rē), *n.* **Patrick,** 1736–1794, American patriot and orator.

Henry IV, 1553–1610, King of France 1589–1610.

Henry VIII, 1491–1547, King of England 1509–1547.

he·pat·i·ca (hi pat′i kə), *n.* a low plant that has delicate purplish, pink, or white flowers.

hepta-, a prefix meaning seven: *heptagon.*

hep·ta·gon (hep′tə gon′), *n.* a polygon having seven sides and seven angles. —**hep·tag·o·nal** (hep tag′ə-nəl), *adj.*

her (hûr), *pron.* **1.** the objective case of **she:** *We saw her this morning. Give it to her.* **2.** the possessive case of **she** (used as an adjective): *Her coat is on the chair.*

He·ra (hēr′ə), *n.* (in Greek mythology) the queen of the gods and wife of Zeus: identified with the Roman goddess Juno.

128 4/7°

Heptagon (regular)

her·ald (her′əld), *n.* **1.** a messenger, esp. one that in former times served a king or lord. **2.** a person or thing that comes before; forerunner: *The returning swallows are heralds of spring.* —*v.* **3.** to give tidings of; announce: *The swallows heralded spring.*

he·ral·dic (he ral′dik), *adj.* of or referring to heralds or heraldry: *a heraldic device.*

her·ald·ry (her′əl drē), *n., pl.* **her·ald·ries. 1.** the science or art of designing coats of arms or of tracing family history. **2.** a coat of arms. **3.** pomp and ceremony: *the heraldry of a royal court.*

herb (ûrb, hûrb), *n.* **1.** a flowering plant whose stem above the ground does not become woody. **2.** a plant of this kind, used in cookery or medicine.

her·ba·ceous (hûr bā′shəs, ûr bā′shəs), *adj.* of, referring to, or characteristic of an herb.

herb·age (ûr′bij, hûr′bij), *n.* grass or green plants, esp. when used as pasturage for cows, horses, etc.

her·biv·o·rous (hûr biv′ər əs), *adj.* feeding on plants: *a herbivorous animal.* See also **carnivorous, omnivorous** (def. 1).

her·cu·le·an (hûr′kyə lē′ən), *adj.* very hard to do: *a herculean task.*

Her·cu·les (hûr′kyə lēz′), *n.* (in Greek mythology) a hero famed for his great strength and endurance. —**Her′cu·le′an,** *adj.*

herd (hûrd), *n.* **1.** a number of animals kept, feeding, or traveling together: *a herd of buffalo; a herd of cows.* **2.** *Informal.* a large group of people; mob; crowd: *a herd of onlookers.* —*v.* **3.** to tend, drive, or lead (cattle, sheep, etc.). **4.** to drive (a group of people) together or to some place: *The teacher herded the children into the classroom.* **5.** to form into a herd or group: *The elephants herded together.* —**herd′er,** *n.*

herds·man (hûrdz′mən), *n., pl.* **herds·men.** a person who herds cattle, sheep, or the like; herder.

here (hēr), *adv.* **1.** in this place or spot (opposite of *there*): *Put the pen here.* **2.** to or toward this place: *Come here.* **3.** at this point: *Here the speaker paused for questions.* **4.** in this life (often fol. by *below*): *Nothing is permanent here below.* —*n.* **5.** this place: *a short distance from here.* —*interj.* **6.** (used as an exclamation to gain attention, give comfort, etc.): *Here, don't cry.* **7.** (used as an exclamation in answering a roll call to show that one is present.) **8. here and now,** at the present moment; immediately: *This dillydallying has got to stop here and now!* **9. here and there,** first in one place and then in another: *We stopped here and there along the way.*

here·a·bout (hēr′ə bout′), *adv.* about this place; near here: *I lost my glasses hereabout.* Also, **here′a·bouts′.**

here·af·ter (hēr af′tər), *adv.* **1.** after this in time; in the future: *Hereafter we will keep our promises.* —*n.* **2.** life after death: *Do you believe in the hereafter?*

here·by (hēr bī′, hēr′bī′), *adv.* by means of this statement, act, etc.: *I hereby resign from the job.*

he·red·i·tar·y (hə red′i ter′ē), *adj.* **1.** passing or capable of being passed from parents to offspring: *hereditary traits.* **2.** passing to one by inheritance: *hereditary wealth.* —**he·red′i·tar′i·ly,** *adv.*

he·red·i·ty (hə red′i tē), *n., pl.* **he·red·i·ties. 1.** the transmission of characteristics from parents to their offspring. **2.** the characteristics transmitted.

here·in (hēr in′), *adv.* **1.** in or into this place, thing, etc.: *the letter enclosed herein.* **2.** in this case or matter: *Herein you are wrong.*

here·of (hēr uv′), *adv.* of or concerning this: *upon the receipt hereof; more hereof later.*

here·on (hēr on′, -ôn′), *adv.* on this object, document, etc.: *Write your signature hereon.*

here's (hērz), contraction of **here is.**

her·e·sy (her′i sē), *n., pl.* **her·e·sies. 1.** a religious belief that does not agree with the accepted doctrine of a religion. **2.** the holding of such a belief: *to be guilty of heresy.* **3.** any belief or opinion that does not agree with an accepted doctrine.

her·e·tic (her′i tik), *n.* **1.** a person who holds a belief or beliefs not acceptable to his church. **2.** anyone who does not conform to the beliefs and attitudes of his group.

he·ret·i·cal (hə ret′i kəl), *adj.* of or referring to heresy or heretics. —**he·ret′i·cal·ly,** *adv.*

here·to·fore (hēr′tə fôr′), *adv.* before this time; until now: *the method that was followed heretofore.*

here·up·on (hēr′ə pon′, -ə pôn′), *adv.* immediately following this: *Hereupon he loudly denied his guilt.*

here·with (hēr with′, -wiŧħ′), *adv.* **1.** along with this: *I enclose my application herewith.* **2.** by means of this; hereby: *I herewith resign.*

her·it·age (her′i tij), *n.* something that comes or belongs to a person as an inheritance, such as property, a right, etc.: *Freedom is a priceless heritage.*

Her·mes (hûr′mēz), *n.* (in Greek mythology) the messenger of the gods and the god of commerce, cunning, and theft: identified with the Roman god Mercury.

her·met·ic (hûr met′ik), *adj.* made airtight by sealing. —**her·met′i·cal·ly,** *adv.*

her·mit (hûr′mit), *n.* a person who lives alone in a remote place, often for the purpose of leading a religious life. —**her′mit·like′,** *adj.*

her·mit·age (hûr′mi tij), *n.* the home of a hermit.

her′mit crab′, any of numerous crabs that protect their soft bodies by living in the castoff shells of other shellfish.

her′mit thrush′, a brown North American thrush noted for its beautiful song.

he·ro (hēr′ō), *n., pl.* **he·roes. 1.** a person who is admired for his courage, ability, and noble deeds: *Washington is an American hero.* **2.** the chief male character in a story, novel, play, etc.

Hermit crab
(length 3 in.)

Her·od (her′əd), *n.* (*"the Great"*) 73?–4 B.C., king of Judea 37–4.

he·ro·ic (hi rō′ik), *adj.* **1.** of or like a hero: *a heroic career; a heroic explorer.* **2.** worthy of a hero; daring; noble: *heroic deeds.* **3.** dealing with heroes and their deeds: *a heroic tale.* —**he·ro′i·cal·ly,** *adv.*

he·ro·ics (hi rō′iks), *n.pl.* actions or words that are meant to seem noble, but are really foolish: *the heroics of a bad actor.*

her·o·in (her′ō in), *n.* a dangerous narcotic drug derived from morphine.

her·o·ine (her′ō in), *n.* **1.** a female hero. **2.** the chief female character in a story, novel, play, etc.

her·o·ism (her′ō iz′əm), *n.* the qualities, actions, etc., of a hero: *The soldiers fought with heroism.*

her·on (her′ən), *n.* any of numerous long-legged, long-billed wading birds that feed on frogs and small fish, including the bitterns and egrets.

Herr (her), *n., pl.* **Her·ren** (her′ən). (in German) a man: used as a term of address for a man, corresponding to *Mr.* or *sir.*

her·ring (her′ing), *n., pl.* **her·rings** *or* **her·ring. 1.** a small food fish of the N Atlantic Ocean. Sardines are young herring. **2.** any of several similar food fishes.

her·ring·bone (her′ing bōn′), *n.* a pattern of rows of slanting lines, forming a V or an upside-down V, used in textiles, embroidery, etc.

Heron
(height
4 to 5 ft.)

hers (hûrz), *pron.* **1.** a form of the possessive case of *she* used as a predicate adjective: *The red umbrella is hers.* **2.** that or those belonging to her: *Hers are the yellow ones.*

her·self (hər self′), *pron.* **1.** a form of *her* or *she* that is used for emphasis: *She herself told me.* **2.** a form of *her* that is used when the subject of the sentence is the same as the object: *She cut herself badly.* **3.** her normal self: *After a few weeks of rest, she will be herself again.* —**Usage.** See myself.

hertz (hûrts), *n., pl.* **hertz.** a unit of frequency equal to one cycle per second. *Abbr.:* Hz [named after H. R. *Hertz* (1857–1894), German physicist]

he's (hēz), **1.** contraction of *he is.* **2.** contraction of *he has.*

hes·i·tan·cy (hez′i t³n sē), *n., pl.* **hes·i·tan·cies.** another word for **hesitation.**

hes·i·tant (hez′i t³nt), *adj.* hesitating; undecided, doubtful, or unwilling. —**hes′i·tant·ly,** *adv.*

hes·i·tate (hez′i tāt′), *v.,* **hes·i·tat·ed, hes·i·tat·ing. 1.** to put off acting because of fear or doubt: *She hesitated before confessing the truth.* **2.** to be unwilling because of scruples: *He hesitated to go through the red light.* **3.** to pause: *He hesitated before reading the next verse.* —**hes′i·tat′ing·ly,** *adv.*

hes·i·ta·tion (hez′i tā′shən), *n.* **1.** the act of hesitating. **2.** a halting in speech. Also, **hesitancy.**

Hes·per·i·des (he sper′i dēz′), *n.* (in Greek mythology) **1.** (*used as pl.*) the nymphs who guarded the golden apples of Hera. **2.** (*used as sing.*) the garden where the golden apples were grown.

Hes·per·us (hes′pər əs), *n.* an evening star, esp. Venus.

Hes·sian (hesh′ən), *n.* **1.** a native or inhabitant of Hesse, a state in W Germany. **2.** a Hessian soldier on the English side during the American Revolution. —*adj.* **3.** of or referring to Hesse or its inhabitants.

het·er·o·dox (het′ər ə doks′), *adj.* not in agreement with accepted doctrines, beliefs, etc., esp. in religion. —**het′er·o·dox′y,** *n.*

het·er·o·ge·ne·ous (het′ər ə jē′nē əs), *adj.* made up of members or parts that are different (opposite of *homogeneous*): *a heterogeneous group of people.*

hew (hyoo), *v.,* **hewed** *or* **hewn** (hyoon); **hew·ing. 1.** to chop or hack with an ax, sword, etc.: *to hew wood.* **2.** to shape or make with cutting blows: *to hew a statue from marble.* —**hew′er,** *n.*

hex (heks), *v.* **1.** to cast a spell on; bewitch. —*n.* **2.** a spell or charm. [from the German word *Hexe* "witch"] —**hex′er,** *n.*

hexa-, a prefix meaning six: *hexagon.*

hex·a·gon (hek′sə gon′, hek′sə gən), *n.* a polygon with six sides and six angles. —**hex·ag·o·nal** (hek sag′ə n³l), *adj.*

120°

Hexagon
(regular)

hey (hā), *interj.* (used as an exclamation to call attention or to show pleasure, surprise, etc.)

hey·day (hā′dā′), *n.* the time or stage of greatest strength, success, etc.: *In his heyday he was a popular artist.*

Hf, *Chem.* the symbol for **hafnium.**

Hg, *Chem.* the symbol for **mercury.** [from the Latin word *hydrargyrum*]

hg, hectogram; hectograms.

hgt., height. Also, **ht.**

hi (hī), *interj. Informal.* hello.

hi·a·tus (hī ā′təs), *n.* a break, blank space, gap, etc.: *a hiatus in a story; a hiatus in the conversation.*

Hi·a·watha·a (hī′ə woth′ə), *n.* the Indian hero of *The Song of Hiawatha* (1855), a poem by Henry Wadsworth Longfellow.

hi·ber·nate (hī′bər nāt′), *v.,* **hi·ber·nat·ed, hi·ber·nat·ing.** to spend the winter in a dormant, sleeplike state, as bears do. —**hi′ber·na′tion,** *n.*

hi·bis·cus (hī bis′kəs), *n.* any of several plants certain species of which have large, colorful flowers.

hic·cup (hik′up), *n.* 1. a quick, involuntary intake of breath ended by a closing of the throat. 2. the sharp sound produced by this. 3. Usually, **hiccups.** the condition of having such spasms. —*v.,* **hic·cuped** *or* **hic·cupped; hic·cup·ing** *or* **hic·cup·ping.** 4. to make the sound of a hiccup. 5. to have hiccups.

hick·o·ry (hik′ə rē), *n., pl.* **hick·o·ries.** 1. any of several tall North American trees that bear large hardshell nuts. 2. the hard, strong wood of this tree, used for tool handles.

hid (hid), *v.* the past tense and a past participle of **hide.**

hid·den (hid′³n), *adj.* concealed from sight; secret: *a hidden meaning; a hidden treasure.*

hide[1] (hīd), *v.,* **hid** (hid); **hid·den** (hid′³n) *or* **hid; hid·ing.** 1. to keep or put out of sight; conceal: *He hid the money in his desk.* 2. to cover up; keep from being seen: *Clouds hid the sun.* 3. to keep secret: *He hid his sadness.* 4. to lie concealed: *He hid in the closet.* [from the Old English word *hȳdan*]

hide[2] (hīd), *n.* 1. the pelt of a large animal, as a cow, buffalo, horse, etc., either raw or tanned. 2. *Informal.* the skin of a person: *He worried only about saving his own hide when the fire broke out.* —*v.,* **hid·ed, hid·ing.** 3. *Informal.* to beat; thrash. [from the Old English word *hȳd*]

Hide

hide-and-seek (hīd′³n sēk′), *n.* a children's game in which one player gives the other players a chance to hide and then tries to find them. Also, **hide-and-go-seek** (hīd′³n gō sēk′).

hide·a·way (hīd′ə wā′), *n.* a place to which one can go for refuge, to be alone, etc.: *a country hideaway.*

hide·bound (hīd′bound′), *adj.* narrow and rigid in one's ideas and opinions; old-fashioned.

hid·e·ous (hid′ē əs), *adj.* ugly or horrible: *a hideous frown; a hideous crime.* —**hid′e·ous·ly,** *adv.*

hide·out (hīd′out′), *n.* a safe place for hiding, esp. from the law. Also, **hide′-out′.**

hid·ing[1] (hī′diŋ), *n.* 1. the act of concealing, or the state of being concealed: *to remain in hiding.* 2. a place of concealment. [from **hide**[1] + *-ing*]

hid·ing[2] (hī′diŋ), *n. Informal.* a whipping or beating. [from **hide**[2] + *-ing*]

hie (hī), *v.,* **hied; hie·ing** *or* **hy·ing.** to hasten or hurry: *He hied to the store. He hied himself home.*

hi·er·ar·chy (hī′ə rär′kē), *n., pl.* **hi·er·ar·chies.** 1. a system of persons or things ranked one above another: *the hierarchy of the army.* 2. a body or group of officials, clergymen, etc., organized in such a system: *The hierarchy gave its approval.* —**hi′er·ar′chi·cal,** *adj.* —**hi′er·ar′chi·cal·ly,** *adv.*

hi·er·o·glyph·ic (hī′ər ə glif′ik), *n.* 1. Also, **hi′er·o·glyph′.** 1. a symbol, used esp. in ancient Egyptian writing, that resembles a picture of a person, animal, or thing. 2. Usually, **hieroglyphics.** writing using such symbols. 3. **hieroglyphics,** writing, figures, etc., that are difficult to read or make out. —*adj.* 4. of or referring to hieroglyphics or to writing in hieroglyphics: *a hieroglyphic inscription.*

hi-fi (hī′fī′), *n.* 1. a radio, phonograph, or the like, that contains high-fidelity equipment. —*adj.* 2. referring to or providing high fidelity: *His new hi-fi set has four speakers.*

high (hī), *adj.* 1. reaching far upward; lofty; tall: *a high wall.* 2. having a certain measurement upward: *a stack of books two feet high.* 3. located a great distance above the ground: *a flock of birds high in the sky.* 4. greater than usual: *high speed.* 5. costly; expensive: *high rents.* 6. lofty in rank, quality, etc.: *high society.* 7. chief; principal: *a high priest.* 8. sharp in musical pitch; shrill. 9. reaching to or coming downward from a height: *a high dive.* 10. important or serious: *high treason.* 11. being at the farthest reach or degree: *high tide; high noon.* 12. merry or joyful: *high spirits.* 13. rich or extravagant: *high living.* 14. *Informal.* under the influence of alcohol or drugs. 15. noble or excellent: *high aims.* 16. (of meat) beginning to spoil; tainted. —*adv.* 17. at or to a high point, place, or level: *The bird flew high in the sky.* —*n.* 18. an arrangement of gears in a motor vehicle that allows the greatest speed. 19. a high level, place, etc.: *a new high in prices.* 20. a region or a mass of air in which the barometric pressure of the air is high. 21. **high and low,** in every possible place; everywhere: *I've hunted high and low for that cat.* 22. **on high, a.** at or to a height; above: *The flag flew on high.* **b.** in heaven: *God on high.*

high·born (hī′bôrn′), *adj.* of high rank by birth.

high·boy (hī′boi′), *n.* a tall chest of drawers on legs.

high·brow (hī′brou′), *n.* 1. a person who has or pretends to have a great interest in art, ideas, serious writing, etc. —*adj.* 2. of, referring to, or characteristic of a highbrow: *a highbrow movie.*

high·fa·lu·tin (hī′fə loot′³n), *adj. Informal.* pompous or pretentious; high-flown: *highfalutin language.*

high′ fidel′ity, the undistorted reproduction of sound. —**high′-fi·del′i·ty,** *adj.*

high-flown (hī′flōn′), *adj.* 1. lofty in aims, ambitions, etc.: *high-flown ideas for reforming the world.* 2. pompous or pretentious.

high-grade (hī′grād′), *adj.* of high quality; superior:

Hieroglyphics

This antique chair shows high-grade workmanship.

high-hand·ed (hī′han′did), *adj.* acting or done without consideration for others; overbearing; arrogant: *a high-handed politician.*

high-hat (hī′hat′), *v.,* **high-hat·ted, high-hat·ting. 1.** to snub or treat in a snobbish way. — *adj.* **2.** snobbish; haughty.

high′ jump′, an athletic contest in which the participants jump for height over a raised crossbar.

high·land (hī′lənd), *n.* **1.** an elevated region; plateau. **2. highlands,** a mountainous region of a country.

High′land fling′. See **fling** (def. 6).

High·lands (hī′ləndz), *n. (used as pl.)* a mountainous region of northern and western Scotland. —**High′land·er,** *n.*

high·light (hī′līt′), *n.* **1.** a point or area where the light is brightest, as in a photograph or painting. **2.** an enjoyable or memorable event, scene, part, or the like: *Our visit to Paris was one of the highlights of our trip.* —*v.,* **high·light·ed, high·light·ing. 3.** to make highlights in (a painting, photograph, etc.) **4.** to assign an important place to: *to highlight the need for education.* **5.** to add interest to: *The play was highlighted by her performance.*

high·ly (hī′lē), *adv.* **1.** in or to a high degree: *highly seasoned food.* **2.** with great approval: *to think highly of someone.* **3.** at or to a high price: *a highly paid worker.* **4.** in a high position: *a highly placed officer.*

high-mind·ed (hī′mīn′did), *adj.* having or showing noble or worthy feelings, ideals, etc.: *a high-minded concern for others.* —**high′mind′ed·ness,** *n.*

High·ness (hī′nis), *n.* a title of honor given to the members of a royal family (usually preceded by *His, Her, Your,* etc.).

high·road (hī′rōd′), *n.* **1.** a main road; highway. **2.** an easy or certain course: *the highroad to success.*

high′ school′, a school following grammar school and coming before college, usually consisting of grades 9 through 12. —**high′-school′,** *adj.*

high′ seas′, the open waters of a sea or ocean that are not under the control of any country.

high-spir·it·ed (hī′spir′i tid), *adj.* **1.** lively or enthusiastic: *a high-spirited horse.* **2.** courageous; bold; daring: *high-spirited adventurers.*

high-strung (hī′strung′), *adj.* highly tense or nervous: *to be high-strung before giving a speech.*

high′ tide′, 1. the tide at its highest level. **2.** the time that the tide reaches this level. **3.** the highest level or point of something: *the high tide of a career.*

high′ time′, the time after the best or proper time, yet before it is too late: *It's high time you wrote her!*

high·way (hī′wā′), *n.* a main road, esp. one between principal cities.

high·way·man (hī′wā′mən), *n., pl.* **high·way·men.** a holdup man, esp. one on horseback, who robs travelers along a public road.

hi·jack (hī′jak′), *v.* **1.** to steal (something) from a moving vehicle by stopping it. **2.** to rob (a moving vehicle) in similar manner. **3.** to seize (a moving vehicle or air-

craft) by force or threat of force. —**hi′jack′er,** *n.*

hike (hīk), *v.,* **hiked, hik·ing. 1.** to walk or march a great distance, esp. in the country or woods: *The scout troop hikes every weekend.* **2.** to rise or raise (often fol. by *up*): *a shirt that hikes up; to hike prices.* —*n.* **3.** a long walk or march. **4.** an increase or rise: *a hike in the cost of living.* —**hik′er,** *n.*

hi·lar·i·ous (hi lâr′ē əs, hi lar′ē əs), *adj.* **1.** boisterously gay, cheerful, or merry: *a hilarious party.* **2.** very funny or comical: *a hilarious joke.* —**hi·lar′i·ous·ly,** *adv.* —**hi·lar′i·ous·ness,** *n.*

hi·lar·i·ty (hi lar′i tē, hi lâr′i tē), *n.* boisterous gaiety.

hill (hil), *n.* **1.** an elevation of the earth's surface, smaller than a mountain. **2.** any heap, pile, or mound, esp. of earth, sand, or the like. **3.** a small mound of earth raised around a plant or plants. **4.** the plant or plants so surrounded: *a hill of beans.* **5. go over the hill,** *Slang.* **a.** to break out of prison. **b.** to leave one's military unit without permission.

hill·bil·ly (hil′bil′ē), *n., pl.* **hill·bil·lies.** *Informal.* a person from the mountains or backwoods, esp. in the southern U.S.

hill·ock (hil′ək), *n.* a small hill. —**hill′ock·y,** *adj.*

hill·side (hil′sīd′), *n.* the side or slope of a hill.

hill·top (hil′top′), *n.* the top or summit of a hill.

hill·y (hil′ē), *adj.,* **hill·i·er, hill·i·est.** covered with hills; having many hills: *hilly territory.* —**hill′i·ness,** *n.*

hilt (hilt), *n.* **1.** the handle of a sword or dagger. **2. to the hilt,** to the greatest extent or degree; completely; fully: *He supported the cause to the hilt.*

him (him), *pron.* the objective case of **he:** *I'll see him tomorrow. Give the message to him.*

Him·a·la·yas (him′ə lā′əz, hi mäl′yəz), *n.* **the,** a mountain range extending along the border of India and Tibet. Highest peak, Mt. Everest, 29,028 ft. —**Him′a·la′yan,** *adj.*

him·self (him self′), *pron.* **1.** a form of *him* or *he* used for emphasis: *He himself would never say such a thing.* **2.** a form of *him* used when the subject of the sentence is the same as the object: *He found himself in a strange town.* **3.** his normal self: *He's not himself today.* —**Usage.** See **myself.**

hind[1] (hīnd), *adj.* in the rear, or at the back: *the hind legs of an animal.* [from the Old English word *hindan* "from behind"]

hind[2] (hīnd), *n., pl.* **hinds or hind.** a female red deer, esp. in and after the third year. [from Old English]

hin·der[1] (hin′dər), *v.* to delay, hamper, or prevent: *His progress was hindered by bad health.* [from the Old English word *hindrian* "to hold back"]

hind·er[2] (hīn′dər), *adj.* in the rear, or at the back; hind: *the hinder part of a ship.* [from the Old English word *hinder* "behind"]

Hin·di (hin′dē), *n.* **1.** any of a group of modern Indic languages spoken in northern India. —*adj.* **2.** of, referring to, or expressed in Hindi.

hind·most (hīnd′mōst′), *adj.* farthest behind; nearest the rear; last: *the hindmost marchers in a parade.*

hind·quar·ter (hīnd′kwôr′tər), *n.* **1. hindquarters,** the back end of an animal. **2.** the back half of a side of meat, including the loin and rear leg.

hin·drance (hin′drəns), *n.* **1.** a person or thing that hinders; obstacle: *Poor health was a hindrance to his progress.* **2.** the act of hindering, or the state of being hindered: *to come and go without hindrance.*

hind·sight (hīnd′sīt′), *n.* the understanding of a situation, event, etc., after it has occurred and when it is too late: *Hindsight is easier than foresight.*

Hin·du (hin′dōō), *n.* **1.** a believer in Hinduism. **2.** a native or inhabitant of Hindustan or India. —*adj.* **3.** of or referring to Hindus or Hinduism.

Hin·du·ism (hin′dōō iz′əm), *n.* the main religion of India, having many gods, of which the chief is Brahma.

Hin·du·stan (hin′dōō stan′, hin′dōō stän′), *n.* northern India.

Hin·du·sta·ni (hin′dōō stä′nē), *n.* **1.** a modern Indic language of northern India, developed from Hindi. —*adj.* **2.** of or referring to Hindustan or its people. **3.** of, referring to, or expressed in the Hindustani language.

hinge (hinj), *n.* **1.** a pivoted or flexible piece on which a door, cover, or other part swings or turns. **2.** a joint like the knee, or that between the halves of a clam shell, that permits only one kind of motion. —*v.*, **hinged, hing·ing.** **3.** to put a hinge or hinges on: *to hinge a door.* **4.** to depend on: *Everything hinges on his playing in the game on Friday.* —**hinge′like′,** *adj.*

Hinges
A, On a door; B, On a gate

hint (hint), *n.* **1.** a slight suggestion; inkling; clue: *He gave us a hint that helped us solve the problem.* **2.** a trace or slight amount: *a hint of spring in the air; a hint of garlic in the salad.* —*v.* **3.** to give a hint of: *He hinted the answer.* **4.** to suggest indirectly: *He hinted that we should leave.*

hin·ter·land (hin′tər land′), *n.* **1.** land lying behind a coastal region. **2.** Often, **hinterlands.** the remote parts of a country, far from towns and settlements.

hip (hip), *n.* **1.** the projecting part on either side of the body just below the waist. **2.** the joint between the thighbone and the hipbone. **3.** a similar part or joint in an animal.

hip·bone (hip′bōn′), *n.* the projecting bone at each side of the pelvis.

hip·po·drome (hip′ə-drōm′), *n.* **1.** an arena for horse shows, circuses, games, etc. **2.** (in ancient Greece and Rome) a stadium for horse races and chariot races.

hip·po·pot·a·mus (hip′ə pot′ə məs), *n.* a very large animal having a thick body, short legs, and a large head, found in and near the rivers and lakes of Africa, and able to remain under water for long peri-

Hippopotamus
(4½ ft. high at shoulder; length 13 ft.)

ods. [from a Greek word meaning "river horse," which comes from *hippos* "horse" + *potamos* "river"]

hire (hīr), *v.*, **hired, hir·ing.** **1.** to employ for wages: *to hire extra help for the summer.* **2.** to pay for the use of; rent: *to hire a car.* **3.** to grant the use or services of for pay (often fol. by *out*): *We hired ourselves out as baby-sitters.* —*n.* **4.** a price paid for the services of a person or the use of something: *The worker was worth his hire.* **5.** the act of hiring, or the state of being hired. **6. for hire,** available for use or service in return for payment.

hire·ling (hīr′ling), *n.* a person who works only for payment, esp. one who can be hired to do low or dishonest things.

Hi·ro·shi·ma (hēr′ō shē′mə, hi rō′shi mə), *n.* a port city in SW Japan: first use of atomic bomb 1945. See also **Nagasaki.**

his (hiz), *pron.* **1.** the possessive form of **he:** *His hat is the brown one. That book is his.* **2.** that or those belonging to him: *I borrowed a tie of his.*

His·pan·ic (hi span′ik), *adj.* **1.** Spanish. **2.** Latin-American. — *n.* **3.** a U.S. citizen or resident of Spanish-speaking descent.

His·pan·io·la (his′pən yō′lə), *n.* an island in the West Indies, made up of Haiti and the Dominican Republic. 29,843 sq. mi.

hiss (his), *v.* **1.** to make a sharp sound like that of the letter *s* drawn out for a long time: *Steam hissed from the spout.* **2.** to express dislike of (something) by making such a sound: *They hissed her performance.* —*n.* **3.** a hissing sound, esp. to show dislike. —**hiss′er,** *n.* —**hiss′ing·ly,** *adv.*

hist (st), *interj.* (a hissing sound used to attract attention, command silence, etc.)

hist., 1. historian. **2.** historical. **3.** history.

his·to·ri·an (hi stôr′ē ən), *n.* an expert in history, or a writer on historical subjects.

his·tor·ic (hi stôr′ik, hi stor′ik), *adj.* well-known or important in history: *a historic spot; a historic flight.*

his·tor·i·cal (hi stôr′i kəl, hi stor′i kəl), *adj.* **1.** of, referring to, or characteristic of history or past events: *This spot has historical associations.* **2.** dealing with past events: *a historical survey of the war.* **3.** based on history: *a historical novel.* —**his·tor′i·cal·ly,** *adv.*

his·to·ry (his′tə rē), *n.*, *pl.* **his·to·ries. 1.** the branch of knowledge dealing with past events. **2.** an account of past events: *to write a history of England.* **3.** the events written about or studied: *a century full of history.* **4.** a past that is interesting or unusual: *This ship has quite a history.*

hit (hit), *v.*, **hit, hit·ting. 1.** to deal a stroke or blow; strike: *Hit the ball. Hit hard.* **2.** to collide or collide with: *His car hit a telephone pole.* **3.** to reach by throwing, shooting, etc.: *He hit the target.* **4.** to succeed in striking: *The arrow hit the target.* **5.** to score (a base hit) in baseball. **6.** See **bat**[1] (def. 3). **7.** to affect severely; hurt: *They were hit by the loss of their friends.* **8.** to attack sharply (often fol. by *out*): *The speech hits out at prejudice.* **9.** to reach or attain: *The* *new train hit 100 mph.* **10.** to come or light (usually fol. by *upon* or *on*): *to hit on a new way.* —*n.* **11.** a stroke or blow: *a hit on the head.* **12.** a base hit. **13.** a successful play, song, book, etc.: *The new movie is a hit.* **14. hit it off,** *Informal.* to get along; agree: *We hit it off the first time we met.* **15. hit or miss,** in a haphazard manner: *to clean house hit or miss.* —**hit′less,** *adj.* —**hit′ter,** *n.*

hit-and-run (hit′°n run′), *adj.* **1.** guilty of leaving the scene of an accident caused by a vehicle driven by oneself: *a hit-and-run driver.* **2.** resulting from this: *a hit-and-run accident.*

hitch (hich), *v.* **1.** to fasten or tie by means of a hook, rope, strap, etc.; tether: *to hitch a horse to a post.* **2.** to raise with jerks; hike up: *to hitch up one's trousers.* —*n.* **3.** a jerk or pull: *He gave a hitch to his trousers.* **4.** a delay or obstacle: *It went off without a hitch.* **5.** a kind of knot used for a temporary fastening.

hitch-hike (hich′hīk′), *v.*, **hitch-hiked, hitch-hik-ing.** to travel by getting free automobile rides and sometimes by walking between rides. —**hitch′hik′er,** *n.*

hith-er (hith′ər), *adv.* **1.** to or toward this place. —*adj.* **2.** being on this or the closer side: *the hither side of the meadow.* **3. hither and thither,** here and there: *We traveled hither and thither.*

hith-er-to (hith′ər too′), *adv.* up to this time; till now: *a hitherto unknown fact.*

Hit-ler (hit′lər), *n.* **Ad-olf** (ad′olf, ā′dolf), 1889–1945, Nazi dictator of Germany, born in Austria.

Hit-tite (hit′īt), *n.* **1.** a member of an ancient people who had a great empire in Asia Minor and Syria. **2.** the ancient language of the Hittites, belonging or related to the Indo-European family. —*adj.* **3.** of or concerning the Hittites or their language.

hive (hīv), *n.* **1.** a man-made shelter or house for honeybees. **2.** the bees that live in a hive. **3.** a place that swarms with busy people: *The stock market is a hive.* —*v.*, **hived, hiv-ing. 4.** to enter or cause to enter a hive: *to hive bees.* **5.** to live together in or as if in a hive.

Hive

hives (hīvz), *n. (used as sing. or pl.)* a disease that produces red, itching patches on the skin.

hl, hectoliter; hectoliters.

hm, hectometer; hectometers.

H.M., His (or Her) Majesty.

H.M.S., **1.** His (or Her) Majesty's Service. **2.** His (or Her) Majesty's Ship.

ho (hō), *interj.* (used as a call to attract attention, esp. to something specified or to a word expressing a destination): *Land ho! Westward ho!*

Ho, *Chem.* the symbol for holmium.

hoar (hôr), *n.* **1.** another word for **hoarfrost.** —*adj.* **2.** an old form of **hoary.**

hoard (hôrd), *n.* **1.** a supply of money, food, etc., that is hidden or carefully guarded for future use.

—*v.* **2.** to gather and save, often secretly and greedily: *The miser hoarded all his money.* —**hoard′er,** *n.*

hoar-frost (hôr′frôst′), *n.* a white frost. Also, **hoar.**

hoarse (hôrs), *adj.*, **hoars-er, hoars-est. 1.** having a rough or husky sound: *a hoarse voice; a hoarse bray.* **2.** having a rough or husky voice: *This cold makes me hoarse.* —**hoarse′ly,** *adv.* —**hoarse′ness,** *n.*

hoar-y (hôr′ē), *adj.*, **hoar-i-er, hoar-i-est. 1.** gray or white with age: *hoary hair.* **2.** white or gray: *a hoary winter landscape.* **3.** old or ancient: *a hoary castle; hoary customs.* —**hoar′i-ly,** *adv.* —**hoar′i-ness,** *n.*

hoax (hōks), *n.* **1.** a mischievous trick or deception: *The report of a landing on Mars was a hoax.* —*v.* **2.** to deceive by a hoax: *The people were hoaxed by promises of wealth.* —**hoax′er,** *n.*

hob¹ (hob), *n.* a shelf at the back or side of a fireplace, used for keeping food warm. [perhaps another form of the word *hub*]

hob² (hob), *n.* **1.** a hobgoblin or elf. **2. play hob with,** to do mischief or harm to: *The thunderstorm played hob with our radio.* [from a Middle English word, a special use of *Hob,* a nickname for *Robert*]

Ho-bart (hō′bärt), *n.* **Gar-ret A.** (gar′it), 1844–1899, 24th Vice President of the U.S. 1897–1899.

hob-ble (hob′əl), *v.*, **hob-bled, hob-bling. 1.** to walk lamely; limp: *His sprained ankle caused him to hobble.* **2.** to fasten together the legs of (a horse, mule, etc.) with rope, in order to prevent free movement. **3.** to hinder or hamper: *to be hobbled by lack of money.* —*n.* **4.** a limp or lame gait: *to walk with a hobble.* **5.** a rope, strap, etc., used to hobble an animal. —**hob′bler,** *n.* —**hob′bling-ly,** *adv.*

hob-by (hob′ē), *n., pl.* **hob-bies.** an interest pursued for pleasure in one's spare time and not as one's main occupation: *The dentist's hobby is painting.*

hob-by-horse (hob′ē hôrs′), *n.* a stick with a horse's head, or a rocking horse, ridden by children.

hob-gob-lin (hob′gob′lin), *n.* **1.** a mischievous goblin. **2.** anything that causes fear; bogy.

hob-nail (hob′nāl′), *n.* a large-headed nail for protecting the soles of heavy boots and shoes.

hob-nob (hob′nob′), *v.*, **hob-nobbed, hob-nob-bing.** to be on very friendly terms: *to hobnob with the rich and famous.*

ho-bo (hō′bō), *n., pl.* **ho-bos** or **ho-boes.** a tramp.

Ho Chi Minh (hō′ chē′ min′), 1892?–1969, Vietnamese political leader: president of North Vietnam 1954–1969.

Ho′ Chi′ Minh′ Cit′y, a port city in S Vietnam. Former name, Saigon.

hock (hok), *n.* a joint in the hind leg of a horse or other animal, related to the ankle in man.

hock-ey (hok′ē), *n.* a game played on ice between two teams, each having six players, who wear skates and compete in scoring goals by shooting the puck into each other's goal cage. Also, **ice hockey.**

Hockey rink

ho·cus-po·cus (hō′kəs pō′kəs), *n.* **1.** meaningless words used by magicians. **2.** trickery or needlessly mysterious actions or talk: *He confused me with that hocus-pocus about extra charges.*

hod (hod), *n.* **1.** a trough for carrying mortar, bricks, etc., fixed crosswise on top of a pole and carried on the shoulder by masons. **2.** a coal scuttle.

hodge·podge (hoj′poj′), *n.* a confused mixture; mess; jumble: *a hodgepodge of loose papers.*

hoe (hō), *n.* **1.** a long-handled tool having a thin, flat blade, used to break up the soil, destroy weeds, etc. —*v.*, **hoed, hoe·ing. 2.** to dig, scrape, weed, etc., with a hoe. —**ho′er,** *n.* —**hoe′like′,** *adj.*

hog (hôg, hog), *n.* **1.** a large pig, esp. one raised for meat. **2.** *Informal.* a selfish, greedy, or filthy person. —*v.*, **hogged, hog·ging. 3.** *Slang.* to take more than one's share of: *My older brother always hogs the bed.* **4. go whole hog,** *Informal.* to do something completely or to the most extreme degree: *We went whole hog and took the deluxe tour.* **5. live high off the hog,** to be in prosperous circumstances: *They've been living high off the hog ever since they won all that money.*

Hog (Domestic)
(length to 4 ft.)

hog·gish (hô′gish, hog′ish), *adj.* like or befitting a hog; selfish, greedy, or filthy: *hoggish table manners.* —**hog′gish·ly,** *adv.* —**hog′gish·ness,** *n.*

hogs·head (hôgz′hed′, hogz′hed′), *n.* **1.** a large cask or barrel. **2.** any of various units of liquid measure, esp. one equivalent to 63 gallons.

hoist (hoist), *v.* **1.** to raise or lift, esp. with a rope, crane, etc.: *to hoist a sail.* —*n.* **2.** the act of hoisting; a lift. **3.** a machine for hoisting, such as an elevator.

hold¹ (hōld), *v.*, **held** (held), **hold·ing. 1.** to have or keep in the hand; grasp: *He held a sword.* **2.** to carry, bear, or support, as with the hands and arms: *The mother held the baby close.* **3.** to set aside; keep in reserve: *The library will hold the book until you call for it.* **4.** to keep or remain in a certain state, position, etc.: *He held them spellbound. She would not hold still.* **5.** to remain fast; cling: *The ivy held to the wall.* **6.** to keep a grasp or grip on something: *Hold tightly to the railing.* **7.** to detain: *The teacher held him after class.* **8.** to carry on, engage in, preside over, or observe: *to hold a meeting.* **9.** to occupy or have the ownership or use of: *to hold political office.* **10.** to contain or be capable of containing: *This bottle holds a quart.* **11.** to think or believe: *We hold this to be true.* **12.** to regard or consider: *I hold you responsible.* **13.** to point or aim: *He held a gun on the prisoner.* **14.** to remain faithful or steadfast (usually fol. by *to*): *He held to his purpose.* **15.** to remain valid; be in force: *This rule no longer holds.* —*n.* **16.** the act of holding fast; grasp; grip. **17.** something to hold a thing by; handle. **18.** a controlling force or strong influence. **19.** (in music) a sign (⌒) indicating that a note or rest is to be made longer than its indicated value. **20.** the lengthening of a note or rest by a performer. **21. hold back, a.** to stop or restrain: *to hold back one's tears.* **b.** to keep in one's possession: *to hold back part of an employee's pay.* **22. hold down, a.** to control or restrain: *Hold down that noise!* **b.** to continue to keep and manage well: *He's held down the same job for 20 years.* **23. hold off, a.** to keep at a distance; resist: *to hold off an enemy attack.* **b.** to postpone or defer: *Let's hold off going till we get a weather report.* **24. hold out, a.** to extend; stretch forth. **b.** to continue to exist; last: *How long will the food hold out?* **c.** to refuse to yield or submit: *He's holding out for a pay increase.* **d.** to withhold something expected or due: *to hold out important information.* **25. hold up, a.** to hinder; delay: *A snowstorm held up the train.* **b.** *Informal.* to rob: *to hold up a bank.* **c.** to maintain one's condition; endure: *to hold up under a severe strain.* [from the Old English word *healdan*]

hold² (hōld), *n.* the cargo space in the hull of a vessel, esp. between the lowest deck and the bottom. [another form of the word *hole*]

hold·er (hōl′dər), *n.* **1.** any device for holding: *a toothbrush holder.* **2.** a person who has the ownership or use of something; owner; tenant.

hold·ing (hōl′ding), *n.* **1.** the act of a person or thing that holds. **2.** Often, **holdings.** property, such as land, stocks and bonds, etc.

hold·up (hōld′up′), *n.* **1.** *Informal.* robbery by the use of force. **2.** a stop or delay in the progress of something: *a holdup in bus service.*

hole (hōl), *n.* **1.** an opening through something: *a hole in the fence.* **2.** a hollow place; cavity: *a hole in the ground.* **3.** a shelter or home dug by an animal; burrow: *a rabbit hole.* **4.** (in golf) a cup in the ground into which the ball is to be played. **5.** a fault or flaw: *They found holes in his alibi.* **6.** a shabby, dreary abode. **7.** a small, dark prison cell. —*v.*, **holed, hol·ing. 8.** to make a hole or holes in: *to hole a mountain with a tunnel.* **9.** to drive into a hole, as a golf ball. **10.** to bore, as a tunnel, passage, etc. **11. hole up,** *Slang.* to hide from pursuers, the police, etc.: *We're going to hole up in the mountains for a long rest.* **12. in the hole,** in debt: *We were $15 in the hole after the Fourth of July picnic.*

hol·i·day (hol′i dā′), *n.* **1.** a day on which most stores, offices, schools, etc., are closed, such as the anniversary of a great event or the birthday of a famous person. **2.** a religious day; a holy day. **3.** *Chiefly British.* a vacation. —*adj.* **4.** festive or joyous: *We were in a holiday mood.*

ho·li·ness (hō′lē nis), *n.* the quality of being holy.

Ho·li·ness (hō′lē nis), *n.* a title of the Pope (usually preceded by *His* or *Your*).

Hol·land (hol′ənd), *n.* See **Netherlands, the.**

hol·ler (hol′ər), *Informal.* —*v.* **1.** to cry aloud: *to holler for help; to holler insults.* —*n.* **2.** a loud cry to attract attention, call for help, etc.

hol·lo (hol′ō, hə lō′), *interj., n., pl.* **hol·los;** *v.,* **hol·loed, hol·lo·ing.** another spelling of **hallo.**

hol·low (hol′ō), *adj.* **1.** having a space inside; not solid; empty: *a hollow ball.* **2.** shaped like a bowl or cup; concave. **3.** sunken, as the cheeks or eyes. **4.** sounding dull, muffled, or deep: *a hollow voice.* **5.** having no meaning or truth; false: *a hollow victory.* —*n.* **6.** an empty space within anything; hole or cavity: *the hollow of a bowl.* **7.** a valley: *a house in the hollow.* —*v.* **8.** to make or become hollow: *to hollow out a log.* **9.** to form by making something hollow (often fol. by *out*): *boats hollowed out of logs.* —*adv.* **10.** in a hollow manner; falsely: *The accusations rang hollow.* —**hol′low·ness,** *n.*

hol·ly (hol′ē), *n., pl.* **hol·lies.** any of several evergreen trees or shrubs having shiny, spine-toothed leaves and bearing red berries.

hol·ly·hock (hol′ē hok′, hol′ē-hôk′), *n.* a tall garden plant that has large flowers of various colors.

Hol·ly·wood (hol′ē wŏŏd′), *n.* the NW part of Los Angeles, California: motion-picture studios.

Holly

hol·mi·um (hōl′mē əm), *n. Chem.* an element of the rare-earth group. *Symbol:* Ho [from a modern Latin word, which comes from *(Stock)holm,* Sweden]

hol·o·caust (hol′ə kôst′, hō′lə kôst′), *n.* great destruction and loss of life, esp. by fire.

ho·log·ra·phy (hə log′rə fē), *n.* a technique of using laser light to produce a three-dimensional image when properly illuminated on a photographic film.

Hol·stein (hōl′stīn), *n.* a black-and-white breed of dairy cattle noted for producing large quantities of milk. [named after a district in N West Germany, where it was bred, although its original home was in Holland]

hol·ster (hōl′stər), *n.* a leather case for a pistol, usually attached to a belt at the hip.

Holstein
(4 ft. high at shoulder)

ho·ly (hō′lē), *adj.,* **ho·li·er, ho·li·est. 1.** coming from or having to do with God: *The Bible is a holy book.* **2.** sacred or consecrated: *holy ground.* **3.** spiritually devoted; saintly; godly: *a holy man.* **4.** inspiring or worthy of great respect.

Ho′ly Ark′, a cabinet in a synagogue containing the scrolls of the Torah.

Ho′ly Commun′ion. See **communion** (def. 5).

Ho′ly Ghost′, the third person of the Trinity; the spirit of God.

Ho′ly Grail′, another name for **Grail.**

Ho′ly Land′, another name for **Palestine.**

Ho′ly Ro′man Em′pire, a loose federation of Germanic states in central Europe, ruled by an emperor A.D. 962 to 1806.

Ho′ly Scrip′ture. See **Scripture** (def. 1). Also, **Ho′ly Scrip′tures.**

Ho′ly Week′, the week preceding Easter Sunday.

Ho′ly Writ′, the Scriptures.

hom·age (hom′ij, om′ij), *n.* **1.** respect; reverence: *to pay homage to the memory of the dead.* **2.** a pledge of loyalty and service made by a feudal vassal to his lord. [from an Old French word, which comes from *home* "man"]

home (hōm), *n.* **1.** a house, apartment, or other place of residence. **2.** family life: *a happy home.* **3.** an institution where the sick, needy, etc., are cared for: *a home for the blind.* **4.** a person's native place or country. **5.** a place or region where an animal or thing is to be found: *Australia is the home of the kangaroo.* **6.** the destination or goal in certain games. **7.** *Informal.* home plate. —*adj.* **8.** of, referring to, or connected with one's home or country: *home problems.* **9.** played or playing in one's own town: *a home game.* **10.** being the headquarters of a business or organization: *The home office is in New York.* —*adv.* **11.** to, toward, or at home: *We drove home in the rain.* **12.** to the heart or the mark aimed at: *Her argument hit home.* —*v.,* **homed, hom·ing. 13.** to go or return home. **14.** to dwell or have a home. **15.** (of guided missiles, aircraft, etc.) to move or be guided toward a destination or target. **16. at home, a.** in one's home or country. **b.** willing to receive social visits: *She was not at home to callers.* **c.** at ease: *He is not at home with strangers.* **17. bring home to,** to make clear or forceful to: *The foolishness of his behavior was brought home to him.* —**home′less,** *adj.*

home·land (hōm′land′), *n.* a person's native land.

home·like (hōm′līk′), *adj.* like home; familiar; comfortable: *a pleasant, homelike hotel.*

home·ly (hōm′lē), *adj.,* **home·li·er, home·li·est. 1.** not beautiful; unattractive: *a homely face.* **2.** plain and simple: *homely manners.* —**home′li·ness,** *n.*

home·made (hōm′mād′), *adj.* **1.** made at home or locally: *homemade bread.* **2.** made by oneself; amateurish: *a crude, homemade table.*

home′ plate′, (in baseball) the base at which the batter stands and which a base runner must reach safely in order to score a run.

hom·er (hō′mər), *n. Informal.* another term for **home run.**

Ho·mer (hō′mər), *n.* 9th century B.C., Greek epic poet: author of the *Iliad* and *Odyssey.*

home·room (hōm′rōōm′, -rŏŏm′), *n.* a school classroom in which pupils of the same grade meet at certain times, as at the beginning of the day.

home′ run′, (in baseball) a hit that allows a batter to score a run by touching all the bases without stop.

home·sick (hōm′sik′), *adj.* longing for home: *After a week at camp he was homesick.* —**home′sick′ness,** *n.*

home·spun (hōm′spun′), *n.* **1.** a coarse, loosely woven cloth made of homespun yarn. —*adj.* **2.** spun or made at home: *homespun cloth.* **3.** made of such cloth: *homespun clothing.* **4.** plain; simple: *homespun humor.*

home·stead (hōm′sted), *n.* **1.** a piece of land granted to a settler by the U.S. government to use as a farm and as a site for a home. **2.** any dwelling with its land and buildings. —v. 3. to settle on a home-stead. —**home′stead·er,** n.

home·stretch (hōm′strech′), n. the straight part of a race track from the last turn to the finish line.

home·ward (hōm′wərd), adv. 1. Also, **home′wards.** toward home. —adj. 2. directed toward home: *the homeward journey.*

home·work (hōm′wûrk′), n. 1. schoolwork to be done outside the classroom. 2. any work to be done at home.

home·y (hō′mē), adj., **hom·i·er, hom·i·est.** like home; cozy; homelike. —**home′y·ness, hom′i·ness,** n.

hom·i·cide (hom′i sīd′), n. 1. the killing of one human being by another. 2. a person who kills another; murderer. —**hom′i·ci′dal,** adj.

hom·i·ly (hom′ə lē), n., pl. **hom·i·lies.** 1. a sermon, usually based on something in the Bible. 2. serious talk or writing on morals or behavior.

hom′ing pi′geon, a pigeon trained to return to its home and used for carrying messages.

hom·i·ny (hom′ə nē), n. corn from which the hull and germ have been removed. [from Algonquian]

ho·mo·ge·ne·ous (hō′mə jē′nē əs), adj. composed of parts that are all of the same kind (opposite of *heterogeneous*): *a group of homogeneous objects.* —**ho′mo·ge′ne·ous·ly,** adv.

ho·mog·e·nize (hə moj′ə nīz′), v., **ho·mog·e·nized, ho·mog·e·niz·ing.** to make the same throughout, esp. to blend (milk and cream) inseparably together. —**ho·mog′e·ni·za′tion,** n. —**ho·mog′e·niz′er,** n.

hom·o·graph (hom′ə graf′), n. a word spelled the same as one or more other words, but of different origin and meaning, whether pronounced the same or differently, as *calf*[1] (young animal) and *calf*[2] (part of the leg), or *lead*[1] (to conduct) and *lead*[2] (the metal).

hom·o·nym (hom′ə nim), n. 1. a word spelled and pronounced the same as one or more other words, but of different origin and meaning, as *mean*[1] (to intend) and *mean*[2] (low). 2. a homophone. 3. a homograph.

hom·o·phone (hom′ə fōn′), n. a word pronounced the same as one or more other words, but of different origin and meaning, whether spelled the same or differently, as *heir* and *air,* or *date*[1] (day) and *date*[2] (the fruit).

Hon., Honorable.

Hon·du·ras (hon dŏŏr′əs), n. a republic in N Central America. 43,277 sq. mi. *Cap.:* Tegucigalpa.

hone (hōn), n. 1. a fine whetstone for sharpening razors. —v., **honed, hon·ing. 2.** to sharpen on a hone: *to hone a razor.*

hon·est (on′ist), adj. 1. honorable in word and deed; upright. 2. showing uprightness and fairness: *honest dealings.* 3. sincere and open: *an honest face.* 4. genuine: *honest weights.*

hon·est·ly (on′ist lē), adv. 1. in an honest manner. —interj. 2. (used as an exclamation of mild annoyance, disbelief, etc.): *Honestly, you are the limit!*

hon·es·ty (on′i stē), n., pl. **hon·es·ties.** the quality or fact of being honest; truthfulness; sincerity: *a man of unquestionable honesty.*

hon·ey (hun′ē), n., pl. **hon·eys. 1.** a sweet substance produced by bees and stored in their nests and hives for food. 2. this substance used in cooking or as a spread or sweetener. 3. anything that is sweet, delightful, pleasant, etc.: *the honey of praise.* 4. darling; sweetheart. 5. *Informal.* something of high quality: *The new bike is a honey.* —v., **honeyed** or **honied; hon·ey·ing. 6.** to sweeten or flavor with or as if with honey: *honeyed words of praise.*

hon·ey·bee (hun′ē bē′), n. a bee that produces and stores honey.

hon·ey·comb (hun′ē kōm′), n. 1. a wax structure of many six-sided cells made by bees for storing honey. 2. anything resembling this in having many rooms, compartments, etc.: *The building was a honeycomb of offices.* —v. 3. to fill with holes like a honeycomb: *a mountain that was honeycombed with mines.* —adj. 4. like a honeycomb in structure or appearance: *a honeycomb pattern.*

Honeycomb

hon·ey·dew (hun′ē dōō′, -dyōō′), n. 1. a sweet material produced by the leaves of certain plants in hot weather. 2. a sugary material produced by aphids and some other insects. 3. a sweet melon having pale green flesh.

hon·eyed (hun′ēd), adj. 1. sweetened with honey: *honeyed beverages.* 2. loving or flattering: *honeyed words.* Also, **hon′ied.**

hon·ey·moon (hun′ē mōōn′), n. 1. a vacation or trip taken by a newly married couple. —v. 2. to go on a honeymoon.

hon·ey·suck·le (hun′ē-suk′əl), n. a climbing plant with very sweet-smelling flowers.

Hong Kong (hong′kong′), a British crown colony on the coast and adjacent islands of SE China. 398 sq. mi.

CHINA — Canton — Limit of Colony — Macao — Hong Kong — SOUTH CHINA SEA

honk (hongk, hôngk), n. 1. the cry of a goose. 2. any sound like this. 3. the sound of an automobile horn. —v. 4. to make a honk: *Geese honked in the pond.* 5. to cause (an automobile horn) to honk.

Hon·o·lu·lu (hon′ə lōō′lōō), n. a seaport and the capital city of Hawaii.

hon·or (on′ər), n. 1. high respect or esteem. 2. fame or glory. 3. honesty in one's beliefs and actions: *a man of honor.* 4. a source or cause of credit or good repute: *He is an honor to his family.* 5. the privilege of receiving a favor from a distinguished person or group: *to have the honor of meeting the queen.* 6. (usually cap.) a title of respect, esp. for judges and mayors (preceded by *his, your,* etc.). 7. **honors, a.**

---

act, āble, dâre, ärt; ebb, ēqual; if, īce; hot, ōver, ôrder; oil; bŏŏk; ōōze; out; up, ûrge; ə = a as in *alone*; ə as in *button* (but′ə n), *fire* (fīər); chief; shoe; thin; that; zh as in *measure* (mezh′ər). See full key inside cover.

special rank granted to an outstanding student. **b.** recognition for outstanding achievement, quality, etc.: *He won the honors in the art show.* —*v.* **8.** to hold in honor or high respect; revere: *to honor heroes.* **9.** to confer honor upon: *She honored us with a visit.* **10.** to accept or pay (a check). **11. be on one's honor,** to accept responsibility for one's actions: *We were on our honor to do the work without help.* **12. do honor to,** to show respect to: *On Memorial Day we do honor to the nation's dead servicemen.* **13. do the honors,** to act as a host or hostess.

hon·or·a·ble (on′ər ə bəl), *adj.* **1.** upright or honest: *honorable behavior.* **2.** worthy of honor and high respect (often used as part of a title): *The Honorable Nelson A. Rockefeller, Governor of New York.* **3.** bringing honor or credit: *an honorable discharge.* —**hon′or·a·ble·ness,** *n.* —**hon′or·a·bly,** *adv.*

hon·or·ar·y (on′ə rer′ē), *adj.* **1.** given for honor only, without the usual duties, privileges, etc.: *an honorary degree.* **2.** holding a position given for honor only: *an honorary officer of the club.*

Hon·shu (hôn′shoo), *n.* the chief island of Japan. 88,851 sq. mi.

hood (hood), *n.* **1.** a loose covering for the head and neck, often fastened to a coat or cloak. **2.** anything that resembles such a covering. **3.** the part of an automobile that covers the engine. —*v.* **4.** to cover with a hood.

-hood, a suffix used to form nouns meaning **1.** a state, quality, or condition: *childhood; likelihood.* **2.** a group or class: *brotherhood; priesthood.*

hood·lum (hood′ləm, hood′ləm), *n.* **1.** a gangster or thug. **2.** a teen-age tough.

hood·wink (hood′wingk′), *v.* to deceive or trick: *He was hoodwinked into buying a worthless car.* —**hood′wink′er,** *n.*

hoof (hoof, hoof), *n., pl.* **hoofs** or **hooves** (hoovz, hoovz). **1.** the hard, horny covering of the feet of horses, donkeys, cattle, etc. **2.** the foot of such an animal. —*v. Slang.* **3.** to walk (often fol. by *it*): *Let's hoof it instead of taking the bus.* **4.** to dance, esp. to tap-dance. —**hoof′less,** *adj.* —**hoof′like′,** *adj.*

hoofed (hooft, hooft), *adj.* having hoofs.

hook (hook), *n.* **1.** a piece of metal or other hard substance, curved or having a sharp angle, used for catching, pulling, holding, or hanging something. **2.** a fishhook. **3.** something having a curved shape, as a cape of land, a bend in a river, etc. **4.** a short blow in boxing, delivered with a curving motion. —*v.* **5.** to attach, fasten, catch hold of, etc., with or as if with a hook. **6.** to catch fish with a fishhook. **7.** to curve or bend like a hook: *The stream hooks to the left.* **8.** to become fastened by or as if by a hook: *This brooch hooks easily.* **9. by hook or by crook,** by any means possible: *I have to get to the World Series by hook or by crook.* **10. hook, line, and sinker,** *Informal.* entirely; completely: *He fell for the idea hook, line, and sinker.* —**hook′less,** *adj.* —**hook′like′,** *adj.*

hook·ah (hook′ə), *n.* a tobacco pipe with a long, flexible tube by which the smoke is drawn through a jar of water and thus cooled.

hook·up (hook′up′), *n.* **1.** the arrangement of parts in a radio, television set, etc. **2.** a network, as of radio or television stations: *a nationwide hookup.*

hook·worm (hook′wûrm′), *n.* a tiny, bloodsucking worm that lives in the intestines of man and some animals, causing anemia.

hook·y (hook′ē), *n. Informal.* absence from school without permission: *Didn't you ever play hooky when you were a boy?*

hoop (hoop, hoop), *n.* **1.** a circular band of wood, metal, etc., used to bind together the staves of a barrel. **2.** a band of wood or plastic used as a toy. **3.** a flexible band used to expand a woman's skirt. **4.** a wicket in croquet. —*v.* **5.** to bind together with or as if with a hoop or hoops. —**hoop′like′,** *adj.*

hoo·poe (hoo′poo), *n.* any of several birds found in Europe, having a fanlike crest.

hoop′ skirt′, **1.** a woman's skirt made to bell out by a framework of flexible hoops. **2.** the framework for such a skirt.

hoo·rah (hoo rä′), *interj., v., n.* another spelling of **hurrah.** Also, **hoo·ray** (hoo rä′).

hoot (hoot), *n.* **1.** the cry of an owl. **2.** a sound like this, esp. a shout or cry of disapproval. —*v.* **3.** to make a hoot, as an owl. **4.** to cry out or shout in disapproval: *The audience hooted when the speaker came on stage.* **5.** to attack or drive away with hoots: *They hooted him as he spoke.* **6.** to express with hoots: *They hooted their disapproval.* —**hoot′er,** *n.*

Hoopoe
(length 11 in.)

Hoo·ver (hoo′vər), *n.* Herbert, 1874–1964, 31st President of the U.S. 1929–1933.

Hoo′ver Dam′, the official name of **Boulder Dam.**

hooves (hoovz, hoovz), *n.* a plural of **hoof.**

hop¹ (hop), *v.,* **hopped, hop·ping. 1.** to make a short, bouncing leap with both or all feet off the ground: *The frog hopped into the pond.* **2.** to spring or leap on one foot. **3.** to jump over with a hop: *to hop a fence.* **4.** *Informal.* to make a quick trip, esp. by plane: *to hop up to Boston.* **5.** *Informal.* to board or get onto, as a car, train, etc. —*n.* **6.** an act of hopping. **7.** *Informal.* **a.** a short trip, esp. by plane: *a hop from Dallas to San Antonio.* **b.** a dancing party. [from the Old English word *hoppian*]

hop² (hop), *n.* **1.** a twining plant that bears cone-shaped green flowers. **2. hops,** the dried flowers of this plant used in flavoring beer. [from the earlier Dutch word *hoppe*]

hope (hop), *n.* **1.** the feeling that what is wanted can be had or that events will turn out for the best: *to be full of hope for the future.* **2.** a particular case of this feeling: *a hope of victory.* **3.** grounds for this feeling: *Is there any hope for his recovery?* **4.** a person or thing looked upon with expectation in time of trouble, need, etc.: *This drug is his only hope.* —*v.,* **hoped, hop·ing. 5.** to look forward to with desire and some confidence: *I hope to see you soon.* **6.** to believe, desire, or trust: *I hope that my work is satisfactory.* **7.** to feel that something desired may happen: *to hope for an early spring.* **8.** to wish for and expect the best: *While we live, we hope.*

hope·ful (hōp′fəl), *adj.* **1.** full of or showing hope: *hopeful words.* **2.** giving hope: *a hopeful sign of improvement.* —*n.* **3.** a promising and ambitious person: *presidential hopefuls.* —**hope′ful·ly,** *adv.* —**hope′ful·ness,** *n.*

hope·less (hōp′lis), *adj.* **1.** giving no hope; beyond hope: *a hopeless illness.* **2.** without hope: *hopeless captives.* —**hope′less·ly,** *adv.* —**hope′less·ness,** *n.*

hop·per (hop′ər), *n.* **1.** a person or thing that hops. **2.** a jumping insect, such as a grasshopper. **3.** a funnel-shaped container in which coal, grain, etc., is stored temporarily, being filled through the top and later emptied through the bottom.

hop·scotch (hop′skoch′), *n.* a children's game in which a player tosses a small stone into one of several numbered sections drawn together on the ground, and then hops on one foot from section to section, picking up the stone on his return.

horde (hôrd), *n.* **1.** a large group; multitude; crowd: *a horde of insects.* **2.** a tribe or troop of wandering people, esp. of Asian nomads in former times: *The hordes of Attila swept over Europe.*

hore·hound (hôr′hound′), *n.* **1.** a European herb used to flavor candy and cough drops. **2.** the candy or cough drops flavored with this.

ho·ri·zon (hə rī′zən), *n.* **1.** the line where the earth or the sea appears to meet the sky. **2.** the limit of one's knowledge, experience, etc.: *Reading widens one's horizons.* [from the Greek phrase *hōrizōn kyklos* "bounding or limiting circle"]

hor·i·zon·tal (hôr′i zon′t[ə]l), *adj.* **1.** parallel to the horizon; at right angles to the vertical. —*n.* **2.** the horizontal direction. —**hor′i·zon′tal·ly,** *adv.*

hor·mone (hôr′mōn), *n.* any of several substances produced by the ductless glands, each of which affects a particular body tissue or organ. Hormones influence almost all body functions, including growth, the absorption of food, and reproduction.

horn (hôrn), *n.* **1.** one of the hard, bony, often curved and pointed growths on the heads of such animals as cattle, sheep, and goats. **2.** any growth resembling this, such as an antler of a deer or the growth on the nose of a rhinoceros. **3.** the substance of which horn is composed. **4.** something made from a hollowed-out horn, such as a container or a musical instrument. **5.** a French horn. **6.** a device that makes a loud noise, esp. as a warning: *an automobile horn.* **7. blow one's own horn,** to boast about oneself. **8. horn in,** *Slang.* to interrupt or intrude: *to horn in on another's conversation.* —**horn′less,** *adj.* —**horn′less·ness,** *n.* —**horn′like′,** *adj.*

Horn (hôrn), *n.* Cape. See Cape Horn.

horned (hôrnd), *adj.* having horns (often used in combination): *a horned beast; a blunt-horned beast.* —**horn·ed·ness** (hôr′nid nis), *n.*

horned′ liz′ard, any of several lizards of western North America, having hornlike spines on the head and a flattened body covered with spiny scales.

horned′ toad′, a small lizard that eats insects and has hornlike spines on its head.

Horned lizard
(length to 4½ in.)

hor·net (hôr′nit), *n.* any of several large kinds of wasps that can give painful stings.

horn′ of plen′ty, another name for **cornucopia.**

horn·pipe (hôrn′pīp′), *n.* **1.** a lively dance for one person, traditionally a favorite of sailors. **2.** a piece of music for this dance.

horn·y (hôr′nē), *adj.,* **horn·i·er, horn·i·est. 1.** having horns: *a horny head.* **2.** composed of the substance of which horns are formed or of a similar substance. **3.** hornlike through hardening; callous: *hands made horny by hard work.* —**horn′i·ness,** *n.*

hor·o·scope (hôr′ə skōp′, hor′ə skōp′), *n.* **1.** a chart showing the position of planets and the signs of the zodiac, used by astrologers to foretell a person's future. **2.** a prediction of the future based on this chart.

hor·ri·ble (hôr′ə bəl, hor′ə bəl), *adj.* **1.** causing or likely to cause horror: *a horrible crime.* **2.** very unpleasant or bad: *horrible weather.* —**hor′ri·bly,** *adv.*

hor·rid (hôr′id, hor′id), *adj.* **1.** causing horror; horrible: *a horrid, ugly beast.* **2.** very unpleasant; nasty: *a horrid remark.* —**hor′rid·ly,** *adv.* —**hor′rid·ness,** *n.*

hor·ri·fy (hôr′ə fī′, hor′ə fī′), *v.,* **hor·ri·fied, hor·ri·fy·ing.** to cause to feel horror: *The bad news horrified them.* —**hor′ri·fy′ing·ly,** *adv.*

hor·ror (hôr′ər, hor′ər), *n.* **1.** great fright and shock caused by something evil or hideous. **2.** anything that causes such a feeling: *the horrors of war.* **3.** the fact of being horrible: *the horror of starvation.* **4.** strong dislike: *She has a horror of snakes.* **5.** *Informal.* something thought to be ugly, in bad taste, etc.: *That carpet is a horror.*

Horse
(to 6 ft. high at shoulder)

horse (hôrs), *n.* **1.** a large four-legged animal with hoofs, a mane, and a tail made up of long hair. Horses eat grass or grain and have been used since prehistoric times for riding and for carrying or pulling loads. **2.** soldiers on horseback; cavalry: *a thousand horse.* **3.** a leather-covered block on legs, used in gymnastic exercises. **4.** a frame, block, etc., on legs, used as a support: *The motor was mounted on horses for repairs.* —*v.,* **horsed, hors·ing. 5.** to provide with or mount on a horse or horses. **6. from the horse's mouth,** *Slang.* from a reliable source; on good authority. **7. hold**

one's horses, to be calm or patient: *Just hold your horses, can't you see I'm busy?* **8. horse of a different color,** something entirely different. **9. look a gift horse in the mouth,** to criticize a gift: *It's not exactly the color you wanted, but don't look a gift horse in the mouth.*

horse·back (hôrs′bak′), *n.* **1.** the back of a horse. —*adv.* **2.** on the back of a horse: *to ride horseback.*

horse′ chest′nut, 1. the shiny, brown seed of a large, spreading shade tree. **2.** the tree itself. [so named because the seeds were used for treating certain diseases of horses]

horse·fly (hôrs′flī′), *n., pl.* **horse·flies.** any of several large, bloodsucking flies that bite horses, cattle, and humans.

horse·hair (hôrs′hâr′), *n.* **1.** a hair or the hair of a horse. **2.** a glossy, strong cloth woven of the hair of a horse.

horse·man (hôrs′mən), *n., pl.* **horse·men. 1.** a man who rides on horseback. **2.** a man skilled in riding or training horses.

Horsefly (length ½ in.)

horse·man·ship (hôrs′mən ship′), *n.* the skill or technique of a horseman.

horse′ op′era, *Slang.* a television show or motion picture dealing with the adventures of settlers, cowboys, etc., in the old West.

horse·play (hôrs′plā′), *n.* rough or noisy play.

horse·pow·er (hôrs′pou′ər), *n.* a unit of power equal to 550 foot-pounds per second, or 745.7 watts.

horse·rad·ish (hôrs′rad′ish), *n.* **1.** a plant whose white, sharp-tasting root is ground for use as a flavoring or relish. **2.** the relish itself.

Horseshoe

horse·shoe (hôrs′shoo′), *n.* **1.** a U-shaped iron plate nailed to a horse's hoof for protection against injury. **2.** something resembling this in shape, as a valley, bend of a river, etc. **3. horseshoes,** *(used as sing.)* a game in which horseshoes or pieces of a similar shape are tossed at a stake in the ground. —*v.,* **horse·shoed, horse·shoe·ing. 4.** to put horseshoes on; shoe. —**horse′sho′er,** *n.*

horse′shoe crab′, any of several sea animals similar to a large crab but having a spikelike tail and a top shell shaped like a horseshoe.

Horseshoe crab (length 2 ft.)

horse′shoe mag′net, a permanent magnet, shaped like a horseshoe, whose magnetic field is concentrated at the open end. See also **bar magnet.**

horse·whip (hôrs′hwip′, -wip′), *n.* **1.** a whip used for controlling horses. —*v.,* **horse·whipped, horse·whip·ping. 2.** to beat with a horsewhip. —**horse′whip′per,** *n.*

horse·wom·an (hôrs′woom′ən), *n., pl.* **horse·wom·en. 1.** a woman who rides on horseback. **2.** a woman skilled in riding or training horses.

hors·y (hôr′sē), *adj.,* **hors·i·er, hors·i·est. 1.** of, referring to, or characteristic of a horse or horses: *The stables had a horsy smell.* **2.** dealing with horses or sports involving them: *horsy society people.*

hor·ti·cul·ture (hôr′tə kul′chər), *n.* the science or art of cultivating flowers, fruits, and vegetables. —**hor′ti·cul′tur·al,** *adj.* —**hor′ti·cul′tur·ist,** *n.*

ho·san·na (hō zan′ə), *interj.* (used as an exclamation of praise to God or Christ.) [from a Hebrew phrase meaning "save, we pray"]

hose (hōz), *n., pl.* for defs. 1, 3 **hose,** for def. 2 **hos·es. 1.** *(used as pl.)* hosiery; stockings. **2.** a flexible tube for carrying liquid, esp. water, to a certain point: *a garden hose.* **3.** tight-fitting, stockinglike breeches worn by men in former times. —*v.,* **hosed, hos·ing. 4.** to spray or drench with a hose.

Ho·se·a (hō zē′ə, hō zā′ə), *n.* (in the Bible) **1.** a Hebrew prophet of the 8th century B.C. **2.** a book of the Old Testament bearing his name.

ho·sier·y (hō′zhə rē), *n.* stockings or socks; hose.

hos·pice (hos′pis), *n.* a house where travelers may stop and rest, esp. one kept by a religious order.

hos·pi·ta·ble (hos′pi tə bəl, ho spit′ə bəl), *adj.* **1.** treating guests warmly and generously: *a hospitable host.* **2.** having an open mind (usually fol. by *to*): *to be hospitable to new ideas.* —**hos′pi·ta·bly,** *adv.*

hos·pi·tal (hos′pi təl), *n.* an institution in which sick or injured people are given medical care.

hos·pi·tal·i·ty (hos′pi tal′i tē), *n., pl.* **hos·pi·tal·i·ties.** friendly treatment of guests.

hos·pi·tal·ize (hos′pi təlīz′), *v.,* **hos·pi·tal·ized, hos·pi·tal·iz·ing.** to place in a hospital for medical or surgical treatment. —**hos′pi·tal·i·za′tion,** *n.*

host¹ (hōst), *n.* **1.** a person who receives or entertains guests in his own home. **2.** the landlord of an inn. **3.** the living animal or plant on which a parasite lives. [from an Old French word, which comes from Latin *hospes* "guest, stranger"]

host² (hōst), *n.* a great number of persons or things: *a host of stars; a host of visitors.* [from an Old French word, which comes from Latin *hostis* "enemy"]

Host (hōst), *n.* the consecrated bread of the Eucharist. [from the Latin word *hostia,* which in pagan times meant "victim, sacrifice"]

hos·tage (hos′tij), *n.* a person given or kept as a pledge, esp. by an enemy in war, until certain conditions are fulfilled.

hos·tel (hos′təl), *n.* a lodging place for hikers and travelers by bicycle, esp. the young.

hos·tel·ry (hos′təl rē), *n., pl.* **hos·tel·ries.** a hostel or inn.

host·ess (hō′stis), *n.* **1.** a female host. **2.** a woman employed in a restaurant to show people to their tables and seat them.

hos·tile (hos′təl), *adj.* **1.** unfriendly in feeling, action, appearance, etc.: *hostile words; a hostile look.* **2.** of, referring to, or characteristic of an enemy: *Hostile forces moved across the border.* —**hos′tile·ly,** *adv.*

hos·til·i·ty (ho stil′i tē), *n., pl.* **hos·til·i·ties. 1.** a hostile attitude or state; unfriendliness: *We were upset by his hostility and suspicion.* **2.** opposition to or rejection of a plan, idea, etc. **3. hostilities,** acts of warfare; war: *a period of hostilities between two nations.*

hos·tler (hos′lər, os′lər), *n.* a person who takes care of horses, esp. at an inn. Also, **ostler.**

hot (hot), *adj.,* **hot·ter, hot·test. 1.** having a high temperature; capable of giving off heat. **2.** causing a burning feeling: *hot mustard.* **3.** excited or violent in feeling: *a hot temper.* **4.** fast, furious, or intense: *a hot battle.* **5.** following very closely: *The police were hot on the thief's trail.* **6.** absolutely new; fresh: *news hot from the press.* **7.** *Informal.* good or excellent: *That story is a hot one.* **8.** charged with electricity: *a hot wire.* **9.** dangerously radioactive. **10.** *Informal.* very uncomfortable or unpleasant: *He'll make it hot for you if you lie.* —*adv.* **11.** in a hot manner; hotly: *The sun shone hot on the roofs.* —**hot′ly,** *adv.*

hot·bed (hot′bed′), *n.* **1.** a bed of earth protected by a glass-covered frame and warmed by fermenting manure, used for growing plants quickly. **2.** a place that causes the rapid growth of something bad: *Slums are hotbeds of crime.*

hot′ cake′, 1. a griddlecake or pancake. **2. sell** (or **go**) **like hot cakes,** to be very much in demand: *Copies of the book sold like hot cakes.*

hot′ dog′, *Informal.* a cooked frankfurter, usually served in a soft roll with mustard, relish, etc.

ho·tel (hō tel′), *n.* an establishment that rents rooms to travelers and others, and that usually has restaurants, shops, etc. [from the French word *hôtel,* which comes from Old French *hostel* "hostel"]

ho·tel·keep·er (hō tel′kē′pər), *n.* a person who owns or manages a hotel.

hot·foot (hot′foot′), *v.* to go in great haste (often fol. by it): *Hotfoot it to the store for some sugar.*

hot·head·ed (hot′hed′id), *adj.* having a hot temper; quick to become angry or take offense: *Be careful what you say to him because he's hotheaded.* —**hot′head′ed·ly,** *adv.* —**hot′head′ed·ness,** *n.*

hot·house (hot′hous′), *n., pl.* **hot·hous·es** (hot′hou′ziz). a heated greenhouse, used esp. for growing fruits and flowers out of season.

hot′ line′, 1. a direct Teletype or telephone line for instant communication between two chiefs of state in case of international crisis. **2.** any direct telephone line used for instant contact, counseling, etc.

hot′ plate′, a small, portable electric stove for cooking, having one or two burners.

hot′ rod′, *Slang.* a car, esp. an old one, whose engine has been altered for greater speed, and whose body has been stripped down.

Hot·ten·tot (hot′ᵊn tot′), *n.* **1.** a member of a people of southern Africa. **2.** the language of the Hottentots.

hot′ wa′ter, *Informal.* a difficult situation; trouble: *He's in hot water after losing his money.*

hound (hound), *n.* **1.** any of several breeds of dog used for hunting, esp. one with a long face and large, drooping ears. **2.** any dog. —*v.* **3.** to chase or pursue without a break: *The actress was hounded by her fans*

wherever she went. **4.** to urge with force: *His mother hounded him to go to the dentist.*

hound's′ tooth′, a pattern of broken or jagged checks, often used on fabrics.

hour (our), *n.* **1.** a unit of time equal to 60 minutes: *There are 24 hours in a day.* **2.** a particular or appointed time: *At what hour are you leaving?* **3.** a customary or usual time: *dinner hour.* **4.** the present time: *the man of the hour.*

Hound's tooth

5. hours, a. the usual time spent at some activity: *working hours; school hours.* **b.** the time one goes to bed: *to keep late hours.* **6.** distance usually covered by an hour of travel: *We live two hours from New York.*

hour·glass (our′glas′), *n.* a device for measuring time, having two bulbs of glass joined by a narrow passage through which an amount of sand runs in just an hour from the upper to the lower bulb.

hour·ly (our′lē), *adj.* **1.** done, happening, taken, etc., every hour: *an hourly dose of medicine.* **2.** for an hour: *an hourly rate of pay.* **3.** frequent or continual: *hourly complaints.* —*adv.* **4.** every hour; hour by hour: *The bells ring hourly.* **5.** frequently; very often. **6.** in the near future; soon.

Hourglass

house (hous), *n., pl.* **hous·es** (hou′ziz). **1.** a building in which people live. **2.** a household: *They set up house in New York.* **3.** *(often cap.)* a family, esp. of royalty or the nobility: *kings of an ancient house.* **4.** a building for any purpose: *a house of worship.* **5.** a theater, concert hall, or the like. **6.** an audience in a theater, concert hall, or the like. **7.** an assembly of people who make laws, or the place where they meet. **8.** a business firm: *a publishing house.* —*v.* (houz), **housed, hous·ing. 9.** to give a dwelling or shelter to; lodge: *to house homeless families.* **10.** to provide storage space for: *The old furniture is housed in the attic.* **11. bring down the house,** to receive tremendous applause from an audience: *Her performance in "Swan Lake" always brings down the house.* **12. on the house,** as a gift from the management; free: *Breakfast is on the house.*

house·boat (hous′bōt′), *n.* a flat-bottomed, bargelike boat fitted for use as a home.

house·break (hous′brāk′), *v.,* **house·broke** (hous′brōk′), **house·bro·ken** (hous′brō′kən), **house·break·ing.** to train (a dog, cat, etc.) not to excrete indoors or to excrete in a certain place.

house·break·ing (hous′brā′king), *n.* the act of breaking into another's house with the purpose of robbing or of committing some other crime. —**house′break′er,** *n.*

Housefly
(length
¼ in.)

house·fly (hous′flī′), *n., pl.* **house·flies.** a medium-sized fly that lives in houses and feeds on food, garbage, etc.

house·hold (hous′hōld′, -ōld′), *n.* **1.** all the people

act, āble, dâre, ärt; ebb, ēqual; if, īce; hot, ōver, ôrder; oil; bŏŏk; ōōze; out; up, ûrge; ə = *a* as in *alone;* ᵊ as in *button* (but′ᵊn), *fire* (fī°r); chief; shoe; thin; ŧħat; zh as in *measure* (mezh′ər). See full key inside cover.

who dwell together in a house, esp. a family: *a large household.* —*adj.* **2.** of or used in a household: *household tasks; a household cleanser.*

house·hold·er (hous′hōl′dər), *n.* **1.** a person who owns or occupies a house. **2.** the head of a family.

house·keep·er (hous′kē′pər), *n.* a person employed to do or direct household work.

house·keep·ing (hous′kē′pin͞g), *n.* the care and management of a house.

house·maid (hous′mād′), *n.* a girl or woman employed as a servant to do housework.

house·moth·er (hous′mu*th*′ər), *n.* a woman who oversees and manages a place of residence, esp. for children, students, or young women.

House′ of Com′mons, the lower and chief lawmaking house of the British Parliament, the members of which are elected by the people.

House′ of Lords′, the upper house of the British Parliament, made up of the nobility and clergymen of high rank.

House′ of Represent′atives, the lower legislative branch in many national and state governments, as in the U.S., Mexico, Japan, etc.

house·top (hous′top′), *n.* the top or roof of a house.

house·warm·ing (hous′wôr′min͞g), *n.* a party held to celebrate moving into a new house or apartment.

house·wife (hous′wif′), *n., pl.* **house·wives** (hous′-wīvz′). a married woman who does or directs the household work of her family.

house·work (hous′wûrk′), *n.* the work of keeping a house, such as cooking, cleaning, etc.

hous·ing (hou′zin͞g), *n.* **1.** any shelter or dwelling place: *The family was without housing.* **2.** houses or lodgings: *to provide housing for students.* **3.** the providing of a home or homes: *Funds are available for workers' housing.* **4.** anything that covers and protects, as a case for a machine or engine.

hous′ing proj′ect. See project (def. 3).

Hous·ton (hyo͞o′stən), *n.* **1. Sam(uel),** 1793–1863, U.S. soldier and president of the Republic of Texas 1836–1838. **2.** a city in SE Texas.

hove (hōv), *v.* a past tense and past participle of **heave.**

hov·el (huv′əl, hov′əl), *n.* **1.** a small, broken-down house. **2.** a wretched, dirty dwelling place.

hov·er (huv′ər, hov′ər), *v.* **1.** to hang fluttering or suspended in the air: *birds hovering in the wake of a ship.* **2.** to linger about; wait near at hand: *The waiter hovered as we ate.* **3.** to be in an uncertain state; waver: *to hover between life and death.* —**hov′er·ing·ly,** *adv.*

how (hou), *adv.* **1.** in what way; by what means: *How do you do this?* **2.** to what extent or degree: *How damaged is your car?* **3.** in what state or condition: *How are you?* **4.** for what reason; why: *How is it that you never visit us?* **5.** in whatever way: *You may travel how you please.* —*n.* **6.** a way or manner of doing something: *He doesn't understand the how or why of it.* **7. and how!** *Informal.* certainly!: *Am I glad? And how!* **8. how about, a.** how do you feel about; would you be interested in: *How about a swim*

before breakfast? **b.** would you like; will you take: *If there's no soda, how about milk?* **9. how come?** *Informal.* why is it that?: *How come we never see you?*

how·dah (hou′də), *n.* a seat, often covered and having railings, for riding on the back of an elephant.

how·e'er (hou âr′), *adv., conj.* however: used esp. in literature.

how·ev·er (hou ev′ər), *adv.* **1.** to whatever degree or extent; no matter how: *However wrong you may be, I will still like you.* **2.** in whatever way, manner, or means: *Arrange your hair however you wish.* **3.** how (used in questions for greater emphasis): *However did it happen?* —*conj.* **4.** nevertheless; yet: *We are winning; however, the game is not over.*

how·itz·er (hou′it sər), *n.* a cannon with a short barrel, used for firing shells at a high angle.

howl (houl), *v.* **1.** to utter a long, loud, mournful cry, such as that of a dog or wolf. **2.** to utter a similar cry in pain, rage, etc.; wail. **3.** *Informal.* to laugh loudly. —*n.* **4.** the cry of a dog, wolf, etc. **5.** a cry or wail of pain, rage, protest, etc. **6.** a sound resembling this: *the howl of the wind.* —**howl′er,** *n.*

hoy·den (hoid′ᵊn), *n.* a bold, boisterous girl; tomboy.

hp, horsepower. Also, **HP**

H.P., 1. (in electricity) high power. **2.** high pressure. **3.** horsepower. Also, **h.p.**

H.Q., headquarters. Also, **h.q., HQ**

hr., hour.

H.R.H., His (or Her) Royal Highness.

hrs., hours.

ht., height. Also, **hgt.**

Hts., Heights (in names of places): *Crown Hts.*

Hua Kuo-feng (hwä′ kwō fun͞g′), born 1920?, Chinese communist leader.

hub (hub), *n.* **1.** the central part of a wheel, into which the spokes are fixed. **2.** a center of activity, interest, etc.: *Paris is the hub of France.*

hub·bub (hub′ub), *n.* a loud, confused noise, as of many voices: *a hubbub in the marketplace.*

huck·le·ber·ry (huk′əl ber′ē), *n., pl.* **huck·le·ber·ries. 1.** a dark blue berry that resembles the blueberry and is often used in pies. **2.** the shrub that bears this berry.

huck·ster (huk′stər), *n.* **1.** a peddler of small articles, esp. of fruits and vegetables. **2.** *Informal.* a forceful salesman, or an advertising man.

hud·dle (hud′ᵊl), *v.,* **hud·dled, hud·dling. 1.** to gather or crowd closely together: *We huddled around the stove to get warm.* **2.** to put closely together: *She huddled her belongings and left the house.* —*n.* **3.** a small, compact gathering of people for discussion, esp. a group of football players gathered together to decide the next play. **4.** a number of persons or things jumbled or crowded together.

Hud·son (hud′sən), *n.* a river in E New York. 306 mi. long.

Hud′son Bay′, a large inland sea in N Canada. 850 mi. long; 600 mi. wide; 400,000 sq. mi.

hue (hyo͞o), *n.* a shade of color; tint: *pale hues of red and green.* [from the Old English word *hīw* "form, appearance, color"]

hue′ and cry′, a loud outcry of alarm: *The public raised a great hue and cry over the election scandal.* [*hue* in this phrase comes from the Old French word *hu* "hoot, outcry," which comes from *huer* "to hoot, shout"]

huff (huf), *n.* **1.** a mood of anger or resentment: *Insulted, she left in a huff.* —*v.* **2.** to make angry: *She was huffed by their rudeness.* **3.** to blow or breathe heavily: *The racers huffed and puffed.*

huff·y (huf′ē), *adj.,* **huff·i·er, huff·i·est. 1.** easily offended; touchy. **2.** offended; sulky: *a huffy mood.* —**huff′i·ly,** *adv.* —**huff′i·ness,** *n.*

hug (hug), *v.,* **hugged, hug·ging. 1.** to clasp tightly in the arms; embrace: *The mother hugged her baby.* **2.** to cling firmly or fondly to: *to hug a belief.* **3.** to keep close to: *The boat hugged the shore.*

huge (hyōōj), *adj.,* **hug·er, hug·est.** extremely large or great: *a huge animal; a huge sum.* —**huge′ly,** *adv.* —**huge′ness,** *n.*

Hu·gue·not (hyōō′gə not′), *n.* a French Protestant, esp. of the 16th and 17th centuries.

hu·la-hu·la (hōō′lə hōō′lə), *n.* a Hawaiian native dance that tells a story, performed with swaying movements of the body.

hulk (hulk), *n.* **1.** an old, broken-down ship. **2.** a bulky or unwieldy person or thing: *a hulk of a man; the hulk of a burned-out building.*

hulk·ing (hul′king), *adj.* bulky; heavy and clumsy: *a tall, hulking man.*

hull[1] (hul), *n.* **1.** the husk, shell, or pod of a seed or fruit. **2.** the calyx, or green fringe of leaves, of a strawberry or raspberry. —*v.* **3.** to remove the hull of: *to hull strawberries.* [from the Old English word *hulu* "husk, pod," related to *helan* "to cover"]

hull[2] (hul), *n.* **1.** the body of a ship, apart from rigging, masts, etc. **2.** the main body of a flying boat, on which it lands or takes off. **3.** the framework of a dirigible. [from a special use of *hull*[1]]

hul·la·ba·loo (hul′ə bə lōō′), *n., pl.* **hul·la·ba·loos.** a loud noise or disturbance; uproar: *He made a hullabaloo when he saw the mistake.*

hum (hum), *v.,* **hummed, hum·ming. 1.** to sing with closed lips: *to hum softly to oneself; to hum a song.* **2.** to make a low, droning sound: *humming voices; a humming motor.* **3.** to bring, put, etc., by humming: *to hum a child to sleep.* **4.** to be busy or active: *Things are humming at the office.* —*n.* **5.** the act or sound of humming: *the hum of bees.* —**hum′mer,** *n.*

hu·man (hyōō′mən), *adj.* **1.** of, referring to, or characteristic of mankind: *human history; the human race.* **2.** sympathetic; humane: *human tolerance.* —*n.* **3.** a human being. —**hu′man·like′,** *adj.*

hu·mane (hyōō mān′), *adj.* kind, gentle, or sympathetic toward men and animals. —**hu·mane′ly,** *adv.* —**hu·mane′ness,** *n.*

hu·man·ist (hyōō′mə nist), *n.* a person who gives first importance to man and the things man has made, and who is concerned with human happiness and improvement.

hu·man·i·tar·i·an (hyōō man′i târ′ē ən), *n.* **1.** a person concerned with human happiness and welfare: *The best doctors are humanitarians.* —*adj.* **2.** concerned with human happiness and welfare: *Charity is humanitarian.*

hu·man·i·ty (hyōō man′i tē), *n., pl.* **hu·man·i·ties. 1.** the human race; mankind: *Humanity has need of peace.* **2.** human nature: *our common humanity.* **3.** kindness or sympathy: *a person who shows humanity toward others.* **4. the humanities,** the studies that include literature, art, philosophy, etc., but not the sciences.

hu·man·ize (hyōō′mə nīz′), *v.,* **hu·man·ized, hu·man·iz·ing. 1.** to make or become humane, kind, or gentle: *Their religious beliefs humanized them.* **2.** to make or become civilized: *Ancient Rome humanized the world.*

hu·man·kind (hyōō′mən kīnd′), *n.* the human race; mankind; humanity.

hu·man·ly (hyōō′mən lē), *adv.* **1.** in a human manner: *We should behave humanly toward others.* **2.** within human power: *We did all that was humanly possible to help him.*

hum·ble (hum′bəl), *adj.,* **hum·bler, hum·blest. 1.** modest; not proud: *He was humble though famous.* **2.** lowly or of little importance: *Great careers often have humble beginnings.* —*v.,* **hum·bled, hum·bling. 3.** to lower in rank, importance, position, etc.: *The enemy was humbled and forced to surrender.* —**hum′ble·ness,** *n.* —**hum′bly,** *adv.*

hum·bug (hum′bug′), *n.* **1.** a trick; hoax; fraud: *a humbug to deceive the public.* **2.** pretense or sham: *to speak without humbug.* **3.** a person who is not what he claims to be: *He was not a doctor but a humbug.* —*v.,* **hum·bugged, hum·bug·ging. 4.** to deceive or trick: *He was humbugged into believing lies.* —*interj.* **5.** nonsense!

hum·ding·er (hum′ding′ər), *n. Slang.* a remarkable or excellent person or thing: *His new bicycle is a humdinger.*

hum·drum (hum′drum′), *adj.* dull, boring, or monotonous: *a rainy, humdrum day spent indoors.*

hu·mid (hyōō′mid), *adj.* moist or damp with water or vapor: *a warm, humid day in August.*

hu·mid·i·fy (hyōō mid′ə fī′), *v.,* **hu·mid·i·fied, hu·mid·i·fy·ing.** to add moisture to (the air). —**hu·mid′i·fi·ca′tion,** *n.* —**hu·mid′i·fi′er,** *n.*

hu·mid·i·ty (hyōō mid′i tē), *n.* **1.** a humid condition; dampness. **2.** the amount of water vapor in the air.

hu·mil·i·ate (hyōō mil′ē āt′), *v.,* **hu·mil·i·at·ed, hu·mil·i·at·ing.** to lower the pride of; put to shame; embarrass: *He was humiliated by the insult.* —**hu·mil′i·at·ing·ly,** *adv.*

hu·mil·i·a·tion (hyōō mil′ē ā′shən), *n.* **1.** the act of humiliating. **2.** the state of being humiliated; loss of pride or self-respect.

hu·mil·i·ty (hyōō mil′i tē), *n.* the quality of being humble; lack of self-importance; modesty: *They were impressed by the great man's humility.*

hum·ming·bird (hum′ing bûrd′), *n.* any of various small, brightly colored American birds whose rapidly beating wings make a humming sound when they hover near flowers to feed.

hum·mock (hum′ək), *n.* a small, low, rounded hill.

hu·mor (hyōō′mər), *n.* 1. the quality of being comic or funny: *The story was full of humor.* 2. the ability to understand what is comic or funny: *a lively sense of humor.* 3. comic or funny writing or talk: *the humor of a comedian.* 4. mood; temper; disposition: *The weather has put me in a bad humor.* —*v.* 5. to put up with the whims or moods of; indulge: *They humored her in order to have a little peace.* 6. **out of humor,** cross; angry; displeased: *He is out of humor because of bad news.* [from the Latin word *hūmor* "fluid." It was formerly believed that a person's disposition was determined by certain fluids in the body]

hu·mor·ist (hyōō′mər ist), *n.* a person skilled in the use of humor, as in writing or acting.

hu·mor·ous (hyōō′mər əs), *adj.* full of humor; comic; funny: *a humorous writer; a humorous situation.* —**hu′mor·ous·ly,** *adv.*

hump (hump), *n.* 1. a rounded bulge on the back: *a camel's hump.* —*v.* 2. to rise or raise in a hump; arch: *The cat humped her back and yawned.* 3. **over the hump,** past the most difficult or tedious part: *If we work hard for another hour, we'll be over the hump.*

hump·back (hump′bak′), *n.* 1. a back that is humped. 2. a hunchback. 3. a kind of whale that has a humped back.

hump·backed (hump′bakt′), *adj.* having a hump on the back; hunchbacked.

Hum·phrey (hum′frē), *n.* Hubert H(oratio), 1911–1978, 38th Vice President of the U.S. 1965–1969.

hu·mus (hyōō′məs), *n.* the material in soil that is formed from decayed plants. Plants will not grow in soil that lacks humus.

Hun (hun), *n.* 1. a member of a warlike Asian people who overran large parts of Europe under their leader, Attila, in the 5th century A.D. 2. *(often l.c.)* a barbaric, destructive person.

hunch·back (hunch′bak′), *n.* a person whose back is humped or crooked.

hunch·backed (hunch′bakt′), *adj.* another word for **humpbacked.**

hun·dred (hun′drid), *n., pl.* **hun·dreds** *or* (after a numeral) **hun·dred.** 1. a number that is ten times ten. 2. this many or about this many persons or things: *A hundred of the soldiers charged the fort.* 3. **hundreds,** the numbers, years, degrees, dollars, etc., between 100 and 199, or between 100 and 999: *The temperature must be in the hundreds.* —*adj.* 4. amounting to one hundred in number: *There must have been a hundred persons in the crowd.*

hun·dred·fold (hun′drid fōld′), *adj.* 1. a hundred times as great or as much: *a hundredfold increase.*

Hummingbird
(length 3½ in.)

—*adv.* 2. in a hundredfold measure (often preceded by *a* or *one*): *The output increased a hundredfold.*

hun·dredth (hun′dridth, hun′dritth), *adj.* 1. being number one hundred in a series: *the hundredth floor.* —*n.* 2. one of a hundred equal parts. 3. a person or thing that is number one hundred.

hun·dred·weight (hun′drid wāt′), *n., pl.* **hun·dred·weights** *or* (after a numeral) **hun·dred·weight.** 1. (in the U.S.) a unit of weight equal to 100 pounds. 2. (in England) a unit of weight equal to 112 pounds.

hung (hung), *v.* a past tense and past participle of **hang.**

—**Usage.** See **hang.**

Hun·gar·i·an (hung gâr′ē ən), *n.* 1. a native or inhabitant of Hungary. 2. Also, **Magyar.** the language of the Hungarians, related to Finnish. —*adj.* 3. of or referring to Hungary, its people, or their language.

Hungar′ian gou′lash, another name for **goulash.**

Hun·ga·ry (hung′gə rē), *n.* a republic in central Europe. 35,926 sq. mi. *Cap.:* Budapest.

hun·ger (hung′gər), *n.* 1. a strong need or desire for food. 2. the pain or weakness caused by a lack of food. 3. a deep craving: *a dictator's hunger for power.* —*v.* 4. to feel hunger.

hun·gry (hung′grē), *adj.,* **hun·gri·er, hun·gri·est.** 1. having a need or desire for food. 2. showing hunger: *a lean and hungry look.* 3. strongly desirous: *to be hungry for knowledge.* —**hun′gri·ly,** *adv.*

hunk (hungk), *n. Informal.* a large piece or lump; chunk.

hunt (hunt), *v.* 1. to chase and try to kill (wild animals): *to hunt buffalo.* 2. to pursue with force (often fol. by *down*): *to hunt down a fugitive.* 3. to make a thorough search: *to hunt for a lost child.* —*n.* 4. the act of hunting: *They gathered at dawn for the hunt.*

hunt·er (hun′tər), *n.* 1. a person who hunts. 2. an animal trained for hunting.

hunts·man (hunts′mən), *n., pl.* **hunts·men.** 1. a man who manages the hounds in a hunt. 2. a hunter.

Hunts·ville (hunts′vil), *n.* a city in N Alabama: rocket and missile center.

hur·dle (hûr′dəl), *n.* 1. a barrier over which a contestant in a race must leap. 2. **hurdles,** *(used as sing.)* a race in which contestants must leap over such barriers. 3. a difficulty to be overcome; obstacle. —**hur′dler,** *n.*

hur·dy-gur·dy (hûr′dē gûr′dē), *n., pl.* **hur·dy-gur·dies.** 1. a musical instrument, esp. a piano or organ, played by turning a crank and used by a street musician. 2. a stringed instrument resembling a lute or guitar, played by pressing strings against a rosined wheel that is turned by a hand crank.

Hurdy-gurdy
(def. 2)

hurl (hûrl), *v.* to throw or fling with great force: *to hurl a javelin.*

Hu·ron (hyoor′ən, hyoor′on), *n.* **Lake,** a lake between the U.S. and Canada: second largest of the Great Lakes. 23,010 sq. mi.

hur·rah (hə rä′, hə rô′), *interj.* **1.** (used as a shout of joy or acclaim.) —*v.* **2.** to shout or cheer with "hurrah." —*n.* **3.** a shout of "hurrah." Also, **hoorah, hooray.**

hur·ri·cane (hûr′ə kān′, hûr′ə kən), *n.* a violent wind and rain storm that starts over the ocean in the tropics and is marked by winds that blow in a circular pattern at speeds of greater than 73 miles an hour. [from the Spanish word *huracán,* which comes from an Indian language of the West Indies]

hur·ried (hûr′ēd, hur′ēd), *adj.* done with hurry; hasty: *a hurried departure.* —**hur′ried·ly,** *adv.*

hur·ry (hûr′ē, hur′ē), *v.,* **hur·ried, hur·ry·ing. 1.** to move or act with haste (often fol. by *up*): *Hurry up, it's starting to rain!* **2.** to make (a person) do something too fast: *If you hurry me, I'll get mixed up.* —*n.* **3.** eager movement or action: *He's in a hurry to get to school.*

hurt (hûrt), *v.,* **hurt, hurt·ing. 1.** to cause bodily injury or pain to (someone). **2.** to offend or cause suffering to: *She hurt his feelings.* —*adj.* **3.** injured or offended: *hurt feelings.* —*n.* **4.** pain or injury.

hurt·ful (hûrt′fəl), *adj.* causing hurt or injury; harmful. —**hurt′ful·ly,** *adv.* —**hurt′ful·ness,** *n.*

hur·tle (hûr′t³l), *v.,* **hur·tled, hur·tling.** to move with great speed: *The car hurtled down the highway.*

hus·band (huz′bənd), *n.* a married man in relation to his wife. [from the Old English word *hūsbonda* "master of the house"]

hus·band·man (huz′bənd mən), *n., pl.* **hus·band·men.** a farmer.

hus·band·ry (huz′bən drē), *n.* **1.** the cultivation of crops and animals. **2.** good management.

hush (hush), *interj.* **1.** (used as a command to be silent.) —*v.* **2.** to become or make silent. —*n.* **3.** silence or quiet: *A hush settled over the audience.*

husk (husk), *n.* **1.** the dry, hard covering of a seed or an ear of corn. **2.** any worthless covering. —*v.* **3.** to remove the husk from: *to husk corn.*

husk·y[1] (hus′kē), *adj.,* **husk·i·er, husk·i·est. 1.** big and strong; burly. **2.** (of the voice) somewhat hoarse and rough. [from *husk* + *-y* (def. 1a)] —**husk′i·ly,** *adv.* —**husk′i·ness,** *n.*

husk·y[2] (hus′kē), *n., pl.* **husk·ies.** *Informal.* a big, strong person: *a football team made up of huskies.* [from *husk* + *-y* (def. 3)]

husk·y[3] (hus′kē), *n., pl.* **husk·ies.** another name for **Eskimo dog.** [perhaps short for *Eskimo*]

hus·sar (hə zär′), *n.* a member of the light cavalry in some European armies. [from the Hungarian word *huszár* "freebooter"]

hus·sy (hus′ē, huz′ē), *n., pl.* **hus·sies.** a mischievous or ill-behaved girl. [from the Middle English word *huswif* "housewife"]

hus·tle (hus′əl), *v.,* **hus·tled, hus·tling. 1.** to work hurriedly or energetically: *She hustled around the kitchen getting dinner.* **2.** *Informal.* to be aggressive, esp. in business. **3.** to force by pushing or shoving: *They hustled him out the door.* —*n.* **4.** energetic

work or activity: *the hustle and bustle of Christmas shopping.* **5.** discourteous shoving or pushing.

hut (hut), *n.* a small dwelling made of logs, mud, or grass.

hutch (huch), *n.* **1.** a pen for small animals: *a rabbit hutch.* **2.** a chest for storage.

huz·zah (hə zä′), *interj.* **1.** (used as an exclamation of joy or appreciation) hurrah! —*n.* **2.** the exclamation "huzzah." —*v.* **3.** to shout "huzzah."

Hwang Ho (hwäng′ hō′), a river in W China. 2800 mi. long. Also, **Yellow River.**

hy·a·cinth (hī′ə sinth), *n.* a plant that grows from a bulb and bears spikes of bell-shaped flowers.

hy·brid (hī′brid), *n.* **1.** an animal or plant whose parents belong to different species, breeds, races, etc. **2.** anything derived from two different sources.

hy·brid·ize (hī′bri dīz′), *v.,* **hy·brid·ized, hy·brid·iz·ing.** to produce or make produce hybrids. —**hy′brid·i·za′tion,** *n.*

hy·dra (hī′drə), *n.* a tiny freshwater animal with a tubelike body having a ring of tentacles at one end.

Hyacinth

Hy·dra (hī′drə), *n.* (in Greek mythology) a snake with nine heads, each of which was replaced by two if cut off. It was killed by Hercules.

hy·dran·gea (hī drān′jə), *n.* a shrub that bears large clusters of white, pink, or blue flowers.

hy·drant (hī′drənt), *n.* an upright pipe with an outlet in the street, used for drawing water from a main.

hy·drau·lic (hī drô′lik, hī drol′ik), *adj.* **1.** operated by liquid in motion or under pressure. **2.** of or concerning hydraulics. **3.** hardening under water, such as cement. —**hy·drau′li·cal·ly,** *adv.*

hy·drau·lics (hī drô′liks, hī drol′iks), *n. (used as sing.)* the science that deals with the motion of water and other liquids.

hydro-, a prefix meaning **1.** water: *hydroelectric.* **2.** containing hydrogen: *hydrochloric.*

hy·dro·car·bon (hī′drə kär′bən), *n. Chem.* a compound composed only of carbon and hydrogen. Many of the useful substances found in petroleum are hydrocarbons or mixtures of hydrocarbons.

hy′dro·chlo′ric ac′id (hī′drə klôr′ik), *Chem.* a strong acid, a compound of hydrogen and chlorine, found in dilute form in gastric juice and used in more concentrated form for etching and cleaning metals.

hy·dro·e·lec·tric (hī′drō i lek′trik), *adj.* referring to electric power produced from the energy of falling or running water.

hy·dro·foil (hī′drə foil′), *n.* a kind of boat having small, winglike structures underneath it by means of which the hull is lifted above the surface of the water when the boat is moving rapidly.

Hydrofoil

hy·dro·gen (hī′drə jən), *n. Chem.* a light, highly inflammable gas. The lightest of the elements, hydrogen was formerly used in balloons and dirigibles. *Symbol:* H

hy′drogen bomb′, a bomb that derives its explosive power from the fusion of hydrogen nuclei. The hydrogen bomb is the most destructive weapon known. Also, **H-bomb.**

hy′drogen perox′ide, *Chem.* a compound of oxygen and hydrogen, dissolved in water for use as a disinfectant and bleach.

hy·drom·e·ter (hī drom′i tər), *n.* a device for measuring the specific gravity of liquids.

hy·dro·pho·bi·a (hī′drə fō′bē ə), *n.* another name for **rabies.** [from a Greek word meaning "fear of water"]

hy·dro·plane (hī′drə plān′), *n.* 1. a light motorboat designed to skim on the surface of the water at high speeds. 2. an airplane that can take off from and land on water.

hy·e·na (hī ē′nə), *n.* a large, doglike animal of Africa and Asia that feeds on the remains of other animals' prey.

hy·giene (hī′jēn), *n.* 1. the science that deals with health. 2. a practice that leads to health. —**hy·gi·en·ic** (hī′jē en′ik, hī·jē′nik), *adj.*

Hyena
(3 ft. high at shoulder)

hy·grom·e·ter (hī grom′i tər), *n.* an instrument for measuring the moisture of the air.

Hy·men (hī′mən), *n.* (in Greek mythology) the god of marriage.

hymn (him), *n.* a song of praise, esp. one for singing by a religious congregation or other group.

hym·nal (him′nəl), *n.* a book of hymns. Also, **hymn′book′.**

hyper-, a prefix meaning over, very, or too much: *hypertension; hypercritical.*

hy·per·bo·le (hī pûr′bə lē), *n.* an exaggerated statement, not intended to be taken literally, such as "I've told you a million times."

hy·per·crit·i·cal (hī′pər krit′i kəl), *adj.* overly critical. —**hy′per·crit′i·cal·ly,** *adv.*

hy·per·sen·si·tive (hī′pər sen′si tiv), *adj.* overly sensitive: *to be hypersensitive to criticism.*

hy·phen (hī′fən), *n.* a punctuation mark (-) used to connect the parts of a compound word, such as *mother-in-law,* or to divide a word at the end of a line. [from a Greek phrase meaning "combined under one," from *hypo* "under" + *hen* "one"]

hy·phen·ate (hī′fə nāt′), *v.,* **hy·phen·at·ed, hy·phen·at·ing.** 1. to join by a hyphen. 2. to write or print

with a hyphen: *"Make-up" is a hyphenated word.* —**hy′phen·a′tion,** *n.*

hyp·no·sis (hip nō′sis), *n.* a state resembling a deep sleep in which one is unusually responsive to what another person commands or suggests. Such a trance may be brought on by a hypnotist or by the person himself. —**hyp·not·ic** (hip not′ik), *adj.*

hyp·no·tism (hip′nə tiz′əm), *n.* 1. the science dealing with hypnosis. 2. the act of putting someone into hypnosis: *hypnotism of a patient.*

hyp·no·tist (hip′nə tist), *n.* a specialist in hypnosis.

hyp·no·tize (hip′nə tīz′), *v.,* **hyp·no·tized, hyp·no·tiz·ing.** to put (someone) into hypnosis.

hy·po (hī′pō), *n., pl.* **hy·pos.** a hypodermic syringe or injection.

hy·po·chon·dri·ac (hī′pə kon′drē ak′), *n.* a person who worries a great deal about his health and often imagines that he has some serious illness.

hy·poc·ri·sy (hi pok′rə sē), *n.* a pretense of being good, noble, moral, etc., when one really is not.

hyp·o·crite (hip′ə krit), *n.* a person who pretends to be what he is not in order to impress others: *I would be a hypocrite if I applauded that speech.* —**hyp′o·crit′i·cal,** *adj.* —**hyp′o·crit′i·cal·ly,** *adv.*

hy·po·der·mic (hī′pə dûr′mik), *adj.* 1. referring to the giving of medicine under the skin. —*n.* 2. a hypodermic injection. 3. a hypodermic syringe.

Hypodermic syringe

hy·pot·e·nuse (hī pot′ə nōōs′, -nyōōs′), *n.* the side of a right triangle opposite the right angle. The hypotenuse is always the longest side of a right triangle.

hy·poth·e·sis (hī poth′i sis), *n., pl.* **hy·poth·e·ses** (hī poth′i sēz′). 1. something that is assumed to be true and is used as the basis for further study or discussion. 2. an assumption.

hy·po·thet·i·cal (hī′pə thet′i kəl), *adj.* assumed by hypothesis; supposed: *a hypothetical question.* —**hy·po·thet′i·cal·ly,** *adv.*

hys·te·ri·a (hi stēr′ē ə, hi ster′ē ə), *n.* 1. a condition caused by emotional problems in which a person suffers from some physical disorder, such as paralysis of the legs, for which there is no physical cause. 2. an uncontrollable outburst of fear or weeping.

hys·ter·i·cal (hi ster′i kəl), *adj.* 1. suffering from hysteria. 2. very excited from fear: *The little girl got hysterical when she couldn't find her mother.* 3. causing very much laughter; extremely funny: *That joke is hysterical.* —**hys·ter′i·cal·ly,** *adv.*

hys·ter·ics (hi ster′iks), *n.pl. (used as sing.)* a fit of uncontrollable laughing or weeping: *The woman had hysterics when she broke her necklace.*

Hz, hertz.

	Semitic	Greek	Latin	Gothic	Modern Roman
DEVELOPMENT OF UPPER-CASE LETTERS	ϟ	⟩	ǀ	ǀ	Ɜ	I
DEVELOPMENT OF LOWER-CASE LETTERS	ι	ǀ	⌡	ι	î	i
	Greek		Medieval	Gothic	Modern Roman

I

I, i (ī), *n., pl.* **I's** *or* **Is, i's** *or* **is.** the ninth letter of the English alphabet.

I (ī), *pron.* the first person singular pronoun, used by the speaker or writer when referring to himself: *I want to ask you something.*

I, 1. the Roman numeral for 1. 2. *Chem.* the symbol for **iodine.**

I., 1. Independent. 2. Island; Islands. 3. Isle; Isles.

i., 1. interest. 2. island; islands. 3. isle; isles.

i·am·bic (ī am′bik), *adj.* referring to poetry that has measures of two syllables, an unaccented one followed by an accented one, as in Come live′/ with me′/ and be′/ my love′.

-ian, another form of the suffix **-an,** used to form adjectives and nouns: *mammalian; Athenian; guardian.*

I·be·ri·a (ī bēr′ē ə), *n.* a peninsula in SW Europe: made up of Spain and Portugal. Also, **Iber′ian Penin′sula.**

I·be·ri·an (ī bēr′ē ən), *adj.* of or concerning Iberia or its people.

i·bex (ī′beks), *n.* any of several wild goats of Europe, North Africa, and Asia having back-curving horns.

-ibility, a suffix used to form nouns from adjectives ending in **-ible:** *reversibility.*

i·bis (ī′bis), *n., pl.* **i·bis·es** *or* **i·bis.** any of several large wading birds related to the storks and having long, thin, downcurving bills. See illus. at **wader.**

-ible, another form of the suffix **-able,** used to form adjectives: *flexible.*

-ic, a suffix used to form

Ibex
(3 ft. high at shoulder)

adjectives meaning of, like, or concerning: *poetic; metallic; Celtic.* Some of these adjectives are used also as nouns: *an anemic; a harmonic.*

-ical, a suffix made up of **-ic** and **-al,** used to form adjectives that may be synonyms of those ending in **-ic** *(poetic, poetical),* or that have a somewhat different meaning *(economic, economical).*

Ic·a·rus (ik′ər əs), *n.* (in Greek mythology) the son of Daedalus, with whom he escaped from the labyrinth of Crete by means of wings made by his father from wax and feathers. The wings melted when he flew too close to the sun, and he drowned in the sea.

ice (īs), *n.* 1. frozen water. 2. any substance resembling ice: *camphor ice.* —*v.,* **iced, ic·ing.** 3. to cool with ice: *to ice a glass of water.* 4. to cover with icing: *to ice a cake.* 5. to cover or become covered with ice (often fol. by *up*): *The window iced up.* 6. **break the ice,** to overcome shyness or awkwardness within a group of people: *The hostess broke the ice by introducing everyone.* 7. **cut no ice,** *Informal.* to fail to make a favorable impression: *Her father may be famous, but that cuts no ice with me.* 8. **on thin ice,** in a risky or delicate situation: *With such a flimsy alibi, he was really on thin ice.* —**ice′like′,** *adj.*

ice′ age′, any of several periods during which large areas of the earth were covered by glaciers.

ice·berg (īs′bûrg), *n.* a large mass of ice, detached from a glacier and floating out to sea.

ice·boat (īs′bōt′), *n.* a vehicle for rapid movement on ice, consisting of a T-shaped frame on runners and driven by sails.

ice·box (īs′boks′), *n.* 1. a cabinet with a compartment for ice and used for keeping foods fresh. 2. *Informal.* a refrigerator.

ice·break·er (īs′brā′kər), *n.* a ship that is specially constructed to open up passages through ice for other ships.

Iceboat

ice·cap (īs′kap′), *n.* a large, permanent sheet of ice, such as that covering the North and South poles.

ice′ cream′, a frozen food made of cream or milk, sugar, eggs, and flavorings.

ice′ hock′ey, another name for **hockey.**

Ice·land (īs′lənd), *n.* an island republic in the N Atlantic near Greenland: formerly Danish. **—Ice·land·er** (īs′lan′dər, īs′lən dər), *n.*

Ice·lan·dic (īs lan′dik), *n.* **1.** the Germanic language of Iceland. **—***adj.* **2.** of or concerning Iceland, its people, or their language.

ice′ skate′. See skate[1] (def. 1).

ice-skate (īs′skāt′), *v.,* **ice-skat·ed, ice-skat·ing.** to glide on ice by using skates. **—ice′-skat′er,** *n.*

ich·neu·mon (ik nōō′mən, -nyōō′-), *n.* a slender, flesh-eating Egyptian mammal that resembles a large weasel.

ich·thy·o·saur·us (ik′thē ə sôr′əs), *n.* any of various extinct fishlike reptiles, from 4 to 40 feet in length.

i·ci·cle (ī′si kəl), *n.* a tapered, hanging stick of ice formed by the freezing of dripping water.

ic·ing (ī′sing), *n.* a mixture of sugar, butter, egg whites, flavoring, etc., for covering cakes; frosting.

Ichthyosaurus (length to 40 ft.)

i·con (ī′kon), *n.* **1.** a picture or image. **2.** an image of Christ or a saint that is considered sacred.

i·con·o·clast (ī kon′ə klast′), *n.* a person who attacks beliefs, thoughts, or practices that most people accept. **—i·con′o·clas′tic,** *adj.*

-ics, a suffix used to form nouns meaning **1.** a field of knowledge or study: *electronics; mathematics.* **2.** a system or practice: *politics; tactics.* **3.** actions of a certain kind: *heroics; hysterics.*

i·cy (ī′sē), *adj.,* **i·ci·er, i·ci·est. 1.** covered with ice: *an icy pavement.* **2.** very cold: *An icy wind was blowing.* **3.** without warmth of feeling: *an icy look.* **—i′ci·ly** (ī′sə lē), *adv.* **—i′ci·ness,** *n.*

I′d (īd), contraction of *I would, I should,* or *I had.*

I.D., **1.** identification. **2.** Intelligence Department.

Ida., Idaho.

I·da·ho (ī′də hō′), *n.* a state in the NW United States. 83,557 sq. mi. *Cap.:* Boise. **—I′da·ho′an,** *n., adj.*

i·de·a (ī dē′ə), *n.* **1.** something pictured, thought, or believed in the mind; concept: *an idea of the nature of the universe.* **2.** an impression or hint: *Give me an idea of what you want.* **3.** a plan of action: *the idea of becoming an engineer.* [from a Greek word, which comes from *idein* "to see"]

i·de·al (ī dē′əl, ī dēl′), *n.* **1.** a perfect model or standard: *the ideals of freedom.* **2.** a person or thing looked upon as a model for imi-

tation: *The judge was his ideal.* **3.** a goal or aim. **—***adj.* **4.** regarded as perfect: *an ideal spot for a house.* **—i·de′al·ly,** *adv.*

i·de·al·ism (ī dē′ə liz′əm), *n.* the pursuit of high and noble goals: *Lincoln never lost his idealism.*

i·de·al·ist (ī dē′ə list), *n.* **1.** a person who pursues high and noble goals. **2.** a person who sees things as they should be and not as they actually are. **—i·de′al·is′tic,** *adj.* **—i·de′al·is′ti·cal·ly,** *adv.*

i·de·al·ize (ī dē′ə līz′), *v.,* **i·de·al·ized, i·de·al·iz·ing.** to consider as the very best: *John idealizes his father.*

i·den·ti·cal (ī den′ti kəl), *adj.* exactly the same; indistinguishable: *identical twins.* **—i·den′ti·cal·ly,** *adv.*

i·den·ti·fi·ca·tion (ī den′tə fə kā′shən), *n.* **1.** the act of identifying: *The identification of the criminal took a long time.* **2.** the state of being identified: *The general's identification with the victory made him popular.* **3.** a document, etc., that identifies one: *He always carries identification with him.*

i·den·ti·fy (ī den′tə fī′), *v.,* **i·den·ti·fied, i·den·ti·fy·ing. 1.** to recognize as being a particular person or thing: *He identified his pen by the initials on it.* **2.** to associate in feeling or action (usually fol. by *with*): *He didn't want to identify himself with their group.* **3.** to put oneself in the place of another: *to identify with the hero.* **—i·den′ti·fi′er,** *n.*

i·den·ti·ty (ī den′ti tē), *n., pl.* **i·den·ti·ties. 1.** the condition of being oneself and not another: *They recognized the author's identity by his style of writing.* **2.** an exact likeness: *an identity of interests.*

i·de·ol·o·gy (ī′dē ol′ə jē), *n., pl.* **i·de·ol·o·gies.** the beliefs and doctrines of a political or religious group.

ides (īdz), *n. (used as sing. or pl.)* (in the ancient Roman calendar) the 15th day of March, May, July, or October, and the 13th day of the other months.

id·i·o·cy (id′ē ə sē), *n.* **1.** the condition of being an idiot. **2.** utterly senseless or foolish behavior: *Running in front of cars is sheer idiocy.*

id·i·om (id′ē əm), *n.* **1.** an expression whose meaning must be learned as a whole, since it cannot be derived from the meanings of the separate words in it, as *to go for,* meaning "to like." **2.** a language or dialect: *the French idiom.*

id·i·o·mat·ic (id′ē ə mat′ik), *adj.* **1.** having the nature of an idiom: *an idiomatic expression.* **2.** having the special characteristics of a certain language: *Translate this into idiomatic English.* **—id′i·o·mat′i·cal·ly,** *adv.*

id·i·o·syn·cra·sy (id′ē ə sing′krə sē), *n., pl.* **id·i·o·syn·cra·sies.** a habit or characteristic that is unusual; peculiarity: *Wearing only yellow socks was an idiosyncrasy of his.* **—id·i·o·syn·crat·ic** (id′ē ō sin krat′ik), *adj.*

id·i·ot (id′ē ət), *n.* **1.** a person who from birth lacks almost all of the ordinary mental powers as a result of injury, disease, etc.; one who cannot develop beyond the mental age of three or four years. **2.** a completely foolish or senseless person.

id·i·ot·ic (id′ē ot′ik), *adj.* completely senseless or foolish: *idiotic behavior.* **—id′i·ot′i·cal·ly,** *adv.*

i·dle (īd′³l), *adj.,* **i·dler, i·dlest. 1.** not working; unemployed: *idle workmen.* **2.** not being used: *idle machinery.* **3.** avoiding work; lazy. **4.** of no real worth: *idle talk.* **—v., i·dled, i·dling. 5.** to pass (time) in idleness: *to idle the hours away.* **6.** (of a machine) to operate without doing useful work: *A car idles when it is out of gear.* **—i′dle·ness,** *n.* **—i′dly,** *adv.*

i·dler (īd′lər), *n.* a person who idles; loafer.

i·dol (īd′əl), *n.* **1.** an image worshiped as a deity. **2.** a person or thing greatly admired: *a movie idol.*

i·dol·a·trous (ī dol′ə trəs), *adj.* **1.** worshiping idols. **2.** blindly adoring; excessively devoted to a person or thing.

i·dol·a·try (ī dol′ə trē), *n.* **1.** religious worship of idols. **2.** excessive devotion to a person or thing.

i·dol·ize (īd′ºlīz′), *v., i·dol·ized, i·dol·iz·ing.* **1.** to worship as an idol. **2.** to admire excessively: *to idolize a movie star.* **—i′dol·i·za′tion,** *n.* **—i′dol·iz′er,** *n.*

i·dyll (īd′ºl), *n.* **1.** a short poem or prose story describing a scene in the country or any charmingly simple event. **2.** any charming and simple scene or event about which an idyll could be written. Also, **i′dyl.**

i·dyl·lic (ī dil′ik), *adj.* reminding one of the simple and charming pleasures of nature: *an idyllic afternoon on the lake.* **—i·dyl′li·cal·ly,** *adv.*

i.e., that is. [from the Latin phrase *id est*]

if (if), *conj.* **1.** in case; granting or supposing that; on condition that: *Stay home if it rains. I'll go if he goes.* **2.** even though: *an appreciative if small crowd.* **3.** whether: *See if anyone is there.* **4.** (used to express a wish): *If only the rain would stop!*

ig·loo (ig′lōō), *n., pl.* **ig·loos.** an Eskimo house or hut built of blocks of hard snow and shaped like a dome.

ig·ne·ous (ig′nē əs), *adj.* produced by intense heat or by volcanic activity: *igneous rock.*

ig·nite (ig nīt′), *v., ig·nit·ed, ig·nit·ing.* **1.** to set on fire; kindle: *to ignite logs.* **2.** to catch fire: *The oil ignited quickly.* **—ig·nit′a·ble,** *adj.*

ig·ni·tion (ig nish′ən), *n.* **1.** the act of setting on fire or catching fire. **2.** the system in a gasoline engine that ignites the fuel in the cylinder.

ig·no·ble (ig nō′bəl), *adj.* of low character; base; shameful: *Treason is an ignoble act.* **—ig·no′bly,** *adv.*

ig·no·min·i·ous (ig′nə min′ē əs), *adj.* causing dishonor; humiliating: *an ignominious defeat.* **—ig′no·min′i·ous·ly,** *adv.*

ig·no·min·y (ig′nə min′ē), *n.* public dishonor and disgrace: *The traitor suffered lasting ignominy.*

ig·no·ra·mus (ig′nə rā′məs, ig′nə ram′əs), *adj.* an ignorant or dull-witted person.

ig·no·rance (ig′nər əns), *n.* lack of knowledge or information.

ig·no·rant (ig′nər ənt), *adj.* **1.** lacking in knowledge or training; unlearned. **2.** uninformed; unaware: *He was ignorant of their intentions.* **3.** showing a lack of knowledge: *an ignorant statement.* **—ig′no·rant·ly,** *adv.*

ig·nore (ig nôr′), *v., ig·nored, ig·nor·ing.* to take no notice of: *They ignored his behavior.*

i·gua·na (i gwä′nə), *n.* any of several large tropical American lizards.

il-, a form of the prefix **in-,** used before words beginning with *l*: *illegal; illiterate.*

Iguana
(length to 6 ft.)

Il·i·ad (il′ē əd), *n.* a long poem of ancient Greece that describes the Trojan War, believed to have been written by Homer around 800 B.C.

ilk (ilk), *n.* family, class, or kind: *he and all his ilk; a person of that ilk.*

ill (il), *adj.,* **worse** (wûrs), **worst** (wûrst). **1.** suffering from a disease or disorder; sick. **2. ill at ease,** uncomfortable; nervous: *I'm always ill at ease at parties.*

Ill., Illinois.

ill-bred (il′bred′), *adj.* showing lack of proper breeding; rude: *ill-bred behavior.*

il·le·gal (i lē′gəl), *adj.* not legal; contrary to existing laws and rules. **—il·le′gal·ly,** *adv.*

il·leg·i·ble (i lej′ə bəl), *adj.* impossible or hard to read: *an illegible handwriting.* **—il·leg′i·bly,** *adv.*

il·le·git·i·mate (il′i jit′ə mit), *adj.* **1.** not legitimate; illegal: *an illegitimate suspension of the constitution.* **2.** born to parents who are not married to each other: *an illegitimate child.* **—il·le·git·i·ma·cy** (il′i jit′ə mə sē), *n.*

ill-fat·ed (il′fā′tid), *adj.* destined to end unhappily: *The captain set out on his ill-fated journey.*

ill-fa·vored (il′fā′vərd), *adj.* **1.** unpleasant to look at; ugly: *an ill-favored girl.* **2.** offensive; unpleasant: *ill-favored remarks.*

il·lib·er·al (i lib′ər əl), *adj.* **1.** narrow-minded; bigoted: *an illiberal community.* **2.** not generous; stingy.

il·lic·it (i lis′it), *adj.* not permitted or authorized; improper: *illicit smuggling of goods.* **—il·lic′it·ly,** *adv.*

il·lim·it·a·ble (i lim′i tə bəl), *adj.* not limited; boundless: *an illimitable quantity.*

Il·li·nois (il′ə noi′), *n.* a state in the midwestern United States. 56,400 sq. mi. *Cap.:* Springfield. **—Il·li·nois·an** (il′ə noi′ən, il′ə·noi′zən), *n., adj.*

il·lit·er·a·cy (i lit′ər ə sē), *n.* the lack of the ability to read and write.

il·lit·er·ate (i lit′ər it), *adj.* **1.** unable to read and write. **2.** showing a lack of education: *He wrote an illiterate paper.* **3.** showing lack of knowledge in a particular field: *He is musically illiterate.* **—n. 4.** an illiterate person: *The army won't accept illiterates.* **—il·lit′er·ate·ly,** *adv.*

WISCONSIN
LAKE MICHIGAN
IOWA
Rockford
Chicago
Rock River
Joliet
Rock Island
Peoria
Illinois
Mississippi R.
Springfield
Decatur
INDIANA
Missouri R.
East St. Louis
St. Louis
MISSOURI
Wabash River
Ohio R.
0 50 100 150
MILES
KENTUCKY

ill-man·nered (il′man′ərd), *adj.* having bad manners; impolite; rude.

ill-na·tured (il′nā′chərd), *adj.* having or showing an

unpleasant character or disposition: *an ill-natured remark; an ill-natured girl.* —**ill′·na′tured·ly,** *adv.*

ill·ness (il′nis), *n.* the state of being ill; sickness: *Illness kept the man out of work.*

il·log·i·cal (i loj′i kəl), *adj.* not logical; not showing good sense or reasoning: *an illogical decision.* —**il·log′i·cal·ly,** *adv.*

ill-tem·pered (il′tem′pərd), *adj.* having or showing a bad temper; irritable.

ill-treat (il′trēt′), *v.* to treat badly; maltreat.

il·lu·mi·nate (i loo′mə nāt′), *v.,* **il·lu·mi·nat·ed, il·lu·mi·nat·ing. 1.** to light up: *The sun illuminated the dark corners of the room.* **2.** to make clear or understandable: *to illuminate the meaning of a sentence.* **3.** to decorate (a manuscript or page) with color, gold, or the like. Also, **illumine.** —**il·lu′mi·na′tor,** *n.*

il·lu·mi·na·tion (i loo′mə nā′shən), *n.* **1.** the act of illuminating, or the state of being illuminated. **2.** lighting; lights: *inadequate illumination to read by.* **3.** intellectual or spiritual enlightenment. **4.** the decoration of a manuscript: *ornate illumination.*

il·lu·mine (i loo′min), *v.,* **il·lu·mined, il·lu·min·ing.** another word for **illuminate.**

illus., 1. illustrated. **2.** illustration.

ill-use (il′yooz′), *v.,* **ill-used, ill-using.** to treat badly or cruelly: *He ill-used his best friends.*

il·lu·sion (i loo′zhən), *n.* **1.** an appearance that deceives by producing a false impression: *Stereo slides create the illusion of depth.* **2.** a false idea: *He was under the illusion that he lived in the biggest house in the world.*

il·lu·so·ry (i loo′sə rē), *adj.* causing illusion; deceptive: *The illusory peace soon ended.* Also, **il·lu·sive** (i loo′siv).

Optical illusion
Line AB equals
line BC

il·lus·trate (il′ə strāt′, i lus′trāt), *v.,* **il·lus·trat·ed, il·lus·trat·ing. 1.** to make clear by examples or comparisons: *to illustrate the problems of the presidency.* **2.** to furnish with drawings or pictures that help to clarify the text: *to illustrate a book.*

il·lus·tra·tion (il′ə strā′shən), *n.* **1.** something that illustrates, such as a picture in a book or magazine. **2.** a comparison or example. **3.** the act of illustrating.

il·lus·tra·tive (i lus′trə tiv, il′ə strā′tiv), *adj.* serving to illustrate: *to add illustrative material to a book.*

il·lus·tra·tor (il′ə strā′tər), *n.* an artist who makes illustrations.

il·lus·tri·ous (i lus′trē əs), *adj.* **1.** highly renowned; famous: *the illustrious Senator.* **2.** made famous by many noble accomplishments: *an illustrious career.* —**il·lus′tri·ous·ly,** *adv.* —**il·lus′tri·ous·ness,** *n.*

ill′ will′, hostile feeling; hostility or hatred: *He no longer bears his opponent any ill will.*

im-, a form of the prefix **in-,** used before words beginning with *m, b,* or *p: immoral; imbed; impolite.*

I'm (īm), contraction of *I am.*

im·age (im′ij), *n.* **1.** a physical likeness of a person, animal, or thing, such as a photograph, painting, or statue. **2.** an appearance of an object produced by reflection: *He saw his image in the lake.* **3.** the picture formed by a mirror or lens. **4.** an idea or concept: *Try to form an image of what happened that night.* **5.** a copy or facsimile: *He is the image of his father.* **6.** a figure of speech: *The poet used the image of a roaring sea.* **7.** an idol or object of worship.

im·age·ry (im′ij rē), *n.* images, esp. as used in poetry: *The poet used the imagery of the sun going to sleep and rising.*

im·ag·i·na·ble (i maj′ə nə bəl), *adj.* capable of being imagined: *the tallest building imaginable.* —**im·ag′i·na·bly,** *adv.*

im·ag·i·nar·y (i maj′ə ner′ē), *adj.* existing only in imagination; not real: *an imaginary trip to Mars.*

im·ag·i·na·tion (i maj′ə nā′shən), *n.* **1.** the ability to form images or thoughts of things or concepts that are not present or that never existed: *The storyteller's imagination created giants and ghosts.* **2.** the creative or skillful use of resources, materials, etc.; resourcefulness: *The house was built with imagination.*

im·ag·i·na·tive (i maj′ə nə tiv, i maj′ə nā′tiv), *adj.* rich in or showing imagination: *an imaginative child; an imaginative color scheme.* —**im·ag′i·na·tive·ly,** *adv.*

im·ag·ine (i maj′in), *v.,* **im·ag·ined, im·ag·in·ing. 1.** to form a mental image of (something not actually present): *to imagine a great castle.* **2.** to believe or suppose: *I imagine you're right.*

im·be·cile (im′bi səl), *n.* **1.** a person lacking the usual capacity for mental growth; one who cannot develop beyond the mental age of seven or eight. **2.** a dull-witted or foolish person. —**im·be·cil·i·ty** (im′bi sil′i tē), *n.*

im·bed (im bed′), *v.,* **im·bed·ded, im·bed·ding.** another spelling of **embed.**

im·bibe (im bīb′), *v.,* **im·bibed, im·bib·ing. 1.** to drink: *to imbibe liquor.* **2.** to absorb or soak up: *The roots imbibed all the water.* **3.** to take into the mind and understand: *to imbibe new ideas.*

im·bro·glio (im brōl′yō), *n.* a confused state of affairs, or a complicated disagreement: *an imbroglio over control of the river.*

im·bue (im byoo′), *v.,* **im·bued, im·bu·ing. 1.** to inspire, as with feelings, opinions, etc.: *to imbue a man with hope.* **2.** to give a certain quality or character to: *Twilight imbued the sky with redness.*

im·i·tate (im′i tāt′), *v.,* **im·i·tat·ed, im·i·tat·ing. 1.** to follow or try to follow: *He imitates his uncle's way of dressing.* **2.** to copy, mimic, or counterfeit: *to imitate a famous singer.* **3.** to have the appearance of: *a plastic made to imitate wood.* —**im′i·ta′tor,** *n.*

im·i·ta·tion (im′i tā′shən), *n.* **1.** the result of imitating; a copy or counterfeit: *That painting is an imitation.* **2.** the act of imitating: *He did a funny imitation of his father.* —*adj.* **3.** designed to imitate a genuine article: *imitation velvet.*

im·i·ta·tive (im′i tā′tiv), *adj.* imitating or copying; made or done in imitation: *Words such as "boom" and "cuckoo" are imitative of sounds.*

im·mac·u·late (i mak′yə lit), *adj.* **1.** free from spot or stain; spotlessly clean: *an immaculate tablecloth.*

2. free from moral blemish; pure: *to lead a life of immaculate goodness.* —im·mac′u·late·ly, *adv.*

im·ma·te·ri·al (im′ə tēr′ē əl), *adj.* 1. of no importance: *It is immaterial to the case whether that witness appears or not.* 2. not material; spiritual: *Ghosts are immaterial beings.* —im′ma·te′ri·al·ly, *adv.*

im·ma·ture (im′ə tŏŏr′, -tyŏŏr′), *adj.* 1. not mature, ripe, or developed: *immature fruit.* 2. not showing maturity: *immature behavior.* —im′ma·ture′ly, *adv.* —im′ma·tu′ri·ty, *n.*

im·meas·ur·a·ble (i mezh′ər ə bəl), *adj.* incapable of being measured; limitless: *the immeasurable expanse of the sky.* —im·meas′ur·a·bly, *adv.*

im·me·di·ate (i mē′dē it), *adj.* 1. occurring or accomplished without delay; instant: *Your immediate reply is requested.* 2. nearest or next: *the immediate future.* 3. being the closest in relation: *a member of the immediate family.* —im·me′di·ate·ly, *adv.*

im·me·mo·ri·al (im′ə môr′ē əl), *adj.* extending back beyond memory or record: *from time immemorial.*

im·mense (i mens′), *adj.* vast; very great: *an immense storehouse of knowledge.* —im·mense′ly, *adv.*

im·men·si·ty (i men′si tē), *n.* an enormous extent; vastness; hugeness: *the immensity of the desert.*

im·merse (i mûrs′), *v.,* im·mersed, im·mers·ing. 1. to put or plunge into a liquid: *to immerse clothes in water.* 2. to involve deeply; absorb: *He totally immersed himself in his studies.* 3. to baptize by immersion. —im·mers′i·ble, *adj.*

im·mer·sion (i mûr′zhən, i mûr′shən), *n.* 1. the act of immersing, or the state of being immersed. 2. baptism in which the whole body of a person is submerged in water. 3. the state of being deeply absorbed: *His total immersion in his business left little time for a hobby.*

im·mi·grant (im′ə grənt), *n.* a person who comes to a country in order to live there permanently (distinguished from *emigrant*): *America became a haven for immigrants.*

im·mi·grate (im′ə grāt′), *v.,* im·mi·grat·ed, im·mi·grat·ing. to come to a country in order to live there permanently (distinguished from *emigrate*).

im·mi·gra·tion (im′ə grā′shən), *n.* 1. the act of immigrating: *He has lived here since his immigration to the New World.* 2. a group or number of immigrants: *There was an increase in immigration last year.*

im·mi·nent (im′ə nənt), *adj.* likely to occur at any moment: *an imminent storm.* —im′mi·nence, *n.* —Usage. See eminent.

im·mo·bile (i mō′bil), *adj.* 1. not mobile; incapable of being moved; immovable. 2. not moving; motionless: *He lay immobile on the bed.* —im′mo·bil′i·ty, *n.*

im·mo·bi·lize (i mō′bə līz′), *v.,* im·mo·bi·lized, im·mo·bi·liz·ing. 1. to make immobile. 2. to prevent from functioning or producing: *A strike immobilized the steel industry.* —im·mo′bi·li·za′tion, *n.*

im·mod·er·ate (i mod′ər it), *adj.* not moderate; exceeding reasonable limits: *The woman was immoderate in her love of candy.* —im·mod′er·ate·ly, *adv.*

im·mod·est (i mod′ist), *adj.* not modest; lacking restraint in conduct or speech; shameless: *immodest words; immodest clothing.* —im·mod′est·ly, *adv.* —im·mod′es·ty, *n.*

im·mo·la·tion (im′ə lā′shən), *n.* a sacrifice to a god or idol.

im·mor·al (i môr′əl, i mor′əl), *adj.* not moral; wicked, sinful, or evil: *immoral behavior; an immoral person.* —im·mo·ral·i·ty (im′ə ral′i tē), *n.* —im·mor′al·ly, *adv.*

im·mor·tal (i môr′təl), *adj.* 1. not subject to death; everlasting: *immortal gods; an immortal poem.* —*n.* 2. a being that is immortal. 3. a person whose fame will last forever: *Shakespeare is one of the immortals of poetry.* —im·mor′tal·ly, *adv.*

im·mor·tal·i·ty (im′ôr tal′i tē), *n.* 1. the state or quality of being immortal; unending life. 2. lasting fame.

im·mor·tal·ize (i môr′t^əlīz′), *v.,* im·mor·tal·ized, im·mor·tal·iz·ing. 1. to make immortal; cause to live forever: *The ancient Greeks immortalized their heroes.* 2. to bestow everlasting fame upon: *The sculptor Phidias was immortalized by the Parthenon.*

im·mov·a·ble (i mōō′və bəl), *adj.* 1. not able to be moved; fixed or stationary: *immovable mountains.* 2. incapable of being changed: *The Senator held to his immovable purpose.* 3. incapable of being affected with feeling: *He remained immovable in spite of our pleading.* —im·mov′a·bly, *adv.*

im·mune (i myōōn′), *adj.* 1. protected from or incapable of catching a disease. 2. exempt; not affected by: *immune to criticism.*

im·mu·ni·ty (i myōō′ni tē), *n., pl.* for def. 2 im·mu·ni·ties. 1. the state of being protected from catching a particular disease: *Vaccination gives immunity to smallpox.* 2. exemption from an obligation: *The clergy has immunity from military service.*

im·mu·nize (im′yə nīz′), *v.,* im·mu·nized, im·mu·niz·ing. to make immune. —im′mu·ni·za′tion, *n.*

im·mu·ta·ble (i myōō′tə bəl), *adj.* not able to be changed or altered: *an immutable decision.* —im·mu′ta·bly, *adv.*

imp (imp), *n.* 1. a little devil or demon; an evil spirit. 2. a mischievous child.

imp., 1. imperative. 2. imperfect. 3. imperial. 4. import. 5. important. 6. imported. 7. improper.

im·pact (im′pakt), *n.* 1. the striking of one object against another: *The impact of the rock broke the window.* 2. influence or effect: *The President's speech had a great impact on Congress.*

im·pair (im pâr′), *v.* to make or cause to become worse; weaken or damage: *Reading in poor light impaired her eyesight.* —im·pair′ment, *n.*

im·pal·a (im pal′ə, im pä′lə), *n.* an African antelope noted for its ability to leap.

Impala
(2½ ft. high
at shoulder)

im·pale (im pāl/), v., **im·paled, im·pal·ing.** 1. to pierce with any pointed object, esp. as a means of torture or execution: *The soldier was impaled on his own spear.* 2. to fix in a position by means of a pointed object: *to mount insects by impaling them.* —**im·pale/ment**, n.

im·pal·pa·ble (im pal/pə bəl), adj. 1. not able to be felt by the sense of touch; intangible. 2. not able to be readily grasped by the mind: *to argue about impalpable differences.* —**im·pal/pa·bly**, adv.

im·pan·el (im pan/əl), v., **im·pan·eled** or **im·pan·elled; im·pan·el·ing** or **im·pan·el·ling.** 1. to enter on a panel or list for jury duty. 2. to select (a jury) from the panel. —**im·pan/el·ment**, n.

im·part (im pärt/), v. 1. to make known; tell; relate: *to impart information.* 2. to give or bestow: *The dim lights impart an air of coziness to the room.* —**im·part/a·ble**, adj.

im·par·tial (im pär/shəl), adj. not partial or biased: *to render an impartial judgment.* —**im·par·ti·al·i·ty** (im pär/shē al/i tē), n. —**im·par/tial·ly**, adv.

im·pass·a·ble (im pas/ə bəl), adj. not passable; not allowing passage over, through, along, etc.: *Floods made the bridge impassable.* —**im·pass/a·bly**, adv.

im·passe (im/pas, im pas/), n. a position from which there is no escape; deadlock: *The negotiations reached an impasse.*

im·pas·sioned (im pash/ənd), adj. filled with emotion; ardent: *an impassioned plea.* —**im·pas/sioned·ly**, adv.

im·pas·sive (im pas/iv), adj. without emotion; untouched or unmoved: *The family's suffering left the neighbors impassive.* —**im·pas/sive·ly**, adv.

im·pa·tience (im pā/shəns), n. lack of patience; eager desire for change: *the people's impatience with corrupt officials.*

im·pa·tient (im pā/shənt), adj. not patient; lacking patience: *to be impatient to get started; to be impatient with latecomers.* —**im·pa/tient·ly**, adv.

im·peach (im pēch/), v. 1. to accuse (an official) before a court, legislative body, etc., of misconduct in office: *The House of Representatives impeached President Andrew Johnson.* 2. to challenge the credibility of: *The lawyer impeached the testimony of the witness.* [from an early French word *empecher*, which comes from Latin *impedicāre* "to restrain"] —**im·peach/er**, n. —**im·peach/ment**, n.

im·pec·ca·ble (im pek/ə bəl), adj. without flaw; faultless: *to have impeccable manners; to speak impeccable French.* —**im·pec/ca·bly**, adv.

im·pe·cu·ni·ous (im/pə kyōō/nē əs), adj. having little or no money: *an impecunious student.*

im·pede (im pēd/), v., **im·ped·ed, im·ped·ing.** to delay or interfere with; hinder; obstruct: *The bumpy road impeded the car's progress.*

im·ped·i·ment (im ped/ə mənt), n. 1. anything that causes delay or difficulty; any obstruction or obstacle: *Illiteracy is an impediment to progress.* 2. any physical defect that impedes speech.

im·pel (im pel/), v., **im·pelled, im·pel·ling.** 1. to drive or urge forward; incite to action: *Fright impelled the cat to hide.* 2. to drive onward: *A strong wind impels the boat toward the shore.*

im·pend (im pend/), v. to be about to occur; threaten: *When negotiations failed, war impended.*

im·pen·e·tra·ble (im pen/i trə bəl), adj. 1. unable to be penetrated, pierced, or entered: *an impenetrable jungle.* 2. incapable of being understood: *an impenetrable mystery.* —**im·pen/e·tra·bly**, adv.

im·pen·i·tent (im pen/i t°nt), adj. not feeling remorse or sorrow for a sin or crime: *an impenitent sinner.* —**im·pen/i·tence**, n. —**im·pen/i·tent·ly**, adv.

im·per·a·tive (im per/ə tiv), adj. 1. absolutely necessary; unavoidable: *It is imperative that you come.* 2. describing the mood of a verb used to express a command or a direct request. In the sentence *Call me at eight,* the verb *call* is in the imperative mood. —n. 3. the imperative mood. 4. a verb form in the imperative mood.

im·per·cep·ti·ble (im/pər sep/tə bəl), adj. 1. very slight or gradual: *an imperceptible change.* 2. not perceived by the senses: *Some sounds heard by dogs are imperceptible to men.* —**im/per·cep/ti·bly**, adv.

im·per·fect (im pûr/fikt), adj. 1. having defects: *an imperfect garment.* 2. not perfect; incomplete: *imperfect knowledge of Spanish.* —**im·per/fect·ly**, adv.

im·per·fec·tion (im/pər fek/shən), n. 1. a flaw or defect: *The material had many imperfections.* 2. the condition of being imperfect: *Imperfection is a human quality.*

im·pe·ri·al (im pēr/ē əl), adj. 1. referring or belonging to an empire or emperor: *the imperial navy; imperial government.* 2. of commanding quality; regal: *She spoke in an imperial voice.* —**im·pe/ri·al·ly**, adv.

im·pe·ri·al·ism (im pēr/ē ə liz/əm), n. the policy of extending the rule of a nation over foreign countries or of acquiring colonies: *The 20th century witnessed the decline of imperialism.* —**im·pe/ri·al·ist**, n., adj. —**im·pe/ri·al·is/tic**, adj.

im·per·il (im per/əl), v., **im·per·iled** or **im·per·illed; im·per·il·ing** or **im·per·il·ling.** to put in peril; endanger: *The heavy rains imperiled the crops.*

im·pe·ri·ous (im pēr/ē əs), adj. 1. marked by haughtiness or arrogance; overbearing: *an imperious command.* 2. urgent; imperative: *an imperious need.* —**im·pe/ri·ous·ly**, adv.

im·per·ish·a·ble (im per/i shə bəl), adj. not perishable; indestructible; enduring. —**im·per/ish·a·bly**, adv.

im·per·son·al (im pûr/sə n°l), adj. 1. having no reference to a particular person; general: *impersonal comments.* 2. having no personality or human traits: *impersonal forces of nature.* 3. describing a verb used in the third person singular without a definite subject. The place of the subject is usually taken by the pronoun *it.* In the sentence *It snows in winter,* *snows* is an impersonal verb. —**im·per/son·al·ly**, adv.

im·per·son·ate (im pûr/sə nāt/), v., **im·per·son·at·ed, im·per·son·at·ing.** 1. to pretend to be: *to impersonate a police officer.* 2. to act the part of, esp. on stage: *The ballerina impersonated a swan.* —**im·per/son·a/tion**, n. —**im·per/son·a/tor**, n.

im·per·ti·nence (im pûr′t³nəns), *n.* unmannerly presumption; insolence: *He ought to apologize for such impertinence.*

im·per·ti·nent (im pûr′t³nənt), *adj.* 1. presumptuous; rude; uncivil: *to ask an impertinent question.* 2. not pertinent; irrelevant or unimportant: *Omit all the impertinent details.* —**im·per′ti·nent·ly,** *adv.*

im·per·turb·a·ble (im′pər tûr′bə bəl), *adj.* incapable of being annoyed or agitated; not easily excited; calm: *She remained imperturbable throughout the crisis.* —**im′per·turb′a·bly,** *adv.*

im·per·vi·ous (im pûr′vē əs), *adj.* 1. not permitting penetration or passage: *to make a coat impervious to rain; a shield impervious to arrows.* 2. incapable of being injured: *a material impervious to abuse.* 3. incapable of being moved or affected: *impervious to criticism.* [from the Latin word *impervius* "having no way through," which comes from *in-* "not, without" + *per* "through" + *via* "way"]

im·pet·u·os·i·ty (im pech′oo os′i tē), *n.* the condition of being impetuous; an action marked by sudden or rash energy or emotion: *The impetuosity of his remarks startled the audience.*

im·pet·u·ous (im pech′oo əs), *adj.* 1. characterized by sudden or rash energy, action, or emotion; impulsive: *His impetuous action took us all by surprise.* 2. moving with great force; violent: *an impetuous wind.* —**im·pet′u·ous·ly,** *adv.*

im·pe·tus (im′pi təs), *n.* a moving force; stimulus: *A long drought gave impetus to the migration.*

im·pi·e·ty (im pī′i tē), *n., pl* for def. 2 **im·pi·e·ties.** 1. a lack of piety or of the proper respect or attention: *the impiety of a son toward his parents.* 2. an impious act: *The prophet denounced the king's impieties.*

im·pinge (im pinj′), *v.,* **im·pinged, im·ping·ing.** 1. to strike; dash; collide (usually fol. by *on, upon,* or *against*): *flashes of light impinging on the eye.* 2. to encroach; infringe (usually fol. by *on* or *upon*): *to impinge on another's rights.*

im·pi·ous (im′pē əs), *adj.* not pious or respectful; irreligious: *The impious son abandoned his aged father.* —**im′pi·ous·ly,** *adv.*

imp·ish (im′pish), *adj.* like an imp; mischievous: *to take impish delight in a prank.* —**imp′ish·ly,** *adv.* —**imp′ish·ness,** *n.*

im·plac·a·ble (im plak′ə bəl, im plā′kə bəl), *adj.* not able to be pleased or appeased; irreconcilable: *implacable enemies; implacable anger.* —**im·plac′a·bly,** *adv.*

im·plant (im plant′), *v.* to impress deeply; instill: *to implant high aspirations in a student.*

im·plau·si·ble (im plô′zə bəl), *adj.* not plausible; lacking the appearance of truth: *an implausible story.* —**im·plau′si·bly,** *adv.*

im·ple·ment (im′plə mənt), *n.* 1. an instrument; tool; utensil: *farm implements.* —*v.* (im′plə ment′). 2. to carry out; fulfill: *to implement a reform.*

im·pli·cate (im′plə kāt′), *v.,* **im·pli·cat·ed, im·pli·cat·ing.** to involve as being closely connected, esp. in a

crime or charge: *Don't implicate me in your schemes.*

im·pli·ca·tion (im′plə kā′shən), *n.* 1. something that is implied or suggested: *Experts are studying the implications of the recent elections.* 2. the act of implying, or the state of being implied: *to make a point by implication.* 3. the act of implicating, or the state of being implicated: *He denied any implication with the hoodlums.*

im·plic·it (im plis′it), *adj.* 1. implied rather than directly stated: *Disapproval was implicit in his father's reaction.* 2. unquestioning; absolute: *implicit obedience; implicit faith.* —**im·plic′it·ly,** *adv.*

im·plore (im plôr′), *v.,* **im·plored, im·plor·ing.** to beg urgently, as for aid or mercy: *I implored him not to take such risks. They implored the queen's help.*

im·ply (im plī′), *v.,* **im·plied, im·ply·ing.** 1. to indicate or suggest without directly saying: *His smile implied approval.* 2. to involve as a necessary condition: *Much knowledge implies much study.* —**Usage. See infer.**

im·po·lite (im′pə līt′), *adj.* not polite or courteous; rude. —**im′po·lite′ly,** *adv.* —**im′po·lite′ness,** *n.*

im·port (im pôrt′), *v.* 1. to bring in (merchandise) from a foreign country: *to import coffee from Brazil.* 2. to signify or imply; mean: *What does his election import for the farmers?* —*n.* (im′pôrt). 3. something imported from abroad: *imports from Japan.* 4. meaning; significance: *The commentators tried to explain the import of this event.* [from the Latin word *importāre* "to carry in"] —**im·port′er,** *n.*

im·por·tance (im pôr′t³ns), *n.* 1. the quality of being important: *the importance of a good education.* 2. important position, rank, or influence: *The advisers were men of importance.*

im·por·tant (im pôr′t³nt), *adj.* 1. of much significance; very meaningful: *an important task.* 2. of much influence, authority, or distinction: *an important artist.* —**im·por′tant·ly,** *adv.*

im·por·ta·tion (im′pôr tā′shən), *n.* 1. the act of importing: *the importation of wine.* 2. something imported: *Her dress is a new importation from Spain.*

im·por·tu·nate (im pôr′chə nit), *adj.* 1. urgently requesting again and again: *an importunate beggar; to avoid importunate bill collectors.* 2. made repeatedly: *importunate requests for funds.*

im·por·tune (im′pôr toon′, -tyoon′, im pôr′chən), *v.,* **im·por·tuned, im·por·tun·ing.** to annoy repeatedly with urgent demands: *They importuned the unwilling mayor to run for the Senate.*

im·por·tu·ni·ty (im′pôr too′ni tē, -tyoo′-), *n., pl.* for def. 2 **im·por·tu·ni·ties.** 1. persistence in making demands: *The beggar's importunity annoyed the tourists.* 2. urgent and persistent requests or demands: *I finally gave in to his importunities.*

im·pose (im pōz′), *v.,* **im·posed, im·pos·ing.** 1. to put or set on as a burden, tax, or obligation: *to impose a fine of $25 on speeders; to impose a tax on silks.* 2. to establish by authority: *The majority imposed its will in the council.* 3. to force or thrust (oneself)

---

act, āble, dâre, ärt; ebb, ēqual; if, īce; hot, ōver, ôrder; oil; book; ooze; out; up, ûrge; ə = *a* as in *alone*; ³ as in *button* (but′³n), *fire* (fi³r); chief; shoe; thin; ᵺat; zh as in *measure* (mezh′ər). See full key inside cover.

upon others. **4. impose on** (or **upon**), to take unfair advantage of (friendship, hospitality, etc.): *I'd stay, but I don't want to impose on you.* —**im·pos′er,** *n.*

im·pos·ing (im pō′zing), *adj.* very impressive; making an impression on the mind by great size, appearance, or importance: *an imposing list of members; an imposing monument.* —**im·pos′ing·ly,** *adv.*

im·po·si·tion (im′pə zish′ən), *n.* **1.** the laying on of something, such as a burden or obligation: *the imposition of new taxes.* **2.** something imposed by authority, such as a task or requirement: *The increase in the bus fare is a new imposition.* **3.** a taking advantage of a person, friendship, etc.: *Would it be too great an imposition to ask you to drive me home?*

im·pos·si·bil·i·ty (im pos′ə bil′i tē), *n., pl.* for def. 2 **im·pos·si·bil·i·ties. 1.** the quality of being impossible: *the impossibility of coming to a quick decision.* **2.** something impossible: *His election was considered an impossibility.*

im·pos·si·ble (im pos′ə bəl), *adj.* **1.** not possible; unable to be, exist, or happen. **2.** incapable of being true; beyond belief: *When I heard the news, I said that such a thing was impossible.* **3.** beyond one's ability to solve, manage, or the like: *an impossible situation; an impossible child.* —**im·pos′si·bly,** *adv.*

im·post (im′pōst), *n.* a tax or duty: *an impost on foreign cars.*

im·pos·tor (im pos′tər), *n.* a person who deceives by pretending to be someone else: *He was not the true heir but an impostor.* Also, **im·pos′ter.**

im·pos·ture (im pos′chər), *n.* the act or practice of deceiving by pretending to be somebody else: *His imposture as a doctor was quickly discovered.*

im·po·tent (im′pə tᵊnt), *adj.* lacking power or ability; ineffective: *The king was impotent against the uprising.* —**im′po·tence,** *n.* —**im′po·tent·ly,** *adv.*

im·pound (im pound′), *v.* **1.** to shut up in a pound: *to impound stray cats.* **2.** to seize and retain in the custody of the law: *The judge impounded the company's records.* —**im·pound′er,** *n.*

im·pov·er·ish (im pov′ər ish), *v.* **1.** to make poor: *Big medical bills impoverished the patient.* **2.** to exhaust the strength or richness of: *Bad farming impoverished the soil.* —**im·pov′er·ish·ment,** *n.*

im·prac·ti·ca·ble (im prak′tə kə bəl), *adj.* not practicable; not suited for practical use: *impracticable ideas.*

im·prac·ti·cal (im prak′ti kəl), *adj.* not practical; useless or foolish: *an impractical plan; an impractical man who never saved a cent.*

im·pre·ca·tion (im′prə kā′shən), *n.* **1.** the act of cursing or of calling down evil upon someone. **2.** an evil wish; curse: *to shout imprecations at an enemy.*

im·pre·cise (im′pri sīs′), *adj.* not precise or exact; vague: *the imprecise use of words; imprecise notions of life in America.* —**im′pre·cise′ly,** *adv.*

im·preg·na·ble (im preg′nə bəl), *adj.* strong enough to resist attack: *an impregnable fortress; an impregnable argument.* —**im·preg′na·bil′i·ty,** *n.* —**im·preg′na·bly,** *adv.*

im·preg·nate (im preg′nāt), *v.,* **im·preg·nat·ed, im·**

preg·nat·ing. **1.** to make pregnant; fertilize. **2.** to fill thoroughly; saturate: *to impregnate a cloth with furniture polish.* —**im′preg·na′tion,** *n.*

im·pre·sa·ri·o (im′pri sär′ē ō′), *n., pl.* **im·pre·sa·ri·os.** a person who organizes or manages public entertainments: *an opera impresario.* [from an Italian word, which comes from *impresa* "undertaking"]

im·press¹ (im pres′), *v.* **1.** to affect deeply in mind or feelings: *The student's recital impressed the audience.* **2.** to fix firmly in the mind: *I want to impress on you the need for promptness.* **3.** to press or stamp upon; imprint: *to impress wax with a seal.* [from the Latin word *impressus,* the past participle of *imprimere* "to press into or upon"]

im·press² (im pres′), *v.* to press or force into service: *The British used to impress American sailors into their navy.* [from *im-* + *press²*]

im·pres·sion (im presh′ən), *n.* **1.** a strong effect produced on the mind or feelings: *The new play made a favorable impression on the audience.* **2.** a vague or indistinct notion or belief: *I was under the impression that he had moved.* **3.** a mark produced by pressure: *the impression of a head on the pillow.*

im·pres·sion·a·ble (im presh′ə nə bəl), *adj.* easily impressed or influenced: *The impressionable child believed any tale.* —**im·pres′sion·a·bly,** *adv.*

im·pres·sive (im pres′iv), *adj.* making a strong impression on the mind; imposing: *an impressive view.* —**im·pres′sive·ly,** *adv.* —**im·pres′sive·ness,** *n.*

im·print (im′print), *n.* **1.** a mark made by pressure: *the imprint of shoes in the snow.* **2.** the influence and effect left by a person or thing: *A great president leaves his imprint on history. Hunger left its imprint on the boy's face.* **3.** the publisher's name together with the place and date of publication printed on the title page of a book. —*v.* (im print′). **4.** to produce a mark by pressure: *to imprint wax with a seal.* **5.** to fix firmly in the mind: *The mountains of Greece are permanently imprinted in my memory.*

im·pris·on (im priz′ən), *v.* to put in prison or in a place like a prison: *to be imprisoned for stealing.* —**im·pris′on·ment,** *n.*

im·prob·a·bil·i·ty (im prob′ə bil′i tē), *n., pl.* for def. 2 **im·prob·a·bil·i·ties. 1.** the quality of being improbable: *the improbability of snow in June.* **2.** something improbable or unlikely: *Events that were once considered improbabilities have become realities.*

im·prob·a·ble (im prob′ə bəl), *adj.* not probable; unlikely to be or happen. —**im·prob′a·bly,** *adv.*

im·promp·tu (im promp′tōō, -tyōō), *adj.* **1.** made or done without previous planning: *an impromptu party.* —*adv.* **2.** without previous preparation; offhand: *to deliver a speech impromptu.*

im·prop·er (im prop′ər), *adj.* not proper; incorrect or unsuitable: *an improper address; clothes that were improper for the occasion.* —**im·prop′er·ly,** *adv.*

improp′er frac′tion, a fraction such as $^3/_2$, $^{12}/_7$, etc., in which the numerator is larger than the denominator. See also **proper fraction.**

im·pro·pri·e·ty (im′prə prī′i tē), *n., pl.* for def. 2 **im·pro·pri·e·ties. 1.** the condition of being improper: *the* *impropriety of talking during a religious service.* **2.** an improper or unsuitable act, expression, etc.

im·prove (im proٯov′), *v.,* **im·proved, im·prov·ing. 1.** to make or become better: *The man improved his house by adding a new room. Has your health improved?* **2.** to make good use of; turn to account: *He improved his free time by reading.* **3. improve on,** to make improvement on: *to improve on old ways.*

im·prove·ment (im proٯov′mənt), *n.* **1.** the act of improving, or the state of being improved: *Her health has shown some improvement.* **2.** a change or addition that adds value: *to make improvements on a house.* **3.** a thing or person that is superior to what went before: *These cool days are a real improvement.*

im·prov·i·dent (im prov′i dənt), *adj.* not provident; neglecting to provide for future needs: *The improvident worker saved no money for his retirement.* —**im·prov′i·dent·ly,** *adv.*

im·prov·i·sa·tion (im prov′i zā′shən, im′prə vi zā′shən), *n.* **1.** the act of improvising. **2.** something that is improvised.

im·pro·vise (im′prə vīz′), *v.,* **im·pro·vised, im·pro·vis·ing.** to perform or make without previous preparation: *to improvise an accompaniment to a song; to improvise a meal from leftovers.*

im·pru·dent (im proٯod′′′nt), *adj.* not prudent; lacking discretion: *The imprudent woman told everyone she had hidden money in her house.* —**im·pru′dence,** *n.* —**im·pru′dent·ly,** *adv.*

im·pu·dent (im′pyə dənt), *adj.* shamelessly bold; showing a complete lack of respect; rude. —**im′pu·dence,** *n.* —**im′pu·dent·ly,** *adv.*

im·pugn (im pyoٯon′), *v.* to question the truth of; cast doubt upon: *The lawyer impugned the witness's story.* —**im·pugn′a·ble,** *adj.*

im·pulse (im′puls), *n.* **1.** a push or pull that makes something move. **2.** a sudden inclination to act: *an impulse to cry.*

im·pul·sive (im pul′siv), *adv.* **1.** having the power to push forward. **2.** acting on impulse; moved by sudden emotion: *The impulsive woman ran forward and gave the violinist some flowers.* **3.** done on impulse: *an impulsive action.* —**im·pul′sive·ly,** *adv.* —**im·pul′sive·ness,** *n.*

im·pu·ni·ty (im pyoٯo′ni tē), *n.* freedom from punishment or bad effects: *You cannot neglect your teeth with impunity.*

im·pure (im pyoٯor′), *adj.* **1.** not pure; dirty: *impure water.* **2.** mixed with some less valuable material: *impure silver.* **3.** not morally pure or proper; obscene: *impure ideas.* —**im·pure′ly,** *adv.*

im·pu·ri·ty (im pyoٯor′i tē), *n., pl.* for def. 2 **im·pu·ri·ties. 1.** the quality of being impure: *The water's impurity makes it undrinkable.* **2.** something that is or makes impure: *to remove impurities from the air.*

im·pute (im pyoٯot′), *v.,* **im·put·ed, im·put·ing.** to lay blame for; attribute: *to impute a crime to someone.* —**im′pu·ta′tion,** *n.*

in (in), *prep.* **1.** (used to indicate location): *walking in*

the park. **2.** (used to indicate movement from outside to within) into: *Let's go in the house.* **3.** (used to specify a limited condition, quality, manner, or time): *to break in half; to speak in a whisper; to sketch in ink.* —*adv.* **4.** inside or into some place: *Bring the packages in. Is the doctor in?* **5.** on good terms: *He's in with his boss.* **6.** in vogue; in style: *Loud ties are in this year.* —*adj.* **7.** *Informal.* understandable only to a special group: *an in joke.* **8.** incoming; inbound: *mail for the in basket.* **9.** plentiful; available: *Strawberries are in now.* **10.** being in power or authority: *the in party.* —*n.* **11.** pull or influence: *He's got an in with important people.* **12.** Usually, **ins.** persons in office or power. **13. be in for,** to be likely to undergo something, esp. an unpleasant experience: *We knew we were in for a long, boring afternoon.* **14. have it in for,** to be mad at: *He has it in for me because I told on him.* **15. ins and outs,** fine points; details: *He knows the ins and outs of tennis.*

In, *Chem.* the symbol for **indium.**

in-, a prefix meaning **1.** not: *inactive;* lack of: *inattention.* **2.** in or into: *indoors; ingrain.* **3.** on or upon: *inscribe.* **4.** toward: *inland.*

in., inch; inches.

in·a·bil·i·ty (in′ə bil′i tē), *n.* lack of ability, power, or means: *the inability to remember names.*

in·ac·ces·si·ble (in′ək ses′ə bəl), *adj.* impossible to reach: *Their house is inaccessible except by helicopter.* —**in′ac·ces′si·bil′i·ty,** *n.* —**in′ac·ces′si·bly,** *adv.*

in·ac·cu·ra·cy (in ak′yər ə sē), *n., pl.* for def. 2 **in·ac·cu·ra·cies. 1.** the quality or state of being inaccurate: *Inaccuracy in the use of words can be corrected by reading.* **2.** something that is inaccurate; error: *The report was full of inaccuracies.*

in·ac·cu·rate (in ak′yər it), *adj.* not accurate; not exact, correct, or true: *an inaccurate description.* —**in·ac′cu·rate·ly,** *adv.*

in·ac·tion (in ak′shən), *n.* a lack of action; idleness.

in·ac·tive (in ak′tiv), *adj.* not active; sluggish; idle: *to lead an inactive life.* —**in·ac′tive·ly,** *adv.* —**in′ac·tiv′i·ty,** *n.*

in·ad·e·qua·cy (in ad′ə kwə sē), *n., pl.* for def. 2 **in·ad·e·qua·cies. 1.** the state or condition of being inadequate; insufficiency. **2.** something inadequate; defect: *The plan has many inadequacies.*

in·ad·e·quate (in ad′ə kwit), *adj.* not adequate; less than is required: *an inadequate supply of food.* —**in·ad′e·quate·ly,** *adv.*

in·ad·mis·si·ble (in′əd mis′ə bəl), *adj.* not admissible; not allowable: *inadmissible evidence.*

in·ad·vert·ent (in′əd vûr′t′′nt), *adj.* not on purpose; unintentional: *an inadvertent glance at a test.* —**in′ad·vert′ent·ly,** *adv.*

in·ad·vis·a·ble (in′əd vī′zə bəl), *adj.* not advisable; unwise: *Talking during the exam would be inadvisable.* —**in′ad·vis′a·bly,** *adv.*

in·al·ien·a·ble (in āl′yə nə bəl), *adj.* not able to be rejected or given to someone else: *Freedom of speech is an inalienable right.* —**in·al′ien·a·bly,** *adv.*

---

act, āble, dâre, ärt; ebb, ēqual; if, īce; hot, ōver, ôrder; oil; bŏŏk; ōōze; out; up, ûrge; ə = *a* as in *alone;* ′ as in *button* (but′′n), *fire* (fī′r); chief; shoe; thin; ŧħat; zh as in *measure* (mezh′ər). See full key inside cover.

in·ane (i nān′), *adj.* lacking meaning or sense; foolish: *That was an inane thing to say.* [from the Latin word *inānis* "empty, vain"] —**in·ane′ly,** *adv.*

in·an·i·mate (in an′ə mit), *adj.* 1. not animate; lifeless: *Rocks are inanimate.* 2. spiritless; dull: *an inanimate reading of a poem.* —**in·an′i·mate·ly,** *adv.*

in·an·i·ty (i nan′i tē), *n., pl.* for def. 2 **in·an·i·ties.** 1. lack of sense or ideas; silliness. 2. something inane, such as a remark or an opinion.

in·ap·pli·ca·ble (in ap′lə kə bəl), *adj.* not applicable or suitable. —**in·ap′pli·ca·bly,** *adv.*

in·ap·pro·pri·ate (in′ə prō′prē it), *adj.* not appropriate; not suitable or proper: *Applause at the concert in the church was inappropriate.* —**in′ap·pro′pri·ate·ly,** *adv.* —**in′ap·pro′pri·ate·ness,** *n.*

in·ar·tic·u·late (in′är tik′yə lit), *adj.* 1. uttered without intelligible meaning: *inarticulate wailing.* 2. not able to use articulate speech: *inarticulate with rage.* 3. not able to express oneself in clear and effective speech. —**in′ar·tic′u·late·ly,** *adv.*

in·ar·tis·tic (in′är tis′tik), *adj.* not artistic; lacking artistic feeling or taste: *an inartistic arrangement of furniture.* —**in′ar·tis′ti·cal·ly,** *adv.*

in·as·much′ as′ (in′əz much′), 1. in view of the fact that; since: *Inasmuch as we're all here, why don't we hold a meeting?* 2. insofar as; to such a degree as: *Let everyone help inasmuch as he is able.*

in·at·ten·tion (in′ə ten′shən), *n.* lack of attention; neglect; carelessness: *Inattention causes accidents.*

in·at·ten·tive (in′ə ten′tiv), *adj.* not attentive; negligent; careless: *The inattentive student didn't follow the instructions.* —**in′at·ten′tive·ly,** *adv.* —**in′at·ten′tive·ness,** *n.*

in·au·di·ble (in ô′də bəl), *adj.* incapable of being heard: *an inaudible whisper.* —**in·au′di·bil′i·ty,** *n.* —**in·au′di·bly,** *adv.*

in·au·gu·ral (in ô′gyər əl), *adj.* 1. being part of an inauguration: *the inaugural ball.* 2. marking the beginning of a series: *the inaugural concert of the fall season.* —*n.* 3. an inaugural address: *He delivered a stirring inaugural.* 4. the inauguration ceremony: *the inaugural of a new president.*

in·au·gu·rate (in ô′gyə rāt′), *v.,* **in·au·gu·rat·ed, in·au·gu·rat·ing.** 1. to begin formally: *to inaugurate a new television series.* 2. to induct into office with a formal ceremony: *to inaugurate a president.* —**in·au′gu·ra′tion,** *n.*

in·aus·pi·cious (in′ô spish′əs), *adj.* not auspicious; unfavorable: *The failure of the first missile was an inauspicious beginning for the program.* —**in′aus·pi′cious·ly,** *adv.* —**in′aus·pi′cious·ness,** *n.*

in·born (in′bôrn′), *adj.* present from birth; not learned; innate: *an inborn musical talent.*

in·bred (in′bred′), *adj.* 1. inborn; natural. 2. produced by inbreeding.

in·breed·ing (in′brē′ding), *n.* the mating of closely related organisms to produce a pure strain.

Inc., Incorporated.

inc., 1. inclosure. 2. included. 3. including. 4. inclusive. 5. income. 6. incorporated. 7. increase.

In·ca (ing′kə), *n.* a member of a South American Indian people who ruled an empire in Peru, Ecuador, and N Chile before being conquered by Pizarro in 1533.

in·cal·cu·la·ble (in kal′kyə lə bəl), *adj.* 1. too great to be calculated: *an incalculable number of stars.* 2. not able to be forecast or predicted: *The outcome of the election is incalculable.* —**in·cal′cu·la·bly,** *adv.*

in·can·des·cent (in′kən des′ənt), *adj.* 1. glowing or white with heat; very bright. 2. brilliant; highly intelligent: *incandescent wit.* —**in′can·des′cence,** *n.*

in′can·des′cent lamp′, a lamp that gives off light because it contains a white-hot filament. The ordinary electric light bulb is an incandescent lamp.

in·can·ta·tion (in′kan tā′shən), *n.* 1. the chanting or uttering of words supposed to have magical power: *The witch doctor's incantation did not heal the sick child.* 2. the words used for this purpose.

in·ca·pa·ble (in kā′pə bəl), *adj.* 1. not capable; not having the necessary power or ability: *an incapable worker.* 2. **incapable of,** not capable of or subject to (a certain action, requirement, etc.): *He's incapable of doing the work.* —**in·ca′pa·bly,** *adv.*

in·ca·pac·i·tate (in′kə pas′i tāt′), *v.,* **in·ca·pac·i·tat·ed, in·ca·pac·i·tat·ing.** to make incapable or unfit; disqualify: *He was incapacitated by a stroke.*

in·ca·pac·i·ty (in′kə pas′i tē), *n.* a lacking of power or ability: *an incapacity to do precise work.*

in·car·cer·ate (in kär′sə rāt′), *v.,* **in·car·cer·at·ed, in·car·cer·at·ing.** to confine in a prison: *to be incarcerated for robbery.* [from the medieval Latin word *incarcerātus* "imprisoned," which comes from *in-* "in" + *carcer* "prison"]

in·car·nate (in kär′nit, in kär′nāt), *adj.* 1. having a human form: *a devil incarnate.* 2. made real or actual; personified: *The soldiers said their general was bravery incarnate.* —*v.* (in kär′nāt), **in·car·nat·ed, in·car·nat·ing.** 3. to be an example of; embody: *a lady who incarnates goodness.*

in·car·na·tion (in′kär nā′shən), *n.* 1. a taking on of human form. 2. a being who embodies a god or spirit: *The Egyptians considered the Pharaoh the incarnation of a god.* 3. **the Incarnation,** (in Christian theology) the taking on of a human body by Christ. 4. a person or thing regarded as the embodiment of some quality: *She's the incarnation of goodness.*

in·case (in kās′), *v.,* **in·cased, in·cas·ing.** another spelling of encase. —**in·case′ment,** *n.*

in·cau·tious (in kô′shəs), *adj.* not cautious; careless; reckless. —**in·cau′tious·ly,** *adv.*

in·cen·di·ar·y (in sen′dē er′ē), *adj.* 1. referring to the intentional burning of property: *an incendiary crime.* 2. inflaming the emotions; stirring up trouble: *an incendiary speech.* 3. igniting upon bursting; causing fires: *incendiary bombs.* —*n., pl.* **in·cen·di·ar·ies.** 4. a person who maliciously sets fire to property.

in·cense[1] (in′sens), *n.* 1. a gum or other substance that produces a sweet odor when burned. 2. the perfume or odor that is produced. 3. any pleasant smell: *the incense of flowers.* [from the Latin word *incensum,* literally "something kindled," which comes from *incendere* "to set on fire"]

in·cense² (in sens′), v., **in·censed, in·cens·ing.** to make angry; enrage: *He was incensed at my remarks.* [from a Middle English word, which comes from Latin *incensus* "set afire." See *incense¹*]

in·cen·tive (in sen′tiv), n. something that makes one want to work or make an effort; stimulus or spur: *A large bonus was her incentive to work harder.*

in·cep·tion (in sep′shən), n. a beginning or start.

in·ces·sant (in ses′ənt), adj. continuing without interruption: *an incessant noise.* —**in·ces′sant·ly,** adv.

in·cest (in′sest), n. sexual relations between persons so closely related that they are forbidden by law or religion to marry.

inch (inch), n. 1. a unit of length equal to ¹/₁₂ foot or 2.54 centimeters. 2. a very small amount: *He wouldn't budge an inch.* —v. 3. to move by small degrees: *He inched his way to victory.*

inch·worm (inch′wûrm′), n. another name for **measuring worm.**

in·ci·dence (in′si dəns), n. the rate at which something occurs: *The incidence of measles was three times greater in New York than in Chicago.*

in·ci·dent (in′si dənt), n. 1. an occurrence or event, often of little importance. 2. a small disturbance or clash which may lead to a larger conflict: *a border incident involving guerrilla fighters.* —adj. 3. likely to happen; occurring naturally: *difficulties incident to changing schools.*

in·ci·den·tal (in′si den′t³l), adj. 1. happening or likely to happen in connection with something else: *problems incidental to opening a new store.* 2. occurring merely by chance; not specifically accounted for: *incidental expenses.*

in·ci·den·tal·ly (in′si den′t³lē), adv. 1. in an incidental manner. 2. apart or aside from the main subject; by the way.

in·cin·er·ate (in sin′ə rāt′), v., **in·cin·er·at·ed, in·cin·er·at·ing.** to burn to ashes. —**in·cin·er·a′tion,** n.

in·cin·er·a·tor (in sin′ə rā′tər), n. a furnace for burning trash or garbage.

in·cip·i·ent (in sip′ē ənt), adj. beginning to exist or appear: *an incipient rebellion.*

in·cise (in sīz′), v., **in·cised, in·cis·ing.** 1. to cut into: *to incise a wound.* 2. to carve (figures, a design, etc.) into; engrave: *to incise a stone with one's initials.*

in·ci·sion (in sizh′ən), n. 1. a cut, gash, or notch: *The surgeon made an incision to drain the wound.* 2. the act of incising.

in·ci·sive (in sī′siv), adj. 1. sharp or keen: *an incisive blade; an incisive tone of voice.* 2. penetrating or acute: *an incisive mind; an incisive wit.* —**in·ci′sive·ly,** adv.

in·ci·sor (in sī′zər), n. one of the four front teeth in each jaw, used for cutting.

in·cite (in sīt′), v., **in·cit·ed, in·cit·ing.** to stimulate or prompt to action; urge on: *The leader's speech incited the soldiers to defend their city.* —**in·cite′ment,** n.

in·ci·vil·i·ty (in′sə vil′i tē), n., pl. for def. 2 **in·ci·vil·i·ties.** 1. the condition of being uncivil; uncivil behav-ior. 2. an uncivil act: *It is an incivility not to rise when being introduced to an elderly person.*

incl., 1. including. 2. inclusive.

in·clem·ent (in klem′ənt), adj. 1. (of the weather) severe; stormy: *an inclement day.* 2. not kind or merciful: *an inclement monarch.* —**in·clem′en·cy,** n.

in·cli·na·tion (in′klə nā′shən), n. 1. a liking or natural preference for something: *an inclination for hiking.* 2. a tendency toward a condition: *the door's inclination to stick.* 3. the act of inclining; a bending: *an inclination of the head.* 4. the state of being inclined; a sloping: *the inclination of a roof.*

in·cline (in klīn′), v., **in·clined, in·clin·ing.** 1. to have a mental tendency or preference: *John inclines to study at night.* 2. to have a natural tendency: *Some people must diet because they incline to heaviness.* 3. to lean or slant: *The road inclines to the left.* 4. to bend or bow: *to incline the head.*

in·clined (in klīnd′), adj. 1. having an inclination or tendency; disposed: *He was inclined to stay all night.* 2. sloping or slanting.

in·close (in klōz′), v., **in·closed, in·clos·ing.** another spelling of **enclose.**

in·clo·sure (in klō′zhər), n. another spelling of **enclosure.**

in·clude (in klŏŏd′), v., **in·clud·ed, in·clud·ing.** to contain as part of the whole: *The rent includes gas and electricity.*

in·clu·sion (in klŏŏ′zhən), n. 1. the act of including, or the state of being included: *The inclusion of books in the tuition saves money.* 2. something included.

in·clu·sive (in klŏŏ′siv), adj. 1. including the limits or extremes mentioned: *You will be paid from the 5th to the 10th inclusive, that is for 6 days.* 2. **inclusive of,** including: *Europe inclusive of England.*

in·cog·ni·to (in kog′ni tō′, in′kog nē′tō), adj. 1. having one's identity concealed to avoid notice: *The king was there, but he was incognito.* —adv. 2. with the real identity concealed: *to travel incognito.* [from an Italian word, which comes from Latin *incognitus* "unknown"]

in·co·her·ent (in′kō hēr′ənt), adj. not logically connected; rambling; confused: *an incoherent description.* —**in′co·her′ence,** n. —**in′co·her′ent·ly,** adv.

in·com·bus·ti·ble (in′kəm bus′tə bəl), adj. not combustible; incapable of being burned.

in·come (in′kum), n. the money that one receives from business, labor, etc.; salary, wages, or revenue.

in′come tax′, a tax on an individual's income.

in·com·ing (in′kum′ing), adj. 1. coming in: *the incoming tide.* 2. referring to an official who is about to take up his office; succeeding: *the incoming mayor.*

in·com·men·su·rate (in′kə men′shər it, in′kə men′sər it), adj. not adequate or in proportion: *The time allowed was incommensurate with the assignment.*

in·com·mu·ni·ca·ble (in′kə myŏŏ′nə kə bəl), adj. unable to be communicated or shared: *an incommunicable secret.*

in·com·mu·ni·ca·do (in/kə myoo/nə kä/dō), *adj.* (esp. of a prisoner) not allowed to communicate with others: *The spy was held incommunicado.* [from the Spanish word *incomunicado,* which comes from *in-* "not" + *comunicar* "to communicate"]

in·com·pa·ra·ble (in kom/pər ə bəl), *adj.* so excellent that it has no equal; matchless: *the incomparable beauty of a lake.* —**in·com/pa·ra·bly,** *adv.*

in·com·pat·i·ble (in/kəm pat/ə bəl), *adj.* 1. not compatible; unable to exist together in harmony: *incompatible roommates.* 2. not going well together; not suited to one another: *incompatible colors.* —**in/com·pat/i·bil/i·ty,** *n.* —**in/com·pat/i·bly,** *adv.*

in·com·pe·tent (in kom/pi tənt), *adj.* 1. not competent; lacking qualification or ability: *The incompetent clerk was dismissed.* 2. not legally qualified: *A forced confession is incompetent evidence.* —**in·com/pe·tence,** *n.* —**in·com/pe·tent·ly,** *adv.*

in·com·plete (in/kəm plēt/), *adj.* not complete; lacking some part. —**in/com·plete/ly,** *adv.*

in·com·pre·hen·si·ble (in/kom pri hen/sə bəl, in·kom/pri hen/sə bəl), *adj.* unable to be understood. —**in/com·pre·hen/si·bil/i·ty,** *n.* —**in/com·pre·hen/si·bly,** *adv.*

in·con·ceiv·a·ble (in/kən sē/və bəl), *adj.* impossible to imagine, conceive, or believe: *inconceivable meanness; inconceivable luxury.* —**in/con·ceiv/a·bly,** *adv.*

in·con·clu·sive (in/kən kloo/siv), *adj.* not conclusive or definite; not clearing up doubts: *The jury found the evidence inconclusive for a conviction.* —**in/con·clu/sive·ly,** *adv.* —**in/con·clu/sive·ness,** *n.*

in·con·gru·i·ty (in/kong groo/i tē), *n., pl.* for def. 2 **in·con·gru·i·ties.** 1. the condition of being incongruous: *the incongruity of mixing modern lamps with Colonial furniture.* 2. something incongruous: *The incongruities in his story made it unbelievable.*

in·con·gru·ous (in kong/groo əs), *adj.* 1. out of place; not suitable or appropriate: *A seven-foot child would be incongruous in a family of midgets.* 2. lacking harmony of parts; not consistent: *He gave an incongruous alibi, one part of which contradicted the other.* —**in·con/gru·ous·ly,** *adv.*

in·con·se·quen·tial (in/kon sə kwen/shəl), *adj.* of little or no importance; trivial: *The amount of money it cost was inconsequential because of the great pleasure it gave the people.* —**in/con·se·quen/tial·ly,** *adv.*

in·con·sid·er·ate (in/kən sid/ər it), *adj.* lacking regard for the rights or feelings of others; thoughtless. —**in/con·sid/er·ate·ly,** *adv.* —**in/con·sid/er·ate·ness,** *n.*

in·con·sist·en·cy (in/kən sis/tən sē), *n., pl.* for def. 2 **in·con·sist·en·cies.** 1. the quality of being inconsistent. 2. something inconsistent: *a report full of inconsistencies.*

in·con·sist·ent (in/kən sis/tənt), *adj.* 1. not consistent; not in agreement or harmony: *His behavior is inconsistent with good citizenship.* 2. not keeping to the same attitudes, standards of conduct, etc.: *You would be inconsistent to vote for the plan after attacking it.* —**in/con·sist/ent·ly,** *adv.*

in·con·sol·a·ble (in/kən sō/lə bəl), *adj.* unable to be comforted or consoled; full of grief or sorrow: *The boy was inconsolable when his dog ran away.* —**in/con·sol/a·bly,** *adv.*

in·con·spic·u·ous (in/kən spik/yoo əs), *adj.* not conspicuous; not noticeable; attracting little attention: *an inconspicuous necktie.* —**in/con·spic/u·ous·ly,** *adv.*

in·con·stant (in kon/stənt), *adj.* not constant; changing often; changeable or fickle: *an inconstant breeze; an inconstant friend.* —**in·con/stan·cy,** *n.* —**in·con/stant·ly,** *adv.*

in·con·test·a·ble (in/kən tes/tə bəl), *adj.* not contestable; not to be argued about or questioned: *Facts are incontestable.* —**in/con·test/a·bly,** *adv.*

in·con·tro·vert·i·ble (in/kon trə vûr/tə bəl), *adj.* indisputable; not deniable or questionable: *an absolute and incontrovertible truth.* —**in/con·tro·vert/i·bly,** *adv.*

in·con·ven·ience (in/kən vēn/yəns), *n.* 1. the state of being inconvenient; trouble, annoyance, or bother: *The delay caused us great inconvenience.* 2. something that causes discomfort, trouble, etc. —*v.,* **in·con·ven·ienced, in·con·ven·ienc·ing.** 3. to cause inconvenience to; trouble, discomfort, or annoy.

in·con·ven·ient (in/kən vēn/yənt), *adj.* not convenient; causing bother or annoyance; troublesome; discomforting: *an inconvenient time for a visit.* —**in/con·ven/ient·ly,** *adv.*

in·cor·po·rate (in kôr/pə rāt/), *v.,* **in·cor·po·rat·ed, in·cor·po·rat·ing.** 1. to put in or introduce into, as part of a whole; include: *He incorporated all the important facts in his speech.* 2. to combine, as parts of a whole: *to incorporate all the ingredients in a recipe.* 3. to form a corporation. [from the Latin word *incorporātus* "embodied," which comes from *in-* "in" + *corpus* "body"] —**in·cor/po·ra/tion,** *n.*

in·cor·po·rat·ed (in kôr/pə rā/tid), *adj.* formed or chartered as a corporation: *an incorporated town.*

in·cor·rect (in/kə rekt/), *adj.* 1. not correct; wrong; inaccurate: *an incorrect answer on a test.* 2. not proper; inappropriate: *incorrect behavior.* —**in/cor·rect/ly,** *adv.* —**in/cor·rect/ness,** *n.*

in·cor·ri·gi·ble (in kôr/i jə bəl), *adj.* so bad or firmly fixed as to be beyond reform or change: *an incorrigible thief.* —**in·cor/ri·gi·bly,** *adv.*

in·cor·rupt·i·ble (in/kə rup/tə bəl), *adj.* 1. not corruptible; honest or trustworthy; not capable of being bribed: *an incorruptible politician.* 2. not capable of decaying; indestructible: *an incorruptible metal.* —**in/cor·rupt/i·bly,** *adv.*

in·crease (in krēs/), *v.,* **in·creased, in·creas·ing.** 1. to make greater or larger; add to: *to increase one's knowledge.* 2. to become greater or more numerous; grow: *The population increases rapidly.* —*n.* (in/krēs). 3. growth in size, numbers, etc.: *an increase in earnings.* 4. the amount by which something is increased: *a 10% tax increase.*

in·creas·ing·ly (in krē/sing lē), *adv.* more and more; to an increasing degree: *As the storm approached, it became increasingly dark.*

in·cred·i·ble (in kred/ə bəl), *adj.* so unusual as to seem impossible; unbelievable: *an incredible plot in a story.* —**in·cred/i·bil/i·ty,** *n.* —**in·cred/i·bly,** *adv.*

in·cred·u·lous (in krej′ə ləs), *adj.* 1. not credulous; skeptical; unwilling to believe. 2. showing unbelief; expressing doubt: *He gave me an incredulous look.* —**in·cred′u·lous·ly**, *adv.* —**in·cre·du·li·ty** (in′kri dōō′li tē, -dyōō′-), *n.*

in·crim·i·nate (in krim′ə nāt′), *v.*, **in·crim·i·nat·ed, in·crim·i·nat·ing.** to involve (someone) in a crime or fault; show (someone) to be guilty: *The testimony of the defendant incriminated many others.* —**in·crim′i·na′tion**, *n.* —**in·crim·i·na·to·ry** (in krim′ə nə tôr′ē), *adj.*

in·crust (in krust′), *v.* 1. to cover with a crust: *His boots were incrusted with mud.* 2. to decorate the surface of (something), as with jewels: *The bracelet was incrusted with diamonds.* Also, **encrust.**

in·cu·bate (iñg′kyə bāt′), *v.*, **in·cu·bat·ed, in·cu·bat·ing.** 1. to keep (eggs) warm so that they will hatch. 2. to grow or develop. —**in′cu·ba′tion**, *n.*

in·cu·ba·tor (iñg′kyə bā′tər), *n.* 1. a heated container for hatching eggs. 2. a heated apparatus for helping to keep premature babies alive.

in·cu·bus (iñg′kyə bəs), *n.* 1. a nightmare. 2. something that oppresses one like a nightmare.

in·cul·cate (in kul′kāt), *v.*, **in·cul·cat·ed, in·cul·cat·ing.** to impress or teach by means of repeated statements or advice: *The teacher inculcated a love of learning in his pupils.* —**in′cul·ca′tion**, *n.*

in·cum·bent (in kum′bənt), *adj.* 1. holding an indicated position, office, etc.: *the incumbent senator.* 2. obligatory (often fol. by *on* or *upon*): *He felt it was incumbent on him to attend the meeting.* —*n.* 3. a person who holds an office. —**in·cum′bent·ly**, *adv.*

in·cur (in kûr′), *v.*, **in·curred, in·cur·ring.** to run or fall into (something undesirable or harmful); bring upon oneself: *to incur someone's displeasure.*

in·cur·a·ble (in kyōōr′ə bəl), *adj.* not curable; lacking a remedy, or not responding to treatment: *an incurable disease.* —**in·cur′a·bly**, *adv.*

in·cur·sion (in kûr′zhən), *n.* a sudden invasion or attack; raid.

Ind., 1. Indian. 2. Indiana.

ind., 1. independent. 2. index. 3. indicated. 4. indirect. 5. industrial. 6. industry.

in·debt·ed (in det′id), *adj.* 1. obligated to repay a loan of money. 2. being under obligation for favors or kindness: *He was indebted to his friend for his good advice.*

in·debt·ed·ness (in det′id nis), *n.* 1. the state of being indebted. 2. an amount owed: *a total indebtedness of $50.*

in·de·cen·cy (in dē′sən sē), *n., pl.* for def. 2 **in·de·cen·cies.** 1. the condition of being indecent. 2. an indecent act, remark, etc.

in·de·cent (in dē′sənt), *adj.* 1. not decent; improper or in bad taste; vulgar: *an indecent lack of respect.* 2. immodest or immoral; obscene: *indecent jokes.* —**in·de′cent·ly**, *adv.*

in·de·ci·sion (in′di sizh′ən), *n.* inability to decide; lack of decision.

in·de·ci·sive (in′di sī′siv), *adj.* 1. not decisive or conclusive; not leading to a solution: *an indecisive battle.* 2. having the quality of indecision; hesitating: *an indecisive person.* —**in′de·ci·sive·ly**, *adv.* —**in′de·ci′sive·ness**, *n.*

in·dec·o·rous (in dek′ər əs, in′di kôr′əs), *adj.* not proper or suitable; not in good taste. —**in·dec′o·rous·ly**, *adv.*

in·deed (in dēd′), *adv.* 1. in fact; in reality; truly: *The book is indeed interesting.* —*interj.* 2. (used as an exclamation of surprise, disbelief, scorn, etc.): *Indeed, I can hardly believe it!*

indef., indefinite.

in·de·fat·i·ga·ble (in′di fat′ə gə bəl), *adj.* not giving in to fatigue; incapable of being tired out. —**in′de·fat′i·ga·bly**, *adv.*

in·de·fen·si·ble (in′di fen′sə bəl), *adj.* 1. incapable of being defended: *The army retreated from an indefensible position in an open field.* 2. inexcusable; unjustifiable: *indefensible tardiness.*

in·de·fin·a·ble (in′di fī′nə bəl), *adj.* not able to be defined; not easily defined, identified, or described: *an indefinable aroma.* —**in′de·fin′a·bly**, *adv.*

in·def·i·nite (in def′ə nit), *adj.* 1. not definite; without fixed limits: *an indefinite postponement.* 2. not clearly defined or certain; vague: *indefinite plans; an indefinite reply.* —**in·def′i·nite·ly**, *adv.*

indef′inite ar′ticle, the article used to point out any one of a class of persons or things. In English, the indefinite article is *a* or *an.*

in·del·i·ble (in del′ə bəl), *adj.* 1. incapable of being removed or erased; permanent: *indelible ink; an indelible impression.* 2. making marks that are hard to remove: *an indelible pencil.* —**in·del′i·bly**, *adv.*

in·del·i·ca·cy (in del′ə kə sē), *n., pl.* for def. 2 **in·del·i·ca·cies.** 1. the quality or state of being indelicate. 2. something indelicate, such as an act or remark.

in·del·i·cate (in del′ə kit), *adj.* 1. not delicate; rough; coarse: *indelicate manners.* 2. impolite or rude; improper; immodest: *indelicate remarks.* —**in·del′i·cate·ly**, *adv.*

in·dem·ni·fy (in dem′nə fī′), *v.*, **in·dem·ni·fied, in·dem·ni·fy·ing.** 1. to compensate (someone) for a loss, damage, injury, etc.: *He was indemnified for his injury.* 2. to insure against future loss, damage, injury, etc. —**in·dem·ni·fi·ca·tion** (in dem′nə fə kā′shən), *n.*

in·dem·ni·ty (in dem′ni tē), *n., pl.* **in·dem·ni·ties.** 1. protection or insurance against damage, loss, etc. 2. payment made for damage, loss, etc. [from the Latin word *indemnitās,* which comes from *indemnis* "without loss"]

in·dent (in dent′), *v.* 1. to set back (the first line of a paragraph) from the margin. 2. to form a cove or bay in: *The sea indents the coast.*

in·den·ta·tion (in′den tā′shən), *n.* 1. a cut or notch. 2. a part or area of something that slopes backward, as a bay or cove. 3. an indenting, or the state of being indented. 4. a dent.

in·den·tion (in den′shən), *n.* 1. the indenting of a

line in writing or printing. **2.** the blank space left by indenting: *an indention of five spaces.*

in·den·ture (in den′chər), *n.* **1.** an agreement or written contract, esp. one in which a person obligates himself to work for another person. *—v.,* **in·den·tured, in·den·tur·ing. 2.** to put (someone) under such a contract: *an indentured servant.*

in·de·pend·ence (in′di pen′dəns), *n.* freedom from the influence or control of others.

Independ′ence Day′, July 4, a national holiday commemorating the adoption of the Declaration of Independence in 1776. Also, **Fourth of July.**

in·de·pend·ent (in′di pen′dənt), *adj.* **1.** free from the control or influence of others; thinking or acting for oneself. **2.** not under the rule or government of another; free: *an independent nation.* **3.** not joined to or associated with something else; separate: *an independent small business.* **4.** not wanting or needing the aid or support of another. **5.** providing enough financial support to free one from work: *She has an independent income.* —**in′de·pend′ent·ly,** *adv.*

in′depend′ent clause′, a clause that can form a complete sentence by itself. An independent clause may be used with one or more other clauses to form a compound or complex sentence. In the sentence *He came in as we were leaving, He came in* is an independent clause.

in·de·scrib·a·ble (in′di skrī′bə bəl), *adj.* **1.** too great, beautiful, terrifying, etc., to be described: *a war of indescribable violence.* **2.** too vague or indefinite to describe: *a shadowy, indescribable shape.* —**in′de·scrib′a·bly,** *adv.*

in·de·struct·i·ble (in′di struk′tə bəl), *adj.* incapable of being destroyed. —**in′de·struct′i·bly,** *adv.*

in·de·ter·mi·nate (in′di tûr′mə nit), *adj.* not precise or definite in amount or extent; vague; uncertain; indefinite: *They will be away for an indeterminate period.* —**in′de·ter′mi·nate·ly,** *adv.*

in·dex (in′deks), *n., pl.* **in·dex·es** or **in·di·ces** (in′di-sēz′). **1.** (in a book) an alphabetical list of names, topics, and places, which gives the page number on which each is mentioned. **2.** something that points out or shows; a sign or token: *His skill in writing is an index of his intelligence.* **3.** a pointer in a scientific instrument: *the index of a dial.* —*v.* **4.** to make an index for: *to index a book.* **5.** to put in an index: *to index all proper names in a book.* [from a Latin word meaning "pointer, indicator," which is related to *indicāre* "to indicate"]

in′dex fin′ger, another name for **forefinger.**

In·di·a (in′dē ə), *n.* a republic in S Asia. 1,246,880 sq. mi. *Cap.:* New Delhi.

In·di·an (in′dē ən), *n.* **1.** a member of any of the peoples living in North and South America before the continent was discovered by Europeans. **2.** a native of India or of the East Indies. **3.** any of the languages of the Ameri-

can Indians. —*adj.* **4.** of, concerning, or characteristic of the American Indians or their languages. **5.** of, concerning, or characteristic of India or the East Indies.

In·di·an·a (in′dē an′ə), *n.* a state in the central United States. 36,291 sq. mi. *Cap.:* Indianapolis. —**In′di·an′an,** *n., adj.*

In·di·an·ap·o·lis (in′dē-ə nap′ə lis), *n.* the capital city of Indiana, in the central part.

In′dian club′, a metal or wooden club shaped like a large bottle, used singly or in pairs for exercising the arms.

In′dian corn′. See **corn**[1] (defs. 1, 2).

In′dian O′cean, the ocean S of Asia, E of Africa, and W of Australia. 28,357,000 sq. mi.

In′dian sum′mer, a period of mild, dry weather occurring in late autumn.

In′dian Ter′ritory, a former territory of the United States reserved for displaced Indian tribes: now part of Oklahoma. about 31,000 sq. mi.

In′dia rub′ber. See **rubber**[1] (def. 1).

In·dic (in′dik), *adj.* **1.** of or concerning India; Indian. **2.** of or concerning a branch of the Indo-European family of languages including Sanskrit, Hindi, Bengali, and other ancient and modern languages of India, Pakistan, and Ceylon. —*n.* **3.** the Indic branch of the Indo-European language family.

in·di·cate (in′də kāt′), *v.,* **in·di·cat·ed, in·di·cat·ing. 1.** to be a sign of: *The fever indicates an infection.* **2.** to point out or point to; direct attention to: *to indicate a place on the map.* **3.** to show; make known: *The thermometer indicates air temperature.*

in·di·ca·tion (in′də kā′shən), *n.* **1.** something that indicates or points out, such as a sign or token. **2.** the act of indicating.

in·dic·a·tive (in dik′ə tiv), *adj.* **1.** indicating or pointing out; suggestive (usually fol. by *of*): *behavior indicative of nervousness.* **2.** describing the mood of a verb used to express ordinary statements or questions. In the sentences *John plays football* and *Have you a pen?,* the verbs *plays* and *have* are in the indicative mood. —*n.* **3.** the indicative mood. **4.** a verb form in the indicative mood.

in·di·ca·tor (in′də kā′tər), *n.* **1.** a person or thing that indicates. **2.** a pointing or directing device, such as a pointer or a dial on an instrument.

in·di·ces (in′di sēz′), *n.* a plural of **index.**

in·dict (in dīt′), *v.* **1.** to charge with an offense or crime. **2.** (of a grand jury) to bring a formal accusation against.

in·dict·ment (in dīt′mənt), *n.* **1.** the act of indicting, or the state of being indicted. **2.** a formal accusation presented by a grand jury.

In·dies (in′dēz), *n., the.* **1.** another name for **East Indies. 2.** a former name for **West Indies.**

in·dif·fer·ence (in dif′ər əns), *n.* **1.** lack of interest or concern. **2.** unimportance: *a matter of indifference.*

in·dif·fer·ent (in dif′ər ənt), *adj.* **1.** without interest or concern; not caring. **2.** having no preference. **3.** not very good: *an indifferent book.* **4.** not important. —**in·dif′fer·ent·ly,** *adv.*

in·dig·e·nous (in dij′ə nəs), *adj.* growing or produced naturally in a particular region or country; native: *Name some plants that are indigenous to Canada.*

in·di·gent (in′di jənt), *adj.* lacking food, clothing, and other necessities; poor; needy: *Many families were indigent during the Great Depression.* —**in′di·gence,** *n.*

in·di·gest·i·ble (in′di jes′tə bəl), *adj.* not capable of being digested, or very difficult to digest. —**in′di·gest′i·bly,** *adv.*

in·di·ges·tion (in′di jes′chən), *n.* discomfort caused by difficulty in digesting food.

in·dig·nant (in dig′nənt), *adj.* feeling or showing indignation: *Why was he so indignant at my suggestion?* —**in·dig′nant·ly,** *adv.*

in·dig·na·tion (in′dig nā′shən), *n.* strong displeasure at something considered unworthy or unjust.

in·dig·ni·ty (in dig′ni tē), *n., pl.* **in·dig·ni·ties.** an injury to one's dignity or self-respect.

in·di·go (in′də gō′), *n., pl.* **in·di·gos** *or* **in·di·goes. 1.** a deep violet-blue dye extracted from various plants. **2.** the color of this dye. **3.** a plant yielding this dye. —*adj.* **4.** of the color indigo.

in·di·rect (in′də rekt′, in′dī rekt′), *adj.* **1.** not following a straight line: *an indirect path.* **2.** not directly connected: *an indirect result.* **3.** not straightforward or to the point: *an indirect answer.* —**in′di·rect′ly,** *adv.*

in′direct ob′ject, a word, phrase, or clause expressing the person or thing to which something is given, or for which the action of a verb is performed. In the sentence *I gave Mother some flowers, Mother* is the indirect object of the verb.

in·dis·creet (in′di skrēt′), *adj.* not discreet; lacking sound judgment: *to make an indiscreet statement.* —**in′dis·creet′ly,** *adv.*

in·dis·cre·tion (in′di skresh′ən), *n.* **1.** lack of discretion. **2.** an indiscreet action.

in·dis·crim·i·nate (in′di skrim′ə nit), *adj.* **1.** not discriminating; choosing at random: *An indiscriminate movie fan goes to see everything.* **2.** not kept apart or divided; thrown together; jumbled: *an indiscriminate pile of books.* —**in′dis·crim′i·nate·ly,** *adv.*

in·dis·pen·sa·ble (in′di spen′sə bəl), *adj.* not dispensable; absolutely necessary or essential: *A good education is indispensable for success in any career.* —**in′dis·pen′sa·bly,** *adv.*

in·dis·posed (in′di spōzd′), *adj.* **1.** slightly sick or ill: *to be indisposed with a cold.* **2.** unwilling: *indisposed to help.*

in·dis·po·si·tion (in′dis pə zish′ən), *n.* **1.** the state of being indisposed; a slight illness. **2.** lack of inclination or willingness.

in·dis·put·a·ble (in′di spyoo′tə bəl), *adj.* not able to be disputed or denied. —**in′dis·put′a·bly,** *adv.*

in·dis·sol·u·ble (in′di sol′yə bəl), *adj.* incapable of being dissolved, undone, or destroyed: *an indissoluble substance; an indissoluble agreement.*

in·dis·tinct (in′di stingkt′), *adj.* not distinct; unclear; vague: *an indistinct sound; an indistinct picture.* —**in′dis·tinct′ly,** *adv.*

in·dis·tin·guish·a·ble (in′di sting′gwi shə bəl), *adj.* not capable of being distinguished: *Blue and green are often indistinguishable in poor light.*

in·di·um (in′dē əm), *n. Chem.* a rare metallic element. *Symbol:* In

in·di·vid·u·al (in′də vij′oo əl), *adj.* **1.** particular; separate: *Each student receives individual attention.* **2.** intended for the use of one person only: *individual portions.* **3.** of, concerning, or characteristic of a particular person or thing: *individual tastes.* —*n.* **4.** a single human being, as distinguished from a group. **5.** a person. [from the Latin word *individuus* "indivisible," which comes from *in-* "not" + *dividere* "to divide"]

in·di·vid·u·al·ist (in′də vij′oo ə list), *n.* a person who thinks or acts with great independence.

in·di·vid·u·al·i·ty (in′də vij′oo al′i tē), *n., pl.* for def. 1 **in·di·vid·u·al·i·ties. 1.** the particular character, or combination of qualities, that distinguishes one person or thing from others. **2.** the state or quality of being individual or unique.

in·di·vid·u·al·ly (in′də vij′oo ə lē), *adv.* **1.** for himself or herself; personally: *Each of us is individually responsible.* **2.** one at a time; separately: *The teacher helped each student individually.*

in·di·vis·i·ble (in′də viz′ə bəl), *adj.* not divisible; unable to be divided into parts. —**in′di·vis′i·bly,** *adv.*

In·do·chi·na (in′dō chī′nə), *n.* a peninsula in SE Asia between the Bay of Bengal and the South China Sea, which includes the nations of Vietnam, Cambodia, Laos, Thailand, Malaysia, and Burma.

in·doc·tri·nate (in dok′trə nāt), *v.,* **in·doc·tri·nat·ed, in·doc·tri·nat·ing.** to instruct (a person or persons) in a doctrine, belief, etc. —**in·doc′tri·na′tion,** *n.*

In·do-Eu·ro·pe·an (in′dō yoor′ə pē′ən), *adj.* **1.** of or concerning a large family of languages, including most of the languages of Europe and of countries colonized by Europeans, and extending as far as southwestern Asia and India. —*n.* **2.** the Indo-European family of languages. **3.** the ancient lost lan-

guage from which all the languages of the
Indo-European family are descended.

in·do·lent (in'd³lənt), *adj.* having or showing a disposition to avoid work; lazy. —**in'do·lence,** *n.*

in·dom·i·ta·ble (in dom'i tə bəl), *adj.* unable to be
overcome: *indomitable pride.* —**in·dom'i·ta·bly,** *adv.*

In·do·ne·sia (in'də nē'zhə), *n.* a republic in the East
Indies, made up of Sumatra, Java, Sulawesi, and

about 3000 other islands. about 580,000 sq. mi. *Cap.:*
Djakarta. Former name, **Dutch East Indies.**

In·do·ne·sian (in'də nē'zhən), *adj.* 1. of or belonging to a group of languages forming a branch of the
Malayo-Polynesian family. 2. of or concerning Indonesia or the Indonesians. —*n.* 3. a member of a
group consisting of the natives of Indonesia, the
Filipinos, and the Malays of Malaya. 4. the Indonesian languages. 5. the official language of Indonesia,
based on Malay and some other related languages.

in·door (in'dôr'), *adj.* occurring or used in a house
or building, rather than out of doors: *an indoor sport.*

in·doors (in dôrz'), *adv.* in or into a house or building: *Stay indoors during the storm.*

in·dorse (in dôrs'), *v.,* **in·dorsed, in·dors·ing.** another
spelling of **endorse.** —**in·dors'er,** *n.*

in·dorse·ment (in dôrs'mənt), *n.* another spelling of
endorsement.

in·du·bi·ta·ble (in dōō'bi tə bəl, -dyōō'-), *adj.* not to
be doubted; unquestionable; certain. —**in·du'bi·ta-
bly,** *adv.*

in·duce (in dōōs', -dyōōs'), *v.,* **in·duced, in·duc·ing.** 1.
to influence or persuade: *Induce him to stay.* 2. to
bring about or cause: *to induce sleep by drugs.* 3. to
reach (a conclusion) on the basis of observations of
particular facts. 4. to produce (magnetism or electricity) by induction.

in·duce·ment (in dōōs'mənt, -dyōōs'-), *n.* 1. something that induces; an incentive: *Praise is a powerful
inducement.* 2. the act of inducing.

in·duct (in dukt'), *v.* 1. to install in an office or position, esp. with formal ceremonies. 2. to enlist (a
draftee) into military service; draft.

in·duc·tion (in duk'shən), *n.* 1. the process by
which a body that is magnetized or has an electric
charge produces magnetic or electric effects in another body without touching it. 2. the act or process
of enlisting a draftee into military service: *to report
for induction.* 3. any form of reasoning in which one
draws a conclusion or general principle from known
facts or statements believed to be true. It is the form
of reasoning used generally in science and everyday

life. 4. a conclusion reached by this process. 5. the
act of inducting; introduction.

in·dulge (in dulj'), *v.,* **in·dulged, in·dulg·ing.** 1. to
yield to or gratify (desires, feelings, etc.): *to indulge
one's love of candy; to indulge in expensive clothes.*
2. to yield to the wishes or whims of (oneself or another): *to indulge a sick person.*

in·dul·gence (in dul'jəns), *n.* 1. the act or practice
of indulging; humoring. 2. something indulged in. 3.
a favor in the form of an extension of time for paying
a bill, finishing a job, etc. 4. (in the Roman Catholic
Church) a pardoning from the punishment due for
sin.

in·dul·gent (in dul'jənt), *adj.* characterized by or
showing indulgence; very permissive; not strict: *indulgent parents.* —**in·dul'gent·ly,** *adv.*

In·dus (in'dəs), *n.* a river in E Pakistan. about 1900 mi.
long.

in·dus·tri·al (in dus'trē-
əl), *adj.* 1. of, concerning,
or resulting from industry.
2. having many and
highly developed indus-
tries: *an industrial region.*
3. of or concerning the
workers in industries.
—**in·dus'tri·al·ly,** *adv.*

in·dus·tri·al·ist (in dus'trē ə list), *n.* a person who
owns or manages an industrial enterprise.

in·dus·tri·al·ize (in dus'trē ə līz'), *v.,* **in·dus·tri·al-
ized, in·dus·tri·al·iz·ing.** to make or become industrial: *to industrialize a rural area.* —**in·dus'tri·al·i·za'
tion,** *n.*

in·dus·tri·ous (in dus'trē əs), *adj.* hard-working;
diligent. —**in·dus'tri·ous·ly,** *adv.*

in·dus·try (in'də strē), *n., pl.* for defs. 1, 2 **in·dus-
tries.** 1. the total of manufacturing enterprises in a
particular field, often named after its main product:
the automobile industry. 2. any general business
field. 3. trade or manufacture in general. 4. hard,
concentrated work; diligence.

-ine, a suffix used to form 1. adjectives meaning of,
like, or concerning: *crystalline; leonine.* 2. feminine
nouns: *heroine.*

in·e·bri·ate (in ē'brē āt'), *v.,* **in·e·bri·at·ed, in·e·bri·at-
ing.** 1. to make drunk; intoxicate. —*n.* (in ē'brē it).
2. an intoxicated person. —**in·e'bri·a'tion,** *n.*

in·ed·i·ble (in ed'ə bəl), *adj.* not edible; not fit to be
eaten.

in·ef·fa·ble (in ef'ə bəl), *adj.* incapable of being expressed or described; inexpressible; unspeakable:
ineffable happiness. —**in·ef'fa·bly,** *adv.*

in·ef·fec·tive (in'i fek'tiv), *adj.* 1. not effective; not
producing results: *an ineffective plan.* 2. inefficient
or incapable: *an ineffective worker.* —**in'ef·fec'tive-
ly,** *adv.* —**in'ef·fec'tive·ness,** *n.*

in·ef·fec·tu·al (in'i fek'chōō əl), *adj.* without satisfactory effect; useless. —**in'ef·fec'tu·al·ly,** *adv.*

in·ef·fi·cien·cy (in'i fish'ən sē), *n.* the quality or
condition of being inefficient.

in·ef·fi·cient (in'i fish'ənt), *adj.* not efficient; wasteful of time or energy: *an inefficient system; an inefficient employee.* —in'ef·fi'cient·ly, *adv.*

in·e·las·tic (in'i las'tik), *adj.* not capable of being stretched or compressed; unyielding.

in·el·e·gant (in el'ə gənt), *adj.* not elegant; lacking in refinement, gracefulness, etc. —in·el'e·gance, *n.* —in·el'e·gant·ly, *adv.*

in·el·i·gi·ble (in el'i jə bəl), *adj.* not eligible or qualified: *ineligible to hold office.* —in·el'i·gi·bil'i·ty, *n.*

in·ept (in ept'), *adj.* 1. without skill or aptitude: *an inept seamstress.* 2. out of place; inappropriate: *an inept remark.* —in·ept·i·tude (in ep'ti tood', -tyood'), *n.* —in·ept'ly, *adv.*

in·e·qual·i·ty (in'i kwol'i tē), *n., pl.* in·e·qual·i·ties. 1. the condition of being unequal in size, status, etc.; lack of equality. 2. the condition of being uneven; unevenness: *inequality of a surface.*

in·eq·ui·ta·ble (in ek'wi tə bəl), *adj.* not equitable; unjust or unfair. —in·eq'ui·ta·bly, *adv.*

in·ert (in ûrt'), *adj.* 1. having no power of action, motion, or resistance: *inert matter.* 2. having little capability of entering into a chemical reaction: *an inert gas.* 3. having no medicinal action. —in·ert'ly, *adv.* —in·ert'ness, *n.*

in·er·tia (in ûr'shə), *n.* 1. inert condition; inactivity; sluggishness. 2. the property of matter that causes it to tend to remain at rest if it is at rest or to continue in straight-line motion if it is in motion.

in·es·cap·a·ble (in'e skā'pə bəl), *adj.* incapable of being escaped, ignored, or avoided: *an inescapable duty.* —in'es·cap'a·bly, *adv.*

in·es·ti·ma·ble (in es'tə mə bəl), *adj.* incapable of being estimated: *inestimable wealth.* —in·es'ti·ma·bly, *adv.*

in·ev·i·ta·ble (in ev'i tə bəl), *adj.* unable to be avoided; certain; necessary. —in·ev'i·ta·bly, *adv.*

in·ex·act (in'ig zakt'), *adj.* not exact; not strictly accurate: *an error due to inexact measurements.* —in'ex·act'ly, *adv.* —in'ex·act'ness, *n.*

in·ex·cus·a·ble (in'ik skyoo'zə bəl), *adj.* not excusable; incapable of being justified or excused: *inexcusable conduct.* —in'ex·cus'a·bly, *adv.*

in·ex·haust·i·ble (in'ig zôs'tə bəl), *adj.* 1. not exhaustible; incapable of being used up: *an inexhaustible supply.* 2. tireless: *an inexhaustible runner.* —in'ex·haust'i·bly, *adv.*

in·ex·o·ra·ble (in ek'sər ə bəl), *adj.* not to be affected or changed by prayers or pleas; unyielding; unrelenting. —in·ex'o·ra·bly, *adv.*

in·ex·pe·di·ent (in'ik spē'dē ənt), *adj.* not expedient; not suitable or advisable.

in·ex·pen·sive (in'ik spen'siv), *adj.* not expensive; not high in price. —in'ex·pen'sive·ly, *adv.*

in·ex·pe·ri·ence (in'ik spēr'ē əns), *n.* lack of experience or of knowledge or skill gained from experience.

in·ex·pe·ri·enced (in'ik spēr'ē ənst), *adj.* not experienced; without knowledge or skill gained from experience: *an inexperienced driver.*

in·ex·pert (in eks'pûrt), *adj.* not expert; unskilled. —in·ex'pert·ly, *adv.*

in·ex·pli·ca·ble (in eks'plə kə bəl, in'ik splik'ə bəl), *adj.* not explicable; incapable of being explained.

in·ex·press·i·ble (in'ik spres'ə bəl), *adj.* not expressible; incapable of being uttered or expressed in words. —in'ex·press'i·bly, *adv.*

in·ex·tri·ca·ble (in eks'trə kə bəl, in'ik strik'ə bəl), *adj.* 1. from which one cannot extricate or disentangle oneself: *an inextricable maze.* 2. incapable of being disentangled or undone: *an inextricable knot.* 3. hopelessly intricate, involved, or puzzling: *an inextricable problem.* —in·ex'tri·ca·bly, *adv.*

Inf., Infantry.

inf., 1. inferior. 2. infinitive. 3. information.

in·fal·li·ble (in fal'ə bəl), *adj.* 1. not fallible; free from error. 2. absolutely sure; certain: *an infallible remedy.* —in·fal'li·bil'i·ty, *n.* —in·fal'li·bly, *adv.*

in·fa·mous (in'fə məs), *adj.* 1. having an extremely bad reputation. 2. deserving or causing a bad reputation; shamefully evil: *an infamous act.* —in'fa·mous·ly, *adv.*

in·fa·my (in'fə mē), *n., pl.* for def. 3 in·fa·mies. 1. evil reputation or strong condemnation as the result of a shameful or criminal act. 2. infamous character or conduct. 3. an infamous act or circumstance.

in·fan·cy (in'fən sē), *n., pl.* in·fan·cies. 1. the state or period of earliest childhood. 2. the very early stages of anything: *Space science is still in its infancy.*

in·fant (in'fənt), *n.* 1. a child during the earliest period of its life; baby. —*adj.* 2. concerning infants or infancy: *infant care; infant food.* 3. in an early stage of development: *an infant industry.* [from the Latin word *infāns,* literally "not speaking," which comes from *in-* "not" + *fāri* "to speak"]

in·fan·tile (in'fən tīl'), *adj.* 1. like an infant; babyish. 2. of or concerning infants or infancy. 3. being in the earliest stage of development.

in'fantile paral'ysis, another name for **poliomyelitis.**

in·fan·try (in'fən trē), *n., pl.* in·fan·tries. soldiers or military units that are equipped to fight on foot.

in·fan·try·man (in'fən trē mən), *n., pl.* in·fan·try·men. a soldier of the infantry.

in·fat·u·ate (in fach'oo āt'), *v.,* in·fat·u·at·ed, in·fat·u·at·ing. to inspire (a person) with foolish or unreasoning love. —in·fat'u·a'tion, *n.*

in·fect (in fekt'), *v.* 1. to contaminate or become contaminated with disease germs. 2. to influence with a mood or feeling: *Her joy infected us all.*

in·fec·tion (in fek'shən), *n.* 1. a disease or condition produced by germs: *A serious infection developed in the wound.* 2. the act or process of infection: *Wounds should be bandaged to prevent infection.*

in·fec·tious (in fek'shəs), *adj.* 1. transmitted by infection: *an infectious disease.* 2. tending to affect or influence others: *an infectious laugh.* —in·fec'tious·ly, *adv.*

in·fer (in fûr'), *v.,* in·ferred, in·fer·ring. 1. to conclude

or derive by reasoning or from evidence: *From what he said I inferred he was happy with the new job.* **2.** to indicate as a conclusion; lead to: *The circumstances infer his guilt.* **3.** to guess or speculate.
—Usage. *Infer,* which means to understand or conclude, should not be used as a synonym of *imply,* which means to hint or suggest: *He implied that I was cheating. I inferred that she was an only child.*

in·fer·ence (in′fər əns), *n.* **1.** the act or process of inferring. **2.** something that is inferred.

in·fe·ri·or (in fēr′ē ər), *adj.* **1.** low or lower in rank, degree, or grade: *A duke is inferior to a prince.* **2.** of little or less importance, value, or excellence: *an inferior material.* **—***n.* **3.** a person who is inferior.

in·fe·ri·or·i·ty (in fēr′ē ôr′i tē), *n.* the state or quality of being inferior.

in·fer·nal (in fûr′nəl), *adj.* **1.** of or concerning hell. **2.** hellish; horrible; terrible: *an infernal plot.*

in·fer·no (in fûr′nō), *n., pl.* **in·fer·nos. 1.** hell; the infernal regions. **2.** a place or region that resembles hell. [from an Italian word, which comes from Latin *infernus* "lower, nether"]

in·fest (in fest′), *v.* to overrun in a troublesome or harmful way: *Mosquitoes infested the campsite.*

in·fi·del (in′fi dəl), *n.* **1.** a person who has no religious faith; unbeliever. **2.** (among Christians) a person who does not accept Christianity. **3.** (among Muslims) a person who does not accept Islam. **—***adj.* **4.** without religious faith. **5.** showing a lack of belief: *infidel ideas.* [from the Latin word *infidēlis* "unfaithful"]

in·fi·del·i·ty (in′fi del′i tē), *n., pl.* for def. 3 **in·fi·del·i·ties. 1.** unfaithfulness or disloyalty, esp. to one's husband or wife. **2.** lack of religious faith. **3.** an act or instance of unfaithfulness.

in·field (in′fēld), *n.* (in baseball) **1.** the diamond; the area bounded by home plate and the three bases. **2.** the positions in the infield, played by the first baseman, second baseman, shortstop, and third baseman: *to play the infield.* **3.** the infielders as a group.

in·field·er (in′fēl′dər), *n.* (in baseball) any of the players stationed in the infield.

in·fil·trate (in fil′trāt, in′fil trāt′), *v.,* **in·fil·trat·ed, in·fil·trat·ing.** to filter or go into or through: *Troops infiltrated the enemy territory.* **—in′fil·tra′tion,** *n.* **—in·fil·tra·tor** (in′fil trā′tər, in fil′trā tər), *n.*

in·fi·nite (in′fə nit), *adj.* **1.** exceedingly great: *a discovery of infinite importance.* **2.** without limits; endless: *God's infinite mercy.* **—***n.* **3.** something that is infinite. **4. the Infinite,** God. **—in′fi·nite·ly,** *adv.*

in·fin·i·tes·i·mal (in′fin i tes′ə məl), *adj.* extremely small; minute.

in·fin·i·tive (in fin′i tiv), *n.* **1.** a verb form that names an action or state of being without specifying a subject. In English, the infinitive may be used as a noun or with an auxiliary verb, and is often preceded by *to.* In the sentences *To swim is pleasant* and *You must eat, to swim* and *eat* are infinitives. **—***adj.* **2.** of or used as an infinitive: *an infinitive construction.*

in·fin·i·ty (in fin′i tē), *n., pl.* **in·fin·i·ties. 1.** the quality or state of being infinite. **2.** something that is in-

finite, such as space or time. **3.** an infinite extent, amount, or number. **4.** an immeasurably great number. *Symbol:* ∞

in·firm (in fûrm′), *adj.* **1.** feeble or weak in body or health, often because of age. **2.** not firm or definite; faltering: *infirm of purpose.*

in·fir·ma·ry (in fûr′mə rē), *n., pl.* **in·fir·ma·ries.** a place for the care of the infirm, sick, or injured.

in·fir·mi·ty (in fûr′mi tē), *n., pl.* **in·fir·mi·ties. 1.** a physical weakness or ailment: *the infirmities of old age.* **2.** a moral weakness or failing.

in·flame (in flām′), *v.,* **in·flamed, in·flam·ing. 1.** to set on fire. **2.** to excite or stir up; arouse: *The politician's speech inflamed the crowd.* **3.** to make or become reddened, swollen, and painful: *Chemical fumes can inflame the eye.*

in·flam·ma·ble (in flam′ə bəl), *adj.* **1.** easily set on fire; flammable. **2.** easily aroused; excitable.

in·flam·ma·tion (in′flə mā′shən), *n.* **1.** the act of inflaming, or the state of being inflamed. **2.** a redness, swelling, pain, or hotness of part of the body, caused by infection, chemicals, or injury.

in·flam·ma·to·ry (in flam′ə tôr′ē), *adj.* **1.** tending to arouse or stir up strong feelings: *an inflammatory speech.* **2.** referring to or accompanied by inflammation: *an inflammatory condition.*

in·flate (in flāt′), *v.,* **in·flat·ed, in·flat·ing. 1.** to swell or puff out with gas: *to inflate an inner tube.* **2.** to puff up with pride, satisfaction, etc. **3.** to increase (currency, prices, etc.) beyond normal limits.

in·fla·tion (in flā′shən), *n.* **1.** a rise of prices caused by the issuing of too much paper money. **2.** the act of inflating, or the state of being inflated. **—in·fla′tion·ar·y,** *adj.*

in·flect (in flekt′), *v.* **1.** to bend or turn from a direct line or course. **2.** to change or modulate the tone or pitch of (the voice). **3.** (in grammar) **a.** to change the form of a word to show differences of meaning or grammatical function. **b.** to conjugate (a verb). **c.** to decline (a noun, pronoun, adjective, or adverb). **d.** to give the inflected forms of a word.

in·flec·tion (in flek′shən), *n.* **1.** a change in the pitch or tone of the voice. **2.** (in grammar) **a.** a listing or reciting of the inflected forms of a word. **b.** the conjugation of a verb. **c.** the declension of a noun, pronoun, adjective, or adverb. **3.** a bend or angle. **—in·flec′tion·al,** *adj.*

in·flex·i·ble (in flek′sə bəl), *adj.* **1.** not flexible; incapable of being bent; rigid: *an inflexible rod.* **2.** of an unyielding temper, purpose, etc.: *an inflexible will to succeed.* **3.** not permitting change: *inflexible rules.* **—in·flex′i·bil′i·ty,** *n.* **—in·flex′i·bly,** *adv.*

in·flict (in flikt′), *v.* **1.** to lay on: *to inflict a blow.* **2.** to impose: *to inflict punishment.* **—in·flic′tion,** *n.*

in·flu·ence (in′floo əns), *n.* **1.** the power to produce effects on others by indirect means: *He used his influence to get me a job.* **2.** a person or thing that has such power: *to be a good influence.* **—***v.,* **in·flu·enced, in·flu·enc·ing. 3.** to exercise influence on.

in·flu·en·tial (in′floo en′shəl), *adj.* having or using

influence: *to have influential friends.* —in′flu·en′
tial·ly, *adv.*

in·flu·en·za (in′floo en′zə), *n.* an extremely contagious disease that causes inflammation in the nose
and throat, aching joints, fever, and, frequently, upset stomach. Also, **flu, grippe.**

in·flux (in′fluks′), *n.* a flowing in: *an influx of tourists.*

in·fold (in fold′), *v.* another spelling of **enfold.**

in·form (in fôrm′), *v.* 1. to give knowledge or information; tell; notify: *He informed them of his arrival.*
2. to supply (oneself) with knowledge: *Before the trip
she informed herself about the island.* 3. to give
damaging evidence: *The thief informed on his gang.*

in·for·mal (in fôr′məl), *adj.* 1. without formality or
ceremony; casual: *informal clothing.* 2. (of language)
suitable for use in ordinary speech or writing, but not
for formal use. —in·for′mal·ly, *adv.*

in·for·mal·i·ty (in′fôr mal′i tē), *n., pl.* for def. 2 in·
for·mal·i·ties. 1. the state of being informal: *The
pleasant informality of a picnic.* 2. an informal act.

in·form·ant (in fôr′mənt), *n.* a person who gives information or news; informer.

in·for·ma·tion (in′fər mā′shən), *n.* 1. knowledge
given or received concerning a particular fact or circumstance; news: *I received my information about
the party from Tom.* 2. the act or fact of informing:
The pamphlet is for the information of voters.

in·form·a·tive (in fôr′mə tiv), *adj.* giving information; instructive: *an informative book.* —in·form′a·
tive·ly, *adv.*

in·form·er (in fôr′mər), *n.* 1. a person who gives information or news; informant. 2. a person who informs against another, esp. for money or other
reward.

in·frac·tion (in frak′shən), *n.* the breaking of a rule
or law; violation.

in·fra·red (in′frə red′), *n.* 1. radiation of longer
wavelength than red light. Infrared rays are invisible
but they can be felt as heat. —*adj.* 2. noting or concerning the infrared or its rays: *infrared radiation.*

in·fre·quent (in frē′kwənt), *adj.* happening or occurring rarely; scarce; rare: *infrequent visits.* —in·
fre′quent·ly, *adv.*

in·fringe (in frinj′), *v.,* in·fringed, in·fring·ing. 1. to
commit a breach or infraction of; violate: *to infringe
a rule.* 2. to trespass (usually fol. by *on* or *upon*): *to
infringe on someone's privacy.* —in·fringe′ment, *n.*

in·fur·i·ate (in fyoor′ē āt′), *v.,* in·fur·i·at·ed, in·fur·i·at·
ing. to make furious; enrage: *His constant nagging
infuriates me.* —in·fur′i·at′ing·ly, *adv.*

in·fuse (in fyooz′), *v.,* in·fused, in·fus·ing. 1. to cause
to penetrate; instill (usually fol. by *into*): *to infuse
loyalty into the new employees.* 2. to inspire (usually
fol. by *with*): *The new coach infused the team with
enthusiasm.* 3. to steep or soak (leaves, bark, roots,
etc.): *to infuse tea leaves.* —in·fu′sion, *n.*

-ing, a suffix used to form 1. nouns meaning a. the
action of a verb or its result: *walking; building.* b.

material used for a certain purpose: *shirting; lining.*
2. the present participles of verbs: *I am eating.* Present participles are often used as adjectives: *shining
eyes; a fighting man.*

in·gen·ious (in jēn′yəs), *adj.* 1. characterized by
cleverness or originality: *an ingenious machine.* 2.
creative; inventive; resourceful: *an ingenious artist.*
—in·gen′ious·ly, *adv.*

in·ge·nu·i·ty (in′jə noo′i tē, -nyoo′-), *n.* the quality
of being ingenious; cleverness: *He has a great deal of
ingenuity when it comes to solving puzzles.*

in·gen·u·ous (in jen′yoo əs), *adj.* innocent, simple,
and natural: *an ingenuous answer.* —in·gen′u·ous·ly,
adv.

in·got (ing′gət), *n.* a mass of metal cast in a convenient form for shaping, remelting, or refining.

in·grain (in grān′), *v.* to fix deeply and firmly: *to ingrain an idea in the mind.*

in·grate (in′grāt), *n.* an ungrateful person.

in·gra·ti·ate (in grā′shē āt′), *v.,* in·gra·ti·at·ed, in·gra·
ti·at·ing. to establish (oneself) in the favor or good
graces of another or others by trying to please (usually fol. by *with*): *He attempted to ingratiate himself
with the boss.* —in·gra′ti·at′ing·ly, *adv.*

in·grat·i·tude (in grat′i tood′, -tyood′), *n.* the state
of being ungrateful; lack of gratitude.

in·gre·di·ent (in grē′dē ənt), *n.* 1. something added
as part of a mixture: *the ingredients of a cake.* 2. a
part that helps make up anything: *the ingredients of
political success.*

in·gress (in′gres), *n.* 1. the act of going in or entering. 2. the right to enter. 3. a place or way of entering; entrance.

in·grown (in′grōn′), *adj.* having grown into the
flesh: *an ingrown toenail.*

in·hab·it (in hab′it), *v.* to live or dwell in (a place):
Many animals inhabit the forest.

in·hab·it·a·ble (in hab′i tə bəl), *adj.* capable of being inhabited: *an inhabitable region.*

in·hab·it·ant (in hab′i t³nt), *n.* a person or an animal
that inhabits a place.

in·hale (in hāl′), *v.,* in·haled, in·hal·ing. to breathe in:
to inhale air. —in·ha·la·tion (in′hə lā′shən), *n.*

in·hal·er (in hā′lər), *n.* a small device for inhaling
medication.

in·har·mo·ni·ous (in′här mō′nē əs), *adj.* 1. not harmonious; discordant; dissonant: *inharmonious sounds.*
2. not in agreement; clashing: *inharmonious ideas.*

in·her·ent (in hēr′ənt, in her′ənt), *adj.* existing in
something as a permanent and inseparable part: *the
inherent hardness of a diamond.* —in·her′ent·ly,
adv.

in·her·it (in her′it), *v.* 1. to take or receive (property,
a right, a title, etc.) as an heir: *to inherit an estate.* 2.
to receive (physical characteristics) from a parent or
grandparent: *She has inherited her father's blue eyes.*
—in·her′i·tor, *n.*

in·her·it·ance (in her′i t³ns), *n.* 1. something that is
or may be inherited: *The farm is his inheritance.* 2.

the act or fact of inheriting: *to receive property by inheritance.*

in·hib·it (in hib′it), *v.* to hold back, check, or restrain: *Shyness inhibited her from speaking up.*

in·hi·bi·tion (in′i bish′ən, in′hi bish′ən), *n.* 1. the act of inhibiting, or the state of being inhibited. 2. the holding back of an action or thought because of fear, caution, etc.

in·hos·pi·ta·ble (in hos′pi tə bəl, in′ho spit′ə bəl), *adj.* 1. not inclined to hospitality; not generous and warm to guests. 2. (of a region, climate, etc.) not offering shelter, favorable conditions, etc.

in·hu·man (in hyoo′mən, -yoo′-), *adj.* 1. lacking sympathy, pity, or compassion; cruel. 2. not human. —**in·hu′man·ly,** *adv.*

in·hu·mane (in′hyoo mān′, -yoo-), *adj.* not humane; lacking humanity or kindness: *inhumane treatment of animals.* —**in′hu·mane′ly,** *adv.*

in·hu·man·i·ty (in′hyoo man′i tē), *n., pl.* for def. 2 **in·hu·man·i·ties.** 1. the state or quality of being inhuman or inhumane; cruelty. 2. an inhuman or inhumane act.

in·im·i·cal (i nim′i kəl), *adj.* 1. unfriendly; hostile: *a cold, inimical stare.* 2. having a bad effect; harmful: *Lack of rain is inimical to crops.*

in·im·i·ta·ble (i nim′i tə bəl), *adj.* incapable of being imitated; matchless: *an inimitable comedian.* —**in·im′i·ta·bly,** *adv.*

in·iq·ui·tous (i nik′wi təs), *adj.* characterized by iniquity; wicked; sinful.

in·iq·ui·ty (i nik′wi tē), *n., pl.* **in·iq·ui·ties.** 1. great injustice; wickedness. 2. a wicked act; sin.

in·i·tial (i nish′əl), *adj.* 1. of or concerning the beginning; first: *the initial step in a process.* —*n.* 2. the first letter of a word or name: *UN are the initials of the United Nations.* —*v.,* **in·i·tialed** *or* **in·i·tialled; in·i·tial·ing** *or* **in·i·tial·ling.** 3. to mark or sign with an initial or the initials of one's name, sometimes to show approval: *The teacher initialed all the corrected papers.* —**in·i′tial·ly,** *adv.*

in·i·ti·ate (i nish′ē āt′), *v.,* **in·i·ti·at·ed, in·i·ti·at·ing.** 1. to begin, get going, or originate: *to initiate a lecture series.* 2. to admit with special ceremonies into a secret society: *to be initiated into a fraternity.* 3. to introduce into the knowledge of some art or subject: *to initiate a person into the study of music.* —*n.* (i·nish′ē it). 4. a person who has been initiated.

in·i·ti·a·tion (i nish′ē ā′shən), *n.* 1. formal admission into a society, club, etc. 2. the ceremonies of admission.

in·i·ti·a·tive (i nish′ē ə tiv, i nish′ə tiv), *n.* 1. an introductory or beginning act or step; leading action: *He took the initiative in organizing the group.* 2. readiness and ability in initiating action: *He's successful because he has a great deal of initiative.* 3. a procedure by which voters may propose new legislation.

in·ject (in jekt′), *v.* 1. to force (a fluid) into a passage, cavity, or tissue: *to inject a serum.* 2. to introduce or throw in: *to inject a remark into a conversation.*

in·jec·tion (in jek′shən), *n.* 1. the act of injecting. 2.

anything that is injected. 3. a liquid injected into the body, esp. for medicinal purposes.

in·ju·di·cious (in′joo dish′əs), *adj.* not judicious; unwise. —**in′ju·di′cious·ly,** *adv.*

in·junc·tion (in jungk′shən), *n.* 1. a legal order requiring a person or persons to do or refrain from doing a particular thing. 2. a command or order.

in·jure (in′jər), *v.,* **in·jured, in·jur·ing.** to do or cause harm to; damage; hurt: *to injure one's hand.*

in·ju·ri·ous (in joor′ē əs), *adj.* causing injury or damage; harmful; hurtful: *Going without sleep is injurious to one's health.* —**in·ju′ri·ous·ly,** *adv.*

in·ju·ry (in′jə rē), *n., pl.* **in·ju·ries.** harm or damage: *injury to one's arm; an injury to his pride.*

in·jus·tice (in jus′tis), *n.* 1. the quality or fact of being unjust or unfair. 2. an unjust act, action, or treatment; unfairness: *You do him an injustice by not paying close attention.*

ink (ingk), *n.* 1. a liquid used for writing or printing. 2. a dark fluid ejected by octopuses and similar sea animals to help them hide from enemies. —*v.* 3. to mark, stain, or smear with ink.

ink·ling (ingk′ling), *n.* a slight suggestion or idea; hint: *She had no inkling we were planning a surprise party.* [from the earlier word *inkle* "to hint," which comes from Middle English *inclen* + *-ing*]

ink·stand (ingk′stand′), *n.* 1. a small stand for holding ink, pens, etc. 2. another name for **inkwell.**

ink·well (ingk′wel′), *n.* a container for ink.

ink·y (ing′kē), *adj.,* **ink·i·er, ink·i·est.** 1. black as ink: *inky shadows.* 2. stained with ink: *inky fingers.* —**ink′i·ness,** *n.*

in·laid (in′lād′, in′lād′), *v.* 1. the past tense and past participle of **inlay.** —*adj.* 2. set in the surface as a decoration: *an inlaid design of flowers.* 3. decorated with an inlaid design: *an inlaid box.*

in·land (in′lənd), *adj.* 1. situated in or referring to the interior part of a country or region: *an inland waterway.* —*adv.* (in′land′, -lənd). 2. in or toward the interior of a country: *to travel inland.* —*n.* (in′land′, -lənd). 3. the interior part of a country, away from the border.

in-law (in′lô′), *n.* a relative by marriage.

in·lay (in′lā′, in′lā′), *v.,* **in·laid, in·lay·ing.** 1. to decorate (an object) with veneers or fine materials set in its surface. 2. to insert or apply (layers of fine materials) in the surface of an object. —*n.* (in′lā′). 3. a veneer of fine material inserted in something else. 4. a design or decoration made by inlaying. 5. a filling of metal or porcelain that is first shaped to fit a cavity in a tooth and then cemented into it.

in·let (in′let, -lit), *n.* 1. an indentation of a shoreline. 2. an entrance.

in·mate (in′māt′), *n.* a person who is confined in a prison, hospital, etc.

in·most (in′mōst′), *adj.* 1. located farthest within: *the inmost regions of the forest.* 2. most personal or private: *one's inmost thoughts.*

inn (in), *n.* a commercial establishment that provides lodging and food for the public, esp. travelers.

in·nate (i nāt′, in′āt′), *adj.* existing within someone or something; native: *innate talent; an innate flaw in her reasoning.* —**in·nate′ly,** *adv.*

in·ner (in′ər), *adj.* **1.** situated farther within; interior. **2.** more intimate, private, or secret: *his inner circle of friends.* **3.** mental; spiritual: *the inner life.*

in′ner ear′, the innermost part of the ear containing the parts that perceive sound and control balance. See illus. at **ear.**

in·ner·most (in′ər mōst′), *adj.* farthest inward; inmost.

in′ner tube′, a doughnut-shaped rubber tube that is inflated inside the thick outer part of a tire. See illus. at **tire².**

in·ning (in′ing), *n.* **1.** a division of a baseball game during which each team has an opportunity to score until three outs have been made against it. **2.** an opportunity for activity; turn or chance: *My inning will come when he wants another favor.*

inn·keep·er (in′kē′pər), *n.* a person who owns or operates an inn.

in·no·cence (in′ə səns), *n.* **1.** freedom from wrong, guilt, or blame: *to prove one's innocence.* **2.** simplicity; freedom from cunning or trickery: *a child's innocence.*

in·no·cent (in′ə sənt), *adj.* **1.** free from wrong, guilt, or blame: *to be innocent of a crime.* **2.** having the simplicity of an unworldly person: *innocent as a child.* **3.** not causing or intending to cause harm or damage: *an innocent remark; innocent fun.* —*n.* **4.** an innocent person. —**in′no·cent·ly,** *adv.*

in·noc·u·ous (i nok′yōō əs), *adj.* not harmful or injurious; harmless: *an innocuous comment.* —**in·noc′u·ous·ly,** *adv.*

in·no·vate (in′ə vāt′), *v.,* **in·no·vat·ed, in·no·vat·ing.** to introduce something new; make changes (often fol. by *on* or *in*). —**in′no·va′tor,** *n.*

in·no·va·tion (in′ə vā′shən), *n.* **1.** something new or different introduced: *the innovation of color television.* **2.** the act of innovating; introduction of new things or methods: *to make innovations in the field of medicine.*

in·nu·en·do (in′yōō en′dō), *n., pl.* **in·nu·en·dos** *or* **in·nu·en·does.** an indirect hint about a person or thing, esp. one that is damaging or mean: *The conversation was full of innuendos about his reputation.* [from a Latin word meaning literally "by signaling," which comes from *innuere* "to nod the head"]

in·nu·mer·a·ble (i nōō′mər ə bəl, -nyōō′-), *adj.* incapable of being numbered or counted; too many to be counted: *innumerable grains of sand.* —**in·nu′mer·a·bly,** *adv.*

in·oc·u·late (i nok′yə lāt′), *v.,* **in·oc·u·lat·ed, in·oc·u·lat·ing.** to inject a substance into (a person's body), esp. a harmless preparation of disease germs for the purpose of producing immunity to the disease. —**in·oc′u·la′tion,** *n.*

in·of·fen·sive (in′ə fen′siv), *adj.* doing no harm; unobjectionable: *an inoffensive joke.* —**in′of·fen′sive·ly,** *adv.*

in·op·er·a·tive (in op′ər ə tiv), *adj.* not working; without effect: *inoperative remedies.*

in·op·por·tune (in op′ər tōōn′, -tyōōn′), *adj.* not appropriate or timely: *an inopportune visit.* —**in·op′por·tune′ly,** *adv.*

in·or·di·nate (in ôr′d³nit), *adj.* not within proper limits; excessive: *He ate an inordinate amount of candy.* —**in·or′di·nate·ly,** *adv.*

in·or·gan·ic (in′ôr gan′ik), *adj.* **1.** not produced by, contained in, or characteristic of living bodies: *The sand and gravel in soil are inorganic matter.* **2.** not concerned with the compounds of which living matter is composed: *inorganic chemistry.*

in·quest (in′kwest), *n.* a legal inquiry before a jury, esp. an investigation into the cause of a death.

in·quire (in kwī³r′), *v.,* **in·quired, in·quir·ing.** **1.** to seek information by questioning; ask: *to inquire about a person.* **2.** to make an investigation (usually fol. by *into*): *to inquire into the accident.* Also, **enquire.** —**in·quir′er,** *n.* —**in·quir′ing·ly,** *adv.*

in·quir·y (in kwī³r′ē, in′kwə rē), *n., pl.* **in·quir·ies. 1.** a seeking for truth, information, or knowledge. **2.** an investigation: *a police inquiry.* **3.** a question; query: *He made many inquiries before finding out about the lost dog.* Also, **enquiry.**

in·qui·si·tion (in′kwi zish′ən), *n.* **1.** an official investigation, esp. one of a political or religious nature. **2.** a judicial or official inquiry. **3. the Inquisition,** (formerly) a special tribunal set up by the Roman Catholic Church to combat and punish heresy.

in·quis·i·tive (in kwiz′i tiv), *adj.* **1.** eager for knowledge; curious: *an inquisitive mind.* **2.** too curious; prying. —**in·quis′i·tive·ly,** *adv.*

in·quis·i·tor (in kwiz′i tər), *n.* a person who makes an official investigation.

in·road (in′rōd′), *n.* **1.** a forcible or serious encroachment: *inroads on our savings.* **2.** a hostile raid or attack.

in·rush (in′rush′), *n.* a rushing in; influx.

in·sane (in sān′), *adj.* **1.** not sane; suffering from mental illness or insanity. **2.** for insane people: *an insane asylum.* **3.** completely senseless: *an insane answer.* —**in·sane′ly,** *adv.*

in·san·i·ty (in san′i tē), *n.* a serious and more or less lasting disorder of the mind; mental illness.

in·sa·tia·ble (in sā′shə bəl), *adj.* incapable of being satisfied: *insatiable ambition.* —**in·sa′tia·bly,** *adv.*

in·scribe (in skrīb′), *v.,* **in·scribed, in·scrib·ing. 1.** to write or engrave (words, characters, etc.): *to inscribe initials on the back of a bracelet.* **2.** to mark (a surface) with words, characters, etc. **3.** to address, autograph, or dedicate (a book, photograph, etc.) to someone. **4.** to enroll; place on an official list.

in·scrip·tion (in skrip′shən), *n.* **1.** something inscribed. **2.** a brief, informal dedication of a book. **3.** the act of inscribing.

in·scru·ta·ble (in skrōō′tə bəl), *adj.* not easily understood; mysterious: *an inscrutable look.* —**in·scru′ta·bly,** *adv.*

in·sect (in′sekt), *n.* **1.** any of a very large class of small, winged animals having six legs and bodies divided into three parts. **2.** (loosely) any of various related animals, such as a spider or tick.

in·sec·ti·cide (in sek′ti·sīd′), *n.* a substance used for killing insects.

Insect (Grasshopper)

in·se·cure (in′si kyŏŏr′), *adj.* **1.** exposed to danger; unsafe. **2.** not firm or steady: *insecure foundations.* **3.** not confident; subject to fear, doubt, etc. **—in′se·cure′ly,** *adv.*

in·se·cu·ri·ty (in′si kyŏŏr′i tē), *n., pl.* for defs. 2, 3 **in·se·cur·i·ties. 1.** the quality or state of being insecure; instability. **2.** lack of confidence or assurance; self-doubt: *His shyness is the result of his insecurity.* **3.** something insecure.

in·sen·sate (in sen′sāt), *adj.* **1.** not able to feel: *insensate stone.* **2.** without feeling; hard; cold: *an insensate remark.* **3.** without sense, understanding, or judgment.

in·sen·si·ble (in sen′sə bəl), *adj.* **1.** incapable of feeling or perceiving; unconscious. **2.** not subject to a particular feeling: *insensible to shame.* **3.** unaware and inappreciative: *insensible of kindness.* **4.** not perceptible to the senses; not easily felt: *an insensible change in temperature.* **—in·sen′si·bil′i·ty,** *n.* **—in·sen′si·bly,** *adv.*

in·sen·si·tive (in sen′si tiv), *adj.* not sensitive; unaware of feeling: *insensitive skin; an insensitive person.* **—in·sen′si·tive·ly,** *adv.* **—in·sen′si·tiv′i·ty,** *n.*

in·sep·a·ra·ble (in sep′ər ə bəl), *adj.* incapable of being separated or parted: *inseparable friends.* **—in·sep′a·ra·bly,** *adv.*

in·sert (in sûrt′), *v.* **1.** to put, place, or set in: *to insert a plug in a socket.* **—***n.* (in′sûrt). **2.** something inserted or to be inserted, such as pages in a book.

in·ser·tion (in sûr′shən), *n.* **1.** the act of inserting. **2.** something inserted. **3.** lace or embroidery inserted between parts of other material.

in·set (in′set′), *n.* **1.** something inserted; an insert. **—***v.* (in set′), **in·set, in·set·ting. 2.** to set in or insert: *to inset a panel in a dress.*

in·shore (in′shôr′), *adj.* **1.** carried on or lying close to the shore. **—***adv.* **2.** toward the shore.

in·side (in′sīd′, in′sīd′), *prep.* **1.** on the inner side or part of; within: *inside the house.* **—***adv.* **2.** in or into the inner part: *to be inside.* **—***n.* (in′sīd′). **3.** the inner part; interior: *the inside of a building.* **—***adj.* (in′sīd′, in′sīd′). **4.** located on the inside; interior: *an inside seat.* **5.** private or confidential; secret: *inside information.* **6. inside of,** within the space or period of: *I'll be there inside of ten minutes.* **7. inside out, a.** with the inner side facing out: *Your sweater is inside out.* **b.** completely; perfectly: *He knows carpentry inside out.*

in·sid·er (in′sī′dər), *n.* **1.** a member of a certain society, circle of friends, etc. **2.** a person who has some special advantage, knowledge, or influence.

in·sid·i·ous (in sid′ē əs), *adj.* **1.** slyly treacherous or deceitful: *an insidious enemy.* **2.** operating in a hidden way but with serious and often dangerous effect: *an insidious disease.* **—in·sid′i·ous·ly,** *adv.*

in·sight (in′sīt′), *n.* the ability to understand the true nature of a thing: *insight into political problems.*

in·sig·ni·a (in sig′nē ə), *n.* a badge or distinguishing mark of office or honor.

in·sig·nif·i·cance (in′sig nif′ə kəns), *n.* the quality or condition of being insignificant; lack of importance.

in·sig·nif·i·cant (in′sig nif′ə kənt), *adj.* having little or no importance, meaning, or value: *an insignificant question.* **—in′sig·nif′i·cant·ly,** *adv.*

in·sin·cere (in′sin sēr′), *adj.* not sincere or honest in the expression of actual feeling: *an insincere compliment.* **—in′sin·cere′ly,** *adv.* **—in·sin·cer·i·ty** (in′sin·ser′i tē), *n.*

in·sin·u·ate (in sin′yŏŏ āt′), *v.,* **in·sin·u·at·ed, in·sin·u·at·ing. 1.** to suggest or hint slyly: *He insinuated that she was lying.* **2.** to introduce into a position by indirect means: *to insinuate oneself into favor.* **—in·sin′u·at′ing·ly,** *adv.*

in·sin·u·a·tion (in sin′yŏŏ ā′shən), *n.* **1.** an indirect suggestion or hint. **2.** the art or power of pleasing and winning affection.

in·sip·id (in sip′id), *adj.* **1.** without interesting or attractive qualities: *an insipid tale.* **2.** without enough taste to be pleasing: *a rather insipid fruit.* **—in·sip′id·ly,** *adv.*

in·sist (in sist′), *v.* **1.** to be firm or determined on some matter: *He insists that he is right.* **2.** to demand firmly: *I insist that you leave.*

in·sist·ent (in sis′tənt), *adj.* **1.** persistent in dwelling upon or demanding something: *He was so insistent that I decided to go.* **2.** demanding attention or notice: *the insistent ring of a telephone.* **—in·sist′ence,** *n.* **—in·sist′ent·ly,** *adv.*

in·snare (in snâr′), *v.,* **in·snared, in·snar·ing.** another spelling of **ensnare.**

in·sole (in′sōl′), *n.* **1.** the inner sole of a shoe or boot. **2.** a thickness of warm or waterproof material laid as an inner sole within a shoe.

in·so·lent (in′sə lənt), *adj.* very rude or disrespectful; impertinent; insulting: *an insolent child; an insolent reply.* **—in′so·lence,** *n.* **—in′so·lent·ly,** *adv.*

in·sol·u·ble (in sol′yə bəl), *adj.* **1.** not capable of being solved: *an insoluble problem.* **2.** not capable of being dissolved: *an insoluble substance.* **—in·sol′u·bil′i·ty,** *n.*

in·sol·vent (in sol′vənt), *adj.* unable to pay one's bills; bankrupt. **—in·sol′ven·cy,** *n.*

in·som·ni·a (in som′nē ə), *n.* inability to sleep; sleeplessness.

in·so·much (in′sō much′), *adv.* **1.** to such an extent or degree; so (usually fol. by *that*): *It rained insomuch that our plans had to be canceled.* **2.** because; inasmuch (usually fol. by *as*): *Insomuch as I was tired, we didn't go to the party.*

in·spect (in spekt′), *v.* **1.** to look carefully at or over: *to inspect every part of a machine.* **2.** to view or examine formally or officially: *to inspect troops.*

in·spec·tion (in spek′shən), *n.* **1.** the act of inspecting or viewing: *The counselor made an inspection of our bunks.* **2.** formal or official viewing or examination: *an inspection of the troops.*

in·spec·tor (in spek′tər), *n.* **1.** an officer who is appointed to inspect. **2.** a police officer, usually ranking next below a superintendent. **3.** a person who inspects.

in·spi·ra·tion (in′spə rā′shən), *n.* **1.** an inspiring action or influence: *I cannot write without inspiration.* **2.** a thought or idea that comes to someone suddenly: *to have an inspiration.* **3.** a person or thing that inspires. **4.** the drawing of air into the lungs; inhalation. —**in′spi·ra′tion·al,** *adj.*

in·spire (in spī′r), *v.,* **in·spired, in·spir·ing. 1.** to fill with life, feeling, or strength: *The teacher inspired him to do well.* **2.** to produce or arouse: *to inspire confidence.* **3.** to inhale. —**in·spir′ing·ly,** *adv.*

in·sta·bil·i·ty (in′stə bil′i tē), *n.* the quality or state of being unstable; lack of stability or firmness: *Because of his instability you can't depend on him.*

in·stall (in stôl′), *v.* **1.** to place in position for service or use: *to install a heating system.* **2.** to establish in an office, position, or place: *to install a new assistant.* **3.** to induct into an office with ceremonies and formalities: *to install a president.* [from the medieval Latin word *installāre,* literally "to place in a stall"]

in·stal·la·tion (in′stə lā′shən), *n.* **1.** something installed, such as a system of machinery placed in position for use. **2.** the act of installing. **3.** any more or less permanent military post, camp, or base.

in·stall·ment[1] (in stôl′mənt), *n.* **1.** any of several parts into which a debt is divided for payment at successive times: *You can pay for the bicycle in 12 monthly installments.* **2.** a single portion of something issued in parts at successive times: *a magazine serial in six installments.* [from *in-* + the earlier word *estall* "to delay payment" + *-ment*]

in·stall·ment[2] (in stôl′mənt), *n.* **1.** the act of installing. **2.** the fact of being installed; installation. [from *install* + *-ment*]

in·stance (in′stəns), *n.* **1.** a case or example of anything: *an instance of success.* —*v.,* **in·stanced, in·stanc·ing. 2.** to give as an example: *He instanced Holland as a country in northern Europe.*

in·stant (in′stənt), *n.* **1.** a very short space of time; a moment. **2.** a particular moment: *At the same instant the telephone rang.* —*adj.* **3.** taking place without any lapse of time; immediate: *instant relief.* **4.** pressing or urgent: *an instant need.* **5.** (of a food) requiring only water, milk, etc., to prepare: *instant coffee.*

in·stan·ta·ne·ous (in′stən tā′nē əs), *adj.* occurring or completed in an instant: *an instantaneous explosion.* —**in′stan·ta′ne·ous·ly,** *adv.*

in·stant·ly (in′stənt lē), *adv.* immediately; at once.

in·stead (in sted′), *adv.* **1.** as a replacement; in the place of someone or something: *We had no coffee, so he drank tea instead.* **2. instead of,** in place of: *I'll take milk instead of cream.*

in·step (in′step′), *n.* **1.** the upper surface of the foot between the ankle and the toes. **2.** the part of a shoe, stocking, etc., covering the instep.

in·sti·gate (in′stə gāt′), *v.,* **in·sti·gat·ed, in·sti·gat·ing. 1.** to provoke or urge on to some action: *She instigated her friend to make the telephone call.* **2.** to bring about by provoking or urging on; incite: *to instigate trouble.* —**in′sti·ga′tion,** *n.* —**in′sti·ga′tor,** *n.*

in·still (in stil′), *v.* **1.** to place or infuse slowly into the mind or feelings: *to instill good manners in a child.* **2.** to put in drop by drop.

in·stinct (in′stingkt), *n.* **1.** a natural or inborn impulse or pattern of behavior; an ability or behavior that comes naturally without being learned: *In the fall birds find their way south by instinct.* **2.** a natural inclination or talent: *She has an instinct for knowing which colors look good together.*

in·stinc·tive (in stingk′tiv), *adj.* of, concerning, or arising from instinct; natural; inborn. —**in·stinc′tive·ly,** *adv.* —**in·stinc′tive·ness,** *n.*

in·sti·tute (in′sti tōōt′, -tyōōt′), *v.,* **in·sti·tut·ed, in·sti·tut·ing. 1.** to set up; establish: *to institute a government.* **2.** to start; get under way: *to institute a project.* —*n.* **3.** a society or organization for carrying on a particular work: *a scientific institute.* **4.** the building or buildings occupied by such a society or organization.

in·sti·tu·tion (in′sti tōō′shən, -tyōō′-), *n.* **1.** an organization or establishment devoted to a particular purpose: *an educational institution.* **2.** the building or buildings used by such an organization or establishment. **3.** any established law, practice, or custom. **4.** the act of instituting or setting up; establishment. —**in′sti·tu′tion·al,** *adj.*

in·struct (in strukt′), *v.* **1.** to furnish with knowledge; teach; train; educate. **2.** to furnish with information; inform: *to instruct a person of his legal rights.* **3.** to direct or command; order: *The man instructed us to remain standing.*

in·struc·tion (in struk′shən), *n.* **1.** the act or practice of instructing or teaching; education. **2.** the knowledge or information given. **3.** Usually, **instructions.** orders or directions.

in·struc·tive (in struk′tiv), *adj.* used to instruct or inform; giving information: *an instructive booklet; an instructive talk.* —**in·struc′tive·ly,** *adv.*

in·struc·tor (in struk′tər), *n.* **1.** a person who instructs; teacher. **2.** a teacher in a college or university who ranks below an assistant professor. Also, *referring to a woman,* **in·struc·tress** (in struk′tris).

in·stru·ment (in′strə mənt), *n.* **1.** a mechanical device, implement, or tool: *a surgical instrument.* **2.** a device for producing musical sounds: *a stringed instrument.* **3.** any means by which something is done: *an instrument of government.* **4.** a formal legal document, such as a contract, deed, or grant.

in·stru·men·tal (in′strə men′t'l), *adj.* **1.** written for or played on musical instruments. **2.** serving as an instrument or means; helpful; useful: *He was instru-*

mental in helping her find an apartment. —in′stru·
men′tal·ly, *adv.*

in·stru·men·tal·ist (in′strə men′t^əlist), *n.* a person
who plays a musical instrument.

in·sub·or·di·nate (in′sə bôr′d^ənit), *adj.* not submitting to authority; disobedient. —in′sub·or′di·nate·ly,
adv. —in′sub·or′di·na′tion, *n.*

in·sub·stan·tial (in′səb stan′shəl), *adj.* 1. not substantial; slight; frail: *an insubstantial net.* 2. without
reality; unreal: *insubstantial dreams.* —in′sub·stan′
tial·ly, *adv.*

in·suf·fer·a·ble (in suf′ər ə bəl), *adj.* not to be endured; intolerable; unbearable: *insufferable manners.*
—in·suf′fer·a·bly, *adv.*

in·suf·fi·cien·cy (in′sə fish′ən sē), *n., pl.* in·suf·fi·
cien·cies a lack of enough of something; deficiency.

in·suf·fi·cient (in′sə fish′ənt), *adj.* not enough;
inadequate: *an insufficient supply of paper.* —in′suf-
fi′cient·ly, *adv.*

in·su·lar (in′sə lər, ins′yə lər), *adj.* 1. of or concerning an island or islands: *insular possessions.* 2. dwelling or located on an island. 3. of, concerning, or
characteristic of people who live on an island; isolated. 4. narrow-minded; not liberal: *insular attitudes.* —in·su·lar·i·ty (in′sə lar′i tē), *n.*

in·su·late (in′sə lāt′), *v.,* in·su·lat·ed, in·su·lat·ing. 1. to
cover or separate with nonconducting material to
prevent or reduce the flow of electricity, heat, or
sound. 2. to place in an isolated situation or condition. [from the Latin word *insulātus* "made into an
island," which comes from *insula* "island"]

in·su·la·tion (in′sə lā′shən), *n.* 1. material used for
insulating: *rubber insulation.* 2. the act of insulating,
or the state of being insulated.

in·su·la·tor (in′sə lā′tər), *n.* 1. a material that blocks
or slows the flow of electricity, heat, or sound: *Asbestos is a good insulator.* 2. a piece of such a material
used to support a current-carrying wire.

in·su·lin (in′sə lin), *n.* 1. a substance secreted by the
pancreas that is required for the proper absorption of
sugar by the body. 2. a preparation of this made
from the glands of animals for the treatment of diabetes.

in·sult (in sult′), *v.* 1. to treat rudely; affront: *He insulted them by making fun of their new car.* —n.
(in′sult). 2. a rude action or speech. —in·sult′ing·ly,
adv.

in·su·per·a·ble (in soo′pər ə bəl), *adj.* incapable of
being passed over, overcome, or surmounted: *an in-
superable barrier.* —in·su′per·a·bly, *adv.*

in·sup·port·a·ble (in′sə pôr′tə bəl), *adj.* not to be
endured; insufferable: *insupportable rudeness.* —in′
sup·port′a·bly, *adv.*

in·sur·ance (in shoor′əns), *n.* 1. the act, system, or
business of protecting against loss or harm by paying
small, regular amounts to a company in exchange for
a promise from that company to pay a certain
amount in case of death, accident, fire, theft, etc. 2.
the contract by which such an agreement for protection is made. 3. the amount for which anything is
insured. Also, *esp. British,* **assurance.**

in·sure (in shoor′), *v.,* in·sured, in·sur·ing. 1. to issue
or obtain insurance on or for: *The company insures
Father's car.* 2. another spelling of **ensure.** —in·sur′
er, *n.*

in·sur·gent (in sûr′jənt), *n.* 1. a person who engages
in armed resistance to a government or to the execution of its laws; rebel. —*adj.* 2. rising in revolt;
rebellious.

in·sur·mount·a·ble (in′sər moun′tə bəl), *adj.* incapable of being surmounted, passed over, or overcome: *an insurmountable obstacle.* —in′sur·mount′a·
bly, *adv.*

in·sur·rec·tion (in′sə rek′shən), *n.* the act or an instance of rising in open rebellion against an established government or authority.

in·tact (in takt′), *adj.* not changed, damaged, or lessened; remaining uninjured, sound, or whole: *The bicycle remained intact after the accident.*

in·take (in′tāk′), *n.* 1. the act or an instance of taking in: *intake of water.* 2. the place at which a fluid
is taken into a channel, pipe, etc. 3. something that
is taken in. 4. a quantity taken in.

in·tan·gi·ble (in tan′jə bəl), *adj.* 1. not tangible; incapable of being touched: *intangible clouds.* 2. not
definite or clear to the mind: *intangible arguments.*
—*n.* 3. something intangible. —in·tan′gi·bly, *adv.*

in·te·ger (in′ti jər), *n.* a whole number: *7, –2, and 0
are integers;* 1 1/2 *is not.*

in·te·gral (in′tə grəl), *adj.* 1. being an essential part
of the whole: *The wire is an integral part of the device.* 2. entire; complete; whole. 3. referring to or
being an integer; not fractional.

in·te·grate (in′tə grāt′), *v.,* in·te·grat·ed, in·te·grat·
ing. 1. to bring together into a whole: *He integrated
the different versions into one story.* 2. to make the
use of (a school, restaurant, etc.) available to persons
of all races: *to integrate housing.* —in′te·gra′tion, *n.*

in·teg·ri·ty (in teg′ri tē), *n.* 1. adherence to moral
and ethical principles; soundness of moral character;
honesty: *a man of integrity.* 2. sound or perfect condition: *the integrity of a ship's hull.*

in·teg·u·ment (in teg′yə mənt), *n.* a natural outer
covering, such as a skin, husk, shell, or rind.

in·tel·lect (in′t^əlekt′), *n.* 1. the power of the mind
by which one knows or understands; the power of
thinking. 2. the capacity for thinking and acquiring
knowledge. 3. a person who has a great capacity for
thought and knowledge.

in·tel·lec·tu·al (in′t^əlek′choo əl), *adj.* 1. appealing
to or using the intellect: *intellectual pursuits.* 2. of or
referring to the intellect: *intellectual powers.* 3. having a notable mental capacity: *an intellectual person.*
—*n.* 4. a person of superior intellect. 5. a person
who pursues things of interest to the intellect. —in′
tel·lec′tu·al·ly, *adv.*

in·tel·li·gence (in tel′i jəns), *n.* 1. a capacity for reasoning or understanding; ability to use thought to
solve problems, to see likenesses between different
things, etc. 2. knowledge of an event, circumstance,
etc.; news or information, esp. of a secret nature:
intelligence obtained from enemy communications.

3. the gathering of information, esp. secret information, or the persons engaged in such work: *to work for military intelligence.*

intel′ligence quo′tient. See IQ.

in·tel·li·gent (in tel′i jənt), *adj.* having or showing intelligence; bright: *an intelligent person; an intelligent answer.* —in·tel′li·gent·ly, *adv.*

in·tel·li·gi·ble (in tel′i jə bəl), *adj.* capable of being understood; understandable: *an intelligible response.* —in·tel′li·gi·bly, *adv.*

in·tem·per·ance (in tem′pər əns), *n.* failure to practice moderation or use self-control, esp. in the consumption of alcoholic beverages.

in·tem·per·ate (in tem′pər it), *adj.* 1. given to too much use of alcoholic beverages. 2. lacking restraint and self-control; not temperate. 3. extreme in temperature. —in·tem′per·ate·ly, *adv.*

in·tend (in tend′), *v.* 1. to have in mind as something to be done or brought about; plan: *What do you intend to do with your old bicycle?* 2. to design or mean for a particular purpose or use: *a fund intended for emergency use only.*

in·tend·ed (in ten′did), *adj.* 1. planned or designed; intentional. 2. prospective: *his intended wife.* —*n.* 3. *Informal.* a person's fiancé or fiancée.

in·tense (in tens′), *adj.* 1. very strong or great: *intense heat; an intense gale.* 2. having or showing great strength, strong feeling, etc.: *an intense face.* —in·tense′ly, *adv.*

in·ten·si·fi·er (in ten′sə fī′ər), *n.* 1. a person or thing that intensifies. 2. (in grammar) a word or phrase that is used to add force or emphasis to the meaning of an adjective or adverb, such as *very, quite, rather, so, too, a bit,* etc.

in·ten·si·fy (in ten′sə fī′), *v.,* in·ten·si·fied, in·ten·si·fy·ing. to make or become intense or more intense: *The storm intensified her fear.* —in·ten′si·fi·ca′tion, *n.*

in·ten·si·ty (in ten′si tē), *n., pl.* in·ten·si·ties. 1. the quality or condition of being intense. 2. the amount or extent of energy, strength, concentration, etc.: *He went at the job with great intensity.* 3. a high or extreme degree: *intensity of heat; intensity of feeling.*

in·ten·sive (in ten′siv), *adj.* 1. done with intensity; thorough and concentrated: *intensive questioning.* 2. (in grammar) giving force or emphasis; intensifying a meaning. In *I myself have suffered most, myself* is an intensive pronoun. *So, too, very, quite* are intensive adverbs. In words such as *belabor* or *berate, be-* is an intensive prefix. —*n.* 3. an intensive word, phrase, or element. —in·ten′sive·ly, *adv.*

in·tent[1] (in tent′), *n.* 1. the act or fact of intending to do something: *criminal intent.* 2. that which is intended; purpose; intention: *He broke into the store with intent to steal.* 3. meaning or significance: *What was the intent of his remark?* [from the Latin word *intentus* "aim, purpose," literally "stretched out." See *intent*[2]]

in·tent[2] (in tent′), *adj.* 1. firmly fixed or directed: *intent concentration.* 2. having the attention sharply fixed on something: *to be intent on one's job; to be intent on revenge.* [from the Latin word *intentus,* literally "stretched out, taut"]

in·ten·tion (in ten′shən), *n.* plan or purpose; that which is intended: *His intention is to travel abroad.*

in·ten·tion·al (in ten′shə nəl), *adj.* done on purpose; deliberate: *an intentional insult.* —in·ten′tion·al·ly, *adv.*

in·ter (in tûr′), *v.,* in·terred, in·ter·ring. to place (a dead body) in a grave or tomb; bury.

inter-, a prefix meaning 1. between or among: *interstate; international.* 2. together: *intermingle.* 3. one with the other: *interact; interchange.*

in·ter·act (in′tər akt′), *v.* to act upon each other or upon one another: *two chemicals that interact.* —in·ter·ac·tion (in′tər ak′shən), *n.*

in·ter·cede (in′tər sēd′), *v.,* in·ter·ced·ed, in·ter·ced·ing. 1. to plead in behalf of a person in difficulty or trouble: *to intercede with the governor for a condemned man.* 2. to attempt to settle differences between two people or groups.

in·ter·cept (in′tər sept′), *v.* 1. to take, seize, or stop: *to intercept a messenger; to intercept an escape.* 2. to mark off or include, such as between two points or lines. —in′ter·cep′tion, *n.*

in·ter·ces·sion (in′tər sesh′ən), *n.* 1. the act or an instance of interceding. 2. a prayer to God on behalf of another or others.

in·ter·change (in′tər chānj′), *v.,* in·ter·changed, in·ter·chang·ing. 1. to put (each of two things) in the place of the other: *He interchanged the cat's and the dog's dishes by mistake.* 2. to give and receive; exchange. —*n.* (in′tər chānj′). 3. the act or an instance of interchanging: *an interchange of letters.* 4. a highway junction consisting of a system of road levels such that vehicles may move from one road to another without crossing the stream of traffic.

in·ter·change·a·ble (in′tər chān′jə bəl), *adj.* 1. (of two things) capable of being put or used in the place of each other: *interchangeable words.* 2. (of one thing) capable of replacing or changing places with something else: *an interchangeable part of a machine.* —in′ter·change′a·bly, *adv.*

in·ter·col·le·giate (in′tər kə lē′jit), *adj.* taking place between colleges: *intercollegiate athletics.*

in·ter·con·ti·nen·tal (in′tər kon′t³nen′t³l), *adj.* 1. between or among continents; involving two or more continents: *intercontinental trade.* 2. traveling between continents: *intercontinental jet airplanes.*

in·ter·course (in′tər kôrs′), *n.* dealings or communication between individuals, groups, countries, etc.

in·ter·de·pend·ent (in′tər di pen′dənt), *adj.* dependent on each other: *interdependent influences.* —in′ter·de·pend′ence, *n.*

in·ter·dict (in′tər dikt′), *n.* 1. a forbidding or prohibiting of something. 2. (in the Roman Catholic Church) a punishment by which a member is prohibited from participation in certain sacred acts. —*v.* (in′tər dikt′). 3. to forbid or prohibit. 4. to forbid (a person) to practice certain religious functions and privileges. —**in'ter·dic'tion,** *n.*

in·ter·est (in'tər ist, in'trist), *n.* **1.** a person's feelings or attitudes of concern, involvement, or curiosity: *He has an interest in music.* **2.** a person or thing that arouses such feelings or attitudes: *Chess is his main interest.* **3.** the power to excite such feelings or attitudes: *questions of great interest.* **4.** a legal share or right in the ownership of property or a business. **5.** benefit or advantage: *Keep your own interests in mind.* **6.** a sum paid for the use of money or charged for borrowing money: *The bank pays 4% interest on savings.* **7.** Often, **interests.** a group of persons having influence on and often involved in an enterprise, industry, or activity: *the labor interests.* —*v.* **8.** to excite the attention or curiosity of: *Mystery stories interest him very much.* **9.** to cause to take a personal concern; involve: *We tried to interest him in the club.* **10. in the interests of,** so as to further or advance; in behalf of: *in the interests of good government.*

in·ter·est·ed (in'tri stid, in'tə res'tid), *adj.* **1.** having or showing an interest in something; concerned: *an interested audience.* **2.** having an interest or share. **3.** influenced by personal reasons: *an interested witness.*

in·ter·est·ing (in'tri sting, in'tə res'ting), *adj.* holding the attention or curiosity: *an interesting book.* —**in'ter·est·ing·ly,** *adv.*

in·ter·fere (in'tər fēr'), *v.,* **in·ter·fered, in·ter·fer·ing.** **1.** to come into opposition; get in the way: *The noise interferes with my studying.* **2.** to take part in the affairs of others; meddle: *She always interferes in other people's business.* —**in'ter·fer'ing·ly,** *adv.*

in·ter·fer·ence (in'tər fēr'əns), *n.* **1.** the act, fact, or an instance of interfering. **2.** something that interferes.

in·ter·im (in'tər im), *n.* **1.** the time elapsing between two events; meantime: *I'll phone you in the interim.* —*adj.* **2.** belonging to or connected with an intervening period of time; temporary: *an interim law.*

in·te·ri·or (in tēr'ē ər), *adj.* **1.** of, referring to, or located within: *the interior part of a house.* —*n.* **2.** the internal part; inside: *the interior of the house.* **3.** the inland parts of a region, country, etc.: *the interior of the forest.* **4.** the domestic affairs of a country: *the Department of the Interior.*

interj., interjection.

in·ter·ject (in'tər jekt'), *v.* to introduce or throw in; insert: *to interject an explanation.*

in·ter·jec·tion (in'tər jek'shən), *n.* **1.** the act of interjecting or inserting: *the interjection of a funny remark into a speech.* **2.** something interjected. **3.** an exclamation, often expressing emotion, and having no grammatical connection with the rest of the sentence, such as *Oh!, Hey!,* or *Darn!*

Interlacing arches

in·ter·lace (in'tər lās'), *v.,* **in·ter·laced, in·ter·lac·ing.** **1.** to cross one another as if woven together; intertwine: *Their hands interlaced.* **2.** to unite or arrange (threads, strips,

branches, etc.) so as to cross one another, passing over and under: *to interlace ribbons.*

in·ter·lard (in'tər lärd'), *v.* to give variety to by mixing in or interjecting something different or unusual: *to interlard a speech with funny stories.*

in·ter·lock (in'tər lok'), *v.* **1.** to interlace, one with another: *The branches of the trees interlock to form a natural archway.* **2.** to lock or fit together: *The machinery parts interlock.*

in·ter·lop·er (in'tər lō'pər), *n.* a person who intrudes or interferes where he is not wanted; meddler; intruder.

in·ter·lude (in'tər lood'), *n.* **1.** an event or period of time that differs from what comes before and after: *an interlude of warm weather between the weeks of bitter cold.* **2.** a piece of music played between the parts of a song, church service, drama, etc.

in·ter·mar·riage (in'tər mar'ij), *n.* marriage between a man and woman of different races, religions, or ethnic groups.

in·ter·mar·ry (in'tər mar'ē), *v.,* **in·ter·mar·ried, in·ter·mar·ry·ing.** **1.** to become connected by marriage: *The tribes intermarried.* **2.** to marry outside one's religion, race, or ethnic group.

in·ter·me·di·ar·y (in'tər mē'dē er'ē), *adj.* **1.** being between; intermediate. **2.** acting between persons, groups, etc.: *an intermediary power.* —*n., pl.* **in·ter·me·di·ar·ies. 3.** a person who acts as a mediator or go-between.

in·ter·me·di·ate (in'tər mē'dē it), *adj.* **1.** being, located, or acting between two points, stages, things, persons, etc.: *the intermediate stages of development.* —*n.* **2.** something intermediate.

in·ter·ment (in tûr'mənt), *n.* the act or a ceremony of interring; burial.

in·ter·mez·zo (in'tər met'sō), *n., pl.* **in·ter·mez·zos** or **in·ter·mez·zi** (in'tər met'sē). a short piece of music to be played between sections of a larger work.

in·ter·mi·na·ble (in tûr'mə nə bəl), *adj.* appearing to have no limit or end; unending: *an interminable trip.* —**in'ter'mi·na·bly,** *adv.*

in·ter·min·gle (in'tər ming'gəl), *v.,* **in·ter·min·gled, in·ter·min·gling.** to mix or mingle together.

in·ter·mis·sion (in'tər mish'ən), *n.* **1.** an interval between periods of action or activity; break: *They studied for hours without an intermission.* **2.** a short interval between the acts of a play or parts of a public performance.

in·ter·mit·tent (in'tər mit'ᵊnt), *adj.* stopping for a time; stopping and starting again: *an intermittent pain.* —**in'ter·mit'tent·ly,** *adv.*

in·ter·mix (in'tər miks'), *v.* to mix together; intermingle.

in·ter·mix·ture (in'tər miks'chər), *n.* **1.** the act of intermixing. **2.** a mass of ingredients mixed together; mixture.

in·tern¹ (in tûrn'), *v.* to confine within certain limits: *to intern refugees.* [from the French word *interner,* which comes from Latin *internus* "inner, within"] —**in·tern'ment,** *n.*

in·tern² (in'tûrn), *n.* **1.** Also, **interne.** a recent medical school graduate who is a member of the medical staff of a hospital, usually serving an apprenticeship under supervision. —*v.* **2.** to perform the duties of an intern. [from the French word *interne,* literally "living within." See *intern*[1]]

in·ter·nal (in tûr′n²l), *adj.* **1.** of, referring to, or located on the inside of something; interior: *internal parts of a machine.* **2.** of or concerning the domestic affairs of a country: *internal politics.* —**in·ter′nal·ly,** *adv.*

in·ter′nal-com·bus′tion en′gine (in tûr′n²l kəm bus′chən), an engine whose power comes from the burning of fuel within the engine itself. Gasoline engines, diesel engines, and jet engines are all internal-combustion engines; steam engines are not.

in·ter·na·tion·al (in′tər nash′ə n²l), *adj.* **1.** between or among nations; involving two or more nations: *international trade.* **2.** referring to the relations between nations: *international legislation.* —**in′ter·na′tion·al·ly,** *adv.*

In′terna′tional Date′ Line′, an imaginary line following approximately the 180th meridian, the regions to the east of which are counted as being one day earlier in their calendar dates than the regions to the west.

in·ter·na·tion·al·ize (in′tər nash′ə n²liz′), *v.,* **in·ter·na·tion·al·ized, in·ter·na·tion·al·iz·ing.** to make international; bring under the control of several nations: *to internationalize a city.*

in·terne (in′tûrn), *n.* See intern² (def. 1).

in·ter·ne·cine (in′tər nes′ēn), *adj.* **1.** very destructive: *internecine fighting.* **2.** of or referring to conflict or struggle within a group.

in·ter·plan·e·tar·y (in′tər plan′i ter′ē), *adj.* existing or happening between planets: *interplanetary space.*

in·ter·play (in′tər plā′), *n.* action or influence on each other.

in·ter·po·late (in tûr′pə lāt′), *v.,* **in·ter·po·lat·ed, in·ter·po·lat·ing.** **1.** to change (a text) by adding new material, often for the purpose of changing the meaning. **2.** to add (new words or phrases). —**in·ter′po·la′tion,** *n.*

in·ter·pose (in′tər pōz′), *v.,* **in·ter·posed, in·ter·pos·ing.** **1.** to place between. **2.** to put in (a remark, question, etc.) in the middle of a conversation. **3.** to come between or intervene in order to help: *to interpose in an argument between two people.* —**in·ter·po·si·tion,** *n.*

in·ter·pret (in tûr′prit), *v.* **1.** to give the meaning of;

explain: *to interpret a poem.* **2.** to understand in a certain way: *to interpret a reply as favorable.* **3.** to perform (a song, role in a play, etc.) according to one's understanding: *She interpreted the song beautifully.* **4.** to translate. —**in·ter′pret·er,** *n.*

in·ter·pre·ta·tion (in tûr′pri tā′shən), *n.* **1.** the act of interpreting; explanation. **2.** the performance of music, a dramatic part, etc., so as to bring out the meaning: *a humorous interpretation of the role.* **3.** a translation.

in·ter·pre·ta·tive (in tûr′pri tā′tiv), *adj.* serving to interpret: *an interpretative essay.* Also, **in·ter·pre·tive** (in tûr′pri tiv).

in·ter·ra·cial (in′tər rā′shəl), *adj.* of or involving members of different races: *interracial cooperation.* —**in′ter·ra′cial·ly,** *adv.*

in·ter·re·lat·ed (in′tər ri lā′tid), *adj.* mutually related: *an interrelated series of experiments.*

in·ter·re·la·tion (in′tər ri lā′shən), *n.* the fact or condition of being mutually related. Also, **in·ter·re·la·tion·ship.**

in·ter·ro·gate (in ter′ə gāt′), *v.,* **in·ter·ro·gat·ed, in·ter·ro·gat·ing.** to examine (a person) by formal or official questioning: *to interrogate a suspect.* —**in·ter′ro·ga′tor,** *n.*

in·ter·ro·ga·tion (in ter′ə gā′shən), *n.* **1.** the act of interrogating; questioning. **2.** an instance of being interrogated: *The prisoner was nervous during his interrogation.* **3.** a question or inquiry.

in·ter·rog·a·tive (in′tə rog′ə tiv), *adj.* **1.** of or referring to a question. **2.** (in grammar) asking a question: *"Did you go?" is an interrogative sentence.* —*n.* **3.** a word used to ask a question, such as *where, how,* or *why.*

in·ter·rog·a·to·ry (in′tə rog′ə tôr′ē), *adj.* containing or asking a question.

in·ter·rupt (in′tə rupt′), *v.* **1.** to break off or cause to stop: *He interrupted the speaker to ask a question.* **2.** to interfere with or break the continuity of: *The wall interrupts the view.* **3.** to interfere with action or speech: *Please don't interrupt.*

in·ter·rup·tion (in′tə rup′shən), *n.* **1.** the act or an instance of interrupting. **2.** the state of being interrupted. **3.** something that interrupts. **4.** an intermission or break.

in·ter·scho·las·tic (in′tər skə las′tik), *adj.* between or among schools: *interscholastic debates.*

in·ter·sect (in′tər sekt′), *v.* **1.** to cut or divide by passing through or across. **2.** to cross, as lines, wires, etc.: *The highways intersect near the town.*

in·ter·sec·tion (in′tər sek′shən), *n.* **1.** a place where two or more roads meet, esp. when at least one is a major highway. **2.** any area or place of intersection. **3.** the act or fact of intersecting.

in·ter·sperse (in′tər spûrs′), *v.,* **in·ter·spersed, in·ter·spers·ing.** **1.** to scatter here and there among other things: *to intersperse flowers among shrubs.* **2.** to change by scattering or placing something here and there: *to intersperse the shrubs with flowers.*

---

act, āble, dâre, ärt; ebb, ēqual; if, īce; hot, ōver, ôrder; oil; bŏŏk; ōōze; out; up, ûrge; ə = *a* as in *alone;* ³ as in *button* (but′²n), *fire* (fī³r); **chief;** shoe; thin; ŧhat; zh as in *measure* (mezh′ər). See full key inside cover.

in·ter·state (in′tər stāt′), *adj.* connecting or jointly involving states of the U.S.: *interstate commerce.*

in·ter·stel·lar (in′tər stel′ər), *adj.* existing or happening between stars: *interstellar space.*

in·ter·twine (in′tər twīn′), *v.,* **in·ter·twined, in·ter·twin·ing.** to twist or twine together; interlace.

in·ter·ur·ban (in′tər ûr′bən), *adj.* connecting two or more cities: *interurban transportation.*

in·ter·val (in′tər vəl), *n.* 1. a period of time between two events: *an interval of 50 years.* 2. a space between things, points, limits, etc.: *an interval of 10 feet between posts.* 3. (in music) the difference in pitch between two tones. 4. **at intervals,** here and there; now and then: *The restaurants are placed at intervals along the highway.*

in·ter·vene (in′tər vēn′), *v.,* **in·ter·vened, in·ter·ven·ing.** 1. to come, be, or occur between two places or times. 2. to come between, as in an action; intercede: *to intervene in a dispute.*

in·ter·ven·tion (in′tər ven′shən), *n.* 1. the act or fact of intervening: *His intervention helped to settle the argument.* 2. interference by one state or nation in the affairs of another.

in·ter·view (in′tər vyōō′), *n.* 1. a meeting for obtaining information by questioning a person or persons, as for a magazine article or a television broadcast. 2. a formal meeting in which a person or persons question, consult, or evaluate another or others: *a job interview.* —*v.* 3. to have an interview with: *The television reporter interviewed the presidential candidates.* —**in′ter·view′er,** *n.*

in·ter·weave (in′tər wēv′), *v.,* **in·ter·wove** (in′tər wōv′); **in·ter·wo·ven** (in′tər wō′vən) *or* **in·ter·wove** (in′tər wōv′); **in·ter·weav·ing.** 1. to weave together: *to interweave blue and red threads.* 2. to combine together: *to interweave truth with fiction.*

in·tes·tate (in tes′tāt, in-tes′tit), *adj.* (of a person) not having made a will: *to die intestate.*

in·tes·ti·nal (in tes′tə-nəl), *adj.* 1. of or referring to the intestines: *intestinal juice.* 2. occurring in or affecting the intestines: *intestinal pains.*

in·tes·tine (in tes′tin), *n.* Often, **intestines.** the long coiled tube that makes up the lower portion of the alimentary canal where most of the digestion and absorption of food takes place and where solid wastes are accumulated and prepared for elimination from the body. See also **large intestine, small intestine.**

Intestines (Human)
A, End of esophagus;
B, Stomach; C, Small intestine; D, Appendix;
E, Large intestine;
F, Colon; G, Rectum

in·ti·ma·cy (in′tə mə sē), *n., pl.* **in·ti·ma·cies.** a close, familiar, and usually affectionate or loving, personal relationship.

in·ti·mate¹ (in′tə mit), *adj.* 1. associated in close personal relations: *an intimate friend.* 2. private; very personal: *intimate thoughts.* 3. arising from close personal connection or familiar experience: *intimate knowledge.* —*n.* 4. an intimate friend or associate. [from the Latin word *intimus* "close friend"] —**in′ti·mate·ly,** *adv.*

in·ti·mate² (in′tə māt′), *v.,* **in·ti·mat·ed, in·ti·mat·ing.** to make known indirectly; suggest: *She intimated that there might be famous people at the meeting.* [from the Latin word *intimātus* "made known"] —**in′ti·ma′tion,** *n.*

in·tim·i·date (in tim′i dāt′), *v.,* **in·tim·i·dat·ed, in·tim·i·dat·ing.** to make timid or fearful; frighten: *Large groups intimidate her.* —**in·tim′i·da′tion,** *n.*

in·to (in′tōō), *prep.* 1. to the inside of; in toward: *He walked into the room.* 2. to the state, condition, or form of: *to go into shock; to be translated into German.* 3. (used to indicate the division of one number into another number): *2 into 20 equals 10.*

in·tol·er·a·ble (in tol′ər ə bəl), *adj.* not tolerable; impossible to endure: *intolerable heat.* —**in·tol′er·a·bly,** *adv.*

in·tol·er·ance (in tol′ər əns), *n.* 1. lack of toleration; unwillingness to tolerate or understand different opinions or beliefs, persons of different races or backgrounds, etc.: *religious intolerance.* 2. inability to bear or endure something: *intolerance of heat.*

in·tol·er·ant (in tol′ər ənt), *adj.* not tolerating political or religious beliefs or opinions different from one's own: *intolerant of other people's customs.* —**in·tol′er·ant·ly,** *adv.*

in·to·na·tion (in′tə nā′shən), *n.* 1. the rising and falling pattern or melody of pitch changes in speech. 2. the correctness in pitch of musical tones. 3. something intoned or chanted.

in·tone (in tōn′), *v.,* **in·toned, in·ton·ing.** to utter in a singing voice; chant.

in·tox·i·cant (in tok′sə kənt), *n.* something that intoxicates, such as alcoholic liquor or certain drugs.

in·tox·i·cate (in tok′sə kāt′), *v.,* **in·tox·i·cat·ed, in·tox·i·cat·ing.** 1. to make drunk. 2. to make enthusiastic: *We were intoxicated by the prospect of going to Europe.*

in·tox·i·ca·tion (in tok′sə kā′shən), *n.* 1. the state of being intoxicated; drunkenness. 2. overpowering excitement.

in·trac·ta·ble (in trak′tə bəl), *adj.* difficult to manage; stubborn; obstinate: *an intractable mule.*

in·tra·mu·ral (in′trə myōōr′əl), *adj.* involving representatives of a single school: *intramural athletics.*

in·tran·si·tive (in tran′si tiv), *adj.* 1. describing a verb that does not have or does not require a direct object. In the sentence *Sit straight, sit* is an intransitive verb. —*n.* 2. an intransitive verb or verb form. See also **transitive.** —**in·tran′si·tive·ly,** *adv.*

in·tra·ve·nous (in′trə vē′nəs), *adj.* into or within a vein: *an intravenous injection.* —**in′tra·ve′nous·ly,** *adv.*

in·trench (in trench′), *v.* another spelling of **entrench.** —**in·trench′ment,** *n.*

in·trep·id (in trep′id), *adj.* very brave; fearless: *an intrepid explorer.* —**in·tre·pid′i·ty,** *n.* —**in·trep′id·ly,** *adv.*

in·tri·ca·cy (in′trə kə sē), *n., pl.* for def. 2 **in·tri·ca·cies.** 1. intricate character or state: *the intricacy of the machine.* 2. an intricate part, action, event, etc.: *the intricacies of the new regulations.*

in·tri·cate (in′trə kit), *adj.* 1. entangled or involved; having many interrelated parts: *intricate machinery.* 2. complicated; hard to understand: *an intricate set of problems.* —**in′tri·cate·ly,** *adv.*

in·trigue (in trēg′), *v.,* **in·trigued, in·tri·guing.** 1. to arouse the curiosity or interest of by unusual or fascinating qualities: *The new game intrigued the whole family.* 2. to accomplish or force by plotting. —*n.* (in trēg′, in′trēg). 3. the use of underhand methods and secret plotting. 4. a secret plot or scheme. 5. a secret love affair.

in·trin·sic (in trin′sik), *adj.* belonging to a thing by its very nature: *The music is pleasant but has little intrinsic worth.* —**in·trin′si·cal·ly,** *adv.*

intro., 1. introduction. 2. introductory. Also, **introd.**

in·tro·duce (in′trə dōōs′, -dyōōs′), *v.,* **in·tro·duced, in·tro·duc·ing.** 1. to make acquainted: *Will you introduce us?* 2. to bring (a person) to first knowledge or experience of something: *to introduce someone to skiing.* 3. to create, propose, advance, or bring into notice for the first time: *to introduce a new idea.* 4. to begin; lead into: *to introduce a speech with a joke.* 5. to bring in or establish: *to introduce a plant into America.* 6. to put in; insert: *to introduce a brighter color in the painting.*

in·tro·duc·tion (in′trə duk′shən), *n.* 1. the act of introducing, or the state of being introduced. 2. a formal presentation of one person to another. 3. something introduced. 4. the opening part, as of a book or musical composition, leading up to the main part.

in·tro·duc·to·ry (in′trə duk′tə rē), *adj.* serving to introduce: *introductory remarks.*

in·tro·spec·tion (in′trə spek′shən), *n.* the examination or observation of one's own thoughts or feelings.

in·tro·vert (in′trə vûrt′), *n.* a person who is concerned mostly with his own thoughts and feelings rather than with the world around him. See also **extrovert.**

in·trude (in trōōd′), *v.,* **in·trud·ed, in·trud·ing.** 1. to thrust or bring in without reason, permission, or welcome: *He intruded his opinions into the discussion.* 2. to thrust oneself without invitation or welcome: *to intrude upon his privacy.* —**in·trud′er,** *n.*

in·tru·sion (in trōō′zhən), *n.* the act or an instance of intruding: *Pardon my intrusion, but have you seen Bill?* —**in·tru′sive,** *adj.*

in·trust (in trust′), *v.* another spelling of **entrust.**

in·tu·i·tion (in′tōō ish′ən, -tyōō-), *n.* 1. knowledge of something that is not based on reasoning: *She knew by intuition that something was wrong.* 2. something known in this way; hunch.

in·tu·i·tive (in tōō′i tiv, -tyōō′-), *adj.* 1. knowing by intuition. 2. resulting from or involving intuition: *intuitive knowledge.* —**in·tu′i·tive·ly,** *adv.*

in·un·date (in′ən dāt′), *v.,* **in·un·dat·ed, in·un·dat·ing.** 1. to flood; overspread with water; overflow. 2. to overspread, as if with a flood: *inundated with letters.* —**in′un·da′tion,** *n.*

in·ure (in yŏŏr′, i nŏŏr′), *v.,* **in·ured, in·ur·ing.** to toughen or harden by use; accustom (usually fol. by *to*): *to inure a person to hardship.*

in·vade (in vād′), *v.,* **in·vad·ed, in·vad·ing.** 1. to enter forcefully as an enemy: *Germany invaded Poland in 1939. Locusts invaded the fields.* 2. to enter as if to take possession: *to invade a neighbor's home.* 3. to enter and spread throughout: *viruses that invade the bloodstream.* 4. to intrude or encroach upon: *to invade one's privacy.* —**in·vad′er,** *n.*

in·va·lid[1] (in′və lid), *n.* 1. a person who is so sick that he cannot care for himself, esp. one who has been sick for a long time. —*adj.* 2. sick and unable to care for oneself. 3. of or for invalids: *an invalid diet.* [from the Latin word *invalidus* "weak," which comes from *in-* "not" + *validus* "strong, healthy"]

in·val·id[2] (in val′id), *adj.* not valid; without force or foundation; worthless: *The coupon is invalid after May 15th.* [from the medieval Latin word *invalidus* "not legally valid"]

in·val·i·date (in val′i dāt′), *v.,* **in·val·i·dat·ed, in·val·i·dat·ing.** to make invalid or worthless: *to invalidate a check.*

in·val·u·a·ble (in val′yōō ə bəl), *adj.* worth more than can be estimated; priceless. —**in·val′u·a·bly,** *adv.*

in·var·i·a·ble (in vâr′ē ə bəl), *adj.* not variable or capable of being varied; unchanging. —**in·var′i·a·bly,** *adv.*

in·va·sion (in vā′zhən), *n.* 1. the act or an instance of invading or entering as an enemy: *the army's invasion.* 2. the entrance of anything troublesome or harmful: *an invasion of mosquitoes.* 3. an intrusion: *invasion of privacy.*

in·vec·tive (in vek′tiv), *n.* harsh and insulting language.

in·veigh (in vā′), *v.* to protest strongly or attack with words: *to inveigh against discrimination.*

in·vei·gle (in vā′gəl, in vē′gəl), *v.,* **in·vei·gled, in·vei·gling.** to entice, lure, or convince by artful, persuasive talk: *to inveigle a person into playing cards.*

in·vent (in vent′), *v.* 1. to make or bring into being for the first time: *to invent the sewing machine.* 2. to make up: *to invent excuses.*

in·ven·tion (in ven′shən), *n.* 1. the act of inventing: *the invention of a new kind of airplane.* 2. something invented: *Television is an invention of this century.* 3. the power of inventing, devising, or originating: *a poet's invention.* 4. something made up or fabricated: *His story was pure invention.*

---

in·ven·tive (in ven′tiv), *adj.* 1. good at inventing: *an inventive poet.* 2. involving or showing invention: *an inventive idea.* —**in·ven′tive·ness**, *n.*

in·ven·tor (in ven′tər), *n.* a person who invents, esp. one who designs a new machine, process, etc.

in·ven·to·ry (in′vən tôr′ē), *n.*, *pl.* **in·ven·to·ries.** 1. a detailed list of merchandise or stock on hand. 2. the objects or items represented on such a list. 3. the act of making such a list: *The store closed early for inventory.* —*v.*, **in·ven·to·ried, in·ven·to·ry·ing.** 4. to make an inventory of: *to inventory a store's stock.*

in·verse (in vûrs′, in′vûrs), *adj.* 1. reversed in position or direction: *inverse order.* 2. related in such a way that as one increases the other decreases: *an inverse relationship between one's speed and the time required to travel a certain distance.* —*n.* 3. something inverse; the direct opposite. —**in·verse′ly**, *adv.*

in·ver·sion (in vûr′zhən), *n.* 1. the act or an instance of inverting: *the inversion of the words in a sentence to form a question.* 2. anything that is inverted: *The number 73 is an inversion of the number 37.*

in·vert (in vûrt′), *v.* 1. to turn upside down. 2. to reverse in position, direction, or relationship.

in·ver·te·brate (in vûr′tə brit, in vûr′tə brāt′), *adj.* 1. without a backbone: *Worms are invertebrate animals.* —*n.* 2. an invertebrate animal.

in·vest (in vest′), *v.* 1. to put (money) to use in expectation of making a profit: *to invest $200 in stocks.* 2. to use, give, or devote in order to achieve something: *to invest time in one's work.* 3. to furnish with power, rank, etc.: *to invest the chairman with veto powers.* 4. to give a certain quality to: *He invested his gestures and words with elegance.* 5. to install in an office or position: *a ceremony to invest the new officers.* 6. to clothe or cover. —**in·ves′tor**, *n.*

in·ves·ti·gate (in ves′tə gāt′), *v.*, **in·ves·ti·gat·ed, in·ves·ti·gat·ing.** to search or look into thoroughly; examine in detail: *to investigate the causes of the fire.* —**in·ves′ti·ga·tor**, *n.*

in·ves·ti·ga·tion (in ves′tə gā′shən), *n.* a thorough search or inquiry to learn the facts about something.

in·vest·ment (in vest′mənt), *n.* 1. the investing of money for profitable returns. 2. the money invested: *an investment of $500.* 3. a property or right in which a person invests.

in·vet·er·ate (in vet′ər it), *adj.* 1. confirmed in a habit, practice, feeling, or the like: *an inveterate gambler.* 2. firmly established by long continuance or use: *an inveterate disease; an inveterate custom.*

in·vid·i·ous (in vid′ē əs), *adj.* causing or tending to cause hard feelings because of unfairness: *invidious comparisons.* —**in·vid′i·ous·ly**, *adv.*

in·vig·or·ate (in vig′ə rāt′), *v.*, **in·vig·or·at·ed, in·vig·or·at·ing.** to give vigor to; fill with life or energy: *Exercise invigorates the body.* —**in·vig′or·at′ing·ly**, *adv.*

in·vin·ci·ble (in vin′sə bəl), *adj.* incapable of being conquered, defeated, or subdued: *an invincible opponent.* —**in·vin′ci·bil′i·ty**, *n.* —**in·vin′ci·bly**, *adv.*

in·vi·o·la·ble (in vī′ə lə bəl), *adj.* prohibiting violation: *an inviolable sanctuary.* —**in·vi′o·la·bil′i·ty**, *n.*

in·vi·o·late (in vī′ə lit), *adj.* not violated; undisturbed or untouched; unbroken.

in·vis·i·ble (in viz′ə bəl), *adj.* not visible; not capable of being seen: *invisible ink.* —**in·vis′i·bil′i·ty**, *n.* —**in·vis′i·bly**, *adv.*

in·vi·ta·tion (in′vi tā′shən), *n.* 1. the act of inviting. 2. the written or spoken form with which a person is invited.

in·vite (in vīt′), *v.*, **in·vit·ed, in·vit·ing.** 1. to ask or request the presence or participation of: *to invite friends to dinner.* 2. to request politely or formally: *to invite donations.* 3. to act so as to cause: *to invite danger by fast driving.* 4. to attract or tempt.

in·vit·ing (in vī′tiñg), *adj.* offering an invitation of an attractive or tempting nature: *an inviting offer for a summer job.* —**in·vit′ing·ly**, *adv.*

in·vo·ca·tion (in′və kā′shən), *n.* 1. the act of calling upon God for help, protection, inspiration, etc. 2. the act of calling upon any spirit or supernatural force for help, protection, etc.

in·voice (in′vois), *n.* 1. a detailed list of goods sold or services provided, together with the charges and terms of payment. —*v.*, **in·voiced, in·voic·ing.** 2. to present an invoice to or for.

in·voke (in vōk′), *v.*, **in·voked, in·vok·ing.** 1. to call for with earnest desire; pray for: *to invoke God's mercy.* 2. to ask for. 3. to declare to be in effect: *to invoke a veto.* 4. to call forth by magic or incantation: *to invoke a spirit.*

in·vol·un·tar·y (in vol′ən ter′ē), *adj.* 1. not voluntary; done without choice or against one's will. 2. unintentional; unconscious: *an involuntary stammer.* —**in·vol·un·tar·i·ly** (in vol′ən târ′ə lē), *adv.*

in·volve (in volv′), *v.*, **in·volved, in·volv·ing.** 1. to include as a necessary part: *The project involved a lot of effort.* 2. to cause to be associated with; implicate: *Don't involve me in your quarrel!* 3. to absorb fully: *He's very involved in politics.* —**in·volve′ment**, *n.*

in·vul·ner·a·ble (in vul′nər ə bəl), *adj.* incapable of being wounded, hurt, or damaged. —**in·vul′ner·a·bil′i·ty**, *n.* —**in·vul′ner·a·bly**, *adv.*

in·ward (in′wərd), *adv.* Also, **in′wards.** 1. toward the inside or center: *The door leads inward.* 2. into or toward the mind or soul: *He turned his thoughts inward.* —*adj.* 3. directed or located toward the inside: *an inward passage; inward feelings.*

in·ward·ly (in′wərd lē), *adv.* 1. in, on, or to the inside or inner part. 2. privately; secretly: *Inwardly, I disliked his idea.* 3. within the self; mentally.

i·o·dine (ī′ə dīn′), *n.* 1. *Chem.* a grayish substance extracted from sea water or seaweed and important in nutrition. Iodine is a chemical element of the halogen family. *Symbol:* I 2. a brownish solution of this substance, used as a disinfectant, esp. on minor cuts.

i·on (ī′ən, ī′on), *n.* an atom or group of atoms having an electric charge due to a loss or gain of electrons.

-ion, a suffix used to form nouns meaning 1. action or process: *inspection; rebellion.* 2. result of an action: *creation; concussion.* 3. state or condition: *depression; location.*

I·on·ic (ī on′ik), *adj.* referring to a style, or order, of ancient Greek architecture characterized by columns having scrollwork at the top. See also **Corinthian** (def. 2), **Doric**. See illus. at **order**.

i·on·ize (ī′ə nīz′), v., **i·on·ized, i·on·iz·ing. 1.** to produce ions in: *to ionize a gas with an electric spark.* **2.** to convert into ions. —**i′on·i·za′tion,** n.

i·on·o·sphere (ī on′ə sfēr′), n. a region in the atmosphere extending from about 50 to 250 miles above the earth's surface, in which much of the air has been ionized by radiation from outer space.

i·o·ta (ī ō′tə), n. a very small quantity: *There wasn't an iota of truth in what he said.* [from the name of the Greek letter *iota*, which is the smallest letter of the Greek alphabet]

IOU, an informal note acknowledging a debt: *I gave him an IOU for ten dollars.* Also, **I.O.U.** [from the phrase *"I owe you"*]

I·o·wa (ī′ə wə), n. a state in the central United States. 56,280 sq. mi. *Cap.:* Des Moines. —**I′o·wan,** *n., adj.*

ipm, inches per minute. Also, **i.p.m.**

ips, inches per second. Also, **i.p.s.**

IQ, intelligence quotient: a measure of intelligence equal to a person's mental age, as shown by a test, divided by his actual age and multiplied by 100. A ten-year-old child whose mental age is that of the average twelve-year-old has an IQ of 120. Also, **I.Q.**

Ir, *Chem.* the symbol for **iridium.**

ir-, a form of the prefix **in-,** used before words beginning with *r: irradiate; irregular.*

I·ran (i ran′, ē rän′), n. a kingdom in SW Asia. about 635,000 sq. mi. *Cap.:* Teheran. Former name, **Persia.**

I·ra·ni·an (i rā′nē ən), *adj.* **1.** of or referring to Iran, its inhabitants, or their language. **2.** of or referring to a branch of the Indo-European family of languages, including ancient Persian, modern Iranian, and several others. —*n.* **3.** the Iranian branch of the Indo-European language family. **4.** the modern language of Iran. **5.** an inhabitant of Iran.

I·raq (i rak′, ē räk′), n. a republic in SW Asia. 172,-000 sq. mi. *Cap.:* Baghdad. —**I·ra·qi** (i rak′ē, ē räkē), *n., adj.*

i·ras·ci·ble (i ras′ə bəl), *adj.* easily made angry. —**i·ras′ci·bly,** *adv.*

i·rate (ī′rāt, ī rāt′), *adj.* angry; enraged.

ire (ī³r), *n.* anger; wrath.

Ire·land (ī³r′lənd), *n.* **1.** a large western island of the British Isles, made up of the Republic of Ireland and Northern Ireland. 32,375 sq. mi. **2. Republic of,** a republic occupying most of the island of Ireland. 27,137 sq. mi. *Cap.:* Dublin. Gaelic name, **Eire.**

ir·i·des·cence (ir′i des′əns), *n.* an iridescent quality; a play or show of lustrous, changing colors.

ir·i·des·cent (ir′i des′ənt), *adj.* displaying lustrous colors like those of the rainbow.

i·rid·i·um (i rid′ē əm, ī rid′ē əm), *n. Chem.* a hard, silvery metallic element. *Symbol:* Ir

i·ris (ī′ris), *n.* **1.** any of various plants having sword-shaped leaves and usually purple, blue, or white flowers. **2.** the colored part of the eye, surrounding the pupil. See illus. at **eye.**

Iris

I·rish (ī′rish), *adj.* **1.** of, referring to, or characteristic of Ireland, its inhabitants, or their language. —*n.* **2.** the Irish people. **3.** the Celtic language of Ireland, spoken by some of its people. **4.** English as spoken by the Irish.

I·rish·man (ī′rish mən), *n., pl.* **I·rish·men. 1.** a man born in Ireland or of Irish ancestry. **2.** a native or inhabitant of Ireland.

I′rish pota′to, the common white potato.

I′rish Sea′, a part of the Atlantic Ocean between Ireland and England.

I′rish set′ter, one of an Irish breed of setters having a reddish-brown coat. See illus. at **setter.**

I′rish ter′rier, one of an Irish breed of terriers having a thick, wiry, reddish coat.

I′rish wolf′hound, one of an Irish breed of large, tall dogs having a rough, wiry coat.

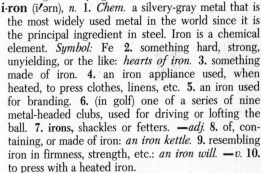

Irish wolfhound
(32 in. high
at shoulder)

irk (ûrk), *v.* to irritate or annoy: *Her constant talking irked me.*

irk·some (ûrk′səm), *adj.* irritating or annoying: *irksome rules.*

i·ron (ī′ərn), *n.* **1.** *Chem.* a silvery-gray metal that is the most widely used metal in the world since it is the principal ingredient in steel. Iron is a chemical element. *Symbol:* Fe **2.** something hard, strong, unyielding, or the like: *hearts of iron.* **3.** something made of iron. **4.** an iron appliance used, when heated, to press clothes, linens, etc. **5.** an iron used for branding. **6.** (in golf) one of a series of nine metal-headed clubs, used for driving or lofting the ball. **7. irons,** shackles or fetters. —*adj.* **8.** of, containing, or made of iron: *an iron kettle.* **9.** resembling iron in firmness, strength, etc.: *an iron will.* —*v.* **10.** to press with a heated iron.

I′ron Age′, the period in the history of mankind, following the Stone Age and Bronze Age, marked by the use of iron tools and weapons.

i·ron·clad (ī′ərn klad′), *adj.* **1.** covered or cased with iron plates. **2.** very rigid or exacting; unbreakable: *an ironclad contract.* —*n.* **3.** a 19th-century warship having iron or steel armor plating.

i′ron cur′tain, a barrier to the exchange of information and ideas created by the hostility of one country to another or others, esp. such a barrier between the Soviet Union, or areas controlled by it, and other countries.

i·ron·ic (ī ron′ik), *adj.* 1. expressing irony or mockery: *an ironic smile.* 2. using irony: *an ironic speaker.* Also, **i·ron′i·cal.** —**i·ron′i·cal·ly,** *adv.*

i′ron lung′, a large machine that forces air in and out of a person's lungs and makes it possible for him to breathe, esp. someone who has been paralyzed by polio.

i′ron py′rites, another name for **pyrite.**

i·ron·work (ī′ərn wûrk′), *n.* objects or parts of objects made of iron.

i·ro·ny (ī′rə nē, ī′ər nē), *n., pl.* **i·ro·nies.** 1. a figure of speech in which the words express a meaning that is often the direct opposite of the intended meaning: *To say "Beautiful weather, isn't it?" when it's raining is irony.* 2. an outcome of events contrary to what was, or might have been, expected. [from the Greek word *eirōneia,* which comes from *eirōn* "a person who says less than he thinks"]

Ir·o·quois (ir′ə kwoi′), *n., pl.* **Ir·o·quois.** a member of the Indian confederacy, the Five Nations, inhabiting the northeastern U.S. and eastern Canada.

ir·ra·di·ate (i rā′dē āt′), *v.,* **ir·ra·di·at·ed, ir·ra·di·at·ing.** 1. to expose to light or other radiation. 2. to shed light upon; illuminate. —**ir·ra′di·a′tion,** *n.*

ir·ra·tion·al (i ra<u>sh</u>′ə n^əl), *adj.* 1. without the faculty or power of reason: *an irrational animal.* 2. lacking sound judgment or common sense: *an irrational argument; an irrational fear.* —**ir·ra′tion·al·ly,** *adv.*

irra′tional num′ber, a number that cannot be represented exactly by the quotient of two whole numbers (distinguished from *rational number*): $\sqrt{2}$ *is an irrational number.*

ir·rec·on·cil·a·ble (i rek′ən sī′lə bəl), *adj.* incapable of being reconciled or brought into harmony; opposed: *irreconcilable enemies.* —**ir·rec′on·cil′a·bly,** *adv.*

ir·re·cov·er·a·ble (ir′i kuv′ər ə bəl), *adj.* incapable of being recovered or regained: *irrecoverable losses.*

ir·re·deem·a·ble (ir′i dē′mə bəl), *adj.* 1. not redeemable; incapable of being bought back or paid off: *irredeemable coupons.* 2. beyond redemption; hopeless: *an irredeemable liar.* —**ir′re·deem′a·bly,** *adv.*

ir·re·duc·i·ble (ir′i dōō′sə bəl, -dyōō′-), *adj.* not reducible; incapable of being reduced, diminished, or simplified. —**ir′re·duc′i·bly,** *adv.*

ir·ref·u·ta·ble (i ref′yə tə bəl, ir′i fyōō′tə bəl), *adj.* not refutable; incapable of being disproved: *irrefutable evidence.* —**ir·ref′u·ta·bly,** *adv.*

ir·reg·u·lar (i reg′yə lər), *adj.* 1. not evenly shaped or formally arranged: *an irregular pattern.* 2. not conforming to established customs: *irregular behavior.* 3. (in grammar) not following the usual rules of inflection. The verbs *keep* and *see* are irregular in their conjugation. The noun *child* has an irregular plural form: *children.* The adjective *bad* has irregu-

lar comparative and superlative forms: *worse, worst.* —**ir·reg′u·lar·ly,** *adv.*

ir·reg·u·lar·i·ty (i reg′yə lar′i tē), *n., pl.* for def. 2 **ir·reg·u·lar·i·ties.** 1. the quality or state of being irregular. 2. something irregular.

ir·rel·e·vant (i rel′ə vənt), *adj.* not relevant; having no relation or connection to the topic: *irrelevant questions.* —**ir·rel′e·vance,** *n.* —**ir·rel′e·vant·ly,** *adv.*

ir·re·li·gious (ir′i lij′əs), *adj.* not religious; not practicing a religion.

ir·re·me·di·a·ble (ir′i mē′dē ə bəl), *adj.* not capable of being remedied, cured, or repaired.

ir·rep·a·ra·ble (i rep′ər ə bəl), *adj.* not reparable; incapable of being corrected or made good: *an irreparable mistake.* —**ir·rep′a·ra·bly,** *adv.*

ir·re·place·a·ble (ir′i plā′sə bəl), *adj.* incapable of being replaced; unique: *an irreplaceable antique.*

ir·re·press·i·ble (ir′i pres′ə bəl), *adj.* incapable of being repressed or restrained: *an irrepressible urge.* —**ir′re·press′i·bly,** *adv.*

ir·re·proach·a·ble (ir′i prō′chə bəl), *adj.* free from blame; without fault: *irreproachable conduct.* —**ir·re·proach′a·bly,** *adv.*

ir·re·sist·i·ble (ir′i zis′tə bəl), *adj.* 1. not resistible; incapable of being resisted or withstood: *an irresistible force.* 2. very tempting: *She saw an irresistible hat in the store window.* —**ir′re·sist′i·bly,** *adv.*

ir·res·o·lute (i rez′ə lōōt′), *adj.* not resolute; doubtful, hesitant, or undecided: *An irresolute person is usually not a good leader.* —**ir·res′o·lute′ly,** *adv.* —**ir·res′o·lu′tion,** *n.*

ir·re·spec·tive (ir′i spek′tiv), *adj.* without regard to; ignoring or discounting (usually fol. by *of*): *Irrespective of the weather, I must go.*

ir·re·spon·si·ble (ir′i spon′sə bəl), *adj.* 1. said, done, or characterized by a lack of a sense of responsibility: *irresponsible behavior.* 2. not responsible, answerable, or accountable to any higher authority. —**ir′re·spon′si·bil′i·ty,** *n.* —**ir′re·spon′si·bly,** *adv.*

ir·re·triev·a·ble (ir′i trē′və bəl), *adj.* not retrievable; that cannot be recovered; irrecoverable. —**ir′re·triev′a·bly,** *adv.*

ir·rev·er·ent (i rev′ər ənt), *adj.* not reverent; lacking reverence or respect. —**ir·rev′er·ence,** *n.* —**ir·rev′er·ent·ly,** *adv.*

ir·re·vers·i·ble (ir′i vûr′sə bəl), *adj.* not reversible; incapable of being reversed or changed: *His decision is irreversible.* —**ir′re·vers′i·bly,** *adv.*

ir·rev·o·ca·ble (i rev′ə kə bəl), *adj.* not to be revoked or recalled: *an irrevocable command.* —**ir·rev′o·ca·bly,** *adv.*

ir·ri·gate (ir′ə gāt′), *v.,* **ir·ri·gat·ed, ir·ri·gat·ing.** 1. to supply (land) with water by artificial methods for the growing of crops. 2. to wash (a wound, the eye, etc.) with a flow of liquid. —**ir′ri·ga′tion,** *n.*

ir·ri·ta·ble (ir′i tə bəl), *adj.* 1. easily irritated; readily excited to impatience or anger: *She's in an irritable mood.* 2. very sensitive: *an irritable wound.* —**ir′ri·ta·bil′i·ty,** *n.* —**ir′ri·ta·bly,** *adv.*

ir·ri·tant (ir′i t^ənt), *n.* 1. something that causes irritation. —*adj.* 2. causing irritation; irritating.

ir·ri·tate (ir/i tāt/), *v.*, **ir·ri·tat·ed, ir·ri·tat·ing. 1.** to become or cause to become impatient or angry: *Teasing irritates her.* **2.** to make sore, swollen, or inflamed: *The wool sweater irritates his skin.* —**ir/ri·tat/ing·ly,** *adv.*

ir·ri·ta·tion (ir/i tā/shən), *n.* **1.** the act or fact of irritating. **2.** the state of being irritated. **3.** a soreness, swelling, or inflammation of part of the body: *an irritation of the skin.*

is (iz), *v.* the third person singular, present tense of **be:** *She is my sister. Is anyone home?*

Is., **1.** Island; Islands. **2.** Isle; Isles. Also, **is.**

I·saac (ī/zək), *n.* (in the Bible) a son of Abraham and Sarah, and father of Jacob.

Is·a·bel·la I (iz/ə bel/ə), *("the Catholic")* 1451–1504, queen of Spain 1474–1504.

I·sa·iah (ī zā/ə), *n.* **1.** (in the Bible) a Hebrew prophet of the 8th century B.C. **2.** a book of the Old Testament bearing his name.

Is·car·i·ot (i skar/ē ət), *n.* (in the Bible) the last name of Judas, the betrayer of Jesus.

-ish, a suffix used to form adjectives meaning **1.** of, from, or belonging to: *British; Spanish.* **2.** like or resembling: *boyish; girlish.* **3.** having the tendency of: *freakish; selfish.* **4.** somewhat; rather: *warmish; biggish.* **5.** approximately: *fortyish; fiftyish.*

i·sin·glass (ī/zin glas/, ī/zing glas/), *n.* **1.** a pure gelatin obtained from the air bladders of fish and used in making glues and jellies. **2.** another name for **mica.**

I·sis (ī/sis), *n.* a goddess in the religion of the ancient Egyptians.

Isl., **1.** Island; Islands. **2.** Isle; Isles. Also, **isl.**

Is·lam (is/ləm, is läm/), *n.* **1.** the religious faith of Muslims, as set forth in the Koran, which teaches that Allah is the only God and that Muhammad is his prophet. **2.** the whole body of Muslim believers, their civilization, and the countries in which theirs is the chief religion. —**Is·lam·ic** (is lam/ik, is lä/mik), *adj.*

Isis

is·land (ī/lənd), *n.* **1.** a land area completely surrounded by water and not large enough to be called a continent. **2.** anything resembling an island because of its isolation.

is·land·er (ī/lən dər), *n.* a native or inhabitant of an island.

isle (īl), *n.* a small island.

is·let (ī/lit), *n.* a very small island.

-ism, a suffix used to form nouns meaning **1.** action or process: *baptism; criticism.* **2.** state or condition: *barbarism; cannibalism.* **3.** system of doctrines or beliefs: *Judaism; socialism.* **4.** quality or condition of: *heroism; Americanism.* **5.** system of related parts: *mechanism; organism.*

isn't (iz/ənt), contraction of *is not.*

i·so·bar (ī/sə bär/), *n.* a line on a weather map that connects points at which the barometric pressure is the same. See also **isotherm.**

i·so·late (ī/sə lāt/), *v.,* **i·so·lat·ed, i·so·lat·ing.** to set or place apart; separate so as to be alone: *The doctor isolated the patients who had contagious diseases.*

i·so·la·tion (ī/sə lā/shən), *n.* **1.** the act or an instance of isolating. **2.** the state of being isolated. **3.** the complete separation from others of a person suffering from contagious or infectious disease; quarantine.

i·so·la·tion·ist (ī/sə lā/shə nist, is/ə lā/shə nist), *n.* a person who believes in isolating one's country from alliances with other nations. —**i/so·la/tion·ism,** *n.*

i·sos·ce·les tri·angle (ī sos/ə lēz/), a triangle having two sides that are the same length.

i·so·therm (ī/sə thûrm/), *n.* a line on a weather map that connects points at which the temperature is the same. See also **isobar.**

i·so·tope (ī/sə tōp/), *n.* any of two or more forms of a chemical element having different atomic weights: *Hydrogen has three isotopes, one of which is radioactive.*

Is·ra·el (iz/rē əl), *n.* **1.** a republic in SW Asia, on the Mediterranean Sea: formed as a Jewish state in 1948. 7984 sq. mi. *Cap.:* Jerusalem. **2.** the people traditionally descended from Jacob; the Hebrew or Jewish people. **3.** (in the Bible) a name given to Jacob after he had wrestled with the angel. **4.** (in ancient times) the northern kingdom of the Hebrews.

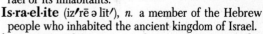

Israel

Is·rae·li (iz rā/lē), *n.* **1.** a native or inhabitant of modern Israel. —*adj.* **2.** of or referring to modern Israel or its inhabitants.

Is·ra·el·ite (iz/rē ə līt/), *n.* a member of the Hebrew people who inhabited the ancient kingdom of Israel.

is·su·ance (ish/ōō əns), *n.* the act of issuing or distributing.

is·sue (ish/ōō), *n.* **1.** the act of sending out or putting forth; distribution. **2.** something that is printed or published and distributed: *the latest issue of a magazine.* **3.** a quantity sent forth at one time: *an issue of commemorative stamps.* **4.** a matter that is in dispute: *They discussed the issue for hours.* **5.** the outcome or result of a proceeding, affair, etc. **6.** offspring; progeny: *to die without issue.* **7.** a discharge of blood, pus, or the like. —*v.,* **is·sued, is·su·ing. 8.** to go, pass, or flow out; come forth; emerge: *Water issued from the open fire hydrant.* **9.** to mint, print, or publish for sale or distribution: *to issue a new book.* **10.** to distribute or give out: *to issue summer uniforms to soldiers.* **11.** to occur as a result: *What issued from the debate?* **12. take issue with,** to disagree with: *He seemed to take issue with everything I said.*

-ist, a suffix used to form nouns meaning **1.** a person who is occupied with or connected with: *machinist;*

novelist. **2.** one who believes in or supports certain ideas: *socialist; Buddhist.*

Is·tan·bul (is′tan bool′, is′tän bool′), *n.* a port city in NW Turkey, on both the European and Asiatic banks of the Bosporus: built by the Romans on the site of Byzantium. Former name (A.D. 330–1930), **Constantinople.**

Isth., Isthmus. Also, **isth.**

isth·mus (is′məs), *n.* a narrow strip of land, bordered on both sides by water, connecting two larger bodies of land: *the Isthmus of Panama.*

it (it), *pron.* **1.** (used to represent a person, animal, group, or thing previously mentioned, or about to be mentioned): *It has red upholstery.* **2.** (used as the impersonal subject of the verb *to be*): *It is foggy.* **3.** (used as the subject of any impersonal verb): *It rained last night.* —*n.* **4.** (in children's games) the player who is to perform some task, for example, in tag, the one who must catch the others. **5.** life in general: *How's it going?* **6. get with it,** *Slang.* to become interested, begin to put forth effort, etc.: *You'd better get with it or you'll flunk spelling.*

ital., italic; italics.

I·tal·ian (i tal′yən), *adj.* **1.** of or concerning Italy, its people, or their language. —*n.* **2.** a native or inhabitant of Italy, or a person of Italian descent. **3.** the Romance language of Italy and part of Switzerland.

Ital′ian Soma′liland, a former Italian colony in E Africa, now part of the Somali Republic.

i·tal·ic (i tal′ik, ī tal′ik), *adj.* **1.** indicating a style of printing type in which the letters usually slant to the right, used esp. for emphasis: *This sentence is in italic type.* —*n.* **2.** Often, **italics.** italic type.

i·tal·i·cize (i tal′i sīz′, ī tal′i sīz′), *v.* **1.** to print in italic type. **2.** to underline (a written word, sentence, or the like) with a single line to indicate italics.

itals., italics.

It·a·ly (it′ᵊlē), *n.* a republic in S Europe. 116,294 sq. mi. *Cap.:* Rome.

itch (ich), *n.* **1.** an unpleasant feeling that causes a desire to scratch. **2.** a restless longing: *an itch for excitement.* —*v.* **3.** to have or cause an itch: *My skin itches. This rough cloth itches.* **4.** to have a desire to do or get something: *to itch after fame and fortune.*

itch·y (ich′ē), *adj.,* **itch·i·er, itch·i·est.** having or causing an itching feeling: *an itchy allergy; an itchy sweater.* —**itch′i·ness,** *n.*

-ite, a suffix used to form nouns meaning **1.** native or inhabitant of: *Brooklynite; Canaanite.* **2.** descendant of: *Semite; Israelite.* **3.** supporter or follower of: *Mennonite.* **4.** rock or mineral: *lignite; bauxite.*

i·tem (ī′təm), *n.* **1.** a separate article: *There are 50 items on the list.* **2.** a separate piece of information or news: *an item about China in the magazine.*

i·tem·ize (ī′tə mīz′), *v.,* **i·tem·ized, i·tem·iz·ing.** to state by items; list the individual units or parts of: *to itemize expenses.* —**i′tem·i·za′tion,** *n.*

it·er·ate (it′ə rāt′), *v.,* **it·er·at·ed, it·er·at·ing.** to utter or say again; repeat. —**it′er·a′tion,** *n.*

Ith·a·ca (ith′ə kə), *n.* an Ionian island W of Greece: home of Ulysses.

i·tin·er·ant (ī tin′ər ənt), *adj.* **1.** traveling from place to place: *an itinerant salesman.* —*n.* **2.** a person who travels from place to place.

i·tin·er·ar·y (ī tin′ə rer′ē), *n.,* *pl.* **i·tin·er·ar·ies. 1.** a detailed plan for a journey, esp. a list of places to visit. **2.** an account of a journey; a record of travel.

it'll (it′ᵊl), contraction of *it will* or *it shall.*

its (its), *pron.* the possessive form of **it,** used as an adjective: *The book has lost its jacket.*

it's (its), **1.** contraction of *it is: It's raining.* **2.** contraction of *it has: It's been a long time.*

it·self (it self′), *pron.* **1.** a form of **it** that is used for emphasis: *The bowl itself is beautiful.* **2.** a form of **it** that is used when the subject of the sentence is the same as the object: *The battery recharges itself.* **3.** its normal or ordinary self: *With good care the dog will soon be itself again.*
—**Usage.** See **myself.**

-ity, a suffix used to form nouns meaning **1.** state or condition: *activity; austerity.* **2.** quality or characteristic: *elasticity; humidity.*

I've (īv), contraction of *I have: I've lost my cap.*

-ive, a suffix used to form adjectives meaning **1.** doing or connected with something: *active; festive.* Some of these adjectives may be used as nouns: *an operative; a detective.* **2.** having a tendency to: *destructive; conductive.*

i·vied (ī′vēd), *adj.* covered or overgrown with ivy: *ivied walls.*

i·vo·ry (ī′və rē, ī′vrē), *n.,* *pl.* **i·vo·ries. 1.** the hard white substance of which the tusks of elephants and walruses are composed. **2.** a creamy or yellowish white. —*adj.* **3.** made of ivory: *an ivory comb.* **4.** of the color ivory: *ivory walls.*

I′vory Coast′, a republic in W Africa. 127,520 sq. mi. *Cap.:* Abidjan.

i·vy (ī′vē), *n.,* *pl.* **i·vies.** any of various climbing or trailing plants, esp. those with shiny green leaves grown in gardens and on the walls of buildings.

Ivy

I·wo Ji·ma (ē′wə jē′mə, ē′wō), an island in the N Pacific Ocean: World War II battle between Japan and U.S.

Ix·ta·ci·huatl (ēs′tä sē′wät°l), *n.* an extinct volcano in S central Mexico. 17,342 ft.

-ize, a suffix used to form verbs meaning **1.** to make or cause to be: *Americanize; civilize.* **2.** to form into: *unionize; colonize.* **3.** to become or become like: *crystallize.* **4.** to treat in a certain way: *tyrannize; idolize.* **5.** to practice or engage in: *theorize; economize.*

	Semitic	Greek	Latin	Gothic	Modern Roman
DEVELOPMENT OF UPPER-CASE LETTERS	See the letter I		I	Ɉ	J
DEVELOPMENT OF LOWER-CASE LETTERS	j (Medieval)			j (Gothic)	j (Modern Roman)

J

J, j (jā), *n., pl.* **J's** *or* **Js, j's** *or* **js.** the 10th letter of the English alphabet.

jab (jab), *v.,* **jabbed, jab·bing. 1.** to poke or thrust sharply: *He jabbed me with his elbow.* —*n.* **2.** a poke or thrust.

jab·ber (jab′ər), *v.* **1.** to speak quickly and in a confused way; chatter; babble. —*n.* **2.** quick, confused talk; chatter; gibberish.

jack (jak), *n.* **1.** a machine for lifting heavy loads a short distance: *an automobile jack.* **2.** Also, **knave.** a playing card bearing the picture of a servant or a soldier, ranking between the ten and the queen. **3.** Also, **jackstone.** one of a set of small, metal objects having six points, used in the game of jacks. **4. jacks.** Also, **jackstones.** *(used as sing.)* a children's game in which one tosses and gathers jacks, usually while bouncing a rubber ball. **5.** a small flag flown at the bow of a vessel, usually showing the vessel's nationality. **6.** an electric socket that accepts a small plug: *a telephone jack.* —*v.* **7.** to lift or move with or as if with a jack: *to jack a car up.* **8.** *Informal.* to increase or raise: *to jack up prices.*

jack·al (jak′əl, jak′ôl), *n.* any of several wild dogs of Asia and Africa, smaller than wolves, that hunt at night in packs.

jack·ass (jak′as′), *n.* **1.** a male donkey. See also **jennet. 2.** a very foolish or stupid person; fool.

jack·boot (jak′boot′), *n.* a large, leather boot reaching up over the knee.

Jackal (total length 3 ft.)

jack·daw (jak′dô′), *n.* a black European bird related to the crow.

jack·et (jak′it), *n.* **1.** a short coat, usually opening down the front. **2.** any outer covering or wrapper: *a book jacket; a record jacket.* **3.** the skin of a cooked potato.

jack-in-the-box (jak′in ᵺə boks′), *n., pl.* **jack-in-the-box·es.** a toy consisting of a box from which an enclosed figure springs up when the lid is released.

jack-in-the-pul·pit (jak′in ᵺə poŏl′pit, -pul′pit), *n., pl.* **jack-in-the-pul·pits.** a North American plant that grows in damp woodlands and has a flower that is surrounded and arched over by a large leaf.

Jack-in-the-pulpit

jack·knife (jak′nīf′), *n., pl.* **jack·knives** (jak′nīvz′). **1.** a large pocketknife. **2.** a fancy dive during which the diver bends in midair to touch his toes and straightens out immediately before entering the water.

jack-of-all-trades (jak′əv ôl′trādz′), *n., pl.* **jacks-of-all-trades** (jaks′əv ôl′trādz′). a man who is good at many different kinds of work or can make all sorts of repairs.

jack-o'-lan·tern (jak′ə lan′tərn), *n.* a hollowed pumpkin with openings cut to look like human eyes, nose, and mouth, and in which a candle or other light may be placed: used at Halloween.

jack·pot (jak′pot′), *n.* the big prize in a game or contest.

jack′ rab′bit, any of various hares of western North America having long ears and very long hind legs.

Jack·son (jak′sən), *n.* **1.** Andrew, 1767–1845, 7th President of the U.S. 1829–1837. **2.** the capital city of Mississippi, in the central part. —**Jack·so·ni·an** (jak sō′nē ən), *n.*

Jack·son·ville (jak′sən vil′), *n.* a port city in NE Florida.

Jack rabbit (length 22 in.; ears 5 in.)

jack·stone (jak′stōn′), *n.* **1.** See **jack** (def. 3). **2. jackstones.** See **jack** (def. 4).

Ja·cob (jā′kəb), *n.* (in the Bible) a son of Isaac and the father of the founders of the 12 tribes of Israel.

jade¹ (jād), *n.* **1.** a hard, usually green stone used in

act, āble, dâre, ärt; ebb, ēqual; if, īce; hot, ōver, ôrder; oil; boŏk; ōoze; out; up, ûrge; ə = a as in *alone;* ᵊ as in *button* (but′ᵊn), *fire* (fīᵊr); chief; ṣhoe; thin; ᵺhat; zh as in *measure* (mezh′ər). See full key inside cover.

jewelry and carvings. **2.** Also, **jade′ green′.** a green, varying from bluish green to yellowish green. —*adj.* **3.** of the color jade. [from the Italian word *giada*, which comes from the earlier Spanish phrase *piedra de ijada* "stone of the flank." It was thought that this stone could cure diseases of the kidneys by being placed or worn on that part of the body]

jade² (jād), *n.* **1.** a worn-out, broken-down, or mean horse. **2.** a worthless or mean woman. —*v.,* **jad·ed, jad·ing. 3.** to make or become dull, worn-out, or tired, as from overwork or overuse: *a jaded plot.*

jag (jag), *n.* a sharp point on an edge or surface.

jag·ged (jag′id), *adj.* having ragged, uneven notches, points, or teeth: *the jagged edge of a saw.*

jag·uar (jag′wär), *n.* a large, ferocious, spotted animal of the cat family found in tropical America.

jai a·lai (hī′ lī′, hī′ ə lī′), a game resembling handball, played on a three-walled court between two, four, or six players equipped with basketlike rackets.

jail (jāl), *n.* **1.** a prison, esp. one for persons awaiting trial or convicted of minor offenses.

Jaguar
(total length 7 ft.)

—*v.* **2.** to put or keep in jail. Also, *British,* **gaol.**

jail·er (jā′lər), *n.* a person who is in charge of a jail. Also, **jail′or.**

Ja·kar·ta (jə kär′tə), *n.* another spelling of **Djakarta.**

ja·lop·y (jə lop′ē), *n., pl.* **ja·lop·ies.** *Informal.* an old, run-down automobile.

jam¹ (jam), *v.,* **jammed, jam·ming. 1.** to press, squeeze, or wedge tightly between bodies or surfaces: *He jammed his shirts in the drawer.* **2.** to bruise or crush by squeezing: *He jammed his hand in the door.* **3.** to press, push, or thrust violently: *She jammed her foot on the brake.* **4.** to make or become stuck or blocked: *to jam a lock.* **5.** to interfere with radio signals. —*n.* **6.** a mass of objects jammed together so as to hinder or prevent movement: *a traffic jam.* **7.** *Informal.* a difficult or embarrassing situation; fix: *His lying got him into a jam.* [perhaps imitative of the sound of squeezing or crushing]

jam² (jam), *n.* a preserve made of whole fruit that has been slightly crushed and then boiled with sugar, used as a spread on bread, rolls, etc. [probably a special use of *jam¹*]

Ja·mai·ca (jə mā′kə), *n.* an island republic in the West Indies, S of Cuba, formerly a British colony. 4413 sq. mi. *Cap.:* Kingston. —**Ja·mai′can,** *n., adj.*

jamb (jam), *n.* either of the upright sides of a doorway or window.

jam·bo·ree (jam′bə rē′), *n.* **1.** *Informal.* any noisy merrymaking; carousal. **2.**

a large gathering of members of the Boy Scouts, usually nationwide or international in scope.

James (jāmz), *n.* **1.** (in the Bible) one of two of Christ's 12 apostles. **2.** a book of the New Testament.

James·town (jāmz′toun′), *n.* a village in E Virginia: first permanent English settlement in North America 1607.

Jan., January.

jan·gle (jang′gəl), *v.,* **jan·gled, jan·gling. 1.** to produce or cause to produce a harsh, often metallic sound. **2.** to speak angrily; quarrel. **3.** to cause to become irritated or upset: *The noise of the sirens jangled my nerves.* —*n.* **4.** a harsh or discordant sound. **5.** an argument, dispute, or quarrel.

jan·i·tor (jan′i tər), *n.* a person employed in an apartment house, office building, etc., to clean the public areas, remove garbage, and serve as a handyman.

Jan·u·ar·y (jan′yoo er′ē), *n., pl.* **Jan·u·ar·ies.** the first month of the year, having 31 days.

Ja·nus (jā′nəs), *n.* (in Roman mythology) the god of gates and doorways, who watched over beginnings and endings, usually pictured as having two faces back to back.

ja·pan (jə pan′), *n.* **1.** any of various hard, durable, black varnishes, originally from Japan. —*adj.* **2.** of or referring to japan: *a japan table.* —*v.,* **ja·panned, ja·pan·ning. 3.** to varnish with japan.

Ja·pan (jə pan′), *n.* a constitutional monarchy on a chain of islands off the E coast of Asia. 141,529 sq. mi. *Cap.:* Tokyo. Japanese name, **Nippon.**

Jap·a·nese (jap′ə nēz′), *adj.* **1.** of, referring to, or characteristic of Japan, its people, or their language. —*n., pl.* **Jap·a·nese. 2.** a native of Japan. **3.** the language of Japan, not known to be related to any other language.

Jap′anese bee′tle, a beetle with a bluish iridescent shell that feeds on the leaves of trees and garden plants.

jar¹ (jär), *n.* a broad-mouthed container usually made of glass or earthenware. [from the French word *jarre,* which comes from Arabic *jarrah* "an earthen vessel for water"]

jar² (jär), *v.,* **jarred, jar·ring. 1.** to produce or cause to produce a harsh, grating sound. **2.** to have an unpleasant, disturbing effect on: *The sudden noise jarred me.* **3.** to vibrate or shake: *The explosion jarred several buildings in the area.* **4.** to conflict, clash, or disagree. —*n.* **5.** a harsh, grating sound. **6.** a jolt or shake; a vibrating movement. **7.** a sudden, unpleasant effect on the mind or feelings; shock. [perhaps from the Old English word *cearran* "to creak"]

jar·gon (jär′gən), *n.* **1.** language or speech peculiar to a profession or class: *medical jargon; teen-agers′ jargon.* **2.** meaningless talk or writing; gibberish. **3.** a mixed language, such as pidgin English.

jas·mine (jaz′min, jas′min), *n.* any of several shrubs or vines that bear fragrant yellow, red, or white flowers. Also, **jessamine.**

Ja·son (jā′sən), *n.* (in Greek mythology) a prince who led the Argonauts in their search for the Golden Fleece.

jas·per (jas′pər), *n.* a hard stone, usually brown, green, or red in color, used for carvings.

jaun·dice (jôn′dis), *n.* 1. a condition that causes yellowing of the skin and the whites of the eyes. 2. a condition or attitude in which one's views are prejudiced. —*v.,* **jaun·diced, jaun·dic·ing.** 3. to distort or prejudice: *an attitude jaundiced by envy.*

jaunt (jônt), *v.* 1. to make a short journey, esp. for pleasure. —*n.* 2. such a journey.

jaun·ty (jôn′tē), *adj.,* **jaun·ti·er, jaun·ti·est.** 1. easy and light in manner or bearing: *a jaunty step.* 2. smartly trim; perky: *a jaunty skirt.* —**jaun′ti·ly,** *adv.* —**jaun′ti·ness,** *n.*

Ja·va (jä′və), *n.* 1. the main island of Indonesia. 48,920 sq. mi. 2. the coffee bean or plant.

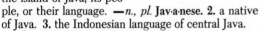

Java

Jav·a·nese (jav′ə nēz′), *adj.* 1. of or referring to the island of Java, its people, or their language. —*n., pl.* **Jav·a·nese.** 2. a native of Java. 3. the Indonesian language of central Java.

jave·lin (jav′lin, jav′ə lin), *n.* a light spear, usually thrown by hand.

jaw (jô), *n.* 1. either of two sets of bones at the lower part of the face in which the teeth are set. 2. the part of the face covering these bones: *His jaw is swollen.* 3. Usually, **jaws.** anything resembling a pair of jaws: *the jaws of a vise.* —*v.* 4. *Slang.* to talk; gossip.

jaw·bone (jô′bōn′), *n.* a bone of the jaw, esp. of the lower jaw.

jay (jā), *n.* any of several birds related to the crow, such as the blue jay.

jay·walk (jā′wôk′), *v.* to cross a street in the middle of the block or against a red light. —**jay′walk′er,** *n.*

jazz (jaz), *n.* 1. a kind of popular music based on African and American folk music. Jazz has catchy tunes and rhythms, mostly made up by the musicians as they play. —*adj.* 2. of, characteristic of, or noting jazz: *a jazz band.*

JD, juvenile delinquent. Also, **J.D.**

jeal·ous (jel′əs), *adj.* 1. feeling resentment and envy of someone's accomplishments or of a person because of his accomplishments, advantages, etc.: *He was jealous of his brother's wealth.* 2. fearful of losing another's affection: *Was he jealous of his girlfriend?* 3. very careful in keeping or guarding something: *to be jealous of one's fame.* —**jeal′ous·ly,** *adv.*

jeal·ous·y (jel′ə sē), *n., pl.* **jeal·ous·ies.** 1. the feeling or state of being jealous. 2. an instance of being jealous: *Petty jealousies can spoil a friendship.* 3. great care in keeping or guarding something.

jean (jēn), *n.* 1. Sometimes, **jeans.** a heavy, twilled cotton fabric. 2. **jeans,** *(used as pl.)* overalls or trousers made of this fabric. See also **Levis.**

Jeanne d'Arc (zhän därk′), the French name of **Joan of Arc.**

jeep (jēp), *n.* a small military motor vehicle.

jeer (jēr), *v.* 1. to speak or shout mockingly or rudely; make fun of. —*n.* 2. a mocking or rude remark or gibe.

Jef·fer·son (jef′ər sən), *n.* **Thomas,** 1743–1826, 2nd Vice President of the U.S. 1797–1801; 3rd President of the U.S. 1801–1809. —**Jef·fer·so·ni·an** (jef′ər sō′nē ən), *adj.*

Jef′ferson Cit′y, the capital city of Missouri, in the central part.

Je·ho·vah (ji hō′və), *n.* a name for God in the Old Testament.

jell (jel), *v.* 1. to thicken and become like jelly. 2. to become clear or definite: *The plan began to jell.*

jel·ly (jel′ē), *n., pl.* **jel·lies.** 1. a food preparation of a soft, elastic consistency made from fruit juice boiled down with sugar, by cooking bones in meat juice, or by using gelatin. 2. anything of the consistency of jelly. —*v.,* **jel·lied, jel·ly·ing.** 3. to bring or come to the consistency of jelly: *Mother jellied the sauce.* —**jel′ly·like′,** *adj.*

jel·ly·bean (jel′ē bēn′), *n.* a bean-shaped, colored candy with a hard coating and a gummy filling.

jel·ly·fish (jel′ē fish′), *n., pl.* **jel·ly·fish·es** *or* **jel·ly·fish.** any of various sea animals having soft, transparent bodies, some of which also have long, trailing tentacles.

jen·net (jen′it), *n.* a female donkey. See also **jackass** (def. 1).

jen·ny (jen′ē), *n., pl.* **jen·nies.** 1. another name for **spinning jenny.** 2. the female of certain animals, esp. a female donkey or female bird: *a jenny wren.*

Jellyfish
(body 8 in. across;
tentacles 30 in. long)

jeop·ard·ize (jep′ər dīz′), *v.,* **jeop·ard·ized, jeop·ard·iz·ing.** to put in danger: *to jeopardize one's health by smoking.*

jeop·ard·y (jep′ər dē), *n.* danger or risk of harm, injury, loss, death, or the like; peril: *The outbreak of war placed their lives in jeopardy.*

jer·bo·a (jər bō′ə), *n.* any of various mouselike animals of North Africa and Asia, with long hind legs used for jumping.

Jer·e·mi·ah (jer′ə mī′ə), *n.* 1. (in the Bible) a Hebrew prophet of the 6th and 7th centuries B.C. 2. a book of the Old Testament bearing his name.

Jer·i·cho (jer′ə kō′), *n.* an ancient walled city of Palestine, N of the Dead Sea.

jerk¹ (jûrk), *n.* 1. a quick, sharp pull, twist, throw, etc.: *The fisherman gave his line a jerk.* 2. a sudden, quick movement caused by a muscle tightening or the like; sudden start or twitch: *His leg gave a jerk when the doctor tapped him on the knee.* 3. *Slang.* a silly or foolish person. —*v.* 4. to pull, twist, hit, or the like, with a sudden, sharp movement, rather than with a smooth movement: *Don't jerk the bat when you swing.* 5. to give a jerk or move with a jerk: *The train jerked into the station.* [perhaps another form of the English dialect word *yerk* "to draw stitches tight (in making a shoe)," which comes from Old English *gearcian* "to prepare"] —jerk′er, *n.* —jerk′ing·ly, *adv.*

jerk² (jûrk), *v.* to preserve (meat) for eating by cutting it in strips and drying it in the sun: *jerked beef.* [from the earlier word *jerky* "dried meat," which comes from Spanish *charqui,* from a Quechuan word]

jer·kin (jûr′kin), *n.* a close-fitting, sleeveless jacket, worn esp. in the 16th and 17th centuries.

jerk·y (jûr′kē), *adj.,* jerk·i·er, jerk·i·est. 1. moving with jerks or sudden starts: *a jerky way of walking.* 2. *Slang.* foolish or silly: *That was a jerky thing to say.* —jerk′i·ly, *adv.* —jerk′i·ness, *n.*

Je·rome (jə rōm′), *n.* Saint, A.D. c340–420, Christian Biblical scholar: prepared Latin version of the Bible.

jer·sey (jûr′zē), *n., pl.* jer·seys. 1. a close-fitting knitted sweater or shirt. 2. a light fabric of wool, silk, nylon, or the like, knitted or woven by machine.

Jer·sey (jûr′zē), *n.* 1. an island in the English Channel. 2. *Informal.* New Jersey. —Jer′sey·ite, *n.*

Jer′sey Cit′y, a port city in NE New Jersey.

Je·ru·sa·lem (ji rōō′sə ləm), *n.* the capital city of Israel: a holy city for Jews, Christians, and Muslims.

jes·sa·mine (jes′ə min), *n.* another spelling of jasmine.

jest (jest), *n.* 1. a funny or teasing remark; joke. 2. a person or thing that is being laughed at; laughingstock. —*v.* 3. to speak in a playful or humorous way; joke or tease. 4. **in jest,** in fun; in a joking or teasing way: *to speak in jest.*

jest·er (jes′tər), *n.* 1. a clown or fool kept by a king or noble for entertainment and amusement, esp. during the Middle Ages. 2. any person given to telling jokes, playing pranks, etc.

Jes·u·it (jezh′ōō it, jez′yōō it, jez′ōō it), *n.* a member of a Roman Catholic religious order (**Society of Jesus**) founded by Ignatius of Loyola in 1534.

Je·sus (jē′zəs), *n.* the founder of the Christian religion. Also, **Je′sus Christ′.**

jet¹ (jet), *n.* 1. a strong or high-speed stream of liquid or gas from a nozzle or other small opening. 2. a spout or nozzle for emitting such a stream: *a gas jet.* 3. a jet engine. 4. Also, **jet′ plane′.** a jet-propelled airplane. —*v.,* jet·ted, jet·ting. 5. to shoot (something) forth in a stream; spout: *jet burning gas.* 6. to be shot forth in a stream: *Water jetted into the air.* 7. to travel by jet plane: *to jet to San Francisco.* [from the French word *jeter* "to throw," which comes from Latin *jactāre*]

jet² (jet), *n.* a very hard, black coal, often polished and used for buttons, beads, etc. [from the Old French word *jaiet,* which comes from the Greek phrase *lithos gagatēs* "Stone of Gagai," a town in the ancient Near East where the stone was found]

jet′ en′gine, an engine that produces forward motion by the rearward exhaust of a jet of gas.

jet-pro·pelled (jet′prə peld′), *adj.* propelled by one or more jet engines.

jet′ propul′sion, propulsion by means of a rearward jet of a liquid or gas.

jet·sam (jet′səm), *n.* goods deliberately thrown from a ship in a storm or other emergency to lighten the ship and prevent it from sinking. See also **flotsam.**

jet′ stream′, a narrow band of high-speed wind that blows from west to east at a high altitude.

jet·ti·son (jet′i sən, jet′i zən), *v.* 1. to throw (goods) overboard from a ship or aircraft in order to lighten it or make it steadier in a storm or other emergency. 2. to discard or abandon: *to jettison a plan.* —*n.* 3. the act of jettisoning something.

jet·ty (jet′ē), *n., pl.* jet·ties. 1. a pier or other structure of stones, timbers, or the like, built out into the water to protect a harbor from waves, strong currents, etc. 2. a wharf or landing pier; dock.

Jew (jōō), *n.* 1. a person whose religion is Judaism or who is a member of a people who trace their descent from the Biblical Hebrews. 2. an Israelite.

jew·el (jōō′əl), *n.* 1. a cut and polished precious stone, such as a diamond, ruby, or emerald; gem. 2. a personal ornament or piece of jewelry, esp. one made of precious metal and set with gems. 3. a bit of precious stone or other very hard material used in the mechanism of a watch or clock. 4. a thing or person that is unusually precious or excellent. —*v.,* jeweled *or* jew·elled; jew·el·ing *or* jew·el·ling. 5. to adorn with or as if with jewels: *Tiny lights jeweled the Christmas tree.* —jew′el·like′, *adj.*

jew·el·er (jōō′ə lər), *n.* a person who makes, sells, or repairs jewelry, watches, etc.

jew·el·ry (jōō′əl rē), *n.* articles of gold, silver, gems, or the like, used as personal ornaments.

Jew·ish (jōō′ish), *adj.* of or concerning the Jews: *Jewish history.*

jew's-harp (jōōz′härp′), *n. (sometimes cap.)* a small musical instrument consisting of a metal frame held between the teeth and a springy metal tongue that is twanged by the finger. Also, **jews′-harp′.**

Jew's harp
(length 3 in.)

Jez·e·bel (jez′ə bel′), *n.* 1. (in the Bible) the wicked wife of Ahab, king of Israel. 2. a wicked, shameless woman.

jib (jib), *n.* (on a sailboat) any of various triangular sails set forward of the foremast.

jibe¹ (jīb), *v.,* jibed, jib·ing. 1. (of a boom, sail, or the like) to shift from one side to the other when the boat is sailing before the wind. 2. to change the course of a boat so that a sail shifts in this way: *to jibe suddenly.* 3. to cause to jibe. —*n.* 4. the act of jibing. [from the Dutch word *gijben*]

jibe² (jīb), *v.,* jibed, jib·ing. another spelling of **gibe.**

jibe³ (jīb), *v.,* jibed, jib·ing. to agree or match; be in accord: *Your story doesn't jibe with the facts.*

jif·fy (jif′ē), *n., pl.* jif·fies. *Informal.* a short time: *I'll be over in a jiffy.*

jig¹ (jig), *n.* a device for guiding a drill or other tool, esp. one used in performing the same operation on

(Caption near jerkin illustration:) Jerkin

many identical pieces of work. [perhaps another form of the word *gauge*]

jig² (jig), *n.* **1.** a lively dance. **2.** a piece of music for this dance. —*v.*, **jigged, jig·ging. 3.** to dance a jig. [perhaps another form of *jog*¹]

jig·gle (jig′əl), *v.*, **jig·gled, jig·gling. 1.** to move up and down or back and forth with short, quick jerks: *He jiggled a carrot in front of the donkey's nose.* —*n.* **2.** a jiggling or jerking movement.

jig·saw (jig′sô′), *n.* a narrow saw, mounted upright in a frame, used to cut curves or other complicated shapes.

jig′saw puz′zle, a set of pieces of wood, cardboard, or the like, cut in irregular shapes, that fit together to form a picture or design.

jilt (jilt), *v.* to stop seeing or cast aside (a sweetheart, boyfriend, etc.): *They were engaged, but then he jilted her.* —**jilt′er,** *n.*

jim·my (jim′ē), *n.*, *pl.* **jim·mies. 1.** a short crowbar. —*v.*, **jim·mied, jim·my·ing. 2.** to force open (a door, window, etc.) with a jimmy or with something resembling a jimmy: *The burglars jimmied the lock.*

jim′son weed′ (jim′sən), a tall, poisonous weed having an unpleasant smell and bearing white or lavender flowers.

jin·gle (jiñg′gəl), *v.*, **jin·gled, jin·gling. 1.** to make clinking or tinkling sounds, as small bells do: *The cowboy's spurs jingled as he walked along.* **2.** to cause (something) to make a jingling sound: *to jingle the coins in one's pocket.* —*n.* **3.** a clinking or tinkling sound: *the jingle of sleigh bells.* **4.** a catchy poem or song having much rhyme and little sense, such as the Mother Goose verses.

jinn (jin), *n.*, *pl.* **jinns** *or* **jinn.** another name for **genie.**

jin·rik·i·sha (jin rik′shô, jin rik′shä), *n.* (in Asian countries) a small, two-wheeled carriage for one or two persons, having a folding top, and pulled along by one or more men. Also, **jin·rik′sha.**

jinx (jiñgks), *n.* **1.** a person or thing supposed to bring bad luck; a bad-luck charm or spell. —*v.* **2.** to bring bad luck to; place a jinx on.

jit·ter (jit′ər), *n.* **1. jitters,** nervousness; a feeling of fright or uneasiness: *to have the jitters about taking a test.* —*v.* **2.** to behave nervously. —**jit′ter·y,** *adj.*

jiu·ji·tsu (jōō ji′tsōō), *n.* another spelling of **jujitsu.**

Joan of Arc (jōn′ əv ärk′), **Saint,** 1412?–1431, French heroine and martyr who led the French army against the English. French name, **Jeanne d'Arc.**

job (job), *n.* **1.** a piece of work, esp. one done as a part of one's regular work or for an agreed price: *the job of mowing a lawn.* **2.** anything one has to do; duty: *It's your job to see that everyone has seats.* **3.** a position of employment; work: *a summer job.*

Job (jōb), *n.* **1.** (in the Bible) a man who patiently suffered great troubles while keeping his faith in God. **2.** a book of the Old Testament bearing his name.

job·ber (job′ər), *n.* a person who buys goods in large quantities and sells them to retail stores or dealers; wholesaler.

jock·ey (jok′ē), *n.*, *pl.* **jock·eys. 1.** a person hired to ride horses in races. —*v.*, **jock·eyed, jock·ey·ing. 2.** to ride (a horse) in a race. **3.** to maneuver cleverly or trickily: *to jockey oneself into a better job.*

jo·cose (jō kōs′), *adj.* humorous or jolly; given to joking: *a smiling, jocose man.* —**jo·cose′ly,** *adv.* —**jo·cose′ness,** *n.*

joc·u·lar (jok′yə lər), *adj.* humorous or joking: *a witty, jocular person; a jocular remark.* —**joc·u·lar·i·ty** (jok′yə lar′i tē), *n.* —**joc′u·lar·ly,** *adv.*

joc·und (jok′ənd), *adj.* cheerful and merry; jovial; gay: *a friendly, jocund host.* —**joc′und·ly,** *adv.*

jodh·purs (jod′pərz), *n.pl.* trousers for horseback riding that have a full shape above the knee and fit tightly from the knee to the ankle. [named after *Jodhpur,* a city in India, where they were used]

Jo·el (jō′əl), *n.* **1.** (in the Bible) a Hebrew prophet. **2.** a book of the Old Testament bearing his name.

jog¹ (jog), *v.*, **jogged, jog·ging. 1.** to move or shake with a small push or jerk; nudge; jar: *The coachman jogged the horse's reins.* **2.** to stir or jolt into action: *Finding the old letters in the attic had jogged his memory.* **3.** to run or ride at a trot: *Mr. Eaton jogs for a mile every morning.* **4.** to move with a jolt or jerk. —*n.* **5.** a shake or slight push; nudge: *to wake someone up with a jog.* **6.** a steady trot: *to ride at a jog.* [a blend of the English dialect words *jot* "to jog" + *shog* "to shake"] —**jog′ger,** *n.*

jog² (jog), *n.* **1.** a jag, bump, or other irregularity, in a smooth surface or straight line. **2.** a bend or turn: *a jog in a road.* —*v.*, **jogged, jog·ging. 3.** to bend; form a jog: *The trail jogged to the right.* [another form of the word *jag*]

jog·gle (jog′əl), *v.*, **jog·gled, jog·gling. 1.** to shake slightly; rattle back and forth; jiggle: *She joggled the key in the lock.* —*n.* **2.** a shake or jolt.

Jo·han·nes·burg (jō han′is bûrg′), *n.* a city in the N part of the Republic of South Africa.

John (jon), *n.* **1.** (in the Bible) one of Christ's 12 apostles and one of the four Evangelists, believed to be the author of the Gospel of St. John, the book of Revelation, and three other books of the New Testament. **2.** the fourth Gospel or any of three other books of the New Testament bearing his name. **3.** 1167?–1216, king of England 1199–1216: signer of the Magna Charta 1215.

John′ Bull′, 1. the English people or nation. **2.** the typical Englishman.

john·ny·cake (jon′ē kāk′), *n.* a cake or bread made of corn meal and water or milk.

John·son (jon′sən), *n.* **1. Andrew,** 1808–1875, 16th Vice President of the U.S. 1865; 17th President of the U.S. 1865–1869. **2. Lyn·don Baines** (lin′dən bānz), 1908–1973, 37th Vice President of the U.S. 1961–1963; 36th President of the U.S. 1963–1969. **3. Richard Men·tor** (men′tər), 1780–1850, 9th Vice President of the U.S. 1837–1841. **4. Samuel** *("Dr. Johnson"),* 1709–1784, English critic and writer: author of one of the first English dictionaries.

---

act, āble, dâre, ärt; ebb, ēqual; if, īce; hot, ōver, ôrder; oil; bŏŏk; ōōze; out; up, ûrge; ə = *a* as in *alone;* ᵊ as in *button* (but′ᵊn), *fire* (fiᵊr); chief; shoe; thin; ŧħat; zḫ as in *measure* (mezh′ər). See full key inside cover.

John′ the Bap′tist, (in the Bible) the forerunner and baptizer of Jesus.

join (join), *v.* **1.** to put or come together; connect; unite: *to join two pieces of rope by tying them together.* **2.** to combine or unite: *The two allied armies joined forces.* **3.** to become a member of (a group, organization, etc.): *She's joining the club.* **4.** to meet or come into the company' of: *We'll join you at the game.* **5.** to take part; participate (often fol. by *in*): *They all joined in the dancing.* **6.** to clash; meet and fight: *Our cavalry joined with the enemy troops and defeated them.* —*n.* **7.** a place or line of joining; seam: *You can see the joins between the planks in the floor.* **8. join up,** to enlist in the armed forces: *When war broke out he joined up right away.*

join·er (joi′nər), *n.* **1.** a person or thing that joins. **2.** a carpenter, esp. one who builds doors, windows, stairs, etc.

joint (joint), *n.* **1.** the place at which two things or parts are joined or united: *joints in woodwork.* **2.** a part that connects two things. **3.** the movable or fixed connection between two bones. **4.** a large piece of meat with a bone, esp. for roasting: *a joint of beef.* **5.** *Slang.* a place that has a bad reputation or is run-down and dirty: *That restaurant is a terrible joint.* —*adj.* **6.** shared or done by two or more persons or groups; combined: *My parents have a joint savings account.* —*v.* **7.** to form or provide with a joint or joints: *to joint a pipe line.*

joint·ly (joint′lē), *adv.* together or in common: *They own their house jointly.*

joist (joist), *n.* any of a number of small parallel beams for supporting a floor or ceiling.

joke (jōk), *n.* **1.** something said or done to cause laughter or amusement; jest: *he put on a clown's hat as a joke.* **2.** a practical joke. **3.** something that is not serious or difficult; something that can be laughed at: *That test was a joke.* —*v.*, **joked, jok·ing. 4.** to make jokes, or act in an amusing way: *He loves to joke.* —**jok′ing·ly,** *adv.*

A, Joists under flooring

jok·er (jō′kər), *n.* **1.** a person who jokes. **2.** one of two extra playing cards in a pack, usually bearing a picture of a jester. **3.** a trick or method for getting the better of someone or getting around something, for example a piece of tricky wording in a contract.

jol·ly (jol′ē), *adj.*, **jol·li·er, jol·li·est.** happy or merry; full of fun: *a cheerful, jolly man; a jolly gathering.*

Jol′ly Rog′er (roj′ər), a pirate's flag, having a white skull and crossbones on a black background. Also, **black flag.**

jolt (jōlt), *v.* **1.** to jar or shake roughly: *That roller coaster really jolted me.* **2.** to move with a sharp jerk or series of jerks: *The car jolted to a stop.* —*n.* **3.** a sudden shock, bump, or jerk: *The train started with a jolt.* —**jolt′ing·ly,** *adv.*

Jo·nah (jō′nə), *n.* **1.** (in the Bible) a Hebrew prophet who was thrown overboard from his ship and was swallowed by a large fish that after three days cast him onto the shore unhurt. **2.** a book of the Old Testament bearing his name.

Jon·a·than (jon′ə thən), *n.* (in the Bible) a son of Saul and a friend of David.

Jones (jōnz), *n.* **John Paul,** 1747–1792, American naval commander in the American Revolution, born in Scotland.

jon·quil (jong′kwil, jon′kwil), *n.* a fragrant yellow narcissus that resembles a daffodil.

Jor·dan (jôr′dən), *n.* **1.** a kingdom in SW Asia. 37,264 sq. mi. *Cap.:* Amman. **2.** a river flowing S from Lebanon into the Dead Sea. 200 mi. long.

Jo·seph (jō′zəf, jō′səf), *n.* (in the Bible) **1.** the first son of Jacob and Rachel, sold into slavery by his brothers. **2.** the husband of Mary who was the mother of Jesus.

josh (josh), *v.* to joke or tease in a friendly way. —**josh′er,** *n.*

Josh·u·a (josh′oo ə), *n.* **1.** (in the Bible) the successor of Moses as leader of the Israelites. **2.** a book of the Old Testament bearing his name.

jos·tle (jos′əl), *v.*, **jos·tled, jos·tling.** to bump or push against (someone); shove: *Don't jostle the person next to you.* —**jos′tler,** *n.*

jot (jot), *v.*, **jot·ted, jot·ting. 1.** to write down quickly; make a note of: *He jotted down the address.* —*n.* **2.** a bit; a tiny part: *I don't care a jot.*

jounce (jouns), *v.*, **jounced, jounc·ing. 1.** to move up and down roughly or with jolts; bounce or bump: *The truck jounced along the bumpy road.* —*n.* **2.** a jolting fall or bounce; bump.

jour·nal (jûr′nəl), *n.* **1.** a daily record of things that happen, one's thoughts, etc.; a diary or official record of business. **2.** a newspaper. **3.** a magazine or periodical, esp. one that is devoted to a field of learning, such as medicine or history. [from an Old French word meaning "daily"]

jour·nal·ism (jûr′nəliz′əm), *n.* the work or profession of reporting, writing, editing, or publishing news in a newspaper or magazine.

jour·nal·ist (jûr′nə list), *n.* **1.** a person whose occupation is journalism. **2.** a person who keeps a diary.

jour·nal·is·tic (jûr′nə lis′tik), *adj.* of or referring to journalists or journalism.

jour·ney (jûr′nē), *n.*, *pl.* **jour·neys. 1.** a trip or voyage, esp. one taking a long time: *to make a journey across the country.* —*v.*, **jour·neyed, jour·ney·ing. 2.** to make a trip or journey; travel: *to journey all over Europe.*

jour·ney·man (jûr′nē mən), *n.*, *pl.* **jour·ney·men.** a person who has learned a trade or handicraft and works for another. In the trade guilds of the Middle Ages, a journeyman ranked above an apprentice but below a master.

joust (joust), *n.* **1.** a battle or contest between two armored knights on horseback fighting with weapons of war such as the lance, sword, or mace. —*v.* **2.** to fight or contend in a joust. —**joust′er,** *n.*

Jove (jōv), *n.* See **Jupiter** (def. 1).

jo·vi·al (jō′vē əl), *adj.* full of friendliness and good spirits; cheerful; jolly: *a jovial leader; jovial laughter.* —**jo·vi·al·i·ty** (jō′vē al′i tē), *n.* —**jo′vi·al·ly,** *adv.*

jowl[1] (joul), *n.* **1.** a jaw, esp. the lower jaw. **2.** See **cheek** (def. 1). [from the Middle English word *chawl,* which comes from Old English *ceafl* "jaw"]

jowl[2] (joul), *n.* a fold of flesh hanging from the lower jaw: *Fat people sometimes have heavy jowls.* [from the Middle English word *cholle,* which comes from Old English *ceole* "throat"]

joy (joi), *n.* **1.** great delight or happiness; great pleasure: *He was full of joy because it was his birthday.* **2.** something or someone that causes great happiness or pleasure: *The new dishwasher is an absolute joy.*

joy·ful (joi′fəl), *adj.* **1.** full of joy; glad; delighted: *We are joyful that you arrived safely.* **2.** showing or expressing joy; happy: *a joyful smile.* **3.** causing or bringing joy; very pleasing: *joyful news.* —**joy′ful·ly,** *adv.* —**joy′ful·ness,** *n.*

joy·less (joi′lis), *adj.* without joy or gladness; unhappy; grim: *a joyless person; a joyless occasion.* —**joy′less·ly,** *adv.* —**joy′less·ness,** *n.*

joy·ous (joi′əs), *adj.* joyful or happy; wonderful: *a joyous time at the beach.*

J.P., Justice of the Peace.

Jr., Junior. Also, **jr.**

ju·bi·lant (jōō′bə lənt), *adj.* expressing or showing joy or triumph; rejoicing: *The sailors gave a jubilant shout when they sighted land.* —**ju′bi·lant·ly,** *adv.*

ju·bi·la·tion (jōō′bə lā′shən), *n.* joy or rejoicing: *a time of happiness and jubilation.*

ju·bi·lee (jōō′bə lē′, jōō′bə lē′), *n.* **1.** the celebration of an anniversary, esp. a 25th, 50th, or 75th anniversary. **2.** any time or occasion of rejoicing. [from an early French word *jubile,* which comes from Greek *iōbēlaios,* from Hebrew *yōbhēl* "ram's horn" (used in Biblical times to announce the festivals)]

Ju·dah (jōō′də), *n.* **1.** (in the Bible) the fourth son of Jacob and Leah. **2.** one of the 12 tribes of Israel, descended from him. **3.** a Biblical kingdom that included the tribes of Judah and Benjamin.

Ju·da·ism (jōō′dē iz′əm, jōō′dā iz′əm), *n.* the religion of the Jews, based on belief in one God and the teachings of the Old Testament and the Talmud.

Ju·das (jōō′dəs), *n.* **1.** (in the Bible) Judas Iscariot, the betrayer of Jesus. **2.** anyone who betrays another; traitor. **3.** (in the Bible) one of Christ's 12 apostles (not Judas Iscariot).

Jude (jōōd), *n.* a book of the New Testament.

Ju·de·a (jōō dē′ə), *n.* the southern part of ancient Palestine. Also, **Ju·dae′a.**

judge (juj), *n.* **1.** a public official who has the authority to hear and decide cases in a court of law. **2.** a person who is in charge of choosing winners, enforcing rules, etc., in a contest or competition: *a judge at a dog show.* **3.** a person who can estimate the worth or quality of something: *He's a good judge of horses.* —*v.,* **judged, judg·ing. 4.** to hear evidence or arguments in (a legal case) in order to pass judgment; try: *to judge a criminal case.* **5.** to act as a judge: *The king must judge between them.* **6.** to pass judgment or legal sentence on (a person): *This court judges you guilty.* **7.** to form an opinion of (a person or thing); decide or make a judgment about (something): *He judges people unfairly.* **8.** to think or guess: *I judge the distance to be about five miles.* —**judge′ship,** *n.*

Judg·es (juj′iz), *n. (used as sing.)* a book of the Old Testament that deals with the history of the Hebrews from the death of Joshua to the birth of Samuel.

judg·ment (juj′mənt), *n.* **1.** the act of judging or making a decision: *judgment in a court case.* **2.** a decision or sentence: *What was the jury's judgment?* **3.** the ability to judge or decide wisely: *He has no judgment in money matters.* **4.** opinion: *In my judgment you ought to apologize.* **5.** a misfortune believed to be sent by God as a punishment: *His sickness was a judgment for his wicked life.*

ju·di·cial (jōō dish′əl), *adj.* **1.** of or referring to judges or the administration of justice: *judicial proceedings.* **2.** capable of making wise decisions; critical and fair: *a judicial mind.* —**ju·di′cial·ly,** *adv.*

ju·di·ci·ar·y (jōō dish′ē er′ē, jōō dish′ə rē), *n., pl.* **ju·di·ci·ar·ies. 1.** the branch of government in charge of administering justice and interpreting law. **2.** the system of courts of justice in a country. **3.** judges as a group: *He's a member of the judiciary.*

ju·di·cious (jōō dish′əs), *adj.* using or showing good judgment; sensible; wise: *a judicious decision.* —**ju·di′cious·ly,** *adv.* —**ju·di′cious·ness,** *n.*

Ju·dith (jōō′dith), *n.* a heroine among the ancient Jews who saved her town from an Assyrian army by cutting off the head of its commander while he slept.

ju·do (jōō′dō), *n.* a kind of Japanese wrestling and method of defending oneself that is based on jujitsu but does not include harmful blows or throws.

jug (jug), *n.* **1.** a container for liquid, made of pottery, glass, or metal, usually having a handle and a short, small neck. **2.** any similar container, such as a pitcher. **3.** the contents of such a container; jugful: *How much is a jug of cider?*

jug·ful (jug′fool), *n., pl.* **jug·fuls.** the amount that a jug can hold: *There's only one jugful of water left.*

jug·gle (jug′əl), *v.,* **jug·gled, jug·gling. 1.** to keep (several objects) in motion in the air by quickly tossing and catching one after the other: *He can juggle four balls at once.* **2.** to change (things) around so as to deceive or trick someone: *The dishonest teller juggled the bank's records to cover up his thefts.* **3.** to come close to dropping and then catch hold of again: *The waiter juggled a tray stacked with plates.*

jug·gler (jug′lər), *n.* a person who performs juggling tricks with balls, plates, knives, etc.

Ju·go·slav (yōō′gō släv′), *n., adj.* another spelling of **Yugoslav.** —**Ju′go·slav′ic,** *adj.*

Ju·go·sla·vi·a (yōō′gō slä′vē ə), *n.* another spelling of **Yugoslavia.** —**Ju′go·sla′vi·an,** *n., adj.*

jug·u·lar (jug′yə lər), *adj.* **1.** of or concerning the neck. —*n.* **2.** the jugular vein.

jug′ular vein′, either of two large veins in the neck.

juice (jōōs), *n.* **1.** the liquid part of a plant or animal material: *orange juice; meat juice.* **2.** a fluid produced by the body: *gastric juice.*

juic·y (jōō′sē), *adj.,* **juic·i·er, juic·i·est. 1.** full of juice. **2.** unusually interesting or colorful: *a juicy bit of news.* —**juic′i·ness,** *n.*

ju·ji·tsu (jōō ji′tsōō), *n.* a kind of Japanese wrestling and method of fighting without weapons in which one uses the force of an opponent's attack against him. Also, **jiujitsu.**

juke·box (jōōk′boks′), *n.* a machine having a phonograph and a selection of records that is worked by putting in a coin and pushing a button for the record one wants to hear.

Ju·li·et (jōō′lē ət, jōō′lē et′), *n.* the heroine of Shakespeare's play *Romeo and Juliet.*

Ju·ly (jōō lī′, jə lī′), *n.* the seventh month of the year, having 31 days. [from the Latin word *Jūlius,* which comes from the name of Julius Caesar]

jum·ble (jum′bəl), *v.,* **jum·bled, jum·bling. 1.** to mix in a confused heap; throw or mix together without order: *You've jumbled all the papers I had arranged on my desk.* —*n.* **2.** a disorderly heap: *a jumble of clothes in a suitcase.* **3.** a confused state; mess; muddle: *Everything is in a jumble in your room.*

jum·bo (jum′bō), *n., pl.* **jum·bos. 1.** *Informal.* a very large person, animal, or object. —*adj.* **2.** very large; giant: *a jumbo hamburger.* [named after *Jumbo,* a large elephant in the Barnum show. The name comes from the Swahili word *jumbe* "chief"]

jump (jump), *v.* **1.** to leap or spring into the air or from a height: *The boy jumped from the top step.* **2.** to leap or spring over (something): *to jump a fence.* **3.** to get up or rise suddenly: *They jumped from their seats when the president came in.* **4.** to move or jerk suddenly from surprise, shock, or the like; start: *He jumped when we all shouted "Boo!"* **5.** to cause to leap or spring: *to jump a horse over a fence.* **6.** to move quickly or skip from one thing to another: *The speaker was running out of time, so he jumped to the end of his speech.* **7.** to rise or increase suddenly: *The price jumped from $5 to $10.* **8.** to cause to do this; raise suddenly: *The landlord jumped the rent.* **9.** to leave (the track or rails): *The train jumped the track.* **10.** to get on board in a hurry: *to jump on a plane for Chicago.* —*n.* **11.** the act of jumping; leap or bound: *With one jump the cat was on top of the bookcase.* **12.** a space, distance, or obstacle that is jumped or is to be jumped: *That ditch is a big jump.* **13.** a sudden rise or increase: *a jump in prices.* **14.** a sudden start or jerk: *He gave a jump when the teacher called his name.* **15.** any sudden change: *a jump from rags to riches.* **16. get the jump on,** *Informal.* to get a head start on (someone): *He got the jump on me by leaving a week early.* **17. jump at,** to

take or accept eagerly: *He jumped at the chance to go to Africa.* **18. jump on (someone),** *Informal.* to scold or criticize: *I jumped on her for keeping me waiting.*

jump·er[1] (jum′pər), *n.* a person, animal, or thing that jumps: *That horse is a wonderful jumper.*

jump·er[2] (jum′pər), *n.* **1.** a sleeveless dress, usually worn over a blouse. **2.** a loose jacket, esp. a workman's jacket. **3. jumpers,** another name for **rompers.** [from the earlier word *jump* "short coat," which comes from Old French *jupe,* from Arabic *jubbah* "long outer garment" + *-er*]

jump′ing bean′, a seed of certain Mexican plants having the larva of a moth living inside it and causing it to move or jump.

jump′ing jack′, a toy, puppetlike figure, having jointed arms and legs, that can be made to move or jump by means of a string or stick attached to it.

jump·y (jum′pē), *adj.,* **jump·i·er, jump·i·est. 1.** nervous; easily upset: *He was jumpy and short-tempered just before his exam.* **2.** moving with sudden jumps or jerks. —**jump′i·ness,** *n.*

Junc., Junction.

jun·co (jung′kō), *n., pl.* **jun·cos.** any of several North American gray-and-white finches that do not migrate in winter. Also, **snowbird.**

junc·tion (jungk′shən), *n.* **1.** a place or point where things join or meet, esp. roads or railroad lines. **2.** a joining or combining: *the junction of two streams to form a river.*

junc·ture (jungk′chər), *n.* **1.** a point of time, esp. one that is important or critical: *At that juncture the general had to make a decision involving many lives.* **2.** the act of joining, or the state of being joined; junction. **3.** a place of joining; joint or junction. **4.** something by which two things are joined.

June (jōōn), *n.* the sixth month of the year, having 30 days. [from the Latin word *Jūnius,* which comes from the name of a Roman family]

Ju·neau (jōō′nō), *n.* a seaport and the capital city of Alaska, in the SE part.

June′ bug′, any of several large, brown beetles that appear in late spring or early summer.

jun·gle (jung′gəl), *n.* wild land overgrown with trees, vines, and other plants, esp. in a tropical region: *Beyond this river lies dangerous, unexplored jungle.* [from the Hindi word *jangal*]

June bug
(length 1 in.)

jun·ior (jōōn′yər), *adj.* **1.** younger (used esp. of a son bearing the same full name as his father, and often written as *Jr.* or *jr.* following the name): *Michael Smith, Jr.* See also **senior** (def. 1). **2.** having a lower rank or position: *a junior partner in a law firm.* **3.** being more recently elected or appointed: *the junior Senator from Kentucky.* **4.** (in a college, school, etc.) indicating a class next below that of the senior or highest class: *junior courses.* —*n.* **5.** a person who is younger than another: *the junior of two brothers.* **6.** a person who is newer or of lower rank in an office, position, class, etc. **7.** a student in the class or year next below the senior: *The juniors play the seniors in basketball tomorrow.*

jun′ior col′lege, a school that covers the first two years of college instruction and grants a certificate instead of a degree.

jun′ior high′ school′, a school for the 7th, 8th, and 9th grades.

ju·ni·per (jōō′nə pər), *n.* an evergreen shrub or tree having cones that form purple berries used in medicine, cooking, and for flavoring gin.

junk¹ (jungk), *n.* **1.** worn-out or useless objects or material; trash; rubbish: *That stuff in the attic is just junk.* —*v.* **2.** *Informal.* to throw out or discard as worthless: *It's time to junk these old clothes.* [from the Middle English word *jonke*]

junk² (jungk), *n.* a seagoing ship used in China and neighboring waters, having square sails, a high stern, and usually a flat bottom. [from the Portuguese word *junco* "sailboat," which comes from Javanese *jon*]

Junk

jun·ket (jung′kit), *n.* **1.** a sweet food resembling custard, made of flavored milk curdled with rennet. **2.** a pleasure trip or outing: *a junket down the Mississippi.* **3.** a trip made by a public official at public expense: *The Senator is on a junket to Europe.* **4.** a feast or picnic. —*v.* **5.** to go on a junket or trip: *to junket in Asia.* **6.** to feast or picnic.

junk·yard (jungk′yärd′), *n.* a yard in which junk is collected.

Ju·no (jōō′nō), *n.* (in Roman mythology) the queen of the gods and wife of Jupiter: identified with the Greek goddess Hera.

jun·ta (hōōn′tə, jun′tə), *n.* **1.** a small group ruling a country, esp. after overthrowing the existing government. **2.** a council or committee.

Ju·pi·ter (jōō′pi tər), *n.* **1.** Also, **Jove.** (in Roman mythology) the supreme god, ruler of gods and men and husband of Juno: identified with the Greek god Zeus. **2.** the planet fifth in order of distance from the sun. Jupiter is the largest of the planets, having a diameter of 88,640 miles; its average distance from the sun is 483,000,000 miles.

ju·ris·dic·tion (jōōr′is dik′shən), *n.* **1.** the right, power, or authority to administer justice. **2.** control or authority: *The mayor has jurisdiction over the police force.* **3.** extent or range of authority: *Your case isn't within the jurisdiction of this court.*

ju·ris·pru·dence (jōōr′is prōōd′³ns), *n.* **1.** the science or philosophy of law. **2.** a system or body of laws.

ju·ror (jōōr′ər), *n.* a member of a jury: *Twelve jurors were selected to hear the evidence.*

ju·ry (jōōr′ē), *n., pl.* **ju·ries. 1.** a group of persons sworn to listen to evidence and to give a fair and just verdict in a trial or hearing in a court of law. See also **grand jury. 2.** a group of persons chosen to act as judges in a contest, competition, or the like.

ju·ry·man (jōōr′ē mən), *n., pl.* **ju·ry·men.** a man who is a member of a jury; juror.

just (just), *adj.* **1.** fair and honest; morally or legally right or correct: *The jury gave a just verdict.* **2.** based on knowledge and understanding; reasonable: *a just estimate of how the voting will turn out.* **3.** well-deserved; given rightly: *a just reward for one's efforts.* **4.** having a basis in fact: *a just complaint.* **5.** according to correct principles; proper: *just proportions in a building.* —*adv.* **6.** a little while ago; very recently: *The sun just set.* **7.** exactly or precisely: *That's just the way it happened.* **8.** by a small amount; barely: *The dart just missed the bull's-eye.* **9.** merely or only: *He's just a private.* **10.** really or positively: *That's just marvelous!*

jus·tice (jus′tis), *n.* **1.** fairness or rightness, esp. in dealing with people, claims, etc.: *Justice requires that the rich and the poor be given equal treatment in courts of law.* **2.** rightfulness or lawfulness of a claim, plea, or the like: *to complain with justice.* **3.** the administering or carrying out of law: *a court of justice.* **4.** that which is fair or is due a person: *to seek justice by suing to recover one's losses.* **5.** a judge or magistrate. **6. do justice, a.** to treat justly or fairly: *That portrait doesn't do her justice.* **b.** to appreciate properly: *There was so much good food, I just couldn't do it justice.*

jus′tice of the peace′, a local public officer, usually having the authority to try minor legal cases, perform marriages, administer oaths, etc.

jus·ti·fi·a·ble (jus′tə fī′ə bəl), *adj.* capable of being justified; capable of being shown to be right or just: *justifiable anger.* —**jus′ti·fi′a·bly,** *adv.*

jus·ti·fi·ca·tion (jus′tə fə kā′shən), *n.* **1.** a fact or explanation used to justify or defend something; excuse or good reason: *His sickness was justification for being late with his work.* **2.** the act of justifying: *He spoke in justification of his beliefs.* **3.** the state of being justified: *The investigation provided justification of their suspicions.*

jus·ti·fy (jus′tə fī′), *v.,* **jus·ti·fied, jus·ti·fy·ing. 1.** to show (an act, claim, statement, etc.) to be just, reasonable, or right: *The cost of the painting is justified by the pleasure it gives us.* **2.** to defend or uphold as blameless; explain or excuse: *The lawyer attempted to justify his client's actions.*

just·ly (just′lē), *adv.* **1.** in a just manner; fairly; honestly: *The teacher graded the papers justly.* **2.** accurately or properly: *to measure something justly.* **3.** as deserved; deservedly: *The poem was justly praised by several of the critics.*

jut (jut), *v.,* **jut·ted, jut·ting. 1.** to stick out; extend beyond the main part (often fol. by *out*): *land jutting out into the sea.* —*n.* **2.** something that juts out: *The lighthouse stood on a jut of land.*

---

act, āble, dâre, ärt; ebb, ēqual; if, īce; hot, ōver, ôrder; oil; bŏŏk; ōōze; out; up, ûrge; ə = a as in *alone;* ³ as in *button* (but′³n), *fire* (fī³r); *chief;* *shoe;* *thin;* *ŧħat;* zh as in *measure* (mezh′ər). See full key inside cover.

jute (jōōt), *n.* a strong fiber obtained from tropical plants and used to make rope, twine, burlap, etc.

ju·ve·nile (jōō′və n^əl, jōō′və nīl′), *adj.* **1.** young, youthful, or childish. **2.** of or for young persons: *juvenile interests; juvenile books.* —*n.* **3.** a young person; youth: *a group of juveniles.* **4.** a book for children.

ju′venile court′, a law court having authority over young persons, generally those under 18 years.

ju′venile delin′quency, behavior by young persons that is illegal or considered harmful enough to require action by a juvenile court.

ju′venile delin′quent, a child or young person who commits illegal or harmful acts against society.

jux·ta·po·si·tion (juk′stə pə zi_s_h′ən), *n.* **1.** the act of placing two or more objects, ideas, colors, etc., close together or side by side for comparison or contrast. **2.** the fact or state of being close together or side by side: *The juxtaposition of their pictures brings out the strong resemblance between father and son.*

	Semitic	Greek	Latin	Gothic	Modern Roman	
DEVELOPMENT OF UPPER-CASE LETTERS	↓	ꓘ	K	ꓘ	𝕶	K

	Greek	Medieval	Gothic	Modern Roman
DEVELOPMENT OF LOWER-CASE LETTERS	κ	κ	ƙ	k

K

K, k (kā), *n., pl.* **K's** *or* **Ks**, **k's** *or* **ks**. the 11th letter of the English alphabet.

K, 1. Kelvin. 2. (in chess) king.

K, *Chem.* the symbol for **potassium**. [from the modern Latin word *kalium*]

k., 1. karat. 2. kilogram; kilograms. 3. knot.

K2, *n.* a mountain in N Kashmir: second highest peak in the world. 28,250 ft.

Ka·bul (kä′bool), *n.* the capital city of Afghanistan, in the NE part.

kai·ak (kī′ak), *n.* another spelling of **kayak.**

kai·ser (kī′zər), *n.* a German emperor. [from a German word, which comes from Latin *Caesar* "emperor"]

kale (kāl), *n.* a plant resembling cabbage and having curled or wrinkled leaves, used as a vegetable.

ka·lei·do·scope (kə lī′də skōp′), *n.* a tube with an eyepiece at one end and two plates of translucent glass loosely holding bits of colored glass at the other end, in which beautiful patterns are formed by multiple reflection in two or three mirrors. [from the Greek words *kalos* "beautiful" + *eidos* "shape" + *skopein* "to view"] **—ka·lei·do·scop·ic** (kə lī′də skop′ik), *adj.*

Kam·chat·ka (kam chat′kə), *n.* a peninsula in the E Soviet Union, extending S in the Bering Sea. 750 mi. long. 104,200 sq. mi. **—Kam·chat′kan,** *n., adj.*

kan·ga·roo (kang′gə roo′), *n., pl.* **kan·ga·roos** *or* **kan·ga·roo.** a large Australian animal having small front limbs, powerful hind legs used for leaping, and a long, powerful tail. The female kangaroo has a pouch in which the young are carried.

Kangaroo
(total length 7½ ft.)

kangaroo′ rat′, any of various small jumping rodents of Mexico and the western U.S.

Kans., Kansas.

Kan·sas (kan′zəs), *n.* a state in the central United States. 82,276 sq. mi. *Cap.:* Topeka. **—Kan′san,** *n., adj.*

Kan′sas Cit′y, 1. a city in W Missouri. 2. a city in NE Kansas, opposite Kansas City, Missouri.

Ka·ra·chi (kə rä′chē), *n.* a port city in S West Pakistan.

kar·a·kul (kar′ə kəl), *n.* an Asian breed of sheep, the young of which have black fleece and the adults brown or gray fleece. See also **caracul.**

kar·at (kar′ət), *n.* a unit for measuring the purity of gold, pure gold being 24-karat.

ka·ra·te (kə rä′tē), *n.* a Japanese method of self-defense using the hands, elbows, knees, or feet.

Kash·mir (kash′mēr, kash mēr′), *n.* a region N of India and West Pakistan: claimed by both countries.

Kash′mir goat′, an Asian goat smaller than the Angora and having smaller horns, raised for its undercoat of short, downy fibers, known as cashmere. Also, **Cashmere goat.**

ka·ty·did (kā′tē did), *n.* any of several large, usually green American grasshoppers, the males of which produce the shrill song for which the insect is named.

Katydid
(length 2 in.)

kay·ak (kī′ak), *n.* 1. an Eskimo boat having a light framework covered with skins and a small opening in the center for the person who is paddling it. 2. a similar boat made of metal and nylon or other materials. Also, **kaiak.**

kc, kilocycle; kilocycles.

Keats (kēts), *n.* **John,** 1795–1821, English poet.

keel (kēl), *n.* 1. a timber or metal bar or part running down the center of a ship's bottom. 2. a similar part in an airplane, dirigible, etc. 3. **keel over, a.** to overturn or capsize: *The boat keeled over in the storm.* **b.**

---

act, āble, dâre, ärt; ebb, ēqual; if, īce; hot, ōver, ôrder; oil; bŏŏk; ōōze; out; up, ûrge; ə = *a* as in *alone;*
ᵊ as in *button* (but′ᵊn), *fire* (fīᵊr); *chief;* ṣhoe; thin; ᵺat; zh as in *measure* (mezh′ər). See full key inside cover.

to faint. **4. on an even keel,** in a state of balance or harmony; steady: *Relations between the two countries are seldom on an even keel.*

keel·haul (kēl′hôl′), *v.* to haul (someone) under the bottom of a ship and up the other side as a punishment.

keen¹ (kēn), *adj.* **1.** extremely sharp; finely sharpened: *a knife with a keen edge.* **2.** sharp, biting, or piercing: *a keen wind; a keen wit.* **3.** very sensitive, alert, or sharp: *keen hearing; a keen mind.* **4.** strong or intense: *keen competition.* **5.** enthusiastic or eager: *He's very keen about going to California.* [from the Old English word *cēne,* which is related to *can¹.* The original sense was "wise, skillful"] —**keen′ly,** *adv.* —**keen′ness,** *n.*

keen² (kēn), *n.* **1.** a wailing lament for the dead. —*v.* **2.** to wail in lament for the dead; grieve by wailing. [from the Irish word *caoine* "lament"] —**keen′er,** *n.*

keep (kēp), *v.,* **kept** (kept), **keep·ing. 1.** to take and hold as one's own; possess: *If you like that picture, you may keep it.* **2.** to have in a certain place until wanted; store: *He keeps his toys in the closet.* **3.** to have in one's care: *Would you keep my dog for the weekend?* **4.** to have, care for, or manage for use or profit: *to keep a store; to keep chickens.* **5.** to cause to stay in a certain place, condition, etc.: *Keep that horse in his stall! Keep the baby quiet.* **6.** to prevent, hold back, or restrain: *laws to keep people from driving too fast.* **7.** to remain at, in, or on: *Please keep your seats. Keep to the left.* **8.** to maintain; cause to be or continue to be in effect: *to keep silence; to keep a lookout.* **9.** to respect, hold to, or hold back; observe: *to keep a secret; to keep one's word.* **10.** to continue or go on: *to keep trying; to keep working.* **11.** to remain without spoiling; stay fresh: *How long will this meat keep?* —*n.* **12.** support, esp. food and lodging: *to work for one's keep.* **13.** the most heavily fortified building in a medieval castle. **14. for keeps, a.** with the understanding that each person keeps his winnings: *to play for keeps.* **b.** permanently or finally: *This time let's settle the matter for keeps.* **15. keep back, a.** to hold in check; restrain: *The sandbags kept back the floodwaters. She tried to keep back her tears.* **b.** to stay away: *The guard says to keep back from the railing.* **c.** to refuse to reveal: *Are you keeping back anything we should know?* **16. keep to oneself, a.** to stay away from the company of others. **b.** to keep (something) secret or confidential: *You must promise to keep this to yourself.* **17. keep up, a.** to maintain the same speed, progress, etc., as another or others: *He went so fast I couldn't keep up with him.* **b.** to maintain (something) in good condition; keep in repair: *It's hard to keep up that big house.*

keep·er (kē′pər), *n.* **1.** a person who tends or guards (often used in combination): *The lion recognized his keeper. His uncle is a zookeeper.* **2.** a person who manages or owns a place of business (often used in combination): *a hotelkeeper.* **3.** a person or thing that holds or keeps: *the keeper of the keys.*

keep·ing (kē′ping), *n.* **1.** logical agreement or harmony: *His actions have not been in keeping with his promises.* **2.** care or charge: *She has ten children in her keeping for the summer.* **3.** the observing of certain rules or customs: *the keeping of the Sabbath.*

keep·sake (kēp′sāk′), *n.* something kept in memory of a person, friendship, special occasion, or the like; a remembrance: *Mother has a trunk full of keepsakes in the attic.*

kees·hond (kās′hond′), *n., pl.* **kees·hond·en** (kās′hon′dən). one of a Dutch breed of small dogs having thick, silver-gray hair tipped with black and a tail carried over the back.

Keeshond
(18 in. high
at shoulder)

keg (keg), *n.* a small barrel or cask, usually having a capacity of from 5 to 10 gallons.

kelp (kelp), *n.* **1.** any large, brown seaweed. **2.** the ash of such a seaweed from which iodine is extracted.

Kel·vin (kel′vin), *adj.* referring to the scale of temperature (**Kel′vin scale′**) in which the degree intervals are the same size as those of the Celsius (centigrade) scale, but 0° is absolute zero, or −273.16°C. *Symbol:* K [named after William Thompson *Kelvin* (1824–1907), English physicist]

ken (ken), *n.* **1.** knowledge or understanding: *Those fine points of law are beyond my ken.* **2.** range of sight or vision: *From here there's not a house within ken.* —*v.,* **kenned** *or* **kent** (kent); **ken·ning. 3.** *Scottish.* to know or understand. **4.** *Archaic.* to see or recognize: *Do you ken John Peel?*

Ken·ne·dy (ken′i dē), *n.* **1. John Fitzgerald,** 1917–1963, 35th President of the U.S. 1961–1963. **2. Cape,** former name (1963–1973) of **Cape Canaveral.**

ken·nel (ken′əl), *n.* **1.** a house for a dog or dogs. **2.** Often, **kennels.** a place where dogs are bred, raised, trained, or boarded. —*v.,* **ken·neled** *or* **ken·nelled; ken·nel·ing** *or* **ken·nel·ling. 3.** to put or keep in a kennel or kennels: *We'll have to kennel our dog when we go away.*

Kent (kent), *n.* a county in SE England.

Ken·tuck·y (kən tuk′ē), *n.* a state in the E central United States. 40,395 sq. mi. *Cap.:* Frankfort. —**Ken·tuck′i·an,** *n., adj.*

Ken·ya (kēn′yə, ken′yə), *n.* a republic in E Africa. 223,478 sq. mi. *Cap.:* Nairobi. —**Ken′yan,** *n., adj.*

ke·pi (kā′pē, kep′ē), *n., pl.* **ke·pis.** a French military cap with a flat top and a nearly straight visor.

kept (kept), *v.* the past tense and past participle of **keep.**

ker·chief (kûr′chif), *n.* a cloth worn as a head covering or scarf, esp. by women.

ker·nel (kûr′nəl), *n.* **1.** the softer, edible part of a nut. **2.** a seed: *a kernel of corn.* **3.** the central part of a story, plan, idea, etc.; core; main point.

ker′nel sen′tence, a simple, active, declarative sentence containing no modifiers or connectives, which may be used in making more elaborate sentences. The sentence *Good tests are short* is made from two kernel sentences: (1) *Tests are short.* (2) *(The) tests are good.* Also, **basic sentence.**

ker·o·sene (ker′ə sēn′, ker′ə sēn′), *n.* a clear liquid made from petroleum that evaporates less easily than gasoline and is burned in lamps and stoves. [from the Greek word *kēros* "wax, paraffin"]

Ker′ry blue′ ter′rier (ker′ē), one of an Irish breed of terriers having a soft, wavy, bluish-gray coat.

ketch (kech), *n.* a sailboat having two masts, the forward one being the mainmast and the rear one being smaller and set forward of the rudderpost. The sails are rigged fore and aft, in a lengthwise direction from bow to stern.

Kerry blue terrier (18½ in. high at shoulder)

ketch·up (kech′əp, kach′əp), *n.* a kind of tomato sauce that is highly seasoned. Also, **catchup, catsup.** [from the Chinese dialect word *ke-tsiap* "brine of pickled fish"]

ket·tle (ket′ᵊl), *n.* **1.** a teakettle. **2.** a container in which to boil liquids, cook foods, etc.; pot: *a soup kettle.*

ket·tle·drum (ket′ᵊl drum′), *n.* a drum consisting of a large metal hemisphere over which a skin is stretched. See also **timpani.**

key¹ (kē), *n., pl.* **keys. 1.** a specially shaped piece of metal for locking and unlocking a lock. **2.** a similar device used for winding, opening, etc.: *a key to tighten roller skates; a key for winding a toy car.* **3.** one of the parts for operating a piano, typewriter, or the like, pressed by the finger. **4.** something that serves as a means of achieving or gaining something: *Hard work was the key to her success.* **5.** something that serves to

Kettledrum

explain, clarify, solve, etc., such as a list of answers or the like: *The key to the puzzle is printed in the back of the book.* **6.** a city, stronghold, place, etc., that is essential for controlling or gaining entrance to an area: *Gibraltar is the key to the Mediterranean.* **7.** a musical scale: *the key of C.* **8.** tone or pitch, esp. of the voice: *She speaks in a high key.* —*adj.* **9.** chief or major; essential or very important: *the key play in a game.* —*v.,* **keyed, key·ing. 10.** to adjust or regulate; fit: *He keyed his speech to the interests of his audience.* **11.** to adjust or regulate the tone or pitch of (an instrument). **12. key up,** to arouse (someone) to a high level of excitement: *The explosion keyed us up so much it was hours before we got to sleep.* [from the Old English word *cǣg*]

key² (kē), *n., pl.* **keys.** a reef, or a small, low island:

the *Florida Keys.* [from the Spanish word *cayo,* which comes from a West Indian language]

Key (kē), *n.* **Francis Scott,** 1780-1843, author of *The Star-Spangled Banner.*

key·board (kē′bôrd′), *n.* a row or set of keys, such as that on a piano or a typewriter.

key·hole (kē′hōl′), *n.* a hole in a lock for a key to enter.

key·note (kē′nōt′), *n.* **1.** (in music) the note or tone on which a key or system of tones is based. **2.** the main idea, point, or principle in a speech, program for action, or the like.

key·stone (kē′stōn′), *n.* **1.** the middle stone at the top of an arch. **2.** something on which related things depend: *the keystone of his plan.*

Key′ West′, a port city on an island south of Florida: southernmost city in U.S.

kg, 1. keg; kegs. **2.** kilogram; kilograms.

khak·i (kak′ē), *n., pl.* **khak·is. 1.** a dull, yellowish brown. **2.** a tough cotton cloth of this color, used esp. in making uniforms. **3. khakis, a.** trousers made of khaki. **b.** a uniform made of khaki.

khan (kän, kan), *n.* **1.** (in the Middle Ages) ruler of the Tatar and Mongol tribes. **2.** a title of respect in India, Iran, Pakistan, and other Asian countries.

Khan (kän), *n.* **Gen·ghis** (jeng′gis). See **Genghis Khan.**

Khru·shchev (krōōsh′chef, krōōsh′chôf), *n.* **Ni·ki·ta S.** (ni kē′tə), 1894–1971, premier of the Soviet Union 1958–1964.

Khy′ber Pass′ (kī′bər), the chief mountain pass between Pakistan and Afghanistan, E of Kabul.

kHz, kilohertz.

kib·butz (ki bōōts′), *n., pl.* **kib·but·zim** (ki bōōt-sēm′). (in Israel) a community settlement, usually devoted to farming. [from the Hebrew word *qibbūs,* literally "a gathering"]

kib·itz (kib′its), *v. Informal.* to act as a kibitzer: *We don't want anyone kibitzing at this game.*

kib·itz·er (kib′it sər), *n. Informal.* someone who looks on and gives unwelcome advice, esp. at a card game.

kick (kik), *v.* **1.** to strike, strike out, or hit forcefully with the foot. **2.** to spring or jump back with force, as a gun does when fired; recoil. **3.** to have a tendency to kick: *That mule kicks, so watch out!* **4.** *Informal.* to complain or grumble: *to kick about a rule.* —*n.* **5.** the act of kicking; a hit with the foot: *He gave the tire a kick.* **6.** a springing back or recoil, esp. of a gun: *the kick of a rifle.* **7.** *Slang.* a thrill; pleasurable excitement: *to get a kick out of flying a plane.* **8. alive and kicking,** well and full of energy: *He's 93, but he's still alive and kicking.* **9. kick in,** *Slang.* to contribute (money) as one's share: *Everyone's kicking in a dollar for the gift.* **10. kick off, a.** (in football) to begin play with a kickoff. **b.** *Slang.* to die. **c.** *Informal.* to begin or start (something): *Why don't you kick off the meeting?* **11. kick out,** *Informal.* to force to leave; oust: *They kicked us out of the movie for throwing popcorn.* —**kick′er,** *n.*

kick·off (kik′ôf′), *n.* (in football) a kick that begins play at the beginning of the game, at the beginning of the second half, or after a touchdown or field goal.

kid¹ (kid), *n.* **1.** a young goat. **2.** leather made from the skin of a kid or goat. **3.** *Informal.* a child or young person. [from the Middle English word *kide,* which comes from Scandinavian]

kid² (kid), *v.,* **kid·ded, kid·ding.** to tease or fool; joke with: *His friends kid him because he's so skinny.* [perhaps a special use of *kid¹*] —**kid′ding·ly,** *adv.*

kid·nap (kid′nap), *v.,* **kid·napped** *or* **kid·naped; kid·nap·ping** *or* **kid·nap·ing.** to carry off (a person) by force, esp. in order to get money for returning him; abduct and hold for ransom. —**kid′nap·per, kid′nap·er,** *n.*

kid·ney (kid′nē), *n., pl.* **kid·neys. 1.** either of a pair of organs in the body that remove liquid wastes from the bloodstream. **2.** the kidney or kidneys of an animal, used as food.

Ki·ev (kē′ef), *n.* a city in the SW Soviet Union, on the Dnieper River.

Kil·i·man·ja·ro (kil′ə mən jär′ō), *n.* a volcanic mountain in N Tanzania: highest peak in Africa. 19,-321 ft.

kill (kil), *v.* **1.** to cause to die or cause death; take life from (a living being). **2.** to destroy or ruin: *That mistake killed his chances of winning.* **3.** to defeat, discard, or discontinue: *to kill a bill in Congress.* **4.** to while away (time): *to kill a couple of hours watching a ball game.* —*n.* **5.** the act of killing, esp. in hunting game: *The hunter made a quick kill.* **6.** an animal or number of animals killed: *The hunters brought back their kill.* **7. kill off,** to destroy completely; wipe out: *Something is killing off the fish in this stream.* —**kill′er,** *n.*

kill·deer (kil′dēr′), *n.* an American plover named for its shrill call.

kill·ing (kil′ing), *n.* **1.** the act of a person or thing that kills. **2.** the game killed on a hunt; kill. **3.** extraordinary financial success; a very large profit: *He made a killing in the stock market.* —*adj.* **4.** causing death: *a killing blow.* **5.** very painful or exhausting: *a killing march.* **6.** *Informal.* very funny. —**kill′ing·ly,** *adv.*

kill-joy (kil′joi′), *n.* a person or thing that spoils the joy or fun of others.

kiln (kil, kiln), *n.* a furnace or oven for burning, baking, or drying, used in making pottery, bricks, etc.

kil·o (kil′ō, kē′lō), *n., pl.* **kil·os.** a kilogram.

kilo-, a prefix meaning thousand: *kilowatt.*

kil·o·cal·o·rie (kil′ə kal′ə rē), *n.* See **calorie** (def. 2).

kil·o·cy·cle (kil′ə sī′kəl), *n.* a unit of frequency equal

to 1000 cycles per second; kilohertz. The term kilohertz is preferred in technical use. *Abbr.:* kc

kil·o·gram (kil′ə gram′), *n.* the basic unit of mass and weight in the metric system: equal to 1000 grams, or 2.2046 pounds. *Symbol:* kg

kil′ogram cal′orie. See **calorie** (def. 2).

kil·o·hertz (kil′ə hûrts′), *n., pl.* **kil·o·hertz.** a unit of frequency equal to 1000 hertz, or 1000 cycles per second. *Abbr.:* kHz

kil·o·li·ter (kil′ə lē′tər), *n.* a unit of volume or capacity in the metric system, equal to 1000 liters. *Symbol:* kl

kil·om·e·ter (ki lom′i tər, kil′ə mē′tər), *n.* a unit of length in the metric system: equal to 1000 meters, or 3280.8 feet (about ⁶/₁₀ mile). *Symbol:* km

kil·o·watt (kil′ə wot′), *n.* a unit of power, used esp. for electricity: equal to 1000 watts. *Abbr.:* kw, kW

kil·o·watt-hour (kil′ə wot′our′), *n.* a unit of energy used esp. for electricity and equivalent to the work done by one kilowatt in one hour. *Abbr.:* kwh, kWh

kilt (kilt), *n.* any short pleated skirt, esp. a plaid skirt that wraps around the waist, worn by men in the Scottish Highlands.

kil·ter (kil′tər), *n.* *Informal.* good condition; order or working order: *Our car is out of kilter.*

ki·mo·no (kə mō′nə), *n., pl.* **ki·mo·nos. 1.** a loose, wide-sleeved robe, fastened at the waist with a wide sash, worn esp. in Japan as an outer garment by men and women. **2.** a woman's loose dressing gown.

kin (kin), *n.* **1.** a person's family or relatives; kinfolk: *She went home to visit her kin.* —*adj.* **2.** of the same family; related: *They look alike, but they're not kin.*

-kin, a suffix forming diminutive nouns: *lambkin.*

kind¹ (kīnd), *adj.* **1.** gentle, tender, and good: *a loving, kind grandmother.* **2.** showing or based on gentleness and consideration: *a kind smile; kind words of encouragement.* [from the Old English word *gecynde* "natural"]

kind² (kīnd), *n.* **1.** sort or type; variety: *What kinds of sports did you learn at camp?* **2.** a class or group of animals, plants, etc., of the same type; family: *There are animals of all kinds in the forest.* **3. in kind, a.** in the same way; with something of the same kind: *His rudeness paid her back in kind for insulting him.* **b.** with farm products or something else useful rather than with money: *The farmer paid the rent in kind by giving the landlord half his cotton crop.* **4. kind of,** *Informal.* to some extent; rather: *Isn't it getting kind of warm in here?* [from the Old English word *gecynd* "nature, race"]

—**Usage.** The use of *kind of* and *sort of* is avoided by careful writers and speakers because both phrases show a lack of clear thinking about what is being expressed. If one wants to be vague in describing something, he may use such expressions as *rather, quite,* or *something like: The movie was rather good* (or *quite good*). *He's feeling somewhat better today* (or *a bit better*). *Their new house is something like a castle* (not *kind of like* or *sort of like*).

kin·der·gar·ten (kin′dər gär′t⁰n, kin′dər gär′d⁰n), *n.* a school for young children that prepares them for attending first grade.

Kidney (Human)
(cross section)
A, Adrenal gland
B, To bladder

kind·heart·ed (kīnd′här′tid), *adj.* having or showing kindness: *a gentle, kindhearted person; a generous, kindhearted act.* —**kind′heart′ed·ness,** *n.*

kin·dle (kin′dəl), *v.,* **kin·dled, kin·dling. 1.** to start (a fire); cause (a flame or the like) to begin burning: *to kindle a fire in the woods.* **2.** to set on fire; light: *to kindle some dead branches.* **3.** to begin to burn; catch fire: *The campfire kindled slowly.* **4.** to excite or arouse; stir up: *to kindle suspicion.*

kind·li·ness (kīnd′lē nis), *n.* **1.** the quality of being kind, full of goodwill, etc.: *She's known for her kindliness and generosity.* **2.** a kind act or good deed.

kin·dling (kind′ling), *n.* **1.** material, such as dry twigs, that burns easily, used in starting a fire. **2.** the act of one who kindles a fire.

kind·ly (kīnd′lē), *adj.,* **kind·li·er, kind·li·est. 1.** of a kind and gentle nature; kind: *a quiet, kindly old man; a thoughtful, kindly visit to someone who is sick.* —*adv.* **2.** in a kind manner: *Speak kindly to children.* **3.** sincerely or heartily: *We thank you kindly.* **4.** with liking or approval; favorably: *He didn't take kindly to my suggestion.* **5.** as a favor; please: *Would you kindly close the door?*

kind·ness (kīnd′nis), *n.* **1.** the quality of being kind; gentleness; considerateness: *He admires kindness and courage in people.* **2.** a kind or generous act: *It would be a kindness to help her.*

kin·dred (kin′drid), *n.* **1.** a person's relatives; family; kinfolk. **2.** a group of persons related to one another; tribe; family. **3.** relationship or kinship. —*adj.* **4.** similar or alike; related: *two friends with kindred interests.* **5.** related by birth; belonging to one's family.

ki·net·ic (ki net′ik), *adj.* of or referring to motion.

kin·folk (kin′fōk′), *n.pl.* relatives; members of one's family. Also, **kin′folks′.**

king (king), *n.* **1.** a male ruler or monarch of a country, esp. one who inherits his title for life. **2.** any person, thing, or animal that is regarded as outstanding in strength, power, importance, etc.; leader: *The lion is the king of the beasts. Mr. Feather is an oil king.* **3.** a playing card bearing the picture of a king. **4.** (in chess) the piece that one tries to checkmate in order to win the game. See illus. at **chess. 5.** (in checkers) a piece that has been moved entirely across the board and can now be moved in any direction.

King (king), *n.* **1. Martin Luther,** 1929–1968, U.S. minister and civil-rights leader: Nobel peace prize 1964. **2. William Ru·fus De·Vane** (rōō′fəs də vān′), 1786–1853, 13th Vice President of the U.S. 1853.

king·bird (king′bûrd′), *n.* any of several grayish-black American birds that catch insects while in flight.

king·dom (king′dəm), *n.* **1.** a state or government having a king or queen as its head: *the kingdom of Morocco.* **2.** anything thought of as an independent area or realm: *the kingdom of art.* **3.** one of the three large divisions of natural things: *the animal kingdom; the plant kingdom; the mineral kingdom.*

king·fish·er (king′fish′ər), *n.* any of numerous brightly colored birds having a crest of feathers on its head. Some species feed on fish and some on insects.

Kingfisher (length 13 in.)

king·ly (king′lē), *adj.,* **king·li·er, king·li·est.** of, referring to, or befitting a king; regal; royal: *a proud, kingly manner.* —**king′li·ness,** *n.*

Kings (kingz), *n. (used as sing.)* **1.** either of two books of the Old Testament used by Protestants, I Kings or II Kings, which contain the history of the kings of Israel and Judah. **2.** any of four books of the Old Testament used by Catholics, including I and II Samuel and I and II Kings of the Protestant version.

king's′ Eng′lish, correct English speech or usage, esp. of England.

king·ship (king′ship), *n.* **1.** the office or power of a king: *The young prince was destined for the kingship.* **2.** rule by a king; monarchy: *to live during the kingship of Henry VIII.*

king·size (king′sīz′), *adj.* larger than the usual size: *a king-size bed.* Also, **king′-sized′.**

King·ston (kingz′tən, king′stən), *n.* a seaport and the capital city of Jamaica.

kink (kingk), *n.* **1.** a twist or curl in a rope, hair, or the like. **2.** sharp pain or stiffness in a muscle. **3.** a flaw or fault in a machine, plan, or the like, that prevents it from working properly. **4.** a mental twist or odd notion; quirk. —*v.* **5.** to form or cause to form a kink or kinks.

kin·ka·jou (king′kə jōō′), *n.* a brownish animal of Central and South America, related to the raccoon, that lives in trees and has a tail that can be used for grasping.

kink·y (king′kē), *adj.,* **kink·i·er, kink·i·est.** having small twists or curls: *The telephone cord is kinky.* —**kink′i·ness,** *n.*

Kinkajou (length 3 ft.)

Kin·sha·sa (kin′shä sä), *n.* seaport and the capital city of Zaïre, located in the W part, on the Zaïre River. Former name (1908–1960), **Leopoldville.**

kin·ship (kin′ship), *n.* **1.** the state or fact of being relations; family relationship: *He was proud of his kinship with the president.* **2.** the state or fact of being related or alike in some way; natural relationship: *There is a kinship between fluorine and chlorine.*

kins·man (kinz′mən), *n., pl.* **kins·men.** a relative, esp. a male to whom one is related by birth.

kins·wom·an (kinz′wŏŏm′ən), *n., pl.* **kins·wom·en.** a female relative.

ki·osk (kē′osk′), *n.* **1.** a small structure resembling a shed or covered stand, having one or more sides open, used as a newspaper stand, a bandstand, or the like. **2.** (in Turkey and Iran) a similar structure serving as a kind of summerhouse or open pavilion. [from the French word *kiosque* "a stand in a public park," which comes from Persian *kūshk* "garden pavilion"]

---

act, āble, dâre, ärt; ebb, ēqual; if, īce; hot, ōver, ôrder; oil; bŏŏk; ōōze; out; up, ûrge; ə = a as in *alone*; ³ as in *button* (but′³n), fire (fī³r); chief; shoe; thin; ŧħat; zh as in *measure* (mezh′ər). See full key inside cover.

Kip·ling (kip′ling), *n.* Rudyard, 1865–1936, English author.

kip·per (kip′ər), *n.* 1. a salted, smoked or dried fish, esp. a herring. —*v.* 2. to salt and dry or smoke (a fish).

kirk (kûrk), *n.* (in Scotland) a church.

kiss (kis), *v.* 1. to touch or press with the lips as a sign of affection, greeting, respect, etc. 2. to join lips: *At the end of the movie the hero and heroine kissed.* 3. to touch lightly; caress gently: *A faint breeze kissed their brows.* —*n.* 4. the act of kissing; a touching with the lips: *Give your grandmother a kiss.* 5. a light touch.

kit (kit), *n.* 1. a set of tools or supplies for a particular purpose. 2. a container for these, such as a box or bag. 3. a set of materials or parts from which something can be put together: *a kit for a model airplane.* 4. whole kit and caboodle, the whole lot or collection of persons or things: *I saved so many comic books that my mother threw out the whole kit and caboodle.*

kitch·en (kich′ən), *n.* 1. a room or place equipped for cooking. —*adj.* 2. of, in, or for use in a kitchen: *the kitchen curtains; a kitchen knife.*

kitch·en·ette (kich′ə net′), *n.* a very small kitchen or area used for cooking.

kitch·en·ware (kich′ən wâr′), *n.* pots, pans, etc., used in the kitchen or for cooking.

kite (kīt), *n.* 1. a light frame covered with paper, plastic, or thin cloth that is flown in the wind at the end of a long string. 2. any of several small hawks having thin, pointed wings.

kith (kith), *n.* friends or acquaintances. The phrase "kith and kin" means "friends and relatives."

kit·ten (kit′ᵊn), *n.* a young cat.

kit·ten·ish (kit′ᵊnish), *adj.* cute or playful like a kitten: *a kittenish little child; a kittenish smile.* —**kit′ten·ish·ly,** *adv.*

kit·ty (kit′ē), *n., pl.* **kit·ties.** 1. a kitten. 2. a pet name for a cat.

ki·wi (kē′wē), *n., pl.* **ki·wis.** any of several large birds of New Zealand that are unable to fly. [from a Maori word]

Kiwi (total length 28 in.)

KKK, Ku Klux Klan. Also, **K.K.K.**

kl, kiloliter; kiloliters.

Klon·dike (klon′dīk), *n.* a region of the Yukon territory in NW Canada: gold rush 1897–1898.

km, kilometer; kilometers.

knack (nak), *n.* talent or ability: *to have a knack for gardening.*

knap·sack (nap′sak′), *n.* a leather or canvas bag for clothes and other supplies, carried on the back by soldiers, campers, or the like.

knave (nāv), *n.* 1. a dishonest or untrustworthy person; scoundrel; villain. 2. See **jack** (def. 2). —**knav′ish,** *adj.*

knav·er·y (nā′və rē), *n., pl.* for def. 2 **knav·er·ies.** 1. trickery or dishonesty; behavior suitable to a knave or scoundrel: *cheating and other knavery.* 2. a knavish or dishonest act: *He was accused of one knavery after another.*

knead (nēd), *v.* 1. to work (clay, dough, etc.) into a well-mixed mass by pressing, folding, and stretching it: *He kneaded the dough with his hands.* 2. to squeeze, press, and rub (a muscle or the like); massage. 3. to shape or make by kneading: *to knead a loaf of bread.* —**knead′er,** *n.*

knee (nē), *n.* 1. the joint in the leg between the thigh and the lower leg. 2. a similar joint in the hind or front leg of an animal. 3. the part of a garment covering the knee.

knee·cap (nē′kap′), *n.* the flat, movable bone at the front of the knee.

kneel (nēl), *v.,* **knelt** (nelt) *or* **kneeled; kneel·ing.** to drop to or rest on one or both knees: *He knelt before the altar and prayed.*

knell (nel), *n.* 1. the sound of a bell rung slowly in mourning. 2. a sound or sign announcing a death, or the end of something: *The barbarian invasions sounded the knell of the Roman Empire.* —*v.* 3. (of a bell) to sound or ring slowly or mournfully; toll. 4. to proclaim or call by or as if by a bell: *The church bells knelled the death of the king.*

knelt (nelt), *v.* a past tense and past participle of **kneel.**

knew (nōō, nyōō), *v.* the past tense of **know.**

knick·ers (nik′ərz), *n. (used as pl.)* short, loosely fitting trousers, gathered in at the knee. Also, **knick·er·bock·ers** (nik′ər bok′ərz).

knick·knack (nik′nak′), *n.* a small article of little value, kept as a decoration; trinket: *a collection of china dogs and other knickknacks.*

knife (nīf), *n., pl.* **knives** (nīvz). 1. a tool for cutting, having a sharp-edged metal blade set into a handle. 2. any blade for cutting, such as a blade in a machine. —*v.,* **knifed, knif·ing.** 3. to cut or stab with a knife: *Two men were knifed in the fight.*

knight (nīt), *n.* 1. (in the Middle Ages) **a.** a mounted soldier. **b.** a man of noble birth who, having served his king or lord as a page and squire, was raised to the honorary rank of officer and sworn to follow the rules of chivalry. 2. a man honored by the British king or queen with a rank similar to that of a medieval knight. He ranks just below a baronet and is given the title *Sir,* as in *Sir John Smith.* 3. (in chess) a piece shaped like a horse's head. See illus. at **chess.** —*v.* 4. to dub or make (a man) a knight: *The queen knighted the famous explorer.* [from the Old English word *cniht* "boy, manservant"]

knight-er·rant (nīt′er′ənt), *n., pl.* **knights-er·rant** (nīts′er′ənt). a medieval knight who traveled in search of adventures.

knight·hood (nīt′hŏŏd), *n.* 1. the character, rank, or calling of a knight: *The scientist was given a knighthood by the queen.* 2. knights as a group.

knight·ly (nīt′lē), *adj.* 1. of or belonging to a knight: *knightly armor.* 2. characteristic of a knight; noble and courageous: *knightly deeds.* —*adv.* 3. in the manner of a knight; in a noble manner.

Knights′ of the Round′ Ta′ble, the knights of King Arthur.

knit (nit), *v.,* **knit·ted** *or* **knit; knit·ting.** 1. to make (a garment, fabric, etc.) by joining loops of yarn, either by hand with knitting needles or by machine: *to knit a sweater.* 2. to join or draw closely together; unite: *Their drive to win knitted together the members of the team.* 3. to draw into folds or wrinkles; wrinkle: *She knits her brow when she's puzzled.* 4. to become closely joined; grow together: *How long will it take the bone to knit?* —**knit′ter,** *n.*

knit·ting (nit′ing), *n.* 1. the act of a person or thing that knits: *She took up knitting when she was ill.* 2. something that is being knitted or has been knitted: *She put her knitting away in a drawer.*

knit′ting nee′dle, a straight, slender rod having a dull point at one or both ends, used for knitting.

knives (nīvz), *n.* the plural of **knife.**

knob (nob), *n.* 1. a rounded handle on a door, drawer, radio, etc.: *The knob fell off the bureau drawer.* 2. a rounded lump or part that sticks out, such as a knot on a tree trunk. 3. a rounded hill or mountain. —**knobbed,** *adj.*

knock (nok), *v.* 1. to strike a blow that makes a rapping or thumping sound; rap, esp. with the knuckles: *to knock on someone's door.* 2. to give a strong blow to; hit; strike: *The swing knocked the boy on the shin.* 3. to bump or strike together: *Fear made her knees knock.* 4. to make by striking or pounding: *to knock a hole in the wall.* 5. to cause to fall by a blow or bump (often fol. by *over* or *down*): *The cat knocked over the lamp.* 6. to hit (a thing) against something else; bump: *He knocked his elbow on the door.* 7. to make a pounding or rattling noise: *The engine of our car is knocking.* —*n.* 8. the sound of knocking; the sound of a blow or rap: *Did you hear a knock?* 9. a hit, rap, or thump: *Give the door a knock.* 10. a pounding or rattling noise: *a knock in the car's engine.* 11. **knock down,** *Slang.* **a.** to lower or reduce: *I can't buy it till they knock down the price.* **b.** to receive as salary; earn: *He knocks down a hundred a week at least.* 12. **knock it off,** *Slang.* stop it: *It's too late to play your radio, so just knock it off.* 13. **knock out, a.** (in boxing) to strike (an opponent) so that he is unable to rise within a certain time: *He knocked out the champ in the third round.* **b.** *Slang.* to produce quickly and efficiently: *We can knock out thirty of these an hour.* **c.** to damage or destroy: *The storm knocked out the electric power.*

knock·er (nok′ər), *n.* 1. a person or thing that knocks. 2. a hinged knob, bar, or the like, set on a door, used for knocking.

knock-kneed (nok′nēd′), *adj.* having legs that curve inward at the knees.

knock·out (nok′out′), *n.* 1. (in boxing) the act of knocking out an opponent: *to win by a knockout.* 2. a blow or hit that knocks out someone: *He was dizzy*

from the knockout. —*adj.* 3. strong enough to knock out someone: *a knockout punch.*

knoll (nōl), *n.* a small, rounded hill.

knot (not), *n.* 1. an interlacing of a cord, rope, or the like, drawn tight into a lump, for fastening two cords together or a cord to something else. 2. a ribbon tied as a bow and worn as an ornament. 3. a small group of persons or things: *a knot of curious bystanders.* 4. a lump or swelling, as in a muscle. 5. a hard, roughly circular spot in wood at the place where a branch joins the trunk of a tree. 6. a unit of speed equal to one nautical mile per hour: *The ship's cruising speed was 18 knots.* 7. a difficult matter; problem. 8. a bond: *the matrimonial knot.* —*v.,* **knot·ted, knot·ting.** 9. to tie in a knot. 10. to fasten by a knot. 11. to become tied or tangled in knots. 12. **tie the knot,** *Informal.* to get married.

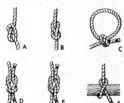

Knots
A, Overhand knot
B, Figure of eight
C, Slipknot
D, Square knot
E, Granny knot
F, Half hitch

knot·hole (not′hōl′), *n.* a hole in a board, plank, or the trunk of a tree where a knot has fallen out.

knot·ty (not′ē), *adj.,* **knot·ti·er, knot·ti·est.** 1. full of knots. 2. intricate or difficult: *a knotty problem.* —**knot′ti·ness,** *n.*

know (nō), *v.,* **knew** (nōō, nyōō), **known** (nōn), **know·ing.** 1. to perceive or understand as fact; be certain. 2. to have fixed in the mind or memory, as from experience or study: *to know a poem by heart.* 3. to be aware of; recognize; be acquainted or familiar with: *to know a classmate; to know carpentry.* 4. to be able to distinguish: *to know right from wrong.* 5. **in the know,** *Informal.* having inside information: *I hear he's in the know about that ship's disappearance.* 6. **know the ropes,** *Informal.* to understand thoroughly a particular subject, business, etc.

know·ing (nō′ing), *adj.* 1. having knowledge or information; intelligent. 2. shrewd; suggesting secret or special knowledge: *a knowing glance.* 3. deliberate or intentional. —**know′ing·ly,** *adv.*

knowl·edge (nol′ij), *n.* 1. the fact or state of knowing: *She was pleased by their knowledge of her success.* 2. familiarity with or understanding of a subject or activity: *a knowledge of swimming; a knowledge of Latin.* 3. something that is or may be known. 4. the sum of what is known by mankind. 5. **to one's knowledge,** as far as one knows: *He hasn't been here, to my knowledge.*

Knox·ville (noks′vil), *n.* a city in E Tennessee.

knuck·le (nuk′əl), *n.* 1. a joint of a finger, esp. one of the joints at the roots of the finger. 2. the small bulge produced by such a joint when the finger is bent. 3. **knuckle down,** to work at something seriously and vigorously: *If you knuckle down, you can* *finish soon.* **4. knuckle under,** to give in; submit or yield: *We won't knuckle under even if we lose the war.*

K.O., (in boxing) knockout. Also, **k.o., KO**

ko·a·la (kō ä′lə), *n.* a gray, furry, tree-dwelling animal of Australia that resembles a small bear. Also, **koa′la bear′.**

Ko·be (kō′bē), *n.* a port city in S Japan.

kohl·ra·bi (kōl rä′bē, kōl′rä′bē), *n., pl.* **kohl·ra·bies.** a plant whose stem has a turnip-shaped swelling above the ground that is eaten as a vegetable.

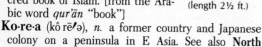

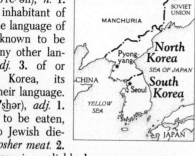

Koalas
(length 2½ ft.)

Ko·ran (kô rän′, kô ran′), *n.* the sacred book of Islam. [from the Arabic word *qur'ān* "book"]

Ko·re·a (kô rē′ə), *n.* a former country and Japanese colony on a peninsula in E Asia. See also **North Korea, South Korea.**

Ko·re·an (kô rē′ən), *n.* **1.** a native or inhabitant of Korea. **2.** the language of Korea, not known to be related to any other language. —*adj.* **3.** of or concerning Korea, its people, or their language.

ko·sher (kō′shər), *adj.* **1.** clean or fit to be eaten, according to Jewish dietary laws: *kosher meat.* **2.** *Informal.* **a.** genuine; reliable. **b.** proper; correct.

kow·tow (kou′tou′), *v.* to act in a very slavish or humble manner in showing obedience, respect, or the like: *to kowtow to one's superior.* [from the Chi-

nese phrase *k'o t'ou,* literally "knock one's head"]

K.P., (in military use) kitchen police: work done as a helper in the kitchen of a military base, either as part of one's regular duties or as punishment.

Kr, *Chem.* the symbol for **krypton.**

Krem·lin (krem′lin), *n.* **1.** the citadel of Moscow, including within its walls the chief office of the Soviet government. **2.** the executive branch of the government of the Soviet Union.

kryp·ton (krip′ton), *n.* a very rare inert gas used to fill special electric light bulbs. Krypton is a chemical element. *Symbol:* Kr

Kt, (in chess) knight.

kt., **1.** karat. **2.** knot.

ku·dos (kōō′dōz, kōō′dos), *n.* praise and glory, esp. for one's deeds or achievements.

ku·du (kōō′dōō), *n.* a large African antelope, the male of which has large corkscrewlike horns.

Kudu
(5 ft. high at shoulder)

kum·quat (kum′kwot), *n.* a small citrus fruit with a sweet, orange rind and a sour pulp. [from the Chinese phrase *kam kwat* "gold orange"]

kung fu (kung′ fōō′), a Chinese method of self-defense involving soft, fluid movements of hands and legs. [from a Chinese phrase, literally "accomplished technique"]

Ku·wait (kōō wāt′, kōō wīt′), *n.* a country in NE Arabia. 8000 sq. mi.

kw, kilowatt. Also, **kW**

kwh, kilowatt-hour. Also, **kWh**

Ky., Kentucky.

Ky·o·to (kē ō′tō), *n.* a city in central Japan.

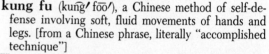

	Semitic	Greek	Latin	Gothic	Modern Roman	
DEVELOPMENT OF UPPER-CASE LETTERS	↙	⌐	∧	↓	L	𝕷	L

	Greek		Medieval	Gothic	Modern Roman	
DEVELOPMENT OF LOWER-CASE LETTERS	λ	ↆ	L	⌐	⌐	l

L

L, l (el), *n., pl.* **L's** *or* **Ls, l's** *or* **ls. 1.** the 12th letter of the English alphabet. **2.** something having the shape of an L.

L (el), *n., pl.* **L's** *or* **Ls.** *Informal.* an elevated railroad.

l , 1. large. **2.** left. **3.** length. **4.** *British.* pound; pounds. [from the Latin word *libra*]

L, 1. *(sometimes l.c.)* the Roman numeral for 50. **2.** inductance.

l, 1. large. **2.** liter; liters.

L., 1. Lady. **2.** Lake. **3.** large. **4.** law. **5.** left. **6.** Liberal. **7.** Lord. **8.** low.

l., 1. large. **2.** law. **3.** leaf. **4.** league. **5.** left. **6.** length. **7.** line. **8.** link.

la (lä), *n.* the sixth note of a musical scale.

La, *Chem.* the symbol for **lanthanum.**

La., Louisiana.

lab., 1. labor. **2.** laboratory. **3.** laborer.

la·bel (lā′bəl), *n.* **1.** a tag, sticker, or the like, giving information about the object to which it is attached: *the label on a bottle.* —*v.,* **la·beled** *or* **la·belled; la·bel·ing** *or* **la·bel·ling. 2.** to attach a label to: *The letter was labeled "confidential." ***3.** to classify or describe; call: *The king's enemies labeled him a tyrant.*

la·bi·al (lā′bē əl), *adj.* **1.** of or concerning the lips. **2.** pronounced with the lips close together, as the sounds of *b, p,* or *m.* —*n.* **3.** a labial sound.

la·bor (lā′bər), *n.* **1.** work, esp. of a hard or tiring kind; toil. **2.** a piece of work; job or task: *the 12 labors of Hercules.* **3.** workers as a group: *organized labor.* **4.** the effort or process of giving birth to an offspring. —*v.* **5.** to perform labor; work. **6.** to move with difficulty: *They labored up the mountain.*

lab·o·ra·to·ry (lab′rə tôr′ē, lab′ər ə tôr′ē), *n., pl.* **lab·o·ra·to·ries. 1.** a place for scientific research, experiments, tests, or demonstrations. **2.** a place where drugs or special devices are made.

La′bor Day′, the first Monday in September, a legal holiday in honor of labor.

la·bored (lā′bərd), *adj.* not easy; done with effort or difficulty: *a labored response to a question.*

la·bor·er (lā′bər ər), *n.* a worker, esp. one whose job requires physical effort rather than an acquired skill.

la·bo·ri·ous (lə bôr′ē əs), *adj.* **1.** requiring much labor or exertion. **2.** diligent; hardworking. —**la·bo′ri·ous·ly,** *adv.*

la′bor un′ion, a group of workers organized to protect and further their interests, as in working conditions, wages, and the like.

Lab·ra·dor (lab′rə dôr′), *n.* **1.** a peninsula in NE North America surrounded by Hudson Bay, the Atlantic Ocean, and the Gulf of St. Lawrence. **2.** the mainland portion of Newfoundland.

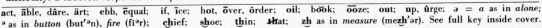

la·bur·num (lə bûr′nəm), *n.* a small tree that bears hanging clusters of yellow flowers.

lab·y·rinth (lab′ə rinth), *n.* an intricate arrangement of passages or paths in which it is difficult to find one's way; maze.

lace (lās), *n.* **1.** a delicate, netlike fabric of threads. **2.** a cord or string for fastening or drawing together two flaps by being passed through holes in their edges: *I need laces for my shoes.* —*v.,* **laced, lac·ing. 3.** to fasten or draw together with a lace.

lac·er·ate (las′ə rāt′), *v.,* **lac·er·at·ed, lac·er·at·ing. 1.** to tear roughly; mangle. **2.** to grieve or hurt: *Their insults lacerated him.*

lac·er·a·tion (las′ə rā′shən), *n.* an injury resulting from lacerating; rough, jagged tear.

lach·ry·mal (lak′rə məl), *adj.* of, referring to, or producing tears.

lack (lak), *n.* **1.** deficiency or absence of something needed: *a lack of money.* **2.** something that is needed or missing. —*v.* **3.** to be short of; be missing: *The book lacked illustrations.*

---

act, āble, dâre, ärt; ebb, ēqual; if, īce; hot, ōver, ôrder; oil; boŏk; ōoze; out; up, ûrge; ə = a as in *alone;* ᵊ as in *button* (but′ᵊn), *fire* (fīᵊr); chief; shoe; thin; that; zh as in *measure* (mezh′ər). See full key inside cover.

lack·a·dai·si·cal (lak′ə dā′zi kəl), *adj.* listless; having little or no vigor or interest: *a lackadaisical attitude toward homework.* —**lack′a·dai′si·cal·ly,** *adv.*

lack·ey (lak′ē), *n., pl.* **lack·eys.** 1. a male servant; footman. 2. a follower who obeys another person as if he were his servant.

lack·lus·ter (lak′lus′tər), *adj.* without brilliance or liveliness; dull.

la·con·ic (lə kon′ik), *adj.* using few words; concise: *a laconic way of expressing oneself.* —**la·con′i·cal·ly,** *adv.*

lac·quer (lak′ər), *n.* 1. a substance that dries to form a hard, glossy coating, used as a finish. —*v.* 2. to coat with lacquer. [from the early Portuguese word *la-car,* which comes from Arabic *lakk*]

la·crosse (lə krôs′), *n.* a game, played with a ball

Lacrosse racquet

and long-handled, netted rackets, in which two teams of ten members each try to send the ball into each other's goal.

lac·tic (lak′tik), *adj.* of or obtained from milk.

lac′tic ac′id, an acid found in sour milk.

lac·y (lā′sē), *adj.,* **lac·i·er, lac·i·est.** of or like lace. —**lac′i·ness,** *n.*

lad (lad), *n.* a boy or youth.

lad·der (lad′ər), *n.* a device for climbing, formed by two long, vertical pieces of wood or metal connected by a number of steps.

lade (lād), *v.,* **lad·ed; lad·en** (lād′ᵊn) *or* **lad·ed; lad·ing.** 1. to load with a cargo. 2. to lift or move, as with a ladle.

lad·en (lād′ᵊn), *adj.* loaded or burdened: *a strawberry bush laden with berries.*

lad·ing (lā′diɳ), *n.* freight or cargo.

la·dle (lād′l), *n.* 1. a long-handled spoon with a cup-shaped bowl used for dipping liquids. —*v.,* **la·dled, la·dling.** 2. to dip out with a ladle, spoon, etc.

la·dy (lā′dē), *n., pl.* **la·dies.** 1. a woman of good family, social position, breeding, etc. 2. a polite term for any woman. 3. one's wife or sweetheart. 4. *(usually cap.)* (in Great Britain) the title of certain women who have noble rank either by birth or by marriage. [from the Old English word *hlæfdige.* The original meaning probably was "kneader of dough"]

la·dy·bug (lā′dē bug′), *n.* any of several small beetles, esp. one with bright-red wings spotted with black that feeds on small insects. Also, **la·dy·bird** (lā′dē bûrd′).

la·dy·like (lā′dē līk′), *adj.* appropriate to a lady; well-bred: *a ladylike appearance.*

la·dy·ship (lā′dē ship′), *n. (often cap.)* the form used in speaking of or to a woman having the title of *Lady* (usually preceded by *her* or *your*).

la·dy's-slip·per (lā′dēz slip′ər), *n.* any of several North American orchids whose flowers have a shape resembling a slipper.

Lady's-slipper

La·fa·yette (lä′fē et′), *n.* **Marquis de,** 1757–1834,

French statesman and soldier who served in the American Revolutionary Army.

lag (lag), *v.,* **lagged, lag·ging.** 1. to move slowly; fail to keep a set speed or pace; loiter: *She lagged behind the other hikers.* 2. to lose strength; become less intense: *Our interest lagged as the meeting went on.* —*n.* 3. a falling behind; delay: *the lag between a sound and its echo.*

lag·gard (lag′ərd), *n.* 1. a person who lags; loiterer. —*adj.* 2. slow or sluggish; backward.

la·goon (lə gōōn′), *n.* 1. a shallow, pondlike body of water, esp. one connected with a larger body of water, such as a lake or the sea. 2. the body of water surrounded by an atoll.

La·gos (lä′gōs, lā′gōs), *n.* a seaport and the capital city of Nigeria, in the SW part.

laid (lād), *v.* the past tense and past participle of **lay.**

lain (lān), *v.* the past participle of **lie²**.

lair (lâr), *n.* a den or resting place of a wild animal.

laird (lârd), *n.* (in Scotland) the owner of an estate.

la·i·ty (lā′i tē), *n.* 1. religious worshipers who are not members of the clergy; laymen. 2. the people outside a particular profession or group, as distinguished from those belonging to it.

lake (lāk), *n.* a large inland body of water.

lam (lam), *Slang.* —*v.,* **lammed, lam·ming.** 1. to run away quickly; flee; escape. —*n.* 2. a fleeing or escaping. 3. **on the lam,** fleeing or hiding, esp. from the police: *a prisoner on the lam.*

la·ma (lä′mə), *n.* (in Tibet and Mongolia) a Buddhist priest or monk.

lamb (lam), *n.* a young sheep.

lam·baste (lam bāst′, lam bast′), *v.,* **lam·bast·ed, lam·bast·ing.** *Informal.* 1. to beat or whip severely. 2. to scold severely: *He was lambasted for his tardiness.*

lamb·kin (lam′kin), *n.* a little lamb.

lame (lām), *adj.,* **lam·er, lam·est.** 1. crippled or disabled, esp. in the foot or leg. 2. sore or painful; stiff: *a lame arm.* 3. weak, clumsy, or inadequate: *a lame excuse.* —*v.,* **lamed, lam·ing.** 4. to make lame; cripple. —**lame′ly,** *adv.* —**lame′ness,** *n.*

la·ment (lə ment′), *v.* 1. to feel or show sorrow over; mourn for: *He lamented the death of his friend.* 2. to feel or show sorrow; weep. —*n.* 3. a sorrowful song or poem.

lam·en·ta·ble (lam′ən tə bəl, lə men′tə bəl), *adj.* 1. that is to be lamented; regrettable: *a lamentable mishap.* 2. so bad as to arouse pity: *He does lamentable work.* —**lam′en·ta·bly,** *adv.*

lam·en·ta·tion (lam′ən tā′shən), *n.* the act of lamenting; a wailing or crying out in grief.

Lam·en·ta·tions (lam′ən tā′shənz), *n. (used as sing.)* a book of the Old Testament, traditionally believed to have been written by Jeremiah.

lam·i·nate (lam′ə nāt′), *v.,* **lam·i·nat·ed, lam·i·nat·ing.** 1. to form by building up from thin layers. 2. to split or roll into thin layers. —**lam′i·na′tion,** *n.*

lamp (lamp), *n.* 1. a device for providing light, such as a holder having a socket for an electric light bulb, a vessel for burning alcohol, oil, etc., through a wick, or a fixture having a gas jet. 2. an incandescent lamp. **3.** a fluorescent lamp. **4.** a device for providing special radiation: *an ultraviolet lamp.*

lamp·black (lamp′blak′), *n.* a fine, black soot used in making paints: an almost pure form of carbon.

lam·poon (lam pōōn′), *n.* **1.** a piece of writing that attacks or ridicules someone. —*v.* **2.** to attack (someone) in a lampoon; ridicule.

lam·prey (lam′prē), *n., pl.* **lam·preys.** any of a group of freshwater fishes that resemble an eel and prey on more valuable food fishes.

lance (lans), *n.* **1.** a weapon made of a long shaft topped by a sharp metal head, formerly used by cavalry soldiers in charging. **2.** a soldier armed with this weapon; lancer. **3.** any instrument resembling or used like this weapon, as a fish spear, a surgical lancet, etc. —*v.,* **lanced, lanc·ing. 4.** to cut open with or as if with a lancet: *to lance a boil.*

Lamprey
(length 21 in.)

Lan·ce·lot (lan′sə lot′), *n.* (in the legend of King Arthur) the bravest of the Knights of the Round Table.

lanc·er (lan′sər), *n.* a mounted soldier armed with a lance.

lan·cet (lan′sit), *n.* a small, sharp surgical instrument for opening boils, abscesses, etc.

land (land), *n.* **1.** the part of the earth's surface above water. **2.** a particular area or part of this; ground; property: *fertile land; to buy land in Florida.* **3.** a nation or region: *the land of one's birth.* —*v.* **4.** to bring to or come to rest on land: *The pilot landed the plane on schedule.* **5.** to bring (a fish) to land, into a boat, etc. **6.** to arrive or cause to arrive in a particular situation or condition: *He landed in jail.* **7.** *Informal.* to obtain or get by effort: *to land a good job.* **8.** **land on,** *Informal.* to scold or criticize severely: *Aunt Jane landed on me for getting home so late.* **9.** **see how the land lies,** to investigate a situation thoroughly before taking action: *You'd better see how the land lies before asking him for a favor.*

lan·dau (lan′dô, lan′dou), *n.* a four-wheeled, two-seated carriage with a two-part folding top.

land·ed (lan′did), *adj.* **1.** owning land: *a landed proprietor.* **2.** consisting of land: *landed property.*

land·hold·er (land′hōl′dər), *n.* a person who owns or occupies land.

land·ing (lan′ding), *n.* **1.** the act of coming or bringing to land: *the landing of the Pilgrims; the landing of an airplane.* **2.** a place where people or goods are landed, as from a ship. **3.** a platform between flights of stairs.

land′ing field′, a field cleared for the landing and takeoff of aircraft.

land·la·dy (land′lā′dē), *n., pl.* **land·la·dies. 1.** a woman who owns lands or buildings that she leases to others. **2.** a woman who manages an inn, boardinghouse, etc.

land·locked (land′lokt′), *adj.* **1.** shut in or nearly shut in by land: *a landlocked bay.* **2.** living in waters shut off from the sea: *landlocked salmon.*

land·lord (land′lôrd′), *n.* **1.** a person who owns lands or buildings that he leases to others. **2.** the manager of an inn, rooming house, etc.

land·lub·ber (land′lub′ər), *n.* a person who lacks experience at sailing or who has no skill on shipboard.

land·mark (land′märk′), *n.* **1.** a well-known or easily seen object that serves as a guide: *The large barns were the landmarks we looked for to find our way home.* **2.** any outstanding feature, fact, event, etc.: *The Empire State Building is a New York City landmark.* **3.** an object, such as a stake or stone, that marks the boundary of a piece of land.

land·own·er (land′ō′nər), *n.* a person who owns land.

land·scape (land′skāp′), *n.* **1.** an expanse of natural scenery that can be seen from one viewpoint: *a mountainous landscape.* **2.** a picture of such scenery: *The painter specializes in landscapes.* —*v.,* **landscaped, land·scap·ing. 3.** to improve the appearance of (a piece of land) by clearing, planting, etc.: *The front lawn was carefully landscaped.*

Land's′ End′, the SW tip of England.

land·slide (land′slīd′), *n.* **1.** a fall or sliding down of soil and rocks on a steep slope. **2.** the mass of soil and rocks that slides down. **3.** an overwhelming majority of votes for a particular party or candidate in an election: *to win by a landslide.*

land·ward (land′wərd), *adv.* **1.** Also, **land′wards.** toward the land. —*adj.* **2.** lying, facing, or tending toward the land; being in the direction of the land.

lane (lān), *n.* **1.** a narrow way or passage between hedges, fences, walls, or houses: *a winding country lane.* **2.** any narrow path, way, track, etc.: *the lanes of a bowling alley.* **3.** a special route followed by ships or airplanes: *the approach lanes to an airport.* **4.** a marked part of a road or highway wide enough for a single line of traffic: *The turnpike has four lanes.*

lan·guage (lang′gwij), *n.* **1.** human speech, or writing representing speech. **2.** a set of symbols expressing meanings generally agreed upon: *the language of mathematics.* **3.** a form of speech belonging exclusively to a nation, tribe, or similar group: *the French language.* **4.** a style of expression of a social or occupational class: *baseball language.* **5.** a particular manner of expression in speech or writing: *flowery language.* **6.** the study of language; linguistics.

lan·guid (lang′gwid), *adj.* **1.** drooping from weakness; faint; lacking vigor or vitality. **2.** sluggish or slow: *a languid way of walking.* —**lan′guid·ly,** *adv.*

lan·guish (lang′gwish), *v.* **1.** to become weak; droop; fade: *to languish from hunger.* **2.** to become weak from suffering or neglect; waste away: *to languish in prison for many years.* **3.** to pine with desire or longing: *to languish for one's home.*

lan·guor (lang′gər), *n.* **1.** physical weakness; fatigue; weariness: *a languor caused by the tropical climate.* **2.** lack of energy or spirit; sluggishness; listlessness. **3.** stillness or inactivity: *the languor of warm summer* *days.* **4.** emotional tenderness: *the languor of soft music.* —lan**/**guor·ous, *adj.*

lank (langk), *adj.* **1.** long or tall and slender; lean; thin: *a lank body; lank grass.* **2.** (of hair) straight and limp; without curls. —lank**/**ness, *n.*

lank·y (lang**/**kē), *adj.,* lank·i·er, lank·i·est. very thin and tall; rawboned; gaunt: *a lanky member of the basketball team.* —lank**/**i·ness, *n.*

lan·o·lin (lan**/**ə lin), *n.* an oily substance found in the wool of sheep and used in ointments, hairdressings, etc.

Lan·sing (lan**/**sing), *n.* the capital city of Michigan, in the S part.

lan·tern (lan**/**tərn), *n.* **1.** a case with sides of glass, paper, or the like, for enclosing a light and protecting it from the wind or rain. **2.** a magic lantern.

lan·tha·num (lan**/**thə nəm), *n.* *Chem.* a metallic element of the rare-earth group. *Symbol:* La

lan·yard (lan**/**yərd), *n.* **1.** a short rope used on ships for fastening or tightening something. **2.** a small cord for holding or suspending small objects, as a whistle around the neck. **3.** a cord with a hook at one end, used in firing certain kinds of cannons.

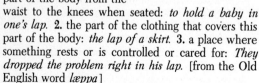

La·os (lä**/**ōs, lā**/**ōs), *n.* a country in SE Asia: formerly part of French Indochina. 91,500 sq. mi. *Cap.:* Vientiane. —La·o·tian (lā ō**/**shən), *n., adj.*

lap[1] (lap), *n.* **1.** the front part of the body from the waist to the knees when seated: *to hold a baby in one's lap.* **2.** the part of the clothing that covers this part of the body: *the lap of a skirt.* **3.** a place where something rests or is controlled or cared for: *They dropped the problem right in his lap.* [from the Old English word *læppa*]

lap[2] (lap), *v.,* lapped, lap·ping. **1.** to fold over or around something; wrap; wind: *to lap a bandage around the head.* **2.** to lay partly over something else; overlap: *to lap the shingles of a roof.* **3.** to lie partly over (something else): *The magazines were arranged to lap over each other.* **4.** to extend beyond a limit: *The first meeting lapped over into the time set for the second.* —*n.* **5.** the act of lapping. **6.** an overlapping amount or part. **7.** a complete circuit around a race track: *This track has four laps to the mile.* [from the Middle English word *lappen* "to fold"]

lap[3] (lap), *v.,* lapped, lap·ping. **1.** to take in (liquid) with the tongue; lick up a liquid: *The dog lapped the water thirstily.* **2.** to wash against (something) with a light, splashing sound: *Waves lapped the shore.* —*n.* **3.** the act or sound of lapping a liquid: *the quiet lap of the sea on the rocks.* **4. lap up, a.** *Informal.* to enjoy with great enthusiasm: *The audience lapped up the entertainment.* **b.** to eat or drink: *The cat lapped up her milk.* [from the Old English word *lapian*]

La Paz (lä päs**/**), the actual capital city of Bolivia, in the W part. See also **Sucre.**

la·pel (lə pel**/**), *n.* the part of a collar that is folded back on the breast.

lap·i·dar·y (lap**/**i der/ē), *n., pl.* lap·i·dar·ies. **1.** a person who cuts, polishes, and engraves precious stones. —*adj.* **2.** of or concerning precious stones or their cutting and engraving.

lap·is laz·u·li (lap**/**is laz**/**yōō lē, laz**/**yōō lī/), a deep-blue semiprecious stone used in jewelry. [from a medieval Latin phrase meaning "stone of azure"]

Lap·land (lap**/**land/), *n.* a region in the N of the Scandinavian countries.

Lapp (lap), *n.* **1.** Also, **Lap·land·er** (lap**/**lan/dər). any member of the people living in Lapland. **2.** the language of the Lapps, closely related to Finnish.

lapse (laps), *n.* **1.** a slip or slight error; failure: *He had a lapse of memory.* **2.** a fall or slipping away from a higher to a lower condition: *a lapse into savagery.* **3.** an interval or passage of time: *a lapse of five years.* **4.** the ending of a right or privilege through neglect: *the lapse of an insurance policy.* —*v.,* lapsed, laps·ing. **5.** to fall, slip, or sink: *to lapse into silence.* **6.** to fall into disuse: *The custom lapsed many years ago.* **7.** to pass away, as time; elapse.

lap·wing (lap**/**wing/), *n.* a bird of Europe and Asia noted for its flapping flight and its shrill cry.

lar·board (lär**/**bôrd/, lär**/**bərd), *n.* **1.** the left side of a ship; port. —*adj.* **2.** located on or toward this side of a ship.

lar·ce·ny (lär**/**sə nē), *n., pl.* lar·ce·nies. the stealing of the personal goods of another; theft. —lar**/**ce·nist, *n.*

larch (lärch), *n.* **1.** a tree that is related to the pine but loses its cones and needles in the fall. **2.** the tough, durable wood of this tree.

lard (lärd), *n.* **1.** the fat of hogs that has been melted down and made clear for use in cooking. —*v.* **2.** to cover with lard or fat. **3.** to prepare (meat) for cooking by inserting strips of pork or fat: *to lard a roast.* **4.** to add to (something) in order to improve or decorate: *to lard a speech with amusing stories.*

lar·der (lär**/**dər), *n.* a room or place where food is kept; pantry.

large (lärj), *adj.,* larg·er, larg·est. **1.** greater than average in size, amount, or number; big. **2.** on a great scale: *a large producer of movies.* **3.** of great scope or range; broad: *a large variety of interests.* **4. at large, a.** not confined; at liberty: *The murderer is still at large.* **b.** as a whole; in its entirety: *The country at large is behind the President.* —large**/**ness, *n.*

large/ **intes**/**tine,** the lower portion of the intestines, shorter but larger in diameter than the upper portion. Solid wastes are accumulated and prepared for elimination from the body in the large intestine. See illus. at **intestine.**

large·ly (lärj′lē), *adv.* to a great extent; chiefly: *His wealth is largely in land.*

lar·go (lär′gō), *adj., adv.* 1. (in music) slow and dignified. —*n., pl.* **lar·gos.** 2. a slow or dignified piece of music or section of a longer work.

lar·i·at (lar′ē ət), *n.* 1. a lasso. 2. a rope for tethering grazing animals.

lark¹ (lärk), *n.* 1. any of numerous small European songbirds, esp. the skylark, noted for the beauty of its song. 2. any of various similar North American birds, esp. the meadowlark. [from the Old English word *lāwerce*]

lark² (lärk), *n.* 1. a merry, carefree adventure; frolic; prank. —*v.* 2. to have fun; play pranks.

lark·spur (lärk′spûr′), *n.* a plant having spikes of blue, pink, or white flowers, the rear part of which has the shape of a pointed spur.

Larkspur

lar·va (lär′və), *n., pl.* **lar·vae** (lär′vē). an insect in the early, wingless stage of its development, during which it feeds and grows. Larvae frequently resemble fat worms. —**lar′val,** *adj.*

Larva of butterfly (length 1½ in.)

lar·yn·gi·tis (lar′ən jī′tis), *n.* an inflammation of the larynx that causes hoarseness and, sometimes, the inability to speak above a whisper.

lar·ynx (lar′iñgks), *n., pl.* **lar·ynx·es** *or* **la·ryn·ges** (lə rin′jēz). the structure at the upper end of the windpipe that contains the vocal cords. See illus. at **lung, mouth.**

La Salle (lə sal′), **Robert Cav·e·lier** (kav′əl yā′), 1643–1687, French explorer of North America.

las·civ·i·ous (lə siv′ē əs), *adj.* indecent or obscene; lewd. —**las·civ′i·ous·ly,** *adv.*

la·ser (lā′zər), *n.* a device that produces a very narrow beam of extremely intense light, used for cutting and drilling, in surgery, and in communications.

lash¹ (lash), *n.* 1. the flexible striking part of a whip. 2. a swift stroke or blow, as with a whip. 3. an eyelash. —*v.* 4. to strike or beat, as with a whip: *to lash a team of horses.* 5. to beat violently against: *The wind lashed the trees.* 6. to fling or switch back and forth: *The cat lashed its tail.* 7. to attack someone or something with harsh words (often fol. by *out*): *to lash out at social injustice.* [from the Middle English word *lasshe,* which is perhaps of imitative origin]

lash² (lash), *v.* to tie or bind with a rope or cord. [from an early Dutch word *lasschen* "to patch, sew together"]

lass (las), *n.* a girl or young woman.

las·sie (las′ē), *n.* a young girl; lass.

las·si·tude (las′i tōōd′, -tyōōd′), *n.* weariness of body or mind; lack of interest or energy.

las·so (las′ō, la sōō′), *n., pl.* **las·sos** *or* **las·soes.** 1. a long rope with a running noose at one end, used for catching horses, cattle, etc.; lariat. —*v.,* **las·soed, las·so·ing.** 2. to catch with a lasso.

last¹ (last), *adj., a superlative of* **late** *with* **later** *as comparative.* 1. coming after all others in time, order, or place: *the last chapter of a novel.* 2. the most recent; latest: *last Tuesday.* 3. being the only one remaining: *a last chance.* 4. least likely or suitable: *He is the last person we'd want to represent us.* —*adv.* 5. after all others: *She arrived last at the party.* 6. most recently: *He was alone when last seen.* 7. finally; in conclusion. —*n.* 8. a person or thing that is last: *to be the last in line.* 9. end or conclusion: *We haven't heard the last of this.* 10. **at last,** after a long pause or delay: *He stopped to look at his notes, and at last he spoke.* 11. **at long last,** after much troublesome delay: *The ship docked at long last.* [from the Old English word *latest,* superlative of *læt* "late"]

last² (last), *v.* 1. to continue or go on in time: *The festival lasted a week.* 2. to remain in good condition: *This suit must last me a year.* 3. to remain unexhausted; hold out: *How long will the water supply last?* [from the Old English word *læstan*]

last³ (last), *n.* 1. a wooden or metal model of the foot on which shoes or boots are made or repaired. 2. **stick to one's last,** to do only that for which one is qualified. [from the Old English word *læste*]

last·ing (las′tiñg), *adj.* continuing a long time; enduring; permanent: *a lasting friendship.* —**last′ing·ly,** *adv.*

last·ly (last′lē), *adv.* in conclusion; finally.

Last′ Sup′per, the supper of Jesus and His disciples on the eve of His Crucifixion.

lat., latitude.

latch (lach), *n.* 1. a device for holding a door, gate, or the like, closed, consisting of a bar that slides or falls into a catch or groove. —*v.* 2. to close or fasten with a latch. 3. **latch onto,** *Informal.* to acquire or obtain: *If I can latch onto some money, I can buy that new fishing tackle.*

late (lāt), *adj.,* **lat·er** *or* **lat·ter** (lat′ər); **lat·est** *or* **last** (last). 1. occurring or appearing after the usual or expected time; tardy: *a late spring; to be late for school.* 2. toward the end, as of a period of time: *in the late nineteenth century.* 3. very recent: *a late bulletin.* 4. recently deceased: *the late Mr. Phipps.* 5. immediately preceding the present one; former: *the late attorney general.* —*adv.,* **lat·er, lat·est.** 6. after the usual or proper time; after delay: *to come home late.* 7. at or to an advanced time: *to talk late into the night.* 8. recently but no longer; lately: *a man, late of Chicago, now living abroad.* 9. **of late,** lately; recently: *You've been looking better of late.* —**late′ness,** *n.*

la·teen′ sail′ (la tēn′, lə tēn′), a triangular sail set on a long yard, used esp. in the Mediterranean.

late·ly (lāt′lē), *adv.* recently; not long since: *I've been walking to school lately.*

la·tent (lāt′ᵊnt), *adj.* present but hidden and not ac-

act, āble, dâre, ärt; ebb, ēqual; if, īce; hot, ōver, ôrder; oil; bŏŏk; ōōze; out; up, ûrge; ə = a as in *alone*; ᵊ as in *button* (but′ᵊn), *fire* (fiᵊr); **chief;** **shoe;** thin; ℋhat; zh as in *measure* (mezh′ər). See full key inside cover.

tive: *a latent ability; latent resources.* —**la′tent·ly,** *adv.*

lat·er·al (lat′ər əl), *adj.* of, placed at, coming from, or aimed toward the side: *a lateral pass in football.* —**lat′er·al·ly,** *adv.*

la·tex (lā′teks), *n.* a sticky, milky liquid produced by certain plants, such as milkweed. Rubber is made from the latex of a tropical plant.

lath (lath), *n., pl.* **laths** (la_t_hz, laths). **1.** one of the thin, narrow strips of wood used as a support for plasterwork, roofing, etc. —*v.* **2.** to cover or line with laths.

lathe (lā_t_h), *n.* a machine for shaping wood, metal, or other material by rotating it against a cutting tool.

lath·er (la_t_h′ər), *n.* **1.** foam or froth made by soap stirred in water. **2.** foam formed in sweating, as on a horse. —*v.* **3.** to become covered with lather, as a horse. **4.** to cover with lather: *He lathered his face before shaving.*

Lathe for working wood

Lat·in (lat′ᵊn, lat′in), *n.* **1.** the Indo-European language of the ancient Romans. Latin is the ancestor of the Romance languages. **2.** any form of Latin used in medieval or modern times. **3.** a member of any of the Latin peoples. —*adj.* **4.** of or concerning Latin. **5.** of or concerning those peoples whose languages come from Latin, such as Spanish, Portuguese, French, Italian, or Rumanian.

Lat′in Amer′ica, the part of the American continents south of the U.S. in which Romance languages are spoken. —**Lat′in-A·mer′i·can,** *adj.* —**Lat′in Amer′ican.**

lat·i·tude (lat′i tōōd′, -tyōōd′), *n.* **1.** the distance on the earth's surface north or south of the equator, stated in degrees. Lines of latitude are circles that run parallel to the equator. See also **longitude. 2.** a place or region as marked by this distance: *tropical latitudes.* **3.** freedom of action, opinion, etc.: *to be allowed latitude in the choice of one's friends.*

lat·ter (lat′ər), *adj.* **1.** being the second mentioned of two (distinguished from *former*): *Of the two versions of the story, I prefer the latter.* **2.** more advanced in time; later: *the latter part of the month.*

Lat′ter-day Saint′ (lat′ər dā′), a Mormon.

lat·tice (lat′is), *n.* **1.** a structure of wooden or metal strips crossed to form a pattern of open spaces. —*v.,* **lat·ticed, lat·tic·ing. 2.** to form into a lattice.

Lat·vi·a (lat′vē ə), *n.* a part of the Soviet Union on the Baltic Sea, formerly an independent country. 25,395 sq. mi. *Cap.:* Riga.

Lat·vi·an (lat′vē ən), *n.* **1.** a native or inhabitant of

Latvia. **2.** the Baltic language of Latvia. —*adj.* **3.** of or concerning Latvia, its people, or their language.

laud (lôd), *v.* to praise; extol: *to laud a new play.*

laud·a·ble (lô′də bəl), *adj.* praiseworthy or commendable: *a laudable effort.* —**laud′a·bly,** *adv.*

laud·a·to·ry (lô′də tôr′ē), *adj.* containing or expressing praise: *a laudatory speech for a candidate.*

laugh (laf), *v.* **1.** to show emotion, such as joy, pleasure, scorn, or nervousness, by smiling and making sounds in the throat that can range from loud bursts to quiet chuckles: *We laughed all through the movie.* **2.** to drive, put, bring, etc., by laughter (usually fol. by *out, away,* etc.): *He laughed away his cares.* —*n.* **3.** the act or sound of laughing. **4. laugh at,** to make fun of; ridicule: *He laughed at my attempts to paint.* **5. laugh off,** to dismiss as absurd; ridicule: *He laughed off the idea that the trip was dangerous.*

laugh·a·ble (laf′ə bəl), *adj.* arousing laughter; funny; ridiculous. —**laugh′a·bly,** *adv.*

laugh·ing·stock (laf′ing stok′), *n.* an object of ridicule; the butt of a joke.

laugh·ter (laf′tər), *n.* the act or sound of laughing.

launch[1] (lônch), *n.* **1.** a heavy, open motorboat. **2.** a large boat carried by a warship. [from a Portuguese word, which comes from Malay *lanchāran*]

launch[2] (lônch), *v.* **1.** to set in the water; float (a vessel) by allowing it to slide down an incline: *to launch a new battleship.* **2.** to cause to start: *to launch a new business.* **3.** to throw; hurl: *to launch a spear.* **4.** to send forth or upward with force: *to launch a spacecraft.* —*n.* **5.** the act or process of launching: *The launch was A-O.K.* [from the Latin word *lanceāre* "to wield a lance," which comes from *lancea* "lance"]

launch′ pad′, a platform from which a rocket is launched. Also, **launch′ing pad′.**

laun·der (lôn′dər), *v.* to wash or wash and iron (clothes).

laun·dress (lôn′dris), *n.* a woman who washes and irons clothes, linens, etc.

laun·dry (lôn′drē), *n., pl.* **laun·dries. 1.** a room or business establishment where clothes, linens, etc., are laundered. **2.** clothes, linens, etc., that have been or are about to be laundered.

laun·dry·man (lôn′drē man′), *n., pl.* **laun·dry·men. 1.** a man who works in or operates a laundry. **2.** a man who collects and delivers laundry.

lau·re·ate (lôr′ē it), *adj.* **1.** having or receiving high honor in a particular field: *a poet laureate.* —*n.* **2.** a person who has been honored in a particular field.

lau·rel (lôr′əl, lor′əl), *n.* **1.** a small, European evergreen tree. The ancient Greeks and Romans used its leaves to crown victors in athletic or poetry contests. **2.** any of various similar trees or shrubs, such as the mountain laurel. **3. look to one's laurels,** to be alert to the fact that someone else may be more skillful, more successful, etc.: *Competing with others will force you to look to your laurels.* **4. rest on one's laurels,** to be content with one's present achievements: *After winning a gold medal, he decided to rest on his laurels.* Also, **bay** (for defs. 1, 2).

la·va (lä′və, lav′ə), *n.* **1.** the molten rock that flows from a volcano. **2.** this rock when it has cooled and hardened. [from an Italian word meaning "avalanche," which comes from Latin *lābēs* "a sliding down, falling"]

lav·a·to·ry (lav′ə tôr′ē), *n., pl.* **lav·a·to·ries. 1.** a room with equipment for washing the hands and face and usually with a toilet. **2.** a bowl or basin with running water for washing.

lave (lāv), *v.,* **laved, lav·ing.** to wash; bathe.

lav·en·der (lav′ən dər), *n.* **1.** a pale, bluish purple. **2.** a European shrub having pale purple, sweet-smelling flowers used in making perfume. **3.** the dried flowers or other parts of this plant, put among linens, clothes, etc., as a scent.

lav·ish (lav′ish), *adj.* **1.** using or giving abundantly or in too great amounts (often fol. by *of* or *with*): *to be lavish with one's money.* **2.** spent or given in abundance: *a lavish serving of food.* —*v.* **3.** to spend or give in great amounts: *to lavish favors on a person.* —**lav′ish·ly,** *adv.*

law (lô), *n.* **1.** a rule, established by a legislative authority or by custom, that a nation or group of people follows. **2.** a system or collection of such rules. **3.** the condition of society brought about by the observance of such rules: *maintaining law and order.* **4.** the group of such rules concerned with a particular subject: *commercial law.* **5.** the profession of a lawyer, judge, or the like: *to practice law.* **6.** an agency enforcing such rules, esp. the police: *The law arrived soon after the burglary.* **7.** legal action in a court: *to go to law over a trifle.* **8.** any rule or custom about which a group of authorities agrees: *the laws of grammar.* **9.** a scientific or mathematical statement that is true under certain circumstances: *the law of gravity.* **10. lay down the law,** to give an opinion, command, etc., forcefully: *She really laid down the law when I got home late.* **11. take the law into one's own hands,** to take revenge or deal out justice without using legal procedures.

law·a·bid·ing (lô′ə bī′ding), *adj.* obedient to the law.

law·break·er (lô′brā′kər), *n.* a person who breaks the law.

law·ful (lô′fəl), *adj.* **1.** permitted by law: *lawful acts.* **2.** recognized by or according to law: *a lawful heir.* —**law′ful·ly,** *adv.* —**law′ful·ness,** *n.*

law·giv·er (lô′giv′ər), *n.* a person who sets up, teaches, or proclaims a law or a code of laws.

law·less (lô′lis), *adj.* **1.** contrary to the law: *lawless violence.* **2.** uncontrollable; unruly; disorderly: *a lawless mob.* **3.** being without law; having no laws: *the lawless frontier of the early West.* —**law′less·ly,** *adv.* —**law′less·ness,** *n.*

law·mak·er (lô′mā′kər), *n.* a person who makes or enacts laws; legislator: *the lawmakers in Washington.* —**law′mak′ing,** *n., adj.*

lawn¹ (lôn), *n.* a piece of grass-covered ground, esp. one kept closely mowed. [from the Old French word *lande* "moor, heath," which comes from Celtic]

lawn² (lôn), *n.* a thin linen or cotton fabric: *a handkerchief made of lawn.* [perhaps named after *Laon,* a city in France noted for the making of linen]

lawn′ mow′er, a machine for cutting grass.

lawn′ ten′nis, tennis, esp. when played on a grass court.

law·ren·ci·um (lô ren′sē əm), *n. Chem.* a manmade, radioactive, metallic element. Lawrencium is the heaviest element known. *Symbol:* Lw

law·suit (lô′sōot′), *n.* the act or process of suing in a court of law.

law·yer (lô′yər, loi′ər), *n.* a person whose profession is to conduct lawsuits for clients and to advise or act for them in other legal matters; attorney.

lax (laks), *adj.* **1.** not strict; careless or negligent: *lax morals.* **2.** not exact or precise; vague: *The terms of the agreement were far too lax.* **3.** loose; slack; not tense or firm: *a lax handshake.* —**lax′ness,** *n.*

lax·a·tive (lak′sə tiv), *n.* a medicine for relieving constipation.

lax·i·ty (lak′si tē), *n.* the state or quality of being lax; looseness, slackness, or carelessness.

lay¹ (lā), *v.,* **laid** *or,* for def. 4, **layed; lay·ing. 1.** to put or place in a horizontal or resting position; set down: *to lay a baby in its crib.* **2.** to beat down; throw to the ground: *The storm laid the grain flat.* **3.** to present; bring forward: *He laid his case before the commission.* **4.** to place as a wager; bet: *He layed $10 on the horse.* **5.** to deposit (an egg or eggs): *The hen laid two eggs.* **6.** to place, set, or cause to be in a particular position, order, state, etc.: *to lay bricks; to lay open a wound.* **7.** to put or place: *to lay stress on good grades.* **8.** to place or locate: *The scene is laid in France.* **9.** to devise or arrange: *to lay plans.* **10.** to quiet or make vanish: *to lay a ghost.* **11.** to cause to subside: *to lay the dust with a spray of water.* —*n.* **12.** the way or position in which a thing lies: *the lay of the south pasture.* **13. lay aside, a.** to stop using or practicing: *to lay aside old-fashioned ideas.* **b.** to save or store up: *to lay aside money.* **14. lay down, a.** to give up; yield: *The soldiers laid down their arms.* **b.** to state firmly and decisively: *to lay down the rules of conduct.* **15. lay in,** to store away for future use: *We laid in a load of canned goods.* **16. lay of the land,** the facts or mood of a situation: *Ask a few questions and try to get the lay of the land.* **17. lay off, a.** to dismiss an employee, esp. temporarily: *I hear that most of the clerks will be laid off after Christmas.* **b.** *Slang.* to stop annoying or teasing: *Lay off me, will you?* **18. lay out, a.** to spread out in order: *Lay out the clothes you're going to wear tomorrow.* **b.** *Informal.* to spend or contribute: *He had to lay out $10 for a new tire.* **19. lay up, a.** to store up or put away. **b.** to confine because of illness; make ill: *He's been laid up with a cold.* [from the Old English word *lecgan* "to lay"] —**Usage.** See **lie².**

lay² (lā), *v.* the past tense of **lie².**

lay³ (lā), *adj.* **1.** belonging to, concerning, or performed by the people or laity, as distinguished from the clergy: *a lay sermon.* **2.** not belonging to a specified profession, esp. law or medicine: *a lay opinion on a legal case.* [from the Latin word *lāicus*]

lay⁴ (lā), *n.* **1.** a short, narrative poem, esp. one to be sung. **2.** a song. [from an Old French word, which comes from Germanic]

lay·er (lā′ər), *n.* **1.** a thickness of some material spread over a surface: *a layer of paint; the layers of a cake.* **2.** a person or thing that lays (usually used in combination): *bricklayer.*

lay·ette (lā et′), *n.* an outfit of clothing, bedding, etc., for a newborn child.

lay·man (lā′mən), *n., pl.* **lay·men. 1.** a person who is not a clergyman. **2.** a person who is not a member of a specified profession, esp. of law or medicine.

lay·out (lā′out′), *n.* **1.** a laying or spreading out. **2.** an arrangement or plan: *the layout of a house.*

Laz·a·rus (laz′ər əs), *n.* (in the Bible) a brother of Mary and Martha whom Jesus raised from the dead.

la·zy (lā′zē), *adj.,* **la·zi·er, la·zi·est. 1.** not willing to work; idle. **2.** slow-moving; sluggish: *a lazy stream.* —**la′zi·ly,** *adv.* —**la′zi·ness,** *n.*

lb., pound; pounds. [short for the Latin word *libra*]

lbs., pounds.

l.c., 1. letter of credit. **2.** lower case.

LD, long distance.

lea (lē, lā), *n.* an open, grassy field; meadow.

leach (lēch), *v.* **1.** to pass water through something so as to remove soluble materials: *to leach lye from ashes.* **2.** to lose soluble materials in this way: *Rain can leach valuable minerals from soil.*

lead¹ (lēd), *v.,* **led** (led), **lead·ing. 1.** to show the way to, esp. by going before or with; guide: *You lead and we'll follow.* **2.** to influence; guide in action, opinion, etc.: *What led him to change his mind?* **3.** to bring or go to a place: *This street leads to the bridge.* **4.** to direct or be in control or command of: *to lead a band; to lead a discussion.* **5.** to be at the head of: *Iowa leads the nation in corn production.* **6.** to go first; be in advance: *to lead in a parade.* **7.** to go through or pass (time, life, etc.): *to lead a full life.* **8.** to result in; tend toward (usually fol. by *to*): *The incident led to his quitting his job.* —*n.* **9.** the first or foremost place: *to take the lead in a race.* **10.** the extent or distance of such an advance: *He had a lead of four yards.* **11.** a guide to a road, course of action, method, etc.; clue: *to be given a lead in solving a problem.* **12.** example; leadership: *They followed his lead in everything they did.* **13.** the principal role in a play, or the person who plays it. **14.** the act or right of playing first in a card game. **15.** (in journalism) a short summarizing introduction to a news story or article. —*adj.* **16.** most important; first: *a lead editorial.* **17. lead off, a.** to begin an action: *He led off with an announcement.* **b.** (in baseball) to be the first batter. **18. lead up to,** to approach (a subject) gradually so as to seem casual or offhand: *She was so nice to me that I could see she was leading up to something.* [from the Old English word *lǣdan*]

lead² (led), *n.* **1.** a soft, heavy, bluish-gray metal used in making pipe, solder, weights, bullets, etc.: a chemical element. *Symbol:* Pb **2.** the graphite of a pencil. **3.** something made of lead. **4.** bullets collectively; shot. —*v.* **5.** to cover, line, weight, or join with lead. —*adj.* **6.** made of lead: *a lead sinker.* [from the Old English word *lēad*]

lead·en (led′ən), *adj.* **1.** heavy; hard to move: *a leaden weight; leaden feet.* **2.** dull; gloomy; oppressive: *a leaden piece of writing; a leaden silence.* **3.** made of lead. **4.** of a dull gray color: *leaden skies.*

lead·er (lē′dər), *n.* a person or thing that leads: *the leader of a Boy Scout troop; the nation's leader.*

lead·er·ship (lē′dər ship′), *n.* **1.** the position of a leader. **2.** ability to lead: *He has shown leadership on several occasions.* **3.** an act or instance of leading: *They prospered under his leadership.*

lead·ing (lē′diṅg), *adj.* **1.** chief; principal; most important: *a leading medical authority.* **2.** coming in advance of others: *He rode the leading car.* **3.** directing; guiding.

leaf (lēf), *n., pl.* **leaves** (lēvz). **1.** one of the thin, green, usually flat parts of a plant that grow from a stalk or stem. **2.** a petal of a flower. **3.** one of the paper sheets in a book, periodical, etc., each side being a page. **4.** a thin sheet of metal: *gold leaf.* **5.** a sliding, hinged, or detachable flat part, as of a door or table. —*v.* **6.** to put forth leaves. **7.** to turn pages quickly (usually fol. by *through*): *to leaf through a catalog.* **8. turn over a new leaf,** to make a fresh start: *Turn over a new leaf and try harder.*

Leaves

leaf·let (lēf′lit), *n.* **1.** a small flat or folded sheet of printed matter; pamphlet. **2.** a small leaf. **3.** one of the blades or divisions of a compound leaf.

leaf·y (lē′fē), *adj.,* **leaf·i·er, leaf·i·est. 1.** having or covered with leaves. **2.** resembling a leaf; leaflike. —**leaf′i·ness,** *n.*

league¹ (lēg), *n.* **1.** a group of persons, parties, nations, etc., united for a common purpose. **2.** a group of athletic teams that compete chiefly among themselves: *a bowling league.* —*v.,* **leagued, lea·guing. 3.** to unite in a league; combine. **4. in league,** having an agreement; allied: *The neighbors were in league against the new highway.* [from the Italian word *lega,* which comes from *legare* "to bind"]

league² (lēg), *n.* an obsolete unit of distance equivalent to about three miles. [from the Latin word *leuca,* which comes from Celtic]

League′ of Na′tions, an international organization, 1919–1946, for promoting world peace.

Le·ah (lē′ə), *n.* (in the Bible) the first wife of Jacob.

leak (lēk), *n.* **1.** a hole, crack, or opening that accidentally lets water, air, light, etc., enter or escape: *a leak in a bucket.* **2.** any means by which something is unintentionally let out or made public: *a leak of military secrets.* **3.** the act or an instance of leaking: *a slow leak in a tire.* —*v.* **4.** to let (water, air, light, etc.) enter or escape: *The pipe was leaking gas. The roof leaks.* 5. to allow to become known: *to leak the news of the ambassador's visit.*

leak·age (lē′kij), *n.* 1. the act or an instance of leaking. 2. the thing that leaks in or out. 3. the amount that leaks.

leak·y (lē′kē), *adj.,* **leak·i·er, leak·i·est.** having a leak or leaks: *a leaky boat.* —**leak′i·ness,** *n.*

lean[1] (lēn), *v.* 1. to bend from a vertical position; slant: *He leaned his head forward.* 2. to rest against or on something for support; prop: *The old lady leaned on her husband's arm.* 3. to incline in feeling, opinion, action, etc.; tend: *to lean toward socialism.* 4. to rely; depend: *He leans too much on others for his views.* 5. **lean over backward,** to do one's utmost: *I've leaned over backward to be friendly with her.* [from the Old English word *hleonian*]

lean[2] (lēn), *adj.* 1. without much flesh or fat; thin: *lean meat; a lean face.* 2. lacking in richness, fullness, quantity, etc.; poor: *a lean diet; lean years.* —*n.* 3. flesh or meat containing little or no fat. [from the Old English word *hlǣne*] —**lean′ness,** *n.*

lean·ing (lē′ning), *n.* inclination; tendency: *strong literary leanings.*

leant (lent), *v. Chiefly British.* a past tense and past participle of lean[1].

lean-to (lēn′tōō′), *n., pl.* **lean-tos.** 1. a shed having a roof with a single slope, the higher end resting against a wall or another building. 2. a shack or shed supported at one side by trees or posts and having a roof sloping downward from them.

leap (lēp), *v.,* **leaped** *or* **leapt** (lept, lēpt); **leap·ing.** 1. to spring or jump: *to leap over a ditch.* 2. to jump over: *to leap a fence.* 3. to move quickly and lightly: *to leap aside.* 4. to rise, pass, come, etc., as if with a jump: *to leap to a conclusion.* 5. to cause to jump: *to leap a horse over a hurdle.* —*n.* 6. a spring, jump, or bound. 7. the distance covered by a jump: *a leap of two yards.* 8. **by leaps and bounds,** very rapidly: *She is progressing by leaps and bounds.*

leap·frog (lēp′frog′, -frôg′), *n.* a game in which players take turns leaping over the back of another player who is bent over from the waist.

leap′ year′, a year of 366 days, with February 29 as an additional day. A year that can be exactly divided by 4 is a leap year. Years that begin a century are not leap years unless they can be exactly divided by 400. The year 2000 will be a leap year; the year 1900 was not.

learn (lûrn), *v.,* **learned** (lûrnd) *or* **learnt** (lûrnt); **learn·ing.** 1. to acquire knowledge of or skill in: *to learn French.* 2. to acquire knowledge or skill: *to learn rapidly.* 3. to find out: *to learn the truth.* 4. to become informed: *to learn of an accident.* 5. to memorize: *to learn a poem.* 6. to become able through study or practice: *to learn to sing.* —**learn′er,** *n.*

learn·ed (lûr′nid), *adj.* having or showing much knowledge: *a learned man.*

learn·ing (lûr′ning), *n.* 1. knowledge gained by careful study: *The professor was a man of learning.* 2. the act or process of gaining knowledge or skill.

lease (lēs), *n.* 1. a written agreement granting the use of land, buildings, or other property for a certain period of time in return for money paid as rent. 2. the period such property is leased: *This lease is up in December.* 3. the property leased. —*v.,* **leased, leas·ing.** 4. to grant the use of by means of a lease: *She leased her apartment to a friend.* 5. to take or hold by means of a lease; rent: *He leased the farm from his uncle.*

leash (lēsh), *n.* 1. a strap or line for leading or holding a dog or other animal. —*v.* 2. to fasten or hold in with or as if with a leash; control: *to leash the dog; to leash the energy of the atom.*

least (lēst), *adj., a superlative of* **little** *with* **less** *or* **lesser** *as comparatives.* 1. smallest in amount, size, degree, etc.: *He ran the least distance of all.* —*n.* 2. someone or something that is least: *the least of one's problems.* —*adv., superlative of* **little** *with* **less** *as comparative.* 3. to the smallest amount or degree: *the least important item.* 4. **at least, a.** at the lowest estimate or figure: *The trip will cost at least $10.* **b.** in any case; anyhow: *At least you could say thank you.*

leath·er (leth′ər), *n.* 1. the skin of an animal prepared for use by tanning. —*adj.* 2. made of leather: *a leather belt.*

leath·ern (leth′ərn), *adj.* made of or resembling leather.

leath·er·y (leth′ə rē), *adj.* like leather; tough: *a tanned, leathery face.* —**leath′er·i·ness,** *n.*

leave[1] (lēv), *v.,* **left** (left), **leav·ing.** 1. to go away or depart from; set out: *to leave a room; to leave for vacation.* 2. to let stay as specified: *to leave a door unlocked.* 3. to let remain without interference: *Leave the puppy alone!* 4. to abandon: *He left politics to study law.* 5. to let remain for another to do or decide: *He left the details to his lawyer.* 6. to let remain in the same place, condition, etc.: *I left the book where I found it.* 7. to have remaining behind as a result of something: *The wound left a scar.* 8. to have remaining after one's death: *He leaves a widow.* 9. to give for use after one's death: *to leave money in a will.* 10. to have as a remainder after subtraction: *2 from 4 leaves 2.* 11. **leave off,** to stop or cease: *This story starts where that one leaves off.* 12. **leave out,** to omit; exclude: *You left out one "o" in "choose."* [from the Old English word *lǣfan*]

leave[2] (lēv), *n.* 1. permission to do something: *to ask leave to go.* 2. permission to be absent: *to be on leave.* 3. the length of time this permission lasts: *30 days' leave.* 4. departure; farewell: *He took leave of the family immediately after dinner.* [from the Old English word *lēaf*]

leave[3] (lēv), *v.,* **leaved, leav·ing.** to put forth leaves.

leav·en (lev′ən), *n.* 1. Also, **leav′en·ing.** something, such as yeast or baking powder, that makes dough rise by producing small bubbles of gas. 2. anything that acts upon something else to improve it, lighten it, or produce a gradual change in it: *a story with the leaven of wit.* —*v.* 3. to cause (dough) to rise.

leaves (lēvz), *n.* the plural of **leaf.**

leave-tak·ing (lēv′tā′kiŋg), *n.* a farewell; the act of saying good-by: *His leave-taking was brief.*

leav·ings (lē′viŋgz), *n.pl.* things that are left; remains; refuse.

Leb·a·non (leb′ə nən), *n.* a republic at the E end of the Mediterranean Sea, N of Israel. 3927 sq. mi. *Cap.:* Beirut.

lec·tern (lek′tərn), *n.* a desk or stand with a slanted top on which a speaker or lecturer may put the books, papers, etc., that he needs to consult or read from.

lec·ture (lek′chər), *n.* 1. a speech given before an audience, esp. for instruction or to set forth a particular subject: *a lecture on modern art.* 2. a speech that warns or rebukes; a long scolding: *He was given a lecture on his rudeness.* —*v.,* **lec·tured, lec·tur·ing.** 3. to give a lecture; teach by giving a series of lectures: *He lectures on art at the university.* 4. to rebuke or scold at length. —**lec′tur·er,** *n.*

led (led), *v.* the past tense and past participle of **lead**[1].

ledge (lej), *n.* 1. a narrow shelf of rock projecting from a cliff or slope. 2. any narrow, projecting part, such as a window sill or a shelflike surface projecting from the wall of a building.

ledg·er (lej′ər), *n.* an account book in which a business keeps the final records for all money received and spent.

lee (lē), *n.* 1. the side or part, esp. of a ship, that is sheltered from the wind. —*adj.* 2. sheltered from the wind: *the lee side of a sailboat.*

Lee (lē), *n.* **Robert E.,** 1807–1870, Confederate general: commander of Confederate forces in the American Civil War.

leech (lēch), *n.* 1. any of various bloodsucking worms, esp. certain freshwater species formerly used by doctors to draw the blood of patients suffering a variety of illnesses. 2. a person who clings to another person in order to gain something; parasite.

Leeds (lēdz), *n.* a city in N England.

leek (lēk), *n.* a plant resembling an onion, eaten as a vegetable or used in soups.

leer (lēr), *n.* 1. a sly, sidelong look suggestive of lust, evil, etc. —*v.* 2. to look with a leer.

Leech
(length
5 to 6 in.)

leer·y (lēr′ē), *adj.,* **leer·i·er, leer·i·est.** wary; suspicious (usually fol. by *of*): *They were leery of the advice the stranger offered.*

lees (lēz), *n.pl.* the sediment that settles to the bottom of a container of liquid, esp. wine; dregs.

lee·ward (lē′wərd, lōō′ərd), *adj.* 1. located or moving in the direction toward which the wind is blowing (opposite of *windward*). —*n.* 2. the lee side; the point toward which the wind blows. —*adv.* 3. toward the lee.

Lee′ward Is′lands (lē′wərd, lōō′ərd), a group of islands in the NE West Indies.

lee·way (lē′wā′), *n.* 1. extra time, space, resources, etc., with which to operate: *With 10 minutes' leeway we can catch the train.* 2. the drift of a ship to leeward from its course.

left[1] (left), *adj.* 1. of or concerning the side of a person or thing that is turned toward the west when the subject faces north (opposite of *right*): *the left hand; the left door.* —*n.* 2. the left side or direction; something on the left side: *Take the seat on his left.* 3. (*usually cap.*) the political parties, groups, etc., that advocate liberal, progressive, or radical policies. —*adv.* 4. toward the left: *to turn left.* [from an Old English word meaning "idle"]

left[2] (left), *v.* the past tense and past participle of **leave**[1].

left-hand (left′hand′), *adj.* 1. on or to the left. 2. of, for, or with the left hand.

left-hand·ed (left′han′did), *adj.* 1. using the left hand with greater ease and skill than the right: *a left-handed pitcher.* 2. made for or done by the left hand: *a left-handed tool; a left-handed punch.* 3. turning from right to left. 4. doubtful, unintentional, or ·sarcastic: *a left-handed compliment.* —*adv.* 5. with or toward the left hand: *He writes left-handed.* —**left′-hand′ed·ness,** *n.*

left·o·ver (left′ō′vər), *n.* 1. something left from a larger amount, such as food remaining after a meal. —*adj.* 2. being left, such as an unused part: *leftover meat.*

leg (leg), *n.* 1. one of the limbs of humans and animals that support and move the body. 2. something resembling a leg in use, appearance, or position: *the leg of a chair.* 3. the part of a garment that covers a leg. 4. either of the sides of a right triangle adjacent to the right angle. 5. one of the distinct parts of a journey: *the last leg of a trip.* 6. **on one's** (or **its**) **last legs,** close to exhaustion, breakdown, or failure: *This old car is on its last legs.* 7. **pull one's leg,** to trick or deceive (a person): *The way he kids around I can't tell when he's pulling my leg.* 8. **shake a leg,** to hurry; move quickly: *If you don't shake a leg, we'll never get there.* —**leg′less,** *adj.*

leg., 1. legal. 2. legend. 3. legislative. 4. legislature.

leg·a·cy (leg′ə sē), *n., pl.* **leg·a·cies.** 1. a gift of property, money, etc., left by a will; bequest. 2. anything handed down from the past, as from an ancestor: *our legacy from ancient Rome.*

le·gal (lē′gəl), *adj.* 1. permitted by law; lawful: *legal acts.* 2. of or having to do with law or lawyers: *legal documents; a legal mind.* —**le′gal·ly,** *adv.*

le·gal·i·ty (lē gal′i tē), *n.* the state or condition of being lawful; lawfulness.

le·gal·ize (lē′gə līz′), *v.,* **le·gal·ized, le·gal·iz·ing.** to make legal.

le′gal ten′der, currency that may be offered in payment of debts and that must be accepted by creditors.

leg·ate (leg′it), *n.* an official representative, esp. of the pope.

leg·a·tee (leg′ə tē′), *n.* a person to whom a legacy is left.

le·ga·tion (li gā′shən), *n.* 1. a diplomatic official and his staff in a foreign mission, when the official ranks below an ambassador. 2. the headquarters of such a representative in a foreign country.

le·ga·to (lə gä′tō), *adj.* (in music) without any break between notes; smooth (opposite of *staccato*).

leg·end (lej′ənd), *n.* 1. a story handed down from earlier times, which many people believe to be historical. 2. a group of these stories, esp. as they have to do with a particular people, nation, tribe, etc.: *a popular hero in American legend.* 3. the inscription on a coin, medal, monument, etc. 4. a table or list explaining a map, chart, or the like.

leg·end·ar·y (lej′ən der′ē), *adj.* 1. of, concerning, or like a legend. 2. celebrated or described in legend: *a legendary hero.*

leg·er·de·main (lej′ər də mān′), *n.* 1. skill in or practice of magical tricks, jugglery, etc. 2. trickery; deception.

leg·ged (leg′id, legd), *adj.* having a certain number or kind of legs (usually used in combination): *two-legged; long-legged.*

leg·gings (leg′ingz), *n.pl.* coverings for the legs, as of leather or canvas.

leg·horn (leg′ərn, -hôrn′), *n.* a breed of chicken raised chiefly for producing eggs.

leg·i·ble (lej′ə bəl), *adj.* capable of being read; easy to read: *a legible inscription on a monument; legible handwriting.* —**leg′i·bil′i·ty,** *n.* —**leg′i·bly,** *adv.*

le·gion (lē′jən), *n.* 1. (in ancient Rome) an army brigade having from 3000 to 6000 foot soldiers and from 300 to 700 horsemen. 2. any large body of armed men; army. 3. any great number or multitude: *The singer had a legion of fans.*

leg·is·late (lej′is lāt′), *v.,* **leg·is·lat·ed, leg·is·lat·ing.** 1. to make laws. 2. to create or control by passing laws: *to legislate an inheritance tax.*

leg·is·la·tion (lej′is lā′shən), *n.* 1. the act of making laws. 2. the law or group of laws made: *legislation passed by Congress.*

leg·is·la·tive (lej′is lā′tiv), *adj.* 1. of or concerning the making of laws: *legislative power.* 2. having the power of making laws: *a legislative body.* 3. ordered by law or by a legislature: *a legislative ruling.*

leg·is·la·tor (lej′is lā′tər), *n.* a person who makes laws, esp. a member of a legislative body: *Congressmen are legislators.*

leg·is·la·ture (lej′is lā′chər), *n.* a body of persons who have power to make, change, or repeal laws.

le·git·i·ma·cy (li jit′ə mə sē), *n.* the state or quality of being legitimate.

le·git·i·mate (li jit′ə mit), *adj.* 1. according to law; lawful: *the legitimate owner of the property.* 2. justified; genuine: *a legitimate complaint.* 3. (of a child) born of married parents. —**le·git′i·mate·ly,** *adv.*

leg·ume (leg′yōōm, li gyōōm′), *n.* 1. a plant that produces its seeds in pods, such as a bean plant. 2. the pod of such a plant. —**le·gu′mi·nous,** *adj.*

Le Ha·vre (lə hä′vrə), a port city in N France, at the mouth of the Seine.

lei·i (lā′ē, lā), *n., pl.* **le·is.** (in the Hawaiian Islands) a wreath of flowers, leaves, etc.

lei·sure (lē′zhər), *n.* 1. free or unoccupied time; freedom from work or duty: *to use one's leisure for reading.* —*adj.* 2. free or unoccupied: *leisure hours.* 3. **at leisure, a.** having time for leisure: *I'm usually at leisure in the afternoons.* **b.** out of work, or between jobs. 4. **at one's leisure,** during one's free time; at one's convenience: *Take this book and read it at your leisure.*

lei·sure·ly (lē′zhər lē), *adj.* 1. done without haste; slow; unhurried: *a leisurely pace.* —*adv.* 2. in a leisurely manner: *to walk leisurely.*

lem·ming (lem′ing), *n.* a small, mouselike animal found in northern Norway and Sweden, and noted for migrating in large numbers, often jumping into the sea and drowning.

lem·on (lem′ən), *n.* 1. a small, egg-shaped, yellow citrus fruit having very sour juice. 2. the tree bearing this fruit. 3. a clear, light yellow. —*adj.* 4. having the color, taste, or odor of lemon.

Lemming
(length 6 in.)

lem·on·ade (lem′ə nād′), *n.* a beverage made of lemon juice, sweetener, and water.

le·mur (lē′mər), *n.* any of various small, tree-dwelling animals similar to monkeys, found chiefly on Madagascar. [from a modern Latin word, which is a special use of a Latin word meaning "ghost, specter"]

lend (lend), *v.,* **lent** (lent), **lend·ing.** 1. to give temporary use of (something) with the understanding that it will be returned: *The bank lends money.* 2. to furnish or give; impart: *Distance lends enchantment to the view.* 3. to give or contribute freely: *He lent his aid to the cause.* —**lend′er,** *n.*

length (lengkth, length), *n.* 1. the extent of anything as measured end to end: *a length of 10 yards.* 2. the longest or longer extent of anything: *The length of the room is 20 feet and the width is 15 feet.* 3. extent of anything from beginning to end: *the length of a book.* 4. a piece or portion of a certain extent: *a length of rope.* 5. **at length,** after a time; finally: *At length he spoke again.* 6. **go to any lengths,** to take extreme measures to accomplish one's purpose: *He would go to any lengths to get that scholarship.*

length·en (lengk′thən, leng′thən), *v.* to make or become longer: *to lengthen a coat.*

length·wise (lengkth′wīz′, length′-), *adv., adj.* in the direction of the length: *to measure a room* *lengthwise; a lengthwise measurement.* Also, **length·ways** (leṅgth′wāz′, leṅgth′-).

length·y (leṅgk′thē, leṅg′thē), *adj.*, **length·i·er, length·i·est.** having great length; very long: *a lengthy trip.* —**length′i·ness,** *n.*

le·ni·ent (lē′nē ənt, lēn′yənt), *adj.* gently tolerant; permissive; indulgent; not harsh or strict: *a lenient teacher.* —**le′ni·en·cy, le′ni·ence,** *n.*

Len·in (len′in), *n.* **Vlad·i·mir Il·yich** (vlad′ə mir′ il′-yich), 1870–1924, Russian revolutionary leader.

Len·in·grad (len′in grad′), *n.* a port city in the NW Soviet Union. Former names, **St. Petersburg** (1703–1914); **Petrograd** (1914–1924).

lens (lenz), *n., pl.* **lens·es.** 1. a piece of glass or transparent plastic whose surfaces are curved so as to bend rays of light.

Lenses (cross section)

Lenses are used in magnifying glasses, telescopes, microscopes, cameras, and eyeglasses. 2. the part of the eye that focuses incoming rays of light onto the retina. See illus. at **eye.**

lent (lent), *v.* the past tense and past participle of **lend:** *She lent him two dollars.*

Lent (lent), *n.* (in the Christian religion) an annual season of fasting and penitence prior to Easter, beginning on Ash Wednesday and lasting 40 days, not counting Sundays. —**Lent′en,** *adj.*

len·til (len′til, len′t³l), *n.* 1. a plant whose round, flattened seeds are used as food. 2. the seed itself.

Le·o (lē′ō), *n.* the Lion: a constellation and sign of the zodiac.

Le·o·nar·do da Vin·ci (lē′ə när′dō də vin′chē). See **Vinci, Leonardo da.**

le·o·nine (lē′ə nīn′), *adj.* of or referring to the lion.

leop·ard (lep′ərd), *n.* 1. a large, ferocious Asian or African member of the cat family, having a yellowish coat with black spots. 2. any of various similar animals, such as the jaguar.

Le·o·pold·ville (lē′ə-pōld vil′), *n.* the former name of **Kinshasa.**

lep·er (lep′ər), *n.* a person who has leprosy.

lep·re·chaun (lep′rə-kôn′, lep′rə kon′), *n.* (in Irish folklore) an elf, often a shoemaker, who is supposed to tell where treasure is hidden if he is caught.

Leopard
(2½ ft. high at shoulder; total length 7½ ft.)

lep·ro·sy (lep′rə sē), *n.* a slightly infectious disease, formerly believed to be highly contagious, that causes sores on the skin, a gradual loss of feeling, the loss of fingers or toes, and deformities of the face.

lep·rous (lep′rəs), *adj.* affected with or resembling the effects of leprosy.

le·sion (lē′zhən), *n.* an injury; hurt; wound.

Le·so·tho (le sō′tō, le sōō′tō), *n.* a kingdom in S Africa, formerly British. 11,716 sq. mi. Former name, **Basutoland.**

less (les), *adv., a comparative of* **little** *with* **least** *as superlative.* 1. to a smaller extent, amount, or degree: *less clearly.* 2. most certainly not: *He could barely pay for his own meal, much less for mine.* —*adj., a comparative of* **little** *with* **least** *as superlative.* 3. smaller in size, amount, degree, etc.; not so large, great, or much: *less warmth.* —*n.* 4. a smaller amount or quantity: *He has less than five dollars.* —*prep.* 5. minus; without: *a year less two days.*
—**Usage.** See **fewer.**

-less, a suffix used to form adjectives meaning 1. without: *homeless; faultless.* 2. unable to do a certain thing: *sleepless; harmless.* 3. not permitting a certain thing to be done: *countless; useless.*

less·en (les′ən), *v.* to make or become less.

less·er (les′ər), *adj., a comparative of* **little** *with* **least** *as superlative.* less; smaller in size, amount, importance, etc.: *a lesser evil.*

Less′er Antil′les. See under **Antilles.**

less′er pan′da. See **panda** (def. 2).

les·son (les′ən), *n.* 1. a part of a book or the like, such as an exercise, a text, etc., assigned a pupil for study. 2. a single session of formal instruction in a subject: *a piano lesson.* 3. something to be learned or studied; an instructive example: *His behavior was a lesson in good manners.* 4. a portion of the Scriptures to be read at a religious service.

lest (lest), *conj.* 1. for fear that: *He kept notes lest he should forget.* 2. that (used after words expressing fear, danger, etc.): *There was danger lest the plan become known.*

let¹ (let), *v.,* **let, let·ting.** 1. to allow or permit: *Let me do that for you.* 2. to allow to pass, go, or come: *The maid let us in.* 3. to rent or be rented: *They let their apartment for the summer.* 4. to cause or make: *to let one know the truth.* 5. **let down, a.** to disappoint or fail: *We need your help, so don't let us down.* **b.** to ease up; slacken: *If we don't let down, we'll finish in an hour.* 6. **let off, a.** to free from duty; excuse: *They let us off for Lincoln's birthday.* **b.** to free or give little punishment to: *They let him off with a light sentence.* 7. **let out, a.** to reveal (something secret or confidential): *I'll tell you if you promise not to let it out.* **b.** to be finished; end: *When does school let out for the summer?* **c.** to enlarge; increase the size of: *to let out the hem of a dress.* 8. **let up,** to slacken or stop: *The heat wave should let up by Saturday.* [from the Old English word *lætan*]

let² (let), *n.* (in tennis, badminton, etc.) any play that is not good and must be replayed, esp. a service that hits the net before dropping into the opponent's court. [from the Old English word *lettan* "to hinder, stand in the way of"]

-let, a suffix used to form 1. diminutive nouns: *ringlet; piglet.* 2. nouns meaning something worn on a certain part of the body: *anklet.*

le·thal (lē′thəl), *adj.* of, referring to, or causing death: *a lethal weapon.* —**le′thal·ly,** *adv.*

le·thar·gic (lə thär′jik), *adj.* 1. affected with lethargy; drowsy; sluggish. 2. producing lethargy: *a lethargic day.* —**le·thar′gi·cal·ly,** *adv.*

leth·ar·gy (leth/ər jē), *n.* the quality or state of being drowsy and dull.

let's (lets), contraction of *let us: Let's eat lunch.*

let·ter (let/ər), *n.* **1.** a communication in writing or printing addressed to a person or a group of persons. **2.** one of the marks used in writing or printing to represent speech sounds: *the letters of the alphabet.* **3.** actual terms or wording (distinguished from *spirit*): *the letter of the law.* **4.** an emblem consisting of the initial of a school, awarded to a student for outstanding performance, esp. in athletics: *a football letter.* **5. letters,** *(used as sing. or pl.)* literature in general: *a man of letters.* —*v.* **6.** to mark or write with letters; inscribe. **7. to the letter,** to the last detail; precisely: *His orders must be carried out to the letter.*

let·ter·head (let/ər hed/), *n.* **1.** a printed heading on stationery, esp. one giving a name and address. **2.** a piece of paper with such a heading.

let·ter·ing (let/ər ing), *n.* **1.** the act or process of inscribing with or making letters: *He's very good at lettering.* **2.** the letters themselves: *fancy lettering.*

let·tuce (let/is), *n.* any of several plants whose broad leaves usually are bunched together in a compact head, often eaten in salads.

let·up (let/up/), *n. Informal.* a pause or relief: *a letup in the bad weather.*

leu·co·cyte (lōō/kə sīt/), *n.* a white blood cell. Leucocytes destroy germs in the bloodstream.

leu·ke·mi·a (lōō kē/mē ə), *n.* a usually fatal disease in which the body produces too many white blood cells.

Le·vant (li vant/), *n.* the lands bordering the E shores of the Mediterranean Sea.

lev·ee (lev/ē), *n.* **1.** an embankment designed to prevent the flooding of a river. **2.** a landing place for vessels; quay.

lev·el (lev/əl), *adj.* **1.** having an even surface, with no part higher than another: *a level floor.* **2.** being parallel to the horizon; horizontal. **3.** equal in quality, height, importance, etc.: *The couch is level with the end table.* —*n.* **4.** a device that shows when something is truly horizontal or truly vertical by means of an air bubble in a small tube of liquid. **5.** a horizontal position or condition: *The second shelf is on a level with the desk.* **6.** a level or flat surface. **7.** a position with respect to a given height: *The water rose to a level of 30 feet.* **8.** a position in a graded scale of values; rank: *a sixth-grade reading level.* —*v.,* **lev·eled** *or* **lev·elled; lev·el·ing** *or* **lev·el·ling. 9.** to make level or even: *to level a board.* **10.** to bring to the level of the ground: *to level trees.* **11.** to aim at a mark or objective: *to level a rifle; to level criticism.* **12. one's level best,** *Informal.* one's very best or utmost: *I did*

Level (def. 4)

A, Glass tube for determining level surfaces;
B, Glass tube for determining vertical surfaces

my level best to talk him out of it. **13. on the level,** *Slang.* honest or reliable: *Is that information on the level?* —**lev/el·ly,** *adv.* —**lev/el·ness,** *n.*

lev·er (lev/ər, lē/vər), *n.* **1.** a bar or handle used to lift a weight or to turn something. **2.** a simple machine consisting of a rigid bar that rests or turns on a pivot or fulcrum, by means of which a small force exerted through a large distance can produce a larger force acting over a smaller distance.

lev·er·age (lev/ər ij, lē/vər ij), *n.* **1.** the action of a lever. **2.** the mechanical power or advantage gained by using a lever.

Le·vi (lē/vī), *n.* **1.** (in the Bible) a son of Jacob and Leah. **2.** one of the 12 tribes of ancient Israel, descended from him.

Le·vi·a·than (li vī/ə thən), *n.* **1.** (in the Bible) an enormous sea monster. **2.** any creature or thing that is unusually large, esp. a whale or ship.

Le·vis (lē/vīz), *n. Trademark.* close-fitting trousers of heavy denim or a similar material.

Le·vite (lē/vīt), *n.* (in the Bible) a member of the tribe of Levi, from which assistants to Jewish priests were chosen.

Le·vit·i·cus (li vit/ə kəs), *n.* the third book of the Old Testament.

lev·i·ty (lev/i tē), *n., pl.* **lev·i·ties.** lightness of mind, character, or behavior: *This is a time for seriousness, not for levity.*

lev·y (lev/ē), *n., pl.* **lev·ies. 1.** a raising or collecting of money, troops, etc., by authority or force. **2.** a person or thing that is collected in this manner. —*v.,* **lev·ied, lev·y·ing. 3.** to make a levy of; collect: *to levy a tax.* **4.** to enlist for military service: *to levy troops.* **5.** to start or wage: *to levy war.*

lewd (lōōd), *adj.* obscene or indecent; vulgar. —**lewd/ly,** *adv.* —**lewd/ness,** *n.*

Lew·is (lōō/is), *n.* **Mer·i·weth·er** (mer/i weth/ər), 1774–1809, leader of Lewis and Clark expedition to explore the NW United States 1804–1806.

lex·i·cog·ra·phy (lek/sə kog/rə fē), *n.* the writing or making of dictionaries. —**lex/i·cog/ra·pher,** *n.*

lex·i·con (lek/sə kon/), *n.* **1.** a wordbook or dictionary, esp. of Greek, Latin, or Hebrew. **2.** the vocabulary of a particular language, field, group, person, etc.: *a lexicon of biology.*

Lex·ing·ton (lek/sing tən), *n.* a town in E Massachusetts, NW of Boston: first battle of American Revolution fought here 1775.

lg., **1.** large. **2.** long.

Li, *Chem.* the symbol for lithium.

L.I., Long Island.

li·a·bil·i·ty (lī/ə bil/i tē), *n., pl.* **li·a·bil·i·ties. 1.** something causing loss, harm, or inconvenience; disadvantage; drawback. **2.** the state or quality of being liable. **3. liabilities,** moneys owed; debts (opposite of *assets*).

li·a·ble (lī/ə bəl), *adj.* **1.** subject, exposed, or open to something possible or likely: *An open wound is liable to infection.* **2.** legally responsible: *If he injures him-*

self on your property, you are liable. **3.** *Informal.* likely: *The dog is liable to bark if he's disturbed.*

li·ai·son (lē′ə zon′, lē ā′zən), *n.* connection or contact maintained between units of any organization to ensure cooperation.

li·ar (lī′ər), *n.* a person who tells lies.

li·bel (lī′bəl), *n.* **1.** something written or printed that damages a person's reputation. —*v.,* **li·beled** *or* li·belled; li·bel·ing *or* li·bel·ling. **2.** to publish a libel against. —**li′bel·ous,** *adj.*

lib·er·al (lib′ər əl, lib′rəl), *adj.* **1.** favorable to progress or reform in religious or political affairs. **2.** open-minded or tolerant. **3.** generous or abundant: *a liberal supply of food.* **4.** not strict or literal: *a liberal interpretation.* —*n.* **5.** a person of liberal opinions or views. —**lib′er·al·ly,** *adv.*

lib′eral arts′, the course of instruction at a college, including the arts, natural sciences, and the humanities, giving a broad, general education.

lib·er·al·ism (lib′ər ə liz′əm), *n.* **1.** the quality or state of being liberal, such as in behavior, attitude, etc. **2.** liberal political or social beliefs and ideas.

lib·er·al·i·ty (lib′ə ral′i tē), *n., pl.* for def. 2 **lib·er·al·i·ties. 1.** the quality or condition of being liberal in giving; generosity. **2.** tolerance; broad-mindedness.

lib·er·al·ize (lib′ər ə līz′), *v.,* **lib·er·al·ized, lib·er·al·iz·ing.** to make or become liberal.

lib·er·ate (lib′ə rāt′), *v.,* **lib·er·at·ed, lib·er·at·ing.** to set free; release: *to liberate slaves; to liberate a gas.* —**lib′er·a′tion,** *n.* —**lib′er·a′tor,** *n.*

Li·be·ri·a (lī bēr′ē ə), *n.* a republic in W Africa: founded by freed American slaves in 1822. about 43,000 sq. mi. *Cap.:* Monrovia. —**Li·be′ri·an,** *n., adj.*

lib·er·tine (lib′ər tēn′), *n.* **1.** a reckless, immoral man. —*adj.* **2.** without moral restraint.

lib·er·ty (lib′ər tē), *n., pl.* **lib·er·ties. 1.** freedom from tyrannical rule or government. **2.** freedom from foreign rule; independence. **3.** freedom from bondage, captivity, or physical restraint. **4.** freedom from outside control or interference; freedom to choose. **5.** Often, **liberties.** an act of boldness or excessive familiarity.

Li·bra (lī′brə, lē′brə), *n.* the Scales or the Balance: a constellation and sign of the zodiac.

li·brar·i·an (lī brâr′ē ən), *n.* **1.** a person in charge of a library. **2.** a person trained for library service.

li·brar·y (lī′brer′ē), *n., pl.* **li·brar·ies. 1.** a room or building containing books and other materials for reading, study, etc. **2.** a collection of manuscripts, books, and other materials for reading, study, etc.

li·bret·to (li bret′ō), *n., pl.* **li·bret·tos** *or* **li·bret·ti** (li bret′ē). **1.** the words of an opera or other musical work. **2.** a booklet containing such a text.

Lib·y·a (lib′ē ə), *n.* a republic in N Africa, covering an area of about 679,400 sq. mi. —**Lib′y·an,** *n., adj.*

Lib′yan Des′ert, a desert in N Africa: eastern part of the Sahara.

lice (līs), *n.* the plural of **louse.**

li·cense (lī′səns), *n.* **1.** formal permission to do a certain thing, such as carrying on some business, driving a car, etc. **2.** a certificate of such permission; an official permit. **3.** intentional departure from rule, convention, or fact, such as for the sake of literary or artistic effect: *poetic license.* **4.** too much freedom or liberty: *License is not freedom, merely the abuse of freedom.* —*v.,* **li·censed, li·cens·ing. 5.** to give a license to or for: *to license a driver.*

li·cen·tious (lī sen′shəs), *adj.* unrestrained by law or morality; lawless; immoral. —**li·cen′tious·ness,** *n.*

li·chen (lī′kən), *n.* any of numerous flat, green, yellow, or brown plants that grow on rocks or tree trunks. Lichens consist of fungus and an alga, each of which helps the other to survive.

lick (lik), *v.* **1.** to pass the tongue over the surface of. **2.** to pass lightly over: *Flames licked the logs.* **3.** *Informal.* to hit, esp. as a punishment; beat. **4.** *Informal.* to overcome or defeat: *The other team licked us badly in yesterday's game.* —*n.* **5.** a stroke of the tongue over something. **6.** a salt lick. **7.** *Informal.* a blow. **8.** *Informal.* a small amount: *He hasn't done a lick of work. She doesn't have a lick of sense.*

lic·o·rice (lik′ə ris, lik′ər ish), *n.* a plant whose dried root is used to flavor candy.

lid (lid), *n.* **1.** a movable cover or the like for closing the opening of a jar, trunk, etc. **2.** an eyelid. **3. blow the lid off,** *Slang.* to make public (something that is scandalous, illegal, or the like): *The newspaper blew the lid off the housing scandal.*

lie[1] (lī), *n.* **1.** a false statement made with intent to deceive; falsehood. —*v.,* **lied, ly·ing. 2.** to speak falsely or utter an untruth on purpose: *He lied about his grades.* [from the Old English word *lēogan*]

lie[2] (lī), *v.,* **lay** (lā), **lain** (lān), **ly·ing. 1.** to be or get into a prone, horizontal position; recline (often fol. by *down*): *to lie down for a nap.* **2.** to be buried in a particular spot. **3.** to rest on a surface: *The book lay on the table.* **4.** to be found or located in a certain area, place, or situation: *The fault lies with both of us. The village lies to the north of the lake.* **5.** to remain or be in a certain condition: *The seeds lay dormant in winter.* [from the Old English word *licgan*]

—**Usage.** The two verbs **lie** and **lay** are not synonymous and should not be confused. *Lie* means "recline" and is not followed by an object: *He is lying on the couch. He lay there yesterday till I called him. He has lain there every afternoon this week. Lay* means "place, put" and requires an object: *Lay the book on the table. She laid her fan on the chair. Where have you laid my napkin?*

Liech·ten·stein (lik′tən stīn′), *n.* a small principality in central Europe between Switzerland and Austria. 65 sq. mi. *Cap:* Vaduz.

lief (lēf), *adv.* gladly; willingly.

liege (lēj), *n.* **1.** a feudal lord entitled to allegiance and service. **2.** a feudal subject who owed such allegiance and service.

MEDITERRANEAN SEA

CRETE

TUNISIA

Tripoli

Benghazi

ALGERIA

Libya

ARAB REPUBLIC OF EGYPT

NIGER   CHAD   SUDAN

lien (lēn), *n.* a legal right to hold property or to have it sold or applied for payment of a debt: *The bank has a lien on the car until it is paid for in full.*

lieu (lōō), *n.* **in lieu of,** instead of: *He gave me his I.O.U. in lieu of cash.*

lieu·ten·ant (lōō ten′ənt), *n.* **1.** a first lieutenant or second lieutenant in the U.S. Army. **2.** an officer in the U.S. Navy, ranking above a lieutenant junior grade and below a lieutenant commander.

lieuten′ant colo′nel, an officer in the U.S. Army, ranking above a major and below a colonel.

lieuten′ant comman′der, an officer in the U.S. Navy, ranking above a lieutenant and below a commander.

lieuten′ant gen′eral, an officer in the U.S. Army, ranking above a major general and below a general.

lieuten′ant gov′ernor, a state officer next in rank to the governor.

lieuten′ant jun′ior grade′, an officer in the U.S. Navy, ranking above an ensign and below a lieutenant.

life (līf), *n., pl.* **lives** (līvz). **1.** the condition that distinguishes animals and plants from rocks or water and which permits them to grow, reproduce, etc. **2.** a living being: *Several lives were lost in the plane crash.* **3.** living things considered altogether, whether animals or plants: *life on another planet.* **4.** the course or period of a person's existence: *a long life.* **5.** the experiences and actions that make up a person's existence: *a happy life.* **6.** the period of time during which something works or functions: *the life of a car.* **7.** a manner of existence: *country life.* **8.** a biography. **9.** liveliness and spirit: *The group was full of life.* **10. for dear life,** with desperate energy or speed: *They ran for dear life when I screamed.*

life′ belt′, a life preserver in the form of a belt.

life·boat (līf′bōt′), *n.* a ship's boat, designed to be readily able to rescue persons from a sinking ship.

life′ buoy′, a device that floats, for supporting a person who has fallen into the water until rescued.

life·guard (līf′gärd′), *n.* a person employed at a beach or pool to protect bathers from drowning.

life′ insur′ance, insurance providing for payment of a sum of money to a person named in the insurance policy upon the death of the policyholder or to the policyholder upon reaching a certain age.

life′ jack′et, a life preserver in the form of a sleeveless jacket.

life·less (līf′lis), *adj.* **1.** without life; dead: *a lifeless body.* **2.** never having been alive; inanimate. —**life′less·ly,** *adv.*

life·like (līf′līk′), *adj.* resembling or imitating real life: *a lifelike statue of a man; a very lifelike story.* —**life′like′ness,** *n.*

life′ line′, **1.** a line or rope for saving life, such as one attached to a lifeboat. **2.** the line by which a diver is lowered and raised. **3.** a route over which supplies must be sent to sustain an area or a group of persons otherwise isolated.

life·long (līf′lông′), *adj.* lasting or continuing through life: *lifelong happiness.*

life′ preserv′er, a buoyant or inflatable jacket, belt, or similar device for keeping a person afloat.

life-size (līf′sīz′), *adj.* of the natural size of an object in life: *a life-size statue.* Also, **life′-sized′.**

life·style (līf′stīl′), *n.* a person's typical way of living, attitudes, preferences, etc.

life·time (līf′tīm′), *n.* the time that the life of someone or something continues: *the lifetime of a dog.*

lift (lift), *v.* **1.** to move or bring upward to some higher position: *to lift a rock; to lift one's head.* **2.** to remove, cancel, or put an end to: *to lift a curfew.* **3.** to raise in rank or condition; elevate: *The good news lifted our spirits.* **4.** to move upward or rise: *The fog lifted.* **5.** *Slang.* to steal. —*n.* **6.** the act of lifting or raising. **7.** a ride in a vehicle: *He gave me a lift home.* **8.** a feeling of happiness or uplift: *The letter gave her a lift.* **9.** *British.* an elevator.

lift-off (lift′ôf′, -of′), *n.* **1.** the action of a rocket or airplane in rising from the ground under its own power. **2.** the instant when this action takes place.

lig·a·ment (lig′ə mənt), *n.* a band of strong fibers that connects bones or holds body organs in place.

lig·a·ture (lig′ə chōōr′), *n.* **1.** the act of binding or tying up. **2.** anything that is used for binding or tying up, such as a band, bandage, or cord.

light¹ (līt), *n.* **1.** the type of radiation that the eye perceives and by means of which we can see. **2.** an agent or source of light, such as the sun, a lamp, or a beacon. **3.** the aspect in which a thing appears or is regarded: *She looked at the problem in a new light after learning more facts.* **4.** a means of igniting or lighting: *He wanted a light for his pipe.* **5.** a person who is a shining example. —*adj.* **6.** having light; well-lighted; bright: *a light, cheery room.* **7.** pale; not deep or dark in color: *a light shade of blue.* —*v.,* **light·ed** *or* **lit** (lit); **light·ing. 8.** to set burning; kindle; ignite: *to light a match.* **9.** to take fire or become kindled: *The fire lighted quickly.* **10.** to turn or switch on (an electric light): *to light the lamp.* **11.** to give light to: *to light a room.* **12.** to cause to brighten: *A smile lit up her face.* **13. come to light,** to be discovered or revealed: *Several new songs came to light after the composer's death.* **14. see the light,** to accept or understand an idea that one formerly opposed. [from the Old English word *lēoht*]

light² (līt), *adj.* **1.** of little weight; not heavy: *a light package.* **2.** of small amount, force, intensity, etc.: *light snow flurries.* **3.** not very deep or serious: *light reading.* **4.** using or applying little or slight pressure: *a light knock at the door.* **5.** airy in movement; graceful: *a light step.* **6.** not rich or heavy: *a light snack.* **7.** characterized by good spirits; cheerful; gay: *a light mood.* **8.** lacking the proper seriousness. **9. make light of,** to treat as unimportant: *to make light of an embarrassing situation.* [from the Old English word *liht*]

light³ (līt), *v.,* **light·ed** *or* **lit** (lit); **light·ing. 1.** to get down or descend: *to light from a horse.* **2.** to come to rest; fall or settle upon: *A bird lighted on the grass.* **3.** to come by chance, happen, or hit (usually fol. by *on* or *upon*): *to light on a clue.* **4. light into,** *Informal.* to attack, either with physical force or with words: *He lit into me the minute I disagreed with him.* **5. light out,** *Slang.* to leave quickly: *When July comes we light out for the mountains.* [from the Old English word *lihtan* "to relieve of weight"]

light·en¹ (līt/ᵊn), *v.* **1.** to make or become light: *The stars lightened the sky.* **2.** to flash as or like lightning: *It thundered and lightened all afternoon.* [from *light¹* + *-en*]

light·en² (līt/ᵊn), *v.* **1.** to make lighter in weight: *I lightened the package by taking out a book.* **2.** to make less troublesome or harsh: *to lighten a punishment.* **3.** to cheer or gladden: *to lighten one's spirits.* [from *light²* + *-en*]

light·er¹ (lī/tər), *n.* **1.** a person or thing that lights or ignites. **2.** a mechanical device used in lighting cigars, cigarettes, or pipes for smoking. [from *light¹* + *-er*]

light·er² (lī/tər), *n.* a flat-bottomed barge used in loading or unloading ships. [from a Dutch word, which is related to *light²*]

light-foot·ed (līt/foot/id), *adj.* stepping lightly or nimbly; graceful. —**light/-foot/ed·ness,** *n.*

light-head·ed (līt/hed/id), *adj.* **1.** having or showing a silly or frivolous nature. **2.** giddy or dizzy; faint. —**light/-head/ed·ly,** *adv.* —**light/-head/ed·ness,** *n.*

light-heart·ed (līt/här/tid), *adj.* gay and cheerful; carefree. —**light/-heart/ed·ly,** *adv.* —**light/-heart/ed·ness,** *n.*

light·house (līt/hous/), *n., pl.* **light·hous·es** (līt/hou/ziz). a tower having a light or lights, used as an aid to navigation or as a warning of some danger.

light·ing (lī/tiñg), *n.* **1.** the act of igniting or illuminating: *the lighting of a fire.* **2.** the arrangement of lights to achieve certain effects: *bright lighting.*

light·ly (līt/lē), *adv.* **1.** with little weight, force, or intensity: *to knock lightly.* **2.** to a small amount or degree; slightly: *lightly buttered bread.* **3.** without trouble or effort; easily: *His good grades did not come lightly.* **4.** nimbly or quickly: *to step lightly.* **5.** without concern; indifferently: *She spoke lightly of the problem.*

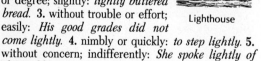
Lighthouse

light·ness¹ (līt/nis), *n.* **1.** the state or quality of being light or illuminated. **2.** thin or pale color. [from the Old English word *līhtnes*]

light·ness² (līt/nis), *n.* **1.** the state or quality of being light in weight. **2.** the quality of being agile or graceful. **3.** lack of pressure or worry. **4.** gaiety of manner, speech, etc.; cheerfulness. **5.** lack of seriousness. [from the Middle English word *lightnesse*]

light·ning (līt/niñg), *n.* a bright flash of electricity in the sky or between a cloud and the ground.

light/ning bug/, another word for **firefly.**

light/ning rod/, a tall, pointed metal rod for conducting lightning directly to the ground, thereby protecting the building to which it is attached.

light·ship (līt/ship/), *n.* a ship anchored in a certain location and displaying a light or lights for the guidance of mariners.

light·weight (līt/wāt/), *adj.* being lighter in weight than the average: *a lightweight suit.* **2.** of or referring to a lightweight boxer. —*n.* **3.** a person of less than average weight. **4.** a professional boxer weighing between 126 and 135 pounds.

light-year (līt/yēr/), *n.* a unit of distance equal to the distance that light travels through empty space in one year, equal to about 6 trillion miles.

lig·nite (lig/nīt), *n.* a dark brown type of coal often having a woody texture.

lik·a·ble (lī/kə bəl), *adj.* readily or easily liked; pleasing: *a likable person.* Also, **like/a·ble.** —**lik/a·ble·ness,** *n.* —**lik/a·bly,** *adv.*

like¹ (līk), *adj.* **1.** of the same or similar form, appearance, kind, quantity, etc.: *He donated a like sum of money to the group.* —*prep.* **2.** similarly to; in the manner characteristic of: *She plays tennis like a professional.* **3.** resembling; similar to. **4.** characteristic of: *It's just like him to do that.* **5.** as if there is a promise of: *It looks like rain.* —*n.* **6.** a like person or thing, or like persons or things: *I don't want to see his like ever again.* **7. the like,** a similar thing or things: *They grow oranges, grapefruit, and the like.* [from the Old English word *gelīc*]

—**Usage.** *Like* should not replace *as* before a subject and verb: *Do as I say, not as I do. The milk shake tastes good as* (not *like*) *a milk shake should.* Similarly, it should never be used to replace *as if: He ran as if he were* (not *like he was*) *frightened.*

like² (līk), *v.,* **liked, lik·ing.** **1.** to take pleasure in; find agreeable to one's taste: *to like cake and ice cream.* **2.** to have a kindly and friendly feeling for; be fond of. **3.** to feel inclined; wish: *You may stay if you like.* —*n.* **4.** Usually, **likes.** a favorable feeling; preference: *likes and dislikes.* [from the Old English word *līcian;* related to *like¹*]

-like, a suffix used to form adjectives meaning **1.** resembling: *childlike; lifelike.* **2.** typical of or proper to: *businesslike; workmanlike.*

like·li·hood (līk/lē hood/), *n.* a probability or chance of something: *a likelihood of snow.*

like·ly (līk/lē), *adj.,* **like·li·er, like·li·est. 1.** probably or apparently destined: *It is likely to pour.* **2.** seeming like truth, fact, or certainty; reasonably to be believed or expected: *a likely story.* **3.** apparently suitable: *a likely place for the party.* **4.** showing promise of excellence: *a likely person for the job.*

lik·en (lī/kən), *v.* to represent as like; compare: *to liken someone to a weasel.*

like·ness (līk/nis), *n.* **1.** a representation, picture, or image, esp. a portrait. **2.** the form or appearance of something; guise: *He appeared in the likeness of a ghost.* **3.** the state or fact of being like: *There is a strong likeness between the cousins.*

like·wise (līk′wīz′), *adv.* 1. in addition; also: *He is tall and likewise very strong.* 2. in like manner; in the same way: *Watch me and then do likewise.*

lik·ing (lī′kiŋ), *n.* preference, favor, or taste: *a liking for popular music.*

li·lac (lī′lək, lī′lak), *n.* a shrub that bears clusters of sweet-smelling lavender or white flowers.

lilt (lilt), *n.* 1. rhythmic swing: *There was a lilt in her voice as she recited the poem.* 2. a lilting song or tune. —*v.* 3. to sing or play in a light, tripping, or rhythmic manner.

lil·y (lil′ē), *n., pl.* **lil·ies.** 1. any of several plants that grow from bulbs and have funnel-shaped or bell-shaped flowers. —*adj.* 2. white as a lily.

lil′y of the val′ley, *pl.* **lilies of the valley.** a low plant that bears clusters of drooping, sweet-smelling, white flowers.

Li·ma (lē′mə), *n.* the capital city of Peru.

li′ma bean′ (lī′mə), a large, flat bean eaten as a vegetable.

limb (lim), *n.* 1. a part of a human being or an animal other than the body or head, such as an arm, leg, or wing. 2. a branch of a tree. 3. **out on a limb,** *Informal.* in a dangerous situation: *With all the money he owes he's really out on a limb.*

lim·ber (lim′bər), *adj.* 1. bending easily; flexible; pliant: *a limber branch.* 2. characterized by ease in bending the body; supple. —*v.* 3. to make or become limber (usually fol. by *up*): *He exercised to limber up before the game.*

lim·bo (lim′bō), *n.* 1. *(often cap.)* a region on the border of hell or heaven, serving as the resting place after death for unbaptized infants and for the righteous who died before the coming of Christ. 2. a place or state for forgotten or unwanted persons or things. [from the Latin phrase *in limbō* "on the edge"]

Lily of the valley

lime¹ (līm), *n.* 1. a white or grayish substance made from limestone by heating. Lime is used as a fertilizer and in making mortar, plaster, bleaching powder, and glass. —*v.,* **limed, lim·ing.** 2. to treat or cover with lime. [from the Old English word *līm*]

lime² (līm), *n.* 1. a green citrus fruit slightly smaller and more sour than a lemon. 2. the tree bearing this fruit. [from a Spanish word, which comes from Arabic *līmah* "citrus fruit"]

lime·light (līm′līt′), *n.* 1. a very bright gaslight formerly used for stage lighting. 2. public interest, notice, or attention: *The author has been in the limelight since his new book was published.*

lim·er·ick (lim′ər ik), *n.* a kind of humorous verse of five lines:

> There was a young lady of Niger
> Who smiled as she rode on a tiger:
> They came back from their ride
> With the lady inside
> And a smile on the face of the tiger.

[named after *Limerick,* a county of Ireland where it originated]

lime·stone (līm′stōn′), *n.* a common white stone from which lime can be made. Limestone is often used for building and making roads.

lim·it (lim′it), *n.* 1. the final or furthest bound or point beyond which something cannot or does not go. 2. a boundary of a country or district. 3. **limits,** the region enclosed within boundaries: *city limits.* —*v.* 4. to restrict by or as if by establishing limits: *to limit spending.* 5. **the limit,** *Informal.* an extremely annoying person or thing: *This delay is really the limit!*

lim·i·ta·tion (lim′i tā′shən), *n.* 1. something that limits, esp. a shortcoming or restriction. 2. the act of limiting. 3. the quality or state of being limited.

lim·it·ed (lim′i tid), *adj.* 1. confined within limits; restricted: *The scientist had limited knowledge of the secret project.* 2. making only a few stops en route: *a limited train.* —*n.* 3. a limited train, bus, etc.

lim·it·less (lim′it lis), *adj.* without limit: *a limitless supply of food.*

limn (lim), *v. Archaic.* 1. to represent in drawing or painting. 2. to portray in words; describe.

lim·ou·sine (lim′ə zēn′, lim′ə zēn′), *n.* a large, luxurious automobile, usually driven by a chauffeur.

limp¹ (limp), *v.* 1. to walk with a jerky movement, as when lame. —*n.* 2. a lame movement or way of walking. [from the Old English word *lemp-,* in the compound *lemphealt* "limping"]

limp² (limp), *adj.* 1. lacking stiffness or firmness: *a limp collar.* 2. lacking vitality or strength; tired: *We all felt limp after the long hike.* [from Scandinavian]

lim·pet (lim′pit), *n.* any of various small, saltwater shellfish found clinging to rocks.

lim·pid (lim′pid), *adj.* clear or transparent, such as water or air.

Lin·coln (liŋ′kən), *n.* 1. **Abraham,** 1809–1865, 16th President of the U.S. 1861–1865. 2. the capital city of Nebraska, in the SE part.

Lin′coln's Birth′day, February 12, a legal holiday in many states of the U.S. in honor of the birth of Abraham Lincoln.

Lind·bergh (lind′bûrg), *n.* **Charles A.,** born 1902, U.S. aviator: made first solo, nonstop, transatlantic flight 1927.

lin·den (lin′dən), *n.* any of various large shade trees having heart-shaped leaves and bearing clusters of sweet-smelling, yellowish-white flowers.

line¹ (līn), *n.* 1. a long, very thin mark: *He drew a line to separate the columns.* 2. something occurring naturally or accidentally that resembles such a line: *The old woman's face had many lines.* 3. a row of persons or things: *a long line in front of the theater.* 4. (in geometry) the path traced by a moving point, having indefinite length and no breadth. 5. a single row of letters or other characters on a page. 6. a series of words written, printed, or recited as one of the parts of a larger piece of writing: *The poem has 10 lines.* 7. a brief written message: *She dropped me* *a line to tell me the news.* **8.** a course of action, belief, method, or explanation of these, such as one adopted by a political group. **9.** a series of ancestors or of animals or plants of preceding generations: *He's from a long line of bankers.* **10.** a transportation company or one of its routes. **11.** a person's occupation or business: *What line is he in?* **12.** a cord or rope, esp. a strong one used for fishing, hauling, hanging clothes, etc., or in rigging. **13.** a wire circuit connecting two or more pieces of electric apparatus: *a telephone line.* **14.** (in football) either of the two front rows of opposing players lined up opposite each other on the line of scrimmage. **15.** Usually, **lines.** the spoken words of a dramatic performance. **16. lines,** the general form or notion: *a work written on traditional lines.* **17.** Often, **lines.** a distribution of troops for the defense of a position or for an attack: *within the enemy's lines.* —*v.,* **lined, lin·ing. 18.** to mark with a line or lines: *to line a piece of paper.* **19. draw the line,** to set a limit or restriction, as for action: *I'll go, but I draw the line at making a speech.* **20. line up, a.** to take a position in a line: *to line up for a fire drill.* **b.** to bring into a line or into line with others: *Line up the target in your sights.* **c.** to arrange for; obtain: *to line up a summer job.* **21. out of line,** *Slang.* **a.** beyond what is reasonable or acceptable: *The prices at that store are way out of line.* **b.** rude or vulgar: *That last remark was certainly out of line.* **22. read between the lines,** to discover a meaning that is hinted at but not expressed: *If you read between the lines you'll see she's not so happy at camp.* [from an Old English word, which comes from Latin *linea* "string, cord"]

line² (līn), *v.,* **lined, lin·ing.** to cover the inner side of: *to line a coat with wool.* [from the Old English word *līn,* which comes from Latin *līnum* "flax"]

lin·e·age (lin′ē ij), *n.* **1.** descent from an ancestor; ancestry. **2.** the line of descendants of a particular ancestor; family.

lin·e·al (lin′ē əl), *adj.* being in the direct line, such as an ancestor.

lin·e·a·ment (lin′ē ə mənt), *n.* Often, **lineaments.** a feature or detail of a face, body, or figure, considered with respect to its outline or contour.

lin·e·ar (lin′ē ər), *adj.* **1.** extended or arranged in a line: *a linear series.* **2.** involving measurement in one direction only; having to do with length.

line·man (līn′mən), *n., pl.* **line·men. 1.** Also, **lines′ man.** a man who installs or repairs telephone, telegraph, or other wires. **2.** (in football) one of the players in the line.

lin·en (lin′ən), *n.* **1.** fabric woven from flax yarns. **2.** Often, **linens.** clothing, bedding, etc., made of linen cloth or a more common substitute, such as cotton. —*adj.* **3.** made of linen: *a linen tablecloth.*

lin·er (lī′nər), *n.* **1.** one of a commercial line of steamships or airplanes. **2.** a person or thing that traces by or marks with lines. **3.** a kind of cosmetic for outlining the eyes.

line-up (līn′up′), *n.* **1.** an orderly arrangement of persons or things in a row. **2.** the persons or things themselves. **3.** a technique used in police investigation in which a victim or eyewitness is asked to identify a suspect from a number of people standing in a line. **4.** (in sports) the list of the participating players in a game together with their positions.

-ling, a suffix used to form **1.** diminutive nouns: *duckling.* **2.** nouns meaning one connected with something, usually in an inferior capacity: *hireling.*

lin·ger (ling′gər), *v.* to remain or stay on in a place, as if from reluctance to leave.

lin·ge·rie (län′zhə rā′, lan′zhə rē′), *n.* undergarments or nightwear worn by women.

lin·go (ling′gō), *n., pl.* **lin·goes.** *Informal.* **1.** language or speech, esp. if strange or foreign. **2.** language or speech peculiar to a profession or class: *jazz lingo.*

lin·guist (ling′gwist), *n.* **1.** a person skilled in several languages. **2.** a specialist in linguistics.

lin·guis·tic (ling gwis′tik), *adj.* **1.** of or concerning a language or languages. **2.** of or concerning linguistics.

lin·guis·tics (ling gwis′tiks), *n. (used as sing.)* the science or study of language.

lin·i·ment (lin′ə mənt), *n.* a liquid, often strong-smelling, that is rubbed on the skin to relieve sprains or bruises.

lin·ing (lī′ning), *n.* a layer of material on the inside of something: *a coat lining; the stomach lining.*

link (lingk), *n.* **1.** any of the separate pieces that form a chain. **2.** anything serving to connect one part or thing with another; bond; tie. —*v.* **3.** to join by or as if by a link or links; unite: *to link arms.*

links (lingks), *n.pl.* another word for **golf course.**

lin·net (lin′it), *n.* a small songbird of Europe.

li·no·le·um (li nō′lē əm), *n.* a floor covering formed of burlap or canvas coated with linseed oil, powdered cork, and rosin.

Lin·o·type (lī′nə tīp′), *n. Trademark.* (in printing) a keyboard machine for molding type characters in hot metal. The metal is ejected from the machine in the form of a single bar containing several characters.

lin·seed (lin′sēd′), *n.* another name for **flaxseed.**

lin′seed oil′, an oil pressed from the seeds of the flax plant, used in making paints, printing inks, and linoleum.

lint (lint), *n.* **1.** small shreds or ravelings of yarn; bits of thread. **2.** a soft material for dressing wounds, obtained by scraping or otherwise treating linen cloth.

lin·tel (lin′t°l), *n.* a horizontal part supporting the weight above a door or window.

li·on (lī′ən), *n.* **1.** a large, powerful, grayish-tan member of the cat family native to Africa and Asia, the male of which usually has a shaggy mane. **2.** a man of great strength and courage. **3.** a famous person; celebrity. **4. the Lion,** another name for **Leo.**

Lion and lioness
(3½ ft. high at shoulder;
total length 9 ft.)

li·on·ess (līʹə nis), *n.* a female lion.

lip (lip), *n.* **1.** either of the two fleshy parts of the face that form an opening to the mouth and cover the teeth. **2.** a protecting rim on a container or other hollow object: *the lip of a pitcher.* **3. keep a stiff upper lip,** to face misfortune bravely and with determination.

lip·stick (lipʹstik'), *n.* a crayonlike cosmetic used in coloring the lips.

liq·ue·fac·tion (lik'wə fakʹshən), *n.* **1.** the act or process of liquefying. **2.** the state of being liquefied.

liq·ue·fy (likʹwə fī'), *v.,* **liq·ue·fied, liq·ue·fy·ing.** to make or become liquid either by melting or by condensing: *to liquefy a solid; to liquefy a gas.*

li·queur (li kûrʹ), *n.* any of a class of alcoholic liquors, usually strong, sweet, and highly flavored.

liq·uid (likʹwid), *adj.* **1.** capable of flowing, like water, but not capable of expanding to fill any container, like air; neither solid nor gaseous. **2.** (of sounds, tones, etc.) having an agreeable, flowing quality. **3.** (of movements, gestures, etc.) graceful and smooth; free. **4.** in cash, or easily changed into cash: *liquid assets.* **5.** pronounced without friction and with only partial stoppage of the breath stream, as the sound of *l* or *r.* —*n.* **6.** a liquid substance. **7.** a liquid sound, such as *l* or *r.*

liq·ui·date (likʹwi dāt'), *v.,* **liq·ui·dat·ed, liq·ui·dat·ing.** **1.** to settle or pay (a debt). **2.** to settle up (accounts). **3.** to break up, abolish, or do away with: *to liquidate a partnership.* —**liq'ui·daʹtion,** *n.*

liq'uid meas'ure, a system of volume or capacity units used in measuring quantities of liquids.

liq·uor (likʹər), *n.* **1.** a distilled beverage, such as brandy or whiskey, as distinguished from a fermented beverage, such as beer or wine. **2.** a liquid, such as broth, from cooked meats, vegetables, etc.

li·ra (lērʹə), *n., pl.* **li·ras** *or* **li·re** (lērʹā). an aluminum coin and monetary unit of Italy.

Lis·bon (lizʹbən), *n.* a seaport and the capital city of Portugal, in the SW part.

lisle (līl), *n.* **1.** Also, **lisle' thread'.** a fine cotton thread, used esp. for hosiery. —*adj.* **2.** made of lisle thread.

lisp (lisp), *n.* **1.** a speech defect consisting in pronouncing *s* and *z* like or nearly like the *th-* sounds of *thin* and *this,* respectively. —*v.* **2.** to pronounce or speak with a lisp.

lis·some (lisʹəm), *adj.* lithe and limber; supple. —**lisʹsome·ness,** *n.*

list¹ (list), *n.* **1.** a series of names or other items written or printed together in a meaningful grouping: *a grocery list.* —*v.* **2.** to set down together or enter in a list. [from the Italian word *lista* "roll of names," earlier "band, strip (of paper)," which comes from Germanic]

list² (list), *n.* **1.** a leaning to one side: *the list of a ship.* —*v.* **2.** (of a vessel) to lean to one side: *The ship listed during the storm.* [from an Old English word meaning "border"]

list³ (list), *v. Archaic.* to listen or listen to. [from the Old English word *hlystan*]

lis·ten (lisʹən), *v.* **1.** to give attention for the purpose of hearing. **2.** to pay attention to what is said: *She never listens when the teacher gives an assignment.* **3. listen in,** to overhear a conversation; eavesdrop. [from the Old English word *hlysnan,* which is related to *list³*] —**lisʹten·er,** *n.*

list·less (listʹlis), *adj.* feeling or showing no interest in anything. —**listʹless·ly,** *adv.* —**listʹless·ness,** *n.*

lists (lists), *n. (used as sing. or pl.)* an enclosed arena for tilting contests between knights.

lit¹ (lit), *v.* a past tense and past participle of **light¹**: *I lit the lamp.*

lit² (lit), *v.* a past tense and past participle of **light³**: *The robin lit on the branch.*

lit., **1.** liter; liters. **2.** literal. **3.** literally. **4.** literary. **5.** literature.

li·ter (lēʹtər), *n.* a unit of volume or capacity in the metric system: equal to 1.1 quarts or 1000 cubic centimeters. *Symbol:* l Also, *esp. British,* **litre.**

lit·er·a·cy (litʹər ə sē), *n.* the quality or state of being able to read and write.

lit·er·al (litʹər əl), *adj.* **1.** following the words of the original as closely as possible: *a literal translation.* **2.** following the strict or usual meaning. **3.** true to fact; not exaggerated: *a literal statement.* —**litʹer·al·ly,** *adv.*

lit·er·ar·y (litʹə rer'ē), *adj.* **1.** referring to literature. **2.** well acquainted with literature; well-read: *a literary person.* **3.** being a writer by profession.

lit·er·ate (litʹər it), *adj.* **1.** able to read and write. **2.** having an education; literary; well-read. —*n.* **3.** a person who is educated.

lit·er·a·ture (litʹər ə choŏr'), *n.* **1.** writing that has permanent worth because of its artistic excellence. **2.** all the writings of a specific language, period, people, etc.: *French literature.* **3.** the writings dealing with a particular subject: *medical literature.* **4.** the profession of a writer or author.

lithe (līth), *adj.,* **lith·er, lith·est.** bending easily; limber; supple.

lith·i·um (lithʹē əm), *n. Chem.* the lightest of all metals. Lithium is a chemical element. *Symbol:* Li

lith·o·graph (lithʹə graf'), *n.* **1.** a print produced by lithography. —*v.* **2.** to produce or copy by lithography.

li·thog·ra·phy (li thogʹrə fē), *n.* the art or process of producing a figure or image on a flat, specially prepared stone or plate in such a way that it will absorb and print with special inks.

Lith·u·a·ni·a (lith'oō āʹnē ə), *n.* a part of the Soviet Union on the Baltic Sea, formerly an independent country. 25,174 sq. mi. *Cap.:* Vilna.

Lith·u·a·ni·an (lith/ōo ā/nē ən), *adj.* **1.** of or concerning Lithuania, its inhabitants, or their language. —*n.* **2.** a native or inhabitant of Lithuania. **3.** the Baltic language of Lithuania.

lit·i·ga·tion (lit/ə gā/shən), *n.* **1.** the act or process of carrying on a lawsuit. **2.** the lawsuit itself.

lit·mus (lit/məs), *n.* a dye obtained from certain lichens that turns blue in alkaline solutions and red in acid solutions.

lit/mus pa/per, a strip of paper that has been soaked in litmus, used to determine whether a solution is acid or alkaline.

li·tre (lē/tər), *n.* a British spelling of **liter.**

lit·ter (lit/ər), *n.* **1.** a variety of objects scattered about; scattered rubbish: *The yard was full of litter.* **2.** a number of young brought forth at one time: *a litter of kittens.* **3.** a stretcher. **4.** a vehicle carried by men or animals, consisting of a bed or couch, often covered and curtained, suspended between shafts. **5.** straw, hay, or the like, used as bedding for animals, protection for plants, etc. —*v.* **6.** to strew or scatter with litter: *to litter the highway.* **7.** to give birth to a litter. [from the Old French word *litiere,* which comes from Latin *lectus* "bed"]

lit·tle (lit/əl), *adj.,* **less** (les) *or* **less·er** (les/ər); **least** (lēst) *or* **lit·tler; lit·tlest.** **1.** not large in size: *a little kitten.* **2.** few in number: *a little group.* **3.** not much: *little hope.* **4.** short in duration: *a little while.* **5.** of small importance, concern, influence, etc.: *a little problem.* **6.** petty or mean: *a little mind.* —*adv.,* **less** (les), **least** (lēst). **7.** not at all (used before a verb): *He little knows what awaits him.* **8.** in only a small amount or degree; not much: *I slept very little last night.* **9.** seldom; rarely; infrequently. —*n.* **10.** a small amount, quantity, or degree: *I did little to help.* **11. little by little,** by degrees; gradually: *Little by little she's learning to play the guitar.* —**lit/tle·ness,** *n.*

Lit/tle Amer/ica, a base on Antarctica, established by Admiral Richard E. Byrd in 1929 for polar explorations.

Lit/tle Bear/, the most northern constellation, containing the seven stars of the Little Dipper.

Lit/tle Dip/per. See under **dipper** (def. 2).

Lit/tle Rock/, the capital city of Arkansas, in the central part.

Little America

lit/tle slam/. See under **slam².**

lit·ur·gy (lit/ər jē), *n., pl.* **lit·ur·gies.** a form of public worship; ritual. —**li·tur·gi·cal** (li tûr/ji kəl), *adj.*

liv·a·ble (liv/ə bəl), *adj.* **1.** suitable for living in; comfortable: *a livable cabin.* **2.** able to be lived with; companionable. **3.** worth living; endurable; bearable: *to make life more livable.* Also, **live/a·ble.**

live¹ (liv), *v.,* **lived** (livd), **liv·ing. 1.** to have life; to be alive. **2.** to remain alive: *to live to a ripe old age.* **3.** to support oneself: *to live on one's income.* **4.** to feed or exist: *to live on fish and rice.* **5.** to dwell or reside: *to live in a city; to live on a farm.* **6.** to pass life in a certain way: *to live happily.* **7.** to represent or put into practice in one's life: *to live a lie; to live one's religion.* **8. live down,** to conduct oneself so as to cause (past mistakes) to be forgiven: *He moved to another town, hoping to live down the scandal.* **9. live high,** to live in luxury. **10. live up to,** to come up to (a certain ideal, standard, etc.): *The movie didn't live up to our expectations.* [from the Old English word *lifian*]

live² (līv), *adj.,* for defs. 2, 3 **liv·er, liv·est. 1.** having life; alive. **2.** of current interest or importance: *a live problem.* **3.** burning or glowing: *live coals.* **4.** loaded or unexploded: *a live cartridge.* **5.** electrically charged: *a live wire.* **6.** broadcast or televised at the moment it is being presented at the studio: *The program is live.* [a shortened form of *alive*]

live·li·hood (līv/lē hŏod/), *n.* a means of maintaining life: *He earns his livelihood by teaching.*

live·long (liv/lông/), *adj.* (of a period of time) whole or entire: *the livelong day.*

live·ly (līv/lē), *adj.,* **live·li·er, live·li·est. 1.** full of life; energetic: *a lively kitten.* **2.** strong, keen, or distinct: *a lively interest.* **3.** animated or spirited: *a lively tune.* **4.** vivid or bright: *lively colors.* **5.** full of bounce; springing back: *a lively ball.* **6.** full of activity: *a lively day.* —*adv.* **7.** with activity or animation; sprightly: *to step lively.* —**live/li·ness,** *n.*

liv·en (lī/vən), *v.* to make or become more lively (often fol. by *up*): *The party began to liven up.*

liv·er¹ (liv/ər), *n.* **1.** a large, reddish-brown organ of the body that produces bile, stores carbohydrates, and is important in other body functions. **2.** an organ in animals, similar to the human liver, often used as food. [from the Old English word *lifer*]

liv·er² (liv/ər), *n.* **1.** a person who lives in a certain way: *a fancy liver.* **2.** a resident or inhabitant: *a city liver.*

liv·er·ied (liv/ə rēd, liv/rēd), *adj.* dressed in livery.

Liv·er·pool (liv/ər pōol/), *n.* a port city in W England.

liv·er·wort (liv/ər wûrt/), *n.* any of a large class of plants related to the mosses that grow chiefly on damp ground, in water, and on tree trunks.

liv·er·y (liv/ə rē, liv/rē), *n., pl.* **liv·er·ies. 1.** a uniform worn by servants. **2.** the keep, feeding, and stabling of horses for pay.

lives (līvz), *n.* the plural of **life.**

live·stock (līv/stok/), *n. (used as sing. or pl.)* the horses, cattle, sheep, etc., kept on a farm or ranch.

liv·id (liv/id), *adj.* **1.** having a discolored, bluish appearance due to a bruise, congestion of blood vessels, etc. **2.** enraged; very angry. —**liv/id·ly,** *adv.*

liv·ing (liv/ing), *adj.* **1.** being alive; not dead. **2.** in actual existence or use: *living languages.* **3.** active or strong: *a living faith.* **4.** lifelike; true to life, such as a picture or story. **5.** of or concerning living persons: *within living memory.* **6.** sufficient for living: *a living wage.* —*n.* **7.** the act or condition of a person or thing that lives. **8.** a particular manner or way of life: *luxurious living.* **9.** the means of maintaining life; livelihood: *to earn one's living.*

liv′ing room′, a room in a house used by a family for various individual and social activities.

liz·ard (liz′ərd), *n.* **1.** any of numerous reptiles having a slim body, a long tail, and two pairs of legs. Some lizards live on the ground, some in water, and some in trees. **2.** leather made from the skin of the lizard.

Lizard
(length 4 to 7½ in.)

lla·ma (lä′mə), *n.* a woolly-haired South American animal related to the camel and used as a beast of burden.

lo (lō), *interj.* look; see; behold.

load (lōd), *n.* **1.** a quantity of material or number of objects that is, or is to be, carried or supported: *a load of rocks.* **2.** the normal maximum amount of something carried by a vehicle, vessel, etc., often used as a unit of measure: *a wagonload of hay.* **3.** something that burdens or oppresses like a heavy weight: *a load on one's mind.* **4.** anything that uses electric power. **5.** a charge of powder, shot, etc., for a firearm. —*v.* **6.** to put a load in or on: *to load a truck with boxes.* **7.** to fill so as to make usable: *to load a camera.* **8.** to give in great abundance: *They loaded us down with gifts.* **9.** to burden or oppress: *to be loaded down with problems.* **10.** to weight (dice) to make them fall in a particular way.

Llama
(4 ft. high at shoulder)

load·star (lōd′stär′), *n.* another spelling of **lodestar.**

load·stone (lōd′stōn′), *n.* a magnetized variety of iron ore formerly used in making compasses. Also, **lodestone.**

loaf¹ (lōf), *n., pl.* **loaves** (lōvz). **1.** a portion of bread or cake baked in a definite form. **2.** a shaped or molded mass of food: *a meat loaf.* [from the Old English word *hlāf* "loaf, bread"]

loaf² (lōf), *v.* to idle away time: *He loafed all weekend.* [see **loafer**]

loaf·er (lō′fər), *n.* **1.** a person who loafs; a lazy person. **2.** a slip-on shoe, similar to a moccasin, for casual wear. [probably short for the earlier word *land-loafer* "vagabond," which comes from the Dutch word *landloper.* See **lope**]

loam (lōm), *n.* a rich soil containing sand, silt, and clay.

loan (lōn), *n.* **1.** the act of lending. **2.** something lent on condition of its being returned, esp. a sum of money lent at interest. —*v.* **3.** to make a loan of; lend (a sum of money): *I loaned him a dollar.*

loath (lōth, lōᴛʜ), *adj.* unwilling; reluctant: *He is loath to go.* Also, **loth.**

loathe (lōᴛʜ), *v.,* **loathed, loath·ing.** to feel disgust or intense dislike for; detest: *to loathe turnips.*

loath·ing (lō′ᴛʜing), *n.* strong dislike mingled with disgust: *a loathing for insects.*

loath·some (lōᴛʜ′səm, lōᴛʜ′səm), *adj.* causing loathing; disgusting: *a loathsome sight.*

lob (lob), *v.,* **lobbed, lob·bing. 1.** to hit a ball in a high arc. —*n.* **2.** a ball hit in a high arc.

lob·by (lob′ē), *n., pl.* **lob·bies. 1.** a corridor or entrance hall, often used as a waiting room. **2.** a group of persons who campaign to influence the voting of legislators. —*v.,* **lob·bied, lob·by·ing. 3.** to try to influence the voting of legislators. —**lob′by·ist,** *n.*

lobe (lōb), *n.* **1.** a rounded projection of a leaf or a body organ. **2.** the soft lower part of the ear.

lob·lol·ly (lob′lol′ē), *n., pl.* **lob·lol·lies. 1.** a pine tree of the southern U.S. **2.** the wood of this tree. Also, **lob′lolly pine′.**

lob·ster (lob′stər), *n., pl.* **lob·sters** *or* **lob·ster. 1.** a sea animal having a hard shell, eight legs, and two large claws. **2.** any of various similar animals, esp. certain large crayfishes. **3.** the flesh of these animals used as food.

Lobster
(length 8 to 12 in.)

lo·cal (lō′kəl), *adj.* **1.** referring to, characteristic of, or restricted to a certain place or certain places: *a local newspaper.* **2.** referring to or affecting a particular part or parts of the body: *a local pain.* **3.** stopping at all stations: *a local train.* —*n.* **4.** a local train, bus, etc. **5.** a local branch of a union, fraternity, etc.

lo′cal an′esthet′ic. See under **anesthetic.**

lo·cal·i·ty (lō kal′i tē), *n., pl.* **lo·cal·i·ties.** a place or area.

lo·cal·ize (lō′kə līz′), *v.,* **lo·cal·ized, lo·cal·iz·ing.** to confine in one place: *to localize an infection.*

lo·cal·ly (lō′kə lē), *adv.* in a particular place, area, location, etc.: *The magazine is published locally.*

lo·cate (lō′kāt, lō kāt′), *v.,* **lo·cat·ed, lo·cat·ing. 1.** to discover the place or location of: *to locate a lost kitten.* **2.** to establish in a position, situation, or locality; place: *The phonograph is located in the den.* **3.** to settle: *to locate in the West.*

lo·ca·tion (lō kā′shən), *n.* **1.** the place where someone or something is at a given moment: *Do you know the location of the box?* **2.** a site for a business, home, etc.: *a good location for a restaurant.* **3.** the act of locating, or the state of being located.

loch (lok), *n.* (in Scotland) **1.** a lake. **2.** a narrow arm of the sea.

lock¹ (lok), *n.* **1.** a mechanical device for securing a door. **2.** any device for fastening or securing something. **3.** (in a firearm) the mechanism that explodes the charge. **4.** an enclosed chamber in a canal, dam, etc., with gates at each end, for raising or lowering vessels by admitting or releasing water. —*v.* **5.** to fasten or secure with a lock or locks: *to lock a suit-case.* **6.** to shut in a place fastened by a lock or locks: *to lock up a prisoner.* **7.** to join or unite: *to lock arms.* **8.** to become locked: *The door locks by itself.* **9. lock, stock, and barrel,** including every part; completely; entirely: *You can have all my ski equipment, lock, stock, and barrel.* [from the Old English word *loc* "fastening, bar"]

lock² (lok), *n.* **1.** a tress or portion of hair. **2.** a small portion of wool, cotton, flax, etc. [from the Old English word *locc* "lock of hair"]

lock·er (lok′ər), *n.* **1.** a chest, drawer, compartment, or closet that may be locked. **2.** a refrigerated compartment that may be rented for storing frozen foods.

lock·et (lok′it), *n.* a small case for a portrait, lock of hair, or other keepsake, usually worn on a necklace.

lock·jaw (lok′jô′), *n.* another name for **tetanus.**

lock·out (lok′out′), *n.* the closing of a business or dismissal of all employees by the employer because of a disagreement over wages, benefits, etc.

lock·smith (lok′smith′), *n.* a person who makes or repairs locks.

lo·co·mo·tion (lō′kə mō′shən), *n.* the act or ability of moving under one's own power.

lo·co·mo·tive (lō′kə mō′tiv), *n.* **1.** an engine for pulling railroad trains. —*adj.* **2.** moving or traveling by means of its own power.

lo·cust (lō′kəst), *n.* **1.** any of several kinds of grasshoppers that have short feelers and migrate in enormous swarms, eating all vegetation in their path. **2.** an American tree having thorny branches and bearing white flowers. **3.** the hard wood of this tree.

lode (lōd), *n.* a vein or deposit of metal ore.

lode·star (lōd′stär′), *n.* a star that shows the way, esp. the North Star. Also, **loadstar.**

lode·stone (lōd′stōn′), *n.* another spelling of **loadstone.**

lodge (loj), *n.* **1.** a roughly built shelter or hut. **2.** a cabin or cottage. **3.** a hotel building or main building at a resort or camp. **4.** a branch of a secret society, or its meeting place. —*v.,* **lodged, lodg·ing. 5.** to live or stay temporarily: *to lodge in a hotel.* **6.** to furnish with a place to stay or live temporarily: *to lodge a guest.* **7.** to be fixed or caught in a place or position: *His foot lodged in the door.* **8.** to fix or bring into a particular place or position: *to lodge a post in the ground.* **9.** to submit or file: *to lodge a complaint.*

lodg·er (loj′ər), *n.* a person who lives in rented quarters in another's house.

lodg·ing (loj′ing), *n.* **1.** a temporary place to stay; temporary quarters. **2. lodgings,** a room or rooms rented for residence in another's house.

loft (lôft), *n.* **1.** a room or area under a sloping roof. **2.** a gallery or upper level in a church, hall, etc., having a special purpose: *a choir loft.* **3.** an upper story of a warehouse or factory. —*v.* **4.** to hit or throw something high in the air: *to loft a ball.*

loft·y (lôf′tē), *adj.,* **loft·i·er, loft·i·est. 1.** extending high in the air; towering. **2.** exalted in rank, dignity, or character. **3.** haughty; proud; arrogant: *a lofty manner.* —**loft′i·ly,** *adv.* —**loft′i·ness,** *n.*

log¹ (lôg, log), *n.* **1.** an unhewn length of the trunk or large limb of a felled tree. **2.** any of various devices for determining the speed of a vessel. **3.** any of various records concerning a trip made by a vessel or aircraft; logbook. —*v.,* **logged, log·ging. 4.** to cut (trees) into logs. **5.** to cut down the trees or timber on (land). [from the Middle English word *logge* "pole, limb of a tree"] —**log′ger,** *n.*

log² (lôg, log), *n.* short for **logarithm.**

Lo·gan (lō′gən), *n.* **Mount,** a mountain in NW Canada: highest peak in Canada and second highest in North America. 19,850 ft.

lo·gan·ber·ry (lō′gən ber′ē), *n., pl.* **lo·gan·ber·ries. 1.** a large, dark-red berry, a cross between a blackberry and a raspberry. **2.** the plant bearing this berry.

log·a·rithm (lô′gə riŧħ′əm, log′ə riŧħ′əm), *n.* the power to which a number must be raised to yield another number. Logarithms are used to simplify complicated calculations, since numbers may be multiplied by adding their logarithms, and any root of a number may be found by dividing its logarithm.

log·book (lôg′book′, log′-), *n.* a book in which details of a trip made by a vessel or aircraft are recorded; log.

log·ger·head (lô′gər hed′, log′ər-), *n.* **1.** a sea turtle that has a large head. **2.** a thickheaded or stupid person. **3. at loggerheads,** engaged in dispute; arguing; quarreling.

log·gia (loj′ə, lô′jē ə), *n.* a gallery or an enclosed area within the body of a building, open to the air on at least one side.

log·ging (log′ing), *n.* the work or business of cutting down trees and transporting the logs to sawmills.

log·ic (loj′ik), *n.* **1.** the science that deals with sound reasoning. **2.** a method of reasoning. **3.** reason or sound judgment.

log·i·cal (loj′i kəl), *adj.* **1.** according to or agreeing with logic: *a logical answer.* **2.** reasonable; that can be expected: *A fight was the logical result of his threats.* —**log′i·cal·ly,** *adv.*

lo·gi·cian (lō jish′ən), *n.* a person skilled in logic.

-logy, a suffix used to form nouns meaning a field of knowledge or study: *biology; geology.*

loin (loin), *n.* **1.** Usually, **loins.** the part of the body of man or a four-legged animal along the spine between the lowest ribs and the hips. **2.** a cut of meat from this region of an animal.

Loire (lwär), *n.* a river in central France. 625 mi. long.

loi·ter (loi′tər), *v.* **1.** to linger aimlessly: *to loiter in the park.* **2.** to pass (time) in an idle or aimless manner (usually fol. by *away*): *to loiter away the afternoon.* —**loi′ter·er,** *n.* —**loi′ter·ing·ly,** *adv.*

loll (lol), *v.* **1.** to recline or lean in a relaxed manner; lounge: *to loll on a sofa.* **2.** to hang or allow to hang loosely; dangle: *The dog's tongue lolled.*

lol·li·pop (lol′ē pop′), *n.* a piece of hard candy or taffy stuck on the end of a stick. Also, **lol′ly·pop′.**

Lon·don (lun′dən), *n.* the capital city of the United Kingdom, in SE England. —**Lon′don·er,** *n.*

lone (lōn), *adj.* being alone; sole; single: *the lone survivor.*

lone·ly (lōn′lē), *adj.,* **lone·li·er, lone·li·est. 1.** without company; lone; solitary. **2.** without friendly companionship; alone. **3.** remote from places of human habitation; isolated. —**lone′li·ness,** *n.*

lone·some (lōn′səm), *adj.* **1.** depressed or sad because of the lack of friends, companionship, etc. **2.** causing such feeling: *a lonesome summer.* **3.** lonely in situation; remote: *a lonesome path.*

long¹ (lông), *adj.,* **long·er** (lông′gər), **long·est** (lông′gist). **1.** having considerable extent from beginning to end; not short: *a long wait.* **2.** extending, lasting, or totaling a number of specified units: *eight miles long.* **3.** (of vowel sounds) taking a longer time to pronounce. *Feed* has a longer vowel sound than *feet* or *fit.* —*n.* **4.** a long time: *They haven't been gone for long.* —*adv.* **5.** for or through a great extent of space or time: *a change long hoped for.* **6.** throughout a certain period of time: *It's been muggy all summer long.* **7.** at a point of time far from another: *long before.* [from the Old English word *lang*]

long² (lông), *v.* to have a strong desire; yearn: *I long to travel.* [from the Old English word *langian* "to grow longer, yearn after"]

long., longitude.

Long′ Beach′, a city in SW California, S of Los Angeles.

long′ dis′tance, telephone service between distant points. —**long′-dis′tance,** *adj.*

lon·gev·i·ty (lon jev′i tē), *n.* **1.** long life. **2.** length of service: *Promotions here are based on longevity.*

Long·fel·low (lông′fel′ō), *n.* **Henry Wads·worth** (wodz′wərth), 1807–1882, U.S. poet.

long·hand (lông′hand′), *n.* writing in which words are written out in full by hand.

Long·horn (lông′hôrn′), *n.* one of a nearly extinct English breed of beef cattle having long horns.

long·ing (lông′ing), *n.* **1.** a strong desire: *a longing to travel.* —*adj.* **2.** having or showing a strong desire.

Long′ Is′land, an island in SE New York. 118 mi. long. 1682 sq. mi.

Long′ Is′land Sound′, an arm of the Atlantic between Connecticut and Long Island. about 90 mi. long.

lon·gi·tude (lon′ji tōōd′, -tyōōd′), *n.* the distance on the earth's surface that is measured east or west of the prime meridian, which passes through Greenwich, England. Longitude is stated in degrees east or west of the prime meridian. Lines of longitude run from the North Pole to the South Pole. See also **latitude** (def. 1).

lon·gi·tu·di·nal (lon′ji tōōd′ⁿl, -tyōōd′-), *adj.* **1.** of or referring to longitude. **2.** running or placed lengthwise. —**lon′gi·tu′di·nal·ly,** *adv.*

long-lived (lông′livd′, lông′livd′), *adj.* having a long life, or lasting a long time: *a long-lived man.*

long-range (lông′rānj′), *adj.* **1.** designed to fire a long distance: *long-range missiles.* **2.** concerned with the more distant future: *long-range plans.*

long·shore·man (lông′shôr′mən), *n., pl.* **long·shore·men.** a man employed on the wharves of a port to load and unload vessels.

long-suf·fer·ing (lông′suf′ər ing), *adj.* enduring injury or provocation long and patiently.

long′ ton′. See under **ton** (def. 1).

long-wind·ed (lông′win′did), *adj.* talking or writing at great length: *a long-winded speech.*

look (lŏŏk), *v.* **1.** to set one's eyes upon something or in some direction in order to see: *Look at the blackboard.* **2.** to use the sight in seeking, searching, examining, watching, etc.: *to look for an apartment.* **3.** to appear or seem: *He looks pale.* **4.** to give (someone) a look: *He looked me straight in the eye.* **5.** to direct the attention: *to look at the facts.* **6.** to have an appearance appropriate to: *The actor looks his part.* **7.** to have an outlook; face: *The window looks upon the street.* —*n.* **8.** the act or an instance of looking: *a look at the house.* **9.** an expressive glance: *a sad look.* **10. looks,** general aspect or appearance: *good looks.* **11. look after,** to take care of: *Look after my sister while I'm gone.* **12. look down on,** to have contempt for; scorn: *She looks down on anyone who can't swim well.* **13. look up, a.** *Informal.* to show improvement: *Business is looking up.* **b.** to search for, esp. in a reference book: *Look up the meaning of this word.* **c.** to visit: *Look me up when you're in town.* **14. look up to,** to admire or respect: *He's a man you can really look up to.*

look′ing glass′, a mirror made of glass.

look·out (lŏŏk′out′), *n.* **1.** a watch kept for someone that may come or something that may happen: *We were on the lookout for her all day.* **2.** a person or group employed to keep such a watch. **3.** a station or place from which a watch is kept.

loom¹ (lōōm), *n.* a hand-operated or power-driven apparatus for weaving fabrics. [from the Old English word *gelōma* "tool, implement"]

loom² (lōōm), *v.* to come into view in indistinct and enlarged form: *The mountainous island loomed on the horizon.*

loon (lōōn), *n.* any of several large, short-tailed water birds that feed on fish, noted for their strange, laughing call.

loon·y (lōō′nē), *adj.,* **loon·i·er, loon·i·est.** *Slang.* lunatic; insane; crazy. —**loon′i·ness,** *n.*

loop (lōōp), *n.* **1.** a portion of a cord, ribbon, etc., folded or doubled upon itself so as to leave an opening between the parts. **2.** anything shaped more or less like a loop, such as a line drawn on paper, a part of a letter, a part of a path, or a line of motion. —*v.* **3.** to form into a loop or loops: *to loop a rope.* **4.** to enfold or encircle in or with something formed into a loop: *to loop the handle with a piece of string.*

loop·hole (loop'hōl'), *n.* **1.** a small or narrow opening in a wall, for looking through, for admitting light and air, or, particularly in a fortification, for firing guns, cannons, etc., against an enemy. **2.** a means of escape or evasion: *There are a number of loopholes in the tax laws whereby taxpayers can save money.* [from the Middle English word *loupe* "window" + *hole*]

loose (loos), *adj.*, **loos·er, loos·est. 1.** free from anything that binds or restrains. **2.** not bound or tied together: *to stack loose papers; to wear one's hair loose.* **3.** not put up in a package or other container: *loose fruit.* **4.** lacking in moral restraint: *loose conduct.* **5.** not firm or tight: *a loose tooth.* **6.** not fitting closely: *a loose sweater.* **7.** not close or compact in structure or arrangement: *a loose weave.* **8.** not strict, exact, or precise: *loose thinking; a loose interpretation.* —*adv.* **9.** in a loose manner; loosely (usually used in combination): *loose-fitting; loose-jointed.* —*v.*, **loosed, loos·ing. 10.** to let loose; free from bonds or restraint: *to loose a dog from a chain.* **11.** to unfasten, undo, or untie: *to loose a knot in a shoelace.* —**loose'ly**, *adv.* —**loose'ness**, *n.*

loose-leaf (loos'lēf'), *adj.* consisting of individual sheets of paper held in a binder in such a way as to allow their removal without tearing: *a loose-leaf notebook.*

loos·en (loo'sən), *v.* to make or become loose or looser: *to loosen one's grip.*

loot (loot), *n.* **1.** spoils or plunder taken by pillaging in a war. **2.** anything taken by dishonesty or force. —*v.* **3.** to plunder or rob. —**loot'er**, *n.*

lop[1] (lop), *v.*, **lopped, lop·ping. 1.** to cut off: *They had to lop off whole pages of the report.* **2.** to cut off branches from: *to lop a bush.* [from the Middle English word *loppe* "a part lopped off"]

lop[2] (lop), *v.*, **lopped, lop·ping. 1.** to hang or let hang loosely or limply; droop. —*adj.* **2.** hanging down limply or droopingly: *a rabbit with lop ears.* [from the earlier words *lop* "spider" or *lop* "dangling limb of a tree"]

lope (lōp), *v.*, **loped, lop·ing. 1.** to move or run with bounding steps, such as a quadruped, or with a long, easy stride, such as a person. —*n.* **2.** a long, easy gait or stride.

lop·sid·ed (lop'sī'did), *adj.* **1.** lopping or leaning to one side. **2.** heavier, larger, or more developed on one side; unbalanced: *a lopsided design.* —**lop'sid'ed·ly**, *adv.* —**lop'sid'ed·ness**, *n.*

lo·qua·cious (lō kwā'shəs), *adj.* very talkative. —**lo·qua'cious·ness**, *n.*

lord (lôrd), *n.* **1.** a person who has power over others; master, chief, or ruler. **2.** a feudal superior; the proprietor of a manor. **3.** a titled nobleman. —*v.* **4.** to assume airs of importance and authority (usually fol. by *it*): *Ever since she won the contest she's lorded it over her friends.*

Lord (lôrd), *n.* **1.** the Supreme Being; God. **2.** the Savior, Jesus Christ. **3.** (in England) the title of certain high officials. **4. Lords**, the House of Lords.

lord·ly (lôrd'lē), *adj.*, **lord·li·er, lord·li·est. 1.** suitable for or befitting a lord; grand, magnificent, or elegant: *lordly manners.* **2.** haughty or arrogant.

lord·ship (lôrd'ship), *n.* **1.** *(often cap.)* a British term of respect used when speaking of or to judges or some noblemen (often preceded by *his* or *your*). **2.** the state or dignity of a lord.

Lord's' Prayer', **the,** the prayer given by Jesus to His disciples. It begins with the words *Our Father.*

Lord's' Sup'per, the, 1. the celebration of Communion or the Eucharist. **2.** the Last Supper.

lore (lôr), *n.* **1.** the body of knowledge, esp. of a traditional or popular nature, on a particular subject: *the lore of herbs.* **2.** learning or knowledge.

lor·gnette (lôrn yet'), *n.* **1.** a pair of eyeglasses mounted on a handle. **2.** a pair of opera glasses held by a handle.

lor·ry (lôr'ē), *n.*, *pl.* **lor·ries. 1.** *British.* a large motor truck. **2.** any of various vehicles running on rails for transporting material in a mine or factory. **3.** a long, low, horse-drawn wagon without sides.

Los An·ge·les (lôs an'jə ləs), a port city in SW California. 452 sq. mi.

lose (looz), *v.*, **lost** (lôst), **los·ing. 1.** to come to be without because of accident, theft, etc.: *I lost my notebook on the bus.* **2.** to suffer the loss or deprivation of: *to lose one's life.* **3.** to fail to keep, preserve, or maintain: *to lose one's balance.* **4.** to fail to win: *to lose a tennis match.* **5.** to bring to destruction or ruin: *Ship and crew were lost.* **6.** to have slip from sight, hearing, attention, etc.: *to lose a speaker's words.* **7.** to stray from by mistake: *He lost his way.* **8.** to cause the loss or defeat of: *The delay lost the battle for them.* **9.** to use to no purpose; waste: *to lose time.* **10. lose out,** *Informal.* to suffer defeat or loss: *Our team lost out in the finals.* —**los'er**, *n.*

los·ing (loo'zing), *adj.* causing or suffering loss or defeat: *a losing battle; the losing team.*

loss (lôs), *n.* **1.** harm or disadvantage from failure to keep, have, or get: *to bear the loss of a robbery.* **2.** an amount or number lost: *a loss of several dollars.* **3.** the state of being without something that one has had: *the loss of a suitcase.* **4.** a losing by defeat; failure to win: *the loss of a bet.* **5.** destruction or ruin: *the loss of a ship by fire.* **6. at a loss, a.** at less than cost; at a financial loss: *We sold the bicycle at a loss.* **b.** in a state of confusion or uncertainty; confused: *I was at a loss for an answer.*

lost (lôst), *adj.* **1.** no longer in one's possession: *lost friends.* **2.** no longer to be found: *lost books.* **3.** having gone astray: *lost children.* **4.** not used to good purpose; wasted: *lost time.* **5.** not won: *a lost battle.* **6.** destroyed; ruined: *lost ships.* **7.** preoccupied; absorbed: *lost in thought.* **8.** desperate; hopeless: *a lost look.* —*v.* **9.** the past tense and past participle of **lose.**

lot (lot), *n.* **1.** one of a set of objects, such as straws or pebbles, drawn or thrown from a container to decide a question or choice by chance. **2.** the casting or drawing of such objects: *to choose a person by lot.* **3.** the decision or choice made by such a method. **4.** an allotted share or portion: *to receive one's lot of an in-*

heritance. **5.** the portion in life assigned by fate: *Her lot was not a happy one.* **6.** a distinct portion or piece of land: *a building lot.* **7.** a distinct portion or parcel of anything: *The furniture was auctioned off in 20 lots.* **8.** Often, **lots.** *Informal.* a great many or a great deal: *a lot of books; lots of money.*

Lot (lot), *n.* (in the Bible) a nephew of Abraham whom God allowed to escape from Sodom with his wife. She was changed into a pillar of salt when she looked back at the burning city.

loth (lōth, lōth), *adj.* another spelling of **loath.**

lo·tion (lō′shən), *n.* a soothing liquid for the skin.

lot·ter·y (lot′ə rē), *n., pl.* **lot·ter·ies.** a gambling game or method of raising money, usually for some public purpose, in which a large number of tickets are sold and a drawing is held for prizes.

Lotus (def. 2)

lo·tus (lō′təs), *n., pl.* **lo·tus·es.** **1.** a water lily that grows in Egypt and Asia. **2.** something resembling a lotus, such as an architectural decoration. **3.** a shrubby herb having pink, red, or white flowers. **4.** (in Greek mythology) a plant yielding a fruit that caused a dreamy and contented forgetfulness in those who ate it.

loud (loud), *adj.* **1.** strong in sound: *loud talking.* **2.** making strong sounds: *loud trombones.* **3.** full of sound or noise; noisy: *a loud party.* **4.** too bright; flashy: *loud ties.* —*adv.* **5.** in a loud manner; loudly: *Please talk louder.* —**loud′ly,** *adv.* —**loud′ness,** *n.*

loud·speak·er (loud′spē′kər), *n.* a device that converts electrical signals into audible sound, as in a hi-fi, radio, or the like. Also, **speaker.**

Lou·i·si·an·a (loo ē′zē an′ə), *n.* a state in the S United States. 48,523 sq. mi. *Cap.:* Baton Rouge. —**Lou·i′si·an′an,** *n., adj.*

Loui′sian′a Pur′chase, the territory that the U.S. purchased from France in 1803: now part of the central U.S.; covered an area of 885,000 sq. mi.

Lou·is·ville (loo′ē vil′), *n.* a port city in N Kentucky, on the Ohio River.

lounge (lounj), *v.,* **lounged, loung·ing.** **1.** to pass time idly. **2.** to recline in a relaxed manner: *We lounged in the sun all afternoon.* —*n.* **3.** a sofa for reclining, sometimes backless, having a headrest at one end. **4.** a large sitting room in a hotel, theater, etc.

louse (lous), *n., pl.* **lice** (līs). a small, wingless insect that lives on man and animals, sucking their blood.

Body louse (length ⅙ in.)

lous·y (lou′zē), *adj.,* **lous·i·er, lous·i·est.** **1.** infested with lice. **2.** *Informal.* very mean or bad: *That was a lousy thing to do to another person.*

lout (lout), *n.* an awkward, stupid person; oaf.

lou·ver (loo′vər), *n.* **1.** any of a series of narrow openings framed at their longer edges with slanting, overlapping slats. **2.** a door or window having adjustable louvers.

lov·a·ble (luv′ə bəl), *adj.* of such a nature as to attract love: *a lovable kitten.* Also, **love′a·ble.** —**lov′a·ble·ness,** *n.* —**lov′a·bly,** *adv.*

love (luv), *n.* **1.** a deeply tender affection for a person of the opposite sex. **2.** a feeling of warm personal attachment or deep affection for a parent, child, relative, or friend. **3.** a strong liking for anything: *her love of books.* **4.** a person whom one loves; beloved person; sweetheart. **5.** something toward which love or great liking is felt: *The theater was her great love.* **6.** (in tennis) a score of zero; nothing. —*v.,* **loved, lov·ing.** **7.** to have love or affection for: *All her pupils love her.* **8.** to have a strong liking for; take great pleasure in: *to love music.*

love·bird (luv′bûrd′), *n.* any of various small parrots that show great affection for their mates.

love·lorn (luv′lôrn′), *adj.* not loved; forsaken by the person one loves.

love·ly (luv′lē), *adj.,* **love·li·er, love·li·est.** **1.** charmingly beautiful: *a lovely flower.* **2.** having a beautiful character or personality: *a lovely person.* **3.** *Informal.* delightful: *I had a lovely time.* —**love′li·ness,** *n.*

lov·er (luv′ər), *n.* **1.** a person who is in love, esp. a man in love with a woman. **2.** a person who has a strong liking for something: *a lover of music.*

lov·ing (luv′ing), *adj.* feeling or showing love; affectionate; fond: *loving glances.* —**lov′ing·ly,** *adv.*

low¹ (lō), *adj.* **1.** situated or occurring not far above the ground, floor, or base: *a low shelf.* **2.** not high or tall: *a low building.* **3.** lying or being below the general level: *low ground.* **4.** bending or passing far downward; deep: *a low bow.* **5.** lacking in usual strength; weak: *to feel low and listless.* **6.** depressed or dejected; unhappy: *low spirits.* **7.** of small amount, degree, force, etc.: *a low number; a low flame.* **8.** below an acceptable standard: *low marks.* **9.** assigning little worth, value, or excellence; unfavorable: *a low opinion.* **10.** mean or base: *a low trick.* **11.** coarse or vulgar: *low entertainment.* **12.** not loud: *a low whisper.* **13.** not high in musical pitch: *a low note.* —*adv.* **14.** in or to a low position, degree, tone, etc.: *to bend low; to speak low.* —*n.* **15.** something that is low. **16.** an arrangement of gears in a truck, automobile, etc., that permits driving at low speeds and provides the greatest power. **17.** a region or a mass of air in which the barometric pressure is low. **18.** **lie low,** to hide oneself or one's true intentions: *You'd better lie low until the scandal dies down.* [from the Middle English word *lāh,* which comes from Scandinavian]

low² (lō), *v.* **1.** to make the sound characteristic of cattle; moo. —*n.* **2.** the act or the sound of lowing. [from the Old English word *hlōwan*]

low·boy (lō′boi′), *n.* a low chest of drawers on short legs.

---

act, āble, dâre, ärt; ebb, ēqual; if, īce; hot, ōver, ôrder; oil; bŏŏk; ōōze; out; up, ûrge; ə = a as in *alone;* ᵊ as in *button* (but′ᵊn), *fire* (fī′ᵊr); chief; shoe; thin; that; zh as in *measure* (mezh′ər). See full key inside cover.

Low′ Coun′tries, Belgium, Luxembourg, and the Netherlands.

low·er[1] (lō′ər), v. **1.** to cause to descend; let down: *to lower a flag.* **2.** to make lower in height or level: *to lower the water in a canal.* **3.** to reduce in amount, price, degree, force, etc. **4.** to make less loud: *to lower one's voice.* —*adj.* **5.** the comparative of **low**[1].

low·er[2] (lou′ər), v. **1.** to be dark and threatening, such as the sky. **2.** to frown or scowl. —*n.* **3.** a dark, threatening appearance. **4.** a frown or scowl. [from the Middle English word *loure* "to frown"]

Low′er Califor′nia (lō′ər), a long, narrow peninsula in NW Mexico, S of California. Spanish name, **Baja California.**

low·er-case (lō′ər kās′), *adj.* **1.** (of a letter of the alphabet) written or printed usually in a different form and smaller than its related capital letter. In the word "John," *J* is a capital letter, while *o, h,* and *n* are lower-case letters. —*v.,* **low·er-cased, low·er-cas·ing. 2.** to print or write with a lower-case letter or letters. —*n.* **3.** a lower-case letter.

low·er·most (lō′ər mōst′), *adj.* another word for **lowest.**

low·land (lō′lənd), *n.* **1.** land that is low or level. **2. the Lowlands,** a low, level region in S, central, and E Scotland. —*adj.* **3.** of, referring to, or characteristic of a lowland or lowlands.

low·ly (lō′lē), *adj.,* **low·li·er, low·li·est. 1.** humble in station, condition, or nature: *a lowly cottage.* **2.** humble in spirit; meek. —*adv.* **3.** in a low position, manner, or degree. **4.** in a quiet voice; softly: *to speak lowly.* —**low′li·ness,** *n.*

low-spir·it·ed (lō′spir′i tid), *adj.* depressed or dejected.

low′ tide′, 1. the tide at the point of maximum ebb. **2.** the time of low water.

lox (loks), *n.* a kind of smoked salmon.

loy·al (loi′əl), *adj.* **1.** faithful to one's sovereign, government, or state: *a loyal subject.* **2.** faithful to one's oath, commitments, or obligations: *to be loyal to a vow.* **3.** faithful to any person or thing: *loyal friends.*

loy·al·ist (loi′ə list), *n.* a person who supports the sovereign or the existing government, esp. in time of revolt.

loy·al·ty (loi′əl tē), *n., pl.* **loy·al·ties.** the state or quality of being loyal; faithfulness.

Loy·o·la (loi ō′lə), *n.* **Saint Ig·na·tius of** (ig nā′shəs), 1491–1556, Spanish founder of the Jesuits.

loz·enge (loz′inj), *n.* **1.** a small, flavored confection of sugar or syrup, often medicated. **2.** a diamond-shaped figure.

LP, *Trademark.* a phonograph record designed to be played at 33⅓ revolutions per minute; a long-playing record. Also, **L-P**

ls, liters. Also, **ls.**

LSD, a highly dangerous drug that produces hallucinations.

Lt., Lieutenant.

Lt. Col., Lieutenant Colonel.

Lt. Comdr., Lieutenant Commander. Also, **Lt. Com.**

Ltd., Limited.

Lt. Gen., Lieutenant General.

Lu, *Chem.* the symbol for **lutetium.**

lu·au (loo ou′, loo′ou), *n.* a feast of Hawaiian food, usually accompanied by Hawaiian entertainment.

lub·ber (lub′ər), *n.* **1.** a big, clumsy, stupid person. **2.** an awkward or unskilled seaman.

Lub·bock (lub′ək), *n.* a city in NW Texas.

lu·bri·cant (loo′brə kənt), *n.* a substance, such as oil or grease, that is used on the moving parts of machinery to reduce friction.

lu·bri·cate (loo′brə kāt′), *v.,* **lu·bri·cat·ed, lu·bri·cat·ing.** to apply a lubricant to in order to reduce friction. —**lu′bri·ca′tion,** *n.* —**lu′bri·ca′tor,** *n.*

lu·cid (loo′sid), *adj.* **1.** shining or bright. **2.** clear; transparent. **3.** easily understood; clear: *a lucid explanation.* **4.** thinking clearly; rational; sane. —**lu·cid′i·ty,** *n.* —**lu′cid·ly,** *adv.*

Lu·ci·fer (loo′sə fər), *n.* an archangel who rebelled and was driven out of heaven; Satan; the Devil.

luck (luk), *n.* **1.** the force that seems to operate for good or ill in a person's life. **2.** good fortune: *He had no luck in finding work.* **3. down on one's luck,** having a spell of bad luck: *to help a friend who is down on his luck.* **4. in luck,** lucky; fortunate: *If the store is still open we're in luck.* **5. out of luck,** unlucky; unfortunate: *All the seats had been sold, so we were out of luck.* **6. push one's luck,** to try to make too much of an opportunity: *You've already won two games, so don't push your luck.*

luck·i·ly (luk′ə lē), *adv.* by good luck; fortunately: *Luckily, we could still buy tickets.*

luck·less (luk′lis), *adj.* having no luck, or troubled with bad luck: *luckless explorers.*

luck·y (luk′ē), *adj.,* **luck·i·er, luck·i·est. 1.** having good luck; fortunate: *to be lucky in life.* **2.** happening fortunately: *a lucky accident.* **3.** bringing good luck: *a lucky penny; a lucky day.*

lu·cra·tive (loo′krə tiv), *adj.* profitable; moneymaking: *a lucrative business.* —**lu′cra·tive·ly,** *adv.*

lu·cre (loo′kər), *n.* monetary gain; money.

lu·di·crous (loo′də krəs), *adj.* amusingly absurd; ridiculous; comical: *a ludicrous situation.* —**lu′di·crous·ly,** *adv.*

lug[1] (lug), *v.,* **lugged, lug·ging.** to pull along or carry with force or effort: *to lug a suitcase upstairs.* [from the Middle English word *luggen,* which comes from Scandinavian]

lug[2] (lug), *n.* a projecting piece by which anything is held or supported. [from Scandinavian]

lug·gage (lug′ij), *n.* suitcases, trunks, etc.; baggage.

lug·sail (lug′sāl′, lug′səl), *n.* a four-cornered sail fastened to a yard that crosses the mast.

lu·gu·bri·ous (loo goo′brē əs), *adj.* mournful or gloomy, esp. in an exaggerated manner: *to wear a lugubrious expression.* —**lu·gu′bri·ous·ly,** *adv.*

Luke (look), *n.* **1.** (in the Bible) an early Christian disciple and companion of Paul, and one of the four Evangelists: believed to be the author of the Gospel of St. Luke and the Acts. **2.** the third Gospel of the New Testament.

luke·warm (lōōk′wôrm′), *adj.* **1.** moderately warm; tepid: *lukewarm water.* **2.** having or showing little enthusiasm: *a lukewarm greeting.*

lull (lul), *v.* **1.** to put to sleep by soothing or quieting: *to lull the baby to sleep.* **2.** to quiet down, let up, or subside: *The storm lulled.* —*n.* **3.** a temporary stillness: *a lull in the traffic.*

lull·a·by (lul′ə bī′), *n.,* *pl.* **lull·a·bies.** a song used to lull a child to sleep.

lum·ba·go (lum bā′gō), *n.* a recurring pain in the lower part of the back.

lum·bar (lum′bər, lum′bär), *adj.* of or referring to the loins or lower back.

lum·ber[1] (lum′bər), *n.* **1.** timber sawed or split into planks, boards, etc. —*v.* **2.** to cut timber and prepare it for market. [from a special use of *lumber*[2]. The original sense is "something heavy or cumbersome"]

lum·ber[2] (lum′bər), *v.* to move clumsily or heavily: *The elephant lumbered around the circus tent.* [from the Middle English word *lomeren,* which comes from Scandinavian]

lum·ber·ing[1] (lum′bər ing), *n.* the business of cutting and preparing timber.

lum·ber·ing[2] (lum′bər ing), *adj.* moving clumsily or heavily; awkward: *a lumbering walk.*

lum·ber·jack (lum′bər jak′), *n.* a person who works at lumbering.

lum·ber·man (lum′bər mən), *n.,* *pl.* **lum·ber·men.** **1.** a person who deals in lumber. **2.** a person who cuts prepared logs into lumber.

lu·mi·nar·y (lōō′mə ner′ē), *n.,* *pl.* **lu·mi·nar·ies.** **1.** a body that gives off light, esp. the sun or the moon. **2.** a famous and respected person.

lu·mi·nous (lōō′mə nəs), *adj.* **1.** giving off or reflecting light: *luminous paint.* **2.** easily understood; clear; lucid: *a luminous report.* —**lu′mi·nous·ly,** *adv.*

lump[1] (lump), *n.* **1.** a piece or mass of solid matter of no particular shape: *a lump of clay.* **2.** a bump or swelling: *She fell and got a lump on her head.* **3.** a small cube of granulated sugar. —*adj.* **4.** in the form of a lump or lumps: *lump sugar.* **5.** made up of several items taken together: *a lump sum.* —*v.* **6.** to unite into one collection or mass (often fol. by *together*): *Last year they lumped all the classes together.* **7.** to form or raise a lump or lumps: *The gravy lumped because we overcooked it.* [from the Middle English word *lumpe*]

lump[2] (lump), *v. Informal.* to put up with: *If you don't like it, you can lump it.* [probably from a special use of *lump*[1]]

lump·y (lum′pē), *adj.,* **lump·i·er, lump·i·est.** **1.** full of lumps: *lumpy sauce.* **2.** covered with lumps. —**lump′i·ness,** *n.*

Lu·na (lōō′nə), *n.* (in Roman mythology) the goddess of the moon: sometimes identified with another Roman moon goddess, Diana.

lu·na·cy (lōō′nə sē), *n.,* *pl.* **lu·na·cies.** **1.** mental illness; insanity; madness. **2.** crazy or reckless behavior, or an instance of it: *Fast driving is lunacy.*

lu·nar (lōō′nər), *adj.* of or concerning the moon.

lu′nar eclipse′. See under **eclipse** (def. 1).

lu·na·tic (lōō′nə tik), *n.* **1.** an insane person; madman. **2.** a person who behaves in an extremely unusual or reckless way. —*adj.* **3.** crazy or reckless: *wild, lunatic behavior.* **4.** intended for or used by insane persons: *a lunatic asylum.*

lunch (lunch), *n.* **1.** a meal between breakfast and dinner. **2.** any light snack: *a picnic lunch.* —*v.* **3.** to eat lunch: *to lunch late.*

lunch·eon (lun′chən), *n.* lunch, esp. a formal lunch in honor of a special occasion.

lunch·room (lunch′rōōm′, -rŏŏm′), *n.* **1.** a restaurant that specializes in serving light meals. **2.** a cafeteria or other eating place in a school or office.

lung (lung), *n.* either of two saclike organs of breathing in the chest of man and other animals. Blood receives oxygen and gives up carbon dioxide in the lungs.

lunge (lunj), *n.* **1.** a sudden forward movement or thrust; plunge: *He made a lunge for the ball.* —*v.,* **lunged, lung·ing.** **2.** to make a lunge or thrust; move with a lunge: *The dog lunged for the bone.*

lung·fish (lung′fish′), *n.,* *pl.* **lung·fish·es** *or* **lung·fish.** any of several fishes that have lungs as well as gills.

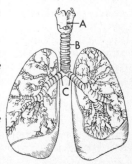

Lungs (Human)
A, Larynx; B, Windpipe;
C, Bronchi

lu·pine (lōō′pin), *n.* a kind of pea plant grown for its blue, pink, or white flowers.

lurch[1] (lûrch), *n.* **1.** an act or instance of swaying or staggering suddenly. —*v.* **2.** to make a lurch, or move in lurches.

lurch[2] (lûrch), *n.* **leave in the lurch,** to leave in an uncomfortable or difficult situation; desert in time of trouble: *He left me in the lurch with all that work to do.* [from an early French word *lourche,* the name of a game, which comes from Germanic]

lure (lŏŏr), *n.* **1.** anything that attracts or tempts. **2.** the power of attracting or tempting. **3.** live or esp. artificial bait used in angling or trapping; decoy. —*v.,* **lured, lur·ing.** **4.** to attract or entice: *to be lured by the smell of roasting meat.*

lu·rid (lŏŏr′id), *adj.* **1.** lighted or shining with an unnatural, fiery glow; brightly red: *a lurid sunset.* **2.** wildly dramatic; sensational: *lurid crimes.* —**lu′rid·ly,** *adv.*

lurk (lûrk), *v.* **1.** to lie or wait in hiding: *The cat lurked in the bushes.* **2.** to sneak or slink.

lus·cious (lush′əs), *adj.* **1.** highly pleasing to the taste or smell: *a luscious ripe peach.* **2.** sweet or attractive to any of the senses or to the mind: *luscious music.* —**lus′cious·ly,** *adv.*

lush (lush), *adj.* 1. (of vegetation, plants, grasses, etc.) growing vigorously; luxuriant. 2. having rich, luxuriant vegetation: *lush forests.* 3. very rich or luxurious: *a lush apartment.*

lust (lust), *n.* 1. a powerful desire, esp. one that is unnatural or uncontrollable: *a lust for wealth.* —*v.* 2. to have a strong desire (often fol. by *for* or *after*): *to lust after power.*

lus·ter (lus′tər), *n.* 1. the state or quality of shining by reflecting light; glitter; sparkle. 2. a substance, such as a coating or polish, used to give a sheen or gloss. 3. brightness or brilliance; radiance: *the luster of polished silver.* 4. excellence, merit, glory, etc.: *The award added luster to his reputation.*

lus·trous (lus′trəs), *adj.* having luster; shining: *a lustrous finish on the vase.*

lust·y (lus′tē), *adj.*, **lust·i·er, lust·i·est.** full of healthy vigor: *a lusty child.* —**lust′i·ly,** *adv.* —**lust′i·ness,** *n.*

lute (loot), *n.* a stringed musical instrument having a wide neck and a body shaped like half a pear. The strings of a lute are plucked by the fingers.

Lute

lu·te·nist (loot′ᵊnist), *n.* a person who plays the lute.

lu·te·ti·um (loo tē′shē əm), *n. Chem.* a metallic element of the rare-earth group. *Symbol:* Lu Also, **lu·te′ci·um.**

Lu·ther (loo′thər), *n.* **Martin,** 1483–1546, German leader of the Protestant Reformation.

Lu·ther·an (loo′thər ən), *adj.* 1. of or concerning Luther and his doctrines, or belonging to one of the Protestant churches that bear his name. —*n.* 2. a follower of Luther, or an adherent of his doctrines; a member of the Lutheran Church.

Lux·em·bourg (luk′səm bûrg′), *n.* a grand duchy surrounded by Germany, France, and Belgium. 999 sq. mi. *Cap.:* Luxembourg. Also, **Lux′em·burg.**

lux·u·ri·ant (lug zhoor′ē ənt, luk shoor′ē ənt), *adj.* 1. growing richly and abundantly; lush: *luxuriant vegetation.* 2. very rich or fancy; elaborate; florid: *luxuriant decoration.* —**lux·u′ri·ance,** *n.* —**lux·u′ri·ant·ly,** *adv.*

lux·u·ri·ate (lug zhoor′ē āt′, luk shoor′ē āt′), *v.,* **lux·u·ri·at·ed, lux·u·ri·at·ing.** 1. to live or indulge in luxury. 2. to grow fully or abundantly; thrive. 3. to take

great delight: *to luxuriate in a hot bath.*

lux·u·ri·ous (lug zhoor′ē əs, luk shoor′ē əs), *adj.* 1. characterized by luxury and great comfort: *a luxurious home.* 2. loving luxury: *a man of luxurious tastes.* —**lux·u′ri·ous·ly,** *adv.*

lux·u·ry (luk′shə rē, lug′zhə rē), *n., pl.* **lux·u·ries.** 1. something enjoyed as an addition to the ordinary necessities and comforts of life: *Expensive jewelry is a luxury.* 2. use of and indulgence in the pleasures offered by such things: *to live in luxury.* —*adj.* 3. providing luxury: *a luxury hotel.*

Lu·zon (loo zon′), *n.* the chief island in the Philippines. 40,420 sq. mi.

lv., leave.

Lw, *Chem.* the symbol for **lawrencium.**

-ly, a suffix used to form 1. adverbs from adjectives: *gladly; greatly.* 2. adjectives or adverbs meaning **a.** once in each period of time: *hourly; weekly.* **b.** in, toward, or from a certain direction: *northerly; westwardly.* 3. adjectives meaning like or resembling: *manly; saintly.*

ly·ce·um (lī sē′əm, lī′sē əm), *n.* a building for public meetings, lectures, etc.

lye (lī), *n.* a highly caustic alkali, sometimes used in cleaning and in making soap.

ly·ing[1] (lī′ing), *n.* 1. the telling of lies. —*adj.* 2. deliberately untruthful: *a lying report.*

ly·ing[2] (lī′ing), *v.* the present participle of **lie**[2].

lymph (limf), *n.* a yellowish fluid containing white blood cells that surrounds body cells and carries their wastes to the bloodstream.

lym·phat·ic (lim fat′ik), *adj.* 1. relating to, containing, or conveying lymph: *a lymphatic vessel.* 2. sluggish, listless, or flabby: *a lymphatic personality.*

lynch (linch), *v.* to hang or otherwise kill (a person) by mob action and without legal authority.

lynx (lingks), *n., pl.* **lynx·es** or **lynx.** any of several North American wildcats having a short tail and tufted ears.

lyre (līr), *n.* an ancient musical instrument resembling a small harp.

lyre·bird (līr′bûrd′), *n.* an Australian bird, the male of which has a long tail that is lyre-shaped when spread.

Lyre

lyr·ic (lir′ik), *adj.* Also, **lyr′i·cal.** 1. (of a poem) having the form and general effect of a song. 2. concerning or writing such poems. 3. having to do with singing. —*n.* 4. a lyric poem. 5. Often, **lyrics.** the words of a song: *He wrote the music and I wrote the lyrics.* —**lyr′i·cal·ly,** *adv.*

NORTH SEA · NETHERLANDS · WEST GERMANY · BELGIUM · FRANCE · Luxembourg · **Luxembourg** · ★Paris · Rhine River · Rhône River

	Semitic	Greek		Latin	Gothic	Modern Roman	
DEVELOPMENT OF UPPER-CASE LETTERS	ϟ	↳	M	↳↳	M	𝔐	M
DEVELOPMENT OF LOWER-CASE LETTERS	μ	∿	ϻ	ϻ	𝔪	m	
	Greek		Medieval		Gothic	Modern Roman	

M

M, m (em), *n., pl.* **M's** *or* **Ms, m's** *or* **ms.** the 13th letter of the English alphabet.

M, 1. the Roman numeral for 1000. 2. (in printing) em.

m, 1. medieval. 2. medium. 3. meter; meters. 4. middle.

M., 1. Majesty. 2. Medicine. 3. Medium. 4. noon. [from the Latin word *merīdiēs*] 5. Monday. 6. mountain.

m., 1. male. 2. married. 3. masculine. 4. mass. 5. (in music) measure. 6. medium. 7. noon. [from the Latin word *merīdiēs*] 8. mile. 9. minute. 10. month. 11. morning.

ma (mä), *n. Informal.* mother.

mA, milliampere; milliamperes. Also, **ma**

ma'am (mam), *n. Informal.* madam.

ma·ca·bre (mə käb′ər, mə käb′), *adj.* gruesome or grim; horrible: *macabre ghost stories.* [from the French phrase *danse macabre* "dance of death"]

mac·ad·am (mə kad′əm), *n.* 1. a macadamized road or pavement. 2. the broken stone used in making such a road. [named after J. L. *McAdam* (1756–1836), its Scottish inventor]

mac·ad·am·ize (mə kad′ə mīz′), *v.,* **mac·ad·am·ized, mac·ad·am·iz·ing.** to pave with layers of broken stone, usually with asphalt or tar as a binder.

Ma·cao (mə kou′), *n.* a Portuguese overseas province in S China.

ma·caque (mə käk′), *n.* any of several monkeys, found chiefly in Asia and the East Indies, having large cheek pouches and, frequently, a short tail.

mac·a·ro·ni (mak′ə rō′nē), *n.* a pasta in the form of dried, hollow tubes, letters of the alphabet, etc. [from Italian]

Macaque
(total length 5½ ft.)

mac·a·roon (mak′ə rōōn′), *n.* a cookie made of egg whites, sugar, almond paste or coconut, and, sometimes, flour. [from the French word *macaron,* which comes from Italian]

Mac·Ar·thur (mə kär′thər), *n.* **Douglas,** 1880–1964, U.S. general: commander of U.S. forces in the Far East 1941–1951.

ma·caw (mə kô′), *n.* any of various large, long-tailed parrots of Central and South America, noted for their brilliantly colored feathers. [from the Portuguese word *macao,* which comes from South American Indian]

Mac·beth (mək beth′, mak beth′), *n.* died 1057, king of Scotland: subject of a play by Shakespeare.

mace[1] (mās), *n.* 1. a clublike weapon of war, often with a spiked metal head, used in the Middle Ages. 2. a ceremonial staff carried by certain officials as a symbol of office. [from an Old French word meaning "large mallet"]

mace[2] (mās), *n.* a spice ground from the layer between a nutmeg shell and its outer husk. [from the Old French word *macis,* which comes from Latin *maccis,* the name of a spice]

Macaw
(length
3 ft.)

Mac·e·do·ni·a (mas′i dō′nē ə), *n.* an ancient country N of Greece. Also, **Mac·e·don** (mas′i don′). —**Mac′e·do′ni·an,** *n., adj.*

ma·chet·e (mə shet′ē, mə chet′ē), *n.* a large, heavy knife used as a tool in cutting sugar cane and clearing underbrush or as a weapon.

mach·i·na·tion (mak′ə nā′shən), *n.* 1. the act or process of plotting. 2. Usually, **machinations.** crafty schemes; plots; intrigues: *the machinations of a conspiracy.*

Machete

ma·chine (mə shēn′), *n.* 1. an assembly of various parts that work together to perform a particular job:

a sewing machine. **2.** something that is mechanically powered, such as an airplane or automobile. **3.** another term for **simple machine. 4.** an organized group of persons that conducts or controls the activities of a political party or other organization. *—v.,* **ma·chined, ma·chin·ing. 5.** to make or process using a machine: *to machine a rod to a precise diameter.* [from a French word, which comes from Greek dialect *machana* "pulley"]

machine′ gun′, a gun that fires a rapid, steady stream of bullets as long as the trigger is pressed.

ma·chin·er·y (mə shē′nə rē), *n., pl.* **ma·chin·er·ies. 1.** a group or assembly of machines. **2.** the parts of a machine. **3.** any system by which action, order, etc., is maintained: *the machinery of government.*

ma·chin·ist (mə shē′nist), *n.* a person who makes, operates, or repairs machines or machine tools.

ma·chis·mo (mä chiz′mō), *n.* a strong or exaggerated quality or sense of being masculine.

Mac·ken·zie (mə ken′zē), *n.* a river in NW Canada, flowing from the Great Slave Lake to the Arctic Ocean. 1120 mi. long.

mack·er·el (mak′ər əl, mak′rəl), *n., pl.* **mack·er·els** or **mack·er·el.** an important North Atlantic food fish whose back is marked with dark, wavy crossbands.

Mack·i·nac (mak′ə nô′, mak′ə nak′), *n.* **Straits of,** a strait between the peninsulas of Upper and Lower Michigan, connecting Lakes Huron and Michigan.

mack·i·naw (mak′ə nô′), *n.* a short coat of thick wool, usually plaid.

mack·in·tosh (mak′in tosh′), *n.* a raincoat made of rubberized cloth.

ma·cron (mā′kron), *n.* a horizontal line over a vowel to show that it has a long sound, as in *fate* (fāt).

mad (mad), *adj.,* **mad·der, mad·dest. 1.** enraged or irritated; angry. **2.** mentally disturbed; insane. **3.** very foolish or unwise: *a mad idea.* **4.** overcome by eagerness or enthusiasm: *mad about tennis.* **5.** having rabies: *a mad dog.* **—mad′ly,** *adv.* **—mad′ness,** *n.*

Mad·a·gas·car (mad′ə gas′kər), *n.* an island off the SE coast of Africa: the main part of the Malagasy Republic. 227,800 sq. mi.

mad·am (mad′əm), *n.* a polite term of address to a woman, originally used only to a woman of rank and authority. [from the Old French word *madame,* which comes from the phrase *ma dame* "my lady"]

mad·ame (mad′əm, mə dam′, mə däm′), *n., pl.* **mes·dames** (mā dam′, mā däm′). a title of respect used in speaking to or of a married woman, esp. one of rank, who is not of American or British origin.

mad·cap (mad′kap′), *adj.* **1.** wild or reckless; impulsive: *a madcap scheme.* **—n. 2.** a madcap person.

mad·den (mad′ᵊn), *v.* **1.** to make or become mad. **2.** to make angry; anger. **—mad′den·ing·ly,** *adv.*

COMORO ISLANDS   Diego Suarez
AFRICA
MOZAMBIQUE CHANNEL
Tananarive★   Tamatave
Madagascar
(MALAGASY REPUBLIC)   INDIAN OCEAN
Fort Dauphin

made (mād), *v.* the past tense and past participle of **make.**

Ma·dei·ra (mə dēr′ə, mə der′ə), *n.* a group of islands off the NW coast of Africa, belonging to Portugal. 308 sq. mi.

mad·e·moi·selle (mad′ə mə zel′, mad′mwə zel′), *n., pl.* **mad·e·moi·selles** or **mes·de·moi·selles** (mā′də mə zel′, mād′mwə zel′). a title of respect used in speaking to or of a girl or unmarried woman who is not of American or British origin.

made-up (mād′up′), *adj.* **1.** concocted or invented: *a made-up story.* **2.** wearing make-up.

mad·house (mad′hous′), *n., pl.* **mad·hous·es** (mad′hou′ziz). **1.** an insane asylum. **2.** a wild, confused, and often noisy place.

Mad·i·son (mad′i sən), *n.* **1. James,** 1751–1836, 4th President of the U.S. 1809–1817. **2.** his wife, **Dolly,** 1768–1849. **3.** the capital city of Wisconsin, in the S part.

mad·man (mad′man′, mad′mən), *n., pl.* **mad·men.** an insane man; lunatic.

Ma·don·na (mə don′ə), *n.* **1.** the Virgin Mary (usually preceded by *the*). **2.** a picture or statue representing the Virgin Mary.

mad·ras (mad′rəs, mə dras′), *n.* a light cotton fabric with woven stripes or figures, often of another color, for shirts, dresses, etc. [named after *Madras,* India, where it was originally woven]

Ma·dras (mə dras′, mə dräs′), *n.* a port city in SE India.

Ma·drid (mə drid′), *n.* the capital city of Spain, in the central part.

mael·strom (māl′strəm), *n.* **1.** a large, powerful, or violent whirlpool. **2.** a wild confusion or disorder; uproar; tumult.

maes·tro (mī′strō), *n., pl.* **maes·tros.** a master of one of the arts, esp. a great composer, performer, conductor, or teacher of music.

mag·a·zine (mag′ə zēn′, mag′ə zēn′), *n.* **1.** a publication that is issued periodically, usually bound in a paper cover, and containing stories, essays, poems, etc., by many writers, and often photographs and drawings. **2.** a room or place for keeping gunpowder and other explosives. **3.** a replaceable container holding bullets for a gun, film for a camera, etc. [from the French word *magasin* "store, storehouse"]

Ma·gel·lan (mə jel′ən), *n.* **1. Ferdinand,** c1480–1521, Portuguese navigator: made first voyage around the world. **2. Strait of,** a strait near the S tip of South America connecting the Atlantic and Pacific oceans.

CHILE   ARGENTINA   ATLANTIC OCEAN
Strait of Magellan
PACIFIC OCEAN
TIERRA DEL FUEGO   FALKLAND ISLANDS
CAPE HORN

ma·gen·ta (mə jen′tə), *n.* **1.** a reddish purple. **—adj. 2.** of the color magenta.

mag·got (mag′ət), *n.* the legless larva of various insects, esp. of the common housefly.

Ma·gi (mā′jī), *n.pl., sing.* **Ma·gus** (mā′gəs). (in the Bible) the three wise men who came to Bethlehem to honor Jesus shortly after His birth.

mag·ic (maj′ik), *n.* 1. the use of various techniques, such as chants, formulas, and rituals, that supposedly give a person supernatural powers. 2. any unusual or exceptional influence, charm, power, etc.: *the magic of his voice.* 3. tricks performed by a magician as a form of entertainment. —*adj.* 4. Also, **mag′i·cal.** of, concerning, or produced by or as if by magic: *magic powers; magic beauty.* [from the Latin word *magica*, which comes from Greek *magos* "seer, wizard"] —**mag′i·cal·ly**, *adv.*

ma·gi·cian (mə jish′ən), *n.* 1. a person skilled in magic. 2. an entertainer who performs magic tricks.

mag′ic square′, a square containing numbers arranged in an equal number of rows and columns so that the sum of the numbers in any row, column, or diagonal is the same.

10	3	8
5	7	9
6	11	4

Magic square

mag·is·te·ri·al (maj′i stēr′ē əl), *adj.* 1. of, concerning, or proper for a master; authoritative; important. 2. domineering and overbearing. 3. of or proper to a magistrate or his office.

mag·is·trate (maj′i strāt′), *n.* 1. a civil officer responsible for administering the law. 2. a minor judicial officer, such as a justice of the peace.

Mag·na Char·ta (mag′nə kär′tə), 1. the "great charter" of English liberties, signed by King John and the English barons at Runnymede, June 15, 1215. 2. any basic constitution or law guaranteeing rights.

mag·na·nim·i·ty (mag′nə nim′i tē), *n., pl.* for def. 2 **mag·na·nim·i·ties.** 1. the quality of being magnanimous. 2. a magnanimous act.

mag·nan·i·mous (mag nan′ə məs), *adj.* generous in forgiving an offense. —**mag·nan′i·mous·ly**, *adv.*

mag·nate (mag′nāt, mag′nit), *n.* a person of great influence, importance, or standing in a particular enterprise, field of business, etc.: *a steel magnate.*

mag·ne·sia (mag nē′zhə, mag nē′shə), *n.* a compound of magnesium used as an antacid and laxative.

mag·ne·si·um (mag nē′zē əm), *n.* a light, silver-white metal that burns with a dazzling white light, used in lightweight alloys and in flares: a chemical element. *Symbol:* Mg

mag·net (mag′nit), *n.* 1. an object, usually a straight or horseshoe-shaped piece of iron or steel, that has the property of attracting pieces of iron or steel and of repelling another magnet. 2. a person or thing that attracts by some power or charm: *The new swimming pool was a magnet for all the children in the neighborhood.* [from the Latin word *magnēta*, from the Greek phrase *ho Magnēs lithos* "the stone of Magnesia (an ancient city in Asia Minor)"]

mag·net·ic (mag net′ik), *adj.* 1. concerning a magnet or magnetism. 2. having the properties of a magnet. 3. capable of being magnetized. 4. having a strong power or charm: *a magnetic personality.* —**mag·net′i·cal·ly**, *adv.*

magnet′ic field′, a region, such as the space around a magnet, containing magnetic forces.

magnet′ic pole′, 1. the points of a magnet, usually the ends, at which its magnetism appears to be concentrated. 2. either of the points on the earth's surface, one in the arctic and one in the antarctic, toward which a magnetic needle points.

mag·net·ism (mag′ni tiz′əm), *n.* 1. the properties of attraction and repulsion possessed by a magnet. 2. magnetic or attractive power or charm.

mag·net·ize (mag′ni tīz′), *v.*, **mag·net·ized, mag·net·iz·ing.** 1. to make a magnet of or to impart magnetic properties to. 2. to have an attracting or compelling influence on: *The speaker magnetized the audience.*

mag·ne·to (mag nē′tō), *n., pl.* **mag·ne·tos.** a small electric generator whose armature rotates in a magnetic field provided by a group of permanent magnets.

mag·ni·fi·ca·tion (mag′nə fə kā′shən), *n.* 1. the act of magnifying, or the state of being magnified. 2. the power to magnify. 3. the amount by which a device can magnify or by which an image is magnified.

mag·nif·i·cence (mag nif′i səns), *n.* the quality or state of being magnificent; splendor: *the magnificence of the Grand Canyon.*

mag·nif·i·cent (mag nif′i sənt), *adj.* 1. making a splendid appearance or show: *a magnificent party; a magnificent mansion.* 2. very fine; superb: *a magnificent orchestra.* —**mag·nif′i·cent·ly**, *adv.*

mag·ni·fy (mag′nə fī′), *v.*, **mag·ni·fied, mag·ni·fy·ing.** 1. to make something appear to be larger, as a lens does. 2. to cause to seem greater or more important; exaggerate: *He magnified his accomplishments to impress his friends.* —**mag′ni·fi′er**, *n.*

mag′nifying glass′, a lens for making things look larger.

mag·ni·tude (mag′ni tood′, -tyood′), *n.* 1. size or extent; dimensions: *a room of great magnitude.* 2. great amount or importance: *problems of great magnitude.* 3. the relative brightness of a star or other heavenly body.

mag·no·lia (mag nōl′yə, mag nō′lē ə), *n.* any of several North American ornamental shrubs or trees having large, usually sweet-smelling flowers. [named after Pierre *Magnol* (1638–1715), French botanist]

mag·pie (mag′pī′), *n.* 1. either of two black-and-white birds related to the crow and noted for their noisy, mischievous habits. 2. a person who talks or chatters a great deal; chatterbox. [from *Mag* "Margaret" + *pie* "magpie," which comes from Latin *pica*]

Mag·yar (mag′yär), *n.* 1. a member of a group of people that make up a main part of the population of Hungary. 2. the Hungarian language. —*adj.* 3. of or concerning the Magyars or their language.

Magpie
(length 18 in.)

ma·ha·ra·jah (mä′hə rä′jə), *n.* the title of a ruling prince in India. Also, **ma′ha·ra′ja.**

ma·ha·ra·nee (mä′hə rä′nē), *n.* **1.** the wife of a maharajah. **2.** an Indian princess.

ma·hat·ma (mə hät′mə), *n.* (in some Asian religions) a wise and holy man.

Ma·hi·can (mə hē′kən), *n., pl.* **Ma·hi·cans** *or* **Ma·hi·can.** a member of a confederacy of Indians formerly located along the upper Hudson River. Also, **Mohi·can.**

ma·hog·a·ny (mə hog′ə nē), *n., pl.* **ma·hog·a·nies. 1.** any of several large tropical trees yielding a hard, reddish-brown wood used for making furniture. **2.** the wood of these trees. **3.** a reddish brown. —*adj.* **4.** made of mahogany. **5.** of the color mahogany.

Ma·hom·et (mə hom′it), *n.* another spelling of **Muhammed.**

maid (mād), *n.* **1.** a girl; young unmarried woman. **2.** a female servant.

maid·en (mād′°n), *n.* **1.** a young, unmarried woman; girl; maid. —*adj.* **2.** of, concerning, or befitting a girl or unmarried woman. **3.** made, tried, appearing, etc., for the first time: *a maiden voyage.*

maid·en·hair (mād′°n hâr′), *n.* any of several species of fern having slender, glossy stalks and delicate, finely divided fronds.

maid·en·hood (mād′°n hŏŏd′), *n.* the state or time of being a maiden.

maid′en name′, the last name of an unmarried woman.

maid′ of hon′or, 1. the chief unmarried attendant of a bride. **2.** an unmarried woman, usually of noble birth, attendant on a queen or princess.

maid·serv·ant (mād′sûr′vənt), *n.* a female servant.

mail¹ (māl), *n.* **1.** letters, packages, etc., that are sent or delivered by means of the post office. **2.** a single collection of such letters, packages, etc., as sent or delivered. **3.** Often, **mails.** the system, usually operated by the national government, for sending or delivering letters, packages, etc.; postal system. —*adj.* **4.** of or concerning mail: *mail delivery.* —*v.* **5.** to send by mail: *to mail a letter.* [from the Old French word *malle,* which comes from Germanic]

mail² (māl), *n.* flexible armor of interlinked rings. [from an Old French word, which comes from Latin *macula* "mesh, spot"]

mail·box (māl′boks′), *n.* **1.** Also, **postbox.** a public box in which mail is placed for delivery by the post office. **2.** a private box into which mail is delivered by the mailman.

Mail²

mail·man (māl′man′), *n., pl.* **mail·men.** a man who delivers mail; postman.

mail′ or′der, an order received or shipped through the mail.

maim (mām), *v.* to deprive of the use of some part of the body by wounding; cripple.

main (mān), *adj.* **1.** most important; principal: *the main idea.* —*n.* **2.** a principal pipe or duct in a system used to distribute water, gas, etc. **3.** (in literature) the open sea; high sea: *the bounding main.*

main′ clause′, a clause that can form a sentence by itself, used with one or more subordinate clauses to form a complex sentence. In the sentence *He went home when the meeting was over,* He went home is the main clause. Also, **principal clause.**

Maine (mān), *n.* a state in the NE United States. 33,-215 sq. mi. *Cap.:* Augusta.

main·land (mān′land′, -lənd), *n.* the principal land of a country, region, etc., as distinguished from nearby islands.

main·ly (mān′lē), *adv.* for the most part; chiefly; principally.

main·mast (mān′mast′, -məst), *n.* (on a sailing ship) the principal mast, usually the second one from the bow. See illus. at **quarter-deck.**

main·sail (mān′sāl′, -səl), *n.* the lowermost sail on a mainmast.

main·spring (mān′spring′), *n.* **1.** the principal spring in a mechanism: *the mainspring of a watch.* **2.** the principal cause: *the mainspring of the plan.*

main·stay (mān′stā′), *n.* **1.** a person or thing that acts as a chief support or part of something: *He is the mainstay of the group.* **2.** (on a sailing ship) the stay that secures the mainmast forward.

main·tain (mān tān′), *v.* **1.** to keep in existence; continue: *to maintain a correspondence.* **2.** to keep in good condition: *to maintain a system of highways.* **3.** to declare or state; affirm: *He maintains he saw a flying saucer.* **4.** to support in speech or argument: *He maintained his position in the debate.* **5.** to provide for the upkeep or support of; support: *to maintain a family.* [from the Old French word *maintenir,* from the Latin phrase *manū tenēre* "to hold in hand"]

main·te·nance (mān′t°nəns), *n.* **1.** the act of maintaining, or the state of being maintained: *the maintenance of friendly relations with England.* **2.** means of upkeep or support; livelihood.

maize (māz), *n.* **1.** See **corn¹** (defs. 1, 2). **2.** a pale yellow resembling the color of corn. [from the Spanish word *maíz,* which comes from West Indian]

Maj., 1. (in the military) Major. **2.** (in music) major (scale).

ma·jes·tic (mə jes′tik), *adj.* characterized by or having majesty; stately; grand: *a majestic manner; the majestic Alps.* —**ma·jes′ti·cal·ly,** *adv.*

maj·es·ty (maj′i stē), *n., pl.* for def. 3 **maj·es·ties. 1.** stately dignity; grandeur: *the majesty of the estate.* **2.** supreme greatness or authority. **3.** *(usually cap.)* a title used when speaking of or to a sovereign (usually preceded by *his, her,* or *your*): *His Majesty's Navy.*

Maj. Gen., Major General.

ma·jor (mā′jər), *n.* **1.** an officer in the U.S. Army, ranking below a lieutenant colonel and above a captain. **2.** a subject upon which a college student concentrates a large share of his efforts: *History was his major.* —*adj.* **3.** greater in size, amount, extent, or rank: *The major part of the project is completed.* **4.**

great in rank or importance: *a major question; a major artist.* **5.** of or referring to a musical interval a half step larger than the corresponding minor interval: *A to C♯ is a major third.* **6.** of or referring to a musical chord, scale, or key having one or more such intervals, reckoned from the lowest note, or tonic: *The key of A major contains C♯ instead of C♮.* —*v.* **7.** to follow a particular course of study: *He majored in chemistry at college.*

ma·jor-do·mo (mā′jər dō′mō), *n., pl.* **ma·jor-do·mos.** a man in charge of a great household.

ma′jor gen′eral, an officer in the U.S. Army, ranking below a lieutenant general and above a brigadier general.

ma·jor·i·ty (mə jôr′i tē, mə jor′i tē), *n., pl.* **ma·jor·i·ties.** **1.** the greater part or number; any number larger than half the total: *the majority of the class.* **2.** the amount by which the greater number of votes is larger than the remainder (distinguished from *plurality*): *If a vote comes out 70, 30, and 10, the winner has a majority of 30 and a plurality of 40.* **3.** the condition or time of being of full legal age.

make (māk), *v.,* **made** (mād), **mak·ing. 1.** to bring into existence by shaping or changing material, combining parts, etc.: *to make a dress.* **2.** to produce; cause to exist; bring about: *to make trouble.* **3.** to cause to be or become: *to make someone happy.* **4.** to put in the proper condition or state for use; fix; prepare: *to make a bed; to make a meal.* **5.** to cause or compel; force: *to make a dog beg.* **6.** to establish; put into existence: *to make laws.* **7.** to be equal to: *Two plus two makes four.* **8.** to deliver or utter: *to make a moving speech.* **9.** to go or travel at a certain speed: *to make 60 miles an hour.* **10.** to arrive in time for: *If you hurry, you can make the next flight.* **11.** to act or behave in a certain way: *to make merry.* —*n.* **12.** style or manner of being made; form; build. **13.** brand or kind: *What make of washing machine did you buy?* **14. make do,** to get along with less of something or with a substitute: *There's no flour, but I can make do with bread crumbs.* **15. make good, a.** to repay or make up for a shortcoming, loss, etc.: *My sweater was soiled, but the store said they'd make good the damage.* **b.** to succeed: *to make good in the poultry business.* **16. make off with,** to steal: *Who made off with my catcher's mitt?* **17. make out, a.** to fill out; complete: *to make out an application.* **b.** to see clearly; distinguish: *I can't make out the letters on the sign.* **c.** to show as being; make known as: *He tried to make me out a liar.* **d.** *Informal.* to succeed; get along: *How are you making out in the new school?* **18. make up, a.** to form; compose: *How many ounces make up a pound?* **b.** to put together; construct: *Shall I make up a new list?* **c.** to become friendly again: *Why don't you two apologize and make up?* **d.** to apply stage make-up, cosmetics, etc. **e.** make good; compensate for: *I have to make up all that work I missed.* [from the Old English word *macian*] —**mak′er,** *n.*

make-be·lieve (māk′bi lēv′), *n.* **1.** something pretended or not true: *the land of make-believe.* —*adj.* **2.** made-up or unreal: *a make-believe story.*

make·shift (māk′shift′), *n.* **1.** a temporary substitute. —*adj.* **2.** used as a makeshift: *The orange crates are makeshift tables.*

make-up (māk′up′), *n.* **1.** facial cosmetics, such as lipstick or powder, used by women. **2.** the manner of being composed or made up; composition: *the make-up of a chemical.* **3.** the physical or mental characteristics of a person: *Generosity is part of her make-up.* **4.** cosmetics, costumes, etc., used by a performer. **5.** the arrangement of the printed material in a page, book, or the like.

mal-, a prefix meaning **1.** bad or badly: *malfunction.* **2.** wrong or wrongly: *malpractice; maltreat.*

Mal·a·chi (mal′ə kī′), *n.* **1.** (in the Bible) a Hebrew prophet of the 5th century B.C. **2.** the book of the Old Testament bearing his name.

mal·ad·just·ed (mal′ə jus′tid), *adj.* poorly adjusted to one's circumstances or environment.

mal·a·dy (mal′ə dē), *n., pl.* **mal·a·dies. 1.** any disorder or disease of the body. **2.** any undesirable or disordered condition: *social maladies.* [from the Old French word *maladie,* which comes from the Latin phrase *male habitus* "ill-conditioned"]

Mal·a·gas′y Repub′lic (mal′ə gas′ē), a republic made up of Madagascar and nearby islands.

ma·lar·i·a (mə lâr′ē ə), *n.* any of a group of lingering diseases producing chills, fever, and sweating. Malaria is caused by the bite of certain tropical mosquitoes. [from an Italian word, which comes from the phrase *mala aria* "bad air"] —**ma·lar′i·al,** *adj.*

Ma·la·wi (mä lä′wē), *n.* a republic in SE Africa. 49,177 sq. mi. Former name, **Nyasaland.**

Ma·lay (mā′lā, mə lā′), *n.* **1.** a member of the Malay Peninsula and neighboring islands. **2.** a language of the Malayo-Polynesian family spoken in the Malay Peninsula and also used widely in the East Indies as a language of commerce. —*adj.* **3.** of or concerning the Malays, their country, or their language. Also, **Ma·lay·an** (mə lā′ən).

Ma·lay·a (mə lā′ə), *n.* **1.** another name for the **Malay Peninsula. 2.** the part of Malaysia on the Malay Peninsula.

Ma′lay Archipel′ago (mā′lā, mə lā′), an extensive island group SE of Asia. It includes Sumatra, Borneo, the Philippines, Sulawesi, and New Guinea. Also, **Malaysia.**

Ma·lay·o-Pol·y·ne·sian (mə lā′ō pol′ə nē′zhən), *adj.* **1.** of or belonging to a family of languages spoken in most of Oceania, the Philippines, Formosa, the East Indies, the Malay Peninsula, and Madagascar. —*n.* **2.** the Malayo-Polynesian family of languages.

Ma′lay Penin′sula, a peninsula in SE Asia, consisting of Malaya and the S part of Thailand. Also, **Malaya.**

Ma·lay·sia (mə lā′zhə), *n.* **1.** an independent federation of SE Asia, made up of many islands of the Malay Archipelago. 126,310 sq. mi. **2.** another name for the **Malay Archipelago.** —**Ma·lay′sian,** *n., adj.*

mal·con·tent (mal′kən tent′), *adj.* **1.** not happy or contented, esp. habitually; dissatisfied. —*n.* **2.** a malcontent person. —**mal′con·tent′ed·ly,** *adv.*

Mal·dives (mal′dīvz), *n.* a republic made up of 2000 small islands in the Indian Ocean, SW of Sri Lanka: formerly British. 115 sq. mi.

male (māl), *adj.* **1.** belonging to the sex that fathers young by fertilizing the female. **2.** of or referring to this sex or to men; masculine: *the male birth rate; male pride.* —*n.* **3.** a man or boy. **4.** a male animal. [from an old French word, which comes from Latin *masculus* "male, masculine"]

mal·e·dic·tion (mal′i dik′shən), *n.* a curse; evil spell: *to put a malediction on one's enemy.*

mal·e·fac·tor (mal′ə fak′tər), *n.* a person who breaks the law or does evil; wrongdoer; criminal.

ma·lev·o·lent (mə lev′ə lənt), *adj.* wishing evil to another or others; showing ill will or malice; malicious. —**ma·lev′o·lence,** *n.* —**ma·lev′o·lent·ly,** *adv.*

mal·fea·sance (mal fē′zəns), *n.* wrongdoing by a public official.

mal·for·ma·tion (mal′fôr mā′shən), *n.* a faulty formation or structure, esp. of a part of the body.

Ma·li (mä′lē), *n.* **Republic of,** a republic in W Africa. 463,500 sq. mi. *Cap.:* Bamako. —**Ma′li·an,** *n., adj.*

mal·ice (mal′is), *n.* the desire to hurt someone; ill will; spite: *a remark full of malice.*

ma·li·cious (mə lish′əs), *adj.* full of or showing malice; malevolent; spiteful: *malicious gossip.* —**ma·li′cious·ly,** *adv.*

ma·lign (mə līn′), *v.* **1.** to tell lies about; slander; defame: *He was maligned as a traitor.* —*adj.* **2.** bad; evil; harmful. **3.** malevolent; malicious. —**ma·lign′er,** *n.*

ma·lig·nant (mə lig′nənt), *adj.* **1.** deadly; tending to produce death: *a malignant tumor.* **2.** causing or wishing harm or suffering; injurious; evil: *a malignant attack on one's reputation.* —**ma·lig′nan·cy,** *n.* —**ma·lig′nant·ly,** *adv.*

ma·lig·ni·ty (mə lig′ni tē), *n.* the state or character of being evil or harmful; ill will; spite: *They feared the malignity of gossip.*

ma·lin·ger (mə ling′gər), *v.* to pretend illness, esp. to avoid duty or work. —**ma·lin′ger·er,** *n.*

mall (môl), *n.* a long, wide avenue or walk, usually lined with trees.

Mallard
(length 2 ft.)

mal·lard (mal′ərd), *n., pl.* **mal·lards** *or* **mal·lard.** a wild duck with brownish feathers, the male of which has a green head.

mal·le·a·ble (mal′ē ə bəl), *adj.* **1.** capable of being shaped by hammering, esp. of being hammered or rolled into thin sheets. **2.** easily led or influenced: *a malleable mind.* —**mal′le·a·bil′i·ty,** *n.*

mal·let (mal′it), *n.* **1.** a wooden hammer used for driving any tool with a wooden handle, such as a chisel. **2.** a long-handled wooden hammer used for striking balls in croquet or polo. **3.** a light hammer with a small, hard head used to play the marimba, xylophone, etc.

Mallet

mal·low (mal′ō), *n.* a tall herb that bears white or colored flowers having five petals.

mal·nu·tri·tion (mal′nōō trish′ən, -nyōō-), *n.* a lack of proper nutrition resulting from a badly balanced diet, not enough food, or poor digestion.

mal·prac·tice (mal prak′tis), *n.* **1.** wrong medical treatment by a doctor, resulting in harm to a patient. **2.** any wrong or improper practice, as by a lawyer, public official, etc.

malt (môlt), *n.* **1.** grain that has sprouted, esp. barley, which is used in making beer. —*v.* **2.** to change (grain) into malt. **3.** to treat or mix with malt.

Mal·ta (môl′tə), *n.* **1.** an island in the Mediterranean Sea between Sicily and Africa. 95 sq. mi. **2.** a republic on Malta and two nearby smaller islands, formerly a British colony. 122 sq. mi. —**Mal·tese** (môl tēz′), *n., adj.*

malt′ed milk′ (môl′tid), **1.** a powder made of dried milk and malt. **2.** Also, **malt′ed.** a drink made by dissolving this powder in milk, often with the addition of ice cream and flavoring.

Mal′tese cat′, a bluish-gray breed of cat.

Mal′tese cross′, a cross having arms of equal length that widen outward, with notches at their ends. See illus. at **cross.**

mal·treat (mal trēt′), *v.* to treat badly; handle roughly: *to maltreat a pet.*

mam·ma (mä′mə), *n. Informal.* mother. Also, **ma′ma.**

mam·mal (mam′əl), *n.* a member of a group of related animals that includes human beings, all four-legged animals, seals, and whales. Mammals are distinguished by suckling their young, having a backbone, and having a body at least partly covered with hair.

mam·mon (mam′ən), *n.* wealth regarded as a cause of greed and other evils. [from the Aramaic word *māmōnā* "riches"]

Mammoth
(9 ft. high at shoulder)

mam·moth (mam′əth), *n.* **1.** a large, extinct, elephantlike animal that had a hairy skin and long, curved tusks. —*adj.* **2.** huge; enormous: *They have a mammoth house.* [from the Russian word *mamont*]

mam·my (mam′ē), *n., pl.* **mam·mies. 1.** *Informal.* mother. **2.** a Negro woman in the South who takes care of the young children of a white family.

man (man), *n., pl.* **men** (men). **1.** an adult male person, as distinguished from a woman or a boy. **2.** the human race; mankind: *the history of man.* **3.** an individual: *It was every man for himself. Give a man a chance.* **4.** a husband: *man and wife.* **5.** a male servant, employee, etc.: *My man will help me.* **6.** a manly male person: *The experience made a man of him.* **7.** one of the pieces used in playing certain games, as chess or checkers. —*v.,* **manned, man·ning. 8.** to supply with men: *to man a job.* **9.** to take one's place or post at: *to man a gun.* **10. to a man,** without exception; everyone: *We're behind you to a man.* [from Old English] —**man′like′,** *adj.*

-man, a suffix used to form nouns meaning **1.** native or inhabitant of: *Chinaman; Englishman.* **2.** a person engaged in some work: *postman; cattleman.*

Man., Manitoba (Canada).

man·a·cle (man′ə kəl), *n.* **1.** a shackle for the hand; handcuff. —*v.,* **man·a·cled, man·a·cling. 2.** to handcuff: *to manacle a criminal.* **3.** to hamper or restrain: *He was manacled by fear.*

man·age (man′ij), *v.,* **man·aged, man·ag·ing. 1.** to succeed in bringing about: *He managed to save enough money.* **2.** to have charge of: *to manage a business.* **3.** to guide the behavior of: *He could not manage the young children.* **4.** to handle or control: *He cannot manage the car.* **5.** to succeed under difficulty: *How will she manage with her husband gone?*

man·age·a·ble (man′i jə bəl), *adj.* capable of being managed or dealt with: *a manageable task.* —**man′age·a·bil′i·ty,** *n.* —**man′age·a·bly,** *adv.*

man·age·ment (man′ij mənt), *n.* **1.** the act or skill of managing: *the management of a business.* **2.** the persons who direct a business: *Management favored the policy.*

man·ag·er (man′i jər), *n.* **1.** a person who manages a team, business, etc.: *the sales manager.* **2.** a person who manages a household: *His wife is a good manager.* —**man′ag·er·ship′,** *n.*

man·a·ge·ri·al (man′i jēr′ē əl), *adj.* having to do with management: *managerial duties.*

Ma·na·gua (mə nä′gwə), *n.* the capital city of Nicaragua, in the W part.

man-at-arms (man′ət-ärmz′), *n., pl.* **men-at-arms** (men′ət ärmz′). **1.** a soldier. **2.** a heavily armed soldier on horseback in the Middle Ages.

Manatee
(length 8 to 13 ft.)

man·a·tee (man′ə tē′, man′ə tē′), *n.* a large sea mammal of Florida, the West Indies, and the Gulf of Mexico, having two front flippers and a spoon-shaped tail; sea cow.

Man·ches·ter (man′ches′tər, man′chi stər), *n.* a city in NW England.

Man·chu (man chōō′), *n., pl.* **Man·chus** or **Man·chu. 1.** a member of a Mongolian people of Manchuria who conquered China and ruled that country from 1644 to 1912. **2.** the language of the Manchus. —*adj.* **3.** of or belonging to the Manchus, their country, or their language.

Man·chu·ri·a (man chōor′ē ə), *n.* a region in NE China. —**Man·chu′ri·an,** *n., adj.*

Man·da·lay (man′dəlā′, man′dəlā′), *n.* a city in central Burma.

man·da·rin (man′də rin), *n.* **1.** a man high in public office in China under the emperors. **2.** a kind of orange having a skin that peels easily. [from the Portuguese word *mandarim,* which comes from Sanskrit *mantrin* "councillor." The fruit is so named from the color of a mandarin's robes]

Man·da·rin (man′də rin), *n.* the Chinese language in its official and most widely used form.

man·date (man′dāt, man′dit), *n.* **1.** control over a territory formerly granted by the League of Nations to a member country. **2.** the territory that is controlled. **3.** a vote that expresses the will of the people in an election: *a mandate favoring the governor's policies.* **4.** any official command: *a royal mandate.* —*v.* (man′dāt), **man·dat·ed, man·dat·ing. 5.** to put (a territory) under a mandate. **6.** to decree by a law or command: *to mandate a change in policy.*

man·da·to·ry (man′də tôr′ē), *adj.* ordered or required.

man·di·ble (man′də bəl), *n.* **1.** the bone of the lower jaw. **2.** either the upper or the lower part of a bird's bill. **3.** either of the biting mouthparts of an insect.

man·do·lin (man′dəlin, man′-dəlin′), *n.* a musical instrument having a pear-shaped body and strings that are plucked with a plectrum.

Mandolin

man·drake (man′drāk), *n.* a European herb that has a forked root formerly used in medicine.

man·drill (man′dril), *n.* a large, ferocious-looking baboon of W Africa, the male of which has bright blue and red markings on its face.

mane (mān), *n.* the long hair that grows on or around the neck of certain animals, such as the horse or lion.

ma·neu·ver (mə nōō′vər), *n.* **1.** a planned and controlled movement of troops, warships, etc. **2.** a skillful or crafty move or way of acting: *His maneuvers got him quick advancement.* —*v.,* **ma·neu·vered, ma·neu·ver·ing. 3.** to change the position of (troops,

Mandrill
(20 in. high at shoulder; length 3 ft.)

warships, etc.) by a maneuver. **4.** to accomplish or control by maneuvers: *He maneuvered his way into power.* **5.** to perform maneuvers: *Ships were maneuvering offshore.* **6.** to plot or scheme. —**ma·neu′ver·a·ble,** *adj.* —**ma·neu′ver·a·bil′i·ty,** *n.*

man·ful (man′fəl), *adj.* having or showing a manly spirit; bold; courageous: *a manful fight.* —**man′ful·ly,** *adv.* —**man′ful·ness,** *n.*

man·ga·nese (mañg′gə nēz′, mañg′gə nēs′), *n.* *Chem.* a hard, brittle metallic element used as an alloy in steel. *Symbol:* Mn

mange (mānj), *n.* any of various diseases of animals that cause loss of hair and the formation of scabs on the skin.

man·ger (mān′jər), *n.* a box or trough from which horses or cattle eat.

man·gle[1] (mañg′gəl), *v.,* **man·gled, man·gling. 1.** to cut, tear, crush, twist, etc., in such a way as to harm or destroy: *The lion mangled his trainer's hand.* **2.** to spoil or botch: *His speech was mangled by stuttering.* [from the early French word *mangler,* which comes perhaps from Greek *manganon* "engine of war"]

man·gle[2] (mañg′gəl), *n.* **1.** a machine for ironing sheets, tablecloths, etc. —*v.,* **man·gled, man·gling. 2.** to smooth with a mangle. [from the Dutch word *mangel,* which comes from Latin *manganum,* from Greek *manganon* "engine of war"]

man·go (mañg′gō), *n., pl.* **man·goes** *or* **man·gos. 1.** the juicy, oblong fruit of a tropical tree, eaten ripe or preserved or pickled. **2.** the tree itself.

man·grove (mañg′grōv, man′grōv), *n.* any tropical tree that sends roots down from its branches, forming dense thickets, esp. in swampy areas.

man·gy (mān′jē), *adj.,* **man·gi·er, man·gi·est.** having, caused by, or like mange. —**man′gi·ness,** *n.*

man·han·dle (man′han′dəl), *v.,* **man·han·dled, man·han·dling.** to handle roughly: *The spy was manhandled by the soldiers.*

Man·hat·tan (man hat′ᵊn, mən hat′ᵊn), *n.* **1.** an island at the mouth of the Hudson River. **2.** a borough of New York City on this island: commercial center.

man·hole (man′hōl′), *n.* a hole, usually with a cover, over the entrance to a sewer, drain, etc.

man·hood (man′hŏŏd), *n.* **1.** the state of being a man. **2.** the qualities a man should have, such as courage, strength, etc. **3.** men as a group: *the manhood of England.*

ma·ni·a (mā′nē ə), *n.* **1.** a form of insanity or mental disorder characterized by extreme excitement or violence. **2.** great enthusiasm for something: *a mania for collecting records.*

ma·ni·ac (mā′nē ak′), *n.* an insane person; madman; lunatic.

ma·ni·a·cal (mə nī′ə kəl), *adj.* of or referring to mania or maniacs: *violent, maniacal behavior.* —**ma·ni′a·cal·ly,** *adv.*

man·i·cure (man′ə kyŏŏr′), *n.* **1.** treatment of the hands, esp. to trim and shape the fingernails. —*v.,* **man·i·cured, man·i·cur·ing. 2.** to give a manicure to. —**man′i·cur′ist,** *n.*

man·i·fest (man′ə fest′), *adj.* **1.** easy to see or under-stand; clear; obvious; evident. —*v.* **2.** to make manifest; show plainly: *He manifested his approval with a smile.* **3.** to prove; put beyond doubt or question: *This action manifests his loyalty.* —*n.* **4.** a list of cargo, passengers, etc., carried by a ship or airplane. —**man′i·fest′ly,** *adv.*

man·i·fes·ta·tion (man′ə fes tā′shən), *n.* **1.** the act of manifesting; appearance or indication: *the manifestation of a disease.* **2.** a public demonstration: *a huge manifestation for a political candidate.*

man·i·fes·to (man′ə fes′tō), *n., pl.* **man·i·fes·toes,** a public announcement by a government, political party, etc., setting forth its opinions, views, or plans.

man·i·fold (man′ə fōld′), *adj.* **1.** of many kinds; numerous and varied: *manifold duties.* **2.** having many different parts, sections, etc.: *a manifold program for clearing slums.* —*n.* **3.** a copy, as of something written. **4.** a pipe with several openings by means of which a liquid or gas is either collected or distributed: *An automobile engine has an intake manifold and an exhaust manifold.* —**man′i·fold′ly,** *adv.*

man·i·kin (man′ə kin), *n.* **1.** a little man; dwarf. **2.** another spelling of **mannequin.**

Ma·ni·la (mə nil′ə), *n.* a seaport and the capital city of the Philippines, on S Luzon.

ma·nip·u·late (mə nip′yə lāt′), *v.,* **ma·nip·u·lat·ed, ma·nip·u·lat·ing. 1.** to handle, manage, or use, esp. with skill: *to manipulate the controls of a machine.* **2.** to manage or influence by artful or crafty means: *He uses flattery to manipulate people.* **3.** to tamper with or change (accounts, figures, etc.) for one's own purpose: *to manipulate an expense account.* —**ma·nip′u·la′tion,** *n.* —**ma·nip′u·la′tor,** *n.*

Man·i·to·ba (man′i tō′bə), *n.* a province in central Canada. 246,512 sq. mi. *Cap.:* Winnipeg.

man·kind (man′kīnd′ *for def. 1;* man′kīnd′ *for def. 2*), *n.* **1.** the human race. **2.** men, as distinguished from women.

man·ly (man′lē), *adj.,* **man·li·er, man·li·est. 1.** having the qualities desirable in a man: *a manly leader.* **2.** suitable for a man: *manly sports.* —**man′li·ness,** *n.*

man-made (man′mād′), *adj.* produced, formed, or made by man; artificial: *a man-made lake.*

man·na (man′ə), *n.* (in the Bible) the miraculous food that fell from heaven to feed the Israelites in the wilderness.

man·ne·quin (man′ə kin), *n.* **1.** a model of the human figure used for displaying clothing and by tailors, dress designers, etc., for fitting or making clothes. **2.** a girl or woman employed to model clothes. Also, **manikin.**

man·ner (man′ər), *n.* **1.** a way in which something happens or is done: *the French manner of cooking asparagus.* **2.** a way of acting or behaving: *His manner showed embarrassment.* **3. manners, a.** a way of behaving with people, judged by rules of politeness: *It is bad manners to blow on your soup.* **b.** the customs, ways of living, etc., of a people, class, etc.: *the manners of the English.* **4.** *(used as pl.)* kind or sort: *In the summer we play all manner of games.*

man·ner·ism (man′ə riz′əm), *n.* a peculiar or affected action, way of behaving, etc.: *He has a mannerism of coughing before he speaks.*

man·ner·ly (man′ər lē), *adj.* **1.** having or showing good manners; polite: *mannerly behavior.* —*adv* **2.** courteously; politely. —**man′ner·li·ness,** *n.*

man·nish (man′ish), *adj.* (of a woman) resembling a man in appearance or behavior: *She wears mannish clothes.* —**man′nish·ly,** *adv.* —**man′nish·ness,** *n.*

man-of-war (man′əv wôr′), *n., pl.* **men-of-war** (men′əv wôr′). a warship.

man·or (man′ər), *n.* **1.** an estate belonging to a lord in the Middle Ages. **2.** the house on such an estate. **3.** any large, imposing house; mansion. —**ma·no·ri·al** (mə nôr′ē əl), *adj.*

man·sard (man′särd), *n.* a roof having four sides, each with two slopes, the lower one steep, the upper one nearly flat. Also, **man′sard roof′.**

man·sion (man′shən), *n.* a large, impressive house.

man·slaugh·ter (man′slô′tər), *n.* the killing of a human being by another, esp. without malice or premeditation, as in an accident.

man·tel (man′t'l), *n.* **1.** a shelf above a fireplace. **2.** the brick, stone, etc., that frames and decorates a fireplace. Also, **man·tel·piece** (man′t'l pēs′).

man·til·la (man tē′ə, man tē′yə), *n.* a silk or lace head scarf, usually covering the shoulders, worn esp. in Spain and Latin America.

Mantilla

man·tis (man′tis), *n.* any of several large insects that are related to the grasshopper. They feed on other insects and often hold their forelegs raised as if in prayer. Also, **praying mantis.** See also **walking stick.** [from a Greek word meaning "prophet"]

man·tle (man′t'l), *n.* **1.** a loose, sleeveless cloak. **2.** something that covers or hides: *the mantle of darkness.* **3.** a fireproof device placed over a gas jet, kerosene wick, etc., that gives off light when heated. **4.** the part of the earth, about 1800 miles thick, between the crust and the core. —*v.,* **man·tled, man·tling. 5.** to cover with or as if with a mantle: *Mist mantled the meadow.*

*Mantis
(length 2 in.)*

man·u·al (man′yōō əl), *adj.* **1.** operated by hand: *a manual gearshift.* **2.** done with or by use of the hands: *manual labor.* —*n.* **3.** a small book, esp. one that gives information or instruction: *a spelling manual.* **4.** drill in handling a rifle or other weapon. —**man′u·al·ly,** *adv.*

man′ual train′ing, training in a handicraft, esp. woodworking.

man·u·fac·ture (man′yə fak′chər), *v.,* **man·u·fac·**

tured, **man·u·fac·tur·ing. 1.** to make (objects or materials), esp. by machinery and in large amounts. **2.** to make up or invent: *to manufacture excuses.* —*n.* **3.** the making of goods and materials, esp. by machinery and on a large scale. **4.** something manufactured: *a tariff on manufactures.* **5.** the making of anything: *the manufacture of blood corpuscles.* —**man′u·fac′tur·er,** *n.*

ma·nure (mə nŏŏr′, -nyŏŏr′), *n.* **1.** a substance, esp. animal excrement, used as a fertilizer. —*v.,* **ma·nured, ma·nur·ing. 2.** to treat or spread with manure.

man·u·script (man′yə skript′), *n.* **1.** the original text of an author's work, written by hand or typewritten, that is submitted to a publisher. **2.** writing, as distinguished from print. **3.** a book or document written by hand before the invention of printing.

Manx′ cat′ (mangks), a tailless variety of domestic cat. [named after the Isle of *Man,* off the W coast of Britain, where first bred]

man·y (men′ē), *adj.,* **more** (môr), **most** (mōst). **1.** forming a large number: *many people.* **2.** noting each one of a large number (usually fol. by *a* or *an*): *It rained for many a day.* —*n.* **3.** a large but indefinite number of persons or things: *A great many of the cattle died.* —*pron.* **4.** many persons or things: *Many left early.*

*Manx cat
(length to 18 in.)*

Ma·o·ri (mä′ô rē, mou′rē), *n., pl.* **Ma·o·ris** or **Ma·o·ri. 1.** a member of a brown-skinned Polynesian people of New Zealand. **2.** the Polynesian language of the Maoris. —*adj.* **3.** of or concerning the Maoris or their language.

Mao Tse-tung (mou′ tsə tōŏng′), 1893–1976, Chinese communist leader.

map (map), *n.* **1.** a drawing, usually flat, of an area on the earth's surface, showing cities, rivers, oceans, etc. **2.** a drawing of an area of the sky, showing stars, planets, etc. —*v.,* **mapped, map·ping. 3.** to make a map of or show on a map: *Early navigators mapped the new lands.* **4.** to sketch or plan (usually fol. by *out*): *to map out a new career.*

ma·ple (mā′pəl), *n.* **1.** a large, spreading shade tree, some varieties of which have a sweet sap used for making syrup. **2.** the light-colored wood of this tree, used for making furniture.

mar (mär), *v.,* **marred, mar·ring.** to spoil, damage, or disfigure to a certain extent: *The surface was marred by stains. The performance was marred by catcalls.*

Mar., March.

mar·a·bou (mar′ə bōō′), *n.* any of several large storks, having under the wings and tail soft, downy feathers that are used in millinery and for making a furlike trimming or material.

*Marabou
(length 5 ft.)*

ma·rac·a (mə rä′kə), *n.* a rattle made of a gourd filled with seeds or pebbles, used, often in pairs, as a rhythm instrument in Latin-American music.

mar′a·schi′no cher′ry (mar′ə skē′nō, mar′ə shē′nō), a cherry preserved in a sweet, red syrup, used to garnish drinks, ice cream, cakes, etc.

mar·a·thon (mar′ə thon′, mar′ə thən), *n.* 1. a long-distance foot race, esp. one measuring 26 miles 385 yards. 2. any long contest to test endurance: *a dance marathon.* [so called after the famous 26-mile run of the messenger Pheidippides from Marathon, a plain in SE Greece, to Athens bearing news of the Greek victory over the Persians in 490 B.C.]

ma·raud·er (mə rôd′ər), *n.* a person who raids for plunder; pirate.

mar·ble (mär′bəl), *n.* 1. a smooth, hard stone sometimes white, sometimes mottled or veined, used in building and in sculpture. 2. a little ball made of glass, agate, etc., for use in games. 3. **marbles,** a game for children using these little balls. —*adj.* 4. made of marble: *marble statues.* —*v.,* **mar·bled, mar·bling.** 5. to color or stain like streaked marble: *The covers of the book were marbled.*

march¹ (märch), *v.* 1. to walk or cause to walk with regular and measured steps. —*n.* 2. the act of marching. 3. the distance covered in marching. 4. any progress: *the march of science.* 5. a piece of music for accompanying marching. [from the Old French word *marchier* "to tread"]

march² (märch), *n.* a tract of land along the border of a country; frontier. [from the Old English word *gemearc* "boundary"]

March (märch), *n.* the third month of the year, having 31 days. [from the Old French word *Marche,* which comes from the Latin phrase *Martius mēnsis* "month of Mars"]

mar·chion·ess (mär′shə nis, mär′shə nes′), *n.* 1. the wife or widow of a marquis. 2. a lady holding in her own right a rank equal to that of a marquis.

Mar·co Po·lo (mär′kō pō′lō). See **Polo, Marco.**

Mar·di gras (mär′dē grä′), the day before Lent, often celebrated as a day of carnival.

mare (mâr), *n.* a female horse.

mar·ga·rine (mär′jər in), *n.* a spread like butter, made of vegetable oils and milk; oleomargarine.

mar·gin (mär′jin), *n.* 1. a border or edge: *the margin of a wood.* 2. the space around the printed matter on a page: *to write in the margins of a book.* 3. an extra amount, as of time, money, etc., beyond what is actually needed: *Allow a margin of safety.*

mar·gin·al (mär′jə nəl), *adj.* 1. referring to a margin: *marginal width.* 2. situated on the border or edge: *the marginal territories of a country.* 3. written or printed in the margin of a page: *marginal notes.* —**mar′gin·al·ly,** *adv.*

mar·gue·rite (mär′gə rēt′), *n.* 1. a European daisy. 2. any of several flowers resembling daisies, esp. a white chrysanthemum having a yellow center.

mar·i·gold (mar′ə gōld′), *n.* a plant with strong-smelling leaves that bears orange or yellow flowers.

ma·ri·jua·na (mar′ə wä′nə), *n.* an Indian hemp plant whose leaves and flowers are extremely intoxicating when dried and taken as a drug. Also, **ma·ri·hua′na.**

ma·rim·ba (mə rim′bə), *n.* a musical instrument consisting of a row of wooden bars that are struck with light mallets. The bars often have resonators under them to increase the tone. [from West African]

Marimba

ma·ri·na (mə rē′nə), *n.* a small harbor or part of a harbor where sailboats and motorboats may be docked and serviced.

mar·i·nate (mar′ə nāt′), *v.,* **mar·i·nat·ed, mar·i·nat·ing.** to let (food) stand in a liquid, such as a mixture of vinegar, oil, and seasonings, before cooking or serving.

ma·rine (mə rēn′), *adj.* 1. of or referring to the sea; living or growing in the sea: *A whale is a marine animal. Seaweed is a marine plant.* 2. referring to shipping or navigation: *marine transportation.* 3. of or referring to the marines. —*n.* 4. *(sometimes cap.)* a member of the U.S. Marine Corps.

Marine′ Corps′, the United States Marine Corps.

mar·i·ner (mar′ə nər), *n.* a sailor or navigator.

mar·i·on·ette (mar′ē ə net′), *n.* a puppet with jointed limbs, operated from above by pulling strings attached to various parts of its body. [from the French word *marionnette,* which comes from *Marion,* a diminutive form of *Marie* "Mary"]

mar·i·tal (mar′i təl), *adj.* of or referring to marriage: *marital happiness.* —**mar′i·tal·ly,** *adv.*

mar·i·time (mar′i tīm′), *adj.* 1. of or referring to the sea, navigation, or seagoing vessels: *maritime laws.* 2. living in the sea; marine: *maritime vegetation.* 3. bordering on or making a living from the sea: *England is a maritime country.*

Mar′itime Prov′inces, the Canadian provinces of Nova Scotia, New Brunswick, and Prince Edward Island.

mar·jo·ram (mär′jər əm), *n.* a plant similar to mint, used in cooking as a seasoning.

mark¹ (märk), *n.* 1. a line, spot, scar, or dent appearing on a surface: *inky marks on a sheet of paper.* 2. a sign or object used in measuring, finding one's way, etc. 3. a label, sign, etc., used in place of a signature, for punctuation, to show ownership or manufacture, etc. 4. some outward sign that shows one's feeling, state of mind, etc.: *to bow as a mark of respect.* 5. a grade given as a rating of a pupil's conduct, study, etc., or a symbol, such as a letter or number, showing this: *low marks in school; a mark of A.* 6. the required standard for something: *His performance is below the mark.* 7. a goal or target: *The arrow hit the mark.* 8. an object of scorn, swindling, etc.: *His innocence made him an easy mark for thieves.* 9. the starting line of a race on foot: *On your mark, get set, go!* —*v.* 10. to be an important feature of: *His work is* marked by great care for detail. **11.** to put a mark or marks on: *The cover was marked with stains.* **12.** to put a figure, tag, or sign on (an object) to show price, brand name, etc. **13.** to trace or form by or as if by marks (often fol. by *out*): *to mark out a plan of attack.* **14.** to point out or show by or as if by marks: *to mark names on a list.* **15.** to single out; destine: *He was marked for success.* **16.** to make known; indicate: *He marked his respect with a bow.* **17.** to give heed or attention to: *Mark my words!* **18. make one's mark,** to achieve success, one's ambition, etc.: *He made his mark in the feed business.* **19. mark down,** to reduce in price: *In January they mark down all linens.* **20. mark off,** to mark the dimensions or boundaries of: *We marked off the limits of our backyard.* **21. mark up, a.** to mark with notes, scribbles, etc.; deface: *If you mark up that book you won't get another one.* **b.** to raise the price of: *You should have bought a kite before they were marked up.* [from the Old English word *mearc* "mark, sign"]

mark² (märk), *n.* a basic unit of money in Germany. [from the medieval Latin word *marca* "unit of weight," which itself comes from a Germanic word related to *mark¹*]

Mark (märk), *n.* **1.** (in the Bible) one of the four Evangelists, believed to have written the Gospel of St. Mark. **2.** the second Gospel of the New Testament.

marked (märkt), *adj.* **1.** having a mark or marks: *The book has a marked cover.* **2.** striking; outstanding: *a marked success.* **3.** watched closely as an object of suspicion or vengeance: *Now that his identity is known, the murderer is a marked man.* —**mark·ed·ly** (mär′kid lē), *adv.* —**mark′ed·ness,** *n.*

mark·er (mär′kər), *n.* **1.** a person or thing that marks. **2.** something used as a mark or indication: *a marker to show the spot where something is buried.*

mar·ket (mär′kit), *n.* **1.** a meeting of people for buying or selling. **2.** a place used for buying and selling. **3.** a store for the sale of food: *a vegetable market.* **4.** trade in a particular item: *the coffee market.* **5.** demand for something that is for sale: *There is no market for ice skates in tropical countries.* **6.** a place where or the group of people to whom goods can be sold: *coffee for the American market.* —*v.* **7.** to buy or sell in a market: *They marketed their cattle. On Saturdays we market for the weekend.* **8. in the market for,** ready or seeking to buy: *Dad is in the market for a station wagon.* **9. on the market,** for sale; available: *Pumpkins are usually on the market in October.* [from an Old English word, which comes from Latin *mercātus* "trade, market"]

mar·ket·a·ble (mär′ki tə bəl), *adj.* fit to be sold or sold without difficulty: *a marketable used car.*

mar·ket·place (mär′kit plās′), *n.* **1.** a building or area where goods are bought and sold. **2.** the world of commerce: *It's hard to earn a living in the marketplace.* Also, **mar′ket place′.**

mark·ing (mär′kiŋ), *n.* **1.** a mark, or a number or pattern of marks: *The bird has black and white markings on its wings.* **2.** the act of a person or thing that marks: *the marking of papers.*

marks·man (märks′mən), *n., pl.* **marks·men.** a person skilled in shooting at targets; one who shoots well. —**marks′man·ship′,** *n.*

Mark Twain. See **Twain, Mark.**

mar·lin (mär′lin), *n., pl.* **mar·lins** *or* **mar·lin.** a large saltwater game fish whose upper jaw is formed into a pointed spike.

mar·line·spike (mär′lin spīk′), *n.* a pointed iron tool used in separating strands of rope in splicing. Also, **mar′lin·spike′.**

mar·ma·lade (mär′mə lād′), *n.* a jellylike preserve of fruit, esp. of oranges, that contains bits of rind.

Mar·ma·ra (mär′mə rə), *n.* **Sea of,** a sea between European and Asian Turkey, connecting the Bosporus and the Dardanelles. 4300 sq. mi.

mar·mo·set (mär′mə zet′), *n.* any of several small South and Central American monkeys, having soft fur and a long tail.

mar·mot (mär′mət), *n.* **1.** any of several bushy-tailed, stocky rodents, such as the woodchuck. **2.** any of certain related animals, such as the prairie dog.

ma·roon¹ (mə rōōn′), *n.* **1.** a dark brownish red. —*adj.* **2.** of the color maroon. [from the French word *marron,* which comes from Italian *marrone* "chestnut"]

Marmoset
(total length
10 in.)

ma·roon² (mə rōōn′), *v.* **1.** to put ashore and leave on an uninhabited island or coast: *The pirates marooned their captives.* **2.** to leave without money, help, hope, etc.: *He was marooned in a strange town.* [from the American Spanish word *cimarrón* "wild"]

mar·quee (mär kē′), *n.* a small roof covering the entrance to a theater, hotel, apartment house, etc.

mar·quess (mär′kwis), *n.* another spelling of **mar·quis.**

Mar·quette (mär ket′), *n.* **Jacques** (zhäk), 1637–1675, French Jesuit missionary and explorer in America.

mar·quis (mär′kwis, mär kē′), *n., pl.* **mar·quis·es** *or* **mar·quis** (mär kēz′). a nobleman ranking just below a duke and above an earl or count. Also, **marquess.** [from a French word, which comes from a Provençal word meaning "ruler of a border district"]

Marquee

mar·quise (mär kēz′), *n.* **1.** the wife or widow of a marquis. **2.** a lady holding in her own right a rank equal to that of a marquis.

mar·riage (mar′ij), *n.* **1.** the state of being married:

a happy marriage. **2.** the ceremony in which a man and woman are married: *Many guests were present at the marriage.* **3.** any close and harmonious relationship: *the marriage of health and beauty.*

mar·riage·a·ble (mar′i jə bəl), *adj.* old enough or suitable for marriage: *of a marriageable age.*

mar·ried (mar′ēd), *adj.* **1.** joined in wedlock; wedded. **2.** of or concerning marriage: *married life.*

mar·row (mar′ō), *n.* **1.** the soft, fatty material that fills the hollow interiors of bones. **2.** the main or central part: *the marrow of the problem.*

mar·ry (mar′ē), *v.*, **mar·ried, mar·ry·ing. 1.** to take as a husband or wife: *She married John.* **2.** to enter into marriage; wed: *When are you planning to marry?* **3.** to join in wedlock: *The priest married them.* **4.** to give in marriage (often fol. by *off*): *They married off their children.* **5.** to join together closely: *a case of beauty married to brains.* [from the Old French word *marier,* which comes from Latin *marītāre*]

Mars (märz), *n.* **1.** (in Roman mythology) the god of war: identified with the Greek god Ares. **2.** the planet fourth in order from the sun, noted for its reddish color. Mars has a diameter of 4230 miles and an average distance from the sun of 142,000,000 miles.

Mar·sa·la (mär sä′lə), *n.* **1.** a seaport in W Sicily. **2.** a sweet, dark wine made near there.

Mar·seil·laise (mär′sā ez′), *n.* the French national anthem, written in 1792.

Mar·seilles (mär sā′), *n.* a port city in SE France.

marsh (märsh), *n.* low, wet land; swamp; bog.

mar·shal (mär′shəl), *n.* **1.** a U.S. federal officer with duties similar to those of a sheriff. **2.** a police or fire chief in some communities. **3.** a person in charge of ceremonies, parades, etc. **4.** a military officer of the highest rank in France and certain other foreign countries. —*v.*, **mar·shaled** *or* **mar·shalled; mar·shaling** *or* **mar·shal·ling. 5.** to arrange in proper order: *to marshal facts.* **6.** to array (troops): *to marshal an army for battle.* [from an Old French word, which comes from a Germanic word meaning "groom," later "master of the stables"]

Mar·shall (mär′shəl), *n.* Thomas R., 1854–1925, 28th Vice President of the U.S. 1913–1921.

Mar′shall Is′lands, a group of 24 atolls in the N Pacific, now under U.S. trusteeship. 74 sq. mi.

marsh·land (märsh′land′), *n.* a region or area that has marshes, swamps, bogs, or the like.

marsh′ mal′low, a marsh plant having pink flowers.

marsh·mal·low (märsh′mel′ō), *n.* a soft, white, spongelike candy made chiefly from gelatin and sugar.

marsh·y (mär′shē), *adj.*, **marsh·i·er, marsh·i·est. 1.** consisting of a marsh; soft and wet; boggy: *marshy lowlands.* **2.** referring to a marsh: *marshy plants.* —**marsh′i·ness,** *n.*

mar·su·pi·al (mär soo′pē əl), *adj.* any of a group of animals, including kangaroos, opossums, etc., the female of which has a pouch for carrying her young.

mart (märt), *n.* a market or marketplace; trade center: *a mart for household goods.*

mar·ten (mär′t⁹n, mär′tin), *n., pl.* **mar·tens** *or* **mar·ten. 1.** any of several slender, usually tree-dwelling animals, having a long, glossy coat and a bushy tail. **2.** the fur of such an animal, usually dark brown in color.

Marten
(total length 2½ ft.)

Mar·tha (mär′thə), *n.* (in the Bible) the sister of Lazarus and Mary.

mar·tial (mär′shəl), *adj.* **1.** fond of war; warlike; brave: *Ancient Rome was a martial state.* **2.** referring to or suitable for war: *martial conquests; martial music.* **3.** befitting a warrior: *a martial stride.*

mar′tial law′, the law imposed by military forces when civil authority has broken down.

Mar·tian (mär′shən), *adj.* **1.** of or concerning the planet Mars. —*n.* **2.** a being that supposedly inhabits the planet Mars.

mar·tin (mär′t⁹n, mär′tin), *n.* any of several birds of the swallow family.

mar·ti·net (mär′t⁹net′), *n.* a person who practices very strict discipline, forcing others to obey rules without question: *Their father was a martinet.* [named after Jean *Martinet* (d. 1672), French general who invented a system of drill]

Mar·ti·nique (mär′t⁹nēk′), *n.* an island in the E West Indies: a department of France. 425 sq. mi.

mar·tyr (mär′tər), *n.* **1.** a person who chooses to suffer or die rather than give up his religion. **2.** a person who suffers or dies for any cause: *a patriotic martyr.* **3.** a person who undergoes great suffering, or one who seeks sympathy by pretending to suffer. —*v.* **4.** to make a martyr of: *The ancient Romans martyred many early Christians.*

mar·tyr·dom (mär′tər dəm), *n.* **1.** the suffering or death of a martyr. **2.** extreme suffering; torment.

mar·vel (mär′vəl), *n.* **1.** a person or thing that causes wonder, admiration, or astonishment: *The picture is a marvel of beauty.* —*v.*, **mar·veled** *or* **mar·velled; mar·vel·ing** *or* **mar·vel·ling. 2.** to be struck with wonder: *We marveled at the beautiful sculpture.*

mar·vel·ous (mär′və ləs), *adj.* **1.** arousing wonder, admiration, or astonishment: *a marvelous discovery.* **2.** superb or excellent; great: *We had a marvelous time at the party.* Also, *esp. British,* **mar′vel·lous.** —**mar′vel·ous·ly, mar′vel·lous·ly,** *adv.*

Marx (märks), *n.* Karl, 1818–1883, German socialist and political theorist: originator of communist doctrines. —**Marx′i·an,** *adj.*

Marx·ism (märk′siz əm), *n.* the theories and teachings of Karl Marx, esp. that governments support the few people who are rich against the many workers who are poor, and that there must be a revolution of the workers to bring about a new and better socialist, or communist, society.

Marx·ist (märk′sist), *n.* **1.** a person who believes in or supports Marxism. —*adj.* **2.** of or concerning Marxism: *Marxist political doctrines.*

Mar·y (mâr′ē), *n.* the Virgin Mary.

Mar·y·land (mer′ə lənd), *n.* a state in the E United States, on the Atlantic coast. 10,577 sq. mi. *Cap.:* Annapolis.

Mar′y, Queen′ of Scots′, 1542–1587, queen of Scotland 1542–1567: beheaded by order of Queen Elizabeth I.

mas·car·a (ma skar′ə), *n.* a dark make-up used to color the eyelashes and sometimes the eyebrows.

mas·cot (mas′kot, mas′kət), *n.* a person, animal, or thing supposed to bring good luck: *The collie was the team's mascot.*

mas·cu·line (mas′kyə lin), *adj.* **1.** having the qualities of a man; manly: *a masculine voice.* **2.** of or for boys or men: *masculine names; masculine sports.* **3.** (in grammar) having the gender of nouns and pronouns that refer to male persons or animals, or to things considered to be male. In the sentences *John lost his hat* and *The enemy did not protect his flank,* the words *John* and *enemy* are treated as masculine nouns.

ma·ser (mā′zər), *n.* a device, operating on the principle of the laser, that amplifies microwaves.

mash (mash), *n.* **1.** a soft, pulpy mass: *a mash of apples and cranberries.* **2.** a mixture of boiled grain, bran, meal, etc., fed warm to horses and cattle. **3.** crushed malt or meal soaked in hot water and used in brewing beer. —*v.* **4.** to crush: *The door mashed his finger.* **5.** to crush into a soft mass: *to mash potatoes.*

mask (mask), *n.* **1.** a covering for all or part of the face as disguise, for protection, etc.: *a welder's mask; a Halloween mask.* **2.** anything that disguises or conceals: *Her smile was a mask for sadness.* **3.** a masquerade. **4.** a copy of a person's face, esp. one cast in a mold made on the face. —*v.* **5.** to cover with or put on a mask: *They masked for the party.* **6.** to hide or conceal: *She masked her sadness with a smile.* —**mask′er,** *n.* —**mask′like′,** *adj.*

ma·son (mā′sən), *n.* **1.** a person whose trade is building with stones, bricks, etc., usually with the use of mortar or cement. **2.** *(often cap.)* a Freemason.

Ma′son-Dix′on line′ (mā′sən dik′sən), the boundary between Pennsylvania and Maryland: regarded as the dividing line between the North and the South. [named after Charles *Mason* and Jeremiah *Dixon,* who partly surveyed the line between the years 1763 and 1767]

ma·son·ic (mə son′ik), *adj. (often cap.)* referring to or characteristic of Freemasons.

ma·son·ry (mā′sən rē), *n., pl.* **ma·son·ries. 1.** the skill or occupation of a mason. **2.** work made by a mason: *a wall of solid masonry.*

masque (mask), *n.* **1.** a fanciful and ornate type of play performed in England in the 16th and 17th centuries, chiefly by amateur actors. **2.** a masquerade.

mas·quer·ade (mas′kə rād′), *n.* **1.** a party where masks and elaborate costumes are worn. **2.** a costume for such a party. **3.** any disguise: *His swaggering is a masquerade for his cowardice.* —*v.,* **mas·quer·ad·ed, mas·quer·ad·ing. 4.** to go about under false pretenses; appear to be another: *He masqueraded as an English lord.* —**mas′quer·ad′er,** *n.*

mass (mas), *n.* **1.** the quantity of matter in a body; the property of matter that causes it to have weight. **2.** a large, formless body of particles, parts, or objects: *a mass of sand; a mass of leaves.* **3.** a large number or quantity: *His hand was covered with a mass of scratches.* **4.** the greater part of anything: *The mass of public opinion was against it.* —*v.* **5.** to gather into or come together in a mass: *He massed his papers together. The crowd massed in the square.* **6. the masses,** the working classes; the common people: *a type of entertainment popular among the masses.*

Mass (mas), *n.* **1.** a service held in the Roman Catholic Church and some other churches, involving the celebration of Holy Communion. **2.** music written for parts of this service.

Mass., Massachusetts.

Mas·sa·chu·setts (mas′ə chōō′sits), *n.* a state in the NE United States, on the Atlantic coast. 8257 sq. mi. *Cap.:* Boston.

mas·sa·cre (mas′ə kər), *n.* **1.** the slaughter of a large number of people, esp. in warfare. —*v.,* **mas·sa·cred, mas·sa·cring. 2.** to kill in large numbers, esp. cruelly and violently.

mas·sage (mə säzh′), *n.* **1.** the act or technique of treating the body by rubbing, kneading, and the like, to improve circulation and loosen the muscles. —*v.,* **mas·saged, mas·sag·ing. 2.** to treat by massage. —**mas·sag′er,** *n.*

mas·sive (mas′iv), *adj.* **1.** forming a large mass; bulky or heavy. **2.** large, as the head or forehead. **3.** solid or substantial: *a massive contribution.* —**mas′sive·ly,** *adv.* —**mas′sive·ness,** *n.*

mast (mast), *n.* **1.** a tall pole rising above the deck of a boat or ship, for supporting sails and rigging. **2.** any tall, upright pole, such as a support for an antenna or the main post of a derrick or crane. —*v.* **3.**

to provide with a mast or masts: *to mast a schooner.*

mas·ter (mas′tər), *n.* **1.** a person who owns, uses, directs, or controls a person, animal, or thing: *the master and his dog; to be master of a situation.* **2.** a skilled workman or artist who works on his own rather than for another. In the trade guilds of the Middle Ages masters were qualified to teach apprentices and to hire journeymen. **3.** the captain of a ship. **4.** a male teacher, esp. in a British school. **5.** a man highly skilled or learned in an art, craft, profession, etc.: *a master of the novel.* **6.** a boy or young man (used chiefly as a term of address). —*adj.* **7.** chief; principal: *a master bedroom.* **8.** directing or controlling: *a master switch.* **9.** being a master of some art, craft, etc.: *a master violinist.* **10.** showing mastery: *a master painting.* —*v.* **11.** to conquer or subdue: *He mastered his anger.* **12.** to become skilled in: *He mastered French.*

mas·ter·ful (mas′tər fəl), *adj.* **1.** having or showing the qualities of a master: *masterful control.* **2.** showing skill or mastery: *a masterful performance.* —**mas′ter·ful·ly,** *adv.* —**mas′ter·ful·ness,** *n.*

mas·ter·ly (mas′tər lē), *adj.* **1.** like or befitting a master, as in skill or art: *a masterly painting.* —*adv.* **2.** in a masterly manner: *to speak masterly.*

mas·ter·mind (mas′tər mīnd′), *v.* **1.** to plan and direct something fully: *She masterminded the program.* —*n.* **2.** a person who has thought up or who directs the fulfillment of something: *He was the mastermind of the government's new policy.*

mas′ter of cer′emonies, a person who directs the entertainment at a party, dinner, or the like.

mas·ter·piece (mas′tər pēs′), *n.* **1.** a great work of art, writing, music, etc., esp. the best single work of its maker: *That book is his masterpiece.* **2.** anything done with great skill: *Mother's cakes are masterpieces.*

mas·ter·y (mas′tə rē), *n., pl.* for def. 2 **mas·ter·ies. 1.** the state of being a master; power of command or control: *He had mastery over the men.* **2.** command or grasp, as of a subject: *mastery of a language.*

mast·head (mast′hed′), *n.* **1.** the top part of a mast. **2.** a space in a newspaper, magazine, or the like, in which is printed the publication's name, the names of the owner and staff, etc.

mas·ti·cate (mas′tə kāt′), *v.,* **mas·ti·cat·ed, mas·ti·cat·ing.** to chew. —**mas′ti·ca′tion,** *n.* —**mas′ti·ca′tor,** *n.*

mas·tiff (mas′tif), *n.* a large, powerful, short-haired dog having a pale tan or brindled coat.

mas·to·don (mas′tə don′), *n.* a large, extinct animal closely resembling an elephant.

mat¹ (mat), *n.* **1.** a piece of cloth, plastic, rubber, etc., used to protect a surface, as an area of a floor. **2.** a smaller piece of material, set under a dish of food, a lamp, vase, etc. **3.** a large, thick pad used on a floor to protect wrestlers and tumblers. **4.** a thick and tangled mass, as of hair or leaves. —*v.,* **mat·ted, mat·ting. 5.** to cover with a mat or mats: *to mat the floor.* **6.** to form

Mastiff
(30 in. high
at shoulder)

into a mat: *to mat rushes.* **7.** to become entangled: *His hair matted in the wind.* [from the Old English word *matte,* which comes from Latin *matta* "mat of rushes," from Semitic]

mat² (mat), *n.* a piece of cardboard that is used to form a border around a picture. [partly from a special use of *mat¹,* and partly from the word *mat* "dull, not shiny"]

mat·a·dor (mat′ə dôr′), *n.* the bullfighter who kills the bull in a bullfight.

match¹ (mach), *n.* **1.** a slender piece of wood or cardboard tipped with a chemical that bursts into flame when the tip is rubbed on a rough or chemically prepared surface. **2.** a wick or cord that burns at an even rate, formerly used as a fuse and to fire guns. [from the Old French word *mesche,* which comes from Latin *myxa* "lamp wick," from a Greek word]

match² (mach), *n.* **1.** a person or thing that resembles or is identical to another: *the blue sock and its match.* **2.** a person or thing that is able to deal with another as an equal: *to meet one's match.* **3.** a pair of persons or things that go well together: *Your red hat and yellow blouse are not a good match.* **4.** a person or thing suitable for another: *A dark tie is a good match for a light jacket.* **5.** a contest or game: *a football match.* **6.** a person who is regarded as a future husband or wife. **7.** a marriage: *Their parents arranged the match.* —*v.* **8.** to go well with or together: *Your tie does not match your jacket.* **9.** to be alike in size, shape, color, etc.: *Your socks don't match.* **10.** to be alike in nature, character, etc.: *Their personalities match.* **11.** to be equal to: *My talents do not match yours.* **12.** to cause to compete against each other: *to match the boxers.* **13.** to put in agreement with; adapt: *to match one's deeds to one's words.* **14.** to join in marriage: *The couple was happily matched.* [from the Old English word *gemæcca* "mate, fellow"] —**match′a·ble,** *adj.* —**match′er,** *n.*

match·book (mach′book′), *n.* a small cardboard folder into which rows of paper matches are stapled.

match·less (mach′lis), *adj.* having no equal; peerless; incomparable: *a woman of matchless beauty.* —**match′less·ly,** *adv.* —**match′less·ness,** *n.*

match·lock (mach′lok′), *n.* an old type of gun fired by a burning match when the trigger was pulled.

mate (māt), *n.* **1.** one of a pair: *I can't find the mate to this glove.* **2.** a husband or wife; spouse. **3.** one of a pair of mated animals: *the hippopotamus and his mate.* **4.** a comrade, partner, fellow worker, etc. (often used in combination): *classmate.* **5.** an officer on a merchant ship ranking just below a captain. **6.** a petty officer in the navy. —*v.,* **mat·ed, mat·ing. 7.** to join as a mate or mates: *Birds mate in the spring.*

ma·te·ri·al (mə tēr′ē əl), *n.* **1.** the substance or substances of which a thing is made or composed: *materials for building a house.* **2.** a group of facts, ideas, etc., that may serve as a basis for a work: *to gather material for a story.* **3.** a fabric. **4. materials,** the articles or equipment for doing something: *writing materials.* —*adj.* **5.** formed or consisting of matter; physical: *the material world.* **6.** concerned with the body rather than with the mind or the spirit: *material comforts.* **7.** important; substantial: *His help made a material difference.* **8.** likely to influence the decision of a court: *a material witness.*

ma·te·ri·al·ism (mə tēr′ē ə liz′əm), *n.* **1.** the belief that nothing exists in the universe that is not matter, including the mind, and that all movement is brought about by material rather than spiritual forces. **2.** concern for comfort, luxury, etc., rather than for things of the mind or spirit.

ma·te·ri·al·ist (mə tēr′ē ə list), *n.* **1.** a person who believes in materialism as explaining the nature of the universe. **2.** one who is concerned primarily with material things rather than with things of the mind or the spirit. —**ma·te′ri·al·is′tic,** *adj.*

ma·te·ri·al·ize (mə tēr′ē ə līz′), *v.,* **ma·te·ri·al·ized, ma·te·ri·al·iz·ing. 1.** to come or bring into existence: *The meeting never materialized.* **2.** to assume a physical form: *The ghost materialized before him.* **3.** to appear all at once, as if out of thin air: *The speeding car materialized out of nowhere.*

ma·te·ri·al·ly (mə tēr′ē ə lē), *adv.* **1.** to an important degree: *He helped us materially.* **2.** with regard to matter or material things: *Things were better materially, but the morale was bad.*

ma·ter·nal (mə tûr′n°l), *adj.* **1.** of, relating to, or like a mother: *maternal love.* **2.** related through a mother: *Mother's parents are our maternal grandparents.* [from the Latin word *māternus,* which comes from *māter* "mother"] —**ma·ter′nal·ly,** *adv.*

ma·ter·ni·ty (mə tûr′ni tē), *n.* **1.** the state of being a mother; motherhood. **2.** motherliness. —*adj.* **3.** of or concerning pregnancy and childbirth: *a maternity dress; a maternity ward.*

math (math), *n. Informal.* mathematics.

math·e·mat·i·cal (math′ə mat′i kəl), *adj.* **1.** of, referring to, or using mathematics. **2.** used in mathematics. **3.** extremely accurate and precise. —**math′e·mat′i·cal·ly,** *adv.*

math·e·ma·ti·cian (math′ə mə tish′ən), *n.* a person who specializes in mathematics.

math·e·mat·ics (math′ə mat′iks), *n.* the study of numbers, quantities, and shapes and of their relationships. Arithmetic, algebra, geometry, and calculus are some of the branches of mathematics.

mat·i·née (mat′°nā′), *n.* a performance of a play, movie, etc., held in the afternoon: *We ordered seats for the Saturday matinée.* Also, **mat·i·nee′.** [from a French word meaning "morning"]

mat·ins (mat′°nz), *n.pl. (often used as sing.)* **1.** a service held in the Roman Catholic Church at midnight or daybreak. **2.** a service of prayer held in the morning in the Church of England.

ma·tri·arch (mā′trē ärk′), *n.* a female head or chief of a family or tribe. —**ma′tri·ar′chal,** *adj.*

ma·tric·u·late (mə trik′yə lāt′), *v.,* **ma·tric·u·lat·ed, ma·tric·u·lat·ing.** to enroll in a college or university. —**ma·tric′u·la′tion,** *n.*

mat·ri·mo·ny (ma′trə mō′nē), *n.* the state of being married; marriage; wedlock. —**mat′ri·mo′ni·al,** *adj.*

ma·trix (mā′triks), *n., pl.* **ma·trix·es** or **ma·tri·ces** (mā′tri sēz′). something that molds, shapes, or gives a form or beginning to another thing: *Ancient Rome was the matrix of Western civilization.*

ma·tron (mā′trən), *n.* **1.** a married woman or a widow, esp. one of high social position who has children: *young society matrons.* **2.** a woman who has charge of inmates in a prison or other institution.

ma·tron·ly (mā′trən lē), *adj.* of, referring to, or like a matron; serious and dignified. —**ma′tron·li·ness,** *n.*

mat·ted (mat′id), *adj.* **1.** tangled together in a thick mass: *matted hair.* **2.** covered with a mat or mats: *a matted floor.*

mat·ter (mat′ər), *n.* **1.** the substance or substances of which something is made: *the hard matter of teeth and bones.* **2.** the substance of which the whole universe is made. **3.** the ideas, information, etc., of something that has been written, such as a book. **4.** something written or printed: *postal matter.* **5.** a situation, state, business, etc.: *He promised to look into the matter.* **6.** an amount or extent reckoned approximately: *a matter of 10 miles.* **7.** importance or significance: *an event of little matter.* **8.** difficulty or trouble (usually preceded by *the*): *What is the matter?* —*v.* **9.** to be of importance: *It doesn't matter what they think.* **10. as a matter of fact,** actually; in reality: *As a matter of fact, I wasn't even there.* **11. no matter,** regardless of: *I want to know when you get home no matter what time it is.*

Mat·ter·horn (mat′ər hôrn′), *n.* a mountain on the border of Switzerland and Italy. 14,780 ft.

mat·ter-of-fact (mat′ər-əv fakt′), *adj.* keeping strictly to facts; not imaginative: *a matter-of-fact account of what happened; a practical, matter-of-fact person.*

Mat·thew (math′yōō), *n.* **1.** (in the Bible) one of the 12 apostles of Christ and one of the four Evangelists, believed to have written the Gospel of St. Matthew. **2.** the first Gospel of the New Testament.

Mat·thi·as (mə thī′əs), *n.* (in the Bible) a disciple chosen to take the place of Judas Iscariot as one of the apostles.

mat·ting (mat′ing), *n.* woven straw, hemp, and other material used for making mats, wrappings, etc.

mat·tock (mat′ək), *n.* a tool similar to a pickax, with the head having a flat blade on one side and a pointed blade on the other: used for loosening soil in digging.

mat·tress (ma′tris), *n.* a large pad used on or for a bed, consisting of a casing of heavy cloth that contains hair, cloth, or other stuffing, or a framework of metal springs.

ma·ture (mə tŏŏr′, -tyŏŏr′), *adj.* **1.** fully developed or grown: *a mature person; a mature plant.* **2.** ripe, such as fruit, cheese, or wine. **3.** completed or perfected: *mature plans.* —*v.*, **ma·tured, ma·tur·ing. 4.** to make or become mature. —**ma·ture′ly,** *adv.*

ma·tu·ri·ty (mə tŏŏr′i tē, -tyŏŏr′-), *n.* **1.** the state of being mature; ripeness: *to reach maturity.* **2.** full development in mind, character, etc.: *He shows a maturity beyond his years.* **3.** the time when an insurance policy, bond, etc., reaches its full value or becomes payable.

mat·zo (mät′sə), *n., pl.* **mat·zos.** unleavened bread in the form of large crackers, eaten by Jews during Passover. Also, **mat′zah.** [from a Yiddish word, which comes from Hebrew *maṣṣāh*]

maud·lin (môd′lin), *adj.* foolishly or tearfully emotional; sentimental: *a maudlin story of a little orphan.*

maul (môl), *n.* **1.** a large, heavy hammer. —*v.* **2.** to handle roughly so as to bruise or injure: *The lion mauled his trainer.* —**maul′er,** *n.*

maun·der (môn′dər), *v.* **1.** to talk in a rambling, foolish, or meaningless way: *The old man maundered about the past.* **2.** to move, go, or act in an aimless or confused way: *He maundered about the house.*

Mau·ri·ta·ni·a (môr′i tā′nē ə), *n.* a republic in W Africa, largely in the Sahara Desert: formerly a French colony. 418,120 sq. mi. —**Mau′ri·ta′ni·an,** *n., adj.*

Mau·ri·tius (mô rish′əs, mô rish′ē əs), *n.* a republic on several islands E of Madagascar, formerly a British colony. 809 sq. mi.

mau·so·le·um (mô′sə lē′əm, mô′zə lē′əm), *n.* **1.** a large, elaborate tomb: *the mausoleum of an ancient king.* **2.** a tomb for many bodies.

mauve (mōv), *n.* **1.** a pale bluish purple. —*adj.* **2.** of the color mauve: *a mauve dress.*

mav·er·ick (mav′ər ik), *n.* **1.** an unbranded calf, cow, or steer, esp. a motherless calf. **2.** a person who acts apart from his group; dissenter: *The governor was a maverick, often defying his party's policies.* [named after Samuel A. *Maverick* (1803–1870), a Texas pioneer who did not brand his cattle]

maw (mô), *n.* **1.** the mouth, throat, or gullet of an animal. **2.** the crop or craw of a fowl.

mawk·ish (mô′kish), *adj.* **1.** sickly sentimental; maudlin: *mawkish concern for the poor.* **2.** having a faint, sickly flavor; insipid: *weak, mawkish tea.* —**mawk′ish·ly,** *adv.* —**mawk′ish·ness,** *n.*

max., maximum.

max·im (mak′sim), *n.* a short saying meant to express the truth about something: *"Handsome is as handsome does" is a maxim.*

max·i·mum (mak′sə məm), *n.* **1.** the greatest amount or degree allowed, reached, etc.: *He increased his efforts to the maximum.* —*adj.* **2.** amounting to a maximum; greatest possible; highest: *What was yesterday's maximum temperature?*

may (mā), *auxiliary verb, past tense* **might** (mīt). **1.** to be likely or possible to: *It may snow today.* **2.** to be allowed to: *You may go if you wish.* **3.** to let it be or happen that: *Long may she reign.* **4.** to have the opportunity to: *They fought so that we might be free.* —Usage. See **can¹.**

May (mā), *n.* the fifth month of the year, having 31 days. [from the Old English word *Maius,* which comes from the Latin phrase *Maius mēnsis* "month of (the goddess) Maia"]

Ma·ya (mä′yə), *n., pl.* for def. 1 **Ma·yas** *or* **Ma·ya. 1.** a highly civilized Indian people of the Yucatan Peninsula, Guatemala, and British Honduras, whose empire flourished from A.D. c300 to A.D. c900 and declined before being conquered by the Spanish in the 16th century. **2.** the language of the Mayas.

Ma·yan (mä′yən), *adj.* **1.** of or concerning the Mayas or their language. —*n.* **2.** a member of the Mayan people.

may·be (mā′bē), *adv.* perhaps; possibly: *Maybe I'll come too.*

May′ Day′, the first day of May, celebrated in many parts of the world with dancing around a maypole and the crowning of a May queen, also, in some countries, with political demonstrations.

May·day (mā′dā′), *n.* a distress signal sent by radio, used by ships and aircraft.

May·flow·er (mā′flou′ər), *n.* **1.** the ship in which the Pilgrims sailed to America in 1620. **2.** any of various plants that bloom in May, as the trailing arbutus in the U.S. and the hawthorn in England.

may·fly (mā′flī′), *n.* a flying insect with delicate transparent wings.

may·hem (mā′hem, mā′əm), *n.* the crime of injuring, maiming, or crippling a person deliberately.

Mayfly
(body length 1 in.)

may·on·naise (mā′ə nāz′, mā′ə nāz′), *n.* a thick dressing for food made of egg yolks, oil, vinegar, and seasonings.

may·or (mā′ər), *n.* the chief official of a city or town. [from the Latin word *major* "greater, elder"]

may·or·al·ty (mā′ər əl tē), *n., pl.* **may·or·al·ties.** the position of a mayor, or the time during which he holds office: *The building was put up during the mayoralty of Mr. La Guardia.*

may·pole (mā′pōl′), *n.* a tall pole, decorated with ribbons and flowers, around which people dance to celebrate May Day.

mayst (māst), *v.* an old form of **may,** found now chiefly in Biblical and poetic writing and used with *thou: Thou mayst come to the feast with thy friend.*

maze (māz), *n.* **1.** a complex and confusing network of passageways, tunnels, etc.: *The old part of town is a maze of little streets.* **2.** a state of confusion or bewilderment.

Mc·Kin·ley (mə kin′lē), *n.* **1. William,** 1843–1901, 25th President of the U.S. 1897–1901. **2. Mount,** a mountain in central Alaska: highest peak in North America. 20,300 ft.

Md, *Chem.* the symbol for **mendelevium.**

Md., Maryland.

M.D., Doctor of Medicine. [from the Latin phrase *Medicinae Doctor*]

mdse., merchandise.

me (mē), *pron.* the objective case of **I**: *They asked me to the party. Give me your hand.*

Me., Maine.

mead¹ (mēd), *n.* an alcoholic liquor made by fermenting honey and water. [from the Old English word *meodu*]

mead² (mēd), *n. Archaic.* a meadow. [from the Old English word *mǣd*]

mead·ow (med′ō), *n.* level, grassy ground used as a pasture or as a source of hay. [from the Old English stem *mǣdw-*, in inflected forms of *mǣd* "mead²"]

mead·ow·lark (med′ō lärk′), *n.* any of several American songbirds, esp. a brownish and black one that is about the size of a robin and has a yellow breast.

mea·ger (mē′gər), *adj.* 1. lacking fullness or richness; slight; scanty: *a meager meal.* 2. thin or lean: *a meager body.* Also, *esp. British,* **mea′gre.** —**mea′ger·ly,** *adv.* —**mea′ger·ness,** *n.*

Meadowlark
(length 9 in.)

meal¹ (mēl), *n.* 1. one of the regular times for eating food, as breakfast, lunch, or dinner. 2. the food served or eaten at such a time: *a hearty meal.* [from the Old English word *mǣl* "measure, fixed time, meal"]

meal² (mēl), *n.* 1. coarse, unsifted powder ground from grain: *wheat meal.* 2. any ground or powdery substance that looks like this: *a meal of bread crumbs.* [from the Old English word *melu*, which is related to Latin *molere* "to grind" and to *mill¹*]

meal·time (mēl′tīm′), *n.* the usual time for a meal: *I have to be back by mealtime.*

meal·y (mē′lē), *adj.,* **meal·i·er, meal·i·est.** 1. like meal; dry and powdery: *mealy potatoes.* 2. containing meal. —**meal′i·ness,** *n.*

mean¹ (mēn), *v.,* **meant** (ment), **mean·ing.** 1. to have in mind as one's purpose; intend: *I meant to tell him, but I forgot.* 2. to intend for a certain purpose: *He was not meant to be a soldier.* 3. to want to express: *He always says what he means.* 4. to signify: *to know what a word means.* 5. to be a sign of: *Frost means that winter is on the way.* 6. to make possible or unavoidable: *This money means security. That act means war.* 7. **mean well,** to try to be kind or helpful: *Her nagging gets on my nerves, but I suppose she means well.* [from the Old English word *mǣnan*]

mean² (mēn), *adj.* 1. low in grade, quality, or character. 2. low in rank: *mean subjects of the king.* 3. of small importance; petty: *mean little details.* 4. smallminded; base: *It is mean not to defend a friend.* 5. stingy or miserly: *He is mean with his money.* 6. rude, selfish, or disagreeable: *You were very mean to keep everything for yourself.* 7. *Informal.* trou-

blesome or vicious, as a horse. 8. *Slang.* excellent: *He plays a mean game of table tennis.* [from the Middle English word *mene,* which is short for Old English *gemǣne* "common"] —**mean′ly,** *adv.* —**mean′ness,** *n.*

mean³ (mēn), *n.* 1. Usually, **means.** a way of doing or getting something: *trains, planes, and other means of travel.* 2. **means, a.** resources, esp. money: *The widow was left without means.* **b.** considerable wealth; riches: *a man of means.* 3. something midway between two extremes: *a mean between hot and cold.* 4. an average. —*adj.* 5. occupying a middle position between two extremes: *a man of mean height.* 6. being of average value or quality. 7. **by all means,** certainly; to be sure: *Go, by all means.* 8. **by means of,** with the help of: *I climbed the wall by means of a rope.* 9. **by no means,** not at all: *Our going is by no means certain.* [from the Old French word *meien,* which comes from Latin *mediānus* "middle"]

me·an·der (mē an′dər), *v.* 1. to go in a winding course: *The river meanders through the valley.* 2. to wander aimlessly; ramble: *The conversation meandered.* —*n.* 3. Usually, **meanders.** turnings or windings: *the meanders of a river.* —**me·an′der·ing·ly,** *adv.*

mean·ing (mē′ning), *n.* 1. what is meant or supposed to be understood: *The meaning of what she said escaped me.* 2. the purpose of something: *What is the meaning of this intrusion?* —*adj.* 3. intentioned (used in combination): *a well-meaning person.* 4. full of meaning: *She gave me a meaning look.*

mean·ing·ful (mē′ning fəl), *adj.* full of meaning; significant: *a meaningful life.* —**mean′ing·ful·ly,** *adv.*

mean·ing·less (mē′ning lis), *adj.* without meaning or purpose: *Life without friends is meaningless.* —**mean′ing·less·ly,** *adv.*

meant (ment), *v.* the past tense and past participle of **mean.**

mean·time (mēn′tīm′), *n.* 1. the time between; meanwhile: *It rained on Monday and Friday, but in the meantime the weather was fine.* —*adv.* 2. another word for **meanwhile.**

mean·while (mēn′hwīl′, -wīl′), *adv.* Also, **meantime.** 1. during the time between: *I'll be back soon, but meanwhile wait for me here.* 2. at the same time: *The weather was fine at the shore, but meanwhile it was raining back home.* —*n.* 3. another word for **meantime.**

mea·sles (mē′zəlz), *n. (used as sing. or pl.)* an infectious disease, common among children, that causes fever and red marks on the skin. See also **German measles.**

mea·sly (mē′zlē), *adj.,* **mea·sli·er, mea·sli·est.** 1. having measles. 2. *Informal.* paltry or skimpy; insufficient: *a measly amount of money.*

meas·ur·a·ble (mezh′ər ə bəl), *adj.* capable of being measured: *The depths of the ocean are measurable.* —**meas′ur·a·bly,** *adv.*

---

act, āble, dâre, ärt; ebb, ēqual; if, īce; hot, ōver, ôrder; oil; bŏŏk; ōōze; out; up, ûrge; ə = a as in *alone;* ᵊ as in *button* (but′ᵊn), *fire* (fī²r); chief; shoe; thin; ᵗhat; zh as in *measure* (mezh′ər). See full key inside cover.

meas·ure (mezh/ər), v., **meas·ured, meas·ur·ing. 1.** to find the size, extent, dimensions, quantity, or capacity of (something), esp. by comparison with a standard: *to measure a rug.* **2.** to have a particular size: *This rug measures 9 by 12 feet.* **3.** to mark off or deal out by or as if by measurement (often fol. by *off* or *out*): *to measure off a yard of cloth.* **4.** to be used in measuring (something): *A barometer measures air pressure.* —n. **5.** something used in measuring, such as a cup, ruler, or tape. **6.** a unit or system of units used in measuring. **7.** a quantity measured out. **8.** a bar of music. **9.** any way of measuring or estimating: *His kindness is beyond measure.* **10.** an extent or degree: *In a measure you are right.* **11.** a moderate or necessary amount: *a measure of prudence is essential.* **12.** reasonable bounds or limits: *His grief knew no measure.* **13.** a law: *a new measure enacted by the legislature.* **14. for good measure,** as something extra: *They fined him and took away his driver's license for good measure.* **15. measure up,** to reach a certain standard: *Attendance didn't measure up to last year's.* —meas/ur·er, n.

M, Measure (def. 8)

meas·ured (mezh/ərd), adj. **1.** determined or regulated by measure: *measured distances; measured ingredients.* **2.** regular or uniform: *a measured gait.* **3.** carefully planned or thought out: *a measured reply.* —meas/ured·ly, adv. —meas/ured·ness, n.

meas·ure·less (mezh/ər lis), adj. without limits or bounds: *the measureless universe.*

meas·ure·ment (mezh/ər mənt), n. **1.** the act or process of measuring. **2.** a measured quantity or dimension. **3.** a system of units of measure.

meas/ur·ing worm/, any of several small caterpillars that move by bringing the rear end of the body forward and then advancing the front end. Also, **inchworm.**

Measuring worm (length 1½ in.)

meat (mēt), n. **1.** the flesh of animals used as food, usually not including fish and fowl. **2.** food in general: *meat and drink.* **3.** the edible part of a fruit, nut, etc. **4.** the most important part; gist: *the meat of a lecture.*

meat·y (mē/tē), adj., **meat·i·er, meat·i·est. 1.** of, like, or full of meat: *a rich, meaty stew.* **2.** rich in meaning; pithy: *a meaty saying.* —meat/i·ness, n.

Mec·ca (mek/ə), n. **1.** a city in W Saudi Arabia: birthplace of Muhammad and spiritual center of Islam. **2.** *(often l.c.)* any place that many people visit or hope to visit: *Paris is a mecca for tourists.* —Mec/can, n., adj.

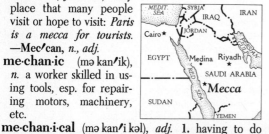

me·chan·ic (mə kan/ik), n. a worker skilled in using tools, esp. for repairing motors, machinery, etc.

me·chan·i·cal (mə kan/i kəl), adj. **1.** having to do

with machinery: *a mechanical failure.* **2.** run by a machine: *a mechanical toy.* **3.** caused by machinery: *mechanical propulsion.* **4.** acting or done without interest, feeling, etc.: *a mechanical smile.* **5.** routine and monotonous: *a day devoted to mechanical tasks.* —me·chan/i·cal·ly, adv.

me·chan·ics (mə kan/iks), n. **1.** *(used as sing.)* the science that deals with the motion of objects and with the forces that produce motion. **2.** *(used as pl.)* the technical part or the ordinary routine of something: *the mechanics of organizing a banquet.*

mech·an·ism (mek/ə niz/əm), n. **1.** a machine. **2.** the mechanical part of something: *the mechanism of a clock.* **3.** any organization of parts working together: *the mechanism of government.*

mech·a·nize (mek/ə nīz/), v., **mech·a·nized, mech·a·niz·ing. 1.** to equip with machinery: *to mechanize an army.* **2.** to make, perform, do, etc., with machinery: *to mechanize the manufacture of cloth.* **3.** to make mechanical. —mech/a·ni·za/tion, n.

med., 1. medical. **2.** medicine. **3.** medium.

med·al (med/əl), n. a flat, badgelike piece of metal, often engraved or stamped with words or a picture, used to celebrate an important event or given to a person as a reward for some noble action.

me·dal·lion (mə dal/yən), n. **1.** a large medal. **2.** a design resembling a medal, used in decoration.

med·dle (med/əl), v., **med·dled, med·dling.** to involve oneself in something without being asked or wanted by those directly concerned: *Please don't meddle in my private affairs.* —med/dler, n.

med·dle·some (med/əl səm), adj. tending to meddle or interfere: *Idle people are often meddlesome.* —med/dle·some·ly, adv. —med/dle·some·ness, n.

Me·de·a (mi dē/ə), n. (in Greek mythology) a witch who helped Jason, her husband, get the Golden Fleece.

me·di·a (mē/dē ə), n. **1.** a plural of **medium. 2.** the **media,** the means of communication that reach very large numbers of people, such as the press, television, and radio.

me·di·ae·val (mē/dē ē/vəl, med/ē ē/vəl), adj. another spelling of **medieval.**

me·di·al (mē/dē əl), adj. **1.** in or of the middle; median. **2.** average or ordinary; mean: *a person of medial height.* —me/di·al·ly, adv.

me·di·an (mē/dē ən), adj. **1.** in or of the middle; medial. —n. **2.** the middle number of a series.

me·di·ate (mē/dē āt/), v., **me·di·at·ed, me·di·at·ing. 1.** to settle (a dispute, strike, etc.) by acting as a judge or go-between. **2.** to bring about (an agreement, peace, etc.) by acting as a judge or go-between. **3.** to act as a judge or go-between. —me/di·a/tion, n.

med·i·cal (med/i kəl), adj. of or relating to the science of medicine. —med/i·cal·ly, adv.

med·ic·a·ment (mə dik/ə mənt, med/ə kə mənt), n. a healing substance; medicine or medication.

Med·i·care (med/ə kâr/), n. a federal program for hospitalization and medical insurance for persons 65 years of age and older.

med·i·cate (med/ə kāt/), v., **med·i·cat·ed, med·i·cat·**

ing. 1. to treat with medicine: *to medicate an illness.*
2. to add medicine to: *to medicate an ointment.*

med·i·ca·tion (med/ə kā/shən), *n.* **1.** the use or application of medicine. **2.** a medicinal substance; medicine.

me·dic·i·nal (mə dis/ə nəl), *adj.* of, referring to, or containing a medicine. **—me·dic/i·nal·ly,** *adv.*

med·i·cine (med/i sin), *n.* **1.** a substance used in treating or preventing disease or illness; drug. **2.** the art or science of restoring, improving, or preserving health. **3.** the medical profession.

med/icine man/, (esp. among American Indians) a man supposed to have magical powers in curing illnesses, fighting evil spirits, etc.

me·di·e·val (mē/dē ē/vəl, med/ē ē/vəl), *adj.* of, like, or characteristic of the Middle Ages: *medieval beliefs; medieval architecture.* Also, **mediaeval.**

Me·di·na (mə dē/nə), *n.* a city in W Saudi Arabia: Muhammad's tomb.

me·di·o·cre (mē/dē ō/kər), *adj.* of merely ordinary quality; neither good nor bad: *a mediocre painting.*

me·di·oc·ri·ty (mē/dē ok/ri tē), *n., pl.* for def. 2 **me·di·oc·ri·ties. 1.** the state or quality of being mediocre: *the mediocrity of so many modern buildings.* **2.** a person who has only ordinary skill, talent, etc.

med·i·tate (med/i tāt/), *v.,* **med·i·tat·ed, med·i·tat·ing. 1.** to think quietly and seriously; reflect. **2.** to plan or intend to do: *He meditated revenge against his enemies.* **—med/i·tat/ing·ly,** *adv.* **—med/i·ta/tor,** *n.*

med·i·ta·tion (med/i tā/shən), *n.* thought; reflection; contemplation: *meditation upon God.*

Med·i·ter·ra·ne·an (med/i tə rā/nē ən), *n.* **1.** the Mediterranean Sea. **—adj. 2.** of or referring to the Mediterranean Sea. **3.** located or dwelling on or near the Mediterranean Sea. [from the Latin word *mediterrāneus* "inland," which comes from *medius* "middle" + *terra* "land, earth"]

Med/iterra/nean Sea/, a sea surrounded by Africa, Europe, and Asia. 1,145,000 sq. mi.

me·di·um (mē/dē əm), *n., pl.* for defs. 1–6 **me·di·a** (mē/dē ə), for defs. 1–7 **me·di·ums. 1.** an intervening substance, such as air, through which something passes or acts. **2.** the substance, such as air or water, in which something lives. **3.** a special solid or liquid material in which bacteria can be grown. **4.** something that occupies a place midway between two extremes: *a happy medium in temperature.* **5.** a means by which something is produced or presented: *the television medium.* **6.** a liquid with which pigments are mixed: *Oil is the medium of oil paints.* **7.** a person through whom the spirits of the dead are supposedly able to contact the living. **—adj. 8.** halfway between two extremes: *a shirt of medium size.*

med·ley (med/lē), *n., pl.* **med·leys.** a piece of music that combines tunes or parts of several other pieces.

me·dul·la (mi dul/ə), *n.* **1.** the soft inner part of the marrow of the bones, the center of a gland, the pith of a plant, etc. **2.** the medulla oblongata.

medul/la ob·long·a/ta (ob/lông gä/tə), the lowest part of the brain, which joins the spinal cord and controls automatic acts, such as the heartbeat and breathing. See illus. at **brain.**

Me·du·sa (mə doo/sə, -dyoo/-), *n.* (in Greek mythology) one of the Gorgons, killed by Perseus.

meek (mēk), *adj.* **1.** humble; without spirit. **2.** very patient and mild. **—meek/ly,** *adv.* **—meek/ness,** *n.*

meer·schaum (mēr/shəm, mēr/shôm), *n.* **1.** a soft, white mineral used for making the bowls of tobacco pipes. **2.** a pipe with a bowl made of meerschaum.

meet¹ (mēt), *v.,* **met** (met), **meet·ing. 1.** to come together or face to face: *We met in the street. The assembly meets today.* **2.** to become acquainted or acquainted with: *Have you two met? We met each other at the party.* **3.** to join at a certain time and place: *Meet me downtown at noon.* **4.** to be present at the arrival of: *I met her at the airport.* **5.** to come to or before: *A curious sight met my eyes.* **6.** to come across or encounter: *We met few people on the way.* **7.** to come together physically: *The two cars met in a head-on collision.* **8.** to satisfy or agree with: *This work does not meet our requirements.* **9.** to face, oppose, or deal with: *We must meet him squarely and frankly on that point.* **10.** to become joined together: *The two highways meet outside of town.* **—n. 11.** a group assembled for a hunt, athletic contest, etc. **12. meet halfway,** to grant some of the requests or demands of (another person): *I can't promise everything, but maybe I can meet you halfway.* **13. meet with, a.** to come across; encounter: *We met with difficulties on the way.* **b.** to experience: *to meet with disaster.* [from the Old English word *gemētan*]

meet² (mēt), *adj.* suitable or proper. [from the Middle English word *mete*, which is short for Old English *gemǣte* "suitable"]

meet·ing (mē/tiñg), *n.* **1.** the act of coming together. **2.** a gathering of persons for some purpose; assembly.

meet/ing house/, a house or building for religious worship, esp. for Quakers.

meg·a·phone (meg/ə fōn/), *n.* a cone-shaped tube for directing the sound of the voice so that it will carry farther.

meg·a·there (meg/ə-thēr/), *n.* any of various huge, slothlike animals that are now extinct.

Me·kong (mā/koñg/), *n.* a river flowing SE from China along the border between Thailand and Laos, through South Vietnam, and into the South China Sea.

mel·an·chol·y (mel/ən-kol/ē), *n., pl.* **mel·an·chol·ies. 1.** a gloomy state of mind; depression. **—adj. 2.** feeling or showing melancholy; mournful; depressed. **3.** causing melancholy; depressing: *the melancholy sight of dark skies* *and falling leaves.* [from the Greek word *melancholia,* literally "black bile." The Greeks believed melancholy was caused by an excess of black bile.]

Mel·a·ne·sia (mel'ə nē'zhə), *n.* the islands in the S Pacific NE of Australia, part of Oceania. —**Mel'a·ne'sian,** *n., adj.*

Mel·bourne (mel'bərn), *n.* a port city in SE Australia.

me·lee (mā'lā, mā lā'), *n.* a confused, hand-to-hand fight; brawl.

mel·lif·lu·ous (mə lif'loo əs), *adj.* sweetly or smoothly flowing; sweet-sounding: *mellifluous music.* —**mel·lif'lu·ous·ly,** *adv.* —**mel·lif'lu·ous·ness,** *n.*

mel·low (mel'ō), *adj.* 1. soft and full-flavored from ripeness, as fruit. 2. having a rich, delicious flavor: *mellow wine; mellow cheese.* 3. soft and rich, such as sound, color, light, etc.: *a painting full of mellow tones.* 4. rich and loamy: *mellow soil.* 5. gentle and kind from age or experience: *The years had made her mellow.* —*v.* 6. to make or become mellow.

me·lod·ic (mə lod'ik), *adj.* 1. melodious or tuneful. 2. of or referring to melody rather than to rhythm or harmony. —**me·lod'i·cal·ly,** *adv.*

me·lo·di·ous (mə lō'dē əs), *adj.* 1. pleasing to the ear: *a melodious voice.* 2. full of melody; tuneful: *a melodious opera.* —**me·lo'di·ous·ly,** *adv.* —**me·lo'di·ous·ness,** *n.*

mel·o·dra·ma (mel'ə drä'mə, mel'ə dram'ə), *n.* 1. a play that portrays violent action, strong feeling, etc. 2. anything in real life that resembles such a play: *She would make a melodrama out of the slightest mishap.* —**mel·o·dra·mat·ic** (mel'ə drə mat'ik), *adj.*

mel·o·dy (mel'ə dē), *n., pl.* **mel·o·dies.** 1. musical sounds in a pleasing order; tune. 2. the principal part in a song or other composition: *I'll play the melody if you'll play the accompaniment.*

mel·on (mel'ən), *n.* the large, fleshy, round or oval fruit of various vines, such as the watermelon or cantaloupe.

melt (melt), *v.,* **melt·ed; melt·ed** *or* **mol·ten** (mōl't³n); **melt·ing.** 1. to change from a solid to a liquid: *The sun melted the ice.* 2. to dwindle or gradually pass (often fol. by *away*): *His fortune melted away.* 3. to dissolve: *Sugar melts in water.* 4. to blend gradually (often fol. by *into*): *Night melted into day.* 5. to soften in feeling: *The music melted his heart.*

mem·ber (mem'bər), *n.* 1. a part or organ of a human or animal body; limb, such as an arm, leg, or wing. 2. any of the persons that make up a club, church, political party, or other group. 3. any part of a whole: *A column is one of the members of a building.*

mem·ber·ship (mem'bər ship'), *n.* 1. the state of being a member: *membership in a club.* 2. the total number of members in a club or other group.

mem·brane (mem'brān), *n.* a thin, flexible sheet or layer that surrounds or lines organs, connects parts, etc., in a plant or animal. —**mem·bra·nous** (mem'brə nəs), *adj.*

me·men·to (mə men'tō), *n., pl.* **me·men·tos** *or* **me·men·toes.** something kept as a reminder of what is past or gone; souvenir: *mementos of travel.*

mem·o (mem'ō), *n., pl.* **mem·os.** *Informal.* a memorandum.

mem·oir (mem'wär), *n.* 1. **memoirs,** the story of one's life written by oneself; autobiography. 2. a biography.

mem·o·ra·ble (mem'ər ə bəl), *adj.* worthy of being remembered; notable: *a memorable occasion.* —**mem'o·ra·bly,** *adv.*

mem·o·ran·dum (mem'ə ran'dəm), *n., pl.* **mem·o·ran·dums** *or* **mem·o·ran·da** (mem'ə ran'də). 1. a brief note serving as a reminder to do something. 2. a note sent between persons employed in the same company.

me·mo·ri·al (mə môr'ē əl), *n.* something meant to preserve the memory of a person, event, etc., such as a monument, holiday, or church service: *a memorial for the soldiers who died in the war.* —*adj.* 2. preserving the memory of a person or thing; commemorative: *a memorial service.* —**me·mo'ri·al·ly,** *adv.*

Memo'rial Day', May 30, a legal holiday in most states of the U.S. in memory of dead servicemen in all wars: now officially observed on the last Monday in May. Also, **Decoration Day.**

mem·o·rize (mem'ə rīz'), *v.,* **mem·o·rized, mem·o·riz·ing.** to learn by heart; fix in the mind: *to memorize a speech.* —**mem'o·ri·za'tion,** *n.* —**mem'o·riz'er,** *n.*

mem·o·ry (mem'ə rē), *n., pl.* **mem·o·ries.** 1. the ability to remember: *I have a bad memory.* 2. the act or fact of remembering: *to speak lines from memory.* 3. the length of time over which remembrance reaches: *an event in the memory of living men.* 4. something remembered; mental impression. 5. fame or reputation, esp. after death: *a ruler of beloved memory.* 6. a remembrance or commemoration: *a monument in memory of Columbus.*

Mem·phis (mem'fis), *n.* 1. a port city in SW Tennessee, on the Mississippi. 2. a ruined city in Upper Egypt, on the Nile, S of Cairo: the ancient capital of Egypt.

men (men), *n.* the plural of **man.**

men·ace (men'is), *n.* 1. something that threatens to cause evil, harm, etc.; threat: *Rocks are a menace to ships.* —*v.,* **men·aced, men·ac·ing.** 2. to threaten: *A storm menaced the town.* —**men'ac·ing·ly,** *adv.*

me·nag·er·ie (mə naj'ə rē, mə nazh'ə rē), *n.* a collection of wild or strange animals kept in cages and shown to the public.

mend (mend), *v.* 1. to make whole, sound, or usable by repairing: *to mend clothes.* 2. to make or become better; improve: *He promised to mend his ways.* —*n.* 3. a part that is mended: *a mend in a shirt.* 4. **on the mend,** showing improvement, esp. in recovery from an illness: *He was sick, but he's on the mend now.*

men·da·cious (men dā'shəs), *adj.* 1. containing lies; false or untrue: *a mendacious report.* 2. tending to lie; dishonest: *a mendacious person.* —**men·dac·i·ty** (men das'i tē), *n.* —**men·da'cious·ly,** *adv.*

men·de·le·vi·um (men'də lē'vē əm), *n. Chem.* a

man-made, radioactive, metallic element. *Symbol:* Md

Men·dels·sohn (men′d'l sən), *n.* **Fe·lix** (fē′liks), 1809–1847, German composer.

men·di·cant (men′də kənt), *adj.* **1.** begging or living by charity: *mendicant friars.* —*n.* **2.** a person who lives by begging. **3.** a mendicant friar.

men·folk (men′fōk′), *n.pl.* men, esp. those of a family or community. Also, **men′folks′.**

men·ha·den (men hād′'n), *n., pl.* **men·ha·den.** a fish found along the eastern coast of the U.S., used for making oil and fertilizer.

me·ni·al (mē′nē əl), *adj.* done by or fit for servants; humble; servile: *menial tasks.* —**me·ni·al·ly,** *adv.*

men·in·gi·tis (men′in jī′tis), *n.* a dangerous inflammation of the membrane of the brain or spinal cord.

Men·non·ite (men′ə nīt′), *n.* a member of a Protestant sect that opposes military service, the taking of oaths, etc., and that practices a simple way of living.

me·nor·ah (mə nôr′ə), *n.* **1.** a candelabrum having nine branches, used in the Jewish celebration of Hanukkah. **2.** a candelabrum having seven branches, used as the symbol of Israel.

men·stru·ate (men′strōō āt′), *v.,* **men·stru·at·ed, men·stru·at·ing.** to undergo menstruation.

men·stru·a·tion (men′strōō ā′shən), *n.* the act of discharging blood from the uterus. Menstruation normally occurs in girls and women approximately every 28 days between puberty and early middle age, except during pregnancy.

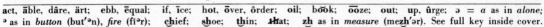
Menorah

-ment, a suffix used to form nouns meaning **1.** an action, or the result of an action: *judgment; punishment.* **2.** a means or instrument: *government; adornment.*

men·tal (men′t'l), *adj.* **1.** of or concerning the mind. **2.** ill in the mind: *a mental patient.* **3.** providing care for persons ill in the mind: *a mental hospital.*

men·tal·i·ty (men tal′i tē), *n., pl.* **men·tal·i·ties.** mental ability or character: *a person of high mentality.*

men·tal·ly (men′t'lē), *adv.* **1.** in or with the mind: *to note something mentally.* **2.** with regard to the mind: *mentally ill.*

men·thol (men′thôl), *n.* a substance obtained from peppermint oil, used in perfumes and candies, and in medicines because of its cooling effect.

men·tion (men′shən), *v.* **1.** to speak about briefly; refer to; name: *He mentioned several places he had visited.* —*n.* **2.** a brief notice; remark: *No mention was made of his absence.* **3. not to mention,** in addition to: *There was chocolate cake, not to mention pie.*

men·tor (men′tər, men′tôr), *n.* a wise and trusted teacher or adviser.

men·u (men′yōō), *n.* a list of the foods available at a restaurant or that will be served at a banquet or similar meal; bill of fare. **2.** the dishes that are served.

me·ow (mē ou′, myou), *n.* **1.** the sound a cat makes. —*v.* **2.** to make such a sound.

mer·can·tile (mûr′kən tēl′, mûr′kən tīl′), *adj.* of or concerning merchants or trade; commercial: *England is a mercantile country.*

mer·ce·nar·y (mûr′sə ner′ē), *adj.* **1.** working or acting merely for money or other reward: *She married for mercenary reasons.* **2.** fighting in an army solely for pay: *mercenary soldiers.* —*n., pl.* **mer·ce·nar·ies. 3.** a professional soldier fighting in a foreign army solely for pay.

mer·chan·dise (mûr′chən dīz′, mûr′chən dīs′), *n.* **1.** goods, esp. manufactured goods. —*v.* (mûr′chən dīz′), **mer·chan·dised, mer·chan·dis·ing.** **2.** to buy and sell; deal in; trade. —**mer′chan·diz′er,** *n.*

mer·chant (mûr′chənt), *n.* **1.** a person who buys and sells goods for profit on a large scale; dealer; trader. **2.** a storekeeper: *the neighborhood merchants.* —*adj.* **3.** concerned with or used for trade or commerce: *a merchant ship.*

mer·chant·man (mûr′chənt mən), *n., pl.* **mer·chant·men.** a commercial ship that carries primarily freight.

mer′chant marine′, 1. the ships of a nation that are engaged in commerce. **2.** the officers and crews of these ships.

mer·ci·ful (mûr′si fəl), *adj.* full of or showing mercy; compassionate. —**mer′ci·ful·ly,** *adv.*

mer·ci·less (mûr′si lis), *adj.* without mercy; pitiless. —**mer′ci·less·ly,** *adv.* —**mer′ci·less·ness,** *n.*

mer·cu·ri·al (mər kyŏŏr′ē əl), *adj.* **1.** of or concerning mercury. **2.** very changeable in mood; sprightly; lively: *a mercurial temper.*

mer·cu·ry (mûr′kyə rē), *n., pl.* **mer·cu·ries.** *Chem.* a heavy, metallic element that is a liquid at ordinary temperatures. Mercury is used in thermometers and ultraviolet lamps, and its compounds are widely used in medicine. *Symbol:* Hg

Mer·cu·ry (mûr′kyə rē), *n.* **1.** (in Roman mythology) the messenger of the gods and god of commerce, having a quick wit and a talent for thievery: identified with the Greek god Hermes. **2.** the planet closest to the sun. Mercury is the smallest of the planets, having a diameter of 3000 miles; its average distance from the sun is 36,000,000 miles.

mer·cy (mûr′sē), *n., pl.* for defs. 3, 4 **mer·cies. 1.** compassion or kindness shown toward an enemy, offender, or other person in one's power: *No mercy was shown to the captives.* **2.** the power to forgive or spare from full punishment: *The judge exercised mercy.* **3.** a blessing or gift, esp. from God: *They thanked God for His infinite mercies.* **4.** a good or lucky thing: *It's a mercy you didn't drown.* —*interj.* **5.** Good heavens!: *Mercy!*

Mercury

---
act, āble, dâre, ärt; ebb, ēqual; if, īce; hot, ōver, ôrder; oil; bŏŏk; ōōze; out; up, ûrge; ə = a as in alone; ' as in button (but′'n), fire (fī'r); chief; shoe; thin; ŧħat; zh as in measure (mezh′ər). See full key inside cover.

Why didn't you call the police? **6. at the mercy of,** entirely in the power of: *The captured soldiers were at the mercy of the enemy.*

mere (mēr), *adj., superlative* **mer·est.** nothing more or better than; only: *All that trouble for a mere cat!*

mere·ly (mēr′lē), *adv.* only; just; no more than: *It is merely a matter of time.*

mer·e·tri·cious (mer′i trish′əs), *adj.* falsely or deceptively showy, flashy, or the like: *a meretricious movie supposedly based on the Bible.* —**mer′e·tri′cious·ly,** *adv.* —**mer′e·tri′cious·ness,** *n.*

merge (mûrj), *v.,* **merged, merg·ing.** to combine or blend so that identity is lost: *The two streams merged, forming a river.*

merg·er (mûr′jər), *n.* the combining of two or more companies into one.

me·rid·i·an (mə rid′ē ən), *n.* **1.** a line of longitude. **2.** the highest point reached by the sun or a star. **3.** the highest point of any course, career, etc.: *the meridian of success.* [from the Latin word *meridiānus* "of or at noon," from *meridiēs* "midday"]

me·ringue (mə rang′), *n.* a topping for pies and cakes made of beaten egg whites and sugar.

Me·ri·no (mə rē′nō), *n., pl.* **Me·ri·nos.** a breed of sheep raised for its fine wool.

mer·it (mer′it), *n.* **1.** claim to respect; worth; value; excellence: *He has the merit of being honest.* **2.** Often, **merits.** the state or fact of deserving; desert: *We treat him according to his merits.* —*v.* **3.** to be worthy of; deserve: *This question does not merit our attention.*

Merino
(2 ft. high at shoulder)

mer·i·to·ri·ous (mer′i tôr′ē əs), *adj.* having merit; deserving praise, reward, etc.; praiseworthy. —**mer′i·to′ri·ous·ly,** *adv.*

Mer·lin (mûr′lin), *n.* a magician and wise man in the court of King Arthur.

mer·maid (mûr′mād′), *n.* an imaginary creature supposed to live in the sea, having the upper body and head of a woman and the tail of a fish. [from a Middle English word, which comes from *mere* "lake, sea" + *mayde* "maid"]

mer·man (mûr′man′), *n., pl.* **mer·men.** an imaginary creature supposed to live in the sea, having the upper body and head of a man and the tail of a fish.

mer·ri·ment (mer′i mənt), *n.* merry gaiety; mirth.

mer·ry (mer′ē), *adj.,* **mer·ri·er, mer·ri·est. 1.** full of cheerfulness and gaiety. **2.** marked by gaiety: *a merry party.* **3. make merry,** to be gay or joyful: *New Year's Eve is a time for making merry.* —**mer′ri·ly,** *adv.*

mer·ry-go-round (mer′ē gō round′), *n.* **1.** Also, **carrousel.** a circular platform rotated by machinery, having wooden horses and seats on which people may ride, as at a carnival or amusement park. **2.** a busy way of living: *Life in a big city can be a merry-go-round.*

mer·ry·mak·ing (mer′ē mā′king), *n.* **1.** the act of taking part gaily in some merry celebration. **2.** a merry party. —**mer′ry·mak′er,** *n.*

me·sa (mā′sə), *n.* a kind of hill having a broad, flat top and steep sides, found esp. in the southwestern United States.

mes·dames (mā däm′, mā dam′), *n.* a plural of **madame.**

mes·de·moi·selles (mā′də mə zel′, mād′mwə zel′), *n.* a plural of **mademoiselle.**

mesh (mesh), *n.* **1.** one of the open spaces in a net, screen, or the like. **2. meshes, a.** the lines, threads, or the like, that are woven together to form such spaces. **b.** anything that catches or traps like a net: *the meshes of the law.* **3.** a loose, open fabric, such as net or screen. —*v.* **4.** to catch or entangle in or as if in a net; enmesh. **5.** to fit together; interlock.

Mes·o·po·ta·mi·a (mes′ə pə tā′mē ə), *n.* an ancient country in W Asia between the Tigris and Euphrates rivers: now part of Iraq. —**Mes′o·po·ta′mi·an,** *n., adj.*

Mes′o·zo′ic e′ra (mez′-ə zō′ik), the geological period following the Pale-ozoic era and extending from about 220 million to about 70 million years ago.

mes·quite (mə skēt′), *n.* a prickly shrub or small tree of the southwestern U.S. and Mexico that bears beanlike pods used as fodder.

mess (mes), *n.* **1.** a dirty or untidy condition: *The kitchen was in a mess after dinner.* **2.** a heap of things jumbled together: *a mess of papers.* **3.** a state of confusion: *His business affairs are in a mess.* **4.** an unpleasant situation: *His lying got him in a mess.* **5.** a group of people that eat regularly together: *the officers' mess.* **6.** the meal eaten by such a group. **7.** the place where such a meal is eaten. **8.** an amount of food that is needed to make up a dish or a meal: *She picked a mess of beans for dinner.* —*v.* **9.** to make dirty or untidy (often fol. by *up*): *Don't mess up my clean floor.* **10.** to make a muddle of (usually fol. by *up*): *He thoroughly messed up the report.* **11.** to eat as a member of a mess.

mes·sage (mes′ij), *n.* **1.** news, facts, etc., sent by mail, radio, a messenger, etc.: *She sent a message saying she was ill.* **2.** an important or official announcement, statement, etc.: *the President's message to Congress.* **3.** the central idea of a play, story, etc.

mes·sen·ger (mes′ən jər), *n.* a person who carries messages, parcels, etc.

mes·si·ah (mi sī′ə), *n.* a person who frees others from hardship, suffering, or the like; deliverer. —**mes·si·an·ic** (mes′ē an′ik), *adj.*

Mes·si·ah (mi sī′ə), *n.* **1.** (in Jewish belief) the person whom God will send to save the Jewish people. **2.** (in Christian belief) Jesus Christ, the savior of mankind. —**Mes·si·an·ic** (mes′ē an′ik), *adj.*

Messrs. (mes′ərz), the plural of **Mr.:** *Present at the meeting were Messrs. Gleason, Strong, and Merrill.* [short for the French word *Messieurs* "sirs"]

mess·y (mes′ē), *adj.*, **mess·i·er, mess·i·est. 1.** being in a dirty, untidy, or confused condition: *a messy, cluttered room.* **2.** embarrassing or unpleasant: *messy situations.* —**mess′i·ly,** *adv.* —**mess′i·ness,** *n.*

met (met), *v.* the past tense and past participle of **meet.**

me·tab·o·lism (mə tab′ə liz′əm), *n.* the complete set of physical and chemical processes by which a living thing uses the materials it takes in to maintain itself, grow, and carry on the other activities of life. —**met·a·bol·ic** (met′ə bol′ik), *adj.*

met·al (met′əl), *n.* **1.** any of a class of substances most of which are good conductors of electricity and heat, are shiny when polished, and generally can be shaped by hammering. Gold, silver, copper, iron, tin, and aluminum are all metals. **2.** an alloy of two or more pure metals, such as brass or bronze. **3.** (in chemistry) an element that gives up electrons and forms positive ions.

me·tal·lic (mə tal′ik), *adj.* of, relating to, consisting of, or reacting like a metal or metals.

met·al·lur·gy (met′ʲəlûr′jē), *n.* **1.** the technique or science of extracting metals from their ores. **2.** the technique or science of making alloys. —**met′al·lur′gi·cal,** *adj.* —**met′al·lur′gist,** *n.*

met·a·mor·pho·sis (met′ə môr′fə sis), *n., pl.* **met·a·mor·pho·ses** (met′ə môr′fə sēz′). **1.** a change or series of changes, such as that which occurs in some insects, involving a complete alteration in form and appearance. **2.** any complete change in appearance, way of acting, etc.: *the metamorphosis of a man into a frog in a fairy tale.*

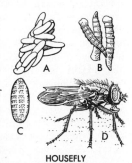

HOUSEFLY

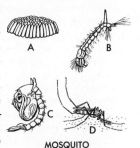

MOSQUITO

Metamorphosis
A, Eggs; B, Larvae;
C, Pupae; D, Adults

met·a·phor (met′ə fôr′), *n.* a kind of comparison in which one thing is said to be another that it resembles in some important way, such as "Her faith is a rock." —**met′a·phor′i·cal,** *adj.* —**met′a·phor′i·cal·ly,** *adv.*

met·a·phys·i·cal (met′ə fiz′i kəl), *adj.* **1.** of or like metaphysics: *a metaphysical question.* **2.** vague, obscure, or hard to understand: *a metaphysical argument full of strange words.* —**met′a·phys′i·cal·ly,** *adv.*

met·a·phys·ics (met′ə fiz′iks), *n. (used as sing.)* the branch of philosophy that deals with questions concerning the real nature of the universe, existence, etc.

mete (mēt), *v.*, **met·ed, met·ing.** to deal out; allot (usually fol. by *out*): *to mete out justice.*

me·te·or (mē′tē ər), *n.* **1.** a streak of light in the sky caused by a particle of matter from outer space entering the earth's atmosphere at high speed and being heated by friction until it glows; shooting star. **2.** the particle causing such a streak of light; meteoroid. **3.** a meteorite. —**me·te·or·ic** (mē′tē ôr′ik), *adj.*

me·te·or·ite (mē′tē ə rīt′), *n.* a piece of stone or metal that has reached the earth from outer space; a fallen meteoroid.

me·te·or·oid (mē′tē ə roid′), *n.* any of the small bodies, often remnants of comets, that become meteors if they enter the earth's atmosphere.

me·te·or·o·log·i·cal (mē′tē ər ə loj′i kəl), *adj.* **1.** having to do with the weather. **2.** having to do with meteorology. —**me′te·or·o·log′i·cal·ly,** *adv.*

me·te·or·ol·o·gy (mē′tē ə rol′ə jē), *n.* the science that deals with the atmosphere, esp. with regard to weather and climate. —**me′te·or·ol′o·gist,** *n.*

me·ter[1] (mē′tər), *n.* the base unit of length in the metric system, equal to 39.37 inches or 3.2808 feet. *Symbol:* m Also, *esp. British,* **metre.** [from the French word *mètre,* from Greek *metron* "measure"]

me·ter[2] (mē′tər), *n.* **1.** (in music) the rhythm of a composition, or the way in which this rhythm is indicated, beaten, or counted. **2.** (in poetry) the arrangement of words in rhythmic lines. Also, *esp. British,* **metre.** [from the Old English word *mēter,* which comes from Latin *metrum* "poetic meter," from Greek *metron* "measure." See *meter*[1]]

me·ter[3] (mē′tər), *n.* an instrument, esp. one with a dial, that automatically measures and indicates an amount, intensity, etc., as of gas, water, or electricity that is being supplied to a user: *The man is here to read the gas meter.* [from *mete* (used in its earlier sense, "to measure") + *-er*]

-meter, a suffix used to form nouns meaning **1.** a measuring instrument: *voltmeter; thermometer.* **2.** a measure of length of so many meters: *kilometer.*

meth·ane (meth′ān), *n.* a colorless, odorless, flammable gas, often used as a fuel for stoves.

me·thinks (mi thiŋks′), *v., past tense* **me·thought** (mi thôt′). *Archaic.* it seems to me.

meth·od (meth′əd), *n.* **1.** a way of doing something: *the French method of cooking chicken.* **2.** order or system in one's actions.

me·thod·i·cal (mə thod′i kəl), *adj.* working, acting, or performed according to a carefully followed plan, order, method, etc.: *a methodical housekeeper.* —**me·thod′i·cal·ly,** *adv.*

Meth·od·ist (meth′ə dist), *n.* a member of a Protestant denomination that grew out of the teachings of John Wesley. —**Meth′od·ism,** *n.*

Me·thu·se·lah (mə thoo′zə lə), *n.* (in the Bible) a man said to have lived 969 years.

me·tic·u·lous (mə tik′yə ləs), *adj.* very careful about details: *a meticulous worker.* —**me·tic′u·lous·ly,** *adv.* —**me·tic′u·lous·ness,** *n.*

me·tre (mē′tər), *n.* the British spelling of **meter**[1] and **meter**[2].

met·ric (me′trik), *adj.* of or concerning the metric system or its units of measure.

met·ri·cal (me′tri kəl), *adj.* **1.** having to do with poetic or musical meter. **2.** having to do with measurement. —**met′ri·cal·ly,** *adv.*

met′ric sys′tem, the decimal system of weights and measures used in scientific work and for all purposes in most countries. The basic units are the meter (equal to 39.37 inches) for length, the kilogram (equal to 2.2 pounds) for mass, and the liter (equal to 1.057 liquid quarts) for volume or capacity. See also table inside back cover.

met′ric ton′. See under **ton** (def. 1).

met·ro·nome (me′trə nōm′), *n.* an instrument for marking time, used esp. as an aid in practicing music by clicking at a fixed rate that is set in advance.

me·trop·o·lis (mə trop′ə lis), *n., pl.* **me·trop·o·lis·es.** **1.** a city of great size. **2.** a city that is the capital of a state or country or the center of a region: *Paris is the metropolis of France.* [from a Greek word meaning "mother city"]

met·ro·pol·i·tan (me′trə pol′i-tᵊn), *adj.* **1.** of or referring to a metropolis. —*n.* **2.** a person who lives in a metropolis or feels at home in one.

Metronome

-metry, a suffix used to form nouns meaning a science or system or process of measuring: *geometry.*

met·tle (met′ᵊl), *n.* spirit; courage: *He proved his mettle in the war.* —**met′tle·some,** *adj.*

mew (myōō), *n.* **1.** the sound a cat makes. —*v.* **2.** to make this sound.

mewl (myōōl), *v.* to cry, as a baby; whimper.

Mex·i·can (mek′sə kən), *adj.* **1.** of or concerning Mexico or its people. —*n.* **2.** a native or inhabitant of Mexico.

Mex′ican War′, the war between the U.S. and Mexico 1846–1848.

Mex·i·co (mek′sə kō′), *n.* **1.** a republic in S North America. 761,530 sq. mi. *Cap.:* Mexico City. **2. Gulf of,** an arm of the Atlantic surrounded by the U.S., Cuba, and Mexico. 700,000 sq. mi.

Mex′ico Cit′y, the capital city of Mexico, in the central part. about 7400 ft. above sea level.

mez·za·nine (mez′ə nēn′, mez′ə nēn′), *n.* **1.** a low story between two main stories in a building. **2.** the lowest balcony in a theater or its front part.

mfg., manufacturing.

mg, milligram; milligrams.

Mg, *Chem.* the symbol for **magnesium.**

Mgr., **1.** Manager. **2.** Monsignor.

mgt., management.

mi (mē), *n.* the third note of a musical scale.

mi., **1.** mile; miles. **2.** mill; mills. Also, **mi**

Mi·a·mi (mī am′ē, mī am′ə), *n.* a city in SE Florida: seaside winter resort.

mi·ca (mī′kə), *n.* a shiny mineral that can be split into thin, nearly transparent sheets sometimes used as windows in high-temperature ovens and as an electric insulator.

Mi·cah (mī′kə), *n.* **1.** (in the Bible) a prophet of the 8th century B.C. **2.** a book of the Old Testament bearing his name.

mice (mīs), *n.* the plural of **mouse.**

Mich., Michigan.

Mi·chael (mī′kəl), *n.* an archangel and leader of all the angels of Heaven.

Mich·ael·mas (mik′əl məs), *n.* a Christian festival celebrated on September 29 in honor of the archangel Michael.

Mi·chel·an·ge·lo (mī′-kəl an′jə lō′, mik′əl an′jə-lō′), *n.* (*Michelangelo Buonarroti*) 1475–1564, Italian sculptor, painter, architect, and poet.

Mich·i·gan (mish′ə-gən), *n.* a state in the N central United States. 58,-216 sq. mi. *Cap.:* Lansing. **2. Lake,** a lake in

the N central United States, between Wisconsin and Michigan: third largest of the Great Lakes. 22,400 sq. mi. —**Mich·i·gan·der** (mish′ə gan′dər), *n.*

micro-, a prefix meaning **1.** small: *microfilm.* **2.** enlarging or magnifying: *microscope.* **3.** a millionth part of: *microgram.*

mi·crobe (mī′krōb), *n.* a germ or other kind of bacterium.

mi·cro·film (mī′krə film′), *n.* a film on which printed or written material is filmed in very small size for storing in a small place.

Micrometer

mi·crom·e·ter (mī krom′i tər), *n.* **1.** Also, **microm′eter cal′iper.** a precision tool for measuring thicknesses. **2.** a device for measuring small distances and angles or for making precise adjustments, esp. one that is controlled by a screw.

mi·cron (mī′kron), *n.* a unit of length in the metric system, equal to one millionth of a meter. *Symbol:* μ, mu

mi·cro·or·gan·ism (mī′krō ôr′gə-niz′əm), *n.* a microscopic plant or animal: *Bacteria and viruses are microorganisms.*

mi·cro·phone (mī′krə fōn′), *n.* a device that converts sounds into electric signals for broadcasting, recording, etc.

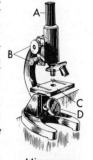

Microscope
A, Eyepiece; B, Adjusting screws; C, Platform for slide; D, Mirror for illumination

mi·cro·scope (mī′krə skōp′), *n.* an optical instrument, usually containing several sets of lenses, that provides great magnification and permits one to see things too small to be seen with the naked eye. [from the Greek words *mĭkros* "small" + *skopein* "to view"]

mi·cro·scop·ic (mī′krə skop′ik), *adj.* **1.** extremely small or fine; tiny. **2.** concerning or seen through a microscope. —**mi′cro·scop′i·cal·ly,** *adv.*

mi·cro·wave (mī′krō wāv′), *n.* a short radio wave having a wavelength between 1 millimeter and 30 centimeters.

mid¹ (mid), *adj.* located at or near the middle point or part: *in mid September; in the mid 1930's.* [from the Old English word *midd*]

mid² (mid), *prep.* another form of **amid.**

mid-, a prefix meaning **1.** middle: *midrib.* **2.** middle part of: *midday.*

Mi·das (mī′dəs), *n.* (in Greek mythology) a king of Phrygia who had the power to change everything he touched into gold.

mid·day (mid′dā′), *n.* **1.** the middle of the day; noon or the time around noon. —*adj.* **2.** referring to or happening during the middle part of the day: *Stay out of the midday sun.*

mid·dle (mid′°l), *adj.* **1.** halfway between two points, sides, etc.: *the middle house on the street.* —*n.* **2.** the part or position halfway between two points, sides, etc.: *the middle of the ocean.* **3.** the middle part of the human body, esp. the waist.

mid′dle age′, the time of life between youth and old age; the years between 45 and 65 or thereabouts. —**mid′dle-aged′,** *adj.*

Mid′dle Ag′es, the time in European history between the fall of Rome and the Italian Renaissance, from about A.D. 476 to around 1400.

Mid′dle Atlan′tic States′, New York, New Jersey, and Pennsylvania.

mid′dle class′, the social class above the working class and lower than the wealthy class or, in some countries, the aristocracy, now often thought of as including all people of average income, education, etc.

mid′dle ear′, the middle portion of the ear: an air-filled chamber directly behind the eardrum, containing three tiny bones called the hammer, anvil, and stirrup. See illus. at **ear.**

Mid′dle East′, (loosely) the area from Libya to Afghanistan. —**Mid′dle East′ern.**

Mid′dle Eng′lish, the English language as spoken and written from about 1150 to 1475.

mid·dle·man (mid′°l man′), *n., pl.* **mid·dle·men.** an intermediary or go-between, esp. a person who buys goods from a producer and sells to a consumer.

mid·dle·weight (mid′°l wāt′), *n.* **1.** a boxer weighing from 147 to 160 pounds, between a welterweight and a light heavyweight. —*adj.* **2.** of or referring to a middleweight or middleweights: *the middleweight championship.*

Mid′dle West′, another name for the **Midwest.** —**Mid′dle West′ern.** —**Mid′dle West′erner.**

mid·dling (mid′liŋg), *adj.* medium or average in size, rank, goodness, etc.: *a man of middling height.*

mid·dy (mid′ē), *n., pl.* **mid·dies. 1.** *Informal.* a mid-

shipman. **2.** Also, **mid′dy blouse′.** a loose blouse with a large, wide collar, worn esp. by sailors.

midge (mij), *n.* **1.** any of numerous tiny flying insects, such as the gnat. **2.** a tiny person.

midg·et (mij′it), *n.* **1.** a person who is very much shorter than normal but whose entire body is normal in proportions. **2.** any animal or thing very small of its kind. —*adj.* **3.** very small or of a kind below the usual size: *a midget variety of corn.*

mid·land (mid′lənd), *n.* **1.** the middle or inward part of a country: *Illinois is in the midland of the U.S.* —*adj.* **2.** in or of the midland: *a midland state.*

mid·most (mid′mōst′), *adj.* being exactly in or very near the middle: *the midmost part of a tunnel.*

mid·night (mid′nīt′), *n.* **1.** the middle of the night; at or around twelve o'clock. —*adj.* **2.** occurring in the middle of the night: *a midnight snack.* **3.** resembling the darkness of midnight: *a midnight blue.*

mid·rib (mid′rib′), *n.* the middle rib of a leaf.

mid·riff (mid′rif), *n.* the middle part of the body between the chest and the waist: *The blow struck him in the midriff.*

M, Midrib

mid·ship·man (mid′ship′mən), *n., pl.* **mid·ship·men.** a student in the U.S. Naval Academy training to become a commissioned officer in the Navy or the Marine Corps. See also **cadet.**

midst¹ (midst), *n.* **1.** a middle part or place; middle; center: *in the midst of the crowd.* **2.** the most important or critical time: *He broke down in the midst of the crisis.* [from the Middle English word *middes,* which comes from *amiddes* "amidst"]

midst² (midst), *prep.* another form of **amidst.**

mid·stream (mid′strēm′), *n.* the middle of a stream.

mid·sum·mer (mid′sum′ər), *n.* **1.** the middle of summer. —*adj.* **2.** occurring in or typical of midsummer: *a midsummer heat wave.*

Mid·way (mid′wā′), *n.* a group of several U.S. islets in the N Pacific.

Mid·west (mid′west′), *n.* the central United States, usually considered to be the area W of the Alleghenies, N of Oklahoma and Arkansas, and E of the Rockies. Also, **Middle West.**

Mid·west·ern (mid′wes′tərn), *adj.* of or referring to the Midwest. —**Mid′west′ern·er,** *n.*

mid·wife (mid′wīf′), *n., pl.* **mid·wives** (mid′wīvz′). a woman who assists women during childbirth.

mid·win·ter (mid′win′tər), *n.* **1.** the middle of winter. —*adj.* **2.** typical of or occurring in the middle of the winter: *a midwinter storm.*

mien (mēn), *n.* the way a person bears or carries himself or herself; bearing: *a ruler of noble mien.*

might¹ (mīt), *v.* the past tense of **may.**

might² (mīt), *n.* power, force, or ability: *He tried with all his might.* [from the Old English word *miht*]

might·y (mī′tē), *adj.,* **might·i·er, might·i·est. 1.** having or showing might or power: *mighty armies.* **2.** of great size; huge: *mighty oaks.* **3.** of great importance or extent: *a mighty accomplishment.* —*adv.* **4.** *Informal.* very; extremely: *I'm mighty pleased to see you.* —**might′i·ly,** *adv.* —**might′i·ness,** *n.*

mi·graine (mī′grān), *n.* a very severe kind of headache, usually on only one side of the head and often accompanied by nausea.

mi·grant (mī′grənt), *adj.* **1.** migrating or migratory. —*n.* **2.** a person or thing that migrates.

mi·grate (mī′grāt), *v.,* **mi·grat·ed, mi·grat·ing. 1.** to go from one country, region, etc., to settle in another, as tribes of people. **2.** to go back and forth regularly from one region to another, as certain birds, fishes, and other animals. —**mi′gra·tor,** *n.*

mi·gra·tion (mī grā′shən), *n.* **1.** the act of migrating. **2.** a migrating movement: *vast migrations of settlers.* **3.** a number of migrating people or animals.

mi·gra·to·ry (mī′grə tôr′ē), *adj.* **1.** migrating by habit or custom: *migratory birds.* **2.** making a migration: *migratory tribes.* **3.** referring to or indicating migration: *migratory movements of birds.*

mi·ka·do (mi kä′dō), *n., pl.* **mi·ka·dos.** a title of the emperor of Japan.

Mi·lan (mi lan′, mi län′), *n.* a city in N Italy.

milch (milch), *adj.* yielding milk; kept for its milk: *a milch cow.*

mild (mīld), *adj.* **1.** gentle in feeling or behavior toward others. **2.** not severe or extreme: *a mild winter.* **3.** not sharp or strong, as in taste: *a mild flavor.* —**mild′ly,** *adv.* —**mild′ness,** *n.*

mil·dew (mil′dōō′, -dyōō′), *n.* **1.** a kind of fungus that grows on cloth, leather, paper, etc., in damp climates. —*v.* **2.** to cause mildew in; be affected with mildew. [from the Old English word *mildēaw,* which comes from *mil-* "honey" + *dēaw* "dew"]

mile (mīl), *n.* **1.** Also, **statute mile.** a unit of distance used in land measurements, equal to 5280 feet or 1760 yards (1.609 kilometers). **2.** Also, **air mile, nautical mile.** a unit of distance used in navigation at sea or in aircraft, equal to about 6076 feet (1.852 kilometers).

mile·age (mī′lij), *n.* **1.** the distance in miles traveled or to be traveled: *the mileage between two cities.* **2.** the number of miles a vehicle can travel on a certain quantity of fuel: *20 miles per gallon is good mileage for that car.* **3.** an allowance for traveling at a fixed rate per mile: *His mileage came to more than $90.*

mile·post (mīl′pōst′), *n.* a post showing the distance in miles to a place.

mile·stone (mīl′stōn′), *n.* **1.** a stone showing the distance in miles to a place. **2.** a significant event, as in history or a person's life: *His first job was a milestone in his career.*

mil·i·tant (mil′i tənt), *adj.* **1.** aggressive or warlike; engaged in warfare: *a militant nation.* —*n.* **2.** a person who is aggressive or ready to fight in behalf of a cause: *a demonstration led by militants.*

mil·i·ta·rism (mil′i tə riz′əm), *n.* **1.** a policy of maintaining a very powerful military force. **2.** a tendency to regard military ideals as supreme. —**mil′i·ta·rist,** *n.* —**mil′i·ta·ris′tic,** *adj.*

mil·i·ta·rize (mil′i tə rīz′), *v.,* **mil·i·ta·rized, mil·i·ta·**

riz·ing. **1.** to equip with armed forces, military supplies, etc. **2.** to inspire with military ideals or spirit. —**mil′i·ta·ri·za′tion,** *n.*

mil·i·tar·y (mil′i ter′ē), *adj.* **1.** of or concerning armed forces, soldiers, or war: *military strength.* **2.** of, suitable to, or referring to a soldier: *military bearing; a military career.* **3.** done by soldiers: *military duty.* —*n., pl.* **mil·i·tar·ies** *or* **mil·i·tar·y. 4.** the armed forces of a nation; military personnel, esp. commissioned officers as a group: *Representatives of the military met with the press.* —**mil′i·tar′i·ly,** *adv.*

mil·i·tate (mil′i tāt′), *v.,* **mil·i·tat·ed, mil·i·tat·ing.** to operate; have effect or influence: *Every fact he gave militated against the plan.*

mi·li·tia (mi lish′ə), *n.* a body of citizens enrolled in military service but serving full time only in emergencies. [from the Latin word *miles* "soldier"]

milk (milk), *n.* **1.** a white or bluish-white liquid produced by female mammals for feeding their young. **2.** this liquid produced by cows, goats, or other domesticated animals and used as food for humans. **3.** any liquid resembling this, as the juice or sap of certain plants, certain medicines, etc.: *coconut milk; milk of magnesia.* —*v.* **4.** to draw milk from (a cow or other animal). **5.** to drain wealth, strength, information, etc., from (someone): *The fortuneteller milked the customers of their savings.* **6. cry over spilt milk,** to grieve over something that cannot be changed.

milk·man (milk′man′), *n., pl.* **milk·men.** a man who sells or delivers milk.

milk′ of magne′sia, a milky mixture of magnesia in water, used as a mild laxative or to soothe an upset stomach.

milk′ shake′, a drink made of cold milk, flavoring, and usually ice cream, mixed together.

milk·weed (milk′wēd′), *n.* a tall plant of down-filled pods and stems filled with a sticky, milky juice.

milk·y (milk′ē), *adj.,* **milk·i·er, milk·i·est. 1.** like milk, as in color or taste: *a milky white.* **2.** made of or containing milk: *a milky sauce.* —**milk′i·ness,** *n.*

Milk′y Way′, a cloudlike band of light stretching across the sky and composed of innumerable stars too far away to be seen

Milkweed

clearly with the naked eye. The Milky Way is the galaxy that contains the solar system.

mill¹ (mil), *n.* **1.** a building in which manufacturing or other mechanical work is done: *a steel mill.* **2.** a building in which grain is ground: *a flour mill.* **3.** a machine for grinding or crushing any solid substance, such as corn, wheat, or coffee. **4.** any of various machines that prepare materials or perform an operation: *a windmill.* —*v.* **5.** to grind, work, treat, or shape (something) in or with a mill. **6.** to move around aimlessly (often fol. by *about* or *around*): *to mill about in the lobby.* **7. through the mill,** suffering severe problems: *Dad has really been through the mill since Mother got sick.* [from the Old English word *mylen,* which comes from Latin *malīna*]

mill² (mil), *n.* one tenth of a cent: used only in figuring. [short for the Latin word *millēsimus* "thousandth," which comes from *mille* "thousand"]

mil·len·ni·um (mi len′ē əm), *n., pl.* **mil·len·ni·ums** *or* **mil·len·ni·a** (mi len′ē ə). **1.** a period of one thousand years. **2. the millennium,** (in the Bible) the period of a thousand years during which Christ will reign on earth. **3.** a period of righteousness and happiness, esp. in the indefinite future. —**mil·len′ni·al,** *adj.*

mill·er (mil′ər), *n.* **1.** a person who owns or operates a mill, esp. a flour mill. **2.** a moth having wings that seem powdered with flour.

mil·let (mil′it), *n.* a grass grown in the U.S. for fodder and in Europe and Asia for its edible grain.

milli-, a prefix meaning a thousandth part of: *millimeter.*

mil·li·gram (mil′ə gram′), *n.* a very small unit of mass or weight in the metric system, equal to ¹/₁₀₀₀ gram, or 0.015 grain. *Symbol:* mg

mil·li·li·ter (mil′ə lē′tər), *n.* a unit of capacity in the metric system, equal to ¹/₁₀₀₀ liter, or 0.034 fluid ounce. *Symbol:* ml

mil·li·me·ter (mil′ə mē′tər), *n.* a unit of length in the metric system, equal to ¹/₁₀₀₀ meter, or 0.039 inch. *Symbol:* mm

mil·li·ner (mil′ə nər), *n.* a person who makes or sells hats for women.

mil·li·ner·y (mil′ə ner′ē), *n.* **1.** women's hats. **2.** the business of a milliner.

mil·lion (mil′yən), *n., pl.* **mil·lions** *or* (after a numeral) **mil·lion. 1.** a number that is a thousand times one thousand (1,000,000). **2.** a group of this many persons or things: *A million voted against the measure.* **3. millions,** the numbers, dollars, etc., between 1,000,000 and 999,999,999: *Some building projects cost in the millions.* —*adj.* **4.** amounting to one million in number: *a million persons.*

mil·lion·aire (mil′yə nâr′), *n.* **1.** a person whose wealth amounts to a million or more dollars, pounds, etc. **2.** any very rich person.

mil·lionth (mil′yənth), *adj.* **1.** coming last in a series of a million. **2.** being one of a million equal parts. — *n.* **3.** the millionth member of a series. **4.** one of a million equal parts.

mil·li·pede (mil′ə pēd′), *n.* a small, wormlike animal resembling a centipede but having more legs.

mill·stone (mil′stōn′), *n.*
1. either of a pair of heavy round stones between which grain is ground. **2.** any heavy burden: *His debts were a millstone around his neck.*

Millipede
(length 1 in.)

Mil·wau·kee (mil wô′kē), *n.* a port city in SE Wisconsin, on Lake Michigan.

mime (mīm), *n.* **1.** an actor who mimics or who performs in a pantomime. **2.** a jester, clown, etc. —*v.,* **mimed, mim·ing. 3.** to mimic; imitate.

mim·e·o·graph (mim′ē ə graf′), *n.* **1.** a machine that makes copies from a typewritten or written stencil.

—*v.* **2.** to make copies of (something) using a mimeograph: *to mimeograph an announcement.*

mim·ic (mim′ik), *v.,* **mim·icked, mim·ick·ing. 1.** to imitate or copy (someone) in action, speech, etc., often playfully or in order to ridicule. **2.** to imitate closely; ape: *He mimicked his older brother's way of walking.* **3.** to resemble closely: *Certain insects mimic leaves or bark.* — *n.* **4.** a person who mimics, esp. with skill. — *adj.* **5.** mock or sham: *a mimic battle.*

mim·ic·ry (mim′ik rē), *n., pl.* **mim·ic·ries. 1.** the act, practice, or art of mimicking. **2.** the close resemblance, as if from imitation, of an animal to some different animal or to surrounding objects, esp. as a means of protection or concealment.

mi·mo·sa (mi mō′sə), *n.* any of numerous plants or trees, native to warm regions, having small flowers and feathery leaves.

min., **1.** minimum. **2.** minute; minutes.

min·a·ret (min′ə ret′), *n.* (in Muslim countries) a slender tower attached to a mosque from which a crier calls the people to prayer. [from a French word, which comes from Arabic *manārah* "lighthouse"]

Minaret

mince (mins), *v.,* **minced, minc·ing. 1.** to cut into very small pieces: *to mince an onion.* **2.** to act or speak with affected elegance. **3.** to walk with short, dainty steps. —*n.* **4.** something cut up in very small pieces; mincemeat. **5. not mince words,** to speak bluntly and frankly: *I never mince words about what I think.*

mince·meat (mins′mēt′), *n.* a mixture of minced apples, suet, and sometimes meat, raisins, currants, spices, etc., used as a filling for pies.

mind (mīnd), *n.* **1.** the part of a human being that thinks, understands, feels, wishes, imagines, remembers, chooses, makes decisions, etc. **2.** the powers of reasoning and understanding, as distinguished from the powers of feeling and wishing. **3.** intellectual ability: *He has a good mind.* **4.** reason or sanity: *to lose one's mind.* **5.** way of thinking and feeling: *To my mind, you made a mistake.* **6.** opinion, intention, or desire: *to change one's mind.* **7.** remembrance or recollection: *Happier days were called to mind.* **8.** attention; thoughts: *He can't keep his mind on his studies.* —*v.* **9.** to pay attention to; heed: *Mind the instructions.* **10.** to obey; heed: *to mind one's parents.* **11.** to attend to; take care of: *to mind the baby.* **12.** to be careful about; take care: *Mind what you say.* **13.** to object to (something); feel concern: *Do you mind the open window? Do you mind if we leave early?* **14. a piece of one's mind,** a scolding or reprimand: *I gave her a piece of my mind for doing such sloppy work.* **15. bear in mind,** to remember: *Bear in mind that we're leaving at 6 a.m.* **16. be of one mind,** to be in agreement; have the same opinion: *They were of one mind about where to go.* **17. have a good mind to,** to feel tempted or inclined to: *I have a good mind to leave town.* **18. make up one's mind,** to decide on a particular action: *Make up your mind and do it.* **19. never mind,** don't bother; disregard it. **20. presence of mind,** ability to think clearly in a crisis: *He had the presence of mind to call the police.* [from the Old English word *gemynd*]

mind·ed (mīn′did), *adj.* **1.** having a certain kind of mind (usually used in combination): *strong-minded.* **2.** inclined or disposed: *He was minded to go home.*

mind·ful (mīnd′fəl), *adj.* attentive or careful (usually fol. by *of*): *mindful of duties.*

mind·less (mīnd′lis), *adj.* **1.** without intelligence. **2.** careless or thoughtless: *mindless of danger.*

mind′ read′ing, the supposed ability to know what other people are thinking. —**mind′ read′er.**

mine[1] (mīn), *pron.* **1.** that which belongs to me: *The yellow sweater is mine. Mine is the car with the flat tire.* **2.** *Archaic.* my (used before a word beginning with a vowel or a silent *h,* or following a noun): *mine eyes; lady mine.* [from the Old English word *mīn*]

mine[2] (mīn), *n.* **1.** a pit or tunnel in the earth for removing metal ores, precious stones, coal, or other minerals. **2.** an abundant supply or source: *She has a mine of information about sports cars.* **3.** (in warfare) **a.** an underground passage, as for placing explosives beneath an enemy's fortifications or position. **b.** an explosive that is buried underground or placed underwater for the purpose of blowing up an enemy's soldiers, vehicles, ships, etc. —*v.*, **mined, min·ing. 4.** to dig for minerals; make a mine. **5.** to remove from a mine: *to mine copper.* **6.** to dig in (earth, rock, etc.) in order to get ores, coal, etc. **7.** to make underground passages in or under. **8.** to lay military mines in or under: *to mine a bridge.* [from a French word, which is perhaps a shortened form of Old French *miniere* "mine," from medieval Latin *minera*]

min·er (mī′nər), *n.* a person who works in a mine.

min·er·al (min′ər əl), *n.* **1.** a substance that is taken from the earth and has a definite chemical composition, such as coal, quartz, or copper. **2.** anything that is not of animal or vegetable origin. —*adj.* **3.** concerning, resembling, or containing minerals.

min·er·al·o·gy (min′ə rol′ə jē), *n.* the science or study of minerals. —**min′er·al′o·gist,** *n.*

Mi·ner·va (mi nûr′və), *n.* (in Roman mythology) the goddess of wisdom and the arts: identified with the Greek goddess Athena.

min·gle (miñg′gəl), *v.*, **min·gled, min·gling. 1.** to mix or combine; blend; unite: *to mingle voices in a chorus.* **2.** to become mixed or blended: *a town where old and new ways mingle.* **3.** to mix or take part with others: *He doesn't mingle with people his own age.*

mini-, a prefix meaning **1.** very short: *miniskirt.* **2.** very small: *minicalculator.*

min·i·a·ture (min′ē ə chər, min′ə chər), *n.* **1.** a representation or image of something on a small or reduced scale: *a miniature of the Eiffel Tower.* **2.** a very small painting, esp. a portrait. —*adj.* **3.** represented on a very small scale; very small.

min·im (min′əm), *n.* the smallest unit of liquid measure, equal to 1/60 of a fluid dram.

min·i·mize (min′ə mīz′), *v.*, **min·i·mized, min·i·miz·ing. 1.** to reduce (something) to the smallest possible amount or degree: *safety rules to minimize accidents.* **2.** to belittle the value or importance of: *He minimized his own accomplishments.*

min·i·mum (min′ə məm), *n.* **1.** the least possible or permissible amount or degree: *Dark shades admit a minimum of light.* **2.** the lowest amount or degree attained or recorded: *The temperature yesterday was the minimum for that date.* —*adj.* **3.** least or lowest possible or permissible: *a minimum shipping charge.*

min·ing (mī′niñg), *n.* **1.** the process or industry of extracting ores, coal, etc., from the earth. **2.** the laying of explosive mines.

min·ion (min′yən), *n.* **1.** a servant or follower, esp. of a person or group holding power: *the minions of the law.* **2.** a person in favor; favorite.

min·is·ter (min′i stər), *n.* **1.** a clergyman, esp. of a Protestant denomination; pastor. **2.** (in some countries) the head of a government department: *a minister of education.* **3.** a person, ranking below an ambassador, who represents his country abroad. —*v.* **4.** to perform the functions of a clergyman or pastor. **5.** to give service, care, or aid: *to minister to the sick and needy.* —**min·is·te·ri·al** (min′i stēr′ē əl), *adj.*

min·is·tra·tion (min′i strā′shən), *n.* **1.** the act of ministering. **2.** any service, care, or aid given.

min·is·try (min′i strē), *n.*, *pl.* **min·is·tries. 1.** the office or functions of a minister. **2.** ministers as a group or class. **3.** a government department headed by a minister. **4.** the building or buildings housing such a department. **5.** the term of office of a minister. **6.** the act of ministering or serving.

Mink
(length 15 in.)

mink (miñgk), *n.*, *pl.* **minks** *or* **mink. 1.** an animal resembling a weasel that is raised for its soft, valuable fur. **2.** the fur of this animal.

Minn., Minnesota.

Min·ne·ap·o·lis (min′ē ap′ə lis), *n.* a city in SE Minnesota, on the Mississippi River.

Min·ne·so·ta (min′i sō′tə), *n.* a state in the N central United States. 84,068 sq. mi. *Cap.:* St. Paul. —**Min′ne·so′tan,** *n.*, *adj.*

min·now (min′ō), *n.*, *pl.* **min·nows** *or* **min·now.** any of various small freshwater fishes.

mi·nor (mī′nər), *adj.* **1.** smaller or less important: *a minor planet; a minor wound.* **2.** of or referring

to a musical interval a half step smaller than the corresponding major interval: *C to E♭ is a minor third.*

3. of or referring to a musical chord, scale, or key having one or more such intervals, reckoned from the lowest note or tonic: *The key of C minor contains E♭ instead of E♮.* —*n.* **4.** a person under legal age: *Liquor is not sold to minors.*

mi·nor·i·ty (mi nôr′i tē), *n.*, *pl.* **mi·nor·i·ties.** **1.** the smaller of two parts making up a whole: *Our candidate received a minority of the votes.* **2.** Also, **minor′ity group′.** a group that differs in race, religion, national origin, etc., from the majority of the population. **3.** the condition or time of being under legal age.

Min·o·taur (min′ə tôr′), *n.* (in Greek mythology) a monster, half bull and half man, that was kept in a labyrinth in Crete and was killed by Theseus.

min·strel (min′strəl), *n.* **1.** a medieval musician who sang or recited to the accompaniment of musical instruments. **2.** any musician, singer, or poet. **3.** (formerly) one of a troupe of singers, dancers, and comedians, usually white men made up as Negroes.

mint¹ (mint), *n.* **1.** any of several herbs having pointed green leaves that have a pleasant smell and taste, used as a flavoring. **2.** a candy flavored with mint. [from the Old English word *minte,* which comes from Latin *mentha,* from Greek *minthē*]

mint² (mint), *n.* **1.** a place where money is coined. **2.** *Informal.* a large amount, esp. of money: *He made a mint in the stock market.* —*adj.* **3.** brand-new: *a book in mint condition.* —*v.* **4.** to make (metal) into coins. **5.** to make (coins) out of metal. [from the Old English word *mynet* "coin," which comes from Latin *monēta,* named after the temple of Juno *Monēta,* where Roman money was coined]

min·u·end (min′yoo end′), *n.* (in arithmetic) the number from which another is subtracted: *In the case of 12 − 7 = 5, 12 is the minuend.* See also **subtrahend.**

min·u·et (min′yoo et′), *n.* **1.** a slow, graceful, formal dance popular in the 17th and 18th centuries. **2.** a piece of music suitable for this dance.

mi·nus (mī′nəs), *prep.* **1.** less by the subtraction of; decreased by: *Nine minus three is six.* **2.** lacking; without: *a silver teapot minus a lid.* —*adj.* **3.** indicating or used in subtraction: *a minus sign.* **4.** less than or lower than zero: *a temperature of minus ten degrees.* **5.** less than or lower than a fixed point: *a grade of B minus.* —*n.* **6.** a minus sign. **7.** a quantity subtracted: *You get a minus for each wrong answer.*

mi′nus sign′, the symbol (−) placed between two numbers to indicate that the second number is to be subtracted from the first.

min·ute¹ (min′it), *n.* **1.** a unit of time equal to ¹⁄₆₀ hour or 60 seconds. **2.** a unit of angular measure equal to ¹⁄₆₀ degree or 60 seconds. *Symbol: ′ The tropic of Cancer is 23 degrees 30 minutes (23°30′) north of the equator.* **3.** a short time; moment: *I'll join you in a minute.* **4.** minutes, an official record of a meeting. **5.** **up to the minute,** up-to-date; modern: *After remodeling, our kitchen will be up to the*

minute. [from the medieval Latin word *minūta,* which comes from Latin *minūtus* "lessened, made smaller." See *minute²*]

mi·nute² (mī noot′, -nyoot′), *adj.* **1.** very small: *a minute amount; minute figures.* **2.** careful and thorough; paying attention to details: *a minute examination.* [from the Latin word *minūtus* "lessened, made smaller," which comes from *minuere* "to diminish"] —**mi·nute′ly,** *adv.* —**mi·nute′ness,** *n.*

Min·ute·man (min′it man′), *n.*, *pl.* **Min·ute·men.** one of a group of civilians at the time of the American Revolution who remained ready to serve as soldiers on very short notice.

minx (mingks), *n.* a pert or saucy girl.

mir·a·cle (mir′ə kəl), *n.* **1.** an event that cannot be explained by natural laws and is therefore believed to be of divine or supernatural origin. **2.** an unusual happening; wonder; marvel: *the miracles of science.*

mi·rac·u·lous (mi rak′yə ləs), *adj.* **1.** of the nature of a miracle: *a miraculous cure.* **2.** seeming to perform miracles: *a miraculous drug.* —**mi·rac′u·lous·ly,** *adv.*

mi·rage (mi räzh′), *n.* **1.** an optical effect occurring sometimes in open spaces, such as the sea or a desert, that causes the reflection of distant objects to appear closer and often upside down. **2.** something unreal or fanciful; illusion.

mire (mī°r), *n.* **1.** an area of wet, marshy ground. **2.** deep mud. —*v.,* **mired, mir·ing.** **3.** to stick or cause to stick fast in mire: *We drove off the road and mired the car.* **4.** to soil or bespatter with mud or filth.

mir·ror (mir′ər), *n.* **1.** a flat piece of glass coated on the back with mercury, silver, or some other reflecting substance. **2.** any polished surface of metal or other smooth material that reflects light. **3.** something that gives a true picture or description: *His books are a mirror of early America.* —*v.* **4.** to reflect: *The pond mirrored the full moon.* **5.** to give a picture or description of: *Her suffering was mirrored in her face.*

mirth (mûrth), *n.* laughing gaiety or amusement. —**mirth′ful,** *adj.* —**mirth′ful·ly,** *adv.*

mis-, a prefix meaning **1.** not: *mistrust.* **2.** bad or badly: *misfortune; misfire.* **3.** incorrectly or mistakenly: *misprint.* **4.** wrong or wrongly: *mistrial; misfit.*

mis·ad·ven·ture (mis′əd ven′chər), *n.* an unfortunate accident; mishap: *We arrived safely, in spite of many misadventures on the way.*

mis·an·thrope (mis′ən throp′, miz′ən throp′), *n.* a person who dislikes or distrusts all mankind. —**mis·an·throp·ic** (mis′ən throp′ik, miz′-), *adj.*

mis·ap·ply (mis′ə plī′), *v.,* **mis·ap·plied, mis·ap·ply·ing.** to use or apply wrongly: *to misapply a word.*

mis·ap·pre·hend (mis′ap ri hend′), *v.* to misunderstand. —**mis′ap·pre·hen′sion,** *n.*

mis·ap·pro·pri·ate (mis′ə prō′prē āt′), *v.,* **mis·ap·pro·pri·at·ed, mis·ap·pro·pri·at·ing.** to put to a wrong use: *to misappropriate public funds.* —**mis′ap·pro′pri·a′tion,** *n.*

mis·be·have (mis′bi hāv′), *v.,* **mis·be·haved, mis·be-**

---

act, āble, dâre, ärt;   ebb, ēqual;   if, īce;   hot, ōver, ôrder;   oil;   book;   ōoze; out;   up, ûrge;   ə = *a* as in *alone;* ᵊ as in *button* (but′ᵊn), *fire* (fī°r);   chief;   shoe;   thin;   ŧħat;   zh as in *measure* (mezh′ər). See full key inside cover.

hav·ing. to behave badly or improperly. —mis·be·ha/vior, *n.*

misc., 1. miscellaneous. 2. miscellany.

mis·cal·cu·late (mis kal/kyə lāt/), *v.*, mis·cal·cu·lat·ed, mis·cal·cu·lat·ing. to calculate or judge incorrectly. —mis/cal·cu·la/tion, *n.*

mis·call (mis kôl/), *v.* to call by a wrong name.

mis·car·riage (mis kar/ij, *or, for def. 2,* mis/kar ij), *n.* 1. failure to achieve a proper or desired result: *The trial was a miscarriage of justice.* 2. the birth of a baby before it is developed enough to live.

mis·car·ry (mis kar/ē), *v.,* mis·car·ried, mis·car·ry·ing. 1. to fail to achieve a desired result: *Our plans miscarried because supplies did not arrive in time.* 2. to have a miscarriage during pregnancy.

mis·cel·la·ne·ous (mis/ə lā/nē əs), *adj.* consisting of different kinds: *miscellaneous pens and pencils.*

mis·cel·la·ny (mis/ə lā/nē), *n.* 1. a collection of things of different kinds: *a miscellany of old books, clothes, and furniture for sale.* 2. a volume of writings by several authors on a variety of subjects.

mis·chance (mis chans/), *n.* an unfortunate occurrence; mishap: *By some mischance, my name was not entered on the list of members.*

mis·chief (mis/chif), *n.* 1. a tendency to tease or annoy: *That little rascal is full of mischief.* 2. an action that causes injury or damage: *A student's mischief caused the fire at the school.* 3. a mischief-maker. 4. harm or trouble: *His careless driving brought him to mischief.*

mis·chief-mak·er (mis/chif mā/kər), *n.* a person who makes mischief or stirs up trouble.

mis·chie·vous (mis/chə vəs), *adj.* 1. full of mischief; playful; teasing: *a mischievous puppy.* 2. harmful or injurious: *Don't listen to mischievous gossip.* —mis/chie·vous·ly, *adv.* —mis/chie·vous·ness, *n.*

mis·con·cep·tion (mis/kən sep/shən), *n.* a wrong idea of something; mistaken notion: *to have a misconception of the size of the world.*

mis·con·duct (mis kon/dukt), *n.* 1. wrong or improper conduct. 2. poor management, esp. of a business. —*v.* (mis/kən dukt/). 3. to manage poorly or inefficiently. 4. to misbehave (oneself).

mis·count (mis kount/), *v.* 1. to count or calculate wrongly. —*n.* 2. a wrong count or calculation.

mis·cre·ant (mis/krē ənt), *n.* 1. a wicked person; villain. —*adj.* 2. like a villain; wicked; evil.

mis·deal (mis dēl/), *v.,* mis·dealt (mis delt/), mis·deal·ing. 1. to deal wrongly, esp. at cards. —*n.* 2. an incorrect deal.

mis·deed (mis dēd/), *n.* a wicked deed; wrongdoing.

mis·de·mean·or (mis/di mē/nər), *n.* 1. a crime that is considered less serious than a felony, usually punishable by a fine or by imprisonment for not more than one year. 2. any misbehavior or wrongdoing.

mis·di·rect (mis/di rekt/), *v.* 1. to give wrong directions or instructions to: *We got lost when a passer-by misdirected us.* 2. to put to a wrong use; misapply: *to misdirect one's talents.* 3. to send (a letter, package, telegram, or the like) to a wrong address. —mis/di·rec/tion, *n.*

mis·do·ing (mis dōō/ing), *n.* a misdeed; wrongdoing.

mi·ser (mī/zər), *n.* 1. a person who dislikes spending or sharing his money or possessions. 2. a person who lives in poverty while saving and hoarding money.

mis·er·a·ble (miz/ər ə bəl), *adj.* 1. living in poverty; needy. 2. of wretched character or quality; mean: *a miserable hut.* 3. depressed in spirit; melancholy: *Rainy days make me miserable.* 4. expressing misery: *I saw the miserable look on his face.* 5. pitiable; deplorable: *a miserable failure.* —mis/er·a·bly, *adv.*

mi·ser·ly (mī/zər lē), *adj.* of or like a miser; stingy. —mi/ser·li·ness, *n.*

mis·er·y (miz/ə rē), *n., pl.* mis·er·ies. 1. very poor or wretched conditions: *They lived in misery in a slum.* 2. great distress of mind; extreme unhappiness. 3. something that causes distress or unhappiness: *His lameness has been a misery to him.*

mis·fire (mis fīʳr/), *v.,* mis·fired, mis·fir·ing. 1. to fail to fire, as a gun, rocket, engine, etc. 2. *Informal.* to fail to achieve a desired result: *Our plans misfired.* —*n.* 3. a failure to fire.

mis·fit (mis/fit, mis fit/), *n.* 1. a person who is badly adjusted to his work or his surroundings. 2. something, such as a garment, that does not fit properly.

mis·for·tune (mis fôr/chən), *n.* 1. bad luck: *He succeeded in spite of misfortune.* 2. an unfortunate accident; mishap: *Our worst misfortune was losing our home in the flood.*

mis·giv·ing (mis giv/ing), *n.* a feeling of doubt, distrust, or anxiety: *I have misgivings about letting Jimmy drive the car.*

mis·gov·ern (mis guv/ərn), *v.* to govern or manage badly. —mis·gov/ern·ment, *n.*

mis·guid·ed (mis gī/did), *adj.* 1. based on a wrong notion; mistaken: *misguided efforts to help the poor.* 2. following wrong influences; misled: *The misguided boy turned to crime.* —mis·guid/ed·ly, *adv.*

mis·han·dle (mis han/dᵊl), *v.,* mis·han·dled, mis·han·dling. 1. to handle roughly or clumsily: *Don't mishandle the glassware.* 2. to manage badly: *to mishandle one's money.*

mis·hap (mis/hap, mis hap/), *n.* an unfortunate accident: *We completed the unloading without mishap.*

mis·in·form (mis/in fôrm/), *v.* to give false or incorrect information to: *You were misinformed about my plans.* —mis·in·for·ma·tion (mis/in fər mā/shən), *n.*

mis·in·ter·pret (mis/in tûr/prit), *v.* to interpret wrongly; misunderstand: *He misinterpreted my offer to help.* —mis/in·ter/pre·ta/tion, *n.*

mis·judge (mis juj/), *v.,* mis·judged, mis·judg·ing. 1. to estimate incorrectly: *to misjudge a distance.* 2. to judge wrongly or unfairly: *to misjudge a good friend.* —mis·judg/ment, mis·judge/ment, *n.*

mis·lay (mis lā/), *v.,* mis·laid (mis lād/), mis·lay·ing. to put (something) in a place and then forget where it is: *to mislay one's glasses.*

mis·lead (mis lēd/), *v.,* mis·led (mis led/), mis·lead·ing. 1. to lead or guide wrongly: *The police were misled by a false trail left by the robbers.* 2. to lead into error or wrongdoing: *He was an honest boy, but his companions misled him.* 3. to give a wrong impression; deceive: *to be misled by lies and deceit.*

mis·man·age (mis man′ij), *v.*, **mis·man·aged, mis·man·ag·ing.** to manage (something) badly or dishonestly: *to mismanage public funds.* —**mis·man′age·ment,** *n.*

mis·name (mis nām′), *v.*, **mis·named, mis·nam·ing.** to call by a wrong or unsuitable name: *a dirty, narrow street misnamed Golden Lane.*

mis·no·mer (mis nō′mər), *n.* a wrong or unsuitable name or term: *"Fish" is a misnomer if applied to a whale.*

mis·place (mis plās′), *v.*, **mis·placed, mis·plac·ing.** 1. to put in a wrong place: *to misplace dishes on a table.* 2. to mislay: *It seems I have misplaced my comb.* 3. to place unsuitably or unwisely: *to misplace one's trust.* —**mis·place′ment,** *n.*

mis·print (mis′print′), *n.* 1. a mistake in printing. —*v.* (mis print′). 2. to print incorrectly.

mis·pro·nounce (mis′prə nouns′), *v.*, **mis·pro·nounced, mis·pro·nounc·ing.** to pronounce incorrectly: *to mispronounce French words.* —**mis·pro·nun·ci·a·tion** (mis′prə nun′sē ā′shən), *n.*

mis·quote (mis kwōt′), *v.*, **mis·quot·ed, mis·quot·ing.** to quote incorrectly: *He said he knew the poem, but he misquoted several lines.* —**mis′quo·ta′tion,** *n.*

mis·read (mis rēd′), *v.*, **mis·read** (mis red′), **mis·read·ing.** 1. to read wrongly: *I couldn't find the house because I had misread the address.* 2. to interpret wrongly; misunderstand: *He failed the test because he misread the instructions.*

mis·rep·re·sent (mis′rep ri zent′), *v.* 1. to represent incorrectly or falsely: *He misrepresented his age in applying for the job.* 2. to give a wrong idea or impression of: *A tourist who behaves badly can misrepresent his country.* —**mis′rep·re·sen·ta′tion,** *n.*

mis·rule (mis rool′), *n.* 1. bad or unwise rule; misgovernment. 2. lack of effective rule; disorder. —*v.*, **mis·ruled, mis·rul·ing.** 3. to rule badly; misgovern.

miss[1] (mis), *v.* 1. to fail to hit, strike, or reach: *The bullet missed the target.* 2. to fail to meet, catch, get, etc.: *I missed the train.* 3. to fail to take advantage of: *I missed my chance.* 4. to fail to attend, fulfill, or comply with: *He has missed school twice.* 5. to notice the loss or absence of: *I missed my wallet when I was about to pay.* 6. to feel the absence or loss of: *We shall miss you when you're gone.* 7. to escape or avoid: *He narrowly missed catching pneumonia.* 8. to fail to see, hear, or understand: *You missed the point of his remark.* 9. to pass over or overlook: *I missed a few spots in shaving this morning.* 10. to fail to hold onto; lose: *to miss one's footing.* —*n.* 11. a failure to hit or reach something. 12. an omission. [from the Old English word *missan* "to miss"]

miss[2] (mis), *n.*, *pl.* **miss·es.** 1. *(usually cap.)* a title used before the name of an unmarried woman: *Our teacher is Miss Richards.* 2. a young unmarried woman; girl: *May I help you, miss?* [short for *mistress*]

Miss., Mississippi.

mis·sal (mis′əl), *n. (sometimes cap.)* a book containing the prayers for the Mass throughout the year, esp. in the Roman Catholic Church.

mis·shap·en (mis shā′pən), *adj.* badly shaped; deformed: *a misshapen body.*

mis·sile (mis′əl), *n.* 1. an object or weapon that is thrown, shot, or propelled in some other way to its target. 2. a guided missile.

miss·ing (mis′ing), *adj.* 1. absent or lacking: *a missing page.* 2. lost; not found or accounted for: *a soldier missing in action.*

mis·sion (mish′ən), *n.* 1. a task that a person or group of persons is sent to perform: *a goodwill mission.* 2. the goal of a military or similar operation: *Our mission was to capture hill 318.* 3. a group of persons representing a government abroad: *the Pakistani mission to the United Nations.* 4. a group of persons sent by a religious body to do missionary work in a foreign land, work in a city's slums, etc. 5. the work performed by such a group, or the place in which it is performed. 6. the principal task of a person's life; calling: *His mission in life is teaching.*

mis·sion·ar·y (mish′ə ner′ē), *n.*, *pl.* **mis·sion·ar·ies.** 1. a person who is sent on a mission. —*adj.* 2. of or concerning a mission or missions.

Mis·sis·sip·pi (mis′i sip′ē), *n.* 1. a state in the southern U.S. 47,716 sq. mi. *Cap.:* Jackson. 2. a river flowing S from N Minnesota to the Gulf of Mexico: the principal river of the U.S. 2470 mi. long. —**Mis′sis·sip′pi·an,** *n., adj.*

mis·sive (mis′iv), *n.* a written message; letter.

Mis·sour·i (mi zoor′ē, mi zoor′ə), *n.* 1. a state in the central United States. 69,674 sq. mi. *Cap.:* Jefferson City. 2. a river flowing from SW Montana into the Mississippi River N of St. Louis, Missouri. 2723 mi. long. —**Mis·sour′i·an,** *n., adj.*

mis·spell (mis spel′), *v.*, **mis·spelled** *or* **mis·spelt** (mis spelt′); **mis·spell·ing.** to spell incorrectly: *You've misspelled my name.*

mis·spell·ing (mis spel′ing), *n.* an incorrect spelling: *"Wierd" is a misspelling of "weird."*

mis·spent (mis spent′), *adj.* spent wrongly or foolishly; wasted: *a misspent life.*

mis·state (mis stāt′), *v.*, **mis·stat·ed, mis·stat·ing.** to state wrongly or falsely. —**mis·state′ment,** *n.*

mis·step (mis step′), *n.* **1.** a wrong step. **2.** an error in conduct; misbehavior: *Just one misstep, and you're off the team!*

mist (mist), *n.* **1.** a thin fog. **2.** a haze that obscures vision or recollection: *a mist of tears; the mists of time.* —*v.* **3.** to make or become misty: *The windows misted with steam.* **4.** to rain in fine drops; drizzle.

mis·take (mi stāk′), *n.* **1.** a wrong action; error: *In learning anything new, we make many mistakes.* **2.** a wrong judgment or idea; misunderstanding: *It is a mistake to believe that.* —*v.*, **mis·took** (mi stŏŏk′), **mis·tak·en** (mi stā′kən), **mis·tak·ing.** **3.** to identify as the wrong person or thing: *I mistook him for his brother.* **4.** to misunderstand: *to mistake a question.*

mis·tak·en (mi stā′kən), *adj.* **1.** wrongly believed or imagined; erroneous: *a mistaken idea.* **2.** making a mistake or misjudgment: *If you believe he did it, you're mistaken.* —**mis·tak′en·ly,** *adv.*

mis·ter (mis′tər), *n.* **1.** *(usually cap.)* a title used before the name of a man or his rank or office (usually abbreviated *Mr.*): *Mr. Philips; Mr. President.* **2.** *Informal.* sir: *Watch where you're going, mister!*

mis·tle·toe (mis′əl tō′), *n.* an evergreen plant with white berries that grows on the trunks and branches of trees. Sprigs of mistletoe are often used as a Christmas decoration.

mis·took (mi stŏŏk′), *v.* the past tense of **mistake.**

mis·treat (mis trēt′), *v.* to treat badly or unfairly; abuse: *to mistreat a pet.* —**mis·treat′ment,** *n.*

mis·tress (mis′tris), *n.* **1.** a woman who has authority or control over a household, an institution, a servant, etc. **2.** the female owner of an animal, a slave, etc. **3.** a woman who unlawfully lives with a man as his wife. **4.** *(usually cap.)* a title formerly used before the name of a married or unmarried woman: now replaced by *Mrs.* or *Miss.*

Mistletoe

mis·tri·al (mis trī′əl), *n.* **1.** a trial that is not completed, or the findings of which are set aside, because of an error in the proceedings. **2.** a trial in which the jury cannot agree.

mis·trust (mis trust′), *n.* **1.** lack of trust or confidence; suspicion: *His mistrust of all strangers makes him almost a hermit.* —*v.* **2.** to be suspicious of; distrust: *I mistrust his promises.* —**mis·trust′ful,** *adj.*

mist·y (mis′tē), *adj.*, **mist·i·er, mist·i·est.** **1.** consisting of or covered with mist: *misty air; a misty landscape.* **2.** indistinct or vague, as if seen through mist: *misty recollections of bygone years.* —**mist′i·ness,** *n.*

mis·un·der·stand (mis′un dər stand′), *v.*, **mis·un·der·stood** (mis′un dər stŏŏd′), **mis·un·der·stand·ing.** to understand wrongly or imperfectly: *I'm late because I misunderstood the directions.*

mis·un·der·stand·ing (mis′un dər stan′ding), *n.* **1.** a failure to understand. **2.** a quarrel or disagreement: *A misunderstanding ended their friendship.*

mis·use (mis yōōs′), *n.* **1.** wrong or improper use: *misuse of words.* —*v.* (mis yōōz′), **mis·used, mis·us·**

ing. **2.** to use wrongly or improperly: *to misuse power.* **3.** to mistreat; abuse: *He misuses the car by changing gears so suddenly.*

mite[1] (mīt), *n.* any of numerous small animals, related to spiders, that live on plants, animals, or stored food. [from the Old English word *mite,* meaning originally "cutter, biter." See *mite*[2]]

mite[2] (mīt), *n.* **1.** a very small coin or sum of money. **2.** a very small object or bit of something: *to have a mite of toast.* **3.** a tiny child or animal. [from an early Dutch word *mite,* meaning originally "piece cut off"; related to *mite*[1]]

mi·ter (mī′tər), *n.* **1.** a tall cap, rising to a point in front and back, and often richly adorned. Miters are worn by bishops and other high-ranking clergymen at special ceremonies. **2.** a surface formed by cutting a piece of wood or other material at an angle, so as to form a joint with another piece similarly cut. —*v.* **3.** to cut a miter in (a piece of wood or other material). **4.** to join (two pieces so cut). **5.** to bestow a miter upon; raise to the rank of bishop. Also, *esp. British,* **mitre.**

Miter

mit·i·gate (mit′ə gāt′), *v.*, **mit·i·gat·ed, mit·i·gat·ing.** to make or become less severe or painful: *circumstances that mitigate a person's guilt.* —**mit′i·ga′tion,** *n.*

mi·to·sis (mī tō′sis), *n.* the process by which a cell divides to produce two identical cells that differ from the parent cell only in size.

mi·tre (mī′tər), *n., v.,* **mi·tred, mi·tring.** a British spelling of **miter.**

mitt (mit), *n.* **1.** a heavy, padded glove worn by some baseball players, esp. a catcher. **2.** a mitten. **3.** a long glove without fingers, worn by women. **4.** *Slang.* a hand.

mit·ten (mit′ᵊn), *n.* a glove that has one pocket for four of the fingers and a separate pocket for the thumb.

mix (miks), *v.,* **mixed** *or* **mixt; mix·ing. 1.** to put together (various things) so as to form a single mass. **2.** to put in as an ingredient: *Mix some sugar into the coffee.* **3.** to form by putting different things together: *to mix a drink.* **4.** to combine or join: *to mix work with play.* **5.** to combine so as to form a single mass: *Oil and water do not mix.* **6.** to join a group or company: *Why don't you mix with the crowd?* —*n.* **7.** something formed by mixing; mixture: *a cake mix.* **8. mix up,** to confuse completely, esp. to mistake one person or thing for another: *to mix up dates; to mix up twins.*

mixed (mikst), *adj.* **1.** put together or formed by mixing: *a mixed drink.* **2.** made up of different kinds: *mixed candies.* **3.** of or including both sexes: *mixed company.* **4.** confused; jumbled: *mixed sizes.*

mixed′ num′ber, a number consisting of a whole number and a fraction, such as $4\frac{1}{2}$ or 4.5.

mix·er (mik′sər), *n.* **1.** a machine or tool used for mixing. **2.** a person who associates well (or badly) with others: *He's a great mixer at parties.*

mix·ture (miks′chər), *n.* **1.** something produced by mixing: *a mixture of cream, eggs, sugar, and spices.* **2.** the act or process of mixing: *The mixture of several fine coffees produced this blend.*

mix-up (miks′up′), *n.* a confused state of things; tangle: *a mix-up in the bus schedules.*

miz·zen (miz′ən), *n.* **1.** a fore-and-aft sail set on a mizzenmast. **2.** a mizzenmast.

miz·zen·mast (miz′ən mast′, -məst), *n.* **1.** the third mast from the bow in a vessel having three or more masts. See illus. at **quarter-deck. 2.** a short mast near the stern in a yawl or ketch.

ml, milliliter; milliliters.

Mlle., mademoiselle. Also, **Mlle.**

mm, millimeter; millimeters.

Mme., madame.

Mn, *Chem.* the symbol for **manganese.**

Mo, *Chem.* the symbol for **molybdenum.**

Mo., Missouri.

mo., month; months.

M.O., **1.** mail order. **2.** method of working. [from Latin *modus operandi*] **3.** money order. Also, **m.o.**

mo·a (mō′ə), *n.* any of several extinct, flightless birds of New Zealand, related to the kiwis but resembling the ostrich.

Mo·ab (mō′ab), *n.* (in the Bible) an ancient kingdom E of the Dead Sea, now in Jordan.

moan (mōn), *n.* **1.** a long, low sound expressing pain, sorrow, disappointment, etc. **2.** any similar sound made by inanimate things: *the moan of the wind.* —*v.* **3.** to utter a moan or moans. **4.** to express by moaning: *He moaned his dismay.* —**moan′ing·ly,** *adv.*

Moa
(height 10 ft.)

moat (mōt), *n.* a deep, wide trench, usually filled with water, dug around a fortress or castle for protection.

mob (mob), *n.* **1.** a disorderly crowd that may easily be moved to riot and violence. **2.** any group of persons or things: *There was a mob at the sale.* **3.** the common people: *Her style of folk singing pleases the mob.* **4.** a gang of criminals. —*v.,* **mobbed, mob·bing. 5.** to crowd around noisily: *The stars were mobbed by fans.* **6.** to attack violently: *If you say that in this town, they'll mob you.* [short for the Latin phrase *mobile vulgus* "the fickle crowd"]

mo·bile (mō′bəl), *adj.* **1.** moving easily; capable of being moved: *mobile troops; a mobile blood bank.* **2.** changing easily; showing changes of mood or expression: *a mobile face.* —*n.* (mō′bēl). **3.** a sculpture made of loosely connected pieces, often hanging from wires, that move easily when stirred by a touch or a slight breeze. —**mo·bil·i·ty** (mō bil′i tē), *n.*

Mo·bile (mō′bēl, mō bēl′), *n.* a port city in SW Alabama.

mo·bi·lize (mō′bə līz′), *v.,* **mo·bi·lized, mo·bi·liz·ing.** to assemble and organize in readiness for action: *to mobilize against attack.* —**mo′bi·li·za′tion,** *n.*

moc·ca·sin (mok′ə sin), *n.* **1.** a low, heelless shoe made of soft leather, originally worn by American Indians. **2.** a similar shoe or slipper for casual wear. **3.** any of several poisonous snakes of the southern U.S.

mo·cha (mō′kə), *n.* **1.** a fine grade of coffee grown originally in Arabia. **2.** a flavoring made from coffee, or a mixture of chocolate and coffee. —*adj.* **3.** flavored with mocha: *mocha icing.*

mock (mok), *v.* **1.** to ridicule or scorn, esp. by imitating: *He mocked my way of speaking.* **2.** to deceive or disappoint: *My high hopes for him were mocked by his poor performance.* —*adj.* **3.** done or made as a model or imitation of something; sham: *a mock trial.* —*n.* **4.** an imitation or mockery: *to say something in mock.* **5.** something that is mocked or ridiculed.

mock·er·y (mok′ə rē), *n., pl.* **mock·er·ies. 1.** the act of mocking; ridicule. **2.** a ridiculous or shameful imitation: *The trial was a mockery of justice.* **3.** a futile or disappointing action: *His refusal to change made a mockery of our efforts.* **4.** an object of ridicule: *His follies made him a mockery in the town.*

mock·ing·bird (mok′ing bûrd′), *n.* any of several gray, black, and white songbirds of the U.S. and Mexico that can imitate the songs of other birds.

mock-up (mok′up′), *n.* a model, often full-size, as of an airplane or space capsule, that enables engineers to see how the parts will fit and work together.

mod., **1.** moderate. **2.** modern.

mode (mōd), *n.* **1.** manner or way of acting or doing something: *various modes of travel.* **2.** a style or fashion in dress, manners, etc.: *the latest mode from Paris.* **3.** (in grammar) another word for **mood².**

mod·el (mod′l), *n.* **1.** a copy of something, usually on a smaller scale: *a model of the new bus terminal.* **2.** a person or thing that is considered worthy of imitation; example: *He is the model of a good teacher.* **3.** a person or thing that serves as an example for an artist or writer: *Raphael used the same model for most of his paintings of the Madonna.* **4.** something made in a particular design or style: *Our car is a sports model.* **5.** a person employed in posing with or displaying clothes or other products: *a fashion model.* —*adj.* **6.** serving as an example or demonstration: *a model home.* **7.** worthy of imitation: *a model student.* —*v.,* **mod·eled** *or* **mod·elled; mod·el·ing** *or* **mod·el·ling. 8.** to form or plan according to a model: *This building is modeled on a classic Greek temple.* **9.** to give shape or form to: *to model clay animals.* **10.** to wear or display as a demonstration: *He models sportswear.* **11.** to be employed as a model: *She has modeled for many photographers.*

mod·er·ate (mod′ər it), *adj.* **1.** of a medium amount or degree; not extreme: *a moderate price; having a moderate success.* **2.** mild; not violent or radical:

moderate political views. —*n.* **3.** a person who is moderate in his opinions and actions. —*v.* (mod′ərāt′), **mod·er·at·ed, mod·er·at·ing. 4.** to make or become less severe or violent: *Moderate your language in company. After March the wind moderated.* **5.** to act as moderator for (a panel discussion, debate, etc.). —**mod′er·ate·ly,** *adv.*

mod·er·a·tion (mod′ə rā′shən), *n.* **1.** the quality or condition of being moderate; avoidance of extremes: *Exercise in moderation can be very beneficial.* **2.** the act of moderating or making less severe: *The rains caused a moderation of the heat wave.*

mod·er·a·tor (mod′ə rā′tər), *n.* **1.** a person or thing that moderates. **2.** a person who presides over (a panel discussion, debate, quiz show, etc.).

mod·ern (mod′ərn), *adj.* **1.** of or referring to present or recent time: *a modern city.* **2.** of or concerning the period following the Middle Ages, from about 1500 up to the present: *modern history.* **3.** of or referring to styles or fashions of the present or the immediate past: *modern sculpture; modern dress.* —*n.* **4.** a person of modern times or of modern opinions and tastes: *The airplane is an invention of the moderns.* —**mod′ern·ly,** *adv.* —**mod′ern·ness,** *n.*

Mod′ern Eng′lish, the English language as spoken and written since about 1475.

mod·ern·ize (mod′ər nīz′), *v.,* **mod·ern·ized, mod·ern·iz·ing.** to adapt to modern styles, ideas, etc.: *to modernize one's kitchen.* —**mod′ern·i·za′tion,** *n.*

mod·est (mod′ist), *adj.* **1.** having a humble opinion of one's worth or importance; not vain or boastful: *a modest hero.* **2.** simple in form or appearance: *a modest house.* **3.** moderate; not excessive: *a modest price.* **4.** decent or reserved in dress, behavior, etc.: *a modest bathing suit.* —**mod′est·ly,** *adv.*

mod·es·ty (mod′i stē), *n., pl.* **mod·es·ties. 1.** the quality of being modest. **2.** simplicity in form or appearance: *modesty in decoration.* **3.** moderation in amount or degree: *the modesty of our contribution.* **4.** decency in dress, behavior, etc.: *the modesty of our grandparents.*

mod·i·cum (mod′ə kəm), *n.* a small or moderate amount: *to pass a test with a modicum of effort.*

mod·i·fi·ca·tion (mod′ə fə kā′shən), *n.* **1.** a modifying or altering: *The plan was approved after some modification.* **2.** a modified form; variety: *The new rifle is a modification of an earlier model.*

mod·i·fi·er (mod′ə fī′ər), *n.* **1.** a person or thing that modifies. **2.** a word or phrase used to modify another word or phrase. Modifiers are usually adjectives or adverbs, and sometimes nouns.

mod·i·fy (mod′ə fī′), *v.,* **mod·i·fied, mod·i·fy·ing. 1.** to make or become partly changed or altered: *We modified the original plan of the house.* **2.** (in grammar) to limit the meaning of, or describe, a word or phrase in the same construction. In *a very small house,* the adjective *small* modifies the noun *house,* and the adverb *very* modifies the adjective *small.* In *broom closet,* the noun *broom* modifies another noun, *closet.* **3.** to reduce in amount or degree; moderate: *to modify one's demands.*

mod·ish (mō′dish), *adj.* following the latest mode; stylish: *a modish hat.* —**mod′ish·ly,** *adv.* —**mod′ish·ness,** *n.*

mod·u·late (moj′ə lāt′, mod′yə lāt′), *v.,* **mod·u·lat·ed, mod·u·lat·ing. 1.** to regulate or adjust, usually to a lesser amount or degree: *Dark glasses will modulate glare.* **2.** to vary the inflection of (the voice) to express changes in emphasis or meaning. **3.** to alter the power or the frequency of (a radio wave) so as to carry a signal. See also **amplitude modulation, frequency modulation. 4.** (in music) to pass from one key to another. —**mod′u·la′tion,** *n.*

mo·gul (mō′gəl), *n.* an important or influential person: *a mogul of the steel industry.*

Mo·gul (mō′gul), *n.* **1.** one of the Mongol conquerors of India, who ruled from 1526 to 1857. **2.** one of their descendants. **3.** a Mongol or Mongolian.

mo·hair (mō′hâr′), *n.* **1.** the fleece of the Angora goat. **2.** a fabric made of yarn from this fleece.

Mo·ham·med (mō ham′id), *n.* another spelling of **Muhammad.**

Mo·ham·med·an (mō ham′i dᵊn), *adj., n.* another word for **Muslim.**

Mo·ham·med·an·ism (mō ham′i dᵊniz′əm), *n.* the Muslim religion; Islam.

Mo·ha′ve Des′ert (mō hä′vē), another spelling of **Mojave Desert.**

Mo·hawk (mō′hôk), *n., pl.* **Mo·hawks** *or* **Mo·hawk.** a member of an Indian tribe formerly located in central New York along the Mohawk River, now in southern Canada.

Mo·hi·can (mō hē′kən), *n., pl.* **Mo·hi·cans** *or* **Mo·hi·can.** another spelling of **Mahican.**

moist (moist), *adj.* slightly wet; damp.

mois·ten (moi′sən), *v.* to make or become moist.

mois·ture (mois′chər, moish′chər), *n.* **1.** water or other liquid condensed as fine drops in the air or on a surface, or contained or mixed in a solid substance. **2.** a small quantity of water or other liquid.

Mo·ja′ve Des′ert (mō hä′vē), a desert in S California. about 13,500 sq. mi. Also, **Mohave Desert.**

mo·lar (mō′lər), *n.* **1.** a tooth with a broad surface adapted for grinding. An adult has twelve molars, three on each side of the upper and lower jaws. —*adj.* **2.** adapted for grinding: *molar teeth.* **3.** of or concerning molar teeth: *a molar crown.*

mo·las·ses (mə las′iz), *n.* a thick, dark-colored syrup produced in the process of refining sugar.

mold¹ (mōld), *n.* **1.** a hollow form for giving a particular shape to material that is put into it in a molten or liquid state. **2.** something that is formed in a mold: *a mold of gelatin.* **3.** shape or form: *the delicate mold of her chin.* **4.** quality, character, or type: *Men of his mold are rare in the business world.* —*v.* **5.** to shape or form in a mold. **6.** to train or develop in a certain way: *to mold the character of young people.* Also, *esp. British,* **mould.** [from the Old French word *modle,* which comes from Latin *modulus* "a small measure"]

mold² (mōld), *n.* **1.** a growth of tiny fungus plants, usually downy or furry in appearance, that forms on food and other substances as they decay. **2.** any of the fungi that produce such a growth. —*v.* **3.** to become spotted or covered with such a growth. Also, *esp. British,* **mould.** [from the Middle English word *mowlde*]

mold³ (mōld), *n.* a soft, crumbly kind of earth that is rich in organic matter and suited for the growth of plants. Also, *esp. British,* **mould.** [from the Old English word *molde* "earth, dust"]

mold·er (mōl′dər), *v.* to turn to dust by natural decay; crumble: *The walls of the old house had moldered to the ground.* Also, *esp. British,* **moulder.**

mold·ing (mōl′ding), *n.* **1.** the act or process of shaping or forming. **2.** something that is molded. **3.** a shaped or carved edge extending around a building, a piece of furniture, a picture frame, etc. **4.** a strip or strips of wood or other material forming a frame around a door, window, the upper part of a wall, etc. Also, *esp. British,* **moulding.**

mold·y (mōl′dē), *adj.,* **mold·i·er, mold·i·est. 1.** overgrown or covered with mold: *Bread becomes moldy if left in the open.* **2.** musty with dampness or decay: *The cellar smells moldy.* Also, *esp. British,* **mouldy.** —**mold′i·ness,** *n.*

mole¹ (mōl), *n.* a small spot on the skin, usually dark, slightly raised, and hairy. [from the Old English word *māl*]

mole² (mōl), *n.* any of various small furry animals with very poor eyesight that live underground and feed on insects. [from the Middle English word *molle*]

Mole²
(total length to 8 in.)

mo·lec·u·lar (mō lek′yə-lər, mə lek′yə lər), *adj.* of, referring to, or caused by molecules.

mol·e·cule (mol′ə-kyool′), *n.* the smallest particle of a substance that can be said to have the properties of that substance. Molecules consist of one or more atoms. A water molecule consists of two hydrogen atoms and one oxygen atom.

mole·hill (mōl′hil′), *n.* **1.** a small mound or ridge raised by a mole burrowing underground. **2. make a mountain out of a molehill,** to worry or fuss about something of little importance.

mo·lest (mə lest′), *v.* to bother or annoy, esp. so as to cause trouble or injury: *The coastal towns were often molested by pirates.* —**mo·les·ta·tion** (mō′le stā′shən, mol′e stā′shən), *n.*

mol·li·fy (mol′ə fī′), *v.,* **mol·li·fied, mol·li·fy·ing.** to make less harsh or violent; calm; appease: *to mollify an angry mob.*

mol·lusk (mol′əsk), *n.* a member of the important group of related animals that includes snails, clams, oysters, squids, and octopuses, having soft bodies without backbones, which are often protected by a shell of one or more pieces.

Mo·loch (mō′lok, mol′ək), *n.* **1.** (in the Bible) a god

that was worshiped by burning children alive in sacrifice. **2.** anything demanding terrible sacrifice and suffering: *the Moloch of war.*

molt (mōlt), *v.* to cast off or shed feathers, horns, skin, etc., that will be replaced by a new growth. Many animals molt, including birds, reptiles, insects, and certain mammals. Also, *esp. British,* **moult.**

mol·ten (mōl′t³n), *adj.* changed to a liquid by heat; melted: *molten glass.*

mo·lyb·de·num (mə lib′də nəm, mol′ib dē′nəm), *n. Chem.* a metallic element used in steel to increase its hardness. *Symbol:* Mo

mom (mom), *n. Informal.* mother.

mo·ment (mō′mənt), *n.* **1.** a short period of time: *Wait here a moment.* **2.** the present or any particular point of time: *He is busy at the moment.* **3.** importance or significance: *questions of great moment.*

mo·men·tar·i·ly (mō′mən târ′ə lē), *adv.* **1.** for a moment; briefly: *The wind ceased momentarily.* **2.** every moment; from one moment to another: *The breach in the dam is widening momentarily.* **3.** at any moment; very shortly: *They are expected momentarily.*

mo·men·tar·y (mō′mən ter′ē), *adj.* **1.** lasting only a moment; very brief: *a momentary outburst of anger.* **2.** likely or expected to occur at any moment: *The besieged town faced momentary destruction.*

mo·men·tous (mō men′təs), *adj.* of great importance or significance: *a momentous decision.* —**mo·men′tous·ly,** *adv.* —**mo·men′tous·ness,** *n.*

mo·men·tum (mō men′təm), *n.* the property of a body that keeps it in motion once it is moving. In physics, the momentum of a body is defined as the product of its mass and its velocity.

Mon., **1.** Monday. **2.** Monsignor.

Mon·a·co (mon′ə kō′), *n.* a principality on the Mediterranean coast, bordering SE France. ¹⁄₂ sq. mi.

mon·arch (mon′ərk), *n.*
1. a hereditary ruler of a state or nation: *Queen Elizabeth II is the present monarch of Great Britain.* **2.** any person or thing that has great power: *The battleship is the monarch of the seas.* **3.** a large butterfly having reddish-brown wings with black markings.

mo·nar·chi·cal (mə när′ki kəl), *adj.* of, like, or belonging to a monarch or monarchy.

mon·ar·chism (mon′ər kiz′əm), *n.* **1.** the principles or system of government by a monarch. **2.** belief in and support of monarchy as a form of government.

mon·ar·chist (mon′ər kist), *n.* **1.** a person who believes in and supports monarchy as a form of government. **2.** a member of a political party or group that seeks to establish or restore a monarchy. —**mon′ar·chist′ic,** *adj.*

mon·ar·chy (mon′ər kē), *n., pl.* **mon·ar·chies. 1.** a government or state that has a monarch at its head. **2.** rule or power exercised by a monarch.

mon·as·ter·y (mon′ə ster′ē), *n., pl.* **mon·as·ter·ies.** a place occupied by a group of persons, esp. monks, living apart and obeying strict religious vows.

mo·nas·tic (mə nas′tik), *adj.* **1.** of or referring to monks or monasteries. **2.** living in seclusion like a monk. —*n.* **3.** a monk or other person living in a monastery. —**mo·nas·ti·cism** (mə nas′ti siz′əm), *n.*

Mon·dale (mon′dāl′), *n.* **Wal·ter F**(rederick), born 1928, 42nd Vice President of the U.S. since 1977.

Mon·day (mun′dē, mun′dā), *n.* the second day of the week, following Sunday. [from the Old English word *Mōnandæg,* which is a translation of the Latin phrase *lūnae diēs* "day of the moon"]

mon·e·tar·y (mon′i ter′ē), *adj.* **1.** of or referring to the coinage or currency of a country: *The monetary unit of Argentina is the peso.* **2.** measured or valued in terms of money: *monetary rewards.*

mon·ey (mun′ē), *n., pl.* **mon·eys** *or* **mon·ies. 1.** pieces of gold, silver, or other metal, or paper bills issued in a certain form by a government for use in payment of goods and services. **2.** anything used and accepted as having the value of money, such as checks, wampum, etc. **3.** wealth measured in terms of money. **4. for one's money,** in one's opinion: *For my money, he's the weakest player on the team.*

mon·eyed (mun′ēd), *adj.* **1.** having money; wealthy: *the moneyed classes of society.* **2.** characteristic of wealth or wealthy persons.

mon′ey or′der, an order for the payment of money, esp. one that is issued by one post office for payment at another.

Mon·gol (mong′gəl), *n.* **1.** a member of an Asiatic people that came originally from Mongolia and in the 13th century conquered most of Asia and eastern Europe. Their modern descendants live chiefly in eastern Mongolia. **2.** the language of the Mongols, belonging to the Mongolian group. —*adj.* **3.** another word for **Mongolian.**

Mon·go·li·a (mong gō′lē ə), *n.* **1.** a region in E central Asia. **2.** another name for **Mongolian People's Republic.**

Mon·go·li·an (mong gō′lē ən), *n.* **1.** a native or inhabitant of Mongolia or of the Mongolian People's Republic. **2.** a member of the Mongoloid race. **3.** any of a group of related languages spoken in Mongolia. —*adj.* Also, **Mongol. 4.** of or concerning Mongolia, its people, or their languages. **5.** of or concerning the Mongols. **6.** of or belonging to the Mongoloid race.

SOVIET UNION
MANCHURIA
MONGOLIAN PEOPLE'S REPUBLIC
Mongolia
INNER MONGOLIA
TIBET
CHINA
INDIA
BURMA
PACIFIC OCEAN

Mongo′lian Peo′ple's Repub′lic, a republic in E central Asia. about 600,000 sq. mi.

Mon·gol·oid (mong′gə loid′), *adj.* **1.** belonging to or characteristic of one of the major traditional races of humankind, whose members often have a yellowish skin, eyes that appear to be slanted, high cheekbones, and straight black hair. The Mongoloid peoples include the Chinese, Japanese, Thais, Eskimos, and some American Indians. —*n.* **2.** a member of the Mongoloid race.

mon·goose (mong′gōōs′), *n., pl.* **mon·goos·es.** an animal resembling a weasel and noted for its ability to kill poisonous snakes.

mon·grel (mong′grəl), *n.* **1.** any animal, esp. a dog, of mixed breed. —*adj.* **2.** of mixed breed or origin: *a mongrel puppy.*

mon·i·tor (mon′i tər), *n.* **1.** a pupil appointed to assist in conducting a class or keeping order: *a hall monitor.* **2.** a person or thing that reminds or warns. **3.** a receiver used in a radio or television

Mongoose
(total length 2½ ft.)

studio to observe the quality of transmission. —*v.* **4.** to observe (a radio or television broadcast) to check the quality of transmission, or for purposes of censorship, to detect propaganda, etc. **5.** to observe, coach, or supervise.

monk (mungk), *n.* a man who lives apart from others or in a monastery and observes the rules and vows of a religious order.

mon·key (mung′kē), *n., pl.* **mon·keys. 1.** any of a group of small, furry, highly intelligent animals that are closely related to man and usually have long tails. See also **ape** (def. 1). **2.** a person who is like a monkey, esp. in behavior: *He's a mischievous little monkey.* —*v.,* **mon·keyed, mon·key·ing. 3.** to play mischievously; meddle; fool: *Don't monkey with that switch.* **4. make a monkey out of,** to make a fool of (someone): *She tried to make a monkey out of me in front of all my friends.*

Monkey (Rhesus)
(total length 2½ ft.)

mon′key wrench′, a wrench having an adjustable jaw, used for grasping nuts of different sizes.

monk·ish (mung′kish), *adj.* of or like a monk: *a person of monkish habits.*

monks·hood (mungks′hŏŏd′), *n.* a poisonous plant whose flowers are shaped like hoods.

mono-, a prefix meaning one, single, or alone: *monoplane; monogram; monologue.*

mon·o·cle (mon′ə kəl), *n.* an eyeglass for one eye.

mo·nog·a·my (mə nog′ə mē), *n.* the practice or custom of marrying only one person at a time. See also **bigamy, polygamy.** —**mo·nog′a·mous,** *adj.*

Monkey wrench

mon·o·gram (mon′ə gram′), *n.* **1.** a design formed by combining or interlacing letters, such as one's initials, used on personal articles, stationery, etc. —*v.,* **mon·o·grammed, mon·o·gram·ming. 2.** to put a monogram on: *to monogram a shirt.*

mon·o·lith (mon′ə lith), *n.* **1.** a large, single block of stone. **2.** a column, statue, etc., cut from a single block of stone. **3.** any large organization, such as a government or a business, under the absolute control of a single person or a small group: *an industrial monolith.* —**mon′o·lith′ic,** *adj.*

mon·o·logue (mon′ə lôg′), *n.* **1.** a long speech by one person. **2.** a scene or part of a play in which one character speaks alone. **3.** a play, skit, or poem performed by one person speaking alone.

mon·o·plane (mon′ə plān′), *n.* an airplane with only one set of wings. All modern airplanes are monoplanes.

mo·nop·o·lize (mə nop′ə līz′), *v.,* **mo·nop·o·lized, mo·nop·o·liz·ing. 1.** to acquire or have a monopoly of: *A few large companies monopolize the steel industry.* **2.** to play the largest role in or enjoy the largest share of; dominate: *to monopolize the conversation.*

mo·nop·o·ly (mə nop′ə lē), *n., pl.* **mo·nop·o·lies. 1.** exclusive or nearly exclusive control of a product, industry, or business activity. The holder of a monopoly can fix prices without fear of competition. **2.** an exclusive privilege granted by a government to provide a service or manufacture a certain article: *His patent gives him a monopoly over his invention.* **3.** a service or product that is under exclusive control of a company, group, or government: *In France, tobacco is a monopoly of the state.* **4.** a company or group that exercises exclusive control: *The government accused that company of being a monopoly.*

mon·o·rail (mon′ə rāl′), *n.* **1.** a railroad whose trains run on a single rail, either on the ground or overhead. **2.** the rail of such a railroad.

mon·o·syl·la·ble (mon′ə sil′ə bəl), *n.* a word of one syllable, such as *he, may,* or *strength.* —**mon·o·syl·lab·ic** (mon′ə si lab′ik), *adj.*

mon·o·the·ism (mon′ə thē iz′əm), *n.* belief in the existence of only one God.

mon·o·tone (mon′ə tōn′), *n.* **1.** a manner of speaking or singing without varying the tone of the voice. **2.** lack of variety in style, color, or form: *The gray monotone of the walls is depressing.*

mo·not·o·nous (mə not′ʰnəs), *adj.* **1.** lacking in variety; dull or boring: *a monotonous trip across the prairie.* **2.** continuing on the same tone: *the monotonous chant of an auctioneer.* —**mo·not′o·nous·ly,** *adv.*

mo·not·o·ny (mə not′ʰnē), *n.* **1.** lack of variety; sameness: *A short vacation broke the monotony of hard work.* **2.** sameness of tone: *The monotony of his voice is irritating.*

mon·ox·ide (mon ok′sīd), *n.* a compound containing only one atom of oxygen in each molecule.

Mon·roe (mən rō′), *n.* **James,** 1758–1831, 5th President of the U.S. 1817–1825.

Monroe′ Doc′trine, the doctrine, contained in a message of President Monroe to Congress in 1823,

prohibiting European intervention in the affairs of Latin America.

mon·sieur (mə syûr′), *n.* a French title of respect used in addressing a man, equivalent to *Mr.* or *sir.*

Mon·si·gnor (mon sē′nyər), *n.* **1.** a title of honor conferred upon certain priests of the Roman Catholic Church. **2.** a priest who has this title.

mon·soon (mon sōōn′), *n.* **1.** the seasonal wind of the Indian Ocean and southern Asia, blowing from the southwest in summer and from the northeast in winter. **2.** the summer rainy season, when the monsoon is blowing from the southwest.

mon·ster (mon′stər), *n.* **1.** a human being, animal, or plant that is misshapen or abnormal in some way: *The cow gave birth to a two-headed monster.* **2.** an imaginary creature that combines features of different animals, or human and animal features, such as a centaur, griffin, or sphinx. **3.** an extremely wicked or fiendish person: *Only a monster would do such an awful thing!* **4.** anything extremely ugly or unnatural. **5.** any animal or thing of huge size: *I caught a seven-pound fluke that was a monster.* —*adj.* **6.** huge; enormous: *a monster celebration.*

mon·stros·i·ty (mon stros′i tē), *n., pl.* for def. 2 **mon·stros·i·ties. 1.** the condition of being monstrous. **2.** a monster or something monstrous: *The new stadium is a monstrosity.*

mon·strous (mon′strəs), *adj.* **1.** extremely ugly, misshapen, or abnormal. **2.** unbelievably cruel or vicious: *a monstrous crime.* **3.** extremely large; huge: *a monstrous banquet.*

Mont., Montana.

Mon·tan·a (mon tan′ə), *n.* a state in the NW United States. 147,138 sq. mi. *Cap.:* Helena. —**Mon·tan′an,** *n., adj.*

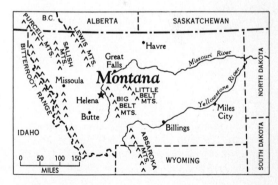

Mont Blanc (mont blängk′), a mountain in SW Europe on the boundary between France and Italy: highest peak of the Alps. 15,781 ft.

Mon·te·vi·de·o (mon′tə vi dā′ō), *n.* a seaport and the capital city of Uruguay.

Mont·gom·er·y (mont gum′ə rē), *n.* the capital city of Alabama, in the central part.

month (munth), *n.* **1.** any of the twelve parts into which the calendar year is divided. **2.** any period that consists of about four weeks or thirty days.

month·ly (munth′lē), *adj.* **1.** taking place or being done, paid, etc., once a month: *a monthly meeting.* **2.** lasting for a month: *a monthly supply of food.* —*n., pl.* **month·lies. 3.** a magazine that is published once a month. —*adv.* **4.** once a month; by the month.

Mont·pel·ier (mont pēl′yər), *n.* the capital city of Vermont, in the central part.

Mont·re·al (mon′trē ôl′), *n.* a port city in S Quebec, in SE Canada, on an island in the St. Lawrence.

mon·u·ment (mon′yə mənt), *n.* **1.** something built or set up in a particular place in honor of a person, event, etc. **2.** a building or a natural site preserved for its beauty or historical interest. **3.** a work of art, literature, etc., of permanent value and interest.

mon·u·men·tal (mon′yə men′t³l), *adj.* **1.** of, like, or serving as a monument: *a monumental arch.* **2.** worthy of being preserved for its cultural or historical interest: *a monumental event.* **3.** very great, impressive, or notable: *a monumental liar.*

moo (mōō), *v.,* **mooed, moo·ing. 1.** to make a sound like that of a cow. —*n., pl.* **moos. 2.** the sound made by a cow, or a sound similar to it.

mood¹ (mōōd), *n.* a person's emotional state or attitude at a particular moment; humor: *If the boss is in a good mood today, I'll ask for a raise.* [from the Old English word *mōd* "mind, spirit, courage"]

mood² (mōōd), *n.* the grammatical construction of a verb in a clause or sentence that shows whether the verb expresses a statement or question *(indicative),* a command or request *(imperative),* or a doubt or supposition *(subjunctive).* Also, **mode.** See also **imperative** (def. 2), **indicative** (def. 2), **subjunctive** (def. 1). [from a special use of *mode,* but spelled as if from *mood¹*]

mood·y (mōō′dē), *adj.,* **mood·i·er, mood·i·est. 1.** having or showing a sad or sullen frame of mind; gloomy: *I can't talk to him when he's moody.* **2.** likely to have frequent changes of mood. —**mood′i·ly,** *adv.* —**mood′i·ness,** *n.*

moon (mōōn), *n.* **1.** the earth's only natural satellite. The moon has a diameter of 2160 miles, and its average distance from the earth is 238,857 miles. It revolves around the earth every 28 days, and shines by reflecting the light of the sun. **2.** a satellite of any of the other planets. **3.** a month, or a period of about a month. —*v.* **4.** to behave, talk, or gaze in an idle or dreamy manner: *to moon about the good old days.* **5.** **once in a blue moon,** once in a great while; rarely: *That kind of chance comes once in a blue moon.*

moon·beam (mōōn′bēm′), *n.* a ray of moonlight.

moon·light (mōōn′līt′), *n.* **1.** the light of the moon. —*adj.* **2.** lighted by the moon: *a moonlight night.* **3.** taking place by the light of the moon, or at night: *a moonlight dance.* —*v.,* **moon·light·ed, moon·light·ing. 4.** *Informal.* to work at another job after one's regular employment, esp. at night.

moon·lit (mōōn′lit′), *adj.* lighted by the moon.

moon·shine (mōōn′shīn′), *n.* **1.** *Informal.* smuggled or illegally distilled whiskey. **2.** the light of the

moon; moonlight. **3.** idle talk; nonsense: *Those reports of flying saucers are just moonshine.*

moon·stone (mōōn′stōn′), *n.* a semiprecious stone, blue in color and nearly transparent, used as a gem.

moon·struck (mōōn′struk′), *adj.* insane, or mentally dazed, supposedly by the influence of the moon.

moor¹ (mōōr), *n.* an area of open wasteland, found mostly in England and Scotland, often marshy and overgrown with heather. [from the Old English word *mōr*]

moor² (mōōr), *v.* **1.** to secure (a ship, dirigible, balloon, etc.) in a particular place by means of ropes or anchors. **2.** to fasten or fix firmly. [from the Middle English word *more*]

Moor (mōōr), *n.* a member of a mixed race of Arab and Berber ancestry, inhabiting NW Africa. The Moors invaded Spain in the 8th century, and held control over that country until they were finally driven out in 1492. —**Moor′ish,** *adj.*

moor·ing (mōōr′ing), *n.* **1.** the act of securing a ship or other craft. **2.** the place where a ship or the like is secured. **3.** Usually, **moorings.** the ropes, anchors, or other means by which a ship or any other object is held secure.

moose (mōōs), *n., pl.* **moose.** a very large animal of the deer family, found in the northern U.S. and Canada, the male of which has very large antlers. [from an Algonquian word meaning "he strips or eats off (trees and shrubs)"]

Moose
(5½ ft. high at shoulder; length 9 ft.)

moot (mōōt), *adj.* **1.** open to argument or discussion; debatable; doubtful: *a moot point.* —*v.* **2.** to present or introduce (a subject) for discussion.

mop (mop), *n.* **1.** a bundle of absorbent material, such as yarn or cloth, fastened at the end of a stick or handle and used for washing floors, dishes, etc. —*v.,* **mopped, mop·ping. 2.** to rub or wipe with or as if with a mop: *to mop a floor.* **3. mop up, a.** (of a military force) to clear a captured area of all remaining enemy resistance. **b.** *Slang.* to dispose of; complete; finish: *to mop up a task.*

mope (mōp), *v.,* **moped, mop·ing.** to be listless, dull, or depressed: *He moped around the house all day.*

mo·ped (mō′ped), *n.* a heavily built motorized bicycle. [from *mo(tor) ped(al)*]

mor·al (môr′əl), *adj.* **1.** of or concerned with right conduct or its principles. **2.** right or virtuous in behavior: *a moral person.* **3.** able to recognize principles of right conduct. **4.** expressing or teaching principles of right conduct: *a moral tale.* **5.** of, concerning, or acting on the mind: *moral support.* — *n.* **6.** the moral teaching or practical lesson contained in a story or experience. **7. morals,** principles or habits with respect to right or wrong conduct.

mo·rale (mə ral′), *n.* a person's state of mind with

respect to cheerfulness, confidence, etc.

mor·al·ist (môr′ə list), *n.* **1.** a person who teaches morality. **2.** a person who practices morality.

mo·ral·i·ty (mə ral′i tē, mô ral′i tē), *n., pl.* for def. 3 **mo·ral·i·ties.** **1.** the quality of conforming to or following the rules of right conduct: *He questioned the morality of the law.* **2.** moral quality or character; virtue. **3.** a system of morals: *religious morality.*

mor·al·ize (môr′ə līz′), *v.,* **mor·al·ized, mor·al·iz·ing.** **1.** to make moral statements or judgments. **2.** to explain (something) in terms of a moral lesson.

mor·al·ly (môr′ə lē), *adv.* **1.** in a moral manner; virtuously. **2.** from a moral point of view: *Morally, he had no right to do it.* **3.** almost; practically: *I am morally sure I closed the windows.*

mo·rass (mə ras′), *n.* a tract of low, soft, wet ground; marsh; bog.

mor·a·to·ri·um (môr′ə tôr′ē əm), *n.* **1.** a legal authorization to delay the payment of debts. **2.** the period during which such authorization is in effect. **3.** the temporary stopping of a hostile or dangerous activity

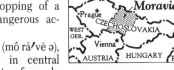
Moravia

Mo·ra·vi·a (mô rā′vē ə), *n.* a region in central Czechoslovakia, formerly belonging to Austria. —**Mo·ra·vi·an,** *n., adj.*

mor·bid (môr′bid), *adj.* **1.** suggesting an unhealthy mental state; very gloomy: *a morbid interest in death.* **2.** affected by, caused by, or causing disease: *a morbid condition of the liver.* —**mor′bid·ly,** *adv.*

mor·dant (môr′d°nt), *adj.* **1.** sarcastic or biting: *a mordant wit.* —*n.* **2.** a substance used in dyeing to make the color permanent.

more (môr), *adj., comparative of* **much** *or* **many** *with* **most** *as superlative.* **1.** in addition to that or those already given, taken, used, etc.: *more time; more pencils.* —*n.* **2.** an additional quantity, amount, or number: *I'm too tired to read any more.* **3.** a greater quantity, amount, or degree: *We bought more than we needed.* —*adv., comparative of* **much** *with* **most** *as superlative.* **4.** in or to a greater extent or degree: *more rapid.* **5.** in addition; further; longer; again: *Let's talk more another time.* **6. more or less,** to some extent; rather: *I'm more or less friendly with him.*

more·o·ver (môr ō′vər, môr′ō′vər), *adv.* beyond what has been said; further; besides.

morgue (môrg), *n.* **1.** a place in which the bodies of unidentified dead persons are kept until they are claimed or released for burial. **2.** a library or file of clippings, photographs, etc., kept for reference in a newspaper office.

mo·ri·on (môr′ē on′), *n.* an open helmet of the 16th and early 17th centuries, usually having a flat or turned-down brim and a crest from front to back.

Morion

Mor·mon (môr′mən), *n.* a member of the Church of Jesus Christ of Latter-day Saints (**Mor′mon Church′**),

founded in the U.S. in 1830 by Joseph Smith.

morn (môrn), *n.* another word for **morning:** used esp. in literature.

morn·ing (môr′ninͦg), *n.* **1.** the beginning of day; dawn. **2.** the first part or period of the day, extending from dawn, or from midnight, to noon. —*adj.* **3.** of or occurring in the morning: *morning exercise.*

morn·ing-glo·ry (môr′ninͦg glôr′ē), *n., pl.* **morn·ing-glo·ries.** a climbing plant having funnel-shaped blue, purple, pink, or white flowers that open in the morning and close when the sun is hot.

morn′ing star′, a bright planet, esp. Venus, seen in the east immediately before sunrise.

Mo·roc·co (mə rok′ō), *n.* a kingdom in NW Africa. —**Mo·roc′can,** *n., adj.*

Morocco

mo·ron (môr′on), *n.* **1.** a person who lacks normal mental powers; one who cannot develop beyond the mental age of about 10. **2.** *Informal.* any stupid person, or a person who lacks good judgment.

mo·rose (mə rōs′), *adj.* gloomy and ill-humored: *a morose person; a morose mood.* —**mo·rose′ly,** *adv.*

Mor·phe·us (môr′fē əs), *n.* (in Greek mythology) the god of dreams.

mor·phine (môr′fēn), *n.* a drug made from opium and sometimes used to relieve intense pain.

Mor′ris chair′ (môr′is, mor′is), a large armchair having an adjustable back and loose cushions.

mor·row (môr′ō, mor′ō), *n.* **1.** the day immediately after this or after some other particular day or night: *We depart on the morrow.* **2.** *Archaic.* another word for **morning:** *Good morrow, my friend.*

Morse (môrs), *n.* **Samuel F. B.,** 1791–1872, U.S. inventor: developed code for telegraph.

Morse′ code′, a signal code of dots, dashes, and spaces, used in telegraphy and for blinker signaling.

mor·sel (môr′səl), *n.* **1.** a bite, mouthful, or small portion of food, candy, etc. **2.** a small piece, quantity, or amount of anything; scrap: *a morsel of news.*

mor·tal (môr′t°l), *adj.* **1.** subject to death: *a mortal being.* **2.** of or referring to man as subject to death: *mortal weaknesses.* **3.** of or concerning death. **4.** involving spiritual death (distinguished from *venial*): *mortal sin.* **5.** to the death: *mortal combat.* **6.** very great; severe: *in mortal fear.* —*n.* **7.** a human being. —**mor′tal·ly,** *adv.*

mor·tal·i·ty (môr tal′i tē), *n., pl.* **mor·tal·i·ties.** **1.** the state or condition of being subject to death. **2.** the relative frequency of death in a district or community; death rate: *an increase in infant mortality.* **3.** death or destruction on a large scale.

mor·tar (môr′tər), *n.* **1.** a bowl in which substances are powdered with a pestle. **2.** a mixture of lime or cement, or a combi-

A, Mortar
B, Pestle

nation of both, with sand and water, for holding bricks or stones together. **3.** a cannon for throwing shells at high angles.

mor·tar·board (môr′tər bôrd′), *n.* **1.** a square board used by masons to hold mortar. **2.** a close-fitting cap with a square flat top and a tassel, worn as part of an academic costume, esp. in a graduation ceremony.

mort·gage (môr′gij), *n.* **1.** a claim on property, given to a creditor as security for a loan. **2.** the deed that establishes such a transaction. —*v.*, **mort·gaged, mort·gag·ing. 3.** to place (property) under a mortgage. **4.** to obligate or pledge.

mor·ti·fi·ca·tion (môr′tə fə kā′shən), *n.* **1.** humiliation in feeling caused by a wound to one's pride. **2.** a cause or source of such humiliation. **3.** the death of part of the body; gangrene.

mor·ti·fy (môr′tə fī′), *v.*, **mor·ti·fied, mor·ti·fy·ing. 1.** to humiliate by wounding the pride or self-respect. **2.** to force (the body or its desires) to undergo strict discipline. **3.** to affect with or undergo death or decay.

mor·tise (môr′tis), *n.* **1.** a square or rectangular hole, esp. one cut to fit a tenon for joining two pieces. —*v.*, **mor·tised, mor·tis·ing. 2.** to join by means of a mortise and tenon.

Mortise joint
M, Mortise
T, Tenon

Mor·ton (môr′t'n), *n.* **Le·vi Par·sons** (lē′vī pär′sənz), 1824–1920, 22nd Vice President of the U.S. 1889–1893.

mor·tu·ar·y (môr′choo er′ē), *n., pl.* **mor·tu·ar·ies.** a funeral home.

mos., months.

mo·sa·ic (mō zā′ik), *n.* **1.** a picture or decoration made of small pieces of stone, glass, etc. —*adj.* **2.** resembling or used for making a mosaic.

Mo·sa·ic (mō zā′ik), *adj.* of or referring to Moses or the writings, laws, and principles attributed to him.

Mos·cow (mos′kō, mos′kou), *n.* the capital city of the Soviet Union, in the central part in Europe.

Mo·ses (mō′ziz, mō′zis), *n.* (in the Bible) a Hebrew leader and lawgiver who brought the Israelites out of Egypt and led them to the Promised Land.

Mos·lem (moz′ləm, mos′ləm), *adj., n., pl.* **Mos·lems** or **Mos·lem.** another spelling of **Muslim.**

mosque (mosk), *n.* a Muslim place of public worship.

Mosque

mos·qui·to (mə skē′tō), *n., pl.* **mos·qui·toes.** any of numerous insects having a slender body and long legs, the females of which suck the blood of animals and man. The bite of a mosquito usually causes redness and itching. Ma-

laria and yellow fever are transmitted by some kinds of mosquitoes. [from a Spanish word meaning "little fly"]

moss (môs), *n.* **1.** any of numerous plants with tiny leaves that grow in tufts, sods, or mats on moist ground, tree trunks, rocks, etc. **2.** a growth of such plants: *a large patch of moss on a rock.*

moss·y (mô′sē), *adj.,* **moss·i·er, moss·i·est.** covered with or appearing as if covered with moss: *the mossy bank of a stream.* —**moss′i·ness,** *n.*

most (mōst), *adj., superlative of* **much** *or* **many** *with* **more** *as comparative.* **1.** in the greatest number, amount, or degree: *the most votes; the most talent.* **2.** in the majority of cases: *Most people are law-abiding.* —*n.* **3.** the greatest amount, number, or part: *Most of his writing is good.* **4.** the majority of persons: *to be happier than most.* **5.** the best that is possible: *the most one can expect.* —*adv., superlative of* **much** *with* **more** *as comparative.* **6.** in or to the greatest extent or degree: *most wisely.* **7. at the most,** at the maximum: *At the most it will cost a few dollars.* **8. make the most of,** to use to the greatest advantage: *to make the most of one's time.*

-most, a suffix used to form adjectives and adverbs meaning **1.** furthest in a certain direction: *easternmost.* **2.** nearest a certain point: *topmost; endmost.*

most·ly (mōst′lē), *adv.* for the most part; mainly; chiefly: *The remaining seats are mostly in the back.*

mote (mōt), *n.* a particle or speck, esp. of dust.

mo·tel (mō tel′), *n.* a hotel, esp. one located near a highway, that provides travelers with lodging and free parking facilities. [from *motor* + *hotel*]

moth (môth), *n., pl.* **moths** (môthz, môths). any of numerous insects that resemble butterflies but have heavier bodies, different types of antennae, and fly mostly at night. The larvae of some moths are destructive to vegetation and to cloth.

Moth
(wingspread
to 4½ in.)

moth·ball (môth′bôl′), *n.* a small ball of some strong-smelling material that repels moths.

moth-eat·en (môth′ēt/'n), *adj.* **1.** eaten or damaged by or as if by moths. **2.** out of fashion or worn out.

moth·er[1] (muth′ər), *n.* **1.** a female parent. **2.** the source of something: *Necessity is the mother of invention.* —*adj.* **3.** being a mother: *a mother bird.* **4.** derived from one's mother; native: *a mother dialect.* **5.** of, concerning, or characteristic of a mother: *mother love.* **6.** like a mother in being a source of origin: *the mother church; the mother country.* —*v.* **7.** to care for or protect as a mother does: *She mothers her little brother.* [from the Old English word *mōdor,* which is related to Latin *māter*] —**moth′er·less,** *adj.*

moth·er[2] (muth′ər), *n.* a slimy substance found on the surface of fermenting liquids, such as cider or vinegar, that causes fermentation if mixed with unfermented liquid. [perhaps from the Dutch word *modder* "dregs," which is related to English *mud*]

Moth′er Goose′, a made-up name for the author of a collection of old English nursery rhymes.

moth·er·hood (muth′ər hŏŏd′), *n.* **1.** the state of being a mother. **2.** mothers as a group.

moth·er-in-law (muth′ər in lô′), *n., pl.* **moth·ers-in-law** (muth′ərz in lô′). the mother of one's husband or wife.

moth·er·land (muth′ər land′), *n.* **1.** a person's native land. **2.** the land of one's ancestors.

moth·er·ly (muth′ər lē), *adj.* of or like a mother; warm; protective. —**moth′er·li·ness,** *n.*

moth·er-of-pearl (muth′ər əv pûrl′), *n.* a hard, iridescent substance that lines the shells of certain mollusks, used for making buttons, jewelry, etc.

moth′er supe′rior, *pl.* **mother superiors** *or* **mothers superior.** the nun in charge of a convent; abbess.

mo·tif (mō tēf′), *n.* **1.** a subject, theme, or idea that recurs in an artistic work, a musical composition, or a novel. **2.** a form, shape, or figure in a design.

mo·tion (mō′shən), *n.* **1.** the action or process of moving. **2.** a bodily movement or change of posture; gesture: *He made a motion with his hand.* **3.** a formal proposal to be discussed and voted on: *a motion to adjourn the meeting.* —*v.* **4.** to make a gesture; signal: *He motioned for us to join him.*

mo·tion·less (mō′shən lis), *adj.* without motion or incapable of motion: *to wait motionless.*

mo′tion pic′ture, **1.** a sequence of pictures that is photographed in motion by a specially designed camera and shown on a screen by a projector in such rapid succession as to give the appearance of natural movement. **2.** a play or event presented in this form. —**mo′tion-pic′ture,** *adj.*

mo·ti·vate (mō′tə vāt′), *v.,* **mo·ti·vat·ed, mo·ti·vat·ing.** to provide with a motive or motives.

mo·ti·va·tion (mō′tə vā′shən), *n.* **1.** the act or an instance of motivating. **2.** the state of being motivated. **3.** something that motivates; incentive.

mo·tive (mō′tiv), *n.* **1.** something that causes a person to act in a certain way: *the motive for a crime.* —*adj.* **2.** tending to cause motion: *motive force.*

mot·ley (mot′lē), *adj.* **1.** made up of different parts or elements; varied. **2.** being a combination of different colors. —*n., pl.* **mot·leys.** **3.** a combination of different colors. **4.** the multicolored garment of a court jester or clown.

mo·tor (mō′tər), *n.* **1.** a small engine: *an outboard motor.* **2.** a device that converts electrical energy to mechanical energy: *an electric motor.* —*adj.* **3.** of or referring to muscular movement: *a motor nerve.* —*v.* **4.** to ride or travel in an automobile.

mo·tor·boat (mō′tər bōt′), *n.* **1.** a boat propelled by an inboard or outboard motor. —*v.* **2.** to travel in or operate a motorboat.

mo·tor·car (mō′tər kär′), *n.* an automobile.

mo·tor·cy·cle (mō′tər sī′kəl), *n.* **1.** a two-wheeled vehicle, similar to but heavier than a bicycle, driven by a gasoline engine. —*v.,* **mo·tor·cy·cled, mo·tor·cy·cling.** **2.** to ride on or operate a motorcycle.

mo·tor·ist (mō′tər ist), *n.* a person who drives or travels in an automobile.

mo·tor·ize (mō′tə rīz′), *v.,* **mo·tor·ized, mo·tor·iz·ing.** **1.** to furnish with a motor or motors. **2.** to supply with motor-driven vehicles in place of horses and horse-drawn vehicles: *to motorize an army.*

mo·tor·man (mō′tər mən), *n., pl.* **mo·tor·men.** **1.** a person who operates an electric vehicle, such as a streetcar or subway train. **2.** a person who operates a motor.

mo′tor scoot′er, a motor vehicle similar to a child's scooter, but larger and heavier and provided with a saddlelike seat.

mot·tle (mot′əl), *v.,* **mot·tled, mot·tling.** **1.** to mark with spots or blotches of a different color or shade. —*n.* **2.** a spot or blotch of color. **3.** spotted coloring or pattern. —**mot′tled,** *adj.*

mot·to (mot′ō), *n., pl.* **mot·toes** *or* **mot·tos.** **1.** a short saying that expresses a guiding principle. **2.** a word or phrase inscribed on a seal, coin, etc.

mould (mōld), *n., v.* the British spelling of **mold.**

mould·er (mōl′dər), *v.* the British spelling of **molder.**

mould·ing (mōl′ding), *n.* the British spelling of **molding.**

mould·y (mōl′dē), *adj.,* **mould·i·er, mould·i·est.** the British spelling of **moldy.** —**mould′i·ness,** *n.*

moult (mōlt), *v.* the British spelling of **molt.**

mound (mound), *n.* **1.** a small hill formed of earth, sand, stones, etc., esp. over a grave or ruins. **2.** a small hill or knoll. **3.** (in baseball) the slightly raised ground from which the pitcher pitches the ball. —*v.* **4.** to furnish or enclose with a mound of earth.

mount¹ (mount), *v.* **1.** to go up; climb; ascend: *He mounted the stairs slowly.* **2.** to rise in amount. **3.** to get up on (a horse or other animal) for riding. **4.** (of a fortress or vessel) to have or carry (guns) in position for use. **5.** to fix on or in a support: *to mount a photograph.* —*n.* **6.** a horse, bicycle, etc., used for riding. [from the Old French word *monter* "to go up, ascend," which comes from Latin *mōns* "hill, mountain"]

mount² (mount), *n.* a hill or mountain. [from the Old English word *munt,* which comes from Latin *mōns* "hill, mountain"]

moun·tain (moun′tən), *n.* **1.** a natural elevation rising to a summit and higher than a hill. **2.** a large mass of something. —*adj.* **3.** living, growing, or located in the mountains: *mountain plants.*

moun·tain·eer (moun′t∂nēr′), *n.* **1.** an inhabitant of a mountainous district. **2.** a climber of mountains. —*v.* **3.** to climb mountains.

Mountain goat
(3½ ft. high
at shoulder)

moun′tain goat′, a goatlike antelope of the mountainous regions of North America, having a white coat and black, pointed horns. Mountain goats are noted for their surefootedness and agility. Also, **Rocky Mountain goat.**

moun′tain li′on, another name for **cougar.**

moun·tain·ous (moun′t^ənəs), *adj.* 1. composed of or having many mountains. 2. very large and high like a mountain.

moun·tain·side (moun′t^ən sīd′), *n.* the side or slope of a mountain.

moun·te·bank (moun′tə baɴk′), *n.* 1. a person who sells worthless medicines by trickery in public places. 2. any quack or swindler.

mount·ing (moun′tiɴg), *n.* something that serves as a mount: *a new mounting for the jewel.*

Mount′ Ver′non, the estate and burial place of George Washington in NE Virginia, on the Potomac River 15 mi. below Washington, D.C.

mourn (môrn), *v.* to feel or express sorrow or grief over (misfortune, someone's death, etc.). [from the Old English word *murnan*] —**mourn′er,** *n.*

mourn·ful (môrn′fəl), *adj.* having, expressing, or showing sorrow or grief: *a mournful cry.* —**mourn′ful·ly,** *adv.*

mourn·ing (môr′niɴg), *n.* 1. the act of a person who mourns; sorrowing or lamentation. 2. a show of sorrow for a person's death, such as the wearing of black, the displaying of flags at half-mast, etc. 3. the outward tokens of such sorrow.

mourn′ing dove′, a North American dove, noted for its sad, plaintive cooing.

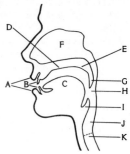

House mouse
(total length
to 7 in.)

mouse (mous), *n., pl.* **mice** (mīs). 1. any of numerous small, furry animals having a long tail. Some species of mice live in fields, others infest buildings, and some are specially bred for use in scientific experiments and as pets. —*v.* (mouz), **moused, mous·ing.** 2. to hunt for or catch mice. 3. to hunt out (prey), as a cat hunts out mice. —**mous·er** (mou′zər), *n.*

mouse·trap (mous′trap′), *n.* a trap for mice, usually consisting of a wooden base on which a metal spring is mounted.

mousse (mōōs), *n.* 1. a dessert made with whipped cream and gelatin, and chilled in a mold. 2. a similar food containing meat, vegetables, or fish.

mous·tache (mə stash′, mus′tash), *n.* another spelling of **mustache.**

mouth (mouth), *n., pl.* **mouths** (mouŧhz). 1. the opening through which animals and humans take in food and drink. The mouth contains the tongue and teeth, which are important in making sounds, eating, etc. 2. any opening resembling a mouth: *the mouth of a cave.* 3. the part of a river where its waters are discharged into some other body of water. —*v.* (mouŧh). 4. to utter or pronounce softly and indistinctly: *Stop mouthing your words and speak up.* 5. to put or take into the mouth. 6. to press, rub, or chew at with the mouth or lips. 7. **down in the mouth,** *Informal.* sad; dejected: *He looks so down in the mouth he must have a serious problem.*

mouth·ful (mouth′fool′), *n., pl.* **mouth·fuls.** 1. the amount a mouth can hold. 2. the amount of food usually taken into the mouth at one time. 3. a word or phrase that is difficult to say.

mouth′ or′gan, another name for **harmonica.**

mouth·parts (mouth′pärts′), *n.pl.* the parts of the head of an insect or other arthropod that surround or are associated with its mouth.

mouth·piece (mouth′pēs′), *n.* 1. the part of something that is placed in or near the mouth: *a trumpet mouthpiece; a telephone mouthpiece.* 2. a person, newspaper, etc., that conveys the opinions or sentiments of another or others; spokesman.

Mouth

A, Lips; B, Teeth;
C, Tongue; D, Hard
palate; E, Soft
palate; F, Nasal
cavity; G, Uvula;
H, Pharynx; I, Epi-
glottis; J, Larynx;
K, Vocal cords

mov·a·ble (mōō′və bəl), *adj.* 1. capable of being moved. 2. changing from one date to another in different years: *a movable holiday.* —*n.* 3. **movables,** movable property. Also, **move′a·ble.**

move (mōōv), *v.,* **moved, mov·ing.** 1. to pass from one place or position to another: *I moved to another part of the auditorium.* 2. to go from one place of residence to another: *We moved from New York to Boston.* 3. to change from one place or position to another: *He moved the table upstairs.* 4. to have a regular motion, as a machine does. 5. to prompt or cause: *What moved him to do that?* 6. to arouse the feelings of: *to move someone to anger.* 7. to affect with tender feelings or emotion: *The poem moved me.* 8. to submit a formal request or proposal: *He moved that the meeting be adjourned.* 9. to advance or progress: *The work on the new school moved slowly.* 10. *Informal.* to start off or leave. —*n.* 11. the act or an instance of moving; movement. 12. a change of residence. 13. an action toward an end; step: *a good move.* 14. (in chess, checkers, etc.) **a.** a player's right or turn to make a play. **b.** the play itself. 15. **on the move,** *Informal.* **a.** busy; active: *to be on the move all day and night.* **b.** going from place to place: *The armed forces are always on the move.*

move·ment (mōōv′mənt), *n.* 1. the act, process, or result of moving. 2. a particular manner of moving: *graceful movements.* 3. a change of position or location of troops, ships, etc. 4. a series of actions or activities directed toward a particular end: *a civil rights movement.* 5. a major section of a long musical work. 6. the working parts of a clock or watch. 7. a bowel movement. 8. Usually, **movements.** actions or activities of a person or a group of persons.

mov·er (mōō′vər), *n.* a person who moves, esp. a person who moves furniture and household belongings from one place to another.

mov·ie (mōo′vē), *n. Informal.* **1.** a motion picture. **2.** a motion-picture theater. **3. movies, a.** motion pictures considered as an industry. **b.** motion pictures considered as a form of art or entertainment. **c.** the showing of a motion picture.

mov·ing (mōo′viṅg), *adj.* **1.** that moves: *a moving target.* **2.** causing or producing motion. **3.** exciting the emotions, esp. in a touching way.

mov′ing pic′ture, a motion picture.

mow[1] (mō), *v.,* **mowed; mowed** *or* **mown** (mōn); **mow·ing. 1.** to cut down (grass, grain, etc.) with a scythe or a machine. **2.** to cut grass, grain, etc., from: *to mow an overgrown lawn.* **3.** to destroy or kill in great numbers: *to mow down the enemy.* [from the Old English word *māwan*] —**mow′er,** *n.*

mow[2] (mou), *n.* **1.** the place in a barn where hay, sheaves of grain, etc., are stored. **2.** a heap or pile of hay or of sheaves of grain in a barn. [from the Old English word *mūwa* "heap"]

mown (mōn), *v.* a past participle of **mow**[1].

Mo·zam·bique (mō′zam bēk′), *n.* an independent country in SE Africa. 303,769 sq. mi. Former name, **Portuguese East Africa.**

Mo·zart (mōt′särt), *n.* **Wolf·gang Am·a·de·us** (wŏŏlf′-gaṅg am′ə dā′əs), 1756–1791, Austrian composer.

MP, 1. Military Police. **2.** Mounted Police. Also, **M.P.**

mph, miles per hour. Also, **m.p.h.**

Mr. (mis′tər), *pl.* **Messrs.** (mes′ərz). Mister: a title of respect written or said before a man's name, or in showing respect for a man's position.

Mrs. (mis′iz, mis′is), *pl.* **Mrs.** *or* **Mmes.** (mā däm′, mā dam′). a title of respect written or said before the name of a married woman: *Mrs. Dallas Goss; Mrs. Jane Murphy.* See also **miss**[2] (def. 1).

Ms. (miz, em′es′), *n., pl.* **Mss., Mses.** (miz′es). a title of respect used before a woman's name regardless of her marital status or when such status is unknown.

MS., manuscript. Also, **ms.**

Msgr., Monsignor.

MSS., manuscripts. Also, **mss.**

Mt., 1. Mount: *Mt. Rainier.* **2.** Mountain. Also, **mt.**

Mts., Mountains. Also, **mts.**

much (much), *adj.,* **more, most. 1.** being of great quantity, amount, measure, or degree: *There is much work to be done.* —*n.* **2.** a great quantity or amount: *There is much to see.* **3.** a great, important, or notable thing or matter: *It wasn't much.* —*adv.,* **more, most. 4.** to a great extent or degree. **5.** nearly or about: *I acted much the same way as you did.*

mu·ci·lage (myōo′sə lij), *n.* any of various gummy substances used to stick things together.

muck (muk), *n.* **1.** moist farmyard dung; manure. **2.** filth; dirt.

muck·rake (muk′rāk′), *v.,* **muck·raked, muck·rak·ing.** to search for and expose corruption or scandal, esp. in politics. —**muck′rak·er,** *n.*

mu·cous (myōo′kəs), *adj.* **1.** of, concerning, or resembling mucus. **2.** containing or secreting mucus.

mu′cous mem′brane, the moist membrane that lines the nose, the mouth, and the respiratory and digestive tracts.

mu·cus (myōo′kəs), *n.* the slimy liquid secreted by the mucous membrane that lubricates the respiratory and digestive tracts.

mud (mud), *n.* wet, soft earth or earthy matter.

mud·dle (mud′əl), *v.,* **mud·dled, mud·dling. 1.** to mix up in a confused or bungling manner; jumble: *to muddle an assignment.* **2.** to think or act in a confused or bungling manner: *He muddled through the problem.* **3.** to cause to become confused: *His strange words muddled me.* —*n.* **4.** a confused mental state. **5.** a confused state of affairs; mess.

mud·dy (mud′ē), *adj.,* **mud·di·er, mud·di·est. 1.** covered with mud: *muddy boots.* **2.** not clear or pure: *a muddy stream.* **3.** not clear in meaning; obscure: *muddy writing.* —*v.,* **mud·died, mud·dy·ing. 4.** to make or become muddy. —**mud′di·ness,** *n.*

mud·pup·py (mud′pup′ē), *n., pl.* **mud·pup·pies.** any of several large salamanders, having bushy, red gills and well-developed limbs.

mud·skip·per (mud′skip′ər), *n.* any of several tropical fishes found from Africa to the East Indies and Japan, noted for their habit of remaining out of water on mud for periods of time and for jumping about when disturbed.

Mudpuppy (length 8 in.)

muff (muf), *n.* **1.** a thick, tubular case of cloth, fur, or the like, carried by women and girls to warm the hands. **2.** (in sports) a failure to catch a ball that may reasonably be expected to be caught. **3.** any failure. —*v.* **4.** (in sports) to fail to catch (a ball). **5.** *Informal.* to bungle; handle clumsily.

muf·fin (muf′in), *n.* a small, round cake made with wheat flour, corn meal, or the like.

muf·fle (muf′əl), *v.,* **muf·fled, muf·fling. 1.** to wrap in a shawl, coat, etc., esp. to keep the face and neck warm. **2.** to wrap with something to deaden or prevent sound. **3.** to deaden (sound) by wrappings or other means. —*n.* **4.** something that muffles.

muf·fler (muf′lər), *n.* **1.** a device that reduces the noise of an engine's exhaust. **2.** a heavy neck scarf.

muf·ti (muf′tē), *n.* civilian clothing, as distinguished from military or other uniform.

mug (mug), *n.* **1.** a large, heavy drinking cup having a handle. **2.** the quantity a mug can hold. **3.** *Slang.* the face. —*v.,* **mugged, mug·ging. 4.** to assault (a victim), usually with intent to rob.

mug·gy (mug′ē), *adj.,* **mug·gi·er, mug·gi·est.** humid and oppressive; damp and close. —**mug′gi·ness,** *n.*

Mu·ham·mad (mōo ham′əd), *n.* A.D. 570–632, founder of Islam. Also, **Mahomet, Mohammed.**

Mu·ham·mad·an (mōo ham′ə dən), *adj., n.* another word for **Muslim.**

mu·lat·to (mə lat′ō, myōo lat′ō), *n., pl.* **mu·lat·toes.** a person having one white and one black parent.

mul·ber·ry (mul′ber′ē), *n., pl.* **mul·ber·ries. 1.** a tree that bears a sweet, berrylike fruit and broad leaves that serve as food for silkworms. **2.** the fruit of this tree. **3.** a dark purple. — *adj.* **4.** of this color.

mulch (mulch), *n.* **1.** a covering of straw, leaves, or the like, spread on the ground to protect plants from cold, drying, etc. —*v.* **2.** to cover with mulch.

mulct (mulkt), *v.* **1.** to deprive (a person) of something, esp. by cheating or fraud; swindle. **2.** to obtain (money or the like) by fraud. **3.** to punish by fine. —*n.* **4.** a fine or penalty.

Mule
(5 ft. high at shoulder)

mule (myōōl), *n.* **1.** a strong but stubborn work animal, the offspring of a male donkey and a female horse. **2.** a machine that spins fibers into yarn and winds the yarn on spindles. **3.** *Informal.* a stubborn person.

mule′ deer′, a deer of western North America, having large ears.

mu·le·teer (myōō′lə tēr′), *n.* a driver of mules.

mul·ish (myōō′lish), *adj.* stubborn or obstinate. —**mul′ish·ness,** *n.*

mull[1] (mul), *v.* to study or ponder (often fol. by *over*): *You'd better mull over that decision.* [perhaps another form of the word *muddle*]

mull[2] (mul), *v.* to heat, sweeten, and spice for drinking, such as ale, wine, etc.: *mulled cider.*

Mule deer
(3½ ft. high at shoulder;
total length 6 ft.)

mul·lein (mul′ən), *n.* a weed having coarse, woolly leaves and spikes of yellow flowers.

mul·let (mul′it), *n., pl.* **mul·lets** or **mul·let.** any of several salt- or freshwater food fishes having a nearly cylindrical body.

multi-, a prefix meaning many: *multimillionaire.*

mul·ti·col·ored (mul′ti kul′ərd), *adj.* of many colors.

mul·ti·far·i·ous (mul′tə fâr′ē əs), *adj.* **1.** having many different parts, elements, forms, etc. **2.** many and varied: *multifarious activities.*

mul·ti·form (mul′tə fôrm′), *adj.* having many forms; of many different forms or kinds.

mul·ti·lat·er·al (mul′ti lat′ər əl), *adj.* **1.** having many sides; many-sided. **2.** participated in by two or more nations: *multilateral treaties.*

mul·ti·mil·lion·aire (mul′tē mil′yə nâr′, mul′tī-), *n.* a person who has several million dollars, pounds, francs, etc.

mul·ti·na·tion·al (mul′ti nash′ə n²l), *adj.* **1.** of or involving many nations. — *n.* **2.** a very large corporation having divisions in many countries.

mul·ti·ple (mul′tə pəl), *adj.* **1.** consisting of, having, or involving many individuals, parts, elements, rela-

tions, etc. —*n.* **2.** a number that contains another number a certain number of times without a remainder: *12 is a multiple of 3.*

mul·ti·pli·cand (mul′tə pli kand′), *n.* (in arithmetic) the number that is added to itself or multiplied by another: *In the case of 4 × 3 = 12, 3 is the multiplicand.*

mul·ti·pli·ca·tion (mul′tə plə kā′shən), *n.* **1.** the act or process of multiplying. **2.** the state of being multiplied. **3.** (in arithmetic) the process or technique of adding a number to itself a given number of times, represented by a multiplication sign (×). 4 × 3 is the same as 3 + 3 + 3 + 3.

mul·ti·plic·i·ty (mul′tə plis′i tē), *n., pl.* **mul·ti·plic·i·ties.** a multitude or great number: *She received a multiplicity of compliments.*

mul·ti·pli·er (mul′tə plī′ər), *n.* **1.** (in arithmetic) the number that shows how many times the multiplicand is to be added to itself: *In the case of 4 × 3 = 12, 4 is the multiplier.* **2.** a person or thing that multiplies.

mul·ti·ply (mul′tə plī′), *v.,* **mul·ti·plied, mul·ti·ply·ing.** **1.** (in arithmetic) to find the product of two or more numbers. **2.** to increase by producing offspring: *to multiply like rabbits.* **3.** to make or become many; increase: *His troubles multiplied.*

mul·ti·tude (mul′ti tōōd′, -tyōōd′), *n.* a great number of persons or things; crowd.

mul·ti·tu·di·nous (mul′ti tōōd′²nəs, -tyōōd′-), *adj.* forming a multitude; existing in great numbers.

mum (mum), *adj.* **1.** silent; not saying a word: *to keep mum.* **2. mum's the word,** do not reveal what you know: *It's a secret, so mum's the word.*

mum·ble (mum′bəl), *v.,* **mum·bled, mum·bling.** **1.** to speak low and unclearly: *He mumbled his name and I didn't catch it.* —*n.* **2.** a low, indistinct utterance.

mum·mer (mum′ər), *n.* **1.** a person who wears a mask or costume, esp. in some countries at Christmas, New Year's, and other festive seasons. **2.** an actor.

mum·mer·y (mum′ə rē), *n., pl.* **mum·mer·ies.** **1.** a performance by mummers. **2.** an empty, ridiculous, or showy ceremony or performance.

mum·mi·fy (mum′ə fī′), *v.,* **mum·mi·fied, mum·mi·fy·ing.** **1.** to make (a dead body) into a mummy. **2.** to dry or shrivel up.

mum·my (mum′ē), *n., pl.* **mum·mies.** a dead body preserved from decay by artificial or natural means.

mumps (mumps), *n. (used as sing.)* a contagious disease that causes painful swelling of the glands in the jaw below the ear and is common among children.

munch (munch), *v.* to chew noisily and with steady working of the jaws.

mun·dane (mun dān′, mun′dān), *adj.* referring to the everyday concerns of this world rather than spiritual matters; ordinary: *a mundane chore.*

Mu·nich (myōō′nik), *n.* a city in SW Germany.

mu·nic·i·pal (myōō nis′ə pəl), *adj.* of or concerning the local government of a town or city.

mu·nic·i·pal·i·ty (myōō nis′ə pal′i tē), *n., pl.* **mu·nic·i·pal·i·ties.** a city, town, or district having local self-government.

mu·nif·i·cent (myōō nif′i sənt), *adj.* characterized

by or showing great generosity. —**mu·nif′i·cence,** *n.*
—**mu·nif′i·cent·ly,** *adv.*

mu·ni·tion (myo͞o nish′ən), *n.* **1.** Usually, **munitions.**
materials used in war, esp. weapons and ammunition.
—*v.* **2.** to provide with munitions.

mu·ral (myo͝or′əl), *adj.* **1.** of, referring to, or resembling a wall. —*n.* **2.** a painting done on or permanently attached to a wall.

mur·der (mûr′dər), *n.* **1.** the unlawful and intentional killing of a human being. **2.** *Slang.* something
very difficult: *That final exam was murder!* —*v.* **3.** to
kill (a person) unlawfully and intentionally. **4.** to
spoil or ruin: *to murder a tune.* —**mur′der·er;** *referring to a woman,* **mur′der·ess,** *n.*

mur·der·ous (mûr′dər əs), *adj.* **1.** relating to murder. **2.** guilty of, intending, or capable of murder.

mu·rex (myo͝or′eks), *n.,* *pl.* **mu·ri·ces** (myo͝or′i sēz′)
or **mu·rex·es.** any various marine mollusks common in
tropical seas.

murk (mûrk), *n.* darkness; gloom.

murk·y (mûr′kē), *adj.,* **murk·i·er, murk·i·
est.** intensely dark or gloomy. —**murk′i·
ness,** *n.*

Mur·mansk (mo͝or mänsk′), *n.* a port city
in the NW Soviet Union.

mur·mur (mûr′mər), *n.* **1.** any low, continuous sound. —*v.* **2.** to make a low or indistinct sound. **3.** to complain in a quiet,
guarded manner.

mus·cle (mus′əl), *n.* **1.** the kind of body
tissue made up of fibers that can lengthen
and shorten to produce movement. **2.** a
mass of such tissue that acts to move a particular part
of the body. **3.** muscular strength; brawn. [from the
Latin word *musculus,* literally "little mouse," which
comes from *mūs* "mouse." The meaning "muscle"
comes from the fancied resemblance of a twitching
muscle to a mouse running back and forth under the
skin]

mus·cu·lar (mus′kyə lər), *adj.* **1.** having well-
developed muscles; strong; brawny. **2.** concerning a
muscle or the muscles.

muse (myo͞oz), *v.,* **mused, mus·ing.** to meditate in silence; ponder: *to muse over a question.*

Muse (myo͞oz), *n.* **1.** (in Greek mythology) any of
nine daughters of Zeus who were goddesses of the
arts and learning. **2.** *(often l.c.)* the power regarded
as inspiring a writer: *a visit from the muse.*

mu·se·um (myo͞o zē′əm), *n.* a building or place
where works of art or other objects of permanent
value are kept and displayed.

mush¹ (mush), *n.* **1.** meal, esp. corn meal, boiled in
water or milk until it forms a thick, soft mass. **2.** any
thick, soft mass. [from the Old English word *mōs*
"food." The *-sh* ending is from *mash*]

mush² (mush), *v.* to go or travel, esp. over snow with
a dog team and sled. [perhaps from the Canadian
French word *moucher* "to hurry," which comes from
mouche "a fly"]

Mushroom

mush·room (mush′ro͞om), *n.* **1.** any of various small
fungi shaped somewhat like an umbrella, esp. those
kinds that are safe to eat. See also
toadstool. —*adj.* **2.** made of or
containing mushrooms: *a mushroom omelet.* **3.** resembling the
shape of a mushroom: *a mushroom
cloud.* —*v.* **4.** to spread, grow, or
develop quickly.

mu·sic (myo͞o′zik), *n.* **1.** the art of
arranging and combining sounds in
ways that express emotion or are pleasant to hear. **2.**
the sounds produced by this art. **3.** a musical composition, or a group of such compositions. **4.** the written or printed signs from which a composition is
played or sung. **5.** any pleasing sound. **6. face the
music,** *Informal.* to take the consequences of one's
actions or mistakes: *to face the music for lying.*

mu·si·cal (myo͞o′zi kəl), *adj.* **1.** concerning or producing music. **2.** resembling music; harmonious. **3.**
fond of or skilled in music. —*n.* **4.** a musical comedy.
—**mu′si·cal·ly,** *adv.*

mu′sical com′edy, a show or play with music and
dancing, usually one having an amusing plot.

mu′sical in′strument, a device on which music
is played, such as a piano, clarinet, violin, or bugle.

mu′sic box′, a box or case containing an apparatus
for producing music mechanically.

mu·si·cian (myo͞o zish′ən), *n.* a person who sings,
plays a musical instrument, conducts an orchestra, or
composes music.

musk (musk), *n.* **1.** a strong-smelling substance, used
in making perfumes, found in a gland in the male
musk deer. **2.** a similar secretion of other animals,
such as the civet or muskrat. **3.** the odor of musk.

musk′ deer′, a small, hornless deer, the male of
which produces musk.

mus·kel·lunge (mus′kə lunj′), *n.,* *pl.* **mus·kel·lunge.**
a large North American freshwater game fish related
to the pike.

mus·ket (mus′kit), *n.* a gun resembling a rifle, formerly used by soldiers.

mus·ket·eer (mus′ki tēr′), *n.* a soldier armed with a
musket.

mus·ket·ry (mus′ki trē), *n.* **1.** the technique of firing
muskets. **2.** muskets or musketeers as a group.

musk·mel·on (musk′mel′ən), *n.* **1.** any of numerous
kinds of melon having a tough rind and sweet
orange, yellow, white, or
green flesh, esp. the cantaloupe. **2.** the vine bearing such melons.

musk′ ox′, a large, oxlike animal with shaggy
brown fur and a musky
odor, found in the arctic
regions of North America.

musk·rat (musk′rat′), *n.,*
pl. **musk·rats** *or* **musk·rat.** **1.** a large North American

Murex
(shell
length
4 to 5 in.)

Murex

Muskrat
(total length
about 2 ft.)

water rat having a musky odor. **2.** its thick, light-brown fur, used esp. for women's coats.

musk·y (mus′kē), *adj.,* **musk·i·er, musk·i·est.** having the odor of musk.

Mus·lim (muz′lim, mŏŏz′lim), *adj.* **1.** of or referring to the religion, law, or civilization of Islam. —*n., pl.* **Mus·lims** *or* **Mus·lim. 2.** a follower of Islam. Also, **Mus′lem, Moslem, Mohammedan.**

mus·lin (muz′lin), *n.* a cotton fabric of plain weave used for sheets and for a variety of other purposes.

muss (mus), *n.* **1.** *Informal.* a state of disorder or untidiness. —*v.* **2.** to put into disorder (usually fol. by *up*): *The wind mussed up my hair.*

mus·sel (mus′əl), *n.* **1.** a saltwater shellfish that resembles a clam but has a blue-black, teardrop-shaped shell. **2.** a kind of freshwater clam.

Mus·so·li·ni (mŏŏs′ə lē′nē), *n.* **Be·ni·to** (bə nē′tō), *("Il Duce"),* 1883–1945, Italian Fascist leader: premier of Italy 1922–1943.

must (must), *auxiliary verb.* **1.** to be forced to, as by instinct or natural law: *One must eat.* **2.** to be required to: *You must drive carefully.* **3.** to feel a strong urge to: *I must try some of that pudding.* **4.** to be certain to: *Man must die.* —*n.* **5.** anything necessary or vital: *Seeing Paris is a must.*

Mussel
(length 4 in.)

mus·tache (mus′tash, mə stash′), *n.* the hair that grows on the upper lip, usually trimmed and shaped in various ways. Also, **moustache.**

mus·tang (mus′tanḡ), *n.* a small, hardy, wild or half-wild horse of the American plains.

mus·tard (mus′tərd), *n.* a brownish powder or paste with a sharp or burning taste and an irritating effect on the skin, made from the small, round seeds of a plant related to cabbage and watercress.

mus·ter (mus′tər), *v.* **1.** to assemble (troops, a ship's crew, etc.) for battle or inspection. **2.** to gather or summon (often fol. by *up*): *to muster up one's courage.* —*n.* **3.** an assembling of troops or men for inspection or other purposes.

must·n't (mus′ənt), contraction of *must not.*

mus·ty (mus′tē), *adj.,* **mus·ti·er, mus·ti·est. 1.** having a moldy odor or flavor. **2.** old and outdated: *musty laws.* —**mus′ti·ness,** *n.*

mu·tant (myōōt′ənt), *adj.* a new kind of animal or plant produced by mutation.

mu·tate (myōō′tāt), *v.,* **mu·tat·ed, mu·tat·ing.** to undergo mutation; change.

mu·ta·tion (myōō tā′shən), *n.* **1.** the act or process of changing. **2.** a change or alteration. **3.** (in biology) the sudden appearance of a characteristic that makes an offspring different from its parents and that can be passed on to future generations. **4.** an animal or plant having such a characteristic; mutant.

mute (myōōt), *adj.* **1.** unable to speak. **2.** refraining from speech; silent. **3.** (of a speech sound) silent; not pronounced, such as the *e* in *bake.* —*n.* **4.** a person who is unable to speak. **5.** a device for muffling the

tone of a musical instrument. —*v.,* **mut·ed, mut·ing. 6.** to deaden or muffle the sound of.

mu·ti·late (myōōt′əlāt′), *v.,* **mu·ti·lat·ed, mu·ti·lat·ing. 1.** to deprive (a person or animal) of a limb or other essential part. **2.** to injure or disfigure by removing or damaging: *He mutilated the book by ripping the pages.* —**mu′ti·la′tion,** *n.*

mu·ti·neer (myōōt′ə nēr′), *n.* a person who mutinies.

mu·ti·nous (myōōt′ə nəs), *adj.* tending to, engaged in, or involving revolt against authority; rebellious.

mu·ti·ny (myōōt′ə nē), *n., pl.* **mu·ti·nies. 1.** revolt or rebellion against authority, esp. by seamen or soldiers against their officers. —*v.,* **mu·ti·nied, mu·ti·ny·ing. 2.** to commit mutiny; revolt against authority.

mutt (mut), *n. Informal.* a dog, esp. a mongrel.

mut·ter (mut′ər), *v.* **1.** to utter words unclearly or in a low tone. **2.** to make a low, rumbling sound. —*n.* **3.** the act or utterance of a person who mutters.

mut·ton (mut′ən), *n.* meat from a sheep.

mu·tu·al (myōō′chōō əl), *adj.* **1.** possessed, experienced, performed, etc., by each of two or more with respect to the other or others: *in mutual agreement.* **2.** having the same relation each toward the other or others: *to be mutual enemies.* **3.** of or concerning each of two or more; having in common: *mutual friends.* —**mu′tu·al·ly,** *adv.*

muz·zle (muz′əl), *n.* **1.** the front part of an animal's head, including the nose, jaws, and mouth. **2.** the open end of a gun barrel. **3.** a device placed over an animal's mouth to prevent biting, eating, etc. —*v.,* **muz·zled, muz·zling. 4.** to put a muzzle on (an animal or its mouth). **5.** to restrain or prevent from speaking or expressing an opinion.

my (mī), *adj.* **1.** belonging to or concerning me: *my pencil; my problems.* —*interj.* **2.** *Informal.* (used as an explanation of surprise): *My, what a big house!*

my·na (mī′nə), *n.* any of several Asian birds of the starling family, some species of which can be taught to mimic speech. Also, **my′nah.**

my·o·pi·a (mī ō′pē ə), *n.* the scientific term for **near-sightedness.**

my·op·ic (mī op′ik), *adj.* the scientific term for **near-sighted.**

myr·i·ad (mir′ē əd), *n.* **1.** a very large and indefinite number. **2.** ten thousand.

myrrh (mûr), *n.* the sweet-smelling resin of certain Asian and African shrubs, used for incense and in perfumes and medicines.

myr·tle (mûr′tᵊl), *n.* **1.** a European evergreen shrub having berries and sweet-smelling white flowers. **2.** any of various American evergreen plants, esp. the periwinkle.

my·self (mī self′), *pron.* **1.** a form of *me* or *I* used for emphasis: *I myself told her.* **2.** a form of *me* used when the subject of the sentence is the same as the object: *I saw myself in the mirror.* **3.** my normal or ordinary self: *A short nap and I was myself again.*

—**Usage.** It is incorrect to use any reflexive pronoun *(myself, yourself, himself, herself, itself, ourselves, yourselves, themselves)* where the nominative or objective form of the pronoun would normally occur:

The award was given to me (not *myself*). *Helen went with Bob and me* (not *Bob and myself*). *My brother and I* (not *My brother and myself*) *thank you.*

mys·te·ri·ous (mi stēr**/**ē əs), *adj.* full of, involving, or suggesting mystery; puzzling: *mysterious words that we could not understand.* —**mys·te/ri·ous·ly,** *adv.*

mys·ter·y (mis**/**tə rē), *n., pl.* **mys·ter·ies.** 1. something that is impossible to understand: *sacred mysteries.* 2. something that arouses curiosity because it is not explained or understood: *This riddle remains a mystery.* 3. secrecy, or the quality of being puzzling: *to have an air of mystery.* 4. Also, **mys/tery sto/ry.** a work of fiction concerned with the identification and capture of a criminal or criminals.

mys·tic (mis**/**tik), *adj.* 1. spiritually important or symbolic. 2. of mysterious character, power, or importance. 3. of or concerning mystics or mysticism. —*n.* 4. a person who believes in the possibility of attaining insight into the knowledge of God and the supernatural by intuition rather than by reason.

mys·ti·cal (mis**/**ti kəl), *adj.* 1. mystic or occult. 2. of or concerning mystics or mysticism: *mystical truth.*

mys·ti·cism (mis**/**ti siz/əm), *n.* 1. the qualities or way of thinking of mystics. 2. the belief that one may have an immediate spiritual understanding of supernatural truths and a direct union of the soul with God through contemplation and love. 3. obscure, confused thought or speculation.

mys·ti·fy (mis**/**tə fī/), *v.,* **mys·ti·fied, mys·ti·fy·ing.** 1. to cause bewilderment in; puzzle: *Her rudeness mystifies me.* 2. to make (something) mysterious or complicated. —**mys/ti·fi·ca/tion,** *n.*

myth (mith), *n.* 1. a traditional or legendary story, usually concerned with gods and the creation of the world and its inhabitants. 2. a made-up story, happening, or person. 3. an unsound belief shared by many people: *It is a myth that hard work always brings success.*

myth·i·cal (mith**/**i kəl), *adj.* 1. concerning or involving a myth or myths. 2. imaginary or made-up.

myth·o·log·i·cal (mith/ə loj**/**i kəl), *adj.* of or concerning mythology: *Hercules was a mythological hero of ancient Greece.*

my·thol·o·gy (mi thol**/**ə jē), *n., pl.* **my·thol·o·gies.** 1. a group of myths, often having a common source or subject. 2. the science or study of myths.

---

act, āble, dâre, ärt; ebb, ēqual; if, īce; hot, ōver, ôrder; oil; bŏŏk; ōōze; out; up, ûrge; ə = *a* as in *alone;*
ə as in *button* (but'ən), *fire* (fiər); çhief; ṣhoe; ţhin; ŧħat; zh as in *measure* (mezh'ər). See full key inside cover.

N
Semitic	Greek	Latin	Gothic	Modern Roman
צ	ר	N	N	N

DEVELOPMENT OF UPPER-CASE LETTERS

ν	~	N	n	n
Greek	Medieval		Gothic	Modern Roman

DEVELOPMENT OF LOWER-CASE LETTERS

N, n (en), *n., pl.* **N's** *or* **Ns, n's** *or* **ns.** the 14th letter of the English alphabet.

N, 1. north. 2. northern.

N, 1. *Chem.* the symbol for **nitrogen.** 2. (in chess) knight. 3. (in printing) en.

n, neutron.

N., 1. noon. 2. north. 3. northern.

n., 1. noon. 2. north. 3. northern. 4. noun. 5. number.

Na, *Chem.* the symbol for **sodium.** [short for the modern Latin word *natrium*]

nab (nab), *v.,* **nabbed, nab·bing.** *Informal.* to capture or arrest. **—nab′ber,** *n.*

na·dir (nā′dər, nā′dēr), *n.* 1. the lowest point or condition: *the nadir of poverty or despair.* 2. the point in the heavens opposite to the zenith. The nadir lies directly beneath an observer's position.

nag¹ (nag), *v.,* **nagged, nag·ging.** to criticize or find fault with: *Please stop nagging me about getting a haircut.* [from Scandinavian]

nag² (nag), *n.* a horse, esp. one that is old or worthless. [from the Middle English word *nagge*]

Na·ga·sa·ki (nä′gə sä′kē, nag′ə-sak′ē), *n.* a port city in SW Japan: second atomic bomb dropped 1945. See also **Hiroshima.**

Na·hum (nā′həm), *n.* (in the Bible) 1. a Hebrew prophet of the 7th century B.C. 2. the book of the Old Testament bearing his name.

nai·ad (nā′ad, nī′ad), *n., pl.* **nai·ads** *or* **nai·a·des** (nā′ə dēz′, nī′ə-dēz′).** (in Greek mythology) a kind of nymph that lived in rivers and streams.

nail (nāl), *n.* 1. a small piece of metal, usually flattened at one end and pointed at the other. Nails are made in many sizes and shapes for hammering into wood and other materials to fasten pieces together. 2. the thin, horny plate on the upper side of the end of a finger or toe. **—v.** 3. to

A B C

Nails
A, Common nail
B, Finishing nail
C, Brad

fasten with a nail or nails. 4. *Informal.* to catch or seize: *to nail a thief.* 5. **hit the nail on the head,** to say or do exactly the right thing: *When you said he was lazy, you hit the nail on the head.* **—nail′like′,** *adj.*

Nai·ro·bi (nī rō′bē), *n.* the capital city of Kenya, in the SW part.

na·ive (nä ēv′), *adj.* 1. having a simple, unaffected nature; childlike; unsophisticated. 2. lacking in experience, judgment, or information. **—na·ive′ly,** *adv.*

na·ïve·té (nä ēv tā′), *n.* 1. the quality or state of being naïve. 2. a naïve action, remark, etc.

na·ked (nā′kid), *adj.* 1. without clothing or covering; nude. 2. without any covering or overlying matter. 3. bare or stripped: *The trees were left naked of leaves.* 4. simply and truthfully revealed; plain: *the naked facts.* **—na′ked·ly,** *adv.* **—na′ked·ness,** *n.*

name (nām), *n.* 1. a word or a group of words by which a person, place, idea, etc., is known or designated. 2. something that a person is called, esp. as an insult or reproach: *to call a person names.* **—v.,** **named, nam·ing.** 3. to give a name to: *Have they named the kitten?* 4. to identify, specify, or mention by name: *to name the planets.* 5. to designate (a person, group, etc.) for some duty or office: *to name a chairman.* 6. **to one's name,** in one's possession: *I haven't a penny to my name.*

name·less (nām′lis), *adj.* 1. having no name. 2. not marked or signed with a name; unnamed. 3. difficult or impossible to describe: *a nameless charm.* 4. too shocking to describe: *nameless crimes.*

name·ly (nām′lē), *adv.* that is to say; specifically: *an item of legislation, namely the housing bill.*

name·sake (nām′sāk′), *n.* a person given the same name as another: *He is his grandfather's namesake.*

Nan·king (nan′king′), *n.* a port in E China: a former capital of China.

nan′ny goat′ (nan′ē), a female goat.

Na·o·mi (nā ō′mē), *n.* (in the Bible) the mother-in-law of Ruth.

nap¹ (nap), *v.,* **napped, nap·ping.** 1. to sleep for a short time; doze. 2. to be off one's guard: *His ques-*

tion caught me napping. —*n.* **3.** a brief period of sleep. [from Old English *hnappian* "to doze"]

nap² (nap), *n.* the short, fuzzy ends of fibers on the surface of cloth. [from the Middle English word *noppe,* related to Old English *hnoppian* "to pluck"]

nape (nāp, nap), *n.* the back part of the neck.

naph·tha (naf/thə, nap/thə), *n.* a colorless liquid distilled from petroleum, used as a solvent, cleaning fluid, fuel, etc.

nap·kin (nap/kin), *n.* **1.** a rectangular piece of cloth or paper for use in wiping the lips and fingers and to protect the clothes while eating. **2.** a small towel of linen or cotton cloth.

Na·ples (nā/pəlz), *n.* a port city in SW Italy.

Na·po·le·on (nə pō/lē ən), *n. (Napoleon Bonaparte) ("the Little Corporal")* 1769–1821, French general born in Corsica: emperor of France 1804–1815. —**Na·po·le·on·ic** (nə pō/lē on/ik), *adj.*

nar·cis·sus (när sis/əs), *n.* a plant that grows from a bulb and has yellow or white flowers in the spring. Daffodils are one kind of narcissus.

Nar·cis·sus (när sis/əs), *n.* (in Greek mythology) a youth who fell in love with his own reflection in a pool and pined away, after which he was changed into a flower.

nar·cot·ic (när kot/ik), *n.* any of a number of dangerous, habit-forming drugs used in small doses to relieve pain or induce sleep.

nar·rate (nar/rāt, na rāt/), *v.,* **nar·rat·ed, nar·rat·ing.** to tell the story of (events, experiences, etc.); recite. —**nar/ra·tor,** *n.*

nar·ra·tion (na rā/shən), *n.* **1.** something that is narrated; an account or story. **2.** the act or process of narrating.

nar·ra·tive (nar/ə tiv), *n.* **1.** a story of events, experiences, or the like; narration. **2.** the art, technique, or process of narrating. —*adj.* **3.** telling a story: *a narrative poem.*

nar·row (nar/ō), *adj.* **1.** of little breadth or width: *a narrow hallway.* **2.** having little room or space: *narrow quarters.* **3.** limited in interests, sympathies, outlook, etc. **4.** limited in amount: *narrow resources.* **5.** barely adequate or successful: *a narrow escape.* —*v.* **6.** to make or become narrower. —*n.* **7.** a narrow part, place, or thing. **8. narrows,** *(used as sing. or pl.)* a narrow part of a strait, river, ocean current, etc. —**nar/row·ly,** *adv.* —**nar/row·ness,** *n.*

Narwhal
(total length 23 ft.; tusk 9 ft.)

nar·row-mind·ed (nar/ō mīn/did), *adj.* not open or receptive to new ideas; biased; conservative. —**nar/row-mind/ed·ly,** *adv.* —**nar/row-mind/ed·ness,** *n.*

nar·whal (när/wəl), *n.* a small whale having a single long, twisted tusk extending from its upper jaw.

NASA (nas/ə), *n.* National Aeronautics and Space Administration.

na·sal (nā/zəl), *adj.* **1.** of or concerning the nose: *the nasal cavity.* **2.** pronounced through the nose, as the sounds of *m, n,* or *ng.* —*n.* **3.** a nasal sound. —**na·sal·i·ty** (nā zal/i tē), *n.* —**na/sal·ly,** *adv.*

Nash·ville (nash/vil), *n.* the capital city of Tennessee, in the central part.

Nas·sau (nas/ô), *n.* a seaport and the capital city of the Bahamas.

Nas·ser (nä/sər, nas/ər), *n.* **Ga·mal Ab·del** (gə mäl/ ab/del), 1918–1970, premier of the United Arab Republic 1954–1958: president 1958–1970.

na·stur·tium (nə stûr/shəm), *n.* a plant having round leaves and funnel-shaped red, yellow, orange, or white flowers.

nas·ty (nas/tē), *adj.,* **nas·ti·er, nas·ti·est. 1.** disgustingly dirty. **2.** disgusting to taste or smell. **3.** very objectionable or disagreeable: *a nasty habit.* **4.** obscene or indecent: *nasty language.* **5.** vicious, spiteful, or ugly: *a nasty temper.* **6.** bad or unpleasant to deal with or experience: *a nasty cut; a nasty incident.* —**nas/ti·ly,** *adv.* —**nas/ti·ness,** *n.*

na·tal (nāt/ᵊl), *adj.* of or concerning one's birth.

na·tion (nā/shən), *n.* **1.** a group of people living in a particular country and having its own government. **2.** the country itself. **3.** (in American history) one of the tribes belonging to an Indian confederation.

na·tion·al (nash/ə nᵊl), *adj.* **1.** of, concerning, maintained by, or common to a whole nation: *national affairs.* —*n.* **2.** a citizen or subject of a particular country. —**na/tion·al·ly,** *adv.*

Na/tional Guard/, state military forces that become an active part of the army when ordered into federal service by the President in times of emergency.

na·tion·al·ism (nash/ə nᵊliz/əm), *n.* **1.** devotion to the interests of one's own nation. **2.** desire for national advancement or independence.

na·tion·al·ist (nash/ə nᵊlist), *n.* **1.** a person who is devoted to nationalism. **2.** one who works for national independence. —*adj.* **3.** Also, **na/tion·al·is/tic.** of, concerning, or promoting nationalism.

Na/tionalist Chi/na. See China, Republic of.

na·tion·al·i·ty (nash/ə nal/i tē), *n., pl.* **na·tion·al·i·ties. 1.** membership in a particular nation or country. **2.** existence as an independent nation. **3.** a nation or people.

na·tion·al·ize (nash/ə nᵊlīz/), *v.,* **na·tion·al·ized, na·tion·al·iz·ing. 1.** to bring under the control or ownership of a nation, such as industries or land. **2.** to make national in extent or scope. **3.** to make into a nation. —**na/tion·al·i·za/tion,** *n.*

na·tion·wide (nā/shən wīd/), *adj.* extending throughout the nation.

na·tive (nā/tiv), *adj.* **1.** being the place of origin of a person or thing: *one's native land.* **2.** belonging to a person at his birth or to a thing at its origin: *native intelligence.* **3.** of, concerning, or belonging to the original inhabitants of a place or country. **4.** belonging to a person by reason of his birthplace: *one's na-*

tive language. **5.** found in nature rather than produced artificially. **6.** originating naturally in a particular country or region: *native vegetation.* —*n.* **7.** one of the original inhabitants of a place or a country. **8.** a person born in a particular place or country.

na·tiv·i·ty (nə tiv′i tē, nā tiv′i tē), *n., pl.* **na·tiv·i·ties.** **1.** a person's birth. **2. the Nativity, a.** the birth of Christ. **b.** the season of Christmas.

natl., national.

NATO (nā′tō), *n.* North Atlantic Treaty Organization: an organization of nations formed in Washington, D.C., in 1949, for the purpose of collective defense against aggression.

nat·ty (nat′ē), *adj.,* **nat·ti·er, nat·ti·est.** neat and stylish in dress or appearance. —**nat′ti·ly,** *adv.*

nat·u·ral (nach′ər əl, nach′rəl), *adj.* **1.** of or concerning nature. **2.** existing in or formed by nature: *a natural waterfall.* **3.** inborn; native: *natural ability.* **4.** being so because of one's nature: *a natural mathematician.* **5.** reproducing the original or the original state closely: *a natural likeness.* **6.** of or referring to the natural sciences. **7.** not forced or affected; sincere: *a natural smile.* **8.** (in music) neither sharp nor flat. —*n.* **9.** *Informal.* any person or thing that is well qualified in some way. **10.** (in music) **a.** a white key on a piano, organ, etc. **b.** the sign (♮) placed to the left of a note to cancel a previous sharp or flat. **c.** the note so marked. —**nat′u·ral·ly,** *adv.*

nat·u·ral·ist (nach′ər ə list, nach′rə list), *n.* a person who specializes in natural history, esp. a botanist or zoologist.

nat·u·ral·ize (nach′ər ə līz′, nach′rə līz′), *v.,* **nat·u·ral·ized, nat·u·ral·iz·ing.** **1.** to make a citizen of (an alien). **2.** to introduce (animals or plants) into a region and cause them to thrive as if native. **3.** to introduce or adopt (foreign customs, words, etc.). —**nat′u·ral·i·za′tion,** *n.*

nat′ural num′ber, a positive whole number, such as 1, 2, 57, etc.

nat′ural re′sources, the natural wealth of a country, consisting of land, forests, minerals, etc.

na·ture (nā′chər), *n.* **1.** the particular combination of qualities belonging to a person, animal, thing, or class by birth, origin, or physical make-up. **2.** the instincts that control conduct. **3.** character, kind, or sort: *two books of the same nature.* **4.** the physical world apart from man and his civilization. **5.** the true appearance of anything: *a portrait true to nature.* **6.** the laws and principles believed to be followed naturally and rightly by living things.

na′ture stud′y, the study of the physical world, esp. plants and animals.

naught (nôt), *n.* **1.** a cipher (0); zero. **2.** not anything; nothing. **3.** complete failure: *Her efforts came to naught.* Also, **nought.**

naugh·ty (nô′tē), *adj.,* **naugh·ti·er, naugh·ti·est.** **1.** badly behaved; disobedient; mischievous. **2.** improper or obscene: *a naughty word.* —**naugh′ti·ly,** *adv.* —**naugh′ti·ness,** *n.*

Na·u·ru (nä ōō′rōō), *n.* **Republic of,** an island republic in the Pacific Ocean, near the equator, governed by Australia before 1968. Its area is 8¼ sq. mi.

nau·se·a (nô′zē ə, nô′zhə), *n.* **1.** sickness of the stomach, esp. with an urge to vomit. **2.** extreme disgust or loathing. [from the Greek word *nausia* "seasickness," which comes from *naus* "ship"]

nau·se·ate (nô′zē āt′, nô′sē āt′), *v.,* **nau·se·at·ed, nau·se·at·ing.** to make or become sick to the stomach.

nau·seous (nô′shəs, nô′zē əs), *adj.* causing nausea; sickening.

naut., nautical.

nau·ti·cal (nô′ti kəl), *adj.* of or referring to seamen, ships, or navigation: *nautical terms.* —**nau′ti·cal·ly,** *adv.*

nau′tical mile′. See mile (def. 2).

nau·ti·lus (nôt′ᵊləs), *n.* **1.** any of various small sea animals having a spiral, chambered shell. **2.** a small sea animal, the female of which has a thin, white shell.

Nav·a·ho (nav′ə hō′, nä′və hō′), *n., pl.* **Nav·a·hos, Nav·a·hoes,** *or* **Nav·a·ho.** **1.** a member of an Indian tribe of northern Arizona and New Mexico. **2.** the language of the Navahos. —*adj.* **3.** of, concerning, or characteristic of the Navaho Indians or their language.

Nautilus (shell length 8 in.)

na·val (nā′vəl), *adj.* **1.** of or concerning ships, esp. warships. **2.** of or connected with a navy. **3.** having a navy: *one of the great naval powers.*

nave (nāv), *n.* the main area of a church between the side aisles.

na·vel (nā′vəl), *n.* the mark or depression at the middle of the abdomen where the umbilical cord was attached.

na′vel or′ange, a large, thick-skinned orange that has a depression resembling a navel at one end.

nav·i·ga·ble (nav′ə gə bəl), *adj.* **1.** (of a body of water) deep and wide enough to allow the passage of ships. **2.** capable of being steered or guided, such as a ship, airplane, or missile. —**nav′i·ga·bil′i·ty,** *n.*

nav·i·gate (nav′ə gāt′), *v.,* **nav·i·gat·ed, nav·i·gat·ing.** **1.** to cross (the sea, a river, etc.) in a vessel or aircraft. **2.** to direct (a ship, airplane, etc.) on its course.

nav·i·ga·tion (nav′ə gā′shən), *n.* **1.** the act or process of navigating. **2.** the art or science of determining or directing the course of a ship, airplane, etc.

nav·i·ga·tor (nav′ə gā′tər), *n.* a person who practices or is skilled in navigation.

na·vy (nā′vē), *n., pl.* **na·vies.** **1.** the total number of warships and other ships belonging to a country or ruler. **2.** *(often cap.)* a combined force of such warships together with their officers and men, equipment, yards, etc. **3.** Also, **na′vy blue′.** a dark blue. —*adj.* **4.** of the color navy: *red with a navy stripe.*

nay (nā), *adv.* **1.** no (used esp. in voting). **2.** and not only so, but; indeed: *He has many good, nay, noble qualities.* —*n.* **3.** a denial or refusal. **4.** a negative vote, or a voter on the negative side: *to count the nays.*

Naz·a·rene (naz′ə rēn′, naz′ə rēn′), *n.* **1.** a native or inhabitant of Nazareth. 2. **the Nazarene,** another name for **Jesus.**

Naz·a·reth (naz′ər əth), *n.* a town in N Israel: the childhood home of Jesus.

Na·zi (nä′tsē, nat′sē), *n., pl.* **Na·zis.** 1. a member of the political party under Adolf Hitler, which controlled Germany from 1933 to 1945. —*adj.* 2. of or referring to the Nazis.

NB, note well; take notice. Also, **N.B.** [from the Latin phrase *notā bene*]

Nb, *Chem.* the symbol for **niobium.**

N.C., North Carolina.

NCO, Noncommissioned Officer. Also, **N.C.O.**

Nd, *Chem.* the symbol for **neodymium.**

N. Dak., North Dakota. Also, **N.D.**

NE, 1. northeast. 2. northeastern.

Ne, *Chem.* the symbol for **neon.**

N.E., 1. New England. 2. northeast. 3. northeastern.

Ne·an′der·thal man′ (nē an′dər thôl′), a powerfully built prehistoric man that lived in caves in Europe and western Asia and used stone tools. [named after *Neanderthal,* a valley near Düsseldorf, Germany, where remains were found]

Ne·a·pol·i·tan (nē′ə pol′i t°n), *adj.* 1. of, referring to, or characteristic of Naples. —*n.* 2. a native or inhabitant of Naples.

neap′ tide′ (nēp), a tide at the time when the difference between low and high tide is smallest.

near (nēr), *adv.* 1. at or to a place a short distance away from a certain person or thing, or from oneself: *The hotel is near the terminal.* 2. almost or nearly: *I was near dead from exhaustion.* —*adj.* 3. being close by; not distant: *the near future.* 4. being relatively closer: *the near side of the road.* 5. being of one's immediate family or circle of friends. 6. coming close; barely avoided: *a near collision.* —*prep.* 7. at, to, or within a short distance or short period of time from: *near the corner.* —*v.* 8. to come or draw near; approach: *We're nearing the house.* —**near′ness,** *n.*

near·by (nēr′bī′), *adj., adv.* close at hand; not far off: *a nearby restaurant; to walk nearby.*

Near′ East′, the region made up of SW Asia and the United Arab Republic, and formerly including the Balkan States. —**Near′ East′ern.**

near·ly (nēr′lē), *adv.* 1. almost; all but: *She nearly drowned.* 2. with close kinship; closely: *He is nearly related to the mayor.*

near·sight·ed (nēr′sī′tid), *adj.* able to see objects that are close-by more clearly than those at a distance (opposite of *farsighted*). —**near′sight′ed·ly,** *adv.* —**near′sight′ed·ness,** *n.*

neat (nēt), *adj.* 1. orderly and clean; tidy. 2. having a simple, pleasing appearance. 3. carefully done; clear and precise: *neat handwriting.* 4. clever or skillful: *a neat trick.* —**neat′ly,** *adv.* —**neat′ness,** *n.*

neath (nēth), *prep.* another form of **beneath:** used chiefly in poetry. Also, **'neath.**

Neb., Nebraska. Also, **Nebr.**

Ne·bras·ka (nə bras′kə), *n.* a state in the central United States. 77,237 sq. mi. *Cap.:* Lincoln. —**Ne·bras′kan,** *n., adj.*

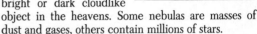

Neb·u·chad·nez·zar (neb′yə kəd nez′ər), *n.* (in the Bible) a king of Babylonia and conqueror of Jerusalem.

neb·u·la (neb′yə lə), *n.* a bright or dark cloudlike object in the heavens. Some nebulas are masses of dust and gases, others contain millions of stars.

neb·u·lous (neb′yə ləs), *adj.* 1. hazy or vague; not clear. 2. cloudy or cloudlike. 3. of or like a nebula. —**neb′u·lous·ly,** *adv.*

nec·es·sar·i·ly (nes′i ser′ə lē), *adv.* 1. by or of necessity; as a need or requirement: *An astronaut must necessarily have special training.* 2. as a necessary result; as a matter of course: *It doesn't necessarily mean they'll win the game.*

nec·es·sar·y (nes′i ser′ē), *adj.* 1. needed or essential; required: *Warm clothes are necessary when you go sledding.* 2. happening as a matter of course; unavoidable: *The flood was a necessary result of the heavy rainfalls.* —*n., pl.* **nec·es·sar·ies.** 3. something that is needed or essential; necessity: *They gave him clothing, food, and other necessaries for his trip.*

ne·ces·si·tate (nə ses′i tāt′), *v.,* **ne·ces·si·tat·ed, ne·ces·si·tat·ing.** to make necessary or unavoidable; compel; force: *The rainy weather necessitated a change in our plans.*

ne·ces·si·ty (nə ses′i tē), *n., pl.* **ne·ces·si·ties.** 1. something that is necessary or essential: *Food is a necessity of life.* 2. the fact of being necessary; need: *He saw the necessity of doing some study in order to pass the test.* 3. a state of emergency or extreme need: *In necessity the pilot can bail out.* 4. an overpowering force that causes a person to act in a certain way. 5. poverty or neediness: *Her family has no money and is in dire necessity.*

neck (nek), *n.* 1. the part of the body that joins the head·to the trunk. 2. the part of a garment going around the neck or lying near it. 3. a slender part that resembles a neck, as on a bottle, violin, etc. 4. a narrow strip of land, such as a peninsula. 5. **break one's neck,** *Informal.* to make a great effort: *We broke our necks to get there on time.* 6. **neck and neck,** just even or very close: *The horses were neck and neck at the finish line.* 7. **stick one's neck out,** *Slang.* to risk one's safety, reputation, etc.: *That's the last time I stick my neck out to help him!*

neck·er·chief (nek′ər chif), *n.* a cloth worn around the neck.

neck·lace (nek′lis), *n.* an ornament or piece of jewelry worn around the neck, for example a string of beads or pearls.

neck·line (nek′līn′), *n.* the shape of the neck of a dress or other garment.

neck·tie (nek′tī′), *n.* a band of fabric worn around

the neck under the collar and knotted under the chin.

nec·tar (nek′tər), *n.* **1.** a sweet liquid secreted by plants and used by bees to make honey. **2.** (in Greek and Roman mythology) the drink of the gods that gave immortality. **3.** fruit juice, esp. when undiluted: *apricot nectar.* **4.** any delicious drink.

nec·tar·ine (nek′tə rēn′), *n.* a kind of peach having a smooth skin.

need (nēd), *n.* **1.** urgent want, esp. of something necessary: *There is a need for a new hospital in this city.* **2.** necessity or obligation: *There is no need to worry about that.* **3.** a requirement, qualification, or the like: *He couldn't meet the needs of the job.* **4.** poverty or extreme want. —*v.* **5.** to require; have need of: *That dog needs a drink of water.* **6.** to be obliged or required (usually fol. by an infinitive): *He needs to work a little harder.* **7.** to be under a necessity or obligation (used as an auxiliary verb in negative statements or in questions): *He need not go. Need I bring extra money?* **8. if need be,** if it should be necessary: *I can lend you one if need be.*

need·ful (nēd′fəl), *adj.* required or needed; necessary: *needful supplies for a camping trip.*

nee·dle (nēd′əl), *n.* **1.** a small, very slender steel rod or piece of wire, having a sharp point at one end and an eye or hole for thread at the other end, used in sewing. **2.** any similar device, such as a knitting needle, used to make stitches. **3.** the pointer on a dial, compass, or the like. **4.** the hollow, pointed tip of a hypodermic syringe that is inserted beneath the skin in giving an injection. **5.** the needle-shaped leaf of various evergreen trees: *a pine needle.* **6.** (on a phonograph) the small, needlelike instrument that transmits vibrations from a revolving record. —*v.,* **nee·dled, nee·dling. 7.** to prick or pierce with or as if with a needle. **8.** *Informal.* to tease, esp. in an annoying way: *We needled her into letting us go with her.* —**nee′dle·like′,** *adj.*

need·less (nēd′lis), *adj.* unnecessary; not needed, useful, or desired. —**need′less·ly,** *adv.* —**need′less·ness,** *n.*

nee·dle·work (nēd′əl wûrk′), *n.* **1.** the art of working with a needle, esp. in embroidery that is unusually intricate or elaborate. **2.** work done with a needle, such as a piece of embroidery.

need·n't (nēd′ənt), contraction of *need not.*

need·y (nē′dē), *adj.,* **need·i·er, need·i·est.** extremely poor; in a state of need or want: *to help needy farm workers.* —**need′i·ness,** *n.*

ne'er (nâr), *adv.* another form of **never**: used esp. in poetry.

ne'er-do-well (nâr′dōō wel′), *n.* a lazy, worthless person; good-for-nothing.

ne·far·i·ous (ni fâr′ē əs), *adj.* extremely wicked; vile; atrocious. —**ne·far′i·ous·ly,** *adv.*

ne·gate (ni gāt′), *v.,* **ne·gat·ed, ne·gat·ing. 1.** to wipe out or destroy the effect of (something): *Bad luck negated his efforts to succeed.* **2.** to deny or disprove the truth or existence of (something); contradict.

ne·ga·tion (ni gā′shən), *n.* **1.** the act of denying; denial. **2.** the absence or opposite of something: *Darkness is the negation of light.*

neg·a·tive (neg′ə tiv), *adj.* **1.** expressing negation, refusal, or denial; saying no: *a negative answer to a request.* **2.** not helpful, enthusiastic, or cooperative: *He showed a negative attitude toward our plan.* **3.** not producing the outcome that was expected or hoped for: *The results of the search were negative.* **4.** (in an experiment, test, etc.) not producing the results or symptoms looked for: *His TB test was negative.* **5.** involving or indicating subtraction or something that is to be subtracted; minus: *a negative number.* **6.** caused by or associated with an excess of electrons: *a negative charge.* —*n.* **7.** an exposed film or plate in which the light portions of the subject that was photographed are dark and the dark portions light. **8.** a word or expression that states refusal, denial, contradiction, or the like: *The words "no" and "nothing" are negatives.* **9.** a person or group of persons arguing against a statement, proposal, or the like, as in a debate. **10. in the negative,** in a way that expresses refusal, rejection, etc.; no: *She replied in the negative.* —**neg′a·tive·ly,** *adv.*

ne·glect (ni glekt′), *v.* **1.** to pay little or no attention to; fail to take care of: *to neglect one's work; to neglect a pet.* **2.** to fail to do or perform: *She neglected to wash the dishes.* —*n.* **3.** an instance of neglecting; lack of care, or failure to do what must be done: *The tools became rusted because of neglect.* **4.** the state of being neglected or not cared for: *The old house has fallen into neglect.* —**ne·glect′ed·ly,** *adv.*

ne·glect·ful (ni glekt′fəl), *adj.* careless, thoughtless, or negligent; inclined to neglect: *to be neglectful of one's duties.* —**ne·glect′ful·ly,** *adv.*

neg·li·gee (neg′li zhā′, neg′li zhā′), *n.* **1.** a woman's dressing gown or robe. **2.** casual, informal dress. Also, **neg′li·gée′.**

neg·li·gence (neg′li jəns), *n.* neglect or lack of attention to what should be done; a being negligent: *Because of your negligence the basement is flooded.*

neg·li·gent (neg′li jənt), *adj.* **1.** guilty of neglect; not carrying out one's responsibilities; neglectful: *a lazy, negligent worker.* **2.** careless or casual: *a negligent way of dressing.* —**neg′li·gent·ly,** *adv.*

neg·li·gi·ble (neg′li jə bəl), *adj.* very small and unimportant. —**neg′li·gi·bly,** *adv.*

ne·go·ti·a·ble (ni gō′shə bəl), *adj.* **1.** (of bills, securities, etc.) capable of being transferred or sold to another owner: *negotiable bonds.* **2.** capable of being negotiated. —**ne·go′tia·bil′i·ty,** *n.*

ne·go·ti·ate (ni gō′shē āt′), *v.,* **ne·go·ti·at·ed, ne·go·ti·at·ing. 1.** to deal or bargain with another or others: *The farm owners are going to negotiate with the striking workers.* **2.** to arrange or bring about by discussion or bargaining: *The two governments negotiated a peace settlement.* **3.** to move through, around, or over in a satisfactory way: *to negotiate a high fence.* **4.** to sell or transfer: *to negotiate bonds.* —**ne·go′ti·a·tor,** *n.*

ne·go·ti·a·tion (ni gō′shē ā′shən), *n.* **1.** Often, **negotiations.** discussion aiming at agreement; bargaining: *The two nations have begun negotiations to settle the dispute.* **2.** the act or process of negotiating: *the negotiation of a truce.*

Ne·gro (nē′grō), *n., pl.* **Ne·groes. 1.** a person having Negroid characteristics. **2.** a person of black African ancestry. — *adj.* **3.** of or concerning blacks or Negroes: *Negro history.*
—**Usage.** Many people today prefer to use *black* rather than *Negro.*

Ne·groid (nē′groid), *n.* **1.** a member of one of the major traditional racial groupings of humankind, including esp. the people of Africa south of the Sahara desert and their descendants, typically having dark skins, dark curly hair, etc., and certain other genetic features. — *adj.* **2.** of or belonging to this group.

Ne·he·mi·ah (nē′ə mī′ə), *n.* **1.** (in the Bible) a Hebrew leader of the 5th century B.C. **2.** the book of the Old Testament bearing his name.

Neh·ru (nā′rōō, ne′rōō), *n.* **Ja·wa·har·lal** (jə wə hər-läl′), 1889–1964, prime minister of India 1950–1964.

neigh (nā), *v.* **1.** to utter the cry of a horse; whinny. —*n.* **2.** the cry of a horse; whinny.

neigh·bor (nā′bər), *n.* **1.** a person who lives near another: *Our nearest neighbors are a mile away.* **2.** any person or thing that is near another: *Canada is a neighbor of the United States.* **3.** one's fellow human being; fellow-man: *Love thy neighbor as thyself.* —*adj.* **4.** living or located near another: *one of our neighbor nations.* [from Old English *nēahbūr,* which comes from *nēah* "near" + *gebūr* "farmer"]

neigh·bor·hood (nā′bər hŏŏd′), *n.* **1.** the area surrounding or near some place, person, etc.: *There are many small farms in the neighborhood of this town.* **2.** a district or area, esp. in a city or suburb. **3.** a number of persons living near one another or in a particular place: *The whole neighborhood came to our picnic.* **4. in the neighborhood of,** nearly or about: *He owes us in the neighborhood of $50.*

neigh·bor·ing (nā′bər ĭng), *adj.* living or located nearby: *to visit a neighboring town.*

neigh·bor·ly (nā′bər lē), *adj.* friendly and helpful; like a good neighbor. —**neigh′bor·li·ness,** *n.*

nei·ther (nē′ther, nī′ther), *conj.* **1.** not either (usually fol. by *nor*): *Neither John nor Betty is at home.* **2.** nor; likewise not; no more: *My sister can't swim, and neither can I.* —*adj.* **3.** not either; not the one or the other: *Neither statement is true.* —*pron.* **4.** not one person or the other; not one thing or the other: *Neither of those plans is workable.*
—**Usage.** When used as an adjective or pronoun, *neither* is generally followed by a singular verb: *Neither book is interesting. Neither is on the shelf.* When joining two subjects, *neither* is always followed by *nor* and used with either a singular or plural verb, depending on the second subject: *Neither John nor Bill is a member. Neither Jane nor I am going to the party. Neither Dad nor the Joneses are here yet.*

nem·e·sis (nem′i sis), *n., pl.* **nem·e·ses** (nem′i sēz′). **1.** something or someone that defeats one; an opponent,

problem, or the like, that cannot be overcome: *The soldiers fought bravely, but the enemy's air strength was their nemesis.* **2.** a person, event, or the like, that is the cause of a just punishment.

Nem·e·sis (nem′i sis), *n.* (in Greek mythology) the goddess of vengeance.

neo-, a prefix meaning new or recent: *neophyte.*,

ne·o·dym·i·um (nē′ō dim′ē əm), *n. Chem.* a metallic element of the rare-earth group. *Symbol:* Nd

ne·on (nē′on), *n.* a rare, inert gas that is used to make colored lights, since it gives off a reddish glow when electricity passes through it. Neon is a chemical element. *Symbol:* Ne

ne·o·phyte (nē′ə fīt′), *n.* **1.** a beginner or novice; newcomer. **2.** a recent convert to a belief or religion.

Ne·pal (nə pôl′, nə päl′), *n.* a constitutional monarchy in the Himalayas between India and Tibet.

neph·ew (nef′yōō), *n.* **1.** a son of one's brother or sister. **2.** a son of one's husband's or wife's brother or sister.

Nep·tune (nep′tōōn, -tyōōn), *n.* **1.** (in Roman mythology) the god of the sea: identified with the Greek god Poseidon. **2.** the planet eighth in order from the sun. Neptune has a diameter of 39,930 miles; its average distance from the sun is 2,793,500,000 miles.

nep·tu·ni·um (nep tōō′nē əm, -tyōō′-), *n. Chem.* a man-made, radioactive, metallic element. *Symbol:* Np

Neptune

Ne·ro (nēr′ō), *n.* A.D. 37–68, emperor of Rome 54–68.

nerve (nûrv), *n.* **1.** one of the bundles of fibers that carry the impulses we recognize as feelings or those that cause muscles to contract and relax. Nerves connect the brain with the spinal cord and all the rest of the body. **2.** courage or great endurance: *It takes nerve to train lions and tigers for the circus.* **3.** impudence; rude boldness: *He had the nerve to suggest that I wasn't telling the truth.* **4. nerves,** nervousness; jitters: *He had an attack of nerves when it was his turn to speak.* — *v.,* **nerved, nerv·ing. 5.** to give strength or courage to; arouse courage in: *to nerve oneself to fight back.* **6. get on one's nerves,** to irritate or provoke one.

nerve′ cell′, one of the specialized cells that make up nerve tissue.

nerve′ fi′ber, any of the long, threadlike parts that extend outward from the center of a neuron.

nerve·less (nûrv′lis), *adj.* **1.** cool and calm; not nervous: *a bold, nerveless pilot.* **2.** lacking strength; feeble or weak: *The pen dropped from his nerveless fingers.* **3.** having no nerves, as a part of the body. —**nerve′less·ly,** *adv.*

nerve-rack·ing (nûrv′rak′ĭng), *adj.* extremely irritating or difficult to bear: *nerve-racking noise; terrible, nerve-racking suspense.* Also, **nerve′-wrack′ing.**

nerv·ous (nûr′vəs), *adj.* **1.** restless or highly excitable; easily made fearful or upset: *a nervous person who cries easily.* **2.** showing fear or uneasiness. **3.** of or concerning the nerves or nervous system: *nervous diseases.* **4.** strong or bold: *a quick, nervous burst of speed.* —**nerv′ous·ly,** *adv.* —**nerv′ous·ness,** *n.*

nerv′ous sys′tem, the system made up of the nerves and nerve centers, including the brain, spinal cord, etc.

nerv·y (nûr′vē), *adj.,* **nerv·i·er, nerv·i·est. 1.** brash or insolent; fresh: *a rude, nervy remark.* **2.** brave or courageous: *a nervy mountain climber.* **3.** nervous; uneasy. —**nerv′i·ly,** *adv.* —**nerv′i·ness,** *n.*

-ness, a suffix used to form nouns meaning a state or quality: *goodness; darkness.*

nest (nest), *n.* **1.** the structure of twigs, grass, mud, etc., formed by a bird as a place to lay eggs and rear its young. **2.** a structure built by insects for similar purposes. **3.** a hole, burrow, or the like, excavated or used by other kinds of animals, such as turtles, rabbits, etc., for similar purposes. **4.** a group of birds or other animals living in a nest. **5.** any refuge or place of safety; a cozy place. **6.** a collection of things lying one inside the other: *a nest of tables.* **7.** a place filled with something bad or wicked: *a robbers' nest.* — *v.* **8.** to build or live in a nest. **9.** to put (things) one inside another: *to nest boxes.* —**nest′er,** *n.*

nest′ egg′, 1. money reserved for an emergency, retirement, etc. **2.** a real or imitation egg left in a nest to encourage a hen to continue laying eggs there.

nes·tle (nes′əl), *v.,* **nes·tled, nes·tling. 1.** to lie close and snug, as a bird in a nest does; snuggle or cuddle. **2.** to lie or be located in a safe, pleasant spot: *The cabin nestled in a clearing in the woods.* **3.** to hold or press in an affectionate or cozy way: *to nestle a baby in one's arms.* —**nes′tler,** *n.*

nest·ling (nest′ling, nes′ling), *n.* a bird that is too young to leave the nest.

net¹ (net), *n.* **1.** a fabric made of knotted or meshed cord, thread, etc., having evenly spaced, large or small holes in it: *She wore a long veil of net.* **2.** something made of this or similar fabric, such as a device for catching fish, butterflies, etc., or the barrier across the center of a tennis court. **3.** anything that serves to trap or ensnare: *a net of roadblocks to catch a criminal.* —*v.,* **net·ted, net·ting. 4.** to catch in or as if in a net: *to net a butterfly; to net a bank robber.* **5.** to cover or provide with a net or netting. [from the Old English word *nett*] —**net′like′,** *adj.*

net² (net), *adj.* **1.** remaining after expenses, taxes, etc., are subtracted (opposite of *gross*): *He took in $100, and his net profit was $75.* **2.** final or ultimate: *the net result of one's efforts.* —*n.* **3.** net profit, income, or the like: *His net on that one deal was $1,-000.* —*v.,* **net·ted, net·ting. 4.** to gain or make as clear profit after taxes, expenses, etc., have been subtracted: *That movie netted a small fortune.* [from an Old French word meaning "neat, clean"]

neth·er (neth′ər), *adj.* **1.** lying, or believed to lie, beneath the earth's surface: *the nether regions of hell.* **2.** lower or under: *his nether lip.*

Neth·er·lands (neth′ər ləndz), *n.* **the,** *(used as sing. or pl.)* a kingdom in W Europe, bordering on the North Sea, West Germany, and Belgium. 13,433 sq. mi. *Capitals:* Amsterdam and The Hague. Also, **Holland.**

Neth′erlands Antil′les, a Netherlands overseas territory consisting of two groups of three islands each in the West Indies. 394 sq. mi.

neth·er·most (neth′ər mōst′), *adj.* lowest or deepest: *a dungeon in the nethermost part of the castle.*

net·ting (net′ing), *n.* any of various kinds of net fabric; net: *mosquito netting.*

net·tle (net′əl), *n.* **1.** any of several herbs having leaves covered with hairs that sting the skin when touched. —*v.,* **net·tled, net·tling. 2.** to irritate or provoke: *to be nettled by someone's remarks.*

net·work (net′wûrk′), *n.* **1.** any netlike, crisscross combination of lines, veins, roads, passages, etc.: *a network of tunnels.* **2.** a group of radio or television stations connected in such a way that the same program can be broadcast by all. **3.** a net or netting.

neu·ral·gia (nŏŏ ral′jə, nyŏŏ-), *n.* a sharp pain along the course of a nerve.

neu·ron (nŏŏr′on, nyŏŏr′-), *n.* a nerve cell, including the branches and threadlike fibers extending from it.

neu·ro·sis (nŏŏ rō′sis, nyŏŏ-), *n., pl.* **neu·ro·ses** (nŏŏ-rō′sēz, nyŏŏ-). an emotional disorder in which one suffers excessively from fears, depression, etc.

neu·rot·ic (nŏŏ rot′ik, nyŏŏ-), *adj.* **1.** of, referring to, or caused by excessive fear, anxiety, etc.: *a neurotic fear of dogs.* **2.** suffering from excessive fear, anxiety, etc.: *a neurotic person.* —*n.* **3.** a person suffering from neurosis. —**neu·rot′i·cal·ly,** *adv.*

neu·ter (nŏŏ′tər, nyŏŏ′-), *adj.* **1.** (in grammar) having the gender of nouns and pronouns that refer to things that are neither male nor female, as in *The door came off its hinges.* Sometimes the neuter gender is applied to human beings or animals when their sex is either not known or not important to distinguish, as in *The baby is in its crib* or *The kitten is chasing its tail.* **2.** having no organs of reproduction, or having organs that are not developed; asexual: *Worker bees and ants are neuter.* —*n.* **3.** the neuter gender, or a word belonging to the neuter gender. **4.** an animal or insect that lacks organs of reproduction.

neu·tral (nŏŏ′trəl, nyŏŏ′-), *adj.* **1.** (of a person, government, etc.) not taking part or giving help to either side in a war, dispute, contest, etc.; not taking sides: *During the war he escaped to a neutral country.* **2.** of no particular kind; not having distinct qualities or characteristics; indefinite: *a dull, neutral personality.* **3.** (of a color or shade) **a.** gray; without hue. **b.** going well with many other colors; not strong: *Beige is a neutral color.* **4.** (in chemistry) neither acid nor alkaline. **5.** (in electricity) neither positively nor negatively charged; not electrified. —*n.* **6.** a person, government, etc., that remains neutral; one that does not take sides. **7.** (in machinery) the position of gears when not engaged. —**neu′tral·ly,** *adv.*

neu·tral·i·ty (nŏŏ tral′i tē, nyŏŏ-), *n.* the position or condition of being neutral.

neu·tral·ize (nōō′trə līz′, nyōō′-), *v.*, **neu·tral·ized, neu·tral·iz·ing.** 1. to put out of action or make ineffective; counteract: *to neutralize an attack by using a strong defense.* 2. to make neutral, for example by adding acid to an alkaline substance. 3. to declare neutral; assign a neutral status to (a government, nation, etc.). **—neu·tral·i·za·tion** (nōō′trə li zā′shən, nyōō′-), *n.* **—neu′tral·iz′er,** *n.*

neu·tron (nōō′tron, nyōō′-), *n.* a subatomic particle, found in the nuclei of atoms, that has a mass slightly greater than that of a proton and no charge.

Nev., Nevada.

Ne·vad·a (nə vad′ə, nə vä′də), *n.* a state in the W United States. 110,540 sq. mi. *Cap.:* Carson City. **—Ne·vad′an,** *n., adj.*

nev·er (nev′ər), *adv.* 1. not ever; at no time: *I'll never go back there again.* 2. not at all; absolutely not: *That hat will never do for church.*

nev·er·more (nev′ər-môr′), *adv.* never again: *He was nevermore seen in that town.*

nev·er·the·less (nev′ər-thə les′), *adv.* in spite of that; nonetheless; still: *He started late, but nevertheless he arrived on time.*

new (nōō, nyōō), *adj.* 1. recently made, grown, done, born, etc.; not having been long in existence: *He has just written a new book.* 2. not used or worn before: *a new pair of shoes.* 3. recently bought or acquired: *The museum is showing its new paintings.* 4. not known before; recently thought of or discovered: *to discover new stars.* 5. having recently come to a place, position, relationship, etc.: *a new minister in town; a new employee.* 6. not used to; unaccustomed (usually fol. by *to*): *The men are new to this kind of work.* 7. further or additional: *The Republicans made new gains in their campaign this week.* 8. different and better: *The medicine made him feel like a new man.* 9. following what came before; beginning or appearing again: *a new year; a new moon.* **—adv.** 10. recently or lately (usually used in combination): *new-planted crops; new-mown hay.* **—new′ness,** *n.*

New·ark (nōō′ərk, nyōō′-), *n.* a city in NE New Jersey.

New′ Bed′ford, a port city in SE Massachusetts: formerly a major whaling port.

new·born (nōō′bôrn′, nyōō′-), *adj.* 1. recently or only just born. 2. born anew; reborn: *a newborn faith.* **—n.** 3. a baby that has just been born.

New′ Bruns′wick, a province in SE Canada, E of Maine. 27,985 sq. mi. *Cap.:* Fredericton.

new·com·er (nōō′kum′ər, nyōō′-), *n.* a person who has recently arrived; new arrival.

New′ Del′hi, the capital city of India, in the N part, next to Delhi.

new·el (nōō′əl, nyōō′-), *n.* 1. the central pillar or column of a winding staircase. 2. a newel post.

new′el post′, a post supporting one end of a handrail or banister at the top or bottom of a flight of steps.

New′ Eng′land, the NE United States, esp. including the states of Connecticut, Maine, Massachusetts, New Hampshire, Rhode Island, and Vermont. **—New′ Eng′land·er.**

new·fan·gled (nōō′fang′gəld, nyōō′-), *adj.* of a new kind or style; very new or modern: *I can't work this newfangled machine. He doesn't like her newfangled ideas.*

N, Newel post

New·found·land (nōō′fənd land′, nyōō′-; nōō′fənd lənd, nyōō′-), *n.* 1. a large island in E Canada. 42,734 sq. mi. 2. a province in E Canada, composed of Newfoundland Island and Labrador. 155,364 sq. mi. *Cap.:* St. John's. 3. a large, powerful dog having a thick, usually black coat.

New′ Guin′ea, 1. a large island N of Australia, divided into the Indonesian province of West Irian and the Territory of New Guinea. about 317,000 sq. mi. 2. **Territory of,** a territory under the trusteeship of Australia on part of the island of New Guinea and other smaller islands. 92,160 sq. mi. (69,095 sq. mi. on the island of New Guinea).

New′ Hamp′shire, a state in the NE United States. 9304 sq. mi. *Cap.:* Concord.

New′ Ha′ven (hā′vən), a city in S Connecticut, on Long Island Sound.

New′ Heb′ri·des (heb′ri dēz′), an island group in the S Pacific, NE of Australia: under joint French and British rule. 5700 sq. mi.

New′ Jer′sey, a state in the E United States. 7836 sq. mi. *Cap.:* Trenton. **—New′ Jer′seyite.**

new·ly (nōō′lē, nyōō′-), *adv.* 1. recently or lately: *a newly discovered drug.* 2. anew or again: *a newly written copy of one's homework.*

New′ Mex′ico, a state in the SW United States. 121,666 sq. mi. *Cap.:* Santa Fe. **—New′ Mex′ican.**

new′ moon′, 1. the moon when the side facing the earth is not illuminated by the sun. 2. the time, roughly every 28 days, when the face of the moon is dark. 3. the moon that one sees for a few days after this time, when it appears as a very thin crescent.

New′ Or′le·ans (ôr′lē-ənz, ôr′lənz, ôr lēnz′), a port city in SE Louisiana, on the delta of the Mississippi River.

New′port News′ (nōō′pôrt′, nyōō′-), a port city in SE Virginia.

news (nōōz, nyōōz), *n. (used as sing. or pl.)* 1. new information; a report on recent events. 2. a report on current events given in a newspaper or on radio, television, etc.: *The news is on at 10 o'clock every evening.*

news·cast (nōōz′kast′, nyōōz′-), *n.* a broadcast of news on radio or television; news program: *the 11 p.m. newscast.* **—news′cast′er,** *n.*

news·deal·er (nōōz′dē′lər, nyōōz′-), *n.* a person who sells newspapers, magazines, and the like.

New′ South′ Wales′, a state in SE Australia. 309,433 sq. mi.

news·pa·per (nōōz′pā′pər, nyōōz′-), *n.* a publication printed on one or more sheets of paper, containing news, reviews, advertisements, etc., and issued every day or every week.

news·pa·per·man (nōōz′pā′pər man′, nyōōz′-), *n., pl.* **news·pa·per·men.** 1. a man employed by a newspaper as a reporter, writer, editor, or the like. 2. a man who owns or manages a newspaper.

news·reel (nōōz′rēl′, nyōōz′-), *n.* a short motion picture on current events, shown on a film program.

news·stand (nōōz′stand′, nyōōz′-), *n.* a stand, stall, or store where newspapers and magazines are sold.

news·y (nōō′zē, nyōō′zē), *adj.,* **news·i·er, news·i·est.** full of news: *a newsy letter from home.*

newt (nōōt, nyōōt), *n.* any of various salamanders, esp. those that are brightly colored.

Newt
(length 3½ in.)

New′ Tes′tament, one of the two main parts of the Bible, which tells of the life and teachings of Christ and contains writings by early Christians.

New·ton (nōōt′ᵊn, nyōōt′ᵊn), *n.* **Sir Isaac,** 1642–1727, English mathematician: formulated laws of gravity.

New′ World′, another name for the **Western Hemisphere.**

new′ year′, 1. the year that is approaching. 2. a year that has just begun.

New′ Year's′, New Year's Day, or the first few days of the year.

New′ Year's′ Day′, January 1, the first day of the year.

New′ Year's′ Eve′, the night of December 31, the last day of the year.

New′ York′, 1. Also, **New′ York′ State′.** a state in the NE United States. 49,576 sq. mi. *Cap.:* Albany.

2. Also, **New′ York′ Cit′y.** a port city in SE New York at the mouth of the Hudson River: largest city in the Western Hemisphere. **—New′ York′er.**

New′ Zea′land (zē′lənd), a country in the S Pacific Ocean, SE of Australia, consisting of North Island, South Island, and nearby islands. 103,416 sq. mi. *Cap.:* Wellington. **—New′ Zea′land·er.**

next (nekst), *adj.* 1. following immediately in time, order, importance, etc.: *Jean will be first, and Bill will be next. The next time we go shopping I must buy a flashlight.* 2. nearest in position, place, rank, etc.: *We'll stop in the next town.* **—adv.** 3. in the nearest place, time, order, etc.: *You go next. This is my next oldest son.* 4. on the first occasion to follow: *when next we meet.* 5. **next door to,** in the next house or apartment: *He lives next door to us.* 6. **next to, a.** almost or nearly: *It's next to impossible to get an A in this course.* **b.** beside or near: *Stay next to me.*

next-door (neks′dôr′, nekst′-), *adv.* 1. at, to, or in the next house, apartment, building, etc.: *I'm going next-door.* **—adj.** (neks′dôr′, nekst′-). 2. being, located, or living in the next house, apartment, building, etc.: *our next-door neighbors.*

N.H., New Hampshire.

Ni, *Chem.* the symbol for **nickel.**

Ni·ag·a·ra (nī ag′rə, nī ag′ər ə), *n.* 1. a river on the boundary between W New York and Ontario, Canada, flowing from Lake Erie into Lake Ontario. 34 mi. long. 2. short for **Niagara Falls.**

Niag′ara Falls′, 1. the falls of the Niagara River between Canada and the U.S. 2. a city in W New York.

nib (nib), *n.* **1.** the point of a pen; penpoint. **2.** a point of anything: *a cutting tool with a diamond nib.* **3.** a bird's bill or beak.

nib·ble (nib′əl), *v.,* **nib·bled, nib·bling. 1.** to eat in small bites: *The parrot nibbled a cracker.* **2.** to bite or nip gently: *The fish nibbled the bait.* —*n.* **3.** a small morsel or bit. **4.** the act of nibbling. —**nib′bler,** *n.*

Nic·a·ra·gua (nik′ə rä′gwə), *n.* a republic in Central America. 57,143 sq. mi. *Cap.:* Managua. —**Nic′a·ra′guan,** *n., adj.*

nice (nīs), *adj.,* **nic·er, nic·est. 1.** pleasing or agreeable; pleasant: *We had a nice time.* **2.** friendly and kind: *She's such a nice person.* **3.** respectable and well-mannered; refined: *A nice person would never say that.* **4.** showing or requiring accuracy, exactness, care, etc.: *nice workmanship; a nice shot.* **5.** very fine or subtle: *a nice distinction.* —**nice′ly,** *adv.* —**nice′ness,** *n.*

Nice (nēs), *n.* a port city in SE France on the Mediterranean Sea: resort.

ni·ce·ty (nī′si tē), *n., pl.* **ni·ce·ties. 1.** a small or fine point; detail: *to understand the niceties of a game.* **2.** Usually, **niceties.** something refined or elegant; luxury. **3.** extreme delicacy or exactness; precision: *the nicety of a jeweler's workmanship.*

niche (nich), *n.* **1.** a hollowed-out place in a wall for a statue or other decorative object. **2.** a place, position, or career that suits someone: *He found his niche in life when he entered politics.*

Nich·o·las (nik′ə ləs), *n.* **Saint,** flourished 4th century A.D., bishop in Asia Minor: patron saint of Russia and protector of children; often referred to as the original Santa Claus.

nick (nik), *n.* **1.** a notch, chip, or small groove: *These dishes are full of nicks.* —*v.* **2.** to put a nick or nicks in (something); notch or scratch: *The guide nicked the tree trunk with his knife.* **3.** to injure by cutting: *He nicked his chin while shaving.* **4. in the nick of time,** at the most desirable time; without a moment to spare: *The fire engines arrived in the nick of time.*

nick·el (nik′əl), *n.* **1.** a hard, silvery metal used in alloys and for plating other metals. Nickel is a chemical element. *Symbol:* Ni **2.** a U.S. coin, made of copper and nickel, and equal to five cents.

nick·name (nik′nām′), *n.* **1.** a shortened or familiar form of a name: *"Bobby" is a nickname for "Robert."* **2.** a name added to or used instead of the proper name of a person, place, etc., such as "Deadeye" Dick.

nic·o·tine (nik′ə tēn′), *n.* a highly poisonous substance found in tobacco.

niece (nēs), *n.* **1.** a daughter of one's brother or sister. **2.** a daughter of one's husband's or wife's brother or sister.

Ni·ger (nī′jər), *n.* **1.** a republic in NW Africa, for-

merly French. 458,976 sq. mi. **2.** a river in W Africa. 2600 mi. long.

Ni·ge·ri·a (nī jēr′ē ə), *n.* a republic in W Africa, formerly British. 360,000 sq. mi. —**Ni·ge′ri·an,** *n., adj.*

nig·gard (nig′ərd), *n.* **1.** an extremely stingy person. —*adj.* **2.** stingy or niggardly.

nig·gard·ly (nig′ərd lē), *adj.* **1.** stingy; unwilling to give or spend: *a niggardly old miser.* **2.** meager or scanty: *a niggardly tip to a waiter.* —*adv.* **3.** in the manner of a stingy person; stingily. —**nig′gard·li·ness,** *n.*

nig·gling (nig′ling), *adj.* **1.** unimportant or petty: *niggling details.* **2.** fussy or picky: *a scolding, niggling woman.*

nigh (nī), *adv.* **1.** near in space or time (often fol. by *on* or *onto*): *The time draws nigh.* **2.** nearly or almost. —*adj.,* **nigh·er, nigh·est. 3.** being near; close; not distant: *The time is nigh.*

night (nīt), *n.* **1.** the period of darkness between sunset and sunrise: *He worked all day and all night.* **2.** the beginning of night; nightfall: *Night comes early in the winter.* **3.** the darkness of night; the dark: *Cats can see in the night.* **4.** a period or state of ignorance, misfortune, confusion, etc.: *the long night following the fall of the Roman Empire.* —*adj.* **5.** of or concerning the night: *the night hours.* **6.** occurring or appearing at night: *a night game; a night lizard.* **7.** designed for use at night: *a night light.* **8.** working at night: *a night nurse.* —**night′like′,** *adj.*

night·cap (nīt′kap′), *n.* **1.** a cap worn with night clothes. **2.** a drink taken at bedtime.

night′ clothes′, garments for wearing in bed; pajamas or the like.

night·club (nīt′klub′), *n.* a restaurant that stays open very late and also provides drinks, music, and often entertainment.

night·fall (nīt′fôl′), *n.* the beginning of night: *Be home by nightfall.*

night·gown (nīt′goun′), *n.* **1.** a loose gown, worn in bed by women or children. **2.** a man's nightshirt.

night·hawk (nīt′hôk′), *n.* any of several birds related to the whippoorwill that fly mostly at night.

Nightingale
(length 6½ in.)

night·in·gale (nīt′ən gāl′, nī′ting gāl′), *n.* any of several small birds of Europe and Asia, the males of which are noted for their beautiful singing.

Night·in·gale (nīt′ən gāl′, nī′ting gāl′), *n.* **Florence,** 1820–1910, English nurse: reformer of hospital conditions.

night·ly (nīt′lē), *adj.* **1.** happening, appearing, or

Niche

done regularly each night: *his nightly walk.* 2. happening, appearing, or done at night: *nightly adventures.* 3. of or resembling night: *a nightly gloom just before the storm.* —*adv.* 4. on every night: *Performances will be given nightly.* 5. at or by night.

night·mare (nīt′mâr′), *n.* 1. a horrible, terrifying dream. 2. an experience, situation, thought, etc., that is horrible or terrifying: *Rescuing the mountain climbers was a nightmare.* —**night′mar′ish,** *adj.*

night′ owl′, *Informal.* a person who usually stays up late.

night·shade (nīt′shād′), *n.* any of several plants related to the potato and tomato that bear black or red berries, some kinds of which are poisonous.

night·shirt (nīt′shûrt′), *n.* a loose shirt reaching to the knees, for wearing in bed.

nil (nil), *n.* nothing or zero: *Our profit was nil.*

Nile (nīl), *n.* the longest river in Africa, flowing N from Lake Victoria to the Mediterranean Sea. 3485 mi. long.

nil·gai (nil′gī), *n., pl.* **nil·gais** *or* **nil·gai.** a large, Indian antelope, the male of which is bluish gray with small horns and the female tawny and hornless.

nim·ble (nim′bəl), *adj.,* **nim·bler, nim·blest.** 1. quick and light in movement; agile: *Acrobats must be nimble.* 2. quick to understand; bright; alert: *a clever, nimble mind.* —**nim′ble·ness,** *n.* —**nim′bly,** *adv.*

nim·bus (nim′bəs), *n., pl.* **nim·bus·es** *or* **nim·bi** (nim′bī). 1. a shining cloud or halo surrounding a divine or holy person in a painting. 2. an aura of brilliance, glory, etc.

Nim·rod (nim′rod), *n.* 1. (in the Bible) a man famous as a great hunter. 2. a devoted hunter.

nin·com·poop (nin′kəm pōōp′), *n.* a fool or blockhead.

nine (nīn), *n.* 1. a number that is eight plus one. 2. a set of this many persons or things: *Only nine will be there.* 3. a baseball team: *the Kansas City nine.* —*adj.* 4. amounting to nine in number: *nine persons.*

nine·pins (nīn′pinz′), *n.* 1. (*used as sing.*) a form of bowling played with nine pins. 2. **ninepin,** a pin or wooden club used in this game.

nine·teen (nīn′tēn′), *n.* 1. a number that is ten plus nine. 2. a set of this many persons or things: *Nineteen of them will be there.* —*adj.* 3. amounting to 19 in number: *a group of 19 persons.*

nine·teenth (nīn′tēnth′), *adj.* 1. being number nineteen in a series: *the nineteenth floor.* —*n.* 2. one of 19 equal parts. 3. a person or thing that is nineteenth.

nine·ti·eth (nīn′tē ith), *adj.* 1. being number ninety in a series: *the ninetieth floor.* —*n.* 2. one of 90 equal parts. 3. a person or thing that is ninetieth.

nine·ty (nīn′tē), *n., pl.* **nine·ties.** 1. a number that is

nine times ten. 2. a set of this many persons or things: *Ninety of them will be there.* 3. **nineties,** the numbers, years, degrees, etc., between 90 and 99: *The temperature was in the nineties.* —*adj.* 4. amounting to 90 in number: *a group of ninety persons.*

Nin·e·veh (nin′ə və), *n.* the ancient capital of Assyria, on the Tigris, in N Iraq.

nin·ny (nin′ē), *n., pl.* **nin·nies.** a fool or simpleton.

ninth (nīnth), *adj.* 1. being number nine in a series: *the ninth floor.* —*n.* 2. one of nine equal parts. 3. a person or thing that is ninth.

Ni·o·be (nī′ō bē′), *n.* (in Greek mythology) a woman whose boastfulness about her children led Apollo and Artemis to slay them. Zeus, to end her grief, turned her to stone.

ni·o·bi·um (nī ō′bē əm), *n.* a gray metal used in making alloy steels; a chemical element. *Symbol:* Nb

nip[1] (nip), *v.,* **nipped, nip·ping.** 1. to pinch or bite tightly and sharply: *The crab nipped his finger.* 2. to take off by pinching, biting, or snipping (often fol. by *off*): *to nip dead leaves from a plant.* 3. to check or stop: *The police nipped the conspiracy.* 4. to cause pain to, as cold does: *The icy wind nipped their bare hands.* —*n.* 5. the act of nipping; a pinch or bite. 6. sharp, stinging cold; a touch of frost: *There's a nip in the air.* 7. **nip and tuck,** *Informal.* (of a race, contest, etc.) so close that predicting a winner is impossible: *It was nip and tuck which boat would reach port first.* [from Scandinavian]

nip[2] (nip), *n.* 1. a small drink of liquor; sip. —*v.,* **nipped, nip·ping.** 2. to drink (liquor) in small sips, esp. repeatedly. [short for *nipperkin* "vessel containing a half pint of liquid"]

nip·per (nip′ər), *n.* 1. a person or thing that nips. 2. Usually, **nippers.** a tool for nipping, such as pincers. 3. one of the large claws of a lobster, crab, or the like. 4. *Chiefly British.* a small child, esp. a boy.

nip·ple (nip′əl), *n.* 1. the small projection on a breast or udder through which the milk passes. 2. a similarly shaped cap for a baby's bottle. 3. a short length of pipe that is threaded at both ends. —**nip′ple·like′,** *adj.*

Nip·pon (ni pon′, nip′on), *n.* the Japanese name of Japan.

nip·py (nip′ē), *adj.,* **nip·pi·er, nip·pi·est.** sharp or biting: *a cold, nippy wind.*

nit (nit), *n.* the egg or the young of a bloodsucking insect, esp. of a louse.

ni·ter (nī′tər), *n.* another name for **saltpeter.** Also, *esp. British,* **ni′tre.**

ni·trate (nī′trāt), *n.* any of a number of chemical compounds containing nitrogen and oxygen, esp. saltpeter, used in making explosives and as fertilizers.

ni′tric ac′id (nī′trik), a colorless liquid composed of hydrogen, nitrogen, and oxygen that dissolves many metals and is used in etching and in making explosives.

ni·tro·gen (nī′trə jən), *n.* a gas that makes up about 4/5 of the earth's atmosphere: a chemical element found in proteins. *Symbol:* N

ni·trog·e·nous (nī troj′ə nəs), *adj.* concerned with or containing nitrogen: *Proteins are nitrogenous compounds.*

ni·tro·glyc·er·ine (nī′trə glis′ər in), *n.* a clear, syrupy, highly explosive liquid used in making dynamite and as a medicine for treating one kind of heart disease.

nit·wit (nit′wit′), *n.* a foolish or slow-witted person.

Nix·on (nik′sən), *n.* **Richard M**(il·hous) (mil′hous), born 1913, 36th Vice President of the U.S. 1953–1961; 37th President of the U.S. 1969–1974.

N.J., New Jersey.

N. Mex., New Mexico. Also, **N.M.**

NNE, north-northeast. Also, **N.N.E.**

NNW, north-northwest. Also, **N.N.W.**

no (nō), *adv.* **1.** (used as a negative reply to show disagreement, refusal, denial, or the like): *No, I won't be able to leave today.* **2.** not at all; not in any degree: *He feels no better than he did last night.* —*adj.* **3.** not any: *There is no food left.* **4.** not at all; far from being: *He's no genius.* — *n., pl.* **noes** *or* **nos. 5.** a negative reply; denial or refusal: *I won't take no for an answer.* **6.** a negative vote or voter: *The noes won.*

No, *Chem.* the symbol for **nobelium.**

No., **1.** north. **2.** number. Also, **no.**

No·ah (nō′ə), *n.* (in the Bible) the Hebrew patriarch who, by the command of God, built the ark in which he saved himself, his family, and animals of all kinds from the Flood.

no·be·li·um (nō bē′lē əm), *n. Chem.* a man-made, radioactive, metallic element. *Symbol:* No

no·bil·i·ty (nō bil′i tē), *n., pl.* for def. 1 **no·bil·i·ties. 1.** the entire group of nobles of a country; the noble class: *dukes, counts, and other members of the nobility.* **2.** the quality of being noble; high moral character: *He had the nobility of spirit not to take revenge on his enemies.* **3.** noble birth or rank. **4.** grandeur or magnificence: *the nobility of a fine stallion.*

no·ble (nō′bəl), *adj.,* **no·bler, no·blest. 1.** of high birth; having a special and distinguished social rank or title: *The king consulted with the noble lords of the realm.* **2.** of a high moral character; honest, just, generous, etc.: *a great and noble leader.* **3.** grand or magnificent: *The lion is a noble beast.* —*n.* **4.** a person of noble birth or rank; nobleman. **5.** a former gold coin of England. —**no′bly,** *adv.*

no·ble·man (nō′bəl mən), *n., pl.* **no·ble·men.** a man of noble birth or rank; noble.

no·bod·y (nō′bod′ē, nō′bə dē), *pron.* **1.** no person; not anyone; no one: *Nobody was hurt in the accident.* —*n., pl.* **no·bod·ies. 2.** a person of no importance.

noc·tur·nal (nok tûr′nəl), *adj.* **1.** of or concerning the night; occurring at night: *the nocturnal sounds of the jungle.* **2.** active by night: *Bats are nocturnal animals.* **3.** (of certain flowers) opening at night and closing by day. —**noc·tur′nal·ly,** *adv.*

noc·turne (nok′tûrn), *n.* a musical composition of a gentle, dreamy character.

nod (nod), *v.,* **nod·ded, nod·ding. 1.** to bow and raise (the head) quickly, esp. in greeting someone or to show agreement, approval, etc.: *to nod the head in agreement; to nod to a friend.* **2.** to express or indicate (something) by such a movement of the head: *to nod one's approval.* **3.** to let the head drop forward suddenly, as when falling asleep: *She was nodding over her homework.* **4.** (of trees, flowers, or the like) to droop or bend with a swaying motion: *The willow trees nodded in the wind.* —*n.* **5.** a short, quick bowing of the head: *He gave a nod to his friends across the room.* **6.** a sudden drooping of the head, esp. when falling asleep. **7.** a bending or swaying movement of a tree, flower, or the like.

node (nōd), *n.* **1.** a bulge, knob, or knot. **2.** a joint in a stem, esp. one from which a leaf grows. **3.** a rounded mass of body tissue: *a lymph node.* —**nod′al,** *adj.*

nod·ule (noj′ōōl), *n.* a small node, knot, or knob.

no·el (nō el′), *n.* a Christmas song or carol.

No·el (nō el′), *n.* Christmas, or the Christmas season.

nog·gin (nog′ən), *n.* **1.** a small cup or mug. **2.** a small amount of liquor, usually about ¼ pint: *The sailors were each given a noggin of rum.* **3.** *Informal.* the head.

noise (noiz), *n.* **1.** loud, harsh, or confused sound: *the noise of a jet plane taking off.* **2.** any sound: *I thought I heard a noise upstairs.* —*v.,* **noised, nois·ing. 3.** to spread as a report or rumor: *The news of their victory was soon noised around the city.*

noise·less (noiz′lis), *adj.* making no noise; silent or very quiet: *the noiseless movements of a cat.* —**noise′less·ly,** *adv.* —**noise′less·ness,** *n.*

nois·y (noi′zē), *adj.,* **nois·i·er, nois·i·est. 1.** making much noise: *a noisy engine; noisy children.* **2.** full of noise: *a crowded, noisy room.* —**nois′i·ly,** *adv.* —**nois′i·ness,** *n.*

no·mad (nō′mad), *n.* **1.** a member of a people or tribe that has no permanent home but moves about from place to place seeking pasture or a new food supply: *Many Arabs are desert nomads.* **2.** any wanderer. —*adj.* **3.** wandering or nomadic: *a nomad tribe.* [from the Greek word *nomas* "one who pastures flocks," which comes from *nemein* "to pasture"] —**no·mad′ic,** *adj.*

Nome (nōm), *n.* a port city in W Alaska.

nom·i·nal (nom′ə nəl), *adj.* **1.** being such in name only; so-called: *Joe is the nominal captain of the team, but Bill really makes the decisions.* **2.** (of a payment, charge, price, etc.) very small in comparison to actual value: *a nominal charge of $10.* **3.** (in grammar) **a.** of or referring to a noun. **b.** used to form nouns: *-ment is a nominal suffix.* **c.** having the function of a noun, as a gerund. —**nom′i·nal·ly,** *adv.*

nom·i·nate (nom′ə nāt′), *v.,* **nom·i·nat·ed, nom·i·nat·ing. 1.** to name (someone) as a candidate for election or appointment to a position or office: *I nominated*

N, Nodes on a stem

Elizabeth for president of the student council. **2.** to appoint to a position or office: *They nominated Bill to be treasurer.*

nom·i·na·tion (nom/ə nā/shən), *n.* **1.** the act or process of nominating: *the nomination of a candidate; to win the Republican nomination.* **2.** the state of being nominated.

nom·i·na·tive (nom/ə nə tiv), *adj.* **1.** (in grammar) belonging to the case of words or phrases used as the subject of a clause or sentence, or in apposition with the subject, or as a predicate complement. In the sentence *Jim, the captain, is the best player on the team,* the words *Jim, captain,* and *player* are all in the nominative case. —*n.* **2.** the nominative case.

nom·i·nee (nom/ə nē/), *n.* a person nominated as a candidate for a particular office or position: *The two nominees for governor debated on television.*

non-, a prefix meaning **1.** not: *nonexistent.* **2.** without or lacking: *nonsense.*

non·al·co·hol·ic (non/al kə hô/lik), *adj.* containing no alcohol: *soda, tea, and other nonalcoholic drinks.*

non·a·ligned (non/ə līnd/), *adj.* **1.** (of a nation or national policy) not aligned with or favoring the U.S., the U.S.S.R., or Communist China: *The outcome of today's vote in the U.N. depends on the nonaligned nations.* **2.** out of alignment.

nonce (nons), *n.* the present time, occasion, or purpose: *We have enough supplies for the nonce.*

non·cha·lance (non/shə läns/), *n.* lack of worry or concern; the state or quality of being casual and nonchalant: *the nonchalance of an experienced actor.*

non·cha·lant (non/shə länt/), *adj.* coolly unexcited or unconcerned; calm and casual: *to be nonchalant during a crisis.* —**non/cha·lant/ly,** *adv.*

non·com (non/kom/), *n. Informal.* a noncommissioned officer.

non·com·bat·ant (non kom/bə t⁹nt, non/kəm bat/-⁹nt), *n.* **1.** a person who is not a combatant, esp. a civilian in time of war or a member of the armed forces whose job does not include actual fighting. —*adj.* **2.** not engaged in or intended for combat.

non/com·mis/sioned of/ficer (non/kə mish/-ənd), (in the U.S. armed forces) an enlisted person who ranks above a private, seaman, etc., but does not hold an officer's commission.

non·com·mit·tal (non/kə mit/⁹l), *adj.* vague and not definite; not committing one to a definite point of view, course of action, etc.: *He gave me a noncommittal answer.*

non·con·duc·tor (non/kən duk/tər), *n.* a substance that does not readily conduct electricity, heat, or sound; insulator.

non·con·form·ist (non/kən fôr/mist), *n.* **1.** a person who does not follow or conform to established customs of behavior, popular opinion, or the like. **2.** *(often cap.)* a Protestant in England who is not a member of the Church of England; dissenter.

non·de·script (non/di skript/), *adj.* lacking any unusual features and therefore difficult to describe; not of any particular type or kind: *The thief had such a nondescript appearance that no one noticed him.*

none (nun), *pron.* **1.** no one; not one: *None of the members is going.* **2.** not any: *None of the business was finished.* **3.** *(used as pl.)* no persons or things: *I wanted some grapes, but none are left.* —*adv.* **4.** to no extent; not at all: *The guide was none too helpful.*

non·en·ti·ty (non en/ti tē), *n., pl.* **non·en·ti·ties.** a person or thing of no importance.

non·es·sen·tial (non/i sen/shəl), *adj.* **1.** not essential; not necessary: *Because we are low on money, we must avoid all nonessential expenses.* —*n.* **2.** a nonessential person or thing: *to economize by cutting down on nonessentials.*

none·the·less (nun/thə les/), *adv.* even so; nevertheless; however: *She wasn't feeling well, but nonetheless she gave a good performance.*

non·ex·ist·ent (non/ig zis/t⁹nt), *adj.* not real or actual; having no existence: *Don't waste time worrying about nonexistent problems.* —**non/ex·ist/ence,** *n.*

non·fic·tion (non fik/shən), *n.* writing or literature that deals with facts and ideas rather than telling a story with imaginary characters: *Textbooks and newspaper articles are nonfiction.* —**non·fic/tion·al,** *adj.*

non·mil·i·tar·y (non mil/i ter/ē), *adj.* not of, concerning, or for military forces or purposes: *a nonmilitary airport.*

non·pa·reil (non/pə rel/), *adj.* **1.** having no equal; unique or greatly superior: *the nonpareil strength of Hercules.* —*n.* **2.** a person or thing that has no equal: *This great ship is the nonpareil of ocean liners.*

non·par·ti·san (non pär/ti zən), *adj.* **1.** not taking sides; objective; not partisan: *The UN sent nonpartisan observers to report on the war.* **2.** not supporting or favoring any established political party. —*n.* **3.** a person who is nonpartisan.

non·plus (non plus/, non/plus), *v.,* **non·plused** *or* **non·plussed; non·plus·ing** *or* **non·plus·sing.** to confuse or puzzle completely; make utterly bewildered: *We were nonplused by the strange and unexpected news.* [from the Latin phrase *nōn plūs* "no more"]

non·pro·duc·tive (non/prə duk/tiv), *adj.* **1.** not productive; not producing desired or useful results, goods, crops, etc. **2.** (of workers or employees) not directly involved in producing goods. —**non/pro·duc/tive·ly,** *adv.* —**non/pro·duc/tive·ness,** *n.*

non·prof·it (non prof/it), *adj.* not yielding financial profits: *Churches and other nonprofit organizations do not pay taxes in this city.*

non·res·i·dent (non rez/i dənt), *adj.* **1.** not living in, or having one's residence in, a particular place: *Nonresident voters must send in their votes by mail.* —*n.* **2.** a nonresident person: *commuters and other nonresidents.*

non·sec·tar·i·an (non/sek târ/ē ən), *adj.* not allied with or representing any particular religious group: *a nonsectarian school; a nonsectarian religious service.*

non·sense (non/sens), *n.* **1.** something that makes no sense, esp. meaningless words or talk. **2.** foolish or silly behavior, ideas, or the like: *Stop the nonsense and get to work!* —**non·sen/si·cal,** *adj.*

non·stop (non/stop/), *adj.* **1.** making no stops on the way: *a nonstop flight to New Orleans.* —*adv.* **2.**

without making a stop: *We drove nonstop to Boston.*

noo·dle (nōod′∂l), *n.* a narrow strip of dried egg dough. Noodles are prepared for eating by boiling them until they are soft.

nook (nŏŏk), *n.* **1.** a corner or secluded area in a room: *Her desk was placed in a cozy little nook.* **2.** any remote, sheltered spot: *The swallows built their nest in a small nook under the roof.*

noon (nōon), *n.* midday; twelve o'clock in the daytime: *The sun is at its highest point at noon.*

noon·day (nōon′dā′), *adj.* **1.** of or at noon or midday: *the noonday meal.* —*n.* **2.** noon or midday.

no′ one′, not anyone; nobody: *No one is home.*

noon·tide (nōon′tīd′), *n.* noon or midday.

noon·time (nōon′tīm′), *n.* noon or midday: *I'll meet you here at noontime.*

noose (nōos), *n.* **1.** a loop, usually of rope, with a running knot that draws the loop tighter when the rope is pulled. Such a loop is characteristic of lassos and snares. **2.** a tie, bond, or anything that snares or traps: *He was caught in the noose of his own lies.* —*v.*, **noosed, noos·ing. 3.** to catch or hold by a noose: *to noose a rabbit.*

nor (nôr), *conj.* **1.** and not (used in negative phrases, esp. after *neither,* to introduce the following member or members of a series): *Neither Tom nor his sister will be there.* **2.** (used to continue the force of a preceding negative phrase): *I did not take their advice, nor did I ask their help again.*
—Usage. See **neither.**

Nor·dic (nôr′dik), *adj.* **1.** of, belonging to, or characteristic of a North European people who typically are tall, fair, and blue-eyed. Scandinavians are generally Nordic. —*n.* **2.** a Nordic person.

Nor·folk (nôr′fək), *n.* a port city in SE Virginia.

norm (nôrm), *n.* **1.** something that is considered average or usual; general level: *Her grades are well above the norm.* **2.** a standard, model, or pattern.

nor·mal (nôr′məl), *adj.* **1.** of the standard or usual kind; regular; natural: *Your temperature is normal.* **2.** average or healthy in physical, mental, and emotional development: *a normal child.* —*n.* **3.** something that is normal or usual; the average: *I think your pulse is faster than normal.* —**nor′mal·cy, nor·mal·i·ty** (nôr·mal′i tē), *n.*

nor·mal·ly (nôr′mə lē), *adv.* **1.** in a normal way: *The wound is healing normally.* **2.** according to rule, general custom, etc.; generally: *Summer is normally hot.*

Nor·man (nôr′mən), *n.* **1.** a member of the group of Northmen or Scandinavians who conquered Normandy in the 10th century. **2.** a member of a people of mixed Scandinavian and French descent who lived in Normandy and conquered England in 1066. **3.** a native or inhabitant of Normandy. —*adj.* **4.** of or concerning the Normans: *the Norman influence on English customs.*

Nor′man Con′quest, the conquest of England by the Normans under William the Conqueror, in 1066.

Nor·man·dy (nôr′mən dē), *n.* a region in N France along the English Channel.

Norse (nôrs), *adj.* **1.** of or concerning Norway, esp. ancient Norway and its colonies. **2.** of or concerning the Northmen or ancient Scandinavia generally: *Norse legends.* **3.** of or concerning the Norse

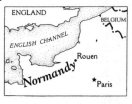

language. —*n.* **4.** *(used as pl.)* the Norwegians, esp. the ancient Norwegians. **5.** *(used as pl.)* the Northmen or ancient Scandinavians generally. **6.** Also, **Old Norse.** the Germanic language of ancient Scandinavia.

Norse·man (nôrs′mən), *n., pl.* **Norse·men.** another word for **Northman.**

north (nôrth), *n.* **1.** one of the four principal compass points; the direction of the North Pole, being one's left when facing the rising sun. *Abbr.:* N **2.** the northern part or region of a country. **3. the North, a.** the arctic regions of the earth. **b.** the part of the U.S. north of the Ohio River, esp. those states that fought against the Confederacy in the Civil War. —*adj.* **4.** Also, **northern.** situated in the north: *the north part of the state.* **5.** coming from the north: *a north wind.* —*adv.* **6.** toward the north: *to sail north.*

North′ Af′rica, the countries of N Africa, esp. those bordering on the Mediterranean Sea. —**North′ Af′rican.**

North′ Amer′ica, the northern continent of the Western Hemisphere. about 8,440,000 sq. mi. —**North′ Amer′ican.**

north·bound (nôrth′-bound′), *adj.* going toward the north: *Most of the traffic is northbound.*

North′ Caroli′na, a state in the SE United States, on the Atlantic coast. 52,712 sq. mi. *Cap.:* Raleigh. —**North′ Carolin′ian.**

North′ Dako′ta, a state in the N central United States. 70,665 sq. mi. *Cap.:* Bismarck. —**North′ Dako′tan.**

north·east (nôrth′ēst′), *n.* **1.** a point on the compass halfway between north and east. *Abbr.:* NE **2.** a region in this direction. **3. the Northeast,** the northeastern part of the U.S., esp. the New England states. —*adj.* **4.** situated toward the

northeast: *the northeast corner of the state.* **5.** directed toward the northeast: *a northeast course.* **6.** coming from the northeast: *a northeast wind.* —*adv.* **7.** toward the northeast: *The whaling ship sailed*

---

northeast. Also, **northeastern** (for defs. 4, 5).

north·east·er (nôrth′ē′stər), *n.* a wind or gale from the northeast.

north·east·er·ly (nôrth′ē′stər lē), *adj.* 1. directed toward the northeast: *in a northeasterly course.* 2. coming from the northeast: *The wind is northeasterly.* —*adv.* 3. toward the northeast: *sailing northeasterly.* 4. from the northeast, as a wind.

north·east·ern (nôrth′ē′stərn), *adj.* See **northeast** (defs. 4, 5).

north·er·ly (nôr′thər lē), *adj.* 1. directed toward the north: *in a northerly course.* 2. coming from the north: *The wind is northerly.* —*adv.* 3. toward the north: *sailing northerly.* 4. from the north, as a wind.

north·ern (nôr′thərn), *adj.* 1. See **north** (def. 4). 2. of or referring to the north, esp. the northern U.S.

North·ern·er (nôr′thər nər), *n. (sometimes l.c.)* a native or inhabitant of the North, esp. of the northern U.S.

North′ern Hem′isphere, the half of the earth between the North Pole and the equator.

North′ern Ire′land, a political division of the United Kingdom, in the NE part of the island of Ireland. 5238 sq. mi. *Cap.:* Belfast.

north′ern lights′, flickering bands or streamers of light sometimes seen in the northern sky. Also, **aurora borealis.**

north·ern·most (nôr′thərn mōst′), *adj.* farthest north: *the northernmost part of Europe.*

North′ern Rhode′sia, former name of **Zambia.**

North′ Is′land, the northern principal island of New Zealand. 44,281 sq. mi.

North′ Kore′a, a country in E Asia, formed in 1948 after the division of Korea. 50,000 sq. mi. —**North′ Kore′an.**

North·man (nôrth′mən), *n., pl.* **North·men.** a member of an ancient Scandinavian people, esp. one of the group that from the 8th to the 11th century established settlements in Great Britain, Ireland, Europe, and probably North America. Also, **Norseman.**

north-north·east (nôrth′nôrth′ēst′), *n.* 1. the point on the compass halfway between north and northeast. *Abbr.:* NNE —*adj.* 2. directed toward this point. 3. coming from this point, as a wind. —*adv.* 4. toward this point. 5. from this point, as a wind.

north-north·west (nôrth′nôrth′west′), *n.* 1. the point on the compass halfway between north and northwest. *Abbr.:* NNW —*adj.* 2. directed toward this point. 3. coming from this point, as a wind. —*adv.* 4. toward this point. 5. from this point, as a wind.

North′ Pole′, the northernmost point on the earth.

North′ Sea′, an arm of the Atlantic Ocean between Great Britain and the European mainland. It covers an area of about 201,000 sq. mi.

North′ Star′, a bright star that does not appear to move as the earth turns on its axis; polestar. The North Star is used by navigators, since its direction is always true north. Also, **Polaris.**

North·um·bri·a (nôr thum′brē ə), *n.* an early English kingdom in N England and S Scotland. —**North·um′bri·an,** *n., adj.*

North′ Vietnam′, a former country in SE Asia, S of China: now part of reunified Vietnam. —**North′ Viet·namese′.**

north·ward (nôrth′wərd), *adj.* 1. directed toward the north. 2. situated in the north. —*adv.* 3. Also, **north′wards.** toward the north: *to sail northward.* —*n.* 4. a northward direction or point.

north·west (nôrth′west′), *n.* 1. a point on the compass halfway between north and west. *Abbr.:* NW 2. a region in this direction. 3. **the Northwest,** the northwestern part of the U.S. —*adj.* 4. situated in the northwest: *the northwest corner of the state.* 5. directed toward the northwest: *to sail a northwest course.* 6. coming from the northwest: *a northwest wind.* —*adv.* 7. toward the northwest: *to sail northwest.* Also, **northwestern** (for defs. 4, 5).

north·west·er (nôrth′wes′tər), *n.* a wind or gale from the northwest.

north·west·er·ly (nôrth′wes′tər lē), *adj.* 1. directed toward the northwest: *in a northwesterly course.* 2. coming from the northwest: *The wind is northwesterly.* —*adv.* 3. toward the northwest: *sailing northwesterly.* 4. from the northwest, as a wind.

north·west·ern (nôrth′wes′tərn), *adj.* See **northwest** (defs. 4, 5).

North′west Pas′sage, a ship route along the Arctic coast of Canada and Alaska, joining the Atlantic and Pacific oceans, long sought by early explorers.

North′west Ter′ritories, a territory N of the central provinces of Canada. 1,304,903 sq. mi.

North′west Ter′ritory, a region between the Ohio and Mississippi rivers, organized by Congress in 1787.

Nor·way (nôr′wā), *n.* a kingdom in N Europe, in the W part of the Scandinavian Peninsula. 124,-555 sq. mi. *Cap.:* Oslo.

Nor·we·gian (nôr wē′jən), *adj.* 1. of or concerning Norway, its people, or their language: *the Norwegian navy.* —*n.* 2. a native or inhabitant of Norway. 3. the Germanic language of Norway.

nose (nōz), *n.* 1. the part of the face in man and certain animals that contains the nostrils and the organs of smell and that serves as the usual path for the air that is breathed in and out. 2. the sense of smell: *A bloodhound should have a good nose.* 3. something that resembles a nose in location or shape, esp. the front end of an airplane. 4. ability to discover or recognize a particular kind of thing: *to have a nose* *for news.* **5.** the length of a nose, esp. of a horse's nose: *to win by a nose.* —*v.,* **nosed, nos·ing. 6.** to sniff or smell. **7.** to touch, rub, or push with the nose; nuzzle: *The mare nosed her colt away from the fence.* **8.** to move or push forward, esp. very carefully: *to nose a car through traffic.* **9.** to meddle or pry (often fol. by *about, into,* etc.): *to nose into other people's private lives.* **10. cut off one's nose to spite one's face,** to harm oneself for the pleasure of hurting someone else: *Canceling the party just to get even with her would be cutting off your nose to spite your face.* **11. look down one's nose at,** *Informal.* to feel oneself superior to: *She looks down her nose at laborers.* **12. on the nose,** *Slang.* **a.** precisely; correctly: *It cost $10 on the nose.* **b.** exactly on time: *I was there at 10 o'clock on the nose.* **13. pay through the nose,** to pay too great a price: *I had to pay through the nose for that new tennis racket.* **14. turn up one's nose at,** to regard with contempt; scorn: *She turned up her nose at the hot dogs.* [from the Old English word *nosu,* which is related to Latin *nāsus*]

nose·bleed (nōz′blēd′), *n.* a flow of blood from the nose.

nose′ cone′, the cone-shaped front section of a rocket or missile, including the heat shield and containing the payload.

nose′ dive′, 1. a sudden drop or plunge of an aircraft. **2.** any sudden drop: *Prices took a nose dive today.*

nose-dive (nōz′dīv′), *v.,* **nose-dived, nose-div·ing.** to go into a nose dive or drop suddenly.

nose·gay (nōz′gā′), *n.* a small bunch of flowers; bouquet.

nos·ey (nō′zē), *adj.,* **nos·i·er, nos·i·est.** another spelling of **nosy.**

nos·tal·gia (no stal′jə), *n.* a longing for pleasures, experiences, etc., that belong to the past: *a feeling of nostalgia for the farm where he grew up.*

nos·tal·gic (no stal′jik),˙ *adj.* full of or expressing nostalgia; longing for what is past: *She was nostalgic for her childhood.* —**nos·tal′gi·cal·ly,** *adv.*

nos·tril (nos′trəl), *n.* one of the two outside openings of the nose. [from the Old English word *nosthyrl,* literally "hole of the nose"]

nos·y (nō′zē), *adj.,* **nos·i·er, nos·i·est.** snooping into other people's business; prying: *a nosy neighbor.* Also, **nosey.** —**nos′i·ly,** *adv.* —**nos′i·ness,** *n.*

not (not), *adv.* (used in negative statements to express disagreement, denial, etc.): *He is not here.*

no·ta·ble (nō′tə bəl),˛ *adj.* **1.** worthy of notice or attention; important, remarkable, or memorable: *a notable speech on foreign policy.* **2.** (of persons) famous, distinguished, or important: *a gathering of notable scientists.* —*n.* **3.** a notable person: *The mayor and other notables appeared on television.* —**no·ta·bil·i·ty** (nō′tə bil′i tē), *n.* —**no′ta·bly,** *adv.*

no·ta·rize (nō′tə rīz′), *v.,* **no·ta·rized, no·ta·riz·ing.** to make (a document) legal by placing the signature and seal of a notary public on it: *to notarize a will.*

no·ta·ry (nō′tə rē), *n., pl.* **no·ta·ries.** a notary public.

no′tary pub′lic, *pl.* **notaries public.** a public official who is authorized to witness the signing of contracts, deeds, statements, etc., and to confirm that the person signing them has sworn that they are truthful. Also, **notary.**

no·ta·tion (nō tā′shən), *n.* **1.** a note, jotting, or record: *to make notations in the margin of a book.* **2.** a system of symbols, letters, or numbers used for a special purpose: *musical notation.* **3.** the process of writing or recording by means of such a system. **4.** the act of making notes in writing.

notch (noch), *n.* **1.** a wedge-shaped cut in a surface or edge: *to cut notches in a stick.* **2.** a deep, narrow opening or pass between mountains. —*v.* **3.** to cut a notch or notches in: *to notch wood with a knife.*

note (nōt), *n.* **1.** a brief written record: *The policeman made a note of our description of the thief.* **2.** a brief, written comment, instruction, reminder, etc.: *Read the notes on the bulletin board.* **3.** a short, informal letter: *a note of thanks.* **4.** a musical sound or tone. **5.** a key on a piano or organ: *The C major scale is played on the white notes.*

Notes (def. 6)
1, Whole note; 2, Half note; 3, Quarter note; 4, Eighth note; 5, Sixteenth note

6. a sign or symbol used to represent a musical tone. **7.** a printed piece of paper accepted as money. **8.** a written promise of payment: *He gave me his note for the loan.* **9.** notice or attention; heed: *an event worthy of note.* **10.** importance or prominence: *a person of note.* **11.** a trace, indication, or quality: *There was a note of optimism in her remarks.* **12.** a formal official communication: *The ambassador delivered his government's note to the prime minister.* —*v.,* **not·ed, not·ing. 13.** to make a note of (something); write or mark down briefly: *to note a telephone number.* **14.** to observe or take notice of: *Please note the instructions.* **15.** to mention specifically: *The senator noted˙ the many letters of encouragement he had received.*

note·book (nōt′book′), *n.* a book in which one may write notes, reminders, or the like.

not·ed (nō′tid), *adj.* famous or widely known.

note·wor·thy (nōt′wûr′t͟hē), *adj.* worthy of attention or notice; notable: *noteworthy discoveries.*

noth·ing (nuth′ing), *n.* **1.** no thing; not anything: *There is nothing left to eat.* **2.** something or someone of no importance: *She scratched herself, but it's nothing.* **3.** a zero quantity; zero: *Nothing from nine leaves nine.* —*adv.* **4.** not at all; in no way or to no degree: *Nothing dismayed by his original failure, he went on to try again.* **5. for nothing, a.** free of charge: *He mended my shoe for nothing.* **b.** in vain; needlessly: *We went to all that expense for nothing.* **6. nothing doing,** *Informal.* **a.** definitely no; certainly not: *I tried to get money for the circus, but nothing* *doing.* **b.** no activity, attractions, etc., worthy of interest: *We went downtown, but there was nothing doing.*

noth·ing·ness (nuth′ing nis), *n.* **1.** the condition of not existing or being: *Their hopes faded to nothingness.* **2.** absence of worth or importance; worthlessness.

no·tice (nō′tis), *n.* **1.** attention or observation; heed (often preceded by *take*): *She took notice of the warning.* **2.** information or warning of something: *to give notice of danger.* **3.** a printed or written announcement giving information or a warning: *We received a notice about the sale.* **4.** a formal statement or warning concerning one's intentions: *You should give notice two weeks before quitting a job.* **5.** a review or critical article or report: *That movie received good notices.* —*v.,* **no·ticed, no·tic·ing. 6.** to be aware of or observe; pay attention to: *Did you notice which way he went?* **7.** to comment on or mention: *This fact was noticed in an earlier chapter.*

no·tice·a·ble (nō′ti sə bəl), *adj.* **1.** capable of attracting attention or of being noticed; easily seen: *a noticeable mistake.* **2.** deserving of notice or attention: *a noticeable beauty.* —**no′tice·a·bly,** *adv.*

no·ti·fi·ca·tion (nō′tə fə kā′shən), *n.* **1.** the act of notifying or informing; a giving notice: *The notification of the club members will take several days.* **2.** a written or printed announcement or notice: *The notifications were mailed yesterday.*

no·ti·fy (nō′tə fī′), *v.,* **no·ti·fied, no·ti·fy·ing.** to inform or give notice of something; make known to: *Did you notify your parents that you are arriving tonight?*

no·tion (nō′shən), *n.* **1.** an idea, esp. a general or vague idea; impression: *I have no notion of how this machine works.* **2.** an opinion, view, or belief: *He has some odd notions about politics.* **3.** a whim or fancy: *a notion of being an actor.* **4. notions,** small articles for sale, such as buttons, pins, ribbons, etc.

no·to·ri·e·ty (nō′tə rī′i tē), *n.* the condition or quality of being notorious; ill fame: *the notoriety of a political dictator.*

no·to·ri·ous (nō tôr′ē əs), *adj.* widely known, esp. as evil or dangerous; infamous: *a notorious criminal.* —**no·to′ri·ous·ly,** *adv.*

not·with·stand·ing (not′with stan′ding, -with-), *prep.* **1.** in spite of: *Notwithstanding the danger of the voyage, he started off boldly.* —*conj.* **2.** although; in spite of the fact that: *He did succeed, notwithstanding his enemies made it difficult for him.* —*adv.* **3.** nevertheless; anyway; yet: *She was nervous, but she continued to speak, notwithstanding.*

nou·gat (nōō′gət), *n.* a chewy or brittle candy containing almonds or other nuts and sometimes fruit.

nought (nôt), *n.* another spelling of **naught.**

noun (noun), *n.* a word used as the name of a person, place, thing, state, or quality. See also **common noun, proper noun.**

nour·ish (nûr′ish, nur′ish), *v.* **1.** to make grow or keep alive and healthy with food. **2.** to strengthen or increase: *The good news nourished our hopes.* —**nour′ish·er,** *n.* —**nour′ish·ing·ly,** *adv.*

nour·ish·ment (nûr′ish mənt, nur′ish mənt), *n.* **1.** something that nourishes, esp. food. **2.** the act of nourishing, or the condition of being nourished: *special food for the nourishment of a weak baby.*

Nov., November.

No·va Sco·tia (nō′və skō′shə), a peninsula and province in SE Canada. 21,068 sq. mi. *Cap.:* Halifax. —**No′va Sco′tian.**

nov·el[1] (nov′əl), *n.* a long story about imaginary people and events, often imitating real life. [from the Italian word *novella* "new (story)"]

nov·el[2] (nov′əl), *adj.* new or different: *Skin-diving was a novel experience for me.* [from the Latin word *novellus* "new, fresh"]

nov·el·ist (nov′ə list), *n.* a person who has written one or more novels.

nov·el·ty (nov′əl tē), *n., pl.* for defs. 2, 3 **nov·el·ties. 1.** the condition or quality of being novel, different, or new; newness; originality: *After a while the novelty of camping wore off.* **2.** a new or unusual experience, occurrence, idea, etc.: *It was a novelty for her to see herself on television.* **3.** a small, inexpensive article that is amusing or attractive: *She bought some little statues and other novelties as gifts.*

No·vem·ber (nō vem′bər), *n.* the eleventh month of the year, having 30 days. [from a Latin word, which comes from *novem* "nine." In the early Roman calendar, November was the ninth month]

nov·ice (nov′is), *n.* **1.** a person who is new to a job, situation, or the like; newcomer; beginner: *He's still a novice, but he's learning the work fast.* **2.** a person who has been received into a religious order, but has not yet taken vows.

no·vi·ti·ate (nō vish′ē it, nō vish′ē āt′), *n.* **1.** the condition or period of being a novice, esp. in a religious order: *the novitiate of a nun.* **2.** the living quarters occupied by novices in a religious order.

now (nou), *adv.* **1.** at this time or moment: *Now the other team has the ball. Don't jump now.* **2.** in the very recent past; a very little while ago (usually preceded by *just* or *only*): *We just now moved into this house.* **3.** at the time or moment mentioned: *Having washed, they were now ready to eat.* **4.** nowadays; in these times: *You seldom hear a waltz now.* **5.** under the present circumstances; as things stand: *Now we're going to have to change our plans.* **6.** (used to introduce a statement or question): *Now, did you really mean to say that?* **7.** (used to strengthen a command, plea, etc.): *Now stop that at once!* —*conj.* **8.** inasmuch as; since: *We can leave, now it's stopped raining.* —*n.* **9.** the present time or moment: *in the here and now.* **10. now and again,** from time to time; occasionally: *We see each other now and again.* Also, **now and then.**

now·a·days (nou′ə dāz′), *adv.* **1.** in these present times: *Nowadays many people travel.* —*n.* **2.** the present: *The manners of nowadays are more casual.*

no·way (nō′wā′), *adv.* in no way; not at all: *The situation has noway improved.* Also, **no′ways′.**

no·where (nō′hwâr′, -wâr′), *adv.* **1.** not anywhere; in, at, or to no place: *Help was nowhere to be found.*

—*n.* **2.** no place in particular; a distant or isolated spot: *Our car broke down in the middle of nowhere.* **3.** a condition of being completely unknown, unfamiliar, etc.; actual or seeming nonexistence: *The news came out of nowhere, and took us all by surprise.*

no·wise (nō′wīz′), *adv.* not at all; in no way: *His condition is nowise improved.*

nox·ious (nok′shəs), *adj.* harmful to physical or moral health; poisonous or unwholesome: *noxious gases; a noxious habit.* —**nox′ious·ly,** *adv.*

noz·zle (noz′əl), *n.* the end of a hose, pipe, etc., that forms an outlet.

Np, *Chem.* the symbol for **neptunium.**

NT, New Testament. Also, **Nt., N.T.**

nt. wt., net weight.

nu·ance (nōō′äns, nōō äns′), *n.* a small but important change of color, meaning, feeling, etc.: *the nuances of a great painting.*

nub (nub), *n.* **1.** a knob or lump on the surface of something. **2.** a lump or small piece: *a nub of coal.* **3.** *Informal.* the gist or main point of something.

Nu·bi·a (nōō′bē ə, nyōō′-), *n.* an ancient kingdom in NE Africa, S of Egypt. —**Nu′bi·an,** *n., adj.*

nu·cle·ar (nōō′klē ər, nyōō′-), *adj.* **1.** of or concerning the nucleus of a cell or an atom. **2.** of, referring to, or using atomic energy: *nuclear weapons.*

nu′clear en′ergy, a scientific term for **atomic energy.**

nu′clear fis′sion. See **fission** (def. 3).

nu′clear fu′sion. See **fusion** (def. 4).

nu·cle·us (nōō′klē əs, nyōō′-), *n., pl.* **nu·cle·us·es** or **nu·cle·i** (nōō′klē ī′, nyōō′-). **1.** a central part around which other parts are grouped; core: *A few hard-working members formed the nucleus of the organization.* **2.** the central portion of most living cells that contains the materials necessary for the cell to reproduce and carry on most of its other activities. See illus. at **cell. 3.** the central part of an atom, which possesses most of the atom's mass but occupies only a small part of its volume. The negatively charged electrons revolve around the positively charged nucleus. [from a Latin word meaning "kernel, little nut," a diminutive of *nux* "nut"]

nude (nōōd, nyōōd), *adj.* **1.** naked or unclothed; bare. —*n.* **2.** an unclothed human figure, esp. as the subject of a painting, sculpture, etc. —**nu′di·ty,** *n.*

nudge (nuj), *v.*, **nudged, nudg·ing. 1.** to push slightly, esp. with the elbow: *Nudge Bill to get his attention.* —*n.* **2.** a slight push, esp. with the elbow.

nug·get (nug′it), *n.* **1.** a lump, esp. of gold or other precious metal as found in nature. **2.** a lump or bit of anything precious: *nuggets of wisdom.*

nui·sance (nōō′səns, nyōō′-), *n.* a highly annoying or obnoxious person, thing, job, etc.: *It's a nuisance to have to clean up after you all the time.*

null (nul), *adj.* **1.** without effect, force, value, etc., esp. without legal force: *The agreement is null unless it is signed.* **2.** being or amounting to nothing or zero. **3. null and void,** without legal force or effect; not valid: *After June 1st the lease is null and void.*

nul·li·fy (nul′ə fī′), *v.*, **nul·li·fied, nul·li·fy·ing. 1.** to take away the value or effectiveness of something: *The penalty nullified the team's gain.* **2.** to make or declare (a law, rule, etc.) void or without legal force; annul. —**nul′li·fi·ca′tion,** *n.*

numb (num), *adj.* **1.** having little or no ability to feel or move: *My fingers grew numb from the cold.* —*v.* **2.** to make numb or without feeling: *The shock numbed him.* —**numb′ly,** *adv.* —**numb′ness,** *n.*

num·ber (num′bər), *n.* **1.** a mathematical unit that has a particular relation to other such units: *2 is an even number.* **2.** a symbol representing such a unit; numeral. **3.** sum or total of a group of persons or things; amount; quantity: *Please find out the number of guests.* **4.** a group or quantity amounting to many or several: *A number of people came.* **5.** a numeral assigned to an object, person, size, etc., for purposes of identification or classification: *a social security number.* **6.** a single act or item in a show, concert, or the like. **7.** one item in a series, such as one issue of a periodical: *the December number of a magazine.* **8.** (in grammar) a form of inflection of nouns, pronouns, verbs, and some adjectives that shows whether a word refers to one (singular) or more than one (plural). —*v.* **9.** to amount to in number; contain; total: *The team numbered nine men.* **10.** to count or enumerate: *The newspapers numbered the crowd at about 3000.* **11.** to mark with numbers: *to number the pages of a notebook.* **12.** to limit in number: *The outlaw knew that his days were numbered.* **13.** to include or be included (often fol. by *with* or *among*): *I number him among my friends.* **14. get** (or **have**) **someone's number,** *Slang.* to understand someone's true motives, character, etc.: *He won't trick me again because I've got his number now.* **15. without** (or **beyond**) **number,** too many to be counted; countless or endless: *stars beyond number.*

num·ber·less (num′bər lis), *adj.* **1.** extremely numerous; countless: *the numberless poor in Asia.* **2.** having no number: *a numberless door.*

Num·bers (num′bərz), *n.* *(used as sing.)* the fourth book of the Old Testament.

nu·mer·al (nōō′mər əl, nyōō′-), *n.* a symbol or group of symbols standing for a number or quantity: *XVIII is a Roman numeral; 18 is an Arabic numeral.*

nu·mer·a·tor (nōō′mə rā′tər, nyōō′-), *n.* the number in a fraction that is written above the line or before the slash and indicates the number of equal parts that the fraction contains: *In the fractions ²/₃ and ²/₅, the numerator is 2.* See also **denominator.**

nu·mer·i·cal (nōō mer′i kəl, nyōō-), *adj.* of, concerning, or expressed in numbers. —**nu·mer′i·cal·ly,** *adv.*

nu·mer·ous (nōō′mər əs, nyōō′-), *adj.* **1.** being or existing in large quantity; many: *Numerous ants were on the picnic table.* **2.** consisting of a large number of persons or things: *The audience was numerous.*

nu·mis·mat·ics (nōō′miz mat′iks, nyōō′-), *n.* *(used*

as sing.) the study or collecting of coins, medals, or the like: *Numismatics is his hobby.*

nu·mis·ma·tist (nōō miz′mə tist, nyōō-), *n.* a specialist in numismatics.

num·skull (num′skul′), *n. Informal.* a stupid person; dunce.

nun (nun), *n.* a woman who is a member of a religious order, usually one who has taken solemn religious vows and lives in a convent.

nun·ci·o (nun′shē ō′), *n., pl.* **nun·ci·os.** an ambassador of the pope.

nun·ner·y (nun′ə rē), *n., pl.* **nun·ner·ies.** a house or group of houses for nuns; convent.

nup·tial (nup′shəl), *adj.* **1.** of or concerning marriage or the marriage ceremony: *The bride and groom made their nuptial vows.* —*n.* **2.** Usually, **nuptials.** a wedding or marriage. —**nup′tial·ly,** *adv.*

nurse (nûrs), *n.* **1.** a person, esp. a woman, who is trained to take care of those who are sick, injured, or the like. **2.** a woman who is employed to take care of a child or children. —*v.,* **nursed, nurs·ing. 3.** to take care of the needs of (a sick or disabled person): *to nurse an invalid.* **4.** to try to cure (an ailment) by taking special care: *to nurse a cold.* **5.** to feed (a baby) at the breast. **6.** to take milk from the breast: *The baby is nursing.* **7.** to take care of (a baby or young child). **8.** to preserve or keep up: *to nurse a grudge.* [from the Old French word *nurice,* which comes from Latin *nūtrīcia* "one who nourishes"]

nurse·maid (nûrs′mād′), *n.* a woman or girl employed to take care of a child or children.

nurs·er·y (nûr′sə rē), *n., pl.* **nurs·er·ies. 1.** a room or place, esp. in a house, set apart for young children. **2.** a nursery school or day nursery. **3.** a place where young trees or other plants are raised and sold.

nurs·er·y·man (nûr′sə rē mən), *n., pl.* **nurs·er·y·men.** a man who owns or manages a nursery for trees or plants.

nurs′er·y rhyme′, a short, simple poem or song for young children.

nurs′er·y school′, a school for children who are too young to attend kindergarten, usually those under five.

nur·ture (nûr′chər), *v.,* **nur·tured, nur·tur·ing. 1.** to provide with the food and care necessary for healthy growth: *to nurture a young child.* **2.** to educate or bring up with care, encouragement, etc.: *to nurture young students.* **3.** to promote the development of (someone or something) by training, support, or the like: *to nurture a new business.* —*n.* **4.** something that nourishes; nourishment. **5.** care that aids growth and development; upbringing, education, or the like.

nut (nut), *n.* **1.** a dry fruit consisting of an edible kernel in a hard or tough shell. **2.** the kernel itself. **3.** a small piece of metal having a threaded hole for screwing onto a bolt. See illus. at **bolt. 4.** *Slang.* **a.** a

crazy or very eccentric person. **b.** an enthusiast or buff; fan: *a racing-car nut.* —*v.,* **nut·ted, nut·ting. 5.** to look for or gather nuts. —**nut′like′,** *adj.*

nut·crack·er (nut′krak′ər), *n.* an instrument for cracking the shells of nuts.

nut·hatch (nut′hach′), *n.* any of numerous small, short-tailed birds with sharp beaks that feed on nuts and insects.

nut·meg (nut′meg), *n.* the hard seed of an East Indian tree, which is grated or ground for use as a spice.

Nuthatch
(length 6 in.)

nu·tri·a (nōō′trē ə, nyōō′-), *n.* **1.** a large, furry South American animal that resembles a beaver and lives in the water. **2.** the pale-brown fur of this animal, similar to beaver.

nu·tri·ent (nōō′trē ənt, nyōō′-), *n.* **1.** a substance that gives nourishment; food. —*adj.* **2.** containing or producing nourishment.

nu·tri·ment (nōō′trə mənt, nyōō′-), *n.* something that nourishes; food.

nu·tri·tion (nōō trish′ən, nyōō-), *n.* **1.** the science that deals with food and the planning of meals. **2.** the act or process of nourishing or being nourished. **3.** nutriment or food. —**nu·tri′tion·al,** *adj.*

nu·tri·tious (nōō trish′əs, nyōō-), *adj.* providing nourishment, esp. to a high degree; nourishing.

nu·tri·tive (nōō′tri tiv, nyōō′-), *adj.* **1.** providing nutriment; nourishing. **2.** of or concerning nutrition.

nut·shell (nut′shel′), *n.* **1.** the shell or covering of a nut. **2. in a nutshell,** in brief: *In a nutshell, his answer was "no."*

nut·ty (nut′ē), *adj.,* **nut·ti·er, nut·ti·est. 1.** full of nuts. **2.** producing or yielding nuts. **3.** nutlike, esp. in taste. **4.** *Slang.* silly or crazy. —**nut′ti·ness,** *n.*

nuz·zle (nuz′əl), *v.,* **nuz·zled, nuz·zling. 1.** to touch, push, or rub with the nose: *The pony nuzzled his shoulder.* **2.** to dig or burrow with the nose, as animals do: *The pig nuzzled in the dirt.* **3.** to dig or root up with the nose. **4.** to snuggle or cuddle.

NW, 1. northwest. **2.** northwestern. Also, **N.W.**

N.Y., New York.

Nya·sa·land (nyä′sä land′, nī as′ə land′), *n.* former name of **Malawi.**

N.Y.C., New York City.

ny·lon (nī′lon), *n.* **1.** a strong, elastic, man-made material used for making cloth, rope, artificial bristles, etc. **2. nylons,** stockings knitted from nylon yarn.

nymph (nimf), *n.* **1.** (in Greek and Roman mythology) one of the nature goddesses, thought of as beautiful maidens, who dwelt in the sea, woods, mountains, etc. **2.** a beautiful or graceful young woman. **3.** the young of certain insects, esp. when closely resembling the adult. —**nymph′like′,** *adj.*

N.Z., New Zealand. Also, **N. Zeal.**

O

O, o (ō), *n., pl.* **O's** *or* **Os, o's** *or* **os** *or* **oes.** the 15th letter of the English alphabet.

O (ō), *interj.* **1.** (used before a name in addressing someone, esp. in poetic language, to emphasize the earnestness of an appeal): *Hear our prayers, O Lord!* **2.** (used as an expression of surprise, pain, gladness, longing, etc.): *O, what a beautiful gift!* —*n., pl.* **O's. 3.** the exclamation "O."

O, 1. the Arabic symbol for zero. **2.** *Chem.* the symbol for **oxygen. 3.** a major blood group or type.

O., 1. Ocean. **2.** Ohio.

oaf (ōf), *n.* a stupid or clumsy person; lout. —**oaf′ish,** *adj.*

O·a·hu (ō ä′hōō), *n.* an island in central Hawaii: location of Honolulu. 589 sq. mi.

oak (ōk), *n.* **1.** any of numerous trees that bear acorns. **2.** the hard, open-grained wood of such trees, used in furniture, for carving, etc.

oak·en (ō′kən), *adj.* made of oak: *an oaken table.*

Oak·land (ōk′lənd), *n.* a port city in W California.

Oak′ Ridge′, a city in E Tennessee, near Knoxville: atomic research center.

oa·kum (ō′kəm), *n.* loose fiber obtained by picking apart old rope, used for caulking the seams between the planks of boats.

oar (ôr), *n.* **1.** a long pole with a broad, flat blade at one end, used for rowing or steering a boat. **2.** a rower or oarsman.

oar·lock (ôr′lok′), *n.* a device, usually a U-shaped piece of metal that swivels, used to hold an oar in place.

oars·man (ôrz′mən), *n., pl.* **oars·men.** a person who rows a boat; rower.

o·a·sis (ō ā′sis), *n., pl.* **o·a·ses** (ō ā′sēz). **1.** a fertile or green area in a desert region, usually having a spring or well. **2.** a place that provides refuge or serves as a pleasant relief or change: *In the past, the universities were oases of learning.*

O, Oarlock

oat (ōt), *n.* **1.** a grass grown for its seeds. **2.** Usually, **oats.** the seed of this plant used as a food for animals and humans. **3. feel one's oats,** to feel lively, gay, or enthusiastic.

oath (ōth), *n., pl.* **oaths** (ōthz, ōths). **1.** a solemn appeal to God or to some highly honored person or thing to witness that one is determined to speak the truth or keep a promise: *He pledged with an oath that he would never betray his country.* **2.** a statement or promise strengthened by such an appeal; pledge or vow: *an oath to tell the whole truth; an oath of office.* **3.** a profane or vulgar expression, esp. an irreverent use of the name of God; curse. **4. take an oath,** to swear solemnly; vow: *He took an oath that he had seen the crime committed.* **5. under (on or upon) oath,** bound by an oath to tell the truth or keep a promise: *to speak under oath.*

Oats

oat·meal (ōt′mēl′), *n.* **1.** meal made from oats. **2.** a cooked breakfast cereal made from this. —*adj.* **3.** made with or containing oatmeal: *oatmeal cookies.*

O·ba·di·ah (ō′bə dī′ə), *n.* (in the Bible) **1.** one of the Hebrew prophets. **2.** a book of the Old Testament bearing his name.

ob·du·rate (ob′dōō rit, -dyōō-), *adj.* **1.** stubborn and unyielding; not touched by pity or tender feelings: *an obdurate refusal.* **2.** stubbornly given over to evil ways; hard-hearted and without remorse. —**ob′du·rate·ly,** *adv.*

o·be·di·ence (ō bē′dē əns), *n.* the act or process of obeying; willingness to follow the orders or wishes of someone in authority.

o·be·di·ent (ō bē′dē ənt), *adj.* obeying or willing to obey; prepared to follow the orders or wishes of someone in authority: *A good hunting dog must be obedient.* —**o·be′di·ent·ly,** *adv.*

o·bei·sance (ō bā′səns, ō bē′səns), *n.* **1.** a bow, curtsy, or other movement of the body expressing respect. **2.** deep respect or homage.

ob·e·lisk (ob′ə lisk), *n.* a four-sided shaft of stone that tapers slightly from bottom to top, the top being shaped like a pyramid.

O·ber·on (ō′bə ron′), *n.* (in medieval folklore) the king of the fairies and husband of their queen, Titania.

o·bese (ō bēs′), *adj.* extremely fat; overweight: *a special diet for obese people.* —**o·bese′ly,** *adv.* —**o·bese′ness, o·bes·i·ty** (ō bē′si tē), *n.*

o·bey (ō bā′), *v.* 1. to follow or comply with the orders, instructions, wishes, etc., of (someone): *Soldiers must obey their commanding officers.* 2. to follow or comply with (an order, law, instruction, etc.): *to obey the rules.* 3. to be obedient; follow the law, rules, orders, etc.: *The marriage ceremony requires the bride to love, honor, and obey.* —**o·bey′er,** *n.*

Obelisk

o·bit·u·ar·y (ō bich′ōō er′ē), *n., pl.* **o·bit·u·ar·ies.** a notice announcing the death of a person, often including a brief account of his life, published in a newspaper or the like.

ob·ject (ob′jikt, ob′jekt), *n.* 1. anything that may be seen or touched and has a particular shape: *Please remove all objects from your desks.* 2. any thing or person toward which thought, action, feeling, etc., is directed: *His family is the object of his affection.* 3. goal or purpose: *What was the object of your trip?* 4. (in grammar) the person or thing that receives the action of a verb or follows a preposition. See also **direct object, indirect object.** —*v.* (əb jekt′). 5. to offer a reason or argument in opposing something; state as a reason for disagreeing or disapproving: *The lawyer objected, but he was overruled.* 6. to express or feel disapproval, dislike, disgust, etc.: *She objects to loud neckties.* —**ob·jec′tor,** *n.*

ob·jec·tion (əb jek′shən), *n.* 1. a reason or cause for objecting; something said or put forward in disagreement, disapproval, or the like: *My objection to the plan is that it will cost too much.* 2. a feeling of disapproval, dislike, or disagreement: *His objection was obvious when he walked out of the room.* 3. the act of objecting: *The way the meeting was run, objection was impossible.*

ob·jec·tion·a·ble (əb jek′shə nə bəl), *adj.* causing or likely to cause objection; offensive, insulting, unfair, or the like: *vulgar, objectionable language.* —**ob·jec′tion·a·bly,** *adv.*

ob·jec·tive (əb jek′tiv), *adj.* 1. not affected by personal feelings or prejudices; unprejudiced: *an objective judge.* 2. real or actual; existing without regard to thought, opinion, imagination, etc. (opposite of *subjective*): *the objective facts of a case.* 3. (in grammar) belonging to the case of words or phrases used as the object of a verb or preposition. In the sentence *I saw the thief, but he did not see me, thief* and *me* are in the objective case. In the phrase *to school, school* is in the objective case. —*n.* 4. something that one intends to achieve or accomplish: *Our first objective is to build a new hospital in this town.*

5. the objective case. —**ob·jec′tive·ly,** *adv.* —**ob·jec′tive·ness,** *n.*

ob·jec·tiv·i·ty (ob′jek tiv′i tē), *n.* the state or quality of being objective or unprejudiced: *The judge was praised for the objectivity of his decisions.*

ob·li·gate (ob′lə gāt′), *v.*, **ob·li·gat·ed, ob·li·gat·ing.** to oblige or bind (someone) legally or morally: *The ruling obligated him to appear in court.*

ob·li·ga·tion (ob′lə gā′shən), *n.* 1. a legal or moral duty; something that binds one to act in a certain way: *Doctors have the obligation to try to cure their patients.* 2. a feeling of indebtedness to someone who has been helpful, kind, or the like. 3. a debt or amount of debt.

ob·lig·a·to·ry (ə blig′ə tôr′ē), *adj.* required or compulsory; morally or legally binding: *Attendance at school is obligatory for everyone under 16.*

o·blige (ə blīj′), *v.*, **o·bliged, o·blig·ing.** 1. to make necessary or require as a moral or legal duty; force: *An injury obliged him to withdraw from the race.* 2. to place under a debt of gratitude: *I am obliged to you for your help.* 3. to favor or help out: *Would you oblige me with some advice?*

o·blig·ing (ə blī′jing), *adj.* willing or eager to help, do favors, or the like. —**o·blig′ing·ly,** *adv.*

ob·lique (ə blēk′), *adj.* 1. slanting, sloping, or diagonal; neither straight up and down nor straight across: *The fireman set the ladder on an oblique line against the house.* 2. not straightforward; indirect or devious: *His remark contained an oblique criticism.* —**ob·lique′ly,** *adv.* —**ob·lique′ness,** *n.*

ob·lit·er·ate (ə blit′ə rāt′), *v.*, **ob·lit·er·at·ed, ob·lit·er·at·ing.** 1. to do away with; destroy completely: *The explosion obliterated the fort.* 2. to blot out or erase.

ob·liv·i·on (ə bliv′ē ən), *n.* 1. the state of being forgotten: *a former movie star, now in oblivion.* 2. a state of forgetting or of not being aware.

ob·liv·i·ous (ə bliv′ē əs), *adj.* 1. not aware; unmindful or unconscious (usually fol. by *of* or *to*): *When he studies, he is oblivious to his surroundings.* 2. forgetful; having no memory (usually fol. by *of*): *to be oblivious of past mistakes.* —**ob·liv′i·ous·ly,** *adv.* —**ob·liv′i·ous·ness,** *n.*

ob·long (ob′lông′), *adj.* 1. elongated, usually from a circular or square form. —*n.* 2. something having an oblong shape: *A football grid is an oblong.*

ob·lo·quy (ob′lə kwē), *n., pl.* **ob·lo·quies.** 1. shame or bad repute; public disgrace. 2. harsh or abusive criticism, esp. when used by the public against someone.

ob·nox·ious (əb nok′shəs), *adj.* extremely disagreeable or offensive; nasty; hateful: *a rude, obnoxious remark.* —**ob·nox′ious·ly,** *adv.*

Oboe

o·boe (ō′bō), *n.* a woodwind instrument having a slender, tubular body and a double reed. [from an Italian word, which comes from French *hautbois,* literally "high wood," that is, a woodwind of high pitch] —**o′bo·ist,** *n.*

ob·scene (əb sēn′), *adj.* offensive to modesty or decency; indecent; lewd.

ob·scen·i·ty (əb sen′i tē), *n., pl.* for def. 2 **ob·scen·i·ties.** 1. indecency; the quality of being offensive to modesty or decency. 2. something obscene, esp. an offensive word or expression.

ob·scure (əb skyoor′), *adj.,* **ob·scur·er, ob·scur·est.** 1. not clear, obvious, or straightforward; uncertain: *The meaning of this poem is obscure.* 2. not expressing one's meaning clearly or plainly: *an obscure writer; an obscure remark.* 3. remote or inconspicuous; not easily noticed or found: *He's visiting an obscure little fishing village.* 4. not well-known or famous: *an obscure 17th-century painter.* 5. indistinct or faint: *a dim, obscure figure in the shadows.* 6. dark or murky: *an obscure back room.* —*v.,* **ob·scured, ob·scur·ing.** 7. to cover or hide from view: *A cloud obscured the moon.* 8. to make confusing or hard to understand: *The vagueness of his language obscured whatever it was he meant to say.* —**ob·scure′ly,** *adv.* —**ob·scure·ness,** *n.*

ob·scu·ri·ty (əb skyoor′i tē), *n., pl.* for def. 2 **ob·scu·ri·ties.** 1. the state or quality of being obscure. 2. something that is obscure: *The critic discussed the obscurities in the book.*

ob·se·qui·ous (əb sē′kwē əs), *adj.* 1. of humble behavior; servile and fawning: *The king chose obsequious advisers.* 2. expressing or showing slavish humility; servile: *an obsequious bow.* —**ob·se′qui·ous·ly,** *adv.* —**ob·se′qui·ous·ness,** *n.*

ob·serv·a·ble (əb zûr′və bəl), *adj.* 1. capable of being observed; visible or noticeable: *an observable difference.* 2. worthy of being celebrated or observed: *an observable holiday.* —**ob·serv′a·bly,** *adv.*

ob·serv·ance (əb zûr′vəns), *n.* 1. the act of following or obeying: *the observance of traffic laws.* 2. a keeping or celebration of a holiday or the like: *the observance of Memorial Day.* 3. a custom, traditional practice, or ceremony: *religious observances.* 4. the act of watching or noticing; observation.

ob·serv·ant (əb zûr′vənt), *adj.* 1. watchful and alert; observing or regarding closely: *an observant and clever detective.* 2. careful in observing or following the law, rules, religious practices, or the like: *an observant Catholic.* —**ob·serv′ant·ly,** *adv.*

ob·ser·va·tion (ob′zûr vā′shən), *n.* 1. the act of observing, noticing, or watching: *They set up a telescope for the observation of ships at sea.* 2. the power or habit of observing or noticing: *to sharpen one's observation.* 3. notice or attention: *That incident escaped her observation.* 4. something that has been observed or learned in the process of observing: *He wrote me his observations on conditions in Russia.* 5. a remark, comment, or statement: *The speaker made some interesting observations.* 6. the condition of being observed or watched: *a suspect under police observation.* —**ob′ser·va′tion·al,** *adj.*

ob·serv·a·to·ry (əb zûr′və tôr′ē), *n., pl.* **ob·serv·a·to·ries.** 1. a specially designed building, usually with a

dome, that houses telescopes and other equipment for observing the moon, planets, and stars. 2. any building or institution concerned with observation.

ob·serve (əb zûrv′), *v.,* **ob·served, ob·serv·ing.** 1. to see, watch, or notice: *Did you observe anything unusual that morning?* 2. to watch carefully and note for the purposes of gathering information: *to observe changes in the tides.* 3. to remark or comment: *"It looks like rain," he observed.* 4. to obey, follow, or carry out: *to observe the law.* 5. to keep or maintain: *to observe a minute of silence.* 6. to celebrate, keep, or show regard for: *to observe a religious holiday.* —**ob·serv′er,** *n.* —**ob·serv′ing·ly,** *adv.*

ob·sess (əb ses′), *v.* to fill and rule the thoughts and feelings of (someone); trouble constantly; haunt: *Fear of being poor obsessed him.*

ob·ses·sion (əb sesh′ən), *n.* 1. an idea, desire, fear, etc., that fills and rules one's thoughts and feelings. 2. the state of being obsessed or ruled by some idea, fear, desire, or the like.

ob·sid·i·an (əb sid′ē ən), *n.* a dark, glassy rock produced by the rapid cooling of lava.

ob·so·les·cent (ob′sə les′ənt), *adj.* being or becoming obsolete; passing out of use; out-of-date. —**ob′so·les′cence,** *n.*

ob·so·lete (ob′sə lēt′, ob′sə lēt′), *adj.* 1. no longer in general use or practice: *an obsolete custom.* 2. of an old-fashioned type; out-of-date: *an obsolete make of automobile.* —**ob′so·lete′ness,** *n.*

ob·sta·cle (ob′stə kəl), *n.* something that stands in the way or interferes with progress: *Laziness is an obstacle to success.*

ob·sti·nate (ob′stə nit), *adj.* 1. stubborn and unyielding, esp. without good reason: *an obstinate refusal to study.* 2. not easily controlled or overcome: *an obstinate cough.* —**ob·sti·na·cy** (ob′stə nə sē), *n.* —**ob′sti·nate·ly,** *adv.*

ob·strep·er·ous (əb strep′ər əs), *adj.* unruly and noisy; disorderly; difficult to control: *rude, obstreperous behavior.* —**ob·strep′er·ous·ly,** *adv.* —**ob·strep′er·ous·ness,** *n.*

ob·struct (əb strukt′), *v.* 1. to block or close up (a passage, road, etc.) with an obstacle or obstacles: *A landslide obstructed the highway.* 2. to hinder or interfere with: *A bad cold obstructed his breathing.* 3. to block from sight: *A pillar obstructed his view of home plate.* —**ob·struc′tive,** *adj.*

ob·struc·tion (əb struk′shən), *n.* 1. something that obstructs; an obstacle, barrier, or hindrance: *An obstruction in the road caused a traffic jam.* 2. the act of obstructing, blocking, or interfering with something: *The obstruction of traffic is against the law.* 3. the state of being obstructed: *The obstruction of the stream was due to a fallen tree.*

ob·tain (əb tān′), *v.* 1. to get or acquire; come into possession of through one's efforts, a request, etc.: *to obtain a train schedule at the station.* 2. to be in effect or use: *The old rules still obtain.*

ob·tain·a·ble (əb tā′nə bəl), *adj.* capable of being

obtained or acquired: *Are tickets for that show still obtainable?*

ob·trude (əb trōod′), *v.*, **ob·trud·ed, ob·trud·ing. 1.** to thrust forward or force upon someone (something not wanted or needed): *to obtrude one's opinions on other people.* **2.** to intrude or interfere: *to obtrude on someone's privacy.* **3.** to thrust forth; push or stick out: *His toes obtruded from the holes in his sneakers.*

ob·tru·sive (əb trōo′siv), *adj.* **1.** tending to intrude or interfere: *a nosy, obtrusive person.* **2.** obtruding or sticking out; easy to see: *an obtrusive error in a report.* —**ob·tru′sive·ly**, *adv.* —**ob·tru′sive·ness**, *n.*

ob·tuse (əb tōos′, ob tōos′), *adj.* **1.** dull or slow in understanding, feeling, etc.: *an obtuse person who never understands a joke.* **2.** blunt or rounded; not sharp, pointed, or acute. —**ob·tuse′ly**, *adv.* —**ob·tuse′ness**, *n.*

obtuse′ an′gle, an angle greater than 90° and less than 180°.

ob·verse (ob′vûrs), *n.* **1.** the side of a coin, medal, or the like, that bears the main design (opposite of *reverse*). **2.** the front or most important side of anything. **3.** a counterpart.

ob·vi·ate (ob′vē āt′), *v.*, **ob·vi·at·ed, ob·vi·at·ing.** to prevent or do away with; avert or make unnecessary: *A letter might obviate the need for a special trip.*

ob·vi·ous (ob′vē əs), *adj.* easily seen, recognized, or understood; clear; unmistakable: *an obvious improvement in his health.* —**ob′vi·ous·ly**, *adv.* —**ob′vi·ous·ness**, *n.*

oc·a·ri·na (ok′ə rē′nə), *n.* a hollow, egg-shaped musical wind instrument with finger holes, used for playing simple tunes.

oc·ca·sion (ə kā′zhən), *n.* **1.** a particular time, esp. of a certain occurrence: *We met on three separate occasions.* **2.** a special or important time, event, celebration, etc.: *His birthday will be quite an occasion.* **3.** an opportunity or convenient time: *I'll do that on the first possible occasion.* **4.** a reason or cause: *What was the occasion for all that noise?* —*v.* **5.** to cause or bring about: *An emergency at home occasioned his leaving the office.* **6. on occasion,** now and then; occasionally: *On occasion we have a picnic in the country.*

Ocarina

oc·ca·sion·al (ə kā′zhə nəl), *adj.* **1.** occurring or appearing from time to time: *An occasional cloud drifted across the moon.* **2.** concerning or intended for a special occasion: *He likes to write birthday poems and other occasional verses.* **3.** used or done from time to time: *He does occasional jobs after school.*

oc·ca·sion·al·ly (ə kā′zhə nəlē), *adv.* at times; now and then: *She likes to go to the movies occasionally.*

Oc·ci·dent (ok′si dənt), *n.* **the, 1.** the West; the countries of Europe and America. **2.** the Western Hemisphere. [from the Latin word *occidēns* "the west, sunset," which is from *occidere* "to fall, set"] —**Oc′ci·den′tal**, *n., adj.*

oc·cult (ə kult′, ok′ult), *adj.* **1.** of or referring to magic, astrology, or other supposed sciences dealing with mysterious or supernatural powers: *a fortuneteller who claims to be skilled in occult powers.* **2.** beyond the range of ordinary knowledge; mysterious: *a supernatural, occult power.* —*n.* **3.** the realm of the supernatural (usually preceded by *the*): *a story dealing with the occult.*

oc·cu·pan·cy (ok′yə pən sē), *n., pl.* **oc·cu·pan·cies. 1.** the act or state of occupying or living in a place. **2.** a taking or having possession, esp. of property. **3.** the time during which a person is an occupant: *The furniture was damaged during your occupancy.*

oc·cu·pant (ok′yə pənt), *n.* a person who occupies, lives in, or takes space in or on something.

oc·cu·pa·tion (ok′yə pā′shən), *n.* **1.** a person's usual work or business; job or trade: *His occupation is teaching.* **2.** the act of occupying or taking possession: *The building will be repaired immediately following our occupation of it.* **3.** the seizure and control of an area, esp. a foreign land, by military force: *the Russian occupation of Hungary in 1956.* **4.** the time during which something is occupied, owned, or controlled. —**oc′cu·pa′tion·al**, *adj.*

oc·cu·py (ok′yə pī′), *v.*, **oc·cu·pied, oc·cu·py·ing. 1.** to take or fill up (space, time, etc.); take space in or on: *The guests will occupy the front row of seats. The film occupied an hour of their time.* **2.** to hold or busy (one's attention, mind, etc.): *The card game occupied him completely.* **3.** to take control of (a place) by military force: *Enemy troops occupied the city.* **4.** to be a resident or tenant of; live in: *to occupy an apartment.* **5.** to hold or have: *She occupies an important position in the city government.*

oc·cur (ə kûr′), *v.*, **oc·curred, oc·cur·ring. 1.** to happen or take place; come to pass: *When did the accident occur?* **2.** to appear or present itself; be found: *Colds occur less often in the summer.* **3.** to appear as a thought; suggest itself (usually fol. by *to*): *A better idea just occurred to me.*

oc·cur·rence (ə kûr′əns, ə kur′əns), *n.* **1.** something that occurs or happens; event; incident: *a frightening occurrence.* **2.** the action or fact of occurring or happening: *to prevent the occurrence of accidents.*

o·cean (ō′shən), *n.* **1.** the vast body of salt water that covers three fourths of the earth's surface. **2.** any one of the geographical divisions of this body of water; the Atlantic Ocean, the Pacific Ocean, the Indian Ocean, the Arctic Ocean, or the Antarctic Ocean.

o·cean·front (ō′shən frunt′), *n.* **1.** land along the shore of an ocean: *a hotel on the oceanfront.* —*adj.* **2.** located on such land: *an oceanfront resort.*

o·cean·go·ing (ō′shən gō′ing), *adj.* **1.** (of a boat, ship, etc.) designed and equipped to go on the open sea: *an ocean-going steamer.* **2.** noting or concerning sea transportation: *ocean-going traffic.*

O·ce·a·ni·a (ō′shē an′ē ə), *n.* the islands of the central and S Pacific Ocean, including Micronesia, Melanesia, and Polynesia. —**O′ce·an′i·an**, *n., adj.*

o·ce·an·ic (ō′shē an′ik), *adj.* **1.** of or concerning the ocean: *oceanic currents.* **2.** living in or produced by the ocean: *oceanic fish.* **3.** resembling an ocean in size or vastness.

o·ce·lot (os′ə lot′, ō′sə lot′), *n.* a large, spotted member of the cat family found from Texas through South America.

o·cher (ō′kər), *n.* **1.** any of various earths used as pigments and containing compounds of iron. Ochers range in color from pale yellow to orange and red. **2.** a color ranging from pale yellow to reddish yellow. —*adj.* **3.** of the color ocher. Also, **o′chre.**

Ocelot
(total length about 4 ft.)

o'clock (ə klok′), *adv.* of or by the clock (used in giving or noting the hour of the day): *The luncheon is on Friday at 12 o'clock.*

Oct., October.

octa-, a prefix meaning eight: *octagon.* Also, **octo-.**

oc·ta·gon (ok′tə gon′), *n.* a polygon with eight sides and eight angles.

oc·tag·o·nal (ok tag′ə nəl), *adj.* concerning or having the shape of an octagon. —**oc·tag′o·nal·ly,** *adv.*

oc·tave (ok′tiv), *n.* **1.** the difference in pitch between one note and the nearest note above or below it that has the same name. When two notes are an octave apart, the higher one has twice the frequency of the lower one. **2.** the musical interval between two such notes. **3.** the sound of two notes separated by this interval. **4.** all the notes within this interval. **5.** a group of eight things.

135°
Octagon
(regular)

octo-, another form of the suffix **octa-.**

Oc·to·ber (ok tō′bər), *n.* the tenth month of the year, having 31 days.

oc·to·pus (ok′tə pəs), *n., pl.* **oc·to·pus·es** *or* **oc·to·pi** (ok′tə pī′). a sea animal having a baglike body and eight long tentacles used to grasp its prey. [from the Greek word *ok-tōpous* "eight-footed"]

oc·u·lar (ok′yə lər), *adj.* **1.** of, concerning, or used by the eye or eyes. —*n.* **2.** the eyepiece of a microscope or other optical instrument.

Octopus
(tentacles 4 ft.)

oc·u·list (ok′yə list), *n.* a doctor who specializes in the examination of the eyes and in treating diseases of the eye.

odd (od), *adj.* **1.** unusual or peculiar; strange: *He was an odd little fellow with a long beard. It's odd that you don't like candy.* **2.** (of a number) not divisible by 2 without leaving a remainder, such as 1, 3, 5, etc. (opposite of *even*). **3.** close to or little more than; roughly (usually used in combination): *30-odd dollars.* **4.** being one of a pair or set; alone without the matching one: *There's an odd shoe under the sofa.* **5.** leftover or extra: *The bill was five dollars and some odd cents.* **6.** occasional or various: *a handyman who does odd jobs.* —**odd′ly,** *adv.* —**odd′ness,** *n.*

odd·i·ty (od′i tē), *n., pl.* for def. 1 **odd·i·ties.** **1.** something or someone that is odd or unusual: *A four-leaf clover is an oddity.* **2.** the quality of being odd; strangeness or peculiarity: *He was struck by the oddity of her costume.*

odds (odz), *n.* *(usually used as pl.)* **1.** the probability or chance that something is so or will happen: *The odds are that it will rain today.* **2.** a ratio of probability. "The odds are 50-50" means that one outcome is as likely as another. **3.** the ratio of probability that a contestant will win or lose a contest, esp. as shown by the betting of money. "Odds of two-to-one" means that two dollars are paid for each dollar bet. **4.** a handicap or advantage given to the weaker person or team in a contest: *We had to give them odds to make it an equal contest.* **5.** an advantage or difference favoring a contestant: *The odds are with the home team.* **6. at odds,** in disagreement; not in harmony: *My figures are at odds with yours.* **7. odds and ends,** stray or miscellaneous items; leftovers: *a box for odds and ends.*

ode (ōd), *n.* a lyric poem that expresses noble or powerful emotions.

O·des·sa (ō des′ə), *n.* a port city in the SW Soviet Union in Europe, on the Black Sea.

O·din (ō′din), *n.* (in Scandinavian mythology) the god of war, poetry, and wisdom; Wotan.

o·di·ous (ō′dē əs), *adj.* deserving or causing hatred or disgust; detestable; loathsome: *an odious crime.* —**o′di·ous·ly,** *adv.* —**o′di·ous·ness,** *n.*

o·di·um (ō′dē əm), *n.* **1.** hatred or strong dislike: *to regard violence with odium.* **2.** the disgrace or blame associated with something hateful or evil: *the odium of being known as a traitor.*

o·dor (ō′dər), *n.* a scent or smell: *the odor of cooking; the sweet odor of perfume.* Also, *esp. British,* **o′dour.** —**o′dor·less,** *adj.*

o·dor·if·er·ous (ō′də rif′ər əs), *adj.* giving off an odor, esp. a fragrant one: *odoriferous blossoms.* —**o′dor·if′er·ous·ly,** *adv.*

o·dor·ous (ō′dər əs), *adj.* having an odor; odoriferous.

O·dys·se·us (ō dis′ē əs), *n.* (in Greek mythology) a wise king of Ithaca and a leader in the Trojan War.

Od·ys·sey (od′i sē), *n.* an epic poem by Homer, describing the adventures of Odysseus during his ten-year attempt to return home to Ithaca after the Trojan War.

Oed·i·pus (ed′ə pəs, ē′də pəs), *n.* (in Greek mythology) a king of Thebes who unwittingly murdered his father and married his mother.

o'er (ôr), *prep., adv.* another form of **over:** used esp. in poetry.

of (uv, ov), *prep.* **1.** from or away from (used to indicate direction or distance): *south of Chicago.* **2.** by or coming from (used to indicate source or origin): *the plays of Shakespeare.* **3.** from or owing to (used to indicate cause, motive, reason, etc.): *to die of hunger.* **4.** containing or having: *a pitcher of milk.* **5.** made with or consisting of: *a dress of silk.* **6.** so as to be rid of or left without: *to be cured of a bad habit; to be robbed of one's money.* **7.** named (used to indicate identity): *the city of Berlin.* **8.** belonging to or living in: *the hem of a dress; the wildlife of the desert.* **9.** (used to indicate inclusion with a group or larger whole): *Is she one of your friends? Is he of the royal family?* **10.** ruling or possessing: *the king of Spain; the owner of the ranch.* **11.** possessed or ruled by: *the property of the government.* **12.** having particular qualities or attributes: *a man of courage.* **13.** about or concerning: *There is talk of peace.* **14.** before or until: *twenty minutes of five.* **15.** set aside for or devoted to: *a minute of prayer.* **16.** on the part of: *It was mean of you to tease him.* **17.** (used to indicate the object of action following a noun or adjective): *the ringing of bells; tired of working.* —**Usage.** See **off.**

off (ôf, of), *adv.* **1.** so as to be no longer attached or supported: *One of my buttons fell off.* **2.** so as to be no longer covering or enclosing: *Take your hat off.* **3.** away from a place, path, course, etc.: *The dog ran off.* **4.** at a distance in space or in the future: *They live two blocks off.* **5.** so as to be discontinued or stopped: *Negotiations have been broken off.* **6.** so as not to be running or operating: *Switch the engine off.* **7.** so as to be less or lower than usual in price, volume, effectiveness, etc.: *Business dropped off this week.* **8.** in absence from work, service, school, etc.: *We get ten days off at Christmas.* **9.** so as to be away or on one's way: *to start off early.* **10.** so as to be divided or separated: *Mark your paper off into three equal parts.* **11.** so as to lose consciousness: *to doze off.* —*prep.* **12.** so as to be no longer attached to, supported by, or covering; away from: *Take the tablecloth off the table.* **13.** away from; turned aside from: *to fly off course.* **14.** below or less than the usual price, volume, standard, etc.: *25 percent off the marked price.* **15.** away from; so as to be free of: *to go off duty.* **16.** away or distant from: *a village off the main road.* **17.** leading into or away from: *an alley off 12th Street.* **18.** at the expense of: *She lives off her parents.* —*adj.* **19.** in error; wrong: *Your addition is off there.* **20.** less or lower: *Business is off this week.* **21.** absent or excused from work or duty: *How do you spend your off hours?* **22.** missing or removed: *One of my buttons is off.* **23.** not running or operating: *Are the lights off?* **24.** canceled or not in effect: *Our agreement is off.* **25.** in a particular state, circumstance, etc.: *to be badly off for money.* **26.** slight or distant: *an off chance that it will rain.* **27.** more distant; farther: *the off side of a wall.* **28.** starting or beginning a trip, errand, outing, etc.: *I'm off to Europe on Monday.* —*interj.* **29.** get away! get down! be off! **30. be off,** depart; leave: *I must be off now.* **31. off and on,** once in a while; now and then: *I worked off and on while I was in school.* —**Usage.** Although *off* is sometimes followed by *of* in informal writing and speaking, such usage is incor-

rect and should be avoided. *Off,* without *of,* is sufficient to express the same idea: *John fell off* (not *off of*) *the ladder.*

of·fal (ô′fəl), *n.* the parts of a butchered animal that are considered unfit for humans to eat.

of·fend (ə fend′), *v.* **1.** to cause displeasure or anger in (someone); hurt or annoy: *Your rudeness offended my mother.* **2.** to be disagreeable to (the senses, good taste, etc.): *Her awful singing offends the ear.* **3.** to do wrong or cause displeasure: *Try not to offend.*

of·fend·er (ə fen′dər), *n.* **1.** a person who offends or causes displeasure. **2.** one who commits an offense.

of·fense (ə fens′, or, esp. for defs. 4, 5, ô′fens), *n.* **1.** a breaking of a law or rule; crime, sin, or fault: *a traffic offense.* **2.** something that offends or displeases: *That junkyard is an offense to the town.* **3.** a feeling of displeasure or resentful anger: *His insults gave offense to everyone.* **4.** attack or assault: *weapons used for offense.* **5.** a person, side, team, etc., that attacks: *Our offense is stronger than our defense.*

of·fen·sive (ə fen′siv, ô′fen siv), *adj.* **1.** causing displeasure or anger: *insulting, offensive behavior.* **2.** unpleasant or disagreeable to the senses: *an offensive smell.* **3.** of or referring to attack or assault: *offensive weapons.* —*n.* **4.** an attack or position of attack: *The allies were ready to take the offensive.* —**of·fen′sive·ly,** *adv.* —**of·fen′sive·ness,** *n.*

of·fer (ô′fər), *v.* **1.** to present for acceptance if wanted: *to offer a cracker to a parrot.* **2.** to put forward or propose: *to offer a suggestion.* **3.** to express willingness to give or perform; volunteer: *to offer to help someone.* **4.** to present solemnly as an act of worship: *to offer prayers to God.* **5.** to present for sale: *to offer one's furniture at a good price.* —*n.* **6.** the act of offering: *Thank you for your offer of help.* **7.** something that is offered, put forward, or volunteered: *I wish we could accept your offer.* **8.** a proposal of marriage. **9.** a statement of a price one is willing to pay; bid: *an offer at an auction.*

of·fer·ing (ô′fər ĭng), *n.* **1.** something that is offered as an act of worship or as a gift or contribution: *generous offerings for a worthy cause.* **2.** the act of someone who offers: *the offering of gifts.*

of·fer·to·ry (ô′fər tôr′ē), *n., pl.* **of·fer·to·ries. 1.** (*sometimes cap.*) the offering to God of unconsecrated bread and wine during a Mass or communion service. **2.** the part of a church service at which offerings are made by the congregation. **3.** the prayers or music used during this part of the service.

off·hand (ôf′hand′, of′-), *adv.* **1.** without previous thought or preparation: *to speak offhand.* —*adj.* **2.** Also, **off′hand′ed.** done or made without previous thought or preparation: *some offhand answers.* **3.** casual or brusque: *an offhand manner.* —**off′hand′ed·ly,** *adv.* —**off′hand′ed·ness,** *n.*

of·fice (ô′fis), *n.* **1.** a place where business is carried on or professional services are available: *the office of a shipping line; a doctor's office.* **2.** the people working in a particular place of business: *a party for the whole office.* **3.** a position of duty, trust, or high authority: *the office of president.* **4.** the duties or services associated with a particular job or position: *to act in the office of adviser.* **5.** Often, **offices.** something done or said for or to someone, esp. as a favor: *the good offices of a friend.* **6.** a church service. [from the Latin word *officium* "service, duty"]

Of·fice (ô′fis), *n.* **1.** an agency or division of certain departments of the federal government: *the Office of Economic Opportunity.* **2.** (esp. in Britain) a major administrative division of the government: *the Foreign Office.*

of·fi·cer (ô′fi sər), *n.* **1.** a person appointed to a position of authority or command in the armed services, esp. one holding a commission. **2.** a person appointed or elected to a position of authority in an organization, public service, etc.: *a police officer.*

of·fi·cial (ə fish′əl), *n.* **1.** a person holding a position of authority in an organization, esp. in the government: *a tax official.* —*adj.* **2.** of or concerning a position of authority: *official duties.* **3.** appointed, authorized, or approved by an organization or the government: *an official investigator.* **4.** formal and public: *an official ceremony.* —**of·fi′cial·ly,** *adv.*

of·fi·ci·ate (ə fish′ē āt′), *v.,* **of·fi·ci·at·ed, of·fi·ci·at·ing. 1.** to perform the duties of some office or position: *The chairman officiated at the meeting.* **2.** to perform the duties of a priest or minister: *to officiate at Mass.*

of·fi·cious (ə fish′əs), *adj.* too forward in offering help or advice; interfering; meddling: *an officious busybody.* —**of·fi′cious·ly,** *adv.* —**of·fi′cious·ness,** *n.*

off·ing (ô′fing, of′ing), *n.* **1.** the more distant part of the sea as seen from the shore. **2.** a location or position at a distance from the shore. **3. in the offing,** a. at a distance but within sight. b. planned or likely to happen: *Some changes are in the offing.*

off·set (ôf′set′, of′-), *v.* **1.** to compensate or make up for: *Our team's strong pitching should offset our weak hitting.* **2.** to set (something) next to something else, for comparison or the like: *to offset gains against losses.* —*n.* (ôf′set′, of′-). **3.** something that compensates or makes up for something else: *She wants to get an A as an offset to that D.* **4.** a part that branches off from the main part, as of a plant, road, pipe, etc. **5.** a printing process in which an inked plate is used to make an impression on a roll of rubber and is transferred from this to paper.

off·shoot (ôf′shoot′, of′-), *n.* **1.** a branch or shoot growing from the main stem of a plant. **2.** something that proceeds from or has developed from something else; branch: *an offshoot of a business.*

off·shore (ôf′shôr′, of′-), *adv.* **1.** off or away from the shore; at a distance from the shore: *to fish offshore.* —*adj.* **2.** moving or tending away from the shore; moving from land toward water: *an offshore breeze.* **3.** located or carried on at some distance from the shore: *offshore oil.*

off·side (ôf′sīd′, of′-), *adv., adj.* (in sports) illegally beyond a particular line or in advance of the ball or puck that is in play: *to run offside.*

off·spring (ôf′spring′, of′-), *n., pl.* **off·spring** *or* **off·springs.** the children or young of a person or any living thing; descendant, or descendants as a group.

off-the-cuff (ôf′thə kuf′, of′-), *adj.* done or said offhand; impromptu: *off-the-cuff remarks.*

oft (ôft), *adv.* another form of **often:** used esp. in poetry.

of·ten (ô′fən), *adv.* many times; frequently: *Did you go to the beach often this summer?*

of·ten·times (ô′fən tīmz′), *adv.* often; many times.

oft·times (ôft′tīmz′, ôf′-), *adv.* another form of **oftentimes:** used esp. in poetry.

o·gle (ō′gəl), *v.,* **o·gled, o·gling.** to look or stare at (someone or something) greedily or with desire: *She couldn't help ogling the diamonds on display.*

o·gre (ō′gər), *n.* **1.** (in legends and fairy tales) an ugly monster, usually a giant, that eats human flesh. **2.** any very ugly or brutal person.

oh (ō), *interj.* **1.** (used as an expression of surprise, pain, disapproval, etc.): *Oh, how could you have made such a mess?* **2.** (used to attract the attention of someone): *Oh, John, will you take these books, please?*

O·hi·o (ō hī′ō), *n.* **1.** a state in the NE central United States. 41,222 sq. mi. *Cap.:* Columbus. **2.** a river flowing SW from Pennsylvania to the Mississippi River in S Illinois. 981 mi. long. —**O·hi′o·an,** *n., adj.*

ohm (ōm), *n.* a unit of electrical resistance. When a potential of one volt causes a current of one ampere to flow in a circuit, the resistance of the circuit is one ohm. [named after Georg Simon *Ohm* (1787–1854), German physicist]

-oid, a suffix used to form **1.** adjectives meaning like or resembling: *Mongoloid.* **2.** nouns meaning something like or resembling: *planetoid.*

oil (oil), *n.* **1.** any of numerous greasy liquids that do not mix with water: *linseed oil; whale oil.* **2.** another name for **petroleum.** —*v.* **3.** to apply oil to; cover with oil: *to oil a squeaky hinge.*

oil·cloth (oil′klôth′), *n., pl.* **oil·cloths** (oil′klôthz′, -klôths′). **1.** a cotton fabric made waterproof by treatment with oil and pigment, for use as tablecloths, shelf coverings, and the like. **2.** a piece of this fabric, used as a tablecloth, etc.

oil′ well′, a well that yields petroleum.

oil·y (oi′lē), *adj.,* **oil·i·er, oil·i·est. 1.** full of or made with oil: *an oily face cream.* **2.** covered with or soaked in oil: *an oily rag.* **3.** of or like oil. **4.** too smooth in manner or speech: *an oily salesman.* —**oil′i·ness,** *n.*

oint·ment (oint′mənt), *n.* a soft, soothing, usually medicated preparation for the skin.

---

act, āble, dâre, ärt; ebb, ēqual; if, īce; hot, ōver, ôrder; oil; book; ooze; out; up, ûrge; ə = *a* as in *alone;* ə as in *button* (but′ən), *fire* (fīər); chief; shoe; thin; ŧħat; zh as in *measure* (mezh′ər). See full key inside cover.

O.K. (ō′kā′, ō′kā′), *adj., adv.* **1.** all right; all correct or satisfactory: *O.K., I'll get it for you. Everything is O.K.* —*v.,* **O.K.'d, O.K.'ing. 2.** to approve by saying or writing "O.K.": *to O.K. a plan.* —*n., pl.* **O.K.'s. 3.** an approval or agreement: *We have to get my mother's O.K. for the party.* Also, **okay.**

o·ka·pi (ō kä′pē), *n., pl.* **o·ka·pis** *or* **o·ka·pi.** an African animal related to the giraffe but smaller and having a much shorter neck.

o·kay (ō′kā′, ō′kā′), *adj., adv., v., n.* another spelling of **O.K.**

O·khotsk (ō kotsk′), *n.* **Sea of,** an arm of the N Pacific Ocean, E of the Soviet Union in Asia. 582,000 sq. mi.

O·ki·na·wa (ō′kə nä′wə), *n.* an island in the N Pacific Ocean, SW of Japan: occupied by the U.S. 1945–1972; returned to Japan 1972. 544 sq. mi. —**O′ki·na′wan,** *n., adj.*

Okla., Oklahoma.

O·kla·ho·ma (ō′klə hō′mə), *n.* a state in the S central United States. 69,919 sq. mi. *Cap.:* Oklahoma City. —**O′kla·ho′man,** *n., adj.*

O′klaho′ma Cit′y, the capital city of Oklahoma, in the central part.

o·kra (ō′krə), *n.* a shrub that bears long, green pods eaten as a vegetable and used in soups, stews, etc.; gumbo. [from a West African language]

old (ōld), *adj.,* **old·er** *or* **eld·er** (el′dər); **old·est** *or* **eld·est** (el′dist). **1.** far advanced in years; having lived or existed for a long time: *My grandfather is very old.* **2.** appearing to be advanced in years: *Worry has made her old.* **3.** having lived or existed for a certain length of time: *a man 30 years old.* **4.** belonging to the past: *the good old days.* **5.** belonging to the historical or very distant past. **6.** having been such for a long time; longstanding: *an old friend.* **7.** used or worn out; not new: *I can't wear this old coat any more.* —*n.* **8.** *(used as pl.)* old persons: *care for the old.* **9.** a person or animal of a particular age or age group (used in combination): *a class for six-year-olds.* **10. of old,** in or of the past: *the days of old.*

Old′ Del′hi, another name for **Delhi.**

old·en (ōl′d^ən), *adj.* old or ancient; of or concerning the distant past: used esp. in literature.

Old′ Eng′lish, the English language as spoken and written from about 450 to 1150. Also, **Anglo-Saxon.**

old·er (ōl′dər), *adj.* a comparative of **old.**

—**Usage.** *Older* is the usual form of the comparative of *old: This building is older than that one. Elder* is used chiefly to indicate the older of two children, esp. those born of the same parents: *The elder brother became king.*

old·est (ōl′dist), *adj.* a superlative of **old.**

—**Usage.** *Oldest* is the usual form of the superlative of *old: This church is the oldest one in town. Eldest* is used chiefly to indicate the oldest of three or more children, esp. those born of the same parents: *The eldest daughter became a nurse.*

old-fash·ioned (ōld′fash′ənd), *adj.* **1.** no longer customary or in style; out-of-date: *an old-fashioned car.* **2.** attached to ways or customs that are considered out-of-date: *an old-fashioned doctor.*

Old′ French′, the French language as spoken and written from about 800 to 1400.

Old′ Glo′ry, another name for **Stars and Stripes.**

old·ish (ōl′dish), *adj.* slightly old or out-of-date.

old′ maid′, **1.** a woman who has never married and is no longer young; spinster. **2.** one who is fussy, prudish, etc.

Old′ Norse′. See **Norse** (def. 6).

Old′ Tes′tament, the first of the two main parts of the Bible, regarded as the complete Bible of the Jews, containing the laws of Moses, the history of the Hebrews, and the writings of the prophets.

old-tim·er (ōld′tī′mər), *n.* **1.** a person who has long been established in a particular line of work, area of residence, etc.: *He is an old-timer with long experience.* **2.** an old or elderly person.

Old′ World′, **1.** Europe, Asia, and Africa. **2.** the Eastern Hemisphere. —**old′-world′,** *adj.*

o·le·an·der (ō′lē an′dər, ō lē an′dər), *n.* a poisonous evergreen plant having pink or white flowers.

o·le·o·mar·ga·rine (ō′lē ō mär′jə rin), *n.* another name for **margarine.**

ol·fac·to·ry (ol fak′tə rē), *adj.* of or concerning the sense of smell: *The nose is an olfactory organ.*

ol·i·gar·chy (ol′ə gär′kē), *n., pl.* **ol·i·gar·chies.** a form of government in which the power is controlled by a small group of persons. —**ol′i·gar′chic,** *adj.*

ol·ive (ol′iv), *n.* **1.** an evergreen tree that grows in warm climates and bears a small rounded fruit that is preserved in brine as a relish or pressed to extract its valuable oil. **2.** the fruit itself. **3.** a dull yellow-green. —*adj.* **4.** of or concerning olives. **5.** of the color olive.

ol′ive branch′, **1.** a branch of the olive tree used as an emblem of peace. **2.** anything offered as a token of peace.

ol′ive oil′, the oil from the olive fruit, used in cooking, salad dressings, medicines, etc.

O·lym·pi·a (ō lim′pē ə), *n.* **1.** the capital city of Washington, in the W part. **2.** a plain in ancient Greece where the Olympic Games were held.

O·lym·pi·an (ō lim′pē ən), *adj.* **1.** of or concerning Mount Olympus or the gods that dwelt there: *the Olympian deities of Greek mythology.* **2.** like or characteristic of the gods or goddesses of Olympus: *an Olympian manner.* **3.** of or concerning Olympia or the Olympic Games; Olympic. —*n.* **4.** a god or goddess of Mount Olympus. **5.** an athlete competing in the Olympic Games.

O·lym·pic (ō lim′pik), *adj.* **1.** of or concerning the Olympic Games: *Olympic competition.* **2.** of or concerning Mount Olympus or its gods and goddesses.

Olym′pic Games′, **1.** the greatest of the games or

festivals of ancient Greece, held every four years in honor of Zeus. **2.** a modern revival of these games consisting of contests for amateur athletes from all nations. The Olympic Games are held every four years, each time in a different country. Also, **Olym′pics.**

O·lym·pus (ō lim′pəs), *n.* **Mount,** a mountain in NE Greece, on the boundary between Thessaly and Macedonia: mythical home of the greater Greek gods and goddesses. 9730 ft.

O·ma·ha (ō′mə hô′, ō′mə hä′), *n.* a city in E Nebraska.

O·man (ō män′), *n.* a country in SE Arabia. 82,-000 sq. mi. *Cap.:* Muscat.

om·buds·man (ôm′bŏŏdz man′), *n., pl.* **om·buds-men.** a public official, originally in Scandinavia, who investigates citizens' complaints against government officials or agencies.

o·me·ga (ō mē′gə, ō mā′gə), *n.* **1.** the 24th, and last, letter of the Greek alphabet. **2.** the last of any series; the end. See also **alpha.**

om·e·let (om′ə lit, om′lit), *n.* eggs beaten until frothy, then cooked, often with cheese, ham, etc.

o·men (ō′mən), *n.* an event believed to be a sign of something good or bad to follow: *She believes that it's a bad omen if a black cat crosses your path.*

om·i·nous (om′ə nəs), *adj.* being a sign of bad luck, evil, harm, danger, etc.; threatening: *ominous storm clouds.* **—om′i·nous·ly,** *adv.* **—om′i·nous·ness,** *n.*

o·mis·sion (ō mish′ən), *n.* **1.** the act of omitting, leaving out, or failing to do something: *the omission of a name from a list.* **2.** something omitted, left out, or not done: *There are several omissions in this list.*

o·mit (ō mit′), *v.,* **o·mit·ted, o·mit·ting.** **1.** to leave out; neglect to include or mention: *He accidentally omitted his return address.* **2.** to fail to do, make, use, etc.; neglect: *She omitted to thank her hostess.*

om·ni·bus (om′nə bus′), *n., pl.* **om·ni·bus·es. 1.** a volume of reprinted works of one author or of works on one subject or of one type: *an omnibus of mystery stories.* **2.** a bus. **—adj. 3.** dealing with numerous objects or items: *Congress passed an omnibus bill on housing.* [from a Latin word meaning "for all"]

om·nip·o·tent (om nip′ə t∂nt), *adj.* unlimited in power; all-powerful; almighty: *an omnipotent god.* **—om·nip′o·tence,** *n.* **—om·nip′o·tent·ly,** *adv.*

om·nis·cient (om nish′ənt), *adj.* having infinite knowledge; knowing all things: *an omniscient god.* **—om·nis′cience,** *n.* **—om·nis′cient·ly,** *adv.*

om·niv·or·ous (om niv′ər əs), *adj.* **1.** eating both plant and animal foods. See also **carnivorous, herbivorous. 2.** eating all kinds of food: *an omnivorous fat man.* **3.** taking in everything, esp. with the mind: *an omnivorous reader.* **—om·niv′or·ous·ly,** *adv.*

on (on, ôn), *prep.* **1.** so as to be supported by: *a hat on a hook.* **2.** attached to or hung from: *the leaves on a tree.* **3.** over or around; so as to be a covering or wrapping for: *Put a blanket on the baby.* **4.** with or among; so as to be associated with: *to play on a team.* **5.** (used to indicate place, location, etc.): *a scar on the face.* **6.** next to or near: *a house on the ocean.* **7.** in the direction of; along: *to go on one's way.* **8.** at the time or occasion of: *The store demands cash on delivery.* **9.** by means of; using: *We coasted on our sleds.* **10.** with respect or regard to; concerning: *to write a book on horses.* **11.** in a condition or process of: *The house is on fire!* **12.** (used to indicate a source): *She depends on her father for money.* **13.** (used to indicate a basis for support or authority): *to swear on one's word of honor.* **14.** subject to: *a doctor on call.* **15.** occupied with; responsible for: *I'm on the switchboard tonight.* **16.** (used to indicate the object of an action, thought, emotion, etc.): *to have mercy on a sinner.* **17.** (used to indicate a meeting or encounter): *to happen on an old friend.* **—adv. 18.** in or into a position of being supported or attached: *Load the suitcases on now.* **19.** in or into a position of covering or wrapping: *Put your clothes on.* **20.** fast or tight to a thing, as for support: *Hold on!* **21.** toward a place, point, activity, etc.: *to look on while others work.* **22.** forward, onward, or along: *Go on now.* **23.** with continuous activity; continuously: *We worked on till late at night.* **24.** in or into operation: *Turn the gas on.* **—adj. 25.** operating or in use: *The radio is on.* **26.** taking place: *There's a war on.* **27. on and on,** so long as to be boring or tiresome.

on·a·ger (on′ə jər), *n.* a wild ass of southwestern Asia.

once (wuns), *adv.* **1.** formerly; at one time in the past: *Once there were Indians living here.* **2.** a single time; one time: *He goes there once a week.* **3.** formerly; at one time having been so: *a once handsome man.* **—conj. 4.** when or if ever: *Once you learn it, you'll never forget it.* **5.** as soon as: *They'll quiet down once the movie starts.* **6. all at once,** suddenly; unexpectedly: *All at once a storm came up.* **7. at once,** immediately; without delay: *Phone him at once.* **8. once in a while,** occasionally; from time to time: *He stops by once in a while.* **9. once upon a time,** at some indefinite time in the distant past.

on·com·ing (on′kum′ing, ôn′-), *adj.* **1.** approaching or nearing: *an oncoming train.* **—n. 2.** approach or onset: *the oncoming of winter.*

one (wun), *n.* **1.** the first and lowest whole number; the number 1. **—adj. 2.** being or amounting to a single person or thing. **3.** being one of a kind: *You are the one person I can trust.* **4.** shared by or common to all: *They shouted with one voice.* **5.** a certain (used in referring to someone who is not known or otherwise described): *One John Smith was chosen.* **—pron. 6.** some indefinite person, used as a typical example: *One could not ask for more.* **7.** a person or thing: *He's a quiet one.* **8.** a person or thing of a certain number or kind: *one of the boys.* **9. one and all,**

everyone: *They arrived, one and all, to congratulate the new president.* **10. one by one,** one person or thing at a time, appearing or happening in a series: *One by one the children got their presents.*

one·ness (wun**′**nis), *n.* **1.** the quality of being one. **2.** unity, agreement, or sameness: *They were brought together by their oneness of purpose.*

one·self (wun self**′**, wunz-), *pron.* **1.** a person's own self: *One can hurt oneself playing football.* **2. be oneself, a.** to be sincere and unaffected: *You don't have to behave in any special way, just be yourself.* **b.** to be in one's normal state of mind or physical condition: *She hasn't been herself all winter.* **3. by oneself, a.** without a companion; alone. **b.** without assistance from anyone: *Can't he eat by himself?*

one-sid·ed (wun**′**sī**′**did), *adj.* considering or favoring just one side of a question or issue; biased: *His one-sided view of the case was very unfair.* —**one′-sid′ed·ly,** *adv.* —**one′-sid′ed·ness,** *n.*

one-way (wun**′**wā**′**), *adj.* moving, or allowing movement, in one direction only: *a one-way street.*

on·ion (un**′**yən), *n.* the round bulb of a plant related to the lily, having a strong smell and taste, eaten as a vegetable and used in cooking to flavor other foods.

on·look·er (on**′**look**′**ər, ôn**′**-), *n.* a person who watches; spectator: *a crowd of onlookers at the fire.*

on·ly (ōn**′**lē), *adv.* **1.** with no other one or anything else besides: *Only he remained.* **2.** no more than; merely; just: *We go there only on weekends.* **3.** as recently as: *I saw him only yesterday.* —*adj.* **4.** being the single one: *He was the only person in the room.* **5.** alone because of some special quality; unique: *the only kind of dog I want.* —*conj.* **6.** except that: *I would have gone, only you objected.* **7. only too,** extremely; very: *I am only too happy to go.*

on·rush (on**′**rush**′**, ôn**′**-), *n.* a strong forward rush.

on·set (on**′**set**′**, ôn**′**-), *n.* **1.** a beginning or start: *the onset of winter.* **2.** an assault or attack.

on·shore (on**′**shôr**′**, ôn**′**-), *adv.* **1.** onto or in the direction of the shore. —*adj.* **2.** moving or going toward shore or onto land. **3.** located on or close to the shore: *an onshore lighthouse.*

on·slaught (on**′**slôt**′**, ôn**′**-), *n.* a vigorous or furious onset, assault, or attack.

Ont., Ontario (Canada).

On·tar·i·o (on târ**′**ē ō**′**), *n.* **1.** a province in S Canada, bordering on the Great Lakes. 412,582 sq. mi. *Cap.:* Toronto. **2. Lake,** a lake between the NE United States and S Canada: the smallest of the Great Lakes. 7540 sq. mi.

on·to (on**′**tōo, ôn**′**tōo), *prep.* **1.** to a place or position upon; on: *to get onto a horse.* **2.** *Informal.* well-informed about; aware of: *I'm onto your little tricks.*

on·ward (on**′**wərd, ôn**′**-), *adv.* **1.** toward or at a position or point ahead or in front: *to walk onward.* —*adj.* **2.** directed or moving onward or forward: *an onward march.* Also, **on′wards.**

on·yx (on**′**iks), *n.* **1.** a hard, glassy stone having straight bands of various colors, used in jewelry. **2.** a similar stone all of one color, esp. black.

ooze¹ (ōoz), *v.,* **oozed, ooz·ing. 1.** to flow or pass slowly through holes or small openings. **2.** to disappear slowly: *His courage oozed away.* [from the Old English word *wōs* "juice, moisture"]

ooze² (ōoz), *n.* **1.** mud composed chiefly of the shells of small organisms, covering parts of the ocean bottom. **2.** soft mud, or slime. [from the Old English word *wāse* "mud"]

o·pal (ō**′**pəl), *n.* a gem, usually white but sometimes almost black, that appears to flash with bright, iridescent colors as it is turned.

o·pal·es·cent (ō**′**pə les**′**ənt), *adj.* having a variety and movement of colors like that of the opal.

o·paque (ō pāk**′**), *adj.* **1.** not transparent or translucent; not allowing light to pass through. **2.** not shining or bright; dark; dull. **3.** hard to understand; not clear. —**o·paque′ly,** *adv.* —**o·paque′ness,** *n.*

ope (ōp), *adj., v.* an old form of **open.**

OPEC (ō**′**pek), *n.* Organization of Petroleum Exporting Countries.

o·pen (ō**′**pən), *adj.* **1.** not closed, barred, or shut: *an open window; an open drawer.* **2.** set so as to permit passage through the opening it otherwise closes: *an open door.* **3.** built or constructed so as not to be fully enclosed: *an open boat.* **4.** not occupied by buildings, fences, trees, etc.: *open country.* **5.** extended or unfolded: *an open newspaper.* **6.** without restrictions as to who may participate: *an open contest.* **7.** available or accessible: *Which job is open? The store is open on Saturday.* **8.** not shy or reserved; frank: *an open person.* **9.** not biased or prejudiced: *an open mind.* —*v.* **10.** to make or become open: *Open your book. The door opened suddenly.* **11.** to give access to or be connected with a place: *This door opens onto a garden.* **12.** to commence or begin: *When does school open?* **13.** to clear of obstructions: *to open a road.* **14.** to make accessible or available: *to open a port for trade.* —*n.* **15.** an open or clear space. **16.** a contest or tournament in which both amateurs and professionals may compete. **17. the open, a.** out of doors, esp. the unenclosed or unobstructed country: *If the weather is nice, we'll have a party in the open.* **b.** the fact or condition of being generally known or made public: *The scandal is now in the open.* —**o′pen·ly,** *adv.* —**o′pen·ness,** *n.*

o′pen air′, the unconfined atmosphere; outdoors. —**o′pen-air′,** *adj.*

o·pen·er (ō**′**pə nər), *n.* **1.** a person or thing that opens. **2.** a device for opening sealed containers: *a can opener.*

o·pen-eyed (ō**′**pən īd**′**), *adj.* **1.** having the eyes open. **2.** having the eyes wide open, as in wonder: *open-eyed amazement.* **3.** watchful, alert, or cautious.

o·pen-hand·ed (ō**′**pən han**′**did), *adj.* generous or liberal. Also, **o′pen·hand′ed.** —**o′pen-hand′ed·ly,** *adv.* —**o′pen-hand′ed·ness,** *n.*

o′pen house′, 1. a party or a time during which a person's home is open to a large group of friends and relatives. **2.** a time during which a school, institution, etc., is open to the public.

o·pen·ing (ō**′**pə ning), *n.* **1.** the act or an instance of making or becoming open. **2.** a gap, hole, or the like, in solid material: *We couldn't find an opening in the wall.* **3.** the first part or beginning of anything. **4.** an unfilled position or job: *There are several openings in the company.* **5.** an opportunity.

o·pen-mind·ed (ō′pən mīn′did), *adj.* having or showing a mind open to new ideas or arguments. —**o′pen-mind′ed·ly,** *adv.* —**o′pen-mind′ed·ness,** *n.*

o·pen·work (ō′pən wûrk′), *n.* any kind of ornamental work showing openings in its design, for example work in metal, wood, or lace.

op·er·a (op′ər ə, op′rə), *n.* a play, usually serious, set to music, with all or most of the words sung to the accompaniment of an orchestra. [from an Italian word meaning "work, opera"]

op′era glass′es, a small, low-power set of binoculars for use at the theater, the opera, etc.

op·er·ate (op′ə rāt′), *v.,* **op·er·at·ed, op·er·at·ing. 1.** to work, perform, or function: *The machine operates well.* **2.** to manage or use: *to operate a machine.* **3.** to put or keep in operation: *He operates a ranch.* **4.** to perform surgery.

op·er·at·ic (op′ə rat′ik), *adj.* **1.** of, referring to, or like opera. **2.** suitable for opera: *an operatic voice.*

op·er·a·tion (op′ə rā′shən), *n.* **1.** the act, process, or manner of functioning or operating: *to watch the operation of a printing press.* **2.** the state of something that operates or is in effect: *a rule no longer in operation.* **3.** a military campaign or action. **4.** a medical treatment or procedure involving surgery.

op·er·a·tive (op′ə rā′tiv, op′ər ə tiv), *adj.* **1.** operating, or exerting force or influence: *My flashlight is not operative.* **2.** being in effect or operation: *laws that are operative in this city.* —*n.* **3.** a person engaged in some branch of work, esp. industrial work. **4.** *Informal.* **a.** a detective. **b.** a secret agent or spy.

op·er·a·tor (op′ə rā′tər), *n.* **1.** a person who operates a machine, apparatus, or the like. **2.** a person who operates a telephone switchboard. **3.** a person who owns or manages an industrial establishment.

op·er·et·ta (op′ə ret′ə), *n.* a light, amusing opera, esp. one in which there is speech as well as singing.

o·pi·ate (ō′pē it, ō′pē āt′), *n.* **1.** a drug containing opium that induces sleep or relieves pain. **2.** any drug with similar properties. **3.** anything that soothes or dulls the mind.

o·pine (ō pīn′), *v.,* **o·pined, o·pin·ing.** to hold or express an opinion.

o·pin·ion (ə pin′yən), *n.* **1.** a belief or judgment of which a person may not be absolutely certain. **2.** the expression of a personal attitude or judgment: *to give an opinion on the elections.* **3.** the expression of a formal or professional judgment: *They've called in another doctor for an opinion.*

o·pin·ion·at·ed (ə pin′yə nā′tid), *adj.* stubborn or conceited with regard to one's opinions.

o·pi·um (ō′pē əm), *n.* the thickened juice of a certain kind of poppy, containing a number of substances that induce sleep and relieve pain, but which are dangerous and habit-forming. [from a Latin word,

which comes from Greek *opion* "poppy juice"]

o·pos·sum (ə pos′əm, pos′əm), *n., pl.* **o·pos·sum.** a small animal of the eastern U.S. that lives mostly in trees and can grasp the branches with its tail. The female has a pouch in which she carries her young. Opossums pretend to be dead when they sense danger. [from Algonquian]

Opossum
(total length 3 ft.)

op·po·nent (ə pō′nənt), *n.* a person who is on an opposing side in a contest, dispute, or the like.

op·por·tune (op′ər tōōn′, -tyōōn′), *adj.* appropriate, favorable, or suitable: *an opportune time to buy a car.* —**op′por·tune′ly,** *adv.*

op·por·tun·ist (op′ər tōō′nist, -tyōō′-), *n.* a person who uses opportunities without concern for moral principles. —**op′por·tun′ism,** *n.*

op·por·tu·ni·ty (op′ər tōō′ni tē, -tyōō′-), *n., pl.* **op·por·tu·ni·ties. 1.** a favorable time or occasion: *an opportunity to go skiing.* **2.** a good position, chance, or prospect for self-advancement.

op·pose (ə pōz′), *v.,* **op·posed, op·pos·ing. 1.** to be or act in opposition to; resist: *to oppose a plan.* **2.** to set in opposition; put facing or opposite each other: *to oppose two armies; to oppose two buildings.*

op·po·site (op′ə zit, op′ə sit), *adj.* **1.** located on the other side or across from another person or object: *I saw him on the opposite side of the room.* **2.** differing greatly; conflicting: *opposite sides in a debate.* —*n.* **3.** a person or thing that is opposite or contrary: *She is the opposite of her sister.* —*prep.* **4.** across from; facing: *The filling station is opposite the library.* —**op′po·site·ly,** *adv.*

op·po·si·tion (op′ə zish′ən), *n.* **1.** the action of opposing, resisting, or combating. **2.** the state of being opposite. **3.** the major political party that is opposed to the party in power. **4.** a person or group that opposes or criticizes an idea, action, etc.

op·press (ə pres′), *v.* **1.** to be as a heavy burden to: *Care and sorrow oppressed him.* **2.** to subject to harsh authority or power; treat harshly: *The tyrant oppressed the people.* —**op·pres′sor,** *n.*

op·pres·sion (ə presh′ən), *n.* **1.** the harsh and unjust use of authority or power. **2.** the act or an instance of oppressing. **3.** the state or feeling of being oppressed.

op·pres·sive (ə pres′iv), *adj.* **1.** unjustly harsh or tyrannical. **2.** causing discomfort: *oppressive heat.* **3.** distressing or upsetting: *oppressive problems.* —**op·pres′sive·ly,** *adv.* —**op·pres′sive·ness,** *n.*

op·pro·bri·ous (ə prō′brē əs), *adj.* **1.** showing reproach or scorn. **2.** disgraceful or shameful.

op·pro·bri·um (ə prō′brē əm), *n.* **1.** the disgrace or reproach resulting from shameful conduct. **2.** a cause of such shame or reproach.

op·tic (op′tik), *adj.* concerning sight or the eye: *the optic nerve.*

op·ti·cal (op′ti kəl), *adj.* **1.** concerning or employing the principles of optics: *The microscope is an optical instrument.* 2. concerning vision: *an optical illusion.* —**op′ti·cal·ly,** *adv.*

op·ti·cian (op tish′ən), *n.* a person who makes or sells eyeglasses or optical instruments.

op′tic nerve′, either of the two nerves that connect the eyes with the brain. See illus. at eye.

op·tics (op′tiks), *n.* *(used as sing.)* the branch of physics that deals with the properties and behavior of light, lenses, and mirrors.

op·ti·mism (op′tə miz′əm), *n.* 1. a tendency to look on the more favorable side of things. 2. the belief that good will always win over evil in the world. 3. the principle or doctrine that the existing world is the best of all possible worlds. [from the Latin word *optimus* "best" + the English suffix *-ism*]

op·ti·mist (op′tə mist), *n.* 1. an optimistic person. 2. a person who favors the principles of optimism.

op·ti·mis·tic (op′tə mis′tik), *adj.* 1. inclined to take a favorable view of occurrences, the future, etc. 2. showing optimism: *an optimistic outlook.* 3. of or concerning optimism. —**op′ti·mis′ti·cal·ly,** *adv.*

op·ti·mum (op′tə məm), *n.* 1. the best or most favorable conditions for obtaining a certain result. —*adj.* 2. best or most favorable: *to work under optimum conditions.*

op·tion (op′shən), *n.* 1. the power or right of choosing. 2. the act of choosing. 3. the right to buy or sell within a specified time and at a stated price.

op·tion·al (op′shə nəl), *adj.* left to one's choice; not required: *Assembly attendance is optional.*

op·tom·e·trist (op tom′i trist), *n.* a person who tests the eyes and prescribes eyeglasses.

op·u·lence (op′yə ləns), *n.* 1. great wealth or riches; affluence. 2. abundance or plenty.

op·u·lent (op′yə lənt), *adj.* 1. rich or affluent. 2. abundant or plentiful: *opulent sunshine.*

o·pus (ō′pəs), *n.* a musical or literary composition or group of compositions.

or (ôr), *conj.* 1. (used to connect words, phrases, or clauses representing choice): *I haven't decided if I will go or if I will stay home.* 2. (used to connect alternative terms for the same thing): *the Hawaiian, or Sandwich, Islands.* 3. (used with *either* or *whether* to show choice): *Either you or I must go. He must decide whether or not to accept.* 4. (used to correct or say differently what was said before): *His book, or rather autobiography, is ready for publication.*

-or, a suffix used to form nouns meaning 1. a person or thing that does something: *conductor; compressor.* 2. an action or condition: *demeanor; candor.*

or·a·cle (ôr′ə kəl, or′ə kəl), *n.* 1. (esp. in ancient Greece) a divine utterance made by a god through a priest or priestess in response to a question. 2. the priest or priestess making such responses, or the shrine or place at which they were made. 3. a person who makes prophecies or speaks wisely.

o·rac·u·lar (ô rak′yə lər), *adj.* 1. of the nature of or suggesting an oracle. 2. making statements or decisions as if by special inspiration or authority. 3. difficult to understand; confusing; obscure.

o·ral (ôr′əl), *adj.* 1. uttered by the mouth; spoken. 2. of or using speech: *oral methods of teaching.* 3. concerning the mouth: *oral hygiene.* —*n.* 4. *Informal.* an examination, esp. for a college degree, that requires spoken answers. —**o′ral·ly,** *adv.*

or·ange (ôr′inj, or′inj), *n.* 1. a round, reddish-yellow citrus fruit valued esp. for its sweet juice. 2. the tree that bears this fruit. 3. a reddish yellow. —*adj.* 4. of or referring to the orange. 5. made or prepared with oranges or orange flavoring: *orange sherbet.* 6. of the color orange. [from a French word, which comes from Persian *nārang*]

or·ange·ade (ôr′inj ād′, or′inj ād′), *n.* a beverage consisting of orange juice, sweetener, and water.

or·ang·u·tan (ô rang′ə tan′), *n.* a large, reddish-brown ape found in Borneo and Sumatra that has very long arms and lives mostly in trees. [from a Malay word meaning "man of the woods"]

Orang-utan (height 4½ ft.)

o·ra·tion (ô rā′shən), *n.* a formal speech, esp. one delivered on a special occasion.

or·a·tor (ôr′ə tər), *n.* a person who delivers an oration or orations.

or·a·tor·i·cal (ôr′ə tôr′i kəl), *adj.* of, referring to, or like an orator or oratory.

or·a·to·ri·o (ôr′ə tôr′ē ō′), *n., pl.* **or·a·to·ri·os.** a large composition for soloists, chorus, and orchestra, usually set to a religious text.

or·a·to·ry¹ (ôr′ə tôr′ē), *n.* the art of public speaking or of speaking eloquently. [from the Latin phrase *ars ōrātōria* "art of the orator"]

or·a·to·ry² (ôr′ə tôr′ē), *n., pl.* **or·a·to·ries.** a small chapel or a room for private devotions. [from the Latin word *ōrātōrium* "place of prayers"]

orb (ôrb), *n.* 1. any of the heavenly bodies, such as the moon or a star. 2. a sphere or globe.

or·bit (ôr′bit), *n.* 1. the curved path that a planet, satellite, or comet takes around the sun, the earth, or some other heavenly body. 2. the path or the energy level of an electron revolving around the nucleus of an atom. —*v.* 3. to travel in or be launched into an orbit. —**or′bit·al,** *adj.*

or·chard (ôr′chərd), *n.* 1. an area, often enclosed, used for cultivating fruit trees. 2. a group or collection of such trees.

or·ches·tra (ôr′ki strə), *n.* 1. a group of performers who play together on various musical instruments, esp. a large group that plays symphonies and other serious music. 2. the space in a theater reserved for the musicians. 3. the entire main-floor space or the front section of seats on the main floor of a theater, used for seating. —**or·ches·tral** (ôr kes′trəl), *adj.*

or·chid (ôr′kid), *n.* 1. any of a large group of plants that bear large, irregularly shaped flowers, esp. certain tropical, climbing varieties. 2. a bluish to reddish purple.

Orchid

or·dain (ôr dān′), *v.* 1. to make (a person) a minister, priest, or rabbi. **2.** to decree or order. **3.** (of God, fate, etc.) to make happen; bring about: *Fate ordained that he would rule the nation.*

or·deal (ôr dēl′), *n.* **1.** any extremely severe or trying test, experience, or trial. **2.** (in former times) a method of determining guilt or innocence by subjecting the accused person to physical danger, the result being considered a divine judgment.

or·der (ôr′dər), *n.* **1.** a message, either written or spoken, that directs a person to do something; command. **2.** a system of arrangement or classification of persons or things: *alphabetical order.* **3.** a state of efficiency or neatness: *I put my papers in order.* **4.** a state of public peace or conformity to law: *to maintain order at the beach.* **5.** a request or set of instructions by which goods or services are sold, made, or furnished: *an order for 50 books.* **6.** something sold, made, or furnished according to a request or set of instructions: *an order of groceries.* **7.** a state of effective operation: *a wrist watch in working order.* **8.** a general classification according to quality or standing: *talents of a high order.* **9.** a major division of plants or animals containing several related families. **10.** a group or body of persons of the same profession, occupation, or pursuits. **11.** a body or society of persons living under the same religious, moral, or social regulations: *an order of monks.* **12.** a style of ancient architecture having a unique design and arrangement of columns: *Doric, Ionic, and Corinthian are the principal orders of ancient Greek architecture.* —*v.* **13.** to give an order to; command. **14.** to give an order for: *Have you ordered dinner yet?* **15.** to put in order; arrange. **16. in order, a.** suitable or appropriate: *Is a present in order?* **b.** in a state of readiness: *Is everything in order for your trip?* **17. in order to,** for the purpose of: *We moved closer in order to hear better.* **18. out of order, a.** not operating properly: *The telephone is out of order.* **b.** not suitable or appropriate: *That remark was out of order.* **19. to order,** according to one's special instructions: *to have shoes made to order.*

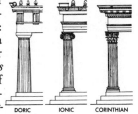

Orders (def. 12)

DORIC   IONIC   CORINTHIAN

or·der·ly (ôr′dər lē), *adj.* **1.** arranged in a neat, tidy manner: *an orderly desk.* **2.** systematic or methodical: *an orderly mind.* **3.** observing rules and discipline: *an orderly meeting; an orderly crowd.* —*n.* **4.** an enlisted man selected to perform various chores for an officer or officers. **5.** a hospital attendant. —**or′der·li·ness,** *n.*

or′di·nal num′ber (ôr′d°n°l), a number that expresses position in a series, as first, second, third, hundredth, etc. See also **cardinal number.**

or·di·nance (ôr′d°nəns), *n.* an authoritative rule or law; decree or command.

or·di·nar·i·ly (ôr′d°nâr′ə lē, ôr′d°nâr′ə lē), *adv.* in ordinary cases; usually: *I ordinarily get up earlier than my brother.*

or·di·nar·y (ôr′d°ner′ē), *adj.* **1.** of the usual kind; not exceptional: *an ordinary day.* **2.** lacking in interest; dull; plain: *an ordinary meal.* **3. out of the ordinary,** exceptional; unusual: *For something out of the ordinary, try a chocolate soda with coffee ice cream.*

or·di·nate (ôr′d°nit), *n.* the distance of a point above or below the horizontal axis of a graph.

or·di·na·tion (ôr′d°nā′shən), *n.* **1.** the ceremony of ordaining a clergyman. **2.** the fact of being ordained.

ord·nance (ôrd′nəns), *n.* **1.** cannon or artillery. **2.** military weapons of all kinds with their equipment, ammunition, etc.

ore (ôr), *n.* a rock or mineral that contains a valuable or useful metal.

Ore., Oregon. Also, **Oreg.**

Or·e·gon (ôr′ə gən, ôr′ə gon′), *n.* a state in the NW United States, on the Pacific coast. 96,981 sq. mi. *Cap.:* Salem. —**Or·e·go·ni·an** (ôr′ə gō′nē ən), *n., adj.*

Or′egon Trail′, a route used during the American westward migrations, from Missouri to Oregon. about 2000 mi. long.

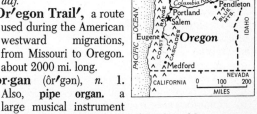

or·gan (ôr′gən), *n.* **1.** Also, **pipe organ.** a large musical instrument played from one or more keyboards and having pipes sounded by compressed air. **2.** any of various similar instruments that produce sounds by electric or electronic means. **3.** a distinct part of a plant or animal composed of different kinds of tissue and having a particular function: *The stomach is a digestive organ.* **4.** a newspaper, magazine, or other publication of interest to a special group.

or·gan·dy (ôr′gən dē), *n.* a fine, thin, cotton fabric usually having a crisp finish and used for blouses, curtains, etc.

or′gan grind′er, a street musician who earns his living by playing a hand organ or hurdy-gurdy.

or·gan·ic (ôr gan′ik), *adj.* **1.** concerning a very large group of chemical compounds containing carbon, many of which are found in living things: *organic chemistry.* **2.** concerning or coming from living things. **3.** concerning or affecting a plant or animal organ. **4.** characterized by the systematic arrangement of parts; organized. —**or·gan′i·cal·ly,** *adv.*

or·gan·ism (ôr′gə niz′əm), *n.* **1.** any form of animal or plant life; any living thing. **2.** any organized body or system made up of related parts that function together: *the governmental organism.*

or·gan·ist (ôr′gə nist), *n.* a person who plays the organ.

or·gan·i·za·tion (ôr′gə ni zā′shən), *n.* **1.** the act or process of organizing: *the organization of a new club.*

2. the state or manner of being organized: *the complicated organization of the files.* **3.** a group of persons organized for some purpose: *a student organization.*

or·gan·ize (ôr′gə nīz′), *v.,* **or·gan·ized, or·gan·iz·ing. 1.** to form into a whole: *to organize a team.* **2.** to arrange or make systematic: *to organize office files.* —**or′gan·iz′er,** *n.*

or·gy (ôr′jē), *n., pl.* **or·gies.** wild, drunken revelry.

o·ri·el (ôr′ē əl), *n.* a bay window projecting out from a wall.

o·ri·ent (ôr′ē ent′), *v.* **1.** to bring into correct relation to surroundings, circumstances, facts, etc.: *to orient soldiers to life in the army.* **2.** to place in any definite position with reference to the points of the compass or other locations. Also, **orientate.**

O·ri·ent (ôr′ē ənt, ôr′ē ent′), *n.* **1.** the Far East. **2.** the Eastern Hemisphere. [from the Latin word *oriēns* "the east, sunrise," which is from *orīrī* "to rise"]

Oriel

O·ri·en·tal (ôr′ē en′t'l), *adj.* **1.** of, referring to, or characteristic of the Orient or East. —*n.* **2.** a native or inhabitant of the Orient.

o·ri·en·tate (ôr′ē en tāt′), *v.,* **o·ri·en·tat·ed, o·ri·en·tat·ing.** another word for **orient.**

o·ri·en·ta·tion (ôr′ē en tā′shən), *n.* **1.** the act or process of orienting: *His first day in camp was taken up with orientation.* **2.** the state of being oriented.

o·ri·fice (ôr′ə fis, or′ə fis), *n.* a mouth or mouthlike opening.

o·ri·gin (ôr′i jin, or′i jin), *n.* **1.** the source from which anything begins or appears: *the origin of a hurricane.* **2.** the first stage of existence; beginning: *the origin of Quakerism in America.* **3.** birth or parentage; extraction: *Scottish origin.*

o·rig·i·nal (ə rij′ə nəl), *adj.* **1.** belonging or referring to the origin or beginning of something, or to a thing at its beginning: *The book still has its original binding.* **2.** having or showing originality; novel; creative: *an original design; an original thinker.* —*n.* **3.** the first form of a work, writing, or the like: *We made 10 copies from the original.* **4.** the person or thing represented by a picture, description, etc.: *The original is said to have been the painter's mother.*

o·rig·i·nal·i·ty (ə rij′ə nal′i tē), *n.* **1.** the quality or state of being original. **2.** ability to think or express oneself independently and individually. **3.** freshness or novelty, as of an idea, method, or performance.

o·rig·i·nal·ly (ə rij′ə nəlē), *adv.* **1.** with respect to origin; by origin: *He is originally from Chicago.* **2.** in the beginning; at first: *Originally the house had ten rooms.* **3.** in an original, unusual, or individual manner: *Originally planned houses are much in demand.*

o·rig·i·nate (ə rij′ə nāt′), *v.,* **o·rig·i·nat·ed, o·rig·i·nat·ing. 1.** to take or have origin; rise or arise: *The practice originated during the Middle Ages.* **2.** to give origin or rise to; initiate; invent: *to originate a new filing system.* —**o·rig′i·na′tor,** *n.*

O·ri·no·co (ôr′ə nō′kō), *n.* a river in Venezuela, flowing N from the Brazilian border, along the E border of Colombia, and E to the Atlantic Ocean. 1600 mi. long.

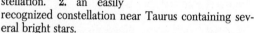

o·ri·ole (ôr′ē ōl′), *n.* any of various songbirds having orange and black plumage.

O·ri·on (ô rī′ən), *n.* **1.** (in Greek and Roman mythology) a giant hunter who was slain by Diana and changed into a constellation. **2.** an easily recognized constellation near Taurus containing several bright stars.

Ork′ney Is′lands (ôrk′nē), an island group off the NE tip of Scotland. 376 sq. mi.

Or·lon (ôr′lon), *n. Trademark.* a man-made fiber, used esp. as a substitute for wool.

or·na·ment (ôr′nə mənt), *n.* **1.** an object or feature intended to improve the appearance of something to which it is added or of which it is a part; decoration. **2.** a person who adds to the credit or glory of a group, society, era, etc. —*v.* (ôr′nə ment′). **3.** to furnish with ornaments: *to ornament shoes with gold buckles.* **4.** to be an ornament to.

or·na·men·tal (ôr′nə men′t'l), *adj.* used or grown for ornament; decorative: *a room decorated with ornamental plants.*

or·na·men·ta·tion (ôr′nə men tā′shən), *n.* **1.** the act of ornamenting, or the state of being ornamented. **2.** the ornaments used in decorating something: *The ornamentation is much too elaborate for this style of coat.*

or·nate (ôr nāt′), *adj.* elaborately or excessively decorated; showy; lavish: *That dress is much too ornate to wear to a christening.* —**or·nate′ly,** *adv.* —**or·nate′ness,** *n.*

or·ni·thol·o·gy (ôr′nə thol′ə jē), *n.* the branch of zoology that deals with birds. —**or′ni·thol′o·gist,** *n.*

o·ro·tund (ôr′ə tund′), *adj.* **1.** (of the voice or speech) characterized by strength, fullness, richness, and clearness. **2.** pompous or bombastic: *an orotund manner of speaking.*

or·phan (ôr′fən), *n.* **1.** a child who has lost one or both of its parents. —*v.* **2.** to deprive of a parent or parents: *The war orphaned many children of Europe.*

or·phan·age (ôr′fə nij), *n.* an institution for the housing and care of orphans.

Or·phe·us (ôr′fē əs, ôr′fyoōs), *n.* (in Greek mythology) a musician who followed his dead wife Eurydice to Hades, where Pluto, charmed by his playing of the lyre, permitted him to return with her to the living world, while warning that he would lose her if he looked back at her before reaching the upper world. At the last moment Orpheus looked back and Eurydice was lost to him forever.

or·tho·dox (ôr′thə doks′), *adj.* **1.** conforming to traditional or established doctrine, esp. in religion. **2.**

of, referring to, or conforming to beliefs, attitudes, or manners that are generally approved; conventional: *This school expects orthodox behavior.*

Or'thodox Church', the Christian religion that developed in the Eastern Roman Empire and divided into several national churches, such as the Greek Orthodox and Russian Orthodox churches. Also, **Eastern Orthodox Church.**

or·tho·dox·y (ôr′thə dok′sē), *n., pl.* for def. 1 **or·tho·dox·ies 1.** an orthodox belief or practice. **2.** the quality of being orthodox.

or·thog·ra·phy (ôr thog′rə fē), *n.* the spelling of words according to accepted usage.

-ory, a suffix used to form **1.** adjectives meaning **a.** of or relating to: *sensory; circulatory.* **b.** having the effect or function of: *promissory; advisory.* **2.** nouns meaning place where something is done, made, or kept: *laboratory; armory.*

Os, *Chem.* the symbol for **osmium.**

os·cil·late (os′ə lāt′), *v.,* **os·cil·lat·ed, os·cil·lat·ing. 1.** to swing or move back and forth as a pendulum does. **2.** to vary or fluctuate between differing opinions, conditions, etc.; waver; vacillate: *to oscillate between optimism and pessimism.* **—os′cil·la′tion,** *n.*

o·sier (ō′zhər), *n.* **1.** any of various willows having tough, flexible twigs used for wicker furniture. **2.** a twig of such a willow.

O·si·ris (ō sī′ris), *n.* the king and judge of the dead in the religion of ancient Egypt.

-osity, a suffix used to form nouns from adjectives ending in **-ous:** *generosity; curiosity.*

Os·lo (oz′lō, os′lō), *n.* a seaport and the capital city of Norway, in the SE part.

os·mi·um (oz′mē əm), *n.* **1.** a hard, heavy metal having the greatest density of any chemical element. *Symbol:* Os **—adj. 2.** made of this metal: *an osmium pen point.*

os·mo·sis (oz mō′sis, os mō′sis), *n.* **1.** a passing of a fluid through a membrane that tends to equalize conditions on both sides of the membrane. **2.** a gradual absorbing, esp. of knowledge.

os·prey (os′prē), *n., pl.* **os·preys.** a large bird of prey that feeds on fish; fish hawk.

os·si·fy (os′ə fī′), *v.,* **os·si·fied, os·si·fy·ing.** to harden into bone: *Cartilage in a baby's skull ossifies as the baby grows older.* **—os′si·fi·ca′tion,** *n.*

os·ten·si·ble (o sten′sə bəl), *adj.* of an outward appearance only; not real or genuine; pretended: *His ostensible cheerfulness concealed a deep sadness.* **—os·ten′si·bly,** *adv.*

os·ten·ta·tion (os′tən tā′shən), *n.* showy or pretentious display for the purpose of impressing others.

os·ten·ta·tious (os′tən tā′shəs), *adj.* showing or inclined toward ostentation: *an ostentatious party; an ostentatious person.* **—os′ten·ta′tious·ly,** *adv.*

os·te·o·path (os′tē ə path′), *n.* a person who practices osteopathy.

os·te·op·a·thy (os′tē op′ə thē), *n.* a system of treating disease based on the idea that health can best be improved or restored by manipulating the bones and muscles.

ost·ler (os′lər), *n.* another word for **hostler.**

os·tra·cize (os′trə sīz′), *v.,* **os·tra·cized, os·tra·ciz·ing.** to exclude, by general consent, from society, privileges, etc.: *He was ostracized by the community for his shocking behavior.* **—os′tra·cism′,** *n.*

os·trich (ô′strich, os′trich), *n.* a very large bird of Africa and Arabia that cannot fly but can run very swiftly; the largest living bird. [from the Old French word *ostruce,* which comes from Greek *strouthiōn*]

Ostrich
(8 ft. high; 6 ft. long)

O·thel·lo (ō thel′ō, ə thel′ō), *n.* the hero of Shakespeare's play *Othello,* a Moor of Venice, who kills his wife out of jealousy.

oth·er (uth′ər), *adj.* **1.** additional or further: *he and one other person.* **2.** different or distinct from the one or ones mentioned or implied: *in some other city.* **3.** different in nature or kind: *I would not want him other than he is.* **4.** being the remaining one of two or more: *the other hand.* **—n. 5.** the other one: *Each praises the other.* **—pron. 6.** Usually, **others.** other persons or things: *others in the medical profession.* **—adv. 7.** otherwise; differently (usually fol. by *than*): *We cannot make the trip other than by driving.* **8. every other,** every second one of a series: *Our club meets every other week.* **9. the other day (night, evening, etc.),** a few days (nights, evenings, etc.) ago; recently.

oth·er·wise (uth′ər wīz′), *adv.* **1.** under other circumstances: *otherwise they may get broken.* **2.** in another manner; differently: *He could not behave otherwise.* **3.** in other respects: *an otherwise nice day.* **—adj. 4.** of another kind; different.

Ot·ta·wa (ot′ə wə), *n.* the capital city of Canada, in SE Ontario.

ot·ter (ot′ər), *n., pl.* **ot·ters** *or* **ot·ter.** any of several furry animals that live in the water, having webbed feet and a long, slightly flattened tail.

Otter
(total length about 4 ft.)

ot·to·man (ot′ə mən), *n., pl.* **ot·to·mans. 1.** a sofa or seat, with or without a back. **2.** a cushioned footstool.

Ot·to·man (ot′ə mən), *adj.* **1.** of or concerning the Ottoman Empire. **—n., pl.** **Ot·to·mans. 2.** a Turk.

Ot′toman Em′pire, a former Turkish Empire (1300–1919), extending at its height over large portions of the Middle East, N Africa, and central Europe: replaced by the republic of Turkey.

ouch (ouch), *interj.* (used as an exclamation of sudden pain.)

ought (ôt), *auxiliary verb.* 1. (used to express duty or obligation): *Everyone ought to help.* 2. (used to express justice or moral rightness): *He ought to be punished.* 3. (used to express something considered appropriate or proper): *You ought to go home.* 4. (used to express probability): *That ought to be the postman.*

ought·n't (ôt/ᵊnt), contraction of *ought not.*

ounce¹ (ouns), *n.* 1. a unit of weight equal to ¹/₁₆ pound (28.35 grams) in ordinary measure. 2. a unit of weight equal to ¹/₁₂ pound (31.103 grams) in the systems of weight used in weighing drugs and precious metals. 3. a fluid ounce. 4. a small quantity or portion: *I haven't an ounce of strength left.* [from an Old French word, which comes from Latin *ūncia* "twelfth part, inch, ounce," from *ūnus* "one"]

ounce² (ouns), *n.* a long-haired, leopardlike animal living in the mountain ranges of central Asia. [from the Old French word *lonce,* which comes from Latin *lynx* "lynx"]

our (our, är), *pron.* of or by us; belonging to us: *our house; our vacation.*

ours (ourz, ärz), *pron.* the one or ones belonging to us: *Which house is ours?*

Ounce
(total length 7 ft.)

our·self (är self/, our-), *pron.* (a form used in place of *myself,* esp. in the regal or formal style, when *we* is used in place of *I*): *The king said, "We have taken unto ourself such powers as may be necessary."*

our·selves (är selvz/, our-), *pron.pl.* 1. (a form of *we* used for emphasis): *We ourselves would never lie.* 2. (a form of *us* used when the subject of the sentence is the same as the object): *We saw ourselves on television.* 3. our normal or ordinary selves: *After a good rest, we're almost ourselves again.*

—**Usage.** See **myself.**

-ous, a suffix used to form adjectives meaning 1. full of: *joyous.* 2. having the quality or nature of: *virtuous.* 3. like or resembling: *fibrous.* 4. having a tendency to: *gluttonous; mutinous.*

oust (oust), *v.* to expel or drive out from a place or position occupied: *We ousted them from the room.*

out (out), *adv.* 1. away from, or not in, the normal or usual place, position, condition, etc.: *You left a letter out of the word.* 2. away from one's home, work, etc.: *We're going out of town.* 3. in or into the outdoors: *to put the cat out.* 4. to exhaustion, extinction, or depletion: *to put the light out.* 5. to the end or conclusion: *to work a problem out.* 6. in or into public notice or knowledge: *The whole story came out.* 7. in or into a condition of neglect, disuse, etc.; not in fashion: *That style has gone out.* 8. so as to project or extend: *to stretch out.* 9. in or into the open; so as to be seen, felt, or experienced: *A rash broke out on her arm.* 10. from a source or material: *made out of cotton.* 11. from a number, stock, or store: *to pick out a shirt.* 12. aloud or loudly: *to call out.* 13. thoroughly;

completely: *to be tired out.* 14. so as to erase, remove, or destroy: *to paint out; to rub out.* —*adj.* 15. exposed; made bare: *The trousers are out at the knees.* 16. absent or missing: *I was out because of illness.* 17. beyond fixed limits: *The ball was declared out.* 18. not correct or accurate: *His calculations are out.* 19. having a financial loss: *I'm out 10 dollars.* 20. removed from or not in effective operation, play, etc.: *The pitcher is out for the season.* 21. unconscious; senseless. 22. finished; ended: *before the week is out.* 23. not operating or functioning; extinguished: *The light is out.* —*prep.* 24. (used to indicate movement or direction from the inside to the outside of something): *He looked out the window.* 25. (used to indicate movement away from a point): *We drove out the old dirt road.* —*interj.* 26. begone! away! —*n.* 27. a means of escape, as from a place, responsibility, etc.: *She's always looking for an out.* 28. (in baseball) a put-out. —*v.* 29. to make or become known: *Out with the truth!* 30. **go all out,** to make an intense effort; do everything possible: *They went all out to make us feel welcome.* 31. **out of,** without or lacking in: *We're out of sugar.*

out-, a prefix meaning 1. out or outside of or away from: *outlaw; outbuilding.* 2. to go beyond or exceed: *outlast; outlive.* 3. to surpass: *outstrip; outsell.*

out-and-out (out/ᵊnout/), *adj.* thorough; complete; absolute: *an out-and-out lie.*

out·bid (out/bid/), *v.*, **out·bid; out·bid·den** (out/bid/ᵊn) *or* **out·bid; out·bid·ding.** to outdo in bidding; bid higher than: *We outbid them at the auction.*

out/board mo/tor (out/bôrd/), a portable gasoline engine clamped on the stern of a boat.

out·bound (out/bound/), *adj.* outward bound; going away from a place: *an outbound plane.*

out·break (out/brāk/), *n.* a sudden and intense display, demonstration, etc.: *an outbreak of rioting.*

out·build·ing (out/bil/ding), *n.* a building smaller than and detached from a main building; outhouse.

out·burst (out/bûrst/), *n.* a sudden and violent outpouring: *an outburst of tears.*

out·cast (out/kast/), *n.* 1. a person who is rejected or cast out, as from home or society. —*adj.* 2. cast out or rejected; discarded.

out·class (out/klas/), *v.* to surpass in class or quality; be superior to or better than.

out·come (out/kum/), *n.* result or consequence.

out·crop (out/krop/), *n.* 1. a cropping out or coming to the surface of the earth: *the outcrop of a mineral.* 2. the part or amount that emerges.

out·cry (out/krī/), *n., pl.* **out·cries.** 1. a crying out. 2. a cry of distress or indignation. 3. loud clamor; noise.

out·date (out/dāt/), *v.*, **out·dat·ed, out·dat·ing.** to put out of date; make old-fashioned.

out·dis·tance (out/dis/tᵊns), *v.*, **out·dis·tanced, out·dis·tanc·ing.** to leave behind in or as if in running.

out·do (out/dŏŏ/), *v.*, **out·did** (out/did/), **out·done** (out/dun/), **out·do·ing.** to surpass in performance; be better than: *He always outdoes me in tennis.*

out·door (out/dôr/), *adj.* located or belonging outdoors: *an outdoor fireplace.*

out·doors (out'dôrz'), *adv.* 1. out of doors; in the open air. —*n.* 2. *(used as sing.)* the world outside of houses; open air.

out·er (ou'tər), *adj.* of, concerning, or located on or toward the outside; farther out; exterior: *the outer limits of the city.*

out'er ear', the external, visible part of the ear. See illus. at **ear**.

out·er·most (ou'tər mōst'), *adj.* farthest out; most distant from the interior or center.

out'er space'. See **space** (def. 1).

out·field (out'fēld'), *n.* (in baseball) 1. the part of the field beyond the diamond or infield. 2. positions in the outfield, played by the right fielder, left fielder, and center fielder. 3. the outfielders as a group. —**out'field'er**, *n.*

out·fit (out'fit'), *n.* 1. a set of articles or equipment for any purpose: *an explorer's outfit; a cooking outfit.* 2. a complete costume, esp. for a woman, usually including shoes, coat, hat, dress, and matching accessories: *a new spring outfit.* 3. *Informal.* a group engaged in an undertaking that requires close cooperation: *a military outfit.* —*v.*, **out·fit·ted, out·fit·ting.** 4. to furnish with an outfit; equip.

out·go (out'gō), *n., pl.* **out·goes.** 1. the act or an instance of going out: *an outgo of warmth and affection.* 2. money paid out; expenditure.

out·go·ing (out'gō'ing), *adj.* 1. going out; departing: *outgoing trains.* 2. interested in and responsive to other people; friendly: *an outgoing personality.*

out·grow (out'grō'), *v.*, **out·grew** (out'grōō'), **out·grown** (out'grōn'), **out·grow·ing.** 1. to grow too large for: *to outgrow a pair of shoes.* 2. to leave behind or lose as one grows older: *to outgrow dolls.* 3. to surpass in growing: *He outgrew his older sister.*

out·growth (out'grōth'), *n.* 1. a development, product, or result: *Crime is often an outgrowth of poverty.* 2. a growing out or forth. 3. something that grows out; offshoot: *an outgrowth of leaves.*

out·guess (out'ges'), *v.* to outwit; be smarter or cleverer than.

out·house (out'hous'), *n., pl.* **out·hous·es** (out'hou'ziz). 1. another word for **outbuilding.** 2. a building separate from a main building with one or more seats and a pit serving as a toilet.

out·ing (ou'ting), *n.* a pleasure trip, picnic, or the like.

out·land·ish (out lan'dish), *adj.* very strange or unusual; odd: *outlandish clothing.* —**out·land'ish·ly,** *adv.* —**out·land'ish·ness,** *n.*

out·last (out'last'), *v.* to last longer than: *These shoes have outlasted the others.*

out·law (out'lô'), *n.* 1. a person, group, or thing excluded from the benefits and protection of the law. 2. a person who defies the law; criminal. —*v.* 3. to deprive of the benefits and protection of the law. 4. to make unlawful; prohibit.

out·lay (out'lā'), *n.* 1. an expending or expenditure of money. 2. an amount spent.

out·let (out'let), *n.* 1. an opening or passage by which anything is let out; vent or exit. 2. a fixture into which the cord of an electrical appliance may be plugged to supply the appliance with electricity. 3. a market for goods: *to seek new outlets for crops.* 4. a retail store selling the goods of a particular manufacturer. 5. a means of expression or satisfaction: *an outlet for one's talent; an outlet for anger.*

out·line (out'līn'), *n.* 1. the line by which a figure or object is defined or bounded. 2. a line drawing or sketch without shading. 3. a general sketch, account, or report of only the main features: *an outline of the story.* —*v.*, **out·lined, out·lin·ing.** 4. to draw or give the outline of: *to outline a plan of action.*

out·live (out'liv'), *v.*, **out·lived, out·liv·ing.** to live or last longer than.

out·look (out'lŏok'), *n.* 1. the view or scene from a place. 2. a person's attitude toward things; mental view: *one's outlook on life.* 3. something that one may expect in the future; expectation: *What is the political outlook for next year?* 4. the place from which a person looks out.

out·ly·ing (out'lī'ing), *adj.* located at a distance from the center or main part; remote: *the outlying parts of town.*

out·mod·ed (out'mō'did), *adj.* 1. gone out of style; no longer fashionable: *an outmoded suit.* 2. not acceptable or usable by present standards: *outmoded equipment.*

out·num·ber (out'num'bər), *v.* to be greater than in number: *The boys outnumber the girls in the class.*

out-of-date (out'əv dāt'), *adj.* gone out of style; outmoded.

out-of-doors (out'əv dôrz'), *adj.* 1. Also, **out'-of-door'.** outdoor. —*n.* 2. *(used as sing.)* outdoors.

out-of-the-way (out'əv thə wā'), *adj.* 1. remote from busy or populated regions; secluded: *an out-of-the-way vacation spot.* 2. seldom encountered; unusual; strange.

out·pa·tient (out'pā'shənt), *n.* a person who is treated at a hospital but who does not stay there.

out·post (out'pōst'), *n.* 1. a station established at a distance from the main body of an army to protect it from surprise attack. 2. the body of troops stationed there. 3. an outlying settlement.

out·put (out'pŏot'), *n.* 1. the act of turning out; production. 2. the quantity or amount produced: *to increase the factory's output.*

out·rage (out'rāj), *n.* 1. an act of violence; any violation of law or decency. 2. anything that insults the feelings: *Her remark was an outrage.* —*v.*, **out·raged, out·rag·ing.** 3. to subject to violence or indignity. 4. to anger or offend; make resentful; shock. [from an Old French word, which comes from *outrer* "to push beyond bounds," from *outre* "beyond," from Latin *ultrā*]

out·ra·geous (out rā'jəs), *adj.* 1. causing great injury or wrong: *an outrageous crime.* 2. extremely rude; offensive; insulting: *an outrageous statement.* 3. passing reasonable limits: *an outrageous price.* —**out·ra′geous·ly,** *adv.*

out·rank (out′rangk′), *v.* to rank above: *A general outranks a major.*

out·rig·ger (out′rig/ər), *n.* a framework supporting a float extended from the side of a boat for adding stability.

out·right (out′rīt′), *adj.* **1.** complete or total: *an outright loss; an outright refusal.* —*adv.* **2.** completely; entirely. **3.** without restraint; openly: *to laugh outright.* **4.** at once; instantly: *to be killed outright.*

out·run (out′run′), *v.,* **out·ran** (out′ran′), **out·run, out·run·ning. 1.** to run faster or farther than. **2.** to exceed or surpass.

out·sell (out′sel′), *v.,* **out·sold** (out′sōld′), **out·sell·ing. 1.** to sell more than: *John outsold the other clerks.* **2.** to sell in greater quantity than: *The plaid skirts outsell the plain skirts.*

out·set (out′set′), *n.* the beginning or start.

out·shine (out′shīn′), *v.,* **out·shone** (out′shōn′), **out·shin·ing. 1.** to shine brighter or more than. **2.** to surpass in splendor, excellence, etc.: *She outshines her brother in school.*

out·side (out′sīd′), *n.* **1.** the outer side, surface, or part: *The outside of the house is painted green.* **2.** the space surrounding or beyond an enclosure or boundary: *We looked in from the outside of the park.* —*adj.* (out′sīd′, out′-). **3.** done or located beyond an enclosure or boundary: *outside noises.* **4.** not belonging to or connected with a certain group, institution, society, etc.: *outside influences.* **5.** extremely unlikely or remote: *an outside chance of our going.* —*adv.* (out′sīd′). **6.** on or to the outside or space without. —*prep.* (out′sīd′, out′sīd′). **7.** on or toward the outside of: *There was a noise outside the door.* **8. outside of,** *Informal.* other than; without taking into consideration: *Outside of Ann, no one else was there.*

out·sid·er (out′sī′dər), *n.* a person not belonging to a particular place or group.

out·skirts (out′skûrts′), *n.pl.* the outlying district or region of a city or town: *He lives on the outskirts of town.*

out·spo·ken (out′spō′kən), *adj.* **1.** expressed with frankness and lack of reserve: *outspoken criticism.* **2.** free or unreserved in speech: *outspoken people.* —**out′spo′ken·ly,** *adv.* —**out′spo′ken·ness,** *n.*

out·spread (out′spred′), *v.,* **out·spread, out·spread·ing. 1.** to spread out; extend. —*adj.* (out′spred′). **2.** spread out; stretched out.

out·stand·ing (out′stan′ding), *adj.* **1.** exceptional; striking: *an outstanding pianist.* **2.** remaining unsettled or unpaid, as debts. —**out′stand′ing·ly,** *adv.*

out·stretched (out′strecht′), *adj.* stretched forth; extended: *I took his outstretched hand.*

out·strip (out′strip′), *v.,* **out·stripped, out·strip·ping. 1.** to outdo or surpass; excel. **2.** to pass or defeat in a race or any other competition.

out·ward (out′wərd), *adj.* **1.** concerning or being what is seen; external or superficial: *outward appearances.* **2.** concerning the outside of the body as distinguished from the mind or spirit. **3.** belonging to or concerning what is outside oneself: *outward influences.* **4.** directed toward the outside or away from a central point. **5.** of or concerning the outside or outer surface. —*adv.* **6.** Also, **out′wards.** toward the outside; out.

out·ward·ly (out′wərd lē), *adv.* **1.** as regards appearance: *to be outwardly calm.* **2.** toward the outside: *to move outwardly.*

out·wear (out′wâr′), *v.,* **out·wore** (out′wôr′), **out·worn** (out′wôrn′), **out·wear·ing. 1.** to wear or last longer than; outlast: *Wool outwears silk.* **2.** to use up or exhaust: *Don't outwear your welcome.*

out·weigh (out′wā′), *v.* **1.** to be greater than in value, importance, influence, etc.: *The advantages outweigh the disadvantages.* **2.** to weigh more than.

out·wit (out′wit′), *v.,* **out·wit·ted, out·wit·ting.** to get the better of by superior intelligence or cleverness.

out·worn (out′wôrn′), *adj.* **1.** out-of-date; obsolete: *outworn opinions.* **2.** worn-out, such as clothes. —*v.* **3.** the past participle of **outwear.**

o·va (ō′və), *n.* the plural of **ovum.**

o·val (ō′vəl), *adj.* **1.** having the general form, shape, or outline of an egg; egg-shaped. —*n.* **2.** an object having an oval shape.

o·va·ry (ō′və rē), *n., pl.* **o·va·ries. 1.** the female organ that produces eggs. **2.** the part of a plant below the flower that encloses the seeds.

o·va·tion (ō vā′shən), *n.* an enthusiastic public reception of a person, esp. loud and prolonged applause.

ov·en (uv′ən), *n.* a heated chamber or compartment, as in a stove, for baking, roasting, etc.

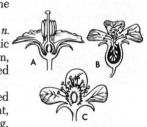

Ovaries (def. 2)
A, Potato flower; B, Rose;
C, Strawberry flower

o·ver (ō′vər), *prep.* **1.** above in place or position: *the roof over one's head.* **2.** above and to the other side of: *to leap over a wall.* **3.** above in authority, rank, or power. **4.** on or on top of: *He hit me over the head.* **5.** through all parts of; throughout: *to wander over the countryside.* **6.** to or on the other side of; across: *to cross over the bridge.* **7.** in excess of; more than: *over 50 people.* **8.** throughout the length or duration of; during: *Schools are closed over the summer.* **9.** in reference to, concerning, or about: *to fight over a silly matter.* **10.** by means of: *I spoke to him over the telephone.* **11.** in preference to: *to be chosen over someone else.* —*adv.* **12.** beyond the top or upper surface or edge of something: *a roof that hangs over.* **13.** so as to cover the surface or affect the whole surface: *to paint the room over.* **14.** from beginning to end; throughout: *to read something over.* **15.** on the other side: *over in Europe.* **16.** to the other side; across: *to sail over; to walk over.* **17.** so as to displace from an upright position: *to knock over a glass of milk.* **18.** once more; again: *She read the letter over before answering.* **19.** across or beyond the edge or rim: *The soup boiled over.*

—adj. 20. remaining or additional; extra: *I still have three dollars and a few cents over.* **21.** ended; done; past: *when the war was over.* **—n. 22.** an amount in excess or addition; extra. **23. all over, a.** done; finished: *We used to be friends, but it's all over now.* **b.** everywhere; in all possible places: *I looked all over for you.* **24. over again,** once more; a second time: *Write this over again neatly.* **25. over and over,** several times; repeatedly: *He tells the same jokes over and over.*

over-, a prefix meaning **1.** over or above: *overcoat; overhang.* **2.** too or too much: *overstocked; overeat.*

o·ver·all (ō/vər ôl/), *adv., adj.* **1.** from one extreme limit of a thing to the other: *the overall distance.* **2.** covering or including everything: *the overall charge.*

o·ver·alls (ō/vər ôlz/), *n.pl.* loose work trousers, usually with a part covering the chest and having straps over the shoulders.

o·ver·awe (ō/vər ô/), *v.,* **o·ver·awed, o·ver·aw·ing.** to gain or keep control of, esp. by inspiring awe; intimidate.

o·ver·bear·ing (ō/vər bâr/iñg), *adj.* rude and arrogant in manner; domineering.

o·ver·board (ō/vər bôrd/), *adv.* **1.** over the side of a ship or boat. **2. go overboard,** to go to extremes, esp. in showing approval or disapproval of a person or thing: *to go overboard in praising a new movie.*

o·ver·bur·den (ō/vər bûr/d°n), *v.* to place too heavy a burden on: *to be overburdened with work.*

o·ver·cast (ō/vər kast/), *adj.* **1.** covered with clouds; cloudy: *a dull, overcast sky.* **—v.** (ō/vər kast/, ō/vər-kast/), **o·ver·cast, o·ver·cast·ing.** **2.** to cloud or make gloomy. **3.** to stitch (the edge of a fabric) to prevent raveling.

o·ver·charge (ō/vər chärj/), *v.,* **o·ver·charged, o·ver·charg·ing.** **1.** to charge (a person) too much. **2.** to fill too full; overload. **—n.** (ō/vər chärj/). **3.** a charge that is greater than a just price.

o·ver·coat (ō/vər kōt/), *n.* a coat worn over the ordinary clothing, esp. one of heavy material worn in winter.

o·ver·come (ō/vər kum/), *v.,* **o·ver·came** (ō/vər kām/), **o·ver·come, o·ver·com·ing.** **1.** to get the better of in a struggle or conflict; conquer: *He overcame his fear of the water.* **2.** to overpower or overwhelm in body or mind: *to be overcome with happiness.*

o·ver·crowd (ō/vər kroud/), *v.* to crowd too much: *to overcrowd an auditorium.*

o·ver·do (ō/vər dōō/), *v.,* **o·ver·did** (ō/vər did/), **o·ver·done** (ō/vər dun/), **o·ver·do·ing.** **1.** to do or perform to excess: *to overdo exercise.* **2.** to exaggerate. **3.** to cook too much or too long.

o·ver·done (ō/vər dun/), *v.* **1.** the past participle of overdo. **—adj. 2.** (of food) cooked too much or too long. **3.** too elaborate; exaggerated: *His politeness is overdone.*

o·ver·dose (ō/vər dōs/), *n.* an excessively large or strong dose of medicine.

o·ver·draw (ō/vər drô/), *v.,* **o·ver·drew** (ō/vər drōō/),

o·ver·drawn (ō/vər drôn/), **o·ver·draw·ing.** **1.** to draw upon (an account, allowance, etc.) in excess of the balance standing to one's credit. **2.** to exaggerate in drawing or describing: *The author has overdrawn his characters.*

o·ver·dress (ō/vər dres/), *v.* to wear clothing that is too elaborate or showy.

o·ver·due (ō/vər dōō/, -dyōō/), *adj.* **1.** having gone past the time when payment was due: *an overdue bill.* **2.** not on time; late: *an overdue train.*

o·ver·eat (ō/vər ēt/), *v.,* **o·ver·ate** (ō/vər āt/), **o·ver·eat·en** (ō/vər ē/t°n), **o·ver·eat·ing.** to eat too much.

o·ver·es·ti·mate (ō/vər es/tə māt/), *v.,* **o·ver·es·ti·mat·ed, o·ver·es·ti·mat·ing.** **1.** to estimate at too high a value, amount, or rate: *He overestimated the importance of the story.* **—n.** (ō/vər es/tə mit). **2.** an estimate that is too high.

o·ver·flow (ō/vər flō/), *v.,* **o·ver·flowed, o·ver·flown** (ō/vər flōn/), **o·ver·flow·ing.** **1.** to flow or run over: *The river overflowed its banks after the heavy rain.* **2.** to have the contents flowing over: *The cup overflowed.* **3.** to pass from one place or part to another as if flowing from a space that is too full: *The population overflowed into the adjoining territory.* **—n.** (ō/vər flō/). **4.** the act of overflowing. **5.** an excess or superabundance. **6.** an outlet for excess liquid.

o·ver·grow (ō/vər grō/), *v.,* **o·ver·grew** (ō/vər grōō/), **o·ver·grown** (ō/vər grōn/), **o·ver·grow·ing.** **1.** to grow over: *The wall of the building is overgrown with ivy.* **2.** to grow too large or too quickly.

o·ver·hand (ō/vər hand/), *adv.* **1.** with the hand and part or all of the arm raised above the shoulder: *to pitch overhand.* **—adj. 2.** thrown or performed overhand: *an overhand stroke.*

o·ver·hang (ō/vər hañg/), *v.,* **o·ver·hung** (ō/vər-huñg/), **o·ver·hang·ing.** **1.** to hang or extend over: *A balcony overhangs the garden.* **—n.** (ō/vər hañg/). **2.** something that extends or juts out over; projection.

o·ver·haul (ō/vər hôl/, ō/vər hôl/), *v.* **1.** to examine thoroughly for repair, revision, etc.: *to overhaul an engine.* **2.** to gain upon or overtake. **—n.** (ō/vər-hôl/). **3.** a general examination and repair.

o·ver·head (ō/vər hed/), *adv.* **1.** over one's head; above: *There's a lot of noise overhead.* **—adj.** (ō/vər-hed/). **2.** located, operating, or passing above or over the head: *an overhead light.* **—n.** (ō/vər hed/). **3.** the general cost of running a business.

o·ver·hear (ō/vər hēr/), *v.,* **o·ver·heard** (ō/vər hûrd/), **o·ver·hear·ing.** to hear (speech or a speaker) without the speaker's intention or knowledge: *to overhear a conversation on a bus.*

o·ver·heat (ō/vər hēt/), *v.* to make or become too hot: *The engine overheated.*

o·ver·joy (ō/vər joi/), *v.* to cause (someone) to feel great joy or delight: *We were overjoyed at the large turnout.*

o·ver·land (ō/vər land/, -lənd), *adv., adj.* over, across, or by land: *to go overland; an overland route.*

o·ver·lap (ō/vər lap/), *v.,* **o·ver·lapped, o·ver·lap·ping.**

1. to lap over; extend over and cover a part of: *The tiles overlap the edge of the roof.* 2. to coincide in part with another thing: *Do our vacations overlap?* —*n.* (ō′vər lap′). 3. the act or an instance of overlapping. 4. the extent or amount of overlapping. 5. an overlapping part.

o·ver·lay (ō′vər lā′), *v.*, **o·ver·laid** (ō′vər lād′), **o·ver·lay·ing.** 1. to lay or place (one thing) over or upon another. 2. to finish with a layer or applied decoration of something: *wood richly overlaid with gold.* —*n.* (ō′vər lā′). 3. something laid over something else; covering. 4. a layer or decoration applied to something: *an overlay of gold.*

o·ver·load (ō′vər lōd′), *v.* 1. to load too heavily; overburden. —*n.* (ō′vər lōd′). 2. a load that is too heavy.

o·ver·look (ō′vər look′), *v.* 1. to fail to notice or consider: *I overlooked a question on the test.* 2. to disregard or ignore: *I overlooked his mistake because he's usually very careful.* 3. to look over from a higher position: *Our house overlooks the lake.* 4. to give a view of: *The room overlooks the garden.*

o·ver·ly (ō′vər lē), *adv.* to an excessive degree; too: *a voyage that was overly long.*

o·ver·night (ō′vər nīt′), *adv.* 1. for or during the night: *to stay overnight.* 2. in a short space of time: *New suburbs appear overnight.* —*adj.* (ō′vər nīt′). 3. done, occurring, or continuing during the night: *an overnight stop.* 4. staying for one night: *an overnight guest.* 5. designed to be used on a trip lasting one night or a very few nights: *an overnight bag.*

o·ver·pass (ō′vər pas′), *n.* a highway or railway bridge crossing some barrier, such as another highway or railroad tracks.

o·ver·pow·er (ō′vər pou′ər), *v.* 1. to overcome or overwhelm in feeling: *We were overpowered with joy at her good fortune.* 2. to overcome or master by superior force: *to overpower an enemy.*

o·ver·rate (ō′vər rāt′), *v.*, **o·ver·rat·ed, o·ver·rat·ing.** to rate or regard too highly; overestimate: *I think we overrated his pitching ability.*

o·ver·reach (ō′vər rēch′), *v.* 1. to reach or extend over or beyond. 2. to reach for or aim at, but go beyond: *to overreach the mark.* 3. to get the better of (someone), esp. by deceit or trickery; outwit. 4. to defeat (oneself) by showing too much eagerness, cunning, etc.

o·ver·ride (ō′vər rīd′), *v.*, **o·ver·rode** (ō′vər rōd′), **o·ver·rid·den** (ō′vər rid′′n), **o·ver·rid·ing.** 1. to trample or crush by riding over. 2. to assert one's will or authority over; dominate: *to override one's advisers.* 3. to be victorious over, esp. by having greater rank, power, or the like: *to override objections.*

o·ver·rule (ō′vər rool′), *v.*, **o·ver·ruled, o·ver·rul·ing.** 1. to rule against or reject the arguments of (a person). 2. to rule or decide against (a plea, argument, etc.). 3. to prevail over: *The group overruled him.*

o·ver·run (ō′vər run′), *v.*, **o·ver·ran** (ō′vər ran′), **o·ver·run, o·ver·run·ning.** 1. to swarm over in great numbers: *Rats overran the warehouse.* 2. to spread over or extend beyond: *Weeds overran the garden.*

o·ver·seas (ō′vər sēz′), *adv.* 1. over, across, or beyond the sea; abroad: *to be sent overseas.* —*adj.* (ō′vər sēz′). 2. of or referring to passage over the sea: *overseas travel.* 3. of or concerning countries across the sea: *overseas trade.*

o·ver·see (ō′vər sē′), *v.*, **o·ver·saw** (ō′vər sô′), **o·ver·seen** (ō′vər sēn′), **o·ver·see·ing.** to direct or supervise; manage: *to oversee workers.*

o·ver·se·er (ō′vər sē′ər), *n.* a person who oversees; supervisor; foreman.

o·ver·shad·ow (ō′vər shad′ō), *v.* 1. to lessen the importance of: *His success overshadowed his past failures.* 2. to cast a shadow over; darken.

o·ver·shoe (ō′vər shoo′), *n.* a shoe or boot, usually worn over another and intended for protection against rain, snow, or the like.

o·ver·shoot (ō′vər shoot′), *v.*, **o·ver·shot** (ō′vər shot′), **o·ver·shoot·ing.** to shoot or go over, beyond, or above; miss: *to overshoot a target.*

o·ver·shot (ō′vər shot′), *adj.* 1. having the upper jaw projecting beyond the lower jaw. 2. (of a water wheel) driven by water falling over the top.

o·ver·sight (ō′vər sīt′), *n.* 1. failure to notice or consider: *The mistakes were the result of his oversight.* 2. supervision; watchful care.

o·ver·size (ō′vər sīz′), *adj.* of a size larger than is usual or necessary: *a box of oversize cigars.* Also, **o′ver·sized′.**

o·ver·sleep (ō′vər slēp′), *v.*, **o·ver·slept** (ō′vər slept′), **o·ver·sleep·ing.** to sleep beyond a certain hour.

o·ver·spread (ō′vər spred′), *v.*, **o·ver·spread, o·ver·spread·ing.** to spread or extend over.

o·ver·state (ō′vər stāt′), *v.*, **o·ver·stat·ed, o·ver·stat·ing.** to state too strongly; exaggerate: *Both sides overstated their positions in that debate.* —**o′ver·state′ment,** *n.*

o·ver·step (ō′vər step′), *v.*, **o·ver·stepped, o·ver·step·ping.** to step or pass over or beyond: *to overstep one's authority.*

o·ver·stock (ō′vər stok′), *v.* 1. to stock with more than is needed: *We are overstocked on pencils.* —*n.* (ō′vər stok′). 2. a stock in excess of what is needed or can be used.

o·ver·sup·ply (ō′vər sə plī′), *n., pl.* **o·ver·sup·plies.** 1. an excessive supply. —*v.* (ō′vər sə plī′), **o·ver·sup·plied, o·ver·sup·ply·ing.** 2. to supply with more than is needed or requested.

o·vert (ō vûrt′, ō′vûrt), *adj.* open to view or knowledge; not hidden or secret. —**o·vert′ly,** *adv.*

o·ver·take (ō′vər tāk′), *v.*, **o·ver·took** (ō′vər took′), **o·ver·tak·en** (ō′vər tā′kən), **o·ver·tak·ing.** 1. to catch up with or pass: *We overtook the car that had been ahead of us.* 2. to happen to or befall suddenly and unexpectedly: *Darkness overtook the hikers.*

o·ver·tax (ō′vər taks′), *v.* 1. to tax too heavily. 2. to make too great demands on: *All that exercise overtaxed his strength.*

o·ver·throw (ō′vər thrō′), *v.*, **o·ver·thrown** (ō′vər thrōn′), **o·ver·throw·ing.** 1. to bring down from a position of power; put an end to: *to overthrow a dictator.* 2. to throw over; upset; overturn. 3. to throw too far: *to overthrow a ball.* —*n.* (ō′vər thrō′). **4.** the condition of being overthrown; defeat; ruin.

o·ver·time (ō′vər tīm′), *n.* **1.** the time during which a person works before or after his normal working hours. **2.** pay earned or received for such time. **3.** (in sports) an additional period of play for deciding the winner of a tied game. —*adv.* **4.** during extra time: *to work overtime.* —*adj.* **5.** of or concerning overtime: *overtime pay.*

o·ver·tone (ō′vər tōn′), *n.* one of the higher tones in a musical sound that give it fullness and a special quality.

o·ver·took (ō′vər tŏŏk′), *v.* the past tense of **overtake.**

o·ver·ture (ō′vər chər, ō′vər chŏŏr′), *n.* **1.** the music played by the orchestra before an opera, oratorio, etc. **2.** an independent composition for orchestra resembling this. **3.** an opening move toward negotiations, establishing relations, etc.: *an overture concerning peace.*

o·ver·turn (ō′vər tûrn′), *v.* **1.** to turn (something) over on its side, face, or back; upset: *to overturn a glass of milk.* **2.** to destroy the power of; overthrow; defeat. —*n.* (ō′vər tûrn′). **3.** the act of overturning.

o·ver·weight (ō′vər wāt′), *n.* **1.** extra weight above what law or regulation allows. **2.** weight in excess of what is considered normal, healthful, etc. —*adj.* **3.** weighing more than is considered normal.

o·ver·whelm (ō′vər hwelm′, -welm′), *v.* **1.** to overcome completely in mind or feeling or by force: *Grief overwhelmed her. The soldiers overwhelmed the enemy.* **2.** to cover or bury beneath a mass of something: *The floodwaters overwhelmed the village.* —**o′ver·whelm′ing,** *adj.*

o·ver·work (ō′vər wûrk′), *v.* **1.** to work or cause to work too hard or too long. —*n.* (ō′vər wûrk′). **2.** too much work.

o·ver·wrought (ō′vər rôt′), *adj.* worked up or excited too much: *to be overwrought because of bad news.*

o·vule (ō′vyōol), *n.* **1.** a body that develops into a plant seed. See illus. at **flower. 2.** a small egg.

o·vum (ō′vəm), *n., pl.* **o·va** (ō′və). a female reproductive cell of a plant or animal, which develops into a new individual after fertilization.

owe (ō), *v.,* **owed, ow·ing. 1.** to be under obligation for the payment or showing of: *He owes me ten dollars. You owe the man respect.* **2.** to be in debt to: *He owes the insurance company.* **3.** to be indebted for: *He owes his fame to hard work and good fortune.*

ow·ing (ō′ing), *adj.* **1.** owed or due: *to pay what is owing.* **2. owing to,** because of: *Owing to poor weather, we decided not to go.*

owl (oul), *n.* any of numerous birds of prey, most of which hunt only at night, usually having a broad head with large eyes that face for-

Owl
(length 2 ft.)

ward and a short, hooked beak. —**owl′like′,** *adj.*

owl·et (ou′lit), *n.* a young owl.

own (ōn), *adj.* **1.** of or belonging to oneself or itself: *He spent only his own money.* —*v.* **2.** to have or hold as belonging to one; possess: *to own a bicycle.* **3.** to admit, acknowledge, or confess: *to own a fault.* —*n.* **4.** something that belongs to one: *This car is my own.* **5. hold one's own, a.** to keep a certain condition or position without becoming worse: *His condition is still serious, but the doctor says he's holding his own.* **b.** to be equal to any competition: *He can hold his own in any fight.* **6. of one's own,** belonging to oneself: *She wants a room of her own.* **7. on one's own,** responsible for one's own actions, livelihood, etc.; independent: *He's been on his own since he was 16.* **8. own up,** to confess: *Whoever did this had better own up.*

own·er (ō′nər), *n.* a person who owns; proprietor.

own·er·ship (ō′nər ship′), *n.* the state or fact of being an owner: *to argue about the ownership of a car.*

ox (oks), *n., pl.* **ox·en** (ok′sən). **1.** an adult castrated bull, used as a draft animal or for food. **2.** any of several similar or related animals.

ox·bow (oks′bō′), *n.* **1.** a U-shaped piece of wood placed under and around the neck of an ox. The oxbow forms a collar and is attached to the yoke. **2.** a U-shaped bend in a river.

ox·cart (oks′kärt′), *n.* a cart drawn by an ox or oxen.

ox·en (ok′sən), *n.* the plural of **ox.**

ox·ford (oks′fərd), *n.* a low shoe laced over the instep.

Ox·ford (oks′fərd), *n.* **1.** a city in S England, NW of London. **2.** a university in Oxford, founded in the 12th century.

ox·ide (ok′sīd), *n.* a chemical compound containing oxygen, esp. one with only one other element.

ox·i·dize (ok′si dīz′), *v.,* **ox·i·dized, ox·i·diz·ing. 1.** to combine chemically with oxygen. **2.** to increase the positive charge on an ion. **3.** to remove one or more electrons from. **4.** to cover or become covered with a coating of oxide or rust. —**ox·i·da·tion** (ok′si dā′shən), *n.* —**ox′i·diz′er,** *n.*

ox·y·gen (ok′si jən), *n.* a gas that makes up about ⅕ of the air we breathe and is essential to life. Oxygen is a chemical element. *Symbol:* O

oys·ter (oi′stər), *n.* any of several edible shellfish having rough, two-part shells, some kinds of which produce pearls.

oz., ounce; ounces.

O′zark Moun′tains (ō′zärk), a group of low mountains in S Missouri, N Arkansas, and NE Oklahoma. Also, **O′zarks.**

o·zone (ō′zōn), *n.* a form of oxygen with a peculiar odor, having three atoms in each molecule instead of two. It is produced when an electric spark passes through oxygen or air.

Oyster (length 2 to 6 in.)

ozs., ounces.

P

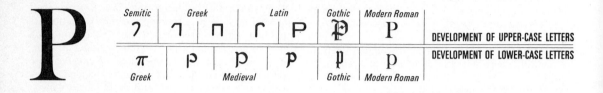

Semitic	Greek	Latin	Gothic	Modern Roman	
פ	ገ	ח	୮	ꟼ	P	**DEVELOPMENT OF UPPER-CASE LETTERS**

| π | ρ | ρ | ρ | ꟼ | p | **DEVELOPMENT OF LOWER-CASE LETTERS** |
| Greek | | Medieval | | Gothic | Modern Roman | |

P, p (pē), *n., pl.* **P's** *or* **Ps, p's** *or* **ps.** 1. the 16th letter of the English alphabet. 2. **mind one's p's and q's, to** be careful of one's behavior: *Mind your p's and q's, or there'll be no picnic tomorrow.*

P, 1. passing (grade). 2. (in chess) pawn. 3. poor.

P, 1. *Chem.* the symbol for **phosphorus.** 2. (in physics) power. 3. (in physics) pressure.

p, (in music) softly. [from the Italian word *piano*]

P., 1. Pastor. 2. post. 3. President. 4. Prince.

p., 1. page. 2. part. 3. participle. 4. past. 5. per. 6. pint. 7. pole. 8. population. 9. after. [from the Latin word *post*]

pa (pä), *n. Informal.* father.

PA, 1. Press Agent. 2. public-address system.

Pa, *Chem.* the symbol for **protactinium.**

Pa., Pennsylvania.

pa·ca (pä′kə, pak′ə), *n.* a large, white-spotted, nearly tailless rodent of Central and South America.

pace (pās), *n.* 1. a rate of movement, esp. in stepping, walking, etc.: *to hike at a rapid pace.* 2. a rate of activity, progress, performance, etc.: *the fast pace of city life.* 3. a single step: *She took three paces forward.* 4. the distance covered in a step. 5. a gait of a horse or other animal in which the feet on the same side are lifted and put down together. —*v.,* **paced, pac·ing.** 6. to set, establish, or regulate the pace for. 7. to take slow, regular steps. 8. to walk up and down or go over with steps: *He paced the floor nervously.* 9. to measure by paces. 10. **put one through one's paces,** to test one's ability or skill: *The coach really put them through their paces during football practice.* 11. **set the pace,** to serve as an example for others to follow: *This typewriter sets the pace in the low-priced field.* [from the Old French word *pas,* which comes from Latin *passus* "step, pace"] —**pac′er,** *n.*

Paca
(length 2½ ft.)

pach·y·derm (pak′i dûrm′), *n.* any of several large, thick-skinned animals including the rhinoceros and the hippopotamus, esp. the elephant.

pa·cif·ic (pə sif′ik), *adj.* 1. tending to make peace: a *pacific proposal.* 2. peaceful; calm. [from the Latin word *pācificus,* which comes from *pāx* "peace" + *facere* "to make"] —**pa·cif′i·cal·ly,** *adv.*

Pacif′ic O′cean, an ocean bordered by the American continents, Asia, and Australia: largest of the oceans; divided by the equator into the North Pacific and the South Pacific. 70,000,000 sq. mi.

pac·i·fism (pas′ə fiz′əm), *n.* 1. opposition to war or violence. 2. the principle or policy of establishing and maintaining universal peace or such relations among all nations that all differences may be settled without war or fighting. —**pac′i·fist,** *n.*

pac·i·fy (pas′ə fī′), *v.,* **pac·i·fied, pac·i·fy·ing.** to bring or restore to a state of peace; quiet; calm: *to pacify a rebel tribe.* —**pac′i·fi·ca′tion,** *n.* —**pac′i·fi′er,** *n.*

pack¹ (pak), *n.* 1. a group of things wrapped or tied up for easy handling or carrying; bundle. 2. a definite quantity of merchandise together with its wrapping or package: *a pack of cigarettes.* 3. a group of people or things: *a pack of fools.* 4. a group of certain animals of the same kind: *a pack of wolves.* 5. a complete set of playing cards, usually 52 in number; deck. —*v.* 6. to make into a pack or bundle: *to pack groceries.* 7. to fill compactly with anything: *to pack a trunk.* 8. to press or crowd together within: *to pack an auditorium.* 9. to become compacted: *Wet snow packs easily.* 10. to cause to go or leave (sometimes fol. by *off, away,* etc.): *We packed her off to her mother.* —*adj.* 11. used in transporting a pack: *pack animals.* [from an early Flemish word *pac*]

pack² (pak), *v.* to choose, collect, arrange, or manipulate so as to serve one's purposes: *to pack a jury.* [perhaps another form of the word *pact*]

pack·age (pak′ij), *n.* 1. a bundle of something that is packed and wrapped or boxed; parcel. 2. a container, such as a box or case, in which something may be packed. —*v.,* **pack·aged, pack·ag·ing.** 3. to put into wrappings or a container.

pack′ an′imal, an animal that carries loads on its back. Horses, mules, donkeys, camels, llamas, etc., are often used as pack animals. See also **draft animal.**

pack·er (pak′ər), *n.* 1. a person or thing that packs.

2. a person or organization that engages in packing food or other goods for market: *a meat packer.*

pack·et (pak′it), *n.* **1.** a small pack or package of anything. **2.** Also, **pack′et boat′.** a boat that carries mail, passengers, and goods regularly on a fixed route.

pact (pakt), *n.* an agreement, treaty, or compact, esp. between two or more nations.

pad¹ (pad), *n.* **1.** a cushionlike mass of soft material, used for comfort, protection, or stuffing. **2.** a number of sheets of paper glued or fastened together at one edge to form a tablet. **3.** a soft, ink-soaked block of absorbent material for inking a rubber stamp. **4.** one of the soft, cushionlike areas on the underside of the feet of certain animals, such as cats, dogs, or foxes. **5.** the large floating leaf of the water lily. —*v.,* **pad·ded, pad·ding. 6.** to furnish, protect, fill out, or stuff with a pad or padding. **7.** to expand or complete with unnecessary or false material: *to pad a term paper; to pad an expense account.* [from an earlier word meaning "bundle to lie on"]

pad² (pad), *n.* **1.** a dull sound, as of footsteps on the ground. —*v.,* **pad·ded, pad·ding. 2.** to travel on foot; walk. **3.** to walk with a soft, dull sound. [from an early Dutch word *paden* "to make or follow a path"]

pad·ding (pad′iṅg), *n.* **1.** material, such as cotton or straw, used to pad something. **2.** unnecessary words used to lengthen a speech, essay, etc.

pad·dle¹ (pad′²l), *n.* **1.** a short, flat oar for propelling and steering a canoe. **2.** any of various similar implements used for mixing, stirring, or beating. **3.** a racket with a short handle and a wide, rounded blade, used in table tennis and similar games. —*v.,* **pad·dled, pad·dling. 4.** to propel with a paddle: *to paddle a canoe.* **5.** to stir, mix, or beat with or as if with a paddle. [from the Middle English word *padell*] —**pad′dler,** *n.*

Table tennis paddle

pad·dle² (pad′²l), *v.,* **pad·dled, pad·dling.** to move the feet or hands playfully in shallow water. —**pad′dler,** *n.*

pad′dle ten′nis, a game similar to tennis, played with wooden paddles and a rubber ball.

pad′dle wheel′, a large wheel having projecting paddles, formerly used as a means of propulsion for ships.

pad·dock (pad′²k), *n.* **1.** a small, enclosed field near a stable or barn, for pasturing or exercising animals. **2.** (in horse racing) the enclosure in which the horses are saddled and mounted.

Paddle wheel

pad·dy (pad′ē), *n., pl.* **pad·dies. 1.** a rice field. **2.** rice in the husk, either harvested or left uncut. [from the Malay word *pādī*]

pad·lock (pad′lok′), *n.* **1.** a portable or detachable lock with a curved bar that is hinged at one end and can be passed through a staple, link, or ring and then snapped shut at the other end. —*v.* **2.** to fasten with or as if with a padlock.

pa·dre (pä′drā, pä′drē), *n.* father (used esp. in addressing or referring to a priest or other clergyman).

pae·an (pē′ən), *n.* any song of praise, joy, or triumph.

pa·gan (pā′gən), *n.* **1.** a person who worships many gods: *The ancient Greeks were pagans.* **2.** a person who is not a Christian, Jew, or Muslim. —*adj.* **3.** of or concerning pagans or their religion.

page¹ (pāj), *n.* **1.** one side of a leaf of something printed or written. **2.** the entire leaf. **3.** an important event or period: *a bright page in English history.* [from a French word, which comes from Latin *pāgina*]

page² (pāj), *n.* **1.** a boy servant or attendant. **2.** a youth in attendance on a person of rank or, in medieval times, a youth being trained for knighthood. **3.** a young male attendant or employee, who carries messages, ushers guests, runs errands, etc. —*v.,* **paged, pag·ing. 4.** to summon by calling out the name of (a person) repeatedly: *The receptionist paged the doctor.* [from Old French]

pag·eant (paj′ənt), *n.* **1.** an elaborate public performance or spectacle that is based on the history of a place, institution, etc. **2.** a costumed procession, parade, or the like, forming part of public or social festivities.

pag·eant·ry (paj′ən trē), *n.* **1.** spectacular display; pomp; ceremony. **2.** pageants, or the performance of pageants.

pa·go·da (pə gō′də), *n.* (in India, Burma, China, etc.) a temple or sacred building, usually a tapering tower having roofs that curve upward over the individual stories.

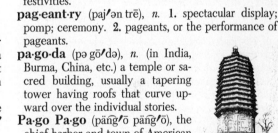
Pagoda

Pa·go Pa·go (päṅg′ō päṅg′ō), the chief harbor and town of American Samoa.

paid (pād), *v.* a past tense and past participle of **pay.**

pail (pāl), *n.* **1.** a round container with a handle and a flat bottom, used for holding or carrying liquids or solids; bucket. **2.** a pailful.

pail·ful (pāl′fool′), *n., pl.* **pail·fuls.** the quantity or amount a pail can hold.

pain (pān), *n.* **1.** an ache or soreness; bodily suffering: *a back pain.* **2.** mental or emotional suffering. **3. pains,** very careful efforts: *He took pains to do a good job.* —*v.* **4.** to cause physical pain to; hurt. **5.** to cause mental or emotional pain to; distress: *Her bad behavior pained him.* **6. on** (or **upon**) **pain of,** liable to suffer the penalty of: *He was forbidden to enter the country on pain of death.*

---

act, āble, dâre, ärt; ebb, ēqual; if, īce; hot, ōver, ôrder; oil; bŏŏk; ōōze; out; up, ûrge; ə = a as in *alone*; ᵊ as in *button* (but′ᵊn), *fire* (fīᵊr); chief; shoe; thin; ᵺat; zh as in *measure* (mezh′ər). See full key inside cover.

pain·ful (pān′fəl), *adj.* 1. affected with or causing pain: *a painful cut.* 2. very difficult or unpleasant; trying; exacting: *a painful duty.* —**pain′ful·ly,** *adv.*

pain·less (pān′lis), *adj.* 1. without pain; causing no pain: *painless dentistry.* 2. *Informal.* not difficult or unpleasant; requiring little work. —**pain′less·ly,** *adv.*

pains·tak·ing (pānz′tā′kiñg), *adj.* using or showing great care, thoroughness, or the like; careful: *a painstaking craftsman; painstaking research.* —**pains′tak′ing·ly,** *adv.*

paint (pānt), *n.* 1. a substance composed of solid coloring matter mixed in a liquid, for applying to various surfaces as a protective or decorative coating, or to canvas or other materials in producing a work of art. —*v.* 2. to coat, cover, or decorate with or as if with paint: *to paint a bookcase; to paint a cut with iodine.* 3. to produce in paint: *to paint a portrait.* 4. to represent in paint: *to paint a sunset.* 5. to describe vividly in words: *He painted an exciting picture of his trip.*

paint·brush (pānt′brush′), *n.* any brush for applying paint.

paint·er¹ (pān′tər), *n.* 1. an artist who paints pictures. 2. a person whose occupation is coating walls or other surfaces with paint. [from *paint* + *-er*]

paint·er² (pān′tər), *n.* a rope for fastening a boat to something. [from the Middle English word *paynter,* which comes probably from earlier French *pentoir* "rope, cord"]

paint·ing (pān′tiñg), *n.* 1. a picture or design made with paint. 2. the act, art, or work of a person who paints.

pair (pâr), *n., pl.* **pairs** *or* **pair.** 1. two identical or similar things that are matched for use together: *a pair of gloves.* 2. something having two parts or pieces joined together: *a pair of scissors; a pair of trousers.* 3. two persons or animals that are similar in some way: *a pair of skaters; a pair of horses.* 4. a married, engaged, or dating couple. —*v.* 5. to arrange or form in pairs or groups of two; match. 6. **pair off,** to separate into pairs; join together in groups of two: *The graduates paired off for the procession.*

pa·jam·as (pə jä′məz, pə jam′əz), *n. (used as pl.)* night clothes consisting of loose-fitting trousers and jacket. Also, *esp. British,* **pyjamas.** [from a Hindi word, which comes from Persian *pāe* "leg" + *jāma* "garment"]

Pa·ki·stan (pak′i stan′, pä′ki stän′), *n.* a republic in S Asia, NW of India, on the Arabian Sea. 310,236 sq. mi. *Cap.:* Islamabad. —**Pa·ki·sta·ni** (pä′ki stä′nē), *n., adj.*

pal (pal), *n. Informal.* a close friend; comrade; chum.

pal·ace (pal′is), *n.* 1. the official residence of a sovereign or bishop. 2. any mansion or large and stately building.

pal·an·quin (pal′ən kēn′), *n.* (in India and other Eastern countries) a passenger carriage consisting of a covered or boxlike litter carried by several men.

pal·at·a·ble (pal′ə tə bəl), *adj.* 1. pleasing or acceptable to the palate or taste. 2. pleasing or acceptable to the mind or feelings: *a palatable idea.*

pal·ate (pal′it), *n.* 1. the roof of the mouth. See illus. at **mouth.** See also **hard palate, soft palate.** 2. the sense of taste. 3. intellectual taste or liking; mental appreciation.

pa·la·tial (pə lā′shəl), *adj.* of, resembling, or suitable for a palace; magnificent. —**pa·la′tial·ly,** *adv.*

pa·lav·er (pə lav′ər, pə lä′vər), *n.* 1. a long conference or discussion, esp. one with primitive natives. 2. long and idle talk; chatter. —*v.* 3. to talk idly.

pale¹ (pāl), *adj.,* **pal·er, pal·est.** 1. lacking strong color; colorless or whitish: *a pale complexion.* 2. light in color: *pale yellow.* 3. not bright or brilliant; dim: *the pale moon.* —*v.,* **paled, pal·ing.** 4. to make or become pale. [from an early French word, which comes from Latin *pallidus* "pallid"] —**pale′ly,** *adv.* —**pale′ness,** *n.*

pale² (pāl), *n.* 1. a stake or picket in a fence. 2. an enclosing or confining barrier; enclosure. 3. a district or region within fixed bounds. —*v.,* **paled, pal·ing.** 4. to enclose with pales; fence. 5. **beyond the pale,** beyond the limits of reason, good taste, etc.: *Such conduct is really beyond the pale.* [from Old English *pāl,* which comes from Latin *pālus* "stake"]

pale·face (pāl′fās′), *n.* a white person, as distinguished from a North American Indian.

Pa′le·o·zo′ic e′ra (pā′lē ə zō′ik, pal′ē ə zō′ik), the geological period following the Proterozoic era: from about 600 million to about 220 million years ago.

Pa·ler·mo (pə lâr′mō, pə lûr′mō), *n.* a seaport and the capital city of Sicily, in the NW part.

Pal·es·tine (pal′i stīn′), *n.* 1. an ancient country in SW Asia, on the E coast of the Mediterranean Sea. 2. a former British territory, made up of part of this country and divided between Israel, Jordan, and the United Arab Republic in 1948: fully occupied by Israel in 1967. Also, **Holy Land.** Biblical name, **Canaan.** —**Pal·es·tin·i·an** (pal′i stin′ē ən), *n., adj.*

pal·ette (pal′it), *n.* 1. a thin board or tablet with a thumb hole at one end, used by painters for holding and mixing colors. 2. the set of colors on such a board or surface.

pal·frey (pôl′frē), *n., pl.* **pal·freys.** 1. a riding horse, as distinguished from a war-horse. 2. a saddle horse, esp. a gentle one.

pal·ing (pā′liñg), *n.* 1. a fence of pales. 2. a pale or picket for a fence. 3. pales as a group.

pal·i·sade (pal′i sād′), *n.* 1. a fence of pales or stakes set firmly in the ground for enclosure or defense. 2. any of a number of pales pointed at the top and set in a row to form a defense. 3. **palisades,** a line of cliffs. —*v.,* **pal·i·sad·ed, pal·i·sad·ing.** 4. to furnish or fortify with a palisade.

pall¹ (pôl), *n.* 1. a covering of darkness, gloom, or the like: *Winter cast its pall over the countryside.* 2. a cloth, often of velvet, for spreading over a coffin, bier, or tomb. [from the Old English word *pæll,* which comes from Latin *pallium* "cloak"]

pall² (pôl), *v.* to become boring, dull, or unpleasant (often fol. by *on*): *The game palled on us after an hour.* [from the Middle English word *pallen,* which is short for *appallen* "to appall"]

pal·la·di·um (pə lā′dē əm), *n. Chem.* a rare, metallic element similar to platinum. *Symbol:* Pd

Pal·las (pal′əs), *n.* another name for **Athena.** Also, **Pal′las Athen′a.**

pall·bear·er (pôl′bâr′ər), *n.* a person who helps carry or walks beside the coffin at a funeral.

pal·let (pal′it), *n.* 1. a bed or mattress of straw. 2. any temporary or makeshift bed.

pal·li·ate (pal′ē āt′), *v.,* **pal·li·at·ed, pal·li·at·ing.** 1. to attempt to lessen the seriousness of (an offense) by excuses and apologies. 2. to relieve (a disease) without curing.

pal·li·a·tive (pal′ē ā′tiv, pal′ē ə tiv), *adj.* 1. serving to palliate. —*n.* 2. something that palliates.

pal·lid (pal′id), *adj.* faint in color; pale; wan: *a pallid face.* —**pal′lid·ly,** *adv.*

pal·lor (pal′ər), *n.* unnatural paleness.

palm¹ (päm), *n.* 1. the part of the inner surface of the hand between the wrist and the fingers. 2. the part of a glove covering this part of the hand. 3. a linear measure of from three to four inches, based on the breadth of the hand. —*v.* 4. to hide or conceal in the palm. 5. **grease someone's palm,** to give money to someone, esp. as a bribe: *The package wasn't delivered until I had greased the doorman's palm.* 6. **palm off,** to dispose of (something), esp. with intent to deceive: *He palmed off his forged painting on the museum officials.* [from the Latin word *palma*]

palm² (päm), *n.* 1. any of numerous tropical plants, most of which are tall, unbranched trees having a crown of large, feathery leaves at the top. 2. a leaf of this tree, used as a symbol of victory. 3. victory; triumph; success: *He won the palm by sheer determination.* [from an Old English word, which comes from Latin *palma* "palm tree"]

palm·er (pä′mər, päl′mər), *n.* a pilgrim, esp. of the Middle Ages, who returned from the Holy Land with a palm branch to show he had been there.

pal·met·to (pal met′ō), *n., pl.* **pal·met·tos** *or* **pal·met·toes.** any of various palm trees having fan-shaped leaves.

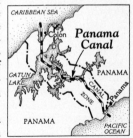
Palm

Palm′ Sun′day, the Sunday before Easter, celebrating Christ's triumphal entry into Jerusalem.

pal·o·mi·no (pal′ə mē′nō), *n., pl.* **pal·o·mi·nos.** a breed of horse, esp. of the southwestern U.S., having a golden color and a pale-yellow mane and tail.

pal·pa·ble (pal′pə bəl), *adj.* 1. easily seen, heard, etc.; obvious. 2. capable of being touched or felt; tangible. —**pal′pa·bly,** *adv.*

pal·pi·tate (pal′pi tāt′), *v.,* **pal·pi·tat·ed, pal·pi·tat·ing.** 1. to pulsate or beat more rapidly than normal; flutter: *His heart palpitated after the exercise.* 2. to beat or pulsate; quiver; throb. —**pal′pi·ta′tion,** *n.*

pal·sied (pôl′zēd), *adj.* suffering from or affected by palsy.

pal·sy (pôl′zē), *n., pl.* **pal·sies.** 1. any of several conditions that produce shaking or quivering of various parts of the body, often the jaw or the hands. —*v.,* **pal·sied, pal·sy·ing.** 2. to paralyze.

pal·try (pôl′trē), *adj.,* **pal·tri·er, pal·tri·est.** trifling; petty; nearly worthless: *a paltry contribution of ten cents.*

pam·pas (pam′pəz), *n.pl., sing.* **pam·pa** (pam′pə). the vast grassy plains of southern South America, esp. of central Argentina.

pam·per (pam′pər), *v.* to treat with extreme indulgence, kindness, or care; spoil: *to pamper a child; to pamper a cold.*

pam·phlet (pam′flit), *n.* 1. a short essay on some subject of current interest: *a political pamphlet.* 2. an unbound booklet of generally less than 80 pages stitched or stapled together.

pam·phlet·eer (pam′fli tēr′), *n.* 1. a person who writes pamphlets. —*v.* 2. to write and issue pamphlets.

pan (pan), *n.* 1. a broad, shallow, metal container used in various forms for frying, baking, washing, etc. 2. a container similar to this, used in industrial or mechanical processes. 3. (in old guns) the part of the lock that is pressed down and holds the priming. —*v.,* **panned, pan·ning.** 4. to wash (gravel, sand, etc.) in a pan to separate gold or other heavy valuable metal. 5. to separate by such washing. 6. *Informal.* to criticize severely: *The critics panned the new play.* 7. **pan out,** to turn out, esp. successfully: *If my trip pans out, I'll bring you a souvenir.*

Pan (pan), *n.* (in Greek mythology) a god of forests, flocks, and shepherds, pictured as having the head, chest, and arms of a man, and the legs and sometimes the horns and ears of a goat.

pan-, a prefix meaning all: *Pan-American; pantheism.*

pan·a·ce·a (pan′ə sē′ə), *n.* a remedy for all diseases or ills; cure-all: *Nobody has a panacea for world problems.*

Pan·a·ma (pan′ə mä′), *n.* 1. a republic in S Central America. 28,575 sq. mi. *Cap.:* Panama. 2. Also, **Pan′ama Cit′y.** the capital city of Panama, at the Pacific end of the Panama Canal. 3. **Isthmus of,** an isthmus linking the continents of North and South America. —**Pan·a·ma·ni·an** (pan′ə mā′nē ən), *n., adj.*

Pan′ama Canal′, a canal extending SE from

the Atlantic Ocean to the Pacific Ocean across the Isthmus of Panama. 40 mi. long.

Pan-A·mer·i·can (pan/ə mer/i kən), *adj.* of, concerning, or representing all the countries or people of North, Central, and South America.

pan·cake (pan/kāk/), *n.* a flat cake of batter cooked in a pan or on a griddle; griddlecake; flapjack.

pan·cre·as (pan/krē əs, pang/krē əs), *n.* a gland located near the stomach, which secretes insulin and a fluid that aids digestion of protein, fat, and starch. —**pan/cre·at/ic,** *adj.*

pan·da (pan/də), *n.* **1.** Also, **giant panda.** a large, black-and-white animal that resembles a bear and is found in Tibet and southern China. **2.** Also, **lesser panda.** a smaller, reddish-brown animal of the Himalayas, having a long, bushy tail.

pan·de·mo·ni·um (pan/də mō/nē əm), *n.* **1.** wild, lawless disturbance or uproar; tumult; chaos. **2.** a place or scene of wild

Giant panda
(2 ft. high at shoulder; length 5 ft.)

uproar or complete chaos. [from the modern Latin word *Pandaemonium* "abode of all demons," coined by John Milton, from the prefix *pan-* "all" + *demon* + a Latin suffix *-ium*]

pan·der (pan/dər), *n.* **1.** a person who profits from the weaknesses or vices of others. —*v.* **2.** to act as a pander: *to pander to people's love of scandal.*

Pan·do·ra (pan dôr/ə), *n.* (in Greek mythology) the first woman on earth, who was given a box holding the troubles that would plague mankind, and which she opened out of curiosity, releasing them.

pane (pān), *n.* one of the divisions of a window, consisting of a single plate of glass in a frame.

pan·e·gyr·ic (pan/i jir/ik, pan/i jī/rik), *n.* **1.** speech or writing in praise of a person or thing. **2.** formal or elaborate praise.

pan·el (pan/əl), *n.* **1.** an area of a wall, door, ceiling, etc., that is distinct from the surrounding or adjoining areas. **2.** a flat, broad piece of wood on which a picture is painted. **3.** the picture itself. **4.** a photograph much longer in one dimension than the other. **5.** a broad, vertical strip of fabric set on a dress, skirt, etc. **6.** a list of persons called to serve as jurors. **7.** the group of persons making up a jury. **8.** a group of persons gathered together to serve as advisers, participate in a quiz game, etc.: *He's on the panel of a TV show.* **9.** a surface or section of a machine containing controls and dials. —*v.,* **pan·eled** *or* **pan·elled; pan·el·ing** *or* **pan·el·ling. 10.** to arrange in or furnish with a panel or panels.

pan-fry (pan/frī/), *v.,* **pan-fried, pan-fry·ing.** to fry in a small amount of fat in a skillet or shallow pan.

pang (pang), *n.* **1.** a sudden feeling of mental or emotional distress: *pangs of loneliness.* **2.** a sudden, brief, sharp pain or physical sensation.

pan·go·lin (pang gō/lin), *n.* any of various mammals of Africa and tropical Asia, having a covering of

broad, overlapping, flattened, horny scales and feeding largely on ants and termites.

pan·han·dle¹ (pan/han/dəl), *n.* **1.** the handle of a pan. **2.** *(sometimes cap.)* a long, narrow, projecting strip of territory that is not a peninsula: *the Texas panhandle.*

pan·han·dle² (pan/han/dəl), *v.,* **pan·han·dled, pan·han·dling.** *Informal.* to beg (money) from passers-by on the street. [from a special use of *panhandle¹* (referring to the outstretched arm in begging)] —**pan/han/dler,** *n.*

pan·ic (pan/ik), *n.* **1.** a sudden, overwhelming fear that produces hysterical behavior, often spreading quickly through a group of persons or animals. —*adj.* **2.** caused by or showing panic: *panic buying of food during a trucker's strike.* —*v.,* **pan·icked, pan·ick·ing. 3.** to affect or be affected with panic. —**pan/ick·y,** *adj.*

pan·nier (pan/yər), *n.* **1.** a large basket to be carried on a person's back. **2.** one of a pair of baskets to be slung across the back of a beast of burden.

pan·o·ply (pan/ə plē), *n., pl.* **pan·o·plies. 1.** a complete suit of armor. **2.** a complete covering or array of something: *to be dressed in a panoply of feathers.*

pan·o·ram·a (pan/ə ram/ə), *n.* **1.** a wide, unobstructed view of a large area. **2.** a wide picture of a landscape or other scene, often shown a part at a time before the spectators. **3.** a continuously passing or changing scene or unfolding of events: *the panorama of recent history.* **4.** a complete view or survey of a subject: *The movie presented an excellent panorama of the Civil War.* [from *pan-* + Greek *horama* "view, sight"] —**pan/o·ram/ic,** *adj.*

pan·pipe (pan/pīp/), *n.* a primitive wind instrument consisting of a row of hollow tubes of different lengths and played by blowing across the upper ends of the tubes.

pan·sy (pan/zē), *n., pl.* **pan·sies. 1.** a plant of the violet family that bears flowers having flat, velvety petals of various colors. **2.** a flower of this plant.

pant (pant), *v.* **1.** to breathe hard and quickly: *He began to pant halfway up the stairs.* **2.** to emit steam or the like in loud puffs. **3.** to long or yearn: *to pant for fame.* —*n.* **4.** a short, quick effort at breathing; gasp. **5.** a noisy puff: *the pant of an engine.*

Panpipe

pan·ta·loon (pan/tə lōōn/), *n.* **1. pantaloons,** a man's close-fitting trousers, worn esp. in the 19th century. **2.** (in modern pantomime) a foolish old man on whom the clown plays tricks. [from the Italian word *Pantalone,* a nickname for a Venetian, from *Pantaleone,* the name of an early patron saint of Venice]

pan·the·ism (pan/thē iz/əm), *n.* the belief that all things are a part of God and that God is the universe as a whole. —**pan/the·is/tic,** *adj.*

Pan·the·on (pan/thē on/), *n.* a domed, circular temple in Rome, built in 27 B.C. to honor all the gods.

pan·ther (pan/thər), *n.* **1.** another name for **cougar. 2.** a black leopard, esp. one found in southern Asia.

pant·ies (pan′tēz), *n. (used as pl.)* underpants or undershorts for women and children.

pan·to·mime (pan′tə mīm′), *n.* **1.** a play or entertainment in which the performers express themselves entirely by gestures. **2.** the art or technique of expressing emotions, actions, feelings, etc., by gestures. —*v.*, **pan·to·mimed, pan·to·mim·ing. 3.** to represent or express in pantomime. —**pan·to·mim·ic** (pan′tə-mim′ik), *adj.*

pan·try (pan′trē), *n., pl.* **pan·tries.** a room or closet for storing food, dishes, utensils, etc.

pants (pants), *n.pl.* **1.** another word for **trousers. 2.** underpants, esp. for women and children; panties.

pap (pap), *n.* soft food for infants or invalids.

pa·pa (pä′pə), *n. Informal.* father.

pa·pa·cy (pā′pə sē), *n., pl.* **pa·pa·cies.** (in the Roman Catholic Church) **1.** the office, dignity, or power of the pope. **2.** the system of Roman Catholic government. **3.** the period during which a certain pope is in office. **4.** the succession or line of the popes.

pa·pal (pā′pəl), *adj.* **1.** of or concerning the pope or the papacy. **2.** of or concerning the Roman Catholic Church.

pa·paw (pô′pô, pə pô′), *n.* **1.** the small, pulpy fruit of a North American shrub or small tree, usually greenish yellow in color. **2.** the tree bearing this fruit. Also, **pawpaw.** [another form of *papaya*]

pa·pa·ya (pə pä′yə), *n.* a large, yellow fruit resembling a melon, which grows on a tropical American shrub or small tree.

pa·per (pā′pər), *n.* **1.** a substance made from rags, straw, wood, or other fibrous material, usually in thin sheets, used to bear writing or printing or for wrapping, covering walls, etc. **2.** a piece, sheet, or leaf of this. **3.** a written or printed document. **4.** Often, **papers.** a document establishing or verifying a person's identity, occupation, or the like: *citizenship papers.* **5.** an essay or article on a particular topic. **6.** a newspaper or journal. —*v.* **7.** to line, cover, or wrap with paper or wallpaper: *to paper the bedroom.* —*adj.* **8.** made of paper: *a paper bag.* **9.** existing on paper only and not in reality: *paper profits.* **10. on paper, a.** in written or printed form. **b.** in theory rather than in practice: *His ideas look good on paper only.* —**pa′per·like′,** *adj.*

pa·per·back (pā′pər bak′), *n.* a book bound in a paper cover.

pa′per clip′, a short piece of wire bent so that it can fasten sheets of paper together; clip.

pa′per wasp′, any of several wasps, such as the yellowjacket or hornet, that builds a nest of a paperlike substance made up of chewed plant material.

pa·pil·la (pə pil′ə), *n., pl.* **pa·pil·lae** (pə pil′ē). a small, nipplelike projection, such as one of those on the tongue.

pa·poose (pa pōōs′, pə pōōs′), *n.* a North American Indian baby or young child.

pap·ri·ka (pa prē′kə), *n.* a red, powdery seasoning made from dried, ripe sweet peppers.

pa·py·rus (pə pī′rəs), *n., pl.* **pa·py·rus·es** *or* **pa·py·ri** (pə pī′rī). **1.** a tall, reedlike plant growing in the Nile valley, whose pith was used by the ancient Egyptians to make a material resembling paper. **2.** the paperlike material made from this plant. **3.** a document or scroll written on this material.

par (pär), *n.* **1.** a condition or quality of being equal in value or standing: *The gains and the losses are on a par.* **2.** an average or normal amount, quality, condition, etc.: *His work has been below par this year.* **3.** (in golf) the number of strokes set as a standard for a hole or a complete course.

par·a·ble (par′ə bəl), *n.* a short story whose purpose is to convey a truth or moral lesson.

pa·rab·o·la (pə rab′ə lə), *n.* the curve formed by the intersection of a cone and plane parallel to one of its sides; the curve formed by all points that are the same distance from a fixed point and a fixed line.

par·a·chute (par′ə shōōt′), *n.* **1.** a large, umbrella-shaped device of fabric that opens in midair and allows a person or an object to descend at a safe speed. **2.** a similar device used to reduce the forward speed of an airplane when it is landing. —*v.*, **par·a·chut·ed, par·a·chut·ing. 3.** to deliver or descend using a parachute.

Parabola

pa·rade (pə rād′), *n.* **1.** a large public procession, usually of a festive nature and accompanied by band music. **2.** a military ceremony involving the formation and marching of troop units. **3.** the orderly assembly of troops for inspection or display. —*v.*, **pa·rad·ed, pa·rad·ing. 4.** to march or appear in a parade. **5.** to show off or display: *to parade one's wealth.* —**pa·rad′er,** *n.*

par·a·dise (par′ə dīs′, par′ə dīz′), *n.* **1.** heaven, as the final resting place of the righteous. **2.** another word for **Eden. 3.** a place of extreme beauty, delight, or happiness.

par·a·dox (par′ə doks′), *n.* **1.** a statement that seems absurd or appears to contradict itself but in reality expresses a possible truth: *It is a paradox that parents punish a child because they love him.* **2.** a self-contradictory and false statement or way of reasoning. **3.** any person, thing, or situation showing an apparently contradictory nature. —**par′a·dox′i·cal,** *adj.*

par·af·fin (par′ə fin), *n.* a white, waxy substance obtained from petroleum and used for making candles, waterproofing paper, etc.

par·a·gon (par′ə gon′, par′ə gən), *n.* a model or pattern of excellence or of a particular excellence: *a paragon of loveliness.*

par·a·graph (par′ə graf′), *n.* **1.** a distinct portion of written or printed matter, dealing with a particular idea, usually beginning with an indentation on a new line. **2.** a note, item, or brief article in a newspaper. —*v.* **3.** to divide into paragraphs.

Par·a·guay (par′ə gwā′, par′ə gwī′), *n.* a republic in

central South America. 157,047 sq. mi. *Cap.:* Asunción. —**Par·a·guay·an,** *n., adj.*

par·a·keet (par/ə kēt/), *n.* any of various small, brightly colored parrots often kept as pets. Also, **parrakeet.**

par·al·lel (par/ə lel/), *adj.* **1.** (of lines, planes, etc.) not meeting at any point however far extended: *Railroad rails are set parallel to each other.* **2.** having the same direction, course, nature, or tendency: *parallel interests.* —*n.* **3.** a parallel line or plane. **4.** a line of latitude. **5.** anything similar in action, effect, nature, or tendency to something else. **6.** a comparison made between two things: *He drew a parallel between his summer vacation and mine.* —*v.,* **par·al·leled** *or* **par·al·lelled; par·al·lel·ing** *or* **par·al·lel·ling. 7.** to make parallel. **8.** to form a parallel to; match; equal. **9.** to go or be in a parallel course, direction, etc., to: *The road parallels the river.*

Parakeet
(length 7 in.)

par/allel bars/, an apparatus made of two wooden bars placed on upright bars, adjustable in height and distance apart, and used for exercising.

par·al·lel·ism (par/ə lel/iz əm), *n.* **1.** the position or relation of parallels. **2.** agreement or close similarity in tendency. **3.** a parallel or comparison.

par·al·lel·o·gram (par/ə lel/ə-gram/), *n.* a four-sided polygon having both pairs of opposite sides parallel.

Parallel bars

pa·ral·y·sis (pə ral/i sis), *n.* **1.** partial or complete loss of the capacity for motion or feeling in some part of the body. **2.** a crippling or stoppage of powers or activity: *The storm caused a paralysis of transportation.*

par·a·lyt·ic (par/ə lit/ik), *adj.* **1.** of or concerning paralysis. —*n.* **2.** a person who is paralyzed.

par·a·lyze (par/ə līz/), *v.,* **par·a·lyzed, par·a·lyz·ing. 1.** to cause (a person) to suffer the loss of movement or feeling in some part of the body. **2.** to make powerless, helpless, ineffective, or inactive.

Par·a·mar·i·bo (par/ə mar/ə bō/), *n.* a seaport and the capital city of Surinam.

par·a·me·ci·um (par/ə mē/shē əm, par/ə mē/sē əm), *n., pl.* **par·a·me·ci·a** (par/ə mē/shē ə, par/ə mē/sē ə). a slipper-shaped, one-celled animal, seen only with a microscope, whose surface is covered with tiny hair-like cilia that propel it through the water.

par·a·med·ic (par/ə med/ik), *n.* a person trained to assist a physician.

par·a·mount (par/ə mount/), *adj.* chief in importance; above others in rank or authority.

par·a·pet (par/ə pit, par/ə pet/), *n.* **1.** a defensive wall or elevation in a fortification. **2.** any low protective wall or barrier at the edge of a balcony, roof, bridge, or the like.

par·a·pher·nal·ia (par/ə fər nāl/yə), *n.* **1.** *(used as pl.)* personal belongings. **2.** *(sometimes used as pl.)*

equipment or apparatus: *camping paraphernalia.*

par·a·phrase (par/ə frāz/), *n.* **1.** a restating of a text or passage that gives the meaning in another form; rewording. —*v.,* **par·a·phrased, par·a·phras·ing. 2.** to restate or reword the meaning of: *He paraphrased the order to make sure everyone understood it.*

par·a·pro·fes·sion·al (par/ə prə fesh/ə n²l), *n.* a person, such as a teacher's assistant, trained to assist a professional.

par·a·site (par/ə sīt/), *n.* **1.** an animal or plant that lives on or in another living organism from which it extracts nourishment. **2.** a person who receives support, advantage, or the like, from another or others without giving proper return. [from the Greek word *parasitos* "one who eats at another's table"]

par·a·sit·ic (par/ə sit/ik), *adj.* of, concerning, or caused by parasites.

par·a·sol (par/ə sôl/), *n.* a woman's small, lightweight umbrella used as a sun shield.

par·a·troop·er (par/ə trōō/pər), *n.* a member of an army infantry unit trained to attack or land in combat areas by parachuting from airplanes.

par·boil (pär/boil/), *v.* to boil partially or for a short time; precook.

par·cel (pär/səl), *n.* **1.** an object, container, or quantity of something wrapped or packed up; package; bundle. **2.** a unit or piece of something for sale; lot: *a parcel of land.* —*v.,* **par·celed** *or* **par·celled; par·cel·ing** *or* **par·cel·ling. 3.** to divide into or distribute in portions (usually fol. by *out*): *to parcel out food.*

par/cel post/, a branch of a postal service that transports and delivers parcels.

parch (pärch), *v.* **1.** to make or become dry: *The sun parched the fields.* **2.** to make or become hot or thirsty: *We were all parched after the long hike.*

parch·ment (pärch/mənt), *n.* **1.** the skin of sheep, goats, etc., prepared for use as a material on which to write. **2.** a manuscript or document on such material. **3.** paper resembling this material.

par·don (pär/d²n), *n.* **1.** forgiveness of an offense or discourtesy: *I beg your pardon.* **2.** a release from the penalty of an offense. —*v.* **3.** to forgive or excuse. **4.** to release from penalty or punishment: *The governor pardoned the prisoner.* —**par/don·a·ble,** *adj.*

pare (pâr), *v.,* **pared, par·ing. 1.** to cut off the outer coating, layer, or part of: *to pare an apple.* **2.** to remove (an outer layer or part) by cutting: *to pare rind from an orange.* **3.** to lessen or decrease gradually: *to pare expenses.*

par·ent (pâr/ənt, par/ənt), *n.* **1.** a father or a mother. **2.** a source, origin, or cause. **3.** any organism that produces or generates another.

par·ent·age (pâr/ən tij, par/ən tij), *n.* descent from parents or ancestors; origin.

pa·ren·tal (pə ren/t²l), *adj.* of, concerning, or like a parent.

pa·ren·the·sis (pə ren/thi sis), *n., pl.* **pa·ren·the·ses** (pə ren/thi sēz/). **1.** either or both of a pair of signs ( ) used to enclose a word, phrase, clause, sentence, or the like, within a sentence. **2.** a word, phrase, clause, sentence, or the like, that interrupts but does not otherwise affect an already complete sentence.

par·ent·hood (pâr′ənt ho͝od′, par′ənt ho͝od′), *n.* the state, condition, or relation of being a parent.

par·fait (pär fā′), *n.* 1. a dessert made of layers of ice cream and fruit, syrup, etc., usually topped with whipped cream. 2. a rich frozen dessert of whipped cream and egg.

pa·ri·ah (pə rī′ə), *n.* an outcast.

par·ing (pâr′iŋ), *n.* 1. the act of a person or thing that pares. 2. a piece or part pared off: *apple parings.*

Par·is (par′is), *n.* the capital city of France, in the N part. —**Pa·ri·sian** (pə rē′zhən, pə rizh′ən), *n., adj.*

par·ish (par′ish), *n.* 1. a church district having its own church or clergyman. 2. (in Louisiana) a county. 3. the people of a church or civil parish.

pa·rish·ion·er (pə rish′ə nər), *n.* a member or inhabitant of a parish.

par·i·ty (par′i tē), *n.* equality, as in amount, status, or character.

park (pärk), *n.* 1. a public area of land having facilities for rest and recreation. 2. an enclosed area or a stadium used for sports: *a baseball park.* 3. a large extent of land forming the grounds of a country house. —*v.* 4. to leave (a vehicle) standing, usually in a lot or on the side of a road, with the intention of not using it again immediately.

par·ka (pär′kə), *n.* a hooded coat or jacket of fur, wool, or other wind-resistant material.

park·way (pärk′wā′), *n.* a wide road with a dividing strip or side strips planted with grass, trees, etc.

par·lance (pär′ləns), *n.* a way or manner of speaking: *legal parlance.*

par·ley (pär′lē), *n., pl.* **par·leys.** 1. a discussion or conference. 2. an informal conference between enemies to discuss terms for ending hostilities. —*v.,* **par·leyed, par·ley·ing.** 3. to hold an informal conference with an enemy. 4. to speak, talk, or confer.

par·lia·ment (pär′lə mənt), *n.* 1. *(usually cap.)* the legislature of Great Britain, consisting of the House of Lords and the House of Commons. 2. *(usually cap.)* the legislature of certain British Commonwealth countries. 3. a similar type of legislative body in other countries.

par·lia·men·ta·ry (pär′lə men′tə rē), *adj.* 1. of or concerning a parliament. 2. enacted by a parliament. 3. having a parliament. 4. according to the rules governing a parliament.

par·lor (pär′lər), *n.* 1. a room for the reception and entertainment of visitors. 2. a room or building forming a business place: *a beauty parlor.*

par′lor car′, (on a railroad) a deluxe passenger car having individual reserved seats.

Par·nas·sus (pär nas′əs), *n.* a mountain in central Greece, considered sacred to Apollo and the Muses in ancient times. 8062 ft.

pa·ro·chi·al (pə rō′kē əl), *adj.* 1. of or concerning a parish or parishes. 2. maintained or operated by a religious organization: *parochial schools.* 3. of very limited or narrow scope; provincial: *parochial ideas.*

par·o·dy (par′ə dē), *n., pl.* **par·o·dies.** 1. a humorous imitation of a serious piece of literature, musical composition, person, event, etc. —*v.,* **par·o·died, par·o·dy·ing.** 2. to imitate for purposes of ridicule.

pa·role (pə rōl′), *n.* 1. the release of a person from prison before the end of his sentence, usually for good behavior and provided that he obey certain regulations. —*v.,* **pa·roled, pa·rol·ing.** 2. to place (a person) on parole. [from the French word *parole,* in the phrase *parole d'honneur* "word of honor"]

par·ox·ysm (par′ək siz′əm), *n.* a severe attack; spasm, fit, or outburst: *a paroxysm of coughing.*

par·quet (pär kā′), *n.* 1. a floor of inlaid design. 2. the main floor of a theater, opera house, etc.

par·ra·keet (par′ə kēt′), *n.* another spelling of **parakeet.**

par·ri·cide (par′i sīd′), *n.* 1. the act of killing one's father, mother, or other close relative. 2. a person who commits such an act.

par·rot (par′ət), *n.* 1. any of numerous tropical birds having hooked bills and, often, brilliant

Parquet

plumage. Parrots can mimic human speech and are often kept as pets. 2. a person who, without thought or understanding, merely repeats the words or imitates the actions of another. —*v.* 3. to repeat or imitate without thought or understanding.

par·ry (par′ē), *v.,* **par·ried, par·ry·ing.** 1. to ward off (a thrust, blow, etc.), as in fencing. 2. to evade or avoid; dodge: *to parry an embarrassing question.* —*n., pl.* **par·ries.** 3. the act or movement of parrying.

parse (pärs, pärz), *v.,* **parsed, pars·ing.** 1. to analyze (a sentence) into its parts, describing the grammatical function and relationship of each part. 2. to describe (a word in a sentence), giving its part of speech, its inflectional form, and its grammatical function.

par·si·mo·ni·ous (pär′sə mō′nē əs), *adj.* showing parsimony; extremely frugal or sparing; stingy.

par·si·mony (pär′sə mō′nē), *n.* extreme economy or frugality; stinginess.

pars·ley (pärs′lē), *n.* a garden herb having frilly leaves used to flavor or garnish food.

pars·nip (pär′snip), *n.* a plant of the carrot family having a large, whitish root that is eaten as a vegetable.

par·son (pär′sən), *n.* a clergyman; minister; preacher.

par·son·age (pär′sə nij), *n.* the residence of a parson or clergyman.

part (pärt), *n.* 1. a portion or division of a whole; piece; fragment; section: *the rear part of the house.* 2. a portion, member, or organ of an animal body. 3. the dividing line formed in combing the hair. 4. a piece of a machine or tool either included at the time of manufacture or provided as a replacement for the original piece. 5. one's share in some action; duty; function. 6. a character or role acted in a play:

She plays the part of the princess. **7.** (in music) a voice or melody, either sung or played: *A quartet is a composition for four parts.* **8.** the music from which a single performer in a group plays: *a first-violin part.* **9.** Usually, **parts. a.** a region or district. **b.** ability or talent: *a man of parts.* —*v.* **10.** to divide into parts. **11.** to comb (the hair) away from a dividing line. **12.** to break off or end (a connection, relationship, etc.): *to part company.* **13.** to put or keep apart; separate. **14.** to go apart from each other: *The friends parted.* **15. for the most part,** usually; mostly: *The boys are well-behaved for the most part.* **16. in part,** to some extent; partly: *The shortage was due in part to poor planning.* **17. part with,** to give up; let go of: *We had to part with some furniture when we moved to a trailer.* **18. take part,** to participate; join in: *to take part in social activities.* **19. take someone's part,** to side with or defend another person: *She always takes his part, even when he's wrong.*

par·take (pär tāk′), *v.,* **par·took** (pär took′), **par·tak·en** (pär tā′kən), **par·tak·ing. 1.** to take part or have a share; participate: *to partake in the celebration.* **2.** to receive, take, or have a share: *to partake of a meal.* **3.** to have something of the nature or quality: *feelings partaking of both joy and regret.*

Par·the·non (pär′thə non′), *n.* the temple of Athena at Athens, completed about 438 B.C.

par·tial (pär′shəl), *adv.* **1.** involving only a part; not total; incomplete: *a partial payment.* **2.** favoring one side; prejudiced; biased. **3. partial to,** having a liking for: *I'm partial to chocolate cake.* —**par′tial·ly,** *adv.*

par·tial·i·ty (pär shal′i tē, pär′shē al′i tē), *n., pl.* for def. 2 **par·tial·i·ties. 1.** the state or condition of being partial. **2.** a special fondness or liking.

par·tic·i·pant (pär tis′ə pənt), *n.* a person who participates or takes part.

par·tic·i·pate (pär tis′ə pāt′), *v.,* **par·tic·i·pat·ed, par·tic·i·pat·ing.** to take or have a part or share: *to participate in the play.* —**par·tic′i·pa′tion,** *n.*

par·ti·ci·pi·al (pär′ti sip′ē əl), *adj.* **1.** of or referring to a participle: *a participial phrase.* **2.** formed from a participle.

par·ti·ci·ple (pär′ti sip′əl), *n.* an inflected form of a verb showing tense and voice, that may be used as an adjective or noun, or with an auxiliary to form certain tenses. See also **past participle, present participle.**

par·ti·cle (pär′ti kəl), *n.* **1.** a tiny portion, piece, or amount; a very small bit: *a particle of dust; a subatomic particle.* **2.** (in grammar) **a.** a prefix or suffix. **b.** a short word used to show a function or relation, such as an article, preposition, or conjunction. **c.** a word having no grammatical connection with other words in a sentence, such as an interjection.

par·tic·u·lar (pər tik′yə lər), *adj.* **1.** of or concerning a single or specific person, thing, occasion, etc.; special rather than general: *His particular interests include skiing and golf.* **2.** distinct or apart from others: *That particular painting is not for sale.* **3.** noteworthy or exceptional; unusual: *Take particular care to do a good job.* **4.** very selective or exacting;

fussy: *to be particular about one's food.* —*n.* **5.** an individual, distinct, or separate part, as an item of a list. **6.** Usually, **particulars.** specific points or details: *the particulars of a case.* **7. in particular,** particularly; especially; above all: *There's one flavor in particular that I like.*

par·tic·u·lar·i·ty (pər tik′yə lar′i tē), *n., pl.* **par·tic·u·lar·i·ties. 1.** a special, peculiar, or individual trait or feature. **2.** attention to details; special care.

par·tic·u·lar·ize (pər tik′yə lə rīz′), *v.,* **par·tic·u·lar·ized, par·tic·u·lar·iz·ing. 1.** to mention or indicate specifically; specify. **2.** to state or treat in detail.

par·tic·u·lar·ly (pər tik′yə lər lē), *adv.* **1.** to a great degree; especially: *His interest in science is particularly strong.* **2.** in a particular manner; specifically: *He studied all the plans, but this one particularly.*

part·ing (pär′ting), *n.* **1.** the act of a person or thing that parts. **2.** a division or separation. **3.** a departure; leave-taking. **4.** a place of division or separation. —*adj.* **5.** given or done at parting: *a parting remark.* **6.** dividing or separating. **7.** departing or leaving: *the parting train.*

par·ti·san (pär′ti zən), *n.* **1.** a supporter of a person, party, or cause. **2.** a member of a group of fighters not part of a regular army; guerrilla. —*adj.* **3.** of, concerning, or like partisans; supporting a particular party, cause, etc.: *partisan politics.*

par·ti·tion (pär tish′ən), *n.* **1.** a division or separation into portions or shares. **2.** something that separates or divides, such as a wall, screen, etc. —*v.* **3.** to divide into parts or portions. **4.** to divide or separate by a partition: *to partition a room with a screen.*

part·ly (pärt′lē), *adv.* in part; to some extent or degree: *His statement is partly true.*

part·ner (pärt′nər), *n.* **1.** a person who shares or partakes; associate. **2.** a person who shares the profits and losses with another or others in a business. **3.** a husband or a wife; spouse. **4.** one's companion in a dance. **5.** a player on the same side or team as another.

part·ner·ship (pärt′nər ship′), *n.* **1.** the state or condition of being a partner; participation; association. **2.** an association of persons joined as partners in business.

part′ of speech′, any of the grammatical classes into which words are divided according to their syntactical function. In English, the parts of speech are noun, pronoun, adjective, verb, adverb, preposition, conjunction, and interjection.

par·took (pär took′), *v.* the past tense of **partake.**

par·tridge (pär′trij), *n., pl.* **par·tridg·es** *or* **par·tridge. 1.** any of several North American game birds including the grouse and the bobwhite. **2.** any of several European pheasants and quails.

Partridge
(length
1 to 1½ ft.)

part-time (pärt′tīm′), *adj.* **1.** working less than the usual number of hours: *a part-time salesman.* **2.** taking up less than the usual time:

a part-time job. —*adv.* **3.** on a part-time basis: *to work part-time.*

par·ty (pär′tē), *n., pl.* **par·ties. 1.** a social gathering for entertainment or to celebrate an occasion: *a birthday party.* **2.** a group of persons gathered together for a particular purpose: *a search party.* **3.** a political organization that controls or seeks to control a government: *the Democratic party.* **4.** a person who takes part in something: *He refused to be a party to the robbery.* **5.** (in law) one of the participants in a lawsuit, contract, etc. **6.** *Informal.* a person: *A certain party called you on the phone.* —*adj.* **7.** suitable for a social gathering: *a party dress.* **8.** of or concerning a political party: *a party primary.*

Pas·a·de·na (pas′ə dē′nə), *n.* a city in SW California, near Los Angeles.

pa·sha (päsh′ə, pash′ə), *n.* a title formerly held by high officials in countries under Turkish rule.

pass (pas), *v.* **1.** to go past or beyond: *We waited until the parade had passed.* **2.** to go by; elapse, as time: *The days passed quickly.* **3.** to spend or use (a period of time): *I passed the time reading.* **4.** to cause or allow to go through: *The guard passed the visitors.* **5.** to come to an end: *The storm passed, and the sun came out.* **6.** to change from one form or state to another: *When water is heated, it passes into steam.* **7.** to go from one place to another: *After dinner, the guests passed into the library.* **8.** to go from one owner to another, esp. by inheritance: *At his death, his property passed to his son.* **9.** to let go without notice; overlook: *He passed my mistakes in spelling.* **10.** to go unnoticed; be disregarded: *Let the insult pass.* **11.** to complete successfully: *to pass an examination.* **12.** to award or receive a satisfactory grade: *The teacher passed the entire class.* **13.** to approve or be approved: *Congress passed the bill. The bill failed to pass.* **14.** to hand from one person to another; hand over: *Please pass me that book.* **15.** to take place; happen: *I forgive all that has passed.* **16.** to give or pronounce (a judgment or opinion): *The judge passed sentence on the convicted murderer.* **17.** to express an opinion or judgment: *I don't know enough about politics to pass on that question.* **18.** to say, esp. in a casual or careless manner: *to pass a remark.* **19.** to go beyond; exceed; surpass: *Jim has passed me in height.* **20.** to be taken, accepted, or recognized, esp. for what one is not: *He can pass for fifty, although he is seventy.* **21.** (in cards) to give up one's chance to bid or play. **22.** (in sports) to throw or hit (a ball, puck, etc.) to a teammate. —*n.* **23.** a narrow road or way, esp. through a gap in a mountain range. **24.** permission to enter or leave a place. **25.** a free ticket. **26.** (in sports) a throwing or hitting of a ball, puck, etc., to a teammate. **27.** a single gesture, stroke, attempt, etc. **28.** a particular state of affairs: *Things have come to a desperate pass.* **29. come to pass,** to occur; happen. **30. pass away,** to die: *He passed away last Friday.* **31. pass off,** to present, offer, or dispose of with the intention of deceiving: *She*

passed herself off as a famous actress. **32. pass on,** to die: *Her relatives have all passed on.* **33. pass out,** *Informal.* to faint: *It was so hot in there I almost passed out.* **34. pass up,** *Informal.* to refuse or neglect to take advantage of: *Don't pass up an opportunity like that.* —**pass′er,** *n.*

pass·a·ble (pas′ə bəl), *adj.* **1.** capable of being traveled on, across, or over: *The roads are passable only in good weather.* **2.** barely adequate or acceptable: *a passable performance of "Hamlet."* —**pass′a·bly,** *adv.*

pas·sage (pas′ij), *n.* **1.** a short portion of a written work or a speech: *He quoted some passages from the Bible.* **2.** a passing from one place, condition, etc., to another: *the passage from riches to poverty.* **3.** permission, right, or freedom to pass: *They were granted passage through the enemy lines.* **4.** the route or course by which a person or thing passes or travels: *a passage through the jungle.* **5.** a narrow space through or along which a person or thing may enter or pass; aisle, corridor, or passageway. **6.** a voyage or journey, esp. across water. **7.** the accommodation, such as a cabin, stateroom, or berth, provided for a passenger on a ship. **8.** the cost of accommodation on a ship; fare. **9.** approval of a bill, law, etc.: *Passage of the housing bill appears certain.*

pas·sage·way (pas′ij wā′), *n.* a narrow space through which a person or thing may pass, such as a hallway, alley, etc.

pas·sen·ger (pas′ən jər), *n.* a person who is carried in a car, train, plane, ship, or other conveyance.

pass·er·by (pas′ər bī′), *n., pl.* **pass·ers·by** (pas′ərz bī′). a person who passes by: *A passer-by helped the blind man cross the street.*

pass·ing (pas′ing), *adj.* **1.** going by or past: *watching the passing crowds.* **2.** elapsing, as time: *the passing years.* **3.** occurring or existing briefly: *a passing fancy.* **4.** adequate or acceptable: *a passing grade.* —*n.* **5.** the act of going by or past. **6.** a lapsing or expiring, esp. of time: *the passing of the seasons.* **7.** a person's death. **8.** ending; extinction: *the passing of the steam locomotive.* —*adv.* **9.** *Archaic.* extremely; very: *His look was passing strange.*

pas·sion (pash′ən), *n.* **1.** a powerful feeling or emotion, such as love, fear, hate, etc. **2.** a strong liking or devotion to a person or thing: *a passion for music.* **3.** the object of a strong liking: *Music is a passion with him.* **4.** (*often cap.*) the sufferings of Christ on the cross or after the Last Supper.

pas·sion·ate (pash′ə nit), *adj.* **1.** filled with or influenced by strong feeling or emotion: *He is a passionate follower of baseball.* **2.** showing or expressing strong feeling: *passionate glances; passionate verses.* —**pas′sion·ate·ly,** *adv.*

pas·sion·flow·er (pash′ən flou′ər), *n.* any of various American climbing vines or shrubs, having showy flowers and a pulpy berry or fruit that is sometimes edible.

Passionflower

pas·sive (pas′iv), *adj.* 1. not reacting or resisting; submissive. 2. acted upon rather than acting or causing action: *He played a passive role in the experiment.* 3. (in grammar) referring to the passive voice. —**pas′sive·ly**, *adv.* —**pas′sive·ness**, *n.*

pas′sive voice′, the inflected form of a verb that shows that the subject receives the action of the verb. In the sentence *Jack was hit by the ball,* the verb *was hit* is in the passive voice.

pass·key (pas′kē′), *n., pl.* **pass·keys.** 1. a key that will open a number of locks. 2. a private key.

Pass·o·ver (pas′ō′vər), *n.* a Jewish festival celebrating the deliverance of the Hebrews from slavery in Egypt.

pass·port (pas′pôrt′), *n.* 1. official written permission granted by a government to one of its citizens by which he may identify himself and prove his right to travel abroad, to have the protection of his government, and to return. 2. anything that enables a person to go somewhere or to achieve something: *Self-confidence is the passport to success.*

pass·word (pas′wûrd′), *n.* a secret word, phrase, or signal that a person must give in order to pass by a guard or sentry.

past (past), *adj.* 1. gone by; finished; ended: *We've had some quarrels, but that's all past now.* 2. having ended just before the present time: *during the past year.* 3. earlier or former: *past mistakes; a past president.* 4. (in grammar) referring to or expressed by the past tense or any verb form expressing action or state of being in past time. —*n.* 5. the time before the present. 6. the earlier history of a nation, person, etc.: *Now that she's famous, she'd like to forget her past.* 7. (in grammar) a. the past tense. b. a verb form in the past tense. —*adv.* 8. so as to pass by or beyond; by: *A column of tanks rumbled past.* —*prep.* 9. beyond in time, distance, number, amount, etc.: *past noon; past the age limit.* 10. beyond the limits or reach of: *The money is past recovery.*

pas·ta (pä′stə), *n.* an Italian food paste that is shaped and dried as spaghetti, macaroni, etc.

paste (pāst), *n.* 1. a mixture of flour and water, often also starch, used for sticking paper, cloth, and similar light materials to other objects. 2. any soft, smooth mixture of solid and liquid ingredients, such as toothpaste, almond paste, etc. 3. dough prepared with shortening and used for making pies, tarts, etc. —*v.,* **past·ed, past·ing.** 4. to stick with paste, glue, or a similar material. 5. *Slang.* to strike hard, esp. with the fists or a heavy weapon.

paste·board (pāst′bôrd′), *n.* a stiff cardboard made by pasting together sheets of paper or by pressing together layers of paper pulp.

pas·tel (pa stel′), *n.* 1. a color having a soft, pale shade. 2. a stick of dried colored paste used in drawing or marking. 3. a drawing made with this kind of stick. —*adj.* 4. of a soft, pale shade: *pastel pink.* 5. drawn with pastels: *a pastel portrait.*

Pas·teur (pa stûr′), *n.* Lou·is (loo′ē), 1822–1895, French chemist and bacteriologist.

pas·teur·ize (pas′chə rīz′), *v.,* **pas·teur·ized, pas·teur·** iz·ing. to heat to a temperature high enough to kill most germs and other microorganisms. [named after Louis *Pasteur*] —**pas′teur·i·za′tion**, *n.*

pas·time (pas′tīm′), *n.* any activity, such as a game, sport, hobby, etc., that makes time pass agreeably.

pas·tor (pas′tər), *n.* a minister or priest in charge of a church or congregation.

pas·to·ral (pas′tər əl), *adj.* 1. of, belonging to, or describing shepherds or rural life: *a pastoral poem; a painting of a quiet, pastoral scene.* 2. of or concerning a minister or priest or his duties: *a pastoral letter.* —*n.* 3. a poem, play, etc., dealing with the life of shepherds or with country life.

pas·tor·ate (pas′tər it), *n.* 1. the position, duties, or jurisdiction of a pastor. 2. the term of office of a pastor. 3. pastors taken together as a group.

past′ par′ticiple, a participle with past meaning, formed in English in one of several ways: by adding one of the endings *-ed, -d, -t, -n,* or *-en* to the stem of the verb *(walked; baked; dreamt; taken; fallen),* or by changing the vowel of the stem *(sung),* or without any change in form *(put).*

past′ per′fect tense′, the form of a verb that expresses action or a state that is completed before some other action or state in the past. In English, the past perfect tense is formed by placing the auxiliary verb *had* before the past participle: *When we got to the station, the train had left.* Also, **pluperfect tense.**

pas·try (pā′strē), *n., pl.* **pas·tries.** 1. a sweet baked food made entirely or largely of paste, such as pies, tarts, etc. 2. any sweet baked foods.

past′ tense′, the form of a verb that expresses action or state in past time. In English, the past tense is formed by adding one of the endings *-ed, -d,* or *-t* to the stem of the verb *(talked; moved; slept),* or by changing the vowel of the stem *(sang),* or without any change in form *(set).*

pas·tur·age (pas′chər ij), *n.* 1. grass or other plants on which livestock feed. 2. land used for feeding of livestock; grazing ground. 3. the business or activity of pasturing livestock.

pas·ture (pas′chər), *n.* 1. land covered with grass or other plants, used for the feeding of livestock. 2. the grass or other plants on which livestock feed. —*v.,* **pas·tured, pas·tur·ing.** 3. to feed (animals) by putting them in a pasture.

past·y (pā′stē), *adj.,* **past·i·er, past·i·est.** 1. of or like paste; sticky; doughy: *a pasty mixture of flour and water.* 2. pale and flabby in appearance: *a pasty complexion.* —**past′i·ness**, *n.*

pat (pat), *v.,* **pat·ted, pat·ting.** 1. to strike lightly with something flat: *Pat the dough into a thin crust.* 2. to stroke or tap gently, showing affection or approval: *That dog loves to have people pat him.* 3. to walk or run with light footsteps: *The children patted about the house.* —*n.* 4. a light stroke or tap with the palm, the fingers, or something flat: *I give the dog a pat when he obeys.* 5. the sound made by patting. 6. a small, flat piece made by patting or cutting: *a pat of butter.* —*adj.* 7. exactly to the point; perfectly suitable: *a pat solution to a problem.* 8. learned perfectly;

thoroughly rehearsed; glib: *pat answers.* —*adv.* **9.** exactly; perfectly: *You must learn this pat.* **10. stand pat,** to remain firm in one's decision or beliefs: *I'm going to stand pat on what I said before.*

Pat·a·go·ni·a (pat/ə gō/nē ə), *n.* a large, level region in S Argentina. —**Pat/a·go/ni·an,** *n., adj.*

patch (pach), *n.* **1.** a small piece of cloth, metal, or other material, used for mending a tear, covering a hole, etc. **2.** a small piece of material used for covering, protecting, etc., or worn as an emblem: *an eye patch; a service patch.* **3.** any of the pieces of cloth sewn together to form patchwork. **4.** a small spot or area that differs from the surrounding area: *a patch of brown on the lawn; a patch of ice on the road.* **5.** a small plot of land on which a particular kind of plant grows or is grown: *a brier patch; a potato patch.* —*v.* **6.** to mend or cover with a patch. **7.** to repair, esp. hastily and in a makeshift way: *We patched the broken axle and started out again.* **8.** to make by joining patches or pieces together: *to patch a quilt.*

patch·work (pach/wûrk/), *n.* **1.** a large piece of material made by sewing or joining together patches of various colors and shapes. **2.** anything made up of pieces or parts of different kinds: *The Soviet Union is a patchwork of many races and languages.* —*adj.* **3.** made of patchwork: *a patchwork quilt.*

pate (pāt), *n.* the top of the head.

pat·ent (pat/ᵊnt), *n.* **1.** the exclusive right granted by a government to an inventor to manufacture, use, or sell his invention for a certain number of years. **2.** an invention or process protected by a patent. **3.** an official document granting a right or privilege, or a title to public land. —*adj.* **4.** protected or granted by a patent. **5.** concerning or dealing with patents: *a patent attorney.* **6.** obvious; evident: *a patent lie.* —*v.* **7.** to secure or protect by a patent: *Have you patented your invention?*

pat/ent leath/er, a smooth, shiny leather, used esp. for making shoes, handbags, etc.

pat·ent·ly (pat/ᵊnt lē), *adv.* openly; clearly; obviously: *His statement is patently false.*

pat/ent med/icine, a medicine that can be sold without a prescription, esp. one having a trade name.

pa·ter·nal (pə tûr/nᵊl), *adj.* **1.** of or like a father; fatherly: *paternal responsibility; paternal advice.* **2.** related on the father's side: *my paternal grandparents.* **3.** received or inherited from a father: *a paternal estate.* [from the Latin word *paternus,* which comes from *pater* "father"] —**pa·ter/nal·ly,** *adv.*

pa·ter·nal·ism (pə tûr/nᵊliz/əm), *n.* a system of government or the conduct of a group, business, etc., resembling a father's treatment of his children, in which strict authority is combined with concern for the welfare of individuals. —**pa·ter/nal·is/tic,** *adj.*

pa·ter·ni·ty (pə tûr/ni tē), *n.* **1.** the state of being a father; fatherhood. **2.** descent from a father; paternal origin: *a foundling of unknown paternity.*

Pat·er·son (pat/ər sən), *n.* a city in NE New Jersey.

path (path), *n., pl.* **paths** (paᵗ͟hz, paths). **1.** a narrow track or way made by the passing of human or animal feet. **2.** a narrow way or lane: *a bicycle path.* **3.** the route or course along which a person or thing moves: *the path of the hurricane; the path to success.* **4.** a way of behaving or thinking: *the path of peace.* **5. cross one's path,** to meet or encounter someone unexpectedly: *I haven't crossed his path in years.*

pa·thet·ic (pə thet/ik), *adj.* arousing feelings of pity or sorrow; pitiful: *a pathetic picture of starving children.* —**pa·thet/i·cal·ly,** *adv.*

path·o·log·i·cal (path/ə loj/i kəl), *adj.* **1.** of or concerning pathology: *pathological studies.* **2.** caused by or involving disease: *a pathological fear of dogs.* **3.** dealing with diseases. —**path/o·log/i·cal·ly,** *adv.*

pa·thol·o·gy (pə thol/ə jē), *n.* **1.** the branch of medicine dealing with the origin, nature, and course of diseases. **2.** the symptoms, conditions, or processes of a disease. —**pa·thol/o·gist,** *n.*

pa·thos (pā/thos), *n.* the quality or power of a literary or artistic work, or a real event, of arousing pity or sympathy: *the pathos of a funeral procession.*

path·way (path/wā/), *n.* **1.** a narrow path or lane, esp. for travelers on foot, bicycle, or horseback. **2.** any route or course: *the pathway to riches.*

pa·tience (pā/shəns), *n.* **1.** the ability to put up with annoyance, misfortune, pain, or delay, without complaint or loss of temper. **2.** diligence; perseverance: *It takes patience to learn to paint portraits.* **3.** See **solitaire** (def. 1).

pa·tient (pā/shənt), *n.* **1.** a person receiving treatment from a physician, dentist, or the like. —*adj.* **2.** having or showing patience. —**pa/tient·ly,** *adv.*

pa·ti·o (pat/ē ō/, pä/tē ō/), *n., pl.* **pa·ti·os. 1.** an open courtyard around which a house or group of houses is built. **2.** an open paved area at the back or side of a house, often furnished with weatherproof chairs and tables, used for outdoor living.

pat·ois (pat/wä), *n., pl.* **pat·ois** (pat/wäz). a dialect spoken chiefly by the people of a rural district.

pa·tri·arch (pā/trē ärk/), *n.* **1.** the father and head of a family or tribe. **2.** the ancestor and founder of a race of people: *Abraham, Isaac, and Jacob are patriarchs of the Jewish people.* **3.** a respected and honored old man. **4.** a high-ranking bishop in the Roman Catholic or Eastern Orthodox Church. —**pa/tri·ar/chal,** *adj.*

pa·tri·cian (pə trish/ən), *n.* **1.** a member of the nobility in ancient Rome. **2.** a highborn or noble person; aristocrat. —*adj.* **3.** aristocratic; noble. **4.** of, belonging to, or like a patrician or patricians. **5.** of cultivated tastes or social manners; refined.

---

act, āble, dâre, ärt; ebb, ēqual; if, īce; hot, ōver, ôrder; oil; book; ōoze; out; up, ûrge; ə = *a* as in *alone*; ᵊ as in *button* (but/ᵊn), *fire* (fiᵊr); chief; shoe; thin; ᵗ͟hat; zh as in *measure* (mezh/ər). See full key inside cover.

Pat·rick (pa′trik), *n.* **Saint,** A.D. 389?–461?, Christian missionary in Ireland: patron saint of Ireland.

pat·ri·mo·ny (pa′trə mō′nē), *n., pl.* **pat·ri·mo·nies. 1.** property inherited from one's father or ancestors. **2.** any quality, trait, or institution that is inherited; heritage: *We must preserve our patrimony of liberty.* **3.** property belonging by endowment to a church or religious institution. —**pat′ri·mo′ni·al,** *adj.*

pa·tri·ot (pā′trē ət, pā′trē ot′), *n.* a person who loves, supports, and defends his country. [from the Greek word *patriōtēs* "countryman," which comes from *patris* "fatherland"]

pa·tri·ot·ic (pā′trē ot′ik), *adj.* **1.** having or expressing loyalty to one's country. **2.** of or like a patriot or patriots. **3.** arousing or inspiring patriotism: *a patriotic hymn.* —**pa′tri·ot′i·cal·ly,** *adv.*

pa·tri·ot·ism (pā′trē ə tiz′əm), *n.* the devoted love, support, and defense of one's country.

pa·trol (pə trōl′), *v.,* **pa·trolled, pa·trol·ing. 1.** to pass regularly through or along (a certain area or route) for the purpose of maintaining order and security: *The police are patrolling the waterfront.* —*n.* **2.** a person, thing, or group that patrols: *A patrol went out to search the area for snipers.* **3.** the act of patrolling: *The police have a thousand men on patrol.* **4.** (in the Boy Scouts and Girl Scouts) a part of a troop, usually consisting of about eight members.

pa·trol·man (pə trōl′mən), *n., pl.* **pa·trol·men. 1.** a policeman assigned to patrol a certain route or area. **2.** a man who patrols.

pa·tron (pā′trən), *n.* **1.** a customer or client of a store, restaurant, hotel, etc. **2.** a person, usually a wealthy person, who supports the work of an artist, writer, composer, etc., or supports an institution such as a museum or a charity.

pa·tron·age (pā′trə nij, pa′trə nij), *n.* **1.** the business brought into a store, restaurant, hotel, etc., by its customers or clients. **2.** the help or support given by a patron to an artist or an institution. **3.** (in politics) control over appointments to public office, government contracts, and awarding of political favors.

pa·tron·ize (pā′trə nīz′, pa′trə nīz′), *v.,* **pa·tron·ized, pa·tron·iz·ing. 1.** to buy or spend at (a store, restaurant, hotel, etc.): *Some people will not patronize a store in which the employees are on strike.* **2.** to give help and support to (an artist or institution). **3.** to behave in a superior manner toward; treat in a condescending way: *Some adults can't talk to a child without patronizing him.* —**pa′tron·iz′ing·ly,** *adv.*

pa′tron saint′, a saint who is looked upon as the special protector of a person, group, or place.

pa·troon (pə trōōn′), *n.* (in the 17th and 18th centuries) a large landowner under the Dutch colonial government of New York and New Jersey who was granted certain privileges and powers.

pat·ter¹ (pat′ər), *v.* **1.** to strike with a series of light, tapping sounds: *the rain pattering on the roof.* **2.** to walk softly and quickly: *The children patter about the house.* —*n.* **3.** a series of light, tapping sounds. **4.** the act of pattering. [from *pat* + the suffix *-er,* expressing repetition]

pat·ter² (pat′ər), *n.* **1.** easy, rapid speech, sometimes meaningless or trivial, used esp. by salesmen, magicians, entertainers, etc.: *The magician distracted our attention with continuous patter.* —*v.* **2.** to speak easily and rapidly. [from the word *pater* in *Paternoster,* Latin name of the Lord's Prayer, because of the resemblance of patter to the muttering of people saying their prayers]

pat·tern (pat′ərn), *n.* **1.** a design made up of a number of things arranged in an orderly manner: *the pattern of the wallpaper.* **2.** a model or guide to be imitated or followed: *the pattern of a happy life; a pattern for a dress.* —*v.* **3.** to make or fashion according to a pattern: *to pattern one's life on that of a great statesman.* **4.** to cover or mark with a pattern: *The walls were patterned with flowers of many colors.*

pat·ty (pat′ē), *n., pl.* **pat·ties. 1.** a flat, round piece of food made by pressing together ground or chopped meat, fish, or other food: *a veal patty.* **2.** a thin, round piece of candy: *a mint patty.* **3.** a small pie made of meat, chicken, or fish, often creamed, and baked in a round shell (**pat′ty shell′**) of pastry.

Paul (pôl), *n.* died A.D. c67, the Christian apostle to the gentiles: author of several books of the New Testament.

Paul VI, born 1897: Pope since 1963.

paunch (pônch), *n.* **1.** the stomach or abdomen. **2.** a large or protruding stomach; potbelly.

pau·per (pô′pər), *n.* **1.** a person who is very poor. **2.** a person supported by charity. —**pau′per·ism,** *n.*

pau·per·ize (pô′pə rīz′), *v.,* **pau·per·ized, pau·per·iz·ing.** to make poor; make a pauper of: *All this buying on installment will pauperize us.*

pause (pôz), *n.* **1.** a brief stop or rest: *After a pause for lunch, we started out again.* **2.** a break or rest in speaking or writing, often for emphasis: *At each pause in his speech, the audience applauded wildly.* **3.** (in music) a hold. —*v.,* **paused, paus·ing. 4.** to make a brief stop or delay: *I paused for a breath before climbing the stairs.* **5. give pause,** to cause to hesitate, as from doubt or surprise: *I wanted to buy it, but the price gave me pause.*

pave (pāv), *v.,* **paved, pav·ing. 1.** to cover (a road, walk, floor, etc.) with concrete, asphalt, stone, tile, or any hard material so as to form a firm, level surface. **2. pave the way for,** to prepare for; lead up to: *Einstein's theory paved the way for the atomic bomb.*

pave·ment (pāv′mənt), *n.* **1.** a paved surface. **2.** material used for paving.

pa·vil·ion (pə vil′yən), *n.* **1.** a lightly constructed, tentlike building used as a temporary shelter in a park or garden, and sometimes for concerts, dancing, etc. **2.** one of the buildings that make up a hospital. **3.** a building, usually of temporary construction, housing an exhibit at a fair or exposition. **4.** a large tent, often with a peaked or rounded top. [from the Old French word *paveillon* "tent," which comes from Latin *pāpiliō* "butterfly." Tents often resemble a butterfly with outspread wings]

pav·ing (pā′viñ), *n.* **1.** a paved surface; pavement.

2. material used for making a pavement. 3. the act or process of making a pavement.

paw (pô), *n.* 1. the foot of an animal, esp. of an animal having claws. —*v.* 2. to strike or scrape with the paws or feet: *The horses pawed the ground restlessly.* 3. to handle roughly or clumsily: *Don't paw the curtains.* 4. to move things about as in searching; rummage: *He pawed through the papers on his desk.*

pawn[1] (pôn), *v.* 1. to deposit as security for a loan; pledge: *I pawned my ring for a hundred dollars.* —*n.* 2. the state of being pawned: *My watch is in pawn.* 3. a person or thing deposited or held as security for a loan or a promise. [from the Middle English word *paun* "pledge," which comes from earlier Flemish *paen*]

pawn[2] (pôn), *n.* 1. (in chess) one of the eight pieces of least value in each of the two colors. See illus. at chess. 2. a person or thing used by someone to further his own purposes: *The children were innocent pawns in the quarrel between the parents.* [from an early French word *paon* "walker," which comes from medieval Latin *pedōnes* "infantry"]

pawn·bro·ker (pôn′brō′kər), *n.* a person engaged in the business of lending money at interest, who accepts and holds articles of value as security.

Paw·nee (pô nē′), *n., pl.* **Paw·nees** *or* **Paw·nee.** a member of an Indian tribe formerly living in Nebraska and Kansas, now in E Oklahoma.

pawn·shop (pôn′shop′), *n.* a pawnbroker's shop.

paw·paw (pô′pô′), *n.* another spelling of **papaw.**

pay (pā), *v.,* **paid** (pād) *or for def. 9* **payed; pay·ing.** 1. to give money or something of equal value in exchange for (something received): *We have to pay the rent.* 2. to give (a certain amount) in exchange for something: *I paid fifty dollars for that watch.* 3. to settle (a debt or other obligation) by giving money or something of equal value: *to pay the bill.* 4. to give money or something of equal value to (a person or organization): *to pay the grocer.* 5. to be profitable or worthwhile (to someone): *It will pay you to study. Crime does not pay.* 6. to bring as earnings or profit: *The job pays a hundred dollars a week. The stock pays four percent.* 7. to give (something due or suitable): *to pay attention; to pay a compliment.* 8. to make (a call, visit, etc.). 9. to let out (a rope, line, etc.) by slackening: *Pay out more cable.* —*n.* 10. wages or salary given for work done. 11. paid employ: *in the pay of the enemy.* 12. anything given in return or as a consequence: *Failure is your pay for being lazy.* —*adj.* 13. (of a machine, accommodation, etc.) requiring deposit of money: *a pay telephone; a pay toilet.* 14. **pay back, a.** to pay the money due on (a debt or other obligation): *He paid back the loan in 6 weeks.* **b.** to pay (someone) whatever is due: *How soon can you pay me back?* **c.** to punish; get even with: *I paid her back by not speaking to her.* 15. **pay off, a.** to pay (a debt) in full: *Next year we expect to pay off the car.* **b.** to result in success: *He took a chance and it paid off.* —**pay′er,** *n.*

pay·a·ble (pā′ə bəl), *adj.* 1. to be paid; due: *This bill is payable within ten days.* 2. that may or can be paid: *payable by check; payable by the month.*

pay·day (pā′dā′), *n.* a day when wages are paid.

pay·ee (pā ē′), *n.* a person to whom money is paid.

pay·load (pā′lōd′), *n.* the useful cargo, bomb load, instrument package, or passenger load carried by an airplane, rocket, missile, etc.

pay·mas·ter (pā′mas′tər), *n.* a person who has the authority or duty of paying out wages or salaries.

pay·ment (pā′mənt), *n.* 1. the act of paying: *We demand payment of the bill.* 2. something paid: *a payment of ten dollars in advance.* 3. reward or punishment: *Success is the payment of hard work.*

pay·roll (pā′rōl′), *n.* 1. a list of employees with the wages or salary to be paid to each. 2. the total amount paid in wages or salaries in a certain period.

Pb, *Chem.* the symbol for **lead.** [from the Latin word *plumbum*]

Pd, *Chem.* the symbol for **palladium.**

pea (pē), *n.* 1. a round, green seed eaten as a vegetable. 2. the vine bearing the pods of these seeds.

peace (pēs), *n.* 1. freedom from war. 2. a time during which there is freedom from war: *a peace of thirty years.* 3. *(often cap.)* a treaty that ends a war: *the Peace of Paris of 1815.* 4. a state of harmony among people or groups: *Settlement of the strike brought peace to the industry.* 5. law and order, esp. in a community: *They were arrested for disturbing the peace.* 6. freedom of the mind from fear, anxiety, or annoyance: *I can't work in peace here.* 7. calm; quiet; silence: *When the children are all at school, there's peace in the house.* 8. **hold one's peace,** to remain quiet: *Speak now, or forever hold your peace.* 9. **keep the peace,** to maintain order or calm: *We look to the UN to keep the peace.* 10. **make peace,** to bring about an end to fighting, quarreling, or the like: *an attempt to make peace between two bitter enemies.*

peace·a·ble (pē′sə bəl), *adj.* 1. inclined to peace; avoiding quarrels: *A peaceable man gets along with his neighbors.* 2. peaceful; harmonious: *a peaceable settlement of the dispute.* —**peace′a·bly,** *adv.*

Peace′ Corps′, a civilian agency, sponsored by the U.S. government, that sends volunteer teachers and workers to developing countries.

peace·ful (pēs′fəl), *adj.* 1. free from war, strife, or disorder: *a peaceful period between wars; a peaceful world.* 2. inclined to peace; peaceable: *a peaceful nation.* 3. calm and tranquil; quiet: *a peaceful mountain village.* —**peace′ful·ly,** *adv.* —**peace′ful·ness,** *n.*

peace·mak·er (pēs′mā′kər), *n.* a person, group, or nation that brings about or tries to bring about peace.

peace′ pipe′, a long tobacco pipe used by North American Indians on special occasions, esp. in celebration of peace. Also, **calumet.**

Peace pipe

peace·time (pēs'tīm'), *n.* a period of peace.

peach (pēch), *n.* **1.** a juicy fruit having a single pit and a fuzzy skin. **2.** the tree bearing this fruit. **3.** a pale yellowish pink. —*adj.* **4.** made with peaches: *peach pie.* **5.** of the color peach: *peach walls.*

pea·cock (pē'kok'), *n.* the male peafowl, noted for its long, spotted, iridescent tail feathers, which can be spread in a fan.

pea·fowl (pē'foul'), *n.* any of several birds originally found in India, Ceylon, southeastern Asia, and the East Indies, the male of which is called a peacock and the female a peahen.

Peacock
(total length to 7½ ft.)

pea·hen (pē'hen'), *n.* a female peafowl.

peak (pēk), *n.* **1.** the pointed top of a mountain or ridge. **2.** a mountain with a pointed summit: *Pikes Peak.* **3.** the pointed top of anything, such as a roof, arch, etc. **4.** the highest point or degree: *the peak of his career.* **5.** the visor of a cap. **6.** a projecting point. **7.** the narrow part of a ship's hull at the bow or the stern.

peaked[1] (pēkt), *adj.* having a peak or point: *a peaked cap.*

peak·ed[2] (pē'kid), *adj.* pale, sickly, or thin: *He looked peaked after losing so much sleep.* [perhaps from *peak,* used with special meaning + *-ed*]

peal (pēl), *n.* **1.** a loud, continued ringing of bells. **2.** any loud sound or series of sounds: *a peal of laughter.* —*v.* **3.** to sound loudly, as a bell.

pea·nut (pē'nut'), *n.* **1.** a plant related to the pea whose seeds ripen in pods under the ground. **2.** the seed of this plant, which resembles the kernel of a nut.

pea'nut but'ter, a smooth paste made from finely ground, roasted peanuts, often eaten as a spread.

pear (pâr), *n.* **1.** a sweet, juicy fruit, usually pointed at the stem and rounded at the bottom. **2.** the tree bearing this fruit.

pearl (pûrl), *n.* **1.** a smooth, rounded body formed inside certain kinds of oysters and enclosing

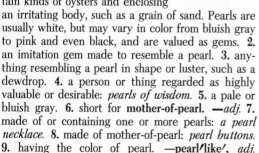
Peanut plant

an irritating body, such as a grain of sand. Pearls are usually white, but may vary in color from bluish gray to pink and even black, and are valued as gems. **2.** an imitation gem made to resemble a pearl. **3.** anything resembling a pearl in shape or luster, such as a dewdrop. **4.** a person or thing regarded as highly valuable or desirable: *pearls of wisdom.* **5.** a pale or bluish gray. **6.** short for **mother-of-pearl.** —*adj.* **7.** made of or containing one or more pearls: *a pearl necklace.* **8.** made of mother-of-pearl: *pearl buttons.* **9.** having the color of pearl. —**pearl'like',** *adj.* —**pearl'y,** *adj.* —**pearl'i·ness,** *n.*

Pearl' Har'bor, a harbor near Honolulu, Hawaii: surprise attack by Japan on U.S. naval base on December 7, 1941, brought U.S. into World War II.

peas·ant (pez'ənt), *n.* **1.** (esp. in Europe and Asia) a farm laborer, or one who owns and works a small farm. **2.** a crude, uneducated person. —*adj.* **3.** of or resembling peasants: *a peasant dance.*

peas·ant·ry (pez'ən trē), *n.* **1.** the class of peasants, or a group of peasants. **2.** the status of peasants.

pease (pēz), *n., pl.* **pease.** *Archaic.* **1.** another form of **pea. 2.** a plural of **pea.**

peat (pēt), *n.* a kind of soil made up principally of decayed plants and found in marshy or damp regions. Peat is sometimes dried for use as fuel.

peat' moss', a spongy kind of moss often found in peat and used to enrich soil in gardening.

peb·ble (peb'əl), *n.* a small · stone, usually made round and smooth by the action of water.

peb·bly (peb'lē), *adj.* **1.** made of or covered with pebbles: *a pebbly path.* **2.** having an uneven texture or surface: *pebbly leather.*

pe·can (pi kän', pi kan', pē'kan), *n.* **1.** an oval, smooth-shelled nut having a sweet, oily kernel. **2.** the tree bearing this nut, common in the southern United States.

pec·ca·ry (pek'ə rē), *n., pl.* **pec·ca·ries** *or* **pec·ca·ry.** any of several piglike animals found from Texas to Paraguay.

Peccary
(about 2 ft. high at
shoulder; length 3 ft.)

peck[1] (pek), *n.* **1.** a unit of dry measure equal to ¼ bushel, or 537.6 cubic inches (8.810 liters). **2.** a container having a capacity of a peck. **3.** *Informal.* a great deal; large amount: *That car has been a peck of worries.* [from the Middle English word *pek,* which comes from Old French]

peck[2] (pek), *v.* **1.** to strike with the beak, in the manner of a bird, or with anything pointed. **2.** to make (a hole) by pecking. **3.** to pick up by pecking: *The chickens pecked the corn.* **4.** to pick or nibble at food. —*n.* **5.** a quick stroke or jab. **6.** a mark or hole made by pecking. **7.** *Informal.* a hurried kiss: *a peck on the cheek.* [from the Middle English word *pekken,* which comes from Flemish] —**peck'er,** *n.*

pec·to·ral (pek'tər əl), *adj.* having to do with the chest or breast: *pectoral muscles; the pectoral fins on a goldfish.*

pe·cu·liar (pi kyool'yər), *adj.* **1.** strange; queer; odd: *There's a peculiar smell in that closet.* **2.** belonging largely to one person, thing, or group; unique: *The igloo is peculiar to Eskimos.* —**pe·cu'liar·ly,** *adv.*

pe·cu·li·ar·i·ty (pi kyoo'lē ar'i tē), *n., pl.* **pe·cu·li·ar·i·ties. 1.** something that is peculiar, unique, or particular: *The ability to change its color is a peculiarity of the chameleon.* **2.** the quality of being peculiar, odd, or unusual: *No one seemed to notice the peculiarity of her costume.*

pe·cu·ni·ar·y (pi kyoo'nē er'ē), *adj.* **1.** of or concerning money: *pecuniary problems of underdeveloped countries.* **2.** having the form of or consisting of money: *the pecuniary rewards of a business career.*

ped·a·gog·ic (ped'ə goj'ik, ped'ə gō'jik), *adj.* of or

concerning teachers and teaching. Also, **ped'a·gog'i·cal.** —**ped'a·gog'i·cal·ly,** adv.

ped·a·gogue (ped'ə gog'), n. 1. a teacher. 2. a person, esp. a teacher, who is strict and formal in his dealings with others.

ped·a·go·gy (ped'ə gō'jē, ped'ə goj'ē), n. 1. the function or work of a teacher; teaching. 2. the art or method of teaching.

ped·al (ped'əl), n. 1. a lever that is operated or pushed by the foot: *a bicycle pedal.* 2. a foot-operated key or keyboard on an organ. —v., **ped·aled** or **ped·alled; ped·al·ing** or **ped·al·ling.** 3. to work or use a pedal or pedals: *You'll have to pedal hard to get up the hill.* 4. to move or work (something) by using a pedal or pedals: *to pedal a bicycle.* —adj. 5. of or concerning a foot or feet. 6. of, concerning, or operated by a pedal or pedals: *Can you fix the pedal mechanism?*

ped·ant (ped'ənt), n. 1. a person who makes too great a show of his knowledge. 2. a person who follows rules strictly and emphasizes minor details. —**pe·dan·tic** (pə dan'tik), adj. —**pe·dan'ti·cal·ly,** adv.

ped·ant·ry (ped'ən trē), n., pl. **ped·ant·ries.** 1. excessive display of knowledge. 2. strict attention to rules and minor details. 3. an instance of being pedantic: *a speech full of pedantries.*

ped·dle (ped'əl), v., **ped·dled, ped·dling.** 1. to carry or cart (goods) from place to place and offer them for sale: *He peddles gadgets for a living.* 2. to deal out or offer, esp. unwelcome ideas: *to peddle gossip.*

ped·dler (ped'lər), n. a person who peddles.

ped·es·tal (ped'i stəl), n. 1. a base or support for a column, vase, lamp, etc. 2. a position of high regard or admiration: *He set his wife on a pedestal.*

pe·des·tri·an (pə des'trē ən), n. 1. a person who travels on foot; walker. —adj. 2. of or for pedestrians: *a pedestrian overpass.* 3. dull and commonplace; lacking imagination: *pedestrian ideas.*

pe·di·a·tri·cian (pē'dē ə trish'ən), n. a doctor who specializes in the care and diseases of children.

ped·i·gree (ped'ə grē'), n. 1. line of descent; ancestry: *tracing the pedigree of George Washington.* 2. a record of descent or ancestry, esp. of animals: *the pedigree of a poodle.* 3. pure or aristocratic descent: *a man of royal pedigree.*

ped·i·greed (ped'ə grēd'), adj. having a pedigree; of pure ancestry: *a pedigreed stallion.*

ped·i·ment (ped'ə mənt), n. 1. a low, triangular gable, usually outlined with cornices, on the front of an ancient Greek building or a building modeled on the Greek style. 2. a similar structure, often used for decoration over a doorway, mantel, etc.

Pediment at top of door

pe·dom·e·ter (pi dom'i tər), n. a device that a person wears in order to determine the distance he has walked.

peek (pēk), v. 1. to look briefly or slyly, esp. from hiding or through a narrow opening; peep: *to peek through a keyhole.* —n. 2. a quick or sly look: *While the teacher was out, some of the students took a peek at the answers.*

peel (pēl), v. 1. to remove the skin or outer covering from: *to peel an apple.* 2. to remove (a skin or outer covering) from something: *He peeled the covers off the bed.* 3. (of skin or a covering) to come off: *Sunburn will make your skin peel.* 4. to lose the skin or outer covering: *The paint on the wall is peeling.* —n. 5. the skin or rind of a fruit, vegetable, etc.; peeling: *a banana peel.* 6. **keep one's eyes peeled,** Slang. to watch carefully; be alert: *Keep your eyes peeled for a parking place.* —**peel'er,** n.

peep¹ (pēp), v. 1. to look through a small opening or from a hiding place; peek. 2. to come partially into view: *The moon peeped out from behind a cloud.* —n. 3. a quick or sly look: *a peep at the inside of the museum.* 4. the first appearance: *at the peep of dawn.* [from the Middle English word *pepe*]

peep² (pēp), n. 1. a short, shrill cry or sound: *the peep of a young robin.* —v. 2. to utter a peep. [from the Middle English word *pipen*]

peer¹ (pēr), n. 1. a person who is one's equal in rank or age, abilities, etc. 2. a member of the nobility; nobleman. 3. a British duke, marquis, earl, viscount, or baron. [from the Old French word *per,* which comes from Latin *pār* "equal"]

peer² (pēr), v. 1. to look closely, esp. out of curiosity or in an effort to see more clearly: *to peer at the shore through a telescope.* 2. to peep out or begin to appear: *The sun peered over the horizon.* [from the Flemish word *pieren* "to look narrowly"]

peer·age (pēr'ij), n. 1. the rank or dignity of a peer. 2. peers taken together as a class. 3. a book recording the names of the nobility.

peer·ess (pēr'is), n. 1. the wife or widow of a peer. 2. a woman having the rank of a peer.

peer·less (pēr'lis), adj. having no equal; matchless: *a peerless leader of men.* —**peer'less·ly,** adv.

peeve (pēv), v., **peeved, peev·ing.** 1. to make peevish; annoy: *It peeves me to wait so long.* —n. 2. something that causes annoyance: *My biggest peeve is the noise.*

peev·ish (pē'vish), adj. cross; irritable; inclined to complain: *Waiting will make most people peevish.* —**peev'ish·ly,** adv. —**peev'ish·ness,** n.

peg (peg), n. 1. a short piece of wood, metal, or other material, inserted into a hole of the same size, for the purpose of fastening two pieces together, keeping score in a game, etc. 2. one of the pins inserted in the neck of a stringed instrument, used for tuning the strings. 3. a step, level, or degree: *He was moved up a peg to the vice presidency.* —v., **pegged, peg·ging.** 4. to fasten or mark with a peg or pegs. 5. to fix at a certain price or level: *Steel is pegged at six dollars a ton.* 6. to work hard and steadily (usually fol. by *away*): *He pegged away at his homework all afternoon.*

Peg·a·sus (peg′ə səs), *n.* (in Greek mythology) a winged horse that stood for poetic inspiration.

Pe·king (pē′king′), *n.* the capital city of the People's Republic of China, in the NE part. Former name, **Pei·ping** (bā′ping′).

Pegasus

Pe·king·ese (pē′kə nēz′), *n., pl.* **Pe·king·ese.** a small, long-haired dog having a flat face, originally bred in China. Also, **Pe·kin·ese′.**

pe·koe (pē′kō), *n.* a superior kind of black tea from Ceylon, India, and Java, made from leaves smaller than those used for orange pekoe.

pelf (pelf), *n.* money or riches, esp. if acquired by greed or dishonesty.

pel·i·can (pel′ə kən), *n.* any of several large, web-footed, fish-eating birds having a large bill with a pouch in which food is stored.

pel′ican hook′, a hooklike device for holding the link of a chain.

pel·la·gra (pə lā′grə, pə lag′rə), *n.* a disease that results from a deficiency in the diet and causes skin changes, nervous disorders, and diarrhea.

pel·let (pel′it), *n.* **1.** a small ball of something, such as food, medicine, clay, paper, etc. **2.** a small ball, usually of lead, used as shot in a gun or pistol. **3.** a bullet.

Pelican
(length 5 ft.)

pell-mell (pel′mel′), *adv.* **1.** in a hasty or confused manner; in a jumbled mass or crowd: *At the sound of gunfire, we ran pell-mell for cover.* —*adj.* **2.** hasty or confused: *a pell-mell rush to the exits.* Also, **pell′mell′.**

pelt¹ (pelt), *v.* **1.** to strike repeated blows at: *He pelted his helpless victim about the face.* **2.** to strike repeatedly with objects thrown or fired: *The rioters pelted the police with stones, bricks, and bottles.* **3.** to throw, hurl, or fire: *to pelt snowballs at the passers-by.* **4.** to beat or strike in quick succession: *Hailstones pelted down on the roof.* —*n.* **5.** speed; quickness: *The chariot approached at full pelt.* **6.** the blow or impact of something that strikes: *the pelt of a hailstone.*

pelt² (pelt), *n.* the skin of an animal before the hair or fur has been removed. [from an Old French word, which is related to *piel* "skin, hide," from Latin *pilus* "hair"]

pel·vic (pel′vik), *adj.* of or belonging to the pelvis.

pel·vis (pel′vis), *n.* **1.** the basinlike cavity in the lower part of the trunk in the body of man and higher animals, formed

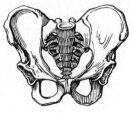
Pelvis (Human)

by the backbone and hipbones. **2.** the bones forming this cavity.

pem·mi·can (pem′ə kən), *n.* a food, originally pre-

pared by American Indians, consisting of shredded dried meat mixed with fat and dried fruits or berries, and pressed or pounded into small cakes.

pen¹ (pen), *n.* **1.** any of various instruments for writing or drawing with ink. **2.** the profession of writing, or things written: *The pen is mightier than the sword.* —*v.,* **penned, pen·ning. 3.** to write: *to pen a letter.* [from the Old English word *pinn,* which comes from Latin *penna* "feather, quill pen"]

pen² (pen), *n.* **1.** a small enclosure for animals. **2.** any enclosure used for confining or enclosing persons or things, such as a place of detention for prisoners, an area for practice and warm-up of athletes, etc. —*v.,* **penned** *or* **pent** (pent); **pen·ning. 3.** to shut up or confine in a pen or other enclosure. [from the Old English word *penn;* perhaps related to *pin*]

pen³ (pen), *n. Slang.* short for **penitentiary.**

pe·nal (pēn′əl), *adj.* **1.** of, concerning, or serving as punishment: *a penal code; penal labor.* **2.** subject to or bringing on punishment: *a penal offense.*

pe·nal·ize (pēn′əlīz′, pen′əlīz′), *v.,* **pe·nal·ized, pe·nal·iz·ing. 1.** to impose a penalty on: *The team was penalized for unnecessary roughness.* **2.** to declare punishable by law or rule: *The city penalizes littering.* **3.** to put under a hardship or disadvantage: *to be penalized by lack of experience.*

pen·al·ty (pen′əl tē), *n., pl.* **pen·al·ties. 1.** punishment for violation of a law, rule, or contract. **2.** something forfeited as a punishment or fine: *a penalty for lateness.* **3.** (in sports) a disadvantage imposed on a player or a team for breaking the rules.

pen·ance (pen′əns), *n.* **1.** a punishment imposed or undertaken as a sign of repentance for a sin or offense. **2.** (in the Roman Catholic Church) a sacrament consisting of confession of a sin, followed by forgiveness.

pence (pens), *n.* a British plural of **penny.**

pen·chant (pen′chənt), *n.* a strong inclination or liking for something: *a penchant for sports.*

pen·cil (pen′səl), *n.* **1.** a thin tube of wood or other material containing a core of graphite, crayon, chalk, etc., used for writing, drawing, coloring, or marking. **2.** anything shaped like a pencil: *a thin pencil of light.* —*v.,* **pen·ciled** *or* **pen·cilled; pen·cil·ing** *or* **pen·cil·ling. 3.** to write, draw, color, or mark with a pencil.

pen·dant (pen′dənt), *n.* **1.** a hanging ornament, such as an earring, locket, or the main piece in a necklace. —*adj.* **2.** another spelling of **pendent.**

pen·dent (pen′dənt), *adj.* **1.** hanging or suspended: *pendent jewels.* **2.** jutting out or overhanging: *a pendent rock.* **3.** undecided; pending. —*n.* **4.** another spelling of **pendant.**

pend·ing (pen′ding), *prep.* **1.** while awaiting; until: *We are holding your deposit pending approval of the lease.* —*adj.* **2.** awaiting decision or settlement: *The lawsuit is pending.* **3.** about to happen; imminent: *the pending visit of the President.*

pen·du·lous (pen′jə ləs, pen′dyə ləs), *adj.* **1.** hanging loosely: *a pendulous palm branch.* **2.** swinging freely: *a boat with pendulous sails.*

pen·du·lum (pen′jə ləm, pen′dyə ləm), *n.* **1.** a string or rod with a weight at one end that swings from a fixed point, used to regulate the speed of clocks and to measure gravity. **2.** something that changes or alternates between extremes: *the pendulum of opinion.*

Pe·nel·o·pe (pə nel′ə pē), *n.* (in Greek mythology) the wife of Odysseus, who remained faithful to him while awaiting his return from the Trojan War.

pen·e·tra·ble (pen′i trə bəl), *adj.* capable of being penetrated. **—pen′e·tra·bil′i·ty,** *n.*

pen·e·trate (pen′i trāt′), *v.,* **pen·e·trat·ed, pen·e·trat·ing. 1.** to pierce and enter or pass through: *The bullet penetrated the wall.* **2.** to spread or soak through: *The heavy rain penetrated our clothes.* **3.** to discover the truth or meaning of: *Science has begun to penetrate the mystery of cancer.* **4.** to make a deep impression on the mind or feelings.

pen·e·trat·ing (pen′i trā′tiñg), *adj.* **1.** having a piercing quality or effect: *a penetrating odor.* **2.** keen; discerning: *a penetrating mind.*

pen·e·tra·tion (pen′i trā′shən), *n.* **1.** the act or power of penetrating: *the penetration of the atmosphere; a light beam of high penetration.* **2.** keenness of mind; insight: *to think with great penetration.* **3.** the distance or extent to which something penetrates: *a penetration of several miles into the earth's crust.*

pen·guin (pen′gwin, peñ′gwin), *n.* any of several black-and-white birds of Antarctica that cannot fly but have wings resembling flippers that are used in swimming.

Penguin
(length
4 ft.)

pen·i·cil·lin (pen′i sil′in), *n.* an antibiotic produced by a certain kind of mold and used against many kinds of disease germs.

pen·in·su·la (pə nin′sə lə, pə nins′yə lə), *n.* a body of land almost entirely surrounded by water. **—pen·in′su·lar,** *adj.*

pe·nis (pē′nis), *n.* the male sex organ.

pen·i·tence (pen′i təns), *n.* the condition or feeling of being penitent; repentance.

pen·i·tent (pen′i tənt), *adj.* **1.** feeling or expressing sorrow for sin or wrongdoing; repentant. **—n. 2.** a penitent person. **3.** (in the Roman Catholic Church) a person who confesses sin and does a penance.

pen·i·ten·tial (pen′i ten′shəl), *adj.* of, concerning, or expressing penitence or repentance.

pen·i·ten·tia·ry (pen′i ten′shə rē), *n., pl.* **pen·i·ten·tia·ries. 1.** a prison, esp. a state or federal prison, where persons convicted of serious crimes are confined. **—adj. 2.** punishable by imprisonment in a penitentiary: *a penitentiary offense.*

pen·knife (pen′nīf′), *n., pl.* **pen·knives** (pen′nīvz′). a small pocketknife.

pen·man (pen′mən), *n., pl.* **pen·men. 1.** a person who writes or copies; scribe; writer. **2.** a person who is skilled in penmanship.

pen·man·ship (pen′mən ship′), *n.* **1.** the art or skill of writing with a pen: *a class in penmanship.* **2.** a person's style of handwriting: *poor penmanship.*

Penn (pen), *n.* **William,** 1644–1718, English Quaker: founder of Pennsylvania 1682.

Penn., Pennsylvania.

pen′ name′, a name used by an author to conceal his real name; pseudonym.

pen·nant (pen′ənt), *n.* **1.** a long, tapering flag used on ships for signaling, or as a decoration, emblem of a school or club, etc. **2.** such a flag serving as an emblem of victory or championship, esp. in sports.

pen·ni·less (pen′ē lis), *adj.* having no money at all.

Penn·syl·va·ni·a (pen′səl vā′nē ə, pen′səl vān′yə), *n.* a state in the E United States. 45,333 sq. mi. *Cap.:* Harrisburg. **—Penn′syl·va′ni·an,** *n., adj.*

pen·ny (pen′ē), *n., pl.* **pen·nies** *or* for def. 2 **pence** (pens). **1.** a bronze coin of the United States, the 100th part of a dollar; cent. **2.** a bronze coin of the British Commonwealth: before February 1971, the 12th part of a shilling; after that date, the 100th part of the British pound. **3.** a name given to various small coins of other countries. **4. a pretty penny,** a great deal of money: *That surfboard cost him a pretty penny.*

pen·ny·weight (pen′ē wāt′), *n.* a unit of weight equal to ¹/₂₀ troy ounce.

pen·ny-wise (pen′ē wīz′), *adj.* **1.** thrifty with small sums. **2. penny-wise and pound-foolish,** thrifty and cautious in small, insignificant matters, but reckless and foolish in important matters.

pen·point (pen′point′), *n.* the point or writing end of a pen, esp. a small device of metal that holds ink for drawing, writing, etc.; nib.

pen·sion (pen′shən), *n.* **1.** an amount of money paid regularly to a person who is retired, disabled, or deserving because of outstanding service, or a sum paid to his dependents or survivors. **—v. 2.** to grant a pension to: *He was pensioned in his old age.*

pen·sion·er (pen′shə nər), *n.* a person who receives a pension.

pen·sive (pen′siv), *adj.* **1.** thoughtful in a serious, sad, or dreamy manner: *a pensive look.* **2.** expressing a pensive idea or mood: *a pensive poem.* **—pen′sive·ly,** *adv.* **—pen′sive·ness,** *n.*

---

pent (pent), v. 1. a past tense and past participle of **pen²**. —adj. 2. shut in; confined (often fol. by *up*): *to be pent up because of illness.*

penta-, a prefix derived from Greek, meaning five: *pentagon.*

pen·ta·gon (pen′tə gon′), n. 1. a polygon having five sides and five angles. 2. **the Pentagon,** a building outside Washington, D.C., in the form of a pentagon, which houses most of the offices of the U.S. Department of Defense. —**pen·tag·o·nal** (pen-tag′ə nəl), adj.

Pen·ta·teuch (pen′tə tōōk′, -tyōōk′), n. the first five books of the Old Testament: Genesis, Exodus, Leviticus, Numbers, and Deuteronomy.

pen·tath·lon (pen tath′lən), n. an athletic contest consisting of five different track and field events and won by the contestant who gains the highest total score. See also **decathlon.**

Pen·te·cost (pen′tə kôst′), n. 1. a Christian festival celebrated on the seventh Sunday after Easter, commemorating the descent of the Holy Ghost upon the apostles; Whitsunday. 2. a Jewish festival celebrating God's giving of the Ten Commandments to Moses.

pent·house (pent′hous′), n., pl. **pent·hous·es** (pent′-hou′ziz). an apartment or other structure built on the roof of a building.

pe·nu·ri·ous (pə nŏŏr′ē əs, -nyŏŏr′-), adj. 1. extremely stingy; miserly: *Repairs were finally made by the penurious landlord.* 2. extremely poor; indigent: *to live in penurious times.* —**pe·nu′ri·ous·ly,** adv.

pen·u·ry (pen′yə rē), n. extreme poverty; indigence: *the penury of the slums.*

pe·on (pē′ən, pē′on), n. 1. (esp. in Mexico) a laborer forced to work to pay off a debt or other obligation. 2. (esp. in Spanish America) a person who does hard labor for low wages.

pe·o·ny (pē′ə nē), n., pl. **pe·o·nies.** 1. a shrub that bears large, many-petaled pink or white flowers. 2. the flower itself.

peo·ple (pē′pəl), n., pl. **peo·ple** or for def. 1 **peo·ples.** 1. a group of persons forming a community, tribe, race, or nation. 2. the persons of a particular group or area: *New York people.* 3. the subjects or followers of a ruler, leader, employer, etc.: *The king addressed his people.* 4. a person's family or relatives: *We invited my wife's people to dinner.* 5. persons in general: *What will people think?* 6. an indefinite number of persons: *The lobby was full of people.* 7. human beings, as distinguished from animals: *Do monkeys have more fun than people?* —v., **peo·pled, peo·pling.** 8. to settle (an area, region, etc.) with people; populate: *Quebec was peopled by immigrants from France.* 9. to dwell in; inhabit: *Indians people the Amazon jungles.*
—**Usage.** See **person.**

Pe·o·ri·a (pē ôr′ē ə), n. a city in central Illinois.

pep (pep), *Informal.* —n. 1. liveliness; vigor; energy: *to be young and full of pep.* —v., **pepped, pep·ping.** 2. to make lively (often fol. by *up*): *He pepped up the party with comic songs.*

pep·per (pep′ər), n. 1. a seasoning with a hot, spicy taste made by grinding the dried berries of a tropical shrub. 2. the shrub itself. 3. any of several plants bearing hollow green or red fruit having either a sweet or a hot taste. 4. the fruit of such a plant. 5. a red powder used in seasoning and made from such fruit. —v. 6. to season with pepper. 7. to cover or decorate: *a dress peppered with tiny flowers.* 8. to spray or pelt with bullets, shot, or other small objects; riddle: *They peppered the house with snowballs.*

pep·per·corn (pep′ər kôrn′), n. the dried berry of the pepper plant.

pep·per·mint (pep′ər mint′), n. 1. an herb grown for its oil, which is used as a flavoring. 2. a piece of candy flavored with this oil.

pep·per·y (pep′ə rē), adj. 1. full of, tasting of, or resembling pepper: *a peppery sauce.* 2. sharp or stinging: *a peppery speech.* 3. hot-tempered; fiery: *a peppery drill sergeant.* —**pep′per·i·ness,** n.

pep·sin (pep′sin), n. 1. an enzyme produced in the stomach that helps in the digestion of proteins. 2. the commercial form of this substance, used in medicines to aid digestion and in making cheese.

per (pûr), prep. 1. to or for each: *one dollar per pound.* 2. during each: *three times per week.* 3. by; by means of: *The TV picture is received per cable.* 4. according to: *I acted per your advice.*

per·am·bu·late (pər am′byə lāt′), v., **per·am·bu·lat·ed, per·am·bu·lat·ing.** 1. to walk through, about, or over. 2. to walk about; stroll.

per·am·bu·la·tor (pər am′byə lā′tər), n. *Chiefly British.* a small baby carriage; stroller.

per an·num (pər an′əm), each year; yearly: *a salary of $12,000 per annum.*

per·cale (pər kāl′), n. a closely woven, smooth cotton cloth, used esp. for sheets, pillowcases, etc.

per cap·i·ta (pər kap′i tə), to, by, or for each person: *a per capita tax; per capita income.*

per·ceive (pər sēv′), v., **per·ceived, per·ceiv·ing.** 1. to observe or become aware of by means of the senses, as to see, hear, taste, smell, or feel: *You can perceive the structure of cells with a good microscope.* 2. to understand or form an idea of: *to perceive the difference between right and wrong.*

per·cent (pər sent′), n. 1. one or more hundredths or hundredth parts: *40 percent of 200 is 80.* 2. a part or fraction of a whole reckoned in hundredths; one of each hundred: *ten percent of the population.* —adj. 3. figured or expressed in hundredths: *a loan at six percent interest. Symbol:* %

per·cent·age (pər sen′tij), n. 1. a part or fraction of a whole expressed as a proportion per hundred: *The percentage of interest on loans is regulated by law.* 2. a share of earnings, profits, etc.: *Our salesmen all work for a percentage.* 3. any part or fraction: *Asian flu attacked a large percentage of the population.*

per·cep·ti·ble (pər sep′tə bəl), adj. capable of being perceived; noticeable: *a perceptible increase in the humidity.* —**per·cep′ti·bly,** adv.

per·cep·tion (pər sep′shən), n. 1. understanding acquired by the mind or the senses; insight: *To under-*

stand war, one must have a perception of the underlying causes. **2.** the ability or power to perceive: *Some animals have a poor perception of distance.* **3.** the act of perceiving: *The pilot's quick perception of danger prevented an accident.*

per·cep·tive (pər sep′tiv), *adj.* **1.** having or showing keen insight or understanding: *a perceptive analysis of the problem.* **2.** of or concerning perception. **3.** having the ability or power to perceive. —**per·cep′tive·ly**, *adv.* —**per·cep′tive·ness**, *n.*

perch[1] (pûrch), *n.* **1.** a pole or rod on which a bird may alight or rest. **2.** any object or elevated place on which a person, animal, or thing may rest. **3.** a measure of length equal to 5½ yards. —*v.* **4.** to alight or rest on a perch or any high object or place: *A sparrow perched on the window sill.* **5.** to set or place on or as if on a perch: *He perched the snapshot on his desk.* [from an Old French word, which comes from Latin *pertica* "pole, staff"]

perch[2] (pûrch), *n., pl.* **perch·es** *or* **perch.** any of various spiny-finned, freshwater fishes. [from an early French word, which comes from Latin *perca*, from Greek *perkē*]

Perch
(length 1 ft.)

per·chance (pər chans′), *adv.* (used esp. in literature) **1.** perhaps; maybe: *We'll find him perchance in his study.* **2.** by chance: *Did you perchance find my umbrella?*

per·co·late (pûr′kə lāt′), *v.,* **per·co·lat·ed, per·co·lat·ing. 1.** to brew or cause to brew in a percolator: *to percolate coffee.* **2.** to pass or cause to pass through a material containing holes or spaces; filter: *The rain percolated the loose soil. You have to percolate the brew through cheesecloth.*

per·co·la·tor (pûr′kə lā′tər), *n.* a coffeepot that brews coffee by forcing boiling water upward through a hollow stem placed in the middle of it, and allowing the water to filter down through ground coffee contained in a porous basket mounted on the stem.

per·cus·sion (pər kush′ən), *n.* **1.** the striking of a sharp blow by one thing against another; impact: *the percussion of the sledge hammer against the wall.* **2.** the striking of sound waves on the eardrum. **3.** a group of percussion instruments in an orchestra.

percus′sion in′strument, a musical instrument whose sound is produced by striking, such as a drum, cymbal, bell, or piano.

per·di·tion (pər dish′ən), *n.* **1.** (in religion) loss of the soul and of heavenly salvation; damnation. **2.** a state or place of damnation; hell. **3.** complete destruction or ruin: *the perdition of one's hopes.*

per·emp·to·ry (pə remp′tə rē), *adj.* **1.** allowing no chance for question or denial: *a peremptory command.* **2.** aggressive or dictatorial: *a peremptory manner.* **3.** (in law) absolute or final: *a peremptory decree.*

per·en·ni·al (pə ren′ē əl), *adj.* **1.** continuing or lasting an indefinitely long time: *the perennial hardships*

of desert life. **2.** (of plants) living more than two years. **3.** lasting or continuing throughout the year: *a perennial stream.* —*n.* **4.** a perennial plant: *Roses are perennials.* —**per·en′ni·al·ly**, *adv.*

per·fect (pûr′fikt), *adj.* **1.** having all the desired qualities; fulfilling all the conditions required: *a perfect circle; a perfect soldier.* **2.** having no defects or shortcomings: *a perfect blossom.* **3.** correct in every detail; without error: *a perfect copy.* **4.** thorough; complete; utter: *a perfect stranger.* **5.** (in grammar) referring to or expressed by a perfect tense. —*n.* **6.** a perfect tense. **7.** a verb form in a perfect tense. —*v.* (pər fekt′). **8.** to bring to completion; finish: *to perfect a plan.* **9.** to bring to perfection: *Practice to perfect your musical skill.* —**per·fect′er**, *n.*

per·fect·i·ble (pər fek′tə bəl), *adj.* capable of becoming or of being made perfect.

per·fec·tion (pər fek′shən), *n.* **1.** the state or quality of being perfect. **2.** a perfect example or specimen of something: *That bracelet is the perfection of the jeweler's art.* **3.** the act or process of perfecting: *We are working on the perfection of a new timing device.*

per·fec·tion·ist (pər fek′shə nist), *n.* a person who strives for perfection in himself and his work or demands it of others. —**per·fec′tion·ism**, *n.*

per·fect·ly (pûr′fikt lē), *adv.* in a perfect manner; thoroughly; completely.

per′fect tense′, any tense of verbs expressing action or state completed at a certain time. See also **future perfect tense, past perfect tense, present perfect tense.**

per·fi·dy (pûr′fi dē), *n., pl.* **per·fi·dies.** a betraying of faith; treachery; deceit. —**per·fid′i·ous**, *adj.*

per·fo·rate (pûr′fə rāt′), *v.,* **per·fo·rat·ed, per·fo·rat·ing.** to punch or bore a hole or holes through; pierce: *The dart perforated the target.*

per·fo·ra·tion (pûr′fə rā′shən), *n.* **1.** a hole or series of holes punched or bored through something, esp. to make tearing apart easy, as in a sheet of postage stamps. **2.** the action or result of perforating.

per·force (pər fôrs′), *adv.* of necessity (used esp. in literature): *We perforce must walk.*

per·form (pər fôrm′), *v.* **1.** to carry out; do; accomplish: *to perform the duties of chairman.* **2.** to act, behave, or work in a certain manner: *The engine is performing satisfactorily.* **3.** to present (a play, musical work, etc.) before an audience: *We performed the play last night.* **4.** to act, sing, dance, etc., before an audience: *The acrobats performed very well.*

per·for·mance (pər fôr′məns), *n.* **1.** a musical, dramatic, or other entertainment. **2.** the act of performing: *the performance of one's duties.* **3.** something done or accomplished: *His new book is a marvelous performance.* **4.** a manner of acting, behaving, or working: *The machine's performance is faulty.*

per·form·er (pər fôr′mər), *n.* **1.** a person or animal that performs, such as an actor, musician, or singer. **2.** a person that does or accomplishes something: *a performer of great deeds.*

per·fume (pûr/fyo͞om, pər fyo͞om/), *n.* **1.** a substance, usually liquid, that has a pleasant smell. **2.** any agreeable odor: *the sweet perfume of the evening breeze.* —*v.* (pər fyo͞om/), **per·fumed, per·fum·ing. 3.** to give a pleasant smell to: *Flowers perfumed the air.*

per·fum·er (pər fyo͞o/mər), *n.* a person who makes or sells perfumes.

per·fum·er·y (pər fyo͞o/mə rē), *n., pl.* **per·fum·er·ies. 1.** a perfume or perfumes: *a new shipment of perfumery.* **2.** the art or business of making or selling perfumes. **3.** a place where perfumes are made or sold.

per·func·to·ry (pər fuŋk/tə rē), *adj.* **1.** done hastily and mechanically, without care or interest: *a perfunctory greeting.* **2.** (of a person) careless or indifferent: *a perfunctory workman.* —**per·func/to·ri·ly,** *adv.*

per·haps (pər haps/), *adv.* maybe; possibly: *Perhaps we'll find him at home.*

Per·i·cles (per/ə klēz/), *n.* c490–429 B.C., a statesman of ancient Athens. —**Per/i·cle/an,** *adj.*

per·i·gee (per/i jē/), *n.* the point in the orbit of the moon or an artificial satellite that is closest to the earth. See also **apogee.**

per·i·he·li·on (per/ə hē/lē ən), *n.* the point in the orbit of a planet or a comet that is closest to the sun. See also **aphelion.**

per·il (per/əl), *n.* **1.** the possibility of suffering injury, damage, or loss; risk; danger: *to face the perils of battle.* —*v.,* **per·iled** *or* **per·illed; per·il·ing** *or* **per·il·ling. 2.** to place in a position of peril; imperil; risk: *to peril one's career by an act of dishonesty.*

per·il·ous (per/ə ləs), *adj.* full of peril; risky; dangerous: *a perilous adventure.* —**per/il·ous·ly,** *adv.*

pe·rim·e·ter (pə rim/i tər), *n.* **1.** the border or boundary around the outside of a two-dimensional figure or an area of ground. **2.** the length or distance of this border.

pe·ri·od (pēr/ē əd), *n.* **1.** a rather large space of time in the life of a person, in history, etc., marked by particular qualities or events: *the Civil War period.* **2.** any definite division or portion of time: *the period that I spent at my uncle's home.* **3.** any of the parts of equal length into which a game, a school day, etc., is divided. **4.** the time required for a cycle to repeat itself: *The period of the moon is about 28 days.* **5.** the point of completion or end of a time during which something lasts or happens: *The arrival of reinforcements put a period to the siege.* **6.** a mark of punctuation (.) used at the end of a sentence, abbreviation, etc. **7.** a pause at the end of a complete sentence or statement.

pe·ri·od·ic (pēr/ē od/ik), *adj.* **1.** occurring or repeating at regular intervals: *Everyone should have a periodic medical examination.* **2.** (of a sentence) long and involved, and usually not complete until the very end is reached. —**pe/ri·od/i·cal·ly,** *adv.*

pe·ri·od·i·cal (pēr/ē od/i kəl), *n.* **1.** a magazine or other publication that is issued at regular intervals. —*adj.* **2.** published at regular intervals: *a periodical review.* **3.** of or concerning such publications: *periodical literature; a periodical index.*

pe·riph·er·al (pə rif/ər əl), *adj.* **1.** of, concerning, located on, or forming an outer boundary or limit: *the peripheral areas of the city.* **2.** of, concerning, or forming a part that is neither essential nor important: *minor, peripheral questions.* —**pe·riph/er·al·ly,** *adv.*

pe·riph·er·y (pə rif/ə rē), *n., pl.* **pe·riph·er·ies. 1.** an outer boundary, limit, or area: *the periphery of the atmosphere.* **2.** the unessential or unimportant aspects of a subject: *So far only the periphery of the tax question has been discussed.*

per·i·scope (per/i skōp/), *n.* an optical instrument containing prisms or mirrors for seeing over or around obstacles. Submarines are equipped with periscopes so that the captain can see objects on the surface when the vessel is submerged.

per·ish (per/ish), *v.* **1.** to die, esp. by withering or decaying: *The crop perished in the drought.* **2.** to vanish; become extinct: *The might of ancient Rome perished.*

per·ish·a·ble (per/i shə bəl), *adj.* **1.** subject to decay or spoilage: *perishable foods.* —*n.* **2.** something perishable, esp. a food: *Store the perishables in the refrigerator.*

per·i·wig (per/i wig/), *n.* a peruke or wig.

per·i·win·kle¹ (per/i wiŋ/kəl), *n.* a small sea snail used for food in Europe. [from the Old English word *pīnewincle,* which comes from Greek *pina,* a kind of mollusk + Old English *wincle,* related to Danish *vinkel* "snail shell"]

Periwinkle (length to 1 in.)

per·i·win·kle² (per/i wiŋ/kəl), *n.* an evergreen plant that grows along the ground, having blue, white, or purple flowers. [from the Middle English word *perwinke,* which comes from Old English *pervincae,* from Latin *pervinca*]

per·jure (pûr/jər), *v.,* **per·jured, per·jur·ing.** to make (oneself) guilty of perjury: *He perjured himself to save his friend from jail.*

per·jured (pûr/jərd), *adj.* **1.** guilty of perjury: *a perjured witness.* **2.** containing or marked by perjury: *perjured testimony.*

per·ju·ry (pûr/jə rē), *n., pl.* **per·ju·ries.** the giving of false testimony under oath before a court of law.

perk¹ (pûrk), *v.* **1.** to move, raise, or thrust forward smartly: *A little boy perked his head out the window.* **2.** to dress smartly: *She was perked out in a new party dress.* **3. perk up,** to make or become livelier, happier, or more attractive: *She started to perk up when I told her about the party.* [from the Middle English word *perken*]

perk² (pûrk), *v. Informal.* to percolate: *Call me when the coffee starts to perk.*

perk·y (pûr/kē), *adj.,* **perk·i·er, perk·i·est.** brisk; saucy; smart. —**perk/i·ness,** *n.*

per·ma·nence (pûr/mə nəns), *n.* the condition or quality of being permanent.

per·ma·nen·cy (pûr/mə nən sē), *n., pl.* for def. 2 **per·ma·nen·cies. 1.** another form of **permanence. 2.** a person or thing that is permanent.

per·ma·nent (pûr/mə nənt), *adj.* **1.** lasting forever or

for an indefinitely long time: *permanent colors.* —*n.*
2. Also, **per′manent wave′.** a wave, artificially set in the hair by the use of heat or chemicals, that lasts for several months. —**per′ma·nent·ly,** *adv.*

per·me·a·ble (pûr′mē ə bəl), *adj.* capable of being penetrated or saturated: *a permeable membrane.* —**per′me·a·bil′i·ty,** *n.*

per·me·ate (pûr′mē āt′), *v.,* **per·me·at·ed, per·me·at· ing.** 1. to pass or penetrate through the pores or spaces of: *The rain permeated our thin clothing.* 2. to spread throughout; saturate: *The smell of frying ba- con permeated the house.* —**per′me·a′tion,** *n.*

per·mis·si·ble (pər mis′ə bəl), *adj.* that may be per- mitted; allowable: *Talking in the halls is permissible only during recess.* —**per·mis′si·bly,** *adv.*

per·mis·sion (pər mish′ən), *n.* 1. the act of permit- ting or giving leave or consent: *He voiced his permis- sion with enthusiasm.* 2. authorization to do something: *I have permission to leave the camp over- night.*

per·mis·sive (pər mis′iv), *adj.* 1. granting or ex- pressing permission: *a permissive nod.* 2. granting permission readily: *permissive parents.* —**per·mis′ sive·ly,** *adv.* —**per·mis′sive·ness,** *n.*

per·mit (pər mit′), *v.,* **per·mit·ted, per·mit·ting.** 1. to allow (a person or thing) to do something: *Will you permit me to join you?* 2. to allow (something) to be done or happen: *The law permits peaceful demon- strations.* 3. to allow opportunity or possibility: *I will go with you if time permits.* —*n.* (pûr′mit). 4. a writ- ten order granting permission to do something; li- cense; pass: *a fishing permit; a press permit.*

per·ni·cious (pər nish′əs), *adj.* harmful; injurious: *a pernicious habit; a pernicious disease.* —**per·ni′cious- ly,** *adv.* —**per·ni′cious·ness,** *n.*

per·ox·ide (pə rok′sīd), *n.* 1. *Chem.* a compound that contains more oxygen than other com- pounds made up of the same chemical elements. 2. short for **hy- drogen peroxide.**

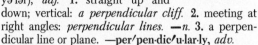

Line AB is perpendicular to line CD

per·pen·dic·u·lar (pûr′pən dik′ yə lər), *adj.* 1. straight up and down; vertical: *a perpendicular cliff.* 2. meeting at right angles: *perpendicular lines.* —*n.* 3. a perpen- dicular line or plane. —**per′pen·dic′u·lar·ly,** *adv.*

per·pe·trate (pûr′pi trāt′), *v.,* **per·pe·trat·ed, per·pe· trat·ing.** to perform, commit, or carry out (a crime, prank, deception, etc.). —**per′pe·tra′tion,** *n.* —**per′ pe·tra′tor,** *n.*

per·pet·u·al (pər pech′oo əl), *adj.* 1. continuing or lasting forever or for an indefinitely long time: *the perpetual hills; perpetual ownership.* 2. uninter- rupted; continuous: *a perpetual stream of sightseers.* —**per·pet′u·al·ly,** *adv.*

per·pet·u·ate (pər pech′oo āt′), *v.,* **per·pet·u·at·ed, per·pet·u·at·ing.** to make perpetual: *His books will perpetuate his name.* —**per·pet′u·a′tion,** *n.*

per·pe·tu·i·ty (pûr′pi too′i tē, -tyoo′-), *n.* 1. the

quality or state of being perpetual. 2. continuous ex- istence forever or for an indefinitely long time: *The money is to be held in trust in perpetuity.*

per·plex (pər pleks′), *v.* to cause confusion in the mind of; puzzle; bewilder: *His remarks perplexed us.*

per·plex·i·ty (pər plek′si tē), *n.,* *pl.* for def. 2 **per- plex·i·ties.** 1. the state of being perplexed; bewilder- ment: *The announcement caused perplexity among the students.* 2. something that causes confusion or uncertainty: *a case filled with perplexities.*

per·se·cute (pûr′sə kyoot′), *v.,* **per·se·cut·ed, per·se- cut·ing.** 1. to pursue or annoy continually with cruel or oppressive treatment; harass: *to persecute someone with criticism.* 2. to oppress, torture, or put to death, esp. for political or religious beliefs: *The early Chris- tians were cruelly persecuted by the Romans.* —**per′ se·cu′tion,** *n.* —**per′se·cu′tor,** *n.*

Per·seph·o·ne (pər sef′ə nē), *n.* (in Greek mythol- ogy) a daughter of Zeus and Demeter who was seized and taken to Hades by Pluto, who made her his queen but permitted her to return to earth for a part of every year. Also, **Proserpina, Proserpine.**

per·se·ver·ance (pûr′sə vēr′əns), *n.* the act or qual- ity of continuing on a particular course or working toward a goal without regard to difficulties or obsta- cles; persistence: *It takes great perseverance to learn to play the piano well.* —**per′se·ver′ing,** *adj.*

per·se·vere (pûr′sə vēr′), *v.,* **per·se·vered, per·se·ver· ing.** to continue at a task or purpose in spite of hard- ships; persist: *Galileo persevered in his investigations despite hardships and persecution.*

Per·sia (pûr′zhə), *n.* 1. a former name of **Iran.** 2. an ancient empire located in W and SW Asia.

Per·sian (pûr′zhən), *adj.* 1. of or belonging to an- cient Persia or modern Iran, their people, or their languages. —*n.* 2. a na- tive or inhabitant of an- cient Persia or modern Iran. 3. the language of ancient Persia, belonging to the Iranian branch of the Indo-European family. 4. the modern language of Iran, descended largely from ancient Persian; Iranian.

Persian cat (8 in. high at shoulder)

Per′sian cat′, a long-haired variety of the domestic cat, originally raised in Persia and Afghanistan.

Per′sian Gulf′, an arm of the Arabian Sea, be- tween SW Iran and Arabia. 600 mi. long.

per·sim·mon (pər sim′- ən), *n.* 1. a red or orange, plumlike fruit that is very bitter and puckers the mouth when not fully rip- ened. 2. the tree bearing this fruit. [from an Algonquian word meaning "dried fruit"]

IRAQ IRAN KUWAIT Persian Gulf GULF OF OMAN UNITED ARAB EMIRATES SAUDI ARABIA

---

act, āble, dâre, ärt; ebb, ēqual; if, īce; hot, ōver, ôrder; oil; book; ooze; out; up, ûrge; ə = *a* as in *alone;* ə as in *button* (but′ən), *fire* (fīr); *chief;* shoe; thin; ŧħat; zh as in *measure* (mezh′ər). See full key inside cover.

per·sist (pər sist′, pər zist′), *v.* 1. to hold steadfastly to a course of action, idea, manner, purpose, etc.; keep on: *He persists in trying to beat me at tennis.* 2. to last or endure: *The leaves of evergreen plants persist throughout the year.*

per·sist·ence (pər sis′təns, pər zis′təns), *n.* 1. the act of persisting. 2. the quality of being persistent: *It takes persistence to be a success.* 3. a lasting or enduring; continuation. Also, **per·sist′en·cy.**

per·sist·ent (pər sis′tənt, pər zis′tənt), *adj.* 1. having the quality or ability to persist: *to be persistent in one's efforts.* 2. lasting or enduring: *a persistent cough.* 3. continuing without interruption: *a persistent knocking.* —**per·sist′ent·ly,** *adv.*

per·son (pûr′sən), *n.* 1. a human being; man, woman, or child. 2. a human being regarded as a particular personality: *He's a very self-conscious person.* 3. the body or outward appearance, clothing, etc., of a human being: *He is very neat about his person.* 4. (in grammar) the division of nouns, pronouns, and verbs into those that refer to the speaker *(first person),* the one spoken to *(second person),* and the person or thing spoken about *(third person).* See also **first person, second person, third person.** 5. **in person,** in the actual physical presence; personally: *You must report to the office in person.*

—**Usage.** Careful writers and speakers usually make a distinction between *persons* and *people. Persons* is used when referring to an exact number: *This table will seat eight persons. People* is used when referring to an indefinite number: *We opened the door and saw a roomful of people.*

per·son·a·ble (pûr′sə nə bəl), *adj.* having a pleasing personal appearance or manner; attractive; charming: *Her brother is a personable young man.* —**per′son·a·ble·ness,** *n.* —**per′son·a·bly,** *adv.*

per·son·age (pûr′sə nij), *n.* 1. an outstanding or important person. 2. any person. 3. a character in a play, story, etc.

per·son·al (pûr′sə nəl), *adj.* 1. of, concerning, or belonging to a particular person: *a personal letter.* 2. done or carried out in person: *a personal appearance.* 3. of or concerning the body, clothing, appearance, etc., of someone: *personal cleanliness.* 4. (in grammar) showing or distinguishing person. *I, you, he, she, it, we, they,* etc., are personal pronouns. The ending *-s* of *he talks* is a personal ending. —*n.* 5. a short paragraph in a newspaper or magazine concerning a particular person: *The personals are on page 12.* 6. a brief, private notice placed in a newspaper or magazine by or on behalf of a particular person.

per·son·al·i·ty (pûr′sə nal′i tē), *n., pl.* **per·son·al·i·ties.** 1. the character of a person as revealed by his appearance, behavior, etc.: *He has a pleasing personality.* 2. pleasing qualities in a person; charm: *She has a great deal of personality.* 3. Often, **personalities.** an uncomplimentary remark or statement about a particular person: *Let's keep personalities out of this dispute.* 4. an outstanding or important person; personage: *personalities of the theater world.*

per·son·al·ize (pûr′sə nəlīz′), *v.,* **per·son·al·ized, per·**

son·al·iz·ing. to make personal; mark or identify with the name, initials, etc., of a person: *personalized stationery.*

per·son·al·ly (pûr′sə nəlē), *adv.* 1. as regards oneself; speaking for oneself: *Personally, I'd rather stay home.* 2. as a person; considering only someone's character or personal qualities: *I like him personally, but he's a poor speaker.* 3. in person; directly: *I told him personally I would not accept his offer.* 4. by oneself; without an agent or go-between: *I will personally take care of all the arrangements.* 5. as if meant for oneself: *I took his remark personally.*

per′sonal pro′noun, any of the pronouns showing person in grammar. In English, *I, you, he, she, it, we, they,* etc., are personal pronouns.

per·son·i·fi·ca·tion (pər son′ə fə kā′shən), *n.* a person or thing that seems an ideal example of a special quality; embodiment: *Your mother is the personification of thoughtfulness.*

per·son·i·fy (pər son′ə fī′), *v.,* **per·son·i·fied, per·son·i·fy·ing.** 1. to represent (an idea or thing) as a person: *In ancient myths, Venus personified love and beauty.* 2. to represent in oneself; be an ideal example of: *Sir Galahad personifies the pure and noble knight.*

per·son·nel (pûr′sə nel′), *n.* all the employees of a company or organization.

per·spec·tive (pər spek′tiv), *n.* 1. the art or method of drawing objects as they appear to the eye, giving the impression of distance and depth. 2. a drawing or painting made in this way. 3. a scene, esp. one extending to a distance; panorama; vista: *From the top of the hill, you can get a perspective of the whole city.* 4. the way things in the distance appear to the eye: *When seen in perspective, the rock formation resembles a human face.* 5. a broad view of the facts, ideas, events, etc., showing them in their true nature and relationships: *to study events in the perspective of history.* —*adj.* 6. of or concerning perspective, or made according to the method of perspective: *a perspective drawing.*

Perspective
H, Horizon

per·spi·ca·cious (pûr′spə kā′shəs), *adj.* having or showing the ability to understand and judge facts or ideas clearly; discerning: *a perspicacious analysis.* —**per′spi·ca′cious·ly,** *adv.*

per·spi·cac·i·ty (pûr′spə kas′i tē), *n.* the ability to understand and judge facts or ideas; discernment; judgment: *The President showed great perspicacity in dealing with the labor crisis.*

per·spi·ra·tion (pûr′spə rā′shən), *n.* 1. moisture that is given off through the pores of the skin; sweat. 2. the act or process of perspiring; sweating.

per·spire (pər spīʳr′), *v.,* **per·spired, per·spir·ing.** to give off perspiration; sweat.

per·suade (pər swād′), *v.,* **per·suad·ed, per·suad·ing.** to get (a person) to do or believe something by reasoning, coaxing, etc.; convince: *I persuaded him to go with us.* —**per·suad′er,** *n.*

per·sua·sion (pər swā′zhən), *n.* **1.** the act of persuading, or the result of being persuaded. **2.** the power or ability to persuade: *a leader of great persuasion.* **3.** a belief, esp. a religious belief: *He is of the Quaker persuasion.*

per·sua·sive (pər swā′siv), *adj.* having the ability to persuade; being of a convincing nature: *a persuasive talker; a persuasive argument.* —**per·sua′sive·ly,** *adv.* —**per·sua′sive·ness,** *n.*

pert (pûrt), *adj.* **1.** bold in speech or behavior; saucy; impudent: *a pert child; a pert remark.* **2.** lively; sprightly: *to feel pert after a swim.* —**pert′ly,** *adv.* —**pert′ness,** *n.*

per·tain (pər tān′), *v.* **1.** to refer or relate (usually fol. by *to*): *a question pertaining to usage.* **2.** to belong (usually fol. by *to*): *the furniture pertaining to the house.* **3.** to be proper or suitable (usually fol. by *to*): *the ceremonies pertaining to a solemn occasion.*

Perth (pûrth), *n.* a city in SW Australia.

per·ti·na·cious (pûr′t³nā′shəs), *adj.* holding stubbornly to an idea or purpose; persevering: *a pertinacious campaigner for mayor.* —**per′ti·na′cious·ly,** *adv.* —**per·ti·nac·i·ty** (pûr′t³nas′i tē), *n.*

per·ti·nent (pûr′t³nənt), *adj.* directly concerning the matter at hand; appropriate; to the point: *pertinent details.* —**per′ti·nence,** *n.* —**per′ti·nent·ly,** *adv.*

per·turb (pər tûrb′), *v.* to make troubled in mind; disturb greatly: *He was perturbed by his son's unruly behavior.* —**per·tur·ba·tion** (pûr′tər bā′shən), *n.*

Pe·ru (pə rōō′), *n.* a republic in W South America. 496,222 sq. mi. *Cap.:* Lima. —**Pe·ru·vi·an** (pə rōō′vē·ən), *n., adj.*

pe·ruke (pə rōōk′), *n.* a wig, esp. of the kind worn by men in the 17th and 18th centuries; periwig.

pe·rus·al (pə rōō′zəl), *n.* a thorough reading of something; scrutiny: *the perusal of a contract before signing one's name.*

pe·ruse (pə rōōz′), *v.,* **pe·rused, pe·rus·ing.** to read or examine, esp. with thoroughness or care: *to peruse the photographs of suspects.*

Peruke

per·vade (pər vād′), *v.,* **per·vad·ed, per·vad·ing.** to spread through every part of; permeate: *The aroma of cooking pervaded the house.* —**per·va·sion** (pər vā′zhən), *n.*

per·va·sive (pər vā′siv), *adj.* capable of or tending to spread widely: *the pervasive odor of fresh flowers.* —**per·va′sive·ly,** *adv.* —**per·va′sive·ness,** *n.*

per·verse (pər vûrs′), *adj.* **1.** holding on stubbornly to wrong or wicked ideas or behavior; contrary: *a perverse child.* **2.** wrong; wicked: *perverse opinions.* **3.** ill-humored; cranky: *He's in a perverse mood today.* —**per·verse′ly,** *adv.* —**per·verse′ness,** *n.*

per·ver·sion (pər vûr′zhən), *n.* **1.** the act of perverting, or the state of being perverted. **2.** an unnatural or abnormal action or condition: *Stealing is a perversion of the natural desire for possessions.*

per·ver·si·ty (pər vûr′si tē), *n., pl.* for def. 2 **per·ver·**

si·ties. **1.** the state or quality of being perverse. **2.** a perverse action or behavior.

per·vert (pər vûrt′), *v.* **1.** to turn away from the right course of action: *to pervert the minds of youth.* **2.** to use for a wrong purpose; misapply: *to pervert one's talents.* **3.** to twist the meaning of; distort: *to pervert a provision of the law.* —*n.* (pûr′vərt). **4.** a person whose behavior is unnatural or abnormal: *a criminal pervert.*

pe·se·ta (pə sā′tə), *n.* a bronze coin and monetary unit of Spain.

pes·ky (pes′kē), *adj.,* **pes·ki·er, pes·ki·est.** *Informal.* annoying; troublesome. —**pes′ki·ness,** *n.*

pe·so (pā′sō), *n., pl.* **pe·sos.** any of various coins and monetary units of Spanish-American countries and the Philippines.

pes·si·mism (pes′ə miz′əm), *n.* **1.** the tendency to see only the gloomy side of things. **2.** the belief that the world contains more evil than good.

pes·si·mist (pes′ə mist), *n.* **1.** a person who tends to be discouraged about things. **2.** a person who believes there is more evil than good in the world. —**pes′si·mis′tic,** *adj.* —**pes′si·mis′ti·cal·ly,** *adv.*

pest (pest), *n.* **1.** a troublesome person or thing; nuisance. **2.** a troublesome or destructive animal, insect, or plant: *The cockroach is a common household pest.* **3.** an epidemic disease; plague.

pes·ter (pes′tər), *v.* to annoy with trifling matters; bother: *Don't pester me now about going to the movies.*

pes·ti·cide (pes′ti sīd′), *n.* a chemical that kills pests, such as flies or mosquitoes.

pes·tif·er·ous (pe stif′ər əs), *adj.* **1.** bringing or spreading disease; pestilential: *pestiferous insects.* **2.** bringing or causing evil; pernicious. **3.** *Informal.* annoying; pesky.

pes·ti·lence (pes′t³ləns), *n.* **1.** a deadly, infectious disease that spreads widely and rapidly; plague. **2.** something harmful or evil. —**pes′ti·len′tial,** *adj.*

pes·ti·lent (pes′t³lənt), *adj.* **1.** bringing or spreading disease; pestilential. **2.** dangerous or destructive to law and order, morals, peace, etc.

pes·tle (pes′əl), *n.* a tool for pounding or grinding substances in a mortar. See illus. at **mortar.**

pet¹ (pet), *n.* **1.** an animal, such as a cat or dog, that is kept as a companion and cared for affectionately. **2.** a person or thing that is given special treatment or preference; favorite: *teacher's pet.* —*adj.* **3.** treated or cared for as a pet: *a pet raccoon.* **4.** preferred or favored, esp. by oneself: *my pet theory.* **5.** used affectionately: *a pet name.* —*v.,* **pet·ted, pet·ting. 6.** to treat or care for as a pet; pamper. **7.** to caress, fondle, or stroke: *Don't pet strange animals.* **8.** *Informal.* to express affection or love by kissing and fondling. [perhaps short for *petty lamb* "little lamb." See *petty*]

pet² (pet), *n.* **1.** a fit of peevishness. —*v.* **2.** to be cross or peevish; sulk. [formed from *pettish*]

pet·al (pet′³l), *n.* one of the leaflike parts of a flower, often brightly colored, that surround the pistil and stamens. See illus. at **flower.** —**pet′al·like′,** *adj.*

Pe·ter (pē′tər), *n.* 1. Also, **Simon Peter.** (in the Bible) died A.D. 67?, one of Christ's 12 apostles. 2. either of two books of the New Testament, believed to have been written by Peter.

pet·i·ole (pet′ē ōl′), *n.* the slender stalk by which a leaf is attached to a stem.

pe·tite (pə tēt′), *adj.* (esp. of a girl or woman) small and dainty.

pe·ti·tion (pə tish′ən), *n.* 1. a formal request: *a petition for a hearing.* 2. a request signed by a number of persons, addressed to a government or other authority: *a petition for lower taxes.* 3. an earnest request; prayer: *a petition for divine assistance.* —*v.* 4. to request (something) by means of a petition: *to petition a change in voting laws.* 5. to address a petition to: *to petition the city council for more playgrounds.* —**pe·ti′tion·er,** *n.*

pet·rel (pe′trəl), *n.* any of numerous small, black-and-white sea birds having long, pointed wings.

pet·ri·fy (pe′trə fī′), *v.,* **pet·ri·fied, pet·ri·fy·ing.** 1. to turn into stone or a stonelike substance: *Wood petrifies by absorbing water that contains minerals.* 2. to strike dumb or paralyze with astonishment, horror, or the like: *I was petrified at the bad news.*

Pet·ro·grad (pe′trə grad′), *n.* a former name (1914–1924) of Leningrad.

pet·rol (pe′trəl), *n.* the British word for **gasoline.**

pe·tro·le·um (pə trō′lē əm), *n.* a dark-colored liquid found in the earth from which many fuels, lubricants, and waxes are made; oil.

pet·ti·coat (pet′ē kōt′), *n.* 1. an underskirt, usually made of decorative material, trimmed and ruffled. 2. a long, full skirt formerly worn by women. —*adj.* 3. of, referring to, or composed of women: *petticoat government.*

pet·tish (pet′ish), *adj.* cross; peevish. [from *pet*[1], in sense of "spoiled child," + -*ish*]

pet·ty (pet′ē), *adj.,* **pet·ti·er, pet·ti·est.** 1. of small importance; trivial: *petty annoyances.* 2. of lower rank: *a petty officer.* 3. narrow-minded or mean: *to be petty about having one's own way.* [from the Middle English word *pety* "small, minor," which comes from Old French *petit* "small, little"] —**pet′ti·ness,** *n.*

pet′ty of′ficer, an enlisted man in the U.S. Navy, ranking above seaman and below an ensign.

pet·u·lant (pech′ə lənt), *adj.* feeling or showing annoyance over minor matters; peevish; fretful. —**pet′u·lance,** *n.* —**pet′u·lant·ly,** *adv.*

pe·tu·ni·a (pə too′nē ə, -tyoo′-), *n.* any of several garden plants bearing brightly colored, funnel-shaped flowers with crinkly petals.

pew (pyoo), *n.* a fixed bench with a back, esp. one of a number of such benches in a church.

Petunia

pe·wee (pē′wē), *n.* 1. any of several small gray or olive-colored birds that feed on insects. 2. another name for **phoebe.**

pew·ter (pyoo′tər), *n.* 1. a gray or silvery alloy of lead and tin, formerly used for making plates, cups, spoons, and other tableware. 2. articles made of pewter. —*adj.* 3. made of pewter: *a pewter mug.* 4. of the color of pewter; dull gray.

pew·ter·er (pyoo′tər ər), *n.* a person who makes pewter utensils or vessels.

Pfc., Private first class.

PG, a designation of a motion picture regarded as unsuitable for children, with parental guidance suggested.

pg., page.

pha·e·ton (fā′i t′n), *n.* a light, four-wheeled carriage, having two or more seats facing forward, often with a top that can be folded back.

pha·lanx (fā′langks), *n.* 1. (in ancient Greece) a body of heavily armed soldiers closely massed together for battle. 2. any closely massed, compact group of persons, animals, or things. 3. a group of persons united for some purpose: *a phalanx of protesters.*

phan·tasm (fan′taz əm), *n.* 1. something imagined, but unreal; fancy: *the phantasms of dreams.* 2. an imagined appearance of a person, esp. of someone dead; ghost; specter.

phan·ta·sy (fan′tə sē, fan′tə zē), *n., pl.* **phan·ta·sies.** another spelling of **fantasy.**

phan·tom (fan′təm), *n.* 1. a ghost or specter. 2. something that seems real, but has no substance, as an image seen in a dream, a mirage, etc. 3. a person or thing that is no longer what it seems to be: *Only the phantom of an empire remained.* —*adj.* 4. of or like a phantom; unreal: *a phantom ship.*

Phar·aoh (fâr′ō, far′ō), *n.* a title of the ancient Egyptian kings.

phar·i·see (far′i sē′), *n.* a hypocritical person who pretends to be religious or moral.

Phar·i·see (far′i sē′), *n.* a member of an ancient Jewish sect that followed religious laws strictly.

phar·ma·ceu·ti·cal (fär′mə soo′ti kəl), *n.* 1. a drug or medicine. —*adj.* 2. of or concerning drugs: *He works for a pharmaceutical house.*

phar·ma·cist (fär′mə sist), *n.* a person who makes, mixes, or sells medicines; druggist.

phar·ma·cy (fär′mə sē), *n., pl.* **phar·ma·cies.** 1. the art and science of making or mixing drugs. 2. the business of selling drugs. 3. a drugstore.

phar·ynx (far′ingks), *n.* the cavity at the back of the mouth that connects with the nose, windpipe, and esophagus. See illus. at **mouth.**

phase (fāz), *n.* 1. the state or condition of a changing thing at a particular time: *a disease in the infectious phase.* 2. any of the steps or stages in a process of change or development: *The war was in its concluding phases.* 3. the appearance of the moon at a particular time, which depends on how much of its illuminated side is visible from the earth. 4. any of the various views or aspects of a subject: *all the phases of a problem.*

Ph.D., Doctor of Philosophy. [from the Latin phrase *Philosophiae Doctor*]

pheas·ant (fez′ənt), *n.* any of numerous game birds having a long tail and brilliantly colored feathers.

phe·nol (fē′nōl), *n.* the scientific name for **carbolic acid.**

phe·nom·e·nal (fi nom′-ə nᵊl), *adj.* 1. extraordinary; remarkable: *A rocket travels at phenomenal speed.* 2. of, concerning, or resembling a phenomenon or phenomena. —**phe·nom′e·nal·ly,** *adv.*

Ring-necked pheasant
(total length to 3 ft.)

phe·nom·e·non (fi nom′ə non′), *n., pl.* for def. 1 **phe·nom·e·na** (fi nom′ə nə); for def. 2 **phe·nom·e·nons.** 1. something that is observed as a fact or event: *Rain is a phenomenon of nature.* 2. an extraordinary thing or person: *The new outfielder is a phenomenon.*

phi·al (fi′əl), *n.* a small flask or bottle; vial.

Phil·a·del·phi·a (fil′ə del′fē ə), *n.* a city in SE Pennsylvania: Declaration of Independence signed here 1776. —**Phil′a·del′phi·an,** *n., adj.*

phil·an·throp·ic (fil′ən throp′ik), *adj.* of, concerning, or engaged in philanthropy; charitable; benevolent. —**phil′an·throp′i·cal·ly,** *adv.*

phi·lan·thro·pist (fi lan′thrə pist), *n.* a person, esp. a wealthy person, who contributes money or other aid to charity, education, or social progress.

phi·lan·thro·py (fi lan′thrə pē), *n., pl.* for defs. 2, 3 **phi·lan·thro·pies.** 1. love of mankind, esp. as shown by working for or donating to charity, education, or social progress. 2. the activity of donating to or working for such purposes. 3. a charitable or benevolent organization.

phi·lat·e·ly (fi lat′ᵊlē), *n.* the collection and study of postage stamps, postmarks, and the like. —**phi·lat′e·list,** *n.*

-phile, a suffix used to form nouns meaning one who loves or is fond of: *Anglophile; bibliophile.*

Phi·le·mon (fi lē′mən, fi le′mən), *n.* a book of the New Testament, written by Paul.

phil·har·mon·ic (fil′här mon′ik), *adj.* 1. devoted to or loving serious music (used esp. in the names of musical organizations, orchestras, etc.). —*n.* 2. a society that supports a symphony orchestra. 3. the symphony orchestra itself: *The orchestra's name is the Rochester Philharmonic.*

Phil·ip (fil′ip), *n.* (in the Bible) one of Christ's 12 apostles.

Phi·lip·pi·ans (fi lip′ē əns), *n.* (used as sing.) a book of the New Testament, written by Paul.

Phil·ip·pines (fil′ə pēnz′, fil′ə pēnz′), *n.* (used as pl.) an independent republic on 7083 islands in the Pacific Ocean, SE of China: formerly under the guardianship of the U.S. Also, **Phil′ippine Is′lands.** —**Phil·ip·pine** (fil′ə pēn′, fil′ə pēn′), *adj.*

Phil·is·tine (fil′i stēn′, fil′i stīn′), *n.* 1. a member of a people inhabiting SW Palestine in Biblical times, often enemies of the Israelites. 2. *(often l.c.)* a person lacking in cultural refinement. —*adj.* 3. *(often l.c.)* having or concerned with commonplace ideas and tastes. 4. of or referring to the ancient Philistines.

phil·o·den·dron (fil′ə den′drən), *n.* a climbing house plant with shiny, evergreen leaves.

phi·lol·o·gy (fi lol′ə jē), *n.* 1. the study of written records, in order to determine their genuineness or their original form, and to explain their meaning. 2. an older name for **linguistics.**

phi·los·o·pher (fi los′ə fər), *n.* 1. a person who studies, teaches, or writes about philosophy. 2. a person who regulates his own life by reason and faces all facts and events with calm and self-assurance.

phil·o·soph·i·cal (fil′ə sof′i kəl), *adj.* 1. of or concerning philosophy or philosophers. 2. calm, patient, and reasonable: *philosophical composure.* Also, **phil′o·soph′ic.** —**phil′o·soph′i·cal·ly,** *adv.*

phi·los·o·phize (fi los′ə fiz′), *v.,* **phi·los·o·phized, phi·los·o·phiz·ing.** 1. to think or reason as a philosopher: *to philosophize about the origin of the universe.* 2. to express opinions that are hastily formed or not one's own: *to philosophize idly about life.*

phi·los·o·phy (fi los′ə fē), *n., pl.* **phi·los·o·phies.** 1. the study of the basic truths and laws of the universe, nature, life, morals, etc. 2. a system of beliefs about basic questions: *the philosophy of Plato.* 3. a calm, patient attitude toward life.

phil·ter (fil′tər), *n.* a drug that is supposed to make a person fall in love; love potion.

phlegm (flem), *n.* 1. thick mucus produced in the nose and throat, as during a cold. 2. a sluggish, indifferent attitude. 3. calmness; coolness.

phleg·mat·ic (fleg mat′ik), *adj.* 1. not easily stimulated; sluggish; indifferent: *a slow, phlegmatic person.* 2. calm; cool; self-assured: *to be phlegmatic in the face of danger.* —**phleg·mat′i·cal·ly,** *adv.*

phlox (floks), *n.* a North American garden plant having clusters of small flowers of various colors, esp. white or pink.

-phobe, a suffix used to form nouns meaning one who fears or dislikes: *Anglophobe.*

pho·bi·a (fō′bē ə), *n.* a strong, unreasonable fear of something: *a phobia about high places.*

phoe·be (fē′bē), *n.* an American flycatcher with a small crest on its head. Also, **pewee.**

Phoe·bus (fē′bəs), *n.* (in Greek and Roman mythology) another name for Apollo as the god of the sun. Also, **Phoe′bus Apol′lo.**

Phoe·ni·cia (fi nish′ə, fi nē′shə), *n.* an ancient kingdom on the Mediterranean Sea, in the region of modern Syria, Lebanon, and Israel. The Phoenicians founded many colonies on the Mediterranean Sea and were famed as traders.

Phoe·ni·cian (fi nish′ən, fi nē′shən), *n.* 1. a native or inhabitant of Phoenicia. 2. the ancient Semitic language of the Phoenicians. —*adj.* 3. of or belonging to Phoenicia, its people, or their language.

Phoe·nix (fē′niks), *n.* 1. the capital city of Arizona, in the central part. 2. (in mythology) a beautiful bird supposed to live about 500 years, then to burn itself to death and rise from its own ashes to begin life anew. It was regarded as a symbol of immortality.

phone (fōn), *Informal.* —*n.* 1. a telephone. —*v.,* **phoned, phon·ing.** 2. to telephone (someone) or make a telephone call.

pho·net·ic (fə net′ik), *adj.* 1. of or referring to speech sounds. 2. representing speech sounds by symbols: *a phonetic alphabet.* 3. agreeing with pronunciation: *phonetic spelling.* —**pho·net′i·cal·ly,** *adv.*

pho·net·ics (fə net′iks), *n. (used as sing.)* the science or study of speech sounds, how they are produced, heard, and understood, and how they are represented by letters or other symbols.

pho·ney (fō′nē), *adj.,* **pho·ni·er, pho·ni·est;** *n., pl.* **pho·neys.** another spelling of **phony.**

phon·ics (fon′iks), *n. (used as sing.)* a method of teaching reading, pronunciation, and spelling by a system of simple phonetic symbols and rules.

pho·no·graph (fō′nə graf′), *n.* a device that reproduces sound from a disk or a cylinder recording; record player. —**pho′no·graph′ic,** *adj.*

pho·ny (fō′nē), *Informal.* —*adj.,* **pho·ni·er, pho·ni·est.** 1. not genuine; fake: *a phony diploma.* —*n., pl.* **pho·nies.** 2. a person or thing that is not genuine; fake: *He's no doctor, he's a phony.* Also, **phoney.** —**pho′ni·ness,** *n.*

phos·phate (fos′fāt), *n.* 1. any of a number of chemical compounds containing phosphorus. Some phosphates are used as fertilizers. 2. a soft drink made of carbonated water and flavored syrup.

phos·pho·res·cence (fos′fə res′əns), *n.* the property of glowing without being heated, esp. after being exposed to light or other radiation. —**phos′pho·res′cent,** *adj.*

phos·pho·rus (fos′fər əs), *n., pl.* **phos·pho·ri** (fos′fə-rī′). *Chem.* a nonmetallic element that exists in two forms, one yellowish white and highly flammable, which glows in the dark, and the other red and less flammable. *Symbol:* P

pho·to (fō′tō), *n., pl.* **pho·tos.** *Informal.* short for **photograph.**

pho′to·e·lec′tric cell′ (fō′tō i lek′trik), an electron tube whose output depends on the amount of light striking it. Photoelectric cells are used to trigger alarms, open doors, regulate camera exposures, etc.

pho·to·graph (fō′tə graf′), *n.* 1. a picture made by photography. —*v.* 2. to take a picture of: *to photograph a landscape.* 3. to be photographed, esp. referring to the way a subject looks in a photograph: *The children photographed very attractively.*

pho·tog·ra·pher (fə tog′rə fər), *n.* a person who takes photographs, esp. as an occupation.

pho·to·graph·ic (fō′tə graf′ik), *adj.* 1. of, concerning, or used in photography: *a photographic lens.* 2. made by or making use of photography: *a photographic display.* 3. clear and accurate in detail: *a*

photographic memory. —**pho′to·graph′i·cal·ly,** *adv.*

pho·tog·ra·phy (fə tog′rə fē), *n.* the art or method of making pictures by the action of light, or some other source of energy, such as x-rays, on a film or glass plate coated with a material that is sensitive to such action.

pho·ton (fō′ton), *n.* the smallest unit of light or other radiant energy. Photons often act in the same way as subatomic particles.

pho·to·syn·the·sis (fō′tə sin′thi sis), *n.* the process by which plants convert water and carbon dioxide into sugars and starches. Photosynthesis requires the presence of chlorophyll and uses light as the source of energy for the complex series of chemical reactions involved.

phrase (frāz), *n.* 1. (in grammar) a group of two or more grammatically related words that does not contain a subject and a predicate, such as a preposition with a noun or pronoun, an adjective with a noun, a verb with an adverb, etc. Examples are *at home; to me; the yellow hat; to drive slow.* 2. a familiar or proverbial expression: *As the old phrase goes, "Haste makes waste."* 3. a brief utterance or remark: *I have time to speak only a few phrases.* 4. (in music) the smallest unit into which a melody is divided, often two to four measures in length. —*v.,* **phrased, phras·ing.** 5. to express in words in a particular way: *to phrase an objection angrily.* 6. (in music) to separate (a melody) or to group (notes) into phrases.

phra·se·ol·o·gy (frā′zē ol′ə jē), *n.* 1. the choice and arrangement of words in speaking or writing: *an author with elaborate phraseology.* 2. the style or manner of expression of a particular person, group, or profession: *legal phraseology.*

Phryg·i·a (frij′ē ə), *n.* an ancient country in central and NW Asia Minor. —**Phryg′i·an,** *n., adj.*

phy·lum (fī′ləm), *n., pl.* **phy·la** (fī′lə). a major division of the animal kingdom consisting of one or more related classes.

phys·ic (fiz′ik), *n.* 1. a medicine, esp. a laxative or cathartic. —*v.,* **phys·icked, phys·ick·ing.** 2. to treat with such a medicine.

phys·i·cal (fiz′i kəl), *adj.* 1. of or concerning the body: *physical exercise.* 2. of or concerning matter or things that exist in nature: *the physical universe.* 3. of or concerning physics. 4. of or concerning those fields of study that do not deal with living things: *the physical sciences.* 5. not chemical: *a physical change.* —**phys′i·cal·ly,** *adv.*

phy·si·cian (fi zish′ən), *n.* a doctor of medicine.

phys·i·cist (fiz′i sist), *n.* a scientist who specializes in physics.

phys·ics (fiz′iks), *n. (used as sing.)* the science that deals with matter, energy, motion, and force, including the study of mechanics, heat, sound, light, electricity, magnetism, and atomic and nuclear structure.

phys·i·og·no·my (fiz′ē og′nə mē, fiz′ē on′ə mē), *n., pl.* **phys·i·og·no·mies.** 1. the kind of features a particular face has: *an unusual physiognomy.* 2. the face itself. 3. the method of guessing a person's character from the appearance of his face. 4. the outward shape of anything: *the physiognomy of a coastline.*

phys·i·ol·o·gist (fiz′ē ol′ə jist), *n.* a scientist who specializes in physiology.

phys·i·ol·o·gy (fiz′ē ol′ə jē), *n.* the science dealing with the functions of living things or parts of living things. —**phys·i·o·log·i·cal** (fiz′ē ə loj′i kəl), *adj.*

phy·sique (fi zēk′), *n.* the build of a person.

pi (pī), *n.* the ratio of the circumference of a circle to its diameter, symbolized by the Greek letter π, approximately equal to 3.1416, or 3¹/₇.

P.I., Philippine Islands.

pi·a·nis·si·mo (pē′ə nis′ə mō′), *adj., adv.* (in music) very soft.

pi·an·ist (pē an′ist, pē′ə nist), *n.* a person who plays the piano.

pi·an·o¹ (pē an′ō), *n., pl.* **pi·an·os.** a musical instrument in which felt-covered hammers, operated from a keyboard, strike metal strings. [short for *piano-forte*, which comes from Italian *piano* "soft" + *forte* "loud"]

pi·an·o² (pē ä′nō), *adj., adv.* (in music) soft. [from Italian]

pi·an·o·for·te (pē an′ə-fôr′tē), *n.* an old name for **piano¹.**

Grand piano

pi·as·ter (pē as′tər), *n.* a coin or monetary unit of the Arab Republic of Egypt, Lebanon, Sudan, and Syria, worth ¹/₁₀₀ of a pound.

pi·az·za (pē az′ə, pē ä′zə), *n.* **1.** (in Italy) a public square. **2.** a porch on a house; veranda.

pi·ca (pī′kə), *n.* **1.** a size of typewriter type in which each character is ¹/₁₀ inch wide. **2.** a similar size of printing type. **3.** a unit of measure used by printers, equal to ¹/₆ inch.

Pic·ar·dy (pik′ər dē), *n.* a region in N France, formerly a province.

Pi·cas·so (pi kä′sō), *n.* **Pa·blo** (pä′blō), 1881–1973, Spanish painter and sculptor in France.

pic·a·yune (pik′ē yōon′), *adj.* **1.** of little value or importance; trifling: *a picayune amount.* **2.** small-minded; petty; mean: *picayune criticism.*

pic·co·lo (pik′ə lō′), *n., pl.* **pic·co·los.** a small flute that plays an octave higher than the ordinary flute.

pick¹ (pik), *v.* **1.** to choose or select: *The coach picked the players for the first team.* **2.** to bring on or cause: *to pick a fight.* **3.** to steal the contents of: *to pick pockets.* **4.** to open (a lock) with some tool or device other than a key. **5.** to scratch, dig, break up, or make holes in, esp. with the fingers or a pointed instrument: *Stop picking at your face.* **6.** to make (a hole or holes) by digging or boring: *The mice picked holes in the bread.* **7.** to clear or clean, using

Piccolo

the fingers or a pointed instrument: *to pick the teeth; to pick the meat from the bones.* **8.** to pluck or gather: *to pick flowers.* **9.** to separate or pull apart: *to pick fibers.* **10.** to pluck (the strings of a musical instrument). **11.** to play by plucking strings: *to pick a guitar.* —*n.* **12.** the act of choosing or selecting: *to take one's pick.* **13.** a person or thing selected: *She's our pick for president.* **14.** the best part: *the pick of the crop.* **15.** the right or opportunity to choose first: *He gave me my pick of the new books.* **16.** a blow or stroke with something pointed. **17.** a plectrum for plucking the strings of a guitar, banjo, etc. **18. pick at, a.** *Informal.* to find fault with; nag: *He's always picking at me about my hair.* **b.** to eat sparingly or without interest: *He was so tired he just picked at his food.* **19. pick on,** *Informal.* to torment, tease, or nag: *The boys pick on him because he's so small.* **20. pick out, a.** to choose or select: *Pick out a half-dozen ripe apples.* **b.** to recognize: *to pick out a face in a crowd.* **21. pick up, a.** to lift: *to pick up a stone.* **b.** to take into a car, ship, etc., or along with one: *I'll pick you up about 8. They stopped to pick up cargo in Rio.* **c.** to receive as a radio or television transmission: *Can you pick up channel 13 on this set?* **d.** to make progress; improve: *Has business picked up yet?* **e.** *Slang.* to take into custody; arrest: *He was picked up for speeding.* **f.** *Slang.* to obtain; purchase: *Pick up a loaf of bread on your way home.* [from the Middle English word *pyke,* which is related to *pekken* "to peck." See *peck²*] —**pick′er,** *n.*

pick² (pik), *n.* **1.** a heavy tool with an iron or steel head, curved and coming to a point at both ends, mounted on a wooden handle, and used for loosening and breaking up soil, rocks, etc. **2.** any pointed instrument used for picking: *an ice pick.* [from the Middle English word *pikke,* which is perhaps related to *pīk* "pick, spike." See *pike⁴*]

pick·ax (pik′aks′), *n., pl.* **pick·ax·es.** a kind of pick having a head with a point at one end and a broad blade at the other end, or both ends pointed. Also, **pick′axe′.**

pick·er·el (pik′ər əl), *n., pl.* **pick·er·els** *or* **pick·er·el.** any of several freshwater game fishes related to but smaller than the pike.

pick·et (pik′it), *n.* **1.** a post, stake, or peg that is driven into the ground to form part of a fence, or to fasten down a tent or the like. **2.** a person, esp. a member of a labor union on strike, who stands or walks in front of a factory, store, etc., to keep workers or shoppers from entering. **3.** a person who demonstrates in a similar manner in protest against the actions of a government or other organization. **4.** a soldier or detachment of soldiers serving as a forward lookout against surprise attack by the enemy. —*v.,* **pick·et·ed, pick·et·ing.** **5.** to enclose or confine with pickets. **6.** to place pickets in front of (a factory, office, etc.). **7.** to march, stand, etc., as a picket.

pick·le (pik′əl), *n.* **1.** a cucumber preserved in brine, vinegar, or the like. **2.** anything preserved in a similar way. **3.** a liquid, such as brine or vinegar, used for preserving various foods. **4.** *Informal.* an awkward situation; embarrassment: *I got into a pickle by forgetting my notebook.* —*v.,* **pick·led, pick·ling. 5.** to preserve in brine, vinegar, or the like.

pick·pock·et (pik′pok′it), *n.* a thief who steals from other people's pockets or purses.

pick·up (pik′up′), *n.* **1.** the act of picking up, esp. for transporting or delivering to some other place: *The school bus makes a pickup at this corner.* **2.** the persons or things that are taken on a bus, truck, etc.: *Did you get the pickup for the cafeteria?* **3.** an increase in activity: *a pickup in business.* **4.** acceleration, or the ability to accelerate: *The car has good pickup.* **5.** (in radio and television) **a.** the reception of sounds and images for conversion into electrical waves for broadcasting. **b.** the apparatus for doing this. **c.** the place where it is done. **6.** the device in a phonograph that converts the vibrations of the stylus into electric signals. **7.** Also, **pick′up truck′.** a small open truck used for deliveries and light hauling.

pick·y (pik′ē), *adj.,* **pick·i·er, pick·i·est.** very fussy or finicky. —**pick′i·ness,** *n.*

pic·nic (pik′nik), *n.* **1.** an outing that includes the eating of food in the open air. **2.** *Informal.* an enjoyable or easy time, occupation, task, etc.: *We had a picnic painting all the walls in different colors.* —*v.,* **pic·nicked, pic·nick·ing. 3.** to go on or take part in a picnic. **4.** to eat a meal in the open air: *Let's picnic out on the patio.* —**pic′nick·er,** *n.*

pic·to·ri·al (pik tôr′ē əl), *adj.* **1.** of, concerning, or expressed by pictures: *a pictorial graph of population growth.* **2.** illustrated by or containing pictures: *a pictorial history.* **3.** of or concerning painters, paintings, or the art of painting: *pictorial art.* **4.** vivid as a picture; graphic: *a pictorial description of the coronation.* —**pic·to′ri·al·ly,** *adv.*

pic·ture (pik′chər), *n.* **1.** a visual representation of a person, object, scene, etc., such as a painting, drawing, or photograph. **2.** a mental image, such as a memory of something seen. **3.** a vivid description: *He gave us a glowing picture of the Olympic Games.* **4.** a motion picture. **5.** a beautiful or interesting person, thing, group, or scene: *The bride was a picture.* **6.** a close resemblance of a person to someone else: *He is the picture of his father.* **7.** a perfect example of some quality or condition: *She is the picture of health.* **8.** the image on a television or motion-picture screen. **9.** a general view or understanding of a situation: *Do you get the picture?* —*v.,* **pic·tured, pic·tur·ing. 10.** to represent in a painting, drawing, or photograph. **11.** to form an idea of in the mind; imagine: *Can you picture Alvin on a surfboard?* **12.** to describe vividly in speech or writing.

pic·tur·esque (pik′chə resk′), *adj.* **1.** attractive or interesting, so as to resemble or be suitable for a painting: *a picturesque mountain village.* **2.** (of speech, writing, etc.) vivid, colorful, and descriptive: *a picturesque account of desert life.* —**pic′tur·esque′ly,** *adv.* —**pic′tur·esque′ness,** *n.*

pie (pī), *n.* a baked food consisting of a pastry crust

filled with fruits, preserves, or meat, and often with strips or a covering of pastry crust.

pie·bald (pī′bôld′), *adj.* **1.** having patches of black and white or other colors. —*n.* **2.** an animal, esp. a horse, of such coloring.

piece (pēs), *n.* **1.** a portion or quantity of any material, forming a unit or whole by itself: *a piece of lumber.* **2.** a part of something forming a larger unit or whole: *a piece of cake.* **3.** a part broken off from something: *Pick up the pieces of the glass.* **4.** an individual thing of a certain kind: *a piece of furniture.* **5.** one of a number of things forming a set: *a chess piece.* **6.** an artistic or literary work, such as a musical composition or a play. **7.** an example or instance of some kind of thought or behavior: *a piece of treachery.* **8.** a firing weapon, such as a pistol or cannon. **9.** a coin: *a five-cent piece.* **10.** a particular amount or unit of work: *The lathe operators are paid by the piece.* —*v.,* **pieced, piec·ing. 11.** to mend by adding or joining pieces; patch: *to piece a torn skirt.* **12.** to make by joining pieces: *to piece a quilt.* **13. go to pieces,** to become upset; lose control of oneself: *He went to pieces when he thought he was lost.*

piece·meal (pēs′mēl′), *adv.* **1.** piece by piece; a little at a time: *He did his homework piecemeal.* **2.** into pieces or fragments: *She tore the letter piecemeal.* —*adj.* **3.** done piece by piece: *a piecemeal job.*

piece·work (pēs′wûrk′), *n.* work done and paid for by the piece, and not by the amount of time spent.

pied (pīd), *adj.* having spots or patches of two or more colors: *a pied horse.*

Pied·mont (pēd′mont), *n.* **1.** a plateau region in the SE United States. **2.** a region in NW Italy.

pier (pēr), *n.* **1.** a large platform or similar structure built out over the water, for use as a landing place for ships, or as an amusement area, strolling place, or breakwater. **2.** a support for the ends of an arch, as in a bridge, door, gateway, etc. **3.** a portion of wall between openings such as doors or windows. **4.** a support of steel or masonry for any structure; pillar.

pierce (pērs), *v.,* **pierced, pierc·ing. 1.** to force a hole or opening through (something); penetrate: *The bullet pierced his lung.* **2.** to make (a hole or opening) by cutting or boring: *to pierce holes in a door.* **3.** to penetrate with the eye or mind; see into or through: *to pierce the difficulties of a problem.* **4.** to have a strong effect on (the senses or emotions): *Her cry pierced our ears. His words pierced their hearts.*

Pierce (pērs), *n.* **Franklin,** 1804–1869, 14th President of the U.S. 1853–1857.

pierc·ing (pēr′sing), *adj.* **1.** loud or shrill: *a piercing voice.* **2.** sharp, intense, and penetrating: *piercing cold; a piercing glance.* —**pierc′ing·ly,** *adv.*

Pierre (pēr), *n.* the capital city of South Dakota, in the central part.

pi·e·ty (pī′i tē), *n., pl.* for def. 4 **pi·e·ties. 1.** strict devotion to religious beliefs and observances. **2.** loyalty and respect toward parents, family, country, etc. **3.** the quality of being pious. **4.** a pious act, remark, belief, or the like: *She practices the Christian pieties.*

pig (pig), *n.* **1.** any of several animals having a thick body, cloven hooves, a long, broad snout, and a short, curly tail, esp. those kinds raised for their meat; hog; swine. **2.** the meat of such animals; pork. **3.** *Informal.* a person of slovenly habits or appearance. **4.** *Informal.* a greedy person; glutton. **5.** a rough, oblong piece of cast metal.

pi·geon (pij′ən), *n.* any of several birds having short legs, a small head, and a thick body. Pigeons are often found in cities, and some are bred for their meat or for racing or carrying messages.

pi·geon·hole (pij′ən hōl′), *n.* **1.** a hole, or one of a row of holes, for pigeons to nest in. **2.** one of a number of small open boxes or slots in a desk or cabinet, used for filing and sorting letters, papers, or the like. —*v.*, **pi·geon·holed, pi·geon·hol·ing. 3.** to file away, as in a pigeonhole. **4.** to put aside or postpone, often indefinitely: *The motion was pigeonholed by the committee.* **5.** to divide into different kinds or classes; sort: *It is hard to pigeonhole people by the way they dress.*

pi·geon-toed (pij′ən tōd′), *adj.* having the toes of the feet turned inward.

pig·gish (pig′ish), *adj.* like a pig, esp. in being greedy or slovenly. —**pig′gish·ly,** *adv.* —**pig′gish·ness,** *n.*

pig·gy·back (pig′ē bak′), *adv.* **1.** on the back or shoulders: *He carried the little girl piggyback.* **2.** by means of a conveyance that travels part of the way mounted on another, such as by truck trailer mounted on a flatcar. —*adj.* **3.** carried on the back or shoulders: *a piggyback ride.* **4.** shipped by piggyback: *piggyback cargo.*

pig·head·ed (pig′hed′id), *adj.* unreasonably stubborn or obstinate: *He's too pigheaded to listen.* —**pig′head′ed·ness,** *n.*

pig′ i′ron, iron in the form of rough oblong castings before it is refined into steel.

pig·let (pig′lit), *n.* a young pig.

pig·ment (pig′mənt), *n.* **1.** any substance used for coloring. **2.** the coloring matter in paint. **3.** any of the substances that give color to living things. —*v.* **4.** to color; add pigment to. —**pig′men·ta′tion,** *n.*

Pig·my (pig′mē), *n., pl.* **Pig·mies.** another spelling of **Pygmy.**

pig·pen (pig′pen′), *n.* **1.** a pen where pigs are kept. **2.** a dirty or untidy place. Also, **pigsty.**

pig·skin (pig′skin′), *n.* **1.** the hide or skin of a pig. **2.** leather made from the hides of pigs. **3.** *Informal.* a football, often made of pigskin.

pig·sty (pig′stī′), *n., pl.* **pig·sties.** another word for **pigpen.**

pig·tail (pig′tāl′), *n.* a long braid of hair that hangs down the back of the head.

Northern pike (length 4½ ft.)

pike¹ (pīk), *n., pl.* **pikes** *or* **pike.** any of several large, slender, freshwater game fishes having a long snout and many sharp teeth. [so called from its pointed snout. See *pike⁴*]

pike² (pīk), *n.* a weapon formerly used by foot soldiers, consisting of a wooden shaft with a sharp metal head. [from the Old French word *pique,* related to *pic* "a pick," which comes from Germanic]

pike³ (pīk), *n.* a toll road; turnpike. [short for *turnpike*]

pike⁴ (pīk), *n.* a sharp point or spike. [from the Old English word *pīc* "pointed tool," related to *pike²*]

Pikes′ Peak′, a mountain in central Colorado, in the Rocky Mountains. 14,108 ft.

pike·staff (pīk′staf′), *n., pl.* **pike·staves** (pīk′stāvz′). **1.** the shaft of a pike or spear. **2.** a staff with a metal point or spike at the lower end, used by travelers on foot, mountain climbers, etc.

pi·las·ter (pi las′tər), *n.* a supporting structure resembling a column, forming part of a wall and projecting slightly outward from it.

Pi·late (pī′lət), *n.* **Pon·tius** (pon′shəs, pon′tē əs), the Roman governor of Judea, who allowed the crucifixion of Jesus.

Pilaster (detail of upper end)

pile¹ (pīl), *n.* **1.** a collection of things laid one upon the other; heap; stack: *a pile of stones.* **2.** a heap of wood on which something is burned, such as a funeral corpse or an animal being sacrificed. **3.** a large building or group of buildings. **4.** *Informal.* a large amount: *a pile of money.* **5.** See **reactor** (def. 2). —*v.*, **piled, pil·ing. 6.** to form into a pile or mass (often fol. by *up*): *Pile up the leaves in the corner. The snow piled up at the door.* **7.** to accumulate; gather (often fol. by *up*): *His only ambition is to pile up money. The bills keep piling up.* **8.** *Informal.* to move as a group in a confused, disorderly fashion; crowd: *The team members piled into the bus.* **9.** to fill or cover with a mass of things: *The desk was piled high with books.* [from an early French word, which comes from Latin *pīla* "pillar"]

pile² (pīl), *n.* a long beam or pillar of wood, steel, concrete, etc., driven into the ground, often under water, as a support for a building, pier, bridge, or other structure. [from the Old English word *pīl* "shaft," which comes from Latin *pīlum* "javelin"]

pile³ (pīl), *n.* **1.** soft, fine hair or down. **2.** a furry or hairy surface formed on some fabrics such as velvet, corduroy, turkish toweling, etc., by short raised loops of yarn, which are sometimes cut and sometimes left as loops. [from the Latin word *pilus* "hair"]

pile′ driv′er, a machine for driving piles into the earth.

pil·fer (pil′fər), *v.* to steal, esp. in small amounts from a larger supply or store: *to pilfer stationery supplies from the office storeroom.* —**pil′fer·age,** *n.*

pil·grim (pil′grim, pil′grəm), *n.* **1.** a person who travels to a religious or historic shrine. **2.** a traveler or wanderer: *a pilgrim along life's way.* **3.** (*usually cap.*) one of the Pilgrim Fathers.

pil·grim·age (pil′grə mij), *n.* **1.** a journey to a religious or historic shrine: *a pilgrimage to Mecca.* **2.** any long journey or wandering.

Pil′grim Fa′thers, the band of Puritans who founded the colony of Plymouth, Massachusetts, in 1620.

pil·ing (pī′lĭng), *n.* a number of piles supporting a structure.

pill (pĭl), *n.* a small ball or tablet containing medicine.

pil·lage (pĭl′ĭj), *v.,* **pil·laged, pil·lag·ing. 1.** to rob with violence, as in time of war; plunder: *The city was pillaged by the invaders.* —*n.* **2.** the act of robbing or plundering, esp. in war. **3.** things taken as plunder; booty: *The bandits carried away vast amounts of pillage.* —**pil′lag·er,** *n.*

pil·lar (pĭl′ər), *n.* **1.** an upright shaft of wood, stone, concrete, etc., usually forming one of the supports of a building, bridge, arch, or other structure. **2.** anything resembling a pillar in shape, such as a natural rock formation. **3.** a person who is an important leader or supporter of an institution or organization: *a pillar of society.* **4. from pillar to post,** from one place, situation, etc., to another, esp. without plan or purpose: *It's time he settled down and stopped going from pillar to post.* —**pil′lared,** *adj.*

pil·lo·ry (pĭl′ə rē), *n., pl.* **pil·lo·ries. 1.** a wooden framework with openings for the neck and wrists, formerly used to punish offenders by exposing them to public ridicule. —*v.,* **pil·lo·ried, pil·lo·ry·ing. 2.** to punish (someone) by means of a pillory. **3.** to ridicule or abuse publicly: *The leaders of the strike were pilloried in the press.*

pil·low (pĭl′ō), *n.* **1.** a bag or case made of cloth, filled with a soft, springy material, such as foam rubber, down, or the like, used as a rest for the head or some other part of the body; cushion. —*v.* **2.**

Pillory

to rest on a pillow or something like a pillow: *The child pillowed his head in his mother's lap.* **3.** to serve as a pillow for: *A soft quilt pillowed his back.*

pil·low·case (pĭl′ō kās′), *n.* a removable covering, usually of cloth, for a pillow. Also, **pil·low·slip** (pĭl′ō slĭp′).

pi·lot (pī′lət), *n.* **1.** a person who flies an airplane or other aircraft. **2.** a person who is trained to steer large ships in and out of harbors or through dangerous stretches of water: *The steamship picked up a pilot at the harbor entrance.* **3.** a person who steers any ship or boat. **4.** a guide or leader. —*v.* **5.** to steer; act as pilot of. **6.** to guide or lead: *The guide piloted a group of tourists through the Forum.*

pi′lot light′, 1. a small flame that is kept burning in a stove, heater, etc., to relight the burners. **2.** a small lamp that indicates whether an appliance, circuit, etc., is turned on.

pi·men·to (pĭ mĕn′tō), *n., pl.* **pi·men·tos. 1.** another name for **allspice. 2.** another spelling of **pimiento.**

pi·mien·to (pĭ myĕn′tō, pĭ mĕn′tō), *n., pl.* **pi·mien-**

tos. a sweet, red pepper used as a vegetable, a garnish, for stuffing olives, etc.

pim·ple (pĭm′pəl), *n.* a small, usually inflamed swelling on the skin; pustule. —**pim′ply,** *adj.*

pin (pĭn), *n.* **1.** a short, thin, usually rounded piece of metal with a point at one end, used for fastening things together. **2.** any long, thin piece of metal, wood, or other material for fastening or supporting things. **3.** an ornament or badge fastened with a pin: *a class pin.* **4.** one of the rounded wooden clubs used as the target in bowling. —*v.,* **pinned, pin·ning. 5.** to fasten or attach with a pin or pins. **6.** to hold fast in one place or position: *Two policemen pinned the struggling suspect to the ground.* **7. on pins and needles,** nervous, tense, or uneasy: *She's always on pins and needles before an exam.* **8. pin down, a.** to hold in one place so as to prevent movement: *The troops were pinned down by enemy fire.* **b.** to determine clearly; fix; establish: *to pin down the cause of a fire.* [from the Old English word *pinn* "peg"]

pin·a·fore (pĭn′ə fôr′), *n.* **1.** a child's apron, worn as a covering for a dress. **2.** a sleeveless house dress worn by women.

pin·cers (pĭn′sərz), *n. (usually used as pl.)* **1.** a tool consisting of two pivoted limbs forming a pair of handles and a pair of jaws, used for gripping, extracting nails, etc. **2.** a claw of a lobster, crab, etc.

pinch (pĭnch), *v.* **1.** to squeeze between two surfaces, such as the finger and thumb, the teeth, the jaws of a tool, etc. **2.** to press upon so as to cause pain or discomfort; cramp: *This shoe pinches my foot.* **3.** to affect in such a way as to cause distress, anxiety, etc.: *to be pinched by hunger.* **4.** to be stingy or sparing with: *to pinch pennies.* **5.** *Informal.* to arrest. **6.** *Slang.* to steal. —*n.* **7.** the act of pinching; nip; squeeze: *He gave her a pinch on the cheek.* **8.** the amount of anything that can be contained between the finger and thumb: *a pinch of salt.* **9.** a feeling of pain or discomfort: *the pinch of hunger.* **10.** a time of trouble or difficulty; emergency: *to help out a friend in a pinch.* **11.** *Informal.* an arrest: *A patrolman made the pinch.* —**pinch′er,** *n.*

pinch-hit (pĭnch′hĭt′), *v.,* **pinch-hit, pinch-hit·ting. 1.** (in baseball) to bat in place of another player, esp. one who is a poor hitter. **2.** to substitute for someone, esp. in an emergency. —**pinch′ hit′ter.**

pin·cush·ion (pĭn′kŏŏsh′ən), *n.* a small cushion or pad into which pins are stuck to store them.

pine[1] (pīn), *n.* **1.** any of numerous cone-bearing evergreen trees having clusters of long, needle-shaped leaves, various kinds of which yield lumber, turpentine, tar, pitch, etc. **2.** the soft, light wood of such a tree. [from the Old English word *pīn,* which comes from Latin *pīnus*]

pine[2] (pīn), *v.,* **pined, pin·ing. 1.** to yearn; long with deep suffering (usually fol. by *for*): *He pined for his lost dog.* **2.** to fail in health or courage (usually fol. by *away*): *She just pined away after her husband died.* [from the Old English word *pīnian* "to torture," which comes from *pīn* "torture," from Latin *pēna* "punishment"]

pine·ap·ple (pīn′ap′əl), *n.* **1.** a large, juicy fruit shaped like a pine cone and having a tart flavor. **2.** the low, tropical plant, with long spiny-edged leaves, that bears this fruit.

pin·feath·er (pin′feŧh′ər), *n.* an undeveloped feather that has just come through the skin.

Ping-Pong (piṅg′poṅg′, piṅg′-pôṅg′), *n. Trademark.* the game of table tennis.

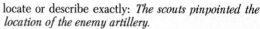

Pineapple

pin·hole (pin′hōl′), *n.* a small hole made by a pin or something as slender as a pin.

pin·ion[1] (pin′yən), *n.* a gear having only a small number of teeth, esp. one that engages a rack or a larger gear. [from the French word *pignon* "cogwheel," which is related to *peigne* "comb"]

pin·ion[2] (pin′yən), *n.* **1.** the outer part of a bird's wing. **2.** the wing of a bird, bat, etc. **3.** a feather. —*v.* **4.** to bind (a person's arms or hands) so as to prevent movement: *The guards pinioned his arms behind his back.* [from the French word *pignon,* which comes from Latin *pinna* "wing, feather"]

pink[1] (piṅgk), *n.* **1.** a pale red. **2.** any of several garden plants having pink, white, or red flowers resembling carnations. **3.** the highest form or degree: *a runner in the pink of condition.* —*adj.* **4.** of the color pink: *pink cheeks.*

pink[2] (piṅgk), *v.* **1.** to cut the edge of (cloth, paper, or the like) in a notched, toothed, or other decorative pattern. **2.** to punch (cloth, leather, or the like) with small holes for decoration. **3.** to pierce with a sharp instrument; prick; stab. [from the Middle English word *pynken* "to prick, pierce"]

pink·eye (piṅgk′ī′), *n.* a contagious disease of man and certain animals that causes soreness and reddening of the eyes.

pink·ish (piṅg′kish), *adj.* slightly pink.

pin′ mon′ey, **1.** a small sum of money set aside for minor expenses. **2.** a small allowance of money given by a husband to his wife for personal expenses.

pin·na·cle (pin′ə kəl), *n.* **1.** a high peak or rock formation. **2.** the highest point; summit; zenith: *His inventions raised him to the pinnacle of fame and success.* **3.** a slender spire or steeple rising above the top of a building or tower.

pin·nate (pin′āt, pin′it), *adj.* resembling a feather, esp. in having parts branching from a central stem: *a pinnate leaf.*

pi·noch·le (pē′nuk əl), *n.* **1.** a card game for two, three, or four persons, played with a deck of 48 cards containing two each of the ace, king, queen, jack, ten, and nine of each suit. **2.** a scoring combination in this game, made up of the queen of spades and the jack of diamonds.

Pinnate leaf

pin·point (pin′point′), *n.* **1.** the point of a pin. **2.** anything very small: *a pinpoint of color.* —*v.* **3.** to

locate or describe exactly: *The scouts pinpointed the location of the enemy artillery.*

pint (pīnt), *n.* **1.** a unit of liquid measure equal to 16 fluid ounces, or 28.875 cubic inches (0.473 liter). **2.** a unit of dry measure equal to half a quart, or 33.6 cubic inches (0.551 liter).

pin·to (pin′tō, pēn′tō), *adj.* **1.** marked with spots of different colors. —*n., pl.* **pin·tos.** **2.** a horse or pony with such markings. [from an American Spanish word meaning "painted"]

pin·up (pin′up′), *n.* **1.** a picture that may be pinned up on a wall, esp. one of a pretty girl. —*adj.* **2.** of, concerning, or appearing in a pinup: *a pinup girl.*

pin·wheel (pin′hwēl′, -wēl′), *n.* **1.** a toy made of a stick with pieces of brightly colored paper, plastic, etc., fastened to it with a pin so that they spin when blown by the wind. **2.** a kind of firework fastened to a pin, on which it spins when lighted.

pin·y (pī′nē), *adj.,* **pin·i·er, pin·i·est. 1.** covered with or consisting of pine trees. **2.** referring to or like pine trees: *a piny odor.*

pi·o·neer (pī′ə nēr′), *n.* **1.** a person who is among the first to enter or settle a region: *The pioneers opened up the West.* **2.** a person who leads the way in a certain field of progress or achievement: *The Wright brothers were pioneers in aviation.* —*v.* **3.** to be a pioneer; lead or show the way: *Pasteur pioneered in preventive medicine.* **4.** to open up or start (a settlement, project, movement, etc.): *Edison pioneered the age of electricity.*

pi·ous (pī′əs), *adj.* **1.** very religious; devout: *a pious missionary.* **2.** of or concerning religious devotion: *pious literature.* **3.** pretending to be devout; hypocritical: *a pious swindler.* —**pi′ous·ly,** *adv.*

pip[1] (pip), *n.* one of the dots or spots on dice, playing cards, or dominoes. [changed from an earlier word *peep*]

pip[2] (pip), *n.* a contagious disease of birds, esp. poultry. [from an early Dutch word, which comes from Latin *pītuīta* "phlegm, pip"]

pip[3] (pip), *n.* **1.** a small seed, such as that of an apple or orange. **2.** *Slang.* someone or something wonderful: *He's a pip!* [short for *pippin* "a seed." See *pippin*]

pipe (pīp), *n.* **1.** a hollow tube made of metal, pottery, or other material for conveying water, gas, steam, etc. **2.** Sometimes, **pipes.** a musical wind instrument consisting of a single tube of wood or other material, esp. a simple or primitive one. **3.** a tube of wood, clay, etc., with a bowl at one end, used for smoking tobacco. **4.** one of the tubes that produce the sound of an organ. **5. pipes,** the bagpipes. **6.** the call or cry of a bird, frog, etc. —*v.,* **piped, pip·ing. 7.** to play on a pipe or bagpipes. **8.** to make a short, shrill sound, like that of a pipe or bird. **9.** to carry by means of pipes: *to pipe water from the mountains.* **10.** to supply with pipes: *to pipe the house for steam heat.* **11. pipe down,** *Slang.* to stop talking; be quiet: *He told us to pipe down and study.*

pipe·line (pīp′līn′), *n.* a long series of pipes for

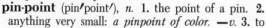

act, āble, dâre, ärt; ebb, ēqual; if, īce; hot, ōver, ôrder; oil; book; ooze; out; up, ûrge; ə = *a* as in *alone;* ə as in *button* (but′ən), *fire* (fīə r); chief; shoe; thin; ŧħat; zh as in *measure* (mezh′ər). See full key inside cover.

transporting oil, water, gas, etc., over great distances.

pipe′ or′gan. See **organ** (def. 1).

pip·er (pī′pər), *n.* a person who plays a wind instrument, esp. the bagpipe.

pi·pette (pī pet′), *n.* a slender tube, usually marked with graduations, for measuring and transferring quantities of liquids in a laboratory.

pip·ing (pī′ping), *n.* **1.** a number of pipes forming a system: *the piping of a building.* **2.** the act or sound of a person or thing that pipes. **3.** a shrill sound or sounds, such as those made by a bird. **4.** the sound or music of a pipe or bagpipes. **5.** a tubelike band of material used for trimming edges and seams of clothing, upholstery, etc. —*adj.* **6.** making a shrill sound: *a piping voice.* **7. piping hot,** very hot; sizzling or steaming: *a piping hot cup of tea.*

pip·pin (pip′in), *n.* any of several kinds of apples. [from the Middle English word *pipin,* which comes from Old French *pepin* "a seed"]

pi·quant (pē′kənt, pē′känt), *adj.* **1.** pleasantly sharp in flavor or aroma: *a piquant sauce.* **2.** lively or stimulating to the mind: *a talk full of piquant phrases.* —**pi′quan·cy,** *n.*

pique (pēk), *v.,* **piqued, piqu·ing. 1.** to cause displeasure in (a person), esp. by an offense to pride, dignity, etc.: *She was piqued at not receiving an invitation.* **2.** to offend (a person's pride, dignity, etc.). **3.** to arouse or stimulate: *to pique one's curiosity.* —*n.* **4.** a feeling of annoyance or displeasure, esp. if caused by a slight or insult; resentment: *She concealed her pique at not being invited.*

pi·qué (pi kā′, pē kā′), *n.* a fabric of cotton, spun rayon, or silk, with raised woven stripes.

pi·ra·cy (pī′rə sē), *n., pl.* **pi·ra·cies. 1.** robbery or other criminal acts committed on the sea. **2.** unauthorized use of a copyrighted or patented work.

pi·ra·nha (pi rän′yə, pi ran′yə), *n.* any of a family of small, freshwater, South American fishes, schools of which are known to attack and devour humans and large animals.

pi·rate (pī′rət), *n.* **1.** a person who commits robbery or crimes of violence on the sea. **2.** a ship used by pirates. **3.** a person who commits piracy of a copyrighted or patented work. —*v.,* **pi·rat·ed, pi·rat·ing. 4.** to print or otherwise reproduce (a copyrighted work) without permission; make use of (a patented invention) for one's own profit without permission. [from the Greek word *peiratēs,* which comes from *peiran* "to attack"]

Piranha
(length
to 1 ½ ft.)

pir·ou·ette (pir′oo et′), *n.* **1.** a whirling movement in dancing performed on one foot or on the points of the toes. —*v.,* **pir·ou·et·ted, pir·ou·et·ting. 2.** to perform a pirouette or a similar movement.

Pi·sa (pē′zə), *n.* a city in NW Italy: leaning bell tower.

Pis·ces (pī′sēz), *n.* the Fishes: a constellation and sign of the zodiac.

pis·ta·chi·o (pi stash′ē ō′, pi stä′shē ō′), *n., pl.* **pis·ta·chi·os. 1.** the nut of a European or Asian tree having a sweet, greenish kernel that is eaten salted or used in candies, ice cream, etc. **2.** the tree bearing this nut.

pis·til (pis′t∂l), *n.* the organ of a flower that produces the seed, consisting of the ovary, style, and stigma. See illus. at **flower.**

pis·tol (pis′t∂l), *n.* a short firearm made to be held and fired with one hand. [from the Czech word *pištal* "pistol, pipe"]

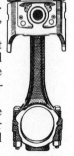

pis·ton (pis′tən), *n.* a disk or cup that moves back and forth inside a tube and exerts pressure on or receives pressure from a liquid or gas in the tube: *the piston of an engine.*

pis′ton ring′, one of two or three springy rings that fit in grooves near the top of a piston and form a tight seal with the cylinder walls.

Piston

pit¹ (pit), *n.* **1.** a hole in the ground. **2.** an excavation made in the earth for mining. **3.** the abode of evil spirits and lost souls; hell. **4.** a small dent or hollow in a surface: *The table top was rough with many small pits.* **5.** a natural hollow at some point on the surface of the body: *the pit of the back.* **6.** a scar on the skin left by smallpox or acne; pockmark. **7.** an enclosure in which animals, such as gamecocks, are set to fight. —*v.,* **pit·ted, pit·ting. 8.** to mark with dents, holes, scars, etc.: *ground pitted by erosion.* **9.** to set or match up against, as in a fight or contest: *to pit one's skill against the experience of a famous golfer.* [from the Old English word *pytt,* which comes from Latin *puteus* "well, pit, shaft"]

pit² (pit), *n.* **1.** the stone of a fruit, such as a peach, plum, cherry, etc. —*v.,* **pit·ted, pit·ting. 2.** to remove the pit or pits from: *The recipe calls for pitted dates.* [from a Dutch word meaning "kernel," which is related to English *pith*]

pitch¹ (pich), *v.* **1.** to erect or set up (a tent, camp, or the like). **2.** to put or set in a particular location or position: *A huge boulder was pitched on the edge of the cliff.* **3.** to throw, hurl, or toss: *to pitch a bottle out the window.* **4.** (in baseball) to throw (the ball) to the batter. **5.** to fall forward or headlong: *He slipped on a rock and pitched into the water.* **6.** to set at a certain point, degree, level, etc.: *He pitched his hopes too high.* **7.** (in music or speech) to set at a certain pitch: *That song is pitched too low for my voice.* **8.** to slope or dip sharply: *a cliff pitching down to the sea.* **9.** to toss or plunge, as a ship, airplane, rocket, etc., so that the bow and stern, or the nose and tail, alternately rise and fall. —*n.* **10.** a certain point, degree, level, etc.: *a high pitch of excitement.* **11.** the degree or angle of slope: *a low roof with a gentle pitch.* **12.** the act or manner of pitching. **13.** (in baseball) a serving of the ball to the batter by the pitcher. **14.** (in music or speech) the degree of height or depth of a tone or sound. The pitch of a note depends on the rapidity of the vibrations that produce it. **15.** a plunging, seesaw movement, as of a ship, airplane, rocket, etc. **16. pitch in,** *Informal.* to begin working in earnest: *We can finish fast if everybody pitches in.* **17. pitch into,** *Informal.* **a.** to begin working on (something) in earnest: *He pitched into his homework, determined to get a good grade.* **b.** to attack, either physically or with words: *He pitched into the other fighter the moment the bell rang.* [from the Middle English word *picchen*]

pitch² (pich), *n.* **1.** any of various dark, sticky substances made from wood, coal, or petroleum, used to coat roofs, pave roads, etc. —*v.* **2.** to cover or seal with pitch. [from the Old English word *pic,* which comes from Latin *pix*]

pitch·black (pich′blak′), *adj.* black as pitch; extremely black.

pitch·blende (pich′blend′), *n.* a black mineral that is the principal ore of uranium.

pitch·er¹ (pich′ər), *n.* **1.** a container for liquids, usually having a handle and a spout for pouring. **2.** Also, **pitcherful.** the amount such a container can hold. [from the Old French word *pichier,* which comes from medieval Latin *bicārium* "beaker"]

pitch·er² (pich′ər), *n.* **1.** a person who pitches. **2.** (in baseball) the player who serves the ball to the opposing batter.

pitch·er·ful (pich′ər foŏl′), *n., pl.* **pitch·er·fuls.** See **pitcher¹** (def. 2).

pitch′er plant′, any of various plants having leaves shaped like a pitcher.

pitch·fork (pich′fôrk′), *n.* a large fork with a long handle, used for lifting and tossing hay, stalks of grain, etc.

pitch′ pipe′, a small flute or reed pipe used for establishing the correct pitch for singing groups or in tuning a musical instrument.

Pitcher plant

pitch·y (pich′ē), *adj.,* **pitch·i·er, pitch·i·est. 1.** full of or covered with pitch. **2.** resembling pitch. **3.** of the color of pitch; extremely black.

pit·e·ous (pit′ē əs), *adj.* arousing a feeling of pity; deserving pity: *the piteous cries of the lost lamb.* —**pit′e·ous·ly,** *adv.*

pit·fall (pit′fôl′), *n.* **1.** a concealed pit for trapping men or animals. **2.** any concealed obstacle or source of danger: *the pitfalls of English grammar.*

pith (pith), *n.* **1.** the soft, spongy tissue at the center of the stem of certain plants. **2.** the soft inner part of a feather, hair, etc. **3.** the important or essential part; gist: *the pith of the argument.*

pith·y (pith′ē), *adj.,* **pith·i·er, pith·i·est. 1.** brief and forceful in expression; full of meaning: *a pithy remark.* **2.** of, like, or full of pith: *the pithy stem of a plant.* —**pith′i·ly,** *adv.* —**pith′i·ness,** *n.*

pit·i·a·ble (pit′ē ə bəl), *adj.* **1.** arousing a feeling of pity; pitiful: *a pitiable beggar.* **2.** arousing or deserving scorn; miserable: *a pitiable attempt to deceive us.* —**pit′i·a·bly,** *adv.*

pit·i·ful (pit′ə fəl), *adj.* **1.** arousing a feeling of pity; deserving pity: *a pitiful plea for help.* **2.** arousing or deserving scorn: *an amateur actor's pitiful performance.* —**pit′i·ful·ly,** *adv.*

pit·i·less (pit′ē lis), *adj.* feeling or showing no pity; merciless: *the dictator's pitiless persecution of his political opponents.* —**pit′i·less·ly,** *adv.*

Pit·man (pit′mən), *n.* a system of shorthand. See illus. at **shorthand.** [named for Sir Isaac *Pitman,* English inventor, who devised it]

pit·tance (pit′ᵊns), *n.* **1.** a small amount or share. **2.** a small allowance, esp. of money.

Pitts·burgh (pits′bûrg), *n.* a port city in SW Pennsylvania, on the Ohio River.

pi·tu·i·tar·y (pi toŏ′i ter′ē, -tyoŏ′-), *adj.* **1.** of, concerning, or obtained from the pituitary gland. —*n., pl.* **pi·tu·i·tar·ies. 2.** the pituitary gland.

pitu′itary gland′, a small oval gland attached to the base of the brain that secretes hormones controlling the growth and many other activities of the body. See illus. at **brain.**

pit·y (pit′ē), *n.* **1.** a feeling of sorrow for the sufferings or misfortune of others. **2.** a cause or reason for sorrow or regret: *It's a pity that he didn't see the car coming.* —*v.,* **pit·ied, pit·y·ing. 3.** to feel pity for; be sorry for: *to pity the sick and helpless.* **4. take pity on,** to show pity for; have sympathy for: *We took pity on them and pulled their car out of the mud.* —**pit′y·ing·ly,** *adv.*

piv·ot (piv′ət), *n.* **1.** a pin or shaft on which something turns or swings. **2.** a person or thing on which something depends: *He is the pivot of the sales department.* **3.** a turning or whirling movement, esp. a turning around on one foot: *A slow pivot brought him around facing the audience.* —*v.* **4.** to turn on a pivot or something resembling a pivot. **5.** to turn around on one foot. **6.** to turn or depend on some particular person or thing: *The whole plan pivots on your being able to go.*

piv·ot·al (piv′ə tᵊl), *adj.* **1.** of, belonging to, or used as a pivot. **2.** highly important; decisive: *a pivotal event in his career.*

pix·y (pik′sē), *n., pl.* **pix·ies.** a mischievous fairy or sprite. Also, **pix′ie.** —**pix′y·ish,** *adj.*

piz·za (pēt′sə), *n.* an Italian dish made of a flat, baked crust of bread dough, topped with tomato sauce and cheese and, sometimes, mushrooms, bacon, sausage, etc.

pkg., package.

pkgs., packages.

pl. 1. place. **2.** plate. **3.** plural.

plac·ard (plak′ärd, plak′ərd), *n.* **1.** a written or printed notice for posting in a public place; poster. —*v.* **2.** to post placards on or in.

pla·cate (plā′kāt, plak′āt), *v.,* **pla·cat·ed, pla·cat·ing.** to calm the anger of (someone); soothe; pacify: *to placate an outraged mob.* —**pla′cat·er,** *n.*

place (plās), *n.* **1.** a particular portion of space: *a place to put the new furniture.* **2.** a portion of space occupied by a person or thing: *to put a book back in its place.* **3.** a space, spot, building, etc., set apart for a particular purpose: *a place of worship.* **4.** any particular spot or point on a body or surface: *a rough place on a road; a torn place on a shirt.* **5.** a particular point or location in a piece of writing: *to lose one's place in a book.* **6.** a space or seat for a person: *Save me a place in the first row.* **7.** position or situation: *If I were in your place, I wouldn't go.* **8.** proper circumstance, position, or location: *A restaurant is not the place for an argument.* **9.** a job or post: *persons in high places of government.* **10.** a function or duty: *It is not your place to criticize them.* **11.** a city, town, or region; locality: *Trains don't stop in that place now.* **12.** position or rank: *The horse finished in second place.* **13.** a dwelling or house: *Please have dinner at my place.* **14.** a short street. **15.** a step or point in order of proceeding: *in the first place.* **16.** (in arithmetic) the position of a figure in a series. —*v.,* **placed, plac·ing. 17.** to put in a particular position, situation, condition, etc.: *Place the vase on the table. He placed an advertisement in the newspaper.* **18.** to identify by connecting with the proper place, circumstances, etc.: *I cannot place her voice.* **19.** to earn a certain standing with relation to others in a race, examination, etc.: *He placed second in a graduating class of 90.* **20. in place,** in the correct or usual place, position, etc.: *The ushers must be in place before the audience is admitted.* **21. in place of,** as a substitute for; instead of: *Would you like milk in place of ginger ale?* **22. out of place, a.** not in the correct or usual place, position, etc.: *Why is this chair out of place?* **b.** not suitable, proper, or in good taste: *That kind of behavior is out of place in the classroom.* **23. take place,** to happen; occur: *Where did the accident take place?*

place·ment (plās′mənt), *n.* **1.** the act of placing. **2.** location or arrangement: *Do you like the placement of the candles?* **3.** the act of an employment office or employer in filling a position.

plac·er (plas′ər), *n.* an exposed deposit of valuable minerals mixed with sand or gravel. [from a Spanish word meaning "sandbank"]

plac·id (plas′id), *adj.* pleasantly calm or peaceful: *placid waters.* —**pla·cid·i·ty** (plə sid′i tē), *n.* —**plac′id·ly,** *adv.*

pla·gia·rism (plā′jə riz′əm), *n.* the act or offense of plagiarizing.

pla·gia·rize (plā′jə rīz′), *v.,* **pla·gia·rized, pla·gia·riz·ing.** to steal and use (the language, ideas, and thoughts of another), representing them as one's own original work. —**pla′gia·rist,** *n.*

plague (plāg), *n.* **1.** any highly contagious fatal disease. **2.** the bubonic plague. **3.** any widespread affliction or evil: *the plague of war.* —*v.,* **plagued, pla·guing. 4.** to trouble, vex, or torment: *The question of his future plagues him with doubt.*

plaid (plad), *n.* **1.** a cloth woven of colored yarns in a pattern of rectangles formed by crossing stripes in various widths. **2.** a long piece of cloth having such a pattern, worn across the shoulder by Scottish High-

landers. —*adj.* **3.** having the pattern of a plaid: *a plaid scarf.*

plain (plān), *adj.* **1.** clear or distinct to the eye or ear: *in plain view.* **2.** clear to the mind; easily understood; obvious: *to make one's meaning plain.* **3.** having little or no decoration or pattern: *a plain fabric.* **4.** direct; sincere; outspoken: *the plain truth.* **5.** not superior or sophisticated; simple; ordinary: *plain people.* **6.** not rich or highly seasoned; simple: *plain food.* **7.** not beautiful: *a plain face.* —*adv.* **8.** clearly and simply: *He's just plain lazy.* —*n.* **9.** an expanse of nearly flat land. —**plain′ness,** *n.*

Plains′ In′dian, a member of any of the nomadic American Indian tribes that formerly inhabited the Great Plains.

plain-spo·ken (plān′spō′kən), *adj.* frank; candid.

plaint (plānt), *n.* a complaint or lament.

plain·tiff (plān′tif), *n.* a person who brings a lawsuit in court (opposite of *defendant*).

plain·tive (plān′tiv), *adj.* expressing sorrow; mournful; sad: *a plaintive melody.*

plait (plāt, plat), *n.* **1.** a braid, as of hair. **2.** a pleat, as of cloth. —*v.* **3.** to braid, as hair. **4.** to pleat.

plan (plan), *n.* **1.** a way of doing or proceeding with something that has been thought out beforehand: *a battle plan; to make plans for the future.* **2.** a drawing showing how the parts or details of a building, machine, garden, street, etc., are arranged: *the floor plan of a house.* —*v.,* **planned, plan·ning. 3.** to arrange the details of (something) beforehand; project a plan or course of action for: *to plan a vacation.* **4.** to intend: *I plan to arrive early.* **5.** to make plans: *to plan ahead.*

pla·nar·i·an (plə nâr′ē ən), *n.* a flatworm capable of swimming about freely in water.

plane¹ (plān), *n.* **1.** a flat, level surface. **2.** a level: *to discuss matters on a serious, moral plane.* **3.** an airplane. —*adj.* **4.** flat or level, as a surface. [from the Latin word *plānum* "level ground"]

plane² (plān), *n.* **1.** any of various woodworking tools for smoothing, shaping, or truing. —*v.,* **planed, plan·ing. 2.** to smooth with a plane. **3.** to remove with or as if with a plane (often fol. by *away* or *off*). [from an early French word, which comes from Latin *plāna*]

Plane

plane³ (plān), *n.* a plane tree.

plan·et (plan′it), *n.* **1.** any of the nine large bodies that revolve in orbits around the sun and shine by reflected light. In order of distance from the sun, the planets are Mercury, Venus, Earth, Mars, Jupiter, Saturn, Uranus, Neptune, and Pluto. **2.** a similar body revolving around any star. [from the Greek word *planētai* "planets," literally "wanderers"]

plan·e·tar·i·um (plan′i târ′ē əm), *n.* **1.** a large machine that projects an image of the heavens onto the inside of a dome, reproducing the motions of the planets, stars, etc. **2.** a building housing such a machine.

plan·e·tar·y (plan′i ter′ē), *adj.* of, concerning, or resembling a planet or the planets.

plane′ tree′, any of several large, spreading shade trees, such as the sycamore. [from the Old French word *plane,* which comes from Greek *platanos,* from *platys* "broad" (referring to the leaves)]

plank (plangk), *n.* **1.** a long, flat piece of timber, thicker than a board. **2.** one of the principles or goals stated in the platform of a political party: *They voted for a plank supporting civil rights.* —*v.* **3.** to cover with planks: *to plank the floors of a house.* **4.** to bake or broil and serve on a board: *to plank a steak.* **5. walk the plank,** to suffer death by drowning after walking off the end of a plank extended from a ship's side: a punishment formerly used by pirates.

plank·ton (plangk′tən), *n.* the tiny animals and plants that float near the surface of a body of water and serve as food for many larger water animals.

plant (plant), *n.* **1.** any member of the vegetable group of living things. Trees, flowers, grasses, mosses, fungi, and algae are all plants. **2.** an herb or other small vegetable growth, in contrast to a tree or shrub: *a potted plant.* **3.** a seedling or shoot, esp. one ready for transplanting. **4.** the buildings and equipment of a factory or other business: *a chemical plant.* **5.** the complete equipment or apparatus for a particular process or operation: *the heating plant of a school.* —*v.* **6.** to put in the ground to grow, as seeds, young trees, etc. **7.** to furnish or stock with plants: *to plant a field of corn.* **8.** to instill or put into the mind (ideas, teachings, etc.): *to plant a love of learning in children.* **9.** to insert or set firmly; put; place: *to plant posts.* **10.** to establish, found, or settle (a colony, city, etc.).

plan·tain[1] (plan′tin, plan′t³n), *n.* **1.** a tropical fruit resembling a banana but eaten cooked. **2.** the tall plant bearing this fruit. [from the Spanish word *plátano* "plantain," also "plane tree," which comes from Greek *platanos.* See *plane tree*]

plan·tain[2] (plan′tin, plan′t³n), *n.* a weed having broad, oval leaves that spread close to the ground and tall, slender spikes covered with small flowers. [from the Old French word *plantein,* which comes from Latin *plantāgō*]

plan·ta·tion (plan tā′shən), *n.* **1.** a large farm or estate on which cotton, tobacco, coffee, or the like, is cultivated, usually by laborers who live on the property. **2.** a group of plants or planted trees: *a rubber plantation.* **3.** a colony or new settlement.

plant·er (plan′tər), *n.* **1.** the owner or manager of a plantation. **2.** a machine for planting seeds in the ground. **3.** a person who plants. **4.** a decorative container for growing flowers and ornamental plants.

plaque (plak), *n.* a flat plate or tablet of metal, porcelain, etc., having a design or picture and intended for ornament, as on a wall, or having an inscription which commemorates something, as on a monument.

plas·ma (plaz′mə), *n.* **1.** the liquid part of the blood or lymph in which the blood or lymph cells are suspended. **2.** a highly ionized gas, consisting almost entirely of free electrons and positive ions.

plas·ter (plas′tər), *n.* **1.** a mixture of lime or gypsum, sand, and water, applied to walls in the form of a paste and allowed to dry and harden. **2.** short for **plaster of Paris. 3.** a preparation for spreading on a cloth and applying to the body for a healing purpose. —*v.* **4.** to cover (walls, ceilings, etc.) with or as if with plaster. **5.** to apply a plaster to (the body, a wound, etc.). **6.** to cover or spread over with something: *to plaster a fence with posters.*

plas′ter of Par′is, a white powder made from gypsum that hardens quickly into a solid after being mixed with water. It is used for making art objects, molds, casts for supporting broken bones, etc.

plas·tic (plas′tik), *n.* **1.** any of numerous materials that may be hardened after being shaped, esp. a man-made material of this kind. Plastics may be molded, shaped while heated, or formed into fibers for making cloth: *Nylon is a plastic.* —*adj.* **2.** made of plastic: *a disposable plastic spoon.* **3.** capable of being molded. **4.** having the power of molding or shaping formless material: *a plastic art.*

plas′tic sur′gery, the branch of surgery dealing with the repair or replacement of malformed, injured, or lost organs and tissues.

Pla·ta (plä′tä), *n.* **Rí·o de la** (rē′ō də lä), an estuary on the SE coast of South America between Argentina and Uruguay. 185 mi. long.

plate (plāt), *n.* **1.** a shallow, usually circular dish from which food is served or eaten. **2.** the contents of such a dish: *She had a vegetable plate for lunch.* **3.** the food and service for one person, as at a banquet: *The wedding breakfast cost $10 a plate.* **4.** household dishes, utensils, etc., of gold or silver. **5.** a dish used for collecting offerings, as in a church. **6.** a flat, polished piece of metal on which something may be or is engraved. **7.** a thin, flat sheet of metal. **8.** a flat or curved sheet of metal, plastic, glass, or the like, on which a picture or text has been etched, molded, or photographically developed. It is inked, as in a press, for printing impressions on other surfaces. **9.** a printed impression from such a piece, as a woodcut. **10.** a full-page illustration in a book. **11.** plated metallic ware: *silver plate.* **12.** (in photography) a sheet of glass, metal, etc., coated with an emulsion sensitive to light, used for taking a photograph. **13.** a set of artificial teeth; denture. —*v.,* **plat·ed, plat·ing. 14.** to coat (metal) with a thin layer of gold, silver, etc. **15.** to cover with metal plates for protection.

Río de la Plata

pla·teau (pla tō′), *n., pl.* **pla·teaus** or **pla·teaux** (pla-tōz′). **1.** a land area having a level surface raised above adjoining land on at least one side; high plain. **2.** any period of slow growth or change: *a plateau in the growth of a business.*

plate′ glass′, a glass formed by rolling the hot glass into a thick plate, which is then ground and polished, used in large windows, mirrors, etc.

plat·form (plat′fôrm), *n.* **1.** a raised, flat structure, as in a hall or meeting place, for use by public speakers, performers, etc. **2.** a set of principles, ideals, or goals on which a person or group, esp. a political party, takes a public stand; program.

plat·i·num (plat′ᵊnəm), *n.* **1.** a hard, heavy, valuable metal, used in jewelry and in making scientific apparatus: a chemical element. *Symbol:* Pt —*adj.* **2.** made of platinum: *a platinum ring.*

plat·i·tude (plat′i tōōd′, -tyōōd′), *n.* a flat, dull remark, esp. one made as if it were fresh and profound, such as "Nobody lives forever."

Pla·to (plā′tō), *n.* 427–347 B.C., Greek philosopher: student of Socrates. —**Pla·ton·ic** (plə ton′ik), *adj.*

pla·toon (plə tōōn′), *n.* **1.** one of the units of a military company, usually consisting of two or more squads and commanded by a lieutenant. **2.** any similar group or company: *a platoon in a football game.* [from the French word *peloton* "little ball, group, platoon," which comes from *pelote* "ball"]

plat·ter (plat′ər), *n.* a large, shallow dish, usually oval in shape, from which food is served.

plat·y·pus (plat′i pəs), *n.* a small, egg-laying mammal of Australia and Tasmania, having webbed feet, a flattened tail, and a duckbill. Also, **duckbill, duckbilled platypus.**

Platypus
(total length
2 ft.)

plau·dit (plô′dit), *n.* Usually, **plaudits.** an enthusiastic expression of approval, such as applause: *The cast of the play won the plaudits of the audience.*

plau·si·ble (plô′zə bəl), *adj.* appearing truthful or reasonable; seemingly worthy of approval or acceptance: *a plausible excuse.* —**plau′si·bil′i·ty,** *n.* —**plau′si·bly,** *adv.*

play (plā), *n.* **1.** a piece of dramatic writing, or a dramatic performance, as on a stage. **2.** exercise or activity for amusement or recreation: *to have time for both work and play.* **3.** fun or jest, as distinguished from seriousness: *Everything he said was said in play.* **4.** a particular action or movement in a game: *A bad play cost him the match.* **5.** the playing or action of a game: *the fourth inning of play.* **6.** one's turn to play in a game: *Whose play is it?* **7.** a playing for stakes; gambling: *to win a bet in play.* **8.** the manner of playing; action of a specified kind: *fair play.* **9.** light, brisk, or changing movement: *the play of a searchlight against the sky.* **10.** action or operation: *The problem made him bring all his intelligence into play.* **11.** freedom of movement or activity: *The steering wheel had too much play.* —*v.* **12.** to amuse oneself; have fun; do or perform in sport: *to play in the street; to play tricks.* **13.** to take part in (a game, pastime, etc.): *to play golf.* **14.** to imitate in jest or sport: *to play house.* **15.** to contend against in a game: *The freshmen played the sophomores in foot-*

ball. **16.** to perform as (a specified player) in a game; use (a piece of equipment, player, etc.) in a game: *Jones played left end. He played his highest card.* **17.** to trifle or toy (often fol. by *with*): *to play nervously with a pencil.* **18.** to act the part of (a person or character); behave in a specified way: *to play Lady Macbeth; to play fair.* **19.** to bet on: *His father likes to play the horses.* **20.** to perform (music); perform on a musical instrument: *to play a sonata; to play the clarinet.* **21.** to be performed: *What is playing at the movie?* **22.** (of instruments, music, etc.) to sound in performance: *Was the radio playing?* **23.** to move or cause to move lightly or quickly: *The lights played over the faces in the crowd.* **24. play down,** to treat as of little importance; minimize; belittle: *The team captain played down his own part in the victory.* **25. play off,** to play an extra game or round in order to settle a tie: *The two teams had to play off for the championship.* **26. play up,** to emphasize the importance of: *to play up science as part of one's education.* **27. play up to,** to try to impress (someone) so as to win favor: *She thinks she can pass by playing up to the teacher.*

play·bill (plā′bil′), *n.* a program of a play.

play·er (plā′ər), *n.* **1.** a person or thing that plays. **2.** a person who plays parts on the stage; actor.

play·fel·low (plā′fel′ō), *n.* a playmate.

play·ful (plā′fəl), *adj.* **1.** full of play; frolicsome: *a playful kitten.* **2.** humorous; not serious: *a playful remark.* —**play′ful·ly,** *adv.* —**play′ful·ness,** *n.*

play·ground (plā′ground′), *n.* an outdoor area used for recreation, esp. by children.

play·house (plā′hous′), *n., pl.* **play·hous·es** (plā′hou′ziz). **1.** a theater. **2.** a small house for children to play in. **3.** a toy house.

play′ing card′, one of a set of 52 cards in four suits, as diamonds, hearts, spades, and clubs, used in playing various games.

play·mate (plā′māt′), *n.* a child's companion in play.

play-off (plā′ôf′, -of′), *n.* (in sports) an extra game, round, etc., to settle a tie.

play·thing (plā′thing′), *n.* a toy.

play·wright (plā′rīt′), *n.* a writer of plays.

pla·za (plä′zə, plaz′ə), *n.* a public square or open space in a city or town.

plea (plē), *n.* **1.** an excuse: *He begged off on the plea that his car wouldn't run.* **2.** (in law) a defendant's answer to a charge: *a plea of not guilty.* **3.** an appeal or request: *a plea for mercy.*

plead (plēd), *v.,* **plead·ed** *or* **plead** (pled) *or* **pled** (pled); **plead·ing.** **1.** to appeal or entreat earnestly: *to plead for time.* **2.** to argue in defense or justification; offer as an excuse: *to plead ignorance.* **3.** to argue (a cause) before a court: *to plead a case.* **4.** to make a plea of a special kind: *The suspect pleaded guilty.* —**plead′er,** *n.*

pleas·ant (plez′ənt), *adj.* **1.** pleasing; agreeable; enjoyable: *a pleasant surprise; pleasant weather.* **2.** (of persons, manners, etc.) polite; friendly. —**pleas′ant·ly,** *adv.* —**pleas′ant·ness,** *n.*

pleas·ant·ry (plez'ən trē), *n., pl.* **pleas·ant·ries.** a good-humored or jesting remark.

please (plēz), *v.,* **pleased, pleas·ing.** **1.** to give (someone) pleasure or satisfaction: *The actress certainly pleased the public.* **2.** to like, wish, or choose: *Go where you please.* **3.** (used as a polite way of requesting, commanding, etc.) be so kind as to: *Please come here.* **4.** to be the pleasure or will of: *May it please your Majesty.* **5. if you please,** if you are willing; if it is convenient: *I would like some more mayonnaise, if you please.*

pleas·ing (plē'zin͡g), *adj.* giving pleasure; agreeable: *a pleasing personality.* —**pleas'ing·ly,** *adv.*

pleas·ur·a·ble (plezh'ər ə bəl), *adj.* agreeable; giving pleasure. —**pleas'ur·a·bly,** *adv.*

pleas·ure (plezh'ər), *n.* **1.** the state or feeling of being pleased; joy; delight: *A good book gives me pleasure.* **2.** a cause or source of enjoyment or delight: *It was a pleasure to see you.* **3.** amusement; gratification; play: *the pursuit of pleasure.* **4.** a person's wish, desire, or choice: *to make known one's pleasure.*

pleat (plēt), *n.* **1.** a flat fold of even width made by doubling cloth on itself and by pressing or stitching it in place. —*v.* **2.** to fold or arrange in pleats.

ple·be·ian (plə bē'ən), *adj.* **1.** of or belonging to the common people; common; vulgar: *a plebeian taste in music.* **2.** of or belonging to the class of common people of ancient Rome. —*n.* **3.** a member of the ordinary or common people. **4.** a member of the class of common people of ancient Rome. [from the Latin word *plēbēius,* which comes from *plēbs* "the common people"]

pleb·i·scite (pleb'i sīt'), *n.* a direct vote by the voters of a state on some important public question.

plec·trum (plek'trəm), *n.* a small piece of ivory, plastic, metal, etc., for plucking the strings of a musical instrument, such as a guitar, banjo, or lyre.

pled (pled), *v.* a past tense and past participle of **plead.**

pledge (plej), *n.* **1.** a solemn promise or agreement: *a pledge of aid; a pledge not to wage war.* **2.** something given or regarded as security: *money given as pledge.* **3.** the state of being given or held as security: *to put a thing in pledge.* —*v.,* **pledged, pledg·ing. 4.** to bind by or as if by a pledge: *to pledge someone to secrecy.* **5.** to promise solemnly: *to pledge one's support.* **6.** to give or deposit as a pledge; pawn.

Ple·ia·des (plē'ə dēz'), *n.pl.* **1.** a cluster of stars in the constellation Taurus, usually thought of as seven, though only six are easily visible. **2.** (in Greek mythology) seven daughters of Atlas who were changed into stars.

ple·na·ry (plē'nə rē, plen'ə rē), *adj.* **1.** full, complete, or absolute: *plenary powers.* **2.** attended by all qualified members: *a plenary session of Congress.*

plen·i·po·ten·ti·ar·y (plen'ē pə ten'shē er'ē), *n., pl.* **plen·i·po·ten·ti·ar·ies. 1.** a person, esp. a diplomatic agent, having full authority to represent a govern-

ment. —*adj.* **2.** having full power or authority, as a diplomatic agent.

plen·i·tude (plen'i tood', -tyood'), *n.* fullness; abundance: *a plenitude of air and sunlight.*

plen·te·ous (plen'tē əs), *adj.* plentiful; abundant: *a plenteous supply of food.* —**plen'te·ous·ly,** *adv.*

plen·ti·ful (plen'ti fəl), *adj.* **1.** existing in great quantity; copious: *a plentiful supply of food.* **2.** yielding abundantly; fruitful: *a plentiful source of inspiration.* —**plen'ti·ful·ly,** *adv.*

plen·ty (plen'tē), *n.* **1.** a full or abundant supply: *You have plenty of time.* **2.** the state or quality of being plentiful; abundance: *to have resources in plenty; a period of peace and plenty.* [from the Latin word *plēnitās* "fullness"]

pleu·ri·sy (ploor'i sē), *n.* an inflammation of the membrane that covers the lungs and lines the chest, causing coughing, discomfort, and fever.

plex·us (plek'səs), *n., pl.* **plex·us·es** *or* **plex·us.** a network of nerves or blood vessels.

pli·a·ble (plī'ə bəl), *adj.* **1.** easily bent; flexible; supple: *pliable leather.* **2.** easily influenced or persuaded: *a pliable young mind.* —**pli'a·bil'i·ty,** *n.*

pli·ant (plī'ənt), *adj.* **1.** bending or yielding easily: *pliant clay.* **2.** easily influenced; compliant: *He has a pliant nature.* —**pli'an·cy,** *n.* —**pli'ant·ly,** *adv.*

pli·ers (plī'ərz), *n.pl. (sometimes used as sing.)* small pincers for bending wire, holding small objects, etc. (usually used with *pair of*): *to buy a pair of pliers.*

plight[1] (plīt), *n.* a condition, state, or situation, esp. an unfavorable one: *the plight of displaced persons after a war.* [from the Middle English word *plit,* which comes from Old French]

plight[2] (plīt), *v.* **1.** to promise; pledge. **2. plight one's troth,** to give one's word, esp. as a promise to marry. [from Old English *pliht* "danger, risk"]

plinth (plinth), *n.* a square slab beneath the base of a column.

PLO, Palestine Liberation Organization.

plod (plod), *v.,* **plod·ded, plod·ding. 1.** to walk or move heavily; trudge: *to plod under the weight of a burden.* **2.** to work slowly and patiently at a task; drudge: *The student plodded along in mathematics.* —**plod'der,** *n.* —**plod'ding·ly,** *adv.*

plot[1] (plot), *n.* **1.** a secret plan or scheme to do something, esp. something unlawful or evil: *a plot to overthrow the government.* **2.** the plan or main story of a play, novel, short story, etc. —*v.,* **plot·ted, plot·ting. 3.** to plan secretly, esp. something evil: *to plot mutiny.* **4.** to draw a plan or map of; mark on a plan, map, or chart, as a ship's course. [from a special use of *plot*[2]; also partly a shortening of the Old French word *complot* "conspiracy"]

plot[2] (plot), *n.* **1.** a small area of ground: *a garden plot.* —*v.,* **plot·ted, plot·ting. 2.** to divide (land) into plots. [from Old English]

plough (plou), *n., v.* another spelling of **plow.**

plov·er (pluv'ər, plō'vər), *n.* any of various birds having a short tail and a bill like that of a pigeon.

plow (plou), *n.* **1.** a farming implement used for cutting and turning over soil. **2.** any implement resembling this, such as a machine for clearing away snow. —*v.* **3.** to turn up (the soil) with a plow. **4.** to work with a plow: *The farmer was still plowing at nightfall.* **5.** to move through something in the manner of a plow; proceed or move laboriously: *a ship plowing through the ocean; to plow through a long book.* Also, **plough.**

plow·man (plou′mən), *n., pl.* **plow·men. 1.** a man who plows. **2.** a farmer.

plow·share (plou′shâr′), *n.* the part of a plow that cuts a furrow in the soil.

pluck (pluk), *v.* **1.** to pull off or out: *to pluck flowers; to pluck the feathers from a chicken.* **2.** to give a pull at: *to pluck someone's sleeve.* **3.** to pull by force; snatch. **4.** to remove the feathers, hairs, etc., from (something) by pulling: *to pluck a chicken.* **5.** to sound (the strings of a musical instrument): *to pluck a guitar.* —*n.* **6.** the act of plucking; tug. **7.** courage; bravery: *to show pluck in a fight.* —**pluck′er,** *n.*

pluck·y (pluk′ē), *adj.,* **pluck·i·er, pluck·i·est.** having or showing courage; brave.

plug (plug), *n.* **1.** a piece of wood or other material used to stop a hole. **2.** a device for making an electrical connection, esp. one that is inserted into a wall socket. **3.** a fireplug. **4.** a cake of pressed tobacco for chewing. **5.** *Informal.* the favorable mention of a commercial product, as on a radio or television program. **6.** *Slang.* a worn-out horse. —*v.,* **plugged, plug·ging. 7.** to stop with or as if with a plug: *to plug a leak; to plug a gap.* **8.** *Informal.* to mention (a product) favorably; publicize: *to plug a new record.* **9.** *Informal.* to work steadily or doggedly; plod (often fol. by *along*): *to plug along at a Spanish lesson.* **10.** **plug in,** to connect (an electrical device) with an outlet: *Plug in the toaster and see if it works.*

plum (plum), *n.* **1.** a round fruit with a smooth skin and a single flat seed. **2.** the tree that bears this fruit. **3.** a raisin, as in a cake or pudding. **4.** a deep purple. —*adj.* **5.** made with or containing plums: *plum cake.* **6.** of the color plum. [from the Old English word *plūme,* which comes from Greek *proumnon*]

plum·age (ploō′mij), *n.* the feathers of a bird.

plumb (plum), *n.* **1.** a small piece of lead or other heavy material that is attached to a cord for measuring the depth of water or to check whether something is truly vertical. —*v.* **2.** to test or measure by a plumb line: *to plumb the depth of a lake.* **3.** to examine closely in order to understand: *to plumb someone's thoughts.* —*adj.* **4.** perpendicular: *a plumb pole.* —*adv.* **5.** *Informal.* completely; absolutely: *You're plumb right.*

plumb·er (plum′ər), *n.* a person who installs and repairs piping, fixtures, etc., esp. in connection with the water supply of a building.

plumb·ing (plum′ing), *n.* **1.** the system of pipes and other apparatus for carrying water, gas, wastes, etc., in a building. **2.** the work or trade of a plumber.

plume (ploōm), *n.* **1.** a feather, esp. a large, long, or fluffy one worn as an ornament. —*v.,* **plumed, plum·**

ing. **2.** (of a bird) to smooth or preen (itself or its feathers). **3.** to cover or adorn with plumes. **4.** to pride (oneself) (often fol. by *on* or *upon*): *She plumed herself on her good looks.*

plum·met (plum′it), *n.* **1.** a weight attached to a line, used for plumbing, sounding, etc. —*v.* **2.** to plunge.

plump¹ (plump), *adj.* **1.** well filled out; rather fleshy or fat. —*v.* **2.** to make or become plump (often fol. by *up*): *to plump up the sofa pillows.* [from the Middle English word *plompe* "dull, rude," which comes from Flemish]

plump² (plump), *v.* **1.** to drop or fall heavily or suddenly: *Since she was tired, she plumped down on the sofa.* —*n.* **2.** a heavy, sudden fall, or the sound of such a fall. —*adv.* **3.** with a heavy or sudden fall or drop: *The skater fell plump on the ice.* —*adj.* **4.** direct; blunt: *a plump refusal to cooperate.* [from the Middle English word *plumpen*]

Plummet

plum′ pud′ding, a rich steamed pudding containing raisins, currants, citron, spices, etc.

plun·der (plun′dər), *v.* **1.** to rob of goods or valuables by force. —*n.* **2.** the act of plundering. **3.** things plundered; loot. —**plun′der·er,** *n.*

plunge (plunj), *v.,* **plunged, plung·ing. 1.** to throw or thrust forcibly or suddenly into a liquid, a place, etc.: *to plunge one's face in cold water.* **2.** to dive, jump, or throw oneself into water, a hole, etc.: *We plunged into the pool.* **3.** to rush or dash with haste: *He plunged through the crowd.* **4.** to throw oneself suddenly into some condition, situation, etc.: *to plunge into debt.* **5.** to pitch violently forward, as a horse, ship, etc. **6.** to bet; gamble: *to plunge on the stock market.* —*n.* **7.** a leap or dive, as into water. **8.** a headlong rush or dash: *a plunge into danger.*

plung·er (plun′jər), *n.* **1.** a part that moves up and down in a tube: *the plunger of a syringe.* **2.** a flexible cup, usually of rubber, on a long handle, used for clearing clogged drains. **3.** a person who plunges.

plu·per′fect tense′ (ploō pûr′fikt), another term for **past perfect tense.**

plu·ral (ploōr′əl), *adj.* **1.** consisting of, containing, or concerning more than one: *a water main with plural connections.* **2.** (in grammar) of or indicating the form or function of nouns, pronouns, verbs, and some adjectives, that refer to more than one person or thing. *Men* is the plural form of *man; we* is the plural form of *I; are* is a plural form of the verb *to be; those* is the plural form of *that.* —*n.* **3.** the plural number. **4.** a plural form or function of a word.

plu·ral·i·ty (ploō ral′i tē), *n., pl.* **plu·ral·i·ties. 1.** the difference between the number of votes received by the leading candidate and those received by the next highest candidate in an election (distinguished from *majority*): *If the vote is 70, 30, and 10, the winner has a plurality of 40 and a majority of 30.* **2.** more than half of the whole; majority. **3.** a large number; multitude. **4.** the state or fact of being plural.

plus (plus), *prep.* **1.** increased by: *Ten plus two equals twelve.* **2.** in addition to; with: *He had wealth plus fame.* —*adj.* **3.** involving or indicating addition: *a plus sign.* **4.** showing a gain or addition; extra: *a plus quantity.* **5.** having a higher or additional value: *a grade of C plus.*

plush (plush), *n.* a fabric resembling velvet but having a deeper pile.

plus′ sign′, the symbol (+) used to indicate that two or more numbers are to be added together.

Plu·to (ploō′tō), *n.* **1.** (in classical mythology) the god ruling the underworld. **2.** the planet farthest away from the sun. Pluto has a diameter of about 3600 miles; its average distance from the sun is 3,-671,000,000 miles.

plu·toc·ra·cy (ploō tok′rə sē), *n.* a form of government in which the wealthy class rules.

plu·to·crat (ploō′tə krat′), *n.* a member of a class or group that rules or has power because of its wealth. —**plu·to·crat·ic** (ploō′tə krat′ik), *adj.*

plu·to·ni·um (ploō tō′nē əm), *n.* a heavy metal used to produce nuclear energy: a man-made, radioactive chemical element. *Symbol:* Pu

ply[1] (plī), *v.*, **plied, ply·ing. 1.** to work with; use: *to ply a needle in sewing.* **2.** to carry on or practice: *to ply a trade.* **3.** to supply with, apply to, or offer something repeatedly to: *to ply a person with drink.* **4.** to address (someone) persistently: *to ply a person with questions.* **5.** to travel regularly over a certain course or between certain places: *The boat plies between here and the island.* [from the Middle English word *plyen,* which is short for *aplyen* "to apply"]

ply[2] (plī), *n., pl.* **plies. 1.** one layer or thickness, as in certain wood products. **2.** any of the strands of which yarn, rope, etc., are made. [from the Old French word *plier* "to fold, bend," which comes from Latin *plicāre*]

Plym·outh (plim′əth), *n.* **1.** a port city in SW England. **2.** a town in SE Massachusetts: oldest town in New England, founded 1620.

Plym′outh Col′ony, the colony established in SE Massachusetts by the Pilgrim Fathers in 1620.

Plym′outh Rock′, 1. a rock at Plymouth, Massachusetts, said to be the place where the Pilgrim Fathers landed in 1620. **2.** an American breed of medium-sized chickens, raised for meat and eggs.

ply·wood (plī′wŏŏd′), *n.* a strong material made by gluing several thin layers of wood together.

Pm, *Chem.* the symbol for **promethium.**

P.M., 1. Paymaster. **2.** Postmaster. **3.** post-mortem. **4.** Prime Minister.

p.m., after noon; the period between 12 noon and 12 midnight. See also **a.m.** [from the Latin phrase *post meridiem*]

pneu·mat·ic (noō mat′ik, nyoō-), *adj.* **1.** of or concerning air, gases, or wind. **2.** operated by compressed air or a vacuum: *a pneumatic drill; pneumatic brakes.* **3.** filled with compressed air, as a tire. —**pneu·mat′i·cal·ly,** *adv.*

pneu·mo·nia (noō mōn′yə, nyoō-), *n.* a disease marked by inflamation of the lungs, caused by germs.

Po (Pō), *n.* a river in N Italy, flowing E. 418 mi. long.

Po, *Chem.* the symbol for **polonium.**

P.O., 1. Petty Officer. **2.** Post Office.

poach[1] (pōch), *v.* **1.** to trespass, esp. on another's game preserve in order to hunt or to steal animals. **2.** to take game or fish illegally. [from an early French word *pocher* "to gouge," which comes from Germanic] —**poach′er,** *n.*

poach[2] (pōch), *v.* to cook (eggs, fish, fruits, etc.) in a hot liquid that is kept just below the boiling point. [from the early French word *pocher,* which comes from *poche* "bag, pocket." When an egg is poached, the white forms a bag or pocket around the yolk]

Po·ca·hon·tas (pō′kə hon′təs), *n.* 1595–1617, American Indian girl who is said to have prevented the execution of Captain John Smith.

pock (pok), *n.* **1.** a skin eruption caused by smallpox, chicken pox, or similar diseases. **2.** a pockmark.

pock·et (pok′it), *n.* **1.** a piece of fabric shaped to form a pouch and attached in or on a garment, used esp. for carrying small articles. **2.** a bag or pouch. **3.** any pouchlike receptacle, envelope, hollow, compartment, etc. **4.** a hole in the earth, esp. one containing gold or other ore. **5.** any air current that can cause an airplane to lose altitude suddenly. —*adj.* **6.** for or carried in the pocket: *a pocket watch.* **7.** small enough to carry in the pocket; relatively small: *a pocket dictionary.* —*v.,* **pock·et·ed, pock·et·ing. 8.** to put into one's pocket: *to pocket one's keys.* **9.** to enclose, as in a pocket; hem in. **10.** to take as one's own, often dishonestly: *to pocket public funds.* **11.** to conceal or suppress: *to pocket one's pride.* **12.** to endure without showing resentment: *to pocket an insult.* —**pock′et·like′,** *adj.*

pock·et·book (pok′it book′), *n.* **1.** a bag or case for money, papers, etc., usually carried in the pocket. **2.** a woman's handbag.

pock·et·ful (pok′it fool′), *n., pl.* **pock·et·fuls.** the amount that a pocket will hold.

pock·et·knife (pok′it nīf′), *n., pl.* **pock·et·knives** (pok′it nīvz′). a small knife with one or more blades that fold into the handle.

pock′et ve′to, a veto brought about by the President's refraining from signing a bill presented to him within ten days of the adjournment of Congress.

pock·mark (pok′märk′), *n.* a small, round scar, such as one resulting from chicken pox or smallpox.

pod (pod), *n.* a long shell or case containing the seeds of certain kinds of plants, such as peas or beans.

Seed pods

po·di·um (pō′dē əm), *n.* a small platform for the conductor of an orchestra, for a public speaker, etc.

Poe (pō), *n.* Edgar Allan, 1809–1849, U.S. poet and short-story writer.

po·em (pō′əm), *n.* a composition in verse and often in rhyme.

po·e·sy (pō′i sē, pō′i zē), *n., pl.* **po·e·sies.** an old word for **poetry.**

po·et (pō′it), *n.* a person who writes poetry.

po·et·ess (pō′i tis), *n.* a female poet.

po·et·ic (pō et′ik), *adj.* 1. of, like, concerning, or suitable for poetry or poets. 2. having the qualities of poetry; imaginative: *a poetic description.* Also, **po·et′i·cal.** —**po·et′i·cal·ly,** *adv.*

poet′ic jus′tice, an ideal justice in which virtue is rewarded and evil punished, as in some literature.

po′et lau′reate, *pl.* **poets laureate.** (in Great Britain) a poet, appointed for life by the king or queen, who is expected to write poems celebrating court and national events.

po·et·ry (pō′i trē), *n.* 1. the art of writing poems. 2. poems collectively: *Elizabethan poetry.* 3. something that has poetic qualities: *the poetry of a sunset.*

poign·ant (poin′yənt), *adj.* 1. keenly distressing to the feelings: *poignant regret.* 2. affecting or moving the emotions: *a poignant scene in a film.* 3. strong in mental appeal; sharp: *a poignant piece of criticism.* —**poign′an·cy,** *n.* —**poign′ant·ly,** *adv.*

poin·set·ti·a (poin set′ē ə, poin set′ə), *n.* a plant native to Mexico and South America, having tiny flowers surrounded by large, bright-red, petallike leaves.

point (point), *n.* 1. a sharp or tapering end: *the point of a dagger.* 2. a projecting part of anything: *a point of land.* 3. a mark made by the sharp end of anything; dot: *The sharp heels left points in the rug.* 4. a mark of punctuation; period. 5. a decimal point. 6. (in geometry) an element having position but not dimensions, as the intersection of two lines. 7. a particular place; spot: *Chicago and points west.* 8. any definite position, as in a scale: *the boiling point.* 9. any of 32 separate directions, as indicated on a compass. 10. a degree or stage: *He was critical to the point of insult.* 11. a particular instant of time: *At that point, I told him he'd said enough.* 12. the important or essential thing; main idea: *the point of a story; to miss the point.* 13. a particular aim or purpose: *There's no point in going now.* 14. a special feature; distinguishing quality: *noble points in someone's character.* 15. a single or separate item; detail: *the fine points in a contract.* 16. a single unit in measuring, counting, scoring a game, etc.: *Our team won by five points.* —*v.* 17. to direct (a finger, weapon, etc.) at or to something: *to point a gun at a target.* 18. to indicate the position of; direct attention to (usually fol. by *out*): *to point out an object in the sky.* 19. to furnish with a point; sharpen. 20. to mark with one or more points, decimal points, etc.; punctuate. 21. to give added force to (usually fol. by *up*): *to point up the need for caution.* 22. to have or face a particular direction: *The sign pointed west.* 23. (of a hunting dog) to indicate the presence and di-

rection of (game) by standing rigid and facing toward the game. 24. **beside the point,** not related to the subject; immaterial: *an interesting remark, but beside the point.* 25. **make a point of,** to regard as important; emphasize: *He makes a point of reading the newspaper every day.* 26. **on the point of,** on the verge of; close to: *She was on the point of graduating when she became ill.* 27. **stretch a point,** to make an extra effort or allowance; make an exception: *He lacked one credit, but they stretched a point and let him graduate.* 28. **to the point,** related to the subject being discussed; suitable; appropriate: *His answer was short and to the point.*

point-blank (point′blangk′), *adj.* 1. aimed or fired straight at a target, as a pistol. 2. direct; straightforward; blunt: *a point-blank denial.* —*adv.* 3. frankly; bluntly.

point·ed (poin′tid), *adj.* 1. having a point or points. 2. sharp; piercing: *pointed wit.* 3. directed particularly, as at a person: *a pointed remark.* 4. directed; aimed: *a pointed gun.*

point·er (poin′tər), *n.* 1. a person or thing that points. 2. a long, tapering stick for pointing out things on a map, blackboard, or the like. 3. the hand of a watch dial, clock, scale, etc. 4. a short-haired hunting dog trained to point game. 5. a piece of advice; useful hint: *I gave him a few pointers on improving his pitching.*

Pointer (26 in. high at shoulder)

point·less (point′lis), *adj.* 1. having no point. 2. not related or pertinent: *a pointless remark.* —**point′less·ly,** *adv.*

point′ of view′, 1. the position from which a person considers or judges a question, problem, situation, etc.: *from the point of view of a doctor.* 2. an opinion, attitude, or judgment.

poise (poiz), *n.* 1. a state of balance or equilibrium. 2. dignified manner; composure. —*v.,* **poised, poising.** 3. to balance evenly; be balanced: *He poised on the board before making his dive.*

poi·son (poi′zən), *n.* 1. a substance that injures the health or destroys life when absorbed into the system. 2. something that is harmful, as to happiness or well-being: *the poison of lies.* —*v.* 3. to kill or injure with or as if with poison. 4. to put poison into or on. 5. to ruin or corrupt: *Hatred had poisoned his mind.* —*adj.* 6. causing poisoning; poisonous.

poi′son i′vy, 1. a vine that bears pointed leaves in clusters of three. Touching the plant may cause a painful rash that itches and tends to spread. 2. the rash caused by touching this plant.

Poison ivy

poi′son oak′, any of several shrubs related to poison ivy that also may cause a rash when they are touched.

poi·son·ous (poi′zə nəs), *adj.* 1. containing poison. 2. having the effect of poison; harmful: *poisonous rumors.*

poi′son su′mac, a kind of poison oak that grows in swamps.

poke[1] (pōk), *v.,* **poked, pok·ing.** 1. to prod or push with something pointed, such as a finger, elbow, or stick: *to poke someone in the ribs.* 2. to make (a hole, passage, etc.) by prodding or pushing: *to poke a hole in a sheet of paper.* 3. to thrust or push: *She poked her head out the window.* 4. to search or pry: *to poke around in a drawer.* 5. to thrust oneself; meddle: *to poke into something that is not one's business.* 6. to go or move in a slow, aimless way: *to poke along.* —*n.* 7. a thrust or push. 8. a slow, dawdling person. 9. **poke fun at,** to ridicule or mock (someone): *to poke fun at someone's way of walking.* [from an early Dutch word *poken* "to thrust"]

poke[2] (pōk), *n.* a bag or sack: a word used esp. in the South and Midwest. [from a Middle English word, which comes from Old French *poque* "bag"]

poke[3] (pōk), *n.* a bonnet with a projecting brim at the front, framing the face. [special use of *poke*[1]]

pok·er[1] (pō′kər), *n.* 1. a metal rod for poking or stirring a fire. 2. a person or thing that pokes. [from *poke*[1] + *-er*]

pok·er[2] (pō′kər), *n.* a card game in which the players bet on the value of their cards, the winner taking the pool. [perhaps from an early Dutch or German word meaning "to play, bluff"]

pok·y (pō′kē), *adj.,* **pok·i·er, pok·i·est.** 1. slow; dull: *a poky driver.* 2. (of a place) small and cramped. 3. (of dress) careless; messy; dowdy. —**pok′i·ness,** *n.*

Po·land (pō′lənd), *n.* a republic in central Europe. 121,000 sq. mi. *Cap.:* Warsaw.

po·lar (pō′lər), *adj.* 1. of, having to do with, or originating at the North or South pole. 2. of or concerning a pole or poles. 3. opposite in character or action: *polar personalities.*

po′lar bear′, a large white bear of the arctic regions.

Po·lar·is (pō lar′is), *n.* 1. the name of the **North Star.** 2. a U.S. ballistic missile that is fired from submerged submarines.

pole[1] (pōl), *n.* 1. a long, slender, tubelike piece of wood, metal, etc.: *a telephone pole; a fishing pole.* —*v.,* **poled, pol·ing.** 2. to push or propel with a pole. [from the Old English word *pāl,* which comes from Latin *pālus*]

Polar bear
(4 ft. high at shoulder; length 7½ ft.)

pole[2] (pōl), *n.* 1. either end of the axis on which the earth, another planet, or a satellite turns. 2. either of the ends of a magnet, where the magnetic properties appear to be concentrated. 3. either of the connec-

tions to an electric cell or battery. [from the Latin word *polus,* which comes from Greek *polos* "pivot, axis, pole"]

Pole (pōl), *n.* a native or inhabitant of Poland.

pole·cat (pōl′kat′), *n., pl.* **pole·cats** or **pole·cat.** 1. a European animal of the weasel family that ejects a foul-smelling fluid when it is attacked or disturbed. 2. another name for **skunk.**

pole·star (pōl′stär′), *n.* another term for **North Star.**

pole′ vault′, a leap or vault over a crossbar performed with the aid of a long pole.

po·lice (pə lēs′), *n.* 1. a force organized, esp. by a city or state government, to maintain order, prevent and detect crime, and enforce the laws. 2. *(used as pl.)* members of such a force. —*v.,* **po·liced, po·lic·ing.** 3. to regulate or keep in order by or as if by means of police. 4. to clean and keep in order (a military camp, post, etc.): *to police the grounds.*

police′ dog′, 1. another name for **German shepherd.** 2. any dog trained to assist policemen.

po·lice·man (pə lēs′mən), *n., pl.* **po·lice·men.** a member of a police force.

po·lice·wom·an (pə lēs′woŏm′ən), *n., pl.* **po·lice·wom·en.** a female member of a police force.

pol·i·cy[1] (pol′i sē), *n., pl.* **pol·i·cies.** 1. a plan or course of action: *a nation's foreign policy.* 2. practical wisdom: *It's good policy to be willing to compromise.* [from the Latin word *politīa* "politics, government," which comes from Greek *politeia* "citizenship"]

pol·i·cy[2] (pol′i sē), *n., pl.* **pol·i·cies.** a written contract by which an insurance company insures a person. [from the Italian word *polizza,* which comes from medieval Latin *apodixa* "receipt," from Greek *apodeixis* "a showing"]

pol·i·cy·hold·er (pol′i sē hōl′dər), *n.* the person or firm in whose name an insurance policy is written.

po·li·o (pō′lē ō′), *n.* short for **poliomyelitis.**

po·li·o·my·e·li·tis (pō′lē ō mī′ə lī′tis), *n.* an infectious disease, esp. of the young, caused by viruses, that affects the nerve cells, producing paralysis.

pol·ish (pol′ish), *v.* 1. to make smooth and glossy, esp. by rubbing: *to polish a brass doorknob.* 2. to improve; make more elegant: *to polish a speech.* —*n.* 3. a substance used to give smoothness or gloss: *shoe polish.* 4. smoothness and gloss of a surface: *a floor with a high polish.* 5. superiority or elegance of manner, performance, etc.: *the polish of a professional singer.* 6. **polish off,** *Slang.* to finish or dispose of quickly: *He polished off six glasses of lemonade after the race.* —**pol′ish·er,** *n.*

Po·lish (pō′lish), *adj.* 1. of or concerning Poland, its inhabitants, or their language. —*n.* 2. the Slavic language of Poland.

po·lite (pə līt′), *adj.* 1. showing good manners toward others, as in behavior, speech, etc.; courteous; gracious. 2. refined or cultured; of a refined or elegant kind: *polite society; polite learning.* —**po·lite′ly,** *adv.* —**po·lite′ness,** *n.*

pol·i·tic (pol′i tik), *adj.* **1.** sagacious; prudent. **2.** expedient; judicious. **3.** referring to politics; political.

po·lit·i·cal (pə lit′i kəl), *adj.* **1.** of, concerning, or belonging to politics or governmental affairs. **2.** of or concerning politicians. —**po·lit′i·cal·ly,** *adv.*

polit′ical sci′ence, the science of the principles and conduct of government.

pol·i·ti·cian (pol′i tish′ən), *n.* **1.** a person who is active or skilled in politics. **2.** a person who engages in politics for his own advantage.

pol·i·tics (pol′i tiks), *n. (used as sing. or pl.)* **1.** political science. **2.** the practice or profession of conducting governmental affairs. **3.** political principles or opinions: *His politics are his own affair.* **4.** the methods or maneuvers of a politician.

Polk (pōk), *n.* **James Knox** (noks), 1795–1849, 11th President of the U.S. 1845–1849.

pol·ka (pōl′kə, pō′kə), *n.* **1.** a lively dance of Bohemian origin. **2.** music for this dance or in its rhythm.

poll (pōl), *n.* **1.** the voting at an election. **2.** the number of votes cast. **3.** a list of individuals, as for purposes of taxing or voting. **4.** Usually, **polls.** the place where votes are taken. **5.** a sampling or collection of opinions on a subject, as in a public survey. **6.** the head, esp. the part on which the hair grows. —*v.* **7.** to take or register the votes of: *to poll the members of a jury.* **8.** to take a sampling of the opinions of. **9.** to receive at the polls, as votes. **10.** to cast at the polls, as a vote. **11.** to cut short or cut off (hair, wool, etc.); crop; shear.

pol·len (pol′ən), *n.* the powdery, yellowish grains that are the male reproductive cells of flowering plants.

pol·li·nate (pol′ə nāt′), *v.,* **pol·li·nat·ed, pol·li·nat·ing.** to convey pollen to (a flower) in order to fertilize it. Many flowers are pollinated by bees gathering nectar. —**pol′li·na′tion,** *n.*

pol·li·wog (pol′ē wog′), *n.* another name for **tadpole.** Also, **pol′ly·wog′.**

Pollen grains (greatly magnified)

poll′ tax′, a tax on every adult individual, esp. one sometimes levied as a requirement for voting.

pol·lu·tant (pə loot′[ə]nt), *n.* something that pollutes, esp. any waste substance that contaminates natural resources.

pol·lute (pə loot′), *v.,* **pol·lut·ed, pol·lut·ing.** to make foul or unclean; defile; desecrate: *to pollute the air with smoke; to pollute a river with sewage and industrial wastes.* —**pol·lu′tion,** *n.*

po·lo (pō′lō), *n.* a game played by two teams on horseback, the object being to score points by driving a wooden ball into the opponents' goal with a long-handled mallet.

Po·lo (pō′lō), *n.* **Mar·co** (mär′kō), c1254–1324, Italian traveler to the Far East.

pol·o·naise (pol′ə nāz′, pō′lə nāz′), *n.* **1.** a slow dance of Polish origin, consisting chiefly of a march for couples. **2.** music for this dance or in its rhythm.

po·lo·ni·um (pə lō′nē əm), *n. Chem.* a radioactive, metallic element. *Symbol:* Po

pol·troon (pol troon′), *n.* a villainous coward.

poly-, a prefix meaning much or many: *polygon.*

pol·y·es·ter (pol′ē es′tər), *n.* a synthetic resin that is light, strong, and resistant to water, used in making textiles, paints, etc.

po·lyg·a·my (pə lig′ə mē), *n.* the practice or condition of having more than one spouse at a time. See also **bigamy, monogamy.** —**po·lyg′a·mous,** *adj.*

pol·y·gon (pol′ē gon′), *n.* a geometrical figure, such as a triangle, square, etc., that is closed, lies in a plane, and has straight sides.

pol·y·he·dron (pol′ē hē′drən), *n.* a solid figure whose faces are all planes, esp. one having many such faces.

Pol·y·ne·sia (pol′ə nē′zhə), *n.* a series of island groups in the Pacific Ocean, extending from the Hawaiian Islands S to New Zealand: part of Oceania.

Pol·y·ne·sian (pol′ə nē′zhən), *adj.* **1.** of or concerning Polynesia, its inhabitants, or their languages. —*n.* **2.** a branch of the Malayo-Polynesian family of languages, including Maori, Tahitian, Samoan, and Hawaiian. **3.** a member of any of the Polynesian peoples.

pol·y·no·mi·al (pol′ē nō′mē əl), *n.* **1.** a mathematical expression consisting of two or more terms, such as $2x^3 + 7x^2 + 4x + 2$. —*adj.* **2.** having two or more parts or terms.

pol·yp (pol′ip), *n.* any of numerous tiny water animals that have no backbones and are related to the sponges. Polyps do not usually move from place to place and often form skeletons of lime around themselves that build up into tropical coral reefs.

pol·y·syl·lab·ic (pol′ē si lab′ik), *adj.* consisting of three or more syllables, such as a word.

pol·y·syl·la·ble (pol′ē sil′ə bəl), *n.* a word having three or more syllables.

pol·y·the·ism (pol′ē thē iz′əm, pol′ē thē′iz əm), *n.* belief in more than one god.

po·made (pə mād′, pə-mäd′), *n.* a perfumed ointment used for the scalp or for dressing the hair.

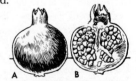
Pomegranate
A, Exterior; B, Interior

pome·gran·ate (pom′-gran′it, pom′ə gran′it), *n.* **1.** a fruit that is slightly smaller than an apple and has a thick red rind and tart red pulp surrounding many small seeds. **2.** the shrub or small tree bearing this fruit, which grows in warm regions.

Pom·er·a·ni·an (pom′ə rā′nē ən), *n.* one of a breed of small dogs having long, straight hair, erect ears, and a tail carried over the back.

pom·mel (pum′əl, pom′əl), *n.* **1.** a knob, as on the hilt of a sword. **2.** the part that sticks up at the front and top of a saddle. See illus. at **saddle.** —*v.,* **pommeled** *or* **pom·melled; pom·mel·ing** *or* **pom·mel·ling. 3.** another spelling of **pummel.**

pomp (pomp), *n.* stately or splendid display; magnificence: *the pomp of a coronation.*

pom·pa·dour (pom′pə dôr′, pom′pə dŏŏr′), *n.* an arrangement of a man's or woman's hair in which it is brushed up and back from, or raised high over, the forehead. [named after the Marquise de *Pompadour* (1721–1764), favorite of King Louis XV of France]

Pom·pei·i (pom pā′), *n.* an ancient city in SW Italy, near present-day Naples: buried by eruption of Mt. Vesuvius in A.D. 79.

pom·pon (pom′pon), *n.* an ornamental tuft or ball of wool or fur, worn on a hat, slippers, etc.

pomp·ous (pom′pəs), *adj.* 1. making a display of dignity or importance; pretentious. 2. high-flown; inflated: *a pompous speech.* —**pomp′ous·ly,** *adv.* —**pom·pos·i·ty** (pom pos′i tē), *n.*

Pon·ce (pōn′sā), *n.* a port city in S Puerto Rico.

Ponce de Le·ón (pons′ də lē′ōn), **Juan** (hwän), c1460–1521, Spanish explorer, esp. in Florida.

pon·cho (pon′chō), *n., pl.* **pon·chos.** a blanketlike cloak with a hole in the center for the head, worn as a raincoat.

pond (pond), *n.* a body of water smaller than a lake.

pon·der (pon′dər), *v.* to consider carefully; meditate: *to ponder one's answer to a question.*

pon·der·ous (pon′dər əs), *adj.* 1. of great weight; very heavy. 2. awkward or unwieldy: *He carried a ponderous burden on his back.* 3. dull; labored: *a ponderous piece of writing.* —**pon′der·ous·ly,** *adv.*

pon·iard (pon′yərd), *n.* a dagger.

pon·tiff (pon′tif), *n.* 1. the Roman Catholic Pope. 2. any high or chief priest.

pon·tif·i·cal (pon tif′i kəl), *adj.* of, concerning, or like a pontiff; papal.

pon·tif·i·cate (pon tif′ə kit′, pon tif′ə kāt′), *n.* 1. the office or term of office of a pontiff. —*v.* (pon tif′ə-kāt′), **pon·tif·i·cat·ed, pon·tif·i·cat·ing.** 2. to perform the duties of a pontiff. 3. to speak in a pompous, arrogant, or opinionated manner.

pon·toon (pon tōōn′), *n.* 1. a boat having a flat bottom. 2. a boat or float used as a support for a temporary bridge over a river. 3. a seaplane float.

po·ny (pō′nē), *n., pl.* **po·nies.** any of various breeds of small horses.

po′ny express′, an early system of carrying mail in the American West, using relays of riders mounted on ponies.

poo·dle (pōōd′ʹl), *n.* a breed of dog having long, thick, curly hair, and noted for its intelligence.

Poodle
(15 in. high
at shoulder)

pooh (pōō), *interj.* (used as an exclamation of contempt or disgust.)

pool[1] (pōōl), *n.* 1. a small body of standing water. 2. a puddle. 3. a small body of standing liquid: *a pool of blood.* 4. a still, deep place in a stream. 5. a swimming pool. [from the Old English word *pōl*]

pool[2] (pōōl), *n.* 1. a game resembling billiards but played on a table having pockets, the object being to drive balls into the pockets with a cue ball. 2. the total amount of money, funds, etc., put together by a group for its common advantage. 3. the total amount staked by bettors in a game, on a race, etc. 4. a facility, resource, or service shared by a group of people: *a car pool; a typing pool.* —*v.* 5. to put (money, interests, etc.) into a pool for common advantage, as in a financial venture. [from the French word *poule* "stakes," literally "hen"]

poop (pōōp), *n.* 1. a raised structure at the stern of a vessel. 2. Also, **poop′ deck′.** a deck at the stern of a vessel that is raised above the main deck. See illus. at **quarterdeck.**

poor (pŏŏr), *adj.* 1. having little or no money, goods, or other means of support: *a poor family.* 2. characterized by or showing poverty: *a poor nation.* 3. lacking something; inferior in quality; meager; inadequate: *poor soil; poor health.* 4. unfortunate; pitiable: *The poor dog was limping.* —*n.* 5. (used as pl.) poor persons as a group: *sympathy for the poor.*

Poop

poor·house (pŏŏr′hous′), *n., pl.* **poor·hous·es** (pŏŏr′-hou′ziz). an institution in which destitute persons are maintained at public expense.

poor·ly (pŏŏr′lē), *adv.* in a poor manner or way; badly: *The team played poorly.*

pop[1] (pop), *v.,* **popped, pop·ping.** 1. to make a short, explosive sound: *The cork popped.* 2. to burst open or cause to burst open with such a sound: *The chestnuts popped while roasting. Don't forget to pop the corn for the party.* 3. to come or go suddenly or unexpectedly; put or thrust suddenly: *We promised to pop in for a visit. Pop the rolls into the oven.* 4. to swell or stick out, as the eyes: *His eyes popped with shock.* 5. to shoot with a firearm; fire. 6. (in baseball) to hit a high fly ball so that it can easily be caught before reaching the ground. —*n.* 7. a short, explosive sound. 8. a flavored, carbonated, bottled beverage; soda. 9. a shot with a firearm. [imitative of the sound]

pop[2] (pop), *adj. Informal.* popular: *pop music; a pop singer.* [short for *popular*]

pop[3] (pop), *n. Informal.* one's father. [short for *papa*]

pop·corn (pop′kôrn′), *n.* 1. any of several kinds of corn whose kernels burst open and puff out when they are heated. 2. such corn when popped.

pope (pōp), *n. (often cap.)* the bishop of Rome, head of the Roman Catholic Church.

---

pop·gun (pop′gun′), *n.* a toy gun from which a pellet is shot, producing a loud pop.

pop·in·jay (pop′in jā′), *n.* a person given to vain, silly displays and chatter.

pop·lar (pop′lər), *n.* 1. any of various rapidly growing trees whose branches spread upward in a slender column. 2. the soft, light, white or greenish wood of such a tree, used for inexpensive furniture and paper pulp.

pop·lin (pop′lin), *n.* a finely corded fabric of cotton, rayon, silk, or wool.

Po·po·cat·e·petl (pō′pə kat′ə pet′əl), *n.* a volcano in S central Mexico. 17,887 ft.

pop·o·ver (pop′ō′vər), *n.* a puffed muffin with a hollow center.

pop·py (pop′ē), *n., pl.* **pop·pies.** any of various plants having cup-shaped red, violet, yellow, or white flowers, one kind of which yields opium.

pop′py seed′, the seed of the poppy plant used as topping or filling in some breads, rolls, and cakes.

pop·u·lace (pop′yə ləs), *n.* the common people of a community, nation, or the like.

Poppy

pop·u·lar (pop′yə lər), *adj.* 1. favored or approved by people in general: *a popular president.* 2. favored or approved by acquaintances. 3. of, concerning, or representing the people as a whole: *the popular vote.* 4. suited to or intended for the general masses of people: *popular music.* 5. suited to the means of ordinary people: *popular prices on all tickets.* —**pop·u·lar·i·ty** (pop′yə lar′i tē), *n.* —**pop′u·lar·ly,** *adv.*

pop·u·lar·ize (pop′yə lə rīz′), *v.,* **pop·u·lar·ized, pop·u·lar·iz·ing.** to make popular.

pop·u·late (pop′yə lāt′), *v.,* **pop·u·lat·ed, pop·u·lat·ing.** 1. to inhabit; live in: *The Great Plains were formerly populated by Indians.* 2. to furnish with inhabitants; people: *to populate a newly discovered continent.*

pop·u·la·tion (pop′yə lā′shən), *n.* 1. the total number of persons living in a country, city, district, etc. 2. the body of inhabitants of a place: *The population of the town was opposed to raising taxes.* 3. the number of inhabitants of a place who belong to a particular race or class: *the native population.* 4. the act or process of populating: *the population of a new state.*

pop·u·lous (pop′yə ləs), *adj.* having many residents; heavily populated.

por·ce·lain (pôr′sə lin), *n.* a fine, strong, translucent type of glazed pottery used for fine dishes, cups, etc.

porch (pôrch), *n.* 1. a covered approach to the doorway of a building. 2. a veranda.

Porcupine
(total length 3 ft.)

por·cu·pine (pôr′kyə pīn′), *n.* any of several slow-moving animals covered with sharp spines, or quills, that stand up when the animal is frightened or attacked. [from the early French phrase *porc d'espine* "thorny pig"]

pore¹ (pôr), *v.,* **pored, por·ing.** to read, study, or ponder steadily and intently (often fol. by *over*): *to pore over a rare old book.* [from the Middle English word *pouren*]

pore² (pôr), *n.* 1. one of the tiny openings by means of which liquids or gases pass through the skin, the surfaces of leaves, etc. 2. any tiny opening or hole, such as one of those in a sponge, certain rocks, etc. [from the Latin word *porus,* which comes from Greek *poros* "passage"]

por·gy (pôr′gē), *n., pl.* **por·gies** *or* **por·gy.** any of various saltwater food fishes of the Mediterranean Sea and the Atlantic coastal waters of Europe and America.

pork (pôrk), *n.* the flesh of hogs used as food.

pork·er (pôr′kər), *n.* a pig, esp. one being fattened for its meat.

po·rous (pôr′əs), *adj.* 1. full of pores. 2. capable of absorbing liquid or allowing the passage of liquids or gases.

por·phy·ry (pôr′fə rē), *n., pl.* **por·phy·ries.** a hard, purplish-red rock containing small white crystals.

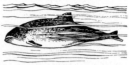

por·poise (pôr′pəs), *n., pl.* **por·pois·es** *or* **por·poise.** 1. a sea mammal resembling a small whale and having a blunt, rounded snout. 2. any of several other sea mammals, such as the dolphin.

Porpoise
(length 5 to 8 ft.)

por·ridge (pôr′ij, por′ij), *n.* a food made of meal or cereal boiled in water or milk until thick.

por·rin·ger (pôr′in jər, por′in jər), *n.* a small dish or cup, often with a handle, from which soup, porridge, or the like, is eaten.

port¹ (pôrt), *n.* 1. a city, town, or other place where ships load or unload. 2. a place along a coast where ships may find refuge from a storm; harbor. [from an Old English word, which comes from Latin *portus* "harbor, haven"]

port² (pôrt), *n.* 1. the left-hand side of a vessel, facing forward (opposite of *starboard*). —*adj.* 2. relating to or located on the left side of a vessel: *the port searchlight.* —*v.* 3. to turn or shift to the left side. [from a special use of *port⁴*]

port³ (pôrt), *n.* a sweet, dark-red wine. [from *Oporto,* a city in Portugal from which the wine is exported]

port⁴ (pôrt), *n.* 1. any of various small, glass-covered openings in the side of a vessel, used for letting in light and air. 2. a small opening in an armored vehicle, aircraft, or vessel, through which a gun can be fired. 3. (in machinery) an opening through which steam, air, water, etc., may pass. [from an Old English word, which comes from Latin *porta* "gate"]

port·a·ble (pôr′tə bəl), *adj.* capable of being easily carried or moved: *a portable typewriter.*

por·tage (pôr′tij), *n.* 1. the carrying of boats, goods, etc., overland from one body of water to another. 2.

the place or route over which this is done. 3. the cost of doing this.

por·tal (pôr′t³l), *n.* a gate, door, or entrance, esp. one of impressive appearance, as to a palace.

Port-au-Prince (pôrt′ō prins′), *n.* a seaport and the capital city of Haiti, in the S part.

port·cul·lis (pôrt kul′is), *n.* a strong grating, as of iron, made to slide along grooves at the sides of a gateway, and let down to prevent entry to a fortress, castle, etc.

por·tend (pôr tend′), *v.* to indicate in advance; give a warning of, as an omen: *The gray skies portend a heavy snow.*

por·tent (pôr′tent), *n.* a sign or warning of something about to happen; omen.

Portcullis

por·ten·tous (pôr ten′təs), *adj.* 1. of the nature of a portent; ominous; threatening: *to speak portentous words.* 2. amazing; prodigious: *an athlete of portentous skill.*

por·ter[1] (pôr′tər), *n.* 1. a person employed to carry baggage, as at a hotel. 2. an attendant in a parlor car or sleeping car. 3. a man employed to clean, sweep, etc., in a place of business. [from the early French word *porteour,* which comes from Latin *portātor* "carrier"]

por·ter[2] (pôr′tər), *n.* a doorkeeper. [from an early French word, which comes from Latin *portārius* "gatekeeper," from *porta* "gate"]

por·ter[3] (pôr′tər), *n.* a heavy, dark-brown ale. [from the phrase *porter's ale.* This originally was an ale favored by London porters]

por·ter·house (pôr′tər hous′), *n., pl.* **por·ter·hous·es** (pôr′tər hou′ziz). a choice cut of beef from between the prime ribs and the sirloin.

port·fo·li·o (pôrt fō′lē ō′), *n., pl.* **port·fo·li·os.** 1. a portable case for carrying loose papers, prints, etc. 2. a list of the stocks, bonds, etc., held by a bank or other investor. 3. the post or office of a minister of state or member of a cabinet.

port·hole (pôrt′hōl′), *n.* 1. any of various small ports in a ship, as for light or air. 2. a small opening in a wall, door, etc., through which to shoot.

por·ti·co (pôr′tə kō′), *n., pl.* **por·ti·coes** *or* **por·ti·cos.** a roof supported by columns, usually attached to a building as a porch.

por·tion (pôr′shən), *n.* 1. a part of a whole: *I read a portion of the book she's writing.* 2. a part of a whole given or belonging to a person or group; share: *His portion is two-thirds of the winnings.* —*v.* 3. to divide into or distribute in portions (usually fol. by *out*): *to portion out the cake.*

Portico

Port·land (pôrt′lənd), *n.* a port city in NW Oregon.

port·ly (pôrt′lē), *adj.,* **port·li·er, port·li·est.** rather heavy or fat; stout. —**port′li·ness,** *n.*

port·man·teau (pôrt man′tō), *n., pl.* **port·man·teaus** *or* **port·man·teaux** (pôrt man′tōz, pôrt man′tō). a trunk or suitcase that opens into two halves.

Por·to Ri·co (pôr′tə rē′kō), former official name of Puerto Rico. —**Por′to Ri′can.**

por·trait (pôr′trit, pôr′trāt), *n.* a painting, photograph, etc., of a person, esp. of the face.

por·trai·ture (pôr′tri chər), *n.* 1. the art of making portraits. 2. a portrait.

por·tray (pôr trā′), *v.* 1. to make a likeness of (a person), as by a drawing, painting, or the like. 2. to picture in words; describe vividly. 3. to act the part of (a character): *He portrayed Napoleon in the play.*

por·tray·al (pôr trā′əl), *n.* 1. the act of portraying. 2. a portrait or description.

Port Sa·id (sä ēd′), a port city in the NE Arab Republic of Egypt, at the Mediterranean end of the Suez Canal.

Ports·mouth (pôrts′məth), *n.* 1. a port city in S England, on the English Channel. 2. a port city in SE Virginia.

Por·tu·gal (pôr′chə gəl), *n.* a republic in SW Europe, on the Iberian Peninsula, W of Spain. 35,414 sq. mi. *Cap.:* Lisbon.

Por·tu·guese (pôr′chə gēz′, pôr′chə gēz′), *adj.* 1. of or concerning Portugal, its inhabitants, or their language. —*n.* 2. the Romance language of Portugal and Brazil.

Por′tuguese East′ Af′rica, former name of Mozambique.

Por′tuguese Guin′ea, former name of **Guinea-Bissau.**

Por′tuguese man-of-war′, any of several ocean animals, having a bladderlike structure by which they are buoyed up and from which are suspended many appendages that gather food and can cause severe injury by stinging.

Por′tuguese West′ Af′rica, former name of **Angola.**

Portuguese man-of-war (body length 8 in.; tentacles 40 to 60 ft.)

pose (pōz), *v.,* **posed, pos·ing.** 1. to assume or hold a physical position: *to pose for a painter.* 2. to place in a position or attitude, as for a picture. 3. to affect or assume a certain character; present oneself insincerely: *to pose as an expert.* 4. to state or put forward: *to pose a problem.* —*n.* 5. a bodily attitude or posture, as for a portrait. 6. an unnatural or studied attitude; affectation: *His friendliness is not a pose.* —**pos′er,** *n.*

Po·sei·don (pə sīd′³n), *n.* (in Greek mythology) the god of the sea: identified with the Roman god Neptune.

posh (posh), *adj. Informal.* elegant or luxurious.

po·si·tion (pə zish′ən), *n.* 1. the location or place of a person or thing: *The house was built in an exposed position in a field.* **2.** the way in which a person or thing is placed or arranged: *a sitting position.* **3.** proper or usual place: *The horses were in position to begin the race.* **4.** situation or condition: *to bargain from a position of strength.* **5.** status or standing, as in society: *a man of wealth and position.* **6.** a job: *a position in a bank.* **7.** mental attitude; stand or opinion: *to define one's position in a debate.* —*v.* **8.** to put in a particular or appropriate place: *to position the pieces for a game of chess.*

pos·i·tive (poz′i tiv), *adj.* **1.** fully and clearly stated; definite: *a positive acceptance of the agreement.* **2.** sure; confident: *Are you positive you will be there?* **3.** allowing no question or denial; leaving no doubt: *positive proof.* **4.** practical; useful; helpful: *to make a positive suggestion.* **5.** showing approval or agreement; affirmative: *a positive answer.* **6.** having a real effect, force, or presence; clearly noticeable: *a small but positive change in the weather.* **7.** (in grammar) of or concerning the initial degree of comparison of adjectives and adverbs, consisting of the simple form of those words, without inflection. *Great* is the positive form of the adjective *great,* of which *greater* and *greatest* are the comparative and superlative forms. *Soon* is the positive form of the adverb *soon,* of which *sooner* and *soonest* are the comparative and superlative forms. **8.** (of a number) greater than zero. **9.** caused by or associated with a deficiency of electrons: *a positive charge; a positive pole.* **10.** (of a test) indicating the presence of the disease or condition tested for. **11.** *Informal.* complete; absolute: *He's a positive fanatic about baseball.* —*n.* **12.** (in grammar) a word in the positive form. **13.** a photographic print or film in which the light portions are the same as the light portions of the subject. —**pos′i·tive·ly,** *adv.*

poss., **1.** possession. **2.** possessive. **3.** possible. **4.** possibly.

pos·se (pos′ē), *n.* a group of men authorized by a sheriff to help him in enforcing the law.

pos·sess (pə zes′), *v.* **1.** to have as one's property; own: *to possess a house and a car.* **2.** to have as an ability, trait, quality, or the like: *to possess courage.* **3.** to control; occupy: *How long did the United States possess Alaska before it became a state?* **4.** to have a powerful influence on; dominate: *The miser was possessed by his greediness.* **5.** (of a spirit, esp. an evil one) to control (a person) from within: *He thought he was possessed by devils.* —**pos·ses′sor,** *n.*

pos·ses·sion (pə zesh′ən), *n.* **1.** the act or fact of possessing. **2.** the fact of owning; ownership: *He came into possession of his father's farm.* **3.** something that one possesses: *He packed all his possessions into one trunk.* **4.** the fact of being in control: *When tackled, he was not in possession of the ball.* **5.** a being dominated or influenced from within, as by a feeling, idea, evil spirit, etc. **6.** a territory belonging to a nation.

pos·ses·sive (pə zes′iv), *adj.* **1.** of, concerning, or showing possession or ownership. **2.** desiring to

dominate or be the only influence on someone: *a possessive husband.* **3.** (in grammar) belonging to the form or case of words or phrases that show possession. In *John's hat, John's* is a noun in the possessive case. —*n.* **4.** the possessive case. **5.** a word or phrase in the possessive case. —**pos·ses′sive·ly,** *adv.* —**pos·ses′sive·ness,** *n.*

posses′sive ad′jective, an adjective formed from a personal pronoun or a relative pronoun, showing a possessor. *My, your, his, her, its, our, their,* and *whose* are possessive adjectives.

posses′sive pro′noun, a pronoun showing possession, used in place of a phrase consisting of a possessive adjective and a noun. *Mine, yours, his, hers, its, ours, theirs,* and *whose* are possessive pronouns. *Whose book is this? It is mine.* In the last sentence *mine* stands for *my book.*

pos·si·bil·i·ty (pos′ə bil′i tē), *n., pl.* for def. 2 **pos·si·bil·i·ties.** **1.** the state or fact of being possible; chance: *There is a possibility of rain today.* **2.** something possible: *Rain is a possibility.*

pos·si·ble (pos′ə bəl), *adj.* **1.** capable of happening, being, being done, being used, etc.: *a possible cure for a disease.* **2.** capable of being true or being the case: *It is possible that he went home.*

pos·si·bly (pos′ə blē), *adv.* **1.** perhaps; maybe: *It may possibly rain today.* **2.** for any possible reason: *She has all the money she can possibly use.* **3.** by any means: *You can't possibly have read that book.*

pos·sum (pos′əm), *n. Informal.* an opossum.

post¹ (pōst), *n.* **1.** a piece of wood, metal, or the like, set upright and usually used as a support: *a fence post; a goal post.* —*v.* **2.** to fasten (a notice, bulletin, etc.) to a post, wall, or the like, in a public place. **3.** to bring to public notice, as by a poster: *to post a reward.* **4.** to publish the name of (someone or something) in a list: *They have posted your train as departing on schedule.* **5.** to put up signs forbidding trespassing on or use of: *to post a farm during the hunting season.* **6.** to cover (a wall, fence, etc.) with notices or posters. [from an Old English word, which comes from Latin *postis* "post, doorpost"]

post² (pōst), *n.* **1.** the place assigned to a person on duty, such as a soldier, sentry, or nurse. **2.** a job, office, or position of trust to which a person is appointed: *to be assigned to a diplomatic post.* **3.** a military camp with permanent buildings: *an army post.* **4.** the troops stationed at such a camp. **5.** a trading post. —*v.* **6.** to station at a post: *The bank had posted guards at every door.* [from the French word *poste,* which comes from Italian *posto,* from Latin *positus* "placed, located"]

post³ (pōst), *n.* **1. a.** a single delivery of mail: *The morning post will come at 10.* **b.** mail: *She is expecting the package by post.* **2.** (formerly) one of a number of places along a route where relays of riders and horses were stationed to carry mail. **3.** a rider who carried mail from one such place to the next. —*v.* **4.** to mail: *Please post this letter right away.* **5.** to travel with speed; hasten. **6. keep posted,** to supply (someone) with up-to-date information; inform: *Keep me* *posted on his activities.* [from the French word *poste*, which comes from Italian *posta*, from Latin *posita* "something put or placed"]

post-, a prefix meaning **1.** after or later than: *postwar.* **2.** behind: *postnasal.*

post·age (pō′stij), *n.* the charge for sending anything by mail.

post′age stamp′, an official, small, paper stamp put on mail to show that the postage has been paid.

post·al (pōs′t°l), *adj.* of or concerning the post office or mail service: *postal delivery; postal employees.*

post·box (pōst′boks′), *n.* See **mailbox** (def. 1).

post′ card′, 1. a small, printed card for sending a message by mail, usually having a picture on one side. **2.** Also, **post′al card′.** a card sold by the post office, with a stamp already printed on it.

post·er (pō′stər), *n.* a printed notice for putting up in a public place, as for advertising.

pos·te·ri·or (po stēr′ē ər), *adj.* **1.** located behind or at the rear (opposite of *anterior*). **2.** coming after in time; later. —*n.* **3.** the buttocks.

pos·ter·i·ty (po ster′i tē), *n.* **1.** all future generations collectively: *poems written for posterity.* **2.** all the descendants of one man.

pos·tern (pō′stərn, pos′tərn), *n.* **1.** a back door or gate; any entrance other than the main one. —*adj.* **2.** located at the back; rear.

post·haste (pōst′hāst′), *adv.* with the greatest possible speed: *to come to a friend's aid posthaste.*

post·hu·mous (pos′chə məs), *adj.* **1.** published after the death of the author: *a posthumous novel.* **2.** born after the death of the father: *a posthumous daughter.* **3.** occurring after one's death: *a posthumous award for bravery.* —**post′hu·mous·ly,** *adv.*

post·man (pōst′mən), *n., pl.* **post·men.** a man who carries and delivers mail.

post·mark (pōst′märk′), *n.* **1.** an official mark stamped on mail to cancel the postage stamp and to indicate the place and date of mailing. —*v.* **2.** to stamp with a postmark.

post·mas·ter (pōst′mas′tər), *n.* the official in charge of a post office. Also, *referring to a woman,* **post′mis′tress.**

post′master gen′eral, *pl.* **postmasters general.** the person who is head of the postal system of a country.

post·mor·tem (pōst môr′təm), *adj.* **1.** of, concerning, or occurring in the time following death. —*n.* **2.** another word for **autopsy.**

post′ of′fice, 1. any of the local offices of a government postal system at which mail is handled and stamps are sold. **2.** *(often cap.)* the department of a government in charge of the mail.

post·paid (pōst′pād′), *adj.* with postage paid by the sender: *They sent me the book postpaid.*

post·pone (pōst pōn′), *v.,* **post·poned, post·pon·ing.** to put off to a later time; defer: *He has postponed his vacation until next week.* —**post·pone′ment,** *n.*

post′ road′, (formerly) a road over which mail was

carried, with stations for furnishing horses for the riders.

post·script (pōst′skript′), *n.* a message added to a letter after the writer has finished and signed it.

pos·tu·late (pos′chə lāt′), *v.,* **pos·tu·lat·ed, pos·tu·lat·ing. 1.** to assume the truth of (something), esp. as a basis for reasoning or arguing; take for granted: *to postulate the existence of God.* **2.** to ask, demand, or claim. —*n.* (pos′chə lit, pos′chə lāt′). **3.** something assumed to be true as a basis for reasoning; fundamental principle.

pos·ture (pos′chər), *n.* **1.** the way a person carries his body; the position of the parts of the body: *poor posture; a sitting posture.* **2.** a particular position of the body; pose: *The model in the art class kept the same posture for 30 minutes.* —*v.,* **pos·tured, pos·tur·ing. 3.** to assume a particular posture; pose: *The actress postured before a mirror, practicing her role.* **4.** to act in an affected or artificial way, as to create an impression: *a child posturing in front of company.*

post·war (pōst′wôr′), *adj.* following a war: *They rebuilt Berlin in the postwar years.*

po·sy (pō′zē), *n., pl.* **po·sies. 1.** a flower. **2.** a bunch of flowers; bouquet. **3.** *Archaic.* a short motto or inscription, as one engraved inside a ring.

pot (pot), *n.* **1.** a container made of earthenware, metal, etc., usually round and deep, used for cooking, serving, growing flowers, and other purposes: *a coffee pot.* **2.** such a container with its contents: *a pot of stew.* **3.** the amount contained in a pot; potful: *a pot of tea.* **4.** a cagelike trap for fish, lobsters, etc. **5.** (in certain games) all the money bet at a single time; pool. —*v.,* **pot·ted, pot·ting. 6.** to put into a pot: *to pot geraniums.* **7.** to preserve or cook (food) in a pot. **8. go to pot,** to become ruined because of neglect: *When the house was sold, the garden went to pot.*

pot·ash (pot′ash′), *n.* a white powder obtained from wood ashes and used in making soap and glass.

po·tas·si·um (pə tas′ē əm), *n.* a very soft, silvery metal that oxidizes rapidly in air: a chemical element whose compounds are used in fertilizers, explosives, soap, glass, etc. *Symbol:* K

po·ta·to (pə tā′tō), *n., pl.* **po·ta·toes. 1.** the thick, rounded, underground stem of a plant originally found in South America, which is eaten as a vegetable. **2.** the plant bearing this underground stem, or tuber. **3.** a sweet potato. —*adj.* **4.** made from potatoes or from potato flour: *potato pancakes.*

pota′to chip′, a thin slice of potato that has been fried until crisp, usually eaten cold.

pot·bel·ly (pot′bel′ē), *n., pl.* **pot·bel·lies.** a protruding belly.

po·ten·cy (pōt′°n sē), *n.* power; effectiveness; strength: *the potency of a medicine.*

po·tent (pōt′°nt), *adj.* **1.** powerful; strong: *a potent fighting force.* **2.** able to persuade; forceful: *The lawyer gave a potent argument for the defense.* **3.** having powerful physical or chemical effects: *a potent drug.* —**po′tent·ly,** *adv.*

po·ten·tate (pōt/ᵊn tāt/), *n.* a person who has great power; monarch or ruler.

po·ten·tial (pə ten/shəl), *adj.* 1. possible, as opposed to actual; capable of being or becoming: *a potential leader.* —*n.* 2. a quality or ability that may be developed or further realized: *He is a musician of great potential.* 3. (in electricity) the energy of an electric charge; voltage. —**po·ten/tial·ly,** *adv.*

po·ten·ti·al·i·ty (pə ten/shē al/i tē), *n., pl.* for def. 2 **po·ten·ti·al·i·ties.** 1. the state or quality of being potential. 2. something potential; possibility.

pot·ful (pot/fŏŏl/), *n.* the amount that a pot can hold.

poth·er (poth/ər), *n.* 1. disturbance; uproar; fuss: *Don't make such a pother about what to wear to the party.* —*v.* 2. to worry; bother.

po·tion (pō/shən), *n.* a drink, esp. one having medicinal or magical powers or that is poisonous: *sleeping potion; love potion.*

pot·luck (pot/luk/), *n.* food that happens to be ready for a meal without being specially prepared: *He was invited to take potluck at his friend's house.*

Po·to·mac (pə tō/mək), *n.* a river flowing SE from the Allegheny Mountains in West Virginia, along the boundary between Maryland and Virginia to the Chesapeake Bay. 287 mi. long.

pot·pie (pot/pī/), *n.* a pie of meat and vegetables topped with a pastry crust and baked.

pot·pour·ri (pō/pŏŏ rē/), *n.* 1. a mixture of dried flower petals and spices, kept in a jar for their fragrance. 2. a musical medley: *a potpourri of songs from Broadway shows.* 3. a collection of miscellaneous pieces of writing.

pot/ shot/, 1. a shot fired at game birds or animals in order to get food, with little concern for skill or sporting rules. 2. a shot fired at an animal or person within easy range, as from ambush.

pot·tage (pot/ij), *n.* a thick soup.

pot·ter¹ (pot/ər), *n.* a person who makes pottery.

pot·ter² (pot/ər), *v. Chiefly British.* another form of **putter**¹.

pot/ter's field/, a burial ground reserved for the poor or those who cannot be identified. [after the account in Matthew 27:1-7, in which Judas, repenting his betrayal of Jesus, returned the thirty pieces of silver to the chief priests and elders, who used it to buy a field from a potter for the burial of strangers and paupers]

pot·ter·y (pot/ə rē), *n., pl.* for def. 3 **pot·ter·ies.** 1. objects, such as dishes, jars, etc., made of clay that is hardened by baking. 2. the art of making such objects. 3. a place where such objects are made.

pouch (pouch), *n.* 1. a bag or sack, esp. a small one: *a tobacco pouch.* 2. the pocket on the abdomen of certain animals, such as kangaroos and opossums, in which the young are carried. 3. any other baglike or pocketlike part, such as the cheeks of a squirrel or the sac below the bill of a pelican.

poul·tice (pōl/tis), *n.* a soft, wet mixture spread on a cloth and applied to the body to soothe inflammation, relieve soreness, etc.

poul·try (pōl/trē), *n.* fowl raised for eggs or meat, including chickens, ducks, turkeys, etc.

pounce (pouns), *v.,* **pounced, pounc·ing.** 1. to swoop down suddenly, as a bird does in seizing its prey. 2. to leap on and seize: *The cat pounced on the bird.* 3. to seize upon: *Unexpectedly the student pounced on the right answer.* —*n.* 4. a sudden swoop, as on prey.

pound¹ (pound), *v.* 1. to strike repeatedly with great force, as with the fist, a hammer, etc.: *to pound on a locked door; to pound a nail into a plank.* 2. to beat or throb violently, as the heart. 3. to crush into a powder or paste by beating repeatedly: *to pound walnuts for a cookie batter.* 4. to go with heavy steps: *The horses pounded down the country road.* —*n.* 5. a heavy blow, or the sound it makes. [from the Old English word *pūnian*]

pound² (pound), *n., pl.* **pounds** *or* **pound.** 1. a unit of weight, in ordinary measure equal to 16 ounces, or about 0.454 kilogram. 2. a unit of weight used for drugs and precious metals, equal to 12 ounces, or about 0.373 kilogram. 3. Also, **pound sterling.** (in England and other parts of the United Kingdom) a unit of money, equal to 20 shillings or 240 pence prior to February, 1971: after that date, consisting of 100 pence. *Symbol:* £ [from the Old English *pund,* which comes from Latin *pondō* "pound," literally "by weight," from *pondus* "weight"]

pound³ (pound), *n.* an enclosed place where stray or homeless animals are kept. [from the Old English word *pund,* which is related to *gepyndan* "to dam up, impound"]

pound/ ster/ling, *pl.* **pounds sterling.** See **pound**² (def. 3).

pour (pôr), *v.* 1. to cause to flow in a stream, as from one container to another, or over or on something: *She poured water on the plants. He poured a glass of milk.* 2. to flow forth, as or as if in a stream: *Water poured over the dam.* 3. to rain heavily. 4. to describe or tell about freely (often fol. by *out* or *forth*): *He poured out his troubles to a friend.* —*n.* 5. the act of pouring. 6. a heavy fall of rain.

pout (pout), *v.* 1. to thrust out the lips in displeasure; look sullen. —*n.* 2. a thrusting out of the lips, as when one is displeased or sulky.

pov·er·ty (pov/ər tē), *n.* 1. the condition of being poor; poorness. 2. lack of something specified: *His writing showed a poverty of imagination.* 3. lack of desirable or necessary qualities: *The farmers moved away because of the poverty of the soil.*

pov·er·ty-strick·en (pov/ər tē strik/ən), *adj.* suffering from poverty; extremely poor.

POW, prisoner of war. Also, **P.O.W.**

pow·der (pou/dər), *n.* 1. a mass of fine, loose particles obtained by grinding, crushing, etc., any solid substance. 2. anything prepared in this way, such as face powder, talcum powder, or gunpowder. 3. short for **gunpowder.** —*v.* 4. to reduce to powder. 5. to sprinkle or cover with powder: *She powdered the cookies with confectioners' sugar.* 6. to sprinkle as if with powder: *A light snowfall powdered the field.* 7. to put powder on (the face, skin, etc.) as a cosmetic.

pow′der horn′, a small container for gunpowder made from the horn of a cow or ox and formerly carried by soldiers and hunters.

pow·der·y (pou′də rē), *adj.* **1.** of or resembling powder: *powdery sand.* **2.** sprinkled or covered with or as if with powder. **3.** easily reduced to powder: *These new walls are made of powdery plaster.*

pow·er (pou′ər), *n.* **1.** ability to do or act; capability of doing something or causing a certain effect: *He will do everything in his power to help his friends. He temporarily lost his power of speech.* **2.** physical strength or force: *It takes power to lift a 200-pound weight.* **3.** control or influence; authority: *The states have the power to tax their citizens.* **4.** a person or thing that has authority or influence, esp. a state or nation: *The major powers held an international conference.* **5.** any particular kind of energy, as mechanical, electrical, etc., used to perform work. **6.** (in physics) the rate at which work is done or energy is transferred. **7.** (in mathematics) the result of multiplying a number by itself a certain number of times, symbolized by a superscript number: *The third power of 3, or 3^3, is 27.* **8.** the magnifying capacity of a lens or other optical instrument. —*adj.* **9.** driven by a motor or engine: *a power mower.* —*v.* **10.** to supply with power: *Atomic energy powers the new submarines.* **11. in power,** holding office or authority: *The Democrats were in power during the war.*

pow·er·ful (pou′ər fəl), *adj.* having great power, authority, or influence: *a large, powerful man; a powerful drug.* —**pow′er·ful·ly,** *adv.*

pow·er·house (pou′ər hous′), *n., pl.* **pow·er·hous·es** (pou′ər hou′ziz). a building where electricity is generated.

pow·er·less (pou′ər lis), *adj.* having no power to act; helpless.

pow′er pack′, a device for supplying power to an electrical or electronic circuit, usually including a transformer.

pow·wow (pou′wou′), *n.* **1.** *Informal.* a meeting or conference. **2.** (among North American Indians) a ceremony performed for the cure of disease, success in a hunt, etc. **3.** a council of or with Indians. —*v.* **4.** to hold a powwow.

pox (poks), *n.* a disease in which the skin breaks out in blisters or pustules, such as chicken pox.

pp., pages.

ppd., **1.** postpaid. **2.** prepaid.

P.P.S., a second or additional postscript. Also, **p.p.s.** [from the Latin phrase *post postscriptum*]

Pr, *Chem.* the symbol for **praseodymium.**

P.R., **1.** public relations. **2.** Puerto Rico.

prac·ti·ca·ble (prak′tə kə bəl), *adj.* **1.** capable of being put into practice: *a practicable way of raising money.* **2.** capable of being used: *a practicable fireplace.* —**prac′ti·ca·bil′i·ty,** *n.* —**prac′ti·ca·bly,** *adv.*

prac·ti·cal (prak′ti kəl), *adj.* **1.** of, concerning, or resulting from practice or action rather than theory or thought: *The old captain gave us much practical in-*formation on sailing that wasn't in books. **2.** suitable for actual use; sensible; useful: *Those shoes aren't practical for summer camp.* **3.** engaged in the actual work of something; working: *As a practical politician, he knows everyone in town.* **4.** inclined toward or suited for actual work or useful activities: *a practical man; a practical mind.* **5.** being such in practice or effect; virtual: *It's a practical certainty our friends will come for a visit though they haven't written us.* —**prac·ti·cal·i·ty** (prak′tə kal′i tē), **prac′ti·cal·ness,** *n.*

prac′tical joke′, a joke that involves playing a trick on someone rather than saying something.

prac·ti·cal·ly (prak′tik lē), *adv.* **1.** in effect; actually: *He's not an officer, but he's practically the leader of the club.* **2.** in a practical manner; usefully. **3.** almost; nearly: *The gas tank is practically empty.*

prac′tical nurse′, a person who is trained and skilled in caring for the sick but is not a graduate of a nursing school.

prac·tice (prak′tis), *n.* **1.** action done repeatedly for the purpose of learning or gaining skill: *Practice makes perfect.* **2.** skill gained by experience or exercise: *to be out of practice.* **3.** the action of performing or doing something: *to put a plan into practice.* **4.** custom; habit: *It is our practice to have dinner at seven.* **5.** the business of a professional man: *The doctor expected his son to take over his practice.* —*v.,* **prac·ticed, prac·tic·ing. 6.** to do exercises in or perform repeatedly in order to gain skill: *to practice the violin.* **7.** to put into action: *He has definite ideas about fair play and he practices them.* **8.** to follow or observe as a matter of habit or custom: *to practice good manners; to practice one's religion.* **9.** to follow as a profession or occupation: *to practice law.* **10.** to perform in a profession or occupation: *Our family doctor has been practicing for 20 years.* Also, **practise** (for defs. 6–10).

prac·ticed (prak′tist), *adj.* experienced; expert: *He has a practiced hand for watercolors.* Also, **prac′tised.**

prac·tise (prak′tis), *v.,* **prac·tised, prac·tis·ing.** another spelling of **practice.**

prac·ti·tion·er (prak tish′ə nər), *n.* a person who practices a profession, art, etc.

prae·tor (prē′tər), *n.* (in the ancient Roman republic) an elected judge, ranking just below a consul.

prae·to·ri·an (prē tôr′ē ən), *adj.* **1.** of or concerning a praetor. **2.** (*often cap.*) of or concerning the bodyguard of the Roman emperors. —*n.* **3.** a praetor. **4.** (*often cap.*) a member of the bodyguard of the Roman emperors.

Prague (präg), *n.* the capital city of Czechoslovakia, in the W part.

prai·rie (prâr′ē), *n.* a large, grassy, level or slightly rolling area of land having few or no trees, esp. the broad plain of central North America.

prai′rie chick′en, either of two North American game birds of the western prairies having brown, black, and white plumage.

---

prai′rie dog′, a small, burrowing animal that lives in large groups and has a cry that resembles a dog's bark.

Prai′rie Prov′inces, the provinces of Manitoba, Saskatchewan, and Alberta, in central Canada.

prai′rie schoon′er, a type of covered wagon used by pioneers in crossing the plains of North America.

Prairie dog
(total length
16 in.)

praise (prāz), *n.* **1.** an expression of approval or admiration. **2.** an expression of honor or reverence; worship: *a hymn of praise to God.* —*v.,* **praised, prais·ing. 3.** to express approval or admiration of; commend. **4.** to worship (God or a deity), as in words or song.

praise·wor·thy (prāz′wûr′t͟hē), *adj.* deserving of praise. —**praise′wor′thi·ness,** *n.*

pra·line (prā′lēn, prā′lēn), *n.* any of various candies made with sugar and nuts, esp. a wafer of pecan meats cooked in brown-sugar syrup.

pram (pram), *n. British Informal.* a perambulator.

prance (prans), *v.,* **pranced, pranc·ing. 1.** to move by springing from the hind legs, as a horse does. **2.** to ride on a horse doing this. **3.** to move or skip in a lively or spirited way; caper: *The small children pranced about in their Halloween costumes.* **4.** to move or walk in a proud, happy way; strut: *The cheerleaders pranced in front of the band.* —*n.* **5.** the act of prancing; a prancing movement.

prank (prangk), *n.* a playful or mischievous trick.

pra·se·o·dym·i·um (prā′zē ō dim′ē əm), *n. Chem.* a metallic element of the rare-earth group. *Symbol:* Pr

prate (prāt), *v.,* **prat·ed, prat·ing.** to talk a great deal in a foolish or pointless manner; babble.

prat·tle (prat′ᵊl), *v.,* **prat·tled, prat·tling. 1.** to talk in a foolish or childish way; chatter. —*n.* **2.** foolish or childish talk; chatter; babble: *the prattle of little children.* **3.** the sound of such talk, or any sound resembling it: *the prattle of water rushing over stones.*

prawn (prôn), *n.* any of various shellfishes related to shrimp, some of which are used for food.

pray (prā), *v.* **1.** to address God with praise, devout pleas, thanksgiving, etc.: *to pray for peace.* **2.** to make an earnest request of (a person); beg: *The captives prayed the king for mercy.* **3.** (used as a polite introduction to questions, requests, etc.) please: *If you change your plans, pray let us know beforehand.* **4.** to get or bring by praying.

Prawn
(length
3 to 4 in.)

prayer (prâr), *n.* **1.** the act or practice of praying. **2.** a speaking to or communing with God, as in worship, entreating, or thanksgiving. **3.** a formula of words used in praying: *the Lord's Prayer.* **4.** a public or private religious service made up mainly of prayers: *morning prayer.* **5.** the thing prayed for: *Their prayer was granted.* **6.** an earnest request; entreaty.

prayer′ book′, a book containing formal prayers.

pray′ing man′tis, another name for **mantis.**

pre-, a prefix meaning **1.** before or earlier than: *prepay; preschool.* **2.** in front or ahead of: *prefix.* **3.** above or over: *preeminent.*

preach (prēch), *v.* **1.** to deliver a sermon; speak on a religious or moral subject. **2.** to plead strongly in favor of (something); recommend publicly: *The political candidate preached the need for higher salaries.* **3.** to give advice on something in a boring or tedious way: *He is always preaching about how to be successful.*

preach·er (prē′chər), *n.* a person who preaches, esp. a member of the clergy.

pre·am·ble (prē′am′bəl), *n.* an introductory statement, as to a formal or legal document, explaining reasons and purposes for what follows.

prec., **1.** preceded. **2.** preceding.

pre·car·i·ous (pri kâr′ē əs), *adj.* **1.** depending on circumstances beyond one's control; uncertain: *He makes a precarious living as a writer.* **2.** dangerous; risky: *The cottage on the island is a precarious place to be during the winter.* —**pre·car′i·ous·ly,** *adv.*

pre·cau·tion (pri kô′shən), *n.* **1.** something done in advance to prevent a possible danger, evil, etc., or to secure good results: *Take the precaution of closing the windows before you leave the house.* **2.** caution taken beforehand; prudent foresight.

pre·cede (pri sēd′), *v.,* **pre·ced·ed, pre·ced·ing.** to go or come before, as in place, rank, importance, time, etc.: *The girls preceded the boys in line.*

prec·e·dence (pres′i dəns, pri sēd′ᵊns), *n.* **1.** the act of preceding. **2.** the state or condition of coming before in place, time, rank, importance, etc.: *Your report has precedence over the others at our next meeting.* **3.** the right to precede other persons in ceremonies or social events.

prec·e·dent (pres′i dənt), *n.* **1.** an act, decision, case, etc., that may serve as a guide or justification for later acts, decisions, cases, etc.: *In making his ruling, the judge mentioned another decision as precedent.* —*adj.* **2.** preceding; previous.

pre·ced·ing (prē sē′ding), *adj.* going or occurring before; previous: *a footnote on the preceding page.*

pre·cept (prē′sept), *n.* a commandment or direction given as a rule of action or conduct; maxim: *One of Benjamin Franklin's precepts is "God helps those who help themselves."*

pre·cinct (prē′singkt), *n.* **1.** a part of a city, town, or the like, marked off as a district for the purposes of voting or police protection. **2.** Often, **precincts.** the space within a definite or understood boundary: *the precincts of a town; the school precincts.* **3.** an enclosing boundary or limit.

pre·cious (presh′əs), *adj.* **1.** of high price or great value: *Gold is a precious metal.* **2.** valuable for some spiritual or moral quality rather than material quality: *Liberty is a precious possession.* **3.** dear; beloved: *a precious friend.* **4.** too delicate, refined, or nice: *a precious style of writing.* **5.** fine; very great (used ironically): *A precious lot of good his education did him!* —*adv.* **6.** very: *She does precious little work.*

prec·i·pice (pres/ə pis), *n.* a cliff having a face that is vertical or nearly vertical.

pre·cip·i·tate (pri sip/i tāt/), *v.,* **pre·cip·i·tat·ed, pre·cip·i·tat·ing. 1.** to bring about suddenly or unexpectedly: *The car accident precipitated a loud argument.* **2.** to throw down, as from a height; hurl, send, or plunge hastily, suddenly, or violently: *to precipitate rocks down the side of a mountain; to precipitate oneself into a fight.* **3.** to separate (a solid substance) from a solution. **4.** (of moisture) to condense from vapor and fall to the earth as rain, snow, etc. —*adj.* (pri sip/i tit). **5.** with great haste; headlong; rash: *a precipitate retreat; precipitate decisions.* —*n.* (pri sip/i tit, pri sip/i tāt/). **6.** a solid substance that has settled out of a solution.

pre·cip·i·ta·tion (pri sip/i tā/shən), *n.* **1.** the act of precipitating, or the state of being precipitated. **2.** a throwing down or falling headlong. **3.** a hurrying in movement or procedure. **4.** sudden or rash haste. **5.** the separation of a substance from a solution. **6.** the depositing of moisture on the earth as a result of condensation in the atmosphere, as rain, snow, hail, etc. **7.** the amount so deposited, usually given in inches of water: *an annual precipitation of 20 inches.*

pre·cise (pri sīs/), *adj.* **1.** exactly stated, defined, or fixed: *to give precise directions.* **2.** being exactly that and neither more nor less; strictly accurate: *The precise amount was $5.47.* **3.** being exactly that one and no other: *In the shop she found the precise dress she wanted.* **4.** carefully distinct: *a precise way of speaking.* **5.** too particular or strict: *His precise following of every little rule can be a bother.* —**pre·cise/ly,** *adv.*

pre·ci·sion (pri sizh/ən), *n.* **1.** the state or quality of being precise; accuracy. —*adj.* **2.** of, concerning, or having precision: *precision instruments.*

pre·clude (pri klood/), *v.,* **pre·clud·ed, pre·clud·ing.** to make impossible; prevent: *A sprained ankle precluded his taking part in the game.*

pre·co·cious (pri kō/shəs), *adj.* more advanced or mature in development than is usual: *a precocious child.* —**pre·co/cious·ly,** *adv.* —**pre·coc·i·ty** (pri kos/i tē), *n.*

pre·cur·sor (pri kûr/sər, prē/kûr sər), *n.* a person or thing that goes before and indicates the approach of someone or something else; forerunner: *The first robin is a precursor of spring.*

pred·a·to·ry (pred/ə tôr/ē), *adj.* **1.** of, concerning, or inclined to robbery, plunder, or the like: *The small tribe made predatory raids on its neighbors.* **2.** preying upon others: *predatory animals.*

pred·e·ces·sor (pred/i ses/ər), *n.* a person who goes before another person, esp. in an office, position, etc.: *Truman was Eisenhower's predecessor as President.*

pre·dic·a·ment (pri dik/ə mənt), *n.* an unpleasant, difficult, or dangerous situation: *He was in a predicament when he found out that all the hotels in town were full.*

pred·i·cate (pred/ə kit), *n.* **1.** (in grammar) the part of a sentence or clause, consisting of the verb and its complement and all their modifiers, that expresses the action performed by or the state of being of the subject. In the sentence *The boy who was sitting in the second row moved up to the head of the class,* the predicate is *moved up to the head of the class.* —*adj.* **2.** (in grammar) belonging to the predicate. —*v.* (pred/ə kāt/), **pred·i·cat·ed, pred·i·cat·ing. 3.** to base (a statement, action, etc.); found (usually fol. by *on*): *His argument was predicated on sound reasoning.*

pre·dict (pri dikt/), *v.* to tell in advance; prophesy: *to predict the weather.*

pre·dic·tion (pri dik/shən), *n.* **1.** the act of predicting. **2.** something that is predicted; prophecy.

pre·dis·pose (prē/di spōz/), *v.,* **pre·dis·posed, pre·dis·pos·ing.** to give a tendency to beforehand; make subject or liable: *John's lack of sleep predisposed him to catching a cold.*

pre·dom·i·nant (pri dom/ə nənt), *adj.* greater or superior in power, importance, number, effect, etc.: *Green is the predominant color in nature.* —**pre·dom/i·nance,** *n.* —**pre·dom/i·nant·ly,** *adv.*

pre·dom·i·nate (pri dom/ə nāt/), *v.,* **pre·dom·i·nat·ed, pre·dom·i·nat·ing.** to be greater in strength, power, influence, number, effect, etc.: *The views of the senior students predominate in the school paper.*

pre·em·i·nent (prē em/ə nənt), *adj.* superior to all others; outstanding: *He is preeminent in his profession.* —**pre·em/i·nence,** *n.* —**pre·em/i·nent·ly,** *adv.*

pre·empt (prē empt/), *v.* **1.** to occupy (public land) in order to establish one's right to buy it. **2.** to take possession of for oneself before others can: *He preempted the best desk in the room.*

preen (prēn), *v.* **1.** (of birds) to smooth or clean (the feathers) with the beak: *The peacock preened itself on the lawn.* **2.** to dress (oneself) carefully; primp.

pref., 1. preface. **2.** prefaced. **3.** preferred.

pre·fab·ri·cate (prē fab/rə kāt/), *v.,* **pre·fab·ri·cat·ed, pre·fab·ri·cat·ing.** to manufacture (a house or building) in standardized parts or sections ready for quick assembly.

pref·ace (pref/is), *n.* **1.** a short introduction to a book, speech, etc. —*v.,* **pref·aced, pref·ac·ing. 2.** to introduce or provide with a preface.

pref·a·to·ry (pref/ə tôr/ē), *adj.* of, concerning, or like a preface; introductory: *The teacher gave some prefatory explanations before the examination.*

pre·fect (prē/fekt), *n.* **1.** (in ancient Rome) any of various civil and military officers. **2.** (in France) the chief administrative official of a department.

pre·fec·ture (prē/fek chər), *n.* the office, jurisdiction, or territory of a prefect.

pre·fer (pri fûr/), *v.,* **pre·ferred, pre·fer·ring. 1.** to like better: *He prefers summer to winter.* **2.** to put forward or present (a statement, claim, charge, etc.) for consideration: *Charges were preferred against the suspect.* **3.** *Archaic.* to put forward or advance, as in rank or office.

---

act, āble, dâre, ärt; ebb, ēqual; if, īce; hot, ōver, ôrder; oil; book; ōoze; out; up, ûrge; ə = a as in alone; ᵊ as in button (but/ᵊn), fire (fiᵊr); chief; shoe; thin; ŧhat; zh as in measure (mezh/ər). See full key inside cover.

pref·er·a·ble (pref′ər ə bəl), *adj.* worthy to be preferred; more desirable. —**pref′er·a·bly,** *adv.*

pref·er·ence (pref′ər əns), *n.* **1.** the act of preferring: *His preference is for coffee rather than tea.* **2.** a thing that is preferred. **3.** the favoring of one person or thing over others: *Preference is given to veterans applying for civil-service jobs.*

pref·er·en·tial (pref′ə ren′shəl), *adj.* of, showing, or giving preference: *preferential treatment.*

pre·fer·ment (pri fûr′mənt), *n.* advancement or promotion, as in rank, office, etc.

pre·fix (prē′fiks), *n.* **1.** (in grammar) an affix placed before a word or stem. Some common prefixes are *anti-, be-, com-, in-, pre-, pro-, re-,* and *un-.* —*v.* (prē fiks′, prē′fiks). **2.** to put before: *He has the right to prefix "Doctor" to his name.* **3.** to add as a prefix.

preg·nan·cy (preg′nən sē), *n., pl.* **preg·nan·cies.** the condition or quality of being pregnant.

preg·nant (preg′nənt), *adj.* **1.** (of a woman or a female animal) having unborn young developing within the body; about to become a mother. **2.** full; filled: *The silence was pregnant with suspense.* **3.** full of meaning; highly significant: *The president's speech contained many pregnant statements.*

pre·his·tor·ic (prē′hi stôr′ik), *adj.* concerning or belonging to a period before recorded history: *The dinosaur is a prehistoric reptile.* Also, **pre′his·tor′i·cal.** —**pre′his·tor′i·cal·ly,** *adv.*

prej·u·dice (prej′ə dis), *n.* **1.** an unfair opinion, judgment, or feeling for or against something, formed beforehand or without knowledge: *Some people have a prejudice against any kind of change.* **2.** hatred or dislike directed against a racial, religious, or national group. **3.** disadvantage or injury resulting from the judgment or action of another: *It is possible for a law to operate to the prejudice of the majority.* —*v.,* **prej·u·diced, prej·u·dic·ing. 4.** to affect or fill with prejudice: *His sincerity prejudiced us in his favor.* **5.** to damage or injure: *The lack of a college education prejudiced his chances for success.*

prej·u·di·cial (prej′ə dish′əl), *adj.* causing prejudice or disadvantage; harmful.

prel·ate (prel′it), *n.* a clergyman of high rank, such as a bishop.

pre·lim·i·nar·y (pri lim′ə ner′ē), *adj.* **1.** coming before or leading up to the main part, event, matter, or business; preparatory: *a preliminary examination.* —*n., pl.* **pre·lim·i·nar·ies. 2.** something preliminary, as an introductory or preparatory step, act, etc.: *He did well in the preliminaries of the contest.*

prel·ude (prel′yood, prā′lood), *n.* **1.** anything that precedes or introduces something of greater importance: *A week of cold, sunny days was the prelude to the first football game of the year.* **2.** a short piece of music, esp. one intended to be played as an introduction to a longer work. —*v.,* **prel·ud·ed, prel·ud·ing. 3.** to serve as a prelude to. **4.** to introduce by a prelude.

pre·ma·ture (prē′mə toor′, -tyoor′; prē′mə choor′), *adj.* coming or happening too soon; before the proper time. —**pre′ma·ture′ly,** *adv.*

pre·med·i·tate (pri med′i tāt′), *v.,* **pre·med·i·tat·ed,** **pre·med·i·tat·ing.** to consider or plan beforehand: *The crime was premeditated.* —**pre·med′i·ta′tion,** *n.*

pre·mier (pri mēr′, prim yēr′), *adj.* **1.** first in rank; leading. **2.** first in time; earliest. —*n.* **3.** the chief officer of a government; prime minister.

pre·mière (pri mēr′, pri myâr′), *n.* a first public performance of a play, opera, movie, etc.

prem·ise (prem′is), *n.* **1.** (in logic) a statement that is assumed to be true and forms the basis for an argument or conclusion: *A premise of earlier astronomy was that the earth was the center of the universe.* **2.** **premises,** a tract of land including the buildings on it: *Don't leave the premises.* —*v.,* **prem·ised, prem·is·ing. 3.** to set forth beforehand as an introduction.

pre·mi·um (prē′mē əm), *n.* **1.** a prize given someone for having bought a product or for having done something in the interests of a business. **2.** an additional amount or bonus above the usual price, wages, interest, or the like: *Seats for the opera were being sold at a premium.* **3.** the amount paid for an insurance policy, usually in installments: *a monthly premium.* **4.** high value: *The teacher put a premium on careful writing.* **5.** **at a premium,** at a very high value because of scarcity: *Good, reliable workers are always at a premium.*

pre·mo·ni·tion (prē′mə nish′ən, prem′ə nish′ən), *n.* a feeling that some event will take place in the future, esp. something harmful or unpleasant; forewarning: *He had a vague premonition of danger.*

pre·oc·cu·pied (prē ok′yə pīd′), *adj.* completely occupied in thought; absorbed.

pre·oc·cu·py (prē ok′yə pī′), *v.,* **pre·oc·cu·pied, pre·oc·cu·py·ing. 1.** to absorb the full attention of: *He preoccupied himself with planning a trip.* **2.** to occupy beforehand or before others. —**pre·oc′cu·pa′tion,** *n.*

prep., **1.** preparation. **2.** preparatory. **3.** prepare. **4.** preposition.

pre·paid (prē pād′), *v.* **1.** the past tense and past participle of **prepay.** —*adj.* **2.** paid for in advance.

prep·a·ra·tion (prep′ə rā′shən), *n.* **1.** the act of preparing: *He spends most of his time in preparation for the tournament.* **2.** the state or condition of being prepared; fitness: *preparation for a career.* **3.** Usually, **preparations.** a plan made or action taken in order to prepare for something: *preparations for a journey.* **4.** something specially prepared or put together, as a medicine, food, or cosmetic: *a preparation for sunburn.*

pre·par·a·to·ry (pri pâr′ə tôr′ē), *adj.* **1.** of or concerned with preparing for something else; serving to prepare: *a preparatory school.* **2.** preliminary; introductory.

pre·pare (pri pâr′), *v.,* **pre·pared, pre·par·ing. 1.** to put in proper condition or readiness; make ready: *to prepare a book report.* **2.** to put things or oneself in readiness; get ready: *to prepare for war.* **3.** to get (something) ready by putting together parts or ingredients or by taking special steps: *to prepare a medicine; to prepare a meal.* —**pre·par′ed·ness,** *n.*

pre·pay (prē pā′), *v.,* **pre·paid** (prē pād′), **pre·pay·**

ing. to pay or pay for in advance: *The company will prepay the postage.*

prep·o·si·tion (prep/ə zish/ən), *n.* a word used with a noun, pronoun, or adjective to form a phrase modifying a verb, noun, or adjective. Some common prepositions are *at, by, for, in, of, on, to,* and *with.*

prep·o·si·tion·al (prep/ə zish/ə n^əl), *adj.* **1.** of or concerning a preposition. **2.** introduced by or containing a preposition: *a prepositional phrase.*

pre·pos·sess·ing (prē/pə zes/ing), *adj.* impressing favorably; attractive. —**pre/pos·ses/sion,** *n.*

pre·pos·ter·ous (pri pos/tər əs), *adj.* completely contrary to reason, common sense, or nature; absurd; foolish. —**pre·pos/ter·ous·ly,** *adv.*

pre·req·ui·site (pri rek/wi zit), *adj.* **1.** required beforehand: *prerequisite courses for entering college.* —*n.* **2.** something required beforehand: *A visa is a prerequisite for travel in many countries.*

pre·rog·a·tive (pri rog/ə tiv), *n.* a right or privilege limited to a specific person or persons: *Voting is a prerogative of adult citizens.*

Pres., President.

pres., **1.** present. **2.** presidency.

pres·age (pres/ij), *n.* **1.** a feeling that something is going to happen; foreboding. **2.** a warning or sign of some future event; omen. —*v.* (pres/ij, pri sāj/), **pres·aged, pres·ag·ing. 3.** to give warning of; foreshadow or predict: *The wind presaged a storm.*

pres·by·ter (prez/bi tər, pres/bi tər), *n.* **1.** an elder in the early Christian church. **2.** a clergyman in certain other churches. **3.** an elder in a Presbyterian church.

Pres·by·te·ri·an (prez/bi tēr/ē ən, pres/bi tēr/ē ən), *adj.* **1.** referring to a Protestant denomination in which the churches are governed by presbyters, or elders, and adhere to modified forms of Calvinism. —*n.* **2.** a member of a Presbyterian church. —**Pres/by·te/ri·an·ism,** *n.*

pres·by·ter·y (prez/bi ter/ē, pres/bi ter/ē), *n., pl.* **pres·by·ter·ies. 1.** (in Presbyterian churches) a church court made up of the ministers and one or two presbyters from each congregation in the district. **2.** a district of the Presbyterian Church. **3.** the part of a church set aside for the clergy.

pre·school (prē/skool/), *adj.* of or concerning a child who has not reached school age.

pre·scribe (pri skrīb/), *v.,* **pre·scribed, pre·scrib·ing. 1.** to set down as a rule or a course of action to be followed; order or direct: *The law prescribes that drivers stay on the right.* **2.** to order (a drug, treatment, etc.) as a remedy for sickness or injury.

pre·scrip·tion (pri skrip/shən), *n.* **1.** a written order for a drug, treatment, etc. **2.** the drug or treatment ordered. **3.** a rule, order, or direction.

pres·ence (prez/əns), *n.* **1.** the state or fact of being present, as with others or in a place: *Her presence at the party was welcome.* **2.** immediate nearness of a person or thing; company: *He signed his will in the presence of witnesses.* **3.** personal appearance or

bearing: *a woman of regal presence.* **4.** something felt to be present but unseen, such as a spirit or ghost. **5. presence of mind,** a calm state of mind that allows a person to act effectively in an emergency: *Did he have the presence of mind to call the police?*

pres·ent¹ (prez/ənt), *adj.* **1.** existing or happening now; at this time: *the present governor.* **2.** being with or near other persons or things, or at a specified or understood place rather than elsewhere: *He was present at the wedding.* **3.** (in grammar) referring to or expressed by the present tense. **4.** being under consideration: *the present topic.* **5.** existing in a place or thing: *Carbon is present in many minerals.* —*n.* **6.** the present time: *They decided they had studied enough for the present.* **7.** (in grammar) **a.** the present tense. **b.** a verb form in the present tense. **8. at present,** at the present time or moment; now: *The building has no vacancies at present.* [from the Latin word *praesēns,* which comes from *praeesse* "to be before, be present"]

pre·sent² (pri zent/), *v.* **1.** to give a gift to, esp. in a formal way: *to present someone with a gold watch.* **2.** to give as a gift: *to present a book to someone.* **3.** to introduce (a person) to another: *Mrs. Smith, I should like to present Mr. Jones.* **4.** to show or exhibit: *The theater will present two new films a week.* **5.** to come to show (oneself) before a person, at a place, etc.: *He presented himself at the unemployment office.* **6.** to bring before the mind for consideration: *Lack of funds presented a problem.* **7.** to set forth in words: *The debating team presented the arguments forcefully.* **8.** to hand or send in, as a bill: *The waiter presented our check for lunch.* —*n.* (prez/ənt). **9.** a thing presented; gift: *Christmas presents.* [from the Old French word *presenter,* which comes from Latin *praesentāre* "to make (someone or something) present." See *present¹*] —**pre·sent/er,** *n.*

pre·sent·a·ble (pri zen/tə bəl), *adj.* **1.** suitable, as in appearance, dress, manners, etc., for being introduced into society or company. **2.** fit to be seen: *Are you presentable now?* **3.** suitable to be given.

pres·en·ta·tion (prez/ən tā/shən, prē/zen tā/shən), *n.* **1.** the act of presenting: *the presentation of a wedding gift.* **2.** introduction, as of a person at court. **3.** an offering for consideration: *a presentation of a plan.* **4.** exhibition or performance, as of a film or play. **5.** a thing presented; gift.

pres·ent-day (prez/ənt dā/), *adj.* current; modern.

pre·sen·ti·ment (pri zen/tə mənt), *n.* a feeling of something about to happen; foreboding.

pres·ent·ly (prez/ənt lē), *adv.* **1.** in a little while; soon: *They will be here presently.* **2.** at the present time: *He is presently abroad.*

pre·sent·ment (pri zent/mənt), *n.* the written statement of an offense by a grand jury, made from their own knowledge or observation.

pres/ent par/ticiple, a participle with present meaning, formed in English by adding the ending -*ing* to the stem of the verb: *walking; taking; sitting.*

pres′ent per′fect tense′, the form of verbs that expresses action or state that is completed before the present. In English, the present perfect tense is formed by placing the present tense of the verb *have* before the past participle: *We have waited three hours. He has been here twice this week.*

pres′ent tense′, the form of verbs that expresses action or state now going on *(He goes)*, something that occurs continually or repeatedly *(I go home every day)*, or something that is permanently true *(Men are mortal).*

pres·er·va·tion (prez′ər vā′shən), *n.* 1. the act of preserving: *the preservation of historical monuments.* 2. the state of being preserved.

pre·serv·a·tive (pri zûr′və tiv), *n.* 1. a substance added to food to prevent it from spoiling, rotting, fermenting, or becoming moldy. —*adj.* 2. tending to preserve.

pre·serve (pri zûrv′), *v.,* **pre·served, pre·serv·ing.** 1. to keep safe from harm or injury: save. 2. to keep up; maintain: *to preserve historical buildings.* 3. to prepare (food or anything perishable) so as to prevent spoiling or decay. —*n.* 4. Usually, **preserves.** fruit, vegetables, etc., cooked with sugar and put in sealed containers. 5. a place set apart for the protection of game or fish. —**pre·serv′er,** *n.*

pre·side (pri zīd′), *v.,* **pre·sid·ed, pre·sid·ing.** 1. to have charge of a meeting, assembly, etc. 2. to have authority or control (often fol. by *over*): *The lawyer presided over the family's estate.*

pres·i·den·cy (prez′i dən sē), *n., pl.* **pres·i·den·cies.** 1. the office of a president. 2. the time during which a president holds office.

pres·i·dent (prez′i dənt), *n.* 1. the highest executive officer of a modern republic. 2. *(usually cap.)* the Chief Executive of the United States. 3. the chief officer of a college, corporation, or other organized group.

pres·i·den·tial (prez′i den′shəl), *adj.* of or concerning a president or presidency: *a presidential office.*

press¹ (pres), *v.* 1. to act upon with steadily applied weight or force; push: *to press the button of a doorbell.* 2. to squeeze juice, sugar, etc., from by pressure: *to press oranges.* 3. to squeeze out, as juice: *to press the juice from oranges.* 4. to flatten; make smooth: *to press clothes.* 5. to hold closely; clasp or hug. 6. to weigh heavily upon; trouble: *Problems pressed him from all sides.* 7. to urge repeatedly; keep asking: *They pressed me to spend the weekend.* 8. to urge insistently or with force: *The store pressed him for payment of his debt.* 9. to urge onward; push forward or hasten: *He pressed his horse to go faster.* 10. to crowd: *After his speech, the audience pressed around the candidate.* —*n.* 11. printed publications collectively, esp. newspapers and periodicals: *freedom of the press.* 12. those who work for such publications, such as reporters or photographers. 13. a business establishment for printing books, magazines, etc. 14. the process or business of printing. 15. any of various machines for exerting pressure, crushing, stamping, etc.: *a printing press; a wine press.* 16. a

crowd or throng. 17. a crowding; a pressing together or forward: *The press of the traffic annoyed the taxi driver.* 18. pressure or urgency, as of business, duties, etc. 19. an upright piece of furniture for holding clothes, books, etc. [from the Middle English word *pressen,* which comes from Latin *pressāre*] —**press′er,** *n.*

press² (pres), *v.* to force into service, esp. naval or military service. [another form of the earlier word *prest* "to recruit," which comes from Old French *prester* "to lend, give an advance on wages"]

press′ a′gent, a person employed to promote the interests of an individual, group, etc., by obtaining favorable publicity.

press·ing (pres′ing), *adj.* urgent; demanding immediate attention: *a pressing engagement.*

pres·sure (presh′ər), *n.* 1. the action of a steady force or weight: *The pressure of the ice broke several limbs off the tree.* 2. the state or condition of being pressed or compressed. 3. (in physics) force per unit area. *Symbol:* P 4. a state of trouble, distress, or strain; oppression: *He was worried because of the pressure of debts.* 5. a strong force or compelling influence: *The old mayor ran for office again because of popular pressure.* 6. urgency, as of affairs or business: *to work under pressure.* —*v.,* **pres·sured, pres·sur·ing.** 7. *Informal.* to influence or seek to influence as if by force: *They pressured him to sign the contract.*

pres′sure cook′er, a strong pot with an airtight cover for cooking foods quickly under the pressure of very hot steam.

pres·su·rize (presh′ə rīz′), *v.,* **pres·su·rized, pres·su·riz·ing.** 1. to maintain normal or near-normal air pressure in (the cabin of an airplane, the interior of a space capsule, etc.). 2. to apply pressure to (a glass, a liquid, the contents of a can, etc.).

pres·tige (pre stēzh′, pre stēj′), *n.* reputation or influence arising from what others or the public know of one's success, achievement, rank, etc.; importance; distinction.

pres·to (pres′tō), *adv.* 1. quickly or immediately. 2. (in music) at a very fast tempo. —*adj.* 3. quick or rapid. —*n., pl.* **pres·tos.** 4. a rapid tempo. 5. a movement or piece of music in a rapid tempo.

pre·sum·a·ble (pri zoo′mə bəl), *adj.* capable of being taken for granted; probable.

pre·sum·a·bly (pri zoo′mə blē), *adv.* most likely; probably: *Presumably he's still at home.*

pre·sume (pri zoom′), *v.,* **pre·sumed, pre·sum·ing.** 1. to take for granted; assume as true without proof: *I presume you're feeling well.* 2. to undertake (to do something) without right or permission; venture: *to presume to speak for someone else.* 3. to rely too much or without reason (often fol. by *on* or *upon*): *Don't presume on my generosity.*

pre·sump·tion (pri zump′shən), *n.* 1. the act of presuming or of taking something for granted. 2. something that is presumed: *The presumption was that it would rain today.* 3. boldness, esp. when unbecoming or impertinent: *He had the presumption to con-*

tradict his father. **4.** reason or grounds for presuming or believing something is true.

pre·sump·tu·ous (pri zump′chōŏ əs), *adj.* too bold; taking liberties; forward: *He is presumptuous to come to my party uninvited.* —**pre·sump′tu·ous·ly,** *adv.*

pre·sup·pose (prē′sə pōz′), *v.,* **pre·sup·posed, pre·sup·pos·ing. 1.** to suppose beforehand; take for granted in advance. **2.** to require as a necessary condition; imply: *An effect presupposes a cause.* —**pre·sup·po·si·tion** (prē′sup ə zish′ən), *n.*

pre·tend (pri tend′), *v.* **1.** to make believe: *Let's pretend that we've landed on the moon.* **2.** to cause (what is not so) to seem so: *to pretend illness.* **3.** to appear falsely, so as to deceive: *to pretend to go to sleep.* **4.** to say or claim (something), esp. insincerely or falsely: *He pretended to know all about everything.* **5.** to make a false claim (usually fol. by *to*): *He pretends to great knowledge.* **6.** to lay claim (usually fol. by *to*): *When the crown prince died, his younger brother pretended to the throne.*

pre·tend·er (pri ten′dər), *n.* **1.** a person who pretends. **2.** a person who lays claim to a throne.

pre·tense (pri tens′, prē′tens), *n.* **1.** the act of pretending; make-believe: *My sleepiness was all pretense.* **2.** a false show of something: *a pretense of friendship.* **3.** a false act, reason, claim, etc.: *He left the table on a pretense of urgent business.* **4.** a claim: *false pretenses.* **5.** a showing off; pretentiousness: *His speech was simple and free from pretense.*

pre·ten·sion (pri ten′shən), *n.* **1.** a claim to something, as a throne, position, etc. **2.** Often, **pretensions.** a claim to some quality, ability, or merit: *He has serious pretensions as a writer.* **3.** a showing off.

pre·ten·tious (pri ten′shəs), *adj.* **1.** making claims to importance or dignity. **2.** making an exaggerated outward show, as of wealth, importance, etc. —**pre·ten′tious·ly,** *adv.* —**pre·ten′tious·ness,** *n.*

pret·er·it (pret′ər it), *n.* (in grammar) **1.** the past tense. **2.** a verb form in the past tense. —*adj.* **3.** describing a past action or state. Also, **pret′er·ite.**

pre·text (prē′tekst), *n.* a false reason put forward to conceal the true one; excuse: *The leaders used the insults as a pretext to declare war.*

Pre·to·ri·a (pri tôr′ē ə), *n.* the administrative capital city of the Republic of South Africa, in the NE part. See also **Cape Town.**

pret·ty (prit′ē), *adj.,* **pret·ti·er, pret·ti·est. 1.** pleasing or attractive in a delicate, dainty, or graceful way: *a pretty face; a pretty tune.* **2.** *Informal.* fine; grand (used ironically): *This is a pretty mess!* —*adv.* **3.** fairly; moderately: *It was a pretty good movie.* **4.** **sitting pretty,** in a very favorable position or situation: *With a good job, nice home, and money in the bank, he's really sitting pretty.* —**pret′ti·ly,** *adv.* —**pret′ti·ness,** *n.*

pret·zel (pret′səl), *n.* a crisp, dry biscuit, usually shaped like a knot and salted on the outside.

pre·vail (pri vāl′), *v.* **1.** to be widespread or current; exist generally: *Freezing temperatures prevailed*

throughout the East. **2.** to be or appear the more important, frequent, usual, etc.: *Green tints prevailed in the color of the upholstery.* **3.** to prove superior in strength or influence; gain control; win out. **4.** **prevail on** (or **upon**), to persuade or induce: *I prevailed on him to usher at the play.*

pre·vail·ing (pri vā′lĭng), *adj.* **1.** of the present time; current: *the prevailing opinion in the newspapers.* **2.** most frequent or usual: *prevailing winds.* **3.** having superior power or influence.

prev·a·lent (prev′ə lənt), *adj.* widespread; in general use. —**prev′a·lence,** *n.*

pre·var·i·cate (pri var′ə kāt′), *v.,* **pre·var·i·cat·ed, pre·var·i·cat·ing.** to speak falsely with deliberate intent; lie. —**pre·var′i·ca′tion,** *n.* —**pre·var′i·ca′tor,** *n.*

pre·vent (pri vent′), *v.* **1.** to keep from occurring: *The vaccine helped to prevent illness.* **2.** to hinder: *There is nothing to prevent us from going.*

pre·ven·tion (pri ven′shən), *n.* **1.** the act of preventing: *the prevention of accidents.* **2.** something that prevents.

pre·ven·tive (pri ven′tiv), *adj.* **1.** serving to prevent injury, disease, evil, etc.: *preventive medicine.* —*n.* **2.** a drug, medicine, vaccine, or the like, for preventing disease.

pre·view (prē′vyōō′), *n.* **1.** an advance showing of a motion picture, play, etc., before its public opening. —*v.* **2.** to view or show beforehand.

pre·vi·ous (prē′vē əs), *adj.* **1.** coming or occurring before something else; earlier; former: *the previous owner.* **2.** **previous to,** prior to; before: *previous to my joining the club.* —**pre′vi·ous·ly,** *adv.*

pre·war (prē′wôr′), *adj.* done or occurring before the war: *prewar prices.*

prey (prā), *n.* **1.** an animal hunted or seized for food, esp. by another animal. **2.** a person or thing that is the victim of an enemy, disease, or the like: *The young man fell prey to a swindler.* **3.** the action or habit of preying: *Hawks are birds of prey.* —*v.* **4.** to seize and devour prey, as animals do (usually fol. by *on* or *upon*): *Foxes prey on rabbits.* **5.** to exert a harmful influence: *Worries preyed on his mind.* **6.** to make raids or violent attacks for plunder: *The Vikings preyed on the coastal settlements of England.*

Pri·am (prī′əm), *n.* (in Greek mythology) a king of Troy, father of Hector, Paris, and Cassandra.

price (prīs), *n.* **1.** the amount of money or its equivalent for which anything is bought or sold. **2.** something that must be given or done in order to obtain a result: *The army won the battle, but at a heavy price in lives.* **3.** a sum offered for the capture of a person alive or dead: *There's a price on the outlaw's head.* —*v.,* **priced, pric·ing. 4.** to set the price of: *This store prices groceries reasonably.* **5.** to ask the price of: *to price furniture.* **6.** **beyond price,** too valuable to set a price on; priceless; invaluable.

price·less (prīs′lis), *adj.* **1.** having a value too high to set a price on; invaluable. **2.** *Informal.* delightfully amusing: *He can tell priceless stories.*

---

act, āble, dâre, ärt; ebb, ēqual; if, īce; hot, ōver, ôrder; oil; bŏŏk; ōoze; out; up, ûrge; ə = *a* as in *alone*; ᵊ as in *button* (but′ᵊn), *fire* (fiᵊr); chief; shoe; thin; ŧħat; zh as in *measure* (mezh′ər). See full key inside cover.

prick (prik), *n.* **1.** a puncture or mark made by a needle, pin, thorn, or the like. **2.** a sharp pain. **3.** the act of piercing with a sharp point. **4.** the state or feeling of being pricked. —*v.* **5.** to pierce or puncture with a sharp point. **6.** to cause a sharp pain to, as from piercing. **7.** to cause distress or anguish to, as from anger, guilt, etc.: *His conscience pricked him suddenly.* **8.** to mark (a surface) with pricks or dots, as in tracing something. **9.** to spur or urge on a horse; ride rapidly. **10. prick up one's ears,** to become very alert; listen closely: *She pricked up her ears when her friends gossiped.*

prick·le (prik′əl), *n.* **1.** a sharp point, as on the bark of a plant or the skin of an animal; spine. **2.** a stinging or tingling sensation: *Alcohol can cause a prickle on tender skin.* —*v.,* **prick·led, prick·ling. 3.** to cause a tingling sensation. **4.** to feel such a sensation.

prick·ly (prik′lē), *adj.,* **prick·li·er, prick·li·est. 1.** having many small, sharp points; full of prickles. **2.** prickling; smarting: *a prickly feeling caused by the heat.* —**prick′li·ness,** *n.*

prick′ly pear′, 1. the pear-shaped, often prickly fruit of certain kinds of cactus. **2.** a cactus bearing this fruit.

pride (prīd), *n.* **1.** too high an opinion of one's importance, superiority, etc.; conceit. **2.** a proper or dignified sense of one's character, worth, position, etc.; self-respect. **3.** pleasure or satisfaction taken in something: *civic pride.* **4.** something that a person is proud of: *His art collection was the pride of the family.* —*v.,* **prid·ed, prid·ing. 5.** to have a feeling of pride in (oneself): *She prides herself on her cooking.*

priest (prēst), *n.* **1.** a person who performs the religious rites of a deity: *a priest of Jupiter.* **2.** (in certain Christian churches) a clergyman or minister.

priest·ess (prē′stis), *n.* a woman who performs sacred rites, esp. of a pagan religion.

priest·hood (prēst′hŏŏd), *n.* **1.** the condition or office of a priest. **2.** priests as a group.

priest·ly (prēst′lē), *adj.,* **priest·li·er, priest·li·est. 1.** of or concerning a priest or the priesthood: *priestly vestments.* **2.** suitable for a priest or the priesthood.

prig (prig), *n.* a person who considers himself superior and is too concerned with or fussy about speech, manners, etc. —**prig′gish,** *adj.*

prim (prim), *adj.,* **prim·mer, prim·mest.** formally precise, proper, neat, etc.: *She's so prim our laughter annoyed her.* —**prim′ly,** *adv.* —**prim′ness,** *n.*

pri·ma·cy (prī′mə sē), *n., pl.* for defs. 2, 3 **pri·ma·cies. 1.** the state of being first in order, rank, importance, etc. **2.** the office or rank of primate. **3.** (in the Roman Catholic Church) the power and authority of the Pope as supreme bishop.

pri·ma don·na (prē′mə don′ə, prim′ə), **1.** the principal female singer in an opera company. **2.** any great female singer.

pri·mal (prī′məl), *adj.* **1.** of the first or early times; first; original. **2.** of first importance; fundamental.

pri·mar·i·ly (prī mâr′ə lē), *adv.* **1.** chiefly; mostly: *They live primarily from farming.* **2.** at first; originally.

pri·ma·ry (prī′mer ē), *adj.* **1.** first in order or time: *the primary grades of school.* **2.** first or highest in importance; chief: *What are your primary goals?* **3.** basic or original; not made from anything else: *The primary colors are red, blue, and yellow.* —*n., pl.* **pri·ma·ries. 4.** something that is first in order, rank, or importance. **5.** Also, **pri′mary elec′tion.** a preliminary election in which voters of each party nominate candidates for office, party officers, etc.

pri′mary stress′, 1. the accent of that syllable of a word that is most strongly pronounced. In the pronunciation of the word *proposition* (prop′ə zish′ən), the third syllable has the primary stress. **2.** the symbol (′) used to mark the primary stress. Also, **pri′mary ac′cent.** See also **secondary stress.**

pri·mate (prī′māt *or, esp. for def. 1,* prī′mit), *n.* **1.** an archbishop or bishop ranking first among the bishops of a province, country, etc. **2.** any member of an important group of related animals including the lemurs, monkeys, apes, and man.

prime (prīm), *adj.* **1.** of first importance or rank; chief: *a prime requirement.* **2.** of greatest value or best quality: *prime ribs of beef.* —*n.* **3.** the beginning or earliest stage of any period. **4.** the best part, stage, condition, etc.: *a man in the prime of his life.* —*v.,* **primed, prim·ing. 5.** to prepare (something) for a particular purpose. **6.** to pour liquid into (a pump) in order to make it ready for action. **7.** to supply (a firearm) with powder. **8.** to cover (a surface) with a preliminary coat, as in painting. **9.** to supply (a person) with information for use: *The aides of the politician primed him for the press conference.*

prime′ merid′ian, the meridian running through Greenwich, England, from which longitude east and west is reckoned.

prime′ min′ister, the first minister and head of government in certain countries.

prime′ num′ber, a number that can be divided evenly only by itself and 1, such as 11, 13, or 17.

prim·er¹ (prim′ər), *n.* **1.** a textbook for teaching children to read. **2.** any textbook for beginners: *a primer of guitar playing.* [from the medieval Latin word *primārium,* which comes from Latin *primārius* "first"]

prim·er² (prī′mər), *n.* **1.** a first coat or layer of paint, size, etc. **2.** a small charge of powder or the like used to explode a larger charge.

pri·me·val (prī mē′vəl), *adj.* of or concerning the first age or ages, esp. of the world; primitive.

prim·ing (prī′ming), *n.* **1.** the explosive or other material used to set off the charge in a gun, mine, etc. **2.** a first coat or layer of paint applied to a surface.

prim·i·tive (prim′i tiv), *adj.* **1.** being the first or earliest of the kind: *primitive man.* **2.** early in the history of the world or of the human race: *primitive art.* **3.** simple, unsophisticated, or crude: *a primitive method of farming; primitive living conditions.* —*n.* **4.** a person or thing that is primitive.

primp (primp), *v.* to groom oneself with extreme or excessive care.

prim·rose (prim′rōz′), *n.* a garden plant with large

leaves at the base of the stem and flowers of various colors that grow at the top of the stem.

prin., 1. principal. 2. principle.

prince (prins), *n.* 1. the son of a king or queen, or the son of a king's son. 2. the ruler of a small state: *Monaco is ruled by a prince.* 3. a person who is chief or preeminent in any class, group, etc.: *a merchant prince; a prince among men.*

Prince′ Ed′ward Is′land, an island in the Gulf of St. Lawrence, forming a province of Canada. 2184 sq. mi. *Cap.:* Charlottetown.

prince·ly (prins′lē), *adj.,* **prince·li·er, prince·li·est.** 1. of or concerning a prince. 2. like or befitting a prince: *princely manners.* 3. lavish or generous; magnificent: *a princely entertainment.*

Prince′ of Wales′, a title conferred on the male heir apparent to the British throne.

prin·cess (prin′sis, prin′ses), *n.* 1. the daughter of a king or queen, or the daughter of a king's son. 2. the wife of a prince.

prin·ci·pal (prin′sə pəl), *adj.* 1. first or highest in rank, importance, value, etc.; chief: *the principal ideas in a book.* —*n.* 2. the chief person or head. 3. something of chief importance. 4. the head or director of a school. 5. (in law) a person who authorizes another to represent him as an agent. 6. (in finance) money or capital, as distinguished from interest or profit.

prin′cipal clause′, another term for **main clause.**

prin·ci·pal·i·ty (prin′sə pal′i tē), *n., pl.* **prin·ci·pal·i·ties.** 1. a state or country, usually a small one, ruled by a prince. 2. the position or authority of a prince; supreme power.

prin·ci·pal·ly (prin′sə pə lē, prin′sip lē), *adv.* largely; chiefly; mainly.

prin′cipal parts′, (in grammar) a set of inflected forms of a verb from which all other forms can be derived. In English, the principal parts of a verb are the infinitive, the past tense, and the past participle, such as *sing, sang, sung* or *smoke, smoked.*

prin·ci·ple (prin′sə pəl), *n.* 1. a general or fundamental rule or truth on which other truths are based: *the principles of modern science.* 2. a scientific rule or law explaining the action of something in nature: *the principle of buoyancy.* 3. a rule of conduct: *He makes it a principle to be polite.* 4. a fundamental doctrine or belief: *the principles of Christianity.* 5. a guiding sense of right conduct; honor: *a man of principle.* 6. **on principle,** because of one's standard of conduct or moral principles: *to object to something on principle.*

print (print), *v.* 1. to produce (a book, newspaper, etc.) by stamping words on paper with inked type, plates, or the like. 2. to cause to be printed; publish: *to print a manuscript.* 3. to form a design or pattern on: *to print calico cloth.* 4. to write in letters like those used in print: *Print your name at the top of the page.* 5. (in photography) to make a positive picture from (a negative). —*n.* 6. words or letters stamped

on paper in ink by type, plates, etc. 7. a design, picture, or the like, printed from an engraved or otherwise prepared plate, block, etc. 8. a mark made by the pressure of one thing on another, as a footprint. 9. cloth stamped with a design or pattern. 10. a garment or other article made of such cloth. 11. a picture, esp. a photographic positive made from a negative. 12. **in print,** available for purchase from the publisher: *Is that book still in print?* 13. **out of print,** no longer available for purchase from the publisher: *The book has been out of print for a year.*

print·er (prin′tər), *n.* a person whose business is the setting of type or running a printing press.

print·ing (prin′ting), *n.* 1. the art or business of producing books, newspapers, etc., by impression from movable types, plates, etc. 2. words, letters, etc., in printed form; printed matter. 3. the total number of copies of anything printed at one time. 4. the act of a person or thing that prints. 5. handwriting in which the letters resemble printed ones.

print′ing press′, a machine for printing on paper from type, plates, etc.

pri·or¹ (prī′ər), *adj.* preceding in time or order; earlier or former: *A prior agreement prevents me from accepting this one.* [from a Latin word meaning "former, before"]

pri·or² (prī′ər), *n.* an officer in a monastery, sometimes ranking just below an abbot. [from a Latin word, which is a special use of *prior* "elder, superior." See *prior¹*]

pri·or·ess (prī′ər is), *n.* a nun who is head of a religious house for women.

pri·or·i·ty (prī or′i tē, prī ôr′i tē), *n., pl.* for defs. 2, 3 **pri·or·i·ties.** 1. the state or condition of being earlier in time or greater in importance. 2. first place in order, rank, privilege, etc. 3. the right of taking first place in order, rank, or importance.

pri·or·y (prī′ə rē), *n., pl.* **pri·or·ies.** a religious house governed by a prior or prioress.

prism (priz′əm), *n.* 1. a piece of glass with flat sides and triangular ends used for reflecting light or for separating it into rays of different colors. 2. (in geometry) a solid having identical, flat, parallel ends and sides that are parallelograms.

pris·mat·ic (priz mat′ik), *adj.* 1. of, concerning, or like a prism. 2. formed by a transparent prism.

pris·on (priz′ən), *n.* 1. a building where persons are confined while awaiting trial or serving sentences for having broken the law. 2. any place where a person is confined against his will.

Prisms

pris·on·er (priz′ə nər, priz′nər), *n.* 1. a person who is confined in prison. 2. Also, **pris′oner of war′.** a person who is captured and held by an enemy during war. 3. any person, animal, etc., that is held captive or deprived of liberty.

prith·ee (prith′ē), *interj. Archaic.* (I) pray thee;

please: *Prithee have mercy on this unhappy man.*

pri·va·cy (prī/və sē), *n.* **1.** the state of being private, alone, or apart from others; seclusion: *to work in privacy.* **2.** the state of being secret; secrecy: *In privacy she told me that she was getting married.*

pri·vate (prī/vit), *adj.* **1.** belonging to some particular person or persons; not for public use: *a private beach.* **2.** limited to some particular person or persons; not public or for public knowledge: *a private discussion that must remain secret.* **3.** intimate or very personal: *His private life is no business of yours.* **4.** not holding public office or employment: *a private citizen.* **5.** of an ordinary citizen; not public or official: *to retire to private life.* —*n.* **6.** an enlisted soldier of one of the lowest ranks in the Army, ranking below a corporal. **7. in private,** away from others: *He does his exercises in private.* —**pri/vate·ly,** *adv.*

pri·va·teer (prī/və tēr/), *n.* **1.** (formerly) a privately owned warship employed by a government to attack enemy shipping. **2.** another name for **privateersman.** —*v.* **3.** to cruise as a privateer searching for and attacking enemy shipping.

pri·va·teers·man (prī/və tērz/mən), *n., pl.* **pri·va·teers·men.** an officer or seaman of a privateer.

pri/vate first/ class/, a soldier ranking just below a corporal in the Army, or just below a lance corporal in the Marines.

pri·va·tion (prī vā/shən), *n.* **1.** lack of the usual comforts or necessities of life: *to suffer from hunger and privation.* **2.** the act of depriving. **3.** a being deprived: *a privation of vitamins in one's diet.*

priv·et (priv/it), *n.* an evergreen shrub with small leaves that is frequently used for hedges.

priv·i·lege (priv/ə lij, priv/lij), *n.* **1.** a special right or benefit enjoyed by a particular person or group: *the privileges of the rich.* —*v.,* **priv·i·leged, priv·i·leg·ing.** **2.** to grant a privilege or special benefit to: *His great fortune privileged him to live in luxury.*

priv·i·leged (priv/ə lijd, priv/lijd), *adj.* **1.** enjoying special privileges, esp. as a result of wealth or social position: *a revolution against the privileged classes of society.* **2.** for or limited to a particular person or group of persons: *privileged information.*

priv·i·ly (priv/ə lē), *adv.* in a privy or private manner; secretly: *to meet privily.*

priv·y (priv/ē), *adj.,* **priv·i·er, priv·i·est.** **1.** having knowledge of something private or secret (usually fol. by *to*): *to be privy to a plot.* **2.** Archaic. private or secret. —*n.* **3.** an outhouse or outdoor toilet.

priv/y coun/cil, a group of personal advisers, esp. of a king or other sovereign.

prize¹ (prīz), *n.* **1.** an award for victory or superior performance in a contest: *The first prize in this race is a silver cup.* **2.** an award offered or won in a game of chance. **3.** something that is valuable or worth trying for: *Fame was the prize he sought.* **4.** something seized or captured, esp. an enemy ship. —*adj.* **5.** having won a prize: *a prize bull.* **6.** worthy of a prize or special notice: *to do a prize job; to make a prize blunder.* **7.** given as a prize: *prize money.* [from the Old French word *prise* "a seizing, capturing," which

comes from Latin *prehensa;* also, in some senses, blended with the Middle English word *pris* "reward," from Latin *pretium* "price, value"]

prize² (prīz), *v.,* **prized, priz·ing.** to value highly; admire or appreciate: *He prizes his children above all else.* [from the Old French word *prisier* "to praise," which comes from Latin *pretiāre* "to value," from *pretium* "price, value"]

prize/ fight/, a contest between boxers for a money prize; a professional boxing match. —**prize/ fight/er. —prize/ fight/ing.**

pro¹ (prō), *adv.* **1.** in favor of a proposal, position, opinion, etc.: *to argue pro and con.* —*n., pl.* **pros. 2.** a person arguing in favor of a proposal in a debate: *The pros have better arguments.* **3.** an argument, point, or consideration in favor of something: *to consider the pros and cons of a proposal.* See also **con¹.** [from the Latin word *prō* "for"]

pro² (prō), *n., pl.* **pros.** *Informal.* a professional or expert: *a golf pro.* [by shortening]

pro-, a prefix meaning **1.** before or forth: *prolong; procreate.* **2.** taking the place of: *proconsul; pronoun.* **3.** favoring or supporting: *pro-British; proslavery.*

pro·a (prō/ə), *n.* a kind of sailboat used in the South Pacific.

prob·a·bil·i·ty (prob/ə-bil/i tē), *n., pl.* for def. 2 **prob·a·bil·i·ties. 1.** the quality or fact of being probable; chance; likelihood: *She carried an umbrella because of the probability of rain.* **2.** something that is proba-

Proa

ble or likely: *His election is now a probability.*

prob·a·ble (prob/ə bəl), *adj.* likely to occur or prove true: *A snowstorm is probable tonight.*

prob·a·bly (prob/ə blē), *adv.* very likely; in all likelihood: *With a ten-point lead, they will probably win the game.*

pro·bate (prō/bāt), *n.* **1.** the legal proving of a will as authentic or valid. —*adj.* **2.** of or concerning a court of probate or the proving of a will: *probate proceedings.* —*v.,* **pro·bat·ed, pro·bat·ing. 3.** to establish the authenticity or validity of (a will).

pro/bate court/, a special court with the power to approve wills, supervise estates, etc.

pro·ba·tion (prō bā/shən), *n.* **1.** a testing or trial, esp. of a person's conduct, character, abilities, etc.: *The first six weeks on this job are a period of probation.* **2.** a method of dealing with persons who have been convicted of a minor crime that allows them to remain out of prison but under the supervision of an official (**proba/tion of/ficer**). **3.** the state of being under special supervision or of being tested as to one's character, abilities, etc.: *to be on probation.* **4.** a process or time of testing or trial.

pro·ba·tion·er (prō bā/shə nər), *n.* a person who is being tested as to character and abilities, esp. one who has been convicted of a crime and is being supervised by a probation officer.

probe (prōb), *v.*, **probed, prob·ing.** 1. to search or investigate: *to probe into the causes of crime.* 2. to examine or explore with or as if with a probe: *to probe a wound.* —*n.* 3. a slender, picklike instrument, used esp. by doctors and dentists to explore wounds, cavities, etc. 4. the act or process of probing or exploring: *a probe into corruption in government.*

pro·bi·ty (prō′bi tē), *n.* honesty or uprightness: *a man of virtue and probity.*

prob·lem (prob′ləm), *n.* 1. any question or matter that is difficult to decide or solve: *The lack of doctors is a serious problem in this community.* 2. someone or something that is puzzling or difficult. 3. (in mathematics) a statement or question requiring a solution: *to have seven problems as homework.* —*adj.* 4. difficult to guide or care for; unruly: *a problem child.*

prob·lem·at·ic (prob′lə mat′ik), *adj.* causing a problem; doubtful; puzzling: *a problematic question.* Also, **prob′lem·at′i·cal.**

pro·bos·cis (prō bos′is), *n.* 1. the trunk of an elephant. 2. any long, flexible snout. 3. the protruding mouthparts of certain insects.

proc., 1. procedure. 2. proceedings. 3. process.

pro·ce·dure (prə sē′jər), *n.* 1. a method or way of doing or proceeding in some action or business: *What is the best procedure for getting into college?* 2. a particular manner of conducting meetings, legal business, or the like: *The chairman had to study parliamentary procedure.* —**pro·ce′dur·al,** *adj.*

pro·ceed (prə sēd′), *v.* 1. to go forward or onward, esp. after stopping: *The policeman signaled the cars to proceed.* 2. to carry on or continue: *He's proceeding slowly in his studies.* 3. to go on to do something: *Then she proceeded to apologize.* 4. to arise or result: *Weakness proceeds from illness.*

pro·ceed·ing (prə sē′diñg), *n.* 1. a particular action, or course of action: *The trial was an unusual proceeding.* 2. the act of a person or thing that proceeds: *a proceeding towards one's goal.* 3. **proceedings,** an activity continuing for some time; a series of events: *the proceedings at a meeting.* 4. Often, **proceedings.** legal action, such as the starting and carrying on of a lawsuit: *Proceedings are under way on his case.*

pro·ceeds (prō′sēdz), *n.* 1. the total sum of money or the profits earned from a sale, investment, etc.: *The proceeds from the auction will be given to charity.* 2. the results of anything.

proc·ess (pros′es), *n.* 1. a series of actions directed toward a certain result; system; method: *a process for producing atomic energy.* 2. a particular series of changes or events: *the process of growth.* 3. the act of carrying out or going through a particular series of actions or changes: *The roast is in the process of cooking.* 4. the act of proceeding or going forward: *the process of time.* 5. (in biology or anatomy) a natural outgrowth or projecting part: *a knoblike process on a bone.* 6. a writ or court order requiring someone to appear in court; summons. —*v.* 7. to treat or pre-

pare by some particular method; make ready to use, eat, etc.: *to process cheese; to process leather.* 8. to handle or deal with according to a particular routine: *to process applications for passports.*

pro·ces·sion (prə sesh′ən), *n.* 1. a line or group of persons, animals, or objects moving along in an orderly way; parade: *a procession of cars.* 2. a continuous or ceremonious movement forward: *the procession of history.*

pro·ces·sion·al (prə sesh′ə nᵊl), *adj.* 1. of, concerning, or resembling a procession or processions. —*n.* 2. a piece of music played or sung during a procession.

pro·claim (prō klām′, prə klām′), *v.* to announce formally or publicly; declare: *The president proclaimed a holiday.* —**pro·claim′er,** *n.*

proc·la·ma·tion (prok′lə mā′shən), *n.* 1. something that is proclaimed or declared: *The king has made an important proclamation.* 2. the act of proclaiming or declaring: *the proclamation of a holiday.*

pro·cras·ti·nate (prō kras′tə nāt′), *v.*, **pro·cras·ti·nat·ed, pro·cras·ti·nat·ing.** to delay or put off action on something: *She procrastinated so long that the opportunity was lost.* —**pro·cras′ti·na′tion,** *n.* —**pro·cras′ti·na′tor,** *n.*

pro·cre·a·tion (prō′krē ā′shən), *n.* the act or process of begetting or bringing forth young.

proc·u·ra·tor (prok′yə rā′tər), *n.* 1. (in ancient Rome) an official of the empire in charge of the management of finances and related matters in a province. 2. any deputy or agent authorized to act for somebody else.

pro·cure (prō kyōōr′), *v.*, **pro·cured, pro·cur·ing.** 1. to obtain or get by effort: *We are having trouble procuring tickets for the circus.* 2. to cause to occur; bring about: *They are working to procure a change in the rules.* —**pro·cure′ment,** *n.*

prod (prod), *v.*, **prod·ded, prod·ding.** 1. to poke or jab, esp. with something pointed: *The boy prodded the cow with a stick.* 2. to rouse or push to do something; nag; goad: *Mother prods us to do better.* —*n.* 3. a pointed instrument or one giving an electric shock, used for prodding animals. 4. a poke or jab: *to give someone a prod in the ribs.* 5. a reminder or speech urging someone to action. —**prod′der,** *n.*

prod., 1. produce. 2. produced. 3. product.

prod·i·gal (prod′ə gəl), *adj.* 1. wasteful in spending or using money, time, resources, etc.: *His prodigal life has brought him to bankruptcy.* 2. bountiful or lavish: *a prodigal harvest.* —*n.* 3. a person who is or has been wasteful with his money; spendthrift. —**prod·i·gal·i·ty** (prod′ə gal′i tē), *n.* —**prod′i·gal·ly,** *adv.*

pro·di·gious (prə dij′əs), *adj.* 1. extraordinary, esp. in size or amount; enormous: *to do a prodigious amount of work.* 2. wonderful or marvelous: *prodigious acts of bravery.* —**pro·di′gious·ly,** *adv.*

prod·i·gy (prod′ə jē), *n.*, *pl.* **prod·i·gies.** 1. a person, esp. a child, having extraordinary talent or ability:

That boy is a prodigy at chess. **2.** something extremely unusual or extraordinary; marvel.

pro·duce (prə do͞os′, -dyo͞os′), *v.,* **pro·duced, pro·duc·ing. 1.** to create or make: *an author who has produced 10 books.* **2.** to give birth to: *Our cat produced a litter of four.* **3.** to provide or supply; yield: *a mine that produces silver.* **4.** to show or present for inspection: *The policeman asked him to produce his driver's license.* **5.** to cause; give rise to: *a drug that produces sleep.* **6.** to act as the producer of (a play, motion picture, television show, etc.). —*n.* (prō′do͞os, -dyo͞os). **7.** agricultural products, esp. vegetables and fruits. [from the Latin word *prōdūcere* "to bring forth"]

pro·duc·er (prə do͞o′sər, -dyo͞o′-), *n.* **1.** someone or something that produces, manufactures, or yields: *The chief producers of steel have raised their prices.* **2.** a person responsible for raising money for and supervising the presentation of a play, motion picture, television show, or the like.

prod·uct (prod′əkt), *n.* **1.** a thing produced, made, or brought forth by labor or thought: *They sell vegetables and other farm products.* **2.** a result or outcome: *The confusion at the meeting was a product of poor planning.* **3.** (in arithmetic) the number obtained by multiplying two or more factors together.

pro·duc·tion (prə duk′shən), *n.* **1.** the act of producing, making, etc.: *the production of automobiles.* **2.** something that is produced, esp. a play, motion picture, or the like: *a new production on Broadway.* **3.** an amount produced: *Production is up this week.*

pro·duc·tive (prə duk′tiv), *adj.* **1.** having the power of producing, yielding, or making something: *The mine was shut down because it was not productive.* **2.** producing in abundance; fertile: *rich, productive farmland.* **3.** producing or yielding economic profit: *productive labor.* **4.** causing or bringing about: *Slum conditions can be productive of crime.* —**pro·duc′tive·ly,** *adv.* —**pro·duc·tiv·i·ty** (prō′duk tiv′i tē, prod′ək tiv′i tē), **pro·duc′tive·ness,** *n.*

Prof., Professor.

prof·a·na·tion (prof′ə nā′shən), *n.* the act of profaning sacred things; sacrilege; blasphemy.

pro·fane (prə fān′), *adj.* **1.** irreverent toward God or sacred things; sacrilegious or blasphemous. **2.** not for or concerned with religious purposes; secular (opposite of *sacred*): *profane music.* —*v.,* **pro·faned, pro·fan·ing. 3.** to treat (something sacred) with irreverence or use for worldly purposes: *The moneylenders profaned the Temple.* —**pro·fane′ly,** *adv.* —**pro·fan′er,** *n.*

pro·fan·i·ty (prə fan′i tē), *n., pl.* for def. 2 **pro·fan·i·ties. 1.** the quality of being profane or disrespectful of sacred things. **2.** profane or irreverent behavior or speech.

pro·fess (prə fes′), *v.* **1.** to express or claim, esp. insincerely: *She professed not to care what people thought.* **2.** to admit openly; acknowledge: *to profess sympathy with a cause.* **3.** to declare openly one's faith in or allegiance to (God, a religion, etc.): *to profess a certain religion.*

pro·fessed (prə fest′), *adj.* **1.** fully admitted by the person himself; acknowledged: *a professed swindler.* **2.** pretended or alleged; insincerely declared: *Don't count on her professed friendship.*

pro·fes·sion (prə fesh′ən), *n.* **1.** an occupation, esp. one that requires advanced education: *Medicine is a profession.* **2.** the persons with such an occupation: *a magazine for the medical profession.* **3.** the act of professing something, esp. religious faith.

pro·fes·sion·al (prə fesh′ə nᵊl), *adj.* **1.** performing or working at something for money rather than simply for pleasure: *a professional golfer.* **2.** of or concerning a profession such as law, medicine, etc.: *professional studies.* **3.** working in a profession: *lawyers, professors, and other professional people.* **4.** of or for professional persons or their business: *a professional apartment.* **5.** expert or skilled: *The carpenter's work was extremely professional.* —*n.* **6.** a person who works in one of the professions. **7.** a person who earns his living in a sport or other occupation frequently engaged in by amateurs: *a tennis tournament for professionals.* **8.** a person who is expert at his work. —**pro·fes′sion·al·ly,** *adv.*

pro·fes·sor (prə fes′ər), *n.* **1.** a college or university teacher, esp. of the highest rank. **2.** a person who has professed his religious faith, deep beliefs, etc.: *a professor of Islam.* —**pro·fes′sor·ship′,** *n.*

pro·fes·so·ri·al (prō′fə sôr′ē əl, prof′ə sôr′ē əl), *adj.* **1.** of or concerning a professor or professors: *His professorial duties include advising students.* **2.** resembling a professor; like that of a professor: *a studious, professorial appearance.* —**pro·fes′so·ri·al·ly,** *adv.*

prof·fer (prof′ər), *v.* **1.** to put forward or offer: *to proffer a suggestion.* —*n.* **2.** the act of proffering; offer: *a proffer of help.*

pro·fi·cient (prə fish′ənt), *adj.* expert or skilled: *to be proficient at taking shorthand; a proficient student.* —**pro·fi′cien·cy,** *n.* —**pro·fi′cient·ly,** *adv.*

pro·file (prō′fīl), *n.* **1.** the outline of something, esp. of the human head viewed from the side. **2.** a picture, engraving, or the like, showing the human head from the side. **3.** a short biography, esp. an article: *Today's newspaper has a profile on our new mayor.*

prof·it (prof′it), *n.* **1.** the amount of money gained from an investment or business venture after all expenses have been paid or subtracted. **2.** an advantage or benefit: *It will be to your profit to take that advice.* —*v.* **3.** to be of benefit or profit to: *It will not profit you to argue further.* **4.** to gain an advantage or benefit: *The other team profited from our mistakes.* —**prof′it·er,** *n.* —**prof′it·less,** *adj.*

prof·it·a·ble (prof′i tə bəl), *adj.* **1.** yielding profit or gain: *The store held a large and profitable sale.* **2.** useful or valuable: *Watching television all night is not a profitable way to spend your time.* —**prof′it·a·ble·ness,** *n.* —**prof′it·a·bly,** *adv.*

prof·it·eer (prof′i tēr′), *n.* **1.** a person who makes too great profits, esp. on inferior products: *profiteers in the black market.* —*v.* **2.** to act as a profiteer.

prof·li·gate (prof′lə git, prof′lə gāt′), *adj.* **1.** completely immoral; evil; corrupt. **2.** extravagant or wasteful: *profligate spending.* —*n.* **3.** a profligate person. —**prof·li·ga·cy** (prof′lə gə sē), *n.*

pro·found (prə found′), *adj.* **1.** having or showing deep understanding; wise: *a profound thinker; a profound judgment.* **2.** deep or severe: *to suffer profound grief; to have a profound influence on someone.* **3.** being far beneath the surface: *the profound depths of the ocean.* **4.** low or deep: *a profound bow.* —**pro·found′ly,** *adv.* —**pro·found′ness,** *n.*

pro·fun·di·ty (prə fun′di tē), *n., pl.* for defs. 2, 3 **pro·fun·di·ties.** **1.** the quality or state of being profound; depth: *the profundity of the ocean.* **2.** Usually, **profundities.** profound or deep matters: *the profundities of life.* **3.** an extremely deep place; abyss.

pro·fuse (prə fyoos′), *adj.* **1.** extremely generous; lavish (often fol. by *in*): *He was profuse in his praise.* **2.** abundant or plentiful: *profuse apologies; a profuse growth of weeds.* —**pro·fuse′ly,** *adv.*

pro·fu·sion (prə fyoo′zhən), *n.* a great quantity or amount; abundance: *a profusion of flowers.*

pro·gen·i·tor (prō jen′i tər), *n.* **1.** an ancestor or forefather: *the progenitors of a nation.* **2.** an original or model; precursor: *the progenitor of steamships.*

prog·e·ny (proj′ə nē), *n., pl.* **prog·e·ny** or (for plants or animals) **prog·e·nies.** **1.** a descendant or offspring of a person, animal, or plant. **2.** such descendants or offspring as a group; children or descendants.

prog·no·sis (prog nō′sis), *n., pl.* **prog·no·ses** (prog-nō′sēz). a prediction or forecast, esp. of whether someone will recover from a disease, injury, etc.: *The doctor's prognosis was favorable.*

prog·nos·tic (prog nos′tik), *adj.* **1.** of or concerning a prognosis or prediction: *The surgeon was famous for his prognostic accuracy.* **2.** serving to predict the course of events: *a prognostic sign.*

prog·nos·ti·cate (prog nos′tə kāt′), *v.,* **prog·nos·ti·cat·ed, prog·nos·ti·cat·ing.** **1.** to forecast or prophesy: *The doctor prognosticated an early recovery.* **2.** to foreshadow or forebode, as an omen does. —**prog·nos′ti·ca′tor,** *n.*

prog·nos·ti·ca·tion (prog nos′tə kā′shən), *n.* **1.** the act of prognosticating or predicting: *the prognostication of the course of a disease.* **2.** a forecast or prediction; prognosis: *His prognostications on the weather are usually wrong.*

pro·gram (prō′gram, prō′grəm), *n.* Also, *esp. British,* **pro′gramme.** **1.** a plan or schedule to be followed: *What is your program for this afternoon?* **2.** (in an entertainment, ceremony, meeting, etc.) a group of things to be done or pieces to be performed. **3.** a printed list of events, acts, performers, etc., in an entertainment, ceremony, or the like: *a theater program.* **4.** a show on radio or television: *There's a good program on at 8:00.* **5.** a plan or set of instructions for the solution of a problem by a computer. —*v.,* **pro·gramed** or **pro·grammed; pro·gram·ing** or **pro·gram·ming. 6.** to plan as part of a program: *They programmed your talk to begin at 9:00.* **7.** to prepare a program for: *to program a computer to play check-*

ers. —**pro′gram·mat′ic,** *adj.*

pro·gram·mer (prō′gram ər), *n.* a person who prepares programs, esp. for a computer. Also, **pro′gram·er.**

prog·ress (prog′res), *n.* **1.** movement forward or an advance, esp. toward a goal or further stage: *The police have made no progress toward solving the crime.* **2.** development or improvements, esp. in a civilization or individual: *Her work shows progress.* —*v.* (prə gres′). **3.** to advance or go forward: *to progress toward a goal.* **4.** to develop or improve: *Has the patient progressed at all?* **5. in progress,** going on; happening: *The meeting is in progress.*

pro·gres·sion (prə gresh′ən), *n.* **1.** the act of progressing. **2.** a sequence or succession; continuous series: *to study the progression of events leading up to the Civil War.* **3.** a series of numbers in which there is a constant relationship between each number and the one following, such as 3, 7, 11, 15, or 3, 6, 12, 24.

pro·gres·sive (prə gres′iv), *adj.* **1.** of, concerned with, or marked by progress: *a progressive community.* **2.** supporting progress and change in politics, science, etc.: *a progressive political party.* **3.** advancing step by step; going on steadily: *a progressive improvement.* **4.** of, concerned with, or following methods that emphasize freedom and experimentation: *a progressive school.* —*n.* **5.** a person who favors progress and reform, esp. in politics. —**pro·gres′sive·ly,** *adv.* —**pro·gres′sive·ness,** *n.*

pro·hib·it (prō hib′it), *v.* **1.** to forbid by authority or law: *Smoking is prohibited in this theater.* **2.** to hinder or prevent: *The deep mud prohibited a rapid march.* —**pro·hib′it·er, pro·hib′i·tor,** *n.*

pro·hi·bi·tion (prō′ə bish′ən), *n.* **1.** the legal forbidding of the manufacture and sale of alcoholic beverages. **2.** *(often cap.)* the period from 1920 to 1933, when the sale of alcoholic beverages in the U.S. was forbidden. **3.** the act of forbidding or prohibiting anything: *the prohibition of slavery.* **4.** a law or decree that forbids or prohibits something: *They protested the many prohibitions on free travel.*

pro·hi·bi·tion·ist (prō′ə bish′ə nist), *n.* a person favoring prohibiting the sale of alcoholic beverages.

pro·hib·i·tive (prō hib′i tiv), *adj.* **1.** that prohibits or forbids: *prohibitive rules.* **2.** tending to prevent the purchase, use, etc., of something: *prohibitive prices.* —**pro·hib′i·tive·ly,** *adv.* —**pro·hib′i·tive·ness,** *n.*

pro·hib·i·to·ry (prō hib′i tôr′ē), *adj.* serving to prohibit; prohibitive. —**pro·hib′i·to′ri·ly,** *adv.*

proj·ect (proj′ekt), *n.* **1.** something that is planned; plan, enterprise, or undertaking: *One of his projects for the summer is to learn French.* **2.** a particular assignment, task, or problem to be worked on: *The science teacher gave each student a project to finish before Christmas.* **3.** Also, **housing project.** a group of apartment buildings. —*v.* (prə jekt′). **4.** to plan or propose: *to project certain changes.* **5.** to extend or stick out: *The diving board projects several feet over the water.* **6.** to throw, cast, or shoot forward: *to pro-*

ject a rocket toward a target. **7.** to calculate or describe (future conditions or events). **8.** to cast (an image, shadow, etc.) onto a surface or into space: *to project a movie onto a screen.*

pro·jec·tile (prə jek′til, prə jek′tīl), *n.* something that is thrown or propelled through the air, esp. a bullet or shell fired from a gun.

pro·jec·tion (prə jek′shən), *n.* **1.** a part that projects or sticks out: *a projection of land into the sea; a projection of rock.* **2.** the act of projecting.

pro·jec·tor (prə jek′tər), *n.* **1.** an apparatus for throwing an enlarged image onto a screen: *a slide projector.* **2.** a person who projects or plans.

pro·le·tar·i·an (prō′li târ′ē ən), *adj.* **1.** of or belonging to the proletariat or working class: *proletarian labor.* **2.** (in ancient Rome) of or belonging to the lowest and poorest class of citizens. —*n.* **3.** a member of the proletariat. [from the Latin word *prōlētārius* "citizen who served the state only by having children," which comes from *prōles* "offspring"]

pro·le·tar·i·at (prō′li târ′ē ət), *n.* **1.** the working class, including esp. those who do not possess their own businesses or land and must labor for a wage from others: *Lenin called for a revolution of the proletariat.* **2.** (in ancient Rome) the lowest class of citizens, including those who did not own property.

pro·lif·ic (prō lif′ik), *adj.* **1.** producing young, offspring, fruit, etc., in abundance; fertile: *a prolific orchard.* **2.** very productive; producing many works: *a prolific author.* —**pro·lif′i·cal·ly,** *adv.*

pro·lix (prō liks′, prō′liks), *adj.* very long and wordy; drawn-out and boring. —**pro·lix·i·ty** (prō lik′si tē), **pro·lix′ness,** *n.* —**pro·lix′ly,** *adv.*

pro·logue (prō′lôg, -log), *n.* **1.** a preface or part that serves to introduce or begin a book, play, poem, etc.: *The prologue is spoken by one of the actors in front of the curtain.* **2.** any event that introduces or leads into something else: *The build-up of arms was the prologue to war.*

pro·long (prə lông′), *v.* to lengthen or extend; make longer: *We decided to prolong our stay in England.*

pro·lon·ga·tion (prō′lông gā′shən), *n.* **1.** the act of prolonging; a lengthening: *the prolongation of a visit.* **2.** the state of being prolonged or extended; a being lengthened. **3.** an added part; extension: *How long will the porch be, including its prolongation?*

prom (prom), *n. Informal.* a formal dance, esp. at a school or college. [short for *promenade*]

prom·e·nade (prom′ə nād′, prom′ə näd′), *n.* **1.** a stroll or walk, esp. in a public place: *to take a promenade down the avenue.* **2.** a place for walking or strolling, in a park, on the deck of a ship, etc.: *a daily walk around the promenade.* **3.** a formal dance; prom. **4.** a march of dancers at a square dance, formal ball, etc. —*v.,* **prom·e·nad·ed, prom·e·nad·ing. 5.** to walk or stroll for pleasure: *to promenade in the park.* **6.** to take part in a promenade at a dance: *The guests promenaded around the ballroom.* —**prom′e·nad′er,** *n.*

Pro·me·the·us (prə mē′thē əs), *n.* (in Greek mythology) a Titan who stole fire from the gods and gave it

to man. As a punishment, Zeus had him chained to a rock, where he was preyed upon by an eagle.

pro·me·thi·um (prə mē′thē əm), *n. Chem.* a metallic element of the rare-earth group. *Symbol:* Pm

prom·i·nence (prom′ə nəns), *n.* **1.** the state of being prominent; distinction, importance, or conspicuousness: *The president held a dinner for people of prominence in the business world.* **2.** something that is prominent, such as a part that juts out: *The eagles built their nest on a prominence of the cliff.*

prom·i·nent (prom′ə nənt), *adj.* **1.** easily seen or very noticeable; conspicuous: *Put up this announcement in a prominent place.* **2.** jutting out or standing out: *Squirrels have prominent teeth.* **3.** important, distinguished, or well-known: *a conference of prominent scientists.* —**prom′i·nent·ly,** *adv.*

pro·mis·cu·ous (prə mis′kyoo əs), *adj.* **1.** not selective or discriminating; showing indifference to value or worth: *a promiscuous reader; promiscuous friendliness.* **2.** made up of a disordered mixture of different things: *a promiscuous heap of rubbish.* —**prom·is·cu·i·ty** (prom′i skyoo′i tē, prō′mi skyoo′i tē), **pro·mis′cu·ous·ness,** *n.* —**pro·mis′cu·ous·ly,** *adv.*

prom·ise (prom′is), *n.* **1.** a statement in which a person declares or pledges that he will or will not do something or that something will or will not happen; pledge: *I have his promise that he will pay back the money.* **2.** a quality that gives reason to expect future success; a cause for expectation or hope: *a young writer who shows promise.* —*v.,* **prom·ised, prom·is·ing. 3.** to pledge or give a promise: *If I promise to be there, I will be there.* **4.** to give cause for expecting; indicate: *Those dark clouds promise a storm.* **5.** to give reason for expectation, esp. of success (often fol. by *well*): *Her new novel promises well.*

Prom′ised Land′, 1. the hereafter; heaven. **2.** (in the Bible) Canaan, the land promised by God to Abraham and his descendants. **3.** *(often l.c.)* a place believed to hold great happiness: *They thought that America would be the promised land.*

prom·is·ing (prom′i sing), *adj.* giving promise of excellence, success, etc.; giving reason to hope for the best: *He's a talented and promising young man.* —**prom′is·ing·ly,** *adv.*

prom·is·so·ry (prom′i sôr′ē), *adj.* containing a promise.

prom′issory note′, a written promise to pay a certain sum of money at a stated time or on demand.

prom·on·to·ry (prom′ən tôr′ē), *n., pl.* **prom·on·to·ries.** a high point of land or rock jutting out into the sea or other body of water; headland: *a lighthouse set high on a promontory.*

pro·mote (prə mōt′), *v.,* **pro·mot·ed, pro·mot·ing. 1.** to work for or toward; help the progress of; further: *Exercise promotes good health.* **2.** to advance in rank, position, grade, etc.: *to promote a student to a higher grade.* **3.** to try to make (a business, product, etc.) successful or popular, esp. by advertising: *a campaign to promote a new brand of toothpaste.*

pro·mot·er (prə mō′tər), *n.* **1.** a person who works to develop or make popular a business, product, personality, etc. **2.** any person or thing that promotes or furthers something.

pro·mo·tion (prə mō′shən), *n.* **1.** advancement in rank, grade, or position: *The teacher recommended Jim for promotion.* **2.** advancement or encouragement; furtherance: *to work for the promotion of peace.* **3.** activities carried on to further a business, product, cause, etc.; advertising; publicity: *promotion for a new movie.*

prompt (prompt), *adj.* **1.** done or given without delay: *a prompt answer; to give prompt service.* **2.** quick to act or react: *She's always prompt to correct the mistakes of others.* **3.** punctual or on time: *You have to be prompt when you have an appointment.* —*v.* **4.** to encourage or urge; inspire to action: *His sad story prompted me to offer my help.* **5.** to inspire or give rise to: *What prompted his change of attitude?* **6.** to supply (an actor, singer, etc.) with lines or words that he has forgotten. —**prompt′ly,** *adv.* —**prompt′ness,** *n.*

prompt·er (promp′tər), *n.* **1.** (in a theater) a person offstage whose job is to supply performers with forgotten lines or to repeat cues. **2.** a person or thing that prompts.

promp·ti·tude (promp′ti tōōd′, -tyōōd′), *n.* the quality of being prompt; promptness.

prom·ul·gate (prom′əl gāt′, prō mul′gāt), *v.,* **prom·ul·gat·ed, prom·ul·gat·ing. 1.** to put (a law, decree, etc.) into operation. **2.** to set forth or teach publicly: *to promulgate a belief.* —**prom·ul·ga·tion** (prom′əl gā′shən, prō′məl gā′shən), *n.* —**prom′ul·ga·tor,** *n.*

pron., **1.** pronoun. **2.** pronunciation.

prone (prōn), *adj.* **1.** having a natural tendency; liable or disposed: *to be prone to anger.* **2.** having the front part facing downward; lying with the face downward: *The wounded soldier was prone on the ground.* —**prone′ly,** *adv.* —**prone′ness,** *n.*

prong (prông, prong), *n.* **1.** one of the points of a fork; tine. **2.** any pointed, projecting part: *the prong of an antler.*

pronged (prôngd, prongd), *adj.* having a prong or prongs.

prong·horn (prông′hôrn′, prong′-), *n., pl.* **prong·horns** *or* **prong·horn.** an animal resembling an antelope found on the plains of western North America.

pro·nom·i·nal (prō nom′ə nəl), *adj.* **1.** of or referring to a pronoun: *a word having a pronominal form.* **2.** derived from a pronoun: *"My" is a pronominal adjective.*

pro·noun (prō′noun′), *n.* a word used in place of a noun or noun phrase. Some common pronouns are *I, you, he, she, it, this, who,* and *what.*

Pronghorn
(3 ft. high at shoulder)

pro·nounce (prə nouns′), *v.,* **pro·nounced, pro·nounc·ing. 1.** to utter the sound or sounds of (a word, name, syllable, etc.); say aloud: *He has trouble pronouncing words with "th" in them.* **2.** to announce or declare, esp. formally: *The doctor pronounced him cured.* —**pro·nounc′er,** *n.*

pro·nounced (prə nounst′), *adj.* quite apparent; decided: *He walked with a pronounced limp.* —**pro·nounc·ed·ly** (prə noun′sid lē), *adv.*

pro·nounce·ment (prə nouns′mənt), *n.* **1.** a formal or official statement: *the pronouncements of a judge.* **2.** the act of declaring or pronouncing.

pro·nun·ci·a·tion (prə nun′sē ā′shən), *n.* **1.** the act or manner of pronouncing words, phrases, syllables, etc.: *The pronunciation of Chinese words is difficult. Her pronunciation is very clear.* **2.** a standard or correct way of pronouncing or saying words, a language, etc.: *What is the pronunciation of your name?*

proof (prōōf), *n.* **1.** facts or evidence showing that something is true or believable: *What proof is there that the earth is round?* **2.** the act or method of establishing that something is true; demonstration: *The proof of your alibi is not going to be easy.* **3.** a trial or test: *to put a new invention to the proof.* **4.** (in printing, lithography, etc.) a trial impression printed to see if corrections are needed. **5.** (in photography) a trial print from a negative. —*adj.* **6.** able to withstand or overcome: *He was proof against all temptations to cheat.*

-proof, a suffix used to form adjectives meaning resistant to or protected against: *waterproof; bombproof.*

proof·read (prōōf′rēd′), *v.,* **proof·read** (prōōf′red′), **proof·read·ing.** to read (printed material) in order to find and correct mistakes. —**proof′read′er,** *n.*

prop¹ (prop), *n.* **1.** a support or object, such as a stick or beam, used to hold something up: *If we can find some props we can make a tent from this sheet.* —*v.,* **propped, prop·ping. 2.** to support with a prop or props: *to prop an old fence.* **3.** to rest (an object) against a support: *Prop the ladder against the wall.* [from the Middle English word *proppe*]

prop² (prop), *n. Informal.* See **property** (def. 5).

prop³ (prop), *n. Informal.* a propeller of a plane, boat, etc.

prop., **1.** properly. **2.** property. **3.** proprietor.

prop·a·gan·da (prop′ə gan′də), *n.* **1.** information, ideas, rumors, etc., deliberately spread in order to influence public opinion: *to publish propaganda against air pollution; to broadcast war propaganda.* **2.** the process and techniques of spreading such information and ideas: *an expert in propaganda.*

prop·a·gan·dist (prop′ə gan′dist), *n.* **1.** a person who creates or spreads propaganda. —*adj.* **2.** of or like propaganda: *propagandist literature.*

prop·a·gan·dize (prop′ə gan′dīz), *v.,* **prop·a·gan·dized, prop·a·gan·diz·ing. 1.** to spread propaganda. **2.** to publicize and spread (ideas, teachings, etc.) by means of propaganda: *The newspapers propagan-*

dized the scientists' views. **3.** to subject (a person, group, etc.) to propaganda; spread propaganda among: *to propagandize soldiers.*

prop·a·gate (prop′ə gāt′), *v.,* **prop·a·gat·ed, prop·a·gat·ing. 1.** to cause (a plant or animal) to multiply or breed. **2.** to multiply or breed. **3.** to transmit (light, sound, heat, etc.) through a medium, such as air, or through empty space. **4.** to spread (information, customs, etc.) from one person or group to another: *to propagate the faith.* —**prop′a·ga′tion,** *n.* —**prop′a·ga′tor,** *n.*

pro·pel (prə pel′), *v.,* **pro·pelled, pro·pel·ling.** to cause to move forward or onward; drive or push forward: *They used a pole to propel their raft.*

pro·pel·lant (prə pel′ənt), *n.* **1.** the substance, usually fuel and oxidizer, that propels a rocket. **2.** the explosive that fires a projectile from a gun.

pro·pel·lent (prə pel′ənt), *adj.* **1.** acting or able to propel or drive something forward: *a propellent force.* —*n.* **2.** another spelling of **propellant.**

pro·pel·ler (prə pel′ər), *n.* **1.** a spinning, fanlike device for driving a boat or airplane. **2.** a person or thing that propels.

pro·pen·si·ty (prə pen′si tē), *n., pl.* **pro·pen·si·ties.** a natural inclination or tendency: *a propensity for dropping things.*

prop·er (prop′ər), *adj.* **1.** appropriate or suitable; right: *the proper time to plant strawberries; the proper tools for the job.* **2.** correct, esp. in meeting the standards of good manners and behavior; decorous: *It's not proper to wear a bathing suit in town.* **3.** belonging to a particular person, thing, group, etc.; special: *Each kind of animal has its proper food.* **4.** in the strict sense of the word: *Shellfish are not among the fishes proper.* **5.** (in grammar) referring to a particular person or thing. Proper nouns and adjectives are usually capitalized, such as *John, Chicago, Monday,* or *American.* **6.** complete or thorough: *The boy got a proper thrashing.* —**prop′er·ness,** *n.*

prop′er frac′tion, a fraction, such as ²/₃, ³/₄, ¹/₆, etc., in which the numerator is smaller than the denominator. See also **improper fraction.**

prop·er·ly (prop′ər lē), *adv.* **1.** in a proper manner. **2.** correctly; without mistakes: *Copy this properly.*

prop′er noun′, a noun used as the name of a particular person, place, or thing, such as *John, London,* or *Chevrolet.* See also **common noun.**

prop·er·ty (prop′ər tē), *n., pl.* for defs 3, 5 **prop·er·ties. 1.** the total of one's possessions: *She will inherit her grandfather's property.* **2.** something that is owned; possession: *Is this pen your property?* **3.** land or a piece of land: *He's bought property near the lake.* **4.** an essential or special quality or characteristic of something: *Heat is a property of fire.* **5.** any movable item used on the set of a play, motion picture, etc.

proph·e·cy (prof′i sē), *n., pl.* **proph·e·cies. 1.** the act or power of foretelling future events: *God granted him the gift of prophecy.* **2.** something that is declared by a prophet, esp. a prediction or message inspired by God. **3.** any prediction of future events.

proph·e·sy (prof′i sī′), *v.,* **proph·e·sied, proph·e·sy·ing. 1.** to foretell or predict: *to prophesy the end of the world.* **2.** to make predictions, esp. by divine inspiration; give God's word to man: *The disciples went among the people prophesying.* —**proph′e·si′er,** *n.*

proph·et (prof′it), *n.* **1.** a person who speaks with or as if with divine inspiration; one who speaks for God to men. **2.** any person who foretells future events or makes predictions. **3.** an inspired teacher or leader. Also, *referring to a woman,* **proph′et·ess.**

pro·phet·ic (prə fet′ik), *adj.* **1.** of or concerning a prophet: *prophetic inspiration.* **2.** of the nature of or containing prophecy: *prophetic writings.* **3.** foretelling or predicting future events, esp. something bad: *No one heeded his prophetic warnings that disaster was near.* —**pro·phet′i·cal·ly,** *adv.*

pro·phy·lac·tic (prō′fə lak′tik, prof′ə lak′tik), *adj.* protecting from disease or infection: *a prophylactic drug.*

pro·pi·ti·ate (prə pish′ē āt′), *v.,* **pro·pi·ti·at·ed, pro·pi·ti·at·ing.** to make favorable or friendly; appease; conciliate: *to offer sacrifices to propitiate the gods.* —**pro·pi′ti·a′tion,** *n.* —**pro·pi′ti·a′tor,** *n.*

pro·pi·tious (prə pish′əs), *adj.* favorable or helpful; providing advantage: *The weather was propitious for boating on the lake.* —**pro·pi′tious·ly,** *adv.* —**pro·pi′tious·ness,** *n.*

prop·jet (prop′jet′), *n.* **1.** a jet engine in which most of the energy produced is used to drive a conventional propeller. **2.** an airplane powered by one or more such engines. See also **fanjet, turbojet.**

pro·po·nent (prə pō′nənt), *n.* a person who puts forward or supports a proposal, plan, theory, etc.: *a proponent of states' rights.*

pro·por·tion (prə pôr′shən), *n.* **1.** the numerical relationship between two things; ratio: *The proportion of sugar to water is greater in syrup than in fruit juice.* **2.** a proper or pleasing balance or relationship; harmony: *The horse's huge head was out of proportion to his small body.* **3. proportions,** dimensions or size: *a building of vast proportions.* **4.** a share or part: *You'll have to do a certain proportion of the work yourself.* **5.** a group of four numbers in which the relationship between the first pair is the same as that between the second pair, such as 6 : 3 = 4 : 2. —*v.* **6.** to adjust in size so as to achieve a proper relationship or balance: *to proportion taxes according to people's ability to pay.* **7.** to balance or harmonize the parts or proportions of: *to proportion a drawing of the human figure.* —**pro·por′tion·ment,** *n.*

pro·por·tion·al (prə pôr′shə nəl), *adj.* **1.** having or being in proportion: *Your rent should be proportional to your income.* **2.** of, relating to, or in the form of a proportion. —**pro·por′tion·al·ly,** *adv.*

pro·por·tion·ate (prə pôr′shə nit), *adj.* **1.** being in proportion; proportional: *a proportionate division of the prize money.* —*v.* (prə pôr′shə nāt′), **pro·por·tion·at·ed, pro·por·tion·at·ing. 2.** to proportion or make proportional. —**pro·por′tion·ate·ly,** *adv.*

pro·pos·al (prə pō′zəl), *n.* **1.** a plan or scheme that is put forward for acceptance: *Will you vote for Bill's* *proposal that we start our own newspaper?* **2.** the act of suggesting a plan or scheme for acceptance; a proposing: *Her proposal of a different plan surprised us all.* **3.** an offer of marriage.

pro·pose (prə pōz′), *v.,* **pro·posed, pro·pos·ing. 1.** to offer (a plan, scheme, etc.) for acceptance or consideration; suggest: *to propose a school budget.* **2.** to suggest or nominate (a person) for office, membership, etc. **3.** to plan or intend: *What do you propose to do now?* **4.** to make an offer of marriage: *Her boyfriend proposed last night.* —**pro·pos′er,** *n.*

prop·o·si·tion (prop′ə zish′ən), *n.* **1.** a plan or scheme; proposal. **2.** an offer of terms for a business transaction: *If he wants to sell his business, we'll make him a proposition.* **3.** anything stated for purposes of discussion; statement: *The proposition you must debate is, "There are no limits to the right of free speech."* **4.** (in mathematics) a statement of a truth to be demonstrated or an operation to be performed. **5.** anything that must be done or dealt with: *Winning this game is going to be a tough proposition.*

pro·pound (prə pound′), *v.* to put forward for consideration or acceptance; propose or suggest: *to propound a new theory.* —**pro·pound′er,** *n.*

pro·pri·e·tar·y (prə prī′i ter′ē), *adj.* **1.** of or like a proprietor or owner: *He has proprietary curiosity about everything that goes on in his store.* **2.** of or concerning property or ownership: *proprietary rights.* **3.** (of a product) manufactured and sold only by the owner of the patent, trademark, etc.: *a proprietary medicine.*

pro·pri·e·tor (prə prī′i tər), *n.* the owner of a business, patent, or the like. Also, *referring to a woman,* **pro·pri′e·tress.** —**pro·pri′e·tor·ship′,** *n.*

pro·pri·e·ty (prə prī′i tē), *n., pl.* **pro·pri·e·ties. 1.** correctness or rightness, esp. with regard to manners and good conduct: *A gentleman behaves with propriety.* **2.** the **proprieties,** customary standards of behavior; manners: *to observe the proprieties.*

pro·pul·sion (prə pul′shən), *n.* **1.** a propelling or driving forward: *an engine for the propulsion of a boat.* **2.** a driving force or impulse.

pro·sa·ic (prō zā′ik), *adj.* **1.** commonplace or dull; lacking imagination or interest: *marketing, housecleaning, and other prosaic tasks.* **2.** of or like prose. —**pro·sa′i·cal·ly,** *adv.* —**pro·sa′ic·ness,** *n.*

pro·scribe (prō skrīb′), *v.,* **pro·scribed, pro·scrib·ing. 1.** to speak or write against; condemn; denounce: *to proscribe unlawful violence.* **2.** to prohibit or forbid: *to proscribe smoking in school.* **3.** to banish or exile. —**pro·scrib′er,** *n.*

pro·scrip·tion (prō skrip′shən), *n.* **1.** the act of proscribing, forbidding, or condemning: *The students protested the proscription of their newspaper.* **2.** the state of being proscribed: *The proscription of all public meetings continued for a month.* **3.** banishment or exile. —**pro·scrip·tive** (prō skrip′tiv), *adj.*

prose (prōz), *n.* spoken or written language that is not poetry; ordinary language without meter or rhyme.

pros·e·cute (pros′ə kyōōt′), *v.,* **pros·e·cut·ed, pros·e·cut·ing. 1.** to bring (a person, case, etc.) to trial in a court of law; carry on a legal action against (someone): *The state is prosecuting him on a charge of blackmail.* **2.** to follow up and complete (something one has undertaken): *to prosecute an investigation.*

pros·e·cu·tion (pros′ə kyōō′shən), *n.* **1.** the act or process of beginning and carrying on a legal action in a court of law: *the prosecution of a criminal.* **2.** the officials who are in charge of such an action. **3.** the continuation and completion of something that one has begun: *the prosecution of a task.*

pros·e·cu·tor (pros′ə kyōō′tər), *n.* **1.** Also, **pros′ecuting attor′ney.** the public officer in charge of the prosecution at a trial. **2.** a person who prosecutes.

pros·e·lyte (pros′ə līt′), *n.* **1.** a person who has changed to a different religion, belief, opinion, etc.; convert. —*v.,* **pros·e·lyt·ed, pros·e·lyt·ing. 2.** to try to convert; proselytize.

pros·e·lyt·ize (pros′ə li tīz′), *v.,* **pros·e·lyt·ized, pros·e·lyt·iz·ing.** to convert or work to convert (a person or persons), esp. to a new religion.

Pro·ser·pi·na (prō sûr′pə nə), *n.* another name for Persephone. Also, **Pro·ser·pi·ne** (prō sûr′pə nē).

pros·o·dy (pros′ə dē), *n.* **1.** the study of poetic meters and the art of writing verse. **2.** a particular system of meter and verse: *Shakespeare's prosody.*

pros·pect (pros′pekt), *n.* **1.** Usually, **prospects.** the probability of success, profit, etc., in the future: *Business prospects are good.* **2.** a looking forward; expectation or hope: *the prospect of visiting Hawaii.* **3.** an outlook or view: *the prospect from a window.* **4.** a possible customer, candidate, client, etc.: *I haven't sold any houses yet, but I've met a few prospects.* —*v.* **5.** to explore (a region) in search of gold, silver, oil, etc. **6.** to work (a mine); take gold or the like from (land one has claimed).

pro·spec·tive (prə spek′tiv), *adj.* **1.** of or in the future: *prospective earnings.* **2.** potential, likely, or expected: *a prospective buyer.* —**pro·spec′tive·ly,** *adv.*

pros·pec·tor (pros′pek tər), *n.* a person who explores a region in search of gold, silver, oil, etc., or who works a mine or claim.

pro·spec·tus (prə spek′təs), *n.* a report describing a forthcoming project.

pros·per (pros′pər), *v.* to be successful or fortunate, esp. financially: *Business is prospering.*

pros·per·i·ty (pro sper′i tē), *n.* the state of flourishing or prospering; good fortune; success: *a happy time of peace and prosperity.*

pros·per·ous (pros′pər əs), *adj.* successful or flourishing; having or marked by good fortune: *a prosperous ranch; a prosperous banker.* —**pros′per·ous·ly,** *adv.* —**pros′per·ous·ness,** *n.*

pros·ti·tute (pros′ti tōōt′, -tyōōt′), *n.* **1.** a woman who engages in sexual acts with men for money; harlot. —*v.,* **pros·ti·tut·ed, pros·ti·tut·ing. 2.** to hire (oneself) out as a prostitute. **3.** to put to an unworthy or immoral use; misuse or cheapen for the sake of money: *to prostitute one's talent as a writer.*

pros·ti·tu·tion (pros'ti tōō'shən, -tyōō'-), *n.* **1.** the act or practice of engaging in sexual acts with men for money: *a campaign to wipe out prostitution.* **2.** base or unworthy use of something valuable, esp. talent or ability.

pros·trate (pros'trāt), *v.*, **pros·trat·ed, pros·trat·ing. 1.** to cast (oneself) face down on the ground: *They prostrated themselves before the emperor.* **2.** to throw or lay flat; flatten: *to prostrate someone with a punch to the head.* **3.** to overthrow or overcome; cause to be helpless: *The terrible heat prostrated her.* —*adj.* **4.** lying flat; stretched out on the ground, esp. with the face or front part downward: *The prostrate prize fighter never even heard the bell.* **5.** overcome or exhausted; helpless: *The soldiers were prostrate after marching all day and all night.*

pros·tra·tion (pro strā'shən), *n.* **1.** the act of prostrating, esp. lying face down on the ground: *the prostration of oneself before an altar in worship of God.* **2.** the state of being prostrated. **3.** extreme physical or mental exhaustion; weakness or depression: *to be in a state of prostration and unable to work.*

pros·y (prō'zē), *adj.*, **pros·i·er, pros·i·est. 1.** of or like prose. **2.** dull, commonplace, or tiresome; prosaic. —**pros'i·ly,** *adv.* —**pros'i·ness,** *n.*

Prot., Protestant.

pro·tac·tin·i·um (prō'tak tin'ē əm), *n.* *Chem.* a radioactive, metallic element. *Symbol:* Pa Also, **pro·toactinium.**

pro·te·an (prō'tē ən, prō tē'ən), *adj.* changing form or appearance readily; variable: *protean clouds.*

pro·tect (prə tekt'), *v.* to defend or guard from attack, harm, danger, etc.; shield from injury: *to protect the kitten from a dog; to wear a helmet to protect one's head.*

pro·tect·ing (prə tek'tiñg), *adj.* giving protection or shelter: *The baby lay in his mother's protecting arms.* —**pro·tect'ing·ly,** *adv.*

pro·tec·tion (prə tek'shən), *n.* **1.** the act of protecting or guarding from harm, loss, etc.: *Your job is the protection of our secret maps.* **2.** the state of being protected: *to be under police protection.* **3.** anything that protects, guards, shields, etc.: *You need a protection for your head in this hot sun.*

pro·tec·tive (prə tek'tiv), *adj.* serving or designed to protect, shield, or guard: *protective armor; a bird's protective coloring.* —**pro·tec'tive·ly,** *adv.* —**pro·tec'tive·ness,** *n.*

protec'tive colora'tion, the coloring possessed by some animals that makes them resemble their surroundings and thus less easily seen by the animals that prey on them. Also, **protec'tive col'oring.**

pro·tec·tor (prə tek'tər), *n.* **1.** a person who protects; defender or guardian. **2.** something that protects; shield or guard. Also, *referring to a woman,* **pro·tec·tress** (prə tek'tris).

pro·tec·tor·ate (prə tek'tər it), *n.* **1.** a territory or state that is protected and partly controlled by a

more powerful state. **2.** the relation between a strong state and its protectorate: *The U.S. holds a protectorate over these islands.*

pro·té·gé (prō'tə zhā'), *n.* a person who is aided and guided in his career by someone of power or influence: *The famous pianist arranged a concert for his protégé.* Also, *referring to a woman,* **pro·té·gée'.**

pro·tein (prō'tēn, prō'tē in), *n.* any of a large group of chemical compounds that contain nitrogen and make up most of the living parts of plants and animals. Proteins are necessary for life and are supplied by meat, fish, eggs, milk, and other foods in the diet.

Prot·er·o·zo·ic e'ra (prot'ər ə zō'ik, prō'tər ə zō'-ik), the geological period following the Archeozoic era and extending from about 1½ billion to about 600 million years ago.

pro·test (prō'test), *n.* **1.** a formal complaint or strong objection; expression of disapproval: *to make a protest against dangerous working conditions.* —*v.* (prə test'). **2.** to make a formal complaint or protest; object to (something): *The players protested the referee's decision.* **3.** to declare earnestly or positively; assert (one's innocence, good intentions, etc.) in answer to an accusation: *The prisoner protested that he was innocent.* —**pro·test'er,** *n.* —**pro·test'ing·ly,** *adv.*

Prot·es·tant (prot'i stənt), *n.* **1.** any Christian of Europe or the Americas who is not a member of the Roman Catholic Church or the Eastern Church. —*adj.* **2.** of or concerning Protestants or their religion. —**Prot'es·tant·ism,** *n.*

Prot'estant Epis'copal Church', a Protestant church in the U.S., related to the Church of England.

prot·es·ta·tion (prot'i stā'shən, prō'ti stā'shən), *n.* **1.** the act of protesting or asserting. **2.** an earnest declaration: *a protestation of innocence.* **3.** a protest or formal objection.

pro·to·ac·tin·i·um (prō'tō ak tin'ē əm), *n.* another spelling of **protactinium.**

pro·to·col (prō'tə kôl'), *n.* the customs and rules of etiquette among diplomats and state officials: *According to protocol, the secretary of state should welcome the visiting prime minister.*

pro·ton (prō'ton), *n.* a particle found in the nucleus of an atom having a positive charge equal to the negative charge on an electron and a mass 1836 times that of an electron. The number of protons in the nucleus is different for each of the elements.

pro·to·plasm (prō'tə plaz'əm), *n.* a cloudy jellylike material that is the basic living substance in all plant and animal cells.

pro·to·type (prō'tə tīp'), *n.* an original or model on which something is patterned: *The Wright brothers built the prototype of many later airplanes.*

pro·to·zo·an (prō'tə zō'ən), *n.*, *pl.* **pro·to·zo·ans** or **pro·to·zo·a** (prō'tə zō'ə). any member of the important group of microscopic animals that consist only of a single cell or colony of similar cells.

pro·tract (prō trakt'), *v.* to draw out or lengthen, esp. in time; prolong: *The discussion period was protracted by numerous questions.* —**pro·tract'ed·ly,** *adv.* —**pro·trac·tion** (prō trak'shən), *n.*

pro·trac·tor (prō trak′tər), *n.* an instrument for measuring or drawing angles.

pro·trude (prō trōōd′), *v.,* **pro·trud·ed, pro·trud·ing.** **1.** to jut or stick out; project: *She noticed a large key protruding from the lock.* **2.** to thrust out or forward: *The cat protruded its claws.*

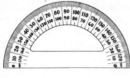

Protractor

pro·tru·sion (prō trōō′zhən), *n.* **1.** the act of protruding or sticking out: *The lizard caught the fly with a quick protrusion of its tongue.* **2.** the state of being protruded; a jutting out: *to have difficulty chewing because of the protrusion of one's front teeth.* **3.** something that protrudes or sticks out: *We took shelter under a narrow protrusion of rock.*

pro·tu·ber·ance (prō tōō′bər əns, -tyōō′-), *n.* **1.** a bulge or swelling: *a protuberance on one's chin.* **2.** the state of being swollen out or bulging: *The protuberance of the frog's eyes gave it a startled expression.*

pro·tu·ber·ant (prō tōō′bər ənt, -tyōō′-), *adj.* bulging out beyond the surrounding surface.

proud (proud), *adj.* **1.** having self-respect; dignified: *a brave and proud people who did not surrender easily.* **2.** feeling honored or greatly pleased because of an achievement or the like (often fol. by *of* or an infinitive): *She is proud of the medal she won.* **3.** thinking too well of oneself; conceited; arrogant. **4.** giving reason to feel pride: *It was a proud moment when we finally reached the top of the mountain.* **5.** majestic or grand: *a proud oak tree; a proud stallion.* —**proud′ly,** *adv.*

Prov., Province.

prove (prōōv), *v.,* **proved; proved** *or* **prov·en** (prōō′vən); **prov·ing. 1.** to show the truth or correctness of (something): *Do you have evidence to prove that statement?* **2.** to show to be genuine or valid: *This contract proves his right to payment.* **3.** to show (oneself) to have certain worthwhile or expected qualities: *She proved herself loyal in times of trouble.* **4.** to test or establish the quality of (something): *methods to prove a new fabric.* **5.** to turn out or be found to be: *The experiment proved successful.* [from the Old French word *prover,* which comes from Latin *probāre* "to try, test, prove"]

Pro·ven·çal (prov′ən säl′), *n.* **1.** a Romance language formerly spoken and written in Provence and other parts of southern France and still spoken today as a local dialect. **2.** a native or inhabitant of Provence. —*adj.* **3.** of or referring to Provence, its people, or their language: *a Provençal folk dance.*

Pro·vence (prə väns′), *n.* a region in SE France, bordering on the Mediterranean Sea.

prov·en·der (prov′ən dər), *n.* **1.** dry food for livestock. **2.** food of any sort; provisions.

prov·erb (prov′ərb), *n.* **1.** a short popular saying that expresses a truth or useful thought, for example "A

stitch in time saves nine." **2.** (in the Bible) a profound saying that requires interpretation.

pro·ver·bi·al (prə vûr′bē əl), *adj.* **1.** of, concerning, or like a proverb: *proverbial wisdom.* **2.** well-known through frequent mention: *He is as poor as the proverbial church mouse.* —**pro·ver′bi·al·ly,** *adv.*

Prov·erbs (prov′ərbz), *n. (used as sing.)* a book of the Old Testament, containing wise sayings.

pro·vide (prə vīd′), *v.,* **pro·vid·ed, pro·vid·ing. 1.** to furnish, supply, or equip: *to provide food to hungry travelers; to provide soldiers with weapons.* **2.** to prepare for in advance: *to provide for a rainy day.* **3.** to take care of the needs of a person, family, etc. (often fol. by *for*): *He has always provided for his family. God will provide.* **4.** to state or arrange as a necessary condition or as something that must be done: *The treaty provides that both countries will withdraw troops from the border.* —**pro·vid′er,** *n.*

pro·vid·ed (prə vī′did), *conj.* on the condition or understanding; if: *I'll go, provided it doesn't rain.*

prov·i·dence (prov′i dəns), *n.* **1.** *(often cap.)* the foreseeing care, guidance, and protection of God or nature: *We must hope that providence will aid us.* **2.** thrifty preparation for the future; prudent care for money or other resources: *Thanks to your providence we shall be comfortable in our old age.*

Prov·i·dence (prov′i dəns), *n.* **1.** God, esp. as the provider of divine guidance and protection to His creatures. **2.** a seaport and the capital city of Rhode Island, in the NE part.

prov·i·dent (prov′i dənt), *adj.* having or showing foresight and care for the future: *a provident father; provident savings.* —**prov′i·dent·ly,** *adv.*

prov·i·den·tial (prov′i den′shəl), *adj.* of, concerning, or due to divine providence: *a providential rescue.* —**prov′i·den′tial·ly,** *adv.*

pro·vid·ing (prə vī′ding), *conj.* on the condition or understanding; provided; if: *He can stay, providing he does his share of the work.*

prov·ince (prov′ins), *n.* **1.** a major division or unit of a country, having its own local government. A province is similar to a state in the U.S. **2. the provinces,** the parts of a country outside of the capital or the largest cities. **3.** a particular area or sphere of activity, authority, knowledge, etc.: *Giving out information to the newspapers is not within my province.*

pro·vin·cial (prə vin′shəl), *adj.* **1.** of, concerning, or coming from a particular province: *a provincial cheese; the provincial government.* **2.** of, concerning, or coming from the hinterlands or provinces: *provincial workers; provincial customs.* **3.** unsophisticated or narrow: *a provincial view of other people's tastes.* —*n.* **4.** a person who lives in or comes from the provinces. —**pro·vin′cial·ly,** *adv.*

pro·vin·cial·ism (prə vin′shə liz′əm), *n.* **1.** lack of sophistication; narrowness of mind or attitude. **2.** a word, expression, or the like, that is characteristic of a particular region: *"Critter" is a provincialism for "creature."*

pro·vi·sion (prə vizh′ən), *n.* 1. the act of supplying or providing: *He is in charge of the provision of food for the soldiers.* 2. **provisions,** a supply of food. 3. an arrangement made beforehand: *What provisions have you made in case it rains on the day of our picnic?* 4. a statement of a condition or requirement to be met: *the provisions of a contract.* —*v.* 5. to supply with food: *to provision troops.* —**pro·vi′sion·er,** *n.*

pro·vi·sion·al (prə vizh′ə nəl), *adj.* 1. temporary or for a limited time only: *a provisional government.* 2. made with certain reservations; conditional: *a provisional agreement.* —**pro·vi′sion·al·ly,** *adv.*

prov·o·ca·tion (prov′ə kā′shən), *n.* 1. the act of provoking or rousing: *Provocation of the enemy would be dangerous.* 2. something that serves to provoke, arouse, etc.: *insults and other provocations.*

pro·voc·a·tive (prə vok′ə tiv), *adj.* provoking or tending to provoke anger, interest, activity, etc.: *The lawyer's provocative questions upset the witness.* —**pro·voc′a·tive·ly,** *adv.* —**pro·voc′a·tive·ness,** *n.*

pro·voke (prə vōk′), *v.,* **pro·voked, pro·vok·ing.** 1. to anger or irritate: *The way he complains always provokes me.* 2. to arouse feelings or activity in: *What finally provoked her into cleaning her room?* 3. to stir up or bring on: *The cruel laws provoked a revolution.* —**pro·vok′er,** *n.* —**pro·vok′ing·ly,** *adv.*

prov·ost (prov′əst, prō′vōst), *n.* 1. a high-ranking official of a college or university who has charge of appointing teachers, scheduling classes, etc. 2. any person appointed to preside or supervise.

prow (prou), *n.* the most forward part of a ship or boat; bow.

prow·ess (prou′is), *n.* 1. unusual bravery, esp. in battle: *a warrior of great prowess.* 2. outstanding ability: *to show prowess as a violinist.*

prowl (proul), *v.* 1. to move about (a place) in a quiet, secret way hunting for food, plunder, etc.: *Thieves prowled the dark streets.* —*n.* 2. the act of prowling; hunt: *The cat went on a prowl through the barn.* 3. **on the prowl,** roving and hunting: *a lion on the prowl.* —**prowl′er,** *n.*

prox·im·i·ty (prok sim′i tē), *n.* nearness in space, time, relation, etc.: *We often go to that park because of its proximity to our school.*

prox·y (prok′sē), *n., pl.* **prox·ies.** 1. the power or function of a person who is authorized to act for another: *If you can't be at the meeting, you can vote by proxy.* 2. a document granting such power. 3. a person who is authorized to act for another: *His proxy will take charge of selling the house.*

prude (prōōd), *n.* a person who is extremely prim and proper, esp. in speech or dress.

pru·dence (prōōd′əns), *n.* care and caution in practical matters; good judgment, esp. in providing for the future: *to use prudence in spending one's money.*

pru·dent (prōōd′ənt), *adj.* 1. wise and careful in practical matters, esp. in providing for the future: *A prudent man doesn't gamble his money away.* 2. showing such care and good judgment: *a prudent decision to learn to swim.* —**pru′dent·ly,** *adv.*

pru·den·tial (prōō den′shəl), *adj.* of, concerning, or showing prudence and care: *prudential savings.* —**pru·den′tial·ly,** *adv.*

prud·er·y (prōō′də rē), *n., pl.* for def. 2 **prud·er·ies.** 1. extreme modesty or primness, esp. in one's dress or behavior: *Her prudery prevented her from enjoying the dancing.* 2. a prudish word, speech, or act: *To say "limb" instead of "leg" is a prudery.*

prud·ish (prōō′dish), *adj.* extremely proper and modest; of or like a prude: *a prudish girl; to have a narrow, prudish attitude.* —**prud′ish·ly,** *adv.* —**prud′ish·ness,** *n.*

prune[1] (prōōn), *n.* 1. a kind of plum that dries without spoiling. 2. such a plum when dried. [from an Old French word, which comes from Greek *proûmnon* "plum." See *plum*]

prune[2] (prōōn), *v.,* **pruned, prun·ing.** 1. to cut off (unwanted twigs, branches, or roots): *to prune dead branches from a tree.* 2. to trim by cutting off twigs, branches, etc.: *to prune a rosebush.* 3. to remove (something unwanted): *to prune the slang from a speech.* 4. to clear of what is unwanted: *to prune an essay.* [from the Middle English word *prouynen,* which comes from Old French *provigner*]

Prus·sia (prush′ə), *n.* a former state in N Europe. It became a military power in the 18th century and was formally abolished in 1947. —**Prus′sian,** *n., adj.*

1871-1914

pry[1] (prī), *v.,* **pried, pry·ing.** 1. to inquire into private matters; snoop: *The detective pried into the man's past.* 2. to look closely or curiously; peer. [from the Middle English word *pryen*]

pry[2] (prī), *v.,* **pried, pry·ing.** 1. to move, raise, or open with a lever: *to pry open a door with a crowbar; to pry a rock out of frozen ground.* 2. to obtain with difficulty: *to pry information out of someone.* [from the dialectal word *prize* "a lever," which comes from Old French *prise* "a seizing." See *prize*[1]]

P.S., 1. postscript. 2. Public School.

p.s., postscript.

psalm (säm), *n.* a sacred song or hymn.

psalm·ist (sä′mist), *n.* 1. the author of a psalm or psalms. 2. **the Psalmist,** David, the traditional author of the Psalms.

Psalms (sämz), *n. (used as sing.)* a book of the Old Testament, containing songs, hymns, and prayers.

Psal·ter (sôl′tər), *n.* 1. the Book of Psalms. 2. *(sometimes l.c.)* a book containing the Psalms, for use in church, private prayer, etc.

psal·ter·y (sôl′tə rē), *n., pl.* **psal·ter·ies.** an ancient musical instrument consisting of a flat box with numerous strings plucked with the fingers or with a plectrum.

Psaltery

pseu·do·nym (sōōd′ə nim), *n.* 1. a name used by a

person in order to conceal his real name. **2.** a pen name. [from the Greek word *pseudōnymon* "false name," which comes from *pseudēs* "false" + *onoma* "name."]

pshaw (shô), *interj.* (used to express disbelief, impatience, contempt, etc.): *"Pshaw," said the old man, "don't believe all the nonsense you hear!"*

psy·che (sī′kē), *n.* the human soul, spirit, or mind; the mental or psychological make-up of a person.

Psy·che (sī′kē), *n.* (in Greek mythology) a beautiful maiden loved by Eros.

psy·chi·a·trist (si kī′ə trist, sī kī′ə trist), *n.* a doctor who practices psychiatry or who treats those who are mentally ill or emotionally disturbed.

psy·chi·a·try (si kī′ə trē, sī kī′ə trē), *n.* (in medicine) the study and treatment of mental illness and emotional disorders. —**psy·chi·at·ric** (sī′kē a′trik), *adj.* —**psy′chi·at′ri·cal·ly,** *adv.*

psy·chic (sī′kik), *adj.* Also, **psy′chi·cal. 1.** of or concerning the human soul or mind; mental: *psychic suffering.* **2.** of, concerning, or caused by forces apparently beyond scientific knowledge; supernatural: *ghosts and other psychic phenomena.* **3.** sensitive to supernatural forces: *The medium claimed to be psychic.* —*n.* **4.** a person who is sensitive to supernatural phenomena. —**psy′chi·cal·ly,** *adv.*

psy·cho·a·nal·y·sis (sī′kō ə nal′i sis), *n.* a method for treating emotional disturbance in which the patient speaks of his feelings, dreams, memories, etc., in order to discover and solve his mental conflicts. —**psy·cho·a·nal·yt·ic** (sī′kō an′/ə lit′ik), **psy′cho·an′a·lyt′i·cal,** *adj.* —**psy′cho·an′a·lyt′i·cal·ly,** *adv.*

psy·cho·an·a·lyst (sī′kō an′/ə list), *n.* a person trained to practice psychoanalysis.

psy·cho·an·a·lyze (sī′kō an′/ə līz′), *v.,* **psy·cho·an·a·lyzed, psy·cho·an·a·lyz·ing.** to treat (a person) by means of psychoanalysis.

psy·cho·log·i·cal (sī′kə loj′i kəl), *adj.* **1.** of or concerning psychology or psychologists: *a psychological textbook.* **2.** of or concerning the mind, feelings, emotions, etc.: *He suffered a psychological shock when he was fired.* —**psy′cho·log′i·cal·ly,** *adv.*

psy·chol·o·gist (sī kol′ə jist), *n.* a specialist in psychology or the study of the mind and the emotions.

psy·chol·o·gy (sī kol′ə jē), *n., pl.* **psy·chol·o·gies. 1.** the study of the human mind and its functions. **2.** the study of human and animal behavior. **3.** the attitudes and behavior typical of a person or group: *The psychology of people changes during wartime.*

psy·cho·sis (sī kō′sis), *n., pl.* **psy·cho·ses** (sī kō′sēz). any major form of mental illness or disease. —**psy·chot·ic** (sī kot′ik), *n., adj.* —**psy·chot′i·cal·ly,** *adv.*

Pt, *Chem.* the symbol for **platinum.**

pt., **1.** part. **2.** payment. **3.** pint.

PTA, Parent-Teacher Association. Also, **P.T.A.**

ptar·mi·gan (tär′mə gən), *n., pl.* **ptar·mi·gans** *or* **ptar·mi·gan.** any of several kinds of grouse that are found in cold, usually mountainous climates and have feathers on the legs and feet.

pter·o·dac·tyl (ter′ə dak′til), *n.* any of various extinct flying reptiles related to the dinosaurs.

pto·maine (tō′mān), *n.* any of various poisonous substances produced when food decays. [from the Italian word *ptomaina,* which comes from Greek *ptoma* "dead body"]

Pterodactyl (wingspread to 20 ft.)

pto′maine poi′soning, an acutely painful stomach or intestinal condition caused by eating poisonous or contaminated food.

pts., **1.** parts. **2.** payments. **3.** pints.

Pu, *Chem.* the symbol for **plutonium.**

pub (pub), *n. British Informal.* a bar or tavern. [short for *public house*]

pu·ber·ty (pyōō′bər tē), *n.* the period or time at which a boy or girl first becomes physically mature and is able to produce offspring, usually between the ages of 12 and 14.

pub·lic (pub′lik), *adj.* **1.** of, concerning, or for the people of a nation, state, city, etc.: *a public holiday; a public outcry.* **2.** open to all persons; not private: *a public beach.* **3.** owned by the people of a community: *public buildings.* **4.** serving or working for the people of a nation, state, city, etc.: *a public official.* **5.** widely known; familiar to many people: *a public figure.* —*n.* **6.** the people who make up a nation, state, city, etc.: *This park is for the public.* **7.** a particular group of people who have something in common: *the book-buying public.* **8. in public,** among or in front of other people: *to appear in public.*

pub′lic-ad·dress′ sys′tem (pub′lik ə dres′), a system of microphones, amplifiers, loudspeakers, etc., for making a speech or music audible to large groups of people.

pub·li·can (pub′lə kən), *n.* **1.** (in ancient Rome) a tax collector. **2.** *British.* the owner or manager of a tavern.

pub·li·ca·tion (pub′lə kā′shən), *n.* **1.** something that is published, such as a magazine, newspaper, book, or the like. **2.** the act of publishing or bringing out a book, magazine, or the like.

pub′lic house′, **1.** *British.* a tavern or bar. **2.** an inn or hostel.

pub·lic·i·ty (pə blis′i tē), *n.* **1.** public notice or attention: *a young actress seeking publicity.* **2.** information given out to the public in order to attract attention to a person, cause, event, etc. **3.** the business or methods of bringing someone or something to the attention of the public: *She will take care of the publicity for our concert.*

pub·li·cize (pub′li sīz′), *v.,* **pub·li·cized, pub·li·ciz·ing.** to bring to the attention of the public; make widely known: *to publicize a new movie.*

pub·lic·ly (pub′lik lē), *adv.* **1.** in a public manner; not secretly or privately; openly: *He was publicly insulted.* **2.** by the public: *a publicly owned park.*

pub′lic opin′ion, the beliefs, opinions, and attitudes of the people of a nation, city, community, or the like, esp. on matters of public interest: *Public opinion favors a change of government.*

pub′lic school′, 1. an elementary school or high school that is paid for by government funds and is open to all students in the community without charge. 2. (in Great Britain) a private boarding school, esp. for boys.

pub·lic-spir·it·ed (pub′lik spir′i tid), *adj.* having or showing an unselfish interest in the well-being of the people of a nation, state, city, etc.: *a public-spirited man who donated parks to the city.*

pub′lic util′ity, a company or other business organization that performs a necessary public service, such as supplying electricity, water, transportation, or the like. Such companies are regulated by the federal, state, or local government.

pub′lic works′, things built for use by the public, out of public funds, such as roads or bridges.

pub·lish (pub′lish), *v.* 1. to print and offer for sale (a book, newspaper, map, engraving, etc.). 2. to print and offer for sale the work of (an author, artist, etc.): *to publish Shakespeare in paperback.* 3. to make publicly or generally known: *to publish the true facts concerning peace talks.*

pub·lish·er (pub′li shər), *n.* a person or company whose business is the printing and offering for sale of books, a newspaper, maps, or the like.

puck (puk), *n.* (in ice hockey) a black disk of hard rubber that is to be hit into the goal.

Puck (puk), *n.* a mischievous elf in folk tales.

puck·er (puk′ər), *v.* 1. to draw or gather together into wrinkles or folds: *Worry puckered his brow. The material puckered when the sewing machine jammed.* —*n.* 2. a puckered part; wrinkle or fold: *a pucker in a seam.*

pud·ding (pŏŏd′ing), *n.* 1. a thick soft dessert, often made of flour, milk, eggs, and sweetening. 2. a similar dish that is unsweetened and eaten as part of the main course: *corn pudding.*

pud·dle (pud′əl), *n.* 1. a small pool of water, esp. muddy or dirty water: *The road was full of puddles after the rain.* 2. a small pool of any liquid: *a puddle of spilled paint.*

pudg·y (puj′ē), *adj.,* **pudg·i·er, pudg·i·est.** short and fat or plump: *pudgy fingers; a pudgy little dog.* —**pudg′i·ness,** *n.*

pueb·lo (pweb′lō), *n., pl.* **pueb·los.** 1. the adobe or stone house or group of houses of certain Indians of Arizona and New Mexico. 2. an Indian village. [from a Spanish word meaning "people, town," which comes from Latin *populus* "people"]

Pueb·lo (pweb′lō), *n.* a member of the Indian people of Arizona and New Mexico who live in pueblos. The Pueblos are descendants of the cliff dwellers.

pu·er·ile (pyŏŏ′ər il, pyŏŏ′ə rīl′), *adj.* childishly foolish; immature: *a silly, puerile trick.*

Puer·to Ri·co (pwer′tə

rē′kō, pôr′tə), an island in the central West Indies: a commonwealth associated with the U.S. 3435 sq. mi. *Cap.:* San Juan. Former official name, **Porto Rico.** —**Puer′to Ri′can.**

puff (puf), *n.* 1. a short, quick forcing out or letting out of air, smoke, steam, or the like: *He blew out the candles with one puff.* 2. a short, quick blast or gust: *A puff of wind blew off her hat.* 3. a sound made by a short, quick blast of air, steam, or the like: *the puff of a steam engine.* 4. a small amount of air, smoke, steam, or the like, released in one blast or gust: *A puff of smoke rose in the distance.* 5. a quick breathing in and out. 6. a light pastry with a filling of whipped cream, jam, etc. 7. a soft pad: *a powder puff.* 8. a small swelling. 9. an arrangement of hair, fabric, etc., in a soft, rounded mass. —*v.* 10. to breathe quick and hard: *The horse was puffing after the race.* 11. to send forth or come forth in puffs or small gusts: *The engine puffed steam. Smoke was puffing from the chimney.* 12. to smoke (a cigar, cigarette, or the like) in puffs. 13. to swell, esp. with a gust or puff of air, wind, steam, or the like: *to puff out one's cheeks.* 14. to blow in gusts or puffs, as the wind does. 15. to move with a puffing sound: *The old train puffed out of the station.* 16. to arrange in puffs: *to puff one's hair.*

puf·fin (puf′in), *n.* any of several sea birds having a short neck and a large, brightly colored bill.

puff·y (puf′ē), *adj.,* **puff·i·er, puff·i·est.** 1. swollen or puffed up: *Her face was puffy from crying.* 2. breathing quick and hard; panting. —**puff′i·ly,** *adv.* —**puff′i·ness,** *n.*

pug (pug), *n.* a small, short-haired dog having a tightly curled tail and a wrinkled face with a short, upturned nose.

Pug
(1 ft. high
at shoulder)

Pu′get Sound′ (pyŏŏ′jit), an arm of the Pacific Ocean in NW Washington.

pu·gil·ism (pyŏŏ′jə liz′əm), *n.* the art or practice of fighting with the fists; boxing.

pu·gil·ist (pyŏŏ′jə list), *n.* a professional boxer. —**pu′gil·is′tic,** *adj.*

pug·na·cious (pug nā′shəs), *adj.* quick to quarrel or fight; quarrelsome: *a fiery, pugnacious man.* —**pug·na′cious·ly,** *adv.*

pug′ nose′, a short, broad, turned-up nose. —**pug-nosed** (pug′nōzd′), *adj.*

pull (pŏŏl), *v.* 1. to use force to cause (something) to move toward or along behind oneself or itself: *a horse pulling a cart.* 2. to use force to try to move something in this way; tug (often fol. by *at* or *on*): *She pulled on the handle, but the door wouldn't open.* 3. to use force to separate (something) from the place where it is lodged or stuck: *to pull a nail out of a board; to pull a tooth.* 4. to tear or rip: *to pull a napkin to pieces.* 5. to move or go: *The car pulled to the side of the road.* 6. to stretch or strain: *to pull a muscle.* —*n.* 7. the act of pulling; tug: *He gave the rope a pull.* 8. a force that pulls or draws: *the pull of a magnet.* 9. effort used in pulling or go-

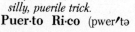

ATLANTIC OCEAN

DOMINICAN
REPUBLIC

BRITISH
VIRGIN
ISLANDS

Mona
Passage

San
Juan

Puerto Rico

VIRGIN
ISLANDS
OF THE U.S.

CARIBBEAN SEA

ing: *It was a long pull to the top of the mountain.* **10.** something used for pulling, such as a handle: *a drawer pull.* **11. pull down, a.** to pull or draw downward: *Pull down the shade.* **b.** to wreck; demolish: *to pull down a building.* **12. pull in, a.** to arrive at a place: *The train pulled in an hour ago.* **b.** *Slang.* to arrest (a person): *to pull someone in for questioning.* **13. pull out,** to leave; depart: *The bus pulled out an hour ago.* **14. pull through,** to come safely through (a crisis, illness, etc.); survive: *He had pneumonia, but luckily he pulled through.* **15. pull up, a.** to come to a halt; stop: *The car pulled up at the curb.* **b.** to bring or draw closer: *Pull up a chair and let's talk.* **c.** to draw out of the ground; uproot: *to pull up weeds.*

pul·let (pŏŏl′it), *n.* a hen that is less than one year old.

pul·ley (pŏŏl′ē), *n., pl.* **pul·leys.** a wheel with a grooved edge over which a rope, chain, or belt passes. Pulleys are used singly to change the direction of a force or in groups to enable one to lift heavy weights.

Pull·man (pŏŏl′mən), *n. Trademark.* **1.** a railroad car equipped with berths for sleeping; sleeping car. **2.** a railroad car equipped with especially comfortable seats that can be reserved in advance.

pull·o·ver (pŏŏl′ō′vər), *n.* a garment, esp. a sweater, that is put on by pulling it over one's head.

pul·mo·nar·y (pul′mə ner′ē, pŏŏl′mə ner′ē), *adj.* of or concerning the lungs.

Pul·mo·tor (pŏŏl′mō′tər), *n. Trademark.* a device that pumps oxygen into the lungs to restore breathing.

pulp (pulp), *n.* **1.** the soft, juicy, edible part of a fruit. **2.** the inner part of a tooth containing blood vessels and nerves. See illus. at **tooth. 3.** a soft, wet mass of ground wood or rags from which paper is made.

pul·pit (pŏŏl′pit, pul′pit), *n.* a platform or small balcony in a church or synagogue, used by the clergyman in speaking to the congregation.

pulp·wood (pulp′wŏŏd′), *n.* any soft wood suitable for making paper pulp.

pulp·y (pul′pē), *adj.*, **pulp·i·er, pulp·i·est.** of or like pulp; soft or fleshy: *pulpy fruit.* —**pulp′i·ness,** *n.*

pul·sate (pul′sāt), *v.*, **pul·sat·ed, pul·sat·ing. 1.** to beat or throb as the heart or an artery does. **2.** to vibrate or quiver. —**pul·sa′tion,** *n.*

pulse[1] (puls), *n.* **1.** the steady throbbing of the arteries caused by the beating of the heart. **2.** a burst of electrical or radiant energy. **3.** any regular beat, stroke, or throb: *the pulse of a ship's engine.* —*v.*, **pulsed, puls·ing. 4.** to beat or throb: *a heart pulsing strongly.* [from the Latin word *pulsus* "a beat"]

pulse[2] (puls), *n.* **1.** any of various plants yielding seeds that are eaten as a vegetable, including peas, beans, and lentils. **2.** the seeds of such a plant. [from the Middle English word *puls,* which comes from a Latin word meaning "thick pap of meal, pulse"]

pul·ver·ize (pul′və rīz′), *v.*, **pul·ver·ized, pul·ver·iz·**

ing. **1.** to pound or grind (something) into dust or powder: *to pulverize sugar cubes.* **2.** to crush or demolish completely: *The bomb pulverized the building.* **3.** to become dust or powder. —**pul′ver·i·za′tion,** *n.* —**pul′ver·iz′er,** *n.*

pu·ma (pyōō′mə), *n.* another name for **cougar.**

pum·ice (pum′is), *n.* a porous, light rock formed when lava cools rapidly, used, esp. when powdered, as a cleaning agent and abrasive.

pum·mel (pum′əl), *v.*, **pum·meled** or **pum·melled; pum·mel·ing** or **pum·mel·ling. 1.** to beat or pound, esp. with the fists: *The fighter pummeled his opponent.* —*n.* **2.** another spelling of **pommel.**

pump[1] (pump), *n.* **1.** any of numerous machines for moving or changing the pressure of a liquid or a gas: *a gasoline pump.* —*v.* **2.** to move (a liquid or gas) with a pump: *to pump water into a pipe.* **3.** to empty of a liquid or gas by using a pump (usually fol. by *out*): *to pump out a small well.* **4.** to fill with air or other gas by using a pump (often fol. by *up*): *to pump up a tire.* **5.** to drive or force in the way that a pump does: *The heart pumps blood through the arteries.* **6.** to question (someone) cleverly or steadily in order to get information. **7.** to obtain (information) by means of clever or steady questioning: *to pump the facts out of someone.* [from the Middle English word *pumpe*]

pump[2] (pump), *n.* a lightweight, low-cut shoe without a fastening or laces, worn esp. by women.

pum·per·nick·el (pum′pər nik′əl), *n.* a dark, coarse, slightly sour bread made of unsifted rye.

pump·kin (pump′kin), *n.* a large, round, yellow-orange fruit of the cucumber family that grows on a trailing vine, used as a vegetable and as a pie filling.

pun (pun), *n.* a humorous use of a word or combination of words so as to emphasize different meanings of the same word or different meanings of words that sound alike. Examples are: A hen scolded her offspring, "If your father could see you, he'd turn over in his gravy." A sign in an auto-repair shop reads, "May we have the next dents?"

punch[1] (punch), *n.* **1.** a hit or blow, esp. with the fist. —*v.* **2.** to hit, esp. with the fist: *to punch a pillow.* **3.** to drive (cattle). [perhaps another form of the word *pounce*] —**punch′er,** *n.*

punch[2] (punch), *n.* **1.** a tool or machine for making holes: *a punch to make holes in paper.* **2.** any similar tool or machine for stamping designs, driving nails, etc. —*v.* **3.** to make holes in with a punch: *to punch bus tickets.* **4.** to stamp with a punch: *to punch prices on cans of food.* [from the early French word *ponçon,* which comes from Latin *punctiō* "a pricking"]

punch[3] (punch), *n.* a drink that is a mixture of two or more other drinks, such as fruit juice, wine, and soda. [perhaps from a Hindi word meaning "five," applied to a drink made of five ingredients]

pun·cheon (pun′chən), *n.* a large barrel or cask.

punc·til·i·ous (pungk til′ē əs), *adj.* careful and exact in one's behavior, manners, or work; proper; precise: *a punctilious, efficient secretary.* —**punc·til′i·ous·ly,** *adv.* —**punc·til′i·ous·ness,** *n.*

punc·tu·al (puṅgk′chōō əl), *adj.* on time or prompt: *Are the trains punctual in this country?* —**punc·tu·al·i·ty** (puṅgk′chōō al′i tē), *n.* —**punc′tu·al·ly,** *adv.*

punc·tu·ate (puṅgk′chōō āt′), *v.,* **punc·tu·at·ed, punc·tu·at·ing.** **1.** to divide and mark (writing) with punctuation marks, such as commas, periods, etc.: *to punctuate a letter.* **2.** to interrupt at times: *His remarks were punctuated with applause.* **3.** to emphasize or give force to: *He used humor to punctuate his sermon.*

punc·tu·a·tion (puṅgk′chōō ā′shən), *n.* **1.** the use of punctuation marks, such as commas, periods, or question marks, to make a piece of writing clear in meaning. **2.** the marks used for this.

punctua′tion mark′, any of the marks or signs, such as a comma (,), period (.), or question mark (?), used in writing to help make the meaning clear.

punc·ture (puṅgk′chər), *n.* **1.** a hole made by a sharp, pointed object, such as a nail: *He put a patch over the puncture in our tire.* **2.** the act of piercing with a sharp, pointed object; a puncturing: *the puncture of a balloon.* —*v.,* **punc·tured, punc·tur·ing. 3.** to pierce or make a hole in: *A piece of glass punctured his foot.* **4.** to cause or show (hope, pride, etc.) to be without force; injure or destroy: *The bad reviews punctured his dream of becoming a writer.*

pun·dit (pun′dit), *n.* **1.** an expert or authority: *a political pundit.* **2.** (in India) a Brahman having a deep knowledge of Hindu law, the writings in Sanskrit, etc.

pun·gent (pun′jənt), *adj.* **1.** sharp or biting to the sense of taste or smell: *a strong, pungent mustard; the pungent odor of burning rubber.* **2.** forceful and sharp; stinging: *a pungent criticism.* —**pun′gen·cy,** *n.*

pun·ish (pun′ish), *v.* **1.** to cause (a person) to suffer pain, loss of freedom, or the like, for a wrongdoing or crime: *The army punished the soldier for being AWOL.* **2.** to make offenders pay a penalty for (a wrongdoing or crime): *This school punishes anyone littering the grounds.* —**pun′ish·er,** *n.*

pun·ish·a·ble (pun′i shə bəl), *adj.* (of a person or act) deserving or liable to punishment or a penalty: *Crossing against the red light is punishable by a fine.*

pun·ish·ment (pun′ish mənt), *n.* **1.** a penalty for a wrongdoing or crime: *As punishment for telling a lie he had to stay in after school.* **2.** the act of punishing: *Do not be too rough in the punishment of a child.* **3.** the fact of being punished: *His punishment was unfair, because he did not know the rules.*

pu·ni·tive (pyōō′ni tiv), *adj.* **1.** imposing punishment or hardship: *harsh, punitive laws.* **2.** serving as a punishment or penalty: *a punitive fine.* **3.** of or concerning punishment: *a discussion of punitive methods.* —**pu′ni·tive·ly,** *adv.* —**pu′ni·tive·ness,** *n.*

Pun·jab (pun jäb′, pun′jäb), *n.* a former state in NW India, now divided between India and West Pakistan.

punk¹ (puṅgk), *Slang.* —*n.* **1.** a worthless or unim-

portant person. **2.** a hoodlum or thug. —*adj.* **3.** poor in quality; worthless: *a punk movie.* **4.** tired or sick; unwell: *He feels punk today.*

punk² (puṅgk), *n.* **1.** a material that burns slowly and is formed into sticks for lighting fireworks, fuses, etc. **2.** dry, decayed wood that can be used as tinder. [perhaps another form of the word *spunk,* which has also this meaning]

punt (punt), *n.* **1.** (in football) a kick in which the ball is dropped and kicked before it hits the ground. **2.** a small, shallow boat that one moves by pushing a long pole against the bottom of a river or lake. —*v.* **3.** to drop and kick (a football) before it touches the ground. **4.** to pole (a small boat) along. **5.** to go boating in a punt. —**punt′er,** *n.*

pu·ny (pyōō′nē), *adj.,* **pu·ni·er, pu·ni·est. 1.** small and weak: *a puny newborn kitten.* **2.** lacking force or importance; feeble or unimportant: *a puny effort.* —**pu′ni·ness,** *n.*

pup (pup), *n.* **1.** a young dog; puppy. **2.** the young of certain other animals, such as foxes and seals.

pu·pa (pyōō′pə), *n., pl.* **pu·pas** or **pu·pae** (pyōō′pē). an insect in the stage between larva and adult, when it usually remains completely inactive. —**pu′pal,** *adj.*

pu·pil¹ (pyōō′pəl), *n.* a person who studies in a school or with a teacher outside of school; student. [from the Old French word *pupille* "orphan, ward," which comes from Latin *pūpillus* "boy" or *pūpilla* "girl"]

pu·pil² (pyōō′pəl), *n.* the dark opening at the center of the iris through which light enters the eye. The pupil expands when there is little light and contracts when the light is bright. See illus. at **eye.** [from the Latin word *pūpilla,* literally "girl, doll" (referring to the small images reflected in the pupils)]

Pupa of fly

pup·pet (pup′it), *n.* **1.** a doll that can be made to move by pulling strings or wires attached to its limbs; marionette. **2.** a doll that can be fitted over one's hand, and is moved by turning one's hand, wiggling one's fingers, etc. **3.** a person who simply follows the commands of another person or group: *The congressman was just a puppet of the local political boss.*

pup·py (pup′ē), *n., pl.* **pup·pies. 1.** a young dog, esp. one that is less than a year old. **2.** See **pup** (def. 2).

pur·blind (pûr′blīnd′), *adj.* partially or nearly blind.

pur·chase (pûr′chəs), *v.,* **pur·chased, pur·chas·ing. 1.** to acquire by the payment of money; buy: *to purchase new clothes for school.* —*n.* **2.** the act of purchasing or buying: *the purchase of a ticket.* **3.** something that is purchased or bought: *Let me show you my new purchases.* **4.** a lever, tackle, or other device that gives one an advantage in moving or raising something. **5.** a good hold or a secure position for lifting something, climbing, etc.; leverage. —**pur′chas·a·ble,** *adj.* —**pur′chas·er,** *n.*

pure (pyōōr), *adj.,* **pur·er, pur·est. 1.** not mixed with anything different, harmful, or of a lower quality: *pure gold; pure water.* **2.** being only that; mere: *pure* *chance.* **3.** absolute; complete: *pure joy.* **4.** free of evil or guilt; innocent; virtuous: *a pure life.* **5.** concerned with theory rather than practical uses; abstract: *pure science.* **—pure′ness,** *n.*

pure·bred (pyŏŏr′bred′), *adj.* of or concerning an animal whose ancestors for many generations were all of the same breed.

pu·rée (pyŏŏ rā′, pyŏŏ rē′), *n.* **1.** a soft mass of food that has been cooked and put through a sieve, usually made with a vegetable or fruit. **2.** a soup made from this. **—v.,** **pu·réed, pu·rée·ing. 3.** to make a purée of: *to purée spinach.*

pure·ly (pyŏŏr′lē), *adv.* **1.** merely or only: *I am going there purely from curiosity.* **2.** entirely or completely: *It's purely your responsibility.* **3.** without evil or guilt: *to live purely.* **4.** in a pure manner; without mixing or becoming mixed with anything different, harmful, or of lower quality: *purely bred horses.*

pur·ga·tive (pûr′gə tiv), *n.* **1.** a strong laxative. **—adj. 2.** having a purging or cleansing effect, esp. by acting as a laxative: *a purgative medicine.*

pur·ga·to·ry (pûr′gə tôr′ē), *n., pl.* **pur·ga·to·ries.** (in the Roman Catholic Church) a condition or place of temporary suffering following death, in which the souls of sinners who have repented may be purified before entering heaven.

purge (pûrj), *v.,* **purged, purg·ing. 1.** to cleanse or rid of whatever is undesirable or impure; purify (often fol. by *of*): *to purge one's soul of sin by prayer; to purge a government of corrupt officials.* **2.** to free or rid (oneself) of guilt, sin, or the like: *The thief purged himself by confessing.* **3.** to cause or undergo emptying of the bowels. **—n. 4.** the act of purging, cleansing, or purifying. **5.** the process of ridding a political party, government, or the like, of all persons who are disloyal or not wanted: *a purge of incompetent officials.* **6.** a strong laxative that causes emptying of the bowels. **—purg′er,** *n.*

pu·ri·fy (pyŏŏr′ə fī′), *v.,* **pu·ri·fied, pu·ri·fy·ing. 1.** to make pure; free from anything harmful or undesirable; cleanse: *to purify city air.* **2.** to free from sin or guilt: *Prayer purifies the soul.* **3.** to become pure or clean. **—pu′ri·fi·ca′tion,** *n.*

pu·ri·tan (pyŏŏr′i t³n), *n.* a person who is extremely strict in moral matters. **—pu·ri·tan·i·cal** (pyŏŏr′i tan′i-kəl), *adj.* **—pu′ri·tan′i·cal·ly,** *adv.*

Pu·ri·tan (pyŏŏr′i t³n), *n.* **1.** a member of the 16th- and 17th-century English sect that wanted the Church of England to simplify its doctrine and worship, and to be stricter in moral matters. **2.** a member of this sect, which settled in New England in the 17th century. **—Pu·ri·tan·i·cal** (pyŏŏr′i tan′i kəl), *adj.* **—Pu′ri·tan·ism,** *n.*

pu·ri·ty (pyŏŏr′i tē), *n.* **1.** the quality of being pure; freedom from anything that is harmful or undesirable: *gold of absolute purity.* **2.** freedom from evil or guilt; innocence: *a life of saintly purity.*

purl¹ (pûrl), *v.* **1.** to knit (a stitch or stitches) in the reverse of the usual way. **—n. 2.** (in knitting) a reverse stitch, used to make ribbing. [from the earlier word *pirl* "to twist into a cord"]

purl² (pûrl), *v.* **1.** to flow with a rippling motion, as a brook or shallow stream does. **2.** to flow with a murmuring sound. **—n. 3.** the motion or sound of purling water. [perhaps from a Scandinavian word, such as Norwegian *purla* "to bubble up, gush"]

pur·loin (pər loin′), *v.* to take dishonestly; steal.

pur·ple (pûr′pəl), *n.* **1.** any color that is a mixture of red and blue; bluish red. **2.** cloth or clothing of this color, esp. as a symbol of royalty: *to wear the purple.* **—adj. 3.** of the color purple: *purple robes.* **4. born to the purple,** of royal or high birth: *He was not born to the purple, but gained great power nevertheless.*

pur·plish (pûr′plish), *adj.* slightly purple.

pur·port (pər pôrt′), *v.* **1.** to claim, esp. falsely: *a forged document purporting to be official.* **2.** to mean or imply: *What does this strange message purport?* **—n.** (pûr′pôrt). **3.** the meaning or sense: *The purport of his letter was that we must be very careful now.* **4.** a purpose or intention.

pur·pose (pûr′pəs), *n.* **1.** a result that one desires or intends to bring about; aim; goal: *What is your purpose in life?* **2.** the reason for which something exists or happens: *What is the purpose of that extra knob on your radio?* **3.** determination or ambition: *a man of purpose.* **—v.,** **pur·posed, pur·pos·ing. 4.** to set as an aim or goal for oneself; intend: *He purposes to visit England next summer.* **5. on purpose,** deliberately; intentionally: *Do you think he did that on purpose?* **—pur′pose·less,** *adj.*

pur·pose·ful (pûr′pəs fəl), *adj.* **1.** having or showing a purpose or aim: *a purposeful plan.* **2.** full of purpose; determined: *a serious, purposeful student.* **—pur′pose·ful·ly,** *adv.* **—pur′pose·ful·ness,** *n.*

pur·pose·ly (pûr′pəs lē), *adv.* deliberately or intentionally: *Did you trip me purposely?*

purr (pûr), *v.* **1.** to make a low murmuring or humming sound, as a cat does when pleased. **—n. 2.** the low murmuring or humming sound made by a cat: *Can you hear the kitten's purr?* **3.** any similar sound: *the purr of a car's motor.* **—purr′ing·ly,** *adv.*

purse (pûrs), *n.* **1.** a small bag or case for carrying money. **2.** a woman's handbag or pocketbook. **3.** a sum of money collected as a present, offered as a prize, or the like: *The horse has won several large purses.* **4.** money available for spending; funds: *the public purse.* **—v.,** **pursed, purs·ing. 5.** to draw into folds or wrinkles; pucker: *to purse the lips.*

purs·er (pûr′sər), *n.* an officer on a ship who is in charge of the financial accounts and official documents.

purs·lane (pûrs′lān), *n.* a plant that grows along the ground and bears yellow flowers. Its leaves are sometimes eaten in salad or cooked as a vegetable.

pur·su·ance (pər sŏŏ′əns), *n.* the following or carrying out of a plan, matter of business, or the like: *In pursuance of our agreement, I have scheduled a general meeting for Monday.*

---

act, āble, dâre, ärt; ebb, ēqual; if, īce; hot, ōver, ôrder; oil; bŏŏk; ōōze; out; up, ûrge; ə = a as in *alone*; ³ as in *button* (but′³n), *fire* (fi³r); chief; shoe; thin; ᵺhat; zh as in *measure* (mezh′ər). See full key inside cover.

pur·su·ant (pər sōō′ənt), *adj.* 1. following, carrying out, or pursuing. —*adv.* 2. in agreement or following (usually fol. by *to*): *Pursuant to local custom, we close from twelve to two every afternoon.*

pur·sue (pər sōō′), *v.,* **pur·sued, pur·su·ing.** 1. to follow in order to catch or overtake; chase: *The hounds pursued the fox.* 2. to try to get or accomplish; seek: *to pursue fame and fortune.* 3. to carry on or engage in; keep on with; practice: *to pursue a hobby.* 4. to follow or carry out: *to pursue a plan of action; to pursue a river to its source.* —**pur·su′er,** *n.*

pur·suit (pər sōōt′), *n.* 1. the act of pursuing; chasing, or following: *the pursuit of a criminal by the police.* 2. an effort to get or accomplish something; a seeking: *the pursuit of pleasure.* 3. an occupation or pastime: *Fishing is one of my favorite pursuits.*

pur·vey (pər vā′), *v.* to provide or supply (food or provisions): *the business of purveying rations to troops.* —**pur·vey′or,** *n.*

pur·vey·ance (pər vā′əns), *n.* 1. the act of purveying or supplying. 2. something that is purveyed or supplied, esp. food.

pus (pus), *n.* a thick, yellow-white liquid produced in sores, abscesses, and infections.

Pu·san (pōō′sän′), *n.* a port city in SE South Korea.

push (pŏŏsh), *v.* 1. to press against (something) in order to move it: *Lean on the door and push hard.* 2. to make (a path, passage, one's way, etc.) by thrusting aside people or objects: *to push one's way through a crowd.* 3. to urge or try to force: *to push someone to make a speech.* 4. to move forward on one's way with effort: *The tired hunters pushed on through the forest.* 5. to try hard to sell or advance (a product, plan, invention, idea, etc.). 6. to thrust or extend: *The tree pushed its roots deep into the soil.* —*n.* 7. the act of pushing; shove: *Give the swing a push.* 8. *Informal.* energy and ambition; drive: *They want a salesman with lots of push.* —**push′er,** *n.*

push·o·ver (pŏŏsh′ō′vər), *n. Slang.* 1. anything done easily: *This test is a pushover.* 2. a person or team that is easily defeated or taken advantage of.

pu·sil·lan·i·mous (pyōō′sə lan′ə məs), *adj.* lacking courage; cowardly. —**pu′sil·lan′i·mous·ly,** *adv.*

puss (pŏŏs), *n.* a cat or kitten.

puss·y (pŏŏs′ē), *n., pl.* **puss·ies.** a cat, esp. a kitten.

puss′y wil′low, a small American willow that bears soft, furry, gray buds in the early spring.

put (pŏŏt), *v.,* **put, put·ting.** 1. to move (something) into some place or position; place or set: *Put the plates on the table.* 2. to bring into some condition, state, or the like: *Put your room in order.* 3. to start (someone) on a task or action: *I put her to sweeping the floor.* 4. to cause to undergo something painful or difficult to endure: *to put a man on trial.* 5. to force or drive to some course or action: *to put an army to flight.* 6. to assign or set: *to*

Pussy
willow

put a high value on honesty. 7. to express or state: *Try to put your questions clearly.* 8. to go or move: *to put out to sea.* 9. to apply for a purpose: *Put your mind to good use.* 10. to propose or submit (a question, plan, etc.): *to put a question to the class.* —*n.* 11. (in sports) a throw of a stone or shot. 12. **put aside, a.** to put to one side or out of the way: *Put aside your work and come for a walk.* **b.** to save; store up: *to put money aside to use in an emergency.* 13. **put down, a.** to write down; record: *Did you put down the correct amount?* **b.** to land an airplane or in an airplane: *We put down at Salem because of fog.* **c.** to put an end to; suppress: *to put down a rebellion.* 14. **put in, a.** to spend (time) in a special way: *I put in an hour fixing that faucet.* **b.** to install: *to put in a new light fixture.* **c.** (of a ship) to come into a port or harbor: *We put in at Newport for three days.* 15. **put off, a.** to postpone: *Let's put off the meeting until next week.* **b.** to stall or delay: *If you can't pay him, maybe you can put him off till next week.* 16. **put on, a.** to dress oneself with (clothing): *to put on a hat.* **b.** to present (a play or other entertainment): *to put on a Christmas show.* **c.** to assume insincerely or without reason: *to put on airs.* 17. **put out, a.** to extinguish (a fire, light, etc.). **b.** disturbed or annoyed: *to be put out about someone's behavior.* **c.** to cause inconvenience to: *Are you sure my staying to dinner won't put you out?* **d.** to prevent from scoring: *We put him out at first base.* 18. **put through, a.** to cause to go into effect: *to put through a request.* **b.** to complete successfully: *to put through a call.* 19. **put up, a.** to construct; erect: *to put up a building.* **b.** to can (fruit, vegetables, etc.); preserve (jellies, jams, etc.). **c.** *Informal.* to provide (someone) with lodging: *Can you put me up for the night?* **d.** to set or arrange (the hair). **e.** to provide or contribute (money): *We each put up fifty cents for the gift.* 20. **put up to,** *Informal.* to encourage (a person) to some action, esp. something mischievous or annoying: *Did Bill put you up to calling me?* 21. **put up with,** *Informal.* to endure; tolerate: *I can't put up with that noise.*

pu·tre·fy (pyōō′trə fī′), *v.,* **pu·tre·fied, pu·tre·fy·ing.** to make or become putrid; decompose; rot. —**pu·tre·fac·tion** (pyōō′trə fak′shən), *n.*

pu·trid (pyōō′trid), *adj.* in a state of decay or decomposition; rotten.

putt (put), *v.* 1. (in golf) to strike or tap (the ball) lightly so that it rolls along the green in the direction of the hole. —*n.* 2. the act of putting; a light stroke or tap of the ball with a putter.

put·tee (put′ē), *n.* 1. a long strip of cloth wound around the leg from ankle to knee, formerly worn by soldiers. 2. a covering for the leg of leather or other tough material, worn by soldiers, riders, etc.; legging.

put·ter[1] (put′ər), *v.* to busy oneself in a casual or absent-minded way with small tasks: *She puttered around the garden all day.* Also, *esp. British,* **potter.** [from the Middle English word *poten* "to push, poke," which comes from Old English *potian*]

put·ter[2] (put′ər), *n.* (in golf) 1. a club for putting, having a rather short, stiff shaft and a small, more or less rectangular head. **2.** a person who putts.

put·ty (put′ē), *n., pl.* **put·ties. 1.** a sticky substance made from powdered chalk and linseed oil that dries hard, used for holding panes of glass in windows, filling cracks, etc. —*v.,* **put·tied, put·ty·ing. 2.** to cover or make secure with putty: *to putty a crack in the wall; to putty the glass in a window.*

puz·zle (puz′əl), *v.,* **puz·zled, puz·zling. 1.** to confuse or perplex; mystify; baffle: *The dog's strange behavior puzzled its master.* **2.** to think about or study some confusing or perplexing matter: *to puzzle over a riddle.* —*n.* **3.** a game or toy that presents a problem to be solved by thought or patient effort: *a jigsaw puzzle.* **4.** something or someone that causes one to be perplexed or puzzled: *Her sudden disappearance certainly is a puzzle.* —**puz′zler,** *n.*

puz·zle·ment (puz′əl mənt), *n.* **1.** a puzzled or perplexed state; a being puzzled: *She's in a puzzlement over what to do next.* **2.** something that puzzles; something perplexing.

Pvt., (in military use) Private.

PW, 1. prisoner of war. **2.** public works.

Pyg·my (pig′mē), *n., pl.* **pyg·mies. 1.** a member of a Negroid race of people, living in central Africa, who are between four and five feet tall. **2.** a member of any similar group of people living in Asia. **3.** *(usually l.c.)* a person or thing that is very small in size or importance. —*adj.* **4.** of or concerning the Pygmies: *a Pygmy village.* **5.** *(usually l.c.)* very small in size or importance: *a pygmy hippopotamus.* Also, **Pigmy.**

py·jam·as (pə jä′məz, pə jam′əz), *n. (used as pl.)* the British spelling of **pajamas.**

py·lon (pī′lon), *n.* **1.** a tall post or tower used to mark a course for aviators. **2.** a steel tower used as a support for high-voltage wires or cable. **3.** a tall, massive gateway at the entrance to an ancient Egyptian temple. **4.** a similar structure used to mark the entrance to a bridge, avenue, or the like.

Pyong·yang (pyuñg′yäñg′), *n.* the capital city of North Korea, in the SW part.

py·or·rhe·a (pī′ə rē′ə), *n.* a disease that causes the formation of pus in the gums and loosening of the teeth.

pyr·a·mid (pir′ə mid), *n.* **1.** a solid having a polygonal base and triangular sides meeting at a point at the top. **2.** any of the very large structures of this shape, built in ancient Egypt as tombs for kings.

py·ram·i·dal (pi ram′i d°l), *adj.* of, referring to, or shaped like a pyramid: *the pyramidal form; a pyramidal structure.*

Pyramid

pyre (pī°r), *n.* a large pile of wood used to burn a dead body, esp. as part of a funeral ceremony.

Pyr·e·nees (pir′ə nēz′), *n.* a mountain range between France and Spain.

Py·rex (pī′reks), *n. Trademark.* a kind of glass used for laboratory and cooking utensils because it does not crack when suddenly heated or cooled.

py·rite (pī′rīt), *n.* a brass-yellow mineral that is sometimes mistaken for gold. Also, **pyrites, iron pyrites, fool's gold.**

py·ri·tes (pə rī′tēz), *n.* **1.** another name for **pyrite. 2.** any compound of a sulfur and metal: *iron pyrites.*

py·ro·ma·ni·ac (pī′rə mā′nē ak), *n.* a person having a mental disorder in which he feels a strong urge to set things on fire. —**py′ro·ma′ni·a,** *n.*

py·ro·tech·nics (pī′rə tek′niks), *n. (used as sing. or pl.)* **1.** the art of making fireworks. **2.** a display of fireworks. —**py′ro·tech′nic, py′ro·tech′ni·cal,** *adj.*

py·thon (pī′thon, pī′thən), *n.* any of several large snakes that crush their prey to death in their powerful coils.

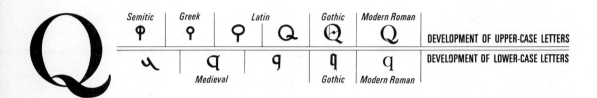

	Semitic	Greek	Latin	Gothic	Modern Roman	
	φ	φ	φ	Q	Q	DEVELOPMENT OF UPPER-CASE LETTERS
	ч	q	q	q	q	DEVELOPMENT OF LOWER-CASE LETTERS
		Medieval		Gothic	Modern Roman	

Q, q (kyōō), *n., pl.* **Q's** *or* **Qs, q's** *or* **qs.** the 17th letter of the English alphabet.

Q, (in chess) queen.

Q., 1. Queen. 2. question.

Qa·tar (kä′tär), *n.* an independent country in E Arabia. 4000 sq. mi. *Cap.:* Doha.

qt., 1. quantity. 2. quart.

qtr., 1. quarter. 2. quarterly.

qts., quarts.

quack[1] (kwak), *n.* 1. the harsh, throaty cry of a duck. 2. any similar sound. —*v.* 3. to give forth a harsh, throaty cry as a duck does. [imitative of the sound]

quack[2] (kwak), *n.* 1. a dishonest or ignorant person who claims to be skilled in medicine. 2. any person who pretends to have skill or knowledge that he does not have; charlatan. —*adj.* 3. being a quack: *a quack doctor.* 4. of or concerning quacks; not genuine: *a quack medicine.* [short for *quacksalver,* an early Dutch word meaning "quack doctor"]

quack·er·y (kwak′ə rē), *n.* the practice or methods of quacks or charlatans.

quad·ran·gle (kwod′rang′gəl), *n.* 1. a four-sided geometrical figure, such as a rectangle; quadrilateral. 2. a square or court surrounded by a building or buildings. —**quad·ran′gu·lar,** *adj.*

quad·rant (kwod′rənt), *n.* 1. one quarter of a circle; an arc or sector of 90°. 2. one of the four areas into which a plane is divided by two perpendicular lines. 3. an instrument for measuring angles in astronomy, navigation, etc.

quad·rat·ic (kwo drat′ik), *adj.* (in mathematics) involving the square and no higher power of the unknown: $4x^2 + 2x + 7 = 0$ *is a quadratic equation.*

quad·ren·ni·al (kwo dren′ē əl), *adj.* 1. occurring or taking place every four years: *The Olympic Games are quadrennial.* 2. lasting for four years. —**quad·ren′ni·al·ly,** *adv.*

Quadrilateral

quad·ri·lat·er·al (kwod′rə lat′ər əl), *n.* a polygon having four sides and four angles.

quad·ru·ped (kwod′rōō ped′), *n.* an animal having four feet, esp. a mammal.

quad·ru·ple (kwo drōō′pəl), *adj.* 1. made up of four parts or members; fourfold: *a quadruple alliance among nations.* 2. four times as great; multiplied four times: *a quadruple amount of work.* —*v.,* **quad·ru·pled, quad·ru·pling.** 3. to make or become four times greater: *We need to quadruple our supply of food.*

quad·ru·plet (kwo drup′lit, kwo drōō′plit), *n.* 1. **quadruplets,** four children born at one time of the same mother. 2. one of a group of quadruplets. 3. any group or combination of four things.

quaff (kwäf, kwaf), *v.* to drink (a beverage) in large amounts and with hearty enjoyment.

quag·mire (kwag′mī°r′), *n.* 1. an area of very soft, muddy ground; bog. 2. a difficult, troublesome, or embarrassing situation.

quail[1] (kwāl), *n., pl.* **quails** *or* **quail.** any of various small, plump game birds, including the bobwhite. [from an Old French word, which comes from Germanic]

quail[2] (kwāl), *v.* to lose heart or courage in the face of danger; shrink with fear: *The hunter quailed at the sight of the charging elephant.* [from a Middle English word meaning "to fail"]

Bobwhite quail (length 9 in.)

quaint (kwānt), *adj.* 1. charmingly old-fashioned: *a quaint old inn.* 2. strange or odd in a pleasing or attractive way; unusual; curious: *She has a quaint, surprising sense of humor. They own a quaint little house in the woods.* [from the Old French word *queinte* "clever, pleasing," which comes from Latin *cognitus* "known"] —**quaint′ly,** *adv.* —**quaint′ness,** *n.*

quake (kwāk), *v.,* **quaked, quak·ing.** 1. to shake or tremble; shiver: *The explosion made the whole house quake.* —*n.* 2. an earthquake. 3. a shaking or trembling. —**quak′ing·ly,** *adv.*

Quak·er (kwā′kər), *n.* another name for a member of the Society of Friends; Friend.

qual·i·fi·ca·tion (kwol′ə fə kā′shən), *n.* **1.** a skill, ability, or accomplishment that is needed or useful in a job or position: *He has all the qualifications for the job.* **2.** something that limits full approval, agreement, enjoyment, or the like; reservation or objection; limitation: *I like your plan, but with one qualification.* **3.** something that must be completed or fulfilled; requirement: *the qualifications to vote.*

qual·i·fied (kwol′ə fīd′), *adj.* **1.** having the necessary skills, ability, or accomplishments for a job, task, position, or the like: *Several qualified men have already applied for this job.* **2.** limited by some objection, reservation, or the like: *qualified approval of a plan.*

qual·i·fi·er (kwol′ə fī′ər), *n.* **1.** a person or thing that qualifies. **2.** (in grammar) a word or phrase used to qualify another word or phrase; modifier.

qual·i·fy (kwol′ə fī′), *v.*, **qual·i·fied, qual·i·fy·ing. 1.** to provide (someone or oneself) with the skills, knowledge, experience, etc., necessary for a job, task, or position; make fitted or competent. **2.** to show that one can fulfill the requirements of a job, task, or position: *to qualify as a lifeguard.* **3.** to limit in some way; make less strong or positive: *to qualify one's praise of a movie.* **4.** (in grammar) to limit or restrict the meaning of; modify. **5.** to call or name; identify or place (something) according to its qualities: *They were not sure whether to qualify sponges as plants or animals.*

qual·i·ta·tive (kwol′i tā′tiv), *adj.* of or concerned with quality or qualities, esp. as opposed to quantity or amount: *You may do less work, but it must show a qualitative improvement.* —**qual′i·ta·tive·ly,** *adv.*

qual·i·ty (kwol′i tē), *n., pl.* **qual·i·ties. 1.** something about a thing or person that helps to recognize or identify it; typical feature or characteristic: *Coldness and hardness are qualities of ice.* **2.** the nature or character of something or someone: *the real quality of life in the old West.* **3.** worth or value; degree of excellence; grade: *work of high quality.* **4.** excellence or high worth: *You must practice in order to achieve quality in playing the guitar.* **5.** high social position or status: *a lady of quality.*

qualm (kwäm), *n.* **1.** a sudden feeling or pang of fear, doubt, or uneasiness; misgiving: *As he stepped onto the train, he began to have qualms about leaving home.* **2.** a feeling that an action is wrong or bad; pang of conscience: *I would report him to the police without a qualm.* **3.** a sudden feeling of illness, esp. that one may faint or vomit. —**qualm′ish,** *adj.*

quan·da·ry (kwon′də rē, kwon′drē), *n., pl.* **quan·da·ries.** a state of uncertainty or puzzlement, esp. as to what to do; dilemma.

quan·ti·ta·tive (kwon′ti tā′tiv), *adj.* **1.** of or relating to quantity; able to be described or measured in terms of quantity or amount: *a quantitative change.* **2.** of or concerned with the describing or measuring of quantity: *a quantitative study of rainfall.*

quan·ti·ty (kwon′ti tē), *n., pl.* **quan·ti·ties. 1.** amount or number; measure: *to serve cake in equal quantities.* **2.** a large amount or number: *There is gold in quantity in that mine.* **3.** something that can be measured or counted: *a physical quantity.*

quan·tum (kwon′təm), *n., pl.* **quan·ta** (kwon′tə). (in physics) a very small, indivisible quantity of energy, such as the energy of a single photon.

quar·an·tine (kwôr′ən tēn′, kwor′ən tēn′), *n.* **1.** a strict isolation to prevent the spread of disease. **2.** a period of time during which persons, animals, or things that have been in contact with a contagious disease are kept apart from others: *The ship was not allowed to unload during the 40-day quarantine.* **3.** a place where infected persons, animals, or things are kept in quarantine. —*v.*, **quar·an·tined, quar·an·tin·ing. 4.** to keep (an infected person, animal, or thing) apart from others; put or hold in quarantine. [from the Italian word *quarantina* "period of forty days," which comes from *quaranta* "forty"]

quar·rel¹ (kwôr′əl, kwor′əl), *n.* **1.** an angry disagreement or fight with words; argument; dispute. **2.** a cause of disagreement, complaint, or angry feelings: *I don't have any quarrel with the way Don ran the meeting.* —*v.*, **quar·reled** *or* **quar·relled; quar·rel·ing** *or* **quar·rel·ling. 3.** to disagree angrily; have a dispute; squabble: *My brothers are quarreling over who gets to use the car tonight.* **4.** to make a complaint; find fault: *She quarrels with everything I do.* [from the Old French word *querele*, which comes from Latin *querēla* "complaint"] —**quar′rel·er,** *n.*

quar·rel² (kwôr′əl, kwor′əl), *n.* a square-headed arrow or bolt, formerly used with a crossbow. [from the Old French word *quarel*, which comes from Latin *quadrus* "square"]

quar·rel·some (kwôr′əl səm, kwor′əl-), *adj.* inclined to quarrel; taking part in many fights and arguments; argumentative: *a short-tempered, quarrelsome boy.* —**quar′rel·some·ly,** *adv.* —**quar′rel·some·ness,** *n.*

quar·ri·er (kwôr′ē ər, kwor′ē ər), *n.* a person who works in a stone quarry. Also, **quarryman.**

quar·ry¹ (kwôr′ē, kwor′ē), *n., pl.* **quar·ries. 1.** a large open pit from which stone is obtained, esp. for use in building. The stone is usually removed by cutting or blasting. —*v.*, **quar·ried, quar·ry·ing. 2.** to take (stone) from a quarry. **3.** to make a quarry or quarries in: *to quarry a small valley.* [from the medieval Latin word *quareia* "place where stone is squared," which comes from Latin *quadrāre* "to square"]

quar·ry² (kwôr′ē, kwor′ē), *n., pl.* **quar·ries. 1.** an animal or bird that is hunted or chased. **2.** any object of search or pursuit: *The detectives closed in on their quarry.* [from the Old French word *cuiree*, which comes from *cuir* "skin, hide," from Latin *corium*]

quar·ry·man (kwôr′ē mən, kwor′ē-), *n., pl.* **quar·ry·men.** another name for **quarrier.**

quart (kwôrt), *n.* **1.** a unit of liquid measure equal to ¼ gallon, or 57.8 cubic inches (0.946 liter). **2.** a unit of dry measure equal to ⅛ peck, or 67.2 cubic inches (1.101 liters). **3.** a container that can hold a quart.

---

act, āble, dâre, ärt; ebb, ēqual; if, īce; hot, ōver, ôrder; oil; bŏŏk; ōōze; out; up, ûrge; ə = a as in alone; ə as in button (but′ən), fire (fī′r); chief; shoe; thin; that; zh as in measure (mezh′ər). See full key inside cover.

quar·ter (kwôr**′**tər), *n.* **1.** any of the four equal parts that make up the whole of something; a fourth part; one fourth: *Cut the pie into quarters.* **2.** one fourth of a dollar, or 25 cents. **3.** a coin worth this amount. **4.** one fourth of an hour, or fifteen minutes; quarter hour: *He stayed an hour and a quarter.* **5.** one fourth of a year, or three months: *He pays taxes every quarter.* **6.** any of the four principal phases of the moon, which are separated by an interval of about seven days, esp. the phases when half the visible face of the moon is illuminated. **7.** any period of time equal to one fourth of the entire time allowed for something: *We made two touchdowns in the last quarter of the game.* **8.** any of the four main points or directions shown by a compass: *During the hurricane, the wind seemed to come from all quarters.* **9.** a region or place, esp. a district of a city or town: *a hotel in the French quarter of the city.* **10.** Usually, **quarters.** a place to live in or spend the night; lodgings: *to find quarters for troops.* **11.** a person or place that is not named or clearly identified: *secret information from a high quarter.* **12.** mercy, esp. as shown to a defeated enemy: *The charging cavalry gave no quarter to the fleeing soldiers.* **13.** one of the four parts of an animal's body, each including a leg: *a quarter of beef.* —*v.* **14.** to divide into four equal parts. **15.** to provide with a place to live or sleep; lodge: *to quarter troops.* **16.** to take up quarters; lodge. —*adj.* **17.** being one of four equal parts that make up the whole of something; equal to one fourth of the whole: *a quarter share.* **18. at close quarters,** at a very short distance; near; close by: *The ships passed each other at close quarters.*

quar·ter·back (kwôr**′**tər bak**′**), *n.* (in football) the player who calls the signals and directs play when the team is on the offense. He usually lines up directly behind the center and receives the ball from him.

quar·ter·deck (kwôr**′**tər dek**′**), *n.* the rear part of the uppermost deck of a ship, running from the midship area or mainmast to the stern. It is usually reserved for officers. Also, **quar′ter·deck′.**

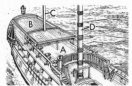

A, Quarter-deck
B, Poop deck
C, Mizzenmast
D, Mainmast

quar·ter·ly (kwôr**′**tər lē), *adj.* **1.** occurring, done, appearing, etc., once every three months: *a quarterly report.* —*n., pl.* **quar·ter·lies. 2.** a magazine or other periodical that is issued once every three months. —*adv.* **3.** each quarter or once every three months.

quar·ter·mas·ter (kwôr**′**tər mas**′**tər), *n.* **1.** a military officer in charge of providing lodging, or quarters, as well as clothing, transportation, etc., for troops. **2.** a naval petty officer responsible for steering the ship, signaling, checking the compasses and other instruments, etc.

quar′ter note′, (in music) a note having one quarter the time value of a whole note. See illus. at **note.**

quar·ter·staff (kwôr**′**tər staf**′**), *n., pl.* **quar·ter·staves** (kwôr**′**tər stāvz**′**, -stavz**′**). a strong pole, about six to eight feet long and having an iron tip, formerly used as a weapon.

quar·tet (kwôr tet**′**), *n.* **1.** a group of four singers or players. **2.** a piece of music composed for such a group. **3.** any group of four persons or things.

quar·to (kwôr**′**tō), *n., pl.* **quar·tos. 1.** a book size of about 9½ x 12 inches, determined by the size of a printed sheet that has been folded into four parts. **2.** a book of this size. —*adj.* **3.** being of this size: *a quarto edition.*

quartz (kwôrts), *n.* a very common mineral composed of silicon and oxygen that occurs in many different forms, including sand, sandstone, amethyst, and agate.

qua·sar (kwā**′**sär, kwā**′**zär), *n.* a small, starlike body that radiates enormous quantities of energy.

quash (kwosh), *v.* **1.** to put down or suppress completely; quell; subdue: *to quash a rebellion.* **2.** to set aside or annul (a law, decree, decision, etc.); make void.

qua·si (kwā**′**zī, kwā**′**sī), *adj.* **1.** resembling or seeming to be, although not being so actually or entirely; halfway: *a quasi comedy with a sad ending.* —*adv.* **2.** seemingly but not actually (usually used in combination): *quasi-scientific ideas.*

qua·ver (kwā**′**vər), *v.* **1.** to shake or tremble; quiver: *Her voice quavered when she tried to sing.* **2.** to say or sing (something) with a quavering or trembling voice. —*n.* **3.** a quavering or trembling, esp. of the voice: *He sang the right note, but with a quaver.* —**qua′ver·ing·ly,** *adv.* —**qua′ver·y,** *adj.*

quay (kē), *n.* a landing place for ships and boats, built of stone, concrete, or the like; wharf.

quea·sy (kwē**′**zē), *adj.,* **quea·si·er, quea·si·est. 1.** slightly ill or sick at the stomach; nauseated: *The sailor began to feel queasy when the sea got rough.* **2.** tending to cause a feeling of sickness or nausea: *the queasy motion of a rolling ship.* **3.** slightly upset or uncomfortable as the result of a guilty conscience, nervousness, or the like; uneasy: *to feel queasy about telling a lie.* **4.** squeamish or delicate: *A queasy person would not enjoy such a brutal movie.* —**quea′si·ness,** *n.*

Que·bec (kwi bek**′**), *n.* **1.** a province in E Canada. 594,860 sq. mi. **2.** a seaport and the capital city of this province, on the St. Lawrence River.

Quech·ua (kech**′**wə), *n., pl.* **Quech·uas** or for def. 2 **Quech·ua. 1.** a South American Indian language spoken by about 4,000,000 people from Ecuador to northern Argentina. **2.** a member of an Indian people of Peru speaking Quechua. —*adj.* **3.** of or concerning the Quechua or their language. Also, **Quech·uan** (kech**′**wən).

queen (kwēn), *n.* **1.** the wife of a king. **2.** a woman ruling a country as its monarch. **3.** a woman who is important or outstanding in some way: *a beauty queen; a queen of society.* **4.** a woman chosen to be the honorary ruler of a festival, ball, or the like. **5.** a playing card bearing a picture of a queen. **6.** (in chess) the most powerful of all the pieces. It is the only piece that can be moved in any direction across as many squares as are empty. See illus. at **chess. 7.** an ant, bee, wasp, or termite that can lay eggs. There is usually only one queen in a nest or hive. See illus. at **bee.**

Queen′ Anne's′ lace′, a wild carrot plant that bears heads of tiny, flat white flowers that look like round pieces of lace.

queen·ly (kwēn′lē), *adj.,* **queen·li·er, queen·li·est. 1.** of or like a queen: *queenly robes.* **2.** befitting or suitable for a queen: *queenly grace.*

queen′ moth′er, a king's widow who is also the mother of a ruling king or queen.

Queens (kwēnz), *n.* a borough of E New York City, on Long Island. 113 sq. mi.

Queens·land (kwēnz′land′, -lənd), *n.* a state in NE Australia. 670,500 sq. mi.

queer (kwēr), *adj.* **1.** different from what is usual or expected; odd or peculiar; unusual: *He has some queer ideas about how to stay healthy.* **2.** suspicious or not completely honest or right: *There's something queer about the way he makes his money.* **3.** slightly ill or faint; queasy; giddy: *to feel queer.* —*v.* **4.** to spoil or ruin; disrupt: *Don't queer our plans by forgetting what you have to do.* **5.** to make unpopular; put in a bad position: *The candidate queered himself with the voters by making too many wild promises.* —**queer′ly,** *adv.* —**queer′ness,** *n.*

quell (kwel), *v.* **1.** to put an end to or put down, esp. with force; suppress: *The army quelled the rebellion.* **2.** to quiet or calm: *to quell someone's fears.*

quench (kwench), *v.* **1.** to put an end to by satisfying; satisfy; slake: *to quench one's thirst.* **2.** to put out (fire, flames, etc.); extinguish, esp. with water. **3.** to overcome or subdue; quell: *to quench anger with kind words.*

quer·u·lous (kwer′ə ləs, kwer′yə ləs), *adj.* **1.** full of complaints; faultfinding; complaining: *a querulous child.* **2.** peevish or complaining: *a querulous tone of voice.* —**quer′u·lous·ly,** *adv.* —**quer′u·lous·ness,** *n.*

que·ry (kwēr′ē), *n., pl.* **que·ries. 1.** a question or inquiry. **2.** doubt or mental uncertainty. —*v.,* **que·ried, que·ry·ing. 3.** to ask or inquire about; question: *I would like to query him about his trip to India.* **4.** to express doubt or confusion about: *The teacher queried some of the facts in my essay.*

quest (kwest), *n.* **1.** a search made in order to find or obtain something; pursuit: *a quest for fame.* **2.** (in stories about knights of the Middle Ages) an adventurous journey or expedition made in order to find or achieve something: *the quest for the Holy Grail.* —*v.* **3.** to search or seek; pursue (often fol. by *for* or *after*): *to quest after hidden treasure.* **4.** (of a knight) to go on a quest. —**quest′er,** *n.*

ques·tion (kwes′chən), *n.* **1.** something asked in order to get information; a request for information; query. A question is written as a sentence followed

by a question mark, such as "Where do you live?" or "When did the Civil War begin?" **2.** a problem or matter for discussion or study: *During this morning's class we shall consider three questions.* **3.** a matter of difficulty or uncertainty; problem: *I would like to buy a car, but there's the question of getting the money.* **4.** a proposal to be debated or voted on at a meeting or the like. **5.** a point of disagreement or doubt; objection: *to raise a question concerning the truthfulness of someone's statements.* —*v.* **6.** to ask (someone) a question or questions; query; interrogate: *The reporters questioned the mayor about the strike.* **7.** to doubt or dispute: *Surely you don't question her honesty.* **8. beyond question,** without doubt; absolutely: *They are beyond question the most beautiful mountains in the world.* **9. out of the question,** not to be considered; impossible: *Your going to Europe this year is out of the question.* —**ques′tion·er,** *n.*

ques·tion·a·ble (kwes′chə nə bəl), *adj.* **1.** of doubtful morality, honesty, etc.; giving one reason for suspicion or disapproval; dubious: *He has certain questionable friendships with known criminals.* **2.** open to question or doubt; not certain; doubtful. —**ques′tion·a·ble·ness,** *n.* —**ques′tion·a·bly,** *adv.*

ques′tion mark′, a punctuation mark (?) showing that a sentence is a question; a mark showing that a question is being asked.

ques·tion·naire (kwes′chə nâr′), *n.* a list of questions used to gather information.

quet·zal (ket säl′), *n.* a Central and South American bird having golden-green and bright-red plumage, the male of which has long, flowing tail feathers.

queue (kyōō), *n.* **1.** a braid of hair worn hanging down from the back of the head; pigtail. **2.** a line of people waiting their turn: *There is a long queue at the entrance to the ball park.* —*v.,* **queued, queu·ing. 3.** to form in a line while waiting (often fol. by *up*): *to queue up to buy tickets.*

Que′zon Cit′y (kā′zon), *n.* a city in the Philippines, NE of Manila.

quib·ble (kwib′əl), *v.,* **quib·bled, quib·bling. 1.** to try to avoid the truth or main point in a discussion by raising unimportant issues, using vague words, trying to confuse the other person, etc.: *to quibble over minor details.* **2.** to criticize or complain for little reason; carp: *She quibbles with her husband over the way he dresses.* —*n.* **3.** a use of petty arguments or vague, confusing language in discussing something; pointless or petty argument: *a lawyer's quibble over the wording in a contract.* **4.** a silly complaint; unimportant criticism or objection. —**quib′bler,** *n.*

quick (kwik), *adj.* **1.** done or happening rapidly or in

Quetzal
(total length
3 ft.; tail
plumes 2 ft.)

a short time; speedy; swift; fast: *She made a quick trip to the store.* **2.** coming or given immediately or in a short time; prompt: *a quick answer to a question.* **3.** moving or able to move with speed; swift: *a quick fox.* **4.** fast to understand, learn, notice, etc.; alert; keen: *a quick mind.* **5.** easily excited; impatient; hasty: *a quick temper.* —*adv.* **6.** speedily or without delay; quickly: *Run quick!* —*n.* **7.** tender, sensitive flesh, esp. under the nails of the fingers or toes. **8.** all living persons (usually preceded by *the*): *the quick and the dead.* [from the Old English word *cwic* "living"] —**quick/ness,** *n.*

quick·en (kwik/ən), *v.* **1.** to make or become faster or more rapid; hurry; hasten: *She quickened her pace.* **2.** to make or become more active, lively, or strong: *His imagination was quickened by his reading.* **3.** to bring life to; revive: *Spring rains quickened the earth.* **4.** to become alive; show signs of life.

quick-freeze (kwik/frēz/), *v.,* **quick-froze** (kwik/-frōz/), **quick-fro·zen** (kwik/frō/zən), **quick-freez·ing.** to freeze (food) rapidly so that it may be safely stored for long periods of time.

quick·lime (kwik/līm/), *n.* See lime[1] (def. 1).

quick·ly (kwik/lē), *adv.* with speed; swiftly or promptly: *to walk quickly; to answer quickly.*

quick·sand (kwik/sand/), *n.* a deep bed of fine, wet sand that swallows up anybody or anything stepping or resting on its surface.

quick·sil·ver (kwik/sil/vər), *n.* metallic mercury in its liquid form.

quick-tem·pered (kwik/tem/pərd), *adj.* easily angered; becoming angry quickly.

quick-wit·ted (kwik/wit/id), *adj.* clever and alert; having or showing a quick mind.

quid (kwid), *n.* a piece of something, esp. tobacco, for chewing.

qui·es·cent (kwē es/ənt), *adj.* at rest; quiet, still, or inactive. —**qui·es/cence,** *n.* —**qui·es/cent·ly,** *adv.*

qui·et (kwī/it), *adj.* **1.** making no noise or disturbing sound; silent or almost silent: *Be quiet or someone will hear you.* **2.** free from noise or disturbance: *a quiet room.* **3.** free from trouble or excitement; calm; peaceful: *a quiet life.* **4.** having no motion, or moving very gently; still: *quiet waters.* **5.** not busy or active: *The doctor told him to rest and be quiet.* **6.** gentle or mild; not rough or high-spirited: *a tame, quiet horse.* **7.** not showy, bright, or loud; soft; subdued: *quiet colors; a quiet style of dressing.* —*v.,* **qui·et·ed, qui·et·ing. 8.** to make or become quiet (often fol. by *down*): *The children quieted down once the movie started.* —*n.* **9.** freedom from noise; silence. **10.** freedom from disturbance or trouble. —**qui/et·ly,** *adv.* —**qui/et·ness,** *n.*

qui·e·tude (kwī/i tōōd/, -tyōōd/), *n.* a state of quiet or rest; stillness; calmness; repose.

quill (kwil), *n.* **1.** a large feather from the wing or tail of a bird. **2.** the hard, hollow part of such a feather. **3.** a pen made from a feather. **4.** a sharp, hollow spine of a porcupine or hedgehog.

quilt (kwilt), *n.* **1.** a cover for a bed, made of two layers of fabric filled with a soft material, such as wool or down, and tufted or stitched together in a pattern of crisscross lines. —*v.* **2.** to stitch together (two pieces of fabric and a soft filling) in this way. **3.** to make quilts.

quilt·ing (kwil/ting), *n.* **1.** the act of a person who quilts. **2.** material for making quilts. **3.** material resembling a quilt; quilted material.

quince (kwins), *n.* **1.** a hard, yellowish, pear-shaped fruit used in jellies and preserves. **2.** the tree that bears this fruit.

qui·nine (kwī/nīn), *n.* a bitter substance obtained from cinchona bark, used to treat malaria.

quin·sy (kwin/zē), *n.* a painful throat condition in which abscesses form on the tonsils.

quin·tes·sence (kwin tes/əns), *n.* **1.** the pure essence of something; purest form: *This sonnet seems to have captured the quintessence of poetry.* **2.** a perfect example of something: *The Parthenon is the quintessence of classical Greek architecture.*

quin·tet (kwin tet/), *n.* **1.** a group of five singers or players. **2.** a piece of music composed for such a group. **3.** any group or set of five persons or things.

quin·tu·plet (kwin tup/lit, kwin tōō/plit), *n.* **1. quintuplets,** five children born at one time of the same mother. **2.** any one of five such children. **3.** any group or set of five persons or things.

quip (kwip), *n.* **1.** a clever or funny remark, often sarcastic. —*v.,* **quipped, quip·ping. 2.** to make a quip or quips.

quire (kwī°r), *n.* a set of 24, or sometimes 25, sheets of paper of the same size and kind or quality.

quirk (kwûrk), *n.* **1.** something odd or peculiar in one's personality or behavior; peculiarity: *One of his little quirks is that he never goes out without an umbrella.* **2.** a sudden twist or turn: *By a quirk of fate, he found himself rich overnight.*

quirt (kwûrt), *n.* a riding whip having a short, thick handle and a lash of braided leather.

quis·ling (kwiz/ling), *n.* a person who betrays his country by helping an invading enemy, often in return for high position in the government set up by the enemy.

quit (kwit), *v.,* **quit** *or* **quit·ted; quit·ting. 1.** to stop or cease: *Quit making so much noise! Don't quit in the middle of the race.* **2.** to leave or depart from: *She quits the city every summer to go to the seashore.* **3.** to let go or give up; abandon or resign: *to quit one's job.* —*adj.* **4.** released from or free of a debt, obligation, or the like; rid (usually fol. by *of*): *He is finally quit of all debts.*

quit·claim (kwit/klām/), *n.* **1.** a legal agreement or deed in which one gives up one's claim or right to property, a privilege, or the like. —*v.* **2.** to quit or give up claim to (a possession, right, etc.).

quite (kwīt), *adv.* **1.** completely or entirely: *I'm not quite finished.* **2.** actually; really; truly: *There was quite a sudden change in the weather.* **3.** to a rather large extent or degree; very: *It is really quite stuffy in here.* **4. quite a,** unusual; exceptional: *Joe is quite a swimmer.* **5. quite a few,** a great many; a large number of: *There were quite a few objections to my plan.*

6. quite a while, a long while: *I had to wait quite a while.*

Qui·to (kē′tō), *n.* the capital city of Ecuador, in the N part.

quits (kwits), *adj.* **1.** being even or on equal terms as a result of repayment or revenge: *We'll be quits, if I beat you in the next game.* **2. call it quits, a.** to stop work or other activity for a while: *The teacher said we could call it quits for this afternoon.* **b.** to give up an effort: *After breaking his leg twice, he decided to call it quits on skiing.*

quit·tance (kwit′ᵊns), *n.* **1.** repayment or revenge. **2.** release or discharge from a debt or obligation. **3.** a document giving proof of such release.

quit·ter (kwit′ər), *n.* a person who quits or gives up too easily or quickly.

quiv·er[1] (kwiv′ər), *v.* **1.** to shake with a slight but rapid motion; tremble; vibrate: *to quiver with excitement.* —*n.* **2.** a quivering; tremble or shiver: *With a quiver of its nostrils, the fox sniffed the breeze.* [from Middle English] —**quiv′er·ing·ly,** *adv.*

quiv·er[2] (kwiv′ər), *n.* a case for holding or carrying arrows. [from the Old French word *quivre,* which comes perhaps from Germanic]

quix·ot·ic (kwik sot′ik), *adj.* extremely chivalrous, romantic, and idealistic in a way that is impractical and often foolish. [after *Don Quixote,* whose character is so described] —**quix·ot′i·cal·ly,** *adv.*

quiz (kwiz), *v.,* **quizzed, quiz·zing. 1.** to examine (a student or class) informally by asking questions or giving a brief test. **2.** to question closely: *The judge quizzed him for an hour about the missing money.* **3.** *British.* to make fun of (someone); mock; tease. —*n., pl.* **quiz·zes. 4.** an informal test or examination. **5.** a questioning on any subject. **6.** *British.* a person who makes fun; tease; joker.

quiz·zi·cal (kwiz′i kəl), *adj.* **1.** questioning or puzzled: *a quizzical expression on her face.* **2.** mocking or teasing: *a quizzical smile.* **3.** odd or comical. —**quiz′zi·cal·ly,** *adv.* —**quiz′zi·cal·ness,** *n.*

quoit (kwoit), *n.* **1. quoits,** a game in which one tries to throw rings of rope or flattened metal over a peg set up in the ground. **2.** a ring used in this game.

Quon′set hut′ (kwon′sit), *Trademark.* a metal building in the shape of half a cylinder set lengthwise on the ground, used esp. as a barracks or storage shed.

quo·rum (kwôr′əm), *n.* the number of members of a group or assembly that must be present at a meeting if any legal or binding business is to be transacted: *We must have a quorum of ten persons.* [from a Latin word meaning "of whom"]

quo·ta (kwō′tə), *n.* a share or portion of a total required of or assigned to a person, group, organization, etc.: *We each have our quota of work to be done.* [from the Latin phrase *quota pars* "how great a part?"]

quot·a·ble (kwō′tə bəl), *adj.* **1.** worth quoting, or easy to remember and quote: *a funny, quotable book.* **2.** suitable to be quoted: *In a terrible temper he made some remarks that are not quotable.*

quo·ta·tion (kwō tā′shən), *n.* **1.** words or a passage from a book, speech, etc., repeated exactly by someone else in speech or writing: *There is a quotation from President Franklin D. Roosevelt on page 20 of your book.* **2.** the act of repeating exactly someone else's words: *His quotation of the patriot's dying words inspired us to fight harder.* **3.** the price of a stock, bond, or the like.

quota′tion mark′, one of the punctuation marks used to show the beginning and end of a quotation, usually printed as (") at the beginning and (") at the end. Single quotation marks, (') and ('), are used for a quotation inserted within a quotation, as *"He said, 'I will go.'"* Also, **quote′ mark′.**

quote (kwōt), *v.,* **quot·ed, quot·ing. 1.** to repeat exactly in speech or writing (words, a passage, phrase, etc.) from an author, book, conversation, or the like: *Paul quoted a verse from the poem we've been studying.* **2.** to repeat exactly the words of (an author, book, etc.): *to quote Shakespeare.* **3.** to enclose (words, a passage, etc.) in quotation marks: *You must quote this phrase.* **4.** to mention or refer to (an authority, ruling, fact, or the like) in support of an argument: *He quoted recent discoveries in science as evidence for his point of view.* **5.** to state (the price) of a stock, bond, or the like. —*n.* **6.** a quotation: *Wasn't that a quote from Robert Browning?* **7.** a quotation mark. —**quot′er,** *n.*

quoth (kwōth), *v. Archaic.* said or spoke (placed before the subject): *Quoth the raven, "Nevermore."*

quo·tient (kwō′shənt), *n.* (in arithmetic) the result obtained by dividing one number into another. In the example $72 \div 3 = 24$, 24 is the quotient. See also **dividend** (def. 2), **divisor.** [from the Latin word *quotiēns* "how many times?"]

R

Semitic	Greek		Latin	Gothic	Modern Roman
𝟫	٩	ꓑ	ꓑ	R	Ꞧ R

DEVELOPMENT OF UPPER-CASE LETTERS

ρ	ᴦ	ꓣ	ᴦ	r	r
Greek		Medieval		Gothic	Modern Roman

DEVELOPMENT OF LOWER-CASE LETTERS

R, r (är), *n., pl.* **R's** *or* **Rs, r's** *or* **rs. 1.** the 18th letter of the English alphabet. **2. the three R's,** reading, 'riting (writing), and 'rithmetic (arithmetic), regarded as the essentials of a person's education.

R, 1. (in electricity) resistance. **2.** a designation of a motion picture to which persons under 17 are admitted only when accompanied by a parent or guardian. **3.** (in chess) rook.

R., 1. radius. **2.** Railroad. **3.** queen. [from the Latin word *Rēgina*] **4.** Republican. **5.** king. [from the Latin word *Rēx*] **6.** right. **7.** River.

r., 1. radius. **2.** railroad. **3.** rare. **4.** residence. **5.** right. **6.** river.

RA, regular army.

Ra, *Chem.* the symbol for **radium.**

rab·bi (rab′ī), *n., pl.* **rab·bis. 1.** the religious leader of a Jewish congregation. **2.** a title of respect for a Jewish scholar or teacher.

rab·bin·i·cal (rə bin′i kəl), *adj.* of or concerning rabbis or their work, writings, etc.: *rabbinical teachings; a rabbinical school.* Also, **rab·bin′ic.**

rab·bit (rab′it), *n.* **1.** a small, furry animal that has long ears and powerful hind legs and lives in burrows. Rabbits are smaller than hares and have shorter ears. **2.** the fur of this animal.

rab·ble (rab′əl), *n.* **1.** a disorderly crowd; mob. **2. the rabble,** the lower classes, or common people, thought of as ignorant and rude.

rab·ble-rous·er (rab′əl rou′zər), *n.* a person who stirs up the fears, feelings, and prejudices of the public; agitator. —**rab′ble-rous′ing,** *adj.*

rab·id (rab′id), *adj.* **1.** violently extreme and unreasonable in opinions or behavior: *a rabid warmonger.* **2.** furious or raging; violently intense: *a rabid hatred.* **3.** affected with or suffering from rabies. —**rab·id′i·ty, rab′id·ness,** *n.* —**rab′id·ly,** *adv.*

ra·bies (rā′bēz), *n.* an infectious disease of dogs, cats, bats, etc., and also of man, that is usually transmitted by the bite of an infected animal and is usu-

Rabbit
(length 15 in.)

ally fatal if not specially treated. Also, **hydrophobia.**

rac·coon (ra kōōn′), *n.* **1.** a small, furry animal having a pointed snout, a bushy, ringed tail, and black markings on its face. Raccoons live in trees and are active chiefly at night. **2.** the fur of this animal. Also, **racoon.**

Raccoon
(total length 3 ft.)

race¹ (rās), *n.* **1.** a contest of speed in running, driving, sailing, etc.: *a horse race; a boat race.* **2.** any contest or competition to achieve something: *the race for the presidency.* **3.** a strong or rapid current of water in the sea, a river, or the like. —*v.,* **raced, rac·ing. 4.** to take part in a contest of speed; run a race: *This horse is racing tomorrow.* **5.** to run a race against: *Jim raced Steve to the corner.* **6.** to enter in a race or races: *He races dogs as a hobby.* **7.** to move, go, or act with speed; hurry: *We'll have to race in order to catch the plane.* **8.** to cause to go fast: *to race the motor of a car.* [from the Middle English word *rase,* which comes from Scandinavian]

race² (rās), *n.* **1.** a division of mankind made up of a very large group of people who share the same ancestry and similar physical characteristics that are passed on through heredity: *The Chinese belong to the Mongoloid race.* **2.** any group of persons related by ancestry and sharing the same culture and homeland: *the race of Vikings.* **3.** a group or kind of living creature: *the race of fishes; the human race.* **4.** a group of persons sharing the same interests, experiences, or the like: *the race of pioneers.* [from a French word, which comes from Italian *razza*]

race·course (rās′kôrs′), *n.* a race track.

race′ horse′, a horse bred or used for racing.

ra·ceme (rā sēm′, rə sēm′), *n.* a cluster of flowers each of which grows on its own short stalk spaced along the stem of a plant, as in the lily of the valley.

rac·er (rā′sər), *n.* **1.** a person or thing that races or takes part in a race. **2.** anything that can move at great speed: *This car is a racer.* **3.** any of several slender American snakes, esp. the blacksnake.

race′ track′, a plot of ground that is used for rac-ing, usually a course having an oval shape.

Ra·chel (rā′chəl), *n.* (in the Bible) a wife of Jacob and the mother of Joseph and Benjamin.

ra·cial (rā′shəl), *adj.* of or referring to race or the races of mankind: *racial migrations; racial pride.* —**ra′cial·ly,** *adv.*

rac·ism (rā′siz əm), *n.* a theory or way of thinking that attempts to explain differences in human behav-ior in terms of race. Racism is usually without any scientific basis and comes from the idea that one's own race is superior and should rule others.

rac·ist (rā′sist), *n.* 1. a person who believes in racism. —*adj.* 2. of or concerning racism: *racist propaganda.*

rack[1] (rak), *n.* 1. a framework or stand on which things may be placed or hung for display or when not being used or worn: *a towel rack; a bicycle rack.* 2. a framework set on a wagon for carrying large loads of hay, straw, or the like. 3. a former instru-ment of torture used to stretch the victim's body, causing great pain and sometimes death. 4. a bar bearing teeth that engage with a gear or pinion. —*v.* 5. to cause great suffering in; torture; torment: *Pain racked his body.* 6. to strain or stretch by effort, force, etc.: *He racked his brains for the answer.* [from the early Dutch word *rec* "framework"]

rack[2] (rak), *n.* 1. *Archaic.* destruction or wreck. 2. **go to rack and ruin,** to become ruined, esp. by ne-glect or decay: *That beautiful estate has gone to rack and ruin since the owners moved out.* [another form of *wrack*[1]]

rack[3] (rak), *n.* a fast pace of a horse in which the legs of the left side move forward together and the legs of the right side move forward together, with the hind foot hitting the ground just before the fore-foot. [perhaps another form of *rock*[2]]

rack·et[1] (rak′it), *n.* 1. a loud, disturbing noise; din; uproar. 2. a dishonest or criminal means of gaining money: *the illegal sale of drugs and other rackets.* [another form of the dialect word *rattick,* which is related to *rattle*]

rack·et[2] (rak′it), *n.* 1. any of various light bats used esp. in tennis and badminton. A racket usually has a fairly long handle and an oval head in which cords of nylon or gut are stretched tight. 2. a short-handled bat or paddle, used in ta-ble tennis, paddle tennis, or similar games. Also, **racquet.** [from the early French word *raquette,* which comes from an Arabic word mean-ing "palm of the hand"]

Rackets
A, Tennis
B, Badminton
C, Squash

rack·et·eer (rak′i tēr′), *n.* a per-son who makes money in an organ-ized illegal activity, such as gambling or drugs.

ra·coon (ra kōōn′), *n.* another spelling of **raccoon.**

rac·quet (rak′it), *n.* 1. another spelling of **racket**[2]. 2. **racquets,** *(used as sing.)* a game played with rackets and a ball on a four-walled court.

rac·y (rā′sē), *adj.,* **rac·i·er, rac·i·est.** 1. lively or vigor-ous; full of zest; spirited: *a racy style of writing.* 2. slightly indecent or improper: *racy stories.* 3. having an agreeably unusual or peculiar taste: *a racy wine; racy fruit.* —**rac′i·ly,** *adv.* —**rac′i·ness,** *n.*

ra·dar (rā′där), *n.* an electronic device for detecting objects, such as ships or airplanes, and determining how far away they are by measuring the direction from which they reflect radio waves and the length of time it takes for the waves to be returned. [from the phrase *ra(dio) d(etecting) a(nd) r(anging)*]

ra·di·al (rā′dē əl), *adj.* 1. extending outward from a central point like rays or radii. 2. of, concerning, or resembling rays or radii. —**ra′di·al·ly,** *adv.*

ra·di·ance (rā′dē əns), *n.* 1. a shining brightness or light: *the radiance of the sun.* 2. warmth; joyful brightness or loveliness: *the radiance of her smile.*

ra·di·ant (rā′dē ənt), *adj.* 1. shining or bright; giving off rays of light: *a radiant bonfire.* 2. shining with joy, hope, happiness, etc.: *a radiant bride.* 3. refer-ring to or transmitted by radiation: *radiant energy.* —**ra′di·ant·ly,** *adv.*

ra′diant en′ergy, energy that is transmitted by means of radiation, esp. in the form of heat, light, ra-dio waves, or x-rays.

ra·di·ate (rā′dē āt′), *v.,* **ra·di·at·ed, ra·di·at·ing.** 1. to give off light, heat, or other radiation: *A fireplace radiates heat into a room.* 2. to be produced or trans-mitted in the form of rays or radiation. 3. to show or spread a feeling of (joy, hope, happiness, etc.): *a smile that radiates happiness.* 4. to spread out or ex-tend in different directions from a center: *roads ra-diating from a city.*

ra·di·a·tion (rā′dē ā′shən), *n.* 1. the process in which energy is given off as particles or waves. 2. the process in which energy is given off by one body and transmitted to and absorbed by another. 3. the particles or waves that are given off or received in this process.

ra·di·a·tor (rā′dē ā′tər), *n.* 1. any of various heating devices, such as a series of pipes in which steam or hot water is circulated. 2. a series of tubes equipped with thin metal fins for cooling a hot liquid or gas, such as the water circulating around an automobile engine.

rad·i·cal (rad′i kəl), *adj.* 1. fundamental or basic; go-ing to the roots or origins of something: *There are radical differences in our points of view.* 2. extreme or drastic, esp. in favoring severe and rapid reforms or changes in politics and society. 3. (in mathemat-ics) of or concerning square roots, cube roots, etc. —*n.* 4. a person who favors severe and rapid reforms or changes in politics and society: *a debate between radicals and conservatives.* 5. a radical sign. 6. *Chem.* a group of atoms that act together as a unit in chemical reactions. —**rad′i·cal·ly,** *adv.*

rad·i·cal·ism (rad′i kə liz′əm), *n.* the beliefs or prac-tices of political radicals.

rad′ical sign′, the sign ($\sqrt{}$), indicating that one is to extract the root of the number following it. $\sqrt{4}$ is read "square root of 4"; $\sqrt[3]{8}$ is read "cube root of 8," etc.

ra·di·i (rā/dē ī/), *n.* the plural of **radius.**

ra·di·o (rā/dē ō/), *n., pl.* **ra·di·os. 1.** the transmitting of messages, music, etc., by means of electric and magnetic waves. **2.** an apparatus for receiving such waves and converting them back to sound. **3.** the business of radio broadcasting: *a career in radio.* —*adj.* **4.** concerning, used in, or sent by radio. —*v.*, **ra·di·oed, ra·di·o·ing. 5.** to transmit (messages, music, etc.) or communicate with (someone) by radio.

ra·di·o·ac·tive (rā/dē ō ak/tiv), *adj.* of, concerning, exhibiting, or caused by radioactivity. —**ra/di·o·ac/tive·ly,** *adv.*

ra·di·o·ac·tiv·i·ty (rā/dē ō ak tiv/i tē), *n.* the property of certain chemical elements causing them to emit radiation as a result of changes in the nuclei of atoms of the element.

ra/dio astron/omy, the branch of astronomy that uses radio waves instead of visible light to study stars, galaxies, etc.

ra·di·om·e·ter (rā/dē om/i tər), *n.* an instrument for showing the transformation of radiant energy into mechanical work.

ra/dio tel/escope, a very large instrument for receiving radio waves from outer space.

ra/dio wave/, one of the electric and magnetic waves that are used to broadcast and transmit radio signals.

rad·ish (rad/ish), *n.* **1.** the crisp, sharp-tasting, red or white root of a garden plant, usually eaten raw, esp. in salads. **2.** a plant having this root.

ra·di·um (rā/dē əm), *n. Chem.* a radioactive metallic element formerly used in the manufacture of luminescent paints and in treating disease. *Symbol:* Ra

Radiometer

ra·di·us (rā/dē əs), *n., pl.* **ra·di·i** (rā/dē ī/). **1.** a straight line drawn from the center to the outside of a circle or sphere. See illus. at **circle. 2.** the length of such a line. **3.** a circular area determined by the length of its radius: *There is no large city within a radius of 50 miles.* **4.** the thicker of the two long bones extending from the elbow to the wrist.

r, Radius

RAdm., Rear Admiral. Also, **R.A.**

ra·don (rā/don), *n.* a rare, chemically inert, radioactive gas produced by the radioactive disintegration of radium: a chemical element. *Symbol:* Rn

RAF, Royal Air Force. Also, **R.A.F.**

raf·fi·a (raf/ē ə), *n.* **1.** the fiber of a palm tree that grows on Madagascar, used for tying and for making baskets, mats, etc. **2.** the palm tree whose leafstalks yield this fiber.

raf·fle (raf/əl), *n.* **1.** a lottery in which a number of persons buy one or more chances to win a prize.

—*v.,* **raf·fled, raf·fling. 2.** to give away as a prize in a raffle (often fol. by *off*): *to raffle off a new car.*

raft (raft), *n.* a platform for floating on water, esp. one made of logs or planks fastened together.

raft·er (raf/tər), *n.* one of a series of sloping timbers or beams used to support the covering of a roof.

rag (rag), *n.* **1.** an almost worthless piece of cloth, esp. one that is torn or worn out: *She tore the old sheet into rags.* **2. rags,** tattered or worn-out clothing: *The beggars wore rags.* —*adj.* **3.** made from rags or small pieces of cloth: *a rag rug; a rag doll.* —*v.,* **ragged, rag·ging.** *Informal.* **4.** to tease; play jokes on. **5.** to scold or lecture.

rag·a·muf·fin (rag/ə muf/in), *n.* a person who is ragged and dirty, esp. a child.

rage (rāj), *n.* **1.** violent anger; fury. **2.** violence, intensity, or fury, as of a storm, fire, disease, etc.: *the rage of a wind; the rage of a fever.* **3.** a violent emotional state; passion: *to be in a rage of excitement.* **4.** a popular fashion; fad; craze: *Knee-length boots are the rage these days.* —*v.,* **raged, rag·ing. 5.** to act or speak with fury; show violent anger: *He was raging because a truck crashed into his new car.* **6.** to move with violent force: *The waves raged against the rocks.* **7.** to continue, proceed, or spread with violence or intensity: *Plague raged through the city.*

rag·ged (rag/id), *adj.* **1.** wearing tattered or worn-out clothes: *a thin, ragged beggar.* **2.** torn or worn out; tattered; shabby: *a ragged old sweater.* **3.** shaggy or uneven: *a ragged haircut.* **4.** having loose or hanging shreds or bits: *a ragged tear in the curtains.* **5.** rough or jagged; not smooth: *ragged stones.* —**rag/ged·ly,** *adv.* —**rag/ged·ness,** *n.*

rag·man (rag/man/, -mən), *n., pl.* **rag·men.** a ragpicker.

ra·gout (ra gōō/), *n.* a highly seasoned stew.

rag·pick·er (rag/pik/ər), *n.* a person who gathers rags, old paper, and other waste material for sale; ragman.

rag·time (rag/tīm/), *n.* a kind of popular music having a fast, syncopated rhythm.

rag·weed (rag/wēd/), *n.* a common weed with ragged leaves. Its pollen is an important cause of hayfever.

raid (rād), *n.* **1.** a sudden attack or invasion, esp. by a group of planes or a small group of soldiers: *to make a raid on an enemy outpost.* **2.** a sudden entry made in order to seize illegal goods, make arrests, or the like: *The police made a raid on the criminals' hideout.* —*v.* **3.** to attack or enter suddenly; make a raid on: *The Indians raided the soldiers' camp at dawn.* **4.** to take part in a raid. —**raid/er,** *n.*

rail¹ (rāl), *n.* **1.** a bar of wood or metal, esp. one set lengthwise as a barrier, banister, part of a fence, or the like. **2.** one of a pair of steel bars set along the ground as a track for the wheels of a railroad train. **3.** a railroad: *to travel by rail.* —*v.* **4.** to enclose with a rail or rails; fence: *to rail off part of a field.* [from the Old French word *raille* "bar, beam," which comes from Latin *regula* "bar, straight piece of wood"]

rail[2] (rāl), v. to complain bitterly; speak harsh, angry words (often fol. by *at* or *against*): *to rail against one's enemies.* [from the French word *railler* "to deride," which comes from Provençal *ralhar* "to chatter," from Latin *ragere* "to shriek"]

rail[3] (rāl), n. any of numerous birds having short wings, a narrow body, long toes, and a harsh cry, which are found in grasslands, forests, and marshes. [from the Old French word *raale,* which comes from Latin *rādere* "to scratch"]

Virginia rail
(length 9½ in.)

rail·ing (rā′lĭng), n. 1. a fencelike barrier made of one or more rails set on upright supports. 2. a rail used as a banister. 3. rails or material for making rails: *We need another load of railing to fix this old fence.*

rail·ler·y (rā′lə rē), n., pl. **rail·ler·ies.** 1. good-humored teasing; banter. 2. a teasing or slightly mocking remark.

rail·road (rāl′rōd′), n. 1. a road or course laid with metal rails for locomotives, trains, etc. 2. such a road together with the locomotives, trains, buildings, and other property and equipment that make up an entire system of transportation. 3. the company of persons owning or operating such a system of transportation: *The railroad is going to run fewer passenger trains.* —v. 4. to work on a railroad. 5. to push (a law, bill, or the like) through so fast that there is not enough time to consider objections: *to railroad a bill through Congress.* 6. *Informal.* to convict (a person) of a crime hastily and unfairly.

rail·way (rāl′wā′), n. 1. a railroad, esp. one using lightweight equipment or operating over short distances. 2. a track for railroad trains.

rai·ment (rā′mənt), n. clothing or attire; apparel.

rain (rān), n. 1. water that is condensed from the air and falls in drops from the sky. 2. a fall of such drops from the sky; rainfall, rainstorm, or shower. 3. **rains,** the rainy season; a time of the year when there is heavy rainfall every day, as in India: *The rains begin next month.* 4. a heavy or thick fall of anything: *a rain of arrows.* —v. 5. (of rain) to fall (usually used with *it* as subject): *It rained all night.* 6. to fall like rain: *Tears rained from her eyes.* 7. to cause to fall down like rain; drop; send down: *The plane rained leaflets over the villages.* 8. to offer or give in great quantity: *to rain compliments upon someone.*

rain·bow (rān′bō′), n. a bow or arc of colors appearing in the heavens opposite the sun and caused by the sun's rays passing through drops of water.

rain·coat (rān′kōt′), n. a waterproof coat worn as protection against rain.

rain·drop (rān′drop′), n. a drop of rain.

rain·fall (rān′fôl′), n. 1. a fall or shower of rain. 2. the amount of water that falls in the form of rain, snow, etc., in a particular area over a specified time, calculated as the total depth of water that would result: *an annual rainfall of 70 inches.*

Rai·nier (rā nēr′, rə nēr′), n. **Mount,** a mountain in W Washington, in the Cascade Range. 14,408 ft.

rain·proof (rān′proof′), adj. 1. keeping out rain, or not damaged by rain: *a rainproof coat.* —v. 2. to make rainproof: *to rainproof a hat.*

rain·storm (rān′stôrm′), n. a storm with a heavy rain.

rain·y (rā′nē), adj., **rain·i·er, rain·i·est.** 1. having rain or much rain: *a rainy morning; a rainy climate.* 2. wet with rain: *rainy streets.* 3. bringing rain: *rainy skies.* —**rain′i·ness,** n.

rain′y day′, a time of need; an emergency: *Save some money for those rainy days.*

raise (rāz), v., **raised, rais·ing.** 1. to lift up; move to a higher position: *to raise a window; to raise one foot.* 2. to set upright: *to raise a ladder against a wall.* 3. to build or set up; construct; erect: *to raise a barn; to raise a monument.* 4. to grow or breed, and care for (plants, animals, etc.): *to raise corn; to raise chickens.* 5. to take care of (a child) for a long period; help to grow up; rear: *She raised two fine boys.* 6. to rouse or arouse; make awake, active, or alive: *a noise that raised the whole neighborhood.* 7. to cause or bring about; stir up: *The harsh laws raised a storm of protest.* 8. to cause to rise: *Yeast raises dough.* 9. to present for discussion or consideration; bring up: *to raise a question.* 10. to increase in value, amount, or force: *to raise prices; to raise one's voice.* 11. to collect or assemble: *to raise money; to raise an army.* 12. to advance in rank or position; promote: *The king raised the soldier to captain of the guard.* 13. to end or lift (a siege, blockade, or the like). —n. 14. an increase, esp. in pay or salary: *He received a raise of ten dollars per week.* —**rais′er,** n.

—Usage. See **rise.**

rai·sin (rā′zin), n. a sweet, dried grape, often used in cakes and cookies.

ra·jah (rä′jə), n. (in India and some other Asian countries) a king, prince, or chief. Also, **ra′ja.**

rake[1] (rāk), n. 1. a garden tool having a long handle attached to a set of metal teeth or prongs: used to smooth out the soil or collect small stones, twigs, leaves, etc. —v., **raked, rak·ing.** 2. to gather with a rake: *to rake leaves.* 3. to smooth, clear, or prepare with a rake; use a rake on: *to rake the lawn; to rake a flower bed.* 4. to search thoroughly: *They raked the house for the missing jewels.* 5. to discover and collect, and bring to light: *to rake up new evidence.* 6. to sweep with gunfire: *Machine guns raked the line of tanks.* 7. to search or observe with a sweeping look: *The sailor's eyes raked the horizon for a sign of land.* [from the Old English word *raca*] —**rak′er,** n.

rake[2] (rāk), n. a man who leads a wild, usually immoral life: *a drunken, rowdy young rake.* [short for the word *rakehell* "dissolute person"]

rake[3] (rāk), n. a slope or sloping angle, esp. of a ship's mast or smokestack. [perhaps from the Old English word *racian* "to take a direction"]

rak·ish[1] (rā′kish), adj. like a rake; wild and immoral;

dissolute: *His friend is a rakish young man.* [from *rake*² + *-ish*]

rak·ish² (rā′kish), *adj.* **1.** dashing or jaunty: *a hat worn at a rakish angle.* **2.** (of a ship) having the appearance of being fast. [from *rake*³ + *-ish*]

Ra·leigh (rô′lē, rä′lē), *n.* **1.** Sir Walter, 1552?–1618, English explorer and writer. **2.** the capital city of North Carolina, in the central part.

ral·ly¹ (ral′ē), *v.*, **ral·lied, ral·ly·ing.** **1.** to bring or gather together again for action: *The captain rallied his scattered troops.* **2.** to bring or come together for a united action or single purpose: *The townspeople rallied to rebuild the bridge.* **3.** to come to the assistance or support of a person, cause, etc.: *The supporters rallied to his cause.* **4.** to recover strength; revive: *The tired runner rallied when he saw the finish line.* **5.** (in tennis, badminton, etc.) to hit the ball or bird back and forth a number of times before a point is scored or a match has begun. —*n., pl.* **ral·lies. 6.** a gathering together of many persons for a single purpose; mass meeting: *a rally of students to cheer the team.* **7.** a recovery from disorder, weakness, etc.; return to strength: *Business should show a rally next month.* **8.** (in tennis, badminton, etc.) the act of hitting the ball or bird back and forth a number of times. [from the French word *rallier* "to rejoin, gather"] —**ral′li·er,** *n.*

ral·ly² (ral′ē), *v.*, **ral·lied, ral·ly·ing.** to tease or ridicule in a good-natured way. [from the French word *railler* "to deride." See **rail²**]

ram (ram), *n.* **1.** a male sheep. **2.** the **Ram,** another name for **Aries. 3.** a device, such as a battering ram, used to batter, crush, or force something: *a ram to knock down a wall; a ram to drive poles into the ground.* —*v.*, **rammed, ram·ming. 4.** to drive or force by heavy blows: *to ram a door open.* **5.** to hit with great force; strike violently against: *The truck rammed the car ahead of it.* **6.** to cram or stuff: *to ram old rags into a hole in the wall.* —**ram′mer,** *n.*

ram·ble (ram′bəl), *v.*, **ram·bled, ram·bling. 1.** to wander or stroll about for pleasure; roam aimlessly: *to ramble through the park.* **2.** to go in a winding course: *The stream rambled through the woods.* **3.** to talk or write in an aimless way: *The speaker rambled on, boring us all.* **4.** to grow or spread in a haphazard way, as many vines do. —*n.* **5.** an aimless walk taken for pleasure: *a ramble through the fields.*

ram·bler (ram′blər), *n.* **1.** a person or thing that rambles or wanders. **2.** any of several kinds of climbing roses that have clusters of small flowers.

ram·bling (ram′bling), *adj.* **1.** wandering aimlessly: *a rambling walk around town.* **2.** having many twists and turns; winding: *a rambling brook.* **3.** spread out irregularly in several directions: *a huge, rambling house.* **4.** wandering or straying from one subject to another: *a rambling sermon.*

ram·bunc·tious (ram bungk′shəs), *adj.* wild and unruly; boisterous: *a noisy, rambunctious little boy.* —**ram·bunc′tious·ly,** *adv.* —**ram·bunc′tious·ness,** *n.*

ram·e·kin (ram′ə kin), *n.* a small dish in which food can be baked and served.

ram·i·fi·ca·tion (ram′ə fə kā′shən), *n.* **1.** the act of ramifying or branching out. **2.** a branch or branching part: *a ramification of a nerve.* **3.** an outgrowth or consequence: *an action that had many ramifications.*

ram·i·fy (ram′ə fī), *v.*, **ram·i·fied, ram·i·fy·ing.** to divide or spread out into branches or branchlike parts; divide or subdivide.

ramp (ramp), *n.* **1.** a sloping surface, such as a walk or roadway, connecting one level or floor with another. **2.** Also, **boarding ramp.** a movable staircase for passengers entering or leaving an airplane.

ram·page (ram′pāj), *n.* **1.** a fit of violent or wild behavior; a furious rushing about: *The angry bull went on a rampage.* —*v.* (ram pāj′), **ram·paged, ram·pag·ing. 2.** to act or rush in a violent, furious manner: *elephants rampaging through the jungle.*

ramp·ant (ram′pənt), *adj.* **1.** existing, growing, or spreading without control; unchecked; widespread: *rampant fear; rampant weeds.* **2.** violent or furious; raging. **3.** (of a four-legged animal) standing on one or both hind legs with the front feet in the air: *a coat of arms showing a lion rampant.* —**ramp′ant·ly,** *adv.*

Rampant (Heraldic lion)

ram·part (ram′pärt, ram′pərt), *n.* **1.** a broad bank or mound of earth raised as a fortification, usually topped by a parapet of earth or stone. **2.** anything serving as a defense or protection: *Faith is his rampart.*

ram·rod (ram′rod′), *n.* **1.** a rod for pushing gunpowder and shot into the barrel of a gun that is loaded through the muzzle. **2.** a rod for cleaning the barrel of a gun.

ram·shack·le (ram′shak′əl), *adj.* loosely held together; rickety; shaky: *He owns a small, ramshackle cabin in the mountains.*

ran (ran), *v.* the past tense of **run.**

ranch (ranch), *n.* **1.** a large farm with land for grazing, used to raise cattle, horses, or other livestock. **2.** any farm, esp. a large farm that is used chiefly to raise one crop or kind of animal: *a chicken ranch; a fruit ranch.* —*v.* **3.** to work on or manage a ranch.

ranch·er (ran′chər), *n.* a person who works on a ranch, esp. an owner or manager.

ranch′ wag′on, another term for **station wagon.**

ran·cid (ran′sid), *adj.* having a strong, unpleasant smell or taste, as a result of staleness, spoilage, or the like: *rancid butter.* —**ran·cid′i·ty,** *n.*

ran·cor (rang′kər), *n.* bitter resentment or spite; hatred; malice: *Being slighted filled him with rancor.* —**ran′cor·ous,** *adj.*

ran·dom (ran′dəm), *adj.* **1.** without plan or order; chance: *He jotted down random thoughts.* **2. at random,** in a random manner; haphazardly: *He chose six marbles at random.*

rang (rang), *v.* the past tense of **ring².**

range (rānj), *n.* **1.** the limits within which something varies: *cloth in a wide range of colors.* **2.** the limits within which something can be done, operate, etc.: *the range of a pistol; a sound out of range of one's* *hearing.* **3.** an area where shooting is practiced: *a rifle range.* **4.** a row or line of persons or things. **5.** a chain of mountains. **6.** a large, open region for grazing livestock. **7.** a large stove with burners and an oven. —*v.,* **ranged, rang·ing. 8.** to vary or change within certain limits: *prices ranging from cheap to expensive.* **9.** to draw up or stretch out in rows or lines, esp. in an orderly fashion: *He ranged the books according to color.* **10.** to place in a certain class or group: *He ranged himself with the winning side.* **11.** to run or go in a certain direction: *a boundary ranging east and west.* **12.** to rove or roam: *Cattle ranged the meadows.* —*adj.* **13.** working or grazing on a range: *Sheep are range animals.*

rang·er (rān′jər), *n.* **1.** a forest ranger. **2.** a member of a body of men who patrol a region as guards. **3.** a person that ranges; rover.

Ran·goon (rang gōōn′), *n.* a seaport and the capital city of Burma, in the S part.

rang·y (rān′jē), *adj.,* **rang·i·er, rang·i·est.** slender and long-limbed: *a rangy animal; a rangy athlete.*

rank¹ (rangk), *n.* **1.** social standing, class, or position: *Dukes are of high rank.* **2.** high social standing: *Persons of rank attended the king.* **3.** official position or grade: *the rank of president.* **4.** grade or class: *a writer of the highest rank.* **5.** a row or line of things or persons placed or standing side by side, esp. a line of soldiers standing abreast. **6.** Usually, **ranks.** the members of an army, navy, or other organization apart from the officers or leaders. —*v.* **7.** to arrange in a rank or ranks. **8.** to hold a certain rank or position: *The United States ranks high as an industrial power.* **9.** to hold the highest rank or position: *The colonel ranks at this camp.* **10. rank and file,** the members of an organization, nation, etc., other than its leaders: *The rank and file will vote on the strike next week.* [from the early French word *ranc,* which comes from Germanic]

rank² (rangk), *adj.* **1.** growing quickly and coarsely: *rank weeds.* **2.** having an unpleasantly strong smell or taste: *a rank cigar.* **3.** utter or complete: *a rank outsider.* [from the Old English word *ranc* "bold, proud"] —**rank′ly,** *adv.* —**rank′ness,** *n.*

ran·kle (rang′kəl), *v.,* **ran·kled, ran·kling. 1.** to be painful to the body or mind: *His wound rankled. Insults sometimes rankle for years.* **2.** to cause pain or soreness in: *The wound rankled him. The decision rankled his conscience.*

ran·sack (ran′sak), *v.* **1.** to search thoroughly through: *He ransacked the house for his glasses.* **2.** to search through for plunder; pillage: *The soldiers ransacked the countryside.* —**ran′sack·er,** *n.*

ran·som (ran′səm), *n.* **1.** the payment of a price for the release of a captive, kidnapped person, etc. **2.** the price paid or demanded: *a ransom of a million dollars.* **3.** the freeing of a captive, kidnapped person, etc., upon the payment of such a price. —*v.* **4.** to free (someone) by the payment of a ransom: *to ransom a kidnapped child.*

rant (rant), *v.* **1.** to speak wildly and loudly: *He ranted about the high cost of living.* —*n.* **2.** wild or loud talk. —**rant′er,** *n.* —**rant′ing·ly,** *adv.*

rap¹ (rap), *v.,* **rapped, rap·ping. 1.** to strike or knock with a quick, light blow: *He rapped the table with his pencil.* **2.** to strike (an object, as a pencil, pen, etc.) against something with such a blow: *He rapped his pencil on the table.* **3.** to say sharply (often fol. by *out*): *to rap out a command.* **4.** *Slang.* to talk or discuss. —*n.* **5.** a quick, light blow. **6.** the sound of such a blow: *the rap of rain upon the roof.* **7.** *Informal.* blame or punishment, esp. for a crime: *He took the rap for a theft he did not commit.* **8.** *Slang.* a talk or discussion. [from the Middle English word *rappen* "to strike, knock"]

rap² (rap), *n.* the least bit: *I don't care a rap what you say.* [the word originally meant a small counterfeit coin]

ra·pa·cious (rə pā′shəs), *adj.* **1.** plundering or taking by force: *rapacious soldiers.* **2.** greedy and grasping: *a rapacious miser.* —**ra·pa′cious·ly,** *adv.* —**ra·pac·i·ty** (rə pas′i tē), **ra·pa′cious·ness,** *n.*

rape¹ (rāp), *n.* **1.** a sexual act committed by force on a woman. **2.** the act of seizing and carrying away by force. —*v.,* **raped, rap·ing. 3.** to commit rape on. **4.** to seize and carry away by force. [from the Latin word *rapere* "to seize, snatch"]

rape² (rāp), *n.* a plant, related to cabbage and watercress, whose leaves are used as food for hogs, sheep, etc. Its seeds contain a useful oil. [from the Latin word *rāpum* "turnip"]

Raph·a·el (raf′ē əl, rā′fē əl), *n.* **1.** 1483–1520, Italian painter. **2.** one of the archangels.

rap·id (rap′id), *adj.* **1.** moving, acting, or happening swiftly or speedily: *a rapid train; rapid growth.* —*n.* **2.** Usually, **rapids.** a part of a river where the current runs swiftly. —**rap′id·ly,** *adv.*

rap·id-fire (rap′id fīゥr′), *adj.* **1.** able to fire shots rapidly, one after the other. **2.** happening or delivered rapidly and without a break: *rapid-fire questions.*

ra·pid·i·ty (rə pid′i tē), *n.* the quality of being rapid; swiftness; speed: *to move with rapidity.*

ra·pi·er (rā′pē ər), *n.* a light sword having a long, narrow blade, used for slashing and thrusting.

rap·ine (rap′in), *n.* the seizure and carrying off of another's property, esp. in a war; plunder.

Rapier and scabbard (17th century)

rap·port (ra pôr′), *n.* a close and harmonious relationship: *a rapport between teacher and students.*

rap·scal·lion (rap skal′yən), *n.* a rascal; rogue; scamp.

rapt (rapt), *adj.* **1.** completely interested; absorbed: *They listened with rapt attention.* **2.** carried away with emotion. **3.** showing rapture: *a rapt smile.* —**rapt′ly,** *adv.* —**rapt′ness,** *n.*

rap·ture (rap′chər), *n.* great joy or delight; bliss.

rap·tur·ous (rap′chər əs), *adj.* full of, feeling, or

showing rapture: *a rapturous smile.* —**rap′tur·ous·ly**, *adv.* —**rap′tur·ous·ness**, *n.*

rare[1] (râr), *adj.*, **rar·er**, **rar·est.** **1.** seldom found; uncommon; scarce: *Water is rare in the desert.* **2.** not dense; thin: *rare gases.* **3.** unusually great or fine: *a pianist of rare talent; a woman of rare beauty.* [from the Latin word *rārus* "loose, thin"] —**rare′ness**, *n.*

rare[2] (râr), *adj.*, **rar·er**, **rar·est.** (of meat) cooked just slightly: *a rare steak.* [from the Old English word *hrēr* "slightly cooked"]

rare·bit (râr′bit), *n.* another name for **Welsh rabbit.**

rar·e·fy (râr′ə fī′), *v.*, **rar·e·fied**, **rar·e·fy·ing.** **1.** to make or become less dense, as air; thin: *The atmosphere is rarefied at high altitudes.* **2.** to make finer or purify: *A life may be rarefied by religious faith.*

rare′-earth′ el′ement (râr′ûrth′), *Chem.* any of a group of related metallic elements: lanthanum, cerium, praseodymium, neodymium, promethium, samarium, europium, gadolinium, terbium, dysprosium, holmium, erbium, thulium, yttrium, ytterbium, or lutetium.

rare·ly (râr′lē), *adv.* **1.** seldom; infrequently. **2.** unusually; exceptionally.

rar·i·ty (râr′i tē), *n., pl.* for def. 1. **rar·i·ties.** **1.** something rare or unusual: *Snow is a rarity in the South.* **2.** the state or quality of being rare: *the rarity of diamonds.* **3.** thinness, as of air or gas.

ras·cal (ras′kəl), *n.* **1.** a bad, dishonest, or mean person; scoundrel: *Did they find the rascal who stole it?* **2.** a mischievous person or animal.

ras·cal·ly (ras′kə lē), *adj.* mean; dishonest; base: *a rascally trick.*

rash[1] (rash), *adj.* **1.** acting too quickly or without due consideration: *Be bold but not rash.* **2.** showing too much haste: *Rash promises are often broken.* [from Middle English] —**rash′ly**, *adv.* —**rash′ness**, *n.*

rash[2] (rash), *n.* a breaking out of red, often itching spots on the skin. [from the Old French word *rasche* "skin eruption," which comes from *raschier* "to scratch," from Latin *rādere*]

rasp (rasp), *n.* **1.** a very coarse file with small, pointed teeth. **2.** a rough, grating sound: *the rasp of a shovel scraping concrete.* —*v.* **3.** to scrape with a rasp or other coarse tool. **4.** to grate upon or annoy: *The loud music rasped his nerves.* **5.** to utter with a rough, grating sound: *The officer rasped a command.* —**rasp′er**, *n.* —**rasp′ing·ly**, *adv.* —**rasp′ish**, *adj.*

rasp·ber·ry (raz′ber′ē), *n., pl.* **rasp·ber·ries.** **1.** a small, rounded, red, black, or pale-yellow fruit containing many seeds. **2.** a prickly shrub bearing this fruit. **3.** *Slang.* a rude sound made with the tongue between the lips to express scorn, dislike, etc.

rat (rat), *n.* **1.** any of several long-tailed, gray, black, brown, or white animals that resemble mice but are much larger and sometimes quite ferocious. **2.** *Slang.* a bad, dishonest person, esp. one who betrays or abandons his friends or partners. —*v.*, **rat·ted**, **rat·ting.** **3.** *Slang.* to tell something that gets another person in trouble; squeal. **4. smell a rat,** to suspect mischief or treachery; be suspicious: *He seems friendly, but I smell a rat.* —**rat′like′**, *adj.*

ratch·et (rach′it), *n.* **1.** a bar or wheel with teeth that are engaged by a pawl, usually to permit motion in only one direction. **2.** a mechanism consisting of such a bar or wheel with a pawl.

Ratchet wheel

rate[1] (rāt), *n.* **1.** a certain quantity or amount of something considered in relation to something else: *at the rate of 60 miles an hour.* **2.** a fixed price per unit: *a rate of 10 cents a pound.* **3.** a degree of speed; pace: *to work at a rapid rate.* **4.** rank or rating: *an athlete of the first rate.* —*v.*, **rat·ed**, **rat·ing.** **5.** to set a value on; appraise: *The buyer rated the jewelry at several thousand dollars.* **6.** to place in a certain class or rank: *He was rated high among the performers.* **7.** to have value, standing, etc.: *He doesn't rate very high as a student.* **8.** to rank very high. **9. at any rate,** at least; nevertheless: *It was a dull movie, but at any rate there was a funny cartoon.* [from the Latin word *rata*, which comes from *rērī* "to judge, reckon"]

rate[2] (rāt), *v.*, **rat·ed**, **rat·ing.** to scold severely; chide; berate. [from the Middle English word *raten*, which comes from Scandinavian] —**rat′er**, *n.*

ra·tel (rāt′ᵊl, rät′ᵊl), *n.* a badgerlike animal of Africa and India.

rath·er (raŧħ′ər, rä′ŧħər), *adv.* **1.** to a certain extent; somewhat: *rather good.* **2.** more properly or justly: *That is true of you rather than of me.* **3.** more accurately or precisely: *He is an artist or, rather, a sculptor.* **4.** more readily or willingly: *to die rather than surrender.* **5.** on the contrary: *It is not cold, rather it is very warm.* —*interj.* (raŧħ′ûr′, rä′ŧħûr′). **6.** *Chiefly British.* yes; certainly.

Ratel
(total length 3 ft.)

rat·i·fy (rat′ə fī′), *v.*, **rat·i·fied**, **rat·i·fy·ing.** to approve or confirm, esp. in a formal or official way: *Congress ratified the bill.* —**rat′i·fi·ca′tion**, *n.* —**rat′i·fi′er**, *n.*

rat·ing (rā′tiñg), *n.* **1.** classification according to rank, merit, etc.: *a rating of the various performances.* **2.** rank, standing, position, etc.: *the rating of a corporal.* **3.** the credit standing of a person or firm.

ra·tio (rā′shō, rā′shē ō′), *n., pl.* **ra·tios.** the numerical relationship between two things, expressed as the number of times the second can be divided into the first: *If there are 12 boys and 6 girls in the classroom, the ratio of boys to girls is 2 to 1.*

ra·tion (rash′ən, rā′shən), *n.* **1.** a fixed allowance of provisions or food, esp. for a soldier or sailor. **2.** an allotted amount of anything: *a ration of money.* **3. rations,** provisions: *We need enough rations to feed 100 persons.* —*v.* **4.** to supply as rations: *to ration food to an army.* **5.** to supply with rations: *to ration an army with food.* **6.** to deal out strictly, as food in wartime: *to ration meat.*

ra·tion·al (rash′ə nᵊl), *adj.* **1.** based on reason; reasonable: *rational behavior.* **2.** able to think and reason: *Man is a rational being.* **3.** (in mathematics) of or referring to a rational number. —**ra·tion·al·i·ty** (ra<u>sh</u>/ə nal/i tē), *n.* —**ra/tion·al·ly,** *adv.*

ra·tion·al·ize (ra<u>sh</u>/ə n⁹līz/), *v.,* **ra·tion·al·ized, ra·tion·al·iz·ing.** 1. to explain (an act, behavior, etc.) in a favorable and seemingly reasonable way while avoiding the true reason, which one is unwilling to admit: *to rationalize stinginess by calling it thrift.* 2. to explain (something supernatural or the like) according to reason or natural laws: *to rationalize a miracle.* —**ra/tion·al·i·za/tion,** *n.* —**ra/tion·al·iz/er,** *n.*

ra/tional num/ber, a number that can be expressed exactly as the quotient of two whole numbers (distinguished from *irrational number*).

rat·line (rat/lin/), *n.* any one of the small ropes that join the shrouds of a ship horizontally and serve as steps for going aloft.

R, Ratline

rat·tan (ra tan/), *n.* 1. any of various palm trees having long, tough stems used for wicker work, canes, etc. 2. the stem of such a tree. 3. a switch or cane made from such a stem.

rat·tle (rat/⁹l), *v.,* **rat·tled, rat·tling.** 1. to make a number of short, sharp sounds rapidly, as by shaking, hitting, etc.: *The pebbles rattled in the cup.* 2. to cause to rattle: *The wind rattled the windows.* 3. to move or go rapidly with a clatter: *The old bus rattled down the road.* 4. to talk rapidly; chatter: *The woman rattled on and on about her trip.* 5. to perform or say in a rapid, easy, mechanical way: *He rattled off a list of names.* 6. to confuse or upset: *The sudden interruption rattled the speaker.* —*n.* 7. a number of short, sharp, rapid sounds: *the rattle of hail on a roof.* 8. a baby's toy that rattles when shaken. 9. any of the horny rings at the end of a rattlesnake's tail.

rat·tler (rat/lər), *n.* a rattlesnake.

rat·tle·snake (rat/⁹l snāk/), *n.* any of several poisonous American snakes having a rattle composed of a series of interlocking horny rings at the end of the tail.

Rattlesnake (length 3 ½ to 6 ft.)

rau·cous (rô/kəs), *adj.* harsh; shrill; grating: *His cold made his voice raucous.* —**rau/cous·ly,** *adv.* —**rau/cous·ness,** *n.*

rav·age (rav/ij), *v.,* **rav·aged, rav·ag·ing.** 1. to cause widespread damage to; lay waste; ruin: *The storm ravaged the coast.* —*n.* 2. widespread damage; destruction; ruin: *the ravages of war.* —**rav/ag·er,** *n.*

rave (rāv), *v.,* **raved, rav·ing.** 1. to talk wildly or insanely: *He raved during his delirium.* 2. to make a furious disturbance, as wind, a storm, etc. 3. to express extravagant praise: *She raved about her baby's beauty.* —*n.* 4. an act of raving. 5. extravagant praise: *The new movie got raves from the critics.* —*adj.* 6. full of praise: *rave reviews.*

rav·el (rav/əl), *v.,* **rav·eled** *or* **rav·elled; rav·el·ing** *or* **rav·el·ling.** 1. to disentangle or undo the threads of (cloth, rope, etc.): *to ravel an old sweater and save the yarn.* 2. to become separated into threads; fray: *The cuffs are beginning to ravel.*

Raven (length 26 in.)

ra·ven (rā/vən), *n.* any of several large black birds related to the crow and having a loud, harsh call.

rav·en·ing (rav/ə niñg), *adj.* greedy for food or prey: *ravening packs of wolves.*

rav·en·ous (rav/ə nəs), *adj.* very greedy or hungry for something, such as food, wealth, or fame. —**rav/en·ous·ly,** *adv.*

ra·vine (rə vēn/), *n.* a narrow, steep-sided valley, esp. one that has been formed by a river or stream.

rav·ing (rā/viñg), *adj.* 1. talking wildly; delirious; frenzied: *a raving maniac.* 2. *Informal.* remarkable; outstanding: *She is a raving beauty.* —*n.* 3. wild, meaningless talk: *the raving of a maniac.* —*adv.* 4. furiously; wildly: *He is stark, raving mad.*

rav·ish (rav/ish), *v.* 1. to seize and carry off by force. 2. to rape. 3. to fill with strong emotion, esp. joy: *They were ravished by the beauty of the landscape.* —**rav/ish·er,** *n.* —**rav/ish·ment,** *n.*

rav·ish·ing (rav/i shiñg), *adj.* extremely pleasing; enchanting: *ravishing beauty.* —**rav/ish·ing·ly,** *adv.*

raw (rô), *adj.* 1. uncooked, as food: *a raw carrot.* 2. being in a natural state; not finished or manufactured: *raw lumber.* 3. painfully open, as a wound. 4. untrained or ignorant: *a raw recruit.* 5. brutal or frank: *a raw statement of the truth.* 6. brutally harsh or unfair: *a raw deal.* 7. damp and chilly: *raw weather.* 8. **in the raw, a.** in the natural, unrefined state: *to look at nature in the raw.* **b.** *Slang.* in the nude; naked.

raw-boned (rô/bōnd/), *adj.* having little flesh; gaunt; thin.

raw·hide (rô/hīd/), *n.* 1. the untanned skin of cattle or other animals. 2. a rope or whip made of rawhide. —*v.* 3. to whip with a rawhide.

raw/ mate/rial, 1. material in its natural state before being prepared, manufactured, etc. 2. a person or persons having talent or promise that needs to be developed: *good raw material for a team.*

ray¹ (rā), *n.* 1. a narrow beam of light or other radiation. 2. the path of such a beam. 3. any form of radiant energy, or a stream of particles that behaves like radiant energy. 4. any of a group of lines that start at a single point. 5. one of the arms of a starfish. 6. a slight amount; trace: *a ray of hope.* [from the Old French word *rai,* which comes from Latin *radius* "ray, beam, radius"]

ray² (rā), *n.* any of numerous fishes related to the shark, but having flattened bodies, very large, flat fins, and often a slender, whiplike tail. [from the Latin word *rāia*]

ray·on (rā/on), *n.* 1. a fiber made by dissolving cellulose and forcing it through tiny holes. 2. fabric made from such fibers.

raze (rāz), *v.*, **razed, raz·ing.** to tear down; demolish: *to raze an old building.*

ra·zor (rā′zər), *n.* 1. a sharp-edged instrument, used esp. for shaving the face or trimming the hair. 2. an electrical instrument, used for the same purpose.

razz (raz), *v.* *Slang.* to make fun of; tease; heckle: *The crowd razzed the player for dropping the ball.*

Rb, *Chem.* the symbol for **rubidium.**

Rd., Road (used in street names): *Torrey Rd.*

re (rā), *n.* the second note of a musical scale: *D is re in the C scale.*

Re, *Chem.* the symbol for **rhenium.**

re-, a prefix meaning 1. again or anew: *rebuild; rewrite.* 2. back or backward: *repay; retrace.*

reach (rēch), *v.* 1. to get to or as far as; arrive at: *The boat reached the shore.* 2. to succeed in touching or getting hold of: *to reach a book on a high shelf.* 3. to make a stretch (often fol. by *out*): *He reached out to touch the book.* 4. to get in contact with: *I called but couldn't reach you.* 5. to amount to: *His fortune reached a million dollars.* 6. to strike or hit: *The bullet reached the mark.* 7. to extend: *a skirt that reaches to the knee.* —*n.* 8. the act or an instance of reaching: *a sudden reach for his gun.* 9. the extent or distance of reaching: *the reach of one's voice.* 10. a stretch or extent of something: *a reach of woodland.* —**reach′a·ble,** *adj.* —**reach′er,** *n.*

re·act (rē akt′), *v.* 1. to respond: *to react favorably to a medicine; to react to a shock by jumping.* 2. to act upon one another. 3. to act in a contrary way; oppose: *The people reacted against the invaders of the country.* 4. to enter into a chemical reaction.

re·ac·tion (rē ak′shən), *n.* 1. an action in response to some other action, event, proposal, etc.: *What was their reaction to your plan?* 2. a return to an earlier state or condition: *a reaction against new ideas.* 3. the action of chemicals upon each other; chemical change. 4. a change in the nucleus of an atom.

re·ac·tion·ar·y (rē ak′shə ner′ē), *adj.* 1. (esp. in politics) favoring a return to former conditions or policies: *a reactionary governor.* —*n.* 2. a person who is reactionary.

re·ac·tor (rē ak′tər), *n.* 1. a person or thing that is undergoing a reaction. 2. a device in which nuclear energy is controlled and converted into some form of energy that is easier to use, such as heat; pile.

read (rēd), *v.*, **read** (red), **read·ing** (rē′diñg). 1. to look at carefully so as to understand the meaning of (something written, printed, etc.): *to read a book.* 2. to speak aloud (something written, printed, etc.): *to read a story to children.* 3. to know (a language) well enough to be able to understand things written in it: *to read French.* 4. to understand the meaning of (signs, symbols, etc.): *to read semaphore.* 5. to understand the meaning of (signs) by touching or feeling: *to read Braille.* 6. to study the movements of (lips) so as to understand what is being said without hearing words, as in deafness. 7. to understand by observing signs, expressions, etc.: *to read a person's thoughts by*

studying his face. 8. to foresee, foretell, or predict: *to read the future in tea leaves.* 9. to find (something not directly stated) from what is read or considered (usually fol. by *into*): *He read fear into her words.* 10. to show or measure: *A thermometer reads the temperature.* 11. to study, as at a university: *to read law.* 12. to be worded as follows: *The sign reads, "Please keep off the grass."* 13. **read between the lines,** to find additional meanings, motives, etc., in something that has been said or written.

read·a·ble (rē′də bəl), *adj.* 1. easy or interesting to read: *a highly readable story.* 2. capable of being read; legible. —**read′a·bil′i·ty, read′a·ble·ness,** *n.*

read·er (rē′dər), *n.* 1. a person who reads, esp. often and with great enjoyment. 2. a schoolbook used for practice in reading.

read·i·ly (red′ə lē), *adv.* 1. promptly; quickly; easily: *The top came off the jar readily.* 2. in a ready manner; willingly: *He answered the door readily.*

read·i·ness (red′ē nis), *n.* 1. the condition of being ready: *Everything is in readiness for the trip.* 2. promptness; quickness; ease: *the readiness of butter to melt.* 3. willingness; cheerful consent.

read·ing (rē′diñg), *n.* 1. the action of a person who reads: *His reading of the book was interrupted.* 2. the recital of something that is written: *The teacher gave a reading of poetry.* 3. the way in which something is interpreted, as a piece of music, a part in a play, etc.: *a beautiful reading of the symphony.* 4. books, magazines, etc., being read or intended to be read. 5. the record shown by an instrument: *The temperature reading is zero.* —*adj.* 6. referring to or used in reading: *a reading lamp; reading matter.* 7. being in the habit of reading: *the reading public.*

re·ad·just (rē′ə just′), *v.* to adjust again or anew: *to readjust a machine; to readjust after a long absence from school.* —**re′ad·just′ment,** *n.*

read·y (red′ē), *adj.*, **read·i·er, read·i·est.** 1. completely prepared for action or use: *Are you ready to go?* 2. willing; agreeable; glad: *ready to forgive.* 3. prompt in understanding, replying, etc.: *a ready wit.* 4. inclined; likely; apt: *She is always ready to find fault.* 5. likely at any moment or time: *a tree ready to fall.* —*v.*, **read·ied, read·y·ing.** 6. to make ready; prepare: *to ready a house for guests.*

read·y-made (red′ē mād′), *adj.* 1. made in advance for sale rather than to order: *a ready-made suit.* 2. not original; trite: *a ready-made answer.*

re·al¹ (rē′əl, rēl), *adj.* 1. genuine; authentic; not imitation: *real pearls.* 2. actual rather than imaginary; true: *real events.* 3. sincere; unfeigned: *a real friend.* —*adv.* 4. *Informal.* very; extremely: *a real nice time.* [from the Latin word *reālis,* which comes from *rēs* "thing"]

re·al² (rē′əl, rēl), *n.* a former silver coin of Spain and Spanish America, the eighth part of a peso. [from a Spanish word meaning "royal," which comes from the Latin word *rēgālis* "regal"]

re′al estate′, property, esp. land or buildings.

re·al·ism (rē′ə liz′əm), *n.* 1. an outlook on life that faces facts and avoids anything that is imagined or is not practical. **2.** (in art and literature) a picturing of life as it is.

re·al·ist (rē′ə list), *n.* **1.** a person who tends to look at things as they really are: *Misfortune made a realist of him.* **2.** an artist or writer whose work is marked by realism.

re·al·is·tic (rē′ə lis′tik), *adj.* **1.** concerned with or based on what is real or practical: *It is realistic to save for the future.* **2.** showing things as they really are, as a novel, painting, or other work of art or literature. —**re′al·is′ti·cal·ly,** *adv.*

re·al·i·ty (rē al′i tē), *n., pl.* for def. 2 **re·al·i·ties. 1.** the state or quality of being real: *the reality of the world.* **2.** a real thing or fact: *Traveling through the air is now a reality.* **3. in reality,** really; actually: *In reality he's taller than I am, but he never stands up straight.*

re·al·i·za·tion (rē′ə li zā′shən), *n.* **1.** understanding; awareness: *He had no realization of what had happened to him.* **2.** the fulfillment or coming into existence of an idea, plan, hope, etc.: *the realization of an old dream.* **3.** something that is realized.

re·al·ize (rē′ə līz′), *v.,* **re·al·ized, re·al·iz·ing. 1.** to understand clearly; grasp: *He realized the importance of the news.* **2.** to make real or fulfill, as an idea, plan, hope, etc.: *He realized his ambition to travel.* **3.** to get as profit: *She realized thousands of dollars on the sale of the property.* —**re′al·iz′a·ble,** *adj.*

re·al·ly (rē′ə lē), *adv.* **1.** actually; truly; in fact: *He is not really a prince.* **2.** indeed: *Really, you shouldn't say that.*

realm (relm), *n.* **1.** kingdom; royal domain. **2.** the region, area, sphere, etc., in which anything exists or happens: *the realm of dreams.*

re·al·tor (rē′əl tər), *n.* a person who sells or manages real estate.

re·al·ty (rē′əl tē), *n.* building and land; real estate.

ream¹ (rēm), *n.* a quantity of paper, usually consisting of 500 sheets. [from the Spanish word *rezma,* which comes from Arabic *rizmah* "bale"]

ream² (rēm), *v.* to enlarge (a bored hole) with a reamer. [from the Old English word *rēman* "to open up, widen"]

ream·er (rē′mər), *n.* any of various tools with sharp cutting edges for enlarging holes.

re·an·i·mate (rē an′ə māt′), *v.,* **re·an·i·mat·ed, re·an·i·mat·ing.** to give new life, spirit, or courage to: *The praise of his friends reanimated him.*

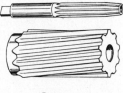

Reamers

reap (rēp), *v.* **1.** to cut (wheat, rye, etc.) with a sickle or other tool or a machine. **2.** to cut (a crop, harvest, etc.) by such means. **3.** to cut a crop from; harvest: *to reap a field.* **4.** to get as a return, result, etc.: *to reap large profits.* —**reap′a·ble,** *adj.*

reap·er (rē′pər), *n.* **1.** a person who reaps. **2.** a

machine for reaping. **3. the Reaper.** Also, **Grim Reaper.** death pictured as a human skeleton holding a scythe.

re·ap·pear (rē′ə pēr′), *v.* to come into sight again; appear again. —**re′ap·pear′ance,** *n.*

rear¹ (rēr), *n.* **1.** the back part of something: *the rear of a building.* **2.** the space or position behind: *The house has a garage in the rear.* **3.** the last or back part of an army, fleet, etc. —*adj.* **4.** of, in, at, or near the back: *the rear door of a bus.* **5. bring up the rear,** to come at the end or follow behind: *You go on ahead, and we'll bring up the rear.* [short for *arrear*]

rear² (rēr), *v.* **1.** to care for and bring up: *to rear a child.* **2.** to raise by building; erect: *to rear a monument.* **3.** to raise upright: *to rear a ladder.* **4.** to rise high, as a building or tower. **5.** to rise up on the hind legs, as a horse. [from the Old English word *rǣran* "to raise"]

rear′ ad′mi·ral, an officer in the U.S. Navy, ranking above a captain and below a vice admiral.

rear′ guard′, a part of a military force that guards the rear from surprise attack, esp. during a retreat.

re·arm (rē ärm′), *v.* to arm again, esp. with new and better weapons. —**re·ar·ma·ment** (rē är′mə mənt), *n.*

re·ar·range (rē′ə rānj′), *v.,* **re·ar·ranged, re·ar·rang·ing.** to arrange again, esp. in a different way: *to rearrange furniture.* —**re′ar·range′ment,** *n.*

rear·ward (rēr′wərd), *adj., adv.* toward or in the rear.

rea·son (rē′zən), *n.* **1.** a cause or motive for some act, event, etc.: *What is your reason for being late?* **2.** something that explains or supports a belief, action, fact, or event: *Give the reason for your answer.* **3.** the power to think, judge, draw conclusions, etc. **4.** sound judgment; good sense: *to act hastily and without reason.* **5.** soundness of mind; sanity: *to lose one's reason.* —*v.* **6.** to think or argue in a logical manner: *to reason about a problem.* **7.** to think through clearly, as a problem: *He reasoned everything out before he acted.* **8.** to conclude (often fol. by *that*): *After studying the map, he reasoned that he must be near home.* **9.** to argue with someone in a calm, reassuring way: *to reason with a child.* **10. by reason of,** because of; on account of: *He was elected chairman by reason of his long experience.* **11. stand to reason,** to be clear, obvious, or logical: *When you always have your own way, it stands to reason that you'll be spoiled.* **12. within reason,** reasonable, proper, or justifiable: *Try to keep your demands within reason.* **13. with reason,** rightfully so; justifiably: *She's worried about her grades, and with reason.*

—**Usage.** Careful writers and speakers avoid the unnecessary use of "because" following the words "the reason is": *He says that the reason he isn't going is that* (not *because*) *he has no money.*

rea·son·a·ble (rē′zə nə bəl, rēz′nə bəl), *adj.* **1.** in agreement with reason; sensible; intelligent; logical: *a reasonable answer.* **2.** having the ability to think and reason: *Man is a reasonable being.* **3.** capable of deciding or behaving with reason: *When he is angry, he is not reasonable.* **4.** fair or just: *reasonable prices.* **5.** moderate in cost; not expensive: *a reasonable restaurant.* —**rea'son·a·bly,** *adv.*

rea·son·ing (rē'zə niñg), *n.* **1.** the act or process of a person who reasons: *a problem that calls for careful reasoning.* **2.** a particular line of argument; train of thought: *The speaker's reasoning was hard to follow.*

re·as·sem·ble (rē'ə sem'bəl), *v.,* **re·as·sem·bled, re·as·sem·bling.** to put, bring, or come together again: *to reassemble a motor.* —**re'as·sem'bly,** *n.*

re·as·sure (rē'ə shŏŏr'), *v.,* **re·as·sured, re·as·sur·ing.** to restore the confidence or assurance of: *His praise reassured me.* —**re'as·sur'ance,** *n.* —**re'as·sur'ing·ly,** *adv.*

re·bate (rē'bāt), *n.* **1.** a refund of part of the money paid for some service or charge: *a rebate on income tax.* —*v.* (rē'bāt, ri bāt'), **re·bat·ed, re·bat·ing. 2.** to allow as a rebate: *to rebate several dollars.* **3.** to make a reduction in: *to rebate a bill.* —**re'bat·er,** *n.*

Re·bek·ah (ri bek'ə), *n.* (in the Bible) the wife of Isaac and the mother of Esau and Jacob.

reb·el (reb'əl), *n.* **1.** a person who refuses to serve his country or who acts against it. **2.** a person who fights against or rejects any authority: *The artist was a rebel against old styles of painting.* —*adj.* **3.** rebellious; defiant: *Rebel acts brought reprisals.* —*v.* (ri bel'), **re·belled, re·bel·ling. 4.** to act as a rebel: *He rebelled against his country.* **5.** to show or feel strong dislike: *He rebelled at the thought of having to leave home.*

re·bel·lion (ri bel'yən), *n.* **1.** an open, armed attack upon one's country or ruler: *a rebellion against a tyrant.* **2.** revolt against any authority, control, or tradition: *a rebellion against old-fashioned customs.*

re·bel·lious (ri bel'yəs), *adj.* **1.** defying or resisting some authority: *rebellious troops.* **2.** resisting treatment or management: *a rebellious horse.* —**re·bel'lious·ly,** *adv.* —**re·bel'lious·ness,** *n.*

re·birth (rē bûrth', rē'bûrth'), *n.* a renewed existence, activity, growth, etc.: *the rebirth of nature in the spring.*

re·born (rē bôrn'), *adj.* as if born again; renewed in life, spirit, etc.: *In the spring, nature is reborn.*

re·bound (ri bound'), *v.* **1.** to spring back or cause to spring back, as a ball: *He caught the ball as it rebounded from the wall.* —*n.* (rē'bound'). **2.** the act of rebounding: *He hit the ball on the rebound.*

re·buff (rē'buf), *n.* **1.** a blunt, often impolite refusal or rejection; snub: *His offer to help met with a rebuff.* **2.** a check to action or progress: *The bad weather was a rebuff to our plans.* —*v.* (ri buf'). **3.** to give a rebuff to; check; reject.

re·build (rē bild'), *v.,* **re·built** (rē bilt'), **re·build·ing.** to remake or build again: *The motor of the car was rebuilt. The town is rebuilding after the flood.*

re·buke (ri byōōk'), *v.,* **re·buked, re·buk·ing. 1.** to scold or reprove: *His father rebuked him for coming home late.* —*n.* **2.** stern disapproval; reprimand.

re·bus (rē'bəs), *n., pl.* **re·bus·es.** a puzzle in which words or phrases are shown by pictures.

re·but (ri but'), *v.,* **re·but·ted, re·but·ting.** to argue against so as to disprove; refute: *He rebutted the claims of his opponent.* —**re·but'ta·ble,** *adj.*

re·but·tal (ri but'əl), *n.* the act of rebutting, as in a debate.

re·cal·ci·trant (ri kal'si trənt), *adj.* stubborn and disobedient: *a recalcitrant boy who would not answer when called.* —**re·cal'ci·trance,** *n.*

re·call (ri kôl'), *v.* **1.** to bring back to mind; remember; recollect: *to recall the past.* **2.** to call back; summon to return: *The ambassador was recalled to his own country.* **3.** to withdraw or revoke: *His license was recalled because of his reckless driving.* —*n.* (ri kôl', rē'kôl'). **4.** recollection or remembrance: *She had no recall of what had happened.* **5.** a calling back or summoning. **6.** the removal or the right of removal of a public official from office by a vote of the people. —**re·call'a·ble,** *adj.*

re·cant (ri kant'), *v.* **1.** to withdraw (a belief, opinion, etc.), esp. publicly or in a formal way; take back; retract: *He recanted the doctrine when threatened by the authorities.* **2.** to confess that one is mistaken or wrong. —**re·can·ta·tion** (rē'kan tā'shən), *n.* —**re·cant'er,** *n.*

re·ca·pit·u·late (rē'kə pich'ə lāt'), *v.,* **re·ca·pit·u·lat·ed, re·ca·pit·u·lat·ing.** to sum up or review briefly, as at the end of a speech, lesson, etc.: *The speaker recapitulated the main points of his argument.* —**re'ca·pit'u·la'tion,** *n.*

re·cap·ture (rē kap'chər), *v.,* **re·cap·tured, re·cap·tur·ing. 1.** to capture again. **2.** to recollect vividly: *Watching the children play, he recaptured his own childhood.* —*n.* **3.** a getting back by capture.

re·cast (rē kast'), *v.,* **re·cast, re·cast·ing. 1.** to cast or shape again: *to recast a statue.* **2.** to work over or rearrange: *to recast an awkward sentence.*

recd., received. Also, **rec'd**

re·cede (ri sēd'), *v.,* **re·ced·ed, re·ced·ing. 1.** to withdraw; move back or away: *The wave broke on the shore and receded.* **2.** to slope backward: *a receding chin.* **3.** to withdraw from a viewpoint, promise, etc.

re·ceipt (ri sēt'), *n.* **1.** the act of receiving, or the state of being received: *the receipt of a package.* **2.** a written statement acknowledging that money, goods, etc., have been received. **3.** **receipts,** the amount or quantity received: *the receipts of a box office.* —*v.* **4.** to acknowledge receiving payment of (a bill).

re·ceiv·a·ble (ri sē'və bəl), *adj.* awaiting receipt of payment: *receivable bills; accounts receivable.*

re·ceive (ri sēv'), *v.,* **re·ceived, re·ceiv·ing. 1.** to have (something) given or sent to one: *to receive a letter.* **2.** to bear, contain, or take up: *The basin receives water from the fountain.* **3.** to catch or be struck by (a blow, shot, etc.): *The house received the full force of the wind.* **4.** to welcome or accept as a guest, member, etc.: *His friends received him warmly.*

re·ceiv·er (ri sē'vər), *n.* **1.** a person or thing that receives. **2.** a device that receives electric signals, waves, or the like, and changes them into sound or light, such as the part of a telephone held to the ear, a radio, television set, etc. **3.** a person appointed by a court to take charge of a business or property involved in a lawsuit.

re·ceiv·er·ship (ri sē′vər ship′), *n.* **1.** the condition of being in the hands of a receiver in law, as property or a business. **2.** the office or duties of a receiver.

re·cent (rē′sənt), *adj.* **1.** appearing, happening, done, etc., in a time just before the present: *a recent discovery; a recent novel.* **2.** not long ago; modern: *a recent period in world history.* —**re′cent·ly,** *adv.*

re·cep·ta·cle (ri sep′tə kəl), *n.* a container or holder for something: *a receptacle for ashes.*

re·cep·tion (ri sep′shən), *n.* **1.** the act of receiving, or the state of being received: *John's mother gave us a warm reception.* **2.** a social affair at which persons are formally received: *a wedding reception.* **3.** the quality of a radio or television broadcast as received.

re·cep·tion·ist (ri sep′shə nist), *n.* a person, usually a girl or woman, who receives callers in an office.

re·cep·tive (ri sep′tiv), *adj.* able, quick, or willing to receive new ideas, knowledge, etc.: *a receptive audience.* —**re·cep·tiv·i·ty** (rē′sep tiv′i tē), *n.*

re·cess (rē′ses, ri ses′), *n.* **1.** a brief period during which work, study, etc., is stopped: *They played games during the school recess.* **2.** a space set in a wall; alcove; niche. **3. recesses,** a hidden, inner area or part: *a small room in the recesses of a house.* —*v.* **4.** to place or set in a recess: *to recess a statue.* **5.** to make a recess or recesses in: *to recess a wall.* **6.** to take a recess or adjourn for a recess.

re·ces·sion (ri sesh′ən), *n.* **1.** the act of receding or withdrawing: *the recession of flood waters.* **2.** a mild but widespread slowdown in business activity.

re·ces·sion·al (ri sesh′ə nəl), *n.* a hymn or other piece of music played at the end of a service.

re·ces·sive (ri ses′iv), *adj.* tending to go, move, or slant back; receding: *a recessive part of a mountain.*

re·charge (rē charj′), *v.,* **re·charged, re·charg·ing.** to restore the electric charge of (a cell or battery).

rec·i·pe (res′ə pē′), *n.* **1.** a set of directions for preparing something to eat or drink. **2.** directions for doing anything: *a recipe for losing weight.* [from a Latin word meaning "take!" imperative of *recipere* "to receive"]

re·cip·i·ent (ri sip′ē ənt), *n.* **1.** a person or thing that receives something: *the recipient of an award.* —*adj.* **2.** receiving or capable of receiving: *The shipments of grain have gone to the recipient nations.*

re·cip·ro·cal (ri sip′rə kəl), *adj.* **1.** given, felt, done, etc., by each toward the other; mutual: *reciprocal affection.* **2.** given, felt, done, etc., in return: *a reciprocal favor.* **3.** working or operating together: *the reciprocal parts of a machine.* —**re·cip′ro·cal·ly,** *adv.*

re·cip·ro·cate (ri sip′rə kāt′), *v.,* **re·cip·ro·cat·ed, re·cip·ro·cat·ing. 1.** to give, feel, etc., in return: *She reciprocated her husband's love.* **2.** to give and receive reciprocally: *to reciprocate gifts.* **3.** to move or cause to move back and forth, as the parts of a machine. —**re·cip′ro·ca′tion,** *n.*

rec·i·proc·i·ty (res′ə pros′i tē), *n.* **1.** a reciprocal condition. **2.** the act of reciprocating; mutual giving and receiving: *Nations practice economic reciprocity when each lowers duty on goods wanted by the other.*

re·cit·al (ri sīt′əl), *n.* **1.** a musical performance, esp. one given by a single performer with or without accompanists: *a piano recital.* **2.** a narration or telling, esp. in detail: *a recital of one's troubles.* —**re·cit′al·ist,** *n.*

rec·i·ta·tion (res′i tā′shən), *n.* **1.** an act of reciting. **2.** a recital of something from memory, esp. before an audience: *the recitation of a poem.* **3.** anything told or narrated. **4.** a lesson recited aloud by a student to a teacher. **5.** a meeting of a class in which students recite aloud.

rec·i·ta·tive (res′i tə tēv′), *n.* a style of music intermediate between speaking and singing, usually accompanied by a series of separated chords.

re·cite (ri sīt′), *v.,* **re·cit·ed, re·cit·ing. 1.** to repeat from memory, as a poem or something else that is written: *He recited the verses to the audience.* **2.** to tell in detail, esp. in class: *to recite a lesson; to recite a list of dates.* **3.** to recite a lesson in class: *She recited without making one mistake.* —**re·cit′er,** *n.*

reck (rek), *v. Archaic.* to heed; pay attention to.

reck·less (rek′lis), *adj.* without caution; heedless; careless (usually fol. by *of*): *to be reckless of danger.* —**reck′less·ly,** *adv.* —**reck′less·ness,** *n.*

reck·on (rek′ən), *v.* **1.** to count; add up: *to reckon the cost of a new building.* **2.** to regard as; consider: *He reckoned himself a lucky man.* **3.** *Informal.* to think or suppose: *I reckon you're tired after your long trip.* **4. reckon with,** to deal or cope with: *There are other problems besides this to reckon with.*

reck·on·ing (rek′ə ning), *n.* **1.** count, computation, or calculation: *a reckoning of a ship's position.* **2.** the settlement of an account: *a reckoning of debts.* **3.** a statement of an amount due; bill.

re-claim (rē klām′), *v.* **1.** to claim or demand the return of: *to re-claim a right.* **2.** to regain possession or ownership of: *He re-claimed his lost jacket.*

re·claim (ri klām′), *v.* **1.** to bring into useful condition, as wild, waste, or neglected land: *to reclaim a desert for farmland.* **2.** to recover for use from refuse or waste material: *to reclaim metal from wrecked automobiles.* **3.** to bring back into right conduct; reform: *to reclaim sinners.* —*n.* **4.** the act of reclaiming or restoring; reclamation: *land beyond reclaim.* —**re·claim′a·ble,** *adj.* —**rec·la·ma·tion** (rek′lə mā′shən), *n.*

re·cline (ri klīn′), *v.,* **re·clined, re·clin·ing.** to lean or lie back; lie down: *She reclined upon the sofa.*

rec·luse (rek′lōōs, ri klōōs′), *n.* a person who lives alone, shut away from the company of others; hermit.

rec·og·ni·tion (rek′əg nish′ən), *n.* **1.** the act of recognizing, or the state of being recognized. **2.** approval and acceptance of one's work, efforts, etc.: *Recognition came to the painter at an early age.* **3.** an act by which one government recognizes the existence of another.

act, āble, dâre, ärt; ebb, ēqual; if, īce; hot, ōver, ôrder; oil; boŏk; ōōze; out; up, ûrge; ə = *a* as in *alone;* ᵊ as in *button* (but′ᵊn), *fire* (fīᵊr); chief; shoe; thin; **th**at; zh as in *measure* (mezh′ər). See full key inside cover.

rec·og·nize (rek′əg nīz′), *v.*, **rec·og·nized, rec·og·niz·ing.** **1.** to identify as someone or something previously seen, known, etc.: *He recognized the face of his friend in the crowd.* **2.** to be aware of as real or true; realize: *He recognized the difficulty of the undertaking.* **3.** to acknowledge as the person having the right to speak: *He waited for the chairman to recognize him.* **4.** to establish diplomatic relations with (a foreign government). **5.** to treat as valid: *The court recognized his claim.* **6.** to acknowledge acquaintance with: *She refused to recognize me at the party.* **7.** to bestow fame or honor upon: *The artist was recognized early by public and critics alike.* —**rec·og·niz·a·ble** (rek′əg nī′zə bəl), *adj.* —**rec′og·niz′a·bly,** *adv.*

re·coil (ri koil′), *v.* **1.** to draw or shrink back, as in alarm, fear, disgust, etc. **2.** to spring back, as a firearm when discharged. **3.** to turn against and harm the doer (usually fol. by *on* or *upon*): *The plot sometimes recoils upon the plotter.* —*n.* (rē koil′, rē′koil′). **4.** an act of recoiling. —**re·coil′ing·ly,** *adv.*

re·col·lect (rē′kə lekt′), *v.* **1.** to collect, gather, or assemble again: *He re-collected the scattered papers.* **2.** to rally or compose (oneself, one's thoughts, etc.): *He re-collected his courage and tried again.*

rec·ol·lect (rek′ə lekt′), *v.* to recall to mind; remember: *to recollect a person's name.*

rec·ol·lec·tion (rek′ə lek′shən), *n.* **1.** the act or power of recollecting; remembrance. **2.** something that is recollected: *recollections of childhood.*

rec·om·mend (rek′ə mend′), *v.* **1.** to present as worthy of trust, use, etc.; mention favorably; approve: *He highly recommended his friend for the job.* **2.** to urge as desirable; advise: *He recommended a good night's sleep.* **3.** to make pleasing, attractive, etc.: *This cold, rainy climate has little to recommend it.* **4.** to entrust, put in the care of, etc. —**rec′om·mend′a·ble,** *adj.*

rec·om·men·da·tion (rek′ə men dā′shən), *n.* **1.** the act of recommending. **2.** something that serves to recommend, as a letter, statement, etc.

rec·om·pense (rek′əm pens′), *v.*, **rec·om·pensed, rec·om·pens·ing.** **1.** to repay or reward, as for aid or service: *He was recompensed for returning the lost purse.* **2.** to make up for: *His insurance recompensed his losses.* —*n.* **3.** something done or given to repay, reward, or make amends: *Their gratitude was an ample recompense for our help.*

rec·on·cile (rek′ən sīl′), *v.*, **rec·on·ciled, rec·on·cil·ing.** **1.** to make friendly again, as after a quarrel, fight, etc.; bring peace between: *to reconcile bitter enemies.* **2.** to cause to accept something unpleasant: *Nothing could reconcile him to his loss.* **3.** to settle or bring into harmony: *to reconcile differences of opinion.* —**rec′on·cil′er,** *n.* —**rec·on·cil·i·a·tion** (rek′-ən sil′ē ā′shən), *n.*

re·con·di·tion (rē′kən dish′ən), *v.* to restore to a good condition; repair; make over: *to recondition the motor of an automobile.*

re·con·nais·sance (ri kon′i səns), *n.* a close examination of a region in order to obtain useful informa-

tion, such as an examination of enemy territory, a geological survey, etc.

re·con·noi·ter (rē′kə noi′tər, rek′ə noi′tər), *v.* **1.** to observe or survey (enemy territory) to obtain useful military information. **2.** to examine or survey (a region) for engineering, geological, or other purposes. —**re′con·noi′ter·er,** *n.*

re·con·sid·er (rē′kən sid′ər), *v.* to consider again, esp. with the possibility of making a change. —**re′con·sid′er·a′tion,** *n.*

re·con·struct (rē′kən strukt′), *v.* **1.** to construct again; rebuild: *to reconstruct a damaged house.* **2.** to form an idea of (something) by using available information: *to reconstruct the daily life of the ancient Romans.* —**re′con·struc′tion,** *n.*

Re·con·struc·tion (rē′kən struk′shən), *n.* the restoration of the former Confederate States to the Union after the Civil War, or the period during which this was done.

re·cord (ri kôrd′), *v.* **1.** to set down in writing or the like for future use or evidence: *to record what was said at a meeting.* **2.** to show or register: *A thermometer records the temperature.* **3.** to register (sound) on a disk or tape for later reproduction: *The orchestra recorded the symphony.* —*n.* (rek′ərd). **4.** the act of recording, or the state of being recorded. **5.** a piece of writing, a chart, etc., that provides information: *to keep a record of absences.* **6.** the facts known about a person or thing: *His record at school is excellent.* **7.** a disk or tape upon which sounds are recorded for later reproduction. **8.** the greatest achievement or performance of its kind to date: *He holds the record in the 100-yard dash.* **9. break a record,** to make a record that is better than the old one: *He broke the record for speed.* **10. off the record,** not included for publication or general knowledge; confidential: *The Senator spoke off the record about our foreign policy.* **11. on record,** existing in a file, document, publication, etc.: *There was no deed to the house on record.*

re·cord·er (ri kôr′dər), *n.* **1.** a person who records, esp. as an official duty. **2.** a device for recording sounds: *a tape recorder.* **3.** a musical wind instrument with a mouthpiece and finger holes. The recorder is a member of the flute family, but is held vertically.

re·cord·ing (ri kôr′ding), *n.* **1.** the act or practice of a person or thing that records. **2.** something that is recorded, as a musical work: *They listened to the new recording of the symphony.* **3.** a phonograph record or tape recording.

Recorder (def. 3)

re·count (rē kount′), *v.* **1.** to count again. —*n.* (rē′kount′, rē kount′). **2.** a second or additional count, as of votes in an election.

re·count (ri kount′), *v.* to relate in detail; describe: *to recount the early days of the West.*

re·coup (ri kōōp′), *v.* **1.** to regain or make up for (something lost): *He recouped all his money.* **2.** to pay back; reimburse: *They recouped him for what he had lost.* —**re·coup′a·ble**, *adj.*

re·course (rē′kôrs, ri kôrs′), *n.* **1.** a turning to a person or thing for help or protection; resort: *His only recourse now is to ask for mercy.* **2.** a person or thing turned to for help or protection: *His family is his recourse in times of trouble.*

re·cov·er (rē kuv′ər), *v.* to cover again or anew.

re·cov·er (ri kuv′ər), *v.* **1.** to get back or regain: *to recover one's health after illness.* **2.** to return to good health or condition: *He soon recovered from the fever.* **3.** to make up for or make good: *to recover wasted time.* **4.** to regain the strength or control over (oneself): *He lost his temper but was able to recover himself.* **5.** to get (something) by legal proceedings: *to recover damages in a suit.*

re·cov·er·y (ri kuv′ə rē), *n., pl.* **re·cov·er·ies. 1.** the regaining of something lost or taken away. **2.** the return to health or normal condition, as after sickness or disaster: *the recovery of a country after a war.*

recpt., receipt. Also, **rcpt., rect.**

rec·re·ant (rek′rē ənt), *adj.* **1.** cowardly; faint-hearted. **2.** unfaithful, disloyal, or traitorous. —*n.* **3.** a coward. **4.** a traitor. —**rec′re·ant·ly**, *adv.*

re·cre·ate (rē′krē āt′), *v.,* **re·cre·at·ed, re·cre·at·ing.** to create or make again, esp. in the mind.

rec·re·a·tion (rek′rē ā′shən), *n.* **1.** a pastime, sport, etc., that brings relaxation and pleasure: *Fishing is his recreation.* **2.** refreshment by means of some pastime, exercise, etc., following work, study, or the like: *He hunts for recreation.* —**rec′re·a′tion·al**, *adj.*

re·crim·i·nate (ri krim′ə nāt′), *v.,* **re·crim·i·nat·ed, re·crim·i·nat·ing.** to accuse or bring charges against (a person) in return: *When they accused us, we should have recriminated.* —**re·crim′i·na′tion**, *n.*

re·cru·des·cence (rē′krōō des′əns), *n.* a fresh outbreak or renewed spell of something, esp. something bad and unwanted: *the recrudescence of a disease; the recrudescence of violence.* —**re′cru·des′cent**, *adj.*

re·cruit (ri krōōt′), *n.* **1.** a newly enlisted or drafted member of the armed forces. **2.** a new member of a club, group, or the like. —*v.* **3.** to enlist for service in the armed forces: *to recruit men for the army.* **4.** to raise or increase (a force) by enlistment: *to recruit a new army.* **5.** to engage or hire, as new employees, members, etc. —**re·cruit′er**, *n.* —**re·cruit′ment**, *n.*

rec·tal (rek′tᵊl), *adj.* of, concerning, or for the rectum: *a rectal thermometer.* —**rec′tal·ly**, *adv.*

rec·tan·gle (rek′tang′gəl), *n.* a parallelogram having four right angles.

rec·tan·gu·lar (rek tang′gyə lər), *adj.* of, concerning, or having the shape of a rectangle. —**rec·tan′gu·lar·ly**, *adv.*

Rectangle

rec·ti·fy (rek′tə fī′), *v.,* **rec·ti·fied, rec·ti·fy·ing. 1.** to set right; correct; remedy: *Try to rectify your mistakes.* **2.** to purify (a spirit or liquor) by repeated distillation. **3.** to convert (alternating current) to direct current. —**rec′ti·fi·ca′tion**, *n.*

rec·ti·tude (rek′ti tōōd′, -tyōōd′), *n.* uprightness in

thought or character; moral goodness; integrity.

rec·tor (rek′tər), *n.* **1.** a clergyman in charge of a parish in the Protestant Episcopal Church. **2.** a clergyman in charge of a college, religious house, or congregation in the Roman Catholic Church. **3.** the head of certain universities, colleges, and schools.

rec·to·ry (rek′tə rē), *n., pl.* **rec·to·ries.** a rector's house; parsonage.

rec·tum (rek′təm), *n.* the lowest portion of the intestine. See illus. at **intestine.**

re·cum·bent (ri kum′bənt), *adj.* lying down; reclining: *a cat recumbent on the hearth.* —**re·cum′ben·cy**, *n.* —**re·cum′bent·ly**, *adv.*

re·cu·per·ate (ri kōō′pə rāt′, -kyōō′-), *v.,* **re·cu·per·at·ed, re·cu·per·at·ing. 1.** to regain health or strength after illness or fatigue: *to recuperate after a cold.* **2.** to recover from a loss: *The business recuperated after being near bankruptcy.* **3.** to restore or get back: *to recuperate one's health; to recuperate a loss.* —**re·cu′per·a′tion**, *n.* —**re·cu′per·a′tive**, *adj.*

re·cur (ri kûr′), *v.,* **re·curred, re·cur·ring. 1.** to occur again, as an event or experience. **2.** to return to the mind: *The idea often recurs to me.* **3.** to come up again for consideration: *The question recurred as to whether we should go.* —**re·cur′ring·ly**, *adv.*

re·cur·rent (ri kûr′ənt, ri kur′ənt), *adj.* occurring or appearing again, esp. repeatedly. —**re·cur′rence**, *n.*

re·cy·cle (rē sī′kəl), *v.,* **re·cy·cled, re·cy·cling.** to treat or process (waste, garbage, etc.) in order to obtain reusable products.

red (red), *n.* **1.** any of various colors resembling the color of blood. **2.** *(often cap.)* someone on the extreme left in politics, esp. a communist. —*adj.,* **red·der, red·dest. 3.** of the color red: *a red rose.* **4.** *(often cap.)* on the extreme left in politics, esp. communist. **5.** **in the red,** losing money; in debt: *a business in the red.* **6.** **see red,** to become angry, esp. suddenly and violently: *When he said I was too short for the team, I saw red.* —**red′ness**, *n.*

red·bird (red′bûrd′), *n.* any of several birds having red plumage, such as the cardinal.

red′ blood′ cell′, a red corpuscle.

red·breast (red′brest′), *n.* any of several birds having a red breast, such as the robin.

red·cap (red′kap′), *n.* a baggage porter in a railroad station.

red′ cell′, a red corpuscle.

Red′ Chi′na. See **China** (def. 1). —**Red′ Chinese′.**

red·coat (red′kōt′), *n.* a British soldier, esp. during the American Revolution.

red′ cor′puscle, one of the round, flattened cells in the blood, which contain hemoglobin. They carry oxygen to all parts of the body and carry carbon dioxide back to the lungs.

Red′ Cross′, an international organization to care for the sick and wounded in war and to help relieve suffering caused by floods, fires, and other disasters.

red′ deer′, 1. a deer of Europe and Asia having a reddish-brown summer coat. **2.** the North American white-tailed deer when in its reddish summer coat.

red·den (red′³n), v. 1. to make or become red. 2. to blush or flush.

red·dish (red′ish), adj. somewhat red; tinged with red: *a reddish sunset.*

re·deem (ri dēm′), v. 1. to buy back: *to redeem a pawned typewriter.* 2. to buy or pay off: *to redeem a mortgage.* 3. to exchange (bonds, trading stamps, etc.) for money or goods. 4. to fulfill, as a pledge, promise, etc. 5. to make up for: *His kindness redeems his lack of tact.* 6. to set free or save: *to redeem a sinner.* —**re·deem′a·ble**, adj.

re·deem·er (ri dē′mər), n. 1. a person who redeems. 2. **the Redeemer,** Jesus Christ.

re·demp·tion (ri demp′shən), n. 1. the act of redeeming, or the state of being redeemed. 2. deliverance from sin; salvation. 3. deliverance; rescue: *The prisoners awaited their redemption.*

red-hand·ed (red′han′did), adj., adv. in the very act of crime, wrongdoing, etc.: *The thieves were caught red-handed.*

red·head (red′hed′), n. a person who has red hair.

red-head·ed (red′hed′id), adj. 1. having red hair: *a red-headed girl.* 2. having a red head, as certain birds. Also, **red′head′ed.**

red′ her′ring, 1. a smoked herring. 2. something meant to draw attention away from the main problem or issue, as in an investigation.

red-hot (red′hot′), adj. 1. glowing red from having been heated to a high temperature, as of iron or steel. 2. very enthusiastic, angry, etc.: *a red-hot temper.* 3. fresh or new: *red-hot information.*

re·dis·cov·er (rē′di skuv′ər), v. to discover again, esp. to find new uses for.

red-let·ter (red′let′ər), adj. memorable; especially important or happy: *a red-letter day.*

red·o·lent (red′³lənt), adj. 1. having a pleasant odor (usually fol. by *of*): *a room redolent of roses.* 2. odorous or smelling: *a kitchen redolent of garlic.* 3. suggestive; reminiscent: *an old house redolent of mystery.* —**red′o·lence,** n. —**red′o·lent·ly,** adv.

re·dou·ble (rē dub′əl), v., **re·dou·bled, re·dou·bling.** 1. to make or become twice as great; double again. 2. to increase greatly: *He redoubled his efforts to win.* 3. to go back over; retrace: *to redouble one's footsteps.*

re·doubt (ri dout′), n. 1. a small fort used to defend a strategic point, as a hill, pass, etc. 2. a small, separate earthwork within a fortification.

re·doubt·a·ble (ri dou′tə bəl), adj. commanding respect, fear, awe, etc.: *a redoubtable commander.* —**re·doubt′a·bly,** adv.

re·dound (ri dound′), v. 1. to have an effect for good or bad (usually fol. by *to*): *The hero's sacrifice redounded to the benefit of all.* 2. to come back or reflect upon a person to his honor or shame (usually fol. by *on* or *upon*): *That lie will redound upon your reputation.*

red′ pep′per, a hot, red seasoning, such as cayenne, or the fruit from which it is made.

re·dress (rē′dres, ri dres′), n. 1. the setting right of what is wrong: *a redress of grievances.* —v. (ri dres′).

2. to set right; remedy or correct: *to redress injuries.* —**re·dress′a·ble, re·dress′i·ble,** adj. —**re·dress′er,** n.

Red′ Riv′er, a river flowing E from Texas along the Texas-Oklahoma border into the Mississippi River in Louisiana. about 1300 mi. long.

Red′ Sea′, an arm of the Indian Ocean, extending NW between Africa and Arabia: connected to the Mediterranean Sea by the Suez Canal. 170,000 sq. mi.

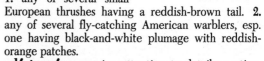

red·skin (red′skin′), n. a North American Indian (often considered an offensive term).

red·start (red′stärt′), n. 1. any of several small European thrushes having a reddish-brown tail. 2. any of several fly-catching American warblers, esp. one having black-and-white plumage with reddish-orange patches.

red′ tape′, excessive attention to details, routine, etc., in business or government: *The report was held up for months by red tape.*

re·duce (ri dōōs′, -dyōōs′), v., **re·duced, re·duc·ing.** 1. to make less in size, number, or amount: *to reduce a price.* 2. to lower in rank or well-being: *The sergeant was reduced to corporal. The family was reduced to poverty.* 3. to bring to destruction (usually fol. by *to*): *a mansion that was reduced to ashes.* 4. to conquer or subdue: *Ancient Rome was reduced by the barbarians.* 5. to lose weight by dieting: *Fat people find it hard to reduce.* 6. to express (a fraction or ratio) in smaller numbers: $^{12}/_{16}$ *may be reduced to* $^6/_8$ *or* $^3/_4$. 7. to remove oxygen from a compound, esp. to extract a metal from its oxide. 8. to lower the positive charge on an ion.

re·duc·tion (ri duk′shən), n. 1. the act of reducing, or the state of being reduced. 2. the amount by which something is reduced: *a 10% reduction in prices.* 3. the result of reducing; a copy on a smaller scale: *This 5 x 8 photograph is a reduction from the 8 x 10.*

re·dun·dan·cy (ri dun′dən sē), n., pl. **re·dun·dan·cies.** 1. the unnecessary repeating of words; verbosity: *a speech marred by redundancy.* 2. too great a supply of anything: *a redundancy of chairs in the room.* 3. something that is redundant, as a word or expression.

re·dun·dant (ri dun′dənt), adj. 1. verbose or repetitious: *a redundant speech.* 2. not necessary or required: *to shed redundant fat.* —**re·dun′dant·ly,** adv.

red′-winged black′bird (red′wiñgd′), a North American blackbird, the male of which has bright red patches on its wings.

red·wood (red′wŏŏd′), n. 1. a cone-bearing tree of California, often more than 300 feet tall. 2. the hard, weather-resistant, reddish wood of this tree.

reed (rēd), n. 1. the hard, hollow, jointed stalk of

various plants that grow in or near water. **2.** any of the plants themselves. **3.** a musical instrument made from the hollow stalk of such a plant. **4.** a thin piece of this stalk or of metal or plastic, whose vibrations produce the sounds of various wind instruments, such as the clarinet, bassoon, or harmonica.

reed·y (rē′dē), *adj.*, **reed·i·er, reed·i·est. 1.** full of reeds: *a reedy marsh.* **2.** like a reed or reeds: *reedy grass.* **3.** having a sound like that of a reed instrument: *a thin, high, reedy voice.* —**reed′i·ness,** *n.*

reef[1] (rēf), *n.* a ridge of rock, sand, or coral at or just below the surface of the water. [from Dutch]

reef[2] (rēf), *n.* **1.** a part of a sail that is rolled and tied down to reduce the area exposed to the wind. —*v.* **2.** to shorten (a sail) by tying a reef. [from the Middle English word *riff,* which comes perhaps from Scandinavian]

reek (rēk), *n.* **1.** a strong, unpleasant smell. —*v.* **2.** to smell strongly and unpleasantly: *The salad reeks of garlic.* —**reek′ing·ly,** *adv.*

reel[1] (rēl), *n.* **1.** a spool or frame that is used to wind up or pay out thread, tape, film, wire, etc. **2.** a quantity of something wound on a reel: *two reels of film.* —*v.* **3.** to wind on a reel: *to reel a hose.* **4.** to pull or draw in by winding a line on a reel (usually fol. by *in*): *to reel in a fish.* **5. reel off,** to say quickly and without effort: *to reel off dates.* [from the Middle English word *rele,* which comes from Old English *hrēol*]

reel[2] (rēl), *v.* **1.** to sway or rock under a blow, shock, etc. **2.** to sway about in standing or walking; stagger: *to reel drunkenly.* **3.** to whirl or seem to whirl: *The room reeled before his eyes when he heard the news.* **4.** to have the feeling of whirling: *His brain reeled.* [from the Middle English word *relen* "to reel, stagger," which comes from *rele* "a reel." See reel[1]]

reel[3] (rēl), *n.* **1.** a lively dance popular in Scotland. **2.** a Virginia reel. [a special use of *reel*[2]]

re·e·lect (rē′i lekt′), *v.* to elect again: *The mayor was reelected for a second term.* Also, **re′-e·lect′.** —**re′e·lec′tion, re′-e·lec′tion,** *n.*

re·en·force (rē′en fôrs′), *v.,* **re·en·forced, re·en·forc·ing.** another spelling of **reinforce.** Also, **re′-en·force′.** —**re′en·force′ment, re′-en·force′ment,** *n.*

re·en·ter (rē en′tər), *v.* **1.** to enter again. **2.** to enroll in again: *He reentered school after a long illness.* Also, **re-en′ter.** —**re·en·trance, re-en·trance** (rē en′trəns), *n.*

re·en·try (rē en′trē), *n., pl.* **re·en·tries. 1.** an act of reentering. **2.** the return into the earth's atmosphere of an artificial satellite, space capsule, rocket, etc.

re·es·tab·lish (rē′e stab′lish), *v.* to establish or set up again; restore: *to reestablish a business.* —**re′es·tab′lish·ment,** *n.*

re·ex·am·ine (rē′ig zam′in), *v.,* **re·ex·am·ined, re·ex·am·in·ing. 1.** to examine again. **2.** to examine (a witness in a legal trial) again after cross-examination. Also, **re′-ex·am′ine.** —**re′ex·am′i·na′tion, re′-ex·am′i·na′tion,** *n.*

ref., **1.** reference. **2.** referred. **3.** reformed.

re·fec·to·ry (ri fek′tə rē), *n., pl.* **re·fec·to·ries.** a dining room in a religious house, a college, etc.

re·fer (ri fûr′), *v.,* **re·ferred, re·fer·ring. 1.** to direct to a person, place, etc., for information or anything needed: *He was referred to a good book on the subject.* **2.** to hand over for consideration, decision, etc.: *to refer a dispute to a judge.* **3.** to allude or call attention to: *He constantly refers to you as his friend.* **4.** to go to for information: *to refer to a dictionary.* —**ref·er·a·ble** (ref′ər ə bəl, ri fûr′ə bəl), *adj.*

ref·er·ee (ref′ə rē′), *n.* **1.** a person who decides or settles a dispute; arbitrator; arbiter. **2.** a judge in a game or sport, as football, basketball, etc.; umpire. —*v.,* **ref·er·eed, ref·er·ee·ing. 3.** to act as a referee for; preside as a referee: *to referee a ball game.*

ref·er·ence (ref′ər əns), *n.* **1.** an act or instance of referring. **2.** a mention; allusion: *a speech full of patriotic references.* **3.** a note or passage in a book referring to an additional source of information: *A list of references appears at the end of each chapter.* **4.** Also, **ref′erence book′.** a book consulted for facts or background information, such as an encyclopedia, dictionary, or atlas. **5.** a person to whom one refers for a statement about one's character or ability: *The maid named her last employers as references.* **6.** a statement, usually written, made by this person. **7.** relation, regard, or respect: *all persons, without reference to age.* —*v.,* **ref·er·enced, ref·er·enc·ing. 8.** to provide (a book, article, etc.) with references.

ref·er·en·dum (ref′ə ren′dəm), *n., pl.* **ref·er·en·dums** *or* **ref·er·en·da** (ref′ə ren′də). **1.** the practice of referring legislative measures to the vote of the people for acceptance or rejection. **2.** a vote on a measure referred in this way.

re·fill (rē fil′), *v.* **1.** to fill again. —*n.* (rē′fil′). **2.** a material, supply, or the like, to replace something that has been used up: *to buy refills for a pen.*

re·fine (ri fīn′), *v.,* **re·fined, re·fin·ing. 1.** to bring to a fine or pure state: *to refine sugar.* **2.** to make more elegant and polished: *to refine one's manners.* —**re·fin′a·ble,** *adj.* —**re·fin′er,** *n.*

re·fined (ri fīnd′), *adj.* **1.** freed from impure matter: *refined sugar; refined oil.* **2.** having or showing breeding, taste, etc.: *refined speech.*

re·fine·ment (ri fīn′mənt), *n.* **1.** fineness or elegance of feeling, taste, manners, etc.: *His choice of pictures shows his refinement.* **2.** an example of refined feeling, manners, etc. **3.** the act of refining, or the state of being refined. **4.** an improvement: *Your plan needs a few refinements.* **5.** an improved form of something.

re·fin·er·y (ri fī′nə rē), *n., pl.* **re·fin·er·ies.** a place where an impure substance or a raw material is purified or processed in some other way in order to make it more useful: *a sugar refinery; an oil refinery.*

re·fin·ish (rē fin′ish), *v.* to give a new surface to (wood, furniture, etc.). —**re·fin′ish·er,** *n.*

re·fit (rē fit′), *v.,* **re·fit·ted, re·fit·ting. 1.** to fit, prepare, or equip again: *The ship was refitted for its return journey.* **2.** to be refitted: *The ship will refit during the holidays.* —*n.* (rē′fit′). **3.** an act of refitting: *The ship is in port for a refit.*

re·flect (ri flekt′), *v.* **1.** to cast back (light, heat, sound, etc.) from a surface: *The silver dish reflected the sunlight.* **2.** to give back or show an image of; mirror: *His face was reflected in the pool.* **3.** to bring (honor, shame, etc.) upon: *His sacrifice reflected glory upon him.* **4.** to bring discredit: *Bad company reflects upon your own character.* **5.** to think, ponder, or meditate: *to reflect on the beauties of nature.* [from the Latin word *reflectere* "to bend back"] —**re·flect′ing·ly,** *adv.*

reflect′ing tel′escope, a telescope that employs a large mirror to gather and focus the light from distant objects, such as planets or stars.

re·flec·tion (ri flek′shən), *n.* **1.** the throwing back or return of light, heat, sound, images, etc., by a surface, such as a mirror, wall, etc. **2.** something that has been reflected: *a reflection in a mirror.* **3.** serious thought: *a matter deserving much reflection.* **4.** a thought that occurs in meditation: *the reflections of philosophers.* **5.** an action or statement that brings blame or doubt: *Your lying is a reflection on your character.* —**re·flec′tion·less,** *adj.*

re·flec·tive (ri flek′tiv), *adj.* **1.** reflecting light, heat, sound, etc.: *a reflective surface.* **2.** given to thinking: *a serious, reflective man.* —**re·flec′tive·ly,** *adv.*

re·flec·tor (ri flek′tər), *n.* **1.** a polished surface that reflects or focuses rays of light, heat, etc. **2.** a reflecting telescope.

re·flex (rē′fleks), *n.* **1.** an action that takes place automatically in response to the stimulation of a nerve and without conscious effort: *The act of pulling back one's hand from a hot stove is a reflex.* —*adj.* **2.** referring to or caused by a reflex: *a reflex action.*

re·flex·ive (ri flek′siv), *adj.* **1.** (in grammar) describing a construction in which the subject and the object are the same. In *I wash myself, wash* is a reflexive verb. In *He cut himself, himself* is a reflexive pronoun. —*n.* **2.** a reflexive pronoun or verb.

re·for·est (rē fôr′ist, rē for′ist), *v.* to replant trees in (a forest or area affected by cutting, fire, etc.). —**re′for·es·ta′tion,** *n.*

re·form (ri fôrm′), *n.* **1.** the improving of what is wrong, evil, or unsatisfactory: *the reform of laws.* **2.** an example of this: *a needed reform in government.* —*v.* **3.** to change for the better: *to reform a thief.* —**re·form′a·ble,** *adj.* —**re·form′ing·ly,** *adv.*

ref·or·ma·tion (ref′ər mā′shən), *n.* **1.** the act of reforming, or the state of being reformed. **2. the Reformation,** the religious movement in the 16th century in Europe that was begun by Martin Luther as a reform in the Catholic Church and led to the founding of the Protestant churches. —**ref′or·ma′tion·al,** *adj.*

re·form·a·to·ry (ri fôr′mə tôr′ē), *adj.* **1.** serving or meant to reform: *reformatory measures.* —*n., pl.* **re·form·a·to·ries. 2.** Also, **reform′ school′.** an institution for reforming young offenders.

re·form·er (ri fôr′mər), *n.* a person devoted to bringing about reforms: *political reformers.*

re·fract (ri frakt′), *v.* to cause (rays of light, radio waves, etc.) to bend.

re·frac·tion (ri frak′shən), *n.* the bending of a ray of light, or of heat or sound waves, that takes place when the ray passes at a slant from one medium to another in which the speed of travel is different. The curved surfaces of a lens enable it to refract the rays of light passing through it.

Refraction
Light ray SP is
refracted by the
water to point R
instead of point L

re·frac·to·ry (ri frak′tə rē), *adj.* **1.** hard to manage; stubbornly disobedient: *a refractory pupil.* **2.** difficult to treat: *a refractory illness.* **3.** very hard and very difficult to melt: *Refractory materials are used in furnace linings.* —**re·frac′to·ri·ly,** *adv.*

re·frain¹ (ri frān′), *v.* to keep oneself from doing, thinking, or saying something; abstain: *Please refrain from talking during the service.* [from the Old French word *refrener,* which comes from Latin *rēfrēnāre* "to bridle, restrain"]

re·frain² (ri frān′), *n.* **1.** a phrase repeated again and again throughout a poem or song, esp. at the end of each stanza. **2.** the music to which such a phrase is set. [from an Old French word, which comes from *refraindre* "to modulate (the voice)"]

re·fresh (ri fresh′), *v.* **1.** to restore the strength and well-being of, as with food, drink, rest, etc.: *The nap completely refreshed him.* **2.** to make fresh again, as by cooling or moistening: *The rain refreshed the parched grass.* **3.** to quicken or arouse: *A brief look at the book refreshed his memory.* —**re·fresh′er,** *n.*

re·fresh·ing (ri fresh′ing), *adj.* **1.** having the power to restore or make fresh again: *a refreshing rest before dinner.* **2.** pleasantly different or unusual: *She was admired for her refreshing outlook on life.* —**re·fresh′ing·ly,** *adv.*

re·fresh·ment (ri fresh′mənt), *n.* **1.** the act of refreshing, or the state of being refreshed. **2.** something that refreshes, esp. food or drink.

re·frig·er·ant (ri frij′ər ənt), *n.* **1.** a substance used for cooling, such as dry ice. **2.** a liquid or gas that circulates in the cooling system of a refrigerator, air conditioner, etc.

re·frig·er·ate (ri frij′ə rāt′), *v.,* **re·frig·er·at·ed, re·frig·er·at·ing.** to make or keep cold or cool, esp. for preservation: *to refrigerate meat.* —**re·frig′er·a′tion,** *n.*

re·frig·er·a·tor (ri frij′ə rā′tər), *n.* a box, room, or cabinet in which foods, chemicals, etc., are kept cool by means of ice or mechanical refrigeration.

re·fu·el (rē fyōō′əl), *v.,* **re·fu·eled** *or* **re·fu·elled; re·fu·el·ing** *or* **re·fu·el·ling. 1.** to supply again with fuel. **2.** to take on a fresh supply of fuel: *The plane can cross the ocean without refueling.*

ref·uge (ref′yōōj), *n.* **1.** shelter from danger, trouble, etc.: *to take refuge from a storm.* **2.** a place of shelter or safety: *The cellar was used as a refuge during the air raids.* **3.** anything or anyone that offers aid, relief, or escape: *Religion is her refuge in times of trouble.*

ref·u·gee (ref'yŏŏ jē'), *n.* a person who flees for refuge or safety, esp. to a foreign country in time of war or political persecution.

re·ful·gent (ri ful'jənt), *adj.* shining; radiant; glowing: *The clouds were refulgent with sunlight.* —**re·ful'gence,** *n.*

re·fund (ri fund'), *v.* 1. to give back (money); repay: *The store refunded the price of the damaged article.* —*n.* (rē'fund). 2. repayment: *The store does not make refunds.* —**re·fund'a·ble,** *adj.* —**re·fund'er,** *n.*

re·fur·bish (rē fûr'bish), *v.* to furbish again; renew; improve: *to refurbish a house with fresh paint.* —**re·fur'bish·ment,** *n.*

re·fus·al (ri fyōō'zəl), *n.* 1. an act or instance of refusing. 2. the right to refuse or accept something before others: *When the house is offered for sale, we have first refusal.*

re·fuse¹ (ri fyōōz'), *v.,* **re·fused, re·fus·ing.** 1. to be unwilling to accept; reject: *He refused our offers to help.* 2. to be unwilling to give; deny: *He refused permission.* 3. to be unwilling to do: *He refuses to go with us.* [from the Old French word *refuser,* which comes from Latin *refūsus* "refused"]

ref·use² (ref'yōōs), *n.* something that is thrown away as worthless or useless; trash; rubbish; garbage. [from the French word *refuser* "to refuse." See *refuse¹*]

re·fute (ri fyōōt'), *v.,* **re·fut·ed, re·fut·ing.** 1. to prove to be wrong or false: *to refute an argument.* 2. to prove to be in the wrong: *to refute one's accusers.* —**re·fu·ta·bil·i·ty** (ri fyōō'tə bil'i tē, ref'yə tə bil'i tē), *n.* —**re·fu·ta·ble** (ri fyōō'tə bəl, ref'yə tə bəl), *adj.*

reg., 1. regiment. 2. region. 3. register. 4. registered. 5. registry. 6. regular. 7. regulation.

re·gain (ri gān'), *v.* 1. to get again; recover: *to regain one's health.* 2. to reach again: *to regain the shore.*

re·gal (rē'gəl), *adj.* 1. of or referring to a king or queen; royal: *regal authority.* 2. befitting or resembling a king: *a regal gait.* 3. stately; splendid: *a regal ship.* —**re'gal·ly,** *adv.*

re·gale (ri gāl'), *v.,* **re·galed, re·gal·ing.** 1. to entertain or amuse thoroughly: *The comedian regaled his audience with jokes.* 2. to feed sumptuously: *The guests were regaled with the choicest foods.*

re·ga·li·a (ri gā'lē ə), *n.pl.* 1. the symbols of royalty, such as the crown, scepter, etc. 2. the decorations of an officer or order. 3. rich clothing.

re·gard (ri gärd'), *v.* 1. to consider in a certain way: *to regard someone with favor.* 2. to show respect or consideration for: *He does not regard the wishes of others.* 3. to hold in esteem; value: *She regards her teacher highly.* 4. to look at; observe: *She regarded the scene with interest.* —*n.* 5. thought; attention; consideration: *He has no regard for others.* 6. respect or esteem: *He has high regard for his friends.* 7. a particular point or subject: *He was quite satisfactory in this regard.* 8. one's look or gaze: *Her regard lingered on the scene.* 9. **regards,** feelings of affection and esteem: *Please give them my regards.* 10. **in** (or **with**) **regard to,** in reference to; concerning: *I'm calling in regard to your advertisement.*

re·gard·ful (ri gärd'fəl), *adj.* 1. observant; heedful (often fol. by *of*): *to be regardful of the law.* 2. showing esteem or respect: *regardful attention.*

re·gard·ing (ri gär'ding), *prep.* with regard to; concerning: *They spoke to us regarding the plan.*

re·gard·less (ri gärd'lis), *adj.* 1. having or showing no regard; heedless; mindless (often fol. by *of*): *He seemed regardless of the danger.* —*adv.* 2. in spite of advice, warning, danger, etc.; anyway: *The journey is difficult, but I must go regardless.* 3. **regardless of,** in spite of; without regard for: *Take a cab, regardless of the cost.*

re·gat·ta (ri gat'ə, ri gä'tə), *n.* a boat race, or a series of boat races.

re·gen·cy (rē'jən sē), *n., pl.* **re·gen·cies.** 1. the office, control, or government of a regent or body of regents. 2. a body of regents. 3. the term of office of a regent: *a long regency during which the prince held power.* 4. a territory or country under the control of a regent or regency: *England was a regency from 1811 to 1820.* —*adj.* 5. of or concerning a regency: *a regency form of government.*

Re·gen·cy (rē'jən sē), *n.* 1. the period in British history (1811–1820) during which George, Prince of Wales, later George IV, was regent. —*adj.* 2. referring to the Regency or to the furnishings, architecture, etc., of this period: *a Regency chair.*

re·gen·er·ate (ri jen'ə rāt'), *v.,* **re·gen·er·at·ed, re·gen·er·at·ing.** 1. to reform completely in spirit: *He was regenerated by his new faith.* 2. to give new force or life to; revive: *Their praise regenerated his hopes.* 3. (of a plant or animal) to grow back (a lost or injured part): *Starfish can regenerate arms that have been cut off.* —**re·gen·er·a'tion,** *n.* —**re·gen'er·a'tor,** *n.*

re·gent (rē'jənt), *n.* 1. a person who rules a kingdom when the sovereign is absent, ill, or underage. 2. a member of a governing board in some state universities. —**re'gent·ship',** *n.*

reg·i·cide (rej'i sīd'), *n.* 1. the killing of a king. 2. a person who kills a king.

re·gime (rə zhēm', rā zhēm'), *n.* 1. a system of rule or government: *a democratic regime.* 2. another word for **regimen.** Also, **ré·gime'.**

reg·i·men (rej'ə mən), *n.* a course of diet, exercises, or manner of living, intended to improve or restore one's health: *His regimen prohibited smoking.*

reg·i·ment (rej'ə mənt), *n.* 1. an army unit consisting of two or more battalions under the command of a colonel. —*v.* (rej'ə ment'). 2. to manage or treat in a strict, systematic manner without respect for individual rights and differences: *The boss was disliked for regimenting his employees.*

reg·i·men·tal (rej'ə men'təl), *adj.* 1. of or referring to a regiment. —*n.* 2. **regimentals,** the uniform of a regiment.

reg·i·men·ta·tion (rej'ə mən tā'shən), *n.* the act or

process of regimenting; strict ordering or control: *the regimentation of people under a dictatorship.*

Re·gi·na (ri jī′nə), *n.* the capital city of Saskatchewan, in S Canada.

re·gion (rē′jən), *n.* **1.** an extensive part of a surface, space, or body: *a region of the earth.* **2.** a part of the earth's surface showing some common characteristic throughout: *a mining region; a forest region.* **3.** an area of interest, activity, etc.; field: *the region of mathematics.* **4.** a part of the body: *the region of the heart.*

re·gion·al (rē′jə nəl), *adj.* of or referring to a region, district, or area, as of a country: *a regional custom; regional cooking.* —**re′gion·al·ly,** *adv.*

reg·is·ter (rej′i stər), *n.* **1.** a book in which records of acts, events, names, etc., are kept: *a register for births.* **2.** a list or record kept in such a book. **3.** an official document showing the nationality of a ship. **4.** registration or registry. **5.** a mechanical device that records automatically: *a cash register.* **6.** the range of a voice or musical instrument. **7.** a device for controlling the flow of warmed air through an opening in a heating system. —*v.* **8.** to enter in a register: *to register the minutes of a meeting.* **9.** to enroll: *to register a student.* **10.** to record (mail) at a post office as a protection against loss, theft, etc. **11.** to show on an instrument or scale: *The thermometer registered zero.* **12.** to show (a mood or emotion) through an expression of the face or a movement of the body: *She registered surprise at the reply.*

reg·is·trar (rej′i strär′), *n.* a person who keeps official records, esp. at a school or college.

reg·is·tra·tion (rej′i strā′shən), *n.* **1.** the act of registering, or an instance of registering. **2.** an entry in a register. **3.** the number registered: *a large registration.* **4.** a certificate showing that someone or something has been registered: *a boat registration.*

reg·is·try (rej′i strē), *n., pl.* **reg·is·tries.** **1.** the act of registering; registration. **2.** a place where registers are kept; an office of registration. **3.** a list or record of names, dates, etc.; register. **4.** the nationality of a ship as shown on its register.

re·gress (ri gres′), *v.* **1.** to move in a backward direction, esp. to an earlier or less advanced state or form. —*n.* (rē′gres). **2.** the act of going back; return: *The step we have taken allows for no regress.* **3.** a movement backward to an earlier or less advanced state or form. —**re·gres′sion,** *n.*

re·gret (ri gret′), *v.,* **re·gret·ted, re·gret·ting. 1.** to feel sorrow or remorse for: *to regret a mistake.* **2.** to think of with a sense of loss: *to regret lost opportunities.* —*n.* **3.** sorrow or remorse for a fault, mistake, etc.: *to feel regret for one's actions.* **4.** a sense of loss: *regret for lost opportunities.* **5. regrets,** a polite refusal of an invitation: *She sent her regrets, saying she could not come.* —**re·gret′ta·ble,** *adj.* —**re·gret′ta·bly,** *adv.*

re·gret·ful (ri gret′fəl), *adj.* full of regret; sorrowful because of what is lost, gone, or done: *to be regretful for wasted time.* —**re·gret′ful·ly,** *adv.* —**re·gret′ful·ness,** *n.*

re·group (rē grōōp′), *v.* **1.** to form into a new group

or groups: *to regroup a class.* **2.** to come together again in the same group: *They regrouped after recess.*

reg·u·lar (reg′yə lər), *adj.* **1.** usual, normal, or customary: *Spring came at its regular time.* **2.** orderly or methodical: *a regular procedure.* **3.** happening at fixed intervals: *to have a regular heartbeat.* **4.** happening again and again at the same time: *regular meals.* **5.** habitual or consistent: *a regular customer.* **6.** following some accepted rule, program, etc.: *a regular member of the party.* **7.** *Informal.* **a.** real; genuine: *a regular fellow.* **b.** absolute; thorough: *a regular scoundrel.* **8.** even or uniform: *a face with regular features.* **9.** (in grammar) following the usual rules of inflection. The verbs *talk* and *push* are regular in their conjugation. The nouns *boy* and *bat* have regular plural forms. The adjective *great* has regular comparative and superlative forms: *greater; greatest.* **10.** (in geometry) having all sides and angles equal: *A square is a regular polygon.* **11.** noting or belonging to the standing army of a state: *a regular officer.* **12.** qualified for or working in an occupation: *a regular clerk.* —*n.* **13.** a customer or client of long standing. **14.** a loyal member of a political party: *the Republican regulars.* —**reg′u·lar′i·ty,** *n.* —**reg′u·lar·ly,** *adv.*

reg·u·late (reg′yə lāt′), *v.,* **reg·u·lat·ed, reg·u·lat·ing. 1.** to control or direct according to a rule, method, etc.: *to regulate one's daily life.* **2.** to adjust or set in proper working order: *to regulate a machine.* **3.** to adjust for amount, degree, etc.: *to regulate the temperature of a room.* —**reg′u·la′tor,** *n.*

reg·u·la·tion (reg′yə lā′shən), *n.* **1.** the act of regulating, or the state of being regulated. **2.** a rule, law, order, etc.: *the regulations of an office.* —*adj.* **3.** conforming to regulation: *a regulation uniform.* **4.** usual or normal: *a regulation procedure.*

re·gur·gi·tate (ri gûr′ji tāt′), *v.,* **re·gur·gi·tat·ed, re·gur·gi·tat·ing.** to surge or cause to surge back, as undigested food from the stomach: *Cows regurgitate their cud.* —**re·gur′gi·ta′tion,** *n.*

re·ha·bil·i·tate (rē′hə bil′i tāt′), *v.,* **re·ha·bil·i·tat·ed, re·ha·bil·i·tat·ing. 1.** to bring back to a condition of good health, ability to work, etc.: *to rehabilitate the handicapped.* **2.** to restore to operation, use, etc.: *to rehabilitate a business.* **3.** to restore the rights, rank, or good reputation of: *The court completely rehabilitated the accused man.* —**re′ha·bil′i·ta′tion,** *n.*

re·hash (rē hash′), *v.* **1.** to bring up or use again; repeat or rework, as old ideas, writing, etc.: *to write a report by rehashing the opinions of others.* —*n.* (rē′hash′). **2.** the act of rehashing. **3.** something that has been rehashed: *His speech was a rehash of all his other speeches.*

re·hears·al (ri hûr′səl), *n.* **1.** a practice performance, usually private, to prepare for the public presentation of an opera, play, etc. **2.** a detailed account or recital: *a rehearsal of one's troubles.*

re·hearse (ri hûrs′), *v.,* **re·hearsed, re·hears·ing. 1.** to practice (a performance) before public presentation. **2.** to drill or train by rehearsal: *to rehearse an actor; to rehearse a dancer.* **3.** to take part in or practice a rehearsal: *The group rehearses every afternoon.* **4.** to tell the facts or details of; recount.

Reich (rīk), *n.* the German nation, esp. the Third Reich ruled by the Nazis (1933–1945).

reign (rān), *n.* **1.** the period during which a sovereign rules: *the reign of Elizabeth I.* **2.** royal power: *to oppose the reign of a despotic king.* **3.** any supreme power or influence: *to live under the reign of justice.* —*v.* **4.** to have royal power: *The king reigned for many years.* **5.** to be widespread; prevail: *Happiness reigned in the house at Christmas.*

re·im·burse (rē'im bûrs'), *v.,* **re·im·bursed, re·im·burs·ing. 1.** to pay back (someone) for an expense or loss: *You will be reimbursed for your services.* **2.** to refund the money for: *Their traveling expenses were reimbursed by the company.* —**re'im·burse'ment,** *n.*

rein (rān), *n.* **1.** one of two leather straps attached to the ends of the bit of a bridle, used by a driver or rider of a horse or other animal to check, control, or guide it. **2.** any means of controlling, curbing, or guiding: *He keeps a tight rein on his spending.* —*v.* **3.** to check, control, or guide by means of reins: *to rein a horse.* **4.** to curb or control: *He reined his anger.* **5. give rein to,** to allow freedom to: *Give rein to your imagination in this assignment.*

re·in·car·nate (rē'in kär'nāt), *v.,* **re·in·car·nat·ed, re·in·car·nat·ing.** to give another body to: *Hindus believe that the soul is reincarnated after death.* —**re'in·car·na'tion,** *n.*

rein·deer (rān'dēr'), *n., pl.* **rein·deer.** any of several large deer of the northern and arctic regions of Europe, Asia, and North America, both male and female of which have antlers. Reindeer are tamed and used as work animals and as a source of milk, meat, and leather.

re·in·force (rē'in fôrs'), *v.,* **re·in·forced, re·in·forc·ing.** to make stronger or more forceful by the addition of something: *to reinforce a wall with cement; to reinforce an argument with facts.* Also, **reenforce.**

European reindeer
(4½ ft. high at shoulder)

re·in·force·ment (rē'in fôrs'mənt), *n.* **1.** the act of reinforcing, or the state of being reinforced. **2.** something that reinforces: *A reinforcement was added to the wall.* **3.** Often, **reinforcements.** an additional supply of men, ships, etc., for a military force.

re·in·state (rē'in stāt'), *v.,* **re·in·stat·ed, re·in·stat·ing.** to put back into a former position or state: *He was reinstated as manager.* —**re'in·state'ment,** *n.*

re·it·er·ate (rē it'ə rāt'), *v.,* **re·it·er·at·ed, re·it·er·at·ing.** to say or do again; repeat (something) often or unnecessarily: *She reiterated the warning about coming straight home.* —**re·it·er·a'tion,** *n.*

re·ject (ri jekt'), *v.* **1.** to refuse to have, take, grant, etc.: *to reject help; to reject a plea.* **2.** to throw away; discard: *to reject useless toys.* —*n.* (rē'jekt). **3.** a person or thing regarded as unfit or imperfect: *He was a reject from the army. The cracked dishes are rejects.*

re·jec·tion (ri jek'shən), *n.* **1.** the act of rejecting, or the state of being rejected. **2.** something that has been rejected.

re·joice (ri jois'), *v.,* **re·joiced, re·joic·ing. 1.** to be glad; take delight (often fol. by *in*): *He rejoiced in his family.* **2.** to make joyful; gladden: *News of the victory rejoiced us.* —**re·joice'ful,** *adj.*

re·join[1] (ri join'), *v.* **1.** to come again into the company of: *I'll rejoin you after lunch.* **2.** to join together again: *to rejoin a broken chain.* [from *re-* + *join*]

re·join[2] (ri join'), *v.* to make a reply; answer: *He rejoined angrily when his request was refused.* [from the Old French word *rejoindre* "to reply"]

re·join·der (ri join'dər), *n.* an answer, esp. to a reply: *He made an angry rejoinder at her remark.*

re·ju·ve·nate (ri jōō'və nāt'), *v.,* **re·ju·ve·nat·ed, re·ju·ve·nat·ing.** to make young again in appearance, health, etc.: *The long rest rejuvenated her.* —**re·ju've·na'tion,** *n.*

rel., **1.** relating. **2.** relative. **3.** relatively. **4.** religion. **5.** religious.

re·lapse (ri laps'), *v.,* **re·lapsed, re·laps·ing. 1.** to fall or slip back into a previous state, esp. one that is wrong or harmful: *Once out of jail, he relapsed into a life of crime.* **2.** to fall back into illness after a partial recovery: *He caught a chill and relapsed.* —*n.* (ri laps', rē'laps). **3.** the act of relapsing, esp. a return to illness after a partial recovery.

re·late (ri lāt'), *v.,* **re·lat·ed, re·lat·ing. 1.** to tell; give an account of: *He related the story of his life.* **2.** to connect in thought or meaning: *to relate two facts.* **3.** to be connected in thought or meaning: *Your suggestions don't relate to our problem.* **4.** to feel close to a person or thing: *He does not relate to the rest of the class.*

re·lat·ed (ri lā'tid), *adj.* **1.** connected by nature, origin, marriage, etc.: *related vegetables; related tribes.* **2.** connected in thought or meaning: *related ideas.*

re·la·tion (ri lā'shən), *n.* **1.** a connection between or among things; relationship: *the relation of health to happiness.* **2.** a person who is related by blood or marriage; relative: *We spend Christmas with our relations.* **3.** reference; regard; respect: *to plan with relation to the future.* **4.** the act of narrating: *a relation of the events in a story.* **5.** a narrative; account: *an interesting relation.* **6. relations,** connections between people, countries, etc.: *The hostile countries broke off relations.*

re·la·tion·ship (ri lā'shən ship'), *n.* **1.** connection or association; relation: *the relationship of two ideas.* **2.** a connection between persons by blood or marriage. **3.** a tie between people: *We have a very close, warm relationship with our minister.*

rel·a·tive (rel/ə tiv), *n.* **1.** a person who is connected with another or others by blood or marriage: *relatives on my mother's side.* **2.** (in grammar) a relative word. —*adj.* **3.** considered in relation to something else; comparative: *the relative merits of democracy and monarchy.* **4.** having meaning only as related to something else: *"Hot" and "cold" are relative terms. Happiness is relative.* **5.** having relation or connection: *He spoke on taxation and relative topics.* **6.** having reference or regard; pertinent: *Your answer is not relative to my question.* **7.** (in grammar) describing a word or construction in which reference is made to some person or thing mentioned or understood in another part of the construction: *a relative pronoun; a relative clause.* **8. relative to,** regarding; concerning: *There was an investigation relative to his disappearance.*

rel/ative clause/, a subordinate clause introduced by a relative pronoun or other relative word, and modifying an antecedent. In the sentence *It was she who saw us, who saw us* is a relative clause.

rel/ative humid/ity, the amount of water vapor in the air, expressed as a percentage of the maximum amount that air at the same temperature can hold.

rel·a·tive·ly (rel/ə tiv lē), *adv.* in a relative manner: *There is relatively little difference between them.*

rel/ative pro/noun, a pronoun that refers to an antecedent. Some relative pronouns are *who, whom, that,* and *which.*

rel·a·tiv·i·ty (rel/ə tiv/i tē), *n.* **1.** the state or fact of being relative: *the relativity of size among different kinds of monkeys.* **2.** a theory formulated by Albert Einstein that is divided into two parts, the first dealing with motion and the second with gravitation. One conclusion, derived from the first part, states that matter and energy are equivalent and form the basis for nuclear energy.

re·lax (ri laks/), *v.* **1.** to make or become less rigid or tense: *The warm sun relaxed his body. His fingers relaxed their grip.* **2.** to make or become less strict or severe, as rules or discipline. **3.** to make or become less worried, anxious, etc.: *The drug quickly relaxed him.* **4.** to leave off work or effort for the sake of rest or recreation: *to relax with a good book.*

re·lax·a·tion (rē/lak sā/shən), *n.* **1.** the removing or reducing of effort, tension, strictness, etc.: *a relaxation of the muscles; a relaxation of discipline.* **2.** rest or diversion from work: *He fishes for relaxation.*

re·lay (rē/lā), *n.* **1.** a team or shift that takes turns with another or others, in doing something: *They worked through the night in relays.* **2.** a relay race. **3.** an electrically operated switch, esp. one that uses a small current to control a much larger one. —*v.* (rē/lā, ri lā/), **re·layed, re·lay·ing. 4.** to pass on; convey: *I will relay your message to her.*

re/lay race/, a race between two or more teams of contestants, each contestant being relieved by another after running part of the distance.

re·lease (ri lēs/), *v.,* **re·leased, re·leas·ing. 1.** to free from pain, confinement, etc.: *Sleep released her from worry. The prisoners were pardoned and released.* **2.**
to let loose; let go: *to release a spring; to release an arrow from a bow.* **3.** to allow to be published, seen, or known: *The office released the information to the newspapers.* —*n.* **4.** an act or instance of release: *the release of a prisoner; release from pain.* **5.** permission to use, publish, sell, etc. **6.** the publication or distribution of something: *the release of a new movie.* **7.** information released to the public in the form of a bulletin, as by a company: *a release describing a new product.* **8.** a device for stopping or starting a machine by releasing a catch, lock, etc.

rel·e·gate (rel/ə gāt/), *v.,* **rel·e·gat·ed, rel·e·gat·ing. 1.** to send or assign to a lower position, place, or rank: *The leading actor was relegated to playing minor roles.* **2.** to assign or turn over (a task, duty, etc.) to someone: *He relegated the task to his assistant.*

re·lent (ri lent/), *v.* **1.** to become more kind, forgiving, understanding, etc.: *He relented and pardoned the mistake.* **2.** to become milder or less severe; slacken: *The cold weather relented and spring came.* —**re·lent/ing·ly,** *adv.*

re·lent·less (ri lent/lis), *adj.* unyieldingly severe, harsh, strict, etc.: *a relentless attack against a foe.* —**re·lent/less·ly,** *adv.*

rel·e·vant (rel/ə vənt), *adj.* related to a particular subject or topic; appropriate: *Your question is not relevant to the topic being discussed.* —**rel/e·vance, rel/e·van·cy,** *n.*

re·li·a·ble (ri lī/ə bəl), *adj.* able to be relied on; dependable or trustworthy: *a reliable friend; a reliable map.* —**re·li·a·bil/i·ty,** *n.* —**re·li/a·bly,** *adv.*

re·li·ance (ri lī/əns), *n.* **1.** trust or confidence: *You can put reliance in his promise.* **2.** trustful or confident dependence: *to have reliance on one's father.* **3.** someone or something that is relied on: *The widow's sister was her only reliance.*

re·li·ant (ri lī/ənt), *adj.* **1.** having or showing dependence; dependent: *Babies are completely reliant upon their parents.* **2.** confident; trustful: *I am reliant on the dealer's guarantee.*

rel·ic (rel/ik), *n.* **1.** a thing, idea, custom, etc., that survives from the past: *This lamp is a relic of the days before electricity.* **2.** something that is of interest because of its age or associations; heirloom; keepsake: *beautiful old relics of grandmother's childhood.* **3.** the body, a part of the body, or a memento of a saint or holy person, regarded as sacred.

re·lief¹ (ri lēf/), *n.* **1.** ease or comfort caused by the removal of pain, distress, etc.: *The medicine brought quick relief.* **2.** something that brings ease from pain, distress, etc.: *The good news was a relief.* **3.** help given to those in poverty or need: *relief for the victims of a flood.* **4.** something that brings a pleasing change, esp. from a monotonous, disagreeable condition: *The warm weather was a relief after the cold, rainy days.* **5.** release from a post of duty: *the relief of a weary sentry by a replacement.* **6.** the person or persons who replace another or others in a post of duty: *Fresh troops were sent to the front as a relief.* [from an Old French word, which comes from *relever* "to raise." See *relieve*]

re·lief[2] (ri lēf′), *n.* **1.** sharpness or vividness due to contrast: *The red house stood in bright relief against the green background.* **2.** a piece of sculpture in which the figures stand out from a flat surface. **3.** differences in the height of land within a certain area. [from a French word, which is a translation of Italian *rilievo*, from *rilevare* "to raise." See *relieve*]

Relief[2]

relief′ map′, a map showing differences in land heights or ocean depths by means of different colors, raised areas or indentations in a surface, etc.

re·lieve (ri lēv′), *v.,* **re·lieved, re·liev·ing. 1.** to ease or lighten (pain, distress, etc.): *The aspirin relieved his headache.* **2.** to free from fear, pain, etc.: *He was relieved when the plane landed safely.* **3.** to free from poverty or need; bring help to: *to relieve the victims of a disaster.* **4.** to break the sameness or monotony of: *The hard work was relieved with short breaks.* **5.** to release (a person on duty) by being or providing a replacement: *The guard is relieved every two hours.* [from the Old French word *relever* "to raise," which comes from Latin *relevāre* "to lift, lighten"]

re·li·gion (ri lij′ən), *n.* **1.** belief in or the worship of God or gods. **2.** a system of belief in and worship of God or gods: *the Christian religion; the Hindu religion.* **3.** something that one believes in, serves, or follows devotedly: *His career was his religion.*

re·li·gious (ri lij′əs), *adj.* **1.** of, referring to, or concerned with religion: *religious beliefs; a religious institution.* **2.** devout; pious: *a deeply religious worshiper.* **3.** very conscientious or faithful: *to be religious about doing one's work.* —*n., pl.* **re·li·gious. 4.** a member of a religious order, as a nun or monk. —**re·li′gious·ly,** *adv.*

re·lin·quish (ri ling′kwish), *v.* **1.** to renounce or surrender: *to relinquish a throne.* **2.** to give up or put aside: *to relinquish a plan.* **3.** to let go; release: *to relinquish one's hold.* —**re·lin′quish·ment,** *n.*

rel·ish (rel′ish), *n.* **1.** a liking or enjoyment of something: *a relish for steak; a relish for adventure.* **2.** a pleasing or enjoyable quality: *Wit adds relish to conversation.* **3.** a spicy food, such as olives, chopped pickles, etc., that stimulates one's appetite for or increases the flavor of other food. —*v.* **4.** to take pleasure in; enjoy: *He relishes traveling to new places.*

re·live (ri liv′), *v.,* **re·lived, re·liv·ing. 1.** to go through an experience again, esp. in memory: *to relive a happy event.* **2.** to live over again: *The old man wished he could relive his youth.*

re·luc·tant (ri luk′tənt), *adj.* **1.** not willing or inclined: *He is reluctant to give his approval.* **2.** showing a lack of willingness or inclination: *reluctant*

consent. —**re·luc′tance,** *n.* —**re·luc′tant·ly,** *adv.*

re·ly (ri li′), *v.,* **re·lied, re·ly·ing.** to depend confidently (usually fol. by *on* or *upon*): *He relies on the opinion of his friends.*

re·main (ri mān′), *v.* **1.** to continue to be; go on being: *We remain friends in spite of our differences.* **2.** to stay behind or in the same place: *He remained after they left.* **3.** to be left: *Nothing remained of the town after the tornado.* **4.** to be left to be done, acted upon, etc.: *The kitchen remains to be cleaned.* —*n.* **5. remains, a.** something that remains; leftovers: *the remains of a picnic.* **b.** ancient ruins: *the remains of a Roman temple.* **c.** a dead body; corpse.

re·main·der (ri mān′dər), *n.* **1.** something that remains or is left: *He took part of the money and left me the remainder.* **2.** (in arithmetic) the quantity that is left over when a number cannot be divided evenly: *In the problem 11÷3, the remainder is 2.*

re·make (rē māk′), *v.,* **re·made** (rē mād′), **re·mak·ing. 1.** to make again or anew: *to remake a dress.* —*n.* (rē′māk′). **2.** something, such as a motion picture, that is made again or anew.

re·mand (ri mand′), *v.* **1.** to send back again, as a legal case to a lower court for further proceedings, or a prisoner to jail to await trial. —*n.* **2.** the act of remanding, or the state of being remanded.

re·mark (ri märk′), *v.* **1.** to say casually, as in making a comment: *He remarked that it was warm for November.* **2.** to note; perceive; observe: *He remarked the lateness of the hour.* —*n.* **3.** the act of remarking. **4.** notice or comment: *The incident passed without remark.* **5.** a casual expression of thought or opinion: *some brief remarks about the election.*

re·mark·a·ble (ri mär′kə bəl), *adj.* worthy of notice; unusual; extraordinary: *a remarkable performance.*

Rem·brandt (rem′brant, rem′bränt), *n.* 1606–1669, Dutch painter.

re·me·di·a·ble (ri mē′dē ə bəl), *adj.* capable of being remedied: *a remediable defect.*

re·me·di·al (ri mē′dē əl), *adj.* for the purpose of remedy or improvement: *remedial exercises; remedial reading.* —**re·me′di·al·ly,** *adv.*

rem·e·dy (rem′i dē), *n., pl.* **rem·e·dies. 1.** something, such as a medicine, that cures or relieves a disease, ailment, etc.: *a remedy for a cold.* **2.** something that corrects or removes an evil: *a remedy for injustice.* —*v.,* **rem·e·died, rem·e·dy·ing. 3.** to cure, relieve, or correct: *to remedy an illness; to remedy an evil.*

re·mem·ber (ri mem′bər), *v.* **1.** to recall to the mind by using the memory: *to remember events of early childhood.* **2.** to keep or have in mind: *Remember your appointment. He would long remember the day.* **3.** to reward; tip: *to remember the staff at Christmas.* **4.** to mention (a person) to another as sending best wishes: *Please remember me to her.*

re·mem·brance (ri mem′brəns), *n.* **1.** the act or fact of remembering; memory: *His remembrance of that time always made him sad.* **2.** a state of being remembered; commemoration: *to hold someone's name in remembrance.* **3.** something that serves to bring to or keep in mind; souvenir; memento: *The faded rose was a remembrance of that happy day.* **4.** remembrances, greetings; regards: *Give her my remembrances.*

re·mind (ri mīnd′), *v.* to cause to remember: *Remind me to buy coffee.* —re·mind′er, *n.*

rem·i·nisce (rem′ə nis′), *v.*, rem·i·nisced, rem·i·nisc·ing. to recall past experiences, events, etc.: *He liked to reminisce about his childhood.*

rem·i·nis·cence (rem′ə nis′əns), *n.* **1.** the act or process of recalling past experience. **2.** something remembered: *an interesting reminiscence.* **3.** Often, reminiscences. a book or other account of one's past experiences: *He wrote his reminiscences of the war.*

rem·i·nis·cent (rem′ə nis′ənt), *adj.* **1.** suggestive of or recalling something because of a certain likeness (usually fol. by *of*): *His way of speaking is reminiscent of my father's.* **2.** fond of recalling the past: *reminiscent old people.*

re·miss (ri mis′), *adj.* **1.** careless, slow, or neglectful in performing one's duty: *The waiters here are very remiss.* **2.** showing negligence: *a thoroughly remiss handling of the matter.* [from the Latin word *remissus* "sent back, relaxed"]

re·mis·sion (ri mish′ən), *n.* **1.** the act of remitting. **2.** pardon or forgiveness: *the remission of a sin; the remission of an offense.* **3.** the temporary decrease of pain, an illness, etc.: *the remission of a fever.* **4.** the cancellation of a debt, duty, etc.

re·mit (ri mit′), *v.*, re·mit·ted, re·mit·ting. **1.** to send (money) in payment: *to remit an amount owed.* **2.** to pardon or forgive: *to remit a sin.* **3.** to free someone from: *to remit a debt; to remit a punishment.* **4.** to make weaker or slacken: *Do not remit your efforts.* —re·mit′ta·ble, *adj.*

re·mit·tance (ri mit′ʰns), *n.* **1.** the sending of money to someone: *a prompt remittance.* **2.** an amount of money sent: *He enclosed his remittance.*

rem·nant (rem′nənt), *n.* **1.** something that is left over, usually a small part, number, or the like: *the remnant of a great fortune.* **2.** a small piece of cloth or other material.

re·mod·el (rē mod′ʰl), *v.*, re·mod·eled *or* re·mod·elled; re·mod·el·ing *or* re·mod·el·ling. to make over in a different way: *to remodel an old house.*

re·mon·strance (ri mon′strəns), *n.* something that is said in disapproval; protest: *a remonstrance against unfair punishment.*

re·mon·strate (ri mon′strāt), *v.*, re·mon·strat·ed, re·mon·strat·ing. to say or plead in protest or disapproval: *to remonstrate against unjust laws.*

rem·o·ra (rem′ər ə), *n.* any of several fishes having a sucking disk on top of the head by which they can attach themselves to sharks, turtles, ships, and other moving objects.

Remora
(length 3 ft.)

re·morse (ri môrs′), *n.* deep and painful regret for

having done something wrong: *The prisoner suffered remorse for his crime.* [from the Latin word *remorsus,* literally "bitten back"]

re·morse·ful (ri môrs′fəl), *adj.* feeling or showing remorse: *a remorseful prisoner; a remorseful mood.* —re·morse′ful·ly, *adv.*

re·morse·less (ri môrs′lis), *adj.* without remorse; merciless; ruthless; cruel: *a remorseless killer.*

re·mote (ri mōt′), *adj.* **1.** far away or distant: *a remote country.* **2.** secluded; set apart: *a remote cottage in the woods.* **3.** far away in time: *a remote period in human history.* **4.** only distantly related: *a remote ancestor.* **5.** slight or faint: *a remote chance.* —re·mote′ly, *adv.*

re·mov·al (ri mōō′vəl), *n.* **1.** the act of removing: *the removal of snow from the streets.* **2.** a change of residence, location, etc.: *the family's removal to a new house.* **3.** dismissal, as from an office: *The people demanded the removal of the incompetent mayor.*

re·move (ri mōōv′), *v.*, re·moved, re·mov·ing. **1.** to take away or off: *to remove books from a shelf; to remove one's coat.* **2.** to move to another place; transfer: *They removed their business to another city.* **3.** to wipe out or get rid of: *to remove a stain.* **4.** to dismiss or force from an office or position: *to remove a corrupt sheriff.* —*n.* **5.** a removal: *the remove of a business to a new location.* **6.** a degree of distance or separation: *a statement at a remove from the exact truth.* —re·mov′a·ble, *adj.* —re·mov′er, *n.*

re·mu·ner·ate (ri myōō′nə rāt′), *v.*, re·mu·ner·at·ed, re·mu·ner·at·ing. **1.** to pay or reward: *He was amply remunerated for mowing the lawn.* **2.** to pay for: *to remunerate a service.*

re·mu·ner·a·tion (ri myōō′nə rā′shən), *n.* **1.** the act of remunerating: *the remuneration of a good deed.* **2.** reward or pay: *to work without remuneration.*

re·mu·ner·a·tive (ri myōō′nə rā′tiv, ri myōō′nər ə tiv), *adj.* profitable or rewarding: *a remunerative job; remunerative reading.*

Re·mus (rē′məs), *n.* (in Roman mythology) the twin brother of Romulus.

Ren·ais·sance (ren′i säns′, ren′i zäns′), *n.* **1.** the intellectual and artistic movement beginning in 14th-century Italy and extending throughout Europe by the 17th century. **2.** the period of history when this occurred. —*adj.* **3.** referring to the styles of painting, architecture, and furniture of the period.

Re·nas·cence (ri nas′əns, ri nās′əns), *n.* the Renaissance.

rend (rend), *v.*, **rent** (rent), **rend·ing. 1.** to tear apart, split, or divide: *The storm rent the ship's sails. The nation was rent by a civil war.* **2.** to tear (one's hair or clothing) in grief, rage, etc. **3.** to pain (the heart, emotions, etc.): *The sight of another's suffering rends our hearts.*

ren·der (ren′dər), *v.* **1.** to cause to be or become; make: *to render someone helpless.* **2.** to do; perform: *She rendered her part in the play with skill.* **3.** to give or supply: *to render aid.* **4.** to pay as due: *to render homage.* **5.** to give in return: *to render blow for blow.* **6.** to deliver by decree; hand down: *The court* *rendered its verdict.* **7.** to give up; surrender: *to render a city to the enemy.* **8.** to translate into another language: *to render a French song into English.* **9.** to melt down, as fat. —**ren′der·a·ble,** *adj.*

ren·dez·vous (rän′dā vōō′), *n.*, *pl.* **·en·dez·vous** (rän′dā vōōz′). **1.** an agreement to meet at a certain time and place. **2.** the place of meeting: *The hotel lobby was our rendezvous.* **3.** the meeting itself: *I look forward to our rendezvous.* **4.** a place where ships, troops, etc., assemble: *a rendezvous for maneuvers.* —*v.,* **ren·dez·voused** (rän′dā vōōd′), **ren·dez·vous·ing** (rän′dā vōō′ing). **5.** to assemble at an agreed time or place: *We rendezvoused at the beach.* [from the French phrase *rendez-vous* "betake yourselves"]

ren·di·tion (ren dish′ən), *n.* **1.** the act of rendering. **2.** a translation: *a French rendition of Shakespeare.* **3.** a performance of a stage role or a piece of music: *a rendition of Hamlet.*

ren·e·gade (ren′ə gād′), *n.* a person who deserts his religious faith, political party, etc., for another.

re·nege (ri nig′, ri neg′), *v.,* **re·neged, re·neg·ing. 1.** to break a rule of play in a card game. **2.** to break a promise; go back on one's word: *He said he would help us, but he reneged.*

re·new (ri nōō′, -nyōō′), *v.* **1.** to begin or take up again: *to renew one's efforts after a break.* **2.** to continue or get again for a further period of time: *to renew a lease; to renew a loan.* **3.** to put in a new supply of: *to renew stock; to renew provisions.* **4.** to revive or make fresh again: *The praise renewed his hopes.* **5.** to put back into a former state; make new or as if new again: *to renew an old house.* —**re·new′ a·ble,** *adj.* —**re·new′al,** *n.*

ren·net (ren′it), *n.* a substance containing rennin that is extracted from the stomach of a calf. It is used in making cheese, junket, etc.

ren·nin (ren′in), *n.* an enzyme found in rennet that curdles milk.

re·nounce (ri nouns′), *v.,* **re·nounced, re·nounc·ing. 1.** to give up or put aside by one's own consent: *He renounced smoking for the sake of his health.* **2.** to disown or cast out: *to renounce a son.* —**re·nounc′er,** *n.*

ren·o·vate (ren′ə vāt′), *v.,* **ren·o·vat·ed, ren·o·vat·ing.** to repair or renew: *to renovate an old house.* —**ren′o·va′tion,** *n.* —**ren′o·va′tor,** *n.*

re·nown (ri noun′), *n.* widespread reputation; fame: *painters of renown.*

re·nowned (ri nound′), *adj.* of a celebrated reputation: *the renowned leaders of history.*

rent¹ (rent), *n.* **1.** a payment regularly made for the use of something, such as a house, automobile, etc. —*v.* **2.** to allow the use of in return for regular payments: *to rent an apartment to a tenant.* **3.** to use in return for such payments: *to rent a new apartment.* **4.** to be leased or let for rent: *The apartment rents for more than we can afford.* **5. for rent,** available for occupancy: *There are no apartments for rent in this building.* [from the Middle English word *rente,* which comes from Old French] —**rent′er,** *n.*

rent² (rent), *n.* **1.** an opening made by rending or tearing: *to mend a rent in a shirt.* **2.** a breach or break in a political party, organization, or the like. —*v.* **3.** the past tense and past participle of **rend.** [another form of the word *rend*]

rent·al (ren′t³l), *n.* **1.** the act of renting. **2.** an amount received or paid as rent. **3.** a house or other property for rent.

re·nun·ci·a·tion (ri nun′sē ā′shən), *n.* an act or instance of renouncing: *the renunciation of a claim.*

re·o·pen (rē ō′pən), *v.* **1.** to open again: *to reopen a box.* **2.** to start or take up again: *to reopen a lawsuit.*

re·or·gan·ize (rē ôr′gə nīz′), *v.,* **re·or·gan·ized, re·or·gan·iz·ing.** to organize again: *to reorganize a business.* —**re′or·gan·i·za′tion,** *n.*

Rep., 1. Representative. **2.** Republic. **3.** Republican.

re·paid (ri pād′), *v.* the past tense and past participle of **repay.**

re·pair¹ (ri pâr′), *v.* **1.** to put back into good condition after wear, decay, damage, etc.: *to repair a motor; to repair one's health.* **2.** to remedy; make up for: *to repair a wrong; to repair a misunderstanding.* —*n.* **3.** an act or process of repairing: *The repair of the car took hours.* **4.** Usually, **repairs.** the work done or to be done in repairing: *to make repairs around the house; a car in need of repairs.* **5.** the condition of something in respect to soundness or fitness for use: *a house in good repair.* [from the early French word *reparer,* which comes from Latin *reparāre*] —**re·pair′a·ble,** *adj.* —**re·pair′er,** *n.*

re·pair² (ri pâr′), *v.* **1.** to go: *He repairs to the beach in the summer.* —*n.* **2.** the act of going: *a weekly repair to the beach.* [from the Old French word *repairier* "to return," which comes from Latin *repatriāre* "to return to one's fatherland"]

re·pair·man (ri pâr′man′, -mən), *n.,* *pl.* **re·pair·men.** a man whose occupation is the repairing of things that are broken, in poor condition, etc.

rep·a·ra·ble (rep′ər ə bəl), *adj.* capable of being repaired or remedied.

rep·a·ra·tion (rep′ə rā′shən), *n.* **1.** an instance of making up for a wrong, damage, etc.: *Money was given in reparation for the offense.* **2.** something done or given to make up for a wrong, damage, etc. **3.** Usually, **reparations.** money or goods that a country defeated in a war must pay to the victor or victors for damages or loss suffered.

rep·ar·tee (rep′ər tē′, rep′är tā′), *n.* **1.** a quick, witty reply. **2.** conversation full of such replies. **3.** skill in making such replies.

re·past (ri past′), *n.* a meal: *a sumptuous repast.*

re·pa·tri·ate (rē pā′trē āt′), *v.,* **re·pa·tri·at·ed, re·pa·tri·at·ing.** to bring or send back (a person) to his own country, esp. after a war. —**re·pa′tri·a′tion,** *n.*

re·pay (ri pā′), *v.,* **re·paid** (ri pād′), **re·pay·ing. 1.** to pay back: *to repay a loan.* **2.** to make a return for: *to repay a favor.* **3.** to return: *to repay a visit.* **4.** to make a return to in any way: *to repay someone for a service.* —**re·pay′a·ble,** *adj.* —**re·pay′ment,** *n.*

re·peal (ri pēl′), *v.* to do away with in a formal way; cancel; annul; revoke: *to repeal an unjust law.* —re·peal′a·ble, *adj.*

re·peat (ri pēt′), *v.* 1. to say again: *to repeat a word over and over.* 2. to say after another: *Please repeat the following sentence.* 3. to tell (something heard): *He repeated the news to his friends.* 4. to do, make, or perform again: *She repeated the concert the next night.* —*n.* 5. the act of repeating: *a repeat of the show.* 6. something repeated; repetition: *The summer shows on TV are all repeats.* —re·peat′a·ble, *adj.*

re·peat·ed (ri pē′tid), *adj.* done, made, or said again and again: *He paid no attention to the repeated warnings.* —re·peat′ed·ly, *adv.*

re·pel (ri pel′), *v.,* re·pelled, re·pel·ling. 1. to drive or force back: *The army repelled the invaders.* 2. to keep off or out: *This fabric repels rain.* 3. to refuse to accept. 4. to disgust: *Her untidiness repelled me.*

re·pel·lent (ri pel′ənt), *adj.* 1. causing dislike or disgust: *repellent behavior.* 2. repelling; driving back: *a repellent military tactic.* —*n.* 3. something that repels: *an insect repellent.* 4. a solution applied to a fabric or garment to increase its resistance, as to water, moths, etc. —re·pel′lent·ly, *adv.*

re·pent (ri pent′), *v.* 1. to feel sorry for something one has said, done, etc. 2. to feel sorry for; regret: *He repented the evil he had done.* —re·pent′er, *n.* —re·pent′ing·ly, *adv.*

re·pent·ance (ri pen′tᵊns), *n.* remorse or regret for having committed a sin, crime, or the like.

re·pent·ant (ri pen′tᵊnt), *adj.* feeling or showing repentance: *a repentant sinner.* —re·pent′ant·ly, *adv.*

re·per·cus·sion (rē′pər kush′ən), *n.* 1. an effect or result, often indirect, of some event or action: *The repercussions of the war were felt throughout ihe world.* 2. an echo or reverberation: *The repercussion of the explosion shook the windows.*

rep·er·toire (rep′ər twär′), *n.* the list of plays, songs, operas, or the like, that a company, actor, singer, etc., is prepared to perform; repertory.

rep·er·to·ry (rep′ər tôr′ē), *n., pl.* rep·er·to·ries. 1. another spelling of **repertoire.** 2. any collection, store, or stock: *a repertory of American plays.*

rep·e·ti·tion (rep′i tish′ən), *n.* 1. the act of repeating: *the repetition of a word.* 2. something repeated: *Today's performance is a repetition of yesterday's.*

rep·e·ti·tious (rep′i tish′əs), *adj.* full of repetition, usually of an unnecessary and tedious kind: *a repetitious speech.* —rep′e·ti′tious·ly, *adv.*

re·pine (ri pīn′), *v.,* re·pined, re·pin·ing. to feel or show annoyance, discontent, etc.; fret.

re·place (ri plās′), *v.,* re·placed, re·plac·ing. 1. to take over the place of: *Electricity has replaced the candle as a source of light.* 2. to put in the place of: *I will replace the cup I broke.* 3. to put back in place. —re·place′a·ble, *adj.*

re·place·ment (ri plās′mənt), *n.* 1. the act of replacing. 2. a person or thing that replaces another, esp. a soldier who replaces another in a military force.

re·plen·ish (ri plen′ish), *v.* to fill up again with food, fuel, or some other necessary item: *to replenish the*

larder; to replenish a fireplace. —re·plen′ish·er, *n.* —re·plen′ish·ment, *n.*

re·plete (ri plēt′), *adj.* 1. abundantly filled: *a story replete with amusing incidents.* 2. stuffed with food and drink. —re·ple′tion, *n.*

rep·li·ca (rep′lə kə), *n.* 1. a close copy of a work of art: *a replica of a famous statue.* 2. any close copy or reproduction.

re·ply (ri plī′), *v.,* re·plied, re·ply·ing. 1. to answer in words or writing; respond: *He replied that he would not go.* 2. to do something in answer: *We replied with bullets to the enemy's attack.* —*n., pl.* re·plies. 3. an answer in words or writing. 4. any answer or response: *a reply to the enemy's attack.*

re·port (ri pôrt′), *n.* 1. a description of an event, action, etc.: *a newspaper report.* 2. a statement or announcement: *a report from the governor.* 3. rumor or gossip: *Is the report of his death true?* 4. repute or fame: *a man of bad report.* 5. a loud noise, as from an explosion: *the report of a gun.* —*v.* 6. to write or give an account of: *to report an event.* 7. to make a report, esp. as a reporter for a newspaper. 8. to make a charge against (a person), as to the police. 9. to announce: *The committee reported its decision.* 10. to present oneself: *to report for work.* 11. to work as a reporter on a newspaper or magazine.

report′ card′, a written report of a pupil's work sent regularly by his school to his parents.

re·port·er (ri pôr′tər), *n.* 1. a person who reports. 2. a person whose work is to gather and report news, as for a newspaper.

re·pose¹ (ri pōz′), *n.* 1. rest or sleep: *a night of repose.* 2. peacefulness; calm: *the repose of the countryside at dusk.* —*v.,* re·posed, re·pos·ing. 3. to lie or be at rest: *to repose in bed.* 4. to lie dead. 5. to rest upon something: *The painting reposes on its easel.* [from the Old French word *reposer,* which comes from Latin *repausāre* "to rest"]

re·pose² (ri pōz′), *v.,* re·posed, re·pos·ing. to put (confidence or trust) in a person or thing. [from the Middle English word *reposen* "to replace," which comes from Latin *repōnere* "to put back"]

re·pos·i·to·ry (ri poz′i tôr′ē), *n., pl.* re·pos·i·tor·ies. a box, room, building, etc., in which things are stored.

re·pos·sess (rē′pə zes′), *v.* to take possession of again, esp. in a case where money due is not paid: *The store repossessed the new furniture.*

rep·re·hen·si·ble (rep′ri hen′sə bəl), *adj.* deserving of blame; blameworthy: *reprehensible behavior.* —rep′re·hen′si·bly, *adv.*

rep·re·sent (rep′ri zent′), *v.* 1. to stand for or symbolize: *Written words represent sounds.* 2. to act in place of; be an agent or substitute for: *He represents our company in Tokyo.* 3. to speak and act for with authority: *An ambassador represents his country abroad.* 4. to act for or on behalf of in a government, such as a congressman: *He represents a district in New York.* 5. to portray or show a likeness of, as a picture does: *The painting represents her faithfully.* 6. to picture to the mind: *He represented his past as having been happier than it actually was.* 7. to show or describe: *The article represented him as being a great leader.* **8.** to act the part of in a play.

rep·re·sen·ta·tion (rep′ri zen tā′shən), *n.* **1.** the act of representing, or the state of being represented. **2.** a picture, figure, statue, etc.: *The painting is a representation of Jupiter.* **3.** a symbol or sign: *Written words are representations of spoken sounds.* **4.** the state, fact, or right of being represented in government. **5.** the representatives of a group in a government: *our representation in the state legislature.* **6.** Often, **representations.** a description or statement of things that are true or are alleged to be true. —**rep′re·sen·ta′tion·al,** *adj.*

rep·re·sen·ta·tive (rep′ri zen′tə tiv), *n.* **1.** a person who represents another or others: *He was the representative of his family at the wedding.* **2.** a member of a legislature, esp. a member of the U.S. House of Representatives. **3.** a typical example or specimen. —*adj.* **4.** serving to represent: *a statue that is representative of peace.* **5.** serving to represent in government, or based upon representation in government. **6.** typical of its kind: *This report is representative of his work.*

re·press (ri pres′), *v.* **1.** to hold back; keep down; check: *He repressed his laughter.* **2.** to put an end to; quell: *to repress a mutiny.* **3.** to keep from thinking about or force out of one's mind: *to repress unhappy thoughts.*

re·pres·sion (ri presh′ən), *n.* **1.** the act of repressing, or the state of being repressed. **2.** the avoiding of painful or unpleasant ideas, memories, etc., by keeping them out of the conscious mind.

re·prieve (ri prēv′), *v.,* **re·prieved, re·priev·ing. 1.** to delay temporarily the punishment of: *The prisoner was reprieved and granted a new trial.* **2.** to relieve temporarily from any harm or affliction: *The medicine reprieved her from the pain.* —*n.* **3.** a temporary delay in carrying out a punishment. **4.** a temporary release from any harm or affliction.

rep·ri·mand (rep′rə mand′), *n.* **1.** a severe reproof or rebuke, esp. by a person in authority: *a reprimand from a judge.* —*v.* **2.** to reprove or rebuke severely, esp. in a formal way.

re·print (rē print′), *v.* **1.** to print again: *to reprint a book.* —*n.* (rē′print′). **2.** a new printing of any printed work, esp. one that is made without any changes: *a cheap reprint of an expensive book.*

re·pris·al (ri prī′zəl), *n.* a loss, injury, etc., inflicted upon an enemy in revenge for harm done, esp. by one nation upon another in war.

re·proach (ri prōch′), *v.* **1.** to find fault with; blame. —*n.* **2.** blame; rebuke; censure: *to deserve reproach for a mistake.* **3.** words expressing blame. **4.** a cause of blame: *He is a reproach to his parents.*

re·proach·ful (ri prōch′fəl), *adj.* showing or expressing reproach. —**re·proach′ful·ly,** *adv.*

rep·ro·bate (rep′rə bāt′), *n.* **1.** a wicked, corrupt person; scoundrel. —*adj.* **2.** wicked; corrupt: *to lead a reprobate life.*

rep·ro·ba·tion (rep′rə bā′shən), *n.* strong disapproval; condemnation; censure.

re·pro·duce (rē′prə dōōs′, -dyōōs′), *v.,* **re·pro·duced, re·pro·duc·ing. 1.** to make a copy, representation, duplicate, or close imitation of. **2.** to produce offspring or young.

re·pro·duc·tion (rē′prə duk′shən), *n.* **1.** the act or process of reproducing. **2.** something made by reproducing: *a faithful reproduction of a painting.* **3.** the natural processes by which plants and animals produce offspring or young.

re·pro·duc·tive (rē′prə duk′tiv), *adj.* of or concerned with reproduction: *reproductive organs.* —**re′pro·duc′tive·ly,** *adv.*

re·proof (ri prōōf′), *n.* **1.** the act of reproving. **2.** a rebuke or scolding: *a reproof for careless work.*

re·prov·al (ri prōō′vəl), *n.* the act of reproving, or something said in reproof; scolding; rebuke.

re·prove (ri prōōv′), *v.,* **re·proved, re·prov·ing. 1.** to speak words of disapproval to; scold; rebuke. **2.** to express disapproval of: *The mistake deserves to be reproved.* —**re·prov′ing·ly,** *adv.*

rep·tile (rep′til, rep′tīl), *n.* a member of a group of cold-blooded animals that includes snakes, lizards, alligators, turtles, etc., whose bodies are covered with scales or bony plates. Reptiles move by crawling on their bellies or by walking on short legs.

rep·til·i·an (rep til′ē ən), *adj.* **1.** of, concerning, or resembling a reptile. —*n.* **2.** a reptile.

re·pub·lic (ri pub′lik), *n.* a country in which the power belongs to the people, who vote for officials to represent them in the government.

re·pub·li·can (ri pub′li kən), *adj.* **1.** of or concerning a republic: *a republican form of government.* **2.** in favor of a republic: *to have republican feelings.* —*n.* **3.** a person who is in favor of a republican form of government.

Re·pub·li·can (ri pub′li kən), *adj.* **1.** of or referring to the Republican party: *the Republican candidates for office.* —*n.* **2.** a person who is a member of the Republican party.

Repub′lican par′ty, one of the two major political parties in the U.S. See also **Democratic party.**

re·pu·di·ate (ri pyōō′dē āt′), *v.,* **re·pu·di·at·ed, re·pu·di·at·ing. 1.** to refuse to accept as right, true, etc.: *to repudiate a treaty.* **2.** to cast off or disown: *to repudiate one's child.* —**re·pu′di·a′tion,** *n.*

re·pug·nance (ri pug′nəns), *n.* **1.** the state of being repugnant: *the repugnance of a difficult task.* **2.** strong dislike or disgust: *to be filled with repugnance.*

re·pug·nant (ri pug′nənt), *adj.* **1.** causing dislike or disgust: *a repugnant task; a repugnant odor.* **2.** contrary; opposed: *to act in a way that is repugnant to one's beliefs.* —**re·pug′nant·ly,** *adv.*

re·pulse (ri puls′), *v.,* **re·pulsed, re·puls·ing. 1.** to drive back or repel: *to repel an invader.* **2.** to drive away with rudeness or coldness: *She repulsed anyone who tried to be friendly.* —*n.* **3.** the act of repelling, or the state of being repelled: *The enemy met with a* *repulse.* **4.** a refusal or rejection: *the repulse of a request.*

re·pul·sion (ri pul/shən), *n.* **1.** the act of repulsing, or the state of being repulsed. **2.** a feeling of being repelled; distaste or disgust: *The sight of the snake caused repulsion.*

re·pul·sive (ri pul/siv), *adj.* causing strong dislike or disgust: *a repulsive odor; a repulsive task.* —**re·pul/sive·ly,** *adv.* —**re·pul/sive·ness,** *n.*

rep·u·ta·ble (rep/yə tə bəl), *adj.* **1.** honorable or respectable: *a reputable old business concern.* **2.** acceptable or standard: *the reputable spelling of a word.* —**rep/u·ta·bil/i·ty,** *n.* —**rep/u·ta·bly,** *adv.*

rep·u·ta·tion (rep/yə tā/shən), *n.* **1.** the esteem or respect in which a person or thing is held: *This restaurant has a poor reputation.* **2.** a favorable name or standing; renown; fame: *His reputation as a painter has grown.* **3.** the way in which a person or thing is known or thought of: *This city has a reputation for vice as well as beauty.*

re·pute (ri pyōōt/), *n.* **1.** regard; standing; reputation. —*v.,* **re·put·ed, re·put·ing. 2.** to consider or regard: *He was reputed to be a millionaire.*

re·put·ed (ri pyōō/tid), *adj.* considered or thought to be a particular thing: *He is the reputed author of the book.* —**re·put/ed·ly,** *adv.*

re·quest (ri kwest/), *n.* **1.** an act or an instance of asking for something to be done: *Her request was promptly heeded.* **2.** something asked for: *The symphony program was made up of requests.* **3.** the state of being asked for or demanded: *a book very much in request.* —*v.* **4.** to ask (someone) for something: *He requested me to leave.* **5.** to ask for: *He requested the book.* **6. on** (or **by**) **request,** in answer to a request: *Additional copies may be had on request.*

re·qui·em (rek/wē əm, rē/kwē əm), *n.* any musical service, hymn, or dirge for the repose of the dead.

Req·ui·em (rek/wē əm, rē/kwē əm), *n.* **1.** the Mass celebrated in the Roman Catholic Church for the repose of the souls of the dead. **2.** the musical setting for this Mass. Also, **Req/uiem Mass/.**

re·quire (ri kwī⁹r/), *v.,* **re·quired, re·quir·ing. 1.** to have need of; need: *I require peace and quiet in order to work.* **2.** to order (someone) to do something: *He required us to stay.* **3.** to demand or exact: *This task will require our best efforts.*

re·quire·ment (ri kwī⁹r/mənt), *n.* **1.** something essential or required: *Intelligence is a requirement for a scientist.* **2.** an act or instance of requiring: *Her one requirement was that they should tell her the truth.* **3.** a need or necessity: *the requirements of daily life.*

req·ui·site (rek/wi zit), *adj.* **1.** required or necessary; indispensable: *Good health is requisite for athletes.* —*n.* **2.** something requisite; a necessary thing.

req·ui·si·tion (rek/wi zish/ən), *n.* **1.** the act of requiring or demanding. **2.** an official or formal demand, esp. one that is in writing: *He filled out a requisition for new supplies.* **3.** the state of being needed or used: *More supplies are in requisition than ever before.* —*v.* **4.** to require or take for use: *to requisition troops.*

re·quit·al (ri kwīt/⁹l), *n.* **1.** the act of requiting. **2.** something done or given as repayment, reward, punishment, etc.: *The money was an ample requital for his services.*

re·quite (ri kwīt/), *v.,* **re·quit·ed, re·quit·ing. 1.** to make repayment or return for: *to requite a kindness with kindness.* **2.** to repay or make return to: *I will requite you for your generosity.*

re·route (rē rōōt/, rē rout/), *v.,* **re·rout·ed, re·rout·ing.** to change the route of: *When the road was closed they rerouted the traffic.*

re·sale (rē/sāl/), *n.* the act of selling something again or secondhand: *the resale of a used car.*

re·scind (ri sind/), *v.* to revoke or repeal; annul: *to rescind an unjust law.*

res·cue (res/kyōō), *v.,* **res·cued, res·cu·ing. 1.** to free or save from danger, captivity, etc.: *to rescue a drowning person.* —*n.* **2.** the act of rescuing: *The firemen performed a heroic rescue.* —**res/cu·er,** *n.*

re·search (ri sûrch/, rē/sûrch), *n.* **1.** careful study of a subject in order to discover or check facts: *to do research in history.* **2.** information or knowledge discovered by such study: *Your paper is an interesting piece of research.* —*v.* **3.** to make researches: *He researches in the library.* **4.** to do research upon: *He thoroughly researched the facts.* —**re·search/er,** *n.*

re·sem·blance (ri zem/bləns), *n.* likeness or similarity: *There is a close resemblance between brother and sister.*

re·sem·ble (ri zem/bəl), *v.,* **re·sem·bled, re·sem·bling.** to be like or similar: *His face resembles his father's.*

re·sent (ri zent/), *v.* to feel or show bitter anger at (a person, act, remark, etc.): *to resent an insult.* —**re·sent/ing·ly,** *adv.*

re·sent·ful (ri zent/fəl), *adj.* full of or marked by resentment: *a resentful enemy; a resentful mood.* —**re·sent/ful·ly,** *adv.* —**re·sent/ful·ness,** *n.*

re·sent·ment (ri zent/mənt), *n.* the feeling of bitter anger aroused by an insult or injury to oneself.

res·er·va·tion (rez/ər vā/shən), *n.* **1.** the act of reserving. **2.** something that keeps one from giving complete approval or acceptance: *to have reservations about the truth of a story.* **3.** an area set aside by the government, as for an Indian tribe or a military installation.

re·serve (ri zûrv/), *v.,* **re·served, re·serv·ing. 1.** to keep back or save for future use: *to reserve money for unexpected expenses.* **2.** to have kept for oneself: *to reserve a seat at a theater.* **3.** to keep as one's own: *I reserve the right to disagree.* —*n.* **4.** something reserved for some future use, purpose, need, etc.: *a reserve of food; a reserve of money.* **5.** an act of reserving. **6.** quietness or coldness in one's dealings with others: *She kept her reserve among her closest friends.* **7. reserves,** part of a military force held in readiness, or the members of such a force enrolled but not on active duty. —*adj.* **8.** kept in reserve; forming a reserve: *reserve funds; reserve troops.*

re·served (ri zûrvd/), *adj.* **1.** set aside for some particular use or purpose: *reserved money.* **2.** kept for some person or persons: *a reserved table in a restau-*

rant. **3.** having or showing formality and reserve in manner: *She was very reserved among strangers.* —re·serv′ed·ly, *adv.*

res·er·voir (rez′ər vwär′), *n.* **1.** a place where water is collected and stored for use. **2.** a part of a machine or any device holding liquid: *The reservoir of a fountain pen holds ink.* **3.** any store, supply, or reserve: *a reservoir of knowledge.*

re·side (ri zīd′), *v.,* **re·sid·ed, re·sid·ing. 1.** to dwell or live in for a considerable time. **2.** to be present or lie in: *Happiness resides in having many friends.* **3.** to belong to as a right: *The choice resides in you.*

res·i·dence (rez′i dəns), *n.* **1.** a dwelling place; house; home. **2.** the act, fact, or time of residing: *a long residence in New York.*

res·i·dent (rez′i dənt), *n.* **1.** a person who resides in a certain place: *She is a resident of Italy.* —*adj.* **2.** residing; dwelling in a place: *a resident guest.*

res·i·den·tial (rez′i den′shəl), *adj.* **1.** of or referring to residence: *a residential hotel.* **2.** suitable or used for residence: *the residential sections of a city.*

re·sid·u·al (ri zij′ōō əl), *adj.* **1.** remaining or left over: *residual time for leisure after one's work is done.* —*n.* **2.** something that remains or is left over; residue: *to live on the residual of one's income after paying debts.*

res·i·due (rez′i dōō′, -dyōō′), *n.* what remains after a part has been taken away, used up, etc.; remainder: *The fire left a residue of ashes.*

re·sign (ri zīn′), *v.* **1.** to give up (an office, position, etc.). **2.** to yield; submit: *The shipwrecked crew resigned themselves to their fate.*

res·ig·na·tion (rez′ig nā′shən), *n.* **1.** the act of resigning. **2.** a formal, written statement that one is resigning: *He sent his resignation to the president of the company.* **3.** meek, uncomplaining acceptance of something: *He endured his lameness with resignation.*

re·signed (ri zīnd′), *adj.* feeling or showing resignation. —re·sign·ed·ly (ri zī′nid lē), *adv.*

re·sil·ient (ri zil′yənt), *adj.* **1.** having the power to return to the original shape or position after being bent, pressed, etc.: *Rubber is a resilient material.* **2.** recovering readily from illness, sorrow, etc.: *His resilient nature helped him to overcome many obstacles.* —re·sil′ience, *n.*

res·in (rez′in), *n.* **1.** any of several sticky brownish or yellowish substances that harden when they dry, obtained esp. from gum trees, pine trees, and the like. Resin is used in making varnishes, medicines, etc. **2.** any of a large class of similar man-made substances used in making plastics, glues, paints, etc.

res·in·ous (rez′ə nəs), *adj.* concerning, resembling, or containing resin.

re·sist (ri zist′), *v.* **1.** to fight against; withstand; oppose: *to resist an invasion.* **2.** to withstand the effect of: *a paint that resists water.* **3.** to try not to give in to: *to resist a desire to laugh; to resist temptation.*

re·sist·ance (ri zis′təns), *n.* **1.** the act or power of resisting: *the body's resistance to disease.* **2.** a force

that opposes another; opposition: *to overcome resistance.* **3.** an underground group in an occupied country, working to overthrow the enemy by the use of sabotage, guerrilla warfare, etc. **4.** the opposition to the flow of an electric current through a circuit or a piece of conducting material.

re·sist·ant (ri zis′tənt), *adj.* resisting; not yielding.

re·sis·tor (ri zis′tər), *n.* a device or part that is used in a circuit to provide opposition to the flow of an electric current.

res·o·lute (rez′ə lōōt′), *adj.* firmly resolved or determined: *a resolute warrior; resolute ambition.* —res′o·lute′ly, *adv.* —res′o·lute′ness, *n.*

res·o·lu·tion (rez′ə lōō′shən), *n.* **1.** the act of resolving: *a slow resolution of a problem.* **2.** a formal decision made after debate and voting by a club or other organization. **3.** a resolve or decision: *a resolution to do better.* **4.** firmness of purpose; determination: *He faced the task with resolution.* **5.** an explanation or solution. **6.** the act of solving a problem.

re·solve (ri zolv′), *v.,* **re·solved, re·solv·ing. 1.** to make up one's mind; decide: *I resolved to speak the truth.* **2.** to make clear; solve: *to resolve a problem after much thought.* **3.** to break or divide into separate parts: *to resolve a topic into three parts.* **4.** to settle by a formal vote or resolution: *The club resolved to support his proposal.* **5.** to turn or change: *This essay is resolving itself into a book.* —*n.* **6.** a resolution or determination: *a resolve to do better.*

re·solved (ri zolvd′), *adj.* determined; resolute.

res·o·nance (rez′ə nəns), *n.* **1.** the property of a string, pipe, bar, room, electric circuit, etc., to respond to vibrations of a particular frequency. **2.** the response itself, esp. the increase in the loudness and richness of the sound produced by a part of a musical instrument, a room, building, etc.

res·o·nant (rez′ə nənt), *adj.* **1.** having a deep, full tone: *a resonant voice.* **2.** concerning or producing resonance. —res′o·nant·ly, *adv.*

re·sort (ri zôrt′), *v.* **1.** to turn for help, protection, or solution, often as a final choice (usually fol. by *to*): *to resort to war when talks fail.* **2.** to go, esp. often or habitually: *We resort to the garden on warm days.* —*n.* **3.** a place to which people go for rest or pleasure: *a vacation resort at the shore.* **4.** use of or appeal to a person or thing for aid, service, etc.: *to have resort to war.* **5.** a person or thing that is resorted to: *Her family is her only resort.*

re·sound (ri zound′), *v.* **1.** to ring with sound or an echo: *The arena resounded with the applause.* **2.** to sound loudly. —re·sound′ing·ly, *adv.*

re·source (rē′sôrs, ri sôrs′), *n.* **1.** a source of supply, support, or aid: *Savings are a resource in time of need.* **2. resources,** the total wealth, power, etc., of a person, group, or country.

re·source·ful (ri sôrs′fəl), *adj.* able to deal skillfully with new problems, situations, etc. —re·source′ful·ly, *adv.* —re·source′ful·ness, *n.*

re·spect (ri spekt′), *n.* **1.** a detail or point: *The two* *vases are alike in all respects.* **2.** relation or reference: *a question with respect to unemployment.* **3.** admiration, honor, or esteem: *The hero won the whole country's respect.* **4.** recognition that a person or thing is worthy of honor or consideration: *respect for the law.* **5. respects,** words or expressions of esteem or friendship: *We paid our respects to the hosts.* **—v. 6.** to hold in esteem or honor: *He respects all his teachers.* **7.** to show regard or consideration for; honor: *to respect someone's privacy.* **—re·spect′er,** *n.*

re·spect·a·ble (ri spek′tə bəl), *adj.* **1.** worthy of respect or esteem: *Medicine is a respectable profession.* **2.** decent or proper: *respectable behavior.* **3.** fairly good or large: *a respectable number.* **—re·spect′a·bil′i·ty,** *n.* **—re·spect′a·bly,** *adv.*

re·spect·ful (ri spekt′fəl), *adj.* full of or showing politeness: *a respectful reply.* **—re·spect′ful·ly,** *adv.*

re·spect·ing (ri spek′tiñg), *prep.* regarding; concerning: *He spoke to us respecting the future.*

re·spec·tive (rē spek′tiv), *adj.* belonging or proper to each person or thing individually: *to put the gifts in their respective boxes.*

re·spec·tive·ly (ri spek′tiv lē), *adv.* in regard to each of a number in the order given: *Ralph and Richard are English and Canadian, respectively.*

res·pi·ra·tion (res′pə rā′shən), *n.* **1.** the act or process of breathing. **2.** the entire set of physical and chemical processes involved in the taking in of oxygen and the giving off of carbon dioxide by a plant or animal.

res·pi·ra·tor (res′pə rā′tər), *n.* **1.** a device, often a gauze filter, worn over the nose and mouth to prevent breathing of dust or other harmful substances. **2.** an apparatus that assists breathing or artificial respiration.

res·pi·ra·to·ry (res′pər ə tôr′ē), *adj.* referring to or used in breathing or respiration.

re·spire (ri spī′r′), *v.,* **re·spired, re·spir·ing.** to breathe.

res·pite (res′pit), *n.* **1.** a short period of time for rest, relief, etc.: *The medicine gave him a respite from pain.* **2.** a delay in the execution of a person condemned to death; reprieve. **—v., res·pit·ed, respit·ing. 3.** to grant a respite to.

re·splend·ent (ri splen′dənt), *adj.* shining brilliantly; gleaming: *a resplendent day in spring.* **—re·splend′ence,** *n.* **—re·splend′ent·ly,** *adv.*

re·spond (ri spond′), *v.* **1.** to reply; answer: *to respond to a letter.* **2.** to react: *He responded favorably to the treatment.*

re·sponse (ri spons′), *n.* **1.** an answer or reply. **2.** something done in answer; reaction: *an enthusiastic response from the audience.* **3.** words sung or spoken by the choir or congregation of a church in reply to the priest or minister.

re·spon·si·bil·i·ty (ri spon′sə bil′i tē), *n., pl.* for defs. 2, 3 **re·spon·si·bil·i·ties. 1.** the state or fact of being responsible: *He assumed responsibility for arranging the meeting.* **2.** something for which a person is responsible: *Cleaning house is her responsibility.* **3.** reliability or dependability.

re·spon·si·ble (ri spon′sə bəl), *adj.* **1.** called upon to do, take care of, or carry out something: *You are responsible for the behavior of your dog.* **2.** demanding responsibility: *a responsible job.* **3.** being the cause or reason: *The cold weather is responsible for the poor crop.* **4.** taking charge of something, carrying out a task, fulfilling a duty, etc.: *The captain of the ship is a responsible man.* **—re·spon′si·bly,** *adv.*

re·spon·sive (ri spon′siv), *adj.* **1.** making answer or reply: *a responsive nod of the head.* **2.** quick to answer or respond: *She has a warm, responsive nature.* **—re·spon′sive·ly,** *adv.* **—re·spon′sive·ness,** *n.*

rest¹ (rest), *n.* **1.** ease and relaxation after a period of activity: *Sleep brings rest to the body and mind.* **2.** relief or freedom from work, troubles, etc.: *His problems gave him no rest.* **3.** one's final peace; death: *eternal rest.* **4.** a stopping or absence of motion: *The ball came to rest in a corner.* **5.** (in music) an interval of silence between notes. **6.** the mark or sign indicating this. **7.** lodging or shelter: *a travelers' rest.* **8.** a piece or thing for something to rest on: *an armrest on a chair.* **—v. 9.** to take one's ease; relax. **10.** to give rest to: *to rest one's eyes.* **11.** to be at ease; have peace: *I will not rest until I learn that you have arrived safely.* **12.** to lie in death. **13.** to stop or lie still: *The ball rests in the corner.* **14.** to remain without further action, discussion, etc.: *Inasmuch as we can't agree, shall we let the matter rest?* **15.** to lay or place: *He rested his arm on the table.* **16.** to be based or founded: *Your argument rests on very doubtful facts.* **17.** to be or be found: *The blame rests with him.* **18.** to be fixed on something, as the eyes, gaze, etc. **19.** to finish presenting evidence on (a case) in a court of law: *The attorney for the defense rested his case.* **20. at rest, a.** sleeping; resting. **b.** not in motion; inactive. **c.** free from worry; peaceful: *to put one's mind at rest.* **21. lay to rest,** to give burial to; bury: *They laid him to rest last Thursday.* [from the Old English word *rest* "a rest, resting" or *restan* "to rest"]

rest² (rest), *n.* **1.** a remaining part; remainder: *The cat ate the rest of the fish.* **2.** the others: *All the rest are going.* **—v. 3.** to go on being; remain: *Rest assured, I will keep my promise.* [from the Middle French word *rester* "to remain," which comes from Latin *restāre* "to remain standing"]

re·state (rē stāt′), *v.,* **re·stat·ed, re·stat·ing.** to state again or in a new way: *He restated the problem, using simpler words.* **—re·state′ment,** *n.*

res·tau·rant (res′tər ənt, res′tə ränt′), *n.* a place where meals are served to customers.

rest·ful (rest′fəl), *adj.* **1.** full of or giving rest: *a restful week in the country.* **2.** at rest; quiet; peaceful: *a restful sea.* **—rest′ful·ly,** *adv.* **—rest′ful·ness,** *n.*

res·ti·tu·tion (res′ti tōō′shən, -tyōō′-), *n.* **1.** the act of making up for a loss, damage, etc.: *The injured man demanded restitution for his hospital expenses.* **2.** the act of giving back property, goods, etc., to the rightful owner; restoration.

res·tive (res′tiv), *adj.* **1.** restless or uneasy: *Having nothing to do makes him restive.* **2.** stubborn; balky;

hard to manage: *a restive horse.* —**res'tive·ly**, *adv.* —**res'tive·ness**, *n.*

rest·less (rest'lis), *adj.* 1. showing or marked by inability to remain at rest: *He grew restless from waiting.* 2. uneasy or nervous: *a worried, restless mind.* 3. never at rest; always in motion: *the restless sea.* —**rest'less·ly**, *adv.* —**rest'less·ness**, *n.*

res·to·ra·tion (res'tə rā'shən), *n.* 1. the act of restoring, or the state of being restored: *the restoration of one's health; the restoration of lost property.* 2. something that is restored: *The house is an interesting restoration dating from colonial times.* 3. **the Restoration,** the period in English history covering the reign of Charles II (1660–1685) and following the end of Puritan rule.

re·stor·a·tive (ri stôr'ə tiv), *adj.* 1. serving to restore: *a restorative operation.* 2. concerned with restoration: *The old building needs restorative work.* —*n.* 3. something that restores, esp. a medicine or drug that brings back health or vigor.

re·store (ri stôr'), *v.,* **re·stored, re·stor·ing.** 1. to bring back into being, use, or the like: *to restore order.* 2. to bring back to a former or normal state: *to restore a building.* 3. to bring back to health or strength: *The long rest restored him.* 4. to put back into a former state or rank: *to restore a book to a shelf.* 5. to return (anything taken away or lost): *The lost child was restored to his mother.* —**re·stor'er**, *n.*

re·strain (ri strān'), *v.* 1. to hold back; keep under control: *to restrain one's anger.* 2. to hamper or limit the freedom or movement of: *The dictator restrained the people. The crowd was restrained by the rope.*

re·straint (ri strānt'), *n.* 1. a restraining action or influence: *They were free to live without restraint.* 2. the act of restraining, or the state of being restrained: *to keep one's feelings in restraint.* 3. something that restrains: *The leash of a dog is used as a restraint.* 4. self-control; reserve of the feelings: *to act with restraint in a disagreeable situation.*

re·strict (ri strikt'), *v.* to confine or keep within limits: *He restricted his comments to a few words.* —**re·strict'ed**, *adj.*

re·stric·tion (ri strik'shən), *n.* 1. the act of restricting, or the state of being restricted: *to enjoy oneself without restriction.* 2. something that restricts, such as a law, rule, or the like.

re·stric·tive (ri strik'tiv), *adj.* tending or serving to restrict: *to impose restrictive measures.*

rest' room', a room in a public building having washing and toilet facilities; lavatory.

re·sult (ri zult'), *v.* 1. to come about as an effect of an action, condition, etc.; to be the outcome: *His illness resulted from an improper diet.* 2. to end in some particular way: *Your efforts are bound to result in success.* —*n.* 3. something that results; an outcome or consequence: *The result of the drought was famine.* 4. the answer to a mathematical problem.

re·sult·ant (ri zul'tənt), *adj.* 1. being a result; following as a result or consequence: *war and its resultant*

hardships. —*n.* 2. something that results; outcome.

re·sume (ri zoom'), *v.,* **re·sumed, re·sum·ing.** 1. to begin again after an interruption: *The applause stopped and the speaker resumed.* 2. to take or occupy again: *They resumed their seats after the intermission.* —**re·sum'a·ble**, *adj.*

ré·su·mé (rez'oo mā'), *n.* 1. a summing up; summary: *a résumé of the main topics of a book.* 2. a brief account of one's education, employment, etc., submitted in application for a job.

re·sump·tion (ri zump'shən), *n.* the act or fact of resuming: *the resumption of school in the fall.*

re·sur·gence (ri sûr'jəns), *n.* a rising or appearing again; revival: *a resurgence of interest in religion.* —**re·sur'gent**, *adj.*

res·ur·rect (rez'ə rekt'), *v.* 1. to raise from the dead; bring to life again. 2. to bring back into use, practice, etc.: *to resurrect the fashions of the 1920's.*

res·ur·rec·tion (rez'ə rek'shən), *n.* 1. the act of rising again from the dead. 2. a bringing back into use, practice, etc.; revival: *the resurrection of a forgotten custom.* 3. **the Resurrection, a.** the rising again of Christ after His death and burial. **b.** the rising again of men on Judgment Day.

re·sus·ci·tate (ri sus'i tāt'), *v.,* **re·sus·ci·tat·ed, re·sus·ci·tat·ing.** to revive from unconsciousness or a state near death: *The man was pulled from the surf and resuscitated by the lifeguard.* —**re·sus'ci·ta'tion**, *n.*

ret., 1. retired. 2. returned.

re·tail (rē'tāl), *n.* the sale of goods directly to consumers (distinguished from *wholesale*). [from the Old French word *retailler* "to cut"] —**re'tail·er**, *n.*

re·tain (ri tān'), *v.* 1. to continue to have; keep. 2. to hold in place: *Props retain the crumbling walls.* 3. to engage the services of: *to retain a lawyer.*

re·tain·er (ri tā'nər), *n.* 1. a fee paid to engage the services of someone, esp. a lawyer. 2. a servant or employee. 3. (in dentistry) a device used in straightening the teeth, attaching a bridge, etc.

retain'ing wall', a wall for holding in place a mass of earth or the like, as at the edge of a terrace or excavation.

re·take (rē tāk'), *v.,* **re·took** (rē took'), **re·tak·en** (rē tā'kən), **re·tak·ing.** 1. to take again; take back: *The army retook the town it had lost to the enemy.* 2. to photograph or film again: *to retake a scene in a motion picture.* —*n.* (rē'tāk'). 3. a picture or scene that is photographed or filmed again.

Retaining wall

re·tal·i·ate (ri tal'ē āt'), *v.,* **re·tal·i·at·ed, re·tal·i·at·ing.** to return like for like, esp. injury for injury: *to retaliate with blows when insulted.* —**re·tal'i·a'tion**, *n.*

re·tal·i·a·to·ry (ri tal'ē ə tôr'ē), *adj.* done to pay back a wrong or injury: *a retaliatory action.*

re·tard (ri tärd'), *v.* to make slow; delay the progress of: *The bad weather retarded work on the new house.*

re·tar·da·tion (rē'tär dā'shən), *n.* 1. the act of retarding, or the state of being retarded. 2. something that retards; hindrance. **3.** slowness or limitation in intellectual or emotional development.

re·tard·ed (ri tär′did), *adj.* slow in intellectual development: *a retarded child.*

retch (rech), *v.* to make efforts to vomit.

re·ten·tion (ri ten′shən), *n.* **1.** the act of retaining, or the state of being retained. **2.** the power or capacity to retain. **3.** the ability to remember; memory.

re·ten·tive (ri ten′tiv), *adj.* **1.** having power or capacity to retain. **2.** having ability to remember; having a good memory. —**re·ten′tive·ly,** *adv.*

ret·i·cent (ret′i sənt), *adj.* inclined to say very little; quiet; reserved. —**ret′i·cence,** *n.* —**ret′i·cent·ly,** *adv.*

ret·i·na (ret′ʰnə), *n.* the lining of the back of the eyeball, which contains the cells that are sensitive to light and receives the images focused upon it by the lens. See illus. at **eye.**

ret·i·nue (ret′ʰnoo′, -nyoo′), *n.* a group of followers serving a king or other important person.

re·tire (ri tī′r), *v.,* **re·tired, re·tir·ing. 1.** to withdraw or go away to a place of shelter or seclusion. **2.** to go to bed. **3.** to withdraw from office, business, or public life: *He retired from political life after 10 years.* **4.** to fall back or retreat: *to retire from battle.* **5.** to withdraw from circulation by taking up and paying: *to retire bonds.* **6.** (in baseball) to put out (a batter or a team at bat). —**re·tire′ment,** *n.*

re·tired (ri tī′rd), *adj.* **1.** no longer occupied with one's business or profession: *a retired engineer.* **2.** withdrawn; secluded: *a retired little village.*

re·tir·ing (ri tī′r′ing), *adj.* avoiding or withdrawing from contact with others; shy; bashful.

re·took (rē took′), *v.* the past tense of **retake.**

re·tort¹ (ri tôrt′), *v.* **1.** to reply sharply. —*n.* **2.** a severe, sharp reply. [from the Latin word *retortus* "bent back," which comes from *re-* "back" + *tortus,* past participle of *torquēre* "to twist, bend"]

re·tort² (ri tôrt′), *n.* a flask used for distilling that has a long, downward-pointing nozzle in which the vapors condense. [from the early French word *retorte,* which comes from a medieval Latin word meaning "bent back." See *retort¹*]

re·touch (rē tuch′), *v.* to improve by new touches or changes: *to retouch a photograph.*

re·trace (ri trās′), *v.,* **re·traced, re·trac·ing.** to go back over: *He retraced his steps trying to find the keys.*

re·tract¹ (ri trakt′), *v.* to draw back or in: *to retract fangs.* [from the Latin word *retractus* "drawn back"] —**re·tract′a·ble,** *adj.*

re·tract² (ri trakt′), *v.* to withdraw or take back: *He retracted his original statement.* [from the Latin word *retractāre,* which comes from *re-* "back" + *tractāre* "to drag, pull"] —**re·trac′tion,** *n.*

re·treat (ri trēt′), *n.* **1.** the withdrawal of a military force before an enemy. **2.** the act of withdrawing into safety or privacy; retirement. **3.** a place of refuge, seclusion, or privacy. —*v.* **4.** to withdraw, retire, or draw back; make a retreat. **5. beat a retreat,** to make a hasty retreat; flee: *Being greatly outnumbered, the army was forced to beat a retreat.*

re·trench (ri trench′), *v.* **1.** to cut down or reduce. **2.**

to reduce expenses; economize: *They retrenched by firing several employees.* —**re·trench′ment,** *n.*

re·tri·al (rē′trīl′), *n.* a second judicial trial of a case that has been tried before.

ret·ri·bu·tion (re′trə byoo′shən), *n.* punishment given in return for some wrong that a person has committed.

re·trieve (ri trēv′), *v.,* **re·trieved, re·triev·ing. 1.** to get back again; recover: *to retrieve a lost glove.* **2.** to make amends for; make up for: *to retrieve an error.* **3.** (of hunting dogs) to fetch and bring back killed or wounded game.

Retriever
(2 ft. high at shoulder)

re·triev·er (ri trē′vər), *n.* any of several kinds of large dogs that have been trained to retrieve game.

ret·ro (re′trō), *n.* short for **retrorocket.**

retro-, a prefix meaning back or backward: *retroactive; retrorocket.*

ret·ro·ac·tive (re′trō ak′tiv), *adj.* being in force from the present back to a previous time: *The law is retroactive to June 1966.*

ret·ro·grade (re′trə grād′), *adj.* **1.** moving backward; having a backward motion or direction. **2.** moving toward a worse condition; degenerating.

ret·ro·gress (re′trə gres′, re′trə gres′), *v.* to go or move backward into an earlier and usually worse condition. —**ret′ro·gres′sion,** *n.*

ret·ro·rock·et (re′trō rok′it), *n.* a rocket that fires forward in order to slow down a space capsule, a large rocket, etc. Also, **ret′ro rock′et, retro.**

ret·ro·spect (re′trə spekt′), *n.* **1.** a survey of past time, events, etc. **2. in retrospect,** in looking back on past events: *In retrospect, I enjoyed the trip.*

re·turn (ri tûrn′), *v.* **1.** to go or come back: *to return from vacation.* **2.** to put, bring, take, give, or send back: *to return a book to a shelf.* **3.** to make a reply; answer. **4.** to give back or repay: *to return borrowed money; to return kindness.* **5.** to yield: *The company returned a large profit.* **6.** to give or announce; render: *The jury returned a verdict.* —*n.* **7.** the act or fact of returning: *his return home.* **8.** a happening again; recurrence: *the return of summer.* **9.** Usually, **returns.** a report on a count of votes, candidates elected, etc.: *election returns.* **10.** Also, **tax return.** an official statement or report of taxable income. **11.** a yield or profit: *He received a good return on his investment.* —*adj.* **12.** of or concerning return or returning: *a return trip.* **13.** sent, given, or done in return: *a return shot.* **14.** done or occurring again: *a return performance.* —**re·turn′a·ble,** *adj.*

re·un·ion (rē yoon′yən), *n.* **1.** the act of reuniting. **2.** the state of being united again. **3.** a gathering of relatives, friends, or associates after a separation.

re·u·nite (rē′yoo nīt′), *v.,* **re·u·nit·ed, re·u·nit·ing.** to unite or come together again after separation.

Rev., Reverend.

rev., 1. revenue. 2. reverse. 3. review. 4. revised. 5. revision. 6. revolution.

re·vamp (rē vamp′), *v.* to make or do over; revise: *to revamp one's plans for the future.*

re·veal (ri vēl′), *v.* 1. to make known; disclose: *to reveal a secret.* 2. to lay open to view; display; exhibit.

rev·eil·le (rev′ə lē), *n.* a signal, as of a drum or bugle, sounded early in the morning to alert military personnel for assembly. [from the French phrase *réveillez-vous!* "wake up!"]

rev·el (rev′əl), *v.,* **rev·eled** *or* **rev·elled; rev·el·ing** *or* **rev·el·ling.** 1. to take great pleasure or delight (usually fol. by *in*): *to revel in success.* 2. to make merry. —*n.* 3. noisy merrymaking. —**rev′el·er,** *n.*

rev·e·la·tion (rev′ə lā′shən), *n.* 1. the act of revealing or making known. 2. something revealed or made known, esp. something surprising and not known before.

Rev·e·la·tion (rev′ə lā′shən), *n.* the last book of the New Testament; the Apocalypse.

rev·el·ry (rev′əl rē), *n., pl.* **rev·el·ries.** noisy or boisterous festivity.

re·venge (ri venj′), *v.,* **re·venged, re·veng·ing.** 1. to inflict punishment or injury in return for a wrong done to. —*n.* 2. the act of revenging; a paying back for injury or wrong. 3. something done in vengeance. 4. the desire to revenge.

re·venge·ful (ri venj′fəl), *adj.* full of revenge.

rev·e·nue (rev′ən yōō′, rev′ə nōō′), *n.* 1. the income of a government from taxation or other sources. 2. the income from any kind of property, service, etc.

re·ver·ber·ate (ri vûr′bə rāt′), *v.,* **re·ver·ber·at·ed, re·ver·ber·at·ing.** (esp. of sound waves) to be reflected; resound. —**re·ver′ber·a′tion,** *n.*

re·vere (ri vēr′), *v.,* **re·vered, re·ver·ing.** to regard with respect; honor: *to revere a scholar.*

Re·vere (ri vēr′), *n.* **Paul,** 1735–1818, American silversmith and patriot: famous for his night horseback ride, April 18, 1775, to warn Massachusetts colonists that British troops were approaching.

rev·er·ence (rev′ər əns), *n.* 1. a feeling or attitude of deep respect. 2. a gesture showing deep respect, such as a bow or curtsy. —*v.,* **rev·er·enced, rev·er·enc·ing.** 3. to regard or treat with reverence.

rev·er·end (rev′ər ənd), *adj.* 1. *(often cap.)* a title of respect placed in front of the name of a clergyman. 2. deserving reverence and respect.

rev·er·ent (rev′ər ənt), *adj.* feeling or showing reverence; deeply respectful. —**rev′er·ent·ly,** *adv.*

rev·er·ie (rev′ə rē), *n.* a state of dreamy thought and meditation: *lost in reverie.*

re·ver·sal (ri vûr′sal), *n.* 1. the act of reversing; a change of direction, opinion, etc. 2. the state of being reversed.

re·verse (ri vûrs′), *adj.* 1. opposite or contrary in position, direction, order, or character: *the reverse side of the argument.* 2. having the back or rear part toward the observer: *the reverse side of a fabric.* 3. producing movement in a mechanism opposite to

that made under ordinary running conditions: *a reverse gear.* —*n.* 4. the opposite or contrary of something. 5. the back or rear of anything. 6. the side of a coin, medal, etc., that does not bear the main design (opposite of *obverse*). 7. a change for the worse; misfortune: *to suffer a reverse in business.* —*v.,* **reversed, re·vers·ing.** 8. to turn in an opposite position. 9. to turn inside out or upside down. 10. to turn in the opposite direction. 11. to change entirely or revoke: *to reverse a verdict.*

re·vers·i·ble (ri vûr′sə bəl), *adj.* 1. able to be worn with either side out: *a reversible coat.* 2. capable of being reversed or of reversing: *a reversible process.*

re·ver·sion (ri vûr′zhən, ri vûr′shən), *n.* 1. an act or instance of reverting; return to a former practice, belief, condition, etc. 2. (in law) the return of an estate to its owner or his heirs.

re·vert (ri vûrt′), *v.* 1. to return or go back to a former habit, practice, belief, condition, etc. 2. to go back to or return to the former owner or his heirs.

re·view (ri vyōō′), *n.* 1. a critical article or report on a recent book, play, recital, or the like. 2. a magazine containing articles on current events, books, art, etc.: *a literary review.* 3. a second or repeated view of something: *a review of the history course.* 4. an inspection of a military force. —*v.* 5. to look at or look over again: *to review notes for a test.* 6. to inspect formally: *to review troops.* 7. to look back upon: *to review the events of the month.* 8. to discuss (a book, play, etc.) in a critical review.

re·view·er (ri vyōō′ər), *n.* a person who writes reviews of new books, plays, etc.

re·vile (ri vīl′), *v.,* **re·viled, re·vil·ing.** to speak of with abuse and contempt; call bad names.

re·vise (ri vīz′), *v.,* **re·vised, re·vis·ing.** 1. to change or alter: *to revise plans because of bad weather.* 2. to change after one or more typings or printings: *to revise a textbook.*

re·vi·sion (ri vizh′ən), *n.* 1. the act, work, or process of revising. 2. a revised form or version, as of a book.

re·viv·al (ri vī′vəl), *n.* 1. the act of reviving, or the state of being revived. 2. restoration or coming back to life, consciousness, strength, etc. 3. restoration or renewal of use or acceptance: *the revival of an old custom.* 4. a new production of an old play. 5. a showing of an old motion picture. 6. a meeting or service for arousing religious interest, usually by enthusiastic singing and preaching.

re·vive (ri vīv′), *v.,* **re·vived, re·viv·ing.** 1. to bring back or return to life or consciousness: *The lifeguard revived the child he had rescued from the lake.* 2. to bring back or give strength or vigor to: *The good news revived his hopes.* 3. to bring back into use or notice: *to revive an old custom.*

rev·o·ca·tion (rev′ə kā′shən), *n.* 1. the act of revoking; annulment; repeal. 2. the state of being revoked.

re·voke (ri vōk′), *v.,* **re·voked, re·vok·ing.** to take back or withdraw; annul; cancel; repeal: *to revoke a driver's license; to revoke a decision.*

re·volt (ri vōlt′), *v.* **1.** to break away from or rise against authority; rebel. **2.** to fill with disgust: *The sight of blood revolts him.* **3.** to turn away in disgust: *to revolt from eating when one is seasick.* —*n.* **4.** an act of revolting; insurrection or rebellion.

rev·o·lu·tion (rev′ə lōō′shən), *n.* **1.** a forcible overthrow of an established government or political system by the people governed. **2.** a complete change in something, often one made quickly: *a revolution in architecture.* **3.** movement in a circular path or orbit: *the revolution of the planets around the sun.* **4.** rotation on an axis: *the revolution of a wheel.* **5.** a single circular movement or rotation.

rev·o·lu·tion·ar·y (rev′ə lōō′shə ner′ē), *adj.* **1.** concerning or like a revolution. **2.** producing or causing complete change: *a revolutionary discovery.* —*n., pl.* **rev·o·lu·tion·ar·ies. 3.** another word for **revolutionist.**

Revolu′tionary War′, another name for the **American Revolution.**

rev·o·lu·tion·ist (rev′ə lōō′shə nist), *n.* a person who favors or takes part in a revolution; revolutionary.

rev·o·lu·tion·ize (rev′ə lōō′shə nīz′), *v.,* **rev·o·lu·tion·ized, rev·o·lu·tion·iz·ing.** to bring about a great change in: *The airplane has revolutionized travel.*

re·volve (ri volv′), *v.,* **re·volved, re·volv·ing. 1.** to move in a curved path; orbit: *The earth revolves around the sun while rotating on its axis.* **2.** to turn around or rotate.

re·volv·er (ri vol′vər), *n.* a pistol having a cylinder that holds a number of bullets and revolves so as to bring a fresh bullet into firing position after each shot.

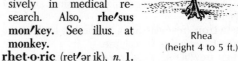
Revolver

re·vue (ri vyōō′), *n.* a group of skits, dances, and songs that poke fun at recent events, famous persons, popular fads, etc.

re·vul·sion (ri vul′shən), *n.* **1.** a strong feeling of disgust, distaste, or dislike. **2.** a sudden and violent change of feeling in sentiment, taste, etc.

re·ward (ri wôrd′), *n.* **1.** something given or received in return for service, merit, etc. **2.** a sum of money offered for the detection or capture of a criminal, the recovery of lost property, etc. —*v.* **3.** to give a reward to or for: *The man rewarded him with 50 dollars. The club agreed to reward his service.*

re·word (rē wûrd′), *v.* to put into other words: *to reword a question.*

re·write (rē rīt′), *v.,* **re·wrote** (rē rōt′), **re·writ·ten** (rē rit′ᵊn), **re·writ·ing.** to write in a different form or manner; revise.

Rey·kja·vik (rā′kyə vēk′), *n.* a seaport and the capital city of Iceland, in the SW part.

Reyn·ard (ren′ərd, rā′närd), *n.* a name given to the fox in many old stories and poems.

RFD, rural free delivery. Also, **R.F.D.**

Rh, *Chem.* the symbol for **rhodium.**

rhap·so·dy (rap′sə dē), *n., pl.* **rhap·so·dies. 1.** an exaggerated expression of feeling or enthusiasm. **2.** a piece of instrumental music of irregular form that sometimes sounds like an improvisation.

rhe·a (rē′ə), *n.* either of two flightless South American birds resembling the African ostrich but smaller.

rhe·ni·um (rē′nē əm), *n. Chem.* a rare, heavy, metallic element. *Symbol:* Re

rhe·o·stat (rē′ə stat′), *n.* an adjustable resistor used to control the current in a circuit, for dimming lights, etc.

rhe·sus (rē′səs), *n.* a small monkey found in India and used extensively in medical research. Also, **rhe′sus mon′key.** See illus. at **monkey.**

Rhea
(height 4 to 5 ft.)

rhet·o·ric (ret′ər ik), *n.* **1.** the study of the effective use of language. **2.** the use of exaggeration or display in language.

rhe·tor·i·cal (ri tôr′i kəl, ri tor′i kəl), *adj.* **1.** of, concerned with, or like rhetoric. **2.** tending to use showy language. —**rhe·tor′i·cal·ly,** *adv.*

rhetor′ical ques′tion, a question asked for effect only and not requiring an answer, as "What could be lovelier than a clear, spring day?"

rheu·mat·ic (rōō mat′ik), *adj.* **1.** concerning, similar to, or caused by rheumatism. **2.** having rheumatism. —*n.* **3.** a person who has or suffers from rheumatism.

rheumat′ic fe′ver, a serious disease, usually affecting children, that causes fever, painful swelling of the joints, and, sometimes, damage to the heart.

rheu·ma·tism (rōō′mə tiz′əm), *n.* a condition that causes pain and stiffness of the joints or back.

Rhine (rīn), *n.* a river flowing from SE Switzerland through West Germany and the Netherlands into the North Sea. 820 mi. long.

rhine·stone (rīn′stōn′), *n.* an imitation gem made of glass, often cut and polished to look like a diamond.

rhi·no (rī′nō), *n., pl.* **rhi·nos** *or* **rhi·no.** short for **rhinoceros.**

rhi·noc·er·os (rī nos′ər əs), *n., pl.* **rhi·noc·er·os·es** *or* **rhi·noc·er·os.** any of several large, thick-skinned animals of Africa and India, having one or two upright horns on the snout. [from the Greek word *rhinokerōs,* which comes from *rhis* "nose" *keras* "horn"]

Rhinoceros (Indian)
(5½ ft. high at shoulder; total length 13 ft.)

Rhode′ Is′land (rōd), a state in the NE United States, on the Atlantic coast: the smallest state in the U.S. 1214 sq. mi. *Cap.:* Providence. —**Rhode′ Is′lander.**

Rhodes (rōdz), *n.* **1.** Cecil John, 1853–1902, British colonial administrator and financier in S Africa. **2.** a Greek island in the SE Aegean, off the SW coast of Turkey. 542 sq. mi.

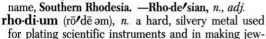

Rho·de·sia (rō dē′zhə), *n.* a former British colony in S Africa: declared its independence in 1965. 150,338 sq. mi. Former name, **Southern Rhodesia.** —**Rho·de′sian,** *n., adj.*

rho·di·um (rō′dē əm), *n.* a hard, silvery metal used for plating scientific instruments and in making jewelry: a chemical element. *Symbol:* Rh

rho·do·den·dron (rō′də den′drən), *n.* any of several evergreen shrubs or trees that bear clusters of pink, purple, or white flowers.

rhom·bus (rom′bəs), *n., pl.* **rhom·bus·es** *or* **rhom·bi** (rom′bī). a parallelogram having four equal sides and four oblique angles.

Rhone (rōn), *n.* a river flowing from the Alps in S Switzerland through SE France into the Mediterranean Sea. 504 mi. long.

Rhombus

rhu·barb (rōo′bärb), *n.* **1.** a plant having thick, reddish stalks and large green leaves. **2.** the stalks of this plant eaten in pies or as stewed fruit. **3.** *Slang.* a quarrel or squabble.

rhyme (rīm), *n.* **1.** identity or similarity in sound of the final part of words or lines of verse. **2.** a word agreeing with another in final sound: *"Find" is a rhyme for "kind."* **3.** verse or poetry having lines ending in the same sound. —*v.,* **rhymed, rhym·ing. 4.** to make rhyme or verse. **5.** to end with the same sound: *The first and the third lines of the poem rhyme.* Also, **rime.** [from the Old French word *rimer* "to rhyme, put in a row," which comes from Germanic *rīm* "series, row"] —**rhym′er,** *n.*

rhythm (riŧħ′əm), *n.* **1.** movement in which there is patterned or regular repetition of a beat, accent, or the like: *the rhythm of a song.* **2.** the pattern of beats or accents in speech or music.

rhyth·mic (riŧħ′mik), *adj.* **1.** having a strong, regular rhythm: *a rhythmic chant.* **2.** of or concerning rhythm. —**rhyth′mi·cal,** *adj.* —**rhyth′mi·cal·ly,** *adv.*

R.I., Rhode Island.

rib[1] (rib), *n.* **1.** one of the curved bones attached to the spine that form the wall of the chest. See illus. at **skeleton. 2.** a similar bone in an animal. **3.** a cut of meat containing one of these bones. **4.** something resembling a rib in form, position, or use, such as a supporting or strengthening part of a building or ship. **5.**

a ridge in knitted fabrics. —*v.,* **ribbed, rib·bing. 6.** to furnish or strengthen with ribs: *to rib a ship.* [from Old English]

rib[2] (rib), *v.,* **ribbed, rib·bing.** to tease; make fun of: *People always rib him about his freckles.* [from a special use of *rib*[1]. The original meaning was probably "to tickle or poke in the ribs"]

rib·ald (rib′əld), *adj.* vulgar or indecent in speech, language, etc. —**rib′ald·ry,** *n.*

rib·bing[1] (rib′ing), *n.* ribs or the arrangement of ribs in cloth, a ship, etc. [from *rib*[1] + *-ing*]

rib·bing[2] (rib′ing), *n.* the act or process of teasing [from *rib*[2] + *-ing*]

rib·bon (rib′ən), *n.* **1.** a woven strip or band of material, used for trimming or tying. **2.** a band of inked material used in a typewriter, adding machine, etc. **3. ribbons,** torn or ragged strips; shreds: *His clothes were torn to ribbons.*

ri′bo·nu·cle′ic ac′id (rī′bō nōo klē′ik, -nyōo-). See **RNA.**

rice (rīs), *n.* the starchy seeds of a cereal grass that grows in warm, wet climates: an important food in many parts of the world.

rich (rich), *adj.* **1.** having wealth or great possessions: *a rich man; a rich nation.* **2.** of great value or worth; valuable: *a rich harvest.* **3.** expensive or costly: *rich jewels.* **4.** containing much butter, sugar, spices, etc.: *rich pastry.* **5.** deep, strong, or full in color or tone: *rich purple; a rich soprano voice.* **6.** abounding (usually fol. by *in* or *with*): *a countryside rich in beauty; a design rich with colors.* **7.** producing or yielding abundantly; fertile: *rich soil.* —*n.* **8. the rich,** rich persons as a group: *The poor depend for help on the rich.* —**rich′ly,** *adv.* —**rich′ness,** *n.*

Rich·ard I (rich′ərd), *("Richard the Lion-Hearted"),* 1157–1199, king of England 1189–1199: went on Third Crusade.

rich·es (rich′iz), *n.pl.* abundant and valuable possessions; wealth.

Rich·mond (rich′mənd), *n.* **1.** a seaport and the capital city of Virginia, in the E part: capital of the Confederacy 1861–1865. **2.** a borough of SW New York City, on Staten Island. 60.3 sq. mi.

rick (rik), *n.* a large stack or pile of hay, corn, or the like, esp. one covered for protection against rain.

rick·ets (rik′its), *n.* a disease of children that is caused by a lack of vitamin D or calcium and produces softening and bending of the bones, esp. in the legs.

rick·et·y (rik′i tē), *adj.* **1.** likely to fall or collapse; shaky: *a rickety chair.* **2.** feeble in the joints: *a rickety old man.* **3.** affected with or suffering from rickets.

rick·shaw (rik′shô′), *n.* short for **jinrikisha.**

ric·o·chet (rik′ə shā′), *n.* **1.** the rebound made by an object after it hits a glancing blow against a surface: *the ricochet of a bullet.* —*v.,* **ric·o·cheted, ric·o·chet·ing. 2.** to move in this way; rebound.

rid (rid), *v.,* **rid** *or* **rid·ded; rid·ding.** to clear or free of something unwanted (usually fol. by *of*): *to rid the house of mice; to rid the mind of doubt.*

rid·dance (rid**/**°ns), *n.* **1.** the act of removing or clearing away something undesirable. **2. good riddance,** (used to express relief that someone or something has been removed).

rid·den (rid**/**°n), *v.* the past participle of **ride.**

rid·dle¹ (rid**/**°l), *n.* **1.** a puzzling question having a tricky answer, as "What do you have sitting down that you don't have standing up?" "A lap." **2.** a puzzling person or thing: *Her actions were a riddle to everyone.* [from the Old English word *rǣdels* "opinion, riddle," which comes from *rǣd* "counsel, advice"]

rid·dle² (rid**/**°l), *v.,* **rid·dled, rid·dling. 1.** to pierce with many holes. **2.** to damage as if by puncturing: *a government riddled by corruption.* —*n.* **3.** a coarse sieve, such as one for sifting sand in a foundry. [from the Old English word *hriddel* "sieve"]

ride (rīd), *v.,* **rode** (rōd), **rid·den** (rid**/**°n), **rid·ing. 1.** to sit on and manage a horse or other animal in motion: *She rides well.* **2.** to sit on and manage so as to be carried along: *to ride a bicycle.* **3.** to be carried along, on, or in: *She rides the bus to work.* **4.** to move or travel: *The new car rides smoothly.* **5.** to carry or transport on or in a vehicle: *She rides me to the bus stop every day.* **6.** to move along in any way; be carried or supported: *riding on his friend's success.* **7.** to depend (usually fol. by *on*): *Our hopes are riding on his performance.* **8.** to control, dominate, or tyrannize over: *The country is ridden by a dictator.* —*n.* **9.** a journey or excursion on a horse, camel, etc., or on or in a vehicle. **10.** a vehicle or device, such as a Ferris wheel, roller coaster, merry-go-round, or the like, on which people ride for amusement. **11. ride out,** to survive or endure (trouble, a storm, etc.) without damage or misfortune: *The ship put to sea to ride out the hurricane.*

rid·er (rī**/**dər), *n.* **1.** a person who rides a horse or other animal, a bicycle, or the like. **2.** an addition or amendment to a bill or document.

ridge (rij), *n.* **1.** a long, narrow elevation of land, such as a chain of hills or mountains. **2.** any raised, narrow strip: *ridges in a plowed field; ridges on corduroy material.* **3.** the back of an animal. **4.** the line where the tops of the rafters of a roof meet. —*v.,* **ridged, ridg·ing. 5.** to form into a ridge or ridges.

ridge·pole (rij**/**pōl**/**), *n.* the horizontal timber at the top of a roof, to which the upper ends of the rafters are fastened.

rid·i·cule (rid**/**ə kyōōl**/**), *n.* **1.** speech or action that mocks someone or something. —*v.,* **rid·i·culed, rid·i·cul·ing. 2.** to make fun of; mock.

ri·dic·u·lous (ri dik**/**yə ləs), *adj.* causing or deserving ridicule; absurd; laughable: *a ridiculous error.* —**ri·dic·u·lous·ly,** *adv.* —**ri·dic·u·lous·ness,** *n.*

rife (rīf), *adj.* **1.** happening frequently or widely: *Crime is rife in the slums.* **2.** current in speech; abounding: *Rumors about her are rife.*

riff·raff (rif**/**raf**/**), *n.* crude, worthless, or low people; rabble.

ri·fle (rī**/**fəl), *n.* **1.** a gun fired from the shoulder whose barrel has spiral grooves cut in its inner surface to make the bullet spin in flight. —*v.,* **ri·fled, ri·fling. 2.** to cut such spiral grooves in (a gun barrel).

Rifle

ri·fle·man (rī**/**fəl mən), *n., pl.* **ri·fle·men. 1.** a soldier armed with a rifle. **2.** an expert in the use of a rifle.

rift (rift), *n.* **1.** an opening made by splitting; cleft; crack. **2.** a break in friendly relations. —*v.* **3.** to burst open; split.

rig (rig), *v.,* **rigged, rig·ging. 1.** to fit (a ship) with the necessary sails, ropes, etc. **2.** to furnish or provide with equipment, clothing, etc. **3.** to arrange dishonestly: *to rig prices.* —*n.* **4.** the arrangement of the masts, spars, sails, etc., on a boat or ship. **5.** *Informal.* unusual costume or dress. **6. rig up,** to equip or set up for use: *to rig up a tree house for the children.*

rig·ging (rig**/**ing), *n.* **1.** the ropes, chains, etc., used to support and work the masts, yards, sails, etc., on a ship. **2.** tackle or equipment for lifting or hauling.

right (rīt), *adj.* **1.** in agreement with what is good, proper, or just: *right conduct.* **2.** in agreement with fact, reason, or some standard or principle; correct: *the right solution.* **3.** sound, normal, or sane, such as a person or his mind. **4.** principal, front, or upper: *the right side of cloth.* **5.** most appropriate, desirable, or suitable: *the right man for the job.* **6.** genuine; authentic: *the right owner.* **7.** noting or concerning the side of a person or thing that is turned toward the east when the face is toward the north (opposite of *left*): *the right hand; the right side of the room.* **8.** *(often cap.)* noting or concerning political conservatives and their beliefs. **9.** having one direction; straight: *a right line.* —*n.* **10.** a legal or moral claim: *She had the right to question him.* **11.** something that is morally or legally proper: *He was taught to do right.* **12.** Sometimes, **rights.** the interest or ownership a person, group, or business has in property: *The author controls the screen rights for the book.* **13.** the side that is normally opposite the side where the heart is; the direction toward that side: *Turn to the right. She was seated on my right.* **14.** a group or party that has conservative political views. —*adv.* **15.** directly, completely, or promptly: *We left right after dinner.* **16.** correctly or accurately: *to guess right.* **17.** properly or correctly: *to act right.* **18.** favorably or well: *to turn out right.* **19.** toward the right hand; on or to the right: *Turn right.* **20.** exactly; precisely: *I put it right on the table.* —*v.* **21.** to put in an upright position: *to right a fallen lamp.* **22.** to bring into agreement with fact; correct: *to right an error.* **23.** to put in proper order, condition, or relationship: *to right a crooked picture.* **24. right away,** immediately; at once: *I knew right away the idea was a mistake.* Also, **right off.**

right′ an′gle, the angle formed at the corners of a square; an angle of 90°

right·eous (rī**/**chəs), *adj.* **1.** morally correct, right, or justifiable: *a righteous decision.* **2.** acting in a morally upright way: *a righteous woman.* [from the Old English word *rihtwis* "in the right way"] —**right′eous·ly,** *adv.* —**right′eous·ness,** *n.*

right·ful (rīt′fəl), *adj.* 1. having a legal or just claim; legitimate: *the rightful owner of the property.* 2. belonging or held by a legal or just claim: *That land is his rightful property.* —**right′ful·ly,** *adv.*

right-hand (rīt′hand′), *adj.* 1. on the right: *the right-hand side of the closet.* 2. of, for, or with the right hand: *the right-hand mitten.* 3. most useful or helpful: *his right-hand man.*

right-hand·ed (rīt′han′did), *adj.* 1. using the right hand or arm more easily than the left. 2. adapted to or performed by the right hand: *a right-handed desk.* 3. rotating clockwise. —*adv.* 4. with the right hand: *to serve a ball right-handed.* —**right′-hand′ed·ness,** *n.*

right-hand·er (rīt′han′dər), *n.* a person who is right-handed, esp. a baseball pitcher who throws with his right hand.

right·ly (rīt′lē), *adv.* 1. in agreement with truth or fact; correctly. 2. in agreement with morality or honesty. 3. properly or suitably.

right′ tri′angle, a triangle having one right angle and two acute angles.

rig·id (rij′id), *adj.* 1. stiff or unyielding; not flexible; hard: *a rigid strip of metal.* 2. very strict or severe: *rigid rules of behavior.* —**ri·gid′i·ty, rig′id·ness,** *n.* —**rig′id·ly,** *adv.*

rig·ma·role (rig′mə rōl′), *n.* 1. an elaborate or complicated procedure. 2. meaningless talk.

rig·or (rig′ər), *n.* 1. strictness or severity: *the rigor of the law.* 2. severity, harshness, or discomfort: *the rigors of winter.* 3. inflexible accuracy; exactness: *the rigor of mathematics.*

rig·or·ous (rig′ər əs), *adj.* 1. very strict: *a rigorous teacher.* 2. very harsh and severe: *a rigorous climate.* 3. exact or accurate; precise: *rigorous calculations.* —**rig′or·ous·ly,** *adv.*

rile (rīl), *v.,* **riled, ril·ing.** 1. to irritate or annoy; vex; roil. 2. another spelling of **roil.**

rill (ril), *n.* a small stream or brook.

rim (rim), *n.* 1. the outer edge, border, or margin of something, esp. of something round: *the rim of a cup.* 2. the outer circle of a wheel. —*v.,* **rimmed, rim·ming.** 3. to provide with a rim or border.

rime¹ (rīm), *n., v.,* **rimed, rim·ing.** another spelling of **rhyme.**

rime² (rīm), *n.* a coating of ice particles; white frost. [from the Old English word *hrim*]

rind (rīnd), *n.* a thick outer covering or skin, found on certain fruits, cheeses, etc.

ring¹ (riṅg), *n.* 1. a circular band of metal or other durable material for wearing on the finger as an ornament. 2. anything having a circular form: *a ring of water; napkin ring.* 3. an enclosed area, often circular, for a sports contest, exhibition, etc.: *a circus ring.* 4. a group of persons cooperating for illegal purposes: *a ring of smugglers.* —*v.,* **ringed, ring·ing.**

5. to surround with a ring; encircle: *The crowd ringed the performers.* 6. to put a ring through the nose of (an animal). 7. (in certain games) to toss a ring over (something). [from the Old English word *hring*]

ring² (riṅg), *v.,* **rang** (raṅg), **rung** (ruṅg), **ring·ing.** 1. to make or cause to make a clear resonant sound, as a bell does: *The telephone rang. He rang the doorbell.* 2. to announce or proclaim; summon; signal: *to ring for the maid; to ring in the New Year.* 3. to sound loudly; be loud or resonant; resound: *His brave words rang out.* 4. to be filled with sound; reverberate with sound: *The room rang with laughter.* 5. to appear to the mind; seem: *His story just doesn't ring true.* 6. to call (someone) on the telephone. 7. (of the ears) to have the sensation of a continued humming sound. —*n.* 8. a ringing sound, as of a bell or bells. 9. a sound or tone similar to the ringing of a bell: *the ring of one's voice.* 10. a telephone call: *Give me a ring tomorrow.* 11. the impression given by a statement, an action, etc.: *Your story has the ring of truth.* [from the Old English word *hringan* "to ring"]

ring·lead·er (riṅg′lē′dər), *n.* a person who leads others, esp. in opposition to authority, law, etc.

ring·let (riṅg′lit), *n.* a curled lock of hair.

ring·mas·ter (riṅg′mas′tər), *n.* a person in charge of the performances in a circus ring.

ring·side (riṅg′sīd′), *n.* 1. the area immediately surrounding a ring, esp. the first few rows of seats on all sides of a boxing or wrestling ring. 2. any place providing a close view.

ring·worm (riṅg′wûrm′), *n.* any of several contagious diseases caused by fungi and producing ring-shaped patches on the skin.

rink (riṅgk), *n.* 1. a smooth expanse of ice for ice skating. 2. a smooth floor, usually of wood, for roller skating.

rinse (rins), *v.,* **rinsed, rins·ing.** 1. to drench in clean water as a final stage in washing or as a light washing: *to rinse a cup.* 2. to remove (soap, dirt, etc.) by such a process: *Rinse the soap off the cups.* —*n.* 3. the act or an instance of rinsing. 4. the water used for rinsing: *Put bluing in the rinse.* 5. any preparation used on the hair after washing to remove any remaining soap or shampoo or to tint the hair.

Ri·o de Ja·nei·ro (rē′ō dä zhə när′ō, jə när′ō, dē), a port city in SE Brazil: formerly the capital.

Rí·o de la Pla·ta (rē′ō dä lä plä′tə). See **Plata, Río de la.**

Ri·o Grande (rē′ō grand′, gran′dē), a river flowing from SW Colorado through central New Mexico and along the boundary between Texas and Mexico into the Gulf of Mexico. 1800 mi. long.

Rí·o Mu·ni (rē′ō mōō′nē), the mainland

province of Equatorial Guinea on the W coast of Africa. 10,045 sq. mi.

ri·ot (rī′ət), *n.* **1.** a noisy, violent public disorder caused by a group or crowd of persons. **2.** a vivid display: *a riot of color.* **3.** *Informal.* something or someone very funny. —*v.* **4.** to take part in a riot or disorderly public outbreak. **5. run riot, a.** to act without control or restraint: *They let their children run riot.* **b.** to grow abundantly or to excess: *Crab grass is running riot in our lawn.* —**ri′ot·er,** *n.*

ri·ot·ous (rī′ə təs), *adj.* **1.** of or like a riot: *riotous behavior.* **2.** taking part in a riot: *a riotous mob.* **3.** loud or boisterous: *riotous shouts.* —**ri′ot·ous·ly,** *adv.*

rip¹ (rip), *v.,* **ripped, rip·ping. 1.** to cut, tear apart, or tear away in a rough manner: *to rip a piece of paper to shreds.* **2.** to become torn apart or split open: *The material ripped easily.* —*n.* **3.** a tear made by ripping. [from Middle English]

rip² (rip), *n.* a stretch of rough water at sea or in a river. [related to *rip¹* and *ripple*]

R.I.P., may he (or she) rest in peace. Also, **RIP** [from the Latin phrase *requiescat in pace*]

ripe (rīp), *adj.,* **rip·er, rip·est. 1.** ready for gathering, eating, or use: *ripe fruit.* **2.** fully developed; mature: *a ripe mind.* **3.** fully prepared or ready to do or undergo something. [from an Old English word, which is related to *ripan* "to reap"] —**ripe′ness,** *n.*

rip·en (rī′pən), *v.* to make or become ripe.

rip·ple (rip′əl), *v.,* **rip·pled, rip·pling. 1.** (of a liquid surface) to form or form into small waves: *The breeze rippled the stream.* **2.** (of a solid surface) to form or have small ruffles or folds. —*n.* **3.** a small wave. **4.** any similar movement or appearance: *ripples in a fabric.* **5.** a sound similar to water flowing in ripples: *a ripple of laughter.*

rip·saw (rip′sô′), *n.* a saw or saw blade for cutting wood parallel to the grain. See also **crosscut saw.**

rip·tide (rip′tīd′), *n.* a tide that opposes another or other tides, causing a violent disturbance in the sea.

Rip Van Win·kle (rip′ van wiñg′kəl), a character in fiction, who slept for 20 years and woke to find a world completely changed.

rise (rīz), *v.,* **rose** (rōz), **ris·en** (riz′ən), **ris·ing. 1.** to get up from a lying or sitting position. **2.** to get up from bed: *to rise at seven o'clock.* **3.** to revolt or rebel: *to rise up against a dictator.* **4.** to move or go upward; ascend: *Smoke rose from the chimney.* **5.** to take place or occur: *A quarrel rose between them.* **6.** to spring up or grow, as plants. **7.** to increase in amount, as prices. **8.** to increase in degree, intensity, or force: *His fever rose during the day.* **9.** to become louder or of higher pitch: *His voice rises when he is angry.* **10.** to become higher: *The land rises sharply.* **11.** to reach a higher rank or level of importance: *He rose to the presidency of the company in only a few years.* **12.** to become lively or cheerful: *Her spirits rose after the vacation.* **13.** to swell or puff up: *Warm dough rises.* **14.** to appear above the horizon. **15.** to prove oneself equal to a demand, emergency, or challenge (usually fol. by *to*): *to rise to the occasion.* **16.** to have a source: *The stream rises in the hills.*

—*n.* **17.** the act or an instance of rising. **18.** an increase in rank, fortune, influence, power, etc. **19.** an increase in height. **20.** an increase in amount. **21.** origin, source, or beginning. **22.** an upward slope, as of ground or a road. **23. give rise to,** to be the cause of; produce: *Higher salaries give rise to higher prices.*
—**Usage.** *Rise* means to get up, arise, appear, grow, etc., and does not take an object: *What time did you rise? The cake rose in the oven. The water has risen two feet. Raise* means to lift, build, collect, increase, etc., and is always used with an object: *Raise your hand. They raised money for the hospital. They have raised our rent again.*

ris·er (rī′zər), *n.* **1.** a person who rises, esp. from bed: *I'm an early riser.* **2.** the vertical face of a stair step.

risk (risk), *n.* **1.** exposure to the chance of injury or loss; hazard; peril. —*v.* **2.** to expose to the chance of injury or loss: *to risk one's life to save another.* **3.** to take or run the chance of: *He risked breaking his leg.* **4. run a** (or **the**) **risk,** to put oneself in danger: *She runs a risk of losing her citizenship.*

risk·y (ris′kē), *adj.,* **risk·i·er, risk·i·est.** involving risk; hazardous; dangerous. —**risk′i·ness,** *n.*

rite (rīt), *n.* a formal act or procedure customary in religious or other solemn use: *They were married according to the rites of their church.*

rit·u·al (rich′ōo əl), *n.* **1.** an established or set form for a religious or other rite. **2.** a system or collection of religious or other rites. —*adj.* **3.** of, concerning, or practiced as a rite or rites: *ritual laws; a ritual dance.* —**rit′u·al·ly,** *adv.*

ri·val (rī′vəl), *n.* **1.** a person who is competing for the same object or goal as another; competitor. —*adj.* **2.** being a rival or rivals; competing: *rival teams.* —*v.,* **ri·valed** *or* **ri·valled; ri·val·ing** *or* **ri·val·ling. 3.** to compete with; try to win from, equal, or outdo: *He rivaled her for the prize.* **4.** to be an equal of; be a match for: *They rival each other in beauty.*

ri·val·ry (rī′vəl rē), *n., pl.* **ri·val·ries.** the action, position, or relation of a rival or rivals; competition.

riv·er (riv′ər), *n.* **1.** a natural stream of water of fairly large size flowing in a definite course. **2.** any stream or outpouring: *rivers of tears; a river of lava.*

riv·er·side (riv′ər sīd′), *n.* **1.** a bank of a river. —*adj.* **2.** on or near a bank of a river.

riv·et (riv′it), *n.* **1.** a metal pin having a head at one end, used to fasten two or more pieces of metal, leather, etc., together. After the rivet is put through holes in the pieces to be fastened, the plain end is hammered to form a second head. —*v.,* **riv·et·ed** *or* **riv·et·ted; riv·et·ing** *or* **riv·et·ting. 2.** to fasten with a rivet or rivets. **3.** to fasten or fix firmly: *He riveted his attention on the speaker.* —**riv′et·er,** *n.*

Riv·i·er·a (riv′ē âr′ə), *n.* a resort area along the Mediterranean coast in S France and NW Italy.

riv·u·let (riv′yə lit), *n.* a small stream or brook.

rm., 1. ream. 2. room.

rms., 1. reams. 2. rooms.

Rn, *Chem.* the symbol for **radon.**

R.N., Registered Nurse. Also, **RN**

RNA, ribonucleic acid: any of a group of complex chemical compounds found in cells that act in conjunction with DNA in the synthesis of proteins.

roach¹ (rōch), *n.* a cockroach.

roach² (rōch), *n., pl.* **roach·es** *or* **roach.** 1. a European freshwater fish related to the carp. 2. any of various similar fishes. [from the Old French word *roche*]

road (rōd), *n.* 1. a long, narrow stretch with a smoothed or paved surface, made for traveling by motor vehicle, carriage, etc., between two or more points. 2. a way or course: *the road to peace.* 3. Also, **roadstead.** a partly sheltered area of water in which ships may anchor. 4. **hit the road,** *Slang.* to begin or resume traveling: *We have to hit the road at 6 a.m.*

road·bed (rōd′bed′), *n.* 1. the foundation for the track of a railroad. 2. the material composing a road.

road·block (rōd′blok′), *n.* an obstruction or barrier placed across a road for stopping or delaying traffic.

road·run·ner (rōd′run′ər), *n.* a cuckoo of the western U.S. that has a crested head and is noted for the speed at which it can run.

road·side (rōd′sīd′), *n.* 1. the side or border of the road. —*adj.* 2. on or near the side of a road: *a roadside restaurant.*

road·stead (rōd′sted′), *n.* See **road** (def. 3).

Roadrunner (length 2 ft.)

road·way (rōd′wā′), *n.* 1. the land over which a road is built. 2. the part of a road over which vehicles travel.

roam (rōm), *v.* to walk, go, or travel without a fixed direction or purpose; wander: *to roam about the world; to roam the countryside.* —**roam′er,** *n.*

roan (rōn), *adj.* 1. (esp. of horses) having a reddish-brown or yellowish-brown coat sprinkled with gray or white. —*n.* 2. a horse having a coat of this color.

roar (rôr), *v.* 1. to make a loud, deep cry or howl: *to roar with pain.* 2. to laugh loudly: *to roar at a joke.* 3. to make a loud sound: *The thunder roared.* —*n.* 4. a loud, deep cry or howl: *the roar of a lion.* 5. a loud, deep sound: *the roar of the surf.*

roast (rōst), *v.* 1. to bake (meat or other food) by exposure to dry heat, esp. in an oven or on a spit. 2. to make or become very hot: *We roasted in the sun.* 3. *Informal.* to make fun of or criticize harshly. —*n.* 4. roasted meat or a piece of meat for roasting. —*adj.* 5. cooked by roasting: *roast beef.* [from the Old French word *rostir,* which comes from Germanic]

roast·er (rō′stər), *n.* 1. a pan or other utensil for roasting something. 2. a chicken or other animal suitable for roasting.

rob (rob), *v.,* **robbed, rob·bing.** 1. to take from by force; steal from: *to rob a bank.* 2. to deprive (someone) of some right or something legally due: *They*

robbed the family of the inheritance. —**rob′ber,** *n.*

rob′ber fly′, any of numerous swift-flying, often large insects that prey on other insects.

rob·ber·y (rob′ə rē), *n., pl.* **rob·ber·ies.** the unlawful taking of another person's property by violence or threat of violence.

robe (rōb), *n.* 1. a long, loose or flowing gown or outer garment worn as ceremonial or official dress: *a judge's robe.* 2. any long, loose garment for wear while lounging, such as a bathrobe or dressing gown. 3. a piece of fur, cloth, etc., used as a blanket, covering, or wrap: *a lap robe.* —*v.,* **robed, rob·ing.** 4. to put a robe on; dress.

Robin (length 10 in.)

rob·in (rob′in), *n.* 1. an American thrush having a brownish-gray back and a reddish breast. 2. any of several small European birds having a reddish breast.

Rob′in Hood′, a legendary English outlaw who robbed from the rich to give to the poor.

ro·bot (rō′bət, rō′bot), *n.* 1. a machine that resembles a human and does mechanical, routine tasks on command. 2. a person who acts and responds without thought.

ro·bust (rō bust′, rō′bust), *adj.* strong and healthy; hardy; vigorous: *robust athletes.* —**ro·bust′ness,** *n.*

roc (rok), *n.* (in Arabian mythology) an imaginary bird of enormous power and strength.

Roch·es·ter (roch′es tər, roch′i stər), *n.* a city in W New York.

rock¹ (rok), *n.* 1. a piece of stone or stony material. 2. the hard, solid mineral matter that makes up the earth's crust. 3. a firm foundation or support. 4. **on the rocks, a.** *Informal.* without funds; bankrupt: *I hear his new business is on the rocks.* **b.** (of a beverage) served in a glass containing ice cubes: *a cocktail on the rocks.* [from the Middle English word *rokke,* which comes from medieval Latin *rocca*]

rock² (rok), *v.* 1. to move or sway to and fro or from side to side: *to rock a baby to sleep.* 2. to shake or disturb violently: *The earthquake rocked the house.* —*n.* 3. a rocking movement: *the gentle rock of the boat.* [from the Middle English word *rocken,* which comes from Old English *roccian*]

rock·a·way (rok′ə wā′), *n.* a light four-wheeled carriage having two or three seats and a fixed top.

rock-bound (rok′bound′), *adj.* enclosed or covered by rocks; rocky: *the rock-bound coast of Maine.*

Rock·e·fel·ler (rok′ə fel′ər), *n.* Nelson A., born 1908, 41st Vice President of the U.S. 1974–1977.

rock·er (rok′ər), *n.* 1. Also, **runner.** one of the curved pieces on which a cradle or a rocking chair rocks. 2. another name for **rocking chair.** 3. any of various devices that operate with a rocking motion.

rock·et (rok′it), *n.* 1. a device that burns solid or liquid fuel to produce a stream of gas that is expelled rearward to drive the device forward. Rockets are used in fireworks and weapons and to propel space-craft. **2.** a missile or spacecraft propelled by a rocket. —*v.*, **rock·et·ed, rock·et·ing. 3.** to move by means of a rocket. **4.** to move like a rocket.

rock·et·ry (rok′i trē), *n.* the science of designing, making, and flying rockets.

Rock·ford (rok′fərd), *n.* a city in N Illinois.

Rock·ies (rok′ēz), *n.* **the,** another name for **Rocky Mountains.**

rock′ing chair′, a chair mounted on rockers or springs so as to permit the sitter to rock back and forth. Also, **rocker.**

rock′ing horse′, a toy horse mounted on rockers or springs on which children may ride.

rock-'n'-roll (rok′ən rōl′), *n.* a style of popular music having a heavily accented rhythm and simple melodies that are repeated over and over again. Rock-'n'-roll performers and dancers often use vigorous, exaggerated movements.

rock′ salt′, common salt in large crystals.

rock·y[1] (rok′ē), *adj.*, **rock·i·er, rock·i·est. 1.** full of rocks. **2.** made of rocks. **3.** full of hazards or difficulties: *The road to success is often rocky.* —**rock′i·ness,** *n.*

rock·y[2] (rok′ē), *adj.*, **rock·i·er, rock·i·est.** tending to rock; shaky; unsteady.

Rock′y Moun′tain goat′, another name for **mountain goat.**

Rock′y Moun′tains, the chief mountain system in North America, extending from central New Mexico to N Alaska. Highest peak, Mount McKinley, 20,300 ft. Also, **the Rockies.**

ro·co·co (rə kō′kō), *n.* **1.** a style of architecture and decoration of the 18th century, marked by very elaborate designs, such as shellwork, foliage, etc. —*adj.* **2.** of, concerning, or like rococo: *a rococo frame for an expensive painting.*

Rococo mirror

rod (rod), *n.* **1.** a stick, wand, or staff of wood or other material. **2.** a stick or a bundle of sticks used for punishing someone. **3.** the punishment given. **4.** a fishing rod. **5.** a unit of length equal to 5½ yards or 16½ feet.

rode (rōd), *v.* the past tense of **ride.**

ro·dent (rōd′ᵊnt), *n.* any member of a group of related animals having sharp teeth that continue to grow as their points are worn away by gnawing. Rats, mice, squirrels, and beavers are all rodents.

ro·de·o (rō′dē ō′, rō dā′ō), *n.*, *pl.* **ro·de·os. 1.** a public exhibition of cowboy skills, such as bronco riding and calf roping. **2.** a roundup of cattle.

roe[1] (rō), *n.* the eggs of a fish, lobster, etc. [from the Middle English word *rowe*]

roe[2] (rō), *n.*, *pl.* **roes** *or* **roe.** another name for **roe deer.** [from the Middle English word *roo,* which comes from Old English *rā*]

roe·buck (rō′buk′), *n.*, *pl.* **roe·bucks** *or* **roe·buck.** a male roe deer.

roe′ deer′, a small, agile deer of Europe and Asia having three-pointed antlers. Also, **roe.**

rogue (rōg), *n.* **1.** a dishonest person; scoundrel. **2.** a playfully mischievous person. **3.** an animal, esp. an elephant, that has been driven from the herd because of its vicious disposition.

ro·guish (rō′gish), *adj.* **1.** dishonest or sneaky. **2.** playfully mischievous: *a roguish smile.* —**ro′guish·ly,** *adv.* —**ro′guish·ness,** *n.*

Roe deer
(2½ ft. high at shoulder)

roil (roil), *v.* **1.** to make (water, wine, etc.) unclear or murky by stirring up sediment; rile. **2.** another spelling of **rile.**

role (rōl), *n.* **1.** a part or character to be played by an actor. **2.** the proper or usual function of a person or thing: *in her role as a teacher.* Also, **rôle.**

roll (rōl), *v.* **1.** to move or cause to move along a surface by turning over and over: *The ball rolled down the hill.* **2.** to move or be moved on wheels: *to roll a shopping cart.* **3.** to flow with a wavy motion, such as waves of water or billows of smoke. **4.** to pass or go on, such as time. **5.** to have a deep, prolonged sound, such as thunder. **6.** to trill: *to roll one's r's.* **7.** to make by forming into a tube or ball: *to roll up string.* **8.** to move from side to side: *She rolled her eyes.* **9.** to spread out flat: *to roll dough.* **10.** to beat (a drum) with rapid, continuous strokes. —*n.* **11.** the act or process of rolling. **12.** a document of paper that is or may be rolled up. **13.** a list of names: *the roll of members.* **14.** an individual cake of bread, often rolled or doubled on itself before baking. **15.** anything rolled up in a round shape: *a roll of wire.* **16.** a rolling motion. **17.** a deep, prolonged sound, as of thunder or drums. **18. roll in,** *Informal.* **a.** to have a large amount of; abound in: *I hear he's rolling in money.* **b.** to go to bed; retire: *to roll in early.* **19. roll up, a.** to gather or collect: *The candidate rolled up a large vote.* **b.** *Informal.* to arrive in a car or other vehicle: *He rolled up in a limousine.*

roll′ call′, the calling of a list of names for checking attendance.

roll·er (rō′lər), *n.* **1.** a person or thing that rolls. **2.** a cylinder, wheel, or caster, upon which something is rolled along. **3.** an object shaped like a tube on which something is rolled up. **4.** an object shaped like a tube for spreading, crushing, or flattening something. **5.** a long, swelling wave.

roll′er coast′er, a small railroad, esp. in an amusement park, having a train with open cars that moves rapidly along a high, sharply winding track built with steep inclines.

roll′er skate′, a device with four wheels or rollers, attached to a shoe or strapped to the feet, for skating on a sidewalk or floor.

roll·er-skate (rō′lər skāt′), *v.*, **roll·er-skat·ed, roll·er-skat·ing.** to glide about on roller skates. —**roll′er-skat′er,** *n.*

rol·lick·ing (rol′i kiŋ), *adj.* moving or acting in a lively, carefree manner; joyous; jolly.

roll′ing mill′, a place where large pieces of metal are passed between rollers to convert them to sheets, bars, etc.

roll′ing pin′, a cylinder of wood or other material, with a handle at each end, for rolling out dough.

ro·ly-po·ly (rō′lē pō′lē), *adj.* **1.** short and plump. —*n., pl.* **ro·ly-po·lies. 2.** a roly-poly person or thing.

Ro·man (rō′mən), *adj.* **1.** of or concerning the ancient or modern city of Rome. **2.** of or concerning the ancient kingdom, republic, or empire of Rome. **3.** *(usually l.c.)* noting the upright style of printing types most often used. —*n.* **4.** a native, inhabitant, or citizen of ancient or modern Rome. **5.** *(usually l.c.)* roman type or lettering.

Ro′man Cath′olic, 1. of or concerning the Roman Catholic Church. **2.** a member of the Roman Catholic Church.

Ro′man Cath′olic Church′, the Christian church of which the Pope, who is bishop of Rome, is the supreme head.

Ro′man Cathol′icism, another name for **Catholicism.**

ro·mance (rō mans′, rō′mans), *n.* **1.** a story that tells of heroic deeds, adventure, and love. **2.** a medieval story or poem telling of heroic or supernatural events. **3.** a love affair. **4.** a made-up, fanciful story. **5.** an appealing or romantic quality: *the romance of travel.* —*v.* (rō mans′), **ro·manced, ro·manc·ing. 6.** to tell fanciful stories. **7.** to think or talk romantically.

Ro′mance lan′guages, a group of languages descended from Latin, including French, Spanish, Italian, Portuguese, and a few others.

Ro′man Em′pire, an ancient empire, extending at its height over most of Europe, the Middle East, and N Africa, lasting from 27 B.C. to A.D. 476.

Ro·man·esque (rō′mə nesk′), *adj.* noting a style of architecture developed in western and southern Europe from the 9th through the 12th centuries, marked by thick masonry construction and the use of round arches and narrow openings.

Ro·ma·ni·a (rō mā′nē ə, rō mān′yə), *n.* another spelling of **Rumania.** —**Ro·ma′ni·an,** *n., adj.*

Ro′man nu′merals, the letters used for numbers by the ancient Romans and still used in numbering introductory pages in books, in inscriptions on buildings, on clock faces, etc. The common symbols are **I** (= 1), **V** (= 5), **X** (= 10), **L** (= 50), **C** (= 100), **D** (= 500), and **M** (= 1000). If a letter is followed by one of the same or smaller value, the two are added: **XX** (= 20), **VI** (= 6); if a letter is followed by one of higher value, the first is subtracted from the second: **IX** (= 9), **XC** (= 90). These rules are combined in reading such numbers as **XIX** (= 19) and **XLVII** (= 47). See also **Arabic numeral.**

Ro′man Repub′lic, the forerunner of the Roman Empire, lasting from c500 B.C. to 27 B.C., when Augustus became emperor.

Ro·mans (rō′mənz), *n.* *(used as sing.)* a book of the New Testament, believed to have been written by Paul to the Christians of Rome.

ro·man·tic (rō man′tik), *adj.* **1.** of or concerning romance: *a romantic story.* **2.** having feelings and thoughts of love and adventure: *a romantic girl.* **3.** impractical; fanciful; unrealistic. **4.** appealing to feelings of romance. **5.** of or concerning Romanticism. —*n.* **6.** a romantic person. **7.** a romantic author, composer, or artist. —**ro·man′ti·cal·ly,** *adv.*

Ro·man·ti·cism (rō man′ti siz′əm), *n.* a style of literature, art, and music of the 19th century, that encouraged freedom of treatment and emphasized imagination and emotion. See also **classicism.**

Rom. Cath., Roman Catholic.

Rome (rōm), *n.* the capital city of Italy, in the central part, on the Tiber River: ancient capital of the Roman Empire; site of Vatican City; seat of the Roman Catholic Church.

Ro·me·o (rō′mē ō′), *n.* the hero of Shakespeare's play, *Romeo and Juliet.*

romp (romp), *v.* **1.** to play or frolic in a lively way. —*n.* **2.** lively or boisterous play or frolic.

romp·ers (rom′pərz), *n.* *(used as pl.)* a loose outer garment combining a shirt and loose, bloused pants, worn esp. by infants. Also, **jumpers.**

Rom·u·lus (rom′yə ləs), *n.* *(in Roman mythology)* the founder of Rome and its first king. He and his twin brother, Remus, were raised by a female wolf.

roof (rōof, roof), *n., pl.* **roofs. 1.** the outside upper covering of a house or other building. **2.** something resembling the roof of a house: *the roof of a car; the roof of the mouth.* —*v.* **3.** to cover with a roof. —**roof′er,** *n.*

Roofs

roof·ing (rōo′fing, roof′ing), *n.* **1.** material for covering roofs. **2.** the trade or activities of a roofer.

roof·tree (rōof′trē′, roof′-), *n.* the ridgepole of a roof.

rook¹ (rook), *n.* **1.** a black European crow that lives in large flocks. **2.** a cheater or swindler. —*v.* **3.** to cheat or swindle: *to be rooked of one's savings.* [from the Old English word *hrōc*]

rook² (rook), *n.* *(in chess)* one of two pieces of the same color, which can be moved any number of unoccupied spaces vertically or horizontally; castle. See illus. at **chess.** [from the Old French word *roc,* which comes from Persian *rukh*]

rook·er·y (rook′ə rē), *n., pl.* **rook·er·ies. 1.** a colony of rooks. **2.** a place where rooks breed. **3.** a place where other kinds of birds or animals breed.

rook·ie (rŏok′ē), *n.* **1.** an athlete playing his first season on a professional sports team. **2.** any new recruit, as on a police force. [another form of *recruit*]

room (rŏom, rŏom), *n.* **1.** a walled or partitioned portion of space within a building or other structure. **2.** the persons present in a room: *The room suddenly became quiet.* **3.** space occupied by or available for something: *There is room for one more chair.* **4.** chance or opportunity for something: *room for improvement.* **5. rooms,** a person's lodgings in a house or building. —*v.* **6.** to lodge in a room or rooms.

room·er (rŏo′mər, rŏom′ər), *n.* a person who lives in a rented room; lodger.

room·ful (rŏom′fŏol, rŏom′-), *n., pl.* **room·fuls.** an amount or number that can fill a room.

room′ing house′, a house with rooms to rent.

room·mate (rŏom′māt′, rŏom′-), *n.* a person who shares a room or apartment with another or others.

room·y (rŏo′mē, rŏom′ē), *adj.* **room·i·er, room·i·est.** offering a large amount of room; spacious: *a roomy house.* —**room′i·ness,** *n.*

Roo·se·velt (rō′zə velt′), *n.* **1. Eleanor,** 1884–1962, U.S. diplomat, author, and lecturer (wife of Franklin Delano Roosevelt). **2. Franklin Del·a·no** (del′ə nō′), *("FDR"),* 1882–1945, 32nd President of the U.S. 1933–1945. **3. Theodore** *(Teddy, "T.R."),* 1858–1919, 25th Vice President of the U.S. 1901; 26th President of the U.S. 1901–1909.

roost (rŏost), *n.* **1.** a perch upon which birds or fowls rest at night. **2.** a large cage, house, or place for fowls or birds to roost in. —*v.* **3.** to sit or rest on a roost, perch, etc. **4.** to settle or stay for the night.

roost·er (rŏo′stər), *n.* a male chicken; cock.

root¹ (rŏot, rŏot), *n.* **1.** the part of a plant that develops and spreads under the ground, anchoring the plant and providing it with water and nourishment from the soil. **2.** any underground part of a plant, such as a bulb. **3.** the hidden base of a hair, tooth, fingernail, etc. **4.** a quantity that, when multiplied by itself a specified number of times, yields a certain number: *The square root of 9 is 3, since 3 x 3 = 9. The cube root of 8 is 2, since 2 x 2 x 2 = 8.* **5.** the basic or most important part: *the root of the matter.* **6.** the source or origin of a thing: *the root of all evil.* **7.** (in grammar) a basic word or stem from which other words are derived. *Cover* is the root of such words as *covering, coverage, coverall, uncover,* and *discover.* —*v.* **8.** to grow roots. **9.** to become fixed or established: *She was rooted to the spot.* **10.** to pull, tear, or dig up by the roots. **11. take root,** to send out roots; begin to grow: *Transplant the bush as soon as it takes root.* [from the Old

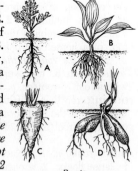

Roots
A, Tap; B, Fibrous;
C, Fleshy (carrot);
D, Tuberous

English word *rōt,* which comes from Scandinavian] —**root′like′,** *adj.*

root² (rŏot, rŏot), *v.* **1.** to turn up the soil with the snout. **2.** to search about; poke; rummage: *She rooted through the drawer to find a red scarf.* [from the Old English word *wrōtan*] —**root′er,** *n.*

root³ (rŏot, rŏot), *v.* to encourage by cheering: *to root for one's team.* [perhaps from Scandinavian]

root′ beer′, a carbonated soft drink flavored with the juices of roots, barks, and herbs.

root·let (rŏot′lit, rŏot′lit), *n.* a small root or a small branch of a root.

rope (rōp), *n.* **1.** a strong, thick line or cord, usually made up of twisted or braided strands of hemp, flax, wire, etc. **2.** a lasso. **3.** a number of things twisted or strung together in the form of a cord: *a rope of tobacco.* **4.** a stringy or sticky thread or mass. —*v.,* **roped, rop·ing. 5.** to tie or fasten with a rope. **6.** to enclose or mark off with a rope or ropes: *to rope off a street.* **7.** to catch with a lasso; lasso: *to rope a calf.* **8. know the ropes,** *Informal.* to be completely familiar with the operation or details of something: *This job needs a man who already knows the ropes.* **9. learn the ropes,** *Informal.* to master the special skills needed in a job or other situation: *He spent six months at the factory learning the ropes.* **10. rope in,** *Slang.* to lure or attract, esp. by deceiving: *The swindler is skilled in roping in victims.* —**rope′like′,** *adj.*

ro·sa·ry (rō′zə rē), *n., pl.* **ro·sa·ries.** (in the Roman Catholic Church) **1.** a series of prayers. **2.** a string of beads used for counting these prayers.

rose (rōz), *n.* **1.** any of various prickly garden plants bearing sweet-smelling flowers of various colors. **2.** a flower of such a plant. **3.** a purplish or pinkish red. —*adj.* **4.** of, for, or containing roses.

ro·se·ate (rō′zē it, rō′zē āt′), *adj.* **1.** tinted with rose; rosy: *a roseate dawn.* **2.** bright or promising: *a roseate future.*

rose·bud (rōz′bud′), *n.* the bud of a rose.

rose·bush (rōz′bŏosh′), *n.* a shrub that bears roses.

rose·mar·y (rōz′mâr′ē), *n., pl.* **rose·mar·ies.** an evergreen European shrub related to mint, whose sweet-smelling leaves are used in cooking and in making medicines and perfumes.

ro·sette (rō zet′), *n.* **1.** a rose-shaped arrangement of ribbon or other material, used as an ornament or badge. **2.** an ornament resembling a rose.

rose′ wa′ter, water mixed with oil of roses.

rose·wood (rōz′wŏod′), *n.* the heavy, hard, reddish wood of various tropical trees, used for making furniture, veneers, etc.

R, Rosettes

Rosh Ha·sha·nah (rŏsh′ hə-shä′nə), (in the Jewish religion) a high holy day, the first day of the Jewish New Year, celebrated in September or October.

ros·in (roz′in), *n.* **1.** the resin left after distilling the turpentine from pine pitch, used chiefly in making varnish, inks, etc., and for rubbing on the bows of stringed instruments. —*v.* **2.** to cover or rub with rosin.

Ross (rôs), *n.* Betsy, 1752–1836, maker of the first U.S. flag.

ros·ter (ros′tər), *n.* **1.** a list of persons or groups, as of military personnel and their assignments of duty. **2.** any list, roll, or register.

ros·trum (ros′trəm), *n.* any platform, stage, or the like, for public speaking.

ros·y (rō′zē), *adj.*, **ros·i·er, ros·i·est. 1.** pink or pinkish-red. **2.** cheerful or optimistic; hopeful. —**ros′i·ly,** *adv.* —**ros′i·ness,** *n.*

rot (rot), *v.*, **rot·ted, rot·ting. 1.** to decompose or decay; spoil: *Water rots wood. The fruit rotted on the tree.* **2.** to fall apart; deteriorate: *The old cabin rotted.* —*n.* **3.** the process of rotting. **4.** rotting or rotten matter. **5.** any of several diseases of plants and animals that cause decay of the living tissues.

ro·ta·ry (rō′tə rē), *adj.* **1.** turning or able to turn on an axis like a wheel. **2.** having one or more parts that rotate. —*n.*, *pl.* **ro·ta·ries. 3.** another name for **traffic circle.**

ro·tate (rō′tāt, rō tāt′), *v.*, **ro·tat·ed, ro·tat·ing. 1.** to turn around a central point: *The earth rotates on its axis while revolving around the sun.* **2.** to cause to happen or follow in a set order or routine: *to rotate farm crops.* **3.** to proceed in a set order or routine: *The players rotated between the outfield and infield.* —**ro′ta·tor,** *n.*

ro·ta·tion (rō tā′shən), *n.* **1.** the act or process of rotating. **2.** one complete turn around an axis. **3.** the act or process of varying the crops grown on the same ground.

R.O.T.C., Reserve Officers' Training Corps. Also, **ROTC**

rote (rōt), *n.* **1.** a fixed or mechanical way of doing something; routine. **2. by rote,** from memory, without thought for meaning: *to recite a poem by rote.*

ro·tis·ser·ie (rō tis′ə rē), *n.* a small broiler having a motor-driven spit.

ro·tor (rō′tər), *n.* **1.** a rotating part in a machine, switch, etc. **2.** a system of rotating blades or airfoils, as on a helicopter.

rot·ten (rot′ⁿn), *adj.* **1.** decomposing or decaying: *rotten apples.* **2.** corrupt or dishonest. **3.** *Informal.* very bad or unpleasant: *This has been a rotten day.* —**rot′ten·ness,** *n.*

Rot·ter·dam (rot′ər dam′), *n.* a port city in the SW Netherlands.

ro·tund (rō tund′), *adj.* **1.** round in shape; rounded: *ripe, rotund fruit.* **2.** plump; fat. **3.** full-toned; deep: *a rotund voice.* —**ro·tun′di·ty,** *n.*

ro·tun·da (rō tun′də), *n.* a round building or hall, esp. one covered by a dome: *the capitol rotunda.*

Rou·en (rōō än′), *n.* a city in N France: cathedral.

rouge (rōōzh), *n.* **1.** a red cosmetic used for coloring the cheeks or lips. **2.** a reddish powder used to polish glass, silver, etc. —*v.*, **rouged, roug·ing. 3.** to color with rouge.

rough (ruf), *adj.* **1.** having a coarse or uneven surface: *rough pavement.* **2.** violent or rugged: *Boxing is a rough sport.* **3.** stormy or violent: *rough weather.* **4.** sharp or harsh: *a rough temper.* **5.** unmannerly or rude: *a rough person.* **6.** difficult or unpleasant: *to have a rough time of it.* **7.** without ordinary comforts: *rough camping.* **8.** done quickly without attention to detail: *a rough drawing.* **9.** not exact; approximate: *a rough guess.* —*n.* **10.** something that is rough, esp. rough ground. **11.** (in golf) any part of the course bordering the fairway on which the grass, weeds, etc., are not trimmed. —*adv.* **12.** in a rough manner; roughly: *to play rough.* —*v.* **13.** to make or become rough; roughen. **14.** to treat violently (often fol. by *up*): *He roughed him up badly during the fight.* **15.** to make or do roughly: *The artist roughed in a few details.* **16. rough it,** to live without the usual comforts and conveniences: *to rough it in the woods.* —**rough′ly,** *adv.* —**rough′ness,** *n.*

rough·age (ruf′ij), *n.* **1.** rough or coarse material. **2.** food that contains a high proportion of indigestible cellulose, such as bran, green vegetables, etc. Roughage stimulates the muscular action that forces food through the system.

rough·en (ruf′ən), *v.* to make or become rough or rougher.

rough·hew (ruf′hyōō′), *v.*, **rough-hewed; rough-hewed** or **rough-hewn** (ruf′hyōōn′); **rough-hewing.** to hew or shape roughly: *to rough-hew stone.*

rough·neck (ruf′nek′), *n. Informal.* a rough, coarse person; tough.

rough·shod (ruf′shod′), *adj.* **1.** shod with horseshoes having projecting nails or points. **2. ride roughshod over,** to treat (someone) harshly or meanly, esp. for selfish reasons: *He got ahead in the world by riding roughshod over his friends.*

rou·lette (rōō let′), *n.* **1.** a game of chance in which players bet on the space into which a spinning ball will come to rest on a rotating wheel. **2.** a small wheel with sharp teeth, for making lines of dots, marks, or perforations.

Rou·ma·ni·a (rōō mā′nē ə), *n.* another spelling of **Rumania.** —**Rou·ma′ni·an,** *n.*, *adj.*

round (round), *adj.* **1.** shaped like a circle or ring: *a round hoop; a round coin.* **2.** shaped like a ball: *a round fruit.* **3.** made up of full, curved lines or shapes: *round handwriting.* **4.** involving circular motion: *a round dance.* **5.** full, complete, or entire: *a round dozen.* **6.** expressed or given to the nearest whole number, or in tens, hundreds, thousands, or the like: *Seven is a round number for six and three-fourths.* **7.** full and rich, such as sound. **8.** (of speech sounds) pronounced with the lips formed in a circle, as the *o* in *bone.* —*n.* **9.** any round shape or object. **10.** Sometimes, **rounds.** a completed course of time, series of events or operations, etc.: *The story has made the rounds of all the newspapers.* **11.** any complete course, series, or succession: *The strike was settled after a long round of talks.* **12.** Often, **rounds.** a going around from place to place, as in a usual or definite route: *The doctor made his rounds.* **13.** a single outburst: *a round of applause.* **14.** a single discharge of shot by each of a number of guns, rifles, etc. **15.** a single discharge by one firearm. **16.** a charge of ammunition for a single shot. **17.** a dance with the dancers arranged or moving in a circle or a ring. **18.** movement in a circle. **19.** the portion of the thigh of beef below the rump and above the leg. **20.** a song for several singers, each of whom sings the same melody starting at a different time: *"Three blind mice" is a well-known round.* —*adv.* **21.** throughout a repeating period of time: *all year round.* **22.** short for **around.** —*prep.* **23.** throughout (a period of time): *a beach you can visit round the year.* **24.** *Informal.* around: *It happened round noon.* —*v.* **25.** to make or become round. **26.** to make a circuit; travel around: *to round the corner.* **27.** to replace by the nearest multiple of 10: *97 can be rounded to 100.* **28.** to pronounce (a vowel) with rounded lips. **29. round out,** to complete or perfect: *That's the stamp I need to round out my collection.* **30. round up, a.** to drive or bring (cattle, sheep, etc.) together. **b.** to assemble; gather: *to round up suspects in a crime.*

round·a·bout (round′ə bout′), *adj.* not straight or direct; indirect: *a roundabout route.*

round·ish (roun′dish), *adj.* almost or nearly round.

round·ly (round′lē), *adv.* **1.** in a round manner. **2.** completely or fully. **3.** outspokenly or severely: *to scold someone roundly.* **4.** vigorously or briskly.

round-shoul·dered (round′shōl′dərd), *adj.* having the shoulders bent forward, giving a rounded form to the upper part of the back.

Round′ Ta′ble, 1. the table around which King Arthur and his knights sat. **2.** King Arthur and his knights as a group.

round′ trip′, a trip to a certain place and back again. —**round′-trip′,** *adj.*

round-up (round′up′), *n.* **1.** the driving together of cattle, horses, etc., for inspection, branding, shipping to market, or the like. **2.** the men and horses that do this. **3.** the gathering together of scattered items or groups of people.

round·worm (round′wûrm′), *n.* any of various worms having a slender, cylindrical body, esp. one that lives as a parasite in the intestines of man and some animals.

rouse (rouz), *v.,* **roused, rous·ing. 1.** to wake up from sleep, inactivity, depression, etc.: *The telephone roused me from my nap.* **2.** to stir up or excite: *to rouse to anger.*

rous·ing (rou′zing), *adj.* **1.** exciting or stirring: *The crowd gave a rousing cheer.* **2.** lively or vigorous: *a rousing welcome.*

rout[1] (rout), *n.* **1.** a disastrous defeat. **2.** confused, disorderly retreat. —*v.* **3.** to cause to scatter in retreat: *to rout the enemy soldiers.* **4.** to defeat completely. [from the Old French word *rute,* which comes from Latin *rupta* "broken"]

rout[2] (rout), *v.* **1.** to turn over or dig up with the

snout, as swine do. **2.** to poke, search, or rummage. **3.** to force or drive out. **4.** to cause to rise from bed. [another form of *root*[2]]

route (rōōt, rout), *n.* **1.** a course, way, or road for travel or shipping. **2.** a specific territory, round, or number of stops regularly visited by a person in the performance of his work or duty: *a milkman's route.* —*v.,* **rout·ed, rout·ing. 3.** to fix the route of: *to route a tour.* **4.** to send or forward by a particular route: *to route goods through Boston.*

rou·tine (rōō tēn′), *n.* **1.** a usual or regular course of procedure or way of doing things: *the routine of an office.* —*adj.* **2.** usual or customary; regular: *routine errands.* **3.** dull or uninteresting: *a routine job.*

rove (rōv), *v.,* **roved, rov·ing.** to wander or roam about: *to rove the woods.*

rov·er[1] (rō′vər), *n.* a person who roves; wanderer.

rov·er[2] (rō′vər), *n.* **1.** a pirate. **2.** a pirate ship. [from a Middle English word, which comes from an earlier Dutch word meaning "robber," from *roven* "to rob"]

row[1] (rō), *n.* a number of persons or things arranged in a line, esp. a straight line: *a row of apple trees; a row of seats.* [from the Old English word *rāw*]

row[2] (rō), *v.* **1.** to propel by using oars: *to row a boat.* **2.** to travel or transport in a boat that is rowed: *to row across the lake.* —*n.* **3.** a trip in a rowboat. [from the Old English word *rōwan*]

row[3] (rou), *n.* a noisy dispute or quarrel.

row·boat (rō′bōt′), *n.* a small boat for rowing.

row·dy (rou′dē), *n., pl.* **row·dies. 1.** a rough disorderly person. —*adj.,* **row·di·er, row·di·est. 2.** rough and disorderly: *rowdy behavior in the park.* —**row′di·ly,** *adv.* —**row′di·ness,** *n.*

roy·al (roi′əl), *adj.* **1.** of or concerning a king, queen, or other sovereign. **2.** descended from or related to a king or queen: *a royal prince.* **3.** coming from or performed by a king or queen: *a royal decree; a royal visit.* **4.** suitable for a king or queen; magnificent: *royal splendor.* —**roy′al·ly,** *adv.*

roy·al·ist (roi′ə list), *n.* **1.** a supporter of a king or royal government. —*adj.* **2.** of or concerning a royalist.

roy·al·ty (roi′əl tē), *n., pl.* **roy·al·ties. 1.** royal persons as a group. **2.** a member of a royal family. **3.** royal status or power. **4.** a portion of the profits paid to the owner of a right, such as a patent, for the use of it. **5.** a portion of the income from a book, play, or the like, paid to its author, composer, etc.

rpm, revolutions per minute. Also, **r.p.m.**

rps, revolutions per second. Also, **r.p.s.**

R.R., 1. Railroad. **2.** Right Reverend.

R.S.V.P., reply requested; please answer. [from the French phrase *r(épondez) s(′il) v(ous) p(laît)* "reply, if you please"]

Rt., route. Also, **Rte.**

rt., right.

Ru, *Chem.* the symbol for **ruthenium.**

rub (rub), *v.,* **rubbed, rub·bing. 1.** to move over the surface of with pressure and friction: *to rub the table with polish.* **2.** to spread or apply with pressure and friction: *to rub wax on the table.* **3.** to move (two things) with pressure and friction over or back and forth over each other: *He rubbed his hands together.* 4. to move with pressure against something: *The cat rubbed against his leg.* 5. to remove or be removed by pressure and friction; erase (often fol. by *off* or *out*): *to rub out a stain.* —*n.* 6. the act or an instance of rubbing: *an alcohol rub.* 7. something that annoys or irritates one's feelings. 8. an obstacle, difficulty, or hindrance: *We like nice things, but the rub is we can't afford them.* 9. **rub it in,** to repeat or emphasize something unpleasant in order to tease or annoy: *He feels bad enough about that, so don't rub it in.* 10. **rub the wrong way,** to offend or annoy: *She has a personality that just rubs people the wrong way.*

rub·ber[1] (rub′ər), *n.* 1. any of several natural or man-made substances that stretch easily, used to make tires, erasers, etc. 2. a low overshoe of this material. 3. an instrument or tool used for rubbing, polishing, scraping, etc. 4. a person who rubs something, esp. to smooth or polish it. —*adj.* 5. made of, containing, or coated with rubber: *a rubber bath mat.* [from *rub* + *-er.* The original meaning was "eraser"] —**rub′ber·y,** *adj.*

rub·ber[2] (rub′ər), *n.* (in certain card games, such as bridge and whist) a series or round played until one side reaches a certain score or wins a certain number of hands.

rub′ber plant′, the tropical plant whose sap is the source of natural rubber, sometimes cultivated as a house plant.

rub′ber stamp′, a device with a rubber printing surface, used for imprinting names, notices, etc.

rub·ber-stamp (rub′ər stamp′), *v.* 1. to imprint with a rubber stamp. 2. *Informal.* to give approval to (something) in a routine way.

rub·bish (rub′ish), *n.* 1. worthless, discarded material; trash. 2. nonsense, as in writing, art, etc.

rub·ble (rub′əl), *n.* 1. rough fragments of broken stone, sometimes used in masonry. 2. broken bits of anything: *Bombing reduced the town to rubble.*

Ru·bi·con (rōō′bə kon′), *n.* a river in N Italy flowing E into the Adriatic Sea. 15 mi. long. By illegally crossing this boundary in 49 B.C., Julius Caesar began a civil war in ancient Rome.

ru·bi·cund (rōō′bə kund′), *adj.* red or reddish; ruddy: *a rubicund complexion.*

ru·bid·i·um (rōō bid′ē əm), *n. Chem.* a metallic element resembling potassium. *Symbol:* Rb

ru·ble (rōō′bəl), *n.* a silver coin and monetary unit of the Soviet Union, roughly equivalent to one U.S. dollar.

ru·by (rōō′bē), *n., pl.* **ru·bies.** 1. a precious stone having a deep-red color. 2. a deep red. —*adj.* 3. of the color ruby.

ruck·sack (ruk′sak′, rōōk′-), *n.* a type of knapsack carried by hikers, bicyclists, etc.

ruck·us (ruk′əs), *n. Informal.* a noisy commotion.

rud·der (rud′ər), *n.* a hinged or pivoted vertical flap that is turned to steer a boat, airplane, etc.

rud·der·post (rud′ər pōst′), *n.* the vertical shaft of a rudder.

rud·dy (rud′ē), *adj.,* **rud·di·er, rud·di·est.** 1. having a fresh, healthy, red color. 2. red or reddish. —**rud′di·ness,** *n.*

rude (rōōd), *adj.,* **rud·er, rud·est.** 1. discourteous or impolite: *a rude reply; a rude person.* 2. roughly built or made; crude: *a rude cottage.* 3. without culture or refinement: *a rude society.* 4. violent or harsh: *a rude storm.* —**rude′ly,** *adv.* —**rude′ness,** *n.*

ru·di·ment (rōō′də mənt), *n.* 1. Usually, **rudiments.** the first rule or step in the process of learning or doing something: *the rudiments of grammar.* 2. an incompletely developed organ or bodily part, esp. one that has no function.

ru·di·men·ta·ry (rōō′də men′tə rē), *adj.* 1. concerning first rules or steps: *a rudimentary knowledge of grammar.* 2. incompletely developed; having no function: *The human embryo has a rudimentary tail.*

rue[1] (rōō), *v.,* **rued, ru·ing.** to feel sorrow over; regret very much: *to rue a foolish remark.* [from the Old English word *brēowan*]

rue[2] (rōō), *n.* any of several strong-smelling plants having yellow flowers and leaves formerly used in medicine. [from an earlier French word, which comes from Latin *rūta,* from Greek *rhytē*]

rue·ful (rōō′fəl), *adj.* 1. causing sorrow or pity: *a rueful story.* 2. feeling or showing sorrow or pity; mournful: *a rueful expression.* —**rue′ful·ly,** *adv.*

ruff (ruf), *n.* 1. a collar of lace gathered or drawn into deep, full, regular folds, worn in the 16th and 17th centuries. 2. a prominent growth of hair or feathers around the necks of certain animals and birds.

ruffed′ grouse′ (ruft), a North American grouse having a tuft of feathers on each side of the neck.

ruf·fi·an (ruf′ē ən, ruf′yən), *n.* 1. a tough, lawless person; brute; bully. —*adj.* 2. tough, lawless, or brutal.

Ruff
(16th century)

ruf·fle (ruf′əl), *v.,* **ruf·fled, ruf·fling.** 1. to destroy the smoothness or evenness of: *The storm ruffled the lake.* 2. to draw up (cloth, lace, etc.) into folds. 3. to disturb or irritate. 4. to make (feathers) stand up straight, as a bird does. —*n.* 5. a break in the smoothness or evenness of some surface; ripple. 6. a strip of cloth, lace, etc., drawn up by gathering along one edge, and used as a trimming on a dress, blouse, etc.

rug (rug), *n.* 1. a thick fabric for covering part of a floor. 2. a piece of thick, warm cloth, used as a coverlet, lap robe, etc. [from Scandinavian]

Rug·by (rug′bē), *n.* 1. a city in central England: site of boys' school. 2. a form of football.

rug·ged (rug′id), *adj.* 1. having a roughly broken, rocky, or jagged surface: *rugged ground.* 2. (of a face) wrinkled or furrowed. 3. strong and robust; sturdy; hardy. 4. rough, harsh, or severe: *rugged ter-*

rain. **5.** rude or unrefined: *rugged manners.* **—rug′ged·ly,** *adv.* **—rug′ged·ness,** *n.*

Ruhr (rŏor), *n.* **1.** a river in W West Germany, flowing into the Rhine. **2.** a mining and industrial area in this region.

ru·in (rŏo′in), *n.* **1. ruins,** the remains of a building, town, or the like, that has been destroyed or that is decayed: *We visited the ruins of ancient Greece.* **2.** a destroyed or decayed building, town, etc. **3.** a fallen and wrecked or decayed condition: *The log cabin went to ruin during the summer.* **4.** the downfall, decay, or destruction of anything: *the ruin of his career.* **5.** something that causes a downfall or destruction: *Alcohol was his ruin.* **—v. 6.** to bring to ruin; damage: *The frost ruined the crops.* **7.** to make poor; bankrupt: *The fire ruined him.*

ru·in·a·tion (rŏo′ə nā′shən), *n.* **1.** the act of ruining, or the state of being ruined. **2.** something that ruins.

ru·in·ous (rŏo′ə nəs), *adj.* **1.** bringing or causing ruin: *a ruinous business venture.* **2.** fallen into ruin. **—ru′in·ous·ly,** *adv.*

rule (rŏol), *n.* **1.** a principle or regulation governing the way in which something is done: *the rules of football.* **2.** the usual or normal condition or practice: *It was her rule to walk to work.* **3.** control or government: *the rule of a king.* **4.** a ruler, esp. one for special measurements: *a pica rule.* **—v., ruled, rul·ing. 5.** to control or direct; govern: *to rule a country.* **6.** to decide or declare; decree: *The court ruled that the case would be tried tomorrow.* **7.** to mark with straight lines: *to rule paper.* **8.** to influence very strongly. **9. as a rule,** as the usual or customary thing; generally: *I get home by five o'clock as a rule.*

rule′ of thumb′, a general principle or rule based on experience rather than on scientific knowledge.

rul·er (rŏo′lər), *n.* **1.** a person who rules or governs. **2.** a strip of wood, metal, etc., having a straight edge and marked off in inches, centimeters, etc.

rul·ing (rŏo′ling), *n.* **1.** a decision made by a person of authority: *a judge's ruling.* **2.** the act of drawing straight lines with a ruler. **3.** the lines so drawn. **—adj. 4.** governing or dominating: *the ruling party.* **5.** controlling; most important: *the ruling concern.*

rum (rum), *n.* an alcoholic liquor made from molasses or some other sugar-cane product.

Ru·ma·ni·a (rŏo mā′nē ə), *n.* a republic in SE Europe, bordering on the Black Sea. 91,654 sq. mi. *Cap.:* Bucharest. Also, **Romania, Roumania.**

Ru·ma·ni·an (rŏo mā′nē ən), *n.* **1.** a native or inhabitant of Rumania. **2.** the Romance language of Rumania. **—adj. 3.** of or concerning Rumania, its inhabitants, or their language. Also, **Romanian, Roumanian.**

rum·ble (rum′bəl), *v.,* **rum·bled, rum·bling. 1.** to make a deep, heavy, rather muffled sound, such as thunder. **2.** to move or travel with such a sound: *The car rumbled down the road.* **—n. 3.** a deep, heavy, rather muffled sound. **4.** a rear part of a carriage containing seats or space for baggage.

ru·men (rŏo′min), *n.* the first of several stomachs in cud-chewing animals, such as cows and sheep. Food is returned from the rumen to the mouth for additional chewing.

ru·mi·nant (rŏo′mə nənt), *n.* **1.** any member of a group of related animals, including cattle, sheep, deer, camels, and giraffes, that have cloven hooves and chew their cud. **—adj. 2.** of or concerning such animals. **3.** inclined toward thought and meditation.

ru·mi·nate (rŏo′mə nāt′), *v.,* **ru·mi·nat·ed, ru·mi·nat·ing. 1.** to chew the cud. **2.** to meditate or think over; ponder; muse. **—ru′mi·na′tion,** *n.*

rum·mage (rum′ij), *v.,* **rum·maged, rum·mag·ing. 1.** to search thoroughly (often fol. by *through*): *to rummage through a closet.* **2.** to find or bring to light (often fol. by *out* or *up*): *to rummage out an old dress.* **—n. 3.** odds and ends. **4.** a thorough search.

rum·my (rum′ē), *n.* any of various card games in which the object is to match cards into related groups.

ru·mor (rŏo′mər), *n.* **1.** a story of doubtful truth that is spread by word of mouth. **2.** gossip or hearsay: *Don't listen to rumor.* **—v. 3.** to tell by rumor.

rump (rump), *n.* **1.** the fleshy back part of an animal's body. **2.** a cut of beef from this part of an animal. **3.** the buttocks.

rum·ple (rum′pəl), *v.,* **rum·pled, rum·pling. 1.** to crumple or crush into wrinkles: *The dress rumpled in the suitcase.* **—n. 2.** a wrinkle or crease.

rum·pus (rum′pəs), *n., pl.* **rum·pus·es.** a noisy disturbance; commotion; uproar.

run (run), *v.,* **ran** (ran), **run, run·ning. 1.** to go quickly by moving the legs more rapidly than at a walk. **2.** to move or act quickly: *Run upstairs and get my sweater.* **3.** to leave quickly; escape. **4.** to make regular trips: *The bus runs from Chicago to St. Louis.* **5.** to perform, compete in, or accomplish by or as if by running: *to run a race.* **6.** to flow or cause to flow: *The water ran down the drain. She ran water into the tub.* **7.** to move under continuing power or force: *The machine runs smoothly.* **8.** to operate; manage or control: *to run a machine.* **9.** to move, glide, turn, or pass easily or freely: *A rope runs in a pulley.* **10.** to cause to pass quickly: *He ran his eyes over the letter.* **11.** to get past or through: *to run a blockade.* **12.** to migrate upstream or inshore, as fish do. **13.** to extend in time: *The play runs two hours.* **14.** to get or become: *The well ran dry.* **15.** to proceed, continue, or go: *The story runs for eight pages.* **16.** to amount, total, or cost: *The bill ran to $100.* **17.** to undergo a spreading of colors: *materials that run when washed.* **18.** to be a candidate for election: *to run for governor.* **19.** to vary within a certain range: *Your work runs from fair to bad.* **20.** to publish, print, or make copies of: *The newspaper ran the story.* **—n. 21.** an act, instance, or period of running: *a run around the block.* **22.** a running pace: *The boys set out at a run.* **23.** a moving or traveling between two places; trip:

We took a run up to the country. **24.** an unraveled place in knitted work: *a run in a stocking.* **25.** the particular course, order, or tendency of something: *the run of events.* **26.** freedom to move around in, pass through, or use something: *We had the run of the house all week.* **27.** a continuous series of performances: *The play had a long run.* **28.** an uninterrupted series of things, events, etc.: *a run of bad luck.* **29.** a fairly large enclosure for domestic animals: *a chicken run.* **30.** a kind or class: *the usual run of speakers.* **31.** a flow, or a flowing movement: *the run of sap.* **32.** the amount that flows during a certain period: *a run of 500 barrels a day.* **33.** a period of time during which something, such as a machine, operates or continues operating. **34.** the movement of a number of fish upstream or inshore from deep water. **35.** (in baseball) the score unit made by safely running around all the bases and reaching home plate. **36. in the long run,** after considerable time or experience; in the end: *In the long run you will succeed.* **37. on the run,** *Informal.* **a.** moving quickly; hurrying about: *With so many activities, she's always on the run.* **b.** while moving or hurrying about: *I'll have to grab a sandwich on the run.* **38. run across, a.** to meet or encounter: *I ran across Helen at the drugstore.* **b.** to find or come upon by chance: *I ran across my old stamp album in the attic.* **39. run after, a.** to follow; chase; pursue: *The dog ran after me for two blocks.* **b.** to try to become friendly with: *She runs after people who are in society.* **40. run down, a.** to collide with and knock down, esp. with a vehicle: *He ran me down with his bicycle.* **b.** to stop functioning: *My watch has run down.* **c.** to search for until found; trace: *to run down the source of a rumor.* **41. run into, a.** to crash into; collide with: *The car ran into a tree.* **b.** to meet accidentally: *to run into an old friend at a party.* **c.** to encounter or experience: *The new project has run into difficulty.* **d.** to amount to: *Our losses ran into the millions.* **42. run out, a.** to come to an end; become finished or used up: *My subscription has run out.* **b.** to force to leave; expel: *They ran him out of the country.* **43. run out of,** to use up a supply of: *to run out of gas.* **44. run over, a.** to hit and knock down, esp. with a vehicle: *The cat was run over by a car.* **b.** to go beyond; exceed: *His speech ran over the time limit.*

run·a·way (run′ə wā′), *n.* **1.** a person who runs away; fugitive; deserter. **2.** a horse or team that has broken away from control. —*adj.* **3.** having run away; escaped. **4.** done by running away.

run-down (run′doun′), *adj.* **1.** fatigued or weary; very tired. **2.** in a state of poor health. **3.** fallen into disrepair: *a run-down house.* **4.** (of a clock, watch, etc.) not running because of not being wound.

rune (rōōn), *n.* **1.** any of the characters of some ancient alphabets used in Scandinavia and Britain. **2.** a mysterious or magic mark shaped like a rune. **3.** an ancient Scandinavian poem, song, or verse. —**ru′nic,** *adj.*

rung¹ (rung), *v.* the past tense and past participle of **ring².**

rung² (rung), *n.* **1.** one of the crosspieces, usually rounded, forming the steps of a ladder. **2.** a rounded or shaped piece fixed between the legs of a chair to increase its sturdiness. [from Old English *hrung*]

run·ner (run′ər), *n.* **1.** a person or thing that runs, esp. as a racer. **2.** either of the long, bladelike strips of metal or wood on which a sled or sleigh rides. **3.** See **rocker** (def. 1). **4.** a long, narrow rug, suitable for a hall or passageway. **5.** a long strip of linen, embroidery, lace, or the like, placed across a table. **6.** a slender stem that runs along the ground and sends out roots at separated points. **7.** a smuggler. **8.** a ship engaged in smuggling.

Runner
of a strawberry plant

run·ner-up (run′ər up′), *n., pl.* **run·ners-up.** a competitor, player, or team finishing in second place.

run·ning (run′ing), *n.* **1.** the act of a person or thing that runs. **2.** managing or directing: *the running of a business.* —*adj.* **3.** galloping, racing, moving, or passing rapidly. **4.** (of a machine) operating or functioning. **5.** performed with or during a run: *a running leap.* **6.** going or carried on continuously: *a running argument.* **7.** discharging pus or other matter: *a running nose; a running sore.*

run′ning knot′, another name for **slipknot.**

run′ning mate′, **1.** a horse entered in the same race as a more important horse from the same stable. **2.** a candidate for an office linked with another and more important office, such as the vice presidency.

run-on (run′on′), *adj.* added at the end of a text: *a run-on entry in a dictionary.*

runt (runt), *n.* **1.** an animal that is small or stunted as compared with others of its kind. **2.** a small, usually mean person.

run·way (run′wā′), *n.* **1.** a way along which something runs. **2.** Also, **airstrip.** a paved or cleared strip on which planes land and take off. **3.** the usual path of deer or other wild animals.

ru·pee (rōō pē′, rōō′pē), *n.* a nickel coin and monetary unit of India and Pakistan.

rup·ture (rup′chər), *n.* **1.** the act of breaking or bursting. **2.** the state of being broken or burst. **3.** a break in friendly or peaceful relations. **4.** a hernia. —*v.,* **rup·tured, rup·tur·ing.** **5.** to break or burst: *to rupture a blood vessel.* **6.** to cause a break in: *to rupture friendly relations.*

ru·ral (rōōr′əl), *adj.* of, concerning, or like the country, country life, or country people.

ru′ral free′ deliv′ery, free mail delivery in outlying country areas. *Abbr.:* R.F.D.

ruse (rōōz), *n.* an action meant to deceive; trick.

rush¹ (rush), *v.* **1.** to move or act with speed: *to rush to catch a train.* **2.** to perform, accomplish, or finish with speed: *He rushed the work.* **3.** to cause to move or act quickly: *I'm doing my best, so don't rush me.* **4.** to act without careful thought: *to rush into difficulties.* **5.** to attack suddenly and violently; charge: *The soldiers rushed the enemy's camp.* —*n.* **6.** the act of rushing. **7.** an eager rushing of persons to some region to be occupied or exploited: *the gold rush to California.* **8.** hurried and busy activity: *the rush of city life.* —*adj.* **9.** requiring or done in haste: *a rush order.* [from an early French word *russher,* which comes from Latin *recūsāre* "to push back"]

rush² (rush), *n.* **1.** any of various grasslike herbs that grow in wet or marshy places. **2.** the stem of such a plant used for making chair seats, mats, baskets, etc. [from the Middle English word *rusch,* which comes from Old English *ryse*]

rusk (rusk), *n.* **1.** a slice of sweet raised bread dried and baked again in the oven. **2.** a light, soft, sweetened biscuit.

rus·set (rus′it), *n.* a yellowish brown, light brown, or reddish brown.

Rus·sia (rush′ə), *n.* **1.** a former empire in E Europe and N Asia: overthrown by the Russian Revolution 1917. *Cap.:* St. Petersburg (1703–1917). **2.** another name for **Soviet Union.**

Rus·sian (rush′ən), *n.* **1.** a native or inhabitant of Russia. **2.** the Slavic language of Russia. —*adj.* **3.** of or concerning Russia, its people, or their language.

Rus′sian Or′thodox Church′, the branch of the Orthodox Church that was the national church of Russia until 1917.

Rus′sian Revolu′tion, the uprising in Russia in 1917, in which the Czarist government collapsed and the Soviet government was established.

rust (rust), *n.* **1.** a red, orange, or brown coating that forms on iron when it is exposed to air or moisture. **2.** any of several diseases of plants that cause reddish-brown spots to appear on the affected parts. **3.** a reddish yellow, reddish brown, or yellowish red. —*v.* **4.** to coat or become coated with rust; corrode. **5.** to deteriorate or weaken through lack of use: *to let a musical talent rust.* —*adj.* **6.** of the color rust.

rus·tic (rus′tik), *adj.* **1.** of, concerning, or living in the country; rural. **2.** simple, plain, or unsophisticated. **3.** rough, rude, or coarse: *rustic manners.* —*n.* **4.** a country person. —**rus′ti·cal·ly,** *adv.*

rus·tle (rus′əl), *v.,* **rus·tled, rus·tling. 1.** to make or cause to make a series of slight, soft sounds: *The leaves rustled in the wind.* **2.** *Informal.* to steal (cattle). —*n.* **3.** a rustling sound: *the rustle of silk.*

rus·tler (rus′lər), *n. Informal.* a cattle thief.

rust·y (rus′te), *adj.,* **rust·i·er, rust·i·est. 1.** covered with or affected by rust: *a rusty pipe.* **2.** of the color rust. **3.** out of practice: *She is rusty in French.* **4.** faulty through lack of use or neglect: *My piano playing is rusty.* —**rust′i·ly,** *adv.* —**rust′i·ness,** *n.*

rut (rut), *n.* **1.** a furrow, track, or groove in the ground, esp. one made by the passage of a vehicle or vehicles. **2.** a fixed and dull way of life; routine. —*v.,* **rut·ted, rut·ting. 3.** to make a rut or ruts in.

ru·ta·ba·ga (rōō′tə bā′gə), *n.* a kind of turnip having a large, yellowish root eaten as a vegetable.

Ruth (rōōth), *n.* **1.** (in the Bible) a woman who left her own people after the death of her husband to live with her mother-in-law, Naomi. She was an ancestor of David. **2.** a book of the Old Testament bearing her name.

ru·the·ni·um (rōō thē′nē əm), *n. Chem.* a rare metallic element. *Symbol:* Ru

ruth·less (rōōth′lis), *adj.* without pity or compassion; cruel. —**ruth′less·ly,** *adv.* —**ruth′less·ness,** *n.*

Rwan·da (rōō än′də), *n.* a republic in central Africa. 10,169 sq. mi. *Cap.:* Kigali.

-ry, another form of the suffix **-ery,** used to form nouns of similar meanings: *dentistry; heraldry; jewelry; circuitry.*

rye (rī), *n.* **1.** a grain used to make flour and whiskey, and as food for livestock. **2.** the plant yielding this grain, a widely cultivated variety of grass.

	Semitic	Greek		Latin	Gothic	Modern Roman
DEVELOPMENT OF UPPER-CASE LETTERS	W	ϟ Σ	ʡ	S	S	S
DEVELOPMENT OF LOWER-CASE LETTERS	σ, s	ʃ	S	s	ß	S
	Greek		Medieval		Gothic	Modern Roman

S

S, s (es), *n., pl.* **S's** *or* **Ss, s's** *or* **ss. 1.** the 19th letter of the English alphabet. **2.** something having the shape of an S.

S, 1. signature. **2.** small. **3.** south. **4.** southern.

S, 1. *(sometimes l.c.)* (in some grading systems) a grade or mark that indicates work of satisfactory or average quality. **2.** *Chem.* the symbol for **sulfur.**

s, 1. satisfactory. **2.** signature. **3.** small.

's, 1. an ending used to form the possessive case of singular nouns and of plural nouns not ending in *-s:* *the boy's coat; the men's hats.* **2.** a contraction of *is: He's here.* **3.** a contraction of *has: He's gone out.* **4.** a contraction of *us: Let's go.*

-s, a suffix used to form **1.** the regular plural of nouns: *boys; birds.* **2.** the third person singular, present tense of verbs: *He asks. She gives.* See also **-es.**

S., 1. Sea. **2.** small. **3.** south. **4.** southern.

s., 1. singular. **2.** small. **3.** south. **4.** southern.

Saar (zär, sär), *n.* **1.** a territory in W West Germany, in the Saar River valley: under French control 1945–1956. 991 sq. mi. **2.** a river in W Europe, flowing from NE France to the Moselle River in West Germany. 150 mi. long.

Sab·bath (sab′əth), *n.* **1.** the seventh day of the week, Saturday, as the day of rest and religious observance among the Jews and in some Christian churches. **2.** the first day of the week, Sunday, as the day of rest and religious observance for most Christians. [from the Hebrew word *shabbat* "rest"]

sa·ber (sā′bər), *n.* **1.** a heavy, one-edged sword, usually curved, used esp. by cavalry. **2.** (in fencing) a sword having two cutting edges and a blunt point.

sa′ber-toothed ti′ger (sā′bər tōōtht′), any of several large, extinct animals having long, saberlike canine teeth.

sa·ble (sā′bəl), *n., pl.* **sa·bles** *or* **sa·ble. 1.** an animal of northern Europe and Asia that resembles a weasel and is valued for its soft, dark-brown fur. **2.** an American marten. **3.** the fur of any of these animals. **4.** the color black. —*adj.* **5.** made of the fur of the sable: *a sable coat.* **6.** very dark; black. [from an Old French word, which comes from Slavic]

Sable
(total length 28 in.)

sa′ble an′telope, a large antelope of Africa, having a black coat and large, curved horns.

sab·ot (sab′ō), *n.* **1.** a shoe made of a single block of wood hollowed out, worn by French, Belgian, and Dutch peasants. **2.** a shoe with a thick wooden sole and sides and a top of coarse leather.

Sable antelope
(5 ft. high at shoulder)

sab·o·tage (sab′ə täzh′), *n.* **1.** any intentional interference with production or work in a plant or factory by enemy agents or by employees during a trade dispute. —*v.,* **sab·o·taged, sab·o·tag·ing. 2.** to injure or attack by sabotage.

sab·o·teur (sab′ə tûr′), *n.* a person who commits or practices sabotage.

sa·bra (sä′brə), *n.* a person born in Israel.

sac (sak), *n.* a baglike organ or part in an animal or plant, often containing a liquid.

SAC, Strategic Air Command. Also, **S.A.C.**

sac·cha·rin (sak′ə rin), *n.* a man-made substance that has 500 times the sweetening power of sugar, used as a substitute for sugar, esp. in low-calorie beverages.

---

act, āble, dâre, ärt; ebb, ēqual; if, īce; hot, ōver, ôrder; oil; bŏŏk; ōōze; out; up, ûrge; ə = *a* as in *alone*; ᵊ as in *button* (but′ᵊn), *fire* (fīᵊr); chief; shoe; thin; ŧhat; zh as in *measure* (mezh′ər). See full key inside cover.

sac·cha·rine (sak′ə rin), *adj.* **1.** of or like sugar. **2.** too sweet or sentimental: *a saccharine smile.*

sac·er·do·tal (sas′ər dōt′ʳl), *adj.* of or concerning priests; priestly.

sa·chem (sā′chəm), *n.* (among some American Indian tribes) the chief of a tribe or of a confederation.

sa·chet (sa shā′), *n.* a small bag, case, or pad containing perfumed powder.

sack¹ (sak), *n.* **1.** a large bag of strong, coarsely woven material for grain, potatoes, coal, etc. **2.** the amount such a bag can hold; sackful. **3.** any bag: *a sack of candy.* **4.** a loose-fitting coat, dress, jacket, or cape. —*v.* **5.** to put into a sack or sacks: *to sack potatoes.* [from the Old English word *sacc,* which comes from Greek *sakkos,* itself from Semitic]

sack² (sak), *v.* **1.** to pillage or loot after capture: *to sack a city.* —*n.* **2.** the plundering of a captured place. [from the Italian word *sacco* "looting, loot," literally "a bag, sack." See *sack¹*]

sack³ (sak), *n.* a kind of strong, light-colored wine formerly imported from Spain. [from the French word *sec,* in the phrase *vin sec* "dry wine"]

sack·cloth (sak′klôth′), *n.* **1.** another word for **sacking. 2.** coarse cloth worn as a sign of mourning or penitence.

sack·ful (sak′fool), *n., pl.* **sack·fuls.** the amount a sack can hold.

sack·ing (sak′ing), *n.* coarse woven material of hemp, jute, or the like, used for making sacks.

sac·ra·ment (sak′rə mənt), *n.* a religious ceremony or practice in Christian churches: *the sacrament of baptism.* —**sac′ra·men′tal,** *adj.*

Sac·ra·men·to (sak′rə men′tō), *n.* a seaport and the capital city of California, in the central part.

sa·cred (sā′krid), *adj.* **1.** dedicated to a deity or to some religious purpose: *a sacred temple.* **2.** inspiring respect; solemn: *a sacred promise.* **3.** concerning or connected with religion (opposite of *profane*): *sacred literature.* [from the Middle English word *sacren* "to consecrate," which comes from Latin *sacer* "holy"] —**sa′cred·ly,** *adv.* —**sa′cred·ness,** *n.*

sac·ri·fice (sak′rə fis′), *n.* **1.** the offering of animal, plant, or human life to a deity as an act of worship. **2.** someone or something that is so offered. **3.** the giving up of something of value for something else: *He made a great sacrifice of time and money to help his friends.* **4.** a loss suffered by selling something below its value: *He sold the house at a sacrifice.* —*v.,* **sac·ri·ficed, sac·ri·fic·ing. 5.** to make a sacrifice or offering of: *to sacrifice an animal.* **6.** to give up for something else: *to sacrifice free time for study.* **7.** to sell at a loss. —**sac·ri·fi·cial** (sak′rə fish′əl), *adj.*

sac·ri·lege (sak′rə lij), *n.* the act of violating or showing disrespect for something sacred. —**sac·ri·le·gious** (sak′rə lij′əs, sak′rə lē′jəs), *adj.*

sac·ris·ty (sak′ri stē), *n., pl.* **sac·ris·ties.** a room in a church for storing sacred vessels, clothing, etc.

sac·ro·sanct (sak′rō sangkt′), *adj.* extremely sacred or holy; that must not be violated or desecrated.

sad (sad), *adj.,* **sad·der, sad·dest. 1.** feeling unhappiness or grief. **2.** expressing sorrow: *a sad song.*

3. causing sorrow: *sad news.* **4.** clumsy; inferior: *a sad performance of a play.* —**sad′ly,** *adv.* —**sad′ness,** *n.*

sad·den (sad′ʳn), *v.* to make or become sad.

sad·dle (sad′ʳl), *n.* **1.** a seat for a rider on the back of a horse or other animal. **2.** a similar seat on a bicycle, tractor, etc. **3.** a part of a harness laid across the back of an animal. **4.** something resembling a saddle in shape or position. **5.** a cut of mutton, lamb, etc., including both loins. **6.** a ridge connecting two hills. —*v.,* **sad·dled, sad·dling. 7.** to put a saddle on: *to saddle a horse.* **8.** to load or burden: *to saddle someone with responsibility.*

English saddle
A, Pommel
B, Seat
C, Stirrup

sad·dle·bag (sad′ʳl bag′), *n.* a large bag, usually one of a pair, hung from or laid over a saddle.

sa·fa·ri (sə fär′ē), *n., pl.* **sa·fa·ris. 1.** an expedition for hunting, esp. in eastern Africa. **2.** any long or adventurous expedition. [from a Swahili word, which comes from Arabic *safara* "to travel"]

Western saddle
A, Pommel
B, Seat
C, Stirrup

safe (sāf), *adj.,* **saf·er, saf·est. 1.** free from injury, danger, or loss: *to arrive safe and sound.* **2.** giving protection from harm, injury, danger, or risk: *a safe place.* **3.** involving little or no risk: *a safe guess.* **4.** dependable or trustworthy: *a safe guide.* **5.** unable to do harm: *The thief is safe in jail.* —*n.* **6.** a box or cabinet of iron or steel for storing valuable articles. —**safe′ly,** *adv.*

safe·guard (sāf′gärd′), *n.* **1.** something that protects, defends, or ensures safety: *a safeguard against crime.* —*v.* **2.** to guard or protect.

safe·keep·ing (sāf′kē′ping), *n.* the act of keeping safe; protection: *Give me the money for safekeeping.*

safe·ty (sāf′tē), *n., pl.* for def. 2 **safe·ties. 1.** freedom from danger, injury, or loss. **2.** a device to prevent injury, such as a lock on a gun to prevent accidental firing.

safe′ty belt′, 1. another term for **seat belt. 2.** a belt or strap worn as a safety precaution by persons working at heights.

safe′ty match′, a match that can be ignited only when rubbed on a specially prepared surface.

safe′ty pin′, a pin bent back on itself to form a spring, with a guard to cover the point.

safe′ty valve′, 1. a valve, such as one in a steam boiler, that opens automatically if the pressure becomes dangerously high. **2.** a harmless outlet for emotion, nervousness, etc.: *Tennis is his safety valve.*

saf·fron (saf′rən), *n.* **1.** the dried, orange-colored stigmas of a kind of crocus used as a dye and a flavoring. **2.** a yellowish orange.

sag (sag), *v.,* **sagged, sag·ging. 1.** to sink or bend downward by weight or pressure: *The shelf sags in the middle because the books are too heavy.* **2.** to hang down unevenly: *The hem on her dress sags.*

3. to lose strength; weaken: *His courage is sagging.*
—*n.* **4.** a place or spot where something sags.

sa·ga (sä′gə), *n.* **1.** a medieval Icelandic or Norse story of the achievements and events of a person or a family. **2.** any story of heroic events.

sa·ga·cious (sə gā′shəs), *adj.* having or showing keen mental understanding and practical sense. —**sa·gac·i·ty** (sə gas′i tē), *n.*

sage¹ (sāj), *n.* **1.** a very wise man. —*adj.*, **sag·er, sag·est. 2.** very wise and shrewd. [from an Old French word, which comes from Latin *sapidus* "wise," from *sapere* "to know"] —**sage′ly,** *adv.*

sage² (sāj), *n.* **1.** an herb related to mint, with grayish-green leaves: used in poultry seasoning. **2.** short for **sagebrush.** [from the Old French word *sauge,* which comes from Latin *salvia*]

sage·brush (sāj′brush′), *n.* any of several bushy plants resembling sage that grow wild on the plains of the western U.S.

Sag·it·ta·ri·us (saj′i târ′ē əs), *n.* the Archer: a constellation and sign of the zodiac.

Sa·har·a (sə har′ə, sə här′ə), *n.* a desert in N Africa, extending from the Atlantic Ocean to the Nile valley. about 3,500,000 sq. mi. —**Sa·har′an,** *adj.*

sa·hib (sä′ib, sä′ēb), *n.* (formerly in India) master.

said (sed), *v.* **1.** the past tense and past participle of **say.** —*adj.* **2.** (in legal documents) named or mentioned before: *the testimony of the said witness.*

sai·ga (sī′gə), *n.* a goatlike antelope of western Asia and eastern Russia, having a very large muzzle.

Sai·gon (sī gon′), *n.* the capital city of former South Vietnam: renamed Ho Chi Minh City.

Saiga
(2½ ft. high at shoulder)

sail (sāl), *n.* **1.** an area of canvas or other fabric extended to the wind in such a way as to cause a ship to move. **2.** some similar piece, such as the part of an arm that catches the wind on a windmill. **3.** sailing ships as a group. —*v.* **4.** to move forward, as a ship. **5.** to travel by water: *to sail to Europe.* **6.** to manage a sailboat, esp. for sport: *to learn to sail.* **7.** to travel through the air: *The kite sailed by.* **8.** to move along in a brisk, easy way: *She sailed into the room.* **9. set sail,** to begin a sea voyage: *We set sail at midnight.*

sail·boat (sāl′bōt′), *n.* a boat moved by sails.

sail·fish (sāl′fish′), *n., pl.* **sail·fish·es** or **sail·fish.** any of several large ocean game fish related to the swordfish and having a very large fin on its back that resembles a sail.

Pacific sailfish
(length to 11 ft.)

sail·or (sā′lər), *n.* **1.** a person whose occupation is sailing or navigation. **2.** a flat-brimmed straw hat with a low, flat crown.

saint (sānt), *n.* **1.** a very holy person formally recognized by the Christian church and given the title of saint. **2.** a person of great holiness, virtue, or kindness. [from an Old French word, which comes from Latin *sanctus* "sacred"] —**saint′like′,** *adj.*

Saint′ Bernard′, a breed of very large tan-and-white dogs that have a large head, long or medium-length hair, and are noted for rescuing travelers in the Swiss Alps.

saint·ed (sān′tid), *adj.* **1.** being among the saints. **2.** like a saint; saintly.

saint·hood (sānt′hŏŏd), *n.* **1.** the condition or status of being a saint. **2.** saints as a group.

saint·ly (sānt′lē), *adj.*, **saint·li·er, saint·li·est.** like or suitable for a saint. —**saint′li·ness,** *n.*

Saint Bernard
(28 in. high at shoulder)

Saint′ Pat′rick's Day′, March 17, observed in honor of St. Patrick, the patron saint of Ireland.

Saint′ Val′entine's Day′, February 14, observed in honor of Saint Valentine as a day for the exchange of valentines.

saith (seth), *v.* an old form of the third person singular, present tense of **say:** *Thus saith the Lord,*

sake (sāk), *n.* **1.** benefit or interest; advantage: *for the sake of your career.* **2.** purpose or end: *for the sake of appearances.*

sal·a·ble (sā′lə bəl), *adj.* suitable for sale. Also, **sale′a·ble.** —**sal′a·bil′i·ty,** *n.*

sal·ad (sal′əd), *n.* **1.** any of various dishes consisting of vegetables, such as lettuce, tomatoes, cucumbers, etc., usually covered with a dressing and sometimes containing seafood, meat, or eggs. **2.** any herb or green vegetable used in such a dish or eaten raw.

sal·a·man·der (sal′ə man′dər), *n.* any of several small amphibians that resemble lizards but have a smooth, moist skin and live in or near water.

Salamander
(length 8 in.)

sa·la·mi (sə lä′mē), *n.* a kind of sausage, originally Italian, often flavored with garlic.

sal·a·ried (sal′ə rēd), *adj.* **1.** receiving a salary: *a salaried employee.* **2.** providing a salary: *a salaried job.*

sal·a·ry (sal′ə rē), *n., pl.* **sal·a·ries.** a fixed amount of money paid at regular times to a person for his work or services: *She receives a salary of $300 a week.*

sale (sāl), *n.* **1.** the act of selling. **2.** a transfer of property for money. **3.** an opportunity to sell something; market. **4.** a selling of goods at reduced prices.

Sa·lem (sā′ləm), *n.* **1.** the capital city of Oregon, in the NW part. **2.** a port city in NE Massachusetts: founded 1626.

sales·man (sālz′mən), *n., pl.* **sales·men.** a man whose job is selling goods, services, etc.

sales·man·ship (sālz′mən ship′), *n.* the ability to sell a product, create interest in new ideas, etc.

sales′ tax′, a tax on articles sold, usually added to the selling price by the seller.

sales·wom·an (sālz′wŏŏm′ən), *n., pl.* **sales·wom·en.** a woman whose job is selling goods, esp. in a store.

sa·li·ent (sā′lē ənt), *adj.* standing out; easily noticed; prominent: *the salient features of the countryside.*

sa·line (sā′līn, sā′lēn), *adj.* of, containing, or resembling salt, esp. common table salt: *a saline solution for gargling.*

sa·li·va (sə li′və), *n.* the watery liquid that flows into the mouth from the salivary glands. Saliva helps in swallowing food and starts the digestion of starches. —**sal·i·var·y** (sal′ə ver′ē), *adj.*

sal′ivary gland′, any of the glands that produce saliva.

sal·let (sal′it), *n.* a light medieval helmet, usually with a slit for vision.

sal·low (sal′ō), *adj.* of a pale, sickly, yellowish color: *a sallow complexion.*

sal·ly (sal′ē), *n., pl.* **sal·lies.** 1. a sudden outward rush: *a sally of troops from the trenches.* 2. an excursion or trip. 3. a clever or witty remark. —*v.,* **sal·lied, sal·ly·ing.** 4. to rush or go forth. [from the Old French word *saillir* "to rush forth," from Latin *salīre* "to leap"]

Sallet
(15th century)

salm·on (sam′ən), *n., pl.* **salm·ons** *or* **salm·on.** 1. any of several food fishes having pink flesh that live in the ocean but swim up rivers to lay their eggs. 2. a light, yellowish pink. —*adj.* 3. of the color salmon.

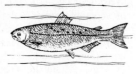

Salmon
(length to 6 ft.)

sa·lon (sə lon′), *n.* 1. a drawing room or reception room in a large house. 2. a gathering of guests in such a room, esp. the leaders in society, art, or politics. 3. a hall used for the exhibition of works of art, or the exhibition itself.

sa·loon (sə lōōn′), *n.* 1. a place where alcoholic drinks are sold. 2. a large room, as on a passenger ship, used as a dining room, lounge, etc.

salt (sôlt), *n.* 1. a white powder, a compound of sodium and chlorine, that is extracted from sea water or mined in underground deposits and used for seasoning and preserving food. Salt is vital to proper functioning of the body. 2. any of a large class of chemical compounds usually produced by neutralizing an acid with a base. 3. **salts,** any of various salts used as a laxative. 4. anything that gives liveliness or humor to something: *the salt of a person's wit.* 5. *Informal.* a sailor, esp. an old or experienced one. —*v.* 6. to season, cure, or treat with salt: *to salt a piece of meat.* —*adj.* 7. containing or having the taste of salt: *salt crackers.* 8. cured or preserved with salt. 9. **salt away,** *Informal.* to store away; keep in reserve; save: *He salts away most of his earnings.* 10. **with a grain of salt,** with suspicion or with allowance for possible exaggeration: *You have to take those stories of hers with a grain of salt.*

salt·cel·lar (sôlt′sel′ər), *n.* a shaker or dish for salt.

sal·tine (sôl tēn′), *n.* a crisp, salted cracker.

Salt′ Lake′ Cit′y, the capital city of Utah, in the N part, near the Great Salt Lake.

salt′ lick′, a place to which animals go to lick natural salt deposits.

salt·pe·ter (sôlt′pē′tər), *n.* a white powder resembling salt that is used in making gunpowder and fertilizers, and in preserving food; niter.

salt·wa·ter (sôlt′wô′tər, -wot′ər), *adj.* of or living in sea water: *Cod are saltwater fish.* Also, **salt′-wa′ter.**

salt·y (sôl′tē), *adj.,* **salt·i·er, salt·i·est.** 1. tasting of or containing salt. 2. very sharp or witty: *salty humor.* —**salt′i·ness,** *n.*

sa·lu·bri·ous (sə lōō′brē əs), *adj.* good for one's health; healthy: *a salubrious climate.*

Sa·lu·ki (sə lōō′kē), *n.* one of a breed of black, white, gold, or black-and-tan dogs resembling the greyhound and having fringes of long hair on the ears, legs, and thighs: raised originally in Egypt and southwestern Asia.

Saluki
(2 ft. high
at shoulder)

sal·u·tar·y (sal′yə ter′ē), *adj.* 1. good for one's health. 2. useful or beneficial: *salutary suggestions.*

sal·u·ta·tion (sal′yə tā′shən), *n.* 1. the act of saluting. 2. something said, written, or done as a greeting. 3. the opening words of a speech or letter, as *Dear Sirs* or *Ladies and Gentlemen.*

sa·lu·ta·to·ri·an (sə lōō′tə tôr′ē ən), *n.* the student ranking second highest in a graduating class.

sa·lute (sə lōōt′), *v.,* **sa·lut·ed, sa·lut·ing.** 1. to address (someone) with friendliness, respect, etc.; greet. 2. to make a bow or other gesture to, as in greeting, farewell, or respect. 3. (in military use) to pay respect to by raising the right hand to the head, presenting arms, firing cannon, etc.; honor. —*n.* 4. the act of saluting or greeting.

Sal·va·dor (sal′və dôr′), *n.* short for **El Salvador.**

sal·vage (sal′vij), *n.* 1. the act of saving a ship or its cargo from the dangers of the sea. 2. the act of saving any property from destruction. 3. the property saved. 4. payment given to those who voluntarily save a ship or its cargo. —*v.,* **sal·vaged, sal·vag·ing.** 5. to save from destruction or loss: *to salvage cargo from a sinking ship.*

sal·va·tion (sal vā′shən), *n.* 1. the act of saving or protecting from harm or loss. 2. the state of being saved or protected. 3. something that saves or protects: *His savings were his salvation when he got sick.* 4. (in religion) the saving of the soul from the power and the penalty of sin; redemption.

Salva′tion Ar′my, an international Christian organization engaged in spreading Christianity and bringing help to the poor.

salve (sav), *n.* 1. a soothing ointment applied to the skin. 2. anything that soothes, calms, or relieves: *His sympathy was a salve to my disappointment.* —*v.,*

salved, salv·ing. 3. to soothe or relieve with or as if with a salve: *to salve a wound; to salve hurt feelings.*

sal·vo (sal′vō), *n., pl.* **sal·vos** *or* **sal·voes. 1.** a discharge of artillery or other firearms at one time. **2.** an outburst of cheers, applause, etc.

Sa·mar·i·a (sə mâr′ē ə), *n.* a district in ancient Palestine: taken by Jordan 1948; occupied by Israeli forces 1967.

Sa·mar·i·tan (sə mar′i t³n), *n.* **1.** an inhabitant of Samaria. **2.** a good Samaritan. —*adj.* **3.** of or concerning Samaria or Samaritans.

sa·mar·i·um (sə mâr′ē əm), *n. Chem.* a metallic element of the rare-earth group. *Symbol:* Sm

same (sām), *adj.* **1.** identical with what is about to be or has just been mentioned: *This street is the same one we were on yesterday.* **2.** being equal or identical though having different names, aspects, etc.: *These are the same rules even though they are differently worded.* **3.** agreeing or corresponding in size, amount, etc.: *two boxes of the same dimensions.* **4.** unchanged in condition or character: *It's the same town after all these years.* —*pron.* **5.** the person or thing just mentioned. **6. the same,** in the same or nearly same way: *Mother doesn't like the idea, and Dad feels the same.*

same·ness (sām′nis), *n.* **1.** the state or quality of being the same; identity. **2.** lack of variety; dullness.

S. Amer., South America.

Sa·mo·a (sə mō′ə), *n.* a group of islands in the S Pacific, part forming an independent republic and the rest belonging to the U.S. See also **American Samoa, Western Samoa.**

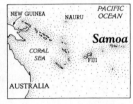

Sa·mo·an (sə mō′ən), *n.* **1.** a native or inhabitant of Samoa. **2.** the Polynesian language of Samoa. —*adj.* **3.** of or concerning Samoa, its people, or their language.

sam·o·var (sam′ə vär′), *n.* a metal urn, used esp. in the Soviet Union to heat water for making tea. [from a Russian word meaning literally "self-boiling"]

sam·pan (sam′pan), *n.* a small boat of the Far East, propelled by a single scull over the stern and having a roofing of mats.

sam·ple (sam′pəl), *n.* **1.** a small part of anything or one of a number of things intended to show the quality, style, or nature of the whole: *a sample of his writing.* —*adj.* **2.** used as a sample: *a sample dress.* —*v.,* **sam·pled, sam·pling. 3.** to test or judge by a sample: *to sample a cake.*

Sampan

sam·pler (sam′plər), *n.* **1.** a person who samples. **2.** an embroidered cloth that shows a beginner's skill in needlework. **3.** a collection of samples or selections.

Sam·son (sam′sən), *n.* **1.** (in the Bible) a Hebrew judge famous for his strength. **2.** any strong man.

Sam·u·el (sam′yōō əl), *n.* **1.** (in the Bible) a judge and prophet of Israel. **2.** either of two books of the Old Testament bearing his name.

San An·to·ni·o (san′ an tō′nē ō′), a city in S Texas: site of the Alamo.

san·a·to·ri·um (san′ə tôr′ē əm), *n., pl.* **san·a·to·ri·ums** *or* **san·a·to·ri·a** (san′ə tôr′ē ə). another spelling of **sanitarium.**

sanc·ti·fy (saṅgk′tə fī′), *v.,* **sanc·ti·fied, sanc·ti·fy·ing. 1.** to make holy; consecrate: *to sanctify a place of worship.* **2.** to purify or free from sin. **3.** to make worthy of respect: *to sanctify a custom by widespread observance.* —**sanc′ti·fi·ca′tion,** *n.*

sanc·ti·mo·ni·ous (saṅgk′tə mō′nē əs), *adj.* pretending to be devout and righteous. —**sanc′ti·mo′ni·ous·ly,** *adv.*

sanc·tion (saṅgk′shən), *n.* **1.** permission or approval granted by an authority: *the sanction of the chairman to go ahead with the project.* **2.** action by one or more nations toward another nation to force it to comply with legal obligations. —*v.* **3.** to authorize, approve, or allow: *to sanction a change in the rules.*

sanc·ti·ty (saṅgk′ti tē), *n.* **1.** holiness or saintliness. **2.** the quality of being sacred: *the sanctity of law.*

sanc·tu·ar·y (saṅgk′chōō er′ē), *n., pl.* **sanc·tu·ar·ies. 1.** a sacred or holy place. **2.** an especially holy place in a temple or church. **3.** a place providing refuge or protection. **4.** safety or protection; refuge: *the sanctuary of a country cabin.* **5.** an area of land where wildlife is protected by law.

sanc·tum (saṅgk′təm), *n.* **1.** a sacred or holy place. **2.** a private place or retreat.

sand (sand), *n.* **1.** tiny, loose grains of worn-down or crushed rock, often found along an ocean shore. **2.** Usually, **sands.** a tract or region composed mostly of sand. —*v.* **3.** to sprinkle, cover, or fill with sand: *to sand an icy road.* **4.** to smooth with sandpaper.

san·dal (san′d³l), *n.* **1.** a shoe consisting of a sole of leather or other material fastened to the foot by thongs or straps. **2.** a low shoe or slipper.

san·dal·wood (san′d³l wŏŏd′), *n.* a sweet-smelling wood of certain Asian trees used for carving and burned as incense.

sand·bag (sand′bag′), *n.* **1.** a bag filled with sand, used in fortification, as ballast, etc. **2.** such a bag used as a blackjack. —*v.,* **sand·bagged, sand·bag·ging. 3.** to supply with sandbags. **4.** to hit or stun with a sandbag.

sand′ bar′, a bar of sand formed in a river or sea by the action of tides or currents.

sand·box (sand′boks′), *n.* a box for holding sand, esp. one for children to play in.

sand′ dol′lar, any of various round, flat sea urchins that live on sandy ocean bottoms off the coasts of the United States.

Sand dollar (width 3 in.)

San Di·e·go (san′ dē ā′gō), a port city in SW California: naval and marine base.

sand·man (sand′man′), *n., pl.* **sand·men.** (in fairy tales and folklore) the man who puts sand in the eyes of children to make them sleepy.

sand·pa·per (sand′pā′pər), *n.* **1.** strong paper coated with a layer of sand or other abrasive, used for smoothing and polishing. —*v.* **2.** to rub with sandpaper; sand.

sand·pi·per (sand′pī′pər), *n.* any of numerous small birds having a slender bill and a piping call that live near the seashore.

sand·stone (sand′stōn′), *n.* a soft, porous rock formed from grains of sand naturally cemented together.

sand·storm (sand′stôrm′), *n.* a windstorm, esp. in a desert, that blows along great clouds of sand.

Sandpiper
(length 7 in.)

sand·wich (sand′wich), *n.* **1.** two or more slices of bread with a layer of meat, fish, cheese, etc., between them. —*v.* **2.** to put into a sandwich. **3.** to insert between two other things: *My bicycle was sandwiched between two cars.* [named after the fourth Earl of *Sandwich* (1718–1792), who had sandwiches brought to him while gambling so that he would not have to stop for meals]

Sand′wich Is′lands, former name of **Hawaiian Islands.**

sand·y (san′dē), *adj.*, **sand·i·er, sand·i·est. 1.** containing, covered with, or like sand: *a sandy beach.* **2.** of a yellowish-red color: *sandy hair.* —**sand′i·ness,** *n.*

sane (sān), *adj.*, **san·er, san·est. 1.** having a sound, healthy mind; not mentally ill. **2.** showing good judgment or good sense: *a sane decision.* —**sane′ly,** *adv.* —**sane′ness,** *n.*

San Fran·cis·co (san′ fran sis′kō), a port city in W California. —**San′ Fran·cis′can.**

sang (sang), *v.* the past tense of **sing.**

san·guine (sang′gwin), *adj.* **1.** cheerful, hopeful, or confident: *a sanguine disposition.* **2.** reddish or ruddy: *a sanguine complexion.*

san·i·tar·i·um (san′i târ′ē əm), *n., pl.* **san·i·tar·i·ums** *or* **san·i·tar·i·a** (san′i târ′ē ə). a hospital for the treatment of lingering illnesses, such as tuberculosis and mental disease. Also, **sanatorium.**

san·i·tar·y (san′i ter′ē), *adj.* **1.** of or concerning health or healthful conditions. **2.** free from dirt, germs, etc.

san·i·ta·tion (san′i tā′shən), *n.* the methods or activities that create healthful, clean conditions.

san·i·ty (san′i tē), *n.* **1.** soundness or health of mind; the state of being sane. **2.** soundness of judgment.

San Jo·se (san′ hō zā′), a city in W California.

San Jo·sé (san′ hō zā′), the capital city of Costa Rica, in the central part.

San Juan (san′ wän′, hwän′), a seaport and the capital city of Puerto Rico, in the N part.

sank (sangk), *v.* the past tense of **sink.**

San Ma·ri·no (san′ mə rē′nō), a small republic in E Italy. 38 sq. mi.

San Mar·tín (san′ mär tēn′), **Jo·sé de** (hō zā′ də), 1778–1850, South American general: led independence movement in S South America.

San Sal·va·dor (san′ sal′və dôr′), the capital city of El Salvador.

San·skrit (san′skrit), *n.* **1.** an ancient Indo-European, Indic language, used in India as the chief language of religion and literature. —*adj.* **2.** of, referring to, or written in Sanskrit.

San·ta (san′tə), *n.* short for **Santa Claus.**

San·ta An·a (san′tə an′ə), a city in SW California.

San·ta Claus (san′tə klôz′), a jolly man of legend, supposed to bring gifts to children on Christmas Eve.

San·ta Fe (san′tə fā′), the capital city of New Mexico, in the N part.

San′ta Fe′ Trail′, an important trade route between Independence, Missouri, and Santa Fe, New Mexico: used from about 1821 to 1880.

San·ti·a·go (san′tē ä′gō), *n.* the capital city of Chile, in the central part.

San·to Do·min·go (san′tō də ming′gō), the capital city of the Dominican Republic, on the S coast.

São Pau·lo (soun′ pou′lōō), a city in S Brazil.

sap¹ (sap), *n.* **1.** the juice of a plant, esp. a tree. **2.** *Slang.* a fool or dunce. [from the Old English word *sæp*]

sap² (sap), *n.* **1.** a deep, narrow trench leading to an enemy fortification or position. —*v.*, **sapped, sapping. 2.** to approach (an enemy fortification or position) by means of a sap or saps. **3.** to undermine; weaken or destroy: *The long illness sapped his strength.* [from the Italian word *zappa* "hoe"]

sap·ling (sap′ling), *n.* a young tree.

sap·phire (saf′ī³r), *n.* **1.** a precious gem usually of a deep blue. **2.** a deep blue. —*adj.* **3.** containing a sapphire or sapphires. **4.** of the color sapphire.

sap·suck·er (sap′suk′ər), *n.* either of two American woodpeckers that drill holes in the bark of maple trees, apple trees, etc., and drink the sap.

sap·wood (sap′wŏŏd′), *n.* the soft wood beneath the inner bark through which the sap flows.

Sar·a·cen (sar′ə sən), *n.* **1.** a name formerly applied to Arabs. **2.** a Muslim, esp. at the time of the crusades. —*adj.* **3.** of or belonging to the Saracens.

Sar·ah (sâr′ə), *n.* (in the Bible) the wife of Abraham and mother of Isaac.

sar·casm (sär′kaz əm), *n.* **1.** a bitter or scornful manner of speaking or writing. **2.** a scornful remark.

sar·cas·tic (sär kas′tik), *adj.* **1.** containing or expressing sarcasm: *a sarcastic remark.* **2.** making use of sarcasm: *a sarcastic critic.* —**sar·cas′ti·cal·ly,** *adv.*

sar·coph·a·gus (sär kof′ə gəs), *n., pl.* **sar·coph·a·gus·es** *or* **sar·coph·a·gi** (sär kof′ə jī′). a stone coffin, esp. one decorated with sculpture, inscriptions, etc., displayed as a monument.

sar·dine (sär dēn′), *n., pl.* **sar·dines** *or* **sar·dine.** any of various small saltwater fishes of the herring family. Sardines are often preserved in oil or sauces for use as food.

Sar·din·i·a (sär din′ē ə, sär din′yə), *n.* an island in the Mediterranean W of Italy: with smaller islands it forms a department of Italy. 9301 sq. mi. —**Sar·din′i·an,** *n., adj.*

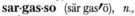

sar·don·ic (sär don′ik), *adj.* bitter or scornful, esp. in a mocking or taunting way; derisive: *His lips curled upward in a sardonic leer.* —**sar·don′i·cal·ly,** *adv.*

sar·gas·so (sär gas′ō), *n., pl.* **sar·gas·sos.** a coarse, olive-brown seaweed that has many berrylike air vessels and is found floating in tropical waters.

Sargas′so Sea′, a relatively calm area of water in the N Atlantic Ocean, NE of the West Indies, noted for its abundance of seaweed.

sa·ri (sär′ē), *n., pl.* **sa·ris.** an outer garment worn by Hindu women, made of a long piece of cotton or silk wound about the body, with one end draped over the head or over one shoulder.

sar·sa·pa·ril·la (sas′pə ril′ə, sär′sə pə ril′ə), *n.* **1.** the root of a tropical American plant used as a medicine and a flavoring. **2.** a soft drink flavored with an extract of this root.

sar·to·ri·al (sär tôr′ē əl), *adj.* **1.** of or concerning tailors or their business. **2.** of or concerning clothing and fashion, esp. men's tailored clothing: *the sartorial splendor of an Easter parade.* —**sar·to′ri·al·ly,** *adv.*

sash[1] (sash), *n.* a long band or scarf of cloth worn over one shoulder or around the waist. [from Arabic]

sash[2] (sash), *n.* a fixed or movable frame in which panes of glass are set, forming part of a door or window. [formed from *sashes* (taken as a plural), another form of the word *chassis*]

Sask., Saskatchewan (Canada).

Sas·katch·e·wan (sas kach′ə won′), *n.* a province in central Canada. 251,700 sq. mi. *Cap.:* Regina.

sass (sas), *Informal.* —*n.* **1.** impudent or disrespectful back talk. —*v.* **2.** to answer impudently.

sas·sa·fras (sas′ə fras′), *n.* **1.** a North American tree related to the laurel. **2.** the dried bark of the root of this tree, used as a flavoring.

sas·sy (sas′ē), *adj.,* **sas·si·er, sas·si·est.** *Informal.* another form of **saucy.**

sat (sat), *v.* the past tense and past participle of **sit.**

Sat., Saturday.

Sa·tan (sāt′ən), *n.* the Devil.

sa·tan·ic (sə tan′ik, sā tan′ik), *adj.* **1.** of, belonging to, or like Satan. **2.** cruel; diabolic: *a satanic laugh.* —**sa·tan′i·cal·ly,** *adv.*

satch·el (sach′əl), *n.* a small bag or suitcase, with a handle or a shoulder strap.

sate (sāt), *v.,* **sat·ed, sat·ing. 1.** to satisfy (a desire or appetite) fully: *We sated our thirst with long gulps of water.* **2.** to supply with an excess of something; glut: *a dictator who was sated with power.*

sa·teen (sa tēn′), *n.* a cotton or linen cloth woven and finished to resemble satin.

sat·el·lite (sat′ə līt′), *n.* **1.** a heavenly body that revolves in an orbit around a planet: *The moon is the only natural satellite of the earth.* **2.** a man-made object launched into an orbit around the earth, the moon, the sun, etc. **3.** an attendant or follower: *The emperor was surrounded by his satellites.* **4.** a country that is dominated by another: *a satellite of the Soviet Union.* [from the Latin word *satelles* "attendant, follower," which comes from Etruscan]

sa·ti·ate (sā′shē āt′), *v.* **1.** to supply with an excess of something; sate. **2.** to satisfy fully.

sat·in (sat′ən), *n.* **1.** a closely woven cloth of silk or similar material, with a smooth, glossy finish on one side. —*adj.* **2.** made of or covered with satin: *a satin dress; a satin cushion.* **3.** like satin; smooth; glossy.

sat·ire (sat′īr), *n.* **1.** a style of writing or speaking that makes witty use of sarcasm or ridicule in exposing or denouncing vice, folly, etc. **2.** a literary work composed in such a style.

sa·tir·i·cal (sə tir′i kəl), *adj.* **1.** of, concerning, or of the nature of satire. **2.** making use of satire: *a satirical novelist.* Also, **sa·tir′ic.** —**sa·tir′i·cal·ly,** *adv.*

sat·i·rist (sat′ər ist), *n.* **1.** a writer of satires. **2.** a person who is in the habit of using satire.

sat·i·rize (sat′ə rīz′), *v.,* **sat·i·rized, sat·i·riz·ing.** to attack or criticize with satire.

sat·is·fac·tion (sat′is fak′shən), *n.* **1.** the act of satisfying, or the state of being satisfied. **2.** a person or thing that makes someone satisfied. **3.** repayment or compensation for a debt or for a wrong or injury done to someone. **4.** the opportunity to obtain revenge or to right a wrong, as by fighting a duel: *to demand satisfaction for an insult.*

sat·is·fac·to·ry (sat′is fak′tə rē), *adj.* **1.** giving or causing satisfaction; good enough: *a satisfactory diet.* **2.** meeting certain requirements or demands: *a satisfactory grade.* —**sat′is·fac′to·ri·ly,** *adv.*

sat·is·fy (sat′is fī′), *v.,* **sat·is·fied, sat·is·fy·ing. 1.** to meet the desires, needs, or demands of (someone or something); make content: *I satisfied him by taking him to the game.* **2.** to put an end to (a craving or appetite): *A good meal satisfied our hunger.* **3.** to pay (a debt or obligation, or the person to whom it is owed): *to satisfy a bill; to satisfy one's creditors.* **4.** to convince; assure: *You will first have to satisfy me of your good intentions.* —**sat′is·fy′ing·ly,** *adv.*

sat·u·rate (sach′ə rāt′), *v.,* **sat·u·rat·ed, sat·u·rat·ing. 1.** to soak thoroughly: *The rain saturated our clothes.* **2.** to fill completely; reach or cover every part of: *A brilliant light saturated the room.* **3.** to cause (a substance) to unite with or dissolve the maximum amount of another substance: *to saturate sugar in a solution.* —**sat′u·ra′tion,** *n.*

Sat·ur·day (sat′ər dē, sat′ər dā′), *n.* the seventh day of the week, following Friday.

Sat·urn (sat′ərn), *n.* **1.** (in Roman mythology) the god of agriculture. **2.** the planet sixth in order from the sun, noted for the series of thin, flat rings that surround it. Saturn has a diameter of 72,000 miles; its average distance from the sun is 886,000,000 miles.

sat·ur·nine (sat′ər nīn′), *adj.* having a gloomy, solemn disposition.

sa·tyr (sā′tər, sat′ər), *n.* **1.** (in Greek and Roman mythology) one of a group of woodland gods, pictured as part man and part goat, given to carousing in the company of Bacchus. **2.** a lewd and lustful man; lecher.

sauce (sôs), *n.* **1.** any sweet or spicy liquid or paste poured or spread over food to add flavor and attractiveness. **2.** anything that increases or stimulates interest: *His lively wit added sauce to the party.* **3.** stewed or preserved fruit: *cranberry sauce.*

sauce·pan (sôs′pan′), *n.* a small metal pot for cooking, usually having a long handle.

sau·cer (sô′sər), *n.* a small, round, shallow dish, esp. one used for holding a cup.

sau·cy (sô′sē), *adj.,* **sau·ci·er,** **sau·ci·est.** **1.** bold in a disrespectful way; forward; impudent. **2.** lively; pert: *a saucy comedian.* **3.** smart; trim: *a saucy hat.* —**sau′ci·ly,** *adv.* —**sau′ci·ness,** *n.*

Sau′di Ara′bia (sou′dē, sä oo′dē, sô′dē), a kingdom in N and central Arabia. about 600,000 sq. mi. —**Sau′di Ara′bian.**

sauer·kraut (sour′-krout′), *n.* shredded cabbage, fermented in brine until sour.

Saul (sôl), *n.* (in the Bible) **1.** the first king of Israel. **2.** Also, **Saul′ of Tar′sus.** the original name of the apostle Paul.

saun·ter (sôn′tər, sän′tər), *v.* **1.** to walk at a leisurely pace; stroll. —*n.* **2.** a leisurely walk; stroll. **3.** a leisurely pace.

sau·ri·an (sôr′ē ən), *adj.* **1.** of, concerning, resembling, or belonging to the same family as a lizard. —*n.* **2.** a dinosaur or lizard.

sau·sage (sô′sij), *n.* chopped beef, pork, or other meats, seasoned and stuffed into a tube or casing made from animal intestine, thin plastic, or the like.

sau·té (sō tā′, sô tā′), *adj.* **1.** lightly fried in a pan with a small quantity of butter, oil, or other fat. —*v.,* **sau·téed,** **sau·té·ing.** **2.** to fry (food) in this way. —*n.* **3.** a dish prepared in this way: *a sauté of veal.*

sav·age (sav′ij), *adj.* **1.** fierce or ferocious: *a savage attack.* **2.** living in a wild state; untamed: *a savage beast.* **3.** living in primitive conditions; uncivilized: *savage tribes of the Amazon jungle.* **4.** wild or rugged, as country or scenery. —*n.* **5.** an uncivilized human being. **6.** a fierce or cruel person. —**sav′age·ly,** *adv.* —**sav′age·ness,** *n.*

sav·age·ry (sav′ij rē), *n., pl.* **sav·age·ries.** **1.** an uncivilized state or condition. **2.** fierce or cruel character or behavior. **3.** a savage act.

sa·van·na (sə van′ə), *n.* a flat, grassy plain with low, scattered trees.

Sa·van·nah (sə van′ə), *n.* a port city in E Georgia.

save¹ (sāv), *v.,* **saved, sav·ing. 1.** to rescue from danger or possible injury or loss: *His quick action saved the child from being struck by the bus.* **2.** to avoid or lessen the use or expenditure of: *We will save fuel with this new furnace.* **3.** to set aside or store: *to save money at a bank.* **4.** to reduce wear, damage, etc., of (something) by careful use: *Proper lighting will save your eyes.* **5.** to be thrifty; economize. **6.** (in religion) to preserve from sin or its consequences: *The Lord will save His people.* [from the Old French word *sauver,* which comes from Latin *salvāre* "to save"] —**sav′er,** *n.*

save² (sāv), *prep., conj.* except; but: *All were lost save one.* [another form of *safe*]

sav·ing (sā′ving), *adj.* **1.** able or tending to save; rescuing; preserving. **2.** compensating; redeeming: *a saving sense of humor.* **3.** thrifty; economical: *a saving housewife.* —*n.* **4.** the act of rescuing or preserving: *the saving of lives.* **5.** the practice or habit of being thrifty. **6.** something saved, or the amount saved: *a saving of half the regular price.* **7.** **savings,** money laid aside, esp. on deposit in a bank. —*prep.* **8.** with the exception of; except: *Saving a few crumbs we put out for them, the birds had nothing to eat all winter.* —**sav′ing·ly,** *adv.*

sav′ings bank′, a bank that receives money for safekeeping and pays interest on it to the depositors.

sav·ior (sāv′yər), *n.* a person who saves or rescues: *a savior of the poor.* Also, *esp. British,* **sav′iour.**

Sav·iour (sāv′yər), *n.* a title of God or Christ. Also, **Sav′ior.**

sa·vor (sā′vər), *n.* **1.** a taste or smell: *a sauce with the savor of garlic.* **2.** a particular quality: *The plan had the savor of treachery.* **3.** an exciting or appealing quality: *The job in Washington tempted him with the savor of politics.* —*v.* **4.** to have a particular taste or smell. **5.** to have a certain quality or appearance (usually fol. by *of*): *His business dealings savor of greed.* **6.** to give a certain taste or smell to; season; flavor. **7.** to enjoy the taste or smell of: *to savor a sizzling steak.* **8.** to take pleasure in; enjoy: *to savor the treasures of a famous art museum.*

sa·vor·y¹ (sā′və rē), *adj.* **1.** having an agreeable taste or smell. **2.** having an exciting or appealing quality. [from *savor* + *-y*]

sa·vor·y² (sā′və rē), *n., pl.* **sa·vor·ies.** a sweet-smelling herb related to mint, often used as a flavoring in cooking. [from the Middle English word *savery,* which comes from Latin *saturēia*]

saw¹ (sô), *n.* **1.** a tool for cutting that consists chiefly of a thin metal blade edged with sharp teeth. —*v.,* **sawed; sawed or sawn** (sôn); **saw·ing. 2.** to cut or shape with a saw or anything resembling or used like a saw. **3.** to make back-and-forth motions like those of a saw: *He*

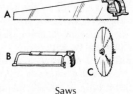

Saws
A, Handsaw; B, Hacksaw; C, Circular saw

sawed the air with his hands as he talked. [from the Old English word *saga,* which is related to Latin *secāre* "to cut"]

saw² (sô), *n.* a saying or proverb, esp. one that is old and too often repeated: *As the old saw goes, "Haste makes waste."* [from the Old English word *sagu,* which is related to English *say*]

saw³ (sô), *v.* the past tense of **see¹.**

saw·dust (sô/dust/), *n.* fine particles of wood made by the action of a saw in cutting.

saw·fish (sô/fish/), *n., pl.* **saw·fish·es** *or* **saw·fish.** a large fish found along tropical coasts and lowland rivers, with a bladelike snout having strong teeth on each side.

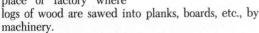
Sawfish
(length to 20 ft.)

saw·horse (sô/hôrs/), *n.* a frame for holding wood while it is being sawed.

saw·mill (sô/mil/), *n.* a place or factory where logs of wood are sawed into planks, boards, etc., by machinery.

sawn (sôn), *v.* a past participle of **saw¹.**

saw·yer (sô/yər), *n.* a person whose occupation is sawing wood.

sax·i·frage (sak/sə frij), *n.* any of various herbs that grow among rocks and bear white, pink, yellow, or purple flowers.

Sax·on (sak/sən), *n.* **1.** a member of a Germanic people, some of whom invaded and occupied parts of Britain in the 5th and 6th centuries A.D. **2.** the Germanic language of the Saxons on the European continent. **3.** the Old English dialects of the regions of Britain settled by the Saxons. **4.** a native or inhabitant of Saxony. —*adj.* **5.** of or concerning the Saxons or their language. **6.** of or referring to Saxony.

Sax·o·ny (sak/sə nē), *n.* a region in S East Germany.

sax·o·phone (sak/sə fōn/), *n.* a musical wind instrument consisting of a wide, curved, conical tube, usually made of brass, having keys for the fingers and a single-reed mouthpiece resembling that of the clarinet. —**sax/o·phon/ist,** *n.*

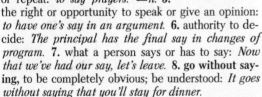
Saxophone

say (sā), *v.,* **said** (sed), **say·ing. 1.** to express in words with the voice; speak: *He says, "Leave at once."* **2.** to express in words, esp. in writing; state: *Jack said in his letter that he would visit us.* **3.** to state as an opinion: *The doctors cannot say if he will recover.* **4.** to recite or repeat: *to say prayers.* —*n.* **5.** the right or opportunity to speak or give an opinion: *to have one's say in an argument.* **6.** authority to decide: *The principal has the final say in changes of program.* **7.** what a person says or has to say: *Now that we've had our say, let's leave.* **8. go without saying,** to be completely obvious; be understood: *It goes without saying that you'll stay for dinner.*

say·ing (sā/ing), *n.* something said, esp. a proverb or familiar expression: *Remember the old saying, "A stitch in time saves nine."*

says (sez), *v.* the third person singular, present tense of **say:** *He says that we should not go.*

Sb, *Chem.* the symbol for **antimony.** [from the Latin word *stibium*]

Sc, *Chem.* the symbol for **scandium.**

S.C., 1. Security Council (of the UN). **2.** Signal Corps. **3.** South Carolina. **4.** Supreme Court.

scab (skab), *n.* **1.** the crust that forms over a sore or wound during healing. **2.** a worker who refuses to join in a labor strike or who takes the place of a worker on strike. —*v.,* **scabbed, scab·bing. 3.** to become covered with a scab. **4.** to act or work as a scab. —**scab/by,** *adj.*

scab·bard (skab/ərd), *n.* a covering or case for the blade of a sword, dagger, etc.; sheath. See illus. at **stiletto.**

sca·bies (skā/bēz, skā/bē ēz/), *n. (used as sing.)* a contagious skin disease of sheep, cattle, and man, caused by tiny insects that burrow beneath the skin, producing severe itching.

scaf·fold (skaf/əld, skaf/ōld), *n.* **1.** a temporary framework for supporting workmen and materials during construction or repair work on a building, monument, or other structure. **2.** a raised platform on which executions, esp. by hanging, are carried out. **3.** any raised framework.

scaf·fold·ing (skaf/əl ding, skaf/ōl ding), *n.* **1.** a scaffold or a framework of scaffolds. **2.** materials for scaffolds.

scald (skôld), *v.* **1.** to burn with hot liquid or steam. **2.** to plunge or cook lightly in a boiling liquid. **3.** to heat almost to the boiling point: *to scald milk.* —*n.* **4.** a burn caused by hot liquid or steam.

scale¹ (skāl), *n.* **1.** one of the thin, flat plates that cover the body of certain animals, such as snakes, lizards, and fishes. **2.** any thin, loose flake: *a scale of paint.* **3.** a hard coating or crust that forms on a surface, for example by the gradual deposit of minerals dissolved in water: *boiler scale.* —*v.,* **scaled, scal·ing. 4.** to remove the scale or scales from: *to scale a fish.* **5.** to come off in flakes or scales: *The paint is scaling from the wall.* [from an early French word *escale,* which comes from Germanic]

scale² (skāl), *n.* **1.** Often, **scales.** a device for weighing. **2. the Scales,** another name for **Libra.** —*v.,* **scaled, scal·ing. 3.** to have a weight of: *My catfish scaled seven pounds.* **4. tip the scales, a.** to weigh: *He tips the scales at 150 pounds.* **b.** to turn the trend of favor, power, etc.: *The recent trouble should tip the scales in favor of our candidate.* [from a Middle English word, which comes from Scandinavian]

scale³ (skāl), *n.* **1.** a series of marks used for measuring: *the scale of a thermometer.* **2.** an instrument, such as a ruler or a protractor, bearing such marks. **3.** the relative size of the representation of something compared to the thing itself: *The scale of a plan may*

act, āble, dâre, ärt; ebb, ēqual; if, īce; hot, ōver, ôrder; oil; bŏŏk; ōōze; out; up, ûrge; ə = *a* as in *alone;* ³ as in *button* (but/³n), fire (fi³r); chief; shoe; thin; ŧħat; zh as in *measure* (mezh/ər). See full key inside cover.

be as large as 1 inch to 1 foot, or 1:12. **4.** a graphic representation of this proportion, such as that shown on a map. **5.** a system of numbering: *the decimal scale.* **6.** (in music) a succession of tones either going up or going down. **7.** a particular succession of tones within an octave; key: *the scale of C.* **8.** an arrangement of things in order of size, amount, number, importance, rank, etc.: *the scale of wages in industry.* —*v.,* **scaled, scal·ing. 9.** to climb up or over: *to scale a fence.* **10.** to make or set according to a scale: *to scale expenses to income.* **11.** to increase or reduce by a certain amount (usually fol. by *up* or *down*): *After bargaining, the union scaled down its demands.* [from the Latin word *scālae* "ladder, stairs"]

sca·lene (skā lēn′), *adj.* (of a triangle) having no equal sides.

scal·lion (skal′yən), *n.* a young onion, or any onion of a kind that does not form a large bulb.

scal·lop (skol′əp, skal′əp), *n.* **1.** any of several nearly round, flat shellfish that swim by clapping their shells together. Their flesh is used as food. **2.** one of a series of rounded curves cut for decoration along the edge of cloth, lace, paper, etc. —*v.* **3.** to cut scallops along the edge of (cloth, lace, paper, etc.). **4.** to bake (food) in a sauce, usually containing milk or cream, with bread crumbs spread over the top.

Scallop
(width to 3 in.)

scalp (skalp), *n.* **1.** the skin and flesh on the top and back of the head, usually covered with hair. —*v.* **2.** to cut or tear the scalp from (a person).

scal·pel (skal′pəl), *n.* a small, light, very sharp knife used in surgery, dissection, etc.

scal·y (skā′lē), *adj.,* **scal·i·er, scal·i·est. 1.** covered with or full of scales: *a scaly fish.* **2.** peeling or flaking off in scales: *a scaly wall.* **3.** resembling a scale or scales: *scaly skin.* —**scal′i·ness,** *n.*

scamp[1] (skamp), *n.* **1.** a worthless person; rogue. **2.** a mischievous, playful person, esp. a child; rascal. [probably from the Old French word *escamper* "to flee, decamp"]

scamp[2] (skamp), *v.* to do (something) in a hasty or careless manner. [perhaps from a Scandinavian word, such as Old Norse *skemma* "to shorten," related to *skammr* "short"]

scamp·er (skam′pər), *v.* **1.** to run or go hastily. **2.** to run about playfully; frolic: *The children scampered about the playground.* —*n.* **3.** a quick run. **4.** a running about playfully; frolic.

scan (skan), *v.,* **scanned, scan·ning. 1.** to examine closely; scrutinize: *She scanned the want ads for weeks looking for a job.* **2.** to glance at or read hastily: *I had only enough time to scan the headlines.* **3.** to find or show the metrical structure of (lines of verse): *The following line is scanned in this way: Twin′kle,/ twin′kle,/ lit′tle/ star′./*

scan·dal (skan′dəl), *n.* **1.** a disgraceful action, occurrence, or situation. **2.** public disgrace or disapproval brought on by such an action, occurrence, or situation: *The arrest of the spies created a scandal in the*

newspapers. **3.** malicious gossip: *She goes all over town spreading scandal about her friends.*

scan·dal·ize (skan′dᵊlīz′), *v.,* **scan·dal·ized, scan·dal·iz·ing.** to shock or horrify by disgraceful conduct.

scan·dal·mon·ger (skan′dᵊl muñ′gər, -moñ′gər), *n.* a person who spreads scandal.

scan·dal·ous (skan′dᵊləs), *adj.* **1.** causing disgrace or offense; shameful: *It was a scandalous costume, even to wear at the beach.* **2.** damaging to the reputation of someone; slanderous: *a scandalous story.*

Scan·di·na·vi·a (skan′də nā′vē ə), *n.* **1.** the countries of Norway, Sweden, Denmark, and sometimes Finland and Iceland. **2.** Also, **Scandina′vian Penin′sula.** the peninsula consisting of Norway and Sweden.

Scan·di·na·vi·an (skan′də nā′vē ən), *n.* **1.** a native or inhabitant of Scandinavia. **2.** any of the Germanic languages of Scandinavia, including Danish, Swedish, Norwegian, Icelandic, and Old Norse. —*adj.* **3.** of or concerning Scandinavia, its inhabitants, or their languages.

scan·di·um (skan′dē əm), *n. Chem.* a rare metallic element. *Symbol:* Sc

scant (skant), *adj.* **1.** barely enough in amount or quantity: *a scant supply of food.* **2.** not full; not complete: *a scant teaspoonful.* **3.** having barely enough (usually fol. by *of*): *to be scant of breath.* —*v.* **4.** to limit the supply of; skimp on: *They had to scant the food in order to meet other expenses.*

scant·y (skan′tē), *adj.,* **scant·i·er, scant·i·est.** not enough or barely enough in amount or quantity: *a scanty meal.* —**scant′i·ly,** *adv.* —**scant′i·ness,** *n.*

scape·goat (skāp′gōt′), *n.* a person, group, or thing made to bear the blame for others or to suffer in their place.

scap·u·la (skap′yə lə), *n., pl.* **scap·u·las** or **scap·u·lae** (skap′yə lē′). the scientific name for **shoulder blade.**

scar (skär), *n.* **1.** the mark that is left on the skin after a wound, sore, or burn has healed. **2.** a mark made on a surface by scratching or scraping: *an old desk full of scars.* **3.** a permanent effect on a person's mind, character, or countenance, made by some painful experience: *the scars of defeat.* —*v.,* **scarred, scar·ring. 4.** to produce or leave a scar on: *The lash scarred his back.* **5.** to heal leaving a scar: *The cut on your cheek will heal, though it may scar.* —**scar′like′,** *adj.*

scar·ab (skar′əb), *n.* **1.** any of several large, dark-shelled beetles, esp. one that was sacred to ancient Egyptians. **2.** a representation of this beetle used by the ancient Egyptians as a seal, charm, or the like.

scarce (skârs), *adj.,* **scarc·er, scarc·est. 1.** not enough to meet the need or demand; hard to obtain: *Sugar and meat were scarce during the war.* **2.** found in very small quantity or amount; rare: *Uranium is a scarce metal.* **3. make oneself scarce,** *Informal.* to leave, stay away, etc.: *I want you to make yourself scarce when company comes.* —**scarce′ness,** *n.*

Scarab
(def. 2)

scarce·ly (skârs′lē), *adv.* **1.** barely; hardly: *I could* *scarcely see its shape in the dim light.* **2.** definitely not: *This is scarcely the time for arguments.*

scar·ci·ty (skâr′si tē), *n., pl.* **scar·ci·ties. 1.** insufficient supply; lack: *There was a scarcity of fuel when the truck drivers were on strike.* **2.** infrequency of occurrence; rarity: *Diamonds are valuable because of their scarcity.*

scare (skâr), *v.,* **scared, scar·ing. 1.** to fill with fear; frighten. **2.** to become frightened: *They can threaten me, but I don't scare easily.* —*n.* **3.** a sudden fright or alarm. **4. scare up,** *Informal.* to find or obtain: *See if you can scare up a screwdriver, will you?*

scare·crow (skâr′krō′), *n.* **1.** a figure resembling a man, dressed in ragged clothes, usually set up in a field of growing crops to frighten away birds and animals. **2.** a thin, ragged person.

scarf (skärf), *n., pl.* **scarfs** *or* **scarves** (skärvz). **1.** a long, broad strip of cloth worn esp. by women as a covering for the head, neck, or shoulders. **2.** a long cover or ornamental cloth for a table, dresser, etc.

scar·let (skär′lit), *n.* **1.** a bright red tinged with orange. **2.** cloth or clothing of this color. —*adj.* **3.** of the color scarlet.

scar′let fe′ver, a contagious disease that causes a fever and a bright-red rash on the skin.

scar·y (skâr′ē), *adj.,* **scar·i·er, scar·i·est.** *Informal.* **1.** causing fright or alarm: *a scary ghost story.* **2.** easily frightened; timid. —**scar′i·ly,** *adv.* —**scar′i·ness,** *n.*

scat (skat), *v.,* **scat·ted, scat·ting.** *Informal.* **1.** to go away quickly: *We had to scat when the rain started coming through the roof.* **2.** (used as an imperative to drive away a person or animal, esp. a cat.)

scath·ing (skā′t͟hing), *adj.* bitterly severe: *scathing criticism.* —**scath′ing·ly,** *adv.*

scat·ter (skat′ər), *v.* **1.** to throw or spread loosely over a wide area: *to scatter seeds.* **2.** to send in different directions: *The wind scatters the leaves.* **3.** to go off in different directions: *The crowd scattered at the end of the game.* —*n.* **4.** the action or result of scattering: *the scatter of bullets on the target.* **5.** a scattering or sprinkling: *We met with only a scatter of fire from the enemy.*

scat·ter·brain (skat′ər brān′), *n.* a flighty or frivolous person; one who does not or cannot think in a serious, orderly manner. —**scat′ter·brained′,** *adj.*

scat·ter·ing (skat′ər ing), *n.* **1.** a small number or quantity, loosely distributed through an area or a larger group: *The audience was mostly children, with a scattering of adults.* —*adj.* **2.** occurring or coming at irregular intervals: *Scattering frost hit the crops in early October.*

scat′ter rug′, a small rug, placed under a table, in front of a chair, etc.

scav·en·ger (skav′in jər), *n.* **1.** any animal, such as a vulture or crab, that feeds on dead or decaying matter. **2.** a person or animal that searches through refuse for usable articles.

sce·nar·i·o (si nâr′ē ō′, si när′ē ō′), *n., pl.* **sce·nar·i·os. 1.** an outline of a play, containing directions about

the scenes, characters, situations, etc. **2.** a script of a motion picture, giving directions for the filming of the scenes and the order in which they are to be filmed; screenplay.

scene (sēn), *n.* **1.** the place where some action or event takes place: *the scene of the accident.* **2.** an arrangement of things seen by the eye as a picture; view; sight. **3.** an incident or situation, esp. an embarrassing or disgraceful one: *Don't make a scene by arguing in public.* **4.** the setting of a story or play: *The scene of the opera is ancient Egypt.* **5.** a division of a play, film, novel, etc., that represents a single episode or incident. **6.** the scenery or a part of the scenery of a play or motion picture.

scen·er·y (sē′nə rē), *n., pl.* **scen·er·ies. 1.** a grouping or arrangement of things in a large view, esp. of a natural setting; landscape. **2.** equipment, such as painted backdrops, platforms, frames, etc., used as a setting for a play or motion picture.

sce·nic (sē′nik), *adj.* **1.** of or concerned with natural scenery: *the scenic attractions of the Alps.* **2.** having pleasing or beautiful scenery: *the scenic lake region.* **3.** of or concerning the stage or motion pictures or the scenery for them: *a scenic production of a novel.*

scent (sent), *n.* **1.** a particular smell, esp. an agreeable one: *the scent of roses.* **2.** an odor left by the passing of a person or animal, by which it can be traced: *The hounds picked up the scent of the fox.* **3.** a trail or trace of any kind: *The customs agents are on the scent of the smugglers.* **4.** a perfume. —*v.* **5.** to smell: *The dog scented a rabbit.* **6.** to get a hint of: *to scent trouble.* **7.** to fill with an odor; perfume: *Roses scented the room.*

scep·ter (sep′tər), *n.* a rod or wand carried or held in the hand by a monarch as an emblem of power. Also, *esp. British,* **scep′tre.**

scep·tic (skep′tik), *n.* another spelling of **skeptic.**

scep·ti·cal (skep′ti kəl), *adj.* another spelling of **skeptical.** —**scep′ti·cal·ly,** *adv.*

scep·ti·cism (skep′ti siz′əm), *n.* another spelling of **skepticism.**

sched·ule (skej′ool, skej′oo əl), *n.* **1.** a list of things to be done or to take place, usually arranged in order of time: *a schedule of football games.* **2.** the time at which something is expected to occur: *The plane reached Paris on schedule.* **3.** a timetable: *a train schedule.* **4.** a list or table of details concerning prices, rates, etc.: *a tax schedule.* —*v.,* **sched·uled, sched·ul·ing. 5.** to arrange in a schedule: *to schedule the lessons of a course.* **6.** to enter in a schedule: *The nurse scheduled my appointment for tomorrow.*

scheme (skēm), *n.* **1.** a plan, design, or program of action to be followed: *a scheme for a new trade center.* **2.** a secret plan, esp. a treacherous one; plot. **3.** a system or arrangement of things: *a scheme of highways.* —*v.,* **schemed, schem·ing. 4.** to devise or put into operation secret or dishonest plans; plot: *to scheme to cheat the taxpayers.* —**schem′er,** *n.*

schem·ing (skē′ming), *adj.* making or carrying out

schemes; crafty: *a scheming politician.* —**schem′ing·ly**, *adv.*

schism (siz′əm), *n.* a division or split into opposing parties or factions brought about by disagreement, esp. among religious groups.

schis·mat·ic (siz mat′ik), *adj.* 1. of, concerned with, or causing schism. —*n.* 2. a person who plans or takes part in a schism.

Schles·wig-Hol·stein (shles′wig hōl′stīn), *n.* two duchies in S Denmark that were annexed by Prussia in the 19th century.

schnau·zer (shnou′zər), *n.* one of a German breed of dogs having a wiry, pepper-and-salt, black, or black-and-tan coat.

schol·ar (skol′ər), *n.* 1. a learned person; one who has devoted much time to study and learning. 2. a person who is preparing himself by study; student; pupil. 3. a student who receives money or other assistance, esp. if earned by outstanding achievement.

Schnauzer
(19 in. high
at shoulder)

schol·ar·ly (skol′ər lē), *adj.* 1. of, like, or suitable for a scholar: *a scholarly appearance.* 2. making or showing effort worthy of a scholar: *a scholarly article.* —*adv.* 3. carefully and thoroughly, in the manner of a scholar.

schol·ar·ship (skol′ər ship), *n.* 1. knowledge gained by study: *The professor is a man of great scholarship.* 2. care and thoroughness in study or work. 3. the quality of a student's work. 4. a grant of money or other assistance given to a worthy student to enable him to continue his studies.

scho·las·tic (skə las′tik), *adj.* of or referring to schools, scholars, teachers, or education: *a scholastic year; scholastic honors.* —**scho·las′ti·cal·ly**, *adv.*

school[1] (skōōl), *n.* 1. a place for teaching and learning. 2. the activities of teaching and learning: *We have no school tomorrow.* 3. a division of a college or university: *business school.* 4. the entire group of persons who study or teach in a particular place: *The whole school came out to see the game.* 5. a group of persons who have similar beliefs or opinions: *My parents are of the conservative school.* 6. a group of artists, writers, scholars, etc., who follow a particular master or leader, or who have similar work, beliefs, and methods: *the impressionist school.* —*adj.* 7. of or belonging to a school or schools: *a school year; a school text.* —*v.* 8. to teach or train: *He was schooled in Germany.* [from the Old English word *scōl,* which comes from Latin *schola,* from Greek *scholē* "leisure used for learning"]

school[2] (skōōl), *n.* 1. a large number of fish or other marine animals that stay together: *a school of herring.* —*v.* 2. to stay together in a school (of fish or other marine life). [from the Dutch word *school* "troop"]

school·book (skōōl′bŏŏk′), *n.* a book used by students in studies at school; textbook.

school·boy (skōōl′boi′), *n.* a boy attending school.

school·girl (skōōl′gûrl′), *n.* a girl attending school.

school·house (skōōl′hous′), *n., pl.* **school·hous·es** (skōōl′hou′ziz). a building where school is held.

school·ing (skōōl′ling), *n.* training or instruction, esp. in a school; education.

school·mas·ter (skōōl′mas′tər), *n.* 1. a man who teaches in a school. 2. a male principal or head of a school.

school·mate (skōōl′māt′), *n.* a companion at school.

school·room (skōōl′room′, -rŏŏm′), *n.* a room in which instruction is carried on; classroom.

school·teach·er (skōōl′tē′chər), *n.* a teacher in a school, esp. a grade school or high school.

school·work (skōōl′wûrk′), *n.* the work done by a student, including work in class and homework: *Finish your schoolwork before watching TV.*

school·yard (skōōl′yärd′), *n.* the yard or playground of a school.

schoon·er (skōō′nər), *n.* 1. a kind of sailing vessel having two or more masts and fore-and-aft sails. 2. *Informal.* a large glass used for beer.

Fishing schooner

Schu·bert (shōō′bərt), *n.* Franz (franz), 1797–1828, Austrian composer.

schwa (shwä), *n.* 1. an indistinct vowel sound heard in many unstressed syllables of English, such as the sound of *a* in *about* or *sofa.* 2. a phonetic symbol (ə) for this sound.

sci·at·i·ca (sī at′i kə), *n.* a pain in the hip and the back of the thigh, sometimes caused by inflammation of the sciatic nerve.

sci·at′ic nerve′ (sī at′ik), a large nerve that runs down the back of the leg, dividing into two branches above the knee and extending down to the foot.

sci·ence (sī′əns), *n.* 1. study or knowledge dealing with a group of facts arranged in an orderly fashion and showing how general laws apply to these facts. 2. any branch of this type of knowledge or study, such as biology, chemistry, physics, or psychology.

sci·en·tif·ic (sī′ən tif′ik), *adj.* 1. of, concerning, produced by, or used in science or the sciences. 2. following the principles or methods of an exact science. —**sci′en·tif′i·cal·ly,** *adv.*

sci·en·tist (sī′ən tist), *n.* a person who specializes in one of the sciences.

scim·i·tar (sim′i tər), *n.* a curved, single-edged sword used chiefly by Turks, Arabs, and Persians.

scin·til·la (sin til′ə), *n.* 1. a spark. 2. a small particle or bit: *There's not a scintilla of evidence.*

A, Scimitar; B, Scabbard

scin·til·late (sin′t[ə]lāt′), *v.,* **scin·til·lat·ed, scin·til·lat·ing.** 1. to give off sparks. 2. to sparkle with interest or enthusiasm. 3. to twinkle, as stars. —**scin′til·la′tion,** *n.*

sci·on (sī′ən), *n.* 1. a shoot, sprout, bud, or twig that is grafted onto another plant. 2. a descendant or offspring.

scis·sors (siz′ərz), *n.pl.* a cutting instrument for paper, cloth, etc., made of two blades fastened together at a point near the handles, so that moving the handles causes the blades to cut by sliding against each other.

scoff (skôf, skof), *v.* **1.** to speak or write scornfully; mock; jeer (often fol. by *at*): *People used to scoff at the idea of space travel.* —*n.* **2.** a scornful expression or remark; jeer. **3.** a person or thing that is ridiculed. —**scoff′er,** *n.*

scold (skōld), *v.* **1.** to criticize or blame angrily; rebuke; reprimand: *The teacher scolded him for not doing his homework.* **2.** to find fault; complain angrily: *You annoy people by scolding all the time.* —*n.* **3.** a person, esp. a woman, who constantly finds fault or complains. —**scold′er,** *n.* —**scold′ing·ly,** *adv.*

sconce (skons), *n.* an ornamental bracket, fastened to a wall, mirror, etc., for holding candles or other lights.

scone (skōn, skon), *n.* a flat, round cake or biscuit, made of a batter containing flour or meal, baked on a griddle.

scoop (skōōp), *n.* **1.** any of various utensils having a deep, rounded or oval container and a short handle, used for picking up or loading loose materials such as flour, sugar, coal, etc. **2.** the bucket of a dredge, steam shovel, etc. **3.** a hollow, rounded cup attached to a handle used for forming or serving balls of a soft material, such as ice cream, potatoes, melon, etc. **4.** the amount that a scoop can hold. **5.** the act of picking up or gathering with a scoop or something like a scoop, such as the arms or hands: *He cleared the table in one scoop.* **6.** a news item first made public in one newspaper, magazine, etc. —*v.* **7.** to pick up or take out with a scoop or something like a scoop: *to scoop ice cream.* **8.** to hollow or dig out.

scoot (skōōt), *Informal.* —*v.* **1.** to go or run swiftly; dart: *Everyone scooted out of the room at the bell.* —*n.* **2.** the act of scooting or darting.

scoot·er (skōō′tər), *n.* **1.** a child's vehicle made of a metal or wooden board supported between two wheels, one in front and one in back, and steered with an upright handlebar. **2.** a motor scooter.

scope (skōp), *n.* **1.** the range or extent of one's understanding: *Such questions are beyond the scope of young children.* **2.** the area or extent covered by or included in something: *an investigation of wide scope.* **3.** opportunity or freedom for movement or action: *to give one's imagination full scope.*

-scope, a suffix used to form nouns meaning an instrument for viewing: *telescope.*

scorch (skôrch), *v.* **1.** to burn slightly or on the surface: *to scorch one's fingers.* **2.** to shrivel or dry up with heat; parch. —*n.* **3.** a slight burn.

score (skôr), *n., pl.* **scores** *or* for def. 5 **score. 1.** the number of points, or the record of them, made in a game or contest, or by any team or individual taking part in it. **2.** the act of making a point or points by a team or individual: *The fumble resulted in a score by the other side.* **3.** a grade received in a test or examination. **4.** a notch or scratch: *The table top was covered with deep scores.* **5.** a group or set of 20: *A score of children were running about the yard.* **6.** an amount owed; account; debt. **7.** *Informal.* the facts of a situation: *If I know what the score is, I may be able to help.* **8.** a written or printed piece of music containing all the separate parts or voices that are to be sung or played in performing a composition. **9.** the music for a play, motion picture, etc. —*v.,* **scored, scor·ing. 10.** to make (a point or points) in a game or contest: *Our team scored two runs.* **11.** to make (a certain score): *I scored 95 on the test.* **12.** to find, keep, or record the score of: *to score a test.* **13.** to make notches or scratches in: *The cardboard is scored for easy folding.* **14.** to win or achieve (success, approval, etc.): *to score a triumph.* **15.** to orchestrate: *to score a piano piece.* **16. settle a score,** to get revenge; retaliate: *In the old West they settled a score with bullets.* —**scor′er,** *n.*

scorn (skôrn), *n.* **1.** a feeling that a person has toward anyone or anything considered mean or worthless; contempt: *I have nothing but scorn for a coward.* **2.** a person or thing that is the object of scorn or contempt. —*v.* **3.** to look down on; despise: *An honest official scorns corruption.* **4.** to refuse or reject with contempt.

scorn·ful (skôrn′fəl), *adj.* feeling or expressing scorn; contemptuous. —**scorn′ful·ly,** *adv.*

Scor·pi·o (skôr′pē ō′), *n.* **1.** the Scorpion: a constellation and a sign of the zodiac. **2.** another name for **Scorpius.**

scor·pi·on (skôr′pē ən), *n.* **1.** an animal, related to the spiders, that looks like a tiny lobster and has a poisonous sting at the end of its tail. **2. the Scorpion, a.** See **Scorpio** (def. 1). **b.** another name for **Scorpius.**

Scorpion
(length
to 3 in.)

Scor·pi·us (skôr′pē əs), *n.* the Scorpion: a constellation. Also, **Scorpio.**

Scot (skot), *n.* a native or inhabitant of Scotland; Scotsman.

scotch (skoch), *v.* **1.** to put an end to; crush; stamp out: *to scotch a rumor.* **2.** to make harmless by injuring or wounding slightly: *to scotch a snake.* **3.** to cut, gash, or score: *to scotch an automobile tire.*

Scotch (skoch), *adj.* **1.** of or concerning Scotland, its inhabitants, or the Scottish dialect. —*n.* **2.** the people of Scotland. **3.** the Scottish dialect. **4.** Also, **Scotch′ whis′ky.** a whiskey distilled in Scotland, esp. from malted barley.

Scotch·man (skoch′mən), *n., pl.* **Scotch·men.** a Scot or Scotsman.

scot-free (skot′frē′), *adj.* free from harm or punishment; safe: *At the trial, he got off scot-free.* [from the earlier word *scot* "payment, tax." The original meaning was "exempt from payment of tax"]

Scot·land (skot′lənd), *n.* a division of the United Kingdom in the N part of Great Britain. 29,796 sq. mi. *Cap.:* Edinburgh.

Scot′land Yard′, 1. headquarters of the London police. 2. the metropolitan police of London, esp. the criminal investigation division.

Scots (skots), *n.* 1. the Scottish dialect. —*adj.* 2. Scotch or Scottish.

Scots′ Gael′ic, the Gaelic dialects spoken in some parts of Scotland.

Scots·man (skots′mən), *n., pl.* **Scots·men.** a native or inhabitant of Scotland; Scot; Scotchman.

Scott (skot), *n.* **Sir Walter,** 1771–1832, Scottish novelist and poet.

Scot·tie (skot′ē), *n.* another name for **Scottish terrier.**

Scot·tish (skot′ish), *adj.* 1. of or concerning Scotland, its people, or the dialect of English spoken there. —*n.* 2. the people of Scotland. 3. the dialect of English spoken in Scotland.

Scot′tish ter′rier, a small terrier having a large head, short legs, and a black, wiry coat, originally bred in Scotland. Also, **Scottie.**

scoun·drel (skoun′drəl), *n.* a mean or dishonorable person; rogue; villain.

scour¹ (skour), *v.* 1. to clean or polish by rubbing, esp. with something hard or rough. 2. to remove (dirt, grease, etc.) from something by rubbing. 3. to clean or dig out by rubbing, esp. by the force of flowing water: *The swollen stream scoured a ravine through the valley.* —*n.* 4. the act of scouring. [from the Middle English word *scouren,* which comes from a Scandinavian word meaning "to rub"]

Scottish terrier
(10 in. high
at shoulder)

scour² (skour), *v.* to range over or through, esp. in searching: *They scoured the woods for the missing children.* [from the Middle English word *scouren,* which comes perhaps from a Scandinavian word meaning "storm, tumult"]

scourge (skûrj), *n.* 1. a whip or lash. 2. a person or thing that causes misery or destruction: *Malaria is the scourge of the tropics.* —*v.,* **scourged, scourg·ing.** 3. to whip with a scourge; lash. 4. to punish or criticize severely.

scout (skout), *n.* 1. a soldier, warship, airplane, etc., that is sent out to observe the position and movements of an enemy. 2. a person sent out to obtain information. 3. a person employed to discover new talent, esp. in sports or entertainment. 4. a member of the Boy Scouts or Girl Scouts. 5. *Informal.* a person, esp. with respect to his or her character: *a good scout.* —*v.* 6. to act as a scout. 7. to examine or observe for the purpose of obtaining information: *to scout the terrain.* 8. *Informal.* to search for (usually fol. by *out* or *up*): *to scout out some firewood.*

scout·ing (skou′ting), *n.* the activities of a scout or scouts.

scout·mas·ter (skout′mas′tər), *n.* the adult leader of a troop of Boy Scouts.

scow (skou), *n.* a large boat with square ends and a flat bottom, used esp. for carrying loads of loose material, such as coal, sand, or gravel.

scowl (skoul), *v.* 1. to draw down or contract the brows in expressing anger or displeasure; frown: *He scowled when he was given the order.* —*n.* 2. a look of anger or displeasure; frown.

scrab·ble (skrab′əl), *v.,* **scrab·bled, scrab·bling.** 1. to scratch or scrape with claws or hands. 2. to grapple or struggle, esp. with the claws or hands. 3. to struggle for possession of something in a disorderly way; scramble: *The children scrabbled for the coins tossed from the windows.* 4. to scrawl or scribble. —*n.* 5. a scratching or scraping with claws or hands. 6. a scrawled or scribbled writing. 7. a disorderly struggle for possession of something; scramble.

scrag·gly (skrag′lē), *adj.,* **scrag·gli·er, scrag·gli·est.** 1. uneven or irregular; jagged: *a scraggly column of recruits.* 2. ragged or shaggy: *a scraggly mustache.*

scrag·gy (skrag′ē), *adj.,* **scrag·gi·er, scrag·gi·est.** 1. lean or thin; scrawny. 2. uneven; rough; jagged. —**scrag′gi·ness,** *n.*

scram·ble (skram′bəl), *v.,* **scram·bled, scram·bling.** 1. to climb, crawl, etc., in a hasty, confused way: *We scrambled down from the roof when the storm broke.* 2. to compete or struggle with other persons to gain something or reach a goal: *A dozen players scrambled for the ball.* 3. to fry (eggs), mixing whites and yolks together. 4. to mix together in a confused way; jumble: *The book split apart, and the pages became scrambled.* —*n.* 5. a hasty, confused crawl, climb, etc. 6. a confused struggle or competition: *There was a scramble for the exits when the bell rang.*

Scran·ton (skran′t³n), *n.* a city in NE Pennsylvania.

scrap¹ (skrap), *n.* 1. a small piece; fragment: *a scrap of cloth.* 2. **scraps,** bits of leftover food. 3. worn or discarded material that can be used over again; junk: *Old cars are melted down for scrap.* —*adj.* 4. made up of scrap or scraps: *scrap paper.* 5. collected to be used over again: *scrap metal.* —*v.,* **scrapped, scrap·ping.** 6. to make into scrap; break up. 7. to discard or reject as useless or worthless: *to scrap a project.* [from the Middle English word *scrappe,* which comes from Scandinavian]

scrap² (skrap), *Informal.* —*n.* 1. a fight or quarrel. —*v.,* **scrapped, scrap·ping.** 2. to fight or quarrel. [another form of the word *scrape*] —**scrap′per,** *n.*

scrap·book (skrap′book′), *n.* a large blank book or folder in which pictures, clippings, etc., are pasted.

scrape (skrāp), *v.,* **scraped, scrap·ing.** 1. to rub (something) with a rough or sharp tool or object to smooth or clean it: *to scrape walls.* 2. to remove by scraping: *to scrape loose paint from the walls.* 3. to injure or damage by rubbing against something rough or sharp: *I fell and scraped my knee on the sidewalk.* 4. to collect or gather with difficulty (usually fol. by *up* or *together*): *The boys finally scraped up enough pennies to buy a football.* 5. to rub roughly on or across (something), often with a grating sound: *The old fiddler scraped his bow across the strings.* 6. to observe strict economy: *We have to scrape to meet* *our expenses.* —*n.* **7.** the act of scraping. **8.** a mark made by scraping, rubbing, or scratching: *a bad scrape along the side of the fender.* **9.** a grating sound made by scraping: *the scrape of wheels on the rails.* **10.** a difficult or embarrassing situation; predicament: *His reckless driving got him into a scrape with the law.* **11. scrape through,** to finish or complete (something) with difficulty: *She scraped through school with very poor grades.*

scrap·er (skrā′pər), *n.* **1.** a person or thing that scrapes. **2.** any of various tools or utensils used for scraping.

scrap·py (skrap′ē), *adj.,* **scrap·pi·er, scrap·pi·est.** *Informal.* fond of fighting or competing: *a scrappy boxer.* —**scrap′pi·ness,** *n.*

scratch (skrach), *v.* **1.** to mark or damage the surface of by rubbing or scraping with something sharp or rough: *to scratch one's hand on a nail.* **2.** to rub or scrape slightly, esp. with the fingernails, to relieve itching: *to scratch a sore spot.* **3.** to scrape, tear, or dig with the nails or claws: *The cat scratched a hole in my shirt.* **4.** to rub or draw along a rough surface: *to scratch a match.* **5.** to cancel or strike out, esp. by drawing a line through (often fol. by *out*). **6.** to withdraw (a horse, candidate, contestant, etc.) from competition. **7.** to write or draw by scratching: *to scratch one's initials in wood.* —*n.* **8.** an act of scratching. **9.** a mark left by scratching. **10.** a slight flesh wound. **11.** the sound of scratching. —*adj.* **12.** used for making quick notes, sketches, etc.: *a scratch pad.* **13.** *Informal.* gathered together hastily: *a scratch team.* **14. from scratch,** from the beginning or starting point: *If this doesn't work, we'll have to start again from scratch.* **15. up to scratch,** up to a certain standard; adequate; satisfactory: *The band sounds better, but it's still not up to scratch.*

scratch·y (skrach′ē), *adj.,* **scratch·i·er, scratch·i·est. 1.** making a scraping or grating sound: *a scratchy pen.* **2.** causing irritation or itching: *a scratchy sweater.* **3.** having the appearance of scratches: *a scratchy drawing.* —**scratch′i·ness,** *n.*

scrawl (skrôl), *v.* **1.** to write or draw in a hasty, awkward manner: *They scrawled their names on the wall. He scrawled a map of the area.* —*n.* **2.** something scrawled, esp. handwriting: *I can't read his scrawl.* —**scrawl′er,** *n.* —**scrawl′y,** *adj.*

scrawn·y (skrô′nē), *adj.,* **scrawn·i·er, scrawn·i·est.** extremely lean or thin; skinny: *a long, scrawny neck.* —**scrawn′i·ness,** *n.*

scream (skrēm), *v.* **1.** to make a loud, shrill, piercing sound or cry. **2.** to say in a loud, piercing voice: *The paper boys screamed the news through the streets.* —*n.* **3.** a loud, shrill, piercing sound or cry. **4.** *Informal.* a very funny person or thing. —**scream′er,** *n.* —**scream′ing,** *adj., n.*

screech (skrēch), *v.* **1.** to make a harsh, shrill sound or cry: *The rusty gate screeched on its hinges.* **2.** to say in a harsh, shrill voice: *The crowd screeched its approval of his speech.* —*n.* **3.** a harsh, shrill sound

or cry: *the screech of a gull.* —**screech′er,** *n.* —**screech′y,** *adj.*

screech′ owl′, any of numerous small American owls having a harsh, screeching cry.

screen (skrēn), *n.* **1.** a framework made of covered folding panels or a thin fixed wall, used as a partition or for shelter or concealment. **2.** anything that provides shelter, concealment, protection, etc.: *a smoke screen; a protective screen of destroyers.* **3.** the reflecting surface onto which moving pictures are projected. **4.** the phosphorescent front surface of the picture tube in a television set, radar set, or oscilloscope. **5.** motion pictures, or the motion-picture industry. **6.** a net or

Screech owl (length 9 in.)

mesh of wire, cloth, plastic, etc., attached to a frame and placed in a window, door, etc., to let in air but keep out insects. **7.** a sieve or coarse wire mesh set in a frame, used for sifting grain, sand, gravel, etc. —*v.* **8.** to shelter, protect, or conceal with a screen or anything used like a screen. **9.** to examine (persons, things, ideas, etc.) in order to classify, select, or assign them: *The personnel department screens all applicants carefully.* **10.** to sift or sort into various sizes by passing through a screen. **11.** to project (a motion picture, slide, etc.) onto a screen.

screen·play (skrēn′plā′), *n.* **1.** the scenario of a motion picture: *an award for the year's best screenplay.* **2.** a story or play written to be produced as a motion picture.

screw (skrōō), *n.* **1.** a fastener that has a spiral ridge winding around it and is driven into wood, metal, etc., by turning its head with a screwdriver, wrench, or the like. **2.** a rod having a similar spiral ridge that fits into a threaded hole, used in clamps, vises, jacks, etc. **3.** a ship or airplane propeller. **4.** anything having a spiral form like that of

Screws

a screw. —*v.* **5.** to fasten or be fastened with a screw or screws: *You have to screw the parts of the table together. These hangers screw into the wall.* **6.** to adjust, loosen, or tighten by means of a screw. **7.** to turn or twist like a screw: *Screw the lid on tight.* **8.** to twist out of shape; contort: *He screwed up his face in disapproval.* **9.** to get or gather with an effort: *to screw a promise out of someone; to screw up courage.* **10. have a screw loose,** *Slang.* to be odd or peculiar; have crazy ideas: *They thought Columbus had a screw loose when he said the earth was round.* **11. put the screws on,** to put pressure on (someone) to do something; force: *They're putting the screws on me to take music lessons.*

screw·driv·er (skrōō′drī′vər), *n.* a tool for turning screws, having one end designed to fit the slotted head of a screw and a handle at the other end. Also, **screw′ driv′er.**

screw·y (skrōō′ē), *adj.,* **screw·i·er, screw·i·est.** *Slang.*

1. crazy; demented. 2. strange and puzzling: *There's something screwy about his story.*

scrib·ble (skrib′əl), *v.,* **scrib·bled, scrib·bling.** 1. to write or draw hastily or carelessly: *to scribble a note; to scribble a sketch.* —*n.* 2. hasty or careless drawing or writing. —**scrib′bler,** *n.*

scribe (skrīb), *n.* 1. a person who works at writing or copying, esp. one who copied manuscripts before the invention of printing. 2. a scholar and teacher of Jewish law in ancient times. 3. an author or writer, esp. a news reporter. 4. a clerk or secretary.

scrim·mage (skrim′ij), *n.* 1. a rough, confused struggle. 2. (in football) **a.** the action that takes place between the teams while the ball is in play. **b.** a practice game, usually between two groups of the same team or squad. —*v.,* **scrim·maged, scrim·mag·ing.** 3. to engage in a scrimmage.

scrimp (skrimp), *v.* 1. to be very sparing or frugal; skimp: *to scrimp on food to pay one's rent.* 2. to use or spend very sparingly: *to scrimp lumber in building a house.*

scrip (skrip), *n.* 1. a receipt or certificate having the value of money. 2. paper money in denominations of less than a dollar, formerly issued in the U.S.

script (skript), *n.* 1. letters or characters written by hand; handwriting. 2. a document or any writing done by hand; manuscript. 3. the written text of a play, motion picture, etc. 4. a particular style or system of writing: *medieval script; Cyrillic script.* 5. a form of printing type that imitates handwriting. [from the Latin word *scrīptum,* which comes from *scrībere* "to write"]

Scrip·ture (skrip′chər), *n.* 1. Often, **Scriptures.** Also, **Holy Scripture, Holy Scriptures.** the sacred writings of the Bible or of the Old Testament or New Testament. 2. *(sometimes l.c.)* a particular passage from the Bible. 3. *(often l.c.)* any sacred book or writing: *Hindu scripture.* —**scrip′tur·al,** *adj.*

scrof·u·la (skrof′yə lə), *n.* a kind of tuberculosis that causes swelling of the lymph glands and inflammation of the joints.

scroll (skrōl), *n.* 1. a roll of parchment, paper, or the like, with writing, painting, or drawing on it. 2. an ornamental figure having a spiral or coiled form, resembling a scroll. —**scroll′-like′,** *adj.*

scroll·work (skrōl′wûrk′), *n.* decorative work made in a pattern of scrolls.

Scrooge (skrooj), *n.* 1. an old miser in Charles Dickens' story, *A Christmas Carol.* 2. *(often l.c.)* any miserly person.

scro·tum (skrō′təm), *n.* the pouch of skin that contains the testicles of a man or male animal.

scrounge (skrounj), *v.,* **scrounged, scroung·ing.** 1. to borrow (small things or amounts) without intention of returning them. 2. to get or take (something) from someone else or at someone else's expense; sponge. **3. scrounge around,** to hunt or forage for something: *to scrounge around for a late snack.* —**scroung′er,** *n.*

scrub¹ (skrub), *v.,* **scrubbed, scrub·bing.** 1. to clean by rubbing with a brush, cloth, etc., or against a rough surface: *to scrub the floors; to scrub one's face.*

2. to remove (something) by hard rubbing: *to scrub the dirt out of one's hands.* —*n.* 3. the act of scrubbing: *to give the pots a scrub.* [from the earlier Dutch word *scrobben*]

scrub² (skrub), *n.* 1. low trees, brush, etc., esp. in a thick growth on uncultivated land. 2. a person, plant, or animal that is smaller than average size or inferior. 3. (in sports) a player who is not a member of the regular team. —*adj.* 4. (esp. of trees or shrubs) small or stunted. 5. (in sports) made up of scrub players: *a scrub team.* [from Scandinavian]

scrub·by (skrub′ē), *adj.,* **scrub·bi·er, scrub·bi·est.** 1. small, stunted, or inferior. 2. covered with scrub: *a scrubby plateau.*

scruff (skruf), *n.* the back part; nape: *the scruff of the neck.*

scru·ple (skroo′pəl), *n.* 1. an idea or principle of conduct arising out of one's conscience, esp. one that prevents doing something evil or harmful: *I have scruples against gambling.* 2. a unit of weight used for weighing drugs, equal to 20 grains (1.296 grams). —*v.,* **scru·pled, scru·pling.** 3. to hesitate or refrain from doing something because of scruples.

scru·pu·lous (skroo′pyə ləs), *adj.* 1. having or following strict rules of conduct; absolutely honest: *a scrupulous public official.* 2. extremely careful and exact; paying attention to details: *a scrupulous investigator; a scrupulous record of events.* —**scru′pu·lous·ly,** *adv.* —**scru′pu·lous·ness,** *n.*

scru·ti·nize (skroot′ᵊnīz′), *v.,* **scru·ti·nized, scru·ti·niz·ing.** to examine closely; inspect carefully: *We scrutinized the car for any possible defects.*

scru·ti·ny (skroot′ᵊnē), *n., pl.* **scru·ti·nies.** 1. careful examination or investigation: *Scrutiny of the records did not reveal any false statements on his part.* 2. close and continuous watching or guarding: *The police have a suspect under scrutiny.*

scu·ba (skoo′bə), *n.* 1. a breathing device used in underwater swimming, which consists of a mouthpiece connected by hoses to air tanks that are strapped to the swimmer's back. —*adj.* 2. done by a swimmer equipped with such a device: *scuba diving.* [from the phrase *s(elf)-c(ontained) u(nderwater) b(reathing) a(pparatus)*]

scud (skud), *v.,* **scud·ded, scud·ding.** 1. to run or move quickly. 2. (of a sailboat) to run before the wind with little or no sail set. 3. to be driven by the wind, as clouds, dry leaves, etc. —*n.* 4. the act of scudding. 5. clouds, spray, or the like, driven by wind. [probably from a Scandinavian word, such as Norwegian *skudda* "to push"]

scuff (skuf), *v.* 1. to walk without raising the feet from the ground; shuffle: *He scuffed along the hall in his slippers.* 2. to make or become marred or scratched by hard use or wear: *He scuffed his shoes on the sharp rocks. These floors scuff easily.* —*n.* 3. the act or sound of scuffing. 4. a flat-heeled slipper open at the back. 5. a scratched or worn spot: *Your new shoes are covered with scuffs.*

scuf·fle (skuf′əl), *v.,* **scuf·fled, scuf·fling.** 1. to struggle or fight in a rough, confused manner: *The pris-*

oner *scuffled with his guards.* **2.** to drag the feet in walking; shuffle. —*n.* **3.** a confused fight or struggle: *There was a scuffle between two spectators over a seat.* **4.** the act or sound of scuffling with the feet.

scull (skul), *n.* **1.** an oar mounted at the stern of a small boat that propels the boat by being moved from side to side. **2.** either of a pair of oars rowed by a single oarsman. **3.** a light, narrow racing boat propelled by one or more oarsmen, each using a pair of oars. —*v.* **4.** to propel (a boat) by means of a scull or sculls.

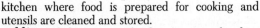

S, Scull

scul·ler·y (skul′ə rē), *n., pl.* **scul·ler·ies.** *Chiefly British.* a small room or section of a pantry or kitchen where food is prepared for cooking and utensils are cleaned and stored.

scul·lion (skul′yən), *n.* a kitchen servant who does rough work, such as scrubbing and cleaning, preparing foods for cooking, etc.

sculp·tor (skulp′tər), *n.* an artist who works in sculpture.

sculp·tress (skulp′tris), *n.* a female sculptor.

sculp·ture (skulp′chər), *n.* **1.** the art of carving or modeling statues, figures, or designs in stone, wood, clay, metal, etc. **2.** a work produced in this way, or a collection of such works. —*v.,* **sculp·tured, sculp·tur·ing. 3.** to carve, model, or otherwise produce a work or works of sculpture. **4.** to make a sculpture of; represent in sculpture: *to sculpture a head in marble.* **5.** to cover or ornament with sculpture: *to sculpture the face of an arch.*

scum (skum), *n.* **1.** a film of dirt or decayed matter that forms on the surface of a liquid: *The pond was covered with green scum.* **2.** a low, worthless person or persons: *Pushers of narcotics are the scum of the earth.* —*v.,* **scummed, scum·ming. 3.** to remove the scum from. **4.** to form scum or become covered with scum. —**scum′my,** *adj.*

scurf (skûrf), *n.* **1.** small, loose scales of skin. **2.** any scaly material on a surface. —**scurf′y,** *adj.*

scur·ril·i·ty (skə ril′i tē), *n., pl.* **scur·ril·i·ties. 1.** scurrilous quality or character. **2.** indecent or vulgar remarks. **3.** a mean, abusive attack on someone's character.

scur·ril·ous (skûr′ə ləs), *adj.* **1.** coarsely abusive: *We were shocked by his scurrilous attack on the mayor.* **2.** using vulgar or indecent language, esp. in joking: *a scurrilous jest.* —**scur′ril·ous·ly,** *adv.* —**scur′ril·ous·ness,** *n.*

scur·ry (skûr′ē, skur′ē), *v.,* **scur·ried, scur·ry·ing. 1.** to go or move quickly: *All the pupils scurried to their seats.* —*n.* **2.** a hasty running; scamper: *the scurry of feet through the hall.*

scur·vy (skûr′vē), *n.* **1.** a disease caused by a lack of vitamin C in the diet that produces swelling and bleeding of the gums, spots on the skin, and severe physical weakness. —*adj.,* **scur·vi·er, scur·vi·est. 2.**

low; contemptible; mean: *a scurvy crew; a scurvy trick.* —**scur′vi·ly,** *adv.* —**scur′vi·ness,** *n.*

scut·tle¹ (skut′ʰl), *n.* a deep bucket with a wide projecting lip, used for holding and carrying coal. [from a Middle English word meaning originally "dish, platter," which comes from Latin *scutella*]

scut·tle² (skut′ʰl), *v.,* **scut·tled, scut·tling. 1.** to run with short, quick steps; scamper: *The puppy scuttled out the door.* —*n.* **2.** a short, quick run: *The lizard slipped away with a smooth scuttle.* [perhaps another form of the word *scuddle,* which comes from *scud*]

scut·tle³ (skut′ʰl), *v.,* **scut·tled, scut·tling. 1.** to sink (a ship) by letting water in through holes in the hull. —*n.* **2.** a small opening with a cover in the deck or hull of a ship. [from the Middle English word *skotel,* which comes from Spanish *escotilla* "hatchway"]

Scyl·la (sil′ə), *n.* **1.** a rock off the coast of Italy near the whirlpool Charybdis. **2. between Scylla and Charybdis,** between two equally dangerous choices: *Faced by chronic illness on the one hand and a risky operation on the other, he was caught between Scylla and Charybdis.*

scythe (sīth), *n.* a tool having a long wooden handle with a long, curved blade attached to it at an angle, used for cutting or mowing grass, grain, etc.

S. Dak., South Dakota. Also, **S.D.**

SE, 1. southeast. **2.** southeastern. Also, **S.E.**

Se, *Chem.* the symbol for **selenium.**

sea (sē), *n.* **1.** the salt waters that cover most of the earth's surface. **2.** one of the largest divisions of these waters; ocean. **3.** a large body of salt water, with more or less definite boundaries of land: *the Mediterranean Sea.* **4.** a large lake or any large body of water entirely enclosed by land: *the Sea of Galilee.* **5.** the condition of the surface of the water at a particular time: *a calm sea.* **6.** a large wave or waves: *The ship was pounded by heavy seas.* **7.** a broad expanse or mass of things: *a sea of faces.* —*adj.* **8.** concerned with, used on, or living in the sea: *sea tales; sea clothing; sea animal.* **9. at sea, a.** on the ocean: *The ship will be at sea for months.* **b.** confused or uncertain: *I'm completely at sea about this assignment.*

sea′ anem′one, a small sea animal having a tubular body and one or more circles of colored tentacles that resemble flower petals surrounding its mouth.

sea·board (sē′bôrd′), *n.* **1.** the line where land and sea meet; coastline; shore. **2.** the region bordering a coast: *the Atlantic seaboard.*

sea′ bread′, ship biscuit; hardtack.

sea′ breeze′, a wind that blows from the sea toward the land.

sea·coast (sē′kōst′), *n.* the land bordering a sea or ocean.

sea′ cow′, another name for **manatee.**

sea′ dog′, a sailor, esp. an old or experienced one.

sea·far·er (sē′fâr′ər), *n.* **1.** a sailor or seaman. **2.** a traveler on the sea.

---

act, āble, dâre, ärt; ebb, ēqual; if, īce; hot, ōver, ôrder; oil; book; ooze; out; up, ûrge; ə = *a* as in *alone*; ᵊ as in *button* (but′ᵊn), *fire* (fīᵊr); chief; shoe; thin; that; zh as in *measure* (mezh′ər). See full key inside cover.

sea·far·ing (sē′fâr′ĭng), *adj.* **1.** traveling by sea: *a seafaring explorer.* **2.** making a living as a sailor or from trading by sea: *a seafaring man; a seafaring nation.* —*n.* **3.** travel by sea. **4.** the occupation of a sailor.

sea·food (sē′fōōd′), *n.* any saltwater fish or shellfish used for food.

sea·go·ing (sē′gō′ĭng), *adj.* **1.** suitable or fit for use on the sea: *a seagoing vessel.* **2.** traveling on the sea; seafaring: *a seagoing orchestra.*

sea′ gull′, a gull, esp. one found at sea or along a seacoast.

sea′ horse′, any of several small fishes having a head slightly resembling that of a horse when seen from the side.

Sea horse
(length
to 4 in.)

seal[1] (sēl), *n.* **1.** an emblem or figure used as a symbol of authority: *the great seal of the United States.* **2.** a stamp, ring, etc., engraved with such a design, used to make an impression in paper, wax, metal, or the like: *a notary's seal.* **3.** the impression made by such a device. **4.** a piece of wax or the like, impressed with a seal and used to close a letter, document, or package in such a way that it must be broken in order to remove or tamper with the contents. **5.** anything that closes or fastens securely. **6.** a decorative stamp, esp. one of a kind given to contributors to a charitable cause: *a Christmas seal.* **7.** anything that confirms or guarantees an agreement or promise: *a seal of secrecy; a seal of brotherhood.* —*v.* **8.** to put a seal on (a letter, document, etc.) as a sign of genuineness or to insure the safety of the contents. **9.** to confirm or guarantee (a promise, agreement, etc.) with some sign or token: *We sealed the bargain with a handshake.* **10.** to close or fasten securely: *to seal a railroad car; to seal someone's lips.* **11.** to settle definitely: *to seal someone's fate.* [from the Old French word *seel,* which comes from Latin *sigillum*]

Great Seal of the United
States of America

seal[2] (sēl), *n., pl.* **seals** or for def. 1 **seal. 1.** any of numerous sea mammals that feed on fish and have limbs reduced to flippers. **2.** the skin or fur of any of these animals. —*v.* **3.** to hunt, kill, or capture seals. —*adj.* **4.** made of sealskin: *a seal cap.* [from the Old English word *seolh*]

sea′ legs′, the ability to adjust one's sense of balance to the rolling and pitching motions of a ship at sea: *After three days out, we found our sea legs.*

sea′ lev′el, the position of the surface of the ocean halfway between high and low tide, from which altitudes on land and depths in the sea are measured.

seal′ing wax′, a kind of wax, soft when heated, used for applying a seal to letters, documents, etc.

sea′ li′on, any of several large seals of the Pacific coast of North America.

seal·skin (sēl′skĭn′), *n.* **1.** the skin or fur of a seal. **2.** a garment made of the fur of a seal.

Seal′y·ham ter′rier (sē′lē ham′, sē′lē əm), one of a Welsh breed of small terriers having short legs and a wiry, mostly white coat.

Sea lion
(length 10 ft.)

seam (sēm), *n.* **1.** a line of stitches joining together two pieces of cloth, leather, or the like. **2.** any line formed by the meeting of two edges: *the seams of a ship's hull.* **3.** a mark or dent forming a line, such as a wrinkle, scar, etc. **4.** a thin layer of rock or mineral deposit in the earth: *a seam of coal.* —*v.* **5.** to join together in a seam. **6.** to furrow; mark with wrinkles, scars, etc.: *His long illness had seamed his face.*

sea·man (sē′mən), *n., pl.* **sea·men. 1.** a man whose job is helping in the sailing, navigating, etc., of a ship, esp. a man below the rank of officer; sailor. **2.** an enlisted man in the U.S. Navy of the lowest rank.

sea·man·ship (sē′mən shĭp′), *n.* knowledge of and skill in sailing and the operation of ships.

sea′ mew′, a gull, esp. a common European species.

seam·stress (sēm′strĭs), *n.* a woman whose occupation is sewing.

seam·y (sē′mē), *adj.,* **seam·i·er, seam·i·est. 1.** having, showing, or resembling a seam or seams: *the seamy side of a dress; the seamy face of a cliff.* **2.** unpleasant, disagreeable, or sordid: *the seamy side of life.*

sé·ance (sā′äns), *n.* a meeting in which people attempt to communicate with the spirits of the dead through a medium.

sea′ ot′ter, a marine otter of northern Pacific shores that has a very valuable fur.

sea·plane (sē′plān′), *n.* an airplane equipped with floats for taking off from and landing on water.

sea·port (sē′pôrt′), *n.* **1.** a port or harbor located on or near a seacoast, with facilities for docking or anchoring seagoing vessels. **2.** a town or city that has such a port.

sear (sēr), *v.* **1.** to burn the surface of: *You sear a steak to seal in the juices.* **2.** to burn or scorch painfully: *He seared his hand on the hot pipe.* **3.** to make unfeeling by some unpleasant experience; harden. **4.** to dry up or wither; parch: *Drought seared the crops.* —*n.* **5.** a mark or scar made by burning.

search (sûrch), *v.* **1.** to examine or investigate carefully in order to find something hidden or lost: *The police searched the suspect for hidden weapons.* —*n.* **2.** the act of searching; careful examination or investigation. **3.** in search of, seeking; looking for: *He went west in search of gold.* **4.** search out, to find or uncover by searching: *to search out the truth.*

search·ing (sûr′chĭng), *adj.* **1.** examining carefully or thoroughly: *a searching review of the evidence.* **2.**

sharply observant; penetrating: *a searching glance.*
—**search′ing·ly,** *adv.*

search·light (sûrch′līt′), *n.* a powerful lamp equipped with a reflector that can shine a narrow beam of light in any desired direction.

sea′ shell′, the shell of any saltwater shellfish.

sea·shore (sē′shôr′), *n.* land along the sea or ocean.

sea·sick (sē′sik′), *adj.* affected with nausea and dizziness due to the rocking motion of a ship in which one is traveling. —**sea′sick′ness,** *n.*

sea·side (sē′sīd′), *n.* 1. land along the sea; seashore. —*adj.* 2. of or at the seaside: *a seaside hotel.*

sea·son (sē′zən), *n.* 1. one of the four major divisions of the year: spring, summer, autumn, or winter. 2. a period of the year in which a particular kind of weather, temperature, etc., prevails: *the rainy season; the hot season.* 3. a period of the year when something is available or at its best condition or quality: *the oyster season.* 4. a period of the year that is most suitable for certain activities: *the harvest season; the tourist season.* 5. a period of the year centering around a holiday or a special occasion: *the Christmas season.* 6. a suitable or proper time: *This is not the season for rejoicing.* —*v.* 7. to add flavor to (food) by the use of seasoning. 8. to add interest or a special quality to: *to season a speech with jokes.* 9. to harden by experience or exposure to difficult conditions: *troops seasoned by battle.* 10. to prepare or make more resistant to use and wear by aging, drying, etc.: *to season lumber; to season a smoking pipe.* 11. **in season, a.** in abundant supply; readily available: *Asparagus is in season now.* **b.** during the period specified by law: *Pheasants may be hunted only in season.* 12. **out of season,** not in season; not readily available or in abundant supply: *Watermelon is out of season in winter.* [from the Old French word *seison,* which comes from Latin *satiō* "sowing time"]

sea·son·a·ble (sē′zə nə bəl), *adj.* 1. suitable or usual for a particular season: *Seasonable cold is predicted for December.* 2. occurring or coming at an appropriate time; timely: *seasonable precautions.* —**sea′son·a·ble·ness,** *n.* —**sea′son·a·bly,** *adv.*

sea·son·al (sē′zə nəl), *adj.* depending on the seasons; coming or appearing at a particular season: *seasonal work; seasonal colds.* —**sea′son·al·ly,** *adv.*

sea·son·ing (sē′zə ning), *n.* 1. any substance, such as salt, herbs, spices, or the like, used for adding flavor to food. 2. anything that adds interest, variety, etc.: *a serious play with a seasoning of comedy.*

seat (sēt), *n.* 1. anything used for sitting on, such as a chair, bench, cushion, etc. 2. the part of a chair, bench, etc., on which a person sits. 3. the part of the body on which a person sits; the buttocks. 4. a part of a garment covering this part of the body: *the seat of one's trousers.* 5. the base or support of an object: *the seat of an anvil; the seat of a statue.* 6. a place in which something is established or has its center: *Detroit is the seat of the automobile industry.* 7. a center of government: *a county seat.* 8. a residence,

usually a mansion or estate: *a country seat.* 9. a place in a theater, stadium, etc., where a spectator has the right to sit, usually by buying a ticket or obtaining a pass. 10. the right of membership in a legislative body or other official group: *a seat in Congress; a seat on the stock exchange.* —*v.* 11. to place on a seat or seats; cause to be seated: *Where will you seat your guests?* 12. to have seats for; accommodate with seats: *The new stadium seats twenty thousand.*

seat′ belt′, a belt or strap attached to a seat of an automobile, airplane, etc., and usually passed around a person's waist to prevent him from being thrown out of the seat in a collision, sudden start or stop, or the like. Also, **safety belt.**

Se·at·tle (sē at′ᵊl), *n.* a port city in W Washington.

sea′ ur′chin, any of various small, round sea animals related to the starfish and having a shell covered with sharp spines.

sea′ wall′, a wall or embankment built along a shore to serve as a breakwater or to prevent the land from being broken down by the force of the waves.

sea·ward (sē′wərd), *adv.* 1. Also, **sea′wards.** toward the sea: *The storm moved seaward.* —*adj.* 2. facing or going in the direction of the sea: *a seaward view; a seaward course.* 3. coming from the sea: *a seaward breeze.* —*n.* 4. the direction toward the sea: *Thick clouds gathered to seaward.*

sea·way (sē′wā′), *n.* 1. a way or route for travel over the sea; shipping lane. 2. a canal or waterway that enables seagoing vessels to reach an inland port.

sea·weed (sē′wēd′), *n.* any plant that grows in the ocean, esp. any of the saltwater algae.

sea·wor·thy (sē′wûr′ŧhē), *adj.* suitable or safe for travel on the sea. —**sea′wor′thi·ness,** *n.*

se·ba′ceous gland′ (si bā′shəs), any of the numerous glands in the skin that secrete an oily substance for lubricating the hair and skin.

se·cede (si sēd′), *v.,* **se·ced·ed, se·ced·ing.** to withdraw from membership in a union or association, esp. a political or religious one: *By 1861 eleven Southern states had seceded from the Union.*

se·ces·sion (si sesh′ən), *n.* 1. the act of seceding. 2. *(often cap.)* (in U.S. history) the withdrawal from the Union of 11 Southern states in the period 1860–1861, which led to the Civil War.

se·clude (si klood′), *v.,* **se·clud·ed, se·clud·ing.** to place or keep apart; shut off; isolate: *He secluded himself in the library to finish his homework.*

se·clud·ed (si kloo′did), *adj.* 1. sheltered or hidden from view; seldom visited: *a secluded spot in the woods.* 2. taking little or no part in worldly activities; withdrawn from society: *a secluded life in a convent.*

se·clu·sion (si kloo′zhən), *n.* 1. the act of secluding. 2. the state of being secluded; solitude: *He found seclusion in his laboratory.* 3. a secluded place.

sec·ond¹ (sek′ənd), *adj.* 1. being number two in a series: *the second floor.* 2. next after the first in grade, rank, quality, or importance: *second mate; the second team.* 3. another: *a second Einstein; a second* *car.* **4.** alternate: *Representatives are elected every second year.* **5.** (in music) being the lower of two parts for the same instrument or voice: *second violin; second soprano.* —*n.* **6.** a person or thing that is second. **7.** a person who aids another as an assistant, esp. in boxing or dueling. **8.** Often, **seconds.** an additional helping of food: *You may have seconds on dessert.* **9.** Usually, **seconds.** a product that is not of the highest quality, usually containing visible flaws. —*v.* **10.** to support in a formal manner: *He seconded my motion at the meeting.* **11.** to help or support: *Her hard work seconded his efforts.* —*adv.* **12.** in the second place, group, etc.: *He will bat second in today's lineup.* [from an Old French word, which comes from Latin *secundus* "following, second"]

sec·ond² (sek′ənd), *n.* **1.** the sixtieth part of a minute of time. **2.** the sixtieth part of a minute of angular measure. *Symbol: ″* [from an early French word, which comes from the medieval Latin phrase *secunda minūta* "second (minute)"]

sec·ond·ar·y (sek′ən der′ē), *adj.* **1.** next after the first in order, place, time, importance, etc. **2.** belonging to a second order, division, period, grade, rank, etc.: *a secondary official.* **3.** derived from something more basic or earlier; not primary or original: *a secondary branch; a secondary meaning of a word.* —*n., pl.* **sec·ond·ar·ies. 4.** a person or thing that is secondary. —**sec·ond·ar·i·ly** (sek′ən dâr′ə lē), *adv.*

sec′ondary school′, a high school, or any school ranking above a primary school and below a college.

sec′ondary stress′, 1. a stress, or accent, that is slightly weaker than a primary stress. In the pronunciation of the word *proposition* (prop′ə ziṣh′ən), the first syllable has a secondary stress. **2.** a symbol (′) used to mark a secondary stress. Also, **sec′-ondary ac′cent.** See also **primary stress.**

sec′ond class′, 1. the class of accommodations on a ship, train, etc., that is less elaborate and less expensive than first class. **2.** (in the U.S. postal system) the class of mail that is not sealed against postal inspection, including newspapers, magazines, etc. **3.** the class ranking just below first class in order, rank, quality, importance, etc. —**sec′ond-class′,** *adj., adv.*

sec′ond-de·gree′ burn′ (sek′ənd di grē′). See under **burn** (def. 11).

sec′ond hand′, the hand that indicates the seconds on a clock or watch.

sec·ond·hand (sek′ənd hand′), *adj.* **1.** not learned by direct study or experience, but from other persons or from books: *My knowledge of electronics is secondhand.* **2.** previously used or owned: *secondhand clothes.* **3.** dealing in used goods: *a secondhand bookseller.*

sec′ond lieuten′ant, a commissioned officer of the lowest rank in the U.S. Army, Air Force, or Marines ranking above a sergeant or warrant officer and below a first lieutenant.

sec·ond·ly (sek′ənd lē), *adv.* in the second place.

sec′ond na′ture, a skill or habit that is so deeply implanted that it seems to be part of one's nature: *Driving is second nature to him.*

sec′ond per′son, 1. the one or ones spoken to by the speaker of a word, phrase, or sentence. **2.** the form of a pronoun or verb that refers to the one or ones spoken to. In English, *you, your,* and *yours* are pronouns of the second person. *Are* is the second person, present-tense form of the verb *to be.*

sec·ond-rate (sek′ənd rāt′), *adj.* of inferior quality, ability, importance, etc.: *a second-rate performance.*

se·cre·cy (sē′kri sē), *n., pl.* for defs. 2, 3 **se·cre·cies. 1.** the state or condition of being secret: *The nation guards the secrecy of its plans.* **2.** a secret or secluded place; privacy: *We spoke in secrecy.* **3.** the ability or habit of keeping something secret: *You can trust him because his secrecy is well known.*

se·cret (sē′krit), *adj.* **1.** kept from the knowledge of others; known only to one or a few persons: *a secret treaty.* **2.** concealed or sealed in such a way as to be accessible only to a person who knows its location or operation: *a secret pocket; a secret panel.* **3.** working or functioning without the knowledge of others: *a secret agent; a secret society.* **4.** isolated or secluded: *a secret retreat.* **5.** keeping knowledge to oneself: *He is very secret about his plans.* **6.** unknown or unknowable; mysterious: *the secret forces of nature.* —*n.* **7.** something kept from the knowledge of others: *The recipe is my own secret.* **8.** something unknown or unknowable; mystery: *the secrets of the universe.* **9.** a reason or explanation, often one not seen or guessed at first: *The secret of the car's amazing speed was a new fuel.* **10.** in **secret,** not known to others; in private; secretly: *The scientists worked on the project in secret.* [from an Old French word, which comes from Latin *secrētus* "hidden"] —**se′cret·ly,** *adv.*

se·cre·tar·i·at (sek′ri târ′ē ət), *n.* **1.** a group of officials and employees that performs the administrative and secretarial duties of a large organization: *the secretariat of the United Nations.* **2.** the building or place housing this group.

se·cre·tar·y (sek′ri ter′ē), *n., pl.* **se·cre·tar·ies. 1.** a person responsible for handling correspondence, keeping records, and performing other general duties for a business office or an association. **2.** *(often cap.)* an official who has charge of a department of government: *the U.S. Secretary of Defense.* **3.** a writing desk with bookshelves built on top of it. [from the medieval Latin word *secrētārius,* originally "keeper of secrets"] —**se·cre·tar·i·al** (sek′ri târ′ē əl), *adj.*

se·crete¹ (si krēt′), *v.,* **se·cret·ed, se·cret·ing.** to produce or give off a useful substance: *Ductless glands secrete hormones.* [formed from *secretion*]

se·crete² (si krēt′), *v.,* **se·cret·ed, se·cret·ing.** to place out of sight; hide; conceal: *She secreted her jewels in the safe.* [from old use of *secret* as a verb]

se·cre·tion (si krē′shən), *n.* **1.** the process by which a cell or gland makes or releases a useful substance. **2.** the substance itself. [from the Latin word *secrētiō,* which comes from *secernere* "to sift, separate"]

se·cre·tive¹ (sē′kri tiv, si krē′tiv), *adj.* having the tendency or habit of keeping things secret: *He is always very secretive about his work.* [from *secret* + -*ive*] —**se′cre·tive·ly,** *adv.* —**se′cre·tive·ness,** *n.*

se·cre·tive² (si krē′tiv), *adj.* 1. of or concerned with secretion. 2. causing or aiding secretion. [from *secret(ion)* + *-ive*]

se′cret serv′ice, 1. a branch of government service engaged in espionage work. 2. *(usually caps.)* a branch of the U.S. Treasury Department that is responsible for tracking down counterfeiters and protecting the President and his family.

secs., seconds.

sect (sekt), *n.* a group, esp. a particular religious denomination, made up of persons holding the same beliefs or opinions or following a certain leader.

sec·tar·i·an (sek târ′ē ən), *adj.* 1. of or belonging to a sect: *a sectarian college.* 2. narrow or limited in interests, purposes, etc.: *a sectarian attitude.* —*n.* 3. a person who is a member of or favors a particular sect. —**sec·tar′i·an·ism,** *n.*

sec·tion (sek′shən), *n.* 1. a part or piece cut off or separated from something: *a section of an orange; a section of the population.* 2. any of the parts or subdivisions of a thing, nation, area, community, class, etc.: *the left section of a drawer; the business section.* 3. a part or subdivision of something written or printed, such as a newspaper, chapter, constitution, etc.: *the sports section; section 2 of the bylaws.* 4. a view or drawing of something showing how it would look if cut straight through: *The drawing shows the human brain in section.* 5. (in some states of the U.S.) one of the 36 parts, each one mile square, into which a township is divided. 6. the act of cutting or dividing. —*v.* 7. to cut or divide into parts.

sec·tion·al (sek′shə nᵊl), *adj.* 1. of or belonging to a particular section, district, or region: *the sectional interests of the Far West.* 2. assembled from a number of separate parts: *a sectional sofa.*

sec·tion·al·ism (sek′shə nᵊliz′əm), *n.* interests and attitudes that are narrowly limited to a particular section or region.

sec·tor (sek′tər), *n.* 1. the part of a circle that is cut off by two radii. 2. a part or division of a military area assigned to a particular unit: *the western sector of Germany.* —*v.* 3. to divide into sectors.

sec·u·lar (sek′yə lər), *adj.* 1. of or concerned with worldly things; not religious or spiritual: *secular education; secular music.* 2. not belonging to a religious or monastic order; not bound by monastic vows: *the secular clergy.* [from the Latin word *saeculāris* "worldly, temporal," which comes from *saeculum* "age, period of time"]

se·cure (si kyŏŏr′), *adj.* 1. free from danger or harm; protected; safe. 2. free from care, anxiety, or uncertainty: *Among my own friends I feel secure.* 3. in safekeeping; not exposed to loss or theft: *Your valuables will be secure in the safe.* 4. firmly or solidly built: *a secure fortress.* 5. firmly fastened: *Everything is secure on deck.* 6. sure; certain: *Victory is now secure.* —*v.,* **se·cured, se·cur·ing.** 7. to get possession of; obtain: *to secure a job.* 8. to free from danger or harm; make safe; protect: *The troops secured the*

business district during the riots. 9. to make sure or certain; ensure: *A good investment will secure your future.* 10. to fix or fasten firmly; put in safekeeping: *to secure all loose objects; to secure a prisoner to prevent his escape.* 11. to protect against loss or risk; place insurance on: *to secure a loan with personal property.* —**se·cure′ly,** *adv.*

se·cu·ri·ty (si kyŏŏr′i tē), *n., pl.* **se·cu·ri·ties.** 1. freedom from danger or harm; protection; safety: *the security of one's home.* 2. something that secures or makes safe; defense: *The radar warning system is our security against attack.* 3. something that insures or protects against loss; guarantee: *Diamonds can be used as security for a loan.* 4. Usually, **securities.** stocks, bonds, or certificates of title to property.

sec′y, secretary. Also, **secy.**

se·dan (si dan′), *n.* 1. an enclosed automobile body having two or four doors and two seats of full width for passengers. 2. a sedan chair.

sedan′ chair′, an enclosed vehicle for one person, supported between two poles which are carried by bearers on foot. It was much used during the 17th and 18th centuries.

Sedan chair

se·date (si dāt′), *adj.* calm, quiet, or solemn: *a sedate dinner party; a sedate old lady.* —**se·date′ly,** *adv.* —**se·date′ness,** *n.*

sed·a·tive (sed′ə tiv), *adj.* 1. relieving pain or tension: *a sedative ointment; a sedative bath.* —*n.* 2. a drug that relieves pain or tension.

sed·en·tar·y (sed′ᵊn ter′ē), *adj.* 1. allowing little freedom of movement; requiring one to remain seated: *Typing is a sedentary job.* 2. not accustomed to moving about much or taking much exercise: *Older persons tend to become more sedentary.*

Se·der (sā′dər), *n.* a ceremonial dinner celebrated by Jews at Passover, in commemoration of the Exodus. [from Hebrew, literally "order, division"]

sedge (sej), *n.* any of numerous rushlike or grasslike plants that grow in wet places.

sed·i·ment (sed′ə mənt), *n.* 1. loose solid matter that settles at the bottom of a liquid; dregs. 2. sand, soil, and the like, carried and deposited by water, wind, glaciers, etc.

sed·i·men·ta·ry (sed′ə men′tə rē), *adj.* 1. of, concerning, or resembling sediment. 2. produced by the depositing of sediment or from deposited sediments: *sedimentary rock.*

sed·i·men·ta·tion (sed′ə mən tā′shən), *n.* the depositing or accumulating of sediment.

se·di·tion (si dish′ən), *n.* the stirring up by speech, writing, or action of public disorder and rebellion against a government.

se·di·tious (si dish′əs), *adj.* 1. full of or causing sedition: *a seditious speech.* 2. inciting to or taking part

in acts of sedition: *a seditious group of students.*
—**se·di′tious·ly,** *adv.*

se·duce (si dōōs′, -dyōōs′), *v.,* **se·duced, se·duc·ing. 1.**
to persuade to do wrong; lead astray; corrupt: *The
promise of a quick fortune seduced him to crime.* **2.**
to win over; attract; entice: *The supermarket chain
seduces customers with special bargains.*

se·duc·tion (si duk′shən), *n.* **1.** the act of seducing.
2. the condition of being seduced. **3.** something that
seduces; enticement.

se·duc·tive (si duk′tiv), *adj.* tending to seduce; en-
ticing; captivating: *a seductive smile.* —**se·duc′tive·
ly,** *adv.* —**se·duc′tive·ness,** *n.*

sed·u·lous (sej′ə ləs), *adj.* **1.** working or acting with
diligence; persevering; persistent: *a sedulous investigator.* **2.** done with diligence and perseverance:
sedulous attempts to win favor. —**sed′u·lous·ly,** *adv.*
—**sed′u·lous·ness,** *n.*

see¹ (sē), *v.,* **saw** (sô), **seen** (sēn), **see·ing. 1.** to perceive with the eyes: *I can't see the blackboard.* **2.** to
view; visit or attend as a spectator: *to see a play.* **3.** to
perceive with the mind; understand: *I can see your
reasons for leaving.* **4.** to form or preserve a mental
picture of: *I can see you as president.* **5.** to find out:
See what the young man wants. **6.** to undergo or experience: *He saw service in the Marines.* **7.** to make
sure: *See that the children go to bed on time.* **8.** to
call on; visit: *I must see my dentist.* **9.** to receive or
attend to as a visitor, patient, petitioner, etc.: *The
doctor will see you in a moment.* **10.** to keep company with; date; court: *He's been seeing my sister for
a month.* **11.** to encourage or support, esp. financially: *He saw his children through college.* **12.** to attend or escort: *I'll see her safely home.* **13.** to have
the power of sight: *Cats can see in the dark.* **14. see
about,** to take care of; attend to: *I have to see about
getting new license plates.* **15. see off,** to go with
(someone) to the place of departure; say good-by to:
We saw Mother off at the depot. **16. see through, a.**
to stay with (something) until completed: *to see a
project through.* **b.** to understand the true nature of:
I saw through her little plan. **17. see to,** to take care
of; attend to: *You wash the dishes, and I'll see to the
ironing.* [from the Old English word *sēon*]

see² (sē), *n.* **1.** the seat or center of authority of a
bishop. **2.** the office or jurisdiction of a bishop. [from
the Old French word *se,* which comes from Latin
sēdēs "seat"]

seed (sēd), *n., pl.* **seeds** *or* **seed. 1.** the grain, pit, nut,
etc., from which a plant grows. Seeds are of many
different sizes and shapes, but most have a hard
outer covering that protects the embryo or undeveloped plant inside. **2.** the source or cause of
anything: *Poverty and oppression are the seeds of discontent.* **3.** offspring; descendants: *the seed of
Abraham.* —*v.* **4.** to sow with seed: *to seed a lawn.* **5.**
to remove the seed or seeds from: *to seed grapes for
a salad.* **6. go to seed, a.** (of a flower) to pass to the
stage of yielding seed. **b.** to decline in energy,
wealth, standing, etc.: *He went to seed soon after his
retirement.* —**seed′er,** *n.* —**seed′less,** *adj.*

seed·case (sēd′kās′), *n.* a hollow body that contains
the seeds of a plant; pod.

seed·ling (sēd′ling), *n.* a young plant or tree, esp.
one grown from seed.

seeds·man (sēdz′mən), *n., pl.* **seeds·men. 1.** a sower
of seed. **2.** a dealer in seed.

seed·y (sē′dē), *adj.,* **seed·i·er, seed·i·est. 1.** full of
seeds: *a seedy orange.* **2.** poorly kept; run-down: *a
seedy shack.* **3.** slovenly in appearance; shabby: *a
seedy old hobo.* —**seed′i·ness,** *n.*

see·ing (sē′ing), *conj.* **1.** in view of the fact; considering (often fol. by *that*): *Seeing that you're staying
home, you can wait for the mailman.* —*n.* **2.** the act
of a person who sees. **3.** the ability to see. —*adj.* **4.**
able to see; sighted: *The blind can often do without
the help of seeing persons.*

See′ing Eye′ dog′, a dog that has been specially
trained to lead or guide a blind person.

seek (sēk), *v.,* **sought** (sôt), **seek·ing. 1.** to try to find;
search for; look for: *to seek a solution to a problem.* **2.**
to try to obtain: *to seek success.* **3.** to try or attempt:
to seek to convince a person. —**seek′er,** *n.*

seem (sēm), *v.* **1.** to appear to be, feel, do, etc.: *It
seems warm outside.* **2.** to appear to oneself: *I seem
unable to get my work done in time.*

seem·ing (sē′ming), *adj.* having a certain appearance, whether real or not; apparent: *His seeming
friendliness concealed his dislike of the stranger.*

seem·ing·ly (sē′ming lē), *adv.* judging from appearances; apparently: *The house is seemingly empty.*

seem·ly (sēm′lē), *adj.,* **seem·li·er, seem·li·est.** suitable
or proper; decent; fitting: *He accepted the award
with seemly modesty.* —**seem′li·ness,** *n.*

seen (sēn), *v.* the past participle of **see¹.**

seep (sēp), *v.* to flow or leak gradually through small
openings or pores; ooze: *Water seeps through the
cracks in the wall.*

seep·age (sē′pij), *n.* **1.** the action of seeping; leakage. **2.** liquid that seeps or leaks through. **3.** the
quantity of liquid that seeps through.

se·er (sē′ər *for def. 1;* sēr *for def. 2*), *n.* **1.** a person
who sees; observer. **2.** a person who foretells future
events; prophet.

seer·suck·er (sēr′suk′ər), *n.* a light fabric of cotton,
linen, or rayon, with crinkled stripes woven into the
material. [from a Persian word meaning literally
"milk and sugar": so called because of the contrast in
textures between the alternating flat and wrinkled
stripes]

see·saw (sē′sô′), *n.* **1.** a device used by children for
play, made of a plank supported at the middle, that
moves up and down at each end as the children sitting on it shift their weight. **2.** a back-and-forth or
up-and-down movement or change: *the seesaw of
wages and prices.* —*adj.* **3.** moving or changing like
a seesaw: *It was a seesaw game, with our team in the
lead about half the time.* —*v.* **4.** to play on a seesaw.
5. to move or change like a seesaw: *Prices of food
seesaw from week to week.*

seethe (sēth), *v.,* **seethed, seeth·ing. 1.** to bubble or
foam in boiling or being stirred up violently: *The cof-*

fee is seething. **2.** to be greatly excited: *The mob seethed with anger.* **—seeth′ing·ly,** *adv.*

seg·ment (seg′mənt), *n.* **1.** one of the parts into which something naturally separates or is divided: *a segment of an orange.* **2.** a part of a circle cut off by a straight line. **3.** a part of a straight line cut off by two points; a line of specified length. **—v.** (seg·ment′). **4.** to separate or divide into segments: *The town is segmented into poor and rich neighborhoods.*

seg·re·gate (seg′rə gāt′), *v.*, **seg·re·gat·ed, seg·re·gat·ing.** **1.** to separate or set apart; isolate: *The sick cattle were segregated from the rest of the herd.* **2.** to separate (a particular racial, religious, or other group) from the rest of society: *It is unlawful to segregate pupils of different races in public schools.*

seg·re·ga·tion (seg′rə gā′shən), *n.* **1.** the act or custom of segregating. **2.** the state or condition of being segregated. **—seg′re·ga′tion·ist,** *n.*

seine (sān), *n.* **1.** a large fishing net having floats at the top ends and weights at the bottom, so that it hangs straight up and down in the water. **—v.,** **seined, sein·ing.** **2.** to fish or catch with a seine.

Seine (sān, sen), *n.* a river in France, flowing NW through Paris to the English Channel. 480 mi. long.

seis·mic (sīz′mik, sīs′mik), *adj.* concerning, resembling, or caused by earthquakes.

seis·mo·graph (sīz′mə graf′, sīs′mə graf′), *n.* any of various instruments for detecting, recording, and measuring the intensity of earth vibrations, esp. those caused by earthquakes.

seize (sēz), *v.*, **seized, seiz·ing.** **1.** to take hold of suddenly or with force; grab; grasp: *to seize a life preserver.* **2.** to grasp with the mind; understand: *to seize a notion.* **3.** to take possession of by force: *to seize a fort.* **4.** to affect suddenly and deeply; overwhelm: *Panic seized the crowd.* **5.** to take possession of by legal order: *The sheriff seized his property to pay off the creditors.* **6.** to arrest; capture: *The police have seized the assassin.* **7.** to take advantage of: *to seize an opportunity.* **8. seize on** (or **upon**), **a.** to grab or take hold of suddenly or with force: *to seize on a rope.* **b.** to resort to frantically or in desperation: *He must seize on some solution to the problem at once.* [from the Old French word *saisir,* which comes from medieval Latin *sacīre* "to set, place"]

sei·zure (sē′zhər), *n.* **1.** the act of seizing. **2.** a sudden attack, esp. of illness: *an epileptic seizure.*

sel·dom (sel′dəm), *adv.* rarely; not often: *The temperature seldom goes below zero in this climate.*

se·lect (si lekt′), *v.* **1.** to take by preference; pick out; choose: *He selected a tie from the rack.* **—adj.** **2.** chosen in preference to others; preferred. **3.** of special excellence; choice: *a select cut of meat.* **4.** careful in

selecting; exclusive: *a select circle of friends.* **5.** carefully chosen: *a select group of volunteers.*

se·lect·ee (si lek tē′), *n.* a person who is selected, esp. one selected by draft for military service.

se·lec·tion (si lek′shən), *n.* **1.** the act of selecting, or the state of being selected. **2.** one or a number of persons or things selected; choice: *Bill Smith is my selection for president.* **3.** a number or variety of things from which a person may choose: *The store has a large selection of summer suits.*

se·lec·tive (si lek′tiv), *adj.* **1.** having the function or power of selecting. **2.** choosing carefully; discriminating: *a selective art collector.* **3.** of or concerning selection.

selec′tive serv′ice, a system for choosing young men for compulsory military service.

se·lect·man (si lekt′mən), *n., pl.* **se·lect·men.** one of a board of town officers in most parts of New England, chosen each year to manage public affairs.

se·lec·tor (si lek′tər), *n.* **1.** a person or thing that selects. **2.** a dial, switch, or other device to select or control the different functions of a machine or apparatus.

se·le·ni·um (si lē′nē əm), *n. Chem.* a nonmetallic element whose electrical resistance varies when light shines on it, used in photoelectric cells, transistors, etc. *Symbol:* Se

self (self), *n., pl.* **selves** (selvz). **1.** a person or thing considered as a complete and separate individual: *one's own self.* **2.** a person's character, or a particular side of his character: *He showed his worst self in that argument.* **3.** personal interest or advantage: *to serve with no thought of self.* **—adj. 4.** of the same material, color, or pattern as the rest: *a self lining.*

self-, a prefix meaning of, by, or for oneself or itself: *self-centered; self-denial; self-propelled.*

self-ad·dressed (self′ə drest′), *adj.* having the address of the sender, to make return easier: *a self-addressed envelope for reply.*

self-ap·point·ed (self′ə poin′tid), *adj.* taking on oneself a function or position, esp. without possessing the required knowledge or skill: *a self-appointed expert on the ballet.*

self-as·ser·tion (self′ə sûr′shən), *n.* insistence on one's importance, opinions, aims, etc. **—self′-as·ser′tive,** *adj.*

self-as·sur·ance (self′ə shŏŏr′əns), *n.* confidence in one's ability; self-confidence. **—self-as·sured** (self′ə shŏŏrd′), *adj.*

self-cen·tered (self′sen′tərd), *adj.* occupied with one's own interests and activities, to the exclusion of others; selfish.

self-con·fi·dence (self′kon′fi dəns), *n.* confidence in one's own abilities, judgment, etc. **—self′-con′fi·dent,** *adj.*

self-con·scious (self′kon′shəs), *adj.* embarrassed in the presence of others; made uneasy by the observation of others; shy. **—self′-con′scious·ly,** *adv.* **—self′-con′scious·ness,** *n.*

self·con·tained (self′kən tānd′), *adj.* 1. having in oneself or itself everything necessary to exist or function independently: *a self-contained house trailer.* 2. keeping one's thoughts and feelings to oneself; reserved. 3. having or showing self-control.

self·con·trol (self′kən trōl′), *n.* control over one's actions, feelings, etc.: *It took all my self-control to keep from hitting him back.*

self·de·fense (self′di fens′), *n.* 1. the use of force in defending oneself against attack: *Carrying a pistol is permitted only for self-defense.* 2. a claim or plea that one's use of force was necessary for one's own safety: *The accused murderer pleaded self-defense.*

self·de·ni·al (self′di nī′əl), *n.* the depriving of oneself; giving up of one's own desires and interests, often for the benefit of others.

self·de·ter·mi·na·tion (self′di tûr′mə nā′shən), *n.* 1. the act or power of making one's own decisions, free of control or influence from outside. 2. the right of a nation to choose its own form of government.

self·dis·ci·pline (self′dis′ə plin), *n.* 1. control over one's actions, feelings, etc.; self-control. 2. discipline and training of oneself. —**self′-dis′ci·plined,** *adj.*

self·ed·u·cat·ed (self′ej′ŏŏ kā′tid), *adj.* educated by one's own efforts, with little or no formal training.

self·es·teem (self′e stēm′), *n.* 1. a proper opinion of one's own person and character; self-respect. 2. too high an opinion of oneself; conceit.

self·ev·i·dent (self′ev′i dənt), *adj.* evident in itself without outside proof: *He told a self-evident lie.*

self·ex·plan·a·to·ry (self′ik splan′ə tôr′ē), *adj.* needing no explanation; entirely clear: *The route marked out on the map is self-explanatory.*

self·ex·pres·sion (self′ik spresh′ən), *n.* expression of one's own ideas, opinions, feelings, etc., esp. through creative acts or works.

self·gov·ern·ing (self′guv′ər niñg), *adj.* having its own government; independent: *Puerto Rico is a self-governing dependency of the United States.*

self·gov·ern·ment (self′guv′ərn mənt, -guv′ər-mənt), *n.* government of a people or other group by its own members; independence.

self·im·por·tant (self′im pôr′t³nt), *adj.* having or showing too high an opinion of one's own worth: *a vain, self-important official.* —**self′-im·por′tance,** *n.*

self·im·posed (self′im pōzd′), *adj.* imposed on oneself; undertaken voluntarily: *a self-imposed task.*

self·in·dul·gent (self′in dul′jənt), *adj.* satisfying one's own desires, whims, etc., often without regard for others. —**self′-in·dul′gence,** *n.*

self·in·flict·ed (self′in flik′tid), *adj.* done to one's person by oneself: *a self-inflicted wound.*

self·in·ter·est (self′in′tər ist, -in′trist), *n.* 1. devotion to one's own interest or advantage, often without regard for others; selfishness. 2. personal interest or advantage.

self·ish (sel′fish), *adj.* 1. caring only for oneself; concerned only with one's own interest or advantage, without regard for others. 2. showing or resulting from one's care and concern only for oneself: *a selfish deed.* —**self′ish·ly,** *adv.* —**self′ish·ness,** *n.*

self·less (self′lis), *adj.* having little or no concern for oneself; unselfish: *selfless service to the poor.* —**self′less·ly,** *adv.* —**self′less·ness,** *n.*

self·made (self′mād′), *adj.* 1. having succeeded in life by one's own efforts: *The head of the company is a self-made man.* 2. made by oneself or itself.

self·pit·y (self′pit′ē), *n.* pity for oneself; a feeling sorry for oneself.

self·pos·sessed (self′pə zest′), *adj.* having or showing control of one's actions, feelings, etc.; calm; poised. —**self′-pos·ses′sion,** *n.*

self·pres·er·va·tion (self′prez′ər vā′shən), *n.* the instinctive desire to preserve one's own life and safety: *Self-preservation is the law of the jungle.*

self·pro·pelled (self′prə peld′), *adj.* moving under its own power; containing within itself the means of producing motion: *a self-propelled mower.*

self·re·li·ance (self′ri lī′əns), *n.* reliance on one's own powers, judgment, etc. —**self′-re·li′ant,** *adj.*

self·re·spect (self′ri spekt′), *n.* respect for oneself; a proper pride in one's own person and character: *If he had any self-respect he wouldn't behave like that.* —**self′-re·spect′ing,** *adj.*

self·re·straint (self′ri strānt′), *n.* control of one's feelings, impulses, etc.; self-control.

self·right·eous (self′rī′chəs), *adj.* confident in one's own claim of being more righteous in thought and action than others. —**self′-right′eous·ly,** *adv.* —**self′-right′eous·ness,** *n.*

self·sac·ri·fice (self′sak′rə fīs′), *n.* sacrifice of one's own desires and interests for the sake of duty or for the benefit of others. —**self′-sac′ri·fic′ing,** *adj.*

self·same (self′sām′), *adj.* the very same; identical: *I still have the selfsame watch that my father carried.*

self·sat·is·fac·tion (self′sat′is fak′shən), *n.* a feeling of being satisfied with oneself or with one's own character, reputation, success, etc.

self·sat·is·fied (self′sat′is fīd′), *adj.* feeling or showing self-satisfaction; smug.

self·seek·ing (self′sē′kiñg), *n.* 1. the seeking of one's own aims and interests; selfishness. —*adj.* 2. tending to or showing self-seeking; selfish. —**self′-seek′er,** *n.*

self·serv·ice (self′sûr′vis), *n.* 1. service of oneself without help, as in a store, cafeteria, etc. —*adj.* 2. requiring or allowing persons to serve themselves: *a self-service elevator.*

self·styled (self′stīld′), *adj.* so-called or considered by oneself: *a self-styled fashion designer.*

self·suf·fi·cient (self′sə fish′ənt), *adj.* 1. able to exist and function without outside help: *The fort is self-sufficient.* 2. having too much confidence in one's own powers and abilities: *He is too self-sufficient to ask anybody's advice.* —**self′-suf·fi′cien·cy,** *n.*

self·sup·port (self′sə pôrt′), *n.* complete support of oneself without outside help: *He has achieved self-support with a steady job.* —**self′-sup·port′ing,** *adj.*

self·taught (self′tôt′), *adj.* taught by oneself, with little or no formal instruction: *a self-taught mechanic.*

self·willed (self′wild′), *adj.* stubborn about having one's way, without regard for the wishes of others.

self-wind·ing (self′wīn′dīng), *adj.* winding itself or keeping wound automatically: *a self-winding watch.*

sell (sel), *v.,* **sold** (sōld), **sell·ing. 1.** to give up or transfer to another for a price: *He sold the car for $600.* **2.** to deal in; have or offer (something) for sale: *to sell pianos.* **3.** to persuade (someone) to buy or accept: *to sell an idea to the public.* **4.** to win the acceptance or approval of (someone): *to sell voters on a candidate.* **5.** to give up or surrender in exchange for something unworthy: *to sell one's soul for gold.* **6.** to betray for one's own gain: *He sold his leader to the enemy.* **7.** to be employed in selling: *He sells for a living.* **8.** to be offered for sale at a certain price (usually fol. by *at* or *for*): *These dresses sell at $25.* **9.** to be in demand by buyers: *Do you think his new book will sell?* **10. sell off,** to sell, esp. at a low price, in order to get rid of: *They were forced to sell off most of their cattle.* **11. sell out, a.** to sell (a stock, supply, etc.) completely: *They sold out the new shoes an hour after the store opened.* **b.** *Informal.* to betray (a comrade, one's country, etc.); turn traitor: *I couldn't believe he would sell out to the enemy.*

sell·er (sel′ər), *n.* **1.** a person who sells; salesman; dealer. **2.** a thing sold, considered with reference to its success in the market: *Strawberries are a good seller this season.*

sel·vage (sel′vij), *n.* the edge of woven fabric, finished so as to prevent raveling. Also, **sel′vedge.**

selves (selvz), *n.* the plural of **self.**

se·man·tic (si man′tik), *adj.* **1.** of or concerned with the meanings of words or other symbols. **2.** of or referring to semantics. —**se·man′ti·cal·ly,** *adv.*

se·man·tics (si man′tiks), *n. (used as sing.)* the study of the meanings of words and how they change and develop.

sem·a·phore (sem′ə fôr′), *n.* **1.** any device or apparatus for signaling by changing the positions of lights, flags, etc. **2.** a system of signaling by changing the positions of two flags of a special kind, held one in each hand. —*v.,* **sem·a·phored, sem·a·phor·ing. 3.** to signal by semaphore.

sem·blance (sem′bləns), *n.* **1.** outward appearance or likeness: *a cloud with the semblance of a dragon.* **2.** unreal appearance; pretense; show: *Under a semblance of calm he was terrified.* **3.** image or copy: *The photograph was only a poor semblance of the parade.*

se·men (sē′mən), *n.* the fluid, produced by males, containing the male reproductive cells.

Semaphore (railroad)

se·mes·ter (si mes′tər), *n.* either of the two terms, of about 15 to 18 weeks each, into which a school year is usually divided.

semi-, a prefix meaning **1.** half: *semicircle.* **2.** twice in each period of time: *semimonthly.* **3.** part or partly: *semiprecious.*

sem·i·an·nu·al (sem′ē an′yōō əl, sem′ī-), *adj.* occurring, appearing, etc., twice each year: *a semiannual inspection.* —**sem′i·an′nu·al·ly,** *adv.*

sem·i·cir·cle (sem′i sûr′kəl), *n.* half of a circle; a half circle: *The class was seated in a semicircle facing the teacher.* —**sem′i·cir′cu·lar,** *adj.*

sem·i·co·lon (sem′i kō′lən), *n.* a punctuation mark (;) used to separate clauses of a sentence or items in a list, when the separation is less than shown by the period, but greater than shown by the comma.

sem·i·con·duc·tor (sem′ē kən duk′tər, sem′ī kən duk′tər), *n.* a substance, such as germanium or silicon, that conducts electricity more easily than an insulator but not as well as a conductor: used in making transistors.

sem·i·fi·nal (sem′ē fin′əl, sem′ī-), *n.* **1.** the next to the last round or contest in a tournament or competition. —*adj.* **2.** of or referring to such an event.

sem·i·month·ly (sem′ē munth′lē, sem′ī-), *adj.* **1.** occurring, appearing, etc., twice each month: *a semimonthly quiz.* —*n., pl.* **sem·i·month·lies. 2.** a publication issued twice each month. —*adv.* **3.** twice each month: *Reports are filed semimonthly.*

sem·i·nar·y (sem′ə ner′ē), *n., pl.* **sem·i·nar·ies. 1.** a special school that trains students for the clergy. **2.** a private school or college, esp. for young women.

Sem·i·nole (sem′ə nōl′), *n., pl.* **Sem·i·noles** *or* **Sem·i·nole.** a member of an Indian tribe formerly located in Florida and now in S Florida and E Oklahoma.

sem·i·pre·cious (sem′ē presh′əs, sem′ī-), *adj.* (of a gem) having far lower value than precious gems. Amethysts, garnets, etc., are semiprecious gems.

Sem·ite (sem′īt), *n.* a member of any of various ancient and modern peoples including the Hebrews, Arabs, Phoenicians, Babylonians, Jews, etc.

Se·mit·ic (sə mit′ik), *n.* **1.** an important family of languages of southwestern Asia and northern Africa, including Arabic, Aramaic, Hebrew, and Phoenician. —*adj.* **2.** of or referring to the Semites or their languages.

sem·i·trop·i·cal (sem′ē trop′i kəl, sem′ī-), *adj.* another word for **subtropical.**

sem·i·week·ly (sem′ē wēk′lē, sem′ī-), *adj.* **1.** occurring, appearing, etc., twice each week: *a semiweekly newspaper.* —*n., pl.* **sem·i·week·lies. 2.** a publication that is issued twice each week. —*adv.* **3.** twice each week: *Meetings are held semiweekly.*

sen·ate (sen′it), *n.* **1.** an assembly having the highest lawmaking or administrative powers, such as the senate of ancient Rome. **2.** (*often cap.*) the upper, and usually smaller, house of a legislative body, such as the Congress of the U.S. or the legislatures of many states. **3.** the place where a senate meets.

sen·a·tor (sen′ə tər), *n.* **1.** a member of a senate. **2.** (*often cap.*) a title of respect given to a person who is or has been a member of the U.S. Senate.

sen·a·to·ri·al (sen′ə tôr′ē əl), *adj.* **1.** of, relating to, or suitable for a senator or senate: *senatorial offices.* **2.** consisting of senators: *a senatorial delegation.* **3.** entitled to elect a senator: *a senatorial district.*

act, āble, dâre, ärt; ebb, ēqual; if, īce; hot, ōver, ôrder; oil; bŏŏk; ōōze; out; up, ûrge; ə = a as in *alone;* ə as in *button* (but′ən), *fire* (fīər); chief; shoe; thin; ŧħat; zh as in *measure* (mezh′ər). See full key inside cover.

send (send), *v.*, **sent** (sent), **send·ing. 1.** to cause, permit, or enable to go: *to send a letter.* **2.** to emit, discharge, utter, etc. (often fol. by *forth, off,* or *out*): *The flowers sent forth a sweet odor.* **3.** to put or bring into a certain condition: *His remarks sent them into a fury.* **4.** to cause to happen, come, be, etc.: *God sent a plague upon them for their wickedness.* **5. send for,** to summon; request the coming or delivery of: *to send for a new catalog.* **6. send in,** to mail (something) to a particular destination: *Send in your contest entry with two box tops.* **7. send out,** to send on the way; dispatch or distribute: *We sent out invitations last week.* —**send′er,** *n.*

Sen·e·ca (sen′ə kə), *n., pl.* **Sen·e·cas** or **Sen·e·ca.** a member of an Indian tribe located in western New York and Canada. The Seneca were one of the tribes of the Iroquois confederacy.

Sen·e·gal (sen′ə gôl′), *n.* a republic in W Africa, formerly French. 76,084 sq. mi. —**Sen·e·ga·lese** (sen′ə gô lēz′), *n., adj.*

se·nile (sē′nīl), *adj.* **1.** showing a decline or weakening of physical and mental powers, caused by old age. **2.** of or belonging to old age or aged persons: *senile diseases.* —**se·nil·i·ty** (si nil′i tē), *n.*

sen·ior (sēn′yər), *adj.* **1.** older or elder (used esp. of a father bearing the same full name as his son, and often written as *Sr.* or *sr.* following the name: *Michael Smith, Sr.*). See also **junior** (def. 1). **2.** having a higher rank or position: *a senior partner in a law firm.* **3.** being elected or appointed earlier: *the senior Senator from Kentucky.* **4.** (in a college, school, etc.) referring to students in their final year, or to their class. —*n.* **5.** a person who is older than another: *the senior of two brothers.* **6.** a person of higher rank or longer service in an office, position, class, etc.: *one's seniors in a company.* **7.** a student in his final year at a school or college.

sen′ior high′ school′, a school attended after junior high school, covering grades 10, 11, and 12.

sen·ior·i·ty (sēn yôr′i tē), *n., pl.* **sen·ior·i·ties. 1.** superiority in age, rank, or length of service. **2.** rights and privileges resulting from length of service: *The policy favors workers with the most seniority.*

sen·na (sen′ə), *n.* **1.** any of several herbs, shrubs, or trees of the bean family whose dried leaves are used as a strong laxative. **2.** the laxative drug made from the leaves of this herb.

se·ñor (sān yôr′), *n.* **1.** a Spanish title of respect used for a man, equivalent to *Mr.* or *Sir.* **2.** a Spanish gentleman.

se·ño·ra (sān yôr′ə), *n.* **1.** a Spanish title of respect used for a married woman, equivalent to *Mrs.* or *Madam.* **2.** a Spanish lady.

se·ño·ri·ta (sān′yə rē′tə), *n.* **1.** a Spanish title of respect used for a girl or an unmarried woman, equivalent to *Miss.* **2.** a Spanish young lady.

sen·sa·tion (sen sā′shən), *n.* **1.** the ability or process of perceiving by the senses; feeling: *His feet were so cold, there was no sensation in them.* **2.** an impression on the body or mind produced by the senses: *a sensation of warmth.* **3.** a state of excitement produced by some unusual act or event: *Her engagement to the prince caused a sensation.* **4.** the cause of such excitement: *The book is a sensation.*

sen·sa·tion·al (sen sā′shə nəl), *adj.* **1.** of or concerning the senses or sensation. **2.** arousing feelings of excitement, interest, etc., esp. by exaggeration of shocking acts or events: *a sensational newspaper.* **3.** extraordinary or outstanding: *a sensational landing on the moon.* —**sen·sa′tion·al·ly,** *adv.*

sense (sens), *n.* **1.** any of the five physical faculties (sight, hearing, taste, smell, and touch) by means of which a living being receives information about itself and its surroundings. **2.** the ability or power to receive impressions through one or more of the five senses; feeling; sensation: *the sense of sight.* **3.** an impression on the body or mind produced by the senses: *a sense of comfort.* **4.** any special ability for understanding, appreciating, etc.: *a sense of humor.* **5.** Usually, **senses.** the ability to think clearly and judge soundly: *Come to your senses.* **6.** intelligent thought, speech, or action: *to talk sense.* **7.** a more or less vague awareness or impression: *a sense of danger.* **8.** the meaning of a word, phrase, or statement: *The word "swell" in its slang sense means "fine" or "elegant."* —*v.,* **sensed, sens·ing. 9.** to become aware of through a sense or the senses: *to sense light and heat.* **10.** to grasp the meaning of; understand: *to sense the importance of a decision.* **11.** to have a more or less vague impression or awareness of: *to sense disaster.* **12. in a sense,** from one viewpoint; according to one explanation: *In a sense there was nothing else I could do.* **13. make sense,** to seem reasonable or sensible: *Your idea doesn't make sense.*

sense·less (sens′lis), *adj.* **1.** without sensation or feeling; unconscious: *He was knocked senseless by the blow.* **2.** stupid or foolish: *to take a senseless risk.* **3.** meaningless or nonsensical: *the senseless lyrics of a song.* —**sense′less·ly,** *adv.* —**sense′less·ness,** *n.*

sense′ or′gan, a part of the body by means of which an organism sees, hears, feels, etc.

sen·si·bil·i·ty (sen′sə bil′i tē), *n., pl.* **sen·si·bil·i·ties. 1.** the ability to feel or be aware: *the sensibility of the ear to sound.* **2.** Often, **sensibilities.** refined tastes in art, literature, social manners, etc.: *to have a fine sensibility for style.* **3.** Often, **sensibilities.** the tendency to feel hurt or offended easily: *The coarse jokes offended everyone's sensibilities.*

sen·si·ble (sen′sə bəl), *adj.* **1.** having or showing good sense or judgment: *a sensible young leader.* **2.** keenly aware (usually fol. by *of*): *sensible of his shortcomings.* **3.** of sufficient size, quantity, or intensity to be noticed: *a sensible change in temperature.* **4.** capable of feeling or perceiving; sensitive: *sensible to pain.* —**sen′si·bly,** *adv.*

sen·si·tive (sen′si tiv), *adj.* **1.** capable of being affected by stimulation or influence from outside: *the* sensitive cells of the retina. 2. easily affected emotionally; easily hurt or offended: *to be sensitive to criticism*. 3. able to respond to or measure very small amounts or changes: *a sensitive barometer*. 4. tender to the touch; sore: *The burn on my arm is still sensitive.* —**sen′si·tive·ly**, *adv.* —**sen′si·tiv′i·ty**, *n.*

sen·so·ry (sen′sə rē), *adj.* of or concerning the senses or sensations: *a sensory nerve.*

sen·su·al (sen′shōō əl), *adj.* 1. of or concerned with the senses, desires, and impulses of the physical body, rather than the mind or spirit: *sensual pleasures.* 2. too much concerned with the satisfaction of desires of the body: *a sensual man.* 3. arousing or exciting the desires or appetites of the senses: *a sensual rhythm.* —**sen′su·al′i·ty**, *n.* —**sen′su·al·ly**, *adv.*

sen·su·ous (sen′shōō əs), *adj.* 1. perceived by or affecting the senses: *sensuous melodies.* 2. deriving pleasure from things that appeal to the senses: *a sensuous love of food.* —**sen′su·ous·ly**, *adv.*

sent (sent), *v.* the past tense and past participle of **send.**

sen·tence (sen′t³ns), *n.* 1. (in grammar) a group of words that contains at least one subject and predicate, and expresses a complete statement, question, exclamation, request, or command: *"If you go" is not a complete sentence. "If you go, I'll wait for you here" is a complete sentence.* 2. a decision, esp. one made by a judge or a court. 3. the punishment pronounced by a judge upon a convicted person: *a sentence of five years in prison.* —*v.,* **sen·tenced, sen·tenc·ing.** 4. to pronounce sentence upon: *The court sentenced the defendant to pay a heavy fine.*

sen·ten·tious (sen ten′shəs), *adj.* 1. saying much in few words; pithy: *a sententious essay.* 2. fond of using familiar sayings or proverbs, often in a dull, self-righteous way: *a sententious lecturer.* —**sen·ten′tious·ly**, *adv.* —**sen·ten′tious·ness**, *n.*

sen·tient (sen′shənt), *adj.* having a sense or senses: *Rocks are not sentient.*

sen·ti·ment (sen′tə mənt), *n.* 1. a mental attitude toward something; opinion: *My letter fully explains my sentiments in this matter.* 2. a feeling or emotion: *a sentiment of pity.* 3. expression of feeling or emotion in an exaggerated or foolish way: *a romantic novel full of sentiment.*

sen·ti·men·tal (sen′tə men′t³l), *adj.* 1. expressing or appealing to tender emotions and feelings: *a sentimental song.* 2. arising from or serving sentiment: *I have kept all those old snapshots for sentimental reasons.* 3. acting in accordance with one's feelings, rather than thought or reason: *Dad is sentimental about his college days.* —**sen′ti·men′tal·ly**, *adv.*

sen·ti·men·tal·ist (sen′tə men′t³list), *n.* a person who is inclined to be sentimental.

sen·ti·men·tal·i·ty (sen′tə men tal′i tē), *n., pl.* for def. 3 **sen·ti·men·tal·i·ties.** 1. the state or quality of being sentimental. 2. the tendency to be influenced by feelings rather than thought or reason. 3. a sentimental act, expression, etc.

sen·ti·nel (sen′t³n³l), *n.* a person or thing that watches or stands guard; a guard or sentry.

sen·try (sen′trē), *n., pl.* **sen·tries.** a guard, esp. a soldier assigned to a certain post to prevent unauthorized persons from going in or out, or to give warning of danger.

S, Sepal

Seoul (sōl, sā ōōl′), *n.* the capital city of South Korea, in the W part.

se·pal (sē′pəl), *n.* one of the leaflike, often green parts of the calyx, which surrounds the petals at the base of a flower. See illus. at **flower.**

sep·a·ra·ble (sep′ər ə bəl, sep′rə bəl), *adj.* capable of being separated.

sep·a·rate (sep′ə rāt′), *v.,* **sep·a·rat·ed, sep·a·rat·ing.** 1. to keep apart; divide by a boundary or something placed between: *The English Channel separates Britain and France.* 2. to set or put apart; divide into parts or groups: *to separate the students into classes.* 3. to go apart or in different directions: *We separated at the station.* 4. to break away; cease to be a part of something: *The branch separated from the tree.* —*adj.* (sep′ər it). 5. not connected or joined: *separate tables.* 6. existing by itself; independent: *a separate nation.* 7. not shared; individual: *separate bedrooms.* —**sep′a·rate·ly**, *adv.*

sep·a·ra·tion (sep′ə rā′shən), *n.* 1. the act of separating: *separation of cream from milk.* 2. the state of being separated: *separation from one's family.* 3. something that separates or divides; boundary: *The river is a separation between the states.* 4. a gap or distance between two things that are separate: *There is a separation of five miles between the two towns.*

sep·a·ra·tist (sep′ə rā′tist, sep′ər ə tist), *n.* a person who takes part in or favors a separation, esp. from a religious or political body.

sep·a·ra·tor (sep′ə rā′tər), *n.* 1. a person or thing that separates. 2. any of various machines or devices for separating one thing from another, such as cream from milk.

se·pi·a (sē′pē ə), *n.* 1. a brown pigment obtained from the inky fluid of cuttlefish and used in drawing. 2. a dark brown. —*adj.* 3. of the color sepia.

Sept., September.

Sep·tem·ber (sep tem′bər), *n.* the ninth month of the year, containing 30 days.

sep·tic (sep′tik), *adj.* of, concerning, or caused by germs or infection.

sep′tic tank′, a tank in which sewage is decomposed and purified by bacteria.

sep·ul·cher (sep′əl kər), *n.* a tomb, grave, or burial place. Also, *esp. British,* **sep′ul·chre.**

se·pul·chral (sə pul′krəl), *adj.* 1. of or referring to a tomb or burial: *a sepulchral vault.* 2. having a deep, hollow sound: *a sepulchral voice.*

se·quel (sē′kwəl), *n.* 1. a book, play, story, etc., that is complete in itself, but continues the story or plot of an earlier work: *"Through the Looking-Glass" is a sequel to "Alice's Adventures in Wonderland."* 2.

something that follows, often as a result: *He lay in bed with a cold as a sequel to his fall through the ice.*

se·quence (sē′kwəns), *n.* **1.** the following of one thing after another; succession: *the sequence of events.* **2.** the order in which things follow one another: *Put the cards in the proper sequence.* **3.** a number of things following one another in a certain order: *a sequence of lectures.*

se·ques·ter (si kwes′tər), *v.* **1.** to withdraw into hiding or solitude; seclude: *He sequestered himself in the library.* **2.** (in law) to seize and hold (property) until debts or other claims are satisfied.

se·quin (sē′kwin), *n.* a small, shiny disk or spangle used as an ornament on dresses, gloves, etc.

se·quoi·a (si kwoi′ə), *n.* either of two very tall evergreen trees, the big tree and the redwood, that grow in California.

se·ra·pe (sə rä′pē), *n.* a blanket, often of brightly colored wool, worn as a shawl or wrap, chiefly by Indians in Latin-American countries.

ser·aph (ser′əf), *n., pl.* **ser·aphs** *or* **ser·a·phim** (ser′ə fim). a member of the highest order of angels. —**se·raph·ic** (si raf′ik), *adj.*

Serb (sûrb), *n.* a native or inhabitant of Serbia; Serbian.

Ser·bi·a (sûr′bē ə), *n.* a former kingdom in S Europe, now part of Yugoslavia. 34,116 sq. mi.

Ser·bi·an (sûr′bē ən), *n.* **1.** a Serb. **2.** the Serbo-Croatian language, esp. as written in Serbia, in the Cyrillic alphabet. —*adj.* **3.** of or referring to Serbia, its people, or their language.

Ser·bo-Cro·a·tian (sûr′bō krō ā′shən), *n.* **1.** the principal Slavic language of Yugoslavia, usually written with Cyrillic letters in Serbia and with Roman letters in Croatia. See also **Croatian** (def. 3), **Serbian** (def. 2). —*adj.* **2.** of or concerning Serbo-Croatian.

sere (sēr), *adj.* dried up; withered.

ser·e·nade (ser′ə nād′), *n.* **1.** a song, addressed to a lady by her lover standing beneath her window. **2.** any of various kinds of light, sentimental songs. —*v.*, **ser·e·nad·ed, ser·e·nad·ing. 3.** to perform a serenade for. **4.** to sing or play a serenade.

se·rene (sə rēn′), *adj.* **1.** calm, peaceful, or tranquil: *a serene setting for a picnic.* **2.** clear; bright; fair: *a serene sky.* —**se·rene′ly,** *adv.*

se·ren·i·ty (sə ren′i tē), *n.* **1.** calmness; peacefulness; tranquillity: *the serenity of a mountain landscape.* **2.** clearness; brightness: *the serenity of the sky.*

serf (sûrf), *n.* **1.** (in feudal times) a person who was bound to the land, and could be sold along with the land, like a slave. **2.** a slave, or any person treated like a slave.

serge (sûrj), *n.* a strong woolen or worsted fabric with slanting ribs woven into it.

ser·geant (sär′jənt), *n.* **1.** a noncommissioned officer ranking above a corporal in an army or similar organization. **2.** (in the U.S. Army and Marine Corps) a noncommissioned officer of any grade above that of corporal. **3.** (in the U.S. Air Force) a noncommissioned officer of any grade above that of airman first class. **4.** a police officer ranking above an ordinary policeman and below a lieutenant.

ser′geant at arms′, an officer whose main duty is to keep order at the meetings of a lawmaking body, in a court of law, etc.

se·ri·al (sēr′ē əl), *n.* **1.** a story published or broadcast in short installments. —*adj.* **2.** published or broadcast in installments: *a serial novel; a serial program.* **3.** arranged or numbered in a series: *serial certificates.* —**se′ri·al·ly,** *adv.*

se·ri·al·ize (sēr′ē ə līz′), *v.*, **se·ri·al·ized, se·ri·al·iz·ing.** to publish or broadcast in serial form.

se′rial num′ber, one of a series of numbers assigned to persons or things of a certain group or class as a means of identification.

se·ries (sēr′ēz), *n., pl.* **se·ries. 1.** a number of similar or related things or events following one another in a certain order: *a series of earthquakes.* **2.** a group or set of similar things: *a series of maps for a book.*

se·ri·ous (sēr′ē əs), *adj.* **1.** thoughtful; grave; solemn: *a serious look.* **2.** sincere; not joking or trifling: *a serious intention.* **3.** requiring careful thought; important: *The choice of a career is a serious matter.* **4.** causing or likely to cause great harm: *a serious illness.* —**se′ri·ous·ly,** *adv.* —**se′ri·ous·ness,** *n.*

ser·mon (sûr′mən), *n.* **1.** a formal talk, usually given by a clergyman or preacher for the purpose of religious or moral instruction. **2.** a serious, often tedious talk on matters of behavior, duty, etc.

se·rous (sēr′əs), *adj.* of, concerning, producing, or resembling serum.

ser·pent (sûr′pənt), *n.* **1.** a snake, esp. a poisonous one. **2.** a sly or treacherous person. **3.** the Devil.

ser·pen·tine (sûr′pən tēn′, sûr′pən tīn′), *adj.* **1.** of or like a serpent: *serpentine fangs.* **2.** winding and twisting: *a serpentine road through the mountains.* **3.** sly or treacherous. —*n.* **4.** a mineral, usually oily green and sometimes spotted like a serpent's skin, used for decorative stonework.

ser·rate (ser′it, ser′āt), *adj.* having notches along the edge, like the teeth of a saw: *a serrate leaf; a serrate knife.* Also, **ser·rat·ed** (ser′ā tid).

ser·ried (ser′ēd), *adj.* crowded or pressed closely together: *serried ranks of soldiers.*

se·rum (sēr′əm), *n.* **1.** any watery fluid from a human or animal body, esp. the pale-yellow liquid that separates from clotted blood. **2.** a fluid of this kind taken from an animal that has been inoculated with disease germs. Serums are used to fight the disease or give immunity to it in humans or in some animals.

Serrate leaf

serv·ant (sûr′vənt), *n.* **1.** a person employed to serve or wait on another, such as a maid, butler, valet, etc.

2. a person who serves devotedly in any capacity: *a servant of liberty.* **3.** a public official or employee: *a civil servant.*

serve (sûrv), *v.,* **served, serv·ing. 1.** to work as a servant: *She has served in this house for ten years.* **2.** to work for; be in the service of: *She has served the Smith family since they came here.* **3.** to be of help to; assist: *to serve the public.* **4.** to give service or aid; be of use; help: *an opportunity to serve.* **5.** to go through a term of service: *He served for four years as treasurer.* **6.** to go through (a term of service, imprisonment, etc.): *She served two terms as president. He served five years for robbery.* **7.** to wait table; work as a waiter. **8.** to provide for customers or guests: *We start to serve at six o'clock. Will you serve coffee on the patio?* **9.** to be enough for: *The recipe will serve six.* **10.** to have a certain use: *A heavy glass mug serves as a paperweight.* **11.** to answer the purpose: *This letter will serve to explain his resignation.* **12.** to provide with a regular supply of something: *Our warehouse in Chicago serves the entire Midwest.* **13.** to treat in a certain way: *His luck has served him badly.* **14.** to deliver or hand over to: *to serve a summons.* **15.** (esp. in tennis) to put (the ball) in play by hitting it. —*n.* **16.** the act, manner, or right of serving, as in tennis: *His serve failed to clear the net.* **17.** **serve one right,** to treat one as he deserves, esp. to punish justly: *It will serve you right if she never speaks to you again.*

serv·er (sûr′vər), *n.* **1.** a person who serves. **2.** something used for serving, such as a tray, a large spoon, spatula, etc.

serv·ice (sûr′vis), *n.* **1.** work performed for another person, a group, organization, etc.: *domestic service; military service.* **2.** assistance given to someone; help; aid: *Thank you for your service to the community.* **3.** goods or utilities that benefit the public: *electric service.* **4.** a company that provides such goods or utilities. **5.** a department of government that serves the public: *the welfare service.* **6.** the armed forces, or any branch of the armed forces: *He was drafted into the service.* **7.** maintenance and repair of machinery, apparatus, etc.: *TV service; brake service.* **8.** the providing of food, drinks, refreshments, etc., or the manner in which this is done: *Service is quicker at the counter.* **9.** Often, **services.** specialized or professional work performed for someone's benefit: *to require the services of a doctor.* **10.** a religious ceremony or ritual: *Sunday morning service.* **11.** a set of dishes, utensils, etc.: *a service for six.* **12.** (in law) the delivering of a legal order to a person. **13.** the act or manner of hitting the ball in certain games, such as tennis. —*adj.* **14.** of, belonging to, or used by persons who serve: *a service cap.* **15.** providing maintenance and repair: *a service truck.* **16.** of or belonging to the armed forces: *a service academy.* —*v.,* **serv·iced, serv·ic·ing. 17.** to maintain or repair: *to service an automobile.* **18.** to supply goods, utilities, etc., to: *This power station services the town.*

serv·ice·a·ble (sûr′vi sə bəl), *adj.* **1.** capable of being used; useful: *a serviceable truck.* **2.** wearing well; durable: *serviceable cloth.*

serv·ice·man (sûr′vis man′, -mən), *n., pl.* **serv·ice·men. 1.** a member of the armed forces. **2.** a person engaged in the maintenance and repair of machinery, equipment, etc.

serv′ice sta′tion, a place where automobiles are provided with gasoline, oil, repairs, etc.

ser·vile (sûr′vil, sûr′vīl), *adj.* **1.** too eager to please; slavish; fawning: *a servile flatterer.* **2.** of or fit for slaves: *servile labor.* —**ser·vil′i·ty** (sûr vil′i tē), *n.*

serv·ing (sûr′ving), *n.* **1.** the act of a person or thing that serves. **2.** a portion of food or drink; helping.

ser·vi·tude (sûr′vi tōōd′, -tyōōd′), *n.* **1.** the condition of a slave; slavery; bondage. **2.** compulsory service or labor as a punishment for criminals.

ses·a·me (ses′ə mē), *n.* a tropical plant whose small seeds are used as food or a source of oil.

ses·sion (sesh′ən), *n.* **1.** the meeting of a court, legislature, class, etc., to conduct its business. **2.** the period of time taken up by such a meeting: *The session lasted until six o'clock.* **3.** a series of such meetings, or the time during which the series continues: *The fall session begins on September 15.* **4.** any meeting of two or more persons: *The teachers had a long session with the principal this afternoon.*

set (set), *v.,* **set, set·ting. 1.** to put in a particular place or position: *Set the ladder against the wall.* **2.** to put into a certain condition: *to set a house on fire.* **3.** to put or apply: *to set a match to a pile of leaves.* **4.** to put in the proper order or arrangement for use: *to set the table for dinner.* **5.** to make or become hard or firm: *He set his body against the blow. Wait until the glue sets.* **6.** to pass below the horizon; sink: *The sun sets early in winter.* **7.** to arrange (the hair) in a particular style, esp. by using rollers, clips, spray, etc. **8.** to put (a price or value) upon something: *He set a price of $20,000 on the house.* **9.** to post or station in a particular place or position for the purpose of performing some duty: *to set a guard at the gate.* **10.** to decide upon or fix definitely: *to set a date for the wedding.* **11.** to establish for others to follow: *to set an example.* **12.** to fix or mount (a gem or the like) in a frame or setting. **13.** to ornament or stud with gems or the like: *a bracelet set with pearls.* **14.** to direct or turn: *to set a course for Hawaii.* **15.** to put (a broken or dislocated part) back in position. **16.** to fit or adapt: *to set a poem to music.* **17.** (in printing) **a.** to arrange (type): *to set type for the next issue.* **b.** to compose in type: *to set a column.* **18.** to urge to attack: *to set dogs on a prowler.* **19.** to place and fasten (a sail) in position to catch the wind. —*n.* **20.** the act of setting, or the state of being set. **21.** a collection of persons or things that belong together: *the social set; a chess set.* **22.** the way that something is set: *the firm set of his jaw.* **23.** an apparatus made up of a number of parts that work together: *a radio set.* **24.** (in tennis) a part of a match, consisting of six or more games, won by a margin of at least two games. **25.** scenery for a particular scene of a play. **26.** (in mathematics) a collection or group of objects, numbers, etc., that have something in common: *the set of odd numbers between 0 and 100.* —*adj.* **27.** definitely fixed or decided: *a set time; set rules.* **28.** fixed in a certain position or condition: *a set smile.* **29.** ready; arranged: *Everything is set for the party.* **30.** stubborn; obstinate: *to be set in one's ways.* **31. set about,** to begin on; start: *to set about painting the garage.* **32. set against, a.** hostile or opposed to: *I'm set against borrowing money for the trip.* **b.** to compare or contrast: *The advantages must be set against the disadvantages.* **33. set aside, a.** to put to one side; reserve: *to set aside money for the future.* **b.** to cancel, overrule, or annul: *to set aside a verdict.* **34. set back, a.** to cause to lag behind, slow down, etc.; hinder: *The strike set our production back six months.* **b.** to turn the hands of (a watch or clock) to show an earlier time: *On the last Sunday in October, set your watch back one hour.* **35. set down, a.** to land an airplane: *We set down in a heavy fog.* **b.** to write or record (something) in writing or printing: *Set down your ideas about the story we just read.* **c.** to attribute; explain as being caused by: *We set the failure down to bad advice.* **36. set forth, a.** to begin a journey; start: *Columbus set forth with three small ships.* **b.** to state or describe: *He set forth those ideas in his latest book.* **37. set in, a.** become widespread; arrive; occur; begin: *Darkness set in.* **b.** (of winds or currents) to blow or flow toward the shore. **38. set off, a.** to ignite or cause to explode: *to set off firecrackers.* **b.** to begin a journey or trip; depart: *to set off for India.* **c.** to increase or improve by contrast: *The light walls set off the dark curtains.* **39. set out, a.** to begin a journey: *to set out for home.* **b.** to make an attempt: *He set out to improve his grades.* **c.** to plant: *to set out geraniums.* **40. set to,** to begin; start: *It's time we set to and worked.* **41. set up, a.** to establish or arrange: *to set up an appointment.* **b.** to provide (someone) with means: *His folks set him up in business.* **c.** to construct or assemble: *We got there early to watch them set up the circus.*

set·back (set′bak′), *n.* **1.** a reverse or defeat: *Losing the game was a setback to our team.* **2.** something that holds back or checks: *a setback to progress.*

set·tee (se tē′), *n.* a seat for two or more persons, usually with a back and arms, and often upholstered.

set·ter (set′ər), *n.* **1.** a person or thing that sets. **2.** any of several kinds of long-haired dogs, often trained to show a hunter the position of hidden game by standing stiffly and pointing with the nose.

Irish setter
(27 in. high at shoulder)

set·ting (set′ing), *n.* **1.** the act of a person or thing that sets. **2.** the surroundings of anything: *a hotel in a mountain setting.* **3.** the frame or mounting of a jewel or the like. **4.** the place or time in which the action of a story or play takes place: *The setting of the play is ancient Greece.* **5.** the scenery and other properties used in a play. **6.** a piece of music composed for a story, poem, etc.

set·tle[1] (set′əl), *v.,* **set·tled, set·tling. 1.** to decide or agree upon: *to settle the terms of a lease.* **2.** to put in a definite order, position, or condition: *to settle one's affairs.* **3.** to pay (a bill, account, etc.). **4.** to move to and populate (a place); colonize: *Quebec was settled by the French.* **5.** to calm; quiet: *This warm milk will settle your stomach.* **6.** to make or become clear, as a liquid, by the sinking of suspended particles to the bottom: *Cooling will settle the drink.* **7.** to sink down gradually: *The foundation has settled. The mud settled out of the water.* **8.** to come to rest: *The mosquito settled on my arm.* **9.** to gather in a particular place: *Fog settled over the city.* **10. settle down, a.** to become calm or quiet: *Settle down and sleep.* **b.** to begin to work seriously: *After recess we have to settle down and study.* **c.** to live a more normal life: *When is Jim going to get married and settle down?* **11. settle on** (or **upon**), to decide on: *After trying on all the coats, I settled on the blue one.* [from the Old English word *setlan*]

set·tle[2] (set′əl), *n.* a long seat or bench, usually wooden, with arms and a high back. [from the Old English word *setle*]

set·tle·ment (set′əl mənt), *n.* **1.** the act of settling, or the state of being settled. **2.** an arrangement or adjustment of a dispute, problem, etc.: *the settlement of a labor strike.* **3.** the settling of persons in a new country or place; a colonizing: *The settlement of New York was begun by the Dutch.* **4.** a community of settlers; colony: *Spanish settlements in the West Indies.* **5.** any small, isolated community; hamlet: *an Eskimo settlement.* **6.** payment of a debt, obligation, etc. **7.** legal transfer of money or property to a person, esp. at the time of marriage, divorce, etc. **8.** the money or property transferred in this way. **9.** an establishment for providing recreation, instruction, personal advice and assistance, etc., to the people of an underprivileged city neighborhood.

Settle

set·tler (set′lər), *n.* **1.** a person or thing that settles. **2.** a new inhabitant of a country or place.

set·up (set′up′), *n.* **1.** a plan or arrangement: *the setup of the production department.* **2.** the state of things; situation: *I'll explain the setup for you.* **3.** a collection or arrangement of tools, utensils, equipment, etc., needed for a particular purpose: *a setup for serving drinks.* **4.** *Informal.* a contest or undertaking in which success is sure; cinch.

sev·en (sev′ən), *n.* **1.** a number that is six plus one. **2.** a set of this many persons or things: *Only seven will be there.* —*adj.* **3.** amounting to seven in number: *seven persons.*

sev′en seas′, all the oceans of the world: the Arctic, Antarctic, North Pacific, South Pacific, North Atlantic, South Atlantic, and Indian oceans.

sev·en·teen (sev′ən tēn′), *n.* **1.** a number that is ten plus seven. **2.** a set of this many persons or things: *Seventeen of them will be there.* —*adj.* **3.** amounting to seventeen in number: *seventeen persons.*

sev·en·teenth (sev′ən tēnth′), *adj.* **1.** being number seventeen in a series: *the seventeenth floor.* —*n.* **2.** one of seventeen equal parts. **3.** a person or thing that is seventeenth.

sev·enth (sev′ənth), *adj.* **1.** being number seven in a series: *the seventh floor.* —*n.* **2.** one of seven equal parts. **3.** a person or thing that is seventh.

sev·en·ti·eth (sev′ən tē ith), *adj.* **1.** being number seventy in a series. — *n.* **2.** one of seventy equal parts. **3.** a person or thing that is seventieth.

sev·en·ty (sev′ən tē), *n., pl.* **sev·en·ties.** **1.** a number that is seven times ten. **2.** a set of this many persons or things: *Seventy of them will be there.* **3. seventies,** the numbers, years, degrees, etc., between 70 and 79: *Grandfather is in his early seventies.* —*adj.* **4.** amounting to seventy in number: *seventy persons.*

Sev′en Won′ders of the World′, the seven most remarkable creations of man in ancient times: the pyramids of Egypt, the Mausoleum at Halicarnassus, the Temple of Artemis (Diana) at Ephesus, the Hanging Gardens of Babylon, the Colossus of Rhodes, the statue of Zeus by Phidias at Olympia, and the lighthouse at Alexandria.

sev·er (sev′ər), *v.* **1.** to separate (a part or piece) from something by cutting or breaking: *to sever a finger.* **2.** to break or cut into parts; split; cleave: *to sever lines of communication.* **3.** to discontinue; put an end to: *to sever a friendship.*

sev·er·al (sev′ər əl), *adj.* **1.** a fairly sizable number: *There were several pupils at the blackboard.* **2.** separate or different; individual: *They went their several ways.* — *n.* **3.** several persons or things: *Several of those present became ill.* —**sev′er·al·ly,** *adv.*

sev·er·ance (sev′ər əns), *n.* **1.** the act of severing: *the severance of a friendship.* **2.** the state of being severed; separation.

se·vere (si vēr′), *adj.,* **se·ver·er, se·ver·est.** **1.** very strict; harsh: *severe discipline.* **2.** serious or stern in manner or appearance; grave: *a severe face.* **3.** very simple or plain: *a severe dress.* **4.** intense; extreme; violent: *severe pain.* **5.** difficult to endure, perform, etc.: *a severe task.*—**se·vere′ly,** *adv.*—**se·vere′ness,** *n.*

se·ver·i·ty (si ver′i tē), *n., pl.* **se·ver·i·ties.** **1.** the state or quality of being severe: *the severity of the climate.* **2.** something severe: *to withstand severities.*

Se·ville (sə vil′), *n.* a port city in SW Spain.

sew (sō), *v.,* **sewed; sewn** (sōn) *or* **sewed; sew·ing.** **1.** to join or attach by stitches: *to sew a ribbon on a hat.* **2.** to make or repair (something) in this way: *to sew a dress.* **3.** to close (a hole, wound, etc.) with stitches (often fol. by *up*): *The surgeon sewed up the cut in the boy's scalp.* **4.** to work with needle and thread, or to operate a sewing machine: *She sews very well.* **5. sew up,** *Informal.* to be certain of; have in one's power or control: *to sew up an election.*

sew·age (sōō′ij), *n.* waste matter that flows through or is carried off by sewers. Also, **sewerage.**

sew·er¹ (sōō′ər), *n.* a pipe or tunnel for carrying off waste water and waste matter, esp. one in a city or town. [from the Middle English word *suere,* which comes from Old French *seuwiere* "overflow channel," from Latin *ex-* "out, away" + *aqua* "water"]

sew·er² (sō′ər), *n.* a person or thing that sews.

sew·er·age (sōō′ər ij), *n.* **1.** the removal of waste water and waste matter by means of sewers. **2.** a system of sewers. **3.** another word for **sewage.**

sew·ing (sō′ing), *n.* **1.** the act or work of a person or thing that sews. **2.** something sewn or to be sewn.

sew′ing machine′, any of various machines for sewing or making stitches, operated by a foot pedal or an electric motor.

sex (seks), *n.* **1.** either of the two groups, male and female, into which people, most kinds of animals, and many kinds of plants can be divided: *Men and boys belong to the male sex, whereas women and girls belong to the female sex.* **2.** the fact or character of being male or female. **3.** the traits that distinguish males and females, or the behavior depending on them. **4.** the activities involved in reproduction, esp. sexual union.

sex·ism (sek′siz əm), *n.* discrimination or bias because of sex, esp. that directed against women.—**sex′ist,** *n., adj.*

sex·tant (seks′tənt), *n.* an instrument that measures the angles between distant objects, used esp. in determining a ship's position at sea by measurement of the height of the sun above the horizon.

sex·tet (seks tet′), *n.* **1.** a group of six singers or players. **2.** a piece of music for such a group.

sex·ton (seks′tən), *n.* an official of a church whose duty is to care for the church building and grounds, ring the bell, etc.

sex·u·al (sek′shōō əl), *adj.* **1.** of, concerning, or depending upon sex or the traits that distinguish the two sexes: *sexual organs; sexual reproduction.* **2.** of or involving union of the organs of reproduction of male and female: *sexual relations.* —**sex·u·al·i·ty** (sek′shōō al′i tē), *n.* —**sex′u·al·ly,** *adv.*

Sgt., Sergeant.

shab·by (shab′ē), *adj.,* **shab·bi·er, shab·bi·est.** **1.** spoiled by much wear or use: *a shabby old coat.* **2.** showing neglect or improper care; run-down: *a shabby apartment.* **3.** slovenly or ragged in dress or appearance: *a shabby beggar.* **4.** mean; unfair; contemptible: *shabby treatment.* —**shab′bi·ly,** *adv.* —**shab′bi·ness,** *n.*

shack (shak), *n.* **1.** a small, crude house or hut; shanty. **2.** a run-down, neglected house or building.

shack·le (shak′əl), *n.* **1.** a ring or other fastening for the wrists, ankles, etc., usually connected by a chain, for preventing escape or freedom of movement; fetter. **2.** any of various devices for fastening or joining. **3.** Often, **shackles.** anything that prevents freedom of thought or action: *the shackles of ignorance.*

—*v.*, **shack·led, shack·ling. 4.** to fasten with a shackle or shackles. **5.** to restrict in thought or action.

shad (shăd), *n.*, *pl.* **shads** *or* **shad.** a food fish of the Atlantic Ocean that swims up rivers to spawn.

shade (shād), *n.* **1.** the darkness caused by something that cuts off the direct rays of the light: *An elm tree provides shade.* **2.** a place or area protected from direct light, esp. sunlight: *to sit in the shade.* **3.** any device that protects from direct light, such as a window shade or lampshade. **4.** the dark part of a painting, photograph, or the like. **5.** the darkness or lightness of a color; the degrees or varieties of a color. **6.** a ghost or specter. **7.** a small amount or degree: *The price of the house was a shade more than we could afford.* **8.** a slight difference; nuance: *the shades of meaning of a word.* **9.** Usually, **shades.** gathering darkness: *the shades of night.* —*v.*, **shad·ed, shad·ing. 10.** to shield or protect from direct light: *Tall trees shade the lawn.* **11.** to darken or dim by means of a shade: *to shade a light bulb.* **12.** to use dark lines or colors in (a painting or drawing) to represent the effects of light and shadow. **13. put in the shade,** to cause to seem slight by comparison; surpass: *Her new dress really puts mine in the shade.*

shad·ing (shā'dĭng), *n.* **1.** a slight difference of color, quality, meaning, etc. **2.** protection against direct light. **3.** the use of dark lines or colors in a painting or drawing to represent the shadow.

shad·ow (shăd'ō), *n.* **1.** a dark figure or image cast on a surface by an object that blocks the light. **2.** a place or area in partial darkness; shade: *I saw him hiding in the shadows.* **3.** Usually, **shadows.** gathering darkness, esp. after sunset: *the shadows of evening.* **4.** a slight amount; trace: *beyond the shadow of a doubt.* **5.** a ghost or specter. **6.** a hint or suggestion: *shadows of things to come.* **7.** a faint image or representation: *He is just a shadow of his former self.* **8.** the dark part of a painting, photograph, or the like. **9.** shelter or protection: *safe in the shadow of the church.* **10.** a threat or influence of fear, sadness, etc.: *the shadow of war.* **11.** a person who follows another constantly, either as a companion or as a spy. —*v.* **12.** to protect from direct light; shade. **13.** to follow (a person) closely, esp. for the purpose of spying on his movements.

shad·ow·y (shăd'ō ē), *adj.* **1.** resembling a shadow; dim; unclear: *shadowy figures moving about.* **2.** unreal; fanciful: *a shadowy hope.* **3.** covered with shadow; dark: *a shadowy corner of the room.*

shad·y (shā'dē), *adj.*, **shad·i·er, shad·i·est. 1.** full of shade; shaded: *a shady path.* **2.** giving shade: *a shady tree.* **3.** *Informal.* not entirely honest or proper; questionable; suspicious: *shady business dealings; a shady character.* —**shad'i·ness,** *n.*

shaft (shăft), *n.* **1.** a long, slender pole forming the handle or stem of various tools, weapons, etc. **2.** a sharp, thin projectile, such as an arrow, dart, or spear. **3.** a sharp, stinging remark directed at a person or thing: *shafts of sarcasm.* **4.** a ray or beam: *a shaft of sunlight.* **5.** a round, straight bar forming part of a machine, for supporting rotating parts or

transmitting motion to other parts. **6.** any tall, slender structure, such as a column, tower, monument, etc. **7.** one of the two poles between which an animal is harnessed to a carriage, wagon, etc. **8.** a long, narrow opening dug into the earth: *a mine shaft.* **9.** an enclosed vertical space in a building: *an elevator shaft.* **10.** the main part of a column.

shag (shăg), *n.* **1.** rough, matted hair, wool, or the like. **2.** a long, rough nap on cloth. **3.** cloth with a long, rough nap.

shag·bark (shăg'bärk'), *n.* a kind of hickory tree with a rough, gray bark: yields a hard, useful wood.

shag·gy (shăg'ē), *adj.*, **shag·gi·er, shag·gi·est. 1.** having long, rough hair or wool: *The yak is a shaggy animal.* **2.** rough and untidy: *a shaggy beard.* **3.** having a rough nap: *shaggy cloth.* —**shag'gi·ness,** *n.*

Shah (shä), *n.* the title of the ruler of Iran.

shake (shāk), *v.*, **shook** (shŏŏk), **shak·en** (shā'kən), **shak·ing. 1.** to move up and down or back and forth with short, rapid motions: *He shook his head. The branches are shaking with the wind.* **2.** to tremble or cause to tremble: *She was shaking with the cold.* **3.** to clasp (a person's hand) in greeting, congratulation, etc. **4.** to come or cause to come off, out, etc., by shaking: *Dry sand shakes off easily. He shook some salt on his meat.* **5.** to disturb or distress deeply: *He was shaken by the sudden death of his friend.* **6.** to get away from; escape from: *The fugitive failed to shake his pursuers.* —*n.* **7.** the act of shaking or being shaken. **8.** a shaking or trembling movement. **9. the shakes,** a fit of trembling, esp. from chills, fever, etc. **10.** something mixed or stirred by shaking, such as a drink: *a milk shake.* **11. no great shakes,** *Informal.* not important; of no special interest or ability: *As a pitcher, he's no great shakes.* **12. shake down, a.** to bring down or cause to fall by shaking: *See if you can shake down some ripe apples.* **b.** to cause to settle: *Shake down the basket of leaves to make it more compact.* **c.** to put in proper condition; test: *to shake down a new ship.* **d.** *Slang.* to force money from (a person) illegally; blackmail: *The gang shook him down when they learned he had been in prison.* **13. shake off, a.** to get rid of by shaking: *Shake off the raindrops and come in.* **b.** to stop worrying about: *to shake off one's cares and worries.* **14. shake up, a.** to mix or loosen by shaking: *to shake up a can of paint.* **b.** to upset or disturb in mind or body: *to be shaken up by bad news.* **15. two shakes,** a very short time; a moment: *I'll be downstairs in two shakes.*

shak·er (shā'kər), *n.* **1.** a person or thing that shakes. **2.** a container with holes in the top, used for holding and sprinkling sugar, flour, etc. **3.** a container for mixing a liquid by shaking: *a cocktail shaker.*

Shak·er (shā'kər), *n.* a member of a Protestant sect in the U.S. that practices celibacy, common ownership of property, and a simple way of life.

Shake·speare (shāk'spēr), *n.* **William,** 1564–1616, English dramatist and poet. —**Shake·spear·e·an** (shāk spēr'ē ən), *adj.*, *n.*

shake-up (shāk'ŭp'), *n.* a sudden and thorough change in the personnel of an organization.

shak·o (shak′ō, shā′kō), *n.*, *pl.* **shak·os** *or* **shak·oes.** a military cap having a tall, stiff crown, a broad visor, and a long plume or tuft on top. [from the Magyar word *czákó,* which comes from German *Zacke* "peak, point"]

shak·y (shā′kē), *adj.,* **shak·i·er, shak·i·est. 1.** shaking or trembling; having a tendency to shake or tremble; weak; unsteady: *a shaky platform.* **2.** unreliable; wavering: *shaky loyalty.* **3.** unsound; of doubtful value: *shaky evidence.* —**shak′i·ly,** *adv.* —**shak′i·ness,** *n.*

shale (shāl), *n.* a kind of rock, formed from clay, that readily splits into layers.

shall (shal), *auxiliary verb, past tense* **should** (shŏŏd). **1.** (used with "I" or "we" to indicate simple future time) plan to or expect to; am going to or are going to: *I shall be at home this evening. We shall visit him tomorrow.* **2.** (used with "you," "he," "she," "it," or "they" to indicate determination or authority) will have to; is determined to; must: *You shall listen to me whether you want to or not.*

—**Usage.** Most educated speakers and writers use *shall* rather than *will* with first-person pronouns in the future tense: *I shall go. We shall be late. Will* is restricted to use with second- and third-person pronouns: *You will be sorry. He will stay home. They will visit her.* In emphatic statements, the use of *shall* and *will* is usually reversed: *I will go, and you can't stop me! They shall be told, whatever happens!*

shal·low (shal′ō), *adj.* **1.** not deep; having little distance between the top and the bottom: *to wade in a shallow pool.* **2.** (of ideas, emotions, etc.) not profound or serious; superficial: *shallow, ignorant thinking.* —*n.* **3.** Usually, **shallows.** *(used as sing. or pl.)* the shallow part of a body of water.

shalt (shalt), *v.* an old form of **shall,** found now chiefly in Biblical and poetic writing and used with *thou: Thou shalt not kill.*

sham (sham), *n.* **1.** an imitation that is meant to deceive; fraud or pretense: *That isn't a real diamond, it's a sham.* —*adj.* **2.** not real; pretended or false; counterfeit: *a sham attack; the sham splendor of a movie theater.* —*v.,* **shammed, sham·ming. 3.** to pretend; put on a false appearance of: *to sham illness.*

sham·ble (sham′bəl), *v.,* **sham·bled, sham·bling. 1.** to walk in an awkward, unsteady way; shuffle: *The prisoner shambled around his cell.* —*n.* **2.** an awkward, unsteady way of walking; a shambling gait: *the shamble of an old dog.*

sham·bles (sham′bəlz), *n. (used as sing. or pl.)* **1.** a slaughterhouse. **2.** any scene of great destruction or disorder: *The flooded town was a shambles.*

shame (shām), *n.* **1.** the painful feeling of guilt or embarrassment that arises when one has done something wrong or ridiculous: *She hung her head in shame when she had to admit that she'd told a lie.* **2.** disgrace or dishonor: *His crime brought shame upon his family.* **3.** something that causes disgrace or dishonor: *The way he cheats people is a shame.* **4.** some-

thing that is cause for regret or sorrow: *It's a shame that you are ill.* —*v.,* **shamed, sham·ing. 5.** to cause to feel shame: *to shame someone by scolding him in public.* **6. for shame!** you should be ashamed of yourself! **7. put to shame, a.** to cause (a person) to be ashamed or disgraced. **b.** to outdo; surpass: *His brilliant playing put the rest of us to shame.*

shame·faced (shām′fāst′), *adj.* **1.** showing shame, guilt, or embarrassment: *a sad, shamefaced expression; shamefaced apologies.* **2.** bashful or shy. —**shame·fac·ed·ly** (shām′fā′sid lē, shām′fāst′lē), *adv.*

shame·ful (shām′fəl), *adj.* causing or deserving shame; disgraceful: *shameful mistreatment of a prisoner.* —**shame′ful·ly,** *adv.* —**shame′ful·ness,** *n.*

shame·less (shām′lis), *adj.* feeling or showing no shame; brazen; indecent: *a wicked, shameless woman.* —**shame′less·ly,** *adv.* —**shame′less·ness,** *n.*

sham·poo (sham pōō′), *n.* **1.** a liquid soap or other preparation for washing the hair. **2.** a washing of the hair: *Give the baby a shampoo.* —*v.,* **sham·pooed, sham·poo·ing. 3.** to wash (the hair or head), esp. with a shampoo. [from Hindi *čāmpnā* "to press"]

sham·rock (sham′rok), *n.* any of several three-leafed plants resembling clover, one of which is the national emblem of Ireland.

shang·hai (shang′hī, shang hī′), *v.,* **shang·haied, shang·hai·ing.** to force (a person) to join the crew of a ship, esp. by using drugs or liquor.

Shamrock

Shang·hai (shang hī′), *n.* a port city in E China, near the mouth of the Yangtze River.

shank (shangk), *n.* **1.** the part of the leg between the knee and the ankle. **2.** a similar part of an animal's leg. **3.** the entire leg of a man including the thigh. **4.** a cut of meat from the upper part of an animal's leg. **5.** a narrow, shaftlike part that connects two portions of a tool: *The shank of a screwdriver connects the blade with the handle.*

Shan·non (shan′ən), *n.* a river flowing SW from N Ireland to the Atlantic Ocean. 240 mi. long.

shan't (shant), contraction of *shall not: I shan't go.*

Shan·tung (shan′tung′ *or, for def. 2,* shan′tung), *n.* **1.** a province in NE China. **2.** *(often l.c.)* a heavy fabric of raw silk.

shan·ty (shan′tē), *n., pl.* **shan·ties.** a small, crudely built cabin or hut; shack.

shape (shāp), *n.* **1.** the outline or outward form of something; appearance with regard to the outline of the surface; figure; contour: *An orange has the same shape as a ball. The ghost appeared in the shape of a man.* **2.** a figure or form seen only in outline: *A vague shape appeared in the fog.* **3.** orderly arrangement: *to give* shape to one's ideas. **4.** condition or physical state: *an old house in bad shape.* —*v.,* **shaped, shap·ing. 5.** to give a definite shape or form to: *to shape clay.* **6.** to develop and bring order to: *to shape young minds.* **7. shape up,** *Informal.* **a.** to assume a definite form; develop, esp. favorably: *Our plans are beginning to shape up.* **b.** to improve one's behavior, performance, etc.: *Shape up or get off the team.* —**shap′a·ble, shape′a·ble,** *adj.* —**shap′er,** *n.*

shape·less (shāp′lis), *adj.* **1.** having no definite shape or form: *shapeless clouds.* **2.** having an unpleasing shape; not shapely: *a dumpy, shapeless figure.* —**shape′less·ly,** *adv.* —**shape′less·ness,** *n.*

shape·ly (shāp′lē), *adj.,* **shape·li·er, shape·li·est.** having a pleasing shape; well formed: *A good horse should have a shapely head.* —**shape′li·ness,** *n.*

share (shâr), *n.* **1.** a part or portion of a whole, given or assigned to one person or one group: *Have you eaten your share of the dessert?* **2.** one of the equal parts into which the capital stocks or ownership of a business or property is divided: *He has ten shares of stock in that company.* —*v.,* **shared, shar·ing. 3.** to use, own, receive, etc., together: *The two chemists shared the Nobel Prize.* **4.** to divide and give out (something) in shares or parts: *I'll share the money with all of you.* **5.** to take part (usually fol. by *in*): *Don't you want to share in the fun?* —**shar′er,** *n.*

share·crop·per (shâr′krop′ər), *n.* a farmer who rents his land, and pays the rent by giving the landowner part of the crop.

share·hold·er (shâr′hōl′dər), *n.* a person who holds one or more shares of stock in a company or corporation; a part owner of a business.

shark¹ (shärk), *n.* any of numerous saltwater fishes ranging in length to over 30 feet, having a rough skin and many rows of sharp teeth. Sharks are extremely dangerous and are known to attack swimmers and divers.

shark² (shärk), *n.* **1.** a person who makes money by cheating other people; swindler. **2.** *Slang.* a person who is outstanding in some activity; expert. [from the German word *Schurke* "rascal"]

Shark¹
(length 30 ft.)

shark·skin (shärk′skin′), *n.* a smooth fabric of rayon or worsted, used for clothing.

Shar·on (shar′ən), *n.* a fertile coastal plain in ancient Palestine, now part of Israel.

sharp (shärp), *adj.* **1.** having a thin cutting edge or a fine point; well-shaped for cutting or piercing: *a sharp knife; a sharp pin.* **2.** ending in a point or thin edge; not blunt or rounded: *a long, sharp nose.* **3.** having or involving a sudden change of direction: *a sharp turn in the road.* **4.** clear and distinct; clearly defined: *a sharp picture on the television set.* **5.** biting in taste or smell: *a sharp cheese.* **6.** piercing or shrill in sound: *a sharp cry of pain.* **7.** keenly cold; piercing; nipping: *a sharp, icy wind.* **8.** severe or in-

tense; felt acutely: *a sharp pain.* **9.** able to perceive very clearly: *a scout with a sharp eye.* **10.** bright; shrewd: *a sharp young man.* **11.** shrewd to the point of being dishonest: *the sharp practices of an unscrupulous loan company.* **12.** angry or harsh: *to use sharp words.* **13.** (in music) above the correct pitch or raised a half step from another note (distinguished from *flat*). **14.** *Slang.* very stylish or fashionable: *a sharp dresser.* —*adv.* **15.** in a sharp manner; keenly, alertly, or closely: *You'll have to look sharp to find the trail.* **16.** abruptly or suddenly: *to pull a horse up sharp.* **17.** promptly or punctually: *Meet me at one o'-clock sharp.* —*n.* **18.** (in music) **a.** a tone a half step above another tone. **b.** the sign (♯) indicating the raising of a tone by a half step. —**sharp′ly,** *adv.* —**sharp′ness,** *n.*

sharp·en (shär′pən), *v.* to make or become sharp or sharper: *to sharpen a knife.* —**sharp′en·er,** *n.*

sharp·shoot·er (shärp′shoo′tər), *n.* a person skilled in shooting, esp. with a rifle; expert marksman.

shat·ter (shat′ər), *v.* **1.** to break into many pieces; smash. **2.** to damage, ruin, or destroy: *to shatter someone's health; to shatter hopes.* —**shat′ter·ing·ly,** *adv.*

shave (shāv), *v.,* **shaved; shaved** *or* **shav·en** (shā′vən); **shav·ing. 1.** to remove (hair, a beard, etc.) by cutting off close to the skin with a razor. **2.** to cut off hair or a growth of beard from (the face, head, legs, etc.) with a razor. **3.** to cut or scrape thin slices from: *to shave a piece of wood with a knife.* **4.** to scrape, graze, or come very close to: *The car shaved the garage door.* **5.** to cut or trim closely: *to shave a lawn.* —*n.* **6.** a cutting off of hair, esp. a growth of beard, with a razor. **7. a close shave,** a narrow escape; close call: *The acrobat had a close shave when the trapeze broke.*

shav·en (shā′vən), *v.* **1.** a past participle of **shave.** —*adj.* **2.** closely cut or trimmed.

shav·er (shā′vər), *n.* **1.** a person or thing that shaves. **2.** an electric razor. **3.** *Informal.* a small boy; youngster.

shav·ing (shā′ving), *n.* **1.** a very thin piece or slice, esp. of wood. **2.** the act of a person or thing that shaves.

shawl (shôl), *n.* a large, heavy scarf of wool or other fabric worn by a woman over the shoulders or head and shoulders.

Shaw·nee (shô nē′), *n., pl.* **Shaw·nees** *or* **Shaw·nee.** a member of a migratory Indian tribe of the eastern and central U.S., now in E Oklahoma.

shay (shā), *n.* a two-wheeled, horse-drawn carriage for two persons; chaise.

she (shē), *pron.* **1.** the female person or animal last mentioned or being spoken of: *As for my sister, she just hates spiders.* **2.** anything regarded as feminine: *She's the finest ship in the fleet.* —*n.* **3.** a female: *Is this kitten a she?*

she-, a prefix meaning female: *she-wolf; she-devil.*

sheaf (shēf), *n., pl.* **sheaves** (shēvz). **1.** a bundle of cut stalks of wheat, rye, or other grain plant, tied around the middle. **2.** any bundle, cluster, or collection of things, bound or tied together: *a sheaf of papers; a sheaf of arrows.*

shear (shēr), *v.,* **sheared; sheared** *or* **shorn** (shôrn); **shear·ing. 1.** to remove (hair, fleece, etc.) by cutting or clipping: *to sheer wool from a sheep.* **2.** to cut or clip the hair, fleece, wool, etc., from: *to shear a sheep.* **3.** to cut or break: *With one stroke of the ax, he sheared the branch from the tree.* **4.** to take something away from; deprive: *The committee sheared the official of his power.* **—n. 5.** Usually, **shears.** a cutting tool resembling a large pair of scissors: *a pair of shears.* **—shear′er,** *n.*

sheath (shēth), *n., pl.* **sheaths** (shēthz). **1.** a case or covering for the blade of a sword, dagger, or the like. **2.** any similar close-fitting case or covering. **3.** a close-fitting dress. **—v. 4.** another spelling of **sheathe.**

sheathe (shēth), *v.,* **sheathed, sheath·ing. 1.** to put (a sword, dagger, etc.) into a sheath or close-fitting case. **2.** to cover or provide with a protective case or covering: *to sheathe one's hands in heavy gloves.* Also, **sheath.**

sheath·ing (shē′thing), *n.* **1.** the act of one who sheathes a sword, dagger, or the like. **2.** a covering or outer layer, such as a layer of metal plates on the bottom of a ship. **3.** material used for such a covering.

sheave (shēv), *v.,* **sheaved, sheav·ing.** to gather or bind into one or more sheaves or bundles.

She·ba (shē′bə), *n.* **Queen of,** (in the Bible) the queen who visited Solomon to find out how wise he was.

shed[1] (shed), *n.* a roughly built, usually small building for storage or shelter. [from the Old English word *sced* "shelter"]

shed[2] (shed), *v.,* **shed, shed·ding. 1.** to pour forth (water or other liquid); let fall in drops or streams: *eyes shedding tears.* **2.** to give or send forth; spread: *This lamp doesn't shed enough light.* **3.** to cast off or let fall: *a tree shedding its leaves.* **4.** (of an animal) to lose hair: *The dog is shedding.* **5. shed blood,** to kill by violence; slaughter: *to shed blood when invading an enemy's country.* [from the Old English word *scēadan*] **—shed′der,** *n.*

she'd (shēd), **1.** contraction of *she had.* **2.** contraction of *she would.*

sheen (shēn), *n.* shining brightness, esp. on a polished surface; gloss; luster.

sheep (shēp), *n., pl.* **sheep. 1.** any of numerous animals related to the goat, various kinds of which are bred for their wool or their meat. **2.** a meek and timid person; one who is easily led by others. **3. separate the sheep from the goats,** to separate the good from the bad; know the difference between what is true and genuine and what is not. **—sheep′like′,** *adj.*

Domestic sheep (about 30 in. high at shoulder)

sheep′ dog′, a dog trained to herd or guard sheep.

sheep·fold (shēp′fōld′), *n.* a pen or enclosure for sheep.

sheep·herd·er (shēp′hûr′dər), *n.* a shepherd. **—sheep′herd′ing,** *n.*

sheep·ish (shē′pish), *adj.* **1.** embarrassed or shy: *With a sheepish smile, he admitted he'd been wrong.* **2.** like a sheep, esp. in being meek and easily led by others. **—sheep′ish·ly,** *adv.* **—sheep′ish·ness,** *n.*

sheep·man (shēp′mən), *n., pl.* **sheep·men. 1.** a man whose occupation is the tending or breeding of sheep, esp. the owner of a sheep ranch. **2.** a shepherd.

sheep·skin (shēp′skin′), *n.* **1.** the skin of a sheep, esp. when processed with the wool left on. **2.** parchment made from the skin of a sheep. **3.** *Informal.* a diploma.

sheer[1] (shēr), *adj.* **1.** extremely thin and fine; transparent or almost transparent: *sheer silk.* **2.** not mixed with anything else; pure: *We had to drill through sheer rock.* **3.** utter or absolute: *sheer nonsense.* **4.** very steep; almost completely vertical: *a sheer cliff.* [from the Old English word *scēr* "clear, undisputed"] **—sheer′ly,** *adv.* **—sheer′ness,** *n.*

sheer[2] (shēr), *v.* **1.** to turn from a course; swerve: *The driver suddenly sheered to the left to avoid the dog.* **—n. 2.** a turning from a course; swerve. [from a special use of *sheer*[1]]

sheet[1] (shēt), *n.* **1.** a large rectangular piece of linen, cotton, or other lightweight fabric, used as a covering on a bed. **2.** a broad, thin layer or covering: *A sheet of ice lay over the driveway.* **3.** a broad flat surface or expanse: *sheets of water.* **4.** a relatively thin, usually rectangular piece or slab: *a sheet of metal.* **5.** a rectangular piece of paper. **6.** a sail for a ship or boat. **—v. 7.** to provide or cover with a sheet or as a layer: *Ice sheeted the pavement.* [from the Old English word *scēat* "corner, sheet"]

sheet[2] (shēt), *n.* a rope or chain for holding or adjusting a sail so that it is set at the desired angle. [from an Old English word meaning "the lower corner of a sail"]

sheet′ light′ning, lightning that appears as a general lighting up of the sky, usually due to the reflection of the lightning of a distant thunderstorm.

sheet′ met′al, metal in sheets or thin plates.

sheet′ mu′sic, music, usually for popular songs, printed on unbound sheets of paper.

sheik (shēk), *n.* (among Arabs and other Muslims) **1.** the head man of a village or tribe; chief. **2.** a religious leader. Also, **sheikh.**

obverse   reverse
Shekel (Hebrew)

shek·el (shek′əl), *n.* **1.** an ancient unit of weight used by the Babylonians, Hebrews, and others, equal to between a quarter and a half ounce. **2.** a coin of this weight, esp. the chief silver coin of the Hebrews.

shel·drake (shel′drāk′), *n.* any of several European and Asian ducks having many-colored plumage.

shelf (shelf), *n., pl.* **shelves** (shelvz).
1. a thin, usually long piece of wood, metal, etc., attached to a wall or set in a frame, and used to hold things: *a bookcase with six shelves.* 2. something resembling a shelf, such as a ledge of rock, a sandbank, reef, or the like. 3. **on the shelf,** not active; useless: *He has been on the shelf ever since his retirement.*

Sheldrake
(length 26 in.)

shell (shel), *n.* 1. the hard outer covering of an animal, such as an oyster, snail, or lobster. 2. the hard outer covering of an egg, nut, or seed. 3. a hollow projectile filled with explosives and fired by a cannon, mortar, etc. 4. a cartridge for a rifle, pistol, shotgun, etc. 5. short for **tortoise shell.** 6. the lower pastry crust of a pie, tart, or the like, before the filling is added. 7. the framework or walls and roof of a building. 8. a long, narrow, lightweight boat for rowing by one or more persons, used esp. in racing. —*v.* 9. to take out of the shell, pod, husk, or the like; remove the shell of: *to shell nuts; to shell peas.* 10. to fire shells or explosives at or on; bombard. 11. **shell out,** *Slang.* to give or contribute (money): *We had to shell out $10 apiece for the bus fare.*

Shell (def. 8)

shel·lac (shə lak′), *n.* 1. a varnish made by dissolving in alcohol the resin secreted by an Asian insect. —*v.,* **shel·lacked, shel·lack·ing.** 2. to coat with this varnish. 3. *Slang.* to defeat soundly; thrash.

Shel·ley (shel′ē), *n.* Percy Bysshe (bish), 1792–1822, English poet.

shell·fire (shel′fīr′), *n.* the firing of explosive shells.

shell·fish (shel′fish′), *n., pl.* **shell·fish·es** *or* **shell·fish.** any freshwater or saltwater animal that has a shell, such as clams, oysters, crabs, lobsters, or crayfish.

shell′ shock′, a nervous or mental disorder resulting from the strain of taking part in modern warfare.

shel·ter (shel′tər), *n.* 1. something that covers or gives protection from storms, falling objects, burning sunlight, etc.; refuge: *The only shelter they had was a small tent.* 2. the condition of being protected or shielded; protection; refuge: *During the storm we took shelter in an old barn.* —*v.* 3. to cover or protect; be a shelter for. 4. to provide with a shelter or protection: *to shelter a fugitive.*

shelve (shelv), *v.,* **shelved, shelv·ing.** 1. to place on a shelf or shelves. 2. to furnish with shelves: *to shelve one wall of a room.* 3. to postpone or put off; set aside for a time or forever: *We'll have to shelve that plan until we have more money.* —**shelv′er,** *n.*

shelv·ing (shel′ving), *n.* 1. material, such as boards, for making shelves. 2. a set of shelves, or shelves collectively.

she·nan·i·gans (shə nan′ə gənz), *n.pl.* mischief or nonsense.

shep·herd (shep′ərd), *n.* 1. a boy or man who herds, tends, and guards sheep. 2. a pastor or priest; clergyman. —*v.* 3. to herd, tend, and guard (sheep). 4. to guide and watch over; lead.

shep·herd·ess (shep′ər dis), *n.* a girl or woman who tends sheep.

sher·bet (shûr′bit), *n.* 1. a frozen dessert made with fruit juice or fruit flavoring, milk, and egg white or gelatin. 2. a drink made of sweetened fruit juice, ice, and water.

sher·iff (sher′if), *n.* 1. the chief law-enforcement officer of a county. 2. (formerly) an important government officer in an English shire.

Sher·man (shûr′mən), *n.* James S., 1855–1912, 27th Vice President of the U.S. 1909–1912.

sher·ry (sher′ē), *n., pl.* **sher·ries.** a strong amber-colored wine, made esp. in southern Spain.

Sher′wood For′est (shûr′wŏŏd′), a former royal forest in central England.

she's (shēz), 1. contraction of *she is.* 2. contraction of *she has.*

Shet′land Is′lands (shet′lənd), a group of islands off the NE coast of Scotland: a county of Scotland. 550 sq. mi. —**Shet′land Is′land·er.**

Shet′land po′ny, a small, sturdy pony having a rough coat, originally raised in the Shetland Islands.

shew (shō), *n.* an old spelling of **show.**

shib·bo·leth (shib′ə leth′), *n.* 1. a special custom or way of pronouncing or using words that is typical of a certain group or class of persons. 2. a watchword or pet phrase of a political party.

shied (shīd), *v.* the past tense and past participle of **shy.**

shield (shēld), *n.* 1. a broad piece of armor, formerly carried on the arm as a defense against swords, lances, arrows, etc. 2. something shaped like such a piece of armor, such as a policeman's badge. 3. a person or thing that protects: *to wear goggles as a shield against flying sparks.* —*v.* 4. to protect or guard with a shield or as if with a shield: *She put up her umbrella to shield herself from the rain.*

shi·er (shī′ər), *adj.* a comparative of **shy.**

shi·est (shī′ist), *adj.* a superlative of **shy.**

shift (shift), *v.* 1. to move from one place, position, direction, etc., to another: *She shifted her chair closer to the fireplace.* 2. to change gears in driving an automobile. —*n.* 3. a change or move from one place, position, direction, etc., to another: *a shift in the wind.* 4. a scheduled period of work: *He works on the night shift.* 5. a group of workers scheduled to work during such a period: *The day shift can leave now.* 6. a woman's straight, loose-fitting dress, sometimes worn with a belt. 7. **shift for oneself,** to take care of oneself; be on one's own: *When his parents* *died, he had to shift for himself.* —**shift′ing·ly,** *adv.*

shift·less (shift′lis), *adj.* lacking in ambition or energy; lazy; good-for-nothing. —**shift′less·ly,** *adv.* —**shift′less·ness,** *n.*

shift·y (shif′tē), *adj.,* **shift·i·er, shift·i·est.** tricky or not straightforward; unreliable; evasive: *a shifty businessman; a shifty answer.* —**shift′i·ness,** *n.*

shil·ling (shil′ing), *n.* a coin of the United Kingdom equal to 12 pence, or ¹/₂₀ of a pound: not used after Feb., 1971. See also **pound²**. [from the Old English word *scilling,* which is related to *scyl* "resonant"]

shil·ly-shal·ly (shil′ē shal′ē), *v.,* **shil·ly-shal·lied, shil·ly-shal·ly·ing. 1.** to be undecided; waver or hesitate: *Stop shilly-shallying, and just say "yes" or "no."* —*n., pl.* **shil·ly-shal·lies. 2.** a going back and forth in one's mind; indecision or hesitation. —*adj.* **3.** unable to decide; wavering; hesitating. —*adv.* **4.** with a lack of decision or conviction; in a hesitating way.

Shi·loh (shī′lō), *n.* a national park in SW Tennessee: site of Civil War battle 1862.

shim·mer (shim′ər), *v.* **1.** to shine with a soft, trembling or quivering light; glimmer: *sunlight shimmering through the curtains.* **2.** to appear to quiver or waver; vibrate with a wavelike motion. —*n.* **3.** a soft, trembling light or gleam: *the shimmer of candlelight.* **4.** a quivering or wavering motion or image resulting esp. from the reflection of waves of heat. —**shim′mer·ing·ly,** *adv.* —**shim′mer·y,** *adj.*

shim·my (shim′ē), *n., pl.* **shim·mies. 1.** a wobbling or shaking, esp. in the front wheels of an automobile, truck, etc. **2.** a ragtime dance in which one shakes one's shoulders and hips. —*v.,* **shim·mied, shim·my·ing. 3.** to wobble or shake. **4.** to dance the shimmy.

shin (shin), *n.* **1.** the front part of the leg between the knee and the ankle. —*v.,* **shinned, shin·ning. 2.** to shinny.

shin·bone (shin′bōn′), *n.* the long bone at the front of the leg between the knee and the ankle.

shin·dig (shin′dig′), *n. Informal.* a large party, dance, or other celebration.

shine (shīn), *v.,* **shone** (shōn) *or* esp. for defs. 4, 5 **shined; shin·ing. 1.** to give off or glow with light; shed or cast light: *The moon shone through the window.* **2.** to be bright with reflected light; gleam; glisten; sparkle: *Polish the silver so that it shines.* **3.** (of light) to appear brightly or strongly, esp. so as to cause discomfort: *The sun is shining in my eyes.* **4.** to cause to shine: *to shine a flashlight in a dark room.* **5.** to make bright or glossy by polishing; polish: *to shine shoes.* **6.** to do very well; be outstanding; excel: *John shines at tennis.* —*n.* **7.** brightness or radiance caused by the giving forth or reflecting of light; glow: *the shine of street lights.* **8.** a gloss or polish; luster: *the shine of patent leather.* **9.** a polishing. **10.** fair weather; sunshine: *rain or shine.* **11.** take a shine

to, *Informal.* to develop a liking for: *I think she's really taken a shine to you.*

shin·er (shī′nər), *n.* **1.** any of various small, American freshwater fishes having glistening scales, esp. one kind of minnow. **2.** *Slang.* a black eye.

shin·gle¹ (shing′gəl), *n.* **1.** a thin, rectangular piece of wood or other material, used in covering the roof or sides of a house. **2.** a small signboard, esp. one hung in front of a doctor's or lawyer's office. **3.** a woman's short haircut. —*v.,* **shin·gled, shin·gling. 4.** to cover with shingles: *to shingle a roof.* **5.** to cut (hair) close to the head. [from the Middle English word *shindle,* which comes from Latin *scindula* "a split piece of wood"] —**shin′gler,** *n.*

shin·gle² (shing′gəl), *n.* **1.** small, rounded stones or pebbles that have been worn down by water, found esp. on beaches and riverbanks. **2.** a beach, riverbank, or other area covered with such small stones. [from an early English word *chingle,* which is related to Norwegian *singel* "coarse sand"]

shin·gles (shing′gəlz), *n. (used as sing. or pl.)* a painful disease of the skin and nerves caused by a virus that produces clusters of blisters.

shin·ny¹ (shin′ē), *n., pl.* **shin·nies. 1.** a simple kind of hockey played with a stick curved at one end and a ball, block of wood, or the like. **2.** the stick used in this game. [probably from *shin ye!,* a cry used in the game]

shin·ny² (shin′ē), *v.,* **shin·nied, shin·ny·ing.** to climb using one's arms and legs; shin (often fol. by *up*): *to shinny up a tree.* [formed from *shin*]

Shin·to (shin′tō), *n.* the native religion of Japan, consisting primarily of the worship of nature and ancestors. Also, **Shin·to·ism** (shin′tō iz′əm).

shin·y (shī′nē), *adj.,* **shin·i·er, shin·i·est. 1.** bright or glossy; shining; gleaming: *a shiny new bicycle.* **2.** (of fabric) worn down or rubbed to a glossy smoothness.

ship (ship), *n.* **1.** a large boat; a vessel moved by sails or an engine, used for traveling on the water, esp. on the ocean. Kinds of ships include steamships, submarines, aircraft carriers, and large sailing vessels. **2.** all the people working or traveling on such a vessel: *The entire ship went ashore.* **3.** any aircraft or spacecraft. —*v.,* **shipped, ship·ping. 4.** to transport by ship, railroad, airplane, etc. **5.** to put or take on board a ship, railroad, airplane, etc.: *At the next port we're shipping grain.* **6.** to take in (water) over the side of a ship or boat. **7.** to go on board to travel by ship; embark. **8.** to fix (an object) in its proper place on a ship or boat: *to ship a tiller.* **9.** ship out, to leave or depart, esp. for another country: *The soldiers will ship out when their training is finished.* **10.** when one's ship comes in, when one's fortune is made: *When my ship comes in I'll buy you a mink coat.*

-ship, a suffix used to form nouns meaning **1.** state or condition: *hardship; friendship.* **2.** skill or art: *statesmanship; horsemanship.* **3.** rank or position: *consulship.* **4.** group or class: *membership.*

ship′ bis′cuit, another name for **hardtack**.

ship·board (ship′bôrd′), *adj.* 1. happening or for use on a ship: *a shipboard telephone; a shipboard romance.* —*n.* 2. *Archaic.* the deck or side of a ship. 3. **on shipboard,** on a ship: *They met on shipboard.*

ship·load (ship′lōd′), *n.* the cargo or load carried by a ship; the amount of cargo or passengers a ship is carrying or can carry.

ship·mate (ship′māt′), *n.* a person who serves with another on the same ship: *Bill and Henry were shipmates in the Navy.*

ship·ment (ship′mənt), *n.* 1. something that is shipped or transported, esp. a quantity of goods sent at one time. 2. the act of shipping or transporting: *The shipment of frozen food requires great care.*

ship′ of the line′, (formerly) a sailing warship equipped to serve in the line of battle, usually having cannons ranged along two or more decks; battleship.

ship·per (ship′ər), *n.* a person who ships goods; one who makes shipments.

ship·ping (ship′ing), *n.* 1. the act or business of one who ships or transports goods. 2. a number of ships, esp. all the merchant ships of a nation, company, port, etc. —*adj.* 3. of or referring to the shipment or transportation of goods: *shipping charges.* 4. of, referring to, or used by a ship: *a shipping lane.*

ship·shape (ship′shāp′), *adj.* in good order; trim or tidy; neat: *Is everything shipshape in your room?*

ship·wreck (ship′rek′), *n.* 1. the destruction or loss of a ship, esp. at sea. 2. the remains of a wrecked ship: *Divers were sent down to explore the shipwreck.* 3. destruction or ruin: *the shipwreck of a business.* —*v.* 4. to cause the destruction or loss of (a ship, boat, etc.). 5. to destroy or ruin: *The scandal shipwrecked his career.*

ship·yard (ship′yärd′), *n.* a place where ships are built or repaired.

shire (shīr), *n.* one of the counties of Great Britain.

shirk (shûrk), *v.* to avoid or get out of doing (a job, duty, etc.): *to shirk a chore.* —**shirk′er,** *n.*

shirr (shûr), *v.* 1. to draw (cloth, material, etc.) into gathers or puckers by pulling it along three or more parallel threads. 2. to bake (eggs removed from the shell) in a shallow dish. —*n.* 3. Also, **shirr′ing.** a shirred or puckered arrangement of cloth.

shirt (shûrt), *n.* 1. a garment for wearing on the upper part of the body, chiefly by men. It usually has a collar, a buttoned opening in the front, and sleeves. 2. an undergarment for the upper part of the body; undershirt. 3. **keep one's shirt on,** *Slang.* to hold back one's anger or impatience; remain calm. 4. **lose one's shirt,** *Slang.* to go broke or bankrupt: *You can lose your shirt in the stock market.*

shirt·ing (shûr′ting), *n.* fabric for making shirts.

shirt·waist (shûrt′wāst′), *n.* 1. a woman's blouse that resembles a shirt. 2. Also, **shirt′waist′ dress′.** a dress having a top resembling a woman's shirt.

shiv·er¹ (shiv′ər), *v.* 1. to shake or tremble, esp. with cold, fear, excitement, etc.; shudder; quiver; quake. —*n.* 2. a shaking or trembling motion; a quiver or shudder. [from the Middle English word *chivere* "a chill"] —**shiv′er·er,** *n.* —**shiv′er·ing·ly,** *adv.*

shiv·er² (shiv′ər), *v.* 1. to break or split into many pieces or fragments; shatter or splinter. —*n.* 2. a fragment or splinter: *to sweep up shivers of glass.* [from the Middle English word *schivere* "fragment"]

shoal¹ (shōl), *n.* 1. a shallow place in a sea, river, or other body of water. 2. a sandbank or sand bar, esp. one in the ocean that is not completely covered at low tide. —*adj.* 3. shallow; not deep: *shoal waters.* [from the Old English word *sceald* "shallow"]

shoal² (shōl), *n.* 1. any group or large number of persons or things. 2. a school of fish. [from the Old English word *scolu* "school (of fish), troop, multitude"]

shoat (shōt), *n.* a young pig after it has stopped living on its mother's milk.

shock¹ (shok), *n.* 1. a sudden and violent blow or impact; a violent jar or collision: *The shock of the explosion broke all the windows in the house.* 2. a sudden and violent disturbance of the mind or feelings: *He received a shock when he found that he had been robbed.* 3. the cause of such a disturbance: *The bad news came as a shock.* 4. the effect on the body produced by an electric current passing through it. 5. a condition of weakness or bodily collapse produced by severe injury, loss of blood, etc. 6. to disturb or upset suddenly and severely; horrify; stun. 7. to undergo a severe disturbance of the mind or feelings; become shocked: *She doesn't shock easily.* 8. to give an electric shock to. [from the French word *choc,* which comes from *choquer* "to clash (in battle)," from Germanic] —**shock′er,** *n.*

shock² (shok), *n.* 1. a group of bundles or sheaves of grain that are placed on end and left leaning against one another in a field. 2. a stack of cornstalks. —*v.* 3. to gather (grain, cornstalks, etc.) into shocks. [from Middle English]

shock³ (shok), *n.* a thick, bushy mass, esp. of ·hair. [probably a special use of *shock²*]

shock′ absorb′er, a device on a vehicle for lessening the effects of sudden jolts, bumps in a road, etc.

shock·ing (shok′ing), *adj.* 1. causing severe surprise, horror, disgust, etc.: *a shocking accident.* 2. very bad; terrible: *shocking manners.* —**shock′ing·ly,** *adv.*

shock′ wave′, a strong, often destructive disturbance, esp. in the air, that spreads outward from an explosion, the path of a supersonic airplane, etc.

shod·dy (shod′ē), *n., pl.* **shod·dies.** 1. material or fibers, esp. of wool, made by shredding rags, waste wool, or the like. 2. cloth made from such material. —*adj.,* **shod·di·er, shod·di·est.** 3. of poor quality or inferior: *shoddy, careless work.* 4. mean or nasty: *a shoddy trick.* 5. (of cloth, a garment, etc.) made of shoddy or containing shoddy. —**shod′di·ness,** *n.*

shoe (shoo), *n.* 1. an outer covering for the human foot, made of leather or other strong material. 2. a horseshoe. 3. the part of a brake that is pressed against a rotating wheel or drum to slow an automobile, train, etc. —*v.,* **shod** (shod) *or* **shoed; shod** *or* **shoed** *or* **shod·den** (shod′⁼n); **shoe·ing.** 4. to provide or fit with a shoe or shoes: *to shoe a horse.* 5. **fill someone's shoes,** to assume another's position, responsibilities, etc.: *We'll never find anyone to fill her shoes.* **6. in someone's shoes,** in another's place, circumstances, etc.: *If I were in your shoes I'd refuse to do it.* —**sho′er,** *n.*

shoe·horn (shoo′hôrn′), *n.* a smooth piece of metal, horn, or the like, shaped so that it can be used to help slip one's heel down into a shoe.

shoe·lace (shoo′lās′), *n.* a string or lace for fastening a shoe.

shoe·mak·er (shoo′mā′kər), *n.* a person who makes or mends shoes.

shoe·string (shoo′string′), *n.* **1.** a shoelace. **2.** *Informal.* very little money: *to live on a shoestring.*

shoe·tree (shoo′trē′), *n.* a foot-shaped object, usually of wood or metal, for placing in a shoe to preserve its shape.

sho·far (shō′fər), *n.* a ram's horn made into a wind instrument, sounded at synagogue services on Rosh Hashanah and Yom Kippur.

shone (shōn), *v.* a past tense and past participle of **shine.**

shoo (shoo), *interj.* **1.** go away! get out! (used esp. to scare or drive away an animal). —*v.,* **shooed, shoo·ing. 2.** to scare or drive away by saying or shouting "shoo": *He shooed the birds out of the garden.*

Shofar

3. to drive away by any means, such as chasing, commanding to go, etc.: *to shoo children out of a kitchen.*

shook (shook), *v.* the past tense of **shake.**

shoot (shoot), *v.,* **shot** (shot), **shoot·ing. 1.** to hit or kill with a bullet, arrow, or other missile sent forth or fired from a weapon: *He raised his rifle and shot the snake.* **2.** to send forth or fire (a bullet, arrow, etc.) from a weapon: *to shoot arrows at a target.* **3.** to send forth or fire a missile from (a weapon): *to shoot a cannon.* **4.** (of a gun) to fire or be discharged: *The gun jammed and would not shoot.* **5.** to send forth rapidly or suddenly: *to shoot questions at someone.* **6.** to move rapidly or suddenly; dash: *The dog shot across the road.* **7.** to spurt or rush forth: *A stream of water shot into the air.* **8.** to pass rapidly through, over, down, or up (something): *A pain shot through his arm.* **9.** to throw, hit, roll, or drive (a ball, puck, etc.) toward a target or goal: *to shoot for a goal.* **10.** to make (a goal) in this way: *to shoot a goal.* **11.** to play (a game): *to shoot pool; to shoot marbles.* **12.** to photograph or film. **13.** to slide (a bolt or the like) into or out of its fastening: *to shoot a bolt in a lock.* **14.** to jut or project; extend: *a piece of land shooting out into the sea.* —*n.* **15.** a young branch, stem, or other new growth of a plant or bud. **16.** a hunting party or shooting contest. **17.** a slide or chute. **18. shoot up, a.** to grow rapidly or suddenly: *In the last year you've really shot up.* **b.** to damage or destroy by reckless shooting: *The cowboys rode in and shot up the town.* —**shoot′er,** *n.*

shoot′ing star′, another term for **meteor.**

shop (shop), *n.* **1.** a store, esp. a small one; a place where foods, clothing, or other goods are sold to the public. **2.** a place where a certain kind of work is done; workshop, factory, or other place of business: *a carpenter's shop.* —*v.,* **shopped, shop·ping. 3.** to go to shops or stores to buy or examine goods: *Mother is out shopping for Christmas presents.* —**shop′per,** *n.*

shop·keep·er (shop′kē′pər), *n.* a person who owns or manages a shop or small store.

shop·lift·er (shop′lif′tər), *n.* a person who steals goods from a shop or store while pretending to be a customer. —**shop′lift′ing,** *n.*

shop·worn (shop′wôrn′), *adj.* soiled or damaged as a result of having been on display in a store or shop: *to buy shopworn furniture at a sale.*

shore¹ (shôr), *n.* **1.** the land along the edge of an ocean, lake, large river, etc.: *a house on the shore.* **2.** land, as distinguished from sea or water: *a marine serving on shore.* [from the Old English word *scora*]

shore² (shôr), *n.* **1.** a post or beam used as a support, esp. one set at an angle against a wall, ship in dry dock, etc. —*v.,* **shored, shor·ing. 2.** to support by one or more posts or beams; prop (usually fol. by *up*): *to shore up a wall.* [from Middle English]

shore·line (shôr′līn′), *n.* the line where shore and ocean meet; outline of a shore.

shore·ward (shôr′wərd), *adv.* **1.** Also, **shore′wards.** toward the shore or land: *to sail shoreward.* —*adj.* **2.** facing or moving toward the shore or land: *to follow a shoreward course.* **3.** (of a wind) coming from the shore.

shorn (shôrn), *v.* a past participle of **shear.**

short (shôrt), *adj.* **1.** having little length; reaching only a little way; not long: *a short path; a short piece of string; a short skirt.* **2.** having little height; not tall: *She's short for her age.* **3.** not lasting a long time; brief in time: *a short visit.* **4.** (of vowel sounds) taking a shorter time to pronounce. *Sit* has a shorter vowel sound than *seed.* **5.** rudely brief or abrupt; curt: *a short refusal of an invitation.* **6.** low in amount; scanty; not enough: *short supplies.* **7.** not long enough to reach a target, mark, etc.: *a throw that was short of the goal.* **8.** less than what is expected or required: *Your payment was a dollar short.* **9.** (of pastry, cake, etc.) crisp or crumbling easily as a result of being made with a large amount of shortening. —*adv.* **10.** suddenly or abruptly: *to stop short.* **11.** in a brief or curt way. **12.** without reaching the desired target, mark, etc.: *The arrow landed short.* —*n.* **13.** something that is short or shorter: *You take the long end, I'll take the short.* **14. shorts, a.** trousers reaching to the knee or above the knee; short pants. **b.** short pants worn as an undergarment by men. **15.** a short circuit. **16. cut short,** to end suddenly and without warning: *My nap was cut short by the phone call.* **17. fall short,** to fail to reach a certain standard, level, etc.: *We fell short of our goal by about $200.* **18. for short,** as an abbreviation: *His name is Patrick, but he's called Pat for short.* **19. short for,** an abbreviation or shortened form of: *"Phone" is short for* *"telephone."* **20. short of, a.** lacking the necessary (food, money, etc.): *I'm short of cash, so I can't go.* **b.** without going to the extreme of: *Short of stealing, I'd do anything for a new bicycle.* **c.** less than; inferior to: *We want nothing short of victory for our team.* —**short′ness,** *n.*

short·age (shôr′tij), *n.* **1.** a lack in quantity: *a shortage of money.* **2.** an amount lacking: *a $10 shortage in the cash register.*

short·cake (shôrt′kāk′), *n.* **1.** a dessert made of a rich biscuit or cake covered with strawberries or other fruit and usually topped with whipped cream. **2.** any cake made with a large amount of shortening.

short′ cir′cuit, an electrical connection that bypasses the normal load in a circuit, causing excessive current to flow, which may lead to a fire.

short-cir·cuit (shôrt′sûr′kit), *v.* **1.** to produce or become a short circuit. **2.** to bypass (something) or cause it to stop functioning.

short·com·ing (shôrt′kum′ing), *n.* a fault, failure, or weakness; defect: *His shortcoming is a quick temper.*

short·cut (shôrt′kut′), *n.* a shorter or quicker route or method; a quicker way: *to take a shortcut going home; a shortcut for solving a problem.*

short·en (shôr′tˀn), *v.* **1.** to make short or shorter: *to shorten a skirt; to shorten a visit.* **2.** to become short or shorter. **3.** to make (pastry, bread, etc.) rich or short by adding extra butter or other shortening.

short·en·ing (shôr′tˀning *or, esp. for def. 1,* shôrt′-ning), *n.* **1.** butter, lard, or other fat, used to make a pastry, cake, etc., crisp or crumbly. **2.** the act or process of making short or shorter.

short·hand (shôrt′hand′), *n.* a method for writing rapidly using simple symbols, strokes, or abbreviations in place of words or phrases.

short-hand·ed (shôrt′han′did), *adj.* having less than the usual or necessary number of workers, helpers, etc.: *They are short-handed at the factory and must hire more men.* —**short′-hand′ed·ness,** *n.*

Shorthand
A, Gregg system
B, Pitman system

short·horn (shôrt′hôrn′), *n.* a breed of cattle having short horns: raised for their meat.

short-lived (shôrt′līvd′, -livd′), *adj.* living or lasting only a little while: *Butterflies are short-lived.*

short·ly (shôrt′lē), *adv.* **1.** in a short time; soon: *I'll leave shortly.* **2.** briefly; not at length: *to speak shortly on a subject.* **3.** in a rudely abrupt or curt manner: *to behave shortly with someone.*

short-sight·ed (shôrt′sī′tid), *adj.* **1.** unable to see far; near-sighted. **2.** lacking in foresight; having or showing little care for the future: *a reckless short-sighted young man; a short-sighted decision.* —**short′-sight′ed·ly,** *adv.* —**short′-sight′ed·ness,** *n.*

short·stop (shôrt′stop′), *n.* (in baseball) **1.** a position between second and third base: *Mark will play shortstop.* **2.** the player playing this position.

short-tem·pered (shôrt′tem′pərd), *adj.* easily angered; having a quick temper.

short′ ton′. See under **ton** (def. 1).

short-wave (shôrt′wāv′), *adj.* of, concerning, using, or receiving shortwaves: *short-wave radio.*

short·wave (shôrt′wāv′), *n.* a radio wave of higher frequency and shorter length than those used in ordinary broadcasting, used for long-distance transmission. Also, **short′ wave′.**

short-wind·ed (shôrt′win′did), *adj.* short of breath; losing one's breath easily.

shot¹ (shot), *n., pl.* **shots** *or for def. 5* **shot. 1.** the act of shooting, esp. the discharge of a weapon or the sound that this makes: *The shot woke the soldiers.* **2.** the distance traveled or to be traveled by a bullet, arrow, or other missile; range: *How long was that shot?* **3.** an attempt to hit a target with a bullet, arrow, or other missile: *That was a good shot.* **4.** any try or attempt: *to have a shot at learning Russian.* **5.** a small lead ball or pebble, used esp. as ammunition for a shotgun. **6.** a person who shoots; marksman: *He's not a good shot.* **7.** (in games) an aimed stroke, throw, hit, etc., esp. toward a goal: *The player took a shot at the basket.* **8.** a metal ball used in shot put. **9.** an injection of medicine with a hypodermic needle. **10.** a photograph taken by a camera. [from the Old English word *sceot,* which is related to *sceōtan* "to shoot"]

shot² (shot), *v.* **1.** the past tense and past participle of **shoot.** —*adj.* **2.** (of fabric) woven so as to have a changeable color: *shot silk.* **3.** streaked with color. **4.** *Slang.* in very bad condition; ruined: *The car is shot.*

shot·gun (shot′gun′), *n.* a gun with a long, smooth barrel, used to fire a charge of shot or small pellets.

shot′ put′, a sports contest in which a heavy metal ball (**shot**) is thrown for distance. —**shot′-put′ter,** *n.*

should (shŏŏd), *auxiliary verb.* **1.** the past tense of **shall. 2.** ought to (used to express obligation or duty): *You should call your mother.* **3.** were or were to; supposing (used to express a possibility): *If it should snow, wear your warm boots.* **4.** ought to; is likely to (used to express probability): *The train should be here any minute now.*

—**Usage.** Most educated speakers and writers use *should* in the conditional tense with first-person pronouns and *would* with second- and third-person pronouns: *I should like to go. You would have to ask him. They would be glad to stay.* See also **shall.**

shoul·der (shōl′dər), *n.* **1.** the part of each side of the body from the side of the neck to the region where the arm begins. **2.** Usually, **shoulders.** these two parts together with the portion of the back that joins them. **3.** a corresponding part in animals. **4.** the joint connecting the arm or the front leg with the body. **5.** a cut of meat that includes the upper part of the front leg: *a shoulder of veal.* **6.** the part of a garment that covers or fits over the shoulder. **7.** an edge or border on the side of a road. **8.** something that resembles a shoulder: *the shoulder of a clothes hanger.* —*v.* **9.** to push or shove with or as if with a shoulder: *to shoulder people aside.* **10.** to take on or take care of; assume: *to shoulder someone else's expenses.* **11.** to put or take on one's shoulder: *to shoulder a pack.* **12. put one's shoulder to the wheel,** to strive toward a particular goal: *If we put our shoulders to the wheel we can finish fast.* **13. shoulder to shoulder,** in a combined effort; with everyone working together: *They all worked shoulder to shoulder to finish the harvest.* **14. straight from the shoulder,** frankly; directly; sincerely: *He told me straight from the shoulder what was wrong.*

shoul′der blade′, either of two flat bones that stand out of the back below the shoulder and contain the socket of the shoulder joint.

shoul′der strap′, 1. a strap worn over the shoulder to hold up a garment, support a rifle or pack, etc. **2.** a strip on the shoulder of an officer's uniform showing his rank.

should·n't (shŏŏd′ʼnt), contraction of *should not.*

shouldst (shŏŏdst), *v.* an old form of **should,** the past tense of **shall,** found now chiefly in Biblical and poetic writing and used with *thou: Thou shouldst not speak in anger.*

shout (shout), *v.* **1.** to call or cry out loudly; yell. **2.** to speak or laugh noisily. —*n.* **3.** a loud call or cry; yell: *a shout for help.* **4.** a sudden, loud outburst: *a shout of laughter.* —**shout′er,** *n.*

shove (shuv), *v.,* **shoved, shov·ing. 1.** to move (a person or thing) by pushing, esp. from behind: *He shoved the people who were standing in front of him. No shoving on the line, please!* —*n.* **2.** the act of shoving; push. **3. shove off, a.** to push a boat from the shore. **b.** *Slang.* to leave; depart: *It's getting late, so we'd better shove off.* —**shov′er,** *n.*

shov·el (shuv′əl), *n.* **1.** a tool having a broad blade or scoop attached to a long handle, used for lifting and moving soil, snow, etc. **2.** a machine with a scoop, used for lifting and moving soil, rocks, etc. —*v.,* **shov·eled** *or* **shov·elled; shov·el·ing** *or* **shov·el·ling. 3.** to lift and throw or remove with a shovel: *to shovel coal.* **4.** to dig or clear with a shovel: *He shoveled a path through the snow.* **5.** to lift and move carelessly, as if with a shovel: *to shovel food into one's mouth.* —**shov′el·er,** *n.*

show (shō), *v.,* **showed, shown** (shōn) *or* **showed; show·ing. 1.** to cause or allow to be seen; display; exhibit: *He showed us the painting he did.* **2.** to be seen; be or become visible or noticeable: *That scar hardly shows.* **3.** to reveal or allow to be seen: *She showed her meanness by not forgiving him.* **4.** to explain or make clear to; inform or teach: *I'll show you how to play chess.* **5.** to make known or point out: *The road signs show the way.* **6.** to guide or usher; direct: *Show Mr. Green into the parlor.* **7.** to grant or give: *to show no mercy.* —*n.* **8.** a showing or presenting to be seen; display; exhibition: *In a show of anger, he quit his job.* **9.** a public exhibition, entertainment, or performance: *a show on television; a dog show.* **10.** a display made to impress others: *a show of wealth.* **11.** a false display; pretense: *He made a show of being tired to get out of working.* **12.** an indication or trace; sign: *There was no show of emotion in her face.* **13. show off, a.** to display so as

to attract attention; flaunt: *Having a party was just an excuse to show off her new clothes.* **b.** to attempt to gain attention by displaying one's talents, knowledge, etc.: *He likes to show off by doing imitations.* **14. show up, a.** *Informal.* to arrive at a place; appear: *We waited for an hour, but he didn't show up.* **b.** *Informal.* to make (someone) seem inferior; outdo: *Do you think he was just trying to show me up?* **c.** to be displayed to advantage; be prominent: *The blue will show up better against a white background.* **15. steal the show,** to be the most pleasing or attractive item or person in a group: *There were lots of beautiful clothes, but the mink bathrobe stole the show.* **16. stop the show,** to win such applause that a theatrical performance is temporarily stopped.

show·boat (shō′bōt′), *n.* a boat, esp. a paddle-wheel steamer, used as a traveling theater.

show·case (shō′kās′), *n.* a glass case for displaying and protecting articles in a shop, museum, etc.

show·down (shō′doun′), *n.* any meeting, argument, battle, etc., in which a conflict or disagreement is openly dealt with and settled.

show·er¹ (shou′ər), *n.* **1.** a brief fall of rain; sprinkle. **2.** something like a shower; a fall or pouring down of anything: *a shower of tears.* **3.** a large supply or amount: *a shower of gifts.* **4.** Also, **show′er bath′. a.** a bath in which water is sprayed on the body: *to take a shower.* **b.** a device for spraying water, esp. a nozzle having many small holes. **c.** a room or cabinet for taking a shower bath. **5.** a party for the giving of gifts, esp. to a girl who is about to be married. —*v.* **6.** to bathe by taking a shower: *He sings while he's showering.* **7.** to wet with rain, water, etc. **8.** to give freely or in large amounts: *to shower praise on someone.* **9.** to fall or pour down in a shower: *Sparks showered all around us.* [from the Middle English word *shour,* which comes from Old English *scūr*] —**show′er·y,** *adj.*

show·er² (shō′ər), *n.* a person or thing that shows or displays.

show·man (shō′mən), *n., pl.* **show·men. 1.** a person who presents or produces a theatrical show. **2.** a person who does things in a dramatic way.

show·man·ship (shō′mən ship′), *n.* the skill or ability of a showman.

shown (shōn), *v.* a past participle of **show.**

show-off (shō′ôf′, -of′), *n.* **1.** a person who shows off, trying to get attention by an exaggerated display of his talents or possessions. **2.** the act of showing off.

show·y (shō′ē), *adj.,* **show·i·er, show·i·est. 1.** making an impressive display; striking; conspicuous: *Orchids are showy flowers.* **2.** gaudy or flashy; too loud or flamboyant to be in good taste: *Tim's boss doesn't approve of his showy clothes.* —**show′i·ness,** *n.*

shrank (shrangk), *v.* a past tense of **shrink.**

shrap·nel (shrap′nʼl), *n.* **1.** a hollow, explosive shell filled with metal pellets or bullets which are released upon explosion, along with jagged pieces of the shell case. 2. shell fragments. [named after H. *Shrapnel* (1761–1842), English army officer, its inventor]

shred (shred), *n.* 1. a piece cut or torn off, esp. a narrow strip: *He tore his napkin into shreds.* 2. a bit: *We haven't got a shred of evidence.* —*v.*, **shred·ded** *or* **shred; shred·ding.** 3. to cut or tear into shreds or narrow strips: *to shred lettuce.* —**shred′der,** *n.*

Shreve·port (shrēv′pôrt′), *n.* a city in NW Louisiana.

shrew[1] (shrōō), *n.* a short-tempered, quarrelsome woman who constantly scolds or nags. [from a special use of *shrew*[2]]

shrew[2] (shrōō), *n.* any of several tiny but fierce mouselike animals that feed on insects and have a long, sharp snout. [from the Old English word *scrēawa*]

shrewd (shrōōd), *adj.* clever and sharp; having or showing keen common sense: *He is a shrewd businessman. You have made a shrewd decision.* —**shrewd′ly,** *adv.* —**shrewd′ness,** *n.*

Shrew (total length 5 in.)

shrew·ish (shrōō′ish), *adj.* having the personality of a shrew; short-tempered and quarrelsome: *a shrewish, nagging wife.* —**shrew′ish·ly,** *adv.* —**shrew′ish·ness,** *n.*

shriek (shrēk), *n.* 1. a sharp, shrill cry. 2. any loud, high or shrill sound; scream: *the shriek of sirens; a shriek of laughter.* —*v.* 3. to cry out in a sharp, shrill voice; screech. 4. to make a loud, shrill sound.

shrift (shrift), *n.* 1. *Archaic.* **a.** the act of shriving or granting absolution of sins following confession and penance. **b.** confession to a priest. 2. **short shrift,** slight attention or consideration given to a person or matter: *to give short shrift to a pest.*

shrike (shrīk), *n.* any of numerous fierce birds having a strong, hooked bill that feed on insects and sometimes other birds and small animals.

shrill (shril), *adj.* 1. having or making a high-pitched and piercing sound: *a shrill whistle; the shrill cry of a bird.* —*v.* 2. to make or give forth such a sound. —**shrill′ness,** *n.* —**shril′ly,** *adv.*

shrimp (shrimp), *n., pl.* **shrimps** *or* for def. 1 **shrimp.** 1. any of several small, long-tailed shellfish most of which live in salt water. Several kinds of shrimp are used as food. 2. *Slang.* a small or unimportant person.

shrine (shrīn), *n.* 1. a place or building where sacred objects or relics are kept. 2. the tomb of a saint. 3. any sacred place or place set aside for prayer. 4. any place that is honored because of important events that have happened there, the memories it arouses, etc.: *a historic shrine.*

Shrimp (length 2 in.)

shrink (shringk), *v.*, **shrank** (shrangk) *or* **shrunk** (shrungk); **shrunk** *or* **shrunk·en** (shrung′kən); **shrink·ing.** 1. to make or become smaller; lessen in size, amount, etc.: *The hot water shrank her sweater. His income has shrunk this year.* 2. to draw back or withdraw in fear, disgust, horror, etc.: *a dog that shrinks at the sound of thunder.* —**shrink′a·ble,** *adj.*

shrink·age (shring′kij), *n.* 1. the act or fact of growing smaller; a shrinking: *These garments have been treated to prevent shrinkage.* 2. a lessening in value. 3. amount or degree of shrinking.

shrive (shrīv), *v.*, **shrove** (shrōv) *or* **shrived; shriv·en** (shriv′ən) *or* **shrived; shriv·ing.** 1. to hear the confession of (a person), giving him a penance and absolution for his sins. 2. to confess, esp. to a priest.

shriv·el (shriv′əl), *v.*, **shriv·eled** *or* **shriv·elled; shriv·el·ing** *or* **shriv·el·ling.** to shrink, dry up, and wrinkle; wither: *Leaves shrivel in the fall.*

shriv·en (shriv′ən), *v.* a past participle of **shrive.**

shroud (shroud), *n.* 1. a cloth or sheet in which a dead body is wrapped for burial. 2. something that covers or conceals like a cloak or veil: *a shroud of darkness.* 3. (on a sailing ship or boat) any of a number of taut ropes or wires running from a masthead to the side of the ship, used to hold the mast steady. —*v.* 4. to wrap or clothe for burial. 5. to cover or hide from view as if with a shroud or veil; conceal: *buildings shrouded in mist.* —**shroud′like′,** *adj.*

shrove (shrōv), *v.* a past tense of **shrive.**

shrub (shrub), *n.* a woody plant, smaller than a tree, with many separate stems branching from near the ground. —**shrub′like′,** *adj.*

shrub·ber·y (shrub′ə rē), *n.* a group of shrubs, or shrubs in general.

shrug (shrug), *v.*, **shrugged, shrug·ging.** 1. to raise or hunch up (the shoulders), esp. to express doubt or lack of interest: *He shrugged his shoulders at my question. She just shrugged and walked away.* —*n.* 2. the movement of raising or hunching up the shoulders: *to answer with a shrug.* 3. a short sweater or jacket that ends at or above the waistline.

shrunk (shrungk), *v.* a past tense and a past participle of **shrink.**

shrunk·en (shrung′kən), *v.* 1. a past participle of **shrink.** —*adj.* 2. grown smaller; shriveled or withered.

shuck (shuk), *n.* 1. a husk, pod, or shell: *corn shucks.* —*v.* 2. to remove a husk or shell from: *to shuck corn.* 3. to take off or cast away, esp. hurriedly: *Shuck your wet boots at the door.* —*interj.* 4. **shucks,** *Informal.* (used to express mild annoyance, regret, etc.): *Shucks, we just missed the bus.* —**shuck′er,** *n.*

shud·der (shud′ər), *v.* 1. to tremble or shake forcefully, as from cold or fright: *He shuddered as he stepped into the icy water.* —*n.* 2. a forceful trembling or shaking; a spasm of trembling: *a shudder of fear.* —**shud′der·y,** *adj.*

shuf·fle (shuf′əl), *v.*, **shuf·fled, shuf·fling.** 1. to drag (the feet) clumsily in walking. 2. to scrape or slide (the feet) in dancing. 3. to mix (playing cards) in a pack. 4. to move (an object or objects) around or back and forth: *He's not really working, he's just shuffling his papers.* —*n.* 5. a clumsy dragging or sliding of the feet: *to walk with a shuffle.* 6. a dance in which one shuffles one's feet. 7. a shuffling or mixing: *Give the cards a shuffle.*

shuf·fle·board (shuf′əl bôrd′), *n.* a game in which players use a long stick to shove disks along a flat surface toward numbered scoring spaces. A shuffleboard court may be painted on a ship's deck, on the pavement of a playground, etc.

Shuffleboard court

shun (shun), *v.*, **shunned, shun·ning.** to keep away from or avoid for reasons of dislike, fear, caution, etc.: *an athlete who shuns tobacco.*

shunt (shunt), *v.* **1.** to turn, move, or push (someone or something) aside or out of the way: *The police shunted traffic off the highway.* **2.** to get rid of or shift: *to shunt the blame onto somebody else.* **3.** to move or switch (a locomotive, railroad car, etc.) onto another track. **4.** to divert part of an electric current by producing an additional conducting path. —*n.* **5.** the additional conducting path. **6.** the act of shunting or turning aside; shift. **7.** a railroad switch.

shush (shush), *interj.* **1.** hush (used as a command to be quiet or silent). —*v.* **2.** to silence or hush by or as if by saying "hush": *He shushed the barking dog.*

shut (shut), *v.*, **shut, shut·ting. 1.** to close (a door, window, cover, etc.): *Shut the gate. He shut the lid of the box.* **2.** to close the doors, windows, covers, etc., of: *to shut a shop for the night.* **3.** to become shut or closed; close: *The door shut behind her.* **4.** to close (something) by folding or bringing its parts together: *to shut a book.* **5.** to enclose or imprison; confine: *to shut a bird in a cage.* —*adj.* **6.** closed or fastened up: *a shut door.* **7. shut down, a.** *Informal.* to cease operating; close: *The factory shut down.* **b.** to cover, surround, or envelop something; close in: *The fog shut down suddenly over the airport.* **8. shut off, a.** to stop the flow of (water, electricity, etc.). **b.** to isolate; separate: *a desert town that was almost shut off from civilization.* **9. shut out, a.** to keep from entering; exclude: *Close the curtains to shut out the light.* **b.** (in sports) to prevent (an opponent or opposing team) from scoring. **10. shut up, a.** to confine or imprison. **b.** to close completely: *to shut up the cabin for the winter.* **c.** *Informal.* to stop talking; be silent.

shut·down (shut′doun′), *n.* a shutting down or closing, esp. of a place of work or business: *a two-week shutdown of a factory.*

shut·in (shut′in′), *adj.* **1.** not allowed to leave one's home, room, etc., esp. as a result of illness. —*n.* **2.** a person who is kept in, esp. because of illness.

shut·out (shut′out′), *n.* **1.** (in sports) a game in which one side or opponent fails to score. **2.** a shutting out or keeping out.

shut·ter (shut′ər), *n.* **1.** a movable panel for covering a window, usually hinged to the wall at each side of the window. **2.** the device on a camera that opens to admit light to the film for a controlled length of time.

shut·tle (shut′əl), *n.* **1.** (in weaving) a device for passing yarn back and forth through the warp, or lengthwise threads. **2.** (in a sewing machine) the sliding container that carries the lower thread. **3.** a train, plane, bus, etc., that goes back and forth on a regular schedule between two destinations. **4.** a shuttlecock. —*v.*, **shut·tled, shut·tling. 5.** to cause to move back and forth with or as if with a shuttle: *to shuttle thread in weaving.* **6.** to travel or move back and forth: *to shuttle between New York and Boston.*

shut·tle·cock (shut′əl kok′), *n.* **1.** (in badminton and battledore) the object that is hit back and forth, having a round cork base and a crownlike top of feathers or light plastic. **2.** an early form of badminton.

Shuttlecock

shy (shī), *adj.*, **shy·er** *or* **shi·er; shy·est** *or* **shi·est. 1.** easily frightened or timid. **2.** timid or nervous when among other people; bashful; self-conscious. **3.** lacking or short: *She will be shy of money until payday.* **4.** distrustful or wary: *I'm shy of doing business with that sort of person.* —*v.*, **shied, shy·ing. 5.** to jump or move quickly back or aside: *The horse shied away from the skunk.* —**shy′er**, *n.* —**shy′ly**, *adv.* —**shy′ness**, *n.*

si (sē), *n.* (in music) another word for **ti.**

Si, *Chem.* the symbol for **silicon.**

Si·am (sī am′), *n.* former name of **Thailand.**

Si·a·mese (sī′ə mēz′), *adj.* **1.** of or concerning Siam (now called Thailand), its people, or their language. —*n., pl.* **Si·a·mese. 2.** a native of Siam; Thai. **3.** the language of Siam, now usually called Thai. **4.** a Siamese cat.

Siamese cat (9 in. high at shoulder)

Si′amese cat′, a breed of slender, short-haired cats, raised originally in Siam, having blue eyes and a pale-brown or grayish body with darker feet, face, and tail.

Si′amese twins′, a pair of twins joined together at some point, sometimes sharing one or more body parts or organs.

Si·be·ri·a (sī bēr′ē ə), *n.* a part of the Soviet Union in N Asia, extending from the Ural Mountains to the Pacific Ocean. —**Si·be′ri·an**, *n., adj.*

sib·yl (sib′il), *n.* any of certain women in ancient Greece or Rome who were thought to be able to predict the future.

Sic·i·ly (sis′ə lē), *n.* an island in the Mediterranean Sea: a part of Italy. 9924 sq. mi. *Cap.:* Palermo. —**Si·cil·ian** (si sil′yən, si sil′ē ən), *n., adj.*

Sicily

sick (sik), *adj.* 1. having disease or poor health; ill; ailing. 2. having nausea. 3. of, for, or concerning a sick person or persons: *to get sick pay when one is in the hospital.* 4. disgusted or very upset: *He was sick about losing his job.* 5. bored or tired: *I am sick of cleaning up after you.* 6. causing or accompanied by nausea: *a sick headache.* —*n.* 7. **the sick,** *(used as pl.)* persons who are sick: *to care for the sick.*

sick·en (sik/ən), *v.* to make or become sick or ill: *The sight of blood sickens him.*

sick·en·ing (sik/ə niñg), *adj.* causing disgust, nausea, or illness: *a sickening crime; a sickening smell.*

sick·le (sik/əl), *n.* a tool for cutting grain, grass, etc., having a curved, hooklike blade and a short handle.

sick·ly (sik/lē), *adj.*, **sick·li·er, sick·li·est.** 1. not strong; unhealthy; ailing. 2. connected with or caused by ill health: *sickly, watery eyes.* 3. causing much sickness or disease: *a sickly climate.* 4. causing disgust or nausea; sickening: *a sickly smell of strong perfume.* 5. lacking force; faint; weak; feeble: *a sickly smile.* —**sick/li·ness,** *n.*

Sickle

sick·ness (sik/nis), *n.* 1. a particular disease or illness: *Mumps is a common sickness among children.* 2. the state or fact of being sick or ill: *He had to stay home all last week because of sickness.* 3. nausea or vomiting.

side (sīd), *n.* 1. one of the surfaces or lines forming the outside or limits of a thing: *A square has four sides.* 2. either of the two broad surfaces of a thin, flat object, such as a door, piece of paper, etc. 3. either of the two longer surfaces of a rectangular object, not forming the front, back, top, or bottom: *the sides of a house.* 4. a part or half of an object, area, body, etc., considered as being in a certain direction, right or left, up or down, etc.: *My left side hurts. He lives on the east side of town.* 5. one of two or more contesting teams, political parties, etc.: *He played on our side in the big game.* 6. the beliefs, opinions, etc., set forth by an opposing person or group: *The arguments for your side are more convincing.* 7. an aspect, phase, or viewpoint: *Consider the question from all sides.* 8. a part or half of a family according to the line of descent through one of the parents: *We're related on my mother's side of the family.* 9. a space next to a person or object: *That dog never leaves her side.* 10. a slope, esp. of a hill or mountain. 11. the left or right half of an animal slaughtered for meat: *a side of beef.* —*adj.* 12. being at or on one side; *the side aisles in a church.* 13. coming from one side: *a side attack.* 14. directed or aimed to or at one side: *a side blow; a side look.* 15. not very important; minor: *side issues.* 16. **on the side,** *Informal.* a. as a side dish: *a hamburger with coleslaw on the side.* b. in addition to one's regular work, duties, etc.: *a policeman who does photography on the side.* 17. **side by side,** next to each other or to one another: *two neighbors who lived side by side for 30 years.* 18. **side with,** to support or sympathize with, esp. in a dispute: *How can you side with a liar?* 19. **take**

sides, to favor one side in a dispute: *A judge can't afford to take sides.*

side/ arm/, a weapon, such as a pistol or a sword, carried at the side or in the belt.

side·arm (sīd/ärm/), *adv.* 1. with the arm extended and moved at or below shoulder level: *Does he pitch sidearm or overhand?* —*adj.* 2. done in this way: *a sidearm throw.*

side·board (sīd/bôrd/), *n.* a piece of furniture for the dining room, usually having shelves and drawers, used to hold silverware, dishes, napkins, etc., for the table.

side·burns (sīd/bûrnz/), *n.pl.* the growth of hair on a man's face that extends downward in front of the ears. [a changed form of the earlier word *burnsides,* named after Gen. A. E. *Burnside* (1824–1881), Union general in the U.S. Civil War]

-sided, a suffix used to form adjectives meaning 1. having a certain number of sides: *six-sided.* 2. having a certain kind of side or sides: *rough-sided.*

side·light (sīd/līt/), *n.* 1. a light coming from or placed at the side. 2. a fact or item of information that is interesting but not of great importance: *The paper printed some sidelights on the election.*

side·line (sīd/līn/), *n.* 1. a line at one side, esp. a line marking a side boundary of a playing field or court for sports. 2. **sidelines,** the area just beyond the sideline on a playing field or court: *The coach stood at the sidelines shouting to his team.* 3. a business, hobby, or other activity done in addition to one's regular business: *He's a banker, but as a sideline he buys and sells antiques.* 4. a stock or line of goods sold by a merchant in addition to his main line of goods: *a shirt salesman who offers a sideline of ties.*

side·long (sīd/lông/), *adj.* 1. directed, moving, slanting, etc., to or along the side; sideways: *The thief gave the policeman a sidelong look.* —*adv.* 2. toward the side; sideways: *She fell sidelong off the sled.*

si·de·re·al (sī dēr/ē əl), *adj.* of, concerning, or determined by the stars: *sidereal time.*

side·sad·dle (sīd/sad/ᵊl), *n.* 1. a saddle for a woman, on which the rider faces front but with both legs on one side of the horse. —*adv.* 2. seated on a sidesaddle: *Formerly, all women rode sidesaddle.*

side/ show/, a small show or exhibition offered in addition to the main show, esp. at a circus.

side·step (sīd/step/), *v.*, **side-stepped, side-stepping.** 1. to step to one side. 2. to avoid or dodge (a person, problem, question, etc.) by or as if by stepping to one side: *The mayor side-stepped the reporters, saying he would meet with them later.*

side·stroke (sīd/strōk/), *n.* (in swimming) a stroke in which the body is turned sideways in the water.

side·swipe (sīd/swīp/), *n.* 1. a sweeping blow or hit on or along the side: *With a sideswipe of his hand, he knocked off my glasses.* —*v.* 2. to hit or scrape with such a blow: *The bus sideswiped two cars.*

side·track (sīd/trak/), *v.* 1. to move (a train, railroad car, etc.) from a main track to a siding. 2. to move or distract from the main issue, course, etc.: *to sidetrack an embarrassing conversation.*

side·walk (sīd′wôk′), *n.* a path or walk, usually paved, at the side of a street or road.

side·wall (sīd′wôl′), *n.* the part of a tire between the edge of the tread and the rim of the wheel. See illus. at tire.

side·ways (sīd′wāz′), *adv.* 1. with one side forward: *You must turn sideways to get through this narrow space.* 2. toward or from one side: *He stepped sideways to avoid the punch.* —*adj.* 3. moving, facing, directed, etc., toward one side: *a sideways glance.* Also, **side·wise** (sīd′wīz′).

side·wind·er (sīd′wīn′dər), *n.* 1. a rattlesnake of the southwestern U.S. and northern Mexico that moves in loose sand by throwing loops of its own body forward. 2. an antiaircraft missile, launched from airplanes, that guides itself to its target by means of the heat the target gives off. 3. a severe swinging blow from the side.

sid·ing (sī′dĭng), *n.* 1. a short railroad, usually connected with the main track at both ends, onto which a train may be switched, esp. to let another train go by. 2. material, such as overlapping boards or sheet metal, used in covering the outside walls of a frame house or building.

si·dle (sīd′ᵊl), *v.,* **si·dled, si·dling.** to move sideways, esp. to edge along in a cautious or sneaky way: *to sidle away from a fight.*

siege (sēj), *n.* 1. the surrounding and attacking of a fortified city, castle, etc., so that it cannot receive help or supplies, and may be more easily captured: *The Union army's siege of Vicksburg lasted eight months.* 2. any long and steady effort to gain or overcome something. 3. any long and dangerous or difficult period: *a siege of illness.*

si·en·na (sē en′ə), *n.* 1. a kind of earth used to make yellowish-brown and reddish-brown pigments. 2. a yellowish or reddish brown.

si·er·ra (sē er′ə), *n.* a chain of hills or mountains having peaks that resemble the teeth of a saw.

Si·er·ra Le·o·ne (sē er′ə lē ō′nē, lē ōn′), an independent country in W Africa, formerly British. 27,925 sq. mi. *Cap.:* Freetown.

Si·er·ra Ne·vad·a (sē er′ə nə vad′ə, nə vä′də), a mountain range in E California. Highest peak, Mt. Whitney, 14,495 ft.

si·es·ta (sē es′tə), *n.* (in Spain and Latin America) a rest or nap taken at midday or in the afternoon.

sieve (siv), *n.* 1. a utensil having a bottom made of mesh or full of small holes, used to sift or separate larger particles from smaller ones or solid matter from liquid: *a sieve for flour.* —*v.,* **sieved, siev·ing.** 2. to put (grain, food, etc.) through a sieve; sift or strain.

sift (sift), *v.* 1. to put (flour, grain, soup, etc.) through a sieve or strainer to separate larger particles from smaller ones or solid matter from liquid. 2. to scatter or sprinkle by using a sieve: *to sift sugar onto a cake.* 3. to examine closely: *The detectives are sifting the evidence.* 4. to pass or fall through or as if through a sieve: *Sawdust sifted down as the carpenters worked.*

sigh (sī), *v.* 1. to let out one's breath with a sound suggestive of weariness, relief, etc.: *She sighed as she started the ironing.* 2. to make a breathy, moaning sound: *wind sighing in the chimney.* 3. to say with a sighing sound: *"We lost," he sighed.* 4. to yearn or long: *to sigh for one's youth.* —*n.* 5. the act or sound of sighing: *to give a loud sigh of relief.*

sight (sīt), *n.* 1. the power of seeing; vision: *Kittens have no sight when they are first born.* 2. the act or fact of seeing: *The sight of planes thrilled him.* 3. a person's range of vision; the distance one can see: *Is there land within sight?* 4. a view or glimpse: *I caught sight of her in the crowd.* 5. something seen or worth seeing; spectacle: *The Grand Canyon is a wonderful sight.* 6. something unusual or dreadful to see: *The town was a sight after the tornado hit it.* 7. any of various devices that help one to view or aim at something: *a sight on a gun.* 8. an observation, esp. one taken with a surveying instrument, to discover an exact position or direction. —*v.* 9. to see or observe: *to sight a ship on the horizon.* 10. to direct or aim (a gun, surveying instrument, etc.) by using a sight or sights. 11. **not by a long sight,** *Informal.* definitely not: *That's not all you have to do, not by a long sight.* 12. **on sight,** immediately upon seeing: *Shoot him on sight.* 13. **out of sight, a.** beyond one's range of vision: *We watched the car till it was out of sight.* **b.** beyond reason; excessively high: *The price of tomatoes is simply out of sight.* 14. **sight unseen,** without examining beforehand: *I bought the radio sight unseen.*

sight·less (sīt′lĭs), *adj.* unable to see; blind. —**sight′less·ly,** *adv.* —**sight′less·ness,** *n.*

sight·ly (sīt′lē), *adj.,* **sight·li·er, sight·li·est.** pleasing to the sight; attractive: *a sightly young girl.* —**sight′li·ness,** *n.*

sight·see·ing (sīt′sē′ĭng), *n.* 1. visiting and looking at places and objects of interest: *to go sightseeing in Europe.* —*adj.* 2. of, concerned with, or used for sightseeing: *a sightseeing bus.* —**sight′see′er,** *n.*

sign (sīn), *n.* 1. a mark, object, emblem, etc., that is used to stand for something else; symbol: *The sign for addition is +.* 2. something that indicates the presence or occurrence of something else; indication: *Smoke is a sign of fire.* 3. a motion or gesture used to express an idea, command, etc.; signal: *His nod is a sign of approval.* 4. a board, metal plate, poster, or the like, bearing an advertisement, place name, warning, etc. 5. something indicating what will happen in the future; omen: *That cough is a bad sign.* 6. a trace: *They found no sign of the lost submarine.* 7. any of the twelve divisions of the zodiac. —*v.* 8. to write one's name on, esp. as a mark of agreement or obligation: *to sign a contract.* 9. to write (one's name) as a signature. **10.** to mark with a sign. **11.** to hire, esp. with a contract: *to sign a football player.* **12. sign off,** to end radio or television broadcasting, esp. till the following day. **13. sign on, a.** to hire or employ: *to sign on a new member of the team.* **b.** to agree to do a job, esp. by signing a contract: *He signed on as a first mate.* **14. sign up, a.** to persuade to join an organization or to sign a contract: *The ball club has signed up a new pitcher.* **b.** to enlist in the armed forces.

sig·nal (sig′nᵊl), *n.* **1.** any sign, sound, gesture, etc., that serves as a warning, command, call for help, or other message: *Red and green lights are used as traffic signals.* —*adj.* **2.** outstanding or notable: *a signal achievement.* **3.** serving as a signal: *a signal light on a car.* —*v.,* **sig·naled** *or* **sig·nalled; sig·nal·ing** *or* **sig·nal·ling. 4.** to make a signal to: *to signal the pitcher to throw a curve.* **5.** to communicate (a command, message, etc.) by using a signal or signals: *to signal a retreat; to signal for help.* —**sig′nal·er,** *n.*

sig·nal·ly (sig′nᵊlē), *adv.* notably or outstandingly: *a signally good year for business.*

sig·nal·man (sig′nᵊl mən), *n., pl.* **sig·nal·men.** one whose occupation or duty is signaling, esp. a man working on a railroad or serving in the armed forces.

sig·na·ture (sig′nə chər), *n.* **1.** a person's name signed or written by himself. **2.** (in music) a group of symbols or signs at the beginning of a staff giving the key or time of a piece of music.

sign·board (sīn′bôrd′), *n.* a board bearing a sign, as an advertisement, announcement, warning, etc.

sig·net (sig′nit), *n.* **1.** a small seal, such as one used to stamp official documents. **2.** the mark made by such a seal.

sig·nif·i·cance (sig nif′ə kəns), *n.* **1.** importance; the quality of having important consequences: *an election of great significance.* **2.** meaning or sense that can be found in something: *facts of no significance.*

sig·nif·i·cant (sig nif′ə kənt), *adj.* **1.** having important consequences; important: *a significant victory.* **2.** having a meaning; meaningful: *a significant remark.* **3.** expressing a secret or special meaning: *a significant wink.* —**sig·nif′i·cant·ly,** *adv.*

sig·ni·fy (sig′nə fī′), *v.,* **sig·ni·fied, sig·ni·fy·ing. 1.** to mean or be a sign of: *A cat's purr signifies its contentment.* **2.** to make known by signs, speech, or action: *He signified his disapproval by frowning.*

si·gnor (sēn′yôr, sin yôr′), *n.* an Italian term of address or title of respect for a man. Also, **si′gnior.**

si·gno·ra (sin yôr′ə), *n.* an Italian term of address or title of respect for a married woman.

si·gno·ri·na (sēn′yô rē′nə), *n.* an Italian term of address or title of respect for an unmarried woman.

sign·post (sīn′pōst′), *n.* a post bearing a sign that gives information, directions, etc.: *a signpost at a fork in the road.*

Sikh (sēk), *n.* a member of a reformed Hindu religious sect that was founded in Punjab, in NW India, around 1500.

si·lage (sī′lij), *n.* food or fodder for livestock, such as hay or cornstalks, stored in a silo.

si·lence (sī′ləns), *n.* **1.** absence of sound; complete quiet or stillness. —*v.,* **si·lenced, si·lenc·ing. 2.** to cause to be silent, quiet, or still: *to silence a barking dog.* **3.** to put down or suppress (a rumor, objection, fear, etc.). —**si′lenc·er,** *n.*

si·lent (sī′lənt), *adj.* **1.** having or making no sound; quiet; still: *an empty, silent house.* **2.** not speaking; saying nothing: *You must remain silent during the lecture.* **3.** speaking or saying very little; not talkative: *a moody, silent man.* **4.** done, made, or appearing without speech or sound: *a silent movie.* **5.** not sounded or pronounced: *The "b" in "doubt" is silent.* **6.** not taking an active part, esp. in a business: *a silent partner.* —**si′lent·ly,** *adv.*

Si·le·sia (si lē′zhə, si lē′shə), *n.* a region in central Europe, now mostly in Poland and Czechoslovakia. —**Si·le′sian,** *n., adj.*

sil·hou·ette (sil′ōo et′), *n.* **1.** a picture or portrait showing the outline of an object, face, etc., filled in with a solid color, usually black. **2.** the outline or general shape of something. **3.** a dark image outlined against a lighter background: *the silhouette of skyscrapers against the sky.* —*v.,* **sil·hou·et·ted, sil·hou·et·ting. 4.** to show in silhouette or outline: *to see someone silhouetted in a window.*

Silhouette

sil·i·ca (sil′ə kə), *n.* a hard compound of silicon and oxygen occurring naturally as quartz and sand, used in making glass, ceramics, abrasives, etc.

sil·i·cate (sil′ə kit, sil′ə kāt′), *n.* any of numerous compounds, including many common minerals, containing silicon, oxygen, and a metal.

sil·i·con (sil′ə kən, sil′ə kon′), *n. Chem.* a nonmetallic element that is found, in combination with other elements, in minerals and rocks, and makes up more than one fourth of the earth's crust. *Symbol:* Si

sil·i·cone (sil′ə kōn′), *n.* any of numerous chemical compounds whose molecules consist of long chains of silicon and oxygen atoms to which other atoms and groups are attached. Silicones can be oily, sticky, or rubbery and are used as adhesives, lubricants, electrical insulators, polishes, etc.

silk (silk), *n.* **1.** the soft, shiny fiber obtained from the cocoons of silkworms. **2.** thread or cloth made from this fiber. **3.** any of various similar fibers, such as those in a spider web or surrounding an ear of corn. —*adj.* **4.** made of or concerned with silk.

silk·en (sil′kən), *adj.* **1.** made of silk: *silken robes.* **2.** like silk; smooth and shiny; silky: *silken hair.*

silk·worm (silk′wûrm′), *n.* the larva, or caterpillar, of a Chinese moth, which produces a fiber for its cocoon from which silk is made.

Silkworm (about 3 in. long) and cocoon

silk·y (sil′kē), *adj.,* **silk·i·er, silk·i·est.** of or like silk; smooth, soft, or shiny: *a silky fabric; a dog with a silky coat.* —**silk′i·ly,** *adv.* —**silk′i·ness,** *n.*

sill (sil), *n.* **1.** a piece of wood, metal, stone, or the like, set along the base of a window frame or doorway. **2.** a horizontal timber, block, or the like, used as a foundation of a wall, house, etc.

sil·ly (sil′ē), *adj.,* **sil·li·er, sil·li·est. 1.** lacking judgment or good sense; foolish; stupid. **2.** ridiculous or absurd: *a silly riddle.* **3.** *Informal.* stunned or dazed: *The fall knocked me silly.* —**sil′li·ness,** *n.*

si·lo (sī′lō), *n., pl.* **si·los.** a structure, usually a tall, round, airtight tower, used for storing fodder such as hay or cornstalks for feeding cattle or other livestock.

silt (silt), *n.* **1.** fine earth or sand carried by streams, rivers, etc., and deposited as sediment. —*v.* **2.** to fill or become filled with silt.

sil·ver (sil′vər), *n.* **1.** a white, shining precious metal, used for making coins, ornaments, table utensils, etc.: a chemical element. *Symbol:* Ag **2.** articles made of silver or a metal resembling silver; silverware: *Put the plates, silver, and glasses on the table.* **3.** coins, esp. ones made of or containing silver. **4.** jewelry made of silver. **5.** a color like that of silver; a shining grayish white. —*adj.* **6.** made of or coated with silver: *a silver cup.* **7.** of a color like that of silver: *silver hairs.* **8.** clear or very pleasing in tone: *a silver voice.* **9.** indicating the 25th event in a series: *a silver wedding anniversary.* —*v.* **10.** to cover with silver or something resembling silver. **11.** to give a silver color to: *Moonlight silvered the fields.* **12.** to become a silver or silvery color: *His hair has silvered.*

sil·ver·fish (sil′vər fish′), *n., pl.* **sil·ver·fish·es** *or* **sil·ver·fish. 1.** a white or silvery goldfish. **2.** a wingless, silvery-gray insect that feeds on starch and damages books, wallpaper, etc.

sil·ver·smith (sil′vər smith′), *n.* a person who makes or repairs articles of silver, as candlesticks, serving bowls, etc.

sil·ver·ware (sil′vər wâr′), *n.* **1.** articles made of or plated with silver, esp. tableware such as spoons, forks, serving bowls, etc. **2.** tableware made of a metal resembling silver, such as stainless steel.

sil·ver·y (sil′və rē), *adj.* **1.** resembling silver; of a shining white or grayish white: *the silvery moon.* **2.** having a clear, ringing tone: *the silvery sound of bells.* —**sil′ver·i·ness,** *n.*

Silverfish (length 1/3 in.)

sim·i·an (sim′ē ən), *adj.* **1.** of or concerning apes or monkeys. **2.** like that of an ape or monkey: *a simian face.* —*n.* **3.** an ape or monkey.

sim·i·lar (sim′ə lər), *adj.* **1.** alike in a general way but not exactly; having some likeness or resemblance: *Brothers often have a similar appearance.* **2.** (in geometry) of the same shape; having corresponding angles equal and corresponding sides in proportion: *similar triangles.* —**sim′i·lar·ly,** *adv.*

sim·i·lar·i·ty (sim′ə lar′i tē), *n., pl.* **sim·i·lar·i·ties. 1.** likeness or resemblance; the state of being alike: *the similarity between two sisters.* **2.** a point of resemblance or likeness: *There are too many similarities between his answers on the test and yours.*

sim·i·le (sim′ə lē), *n.* a figure of speech that compares one thing to another that is quite different from it, esp. by using the words "like" or "as." Examples are "He's as busy as a beaver" and "Her eyes were like jewels."

si·mil·i·tude (si mil′i tōōd′, -tyōōd′), *n.* likeness or sameness: *a similitude in our likes and dislikes.*

sim·mer (sim′ər), *v.* **1.** to keep (a liquid) just at or below the boiling point; boil gently: *to simmer soup.* **2.** to cook (food) in a liquid by gentle boiling: *to simmer vegetables.* **3.** to boil gently with a slight murmuring sound: *simmering water.* **4.** to be just at the point of breaking out into violence, action, etc.: *to simmer with rage.* **5. simmer down,** *Slang.* to become calm or quiet: *The speaker waited for the crowd to simmer down before continuing.*

Si′mon Pe′ter (sī′mən). See **Peter** (def. 1).

sim·per (sim′pər), *n.* **1.** a silly, insincere, or self-conscious smile. —*v.* **2.** to put on such a smile: *She always simpers when she gets a compliment.*

sim·ple (sim′pəl), *adj.,* **sim·pler, sim·plest. 1.** easy to solve, learn, do, answer, etc.: *Checkers is a simple game.* **2.** not having many parts; of a basic kind; not complex: *A hammer is a simple tool.* **3.** plain and straightforward: *a simple, honest answer.* **4.** not rich or sophisticated; ordinary; humble: *simple folk.* **5.** bare or plain; not fancy: *a simple cabin in the woods.* **6.** having nothing added; pure: *the simple truth.* **7.** lacking in intelligence; ignorant or foolish: *a simple man who is easily fooled.*

sim·ple-heart·ed (sim′pəl här′tid), *adj.* having a sincere and honest nature: *a kindly, simple-hearted girl.*

sim′ple machine′, any of several basic devices for modifying force or motion, including the inclined plane, the lever, the wheel and axle, the pulley, etc.

sim·ple-mind·ed (sim′pəl mīn′did), *adj.* **1.** foolish or stupid: *What a simple-minded idea!* **2.** lacking in intelligence; feeble-minded. —**sim′ple-mind′ed·ly,** *adv.* —**sim′ple-mind′ed·ness,** *n.*

sim′ple sen′tence, a sentence that consists of only one independent clause, with no dependent clause.

sim·ple·ton (sim′pəl tən), *n.* a foolish or silly person; one who is easily fooled.

sim·plic·i·ty (sim plis′i tē), *n., pl.* for defs. 2–4 **sim·plic·i·ties. 1.** the quality of being simple and easily understood: *Strive for simplicity when you're explaining something.* **2.** lack of complexity; the condition of being simple in design or structure: *the simplicity of the tools invented by the Indians.* **3.** absence of luxury, adornment, or the like; plainness: *the simplicity of life on a pioneer farm.* **4.** sincerity and straightforwardness: *I liked the simplicity of her manner.*

sim·pli·fy (sim′plə fī′), *v.,* **sim·pli·fied, sim·pli·fy·ing.** to make (something) simple or simpler; make plainer or easier: *Can you simplify those instructions?* —**sim′pli·fi·ca′tion,** *n.* —**sim′pli·fi′er,** *n.*

sim·ply (sim′plē), *adv.* 1. in a simple manner; clearly: *Explain it to me simply.* 2. plainly; without luxury, adornment, etc.: *to live simply.* 3. merely or only: *I simply wanted to know what time it was.* 4. absolutely or utterly: *simply beautiful.*

sim·u·late (sim′yə lāt′), *v.,* **sim·u·lat·ed, sim·u·lat·ing.** 1. to pretend or put on the appearance of: *The officer simulated cheerfulness in order to encourage his men.* 2. to have the appearance of; look like: *The air-raid drill simulated a real attack.*

si·mul·ta·ne·ous (sī′məl tā′nē əs), *adj.* existing or happening at the same time: *Two simultaneous fires kept the firemen busy.* —**si′mul·ta′ne·ous·ly,** *adv.*

sin (sin), *n.* 1. any act that breaks a law of God or a religious law: *the sin of Adam.* 2. any wrong or evil act, such as stealing or deliberately harming others. —*v.,* **sinned, sin·ning.** 3. to commit such an act; offend against God or morality.

Si·nai (sī′nī, sī′nē ī′), *n.* 1. a peninsula in the NE Arab Republic of Egypt, occupied by Israel since 1967. 2. **Mount,** (in the Bible) the mountain upon which Moses received the Ten Commandments from God.

since (sins), *conj.* 1. in the period following the time when: *He has written only once since he went to camp.* 2. continuously from; counting from the time when (often preceded by *ever*): *She has been busy ever since she arrived.* 3. because; inasmuch as: *You had better eat something now, since dinner will be very late.* —*adv.* 4. from then till now (often preceded by *ever*): *He was elected in 1950 and has been a congressman ever since.* 5. ago; before now: *They moved away long since.* —*prep.* 6. continuously from or counting from: *It has been raining since last night.* 7. between a past time or event and the present: *There have been many changes since the war.*

sin·cere (sin sēr′), *adj.,* **sin·cer·er, sin·cer·est.** 1. free from pretense or falseness; honest: *a sincere letter of thanks.* 2. real or genuine: *sincere love.* —**sin·cere′ly,** *adv.*

sin·cer·i·ty (sin ser′i tē), *n., pl.* **sin·cer·i·ties.** freedom from pretense or falseness; honesty or earnestness: *The jury was impressed by the witnesses' sincerity.*

si·ne·cure (sī′nə kyŏŏr′, sin′ə kyŏŏr′), *n.* a job or position requiring little or no work, esp. one that pays well.

sin·ew (sin′yŏŏ), *n.* 1. a cord of strong, tough tissue by which a muscle is attached to a bone; tendon. 2. Often, **sinews.** a source of strength or power: *the sinews of the nation.* 3. strength or power.

sin·ew·y (sin′yŏŏ ē), *adj.* 1. having strong sinews: *an athlete with a lean, sinewy body.* 2. full of sinews; stringy: *tough, sinewy meat.* 3. forceful or vigorous: *a sinewy debate.*

sing (sing), *v.,* **sang** (sang), **sung** (sung), **sing·ing.** 1. to use the voice to produce musical sounds. 2. to per-

form (a song). 3. to produce musical or pleasing sounds, as certain birds and insects do. 4. to bring to a certain state with or by singing; lull: *She sang the baby to sleep.* 5. to tell about or praise in song or verse. 6. to express enthusiastically: *to sing someone's praises.* 7. to make a whistling, ringing, humming, or whizzing sound: *The kettle is singing.* —*n.* 8. *Informal.* a gathering or party for the purpose of singing. 9. **sing out,** *Informal.* to call in a loud voice; shout: *If you need any help, just sing out.*

sing., singular.

Sin·ga·pore (sing′gə pôr′, sing′ə pôr′), *n.* 1. an independent island republic in the South China Sea: formerly British. 220 sq. mi. 2. a port city on this island.

singe (sinj), *v.,* **singed, singe·ing.** 1. to burn slightly; scorch. 2. to burn the ends of (hair or the like). 3. to burn bristles, feathers, fine hair, etc., from (the skin of a dead animal or bird): *The cook first plucked the chicken and then singed it.*

sing·er (sing′ər), *n.* 1. a person who sings, esp. one whose profession is singing. 2. a bird that sings.

Sin·gha·lese (sing′gə lēz′), *adj.* 1. of or concerning Ceylon, its people, or their language. —*n., pl.* **Sin·gha·lese.** 2. a member of the Singhalese people; a native of Ceylon. 3. the Indic language spoken in most of Ceylon. Also, **Sinhalese.**

sin·gle (sing′gəl), *adj.* 1. one only; sole: *A single button held his jacket together.* 2. of or for one person only: *a single room at a hotel.* 3. unmarried; not married. 4. between two persons only; of one against one: *single combat.* 5. sincere and undivided: *a single devotion.* —*v.,* **sin·gled, sin·gling.** 6. to choose or pick (one) from among others (usually fol. by *out*): *She singled out Bob for punishment.* 7. (in baseball) to make a hit that advances one to first base. —*n.* 8. one person or thing; a single one. 9. a room, cabin, etc., for one person. 10. (in baseball) a hit that advances the batter to first base. 11. **singles,** *(used as sing.)* a match or game with one person on each side, esp. a tennis match. —**sin′gle·ness,** *n.*

sin·gle-breast·ed (sing′gəl bres′tid), *adj.* (of a suit, jacket, coat, etc.) having a single button or row of buttons in the front. See also **double-breasted.**

sin′gle file′, a line of persons or things arranged one behind the other.

sin·gle-hand·ed (sing′gəl han′did), *adj.* 1. done by one person alone: *a single-handed rescue.* —*adv.* 2. Also, **sin′gle-hand′ed·ly.** by oneself; without help from others: *He fought them single-handed.*

sin·gle-mind·ed (sing′gəl mīn′did), *adj.* 1. having a single aim or purpose: *a single-minded crusade against disease.* 2. sincere or steadfast: *a single-minded devotion.* —**sin′gle-mind′ed·ly,** *adv.* —**sin′gle-mind′ed·ness,** *n.*

sin·gly (sing′glē), *adv.* 1. one by one; one at a time;

separately: *to pick up marbles singly.* **2.** single-handed; alone: *I'll take care of that problem singly.*

sing·song (sĭng′sông′), *adj.* having a monotonous, up-and-down rhythm and tone: *to recite in a singsong voice.*

sin·gu·lar (sĭng′gyə lər), *adj.* **1.** remarkable or exceptional; extraordinary: *to have singular luck.* **2.** unusual or strange; odd; different: *a house of singular appearance.* **3.** being the only one of its kind; unique: *a singular example.* **4.** (in grammar) of or concerning the form or function of nouns, pronouns, verbs, and some adjectives, that refer to only one person or thing. *Man* is a singular noun; *I* is a singular pronoun; *goes* is a singular form of the verb *to go; that* is a singular demonstrative adjective. **—sin′gu·lar·ly,** *adv.*

sin·gu·lar·i·ty (sĭng′gyə lar′ĭ tē), *n., pl.* for def. 2 **sin·gu·lar·i·ties. 1.** the quality or fact of being singular. **2.** something that is singular, unusual, or unique; peculiarity.

Sin·ha·lese (sĭn′hə lēz′), *adj., n.* another spelling of **Singhalese.**

sin·is·ter (sĭn′ĭ stər), *adj.* **1.** threatening or foreshadowing danger or trouble; ominous: *sinister storm clouds.* **2.** evil or wicked: *a sinister criminal.*

sink (sĭngk), *v.,* **sank** (săngk); **sunk** (sŭngk) *or* **sunk·en** (sŭng′kən); **sink·ing. 1.** to fall or descend gradually to a lower level; drop slowly: *The sun sank in the west.* **2.** to drop or descend below the surface: *The boat sank in the lake.* **3.** to cause to become submerged: *A torpedo can sink a battleship.* **4.** to bury, set, or lay (a pipe line, fence, etc.) in or into the ground. **5.** to dig, bore, or excavate (a mine shaft, well, hole, etc.): *to sink a well.* **6.** to fail gradually in strength or health: *The old man is sinking rapidly.* **7.** to pass or drop gradually into a particular state (usually fol. by *in* or *into*): *to sink into sleep.* **8.** to become lower or less in amount, degree, loudness, etc.: *Her voice sank to a whisper.* **9.** to cause to descend or drop slowly; lower: *He sank his head onto the pillow.* **10.** to lower or degrade oneself: *to sink to stealing.* **11.** to cause to pierce or penetrate: *He sank his teeth into an apple.* **12.** to become absorbed; seep: *The wax sank into the wood.* **13.** to invest (money) in a business venture. *—n.* **14.** a basin having faucets and a drain, used for washing. **15.** a sinkhole.

sink·er (sĭng′kər), *n.* **1.** a person or thing that sinks. **2.** a weight, esp. of lead, for sinking a fishing line or net.

sink·hole (sĭngk′hōl′), *n.* **1.** a hole formed in rock by the action of water, through which surface water flows into an underground passage. **2.** a hollow or sunken area in which water collects; sink.

sin·less (sĭn′lĭs), *adj.* free from or without sin: *a sinless life.* **—sin′less·ly,** *adv.* **—sin′less·ness,** *n.*

sin·ner (sĭn′ər), *n.* a person who sins or does wrong.

sin·u·ous (sĭn′yōō əs), *adj.* **1.** having or making many bends or turns; winding: *a sinuous vine.* **2.** sneaky or dishonest. **—sin′u·ous·ly,** *adv.*

si·nus (sī′nəs), *n.* a hollow place in a bone or other tissue, esp. any of several cavities in the skull that connect with the nasal passages.

-sion, a suffix used to form nouns meaning **1.** action or process: *delusion.* **2.** result of an action: *conclusion.* **3.** state or condition: *derision.*

Sioux (sōō), *n., pl.* **Sioux** (sōō, sōōz). a member of any of several Indian tribes of the central U.S.

sip (sĭp), *v.,* **sipped, sip·ping. 1.** to drink bit by bit; take small tastes of (a liquid): *She was sipping hot tea.* *—n.* **2.** a small taste of liquid: *to try a sip of wine.* **3.** a small quantity of liquid: *Leave me a sip.*

si·phon (sī′fən), *n.* **1.** a tube that is bent to form legs of unequal length for use in transferring a liquid over the edge of a container to a point at a lower level. **2.** a bottle from which liquid is forced by a compressed gas. *—v.* **3.** to pass or move through a siphon: *to siphon gasoline from the tank of an automobile.* Also, **syphon.**

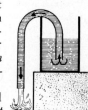

Siphon

sir (sûr), *n.* **1.** a respectful or formal term of address for a man: *What do you think, sir? Yes, sir!* **2.** a lord or gentleman: *Kind sirs and ladies, please be seated.* [a shortened form of *sire*]

Sir (sûr), *n.* a title of a knight or baronet, used before the name: *Sir Francis Drake.*

sire (sīªr), *n.* **1.** the male parent of an animal: *a race horse from a famous sire.* **2.** a respectful form of address, now used only in speaking to a king. **3.** a father or forefather. *—v.,* **sired, sir·ing. 4.** to have as an offspring; beget: *The stallion sired a fine colt.*

si·ren (sī′rən), *n.* **1.** a device for producing a loud, piercing, wailing or whistling sound, used esp. as a warning signal: *Ambulances and police cars have sirens.* **2.** (in Greek mythology) one of a group of beautiful sea nymphs, part woman and part bird, whose singing lured sailors to death and shipwreck. **3.** a woman who uses her beauty to deceive men.

Sir·i·us (sĭr′ē əs), *n.* the brightest star in the heavens.

sir·loin (sûr′loin), *n.* a cut of meat from the part of the loin next to the rump.

si·roc·co (sə rok′ō), *n., pl.* **si·roc·cos.** a hot, dry, dusty wind blowing from northern Africa across the Mediterranean Sea into southern Europe.

sir·rah (sĭr′ə), *n.* an old term of address used to people of lower rank or to children to express annoyance, contempt, etc.

sir·up (sĭr′əp, sûr′əp), *n.* another spelling of **syrup.** **—sir′up·y,** *adj.*

si·sal (sī′səl, sĭs′əl), *n.* **1.** a strong fiber made from the leaves of a Mexican and West Indian plant that resembles a cactus: used for making rope. **2.** the plant yielding this fiber.

sis·sy (sĭs′ē), *n., pl.* **sis·sies. 1.** a timid or cowardly person, esp. a boy or man. **2.** a boy or man who seems too much like a girl, esp. in being weak or delicate. **3.** a little girl, esp. a sister.

---

act, āble, dâre, ärt; ebb, ēqual; if, īce; hot, ōver, ôrder; oil; bŏŏk; ōōze; out; up, ûrge; ə = a as in alone; ª as in button (but′ªn), fire (fīªr); chief; shoe; thin; ŧħat; zh as in measure (mezh′ər). See full key inside cover.

sis·ter (sis′tər), *n.* 1. a girl or woman having the same parents as another person. 2. Also, **half sister.** a girl or woman having either the same mother or the same father as another person. 3. a nun. 4. a girl or woman who is a fellow member with another or others, esp. in a church. 5. a girl or woman who is a close friend: *She was a sister to me.*

sis·ter·hood (sis′tər hŏŏd′), *n.* 1. the state of being a sister. 2. a group of sisters, esp. of nuns or female members of a church. 3. an organization of women having a mutual interest or purpose.

sis·ter-in-law (sis′tər in lô′), *n., pl.* **sis·ters-in-law** (sis′tərz in lô′). 1. the sister of one's husband or wife. 2. the wife of one's brother. 3. the wife of one's wife's or husband's brother.

sis·ter·ly (sis′tər lē), *adj.* of, like, or befitting a sister or sisters: *sisterly affection.* **—sis′ter·li·ness,** *n.*

sis′ter ship′, a ship that is regarded as related to another ship, esp. by having the same design.

Sis·y·phus (sis′ə fəs), *n.* (in Greek mythology) a king of Corinth noted for his trickery, who was punished in Hades by being forced to roll a large stone up a hill. After nearly reaching the top, the stone always rolled down again.

sit (sit), *v.,* **sat** (sat), **sit·ting.** 1. to rest with one's weight off one's feet and supported on the buttocks and back of the thighs; be seated: *The dog sat on the doorstep.* 2. to cause to sit; seat (often fol. by *down*): *to sit oneself down at the table.* 3. to be located or situated: *Our house sits on the hill.* 4. to rest or lie (usually fol. by *on* or *upon*): *His responsibilities sat heavily upon him.* 5. to keep one's seat astride (a horse or other animal): *She sits that horse well.* 6. to pose for an artist, photographer, etc.: *to sit for one's portrait.* 7. to occupy a place or have a seat as a member of an official assembly: *to sit in Congress.* 8. to be in session: *Congress is sitting at this moment.* 9. to keep company or baby-sit: *to sit with a sick friend.* 10. to remain in one place or position: *The work just sat on his desk for weeks.* 11. **sit down,** to take a seat: *to sit down on a bench.* 12. **sit in on,** to be a spectator or visitor at: *We sat in on a session at the U.N.* 13. **sit pretty,** *Informal.* to be in a comfortable or advantageous position: *With three jobs offered him, he's really sitting pretty.* 14. **sit up, a.** to rise from a reclining to a sitting position: *to sit up in bed.* **b.** to sit erect: *Sit up and get your elbows off the table.* **c.** to delay one's going to bed past the usual time: *We sat up late and watched TV.*

sit′-down strike′ (sit′doun′), a labor strike during which workers occupy their place of employment and refuse to work until the strike is settled.

site (sīt), *n.* 1. the position or location of a town, building, etc.: *the site of ancient Troy.* 2. the place where an event occurred: *a battle site.* 3. an area or plot of ground set aside for a house, building, etc.

sit-in (sit′in′), *n.* an organized protest in which demonstrators occupy some place that is forbidden to them, such as a government office.

sit·ting (sit′tĭng), *n.* 1. the act of a person or thing that sits. 2. a period of time during which one is

seated: *He did his homework in one sitting.* 3. a session of a legislature, court, or the like.

Sit′ting Bull′, 1834–1890, Sioux Indian chief and warrior: led massacre of General Custer and his troops 1876.

sit′ting room′, a small living room; parlor.

sit·u·ate (sich′ŏŏ āt′), *v.,* **sit·u·at·ed, sit·u·at·ing.** to put in or on a particular place or site: *to situate a fort high on a cliff; a house situated in the woods.*

sit·u·a·tion (sich′ŏŏ ā′shən), *n.* 1. state of affairs: *We shall be in an embarrassing situation if we can't pay our bills.* 2. location or position: *The situation of the house assures you a beautiful view.* 3. a job or position of employment: *to find a situation as a cook.*

six (siks), *n.* 1. a number that is five plus one. 2. a set of this many persons or things: *Only six will be there.* **—adj.** 3. amounting to six in number: *six persons.*

six·pence (siks′pəns), *n., pl.* **six·pence** or for def. 2 **six·penc·es.** (in Great Britain) 1. the sum of six pennies. 2. a small coin equal to six pennies or half a shilling: not used after Feb. 1971., See also **pound²**.

six-shoot·er (siks′shŏŏ′tər, -shŏŏt′ər), *n.* a revolver from which six shots can be fired without reloading.

six·teen (siks′tēn′), *n.* 1. a number that is ten plus six. 2. a set of this many persons or things: *Sixteen of them will be there.* **—adj.** 3. amounting to sixteen in number: *sixteen persons.*

six·teenth (siks′tēnth′), *adj.* 1. being number sixteen in a series: *the sixteenth floor.* **—n. 2.** one of sixteen equal parts. 3. a person or thing that is sixteenth.

six′teenth′ note′, (in music) a note having one-sixteenth the time value of a whole note. See illus. at **note.**

sixth (siksth), *adj.* 1. being number six in a series: *the sixth floor.* **—n. 2.** one of six equal parts. 3. a person or thing that is sixth.

six·ti·eth (siks′tē ith), *adj.* 1. being number sixty in a series: *the sixtieth floor.* **—n. 2.** one of sixty equal parts. 3. a person or thing that is sixtieth.

six·ty (siks′tē), *n., pl.* **six·ties.** 1. a number that is six times ten. 2. a set of this many persons or things. 3. **sixties,** the numbers, years, degrees, etc., between 60 and 69: *Mr. Smith is in his early sixties.* **—adj. 4.** amounting to sixty in number: *sixty persons.*

siz·a·ble (sī′zə bəl), *adj.* of considerable size; fairly large: *a sizable crowd.* Also, **sizeable.** **—siz′a·ble·ness,** *n.* **—siz′a·bly,** *adv.*

size¹ (sīz), *n.* 1. the measurements of a thing in terms of length, width, height, or thickness: *the size of one's desk.* 2. largeness with regard to the number of persons or things included: *a town that is growing in size.* 3. extent or amount: *a fortune of great size.* 4. any of a series of measures for articles of manufacture or trade: *sizes of shoes.* **—v.,** **sized, siz·ing.** 5. to arrange or sort according to size: *to size eggs.* 6. **size up,** *Informal.* to form an estimate or opinion of (a person, situation, etc.); judge: *to size up one's opponent.* [from the Old French word *sise*]

size² (sīz), *n.* 1. a thin, jellylike or gluelike substance, used to glaze paper, stiffen canvas, cover plastered walls, etc. —*v.*, **sized, siz·ing. 2.** to coat or treat with size. [from a special use of *size*[1]]

size·a·ble (sī′zə bəl), *adj.* another spelling of **sizable.** —**size′a·ble·ness,** *n.* —**size′a·bly,** *adv.*

sized (sīzd), *adj.* of the size mentioned (usually used in combination): *medium-sized.*

siz·zle (siz′əl), *v.*, **siz·zled, siz·zling. 1.** to make a hissing sound, as fat does when frying: *bacon sizzling in the pan.* —*n.* **2.** a sizzling or hissing sound.

skate[1] (skāt), *n.* **1.** Also, **ice skate.** a shoe fitted with a metal blade for gliding on ice. **2.** the blade itself: *Sharpen your skates.* **3.** a roller skate. —*v.*, **skat·ed, skat·ing. 4.** to glide or move along on or as if on skates. [from the Dutch *schaats* "skate"] —**skat′er,** *n.*

skate[2] (skāt), *n.*, *pl.* **skates** or **skate.** any of several ocean flatfishes with broad fins; ray. [from the Middle English word *scate,* which comes from Scandinavian]

skate·board (skāt′bôrd′), *n.* a short, oblong board mounted on roller-skate wheels for gliding on a paved surface.

skein (skān), *n.* a length of yarn or thread wound on a reel or in a loose coil.

skel·e·ton (skel′i t³n), *n.* **1.** the bony framework that supports the body of man and many kinds of animals. **2.** the bones of man or an animal after all the flesh has decayed or been removed: *A skeleton was found buried with the pirate's gold.* **3.** any supporting framework, as of a house, ship, leaf, etc. **4.** an outline, esp. of a literary work: *the skeleton of the plot.* **5.** *Informal.* a very thin person or animal. **6. skeleton in the closet,** a shameful secret, esp. a family scandal kept concealed to avoid public disgrace. —**skel′e·tal,** *adj.*

skel′eton key′, a key filed down in such a way that it can open many locks.

skep·tic (skep′tik), *n.* a person who frequently doubts or questions ideas, facts, etc., that others accept as true. Also, **sceptic.**

skep·ti·cal (skep′ti kəl), *adj.* **1.** inclined to doubt or question ideas, facts, etc., that others accept as true. **2.** showing such a doubt: *a skeptical smile.* Also, **sceptical.** —**skep′ti·cal·ly,** *adv.*

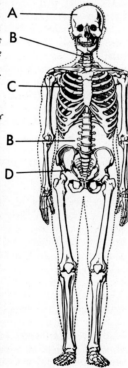

Skeleton (Human)
A, Skull; B, Backbone;
C, Ribs; D, Pelvis

skep·ti·cism (skep′ti siz′əm), *n.* an attitude of doubting or not believing, esp. with regard to truths set forth by a religion. Also, **scepticism.**

sketch (skech), *n.* **1.** a drawing made very quickly or left unfinished. **2.** a brief, general plan, outline, or description: *a sketch of events.* **3.** a short play, esp. a comic one: *a sketch that makes fun of social customs.* — *v.* **4.** to make a sketch or quick drawing of: *to sketch a landscape.* **5.** to make one or more sketches: *to spend an afternoon sketching.* **6.** to give a brief outline or description of: *to sketch the events of the day.* —**sketch′er,** *n.*

sketch·y (skech′ē), *adj.*, **sketch·i·er, sketch·i·est.** like a sketch; giving only outlines or bare essentials; incomplete: *He gave a sketchy account of the accident.* —**sketch′i·ly,** *adv.* —**sketch′i·ness,** *n.*

skew·er (skyōō′ər), *n.* **1.** a long, thick pin, esp. of metal, for holding meat together while it is being cooked. **2.** any similar pin for fastening or holding something in place. —*v.* **3.** to fasten or pierce with or as if with a skewer: *to skewer a turkey.*

ski (skē), *n.*, *pl.* **skis** or **ski. 1.** one of a pair of long, narrow, thin pieces of wood or metal worn clamped to boots, used for gliding over snow. **2.** a water ski. —*v.*, **skied, ski·ing. 3.** to glide over snow on skis. —**ski′er,** *n.*

skid (skid), *n.* **1.** a plank, log, platform, or the like, on which something heavy may be slid or rolled. **2.** a device used to prevent a wheel from turning. **3.** a slipping or sliding motion, esp. sideways: *a skid of a car.* —*v.*, **skid·ded, skid·ding. 4.** to slip or slide, esp. sideways: *to skid on the ice.* **5.** (of a wheel) to slide along the ground without turning. **6.** to move (something heavy) by sliding it on a skid or skids.

skies (skīz), *n.* the plural of **sky.**

skiff (skif), *n.* any of various types of boats small enough for sailing or rowing by one person.

ski·ing (skē′iñg), *n.* the act or sport of gliding over snow on skis.

skill (skil), *n.* **1.** the ability to do something well: *to develop skill in driving a car.* **2.** a particular craft, art, or ability; accomplishment: *reading skills.*

skilled (skild), *adj.* **1.** having skill or the ability to do something well: *a skilled mountain climber.* **2.** showing or requiring skill: *skilled labor.*

skil·let (skil′it), *n.* a frying pan.

skill·ful (skil′fəl), *adj.* **1.** having or using skill or expert ability: *a skillful juggler.* **2.** showing or requiring skill: *a skillful display of fancy driving.* Also, **skil′ful.** —**skill′ful·ly,** *adv.* —**skill′ful·ness,** *n.*

skim (skim), *v.*, **skimmed, skim·ming. 1.** to remove (fat, cream, or the like) from the surface of a liquid. **2.** to clear (a liquid) in this way: *to skim milk.* **3.** to move or glide lightly over or along (a surface): *The seaplane skimmed the waves as it took off.* **4.** to read hurriedly, skipping some parts; glance through (usually fol. by *over* or *through*): *to skim through a book.* **5.** to throw (a stone, stick, etc.) so that it skips along the surface of water.

skim·mer (skim′ər), *n.* **1.** a person or thing that skims. **2.** a shallow, spoonlike utensil, usually having holes in it, used for skimming a liquid. **3.** any of several sea birds resembling gulls that glide with the lower half of the bill in the water in search of food.

skim′ milk′, milk from which the cream has been removed. Also, **skimmed′ milk′.**

skimp (skimp), *v.* **1.** to give or use (something) in sparing or stingy amounts: *She skimped the food when we came to dinner.* **2.** to be frugal or stingy; economize; scrimp: *We can get by, if we skimp on a few things.* **3.** to give too little effort, attention, or money to: *They would never skimp their children.* —**skimp′ing·ly,** *adv.*

skimp·y (skim′pē), *adj.*, **skimp·i·er, skimp·i·est. 1.** not quite large or full enough; scanty: *a skimpy meal.* **2.** too thrifty: *a skimpy manager.* —**skimp′i·ness,** *n.*

skin (skin), *n.* **1.** the outer covering of the body of man or an animal. **2.** the hide or pelt of an animal. **3.** any thin, smooth covering, such as the peel or rind of a fruit. **4.** a container for liquid made of animal skin. —*v.*, **skinned, skin·ning. 5.** to remove or strip the skin, hide, or husk from: *to skin a rabbit.* **6.** to scrape a small amount of skin from: *to skin one's elbow.* **7. by the skin of one's teeth,** *Informal.* by an extremely narrow margin; just barely: *We caught the last bus by the skin of our teeth.* **8. save one's skin,** *Informal.* to avoid harm, esp. to escape death: *He betrayed his friends to save his skin.* —**skin′less,** *adj.*

skin-dive (skin′dīv′), *v.*, **skin-dived** or **skin-dove** (skin′dōv′); **skin-div·ing.** to engage in skin diving. —**skin′-div·er,** *n.*

skin′ div′ing, a sport or pastime in which one swims underwater with a mask and equipment for breathing, such as a snorkel or air cylinder.

skin·flint (skin′flint′), *n.* a stingy person; miser.

skin·ny (skin′ē), *adj.*, **skin·ni·er, skin·ni·est.** very thin or lean; scrawny. —**skin′ni·ness,** *n.*

skip (skip), *v.*, **skipped, skip·ping. 1.** to jump or leap lightly; move by leaps: *to skip over a puddle.* **2.** to move by stepping and hopping first on one foot and then on the other. **3.** to jump lightly over (a swinging rope): *to skip rope.* **4.** to pass over without reading, doing, noticing, etc.; leave out; omit: *to skip a chapter in a book.* **5.** to pass quickly from one point, subject, thing, etc., to another: *to skip from one station to another while watching TV.* **6.** to cause to bounce or skim along a surface: *to skip stones on a pond.* **7.** *Informal.* to be absent from, esp. for no good reason: *to skip school.* **8.** *Informal.* to leave (a place) hurriedly and secretly: *The gangster skipped town.* —*n.* **9.** a skipping movement; light jump or leap. **10.** a gait or way of moving in which one steps and hops first on one foot and then on the other. **11.** the act of passing over or omitting something.

skip·per¹ (skip′ər), *n.* **1.** the master or captain of a boat or ship. —*v.* **2.** to act as a skipper; be captain of (a ship or boat). [from the Dutch word *schipper,* which comes from *schip* "ship"]

skip·per² (skip′ər), *n.* a person or thing that skips.

skir·mish (skûr′mish), *n.* **1.** a brief, often unplanned fight between small groups of soldiers. **2.** any brief fight or conflict. —*v.* **3.** to engage in a skirmish; fight briefly. —**skir′mish·er,** *n.*

skirt (skûrt), *n.* **1.** the part of a dress, slip, or coat that hangs downward from the waist. **2.** a garment for a woman or girl that hangs downward from the waist and is not joined between the legs. **3.** something that resembles a skirt in shape or use, such as the leather flap that hangs down on each side of a saddle. **4.** Usually, **skirts.** outer edge or area; border; outskirts. —*v.* **5.** to pass along the edge or border of: *a highway skirting a city.* **6.** to avoid dealing with or speaking about (something risky, difficult, etc.): *The senator skirted the issue of higher taxes.*

skit (skit), *n.* **1.** a short play, usually comical; sketch. **2.** a short, humorous piece of writing.

skit·tish (skit′ish), *adj.* **1.** easily startled or frightened; apt to shy: *a skittish horse.* **2.** restless, nervous, or overly excited: *a skittish mood.* —**skit′tish·ness,** *n.*

skit·tle (skit′əl), *n.* **1. skittles,** *(used as sing.)* a form of the game of ninepins, in which a wooden ball or disk is used to knock down the pins. **2.** one of the pins used in this game.

skul·dug·ger·y (skul dug′ə rē), *n.* trickery or dishonesty: *the skulduggery of thieves.*

skulk (skulk), *v.* **1.** to stay in hiding, esp. for an evil purpose; lurk: *The bandit skulked in his hideout waiting for night to fall.* **2.** to move stealthily or sneakily; slink: *The tiger skulked in the tall grass.*

skull (skul), *n.* the bony framework of the head, which encloses the brain and gives shape to the face. See illus. at **skeleton.**

skull′ and cross′bones, a picture of a human skull above two crossed bones, formerly used on pirates' flags and now used as a warning sign, esp. on containers of poisonous substances.

skull·cap (skul′kap′), *n.* a small cap without a brim, worn on the top or crown of the head, sometimes for religious observances.

skunk (skuñgk), *n.*, *pl.* **skunks** or **skunk. 1.** a small, black, furry animal having a white stripe running down its back and its bushy tail. The skunk shoots out a vile-smelling liquid when it is alarmed or attacked. **2.** *Informal.* a mean, hateful person.

sky (skī), *n.*, *pl.* **skies. 1.** Often, **skies.** the upper atmosphere or space beyond the earth that appears to form a vast dome overhead: *clouds in the sky; starry skies at night.* **2. out of a clear blue sky,** suddenly and without warning: *Out of a clear blue sky he got up and left.*

Skunk (total length 2 ft.)

sky′ blue′, the color of a clear sky in daytime; a clear, light blue; azure. —**sky′-blue′,** *adj.*

sky·dive (skī′dīv′), *v.*, **sky·dived** or **sky·dove** (skī′dōv′); **sky·dived; sky·div·ing.** to jump from an airplane and delay opening the parachute until various bodily maneuvers have been performed. —**sky′div·er,** *n.*

sky·lark (skī′lärk′), *n.* **1.** either of two small European or Asian birds noted for their song while in flight. —*v.* **2.** to play or frolic.

sky·light (skī′līt′), *n.* an opening in a roof or ceiling, covered with glass, for letting in daylight.

sky·line (skī′līn′), *n.* **1.** the boundary line where the earth and sky appear to meet; horizon. **2.** an outline, esp. of buildings, seen against the sky: *the skyline of a city.*

Skylark
(length 7 in.)

sky·rock·et (skī′rok′it), *n.* **1.** a firework rocket that explodes high in the air, usually with a burst of bright, colored sparks. —*v.* **2.** to rise rapidly or suddenly: *He skyrocketed to success.*

sky·scrap·er (skī′skrā′pər), *n.* an extremely tall building of many stories, usually containing offices.

sky·ward (skī′wərd), *adv.* **1.** Also, **sky′wards.** toward the sky: *to look skyward.* —*adj.* **2.** directed or going toward the sky: *the skyward ascent of a balloon.*

sky·writ·ing (skī′rī′tĭng), *n.* **1.** the act or technique of tracing letters and words in the sky by releasing a special smoke from a moving airplane. **2.** a word, message, etc., produced in this way.

slab (slab), *n.* **1.** a broad, thick, flat piece of some solid material: *They used slabs of stone to make the steps.* **2.** a thick slice: *a slab of bread.*

slack (slak), *adj.* **1.** not tight, taut, or firm; loose: *a slack rope; a slack handshake.* **2.** careless or lazy: *a slack worker.* **3.** slow or sluggish. **4.** not active or busy; dull; slow: *Summer is a slack season for the fur trade.* —*adv.* **5.** in a slack manner: *The rope hung slack.* —*n.* **6.** a part that is slack or loose: *the slack in a rope.* **7.** the condition of being slack or loose. **8.** a lessening in activity, sales, etc.: *a slack in business.* —*v.* **9.** to slacken. —**slack′ly,** *adv.* —**slack′ness,** *n.*

slack·en (slak′ən), *v.* **1.** to make or become less active, rapid, vigorous, etc.: *He told his men not to slacken their efforts.* **2.** to make or become loose or looser: *His grip on the rope suddenly slackened.*

slack·er (slak′ər), *n.* a person who avoids his duty, work, or military service.

slacks (slaks), *n. (used as pl.)* men's or women's trousers for informal wear.

slag (slag), *n.* **1.** a hard, stony waste material produced in separating a metal from its ore. **2.** a kind of lava that looks like cinders.

slain (slān), *v.* the past participle of **slay.**

slake (slāk), *v.,* **slaked, slak·ing. 1.** to satisfy or relieve (thirst, hunger, anger, etc.); quench: *to slake one's thirst by drinking iced tea.* **2.** to cause the disintegration of (lime) by treating it with water.

sla·lom (slä′ləm), *n.* a downhill skiing race in which one must zigzag between poles stuck in the snow.

slam¹ (slam), *v.,* **slammed, slam·ming. 1.** to shut with force and noise: *She slammed the door. The gate slammed behind him.* **2.** to throw or thrust with sud-

den force: *to slam one's books onto the table.* **3.** to hit or strike with force; crash: *The car slammed into the truck.* —*n.* **4.** the act or sound of slamming: *We heard the slam of a door.* [from Scandinavian]

slam² (slam), *n.* (in a bridge game) the winning of all the tricks (**grand slam**) or all but one (**little slam**). [perhaps from a special use of *slam¹*]

slan·der (slan′dər), *n.* **1.** a false statement made deliberately to harm a person's reputation. —*v.* **2.** to utter slander against (a person): *to slander a politician.* —**slan′der·er,** *n.*

slan·der·ous (slan′dər əs), *adj.* containing, involving, or spreading slander: *slanderous statements; a slanderous busybody.* —**slan′der·ous·ly,** *adv.*

slang (slang), *n.* **1.** an informal style of speech or writing, containing colorful expressions, invented words and phrases, and unusual or special meanings for ordinary words. *Scram* and *to blow one's top* are slang expressions. The word *dough* in slang may mean "money." —*adj.* **2.** referring to or of the nature of slang: *a slang term.*

slang·y (slang′ē), *adj.,* **slang·i·er, slang·i·est. 1.** of, like, or full of slang: *slangy talk.* **2.** using much slang: *He is a slangy writer.* —**slang′i·ness,** *n.*

slant (slant), *v.* **1.** to slope or tilt; be at an angle away from a level position: *a shelf that slants instead of being straight.* **2.** to cause to slope or tilt: *to slant a roof so that rain will run off it.* **3.** to present (information, a story, etc.) in a way that favors a particular point of view: *a newspaper that slants the facts.* —*n.* **4.** a slanting position or direction; slope: *to set a ladder at a slant against a wall.* **5.** an attitude or viewpoint: *a story written with a humorous slant.* —**slant′ing·ly,** *adv.*

slant·wise (slant′wīz′), *adv.* **1.** at a slant or angle; in a sloping manner. —*adj.* **2.** slanting or sloping: *a slantwise position.*

slap (slap), *n.* **1.** a sharp blow or smack, esp. with the open hand or something flat: *to give someone a slap on the back.* **2.** a sound made by such a blow. **3.** an insult or sharp criticism: *Her remark was a slap at her lazy brother.* —*v.,* **slapped, slap·ping. 4.** to hit or strike sharply, esp. with the open hand or something flat. **5.** to throw, put, etc., with a slap or smack: *She slapped her notebook down on the desk.*

slap·stick (slap′stik′), *n.* a type of comedy based on wild action, such as chases and ridiculous fights, and exaggerated performances by the actors.

slash (slash), *v.* **1.** to cut or mark with a powerful swinging or sweeping stroke: *They used large knives to slash a path through the jungle.* **2.** to strike or lash out with a powerful swinging or sweeping motion: *The swordsman slashed at the bandits.* **3.** to reduce or lower severely: *to slash prices.* —*n.* **4.** a sweeping stroke made with a knife, sword, pen, etc. **5.** a cut or mark made with such a stroke; gash. **6.** a severe reduction in a price or the like. **7.** a slanting line (/) used as a dividing line in fractions or to separate numbers in writing dates, sums of money, etc.

slat (slat), *n.* **1.** a long, thin, narrow strip of wood, metal, or the like. —*v.*, **slat·ted, slat·ting. 2.** to furnish or make with slats: *to slat a Venetian blind.*

slate (slāt), *n.* **1.** a dark, blue-gray rock that can be split into smooth layers. **2.** a thin piece of this rock, used as a roofing material, to make blackboards, etc. **3.** a blackboard, esp. a small one that is held in the hand. **4.** a dull, dark, bluish gray. **5.** a list of candidates to be considered for nomination, election, or appointment. —*v.*, **slat·ed, slat·ing. 6.** to choose or select: *He is slated to be captain.* **7.** to schedule or arrange: *We have a game slated with your school this year.* **8. a clean slate,** a good record, esp. of honorable conduct: *The candidate has a clean slate.*

slat·tern (slat′ərn), *n.* a dirty, untidy woman or girl. —**slat′tern·ly,** *adj., adv.*

slaugh·ter (slô′tər), *n.* **1.** the killing or butchering of cattle, sheep, etc., esp. for food. **2.** a brutal, violent killing, esp. of many persons. **3.** *Informal.* a thorough defeat; trouncing. —*v.* **4.** to kill or butcher animals, esp. for food. **5.** to kill brutally or massacre. **6.** to defeat thoroughly; trounce. —**slaugh′ter·er,** *n.*

slaugh·ter·house (slô′tər hous′), *n., pl.* **slaugh·ter·hous·es** (slô′tər hou′ziz). a building or place where animals are butchered for food.

Slav (släv, slav), *n.* **1.** one of a group of peoples in eastern, southeastern, and central Europe, including the Russians, Poles, Czechs, Bulgars, Yugoslavs, and others. —*adj.* **2.** of or concerning the Slavs; Slavic.

slave (slāv), *n.* **1.** a person who is owned by another, and can be bought and sold like a piece of property. **2.** a person who is controlled by some powerful need, influence, fear, etc.: *a slave to a drug.* **3.** a person who works hard for little reward; drudge. —*v.*, **slaved, slav·ing. 4.** to work like a slave; drudge.

slave·hold·er (slāv′hōl′dər), *n.* a person who owns slaves. —**slave′hold′ing,** *n.*

slav·er (slav′ər, slā′vər), *v.* **1.** to slobber or drool; let saliva run from the mouth. —*n.* **2.** saliva coming from the mouth.

slav·er·y (slā′və rē), *n.* **1.** the practice of keeping slaves, esp. when allowed or approved by the government: *In what year did slavery end in the U.S.?* **2.** the condition of being a slave; bondage: *to be sold into slavery.* **3.** the condition of being controlled by some powerful need, influence, person, etc.: *his slavery to liquor.* **4.** extremely hard and unrewarding work; drudgery.

Slav·ic (slav′ik, slä′vik), *n.* **1.** a branch of the Indo-European family of languages, including Russian, Ukrainian, Polish, Czech, Slovak, Serbo-Croatian, Bulgarian, and several others. —*adj.* **2.** of or concerning the Slavs, their languages, or their cultures. Also, **Sla·von·ic** (slə von′ik).

slav·ish (slā′vish), *adj.* **1.** of or befitting a slave; base or servile: *slavish submission.* **2.** lacking originality; deliberately imitating something else: *a slavish imitation.* —**slav′ish·ly,** *adv.* —**slav′ish·ness,** *n.*

slaw (slô), *n.* short for **coleslaw.**

slay (slā), *v.*, **slew** (slōō), **slain** (slān), **slay·ing.** to kill by violence: *soldiers slain in battle.* —**slay′er,** *n.*

slea·zy (slē′zē), *adj.*, **slea·zi·er, slea·zi·est. 1.** (of a fabric) too thin or poor in quality; flimsy. **2.** cheap, vulgar, or low: *a sleazy nightclub; a sleazy little pickpocket.* —**slea′zi·ness,** *n.*

sled (sled), *n.* **1.** a small vehicle having a platform set on runners, used for sliding on snow or ice. **2.** a sledge. —*v.*, **sled·ded, sled·ding. 3.** to coast, ride, or be carried on a sled: *to go sledding in winter.*

sledge[1] (slej), *n.* **1.** a heavy or solidly built vehicle mounted on runners, often drawn by a horse or other animal, and used esp. for moving loads across snow or ice. **2.** a sled. **3.** a sleigh. —*v.*, **sledged, sledg·ing. 4.** to travel or carry by sledge. [from the Dutch word *sleedse*]

sledge[2] (slej), *n.* **1.** short for **sledge hammer.** —*v.*, **sledged, sledg·ing. 2.** to sledge-hammer. [from the Old English word *slecg*]

sledge′ ham′mer, a large, heavy hammer, swung with both hands.

sledge-ham·mer (slej′ham′ər), *v.* **1.** to strike, hammer, or beat with or as if with a sledge hammer: *to sledge-hammer a boulder to break it up.* —*adj.* **2.** powerful; ruthless: *a sledge-hammer attack.*

sleek (slēk), *adj.* **1.** smooth and glossy: *a dog with a sleek coat.* **2.** having a smooth and glossy coat; appearing healthy and well-groomed: *a sleek horse.* **3.** smooth and polished in manners, speech, etc. —*v.* **4.** Also, **sleek′en.** to make sleek or smooth: *a cat sleeking itself.* —**sleek′ly,** *adv.* —**sleek′ness,** *n.*

sleep (slēp), *n.* **1.** a state or time of rest in which one loses awareness or consciousness at least partly and the body relaxes: *A tired man needs sleep.* **2.** a state of inactivity resembling sleep: *the sleep of a hibernating animal.* **3.** the repose of death. —*v.*, **slept** (slept), **sleep·ing. 4.** to take rest in sleep; be asleep: *A kitten sleeps most of the day.* **5.** to be inactive; be in a state resembling sleep: *Nature sleeps during the winter.* **6.** to lie in death: *warriors sleeping in their graves.* **7.** to get rid of (a headache, worry, etc.) by sleeping (usually fol. by *off* or *away*): *to sleep off a bad mood.* **8.** to spend or pass in sleep (usually fol. by *away*): *to sleep away the morning.*

sleep·er (slē′pər), *n.* **1.** a person or thing that sleeps. **2.** a sleeping car on a railroad train. **3.** *Informal.* a movie, book, person, etc., that becomes successful after a slow start.

sleep′ing car′, a railroad car having berths for passengers to sleep in; sleeper.

sleep′ing sick′ness, a disease that causes abnormal sleepiness, esp. a generally fatal African disease transmitted by the bite of the tsetse fly.

sleep·less (slēp′lis), *adj.* **1.** without sleep: *to spend a sleepless night.* **2.** always active: *a sleepless vigilance.* —**sleep′less·ly,** *adv.* —**sleep′less·ness,** *n.*

sleep·walk·ing (slēp′wô′king), *n.* the act of walking about while asleep. —**sleep′walk′er,** *n.*

sleep·y (slē′pē), *adj.*, **sleep·i·er, sleep·i·est. 1.** ready to sleep, or not quite awake; desiring to sleep; drowsy: *to put a sleepy baby to bed.* **2.** showing drowsiness: *a sleepy smile.* **3.** inactive; not busy: *a sleepy little town.* —**sleep′i·ly,** *adv.* —**sleep′i·ness,** *n.*

sleet (slēt), *n.* **1.** frozen or freezing rain; a mixture of hail or snow and rain. **2.** a thin coating of ice formed by freezing rain. —*v.* **3.** to fall as sleet.

sleet·y (slē/tē), *adj.,* **sleet·i·er, sleet·i·est.** of or sending down sleet: *sleety weather.*

sleeve (slēv), *n.* **1.** the part of a garment that covers or partly covers the arm. **2.** an envelope, usually of paper, for protecting a phonograph record. **3.** a tube that fits inside a hole or over a rod, a shaft, or another tube. **4. up one's sleeve,** kept secretly ready or close at hand: *I knew by his smile that he had something up his sleeve.* —**sleeve/less,** *adj.*

sleigh (slā), *n.* **1.** a light, usually open vehicle on runners, generally drawn by a horse and used for traveling over snow or ice. —*v.* **2.** to travel or ride in a sleigh: *to go sleighing.* —**sleigh/er,** *n.*

sleight (slīt), *n.* skill or nimbleness, esp. in using one's hands.

sleight/ of hand/, 1. skill in performing feats or tricks, such as juggling or card tricks, that require quick and clever movement of the hands. **2.** the performance of such feats or tricks.

slen·der (slen/dər), *adj.* **1.** thin or slim; not wide or thick in proportion to the height or length: *a frail, slender girl; a tall, slender tree.* **2.** small in size, amount, extent, etc.; meager: *a slender income.* **3.** having little basis, value, or force; slight: *We have only a slender hope of success.* —**slen/der·ly,** *adv.* —**slen/der·ness,** *n.*

slept (slept), *v.* the past tense and past participle of **sleep.**

sleuth (slo͞oth), *n.* **1.** *Informal.* a detective. **2.** a bloodhound. —*v.* **3.** to track or trail (a criminal or the like) as a detective does.

slew¹ (slo͞o), *v.* the past tense of **slay.**

slew² (slo͞o), *v., n.* another spelling of **slue¹.**

slew³ (slo͞o), *n. Informal.* a great number; lot: *a whole slew of people.* [from the Irish word *sluagh* "multitude, army"]

slice (slīs), *n.* **1.** a thin, broad, flat piece cut from something: *a slice of bread.* **2.** a piece or portion: *a slice of land.* **3.** (in golf, baseball, etc.) a stroke that causes the ball to curve to the right or left. —*v.,* **sliced, slic·ing. 4.** to cut into slices: *to slice a turkey.* **5.** to separate or cut off in a slice or slices (sometimes fol. by *off, away,* etc.): *to slice off a piece of cheese.* **6.** to cut with or as if with a sharp edge: *The ship sliced through the waves.* **7.** to hit (a golf ball, baseball, etc.) in such a way that it curves to the right or left. —**slic/er,** *n.*

slick (slik), *adj.* **1.** smooth and glossy; sleek: *slick hair.* **2.** slippery, esp. from being covered with oil, ice, or water: *The road is slick with rain.* **3.** smooth or sly in manners, speech, etc.: *I don't trust slick salesmen.* **4.** clever or tricky: *a slick escape; a slick answer.* —*n.* **5.** a smooth or slippery place or spot: *an oil slick on the road.* —*v.* **6.** to make sleek or smooth: *to slick one's hair.* —*adv.* **7.** smoothly or cleverly.

slick·er (slik/ər), *n.* **1.** a long, loose raincoat of oilskin or a similar material. **2.** Also, **city slicker. a.** a sly, clever person, esp. a swindler. **b.** a person from a large city who has smooth manners.

slide (slīd), *v.,* **slid** (slid); **slid** *or* **slid·den** (slid/³n); **slid·ing. 1.** to move along smoothly on a surface; move in continuous contact with a smooth surface: *to slide down an icy hill.* **2.** to cause to move in this way: *to slide a book across a table.* **3.** to slip or skid. **4.** to move easily or quietly (usually fol. by *in, into, out,* etc.): *to slide into a chair.* **5.** to pass or fall gradually: *to slide into a bad habit.* —*n.* **6.** the act of sliding; a sliding motion or movement: *He took a slide on the ice.* **7.** a smooth, usually sloping surface for sliding: *a slide in a playground.* **8.** an object or part that slides. **9.** a mass of fallen rocks, dirt, or the like; landslide or avalanche. **10.** a small transparent photograph for throwing onto a screen by a projector. **11.** a small piece of glass for mounting objects to be viewed through a microscope.

slide/ rule/, a device resembling a ruler but having a sliding center strip, used for rapid multiplication, division, solving of trigonometry problems, etc.

sli·er (slī/ər), *adj.* a comparative of **sly.**

sli·est (slī/ist), *adj.* a superlative of **sly.**

slight (slīt), *adj.* **1.** small in amount, force, degree, etc.: *a slight change; a slight bump.* **2.** of little importance; trivial or small: *a slight disagreement.* **3.** slender or slim; not heavily built. —*v.* **4.** to treat (someone) as being of little importance; snub or insult: *He slighted his cousin by not answering her letter.* **5.** to give little attention or effort to; neglect: *Students with spring fever slight their studies.* —*n.* **6.** a snub or insult. —**slight/ly,** *adv.*

slim (slim), *adj.,* **slim·mer, slim·mest. 1.** slender or thin: *a slim girl.* **2.** small or scanty: *a slim chance.* —*v.,* **slimmed, slim·ming. 3.** to make or become slim or thin (often fol. by *down*): *She went on a diet to slim down.* —**slim/ly,** *adv.* —**slim/ness,** *n.*

slime (slīm), *n.* **1.** thin, oozy, sticky mud. **2.** any thin, slippery or slightly sticky liquid matter, esp. of an unpleasant kind. **3.** a thin, sticky liquid given off by certain animals and plants: *The snail left a trail of slime behind it.*

slim·y (slī/mē), *adj.,* **slim·i·er, slim·i·est. 1.** of or like slime: *slimy stuff.* **2.** full of or covered with slime. **3.** nasty and unpleasant: *a slimy, sneaky person.* —**slim/i·ly,** *adv.* —**slim/i·ness,** *n.*

sling (sling), *n.* **1.** a broad strap with a string at each end, used for hurling a rock or other object by hand. **2.** a slingshot. **3.** a large bandage used to support an injured part of the body, esp. one tied around the neck and looped under an arm. **4.** a strap for carrying a rifle or other gun. **5.** any strap, band, or the like, that is looped and used to support something. —*v.,* **slung** (slung), **sling·ing. 6.** to fling or throw, esp. with a swinging motion of the hand: *He slung the newspaper across the room.* **7.** to hang or support by means of a sling, strap, or the like: *The soldier slung the rifle over his shoulder.*

sling·shot (sling'shot'), *n.* a Y-shaped stick with an elastic strip between the prongs, used for shooting stones or other small objects.

slink (slingk), *v.,* **slunk** (slungk), **slink·ing.** to move in a sneaky, frightened, or guilty way; creep secretively: *The cat was slinking through the bushes.*

slip¹ (slip), *v.,* **slipped, slip·ping. 1.** to move smoothly or easily; slide or glide: *He slipped the glove onto his hand. The lock slipped into place.* **2.** to slide or drop suddenly, esp. accidentally: *He slipped on the ice. The cup slipped from her fingers.* **3.** to move or pass quickly and quietly: *He slipped a note to me. She slipped out of the room.* **4.** to pass or go without being noticed, used, etc. (often fol. by *away* or *by*): *Time slipped away.* **5.** to fall below some usual standard or level; fail or worsen: *Her work is slipping.* **6.** to escape or free oneself from: *The dog slipped his collar and ran away.* **7.** to be said or revealed accidentally (usually fol. by *out*): *That remark just slipped out.* —*n.* **8.** the act of slipping, esp. a sudden slide: *a slip on the ice.* **9.** a mistake or oversight: *a slip in doing addition.* **10.** a drop from some usual standard or level: *a slip in the price of cotton.* **11.** a woman's undergarment resembling a light, sleeveless dress or a light skirt. **12.** a space between two wharves or in a dock for a ship or boat to lie in: *The ship maneuvered into the slip without the aid of tugboats.* **13. give someone the slip,** to escape from someone: *We hid behind a fence and gave him the slip.* **14. slip something over on,** *Informal.* to deceive or trick someone: *He tried to slip something over on me by selling me a broken watch.* **15. slip up,** to make an error; fail: *He was supposed to remind me, but he slipped up.* [from a Middle English word, which comes from the earlier Dutch word *slippen* "to slip"]

slip² (slip), *n.* **1.** a piece or cutting from a plant, which can be used to grow a new plant. **2.** any long, narrow piece or strip: *a slip of land.* **3.** a small piece of paper, esp. one bearing information. **4.** a young, usually slender person: *a slip of a girl.* [from a Middle English word, which comes from the earlier Flemish word *slippe* "cut piece, strip"]

slip·cov·er (slip'kuv'ər), *n.* **1.** an easily removable cloth covering for a piece of furniture. **2.** a book jacket. Also, **slip' cov'er.**

slip·knot (slip'not'), *n.* a knot that slips easily along the line around which it is made, forming a loop that may be tightened or loosened. Also, **running knot.** See illus. at knot.

slip·per (slip'ər), *n.* any light, low-cut shoe that may be slipped on or off the foot easily.

slip·per·wort (slip'ər wûrt'), *n.* a plant of tropical America that is related to the snapdragon and has slipper-shaped flowers.

Slipperwort

slip·per·y (slip'ə rē), *adj.* **1.** causing or likely to cause slipping or sliding as a result of being smooth or slick: *Rain can make a road slippery.* **2.** likely to slip from one's grasp: *a slippery bar of soap.* **3.** not trustworthy; tricky: *a clever but slippery fellow.* —**slip'per·i·ness,** *n.*

slip·shod (slip'shod'), *adj.* **1.** careless or sloppy: *He did a slipshod job of repairing my bicycle.* **2.** seedy or shabby: *a slipshod beggar.* —**slip'shod'ness,** *n.*

slit (slit), *n.* **1.** a straight, narrow cut or opening: *Sunlight shone through the slits in the shutters.* —*v.,* **slit, slit·ting. 2.** to make a slit or slits in (something). **3.** to cut into long strips.

slith·er (slith'ər), *v.* to move or slide with a side-to-side motion: *The snake slithered through the grass.*

sliv·er (sliv'ər), *n.* **1.** a small, slender piece broken or cut off from something: *a sliver of glass.* —*v.* **2.** to split into slivers.

slob·ber (slob'ər), *v.* **1.** to let saliva or liquid run from the mouth; drool; slaver. **2.** to express one's feelings in a foolishly sentimental way; gush. —*n.* **3.** saliva or liquid dribbled from the mouth.

sloe (slō), *n.* **1.** a small, sour fruit, resembling a plum, that grows on a thorny shrub or small tree. **2.** the shrub or tree that bears this fruit.

slo·gan (slō'gən), *n.* **1.** a phrase or motto used repeatedly in advertisements, a political campaign, etc.: *"I like Ike" was a slogan used during the presidential campaign of 1952.* **2.** a war cry or gathering cry, as formerly used among the Scottish clans. [from the Gaelic word *sluagh-ghairm* "army cry"]

sloop (sloop), *n.* a single-masted sailboat rigged fore-and-aft, having a mainsail and a jib or other small sail.

slop (slop), *v.,* **slopped, slop·ping. 1.** to spill or splash (liquid): *to slop soup onto one's clothing.* **2.** (of liquid) to spill or splash: *The milk slopped all over the table.* **3.** to feed slop or swill to: *to slop pigs.* **4.** to walk or go through mud, slush, or water: *The soldiers slopped through the valley.* —*n.* **5.** liquid carelessly spilled or splashed about. **6.** liquid feed or swill for pigs or other livestock. **7.** Often, **slops.** the dirty water, liquid waste, etc., from a kitchen, ship's galley, or the like. **8.** watery mud. **9.** *Slang.* badly cooked or unpleasant food or drink.

slope (slōp), *v.,* **sloped, slop·ing. 1.** to slant or incline: *a hill that slopes down to the sea; a sloping roof.* **2.** to form or build with a slope or slant: *to slope a road.* —*n.* **3.** a slant, esp. upward or downward. **4.** a portion of land having such a slant, such as the side of a hill: *to ski down a slope.*

slop·py (slop'ē), *adj.,* **slop·pi·er, slop·pi·est. 1.** muddy, slushy, or very wet: *a sloppy football field.* **2.** messy or soiled: *a sloppy kitchen.* **3.** careless or slipshod: *a sloppy housekeeper; a sloppy piece of work.* —**slop'pi·ly,** *adv.* —**slop'pi·ness,** *n.*

slosh (slosh), *n.* **1.** watery mud or partly melted snow; slush. **2.** the lap or splash of liquid: *the slosh of water in a bathtub.* —*v.* **3.** to splash in mud, slush, or water: *to slosh through melting snow.* **4.** to splash about: *to slosh water onto the floor; suds sloshing in a washing machine.*

slot (slot), *n.* **1.** a narrow, straight opening, slit, or groove: *a coin slot; a letter slot.* —*v.,* **slot·ted, slot·ting. 2.** to make or cut a slot or slots in (something).

sloth (slôth, slŏth), *n.* **1.** extreme laziness or indolence. **2.** any of several tropical American animals that hang from the branches of trees and move along them in an upside-down position.

sloth·ful (slôth′fəl, slŏth′fəl), *adj.* extremely lazy. —**sloth′ful·ly,** *adv.* —**sloth′ful·ness,** *n.*

Sloth
(length 2 ft.)

slouch (slouch), *v.* **1.** to sit, stand, or move with an awkward, drooping posture: *Soldiers are not supposed to slouch.* —*n.* **2.** an awkward drooping or slumping posture: *to walk with a slouch.* **3.** a clumsy or lazy person. —**slouch′er,** *n.* —**slouch′ing·ly,** *adv.*

slouch·y (slou′chē), *adj.,* **slouch·i·er, slouch·i·est.** of, with, or having a slouch; drooping: *a slouchy way of walking.* —**slouch′i·ly,** *adv.* —**slouch′i·ness,** *n.*

slough¹ (slou *for defs. 1, 2;* slōō *for def. 3*), *n.* **1.** a swamp, bog, or swamplike area. **2.** a hole full of watery mud. **3.** a marshy pond, backwater, inlet, or the like. Also, **slue.** [from the Old English word *slōh*]

slough² (sluf), *v.* **1.** to shed or cast off (dead skin or other tissue). **2.** to cast off or get rid of (something unwanted). —*n.* **3.** the skin or tissue cast off: *the slough of a snake.* [from the Middle English word *slughe*]

Slo·vak (slō′väk, slō′vak), *n.* **1.** a member of the Slavic people living in Slovakia. **2.** the Slavic language of Slovakia, similar to Czech. —*adj.* **3.** of or concerning the Slovaks, their culture, or their language.

Slo·va·ki·a (slō vä′kē ə, slō vak′ē ə), *n.* a region in central Europe, now in E Czechoslovakia. 18,921 sq. mi. —**Slo·va′ki·an,** *n., adj.*

slov·en·ly (sluv′ən lē), *adj.* **1.** dirty or extremely untidy; not neat. **2.** careless or slipshod: *slovenly work.* —**slov′en·li·ness,** *n.*

slow (slō), *adj.* **1.** having little speed; not fast: *a slow walk; a slow dance.* **2.** not moving or able to move fast or quickly: *a slow runner; a slow car.* **3.** requiring or taking a long time: *a slow journey.* **4.** not clever or quick to learn; mentally dull. **5.** not quickly excited or moved (usually fol. by *to* or an infinitive): *slow to anger.* **6.** going or working at less than the proper or usual speed: *The subway trains are slow this morning.* **7.** showing less than the proper time: *Your watch is slow.* **8.** inactive or dull; not busy or lively: *Business was slow this week.* —*adv.* **9.** in a slow manner; slowly (sometimes used in combination): *to drive slow; a slow-moving car.* —*v.* **10.** to make or become slow or slower (often fol. by *up* or *down*): *They slowed down the music. The car slowed up.* —**slow′ly,** *adv.* —**slow′ness,** *n.*

slow′ mo′tion, a motion-picture technique in which the film runs through the projector at a slower speed than it ran through the camera, making the images on the screen appear to move more slowly than the object that was photographed. —**slow′-mo′tion,** *adj.*

slow·poke (slō′pōk′), *n.* a person who does things very slowly.

slow-wit·ted (slō′wit′id), *adj.* mentally slow or dull; not quick to learn or understand. —**slow′-wit′ted·ness,** *n.*

sludge (sluj), *n.* **1.** mud or ooze. **2.** a muddy deposit at the bottom of a lake, a tank, or a pipe.

slue¹ (slōō), *v.,* **slued, slu·ing. 1.** to turn or swing (something) around. —*n.* **2.** the act of sluing or swinging around. **3.** a position slued to. Also, **slew.**

slue² (slōō), *n.* another spelling of **slough¹.**

slug¹ (slug), *n.* **1.** any of various slimy, slow-moving animals that resemble snails but have no shell. **2.** a caterpillar that resembles this animal. **3.** a piece of lead or other metal for firing from a gun; bullet or shot. **4.** any lump or piece of metal, esp. a small disk used in place of a coin. [from the Middle English word *slugge* "sluggard," which comes from Scandinavian]

Slug
(length 4 in.)

slug² (slug), *Informal.* —*v.,* **slugged, slug·ging. 1.** to hit hard, esp. with the fist. **2.** to hit (a baseball) to a great distance or very hard. —*n.* **3.** the act of slugging; a hard hit. [from a special use of *slug¹*]

slug·gard (slug′ərd), *n.* a lazy, slow person who dislikes any sort of work. —**slug′gard·ly,** *adj.*

slug·gish (slug′ish), *adj.* **1.** lazy or lacking in energy. **2.** moving slowly; having little motion: *a sluggish river.* **3.** not acting or working with full vigor or efficiency. —**slug′gish·ly,** *adv.* —**slug′gish·ness,** *n.*

sluice (slōōs), *n.* **1.** a man-made channel or canal for water, having a gate (**sluice′ gate′**) at the upper end for regulating the flow. **2.** the water held back or regulated by a sluice. **3.** a man-made stream or water channel. **4.** a long, sloping trough for washing or separating ores. —*v.,* **sluiced, sluic·ing. 5.** to let out (water) by or as if by opening a sluice. **6.** to drain (a pond, lake, etc.), esp. by using a sluice. **7.** to wash or drench with water.

slum (slum), *n.* Often, **slums.** a run-down, overcrowded part of a city or town.

slum·ber (slum′bər), *v.* **1.** to sleep, esp. lightly; doze. **2.** to be inactive or calm: *a volcano that has slumbered for many years.* —*n.* **3.** Sometimes, **slumbers.** sleep, esp. light sleep. **4.** a state of inactivity or calm. —**slum′ber·er,** *n.*

slum·ber·ous (slum′bər əs), *adj.* **1.** sleepy or drowsy. **2.** causing or bringing on sleep. Also, **slumbrous** (slum′brəs).

slump (slump), *v.* **1.** to drop or fall heavily; collapse: *Suddenly she slumped to the floor.* **2.** to slouch or sag; take a bowed or bent position or posture: *to slump in a chair.* **3.** to decline or drop sharply: *Business has slumped this month.* —*n.* **4.** the act of slumping. **5.** a slumping or slouching position or posture; sag. **6.** a decline or drop: *a slump in business.*

slung (slung), *v.* the past tense and past participle of **sling.**

slunk (slungk), *v.* the past tense and past participle of **slink.**

slur (slûr), *v.,* **slurred, slur·ring.** 1. to pass over lightly or without proper mention or consideration (often fol. by *over*): *The report slurred over many important facts.* 2. to pronounce (a word, syllable, etc.) indistinctly: *When she tries to speak quickly she slurs her words.* 3. to belittle or insult; damage the reputation of (someone): *His remarks slurred the officer's good name.* 4. to sing a single syllable or play without a break (two or more tones of different pitch). —*n.* 5. an indistinctly pronounced word, syllable, phrase, etc. 6. an insult, slight, or belittling remark. 7. a blot or stain, as upon one's reputation. 8. (in music) the combination of two or more tones of different pitch, sung to a single syllable or played without a break.

slush (slush), *n.* 1. partly melted snow. 2. watery mud.

slush·y (slush′ē), *adj.,* **slush·i·er, slush·i·est.** of or full of slush: *slushy streets.* —**slush′i·ness,** *n.*

slut (slut), *n.* 1. a dirty, slovenly woman. 2. an immoral woman.

sly (slī), *adj.,* **sly·er** *or* **sli·er; sly·est** *or* **sli·est.** 1. clever in a crafty or tricky way; cunning. 2. stealthy or secret; having to do with some secret understanding, trick, etc.: *a sly wink.* 3. playfully clever or mischievous: *a sly joke.* 4. **on the sly,** secretly; underhandedly: *I caught him wearing my cuff links on the sly.* —**sly′ly,** *adv.* —**sly′ness,** *n.*

Sm, *Chem.* the symbol for **samarium.**

smack¹ (smak), *n.* 1. a flavor or trace: *The stew had just a smack of garlic.* 2. a touch, trace, or suggestion: *a smack of a Southern accent.* —*v.* 3. to have a flavor or trace (often fol. by *of*): *a soup that smacks of curry.* 4. to have a touch or suggestion (often fol. by *of*): *His humor smacks of cruelty.* [from the Old English word *smæc*]

smack² (smak), *v.* 1. to strike or slap sharply, esp. with the open hand or something flat. 2. to close and open (the lips) smartly so as to make a quick popping noise, esp. as a sign that one is hungry. —*n.* 3. a sharp slap or blow. 4. a smacking of the lips. 5. *Informal.* a hearty or loud kiss. —*adv.* 6. *Informal.* suddenly and violently: *He ran smack into the wall.* 7. directly or squarely: *The house stands smack opposite the church.* [imitative of the sound]

smack³ (smak), *n.* a small sailing or fishing boat. [perhaps from the Dutch word *smak*]

smack·ing (smak′ing), *adj.* smart or brisk: *a smacking breeze.*

small (smôl), *adj.* 1. not great or large in size; little; not big: *The puppy was too small to jump on the chair.* 2. not great in amount, degree, value, etc.: *Her work shows a small improvement.* 3. not great in number of members, inhabitants, etc.: *a small town.* 4. not very important; minor, petty, or insignificant: *It was only a small disagreement.* 5. mean or petty; not generous: *It was small of you not to forgive him.* 6. of little strength or force; slight or faint: *a small voice.* —*n.* 7. the smallest or most slender part: *the small of the back.* 8. something that is small: *Do you*

prefer the large size or the small? —**small′ness,** *n.*

small′ arms′, firearms, such as pistols or rifles, designed to be held in one or both hands.

small′ cal′orie. See **calorie** (def. 1).

small′ intes′tine, the upper portion of the intestines, longer but smaller in diameter than the lower portion. Most of the digestion and absorption of food takes place in the small intestine. See illus. at **intestine.**

small·pox (smôl′poks′), *n.* a highly contagious disease that causes high fever and spots on the skin that leave permanent scars.

smart (smärt), *adj.* 1. having or showing quick intelligence; bright; clever: *a smart student.* 2. strikingly neat and trim in appearance: *An officer's uniform should be smart.* 3. elegant or fashionable: *a smart shop.* 4. brisk or vigorous: *to walk at a very smart pace.* 5. saucy or witty: *This is no time for smart remarks.* 6. sharply severe; keen or stinging: *a smart pain.* —*v.* 7. to feel a sharp, stinging pain: *My arm smarts from the flu shot.* 8. to cause a sharp, stinging pain: *That slap smarted.* 9. to suffer from hurt feelings: *He's still smarting from their insults.* —*n.* 10. a sharp, stinging pain, as from a wound or blow. —**smart′ly,** *adv.* —**smart′ness,** *n.*

smart·en (smär′t'n), *v.* 1. to make more neat or trim (often fol. by *up*): *A shave would smarten up your appearance.* 2. to make or become brisker or more vigorous. 3. **smarten up,** to make or become aware of certain facts; become smarter or wiser: *The bad experience smartened him up.*

smash (smash), *v.* 1. to break violently into pieces; shatter: *The vase smashed when it hit the floor.* 2. to hit, go, etc., with a shattering force; crash (usually fol. by *against, into, through,* etc.): *His car smashed into mine.* 3. to hit or strike (someone or something) with great force. 4. to destroy completely; crush; ruin: *Her hopes were smashed.* —*n.* 5. the act of smashing or shattering something. 6. the sound of something smashing or shattering: *I heard a smash in the kitchen.* 7. a forceful blow or hit. 8. a violent collision, as between automobiles; smash-up. 9. a smashed or ruined condition; collapse or destruction. 10. *Informal.* something that achieves great success; hit: *Her play was a smash on Broadway.*

smash-up (smash′up′), *n.* a violent crash, smash, or collision, esp. a wreck of one or more automobiles.

smat·ter·ing (smat′ər ing), *n.* a slight knowledge of something: *He has a smattering of Spanish.*

smear (smēr), *v.* 1. to spread (something oily, greasy, wet, etc.) on or over something else: *to smear paint on a canvas.* 2. to spread something oily, greasy, wet, etc., on or over: *to smear bread with jam.* 3. to stain or make dirty: *fingers smeared with ink.* 4. to smudge or blur: *to smear the signature on a check.* 5. to harm (someone's reputation) by spreading lies and damaging stories about him. —*n.* 6. a dab or streak of something oily, greasy, wet, etc.: *a smear of paint.* 7. an attack on someone's reputation, using lies, rumors, etc. —**smear′er,** *n.*

smell (smel), *v.,* **smelled** *or* **smelt** (smelt); **smell·ing.** 1.

to be aware of or perceive the odor of (something) through the nose and its nerves; breathe in or sniff the scent of: *to smell perfume.* **2.** to give off or have an odor or scent: *The room smelled of roses.* **3.** to give off or have an unpleasant odor; stink: *The city dump smells.* **4.** to detect or be aware of by shrewdness: *The policeman smelled trouble.* —*n.* **5.** the sense or faculty by which one smells; ability to smell odors. **6.** an odor or scent.

smell′ing salts′, a strong-smelling substance whose vapors are inhaled to relieve headache, and in cases of fainting or shock.

smell·y (smel′ē), *adj.,* **smell·i·er, smell·i·est.** giving off a strong or unpleasant odor: *a smelly garbage can.*

smelt¹ (smelt), *v.* **1.** to melt (ore) to release the metal it contains. **2.** to obtain (metal) in this way. [probably from an earlier Dutch word]

smelt² (smelt), *n.* any of several small, silvery, salt-water fishes used as food. [from Old English]

smelt³ (smelt), *v.* a past tense and past participle of **smell.**

smelt·er (smel′tər), *n.* **1.** a person or thing that smelts. **2.** a person who owns or works in a place where ores are smelted. **3.** a place where ores are smelted.

smile (smīl), *n.* **1.** an expression of the face marked by a turning up of the corners of the mouth, usually indicating pleasure or amusement but sometimes scorn or bitterness. —*v.,* **smiled, smil·ing. 2.** to have or give a smile. **3.** to express with a smile: *to smile one's thanks.* **4.** to show favor (often fol. by *on* or *upon*): *Fortune smiled on her.* —**smil′er,** *n.* —**smil′-ing·ly,** *adv.*

smirch (smûrch), *v.* **1.** to soil or smudge with or as if with dirt, soot, dust, etc.: *Grime smirched his clothes.* **2.** to disgrace or stain (one's reputation, good name, etc.). —*n.* **3.** a dirty mark or smear. **4.** a disgrace or stain, esp. on one's reputation or good name, etc.

smirk (smûrk), *n.* **1.** an unpleasant, self-satisfied, sarcastic, or knowing smile. —*v.* **2.** to have or give such a smile. —**smirk′er,** *n.*

smite (smīt), *v.,* **smote** (smōt); **smit·ten** (smit′³n) *or* **smit** (smit); **smit·ing. 1.** to strike or hit extremely hard, esp. with the hand, a club, or other weapon: *He smote the dragon with his sword.* **2.** to afflict or affect fatally or seriously: *to be smitten by a disease.* **3.** to strike or affect with sudden and strong feeling: *His conscience smote him. She was smitten with love.*

smith (smith), *n.* **1.** a person who works in metal; one who makes or repairs metal objects. **2.** a blacksmith.

Smith (smith), *n.* **1. John,** 1580–1631, English colonist in Virginia. **2. Joseph,** 1805–1844, U.S. founder of the Mormon Church.

smith·y (smith′ē, smith′ē), *n., pl.* **smith·ies. 1.** the workshop of a smith, esp. a blacksmith. **2.** a blacksmith.

smock (smok), *n.* **1.** a loose, lightweight garment worn over one's clothes to protect them from being stained or soiled. —*v.* **2.** to clothe in a smock; provide with a smock.

smog (smog), *n.* a mixture of fog and smoke often found in the air of cities. It irritates the eyes and harms the respiratory system.

smoke (smōk), *n.* **1.** the grayish, blackish, or brownish cloud of vapors and small solid particles, esp. of carbon, that results from burning wood, coal, oil, etc. **2.** something resembling this, such as mist or a cloud. **3.** a cigarette, cigar, or the like. **4.** the act of inhaling or puffing the smoke from a cigarette, cigar, or the like. —*v.,* **smoked, smok·ing. 5.** to give off smoke: *Their campfire was still smoking.* **6.** to inhale or puff tobacco smoke; take in smoke from a cigarette, cigar, or the like. **7.** to expose (meat, fish, etc.) to smoke so that it can be preserved; cure (food) with smoke. **8.** to color or darken by exposing to smoke: *to smoke glass.* **9. go up in smoke,** to be destroyed by or as if by fire: *We watched the house go up in smoke.* **10. smoke out, a.** to drive from a hiding place by means of smoke: *to smoke the hornets out of a tree.* **b.** to reveal, uncover, or make known: *to smoke out the true leader of the conspiracy.*

smoke·house (smōk′hous′), *n., pl.* **smoke·hous·es** (smōk′hou′zis). a building or place in which meat, fish, etc., are treated or cured with smoke.

smoke·less (smōk′lis), *adj.* having or producing little or no smoke: *a smokeless oven.*

smok·er (smō′kər), *n.* **1.** a person or thing that smokes. **2.** Also, **smok′ing car′.** a car on a railroad train in which passengers may smoke. **3.** an informal gathering or meeting at which one may smoke.

smoke′ screen′, 1. a mass of dense smoke used to hide an area, ship, plane, etc., from the enemy. **2.** anything intended to hide or deceive: *His laughter was just a smoke screen to cover his fear.*

smoke·stack (smōk′stak′), *n.* a tall pipe for the escape of smoke or gases on a steamboat, locomotive, or factory.

smok·y (smō′kē), *adj.,* **smok·i·er, smok·i·est. 1.** giving off smoke or too much smoke: *a smoky fire.* **2.** full of smoke or containing smoke: *a smoky room.* **3.** dark or soiled with smoke: *a smoky ceiling.* **4.** referring to or like smoke: *smoky colors.* —**smok′i·ness,** *n.*

smol·der (smōl′dər), *v.* **1.** to burn or smoke without flame: *smoldering coals.* **2.** to exist or continue in a hidden state without showing outwardly: *Anger smoldered behind his smile.* Also, **smoulder.**

smooth (smooth), *adj.* **1.** free from roughness, bumps, splinters, etc.; having an even surface or texture: *to skate on smooth ice; a smooth piece of wood.* **2.** free from lumps: *a smooth sauce.* **3.** free from hair, a beard, etc.: *the smooth chin of a boy.* **4.** free from jolts, jerks, etc.: *a smooth landing.* **5.** free from difficulties or trouble: *a smooth day at the office.* **6.** calm and even-tempered: *She has a smooth disposition.* **7.** polished and agreeable in manner: *a smooth diplomat.* **8.** free from harshness; bland or mellow: *a smooth voice.* —*adv.* **9.** in a smooth manner;

smoothly. —*v.* **10.** to make the surface of (something) smooth or even: *to smooth wood with sandpaper.* **11.** to free from difficulties or obstacles: *to smooth the way for someone.* **12.** to refine or polish: *His manners need smoothing.* **13.** to remove (wrinkles, lumps, etc.) from something (often fol. by *out* or *away*): *to smooth out wrinkles with an iron.* **14.** to soothe or calm. **15. smooth over,** to cause (something) to seem less harmful, objectionable, or the like: *to smooth over a dispute between children.* —**smooth′er,** *n.* —**smooth′ly,** *adv.* —**smooth′ness,** *n.*

smooth·bore (smooth′bôr′), *adj.* **1.** (of a gun) having a smooth bore like that of a shotgun; not rifled. —*n.* **2.** a smoothbore gun.

smor·gas·bord (smôr′gəs bôrd′), *n.* a Swedish meal with many different kinds of hot and cold foods, set out as a buffet.

smote (smōt), *v.* the past tense of **smite.**

smoth·er (smuth′ər), *v.* **1.** to prevent or be prevented from breathing; suffocate: *The smoke almost smothered the firemen.* **2.** to prevent from burning by covering: *to smother a fire with sand.* **3.** to cover closely or thickly: *to smother liver with onions.* **4.** to hide or keep back: *to smother one's anger.*

smoul·der (smōl′dər), *v.* another spelling of **smolder.**

smudge (smuj), *n.* **1.** a dirty mark or smear: *a smudge of ink.* **2.** dense smoke. **3.** a smoky fire, esp. one used to drive away mosquitoes or protect fruit trees from frost. —*v.,* **smudged, smudg·ing. 4.** to dirty with a smudge or smear.

smudge′ pot′, a container for burning fuel to produce dense smoke, used esp. to protect fruit trees from frost.

smudg·y (smuj′ē), *adj.,* **smudg·i·er, smudg·i·est. 1.** marked with smudges or smears: *smudgy fingers.* **2.** giving off dense smoke; smoky.

smug (smug), *adj.,* **smug·ger, smug·gest.** extremely self-satisfied; contentedly confident: *a smug little smile.* —**smug′ly,** *adv.* —**smug′ness,** *n.*

smug·gle (smug′əl), *v.,* **smug·gled, smug·gling. 1.** to take or transport (goods) into or out of a country, state, etc., illegally: *to smuggle gold.* **2.** to bring, take, put, etc., secretly: *to smuggle a message to a prisoner.* —**smug′gler,** *n.*

smut (smut), *n.* **1.** a bit of soot or grime. **2.** a black or dirty mark; smudge. **3.** a disease of plants that produces black powdery spots on the affected parts. **4.** a fungus that causes such a disease. **5.** indecent or vulgar writing, language, etc. —*v.,* **smut·ted, smut·ting. 6.** to soil or smudge. **7.** (of a plant) to become affected with smut.

smut·ty (smut′ē), *adj.,* **smut·ti·er, smut·ti·est. 1.** soiled with smut, soot, grime, etc. **2.** indecent or vulgar: *a smutty joke.* **3.** (of a plant) affected with smut. —**smut′ti·ness,** *n.*

Sn, *Chem.* the symbol for **tin.** [from the Latin word *stannum*]

snack (snak), *n.* **1.** a small portion of food or drink; a light meal: *a snack of soup and crackers.* —*v.* **2.** to have a snack or light meal.

snag (snag), *n.* **1.** a sharp or rough part that sticks out from something, such as a rough end of a broken branch. **2.** a tree or part of a tree stuck in the bottom of a river, lake, etc., and dangerous to boats or ships. **3.** any obstacle or difficulty: *to strike a snag in carrying out one's plans.* —*v.,* **snagged, snag·ging. 4.** to catch or tear on a snag: *He snagged his trousers while climbing the fence.* **5.** to obstruct, stop, or get hold of: *The reporters snagged the governor to ask him some questions.*

snail (snāl), *n.* a small animal with a soft body and a spiral shell that moves on a single muscular foot.

snake (snāk), *n.* any of numerous long, slender, legless reptiles having a scaly skin and ranging in length from a few inches to more than 20 feet.

Snake (snāk), *n.* a river in the NW United States, flowing from Wyoming to the Columbia River in Washington. 1038 mi. long.

snake·skin (snāk′skin′), *n.* **1.** the skin of a snake. **2.** leather made from the skin of a snake.

Snail
(shell length
to 3 in.)

snak·y (snā′kē), *adj.,* **snak·i·er, snak·i·est. 1.** of or concerning snakes. **2.** full of snakes: *a snaky swamp.* **3.** like a snake, esp. in being treacherous: *He had snaky eyes.*

snap (snap), *v.,* **snapped, snap·ping. 1.** to make a sudden, sharp sound; crack or click: *The burning wood snapped and crackled.* **2.** to cause to make such a sound: *to snap a whip; to snap one's fingers.* **3.** to move, strike, shut, etc., with a sharp clicking or cracking sound: *The lock snapped shut.* **4.** to break suddenly, esp. with a sharp cracking: *He snapped the pencil in two.* **5.** to make a quick, sudden bite or grab (often fol. by *at*): *The dog snapped at the mailman.* **6.** to act or move quickly or smartly: *to snap to attention.* **7.** to seize or take with or as if with a quick bite or grab (usually fol. by *up*): *She's always ready to snap up a bargain.* **8.** to speak to (a person) quickly and sharply (usually fol. by *at*): *I'm sorry I snapped at you.* **9.** to say (something) quickly and sharply (often fol. by *out*): *to snap out an order.* **10.** to close or open with snap fasteners. **11.** to take a photograph of (someone or something), esp. quickly: *I snapped that one as we got off the ferryboat.* **12.** (in football) to put (the ball) in play by handing or passing it backward through one's legs. The ball is generally snapped from the center to the quarterback or a kicker. —*n.* **13.** a quick, sudden action or movement, such as a flick of a whip or the breaking of a twig. **14.** a short, sharp sound; click or crack. **15.** a snap fastener. **16.** a quick sudden bite or grab: *The fish made a snap at the bait.* **17.** a short spell or period, as of cold weather: *an unexpected cold snap.* **18.** a photograph or snapshot. **19.** (in football) the act of snapping the ball. **20.** *Informal.* a job, task, etc., that is extremely easy: *That test was a snap.* —*adj.* **21.** made, done, taken, etc., suddenly or without much thought: *a snap decision.* **22.** easy; not difficult: *a snap course at college.* **23. snap out of it,** *Informal.*

to return to one's health, energy, good spirits, etc.; recover: *He was resentful at first, but later he snapped out of it.*

snap·drag·on (snap′drag′ən), *n.* a garden plant bearing brightly colored flowers whose shape suggests the mouth of a mythical beast.

snap′ fas′tener, a fastening device in two pieces having a projecting part in one piece that fits into a hole in the other, used esp. on garments.

snap·per (snap′ər), *n., pl.* **snap·pers** *or* for def. 1 **snap·per.** 1. any of several large, saltwater food fishes, esp. one with reddish scales caught in the Gulf of Mexico. 2. a snapping turtle. 3. a person or thing that snaps.

snap′ping tur′tle, any of several large, vicious turtles having powerful jaws with which it inflicts serious bites.

snap·pish (snap′ish), *adj.* 1. apt to snap or bite, as a dog. 2. tending to be irritable and impatient, esp. in speech.

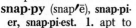

Snapping turtle
(shell length 1 ft.)

snap·py (snap′ē), **snap·pi·er, snap·pi·est.** 1. apt to snap or bite; snappish. 2. *Informal.* **a.** quick, brisk, or lively: *a snappy tune.* **b.** stylish: *a snappy suit.* 3. **make it snappy,** *Slang.* to speed up; hurry: *If you don't make it snappy, we'll leave without you.*

snap·shot (snap′shot′), *n.* an informal photograph, esp. one taken with a simple, inexpensive camera.

snare (snâr), *n.* 1. a noose for catching birds and small animals. 2. anything that entangles, traps, or deceives: *Her obvious charm is a snare in which many people have been caught.*

snare′ drum′, a small drum that produces a crisp, rattling sound by means of cords or fine wire coils stretched across the lower head.

snarl[1] (snärl), *v.* 1. to growl angrily, showing the teeth, as a dog. 2. to speak in a sharp or angry manner. —*n.* 3. an angry growl. 4. an angry or savage tone of voice. [imitative of the sound]

Snare drum

snarl[2] (snärl), *n.* 1. a tangle, as of thread or hair. 2. a complicated or confused condition: *a traffic snarl.* —*v.* 3. to tangle; make complicated or confused. [from a Middle English word, which comes from Scandinavian]

snatch (snach), *v.* 1. to seize or try to seize at something suddenly; grab (usually fol. by *at*): *He snatched at his hat when the wind blew it off his head.* 2. to seize by a sudden grasp: *The thief snatched the lady's purse and ran.* 3. to take or get quickly or when possible: *to snatch a few minutes of sleep.* —*n.* 4. the act or an instance of snatching; a sudden grab: *He made a snatch at the string of the kite.* 5. a small bit or fragment: *to overhear snatches of a con-*

versation. 6. a short period of time: *to study in snatches.*

sneak (snēk), *v.* 1. to go or move in a quiet, secretive, or sly way: *He sneaked out of the room while no one was looking.* 2. to move, put, etc., in a secretive or sly way: *He sneaked the dog into his room.* 3. *Informal.* to take in a secret or sly way; steal: *While our backs were turned, he sneaked another piece of pie.* —*n.* 4. one who sneaks; a cowardly, underhanded person.

sneak·er (snē′kər), *n.* 1. a person who sneaks. 2. a shoe, usually made of canvas, with a rubber or synthetic sole.

sneak·ing (snē′king), *adj.* 1. deceitfully underhanded; contemptible. 2. secret; not fully admitted or expressed, as a feeling, notion, etc.: *I have a sneaking suspicion that it's time to leave.*

sneak·y (snē′kē), *adj.,* **sneak·i·er, sneak·i·est.** deceitful, cowardly, or mean. —**sneak′i·ness,** *n.*

sneer (snēr), *v.* 1. to show scorn, contempt, etc., by look, speech, or writing. —*n.* 2. a look or expression of scorn or contempt. 3. a scornful remark.

sneeze (snēz), *v.,* **sneezed, sneez·ing.** 1. to force out air suddenly and audibly through the nose and mouth by an involuntary action. —*n.* 2. the act or sound of sneezing.

snick·er (snik′ər), *v.* 1. to laugh in a half-suppressed, often disrespectful manner. —*n.* 2. a snickering laugh. Also, **snig′ger.** —**snick′er·ing·ly,** *adj.*

sniff (snif), *v.* 1. to draw air through the nose in short, audible breaths. 2. to smell or try to smell by drawing in short breaths through the nose: *We sniffed the roses. The dog sniffed excitedly at the cupboard door.* 3. to draw in through the nose by sniffing, as air, an odor, powdered tobacco, etc. 4. to show disdain or contempt (usually fol. by *at*): *He sniffed at my offer of $5,000 for the house.* —*n.* 5. the act or sound of sniffing. 6. a scent or odor: *There was a sniff of perfume in the air.*

snif·fle (snif′əl), *v.,* **snif·fled, snif·fling.** 1. to sniff repeatedly, as from a cold or in trying not to cry. —*n.* 2. the act or sound of sniffing. 3. **sniffles,** a condition, as a cold, marked by sniffing (usually preceded by *the*): *This draft is giving me the sniffles.*

snip (snip), *v.,* **snipped, snip·ping.** 1. to cut with a small, quick stroke or strokes of scissors or the like: *to snip a string in two.* —*n.* 2. the act of snipping, as with scissors. 3. a small piece snipped off: *a snip of thread.* 4. *Informal.* a small or impertinent person. 5. **snips,** small, strong shears for cutting metal.

snipe (snīp), *n., pl.* **snipes** *or* **snipe.** 1. any of several game birds living in marshy areas and having a long pointed bill. —*v.,* **sniped, snip·ing.** 2. to shoot or hunt snipe. 3. to shoot at individuals from a concealed position: *The enemy was sniping from the roofs.* —**snip′er,** *n.*

Snipe
(length 11 in.)

sniv·el (sniv/əl), v., **sniv·eled** or **sniv·elled; sniv·el·ing** or **sniv·el·ling. 1.** to weep or cry with sniffling. **2.** to pretend to be tearful; whine. **3.** to run at the nose; sniffle: *She sniveled from the cold all winter.* —n. **4.** whining or pretended weeping. **5.** mucus running from the nose.

snob (snob), n. **1.** a person who looks up to, imitates, and seeks the company of those who have social rank, wealth, etc., and looks down on others whom he considers inferior. **2.** a person who believes himself superior to others in a certain way and is disdainful of those who have different opinions or tastes: *a music snob.*

snob·ber·y (snob/ə rē), n., pl. **snob·ber·ies. 1.** a snobbish act. **2.** the behavior or character of a snob.

snob·bish (snob/ish), adj. of, concerning, or like a snob: *She's too snobbish to eat a hot dog.* —**snob/ bish·ly**, adv. —**snob/bish·ness**, n.

snoop (snōōp), Informal. —v. **1.** to go about in a sneaking, prying way; prowl or pry. —n. **2.** Also, **snoop/er.** a person who snoops. —**snoop/y**, adj.

snooze (snōōz), v., **snoozed, snooz·ing. 1.** to sleep; doze; nap. —n. **2.** a short sleep; nap.

snore (snôr), v., **snored, snor·ing. 1.** to breathe during sleep with harsh or hoarse sounds. —n. **2.** the act or sound of snoring.

snor·kel (snôr/kəl), n. **1.** a device that permits a submarine to remain submerged for long periods, consisting of a series of tubes that extend above the surface for taking in fresh air and discharging engine exhaust and stale air. **2.** a tube through which a person can breathe while swimming face down on or near the surface of the water. —v. **3.** to swim while breathing through such a tube.

snort (snôrt), v. **1.** to force the breath violently through the nostrils with a loud, harsh sound: *The horse snorted at us.* **2.** to make a sound like a snort: *The engine of the old car snorted once and stopped.* **3.** to say (something) with a snort: *"You're late," he snorted.* —n. **4.** the act or sound of snorting.

snout (snout), n. **1.** the front, projecting part of an animal's head, which contains the nose and jaws; muzzle. **2.** something resembling this, as a nozzle, spout, etc.

snow (snō), n. **1.** white flakes or crystals of ice formed from the water vapor in the air. **2.** a fall or layer of these flakes. —v. **3.** to fall or let fall as snow: *It's snowing! It snowed six inches.* **4.** to cover, obstruct, etc., with snow (usually fol. by *under, over, in,* etc.): *Our street was completely snowed under.*

snow·ball (snō/bôl/), n. **1.** a ball of snow pressed together for throwing. **2.** a shrub having clusters of white flowers resembling snowballs. —v. **3.** to throw snowballs at. **4.** to become larger, greater, etc., very rapidly: *Business snowballed just before Christmas.*

snow·bird (snō/bûrd/), n. another name for **junco.**

snow·bound (snō/bound/), adj. shut in by snow: *The farm was snowbound for a month last winter.*

snow·drift (snō/drift/), n. **1.** a bank of snow driven together by the wind. **2.** snow driven before the wind.

snow·drop (snō/drop/), n. a low herb that blooms in the spring and has drooping, white flowers.

snow·fall (snō/fôl/), n. **1.** a fall of snow. **2.** the amount of snow at a certain place or time: *The snowfall was 12 inches yesterday.*

snow·flake (snō/flāk/), n. one of the small feathery clusters of ice crystals that are the form in which snow falls.

snow·man (snō/man/), n., pl. **snow·men.** a figure, resembling a man, made out of packed snow.

snow·plow (snō/plou/), n. a machine for clearing away snow from highways, railroad tracks, etc.

snow·shoe (snō/shōō/), n. a frame resembling a racket across which a network of leather strips is stretched, worn on the feet to keep the wearer from sinking in deep snow.

Snowshoes

snow·storm (snō/stôrm/), n. a storm in which there is a heavy fall of snow.

snow·y (snō/ē), adj., **snow·i·er, snow·i·est. 1.** full of or covered with snow: *snowy fields.* **2.** having much snow: *a snowy day.* **3.** like snow, esp. in whiteness: *a snowy cloth; snowy skin.*

snub (snub), v., **snubbed, snub·bing. 1.** to treat (someone) with disdain or contempt, esp. by ignoring. **2.** to stop suddenly (a rope or cable that is running out). **3.** to check or stop (a boat, a horse, etc.) by means of a rope tied to a post. —n. **4.** the act or an instance of snubbing. **5.** a slight or rebuff. **6.** a sudden check or stop. —adj. **7.** (of the nose) short and turned up at the tip.

snuff¹ (snuf), v. **1.** to draw in (air, odor, etc.) through the nose. **2.** to draw air into the nose, as in order to smell something; examine by sniffing, as an animal does: *After snuffing around, he located the gas leak.* —n. **3.** an act of snuffing; a sniff. **4.** powdered tobacco, usually taken by inhaling into the nostrils. **5. up to snuff,** Informal. up to a certain level or standard, as of health, performance, etc.; satisfactory: *I'm not feeling up to snuff these days.* [from the early Dutch word *snuffen* "to sniff"]

snuff² (snuf), v. **1.** to cut off or remove the burned part of a candlewick. **2.** to extinguish (a candle). **3. snuff out, a.** to extinguish: *to snuff out a candle.* **b.** to suppress; crush: *The government snuffed out all opposition.* [from the Middle English word *snoffe*]

snuff·box (snuf/boks/), n. a small box for snuff.

snuff·er (snuf/ər), n. an instrument for trimming candlewicks or for extinguishing candles.

snuf·fle (snuf/əl), v., **snuf·fled, snuf·fling. 1.** to draw the breath through the nostrils in a noisy way, as when one has a cold. —n. **2.** the act or sound of snuffling. **3. snuffles,** a condition, as from a cold, that causes snuffling.

Snuffer

snug (snug), adj., **snug·ger, snug·gest. 1.** warmly comfortable, sheltered, or cozy: *a snug little house; a snug harbor.* **2.** trim, neat, or compactly arranged: *a* *snug ship.* **3.** fitting tightly: *a snug jacket.* —*adv.* **4.** in a snug manner; snugly: *The shirt fit snug around the neck.* —**snug′ly,** *adv.*

snug·gle (snug′əl), *v.,* **snug·gled, snug·gling.** to lie closely or press closely against a person or thing, as for warmth or comfort or from affection: *The kittens snuggled together. She snuggled the child in her arms.*

so¹ (sō), *adv.* **1.** in the way shown, stated, or understood: *Hold your tennis racket so.* **2.** in the same condition as stated: *The clock is broken and has been so for a week.* **3.** to the degree stated or understood: *Don't walk so fast.* **4.** as (used with a negative in comparisons): *She is not so tall as he.* **5.** very or extremely: *You have been so kind.* **6.** very greatly: *My head aches so!* **7.** for this or that reason; therefore: *She is sick and so cannot come to the party.* **8.** most certainly; indeed: *I was so here on time!* **9.** likewise; also: *If he is going, then so am I.* —*conj.* **10.** in order that; with the purpose that (often fol. by *that*): *Check your paper carefully, so there will be no mistakes.* **11.** with the result that (often fol. by *that*): *He checked his paper carefully, so there were no mistakes in it.* —*pron.* **12.** such or the same as stated: *He tried to be good and remain so.* **13.** approximately that, as in number, amount, length, etc.; more or less: *I'll be away a week or so.* —*interj.* **14.** (used as an exclamation of surprise, shock, discovery, etc.): *So! You've been eating between meals again!* —*adj.* **15.** true as stated or reported: *What you've said just isn't so.* **16. so as,** for the purpose; with the intention: *We sat close to the stage so as to hear better.* [from the Old English word *swā*]

so² (sō), *n.* another word for **sol.**

soak (sōk), *v.* **1.** to lie in and become completely wet with water or some other liquid: *The clothes are soaking in the sink.* **2.** to put or keep in a liquid so as to wet thoroughly; steep. **3.** to take up or in; absorb (often fol. by *up*): *Blotting paper soaks up ink.* **4.** to wet thoroughly: *The sudden shower soaked his clothing.* **5.** to pass, as a liquid, through pores, holes, or the like (usually fol. by *in, through,* etc.): *The rain soaked through the canvas.* **6.** to penetrate the mind or feelings (usually fol. by *through, in,* etc.): *The lesson didn't soak in.* —*n.* **7.** the act of soaking, or the state of being soaked.

so-and-so (sō′ən sō′), *n., pl.* **so-and-sos.** someone or something not definitely named: *Mr. So-and-so.*

soap (sōp), *n.* **1.** a substance used for washing and cleaning, usually made by treating fat with an alkali. —*v.* **2.** to rub or lather with soap. **3. no soap,** *Slang.* absolutely not; nothing doing: *He wanted to borrow a dollar, but I told him no soap.*

soap·box (sōp′boks′), *n.* any platform, such as a wooden box, used by a speaker in the street.

soap·stone (sōp′stōn′), *n.* a very soft grayish or greenish stone whose surface feels soapy or greasy.

soap·suds (sōp′sudz′), *n. (used as pl.)* suds made with soap and water.

soap·y (sō′pē), *adj.,* **soap·i·er, soap·i·est. 1.** of or like soap: *soapy water; a clean, soapy smell.* **2.** covered with soap: *soapy dishes.* **3.** containing or full of soap. —**soap′i·ness,** *n.*

soar (sôr), *v.* **1.** to fly upward or fly at a great height, as a bird or airplane does. **2.** to rise to a higher level: *Prices soared before the holidays.* **3.** to aspire to a higher level: *His hopes soared.*

sob (sob), *v.,* **sobbed, sob·bing. 1.** to weep with short catches of the breath. **2.** to make a sound like this: *The wind sobbed in the trees.* **3.** to utter with sobs: *"He's gone," she sobbed.* **4.** to put, send, etc., by sobbing: *to sob oneself to sleep.* —*n.* **5.** the act of sobbing. **6.** the sound of sobbing, or any similar sound.

so·ber (sō′bər), *adj.* **1.** quiet or solemn in manner or appearance: *a sober young man.* **2.** grave and serious: *a sober occasion.* **3.** subdued in tone or color; not gay or showy: *sober clothing.* **4.** free from excess or exaggeration: *a sober judgment.* **5.** not drunk. **6.** temperate or moderate, esp. in the use of liquor. —*v.* **7.** to make or become sober. —**so·bri·e·ty** (sō-brī′i tē), *n.*

so-called (sō′kôld′), *adj.* called thus but often falsely or incorrectly: *His so-called friends did not visit him in the hospital.*

soc·cer (sok′ər), *n.* a form of football, played between two teams, in which the ball is moved toward the goal by kicking or by bouncing it off any part of the body except the hands and arms.

so·cia·ble (sō′shə bəl), *adj.* **1.** liking company; friendly or agreeable in company: *She's much more sociable than her husband.* **2.** filled with pleasant conversation and companionship: *a sociable evening at a friend's house.* —*n.* **3.** an informal social gathering. —**so′cia·bil′i·ty,** *n.* —**so′cia·bly,** *adv.*

so·cial (sō′shəl), *adj.* **1.** concerning or devoted to friendly relations or companionship: *a social club.* **2.** friendly or sociable, as persons. **3.** of, concerning, or connected with fashionable society: *a social event.* **4.** living or tending to live with others in a community rather than alone: *Man is a social being.* **5.** living together in colonies, hives, etc.: *Bees are social insects.* **6.** of or concerning human beings living together as a community: *social problems.* —*n.* **7.** a social gathering; party: *a church social.* [from the Latin word *sociālis,* which comes from *socius* "comrade"]

so·cial·ism (sō′shə liz′əm), *n.* **1.** the theory that the community as a whole rather than individuals or private interests should own or control the means of producing goods, land, capital, etc. **2.** a political movement that seeks to put this theory into practice.

so·cial·ist (sō′shə list), *n.* **1.** a person who favors socialism. —*adj.* **2.** another form of **socialistic.**

so·cial·is·tic (sō′shə lis′tik), *adj.* **1.** of or concerning socialists or socialism. **2.** favoring or supporting socialism: *The Senator attacked socialistic teachings.*

so·cial·ize (sō′shə līz′), *v.,* **so·cial·ized, so·cial·iz·ing. 1.** to establish or run (something) according to the principles of socialism. **2.** to make fit for life with others; make social. **3.** to associate or mingle sociably with others: *to socialize with one's friends.*

so·cial·ly (sō′shə lē), *adv.* **1.** in a social manner. **2.** in regard to a social group, social relations, or society: *They are quite old and are not active socially.*

so′cial sci′ence, the study of human society and of the behavior of man in relation to his family, government, and other social institutions. History, politics or civics, economics, anthropology, and sociology are social sciences.

so′cial secu′rity, *(often caps.)* a plan by which the federal government makes payments to elderly persons, the unemployed, and others from funds collected from employers and employees.

so′cial stud′ies, (in elementary and secondary schools) a course of studies made up of history, geography, civics, and the like.

so′cial work′, work aimed at improving social conditions in a community, as by improving housing, job opportunities, care for children and the aged, etc.

so·ci·e·ty (sə sī′i tē), *n., pl.* **so·ci·e·ties. 1.** a group of persons joined together for a particular purpose or common interest: *a scientific society.* **2.** the total number of human beings, viewed as members of a community: *to work for the good of society.* **3.** the total number of human beings living together at a particular place and time: *ancient Egyptian society.* **4.** a community regarded in terms of its dominant economic form or class: *an industrial society.* **5.** the fashionable or wealthy class of a community: *a leader of New York society.* **6.** company; companionship.

Soci′ety of Friends′, a Protestant denomination founded in England in the 17th century, opposed to oath-taking and war. The members are commonly called Quakers or Friends.

Soci′ety of Je′sus. See under **Jesuit.**

so·ci·ol·o·gy (sō′sē ol′ə jē, sō′shē ol′ə jē), *n.* the study of the origin, development, organization, and functioning of human society. Sociology deals especially with family relationships, the causes of crime, marriage customs, religion, and the like. —**so·ci·o·log·i·cal** (sō′sē ə loj′i kəl), *adj.* —**so·ci·ol′o·gist,** *n.*

sock¹ (sok), *n., pl.* **socks** *or* **sox** (soks). a short stocking. [from the Old English word *socc,* which comes from Latin *soccus*]

sock² (sok), *Slang.* —*v.* **1.** to strike or hit hard, esp. with the fist. —*n.* **2.** a hard blow.

sock·et (sok′it), *n.* a hollow into which something fits or is fitted: *electric socket; eye socket.*

Soc·ra·tes (sok′rə tēz′), *n.* 469?–399 B.C., Greek philosopher: teacher of Plato.

sod (sod), *n.* **1.** the surface of the ground, esp. when covered with grass; turf. **2.** a section of this surface, usually cut in a square, containing the matted roots of grass. —*v.,* **sod·ded, sod·ding. 3.** to cover with sods.

so·da (sō′də), *n.* **1.** any of several compounds containing sodium, such as washing soda or baking soda. **2.** soda water. **3.** a drink made of soda water flavored with fruit juice or syrup or mixed with ice cream. [from a medieval Latin word, which comes

from Arabic *suwwād,* the name of a plant that yields an ash from which sodium is extracted]

so′da foun′tain, a counter, as in a restaurant or drugstore, where sodas, ice cream, etc., are served.

so′da wa′ter, a bubbly beverage consisting of water charged with carbon dioxide and often flavored.

sod·den (sod′ən), *adj.* **1.** soaked with liquid or moisture: *The clothes hanging on the line were sodden after the rain.* **2.** heavy, lumpy, or soggy, as poorly baked food. **3.** lacking spirit; dull; listless: *He was feeling sodden after staying up all night.*

so·di·um (sō′dē əm), *n.* a soft, silvery metal that oxidizes rapidly in air: a chemical element found in nature only in combination with other elements. *Symbol:* Na

so′dium bicar′bonate, the scientific name for **bicarbonate of soda.**

so′dium chlo′ride, the scientific name for ordinary salt.

Sod·om (sod′əm), *n.* (in the Bible) a city that was destroyed, with Gomorrah, for its wickedness.

-soever, a suffix meaning in any way, or at all, added to certain words: *howsoever; whosoever.*

so·fa (sō′fə), *n.* a long, upholstered couch, usually having a back and two arms. [from the Arabic word *suffah* "platform used as a seat"]

So·fi·a (sō′fē ə, sō fē′ə), *n.* the capital city of Bulgaria, in the W part.

soft (sôft), *adj.* **1.** yielding readily to touch or pressure; easily divided or changed in shape; not hard or stiff: *a soft pillow.* **2.** relatively lacking in hardness: *Gold is a soft metal compared to iron.* **3.** smooth and agreeable to the touch; not rough or coarse: *a soft fabric; soft skin.* **4.** pleasantly low or subdued in sound: *soft music; a soft voice.* **5.** gentle or mild; not harsh: *a soft breeze; a soft light.* **6.** kind or sympathetic; tender: *a soft heart.* **7.** delicate or weak; not strong. **8.** describing the pronunciation of the consonant *c* as in *cent* and of *g* as in *gem.* See also **hard** (def. 10). **9.** *Informal.* requiring little effort; easy: *a soft job.* —*adv.* **10.** in a soft manner; softly. —**soft′ly,** *adv.* —**soft′ness,** *n.*

soft·ball (sôft′bôl′), *n.* **1.** a form of baseball played on a smaller diamond with a larger, softer ball. **2.** the ball itself.

soft′ coal′, another name for **bituminous coal.**

sof·ten (sô′fən), *v.* to make or become soft or softer: *The candles softened in the hot room. The blinds softened the bright sunlight.*

soft-heart·ed (sôft′här′tid), *adj.* kind or tender; sympathetic: *a soft-hearted judge.* —**soft′-heart′ed·ly,** *adv.* —**soft′-heart′ed·ness,** *n.*

soft′ pal′ate, the back part of the roof of the mouth, which lacks the bone present in the front part. See also **hard palate.** See illus. at **mouth.**

soft·wood (sôft′wŏŏd′), *n.* the light, porous wood of various trees, esp. pine, fir, etc., used in carpentry. See also **hardwood.**

sog·gy (sog′ē), *adj.,* **sog·gi·er, sog·gi·est. 1.** thoroughly wet; soaked. **2.** pasty, as poorly baked bread. —**sog′gi·ly,** *adv.* —**sog′gi·ness,** *n.*

soil¹ (soil), *n.* **1.** the material covering much of the earth's surface, made up of disintegrated rock and humus, esp. those kinds in which plants grow; ground; earth. **2.** a country, land, or region: *our native soil.* **3.** any place or condition regarded as suitable for the growth of something: *Poverty is the soil for crime.* [from the early French word *soyl,* which comes from Latin *solium* "seat, base, bottom"]

soil² (soil), *v.* **1.** to make or become dirty: *She soiled her clothes while gardening. White soils easily.* **2.** to spot or stain: *He soiled his hands with ink.* **3.** to disgrace: *to soil one's good name.* —*n.* **4.** a spot or stain. [from the Old French word *souiller* "to dirty"]

so·journ (sō′jûrn), *v.* **1.** to stay for a time in a place: *to sojourn at the beach for a month.* —*n.* **2.** a short stay or visit: *It happened during his sojourn in Paris.*

sol (sōl), *n.* the fifth note of a musical scale.

Sol (sol), *n.* the sun.

sol·ace (sol′is), *n.* **1.** comfort in sorrow or trouble; consolation: *The old man found solace in the visit of his grandchildren.* —*v.,* **sol·aced, sol·ac·ing. 2.** to comfort, console, or cheer. —**sol′ac·er,** *n.*

so·lar (sō′lər), *adj.* of, based on, or operated by the sun or sunlight: *solar heat; solar time; a solar battery.*

so′lar eclipse′. See under **eclipse** (def. 1).

so′lar plex′us, 1. a network of nerves behind the stomach. **2.** a point just below the breastbone, where a blow will affect this nerve center.

so′lar sys′tem, the sun and all the planets, moons, etc., that revolve in orbits around it.

sold (sōld), *v.* the past tense and past participle of **sell.**

sol·der (sod′ər), *n.* **1.** any of various alloys, esp. of tin and lead, that are melted and applied to two pieces of metal to join them together. —*v.* **2.** to join or repair with solder: *The plumber soldered the pipes.*

sol·dier (sōl′jər), *n.* **1.** a person who serves in an army. **2.** an enlisted man as distinguished from a commissioned officer. **3.** a man of military skill or experience: *Napoleon was a great soldier.* **4.** a person who serves in any cause: *a soldier of the Lord.* **5.** *Informal.* a person who avoids work or only pretends to work; loafer. —*v.* **6.** to act or serve as a soldier.

sol·dier·ly (sōl′jər lē), *adj.* of or like a soldier; brave.

sole¹ (sōl), *adj.* **1.** being the only one or ones; only: *He is the sole living relative of the family.* **2.** belonging to one individual or group; exclusive: *He has the sole right to the property.* [from the Old French word *sol,* which comes from Latin *sōlus*]

sole² (sōl), *n.* **1.** the bottom or underside of the foot. **2.** the underside of a shoe, boot, or the like. —*v.,* **soled, sol·ing. 3.** to furnish (a shoe or the like) with a sole. [from an Old English word, which comes from a Latin word meaning "sandal"]

sole³ (sōl), *n.* **1.** a European flatfish used for food. **2.** any of various other flatfishes, esp. flounder. **3.** the flesh of any of these fishes. [from an early French word, which comes from a Latin word meaning "sandal." The fish is so named for its flat shape]

sole·ly (sōl′lē), *adv.* **1.** as the only one or ones: *They are solely responsible for the mistake.* **2.** only or exclusively: *plants found solely in the tropics.*

sol·emn (sol′əm), *adj.* **1.** grave, sober, or serious: *a solemn judge; solemn remarks.* **2.** made or done with great seriousness: *a solemn oath.* **3.** having or done with dignity, formality, or the like: *a solemn occasion; a solemn procession.* **4.** having a religious or sacred character: *a solemn holy day.* **5.** somber or gloomy: *dark, solemn colors.* —**sol′emn·ly,** *adv.*

so·lem·ni·ty (sə lem′ni tē), *n., pl.* for def. 2 **so·lem·ni·ties. 1.** the state or quality of being solemn: *the solemnity of a state funeral.* **2.** Often, **solemnities.** a solemn observance or ceremony: *the solemnities of the Easter season.*

sol·em·nize (sol′əm nīz′), *v.,* **sol·em·nized, sol·em·niz·ing. 1.** to observe with ceremonies: *to solemnize an occasion with speeches and prayers.* **2.** to hold or perform (rites, ceremonies, etc.): *to solemnize a marriage.* **3.** to make solemn or serious; dignify.

so·lic·it (sə lis′it), *v.* to ask or ask for earnestly; entreat or petition for something; urge: *to solicit funds for a charity; to solicit support for a housing bill.* —**so·lic′i·ta′tion,** *n.*

so·lic·i·tor (sə lis′i tər), *n.* **1.** a person who solicits. **2.** a person employed to solicit trade, business, etc. **3.** an officer having charge of the legal business of a city, town, etc. **4.** *British.* a lawyer who advises clients and represents them in lower courts, and who prepares cases for barristers to try in higher courts.

so·lic·i·tous (sə lis′i təs), *adj.* **1.** anxious or concerned (usually fol. by *about, for,* etc.): *to be solicitous about a person's health.* **2.** eager; desirous: *He was always solicitous to please.* —**so·lic′i·tous·ly,** *adv.*

so·lic·i·tude (sə lis′i tōōd′, -tyōōd′), *n.* anxiety or concern; anxious desire or care: *to show solicitude about someone's health.*

sol·id (sol′id), *adj.* **1.** having length, width, and thickness: *A sphere is a solid figure.* **2.** of or concerning bodies or figures having three dimensions: *solid geometry.* **3.** having the inside completely filled; not hollow: *a solid piece of chocolate.* **4.** having definite shape and size; neither liquid nor gaseous. **5.** without openings, breaks, or interruptions; continuous: *a solid wall; a solid hour of studying.* **6.** firm, hard, or compact: *solid ground.* **7.** not flimsy or slight; substantial: *a house of solid construction; good, solid food.* **8.** consisting entirely of one substance, material, color, etc.: *solid gold; a solid blue dress.* **9.** real or genuine: *solid comfort.* **10.** fully reliable or sensible: *a solid citizen.* **11.** firmly united; unanimous in opinion, policy, etc.: *The President won the solid support of Congress.* —*n.* **12.** a body or object having three dimensions. **13.** a solid substance.

sol·i·dar·i·ty (sol′i dar′i tē), *n., pl.* **sol·i·dar·i·ties.** union or fellowship arising from common interests, duties, etc.

so·lid·i·fy (sə lid′ə fī′), *v.,* **so·lid·i·fied, so·lid·i·fy·ing.** to make or become solid.

so·lid·i·ty (sə lid′i tē), *n.* the state or quality of being solid; firmness and strength.

so·lil·o·quy (sə lil′ə kwē), *n., pl.* **so·lil·o·quies.** 1. the act of talking while or as if alone. 2. a speech that an actor makes to himself while alone on the stage: *Hamlet's soliloquy, "To be or not to be."*

sol·i·taire (sol′i târ′), *n.* 1. Also, **patience.** a game of cards played by one person. 2. a precious stone, esp. a diamond, set by itself, usually in a ring.

sol·i·tar·y (sol′i ter′ē), *adj.* 1. alone; without companions: *a solitary passer-by; a solitary journey.* 2. by itself: *one solitary house.* 3. made or done alone or without assistance: *solitary chores.* 4. secluded or lonely: *a solitary cabin in the woods.* 5. being the only one; single: *Not one solitary person spoke up.*

sol·i·tude (sol′i tōōd′, -tyōōd′), *n.* 1. the state of being or living alone; seclusion: *A hermit loves solitude.* 2. a lonely place or one not often visited.

so·lo (sō′lō), *n., pl.* **so·los.** 1. a musical composition for one singer or player with or without accompaniment. 2. a performance by one person. —*adj.* 3. performing or performed alone: *a part for solo trumpet.* 4. done by one person: *a solo flight in an airplane.* —*adv.* 5. by oneself; alone: *After six lessons, he was flying solo.* —*v.* 6. to perform or do a solo.

so·lo·ist (sō′lō ist), *n.* a person who sings or plays a solo or solos.

Sol·o·mon (sol′ə mən), *n.* (in the Bible) a wise king of Israel, the son of David, who lived in the 10th century B.C.

sol·stice (sol′stis, sōl′stis), *n.* either of two times of year when day and night have the most unequal lengths. The summer solstice occurs about June 21st, when the sun is farthest north of the equator, directly over the tropic of Cancer; the winter solstice occurs about December 21st, when the sun is farthest south of the equator, directly over the tropic of Capricorn. See also **equinox.**

sol·u·ble (sol′yə bəl), *adj.* 1. capable of being dissolved. 2. capable of being solved; solvable: *a soluble problem.* —**sol′u·bil′i·ty,** *n.*

so·lu·tion (sə lōō′shən), *n.* 1. the act of solving a problem, question, etc.: *The solution of the problem took us 30 minutes.* 2. a particular instance of solving; explanation or answer: *What is the solution of this problem?* 3. the act or process by which a gas, liquid, or solid breaks into individual molecules and spreads uniformly throughout another gas, liquid, or solid. 4. the uniform mixture formed in this way: *Syrup is a solution of sugar in water.* 5. the state of being dissolved: *to hold sugar in solution.*

solve (solv), *v.,* **solved, solv·ing.** to find the answer, explanation, or solution to (a problem, difficulty, etc.). —**solv′a·ble,** *adj.*

sol·ven·cy (sol′vən sē), *n.* ability to pay one's debts.

sol·vent (sol′vənt), *adj.* 1. able to pay all one's debts. 2. having the power of dissolving. —*n.* 3. a substance that dissolves another to form a solution.

So·ma·li·a (sō mä′lē ə), *n.* an independent republic on the E coast of Africa, formed from the former British Somaliland and former Italian Somaliland. 246,198 sq. mi. *Cap.:* Mogadiscio. Also, **Soma′li Democrat′ic Repub′lic.** —**So·ma′li·an,** *n., adj.*

So·ma·li·land (sō mä′lē land′), *n.* a coastal region in E Africa, including the Afars and Issas Territory, Somalia, and part of Ethiopia.

Sombrero

som·ber (som′bər), *adj.* 1. gloomily dark; dark, as in color; dimly lighted: *a somber hallway; a somber dress.* 2. gloomy; depressing: *a somber mood.*

som·bre·ro (som brâr′ō), *n., pl.* **som·bre·ros.** a hat with a broad brim, used in Spain, Mexico, and the southwestern U.S. [from a Spanish word, which comes from *sombra* "shade"]

some (sum), *adj.* 1. being an unknown or unspecified one: *Some man called you on the telephone today.* 2. (used with plural nouns) certain: *Some days I stay at home.* 3. of an indefinite or unspecified number: *Some students do not like to study.* 4. of an unspecified amount or quantity: *Have some cake.* 5. unspecified but considerable in number, amount, etc.: *We talked for some time.* 6. *Informal.* notable for its kind: *That was some storm!* —*adv.* 7. about; approximately: *Some 300 were present.* —*pron.* 8. an indefinite number, amount, etc.; a certain number: *Some of the guests came late.*

-some, a suffix used to form 1. adjectives meaning **a.** having the quality of: *burdensome.* **b.** having a tendency to: *quarrelsome.* 2. nouns meaning a group of a certain number: *threesome; foursome.*

some·bod·y (sum′bod′ē, -bə dē), *pron.* 1. an unknown or unspecified person: *Somebody left this package for you.* —*n., pl.* **some·bod·ies.** 2. a person of importance: *He always wanted to be somebody.*

some·day (sum′dā′), *adv.* at an indefinite future time.

some·how (sum′hou′), *adv.* 1. in some way not specified or known. 2. **somehow or other,** by any possible means: *We got out somehow or other.*

some·one (sum′wun′, -wən), *n.* some person; somebody.

som·er·sault (sum′ər sôlt′), *n.* 1. an acrobatic movement, in which a person rolls or jumps completely over, heels over head. —*v.* 2. to perform a somersault.

some·thing (sum′thing′), *pron.* 1. some thing; a certain thing that is not known or specified: *Something is wrong here. Did you say something?* 2. a certain part or amount that is not specified: *Our train arrives at two something. She is something of a snob.* —*n.* 3. *Informal.* a thing or person of some value or importance: *His new car is really something!* —*adv.* 4. in some degree; to some extent (often fol. by *like*): *The bird looked something like a hawk.*

some·time (sum′tīm′), *adv.* 1. at some indefinite or unspecified time: *He arrived sometime last week.* 2. at an indefinite future time: *Come to see me sometime.* —*adj.* 3. having been formerly; former: *a sometime resident of Chicago.*

some·times (sum′tīmz′), *adv.* at times; on some occasions; now and then: *We sometimes sleep late.*

some·what (sum′hwot′, -wot′), *adv.* 1. in some measure or degree; to some extent; rather; slightly: *He isn't angry, just somewhat disturbed.* —*pron.* 2. some part, amount, portion, etc.: *The cake lost somewhat of its flavor.*

some·where (sum′hwâr′, -wâr′), *adv.* 1. in, to, or at a place not specified or known: *They live somewhere in Michigan.* 2. at some point of time not named (usually fol. by *about, in, between,* etc.): *It happened somewhere in the 1930's.*

som·no·lent (som′nə lənt), *adj.* 1. sleepy; drowsy. 2. tending to cause sleep.

son (sun), *n.* 1. a male child or person in relation to his parents. 2. any male descendant: *a son of the American Indians.* 3. a male person regarded as the product of particular influences, forces, etc., or as being closely associated with a country, cause, etc.: *a son of the soil; a patriotic son of America.* 4. the Son, the second person of the Trinity; Jesus Christ.

so·nar (sō′när), *n.* 1. a method of detecting and locating objects underwater by means of the sound waves they reflect or by picking up the sounds they produce. 2. the apparatus used in this search. [from the phrase *so(und) na(vigation) r(anging)*]

so·na·ta (sə nä′tə), *n.* a musical composition usually for one or two instruments and typically in three or four movements of contrasting tempos.

song (sông), *n.* 1. a musical composition for one or more singers. 2. something that is sung. 3. the act or art of singing. 4. the musical sounds produced by certain birds or insects. 5. poetic composition; poetry. 6. **for a song,** at a very low price; for almost nothing: *He sold the car for a song.*

song·bird (sông′bûrd′), *n.* a bird that sings: *Larks and nightingales are songbirds.*

Song′ of Sol′omon, a book of the Old Testament. Also, **Song′ of Songs′.**

song·ster (sông′stər), *n.* 1. a person who sings; a singer. 2. a writer of songs or poems. 3. a songbird.

son·ic (son′ik), *adj.* 1. of or concerning sound. 2. noting speeds equal to the speed of sound.

son-in-law (sun′in lô′), *n., pl.* **sons-in-law** (sunz′in-lô′). the husband of one's daughter.

son·net (son′it), *n.* a poem that expresses a single, complete thought or idea and has fourteen lines that are rhymed according to certain definite schemes.

son·ny (sun′ē), *n.* a young boy (often used as a familiar term of address).

so·no·rous (sə nôr′əs, son′ər əs), *adj.* 1. giving out a sound, esp. a deep, resonant sound: *a sonorous gong.* 2. loud, deep, or full in sound: *a sonorous bass voice.* 3. eloquent or impressive in sound, style, etc.

soon (sōon), *adv.* 1. within a short time after this or that time, event, etc.: *We shall know soon after he calls.* 2. before long; in the near future: *Let's leave soon.* 3. before the usual or expected time; early: *We didn't think the letter would arrive so soon.* 4. promptly or quickly: *They came as soon as they could.* 5. readily or willingly: *I would as soon walk as ride.* 6. **sooner or later,** at some future time; eventually: *Sooner or later I'll get even with him.*

soot (sŏŏt), *n.* a black, powdery substance, consisting mostly of carbon, made by the burning of wood, coal, etc.

sooth (sōōth), *n. Archaic.* truth or fact: *In sooth, he is King Arthur.*

soothe (sōōth), *v.,* **soothed, sooth·ing.** 1. to calm, relieve, or comfort: *to soothe someone's anger.* 2. to lessen or soften, as pain, sorrow, doubt, etc.: *to soothe sunburned skin with a lotion.* 3. to have a calming influence; bring quiet, ease, comfort, etc.: *The soft music was soothing after a busy day.*

sooth·say·er (sōōth′sā′ər), *n.* a person who claims to predict future events.

soot·y (sŏŏt′ē), *adj.,* **soot·i·er, soot·i·est.** 1. covered or blackened with soot. 2. consisting of or resembling soot. 3. of a black or dusky color.

sop (sop), *n.* 1. a piece of bread or other food, for dipping in soup, milk, etc. 2. something given to quiet or calm, or as a bribe: *The political boss gave him some cash as a sop.* —*v.,* **sopped, sop·ping** 3. to dip or soak in liquid: *to sop bread in gravy.* 4. to drench or wet thoroughly. 5. to take up (liquid) by absorption (usually fol. by *up*): *He used a sponge to sop up the water.* 6. to be or become thoroughly wet.

so·phis·ti·cat·ed (sə fis′tə kā′tid), *adj.* 1. having or showing worldly experience, education, culture, etc.: *a sophisticated writer.* 2. pleasing or satisfactory to the tastes of persons who are worldly, educated, etc.: *sophisticated music.* 3. artificial; not natural or simple. 4. complex or difficult to operate or understand, such as a piece of machinery.

so·phis·ti·ca·tion (sə fis′tə kā′shən), *n.* 1. sophisticated manners, ideas, tastes, etc., as the result of worldly experience, education, etc. 2. change from natural character or simplicity.

soph·o·more (sof′ə môr′), *n.* a student in his second year at a high school or college.

sop·ping (sop′ing), *adj.* soaked; drenched: *Her clothes were sopping from the rain.*

sop·py (sop′ē), *adj.,* **sop·pi·er, sop·pi·est.** 1. soaked; very wet: *soppy ground.* 2. rainy, as weather: *a soppy day.* —**sop′pi·ness,** *n.*

so·pran·o (sə pran′ō, sə prä′nō), *n., pl.* **so·pran·os.** 1. the highest female voice. 2. a singer with such a voice. 3. the highest musical part in a composition. —*adj.* 4. of a smaller size and higher pitch than alto: *a soprano saxophone.*

sor·cer·er (sôr′sər ər), *n.* a person who is supposed to have supernatural powers through the aid of evil spirits; black magician; wizard.

sor·cer·ess (sôr′sər is), *n.* a female sorcerer; witch.

sor·cer·y (sôr′sə rē), *n.* the use of magic supposedly through the aid of evil spirits; witchcraft.

sor·did (sôr′did), *adj.* 1. dirty or filthy. 2. morally low; vile or depraved.

sore (sôr), *adj.,* **sor·er, sor·est.** 1. physically painful or sensitive, as a wound, diseased part, etc.: *a sore arm.*

2. feeling physical pain: *He is sore from all that exercise.* **3.** causing mental pain. distress, or sorrow: *a sore loss of one's friend.* **4.** feeling mental pain; grieved or sorrowful: *to be sore at heart.* **5.** severe or extreme: *He is in sore need of advice.* **6.** *Informal.* annoyed; angered; offended: *He was sore because he had to wait.* —*n.* **7.** a sore spot or place on the body. —**sore′ly,** *adv.* —**sore′ness,** *n.*

sor·ghum (sôr′gəm), *n.* **1.** a kind of grain having broad leaves and a tall stem grown for use as fodder and for the sweet juice that can be extracted from the stem. **2.** a syrup made from this juice.

so·ror·i·ty (sə rôr′i tē, sə ror′i tē), *n., pl.* **so·ror·i·ties.** a society or club of women or girls, esp. in a college.

sor·rel¹ (sôr′əl, sor′əl), *n.* **1.** a light reddish brown. **2.** a horse of this color. —*adj.* **3.** of the color sorrel. [from the Old French word *sorel,* which comes from a Germanic word meaning "brown"]

sor·rel² (sôr′əl, sor′əl), *n.* a plant having sour leaves that are used in salads, sauces, etc. [from the Old French word *surele,* which comes from a Germanic word meaning "sour"]

sor·row (sor′ō), *n.* **1.** grief, sadness, or regret caused by loss, disappointment, etc. **2.** a cause or occasion of grief or regret; misfortune or trouble: *He had many sorrows in his life.* — *v.* **3.** to feel sorrow.

sor·row·ful (sor′ə fəl), *adj.* **1.** full of or feeling sorrow; sad: *a sorrowful farewell; a sorrowful person.* **2.** showing, expressing, or causing sorrow: *a sorrowful song; a sorrowful event.* —**sor′row·ful·ly,** *adv.*

sor·ry (sor′ē), *adj.,* **sor·ri·er, sor·ri·est. 1.** sorrowful, grieved, or sad: *Was she sorry for her mistake?* **2.** feeling regret, sympathy, pity, etc.: *to be sorry to leave one's friends.* **3.** causing sorrow, pity, contempt, etc.: *a sorry sight.* — *interj.* **4.** (used in apology or regret): *Did I bump you? Sorry.*

sort (sôrt), *n.* **1.** a type, kind, class, or group of persons or things: *What sort of business is he in?* **2.** character, quality, or nature: *girls of a good sort.* **3.** individual or person: *Mr. Smith, the coach, is not a bad sort.* **4.** an example of something that is barely adequate: *He is a sort of writer.* —*v.* **5.** to arrange according to kind or class; classify: *to sort eggs by size.* **6.** to separate or take from other sorts: *to sort the good from the bad.* **7. of sorts,** ordinary; mediocre: *a tennis player of sorts.* **8. out of sorts,** in a bad temper; irritable: *Everyone is out of sorts because of the gloomy weather.* **9. sort of,** *Informal.* in some ways; rather; quite: *She's sort of like a girl I used to know.* —**Usage.** See **kind.**

sor·tie (sôr′tē), *n.* **1.** a rapid movement of troops from a besieged place to attack the besiegers. **2.** a combat mission made by a single airplane.

SOS, **1.** a radio signal used, esp. by ships in distress, as a call for help. **2.** any call for help.

so-so (sō′sō′), *adj.* **1.** neither very good nor very bad; indifferent: *The dinner was so-so.* —*adv.* **2.** in a passable manner; indifferently.

sot (sot), *n.* a person who is habitually drunk.

sou (sōō), *n.* a French coin, no longer in use, that was equal to 5 centimes, or ¹/₂₀ of a franc.

souf·flé (sōō flā′), *n.* a light baked dish made fluffy with beaten egg whites combined with egg yolks, often containing fish, cheese, or other ingredients.

sought (sôt), *v.* the past tense and past participle of **seek.**

soul (sōl), *n.* **1.** the spiritual part of man, as distinct from the physical, that thinks, feels, causes the body to act, and is often regarded as having an existence separate from the body. **2.** the emotional part of man's nature; energy or vitality of feeling or mind: *He put his whole soul into winning the game.* **3.** a person: *Not a soul came because of the rain.* **4.** a person or thing that is the example of or embodies the essential quality of something: *He is the soul of tact.* **5.** a person who inspires some action, cause, etc.— *adj.* **6.** *Slang.* of or characteristic of black Americans or their culture: *soul music.*

soul·ful (sōl′fəl), *adj.* expressive of deep feeling or emotion: *a soulful look.* —**soul′ful·ly,** *adv.* —**soul′ful·ness,** *n.*

soul·less (sōl′lis), *adj.* **1.** without a soul. **2.** lacking nobility of soul; without feeling or spirit.

sound¹ (sound), *n.* **1.** the sensation produced by vibrations reaching the organs of hearing through the air, through liquids, or through solids: *a loud sound.* **2.** the vibrations themselves, which can be heard if their frequency is between 16 cycles per second and about 20,000 cycles per second. **3.** the audible result of an utterance or part of an utterance: *the "s" sound of "slight."* **4.** the quality of an event, letter, etc., as it affects a person: *The news tonight had a good sound.* **5.** the distance within which the noise of something may be heard: *within sound of a waterfall.* —*v.* **6.** to make or cause to make a sound: *The bells sounded loudly at noon. The postman sounded the doorbell.* **7.** to announce or direct by or as if by a sound: *The bugle sounded retreat.* **8.** to convey a certain impression when heard or read; seem: *to sound true.* **9.** to utter audibly; pronounce: *to sound each letter.* **10.** to examine by causing to make sound: *to sound a patient's chest.* **11. sound off,** *Slang.* **a.** to call out one's name, number, etc., as in answer to roll call. **b.** to speak frankly or bluntly: *I shouldn't have sounded off, but he had it coming to him.* **c.** to boast; brag: *Has she been sounding off again about her rich relatives?* [from the Old French word *son,* which comes from Latin *sonus*]

sound² (sound), *adj.* **1.** in good health or condition: *sound in body and mind.* **2.** free from defect, decay, damage, etc.: *sound floors.* **3.** financially secure: *a sound business.* **4.** competent or sensible: *sound judgment.* **5.** having no defect as to truth, justice, wisdom, etc.: *sound advice.* **6.** upright, honest, or honorable. **7.** untroubled or deep: *sound sleep.* **8.** thorough or severe: *a sound thrashing.* —*adv.* **9.** completely or deeply: *sound asleep.* [from the Middle English word *sund,* which comes from Old English *(ge)sund*] —**sound′ly,** *adv.* —**sound′ness,** *n.*

sound³ (sound), *v.* **1.** to measure the depth of (water, a deep hole, etc.) by means of a weighted line, sonar, etc. **2.** to measure (depth) in such a manner, as at sea. **3.** to plunge downward or dive, as a whale. **4.** to seek to find out the views or feelings of (a person) by inquiries, conversation, etc. (often fol. by *out*): *We sounded out his opinion of the plan.* [from an Old English word meaning "channel"]

sound⁴ (sound), *n.* **1.** a relatively narrow passage of water between larger bodies of water or between the mainland and an island: *Puget Sound.* **2.** an inlet of the sea. **3.** the air bladder of a fish. [from the Old English word *sund* "swimming, channel, sea"]

sound·er¹ (soun/dər), *n.* a person or thing that makes a sound or sounds something.

sound·er² (soun/dər), *n.* a person or thing that measures depth.

sound·proof (sound/prŏŏf/), *adj.* **1.** not permitting sound to enter or leave: *a soundproof studio.* —*v.* **2.** to make soundproof: *to soundproof a room.*

sound' wave', a series of vibrations in air, a liquid, or a solid by means of which a sound travels.

soup (sŏŏp), *n.* a liquid food made by boiling meat, fish, or vegetables with various added ingredients.

sour (sour), *adj.* **1.** having an acid taste resembling that of vinegar, lemon juice, etc. **2.** made acid; spoiled or fermented: *sour milk.* **3.** suggesting something spoiled or fermented: *a sour smell.* **4.** disagreeable or unpleasant: *a sour stare.* **5.** peevish; bad-tempered: *sour comments.* **6.** (of soil) too acid. —*v.* **7.** to make or become sour: *Milk sours quickly in warm weather.* **8.** to spoil; cause spoilage in. **9.** to make or become bitter or disagreeable: *Bad luck soured him.* —**sour/ly,** *adv.* —**sour/ness,** *n.*

source (sôrs), *n.* **1.** any person, place, or thing from which something comes or is obtained; a book, person, etc., supplying information; origin: *The newspaper quoted the mayor as the source of the story.* **2.** the beginning or place of origin of a stream or river.

souse (sous), *v.*, **soused, sous·ing. 1.** to drench with or soak in a liquid, such as water. **2.** to steep in pickling brine; pickle. —*n.* **3.** the act of sousing. **4.** *Slang.* a drunkard.

south (south), *n.* **1.** one of the four principal compass points, the direction of the South Pole, being one's right when one faces the rising sun. *Abbr.:* S **2.** the southern part of a region or country. **3. the South, a.** the part of the United States south of Pennsylvania and the Ohio River and east of the Mississippi River, mainly those states that formed the Confederate States. **b.** another name for **Confederate States of America.** —*adj.* **4.** Also, **southern.** situated in the south: *the south part of the state.* **5.** coming from the south: *a south wind.* —*adv.* **6.** toward the south: *to sail south.*

South' Af'rica, Repub'lic of, a country in S Africa, formerly a British colony. 472,000 sq. mi. *Capitals:* Pretoria and Cape Town. —**South' Af'rican.**

South' Amer'ica, a continent in the S part of the Western Hemisphere. about 6,900,000 sq. mi. —**South' Amer'ican.**

South·amp·ton (south amp/tən, south hamp/tən), *n.* a port city in S England.

South' Ara'bia, a former federation in S Arabia, now part of the People's Democratic Republic of Yemen. —**South' Ara'bian.**

South' Austral'ia, a state in S Australia. 380,070 sq. mi.

South' Bend', a city in N Indiana.

south·bound (south/-bound/), *adj.* going toward the south: *southbound traffic.*

South' Caroli'na, a state in the SE United States, on the Atlantic coast. 31,055 sq. mi. *Cap.:* Columbia. —**South' Carolin'ian.**

South' Chi'na Sea', a part of the W Pacific, bounded by SE China, Vietnam, the Malay Peninsula, Borneo, and the Philippines.

South' Dako'ta, a state in the N central United States. 77,047 sq. mi. *Cap.:* Pierre. —**South' Dako'tan.**

south·east (south/ēst/), *n.* **1.** a point on the compass halfway between south and east. *Abbr.:* SE **2.** a region in this direction. —*adj.* **3.** situated toward the southeast: *the southeast corner of the state.* **4.** directed toward the southeast: *to sail a southeast course.* **5.** coming from the southeast: *a southeast wind.* —*adv.* **6.** toward the southeast: *to sail southeast.* Also, **southeastern** (for defs. 4, 5).

South'east A'sia, the countries and islands between India and the Philippines. —**South'east A'sian.**

south·east·er (south/ē/stər), *n.* a wind or gale from the southeast.

south·east·er·ly (south/ē/stər lē), *adj.* **1.** directed toward the southeast: *in a southeasterly course.* **2.** coming from the southeast: *the wind is southeasterly.* —*adv.* **3.** toward the southeast: *sailing southeasterly.* **4.** from the southeast, as a wind.

south·east·ern (south/ē/stərn), *adj.* See **southeast** (defs. 4, 5).

south·er·ly (suth/ər lē), *adj.* **1.** directed toward the south: *in a southerly course.* **2.** coming from the south: *The wind is southerly.* —*adv.* **3.** toward the south: *sailing southerly.* **4.** from the south, as a wind.

south·ern (suth/ərn), *adj.* **1.** See **south** (def. 4). **2.** (*often cap.*) of or concerning the south, esp. the South: *to enjoy Southern hospitality.*

South'ern Cross', a constellation in the southern sky containing four bright stars that form a cross.

South·ern·er (suth/ər nər), *n.* (*sometimes l.c.*) a native or inhabitant of the South, or of a southern region or country.

South'ern Hem'isphere, the half of the earth between the South Pole and the equator.

south·ern·most (suŧħ'ərn mōst'), *adj.* farthest south.

South'ern Rhode'sia, former name of **Rhodesia.**

South'ern Yem'en, former name of **Yemen** (def. 1).

South' Is'land, the largest island of New Zealand. 58,093 sq. mi.

South' Kore'a, a country in E Asia: formed in 1948 when the former country of Korea was divided into North and South Korea. 36,600 sq. mi. *Cap.:* Seoul. **—South' Kore'an.**

south·paw (south'pô'), *Informal.* **—n.** **1.** a person who is left-handed. **2.** (in baseball) a left-handed pitcher. **—adj. 3.** left-handed.

South' Pole', the southernmost point of the earth.

South' Sea' Is'lands, the islands in the S Pacific Ocean. **—South' Sea' Is'lander.**

south-south·east (south'south'ēst'), *n.* **1.** the point on the compass halfway between south and southeast. *Abbr.:* SSE **—adj. 2.** directed toward this point. **3.** coming from this point, as a wind. **—adv. 4.** toward this point. **5.** from this point, as a wind.

south-south·west (south'south'west'), *n.* **1.** the point on the compass halfway between south and southwest. *Abbr.:* SSW **—adj. 2.** directed toward this point. **3.** coming from this point, as a wind. **—adv. 4.** toward this point. **5.** from this point, as a wind.

South' Vietnam', a former country in SE Asia: now part of reunified Vietnam. **—South' Viet'namese'.**

south·ward (south'wərd, suŧħ'ərd), *adj.* **1.** directed toward the south. **2.** situated in the south. **—adv. 3.** Also, **south'wards.** toward the south: *to sail southward.* **— n. 4.** a southward direction or point.

south·west (south'west'), *n.* **1.** a point on the compass halfway between south and west. *Abbr.:* SW **2.** a region in this direction. **3. the Southwest,** the southwestern part of the U.S. **—adj. 4.** situated in the southwest: *the southwest corner of the state.* **5.** directed toward the southwest: *to sail a southwest course.* **6.** coming from the southwest: *a southwest wind.* **—adv. 7.** toward the southwest: *to sail southwest.* Also, **southwestern** (for defs. 4, 5).

south·west·er (south'wes'tər), *n.* a wind or gale from the southwest.

south·west·er·ly (south'wes'tər lē), *adj.* **1.** directed toward the southwest: *in a southwesterly course.* **2.** coming from the southwest: *The wind is southwesterly.* **—adv. 3.** toward the southwest: *sailing southwesterly.* **4.** from the southwest, as a wind.

south·west·ern (south'wes'tərn), *adj.* See **southwest** (defs. 4, 5).

sou·ve·nir (sōō'və nēr', sōō'və nēr'), *n.* something given or kept as a reminder of a place visited, an incident, etc.; memento.

sov·er·eign (sov'rin, sov'ər in), *n.* **1.** a monarch; a king, queen, or other supreme ruler. **2.** a gold coin formerly used in Great Britain, worth 20 shillings or 1 pound. **—adj. 3.** having supreme rank, power, or authority. **4.** greatest or highest; chief; utmost: *a matter of sovereign importance.* **5.** having independent power or authority: *a sovereign state.*

sov·er·eign·ty (sov'rin tē), *n., pl.* for defs. 2, 3 **sov·er·eign·ties. 1.** the quality or condition of being sovereign; supreme power. **2.** royal status or power. **3.** supreme and independent power in government as possessed or claimed by a state or community.

so·vi·et (sō'vē et'), *n.* (in the Soviet Union) any of a number of elected governing councils.

So·vi·et (sō'vē et'), *adj.* of the Soviet Union: *a Soviet statesman.*

So'viet Rus'sia, another name for **Soviet Union.**

So'viet Un'ion, a large country in E Europe and N Asia, composed of 15 republics: formed from Russia. 8,650,069 sq. mi. *Cap.:* Moscow. Also, **Russia.** Official name, **Union of Soviet Socialist Republics.**

sow[1] (sō), *v.,* **sowed; sown** (sōn) *or* **sowed; sow·ing. 1.** to scatter or plant (seeds). **2.** to introduce, spread about, or implant: *to sow distrust.* [from the Old English word *sāwan*]

sow[2] (sou), *n.* a full-grown female pig. [from the Old English word *sugu*]

sox (soks), *n.* a plural of **sock**[1].

soy (soi), *n.* **1.** Also, **soy' sauce'.** a salty sauce made from fermented soybeans. **2.** the soybean.

soy·bean (soi'bēn'), *n.* **1.** a bushy plant of the bean family grown for its seeds, as fodder, and to enrich the soil. **2.** the seed itself, a source of a useful oil.

spa (spä), *n.* **1.** a spring of mineral water. **2.** a place, such as a health resort, having such a spring.

space (spās), *n.* **1.** the portion of the universe outside the earth's atmosphere; outer space. **2.** the unlimited expanse of length, breadth, and height in which the universe and all material things are contained. **3.** extent or area in three dimensions: *The kitchen has plenty of space for working.* **4.** extent or area in two dimensions; a particular distance: *The trees were planted at equal spaces apart.* **5.** a particular extent of time: *a space of two days.* **6.** a seat or room on a train, airplane, etc. **7.** a place available for a particular purpose: *a parking space.* **8.** (in music) the interval between two adjacent lines of the staff. **—v.,** **spaced, spac·ing. 9.** to divide into spaces. **10.** to set some distance apart: *Space the roses every two feet.*

space' cap'sule, a container or vehicle for launching into space, designed to be recovered after its return to earth. Space capsules may carry astronauts, animals, or instruments.

space·craft (spās'kraft'), *n., pl.* **space·craft.** any vehicle, such as a rocket, artificial satellite, or space capsule that can travel in outer space.

space·man (spās'man', -mən), *n., pl.* **space·men.** an astronaut.

space·ship (spās′ship′), *n.* a rocket-powered vehicle designed to carry men to the moon or the planets.

space′ shut′tle, a large spacecraft combining a rocket and a glider airplane, planned for eventual routine ferrying of passengers and equipment into space orbit and back.

space′ sta′tion, a large artificial satellite in orbit around the earth, designed as an observation and launching platform for spaceships.

space′ suit′, a sealed suit in which normal air pressure is maintained to allow the wearer to live in outer space.

spac·ing (spā′sing), *n.* 1. the fixing or arranging of spaces. 2. the way in which spaces are arranged, as in printed matter.

spa·cious (spā′shəs), *adj.* containing or occupying much space; of great extent; vast: *a spacious house; the spacious Western prairies.* —**spa′cious·ly,** *adv.* —**spa′cious·ness,** *n.*

spade¹ (spād), *n.* 1. a tool for digging, having a flat blade for pressing in the earth with the foot and a long handle. —*v.,* **spad·ed, spad·ing.** 2. to dig with a spade (sometimes fol. by *up*): *Let's spade up the garden and plant flowers.* 3. **call a spade a spade,** to speak plainly or bluntly. [from Old English *spadu*]

spade² (spād), *n.* 1. a black figure that resembles an upside-down heart with a short stem, used to indicate one suit in a deck of playing cards. 2. any card of the suit so marked. 3. **spades,** *(used as sing. or pl.)* the suit so marked: *Spades are trumps.* [from the Italian word *spada* "sword" (used as the mark of this suit in the Italian deck)]

spa·ghet·ti (spə get′ē), *n.* a white food paste made of flour and formed into long, thin strings for boiling.

Spain (spān), *n.* a kingdom in SW Europe. 194,988 sq. mi. *Cap.:* Madrid.

spake (spāk), *v.* an old form of **spoke,** found now chiefly in Biblical and poetic writing.

span¹ (span), *n.* 1. the distance between the tip of the thumb and the tip of the little finger when the hand is fully extended, about 9 inches. 2. a short or limited distance or space of time: *the span of a river; a span of two weeks.* 3. the distance between two supports of a bridge. —*v.,* **spanned, span·ning.** 4. to measure by or as if by the fully extended hand. 5. to extend across: *The bridge spans the river at the narrowest point.* 6. to reach or pass over (space or time): *a memory that spans 50 years.* [from Old English]

span² (span), *n.* a pair of horses, oxen, or the like, harnessed and driven together. [from a Flemish word meaning "to fasten, unite"]

span·gle (spang′gəl), *n.* 1. a small, often round piece of glittering metal or other material, used esp. for decorating clothing. 2. any small, bright drop, object, or spot. —*v.,* **span·gled, span·gling.** 3. to decorate with spangles. 4. to sprinkle with small, bright pieces, spots, etc.: *Sequins spangled the dress.*

Span·iard (span′yərd), *n.* a native or inhabitant of Spain.

span·iel (span′yəl), *n.* any of several breeds of small or medium-sized long-haired dogs having long ears.

Span·ish (span′ish), *n.* 1. the Romance language of Spain and Spanish America. 2. the Spanish people. —*adj.* 3. of or referring to Spain, its people, or their language.

Span′ish Amer′ica, the Spanish-speaking countries south of the U.S. —**Span′ish Amer′ican.**

Span′ish-A·mer′i·can War′ (span′ish ə mer′i-kən), the war between the U.S. and Spain in 1898.

Span′ish Arma′da, the fleet sent against England by Spain in 1588, defeated by the English navy.

Span′ish Main′, (formerly) the Caribbean Sea: route of the Spanish treasure galleons from South America and a region frequented by pirates.

spank (spangk), *v.* 1. to punish (a person, usually a child) by striking, esp. on the buttocks, with the open hand, a slipper, etc. —*n.* 2. a slap, esp. on the buttocks, given with the open hand, a slipper, etc.

spank·ing¹ (spang′king), *n.* a series of spanks, as in punishment.

spank·ing² (spang′king), *adj.* 1. blowing briskly: *a spanking breeze.* 2. moving rapidly and smartly; vigorous: *He rode the horse at a spanking pace.* 3. *Informal.* unusually fine, great, large, etc.; remarkable: *He won the race with a spanking performance.* —*adv.* 4. *Informal.* extremely or unusually; very: *three spanking new dresses.* [perhaps from a Scandinavian word, such as Danish *spank* "to strut"]

spar¹ (spär), *n.* 1. a stout pole, such as those used for masts, to which a sail is attached; mast, yard, boom, or the like. —*v.,* **sparred, spar·ring.** 2. to provide or equip with spars. [from the Middle English word *sparre*]

spar² (spär), *v.,* **sparred, spar·ring.** 1. (of boxers) to make the motions of attack and defense with the arms and fists, esp. as a part of training. 2. to box, esp. with light blows. 3. to argue or dispute; wrangle. —*n.* 4. a boxing match. 5. an argument or dispute. [from a Middle English word originally meaning "to thrust"]

spar³ (spär), *n.* any of various shiny minerals that may be easily split. [from the Old English word *spærstan* "gypsum"]

spare (spâr), *v.,* **spared, spar·ing.** 1. to refrain from hurting or destroying: *to spare one's enemies.* 2. to save from discomfort, annoyance, or pain: *to spare him embarrassment.* 3. to give up or do without: *Can you spare a dollar till payday?* 4. to refrain from using, as some instrument, means, aid, etc.: *to spare the rod and spoil the child.* 5. to omit, as from speech or action: *Spare us the details!* 6. to use frugally or economically: *He didn't spare time or effort on his studies.* —*adj.,* **spar·er, spar·est.** 7. kept in reserve; free for other use: *a spare tire; spare time.* 8. lean or thin; scanty, as in amount, fullness, etc.: *a tall, spare man; a spare serving of food.* —*n.* 9. a spare thing, such as an extra tire for emergency use. 10. (in bowling) the knocking down of all pins with two bowls.

spare·rib (spâr′rib′), *n.* a cut of pork containing ribs having only a small amount of meat on them.

spar·ing (spâr′ing), *adj.* economical or frugal.

spark (spärk), *n.* **1.** a small, glowing particle, such as one thrown off by burning wood: *sparks from a fire-place.* **2.** a flash of light caused by an electric current passing through air or any other gas. **3.** a small amount or trace: *a spark of life.* —*v.* **4.** to send forth sparks. **5.** to send forth gleams or flashes. **6.** to stimulate: *to spark interest in a project.*

spar·kle (spär′kəl), *v.,* **spar·kled, spar·kling. 1.** to send forth in or as if in little sparks or gleams of light; glitter: *The flames leaped and sparkled.* **2.** to bubble, as a carbonated drink, wine, etc. **3.** to be brilliant or lively: *The conversation sparkled with wit.* —*n.* **4.** a little spark or flash. **5.** a sparkling appearance or play of light: *the sparkle of a diamond.* **6.** brilliance or liveliness: *the sparkle of conversation.*

spar·kler (spär′klər), *n.* **1.** a person or thing that sparkles. **2.** a firework shaped like a thin stick that throws off bright sparks when lighted.

spark′ plug′, a device for igniting the mixture of fuel and air in a gasoline engine by means of an electric spark.

spar·row (spar′ō), *n.* any small, brownish or grayish birds of the finch family, esp. one variety commonly found in U.S. cities.

spar′row hawk′, either of two small birds of prey used in falconry.

sparse (spärs), *adj.,* **spars·er, spars·est.** thinly scattered or distributed; not thick or dense: *a sparse population; sparse hair.* —**sparse′ly,** *adv.*

Spar·ta (spär′tə), *n.* an ancient city in S Greece. —**Spar′tan,** *n., adj.*

spasm (spaz′əm), *n.* **1.** a sudden, involuntary tightening of a muscle or muscles. **2.** any sudden, brief spell of energy, activity, etc.: *a spasm of hard work.*

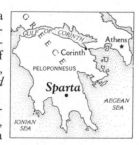

spas·mod·ic (spaz mod′-ik), *adj.* **1.** of, concerning, or characterized by a spasm or spasms: *a spasmodic trembling; a spasmodic pain.* **2.** resembling spasms; sudden but brief: *spasmodic efforts.* —**spas·mod′i·cal·ly,** *adv.*

spas·tic (spas′tik), *adj.* **1.** concerning, resembling, or having spasms. —*n.* **2.** a person afflicted with spasms, palsy, etc.

spat[1] (spat), *n.* **1.** a petty quarrel. **2.** a light blow or slap. —*v.,* **spat·ted, spat·ting. 3.** to have a petty quarrel or dispute. **4.** to strike lightly; slap. [perhaps imitative of the sound of a blow]

spat[2] (spat), *v.* a past tense and past participle of **spit.**

spat[3] (spat), *n.* a short cloth or leather covering worn over the instep and usually fastened under the shoe with a strap. [short for *spatterdash,* from *spatter* + *dash*]

spa·tial (spā′shəl), *adj.* **1.** of or concerning space. **2.** existing or occurring in space.

spat·ter (spat′ər), *v.* **1.** to scatter or splash (something) in small particles or drops: *The dog spattered mud on everyone.* **2.** to splash with something in small drops: *to spatter the ground with water.* **3.** to fall, strike, or spurt in drops: *Rain spattered on the roof.* **4.** to spot with something that soils or stains: *He spattered his fingers with the ink.* **5.** to strike as if in a shower: *Bullets spattered the streets.* —*n.* **6.** the act or sound of spattering: *the spatter of rain on a roof.* **7.** a splash or spot of something spattered.

spat·u·la (spach′ə lə), *n.* a tool having a broad, flat, usually flexible blade, used for blending or lifting foods, mixing drugs, spreading paints, etc.

spav·in (spav′in), *n.* a disease affecting the lower joint in the leg of a horse, causing lameness.

spav·ined (spav′ind), *adj.* **1.** (of a horse) suffering from spavin; lame. **2.** being in poor mechanical or physical condition: *a spavined old car.*

spawn (spôn), *v.* **1.** to deposit eggs directly into the water, as fishes do: *Salmon swim upstream to spawn.* **2.** to produce (masses of eggs or numerous offspring), as fishes, crustaceans, etc., do. **3.** to give birth to; give rise to: *Poor living conditions spawn crime.* —*n.* **4.** the mass of eggs produced by a fish, amphibian, mollusk, crustacean, etc.

spay (spā), *v.* to remove the ovaries of (a female animal) to prevent its producing offspring.

speak (spēk), *v.,* **spoke** (spōk), **spo·ken** (spō′kən), **speak·ing. 1.** to utter words; talk: *He was too hoarse to speak.* **2.** to express or make (something) known; tell: *to speak the truth.* **3.** to deliver a public talk, address, etc.: *to speak at a meeting.* **4.** to communicate orally or in writing; mention: *We spoke of various matters.* **5.** to use or be able to use, as a language: *to speak French.* **6. so to speak,** in a way, or in a manner of speaking: *I've been going around in circles, so to speak.* **7. speak for, a.** to speak in defense or on behalf of: *Mr. Jones will speak for the opposing side.* **b.** to choose or select for oneself: *The blue convertible is already spoken for.* **8. speak out,** to speak one's thoughts, opinions, etc., openly and without fear: *If you disagree, speak out.* **9. to speak of,** worth mentioning: *The town has no parks to speak of.*

speak·er (spē′kər), *n.* **1.** a person who speaks. **2.** *(usually cap.)* the presiding officer of a legislative assembly, such as the U.S. House of Representatives or the British House of Commons. **3.** a loudspeaker.

spear (spēr), *n.* **1.** a weapon for throwing or thrusting, consisting of a long, wooden pole to which a sharp, pointed metal head is attached. —*v.* **2.** to pierce with or as if with a spear.

spear·head (spēr′hed′), *n.* **1.** the sharp, piercing point of a spear. **2.** any person or thing that leads an attack, undertaking, etc. —*v.* **3.** to act as the leader of an attack, undertaking, etc.

spear·mint (spēr′mint′), *n.* an herb, a common kind of mint, used for flavoring chewing gum, candy, etc.

spec., 1. special. **2.** specially. **3.** specification.

spe·cial (spesh′əl), *adj.* **1.** of a distinct or particular kind: *This lock has a special key.* **2.** different from what is ordinary or usual: *Birthdays are special occasions.* **3.** concerning or peculiar to a particular person, thing, or instance: *the special features of a plan.* **4.** having a particular function, purpose, etc.: *a special messenger.* **5.** being such to an exceptional degree; great: *a special friend.* —*n.* **6.** a person or thing having a special purpose, function, etc.: *What is the special on the menu?* —**spe′cial·ly,** *adv.*

spe·cial·ist (spesh′ə list), *n.* a person who devotes himself to one subject or to one particular branch of a subject: *Dr. Jones is a specialist in tropical diseases.*

spe·cial·ize (spesh′ə līz′), *v.,* **spe·cial·ized, spe·cial·iz·ing. 1.** to pursue some special line of study, work, etc.: *In college he specialized in French.* **2.** to change or adapt to a special function or special living conditions: *Camels have specialized so as to survive in the desert.* —**spe′cial·i·za′tion,** *n.*

spe·cial·ty (spesh′əl tē), *n., pl.* for defs. 1, 2 **spe·cial·ties. 1.** a special subject of study, line of work, or the like: *His specialty is art.* **2.** an article, product or line of products, service, etc., that is specially featured or dealt in: *Men's clothing is the specialty of this shop.* **3.** the state or condition of being special.

spe·cie (spē′shē, spē′sē), *n.* coin; coined money.

spe·cies (spē′shēz, spē′sēz), *n., pl.* **spe·cies. 1.** a group of related plants or animals that can interbreed to produce offspring: *Dogs are all members of a single species, but dogs and cats are members of different species.* **2.** sort or kind.

spe·cif·ic (spi sif′ik), *adj.* **1.** definite, precise, or particular: *a specific amount of money.* **2.** peculiar to something or someone: *His specific problems got him in trouble.* **3.** (in biology) of or concerning a species. —*n.* **4.** something specific, as a statement, quality, etc.: *Be sure to give all the specifics in your report.* **5.** (in medicine) a specific remedy: *There is no specific for the common cold.* —**spe·cif′i·cal·ly,** *adv.*

spec·i·fi·ca·tion (spes′ə fə kā′shən), *n.* **1.** the act of specifying; a detailed statement of particular items, requirements, etc. **2.** something specified. **3.** Usually, **specifications.** a detailed description of measurements, materials, etc., as of something to be made.

specif′ic grav′ity, the ratio of the density of one substance to the density of another substance taken as a standard. For solids and liquids, the specific gravity is the ratio of their density to that of water; for gases the density of air or of hydrogen is used as a standard.

spec·i·fy (spes′ə fī′), *v.,* **spec·i·fied, spec·i·fy·ing. 1.** to mention or name definitely; state in detail: *He did not specify his plans for the summer.* **2.** to include (an item) in a list of specifications: *The architect specified a tile for the roof.*

spec·i·men (spes′ə mən), *n.* a part or individual taken as an example of a whole group or number; an animal, plant, mineral, etc., typical of a group.

speck (spek), *n.* **1.** a small spot or stain: *specks of soot on the window sill.* **2.** a very little bit or parti-

cle: *We don't have a speck of sugar.* —*v.* **3.** to mark with or as if with specks.

speck·le (spek′əl), *n.* **1.** a small speck, spot, or mark: *The egg had green speckles.* —*v.,* **speck·led, speck·ling. 2.** to mark with or as if with speckles.

spec·ta·cle (spek′tə kəl), *n.* **1.** anything to be viewed, esp. something of an unusual or impressive kind: *The stars make a fine spectacle.* **2.** a public show: *The coronation was a colorful spectacle.* **3. spectacles.** See eyeglass (def. 1). **4. make a spectacle of oneself,** to behave badly in public: *He made a spectacle of himself, so they sent him home.*

spec·tac·u·lar (spek tak′yə lər), *adj.* **1.** of or like a spectacle; marked by an impressive display: *a spectacular scene in a movie.* **2.** daring or thrilling: *a spectacular dive from a cliff.* —*n.* **3.** a large, elaborate production, as of a film; spectacle: *a Hollywood spectacular.* —**spec·tac′u·lar·ly,** *adv.*

spec·ta·tor (spek′tā tər), *n.* a person who looks on or watches; observer.

spec·ter (spek′tər), *n.* a ghost. Also, **spec′tre.**

spec·tral (spek′trəl), *adj.* **1.** of, concerning, or like a specter; ghostly. **2.** of or concerning a spectrum or spectra.

spec·tro·scope (spek′trə skōp′), *n.* an instrument for observing and making measurements of spectra, consisting of a prism or grating that disperses incoming light to form a spectrum and a small telescope through which the spectrum is examined.

spec·trum (spek′trəm), *n., pl.* **spec·tra** (spek′trə) *or* **spec·trums.** the band of different colors produced when light is dispersed by a prism or other means. A rainbow is the spectrum of sunlight produced by dispersion due to raindrops.

spec·u·late (spek′yə lāt′), *v.,* **spec·u·lat·ed, spec·u·lat·ing. 1.** to think or reflect; form opinions or theories without having full knowledge; ponder; meditate: *Astronomers speculate about the creation of the universe.* **2.** to buy and sell commodities, stocks, etc., at considerable risk, but with the hope of making a large profit from a change of prices: *to speculate on war materials.* —**spec′u·la′tor,** *n.*

spec·u·la·tion (spek′yə lā′shən), *n.* **1.** consideration of some subject; meditation; thought. **2.** an opinion or theory. **3.** trading in commodities, stocks, etc., with the hope of making a large profit from a change of prices. **4.** any business venture involving risk.

spec·u·la·tive (spek′yə lā′tiv), *adj.* **1.** of, concerning, or characterized by speculation; thoughtful; reflective: *to approach a problem in a speculative way.* **2.** theoretical, rather than practical: *a speculative conclusion.* **3.** of or involving financial speculation: *He lost a fortune in speculative ventures.*

speech (spēch), *n.* **1.** the power of speaking; ability to communicate or express thoughts by spoken words. **2.** the act of speaking: *He expresses himself better in speech than in writing.* **3.** remarks or spoken words: *There was nothing in his speech to make us think he was afraid.* **4.** a formal or public talk or address: *a campaign speech; a speech in a play.* **5.** manner of speaking, as of a person or group: *educated speech; Southern speech.* **6.** a language or dialect: *the speech of France.*

speech·less (spēch′lis), *adj.* **1.** temporarily at a loss for words, as from strong emotion, weakness, etc.; silent: *speechless with fear.* **2.** lacking the power of speech; dumb. —**speech′less·ly,** *adv.*

speed (spēd), *n.* **1.** rapidity in moving, going, performing, etc.; swiftness: *with the speed of lightning.* **2.** rate of motion or progress: *to drive at full speed.* **3.** a transmission gear of a motor vehicle: *This car has three forward speeds.* **4.** *Archaic.* success or prosperity. —*v.,* **sped** (sped) *or* **speed·ed; speed·ing. 5.** to move or cause to move rapidly: *The bicycle sped down the hill.* **6.** to drive a vehicle faster than the maximum rate allowed by law: *He was arrested for speeding.* **7.** to increase the rate of speed (usually fol. by *up*): *to speed up one's reading.* **8.** to promote the success of (an affair, undertaking, etc.); further. **9.** to wish success or good luck to (a person): *to speed a friend on a journey.*

speed·boat (spēd′bōt′), *n.* a motorboat built to move rapidly through the water.

speed·er (spē′dər), *n.* a person or thing that speeds, esp. a person who drives an automobile at a recklessly high or illegal speed.

speed·om·e·ter (spē dom′i tər), *n.* a device on a motor vehicle that indicates the speed at which it is traveling and, often, the distance traveled.

speed·way (spēd′wā′), *n.* **1.** a road for fast driving. **2.** a track on which motorcycle or automobile races are held.

speed·y (spē′dē), *adj.,* **speed·i·er, speed·i·est.** characterized by speed; rapid; swift; fast. —**speed′i·ly,** *adv.*

spell[1] (spel), *v.,* **spelled** *or* **spelt** (spelt); **spell·ing. 1.** to name or write the letters of (a word, syllable, etc.) in order: *to spell one's name; to know how to spell.* **2.** (of letters) to form or be (a word, syllable, etc.): *M-a-n spells man.* **3.** to mean; amount to or be equivalent to: *John's athletic ability spelled victory for our team.* **4. spell out, a.** to write out in full or say one by one the letters that compose (a word): *The word "Mrs." is seldom spelled out.* **b.** *Informal.* to state in detail so that the meaning cannot be mistaken: *Do I have to spell it out for you?* [from the Old French word *espeller,* which comes from Germanic]

spell[2] (spel), *n.* **1.** a word or phrase supposed to have magic power; charm: *The wizard used a spell to change the prince into a toad.* **2.** a state or period of enchantment: *She was under a spell.* **3.** any irresistible influence; fascination: *the spell of good music.* [from the Old English word meaning "discourse"]

spell[3] (spel), *n.* **1.** a period of work or other activity: *to take a spell at the wheel.* **2.** an indefinite space of time: *He's been out of town for a spell.* **3.** a period or bout of anything: *a spell of coughing.* **4.** a period of weather of a specified kind: *a hot spell.* —*v.* **5.** to take the place of (someone) for a time; relieve: *Let me spell you at the wheel.* [from the Old English word *spelian* "to be a substitute for"]

spell·bind·er (spel′bīn′dər), *n.* a speaker who holds his audience spellbound.

spell·bound (spel′bound′), *adj.* bound by or as if by a spell; fascinated: *a spellbound audience.*

spell·er (spel′ər), *n.* **1.** a person who spells words. **2.** Also, **spell′ing book′.** a textbook for spelling.

spell·ing (spel′ing), *n.* **1.** the way in which a word or words are spelled: *What is the spelling of your last name?* **2.** the act of naming or writing the letters of a word in order: *Mary is very good at spelling.*

spell′ing bee′, a spelling contest won by the individual or team that spells the most words correctly.

spelt (spelt), *v.* a past tense and past participle of **spell**[1].

spend (spend), *v.,* **spent** (spent), **spend·ing. 1.** to pay out; dispose of (money, wealth, resources, etc.): *to spend a fortune.* **2.** to pay out money: *He has been spending a lot on clothes.* **3.** to use (thought, words, time, etc.) on some object, in some act, etc.: *Don't spend much time on it.* **4.** to use up, consume, or exhaust: *The storm had spent its fury.* **5.** to pass (time) in a particular manner, place, etc.: *to spend the day in the country.* **6.** to give (one's blood, life, etc.) for a cause.

spend·thrift (spend′thrift′), *n.* **1.** a person who wastes his money. —*adj.* **2.** wastefully extravagant.

spent (spent), *v.* **1.** the past tense and past participle of **spend.** —*adj.* **2.** used up or exhausted.

sperm (spûrm), *n.* **1.** a male reproductive cell. **2.** the fluid containing these cells; semen.

sper·ma·cet·i (spûr′mə set′ē, spûr′mə sē′tē), *n.* a waxy substance obtained from the oil in the head of the sperm whale and used in making cosmetics and ointments.

sperm′ whale′, a large, square-headed, toothed whale valued as a source of spermaceti and oil.

spew (spyōō), *v.* to vomit, throw out, or pour forth: *The volcano spewed smoke and lava.*

sphere (sfēr), *n.* **1.** a round object whose surface is the same distance from the center at all points. **2.** any object having a similar shape, such as a ball, planet, globe, or the like. **3.** a place or range within which a person or thing exists, acts, operates, etc.: *a doctor's professional sphere; a nation's sphere of influence.*

Sphere

spher·i·cal (sfer′i kəl), *adj.* **1.** having the shape of a sphere; globular. **2.** of or concerning a sphere or spheres. —**spher′i·cal·ly,** *adv.*

sphinx (sfingks), *n.* **1.** a mysterious, secretive person or thing. **2.** a type of statue in ancient Egypt having a man's head and a lion's body.

Sphinx

Sphinx (sfingks), *n.* (in Greek mythology) a monster, part woman, part lion, having the wings of an eagle, that asked difficult riddles and killed those who did not answer correctly.

spice (spīs), *n.* **1.** any of various substances taken from plants and used as seasonings and flavorings, such as pepper, cloves, cinnamon, and the like. **2.** something that gives interest, liveliness, or zest: *the spice of humor.* —*v.,* **spiced, spic·ing. 3.** to season with a spice or spices. **4.** to give interest or zest to.

spick-and-span (spik′ən span′), *adj.* **1.** spotlessly clean and neat: *a spick-and-span kitchen.* **2.** perfectly new; fresh.

spic·y (spī′sē), *adj.,* **spic·i·er, spic·i·est. 1.** seasoned with spice: *a spicy salad dressing.* **2.** bright, interesting, or lively: *spicy talk.* **3.** slightly improper or scandalous: *a spicy novel.* —**spic′i·ness,** *n.*

Spider
(length ¾ in.)

spi·der (spī′dər), *n.* **1.** any of numerous small animals resembling insects but having eight legs and no wings. Most spiders spin webs that serve as nests and as traps for insects on which they feed. **2.** a heavy frying pan, originally one having feet.

spi′der mon′key, any of several tropical American monkeys having a slender body, long slender limbs, and a long tail that can be wrapped around objects.

spi·der·y (spī′də rē), *adj.* **1.** like a spider. **2.** long, slender, or fine like a spider's legs or web.

spied (spīd), *v.* the past tense and past participle of **spy.**

spies (spīz), *n.* **1.** the plural of **spy.** —*v.* **2.** the third person singular, present tense of **spy.**

spig·ot (spig′ət), *n.* **1.** a small faucet. **2.** a plug for closing the hole in a cask.

Spider monkey
(total length 4½ ft.;
tail 2½ ft.)

spike¹ (spīk), *n.* **1.** a very large nail, for fastening together heavy timbers or railroad track. **2.** something resembling such a nail, for example the pointed projections on top of a fence. **3.** any one of the naillike metal projections on the heel or sole of a shoe. —*v.,* **spiked, spik·ing. 4.** to fasten with a spike or spikes. **5.** to provide with a spike or spikes. **6.** to pierce with or impale on a spike. **7.** to make ineffective; frustrate the action or purpose of: *to spike a rumor of impending war.* [from a Scandinavian word, which comes from Latin *spica*]

spike² (spīk), *n.* **1.** an ear of grain. **2.** a pointed cluster of flowers growing along a stalk. [from the Latin word *spica* "spike, sharp point, ear of grain"]

spill (spil), *v.,* **spilled** *or* **spilt** (spilt); **spill·ing. 1.** to cause or let run or fall, esp. accidentally: *to spill milk.* **2.** (of a liquid, loose particles, etc.) to run, fall, or flow, esp. accidentally: *Water spilled from the bucket.* **3.** to shed (blood). **4.** *Informal.* to cause to

fall from a horse, vehicle, or the like. **5.** *Informal.* to tell or disclose: *Don't spill the secret!* —*n.* **6.** a spilling, as of a liquid. **7.** a quantity spilled. **8.** *Informal.* a fall from a horse, vehicle, or the like.

spill·way (spil′wā′), *n.* a passageway for letting surplus water escape from a lake, reservoir, or the like.

spilt (spilt), *v.* a past tense and past participle of **spill.**

spin (spin), *v.,* **spun** (spun), **spin·ning. 1.** to make (yarn) by drawing out and twisting fibers: *Pioneer women spun yarn on spinning wheels.* **2.** to form (fibers of any material) into thread or yarn: *This machine spins nylon.* **3.** (of spiders, silkworms, etc.) to produce (a thread, cobweb, silk, etc.) by secreting a filament from the body. **4.** to cause to turn around rapidly; twirl: *to spin a coin.* **5.** to turn around rapidly, as the earth, a top, etc. **6.** to tell or narrate: *to spin a tale.* **7.** to draw out or prolong (often fol. by *out*): *to spin out an explanation.* **8.** to have a sensation of whirling; reel: *My head began to spin and I fainted.* —*n.* **9.** a rapidly whirling motion, as given to a ball, top, etc. **10.** a rapid ride, drive, etc., as for exercise or enjoyment: *to go for a spin in the car.* **11.** short for **tailspin.** —**spin′ner,** *n.*

spin·ach (spin′ich), *n.* an herb having large, green leaves eaten as a vegetable.

spi·nal (spīn′əl), *adj.* of or concerning the spine.

spi′nal col′umn. See **backbone** (def. 1).

spi′nal cord′, the cord of nerve tissue running through the center of the backbone, which, together with the brain, forms the central nervous system. See illus. at **brain.**

spin·dle (spin′dəl), *n.* **1.** a rounded, wooden rod, esp. one on which thread is wound in spinning. **2.** a rodlike part of a machine, esp. one that rotates. See illus. at **valve.** —*v.,* **spin·dled, spin·dling. 3.** (of a plant) to grow into a tall, slender stalk.

spin·dle-leg·ged (spin′dəl leg′id, -legd′), *adj.* having long, thin legs.

spin·dling (spind′ling), *adj.* long or tall and slender and often weak. Also, **spin′dly.**

spine (spīn), *n.* **1.** See **backbone** (def. 1). **2.** a stiff, pointed growth on an animal, such as the quill of a porcupine. **3.** a stiff, pointed growth on a plant; thorn.

spine·less (spīn′lis), *adj.* **1.** having no spines or quills. **2.** having no spine or backbone. **3.** without courage or moral force: *a spineless coward.*

spin·et (spin′it), *n.* **1.** a small upright piano. **2.** a small harpsichord.

spin·na·ker (spin′ə kər), *n.* a large, triangular sail carried by racing yachts when running before the wind, attached on the side of the mast opposite the mainsail.

spin·ner·et (spin′ə ret′), *n.* the organ of a caterpillar or spider by which a fine thread is spun to make a cocoon or web.

spin′ning jen′ny, an early spinning machine having more than one spindle.

---

act, āble, dâre, ärt; ebb, ēqual; if, īce; hot, ōver, ôrder; oil; bŏŏk; ōōze; out; up, ûrge; ə = a as in *alone*;
ə as in *button* (but′ən), *fire* (fiər); chief; shoe; thin; that; zh as in *measure* (mezh′ər). See full key inside cover.

spin′ning wheel′, a device formerly used for spinning wool, flax, etc., into yarn or thread. It consisted chiefly of a spindle that was driven by a large wheel, which was operated by a foot pedal or by hand.

Spinning wheel

spin·ster (spin′stər), *n.* an unmarried woman, esp. one who is beyond the usual age of marrying; an old maid.

spin·y (spī′nē), *adj.,* **spin·i·er, spin·i·est. 1.** covered with thorns, quills, or the like. **2.** resembling a spine or thorn.

spi·ral (spī′rəl), *n.* **1.** the curve traced by a point moving around and away from a central point. **2.** a helix. —*adj.* **3.** running continuously around a center while constantly moving away from or approaching it: *a spiral curve.* **4.** coiling around a fixed line in a constantly changing series of planes: *a spiral staircase.* —*v.,* **spi·raled** *or* **spi·ralled; spi·ral·ing** *or* **spi·ral·ling. 5.** to take a spiral form or course. **6.** to cause to take a spiral form.

Spirals

spire (spī°r), *n.* **1.** a tall, sharply pointed part of a tower, roof, etc. See illus. at **steeple. 2.** any tapering, pointed part or top of something: *the spires of mountains.* **3.** a sprout or shoot of a plant, such as a blade of grass.

spir·it (spir′it), *n.* **1.** the human soul. **2.** a supernatural being, such as an angel, demon, ghost, or the like: *evil spirits.* **3.** the moral or emotional nature of man: *Poverty can kill the spirit.* **4. spirits,** feelings, mood, or disposition: *low spirits.* **5.** vigor, courage, etc; liveliness: *He played the game with spirit.* **6.** an individual as characterized by a certain attitude, action, etc.: *A few brave spirits faced the danger.* **7.** a widespread feeling, outstanding characteristic, etc.: *the spirit of the age.* **8.** vigorous sense of membership in a group; loyalty: *school spirit.* **9.** the real meaning or intent (distinguished from *letter*): *the spirit of the law.* **10.** Often, **spirits. a.** alcohol or an alcoholic liquor. **b.** a highly refined or purified substance, esp. one obtained by distillation: *spirits of turpentine.* **11.** a solution in alcohol. —*v.* **12.** to carry off mysteriously or secretly (often fol. by *away* or *off*): *His captors spirited him away.* —*adj.* **13.** of or concerning supernatural beings. **14.** containing or burning alcohol.

Spir·it (spir′it), *n.* the divine influence of God working in the life of man; the third person of the Trinity; Holy Spirit.

spir·it·ed (spir′i tid), *adj.* having or showing courage, vigor, liveliness, etc.

spir·it·less (spir′it lis), *adj.* lacking vigor, courage, liveliness, etc.

spir·it·u·al (spir′i choo əl), *adj.* **1.** of, concerning, or consisting of spirit. **2.** of or concerning the spirit or soul. **3.** of or concerning sacred things; religious. —*n.* **4.** a religious folk song, esp. any of the songs originally sung by the Negroes of the southern U.S. —**spir′it·u·al·ly,** *adv.*

spir·it·u·al·ism (spir′i choo ə liz′əm), *n.* the belief that the spirits of the dead communicate with the living, esp. through mediums. —**spir′it·u·al·ist,** *n.*

spi·ro·chete (spī′rə kēt′), *n.* any of several spiral-shaped bacteria, certain of which cause diseases in man and animals.

spirt (spûrt), *v., n.* another spelling of **spurt.**

spit¹ (spit), *v.,* **spit** *or* **spat** (spat); **spit·ting. 1.** to eject saliva or other matter from the mouth. **2.** to throw out or emit like saliva: *The kettle was spitting boiling water on the fire.* **3.** to express as if by ejecting saliva from the mouth: *to spit out an insult.* **4.** to hiss or sputter: *grease spitting on the fire.* —*n.* **5.** saliva, esp. when ejected from the mouth. **6.** the act of spitting. **7. spit and image,** *Informal.* exact likeness: *He's the spit and image of his father.* Also, **spit′ting im′age.** [from the Old English word *spittan* "to spit"]

spit² (spit), *n.* **1.** a pointed rod for thrusting through and holding meat that is to be cooked over a fire. **2.** a narrow point of land projecting into the water. —*v.,* **spit·ted, spit·ting. 3.** to pierce with a spit. [from the Old English word *spitu*]

spite (spīt), *n.* **1.** bitter ill will with the desire to hurt, annoy, or humiliate another person; malice: *He hid my notebook out of spite.* —*v.,* **spit·ed, spit·ing. 2.** to treat with spite. **3. in spite of,** regardless of; despite: *She came to school in spite of the blizzard.*

spite·ful (spīt′fəl), *adj.* full of spite; showing spite. —**spite′ful·ly,** *adv.* —**spite′ful·ness,** *n.*

spit·fire (spit′fīºr′), *n.* a person, esp. a girl or woman, who has a fiery temper.

spit·tle (spit′ºl), *n.* saliva or spit.

spit·toon (spi tōōn′), *n.* a bowl used as a container to spit into.

splash (splash), *v.* **1.** to dash (water, mud, etc.) or scatter about: *to splash water on a fire.* **2.** to dash a liquid or semi-liquid substance about: *The children splashed happily in the pool.* **3.** to wet or soil by dashing water, mud, etc.; spatter: *Don't splash your dress!* **4.** to fall, move, or go with a splash: *The dog splashed across the stream.* **5.** to cause to appear prominently: *The story was splashed across the front page.* —*n.* **6.** the act or sound of dashing or scattering water, mud, etc., about. **7.** a quantity of something splashed upon or in a thing: *coffee with a splash of cream.* **8.** a spot caused by something splashed. **9.** a patch, as of color or light: *The rabbit's fur had splashes of brown.* **10.** a striking display, impression, or success: *The new movie made quite a splash.*

splash·y (splash′ē), *adj.,* **splash·i·er, splash·i·est. 1.** making a splash or splashes. **2.** marked by splashes or spots. **3.** *Informal.* showy; attracting attention: *an expensive, splashy car.*

splat·ter (splat′ər), *v.* **1.** to spatter or splash. —*n.* **2.** a spatter or splash.

splay (splā), *v.* **1.** to spread out or extend. **2.** to make slanting, as a window, doorway, etc. —*n.* **3.** a slanting surface. —*adj.* **4.** spread out; wide and flat; turned outward: *splay feet.* **5.** clumsy or awkward.

spleen (splēn), *n.* **1.** an organ near the stomach that produces lymph cells and destroys worn-out red blood cells. **2.** ill humor, bad temper, or spite.

splen·did (splen′did), *adj.* **1.** gorgeous; magnificent; grand: *a splendid view; a splendid mansion.* **2.** distinguished or glorious, as a name, reputation, etc. **3.** strikingly admirable or fine: *a splendid talent.* **4.** fine, very good, or excellent: *to have a splendid time.* —**splen′did·ly,** *adv.*

splen·dor (splen′dər), *n.* **1.** great brightness; brilliant light or luster. **2.** magnificence, grandeur, or glory: *the splendor of a coronation.*

splice (splīs), *v.,* **spliced, splic·ing. 1.** to join (two ropes) by weaving the strands together. **2.** to unite (timbers) by overlapping the ends and fastening. **3.** to join (two pieces of film, magnetic tape, etc.) end to end by cementing or using an adhesive tape. —*n.* **4.** a joining of two ropes, timbers, pieces of film, etc., by splicing.

splint (splint), *n.* **1.** a thin piece of wood or other stiff material for holding a broken bone in position while it knits. **2.** one of a number of thin strips of wood woven into a chair seat, basket, etc.

splin·ter (splin′tər), *n.* **1.** a small, thin, sharp piece of wood, glass, bone, etc., split or broken off from the main part. —*v.* **2.** to split or break off in splinters.

split (split), *v.,* **split, split·ting. 1.** to divide from end to end, lengthwise, or into layers: *to split a log in two.* **2.** to become divided: *The fabric split. The political party split on the question of civil rights.* **3.** to tear or break apart; burst: *The wind split the sail.* **4.** to divide into distinct parts or portions: *We split up our rations.* **5.** to divide between two or more persons, groups, etc.; share: *We split a bottle of milk.* **6.** to separate into parts by putting something in between: *to split an infinitive.* —*n.* **7.** the act of splitting. **8.** a crack, tear, break, or the like. **9.** a break in unity, as between persons or within a group. **10.** the acrobatic feat of lowering oneself to the floor with the legs extending in opposite directions to form a straight line. —*adj.* **11.** divided, parted, or separated by or as if by splitting: *a split board; a split ballot.*

split′ infin′itive, an infinitive that has the verb separated from *to,* usually by an adverb or adverbial phrase, such as *to really know* or *to never again return.* It is usually avoided by careful speakers and writers.

splotch (sploch), *n.* **1.** a large, irregular spot; blot. —*v.* **2.** to mark with splotches. —**splotch′y,** *adj.*

splurge (splûrj), *v.,* **splurged, splurg·ing. 1.** to show off; indulge oneself in some luxury or pleasure, esp. a costly one. —*n.* **2.** a showy display; a showing off by spending money lavishly.

splut·ter (splut′ər), *v.* **1.** to talk rapidly and incoherently, as when confused, excited, or embarrassed: *When he is asked a question in class, he always splutters.* **2.** to make a sputtering sound; hiss or spit: *The bacon was spluttering in the pan.* —*n.* **3.** the sound or an instance of spluttering.

spoil (spoil), *v.,* **spoiled** *or* **spoilt** (spoilt); **spoil·ing. 1.** to damage or harm the quality, value, usefulness, etc., of (something): *to spoil a sheet of paper with ink blots; to spoil a friendship by arguing.* **2.** to become bad or unfit for use, as food: *Meat spoils if not refrigerated.* **3.** to damage or harm the character of (someone) by unwise treatment or pampering: *to spoil a child.* **4.** to rob or plunder (persons, places, etc.): *Thieves spoiled the palace of its treasures.* —*n.* **5.** Often, **spoils.** booty or plunder taken in war or robbery. **6.** Usually, **spoils.** public offices that are filled by the persons who have worked for a victorious political party. —**spoil′er,** *n.*

spoils′ sys′tem, the system or practice in which public offices with their advantages are controlled by the victorious political party.

spoilt (spoilt), *v.* a past tense and past participle of **spoil.**

Spo·kane (spō kan′), *n.* a city in E Washington.

spoke¹ (spōk), *v.* the past tense of **speak.**

spoke² (spōk), *n.* **1.** one of the bars or rods connecting the rim of a wheel to the hub. **2.** a rung of a ladder. [from a Middle English word, which comes from Old English *spāca*]

spo·ken (spō′kən), *v.* **1.** the past participle of **speak.** —*adj.* **2.** expressed by speaking; oral: *the spoken word.* **3.** speaking in a specified way: *a plain-spoken man.*

spoke·shave (spōk′shāv′), *n.* a tool having an adjustable blade set between two handles and used for shaping curved ledges on wood or for forming round sticks.

Spokeshave

spokes·man (spōks′mən), *n., pl.* **spokes·men.** a person who speaks for another or others.

sponge (spunj), *n.* **1.** any of various simple water animals that live together in large clumps. **2.** the porous skeleton of such a clump, which readily absorbs water and is used in cleaning. **3.** any of various manmade materials resembling this. —*v.,* **sponged, spong·ing. 4.** to wipe, rub, moisten, or clean with or as if with a wet sponge. **5.** *Informal.* to live or obtain (something) at the expense of others: *He sponged off his family for a year.* **6. throw in the sponge,** *Slang.* to admit defeat; give up: *The election was going against him, but he refused to throw in the sponge.*

spon·gy (spun′jē), *adj.,* **spon·gi·er, spon·gi·est.** of or like a sponge; light and porous; full of holes; absorbing, holding, or yielding liquid. —**spon′gi·ness,** *n.*

spon·sor (spon′sər), *n.* **1.** a person who promotes, pays for, or is responsible for a person or thing: *What company is the sponsor of this television show? The Senator was sponsor of the bill.* **2.** a person who answers for a child at baptism, taking responsibility for its religious upbringing. —*v.* **3.** to act as a sponsor for. —**spon′sor·ship′,** *n.*

spon·ta·ne·i·ty (spon′tə nē′i tē, spon′tə nā′i tē), *n.* the state or quality of being spontaneous.

spon·ta·ne·ous (spon tā′nē əs), *adj.* **1.** coming or resulting from a natural impulse; done freely without effort; unplanned: *spontaneous applause.* **2.** acting or arising from internal forces or causes only. **—spon·ta′ne·ous·ly,** *adv.*

sponta′neous combus′tion, the bursting into flames of a substance without the application of heat or a flame: *Oily rags are a fire hazard, since they are capable of spontaneous combustion.*

spoof (spo͞of), *n.* **1.** a joke, prank, or humorous, mocking imitation of someone or something: *The show was a spoof of college life.* **—v. 2.** to make good-humored fun of (something or someone).

spook (spo͞ok), *n. Informal.* a ghost; specter.

spook·y (spo͞o′kē), *adj.,* **spook·i·er, spook·i·est.** like a spook; suggestive of spooks: *a spooky face at the window; a spooky old house.* **—spook′i·ness,** *n.*

spool (spo͞ol), *n.* **1.** a small cylinder of wood or other material, with a rim at each end, on which thread, wire, or tape is wound. **—v. 2.** to wind on a spool.

spoon (spo͞on), *n.* **1.** a utensil for eating, stirring, measuring, etc., consisting of a shallow bowl with a handle. **—v. 2.** to eat with or take up in a spoon.

spoon·bill (spo͞on′bil′), *n.* any of various birds having a flat, spoon-shaped bill, esp. certain large African and Asian wading birds.

spoon·ful (spo͞on′fo͝ol), *n., pl.* **spoon·fuls.** the amount that a spoon can hold.

spoor (spo͝or, spôr), *n.* the track or trail of a wild animal.

spo·rad·ic (spô rad′ik, spə rad′ik), *adj.* appearing or occurring now and then or here and there; scattered; occasional: *sporadic cheers from the audience; the sporadic growth of plants.* **—spo·rad′i·cal·ly,** *adv.*

Spoonbill
(length 3 ft.)

spore (spôr), *n.* the tiny cell by means of which simple plants that have no seed reproduce. Molds, ferns, mushrooms, etc., reproduce by means of spores.

spor·ran (spor′ən), *n.* a large purse for men, made completely of fur and worn suspended from a belt in front of a kilt: part of the costume of the Scottish Highlands.

sport (spôrt), *n.* **1.** a game, athletic contest, or physical activity, often one performed out of doors, such as baseball, tennis, golf, hunting, etc. **2.** fun or play; recreation; pastime. **3.** playful trifling or jesting. **4.** mockery or ridicule. **5.** an object of mockery; laughingstock. **6.** *Informal.* a sportsman; one who plays fair. **7.** *Informal.* a person who leads a lively life and is willing to take risks. **—adj. 8.** suitable for outdoor or informal wear: *sport clothes.* **—v. 9.** to amuse oneself with some pastime or recreation. **10.** to play or frolic, as a child or an animal does. **11.** to trifle or treat lightly. **12.** *Informal.* to display; show off: *to sport a new fur coat.* **13. make sport of,** to mock or ridicule: *to make sport of someone who speaks with an accent.*

S, Sporran

sport·ing (spôr′ting), *adj.* **1.** taking part in, interested in, concerned with, or suitable for sports: *a sporting man; sporting equipment.* **2.** playing fair; sportsmanlike. **3.** willing to gamble; concerned with betting: *the sporting life of a famous resort.* **4.** *Informal.* involving risk, as in a game or sport: *to give a weaker opponent a sporting chance.*

spor·tive (spôr′tiv), *adj.* playful or frolicsome: *a sportive puppy.*

sports (spôrts), *adj.* **1.** of or concerning a sport or sports: *a sports festival.* **2.** suitable for sports or for informal, outdoor use: *sports jacket.*

sports·man (spôrts′mən), *n., pl.* **sports·men. 1.** a man who takes part in sports, esp. those such as hunting, fishing, etc. **2.** a person who is interested in sports. **3.** a person whose conduct in sports is characterized by fair play, courtesy, good temper, etc. **—sports′man·like′,** *adj.*

sports·man·ship (spôrts′mən ship′), *n.* **1.** skill in sports. **2.** sportsmanlike conduct, such as fair play, courtesy, being a cheerful loser, etc.

spot (spot), *n.* **1.** a mark, stain, or blot, made by dirt, blood, paint, ink, etc. **2.** a stain or blemish, as on a person's character or reputation. **3.** a small part of a surface or whole that differs from the rest in color, texture, etc.: *a bald spot.* **4.** a place or locality: *Washington once slept at this spot.* **5.** (on playing cards) a figure whose number determines the value and whose shape determines the suit. **—v.,** **spot·ted, spot·ting. 6.** to stain with spots; make a spot: *The grease spotted my dress. Ink spots badly.* **7.** to recognize; locate or identify by seeing: *to spot a familiar face in a crowd.* **—adj. 8.** made, paid, delivered, etc., at once: *a spot sale.* **9. hit the spot,** *Slang.* to satisfy a want or need, esp. to quench one's thirst: *That lemonade sure hits the spot.* **10. in a spot,** *Slang.* in a difficult or dangerous situation: *If you're in a spot, you can write home for money.* **11. on the spot, a.** at once; instantly: *We agreed on the spot.* **b.** at the place mentioned: *I was on the spot when the store opened.* **c.** *Slang.* in a difficult or embarrassing situation: *His asking to borrow money put me on the spot.*

spot·less (spot′lis), *adj.* **1.** free from any spot, stain, etc.: *a spotless kitchen.* **2.** pure; without blemish: *a spotless reputation.* **—spot′less·ly,** *adv.*

spot·light (spot′līt′), *n.* **1.** a strong light thrown upon a particular spot, as on a stage, for making some object or person especially clear to the view. **2.** the lamp that produces this light. **3.** public view or attention: *The famous actor is often in the spotlight.* **—v. 4.** to light with a spotlight. **5.** to call attention to: *Newspapers spotlighted the story all week.*

spot·ty (spot′ē), *adj.,* **spot·ti·er, spot·ti·est. 1.** full of, having, or occurring in spots: *spotty coloring.* **2.** irregular or uneven, esp. in quality: *spotty efforts.*

spouse (spous, spouz), *n.* a husband or wife.

spout (spout), *v.* **1.** to discharge forcibly, as a liquid, in a stream or jet: *The teapot was spouting steam.* **2.** to flow forth with force, as liquid or other material through a narrow opening: *Water spouted from the faucet.* **3.** *Informal.* to speak or state (something) lengthily in a pompous manner: *We spent an hour listening to him spout his theories.* —*n.* **4.** a pipe, tube, or channel through or by which liquid is discharged or poured: *the spout of a coffeepot.* **5.** a jet or continuous stream of liquid, steam, etc.

sprain (sprān), *n.* **1.** the violent straining or wrenching of the muscles or ligaments around a joint. **2.** the condition of being sprained. —*v.* **3.** to strain or wrench (the ankle, wrist, or other part of the body).

sprang (sprang), *v.* a past tense of **spring.**

sprat (sprat), *n.* a small, saltwater, European fish resembling a herring.

sprawl (sprôl), *v.* **1.** to be spread out in an unnatural or awkward manner: *The puppy's legs sprawled in all directions.* **2.** to sit or lie with the limbs spread out carelessly or awkwardly: *He sprawled across the bed.* **3.** to spread out in an irregular, straggling manner, as vines, buildings, handwriting, etc. —*n.* **4.** the act of sprawling; a sprawling posture.

spray[1] (sprā), *n.* **1.** water or other liquid blown or falling through the air in fine drops: *ocean spray.* **2.** a jet of liquid in fine drops, such as medicine, perfume, etc., discharged from an atomizer. **3.** a device, such as an atomizer, for discharging such liquid. **4.** a quantity of small objects discharged or flying through the air: *a spray of shattered glass; a spray of bullets.* —*v.* **5.** to apply as a spray: *to spray insecticide on plants.* **6.** to sprinkle or treat with a spray: *to spray the plants.* [from an early Dutch word *spraeien*]

spray[2] (sprā), *n.* a single shoot, twig, or branch of a plant with its leaves, flowers, or berries. [from Middle English]

spray′ gun′, a device consisting of a container with a nozzle through which liquid is sprayed.

spread (spred), *v.,* **spread, spread·ing. 1.** to stretch or open out; unfurl: *to spread a tablecloth; to spread wings.* **2.** to extend or lie stretched out: *The factories spread along the river.* **3.** to distribute or extend over an area of space or time: *to spread papers out on the table.* **4.** to make or become known; pass from a person or persons to others; communicate: *Don't spread rumors. Colds spread rapidly in winter.* **5.** to put in a sheet or layer: *to spread hay to dry.* **6.** to apply a thin layer of (something) as a cover, coating, etc.: *to spread butter on bread.* **7.** to cover with something: *to spread bread with jam.* **8.** to move or force apart: *He spread his arms out in welcome.* **9.** to set (a table). —*n.* **10.** the act of spreading: *the spread of knowledge.* **11.** stretch, expanse, or extent of something: *the spread of an eagle's wings; a spread of timber.* **12.** a cloth covering for a bed, table, or the like. **13.** *Informal.* an abundance of food set out on a table; feast. **14.** any food for spreading on bread, crackers, etc. **15.** (in a newspaper or magazine) an advertisement, photograph, or the like, covering several columns, a full page, etc.: *a two-page spread.* **16.** *Informal.* landed property, as a farm or ranch: *a spread of 1000 acres.* **17. spread oneself thin,** to attempt more activities at one time than can be done

well: *You're spreading yourself thin joining so many clubs.*

spree (sprē), *n.* **1.** a lively frolic or outing. **2.** a spell of drinking to intoxication.

sprig (sprig), *n.* a shoot, twig, or small branch of a plant.

spright·ly (sprīt′lē), *adj.,* **spright·li·er, spright·li·est.** spirited, lively, or gay. —**spright′li·ness,** *n.*

spring (spring), *v.,* **sprang** (sprang), **sprung** (sprung), **spring·ing. 1.** to rise, leap, or move suddenly upward, forward, or outward: *to spring into the air.* **2.** to be released quickly from a confined position, as by elastic force: *The trap sprang shut.* **3.** to cause to fly back, move, act, etc.: *to spring a lock.* **4.** to appear suddenly, come into being, or arise (often fol. by up): *New businesses sprang up in the town. Tears sprang to her eyes.*

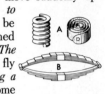

Springs
A, Coil; B, Leaf

5. to develop by or as if by splitting or cracking: *The boat sprang a leak.* **6.** to come into being by growth; be descended: *Oaks spring from acorns. He springs from a prominent family.* **7.** to originate, as from a source or cause. **8.** to bring out, produce, make, etc., suddenly: *to spring a joke on a friend.* —*n.* **9.** a leap, jump, or bound. **10.** an elastic or bouncing quality or movement: *There is a spring in his walk.* **11.** an elastic device, such as a strip of coiled wire, that recovers its shape after being compressed, bent, etc. **12.** the season between winter and summer, usually from March 21 to June 21. **13.** a flow of water coming from the earth, forming a small stream or standing as a pool. **14.** a source or cause of something: *a spring of inspiration.* **15.** the first or freshest stage; a period of growth: *the spring of life.* —*adj.* **16.** of or concerning the season of spring: *spring flowers; a new spring hat.*

spring·board (spring′bôrd′), *n.* **1.** a flexible board used in vaulting, tumbling, or diving. **2.** *Informal.* something that supplies the moving force or conditions for a beginning or change; a point of departure: *Hard work was his springboard to success.*

spring·bok (spring′bok′), *n.* a gazelle of southern Africa, noted for its habit of springing into the air when frightened.

spring′er span′iel (spring′ər), a medium-sized spaniel, used for flushing and retrieving game.

Spring·field (spring′fēld′), *n.* **1.** a city in S Massachusetts. **2.** the capital city of Illinois, in the central part.

Springer spaniel
(18½ in. high
at shoulder)

spring′ tide′, the largest rise and fall of the tide, which occurs at or soon after the new or full moon.

spring·tide (spring′tīd′), *n.* another word for **springtime.**

spring·time (spring′tīm′), *n.* the season of spring.

spring·y (spring′ē), *adj.*, **spring·i·er, spring·i·est.** flexible, elastic, or bouncy: *He walks with a springy step.* —**spring′i·ness,** *n.*

sprin·kle (spring′kəl), *v.*, **sprin·kled, sprin·kling. 1.** to scatter in drops or particles: *to sprinkle water on the roses.* **2.** to spread over with drops or particles of liquid, powder, etc.: *to sprinkle the lawn.* **3.** to rain slightly: *It may sprinkle today.* —*n.* **4.** the act or an instance of sprinkling. **5.** a light rain. **6.** a small quantity or number.

sprink·ler (spring′klər), *n.* **1.** any of various devices for sprinkling, esp. one to which a hose is attached for watering a lawn. **2.** a person who sprinkles.

sprin·kling (spring′kling), *n.* a small quantity or number scattered here and there.

sprint (sprint), *v.* **1.** to race or move at full speed for a short distance, as in running or rowing. —*n.* **2.** a short race at full speed. —**sprint′er,** *n.*

S, Sprit

sprit (sprit), *n.* (on sailboats) a small pole that supports and extends a fore-and-aft sail from the mast.

sprite (sprīt), *n.* an elf, fairy, or goblin.

sprock·et (sprok′it), *n.* a wheel having teeth around the rim that interlock with a conveyor or power chain.

sprout (sprout), *v.* **1.** to begin to grow; shoot forth, as a plant from a seed. **2.** to cause to sprout: *The trees sprouted new leaves.* —*n.* **3.** a shoot of a plant.

Sprockets

spruce[1] (sprōōs), *n.* **1.** any of various cone-bearing, evergreen trees that have short needle-shaped leaves. **2.** the wood of any such tree. [from Middle English *Spruce,* another form of the name *Pruce* "Prussia," from which the timber of this tree was exported]

spruce[2] (sprōōs), *adj.*, **spruc·er, spruc·est. 1.** trim or neat in dress or appearance. —*v.*, **spruced, spruc·ing. 2.** to make spruce; make oneself spruce (often fol. by *up*): *Spruce up the children before the company arrives. He spruced up for his interview.* [short for *Spruce leather,* a fine smooth leather imported from Prussia. See *spruce*[1]]

sprung (sprung), *v.* a past tense and the past participle of **spring.**

spry (sprī), *adj.*, **spry·er** *or* **spri·er; spry·est** *or* **spri·est.** active, nimble, energetic, or lively. —**spry′ness,** *n.*

spud (spud), *n.* **1.** a tool resembling a spade, with a narrow blade, for digging up or cutting the roots of weeds. **2.** a tool resembling a chisel, for removing bark. **3.** *Informal.* a potato.

spume (spyōōm), *n.* **1.** foam, froth, or scum. —*v.*, **spumed, spum·ing. 2.** to foam or froth.

spun (spun), *v.* **1.** the past tense and past participle of **spin.** —*adj.* **2.** formed by or as if by spinning: *spun glass.*

spunk (spungk), *n. Informal.* pluck or spirit.

spur (spûr), *n.* **1.** a U-shaped device worn on the heel of a boot, having a pointed projection or a small wheel with points, for use by a rider in urging a horse forward. **2.** anything that urges on to action or achievement: *His past success was a spur to greater effort.* **3.** a ridge projecting from the main mountain range. **4.** a stiff, sharp, horny projection, as on the leg of a rooster. **5.** a short branch track leading from the main track of a railroad. —*v.*, **spurred, spur·ring. 6.** to pick with or as if with spurs; urge on: *to spur a horse; to spur oneself to greater effort.* **7. on the spur of the moment,** on an impulse; suddenly: *We decided to go on the spur of the moment.* **8. win one's spurs,** to win honor or success: *He won his spurs as captain of the team.*

Spurs

spu·ri·ous (spyoor′ē əs), *adj.* not genuine, authentic, or true; counterfeit: *a spurious Roman coin.*

spurn (spûrn), *v.* **1.** to reject with scorn: *to spurn an offer of assistance.* **2.** to kick away or out of the way.

spurt (spûrt), *v.* **1.** to gush suddenly in a stream or jet, as a liquid: *Oil spurted from the well.* **2.** to show sudden, usually increased, activity or energy for a short period: *The runners spurted forward in the last lap of the race.* —*n.* **3.** a sudden, forceful gush or jet, as of liquid. **4.** a marked increase of effort or activity for a short period. Also, **spirt.**

sput·nik (spoot′nik, sput′nik), *n.* any of several man-made satellites launched by the Soviet Union.

sput·ter (sput′ər), *v.* **1.** to make explosive, popping sounds: *The bacon sputtered in the pan.* **2.** to spit out drops of saliva, bits of food, etc., as when talking excitedly. **3.** to utter (words or sounds) in an excited, angry, or incoherent way: *The old man sputtered his objections at being disturbed.* —*n.* **4.** the act or sound of sputtering. **5.** explosive, confused talk.

spy (spī), *n., pl.* **spies. 1.** a person who keeps close and secret watch on the actions of others. **2.** a person employed by a government to obtain secret information about another country, esp. military information about an enemy. —*v.*, **spied, spy·ing. 3.** to observe secretively; act as a spy: *to spy on an enemy army.* **4.** to search for or find out by careful observation: *to spy out the solution to a puzzle.* **5.** to catch sight of suddenly: *to spy a rare bird overhead.*

spy·glass (spī′glas′), *n.* a small telescope.

Sq., 1. Squadron. **2.** Square (used in street names).

sq. ft., square foot; square feet.

sq. in., square inch; square inches.

sq. mi., square mile; square miles.

squab (skwob), *n., pl.* **squabs** *or* **squab.** a young pigeon.

squab·ble (skwob′əl), *v.*, **squab·bled, squab·bling. 1.** to quarrel, esp. over trifles. —*n.* **2.** a petty quarrel.

squad (skwod), *n.* **1.** the smallest military unit, usually ten men led by a sergeant. Several squads form a company. **2.** a small group of persons engaged in a common enterprise: *A squad of children raided the kitchen for cookies.* [from the French word *esquadre,* which comes from Spanish *escuadra* "squad," literally "a square" (from the square formation)]

squad·ron (skwod′rən), *n.* **1.** a portion of a naval fleet. **2.** a cavalry unit. **3.** (in the Air Force) a group of eight or more airplanes. **4.** a group of persons united together for some purpose.

squal·id (skwol′id), *adj.* **1.** filthy and repulsive, as from lack of care and cleanliness. **2.** wretched, miserable, or degraded.

squall¹ (skwôl), *n.* a sudden, violent gust of wind, often accompanied by rain, snow, or sleet. [perhaps from a special use of *squall²*]

squall² (skwôl), *v.* **1.** to cry or scream loudly or violently: *The hungry baby began to squall.* —*n.* **2.** the act or sound of squalling. [from Scandinavian]

squal·or (skwol′ər), *n.* the state or condition of being squalid.

squan·der (skwon′dər), *v.* to spend or use (money, time, etc.) extravagantly or wastefully (often fol. by *away*): *He squandered his income on gadgets.*

square (skwâr), *n.* **1.** a rectangle having all four sides of equal length. **2.** anything having this shape. **3.** an open area or plaza in a city or town. **4.** an instrument in the form of an L or a T, used for drawing right angles. **5.** (in mathematics) the product obtained when a number is multiplied by itself. **6.** *Slang.* a person who is conservative or behind the times in fads, ideas, manners, tastes, etc. —*v.*, **squared, squar·ing. 7.** to make square in form. **8.** to mark out in one or more squares or rectangles. **9.** (in mathematics) to multiply (a number) by itself. **10.** to form into a right angle or right angles. **11.** to even the score of (a contest). **12.** to set (the shoulders and back) erect so that they form an angle similar to a right angle. **13.** to make straight, level, or even: *Square the cloth on the table.* **14.** to agree or accord (often fol. by *with*): *His story does not square with the facts.* **15.** to pay off; settle (often fol. by *up*): *to square a debt.* —*adj.* **16.** formed with or as if with a right angle. **17.** noting any unit of area measurement having the form of a square and designated by a unit of linear measurement forming a side of the square: *One square foot is the area of a square one foot wide and one foot long.* **18.** having a solid, sturdy form: *a square jaw.* **19.** even, equal, or fair. **20.** *Informal.* substantial or satisfying: *a square meal.* **21.** *Slang.* conventional or behind the times: *square taste in music.* **22. square off,** to assume a posture for fighting, as in boxing: *The champion and the challenger squared off when the round began.*

square′ dance′, a dance by a set of couples arranged in a square or in some set form.

square′ knot′, a common knot that resembles two intertwined loops. See illus. at **knot.**

square-rigged (skwâr′rigd′), *adj.* (of sailing ships) having square sails as the principal sails.

square′ root′, a number that must be multiplied by itself to yield a particular number: *The square root of 16 is 4.*

squash¹ (skwosh), *v.* **1.** to press into a flat mass or pulp; crush or become crushed: *He squashed the flower under his heel.* **2.** to put down or suppress; quash: *to squash a rebellion.* —*n.* **3.** the fall of a heavy, soft body, or the sound such a fall makes. **4.** something squashed. **5.** a game for two or four persons, played with a ball and rackets on a court having four walls. [from an early French word *esquasser*]

squash² (skwosh), *n., pl.* **squash·es** *or* **squash.** the fruit of any of various gourdlike plants, used as a vegetable. [from the American Indian word *askútasquash,* literally "vegetables eaten green"]

squat (skwot), *v.,* **squat·ted** *or* **squat; squat·ting. 1.** to sit in a crouching position with the legs drawn up closely beneath or in front of the body. **2.** to settle without any right or title on another's land. **3.** to settle on public land in order to acquire a title to it. —*adj.* **4.** short or low and thick and broad: *a squat person.* **5.** being in a squatting position; crouching. —*n.* **6.** the act of squatting. **7.** a squatting position. —**squat′ter,** *n.*

squaw (skwô), *n.* (*Often Offensive*) a North American Indian woman, esp. a wife.

squawk (skwôk), *v.* **1.** to utter a loud, harsh cry, as a duck or other fowl when frightened. **2.** *Slang.* to complain loudly. —*n.* **3.** a loud, harsh cry or sound. **4.** *Slang.* a loud complaint.

squeak (skwēk), *n.* **1.** a short, sharp, shrill cry; a sharp, high-pitched sound. —*v.* **2.** to make such a sound: *The mouse squeaked.* **3. squeak by** (or **through**), to win, succeed, etc., by a very narrow margin: *He managed to squeak by in the exam.*

squeak·y (skwē′kē), *adj.,* **squeak·i·er, squeak·i·est.** squeaking; tending to squeak: *squeaky new shoes.*

squeal (skwēl), *n.* **1.** a prolonged, sharp, shrill cry, as of pain, fear, surprise, etc. —*v.* **2.** to utter a squeal.

squeam·ish (skwē′mish), *adj.* **1.** easily shocked; prudish. **2.** easily made sick at the stomach; easily disgusted: *She's squeamish at the sight of blood.* —**squeam′ish·ly,** *adv.* —**squeam′ish·ness,** *n.*

squeeze (skwēz), *v.,* **squeezed, squeez·ing. 1.** to press forcibly together; apply pressure; compress. **2.** to press (something) in order to extract juice, sap, or the like: *to squeeze an orange.* **3.** to force out by pressure: *to squeeze juice from a lemon.* **4.** to thrust forcibly; cram: *He squeezed three suits into the suitcase.* **5.** to give (someone) a hug; embrace. **6.** to force a way (usually fol. by *through, in, out,* etc.): *to squeeze into a crowded room.* —*n.* **7.** the act or an instance of squeezing. **8.** a clasping of one's hand around another's hand, arm, etc., as a token of affection. **9.** a hug or close embrace. —**squeez′er,** *n.*

squelch (skwelch), *v.* **1.** to crush down; squash. **2.** *Informal.* to silence or suppress, as with a crushing argument or reply.

squib (skwib), *n.* **1.** a short and witty or sarcastic saying or piece of writing. **2.** a firework that burns with a hissing noise before exploding. **3.** a firecracker broken in the middle.

act, āble, dâre, ärt; ebb, ēqual; if, īce; hot, ōver, ôrder; oil; bŏok; ōōze; out; up, ûrge; ə = *a* as in *alone;* ᵊ as in *button* (but′ᵊn), *fire* (fī³r); chief; shoe; thin; ŧħat; zh as in *measure* (mezh′ər). See full key inside cover.

squid (skwid), *n., pl.* **squids** *or* **squid.** a sea animal having a slender body and ten arms, or tentacles.

squint (skwint), *v.* **1.** to look with the eyes partly closed: *to squint at the bright lights.* **2.** to look or glance sideways. **3.** to be cross-eyed. —*n.* **4.** the act or an instance of squinting. **5.** the condition of being cross-eyed.

squire (skwīʳr), *n.* **1.** (in England) a country gentleman, esp. the chief landowner in a district. **2.** a young man of noble birth who, as an aspirant to knighthood, served a knight; esquire. **3.** a man who escorts a woman. **4.** (in the U.S.) a title applied to a justice of the peace or local judge of a rural district or small town. —*v.*, **squired, squir·ing.** **5.** to escort (a woman), as to a dance.

squirm (skwûrm), *v.* **1.** to wriggle; turn or twist the body, as from discomfort, pain, etc. **2.** to feel or show discomfort, as from embarrassment. —*n.* **3.** a squirming movement.

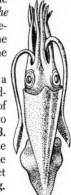

Squid
(total length
8 in.)

squir·rel (skwûr′əl), *n., pl.* **squir·rels** *or* **squir·rel.** **1.** a small, usually reddish-brown or gray animal, that has a bushy tail and lives in or among trees. **2.** the pelt or fur of such an animal.

squirt (skwûrt), *v.* **1.** to eject liquid in a jet from a narrow opening: *The hose squirted all over us.* **2.** to cause (liquid) to come out in a jet: *Squirt the water over that way.* **3.** to wet with a liquid that is squirted: *Don't squirt me with that hose!* —*n.* **4.** the act of squirting. **5.** a spurt or jet, as of water. **6.** an instrument for squirting. **7.** *Informal.* a small or young person who is impudent or self-important.

Gray squirrel
(total length
21 in.)

sq. yd., square yard; square yards.

Sr, *Chem.* the symbol for **strontium.**

Sr., **1.** Senior. **2.** Sir.

Sri Lan·ka (srē′ lang′kə), an island republic in the Indian Ocean, S of India. 25,332 sq. mi. *Cap.:* Colombo. Former name, **Ceylon.** —**Sri′ Lan′kan.**

INDIA
Madras
BAY OF BENGAL
ARABIAN SEA
Sri Lanka
Colombo
INDIAN OCEAN

SS, **1.** steamship. **2.** supersonic.

SSE, south-southeast. Also, **S.S.E.**

SST, supersonic transport.

SSW, south-southwest. Also, **S.S.W.**

-st, another form of the suffix -est: *latest; hadst; dost.*

St., **1.** Saint. **2.** Strait. **3.** Street.

Sta., Station. Also, **sta.**

stab (stab), *v.*, **stabbed, stab·bing.** **1.** to pierce, wound, or thrust with or as if with a pointed weapon: *He stabbed the shark with his knife.* **2.** to hurt (the feelings): *Their misery stabbed his conscience.* —*n.* **3.** a thrust with or as if with a pointed weapon. **4.** a

wound made by stabbing. **5.** a sudden, brief, usually painful, sensation: *a stab of pain.* **6.** *Informal.* a brief attempt; try: *to make a stab at an answer.*

sta·bil·i·ty (stə bil′i tē), *n., pl.* **sta·bil·i·ties.** **1.** the state or quality of being stable. **2.** steadiness or constancy, as of purpose or character. **3.** firmness in position. **4.** permanence; continuance without change.

sta·bi·lize (stā′bə līz′), *v.,* **sta·bi·lized, sta·bi·liz·ing.** **1.** to make or hold stable, firm, or steadfast. **2.** to maintain at a given level or quantity: *to stabilize the price of food.* —**sta′bi·liz′er,** *n.*

sta·ble[1] (stā′bəl), *n.* **1.** a building in which horses, cattle, etc., are fed and kept. **2.** (in horse racing) the group of horses belonging to a single owner or establishment. —*v.,* **sta·bled, sta·bling.** **3.** to put or lodge in a stable. [from the Old French word *estable,* which comes from Latin *stabulum* "standing room"]

sta·ble[2] (stā′bəl), *adj.* **1.** able or likely to last; firmly established; enduring; permanent: *a stable government.* **2.** not likely to fall or give way, as a structure, support, foundation, etc. **3.** resistant to sudden change or fluctuation: *a stable economy.* **4.** steadfast or reliable. [from the Old French word *estable,* which comes from Latin *stabilis* "steady, firm"]

stac·ca·to (stə kä′tō), *adj.* (in music) played or sung so that each note is sounded as briefly as possible and there is a clear break between notes (opposite of *legato*).

stack (stak), *n.* **1.** a large, usually conical, pile of hay, straw, or the like. **2.** a more or less orderly pile or heap: *a stack of books.* **3.** Often, **stacks.** a set of bookshelves ranged one above the other, as in a library. **4.** a smokestack. **5.** a group of rifles placed on their butts and arranged to form a cone. —*v.* **6.** to pile, arrange, or place in a stack. **7.** to arrange (playing cards) so as to cheat: *He stacked the deck and won.* **8. stack up,** *Slang.* **a.** to compare: *How does our team stack up with yours?* **b.** to appear to be true: *His story doesn't stack up.* —**stack′er,** *n.*

Staccato notes

sta·di·um (stā′dē əm), *n.* a sports arena, usually oval or horseshoe-shaped, with tiers of seats.

staff (staf), *n., pl.* for defs. 1–3, 7 **staves** (stāvz) *or* **staffs;** for defs. 4–6 **staffs. 1.** a stick, pole, or rod, for aid in walking, for use as a weapon, etc. **2.** a pole on which a flag is hung. **3.** something that sustains: *Bread is the staff of life.* **4.** a group of assistants to a manager, chief, or executive. **5.** a group of persons, such as employees, who work together on some task. **6.** a body of officers of an army concerned with planning rather than with actual participation in combat. **7.** Also, **stave.** a set of five horizontal lines, together with the corresponding four spaces be-

Stag (red deer)
(4 ft. high at shoulder)

tween them, on which music is written.

stag (stag), *n.* **1.** a full-grown male deer. **2.** *Informal.* a man unaccompanied by a woman at a social gathering. —*adj.* **3.** for or of men only: *a stag dinner.*

stage (stāj), *n.* **1.** a single step, phase, period, or degree in a process, development, or series: *an early stage of life.* **2.** a raised platform, as for speakers, actors in a play, or the like. **3. the stage,** the theater, drama, or the acting profession. **4.** the scene or plan of an action: *France has been the stage of many famous battles.* **5.** a stagecoach. **6.** a place of rest or stopping place on a journey. **7.** the distance between two places of rest on a journey. **8.** a section of a rocket containing a rocket engine, usually separated from other sections of a rocket when its fuel is exhausted. —*v.,* **staged, stag·ing. 9.** to present on a stage: *to stage a play.* **10.** to plan, organize, or carry out (an activity): *The students staged a sit-in.*

stage·coach (stāj′kōch′), *n.* a horse-drawn coach traveling regularly over a fixed route with passengers, parcels, etc.

Stagecoach

stag·ger (stag′ər), *v.* **1.** to walk or move unsteadily. **2.** to cause to reel or become unsteady: *This weight would stagger an elephant!* **3.** to cause to waver or begin to doubt; shock; astonish: *His first view through a big telescope staggered him.* **4.** to arrange in a zigzag order on each side of a center: *The captain staggered his troops along the road.* **5.** to arrange otherwise than at the same time, esp. in a series of alternating or overlapping intervals: *to stagger lunch hours.* —*n.* **6.** the act of staggering; reeling or tottering movement. **7. staggers,** a disease in horses, cattle, etc., that causes blindness, staggering, sudden falling, etc. —**stag′ger·ing·ly,** *adv.*

stag·nant (stag′nənt), *adj.* **1.** not flowing or running, as water, air, etc; stale or foul from standing still. **2.** sluggish, dull, or inactive: *a stagnant business.*

stag·nate (stag′nāt), *v.,* **stag·nat·ed, stag·nat·ing.** to make or become stagnant. —**stag·na′tion,** *n.*

staid (stād), *adj.* **1.** of settled or dignified character; not flighty: *a staid way of speaking; staid behavior.* —*v.* **2.** a past tense and past participle of **stay**[1].

stain (stān), *n.* **1.** a spot or discoloration: *an ink stain.* **2.** a cause of reproach; blemish: *a stain on one's honor.* **3.** a dye for coloring fabrics, woods, etc. —*v.* **4.** to make or become soiled, spotted, or discolored: *You have stained your dress. This white cloth stains easily.* **5.** to color or dye (cloth, wood, etc.) with a stain. **6.** to bring reproach upon; blemish.

stain·less (stān′lis), *adj.* **1.** having no stain; spotless. **2.** resistant to stains, rust, or the like: *stainless steel.*

—*n.* **3.** knives, forks, etc., of stainless steel.

stair (stâr), *n.* **1.** one of a flight or series of steps for going from one level to another, as in a building. **2. stairs,** a flight or series of such steps: *He ran all the way up the stairs.* **3.** a stairway: *a winding stair.*

stair·case (stâr′kās′), *n.* a flight of stairs with its framework, banisters, etc.

stair·way (stâr′wā′), *n.* a passageway from one level of a building to another by a series of stairs.

stake (stāk), *n.* **1.** a post pointed at one end for driving into the ground as part of a fence, support for a plant, etc. **2.** a post to which a person is tied for execution, usually by burning. **3. the stake,** execution by burning: *Joan of Arc was sentenced to the stake.* **4.** a bet or wager in a game, race, or contest. **5.** Often, **stakes.** a prize or reward, as in a contest. **6.** a share, interest, or investment: *He has a large stake in the company.* **7.** any personal involvement or concern: *Parents have a big stake in their children's happiness.* —*v.,* **staked, stak·ing. 8.** to mark with or as if with stakes (often fol. by *off* or *out*): *He staked out the boundaries of the garden.* **9.** to fasten to or support with a stake or stakes: *to stake tomato vines.* **10.** to risk or bet, as upon an uncertain outcome or the result of a game: *to stake one's reputation.* **11.** *Informal.* to furnish (someone) with what is necessary, esp. money: *He staked me to a meal.* **12. pull up stakes,** *Informal.* to leave one's job, place of residence, etc.: *They pulled up stakes and moved West.*

sta·lac·tite (stə lak′tīt), *n.* an icicle-shaped deposit, usually of lime, hanging from the roof of a cave or the like, and formed by the dripping of water.

sta·lag·mite (stə lag′mīt), *n.* a tall, often pointed deposit, usually of lime, formed on the floor of a cave or the like by dripping water.

stale (stāl), *adj.,* **stal·er, stal·est. 1.** not fresh; flat, as beverages; dry or hardened, as bread. **2.** having lost interest; trite; not new: *a stale joke.* **3.** having lost freshness, vigor, intelligence, initiative, or the like, as from strain, boredom, etc.: *He had grown stale on the job.* —*v.,* **staled, stal·ing. 4.** to make or become stale. —**stale′ness,** *n.*

A, Stalactite
B, Stalagmite

stale·mate (stāl′māt′), *n.* **1.** (in chess) a position in which a player cannot move any piece except his king and cannot move his king without putting it in check, the result being a draw **2.** any situation in which no action can be ta'. . . —*v.,* **stale·mat·ed, stale·mat·ing. 3.** to bring to a stalemate or standstill.

Sta·lin (stä′lin), *n.* **Joseph V.,** 1879–1953, Soviet Communist leader: chief of state 1924–1953.

Sta·lin·grad (stä′lin grad′), *n.* a former name of **Volgograd.**

stalk[1] (stôk), *n.* **1.** the stem or any slender supporting part of a plant. **2.** a stem or slender supporting part of anything. [from the Middle English word *stalke*, which comes from Old English *stæla*]

stalk² (stôk), *v.* **1.** to pursue or approach (a person, animal, etc.) stealthily: *to stalk a deer.* **2.** to walk with measured, stiff, or haughty steps: *He stalked away without saying good-by.* **3.** to go through in a steady or sinister manner: *Famine stalked the nation.* —*n.* **4.** the act of stalking. [from the Middle English word *stalken*, which comes from Old English *(be)stealcian* "to move stealthily"]

stall¹ (stôl), *n.* **1.** a compartment in a stable or shed for an animal, such as a cow or horse. **2.** a booth or stand in which merchandise is displayed or sold or some business is carried on: *a butcher's stall.* **3.** a seat in the choir of a church. **4.** a rectangular space marked off, as for parking a car in a parking lot. **5.** a chairlike seat in a theater, esp. one in the front section. —*v.* **6.** to put or keep in a stall. **7.** to stop or cause to stop, esp. unintentionally: *to stall a motor.* [from the Old English word *steall*]

stall² (stôl), *Informal.* —*n.* **1.** a ruse or trick used to delay or deceive. —*v.* **2.** to delay or put off, esp. by evasion or deception: *The thief stalled the police so that his accomplice could get away.* [from an Old English word meaning "decoy"] —**stall′er,** *n.*

stal·lion (stal′yən), *n.* a full-grown male horse, esp. one used for breeding.

stal·wart (stôl′wərt), *adj.* **1.** strongly built; sturdy and robust. **2.** strong and brave: *a stalwart knight.* **3.** firm or steadfast: *a stalwart supporter of the UN.*

sta·men (stā′mən), *n., pl.* **sta·mens** *or* **stam·i·na** (stam′ə nə). the pollen-bearing organ of a flower, consisting of the anther and its stem. See illus. at **flower.**

stam·i·na (stam′ə nə), *n.* physical strength; power to endure disease, fatigue, etc.

stam·mer (stam′ər), *v.* **1.** to speak with involuntary breaks or pauses, or with repetitions of syllables or sounds. **2.** to say with a stammer (sometimes fol. by *out*): *He stammered out his excuse.* —*n.* **3.** the act or an instance of stammering. —**stam′mer·er,** *n.* —**stam′mer·ing·ly,** *adv.*

stamp (stamp), *v.* **1.** to strike forcibly with a downward thrust of the foot. **2.** to bring the foot down forcibly, as in crushing something, expressing rage, etc. **3.** to extinguish, crush, suppress, etc., by or as if by stamping with the foot (often fol. by *out*): *to stamp out a fire; to stamp out a rebellion.* **4.** to walk with heavy, resounding steps: *He stamped out of the room in anger.* **5.** to mark or imprint with a design, word, etc.: *to stamp cloth with colorful patterns.* **6.** to mark or imprint (a design, word, etc.) on: *to stamp one's initials on a document.* **7.** to put a stamp on (a letter, envelope, etc.). **8.** to characterize, distinguish, or reveal: *His earliest work stamped him as a great writer.* —*n.* **9.** the act or an instance of stamping. **10.** a postage stamp. **11.** a die or block with engraved letters, a design, seal, or the like, for imprinting: *a rubber stamp.* **12.** the letters, design, figures, or the like, made with such a die or block. **13.** an official mark indicating genuineness, validity, etc., or pay-

ment of a fee or charge. **14.** a trading stamp. **15.** an instrument or machine for stamping, crushing, or pounding ore or other material. **16.** character, kind, or type: *a man of serious stamp.* —**stamp′er,** *n.*

stam·pede (stam pēd′), *n.* **1.** a sudden, frenzied rush or flight of a herd of frightened animals, esp. horses or cattle. **2.** a general headlong rush or flight, as of a crowd of people: *a stampede to the bargain counter.* —*v.,* **stam·ped·ed, stam·ped·ing. 3.** to scatter or flee in a stampede. **4.** to cause to stampede. **5.** to rush or overrun: *Customers stampeded the stores.* [from the Spanish word *estampar* "to stamp"]

stance (stans), *n.* **1.** the position of the body while standing; posture: *the proud stance of a victor.* **2.** a mental or emotional position adopted in respect to something: *The nation assumed a cautious stance in its foreign policy.* **3.** (in sports) the position of the feet, as when one is golfing or batting a ball.

stanch¹ (stônch, stänch), *v.* **1.** to stop the flow of (a liquid, esp. blood). **2.** to stop the flow of blood or other liquid from (a wound, leak, etc.). Also, **staunch.** [from the Old French word *estanchier* "to close, stop"]

stanch² (stônch, stänch), *adj.* another spelling of **staunch².**

stand (stand), *v.,* **stood** (stŏŏd), **stand·ing. 1.** to assume or keep an upright position on the feet. **2.** to set upright; place: *Stand the chair by the lamp.* **3.** (of things) to be in an upright position. **4.** to have a certain height when upright on the feet: *He stands six feet tall.* **5.** to take a certain position or place: *to stand aside.* **6.** to maintain a steadfast position or attitude, as of support or opposition: *to stand for free speech; to stand as sponsor for someone.* **7.** to be placed or situated: *The house stood two blocks from the school.* **8.** to resist change or decay; remain whole or erect (often fol. by *up*): *The old building has stood up well.* **9.** to continue in force; remain valid: *The agreement stands as signed.* **10.** to remain unchanged or unused: *The bicycle stood in the basement all winter.* **11.** to be or remain in a certain state or condition: *He stands in need of help.* **12.** to be in a certain position or rank: *He stands third in line for promotion.* **13.** to cease moving; halt; stop. **14.** to undergo or submit to: *to stand trial.* **15.** to endure or undergo without harm or without giving way: *My eyes can't stand this glare.* **16.** (of ships) to take a particular course at sea or move in a certain direction: *The ship stood to the south.* **17.** to perform the duty of or take part in as one's job or duty: *to stand guard.* **18.** to treat or pay for: *to stand the cost of a dinner.* —*n.* **19.** the act of standing; a taking or remaining in an upright position. **20.** a stop or halt. **21.** a determined effort for or against something, esp. a defensive effort: *the last stand of weary troops.* **22.** a policy, opinion, or attitude taken or maintained: *We must take a stand on these issues.* **23.** the place in which a person or thing stands; station. **24. the stand,** the place occupied by a person giving testimony in court. **25.** a raised platform, as for a speaker, a band, etc. **26. stands,** a raised section of seats for spectators at a race track, arena, or the like; grandstand. **27.** a framework on or in which articles are put: *a hat stand.* **28.** a piece of furniture, such as a small table, on or in which to put articles (often used in combination): *a nightstand; a washstand.* **29.** a stall, booth, or counter where articles are displayed for sale or business is carried on: *a fruit stand.* **30.** the trees, crops, or the like, growing in a certain area: *a stand of oaks.* **31. stand a chance,** to have a chance or possibility: *We don't stand a chance of winning.* **32. stand by, a.** to support; show confidence in: *to stand by one's friends.* **b.** to continue to honor or accept: *to stand by an agreement.* **c.** to wait, esp. in readiness: *Stand by for an announcement.* **33. stand for, a.** to be a symbol of; represent: *P.S. stands for "postcript."* **b.** to be in favor of; advocate: *Our candidate stands for lower taxes.* **c.** *Informal.* to allow or tolerate: *I won't stand for any more sass!* **34. stand out, a.** to extend outward; project; stick out: *The balcony stands out from the wall.* **b.** to attract notice; be prominent: *a pretty girl who stands out in a crowd.* **35. stand up, a.** to rise to or remain in a standing position: *A man always stands up when being introduced.* **b.** to remain strong, convincing, or durable: *Wool stands up better than silk. His case will never stand up in court.* **c.** *Slang.* to fail to keep an appointment with (someone): *We had a date, but he stood me up.* **36. stand up for,** to give support to; defend: *to stand up for states' rights.* **37. stand up to,** to meet or deal with fearlessly; confront: *to stand up to a bully.*

stand·ard (stan/dərd), *n.* **1.** anything that serves as a rule or principle for making judgments or as a basis for comparison; an approved model: *standards of good writing.* **2.** anything authorized as the measure of quantity or quality: *a standard of weight.* **3.** a flag indicating the presence of the ruler of a state or a public official. **4.** a flag or emblem of an army, navy, nation, etc. **5.** an upright support, such as a timber, bar, or rod: *the standard of a lamp.* —*adj.* **6.** serving as a basis of weight, measure, value, comparison, or judgment: *a standard weight.* **7.** of recognized excellence or authority: *a standard author.* **8.** usual or common; widely used or accepted: *His standard lunch was a sandwich.* **9.** conforming in pronunciation, grammar, vocabulary, etc., to the usage considered correct and acceptable by good speakers and writers of a language.

stand·ard·ize (stan/dər dīz/), *v.,* **stand·ard·ized, stand·ard·iz·ing. 1.** to make of a standard size, weight, quality, or the like: *to standardize manufactured parts.* **2.** to regulate or test by a standard. —**stand/ard·i·za/tion,** *n.*

stand-in (stand/in/), *n.* a person who substitutes for another, esp. a person who substitutes for a motion-picture star during the preparation of lighting, cameras, etc.

stand·ing (stan/ding), *n.* **1.** rank or status; personal position; reputation; credit: *a person of good stand-*

ing. **2.** length of existence, service, membership, experience, etc.: *a friend of long standing.* **3.** the act or position of a person or thing that stands.

Stan·dish (stan/dish), *n.* **Miles** (mīlz), c1584–1656, leader in Plymouth Colony, born in England.

stand·point (stand/point/), *n.* **1.** the point or place where a person stands to view something. **2.** the mental position or attitude from which a person views and judges things; point of view.

stand·still (stand/stil/), *n.* an absence of movement or action; stop; halt.

stank (stangk), *v.* a past tense of **stink.**

stan·za (stan/zə), *n.* an arrangement of a certain number of lines, usually four or more, forming a division of a poem.

sta·ple¹ (stā/pəl), *n.* **1.** a short piece of wire that is bent so as to bind together papers, sections of a book, or the like. **2.** a similar U-shaped piece of metal or wire with pointed ends for driving into a surface to hold a hook, pin, bolt, or the like. —*v.,* **sta·pled, sta·pling. 3.** to fasten by a staple or staples. [from the Old English word *stapol* "support, post"] —**sta/pler,** *n.*

sta·ple² (stā/pəl), *n.* **1.** a principal raw material or commodity grown or manufactured in a locality: *Tobacco is the staple of several Southern states.* **2.** a basic or necessary item of food: *She bought salt, flour, sugar, and other staples.* **3.** the fiber of wool, cotton, or flax. **4.** a basic or principal item, feature, element, or part: *Cowboy dramas are a staple on television.* —*adj.* **5.** chief or prominent among the products of a country or district; chiefly dealt in or consumed. **6.** basic, chief, or principal: *staple industries.* [from the Middle English word *stapel,* which comes from Dutch]

star (stär), *n.* **1.** any of the heavenly bodies, except the moon and planets, appearing as luminous points in the sky at night. **2.** a figure having five or six points radiating from a center. **3.** (in printing) an asterisk. **4.** a person who has a leading part in a theatrical performance or other entertainment. **5.** a person who is prominent in some field: *a baseball star.* —*adj.* **6.** prominent or distinguished: *a star basketball player; a star reporter.* —*v.,* **starred, star·ring. 7.** to set with or as if with stars; decorate with stars. **8.** to feature as a star: *The movie will star a famous actor.* **9.** to appear as a star: *He will star in the new movie.*

star·board (stär/bərd), *n.* **1.** the right-hand side of a vessel or aircraft when one is facing forward (opposite of *port*). —*adj.* **2.** of, concerning, or located to the starboard. —*adv.* **3.** toward the right side. —*v.* **4.** to turn (the helm) to starboard.

starch (stärch), *n.* **1.** a white, tasteless, solid substance, containing carbon, hydrogen, and oxygen, and found in the seeds, tubers, and other parts of plants. **2.** a preparation of this substance used to stiffen fabrics in laundering. —*v.* **3.** to stiffen or treat with starch, such as a shirt collar.

starch·y (stär′chē), *adj.*, **starch·i·er, starch·i·est. 1.** of or like starch. **2.** containing starch. **3.** stiffened with starch. **4.** stiff and formal, as in manner. —**starch′i·ness,** *n.*

stare (stâr), *v.*, **stared, star·ing. 1.** to gaze fixedly and intently, esp. with the eyes wide open, as from curiosity, amazement, etc. **2.** to stare at. **3.** to be boldly conspicuous; stand out. —*n.* **4.** a fixed look with the eyes wide open: *She greeted him with a cold stare.*

Starfish
(diameter to 8 in.)

star·fish (stär′fish′), *n., pl.* **star·fish·es** *or* **star·fish.** a small sea animal having a body shaped like a star, with five or more rays or arms.

stark (stärk), *adj.* **1.** utter, downright, or complete: *stark madness.* **2.** extremely simple, bare, or severe: *a stark interior in a house.* **3.** harsh, grim, or desolate: *a stark landscape.* **4.** stiff or rigid in substance, muscles, etc.; rigid in death. —*adv.* **5.** utterly, completely, or quite: *stark mad.*

Starling
(length 8½ in.)

star·light (stär′līt′), *n.* **1.** the light coming from the stars. —*adj.* **2.** of or concerning starlight.

star·ling (stär′ling), *n.* any of numerous birds introduced into North America from Europe, often having a black body and traveling in large flocks.

star·lit (stär′lit), *adj.* lighted by the stars: *a starlit night.*

star·ry (stär′ē), *adj.*, **star·ri·er, star·ri·est. 1.** full of or lighted by stars: *a starry night.* **2.** of, concerning, or proceeding from stars. **3.** shining like stars: *bright, starry eyes.*

Stars′ and Stripes′, the flag of the United States, having 13 horizontal stripes of red and white, representing the first group of states, and a blue field with 50 stars, representing the present states. Also, **Old Glory.**

Star′-Span·gled Ban′ner, The (stär′spang′-gəld), **1.** the Stars and Stripes. **2.** the national anthem of the United States.

start (stärt), *v.* **1.** to begin or set out on a course of action, procedure, etc.: *to start on a journey; to start on time.* **2.** to set moving or acting; set in operation: *to start a car; to start a fire.* **3.** to enter upon or begin: *to start writing a letter.* **4.** to establish or found: *to start a new business.* **5.** to spring or move suddenly from a position or place: *The rabbit started from the bush.* **6.** to rouse (game) from a place; flush. **7.** to give a sudden jerk, jump, or twitch, as from surprise, pain, etc.: *The loud explosion made us start.* **8.** to protrude: *eyes seeming to start from their sockets.* —*n.* **9.** the beginning of an action, journey, etc.; a setting in motion. **10.** a place from which something begins, as a line marking the beginning point of a race. **11.** a time at which something begins. **12.** the first part of anything: *The start of the book was interesting.* **13.** a sudden springing movement from a po-

sition. **14.** a sudden involuntary jerking movement of the body: *to awake with a start.* **15.** the lead or advantage given to or held by the person or thing that starts first, as at a race or competition. **16.** a chance, opportunity, aid, etc., given to a person starting on a career: *The bride's parents gave the couple a start by buying them a house.* **17. start in,** to begin; commence: *You can start in by sweeping the garage.* **18. start out, a.** to begin a trip: *We started out at six in the morning.* **b.** to begin anything, esp. a career: *He started out as a delivery boy.*

start·er (stär′tər), *n.* **1.** a person or thing that starts. **2.** a person who gives the signal to begin, as for a race, the running of a train or bus, etc.

star·tle (stär′təl), *v.*, **star·tled, star·tling. 1.** to frighten or disturb suddenly. **2.** to cause (someone) to start, by or as if by a sudden shock.

star·va·tion (stär vā′shən), *n.* the act or state of starving; condition of being starved.

starve (stärv), *v.*, **starved, starv·ing. 1.** to suffer or die from lack of food or nourishment. **2.** to cause to suffer or die from lack of food or nourishment. **3.** to subdue, or force to some condition or action, by hunger: *to starve a surrounded fort into surrender.* **4.** to feel a strong need or desire (usually fol. by *for*): *a child who is starved for affection.* [from the Old English word *steorfan* "to die"]

state (stāt), *n.* **1.** the condition of a person or thing, as with respect to manner of existence, circumstances, structure, phase, etc.: *the state of one's health; a liquid state.* **2.** the style of living suitable to a person of high rank and wealth: *to travel in state.* **3.** a particular condition of mind or feeling: *to be in an excited state.* **4.** a nation or its government: *the state of Italy.* **5.** one of the political units or commonwealths that together make up a federal union: *California is a state of the U.S.* **6.** the territory or territories of a state or nation. —*adj.* **7.** accompanied by or involving ceremony: *a state dinner.* —*v.*, **stat·ed, stat·ing. 8.** to set forth definitely or specifically in speech or writing; declare; say: *to state one's position on an issue; to state one's name and age.*

stat·ed (stā′tid), *adj.* fixed or settled: *a stated price.*

state·house (stāt′hous′), *n., pl.* **state·hous·es** (stāt′-hou′ziz). *(sometimes cap.)* the building in which a state legislature sits; the capitol of a state.

state·ly (stāt′lē), *adj.*, **state·li·er, state·li·est. 1.** majestic or imposing: *a stately home.* **2.** extremely dignified: *a stately procession.* —**state′li·ness,** *n.*

state·ment (stāt′mənt), *n.* **1.** something stated: *This statement is false.* **2.** a report, announcement, etc., in speech or writing, setting forth facts, particulars, etc. **3.** the act or manner of stating something.

Stat′en Is′land (stat′ᵊn), *n.* an island at the mouth of the Hudson River: forming Richmond borough of New York City. 64½ sq. mi. —**Stat′en Is′lander.**

state·room (stāt′rōōm′, -rŏŏm′), *n.* a private room or compartment on a train or ship.

states·man (stāts′mən), *n., pl.* **states·men.** a man who is experienced or has great ability in directing the affairs of a government.

stat·ic (stat′ik), *adj.* **1.** not moving or changing; fixed. **2.** of or referring to the electricity contained in or given off by charged bodies. **3.** (in physics) acting by weight alone without producing motion: *static pressure.* —*n.* **4.** electricity contained in or given off by charged bodies or by the atmosphere. **5.** interference, such as a crackling noise, with radio or radar signals as a result of electrical disturbances. —**stat′i·cal·ly,** *adv.*

stat·ics (stat′iks), *n. (used as sing.)* the branch of mechanics that deals with bodies at rest or forces in equilibrium.

sta·tion (stā′shən), *n.* **1.** a place or position in which a person or thing stands or is assigned to stand: *The sentry was at his station.* **2.** a regular stopping place, or the building or buildings at such a stopping place: *a bus station.* **3.** the headquarters of certain public services: *a police station.* **4.** a place equipped for a certain kind of work, service, or the like: *a gasoline station.* **5.** rank or dignity; social standing: *persons of high station.* **6.** (in radio or television companies) the studios, offices, buildings, or equipment used for broadcasts. —*v.* **7.** to assign a station to; place or post in a station: *His unit is stationed in Alaska.*

sta·tion·ar·y (stā′shə ner′ē), *adj.* **1.** standing still; having a fixed position; not moving or movable. **2.** remaining in the same condition or state; not changing: *Prices have remained stationary for a week.*

sta·tion·er (stā′shə nər), *n.* a person who sells stationery.

sta·tion·er·y (stā′shə ner′ē), *n.* **1.** paper and envelopes, esp. for writing letters. **2.** writing materials, as pens, pencils, notebooks, etc.

sta′tion wag′on, an automobile having one or more rows of seats behind the driver and an open area behind the seats for carrying suitcases, parcels, etc.

sta·tis·tic (stə tis′tik), *n.* a fact, item of information, etc., expressed in numbers: *It is a statistic that 3 out of 4 serious accidents occur in the home.*

sta·tis·ti·cal (stə tis′ti kəl), *adj.* of, concerning, or based on statistics. —**sta·tis′ti·cal·ly,** *adv.*

stat·is·ti·cian (stat′i stish′ən), *n.* an expert in or compiler of statistics.

sta·tis·tics (stə tis′tiks), *n.* **1.** *(used as pl.)* numbers, or numerical facts. **2.** *(used as sing.)* the collection, study, and interpretation of such data.

stat·u·ar·y (stach′ōō er′ē), *n.* statues as a group, or a collection of statues.

stat·ue (stach′ōō), *n.* a likeness of a person, animal, or thing, carved in stone, wood, etc., or cast in some metal, as bronze.

stat·u·esque (stach′ōō esk′), *adj.* like or resembling a statue in beauty or dignity of form.

stat·u·ette (stach′ōō et′), *n.* a small statue.

stat·ure (stach′ər), *n.* **1.** the height of a person or animal: *the great stature of a giraffe; a man of average stature.* **2.** standing or achievement: *high moral stature.*

sta·tus (stā′təs, stat′əs), *n.* **1.** the position or rank of a person in relation to another or others in a group: *The banker is a man of high status in our town.* **2.** highly regarded position or rank: *He tried to achieve status by joining the club.* **3.** a state of affairs: *In its present status the business looks hopeless.*

sta′tus quo′ (kwō), the present state of affairs: *People who fear change try to keep the status quo.*

stat·ute (stach′ōōt), *n.* a law or rule, esp. a law passed by a legislative body.

stat′ute mile′. See mile (def. 1).

stat·u·to·ry (stach′ə tôr′ē), *adj.* **1.** of or concerning a statute: *a statutory decree.* **2.** fixed by statute: *a statutory limit.* **3.** punishable by statute: *a statutory offense.*

St. Au·gus·tine (ô′gə stēn′), a seacoast city in NE Florida: founded by the Spanish in 1565; oldest city in the U.S.

staunch[1] (stônch), *v.* another spelling of **stanch**[1].

staunch[2] (stônch, stänch), *adj.* **1.** firm, steadfast, or loyal: *a staunch friend.* **2.** strong or well built: *a staunch ship.* Also, **stanch.** [from a Middle English word meaning "watertight," which comes from Old French *estanchier* "to close, stop." See *stanch*[1]]

stave (stāv), *n.* **1.** one of the thin, narrow pieces of wood that form the sides of a barrel, cask, or the like. **2.** a stick, rod, pole, or the like. **3.** a verse or stanza of a poem or song. **4.** See **staff** (def. 7). —*v.,* **staved** *or* **stove** (stōv); **stav·ing. 5.** to break (a hole) in, esp. in the hull of a boat. **6.** to supply with a stave or staves: *to stave a barrel.* **7. stave off,** to prevent; ward off: *The company hopes to stave off a strike.*

staves (stāvz), *n.* **1.** a plural of **staff**[1]. **2.** the plural of **stave.**

stay[1] (stā), *v.,* **stayed** *or* **staid** (stād); **stay·ing. 1.** to remain at a place, in someone's company, etc.: *Can't you stay awhile?* **2.** to spend some time at a place, in a situation, with a person or group, etc.: *to stay at a hotel; to stay in the army for several years.* **3.** to go on being: *Stay well!* **4.** *Informal.* to remain steadfast, as in performing a task (usually fol. by *with*): *Stay with the job till it's finished.* **5.** to hold back or stop: *He stayed his anger.* **6.** to remain through or during: *They stayed several weeks in Europe.* **7.** to last through: *The horse stayed the race.* **8.** to delay or postpone: *to stay a sentence of execution.* —*n.* **9.** the length of time of a visit or temporary residence: *a brief stay in France.* **10.** a delay or postponement. [from the Old French word *estaier,* which comes from Latin *stāre* "to stand"]

stay[2] (stā), *n.* **1.** something used to support or steady a thing; prop: *a stay for a swaying pole.* **2.** any support or source of strength: *He is her stay in times of trouble.* **3.** a flat strip of steel, plastic, etc., used to stiffen corsets, collars, etc. —*v.,* **stayed, stay·ing. 4.** to support, prop, or hold up. **5.** to give strength or courage to: *Her religion stayed her in her time of need.* [from a special use of *stay*[3]]

stay[3] (stā), *n.* **1.** any of various strong ropes or cables used on a ship to steady masts, funnels, etc. —*v.*, **stayed, stay·ing. 2.** to support or steady with a stay or stays. [from the Old English word *stæg*]

stay·sail (stā′sāl′, stā′səl), *n.* any sail set on a stay, such as a triangular sail between two masts.

stead (sted), *n.* **1.** the place of a person or thing as occupied by a substitute or follower: *The king died, and the queen ruled in his stead.* **2. stand in good stead,** to be useful in a time of need: *In Paris his knowledge of French stood him in good stead.*

stead·fast (sted′fast′, -fəst), *adj.* **1.** fixed firmly; steady: *a steadfast gaze straight ahead.* **2.** firm and unwavering in purpose, loyalty, etc.: *a steadfast friend.* —**stead′fast′ly,** *adv.* —**stead′fast′ness,** *n.*

stead·y (sted′ē), *adj.*, **stead·i·er, stead·i·est. 1.** firmly placed or fixed: *a steady ladder; a steady table.* **2.** even, regular, or free from change: *the steady flow of a fountain.* **3.** regular or habitual: *a steady customer.* **4.** firm or unfaltering: *a steady hand at the wheel.* **5.** steadfast or unwavering: *to be steady in one's purpose.* **6.** reliable and careful: *a steady worker.* —*n.*, *pl.* **stead·ies. 7.** *Informal.* a person of the opposite sex whom one dates exclusively. —*v.*, **stead·ied, stead·y·ing. 8.** to make or become steady: *He shortened one leg of the table to steady it.* **9. go steady,** *Informal.* to date only one person of the opposite sex: *She has been going steady with Jim for over a year now.* —**stead′i·ly,** *adv.* —**stead′i·ness,** *n.*

steak (stāk), *n.* **1.** a slice of meat or fish cooked by broiling or frying. **2.** a patty of ground meat, esp. beef, broiled or fried.

steal (stēl), *v.*, **stole** (stōl), **sto·len** (stō′lən), **steal·ing. 1.** to take or get by theft: *to steal a car.* **2.** to practice theft: *He was jailed for stealing.* **3.** to take or get by sly or clever means: *to steal a glance.* **4.** to move or bring secretly or quietly (usually fol. by *away, from, up, in,* etc.): *He stole from the room without our seeing him.* **5.** to pass or happen gently or without notice: *The hours stole by and suddenly it was time to go.* **6.** (in baseball) to gain (a base) without the help of a hit or error. —*n.* **7.** an act or instance of stealing: *He could not muster courage for the steal.* **8.** *Informal.* something that is sold at a bargain: *That new coat was a steal.* —**steal′er,** *n.*

stealth (stelth), *n.* secret or sly means or action: *They met by stealth to hatch their plot.*

stealth·y (stel′thē), *adj.*, **stealth·i·er, stealth·i·est.** done, showing, or acting by stealth: *No one heard their stealthy footsteps in the dark.* —**stealth′i·ly,** *adv.* —**stealth′i·ness,** *n.*

steam (stēm), *n.* **1.** the invisible gas, or vapor, produced when water boils. **2.** the grayish mist of tiny water droplets formed when this gas condenses in the air. **3.** *Informal.* power or energy: *He'll do the job once he gets up enough steam.* —*v.* **4.** to give off steam or vapor: *a steaming kettle.* **5.** to rise or pass off in the form of steam or vapor: *Moisture steamed from the hot pavement.* **6.** to become covered with steam (often fol. by *up*): *The kitchen windows steamed up.* **7.** to move or travel by means of a steam engine: *The ship steamed into port.* **8.** to cook,

heat, or soften by means of steam: *to steam clams.* **9.** *Informal.* to be angry: *He's steaming because you kept him waiting.* —*adj.* **10.** operated by or using steam: *a steam locomotive; steam heat.* **11. blow off steam,** *Slang.* to express one's feelings freely after restraint: *After hours of holding his temper, he had to blow off steam.* Also, **let off steam. 12. steamed up,** *Slang.* angry: *Don't get steamed up just because you can't have your own way.*

steam·boat (stēm′bōt′), *n.* a boat driven by steam.

steam′ en′gine, 1. an engine worked by steam, esp. one in which a piston is pushed by the action of expanding steam generated in a boiler. **2.** a locomotive powered by steam.

steam·er (stē′mər), *n.* **1.** a machine or vehicle driven by steam, such as a steamship. **2.** a container in which something is steamed. **3.** a clam having a thin, light, oval shell, usually cooked by steaming.

steam′ roll′er, 1. a steam-driven machine having a roller for crushing or leveling materials, used esp. in paving roads. **2.** a power that overcomes everything that lies in its way.

steam-roll·er (stēm′rō′lər), *v.* **1.** to crush with a steam roller. **2.** to overcome, bring about, or move with a force that cannot be resisted: *He steam-rollers everyone into agreeing with him.* —*adj.* **3.** ruthlessly overpowering: *to use steam-roller tactics.*

steam·ship (stēm′ship′), *n.* a large, commercial vessel driven by steam.

steam′ shov′el, a steam-driven machine equipped with a large shovel, used for excavations.

steam·y (stē′mē), *adj.*, **steam·i·er, steam·i·est. 1.** of or like steam: *steamy breath.* **2.** full of steam: *a steamy kitchen.* **3.** covered with steam: *steamy windows.* **4.** hot and humid: *the steamy tropics.*

Steam shovel

steed (stēd), *n.* a horse, esp. a high-spirited horse for riding.

steel (stēl), *n.* **1.** any of various alloys consisting principally of iron and containing carbon and sometimes other metals. Steels are the most widely used of all metals and are made in many degrees of hardness, strength, elasticity, etc. **2.** something made of steel, as a weapon. **3.** great strength or toughness: *muscles of steel; nerves of steel.* —*adj.* **4.** of or concerning steel: *steel knives; the steel industry.* **5.** like steel in color, hardness, or strength: *steel gray; steel nerves.* —*v.* **6.** to make firm or strong: *He steeled himself for the bad news.*

steel′ wool′, a mass of fine, threadlike steel fibers, used for cleaning, scouring, polishing, etc.

steel·work·er (stēl′wûr′kər), *n.* a person employed in the manufacturing of steel.

steel·y (stē′lē), *adj.*, **steel·i·er, steel·i·est. 1.** made of steel. **2.** like steel in color, strength, or hardness: *steely gray skies; steely determination.*

steel·yard (stēl′yärd′, stil′yərd), *n.* a weighing device consisting of a steel bar suspended from a point near one end. The object to be weighed is suspended from the shorter part of the bar and is balanced by moving a weight over the longer part.

steep[1] (stēp), *adj.* **1.** having a sharp slant up and down: *a steep hill.* **2.** *Informal.* (of a price or amount) too high; above what is normal: *He pays a steep rent for his apartment.* [from the Old English word *stēap*] —**steep′ly,** *adv.* —**steep′ness,** *n.*

steep[2] (stēp), *v.* **1.** to soak or be soaked in water or another liquid: *to steep tea leaves.* **2.** to involve deeply: *He steeped himself in study. The matter is steeped in mystery.* [from the Middle English word *stepe*]

stee·ple (stē′pəl), *n.* **1.** a high tower on a building, esp. a church, usually ending in a spire. **2.** a spire.

stee·ple·chase (stē′pəl chās′), *n.* a horse race over a course set with obstacles, such as hurdles, ditches, etc.

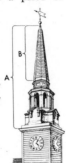

A, Steeple
B, Spire

stee·ple·jack (stē′pəl jak′), *n.* a person who builds or repairs steeples, towers, or the like.

steer[1] (stēr), *v.* **1.** to guide the course of (something in motion): *to steer a bicycle.* **2.** to proceed in a certain direction: *to steer a course westward.* **3.** to be guided in motion in a certain manner: *The new car steers easily.* —*n.* **4.** *Slang.* a piece of information or advice; tip: *His father gave him a good steer about fishing rods.* [from the Old English word *steoran*]

steer[2] (stēr), *n.* a castrated male animal of the ox family, esp. one raised for beef. [from the Old English word *stēor*]

steer·age (stēr′ij), *n.* the part of a ship occupied by passengers paying the lowest fares.

steers·man (stērz′mən), *n., pl.* **steers·men.** a person who steers a ship.

steg·o·saur·us (steg′ə-sôr′əs), *n.* any of several large, heavily armored, plant-eating dinosaurs that lived in what is now the western United States.

Stegosaurus
(length 18 ft.)

stein (stīn), *n.* a mug for beer.

stel·lar (stel′ər), *adj.* **1.** of, concerning, or consisting of stars. **2.** chief; leading; prominent: *a famous actress who played the stellar role.*

stem[1] (stem), *n.* **1.** the main stalk of a plant, which supports all the other parts that are above the ground. **2.** a smaller stalk, such as that of a flower or leaf. **3.** a long, slender part: *the stem of a pipe.* **4.** the stock or line of descent of a family; ancestry. **5.** the form of a word to which inflectional endings are added. The stem of *taking* is *tak-.* The stem of *running* is *run.* **6.** a form that does not exist by itself as a word, but forms words by the addition of prefixes or suffixes. The stem *-ceive* is used to form words like *conceive, deceive, perceive, receive,* etc. —*v.,* **stemmed, stem·ming. 7.** to remove the stem from (a leaf, fruit, etc.): *to stem cherries.* **8.** to arise or have as a source: *This action stems from careful planning.* [from the Old English word *stemn*] —**stem′less,** *adj.* —**stem′like′,** *adj.*

stem[2] (stem), *v.,* **stemmed, stem·ming.** to stop or check: *to stem the flood.* [from the Middle English word *stemme,* which comes from Scandinavian]

stem[3] (stem), *v.,* **stemmed, stem·ming.** to make headway against: *They rowed upstream, stemming the current.* [from a verbal use of *stem*[4]]

stem[4] (stem), *n.* the forward part of a ship or boat: *The ship was painted from stem to stern.* [from the Old English word *stemn,* which was used also with the meanings "prow, stern." See *stem*[1]]

stemmed (stemd), *adj.* **1.** having a stem or a certain kind of stem (often used in combination): *longstemmed roses.* **2.** having the stems taken off: *a cup of stemmed cherries.*

stench (stench), *n.* a bad smell or odor; stink: *the stench of a swamp.*

sten·cil (sten′səl), *n.* **1.** a thin sheet of cardboard, metal, etc., having letters or a design cut into it, through which ink, paint, etc., brushed on one side will come out on a surface against which the sheet is pressed. **2.** letters or a design made in this way. —*v.,* **sten·ciled** or **sten·cilled; sten·cil·ing** or **sten·cil·ling. 3.** to mark with a stencil: *The door was stenciled with his name.* **4.** to make with a stencil: *His name was stenciled on the door.* —**sten′cil·er,** *n.*

Stencil

ste·nog·ra·pher (stə nog′rə fər), *n.* a person who is skilled in taking dictation in shorthand.

ste·nog·ra·phy (stə nog′rə fē), *n.* the art of writing in shorthand. —**sten·o·graph·ic** (sten′ə graf′ik), *adj.* —**sten′o·graph′i·cal·ly,** *adv.*

Sten·o·type (sten′ə tīp′), *n. Trademark.* a keyboard machine similar to a typewriter, used in writing a special kind of shorthand.

sten·to·ri·an (sten tôr′ē ən), *adj.* powerful in sound; very loud: *a stentorian voice.*

step (step), *n.* **1.** a movement made by lifting one foot and setting it down again in a new position, with the body and the other foot following. **2.** the distance covered by such a movement: *He stood a few steps away from us.* **3.** the sound made by the foot in making such a movement: *We heard steps in the dark.* **4.** a mark made by the foot on the ground; footprint: *steps in the wet sand.* **5.** the manner of walking; gait; stride: *a young woman with a lively step.* **6.** a rhythm or pattern in walking, marching, or dancing: *the step of a waltz.* **7.** one of a number of stages toward reaching a goal, making something, etc.: *The next step is to add the butter.* **8.** rank, degree, or grade: *to advance to a higher step in one's career.* **9.** a place for the foot in climbing or going down, as a stair or the rung of a ladder. **10.** a very short distance: *He lives only a few steps away.* —*v.,* **stepped, step·ping. 11.** to move in steps: *They were stepping down the street.* **12.** to move a short distance: *Please step up to the counter.* **13.** to move or act briskly: *We'll have to be stepping now, as it's getting late.* **14.** to put the foot down: *to step on the cat's tail.* **15.** to measure by steps (sometimes fol. by *off*): *He stepped off the length of the room.* **16. in step, a.** moving in time to a rhythm or with the same step or cadence as others: *Keep in step with the music.* **b.** in harmony or accordance: *to be in step with the changing times.* **17. out of step, a.** not moving in time to a rhythm or with the same step or cadence as others. **b.** not in harmony or accordance: *He's always been out of step with others of his age.* **18. step by step,** from one stage to the next in a certain order: *I'll show you step by step how to make a cake.* **19. step in,** to become involved; intervene: *The fight had become a riot by the time the police stepped in.* **20. step on it,** *Slang.* to hurry up: *If you don't step on it we're going to be late!* **21. step out, a.** to leave a place briefly: *I have to step out for a few minutes.* **b.** to go out for an evening of entertainment: *We're stepping out tonight.* **22. step up,** to increase: *to step up production.* **23. watch one's step,** *Informal.* to be careful of one's actions, words, or the like: *Watch your step when you're working with electricity.*

step-, a prefix meaning related by remarriage: *step-brother; stepmother.*

step·child (step′chīld′), *n., pl.* **step·chil·dren.** a child of one's husband or wife by a former marriage.

step·fa·ther (step′fä′ŧhər), *n.* a man who follows one's father as the husband of one's mother after death or divorce.

step·lad·der (step′lad′ər), *n.* a ladder having steps instead of rungs, esp. one having a hinged frame upon which it rests.

step·moth·er (step′muŧh′ər), *n.* a woman who follows one's mother as the wife of one's father after death or divorce.

steppe (step), *n.* a vast plain without trees, esp. one like those found in the western Soviet Union.

step′ping stone′, a stone, usually one of a number, sticking out above the surface of a stream, pond, etc., that is stepped on in crossing.

-ster, a suffix used to form nouns meaning a person who performs or engages in something: *songster; gangster; trickster.*

ster·e·o (ster′ē ō′, stēr′ē ō′), *n., pl.* **ster·e·os. 1.** a stereophonic sound system. **2.** stereophonic reproduction of sound.

ster·e·o·phon·ic (ster′ē ə fon′ik, stēr′ē ə fon′ik), *adj.* of or concerning the recording or reproduction of sound using two or more microphones, amplifiers, loudspeakers, etc., to produce a more realistic effect.

ster·e·op·ti·con (ster′ē op′tə kən, stēr′ē op′tə-kən), *n.* a slide projector, esp. one capable of causing the image of one slide to fade into the image of the next.

ster·e·o·scope (ster′ē ə skōp′, stēr′ē ə skōp′), *n.* a device through which one looks at two pictures of the same object taken from slightly different angles. The combined image gives a three-dimensional effect. —**ster·e·o·scop·ic** (ster′ē ə skop′ik), *adj.*

ster·e·o·type (ster′ē ə tīp′, stēr′ē ə tīp′), *n.* **1.** a metal plate from which a page is printed. **2.** a way of thinking about or describing a person or thing that is lacking in truth, freshness, or originality: *The idea that heroes are always handsome and villains ugly is a stereotype.* —*v.,* **ster·e·o·typed, ster·e·o·typing. 3.** to make a stereotype of. —**ster′e·o·typ′er,** *n.*

ster·ile (ster′il), *adj.* **1.** free from dirt or germs: *a sterile bandage.* **2.** unable to produce offspring. **3.** unable to produce plants; barren: *sterile soil.* **4.** without purpose, meaning, or interest: *a sterile conversation.* —**ste·ril·i·ty** (stə ril′i tē), *n.*

ster·i·lize (ster′ə līz′), *v.,* **ster·i·lized, ster·i·liz·ing. 1.** to make clean and free of germs. **2.** to destroy the ability of a plant or animal to produce offspring. —**ster′i·li·za′tion,** *n.* —**ster′i·liz′er,** *n.*

ster·ling (stûr′ling), *adj.* **1.** of or concerning British money: *sterling currency.* **2.** (of silver) **a.** having a high degree of fineness. **b.** made of silver of this quality: *a sterling sugar bowl.* **3.** very good, fine, or genuine: *a man of sterling character.* —*n.* **4.** silver of fine quality. **5.** British money.

stern¹ (stûrn), *adj.* **1.** firm or strict: *a stern resolve.* **2.** harsh or severe: *stern treatment of a prisoner.* **3.** forbidding or grim: *a stern face.* [from the Old English word *styrne*] —**stern′ly,** *adv.* —**stern′ness,** *n.*

stern² (stûrn), *n.* the back part of a ship: *The ship was afire from stem to stern.* [from the Middle English word *sterne,* which comes from Scandinavian]

ster·num (stûr′nəm), *n.* the scientific name for **breastbone.**

stern·wheel·er (stûrn′-hwē′lər, -wē′lər), *n.* a boat propelled by a paddle wheel at the stern.

Stern wheeler

steth·o·scope (steth′ə skōp′), *n.* an instrument used by doctors to hear sounds produced by the body, esp. those of the lungs and heart.

ste·ve·dore (stē′vi dôr′), *n.* a person employed to load or unload a ship.

Ste·ven·son (stē′vən sən), *n.* **1. Ad·lai E.** (ad′lā), 1835–1914, 23rd Vice President of the U.S. 1893–1897. **2. Robert Louis,** 1850–1894, Scottish novelist.

Stethoscope

stew (stōō, styōō), *v.* **1.** to cook (food) by simmering in a liquid: *to stew meat and vegetables.* **2.** to undergo cooking in this way: *The meat has been stewing for an hour.* **3.** *Informal.* to fret or worry: *He is stewing because he can't find his glasses.* —*n.* **4.** meat, fish, or other food cooked by stewing, usually with vegetables: *a beef stew.* **5.** *Informal.* a state of worry: *Missing the train put him in a stew.* **6. stew in one's own juice,** to suffer the consequences of one's own wrong actions: *Since he won't listen to advice, let him stew in his own juice.*

stew·ard (stōō′ərd, styōō′-), *n.* **1.** a person who takes care of the property or business of another: *He appointed a steward to watch over his estate.* **2.** an attendant on a passenger ship: *The steward made the beds and cleaned the cabin.* **3.** a person on a plane or train who serves food and looks after the comfort of passengers. —**stew′ard·ship′,** *n.*

stew·ard·ess (stōō′ər dis, styōō′-), *n.* a woman who works as a steward.

St. He·le·na (hə lē′nə), a British island in the S Atlantic Ocean: Napoleon's place of exile 1815–1821. 47 sq. mi.

stick¹ (stik), *n.* **1.** a twig or branch from a tree or shrub: *to gather sticks for a fire.* **2.** any slender, long piece of wood, as a cane, club, drumstick, etc. **3. the sticks,** *Informal.* any place far from cities, esp. a country region: *She left Chicago to live in the sticks.* [from the Old English word *sticca*]

stick² (stik), *v.,* **stuck** (stuk), **stick·ing. 1.** to pierce or puncture with something pointed: *to stick a balloon with a pin.* **2.** to thrust in (something sharp) so as to pierce or puncture: *to stick a nail into a tire.* **3.** to fix in place: *to stick a painting on the wall.* **4.** to fasten or attach by glue, moisture, etc.: *to stick a stamp on a letter.* **5.** to have the point or points embedded: *an arrow stuck in the tree.* **6.** to be or become fastened, hindered, checked, etc.: *The car was stuck in the mud.* **7.** to keep or stay firmly or steadily: *to stick to a task.* **8.** to put up with or carry on: *He couldn't stick the job for more than three days.* **9.** to puzzle or confuse: *The problem stuck him.* **10.** *Informal.* to impose something upon (a person or persons): *I was stuck with feeding the cat when they went on vacation.* **11. stick around,** *Slang.* to remain; stay; linger: *Do you want to stick around for refreshments?* **12. stick by,** to remain loyal or faithful to: *She promised to stick by him while he was in prison.* **13. stick up for,** *Informal.* to speak on behalf of; support; defend: *He stuck up for me when I was accused of cheating.* [from the Old English word *stician*]

stick·er (stik′ər), *n.* a gummed label or sign.

stick·le (stik′əl), *v.,* **stick·led, stick·ling.** to argue or haggle, esp. over very slight matters: *She stickled over a small mistake on her bill.*

stick·le·back (stik′əl-bak′), *n., pl.* **stick·le·backs** *or* **stick·le·back.** any of various small fishes having spines on the back, found in fresh waters and sea inlets and

Stickleback
(length 2½ in.)

noted for the ferocity with which the male protects its nest.

stick·ler (stik′lər), *n.* **1.** a person who insists upon exactness: *He's a stickler for obeying the rules.* **2.** any puzzling or difficult problem: *This riddle is a stickler.*

stick·pin (stik′pin′), *n.* a pin used to hold a necktie in place.

stick·y (stik′ē), *adj.,* **stick·i·er, stick·i·est. 1.** clinging or sticking: *Glue is a sticky substance.* **2.** covered or coated with glue or a gluey substance: *the sticky flap of an envelope.* **3.** hot and humid: *sticky August weather.* —**stick′i·ly,** *adv.* —**stick′i·ness,** *n.*

stiff (stif), *adj.* **1.** difficult to bend: *a stiff collar.* **2.** not working or moving easily: *a stiff motor.* **3.** not supple or limber, as a person, animal, or part of the body: *a stiff neck.* **4.** strong; forceful: *stiff winds.* **5.** stubborn; firm: *stiff resistance.* **6.** cold and formal: *a stiff bow.* **7.** lacking ease or grace: *a stiff style of writing.* **8.** difficult, as a task. **9.** harsh or severe: *stiff punishment.* **10.** too high or great: *a stiff price.* **11.** not liquid; thick: *Beat the egg whites till they're stiff.* —*n.* **12.** *Slang.* a dead body; corpse. **13.** *Slang.* fellow; guy: *a poor stiff.* —*adv.* **14.** completely; thoroughly: *to be bored stiff.* —**stiff′ly,** *adv.* —**stiff′ness,** *n.*

stiff·en (stif′ən), *v.* **1.** to make or become stiff: *She stiffened the collar with starch. The enemy's resistance stiffened.* **2.** to become tense, as in bracing oneself for drawing back from a shock: *She stiffened, expecting the worst.* —**stiff′en·er,** *n.*

stiff-necked (stif′nekt′), *adj.* **1.** having a stiff neck. **2.** stubborn; unyielding: *stiff-necked opposition.*

sti·fle (stī′fəl), *v.,* **sti·fled, sti·fling. 1.** to kill by stopping the breath; smother. **2.** to die from lack of air. **3.** to suffer from lack of air: *We were stifling in that little room.* **4.** to curb or check: *to stifle a yawn.*

stig·ma (stig′mə), *n., pl.* **stig·mas** *or* **stig·ma·ta** (stig′mə tə, stig mä′tə). **1.** a stain or bad mark on one's record or reputation: *the stigma of having been in prison.* **2. stigmata,** the wounds of Christ or marks resembling them, supposedly caused by supernatural means, on the bodies of certain holy persons. **3.** the part of the pistil of a flower that receives the pollen when the plant is pollinated. See illus. at **flower.**

stig·ma·tize (stig′mə tīz′), *v.,* **stig·ma·tized, stig·ma·tiz·ing.** to set a mark of disgrace upon: *He was stigmatized as a cruel father.*

stile (stīl), *n.* **1.** a number of steps or rungs for passing over a fence or wall: *We climbed the stile and went into the meadow.* **2.** a turnstile.

sti·let·to (sti let′ō), *n., pl.* **sti·let·tos** *or* **sti·let·toes. 1.** a small, sharp dagger with a slender blade. **2.** a small, sharply pointed tool for making eyelets in cloth, leather, etc.

Stiletto
with scabbard

still¹ (stil), *adj.* **1.** without movement: *He stood still, waiting.* **2.** without noise; silent: *Please be still.* —*n.* **3.** stillness or silence: *the still of the night.* **4.** a single photograph, esp. one from a motion-picture film. —*adv.* **5.** up to or at the time spoken about: *Is he still waiting?* **6.** in spite of that; nevertheless: *They were poor, still they didn't complain.* **7.** even; yet: *You are beautiful, but she is still more beautiful.* —*v.* **8.** to make or become still, calm, or quiet: *He stilled the restless mob with promises.* [from the Old English word *stille*] —**still′ness**, *n.*

still² (stil), *n.* a distilling apparatus consisting of a closed container for heating a liquid and a coil in which the resulting vapors are condensed. [short for *distill*]

still-born (stil′bôrn′), *adj.* dead at birth.

stilt (stilt), *n.* **1.** one of a pair of poles, each with a support for the foot at some distance from the bottom end, enabling a person to walk or stand several feet above the ground. **2.** one of a number of posts supporting a building or dock above the ground or surface of the water. —**stilt′like′**, *adj.*

stilt-ed (stil′tid), *adj.* stiff and pompous in speech, writing, behavior, etc.: *stilted, snobbish manners.*

stim-u-lant (stim′yə lənt), *n.* **1.** a food, drink, medicine, etc., that awakens or speeds up the activity of the mind or body: *Coffee is a common stimulant.* **2.** anything that stimulates: *Travel is a stimulant to the mind.*

stim-u-late (stim′yə lāt′), *v.,* **stim-u-lat-ed, stim-u-lat-ing.** to arouse or awaken; make active: *A glass of juice will stimulate the appetite.* —**stim′u-la′tion,** *n.*

stim-u-lus (stim′yə ləs), *n., pl.* **stim-u-li** (stim′yə lī′). **1.** something that produces a reaction in a living thing or in some part of a living thing: *the stimulus of light on a growing plant.* **2.** anything that stimulates: *Praise is a stimulus to action.*

sting (sting), *v.,* **stung** (stung), **sting-ing. 1.** to prick or wound, as a bee or hornet does. **2.** to cause sharp pain to: *The hail stung my face. The insult stung me.* **3.** to feel sharp pain: *My face stung.* **4.** to cause to feel sharp pain: *Unkind words sting.* **5.** to goad or drive by harsh words, insults, etc.: *His reproach stung me to make an angry reply.* **6.** *Informal.* to cheat or overcharge: *They stung him for all he was worth.* —*n.* **7.** a sharp-pointed, often venom-bearing organ on an insect or other animal that can inflict a painful or dangerous wound. **8.** the act of stinging with such an organ, or the hurt caused by stinging: *the sting of a bee.* **9.** any sharp pain to the feelings or the body: *the sting of an insult.* —**sting′er,** *n.*

sting-ray (sting′rā′), *n.* any of several broad, flat ocean fishes having a long, flexible tail near the base of which is a sharp, toothed spine that can inflict painful wounds.

stin-gy (stin′jē), *adj.,* **stin-gi-er, stin-gi-est. 1.** unwilling to give, lend, or spend: *to be stingy with money.* **2.** scanty; meager: *a stingy dinner.* —**stin′gi-ly,** *adv.* —**stin′gi-ness,** *n.*

stink (stingk), *v.,* **stank** (stangk) *or* **stunk** (stungk); **stunk; stink-ing. 1.** to give off a strong, unpleasant smell. **2.** *Slang.* to be worthless, boring, etc. **3.** to cause to stink (often fol. by *up*): *to stink up the kitchen with garlic.* —*n.* **4.** a strong, unpleasant smell. **5.** *Slang.* a scandal: *There was a stink about his accepting a bribe.*

stink-er (sting′kər), *n.* **1.** a person or thing that

Stingray
(width 5 ft.; total
length 10 ft.)

stinks. **2.** *Slang.* **a.** a spiteful, nasty person. **b.** something that is inferior, such as a movie or book. **c.** something difficult: *a real stinker of an exam.*

stint (stint), *v.* **1.** to give (something) in small amounts: *to stint money.* **2.** to be frugal or sparing: *Don't stint on the dessert.* —*n.* **3.** a task or chore: *His daily stint is to wash the dishes.*

sti-pend (stī′pend), *n.* fixed pay or allowance: *His scholarship provides him with a monthly stipend.*

stip-ple (stip′əl), *v.,* **stip-pled, stip-pling. 1.** to paint, engrave, or draw by means of dots or small touches rather than lines. —*n.* **2.** the result of stippling: *a stipple of yellow paint over green.*

stip-u-late (stip′yə lāt′), *v.,* **stip-u-lat-ed, stip-u-lat-ing.** to require as a part of an agreement: *His contract stipulated extra money for expenses.*

stip-u-la-tion (stip′yə lā′shən), *n.* a requirement in an agreement or contract: *The work was assigned with the stipulation that it would be begun at once.*

stir (stûr), *v.,* **stirred, stir-ring. 1.** to move, esp. lightly or slightly: *leaves stirring in the breeze.* **2.** to move with the hand or a tool: *to stir one's tea.* **3.** to move briskly: *It is late, and we must stir ourselves.* **4.** to arouse; excite: *The hero's example stirred the nation.* **5.** to be active: *Is anything stirring in town?* —*n.* **6.** a slight movement: *the stir of a leaf.* **7.** a motion of mixing, prodding, etc.: *to give the pot of soup a stir.* **8.** a state of excitement: *The news caused a stir.*

stir-ring (stûr′ing), *adj.* moving, exciting, or thrilling: *a stirring song; a stirring victory.*

stir-rup (stûr′əp), *n.* **1.** either of two rings of metal, wood, leather, etc., that hang by straps from the sides of a saddle and are used as supports for the rider's feet. See also **saddle. 2.** one of three small bones in the middle ear that transmit the vibrations of the eardrum to the inner ear.

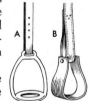
Stirrups
A, Metal
B, Leather

stitch (stich), *n.* **1.** a complete movement of a threaded needle into and out of a piece of cloth, leather, etc. **2.** a loop of thread left in place by such a movement. **3.** a particular way of sewing: *She has a very fine stitch.* **4.** the slightest bit of clothing: *I haven't a stitch to wear.* **5.** the slightest bit of anything: *He won't do a stitch of work.* **6.** a sudden, sharp pain: *a stitch in one's side.* —*v.* **7.** to make stitches; sew. **8.** to work upon, mend, or fasten with stitches: *to stitch a tear.*

St. John's, a seaport and the capital city of Newfoundland, on the SE part of the island.

St. Law-rence (lôr′əns, lor′əns), **1.** a river in SE Canada, flowing from Lake Ontario along the border between New York and Ontario, and entering into the Gulf of St. Lawrence. **2. Gulf of,** an arm of the Atlantic Ocean between SE Canada and Newfoundland.

St. Lawrence Seaway, a waterway system that allows ships to travel up the St. Lawrence River to all Great Lakes ports.

St. Lou·is (loō′is, loō′ē), a port city in E Missouri, on the Mississippi River.

stoat (stōt), *n.* the ermine, esp. when the fur is brown, as it is in summer.

stock (stok), *n.* **1.** a supply of goods kept for use or sale: *a stock of food.* **2.** a theatrical company that puts on a variety of plays. **3.** shares in a business: *to own stock in several companies.* **4.** short for livestock. **5.** the principal stem or trunk of a plant. **6.** ancestry or descent. **7.** a type or breed of plant or animal. **8.** the handle of a whip, fishing rod, rifle, etc. **9. stocks,** a framework with holes that locked around the ankles and sometimes the wrists of a person, formerly used as a means of punishment. **10.** a broth of meat, fish, etc. **11.** any of several garden plants having fragrant white, blue, purple, reddish, or yellowish flowers. —*adj.* **12.** kept regularly on hand: *a stock item.* **13.** having as one's job the care of stock: *a stock clerk.* **14.** common or ordinary: *to give a stock answer.* **15.** of or concerned with the breeding and raising of livestock. **16.** of or referring to the stock of a company: *stock prices.* —*v.* **17.** to supply with a stock: *to stock a refrigerator.* **18.** to supply with livestock: *to stock a farm.* **19.** to lay up in store: *to stock potatoes.* **20.** to lay in a stock of something (often fol. by *up*): *to stock up on canned goods.* **21. put stock in,** to put confidence in: *I don't put stock in anything he says.* **22. take stock, a.** to make an inventory of stock on hand: *The store will be closed while they take stock.* **b.** to estimate the value of something: *to take stock of one's progress.*

Stocks (def. 9)

stock·ade (sto kād′), *n.* **1.** a fence made of strong posts set upright in the ground, used as a defensive barrier. **2.** an area enclosed by such stakes. **3.** a military prison.

stock·brok·er (stok′brō′kər), *n.* a broker who buys and sells stocks and bonds for his customers.

stock′ exchange′, 1. a place where stocks and bonds are bought and sold. **2.** a group of brokers who deal in stocks and bonds.

stock·hold·er (stok′hōl′dər), *n.* a person who owns stock in a company.

Stock·holm (stok′hōm), *n.* a seaport and the capital city of Sweden, in the SE part.

stock·ing (stok′ing), *n.* a close-fitting covering for the foot and part of the leg, usually knitted.

stock′ing cap′, a long, tapering, knitted cap with a tassel at the tip, usually worn in winter.

stock′ mar′ket, 1. a particular place where stocks and bonds are bought and sold; stock exchange. **2.** the trading in stocks and bonds throughout a nation.

stock·pile (stok′pīl′), *n.* **1.** a large supply of food, material, etc., kept in reserve, esp. for use during a shortage. **2.** a supply of munitions kept by a nation for possible use: *an atomic stockpile.* —*v.,* **stock·piled, stock·pil·ing. 3.** to collect for future use.

stock·room (stok′roōm′, -roōm′), *n.* a room in which a stock of material or goods is kept for use or sale.

stock-still (stok′stil′), *adj.* completely motionless: *He stood stock-still.*

stock·y (stok′ē), *adj.,* **stock·i·er, stock·i·est.** solidly built and, usually, short: *a stocky, athletic man.* —**stock′i·ly,** *adv.* —**stock′i·ness,** *n.*

stock·yard (stok′yärd′), *n.* a yard with pens, sheds, etc., in which livestock is kept temporarily.

stodg·y (stoj′ē), *adj.,* **stodg·i·er, stodg·i·est. 1.** heavy and dull; boring: *a long, stodgy book.* **2.** heavy, as food: *a stodgy, indigestible meal.* **3.** old-fashioned: *stodgy ideas.* —**stodg′i·ness,** *n.*

sto·ic (stō′ik), *n.* **1.** a person who remains calm and unmoved by either joy or grief. —*adj.* **2.** another form of stoical.

sto·i·cal (stō′i kəl), *adj.* showing or marked by calmness and self-control; like a stoic: *stoical courage.* —**sto′i·cal·ly,** *adv.* —**sto′i·cal·ness,** *n.*

sto·i·cism (stō′i siz′əm), *n.* great self-control in the face of joy or grief: *His stoicism helped him to endure many hardships.*

stoke (stōk), *v.,* **stoked, stok·ing.** to poke, stir up, and feed (a fire).

stok·er (stō′kər), *n.* **1.** a person employed to tend a furnace, esp. on a ship. **2.** a device that feeds coal or other fuel to a furnace.

stole¹ (stōl), *v.* the past tense of steal.

stole² (stōl), *n.* **1.** a narrow strip of cloth worn over the shoulders by some clergymen during services. **2.** a woman's shoulder scarf of fur or other material. [from an Old English word, which comes from Latin *stola* "clothing, robe," from Greek *stolē*]

sto·len (stō′lən), *v.* the past participle of steal.

stol·id (stol′id), *adj.* not easily excited: *a stolid, practical man.* —**stol′id·ly,** *adv.* —**stol′id·ness,** *n.*

stom·ach (stum′ək), *n.* **1.** the saclike, enlarged part of the digestive tract in man and certain animals where food is stored and partly digested. **2.** the front part of the body between the chest and the hips; belly; abdomen. **3.** appetite for food: *He has no stomach for rich desserts.* **4.** desire or liking: *She has no stomach for the trip.* —*v.* **5.** to take into and keep in the stomach: *He could not stomach the medicine.* **6.** to put up with: *to stomach an insult.*

Human stomach
A, Esophagus;
B, Small
intestine

stom·ach·er (stum′ə kər), *n.* a garment covering the stomach and part of the chest, formerly worn by women.

stomp (stomp), *v.* **1.** *Informal.* to stamp with the foot. —*n.* **2.** a fast jazz dance having a strong beat.

stone (stōn), *n., pl.* **stones** or for def. 6 **stone. 1.** the hard substance, formed from minerals, of which rocks are composed. **2.** a piece of rock; pebble. **3.** a jewel or gem. **4.** a hard body formed in the kidneys, gall bladder, etc., that can cause serious illness and great pain. **5.** the hard pit or seed of certain fruits, such as cherries. **6.** *British.* a unit of weight equal to 14 pounds. —*adj.* **7.** of or referring to stone: *a stone wall.* —*v.,* **stoned, ston·ing. 8.** to throw stones at: *The rioters stoned the palace.* **9.** to kill by striking with stones: *Murderers were stoned in ancient times.* **10.** to cover or set with stones: *to stone a path.* **11.** to remove the stones from: *to stone cherries.* **12. leave no stone unturned,** to put forth every possible effort, as to solve, achieve, or find something: *They left no stone unturned in their search.* —**stone′like′,** *adj.*

Stone′ Age′, the period in the history of mankind, preceding the Bronze Age and the Iron Age, marked by the use of stone tools and weapons.

stone·cut·ter (stōn′kut′ər), *n.* **1.** a person who cuts or carves stone. **2.** a machine for cutting stone.

stone-deaf (stōn′def′), *adj.* completely unable to hear. —**stone′-deaf′ness,** *n.*

stone·wall (stōn′wôl′), *v. Informal.* to block, evade, or stall, esp. intentionally.

stone·ware (stōn′wâr′), *n.* a hard, heavy, glazed pottery.

stone·work (stōn′wûrk′), *n.* **1.** something built of stone, such as a wall. **2.** the skill or process of building with stone.

ston·y (stō′nē), *adj.,* **ston·i·er, ston·i·est. 1.** full of or covered with stones or rocks: *stony soil; a stony beach.* **2.** like stone in hardness or appearance: *stony pavements.* **3.** without feeling: *a stony heart.* **4.** fixed or rigid: *a stony stare.* —**ston′i·ness,** *n.*

stood (stŏŏd), *v.* the past tense and past participle of **stand.**

stool (stŏŏl), *n.* **1.** a single seat without arms or a back: *tall stools along a counter.* **2.** a low seat without arms or a back.

stool′ pi′geon, 1. a pigeon used as a decoy to trap other pigeons. **2.** *Slang.* a person who spies or informs on others, esp. one who works for the police.

stoop[1] (stŏŏp), *v.* **1.** to bend the body forward and downward: *He stooped to tie his shoe.* **2.** to stand or walk with the head and shoulders bent forward: *to stoop from age.* **3.** to lower oneself in dignity: *I will not stoop to cheating.* —*n.* **4.** an act or instance of stooping. **5.** a stooping posture: *He walks with a stoop.* [from the Old English word *stūpian*]

stoop[2] (stŏŏp), *n.* a small staircase at the front entrance of a house. [from the Dutch word *stoep*]

stop (stop), *v.,* **stopped, stop·ping. 1.** to halt; keep from going on: *to stop the car.* **2.** to hold back; restrain (usually fol. by *from*): *They stopped him from throwing the ball.* **3.** to close up; fill: *to stop a hole.* **4.** to fill the holes in: *to stop a leaking kettle.* **5.** (in boxing) to defeat by a knockout: *He was stopped in the second round.* **6.** to close (a finger hole) or press (a string) to change the pitch of a musical instrument. **7.** to come to a halt or an end: *The rain finally stopped.* **8.** to halt for a brief visit (often fol. by *at, in,* or *by*): *We stopped in Boston on the way north.* —*n.* **9.** the act or fact of stopping: *to put a stop to something; to come to a stop.* **10.** a visit or stay at a

place, made during the course of a journey: *a brief stop at Boston.* **11.** a place where buses and other vehicles stop to pick up passengers. **12.** a stopper or plug: *a stop for a bottle.* **13.** something that acts as a check to movement: *a stop to keep a door from closing.* **14.** a part of a musical instrument that regulates pitch, as a hole, key, or peg: *the stops of a flute.* **15.** a punctuation mark, esp. a period. **16. stop by,** to make a brief visit on one's way elsewhere: *They asked me to stop by after the game.* **17. stop off,** to stop at some point, esp. on a journey: *We stopped off at Atlanta on our way to Miami.* **18. stop over,** to stay briefly in a certain place while on one's way elsewhere: *We stopped over in Boston for the night.*

stop·gap (stop′gap′), *n.* a temporary substitute.

stop·light (stop′līt′), *n.* **1.** a light on the rear of a motor vehicle that lights when the driver applies pressure to the brake pedal. **2.** a traffic light.

stop·o·ver (stop′ōv′ər), *n.* a brief stop at a place during a trip, esp. a stop made with the privilege of proceeding later on the same ticket.

stop·page (stop′ij), *n.* **1.** an act or instance of stopping: *a work stoppage.* **2.** the state of being stopped, blocked, etc.: *a stoppage in a drain.*

stop·per (stop′ər), *n.* **1.** a person or thing that stops. **2.** a plug, cork, etc., for closing a bottle, drain, or the like. —*v.* **3.** to close with a stopper.

stop·watch (stop′woch′), *n.* a watch with a hand that measures seconds by fractions, and that can be stopped or started at any instant, used to time races.

stor·age (stôr′ij), *n.* **1.** the act of storing, or the state or fact of being stored. **2.** a place for storing: *All of their furniture is in storage.* **3.** the price charged for storing: *to pay a high storage.*

stor′age bat′tery, an electric battery or cell that can be recharged by passing an electric current through it when its charge has been depleted by use.

store (stôr), *n.* **1.** a place where goods are sold: *a grocery store.* **2.** a supply or stock of something: *a store of food for the winter.* **3. stores,** supplies of anything that is needed: *Our gasoline stores are almost exhausted.* **4.** a plentiful supply of anything: *a store of wisdom.* —*v.,* **stored, stor·ing. 5.** to gather and put away for future use (usually fol. by *up* or *away*): *The squirrel stores up nuts for the winter.* **6.** to put in storage: *They stored their furniture.* **7.** to stay fresh and usable for some time after being stored: *Potatoes store well.* **8. in store, a.** in readiness or reserve: *You'd better keep another supply in store.* **b.** about to happen; likely to occur: *What's in store for him in the army?* **9. set** (or **lay**) **store by,** to value or esteem: *She sets great store by courtesy.*

store·house (stôr′hous′), *n., pl.* **store·hous·es** (stôr′hou′ziz). **1.** a building in which things are stored. **2.** any abundant source: *He is a storehouse of wisdom.*

store·keep·er (stôr′kē′pər), *n.* a person who owns or operates a store. —**store′keep′ing,** *n.*

store·room (stôr′rŏŏm′, -rŏŏm′), *n.* a room in which supplies and goods are stored.

sto·ried (stôr′ēd), *adj.* famous in story, legend, or history: *the storied cities of ancient Greece.*

stork (stôrk), *n.* any of several large wading birds having long legs and a long neck and bill. Storks sometimes nest on roofs or chimneys.

storm (stôrm), *n.* **1.** a violent disturbance of the atmosphere causing high winds and often rain, snow, hail, etc. **2.** any outburst of violence, strong emotion, etc.: *a storm of tears.* **3.** violent attack: *to take a city by storm.* —*v.* **4.** (of the wind or the weather) to blow, rain, snow, hail, etc., with violence: *It stormed all day.* **5.** to show great anger; rage: *He stormed over the delay.* **6.** to rush violently: *He stormed out of the room.* **7.** to attack: *The enemy stormed the city.*

Stork
(length 3½ ft.)

storm·y (stôr′mē), *adj.*, **storm·i·er, storm·i·est.** having storms, or troubled by storms: *a period of stormy weather.* —**storm′i·ly,** *adv.* —**storm′i·ness,** *n.*

sto·ry[1] (stôr′ē), *n.*, *pl.* **sto·ries. 1.** a written or spoken account of something that has happened: *He told us the story of his life.* **2.** a work of fiction, esp. one that is shorter than a novel. **3.** *Informal.* a lie: *What he said about being robbed was only a story.* [from the early French word *estorie,* which comes from Latin *historia* "history"]

sto·ry[2] (stôr′ē), *n.*, *pl.* **sto·ries.** one of the floors of a building. [from a special use of *story*[1]]

sto·ry·tell·er (stôr′ē tel′ər), *n.* **1.** a person who writes or tells stories. **2.** *Informal.* a person who tells lies.

stoup (stoōp), *n.* a basin for holy water, usually at the entrance of a church.

stout (stout), *adj.* **1.** fat in body: *a short, stout woman.* **2.** brave; courageous: *a stout heart.* **3.** strong; sturdy: *stout seamen; a stout rope.* —*n.* **4.** a strong, dark beer. —**stout′ly,** *adv.* —**stout′ness,** *n.*

stout-heart·ed (stout′här′tid), *adj.* brave; dauntless: *stout-hearted troops.* —**stout′-heart′ed·ly,** *adv.* —**stout′-heart′ed·ness,** *n.*

stove[1] (stōv), *n.* a device for heating or cooking that uses coal, oil, gas, or electricity as fuel. [from the Old English word *stofa* "hot-air bathroom"]

stove[2] (stōv), *v.* a past tense and past participle of **stave.**

stove·pipe (stōv′pīp′), *n.* **1.** a metal pipe used to carry away smoke from a stove. **2.** *Informal.* a tall silk hat.

stow (stō), *v.* **1.** to pack or store: *to stow cargo in a ship's hold.* **2. stow away,** to hide aboard a ship, plane, or the like, to obtain free transportation: *He escaped by stowing away on a freighter.*

stow·a·way (stō′ə wā′), *n.* a person who hides on a ship or plane in order to get free passage.

St. Paul, the capital city of Minnesota, in the SE part, on the Mississippi River.

St. Pe·ters·burg (pē′tərz bûrg′), **1.** a port city in W Florida: seaside winter resort. **2.** a former name (1703–1914) of **Leningrad.**

strad·dle (strad′°l), *v.*, **strad·dled, strad·dling. 1.** to walk, stand, or sit with one leg on each side of: *to straddle a horse; to straddle a chair.* **2.** to support or appear to support both sides of: *to straddle an issue.* —**strad′dler,** *n.* —**strad′dling·ly,** *adv.*

strafe (strāf), *v.*, **strafed, straf·ing.** to attack with machine-gun fire from an airplane flying low.

strag·gle (strag′əl), *v.*, **strag·gled, strag·gling. 1.** to wander about in a scattered way; ramble; stray: *Sheep were straggling over the meadow.* **2.** to lag or trail behind: *a group of weary, straggling marchers.* **3.** to grow or spread unevenly: *Vines straggled over the porch.* —**strag′gler,** *n.* —**strag′gling·ly,** *adv.*

straight (strāt), *adj.* **1.** without a bend, angle, or curve: *a straight road.* **2.** exactly level or vertical: *a straight pole; a picture not straight on the wall.* **3.** honest; sincere; frank: *a straight answer.* **4.** direct; unwavering: *a straight course of action.* **5.** complete or absolute; thoroughgoing: *He is a straight Republican.* **6.** having no break or interruption: *in straight succession.* **7.** being in good or proper order: *My room is straight now.* —*adv.* **8.** in a straight line: *to walk straight.* **9.** in an upright or level position or posture: *Stand straight. Set the picture straight.* **10.** without detour; directly: *to go straight home.* **11.** honestly; sincerely; frankly: *to talk straight.* **12. straight off** (or **away**), without delay; at once; immediately: *I knew straight off that I wouldn't like history.* —**straight′ness,** *n.*

straight·a·way (strāt′ə wā′), *adj.* **1.** straight onward, without turning or curving, such as a race course. —*n.* **2.** a straight road, path, or part of a race track. —*adv.* **3.** Also, **straight′way′.** at once; right away.

straight·en (strāt′°n), *v.* to make or become straight: *to straighten curly hair; to straighten a room.*

straight′ face′, a serious look that hides one's true feelings, esp. the desire to laugh: *He told jokes with a straight face.* —**straight′-faced′,** *adj.*

straight·for·ward (strāt′fôr′wərd), *adj.* **1.** going straight ahead; direct; not roundabout: *a straightforward way of solving a problem.* **2.** honest and frank: *a straightforward answer.* —**straight′for′ward·ly,** *adv.* —**straight′for′ward·ness,** *n.*

strain[1] (strān), *v.* **1.** to draw tight; stretch: *to strain a rope.* **2.** to pull with force: *a dog straining at a leash.* **3.** to push or drive to the utmost: *She strained herself to finish on time.* **4.** to try as hard as possible: *She strained to finish.* **5.** to hurt or weaken (a muscle, tendon, etc.) by too much exertion; sprain: *He strained his back lifting the piano.* **6.** to stretch beyond the proper point or limit: *to strain the meaning of a word.* **7.** to pass (liquid) through a sieve, strainer, or the like: *to strain tea.* —*n.* **8.** any strong force or pressure: *The building collapsed under the strain caused by the heavy roof.* **9.** great effort or striving: *a great strain to finish on time.* **10.** an injury to a muscle, tendon, etc., caused by too much exertion: *a strain of the back.* **11.** injury to the mind or the nerves caused by worry, hard work, etc.: *nervous strain.* **12.** Often, **strains.** a melody or tune: *the strains of an old hymn.* [from the Old French word *estreindre* "to press tightly," which comes from Latin *stringere* "to bind"]

strain² (strān), *n.* **1.** a line of ancestry or descent; family. **2.** a particular variety of plants or animals; family; breed. **3.** an inherited characteristic: *a strain of madness in the family.* [from the Old English word *strēon* "lineage, race, tribe"]

strained (strānd), *adj.* not natural; forced: *a strained smile.* —**strained·ly** (strānd′lē, strā′nid lē), *adv.*

strain·er (strā′nər), *n.* a sieve, filter, etc., used for straining: *a soup strainer.*

strait (strāt), *n.* **1.** a narrow passage of water connecting two large bodies of water. **2.** Often, **straits.** a difficult or bad position: *His reckless spending has put him in bad straits.*

strait·en (strāt′ⁿn), *v.* to put into difficulties, esp. financial ones: *He lives in straitened circumstances.*

strait′ jack′et, a garment made of strong cloth and tied at the arms, used to control a person who is violent, delirious, etc.

strait-laced (strāt′lāst′), *adj.* very strict and proper in behavior and opinions: *His strait-laced aunt believed that children should be seen and not heard.*

strand¹ (strand), *v.* **1.** to drive or leave (a ship, fish, etc.) ashore: *The storm stranded the whale on the beach.* **2.** to put in a helpless position: *I was stranded without train fare.* —*n.* **3.** the border of a lake, sea, or river; shore; beach. [from Old English]

strand² (strand), *n.* **1.** a number of fibers or threads twisted together to form a rope, cord, or the like. **2.** a tress of hair. **3.** a string of pearls, beads, etc.

strange (strānj), *adj.,* **strang·er, strang·est. 1.** unusual, extraordinary, or curious: *That was a strange thing to say.* **2.** out of place: *I feel strange in foreign cities.* **3.** unfamiliar; unknown: *They were speaking a strange language.* **4.** not accustomed: *to be strange to a job.* —**strange′ly,** *adv.* —**strange′ness,** *n.*

stran·ger (strān′jər), *n.* **1.** a person whom one does not know: *He is a perfect stranger to me.* **2.** a newcomer in a place: *a stranger in town.* **3.** a person who is unused to something (usually fol. by *to*): *He is no stranger to poverty.*

stran·gle (straṅg′gəl), *v.,* **stran·gled, stran·gling. 1.** to kill by squeezing the throat so as to stop breathing. **2.** to kill by stopping the breath in any manner; choke; stifle; suffocate: *He was strangled by the bone.* **3.** to be choked, stifled, etc.: *He strangled when the rope was drawn tight.* **4.** to stop the growth, progress, or action of: *The suburbs strangled the city.* —**stran′gler,** *n.*

stran·gu·la·tion (straṅg′gyə lā′shən), *n.* the act of strangling, or the state of being strangled.

strap (strap), *n.* **1.** a narrow strip of leather or other material, used for fastening or holding things together. —*v.,* **strapped, strap·ping. 2.** to fasten or hold in place with a strap or straps: *to strap books together; to strap a watch to one's wrist.* **3.** to beat or flog with a strap.

strap·ping (strap′iṅg), *adj.* strongly built; robust: *a tall, strapping man.*

Stras·bourg (stras′bûrg, sträz′bŏŏrg), *n.* a city in NE France, near the Rhine River.

stra·ta (strā′tə, strat′ə), *n.* the plural of **stratum.**

strat·a·gem (strat′ə jəm), *n.* a plan, scheme, or trick for deceiving an enemy or opponent.

stra·te·gic (strə tē′jik), *adj.* **1.** of or referring to strategy: *The enemy's bridges were destroyed for strategic reasons.* **2.** using or showing strategy: *a strategic move.* —**stra·te′gi·cal·ly,** *adv.*

strat·e·gist (strat′i jist), *n.* an expert in strategy.

strat·e·gy (strat′i jē), *n., pl.* **strat·e·gies. 1.** a detailed plan or number of stratagems for reaching a goal or result: *The captain's strategy brought victory for the team.* **2.** the science or art of planning and directing military movements and operations. **3.** skill in using stratagems: *We must have strategy if we are to win.*

Strat·ford-on-A·von (strat′fərd ôn ā′vən), *n.* a town in central England: birthplace and burial place of Shakespeare. Also, **Strat′ford.**

strat·i·fi·ca·tion (strat′ə fə kā′shən), *n.* **1.** the act or process of stratifying or becoming stratified. **2.** an arrangement in layers or levels: *stratifications in rock; stratifications in society.*

strat·i·fy (strat′ə fī′), *v.,* **strat·i·fied, strat·i·fy·ing.** to form or become arranged in layers or levels.

strat·o·sphere (strat′ə sfēr′), *n.* the part of the atmosphere, extending upward from a height of about 7 miles to a height of about 15 miles, where temperatures are fairly uniform and there are few clouds. —**strat·o·spher·ic** (strat′ə sfer′ik), *adj.*

stra·tum (strā′təm, strat′əm), *n., pl.* **stra·tums** *or* **stra·ta** (strā′tə, strat′ə). **1.** a layer of rock or earth: *Sedimentary rocks are often laid down in strata of different colors.* **2.** a social level.

Strauss (strous), *n.* **Jo·hann** (yō′hän), 1825–1899, Austrian composer.

straw (strô), *n.* **1.** a stalk or stem of wheat, rye, oats, or other grass. **2.** a mass of such stalks: *a scarecrow filled with straw.* **3.** a tube, usually of paper or glass, for sucking up a liquid from a container into the mouth. **4.** something almost worthless: *He doesn't care a straw for what people think.* —*adj.* **5.** of, referring to, or containing straw: *a straw hat.* **6. clutch at any straw,** to seize at any chance, no matter how slight, to escape trouble, misery, or the like: *He was clutching at any straw to save his business from bankruptcy.* —**straw′like′,** *adj.*

straw·ber·ry (strô′ber′ē), *n., pl.* **straw·ber·ries. 1.** a red, juicy, pear-shaped berry that grows on a low plant related to the rose. **2.** the plant itself.

straw′ vote′, an unofficial vote taken to find out what the public feels about a certain matter.

stray (strā), *v.* **1.** to leave the proper course, place, etc.; wander: *We strayed from the main road and became lost.* **2.** to go astray from the right or true way of belief, conduct, etc.: *They strayed from their religion.* **3.** to wander in thought, speech, etc. —*n.* **4.** a lost or homeless person or animal: *My cat was a stray I found in the street.* —*adj.* **5.** lost or homeless:

a stray dog. **6.** casual or unplanned; chance: *stray remarks on the weather; a stray bullet.*

streak (strēk), *n.* **1.** a long, narrow mark, smear, band of color, or the like: *a sunset with streaks of bright red.* **2.** a layer: *streaks of fat in meat.* **3.** a strain or trace of anything: *a streak of humor.* **4.** *Informal.* a spell or run: *a streak of good luck.* —*v.* **5.** to mark with a streak or streaks: *to streak a wall with paint.* **6.** to arrange, smear, etc., in the form of streaks: *to streak paint on a wall.* **7.** to make a streak or streaks: *Lightning streaked above the city.* **8.** to move rapidly: *The train streaked over the rails.*

stream (strēm), *n.* **1.** a flowing body of water, esp. a small river. **2.** a flow of anything: *a stream of blood; a stream of light; a stream of words.* —*v.* **3.** to flow or move steadily: *Water streamed from the pipe. The crowd streamed out of the building.* **4.** to send forth or throw off a stream: *Her eyes streamed with tears.* **5.** to wave or flutter in the wind: *Banners streamed from the masts.* **6.** to send forth in a stream: *His wound streamed blood.* —**stream′like′**, *adj.*

stream·er (strē′mər), *n.* **1.** something that streams: *streamers of flame; streamers of light.* **2.** a long, narrow flag or pennant. **3.** a long, flowing ribbon.

stream·let (strēm′lit), *n.* a small stream; rivulet.

stream·line (strēm′līn′), *n.* **1.** a shape resembling that of a teardrop, which offers little resistance to a current of air or water. **2.** the path of a particle in a smoothly flowing current of a liquid or a gas. —*v.*, **stream·lined, stream·lin·ing.** **3.** to make streamlined. **4.** to make simpler and more efficient: *The post office is streamlining its delivery service.*

stream·lined (strēm′līnd′), *adj.* **1.** having a shape that offers the least possible resistance to a current of air or water. **2.** brought up to date, or made more efficient: *a streamlined service to meet modern needs.*

street (strēt), *n.* **1.** a public road, usually paved, in a city or town. **2.** such a road together with the sidewalks and buildings along it: *an attractive residential street.* **3.** the people who live or work on a street: *The noise woke up the whole street.*

street·car (strēt′kär′), *n.* a trolley car.

strength (strengkth, strength), *n.* **1.** power of mind or body; vigor: *strength of will; muscular strength.* **2.** force in numbers: *an army with a strength of many thousands of men.* **3.** effectiveness: *a drug of great strength; an argument with no strength.* **4.** vividness, sharpness, richness, etc.: *coffee of full strength; the strength of a color.* **5.** a source or cause of power: *Knowledge is his strength.* **6. on the strength of,** on the basis of; as a result of: *He was convicted on the strength of her testimony.*

strength·en (strengk′thən, streng′thən), *v.* to make or become strong or stronger: *Exercise will strengthen your muscles.* —**strength′en·er,** *n.*

stren·u·ous (stren′yōō əs), *adj.* **1.** vigorous; energetic: *a strenuous person; a strenuous mind.* **2.** marked by or requiring vigor or energy: *a strenuous sport.* —**stren′u·ous·ly,** *adv.* —**stren′u·ous·ness,** *n.*

strep·to·coc·cus (strep′tə kok′əs), *n., pl.* **strep·to·coc·ci** (strep′tə kok′sī). any of various round bacteria that occur in pairs or long chains. Some types cause diseases.

strep·to·my·cin (strep′tō mī′sin), *n.* an antibiotic produced by a fungus found in soil and used in the treatment of tuberculosis.

stress (stres), *n.* **1.** emphasis or importance: *to lay stress upon good manners.* **2.** emphasis in the form of greater force or loudness in the pronunciation of a part of a word or phrase. In the word *detect,* the stress is on the second syllable. In the phrase *pin money,* the stress is on the word *pin.* **3.** accent or emphasis upon syllables in poetry, or upon notes in music. **4.** the pressure put upon one thing by another; strain: *Steel can endure great stress.* **5.** strain or pressure upon the body, mind, or feelings: *to undergo great emotional stress.* —*v.* **6.** to lay stress upon; emphasize: *She stressed good manners.* **7.** to give emphasis to (a syllable or a word).

stretch (strech), *v.* **1.** to draw out to full or greater length: *to stretch the arms; to stretch rubber bands.* **2.** to reach forth: *He stretched his head to see.* **3.** to extend or spread: *They stretched a rope across the road.* **4.** to cover or lie over a particular place or reach in a certain direction: *The forest stretches for miles.* **5.** to lie at full length (usually fol. by *out*): *He stretched out on the sofa.* **6.** to strain the body so as to draw out the muscles: *to stretch and yawn.* **7.** to be capable of being drawn out: *Rubber stretches easily.* **8.** to make go beyond the normal or proper limits: *to stretch the imagination; to stretch a dollar.* —*n.* **9.** the act of stretching, or the state of being stretched. **10.** unbroken space or time: *to work for many hours at a stretch; a stretch of fertile land in the desert.* **11.** elastic quality: *The rubber has lost its stretch.* —**stretch′a·bil′i·ty,** *n.* —**stretch′a·ble,** *adj.*

stretch·er (strech′ər), *n.* **1.** a litter, usually of canvas stretched on a frame, for carrying the sick, wounded, or dead. **2.** any of various frames or devices for stretching something: *a curtain stretcher.*

strew (strōō), *v.,* **strewed; strewn** (strōōn) *or* **strewed; strew·ing.** **1.** to scatter or sprinkle: *He strewed his clothes around the room.* **2.** to cover with something scattered or sprinkled: *Sawdust strewed the floor.*

strick·en (strik′ən), *adj.* **1.** a past participle of **strike.** **2.** afflicted with disease, trouble, sorrow, etc.: *to send relief to stricken areas after a flood.*

strict (strikt), *adj.* **1.** severe or stern in following or enforcing a rule: *a strict judge.* **2.** rigid; unchanging: *a strict rule of procedure.* **3.** perfect or complete: *strict privacy.* —**strict′ly,** *adv.* —**strict′ness,** *n.*

stric·ture (strik′chər), *n.* **1.** a harsh criticism; censure: *His scandalous behavior brought down strictures from the senate.* **2.** something that limits or restricts: *to live without strictures.* **3.** an unhealthy narrowing of a tube or passage in the body.

stride (strīd), *v.,* **strode** (strōd), **strid·den** (strid′ən), **strid·ing.** **1.** to walk with long steps: *He strode vigor-*

ously along the boardwalk. **2.** to take a long step: *to stride across a puddle.* **3.** to cross over in one long step: *to stride a puddle.* **4.** to straddle: *to stride a horse.* —*n.* **5.** a long step, or the distance covered: *a stride ahead of someone.* **6.** a striding gait: *a vigorous stride.* **7.** a step forward in progress or growth: *Science has made enormous strides.* **8. hit one's stride,** to reach one's regular pace in doing something: *As the game progressed, the players hit their stride.* **9. take (something) in one's stride,** to deal with (something) calmly or easily: *He could take both good and bad luck in his stride.*

stri·dent (strīd/³nt), *adj.* making or having a harsh sound; grating; creaking: *a strident cry for help.* —**stri/dent·ly,** *adv.*

strife (strīf), *n.* **1.** the state of bitter conflict or fighting: *a career marked by strife.* **2.** a conflict, quarrel, fight, etc.: *The strife between them went on for years.*

strike (strīk), *v.,* **struck** (struk); **struck** or *(esp. for def. 18)* **strick·en** (strik/ən); **strik·ing.** **1.** to hit, as with the fist, a weapon, hammer, etc.: *to strike a nail; to strike someone in the nose.* **2.** to deal (a blow). **3.** to attack: *The enemy struck the helpless country.* **4.** to hit or dash against: *The ship struck a rock.* **5.** to make (fire, sparks, a light, etc.) by hitting, rubbing, etc.: *to strike fire from flint.* **6.** to light (a match). **7.** to reach or fall upon (the eyes, ears, etc.): *A strange sight struck their eyes.* **8.** to come to the mind of; occur to: *A happy thought struck him.* **9.** to make an impression on: *How does my plan strike you?* **10.** to come suddenly or unexpectedly (often fol. by *on* or *upon*): *He struck on a new way of making steel.* **11.** to come upon or find (gold, ore, etc.) by digging or drilling. **12.** to reach by agreement: *to strike a bargain.* **13.** to take apart or pull down: *to strike a tent; to strike a sail.* **14.** to cancel or cross out: *to strike a name from a list.* **15.** to stamp (a coin, medal, etc.) by printing or punching. **16.** to sound the hour, as a clock. **17.** to show or be shown by sounding: *The clock struck noon.* **18.** to afflict suddenly (often fol. by *down*): *Disease struck him down.* **19.** to take on (a certain way of appearing): *to strike a silly pose.* **20.** to leave off work in order to have certain demands met: *to strike for higher wages.* **21.** to go or set forth (often fol. by *out*): *They struck out at dawn.* **22.** (of fish) to swallow or take the bait. —*n.* **23.** the act or an instance of striking. **24.** a deliberate stoppage of work until certain demands are met. **25.** a pull made by a fish on a line as it takes the bait. **26.** (in baseball) a pitch that is swung at and missed by the batter, or a pitch that passes over the plate between his shoulders and his knees and is not swung at. **27.** the discovery of a rich supply of oil or ore. **28. strike it rich,** to make or get a great deal of money suddenly or unexpectedly: *He struck it rich with his new oil well.* **29. strike out,** (in baseball) to put out or be put out by means of three strikes: *He struck out 14 batters in a row.* **30. strike up, a.** to begin or commence: *to strike up a friendship.* **b.** to begin to play or sing: *The band struck up a march.* —**strik/er,** *n.*

strik·ing (strī/king), *adj.* **1.** that strikes. **2.** outstand-

ing: *a woman of striking beauty.* **3.** noticeable; conspicuous: *a striking defect.* —**strik/ing·ly,** *adv.*

string (string), *n.* **1.** a slender cord or thick thread for tying. **2.** a strip of cloth, leather, etc., for tying something: *the strings of a bonnet.* **3.** a necklace of beads, pearls, or the like. **4.** a number of things in a line or set close together: *a string of cars; a string of lights.* **5.** a tightly stretched cord or wire on a musical instrument, that sounds when plucked, struck, etc. **6. strings,** stringed musical instruments, esp. those played with a bow. **7.** a group of players classed according to skill: *He made the second string on the football team.* —*v.,* **strung** (strung), **string·ing.** **8.** to put a string or strings on: *to string a violin.* **9.** to thread on or as if on a string: *to string beads.* **10.** to stretch (a cord, thread, etc.) from one point to another. **11.** to arrange in a line or series: *to string words together.* **12.** to strip the fibers from: *to string beans.* **13. pull strings,** to use one's influential friends, business connections, or the like, to get something that one wants or needs: *He pulled strings to get his son that job.* **14. string out,** to extend, prolong, or stretch out: *The parade strung out for miles.*

string/ bean/, any of various kinds of beans cultivated for their long, slender pods, which are eaten as a vegetable after removing a stringlike fiber running along the side.

stringed (stringd), *adj.* (esp. of a musical instrument) having strings (often used in combination): *a five-stringed banjo.*

stringed/ in/strument, a musical instrument that has strings and is played with a bow, such as a violin or cello, or by plucking the strings with the fingers or a plectrum, such as a harp or banjo.

strin·gent (strin/jənt), *adj.* **1.** severe, demanding, or strict: *stringent rules.* **2.** urgent or compelling: *Stringent need forced him to take the job.* **3.** forceful and convincing: *a stringent argument.* **4.** short in money for loans; tight: *a stringent money market.* —**strin/gen·cy,** *n.* —**strin/gent·ly,** *adv.*

string·er (string/ər), *n.* **1.** a person or thing that strings. **2.** a long piece of timber used to connect upright posts.

string·y (string/ē), *adj.,* **string·i·er, string·i·est.** **1.** like string: *stringy vines.* **2.** having tough fibers: *stringy meat; stringy vegetables.* —**string/i·ness,** *n.*

strip¹ (strip), *v.,* **stripped** or **stript** (stript); **strip·ping.** **1.** to take off one's clothing; undress: *They stripped and jumped into the water.* **2.** to take away or remove: *to strip the bark from a tree.* **3.** to deprive: *to strip a soldier of his rank.* **4.** to empty or clear out: *to strip a house of its furniture.* **5.** to rob or plunder: *The invaders stripped the town.* [from the Middle English word *strippe*] —**strip/per,** *n.*

strip² (strip), *n.* **1.** a long, narrow, flat piece of something: *a strip of ribbon.* **2.** an airstrip. [from the German dialect word *strippe* "strap"]

stripe (strīp), *n.* **1.** a band, line, or streak different in color, material, etc., from the rest of a surface or thing: *the stripes of a zebra; stripes of gray in black rock.* **2.** a strip of braid, tape, or the like, worn on the sleeve of a uniform as a badge of rank, service, etc. **3.** sort or kind: *a person of a different stripe from the ordinary.* —**stripe′less,** *adj.*

striped (strīpt, strī′pid), *adj.* having stripes or bands.

strip·ling (strip′ling), *n.* a youth.

strip′ min′ing, mining of coal in an open pit at or near the surface, after removal of the covering earth and rock.

strive (strīv), *v.,* **strove** (strōv), **striv·en** (striv′ən), **striv·ing. 1.** to make a strong effort; try hard: *They strove to succeed.* **2.** to struggle: *They strove against the enemy.* —**striv′er,** *n.* —**striv′ing·ly,** *adv.*

strode (strōd), *v.* the past tense of **stride.**

stroke¹ (strōk), *n.* **1.** the act of striking a blow, or the blow itself: *He chopped the log in half with a single stroke.* **2.** the sound of a striking clock or the hour indicated by such a sound: *the stroke of midnight.* **3.** a sudden attack of a disease, esp. the bursting of a blood vessel in the brain leading to impairment of speech, paralysis, etc. **4.** a throb or beat of the heart. **5.** one of a number of complete movements, as in swimming, rowing, etc.: *the stroke of an oar.* **6.** a movement of a pen, pencil, brush, etc.: *He painted with swift, bold strokes.* **7.** a mark made by such a movement. **8.** a single bit or piece of work, activity, etc: *He refused to do a stroke of work.* **9.** a feat or achievement: *a stroke of genius.* **10.** a sudden action or event: *a stroke of good luck.* —*v.,* **stroked, strok·ing. 11.** to make a single movement of the arm, an oar, etc., as in swimming or rowing. [from a Middle English word, which is related to Old English *strācian* "to stroke." See *stroke²*]

stroke² (strōk), *v.,* **stroked, strok·ing. 1.** to pass the hand or an object lightly over the surface of; caress: *to stroke a cat.* —*n.* **2.** a stroking movement. [from the Old English word *strācian*]

stroll (strōl), *v.* **1.** to walk in a slow, easy way here and there: *to stroll in the park.* **2.** to wander or rove from place to place: *strolling Gypsies.* —*n.* **3.** a slow, easy walk: *to take a stroll on the beach.*

stroll·er (strō′lər), *n.* **1.** a person who strolls. **2.** a chairlike carriage in which a child rides sitting up.

strong (strông), *adj.,* **strong·er** (strông′gər), **strong·est** (strông′gist). **1.** powerful or forceful: *strong muscles; strong winds.* **2.** very able in a certain way: *She is strong in arithmetic.* **3.** having great courage or firmness: *to be strong enough to resist temptation.* **4.** convincing; effective: *strong arguments.* **5.** close, as in appearance: *He bears a strong resemblance to his father.* **6.** bright, as light or color: *strong sunlight.* **7.** devoted or faithful: *He's a strong supporter of his party.* **8.** having a concentrated flavor, aroma, or other quality: *strong tea.* —*adv.* **9.** in a strong manner: *You must act strong.* —**strong′ly,** *adv.*

strong·box (strông′boks′), *adj.* a strongly made box with a lock, used for storing money or valuables.

strong·hold (strông′hōld′), *n.* **1.** a well-fortified place; fortress. **2.** a place where a certain idea or viewpoint is very strong: *a stronghold of liberalism.*

strong′ verb′, a verb that forms its past tense, and often also its past participle, by changing the vowel of the stem, such as *sing, sang, sung* or *ride, rode, ridden.* See also **weak verb.**

stron·ti·um (stron′shē əm, stron′tē əm), *n. Chem.* a metallic element that forms compounds similar to those of calcium. *Symbol:* Sr

strop (strop), *n.* **1.** a thick, wide strap, usually of leather, on which a razor is sharpened. —*v.,* **stropped, strop·ping. 2.** to sharpen (a razor) on a strop.

stro·phe (strō′fē), *n.* a section of a poem, differing from a stanza in not having a fixed number of lines. —**stroph·ic** (strof′ik, strō′fik), *adj.*

strove (strōv), *v.* the past tense of **strive.**

struck (struk), *v.* the past tense and a past participle of **strike.**

struc·tur·al (struk′chər əl), *adj.* **1.** of or concerning a structure or structures: *structural design.* **2.** used in building: *structural steel.* —**struc′tur·al·ly,** *adv.*

struc·ture (struk′chər), *n.* **1.** a building or anything constructed, such as a bridge, dam, etc. **2.** the way in which something is put together: *the structure of a sentence.* —*v.,* **struc·tured, struc·tur·ing. 3.** to organize or give a structure to: *to structure a play.*

strug·gle (strug′əl), *v.,* **strug·gled, strug·gling. 1.** to fight hard: *to struggle against an enemy; to struggle against poverty.* **2.** to try hard; strive: *to struggle for victory.* **3.** to move with effort: *to struggle through mud.* —**strug′gler,** *n.*

strum (strum), *v.,* **strummed, strum·ming. 1.** to play on (a stringed instrument) lightly: *to strum a guitar.* **2.** to make (notes, a melody, etc.) by such playing: *to strum a tune.* —*n.* **3.** the act of strumming. **4.** the sound made by strumming: *the strum of a guitar.*

strung (strung), *v.* the past tense and past participle of **string.**

strut¹ (strut), *v.,* **strut·ted, strut·ting. 1.** to walk in a vain, pompous way: *They strutted down the street in their Easter finery.* —*n.* **2.** the act of strutting, or a strutting walk. [from the Old English word *strutian* "to stand out stiffly"]

strut² (strut), *n.* a long piece of wood or metal set at an angle into a framework for support. [from an earlier word, which is related to *strut¹*]

strych·nine (strik′nīn, strik′nin), *n.* a very poisonous substance sometimes used in medicine as a stimulant.

stub (stub), *n.* **1.** a short piece that is left, as of a pencil, cigar, candle, etc. **2.** the stump of a shrub, tree, plant, etc. **3.** a short part of a check, ticket, etc., kept as a record. —*v.,* **stubbed, stub·bing. 4.** to strike accidentally: *I stubbed my toe against the door.*

stub·ble (stub′əl), *n.* **1.** the stumps of stalks of grain left standing in a field after harvest. **2.** anything that looks like this, such as a short growth of beard. —**stub′bled, stub′bly,** *adj.*

stub·born (stub′ərn), *adj.* **1.** unyielding or obstinate in one's ways; not willing to change: *He was too stub-*

born to admit that he was wrong. **2.** strong and purposeful: *a stubborn fight.* **3.** hard to handle, manage, treat, etc.: *dry, stubborn soil; a stubborn cough.* —**stub′born·ly**, *adv.* —**stub′born·ness**, *n.*

stub·by (stub′ē), *adj.*, **stub·bi·er, stub·bi·est. 1.** short and thick: *stubby fingers.* **2.** covered with stubs or stubble: *stubby land.* **3.** bristly, as the hair or beard. —**stub′bi·ness**, *n.*

stuc·co (stuk′ō), *n.* **1.** a kind of plaster or cement used to coat walls. —*v.*, **stuc·coed, stuc·co·ing. 2.** to cover with stucco: *The brick walls of the house were stuccoed and painted.*

stuck (stuk), *v.* the past tense and past participle of **stick².**

stuck-up (stuk′up′), *adj. Informal.* vain; conceited: *She was stuck-up about her looks.*

stud¹ (stud), *n.* **1.** a small knob or a nail with a rounded head, used as an ornament: *leather decorated with brass studs.* **2.** a buttonlike object used to fasten clothes: *a stud for a collar.* **3.** one of a number of upright beams in a wall forming a frame for an outer surface of wood, plaster, etc. —*v.*, **stud·ded, stud·ding. 4.** to set with studs or the like: *to stud a wall with nails.* **5.** to scatter or lie scattered over: *She studded raisins over the cake. Stars studded the sky.* [from the Old English word *studu* "post"]

stud² (stud), *n.* **1.** a male animal, esp. a horse, kept for breeding purposes. **2.** a number of horses for breeding, or the farm where they are kept. [from the Old English word *stōd*]

stu·dent (stōōd′ənt, styōōd′-), *n.* **1.** a person who studies at a school or college. **2.** any person who studies or examines something carefully: *a student of world affairs.* —*adj.* **3.** of, by, or concerning students: *a program of student songs; student activities.*

stud·ied (stud′ēd), *adj.* carefully planned or thought out: *an air of studied naturalness.*

stu·di·o (stōō′dē ō′, styōō′-), *n.*, *pl.* **stu·di·os. 1.** a room, building, etc., where an artist works. **2.** a place where television or radio programs are broadcast or where motion pictures are made.

stu·di·ous (stōō′dē əs, styōō′-), *adj.* **1.** liking or devoted to study: *a studious pupil.* **2.** giving or showing careful attention: *a studious host; studious planning.* —**stu′di·ous·ly**, *adv.*

stud·y (stud′ē), *n.*, *pl.* **stud·ies. 1.** the pursuit of knowledge of some subject by reading, thinking, etc.: *the study of foreign languages.* **2.** Often, **studies.** work at school or college; education: *to complete one's studies.* **3.** an investigation of some matter, problem, etc., or a written report of this: *The mayor ordered a study of traffic problems.* **4.** a branch of knowledge: *Geography can be a fascinating study.* **5.** deep thought: *He was lost in study and did not hear the bell.* **6.** a room in a house or apartment set apart for study, reading, writing, or the like. **7.** a story or novel in which one subject is dealt with in great detail. —*v.*, **stud·ied, stud·y·ing. 8.** to set oneself to learn: *He studies for hours every night.* **9.** to set oneself to learn (a subject): *He is studying history now.* **10.** to examine or give careful thought to: *to study a*

problem. **11.** to look at carefully in order to learn something: *to study a map.* **12.** to try to memorize or learn by heart: *to study a part in a play.*

stuff (stuf), *n.* **1.** the material of which anything is made: *stuff for building a house.* **2.** things or belongings: *They moved their stuff to their new apartment.* **3.** personal qualities; character: *He has good stuff in him.* **4.** talk or action of a certain kind: *rough stuff.* **5.** worthless or foolish ideas, talk, etc.: *stuff and nonsense.* **6.** *Informal.* something that one is good at: *The dancers did their stuff.* —*v.* **7.** to fill up: *to stuff a valise with clothing.* **8.** to fill with stuffing: *to stuff a pillow; to stuff a chicken.* **9.** to fill or cram with food: *They stuffed themselves with the dessert.* **10.** to thrust or cram into an opening, container, etc.: *He stuffed the money into his pocket.* **11.** to pack tightly; crowd together: *to stuff people into a little room.* **12.** to stop up or plug (usually fol. by *up*): *a nose stuffed up from a cold.*

stuf·fing (stuf′ĭng), *n.* **1.** material used to stuff a mattress, pillow, sofa, etc. **2.** a mixture of bread, seasonings, chopped vegetables, etc., used to stuff poultry or other food.

stuff·y (stuf′ē), *adj.*, **stuff·i·er, stuff·i·est. 1.** lacking fresh air: *a stuffy room.* **2.** stopped up or feeling stopped up: *a stuffy nose; a stuffy head.* **3.** dull or boring: *a stuffy lesson.* **4.** smug and pompous: *stuffy manners.* —**stuff′i·ly**, *adv.* —**stuff′i·ness**, *n.*

stul·ti·fy (stul′tə fī′), *v.*, **stul·ti·fied, stul·ti·fy·ing.** to make or cause to seem foolish, useless, etc.; frustrate; degrade: *a boring routine that stultifies the mind.*

stum·ble (stum′bəl), *v.*, **stum·bled, stum·bling. 1.** to trip or stagger while walking or running: *His foot hit a stone, and he stumbled.* **2.** to walk or go unsteadily: *He stumbled down the street.* **3.** to make a slip, mistake, or blunder: *He stumbled when he came to the difficult word.* **4.** to act or speak in a confused, hesitating way (often fol. by *along*): *He forgot his lines and had to stumble along as best he could.* **5.** to find or come upon by chance (usually fol. by *on, upon, across,* etc.): *We stumbled upon a bargain.* —*n.* **6.** the act of stumbling: *a stumble over a stone.* **7.** a slip, mistake, or blunder: *stumbles in grammar and spelling.* —**stum′bler**, *n.*

stum′bling block′, something that gets in the way of or stops progress; obstacle: *His illness was a stumbling block in his career.*

stump (stump), *n.* **1.** the lower end of a tree or plant after the main part has fallen or been cut off. **2.** the part of an arm, leg, finger, etc., that remains after the rest has been cut off. **3.** a butt or stub: *the stump of a candle.* **4.** a platform for making political speeches. **5.** a heavy step or gait, as of a lame person: *to walk with a stump.* —*v.* **6.** to baffle or puzzle: *Your question stumps me completely.* **7.** to make political speeches in: *The governor stumped the state.* **8.** to walk with a heavy step: *He stumped into the room.*

stump·y (stum′pē), *adj.*, **stump·i·er, stump·i·est. 1.** like a stump; short and thick; stubby: *stumpy fingers.* **2.** full of stumps: *a stumpy field.*

stun (stun), *v.*, **stunned, stun·ning. 1.** to daze or make unconscious, as by a blow, fall, etc. **2.** to amaze or shock: *The bad news stunned us.*

stung (stung), *v.* the past tense and past participle of **sting.**

stunk (stungk), *v.* a past tense and the past participle of **stink.**

stun·ning (stun′ing), *adj.* **1.** that stuns, as a blow. **2.** strikingly good, beautiful, etc.: *a stunning girl.* —**stun′ning·ly,** *adv.*

stunt¹ (stunt), *v.* to stop or slow down the growth or development of: *Lack of rain and poor soil stunted the plants.* [from a Middle English word meaning "stupid," originally "short"]

stunt² (stunt), *n.* **1.** a display of skill or daring: *athletic stunts.* **2.** an act or trick to get attention.

stu·pe·fac·tion (stōō′pə fak′shən, styōō′-), *n.* **1.** the act of stupefying, or the state of being stupefied: *The drug caused stupefaction.* **2.** great amazement: *They received the news with stupefaction.*

stu·pe·fy (stōō′pə fī′, styōō′-), *v.*, **stu·pe·fied, stu·pe·fy·ing. 1.** to dull the senses of: *The drug stupefied him.* **2.** to amaze; astound: *They were stupefied by the announcement.*

stu·pen·dous (stōō pen′dəs, styōō-), *adj.* **1.** amazing; astounding; marvelous: *stupendous news.* **2.** amazingly large or great: *the stupendous buildings of New York.* —**stu·pen′dous·ly,** *adv.*

stu·pid (stōō′pid, styōō′-), *adj.* **1.** lacking intelligence; dull: *Stupid people are slow to learn.* **2.** showing or proceeding from a lack of intelligence: *a stupid thing to do; a stupid idea.* **3.** boring and senseless: *a stupid book.* —**stu′pid·ly,** *adv.*

stu·pid·i·ty (stōō pid′i tē, styōō-), *n., pl.* for def. 2 **stu·pid·i·ties. 1.** lack of intelligence. **2.** a stupid act, remark, idea, etc.: *a speech full of stupidities.*

stu·por (stōō′pər, styōō′-), *n.* a dazed or stunned condition: *to be in a stupor for lack of sleep.*

stur·dy (stûr′dē), *adj.*, **stur·di·er, stur·di·est. 1.** strong; robust; hardy: *sturdy bodies.* **2.** firm; resolute; courageous: *sturdy resistance.* —**stur′di·ness,** *n.*

stur·geon (stûr′jən), *n., pl.* **stur·geons** or **stur·geon.** any of various large food fishes having bony plates along the sides. Sturgeon are found in both fresh and salt waters of the north and are valued as a source of caviar.

Sturgeon
(length to 12 ft.)

stut·ter (stut′ər), *v.* **1.** to speak in a halting manner, repeating sounds and syllables: *He stuttered with embarrassment.* —*n.* **2.** a way of speaking marked by stuttering. —**stut′ter·er,** *n.* —**stut′ter·ing·ly,** *adv.*

Stuy·ve·sant (stī′vi sənt), *n.* Peter, 1592–1672, Dutch colonial administrator in the Americas.

sty¹ (stī), *n., pl.* **sties. 1.** a pigpen. **2.** any filthy place. [from the Old English word *stig*]

sty² (stī), *n., pl.* **sties.** an inflamed swelling on the edge of an eyelid. [from the Middle English word *styanye,* literally "swollen eye"]

style (stīl), *n.* **1.** a particular manner of writing, painting, speaking, building, etc.: *a church in Gothic style; Rembrandt's style of painting.* **2.** elegance or luxury: *The duchess liked to travel in style.* **3.** grace or polish in one's manners, actions, etc.: *to do one's work with style.* **4.** mode or fashion, esp. in dress: *the latest style in gowns; a word that is out of style.* **5.** Also, **stylus.** a pointed instrument used in ancient times for writing on waxed tablets. **6.** the rules according to which printed matter is spelled, punctuated, arranged, etc.: *Our style requires that foreign words be put in italics.* **7.** the slender stalk in a flower forming part of the pistil and having the stigma at its top. See illus. at **flower.** —*v.*, **styled, styl·ing. 8.** to design according to a particular fashion: *to style a dress.*

styl·ish (stī′lish), *adj.* in the latest style; fashionable; smart: *a stylish Paris dress.* —**styl′ish·ly,** *adv.* —**styl′ish·ness,** *n.*

sty·lus (stī′ləs), *n.* **1.** See **style** (def. 5). **2.** a phonograph needle.

Styx (stiks), *n.* (in Greek mythology) a river in Hades over which Charon rowed the spirits of the dead.

suave (swäv), *adj.* smoothly polite or gracious: *suave manners.* —**suave′ly,** *adv.* —**suav·i·ty** (swä′vi tē), **suave′ness,** *n.*

sub (sub), *n.* **1.** a submarine. **2.** a substitute. —*v.*, **subbed, sub·bing. 3.** to act as a substitute.

sub-, a prefix meaning **1.** under or beneath: *subcellar; submarine.* **2.** nearly; less than: *subtropical.* **3.** secondary or subordinate: *subcommittee; subplot.*

sub·al·tern (sub ôl′tərn), *n.* **1.** any officer in the British army below the rank of captain. **2.** a person in a lower rank or position. —*adj.* **3.** lower in rank or position: *a subaltern employee.*

sub·com·mit·tee (sub′kə mit′ē), *n.* a committee that is part of a larger committee.

sub·con·scious (sub kon′shəs), *n.* **1.** that part of the mind of which the individual is usually not aware. —*adj.* **2.** of, concerning, or existing in the subconscious: *subconscious memories; subconscious motives.* —**sub·con′scious·ly,** *adv.* —**sub·con′scious·ness,** *n.*

sub·con·ti·nent (sub kon′t³nənt), *n.* a large land mass forming a more or less separate part of a continent: *the subcontinent of India.*

sub·di·vide (sub′di vīd′, sub′di vīd′), *v.*, **sub·di·vid·ed, sub·di·vid·ing. 1.** to divide into smaller parts: *Each chapter is subdivided into several sections.* **2.** to divide (a plot of land) into building lots.

sub·di·vi·sion (sub′di vizh′ən), *n.* **1.** the act or fact of subdividing. **2.** a division of a division: *Each chapter has several subdivisions.* **3.** a plot of land divided into building lots.

sub·due (səb dōō′, -dyōō′), *v.*, **sub·dued, sub·du·ing. 1.** to overcome; conquer: *to subdue an enemy.* **2.** to control or calm: *to subdue one's anger.* **3.** to tone down; soften: *The dark carpet subdued the color scheme of the room.* —**sub·du′er,** *n.*

sub·head (sub′hed′), *n.* **1.** a title after a main title, as for a section of a chapter. **2.** the smaller part of a newspaper headline, coming at the end. Also, **sub/head/ing.**

sub·ject (sub/jikt), *n.* **1.** a matter or topic dealt with in writing, painting, conversation, etc.: *What is the subject of your essay?* **2.** a branch of knowledge or a course of study: *History is his favorite subject.* **3.** a cause or ground: *a subject for complaint.* **4.** a person who owes loyalty to a king or queen: *The people of England are British subjects.* **5.** a person who is treated or experimented upon by others: *The subject responded favorably to the medicine.* **6.** (in grammar) the one or ones that perform or (in the passive voice) receive the action or have the state of being expressed in the predicate. In the sentence *My brother and I went there, My brother and I* is the subject. —*adj.* **7.** being under control or domination (often fol. by *to*): *to be subject to a king.* **8.** being dependent upon or influenced by something (usually fol. by *to*): *This plan is subject to his approval.* **9.** liable or prone (often fol. by *to*): *to be subject to headaches.* —*v.* (səb jekt/). **10.** to bring under control or influence (usually fol. by *to*): *The country was subjected to enemy rule.* **11.** to cause to undergo; expose (usually fol. by *to*): *to subject metal to heat.* **12.** to make liable or open (usually fol. by *to*): *to subject oneself to ridicule.*

sub·jec·tion (səb jek/shən), *n.* **1.** the act of subjecting: *the subjection of an enemy.* **2.** the state or fact of being subjected: *to live in subjection.*

sub·jec·tive (səb jek/tiv), *adj.* **1.** of or referring to thoughts or feelings rather than to outside objects; existing in the mind; personal; inner (opposite of *objective*): *Our judgments are mostly subjective.* **2.** relying upon one's feelings, moods, etc., rather than upon reason. —**sub·jec/tive·ly,** *adv.*

sub/ject mat/ter, the subject of a book, talk, etc.: *The author handles his subject matter expertly.*

sub·ju·gate (sub/jə gāt/), *v.,* **sub·ju·gat·ed, sub·ju·gat·ing.** to bring under control; conquer: *Ancient Rome subjugated most of Europe.* —**sub/ju·ga/tion,** *n.*

sub·junc·tive (səb jungk/tiv), *adj.* **1.** describing the mood of a verb used to express an emotion, wish, doubt, or possibility. In *if this be treason,* the verb *be* is in the subjunctive mood. —*n.* **2.** the subjunctive mood. **3.** a verb form in the subjunctive mood.

sub·lease (sub/lēs/), *n.* **1.** a lease given by a person who has leased a house, apartment, etc. —*v.* (sub·lēs/), **sub·leased, sub·leas·ing. 2.** to give or take a sublease of (property).

sub·let (sub let/), *v.,* **sub·let, sub·let·ting. 1.** to sublease. —*n.* (sub/let/). **2.** a house, apartment, etc., that is subleased: *He lived in a sublet for a few months.*

sub·li·mate (sub/lə māt/), *v.* **1.** to change the energy of a physical impulse or desire in such a way that it is used for a higher or more acceptable form of behavior. **2.** to sublime (a substance). **3.** (of a physical impulse) to be changed into a worthier or more useful goal. —**sub/li·ma/tion,** *n.*

sub·lime (sə blīm/), *adj.* **1.** inspiring awe or wonder;

lofty; noble: *sublime mountain scenery; sublime music.* **2.** extremely good; excellent: *a sublime dinner.* —*n.* **3.** the state of being lofty, noble, etc.: *to go from the sublime to the ridiculous.* —*v.,* **sub·limed, sub·lim·ing. 4.** to change (a solid substance) by heat to a gas, which on cooling returns to a solid form again. —**sub·lime/ly,** *adv.*

sub·ma·rine (sub/mə rēn/, sub/mə rēn/), *n.* **1.** a warship able to travel underwater. —*adj.* (sub/mə rēn/). **2.** living or growing underwater: *Seaweed is a submarine plant.* **3.** referring to or carried out by a submarine or submarines: *submarine warfare.*

sub·merge (səb mûrj/), *v.,* **sub·merged, sub·merg·ing. 1.** to sink or plunge beneath the surface of water or any liquid: *He submerged his hands in the basin.* **2.** to cover or overflow with water: *High tides submerged the coastal towns.* —**sub·mer/gence,** *n.*

sub·mer·sion (səb mûr/zhən, səb mûr/shən), *n.* the act of submerging, or the state of being submerged.

sub·mis·sion (səb mish/ən), *n.* **1.** the act or an instance of submitting: *the submission of an enemy; the submission of a plan.* **2.** submissive behavior, or the condition of having submitted: *to act with submission; to live in submission.* **3.** something that is submitted, as for consideration: *He made many useful submissions and proposals.*

sub·mis·sive (səb mis/iv), *adj.* obedient; humble: *a submissive servant.* —**sub·mis/sive·ly,** *adv.*

sub·mit (səb mit/), *v.,* **sub·mit·ted, sub·mit·ting. 1.** to yield or give in to the power of another: *They submitted to the enemy's superior force.* **2.** to undergo or cause to undergo some kind of treatment: *to submit metal to heat.* **3.** to present for consideration: *The artist submitted his work to the panel of judges.*

sub·nor·mal (sub nôr/məl), *adj.* **1.** below or inferior to the normal: *a person of subnormal intelligence.* —*n.* **2.** a person who is subnormal.

sub·or·di·nate (sə bôr/d³nit), *adj.* **1.** placed in or belonging to a lower order or rank: *He was subordinate to the manager of the company.* **2.** of less importance: *He believed that wealth was subordinate to health.* **3.** dependent upon: *Our actions are subordinate to his plans.* —*n.* **4.** a subordinate person or thing. —*v.* (sə bôr/d³nāt/), **sub·or·di·nat·ed, sub·or·di·nat·ing. 5.** to put in a lower or less important position: *to subordinate wealth to health.* **6.** to make dependent upon: *We will subordinate our wishes to yours.* —**sub·or/di·na/tion,** *n.*

subor/dinate clause/, another term for **dependent clause.**

sub·poe·na (sə pē/nə), *n.* **1.** a written order to a person to appear in court. —*v.,* **sub·poe·naed, sub·poe·na·ing. 2.** to give (someone) a subpoena.

sub·scribe (səb skrīb/), *v.,* **sub·scribed, sub·scrib·ing. 1.** to give or pledge (money): *He subscribed a large sum to the Red Cross.* **2.** to sign one's name to (something written) to show that one approves: *He subscribed the petition.* **3.** to obtain a subscription to a magazine, newspaper, etc. **4.** to agree or give one's approval: *I will not subscribe to those foolish notions.* —**sub·scrib/er,** *n.*

sub·scrip·tion (səb skrip′shən), *n.* **1.** the right to receive a number of issues of a magazine, newspaper, etc., for a sum of money paid. **2.** a sum of money given or pledged: *a large subscription to a charity.*

sub·se·quent (sub′sə kwənt), *adj.* coming or happening later or after: *Subsequent events proved us wrong.* —**sub′se·quent·ly,** *adv.*

sub·ser·vi·ent (səb sûr′vē ənt), *adj.* **1.** useful or helpful in serving a higher purpose or goal: *Our aims are subservient to the nation's goals.* **2.** too eager to please or be of use; overly obedient: *subservient waiters.* —**sub·ser′vi·ence,** *n.* —**sub·ser′vi·ent·ly,** *adv.*

sub·set (sub′set′), *n.* (in mathematics) a set made up of elements of a larger set.

sub·side (səb sīd′), *v.,* **sub·sid·ed, sub·sid·ing. 1.** to sink to a low or lower level: *The river subsided after the storm.* **2.** to become quiet, calm, or less active: *The applause at last subsided.*

sub·sid·i·ar·y (səb sid′ē er′ē), *adj.* **1.** helping in addition; supplementary: *a subsidiary grant of money.* **2.** of less importance; secondary. —*n., pl.* **sub·sid·i·ar·ies. 3.** a subsidiary person or thing. **4.** a company owned or controlled by another company.

sub·si·dize (sub′si dīz′), *v.,* **sub·si·dized, sub·si·diz·ing.** to give help to with a subsidy: *The group was subsidized by the government.* —**sub′si·diz′er,** *n.*

sub·si·dy (sub′si dē), *n., pl.* **sub·si·dies.** a grant of money, esp. by a government to help a business or other organization: *subsidies to charities.*

sub·sist (səb sist′), *v.* **1.** to remain alive: *The shipwrecked crew subsisted on fish.* **2.** to continue to exist: *Old customs subsist in parts of the country.*

sub·sist·ence (səb sis′təns), *n.* **1.** the state or fact of subsisting or existing. **2.** a means of subsisting; a living or livelihood: *The farm provided a fair subsistence.*

sub·soil (sub′soil′), *n.* a layer of earth below the topsoil.

sub·stance (sub′stəns), *n.* **1.** matter or material: *An object has form and substance.* **2.** a kind of matter: *a metallic substance.* **3.** the meaning or most important part of something: *What is the substance of his letter?* **4.** wealth; riches: *a man of substance.*

sub·stan·tial (səb stan′shəl), *adj.* **1.** ample; considerable: *a substantial supply of food.* **2.** strong or solid: *a substantial fabric; a substantial building.* **3.** wealthy; rich: *a substantial landlord.* **4.** fundamental; essential: *I am in substantial agreement with your point of view.* —**sub·stan′tial·ly,** *adv.*

sub·stan·ti·ate (səb stan′shē āt′), *v.,* **sub·stan·ti·at·ed, sub·stan·ti·at·ing.** to give proof of; show to be true: *They were unable to substantiate their charges.*

sub·stan·tive (sub′stən tiv), *n.* **1.** a noun, or a word, phrase, or clause used as a noun. —*adj.* **2.** of, relating to, or used as a substantive.

sub·sti·tute (sub′sti tōōt′, -tyōōt′), *n.* **1.** a person or thing that acts or serves in place of another: *She will be a substitute while Miss Brown is ill.* —*v.,* **sub·sti·tut·ed, sub·sti·tut·ing. 2.** to put (a person or thing) in the place of another: *to substitute margarine for butter.* **3.** to act as a substitute: *Miss Smith will substitute during the illness of Miss Davis.* —*adj.* **4.** of or referring to a substitute or substitutes: *a substitute pitcher; substitute teaching.* —**sub′sti·tu′tion,** *n.*

sub·stra·tum (sub strā′təm, sub strat′əm), *n., pl.* **sub·stra·ta** (sub strā′tə, sub strat′ə). **1.** a stratum or layer lying under another: *a substratum of rock.* **2.** a basis or foundation: *Laws are the substratum of society.*

sub·ter·fuge (sub′tər fyōōj′), *n.* a trick, scheme, or lie for getting out of something unpleasant: *His excuse was a subterfuge to escape blame.*

sub·ter·ra·ne·an (sub′tə rā′nē ən), *adj.* **1.** existing or situated under the surface of the earth; underground: *a subterranean tunnel.* **2.** hidden or secret: *subterranean activities of spies.*

sub·ti·tle (sub′tīt′ᵊl), *n.* **1.** a second title of a book, poem, essay, etc. **2.** a printed translation of words spoken in a foreign-language motion picture, appearing at the bottom of the screen. —*v.,* **sub·ti·tled, sub·ti·tling. 3.** to provide a subtitle or subtitles for.

sub·tle (sut′ᵊl), *adj.* **1.** fine or delicate in meaning: *a subtle idea.* **2.** difficult to understand; mysterious: *a subtle smile.* **3.** able to see or understand fine differences in meaning: *a subtle mind.* **4.** crafty; sly. —**sub′tle·ness,** *n.* —**sub′tly,** *adv.*

sub·tle·ty (sut′ᵊl tē), *n., pl.* for def. 2 **sub·tle·ties. 1.** the state or quality of being subtle. **2.** something subtle, as a thought: *the subtleties of nuclear theory.*

sub·tract (səb trakt′), *v.* **1.** to take something away. **2.** to take one number away from another; perform the operation of subtraction.

sub·trac·tion (səb trak′shən), *n.* **1.** (in arithmetic) the process or technique of finding the difference between two numbers: represented by a minus sign (–). **2.** the act or an instance of taking one thing away from another.

sub·tra·hend (sub′trə hend′), *n.* (in arithmetic) the number that is subtracted from another: *In the case of 12–7=5, 7 is the subtrahend.* See also **minuend.**

sub·trop·i·cal (sub trop′i kəl), *adj.* **1.** bordering on the tropics; nearly tropical: *subtropical regions.* **2.** referring to or occurring in a region near the tropics: *subtropical temperatures.* Also, **semitropical.**

sub·urb (sub′ûrb), *n.* **1.** a residential area or district outside a city or town: *a quiet suburb of London.* **2.** **suburbs,** the residential area surrounding a city.

sub·ur·ban (sə bûr′bən), *adj.* of, concerning, or living in a suburb or suburbs: *a suburban neighborhood; a suburban family.*

sub·ver·sion (səb vûr′zhən), *n.* **1.** the act of subverting, or the state of being subverted: *the subversion of a country's morale by an enemy.* **2.** something that undermines or corrupts: *Their propaganda was a subversion of the truth.*

sub·ver·sive (səb vûr′siv), *adj.* **1.** tending or trying to subvert; working to undermine or corrupt: *to be guilty of subversive activity against a government.* —*n.* **2.** a person who tries to subvert; one whose aim

---

act, āble, dâre, ärt; ebb, ēqual; if, īce; hot, ōver, ôrder; oil; bŏŏk; ōōze; out; up, ûrge; ə = a as in alone; ᵊ as in button (but′ᵊn), fire (fīᵊr); chief; shoe; thin; that; zh as in measure (mezh′ər). See full key inside cover.

is to destroy, undermine, or corrupt. —sub·ver′sive·ly, *adv.* —sub·ver′sive·ness, *n.*

sub·vert (səb vûrt′), *v.* 1. to overthrow or bring to ruin, esp. in a gradual and underhanded way: *The government was subverted from within by its enemies.* 2. to undermine or corrupt: *to subvert someone's morals.* —sub·vert′er, *n.*

sub·way (sub′wā′), *n.* 1. an underground electric railroad, usually in a large city. 2. *Chiefly British.* a short underground passage, esp. one under a street or highway.

suc·ceed (sək sēd′), *v.* 1. to end as desired; turn out well: *Our efforts succeeded.* 2. to achieve one's aim: *I succeeded in convincing him.* 3. to attain wealth, fame, etc.: *He succeeded after years of hardship.* 4. to take over a position, rank, etc. (often fol. by *to*): *The prince succeeded to the throne when the king died.* 5. to follow; come after: *He succeeded his father as head of the company.*

suc·cess (sək ses′), *n.* 1. a result that one has hoped for: *Our efforts met with success.* 2. the attainment of wealth, fame, etc.: *Success came early to the actress.* 3. a successful person or thing: *He made a success of himself. Her party was a great success.*

suc·cess·ful (sək ses′fəl), *adj.* 1. finding or having success: *We were successful in our efforts. The plan was successful.* 2. having attained wealth, fame, etc.: *a successful novelist.* —suc·cess′ful·ly, *adv.*

suc·ces·sion (sək sesh′ən), *n.* 1. the coming of one person or thing after another: *the succession of days.* 2. a number of persons or things following one another: *a succession of marchers; a succession of numbers.* 3. the taking over of a position, rank, etc., according to right: *succession to a throne.* 4. the order or system according to which one person succeeds another to a position, rank, etc.: *The princess is second in succession to the throne.*

suc·ces·sive (sək ses′iv), *adj.* following one after the other: *It rained for three successive days.* —suc·ces′sive·ly, *adv.*

suc·ces·sor (sək ses′ər), *n.* 1. a person who succeeds another in position or rank: *The president named his successor.* 2. any person or thing that succeeds or follows.

suc·cinct (sək singkt′), *adj.* clearly stated in few words; to the point; brief: *a succinct statement of his beliefs.* —suc·cinct′ly, *adv.* —suc·cinct′ness, *n.*

suc·cor (suk′ər), *n.* 1. help, relief, or aid: *to give succor to the needy.* 2. a person who gives help, relief, or aid: *He is their succor in times of trouble.* —*v.* 3. to help, relieve, or aid.

suc·co·tash (suk′ə tash′), *n.* a cooked dish of corn kernels and beans, usually lima beans.

suc·cu·lent (suk′yə lənt), *adj.* full of juice; juicy. —suc′cu·lence, *n.* —suc′cu·lent·ly, *adv.*

suc·cumb (sə kum′), *v.* 1. to yield; give in: *to succumb to a temptation.* 2. to die: *He succumbed after a long illness.*

such (such), *adj.* 1. of the same kind, quality, or degree as that or those named or meant: *I could never do such a thing.* 2. like or similar: *pots, pans, and*

such utensils. 3. being as shown, described, etc.: *Such is the case.* 4. of so great a kind: *He is such a liar that nobody believes him.* 5. so very: *Such terrible deeds were done!* 6. not named but definite: *Allow such an amount of money for expenses.* —*n.* 7. such a person or thing, or such persons or things: *pens, pencils, and such.*

suck (suk), *v.* 1. to draw into the mouth by action of the lips and tongue: *to suck a beverage through a straw.* 2. to draw liquid from (something) by action of the lips and tongue: *to suck an orange.* 3. to put in the mouth and draw upon: *to suck a piece of candy.* 4. to draw liquid, esp. milk, into the mouth. 5. to draw (water, moisture, etc.) by or as if by suction: *Plants suck their nourishment from the earth.* —*n.* 6. the act or an instance of sucking.

suck·er (suk′ər), *n.* 1. a person or thing that sucks. 2. a part of an animal used for sucking nourishment or holding fast to something: *the suckers of an octopus.* 3. any of several thick-lipped North American freshwater fishes. 4. a shoot from the root of a tree or plant. 5. *Informal.* a lollipop. 6. *Informal.* a person who is easily cheated.

Sucker (length to 2½ ft.)

suck·le (suk′əl), *v.*, suck·led, suck·ling. 1. to nurse at the breast: *Mammals suckle their young.* 2. to suck at the breast: *The kittens lay suckling at their mother's side.*

suck·ling (suk′ling), *n.* an infant or a young animal that suckles.

Su·cre (sōō′krē), *n.* the official capital city of Bolivia, in the S part. Government offices are at La Paz.

su·crose (sōō′krōs), *n.* See sugar (def. 1).

suc·tion (suk′shən), *n.* 1. the act or process of sucking. 2. the force created by a vacuum or by reducing the pressure of a gas: *Liquid rises in a soda straw by the force of suction created in the mouth.*

Su·dan (sōō dan′), *n.* 1. a region in N Africa, S of the Sahara and Libyan deserts, extending from the Atlantic Ocean to the Red Sea. 2. a republic in NE Africa, S of the Arab Republic of Egypt: formerly British. 967,500 sq. mi. *Cap.:* Khartoum. —Su·da·nese (sōō′də nēz′), *n., adj.*

sud·den (sud′ən), *adj.* 1. happening quickly and unexpectedly: *a sudden attack.* 2. made or done without warning; abrupt: *a sudden bend in a road.* 3. all of a sudden, without warning; suddenly and unexpectedly: *All of a sudden the boat started to leak.* —sud′den·ly, *adv.* —sud′den·ness, *n.*

suds (sudz), *n.* *(used as pl.)* 1. soapy water. 2. foam made of soap; lather.

sue (sōō), *v.*, sued, su·ing. 1. to bring a lawsuit against: *to sue someone for libel.* 2. to start a lawsuit: *He threatened to sue.* 3. to plead or beg: *The harassed country sued for peace.*

suede (swād), *n.* **1.** leather finished with a soft, velvety surface on the flesh side. **2.** a cloth resembling this. [from the French phrase *(gants de) Suède* "(gloves from) Sweden"]

su·et (sōō′it), *n.* hard fat about the loins and kidneys of beef, sheep, etc., used in cooking.

Su·ez (sōō ez′, sōō′ez), *n.* **1. Gulf of,** a NW arm of the Red Sea. **2. Isthmus of,** the isthmus joining Africa and Asia, in the NE Arab Republic of Egypt. 72 mi. wide.

Su′ez Canal′, a canal across the Isthmus of Suez, connecting the Mediterranean Sea and the Red Sea. 107 mi. long.

suf·fer (suf′ər), *v.* **1.** to undergo or feel pain or distress: *The patient is still suffering.* **2.** to undergo loss, harm, damage, etc.: *One's health suffers from overwork.* **3.** to feel or endure (pain, distress, loss, harm, etc.): *He suffered his loss in silence.* **4.** to undergo (any action, process, etc.): *to suffer change.* **5.** to put up with; tolerate: *The boss will not suffer disagreement.* **6.** to allow; permit; let: *Will you suffer us to leave a few minutes early?* —**suf′fer·er,** *n.*

suf·fer·ing (suf′ər ing), *n.* **1.** the state of a person who suffers: *to live in suffering.* **2.** something suffered; pain: *the sufferings of war victims.*

suf·fice (sə fīs′), *v.,* **suf·ficed, suf·fic·ing. 1.** to be enough or sufficient: *A bit of dessert will suffice for me.* **2.** to be enough for; satisfy: *A cup of tea will suffice me completely.*

suf·fi·cien·cy (sə fish′ən sē), *n., pl.* **suf·fi·cien·cies. 1.** the state or fact of being sufficient: *There was food in sufficiency.* **2.** a sufficient number or amount: *a sufficiency of food; a sufficiency of money.*

suf·fi·cient (sə fish′ənt), *adj.* adequate or enough: *a sufficient amount of money.* —**suf·fi′cient·ly,** *adv.*

suf·fix (suf′iks), *n.* **1.** an affix placed at the end of a word or stem. Some common suffixes are *-al, -ate, -ence, -ful, -ic, -ity, -ment,* and *-ness.* —*v.* (suf′iks, sə fiks′). **2.** to add as a suffix.

suf·fo·cate (suf′ə kāt′), *v.,* **suf·fo·cat·ed, suf·fo·cat·ing. 1.** to kill by cutting off the supply of air to the lungs or gills; stifle; smother. **2.** to be uncomfortable because of a lack of cool or fresh air: *We were suffocating in that crowded room.* —**suf′fo·ca′tion,** *n.*

suf·frage (suf′rij), *n.* **1.** the right to vote; franchise. **2.** a vote for a candidate or proposed measure.

suf·fuse (sə fyōōz′), *v.,* **suf·fused, suf·fus·ing.** to spread over, as a liquid, color, etc.: *The sunset suffused the sky with red. Tears suffused her eyes.*

sug·ar (shŏŏg′ər), *n.* **1.** a sweet, white powder obtained from the juice of sugar cane or sugar beets; sucrose. **2.** any of various similar substances having different chemical composition: *grape sugar.* —*v.* **3.** to sprinkle or mix with sugar; sweeten: *to sugar one's*

cereal. **4.** to make seem less bad or unpleasant: *to sugar criticism with words of praise.* [from the Arabic word *sukkar,* which comes from Sanskrit]

sug′ar beet′, a kind of beet having a white root and cultivated as a source of sugar.

sug′ar cane′, a tall plant, similar to bamboo, whose sweet juice is a principal source of sugar.

sug·ar-coat (shŏŏg′ər kōt′), *v.* **1.** to cover with sugar: *to sugar-coat a pill.* **2.** to make (something difficult or unpleasant) seem easier or more pleasant: *to sugar-coat a lesson by showing pictures.*

sug′ar plum′, a small, rounded piece of candy; bonbon.

sug·ar·y (shŏŏg′ə rē), *adj.* **1.** of, containing, or resembling sugar: *cake with a sugary crust; sugary snow.* **2.** sweetly flattering or false: *She concealed the truth with sugary words.* —**sug′ar·i·ness,** *n.*

sug·gest (səg jest′, sə jest′), *v.* **1.** to bring up for consideration; propose: *She suggested that we come to her house.* **2.** to bring to mind by resemblance or a natural connection of ideas: *The yellow walls of the room suggested sunlight.* **3.** to hint at without words: *His appearance suggested good health.*

sug·ges·tion (səg jes′chən, sə jes′chən), *n.* **1.** the act of suggesting, or the state of being suggested. **2.** something suggested, as a piece of advice: *Your suggestion is excellent.* **3.** a slight trace or hint: *He speaks English with a suggestion of a foreign accent.* **4.** an idea brought to mind by a smell, sight, etc.: *The smell of roses carries a suggestion of summer.* **5.** a way of influencing behavior by hints rather than by arguments, so that a person acts without thinking.

sug·ges·tive (səg jes′tiv, sə jes′tiv), *adj.* **1.** rich in ideas; leading to thought: *a suggestive article.* **2.** bringing something to mind: *weather suggestive of spring.* **3.** improper; indecent: *a suggestive movie.*

su·i·cid·al (sōō′i sīd′əl), *adj.* **1.** involving, suggesting, or referring to suicide: *His death was suicidal.* **2.** tending or leading to suicide: *suicidal thoughts.* **3.** foolishly or rashly dangerous: *suicidal driving.*

su·i·cide (sōō′i sīd′), *n.* **1.** the act of deliberately taking one's own life. **2.** the ruin of one's own interests, hopes, etc.: *It would be suicide to refuse the offer.* **3.** a person who deliberately takes his own life.

suit (sōōt), *n.* **1.** a set of clothing, armor, or the like, esp. a man's matching jacket and trousers, often with a vest, or a woman's matching jacket and skirt. **2.** a case in court; lawsuit: *to bring a suit for libel.* **3.** one of the four sets or classes (spades, hearts, diamonds, and clubs) into which a deck of playing cards is divided. **4.** the courtship of a woman. **5.** a plea or appeal, esp. to a person of high rank: *a suit to the king.* —*v.* **6.** to match or make appropriate to: *to let the punishment suit the crime.* **7.** to be becoming to: *Blue suits you very well.* **8.** to satisfy or please: *Your arrangement suits me completely.* **9.** to provide with a suit or suits: *He is suited by an excellent tailor.* **10. follow suit, a.** to play a card of the same suit as that which was led. **b.** to follow someone else's example:

He bought a red cap, and we all followed suit. [from a Middle English word, which comes from Old French *suite* "series, succession"]

suit·a·ble (sōō′tə bəl), *adj.* fitting, proper, becoming, etc.: *to wear clothes suitable for winter.* —**suit′a·bil′i·ty, suit′a·ble·ness,** *n.* —**suit′a·bly,** *adv.*

suit·case (sōōt′kās′), *n.* a small piece of luggage for carrying clothing, toilet articles, etc.; valise.

suite (swēt), *n.* **1.** a number of things forming a series or set: *a suite of rooms; a suite of furniture.* **2.** a group of followers; retinue: *the president and his suite.* **3.** a musical composition consisting of several short movements, esp. a series of dances. [from a French word meaning "series, succession"]

suit·or (sōō′tər), *n.* a man who courts a woman.

sul′fa drug′ (sul′fə), any of a group of chemically similar drugs containing sulfur and used in the treatment of infections and diseases caused by bacteria.

sul·fate (sul′fāt), *n.* any of a number of chemical compounds containing sulfur and oxygen.

sul·fide (sul′fīd), *n.* any of a number of chemical compounds containing sulfur and one other element, usually a metal.

sul·fur (sul′fər), *n.* a yellow powder used in making matches, explosives, and medicines: a chemical element. *Symbol:* S

sul·fur′ic ac′id (sul fyōōr′ik), an oily, colorless liquid composed of hydrogen, sulfur, and oxygen, used in many industrial processes, esp. because of its ability to extract unwanted water from other substances.

sul·fur·ous (sul′fər əs, sul fyōōr′əs), *adj.* of, referring to, or containing sulfur: *a sulfurous odor.*

sulk (sulk), *v.* **1.** to be sulky. —*n.* **2.** a mood of sullen ill humor; sulkiness: *The remark put her in a sulk.* **3.** **the sulks,** a period or fit of sulking: *She gets the sulks if she can't have her way.*

sulk·y (sul′kē), *adj.,* **sulk·i·er, sulk·i·est. 1.** sullenly ill-humored or resentful: *She was sulky because she was not invited to the party.* —*n., pl.* **sulk·ies. 2.** a light, two-wheeled, one-horse carriage for one person. —**sulk′i·ly,** *adv.* —**sulk′i·ness,** *n.*

sul·len (sul′ən), *adj.* **1.** showing ill humor or resentment in a gloomy and silent way: *The heat makes me sullen.* **2.** gloomy or dismal: *a sullen, rainy day in November.* —**sul′len·ly,** *adv.* —**sul′len·ness,** *n.*

sul·ly (sul′ē), *v.,* **sul·lied, sul·ly·ing.** to soil, stain, or tarnish; mar the goodness or value of: *Smoke sullied the white walls. Scandal sullied his reputation.*

sul·phur (sul′fər), *n.* another spelling of **sulfur.**

sul·tan (sul′t³n), *n.* a ruler of a Muslim country: *Turkey was at one time ruled by sultans.*

sul·tan·a (sul tan′ə, sul tä′nə), *n.* a wife, sister, daughter, or mother of a sultan.

sul·tan·ate (sul′t³nāt′), *n.* **1.** the office or rule of a sultan. **2.** the territory ruled by a sultan.

sul·try (sul′trē), *adj.* very hot and humid; sweltering: *a sultry August day.* —**sul′tri·ness,** *n.*

sum (sum), *n.* **1.** the result obtained by adding two or more numbers together. In the case of $6 + 3 = 9$, 9 is the sum. See also **addend. 2.** the total of two or more things or amounts: *The price of the various*

items was quite a sum. **3.** a certain amount of money: *to lend small sums.* **4.** a problem in arithmetic: *to do one's sums.* **5.** the total amount; whole: *the sum of human knowledge.* **6.** a brief or concise summary; gist: *I will give you the sum of his remarks.* —*v.,* **summed, sum·ming. 7.** to add together (often fol. by *up*). **8. sum up,** to repeat the main points of (a speech, discussion, etc.); make a summary of (something): *The attorney summed up the case for the defense.* [from the Latin word *summa,* which comes from the adjective *summus* "highest"]

su·mac (shōō′mak, sōō′mak), *n.* **1.** any of various shrubs or small trees having feathery leaves that turn brilliant red in the autumn and bearing cone-shaped clusters of berries. One variety of sumac, growing in swamps, is highly poisonous. **2.** a preparation made from the leaves and bark of certain sumac plants, used in tanning. [from the Arabic word *summāq*]

Su·ma·tra (sōō mä′trə), *n.* a large island in the W part of Indonesia. 164,147 sq. mi. —**Su·ma′tran,** *n., adj.*

sum·ma·rize (sum′ə rīz′), *v.,* **sum·ma·rized, sum·ma·riz·ing.** to make a summary of.

sum·ma·ry (sum′ə rē), *n., pl.* **sum·ma·ries. 1.** a brief, concise statement of something that has been treated in detail: *a summary of the chapter.* —*adj.* **2.** brief or concise: *summary statements.* **3.** done without due consideration and delay: *summary dismissal.*

sum·mer (sum′ər), *n.* **1.** the warm season between spring and autumn, usually from June 21 to September 21. —*adj.* **2.** characteristic of or suitable for summer: *summer sports.* —*v.* **3.** to spend or pass the summer: *Animals summer in the highlands.*

sum·mer·time (sum′ər tīm′), *n.* the summer season.

sum·mit (sum′it), *n.* **1.** the highest point, part, or degree: *the summit of a mountain; the summit of success.* **2.** the highest level of relations between governments: *The president and the prime minister had a meeting at the summit.* —*adj.* **3.** between heads of state: *a summit conference.*

sum·mon (sum′ən), *v.* **1.** to call or send for: *to summon a doctor.* **2.** to order to appear before a court. **3.** to arouse; call forth (often fol. by *up*): *He summoned up all his courage.*

sum·mons (sum′ənz), *n., pl.* **sum·mons·es. 1.** an order to appear before a court, as for trial. **2.** any official order to appear at a certain place for some duty: *a military summons.*

sump·tu·ous (sump′chōō əs), *adj.* costly and magnificent; splendid; rich: *a sumptuous feast.* —**sump′tu·ous·ly,** *adv.* —**sump′tu·ous·ness,** *n.*

sun (sun), *n.* **1.** the star that is the central body of our solar system, around which the earth and the other planets revolve and from which they receive light and heat. The sun has a diameter of 864,000 miles; its average distance from the earth is 93,000,000 miles. **2.** warmth of the sun; sunshine: *to soak up the sun.* —*v.,* **sunned, sun·ning. 3.** to expose to sunshine: *Cats love to sun themselves.* **4. under the sun,** on earth; anywhere: *the brightest jewel under the sun.*

Sun., Sunday.

sun·beam (sun′bēm′), *n.* a beam or ray of sunlight.

Sun·belt (sun′belt′), *n.* (*sometimes l.c.*) *Informal.* the southwest region of the U.S.

sun·bon·net (sun′bon′it), *n.* a bonnet with a very wide brim, worn for protection from the sun.

sun·burn (sun′bûrn′), *n.* **1.** a painful reddening of the skin caused by overexposure to the sun. —*v.*, **sun·burned** *or* **sun·burnt** (sun′bûrnt′); **sun·burn·ing.** **2.** to affect or be affected by sunburn: *skin that sunburns easily.*

sun·dae (sun′dē, sun′dā), *n.* ice cream topped with fruit, syrup, whipped cream, nuts, etc. [probably another spelling of *Sunday.* It is said that this confection was served originally on Sunday, because of a law forbidding the sale of sodas on that day]

Sun·day (sun′dē, sun′dā), *n.* the first day of the week: the day of rest for most Christians. [from the Old English word *Sunnandæg,* which is a translation of Latin *diēs sōlis* "day of the sun"]

Sun′day school′, classes in religious education, sponsored by a church and held on Sunday.

sun·der (sun′dər), *v.* to break apart; divide: *The ship sundered in the storm.*

sun·dew (sun′dōō′, -dyōō′), *n.* any of several small plants that grow in swampy areas and bear balls of sticky hairs that trap insects, on which the plant feeds.

sun·di·al (sun′dī/əl, -dīl′), *n.* an instrument that shows the time of day by means of the position of a shadow cast by a pointer on a dial marked in hours.

Sundial

sun·down (sun′doun′), *n.* sunset, esp. the time of sunset: *We must be home by sundown.*

sun·dries (sun′drēz), *n.pl.* sundry things, esp. various small items for sale: *The store sells combs, handkerchiefs, thread, and other sundries.*

sun·dry (sun′drē), *adj.* various or different: *There are sundry tasks to perform.*

sun·fish (sun′fish′), *n., pl.* **sun·fish** *or* **sun·fish·es.** **1.** a large, brown-and-gray ocean fish, having a flattened body. **2.** any of several small, freshwater fishes of North America having a deep, compressed body.

sun·flow·er (sun′flou/ər), *n.* any of several herbs having showy, yellow-petaled flowers and edible, oil-producing seeds.

sung (sung), *v.* a past tense and the past participle of **sing.**

sun·glass·es (sun′glas/iz), *n., pl.* eyeglasses with colored lenses to protect the eyes from glare.

sunk (sungk), *v.* **1.** a past tense and the past participle of **sink.** **2.** *Slang.* beyond help: *If our call for help is not answered, we're sunk.*

sunk·en (sung′kən), *adj.* **1.** having sunk or lying beneath the surface of the water: *a sunken ship; sunken rocks.* **2.** situated on a lower level: *The house has a sunken living room.* **3.** hollow; pressed inward: *an invalid's sunken eyes and cheeks.*

sun′ lamp′, a lamp that gives off ultraviolet rays, used as a health device, to produce an artificial sun tan, etc.

sun·less (sun′lis), *adj.* without sunlight; dark; gloomy: *a sunless room; a sunless winter day.*

sun·light (sun′līt′), *n.* light of the sun; sunshine.

sun·lit (sun′lit′), *adj.* lighted by the sun: *a lovely, sunlit scene.*

sun·ny (sun′ē), *adj.,* **sun·ni·er, sun·ni·est. 1.** filled with or warmed by sunshine: *a large, sunny room.* **2.** of, like, or from the sun: *sunny beams.* **3.** cheerful or joyous: *a sunny disposition.* —**sun′ni·ness,** *n.*

sun·rise (sun′rīz′), *n.* **1.** the rise of the sun above the horizon in the morning; sunup. **2.** the time when this occurs: *to get up at sunrise.* **3.** the appearance of the sky at this time: *a beautiful sunrise.*

sun′ porch′, a porch or room having large windows or glass panels for letting in sunshine.

sun·set (sun′set′), *n.* **1.** the setting of the sun below the horizon in the evening. **2.** the time when this occurs. **3.** the appearance of the sky at this time: *a fiery sunset.*

sun·shade (sun′shād′), *n.* something used as a protection from the sun, as an awning or parasol.

sun·shine (sun′shīn′), *n.* **1.** the direct light of the sun. **2.** a place where the rays of the sun fall: *to stand in the sunshine.* **3.** cheerfulness or happiness: *a life full of sunshine.* —**sun′shin′y,** *adj.*

sun·spot (sun′spot′), *n.* one of the dark patches that appear periodically on the surface of the sun.

sun·stroke (sun′strōk′), *n.* a sudden and often fatal condition due to prolonged exposure to the sun's rays or to too much heat.

sun′ tan′, a browning of the skin caused by the sun.

sun·up (sun′up′), *n.* sunrise, esp. the time of sunrise.

sup[1] (sup), *v.,* **supped, sup·ping.** to eat supper. [from the Old French word *souper* "to take supper," which comes from Germanic]

sup[2] (sup), *v.,* **supped, sup·ping.** to drink a little at a time; sip. [from the Old English word *supan*]

su·per (sōō′pər), *Informal.* —*n.* **1.** a superintendent. —*adj.* **2.** very good; first-rate.

super-, a prefix meaning **1.** over or above: *superstructure.* **2.** beyond or to excess: *supercharged; superpatriot.* **3.** superior: *superman; superhighway.*

su·per·a·bun·dant (sōō/pər ə bun′dənt), *adj.* very abundant; much more than is necessary: *a superabundant harvest.* —**su′per·a·bun′dance,** *n.* —**su′per·a·bun′dant·ly,** *adv.*

su·per·an·nu·at·ed (sōō/pər an′yōō ā/tid), *adj.* **1.** too old for use or service: *a superannuated car.* **2.** retired because of age or illness: *a superannuated employee.* **3.** out-of-date: *superannuated ideas.*

su·perb (sōō pûrb′), *adj.* **1.** very fine; excellent: *a superb performance.* **2.** sumptuous; rich; grand: *superb furniture.* **3.** majestic; imposing: *The lion is a superb animal.* —**su·perb′ly,** *adv.*

su·per·charg·er (sōō/pər chär/jər), *n.* a powerful

fan for forcing air into an automobile or airplane engine in order to increase its power.

su·per·cil·i·ous (soo/pər sil/ē əs), *adj.* proudly disdainful; haughty: *a supercilious sneer.* —**su/per·cil/i·ous·ly,** *adv.*

su·per·fi·cial (soo/pər fish/əl), *adj.* **1.** on or at the surface; not deep: *a superficial cut.* **2.** slight; not complete or thorough: *a superficial knowledge of German.* **3.** shallow; lacking depth: *a superficial person.* [from the Latin word *superficiālis* "of or on the surface," which comes from *superficiēs* "surface"] —**su·per·fi·ci·al·i·ty** (soo/pər fish/ē al/i tē), **su/per·fi/cial·ness,** *n.* —**su/per·fi/cial·ly,** *adv.*

su·per·fine (soo/pər fīn/), *adj.* **1.** extra fine: *superfine sugar.* **2.** too refined: *superfine manners.*

su·per·flu·i·ty (soo/pər floo/i tē), *n., pl.* for def. 2 **su·per·flu·i·ties. 1.** too great an amount: *a superfluity of rain.* **2.** something superfluous: *to live a simple life without superfluities.*

su·per·flu·ous (sə pûr/floo əs), *adj.* **1.** more than enough; too much: *a superfluous amount of rain.* **2.** needless; unnecessary: *The sentence has several superfluous words.* —**su·per/flu·ous·ly,** *adv.*

su·per·high·way (soo/pər hī/wā/), *n.* a wide highway designed for travel at high speeds.

su·per·hu·man (soo/pər hyoo/mən), *adj.* **1.** above or beyond what is human; divine: *Angels are supposed to be superhuman beings.* **2.** beyond ordinary human power, ability, etc.: *superhuman efforts.*

su·per·im·pose (soo/pər im pōz/), *v.,* **su·per·im·posed, su·per·im·pos·ing.** to place over, above, or on something else: *He superimposed a red design over the blue background.*

su·per·in·tend (soo/pər in tend/), *v.* to take charge of; oversee; direct: *to superintend workers; to superintend a school.*

su·per·in·tend·ent (soo/pər in ten/dənt), *n.* **1.** a person who directs or oversees some work, organization, etc.; supervisor. **2.** a person in charge of the maintenance of a building, esp. an apartment house.

su·pe·ri·or (sə pēr/ē ər), *adj.* **1.** above the average in worth, intelligence, etc.: *a superior student; a superior product.* **2.** greater in quantity or amount: *superior strength.* **3.** showing a feeling of being better than others: *I don't like his superior attitude.* **4.** not yielding or stopping (usually fol. by *to*): *to be superior to temptation.* **5.** higher in place: *superior ground.* **6.** higher in rank, position, etc.: *superior officials.* —*n.* **7.** a person who is superior to another or others. **8.** the head of a monastery, convent, etc.

Su·pe·ri·or (sə pēr/ē ər), *n.* **Lake,** a lake between the U.S. and Canada: largest body of fresh water in the world. 31,820. sq. mi.

su·pe·ri·or·i·ty (sə pēr/ē ôr/i tē, sə pēr/ē or/i tē), *n.* the quality or condition of being superior.

su·per·la·tive (sə pûr/lə tiv), *adj.* **1.** of the highest kind or order: *a superlative dinner; a superlative performance.* **2.** of or referring to the highest degree of comparison of adjectives and adverbs. *Best* and *most beautiful* are superlative forms of the adjectives *good* and *beautiful. Soonest* and *most carefully* are superlative forms of the adverbs *soon* and *carefully.* —*n.* **3.** the superlative degree. **4.** a form in the superlative. —**su·per/la·tive·ly,** *adv.*

su·per·man (soo/pər man/), *n., pl.* **su·per·men.** a man of more than human powers.

su·per·mar·ket (soo/pər mär/kit), *n.* a large store selling food and household items, in which the customer can wait on himself.

su·per·nat·u·ral (soo/pər nach/ər əl), *adj.* **1.** beyond or above what can be explained by the laws of nature: *ghosts and other supernatural creatures.* —*n.* **2.** **the supernatural,** supernatural forces: *Ghosts are supposed to exist in the realm of the supernatural.*

su·per·pow·er (soo/pər pou/ər), *n.* a nation capable of influencing the acts and policies of other nations.

su·per·script (soo/pər skript/), *adj.* written or printed high on a line, as the "2" in a^2b.

su·per·scrip·tion (soo/pər skrip/shən), *n.* **1.** the act of writing words, letters, one's name, etc., above or on something: *the superscription of an address on an envelope.* **2.** that which is written above or on something, such as an address on an envelope.

su·per·sede (soo/pər sēd/), *v.,* **su·per·sed·ed, su·per·sed·ing.** to take the place of; replace; succeed: *The new rules supersede those of last year.*

su·per·son·ic (soo/pər son/ik), *adj.* noting or concerning speeds greater than the speed of sound: *supersonic flight; a supersonic plane.*

su·per·sti·tion (soo/pər stish/ən), *n.* **1.** fearful belief caused by what is unknown or mysterious: *Savages have laws and religions based on superstition.* **2.** a particular belief or practice based on fear of what is unknown or mysterious: *It is a superstition to believe that a broken mirror will cause bad luck.*

su·per·sti·tious (soo/pər stish/əs), *adj.* **1.** of, referring to, or caused by superstition: *superstitious legends.* **2.** believing in superstitions: *superstitious savages.* —**su/per·sti/tious·ly,** *adv.*

su·per·struc·ture (soo/pər struk/chər), *n.* **1.** the part of a building above its foundation or basement. **2.** the parts of a ship built above the main deck. **3.** any structure built above another.

su·per·vise (soo/pər vīz/), *v.,* **su·per·vised, su·per·vis·ing.** to direct or oversee: *to supervise a job; to supervise workers.*

su·per·vi·sion (soo/pər vizh/ən), *n.* the act or function of supervising; superintendence.

su·per·vi·sor (soo/pər vī/zər), *n.* a person who supervises; superintendent. —**su/per·vi/so·ry,** *adj.*

su·pine (soo pīn/), *adj.* **1.** lying on the back. **2.** passive; lazy; inactive: *a supine attitude toward life.* —**su·pine/ly,** *adv.* —**su·pine/ness,** *n.*

sup·per (sup/ər), *n.* the last meal of the day, esp. when dinner is eaten at midday.

sup·plant (sə plant/), *v.* **1.** to take the place of; replace; supersede: *Harvesting machines are supplanting harvesting by hand.* **2.** to take the place of (another) by force, scheming, or the like: *The dictator supplanted the exiled president.*

sup·ple (sup/əl), *adj.,* **sup·pler, sup·plest. 1.** able to bend without damage; pliant; flexible: *a supple reed.*

2. limber; lithe: *a supple dancer.* **3.** able to change freely to meet new situations; adaptable: *a supple mind.* —**sup′ple·ness,** *n.*

sup·ple·ment (sup′lə mənt), *n.* **1.** something added to complete a thing, make up for a lack, etc.: *Vitamins are a supplement to one's diet.* **2.** a part added to a book or an extra section of a newspaper. —*v.* (sup′lə ment′). **3.** to complete or add to: *to supplement one's diet by taking vitamin pills.*

sup·ple·men·ta·ry (sup′lə men′tə rē), *adj.* forming a supplement; additional: *The new witness provided supplementary evidence at the trial.*

sup·pli·ant (sup′lē ənt), *n.* **1.** a person who supplicates. —*adj.* **2.** supplicating; beseeching: *a suppliant look.*

sup·pli·cant (sup′lə kənt), *adj.* **1.** supplicating; beseeching; entreating. —*n.* **2.** a suppliant.

sup·pli·cate (sup′lə kāt′), *v.,* **sup·pli·cat·ed, sup·pli·cat·ing.** to beg humbly; beseech; pray: *He supplicated the governor for pardon.*

sup·pli·ca·tion (sup′lə kā′shən), *n.* the act of supplicating; entreaty: *a supplication for pardon.*

sup·ply (sə plī′), *v.,* **sup·plied, sup·ply·ing.** **1.** to provide or furnish: *to supply someone with clothing; to supply information.* **2.** to make up for or fill: *to supply a need.* —*n., pl.* **sup·plies. 3.** the act of providing or furnishing: *He is generous in his supply of money.* **4.** an amount on hand or available for use: *a large supply of fuel.* **5.** Usually, **supplies.** a stock or store of food or necessary items: *to buy supplies for a camping trip.* [from the Old French word *souplier,* which comes from Latin *supplēre* "to fill up"] —**sup·pli′er,** *n.*

sup·port (sə pôrt′), *v.* **1.** to bear or hold up: *The roof is supported by pillars.* **2.** to provide with the means of living: *to support a family.* **3.** to help or comfort: *She supported him in times of sorrow.* **4.** to uphold (a person, cause, etc.); back: *to support civil rights.* **5.** to help prove: *The will supports his claim to the property.* **6.** to put up with; endure; tolerate: *I will not support this delay.* —*n.* **7.** the act of supporting, or the state of being supported. **8.** a means of holding something up: *The pillars are strong supports for the ceiling.* **9.** upkeep, as of a person or family. **10.** a person or thing that provides upkeep: *He is the family's only support.* **11.** a person or thing that provides help or comfort: *Religion is her support.* **12.** backing or approval: *Our cause needs your support.* —**sup·port′er,** *n.*

sup·port·a·ble (sə pôr′tə bəl), *adj.* capable of being supported; endurable: *a supportable pain.*

sup·pose (sə pōz′), *v.,* **sup·posed, sup·pos·ing. 1.** to consider as possible; assume: *Supposing it were true, what would you say then?* **2.** to take for granted: *I suppose you are tired after that long trip.* **3.** to think or imagine: *What do you suppose will happen next?* **4.** to imply: *A fire supposes a fuel of some kind.*

sup·posed (sə pōzd′, sə pō′zid), *adj.* **1.** thought to be; assumed: *The supposed thief is under arrest.*

2. wrongly thought to be: *to sacrifice real for supposed gains.* —**sup·pos·ed·ly** (sə pō′zid lē), *adv.*

sup·po·si·tion (sup′ə zish′ən), *n.* **1.** the act of supposing. **2.** something supposed: *My supposition proved to be completely wrong.*

sup·press (sə pres′), *v.* **1.** to crush or put down by force: *The rioters were brutally suppressed.* **2.** to do away with; stop: *to suppress an old custom.* **3.** to hold back; restrain: *She could not suppress her tears.* **4.** to keep from being published or known; censor: *The bad news was suppressed by an official in the government.*

sup·pres·sion (sə presh′ən), *n.* the act of suppressing, or the state of being suppressed.

sup·pu·rate (sup′yə rāt′), *v.,* **sup·pu·rat·ed, sup·pu·rat·ing.** to discharge pus. —**sup·pu·ra′tion,** *n.*

su·prem·a·cy (sə prem′ə sē), *n.* **1.** the state of being supreme: *Michelangelo's supremacy among artists.* **2.** supreme power or authority: *the supremacy of a dictator.*

su·preme (sə prēm′, soo-), *adj.* **1.** highest in rank or power: *The emperor was supreme.* **2.** of highest quality or degree: *an act of supreme heroism.* **3.** greatest or extreme: *supreme joy.* —**su·preme′ly,** *adv.*

Supreme′ Be′ing, another name for **God.**

Supreme′ Court′, 1. the highest court in the nation. **2.** the highest court in some states.

Supt., superintendent. Also, **supt.**

sur-, a prefix meaning **1.** above or over: *surmount.* **2.** beyond: *surpass.* **3.** additional: *surtax.*

sur·charge (sûr′chärj′), *n.* **1.** an additional charge, tax, or cost. **2.** too great a charge or price; overcharge. **3.** too heavy a load or burden; overload. —*v.* (sûr chärj′, sûr′chärj′), **sur·charged, sur·charg·ing. 4.** to subject to an additional charge, tax, etc. **5.** to overcharge or overload.

sur·coat (sûr′kōt′), *n.* **1.** a garment formerly worn over armor. **2.** an outer coat.

sure (shŏor), *adj.,* **sur·er, sur·est. 1.** free from doubt; confident: *Always be sure of your facts.* **2.** certain beyond doubt: *He is sure to come.* **3.** reliable; trustworthy: *a sure friend.* **4.** certain to work or give the desired result: *a sure cure.* **5.** firm or stable: *a sure grip.* **6.** accurate; unerring: *a sure aim.* —*adv.* **7.** *Informal.* surely; certainly: *Sure, I'll come.* **8. be sure,** to make certain (to do something mentioned): *Be sure to close the windows when you leave.* **9. for sure,** as a certainty; surely: *I'll see you next week for sure.* **10. make sure,** to be or become absolutely certain: *Call me to make sure I get up in time.* **11. sure enough,** *Informal.* as might have been expected: *Sure enough, she came late.* —**sure′ness,** *n.*

Surcoat

—**Usage.** Most careful writers and speakers avoid the use of *sure* in place of *surely* in all but the most informal situations: *It surely* (not *sure*) *is hot today.*

He'll come, as surely (not *sure*) *as night follows day.*

sure-foot·ed (shŏŏr′fŏŏt′id), *adj.* not likely to stumble, trip, or fall: *The cat is a sure-footed animal.* —**sure′-foot′ed·ly,** *adv.* —**sure′-foot′ed·ness,** *n.*

sure·ly (shŏŏr′lē), *adv.* 1. without missing, slipping, etc.; firmly: *The arrow shot surely to the mark.* 2. certainly; without doubt: *He surely will come.* 3. assuredly; emphatically: *Surely you must be mistaken.*

sure·ty (shŏŏr′i tē), *n., pl.* **sure·ties.** 1. sureness; certainty. 2. something that is a guarantee against loss, damage, etc.; security: *His insurance policy was a surety against fire damage.* 3. a person who is legally responsible for the debts or actions of another.

surf (sûrf), *n.* 1. the waves of the sea that break and foam upon the shore. —*v.* 2. to ride a surfboard; engage in surfing. —**surf′er,** *n.*

sur·face (sûr′fis), *n.* 1. the outer face of anything: *the surface of the water.* 2. any face of a thing: *the six surfaces of a cube.* 3. outward appearance: *She was cheerful on the surface, but sad within.* —*adj.* 4. of, on, or referring to the surface; outward: *a surface view.* 5. slight; not deep: *a surface interest in art.* —*v.,* **sur·faced, sur·fac·ing.** 6. to put a surface on, or finish the surface of: *to surface a road.* 7. to rise to the surface: *The submarine surfaced.*

surf·board (sûrf′bôrd′), *n.* a long, narrow board on which a person stands, kneels, or lies, used in the sport of surfing.

sur·feit (sûr′fit), *n.* 1. too much of something; excess: *a surfeit of rain.* 2. overindulgence in eating or drinking. 3. the uncomfortable feeling that comes from eating or drinking too much. —*v.* 4. to give too much of something to: *He was surfeited with reading.* 5. to feed too much: *to be surfeited with food.*

surf·ing (sûr′fĭng), *n.* a sport in which a person stands or lies prone on a surfboard and rides the crest of a breaking wave toward the shore. Also, **surf′board′ing.**

surge (sûrj), *n.* 1. a strong, wavelike movement: *the surge of a crowd toward an exit.* 2. a swelling wave; billow: *the surge of the sea.* —*v.,* **surged, surg·ing.** 3. (of a ship) to rise and fall with the waves: *to surge at anchor.* 4. to move in or like waves: *The surf surged over us. The crowd surged toward the exit.*

sur·geon (sûr′jən), *n.* a physician who is skilled in surgery.

sur·ger·y (sûr′jə rē), *n., pl.* for def. 3 **sur·ger·ies.** 1. the science of treating diseases by operation upon the body, usually with instruments: *Tonsils are removed by surgery.* 2. treatment, such as an operation, performed by a surgeon. 3. a room or place where such operations are performed.

sur·gi·cal (sûr′ji kəl), *adj.* 1. concerning or involving surgery: *the surgical ward of a hospital.* 2. used in surgery: *surgical instruments.* —**sur′gi·cal·ly,** *adv.*

Su·ri·nam (sŏŏr′ə näm′), *n.* a republic on the NE coast of South America. 60,230 sq. mi. *Cap.:* Paramaribo. Former name, **Dutch Guiana.**

sur·ly (sûr′lē), *adj.,* **sur·li·er, sur·li·est.** 1. very rude or bad-tempered: *a sharp, surly answer.* 2. hostile; not friendly: *a surly dog.* —**sur′li·ness,** *n.*

sur·mise (sər mīz′), *v.,* **sur·mised, sur·mis·ing.** 1. to guess: *I surmised from his look that he was lying.* —*n.* 2. an opinion or guess: *It is my surmise that it will rain tomorrow.*

sur·mount (sər mount′), *v.* 1. to get over or across: *to surmount a fence.* 2. to overcome or conquer: *to surmount grave difficulties.* 3. to be on top of or above: *The peak is surmounted by a castle.*

sur·name (sûr′nām′), *n.* 1. the last name, or family name, of a person: *"Keats" is the surname of John Keats.* 2. a word or phrase added to a person's name to describe him: *King Alfred's surname was "the Great."* —*v.* (sûr′nām′, sûr nām′), **sur·named, sur·nam·ing.** 3. to give a surname to; call by a surname.

sur·pass (sər pas′), *v.* 1. to go beyond in amount, degree, etc.: *His efforts surpassed mine.* 2. to be better than: *This performance surpasses the last.* —**sur·pass′a·ble,** *adj.*

sur·plice (sûr′plis), *n.* a loose, white garment with wide sleeves, worn over other clothing by clergymen and members of a choir.

Surplice

sur·plus (sûr′plus), *n.* 1. an amount or quantity that remains above what is needed or used: *a surplus of wheat.* —*adj.* 2. more than is needed or used: *surplus wheat.*

sur·prise (sər prīz′), *v.,* **sur·prised, sur·pris·ing.** 1. to strike with sudden wonder or astonishment: *Their unplanned visit surprised us.* 2. to come upon or discover suddenly or without warning: *We surprised him stealing.* 3. to attack without warning: *The enemy surprised us in the middle of the night.* —*n.* 4. the act or an instance of surprising. 5. something completely unexpected: *The visit was a surprise.* 6. a feeling of sudden wonder or astonishment: *to be filled with surprise.* 7. **take by surprise,** to astonish or amaze: *The size of their house took us by surprise.*

sur·pris·ing (sər prī′zĭng), *adj.* causing surprise, wonder, or astonishment: *a surprising confession.* —**sur·pris′ing·ly,** *adv.*

sur·ren·der (sə ren′dər), *v.* 1. to give (oneself) up, esp. as a prisoner: *He surrendered himself to the police.* 2. to abandon: *to surrender hope; to surrender a claim.* 3. to yield to an emotion or influence: *He surrendered himself to the beauty of the music.*

sur·rep·ti·tious (sûr′əp tish′əs), *adj.* done in a secret, stealthy way: *Spying is a surreptitious act.* —**sur′rep·ti′tious·ly,** *adv.* —**sur′rep·ti′tious·ness,** *n.*

sur·rey (sûr′ē), *n., pl.* **sur·reys.** a light carriage with four wheels and two seats.

Surrey

sur·ro·gate (sûr′ə gāt′, sûr′ə git), *n.* 1. a person who acts for another; deputy. 2. (in some states) the judge of a probate court. 3. any substitute.

sur·round (sə round′), *v.* to enclose on all sides; shut in; encircle: *Hills surrounded the town. The troops surrounded the enemy camp.*

sur·round·ings (sə roun′diñgz), *n.pl.* the things, people, conditions, etc., that surround one: *He wanted to live in more pleasant surroundings.*

sur·tax (sûr′taks′), *n.* an extra tax on something already taxed.

sur·veil·lance (sər vā′ləns), *n.* a watch kept over a person, group, etc., esp. over a suspect or prisoner.

sur·vey (sər vā′), *v.* 1. to take a broad view of: *He surveyed his past. They surveyed their surroundings.* 2. to look at in detail: *She surveyed the coat thoroughly before she bought it.* 3. to measure (a piece of land, part of a country, etc.) for size, shape, or the position of boundaries. 4. to work as a surveyor. —*n.* (sûr′vā, sər vā′), *pl.* **sur·veys.** 5. the act or an instance of surveying. 6. a detailed examination of a problem or situation: *to conduct a survey of housewives.* 7. a written work that deals with an entire subject, field of study, etc.: *a survey of English poetry.* 8. the measurement of land for size, shape, or the position of boundaries.

sur·vey·ing (sər vā′iñg), *n.* 1. the science of surveying land. 2. the work of a surveyor.

sur·vey·or (sər vā′ər), *n.* a person whose work is surveying land.

sur·viv·al (sər vī′vəl), *n.* 1. the act or fact of surviving. 2. a person or thing that survives: *The house is a survival from the last century.*

sur·vive (sər vīv′), *v.*, **sur·vived, sur·viv·ing.** 1. to remain alive after the death of: *She survived her husband by twenty years.* 2. to continue to exist or be in use: *a building that survives after centuries.* 3. to live through or in spite of: *to survive great hardships.*

sur·vi·vor (sər vī′vər), *n.* a person or thing that continues to live or exist: *the survivors of a storm.*

sus·cep·ti·ble (sə sep′tə bəl), *adj.* 1. capable of being treated in a certain way (often fol. by *to* or *of*): *metal susceptible of a high polish.* 2. easily affected or moved (usually fol. by *to*): *He is susceptible to beautiful music.* —**sus·cep′ti·bil′i·ty,** *n.*

sus·pect (sə spekt′), *v.* 1. to believe to be guilty without proof: *I suspect him of lying.* 2. to doubt or question: *I suspect his honesty.* 3. to surmise or imagine: *I suspect you must be tired after your trip.* —*n.* (sus′pekt). 4. a person who is suspected of a crime or other offense: *The murder suspect was placed under arrest.* —*adj.* (sus′pekt, sə spekt′). 5. open to suspicion; suspicious: *His sudden change of heart is highly suspect.*

sus·pend (sə spend′), *v.* 1. to support from above; hang: *to suspend a picture from a nail.* 2. to put off to a later time: *His sentence was suspended by the judge.* 3. to hold in place in a liquid or the air: *Particles of fat are suspended in milk.* 4. to halt for a time: *to suspend work until after Christmas.* 5. to stop from operating for a time: *to suspend a rule.* 6. to keep out for a time: *He was suspended from school for a term.*

sus·pend·ers (sə spen′dərz), *n.pl.* bands of cloth or elastic material worn over the shoulders and buttoned or clipped to the waist of the trousers to hold them up. Also, *esp. British,* **braces.**

sus·pense (sə spens′), *n.* a state of doubt and nervous excitement that one feels while waiting for some decision or outcome: *The movie kept us in suspense till the end.* —**sus·pense′ful,** *adj.*

sus·pen·sion (sə spen′shən), *n.* 1. the act of suspending, or the state of being suspended. 2. a mixture in which particles of a substance are present in a fluid without being dissolved.

suspen′sion bridge′, a bridge having a deck hung from cables that pass over towers and are anchored at each end.

sus·pi·cion (sə spish′ən), *n.* 1. the act of suspecting, or the state of being suspected: *His honesty puts him above suspicion.* 2. the state of mind of a person who suspects: *Suspicion kept him awake at night.* 3. the feeling or idea of a person who suspects: *I have a suspicion that he was lying.* 4. a slight trace; hint: *a suspicion of a smile.*

sus·pi·cious (sə spish′əs), *adj.* 1. causing suspicion: *a suspicious action.* 2. full of or feeling suspicion: *I am suspicious of your promises.* 3. showing suspicion: *a suspicious glance.* —**sus·pi′cious·ly,** *adv.*

Sus·que·han·na (sus′kwə han′ə), *n.* a river flowing S from New York through Pennsylvania and Maryland into the Chesapeake Bay. 444 mi. long.

sus·tain (sə stān′), *v.* 1. to support from below; bear up: *The building is sustained by a strong foundation.* 2. to bear (a burden, responsibility, etc.). 3. to undergo (injury, loss, etc.). 4. to keep from giving way: *Her faith sustains her.* 5. to keep up or keep going: *to sustain interest.* 6. to nourish and support: *to sustain a family.* 7. to support with aid or approval: *to sustain a worthy cause.* 8. to uphold as right, true, etc.: *My story was sustained by the witness.*

sus·te·nance (sus′tə nəns), *n.* 1. anything that sustains life, such as food and drink. 2. the process of sustaining, or the state of being sustained.

su·ture (sōō′chər), *n.* 1. a joining of the edges of a wound or the like by stitching. 2. one of the stitches or fastenings used in joining the edges of a wound together. 3. the line where two bones, esp. of the skull, meet. —*v.,* **su·tured, su·tur·ing.** 4. to join by or as if by a suture.

SW, 1. southwest. 2. southwestern. Also, **S.W.**

swab (swäb), *n.* 1. a large mop for cleaning floors, decks, etc. 2. a piece of sponge, cloth, cotton, or the like, sometimes fixed to a stick, for applying medicine to or cleaning the mouth, throat, etc. 3. a brush for cleaning the barrel of a gun. —*v.,* **swabbed, swab·bing.** 4. to apply medicine to or clean (a part of the body) with a swab: *to swab one's throat with antiseptic.* 5. to mop: *to swab the decks.*

swad·dle (swod′əl), *v.,* **swad·dled, swad·dling.** 1. to wrap (a baby) with strips of cloth so as to limit movement. **2.** to wrap (anything) with cloth, bandages, etc.: *His head was swaddled in a towel.*

swag (swag), *n. Slang.* stolen goods; plunder; booty.

swag·ger (swag′ər), *v.* **1.** to walk or strut in a bold, haughty way. **2.** to boast or brag noisily. —*n.* **3.** a swaggering walk or manner. —**swag′ger·ing·ly,** *adv.*

Swa·hi·li (swä hē′lē), *n., pl.* **Swa·hi·lis** *or* for def. 1 **Swa·hi·li. 1.** a member of a Bantu people of East Africa. **2.** a mixed language based on Bantu and Arabic, spoken in East Africa and parts of the Congo. —*adj.* **3.** of or referring to the Swahili people or the Swahili language.

swain (swān), *n.* **1.** a lover. **2.** a country lad.

swal·low[1] (swol′ō), *v.* **1.** to move (food, drink, etc.) from the mouth to the stomach through the throat. **2.** to take in (often fol. by *up*): *The crowd swallowed him up.* **3.** to hold in: *to swallow tears.* **4.** to accept without opposition: *to swallow insults.* **5.** *Informal.* to accept without question: *He swallowed the story.* —*n.* **6.** the act or an instance of swallowing. **7.** a quantity swallowed. [from the Old English word *swelgan*]

swal·low[2] (swol′ō), *n.* any of numerous small birds having long wings and a forked tail, noted for their swift, graceful flight. [from the Old English word *swealwe*]

swal·low·tail (swol′ō tāl′), *n.* any of several butterflies whose long lower wings resemble the forked tail of the swallow.

swam (swam), *v.* the past tense of **swim.**

swa·mi (swä′mē), *n., pl.* **swa·mies.** a title of honor given to a Hindu religious teacher.

swamp (swomp), *n.* **1.** a tract of wet, spongy land; marsh; bog. —*v.* **2.** to flood or drench with water. **3.** to sink by flooding with water: *to swamp a boat.* **4.** to overwhelm or flood: *to be swamped with work.*

Swallowtail (wingspread to 4 in.)

swamp·y (swom′pē), *adj.,* **swamp·i·er, swamp·i·est. 1.** having many swamps: *a swampy country.* **2.** like a swamp; muddy: *swampy land.* —**swamp′i·ness,** *n.*

swan (swon), *n.* any of several large, beautiful, swimming birds having a long, slender neck and, usually, pure white plumage.

swan's-down (swonz′doun′), *n.* the soft underfeathers of a swan.

swan′ song′, the last work, act, utterance, or achievement of a person or group before death, retirement, etc.

Swan (length 5 ft.)

swap (swop), *v.,* **swapped, swap·ping. 1.** to exchange or trade one thing for another: *to swap a record player for a typewriter.* —*n.* **2.** an exchange: *He got the radio in a swap.*

sward (swôrd), *n.* the grassy surface of land; turf.

swarm (swôrm), *n.* **1.** a group of honeybees that leave a hive together to form a new colony. **2.** a group of insects clustered closely together: *a swarm of flies.* **3.** a great number of things or persons, esp.

in motion. —*v.* **4.** (of bees) to leave a hive. **5.** to move about in great numbers: *People swarmed to the circus.* **6.** (of a place) to be full; teem or abound: *The park swarms with children.*

swarth·y (swôr′thē, swôr′thē), *adj.,* **swarth·i·er, swarth·i·est.** (of the skin, complexion, etc.) being of a dark color. —**swarth′i·ness,** *n.*

swash·buck·ler (swosh′buk/lər, swôsh′-), *n.* a swaggering swordsman, soldier, or adventurer; daredevil.

swas·ti·ka (swos′ti kə), *n.* **1.** a geometrical figure used as a symbol or an ornament in the Old World and America, consisting of a cross with arms of equal length bent at right angles. **2.** this figure with clockwise arms as the official emblem of the Nazi party.

Swastikas
A, American Indian;
B, Nazi

swat (swot), *v.,* **swat·ted, swat·ting. 1.** to hit, slap, or smack: *to swat a fly.* —*n.* **2.** a blow, slap, or smack. —**swat′ter,** *n.*

swath (swoth), *n.* **1.** the space covered by the stroke of a scythe or the cut of a mowing machine. **2.** the piece or strip so cut. **3.** a strip, belt, or long and narrow extent of anything.

swathe (swoth), *v.,* **swathed, swath·ing. 1.** to wrap or bind with bands. **2.** to bandage. **3.** to enfold or envelop. —*n.* **4.** a wrapping or bandage.

sway (swā), *v.* **1.** to move or swing to and fro: *The sign swayed in the wind.* **2.** to cause to move to one side: *The storm swayed the boat.* **3.** to influence: *The high salary swayed him to accept the job.* **4.** to change from one opinion to another; fluctuate: *He cannot be swayed from his position.* —*n.* **5.** the act of swaying; a swaying movement: *the sway of branches.* **6.** rule or dominion: *under the government's sway.* **7.** dominating power or influence: *His brother seems to have sway over him.*

sway-backed (swā′bakt′), *adj.* (of horses) having a deep downward curve in the back.

Swa·zi·land (swä′zē land′), *n.* a kingdom in SE Africa, formerly a British protectorate. 6704 sq. mi.

swear (swâr), *v.,* **swore** (swôr), **sworn** (swôrn), **swear·ing. 1.** to make a solemn oath by some sacred being or object: *He swore on the Bible to tell the truth.* **2.** to bind by an oath; promise or cause to promise: *He swore me to secrecy.* **3.** to use profane language. **4. swear by, a.** *Informal.* to have confidence in; rely on: *She swears by this new toothpaste.* **b.** Also, **swear to.** to be certain of (something): *I thought he left, but I won't swear by it.* **5. swear in,** to admit (a person) to office or service by administering an oath: *to swear in a new president.* **6. swear off,** *Informal.* to promise or decide to give up (something), esp. for a certain period of time: *to swear off candy bars during Lent.* **7. swear out,** to obtain (a warrant for arrest) by making an accusation under oath: *We swore out a complaint against the reckless driver.*

sweat (swet), *v.,* **sweat** *or* **sweat·ed; sweat·ing. 1.** to perspire. **2.** to gather drops of moisture from the air by condensation: *A glass of ice water sweats on a* *warm day.* **3.** to work or cause to work hard: *to sweat over a report; to sweat employees.* **4.** to cause to lose (weight) by perspiring or hard work (often fol. by *off* or *out*): *to sweat off ten pounds.* **5.** *Informal.* to worry or be concerned about: *to sweat an exam.* —*n.* **6.** See **perspiration** (def. 1). **7.** moisture coming from something or gathered on a surface. **8.** **sweat out,** *Slang.* to wait for anxiously or with great interest: *We sweated out the election returns all night.*

sweat·er (swet′ər), *n.* a knitted jacket or jersey, in pullover or cardigan style, with or without sleeves.

sweat′ gland′, one of the numerous, tiny glands in the skin that secrete perspiration.

sweat′ shirt′, a loose, collarless, cotton-jersey pullover, worn esp. by athletes to prevent chill or, while exercising, to cause sweating.

sweat·shop (swet′shop′), *n.* a shop employing workers at low wages, for long hours, and under poor conditions.

sweat·y (swet′ē), *adj.,* **sweat·i·er, sweat·i·est. 1.** covered, moist, or stained with sweat. **2.** causing sweat. —**sweat·i·ness,** *n.*

Swede (swēd), *n.* a native or inhabitant of Sweden.

Swe·den (swēd′ən), *n.* a kingdom in N Europe, in the E part of the Scandinavian Peninsula. 173,394 sq. mi. *Cap.:* Stockholm.

Swed·ish (swē′dish), *adj.* **1.** of or concerning Sweden, its inhabitants, or their language. —*n.* **2.** the people of Sweden as a group. **3.** the Germanic language of the Swedes.

sweep (swēp), *v.,* **swept** (swept), **sweep·ing. 1.** to move or remove by passing a broom, brush, or the like, back and forth over a surface: *to sweep up dirt.* **2.** to clear or clean of dirt, litter, or the like, by means of a broom or brush: *to sweep the garage floor.* **3.** to pass in swift but stately manner: *She swept into the room.* **4.** to move by or as if by a steady, driving force: *The wind swept the snow into drifts.* **5.** to move or pass in a continuous course: *His glance swept around the room.* **6.** to clear (a surface, place, etc.) of something on or in it: *to sweep a sea of enemy ships.* **7.** to pass over (a surface, region, etc.) with a steady driving force: *sandstorms sweeping the plains.* **8.** to extend in a continuous or curving stretch: *The road sweeps by the dunes.* —*n.* **9.** the act of sweeping, esp. a moving, removing, or clearing by or as if by the use of a broom. **10.** a continuous extent or stretch. **11.** the steady, driving motion of something moving with force, such as the wind. **12.** a swinging or curving movement or stroke: *a sweep of a scythe.* **13.** an overwhelming victory in a contest: *a sweep of all the important prizes.* **14.** a large oar for moving or steering a boat. —**sweep′er,** *n.*

sweep·ing (swē′ping), *adj.* **1.** of wide range or scope: *sweeping reforms.* **2.** moving or passing over a wide area: *a sweeping glance.* **3.** overwhelming; complete: *a sweeping victory.* —*n.* **4.** the act of a person or thing that sweeps. **5.** **sweepings,** trash, or other matter swept out or up: *carpet sweepings.*

sweep·stakes (swēp′stāks′), *n. (used as sing. or pl.)* **1.** a race or other contest for which the prize consists of the stakes contributed by the various competitors. **2.** a lottery or any similar contest.

sweet (swēt), *adj.* **1.** having the taste or flavor of sugar, honey, etc. **2.** not stale; fresh: *sweet milk.* **3.** not salty or salted: *sweet butter.* **4.** pleasing to the ear; musical: *sweet sounds.* **5.** pleasing or fresh to the smell; fragrant: *sweet flowers.* **6.** pleasant in disposition or manners. —*n.* **7.** Usually, **sweets.** pie, cake, candy, or other foods containing sugar. **8.** a beloved person; dear; darling. —**sweet′ly,** *adv.*

sweet·bread (swēt′bred′), *n.* the pancreas or the thymus gland of a calf, sheep, etc., used for food.

sweet·bri·er (swēt′brī′ər), *n.* a rose of Europe and central Asia having a tall stem with strong thorns, often mixed with bristles, and pink flowers.

sweet′ corn′, any of several kinds of corn having sweet kernels and eaten when young.

sweet·en (swēt′ən), *v.* **1.** to make sweet or sweeter, as by adding sugar. **2.** to become sweet or sweeter. **3.** to make mild, soft, or more pleasant: *My compliment sweetened her disposition.* —**sweet′en·er,** *n.*

sweet·en·ing (swēt′ə·ning, swēt′ning), *n.* **1.** something that sweetens food, beverages, etc., such as sugar, saccharin, etc. **2.** the process of causing something to be or become sweet.

sweet·heart (swēt′härt′), *n.* a person who is loved; beloved.

sweet·meat (swēt′mēt′), *n.* any highly sweetened delicacy, such as candied fruit, bonbons, preserves, etc.

sweet′ pea′, a climbing plant of the pea family having sweet-smelling flowers of many colors.

sweet′ pota′to, 1. a vine that grows along the ground and has a yellowish, sweet, starchy root that is eaten as a vegetable. **2.** the root itself.

sweet′ wil′liam, a garden plant bearing clusters of small, many-colored flowers.

swell (swel), *v.,* **swelled; swelled** *or* **swol·len** (swō′lən); **swell·ing. 1.** to increase in size: *My ankle swelled after I sprained it.* **2.** to rise in waves, as the sea. **3.** to bulge out: *The sails swelled in the wind.* **4.** to increase gradually in volume or intensity, such as sound. **5.** to arise and grow within a person, as a feeling or emotion. **6.** to puff up or become puffed up with pride. —*n.* **7.** the act of swelling or the condition of being swollen. **8.** a long and unbroken wave, or a series of such waves. **9.** a gradually rising elevation of land. **10.** a gradual increase in loudness of sound. —*adj. Slang.* **11.** stylish or elegant: *a swell hotel.* **12.** excellent or first-rate: *a swell vacation.*

swell·ing (swel′ing), *n.* a swollen part or place.

swel·ter (swel′tər), *v.* **1.** to suffer from oppressive heat. **2.** to oppress with heat. —*n.* **3.** a sweltering condition.

swept (swept), *v.* the past tense and past participle of **sweep.**

swerve (swûrv), *v.,* **swerved, swerv·ing. 1.** to turn aside abruptly: *The car swerved to avoid the truck.* —*n.* 2. an act of swerving.

swift (swift), *adj.* 1. moving with great speed: *a swift runner.* 2. coming, happening, or performed quickly: *He received a swift reply.* 3. quick to act or respond. —*n.* 4. any of numerous birds resembling swallows but related to the hummingbirds, noted for their rapid flight. —**swift′ly,** *adv.* —**swift′ness,** *n.*

swig (swig), *n.* 1. a swallow of liquid. —*v.*, **swigged, swig·ging.** 2. to drink greedily.

swill (swil), *n.* 1. liquid or partly liquid food, esp. kitchen refuse, for animals. 2. kitchen refuse in general; garbage. —*v.* 3. to drink greedily. 4. to feed (animals) with swill: *to swill the hogs.*

swim (swim), *v.*, **swam** (swam), **swum** (swum), **swim·ming.** 1. to move in water by using the limbs, fins, tail, etc. 2. to move along in or cross by swimming: *to swim a lake.* 3. to float on the surface of water or some other liquid. 4. to move or glide smoothly: *The clouds swam by.* 5. to be surrounded by or covered with a liquid: *The green beans are swimming in butter.* 6. to be dizzy or giddy: *Her head swam from fatigue.* —*n.* 7. the act or a period of swimming. 8. **in the swim,** interested in or informed about current trends, events, etc.; up-to-date: *My grandmother keeps in the swim by going to all the new movies.* —**swim′mer,** *n.*

swim·ming (swim′ing), *n.* 1. the act of a person or thing that swims. 2. the skill or technique of a person who swims: *to teach swimming.* —*adj.* 3. propelling oneself in water by moving the limbs, fins, tail, etc.: *a swimming animal.* 4. used in or for swimming: *a swimming pool.* 5. feeling dizzy.

swim·ming·ly (swim′ing lē), *adv.* without difficulty; with great success: *Mary and I get along swimmingly.*

swin·dle (swin′dᵊl), *v.*, **swin·dled, swin·dling.** 1. to cheat (someone) out of money or other property. 2. to defraud or cheat: *to swindle $100.* —*n.* 3. the act of swindling; a dishonest scheme. —**swin′dler,** *n.*

swine (swin), *n.*, *pl.* **swine.** 1. a pig or hog. 2. a coarse, crude, or mean person.

swine·herd (swin′hûrd′), *n.* a man who takes care of swine.

swing (swing), *v.*, **swung** (swung), **swing·ing.** 1. to move or cause to move back and forth, as something suspended from above. 2. to move or cause to move with a circular or sweeping movement: *to swing a club around one's head.* 3. to hang or cause to hang freely: *The light swings from the ceiling. He swung the hammock between the post and a tree.* 4. to cause to move or turn around a fixed point: *to swing a door shut.* 5. to move to and fro in a swing. 6. *Informal.* to influence or manage as desired: *to swing votes.* —*n.* 7. the act or manner of swinging. 8. the amount or extent of such movement: *to correct the swing of a pendulum.* 9. a curving movement or course: *the swing of a golf club.* 10. a blow or stroke with the hand or an object grasped in the hand: *He took a swing at me.* 11. a smooth style of jazz popular esp. in the 1930's. 12. a seat suspended from

above by ropes or rods on which a person may move to and fro for recreation. 13. **in full swing,** *Informal.* in full operation or progress: *Automobile production is now in full swing.* —**swing′er,** *n.*

swipe (swip), *n.* 1. *Informal.* a strong sweeping blow: *the swipe of a golf club.* —*v.*, **swiped, swip·ing.** 2. *Informal.* to strike with a sweeping blow. 3. *Slang.* to steal.

swirl (swûrl), *v.* 1. to move with a whirling motion: *The snowflakes swirled through the air.* —*n.* 2. a whirling movement. 3. a twist or curl, as of hair.

swish (swish), *v.* 1. to move with a hissing or rustling sound: *The waves swished up on the shore.* 2. to rustle: *Her silk dress swished as she walked.* —*n.* 3. a swishing movement or sound.

Swiss (swis), *adj.* 1. of, concerning, or like Switzerland or its inhabitants. —*n.* 2. a native or inhabitant of Switzerland. 3. Also, **Swiss′ cheese′.** a firm pale-yellow cheese containing many holes.

switch (swich), *n.* 1. a slender, flexible rod, used esp. in whipping. 2. the act of whipping or beating with or as if with such an object. 3. a bunch or tress of long hair to be added to a woman's own hair. 4. a set of movable rails allowing a railroad train to move from one track to another. 5. a device for turning an electric appliance on or off or for changing an electrical connection. 6. a turning, shifting, or changing: *a switch in plans.* 7. a tuft of hair at the end of the tail of some animals. —*v.* 8. to whip or strike with or as if with a switch. 9. to move, swing, or whisk: *to switch a cane.* 10. to shift or exchange: *to switch seats.* 11. to change: *to switch direction.* 12. to turn or change by operating an electrical switch: *to switch off the light.* 13. to move or transfer from one set of tracks to another: *to switch a train.*

switch·board (swich′bôrd′), *n.* a unit containing switches and instruments necessary to complete telephone circuits by hand.

switch·man (swich′mən), *n.*, *pl.* **switch·men.** a person who has charge of a switch or switches on a railroad.

Swit·zer·land (swit′sər lənd), *n.* a republic in central Europe. 15,944 sq. mi. *Cap.:* Bern.

swiv·el (swiv′əl), *n.* 1. a fastening device that allows the thing fastened to turn around freely upon it. 2. such a device consisting of two parts, each of which turns around by itself. 3. a support on which a gun may be turned around in any direction. —*v.*, **swiv·eled** *or* **swiv·elled; swiv·el·ing** *or* **swiv·el·ling.** 4. to turn on or as if on a swivel.

swol·len (swo′lən), *v.* 1. a past participle of swell. —*adj.* 2. enlarged by or as if by swelling: *a swollen ankle.*

swoon (swoon), *v.* 1. to faint. —*n.* 2. a faint.

swoop (swoop), *v.* 1. to sweep down through the air: *The hawk swooped down on the chicken.* —*n.* 2. the act or an instance of swooping.

sword (sôrd), *n.* 1. a weapon consisting of a long, pointed, straight or slightly curved blade with a sharp edge or edges, fixed in a handle. 2. this weapon as the symbol of military power, authority,

punishment, etc.: *The pen is mightier than the sword.*
3. cross swords, to disagree violently; argue or fight: *The two teams crossed swords over the umpire's decision.* —**sword′like′,** *adj.*

sword·fish (sôrd′fish′), *n., pl.* **sword·fish·es** *or* **sword·fish.** a large saltwater game and food fish whose upper jaw is lengthened into a long, swordlike point.

Swordfish
(length to 15 ft.)

swords·man (sôrdz′mən), *n., pl.* **swords·men.** a person who is skilled in the use of a sword.

swore (swôr), *v.* the past tense of **swear.**

sworn (swôrn), *v.* the past participle of **swear.**

swum (swum), *v.* the past participle of **swim.**

swung (swung), *v.* the past tense and past participle of **swing.**

syc·a·more (sik′ə môr′), *n.* **1.** a North American shade tree with smooth bark that is easy to flake off; buttonwood. **2.** a European and Asian maple tree. **3.** a kind of fig tree that grows in the Near East.

Syd·ney (sid′nē), *n.* a port city in SE Australia.

syl·lab·ic (si lab′ik), *adj.* **1.** of or referring to a syllable or syllables. **2.** consisting of a syllable or syllables.

syl·lab·i·cate (si lab′ə kāt′), *v.,* **syl·lab·i·cat·ed, syl·lab·i·cat·ing.** another word for **syllabify.** —**syl·lab′i·ca′tion,** *n.*

syl·lab·i·fy (si lab′ə fī′), *v.,* **syl·lab·i·fied, syl·lab·i·fy·ing.** to form or divide into syllables. —**syl·lab′i·fi·ca′tion,** *n.*

syl·la·ble (sil′ə bəl), *n.* **1.** a unit of speech consisting of a single vowel or diphthong, with or without one or more consonants, pronounced in a single pulse of breath, and forming a word or part of a word. *Man* and *eye* are words of one syllable. *Writing, beautiful,* and *dictionary* are words of more than one syllable. **2.** one or more letters representing a syllable. **3.** any of the parts into which a written word may be divided, esp. at the end of a line. In this dictionary, these divisions of a word are shown by centered dots: *sym·me·try.* **4.** the least portion or amount of speech or writing: *Don't breathe a syllable of this.*

syl·la·bus (sil′ə bəs), *n.* an outline of the main points of a speech, the subjects of a course of lectures, etc.

sylph (silf), *n.* **1.** a slender, graceful girl or woman. **2.** one of a race of light, dainty creatures supposed to inhabit the air.

syl·van (sil′vən), *adj.* **1.** of, concerning, or living in the woods: *sylvan creatures.* **2.** consisting of or full of woods and trees: *a sylvan region.*

sym·bol (sim′bəl), *n.* **1.** something used to represent something else: *An olive branch is a symbol of peace.* **2.** a letter, figure, or other mark used to represent something: *The chemical symbol Au represents gold.*

sym·bol·ic (sim bol′ik), *adj.* **1.** serving as a symbol of something: *a symbolic design.* **2.** of, concerning, or

expressed by a symbol. Also, **sym·bol′i·cal.** —**sym·bol′i·cal·ly,** *adv.*

sym·bol·ism (sim′bə liz′əm), *n.* **1.** the use of symbols to represent things. **2.** a set or system of symbols: *religious symbolism.*

sym·bol·ize (sim′bə līz′), *v.,* **sym·bol·ized, sym·bol·iz·ing. 1.** to be a symbol of; stand for or represent: *A sword symbolizes war.* **2.** to represent by a symbol or symbols: *The artist symbolized war with a sword.*

sym·met·ri·cal (si me′tri kəl), *adj.* having or showing symmetry; well-proportioned; balanced in arrangement of parts. Also, **sym·met′ric.** —**sym·met′ri·cal·ly,** *adv.*

sym·me·try (sim′i trē), *n., pl.* **sym·me·tries. 1.** the correspondence in size, form, and arrangement of parts on opposite sides of a plane, line, or point; regularity of form or arrangement: *the symmetry of a leaf.* **2.** the proper proportion of the parts of a whole to one another with regard to size and form: *the symmetry of a handsome face.*

sym·pa·thet·ic (sim′pə thet′ik), *adj.* **1.** feeling or showing sympathy; compassionate: *a sympathetic listener.* **2.** sharing one's ideas, feelings, etc.: *a sympathetic classmate.* **3.** looking upon with favor (often fol. by *to* or *toward*): *He is sympathetic to the project.* —**sym′pa·thet′i·cal·ly,** *adv.*

sym·pa·thize (sim′pə thīz′), *v.,* **sym·pa·thized, sym·pa·thiz·ing. 1.** to share in a feeling or feelings: *He sympathized with his sister's plans.* **2.** to feel or express sympathy, as for suffering or trouble. —**sym′pa·thiz′er,** *n.*

sym·pa·thy (sim′pə thē), *n., pl.* **sym·pa·thies. 1.** agreement in feeling, as between persons or on the part of one person with respect to another: *sympathy between companions.* **2.** a relationship between persons or things whereby whatever affects one also affects the other. **3.** the ability to share the feelings of another, esp. in sorrow or trouble; compassion: *He expressed his sympathy to the victim's family.* **4.** favor or approval: *to view a plan with sympathy.*

sym·pho·ny (sim′fə nē), *n., pl.* **sym·pho·nies. 1.** a large composition for orchestra, usually in four movements of contrasting tempos. **2.** harmony, as of sounds or colors: *The forest is a symphony of red, gold, and orange.* —**sym·phon·ic** (sim fon′ik), *adj.*

symp·tom (simp′təm), *n.* a sign or indication of something, esp. of a particular disease: *High fever is a symptom of malaria.*

syn·a·gogue (sin′ə gog′), *n.* **1.** a Jewish house of worship. **2.** an assembly or congregation of Jews for the purpose of religious worship.

syn·chro·nize (sing′krə nīz′), *v.,* **syn·chro·nized, syn·chro·niz·ing. 1.** to occur at the same time; agree in time. **2.** to go on, move, etc., at the same rate and exactly together: *The gears must synchronize for efficient operation.* **3.** to cause to show the same time: *to synchronize watches.* —**syn′chro·niz′er,** *n.*

syn·co·pate (sing′kə pāt′), *v.,* **syn·co·pat·ed, syn·co·pat·ing. 1.** (in music) to accent (notes) that occur on

unaccented beats. **2.** to play (a passage) in this way.
—**syn′co·pa′tion,** *n.*

syn·di·cate (sin′də kit), *n.* **1.** a group of individuals or organizations combined or making a joint effort to complete some job or carry out certain negotiations or transactions. **2.** an agency that buys articles, photographs, comic strips, etc., and sells and distributes them for publication in a number of newspapers. —*v.* (sin′də kāt′), **syn·di·cat·ed, syn·di·cat·ing. 3.** to form a syndicate. **4.** to supply for publication in a number of newspapers. —**syn′di·ca′tion,** *n.*

syn·od (sin′əd), *n.* an assembly called together for the discussion and decision of church affairs.

syn·o·nym (sin′ə nim), *n.* a word that is the same or similar in meaning to another: *"Large" and "big" are synonyms.*

syn·on·y·mous (si non′ə məs), *adj.* having the same or similar meaning. —**syn·on′y·mous·ly,** *adv.*

syn·op·sis (si nop′sis), *n., pl.* **syn·op·ses** (si nop′sēz). a brief summary giving a general view of some subject, the plot of a novel, etc.

syn·tax (sin′taks), *n.* **1.** the pattern of grammatical relations of the words and phrases in a clause or sentence. **2.** the grammatical relation of one word or phrase to the others in a clause or sentence. **3.** the study of the structure of grammatical sentences in a language.

syn·the·sis (sin′thi sis), *n., pl.* **syn·the·ses** (sin′thi-sēz′). the combining of separate parts or elements to form a whole: *The synthesis of water requires combining hydrogen and oxygen.*

syn·thet·ic (sin thet′ik), *adj.* **1.** of, concerning, or involving synthesis: *a synthetic process.* **2.** made by artificial, esp. chemical, means: *synthetic rubber.* **3.** not real or genuine; artificial: *a synthetic smile.* —*n.* **4.** something made by a synthetic process. —**syn·thet′i·cal·ly,** *adv.*

syph·i·lis (sif′ə lis), *n.* a serious venereal disease that can affect almost any part of the body.

sy·phon (sī′fən), *n., v.* another spelling of **siphon.**

Syr·a·cuse (sir′ə kyōōs′), *n.* **1.** a city in central New York. **2.** a city in SE Sicily: founded in ancient times by the Carthaginians.

Syr·i·a (sir′ē ə), *n.* **1.** a republic in SW Asia at the E end of the Mediterranean Sea. 71,227 sq. mi. *Cap.:* Damascus. **2.** an ancient country in SW Asia, including the present Syria, Lebanon, Israel, and adjacent areas. —**Syr′i·an,** *n., adj.*

sy·rin·ga (sə riñg′gə), *n.* a garden shrub having clusters of sweet-smelling white flowers.

sy·ringe (sə rinj′, sir′inj), *n.* **1.** a device consisting of a tube and either a plunger or a bulb for taking up or injecting liquids. —*v.,* **sy·ringed, sy·ring·ing. 2.** to cleanse, wash, inject, etc., by means of a syringe.

syr·up (sir′əp, sûr′əp), *n.* **1.** a thick, sweet liquid prepared for cooking or table use from molasses, glucose, etc., mixed with water and often a flavoring agent. **2.** a liquid made of fruit juices, water, etc., boiled with sugar. Also, **sirup.** —**syr′up·y,** *adj.*

sys·tem (sis′təm), *n.* **1.** a group or combination of things or parts forming a whole: *a mountain system; a railroad system.* **2.** an orderly grouping of facts, principles, theories, methods, etc., in a certain field: *a system of philosophy.* **3.** a regular or special method or plan of procedure: *She has a good system for doing housework.* **4.** the human body considered as a functioning unit.

sys·tem·at·ic (sis′tə mat′ik), *adj.* **1.** having, showing, or involving a system, method, or plan: *a systematic course of reading.* **2.** orderly; methodical: *systematic habits.* —**sys′tem·at′i·cal·ly,** *adv.*

sys·tem·a·tize (sis′tə mə tīz′), *v.,* **sys·tem·a·tized, sys·tem·a·tiz·ing.** to arrange in or according to a system. —**sys′tem·a·tiz′er,** *n.*

	Semitic	Greek	Latin	Gothic	Modern Roman
DEVELOPMENT OF UPPER-CASE LETTERS	+	X	T	T	𝕿	T

DEVELOPMENT OF LOWER-CASE LETTERS	τ	ɾ	T	τ	t	t
	Greek		Medieval		Gothic	Modern Roman

T

T, t (tē), *n., pl.* **T's** *or* **Ts, t's** *or* **ts. 1.** the 20th letter of the English alphabet. **2.** something having the shape of a T. **3. to a T,** exactly; perfectly: *That hat suits you to a T.*

T., 1. tablespoon; tablespoonful. **2.** Territory. **3.** township.

t., 1. teaspoon; teaspoonful. **2.** time. **3.** ton.

Ta, *Chem.* the symbol for **tantalum.**

tab (tab), *n.* **1.** a small flap, strap, or loop, as on a garment, used for pulling, hanging, decoration, etc. **2. keep tabs on,** *Informal.* to observe closely; watch; supervise: *The police kept tabs on the suspect.*

tab·ard (tab′ərd), *n.* **1.** a loose garment, sleeveless or with short sleeves, worn by a knight over his armor. **2.** an official garment of a herald, showing his master's coat of arms.

tab·by (tab′ē), *n., pl.* **tab·bies.** a cat with striped fur.

tab·er·nac·le (tab′ər nak′əl), *n.* **1.** a temporary dwelling, such as a tent or a hut. **2.** (in the Bible) a portable shrine carried by the Jews during their wanderings with Moses after the Exodus. **3.** any place or house of worship. **4.** a box for the Eucharist.

ta·ble (tā′bəl), *n.* **1.** a piece of furniture consisting of a flat top supported by one or more legs. **2.** such a piece of furniture used for serving food to those seated at it. **3.** the food served at a table. **4.** a group of persons at a table. **5.** an orderly arrangement of words, numbers, or signs, or a combination of them: *a table of population statistics.* **6. tables,** tablets on which laws were formerly inscribed. —*v.,* **ta·bled, ta·bling. 7.** to lay aside for discussion in the indefinite future: *to table a proposal.* **8. turn the tables on,** to reverse a situation on (someone); get even with: *He tried to cheat me, but I turned the tables on him.* **9. under the table,** secretly or unofficially, esp. in order to bribe someone: *We had to pay money under the*

Tabard
(def. 2)

table to get our new apartment. **10. wait table,** to work as a waiter; serve food: *He worked his way through college by waiting table.*

tab·leau (tab′lō, ta blō′), *n., pl.* **tab·leaux** (tab′lōz, ta-blōz′) *or* **tab·leaus. 1.** a picture, as of a scene. **2.** a representation of a picture, statue, scene, etc., by one or more persons dressed in costume: *The class presented several Biblical tableaux.*

ta·ble·cloth (tā′bəl klôth′), *n., pl.* **ta·ble·cloths** (tā′-bəl klôthz′, -klôths′). a cloth for covering a table top.

ta·ble·land (tā′bəl land′), *n.* an elevated and usually level region; plateau.

ta·ble·spoon (tā′bəl spoon′), *n.* **1.** a spoon larger than a teaspoon or a dessert spoon, used in serving food at the table and as a standard measuring unit in recipes. **2.** a tablespoonful.

ta·ble·spoon·ful (tā′bəl spoon fool′), *n., pl.* **ta·ble·spoon·fuls. 1.** the amount a tablespoon can hold. **2.** ½ fluid ounce (14.8 milliliters); three teaspoonfuls.

tab·let (tab′lit), *n.* **1.** a number of sheets of writing paper, office forms, etc., fastened together at the edge; pad. **2.** a flat slab or surface, esp. one bearing an inscription, carving, or the like. **3.** a thin, flat sheet or leaf of hard material, used for writing or marking. **4.** a small, flat piece of some solid, such as a drug, chemical, soap, or the like: *vitamin tablets.*

ta′ble ten′nis, a variety of tennis played on a table, using paddles and a small, hollow plastic ball.

ta·ble·ware (tā′bəl wâr′), *n.* the dishes, utensils, etc., used at the table.

tab·loid (tab′loid), *n.* **1.** a newspaper whose pages are about half the size of a standard-size newspaper page. **2.** such a newspaper that reports mostly sensational news and is heavily illustrated: *The scandal was reported in the evening tabloid.* —*adj.* **3.** compressed or condensed: *a tabloid report.*

ta·boo (tə boo′, ta boo′), *adj.* **1.** forbidden by society as improper and unacceptable: *taboo words.* —*n., pl.* **ta·boos. 2.** a prohibition of anything; exclusion from general use or practice. —*v.,* **ta·booed, ta-**

act, āble, dâre, ärt; ebb, ēqual; if, īce; hot, ōver, ôrder; oil; book; ooze; out; up, ûrge; ə = a as in alone; ᵊ as in button (but′ᵊn), fire (fiᵊr); chief; shoe; thin; ŧhat; zh as in measure (mezh′ər). See full key inside cover.

boo·ing. **3.** to put under a taboo; prohibit or forbid. Also, **ta·bu′.**

ta·bor (tā′bər), *n.* a small drum formerly used to accompany oneself on a pipe or fife.

tab·u·lar (tab′yə lər), *adj.* **1.** of, concerning, or arranged in a table or systematic arrangement by columns, rows, etc. **2.** having the form of a table or tablet.

tab·u·late (tab′yə lāt′), *v.,* **tab·u·lat·ed, tab·u·lat·ing.** to put or arrange in a table or systematic form: *to tabulate election results.* **—tab′u·la′tion,** *n.*

T, Tabor

tac·it (tas′it), *adj.* **1.** silent; saying nothing. **2.** understood without being openly expressed: *tacit approval.* **—tac′it·ly,** *adv.*

tac·i·turn (tas′i tûrn′), *adj.* inclined to silence; speaking very little. **—tac′i·turn′i·ty,** *n.*

tack (tak), *n.* **1.** a short, sharp-pointed nail, usually with a wide, flat head. **2.** a long, temporary stitch used in sewing. **3.** the direction of a sailing vessel sailing close to the wind. **4.** one movement in the zigzag course of a ship sailing into the wind. **5.** a course of action: *He took a different tack to solve the problem.* **—v. 6.** to fasten by a tack or tacks: *to tack a picture on the wall.* **7.** to secure by some temporary fastening: *to tack a hem.* **8.** to add something extra: *He tacked the service charge onto the bill.* **9.** to change the course of a sailing vessel. **10.** to take or follow a zigzag course. **11. on the wrong tack,** in the wrong way or by using the wrong method: *He started out on the wrong tack, making accusations before he knew the facts.*

tack·le (tak′əl), *n.* **1.** equipment or gear, esp. for fishing. **2.** a system of ropes and pulleys for hoisting, lowering, or shifting objects. **3.** an act of tackling, as in football. **4.** (in football) either of the linemen stationed between a guard and the end. **—v., tack·led, tack·ling. 5.** to undertake to handle, master, solve, etc.: *to tackle a difficult problem.* **6.** (in football) to seize, stop, or throw down (a player carrying the ball).

Ta·co·ma (tə kō′mə), *n.* a port city in W Washington.

tact (takt), *n.* a keen sense of the right thing to say or do in dealing with people or situations.

tact·ful (takt′fəl), *adj.* having or showing tact: *a tactful person; a tactful answer.* **—tact′ful·ly,** *adv.*

tac·tic (tak′tik), *n.* **1.** a method of getting one's way or achieving one's goal: *She's using a new tactic to make the children mind.* **2.** Usually, **tactics. a.** a method of using military forces in battle. **b.** the military operations or maneuvers themselves. **c.** any operations or maneuvers for gaining advantage or success: *She changed her tactics and stopped crying.*

tac·ti·cal (tak′ti kəl), *adj.* **1.** of or concerning tactics, esp. military tactics. **2.** showing skill in maneuvering or handling a situation.

tac·ti·cian (tak tish′ən), *n.* a person who is skilled in planning tactics.

tac·tile (tak′til), *adj.* **1.** of or concerning the sense of touch. **2.** capable of being touched.

tact·less (takt′lis), *adj.* lacking tact: *a tactless remark.* **—tact′less·ly,** *adv.* **—tact′less·ness,** *n.*

tad·pole (tad′pōl′), *n.* a very young frog or toad, esp. when it still has a tail and lives entirely in water. Also, **polliwog.** [from the Middle English word *taddepol,* which comes from *taddle* "toad" + *pol* "head"]

taf·fe·ta (taf′i tə), *n.* a smooth, crisp fabric of acetate, nylon, rayon, or silk in plain weave.

taf·fy (taf′ē), *n.* a candy made of sugar or molasses boiled down, often with butter, nuts, etc. Also, *esp. British,* **toffee.**

Tadpole in early stages of growth (length to 1 in.)

Taft (taft), *n.* **William Howard,** 1857–1930, 27th President of the U.S. 1909–1913; Chief Justice of the U.S. Supreme Court 1921–1930.

tag¹ (tag), *n.* **1.** a piece or strip of strong paper for attaching by one end to something as a mark or label: *The price is on the tag.* **2.** any small, loosely attached, or hanging part or piece. **3.** a hard tip at the end of a shoelace, cord, or the like. **—v., tagged, tag·ging. 4.** to attach a tag to: *to tag a suitcase.* **5.** to add as an afterthought: *He tagged a joke on at the end of his speech.* **6.** *Informal.* to follow closely: *to tag after someone.* [from the Middle English word *tagge*]

tag² (tag), *n.* **1.** a children's game in which one player chases the others till he touches one of them, the one caught then becoming pursuer. **—v., tagged, tag·ging. 2.** to touch in or as if in the game of tag. [perhaps from a special use of *tag¹*]

Ta·ga·log (tä gä′log, tag′ə log′), *n.* an Indonesian language, the official language of the Philippines.

Ta·hi·ti (tə hē′tē), *n.* an island in the southern Pacific Ocean. 402 sq. mi.

Ta·hi·tian (tə hē′shən, tə hē′tē ən), *adj.* **1.** of or concerning Tahiti, its inhabitants, or their language. **—n. 2.** a native or inhabitant of Tahiti. **3.** the Polynesian language of Tahiti.

tail (tāl), *n.* **1.** the rearmost part of an animal, esp. a flexible part that extends from the back end of the body. **2.** anything that looks like this: *the tail of a kite.* **3.** the bottom or end part of anything. **4. tails,** the reverse side of a coin (opposite of *heads*). **—adj. 5.** coming from behind: *a tail breeze.* **6.** being in the rear: *a tail gun on an airplane.* **—v. 7.** to form or furnish with a tail. **8.** *Informal.* to follow close behind. **9. turn tail,** to run away from difficulty or danger, esp. in a cowardly way: *When the police arrived, the hoodlums turned tail.* **—tail′less,** *adj.*

tail·gate (tāl′gāt′), *n.* **1.** the board or gate at the back of a wagon, truck, station wagon, etc., which can be removed or let down for convenience in loading or unloading. **—v., tail·gat·ed, tail·gat·ing. 2.** to drive too close to the rear of another vehicle.

tai·lor (tā′lər), *n.* **1.** a person whose occupation is the making, mending, or altering of suits, coats, and other outer garments. **—v. 2.** to do the work of a tailor. **3.** to make or alter (suits, dresses, etc.). **4.** to adapt to a certain taste, purpose, etc.: *The vacation plans were tailored to fit our needs.*

tail·spin (tāl′spin′), *n.* a diving maneuver of an airplane in which the tail moves in a circle; spin.

tail·wind (tāl′wind′), *n.* a wind coming from directly behind a moving aircraft or vessel.

taint (tānt), *n.* **1.** a trace of something bad, offensive, or harmful. —*v.* **2.** to ruin or damage: *to taint a reputation.* **3.** to become spoiled or damaged: *The meat tainted after a few days.*

Tai·pei (tī′pā′), *n.* the capital city of the Republic of China, on the island of Taiwan.

Tai·wan (tī′wän′), *n.* an island SE of China: seat of the Republic of China since 1949. 13,890 sq. mi. *Cap.:* Taipei. Also, **Formosa.**

take (tāk), *v.,* **took** (took), **tak·en** (tā′kən), **tak·ing.** **1.** to get into one's hands for possession by voluntary action: *to take a book from the table.* **2.** to get into one's possession by force: *to take a bone from*

a snarling dog. **3.** to seize or capture. **4.** to hold, grasp, or grip: *Take my hand.* **5.** to accept willingly: *to take advice.* **6.** to receive or respond to in a certain way: *She took the news hard.* **7.** to gain for use by payment: *I'll take two boxes of cookies.* **8.** to receive regularly by payment; subscribe to: *to take a news magazine.* **9.** to have for one's benefit or use: *to take a nap.* **10.** to subtract or deduct: *If you take 3 from 5, that leaves 2.* **11.** to carry: *I took my suitcase with me.* **12.** to convey or transport: *Will this bus take me to Main Street?* **13.** to conduct or escort: *to take someone out for dinner.* **14.** to get or catch: *He took cold over the weekend.* **15.** to require or demand: *It takes courage to do that.* **16.** to study: *to take ballet.* **17.** to use up or consume: *Studying takes a lot of time.* **18.** to feel or experience: *She took pride in her accomplishments.* **19.** to have the intended result or effect: *The vaccination took.* **20.** to occupy: *to take up room.* **21.** to assume the obligation of: *to take responsibility.* **22.** to do, perform, etc.: *to take a walk.* **23.** (in grammar) to be used with or require the use of (a certain form, case, tense, etc.): *A transitive verb takes an object.* **24.** *Slang.* to cheat. —*n.* **25.** the act of taking. **26.** something that is taken. **27.** the quantity of fish, game, etc., taken at one time. **28.** a scene of a motion picture photographed at one time. **29.** money taken in, esp. profits. **30. take after, a.** to resemble (another person, esp. a parent) in appearance, behavior, etc.: *He takes after his father.* **b.** Also, **take off after.** to follow; chase: *The police car took after the burglars.* **31. take back, a.** to regain possession of: *The store took back our lawn mower.* **b.** to return, as for exchange: *The handle was broken, so I took it back to the store.*

c. to withdraw; retract: *to take back something one has said.* **32. take down, a.** to move (something) from a higher to a lower level: *Take down a can of beans from the shelf.* **b.** to write down; record: *The reporter took down a statement by the mayor.* **c.** to lessen the pride of; humble: *to take someone down a notch or two.* **33. take for,** to mistake (a person or thing) for (someone or something else): *I took you for your mother.* **34. take in, a.** to make (an article of clothing) smaller: *to take in the waist of a dress.* **b.** to provide shelter for: *They took me in when I had no place to stay.* **c.** to include: *The city takes in three of the nearby towns.* **d.** to deceive; trick; cheat: *Don't be taken in by his hard-luck story.* **e.** to understand; comprehend: *I can't take in such large numbers.* **35. take it, a.** *Slang.* to be able to stand hardship, abuse, etc.: *If you can't take it, you shouldn't go hiking.* **b.** to understand: *I take it that you don't like the idea.* **36. take it out of,** *Informal.* to exhaust or fatigue: *This hot weather really takes it out of you.* **37. take it out on,** *Informal.* to cause (someone else) to suffer because of one's unhappiness, misfortune, etc.: *Just because you're angry about the election, don't take it out on me!* **38. take off, a.** to remove: *Take off those wet shoes.* **b.** to leave the ground, as an airplane. **c.** *Informal.* to leave or depart quickly or suddenly: *He took off for the drugstore about 10 minutes ago.* **d.** to withdraw, as from service: *My uncle has been taken off the night shift.* **39. take out, a.** to remove or withdraw: *to take out the garbage.* **b.** to obtain or secure by application: *to take out an insurance policy.* **40. take over,** to assume management of, esp. suddenly or by force: *The crew mutinied and took over the ship.* **41. take to, a.** to respond favorably to; begin to like: *Your dog really takes to me.* **b.** to go to: *She took to her bed with a cold.* **c.** to begin or start: *He took to staying up late when he was in college.* **42. take up, a.** to occupy; cover: *Move over, you're taking up the whole seat.* **b.** to begin to study or practice: *I took up archery last summer.* **c.** to use up; consume: *Studying takes up most of my evening.* **d.** to continue; resume: *We're going to take up where we left off yesterday.* —**tak′er,** *n.*

take·off (tāk′ôf′, -of′), *n.* **1.** the leaving of the ground, as in leaping or beginning a flight in an airplane. **2.** *Informal.* a humorous imitation.

tak·ing (tā′king), *n.* **1.** the act of a person or thing that takes. **2.** something that is taken. **3. takings,** receipts, esp. as a profit. —*adj.* **4.** winning or pleasing; attractive: *a taking smile.*

talc (talk), *n.* a very soft, greenish or gray mineral used in making talcum powder.

tal′cum pow′der (tal′kəm), a powder made from talc and usually perfumed for use as a cosmetic, to absorb perspiration, etc. Also, **tal′cum.**

tale (tāl), *n.* **1.** a story; narrative. **2.** a falsehood or fib. **3.** a rumor or piece of gossip.

tal·ent (tal′ənt), *n.* **1.** a special natural ability: *a talent for drawing.* **2.** a group of persons with special ability: *paintings by local talent.* **3.** any of various ancient units of weight or money. —**tal′ent·ed,** *adj.*

tal·is·man (tal′is mən, tal′iz mən), *n., pl.* **tal·is·mans.** an object, such as a stone, ring, etc., supposed to bring good luck and guard against evil.

talk (tôk), *v.* **1.** to communicate or exchange ideas, information, etc., by speaking: *to talk about a book.* **2.** to consult or confer: *Talk with your adviser.* **3.** to express in words: *to talk sense.* **4.** to use in speaking: *to talk French.* **5.** to discuss: *to talk politics.* **6.** to spread a rumor; gossip. **7.** to give a speech, lecture, etc. **8.** to bring, put, influence, etc., by talk: *to talk a person to sleep.* —*n.* **9.** the act of talking; speech; conversation. **10.** an informal speech or lecture. **11.** rumor or gossip. **12.** mere empty speech: *That's just a lot of talk.* **13.** language, dialect, or lingo. **14.** a subject of talk, esp. of gossip: *Her outfit was the talk of the party.* **15. talk back,** to answer in a rude or disrespectful manner: *I always get punished when I talk back.* **16. talk down to,** to speak to (a person) as though he were not old enough or intelligent enough to understand. **17. talk of,** to discuss (something) as a possibility: *We talked of going swimming, but it was too hot.* **18. talk over,** to discuss thoroughly: *Maybe if you talked it over with your parents they could help.* **19. talk up, a.** to speak openly and without hesitation: *You'd better talk up and let them know how you feel about it.* **b.** to talk of with enthusiasm; promote: *They're talking up a class picnic for next week.* —**talk′er,** *n.*

talk·a·tive (tô′kə tiv), *adj.* inclined to talk a great deal.

tall (tôl), *adj.* **1.** of more than average height: *a tall building.* **2.** having a certain height: *a man six feet tall.* **3.** *Informal.* difficult to believe: *a tall tale.*

Tal·la·has·see (tal′ə has′ē), *n.* the capital city of Florida, in the N part.

tal·low (tal′ō), *n.* the fat from certain animals, used to make candles, soap, etc.

tal·ly (tal′ē), *n., pl.* **tal·lies. 1.** a stick of wood with notches to show the amount of a debt or payment. **2.** anything on which a score or account is kept. **3.** an account, record, or score. —*v.,* **tal·lied, tal·ly·ing. 4.** to mark or enter on a tally; register. **5.** to count or reckon up. **6.** to correspond or agree; match: *The two versions of the story don't tally.*

tal·ly·ho (tal′ē hō′), *interj.* the cry of a huntsman on first sighting a fox.

Tal·mud (täl′mŏŏd, tal′mŏŏd), *n.* the collection of writings on Jewish law and tradition.

tal·on (tal′ən), *n.* a claw, esp. of a bird of prey.

tam (tam), *n.* a tam-o'-shanter.

ta·ma·le (tə mä′lē), *n.* a Mexican dish made of chopped meat that has been packed in cornmeal dough, wrapped in cornhusks, and steamed.

Tambourine

tam·bou·rine (tam′bə rēn′), *n.* a small drum consisting of a circular frame with skin stretched over one side and several pairs of metal disks that jingle when the instrument is struck or shaken.

tame (tām), *adj.,* **tam·er, tam·est. 1.** changed from the wild or savage state; domesticated: *a tame bear.* **2.** harmless; gentle. **3.** lacking excitement; dull: *a tame party.* —*v.,* **tamed, tam·ing. 4.** to make tame: *to tame a lion.* **5.** to control or subdue so as to make useful: *to tame a river.*

tam-o'-shan·ter (tam′ə shan′tər), *n.* a usually woolen cap of Scottish origin, having a round, flat top and often a pompon at its center. Also, **tam.** [named after *Tam O'Shanter,* the hero of a poem by Robert Burns]

tamp (tamp), *v.* **1.** to pack in tightly by tapping: *He tamped the tobacco in his pipe.* **2.** (in blasting) to fill (a hole containing explosives) with earth, clay, or the like.

Tam·pa (tam′pə), *n.* a port city in W Florida.

tam·per (tam′pər), *v.* to meddle, esp. for the purpose of changing, damaging, or misusing: *to tamper with another person's camera.*

tan (tan), *v.,* **tanned, tan·ning. 1.** to convert (an animal hide) to leather, esp. by soaking in a solution containing tanbark. **2.** to make or become brown by exposure to ultraviolet rays, as of the sun. —*n.* **3.** the brown color given to the skin by exposure to the sun or open air. **4.** a yellowish or light brown.

tan·a·ger (tan′ə jər), *n.* any of several small American songbirds, the males of which are usually brightly colored.

tan·bark (tan′bärk′), *n.* the bark of such trees as the oak or hemlock, used in tanning hides and for spreading on the floors of indoor riding rings, race tracks, etc.

Scarlet tanager (length 7 in.)

tan·dem (tan′dəm), *adv.* **1.** one following the other: *to drive horses tandem.* —*adj.* **2.** having animals, seats, parts, etc., arranged tandem or one behind another. —*n.* **3.** a team of horses harnessed in this way. **4.** a two-wheeled carriage with a high driver's seat, drawn by two or more horses harnessed one behind the other. **5.** a tandem bicycle. [from a Latin word meaning "at length"]

tan′dem bi′cycle, a bicycle for two or more persons, having seats and corresponding sets of pedals arranged one behind the other.

tang (tang), *v.* **1.** a strong taste, flavor, or odor. **2.** a touch or trace: *a tang of autumn.* **3.** the part of a chisel or knife attached to the handle or stock.

Tan·gan·yi·ka (tang′gən yē′kə), *n.* the mainland part of Tanzania, in E Africa: formerly German, then British (1920–1961), then a separate republic until union with Zanzibar in 1964. —**Tan′gan·yi′kan,** *n., adj.*

tan·gent (tan′jənt), *adj.* **1.** touching at a single point. —*n.* **2.** a straight line that touches a curve at a single point.

tan·ge·rine (tan′jə rēn′), *n.* a small, sweet orange with a loose skin that is easily removed.

tan·gi·ble (tan′jə bəl), *adj.* **1.** capable of being

touched. 2. real or actual, rather than imaginary: *the tangible benefits of sunshine.* —**tan′gi·bly**, *adv.*

Tan·gier (tan jēr′), *n.* a port city in N Morocco.

tan·gle (taṅg′gəl), *v.,* **tan·gled, tan·gling. 1.** to twist or become twisted into a mass of confusedly inter-laced parts; snarl: *She tangled the yarn. The string tangles easily.* —*n.* **2.** a complicated condi-tion or situation. **3.** a con-fused jumble: *a tangle of ropes.*

tank (taṅgk), *n.* **1.** a large container for holding a liq-uid or gas. **2.** an armored combat vehicle, armed with cannon and machine guns.

tank·ard (taṅg′kərd), *n.* a large drinking mug, usu-ally with a hinged cover.

tank·er (taṅg′kər), *n.* a ship, air-plane, or truck designed to carry oil or other liquid.

tan·ner (tan′ər), *n.* a person whose occupation is to tan hides.

tan·ner·y (tan′ə rē), *n., pl.* **tan·ner·ies.** a place where tanning is done.

tan·nin (tan′in), *n.* a substance ob-tained from the bark of such trees as the oak and hemlock and used to tan hides and to make ink and medicines. Also, **tan′nic ac′id** (tan′ik).

Tankard
(18th century)

tan·ta·lize (tan′t⁹līz′), *v.,* **tan·ta·lized, tan·ta·liz·ing.** to torment with the sight or prospect of something desired that cannot be had: *The apples at the top of the tree tantalized him.* [from *Tantalus,* the name of a Phrygian king who was tormented in Hades by having water and food kept just beyond his reach]

tan·ta·lum (tan′t⁹ləm), *n.* a gray, hard metal that re-sists corrosion and has a very high melting point, used for chemical and surgical instruments and for replacing missing parts of bones: a chemical element. *Symbol:* Ta

tan·ta·mount (tan′tə mount′), *adj.* equivalent, as in value, force, effect, or meaning: *The dictator's angry speech was tantamount to a declaration of war.*

tan·trum (tan′trəm), *n.* a sudden burst of bad tem-per.

Tan·za·ni·a (tan′zə nē′ə, tan zā′nē ə), *n.* a republic in E Africa, formed from the union of Tanganyika and Zanzibar in 1964. 362,820 sq. mi. —**Tan·za·ni·an** (tan′zə nē′ən, tan zā′nē ən), *n., adj.*

tap¹ (tap), *v.,* **tapped, tap·ping. 1.** to strike or touch gently: *to tap someone on the shoulder.* **2.** to make, put, etc., with light blows: *to tap a nail into the wall.* **3.** to strike upon something with light blows: *Stop tapping your feet!* **4.** to add a thickness of leather to the sole or heel of (a boot or shoe). —*n.* **5.** a light blow or rap. [from the Middle English word *tappen* "to tap"]

tap² (tap), *n.* **1.** another word for **faucet. 2.** a stick, long plug, or stopper for closing an opening through which liquid is drawn. **3.** a tool for cutting screw threads inside a hole. —*v.,* **tapped, tap·ping. 4.** to draw liquid from: *to tap a barrel.* **5.** to draw off by removing or opening a tap: *to tap beer.* **6.** to draw upon (resources); use: *to tap talent.* **7.** to connect into (something) secretly so as to receive the message being transmitted: *to tap a telephone.* **8.** to cut a screw thread inside (a hole). [from the Old English word *tæppa*]

tap′ dance′, a dance in which the rhythm is marked by tapping the heels and toes on the floor.

tap-dance (tap′dans′), *v.,* **tap-danced, tap-danc·ing.** to perform a tap dance. —**tap′-danc·er**, *n.*

tape (tāp), *n.* **1.** a long, narrow strip of cloth, mainly used as a means of attaching or binding, and in many forms having one sticky surface. **2.** a long, narrow strip of paper, metal, etc. **3.** a string stretched across the finishing line in a race and broken by the win-ning contestant as he crosses. **4.** a plastic ribbon coated with finely powdered magnetic material on which tape recordings of sound or television signals are made. —*v.,* **taped, tap·ing. 5.** to tie up, bind, or attach with tape. **6.** to measure with or as if with a tape measure. **7.** to record on magnetic tape.

tape′ meas′ure, a long, flexible strip or ribbon of cloth, metal, etc., marked with subdivisions of the foot or meter and used for measuring.

ta·per (tā′pər), *v.* **1.** to make or become smaller or thinner toward one end: *The tailor tapered the legs of the trousers. The church spire tapers gradually.* —*n.* **2.** a gradual tapering off of width or thickness. **3.** a long, slender candle. **4. taper off,** to decrease gradually; diminish: *I think the storm is tapering off.*

tape′ record′er, an electronic machine for record-ing and playing back sounds, television signals, com-puter data, etc., in the form of magnetic impulses on a specially coated plastic tape.

tap·es·try (tap′i strē), *n., pl.* **tap·es·tries.** a decorative fabric upon which colored designs are woven.

tape·worm (tāp′wûrm′), *n.* any of various long, flat worms that live as parasites in the digestive tract of man and some animals.

tap·i·o·ca (tap′ē ō′kə), *n.* a starchy food substance prepared from cassava and used in puddings, as a thickener, etc.

ta·pir (tā′pər), *n., pl.* **ta·pirs** *or* **ta·pir.** any of sev-eral large, hoofed South and Central American animals somewhat resembling pigs but having a long flexible snout.

Tapir
(3 ft. high at shoulder)

tap·root (tap′rōōt′, -rŏŏt′), *n.* a large root that ex-tends downward and has small branches extending sideways from it. See illus. at **root.**

taps (taps), *n., pl.* **taps.** *(used as sing.)* a bugle call, or sometimes a drum signal, sounded at night as an order to turn out lights, or performed at a military funeral or memorial service.

tar¹ (tär), *n.* **1.** any of various dark, sticky substances obtained from wood or petroleum and used for surfacing roads, caulking joints, etc. —*v.,* **tarred, tar·ring. 2.** to smear or cover with or as if with tar. [from the Middle English word *tarre,* which comes from Old English *teru*]

tar² (tär), *n. Informal.* a sailor. [perhaps short for *tarpaulin*]

tar·an·tel·la (tar/ən tel/ə), *n.* **1.** a rapid, whirling dance of southern Italy. **2.** a piece of music for this dance.

ta·ran·tu·la (tə ran/chə lə), *n.* any of various large, hairy spiders that give a painful but not highly poisonous bite.

tar·dy (tär/dē), *adj.,* **tar·di·er, tar·di·est. 1.** late; not on time. **2.** moving or acting slowly: *tardy development.* —**tar/di·ly,** *adv.* —**tar/di·ness,** *n.*

Tarantula
(body length 2 in.)

tare¹ (târ), *n.* **1.** any of various climbing or trailing herbs grown principally for fodder and for improving the soil. **2.** (in the Bible) a harmful weed growing in wheat fields. [from a Middle English word meaning "vetch"]

tare² (târ), *n.* the weight of the container or wrapping of a package, which must be subtracted to give the net weight of the goods inside. [from an Old French word, which comes from Arabic *ṭarhah* "what one throws away"]

tar·get (tär/git), *n.* **1.** an object to be aimed at in shooting practice or competitions. **2.** anything to be struck with missiles. **3.** a goal or aim: *The presidency is his target.* **4.** an object of scorn or abuse: *Famous people are often targets of malicious gossip.*

tar·iff (tar/if), *n.* **1.** an official list of duties or taxes imposed by a government on imported and exported goods. **2.** any duty or tax in such a list: *a tariff on automobiles.* **3.** any charge or fare, as of a railroad.

tar·nish (tär/nish), *v.* **1.** to dull the shine of; discolor. **2.** to become dull or discolored: *Silver tarnishes quickly.* **3.** to destroy the purity of; stain; disgrace: *The scandal tarnished his reputation.* —*n.* **4.** a dull coating on metal, caused by tarnishing.

tar·pau·lin (tär pô/lin, tär/pə lin), *n.* a protective covering of waterproofed canvas or other material.

tar·pon (tär/pən), *n., pl.* **tar·pons** *or* **tar·pon.** a large game fish found in the warmer waters of the Atlantic Ocean.

tar·ry¹ (tar/ē), *v.,* **tar·ried, tar·ry·ing. 1.** to remain or stay. **2.** to delay, wait, or be tardy in acting, starting, etc.; linger. [from the Middle English word *tarye*]

Tarpon
(length to 8 ft.)

tar·ry² (tär/ē), *adj.,* **tar·ri·er, tar·ri·est.** of or like tar; smeared with tar.

tar·si·er (tär/sē ər), *n.* a small animal of Indonesia and the Philippines that lives in trees and has a long, thin tail and very large eyes.

tart¹ (tärt), *adj.* **1.** sharp to the taste; sour: *tart apples.* **2.** sharp and biting; cutting: *a tart remark.* [from the Old English word *teart* "sharp, rough"] —**tart/ness,** *n.*

tart² (tärt), *n.* a small pie filled with fruit, usually having no top crust. [from the Old French word *tarte*]

tar·tan (tär/t³n), *n.* **1.** a plaid, woolen cloth, worn chiefly by the Scottish Highlanders, each clan having one or more of its own plaids. **2.** a design of such a plaid known by the name of the clan wearing it. **3.** any plaid.

Tartan

tar·tar (tär/tər), *n.* **1.** a hard, yellowish or brownish substance that collects on the teeth. **2.** a pinkish substance that collects on the inside of wine barrels and is used to make baking powders.

Tar·tar (tär/tər), *n.* **1.** a member of any of the various tribes, mostly Mongolian and Turkish, that overran Asia and much of eastern Europe in the Middle Ages. —*adj.* **2.** of or concerning the Tartars or their language.

task (task), *n.* **1.** a piece of work to be done; chore; duty. —*v.* **2.** to put a strain upon; burden: *All the disturbances tasked his patience.*

task·mas·ter (task/mas/tər), *n.* a person who assigns tasks to others.

Tas·ma·ni·a (taz mā/nē ə), *n.* an island S of Australia, forming a state. 26,215 sq. mi. —**Tas·ma/ni·an,** *n., adj.*

tas·sel (tas/əl), *n.* **1.** a dangling ornament, consisting of small cords or strands hanging from a roundish knob. **2.** something resembling this, such as the flowering part of certain plants: *the tassels on corn.* —*v.,* **tasseled** *or* **tas·selled; tas·sel·ing** *or* **tas·sel·ling. 3.** to supply or decorate with tassels. **4.** to form into a tassel or tassels. **5.** to remove the tassel from (growing corn) in order to improve the crop.

taste (tāst), *v.,* **tast·ed, tast·ing. 1.** to experience or try the flavor of: *She tasted the meat before adding salt.* **2.** to eat or drink a little of. **3.** to experience (pleasures, sorrows, etc.): *to taste happiness.* **4.** to have a certain flavor: *The milk tastes sour.* —*n.* **5.** the act of tasting food or drink. **6.** the sense by which the flavors of things are perceived. **7.** the quality perceived by this sense; flavor: *Candy has a sweet taste.* **8.** a small quantity tasted; morsel; bit: *a taste of your dessert.* **9.** a personal liking (often fol. by *for*): *a taste for jazz.* **10.** the sense of what is proper, good, or beautiful: *She has excellent taste in clothes.* **11.** the sense of what may properly be said or done: *That remark was in bad taste.* **12.** a slight experience of pleasure, sorrow, etc.: *a taste of triumph.* —tast′er, *n.*

taste′ bud′, one of the numerous groups of specialized cells on the covering of the tongue that detect the flavors of dissolved substances.

taste·ful (tāst′fəl), *adj.* having or showing good taste: *tasteful decorations.* —taste′ful·ly, *adv.*

taste·less (tāst′lis), *adj.* 1. having no taste or flavor: *tasteless soup.* 2. lacking in good taste: *tasteless conduct.* —taste′less·ly, *adv.*

tast·y (tā′stē), *adj.,* tast·i·er, tast·i·est. having a good flavor; good-tasting: *a tasty dessert.* —tast′i·ness, *n.*

tat·ter (tat′ər), *n.* 1. a torn piece hanging loose from or torn off the main part: *a tatter of cloth.* 2. tatters, torn or ragged clothing. —*v.* 3. to tear or wear to tatters.

tat·tered (tat′ərd), *adj.* 1. torn to tatters; ragged: *a tattered flag.* 2. wearing ragged clothing.

tat·ting (tat′ing), *n.* 1. the act or process of making a kind of knotted lace of cotton or linen thread with a shuttle. 2. the lace made in this way.

tat·tle (tat′ᵊl), *v.,* tat·tled, tat·tling. 1. to tell secrets. 2. to gossip or chatter. —*n.* 3. idle talk; chatter; gossip. 4. **tattle on,** to betray by tattling: *She tattled on her brother.* —tat′tler, *n.*

tat·tle·tale (tat′ᵊl tāl′), *n.* a person who reveals secrets.

tat·too¹ (ta tōō′), *n., pl.* tat·toos. 1. a strong beating on or as if on a drum: *The drummers kept up a steady tattoo.* 2. a signal on a drum, bugle, or trumpet, ordering soldiers or sailors to their quarters: usually sounded shortly before taps. 3. *British.* a military pageant or display. [from the earlier word *taptoo,* which comes from Dutch *taptoe* "the tavern is closed"]

tat·too² (ta tōō′), *n., pl.* tat·toos. 1. the act or practice of marking the skin with patterns, pictures, etc., by puncturing it and inserting colored inks. 2. a pattern or picture so made. —*v.,* tat·tooed, tat·too·ing. 3. to mark with tattoos: *to tattoo an arm.* 4. to put (patterns or pictures) on the skin. [from Polynesian]

taught (tôt), *v.* the past tense and past participle of **teach.**

taunt (tônt), *v.* 1. to jeer at or mock; insult. —*n.* 2. an insulting, scornful, or sarcastic remark.

Tau·rus (tôr′əs), *n.* the Bull: a constellation and sign of the zodiac.

taut (tôt), *adj.* 1. tightly drawn; tense: *a taut rope.* 2. emotionally strained or tense: *taut nerves.* 3. in good order or condition; tidy; neat.

tav·ern (tav′ərn), *n.* 1. a place where people buy and drink liquors. 2. a public house for travelers; inn.

taw (tô), *n.* 1. a playing marble used as a shooter. 2. a game in which marbles are arranged in the center of a circle drawn on the ground, the object being to knock as many as possible out of the circle. 3. the line from which the players shoot.

taw·dry (tô′drē), *adj.,* taw·dri·er, taw·dri·est. gaudy; showy and cheap. —taw′dri·ness, *n.*

taw·ny (tô′nē), *adj.,* taw·ni·er, taw·ni·est. of a dark yellowish or dull yellowish-brown color.

tax (taks), *n.* 1. a sum of money imposed on incomes, property, sales, etc., by a government for its support or for certain facilities or services. 2. a burdensome charge, obligation, duty, or demand. —*v.* 3. to impose a tax on: *to tax a person; to tax income.* 4. to lay a burden on: *Those expenses taxed our resources.* 5. to blame or accuse: *to tax a person with laziness.*

tax·a·ble (tak′sə bəl), *adj.* subject to tax: *taxable earnings.*

tax·a·tion (tak sā′shən), *n.* 1. the act of taxing. 2. the amount of money raised by taxes.

tax·i (tak′sē), *n., pl.* tax·is *or* tax·ies. 1. a taxicab. —*v.,* tax·ied; tax·i·ing *or* tax·y·ing. 2. to ride or travel in a taxicab. 3. (of an airplane) to move or cause to move on the ground or on water under its own power.

tax·i·cab (tak′sē kab′), *n.* a public passenger vehicle usually having a meter that records the fare due.

tax·i·der·my (tak′si dûr′mē), *n.* the method of preparing and preserving the skins of animals and of stuffing and mounting them in a lifelike manner. —tax′i·der′mist, *n.*

tax′ return′. See **return** (def. 10).

Tay·lor (tā′lər), *n.* **Zach·a·ry** (zak′ə rē), 1784–1850, U.S. general, 12th President of the U.S. 1849–1850.

TB, tuberculosis. Also, **T.B., t.b.**

Tb, *Chem.* the symbol for **terbium.**

tbs., 1. tablespoon. 2. tablespoonful. Also, **tbsp.**

Tc, *Chem.* the symbol for **technetium.**

Tchai·kov·sky (chī kôf′skē), *n.* **Peter Il·yich** (il′yich), 1840–1893, Russian composer. Also, **Tschaikowsky.**

Te, *Chem.* the symbol for **tellurium.**

tea (tē), *n.* 1. the dried leaves of an Asian shrub used in making a drink. 2. the drink made by soaking these leaves in boiling water, served either hot or iced: *a cup of tea.* 3. the shrub that bears these leaves. 4. a social gathering at which tea is served: *We're invited to a tea.* 5. *British.* a light meal served in the late afternoon.

teach (tēch), *v.,* **taught** (tôt), teach·ing. 1. to give instruction in: *He teaches mathematics.* 2. to give instruction to: *He teaches a large class.* 3. to be employed as a teacher: *He has been teaching for several years.*

teach·a·ble (tē′chə bəl), *adj.* capable of being taught: *a teachable child; a teachable subject.*

teach·er (tē′chər), *n.* a person who teaches or instructs, esp. as a profession; instructor.

teach·ing (tē′ching), *n.* 1. the act or profession of a person who teaches. 2. something that is taught.

tea·cup (tē′kup′), *n.* a cup in which tea is served.

teak (tēk), *n.* 1. a large East Indian tree that yields a hard, reddish-brown wood. 2. the wood of this tree, used for flooring, decks of ships, and furniture.

tea·ket·tle (tē′ket′ᵊl), *n.* a kettle with a cover, spout, and handle, used for boiling water.

---

act, āble, dâre, ärt; ebb, ēqual; if, īce; hot, ōver, ôrder; oil; bŏŏk; ōōze; out; up, ûrge; ə = *a* as in *alone;* ᵊ as in *button* (but′ᵊn), *fire* (fīᵊr); chief; shoe; thin; ᵺhat; zh as in *measure* (mezh′ər). See full key inside cover.

teal (tēl), *n., pl.* **teals** *or* for def. 1 **teal. 1.** any of several small, wild, freshwater ducks having a short neck and noted for their rapid flight. **2.** Also, **teal′ blue′.** a medium or dark greenish blue.

team (tēm), *n.* **1.** a group of persons joined together in some action or contest. **2.** two or more animals harnessed together. —*v.* **3.** to join together in a team.

team·mate (tēm′māt′), *n.* a member of the same team.

team·ster (tēm′stər), *n.* a person who drives teams or trucks for hauling, esp. as an occupation.

team·work (tēm′wûrk′), *n.* cooperative effort by a group of persons acting together as a team or for a common cause: *It takes teamwork to win a pennant.*

tea·pot (tē′pot′), *n.* a container with a lid, spout, and handle, in which tea is made and served.

tear¹ (tēr), *n.* **1.** a drop of salty, watery fluid coming from the eye. —*v.* **2.** to fill up and overflow with tears: *Her eyes teared from cutting onions.* **3. in tears,** in the act of weeping; crying: *The teacher's rebuke left the child in tears.* [from the Old English word *tēar*]

tear² (târ), *v.,* **tore** (tôr), **torn** (tôrn), **tear·ing. 1.** to pull apart or in pieces by force: *to tear cloth into rags.* **2.** to pull or snatch violently: *to tear a book from someone's hands.* **3.** to produce or make by tearing: *to tear a hole in a shirt.* **4.** to make wounds or scratches in: *The nail tore his hand.* **5.** to divide or disrupt: *a country torn by civil war.* **6.** to become torn or shredded: *The cloth tears easily.* **7.** to move with great speed: *He tore out of the room.* —*n.* **8.** the act of tearing. **9.** a rip or hole; rent. **10. tear down,** to pull down; demolish: *They tore down the old house and put up a new one.* **11. tear up, a.** to tear (something) into small pieces: *She tore up the drawing after spoiling it.* **b.** to cancel or annul: *to tear up a contract.* [from the Old English word *teran*]

tear·ful (tēr′fəl), *adj.* **1.** full of tears; weeping. **2.** causing tears: *a tearful story.* —**tear′ful·ly,** *adv.*

tear′ gas′ (tēr), a gas that causes smarting and watering of the eyes.

tease (tēz), *v.,* **teased, teas·ing. 1.** to annoy or irritate with constant demands, questions, etc., often in fun: *Her friends tease her about her freckles.* **2.** to pull apart or separate the fibers of (wool or the like), as in combing. **3.** to ruffle (the hair) by holding it at the ends and combing toward the scalp so as to give body to a hairdo. —*n.* **4.** a person who teases or annoys. **5.** the act of teasing. —**teas′ing·ly,** *adv.*

tea·spoon (tē′spōōn′), *n.* **1.** a small spoon for stirring tea, coffee, etc. **2.** a teaspoonful.

tea·spoon·ful (tē′spōōn fōōl′), *n., pl.* **tea·spoon·fuls. 1.** the amount a teaspoon can hold. **2.** ⅙ fluid ounce (4.9 milliliters); ⅓ tablespoonful.

teat (tit, tēt), *n.* a nipple on an udder or breast.

tech·ne·ti·um (tek nē′shē əm, tek nē′shəm), *n. Chem.* a man-made, metallic element. *Symbol:* Tc

tech·ni·cal (tek′ni kəl), *adj.* **1.** of or concerning a particular art, science, trade, profession, etc.: *technical knowledge.* **2.** concerned with the mechanical or industrial arts and the applied sciences: *technical schools.* **3.** concerned with or strictly following the rules of a certain science, art, etc. —**tech′ni·cal·ly,** *adv.*

tech·ni·cal·i·ty (tek′nə kal′i tē), *n., pl.* for defs. 2, 3 **tech·ni·cal·i·ties. 1.** the condition of being technical. **2.** the use of technical methods or terms. **3.** a technical point, detail, or expression.

tech·ni·cian (tek nish′ən), *n.* a person who is skilled in the methods of a certain field: *a laboratory technician.*

Tech·ni·co·lor (tek′nə kul′ər), *n. Trademark.* a system of making color motion pictures by superimposing the three primary colors to produce a final colored print.

tech·nique (tek nēk′), *n.* **1.** the manner and ability with which an artist, writer, dancer, athlete, or the like, uses his or her skills: *the technique of a ballerina.* **2.** the group of procedures and methods used in any specific field: *new techniques of heart surgery.*

tech·nol·o·gy (tek nol′ə jē), *n.* **1.** the branch of knowledge that deals with industrial arts, applied science, engineering, etc. **2.** the practical application of knowledge: *educational technology.*

te·di·ous (tē′dē əs), *adj.* long and tiresome: *tedious work.* —**te′di·ous·ly,** *adv.*

te·di·um (tē′dē əm), *n.* the quality or condition of being tedious; monotony.

tee (tē), *n.* (in golf) **1.** the starting place, usually a hard mound of earth, at the beginning of play for each hole. **2.** a small wooden, plastic, metal, or rubber peg from which the ball is driven. **3. tee off,** to strike a golf ball from a tee.

teem (tēm), *v.* to abound or swarm; be full of: *The pond teems with minnows.*

teen·age (tēn′āj′), *adj.* of, concerning, or like a teen-ager.

teen·ag·er (tēn′ā′jər), *n.* a person in his or her teens.

teens (tēnz), *n.pl.* the numbers 13 through 19, esp. the years of life: *to be in one's teens.*

tee·pee (tē′pē), *n.* another spelling of **tepee.**

tee·ter (tē′tər), *v.* **1.** to seesaw. **2.** to move unsteadily from side to side. —*n.* **3.** a seesaw. Also, **tee·ter-tot·ter** (tē′tər tot′ər) (for defs. 1, 3).

teeth (tēth), *n.* the plural of **tooth.**

teethe (tē*th*), *v.,* **teethed, teeth·ing.** to grow, develop, or cut teeth: *The baby is teething.*

Te·gu·ci·gal·pa (tā gōō′sē gäl′pä), *n.* the capital city of Honduras, in the S part.

Te·he·ran (te′hə ran′, te′hə rän′), *n.* the capital city of Iran, in the N part. Also, **Te·hran** (te hrän′).

Tel A·viv (tel′ ə vēv′), a city in W Israel.

tele-, a prefix meaning distant or at a distance: *telegraph; television.*

tel·e·cast (tel′ə kast′), *n.* **1.** a television broadcast. —*v.,* **tel·e·cast, tel·e·cast·ing. 2.** to broadcast by television.

teleg., **1.** telegram. **2.** telegraph. **3.** telegraphy.

tel·e·gram (tel′ə gram′), *n.* a message sent by telegraph.

tel·e·graph (tel′ə graf′), *n.* **1.** a system of sending messages over long distances, using a device that transmits electrical signals over a conducting wire. —*v.* **2.** to send by telegraph: *to telegraph an important message.* **3.** to send a message to (someone) by telegraph. —**tel′e·graph′ic**, *adj.*

te·leg·ra·phy (tə leg′rə fē), *n.* the technique or practice of constructing or operating telegraphs.

te·lep·a·thy (tə lep′ə thē), *n.* communication between minds without the use of sight, hearing, or any other sense. —**tel·e·path·ic** (tel′ə path′ik), *adj.*

tel·e·phone (tel′ə fōn′), *n.* **1.** an electrical apparatus or system for transmitting sound to a distant point. —*v.*, **tel·e·phoned, tel·e·phon·ing.** **2.** to speak to by telephone. **3.** to send by telephone.

tel·e·scope (tel′i skōp′), *n.* **1.** an instrument that uses lenses or mirrors to make distant objects appear larger and therefore nearer. Telescopes are used to study stars, planets, and the like. —*v.*, **tel·e·scoped, tel·e·scop·ing.** **2.** to force together, one into another, or force into something else: *to telescope three tubes into one.* **3.** to shorten or condense: *The broadcaster telescoped the events of the past year.*

tel·e·scop·ic (tel′i skop′ik), *adj.* **1.** of, concerning, or like a telescope. **2.** seen by means of a telescope: *a telescopic view of the moon.* **3.** visible only through a telescope. **4.** farseeing: *a telescopic eye.* **5.** having parts that slide one within another.

tel·e·type (tel′i tīp′), *n.* **1.** the message sent on a Teletype. —*v.*, **tel·e·typed, tel·e·typ·ing.** **2.** to send (a message) by Teletype.

Tel·e·type (tel′i tīp′), *n. Trademark.* a telegraphic apparatus for sending and receiving messages, having a keyboard like that of a typewriter.

tel·e·vise (tel′ə vīz′), *v.*, **tel·e·vised, tel·e·vis·ing.** to broadcast or show (a program) on television.

tel·e·vi·sion (tel′ə vizh′ən), *n.* **1.** the broadcasting of images and often sound by means of radio waves to receivers that project the images on a picture tube for viewing at a distance from the point of origin. **2.** the field or industry of television broadcasting. **3.** a set for receiving television broadcasts.

tell (tel), *v.*, **told** (tōld), **tell·ing.** **1.** to give an account of; narrate; relate: *to tell a story.* **2.** to make known or express by speech or writing: *to tell the truth.* **3.** to reveal or disclose (information): *She told the secret. I know, but I won't tell.* **4.** to distinguish: *I can't tell the twins apart.* **5.** to bid or command; order: *Tell him to stop.* **6.** to determine or predict: *Who can tell what tomorrow will bring?* **7.** to count off: *to tell rosary beads.* **8.** to produce a severe effect: *The strain on him was beginning to tell.* **9. tell off,** *Informal.* to criticize severely; scold; rebuke: *He was always interrupting me, but I finally told him off.*

tell·er (tel′ər), *n.* **1.** a person employed in a bank to receive or pay out money over the counter. **2.** a person or thing that tells or relates; narrator.

tell·ing (tel′iñg), *adj.* having force or effect; effective: *a telling blow; a telling speech.*

tell·tale (tel′tāl′), *n.* **1.** a person who reveals private matters; tattletale; tattler. —*adj.* **2.** revealing what is not intended to be known: *a telltale blush.*

tel·lu·ri·um (te lŏŏr′ē əm), *n. Chem.* a rare element having properties resembling those of sulfur. *Symbol:* Te

te·mer·i·ty (tə mer′i tē), *n.* reckless boldness; rashness.

temp., **1.** temperature. **2.** temporary.

tem·per (tem′pər), *n.* **1.** a state of mind or feelings; mood: *She has an even temper.* **2.** heat of mind or passion, shown in outbursts of anger: *He has quite a temper.* **3.** calm mood or state of mind: *to lose one's temper.* **4.** the degree of hardness given to a metal. —*v.* **5.** to soften or moderate: *to temper justice with mercy.* **6.** to bring to a desired consistency: *to temper clay.* **7.** to give strength or toughness to (steel or cast iron) by heating it and then cooling it.

tem·per·a·ment (tem′pər ə mənt, tem′prə mənt), *n.* the make-up of an individual that affects his manner of thinking, feeling, and acting; natural disposition or mood.

tem·per·a·men·tal (tem′pər ə men′t[ə]l, tem′prə men′t[ə]l), *adj.* **1.** showing a strongly marked individual temperament. **2.** moody, irritable, or sensitive. **3.** of or concerning temperament. —**tem′per·a·men′tal·ly,** *adv.*

tem·per·ance (tem′pər əns, tem′prəns), *n.* **1.** moderation or self-control in action, statement, etc. **2.** moderation or complete abstinence from drinking alcoholic liquors.

tem·per·ate (tem′pər it, tem′prit), *adj.* **1.** moderate or self-restrained; not extreme. **2.** moderate in respect to temperature: *a temperate climate.*

tem·per·a·ture (tem′pər ə chər, tem′prə chər), *n.* **1.** a measure of the warmth or coldness of an object or substance. **2.** the degree of heat in a living body, esp. the human body. **3.** the degree of heat in a living body above the normal. In man the normal temperature is about 98.6°F, or about 37°C.

tem·pered (tem′pərd), *adj.* **1.** having a certain temper or disposition (usually used in combination): *a good-tempered child.* **2.** of or concerning steel or cast iron that has been tempered.

tem·pest (tem′pist), *n.* **1.** a severe storm, esp. one with high winds. **2.** a violent commotion. **3. tempest in a teapot** (or **teacup**), a great to-do about nothing: *This squabble is only a tempest in a teapot.*

tem·pes·tu·ous (tem pes′chōō əs), *adj.* violent; stormy; turbulent: *a tempestuous wind; a tempestuous argument.* —**tem·pes′tu·ous·ly,** *adv.*

Tem·plar (tem′plər), *n.* a member of a religious military order founded by Crusaders in Jerusalem during the Middle Ages.

tem·ple¹ (tem′pəl), *n.* **1.** a building or place dedicated to the worship of a god or gods. **2.** *(usually cap.)* any of the three houses of worship built one after another in Jerusalem and in use by the Jews in Biblical times. **3.** a Reform or Conservative synagogue. **4.** a large building devoted to some public use: *a temple of music.* [from the Old English word *tempel,* which comes from Latin *templum* "holy place"]

tem·ple² (tem′pəl), *n.* either of the flattened areas of the skull at each side of the forehead. [from an early French word, which comes from Latin *tempora* "temples," from the plural of *tempus* "time." The original meaning was "a part (of space or time) marked out or cut off"]

tem·po (tem′pō), *n., pl.* **tem·pos.** the rate or speed at which a piece of music is played or sung: *A polka is a dance in quick tempo.*

tem·po·ral¹ (tem′pər əl), *adj.* **1.** of or concerning time. **2.** concerned with the present life or this world. **3.** lasting for a time only; temporary. **4.** not sacred or religious; secular. [from the Latin word *temporālis,* which comes from *tempus* "time"]

tem·po·ral² (tem′pər əl), *adj.* of, concerning, or located near the flat areas of the skull that are on each side of the forehead. [from the Latin word *temporālis,* which comes from *tempora* "temples." See *temple²*]

tem·po·rar·y (tem′pə rer′ē), *adj.* lasting or existing for a time only; not permanent. —**tem·po·rar·i·ly** (tem′pə râr′ə lē), *adv.*

tem·po·rize (tem′pə rīz′), *v.,* **tem·po·rized, tem·po·riz·ing. 1.** to delay making a decision to gain time. **2.** to fit one's words or action to the time or occasion.

tempt (tempt), *v.* **1.** to try to persuade (a person) to do something unwise or wrong. **2.** to appeal strongly to; attract; invite: *The offer tempts me.* **3.** to put to the test in a daring way; provoke: *to tempt one's fate.* —**tempt′er,** *n.*

temp·ta·tion (temp tā′shən), *n.* **1.** the act of tempting. **2.** something that tempts or entices. **3.** the state of being tempted, esp. to evil.

tempt·ing (temp′tiṅg), *adj.* that tempts; inviting: *a tempting offer.* —**tempt′ing·ly,** *adv.*

ten (ten), *n.* **1.** a number that is nine plus one. **2.** a set of this many persons or things: *Ten will be there.* —*adj.* **3.** amounting to ten in number: *ten persons.*

ten·a·ble (ten′ə bəl), *adj.* capable of being held, maintained, or defended: *a tenable fortress; a tenable position in an argument.*

te·na·cious (tə nā′shəs), *adj.* **1.** holding fast; keeping a firm hold: *a tenacious grip; tenacious habits.* **2.** able to retain: *a tenacious memory.* **3.** stubborn or obstinate. **4.** adhesive or sticky. **5.** holding together; not easily pulled apart. —**te·na′cious·ly,** *adv.*

te·nac·i·ty (tə nas′i tē), *n.* the quality or property of being tenacious.

ten·an·cy (ten′ən sē), *n., pl.* for defs. 2, 3 **ten·an·cies. 1.** the condition of being a tenant. **2.** the period of a tenant's occupancy. **3.** occupancy, enjoyment, or use of a position, post, situation, etc.

ten·ant (ten′ənt), *n.* **1.** a person or group that rents and occupies land, a house, an office, or the like, from another for a time. **2.** an occupant or inhabitant of any place. —*v.* **3.** to hold or occupy as a tenant.

Ten′ Command′ments, (in the Bible) the ten laws that were given by God to Moses; Decalogue.

tend¹ (tend), *v.* **1.** to be inclined in action or operation to do something: *The particles tend to unite.* **2.** to favor an idea, emotion, way of thinking, etc.: *He tends to agree with my political ideas.* **3.** to lead in a particular direction: *The road tends to the north.* [from the Old French word *tendre,* which comes from Latin *tendere* "to stretch, extend"]

tend² (tend), *v.* **1.** to attend to by work or services, care, etc.: *to tend a fire.* **2.** to look after; watch over and care for: *to tend the sick.* [short for *attend*]

ten·den·cy (ten′dən sē), *n., pl.* **ten·den·cies. 1.** a natural disposition to move or set in some direction or toward some point: *the tendency of falling bodies toward the earth.* **2.** an inclination or natural bent to something: *He has a tendency to disagree.*

ten·der¹ (ten′dər), *adj.* **1.** soft or delicate; not hard or tough: *a tender steak.* **2.** weak; not strong or hardy: *a tender plant.* **3.** young or immature: *children of tender age.* **4.** delicate, soft, or gentle: *the tender touch of her hand.* **5.** easily moved; kind; compassionate: *a tender heart.* **6.** sensitive to pain: *a tender bruise.* **7.** likely to arouse strong feelings; ticklish; requiring careful handling: *a tender subject.* [from an Old French word, which comes from Latin *tener* "tender"] —**ten′der·ly,** *adv.* —**ten′der·ness,** *n.*

ten·der² (ten′dər), *v.* **1.** to present formally for acceptance. —*n.* **2.** the act of tendering; an offer of something for acceptance. [from an earlier French word meaning "to extend," which comes from Latin *tendere* "to stretch, extend"]

ten·der³ (ten′dər), *n.* **1.** a person who tends; one who cares for or takes charge of someone or something. **2.** a vessel that attends one or more other vessels, as for supplying provisions. **3.** a car attached to a steam locomotive for carrying fuel and water.

ten·der·foot (ten′dər foot′), *n., pl.* **ten·der·foots** or **ten·der·feet** (ten′dər fēt′). **1.** an inexperienced person. **2.** a newcomer to the ranching and mining regions of the western U.S., not used to hardships. **3.** a person in the lowest rank of the Boy Scouts of America or Girl Scouts of America.

ten·der·heart·ed (ten′dər här′tid), *adj.* easily moved to sympathy; kindly. —**ten′der·heart′ed·ly,** *adv.* —**ten′der·heart′ed·ness,** *n.*

ten·der·loin (ten′dər loin′), *n.* (in beef or pork) the tender meat of the muscle running through the sirloin and ending before the ribs.

ten·don (ten′dən), *n.* See **sinew** (def. 1).

ten·dril (ten′dril), *n.* a slender part of climbing plants, which attaches itself to or twines around some other body to support the plant.

T, Tendrils on grape

ten·e·ment (ten′ə mənt), *n.* **1.** any house or building to dwell in. **2.** a portion of a house or building occupied by a tenant as a separate dwelling. **3.** an apartment house, esp. one in the poorer, crowded parts of a large city.

ten·et (ten′it), *n.* any opinion, doctrine, belief, etc., held as true: *the tenets of Christianity.*

ten·fold (ten′fōld′), *adj.* 1. made up of ten parts: *a tenfold plan.* 2. ten times as large or as much: *a tenfold increase.* —*adv.* (ten′fōld′). 3. in tenfold measure.

Tenn., Tennessee.

Ten·nes·see (ten′i sē′), *n.* a state in the SE United States. 42,246 sq. mi. *Cap.:* Nashville. —**Ten′nes·se′an,** *n., adj.*

ten·nis (ten′is), *n.* a game played on a court by two players or two pairs of players using rackets, in which a ball is driven back and forth across a net.

Ten·ny·son (ten′i sən), *n.* **Alfred, Lord,** 1809–1892, English poet: poet laureate 1850–1892.

ten·on (ten′ən), *n.* a projection, esp. a square or rectangular one, that is fitted into a hole of the same shape called a mortise. See illus. at **mortise.**

ten·or (ten′ər), *n.* 1. a high male voice. 2. a singer with such a voice. 3. a musical part for such a voice or having a similar range. —*adj.* 4. of a size and pitch between alto and baritone or bass: *a tenor saxophone.*

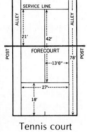

Tennis court

ten·pin (ten′pin′), *n.* 1. one of the pins or wooden clubs used in tenpins. 2. tenpins, *(used as sing.)* a form of bowling played with ten wooden pins.

tense[1] (tens), *adj.,* **tens·er, tens·est.** 1. showing mental or nervous strain: *to be tense before an exam; a tense moment.* 2. stretched tight; drawn taut. —*v.,* **tensed, tens·ing.** 3. to make or become tense. [from the Latin word *tensus* "stretched"] —**tense′ly,** *adv.* —**tense′ness,** *n.*

tense[2] (tens), *n.* 1. the inflected form of a verb that shows the time in which the action or state expressed by the verb takes place. *I give* is present tense; *I gave* is past tense; *I shall give* is future tense. 2. a set of inflections in a given language including all forms of a verb for a certain tense. In English, the present tense of *to take* is *I take, you take, he, she* or *it takes, we take, they take.* [from the Old French word *tens* "time," which comes from Latin *tempus*]

ten·sile (ten′səl), *adj.* of or concerning tension or the act of stretching or pulling: *Nylon thread has great tensile strength.*

ten·sion (ten′shən), *n.* 1. the act of stretching or straining. 2. the state of being stretched or strained. 3. mental or emotional strain; suspense; anxiety: *She felt some tension before taking the exam.* 4. a strained relationship: *tension between two rivals.*

tent (tent), *n.* 1. a portable shelter of canvas, skins, etc., supported by one or more poles and usually extended by ropes fastened to pegs in the ground. —*v.* 2. to camp out or live in a tent.

ten·ta·cle (ten′tə kəl), *n.* 1. any of various slender organs in animals that are used for feeling, grasping, etc.: *An octopus has eight tentacles.* 2. a sensitive hairlike growth on the leaves of certain plants.

ten·ta·tive (ten′tə tiv), *adj.* made or done as a trial, experiment, or attempt; not definite or permanent; experimental: *a tentative plan.* —**ten′ta·tive·ly,** *adv.*

tenth (tenth), *adj.* 1. being number ten in a series: *the tenth floor.* —*n.* 2. one of ten equal parts. 3. a person or thing that is tenth.

ten·u·ous (ten′yōō əs), *adj.* 1. thin or slender in form. 2. thin in consistency. 3. poorly supported; weak: *a tenuous argument.* —**ten′u·ous·ly,** *adv.*

ten·ure (ten′yər), *n.* 1. the holding or possessing of anything, esp. property or an office. 2. the period or term of holding something.

te·pee (tē′pē), *n.* a tent or wigwam of the American Indians. Also, **teepee.**

tep·id (tep′id), *adj.* moderately warm; lukewarm. —**tep′id·ness,** *n.*

ter·bi·um (tûr′bē əm), *n. Chem.* a metallic element of the rare-earth group. *Symbol:* Tb

Tepee

term (tûrm), *n.* 1. a word or group of words having a certain meaning, esp. in a particular field, such as *atom* in physics. 2. the time or period through which something lasts: *a school term.* 3. (in mathematics) a group of numbers or symbols separated from the rest of an equation by a plus, minus, or equal sign. 4. the numerator or denominator of a fraction. 5. **terms, a.** conditions and stipulations: *the terms of a contract.* **b.** footing or standing; relations: *We're on friendly terms.* —*v.* 6. to apply a term to; name; call: *He has been termed the best painter alive.* 7. **come to terms, a.** to reach an agreement: *to come to terms with one's bill collectors.* **b.** to become resigned: *to come to terms with poverty.*

ter·mi·nal (tûr′mə nəl), *adj.* 1. located at or forming the end of something. 2. occurring at or causing the end of life: *a terminal disease.* —*n.* 3. the station at the end of a railway or bus route. 4. the mechanical device by means of which an electric connection is established. 5. the point at which a current may enter or leave an electric circuit or device.

ter·mi·nate (tûr′mə nāt′), *v.,* **ter·mi·nat·ed, ter·mi·nat·ing.** 1. to bring or come to an end: *We terminated the debate.* 2. to form the boundary of: *The lake terminates our property.* —**ter′mi·na′tion,** *n.*

ter·mi·nol·o·gy (tûr′mə nol′ə jē), *n., pl.* **ter·mi·nol·o·gies.** the system of terms belonging to a science, art, or other subject: *the terminology of chemistry.*

ter·mi·nus (tûr′mə nəs), *n.* 1. the end of anything. 2. either end of a railway or bus line.

ter·mite (tûr′mīt), *n.* any of various pale-colored, soft-bodied social insects that feed on wood, some being very destructive to buildings, furniture, etc. Also, **white ant.**

tern (tûrn), *n.* any of numerous sea birds, related to the gulls but usually having a more slender body and bill and a long, deeply forked tail.

ter·race (ter′əs), *n.* **1.** a raised level of earth, esp. one of a series of levels rising one above another. **2.** a nearly level strip of land with a sharp descent along the edge of a sea, lake, or river. **3.** the flat roof of a house. **4.** an open, often paved area connected to a house or apartment and serving as an outdoor living area. —*v.,* **ter·raced, ter·rac·ing. 5.** to form into or furnish with a terrace or terraces.

Tern
(length 15 in.;
wingspread 2½ ft.)

ter·ra cot·ta (ter′ə kot′ə), **1.** a hard, fired clay, brownish-red in color when unglazed, that is used for building, sculpture, and pottery. **2.** something made of terra cotta. **3.** a brownish orange.

ter·rain (tə rān′), *n.* a tract of land, esp. as considered with respect to its natural features.

ter·ra·pin (ter′ə pin), *n.* any of several North American turtles, found in fresh or partly salt water, whose flesh is used for food.

ter·rar·i·um (tə râr′ē əm), *n.* a box or enclosure in which land animals or small plants are kept.

ter·res·tri·al (tə res′trē əl), *adj.* **1.** concerning, made of, or representing the earth as distinct from other planets. **2.** of or concerning land as distinct from water. **3.** of or concerning the earth or this world; earthly or worldly.

ter·ri·ble (ter′ə bəl), *adj.* **1.** severe or harsh: *a terrible winter.* **2.** extremely bad: *terrible behavior.* **3.** causing terror or great fear. —**ter′ri·bly,** *adv.*

ter·ri·er (ter′ē ər), *n.* one of any of several breeds of usually small dogs, used originally to pursue game and drive it out of its hole or burrow.

ter·rif·ic (tə rif′ik), *adj.* **1.** unusually great, intense, or good: *terrific speed; a terrific party.* **2.** causing terror; terrifying: *a terrific storm.* —**ter·rif′i·cal·ly,** *adv.*

ter·ri·fy (ter′ə fī′), *v.,* **ter·ri·fied, ter·ri·fy·ing.** to fill with terror; make greatly afraid.

ter·ri·to·ri·al (ter′i tôr′ē əl), *adj.* **1.** of or concerning territory or land. **2.** of, concerning, or limited to a certain territory or district: *a nation's territorial waters.*

ter·ri·to·ry (ter′i tôr′ē), *n., pl.* **ter·ri·to·ries. 1.** any area of land; region or district. **2.** the land and waters belonging to or under the jurisdiction of a state, sovereign, etc. **3.** the region or district assigned to a representative, agent, salesman, or the like.

ter·ror (ter′ər), *n.* **1.** intense, sharp, overpowering fear: *to be frantic with terror.* **2.** a cause of great fear: *The big dog is a terror to the children.*

ter·ror·ism (ter′ə riz′əm), *n.* **1.** the use of violence and threats to frighten people into submission. **2.** the state of fear and submission produced by these methods. —**ter′ror·ist,** *n.*

ter·ror·ize (ter′ə rīz′), *v.,* **ter·ror·ized, ter·ror·iz·ing. 1.**

to fill or overcome with terror; make very frightened: *The bandits terrorized the town.* **2.** to control or dominate by threats.

ter′ry cloth′ (ter′ē), a pile fabric with loops on both sides, used for towels, bathrobes, etc.

terse (tûrs), *adj.,* **ters·er, ters·est.** brief and to the point: *a terse report on the war.* —**terse′ly,** *adv.*

ter·ti·ar·y (tûr′shē er′ē, tûr′shə rē), *adj.* of the third order, rank, formation, etc.; third.

test (test), *n.* **1.** the means by which the presence, quality, or genuineness of anything is determined: *Medical tests are given to diagnose an illness. The hike was a test of strength.* **2.** a form of examination for judging the performance, capabilities, or achievements of an individual: *a grammar test.* **3.** (in chemistry) the process of detecting the presence of an ingredient in a substance or of identifying a substance: *a test for sodium.* —*v.* **4.** to subject to a test of any kind; try: *The teacher tested us on the assignments.* **5.** to undergo a test or trial. —**test′er,** *n.*

Test., Testament.

tes·ta·ment (tes′tə mənt), *n.* **1.** (in law) a will, esp. one that relates to the handling of personal property. **2.** a covenant, esp. between God and man. —**tes′ta·men′ta·ry,** *adj.*

Tes·ta·ment (tes′tə mənt), *n.* either the New Testament or the Old Testament.

tes·ta·tor (tes′tā tər, te stā′tər), *n.* a person who makes a will.

tes·ti·cle (tes′ti kəl), *n.* one of two male reproductive glands, located in the scrotum, in which sperm is formed. Also, **testis.**

tes·ti·fy (tes′tə fī′), *v.,* **tes·ti·fied, tes·ti·fy·ing. 1.** to bear witness or give evidence under oath: *The witness testified during the trial.* **2.** to serve as evidence or proof: *Her smile testifies to her happiness.* —**tes′ti·fi′er,** *n.*

tes·ti·mo·ni·al (tes′tə mō′nē əl), *n.* **1.** a written declaration recommending a person or thing. **2.** something given or done as an expression of esteem, admiration, or gratitude. —*adj.* **3.** concerning or serving as a testimonial: *a testimonial dinner.*

tes·ti·mo·ny (tes′tə mō′nē), *n., pl.* **tes·ti·mo·nies. 1.** (in law) the statement made by a witness under oath. **2.** evidence in support of a fact or statement; proof. **3.** a declaration or open statement of one's faith.

tes·tis (tes′tis), *n., pl.* **tes·tes** (tes′tēz). another word for testicle.

test′ tube′, a glass tube closed at one end, used in chemical and biological laboratories.

tes·ty (tes′tē), *adj.,* **tes·ti·er, tes·ti·est.** irritable; touchy. —**tes′ti·ly,** *adv.* —**tes′ti·ness,** *n.*

tet·a·nus (tet′ᵊnəs), *n.* an infectious, often fatal disease, caused by a bacterium that enters the body through wounds. The disease is marked by spasms and rigidity of muscles, esp. the muscles of the neck and lower jaw; lockjaw.

teth·er (teŧħ′ər), *n.* **1.** a cord, chain, or the like, used as a fastener. —*v.* **2.** to fasten or confine with or as if with a tether. **3. at the end of one's tether,** at the end of one's strength, patience, etc.

Teu·ton (tōōt′ˀn, tyōōt′ˀn), *n.* **1.** a member of an ancient Germanic people or tribe. **2.** a native of Germany, or a person of German origin. —*adj.* **3.** referring to the Teutons; Teutonic.

Teu·ton·ic (tōō ton′ik, tyōō-), *adj.* **1.** of or concerning the ancient Teutons. **2.** of, concerning, or like the Teutons, or Germans. **3.** noting or concerning the German, Dutch, Scandinavian, British, and related peoples. **4.** (of languages) of Germanic origin. —*n.* **5.** the Germanic languages, esp. the ancient ones.

Tex., Texas.

Tex·as (tek′səs), *n.* a state in the S United States. 267,339 sq. mi. *Cap.:* Austin. —**Tex′an,** *n., adj.*

text (tekst), *n.* **1.** the main body of writing in a manuscript, book, etc., as distinguished from notes, headings, etc. **2.** the actual words of an author or speaker. **3.** any theme or topic; subject: *the text of a speech.* **4.** a textbook. **5.** a short passage of the Scriptures, esp. one chosen as the subject of a sermon: *The minister's text was from Isaiah.*

text·book (tekst′bŏŏk′), *n.* a book used by students for the study of a particular subject.

tex·tile (teks′til, teks′tīl), *n.* **1.** any material that is woven. **2.** a material, such as a fiber or yarn, used in weaving. —*adj.* **3.** woven or capable of being woven. **4.** of or concerning weaving: *textile mills.*

tex·tu·al (teks′chōō əl), *adj.* **1.** of or concerning the text: *textual errors.* **2.** based on or conforming to the text: *a textual interpretation of the Bible.*

tex·ture (teks′chər), *n.* **1.** the structure of the interwoven or intertwined threads, strands, or the like, that make up a textile fabric: *rough texture.* **2.** the look and feel given to a material by the size, shape, hardness, etc., of its parts: *soil of a sandy texture.*

Th, *Chem.* the symbol for thorium.

-th, a suffix used to form **1.** nouns expressing a quality or condition: *warmth; width.* **2.** ordinal numbers: *fourth; tenth.* **3.** an old form of the third person singular, present tense of some verbs: *he doth; he saith.* See also **-eth.**

Thai (tī), *n.* **1.** a native or descendant of a native of Thailand. **2.** the official language of Thailand. —*adj.* **3.** of or concerning Thailand, its people, or their language.

Thai·land (tī′land′, tī′lənd), *n.* a kingdom in SE Asia. 198,242 sq. mi. *Cap.:* Bangkok. Former name, Siam.

thal·li·um (thal′ē əm), *n. Chem.* a rare metallic element. *Symbol:* Tl

Thames (temz), *n.* a river in S England, flowing E through London to the North Sea. 209 mi. long.

than (ҭhan), *conj.* **1.** in comparison with: *He is taller than I am.* **2.** except for; but: *I had no choice other than that.*

thane (ҭhān), *n.* (in early English history) a member of a class of men ranking between earls and ordinary freemen.

thank (thangk), *v.* **1.** to express gratitude or appreciation to: *I thanked him for his help.* —*n.* **2.** Usually, **thanks.** a grateful feeling or acknowledgment of a benefit, favor, or the like: *He expressed his thanks to everyone who had worked with him.* **3. thanks,** I thank you. **4. thanks to,** because of; as a result of: *Thanks to careful planning, the program was a success.*

thank·ful (thangk′fəl), *adj.* feeling or expressing gratitude or appreciation. —**thank′ful·ly,** *adv.* —**thank′ful·ness,** *n.*

thank·less (thangk′lis), *adj.* **1.** not likely to be appreciated or rewarded: *a thankless job.* **2.** not feeling or showing appreciation; ungrateful: *a thankless child.*

thanks·giv·ing (thangks′giv′ing), *n.* **1.** the act of giving thanks. **2.** an expression of thanks, esp. to God.

Thanksgiv′ing Day′, a national holiday for giving thanks to God, observed on the fourth Thursday of November.

that (ҭhat), *pron., pl.* **those** (ҭhōz). **1.** (used to indicate a person, thing, etc., as pointed out or present, mentioned before, supposed to be understood, or sometimes used for emphasis): *That is her mother.* **2.** (used to indicate one of two or more persons, things, etc., already mentioned, referring to the one more remote in place, time, or thought (opposite of *this*): *That is Susan and this is Barbara.* **3.** who, whom, or which: *the horse that he bought.* —*adj., pl.* **those** (ҭhōz). **4.** (used to indicate a person, place, or thing as mentioned before, present, or well-known): *That car is mine.* **5.** (used to indicate the more remote in time, place, or thought): *This room is his and that one is mine.* —*adv.* **6.** (used with adjectives and adverbs of quantity) to the extent or degree indicated: *Don't* take that much. —*conj.* **7.** (used to introduce certain kinds of clauses): *I didn't know that he would be there.* **8. with that,** following that; at that point or moment: *With that, he turned around and left the room.*

thatch (thach), *n.* **1.** a material, such as straw, rushes, leaves, or the like, used to cover roofs, grain stacks, etc. **2.** a covering of such a material. **3.** a thick, unruly growth of hair on the head. —*v.* **4.** to cover with or as if with thatch.

thaw (thô), *v.* **1.** to melt or cause to melt: *The ice will thaw by tomorrow. The warm sun thawed the snow.* **2.** to become warm enough to melt ice and snow. **3.** to make or become less unfriendly or cold: *Her kindness thawed us.* **4.** to free or become free from the effect of cold: *Sit by the fire and thaw out.* —*n.* **5.** the act or process of thawing. **6.** weather warm enough to melt ice and snow.

the¹ (thē, thə), *definite article.* **1.** (used, esp. before a noun, to indicate a specific or particular person or thing): *the book you gave me.* **2.** (used with or as part of a title): *the Duke of Wellington.* **3.** (used to mark a noun as indicating the best-known, most important, etc.): *the skiing center of America.* **4.** (used to mark a noun as being used as a group): *The wolf is a wild animal.* **5.** (used to note a part of the body or a personal belonging): *Has the leg mended?* **6.** (used before an adjective to note an individual or a group of individuals): *to visit the sick.* [from Old English]

the² (thə, thē), *adv.* (used to mean "by how much... by so much" or "in what degree...by that degree"): *the more the merrier.* [from the Old English word *thē,* an inflected form of *that* "that," used as an adverb]

the·a·ter (thē′ə tər), *n.* **1.** a building, part of a building, or outdoor area for presenting dramatic performances, motion-picture shows, etc. **2.** the audience at a theatrical or motion-picture performance: *The theater wept.* **3.** a room or hall, fitted with rows of seats rising like steps, used for lectures, demonstrations, etc. **4.** a place of action; field of operations. **5.** the theater, dramatic performances as a branch of art, an occupation, etc.

the·at·ri·cal (thē a′tri kəl), *adj.* **1.** of or concerning the theater. **2.** artificial and exaggerated: *a theatrical way of speaking.* —*n.* **3. theatricals,** dramatic performances, esp. given by amateurs. —**the·at′ri·cal·ly,** *adv.*

Thebes (thēbz), *n.* **1.** an ancient city in upper Egypt, on the Nile. **2.** a city in ancient Greece. —**The·ban** (thē′bən), *n., adj.*

thee (thē), *pron.* the objective case of **thou.**

theft (theft), *n.* the act or crime of stealing.

their (thâr), *pron.* of or belonging to them (used as an attributive adjective): *We visited their home.*

theirs (thârz), *pron.* of or belonging to them (used as a predicate adjective, after or without a noun): *Are you a friend of theirs?*

them (them), *pron.* the objective case of **they:** *We saw them yesterday. I gave them the books.*

theme (thēm), *n.* **1.** a subject or topic to be discussed in speech or writing. **2.** a short, informal essay, esp. a school composition. **3.** (in music) the main melody of a musical composition.

theme′ song′, a melody identifying or identified with a radio or television program, dance band, etc.

them·selves (them selvz′), *pron.pl.* **1.** a form of **them** or **they** that is used for emphasis: *The authors themselves could not agree.* **2.** a form of **them** that is used when the subject of the sentence is the same as the object: *They dressed themselves quickly.* **3.** their usual, normal selves: *After a hot meal and a few hours' rest, they were themselves again.* —**Usage.** See **myself.**

then (then), *adv.* **1.** at that time: *Prices were lower then.* **2.** immediately or soon afterward: *She smiled and then laughed.* **3.** next in order of time: *We ate, then we started home.* **4.** next in order of place: *Standing beside Charlie is Joe, then Sam, and then Bob.* **5.** in addition; besides; also: *She loves her job, and then it pays so well.* **6.** in that case; as a consequence: *If you pass the test then you'll graduate.* —*n.* **7.** that time: *We have been back since then.* **8. then and there,** at once; at that precise moment: *I told her then and there I wouldn't stand for any more rudeness.*

thence (thens), *adv.* **1.** from that place. **2.** from that time: *three days thence.* —**Usage.** Because "from" is contained in the meaning of *thence,* the two words should not be used together: *to Dublin and thence to London* (not *from thence to London*).

thence·forth (thens′fôrth′), *adv.* from that time onward: *They quarreled and thenceforth were enemies.* Also, **thence·for·ward** (thens′fôr′wərd).

the·oc·ra·cy (thē ok′rə sē), *n., pl.* **the·oc·ra·cies. 1.** a form of government in which God or a deity is recognized as the supreme civil ruler. **2.** a system of government by priests. **3.** a state under such a form of government.

the·o·lo·gian (thē′ə lō′jən), *n.* a person who is learned in theology.

the·ol·o·gy (thē ol′ə jē), *n., pl.* **the·ol·o·gies. 1.** the study of God and His relations to the universe; the study of religion and religious truth. **2.** a particular form, system, or branch of this science or study: *Christian theology.* —**the·o·log·i·cal** (thē′ə loj′i·kəl), *adj.*

the·o·rem (thē′ə rəm), *n.* (in mathematics) a proposition or formula containing something to be proved from other propositions or formulas.

the·o·ret·i·cal (thē′ə ret′i kəl), *adj.* **1.** of or concerning theory: *a theoretical solution.* **2.** existing only in theory; not practical: *My knowledge of football is purely theoretical.* **3.** forming or dealing with theories. —**the′o·ret′i·cal·ly,** *adv.*

the·o·rize (thē′ə rīz′), *v.,* **the·o·rized, the·o·riz·ing.** to form a theory or theories.

the·o·ry (thē′ə rē), *n., pl.* **the·o·ries. 1.** a group of ideas or principles used to explain the nature of some phenomenon, event, occurrence, etc., and to predict its behavior, recurrence, etc.: *Newton's theory of gravitation.* **2.** the branch of a science or art that deals with its principles or methods rather than its practice: *music theory.* **3.** an explanation that has not yet been proved true: *The scientist had several theories about the disease.* **4.** a guess or conjecture: *What's your theory about how the story will end?*

ther·a·peu·tic (ther'ə pyoo'tik), *adj.* of or concerning the treatment or cure of disease.

ther·a·py (ther'ə pē), *n., pl.* **ther·a·pies.** the treatment of a disease or other disorder: *speech therapy.*

there (thâr), *adv.* **1.** in or at that place (opposite of *here*): *He is there now.* **2.** at that point in an action, speech, etc.: *He stopped there for applause.* **3.** in that matter or at that time: *I agree with you there.* **4.** in or into that place: *We went there last year.* —*pron.* **5.** (used to introduce a sentence or clause in which the verb comes before its subject): *There is no hope.* **6.** that place: *He comes from there also.* —*interj.* **7.** (used as an exclamation of satisfaction, relief, encouragement, etc.): *There! It's done.*

there-, a prefix used in combination with certain adverbs and prepositions, standing for a thing, an event, a time, or a place previously mentioned or understood: *therefore; thereupon; thereafter; therein.*

there·a·bouts (thâr'ə bouts'), *adv.* **1.** about or near that place or time: *last June or thereabouts.* **2.** about that number, amount, etc.: *a dozen or thereabouts.* Also, **there'a·bout'.**

there·af·ter (thâr'af'tər), *adv.* after that; afterward.

there·by (thâr'bī', thâr'bī'), *adv.* **1.** by that; by means of that: *She consented and thereby avoided an argument.* **2.** in that connection or relation: *Thereby hangs a tale.* **3.** by or near that place.

there·for (thâr'fôr'), *adv.* for or in exchange for that or this; for it: *a refund therefor.*

there·fore (thâr'fôr'), *adv.* in consequence of that; as a result: *I was hungry, therefore I ate.*

there·from (thâr'frum'), *adv.* from that place, thing, etc.

there·in (thâr'in'), *adv.* **1.** in or into that place or thing. **2.** in that matter, circumstance, etc.

there·of (thâr'uv'), *adv.* **1.** of that or it. **2.** from or out of that origin or cause.

there·on (thâr'on', -ôn'), *adv.* **1.** on or upon that or it. **2.** immediately after that.

there's (thârz), **1.** contraction of *there is.* **2.** contraction of *there has.*

there·to (thâr'too'), *adv.* **1.** to that place, thing, etc. **2.** to that matter, circumstance, etc.

there·un·to (thâr'un too', -un'too), *adv.* in addition to that; thereto.

there·up·on (thâr'ə pon'), *adv.* **1.** immediately following that. **2.** upon that or it. **3.** as a result of that.

there·with (thâr'with'), *adv.* **1.** with that. **2.** in addition to that. **3.** following upon that; thereupon.

there·with·al (thâr'with ôl'), *adv.* **1.** together with that; in addition to that. **2.** following upon that.

ther·mal (thûr'məl), *adj.* **1.** of, concerning, or caused by heat or temperature. **2.** warm; hot: *thermal waters.* —*n.* **3.** a rising current of warm air.

ther·mom·e·ter (thər mom'i tər), *n.* an instrument for measuring temperature, usually consisting of a sealed glass tube containing a column of liquid, such as mercury, that rises and falls with temperature changes. The temperature is read on a scale marked in degrees on the tube or its mounting.

ther·mo·nu·cle·ar (thûr'mō noo'-klē ər, -nyoo'-), *adj.* of, concerning, or involving the fusion of atomic nuclei, esp. of a gas, heated to a temperature of several million degrees.

Ther·mos (thûr'məs), *n. Trademark.* a vacuum bottle.

ther·mo·stat (thûr'mə stat'), *n.* a device that turns a heating or cooling system on and off to maintain a desired temperature automatically.

the·sau·rus (thi sôr'əs), *n.* **1.** a dictionary of synonyms and antonyms. **2.** any dictionary, encyclopedia, or other reference book. **3.** a storehouse or treasury.

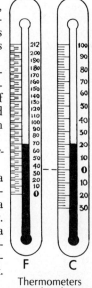

Thermometers
F, Fahrenheit;
C, Celsius
(Centigrade)

these (thēz), *pron., adj.* the plural of **this.**

The·se·us (thē'sē əs, thē'soos), *n.* (in Greek mythology) a hero whose many adventures included slaying the Minotaur.

the·sis (thē'sis), *n., pl.* **the·ses** (thē'sēz). **1.** a proposition stated or put forward for consideration, esp. one to be defended against argument. **2.** a subject for a composition or essay. **3.** a long essay or composition, esp. one by a candidate for a master's or doctor's degree.

thes·pi·an (thes'pē ən), *adj.* **1.** concerning tragedy or drama in general. —*n.* **2.** an actor or actress.

Thes·sa·lo·ni·ans (thes'ə lō'nē ənz), *n.* (*used as sing.*) either of two books of the New Testament, written by Paul.

thew (thyoo), *n.* **1.** Usually, **thews.** a muscle or sinew. **2. thews,** physical strength.

they (thā), *pron.pl.* **1.** the plural of **he, she,** and **it. 2.** people in general: *They say he'll be famous.*

they'd (thād), **1.** contraction of *they had: They'd hoped to see you.* **2.** contraction of *they would: They'd never have known if you hadn't told them.*

they'll (thāl), **1.** contraction of *they will.* **2.** contraction of *they shall.*

they're (thâr), contraction of *they are.*

they've (thāv), contraction of *they have.*

thick (thik), *adj.* **1.** having much extent or space between two surfaces: *a thick board.* **2.** measured between opposite surfaces: *a board one inch thick.* **3.** made of or containing objects, particles, etc., close together; dense: *a thick forest; a thick fog.* **4.** (of a liquid) heavy or dense: *thick soup.* **5.** extreme; decided; heavy: *a thick German accent.* **6.** not properly spoken: *thick speech.* **7.** slow; stupid; dull. **8.** *Informal.* close in friendship. —*adv.* **9.** in a manner to produce something thick: *Slice the cheese thick.* —*n.* **10.** the thickest, densest, or most crowded part: *in the thick of the fight.* **11. through thick and thin,** firmly and faithfully: *We've been friends for years through thick and thin.* —**thick′ly,** *adv.*

thick·en (thik′ən), *v.* **1.** to make or become thick or thicker: *to thicken a gravy.* **2.** to make or become more intense or complicated: *The plot thickens.*

thick·et (thik′it), *n.* a thick or dense growth of shrubs, bushes, or small trees.

thick·head·ed (thik′hed′id), *adj.* dull; stupid.

thick·ness (thik′nis), *n.* **1.** the state or quality of being thick. **2.** the measurement of the smallest dimension of a solid figure: *a board of two-inch thickness.* **3.** a layer: *three thicknesses of cloth.*

thick·set (thik′set′), *adj.* **1.** set thickly or closely together: *a thickset hedge.* **2.** heavily or solidly built; stocky: *a thickset young man.*

thick·skinned (thik′skind′), *adj.* **1.** having a thick skin. **2.** not sensitive to criticism or insults.

thief (thēf), *n., pl.* **thieves** (thēvz). a person who steals, esp. secretly or without open force.

thieve (thēv), *v.,* **thieved, thiev·ing.** to commit theft; steal.

thiev·er·y (thē′və rē), *n., pl.* **thiev·er·ies.** the practice or an instance of thieving; theft.

thiev·ish (thē′vish), *adj.* **1.** inclined to be a thief. **2.** of, concerning, or like a thief.

thigh (thī), *n.* **1.** the part of the lower limb, or leg, in man between the hip and the knee. **2.** a similar part of the hind limb in certain animals.

thigh·bone (thī′bōn′), *n.* a bone in the leg, extending from the pelvis to the knee.

thim·ble (thim′bəl), *n.* a small cap, usually of metal, worn to protect the fingertip when sewing.

thin (thin), *adj.,* **thin·ner, thin·nest. 1.** having little extent or space between two surfaces: *a thin wire.* **2.** having little flesh; lean: *a thin man.* **3.** made of or containing objects, particles, etc., widely separated: *thin vegetation.* **4.** of low consistency: *a thin sauce.* **5.** without solidity, substance, fullness, etc.; weak: *a thin voice; a thin excuse.* —*adv.* **6.** so as to produce something thin: *Slice the ham thin.* —*v.,* **thinned, thin·ning. 7.** to make or become thin or thinner (sometimes fol. by *out*): *Let's wait till the crowd thins out.* —**thin′ly,** *adv.* —**thin′ness,** *n.*

thine (thīn), *pron.* the possessive case of **thou,** used as an adjective: *The book is thine.*

thing (thing), *n.* **1.** a material object without life or consciousness: *That ring is a beautiful thing.* **2.** some object or creature that cannot be named or described exactly: *The stick has a brass thing on it.* **3.** a thought or statement: *I have just one thing to say.* **4.** an action, deed, or event: *to do interesting things.* **5.** a useful object, method, etc.: *This is just the thing for your cold.* **6.** a living being or creature: *She's such a pretty thing.* **7. things, a.** matters; affairs: *Things are going well now.* **b.** clothing or belongings: *She packed her things and left.*

think (thingk), *v.,* **thought** (thôt), **think·ing. 1.** to use the mind in dealing with a certain situation: *He wanted a little time to think before deciding.* **2.** to have in the mind as the subject of one's thoughts (usually fol. by *of* or *about*): *to think about vacation plans.* **3.** to have as an opinion or belief: *I think you're wrong.* **4.** to call something to one's mind (usually fol. by *about* or *of*): *I thought about going shopping today.* **5.** to consider as being: *He thought me unkind.* **6.** to anticipate or expect: *I think I'll be home early.* **7. think twice,** to consider a matter very carefully, esp. before taking action: *You'd better think twice before spending so much money.* **8. think up,** to devise or concoct by thinking: *He thought up a way of cooling the auditorium.* —**think′er,** *n.*

thin-skinned (thin′skind′), *adj.* **1.** having a thin skin. **2.** easily offended; touchy.

third (thûrd), *adj.* **1.** being number three in a series: *the third floor.* —*n.* **2.** one of three equal parts. **3.** a person or thing that is third. —**third′ly,** *adv.*

third′ class′, 1. the class, grade, or rank immediately following the second. **2.** the least expensive class of accommodations on trains, in hotels, etc. **3.** (in the U.S. postal system) the class of mail consisting of merchandise weighing not more than 16 ounces and of written or printed material, such as books, circulars, or the like, not sealed against postal inspection. —**third′-class′,** *adj., adv.*

third′ degree′, harsh, continual questioning, esp. by the police, to obtain information or a confession.

third′-de·gree burn′ (thûrd′də grē′). See under **burn** (def. 11).

third′ per′son, 1. the one or ones spoken about in a grammatical construction. **2.** the form of a pronoun or verb that refers to the one or ones spoken about. In English, *he, she, it, they, their,* and *theirs,* are pronouns of the third person. *Does* is the third person singular, present-tense form of the verb *to do.*

Third′ World′, nonaligned, developing nations, esp. of Africa and Asia, considered as a political force.

thirst (thûrst), *n.* **1.** a feeling of dryness in the mouth and throat caused by need of liquid. **2.** a strong or eager desire: *a thirst for knowledge.* —*v.* **3.** to be thirsty. **4.** to have a strong desire; yearn.

thirst·y (thûr′stē), *adj.,* **thirst·i·er, thirst·i·est. 1.** feeling or having thirst; craving liquid. **2.** needing moisture: *thirsty soil.*

thir·teen (thûr′tēn′), *n.* **1.** a number that is ten plus three. **2.** a set of this many persons or things: *Thirteen will be there.* —*adj.* **3.** amounting to thirteen in number: *thirteen persons.*

thir·teenth (thûr′tēnth′), *adj.* **1.** being number thirteen in a series: *the thirteenth floor.* —*n.* **2.** one of thirteen equal parts. **3.** a person or thing that is thirteenth.

thir·ti·eth (thûr′tē ith), *adj.* **1.** being number thirty in a series: *the thirtieth floor.* —*n.* **2.** one of thirty equal parts. **3.** a person or thing that is thirtieth.

thir·ty (thûr′tē), *n., pl.* **thir·ties. 1.** a number that is three times ten. **2.** a set of this many persons or things: *Thirty of them will be there.* **3. thirties,** the numbers, years, degrees, etc., between 30 and 39: *The woman was in her early thirties.* —*adj.* **4.** amounting to thirty in number: *thirty persons.*

this (ŧẖis), *pron., pl.* **these** (ŧẖēz). **1.** (used to indicate a person, thing, etc., as present, just mentioned, supposed to be understood, or sometimes used for emphasis): *This is my hat.* **2.** (used to indicate one of two or more persons, things, etc., already mentioned, referring to the one nearer in place, time, or thought; opposite of *that*): *This is Liza and that is Amy.* **3.** what is about to follow: *Now hear this!* —*adj., pl.* **these** (ŧẖēz). **4.** (used to indicate a person, place, or thing as present, near, just mentioned, or as well-known): *This man is my friend.* **5.** (used to indicate the nearer in time, place, or thought): *This house is ours and that one is theirs.* —*adv.* **6.** to the extent or degree indicated: *this far.* **7. with this,** following this: *With this, he turned and ran from the room.*

this·tle (this′əl), *n.* any of various prickly plants having purple flower heads.

thith·er (thiŧẖ′ər), *adv.* to or toward that place or point; there.

tho (ŧẖō), *conj., adv. Informal.* short for **though.**

thole (thōl), *n.* a pin or peg, sometimes one of a pair, placed into a gunwale to hold an oar in rowing.

Thom·as (tom′əs), *n.* (in the Bible) an apostle who demanded proof of Christ's resurrection.

Thistle
(height to 9 ft.)

thong (thông), *n.* a narrow strip of leather used as a fastening, as on a sandal, or as the lash of a whip.

Thor (thôr), *n.* (in Scandinavian mythology) the god of thunder, rain, and farming.

tho·rac·ic (thô ras′ik), *adj.* of or concerning the thorax.

tho·rax (thôr′aks), *n.* **1.** the part of the body between the neck and the abdomen containing the cavity in which the heart, lungs, etc., are located; chest. **2.** (in insects) the portion of the body between the head and the abdomen.

tho·ri·um (thôr′ē əm), *n. Chem.* a greenish-white metallic element, used as a source of nuclear energy, in filament coatings, and in alloys. *Symbol:* Th

thorn (thôrn), *n.* **1.** a sharp spine or prickle on a plant. **2.** any of various thorny shrubs or trees. **3. thorn in one's flesh** (or **side**), a source of constant irritation or suffering: *This debt is a thorn in my flesh.*

thorn·y (thôr′nē), *adj.,* **thorn·i·er, thorn·i·est. 1.** full of or overgrown with thorns. **2.** full of difficulties: *a thorny question.* —**thorn′i·ness,** *n.*

thor·ough (thûr′ō, thur′ō), *adj.* **1.** complete; neglecting nothing: *a thorough search.* **2.** very careful; omitting or leaving out nothing: *a thorough worker.* **3.** complete or perfect in all respects: *thorough enjoyment.* —**thor′ough·ly,** *adv.* —**thor′ough·ness,** *n.*

thor·ough·bred (thûr′ō bred′, thur′ō-), *adj.* **1.** of pure or unmixed breed, stock, or race, such as a horse or other animal; bred from the purest and best

blood. **2.** *(sometimes cap.)* of or concerning the Thoroughbred breed of horses. —*n.* **3.** a thoroughbred animal. **4.** a well-bred or well-educated person.

Thor·ough·bred (thûr′ō bred′, thur′ō-), *n.* any of a breed of horses to which all race horses belong.

thor·ough·fare (thûr′ō fâr′, thur′ō-), *n.* **1.** a road, street, or the like, that leads at each end into another street. **2.** a major road or highway.

thor·ough·go·ing (thûr′ō gō′ing, thur′ō-), *adj.* thorough; complete.

those (ŧẖōz), *pron., adj.* the plural of **that.**

thou (ŧẖou), *pron.* an old form of **you,** found now chiefly in Biblical and poetic writing: *What wouldst thou choose for thyself?*

though (ŧẖō), *conj.* **1.** in spite of the fact that: *Though he tried very hard, he lost.* **2.** granting that (often preceded by *even*): *Even though I can't do it the first time, I'll try again.* —*adv.* **3.** for all that; however: *I can only stay for a few minutes though.* **4. as though,** as if: *You look as though you were ill.*

thought¹ (thôt), *n.* **1.** that which one thinks; idea; notion: *to collect one's thoughts.* **2.** the act or process of thinking; mental activity. **3.** consideration or reflection: *Give the problem some thought.* **4.** meditation or contemplation: *deep in thought.* **5.** the ideas of a particular place, class, or time: *ancient Greek thought.* **6.** intention or purpose: *We had some thought of going to Alaska.* **7.** an opinion or belief: *What are his thoughts on the subject?* [from the Old English word *(ge)thōht,* which is related to *think*]

thought² (thôt), *v.* the past tense and past participle of **think.**

thought·ful (thôt′fəl), *adj.* **1.** occupied with or inclined toward thought; reflective: *in a thoughtful mood.* **2.** showing careful thought: *a thoughtful essay.* **3.** showing consideration for others; considerate. —**thought′ful·ly,** *adv.* —**thought′ful·ness,** *n.*

thought·less (thôt′lis), *adj.* **1.** not thinking enough; careless: *It was thoughtless of him to forget.* **2.** inconsiderate or rude: *a thoughtless remark.* —**thought′less·ly,** *adv.* —**thought′less·ness,** *n.*

thou·sand (thou′zənd), *n., pl.* **thou·sands** or (after a numeral) **thousand. 1.** a number that is ten times one hundred. **2.** a group of this many persons or things: *A thousand of the employees were on strike.* **3. thousands,** the numbers, dollars, degrees, etc., between 1000 and 999,999: *to cost thousands; a cast of thousands.* —*adj.* **4.** amounting to one thousand in number: *a thousand people.*

thou·sand·fold (thou′zənd fōld′), *adj.* **1.** one thousand times as great or as much: *a thousandfold increase.* —*adv.* (thou′zənd fōld′). **2.** in thousandfold measure: *The output increased thousandfold.*

thou·sandth (thou′zənth), *adj.* **1.** being number one thousand in a series: *the thousandth revolution of the engine.* —*n.* **2.** one of a thousand equal parts. **3.** a person or thing that is number one thousand.

thrall (thrôl), *n.* **1.** a person in bondage; slave. **2.** slavery; bondage.

thrash (thrash), *v.* **1.** to beat soundly in punishment; flog. **2.** to toss or plunge about wildly or violently: *The animals thrashed about in the cage.* **3.** another spelling of **thresh.**

thrash·er (thrash′ər), *n.* **1.** a person or thing that thrashes. **2.** any of several long-tailed, thrushlike birds, related to the mockingbird.

thread (thred), *n.* **1.** a fine cord of flax, cotton, etc., used for sewing. **2.** anything that resembles a thread: *a thread of smoke.* **3.** a spiral ridge or groove cut into a screw, bolt, nut, or the like. **4.** something that runs throughout something else: *the thread of a story.* —*v.* **5.** to pass the end of a thread through the eye of (a needle). **6.** to arrange on a thread; string: *to thread beads.* **7.** to make (one's way) as among obstacles: *to thread one's way through a crowd.* —**thread′like′,** *adj.*

thread·bare (thred′bâr′), *adj.* **1.** worn out so as to lay bare the threads: *threadbare slipcovers.* **2.** wearing threadbare clothes. **3.** commonplace; hackneyed; trite.

threat (thret), *n.* **1.** a declaration of an intention to inflict punishment or cause harm: *He confessed under the threat of imprisonment.* **2.** a warning of probable trouble: *the threat of a storm.*

threat·en (thret′ən), *v.* **1.** to utter a threat against: *He threatened the boy with a beating.* **2.** to utter or use threats: *He threatened to punish the strikers.* **3.** to be a source of danger to: *Fire threatened the house.* **4.** to give warning of: *The clouds threatened rain.* —**threat′en·ing·ly,** *adv.*

three (thre), *n.* **1.** a number that is two plus one. **2.** a set of this many persons or things: *Only three will be there.* —*adj.* **3.** amounting to three in number: *three persons.*

three-di·men·sion·al (thre′di men′shə n°l), *adj.* having or seeming to have the dimension of depth as well as width and height.

three·fold (thre′fold′), *adj.* **1.** made up of three parts: *a threefold plan.* **2.** three times as great or as much; triple: *a threefold increase.* —*adv.* **3.** in three-fold measure: *The work has increased threefold.*

three·score (thre′skôr′), *adj.* being or containing three times twenty; sixty.

thresh (thresh), *v.* **1.** to separate the grain or seeds from (a cereal plant or the like), esp. with a flail or a threshing machine. **2.** to beat repeatedly or violently as if with a flail: *to thresh the water with one's arms.* Also, **thrash.**

thresh·er (thresh′ər), *n.* **1.** a person or thing that threshes. **2.** a large shark that threshes the water with its long tail to drive together the small fish on which it feeds.

thresh′ing machine′, a machine for removing the grains and seeds from straw or chaff.

thresh·old (thresh′old, thresh′hold), *n.* **1.** the stone or piece of wood under a door; sill of a doorway. **2.** the entrance to a house or building. **3.** any point of entering or beginning: *the threshold of his career.*

threw (throo), *v.* the past tense of **throw.**

thrice (thris), *adv.* three times.

thrift (thrift), *n.* care and economy in handling money or finances; economical management.

thrift·y (thrif′te), *adj.,* **thrift·i·er, thrift·i·est.** practicing thrift or economical management: *a thrifty housewife.* —**thrift′i·ly,** *adv.* —**thrift′i·ness,** *n.*

thrill (thril), *v.* **1.** to feel or cause to feel keen emotion or excitement: *The singing star thrilled his audience.* —*n.* **2.** a sudden feeling of keen emotion or excitement. **3.** something that causes such a feeling: *a story full of thrills.* —**thrill′ing,** *adj.*

thrill·er (thril′ər), *n.* **1.** a person or thing that thrills. **2.** *Informal.* an exciting play, movie, or story, esp. one involving mystery, spying, etc.

thrive (thriv), *v.,* **throve** (throv) *or* **thrived; thrived** *or* **thriv·en** (thriv′ən); **thriv·ing. 1.** to prosper; be fortunate or successful: *The business is thriving.* **2.** to grow vigorously; flourish: *The plants are thriving.*

throat (throt), *n.* **1.** the passage from the mouth to the stomach or to the lungs. **2.** the front of the neck. **3.** any narrow opening or passage resembling the throat: *the throat of a vase.*

throat·y (thro′te), *adj.,* **throat·i·er, throat·i·est.** produced in the throat, such as sounds; husky; hoarse.

throb (throb), *v.,* **throbbed, throb·bing. 1.** to beat with increased force or speed, such as the heart under the influence of emotion or excitement. **2.** to pulsate or vibrate. —*n.* **3.** the act of throbbing. **4.** a violent beat or pulsation.

throe (thro), *n.* **1.** a violent spasm or pang. **2. throes,** any violent struggle: *the throes of battle.*

throne (thron), *n.* **1.** the raised chair or seat occupied by a sovereign, bishop, pope, etc., on ceremonial occasions. **2.** the office or dignity of a sovereign: *He succeeded to the throne when his father died.*

throng (thrông, throng), *n.* **1.** a great number of persons or things crowded or considered together. —*v.* **2.** to gather, go, or move about in large numbers. **3.** to crowd into: *They thronged the small room.*

throt·tle (throt′°l), *n.* **1.** a valve for controlling the flow of fuel to an engine. **2.** the lever, pedal, handle, etc., that controls this valve. —*v.,* **throt·tled, throt·tling. 3.** to choke or strangle. **4.** to silence as if by choking: *His message was throttled by censorship.* **5.** to block or check the flow of (a fluid) so as to control the speed of an engine.

through (throo), *prep.* **1.** in at one end, side, or surface and out at the other: *to pass through a tunnel.* **2.** past: *to go through a stop sign without stopping.* **3.** from one end to the other of: *to swing through the trees.* **4.** having reached the end of: *to be through one's work.* **5.** to and including: *from 1900 through 1950.* **6.** by means of: *It was through him they found out.* —*adv.* **7.** in at one end, side, or surface and out at the other: *to push a needle through.* **8.** all the way: *This train goes through to Boston.* **9.** from the beginning to the end: *to read a letter through.* —*adj.* **10.** having completed an action, process, etc.; finished. **11.** traveling or extending the full distance with little or no interruption: *a through train.* **12. through and through,** through every part; thoroughly: *to be wet* *through and through.* **13. through with, a.** finished with: *Are you through with the sports page?* **b.** at the end of all relations or dealings with: *My sister says she's through with men.*

through·out (thrōō out´), *prep.* **1.** in or to every part of: *They searched throughout the house.* —*adv.* **2.** in every part: *red throughout.*

throve (thrōv), *v.* a past tense of **thrive.**

throw (thrō), *v.,* **threw** (thrōō), **thrown** (thrōn), **throw·ing. 1.** to cast, esp. with the hand; toss; fling: *to throw a ball.* **2.** to project or cast (light, a shadow, etc.). **3.** to put or cause to go or come as if by hurling: *to throw a man into prison.* **4.** to put on, off, or away hastily: *to throw a scarf over one's head.* **5.** to move (a lever or the like) in order to connect or disconnect parts of a mechanism: *to throw a switch.* **6.** to cause to fall to the ground: *The wrestler threw his opponent.* **7.** *Informal.* to lose (a game, race, or other contest) on purpose, as for a bribe. —*n.* **8.** the act or an instance of throwing. **9.** the distance to which anything is or may be thrown: *a stone's throw.* **10. throw away, a.** to dispose of; discard: *to throw away an old shirt.* **b.** to fail to use or take advantage of: *to throw away an opportunity.* **11. throw in, a.** to add as a bonus, gift, or the like: *Buy the car, and I'll throw in an extra set of tires.* **b.** to inject or introduce, as into a discussion, report, etc.: *He threw in a joke to ease the tension of the meeting.* **12. throw out, a.** to cast out; discard: *Let's throw out these old rags and bottles.* **b.** to eject or remove forcibly from a place: *Did they really throw him out of the hotel?* **c.** (in baseball) to put (a runner) out by throwing the ball in time to a baseman: *The batter was thrown out at first.* **13. throw up, a.** to vomit. **b.** to build quickly and haphazardly: *They threw up a row of shanties along the riverbank.* **c.** to reproach with; criticize because of: *She's always throwing it up to me that I lost her key ring.* —**throw´er,** *n.*

thrown (thrōn), *v.* the past participle of **throw.**

thru (thrōō), *prep., adv., adj. Informal.* through.

thrum (thrum), *v.,* **thrummed, thrum·ming. 1.** to play on a stringed instrument, such as a guitar, by plucking the strings; strum. **2.** to drum or tap idly with the fingers. —*n.* **3.** the act or sound of thrumming.

thrush (thrush), *n.* any of various songbirds, sometimes having spotted underparts.

thrust (thrust), *v.,* **thrust, thrust·ing. 1.** to push, put, or drive with force; shove: *He thrust the book aside.* **2.** to put boldly into some position, condition, etc.: *to thrust oneself into a conversation.* **3.** to stab or pierce, as with a sword. —*n.* **4.** the act or an instance of thrusting. **5.** an organized military attack; assault. **6.** a force exerted by a propeller, propulsive gases, etc., to propel a ship, aircraft, or spacecraft.

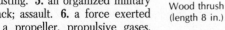

Wood thrush (length 8 in.)

thud (thud), *n.* **1.** a dull sound, as of a heavy blow or fall. —*v.,* **thud·ded, thud·ding. 2.** to beat or strike with a dull sound.

thug (thug), *n.* a vicious ruffian, robber, or murderer.

thu·li·um (thōō´lē əm), *n. Chem.* a metallic element of the rare-earth group. *Symbol:* Tm

thumb (thum), *n.* **1.** the short, thick finger of the hand of man, next to the forefinger. **2.** the part of a glove or mitten for containing the thumb. —*v.* **3.** to soil or damage with the fingers in handling, such as the pages of a book. **4.** to glance through quickly (often fol. by *through*): *to thumb through a magazine.* **5.** (of a hitchhiker) to ask for or get (a ride) by pointing the thumb in the desired direction of travel. **6. all thumbs,** awkward or clumsy: *I'm all thumbs when I try to do embroidery.* **7. thumbs up,** an expression of encouragement or approval: *"Thumbs up," he said, "we're not licked yet!"* **8. turn thumbs down,** to show or indicate disagreement or disapproval, esp. by a rejection, veto, or the like: *They turned thumbs down on our request for a skating rink.* **9. under one's thumb,** under another's absolute control: *He's under the thumb of his older brother.*

thumb·nail (thum´nāl´), *n.* the hard, horny covering of the end of the thumb.

thumb·screw (thum´skrōō´), *n.* **1.** a screw that may be easily turned with the thumb and a finger. **2.** Often, **thumbscrews.** an old instrument of torture by which one or both thumbs were compressed by the tightening of a screw.

thumb·tack (thum´tak´), *n.* a tack with a large, flat head, designed to be thrust into a board or other fairly soft object by the pressure of the thumb.

thump (thump), *n.* **1.** a blow with something thick and heavy, producing a dull sound; a heavy knock. **2.** the sound made by such a blow. —*v.* **3.** to strike or beat with something heavy, so as to produce a dull sound: *He thumped the desk with his fist.* **4.** to strike, beat, or fall heavily with a dull sound: *He thumped down on the bed.*

thun·der (thun´dər), *n.* **1.** a loud, explosive or rumbling noise produced by the sudden expansion of air heated by a lightning discharge. **2.** any loud, resounding noise: *the thunder of applause.* —*v.* **3.** to give forth thunder. **4.** to make a loud noise like thunder: *The gunfire thundered in the hills.* **5.** to utter with loud threats: *to thunder a warning.*

thun·der·bolt (thun´dər bōlt´), *n.* **1.** a flash of lightning accompanied by thunder. **2.** something very destructive or terrible: *the thunderbolts of war.*

thun·der·clap (thun´dər klap´), *n.* a crash of thunder.

thun·der·cloud (thun´dər kloud´), *n.* a tall, dense cloud, charged with electricity and producing lightning and thunder.

thun·der·head (thun´dər hed´), *n.* a thundercloud, esp. one having a flattened, anvil-shaped top.

thun·der·ous (thun´dər əs), *adj.* producing thunder or a loud noise like thunder: *thunderous applause.* —**thun´der·ous·ly,** *adv.*

thun·der·show·er (t͟hun′dər shou′ər), *n.* a shower accompanied by thunder and lightning.

thun·der·storm (t͟hun′dər stôrm′), *n.* a storm with lightning, thunder, rain, and usually gusty winds.

thun·der·struck (t͟hun′dər struk′), *adj.* overcome with amazement; astounded: *We were thunderstruck when we heard the news.*

Thur., Thursday. Also, **Thurs.**

Thurs·day (t͟hûrz′dē, t͟hûrz′dā), *n.* the fifth day of the week, following Wednesday.

thus (t͟hus), *adv.* 1. in this way: *Stated thus, the question is easier to answer.* 2. in accordance with this; so: *It is late, and thus you must go.* 3. to this extent or degree: *thus far.*

thwack (t͟hwak), *v.* 1. to strike or beat with something flat; whack. —*n.* 2. a sharp blow with something flat.

thwart (t͟hwôrt), *v.* 1. to oppose successfully: *to thwart the enemy's attack.* —*n.* 2. a seat across a boat, esp. one used by oarsmen. —*adj.* 3. passing or lying crosswise; across.

thy (t͟hī), *pron.* the possessive case of **thou** (used as an adjective before a noun beginning with a consonant sound): *thy kingdom.*

thyme (tīm), *n.* a plant related to mint. Its leaves are used in cooking as a seasoning.

thy·mus (thī′məs), *n.* a gland near the base of the neck in man, believed to be important in combating infection.

thy·roid (thī′roid), *n.* a ductless gland in the neck. The thyroid secretes a hormone that regulates the rate of body growth and the way in which the body uses the energy from food. Also, **thy′roid gland′.**

thy·self (t͟hī self′), *pron.* an old form of **yourself,** found now chiefly in Biblical and poetic writing: *Thou shalt love thy neighbor as thyself.*

ti (tē), *n., pl.* **tis.** the seventh note of a musical scale: *B is ti in the C scale.*

Ti, *Chem.* the symbol for **titanium.**

ti·ar·a (tē ar′ə, tē är′ə), *n.* 1. a small, jeweled crown worn as an ornament by women. 2. the triple crown of the pope, worn on special occasions.

Ti·ber (tī′bər), *n.* a river in central Italy, flowing through Rome into the Mediterranean Sea. 244 mi. long.

Ti·bet (ti bet′), *n.* a country in S Asia, N of the Himalayas: under control of China. 471,660 sq. mi.

Ti·bet·an (ti bet′ᵊn), *adj.* 1. of or concerning Tibet, its people, or their language. —*n.* 2. a member of the native Mongolian race of Tibet. 3. the language of Tibet, related to Burmese and more distantly to Chinese.

tib·i·a (tib′ē ə), *n., pl.* **tib·i·as** *or* **tib·i·ae** (tib′ē ē′). the scientific term for **shinbone.**

tic (tik), *n.* an involuntary twitch of a muscle, esp. a muscle in the face.

tick[1] (tik), *n.* 1. a slight, sharp, repeated sound, such as a clock makes. 2. a small mark or check. —*v.* 3. to make a sound like that of a clock. 4. to check or mark (usually fol. by *off*): *to tick off the items on the bill.* [from the Middle English word *tek* "little touch"]

tick[2] (tik), *n.* any of numerous small animals that are related to the spiders and mites and feed on the blood of man and animals. Some ticks transmit disease. [from the Old English word *ticia*]

tick[3] (tik), *n.* a cloth covering or case for a mattress or pillow. [from the Middle English word *tikke*, which comes from Latin *tēca*, from Greek *thēkē* "case"]

Dog tick (length ¼ in.)

tick·et (tik′it), *n.* 1. a printed slip of paper or cardboard giving the holder of it the right to receive certain services or benefits: *a theater ticket; a railroad ticket.* 2. a written or printed slip attached to something to identify it or to show its size, price, etc.; label; tag. 3. a list of candidates nominated by a political party. 4. a summons or warning given to a person, esp. for violating traffic and parking rules. —*v.,* **tick·et·ed, tick·et·ing.** 5. to attach or serve a summons to: *to ticket a parked car; to ticket a speeder.* 6. to put a label or tag on: *to ticket a coat for sale.*

tick·ing (tik′ing), *n.* a strong cotton or linen cloth used for making ticks for mattresses or pillows.

tick·le (tik′əl), *v.,* **tick·led, tick·ling.** 1. to rub or stroke lightly with the fingers, a feather, or the like, so as to produce a feeling of tingling or twitching. 2. to poke or scratch in some sensitive part of the body so as to cause laughter. 3. to have or cause a feeling of tingling or twitching from being rubbed or stroked: *The grass makes my feet tickle.* 4. to amuse; excite agreeably: *The clown's tricks tickled the crowd.* —*n.* 5. the act of tickling. 6. a tickling sensation. 7. **tickled pink,** *Informal.* greatly pleased; delighted: *I'm tickled pink that you could be here.* —**tick′ler,** *n.*

tick·lish (tik′lish), *adj.* 1. sensitive to tickling. 2. requiring careful handling; difficult: *a ticklish problem.* 3. easily offended; touchy: *Dad is ticklish about being interrupted.* —**tick′lish·ness,** *n.*

tid·al (tīd′ᵊl), *adj.* of, referring to, or caused by the tides: *a tidal current; a tidal swell.*

tid′al wave′, a large, destructive ocean wave produced by an earthquake, hurricane, very strong wind, etc.

tid·bit (tid′bit′), *n.* 1. a delicate bit of food. 2. a choice bit of anything, such as news or gossip.

tide (tīd), *n.* 1. the regular rise and fall of the ocean, usually occurring twice a day, produced by the gravitational attraction of the sun and especially the moon. 2. anything that rises and falls like the tide: *the tides of business activity.* 3. a current, tendency, drift, etc.: *the tide of public opinion.* 4. **tide over,** to assist (someone) in getting through a period of difficulty or distress: *The loan will tide us over until the* *crops are sold.* **5. turn the tide,** to reverse the trend of events, esp. favorably: *The Battle of Saratoga turned the tide of the American Revolution.*

tide·land (tīd′land′), *n.* land that is regularly exposed and then covered by the ebb and flow of the tide.

tide·wa·ter (tīd′wô′tər, -wot′ər), *n.* **1.** water that is affected by the rise and fall of the tide. **2.** the water covering an area of land at high tide. **3.** a seacoast where there are tidewaters.

ti·dings (tī′dĭngz), *n.* *(sometimes used as sing.)* news, information, or a report: *the sad tidings of a death in the family.*

ti·dy (tī′dē), *adj.,* **ti·di·er, ti·di·est. 1.** neat and orderly: *a tidy room.* **2.** *Informal.* fairly large; considerable: *a tidy sum.* —*v.,* **ti·died, ti·dy·ing. 3.** to make tidy; put in order (often fol. by *up*): *Tidy up your room before dinner.* —**ti′di·ly,** *adv.* —**ti′di·ness,** *n.*

tie (tī), *v.,* **tied, ty·ing. 1.** to bind or fasten with a cord, string, or the like, drawn together and knotted. **2.** to form by looping and drawing tight: *to tie a knot.* **3.** to form a knot or bow in: *to tie a necktie.* **4.** to fasten or join in any way: *Bricks are tied together with mortar.* **5.** to bind closely or firmly: *The two friends were tied by great affection.* **6.** to limit or confine: *The storm tied us to the harbor.* **7.** to make the same score as (an opponent): *The visiting team tied us in our last game. Two teams tied for second place.* —*n.* **8.** anything used to fasten or bind something. **9.** a necktie or bow tie. **10.** a common interest shared by two or more people, nations, etc.: *political ties.* **11.** equality of scores or votes: *The game ended in a tie.* **12.** a beam or rod used as a brace in a building or other structure. **13.** (in music) a curved line connecting two notes of the same pitch and indicating that they are to be played as a single, long note. **14.** any of a number of closely spaced crossbeams used for supporting and fastening the rails of a track. **15. tie in,** to connect or be connected; be consistent: *His story seems to tie in with the facts.* **16. tie up, a.** to fasten securely by tying: *to tie up a package.* **b.** to impede or stop: *An accident tied up traffic.* **c.** to engage or occupy the attention of: *I'll be tied up in meetings all afternoon.* **d.** to invest or place (money) so as not to be available for other uses: *All my money is tied up in real estate.*

Ties (def. 13)

Tien·tsin (tĭn′tsĭn′), *n.* a port city in NE China.

tier (tēr), *n.* any of a series of rows, ranks, or levels arranged one above another: *the first tier of seats in the balcony.*

Tier·ra del Fue·go (tyär′ə del fwā′gō), a group of islands at the S tip of South America, belonging to Argentina and Chile.

tie-up (tī′up′), *n.* **1.** a temporary stoppage or slowing of work, traffic, etc.: *A derailment caused a tie-up of commuter service.* **2.** a connection or relation: *to have a tie-up with the shipping companies.*

tiff (tĭf), *n.* **1.** a minor quarrel; spat. **2.** a slight fit of annoyance or anger.

ti·ger (tī′gər), *n.,* *pl.* **ti·gers** *or* **ti·ger.** a large, ferocious member of the cat family found in southern Asia and having a tawny or orange coat with narrow black stripes.

ti′ger lil′y, a lily having orange flowers with black spots.

Tiger
(total length 10 ft.)

tight (tīt), *adj.* **1.** firmly fixed in place; secure: *a tight knot.* **2.** stretched as far as possible; tense; taut: *a tight cable.* **3.** fitting closely or too closely to some part of the body: *a tight skirt; tight shoes.* **4.** difficult to deal with; troublesome: *to be in a tight situation.* **5.** closely constructed or fitted together, so as to prevent the passage of air, water, steam, etc.: *a good, tight roof.* **6.** firm; strict: *tight discipline.* **7.** packed closely or full: *a tight schedule.* **8.** set closely together; compact: *a tight formation.* **9.** difficult to buy or obtain; scarce: *Mortgage loans are tight this year.* **10.** *Informal.* nearly even; close: *a tight race.* **11.** *Informal.* miserly; stingy. —*adv.* **12.** in a tight manner; securely; closely: *Shut the door tight.* —**tight′ly,** *adv.* —**tight′ness,** *n.*

tight·en (tīt′ən), *v.* to make or become tight: *I tightened the connection to stop the leak.*

tight·fist·ed (tīt′fĭs′tĭd), *adj.* miserly; stingy.

tight·rope (tīt′rōp′), *n.* a rope or wire cable stretched tight, on which acrobats perform.

tights (tīts), *n.pl.* a tight garment, usually made of a stretch fabric, covering the lower part of the body and the legs, worn by acrobats, dancers, etc.

tight·wad (tīt′wod′), *n.* *Informal.* a stingy person; miser.

ti·gress (tī′grĭs), *n.* a female tiger.

Ti·gris (tī′grĭs), *n.* a river in SW Asia, flowing SE from Turkey through Iraq to the Euphrates. 1150 mi. long.

tike (tīk), *n.* another spelling of **tyke.**

til·de (til′də), *n.* a mark (˜) placed over certain letters, as in Spanish over the *n* of *señor* "sir, gentleman," to show that the letter is to be pronounced *ny.*

tile (tīl), *n.* **1.** a thin piece of any of various materials, such as baked clay, stone, wood, metal, asphalt, plastic, etc., used for covering roofs, walls, floors, etc. **2.** one of the small, thin blocks with special markings used in certain games. **3.** a tube or pipe of baked clay used for draining land. —*v.,* **tiled, til·ing. 4.** to cover with tiles.

Roofing tiles

till[1] (tĭl), *prep.* **1.** up to the time of; until: *to fight till death.* **2.** before (used in negative sentences): *He won't arrive till noon.* —*conj.* **3.** to the time when; until: *We ran till we were exhausted.* [from the Old English word *til,* which comes from Scandinavian]

---

act, āble, dâre, ärt; ebb, ēqual; if, īce; hot, ōver, ôrder; oil; bŏŏk; ōōze; out; up, ûrge; ə = *a* as in *alone;*
ᵊ as in *button* (but′ᵊn), *fire* (fīᵊr); chief; shoe; thin; ŧħat; zh as in *measure* (mezh′ər). See full key inside cover.

till² (til), *v.* to work (the soil) by plowing, planting, etc.; cultivate. [from the Old English word *tilian* "to strive after, till"]

till³ (til), *n.* a drawer, box, tray, or the like, for keeping money or valuables, esp. in a store, bank, hotel, etc. [from the Middle English word *tylle,* which comes from Old English *tyllan* "to draw"]

till·age (til′ij), *n.* 1. the act or process of cultivating land. 2. cultivated land.

till·er¹ (til′ər), *n.* a person who cultivates land; farmer. [from the Middle English word *tiliere.* See *till²*]

till·er² (til′ər), *n.* a bar or lever for turning the rudder in steering a boat. [from the early French word *teiler* "weaver's beam," which comes from Latin *tēla* "warp"]

tilt (tilt), *v.* 1. to lean; slant; incline: *The shack tilted from age.* 2. to fight on horseback with lances; joust. 3. to strike or attack with a lance or other weapon or with words (usually fol. by *at*): *to tilt at the evils of society.* —*n.* 4. a slope or slant: *a roof with a sharp tilt.* 5. the act of tilting, or the state of being tilted. 6. a medieval sport in which knights in armor on horseback attacked each other with lances; joust. 7. any contest or dispute. 8. **full tilt,** with full force or speed: *The factory is going full tilt to fill all the Christmas orders.*

tim·ber (tim′bər), *n.* 1. wood suitable for building, making furniture, and other uses. 2. a piece of such wood; log. 3. wooded land; timberland. 4. a piece of wood forming part of a building, ship, etc. —*v.* 5. to provide, cover, or support with timber.

tim′ber line′, 1. the altitude above sea level at which trees no longer grow. 2. the latitude in arctic or antarctic regions beyond which trees do not grow.

tim·bre (tim′bər, tam′bər), *n.* the distinctive tone quality of a sound, esp. that of a voice or musical instrument.

time (tīm), *n.* 1. the duration of all existence, past, present, and future. 2. a period or interval: *a long time; an hour's time.* 3. a system or method of measuring the passing of time: *solar time; standard time.* 4. a particular period considered as separate from other periods: *the time of youth.* 5. Often, **times. a.** an age or era: *ancient times.* **b.** the present period or era: *a sign of the times.* **c.** a period or era in which certain conditions, ideas, etc., prevail: *hard times.* 6. the period during which something lasts or is expected to last: *to live out one's time.* 7. the moment when something is to occur: *a time for action.* 8. a period of work of an employee: *to work full time.* 9. the rate of pay for a particular period of work: *to pay double time for work done on holidays.* 10. a period or occasion considered as providing a certain kind of experience: *We all had a good time at the party.* 11. leisure; spare time: *I don't have time to go to ball games.* 12. a particular point in time: *The time is now 5:29 p.m.* 13. a particular part of a day, year, etc.; season or period: *lunch time; Easter time.* 14. the proper moment for something: *It's time for bed.* 15. each of the occurrences of an act or event that is

repeated: *I saw the picture three times.* 16. (in arithmetic) the number of things that are or can be multiplied: *Two goes into six three times.* 17. (in music) **a.** the relative speed of movement; tempo. **b.** the speed and rhythm of a particular kind of music: *waltz time.* 18. the speed or tempo at which anything is done: *Get over here in the fastest time possible.* —*v.,* **timed, tim·ing.** 19. to measure or record the duration or speed of: *to time a race.* 20. to set the rhythm or sequence of: *Time your steps to the music.* 21. to choose the proper moment for: *He timed his attack perfectly.* —*adj.* 22. of or referring to time: *a time signal.* 23. set to operate or explode at a certain time: *a time bomb.* 24. **ahead of time,** before the time due; early: *I was there 10 minutes ahead of time.* 25. **at one time, a.** once; in a former time: *At one time we were both in the same class.* **b.** at the same time; at once: *They all tried to talk at one time.* 26. **at times,** occasionally; now and then: *At times this neighborhood is very noisy.* 27. **behind the times,** old-fashioned; dated: *Attitudes like that are behind the times.* 28. **for the time being,** for the present; temporarily: *For the time being, sit anywhere you want to.* 29. **from time to time,** on occasion; occasionally: *I see her from time to time.* 30. **in no time,** in a very brief time; almost at once: *The cut will be healed in no time.* 31. **in time, a.** early enough: *Plan to come in time for dinner.* **b.** in the future; eventually: *In time you'll see that I was right.* **c.** in the correct rhythm: *to march in time to the music.* 32. **kill time,** to do something to make time pass more quickly: *We killed time on the bus by counting telephone poles.* 33. **on time, a.** at the specified time; punctually: *to get to school on time.* **b.** on credit: *to buy a new car on time.* 34. **take one's time,** to be slow or leisurely: *Take your time eating.* 35. **time after time,** again and again; repeatedly: *I've warned you time after time.* 36. **time and time again,** on numerous occasions; often: *Time and time again you've ignored me.* Also, **time and again.**

time-hon·ored (tīm′on′ərd), *adj.* held in esteem because of long continuance or use: *Hanging mistletoe at Christmas is a time-honored custom.*

time-keep·er (tīm′kē′pər), *n.* 1. an official who keeps and records the time of a sports event. 2. an employee who records the hours worked by other employees.

time-less (tīm′lis), *adj.* 1. without beginning or end; eternal: *the timeless universe.* 2. true or valid at all times: *the timeless appeal of a marching band.* —**time′less·ness,** *n.*

time·ly (tīm′lē), *adj.* occurring at a suitable time; seasonable: *a timely warning.* —**time′li·ness,** *n.*

time·piece (tīm′pēs′), *n.* any instrument for measuring or recording the passing of time, such as a watch, clock, chronometer, or the like.

tim·er (tī′mər), *n.* 1. a person or thing that times. 2. a device, such as a stopwatch, for measuring time. 3. a device for controlling machinery, an appliance, etc.: *The timer shuts off the oven when the roast is done.*

times (tīmz), *prep.* multiplied by: *Two times two is four.*

time·ta·ble (tīm′tā′bəl), *n.* **1.** a schedule showing the times of arrival and departure of trains, airplanes, buses, etc. **2.** any schedule or plan for the progress and completion of a project: *the timetable for replacing streetcars with buses.*

time′ zone′, any of the 24 zones into which the earth's surface is divided, at intervals of approxi-

Time zones
of the United States

mately 15 degrees of longitude from Greenwich, England, and in which the standard time is one hour earlier or later than that in the next zone.

tim·id (tim′id), *adj.* lacking in self-assurance or courage; fearful; shy. **—ti·mid′i·ty, tim′id·ness,** *n.* **—tim′id·ly,** *adv.*

tim·ing (tī′ming), *n.* **1.** (in the theater) the adjustment of the various parts of a performance in sequence of time so as to produce the most satisfactory effect: *Poor timing spoiled the dance act.* **2.** (in sports) control of the speed and force of a stroke, blow, or other movement, so that it will have its greatest effect at the right moment: *A tennis player needs good timing to return a fast serve.* **3.** the adjustment of the time or speed of any action so as to achieve the greatest effect: *It was clever timing for the President to announce a tax cut just before the election.* **4.** the act of measuring and recording the time of any event, contest, etc.

tim·or·ous (tim′ər əs), *adj.* **1.** easily frightened; timid: *Mice are timorous animals.* **2.** feeling or showing fear; fearful: *a timorous glance.* **—tim′or·ous·ly,** *adv.* **—tim′or·ous·ness,** *n.*

Tim·o·thy (tim′ə thē), *n.* **1.** (in the Bible) a Christian disciple and companion of Paul. **2.** either of two books of the New Testament, written as letters from Paul to Timothy.

tim·pa·ni (tim′pə nē), *n.pl. (sometimes used as sing.)* the group of two or more kettledrums in an orchestra. **—tim′pa·nist,** *n.*

tin (tin), *n.* **1.** a soft, silvery metal that does not corrode easily, used for plating and in making solder: a chemical element. *Symbol:* Sn **2.** tin plate. **3.** a box

or container made from tin plate. **4.** *Chiefly British.* a tin can. **—adj. 5.** made of tin or tin plate. **—v.,** **tinned, tin·ning. 6.** to cover or coat with tin. **7.** *Chiefly British.* to preserve or pack in a can; can.

tin′ can′, a sealed metal container for food or things that spoil easily, esp. one made of tin-plated sheet steel.

tinc·ture (tingk′chər), *n.* **1.** a solution of a drug or other substance in alcohol: *tincture of iodine.* **2.** a slight trace; tinge; tint: *a tincture of red; a tincture of sadness.* **—v.,** **tinc·tured, tinc·tur·ing. 3.** to give a slight trace or tinge to.

tin·der (tin′dər), *n.* any dry material that catches fire easily from the spark of a flint, used for starting a fire.

tin·der·box (tin′dər boks′), *n.* **1.** a box for holding tinder, and usually also a flint and steel for starting fires. **2.** a country, condition, etc., that is likely to break out in violence, war, etc.

tine (tīn), *n.* a sharp point or prong, as on a fork.

tin′ foil′, tin, or an alloy of tin and lead, in the form of a thin, flexible sheet for use as a wrapping.

tinge (tinj), *v.,* **tinged; tinge·ing** *or* **ting·ing. 1.** to give a trace of some color to: *The sky was tinged with red.* **2.** to give a slight quality to: *His political views are tinged with socialism.* **—n. 3.** a slight coloration; tint. **4.** a slight trace of any quality.

tin·gle (ting′gəl), *v.,* **tin·gled, tin·gling. 1.** to have or cause a slight prickling or stinging sensation, as from cold, excitement, a blow, etc.: *Our ears tingled with the cold.* **—n. 2.** a prickling or stinging sensation.

tink·er (ting′kər), *n.* **1.** a person who mends pots and pans. **—v. 2.** to work as a tinker. **3.** to work unskillfully or clumsily at anything: *to tinker with the furnace.* **4.** to busy oneself in a casual or idle way: *to tinker around the house.* **—tink′er·er,** *n.*

tin·kle (ting′kel), *v.,* **tin·kled, tin·kling. 1.** to make or cause to make a series of light, ringing sounds: *Cowbells tinkled in the distance.* **—n. 2.** a tinkling sound.

tin·ny (tin′ē), *adj.,* **tin·ni·er, tin·ni·est. 1.** made of or containing tin. **2.** like tin in appearance, quality, sound, taste, etc. **—tin′ni·ness,** *n.*

tin′ plate′, thin sheet steel or iron coated with tin. Also, **tin′plate′.**

tin-plate (tin′plāt′), *v.,* **tin-plat·ed, tin-plat·ing.** to coat with tin.

tin·sel (tin′səl), *n.* **1.** thin strips or threads of shiny, inexpensive metal or foil, used for decoration. **2.** anything showy or gaudy, made of cheap materials. **3.** any pretense or sham. **—adj. 4.** made of or decorated with tinsel. **5.** showy; gaudy: *a tinsel palace.* **—v.,** **tin·seled** *or* **tin·selled; tin·sel·ing** *or* **tin·sel·ling. 6.** to decorate with tinsel. **7.** to make showy or gaudy.

tin·smith (tin′smith′), *n.* a person who makes or repairs articles of tin or other light metals.

tint (tint), *n.* **1.** a variety of a color; shade: *The rug contained several tints of green.* **2.** any delicate or pale color; tinge: *a tint of red in her cheeks.* **—v. 3.** to color slightly; tinge: *gray hair tinted with blue.*

tin·ware (tin'wâr'), *n.* articles made of tin or tin plate.

ti·ny (tī'nē), *adj.*, **ti·ni·er, ti·ni·est.** very small; minute.

-tion, a suffix used to form nouns meaning 1. action or process: *convention; reception.* 2. result of an action: *reflection; concoction.* 3. state or condition: *affliction; dejection.*

tip¹ (tip), *n.* 1. a slender or pointed end of anything: *the tip of a pencil.* 2. top or highest point: *the tip of the roof.* 3. a small protective cover of metal, leather, rubber, etc., placed over or attached to the end of something: *The rubber tips have come off the chair legs.* —*v.*, **tipped, tip·ping.** 4. to furnish with a tip: *to tip a fishing rod with metal.* 5. to serve as or form the tip of: *A brass ball tipped the flagpole.* 6. to mark, cover, or adorn the tip of: *a cane tipped with silver.* [from Middle English]

tip² (tip), *v.*, **tipped, tip·ping.** 1. to lean; slant; tilt: *The table tipped, causing the glasses to spill over.* 2. to overturn; topple (often fol. by *over*): *The garbage can tipped over with the wind.* 3. to raise or remove (one's) hat), esp. in greeting. —*n.* 4. the act of tipping, or the state of being tipped; tilt. [from the Middle English word *type* "to upset, overturn"]

tip³ (tip), *n.* 1. a small gift of money or something of equal value, in return for some service; gratuity: *Give the newsboy a tip.* 2. a piece of secret or private information: *I gave the reporter a tip for his story.* 3. a useful hint or suggestion: *a book of helpful tips on woodworking.* 4. a light, smart blow; tap. —*v.*, **tipped, tip·ping.** 5. to give a small present or gratuity: *You didn't tip the waiter enough.* 6. to strike or hit lightly: *The batter tipped the ball foul.* 7. **tip off,** *Informal.* to give secret information to, esp. as a warning: *Somebody tipped off the thieves that the police were waiting.* [perhaps from a special use of *tip¹*] —**tip'per,** *n.*

tip·ple (tip'əl), *v.*, **tip·pled, tip·pling.** 1. to drink (intoxicating liquor) often, esp. in small amounts. —*n.* 2. intoxicating liquor. —**tip'pler,** *n.*

tip·sy (tip'sē), *adj.*, **tip·si·er, tip·si·est.** 1. slightly intoxicated or drunk. 2. unsteady, uneven, or crooked. —**tip'si·ly,** *adv.* —**tip'si·ness,** *n.*

tip·toe (tip'tō'), *n.* 1. the tip or end of a toe or the toes. —*adj., adv.* 2. on the tips of the toes, esp. due to eagerness. —*v.*, **tip·toed, tip·toe·ing.** 3. to walk on the tips of the toes; walk softly or stealthily: *I tiptoed in so I wouldn't wake her.*

tip·top (tip'top'), *n.* 1. the highest point; top. —*adj.* 2. at the highest point. 3. *Informal.* of the highest quality; excellent: *to be in tiptop shape.* —*adv.* 4. *Informal.* very well: *The two of them get along tiptop.*

ti·rade (tī'rād), *n.* a long, angry speech or writing, usually denouncing someone or something.

tire¹ (tī³r), *v.*, **tired, tir·ing.** 1. to make or become weary or sleepy; fatigue: *The long trip has tired the children.* 2. to exhaust the patience or interest of; bore: *This kind of talk tires me.* 3. to lose patience; become bored: *I tired of waiting.* [from the Old English word *tyrian* "to weary, be wearied"]

tire² (tī³r), *n.* 1. a ring or band, usually of rubber, either solid or filled with air, that is fitted around the rim of a wheel to provide traction, absorb shock, etc. 2. an iron band or hoop attached to the rim of a wagon wheel to serve as a tread and prevent wear. —*v.*, **tired, tir·ing.** 3. to furnish or equip with a tire or tires. [from the Middle English word *tyre*]

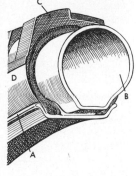

Tire
A, Rim of wheel; B, Inner tube; C, Tread; D, Sidewall

tired (tī³rd), *adj.* exhausted; weary; fatigued.

tire·less (tī³r'lis), *adj.* not becoming tired or exhausted: *a tireless worker for the cause of civil rights.* —**tire'less·ly,** *adv.*

tire·some (tī³r'səm), *adj.* 1. causing fatigue; wearying: *tiresome labor.* 2. uninteresting; boring: *a long, tiresome tale.* 3. annoying; bothersome: *a tiresome habit of playing jokes.* —**tire'some·ness,** *n.*

'tis (tiz), a contraction of *it is.*

tis·sue (tish'oo), *n.* 1. a group of cells in the body of man or in that of a plant or animal that form a particular kind of material with a definite function: *muscle tissue.* 2. any of several kinds of light, soft paper: *cleansing tissue.* 3. a light, woven fabric. 4. an interwoven mass; network; mesh: *a tissue of lies.*

tit¹ (tit), *n.* titmouse or titlark. [from Middle English *tite-* in *titemose* "titmouse." See *titmouse*]

tit² (tit), *n.* a teat. [from Old English *titt*]

Ti·tan (tīt'³n), *n.* 1. (in Greek mythology) one of a race of giant gods, who were overthrown by the gods of Olympus. 2. *(usually l.c.)* any person or thing of great size, strength, importance, etc.; giant: *Dante and Shakespeare are titans of literature.*

Ti·ta·ni·a (ti tā'nē ə), *n.* (in medieval folklore) the queen of the fairies and wife of Oberon.

ti·tan·ic (tī tan'ik), *adj.* of great size, strength, etc.; gigantic; huge: *a titanic military force.*

ti·ta·ni·um (tī tā'nē əm), *n.* a hard, dark-gray or silvery metal that does not corrode easily and is used to harden steel alloys: a chemical element. *Symbol:* Ti

tithe (tīth), *n.* 1. a tenth part of one's income or of the produce of one's land, paid as a tax to support a religious or charitable organization. 2. a tenth part of anything. 3. any small part or portion. —*v.*, **tithed, tith·ing.** 4. to give or pay a tenth of (one's income). 5. to levy a tithe on.

Ti·ti·ca·ca (tē'tē kä'kä), *n.* **Lake,** a lake on the boundary between Peru and Bolivia. 3200 sq. mi.; 12,508 ft. above sea level.

tit·il·late (tit'³lāt'), *v.*, **tit·il·lat·ed, tit·il·lat·ing.** to tickle or excite pleasantly: *to titillate someone's curiosity.* —**tit'il·la'tion,** *n.*

ti·tle (tīt'³l), *n.* 1. the name of a particular thing, such as a book, poem, song, play, organization, etc. 2. a word applied to a person, indicating his rank, occupation, position, etc.: *"Mr.," "Lord Mayor,"* and *"Senator"* are titles. **3.** a championship, in sports or other competition: *the heavyweight title.* **4.** the legal right or claim to possession of property: *to receive title to a house.* —*v.,* **ti·tled, ti·tling. 5.** to give a title to; name; entitle: *to title a book.*

ti·tled (tīt′əld), *adj.* having a title, esp. one of nobility: *The rich heiress married a titled pauper.*

tit·mouse (tit′mous′), *n., pl.* **tit·mice** (tit′mīs′). any of numerous small songbirds, including the chickadee, having soft feathers and a short bill. [from the Middle English word *titemose,* which comes from *tite-,* possibly meaning "small," + *mose* "titmouse." The change in spelling of the last part of the word is by confusion with *mouse*]

tit·ter (tit′ər), *v.* **1.** to laugh in a nervous, uneasy, or self-conscious manner; giggle. —*n.* **2.** a tittering laugh; giggle.

tit·tle (tit′əl), *n.* a very small bit; particle; jot.

tit·tle-tat·tle (tit′əl tat′əl), *n.* **1.** idle talk; gossip; chatter. —*v.,* **tit·tle-tat·tled, tit·tle-tat·tling. 2.** to indulge in idle talk; gossip; chatter.

tit·u·lar (tich′ə lər), *adj.* **1.** of or referring to a title: *the titular role in "Hamlet."* **2.** having a title, esp. of rank. **3.** in title only; having the title, but not the powers or duties, of an office: *The king is only the titular head of the government.*

Ti·tus (tī′təs), *n.* **1.** (in the Bible) a Christian disciple and companion of Paul. **2.** a book of the New Testament, written as a letter from Paul to Titus.

Tl, *Chem.* the symbol for **thallium.**

Tm, *Chem.* the symbol for **thulium.**

TNT, a powerful explosive used in warfare and for blasting. [from *trinitrotoluene,* its chemical name]

to (tōō), *prep.* **1.** so as to reach; as far as: *He came to the house.* **2.** in the direction of; toward: *They went to the east.* **3.** to the extent or limit of: *These trees grow to a hundred feet.* **4.** on or upon: *Apply varnish to the surface.* **5.** until: *I studied from three to six.* **6.** (in telling time) before: *It is ten minutes to two.* **7.** (used to express purpose or intention): *Rush to the rescue.* **8.** (used to express destination or end): *He was sentenced to prison.* **9.** so as to result in: *He failed, to his dismay. I tore the paper to pieces.* **10.** in honor of: *a toast to your health.* **11.** in recognition of: *a monument to their bravery.* **12.** (used to express addition) with; together with: *14 added to 16.* **13.** suitable for; belonging with: *I have the key to the door.* **14.** for the use or possession of; limited to or reserved for: *We have a table to ourselves.* **15.** for the benefit of; into the possession of: *a gift to the university.* **16.** in accordance or agreement with; satisfying the requirements of: *a suit made to measure; an apartment to our liking.* **17.** compared with: *2 is to 10 as 20 is to 100.* **18.** opposed to: *The score is 10 to 6.* **19.** about; concerning: *What did your father say to that?* **20.** as regards; with respect or relation to: *kindness to animals; parallel to the main road.* **21.** with; accompanying or accompanied by: *a ballad*

sung to a guitar. **22.** contained or included in: *12 eggs to a dozen; 60 beats to the minute.* **23.** (used to indicate the indirect object): *Give it to me.* **24.** (used to indicate the infinitive of a verb, and sometimes replacing the infinitive): *Do you want to go? I don't want to.* —*adv.* **25.** into a closed or attached position: *Pull the door to.* **26.** into action or work: *The crew turned to with a will.* **27.** into a state of consciousness: *When he came to, the room was dark.* **28. to and fro,** first in one direction and then in the other; back and forth: *The porch swing moved to and fro.*

toad (tōd), *n.* any of numerous small amphibians resembling frogs but having a dry, bumpy skin and spending most of their lives out of water.

toad·stool (tōd′stōōl′), *n.* **1.** any mushroom with a cap shaped like an umbrella. **2.** a poisonous mushroom, as distinguished from one that is safe to eat.

Toad
(length to 4 in.)

toad·y (tō′dē), *n., pl.* **toad·ies. 1.** a person who flatters others to gain favors from them. —*v.,* **toad·ied, toad·y·ing. 2.** to act like a toady: *He toadies to anyone in authority.*

toast[1] (tōst), *n.* **1.** sliced bread made brown and crisp by heating. —*v.* **2.** to turn into toast; make brown and crisp by heat. **3.** to warm thoroughly; make comfortably warm: *to toast one's feet by the fire.* [from the Old French word *toster* "to toast, scorch," which comes from Latin *torrēre* "to roast, parch"]

toast[2] (tōst), *n.* **1.** a salutation or compliment addressed to a person before taking a drink in his honor. **2.** the act of drinking or proposing a drink in honor of someone. **3.** the person who is honored in this way. **4.** any person, group, event, etc., that is celebrated: *The swimming champions are the toast of the town.* —*v.* **5.** to drink or propose a drink in honor of (someone). [from a special use of *toast*[1], perhaps originally from the custom of putting a bit of toast in a drink, to add zest]

toast·er (tō′stər), *n.* a device for making toast.

toast·mas·ter (tōst′mas′tər), *n.* a person who presides at a banquet, introduces the speakers, and proposes toasts.

to·bac·co (tə bak′ō), *n., pl.* **to·bac·cos. 1.** any of several plants having large, flat leaves that are specially prepared for making cigars, cigarettes, snuff, etc. **2.** the prepared leaves, for smoking, chewing, etc.: *pipe tobacco.* [from the Spanish word *tabaco,* which comes from a word in a West Indian language]

to·bac·co·nist (tə bak′ə nist), *n.* a dealer in tobacco, cigars, and cigarettes.

To·ba·go (tō bā′gō), *n.* an island in the SE West Indies, formerly British: now a part of Trinidad and Tobago; 116 sq. mi.

to·bog·gan (tə bog′ən), *n.* **1.** a long, narrow sled, having a flat bottom, used for coasting. —*v.* **2.** to coast on a toboggan. **3.** to fall or decline rapidly.

to·day (tə dā′), *n.* **1.** the present day: *Today is Monday.* **2.** the present time or age: *the world of today.* —*adv.* **3.** on the present day: *I got up late today.* **4.** in these times; nowadays: *Today more people travel than ever before.*

tod·dle (tod′əl), *v.*, **tod·dled, tod·dling. 1.** to walk with short, unsteady steps, as a child or an old person. —*n.* **2.** the act of toddling. **3.** an unsteady manner of walking. —**tod′dler,** *n.*

tod·dy (tod′ē), *n., pl.* **tod·dies.** a drink made of liquor, hot water, sugar, and sometimes spices.

to-do (tə dōō′), *n., pl.* **to-dos.** *Informal.* bustle; fuss: *There was a great to-do when company arrived.*

toe (tō), *n.* **1.** one of the five fingerlike parts at the end of the foot. **2.** a similar part of an animal's foot. **3.** the part of a shoe, stocking, etc., that covers the toes. **4.** any part of a tool or machine that resembles a toe in shape or position: *the toe of a clamp.* —*v.*, **toed, toe·ing. 5.** to touch or reach with the toes: *to toe the starting line.* **6. on one's toes,** *Informal.* alert; ready; energetic: *The fast game kept us on our toes.*

toe·nail (tō′nāl′), *n.* the hard, horny covering at the end of a toe.

tof·fee (tô′fē), *n.* a British form of **taffy.** Also, **tof′fy.**

to·ga (tō′gə), *n.* a loose outer garment worn in public by citizens of ancient Rome.

to·geth·er (tə geth′ər), *adv.* **1.** in or into one group or mass: *to live together; to pile boxes together.* **2.** in or into the same place: *The two roads come together here.* **3.** in or into contact or association with each other: *to sew the seams together; to bring strangers together.* **4.** taken as a whole or sum: *This painting cost more than the other three together.* **5.** at the same time: *Everybody was shouting together.* **6.** one after the other; in succession: *I waited for months together without a letter from you.* **7.** in or into cooperation, agreement, etc.: *to work together for a cause; to get together on the terms of the contract.* —**to·geth′er·ness,** *n.*

Toga

To·go (tō′gō), *n.* **Republic of,** an independent country in W Africa; 21,830 sq. mi.

togs (togz), *n.pl. Informal.* clothes: *riding togs.*

toil (toil), *n.* **1.** hard work; exhausting labor: *After much toil, we reached the top of the mountain.* —*v.* **2.** to work hard; labor. **3.** to move with difficulty; plod: *to toil along the muddy road.* —**toil′er,** *n.*

toi·let (toi′lit), *n.* **1.** a bathroom fixture for disposal of human wastes, usually consisting of a porcelain bowl having a hinged seat, and a device for flushing with water. **2.** a room containing such a fixture; bathroom. **3.** Also, **toi·lette′.** the act or process of dressing oneself, washing or bathing, arranging the hair, etc.: *to make one's toilet before leaving for school.*

toi′let wa′ter, any of various scented liquids used as after-shave lotion, light perfume, etc.

to·ken (tō′kən), *n.* **1.** something used to represent an act, event, feeling, etc.; a sign or symbol: *to give a* ring as a token of friendship. **2.** a souvenir; keepsake; memento: *The samurai sword is a token of our trip to Japan.* **3.** a metal piece resembling a coin, used in place of money for payment of a fare, a local tax, etc. —*adj.* **4.** of little or no real value; serving only as an indication or sample; minimal: *token compliance with the law.* **5. in token of,** as evidence or a sign of: *I gave her a ring in token of my affection.*

To·ky·o (tō′kē ō′), *n.* a seaport and the capital city of Japan.

told (tōld), *v.* the past tense and past participle of **tell.**

To·le·do (tə lē′dō), *n.* a port city in NW Ohio, on Lake Erie.

tol·er·a·ble (tol′ər ə bəl), *adj.* **1.** able to be tolerated; bearable: *The heat is more tolerable in areas of low humidity.* **2.** fairly good; passable: *He got tolerable marks this term.* —**tol′er·a·bly,** *adv.*

tol·er·ance (tol′ər əns), *n.* **1.** a fair, understanding attitude toward persons whose beliefs, race, nationality, etc., differ from one's own. **2.** the act of tolerating, or the power to tolerate. **3.** the capacity of the body to resist the action of a drug, poison, etc.: *tolerance to alcohol.*

tol·er·ant (tol′ər ənt), *adj.* having or showing tolerance: *a tolerant ruler; a tolerant attitude.* —**tol′er·ant·ly,** *adv.*

tol·er·ate (tol′ə rāt′), *v.*, **tol·er·at·ed, tol·er·at·ing. 1.** to allow without hindrance; permit: *A democratic government tolerates political opposition.* **2.** to put up with; bear; endure: *I can't tolerate that noise.* **3.** to resist the action of (a poison, drug, etc.).

tol·er·a·tion (tol′ə rā′shən), *n.* tolerance, esp. of religious beliefs and practices.

toll¹ (tōl), *v.* **1.** to ring (a bell) with slow, repeated strokes. **2.** to announce (the hour, a death, an alarm) by ringing a bell: *The church bell tolled the hour. The bells tolled the death of the President.* —*n.* **3.** the slow, regular striking of a bell. **4.** the sound so made. [from the Middle English word *tollen*]

toll² (tōl), *n.* **1.** a charge or tax paid for some privilege or service, such as the use of a bridge, tunnel, or highway, a long-distance telephone call, etc. **2.** the amount or extent of loss, damage, injury, etc., caused by an accident or a natural catastrophe: *The earthquake took a toll of 300 dead and injured.* [from an Old English word, which comes from Latin *tolōnēum,* from Greek *telōnion* "tollhouse"]

toll·gate (tōl′gāt′), *n.* a gate where toll is collected for the right to use a bridge, road, etc.

Tol·tec (tōl′tek, tol′tek), *n., pl.* **Tol·tecs** or **Tol·tec.** a member of an advanced Indian civilization of central Mexico that was conquered by the Aztecs.

tom·a·hawk (tom′ə hôk′), *n.* **1.** a light ax formerly used by North American Indians as a weapon and tool. —*v.* **2.** to attack or kill with a tomahawk. [from Algonquian]

Tomahawk

to·ma·to (tə mā′tō, tə mä′tō), *n., pl.* **to·ma·toes. 1.** a climbing vine that bears a round red or yellow, smooth-skinned fruit eaten in salads and as a vegetable. **2.** the fruit of this plant. [from the Spanish word *tomate,* which comes from Nahuatl]

tomb (tōōm), *n.* **1.** a vault or chamber used as a burial place. **2.** a monument or other structure for housing a corpse or commemorating a dead person.

tom·boy (tom′boi′), *n.* a very active young girl who prefers the games, clothes, etc., of boys.

tomb·stone (tōōm′stōn′), *n.* a stone placed on the tomb or grave, usually inscribed with the name, dates of birth and death, etc., of the dead person.

tom·cat (tom′kat′), *n.* a male cat.

tome (tōm), *n.* **1.** a book, esp. a large, heavy one. **2.** one of two or more volumes making up a single work.

tom·fool·er·y (tom′fōō′lə rē), *n., pl.* **tom·fool·er·ies.** foolish behavior; silliness.

to·mor·row (tə môr′ō, tə mor′ō), *n.* **1.** the day following today. **2.** a future day or time: *the new world of tomorrow.* —*adv.* **3.** on the day following today. **4.** at some future time: *We look forward to greater prosperity tomorrow.*

Tomp·kins (tomp′kinz), *n.* **Daniel D.,** 1774–1825, 6th Vice President of the U.S. 1817–1825.

tom·tit (tom′tit′), *n.* any of various small birds, such as the titmouse or the wren.

tom-tom (tom′tom′), *n.* a primitive kind of drum, usually beaten with the hands. [from Hindi *tamtam,* which imitates a drum's sound]

ton (tun), *n.* **1.** any of three units of weight, one equal to 2000 pounds (907.2 kilograms) (**short ton**), one equal to 2240 pounds (1016 kilograms) (**long ton**), or one equal to 2204 pounds (1000 kilograms) (**metric ton**). **2.** Often, **tons.** *Informal.* a great quantity: *I have tons of work to do.*

tone (tōn), *n.* **1.** a sound of a definite pitch, quality, or strength: *the wailing tone of a fire siren.* **2.** a musical sound; note. **3.** a musical interval equivalent to two semitones, such as from A to B or C to D. **4.** a particular way of expressing one's feelings or attitude in speech or writing: *He answered in an annoyed tone.* **5.** a tint or shade of a color: *The room was decorated in several tones of green.* **6.** the state of health of the body, esp. with regard to the firmness and elasticity of the various organs and tissues: *You need more exercise to give your body tone.* **7.** a particular style, characteristic, or the like: *the carefree tone of the 1920's.* **8.** elegance; distinction: *This restaurant has a lot of tone.* —*v.,* **toned, ton·ing. 9.** to give a certain tone to (colors, sounds, etc.). **10.** to improve the tone of (the body, its tissues, organs, etc.). **11. tone down, a.** to make (a color) less vivid; subdue. **b.** to make less intense or violent; moderate: *The newspaper toned down its attack on the mayor.* —**ton′al,** *adj.*

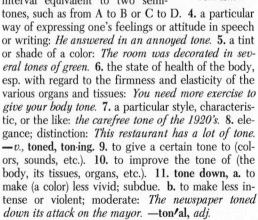

Tom-tom

tongs (tongz, tôngz), *n. (usually used as pl.)* an implement for holding or lifting things, consisting of a pair of arms hinged together, often at one end, with a handle or grip on each arm for bringing the ends together in a jawlike grip: *sugar tongs.*

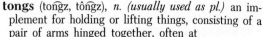

tongue (tung), *n.* **1.** the movable organ in the mouth of man and most vertebrate animals. It is used in eating and tasting and, esp. in man, is important in forming speech sounds. **2.** the tongue

Tongue-and-groove joint

of an animal, used as food: *beef tongue.* **3.** anything resembling a tongue in shape or function: *a tongue of flame.* **4.** a strip or flap of leather under the lacing or fastening of a shoe. **5.** (in carpentry) a projecting strip along the edge of a board, for fitting into a groove in another board. **6.** the clapper of a bell. **7.** the pole of a carriage, wagon, or the like. **8.** a narrow strip of land projecting into the water. **9.** the power of speech: *Have you lost your tongue?* **10.** a manner or style of speech: *a sarcastic tongue.* **11.** a language or dialect: *the English tongue.* —*v.,* **tongued, tongu·ing. 12.** to separate (notes played on a wind instrument) by moving the tongue. **13. hold one's tongue,** to be or keep silent: *I started to say something about her hat, but I held my tongue.* **14. on the tip of one's tongue, a.** on the verge of being said: *A nasty remark was on the tip of my tongue.* **b.** about to be recalled; barely escaping one's memory: *His name is on the tip of my tongue.* **15. slip of the tongue,** an unintentional remark; mistake in speaking: *It was a slip of the tongue to call him Red instead of Ned.* —**tongue′less,** *adj.* —**tongue′like′,** *adj.*

tongue-lash·ing (tung′lash′ing), *n.* a severe scolding or reprimand.

tongue-tied (tung′tīd′), *adj.* **1.** temporarily unable to speak, as the result of surprise, shock, shyness, etc.; struck dumb. **2.** having a defect in speech caused by shortness of the membrane connecting the tongue to the bottom of the mouth.

ton·ic (ton′ik), *n.* **1.** a medicine that builds up one's strength. **2.** anything that refreshes or stimulates: *A brisk walk in the woods is a great tonic for boredom.* **3.** a carbonated quinine water, used esp. as a mixer for highballs. **4.** (in music) the first note of the scale; keynote. —*adj.* **5.** giving or restoring vigor; stimulating: *The sea breezes have a tonic effect.*

to·night (tə nīt′), *n.* **1.** this present night; the night of today: *Tonight will mark the end of our journey.* —*adv.* **2.** on or during this present night: *We'll meet you at seven tonight.* Also, **to-night′.**

ton·nage (tun′ij), *n.* **1.** the amount of cargo that a merchant vessel can carry, measured as one ton for each 100 cubic feet of cargo space. **2.** the total amount of shipping of a country or a port, measured in tons. **3.** a duty on cargo ships based on the weight of the cargo or the carrying capacity, measured in tons. **4.** the total weight of anything, expressed in tons.

ton·sil (ton′səl), *n.* either of a pair of soft, oval masses of tissue at the back of the throat.

ton·sil·lec·to·my (ton′sə lek′tə-mē), *n., pl.* **ton·sil·lec·to·mies.** the surgical operation of removing the tonsils.

ton·sil·li·tis (ton′sə li′tis), *n.* an inflammation of the tonsils.

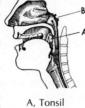

A, Tonsil
B, Adenoids

ton·sure (ton′shər), *n.* 1. the shaving of the head, or a part of it, esp. as a custom of priests or monks. 2. the part of the head, usually the top, or crown, left bare by shaving the hair. —*v.,* **ton·sured, ton·sur·ing.** 3. to shave the head of.

too (tōō), *adv.* 1. in addition; also; besides: *Take along a raincoat, and an umbrella, too.* 2. excessively; to a greater extent than necessary or expected: *These shoes are too large for me.* 3. extremely; very: *You are too kind to do this for me.* 4. indeed; to be sure: *I am too going!*

took (tŏŏk), *v.* the past tense of **take.**

tool (tōōl), *n.* 1. an instrument, esp. one held in the hand, such as a hammer, saw, screwdriver, etc., used in performing some kind of work. 2. the cutting or working part of a machine, such as a lathe, drill, etc. 3. a person who is used by another to further his own purposes: *The labor leader became a tool of the corporations.* 4. anything used to accomplish a definite purpose: *Reading is a necessary tool of learning.* —*v.* 5. to equip with tools or machinery: *to tool a new factory.* 6. to cut, shape, decorate, etc., with a tool: *to tool leather.*

toot (tōōt), *n.* 1. a short sound produced by a whistle, horn, or the like. —*v.* 2. to make such a sound: *Ships toot three times to signal the operator of a drawbridge.* 3. to cause (a horn, whistle, etc.) to sound: *Toot your horn when you're rounding a curve.*

tooth (tōōth), *n., pl.* **teeth** (tēth). 1. any of the hard, white, bony parts growing from the jaws and used to bite and chew. 2. something resembling this, such as one of the points on a saw, comb, or gear. 3. a liking or craving for something: *a sweet tooth.* —*v.,* **toothed** (tōōtht, tōōthd), **tooth·ing** (tōō′thing, tōō′thing). 4. to furnish with teeth: *to tooth a saw.* 5. **by the skin of one's teeth,** by the narrowest margin; barely: *He escaped injury by the skin of his teeth.* 6. **to the teeth,** completely; fully; entirely: *The soldiers were armed to the teeth.*

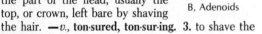

Tooth (Human)
A, Enamel
B, Dentin
C, Pulp
D, Root

tooth·ache (tōōth′āk′), *n.* a pain in or around a tooth.

tooth·brush (tōōth′brush′), *n.* a small brush with a long handle, for cleaning the teeth.

toothed (tōōtht, tōōthd), *adj.* 1. having teeth, esp. of a certain kind or a certain number (often used in combination): *bucktoothed; many-toothed.* 2. having projections or notches like teeth: *a toothed edge.*

tooth·less (tōōth′lis), *adj.* having no teeth.

tooth·paste (tōōth′pāst′), *n.* a paste used for cleaning the teeth, usually applied with a toothbrush.

tooth·pick (tōōth′pik′), *n.* a short, pointed piece of wood or other material, used for removing particles of food from the spaces between the teeth.

tooth·some (tōōth′səm), *adj.* 1. pleasant to the taste; tasty. 2. attractive; pretty.

top[1] (top), *n.* 1. the highest point, part, or surface of anything: *the top of a mountain; the top af a table.* 2. a lid or cover for a box, jar, or other container. 3. highest or greatest degree, amount, etc.: *He shouted at the top of his voice.* 4. highest rank, position, quality, etc.: *He is at the top of his profession.* 5. the part of a plant that grows above ground, esp. of a plant with an edible root: *carrot tops.* —*adj.* 6. of, located at, or forming the top; highest; uppermost: *the top shelf.* 7. highest or greatest in degree, amount, etc.: *the top speed; the top price.* 8. of the highest rank, position, quality, etc.: *the top musicians of the country; the top cut of meat.* —*v.,* **topped, top·ping.** 9. to put a top or topping on: *to top a monument with a statue; to top a cake with strawberries.* 10. to be at the top of: *He topped the class in geography.* 11. to exceed; surpass: *to top the world's speed record.* 12. to remove the top of: *to top a tall tree.* 13. to complete; add a finishing touch to (often fol. by *off*): *to top off a dinner with ice cream.* 14. **on top,** successful; victorious; influential: *It is hard to stay on top in politics.* 15. **on top of, a.** in addition to: *On top of everything else, I've caught a cold.* **b.** immediately after: *Gale winds came on top of the floods.* [from an Old English word meaning "top, summit, tuft of hair"]

top[2] (top), *n.* a child's toy, usually cone-shaped, with a point at the bottom on which it is made to spin. [from Old English]

to·paz (tō′paz), *n.* a clear yellow or brownish mineral used as a gem.

top·coat (top′kōt′), *n.* a lightweight overcoat.

To·pe·ka (tə pē′kə), *n.* the capital city of Kansas, in the NE part.

top·gal·lant (top′gal′ənt), *n.* 1. a mast (**topgal′lant mast′**) fixed to the head of a topmast on a square-rigged ship. 2. a sail (**topgal′lant sail′**) set on a yard of the topgallant mast. —*adj.* 3. of or referring to a topgallant mast.

top′ hat′, a hat, usually black, with a tall, cylindrical crown and a stiff, narrow brim, worn by men esp. on formal occasions.

top·ic (top′ik), *n.* 1. a subject of discussion in speech or writing: *The topic of finances was discussed by the committee.* 2. the title of a talk or discussion: *His topic was "What Is Good Citizenship?"*

top·i·cal (top′i kəl), *adj.* 1. of or concerning matters of current or local interest: *a topical news item.* 2. of, referring to, or arranged by topics: *a topical outline.*

top·knot (top′not′), *n.* 1. a knot or tuft of hair on the top of the head. 2. a tuft or crest of feathers on the head of a bird.

top·mast (top′mast′, top′məst), *n.* the section of a mast just above the lowest section, on a sailing ship.

top·most (top′mōst′), *adj.* highest; uppermost: *the topmost bough of the tree.*

top·notch (top′noch′), *adj. Informal.* of the highest quality; first-rate: *a topnotch salesman.*

to·pog·ra·phy (tə pog′rə fē), *n., pl.* **to·pog·ra·phies.** 1. the physical features of an area, such as mountains, rivers, valleys, etc. 2. the art or science of describing and representing these features on maps and charts. —**to·pog′ra·pher,** *n.* —**top·o·graph·i·cal** (top′ə graf′i-kəl), *adj.* —**top′o·graph′i·cal·ly,** *adv.*

top·ple (top′əl), *v.,* **top·pled, top·pling.** 1. to fall over; tumble: *The wall toppled under blows from the battering ram.* 2. to push over; overturn: *The rioters toppled a number of cars that were parked in the street.* 3. to remove from a position of authority; overthrow: *to topple a government.*

tops (tops), *adj. Informal.* of the highest quality, most pleasing, etc.: *His performance was tops.*

top·sail (top′sāl′, top′səl), *n.* the sail next above the lowest sail on a mast of a sailing ship.

top·soil (top′soil′), *n.* the upper, fertile layer of soil, which contains humus as well as mineral matter.

top·sy-tur·vy (top′sē tûr′vē), *adv.* 1. upside down. 2. in or into a confused or disordered state: *We turned the house topsy-turvy looking for his golf clubs.* —*adj.* 3. turned upside down; inverted. 4. confused or disorderly. —*n.* 5. confusion; disorder.

To·rah (tôr′ə), *n.* (in the Jewish religion) the first section of the Bible containing the first five books of the Old Testament; Pentateuch.

torch (tôrch), *n.* 1. a light, usually carried in the hand, made from a burning piece of wood, often soaked in pitch, resin, oil, or some inflammable substance. 2. such a light used as a symbol of truth, wisdom, loyalty, etc.: *to carry the torch of learning.* 3. any of various devices that produce a hot flame, used for welding, cutting through metal, etc.: *an acetylene torch.* 4. *British.* a flashlight. [from the Old French word *torche,* which comes from Latin *torquēre* "to twist." Torches are often made by twisting some combustible material into a tight roll]

torch·light (tôrch′līt′), *n.* the light of a torch or torches.

tore (tôr), *v.* the past tense of **tear**[2].

tor·e·a·dor (tôr′ē ə dôr′), *n.* a bullfighter.

tor·ment (tôr ment′), *v.* 1. to cause to suffer greatly in body or mind: *The savages tormented their prisoners.* 2. to worry or annoy: *to torment someone with questions.* —*n.* (tôr′ment). 3. great suffering of body or mind; agony: *the torment of poison ivy.* 4. a cause of pain, worry, etc.: *His behavior is a torment to his parents.* —**tor·men′tor,** *n.*

torn (tôrn), *v.* the past participle of **tear**[2].

tor·na·do (tôr nā′dō), *n., pl.* **tor·na·does,** *or* **tor·na·dos.** a violent storm in which the whirling winds form a funnel-shaped cloud and cause great destruction in a narrow area of the storm's path.

To·ron·to (tə ron′tō), *n.* the capital city of Ontario, in SE Canada, on Lake Ontario.

tor·pe·do (tôr pē′dō), *n., pl.* **tor·pe·does.** 1. an underwater missile containing an explosive that travels to its target under its own power. Torpedoes are often used to sink enemy ships. 2. a kind of firework made of gunpowder and gravel wrapped in paper, that explodes when thrown against a hard surface. 3. a broad, flat fish found in the Atlantic Ocean that is capable of stunning its prey with an electric shock. —*v.,* **tor·pe·doed, tor·pe·do·ing.** 4. to attack or destroy (a ship) with a torpedo or torpedoes. 5. to attack or destroy (a person or thing) by any forceful means: *The committee torpedoed the plan for a housing project.*

torpe′do boat′, a small, fast naval craft equipped with tubes for firing torpedoes.

tor·pid (tôr′pid), *adj.* 1. slow in movement or thought; sluggish; dull: *The heat made us torpid.* 2. not moving or feeling; inactive; dormant: *torpid bears hibernating in their dens.* —**tor′pid·ly,** *adv.*

tor·por (tôr′pər), *n.* the state or condition of being torpid; sluggishness; inactivity.

Tor·rance (tôr′əns), *n.* a city in SW California, near Los Angeles.

tor·rent (tôr′ənt), *n.* 1. a stream of water flowing with great rapidity and violence. 2. anything that flows rapidly and in abundance: *a torrent of mail.* 3. a violent downpour of rain.

tor·ren·tial (tô ren′shəl), *adj.* of or like a torrent; rushing; violent: *torrential rains.*

tor·rid (tôr′id), *adj.* very hot and dry; scorching; burning: *a torrid climate.* —**tor′rid·ly,** *adv.*

tor·sion (tôr′shən), *n.* the act of twisting, or the state of being twisted.

tor·so (tôr′sō), *n.* 1. the human body except for the head, arms, and legs; trunk. 2. a sculpture of this part of the body.

tor·til·la (tôr tē′yə), *n.* a round, flat bread made from coarse cornmeal, eaten chiefly in Mexico.

tor·toise (tôr′təs), *n.* 1. a turtle, esp. one that lives on dry land. 2. a very slow person or thing. [from the Middle English word *tortuca,* from medieval Latin *tortuca,* which comes from Greek *tartarouchos* "of Tartarus." The tortoise was thought to be an animal of the lower world]

tor′toise shell′, the horny material that forms the upper shell of certain turtles, used for making combs and ornaments. —**tor′toise-shell′,** *adj.*

tor·tu·ous (tôr′chōō əs), *adj.* 1. full of twists and turns; winding; crooked: *a tortuous trail.* 2. not direct or straightforward; sly; tricky: *a tortuous explanation.* —**tor′tu·ous·ly,** *adv.* —**tor′tu·ous·ness,** *n.*

tor·ture (tôr′chər), *n.* 1. the act of causing severe pain, esp. as a means of punishing a person, or getting a confession or information from him. 2. intense suffering of body or mind; torment; agony. —*v.,* **tor·tured, tor·tur·ing.** 3. to cause to suffer severe pain, anxiety, etc.: *to be tortured by uncertainty.* 4. to subject (someone) to torture. —**tor′tur·er,** *n.* —**tor′tur·ous,** *adj.*

---

act, āble, dâre, ärt; ebb, ēqual; if, īce; hot, ōver, ôrder; oil; bŏŏk; ōōze; out; up, ûrge; ə = *a* as in *alone;* ə as in *button* (but′ən), *fire* (fīr); chief; shoe; thin; ŧħat; zh as in *measure* (mezh′ər). See full key inside cover.

To·ry (tôr′ē), *n., pl.* **To·ries. 1.** a member of a former British political party that favored the authority of the king over Parliament and held conservative political and social views: called the Conservative party since 1832. **2.** *(often l.c.)* a conservative, esp. in politics. **3.** (during the American Revolution) a colonist who remained loyal to the British crown.

toss (tôs), *v.* **1.** to throw, esp. with little force or carelessly: *to toss a paper into the wastebasket.* **2.** to throw from one person to another: *to toss a ball.* **3.** to move with rapid, jerky motions in various directions: *The waves tossed the boat. He tossed in his sleep.* **4.** to raise or jerk upward suddenly: *to toss one's head.* **5.** to throw (a coin) into the air, in order to decide something by the side that faces up when it falls. **6.** to stir or mix lightly: *to toss a salad.* —*n.* **7.** the act of tossing. **8. toss off, a.** to finish very quickly or easily: *He tossed off that book report in 15 minutes.* **b.** to eat or drink (something) rapidly: *He tossed off three glasses of soda in a row.*

tot (tot), *n.* **1.** a small child. **2.** a small amount, esp. of liquor.

to·tal (tōt′²l), *adj.* **1.** being or making up the whole of something; entire: *the total population.* **2.** complete; absolute; utter: *The car was a total wreck.* —*n.* **3.** the whole amount; sum. —*v.,* **to·taled** *or* **to·talled; to·tal·ing** *or* **to·tal·ling. 4.** to add up; find the sum of: *to total the week's receipts.* **5.** to reach a total of: *Our expenses total $625.* —**to′tal·ly,** *adv.*

to·tal·i·tar·i·an (tō tal′i târ′ē ən), *adj.* **1.** of or belonging to a form of government in which political control is concentrated in one group or party, and opposing parties are not recognized or permitted to function. —*n.* **2.** a person who supports or favors such a form of government.

to·tal·i·ty (tō tal′i tē), *n., pl.* **to·tal·i·ties.** the whole of something; entirety: *The plan was rejected in its totality.*

tote (tōt), *v.,* **tot·ed, tot·ing.** *Informal.* **1.** to carry or haul: *Tote your bags out to the car.* **2.** to carry on one's person: *to tote a gun.*

to·tem (tō′təm), *n.* **1.** an animal, plant, or other natural object adopted by a tribe or family as an emblem, and held sacred by the members of the group. **2.** a sculpture, carving, or drawing of such an object.

to′tem pole′, a tall pole carved and painted with figures of totems, erected esp. by Indians of the northwest coast of North America.

Totem pole

tot·ter (tot′ər), *v.* **1.** to walk or move in an unsteady way; stagger: *The old man tottered down the steps.* **2.** to tremble or sway as if about to fall or collapse: *A big boulder tottered on the edge of the cliff.* —*n.* **3.** the act of tottering.

tou·can (tōō′kan, tōō′kän), *n.* any of several brightly colored, fruit-eating, tropical birds having a very large bill. [from a French word, which comes from South American Indian]

Red-billed toucan (length 22 in.)

touch (tuch), *v.* **1.** to put the hand, finger, etc., on or against (something); feel. **2.** to bring (something) into contact with an object or surface: *to touch a match to the powder fuze.* **3.** to be in or come into contact with (something); be or come next to (something): *Our hands touched in greeting. Our land touches the lake.* **4.** to eat, drink, or use in some way: *He does not touch meat.* **5.** to get possession of: *We can't touch the inheritance until the case is settled in court.* **6.** to have an effect on; move: *Their plea for aid touched us deeply.* **7.** to mention or discuss briefly, or in passing (often fol. by *on* or *upon*): *The speaker touched on the question of sales taxes.* **8.** to make a brief stop, esp. at a port (usually fol. by *at*): *The cruise ship will touch at Jamaica.* **9.** to be the equal of; compare with: *There's nobody that can touch him in riding skill.* **10.** *Slang.* to ask or obtain a contribution or loan from: *He touched me for ten dollars.* —*n.* **11.** the sense by which objects are perceived by physical contact, esp. with the fingers. **12.** the quality of an object or material when it is felt, esp. with the fingers; feel: *Velvet has a soft touch.* **13.** the act of touching: *The bubbles burst at a touch.* **14.** communication; correspondence: *Keep in touch with us.* **15.** awareness; understanding: *I'm out of touch with recent events.* **16.** skill with the hands or fingers: *The pianist has a fine touch.* **17.** a light stroke, esp. one that changes or improves something slightly: *The artist put the final touches to his painting.* **18.** a mild attack (of an illness): *a touch of flu.* **19.** a small amount; trace: *a touch of garlic.* **20.** a particular manner of doing things; style: *the touch of a master.* **21.** *Slang.* the act of asking for or obtaining a contribution or loan. **22. touch off, a.** to cause to ignite or explode: *to touch off a charge of dynamite.* **b.** to bring about; cause: *The incident almost touched off a war.* **23. touch up,** to improve or alter (a photograph, painting, etc.) by making slight changes: *They touched up her picture to remove the wrinkles.*

touch·down (tuch′doun′), *n.* a score of six points made in the game of football by carrying or passing the ball safely across the opponent's goal line.

touch·ing (tuch′ing), *adj.* **1.** affecting the emotions deeply; moving: *a touching plea for help.* —*prep.* **2.** with reference to; concerning: *We had a discussion touching our plans for college.* —**touch′ing·ly,** *adv.*

touch·stone (tuch′stōn′), *n.* **1.** a black stone formerly used to test the purity of gold and silver by the color of the streak made on it by rubbing a sample of metal against it. **2.** anything used for testing or measuring the qualities of something.

touch·y (tuch′ē), *adj.,* **touch·i·er, touch·i·est. 1.** easily hurt or offended; sensitive: *She is touchy about her* *short size.* **2.** difficult to handle or manage; delicate: *a touchy operation.* **—touch′i·ness,** *n.*

tough (tuf), *adj.* **1.** strong and durable; not easily broken or cut. **2.** hard to chew: *a tough steak.* **3.** having great endurance; sturdy; hardy: *tough combat veterans.* **4.** not easily influenced or persuaded; stubborn: *He's a tough man to do business with.* **5.** difficult to accomplish or perform; severe: *Being a policeman is a tough job.* **6.** vicious; rough; rowdyish: *a gang of tough youngsters.* **—***n.* **7.** a rough person; rowdy. **—tough′ly,** *adv.* **—tough′ness,** *n.*

tough·en (tuf′ən), *v.* to make or become tough or tougher: *Cycling toughens the leg muscles. The troops toughened under fire.* **—tough′en·er,** *n.*

tou·pee (tōō pā′), *n.* a small wig for covering a bald spot.

tour (tŏŏr), *n.* **1.** a trip undertaken for the purpose of visiting a number of places, usually in a definite order, for sightseeing, inspection, etc.: *a tour of the assembly plant.* **2.** a trip undertaken by entertainers, athletes, etc., often traveling as a group or company, for the purpose of performing in a number of places: *The show went on tour this summer.* **—***v.* **3.** to travel from place to place; go on a tour: *Last year we toured through Canada.* **4.** to travel through; make a tour of: *We are going to tour France next summer.*

tour·ist (tŏŏr′ist), *n.* **1.** a person who makes a tour, esp. for pleasure and sightseeing. **—***adj.* **2.** of or for tourists: *tourist class.*

tour·ma·line (tŏŏr′mə lin, tŏŏr′mə lēn′), *n.* a mineral found in several transparent forms and a variety of colors: used as a gem.

tour·na·ment (tŏŏr′nə mənt), *n.* **1.** a contest in which a number of competitors take part in a series of matches: *a tennis tournament.* **2.** (in medieval times) a contest of skill in which knights were on horseback and armed with lances.

tour·ney (tŏŏr′nē, tûr′nē), *n., pl.* **tour·neys.** **1.** another word for **tournament.** **—***v.,* **tour·neyed, tour·ney·ing. 2.** to take part in a tournament.

tour·ni·quet (tûr′nə kit), *n.* any device for stopping bleeding by pressing on a blood vessel, esp. a bandage that is tightened by twisting with a stick.

tou·sle (tou′zəl), *v.,* **tou·sled, tou·sling. 1.** to disorder; muss up; rumple: *The wind tousled our hair.* **—***n.* **2.** a disordered mass; tangle: *A tousle of hair hung over his face.*

tow[1] (tō), *v.* **1.** to drag or pull (a boat, car, trailer, etc.) by means of a rope, chain, or other device; haul: *A wrecking truck towed the disabled car away.* **—***n.* **2.** the act of towing: *We got a tow from a passing boat.* **3.** the state of being towed: *The pickup truck had a car in tow.* **4.** something that is towed: *The tugboat was pulling a tow of coal barges.* **5.** a rope, chain, or other device used in towing. [from the Old English word *togian* "to pull by force, drag"]

tow[2] (tō), *n.* **1.** the fiber of flax, hemp, or jute after it has been prepared for spinning into yarn or rope. **2.** the shorter, less desirable fibers separated from the

longer ones by combing. [from an Old English word meaning "thread, fiber"]

to·ward (tôrd, tə wôrd′), *prep.* **1.** in the direction of: *We were running toward the school.* **2.** with the purpose of having or getting; for: *We're saving toward new baseball uniforms.* **3.** in the area or vicinity of; near: *They live toward the park.* **4.** turned to; facing: *He had his back toward the entrance.* **5.** shortly before; close to: *We awoke toward sunrise.* **6.** with respect to; regarding: *What is his feeling toward our proposal?* Also, **to·wards′.**

tow·el (tou′əl), *n.* **1.** a piece of cloth or soft paper used for wiping and drying something, esp. the hands, face, or body after washing or bathing. **—***v.,* **tow·eled** *or* **tow·elled; tow·el·ing** *or* **tow·el·ling. 2.** to wipe or dry with a towel. **3. throw in the towel,** *Slang.* to admit defeat; give up: *This assignment is so hard I'm about to throw in the towel.*

tow·er (tou′ər), *n.* **1.** any building or structure that is tall compared to its width and length, either standing alone or forming part of a building: *a water tower; a clock tower.* **2.** any tall structure used as a fort or stronghold: *a prison tower.* **3.** a person or thing that rises high above its surroundings or environment: *My grandmother is a tower of strength.* **—***v.* **4.** to rise high: *White mountain peaks that tower to the sky.* **5.** to rise above other persons or things: *The cathedral towers above the buildings in the square.*

tow·er·ing (tou′ər ing), *adj.* **1.** very high or tall; lofty: *towering pines.* **2.** surpassing others: *a towering genius.* **3.** extreme; intense: *a towering rage.*

Tow′er of Ba′bel. See under **Babel** (def. 1).

tow·head (tō′hed′), *n.* **1.** a head of very blond hair. **2.** a person with such hair. **—tow′head′ed,** *adj.*

town (toun), *n.* **1.** a populated place, usually smaller than a city and larger than a village, having fixed boundaries and a certain amount of self-government. **2.** any city or center of population: *New York is a wonderful town.* **3.** an urban area, as opposed to the countryside: *We'd like to get a house in town.* **4.** the inhabitants of a town; townspeople: *The whole town knew about it.* **5.** the main business or shopping district in a town or city: *I have to go into town to buy some clothes.* **6. go to town,** *Slang.* to do something quickly, efficiently, or successfully: *Now that we have the bricks, we can really go to town on the new chicken coop.* **7. on the town,** *Slang.* out to have a good time; in search of entertainment: *Several of the college boys were out on the town last night.*

town′ cri′er, (in former times) a person employed by a town to make public announcements and proclamations to the people gathered in the streets.

town′ hall′, a hall or building belonging to a town, in which the offices of the town government are located, and often public meetings are held.

town′ meet′ing, **1.** a general meeting of the inhabitants of a town. **2.** (esp. in New England) a meeting of the qualified voters of a town.

town·ship (toun′ship), *n.* **1.** a division of a county having some powers of government. **2.** (in surveys of public land) a district approximately six miles square, divided into 36 sections of approximately one square mile each.

towns·man (tounz′mən), *n., pl.* **towns·men. 1.** a native or inhabitant of a town. **2.** a native or inhabitant of one's own town; fellow citizen.

towns·peo·ple (tounz′pē′pəl), *n.pl.* **1.** the inhabitants of a town. **2.** people who were brought up in a town or city, rather than in the country. Also, **towns·folk** (tounz′fōk′).

tox·ic (tok′sik), *adj.* **1.** of, concerning, or caused by poisoning: *a toxic condition.* **2.** having the effect of a poison; poisonous.

tox·in (tok′sin), *n.* a poisonous substance produced by a plant, animal, or microorganism.

toy (toi), *n.* **1.** an object used for play or amusement; plaything. **2.** something small or of little value; trifle. **3.** an animal of a small breed or variety: *The winning poodle at the dog show was a toy. —adj.* **4.** made or designed for use as a toy: *a toy train.* **5.** of small size: *a toy poodle. —v.* **6.** to play or trifle (often fol. by *with*): *Stop toying with your food!*

trace[1] (trās), *n.* **1.** a mark, sign, or other indication of a person or thing that has existed or passed by: *The ship sank without a trace.* **2.** the track left by a person, animal, or object in passing; trail. **3.** a very small amount: *The drink contained traces of poison. —v.,* **traced, trac·ing. 4.** to follow the track or trail of: *to trace a lost package.* **5.** to follow the course, development, or history of: *to trace the beginnings of the atomic age.* **6.** to make a plan, diagram, or map of: *to trace the location of a mine.* **7.** to make a copy of, by drawing on a sheet of transparent paper placed on top of the original. [from the Old French word *tracier* "to leave or follow a trace"] **—trace′a·ble,** *adj.* **—trac′er,** *n.*

trace[2] (trās), *n.* either of the two straps, chains, or the like, by which a carriage, wagon, sled, etc., is pulled by a draft animal. [from the Old French word *trais,* plural of *trait* "a strap for harness"]

trac·er·y (trā′sə rē), *n., pl.* **trac·er·ies.** ornamental work made in a design of delicate interlacing lines, threads, etc., as in stonework or embroidery.

tra·che·a (trā′kē ə), *n., pl.* **tra·che·ae** (trā′kē ē′). the scientific term for **windpipe.**

Window tracery

trac·ing (trā′sing), *n.* **1.** the act of a person or thing that traces. **2.** something made by tracing, esp. a copy of a drawing, sketch, or the like, made by following the lines of the original on a sheet of transparent paper placed on top of it.

track (trak), *n.* **1.** a rail, or a pair of parallel rails fastened together with crossties, used as a support and guide for the wheels of trains. **2.** any similar structure along which a conveyance or a movable object, such as a door, drawer, etc., may roll or slide. **3.** either or both of the endless metal treads of a tank,

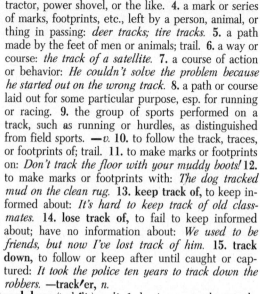

tractor, power shovel, or the like. **4.** a mark or series of marks, footprints, etc., left by a person, animal, or thing in passing: *deer tracks; tire tracks.* **5.** a path made by the feet of men or animals; trail. **6.** a way or course: *the track of a satellite.* **7.** a course of action or behavior: *He couldn't solve the problem because he started out on the wrong track.* **8.** a path or course laid out for some particular purpose, esp. for running or racing. **9.** the group of sports performed on a track, such as running or hurdles, as distinguished from field sports. *—v.* **10.** to follow the track, traces, or footprints of; trail. **11.** to make marks or footprints on: *Don't track the floor with your muddy boots!* **12.** to make marks or footprints with: *The dog tracked mud on the clean rug.* **13. keep track of,** to keep informed about: *It's hard to keep track of old classmates.* **14. lose track of,** to fail to keep informed about; have no information about: *We used to be friends, but now I've lost track of him.* **15. track down,** to follow or keep after until caught or captured: *It took the police ten years to track down the robbers.* **—track′er,** *n.*

track·less (trak′lis), *adj.* **1.** having no track or path: *a trackless desert.* **2.** not running on tracks: *a trackless trolley.*

tract[1] (trakt), *n.* **1.** a stretch of land, water, etc.; region; expanse. **2.** a definite region of the body, esp. a group of related parts or organs: *the digestive tract.* [from the Latin word *tractus* "stretch (of space or time)"]

tract[2] (trakt), *n.* a pamphlet or leaflet for general circulation, usually on a religious or political subject. [from the Latin word *tractātus* "treatise"]

trac·ta·ble (trak′tə bəl), *adj.* **1.** easy to manage, control, or deal with: *a tractable client.* **2.** easy to work with, shape, etc.; malleable: *a tractable metal.*

trac·tion (trak′shən), *n.* **1.** the friction between a moving object and the surface over which it travels: *Throwing sand on icy roads improves the traction of automobile tires.* **2.** the act of pulling or dragging something. **3.** the intentional pulling of a muscle, limb, etc., for a prolonged period to correct an abnormality, insure proper healing, etc.

trac·tor (trak′tər), *n.* **1.** a powerful motor vehicle with large, heavy treads or metal tracks, used for pulling farm machinery or drawing heavy loads. **2.** a short motor vehicle with a powerful engine and a cab for the driver, used for pulling a trailer.

trade (trād), *n.* **1.** the act or process of buying, selling, or exchanging goods or services; commerce. **2.** a purchase, sale, or exchange. **3.** an occupation, esp. one of skilled manual or mechanical work: *building trades.* **4.** the customers of a store or business: *an antique shop serving a select trade.* **5. trades,** the trade winds. *—v.,* **trad·ed, trad·ing. 6.** to buy and sell; carry on trade: *It is unlawful to trade with enemy nations.* **7.** to exchange: *I traded a pocketknife for a compass.* **8.** to be a customer; shop: *We don't trade at the very expensive shops.*

trade·mark (trād′märk′), *n.* a name or symbol used by a manufacturer or merchant for his own goods or services, to distinguish them from those made or sold by others. A trademark is usually registered, and its use is forbidden by law to anyone except its owner.

trad·er (trā′dər), *n.* **1.** a person who trades; merchant or businessman. **2.** a ship used in trade.

trades·man (trādz′mən), *n., pl.* **trades·men. 1.** a man engaged in trade. **2.** a storekeeper.

trade′ un′ion, 1. a union of workers in a particular craft or trade. **2.** any labor union.

trade′ winds′, winds that blow regularly toward the equator in tropical regions, coming from the northeast in the Northern Hemisphere, and from the southeast in the Southern Hemisphere. Also, **trades.**

trad′ing post′, a store operated by a trader or trading company, esp. in a frontier region, where goods are obtained by bartering local products.

trad′ing stamp′, one of a number of stamps given to a customer at the time of a purchase and which may be saved to exchange for various articles.

tra·di·tion (trə dish′ən), *n.* beliefs, legends, customs, etc., handed down from generation to generation, esp. by word of mouth.

tra·di·tion·al (trə dish′ə nəl), *adj.* of, according to, or handed down by tradition: *Giving of gifts at Christmas is traditional.* **—tra·di′tion·al·ly,** *adv.*

traf·fic (traf′ik), *n.* **1.** the movement of vehicles, ships, airplanes, pedestrians, etc., within a place or between one place and another. **2.** the quantity, intensity, or rate of such movement: *Air traffic is heavy at holiday seasons.* **3.** the transportation of goods for the purpose of trade. **4.** trade or dealing in a particular class of goods or services: *traffic in narcotics.* **5.** dealings or relations: *Avoid traffic with criminal elements.* **6.** the amount of freight or passengers transported. **—v., traf·ficked, traf·fick·ing. 7.** to carry on trade or commercial dealings. **8.** to trade or deal in a particular class of goods or services: *to traffic in arms for guerrilla forces.* **—traf′fick·er,** *n.*

traf′fic cir′cle, a circular arrangement of roadways placed at the intersection of two or more roads, around which traffic moves in a counterclockwise direction in passing from one road to another.

traf′fic light′, a signal light or set of lights that controls the flow of traffic along a street or highway.

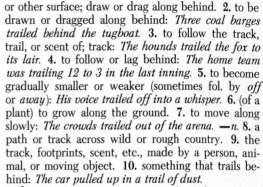
Traffic circle

tra·ge·di·an (trə jē′dē ən), *n.* **1.** an actor in tragedies. **2.** a writer of tragedies. Also, *esp. referring to a woman,* **tra·ge·di·enne** (trə jē′dē en′) for def. 1.

trag·e·dy (traj′i dē), *n., pl.* **trag·e·dies. 1.** a serious play with an unhappy ending. **2.** an unfortunate or dreadful happening; disaster: *The holiday outing ended in tragedy when the bus collided with a truck.*

trag·ic (traj′ik), *adj.* **1.** of, concerning, or engaged in the writing, production, or performance of tragedy: *a tragic poet; a tragic actor.* **2.** unfortunate; dreadful; disastrous: *a tragic accident.* **—trag′i·cal·ly,** *adv.*

trail (trāl), *v.* **1.** to drag or let drag along the ground

or other surface; draw or drag along behind. **2.** to be drawn or dragged along behind: *Three coal barges trailed behind the tugboat.* **3.** to follow the track, trail, or scent of; track: *The hounds trailed the fox to its lair.* **4.** to follow or lag behind: *The home team was trailing 12 to 3 in the last inning.* **5.** to become gradually smaller or weaker (sometimes fol. by *off* or *away*): *His voice trailed off into a whisper.* **6.** (of a plant) to grow along the ground. **7.** to move along slowly: *The crowds trailed out of the arena.* **—n. 8.** a path or track across wild or rough country. **9.** the track, footprints, scent, etc., made by a person, animal, or moving object. **10.** something that trails behind: *The car pulled up in a trail of dust.*

trail·er (trā′lər), *n.* **1.** a person or thing that trails. **2.** a large vehicle drawn by another vehicle, used esp. for hauling freight. **3.** a vehicle equipped for use as a movable dwelling or office, drawn by another vehicle. **4.** a vine that grows along the ground.

train (trān), *n.* **1.** a group of two or more cars connected together and running on rails, drawn by a locomotive, or powered by electricity. **2.** a line or file of persons, vehicles, animals, etc., traveling together: *a wagon train.* **3.** an elongated part of a gown or robe that trails along the ground. **4.** a succession or series of events, ideas, etc. **5.** a group of followers or attendants; retinue. **—v. 6.** to develop or form the habits, thought, behavior, etc., of; rear: *to train an unruly boy.* **7.** to instruct (a person) or acquire skill in some art, craft, or profession: *Medical schools train physicians and surgeons. He is training to be an engineer.* **8.** to instruct (an animal) to perform certain tasks or tricks: *Jack has trained his dog to stand up and beg.* **9.** to make or become fit by exercise, diet, practice, etc., for an athletic performance or competition: *The boxers are training for their championship bout.* **10.** to bring to bear; aim; point: *to train a telescope on a star.*

train·ee (trā nē′), *n.* **1.** a person receiving training for a particular job; learner; apprentice. **2.** an enlisted man or woman undergoing military training.

train·er (trā′nər), *n.* **1.** a person who trains. **2.** a person who trains athletes for performance or competition. **3.** a person who trains animals for performing certain tasks or tricks, or for animal shows.

train·ing (trā′ning), *n.* **1.** a course of instruction or discipline: *teacher training; military training.* **2.** the condition of a person or animal who has been trained: *He was out of training and lost the race.*

traipse (trāps), *v.,* **traipsed, traips·ing.** *Informal.* to walk or go about aimlessly or idly: *We traipsed all over town looking for them.*

trait (trāt), *n.* a special quality or characteristic: *Patience and originality are traits that lead to success.*

trai·tor (trā′tər), *n.* **1.** a person who betrays a friend, a cause, or a trust or duty. **2.** a person who betrays his country; one who commits treason. Also, *referring to a woman,* **trai·tress** (trā′tris).

trai·tor·ous (trā′tər əs), *adj.* **1.** of or like a traitor;

treacherous. **2.** of the nature of treason; treasonable. —**trai′tor·ous·ly,** *adv.*

tra·jec·to·ry (trə jek′tə rē), *n., pl.* **tra·jec·to·ries.** the curved path of a bullet, rocket, or other flying object.

tram (tram), *n.* **1.** *British.* a streetcar; trolley. **2.** a truck or car running on rails, used for carrying loads in a mine.

tram·mel (tram′əl), *n.* **1.** a fetter or shackle, esp. one used in training a horse to pace. **2.** Usually, **trammels.** anything that hinders freedom of action: *the trammels of ignorance.* —*v.,* **tram·meled** *or* **trammelled; tram·mel·ing** *or* **tram·mel·ling. 3.** to hinder; hamper; restrain: *The committee was trammeled by outmoded regulations.*

tramp (tramp), *v.* **1.** to walk with heavy, noisy steps: *He tramped up the stairs.* **2.** to step heavily; trample (usually fol. by *on* or *upon*): *to tramp on someone's toes.* **3.** to travel on foot; hike; march. —*n.* **4.** the act or sound of tramping. **5.** a long walk; hike: *to go for a tramp through the woods.* **6.** a person who travels about on foot, begging his living or working at occasional jobs; vagabond; vagrant. **7.** a cargo ship that does not have a regular run, but takes on and discharges cargo wherever the shippers desire.

tram·ple (tram′pəl), *v.,* **tram·pled, tram·pling. 1.** to step heavily and noisily; stamp. **2.** to step heavily upon; crush: *to trample a flower; to trample a person's feelings.* —*n.* **3.** the act or sound of trampling.

tram·po·line (tram′pə lēn′), *n.* a sheet, usually of heavy canvas, attached by cords or springs to a frame, used as a springboard in tumbling. [from the Italian word *trampolino* "springboard"]

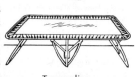

trance (trans), *n.* **1.** a dreamlike state between sleeping and waking, brought on by illness, shock, hypnosis, etc. **2.** a dazed or bewildered condition. **3.** a condition of being completely absorbed in thought.

Trampoline

tran·quil (traṅg′kwil), *adj.* calm; quiet; peaceful: *a tranquil spot; a tranquil life.* —**tran′quil·ly,** *adv.*

tran·quil·iz·er (traṅg′kwə lī′zər), *n.* any of various drugs that have a calming effect without producing sleepiness.

tran·quil·li·ty (traṅg kwil′i tē), *n.* the quality or state of being tranquil; calmness; peacefulness; quiet. Also, **tran·quil′i·ty.**

trans-, a prefix meaning **1.** across or over: *transatlantic; transport.* **2.** changing thoroughly: *transform; transfigure.*

trans·act (tran sakt′, tran zakt′), *v.* to carry on or conduct (business, negotiations, etc.) to conclusion or completion: *to transact a sale of property.*

trans·ac·tion (tran sak′shən, tran zak′shən), *n.* **1.** the act or process of transacting. **2.** something transacted; a business deal.

trans·at·lan·tic (trans′ət lan′tik, tranz′-), *adj.* **1.** crossing the Atlantic Ocean: *a transatlantic liner; a*

transatlantic cable. **2.** located on the other side of the Atlantic Ocean: *transatlantic missile bases.*

tran·scend (tran send′), *v.* **1.** to rise above or go beyond the limits of; exceed: *a mystery that transcends understanding.* **2.** to be greater than or superior to; surpass; excel: *a sculpture that transcends all others in beauty.*

tran·scend·ent (tran sen′dənt), *adj.* going beyond the usual or ordinary; extraordinary: *a light of transcendent brilliance.* Also, **tran·scen·den·tal** (tran′sen den′t³l), *adj.* —**tran·scend′ence,** *n.* —**tran·scend′ent·ly,** *adv.*

trans·con·ti·nen·tal (trans′kon t³nen′t³l), *adj.* **1.** crossing a continent: *a transcontinental railroad.* **2.** located on the other side of a continent.

tran·scribe (tran skrīb′), *v.,* **tran·scribed, tran·scrib·ing. 1.** to make a written or typewritten copy of (shorthand notes, a tape recording, etc.). **2.** (in radio) to make a recording of (a program, announcement, etc.) for later use in broadcasting.

tran·script (tran′skript), *n.* **1.** a written, typewritten, or printed copy; something transcribed. **2.** an exact copy or reproduction of an official document.

tran·scrip·tion (tran skrip′shən), *n.* **1.** the act or process of transcribing. **2.** something transcribed; transcript; copy. **3.** (in radio) a recording of a program, announcement, etc., for later broadcasting.

tran·sept (tran′sept), *n.* **1.** (in churches built in the shape of a cross) the shorter of the two sections that make up the cross. **2.** either of the two arms of this section that extend outward at the sides of the nave.

trans·fer (trans fûr′, trans′fər), *v.,* **trans·ferred, trans·fer·ring. 1.** to move, carry, hand over, change, etc., from one person, place, etc., to another: *to transfer a cargo from ship to truck.* **2.** to imprint or impress (a drawing, design, pattern, etc.) from one surface to another, esp. by use of specially treated paper. **3.** to change from one bus, streetcar, train, etc., to another. —*n.* (trans′fər). **4.** the act or process of transferring. **5.** the state of being transferred. **6.** a means or system of transferring or conveying: *The trucking company operates an interstate transfer.* **7.** a ticket issued to a passenger, enabling him to continue his trip on another bus, streetcar, train, etc. **8.** a drawing, design, pattern, etc., that can be transferred to another surface by heat, pressure, or other means. **9.** a person or thing that transfers or is transferred. **10.** a point or place for transferring.

trans·fer·a·ble (trans fûr′ə bəl), *adj.* capable of being transferred, esp. to another person's ownership: *Your library card is not transferable.*

trans·fer·ence (trans fûr′əns), *n.* **1.** the act or process of transferring. **2.** the fact of being transferred.

trans·fig·u·ra·tion (trans′fig yə rā′shən), *n.* **1.** the act or result of transfiguring; a change in form or appearance. **2. the Transfiguration, a.** (in the Bible) the supernatural change in the appearance of Jesus on the mountain before three of the apostles. **b.** the church festival commemorating this.

trans·fig·ure (trans fig′yər), *v.,* **trans·fig·ured, trans·fig·ur·ing. 1.** to change in outward form or appearance; transform: *Her new clothes transfigured her into a lady of fashion.* **2.** to change so as to glorify or exalt; idealize: *His ambitions were transfigured by the call to high office.*

trans·fix (trans fiks′), *v.*, **trans·fixed** *or* **trans·fixt; trans·fix·ing. 1.** to pierce through; impale: *a roast suckling pig transfixed on a skewer.* **2.** to make or hold motionless with amazement, terror, etc.: *The crowd was transfixed by the man on a tightrope.*

trans·form (trans fôrm′), *v.* **1.** to change in form, appearance, or structure: *Heat transforms water into steam.* **2.** to change in condition, nature, or character: *The barn was transformed into a summer theater.*

trans·for·ma·tion (trans′fər mā′shən), *n.* **1.** the act or process of transforming. **2.** the state of being transformed. **3.** a change in form, appearance, nature, character, etc. **4.** a wig for a woman.

trans·form·er (trans fôr′mər), *n.* **1.** a person or thing that transforms. **2.** a device for altering the voltage in an electric circuit.

trans·fuse (trans fyōōz′), *v.*, **trans·fused, trans·fus·ing. 1.** to transfer or pass from one person or thing to another; transmit; impart: *He transfused his enthusiasm to his followers.* **2.** to transfer (blood) from the body of a person or animal to that of another. —**trans·fu′sion,** *n.*

trans·gress (trans gres′), *v.* **1.** to break or violate a law, rule, command, etc.; offend; sin. **2.** to pass over or go beyond (a limit or bound): *His behavior transgressed the bounds of decency.* —**trans·gres′sor,** *n.*

trans·gres·sion (trans gresh′ən), *n.* the act of transgressing; violation of a law, rule, etc.; offense; sin.

tran·sient (tran′shənt), *adj.* **1.** not lasting or permanent; temporary: *the transient vigor of youth.* **2.** staying only a short time: *a transient guest.* —*n.* **3.** a person or thing that remains only a short time, esp. a temporary guest at a hotel. [from the Latin word *transiēns,* which comes from *transīre* "to pass by, go through or across"] —**tran′sience, tran′sien·cy,** *n.* —**tran′sient·ly,** *adv.*

tran·sis·tor (tran zis′tər), *n.* a small electronic device used to amplify signals and to control the flow of current in radios, computers, television sets, etc.

trans·it (tran′sit), *n.* **1.** a passing across or through, or from one place to another: *The ship made the transit of the Panama Canal.* **2.** conveyance or transportation of persons or goods from one place to another: *The mail is sorted in transit.* **3.** a system of public transportation, including subways, buses, etc., used esp. in large cities. **4.** an instrument used by surveyors for measuring angles.

tran·si·tion (tran zish′ən), *n.* a passing from one place, state, subject, etc., to another; change: *the transition from war to peace.* —**tran·si′tion·al,** *adj.*

tran·si·tive (tran′si tiv), *adj.* **1.** describing a verb that takes a direct object. In the sentence *I need a hammer, need* is a transitive verb. —*n.* **2.** a transitive verb or verb form. See also **intransitive.** —**tran′si·tive·ly,** *adv.*

tran·si·to·ry (tran′si tôr′ē), *adj.* lasting only a short time; brief: *transitory fame.* —**tran′si·to′ri·ness,** *n.*

trans·late (trans lāt′, trans′lāt), *v.*, **trans·lat·ed, trans·lat·ing. 1.** to express (something spoken or written) in another language: *to translate a letter from French into English.* **2.** to change the form, condition, place, or character of: *to translate wishes into deeds.* **3.** to explain in simpler terms; interpret: *The book translates evolution into everyday language.*

trans·la·tion (trans lā′shən), *n.* **1.** the act or process of translating. **2.** something translated: *an English translation of Homer's "Iliad."* **3.** a change of form, condition, place, or character: *translation of thought into action.*

trans·la·tor (trans lā′tər, trans′lā tər), *n.* a person who translates from one language into another.

trans·lu·cent (trans lōō′sənt), *adj.* permitting light to pass through, but not allowing objects on the other side to be seen clearly: *Frosted window glass is translucent but not transparent.* —**trans·lu′cence,** *n.* —**trans·lu′cent·ly,** *adv.*

trans·mi·gra·tion (trans′mī grā′shən), *n.* **1.** the act of moving from one place or country to another in order to settle there; migration. **2.** (in some religions) the passing of a soul at death into another body or another form of life.

trans·mis·sion (trans mish′ən), *n.* **1.** the act or process of transmitting. **2.** something transmitted. **3.** transfer of force between machines or mechanisms. **4.** an enclosed unit of gears or the like for this purpose, as in an automobile. **5.** the broadcasting of radio waves from a transmitter.

trans·mit (trans mit′), *v.*, **trans·mit·ted, trans·mit·ting. 1.** to send or convey from one person, place, or thing to another: *to transmit a message; to transmit a disease.* **2.** to pass on by heredity: *Tall parents usually transmit tallness to their children.* **3.** to pass or cause to pass through: *Glass transmits light.* **4.** to send out (radio or television signals).

trans·mit·ter (trans mit′ər), *n.* **1.** a person or thing that transmits. **2.** (in radio and television) a device for sending electromagnetic waves. **3.** the part of a telephone or telegraph system that converts sound waves into electrical signals.

trans·mute (trans myōōt′), *v.*, **trans·mut·ed, trans·mut·ing.** to change from one form, condition, or substance into another; transform: *The alchemists believed that they could transmute lead into gold.* —**trans·mu·ta·tion** (trans′myōō tā′shən), *n.*

tran·som (tran′səm), *n.* **1.** a crosspiece separating a door or window from a window above it. **2.** a small window above a door or other window.

trans·par·en·cy (trans pâr′ən sē), *n., pl.* for def. 2 **trans·par·en·cies. 1.** the quality or state of being transparent. **2.** a picture, design, or the like, on glass, film, or some translucent material, that may be viewed by light shining through it.

trans·par·ent (trans pâr′ənt), *adj.* **1.** permitting light to pass through, so that objects on the other side can be seen clearly. **2.** so sheer as to permit light to pass through: *a transparent fabric.* **3.** easily recognized or detected; obvious: *a transparent trick.* —**trans·par′ent·ly**, *adv.*

tran·spire (tran spī°r′), *v.,* **tran·spired, tran·spir·ing. 1.** to give off or pass off, as vapor, moisture, odor, etc., through a porous surface. **2.** to be revealed or become known: *It transpired that his best friend had betrayed him.* **3.** *Informal.* to take place; occur; happen. —**tran·spi·ra·tion** (tran′spə ra′shən), *n.* —**Usage.** Careful speakers and writers of English do not use *transpire* to mean "happen" or "occur": *Tell me what happened* (not *what transpired*) *at the meeting this afternoon.*

trans·plant (trans plant′), *v.* **1.** to remove (a plant) from one place and plant in another. **2.** (in surgery) to transfer (an organ or other bodily part) from one part of the body to another or from one person or animal to another. —*n.* (trans′plant′). **3.** the act or process of transplanting: *The surgical team performed a heart transplant.* **4.** a person or thing that is transplanted: *Some roses grow well as transplants.* —**trans′plan·ta′tion**, *n.*

trans·port (trans pôrt′), *v.* **1.** to carry, move, or convey from one place to another. **2.** to carry away by strong emotion; move deeply; thrill: *The crowd was transported with delight.* —*n.* (trans′pôrt′). **3.** the act or process of transporting or conveying; transportation: *Ships are used for transport of iron ore.* **4.** a vehicle or means of transporting, such as a truck, bus, airplane, ship, etc. **5.** a strong emotion; thrill: *a transport of joy.* —**trans·port′er**, *n.*

trans·por·ta·tion (trans′pər tā′shən), *n.* **1.** the act or process of transporting. **2.** a means of transport; conveyance: *One truck is our only transportation.* **3.** the business or activity of transporting passengers and freight. **4.** the cost or price of transport; fare.

trans·pose (trans pōz′), *v.,* **trans·posed, trans·pos·ing. 1.** to change the order or position of; interchange: *Be careful not to transpose the "a" and "u" of the word "gauge."* **2.** to put (a piece of music) into a different key. —**trans·po·si·tion** (trans′pə zish′-ən), *n.*

trans·verse (trans vûrs′, trans′vûrs), *adj.* **1.** lying or reaching across; placed crosswise: *transverse timbers.* —*n.* **2.** something, as a road, that is transverse.

trap (trap), *n.* **1.** a device for catching animals, such as a spring that snaps shut when stepped on, a pitfall, snare, etc. **2.** any device or trick for catching a person unawares: *The police set a trap for the thieves.* **3.** a curve or a U-shaped section in a pipe in which liquid remains and forms a seal for preventing the passage or escape of air or gases through the pipe from behind or below. **4. traps,** the drums and certain other percussion instruments of a jazz or dance band. **5.** a light, two-wheeled carriage. **6.** a trap door. —*v.,* **trapped, trap·ping. 7.** to catch in a trap or

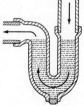

Trap (def. 3)

snare: *to trap beavers for their fur.* **8.** to catch unawares by a trick or device: *The thief was trapped by means of a burglar alarm.* **9.** to set traps to catch wild animals. **10.** to stop or hold back by a trap or seal: *to trap water in a canal lock.*

trap′ door′, a door set in the surface of a floor, ceiling, roof, etc.

tra·peze (tra pēz′), *n.* a short crossbar attached to the ends of two swinging ropes, used for performing acrobatic stunts and gymnastics.

Trapezoid

trap·e·zoid (trap′i zoid′), *n.* a four-sided figure having two sides parallel and two sides not parallel.

trap·per (trap′ər), *n.* a person whose occupation is the trapping of wild animals, esp. for their furs.

trap·pings (trap′ingz), *n. (used as pl.)* articles of equipment or dress, esp. of an elaborate or ornamental kind: *The king wore all the trappings of royalty.*

trash (trash), *n.* **1.** anything worthless or useless; rubbish; refuse. **2.** foolish or worthless talk or writing; nonsense. **3.** worthless, disreputable persons.

trash·y (trash′ē), *adj.,* **trash·i·er, trash·i·est.** consisting of or like trash; worthless; useless. —**trash′i·ness**, *n.*

tra·vail (trə vāl′, trav′āl), *n.* **1.** difficult or burdensome work; toil. **2.** severe mental or physical suffering; anguish. **3.** the pains of childbirth; labor. —*v.* **4.** to suffer the pains of childbirth; be in labor. **5.** to work hard; toil.

trav·el (trav′əl), *v.,* **trav·eled** *or* **trav·elled; trav·el·ing** *or* **trav·el·ling. 1.** to go from one place to another; journey; take a trip. **2.** to go from place to place for the purpose of selling or representing a business firm, government, etc. **3.** to pass through or over; traverse: *I traveled a hundred miles on horseback.* **4.** to move along a fixed path or course: *The sliding doors travel on a track.* —*n.* **5.** the act or process of traveling; journeying. **6. travels,** journeys; wanderings: *We're back from our travels in South America.* **7.** the movement of persons or conveyances along a road or route; traffic: *There is always much travel on a holiday weekend.* [from the Old French word *travaillier* "to labor, torment," which comes from Latin *trepālium* "torture chamber." Before modern times, most travel was done on foot, very laboriously]

trav·eled (trav′əld), *adj.* **1.** having traveled much; experienced in travel: *a traveled diplomat.* **2.** used by travelers: *a well-traveled road.*

trav·el·er (trav′ə lər), *n.* **1.** a person who travels, esp. one who travels much. **2.** a person who travels as a salesman or business representative.

trav·e·logue (trav′ə lôg′, trav′ə log′), *n.* a motion picture or an illustrated lecture describing travels.

tra·verse (trə vûrs′), *v.,* **tra·versed, tra·vers·ing. 1.** to pass or move over, along, or through: *to traverse the sea by ship.* **2.** to extend or reach across or over; cross: *An old bridge traverses the river.* —*n.* (trav′-ərs). **3.** the act of passing across, over, or through: *the traverse of the plains by covered wagon.* **4.** the route or distance traveled in going or moving across or through. **5.** a part or piece placed or extending across; crosspiece; crossbar. —*adj.* (trav′ərs). **6.** lying, extending, or passing across; transverse.

trav·es·ty (trav′i stē), *n., pl.* **trav·es·ties. 1.** an imitation of an artistic or literary work, done in a ludicrous or mocking manner; burlesque. **2.** any ridiculous or shameful imitation: *The trial was a travesty of justice.* —*v.,* **trav·es·tied, trav·es·ty·ing. 3.** to imitate in a mocking manner; burlesque.

trawl (trôl), *n.* **1.** a large cone-shaped fishing net that is dragged along the sea bottom by a boat, for catching fish that stay in deep waters. **2.** a long fishing line held up by buoys or floats, from which are suspended a number of short lines with baited hooks attached. —*v.* **3.** to fish or catch with a trawl.

trawl·er (trô′lər), *n.* a boat used in fishing with a trawl.

tray (trā), *n.* **1.** a flat, shallow receptacle, usually made of wood, metal, etc., for holding, carrying, serving, or displaying various things. **2.** a removable or hinged box or compartment, often forming a part of the inside of a cabinet, chest, trunk, etc.: *a tool chest with trays for screws and bolts.*

treach·er·ous (trech′ər əs), *adj.* **1.** likely to betray; disloyal; untrustworthy: *A treacherous guide led them into an ambush.* **2.** dangerous; hazardous; unsafe: *a treacherous mountain trail.* —**treach′er·ous·ly,** *adv.*

treach·er·y (trech′ə rē), *n., pl.* **treach·er·ies. 1.** betrayal of trust; unfaithfulness; disloyalty. **2.** violation of allegiance; treason.

trea·cle (trē′kəl), *n.* a British word for **molasses.**

tread (tred), *v.,* **trod** (trod); **trod·den** (trod′′n) *or* **trod; tread·ing. 1.** to step or walk on, over, or along: *to tread the pavements looking for a job.* **2.** to trample or crush under foot (usually fol. by *on* or *upon*): *to tread on grapes to make wine; to tread upon a person's foot.* **3.** to make or form by walking or trampling: *to tread a path.* **4.** to perform by walking or dancing: *to tread a lively polka.* **5.** to set down the foot or feet in walking; step; walk: *to tread carefully on the loose boards.* —*n.* **6.** the action of treading, stepping, or walking. **7.** the sound of footsteps. **8.** a manner of treading or walking: *a weary tread.* **9.** a thing or part on which a person or thing treads, stands, or moves, such as the upper surface of a step in a stair. **10.** the part of a wheel, tire, or runner that touches the ground, rail, etc. See illus. at **tire².**

trea·dle (tred′′l), *n.* **1.** a lever or similar device operated by the action of the foot, usually for turning the wheel of a machine. —*v.,* **trea·dled, trea·dling. 2.** to work a treadle.

tread·mill (tred′mil′), *n.* **1.** a mill or other apparatus that is turned by the action of men or animals walking on moving steps or an endless belt. **2.** any monotonous work or routine.

trea·son (trē′zən), *n.* betrayal of one's country; violation of one's allegiance to one's country, esp. by attempting to overthrow the government or by giving aid to an enemy in time of war.

trea·son·a·ble (trē′zə nə bəl), *adj.* of or having to do with treason; traitorous.

trea·son·ous (trē′zə nəs), *adj.* another word for **treasonable.** —**trea′son·ous·ly,** *adv.*

treas·ure (trezh′ər), *n.* **1.** accumulated or stored wealth, esp. in the form of precious metals, jewels, money, etc. **2.** a person or thing that is highly valued or admired: *The faithful old servant was a treasure to the family.* —*v.,* **treas·ured, treas·ur·ing. 3.** to regard as precious; cherish: *to cherish happy memories.* **4.** to store away; hoard: *The boys treasured their pennies in order to buy baseball uniforms.*

treas·ur·er (trezh′ər ər), *n.* an officer of a government, business firm, or society who is responsible for receiving, caring for, and paying out funds.

treas·ur·y (trezh′ə rē), *n., pl.* **treas·ur·ies. 1.** a place where the funds of a government, business firm, etc., are received, kept, and paid out. **2.** the amount of money received or held by a government, business firm, or society: *Do we have enough money in the treasury?* **3.** *(often cap.)* the department of government that has charge of the collection of taxes and the safekeeping and paying out of public funds. **4.** a collection of valuable or outstanding works of art, literature, etc.: *a treasury of modern poetry.*

treat (trēt), *v.* **1.** to act or behave toward (a person or thing) in a certain way: *to treat one's elders with respect.* **2.** to consider or look upon in a certain way: *He treated our complaints as a nuisance.* **3.** to try to relieve or cure (a patient, disease, etc.): *The doctor treated my sore shoulder.* **4.** to speak or write about; discuss (often fol. by *of*): *The book treats of the problems of farm workers.* **5.** to apply some action or substance to, for a particular purpose: *Steel is tempered by being treated with heat.* **6.** to entertain as a guest; give food, lodging, gifts, etc., to: *I'll treat you to a soda.* —*n.* **7.** food, drink, entertainment, etc., given by a person at his own expense to another. **8.** something that gives pleasure or enjoyment: *A dip in the pool was a real treat.* **9.** the act of treating. **10.** a person's turn to treat: *It's your treat for lunch today.*

trea·tise (trē′tis), *n.* a long, formal essay discussing a single subject thoroughly and in detail.

treat·ment (trēt′mənt), *n.* **1.** the act or manner of treating. **2.** a course of actions, such as use of medicines, surgery, etc., for the purpose of curing or relieving a patient or a disease.

trea·ty (trē′tē), *n., pl.* **trea·ties.** a formal agreement reached by negotiation, esp. one entered into by two or more countries establishing peace, alliance, international trade or cooperation, etc.

tre·ble (treb′əl), *adj.* **1.** threefold; triple. **2.** of or concerning the highest part in harmonized music; soprano. **3.** (in music) of the highest pitch or range, such as a voice part, singer, or instrument. —*n.* **4.** a treble voice, instrument, or part. **5.** the upper range of an instrument or voice. —*v.,* **tre·bled, tre·bling. 6.** to increase three times or threefold; triple.

tre′ble clef′, the sign indicating that the second line of the staff is G above middle C. Also, **G clef.** See illus. at **clef.**

tre·bly (treb′lē), *adv.* three times; threefold; triply.

tree (trē), *n.* **1.** a tall plant having a permanent, woody stem or trunk, usually developing branches at some distance from the ground. **2.** any of various plants that resemble a tree in size and shape: *a banana tree.* **3.** any frame or structure having the shape of a tree: *a clothes tree.* **4.** a diagram or drawing showing certain relationships by means of branching lines: *a family tree.* **5.** a pole, beam, bar, or the like, forming part of some structure or used for a special purpose. —*v.*, **treed, tree·ing. 6.** to drive into or up a tree: *The dog treed the cat.* —**tree′like′,** *adj.*

tre·foil (trē′foil), *n.* **1.** any of various plants, such as the clovers, having leaves divided into three leaflets. **2.** an ornamental figure or structure resembling such a leaf.

trek (trek), *v.*, **trekked, trek·king. 1.** to travel slowly or with difficulty. **2.** (in South Africa) to travel by ox wagon. —*n.* **3.** a journey, esp. a long or difficult one. [from the Dutch word *trekken* "to draw, travel"] —**trek′ker,** *n.*

Trefoils (def. 2)

trel·lis (trel′is), *n.* **1.** a frame or structure of latticework, used as a screen or as a support for vines, climbing plants, etc. —*v.* **2.** to train or support (plants) on a trellis.

trem·ble (trem′bəl), *v.*, **trem·bled, trem·bling. 1.** to shake uncontrollably with quick, short movements, as from fear, excitement, weakness, or cold; quiver; quake. **2.** to be troubled with anxiety or concern over a person or thing: *I tremble for her safety.* **3.** to vibrate; waver; be tremulous: *His voice trembled as he announced the tragic news.* —*n.* **4.** the act of trembling. **5.** a state or fit of trembling.

tre·men·dous (tri men′dəs), *adj.* **1.** extremely large, great, or strong; enormous; huge: *a tremendous whale.* **2.** extremely terrifying; awful; dreadful: *a tremendous disaster.* **3.** *Informal.* extraordinary; excellent: *a tremendous singer.* —**tre·men′dous·ly,** *adv.*

trem·or (trem′ər), *n.* **1.** a shaking of the body or limbs, as from fear, excitement, weakness, etc.; a quivering or trembling. **2.** a trembling movement; vibration: *a slight earth tremor; a tremor in one's voice.*

trem·u·lous (trem′yə ləs), *adj.* **1.** trembling; shaking; quivering: *a tremulous voice.* **2.** fearful; timid: *a tremulous orphan child.* —**trem′u·lous·ly,** *adv.* —**trem′u·lous·ness,** *n.*

trench (trench), *n.* **1.** a long, narrow excavation in the ground, for protecting soldiers from enemy fire. **2.** any long, narrow ditch or furrow. —*v.* **3.** to dig trenches in. [from the Old French word *trenche* "a cut," which comes from *trenchier* "to cut"]

trench·ant (tren′chənt), *adj.* **1.** sharp; penetrating; keen: *trenchant wit.* **2.** vigorous; effective; energetic: *a trenchant program for economic development.* —**trench′ant·ly,** *adv.*

trench′ coat′, a waterproof overcoat with a belt, usually cut in military style.

trend (trend), *n.* **1.** a general course or tendency; drift: *The trend is toward larger and faster airplanes.*

—*v.* **2.** to have a certain tendency or direction; tend: *The cost of living has trended upward.*

Tren·ton (tren′t³n), *n.* the capital city of New Jersey, in the W part.

trep·i·da·tion (trep′i dā′shən), *n.* **1.** a feeling of fear or alarm; anxiety: *They entered the deserted house with some trepidation.* **2.** a trembling or quivering movement; tremor.

tres·pass (tres′pəs, tres′pas′), *n.* **1.** unlawful entry upon the property of another. **2.** an offense, sin, or wrongdoing. —*v.* **3.** to enter unlawfully or without permission upon the property of another. **4.** to intrude; infringe; encroach (often fol. by *on*): *to trespass on someone's privacy.* **5.** to commit an offense, sin, or wrongdoing. —**tres′pass·er,** *n.*

tress (tres), *n.* Usually, **tresses.** long, loose curls or locks of hair.

tres·tle (tres′əl), *n.* **1.** a frame like a sawhorse, used for forming a barrier, supporting a table top or platform, etc. **2.** a similar framework of metal or timber, used for supporting a bridge. **3.** a bridge built on trestles.

Trestle (def. 3)

tri-, a prefix meaning **1.** having or consisting of three: *tricolor; triangle; triad.* **2.** into three parts: *trisect.* **3.** every three: *triweekly; trimonthly.*

tri·ad (trī′ad), *n.* **1.** a group of three, esp. of three closely related or associated persons or things. **2.** (in music) a chord of three tones, esp. the first, third, and fifth degrees of a scale.

tri·al (trī′əl, trīl), *n.* **1.** the act or process of hearing and deciding a civil or criminal case in a court of law: *The trial ended in acquittal for the defendant.* **2.** the act of trying, testing, or putting to the proof; test: *The new destroyer is undergoing sea trials.* **3.** an attempt or effort to do something; try. **4.** the condition of being tried or tested; probation: *He was promoted on trial.* **5.** a person, thing, or event that tries one's patience, courage, etc.: *That child is a trial to his parents.* —*adj.* **6.** of or concerned with a trial: *a trial judge; a trial offer.*

tri·al and er·ror, a method or process of solving problems by trying various solutions and discarding the ones that do not work.

tri·an·gle (trī′ang′gəl), *n.* **1.** a plane figure having three sides and three angles. **2.** a flat, triangular piece, often of plastic, with straight edges, used with a T square for drawing lines, geometric figures, etc. **3.** any three-cornered or three-sided figure, object, or piece: *a triangle of land.* **4.** a musical instrument made of a steel rod bent into triangular shape, that produces a high, tinkling sound when struck with a small steel rod.

Triangles

tri·an·gu·lar (trī ang′gyə lər), *adj.* concerning or having the form of a triangle; three-cornered.

trib·al (trī′bəl), *adj.* of or belonging to a tribe or tribes: *a tribal war; tribal customs.*

tribe (trīb), *n.* 1. a group of people descended from a single ancestor or set of ancestors, following the same leader or leaders, sharing the same customs, and often living in the same region. 2. a group of persons of the same class, profession, interests, etc.: *the theatrical tribe.* 3. a group of related animals or plants. [from the Latin word *tribus,* which comes from *tri-* "three." The Roman people were originally divided into three tribes]

tribes·man (trībz′mən), *n., pl.* **tribes·men.** a member of a tribe.

trib·u·la·tion (trib′yə lā′shən), *n.* 1. severe trouble or suffering; distress: *the tribulations of the poor.* 2. something that causes suffering; affliction: *The pioneers had to overcome many tribulations in the new territory.*

tri·bu·nal (trī byōōn′əl), *n.* 1. a court of justice. 2. the bench on which a judge or judges sit. 3. anything that tries or decides: *the tribunal of public opinion.*

trib·une[1] (trib′yōōn), *n.* 1. a person who upholds or defends the rights of the people. 2. (in ancient Rome) one of a number of officials elected to protect the interests and rights of the common people. [from the Latin word *tribūnus,* originally "the head of the tribe." See *tribe*]

trib·une[2] (trib′yōōn), *n.* a raised platform for a speaker; dais; rostrum. [from the medieval Latin word *tribūna,* originally "place where the officials sat." See *tribune*[1]]

trib·u·tar·y (trib′yə ter′ē), *n., pl.* **trib·u·tar·ies.** 1. a stream flowing into a larger stream or other body of water: *The Arkansas River is a tributary of the Mississippi River.* 2. a person or nation that pays tribute to or is subject to another. —*adj.* 3. flowing into a larger stream or body of water. 4. paying tribute; subject: *a tributary nation.*

trib·ute (trib′yōōt), *n.* 1. a gift, compliment, praise, or the like, given as a token of gratitude or respect: *The library is a tribute to the late president.* 2. a sum of money or something of equal value paid by one nation or person to another, often as a result of conquest, or as the price of peace, protection, or the like. 3. any enforced payment or contribution.

trice[1] (trīs), *n.* a very short time; instant: *We called and he appeared in a trice.* [from the Middle English word *tryse,* which is related to *trice*[2]]

trice[2] (trīs), *v.,* **triced, tric·ing.** (in nautical use) 1. to pull or haul with a rope. 2. to haul up and fasten with a rope (usually fol. by *up*): *to trice up a sail.* [from an early Dutch word *trīsen* "to hoist"]

tri·cer·a·tops (trī ser′ə-tops′), *n.* a dinosaur that had a large, bony crest on the neck, a long horn

Triceratops
(total length 20 ft.)

over each eye, and a shorter horn on the nose.

trick (trik), *n.* 1. an act or device intended to deceive or cheat; stratagem; ruse: *Advertised bargains are often just a trick to get customers into the store.* 2. a mischievous act; practical joke; prank: *He loves to play tricks on his schoolmates.* 3. an unfair or dishonest act: *That was a low trick, stealing the blind man's cane.* 4. a clever or skillful act: *Can your dog do tricks?* 5. a feat of magic or sleight of hand: *The magician performed the trick of the disappearing table.* 6. a peculiar habit; mannerism: *He has the trick of puffing out his cheeks before he starts to speak.* 7. the art or knack of doing something: *The trick of making good spaghetti is in the sauce.* 8. (in cards) the group or set of cards played in one round. —*adj.* 9. of, concerning, or making use of tricks: *a trick show; a trick cigar.* 10. intended to trick or deceive: *a trick question.* —*v.* 11. to cheat or deceive: *They tricked the enemy by approaching from the rear.* 12. to dress or decorate, esp. in an elaborate way (often fol. by *out* or *up*): *They were all tricked out in their best clothes.*

trick·er·y (trik′ə rē), *n., pl.* **trick·er·ies.** 1. the use of tricks to cheat or deceive: *He got the job by trickery.* 2. a trick used to deceive: *She got the money from me by a clever trickery.*

trick·le (trik′əl), *v.,* **trick·led, trick·ling.** 1. to flow or fall in drops, or in a small, slow stream: *Water trickled from the leaky faucet.* 2. to cause to flow or fall in such a manner: *He trickled water on the floor.* 3. to move or pass slowly or bit by bit: *Orders trickled in during the slow season.* —*n.* 4. a small, slow stream: *A trickle of water came out of the rocks.* 5. a small, slow, or irregular quantity of persons or things moving along: *The store had only a trickle of customers.*

trick·ster (trik′stər), *n.* a person who plays tricks; deceiver; cheat.

trick·y (trik′ē), *adj.,* **trick·i·er, trick·i·est.** 1. full of or fond of tricks; crafty; sly. 2. difficult to deal with or handle: *a tricky elevator.* 3. unreliable or unsafe: *a tricky ladder.* —**trick′i·ness,** *n.*

tri·col·or (trī′kul′ər), *adj.* 1. Also, **tri′col′ored.** having three colors. —*n.* 2. a flag having three colors. 3. *(often cap.)* the national flag of France, having vertical bands of blue, white, and red.

tri·cy·cle (trī′si kəl), *n.* a three-wheeled vehicle, usually propelled by foot pedals, and used esp. by small children.

tri·dent (trīd′ənt), *n.* 1. a spear having three prongs. 2. (in Greek and Roman mythology) the three-pronged spear carried by Poseidon or Neptune.

Trident held
by Neptune

tried (trīd), *v.* 1. the past tense and past participle of **try.** —*adj.* 2. tested and proved to be good, trustworthy, etc.: *a tried remedy.*

---

act, āble, dâre, ärt; ebb, ēqual; if, īce; hot, ōver, ôrder; oil; bŏŏk; ōōze; out; up, ûrge; ə = *a* as in *alone*; ə as in *button* (but′ən), *fire* (fīər); chief; shoe; thin; ᵺat; zh as in *measure* (mezh′ər). See full key inside cover.

tri·en·ni·al (trī en′ē əl), *adj.* 1. occurring every three years. —*n.* 2. something that occurs every three years. —**tri·en′ni·al·ly,** *adv.*

tries (trīz), *v.* 1. the third person singular, present tense of **try**: *She tries hard to get good grades.* —*n.* 2. the plural of **try.**

Tri·este (trē est′), *n.* a port city in NE Italy.

tri·fle (trī′fəl), *n.* 1. something of little value or importance. 2. a small quantity or amount of anything; bit. —*v.,* **tri·fled, tri·fling.** 3. to treat lightly or without proper respect (usually fol. by *with*): *The captain is not a man to trifle with.* 4. to pass the time idly; dally: *If we trifle here any longer, we'll miss the train.* 5. to play or toy (usually fol. by *with*): *He was trifling with a penknife as he waited.* 6. to spend (time, money, etc.) idly or foolishly. —**tri′fler,** *n.*

tri·fling (trī′fling), *adj.* 1. of little importance; trivial: *a trifling matter.* 2. of small value or amount: *a trifling reward.*

trig·ger (trig′ər), *n.* 1. a small tongue or lever in a pistol, rifle, or other firearm, that fires the weapon when it is squeezed by the finger. 2. any lever or other device that releases a spring, catch, or the like. 3. any act or event that sets off a series of consequences. —*v.* 4. to set off; start: *The attack on Fort Sumter triggered the Civil War.*

trig·o·nom·e·try (trig′ə nom′i trē), *n.* the branch of mathematics that deals with the relations between the sides and angles of triangles and with calculations based on these relations.

trill (tril), *v.* 1. to sing or play with a vibratory or quavering effect. 2. to pronounce, esp. a sound like *r,* with rapid vibration of the tongue or uvula. —*n.* 3. the act or sound of trilling. 4. (in music) the rapid changing back and forth from one tone to

Written   Played

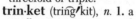

Trill

the tone next to it. 5. a similar sound, such as the warble of a bird. 6. a sound, esp. *r,* produced with rapid vibration of the tongue or uvula.

tril·lion (tril′yən), *n., pl.* **tril·lions,** *or* (after a numeral) **tril·lion.** 1. (in the U.S. and France) a number that is one thousand times one billion (1,000,000,-000,000). 2. (in Great Britain and Germany) a number that is one billion times one billion (1,000,000,000,000,000,000). —*adj.* 3. amounting to one trillion in number: *a trillion dollars.* —**tril′lionth,** *n., adj.*

tril·li·um (tril′ē əm), *n.* any of various plants related to the lily, having three leaves and a single flower.

trim (trim), *v.,* **trimmed, trim·ming.** 1. to make neat and orderly by clipping, pruning, etc. 2. to remove by cutting, plucking, etc. (often fol. by *off* or *away*): *to trim off the fat from a steak.* 3. to decorate; adorn: *to trim a Christmas tree.* 4. to balance (a ship, airplane, etc.) by distributing or rearranging the load of passengers or cargo. 5. to adjust (the sails or yards of a ship) to the direction of the wind and the course of the ship. 6. *Informal.* to beat; defeat: *The visiting team trimmed us 12 to 0.* —*n.* 7. the condition or

fitness of a person or thing for action, work, use, etc.: *The team is in good trim for the game.* 8. the condition or balance of a ship in the water, an airplane in the air, etc. 9. the adjustment of the sails, rigging, etc., of a ship to sailing conditions. 10. material used for ornament or decoration; trimming. 11. the action or result of trimming by cutting, clipping, or the like: *My hair needs a trim.* —*adj.,* **trim·mer, trim·mest.** 12. neat and orderly in appearance; tidy: *a trim lawn.* 13. in good condition or fitness: *a trim ship.* —**trim′ly,** *adv.* —**trim′mer,** *n.* —**trim′ness,** *n.*

trim·ming (trim′ing), *n.* 1. material used for decoration or ornament: *the trimmings for a Christmas tree.* 2. Usually, **trimmings.** foods or other things that are served together with or used to decorate a main dish: *roast turkey with all the trimmings.* 3. **trimmings,** pieces that are cut off or cut away from a larger piece or amount. 4. the action or result of trimming by cutting, clipping, pruning, etc.: *The lawn needs a trimming.* 5. *Informal.* a beating or defeat: *The home team got a trimming in their last game.*

tri·month·ly (trī munth′lē), *adj.* 1. occurring every three months: *a trimonthly inspection.* —*adv.* 2. every three months: *The committee meets trimonthly.*

Trin·i·dad (trin′i dad′), *n.* an island in the E West Indies, formerly British; now part of Trinidad and Tobago. 1864 sq. mi.

Trin′idad and Toba′go, an independent republic in the West Indies. 1980 sq. mi.

trin·i·ty (trin′i tē), *n., pl.* for def. 1 **trin·i·ties.** 1. a group or set of three. 2. the quality of being threefold or triple.

trin·ket (tring′kit), *n.* 1. a small ornament, piece of jewelry, etc. 2. any small object of little value.

tri·o (trē′ō), *n., pl.* **tri·os.** 1. a group of three singers or players. 2. a piece of music composed for such a group. 3. any group of three persons or things.

trip (trip), *n.* 1. a journey or voyage: *to take a trip to Europe.* 2. a course of travel to a particular place, or for a particular purpose: *a shopping trip in town.* 3. a stumble; misstep. 4. a slip, mistake, or blunder. 5. a quick, light step. 6. a device for releasing a spring or lever that controls the action of a machine. —*v.,* **tripped, trip·ping.** 7. to lose one's footing; stumble: *He tripped on the stairs.* 8. to cause to stumble (often fol. by *up*): *The rug tripped him up.* 9. to make a mistake; slip; err: *In reciting, she tripped on some difficult words.* 10. to cause to make a slip or error (often fol. by *up*): *The long runs in the piano piece tripped me up.* 11. to catch in a slip or error (often fol. by *up*): *The lawyer tripped up the witness and proved that she had lied.* 12. to step lightly; skip: *The children tripped into the room.* 13. to release (a spring, lever, or the like). 14. to start or activate (a machine or apparatus).

tripe (trīp), *n.* 1. a part of the stomach of certain ani-

mals such as cows, sheep, or goats, used as food. **2.**
Slang. anything false, worthless, or foolish; nonsense.

tri·ple (trip′əl), *adj.* **1.** consisting of three parts;
threefold: *a triple window.* **2.** repeated three times:
a triple knock at the door. **3.** three times as great or
as many: *to earn triple pay for dangerous duty.* —*n.*
4. an amount, number, etc., that is three times as
great as another: *The enemy force is the triple of
ours.* **5.** (in baseball) a hit that enables the batter to
reach third base safely. —*v.*, **tri·pled, tri·pling. 6.** to
make or become three times as great or as many: *En-
rollments have tripled in the last year.* **7.** (in baseball) to hit a triple. —**tri′ply,** *adv.*

tri·plet (trip′lit), *n.* **1. triplets,** three children born at
one time of the same mother. **2.** any one of three
such children. **3.** any group or set of three persons or
things. **4.** (in music) a group of three notes played or
sung in the time allowed for two. **5.** a stanza of three
rhyming lines of verse.

trip·li·cate (trip′lə kit), *n.* **1.** a group or set of three
identical copies (usually preceded by *in*): *Fill out the
application in triplicate.* —*adj.* **2.** having or made up
of three identical parts, copies, etc.: *a triplicate questionnaire.* —*v.* (trip′lə kāt′), **trip·li·cat·ed, trip·li·cat-
ing. 3.** to make three copies of: *to triplicate a letter.*

tri·pod (trī′pod), *n.* **1.** a stool, table, pedestal, etc.,
with three legs. **2.** a three-legged stand or support,
as for a camera, telescope, etc.

Trip·o·li (trip′ə lē), *n.* **1.** a seaport and the capital
city of Libya, in the NW part. **2.** a former state in N
Africa, now part of Libya.

trip·ping (trip′ing), *adj.* **1.** light and quick; nimble: *a
tripping pace.* **2.** moving with a light, easy rhythm: *a
tripping waltz.* —**trip′ping·ly,** *adv.*

tri·reme (trī′rēm), *n.* (in ancient times) a ship with
three banks of oars on each side, used esp. as a warship.

trite (trīt), *adj.*, **trit·er, trit·
est.** made stale and uninteresting by repeated use;
commonplace: *"Light as
a feather" is a trite ex-
pression.* [from the Latin word *trītus,* literally "worn
down," which comes from *terere* "to rub, wear
down"] —**trite′ly,** *adv.* —**trite′ness,** *n.*

Trireme (cross section)

Tri·ton (trīt′ən), *n.* (in Greek mythology) a son of
Poseidon, pictured as having the head and torso of a
man and the tail of a fish, and blowing a trumpet
made of a conch shell.

tri·umph (trī′əmf), *n.* **1.** victory; success: *triumph in
battle; triumph over disease.* **2.** rejoicing or celebration of a victory: *The returning heroes were received
in triumph.* —*v.* **3.** to win a victory; be successful: *to
triumph over the opponents.* **4.** to celebrate or rejoice over a victory: *The whole nation triumphed at
the news of peace.*

tri·um·phal (trī um′fəl), *adj.* of or celebrating a triumph: *a triumphal entry into a city.*

tri·um·phant (trī um′fənt), *adj.* **1.** victorious; suc-

cessful: *a triumphant army.* **2.** celebrating or rejoicing over a victory: *a triumphant welcome.* —**tri·um′
phant·ly,** *adv.*

triv·et (triv′it), *n.* **1.** a small metal plate with short
legs, esp. one put under a hot dish or platter to protect a table. **2.** a three-legged metal stand used for
supporting cooking vessels over an open fire.

triv·i·al (triv′ē əl), *adj.* **1.** of very little importance or
value; trifling: *I don't have time for trivial questions.*
2. ordinary; commonplace: *the trivial routine of daily
living.* —**triv′i·al·ly,** *adv.*

triv·i·al·i·ty (triv′ē al′i tē) *n., pl.* for def. 1 **triv·i·al·i-
ties. 1.** something trivial; trifle. **2.** the state or quality of being trivial: *He was annoyed at the triviality
of her objections.*

trod (trod), *v.* the past tense and a past participle of
tread.

trod·den (trod′ən), *v.* a past participle of **tread.**

Tro·jan (trō′jən), *adj.* **1.** of or referring to Troy or its
inhabitants. —*n.* **2.** a native or inhabitant of Troy. **3.**
a person who works hard and diligently.

Tro′jan War′, (in classical mythology) the ten-year
war waged by the Greeks against the Trojans to win
back Helen, who had been taken away by Paris, a
prince of Troy.

troll¹ (trōl), *v.* **1.** to sing in a loud, full voice. **2.** to
sing the parts of (a song) in succession, as in a round.
3. to fish or catch with a moving line, drawn through
the water or trailed behind a boat. —*n.* **4.** a song
whose parts are sung in succession; round. **5.** a fishing line with a lure and hook for use in trolling. [from
the early French word *troller* "to run about," which
comes from Germanic] —**troll′er,** *n.*

troll² (trōl), *n.* (in folklore) a giant or dwarf that lives
in a cave or underground. [from Scandinavian]

trol·ley (trol′ē), *n., pl.* **trol·leys. 1.** a trolley car. **2.** a
pulley, or a carriage, basket, or other conveyance in
which objects are carried, suspended from an overhead track. **3.** a grooved wheel or pulley mounted at
the end of a pole on top of an electric car or locomotive, that makes contact with an overhead wire, from
which it draws electric current.

trol′ley car′, a streetcar that is powered by electric current drawn by means of a trolley, usually from
a wire suspended overhead.

trom·bone (trom bōn′, trom′bōn), *n.* a brass wind
instrument consisting of a long, U-shaped metal tube
expanding into a bell,
with a sliding portion that
is moved by the hand to
produce different pitches.

troop (troop), *n.* **1.** a
gathering or collection of
persons or things; com-
pany; band. **2.** a unit of
cavalry about the size of
an infantry company. **3.**

Slide trombone

troops, soldiers, police, militia, etc., considered as
a group: *The governor called out the troops to put*

down the riot. **4.** a unit of Boy Scouts or Girl Scouts containing up to 32 members. —*v.* **5.** to gather or move in a company or crowd: *The class trooped into the auditorium.* **6.** to walk briskly; march.

troop·er (trōō′pər), *n.* **1.** a soldier in the cavalry. **2.** a mounted policeman. **3.** a member of the state police in one of the states of the U.S.

tro·phy (trō′fē), *n., pl.* **tro·phies. 1.** anything taken or won in battle, hunting, competition, etc.; prize; award: *The champion golfer has a roomful of trophies and medals.* **2.** anything that serves as a reminder or memento: *The scars on his face were the trophies of his many street brawls.*

trop·ic (trop′ik), *n.* **1.** the tropic of Cancer or the tropic of Capricorn. **2.** the tropics, the regions lying between the tropic of Cancer and the tropic of Capricorn. They are generally warm and humid. —*adj.* **3.** of or belonging to the tropics; tropical: *tropic heat.*

trop·i·cal (trop′i kəl), *adj.* **1.** of, belonging to, or found in the tropics: *a tropical climate; tropical fish.* **2.** resembling or suggestive of the tropics: *tropical heat; a tropical background.* **3.** used in or suitable for the tropics: *tropical dress.* —**trop′i·cal·ly,** *adv.*

trop′ic of Can′cer, an imaginary line around the earth 23½° N of the equator.

trop′ic of Cap′ricorn, an imaginary line around the earth 23½° S of the equator.

trot (trot), *v.,* **trot·ted, trot·ting. 1.** (of a horse) to go at a gait between a walk and a gallop, in which one front leg and the opposite hind leg move forward at almost the same time. **2.** to ride at a trot. **3.** to cause (a horse) to trot. **4.** to go at a brisk, steady pace; hurry: *Trot down to the store for some milk.* **5.** to run at less than full speed, with long, loose strides: *The boys started to trot, and then broke into a sprint.* —*n.* **6.** the gait of a person or animal when trotting.

troth (trôth, trōth), *n. Archaic.* **1.** faithfulness; loyalty: *by my troth.* **2.** truth: *in troth.* **3.** a promise or pledge, esp. a promise to marry. **4. plight one's troth.** See **plight²** (def. 2).

trot·ter (trot′ər), *n.* a person or animal that trots, esp. a horse bred and trained for harness racing.

trou·ba·dour (trōō′bə dôr′), *n.* **1.** one of a class of poets and minstrels of southern France and northern Italy during the 11th to 13th centuries, who composed and sang songs and ballads on themes of love and chivalry. **2.** any wandering singer or minstrel.

trou·ble (trub′əl), *v.,* **trou·bled, trou·bling. 1.** to disturb in mind; cause to worry or be anxious; distress: *His failure to return home at this late hour troubles me.* **2.** to cause inconvenience or effort to: *May I trouble you to shut the door?* **3.** to cause pain or discomfort to; afflict: *His rheumatism is troubling him again.* **4.** to stir up (a liquid); make murky; agitate: *The storm troubled the waters.* **5.** to put oneself to inconvenience, extra effort, or the like: *If you don't trouble to do your homework, you won't pass.* **6.** to be distressed; worry: *It doesn't pay to trouble about past mistakes.* —*n.* **7.** difficulty, annoyance, or inconvenience: *It would be no trouble at all to mail the book to you.* **8.** a state or condition of distress or

hardship: *to be in financial trouble.* **9.** a misfortune or affliction. **10.** civil disorder or disturbance. **11.** a physical disorder or ailment: *to suffer from heart trouble.* **12.** a mechanical defect or breakdown: *engine trouble.*

trou·ble·some (trub′əl səm), *adj.* **1.** causing inconvenience, annoyance, etc.: *a troublesome car.* **2.** difficult; laborious: *a troublesome job.*

trough (trôf, trof), *n.* **1.** a long, narrow, open container, usually shaped like a box or a basin, used chiefly to hold water or feed for animals. **2.** a channel for carrying off water, as from the roof of a building; gutter. **3.** any long depression or hollow, as between two ridges or waves.

trounce (trouns), *v.,* **trounced, trounc·ing. 1.** to beat; thrash. **2.** to defeat decisively: *We trounced them by a score of 13 to 0.*

troupe (trōōp), *n.* **1.** a company of actors, singers, or other performers, esp. a traveling company. —*v.* **2.** to perform with a traveling company: *to troupe throughout the Midwest.* —**troup′er,** *n.*

trou·sers (trou′zərz), *n.pl.* an outer garment worn chiefly by men and boys, covering the body from the waist to the ankles or knees, divided so as to provide a separate covering around each leg. Also, **pants.**

trous·seau (trōō′sō, trōō sō′), *n., pl.* **trous·seaux** (trōō′sōz, trōō sōz′). an outfit of personal clothing, household linens, etc., collected by a bride in preparation for housekeeping.

trout (trout), *n., pl.* **trouts** *or* **trout.** any of various food or game fishes related to the salmon.

trow (trō), *v. Archaic.* to believe, think, or suppose.

trow·el (trou′əl), *n.* **1.** any of various tools having a flat blade with a handle, used for laying or spreading mortar, plaster, etc. **2.** a similar tool with a scooplike blade, used in gardening for light digging, setting plants, etc.

Brook trout (length 1½ ft.)

troy (troi), *adj.* measured or expressed in units of troy weight.

Troy (troi), *n.* an ancient ruined city in NW Asia Minor: site of the Trojan War.

troy′ weight′, a system of weights in use for precious metals and gems, in which 12 ounces equal one pound. [from *Troyes,* the name of a city in France, where it was originally used]

tru·ant (trōō′ənt), *n.* **1.** a student who stays away from school without permission. **2.** a person who neglects his duty. —*adj.* **3.** absent from school or duty without permission. **4.** neglectful of one's duties; idle; lazy. **5.** of or concerned with truancy or truants: *a truant officer.* —**tru′an·cy,** *n.*

truce (trōōs), *n.* **1.** a temporary halt in warfare or fighting, by agreement of both sides. **2.** temporary rest or relief from pain, illness, etc.

truck[1] (truk), *n.* **1.** any of various large motor vehicles for carrying loads, freight, etc. **2.** such a vehicle consisting of a trailer drawn by a tractor. **3.** a long, low frame with handles and two small wheels, pushed or pulled by hand, used for moving baggage, crates, bales, etc. **4.** a low platform mounted on wheels, propelled by hand or motor, used for moving heavy objects. **5.** a frame with two or more pairs of wheels, for supporting one end of a railroad car, locomotive, etc. **6.** a small wheel. —*v.* **7.** to transport by truck. **8.** to drive a truck. [short for *truckle* "a wheel"] —**truck′er,** *n.*

truck[2] (truk), *n.* **1.** vegetables grown for sale in the market. **2.** barter; goods used for bartering. **3.** *Informal.* trash; rubbish. **4.** *Informal.* dealings; association: *I'll have no truck with the likes of them.* —*v.* **5.** to exchange (goods); barter. [from the Middle English word *trukien,* which comes from Old French *troquer* "to exchange"]

truck′ farm′, a farm on which vegetables are grown for sale in the market.

truck·le (truk′əl), *v.,* **truck·led, truck·ling.** to give in or yield easily; submit weakly: *to truckle to unreasonable demands.*

truck·load (truk′lōd′), *n.* a full or nearly full load on a truck.

truc·u·lent (truk′yə lənt), *adj.* **1.** fierce; cruel; savage: *a truculent beast.* **2.** aggressively hostile; belligerent: *a truculent opponent.* —**truc′u·lence,** *n.* —**truc′u·lent·ly,** *adv.*

trudge (truj), *v.,* **trudged, trudg·ing. 1.** to walk, esp. at a slow, weary pace; plod. —*n.* **2.** a slow, tiresome walk or pace.

true (trōō), *adj.,* **tru·er, tru·est. 1.** in accordance with or based on fact or reality: *a true story.* **2.** genuine; not imitation or artificial: *true vanilla flavoring.* **3.** being the best or highest form of something: *true statesmanship.* **4.** loyal; faithful: *a true friend.* **5.** exact; accurate: *a true copy.* **6.** having the right form, fit, etc.: *a true fit of the piston in the cylinder.* **7.** legitimate or rightful: *the true heirs.* **8.** rightly or properly so called; having the characteristics of a certain group or class: *The starfish is not a true fish.* —*n.* **9.** exact or accurate formation, fit, adjustment, etc.: *The wall is out of true.* —*adv.* **10.** in a true manner; truly; truthfully: *I tell you true, it's his handwriting.* **11.** exactly or accurately: *The frame fits true. This rifle does not fire true.* —*v.,* **trued; tru·ing** *or* **true·ing. 12.** to make true or accurate in shape, fit, adjustment, etc.: *to true the corners of a door frame.* —**true′ness,** *n.*

true′ north′, the direction in which the North Pole lies from any point on the earth's surface.

truf·fle (truf′əl), *n.* any of several edible fungi that grow underground.

tru·ism (trōō′iz əm), *n.* a self-evident, obvious truth: *It is a truism that children resemble their parents.*

tru·ly (trōō′lē), *adv.* **1.** in accordance with fact or truth: *He is truly a credit to his family.* **2.** exactly;

accurately; correctly: *a drawing truly copied from the original.* **3.** rightly; properly; legitimately: *He is truly the heir to the throne.* **4.** really; genuinely; sincerely: *I am truly sorry.*

Tru·man (trōō′mən), *n.* **Harry S,** 1884–1972, 34th Vice President of the U.S. 1945; 33rd President of the U.S. 1945–1953.

trump (trump), *n.* **1.** (in cards) **a.** any card of the suit that outranks all other suits during the playing of a particular hand or round. **b.** Often, **trumps.** the suit itself. —*v.* **2.** to play a trump. **3. trump up,** to make up falsely or deceitfully; fabricate: *to trump up charges against an innocent man.* [another form of the word *triumph*]

trum·pet (trum′pit), *n.* **1.** a brass wind instrument with a powerful tone, made of a curved tube and having a cup-shaped mouthpiece at one end and a flaring bell at the other, and equipped with valves for producing different pitches. **2.** something used as or that resembles a trumpet, esp. in shape or sound.

Trumpet

—*v.,* **trum·pet·ed, trum·pet·ing. 3.** to blow a trumpet. **4.** to proclaim loudly or widely: *to trumpet good news.* **5.** to make a sound like a trumpet: *The elephant trumpeted in rage.* —**trum′pet·er,** *n.*

trun·cheon (trun′chən), *n.* **1.** a policeman's club; billy. **2.** a short staff carried by an official as an emblem of authority; baton.

trun·dle (trun′dᵊl), *v.,* **trun·dled, trun·dling. 1.** to roll or cause to roll along, as on wheels: *The heavy carts trundled past.* **2.** to carry or move in a wagon, cart, or the like: *to trundle baggage off the ship.* —*n.* **3.** a small wheel, roller, or the like. [another form of the earlier word *trindle* "to roll, trundle," which comes from Old English *tryndel* "circle, ring"]

trun′dle bed′, a low bed mounted on wheels or casters, so that it can be rolled under another bed when not in use.

trunk (trungk), *n.* **1.** the main stem of a tree, not including the branches and roots. **2.** a large box or chest, used for storing and transporting clothes, personal articles, etc. **3.** a large compartment in an automobile, usually built into the rear and having a hinged lid, used for luggage, tools, a spare tire, etc. **4.** the body of a man or animal, not including the head and limbs. **5.** a telephone line or channel between two central offices or switching devices. **6.** the main body of an artery, nerve, or the like. **7.** the long nose or snout of an elephant. **8. trunks,** very short trousers worn by men for swimming, boxing, athletics, etc. [from the Latin word *truncus* "stem, trunk"]

trunk′ line′, the main line of a railroad, telephone network, etc.

truss (trus), *v.* **1.** to tie, bind, or fasten. **2.** to tie (the body of a person or animal) with the limbs held tightly to the side (often fol. by *up*): *to truss up a turkey for the oven; to truss up a prisoner.* —*n.* **3.** a rigid frame or framework for supporting a bridge, roof, etc. **4.** a pad, usually held in place by a belt, for supporting a hernia.

trust (trust), *n.* **1.** a strong belief in the honesty, reliability, strength, etc., of a person or thing; faith: *We have put our trust in our leaders.* **2.** confidence in the ability of a person to pay at a later time for goods or services received; credit: *to sell merchandise on trust.* **3.** a person or thing that can be relied upon: *Democracy is our trust.* **4.** the obligation or responsibility of a person in whom confidence or authority is placed: *a position of trust.* **5.** charge; custody; care: *I put my business affairs in your trust.* **6.** something given to a person to keep in safety or to use honestly; responsibility: *A public office is a public trust.* **7.** (in law) **a.** the care and management of property or funds by a person, bank, etc., for the benefit of another. **b.** the property or funds so held. **8.** an illegal combination of business firms for the purpose of controlling prices, eliminating competition, etc.; monopoly. —*adj.* **9.** of or referring to a trust or trusts: *a trust fund; a trust company.* —*v.* **10.** to rely upon or place confidence in someone or something (usually fol. by *in* or *to*): *Trust in me, and everything will turn out well.* **11.** to expect confidently; hope: *I trust that you will reply promptly.* **12.** to rely on: *Trust your doctor.* **13.** to rely on the truth of; believe: *I don't trust his story.* **14.** to commit (a person or thing) to the care of; entrust: *Would you trust him with your life?* **15.** to give credit to (a person) for goods or services: *The bank will trust you for the loan.*

trus·tee (tru stē′), *n.* **1.** a person, usually one of a group of persons, appointed or elected to manage the affairs of a company or organization such as a college, hospital, foundation, church, etc. **2.** a person who cares for and manages the property of another. **3.** a trusty.

trus·tee·ship (tru stē′ship), *n.* **1.** the office or duties of a trustee. **2.** the administrative control of a territory (**trust′ ter′ritory**), given to a country by the United Nations.

trust·ful (trust′fəl), *adj.* full of trust or confidence; believing; trusting: *a trustful friend.* —**trust′ful·ly,** *adv.* —**trust′ful·ness,** *n.*

trust′ fund′, money, securities, property, etc., held and managed by one person or group of persons for the benefit of another.

trust·ing (trus′ting), *adj.* having trust or confidence; trustful: *a trusting child.* —**trust′ing·ly,** *adv.*

trust·wor·thy (trust′wûr′thē), *adj.* deserving of trust or confidence; dependable; reliable: *a trustworthy person.* —**trust′wor′thi·ness,** *n.*

trust·y (trus′tē), *adj.,* **trust·i·er, trust·i·est. 1.** that can be trusted or relied on; dependable: *He has gone hunting with his trusty dog.* —*n.* **2.** Also, **trustee.** a person or thing that is trusted, esp. a convict in a prison who has proved to be reliable, and is given special privileges. —**trust′i·ness,** *n.*

truth (trōōth), *n., pl.* **truths** (trōōthz). **1.** the true state of a matter; the real facts: *to tell the truth.* **2.** the quality or state of being true: *His story has the appearance of truth.* **3.** a statement, principle, etc., that has been proved; fact: *scientific truths.*

truth·ful (trōōth′fəl), *adj.* **1.** telling the truth; honest; sincere: *a truthful reporter on foreign affairs.* **2.** in accordance with truth or fact: *a truthful statement.* —**truth′ful·ly,** *adv.* —**truth′ful·ness,** *n.*

try (trī), *v.,* **tried, try·ing. 1.** to make an attempt or effort; strive: *to try harder.* **2.** to put to a test or trial: *to try a new cough remedy.* **3.** (in law) **a.** to hear and decide (a case). **b.** to examine and establish the guilt or innocence of (an accused person). **4.** to put to a severe test; strain; tax to the limit: *to try one's patience.* —*n., pl.* **tries. 5.** an attempt; effort: *He hit the target on the first try.* **6.** a trial; test: *I'll give the job a try for a week.* **7. try on,** to put on (a hat, dress, etc.) so as to judge the appearance or fit: *Try this on and see how it looks.* **8. try out,** to test the effectiveness of: *Have you tried out your new roller skates?* **9. try out for,** to compete for (a place on a team, role in a play, etc.): *to try out for the soccer team.*

try·ing (trī′ing), *adj.* hard to bear or endure; difficult: *a trying experience.*

try·out (trī′out′), *n.* a trial or test of fitness, strength, skill, etc.: *tryouts for parts in a play.*

try′ square′, a device consisting of a pair of straightedges fixed at right angles to each other, used for testing the squareness of carpentry work or for laying out right angles.

tsar (zär, tsär), *n.* another spelling of **czar.**

tsa·ri·na (zä rē′nə, tsä rē′nə), *n.* another spelling of **czarina.**

Tschai·kow·sky (chī kôf′skē), *n.* Peter Il·yich. See **Tchaikovsky, Peter Ilyich.**

tset′se fly′ (tset′sē, tsē′tsē), any of several bloodsucking African flies that can transmit sleeping sickness and other infections to human beings and animals. [from Bantu]

Tsetse fly (length ¼ in.)

T-shirt (tē′shûrt′), *n.* a lightweight pullover shirt having short sleeves and no collar, usually worn as an undershirt by men and boys.

tsp., **1.** teaspoon. **2.** teaspoonful.

T-square (tē′skwâr′), *n.* a T-shaped ruler used in mechanical drawing for making parallel lines, right angles, etc.

T-square on drawing board

tub (tub), *n.* **1.** a broad, open container, usually made of wood or metal, of round or oval shape, used for washing, holding or storing liquids or loose material, etc. **2.** the amount a tub will hold. **3.** a bathtub. **4.** an old, slow, or clumsy boat. **5.** *Chiefly British Informal.* a bath in a bathtub. —*v.,* **tubbed, tub·bing. 6.** to place or store in a tub.

tu·ba (too′bə, tyoo′-), *n.* a brass wind instrument with valves, having a low range. Also, **bass horn.**

tube (toob, tyoob), *n.* **1.** a long, hollow pipe of metal, glass, rubber, or other material, used esp. for holding or carrying liquids or gases. **2.** a small cylindrical container, made of soft metal, plastic, or other material, sealed at one end and having a cap that screws onto the other end, from which a paste or liquid may be squeezed out. **3.** any hollow, cylindrical vessel or organ in the body of a plant or animal: *the bronchial tubes.* **4.** a subway or tunnel for cars or trains. **5.** an electron tube. **6.** an inner tube. —**tube′less,** *adj.*

Tuba

tu·ber (too′bər, tyoo′-), *n.* a fleshy oblong or rounded thickening or outgrowth of an underground stem or shoot, such as the potato.

tu·ber·cle (too′bər kəl, tyoo′-), *n.* **1.** a small rounded projection or bump, as on a bone, on the surface of the body, or on a plant. **2.** a small, firm, rounded swelling caused by tuberculosis.

tu·ber·cu·lar (too bûr′kyə lər, tyoo-), *adj.* **1.** of, referring to, or suffering from tuberculosis. **2.** of, referring to, or having tubercles. —*n.* **3.** a person suffering from tuberculosis.

tu·ber·cu·lo·sis (too bûr′kyə lo′sis, tyoo-), *n.* a disease that may affect almost any tissue of the body, esp. the lungs, and is characterized by small, rounded swellings, or tubercles.

tube·rose (toob′roz′, tyoob′-), *n.* a plant that grows from a bulb, and has creamy-white, lilylike flowers.

tu·ber·ous (too′bər əs, tyoo′-), *adj.* **1.** of, resembling, or having rounded swellings; knobby. **2.** of, resembling, or having a tuber or tubers.

tub·ing (too′bing, tyoo′-), *n.* **1.** material in the form of a tube: *copper tubing.* **2.** a system of tubes: *the tubing of a refrigerator.* **3.** a piece of tube.

tu·bu·lar (too′byə lər, tyoo′-), *adj.* **1.** of or referring to a tube or tubes. **2.** having the form of a tube.

tuck (tuk), *v.* **1.** to thrust or gather in the loose end or edge of (a garment, covering, etc.) so as to hold it closely in place: *Tuck your shirt into your trousers.* **2.** to cram or hide in a close place: *He tucked the money into his pocket.* **3.** to cover or wrap snugly: *She tucked the children into bed.* **4.** to pull up or gather into folds, usually in order to shorten: *to tuck up a hem.* **5.** (in sewing) to make tucks in. —*n.* **6.** something tucked or folded in. **7.** a fold sewn into a piece of cloth or a garment, for the purpose of decoration, shortening, or making a tighter fit.

tuck·er[1] (tuk′ər), *n.* a piece of fine linen, muslin, lace, or the like, worn by women to cover the neck and shoulders. [from *tuck* (verb) + *-er*]

tuck·er[2] (tuk′ər), *v. Informal.* to weary, tire, or exhaust (often fol. by *out*): *Christmas shopping tuckered us out.* [from *tuck* (verb) + *-er,* a suffix expressing intensity or repetition of an action]

Tuc·son (too′son, too son′), *n.* a city in S Arizona.

Tu·dor (too′dər, tyoo′-), *n.* **1.** a member of the royal family that ruled in England from 1485 to 1603. —*adj.* **2.** of or referring to the Tudor sovereigns or their reigns: *Tudor architecture.*

Tues., Tuesday.

Tues·day (tooz′dē, tooz′dā, tyooz′-), *n.* the third day of the week, following Monday.

tuft (tuft), *n.* **1.** a bunch or cluster of hairs, feathers, grass, threads, etc., growing or fastened closely together at one end and loose at the other end. **2.** a cluster of threads drawn tightly through a mattress, quilt, upholstery, or the like, for holding the stuffing in place, and cut off so as to form a tuft at one or both ends. —*v.* **3.** to provide or decorate with a tuft or tufts. **4.** to form or arrange into a tuft or tufts.

tug (tug), *v.,* **tugged, tug·ging. 1.** io pull or pull at with force or effort: *The dog tugged at the leash.* **2.** to move by pulling; drag; haul: *to tug a piano across the floor.* **3.** to tow with a tugboat. —*n.* **4.** the act of tugging; pull: *to open a drawer with a tug.* **5.** a tugboat. **6.** another word for **trace**[2].

tug·boat (tug′bot′), *n.* a small, powerful boat used for towing or pushing ships, barges, etc. Also, **tug.**

tug′ of war′, 1. an athletic contest between two teams pulling on opposite ends of a rope, each team striving to draw the other across a center line. **2.** any hard struggle, esp. between two persons or groups striving to gain control or possession of something.

tu·i·tion (too ish′ən, tyoo-), *n.* **1.** the charge or fee for instruction, esp. at a college or private school. **2.** teaching; instruction.

tu·lip (too′lip, tyoo′-), *n.* **1.** a plant related to the lily, having large, cup-shaped flowers of various colors. **2.** a flower or bulb of such a plant.

Tul·sa (tul′sə), *n.* a city in NE Oklahoma.

tum·ble (tum′bəl), *v.,* **tum·bled, tum·bling. 1.** to fall or roll end over end: *The boulder tumbled down the hill.* **2.** to fall rapidly; drop: *The temperature tumbled during the night.* **3.** to perform acrobatic leaps, somersaults, or the like. **4.** to toss, mix, or whirl about: *to tumble the ingredients of a salad.* **5.** to knock down; topple: *to tumble a pile of logs.* **6.** to move in a hasty, confused mass; swarm: *The children tumbled out of the classroom.* **7.** *Informal.* to understand or become aware (often fol. by *to*): *They've tumbled to the secret.* —*n.* **8.** an act of tumbling or falling. **9.** an acrobatic or gymnastic feat, such as a leap, somersault, or the like. **10.** a confused state; jumble.

Tulip

tum·bler (tum′blər), *n.* **1.** a performer of acrobatic or gymnastic feats, such as leaps, somersaults, or the like. **2.** a part of the inner workings of a lock, that is lifted or released when the key is inserted, allowing the bolt to move. **3.** a drinking glass without a stem or handle. **4.** any revolving device or apparatus for mixing or tumbling, such as the drum or cage of a clothes dryer or washing machine.

act, āble, dâre, ärt; ebb, ēqual; if, īce; hot, ōver, ôrder; oil; boŏk; ooze; out; up, ûrge; ə = a as in *alone*; ᵊ as in *button* (but′ᵊn), *fire* (fiᵊr); chief; shoe; thin; that; zh as in *measure* (mezh′ər). See full key inside cover.

tum·ble·weed (tum′bəl wēd′), *n.* any of various plants whose branching upper part becomes detached from the roots in autumn and is driven about by the wind.

tum·brel (tum′brəl), *n.* **1.** one of the carts used during the French Revolution to carry condemned prisoners to the guillotine. **2.** a dumpcart used by farmers for carrying manure. Also, **tum′bril.**

tu·mor (tōō′mər, tyōō′-), *n.* an abnormal or diseased swelling or growth in any part of the body.

tu·mult (tōō′məlt, tyōō′-), *n.* **1.** a violent and noisy commotion; uproar: *the tumult of crowds.* **2.** a highly disturbed state of the mind or feelings.

tu·mul·tu·ous (tōō mul′chōō əs, tyōō-), *adj.* **1.** full of tumult or commotion: *a tumultuous welcome.* **2.** highly disturbed in mind or feelings; agitated: *tumultuous passions.* —**tu·mul′tu·ous·ly,** *adv.*

tu·na (tōō′nə, tyōō′-), *n., pl.* **tu·nas** *or* **tu·na. 1.** any of several large food and game fishes found in warm seas. **2.** Also, **tu′na fish′.** the flesh of the tuna, used as food.

tun·dra (tun′drə), *n.* a vast, treeless plain of the northern arctic regions. [from a Russian word meaning "marshy plain"]

Tuna
(length to 14 ft.)

tune (tōōn, tyōōn), *n.* **1.** a series of musical sounds forming a melody. **2.** the state of being in the proper pitch: *to be in tune.* **3.** agreement; accord; harmony: *to be in tune with the latest developments.* —*v.,* **tuned, tun·ing. 4.** to put (a musical instrument) in tune: *to tune a piano.* **5.** to adjust musical instruments, as in an orchestra, to the correct pitch, in preparation for playing (often fol. by *up*): *The violinist tuned up before the recital.* **6.** to bring into harmony: *to tune oneself to the times.* **7.** to adjust (a motor, mechanism, etc.) for proper functioning (often fol. by *up*): *to tune up an engine.* **8.** to adjust (a radio or television set) so as to receive transmitted signals properly. **9. change one's tune,** to change one's mind or opinion: *She changed her tune about skiing after she broke her leg.* **10. to the tune of,** *Informal.* at a cost of: *They fixed my bicycle to the tune of $19.62.* **11. tune in,** to adjust a radio to receive (a station): *Tune in WQXR at 2 p.m.* —**tune′less,** *adj.*

tune·ful (tōōn′fəl, tyōōn′-), *adj.* full of melody; melodious; musical: *a tuneful opera.* —**tune′ful·ly,** *adv.* —**tune′ful·ness,** *n.*

tune·less (tōōn′lis, tyōōn′-), *adj.* without tune; not musical or melodious: *a tuneless whistling.*

tung·sten (tung′stən), *n.* a hard metal having a high melting point. Tungsten is used in alloys, and in electric-lamp filaments. It is a chemical element. *Symbol:* W

tu·nic (tōō′nik, tyōō′-), *n.* **1.** a loose outer garment, usually reaching to the knees, with or without sleeves, and sometimes belted, worn by men and women in ancient Greece and Rome. **2.** a military coat or blouse, usually reaching to or just below the hips. **3.** a similar coat or blouse for women.

tun′ing fork′, a steel instrument consisting of a stem with two prongs, producing a musical tone of constant pitch when struck, and used as a standard for tuning musical instruments.

Tu·nis (tōō′nis, tyōō′-), *n.* the capital city of Tunisia, in the NE part.

Tu·ni·sia (tōō nē′zhə, tōō nē′shə), *n.* a republic in N Africa, on the Mediterranean Sea, formerly French. 48,330 sq. mi. *Cap.:* Tunis. —**Tu·ni′sian,** *n., adj.*

Tuning fork

tun·nel (tun′əl), *n.* **1.** an underground passageway for cars, trains, or pedestrians, made by digging or boring beneath a street, mountain, river, etc. **2.** any similar structure, such as the burrow of an animal. —*v.,* **tun·neled** *or* **tun·nelled; tun·nel·ing** *or* **tun·nel·ling. 3.** to make a tunnel: *The workmen are tunneling under the river.* **4.** to make (a passageway) by digging underground: *to tunnel a subway.*

tun·ny (tun′ē), *n., pl.* **tun·nies** *or* **tun·ny.** another word for **tuna.**

tu·pe·lo (tōō′pə lō′), *n., pl.* **tu·pe·los. 1.** any of several trees that grow in the deep swamps and river bottoms of the southern U.S. **2.** the strong, tough wood of these trees.

tup·pence (tup′əns), *n.* another spelling of **twopence.**

tur·ban (tûr′bən), *n.* **1.** a covering for the head worn chiefly by men in Muslim countries, made of a long sash or scarf wound about the head. **2.** any similar headdress, esp. a brimless hat worn by women.

tur·bid (tûr′bid), *adj.* **1.** (of a liquid) unclear from having sediment stirred up from the bottom; clouded; murky: *turbid waters.* **2.** thick or dense: *turbid smoke.* **3.** confused; muddled: *turbid thinking.*

Turban

tur·bine (tûr′bin, tûr′bīn), *n.* any of various machines having a rotor, usually with vanes or blades, driven by the pressure of moving steam, water, hot gases, or air.

tur·bo·jet (tûr′bō jet′), *n.* **1.** a jet engine in which the incoming air is compressed by a fan of relatively small diameter driven by a turbine in the path of the exhaust gases. **2.** an airplane powered by one or more such engines. See also **fanjet, propjet.**

tur·bo·prop (tûr′bō prop′), *n.* an airplane equipped with one or more jet engines having turbine-driven propellers.

tur·bot (tûr′bət), *n., pl.* **tur·bots** *or* **tur·bot.** a European flatfish having a diamond-shaped body and flesh that is valued as food.

tur·bu·lent (tûr′byə lənt), *adj.* **1.** violently disturbed: *turbulent winds; turbulent emotions.* **2.** causing violence or disturbance; disorderly: *a turbulent mob.* —**tur′bu·lence,** *n.* —**tur′bu·lent·ly,** *adv.*

tu·reen (tōō rēn′, tyōō-), *n.* a large, deep dish with a lid, for serving soup, stew, or other foods.

turf (tûrf), *n.* **1.** the top layer of soil, bound into a tight mass by grass and roots of plants; sod. **2.** a piece cut from this. **3.** a block or piece of peat dug for fuel. **4. the turf, a.** a track for horse racing. **b.** horse racing. —v. **5.** to cover with turf.

tur·gid (tûr′jid), *adj.* **1.** puffed up; swollen. **2.** pompous; bombastic: *turgid writing.* —**tur′gid·ly,** *adv.*

Tu·rin (tŏŏr′in, tyŏŏr′-), *n.* a city in NW Italy, on the Po River.

Turk (tûrk), *n.* **1.** a native or inhabitant of Turkey. **2.** a member of any of the peoples speaking Turkic languages.

tur·key (tûr′kē), *n., pl.* **tur·keys** or **tur·key. 1.** a large bird of America that usually has green and reddish-brown feathers, and that is domesticated in most parts of the world. **2.** the flesh of this bird, used as food.

Tur·key (tûr′kē), *n.* a republic in W Asia and SE Europe. 296,184 sq. mi. *Cap.:* Ankara.

Tur·kic (tûr′kik), *n.* **1.** a group of related languages of central and southwest Asia and eastern Europe, including Turkish, the languages of the Tartars, and several others. —*adj.* **2.** of or referring to Turkic or the peoples speaking Turkic languages.

Turkey
(length to 4 ft.)

Turk·ish (tûr′kish), *adj.* **1.** of or belonging to Turkey or the Turks. **2.** of or referring to the Turkish language. —*n.* **3.** the language of Turkey, belonging to the Turkic group of languages.

tur·moil (tûr′moil), *n.* a condition of great confusion or disturbance; tumult: *His sudden departure left the office in a turmoil.*

turn (tûrn), *v.* **1.** to move or cause to move around an axis or about a center; revolve; rotate: *Water power turns the wheel of the mill.* **2.** to shift or move around so as to face or proceed in a different direction: *Turn your head to the left.* **3.** to reverse or be reversed in placement or position (often fol. by *over*): *The baby turned over in his sleep.* **4.** to change or be changed in nature, character, appearance, color, etc.: *Success turned him into a snob.* **5.** to make or become sour, spoiled, etc.: *The hot sun turned the milk.* **6.** to hinge or depend (usually fol. by *on* or *upon*): *Victory in the battle turned on the speed of their ships.* **7.** to make or become sick or nauseated; upset: *His stomach turns at the mere mention of squid.* **8.** to direct one's thought or attention toward or away from someone or something: *to turn to the governor for help.* **9.** to put or apply to some other use or purpose: *to turn an opponent's error to one's advantage.* **10.** to go or pass around or beyond: *The bus turned the corner. She turned 12 last month.* **11.** to give a rounded form to, esp. by cutting or grinding: *to turn a table leg on a lathe.* **12.** to make, perform, or accomplish with skill: *to turn a phrase.* **13.** to cause to go; send; drive: *He turned the dogs loose.* **14.** to twist out of position; wrench: *He turned his*

ankle. **15.** to attack suddenly (usually fol. by *on*): *The dog turned on his master.* **16.** to earn as wages or profit; gain: *He turned a huge profit on the sale.* —*n.* **17.** the act of rotating or revolving around an axis or center: *a slight turn of the handle.* **18.** the act of changing or reversing position by turning: *a turn of the head.* **19.** one's time or chance to do something: *It's your turn to treat for lunch.* **20.** the act of changing course or direction: *a turn to the left.* **21.** the place at which one changes course or direction: *a turn in the road.* **22.** a change of character, nature, condition, etc.: *a turn for the better.* **23.** the point or time of change: *the turn of the century.* **24.** a single twist or coil of one thing about another: *two turns of rope around the post.* **25.** a short walk or ride: *a turn through the park.* **26.** a spell or period of work; shift: *Will you take a turn at the switchboard?* **27.** an act or action that affects someone else, for good or ill: *to do a good turn.* **28.** *Informal.* a shock of surprise or distress; start. **29. in turn,** in order; during his or her turn: *Each person will go to the blackboard in turn.* **30. out of turn,** out of order: *He gave the answer out of turn.* **31. take turns,** to follow one another in order; alternate: *Everyone will take turns feeding the goldfish.* **32. turn back, a.** to turn and go in the opposite direction: *We decided to turn back when it got dark.* **b.** to fold back (a blanket, sheet of paper, etc.): *Turn back the covers of the bed.* **33. turn down, a.** to turn over; fold down: *Turn down the covers.* **b.** to lessen the intensity of: *Turn down the volume on the radio.* **c.** to refuse or reject (a person, request, etc.). **34. turn in, a.** to go to bed. **b.** to hand in; submit: *to turn in an assignment.* **c.** to turn from one course to another: *Turn in at the next driveway.* **d.** to deliver over to the authorities; inform on: *They turned him in to the police.* **35. turn off, a.** to stop (water, gas, etc.) by closing a valve. **b.** to extinguish (a light). **c.** to drive a vehicle onto another road: *Turn off at Exit 39.* **36. turn on, a.** to cause (water, gas, etc.) to flow by opening a valve. **b.** to switch on (a light). **c.** to put into operation. **d.** to show or use suddenly: *to turn on the charm.* **37. turn out, a.** to extinguish (a light). **b.** to produce (something) as the result of work: *They turn out 1000 cars a day.* **c.** to result or end: *How did the game turn out?* **d.** *Informal.* to be present; appear: *How many members turned out?* **38. turn over, a.** to turn upside down: *The car turned over when it was struck.* **b.** to turn from one side to the reverse side: *to turn over pages in a book.* **c.** to consider; ponder: *to turn over a plan in one's mind.* **d.** to transfer; give: *to turn over a dog to its owner.* **39. turn to, a.** to appeal to for help. **b.** to begin working in earnest: *If everyone turns to, we can do the job in an hour.* **40. turn up, a.** to uncover; find: *to turn up a lost ring.* **b.** to increase or intensify: *Turn up the volume on the TV set.* **c.** to happen; occur: *Let's just wait around and see what turns up.* **d.** to appear; arrive: *to turn up late.* **e.** to be recovered: *I'm sure your watch will turn up eventually.*

act, āble, dâre, ärt; ebb, ēqual; if, īce; hot, ōver, ôrder; oil; bŏŏk; ōōze; out; up, ûrge; ə = *a* as in *alone*; ə as in *button* (but′ə n), *fire* (fīə r); chief; shoe; thin; ŧħat; zh as in *measure* (mezh′ə r). See full key inside cover.

turn·buck·le (tûrn'buk'əl), *n.* a rotating link having one or two internal screw threads, used to connect or unite two threaded parts.

turn·coat (tûrn'kōt'), *n.*
1. a person who goes over to the opposite party or side; renegade. 2. a person who joins the enemy; traitor; deserter.

Turnbuckle

tur·nip (tûr'nip), *n.* 1. the thick, fleshy root of a plant related to the cabbage and used as a vegetable. 2. the plant itself.

turn·key (tûrn'kē'), *n., pl.* **turn·keys.** a person who has charge of the keys of a prison; jailer.

turn·out (tûrn'out'), *n.* 1. a gathering of persons for a meeting, party, show, etc. 2. an output of work. 3. the manner or style in which a person or thing is equipped, dressed, etc. 4. a short sidetrack or a short, widened stretch of road where trains, automobiles, etc., may pass one another.

turn·o·ver (tûrn'ō'vər), *n.* 1. the act or result of turning over; upset. 2. the rate at which persons or things are dismissed, released, sold, etc., and replaced, such as workers, patients, merchandise, etc. 3. a sweet pastry made by placing filling on half of a piece of dough, and folding the other half over. —*adj.* 4. able to be turned over: *a turnover collar.*

turn·pike (tûrn'pīk'), *n.* 1. a highway for fast traffic, having a limited number of entrances and exits, and often tollgates. 2. (formerly) a tollgate. [from the Middle English word *turnepike* "road barrier." See *pike*². Originally, a pike or pole was placed across the road as a barrier where the toll was paid]

turn·stile (tûrn'stīl'), *n.* a structure of four, or sometimes three, revolving arms, set in the opening of an entrance or exit for collecting fares or admission charges, controlling the passage of people, or recording the number of persons passing through it.

turn·ta·ble (tûrn'tā'bəl), *n.* 1. a rotating disk on which a phonograph record rests. 2. a rotating platform provided with one or more tracks running across it, used for turning railroad cars or locomotives around. 3. any rotating stand or platform for holding or serving various things.

tur·pen·tine (tûr'pən tīn'), *n.* 1. a colorless, strong-smelling liquid distilled from the sap of cone-bearing trees and used chiefly to thin paints and varnishes. 2. a mixture of oil and resin obtained from cone-bearing trees.

tur·pi·tude (tûr'pi tōōd', -tyōōd'), *n.* 1. wickedness or baseness of character; depravity. 2. a wicked or base act.

tur·quoise (tûr'koiz, tûr'kwoiz), *n.* 1. a sky-blue or greenish-blue mineral, often used as a gem. 2. a greenish blue, or a bluish green. —*adj.* 3. of the color turquoise.

Turret

tur·ret (tûr'it, tur'it), *n.* 1. a small tower, usually one forming part of a building, castle, or fortress. 2. a part of a lathe that holds any of the cutting tools being used on the lathe at a particular time. 3. a low, heavily armored structure, usually revolving horizontally, forming part of a warship, tank, airplane, etc., in which guns are mounted. —*tur'ret·ed, adj.*

tur·tle (tûr't³l), *n.* 1. any of various reptiles, living on land or in water and having the body enclosed in a shell. The turtle protects itself by drawing the head and legs inside the shell. See also **tortoise** (def. 1). 2. **turn turtle,** to overturn: *My rowboat turned turtle in the storm.*

Box turtle
(length 6 in.)

tur·tle·dove (tûr't³l duv'), *n.* any of several small to medium-sized doves of Europe, having a long tail.

tur·tle·neck (tûr't³l nek'), *n.* 1. a high, soft collar that turns down, used esp. on pullover sweaters and shirts. 2. a sweater or shirt having such a collar. —*adj.* 3. provided with such a collar.

Tus·can (tus'kən), *adj.* 1. of or referring to Tuscany, its people, or their dialects. —*n.* 2. a native of Tuscany. 3. any of the dialects of Italian spoken in Tuscany. 4. a name sometimes used for the standard literary form of the Italian language.

Tus·ca·ny (tus'kə nē), *n.* a region in W central Italy. 8879 sq. mi.

tusk (tusk), *n.* (in certain animals) a tooth developed to great length, usually one of a pair, as in the elephant, walrus, etc.

tus·sle (tus'əl), *v.,* **tus·sled, tus·sling.** 1. to struggle or fight roughly; scuffle. —*n.* 2. a short, vigorous fight or struggle; scuffle.

tus·sock (tus'ək), *n.* a tuft or clump of growing grass or the like.

tut (tut), *interj.* 1. (used as an exclamation of annoyance, impatience, disapproval, etc.) —*n.* 2. an exclamation of "tut." —*v.,* **tut·ted, tut·ting.** 3. to utter the exclamation "tut."

Walrus tusks

tu·te·lage (tōōt'³lij, tyōōt'-), *n.* 1. protection, care, or guardianship: *The orphan was placed under the tutelage of his uncle.* 2. instruction; teaching: *He studied art under the tutelage of the masters.*

tu·te·lar·y (tōōt'³ler'ē, tyōōt'-), *adj.* 1. guarding or protecting: *a tutelary saint.* 2. of or referring to a guardian or guardianship: *tutelary duties.* Also, **tu·te·lar** (tōōt'³lər, tyōōt'-).

tu·tor (tōō'tər, tyōō'-), *n.* 1. a private teacher or coach: *a tutor of French.* —*v.* 2. to teach or coach, esp. privately: *A college student can tutor you in chemistry.* 3. to take lessons from a tutor: *He is tutoring in French.* —*tu·to·ri·al* (tōō tôr'ē əl, tyōō-), *adj.*

tux·e·do (tuk sē'dō), *n., pl.* **tux·e·dos.** 1. a man's jacket for formal wear, usually black and without tails. 2. a man's suit for formal wear, including such a jacket, trousers, and bow tie.

TV, television.

twad·dle (twod'³l), *n.* 1. silly, idle, or boring talk or writing. —*v.,* **twad·dled, twad·dling.** 2. to talk or write in a trivial or tiresome manner.

twain (twān), *n.* an old word for **two**, now used chiefly in poetry: *Never the twain shall meet.*

Twain (twān), *n.* **Mark** (pen name of *Samuel Langhorn Clemens),* 1835–1910, U.S. author and humorist.

twang (twang), *n.* **1.** a sharp, ringing sound, such as that made by plucking a string of a musical instrument. **2.** a speech sound made by allowing the flow of breath to pass through and resound in the nasal passages. —*v.* **3.** to sound or cause to sound with a twang. **4.** to speak or utter with a nasal twang.

'twas (twuz), contraction of **it was.**

tweak (twēk), *v.* **1.** to pinch or pull with a sudden twist: *to tweak someone's nose.* —*n.* **2.** an act of tweaking; sudden pinch or twist.

tweed (twēd), *n.* **1.** a coarse wool cloth, usually woven in two or more colors. **2. tweeds,** clothing made of this cloth. —**tweed′y,** *adj.*

tweet (twēt), *n.* **1.** a feeble chirping sound, such as that made by a small bird. —*v.* **2.** to make such a sound; chirp.

tweez·ers (twē′zərz), *n.pl.* small pincers or nippers for plucking out hairs, picking up or holding small objects, etc.

twelfth (twelfth), *adj.* **1.** being number twelve in a series: *the twelfth floor.* —*n.* **2.** one of twelve equal parts. **3.** a person or thing that is twelfth.

Twelfth′ Night′, the evening before Epiphany, which is the twelfth day after Christmas.

Tweezers

twelve (twelv), *n.* **1.** a number that is ten plus two. **2.** a set of this many persons or things: *Twelve will be there.* —*adj.* **3.** amounting to twelve in number: *twelve persons.*

twen·ti·eth (twen′tē ith), *adj.* **1.** being number twenty in a series: *the twentieth floor.* —*n.* **2.** one of twenty equal parts. **3.** a person or thing that is twentieth.

twen·ty (twen′tē), *n., pl.* **twen·ties. 1.** a number that is two times ten. **2.** a set of this many persons or things: *Twenty of them will be there.* **3. twenties,** the numbers, years, degrees, etc., between 20 and 29: *She is in her early twenties.* —*adj.* **4.** amounting to twenty in number: *twenty persons.*

twenty-one (twen′tē wun′), *n.* a card game, the object of which is to draw cards adding up to a higher total than the dealer's cards, but not higher than 21.

twice (twīs), *adv.* **1.** two times. **2.** in double the amount or degree: *He works twice as hard as you do.*

twid·dle (twid′l), *v.,* **twid·dled, twid·dling. 1.** to twirl or play with (something) lightly or idly, esp. with the fingers. —*n.* **2.** an idle twirling motion, esp. of the fingers. **3. twiddle one's thumbs,** to do nothing; be idle: *I twiddled my thumbs all morning waiting for him to show up.* —**twid′dler,** *n.*

twig (twig), *n.* a slender shoot or branch of a tree or other plant.

twi·light (twī′līt′), *n.* **1.** the dim, scattered light from the sky when the sun is below the horizon, just after sunset. **2.** the period in early evening or early morning, when this light is seen. **3.** a period of decline: *the twilight of the Roman Empire.* **4.** a state of uncertainty or gloom. —*adj.* **5.** of, referring to, or resembling twilight: *the twilight hours.*

twill (twil), *n.* **1.** a weave made in such a way as to produce a pattern of diagonal lines or ribs. **2.** a fabric with such a weave. —*v.* **3.** to weave (cloth) in the pattern of a twill. —*adj.* **4.** made of or resembling twill: *twill trousers.*

'twill (twil), contraction of **it will.**

twin (twin), *n.* **1. twins,** two children born at one time of the same mother. **2.** either of two such children. **3.** either of two persons or things that are closely related or very similar: *I have a watch that is the twin of yours.* **4. the Twins.** See **Gemini** (def. 1). —*adj.* **5.** born as one of a pair at the same time and of the same mother: *twin brothers.* **6.** being one of a pair; identical: *twin beds.* **7.** made up of two similar or connected parts: *an egg with a twin yolk.* —*v.,* **twinned, twin·ning. 8.** to give birth to twins.

twine (twīn), *n.* **1.** a strong thread or string made of two or more strands twisted together. **2.** the act or result of twisting or interweaving. —*v.,* **twined, twin·ing. 3.** to twist together; interweave: *to twine locks of hair.* **4.** to coil, wind, or wrap around (something): *She twined her arms about his neck.* **5.** to follow a winding course: *The river twines through the valleys.*

twinge (twinj), *n.* **1.** a sudden, sharp pain: *a muscular twinge.* **2.** a sudden, sharp onset of feeling; pang: *a twinge of regret.* —*v.,* **twinged, twing·ing. 3.** to feel or cause to feel a sudden, sharp pain or pang.

twin·kle (twing′kəl), *v.,* **twin·kled, twin·kling. 1.** to shine with a flickering or flashing light: *The stars twinkled in the sky.* **2.** to sparkle; gleam: *jewels twinkling in the light.* **3.** to move rapidly; flutter: *The dancers' feet twinkled across the stage.* —*n.* **4.** a flickering or flashing light. **5.** a sparkle or gleam: *the twinkle of jewels; a twinkle of joy in the eyes.*

twin·kling (twing′kling), *n.* **1.** the act of something that twinkles. **2.** a very short time: *I was dressed and ready in a twinkling.*

twirl (twûrl), *v.* **1.** to rotate or cause to rotate rapidly; whirl; spin: *She twirled about the room. She learned to twirl a baton.* —*n.* **2.** the act of rotating rapidly; whirl. [a blend of *tw(ist)* + *(wh)irl*]

twist (twist), *v.* **1.** to combine (two or more strands or threads) by winding together. **2.** to form by or as if by winding strands together: *to twist thread.* **3.** to wind or twine about something: *She twisted the scarf around her neck.* **4.** to turn sharply or wrench out of shape: *to twist an ankle.* **5.** to distort the meaning of: *He twisted my words.* **6.** to curve or bend: *The river twists through the hills.* **7.** to contort: *His face was twisted with anger.* —*n.* **8.** a curve or bend. **9.** a rotary motion or spin. **10.** anything formed by or as if by twisting. **11.** the act or process of twining things together. **12.** a distortion, esp. of meaning. **13.** a sudden, unexpected change. **14.** a different treatment, method, idea, system, etc.: *He gave the old plot a new twist.* **15. twist one's arm,** to use force, threats, etc., to make a person do one's bidding: *I didn't want to go, but she twisted my arm.*

twist·er (twis′tər), *n.* **1.** a person or thing that twists. **2.** *Informal.* a tornado.

twit (twit), *v.*, **twit·ted, twit·ting. 1.** to taunt, tease, or annoy. —*n.* **2.** a reproach; taunt.

twitch (twich), *v.* **1.** to tug or pull at with a quick, short movement; pluck: *He twitched off the cover.* **2.** (of a muscle or part of the body) to move with a sudden, jerky motion: *His eyelid twitches when he's nervous.* —*n.* **3.** a quick, jerky movement of the body, a limb, etc. **4.** a short, sudden pull or tug.

twit·ter (twit′ər), *v.* **1.** to utter a series of small, high sounds, such as a bird does. **2.** to talk lightly and rapidly; chatter. **3.** to titter; giggle. **4.** to tremble with excitement. —*n.* **5.** a twittering sound. **6.** a state of nervous excitement.

two (tōō), *n.* **1.** a number that is one plus one. **2.** a set of this many persons or things: *Only two of them will be there.* —*adj.* **3.** amounting to two in number: *two persons.* **4. put two and two together,** to arrive at a correct conclusion from certain facts that are known: *He wouldn't tell me the news, but I could put two and two together.*

two-edged (tōō′ejd′), *adj.* **1.** having two edges, such as a sword. **2.** cutting or effective both ways.

two-faced (tōō′fāst′), *adj.* **1.** having two faces. **2.** dishonest; hypocritical.

two·fold (tōō′fōld′), *adj.* **1.** made up of two parts: *a twofold plan.* **2.** two times as great or as much; double: *a twofold increase.* —*adv.* **3.** in twofold measure: *The output increased twofold.*

two·pence (tup′əns), *n.* a sum of two British pennies. Also, **tuppence.**

two·pen·ny (tup′ə nē), *adj. British.* amounting to or valued at twopence.

two-step (tōō′step′), *n.* a ballroom dance, marked by sliding steps.

two-way (tōō′wā′), *adj.* **1.** allowing for movement or communication in opposite directions, or both to and from a place: *a two-way street; a two-way radio.* **2.** involving two participants: *a two-way agreement.*

-ty, a suffix used to form **1.** nouns expressing a quality or state: *safety; sovereignty.* **2.** numerals that are multiples of ten: *sixty; ninety.*

ty·coon (tī kōōn′), *n.* a businessman having great wealth and power. [from the Japanese word *taikun,* which comes from Chinese *tai* "great" + *kiun* "prince"]

ty·ing (tī′ing), *v.* the present participle of **tie.**

tyke (tīk), *n.* **1.** a mongrel dog. **2.** a small child. Also, **tike.**

Ty·ler (tī′lər), *n.* **John,** 1790–1862, 10th Vice President of the U.S. 1841; 10th President of the U.S. 1841–1845.

tym·pa·num (tim′pə nəm), *n.* **1.** the scientific term for **eardrum. 2.** the scientific term for **middle ear.**

type (tīp), *n.* **1.** a number of things or persons sharing certain characteristics that cause them to be considered as a group; class. **2.** a thing or person considered as a member of a class or category: *This is some type of mushroom.* **3.** a thing or person that is typical of a class; model; example: *This test is the type the teacher usually gives.* **4.** a block having on its upper surface a raised letter or character. **5.** a group of such pieces. —*v.*, **typed, typ·ing. 6.** to typewrite. **7.** to typify, symbolize, or represent.

Type
(def. 4)

type·write (tīp′rīt′), *v.*, **type·wrote** (tīp′rōt′), **type·writ·ten** (tīp′rit/′ᵊn), **type·writ·ing.** to write by means of a typewriter; type.

type·writ·er (tīp′rī′tər), *n.* a machine for writing in letters and characters that resemble printers' type.

ty·phoid (tī′foid), *n.* a serious, often fatal disease marked by fever and intestinal inflammation.

ty·phoon (tī fōōn′), *n.* a tropical hurricane of the western Pacific area and the China seas.

ty·phus (tī′fəs), *n.* a serious disease caused by a germ transmitted by lice and fleas, and marked by extreme weakness, severe nervousness, and the eruption of reddish spots on the skin.

typ·i·cal (tip′i kəl), *adj.* **1.** having or showing the characteristics or features of its type: *a typical office building.* **2.** showing distinctive, recognizable features; individual; characteristic: *a person's typical walk.* —**typ′i·cal·ly,** *adv.*

typ·i·fy (tip′ə fī′), *v.*, **typ·i·fied, typ·i·fy·ing.** to serve as an example of: *She typifies the girls in that school.*

typ·ist (tī′pist), *n.* a person who operates a typewriter.

ty·pog·ra·phy (tī pog′rə fē), *n.* **1.** the art or process of printing with type. **2.** the work of setting and arranging types and of printing from them. **3.** the general appearance of printed matter.

ty·ran·ni·cal (ti ran′i kəl), *adj.* unjustly cruel, harsh, or severe. —**ty·ran′ni·cal·ly,** *adv.*

tyr·an·nize (tir′ə nīz′), *v.*, **tyr·an·nized, tyr·an·niz·ing. 1.** to rule as a tyrant. **2.** to be cruel and tyrannical.

ty·ran·no·saur·us (ti ran′ə sôr′əs), *n.* a large, flesh-eating dinosaur that walked upright on its hind feet.

tyr·an·ny (tir′ə nē), *n., pl.* **tyr·an·nies. 1.** the government or rule of a tyrant. **2.** cruel or unjust use of power.

ty·rant (tī′rənt), *n.* **1.** a king or ruler who uses his power cruelly and unjustly. **2.** any person who misuses power. **3.** a ruler who has absolute power.

Tyre (tī³r), *n.* an ancient port city of Phoenicia. —**Tyr·i·an** (tir′ē ən), *adj.*

ty·ro (tī′rō), *n., pl.* **ty·ros.** a beginner in learning anything; novice.

Tyr·ol (tir′ol, ti rōl′), *n.* an alpine region in W Austria and N Italy. —**Ty·ro·le·an** (ti rō′lē an), *n., adj.*

	Semitic	Greek	Latin	Gothic	Modern Roman
DEVELOPMENT OF UPPER-CASE LETTERS	Ɣ	Ч	Ɣ	V	ᴜ	U

	Greek	Medieval	Gothic	Modern Roman
DEVELOPMENT OF LOWER-CASE LETTERS	υ	u	u	u	u

U

U, u (yōō), *n., pl.* **U's** *or* **Us, u's** *or* **us.** **1.** the 21st letter of the English alphabet. **2.** something having the shape of a U: *a U-turn.*

U, *Chem.* the symbol for **uranium.**

U., **1.** union. **2.** unit. **3.** united. **4.** university. **5.** upper.

u., **1.** unit. **2.** upper.

UAM, underwater-to-air missile.

U.A.R., United Arab Republic.

u·biq·ui·tous (yōō bik′wi təs), *adj.* being everywhere at the same time: *ubiquitous little ants.*

U-boat (yōō′bōt′), *n.* a German submarine.

u.c., (in printing) upper case.

ud·der (ud′ər), *n.* the large gland of a cow, goat, etc., that produces milk.

UFO, unidentified flying object. See also **flying saucer.**

U·gan·da (yōō gan′də, ōō gän′də), *n.* an independent republic in E Africa, formerly British. 93,981 sq. mi. **—U·gan′dan,** *n., adj.*

ugh (u, ōō, ug), *interj.* (used as an exclamation of disgust, horror, or the like.)

ug·ly (ug′lē), *adj.,* **ug·li·er, ug·li·est.** **1.** very unattractive or unpleasant to look at. **2.** disagreeable or unpleasant: *ugly remarks; ugly weather.* **3.** threatening trouble or danger: *an ugly wound.* **4.** mean or quarrelsome: *an ugly mood.* **—ug′li·ness,** *n.*

UHF, ultrahigh frequency. Also, **uhf**

U.K., United Kingdom.

U·kraine (yōō krān′, yōō′krān), *n.* a republic in the Soviet Union, in S Europe. 223,000 sq. mi.

U·krain·i·an (yōō krā′nē ən), *n.* **1.** a native or inhabitant of the Ukraine. **2.** the Slavic language of the Ukraine, closely related to Russian. **—***adj.* **3.** of or concerning the Ukraine, its people, or their language.

u·ku·le·le (yōō′kə lā′lē), *n.* a musical instrument resembling a guitar but smaller and having four strings. [from Hawaiian]

ul·cer (ul′sər), *n.* **1.** a sore on the surface of the body or in the stomach, intestines, etc., usually containing pus: *a stomach ulcer.* **2.** any rotten or corrupting condition, element, etc.

ul·cer·ate (ul′sə rāt′), *v.,* **ul·cer·at·ed, ul·cer·at·ing.** **1.** to form an ulcer. **2.** to cause an ulcer on or in: *Worry ulcerated his stomach.* **—ul′cer·a′tion,** *n.*

Ukulele

ul·cer·ous (ul′sər əs), *adj.* **1.** of or like an ulcer. **2.** affected with an ulcer or ulcers.

ul·na (ul′nə), *n.* the thinner of the two long bones extending from the elbow to the wrist.

Ul·ster (ul′stər), *n.* a province in the N part of the Republic of Ireland. 3123 sq. mi.

ul·te·ri·or (ul tēr′ē ər), *adj.* **1.** being beyond what is seen or intentionally kept hidden: *ulterior motives.* **2.** coming at a later time or stage: *ulterior action.* **3.** lying beyond or outside of a boundary; more remote: *ulterior regions.*

ul·ti·mate (ul′tə mit), *adj.* **1.** last or final: *The ultimate cost may be more than we can afford.* **2.** highest possible; greatest: *the ultimate good.* **3.** basic; fundamental: *ultimate principles.* **—***n.* **4.** the final point; final result. **5.** a fundamental fact or principle. **—ul′ti·mate·ly,** *adv.*

ul·ti·ma·tum (ul′tə mā′təm), *n.* a final, uncompromising demand or set of terms issued by a person or group involved in a dispute.

ul·tra (ul′trə), *adj.* going beyond what is usual or ordinary; extreme: *ultra conservative.*

ultra-, a prefix meaning **1.** beyond: *ultraviolet.* **2.** extreme or excessive: *ultramodern; ultranationalism.*

ul′tra·high fre′quency (ul′trə hī′), (in radio) any frequency between 300 and 3000 megahertz. *Abbr.:* UHF, uhf

ul·tra·ma·rine (ul′trə mə rēn′), *n.* **1.** a blue pigment made of powdered lapis lazuli. **2.** an artificial blue pigment. **3.** a deep blue. —*adj.* **4.** beyond the sea. **5.** of the color ultramarine.

ul·tra·son·ic (ul′trə son′ik), *adj.* noting or concerning a frequency above the range of human hearing.

ul·tra·vi·o·let (ul′trə vī′ə lit), *n.* radiation of shorter wavelength than visible violet light. Ultraviolet rays are invisible, but they produce sunburn and can make fluorescent materials glow.

U·lys·ses (yōō lis′ēz), *n.* the Latin name for **Odysseus.**

um·bel (um′bəl), *n.* a flower cluster in which a number of flower stalks, nearly equal in length, spread from a common center.

um·ber (um′bər), *n.* **1.** a brown or reddish-brown pigment, used in painting. **2.** a dark, reddish brown.

um·bil·i·cal cord′ (um bil′i kəl), *adj.* a cord connecting an unborn child with its mother.

um·brel·la (um brel′ə), *n.* a light, small, portable, usually circular cover for protection from rain or sun, made of a fabric held on a frame of thin ribs branching out from the top of a carrying stick or handle.

u·mi·ak (ōō′mē ak′), *n.* an open Eskimo boat made of a wooden frame covered with skins.

Umiak

um·pire (um′pīˠr), *n.* **1.** a person selected to rule on the plays in a game. **2.** a person selected to settle a dispute. —*v.,* **um·pired, um·pir·ing. 3.** to act as umpire in (a game, dispute, etc.).

UN, United Nations. Also, **U.N.**

un-, a prefix meaning **1.** not: *unfair.* **2.** opposite of: *un-American.* **3.** lacking or without: *unarmed.* **4.** reversal of an action: *unbend.* **5.** removal or depriving: *unclog.* **6.** completely: *unloose.*

un·a·bashed (un′ə basht′), *adj.* not embarrassed or ashamed: *to speak with unabashed frankness.*

un·a·ble (un ā′bəl), *adj.* lacking the necessary power, ability, etc., to do something.

un·a·bridged (un′ə brijd′), *adj.* not abridged or shortened, such as a book.

un·ac·cent·ed (un ak′sen tid, un′ak sen′tid), *adj.* without an accent mark; not stressed.

un·ac·cep·ta·ble (un′ak sep′tə bəl), *adj.* not acceptable. —**un′ac·cep′ta·bly,** *adv.*

un·ac·count·a·ble (un′ə koun′tə bəl), *adj.* **1.** unexplained; strange. **2.** not responsible: *He is unaccountable for his actions.* —**un′ac·count′a·bly,** *adv.*

un·ac·cus·tomed (un′ə kus′təmd), *adj.* **1.** unusual; unfamiliar: *an unaccustomed sight.* **2.** not accustomed or used to: *We're unaccustomed to such heat.*

un·af·fect·ed[1] (un′ə fek′tid), *adj.* sincere; genuine.

un·af·fect·ed[2] (un′ə fek′tid), *adj.* not influenced; unchanged: *He was unaffected by her tears.*

un·aid·ed (un āˠ′did), *adj.* not aided or helped.

un-A·mer·i·can (un′ə mer′i kən), *adj.* not characteristic of or proper to the U.S., its standards, ideals, etc.

u·na·nim·i·ty (yōō′nə nim′i tē), *n.* the state or quality of being unanimous or in complete agreement; undivided opinion.

u·nan·i·mous (yōō nan′ə məs), *adj.* **1.** being in complete agreement: *The class was unanimous in its approval.* **2.** showing complete agreement: *a unanimous vote.* —**u·nan′i·mous·ly,** *adv.*

un·an·swer·a·ble (un an′sər ə bəl), *adj.* **1.** not having a known answer: *an unanswerable question.* **2.** not open to dispute: *unanswerable proof.*

un·ap·pe·tiz·ing (un ap′i tī′zing), *adj.* not appealing or appetizing: *an unappetizing meal.*

un·ap·pre·cia·tive (un′ə prē′shə tiv), *adj.* not feeling or showing appreciation.

un·ap·proach·a·ble (un′ə prō′chə bəl), *adj.* **1.** not capable of being approached or reached; distant: *an unapproachable person.* **2.** impossible to equal or rival: *unapproachable goodness.*

un·armed (un ärmd′), *adj.* **1.** without weapons or armor. **2.** not having claws, thorns, scales, etc., as animals or plants.

un·as·sist·ed (un′ə sis′tid), *adj.* not assisted; without help: *He rode the bicycle unassisted.*

un·as·sum·ing (un′ə sōō′ming), *adj.* not vain; modest: *a pleasant, unassuming young man.*

un·at·tached (un′ə tacht′), *adj.* **1.** not attached. **2.** not associated with any group, organization, or the like; independent. **3.** not engaged or married.

un·at·tend·ed (un′ə ten′did), *adj.* **1.** not accompanied; alone: *She went to the party unattended.* **2.** not taken care of; receiving no attention: *He left the store unattended for a few minutes.*

un·a·vail·ing (un′ə vā′ling), *adj.* without success; useless; futile: *unavailing efforts.*

un·a·void·a·ble (un′ə voi′də bəl), *adj.* impossible to avoid or escape: *unavoidable delays.* —**un′a·void′a·bly,** *adv.*

un·a·wares (un′ə wârz′), *adv.* **1.** while not aware or conscious of a thing oneself; unknowingly: *He walked into his surprise party unawares.* **2.** without warning; suddenly: *to come upon someone unawares.*

un·bal·anced (un bal′ənst), *adj.* **1.** not balanced: *an unbalanced scale; an unbalanced checkbook.* **2.** mentally disturbed; not sane: *unbalanced judgment.*

un·bar (un bär′), *v.,* **un·barred, un·bar·ring. 1.** to remove a bar or bars from. **2.** to open; unbolt.

un·bear·a·ble (un bâr′ə bəl), *adj.* not bearable; impossible to bear or tolerate; intolerable: *unbearable suffering.* —**un·bear′a·bly,** *adv.*

un·be·com·ing (un′bi kum′ing), *adj.* not suitable or becoming; unattractive: *an unbecoming hat.*

un·be·liev·a·ble (un′bi lē′və bəl), *adj.* impossible to believe. —**un′be·liev′a·bly,** *adv.*

un·be·liev·er (un′bi lē′vər), *n.* **1.** a person who does not believe. **2.** a person who does not accept any, or some particular, religious belief. —**un′be·liev′ing,** *adj.*

un·bend (un bend′), *v.,* **un·bent** (un bent′), **un·bend·ing. 1.** to straighten from a bent form or position. **2.** to relax by being informal or casual: *After an hour or so everyone at the party began to unbend.*

un·bend·ing (un ben′diṅg), *adj.* **1.** not bending; rigid; stiff. **2.** not yielding; firm; strict.

un·bi·ased (un bī′əst), *adj.* not biased or one-sided; impartial; fair: *an unbiased opinion.*

un·blem·ished (un blem′isht), *adj.* not blemished; flawless; perfect: *His attendance record is unblemished.*

un·bolt (un bōlt′), *v.* to open (a door, window, etc.) by or as if by removing a bolt; unlock; unfasten.

un·born (un bôrn′), *adj.* not yet born; yet to come; future: *unborn generations.*

un·bound (un bound′), *v.* **1.** the past tense and past participle of **unbind. 2.** not bound, such as a book. **3.** freed from bonds; not confined.

un·bound·ed (un boun′did), *adj.* **1.** unlimited; boundless: *unbounded hope.* **2.** not restrained or controlled: *unbounded freedom.*

un·bro·ken (un brō′kən), *adj.* **1.** not broken; whole; intact: *an unbroken seal.* **2.** uninterrupted; continuous: *unbroken sleep.* **3.** (esp. of a horse) not tamed.

un·buck·le (un buk′əl), *v.,* **un·buck·led, un·buck·ling.** to undo the buckle or buckles of: *to unbuckle a belt.*

un·bur·den (un bûr′d³n), *v.* **1.** to free from a burden. **2.** to relieve (one's mind, conscience, etc.) by revealing or confessing something.

un·but·ton (un but′³n), *v.* to unfasten the button or buttons of.

un·called-for (un kôld′fôr′), *adj.* **1.** not called for; not required or wanted. **2.** not justified; improper.

un·can·ny (un kan′ē), *adj.* **1.** having or seeming to have a supernatural basis; beyond the ordinary or normal: *to shoot with uncanny accuracy.* **2.** mysterious; uncomfortably strange: *uncanny sounds.*

un·cap (un kap′), *v.,* **un·capped, un·cap·ping.** to remove a cap or cover from: *to uncap a bottle.*

un·cer·tain (un sûr′t³n), *adj.* **1.** not certain or sure; doubtful: *She is uncertain of the answer.* **2.** not definite or fixed: *an uncertain amount.* **3.** not capable of being known or predicted: *an uncertain outcome.* **4.** not dependable: *uncertain weather.*

un·cer·tain·ty (un sûr′t³n tē), *n., pl.* for def. 2 **un·cer·tain·ties. 1.** the state of being uncertain; doubt; hesitancy. **2.** something uncertain: *to face the uncertainties of life.*

un·civ·il (un siv′əl), *adj.* without good manners; rude; impolite.

un·civ·i·lized (un siv′ə līzd′), *adj.* not civilized; savage; barbarous.

un·cle (uṅg′kəl), *n.* **1.** a brother of one's father or mother. **2.** an aunt's husband.

un·clean (un klēn′), *adj.* **1.** not clean; dirty. **2.** morally impure; evil.

Un′cle Sam′, a personification of the government or people of the United States: represented as a tall man with white whiskers, wearing a blue tailcoat, red-and-white-striped trousers, and a top hat with a band of stars.

un·com·fort·a·ble (un kum′fər tə bəl), *adj.* **1.** causing discomfort or distress; painful: *an uncomfortable chair.* **2.** in a state of discomfort; uneasy: *She's uncomfortable with strangers.* **—un·com′fort·a·bly,** *adv.*

un·com·mon (un kom′ən), *adj.* **1.** not common; unusual; rare. **2.** exceptional or remarkable; outstanding: *uncommon beauty.* **—un·com′mon·ly,** *adv.*

un·com·pro·mis·ing (un kom′prə mī′ziṅg), *adj.* not making or accepting compromise; unyielding; firm.

un·con·cern (un′kən sûrn′), *n.* freedom from concern or anxiety: *He bore their insults with seeming unconcern.*

un·con·cerned (un′kən sûrnd′), *adj.* not involved or interested; not caring.

un·con·di·tion·al (un′kən dish′ə n³l), *adj.* not limited by conditions; absolute: *unconditional surrender.* **—un′con·di′tion·al·ly,** *adv.*

un·con·scious (un kon′shəs), *adj.* **1.** not conscious; without awareness or feeling: *He was unconscious for several hours after the operation.* **2.** not aware: *She was unconscious of her mistake.* **3.** done accidentally or unintentionally: *an unconscious compliment.* **—un·con′scious·ly,** *adv.* **—un·con′scious·ness,** *n.*

un·con·sti·tu·tion·al (un′kon sti tōō′shə n³l, -tyōō′-), *adj.* not constitutional; unauthorized by or inconsistent with the constitution. **—un′con·sti·tu′tion·al·ly,** *adv.*

un·con·trol·la·ble (un′kən trō′lə bəl), *adj.* impossible to control or restrain: *an uncontrollable horse.* **—un′con·trol′la·bly,** *adv.*

un·con·ven·tion·al (un′kən ven′shə n³l), *adj.* not conventional; not conforming to convention or rule: *unconventional clothing; an unconventional artist.*

un·cork (un kôrk′), *v.* to draw the cork from.

un·couth (un kōōth′), *adj.* awkward, clumsy, or unmannerly.

un·cov·er (un kuv′ər), *v.* **1.** to lay bare; disclose; reveal: *to uncover a plot.* **2.** to remove the cover or covering from. **3.** to remove a hat from (the head).

unc·tion (uṅgk′shən), *n.* **1.** an act of anointing, esp. as a medical treatment or religious rite. **2.** the oil used in religious rites. **3.** something soothing. **4.** a soothing and persuasive quality in speaking.

unc·tu·ous (uṅgk′chōō əs), *adj.* **1.** resembling an unguent or ointment; oily; greasy. **2.** too smooth, smug, or persuasive in speech or action. **—unc′tu·ous·ly,** *adv.*

un·cut (un kut′), *adj.* **1.** not cut. **2.** not shortened or condensed: *the uncut version of the play.*

un·daunt·ed (un dôn′tid), *adj.* not discouraged: *His defeat left him undaunted.*

un·de·cid·ed (un′di sī′did), *adj.* **1.** not decided or determined: *Plans are still undecided.* **2.** not having one's mind firmly made up.

un·de·clared (un′di klârd′), *adj.* not openly declared or announced: *an undeclared war.*

un·de·ni·a·ble (un′di nī′ə bəl), *adj.* impossible to be questioned or denied: *a man of undeniable talent; an undeniable story.* **—un′de·ni′a·bly,** *adv.*

un·der (un′dər), *prep.* **1.** beneath and covered by: *under a tree.* **2.** below the surface of: *under water.* **3.**

in the position or state of supporting, enduring, etc.: *to sink under a heavy load.* **4.** beneath the heading or within the category of: *He arranged the books under "Fiction" and "General."* **5.** below in degree, amount, etc.; less than: *under ten dollars.* **6.** subject to the instruction or advice of: *to study dance under a famous teacher.* **7.** subject to the influence, condition, or force of: *under these circumstances.* **8.** protected, controlled, or watched by: *under guard.* —*adv.* **9.** below or beneath something: *Go over the fence, not under.* **10.** beneath the surface. **11.** in or to a lower place. **12.** in or to a lower degree, amount, etc.: *selling blouses for $6 and under.* —*adj.* **13.** located on the underside: *a bird's under feathers.*

un·der·age (un'dər āj'), *adj.* of less than the required or legal age.

un·der·bid (un'dər bid'), *v.*, **un·der·bid, un·der·bid·ding.** to make a bid lower than that of (another bidder).

un·der·brush (un'dər brush'), *n.* shrubs, small trees, etc., growing under large trees in a wood or forest.

un·der·clothes (un'dər klōz', -klōᵺz'), *n.pl.* another word for **underwear.** Also, **un·der·cloth·ing** (un'dər klō'ᵺiñg).

un·der·cov·er (un'dər kuv'ər), *adj.* working or done in secret: *an undercover detective.*

un·der·cur·rent (un'dər kûr'ənt, -kur'ənt), *n.* **1.** a current of air or water flowing beneath another current. **2.** an underlying or hidden tendency, attitude, or feeling: *an undercurrent of sadness.*

un·der·dog (un'dər dôg'), *n.* **1.** a person who is expected to lose in a contest or conflict. **2.** a victim of social or political injustice.

un·der·done (un'dər dun'), *adj.* (of food) not thoroughly cooked or not cooked enough.

un·der·es·ti·mate (un'dər es'tə māt'), *v.*, **un·der·es·ti·mat·ed, un·der·es·ti·mat·ing.** to estimate at too low a value, rate, or the like: *We underestimated the cost.*

un·der·foot (un'dər foot'), *adv.* **1.** under the foot or feet; on the ground; underneath or below: *The ground is damp underfoot.* —*adj.* **2.** in the way: *The puppy is always underfoot.*

un·der·gar·ment (un'dər gär'mənt), *n.* an article of underwear.

un·der·go (un'dər gō'), *v.*, **un·der·went** (un'dər-went'), **un·der·gone** (un'dər gôn', -gon'), **un·der·go·ing. 1.** to go through; experience: *to undergo surgery.* **2.** to suffer or endure: *to undergo hardship.*

un·der·grad·u·ate (un'dər graj'ōō it), *n.* **1.** a student at a college or university who has not taken his bachelor's degree. —*adj.* **2.** having the standing of an undergraduate. **3.** of, for, or concerning undergraduates: *undergraduate courses.*

un·der·ground (un'dər ground'), *adj.* **1.** existing, placed, or operating underground: *an underground lake.* **2.** hidden or secret; not open: *Spying is an underground activity.* —*adv.* **3.** beneath the surface of the ground: *Miners work underground.* **4.** in hiding or secret; not openly: *The plotters schemed underground.* —*n.* (un'dər ground'). **5.** the place or region beneath the surface of the ground. **6.** a secret group

working against the government of a country or an occupying enemy.

un·der·growth (un'dər grōth'), *n.* shrubs, plants, vines, etc., growing thickly among trees.

un·der·hand (un'dər hand'), *adj.* **1.** Also, **underhanded.** not open and aboveboard; sly and crafty: *underhand business methods.* **2.** done with the hand below the level of the shoulder and the palm turned upward and forward: *an underhand pitch of a ball.* —*adv.* **3.** with an underhand motion. **4.** secretly; slyly: *to work underhand against the government.*

un·der·hand·ed (un'dər han'did), *adj.* another form of **underhand.** —**un'der·hand'ed·ly,** *adv.* —**un'der·hand'ed·ness,** *n.*

un·der·lie (un'dər lī'), *v.*, **un·der·lay** (un'dər lā'), **un·der·lain** (un'dər lān'), **un·der·ly·ing. 1.** to lie under or beneath: *A bed of rock underlies the soil.* **2.** to form the basis of; support: *What reasons underlie your choice?*

un·der·line (un'dər līn', un'dər līn'), *v.*, **un·der·lined, un·der·lin·ing. 1.** to mark with a line or lines underneath; underscore. **2.** to show the importance of; emphasize: *He underlined his message by repeating it several times.*

un·der·ling (un'dər liñg), *n.* a person of low rank who must obey orders.

un·der·ly·ing (un'dər lī'iñg), *adj.* **1.** lying under or beneath: *The drill pierced the underlying rock.* **2.** basic; fundamental: *the underlying reasons for a choice.*

un·der·mine (un'dər mīn' *or, esp. for def.* 2, un'-dər mīn'), *v.*, **un·der·mined, un·der·min·ing. 1.** to dig a tunnel or hole beneath: *to undermine a mountain.* **2.** to weaken or cause to collapse by wearing away at the base: *The flood waters undermined the houses.*

un·der·neath (un'dər nēth'), *prep., adv.* below the level or surface of; under; beneath: *underneath the table.*

un·der·nour·ished (un'dər nûr'isht, -nur'isht), *adj.* not nourished with enough or the right food for good health or normal growth.

un·der·pants (un'dər pants'), *n.pl.* drawers or shorts worn under the outer clothing.

un·der·part (un'dər pärt'), *n.* the lower part or side of an animal, object, etc.

un·der·pass (un'dər pas'), *n.* a passage running underneath a highway, bridge, railroad, etc.

un·der·pay (un'dər pā'), *v.*, **un·der·paid** (un'dər-pād'), **un·der·pay·ing.** to pay less than the usual or right amount.

un·der·pin·ning (un'dər pin'iñg), *n.* supports placed beneath a wall, foundation, etc.

un·der·priv·i·leged (un'dər priv'ə lijd), *adj.* lacking normal privileges, rights, etc., because of poor education, poverty, or low social standing.

un·der·rate (un'dər rāt'), *v.*, **un·der·rat·ed, un·der·rat·ing.** to rate too low; underestimate: *to underrate someone's ability.*

un·der·score (un'dər skôr'), *v.*, **un·der·scored, un·der·scor·ing. 1.** to draw a line or lines underneath; underline. **2.** to emphasize: *He underscored his warning.*

un·der·sea (un′dər sē′), *adj.* situated, used, or taking place under the surface of the sea.

un·der·seas (un′dər sēz′), *adv.* beneath the surface of the sea: *Submarines travel underseas.*

un·der·sec·re·tar·y (un′dər sek′ri ter′ē), *n., pl.* **un·der·sec·re·tar·ies.** a secretary next in rank below a secretary in a department of the government.

un·der·sell (un′dər sel′), *v.,* **un·der·sold** (un′dər-sōld′), **un·der·sell·ing.** to sell something at a lower price than: *The store undersold its competitors.*

un·der·shirt (un′dər shûrt′), *n.* a collarless undergarment, usually without sleeves, worn over the upper part of the body.

un·der·shot (un′dər shot′), *adj.* 1. having the front teeth of the lower jaw projecting beyond those of the upper jaw, like those of a bulldog. 2. (of a water wheel) driven by water passing beneath.

un·der·side (un′dər sīd′), *n.* an under or lower side.

un·der·signed (un′dər sīnd′), *adj.* 1. signed at the end of: *undersigned names.* —*n.* (un′dər sīnd′). 2. **the undersigned,** a person or persons whose names are signed at the end of a letter or document: *The undersigned agrees to abide by the rules of the contract.*

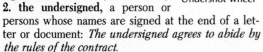
Undershot wheel

un·der·stand (un′dər stand′), *v.,* **un·der·stood** (un′dər stood′), **un·der·stand·ing.** 1. to grasp the meaning of; know: *to understand what is being said.* 2. to have a thorough knowledge of: *to understand one's job.* 3. to see clearly or grasp the importance of: *to understand the consequences of one's actions.* 4. to give a meaning to: *He understood her silence as a refusal.* 5. to learn or hear: *I understand that you have been ill.* 6. to regard as agreed or settled: *I understand that you will repay the loan within a month.* 7. to supply in thought (something that is not stated): *In "I am older than you," "are" is understood at the end.* 8. to feel sympathy toward or be sympathetic in a thoughtful way: *My parents do not understand me. If you can't finish, I will understand.*

un·der·stand·a·ble (un′dər stan′də bəl), *adj.* capable of being understood or accepted with sympathy. —**un′der·stand′a·bly,** *adv.*

un·der·stand·ing (un′dər stan′ding), *n.* 1. the fact of grasping what is meant; knowledge: *My understanding of the problem is limited.* 2. the ability to understand: *a person of great understanding.* 3. an agreement between people: *After hours of argument we came to a friendly understanding.* —*adj.* 4. based on, having, or showing intelligence, sympathy, knowledge, etc.: *an understanding, loving person.* —**un′der·stand′ing·ly,** *adv.*

un·der·stood (un′dər stood′), *v.* 1. the past tense and past participle of **understand.** —*adj.* 2. agreed upon: *It is understood that you will be there.* 3. unstated but implied, as a word left out of a sentence.

un·der·stud·y (un′dər stud′ē), *n., pl.* **un·der·stud·**

ies. 1. a person trained to replace an actor or actress if necessary. —*v.,* **un·der·stud·ied, un·der·stud·y·ing.** 2. to be an understudy to.

un·der·take (un′dər tāk′), *v.,* **un·der·took** (un′dər-took′), **un·der·tak·en** (un′dər tā′kən), **un·der·tak·ing.** 1. to take upon oneself; attempt: *to undertake a difficult task.* 2. to promise or agree to perform a task, duty, or the like: *He undertook to finish the job.*

un·der·tak·er (un′dər tā′kər), *n.* a person whose business is to prepare the dead for burial and to arrange funerals.

un·der·tak·ing (un′dər tā′king *for defs. 1, 2;* un′dər tā′king *for def. 3*), *n.* 1. the act of a person who undertakes something. 2. a task, duty, or the like: *Fortune favored the undertaking.* 3. the business of an undertaker.

un·der·tone (un′dər tōn′), *n.* 1. a low tone of voice: *We spoke in an undertone so that we would not disturb the others.* 2. a quality that does not appear directly: *an undertone of sadness in his voice.*

un·der·tow (un′dər tō′), *n.* a strong current under the surface of the water that moves in a different direction from the surface current, esp. at a beach.

un·der·wa·ter (un′dər wô′tər, -wot′ər), *adj.* placed, existing, used, or happening under water: *an underwater plant; underwater swimming.*

un·der·wear (un′dər wâr′), *n.* clothing worn next to the skin under one's outer clothes. Also, **underclothes, underclothing.**

un·der·weight (un′dər wāt′), *adj.* 1. weighing less than is normal: *to be underweight from hunger.* —*n.* (un′dər wāt′). 2. weight below what is normal.

un·der·went (un′dər went′), *v.* the past tense of **undergo.**

un·der·world (un′dər wûrld′), *n.* 1. the class of people made up of criminals, gangsters, etc. 2. the abode of the dead, esp. in Greek and Roman mythology; Hades.

un·der·write (un′dər rīt′), *v.,* **un·der·wrote** (un′dər-rōt′), **un·der·writ·ten** (un′dər rit′ən), **un·der·writ·ing.** 1. to grant (an insurance policy) by assuming responsibility for any losses named in the agreement. 2. to agree to buy (the unsold part of an issue of stock). 3. to agree to back (an undertaking) with money. —**un′der·writ′er,** *n.*

un·de·served (un′di zûrvd′), *adj.* not deserved or merited. —**un·de·serv·ed·ly** (un′di zûr′vid lē), *adv.*

un·de·sir·a·ble (un′di zī′r ə bəl), *adj.* 1. not desirable or attractive: *an undesirable habit.* —*n.* 2. a person who is found objectionable by others: *beggars and other undesirables.* —**un′de·sir′a·bly,** *adv.*

un·de·vel·oped (un′di vel′əpt), *adj.* 1. (of film) not developed. 2. not fully grown or put to use: *undeveloped fruit; undeveloped resources.*

un·dig·ni·fied (un dig′nə fīd′), *adj.* lacking dignity: *undignified behavior.*

un·di·lut·ed (un′di loo′tid, -dī loo′tid), *adj.* 1. not diluted. 2. pure or complete: *undiluted happiness.*

un·dis·guised (un′dis gīzd′, un′di skīzd′), *adj.* without disguise or concealment; open: *undisguised anger.*

un·dis·put·ed (un'dis pyōō'tid), *adj.* not to be disputed or denied: *Bill is the undisputed champion.*

un·dis·tin·guished (un'di sting'gwisht), *adj.* not distinguished; ordinary or commonplace: *an undistinguished performance.*

un·di·vid·ed (un'di vī'did), *adj.* not divided; whole; entire: *Give me your undivided attention.*

un·do (un dōō'), *v.,* **un·did** (un did'), **un·done** (un dun'), **un·do·ing.** 1. to do away with; cancel; wipe out: *to undo a damage.* 2. to loosen, unfasten, or untie; open. 3. to ruin; destroy: *His carelessness will undo him.*

un·do·ing (un dōō'ing), *n.* 1. the reversal or cancellation of what has been done. 2. destruction, ruin, or disaster: *the undoing of a ship by a storm.* 3. a cause of destruction or ruin: *His pride was his undoing.*

un·done[1] (un dun'), *adj.* not done or completed.

un·done[2] (un dun'), *v.* 1. the past participle of **undo.** —*adj.* 2. brought to destruction or ruin: *They were undone by the war.* 3. unfastened: *The package became undone.*

un·doubt·ed (un dou'tid), *adj.* not doubted or disputed; beyond doubt: *a person of undoubted ability.* —**un·doubt'ed·ly,** *adv.*

un·dreamed-of (un drēmd'uv'), *adj.* not dreamed of or imagined: *undreamed-of wealth.* Also, **un·dreamt-of** (un dremt'uv'),

un·dress (un dres'), *v.,* **un·dressed** *or* **un·drest; un·dress·ing.** 1. to take one's clothes off. 2. to remove the clothes from.

un·due (un dōō', -dyōō'), *adj.* 1. more than is necessary; excessive; too much: *undue haste.* 2. not proper or suitable: *undue influence.*

un·du·lant (un'jə lənt, un'dyə lənt), *adj.* undulating; wavy: *undulant lines.*

un·du·late (un'jə lāt', un'dyə lāt'), *v.,* **un·du·lat·ed, un·du·lat·ing.** 1. to move or cause to move in waves or with a wavelike motion. 2. to have a wavy form or surface: *undulating land.* 3. (of a sound) to rise and fall in pitch. —**un'du·la'tion,** *n.*

un·du·ly (un dōō'lē, -dyōō'-), *adv.* 1. excessively; too much: *unduly worried.* 2. in an improper manner: *unduly harsh.*

un·dy·ing (un dī'ing), *adj.* deathless; immortal; unending: *undying words.*

un·earth (un ûrth'), *v.* 1. to dig out of the earth. 2. to discover or bring to light: *to unearth facts.*

un·earth·ly (un ûrth'lē), *adj.* 1. not of this world; supernatural; weird: *unearthly creatures from outer space.* 2. unusual; extreme; absurd: *to get up at an unearthly hour.* —**un·earth'li·ness,** *n.*

un·eas·y (un ē'zē), *adj.,* **un·eas·i·er, un·eas·i·est.** 1. not easy in body or mind; restless: *Fear of a strike made everyone uneasy.* 2. not easy in manner; awkward: *He feels uneasy among strangers.* 3. worrying; disturbing; upsetting: *uneasy doubts.* —**un·eas'i·ly,** *adv.* —**un·eas'i·ness,** *n.*

un·em·ployed (un'em ploid'), *adj.* 1. not employed; out of work. 2. not in use: *unemployed talents.* —*n.*

3. **the unemployed,** persons who do not have jobs.

un·em·ploy·ment (un'em ploi'mənt), *n.* the condition of being without a job.

un·end·ing (un en'ding), *adj.* having or seeming to have no end; endless: *an unending stream of traffic.*

un·en·dur·a·ble (un'en dŏŏr'ə bəl, -dyŏŏr'-), *adj.* not to be endured or supported: *unendurable pain.*

un·e·qual (un ē'kwəl), *adj.* 1. not equal in size, degree, amount, etc.: *lines of unequal length.* 2. uneven: *an unequal surface.* 3. not right or just; unfair: *unequal laws.* 4. **unequal to,** lacking the strength, ability, etc., required for: *to be unequal to a job.* —**un·e'qual·ly,** *adv.*

un·e·qualed (un ē'kwəld), *adj.* not equaled; supreme; matchless: *an unequaled opportunity.*

UNESCO (yōō nes'kō), *n.* an agency of the United Nations that carries out programs in education, science, and the arts. [from the name *U(nited) N(ations) E(ducational), S(cientific, and) C(ultural) O(rganization)*]

un·e·ven (un ē'vən), *adj.* 1. not level or flat; rough: *an uneven floor.* 2. not equal in amount, size, etc.: *pencils of uneven length.* 3. not fair or balanced: *an uneven contest.* 4. (of a number) odd: *The number 3 is uneven.* —**un·e'ven·ly,** *adv.* —**un·e'ven·ness,** *n.*

un·e·vent·ful (un'i vent'fəl), *adj.* not eventful; routine or ordinary: *a peaceful, uneventful day.*

un·ex·celled (un'ik seld'), *adj.* supreme; unequaled: *an unexcelled beauty.*

un·ex·cit·ing (un'ik sī'ting), *adj.* not exciting; ordinary; dull: *an unexciting life.*

un·ex·pect·ed (un'ik spek'tid), *adj.* not expected; unforeseen; surprising. —**un'ex·pect'ed·ly,** *adv.*

un·fail·ing (un fā'ling), *adj.* 1. not failing; inexhaustible: *an unfailing supply of water.* 2. completely dependable; reliable; faithful: *an unfailing friend.* —**un·fail'ing·ly,** *adv.*

un·fair (un fâr'), *adj.* not fair or right; unjust: *unfair prices.* —**un·fair'ly,** *adv.*

un·faith·ful (un fāth'fəl), *adj.* 1. not faithful or true; disloyal; false: *to be unfaithful to one's friends.* 2. not accurate or complete; inexact: *an unfaithful account of an event.* —**un·faith'ful·ness,** *n.*

un·fa·mil·iar (un'fə mil'yər), *adj.* 1. not familiar; not acquainted: *I am unfamiliar with this neighborhood.* 2. unusual or strange: *an unfamiliar experience.*

un·fas·ten (un fas'ən), *v.* to undo or open (something fastened): *Unfasten your seat belts.*

un·fath·om·a·ble (un fath'əm ə bəl), *adj.* 1. too deep to fathom or measure. 2. not able to be understood or explained: *an unfathomable mystery.*

un·fa·vor·a·ble (un fā'vər ə bəl), *adj.* not favorable or advantageous: *unfavorable working conditions; unfavorable comments.* —**un·fa'vor·a·bly,** *adv.*

un·feel·ing (un fē'ling), *adj.* 1. without sympathy, pity, kindness, etc. 2. lacking feeling: *numb, unfeeling fingers.* —**un·feel'ing·ly,** *adv.*

un·fin·ished (un fin'isht), *adj.* 1. not finished; incomplete: *He left the story unfinished.* 2. left in a rough state: *unfinished furniture.*

un·fit (un fit'), *adj.* 1. not suitable or adapted: *A* *knife is unfit for opening a can.* **2.** not qualified or physically fit: *to be unfit for military service.*

un·flinch·ing (un flin′chǐng), *adj.* not flinching; steadfast; unyielding: *He faced the future with unflinching courage.* —**un·flinch′ing·ly,** *adv.*

un·fold (un fōld′), *v.* **1.** to spread or open out: *to unfold a map.* **2.** to spread out to view: *The land unfolded before them.* **3.** to make or become known: *He unfolded his plan point by point.*

un·fore·seen (un′fôr sēn′), *adj.* not foreseen; unexpected: *an unforeseen difficulty.*

un·for·get·ta·ble (un′fər get′ə bəl), *adj.* impossible to forget. —**un′for·get′ta·bly,** *adv.*

un·for·giv·a·ble (un′fər giv′ə bəl), *adj.* not able to be forgiven: *unforgivable rudeness.* —**un′for·giv′a·bly,** *adv.*

un·for·tu·nate (un fôr′chə nit), *adj.* **1.** suffering from bad luck: *an unfortunate life.* **2.** not favorable or successful: *an unfortunate attempt.* **3.** to be regretted: *an unfortunate remark.* —*n.* **4.** an unfortunate or unhappy person. —**un·for′tu·nate·ly,** *adv.*

un·found·ed (un foun′did), *adj.* without any basis in fact: *unfounded rumors.*

un·friend·ly (un frend′lē), *adj.,* **un·friend·li·er, un·friend·li·est. 1.** not friendly or kind; aloof: *unfriendly neighbors.* **2.** causing trouble; hostile: *unfriendly nations.* **3.** not favorable: *an unfriendly climate.* —**un·friend′li·ness,** *n.*

un·fruit·ful (un frōōt′fəl), *adj.* failing to produce results, offspring, crops, etc.: *an unfruitful search; unfruitful land.*

un·furl (un fûrl′), *v.* to spread out or unroll: *The flags unfurled in the wind.*

un·gain·ly (un gān′lē), *adj.* not graceful; awkward; clumsy: *a tall, ungainly person.*

un·gen·er·ous (un jen′ər əs), *adj.* **1.** not generous; stingy; miserly. **2.** not kind or considerate: *an ungenerous remark.* —**un·gen′er·ous·ly,** *adv.*

un·god·ly (un god′lē), *adj.,* **un·god·li·er, un·god·li·est. 1.** not religious; sinful or wicked: *ungodly behavior.* **2.** *Informal.* dreadful: *an ungodly noise.* —**un·god′li·ness,** *n.*

un·gra·cious (un grā′shəs), *adj.* not courteous; rude: *ungracious manners.* —**un·gra′cious·ly,** *adv.*

un·grate·ful (un grāt′fəl), *adj.* **1.** not showing gratitude: *Though they saved his life, he was ungrateful to them.* **2.** unrewarding or unpleasant: *an ungrateful task.* —**un·grate′ful·ly,** *adv.*

un·guent (ung′gwənt), *n.* an ointment or salve for use on wounds or sores.

un·hand (un hand′), *v.* to take the hand or hands from; release; let go.

un·hap·py (un hap′ē), *adj.,* **un·hap·pi·er, un·hap·pi·est. 1.** not happy or cheerful; sad. **2.** unlucky; unfortunate: *an unhappy business venture.* **3.** unsuitable; inappropriate: *an unhappy combination of colors.* —**un·hap′pi·ly,** *adv.* —**un·hap′pi·ness,** *n.*

un·harmed (un härmd′), *adj.* not hurt or injured; safe and sound.

un·health·y (un hel′thē), *adj.,* **un·health·i·er, un·health·i·est. 1.** not in good health; not well; sickly. **2.** indicating poor physical or mental health: *an unhealthy attitude.* **3.** harmful to good health: *an unhealthy dampness.* **4.** morally bad or harmful: *an unhealthy influence.* —**un·health′i·ness,** *n.*

un·heard-of (un hûrd′uv′), *adj.* **1.** never heard of; unknown: *an unheard-of artist.* **2.** never heard of or done before; previously unknown: *Spaceships travel at unheard-of speeds.* **3.** shocking; outrageous: *He spoke with unheard-of insolence.*

un·hes·i·tat·ing (un hez′i tā′tǐng), *adj.* **1.** without hesitation; immediate: *an unhesitating response to my orders.* **2.** without doubt or misgiving; wholehearted: *He gave unhesitating approval to the plan.* —**un·hes′i·tat′ing·ly,** *adv.*

un·hinge (un hinj′), *v.,* **un·hinged, un·hing·ing. 1.** to remove from its hinges: *to unhinge a door.* **2.** to take apart or separate: *The attack on the center unhinged the enemy line.* **3.** to throw into confusion; upset; unbalance: *The disaster unhinged his mind.*

un·hitch (un hich′), *v.* to unfasten; set loose; free.

un·ho·ly (un hō′lē), *adj.,* **un·ho·li·er, un·ho·li·est. 1.** not holy or sacred; unhallowed. **2.** wicked, depraved, or sinful: *an unholy conspiracy.* **3.** dreadful or disagreeable: *an unholy noise.* —**un·ho′li·ness,** *n.*

un·hook (un hŏŏk′), *v.* to detach, unfasten, or open by releasing a hook: *to unhook a screen door.*

un·horse (un hôrs′), *v.,* **un·horsed, un·hors·ing.** to dislodge or unseat (a rider) from a horse; cause to fall from a horse.

uni-, a prefix meaning one or only one: *unilateral.*

UNICEF (yōō′ni sef′), *n.* a branch of the United Nations that is concerned with the health and welfare of children in distressed areas of the world. [from the name *U(nited) N(ations) I(nternational) C(hildren's) E(mergency) F(und)*]

u·ni·corn (yōō′nə kôrn′), *n.* an imaginary animal resembling a horse and having a single horn in the center of its forehead.

u·ni·form (yōō′nə fôrm′), *n.* **1.** a suit of clothing, often including certain accessories and equipment, that is required to be worn by all members of a certain rank, organization, or occupation: *a nurse's uniform.* —*adj.* **2.** having the same form, appearance, amount, quality, etc., as others of its kind: *a row of uniform desks.* **3.** the same throughout or at all times; not varying: *a board of uniform thickness.* —*v.* **4.** to clothe in or provide with a uniform.

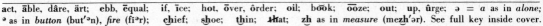

Unicorn

u·ni·form·i·ty (yōō′nə fôr′mi tē), *n.* the state or quality of being uniform; sameness.

u·ni·form·ly (yōō′nə fôrm′lē), *adv.* in a uniform manner; without variation or difference.

u·ni·fy (yōō′nə fī′), *v.,* **u·ni·fied, u·ni·fy·ing.** to make into or become a single unit; unite: *The war unified* *the colonies.* —**u·ni·fi·ca·tion** (yōō/nə fə kā/shən), *n.*

u·ni·lat·er·al (yōō/nə lat/ər əl), *adj.* **1.** of or on one side only. **2.** referring to or done by only one person, group, nation, etc.: *a unilateral reduction of tariffs.* —**u/ni·lat/er·al·ly,** *adv.*

un·im·ag·i·na·ble (un/i maj/ə nə bəl), *adj.* impossible to imagine; unthinkable: *unimaginable suffering* —**un/im·ag/i·na·bly,** *adv.*

un·im·peach·a·ble (un/im pē/chə bəl), *adj.* not subject to doubt or blame; faultless: *an unimpeachable reputation; a report from an unimpeachable source.* —**un/im·peach/a·ble·ness,** *n.*—**un/im·peach/a·bly,** *adv.*

un·im·por·tant (un/im pôr/t³nt), *adj.* not important; of little significance.

un·in·hab·it·ed (un/in hab/i tid), *adj.* without inhabitants or occupants: *an uninhabited house.*

un·in·hib·it·ed (un/in hib/i tid), *adj.* not inhibited; not restrained or restricted: *uninhibited freedom; uninhibited conduct.* —**un/in·hib/it·ed·ly,** *adv.*

un·in·tel·li·gi·ble (un/in tel/i jə bəl), *adj.* not able to be understood. —**un/in·tel/li·gi·bly,** *adv.*

un·in·ter·est·ed (un in/tə res/tid, un in/tris tid), *adj.* **1.** not interested; having or showing no interest; indifferent. **2.** not having an interest, as in a dispute; impartial: *An uninterested person was called in to help settle the strike.* —**un/in/ter·est·ed·ly,** *adv.* —**un/in/ter·est·ed·ness,** *n.* —Usage. See disinterested.

un·in·ter·rupt·ed (un/in tə rup/tid), *adj.* without interruption; continuous. —**un/in·ter·rupt/ed·ly,** *adv.*

un·in·vit·ed (un/in vī/tid), *adj.* not invited; unexpected: *an uninvited visitor.*

un·ion (yōōn/yən), *n.* **1.** the act or process of uniting: *An army was formed by the union of several regiments.* **2.** the state of being united; unity: *In union there is strength.* **3.** something formed by uniting two or more things; combination: *Purple is a union of blue and red.* **4.** a number of persons, nations, states, etc., joined together for a common purpose: *a federal union.* **5.** the act of uniting, or the state of being united in marriage. **6.** an organization of workers; labor union or trade union. **7. the Union, a.** the United States of America. **b.** the Federal government during the Civil War, as opposed to the Confederacy.

un·ion·ize (yōōn/yə nīz/), *v.,* **un·ion·ized, un·ion·iz·ing. 1.** to form or be formed into a union, esp. a labor union or trade union: *to unionize farm workers.* **2.** to put under the rules of a union: *to unionize a factory.* —**un/ion·i·za/tion,** *n.*

Un/ion Jack/, the British national flag.

Un/ion of So/viet So/cialist Repub/lics, official name of the Soviet Union.

u·nique (yōō nēk/), *adj.* **1.** being the only one of its kind: *a unique specimen of an early postage stamp.* **2.** having no like or equal; incomparable: *a unique collection of crown jewels.* —**u·nique/ly,** *adv.* —**u·nique/ness,** *n*

u·ni·sex (yōō/nə seks/), *adj.* worn or used by both sexes alike: *unisex clothes.*

u·ni·son (yōō/ni sən, yōō/ni zən), *n.* **1.** agreement in pitch of two or more musical voices, tones, etc. **2.** harmony; accord; agreement: *The committee acted in*

unison on the proposed plan.

u·nit (yōō/nit), *n.* **1.** any of a number of things, parts, etc., that are alike or equivalent: *The city has built three new housing units.* **2.** something that forms a united whole: *The group of islands forms a political unit.* **3.** a definite quantity, as of space, time, money, etc., used as a standard of measurement: *An hour is a unit of time.* **4.** the smallest whole number; one. **5.** a single part or group of parts that serves a particular purpose: *the exhaust unit of a gas engine.*

U·ni·tar·i·an (yōō/ni lâr/ē ən), *n.* a member of a Protestant denomination that rejects the doctrine of the Trinity and emphasizes tolerance of religious opinion.

u·nite (yōō nīt/), *v.,* **u·nit·ed, u·nit·ing. 1.** to join or combine so as to form a single unit or whole: *The city united its health and welfare agencies into one department.* **2.** to join together for a common purpose: *We must unite all the nations in stamping out hunger and disease.* **3.** to join in marriage.

u·nit·ed (yōō nī/tid), *adj.* **1.** joined or combined into one: *a united system of highways.* **2.** joined together for a common purpose: *a united people; united efforts.* —**u·nit/ed·ly,** *adv.*

Unit/ed Ar/ab Em/ir·ates (em/ə rits), a federation of seven independent Arab states on the S coast of the Persian Gulf. 32,278 sq. mi. *Cap.:* Abu Dhabi.

Unit/ed Ar/ab Repub/lic, former name (1958–1971) of Arab Republic of Egypt.

Unit/ed King/dom, a kingdom in NW Europe, made up of Great Britain and Northern Ireland. 93,377 sq. mi. *Cap.:* London.

Unit/ed Na/tions, an international organization with headquarters in New York City, formed to promote international peace, security, and cooperation: formed in San Francisco in 1945.

Unit/ed States/, a nation of 50 states, located on the continent of North America, except for Hawaii in the N Pacific. *Cap.:* Washington, D.C. Also, **Unit/ed States/ of Amer/ica.** *Abbr.:* U.S., U.S.A.

Unit/ed States/ Air/ Force/, a branch of the U.S. armed forces that controls nearly all military aircraft.

Unit/ed States/ Ar/my, a branch of the U.S. armed forces, including infantry, artillery, armored divisions, and all other forces that operate on land.

Unit/ed States/ Marine/ Corps/, a branch of the U.S. Navy made up of men who are organized and equipped like soldiers, and specially trained for combat landing operations overseas.

Unit/ed States/ Na/vy, a branch of the U.S. armed forces, responsible for defense of the nation from attack by sea.

u·ni·ty (yōō/ni tē), *n., pl.* for defs. 4, 5 **u·ni·ties. 1.** the state or quality of being united into a single whole; oneness: *The unity of the solar system.* **2.** the state of being combined with one or more other persons, things, groups, etc.: *The local union voted in favor of unity with the national organization.* **3.** the state of being in harmony or agreement: *unity among nations.* **4.** a harmonious combination of different parts, esp. in art or literature: *The unity of a well-planned group of buildings.* **5.** the number one.

Univ., **1.** Universalist. **2.** University.

u·ni·valve (yōō′nə valv′), *adj.* **1.** having one valve. **2.** (of a shell) having a single valve or piece: *a univalve mollusk.* —*n.* **3.** a mollusk having a single valve.

u·ni·ver·sal (yōō′nə vûr′səl), *adj.* **1.** of, concerning, or affecting all: *universal education.* **2.** existing or prevailing everywhere. —**u·ni·ver·sal·i·ty** (yōō′nə vər-sal′i tē), *n.*

U·ni·ver·sal·ism (yōō′nə vûr′sə liz′əm), *n.* the Protestant denomination that emphasizes the universal fatherhood of God and the final salvation of all men. —**U′ni·ver′sal·ist,** *n., adj.*

u′niver′sal joint′, a coupling between rotating shafts that permits them to rotate when placed at an angle to each other.

u·ni·ver·sal·ly (yōō′nə vûr′sə lē), *adv.* **1.** in every instance; without exception: *War is universally destructive.* **2.** in all places; everywhere: *Bacteria are universally present in decaying matter.*

Universal joint

u·ni·verse (yōō′nə vûrs′), *n.* everything that is known or believed to exist, including the earth, all heavenly bodies, and outer space; the cosmos; creation.

u·ni·ver·si·ty (yōō′nə vûr′si tē), *n., pl.* **u·ni·ver·si·ties.** an institution that offers instruction at the regular college level and beyond, usually including one or more graduate or professional schools.

un·just (un just′), *adj.* not just; unfair: *an unjust law.*

un·kempt (un kempt′), *adj.* **1.** not combed. **2.** not neat or tidy; messy: *to have an unkempt appearance.*

un·kind (un kīnd′), *adj.* **1.** not kind or considerate: *an unkind refusal.* **2.** without sympathy or mercy; harsh; cruel: *unkind treatment of animals.*

un·kind·ly (un kīnd′lē), *adj.* **1.** not kindly; unkind; unsympathetic: *an unkindly attitude.* —*adv.* **2.** in an unkind manner; harshly; cruelly: *The dog was treated unkindly by its master.* —**un·kind′li·ness,** *n.*

un·kind·ness (un kīnd′nis), *n.* **1.** lack of kindness; harshness; cruelty. **2.** an unkind act: *It would be an unkindness to refuse to help.*

un·know·ing (un nō′ing), *adj.* not knowing; ignorant or unaware: *unknowing aid to the enemy.* —**un·know′ing·ly,** *adv.*

un·known (un nōn′), *adj.* **1.** not known; unidentified: *an unknown assassin; an unknown quantity.* **2.** strange; unfamiliar: *That town is unknown to me.* **3.** unheard-of; not publicly recognized: *an unknown artist.* —*n.* **4.** a person or thing that is unknown.

un·lace (un lās′), *v.,* **un·laced, un·lac·ing.** to loosen or unfasten the laces of: *to unlace a shoe.*

un·latch (un lach′), *v.* to open by lifting or releasing a latch: *to unlatch a window.*

un·law·ful (un lô′fəl), *adj.* not lawful; against the law; illegal. — **un·law′ful·ly,** *adv.* — **un·law′ful·ness,** *n.*

un·learn·ed (un lûr′nid *for def. 1;* un lûrnd′ *for*

defs. 2, 3), *adj.* **1.** not educated; ignorant. **2.** acquired without study or training; natural: *an unlearned skill.* **3.** indicating ignorance or lack of education: *unlearned behavior.*

un·leash (un lēsh′), *v.* to release from a leash or other bond; let loose; set free: *Unleash the dogs. The attackers unleashed the full fury of war.*

un·leav·ened (un lev′ənd), *adj.* baked without yeast or other leaven: *unleavened bread.*

un·less (un les′), *conj.* except in the case that: *Don't shoot unless you're attacked.*

un·like (un līk′), *adj.* **1.** not the same or similar; different: *He wore a coat and trousers of unlike colors.* —*prep.* **2.** different from: *He is unlike his brother.* **3.** not typical or characteristic of: *It's unlike him to be this late.* —**un·like′ness,** *n.*

un·like·ly (un līk′lē), *adj.* **1.** not likely to exist or happen; improbable: *Rain is unlikely this afternoon.* **2.** not likely to succeed; unpromising: *They picked the most unlikely candidate.* —**un·like′li·hood′,** *n.*

un·lim·it·ed (un lim′i tid), *adj.* **1.** without restriction or hindrance: *unlimited use of the gymnasium.* **2.** boundless; infinite: *unlimited outer space.*

un·load (un lōd′), *v.* **1.** to take the load from: *to unload a ship.* **2.** to remove or discharge (goods, passengers, etc.) from a conveyance: *The tanker is unloading oil.* **3.** to remove the charge from (a firearm). **4.** to get rid of; relieve oneself of: *to unload surplus goods.*

un·lock (un lok′), *v.* **1.** to open or unfasten (a door, chest, etc.) by releasing a lock. **2.** to lay open; reveal: *to unlock the secrets of the ocean depths.* **3.** to let loose; release: *to unlock pent-up feelings.*

un·looked-for (un lŏŏkt′fôr′), *adj.* not expected; unforeseen: *to reap unlooked-for profits.*

un·luck·y (un luk′ē), *adj.,* **un·luck·i·er, un·luck·i·est. 1.** not lucky; unfortunate: *an unlucky gambler; an unlucky expedition.* **2.** bringing bad luck: *an unlucky number; an unlucky day.* —**un·luck′i·ly,** *adv.*

un·man·ly (un man′lē), *adj.* **1.** not manly; weak, timid, or cowardly. **2.** not expected of a man; effeminate. —**un·man′li·ness,** *n.*

un·manned (un mand′), *adj.* without a human crew; operating without men physically present and in control: *an unmanned spacecraft.*

un·man·ner·ly (un man′ər lē), *adj.* having bad manners; rude; impolite. —**un·man′ner·li·ness,** *n.*

un·mask (un mask′), *v.* **1.** to remove a mask or disguise. **2.** to reveal the true character of; expose: *to unmask a jewel thief.*

un·men·tion·a·ble (un men′shə nə bəl), *adj.* not fit or proper to be mentioned.

un·mer·ci·ful (un mûr′si fəl), *adj.* without mercy or pity; cruel; relentless. —**un·mer′ci·ful·ly,** *adv.*

un·mind·ful (un mīnd′fəl), *adj.* not mindful; careless; forgetful: *to be unmindful of one's duties.* —**un·mind′ful·ly,** *adv.* —**un·mind′ful·ness,** *n.*

un·mis·tak·a·ble (un′mi stā′kə bəl), *adj.* not capable of being mistaken or misunderstood; clear; obvious:

He bears an unmistakable resemblance to his father.
—un'mis·tak'a·bly, *adv.*

un·mit·i·gat·ed (un mit'ə gā'tid), *adj.* 1. not lessened or eased: *the unmitigated glare of lights.* 2. absolute; complete: *an unmitigated scoundrel.*

un·mixed (un mikst'), *adj.* not mixed with anything else; pure; complete: *days of unmixed pleasure.*

un·moved (un mōovd'), *adj.* 1. not moved; without change of place or position. 2. firm or unyielding in attitude or purpose; resolute: *Both sides remained unmoved after two long days of bargaining.* 3. not emotionally affected; indifferent: *The play left the audience unmoved.*

un·nat·u·ral (un nach'ər əl), *adj.* 1. not natural or normal; abnormal. 2. not in keeping with character or type; unusual: *Our cat has an unnatural liking for dogs.* 3. not real or genuine; artificial or affected: *an unnatural style of speaking.* 4. lacking sympathy, pity, warmth, or the like; cruel; inhuman: *an unnatural delight in the sufferings of others.* —un·nat'u·ral·ly, *adv.*

un·nec·es·sar·y (un nes'i ser'ē), *adj.* not necessary or essential; needless. —un·nec·es·sar·i·ly (un nes'i sâr'ə lē), *adv.*

un·nerve (un nûrv'), *v.,* un·nerved, un·nerv·ing. to deprive of courage, strength, or determination: *The loss of their commander unnerved the troops.*

un·ob·tru·sive (un'əb trōō'siv), *adj.* not obtrusive; inconspicuous or modest: *Black is an unobtrusive color for an automobile.* —un'ob·tru'sive·ly, *adv.* —un'ob·tru'sive·ness, *n.*

un·oc·cu·pied (un ok'yə pīd'), *adj.* 1. without occupants; empty; vacant. 2. not busy or at work; idle: *I like to read in unoccupied moments.* 3. not under military occupation.

un·of·fi·cial (un'ə fish'əl), *adj.* not official; not properly authorized; informal: *an unofficial announcement.* —un'of·fi'cial·ly, *adv.*

un·pack (un pak'), *v.* 1. to empty (a box, trunk, etc.) of its contents: *to unpack a suitcase.* 2. to remove (something) from a container: *Unpack your clothes.*

un·paid (un pād'), *adj.* 1. not paid; still owed: *unpaid bills.* 2. working without pay: *an unpaid worker.*

un·par·al·leled (un par'ə leld'), *adj.* without parallel; unequaled; matchless: *a building of unparalleled beauty.*

un·par·don·a·ble (un pär'd°nə bəl), *adj.* not able to be pardoned or forgiven; inexcusable: *an unpardonable insult.* —un·par'don·a·bly, *adv.*

un·pin (un pin'), *v.,* un·pinned, un·pin·ning. 1. to remove a pin or pins from. 2. to unfasten or take off by removing a pin or pins: *to unpin a dress.*

un·pleas·ant (un plez'ənt), *adj.* not pleasant; depressing; disagreeable. —un·pleas'ant·ly, *adv.* —un·pleas'ant·ness, *n.*

un·pop·u·lar (un pop'yə lər), *adj.* not popular; generally disliked: *an unpopular president; an unpopular law.* —un·pop·u·lar·i·ty (un'pop yə lar'i tē), *n.*

un·prec·e·dent·ed (un pres'i den'tid), *adj.* without precedent; not previously done or known: *an unprecedented space flight.*

un·pre·dict·a·ble (un'pri dik'tə bəl), *adj.* not predictable; not capable of being foreseen or foretold: *This is a season of unpredictable storms.* —un'pre·dict'a·bil'i·ty, *n.* —un'pre·dict'a·bly, *adv.*

un·prej·u·diced (un prej'ə dist), *adj.* without prejudice; fair; impartial: *an unprejudiced witness.*

un·pre·med·i·tat·ed (un'prē med'i tā'tid), *adj.* without premeditation; not planned or thought out beforehand: *an unpremeditated attack.*

un·pre·pared (un'pri pârd'), *adj.* not ready; not properly trained or equipped: *The attack caught the soldiers unprepared.* —un'pre·par'ed·ness, *n.*

un·pre·ten·tious (un'pri ten'shəs), *adj.* not pretentious; simple; plain: *an unpretentious cottage.* —un'pre·ten'tious·ly, *adv.* —un'pre·ten'tious·ness, *n.*

un·prin·ci·pled (un prin'sə pəld), *adj.* lacking moral scruples or principles; unscrupulous: *an unprincipled swindler.*

un·print·a·ble (un prin'tə bəl), *adj.* unfit to be printed or published; indecent or obscene.

un·prof·it·a·ble (un prof'i tə bəl), *adj.* not profitable; not yielding profit or advantage: *an unprofitable investment.* —un·prof'it·a·bly, *adv.*

un·pro·voked (un'prə vōkt'), *adj.* 1. (of an attack or the like) not provoked or brought on by one's own words or actions: *an unprovoked bombing raid.* 2. not feeling provoked, annoyed, or the like.

un·qual·i·fied (un kwol'ə fīd'), *adj.* 1. lacking the necessary qualifications; not fit: *to be unqualified for a job.* 2. not qualified or restricted in any way; absolute; complete: *an unqualified victory.*

un·quench·a·ble (un kwen'chə bəl), *adj.* not capable of being quenched or satisfied: *unquenchable thirst; unquenchable enthusiasm.*

un·ques·tion·a·ble (un kwes'chə nə bəl), *adj.* not open to question; above doubt or criticism; absolute; certain: *an unquestionable fact; a man of unquestionable honesty.* —un·ques'tion·a·bly, *adv.*

un·ques·tioned (un kwes'chənd), *adj.* not open to doubt or dispute: *His authority is unquestioned.*

un·quote (un kwōt'), *v.,* un·quot·ed, un·quot·ing. to close a quotation (often used with the word *quote* opening the quotation): *The candidate said, quote, I am absolutely opposed to this policy, unquote.*

un·rav·el (un rav'əl), *v.,* un·rav·eled *or* un·rav·elled; un·rav·el·ing *or* un·rav·el·ling. 1. to separate or disentangle the threads of (a fabric, rope, etc.): *to unravel a knitted scarf.* 2. to free from complications; make clear; solve: *to unravel a mystery.*

un·read (un red'), *adj.* 1. not read: *an unread report.* 2. not knowledgeable; having little knowledge.

un·read·y (un red'ē), *adj.* not ready or prepared: *to be unready for a test.* —un·read'i·ness, *n.*

un·re·al (un rē'əl, -rēl'), *adj.* not real or actual; imaginary or fantastic: *the unreal world of dreams.*

un·re·al·is·tic (un'rē ə lis'tik), *adj.* not realistic; not based on reality: *unrealistic hopes; an unrealistic story.* —un're·al·is'ti·cal·ly, *adv.*

un·re·al·i·ty (un'rē al'i tē), *n.* 1. lack of reality; the quality of being imaginary or unreal: *the unreality of a dream.* 2. lack of practicality; the quality of being impractical or unreasonable: *the unreality of a plan.*

un·rea·son·a·ble (un rē′zə nə bəl), *adj.* 1. not guided by or based on reason or good sense: *an unreasonable request.* 2. excessive; too great: *an unreasonable price.* —**un·rea′son·a·bly,** *adv.*

un·re·gen·er·ate (un′ri jen′ər it), *adj.* 1. not repentant or reformed: *an unregenerate sinner.* 2. stubborn or unyielding: *an unregenerate conservative.* —**un′re·gen′er·ate·ly,** *adv.*

un·re·lent·ing (un′ri len′tiñg), *adj.* not relenting, yielding, or lessening: *an unrelenting opposition.*

un·re·li·a·ble (un′ri lī′ə bəl), *adj.* not reliable or dependable: *an unreliable witness.* —**un′re·li′a·bly,** *adv.*

un·re·mit·ting (un′ri mit′iñg), *adj.* not lessening or slackening; incessant: *unremitting applause.*

un·re·quit·ed (un′ri kwī′tid), *adj.* 1. not returned or given in turn: *unrequited love.* 2. not avenged: *an unrequited insult.*

un·re·served (un′ri zûrvd′), *adj.* 1. without reservation or doubt; unqualified: *The plan has my unreserved approval.* 2. free from reserve; frank; open: *unreserved friendliness.* —**un·re·serv·ed·ly** (un′ri zûr′vid lē), *adv.*

un·rest (un rest′), *n.* 1. uneasiness or restlessness: *to be nervous and full of unrest.* 2. dissatisfaction and disturbance: *a time of political unrest.*

un·right·eous (un rī′chəs), *adj.* not righteous; wicked; sinful; evil.

un·ri·valed (un rī′vəld), *adj.* having no rival or competitor; having no equal: *His excellence is unrivaled.*

un·roll (un rōl′), *v.* 1. to open or spread out (something rolled or coiled): *to unroll a bolt of fabric.* 2. to lay open; display; reveal. 3. to become unrolled or spread out.

un·ru·ly (un rōō′lē), *adj.,* **un·ru·li·er, un·ru·li·est.** difficult to discipline or rule; disobedient. —**un·ru′li·ness,** *n.*

un·sad·dle (un sad′ʼl), *v.,* **un·sad·dled, un·sad·dling.** 1. to take the saddle from. 2. to cause (a person) to fall from a saddle.

un·safe (un sāf′), *adj.* not safe; dangerous.

un·san·i·tar·y (un san′i ter′ē), *adj.* not sanitary; unclean; unhealthy: *unsanitary living conditions.*

un·sat·is·fac·to·ry (un′sat is fak′tə rē), *adj.* not satisfactory; not meeting one's needs or expectations.

un·sa·vor·y (un sā′və rē), *adj.* 1. unpleasant in taste or smell. 2. socially or morally objectionable: *unsavory language.*

un·schooled (un skōōld′), *adj.* not schooled, taught, or trained.

un·sci·en·tif·ic (un′sī ən tif′ik), *adj.* not meeting the requirements of science, or not using scientific methods: *an unscientific experiment.* —**un′sci·en·tif′i·cal·ly,** *adv.*

un·screw (un skrōō′), *v.* 1. to draw or loosen a screw or screws from. 2. to open or remove (something) by turning: *to unscrew the lid from a jar.*

un·scru·pu·lous (un skrōō′pyə ləs), *adj.* having no

scruples, principles, or conscience. —**un·scru′pu·lous·ly,** *adv.* —**un·scru′pu·lous·ness,** *n.*

un·sealed (un sēld′), *adj.* not sealed or closed: *an unsealed letter.*

un·seat (un sēt′), *v.* 1. to dislodge from a seat or a saddle. 2. to remove from political office.

un·seem·ly (un sēm′lē), *adj.* 1. not seemly; unbecoming or improper: *unseemly behavior.* —*adv.* 2. in an unseemly manner. —**un·seem′li·ness,** *n.*

un·seen (un sēn′), *adj.* not seen; invisible.

un·self·ish (un sel′fish), *adj.* not selfish; generous. —**un·self′ish·ly,** *adv.* —**un·self′ish·ness,** *n.*

un·set·tle (un set′ʼl), *v.,* **un·set·tled, un·set·tling.** 1. to change from a settled state; make unstable. 2. to become or cause to become uncertain or disturbed: *The bad news unsettled him.*

un·set·tled (un set′ʼld), *adj.* 1. not settled; not fixed or stable; unorganized. 2. continuously moving or changing; not situated in one place. 3. wavering or uncertain, as in opinions, behavior, etc. 4. not populated or settled, as a region.

un·sheathe (un shēth′), *v.,* **un·sheathed, un·sheath·ing.** to draw (a sword, dagger, etc.) from a sheath.

un·shod (un shod′), *adj.* not wearing shoes: *an unshod horse.*

un·sight·ly (un sīt′lē), *adj.* distasteful or unpleasant to look at: *to straighten up an unsightly room.*

un·skilled (un skild′), *adj.* 1. having no technical training or skill: *unskilled workers.* 2. not demanding special training or skill: *unskilled jobs.*

un·skill·ful (un skil′fəl), *adj.* not skillful; clumsy or bungling. —**un·skill′ful·ly,** *adv.*

un·so·phis·ti·cat·ed (un′sə fis′tə kā′tid), *adj.* not sophisticated; simple; natural.

un·sound (un sound′), *adj.* 1. not sound; diseased, such as the body or mind. 2. not solid or firm, such as foundations. 3. not well-founded or valid: *an unsound argument.* 4. easily broken; light: *an unsound sleep.* 5. not financially strong: *an unsound company.*

un·speak·a·ble (un spē′kə bəl), *adj.* 1. too great to express in words: *unspeakable beauty.* 2. too bad or horrible to talk about: *unspeakable suffering.* —**un·speak′a·bly,** *adv.*

un·spo·ken (un spō′kən), *adj.* understood without being spoken or uttered: *an unspoken agreement.*

un·sta·ble (un stā′bəl), *adj.* 1. not stable or firm; unsteady: *an unstable chair.* 2. not emotionally stable. 3. (in chemistry) noting compounds that decompose easily or change into other compounds.

un·stead·y (un sted′ē), *adj.* 1. not steady or firm; shaky. 2. not regular; wavering: *unsteady steps.*

un·stressed (un strest′), *adj.* without stress or emphasis, such as a syllable in a word.

un·sub·stan·tial (un′səb stan′shəl), *adj.* 1. not substantial; not supported by fact: *unsubstantial hopes.* 2. not real; without material substance: *an unsubstantial ghost.* 3. lacking strength or solidity; flimsy: *an unsubstantial wall of cardboard.*

---

act, āble, dâre, ärt; ebb, ēqual; if, īce; hot, ōver, ôrder; oil; bŏŏk; ōōze; out; up, ûrge; ə = a as in alone; ʼ as in button (but′ʼn), fire (fī′ʼr); chief; shoe; thin; ᴛ̶ʜat; zh as in measure (mezh′ər). See full key inside cover.

un·suit·a·ble (un sōō′tə bəl), *adj.* not suitable; unbecoming: *That chair is unsuitable for the bedroom.*

un·sung (un suñg′), *adj.* 1. not sung. 2. not celebrated in song or verse; not praised: *an unsung hero.*

un·tan·gle (un tañg′gəl), *v.,* **un·tan·gled, un·tan·gling.** 1. to bring out of a tangled state; unsnarl: *to untangle two lengths of rope.* 2. to straighten out or clear up: *to untangle a problem.*

un·taught (un tôt′), *adj.* 1. not taught; not acquired by teaching; natural: *untaught skills.* 2. not educated; ignorant.

un·think·a·ble (un thiñg′kə bəl), *adj.* impossible to imagine or consider: *It is unthinkable that she could be so rude.*

un·think·ing (un thiñg′kiñg), *adj.* thoughtless; inconsiderate: *an unthinking remark.*

un·ti·dy (un tī′dē), *adj.,* **un·ti·di·er, un·ti·di·est.** not tidy or neat; messy: *an untidy desk.*

un·tie (un tī′), *v.,* **un·tied, un·ty·ing.** 1. to loose or undo (anything tied): *to untie shoelaces.* 2. to let or set loose: *to untie a dog.*

un·til (un til′), *conj.* 1. up to the time that or when: *He read until his guests arrived.* 2. before: *I cannot leave until I finish studying.* —*prep.* 3. onward to or till: *He worked until six o'clock.* 4. before: *He did not go until night.*

un·time·ly (un tīm′lē), *adj.* 1. not happening at a suitable time or season: *an untimely visit.* 2. happening too soon or too early.

un·tir·ing (un tī°r′iñg), *adj.* not becoming tired or exhausted: *his untiring efforts to help the poor.*

un·to (un′tōō, un′tə), *prep.* an old form of **to:** *The people went unto the temple.*

un·told (un tōld′), *adj.* 1. not told, related, or revealed: *an untold story.* 2. not numbered or counted: *Untold thousands watched the parade.* 3. too many or too much to be counted or measured: *untold suffering.*

un·touch·a·ble (un tuch′ə bəl), *adj.* 1. that may not be touched. 2. too distant to be touched. 3. unpleasant to the touch. 4. beyond criticism, control, or investigation: *Modern science considers nothing untouchable.* —*n.* 5. (formerly) a member of a caste in India whose touch was believed to defile a high-caste Hindu.

un·touched (un tucht′), *adj.* 1. not touched or handled. 2. not explored or visited: *untouched lands.* 3. not eaten or drunk: *She left the dessert untouched.* 4. not injured or hurt; undamaged. 5. not affected or changed: *She was untouched by the suffering around her.*

un·to·ward (un tôrd′), *adj.* 1. unfavorable or unfortunate: *Untoward circumstances forced him into bankruptcy.* 2. improper; not suitable: *untoward social behavior.*

un·tried (un trīd′), *adj.* 1. not tried or attempted. 2. not proved or tested. 3. not yet tried by law: *an untried case.*

un·true (un trōō′), *adj.* 1. not true; false: *an untrue rumor.* 2. not loyal; unfaithful. 3. incorrect or inaccurate: *untrue measurements.*

un·truth (un trōōth′), *n., pl.* for def. 2 **un·truths** (un-trōōthz′, -trōōths′). 1. the state or character of being untrue. 2. something untrue; a falsehood or lie.

un·truth·ful (un trōōth′fəl), *adj.* not truthful: *an untruthful story.* —**un·truth′ful·ness,** *n.*

un·used (un yōōzd′), *adj.* 1. not used; not put to use: *unused equipment; unused talent.* 2. not accustomed: *She's unused to this climate.*

un·u·su·al (un yōō′zhōō əl), *adj.* not usual, common, or ordinary; rare; strange. —**un·u′su·al·ly,** *adv.*

un·ut·ter·a·ble (un ut′ər ə bəl), *adj.* 1. not utterable; not pronounceable: *an unutterable foreign word.* 2. not communicable by speaking; unspeakable: *unutterable joy.*

un·veil (un vāl′), *v.* 1. to remove a veil or other covering from. 2. to reveal or disclose, esp. for the first time: *to unveil a monument; to unveil a plan.*

un·war·y (un wâr′ē), *adj.* not wary; not cautious or watchful. —**un·war′i·ness,** *n.*

un·well (un wel′), *adj.* not well; ailing; ill.

un·whole·some (un hōl′səm), *adj.* 1. not wholesome; dangerous to physical or mental health. 2. unhealthy, esp. in appearance: *an unwholesome skin.* 3. morally harmful: *unwholesome activities.*

un·wield·y (un wēl′dē), *adj.* not easily handled or managed; awkward; clumsy: *an unwieldy package.*

un·will·ing (un wil′iñg), *adj.* not willing; reluctant: *She's unwilling to agree.* —**un·will′ing·ly,** *adv.* —**un·will′ing·ness,** *n.*

un·wind (un wīnd′), *v.,* **un·wound** (un wound′), **un·wind·ing.** 1. to undo from or as if from a coiled condition. 2. to become unwound.

un·wise (un wīz′), *adj.* not wise; foolish; lacking in good sense. —**un·wise′ly,** *adv.*

un·wit·ting (un wit′iñg), *adj.* 1. not knowing; unaware. 2. not done on purpose; unintentional. —**un·wit′ting·ly,** *adv.*

un·wont·ed (un wôn′tid), *adj.* not customary or usual; rare: *She danced with unwonted grace.*

un·wor·thy (un wûr′thē), *adj.* 1. not worthy; not deserving or qualified. 2. not suitable or proper: *behavior unworthy of a king.* —**un·wor′thi·ness,** *n.*

un·wound (un wound′), *v.* the past tense and past participle of **unwind.**

un·wrap (un rap′), *v.,* **un·wrapped, un·wrap·ping.** 1. to remove or open the wrapping of: *to unwrap a package.* 2. to become unwrapped.

un·writ·ten (un rit′°n), *adj.* 1. not written; not put in writing or print. 2. not actually expressed; customary; traditional: *an unwritten law.*

un·yield·ing (un yēl′diñg), *adj.* not yielding or giving in; stubborn.

un·yoke (un yōk′), *v.,* **un·yoked, un·yok·ing.** to free from or as if from a yoke: *to unyoke oxen.*

un·zip (un zip′), *v.,* **un·zipped, un·zip·ping.** 1. to open the zipper of. 2. to become unzipped.

up (up), *adv.* 1. to, toward, or in a higher position. 2. to or in an erect position: *to stand up.* 3. out of bed: *to get up.* 4. to or at a source, origin, center, or the like: *to follow a stream up to its source.* 5. to or at a point of equal advance, extent, etc.: *to catch up.* 6. to an end; completely: *to pay up one's debts; to be used up.* **7.** into view or consideration: *The papers turned up. New problems have come up.* **8.** into or in activity, operation, etc.: *to stir up a fire.* —*prep.* **9.** to, toward, or at a higher place on or in: *The cat went up the tree.* **10.** at or to a farther point on: *He is going up the street.* **11.** toward the source, origin, etc., of: *up the river.* —*adj.* **12.** moving in or related to a direction that is up or is regarded as up. **13.** concluded; ended: *Your time is up.* **14.** going on or happening: *What's up over there?* **15.** in a high condition or position: *up on the social scale.* **16.** in an erect or raised position: *The tent is up.* **17.** facing upward. **18.** higher than previously: *The price of meat was up.* **19.** *Informal.* informed; familiar; aware (usually fol. by *on* or *in*): *He is up on current events.* —*n.* **20.** an upward movement; ascent. —*v.,* **upped, up·ping. 21.** *Informal.* to make larger; increase: *to up production.* **22.** *Informal.* to start up; begin something abruptly (usually fol. by *and*): *Then he upped and ran away from home.* **23. on the up and up,** *Slang.* honest; sincere; truthful. **24. up against it,** *Informal.* suffering hardship, esp. because of lack of money: *When his father lost his job they were really up against it.* **25. up and around,** recovered from an illness; well enough to be out of bed: *She should be up and around again in about a week.* Also, **up and about. 26. ups and downs,** good and bad periods: *Every business has its ups and downs.* **27. up to, a.** as far as; reaching: *I was in water up to my chin.* **b.** as many as, but no more: *Take up to five marbles each.* **c.** *Informal.* capable of; equal to: *I'm not up to three hours of skating.* **d.** busy with; doing, esp. of a mischievous nature: *Go see what your little brother is up to.*

up·braid (up brād/), *v.* to find fault with or scold severely.

up·bring·ing (up/bring/ing), *n.* the care and training of the young: *a strict upbringing.*

up·date (up dāt/, up/dāt/), *v.,* **up·dat·ed, up·dat·ing.** to bring (a book, figures, or the like) up to date by adding new information, making corrections, etc.

up·end (up end/), *v.* to set on end, as a barrel, boat, etc.

up·grade (up/grād/), *n.* **1.** an upward incline or slope. —*v.* (up/grād/), **up·grad·ed, up·grad·ing. 2.** to raise to a higher rank, position, value, etc.: *to upgrade workers to supervisors.* **3. on the upgrade,** showing an increase or improvement: *So far this year business is on the upgrade.*

up·heav·al (up hē/vəl), *n.* **1.** a thrusting upward, esp. of a part of the earth's crust. **2.** the state of being upheaved. **3.** strong or violent change or disturbance: *The war has caused great social upheaval.*

up·hill (up/hil/), *adv.* **1.** up or as if up the slope of a hill; upward: *to march uphill.* —*adj.* **2.** going upward on or as if on a hill: *an uphill road.* **3.** tiring or difficult: *an uphill struggle to become successful.*

up·hold (up hōld/), *v.,* **up·held** (up held/), **up·hold·**

ing. **1.** to lift upward; raise. **2.** to give support to: *Columns uphold the heavy roof. Her faith upheld her in that time of sadness.*

up·hol·ster (up hōl/stər), *v.* to provide (chairs, sofas, etc.) with coverings, cushions, stuffings, springs, etc. [originally a noun meaning "upholsterer," literally "a person who upholds" (that is, adds support or padding), from *uphold* + *-ster*] —**up·hol/ster·er,** *n.*

up·hol·ster·y (up hōl/stə rē, ə pōl/stə rē), *n.* **1.** the material supplied by an upholsterer, such as cushions or furniture coverings. **2.** the work or business of an upholsterer.

up·keep (up/kēp/), *n.* **1.** the process or activity of providing an establishment, machine, person, etc., with necessary or proper maintenance, repairs, support, or the like. **2.** the total costs or expenses for this.

up·land (up/lənd, -land/), *n.* **1.** the higher ground of a region or district. —*adj.* **2.** of or concerning uplands or higher regions: *an upland village.*

up·lift (up lift/), *v.* **1.** to lift up; raise. **2.** to improve socially, culturally, or morally. —*n.* (up/lift/). **3.** an act of lifting up or raising. **4.** the process of improving socially, culturally, morally, or the like.

up·on (ə pon/), *prep.* **1.** up and on; upward and onto: *He climbed upon his horse.* **2.** in or into contact with: *The enemy was upon us.*

up·per (up/ər), *adj.* **1.** higher, as in place, position, pitch, etc.: *the upper stories of a house.* **2.** superior, as in rank, dignity, or station: *the upper classes of society.* **3.** (of places) at a higher level, more northerly, or farther from the sea: *upper New York State.* —*n.* **4.** the part of a shoe or boot above the sole.

up·per·case (up/ər kās/), *adj.* **1.** (of a letter of the alphabet) written or printed as a capital letter. —*v.,* **up·per·cased, up·per·cas·ing. 2.** to print or write with an upper-case letter or letters. —*n.* **3.** an upper-case letter; capital.

Up/per E/gypt, the part of ancient Egypt S of the Nile Delta.

up/per hand/, the dominating or controlling position; the advantage: *to fight to get the upper hand.*

up·per·most (up/ər mōst/), *adj.* highest in place, order, rank, power, etc.: *the uppermost row of seats.*

Up/per Vol/ta, a republic in W Africa: formerly French. 106,111 sq. mi.

up·raise (up rāz/), *v.,* **up·raised, up·rais·ing.** to raise up; lift; elevate.

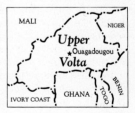

up·right (up/rīt/, up rīt/), *adj.* **1.** erect or vertical; straight up and down: *an upright position.* **2.** righteous, honest, or just: *an upright man.* —*n.* **3.** the state of being upright or vertical. **4.** something standing erect or upright, such as a piece of timber. —*adv.* **5.** in an upright position or direction: *to stand upright.*

up·right pian·o, a piano with a rectangular vertical case, esp. one more than four feet tall. See also **grand piano.**

up·ris·ing (up′rī′zĭñg), *n.* **1.** a rebellion or revolt. **2.** an act of rising up.

up·roar (up′rôr′), *n.* violent and noisy disturbance; turmoil. [from the Dutch word *oproer* "tumult, uprising." The sense and spelling have been affected by the word *roar*]

up·roar·i·ous (up rôr′ē əs), *adj.* **1.** in a state of uproar and turmoil. **2.** making an uproar; confused and noisy. **3.** very funny. —**up·roar′i·ous·ly,** *adv.*

up·root (up rōot′, -rŏot′), *v.* **1.** to pull out by or as if by the roots, esp. so as to destroy: *to uproot weeds; to uproot a bad habit.* **2.** to remove violently or tear away from a native place or environment: *The war uprooted many families from their homes.*

up·set (up set′), *v.,* **up·set, up·set·ting. 1.** to overturn: *to upset a pitcher of milk.* **2.** to disturb mentally or emotionally: *The accident upset him.* **3.** to disturb completely; put out of order: *to upset a filing system.* **4.** to disturb physically: *The spicy food upset his stomach.* **5.** to defeat or overcome an opponent that is favored. —*n.* (up′set′). **6.** an instance of being upset; overturn; overthrow. **7.** the unexpected defeat of a person or group that is favored. —*adj.* (up set′). **8.** overturned: *an upset milk pail.* **9.** disordered or disorganized: *The house is upset.* **10.** distressed or disturbed: *to be emotionally upset; an upset stomach.*

up·shot (up′shŏt′), *n.* the final issue; conclusion or result: *The upshot of the debate was a new law.*

up·side (up′sīd′), *n.* the upper side or part.

up′side down′, 1. with the upper part down: *She turned the chair upside down to dust it.* **2.** in or into complete disorder; mixed up: *We turned the house upside down looking for the tickets.*

up·stairs (up′stârz′), *adv.* **1.** up the stairs; to or on a higher floor: *to walk upstairs.* —*adj.* **2.** located on an upper floor: *an upstairs apartment.* —*n.* **3.** *(used as sing.)* the upper floor or floors of a building.

up·stand·ing (up stan′dĭñg), *adj.* **1.** standing erect; erect and tall. **2.** upright; honorable; just.

up·start (up′stärt′), *n.* **1.** a person who has risen suddenly from a humble position to a position of power or importance. **2.** a person who is haughty because of his sudden success.

up·stream (up′strēm′), *adv.* **1.** toward or in the higher part of a stream; against the current. —*adj.* **2.** directed or located upstream.

up-to-date (up′tə dāt′), *adj.* **1.** having the latest information; current: *an up-to-date report.* **2.** according to the latest ideas, styles, etc.: *an up-to-date suit.*

up·town (up′toun′), *adv.* **1.** toward, to, or in the upper part of a town or city: *He rode uptown on the bus.* —*adj.* (up′toun′). **2.** moving toward, located in, or referring to the upper part of a city or town: *an uptown train.* —*n.* (up′toun′). **3.** the uptown section of a town or city.

up·turn (up tûrn′), *v.* **1.** to turn up or over. —*n.* (up′tûrn′). **2.** a changing or rising movement, as in prices, business, etc.

up·ward (up′wərd), *adv.* Also, **up′wards. 1.** toward a higher place or position: *to look upward.* **2.** toward the source or origin of a stream, the interior of a country or region, etc. **3.** toward a higher or more distinguished condition, rank, level, etc. **4.** more: *twenty dollars and upward.* **5.** in the upper parts; above. —*adj.* **6.** moving or tending upward; directed at or located in a higher place or position. **7. upwards of,** more than; above: *New tires will cost upwards of a hundred dollars.*

Ur (ûr), *n.* an ancient Sumerian city on the Euphrates River, in S Iraq.

U·ral (yŏor′əl), *n.* a river in the Soviet Union, flowing S from the Ural Mountains to the Caspian Sea. 1400 mi. long.

U′ral Moun′tains, a mountain range in the W Soviet Union, extending S from the Arctic Ocean and forming the boundary between Europe and Asia.

u·ra·ni·um (yŏo rā′nē əm), *n. Chem.* a radioactive element that is used as an important source of nuclear energy. *Symbol:* U

U·ra·nus (yŏor′ə nəs; *esp. for def. 2* yŏo rā′nəs), *n.* **1.** (in Greek mythology) a god who was the father of the Titans and the Cyclopes. **2.** the planet seventh in order from the sun. Uranus has a diameter of 30,-880 miles; its average distance from the sun is 1,783,-000,000 miles.

ur·ban (ûr′bən), *adj.* **1.** of, concerning, or like a city or town: *urban problems.* **2.** living in a city or cities: *urban workers.* [from the Latin word *urbānus,* which comes from *urbs* "city"]

ur·bane (ûr bān′), *adj.* elegant, suave, and sophisticated; polished. —**ur·bane′ly,** *adv.*

ur·chin (ûr′chĭn), *n.* a mischievous boy, or any small boy or youngster. [from the Middle English word *urchon* "hedgehog," which comes from Old French]

-ure, a suffix used to form nouns meaning **1.** action or result of an action: *pressure; seizure.* **2.** means or instrument: *legislature.* **3.** group or collection of persons or things: *prefecture; portraiture.*

u·re·a (yŏo rē′ə), *n.* **1.** a chemical compound found in urine. **2.** a commercial form of this compound used as a fertilizer and animal feed.

urge (ûrj), *v.,* **urged, urg·ing. 1.** to push, force, or drive: *to urge dogs on with shouts.* **2.** to try to persuade: *to urge a person to greater caution.* **3.** to recommend strongly: *to urge the passage of a new law.* —*n.* **4.** a strong desire or impulse.

ur·gent (ûr′jənt), *adj.* **1.** pressing; requiring immediate action or attention: *an urgent matter.* **2.** insistent or earnest: *an urgent pleader.* **3.** expressed with insistence: *an urgent tone of voice.* —**ur′gen·cy,** *n.* —**ur′gent·ly,** *adv.*

u·ri·nal (yŏor′ə nəl), *n.* a building, enclosure, or bathroom fixture where a person may urinate.

u·ri·nate (yŏor′ə nāt′), *v.,* **u·ri·nat·ed, u·ri·nat·ing.** to pass or discharge urine.

u·rine (yŏor′ĭn), *n.* the liquid excreted by the kidneys and discharged from the body as waste matter. —**u′ri·nar′y,** *adj.*

urn (ûrn), *n.* **1.** a large or decorative vase, esp. one with an ornamental foot or pedestal. **2.** a vase for holding the ashes of the cremated dead. **3.** a container with a spigot, used for making a large quantity of tea or coffee.

Ur·sa Ma·jor (ûr′sə mā′jər), another name for the constellation **Great Bear.**

Ur·sa Mi·nor (ûr′sə mī′nər), another name for the constellation **Little Bear.**

U·ru·guay (yŏŏr′ə gwā′, ŏŏr′ə gwī′), *n.* a republic in SE South America. 72,172 sq. mi. *Cap.:* Montevideo. —**U′ru·guay′an,** *n., adj.*

U·run·di (ŏŏ rŏŏn′dē), *n.* former name of **Burundi.**

us (us), *pron.* the objective case of **we,** used as direct or indirect object: *Will you come with us?*

U.S., United States. Also, **US**

USA, 1. United States Army. **2.** United States of America. Also, **U.S.A.**

us·a·ble (yŏŏ′zə bəl), *adj.* **1.** available for use. **2.** convenient and capable of being used.

USAF, United States Air Force. Also, **U.S.A.F.**

us·age (yŏŏ′sij, yŏŏ′zij), *n.* **1.** the customary or usual way of doing something; custom or practice: *the usages of the last 50 years.* **2.** the customary manner of using words and phrases, speech sounds, and grammatical constructions in any language or form of a language: *standard usage; British or American usage.* **3.** manner of doing or handling something; treatment: *rough usage.*

USCG, United States Coast Guard. Also, **U.S.C.G.**

use (yŏŏz), *v.,* **used, us·ing. 1.** to employ for some purpose; put into service; make use of: *to use a knife.* **2.** to avail oneself of; apply to one's own purposes: *May I use your telephone?* **3.** to finish completely; consume (often fol. by *up*): *We have used up the entire allowance.* **4.** to treat or behave toward. —*n.* (yŏŏs). **5.** the act of employing, using, or putting into service: *the use of tools.* **6.** the state of being employed or used: *The telephone is in use.* **7.** a way of employing or using something: *the painter's use of color.* **8.** the power, right, or privilege of employing or using something: *to lose the use of the right eye.* **9.** service or advantage in being employed or used: *of no practical use.* **10.** help; profit; resulting good: *What's the use?* **11. have no use for, a.** to have no need for: *I have no use for this old sweater.* **b.** to dislike; refuse to tolerate: *I have no use for anyone who talks that way.* **12. make use of,** to find a use for; utilize; employ to advantage: *Did he make use of his spare time?* **13. put to use,** to use to advantage; utilize: *a big empty house that could be put to use as a hospital.* **14. used to, a.** was in the habit of; did a particular thing regularly: *We used to build a snowman every winter.* **b.** accustomed to; in the habit of: *She is used to studying by herself.* [the verb is from the Old French word *user* "to use," and the noun is from Old French *us* "use." Both come from Latin *ūsus,* past participle of *ūti* "to use"] —**us′er,** *n.*

used (yŏŏzd), *adj.* having former ownership; secondhand: *a used car.*

use·ful (yŏŏs′fəl), *adj.* being of use or service; serving some purpose: *a useful member of society; a useful book.* —**use′ful·ly,** *adv.* —**use′ful·ness,** *n.*

use·less (yŏŏs′lis), *adj.* of no use; not serving any purpose: *It is useless to complain. That is a useless gadget.* —**use′less·ly,** *adv.* —**use′less·ness,** *n.*

ush·er (ush′ər), *n.* **1.** a person who escorts people to seats in a church, theater, etc. —*v.* **2.** to act as an usher to; escort; lead: *He ushered the ladies to their seats.* [from the Old French word *huissier* "doorman, bailiff"]

USMC, United States Marine Corps. Also, **U.S.M.C.**

USN, United States Navy. Also, **U.S.N.**

USO, United Service Organizations. Also, **U.S.O.**

USS, 1. United States Ship. **2.** United States Steamship. Also, **U.S.S.**

USSR, Union of Soviet Socialist Republics. Also, **U.S.S.R.**

u·su·al (yŏŏ′zhŏŏ əl), *adj.* **1.** expected or customary: *his usual skill.* **2.** ordinary or common: *the usual January weather.* **3. as usual,** as is the custom; as it most often happens: *As usual, Bill was 10 minutes late.* —**u′su·al·ly,** *adv.*

u·su·rer (yŏŏ′zhər ər), *n.* a person who lends money at a very high or unlawful rate of interest.

u·surp (yŏŏ sûrp′, yŏŏ zûrp′), *v.* to seize and hold (a position, office, power, etc.) by force or without legal right: *The king's uncle tried to usurp the throne.*

u·su·ry (yŏŏ′zhə rē), *n., pl.* for def. 1 **u·su·ries. 1.** a very high or illegal interest rate. **2.** the lending of money at a very high or illegal interest rate.

U·tah (yŏŏ′tô, yŏŏ′tä), *n.* a state in the W United States. 84,916 sq. mi. *Cap.:* Salt Lake City. —**U′tah·an,** *n., adj.*

u·ten·sil (yŏŏ ten′səl), *n.* a tool or instrument serving a useful purpose: *cooking utensils.* [from the Old French word *utensile,* which comes from Latin *ūtēnsilis* "useful," from *ūtī* "to use"]

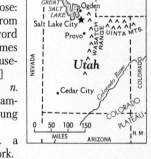

Utah

u·ter·us (yŏŏ′tər əs), *n.* the organ of female mammals in which the young develop before birth.

U·ti·ca (yŏŏ′ti kə), *n.* a city in central New York.

u·til·i·tar·i·an (yŏŏ til′i târ′ē ən), *adj.* **1.** concerning utility. **2.** useful rather than beautiful, decorative, or the like.

u·til·i·ty (yŏŏ til′i tē), *n., pl.* for defs. 2, 3 **u·til·i·ties. 1.** the state or quality of being useful. **2.** something useful. **3.** a public service, such as a bus or rail line, a telephone or electric-light system, or the like.

u·ti·lize (yŏŏt′l īz′), *v.,* **u·ti·lized, u·ti·liz·ing.** to put to use: *to utilize steam to drive an engine.*

ut·most (ut′mōst′), *adj.* **1.** of the greatest or highest degree, quantity, or the like: *of the utmost impor-*

tance. —*n.* **2.** the greatest degree or amount: *The hotel provides the utmost in comfort.* **3.** the most or best of one's abilities, powers, etc.: *He did his utmost to pass the course.* Also, **uttermost.**

U·to·pi·a (yo͞o tō′pē ə), *n.* *(sometimes l.c.)* **1.** a place or state of political or social perfection: *Utopia has never existed on earth, but it's worth working toward.* **2.** any visionary or impractical system or plan for political or social perfection. [from a modern Latin word meaning literally "no place"] —**U·to′pi·an,** *n., adj.*

ut·ter[1] (ut′ər), *v.* **1.** to speak or pronounce. **2.** to give forth (a sound): *She uttered a groan.* [from the Middle English word *outre* "to pronounce, emit"]

ut·ter[2] (ut′ər), *adj.* complete; total: *utter darkness;* *an utter denial.* [from the Old English word *uttra* "outer"] —**ut′ter·ly,** *adv.*

ut·ter·ance (ut′ər əns), *n.* **1.** something uttered; a word or words uttered. **2.** an act of uttering; vocal expression. **3.** a manner of speaking: *to have a dramatic utterance.*

ut·ter·most (ut′ər mōst′), *adj., n.* another word for **utmost.**

U-turn (yo͞o′tûrn′), *n.* a U-shaped turn as made by an automobile to change direction.

u·vu·la (yo͞o′vyə lə), *n.* the small, fleshy, cone-shaped body hanging downward from the middle of the soft palate. See illus. at **mouth.** [from a medieval Latin word meaning literally "little grape," referring to its shape]

	Etruscan	Latin	Gothic	Modern Roman
DEVELOPMENT OF UPPER-CASE LETTERS	V	V	𝔙	V
DEVELOPMENT OF LOWER-CASE LETTERS		Y	ʋ	v
		Medieval	Gothic	Modern Roman

V, v (vē), *n., pl.* **V's** *or* **Vs, v's** *or* **vs.** the 22nd letter of the English alphabet.

V, 1. velocity. 2. victory. 3. volt; volts. Also, **v**

V, 1. the Roman numeral for 5. 2. *Chem.* the symbol for **vanadium.**

V., 1. verb. 2. versus. 3. very. 4. Vice. 5. village. 6. Volume.

v., 1. verb. 2. versus. 3. very. 4. vice. 5. volt. 6. voltage. 7. volume.

Va., Virginia.

va·can·cy (vā′kən sē), *n., pl.* **va·can·cies.** 1. the state of being vacant; emptiness. 2. a vacant or unoccupied place, esp. one for rent. 3. an unoccupied position or office. 4. a gap; opening; empty space.

va·cant (vā′kənt), *adj.* 1. having no contents; empty. 2. not occupied or taken: *a vacant job; a vacant chair.* 3. free from work, business, or care: *vacant hours.* —**va′cant·ly,** *adv.*

va·cate (vā′kāt), *v.,* **va·cat·ed, va·cat·ing.** to make vacant or empty; give up possession or occupancy of: *We have to vacate our apartment in May.*

va·ca·tion (vā kā′shən, və kā′shən), *n.* 1. a period of time during which regular work, study, or other activity is suspended. —*v.* 2. to have or take a vacation: *Next year we'll vacation in Maine.*

vac·ci·nate (vak′sə nāt′), *v.,* **vac·ci·nat·ed, vac·ci·nat·ing.** 1. to inoculate with the virus of cowpox to protect against smallpox. 2. to inoculate with the virus of any of various other diseases as a protection.

vac·ci·na·tion (vak′sə nā′shən), *n.* the act or practice of vaccinating; inoculation with vaccine.

vac·cine (vak sēn′, vak′sēn), *n.* 1. the virus of cowpox used in vaccination. 2. the weakened virus of any of other various diseases used in vaccinations. [from the medical Latin phrase *(variolae) vaccinae* "cowpox," which comes from Latin *vacca* "cow"]

vac·il·late (vas′ə lāt′), *v.,* **vac·il·lat·ed, vac·il·lat·ing.** 1. to waver in decision or opinion; change one's mind often. 2. to sway unsteadily. —**vac·il·la·tion** (vas′ə lā′shən), *n.*

va·cu·i·ty (va kyōō′i tē), *n., pl.* **va·cu·i·ties.** 1. the state of being vacuous. 2. an empty space; void; vacuum. 3. absence of thought or intelligence. 4. a statement revealing such absence.

vac·u·ous (vak′yōō əs), *adj.* 1. without contents; empty. 2. lacking in ideas or intelligence: *a vacuous mind.* 3. without purpose; idle: *a vacuous pastime.* —**vac′u·ous·ly,** *adv.*

vac·u·um (vak′yōō əm, vak′yōōm), *n.* 1. a space entirely empty of matter. 2. an enclosed space from which air has been partially removed. 3. anything suggesting or resembling emptiness. —*v.* 4. to clean with or use a vacuum cleaner.

vac′uum bot′tle, a bottle or flask having a double wall enclosing a vacuum to slow down temperature change: used for keeping liquids hot or cold.

vac′uum clean′er, a machine for cleaning carpets, floors, furniture, etc., by suction.

vac′uum tube′, an electron tube in which the bulb has had as much air as possible removed from it.

vag·a·bond (vag′ə bond′), *adj.* 1. wandering from place to place without any settled home. 2. leading an unsettled or carefree life. —*n.* 3. a person, usually without a permanent home, who wanders from place to place; nomad. 4. an idle wanderer; tramp. 5. a carefree, worthless, or irresponsible person.

va·ga·ry (vā′gə rē, və gâr′ē), *n., pl.* **va·ga·ries.** an unpredictable or odd action or occurrence.

va·gi·na (və jī′nə), *n.* the passage leading to the uterus in female mammals.

va·grant (vā′grənt), *n.* 1. a person with no permanent home and usually without means of support. —*adj.* 2. wandering from place to place. —**va′gran·cy,** *n.*

vague (vāg), *adj.,* **va·guer, va·guest.** 1. not expressed, known, or understood in a clear or definite way: *a vague agreement.* 2. not clearly noticed or perceived: *a vague odor.* 3. (of persons) not clear or definite in thought, understanding, or expression. —**vague′ly,** *adv.* —**vague′ness,** *n.*

vain (vān), *adj.* **1.** too proud of or concerned about one's own appearance, qualities, achievements, etc. **2.** unsuccessful; futile: *a vain attempt.* **3.** without value or importance: *vain gossip.* **4. in vain,** without result or effect: *They tried in vain to rescue the child.* [from an Old French word, which comes from Latin *vānus* "empty, vain"] —**vain′ly,** *adv.*

vain·glo·ri·ous (vān glôr′ē əs), *adj.* filled with vanity; showing too much pride.

vain·glo·ry (van′glôr′ē), *n.* **1.** too much elation or pride over one's own achievements, abilities, etc.; boastful vanity. **2.** empty pomp or show.

val·ance (val′əns, vā′ləns), *n.* **1.** a short curtain or piece of drapery that is hung from the edge of a canopy, from the frame of a bed, etc. **2.** a short curtain placed across the top of a window.

vale (vāl), *n.* a valley.

val·e·dic·to·ri·an (val′i dik tôr′ē ən), *n.* the student ranking highest in a graduating class, who delivers the valedictory at the commencement exercises.

val·e·dic·to·ry (val′i dik′tə rē), *adj.* **1.** bidding good-by; saying farewell: *a valedictory speech.* —*n., pl.* **val·e·dic·to·ries. 2.** an address or oration delivered at commencement exercises on behalf of the graduating class. **3.** any farewell speech.

va·lence (vā′ləns), *n. Chem.* a number that indicates how many electrons an atom can give up or take on in forming a chemical compound.

val·en·tine (val′ən tīn′), *n.* **1.** a sentimental card or message or a gift sent by one person to another on St. Valentine's Day. **2.** a sweetheart chosen or greeted on St. Valentine's Day.

Val·en·tine (val′ən tīn′), *n.* **Saint,** died A.D. c270, Christian martyr at Rome.

val·et (val′it, va lā′), *n.* **1.** a male servant who attends to the personal needs of his employer, as by taking care of clothing. **2.** a man who is employed to care for the clothing of patrons of a hotel, passengers on a ship, etc. —*v.,* **val·et·ed, val·et·ing. 3.** to serve as a valet.

Val·hal·la (val hal′ə), *n.* (in Scandinavian mythology) the hall of Odin into which the souls of heroes slain in battle were brought to feast.

val·iant (val′yənt), *adj.* boldly courageous; brave. —**val′iant·ly,** *adv.*

val·id (val′id), *adj.* **1.** based on fact; sound: *a valid objection.* **2.** producing the desired result; effective: *a valid remedy.* **3.** legally binding: *a valid passport.*

val·i·date (val′i dāt′), *v.,* **val·i·dat·ed, val·i·dat·ing. 1.** to make valid; confirm: *to validate an excuse.* **2.** to make legal: *to validate a contract.*

va·lid·i·ty (və lid′i tē), *n.* **1.** the state or quality of being valid. **2.** legal soundness or force: *to question the validity of a contract.*

va·lise (və lēs′), *n.* a small piece of luggage that can be carried by hand.

Val·kyr·ie (val kēr′ē), *n.* (in Scandinavian mythology) any of the beautiful, warlike maidens who brought the souls of fallen heroes to Valhalla.

val·ley (val′ē), *n., pl.* **val·leys. 1.** a long, flat area of land between uplands, hills, or mountains, often fol-lowing the course of a stream: *We skied down the mountain into the valley.* **2.** a large, flat region drained by a river system: *the Mississippi River valley.*

val·or (val′ər), *n.* boldness or determination in facing great danger, hardship, etc.; courage; bravery.

val·or·ous (val′ər əs), *adj.* having or showing valor; courageous; brave.

val·u·a·ble (val′yōo ə bəl), *adj.* **1.** being worth a great deal of money: *a valuable piece of jewelry.* **2.** of use, service, worth, or importance: *valuable experience.* —*n.* **3.** Usually, **valuables.** articles that are worth a great deal of money, such as jewelry.

val·u·a·tion (val′yōo ā′shən), *n.* **1.** the act of estimating or setting the value of something. **2.** an estimated value or worth.

val·ue (val′yōo), *n.* **1.** relative worth, merit, or usefulness: *the value of a college education.* **2.** monetary worth: *an increase in value.* **3.** meaning, as of a word or expression. **4.** (in mathematics) the quantity or number represented by a figure, symbol, or the like: *Find the value of* x. **5. values,** ideals, customs, institutions, etc., of a person or of a society. —*v.,* **val·ued, val·u·ing. 6.** to calculate or rate the monetary value of; assess: *to value a property.* **7.** to regard or esteem highly: *to value a friendship.* —**val′ue·less,** *adj.*

val·ued (val′yōod), *adj.* **1.** highly regarded or esteemed. **2.** estimated; appraised: *a loss of jewels valued at $100,000.*

valve (valv), *n.* **1.** any device for controlling the flow of a fluid. **2.** a movable part that closes or regulates the passage in such a device. **3.** one of the folds of tissue that control the flow of a fluid in the body, such as one that permits blood to flow in one direction only. **4.** (in musical wind instruments) a device for changing the length of the air column to change the pitch of a tone. **5.** one of the two or more separable pieces that make up certain shells.

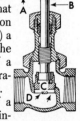

Valve
A, Wheel;
B, Spindle;
C, Disk that
stops flow
of liquid;
D, Liquid

vamp (vamp), *n.* **1.** the portion of a shoe or boot upper that covers the instep and toes. **2.** something patched up or pieced together. —*v.* **3.** to furnish or repair with a vamp.

vam·pire (vam′pīᵊr), *n.* **1.** (in folklore) a corpse that wanders at night, sucking the blood of living persons. **2.** a person who preys ruthlessly upon others. **3.** Also, **vam′pire bat′.** any of various bats that feed on or are believed to feed on blood.

van[1] (van), *n.* **1.** the front division of a military or naval force. **2.** the forefront of any movement, course of progress, or the like. [short for *vanguard*]

van[2] (van), *n.* a covered vehicle, usually a large truck or trailer, used for moving furniture, goods, animals, etc. [short for *caravan*]

va·na·di·um (və nā′dē əm), *n.* a silvery metal used as a toughening ingredient in steel: a chemical element. *Symbol:* V

Van Bu·ren (van byŏŏr′ən), **Martin**, 1782–1862, 8th Vice President of the U.S. 1833–1837; 8th President of the U.S. 1837–1841.

Van·cou·ver (van kōō′vər), *n.* **1.** a large island in SW Canada, off the SW coast of British Columbia. 12,408 sq. mi. **2.** a port city in SW British Columbia, opposite Vancouver Island.

CANADA
Vancouver Island
Vancouver
Victoria
Seattle
PACIFIC OCEAN
WASHINGTON
OREGON

van·dal (van′dᵊl), *n.* a person who willfully destroys or damages public or private property. [after the *Vandals,* a Germanic people that invaded and sacked Rome in A.D. 455]

van·dal·ism (van′dᵊliz′əm), *n.* **1.** a mischievous or malicious destruction or damage of property. **2.** an act of such destruction.

Van·dyke′ beard′ (van dīk′), a short, pointed beard. [named after Sir Anthony *Vandyke* (1599–1641), Flemish painter, in whose portraits it often appears]

vane (vān), *n.* **1.** a weather vane. **2.** a blade on a windmill, turbine, fan, etc.

van·guard (van′gärd′), *n.* **1.** the foremost division or the front part of an army; advance guard. **2.** the forefront of any movement, activity, etc.

va·nil·la (və nil′ə), *n.* **1.** any tropical, climbing orchid, bearing fruit that yields an extract used in flavoring food, in making perfumes, etc. **2.** Also, **vanil′la bean′.** the fruit or bean of this orchid. **3.** the extract of this fruit.

van·ish (van′ish), *v.* **1.** to disappear from sight, esp. quickly; become invisible. **2.** to cease to exist: *His unhappiness vanished when he heard the good news.*

Vanilla
A, Branch with flowers; B, Fruit

van·i·ty (van′i tē), *n., pl.* **van·i·ties.** **1.** too much pride in one's appearance, qualities, achievements, etc.; conceit. **2.** lack of real value or worth: *the vanity of a selfish life.* **3.** something worthless or unimportant. **4.** a vanity case. **5.** a dressing table.

van′ity case′, a small luggage bag or case for holding cosmetics, used or carried by women.

van·quish (vang′kwish), *v.* to defeat or overcome: *to vanquish an enemy; to vanquish one's fears.*

van·tage (van′tij), *n.* **1.** a position, condition, or place giving some advantage. **2.** an advantage or superiority: *a position of vantage.*

vap·id (vap′id), *adj.* lacking life or flavor; dull.

va·por (vā′pər), *n.* **1.** the gaseous state of a substance, esp. of one that is a liquid under normal conditions: *water vapor.* **2.** a visible matter spread in the air, such as fog or smoke. —**va′por·ous,** *adj.*

va·por·ize (vā′pə rīz′), *v.,* **va·por·ized, va·por·iz·ing.**

to change or cause to change into vapor.

var·i·a·ble (vâr′ē ə bəl), *adj.* **1.** apt or likely to vary or change; changeable: *variable wind direction.* **2.** capable of being varied or changed: *The height of the lamp is variable.* —*n.* **3.** something that varies. **4.** a quantity that may assume any given value or set of values. —**var′i·a·bil′i·ty,** *n.* —**var′i·a·bly,** *adv.*

var·i·ance (vâr′ē əns), *n.* **1.** the state or fact of being variable or different: *a temperature variance.* **2.** at variance, in disagreement; not agreeing or conforming: *Your story of the fight is at variance with his.*

var·i·ant (vâr′ē ənt), *adj.* **1.** showing variety or difference: *a variant spelling.* —*n.* **2.** something that differs from the standard or usual form of its kind: *"Grey" is a variant of "gray."*

var·i·a·tion (vâr′ē ā′shən), *n.* **1.** the act, process, or accident of varying or changing. **2.** the amount or rate of change: *a temperature variation of 20 degrees.* **3.** a different form of something; variant.

var·i·col·ored (vâr′i kul′ərd), *adj.* having various colors.

var·ied (vâr′ēd), *adj.* **1.** showing variety; various: *a varied menu.* **2.** having several different colors.

var·i·e·gat·ed (vâr′ē ə gā′tid), *adj.* varied in appearance or color; marked with patches or spots of different colors: *a variegated camellia.*

va·ri·e·ty (və rī′i tē), *n., pl.* **va·ri·e·ties.** **1.** the state or quality of being varied or changing. **2.** a number of different types of things: *a variety of fruits.* **3.** a kind or sort: *a variety of plum.* **4.** Also, **vari′ety show′.** entertainment consisting of a number of brief, unrelated performances or acts.

var·i·ous (vâr′ē əs), *adj.* **1.** being different ones or ones of different kinds: *various remedies.* **2.** numerous; many: *various persons.*

var·let (vär′lit), *n.* *Archaic.* **1.** an attendant or servant; page. **2.** a scoundrel; rascal.

var·nish (vär′nish), *n.* **1.** a preparation for finishing or coating wood, cloth, etc., made of resins dissolved in an oil or in alcohol. **2.** something resembling or suggesting a coat of varnish; shine; gloss. —*v.* **3.** to apply varnish to: *to varnish a floor.* **4.** to give a pleasing appearance to, esp. in order to deceive: *to varnish a fault.*

var·si·ty (vär′si tē), *n., pl.* **var·si·ties.** any principal team, esp. in sports, that represents a school or college: *He is on the varsity in tennis and in debating.*

var·y (vâr′ē), *v.,* **var·ied, var·y·ing.** **1.** to change or alter; make different in some way: *She varied her wardrobe by adding scarves and jewelry.* **2.** to be different from one instance to the next: *The coats vary in size.* **3.** to differ or deviate (usually fol. by *from*): *to vary from the norm.*

vas·cu·lar (vas′kyə lər), *adj.* concerning, composed of, or provided with vessels or ducts that carry fluids, such as blood, lymph, or sap.

vase (vās, vāz), *n.* a hollow container, as of glass, porcelain, or earthenware, usually higher than it is wide, used to hold cut flowers or for decoration.

Vas·e·line (vas′ə lēn′, vas′ə lēn′), *n. Trademark.* a yellowish or whitish jelly obtained from petroleum, used as a lubricant, ointment, etc.

vas·sal (vas′əl), *n.* **1.** (in the Middle Ages) a person granted the use of land, in return for allegiance to a lord and usually military service. **2.** any person owing homage to a superior. **3.** a servant or slave. —*adj.* **4.** of, concerning, or like a vassal.

vast (vast), *adj.* **1.** of very great area or size: *vast desert regions.* **2.** very great: *of vast importance.* —**vast′ly**, *adv.* —**vast′ness**, *n.*

vat (vat), *n.* a large container, such as a tub or tank, used for storing or holding liquids: *a wine vat.*

Vat·i·can (vat′i kən), *n.* **1.** the chief residence of the popes in Vatican City. **2.** the authority and government of the pope.

Vat′ican Cit′y, an independent state within the city of Rome: established in 1929; ruled by the pope. 109 acres.

vaude·ville (vôd′vil, vōd′vil), *n.* theatrical entertainment consisting of a number of individual performances, acts, or mixed numbers.

vault¹ (vôlt), *n.* **1.** a structure shaped like an arch so as to form a ceiling or roof. **2.** a chamber, passage, or room with an arched ceiling or roof. **3.** a strongly built chamber for keeping money or valuable articles. **4.** a burial chamber. —*v.* **5.** to make or build in the form of a vault. [from the early French word *voute,* which comes from Latin *volvere* "to turn"]

vault² (vôlt), *v.* **1.** to leap or spring, as to or from a position or over something. **2.** to leap or spring over: *to vault a fence.* —*n.* **3.** the act of vaulting; leap. [from the Italian word *voltare* "to turn"]

vaunt (vônt), *v.* **1.** to boast of: *to vaunt one's achievements.* —*n.* **2.** a boastful action or utterance.

veal (vēl), *n.* **1.** a calf raised for its meat. **2.** the flesh of the calf as used for food.

veer (vēr), *v.* **1.** to change direction or turn about or aside. **2.** to change the direction or course of; turn: *to veer a ship.*

veg·e·ta·ble (vej′tə bəl, vej′i tə bəl), *n.* **1.** any plant whose fruit, seeds, roots, tubers, bulbs, stems, leaves, or flower parts are used as food. **2.** any plant. —*adj.* **3.** of or made from vegetables: *a vegetable salad.* **4.** of, concerning, or like plants: *the vegetable kingdom.* **5.** made from plants or parts of plants.

veg·e·tar·i·an (vej′i târ′ē ən), *n.* **1.** a person who refuses to eat meat, fish, or fowl, for health reasons or because of moral opposition to the killing of animals. —*adj.* **2.** of, for, or concerning vegetarians. **3.** consisting only of vegetables: *a vegetarian dinner.*

veg·e·tate (vej′i tāt′), *v.,* **veg·e·tat·ed, veg·e·tat·ing. 1.** to grow as or in the manner of a plant. **2.** to live in an inactive or unthinking way: *We've been vegetating ever since we moved away from the city.*

veg·e·ta·tion (vej′i tā′shən), *n.* **1.** all the plant life of a place. **2.** the act or process of vegetating.

veg·e·ta·tive (vej′i tā′tiv), *adj.* **1.** growing or developing as or like plants. **2.** of or concerning vegetation or plants. **3.** with very little action or energy; inactive: *a vegetative existence.*

ve·he·mence (vē′ə məns), *n.* **1.** the quality of being vehement. **2.** violence; fury.

ve·he·ment (vē′ə mənt), *adj.* **1.** marked by strong feeling; intense; ardent: *vehement demands for better working conditions.* **2.** marked by great energy: *vehement clapping.* —**ve′he·ment·ly,** *adv.*

ve·hi·cle (vē′i kəl), *n.* **1.** any means in or by which someone or something is carried or conveyed: *a motor vehicle; a space vehicle.* **2.** a means of transmission or passage: *Air is the vehicle of sound.* **3.** a medium of communication, expression, or display: *a vehicle for political ideas.* **4.** a liquid, such as oil, in which a pigment is mixed. [from the Latin word *vehiculum,* which comes from *vehere* "to convey"]

veil (vāl), *n.* **1.** a piece of opaque or transparent material worn over the face. **2.** a piece of material worn so as to fall over the head and shoulders on each side of the face, forming a part of the headdress of a nun. **3.** something that covers, separates, screens, or hides: *a veil of smoke.* —*v.* **4.** to cover or hide with or as if with a veil.

vein (vān), *n.* **1.** one of the system of branching vessels or tubes carrying blood from various parts of the body to the heart. **2.** one of the riblike thickenings that form the framework of the wing of an insect. **3.** one of the strands or bundles of tissues forming the framework of a leaf. **4.** a body or mass of rock containing a mineral deposit; lode. **5.** a natural channel or a watercourse beneath the surface of the earth. **6.** a streak or marking, as in marble. **7.** a condition, mood, or manner: *conversation in a serious vein.* —*v.* **8.** to furnish with veins. **9.** to mark with lines or streaks suggesting veins.

V, Veins in leaves

veld (velt, felt), *n.* (in S Africa) the open country, bearing grass, bushes, or shrubs, or thinly forested. Also, **veldt.**

vel·lum (vel′əm), *n.* **1.** calfskin, lambskin, kidskin, etc., treated for use as a writing surface. **2.** a texture of paper or cloth suggesting vellum.

ve·loc·i·pede (və los′i pēd′), *n.* **1.** a vehicle, usually having two or three wheels, that is propelled by the rider. **2.** a light, pedal-driven vehicle used for carrying one person on a railroad track.

ve·loc·i·ty (və los′i tē), *n., pl.* **ve·loc·i·ties. 1.** rapidity of motion or operation; swiftness; speed. **2.** the rate of motion of a body in a certain direction.

ve·lour (və lŏŏr′), *n.* a velvetlike fabric of rayon, wool, or other fiber. Also, **ve·lours** (və lŏŏr′).

vel·vet (vel′vit), *n.* **1.** a fabric of silk, nylon, etc., with a thick, soft pile. —*adj.* **2.** made of or covered with velvet: *a velvet dress.* **3.** Also, **vel′vet·like′.** like velvet; smooth; soft.

vel·vet·een (vel′vi tēn′), *n.* a cotton fabric with short pile, resembling velvet.

vel·vet·y (vel′vi tē), *adj.* like velvet; soft; smooth.

ve·nal (vēn′əl), *adj.* **1.** willing to accept a bribe. **2.** influenced by bribery: *a venal agreement.*

vend (vend), *v.* to sell, esp. by peddling.

ven·det·ta (ven det′ə), *n.* a private feud, such as occurred formerly in Corsica and Italy, in which the family of a murdered person seeks to avenge his death by killing the murderer or members of his family.

ven·dor (ven′dər), *n.* a person who sells small items on street corners, at ball games, etc. Also, **ven′der.**

ve·neer (və nēr′), *n.* 1. a very thin layer of wood or other material for facing or inlaying wood. 2. any of the thin layers of wood glued together to form plywood. 3. a facing of a certain material applied to a different one: *a building with a brick veneer.* 4. an outward, deceptive appearance: *He has a thin veneer of self-confidence.* —*v.* 5. to cover with a veneer.

ven·er·a·ble (ven′ər ə bəl), *adj.* worthy of respect because of great age, high office, or noble character.

ven·er·ate (ven′ə rāt′), *v.,* **ven·er·at·ed, ven·er·at·ing.** to regard or treat with reverence or respect. —**ven′er·a′tion,** *n.*

ve·ne′re·al disease′ (və nēr′ē əl), any of several infectious diseases spread esp. by sexual contact.

Ve·ne·tian (və nē′shən), *adj.* 1. of or concerning Venice or its inhabitants. —*n.* 2. a native or inhabitant of Venice.

Vene′tian blind′, a shade for a window having overlapping slats that may be opened or closed.

Ven·e·zue·la (ven′i zwā′lə), *n.* a republic in N South America. 352,143 sq. mi. *Cap.:* Caracas. —**Ven′e·zue′lan,** *n., adj.*

venge·ance (ven′jəns), *n.* 1. punishment inflicted on a person by another who has been harmed by him; revenge. 2. **with a vengeance,** with force, intensity, or determination: *Winter began this year with a vengeance.*

venge·ful (venj′fəl), *adj.* desiring, seeking, or showing vengeance: *a vengeful act.* —**venge′ful·ly,** *adv.*

ve·ni·al (vē′nē əl), *adj.* (esp. of a sin) able to be forgiven or pardoned (distinguished from *mortal*).

Ven·ice (ven′is), *n.* a port city in N Italy, built on numerous small islands.

ven·i·son (ven′i sən, ven′i zən), *n.* the flesh of a deer as used for food. [from the Old French word *venaison,* which comes from Latin *vēnātiō* "hunting," from *vēnārī* "to hunt"]

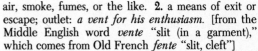

ITALY YUGO-SLAVIA
Venice Trieste
GULF OF VENICE
Po River
ADRIATIC SEA

ven·om (ven′əm), *n.* 1. the poisonous fluid that some animals, such as certain snakes or spiders, secrete and introduce into the bodies of their victims by biting, stinging, etc. 2. something suggesting this, such as ill will or jealousy.

ven·om·ous (ven′ə məs), *adj.* 1. (of an animal) capable of giving a poisoned bite, sting, or wound; poisonous: *a venomous snake.* 2. spiteful; malicious: *a venomous, insulting speech.* —**ven′om·ous·ly,** *adv.*

vent¹ (vent), *n.* 1. an opening serving as an outlet for air, smoke, fumes, or the like. 2. a means of exit or escape; outlet: *a vent for his enthusiasm.* [from the Middle English word *vente* "slit (in a garment)," which comes from Old French *fente* "slit, cleft"]

vent² (vent), *n.* 1. expression; utterance: *to give vent to one's emotions.* —*v.* 2. to give expression to: *She vented her anger on her friends.* 3. to release or discharge (liquid, smoke, etc.). [from the Middle English word *venten,* which comes from Old French *esventer* "to blow out," from Latin *ex-* "out" + *ventus* "wind"]

ven·ti·late (ven′tᵊlāt′), *v.,* **ven·ti·lat·ed, ven·ti·lat·ing.** 1. to provide (a room or other enclosed space) with fresh or cool air. 2. to discuss and examine (a question, problem, etc.) openly and freely. [from the Latin word *ventilāre* "to fan," from *ventus* "wind"]

ven·ti·la·tion (ven′tᵊlā′shən), *n.* 1. the act of ventilating, or the state of being ventilated. 2. facilities or equipment for providing ventilation.

ven·ti·la·tor (ven′tᵊlā′tər), *n.* a device for replacing foul or stale air with fresh air.

ven·tral (ven′trəl), *adj.* of or concerning the belly or abdomen; abdominal.

ven·tri·cle (ven′tri kəl), *n.* 1. any of various hollow organs or parts in an animal body. 2. either of the two lower chambers on each side of the heart that force blood into the arteries. See illus. at **heart.**

ven·tril·o·quism (ven tril′ə kwiz′əm), *n.* the art or practice of speaking so that the voice appears to come from a source other than the speaker.

ven·tril·o·quist (ven tril′ə kwist), *n.* a person who performs or is skilled in ventriloquism. [from the Latin word *ventriloquus,* literally "belly speaker," from *venter* "belly" + *loquī* "to speak"]

ven·ture (ven′chər), *n.* 1. an undertaking involving risk or uncertainty. —*v.,* **ven·tured, ven·tur·ing.** 2. to expose to hazard; risk: *to venture one's career.* 3. to take the risk of: *to venture a voyage.* 4. to express in spite of possible contradiction or opposition: *to venture a guess.* 5. to travel, undertake a project, etc., as part of a venture or as an adventure: *to venture into strange places.*

ven·ture·some (ven′chər səm), *adj.* 1. having or showing a disposition to undertake ventures; adventurous. 2. attended with risk; dangerous; hazardous.

ven·tur·ous (ven′chər əs), *adj.* 1. willing to face risky situations; bold; daring. 2. hazardous; risky; dangerous: *a venturous voyage.*

Ve·nus (vē′nəs), *n.* 1. (in Roman mythology) the goddess of love and beauty: identified with the Greek goddess Aphrodite. 2. the planet second in order from the sun, often the brightest object in the sky except for the sun and the moon. Venus has a diameter of 7700 miles; its average distance from the sun is 67,000,000 miles.

Venus's-flytrap

Ve·nus's-fly·trap (vē′nə siz flī′trap′), *n.* a plant

---

act, āble, dâre, ärt; ebb, ēqual; if, īce; hot, ōver, ôrder; oil; bŏŏk; ōōze; out; up, ûrge; ə = *a* as in *alone;* ᵊ as in *button* (but′ᵊn), *fire* (fīᵊr); *chief;* *shoe;* *thin;* *that;* zh as in *measure* (mezh′ər). See full key inside cover.

having leaves with two lobes that close like a trap when hairs on them are touched by a fly or other insect, which the plant then digests.

ve·ra·cious (və rā′shəs), *adj.* 1. speaking the truth; truthful. 2. true; correct: *a veracious report.*

ve·rac·i·ty (və ras′i tē), *n.* 1. truthfulness; honesty: *to doubt someone's veracity.* 2. truth; accuracy: *to check the veracity of a story.*

Ver·a·cruz (ver′ə krōōz′), *n.* a port city in E Mexico.

ve·ran·da (və ran′də), *n.* a porch, sometimes partly enclosed. [from the Portuguese word *varanda* "railing," which comes from Hindi]

verb (vûrb), *n.* a word or phrase that expresses action or state of being. A verb usually forms the main element of a predicate, is inflected for tense, voice, mood, etc., and is in grammatical agreement with the subject. *Be, come, go,* and *have* are typical verbs.

ver·bal (vûr′bəl), *adj.* 1. of or concerning words: *verbal ability.* 2. expressed in words: *a verbal picture; a verbal agreement.* 3. of or referring to a verb: *The "-s" in "walks" is a verbal ending.* 4. derived from a verb: *In "a fighting man," "fighting" is a verbal adjective. In "there was fierce fighting," "fighting" is a verbal noun.* —*n.* 5. a word derived from a verb, esp. a noun or adjective. —**ver′bal·ly,** *adv.*

ver·ba·tim (vər bā′tim), *adv., adj.* in exactly the same words; word for word: *He repeated the conversation verbatim.*

ver·be·na (vər bē′nə), *n.* any of various plants having brightly colored flowers.

ver·bi·age (vûr′bē ij), *n.* the use of too many words.

ver·bose (vər bōs′), *adj.* using too many words; wordy. —**ver·bose′ly,** *adv.* —**ver·bos·i·ty** (vər bos′i tē), *n.*

ver·dant (vûr′dənt), *adj.* 1. green with vegetation: *verdant fields.* 2. of the color green: *a verdant coat.*

Verde (vûrd), *n.* **Cape,** a cape in Senegal: the westernmost point in Africa.

ver·dict (vûr′dikt), *n.* 1. (in law) the decision reached by a jury concerning an alleged crime, a suit for damages, etc.: *The verdict of the jury was "not guilty."* 2. any judgment or decision. [from the medieval Latin word *vērēdictum,* literally "something truly said"]

ver·di·gris (vûr′də grēs′), *n.* a green or bluish coating formed on copper, brass, or bronze surfaces.

ver·dure (vûr′jər), *n.* green vegetation.

verge (vûrj), *n.* 1. the edge or border of something. 2. the limit or point beyond which something begins or occurs: *on the verge of tears.* —*v.,* **verged, verg·ing.** 3. to be on the verge or border.

Ver·gil (vûr′jil), *n.* 70–19 B.C., Roman poet: author of *The Aeneid.*

ver·i·fi·ca·tion (ver′ə fə kā′shən), *n.* 1. the act or process of verifying. 2. the state of being verified. 3. evidence that verifies something.

ver·i·fy (ver′ə fī′), *v.,* **ver·i·fied, ver·i·fy·ing.** 1. to prove the truth of; confirm. 2. to determine or check the truth or correctness of: *to verify one's addition by the use of an adding machine.*

ver·i·ly (ver′ə lē), *adv. Archaic.* in truth; really.

ver·i·ta·ble (ver′i tə bəl), *adj.* being truly or very much so; genuine or real: *a veritable triumph.* —**ver′i·ta·bly,** *adv.*

ver·i·ty (ver′i tē), *n., pl.* for def. 2 **ver·i·ties.** 1. the state or quality of being true. 2. something that is true, such as a principle or belief.

ver·mi·cel·li (vûr′mi chel′ē, vûr′mi sel′ē), *n.* a kind of pasta resembling spaghetti but thinner. [from an Italian word meaning literally "little worms"]

ver·mil·ion (vər mil′yən), *n.* 1. a brilliant scarlet red. 2. a bright red pigment. Also, **ver·mil′lion.**

ver·min (vûr′min), *n., pl.* **ver·min.** *(used as pl.)* small, troublesome, and often harmful animals or insects: *rats, cockroaches, and other vermin.*

Ver·mont (vər mont′), *n.* a state in the NE United States. 9609 sq. mi. *Cap.:* Montpelier. —**Ver·mont′er,** *n.*

ver·nac·u·lar (vər nak′yə lər), *n.* 1. the common native language of a country or region. 2. the language of ordinary speech. 3. the language or speech peculiar to a profession or class; jargon: *the vernacular of the advertising industry.* —*adj.* 4. of, referring to, or expressed in vernacular.

ver·nal (vûr′nᵊl), *adj.* of, concerning, or happening in spring.

Ver·sailles (ver sī′), *n.* a royal palace and city near Paris, France: treaty ending World War I signed at palace 1919.

ver·sa·tile (vûr′sə til), *adj.* 1. capable of doing many things well: *a versatile performer.* 2. having many uses or applications: *a versatile new plastic.* —**ver′sa·til′i·ty,** *n.*

verse (vûrs), *n.* 1. one of the lines of a poem. 2. a particular type of line: *an iambic verse.* 3. a poem, or a piece of poetry. 4. a short division of a chapter in the Bible. 5. poetic composition; poetry: *the Muse of verse.* [from the Latin word *versus* "a row, line (of poetry)," which comes from *vertere* "to turn"]

versed (vûrst), *adj.* experienced or practiced; skilled; learned (usually fol. by *in*): *to be versed in skin diving.*

ver·si·fy (vûr′sə fī′), *v.,* **ver·si·fied, ver·si·fy·ing.** 1. to put into verses: *to versify a story.* 2. to compose verses. —**ver′si·fi·ca′tion,** *n.*

ver·sion (vûr′zhən), *n.* 1. an account or description, esp. from one person's point of view. 2. a form or variety of something: *a modern version of an antique lamp.* 3. a translation.

ver·sus (vûr′səs), *prep.* 1. against (used esp. to join the names of parties in a legal case, sports contest, etc.): *Smith versus Jones; Army versus Navy.* 2. as compared to; in contrast with: *traveling by plane versus traveling by train.*

ver·te·bra (vûr′tə brə), *n., pl.* **ver·te·brae** (vûr′tə brē′) *or* **ver·te·bras.** any of the bones or segments composing the spinal column in man and higher animals. —**ver′te·bral**, *adj.*

ver·te·brate (vûr′tə brāt′, vûr′tə brit), *adj.* **1.** having a backbone or spinal column. **2.** belonging to or concerning a group of animals that have both a spinal column and a brain that is enclosed in a skull, including mammals, birds, amphibians, and fishes. —*n.* **3.** a vertebrate animal.

Vertebra

ver·tex (vûr′teks), *n., pl.* **ver·tex·es** *or* **ver·ti·ces** (vûr′ti sēz′). **1.** the highest point of something. **2.** (in mathematics) **a.** the point farthest from the base. **b.** the point at which two sides of a figure intersect.

ver·ti·cal (vûr′ti kəl), *adj.* **1.** being in a position or direction at right angles to the horizon; upright. —*n.* **2.** something that is vertical. **3.** the vertical or upright position. —**ver′ti·cal·ly**, *adv.*

ver·ti·go (vûr′tə gō′), *n.* a condition in which a person feels dizzy; dizziness.

verve (vûrv), *n.* vivacity or liveliness; animation: *She's a girl with plenty of verve.*

ver·y (ver′ē), *adv.* **1.** in a high degree: *It is very kind of you to do this.* **2.** absolutely; exactly; *the very best thing to be done; in the very same place as before.* —*adj.* **3.** precise; exact: *This is the very item we have been looking for.* **4.** mere: *The very thought of it is upsetting.* **5.** actual: *He was caught in the very act of stealing.* [from the Old French word *verai* "true," which comes from Latin *vērus*]

ves·i·cle (ves′i kəl), *n.* **1.** a small sac or bladderlike cavity, esp. one filled with fluid. **2.** a blister on the skin.

ves·per (ves′pər), *n.* **1.** the evening star, esp. Venus. **2.** a bell rung at evening. **3. vespers,** *(sometimes cap.)* a religious service in the late afternoon or early evening. —*adj.* **4.** of or concerning vespers.

Ves·puc·ci (ve spoo′chē, -spyoo′-), *n.* **Amerigo,** 1451–1512, Italian explorer after whom America was named.

ves·sel (ves′əl), *n.* **1.** a craft for traveling on water, esp. a fairly large one; ship or boat. **2.** a hollow utensil used esp. for holding liquids. **3.** a tube or duct, such as an artery or vein, containing or carrying blood or some other body fluid.

vest (vest), *n.* **1.** a close-fitting, waist-length, sleeveless garment for men, designed to be worn under a jacket. **2.** a similar garment worn by women. —*v.* **3.** to clothe; dress; robe. **4.** to place in the possession or control of a person or persons (usually fol. by *in*): *to vest authority in a committee.* **5.** to give powers, functions, etc., to: *to vest a committee with power.*

vest·ed (vest′id), *adj.* **1.** held completely and permanently: *vested rights.* **2.** clothed or robed, esp. in church vestments: *a vested priest.*

ves·ti·bule (ves′tə byool′), *n.* **1.** a passage or hall between the outer door and the interior parts of a house or building. **2.** an enclosed entrance at the end of a railroad passenger car.

ves·tige (ves′tij), *n.* **1.** a mark, trace, or visible evidence of something that is no longer present or in existence. **2.** an imperfectly developed organ or part having little or no use. —**ves·tig·i·al** (ve stij′ē əl), *adj.*

vest·ment (vest′mənt), *n.* **1.** a garment, esp. an outer garment. **2.** one of the garments worn by the clergy and their assistants, esp. during divine service. **3. vestments,** clothing: used esp. in literature.

ves·try (ves′trē), *n., pl.* **ves·tries. 1.** a room in or a building attached to a church, in which the vestments, and sometimes other religious objects, are kept. **2.** (in some churches) a similar room used as a chapel, for the Sunday school, etc. **3.** (in the Protestant Episcopal Church) a committee that manages the business affairs of the church.

Ve·su·vi·us (və soo′vē əs), *n.* **Mount,** an active volcano in SW Italy, near Naples. about 3900 ft.

vetch (vech), *n.* any of several climbing plants grown as food for livestock.

vet·er·an (vet′ər ən, ve′trən), *n.* **1.** a person who has had long service or experience in an occupation or office. **2.** a person who has served in a military force, esp. in a war. —*adj.* **3.** experienced through long service or practice: *a veteran member of Congress.* **4.** (of soldiers) having had service or experience in warfare: *veteran troops.*

Vet′erans Day′, November 11, a legal holiday in the U.S. in commemoration of the end of hostilities in World War I and World War II and in honor of service veterans: now officially observed on the fourth Monday in October. Formerly, **Armistice Day.**

vet·er·i·nar·i·an (vet′ər ə nâr′ē ən), *n.* a person who practices veterinary medicine or surgery.

vet·er·i·nar·y (vet′ər ə ner′ē), *n., pl.* **vet·er·i·nar·ies. 1.** another word for **veterinarian.** —*adj.* **2.** noting or concerning the medical and surgical treatment of animals.

ve·to (vē′tō), *n., pl.* **ve·toes. 1.** Also, **ve′to pow′er.** the power vested in one branch of a government to cancel or postpone the decisions, enactments, etc., of another branch. **2.** the use of this right. **3.** a prohibition of any kind. —*v.,* **ve·toed, ve·to·ing. 4.** to reject by exercising a veto: *The President vetoed the bill.* **5.** to prohibit: *She vetoed the party.* [from a Latin word meaning "I forbid"]

vex (veks), *v.* **1.** to irritate or annoy. **2.** to trouble or worry: *The problem vexed him.*

vex·a·tion (vek sā′shən), *n.* **1.** the act of vexing, or the state of being vexed. **2.** something that vexes.

vi·a (vī′ə, vē′ə), *prep.* by way of: *He went to Rome via Paris.*

vi·a·ble (vī′ə bəl), *adj.* **1.** capable of living, growing, and developing, such as an infant, seed, or plant. **2.** practical; workable: *a viable plan.*

vi·a·duct (vī′ə dukt′), *n.* a bridge made up of several short spans for carrying a road, railroad, etc., over a valley or the like.

vi·al (vī′əl), *n.* a small container, as of glass, for holding liquids.

vi·and (vī′ənd), *n.* **1.** an article of food. **2. viands,** articles or dishes of food, esp. choice food. [from the Old French word *viande* "food, meat," which comes from Latin *vivenda* "things to be lived on"]

vi·brant (vī′brənt), *adj.* **1.** moving to and fro rapidly; vibrating. **2.** rich in sound; resonant; resounding. **3.** full of vigor and energy: *a man with a vibrant personality.* —**vi′brant·ly,** *adv.*

vi·brate (vī′brāt), *v.,* **vi·brat·ed, vi·brat·ing. 1.** to move rhythmically and steadily to and fro, as a pendulum does. **2.** to move to and fro or up and down quickly and repeatedly; quiver; tremble. **3.** (of sounds) to produce or have a quivering effect; resound. **4.** to be moved; thrill.

vi·bra·tion (vī brā′shən), *n.* **1.** the act of vibrating, or the state of being vibrated. **2.** a quivering or trembling motion from side to side or up and down. —**vi·bra·to·ry** (vī′brə tôr′ē), *adj.*

vi·bra·tor (vī′brā tər), *n.* **1.** a person or thing that vibrates. **2.** a machine or device causing a vibratory motion, esp. one used to massage parts of the body.

vi·bur·num (vī bûr′nəm), *n.* any of various shrubs such as the cranberry bush or snowball, having clusters of small, white flowers.

vic·ar (vik′ər), *n.* **1.** a clergyman in charge of a chapel in a parish. **2.** (in the Roman Catholic Church) a person representing the pope or a bishop. **3.** a person authorized to perform the functions of another; deputy. [from the Latin word *vicarius* "a substitute," which comes from *vice* "in place of"]

vic·ar·age (vik′ər ij), *n.* **1.** the residence of a vicar. **2.** the salary, office, or duties of a vicar.

vi·car·i·ous (vī kâr′ē əs), *adj.* **1.** performed, received, or suffered in place of another: *vicarious punishment.* **2.** taking the place of another person or thing. **3.** felt or enjoyed by imagining oneself to participate in the experience of others: *vicarious happiness.* —**vi·car′i·ous·ly,** *adv.*

vice (vīs), *n.* **1.** an immoral habit or practice. **2.** immoral conduct.

vice-, a prefix meaning one who acts as a subordinate or substitute for another: *vice-chairman.*

vice′ ad′miral, an officer in the U.S. Navy, ranking above a rear admiral and below an admiral.

vice′ pres′ident, 1. an officer who is next in rank to a president. **2.** *(often caps.)* the elected officer who is next in authority to the President of the U.S. Also, **vice′-pres′ident.** —**vice′ pres′idency.**

vice·roy (vīs′roi), *n.* a person appointed by a sovereign to rule a country or province.

vi·ce ver·sa (vī′sə vûr′sə, vīs′), in reverse order from what has been said or written before: *She dislikes me and vice versa.*

vi·cin·i·ty (vi sin′i tē), *n., pl.* **vi·cin·i·ties.** the area or region near or about a place: *He lives in the vicinity of the post office.*

vi·cious (vish′əs), *adj.* **1.** wicked; evil; bad: *a vicious criminal.* **2.** spiteful; malicious; mean: *a vicious lie.* **3.** savage; ferocious: *a vicious animal.* —**vi′cious·ly,**

adv. —**vi′cious·ness,** *n.*

vi·cis·si·tude (vi sis′i tōōd′, -tyōōd′), *n.* **1.** a change or variation. **2. vicissitudes,** alternating or changing phases or conditions, as of life or fortune: *They have shared the vicissitudes of 40 years.*

vic·tim (vik′tim), *n.* **1.** a person who suffers from a destructive or injurious action or agency: *an accident victim.* **2.** a person who is deceived or cheated. **3.** a living being sacrificed in religious rites.

vic·tim·ize (vik′tə mīz′), *v.,* **vic·tim·ized, vic·tim·iz·ing. 1.** to make a victim of. **2.** to swindle or cheat; take advantage of.

vic·tor (vik′tər), *n.* a person who has won in any struggle or contest.

Vic·to·ri·a (vik tôr′ē ə), *n.* **1.** 1819–1901, queen of Great Britain 1837–1901. **2.** a state in SE Australia. 87,884 sq. mi. *Cap.:* Melbourne. **3.** a seaport and the capital city of British Columbia, on Vancouver Island, in SW Canada. **4. Lake,** a large lake in E Africa. 26,828 sq. mi.

Victo′ria Falls′, falls of the Zambezi River in S Africa. 420 ft. high; more than a mile wide.

Vic·to·ri·an (vik tôr′ē ən), *adj.* **1.** of or concerning Queen Victoria or the period of her reign. **2.** noting the architecture and furniture of this period, which was generally heavy, stiffly formal, and very elaborate. —*n.* **3.** a person, esp. an author or other famous person, who lived during the Victorian period: *Tennyson, Browning, and other Victorians.*

vic·to·ri·ous (vik tôr′ē əs), *adj.* **1.** having achieved a victory; conquering: *our victorious army.* **2.** of or concerning victory. —**vic·to′ri·ous·ly,** *adv.*

vic·to·ry (vik′tə rē), *n., pl.* **vic·to·ries. 1.** a success or triumph over an enemy in battle or war. **2.** a success or triumph in any struggle or contest.

vict·ual (vit′əl), *n.* **1. victuals,** food supplies; provisions. —*v.,* **vict·ualed** *or* **vict·ualled; vict·ual·ing** *or* **vict·ual·ling. 2.** to supply with victuals.

vi·cu·ña (vī kōō′nə, və kōō′nyə), *n.* **1.** a South American animal of the Andes, related to the llama, and yielding a soft, fine wool. **2.** a fabric made from this wool. [from the Spanish word *vicuña,* which comes from Quechuan]

Vicuña
(2½ ft. high
at shoulder)

vid·e·o (vid′ē ō′), *n.* **1.** the picture portion of television, as distinguished from the audio, or sound, portion. —*adj.* **2.** of or concerning television, esp. its visual elements.

vid·e·o·tape (vid′ē ō tāp′), *n.* **1.** a magnetic tape with tracks for recording or reproducing motion pictures and sound, esp. for television. —*v.,* **vid·e·o·taped, vid·e·o·tap·ing. 2.** to record on videotape.

vie (vī), *v.*, **vied, vy·ing.** to strive in competition or rivalry with another; compete.

Vi·en·na (vē en′ə), *n.* a river port and the capital city of Austria, in the NE part, on the Danube River. —**Vi′en·nese′**, *n., adj.*

Vi·et·nam (vē′et näm′, vyet′näm′), *n.* a country in SE Asia, bordering the South China Sea: formerly part of French Indochina; divided in 1954 into North Vietnam and South Vietnam but reunified in 1976. 126,436 sq. mi. *Cap.:* Hanoi.

Vi·et·nam·ese (vē′et nä mēz′, vyet′nə mēz′), *n., pl.* **Vi·et·nam·ese.** 1. a native or inhabitant of Vietnam. 2. the language of Vietnam. —*adj.* 3. of or concerning Vietnam, its people, or their language.

view (vyōō), *n.* 1. the act or an instance of looking at something. 2. the range of one's vision: *to come into view.* 3. an unobstructed sight of something: *a view of the mountains through the window.* 4. a picture or photograph of something. 5. a personal attitude or opinion: *I disagree with his view.* —*v.* 6. to see; behold: *to view a movie.* 7. to look at; survey; inspect: *to view the construction of a road.* 8. to consider; think of: *He viewed the problem with concern.* 9. **in view of**, because of; due to; considering: *In view of the long trip tomorrow, we should get to bed early.* 10. **on view**, available for the public to see: *The paintings will be on view starting Saturday.*

view·find·er (vyōō′fīn′dər), *n.* See **finder** (def. 2).

view·point (vyōō′point′), *n.* 1. a place offering a view of something. 2. a mental attitude.

vig·il (vij′əl), *n.* 1. a period of watchfulness or wakefulness that is kept through the night: *a vigil over a sick person.* 2. the eve, or day and night, before a church festival, esp. an eve that is a fast.

vig·i·lant (vij′ə lənt), *adj.* keenly watchful; alert. —**vig′i·lance**, *n.* —**vig′i·lant·ly**, *adv.*

vig·i·lan·te (vij′ə lan′tē), *n.* a person who belongs to a group that, without legal authority, maintains order and punishes crime when the law seems inadequate.

vig·or (vig′ər), *n.* 1. active strength or force. 2. healthy physical or mental energy.

vig·or·ous (vig′ər əs), *adj.* 1. full of vigor; energetic. 2. strong or active. —**vig′or·ous·ly**, *adv.*

Vi·king (vī′kiṅg), *n.* (*sometimes l.c.*) any of the Scandinavian pirates who plundered the northern and western coasts of Europe from the 8th to the 10th centuries.

vile (vīl), *adj.*, **vil·er, vil·est.** 1. very unpleasant; extremely bad: *a vile odor; vile weather.* 2. morally bad; depraved; foul: *vile behavior; vile language.* 3. degrading or humiliating.

vil·i·fy (vil′ə fī′), *v.*, **vil·i·fied, vil·i·fy·ing.** to defame or slander: *The author vilified the famous statesman.*

vil·la (vil′ə), *n.* a large, luxurious country residence.

vil·lage (vil′ij), *n.* 1. a small community in a rural area, usually smaller than a town. 2. the inhabitants of such a community, considered as a group.

vil·lag·er (vil′i jər), *n.* an inhabitant of a village.

vil·lain (vil′ən), *n.* 1. a cruel person; scoundrel. 2. a character in a play, novel, or the like, who opposes the hero. 3. another spelling of **villein.** [from the Latin word *villānus* "a farm servant," which comes from *villa* "farm"]

vil·lain·ous (vil′ə nəs), *adj.* 1. having a cruel nature. 2. of, concerning, or like a villain: *villainous behavior.* 3. very unpleasant: *villainous weather.*

vil·lain·y (vil′ə nē), *n., pl.* **vil·lain·ies.** 1. the actions or conduct of a villain; wickedness. 2. a villainous act or deed.

vil·lein (vil′ən), *n.* (in the feudal system) a member of a class of persons who were serfs with respect to the lord but had the rights and privileges of freemen with respect to others. Also, **villain.**

vim (vim), *n.* lively or energetic spirit; enthusiasm.

Vin·ci (vin′chē), *n.* **Leonardo da,** 1452–1519, Italian painter, sculptor, architect, engineer, and scientist.

vin·di·cate (vin′də kāt′), *v.*, **vin·di·cat·ed, vin·di·cat·ing.** 1. to clear, as from an accusation or suspicion: *The new evidence vindicated the suspect.* 2. to uphold or justify by argument or evidence: *The prince vindicated his claim to the throne.*

vin·di·ca·tion (vin′də kā′shən), *n.* 1. the act of vindicating, or the state of being vindicated. 2. an excuse or justification.

vin·dic·tive (vin dik′tiv), *adj.* filled with a desire for revenge; vengeful. —**vin·dic′tive·ly**, *adv.* —**vin·dic′tive·ness**, *n.*

vine (vīn), *n.* 1. any plant having a long, slender stem that trails or creeps on the ground or climbs by winding itself about a support. 2. a grape plant.

vin·e·gar (vin′ə gər), *n.* a sour liquid containing acetic acid, produced by the fermentation of wine, cider, etc., used to flavor or preserve food. [from the Old French word *vinegre* "sour wine"] —**vin′e·gar·y**, *adj.*

vine·yard (vin′yərd), *n.* a piece of land where grapes are grown.

Climbing vine

Vin·land (vin′lənd), *n.* a region in E North America, somewhere between Newfoundland and Virginia: visited and described by Norsemen around the year 1000. Also, **Vine·land** (vīn′lənd).

vin·tage (vin′tij), *n.* 1. the wine from a particular harvest or crop. 2. the crop of grapes of one year. 3. the date to which some old-fashioned thing belongs: *a wedding dress of 19th-century vintage.* —*adj.* 4. of good quality; choice: *a vintage crop.* 5. old-fashioned; out-of-date: *a vintage automobile.*

vint·ner (vint′nər), *n.* a wine seller or maker.

vi·nyl (vīn′əl), *n.* 1. one of a group of chemical compounds used in manufacturing plastics that are made into tile, phonograph records, clothing, etc. —*adj.* **2.** of, referring to, or made of vinyl: *a vinyl floor.*

vi·ol (vī′əl), *n.* any of a group of stringed instruments that were used in the 16th and 17th centuries and were replaced by the violin family.

vi·o·la (vē ō′lə), *n.* a four-stringed instrument similar to a violin but slightly larger and deeper in tone. —**vi·o′list,** *n.*

vi·o·late (vī′ə lāt′), *v.,* **vi·o·lat·ed, vi·o·lat·ing. 1.** to break or disregard: *to violate a law; to violate an agreement.* **2.** to disturb: *to violate the peace.* **3.** to act with disrespect toward (something sacred or held in honor): *to violate a flag.* —**vi′o·la·tor,** *n.*

vi·o·la·tion (vī′ə lā′shən), *n.* **1.** a breach, as of a law or an agreement. **2.** an interruption or disturbance: *a violation of privacy.* **3.** an act that shows disrespect for something that is sacred or held in honor: *the violation of a church.*

vi·o·lence (vī′ə ləns), *n.* **1.** swift and great force, esp. that which causes damage or injury: *the violence of the enemy's attack.* **2.** great force of feeling: *He answered the charges against him with violence.* **3.** damage or injury: *the violence done by a storm.* **4.** rough, brutal force: *crimes of violence.*

vi·o·lent (vī′ə lənt), *adj.* **1.** acting with or characterized by great force: *a violent storm.* **2.** resulting from the use of force: *a violent death.* **3.** having or showing great force of feeling: *a violent outburst of anger.* —**vi′o·lent·ly,** *adv.*

vi·o·let (vī′ə lit), *n.* **1.** a small, low, leafy plant that grows in the spring and has purple, blue, yellow, or white flowers. **2.** a flower of this plant. **3.** a bluish purple. —*adj.* **4.** of the color violet; bluish-purple.

vi·o·lin (vī′ə lin′), *n.* a four-stringed instrument, played with a bow. The violin is related to the viola, cello, and double bass, but is smaller and of higher pitch. —**vi′o·lin′ist,** *n.*

Violin

vi·o·lon·cel·lo (vī′ə lən chel′ō), *n., pl.* **vi·o·lon·cel·los.** a cello. —**vi′o·lon·cel′list,** *n.*

VIP, *Informal.* very important person. Also, **V.I.P.**

vi·per (vī′pər), *n.* **1.** any of various poisonous snakes. **2.** a nasty, spiteful person.

vi·ra·go (vi rā′gō, vi rä′gō), *n., pl.* **vi·ra·goes** *or* **vi·ra·gos.** a loud, bad-tempered, scolding woman; shrew.

vir·e·o (vir′ē ō′), *n., pl.* **vir·e·os.** any of several small, insect-eating American birds, having olive-green or gray feathers above and white or yellow feathers below.

Red-eyed vireo
(length 6 in.)

vir·gin (vûr′jin), *n.* **1.** a girl or woman who has never had sexual relations. **2. the Virgin, a.** another name for **Virgin Mary. b.** another name for **Virgo.** —*adj.* **3.** of, referring to, or characteristic of a virgin: *virgin purity.* **4.** pure: *virgin snow.* **5.** untouched or unused: *a virgin forest.* **6.** used for the first time: *virgin wool.* —**vir·gin·i·ty** (vər jin′i tē), *n.*

vir·gin·al[1] (vûr′jə nəl), *adj.* of, referring to, or befitting a virgin: *virginal modesty.*

vir·gin·al[2] (vûr′jə nəl), *n.* a small, box-shaped harpsichord, popular in the 16th and 17th centuries. [from a special use of *virginal*[1]]

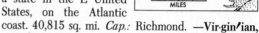

Vir·gin·ia (vûr jin′yə), *n.* a state in the E United States, on the Atlantic coast. 40,815 sq. mi. *Cap.:* Richmond. —**Vir·gin′ian,** *n., adj.*

Virgin′ia Cit′y, a mining town in W Nevada: famous for rich silver deposits.

Virgin′ia creep′er, a climbing plant of North America, having five-pointed leaves and bluish-black berries.

Virgin′ia reel′, an American country dance in which partners face each other and perform various steps together.

Vir′gin Is′lands, a group of islands in the E West Indies belonging to the U.S. and Great Britain.

Vir′gin Mar′y, the mother of Jesus.

Vir·go (vûr′gō), *n.* the Virgin: a constellation and sign of the zodiac.

vir·ile (vir′əl), *adj.* **1.** characteristic of or befitting a man; masculine; manly: *virile sports; a virile personality.* **2.** capable of begetting children. —**vi·ril·i·ty** (və ril′i tē), *n.*

vir·tu·al (vûr′choo əl), *adj.* being so in force or effect though not openly so: *The acts of hostility were a virtual declaration of war.*

vir·tu·al·ly (vûr′choo ə lē), *adv.* for the most part; almost wholly: *The job is virtually finished.*

vir·tue (vûr′choo), *n.* **1.** moral goodness; righteousness. **2.** a particular good moral quality: *Honesty is a virtue.* **3.** chastity. **4.** a good or admirable quality: *Your story has the virtue of being very well written.* **5. by virtue of,** because of; by reason of: *By virtue of his authority, he can end the strike.*

vir·tu·o·so (vûr′choo ō′sō), *n., pl.* **vir·tu·o·sos.** a person who has great skill in some art, esp. in the performance of music: *a piano virtuoso.*

vir·tu·ous (vûr′choo əs), *adj.* **1.** morally good; righteous: *a virtuous life.* **2.** chaste; pure. —**vir′tu·ous·ly,** *adv.* —**vir′tu·ous·ness,** *n.*

vir·u·lent (vir′yə lənt, vir′ə lənt), *adj.* **1.** very poisonous. **2.** very infectious and dangerous: *a virulent disease.* **3.** very spiteful, bitter, or malicious: *a virulent gossip.* —**vir′u·lence,** *n.* —**vir′u·lent·ly,** *adv.*

vi·rus (vī′rəs), *n.* a form of matter smaller than bacteria, that multiplies in the body and causes diseases such as measles or mumps.

vi·sa (vē′zə), *n.* **1.** a permit entered on a passport by an official of a foreign country, allowing the owner of the passport to travel in that country. —*v.,* **vi·saed, vi·sa·ing. 2.** to put a visa on or give a visa to.

vis·age (viz′ij), *n.* **1.** the face: *a sad visage.* **2.** the look or appearance of something: *the cheerful visage of a spring day.*

vis·cer·a (vis′ər ə), *n.pl.* the organs inside the body, esp. the stomach, liver, and intestines. —**vis′cer·al,** *adj.*

vis·count (vī′kount′), *n.* a nobleman ranking just below an earl or count and just above a baron. Also, *referring to a woman,* **vis′count·ess.**

vis·cous (vis′kəs), *adj.* **1.** having a thick, sticky nature; gluey. **2.** resisting flow. —**vis·cos·i·ty** (vi skos′i tē), *n.*

vise (vīs), *n.* any of various devices with two jaws that close together by means of a screw, used to hold an object in place while work is being done on it.

Vise

vis·i·bil·i·ty (viz′ə bil′i tē), *n.* **1.** the state or fact of being visible. **2.** the degree or distance to which things can be seen under certain conditions of weather, light, etc.

vis·i·ble (viz′ə bəl), *adj.* **1.** able to be seen: *a ship visible on the horizon.* **2.** easily noticed; obvious: *His annoyance was visible.* —**vis′i·bly,** *adv.*

Vis·i·goth (viz′ə goth′), *n.* a member of the group of western Goths that overran the Roman Empire in the 5th century and later settled in Spain and southern France.

vi·sion (vizh′ən), *n.* **1.** the sense of sight. **2.** the ability to foresee; foresight: *planners with vision.* **3.** an image or idea that is dreamed or imagined: *a vision of the future.* **4.** a person or thing of great beauty: *She was a vision of loveliness.* —*v.* **5.** to envision. —**vi′sion·less,** *adj.*

vi·sion·ar·y (vizh′ə ner′ē), *adj.* **1.** given to or characterized by fanciful or impractical ideas: *a visionary dreamer.* **2.** belonging to or seen in a vision. **3.** unreal or impractical: *visionary plans.* —*n., pl.* **vi·sion·ar·ies. 4.** a person who sees visions. **5.** a person who indulges in impractical ideas; dreamer.

vis·it (viz′it), *v.* **1.** to go and stay with (a person or persons) or at (a place) for a short time: *to visit one's family; to visit Paris.* **2.** to be a guest of: *to visit a friend for a month.* **3.** to come upon; assail; afflict: *a country visited by the plague.* —*n.* **4.** a call or stay.

vis·it·a·tion (viz′i tā′shən), *n.* **1.** a visit, esp. an official visit for examination or inspection. **2.** a punishment or reward from God: *a divine visitation.*

vis·i·tor (viz′i tər), *n.* a person who pays a visit.

vi·sor (vī′zər), *n.* **1.** a movable covering for the eyes and face, attached to the helmet of a suit of armor. **2.** the front brim of a cap. **3.** a stiff, movable flap over the windshield of a vehicle for protecting the eyes of the driver. Also, **vizor.**

vis·ta (vis′tə), *n.* **1.** a view or outlook, esp. one seen through a long, narrow street or passage. **2.** a mental view or prospect: *a vista of future happiness.*

Vis·tu·la (vis′chōō lə), *n.* a river in Poland, flowing N to the Baltic. 650 mi. long.

vis·u·al (vizh′ōō əl), *adj.* **1.** of or concerning seeing or sight: *a visual image.* **2.** able to be seen; visible. —**vis′u·al·ly,** *adv.*

vis·u·al·ize (vizh′ōō ə līz′), *v.,* **vis·u·al·ized, vis·u·al·iz·ing.** to form a picture of in the mind: *to visualize the future.* —**vis′u·al·i·za′tion,** *n.*

vi·tal (vīt′ᵊl), *adj.* **1.** of, referring to, or necessary to life: *vital processes.* **2.** energetic, lively, or forceful: *a vital leader.* **3.** of first importance; essential: *a vital decision.* —**vi′tal·ly,** *adv.*

vi·tal·i·ty (vī tal′i tē), *n.* **1.** great physical or mental strength: *a player of tremendous vitality.* **2.** ability to go on living or thriving: *the vitality of the nation.*

vi·tal·ize (vīt′ᵊl īz′), *v.,* **vi·tal·ized, vi·tal·iz·ing.** to give life or vigor to: *The mountain air vitalized us all.*

vi·tals (vī′t°ls), *n.pl.* the organs of the body that are necessary to life, such as the heart, liver, etc.

vi·ta·min (vī′tə min), *n.* any of a group of organic substances necessary for the health of the body, found in foods and also produced artificially.

vi·ti·ate (vish′ē āt′), *v.,* **vi·ti·at·ed, vi·ti·at·ing. 1.** to weaken the strength or goodness of; make bad: *Smoke vitiated the air. His character was vitiated by bad habits.* **2.** to remove the legal force of: *to vitiate a contract.* —**vi′ti·a′tion,** *n.*

vit·re·ous (vi′trē əs), *adj.* of, like, or containing glass: *vitreous sand.*

vit′reous hu′mor, the transparent jellylike substance that fills the eyeball behind the lens.

vit·ri·fy (vi′trə fī′), *v.,* **vit·ri·fied, vit·ri·fy·ing.** to change or become changed into glass or a glassy substance: *sand vitrified by fire.* —**vit′ri·fi·ca′tion,** *n.*

vit·ri·ol (vi′trē əl), *n.* **1.** sulfuric acid. **2.** a sulfate made by the action of sulfuric acid on certain metals. **3.** something very severe or caustic: *the vitriol of his criticism.*

vi·va·cious (vi vā′shəs, vī vā′shəs), *adj.* lively; gay; sprightly. —**vi·va′cious·ly,** *adv.* —**vi·vac·i·ty** (vi vas′i tē, vī vas′i tē), *n.*

viv·id (viv′id), *adj.* **1.** very bright or intense, as color or light: *vivid green leaves.* **2.** full of life; lively: *a vivid imagination.* **3.** having the freshness, spirit, appearance, etc., of life: *a vivid painting; a vivid description.* **4.** strong, clear, or distinct: *a vivid memory.* —**viv′id·ly,** *adv.* —**viv′id·ness,** *n.*

viv·i·fy (viv′ə fī′), *v.,* **viv·i·fied, viv·i·fy·ing. 1.** to give life or spirit to: *His gaiety vivified the party.* **2.** to make vivid; brighten or sharpen: *The story was vivified by beautiful descriptions.*

vi·vip·a·rous (vī vip′ər əs), *adj.* bringing forth living animals rather than eggs, as most mammals and some reptiles and fishes do. —**vi·vip′a·rous·ly,** *adv.*

viv·i·sec·tion (viv′i sek′shən), *n.* the act or practice of cutting into or dissecting living bodies, as for the purpose of medical research. —**viv′i·sec′tion·ist,** *n.*

vix·en (vik′sən), *n.* 1. a female fox. 2. a woman who is ill-tempered or quarrelsome.

vi·zor (vī′zər), *n.* another spelling of **visor.**

Vla·di·vos·tok (vlad′ə-vos′tok), *n.* a port city in the SE Soviet Union in Asia.

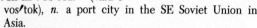

vo·cab·u·lar·y (vō kab′yə ler′ē), *n., pl.* **vo·cab·u·lar·ies.** 1. the words of a language: *English has an enormous vocabulary.* 2. the words used or known by a particular person, group, profession, etc.: *a limited vocabulary; the vocabulary of medicine.* 3. an alphabetical list of words.

vo·cal (vō′kəl), *adj.* 1. of, referring to, or uttered with the voice: *vocal criticism.* 2. sung or meant to be sung: *vocal music.* 3. speaking loudly or openly: *a vocal advocate for reform.* —**vo′cal·ly,** *adv.*

vo′cal cords′, either of two pairs of membranes in the larynx that vibrate with air from the lungs, producing the sound of the voice. See illus. at **mouth.**

vo·cal·ist (vō′kə list), *n.* a singer.

vo·ca·tion (vō kā′shən), *n.* 1. the occupation, profession, or business of a person: *His vocation is law.* 2. a strong impulse or desire to follow a particular career. 3. a religious calling: *to receive one's vocation.*

vo·ca·tion·al (vō kā′shə nəl), *adj.* referring to or connected with a vocation or occupation.

vo·cif·er·ous (vō sif′ər əs), *adj.* making a loud outcry; noisy; clamorous: *a vociferous, angry crowd.* —**vo·cif′er·ous·ly,** *adv.* —**vo·cif′er·ous·ness,** *n.*

vod·ka (vod′kə), *n.* a colorless alcoholic liquor originally made in Russia.

vogue (vōg), *n.* 1. the fashion or style of a particular time: *Short skirts are currently in vogue.* 2. popularity or favor: *That novel had a great vogue.*

voice (vois), *n.* 1. the sound or sounds uttered through the mouth, esp. the human mouth in speaking, singing, etc. 2. the quality or range of such sounds: *a deep voice.* 3. the ability to speak or sing: *The soprano lost her voice.* 4. expression in words or uttered sounds: *to give voice to one's feelings.* 5. the right or power to be heeded, obeyed, etc.: *to have a voice in making decisions.* 6. a will or desire that has been made known: *the voice of the people.* 7. a sound that resembles speech or a quality that seems to have a message or meaning: *the voice of the wind; the voice of one's conscience.* 8. (of speech sounds) the quality produced by vibration of the vocal cords. 9. (in grammar) the inflected form of a verb that shows whether the subject performs or receives the action of the verb. See also **active voice, passive**

voice. 10. a singer or singers: *a musical piece for voice and orchestra.* —*v.,* **voiced, voic·ing.** 11. to express; declare; proclaim: *to voice one's approval.* 12. to utter with the voice. 13. to pronounce (a speech sound) with vibrations of the vocal cords. 14. **with one voice,** in full agreement; unanimously: *With one voice they cheered his speech.*

voiced (voist), *adj.* 1. having a voice of a certain kind (usually used in combination): *gruff-voiced.* 2. expressed with the voice: *voiced disapproval.* 3. (of speech sounds) pronounced with vibration of the vocal cords. The sounds *b, d,* and *g* are voiced. See also **voiceless** (def. 4).

voice·less (vois′lis), *adj.* 1. having no voice; mute; dumb. 2. unspoken; unuttered: *voiceless sympathy.* 3. having no vote or right of choice: *to be voiceless in the government.* 4. (of speech sounds) pronounced without vibration of the vocal cords. The sounds *p, t,* and *k* are voiceless. See also **voiced** (def. 3). —**voice′less·ly,** *adv.* —**voice′less·ness,** *n.*

voice·print (vois′print′), *n.* a graph, made by electronic means, showing the unique characteristics of a person's voice: used as a means of identification.

void (void), *adj.* 1. having no legal force or effect: *a void agreement.* 2. devoid; empty: *a life void of meaning.* 3. without contents; empty. —*n.* 4. an empty space or emptiness: *the immense void of outer space.* —*v.* 5. to cancel or annul: *to void a contract.* 6. to empty or clear out: *to void a room of people.*

voile (voil), *n.* a light dress fabric of wool, silk, rayon, or cotton, having an open weave.

vol., 1. volume. 2. volunteer.

vol·a·tile (vol′ə təl), *adj.* 1. evaporating quickly or easily. 2. tending or likely to break into violence or fall into disorder: *a volatile political situation.* 3. flighty; fickle; changeable: *a volatile personality.* 4. fleeting; passing: *the volatile beauty of flowers.* —**vol·a·til·i·ty** (vol′ə til′i tē), *n.*

vol·can·ic (vol kan′ik), *adj.* 1. of or referring to a volcano: *volcanic activity.* 2. discharged or produced by a volcano: *volcanic mud.* 3. like a volcano in violence; explosive: *a volcanic temper.*

vol·ca·no (vol kā′nō), *n., pl.* **vol·ca·noes** *or* **vol·ca·nos.** 1. an opening in the earth's surface through which lava, steam, ashes, etc., are thrown up. 2. a mountain or hill of ashes or lava thrown up around such an opening.

vole (vōl), *n.* any of several small, mouselike or ratlike rodents having short limbs and a short tail.

Vol·ga (vol′gə), *n.* a river in the Soviet Union, flowing E, then S to the Caspian Sea.

Vol·go·grad (vol′gə-grad′), *n.* a city in the S Soviet Union in Europe, on the Volga River. Former name, **Stalingrad.**

vo·li·tion (vō lish′ən), *n.* 1. the act of willing or choosing: *He came of his own volition.* 2. the power of determining one's actions; will: *The drug deprived him of his volition.*

vol·ley (vol′ē), *n., pl.* **vol·leys. 1.** the discharge of many bullets or other missiles at one time: *a volley of spears.* **2.** the bullets or other missiles so discharged. **3.** a burst or outburst of many things at once: *a volley of protests; a volley of hail.* **4.** (in tennis) the flight of the ball before it hits the ground. **5.** (in soccer) a kick of the ball before it bounces on the ground. —*v.,* **vol·leyed, vol·ley·ing. 6.** to discharge in or as if in a volley. **7.** (in tennis) to return (the ball) before it hits the ground. **8.** (in soccer) to kick the ball before it bounces on the ground.

vol·ley·ball (vol′ē bôl′), *n.* **1.** a game for two teams in which the object is to keep a large ball in motion, from side to side, over a high net, by striking it with the hands before it touches the ground. **2.** the ball used in this game.

vols., volumes.

volt (vōlt), *n.* a unit for measuring the force that causes the movement of electrons in an electric circuit.

volt·age (vōl′tij), *n.* electromotive force, measured in volts.

volt·me·ter (vōlt′mē′tər), *n.* an instrument for measuring the voltage between two points of a circuit.

vol·u·ble (vol′yə bəl), *adj.* speaking with a ready and easy flow of words; fluent; talkative. —**vol′u·bil′i·ty,** *n.* —**vol′u·bly,** *adv.*

vol·ume (vol′yŏŏm, vol′yəm), *n.* **1.** a book. **2.** one book of a set: *an encyclopedia of many volumes.* **3.** all of the issues of a magazine or newspaper that appear in a single year, often bound together into one book. **4.** the amount of space occupied by an object or substance, measured in cubic inches, cubic feet, etc.: *the volume of liquid in a bottle.* **5.** a large mass or quantity: *a volume of mail.* **6.** amount; total: *the volume of sales.* **7.** the degree of sound; loudness.

vo·lu·mi·nous (və lōō′mə nəs), *adj.* **1.** large in quantity, supply, or bulk: *a voluminous amount of mail.* **2.** filling many volumes: *the voluminous works of Shakespeare.* —**vo·lu′mi·nous·ly,** *adv.*

vol·un·tar·y (vol′ən ter′ē), *adj.* **1.** done, made, brought about, etc., by one's own free will or choice: *a voluntary contribution.* **2.** intended or done on purpose: *Was it an accident or a voluntary action?* **3.** done or operated by volunteers: *a voluntary service; a voluntary hospital.* **4.** controlled by the will: *Some muscles are voluntary.* —**vol′un·tar′i·ly,** *adv.*

vol·un·teer (vol′ən tēr′), *n.* **1.** a person who offers to do something of his own free will and usually without pay: *volunteers for hospital work.* **2.** a person who enlists in the military service. —*adj.* **3.** of, concerning, or done by a volunteer or volunteers; voluntary: *volunteer work.* —*v.* **4.** to offer oneself for some service or undertaking. **5.** to enlist in the military service. **6.** to say, tell, offer, etc., voluntarily: *He volunteered the information.*

vo·lup·tu·ous (və lup′chŏŏ əs), *adj.* **1.** full of, giving, or seeking pleasure and luxury: *a voluptuous life.* **2.** pleasing or delightful to the senses: *voluptuous beauty.* —**vo·lup′tu·ous·ly,** *adv.* —**vo·lup′tu·ous·ness,** *n.*

vom·it (vom′it), *v.* **1.** to throw up the contents of one's stomach through the mouth. **2.** to throw out or be thrown out with force: *The volcano vomited smoke and flame.* —*n.* **3.** the matter ejected in vomiting.

voo·doo (vōō′dōō), *n., pl.* **voo·doos. 1.** a type of witchcraft of West African origin, now practiced in the West Indies. —*adj.* **2.** of, referring to, or practicing voodoo.

vo·ra·cious (vô rā′shəs, və rā′shəs), *adj.* **1.** craving or eating large amounts of food. **2.** eager to possess, absorb, etc.: *voracious readers.* —**vo·ra′cious·ly,** *adv.* —**vo·rac·i·ty** (vô ras′i tē, və ras′i tē), *n.*

vor·tex (vôr′teks), *n., pl.* **vor·tex·es** *or* **vor·ti·ces** (vôr′ti sēz′). **1.** a whirling mass of water, as a whirlpool. **2.** a whirling mass of air, fire, etc.: *the vortex of a tornado.* **3.** a state of affairs resembling a whirlpool in violence and power to involve: *the vortex of war.*

vo·ta·ry (vō′tə rē), *n., pl.* **vo·ta·ries. 1.** a person who is bound by religious vows, as a monk or a nun. **2.** a person who is devoted to some person, subject, or pursuit: *a votary of art.*

vote (vōt), *n.* **1.** the expression of opinion or choice by a person or group of persons: *He gave his vote to the other candidate.* **2.** a ballot, ticket, etc., used in making such an expression. **3.** the right to such an expression: *to give women the vote.* **4.** the total number of expressions: *a large vote.* **5.** the decision reached by voting: *Was the vote for or against the measure?* **6.** the expressed choice of a particular group: *to win the labor vote.* —*v.,* **vot·ed, vot·ing. 7.** to cast a ballot. **8.** to elect, enact, etc., by vote: *He was voted into office.* **9.** to support by one's vote: *to vote Republican.* **10.** to declare or decide: *They voted the dinner a great success.*

vot·er (vō′tər), *n.* a person who votes or has the right to vote.

vo·tive (vō′tiv), *adj.* done or given with a vow or as a result of a vow: *a votive offering.*

vouch (vouch), *v.* to support someone or something as being true, right, reliable, etc.; guarantee (usually fol. by *for*): *I will vouch for his honesty.*

vouch·er (vou′chər), *n.* **1.** a record of an expense paid: *This receipt is a voucher for the bill.* **2.** a person or thing that vouches: *His record is a voucher for his honesty.*

vouch·safe (vouch sāf′), *v.,* **vouch·safed, vouch·saf·ing.** to give or grant with graciousness; deign: *The queen vouchsafed a friendly answer.*

vow (vou), *n.* **1.** a solemn promise or pledge: *marriage vows; a vow of secrecy.* **2.** a solemn promise made to God. —*v.* **3.** to make a vow. **4.** to pledge or promise: *to vow revenge.*

vow·el (vou′əl), *n.* **1.** a speech sound produced without obstruction of the flow of the breath, as English *a, e, i, o, u,* and sometimes *w* and *y.* **2.** a letter or group of letters representing a vowel sound, as *ie* in *mischief* or *oo* in *look.* —*adj.* **3.** of, referring to, or consisting of a vowel or vowels.

voy·age (voi′ij), *n.* **1.** a journey, esp. a long one by ship: *a voyage to Borneo.* —*v.,* **voy·aged, voy·ag·ing. 2.** to make a voyage; travel; journey: *to voyage around the world.* —**voy′ag·er,** *n.*

V.P., Vice President. Also, **V. Pres.**

vs., **1.** verse. **2.** versus.

Vt., Vermont.

Vul·can (vul′kən), *n.* (in Roman mythology) the god of fire and the forge.

vul·can·ize (vul′kə nīz′), *v.,* **vul·can·ized, vul·can·iz· ing.** to treat heated rubber with sulfur or some compound of sulfur in order to make it tougher and more lasting. —**vul′can·i·za′tion,** *n.* —**vul′can·iz′er,** *n.*

vul·gar (vul′gər), *adj.* **1.** lacking good taste or breeding; coarse: *Eating with one's fingers is considered vulgar.* **2.** of or referring to the ordinary people of a society: *the vulgar masses.* **3.** (of language) spoken by the common people: *the vulgar tongue.* —**vul′ gar·ly,** *adv.*

vul·gar·ism (vul′gə riz′əm), *n.* **1.** vulgar behavior or character. **2.** a word or phrase used chiefly in the speech of uneducated people, but not considered proper or acceptable in formal or standard speech.

vul·gar·i·ty (vul gar′i tē), *n., pl.* for def. 2 **vul·gar·i· ties. 1.** the state or quality of being vulgar. **2.** something vulgar, as an act or expression.

vul·gar·ize (vul′gə rīz′), *v.,* **vul·gar·ized, vul·gar·iz· ing. 1.** to make vulgar; coarsen; cheapen: *Keeping unrefined company had vulgarized her manners.* **2.** to make (a book, topic, etc.) easier to understand by rewriting; popularize: *to vulgarize a Beethoven symphony.* —**vul′gar·i·za′tion,** *n.*

Vul·gate (vul′gāt), *n.* the Latin version of the Bible used in the Roman Catholic Church.

vul·ner·a·ble (vul′nər ə bəl), *adj.* **1.** open to attack or destruction: *a vulnerable country; to be vulnerable to criticism.* **2.** easily hurt or wounded: *a vulnerable part of the body; vulnerable feelings.* —**vul′ ner·a·bil′i·ty,** *n.* —**vul′ner·a·bly,** *adv.*

vul·ture (vul′chər), *n.* any of several large birds of prey that feed on dead animals.

Vulture
(length 2½ ft.;
wingspread
to 6 ft.)

vy·ing (vī′iñg), *adj.* **1.** competing; contending: *vying teams.* —*v.* **2.** the present participle of **vie.** —**vy′ing·ly,** *adv.*

	Developed in the Middle Ages to represent two U's	Gothic	Modern Roman
DEVELOPMENT OF UPPER-CASE LETTERS		𝔀	W
DEVELOPMENT OF LOWER-CASE LETTERS	ɯ Medieval	𝔴 Gothic	w Modern Roman

W

W, w (dub′əl yoo′), *n., pl.* **W's** *or* **Ws, w's** *or* **ws.** the 23rd letter of the English alphabet.

W, 1. watt; watts. 2. West. 3. western.

W, *Chem.* the symbol for **tungsten.** [abbreviation of *wolfram,* another name for tungsten]

w, watt; watts.

W., 1. watt; watts. 2. weight. 3. West. 4. western. 5. width. 6. (in physics) work.

w., 1. watt; watts. 2. week; weeks. 3. weight. 4. west. 5. western. 6. width. 7. (in physics) work.

wab·ble (wob′əl), *v.,* **wab·bled, wab·bling.** another spelling of **wobble.**

Wac (wak), *n.* a member of the Women's Army Corps, a branch of the U.S. Army.

wad (wod), *n.* 1. a small mass, lump, or ball of something soft: *a wad of cotton; a wad of clay.* 2. a roll of money in bills. 3. *Slang.* a large amount of something, esp. money: *He made a wad in the stock market.* —*v.,* **wad·ded, wad·ding.** 4. to form into a wad or wads: *to wad cotton into balls.* 5. to put a wad or wads into; pad: *to wad a pillow.*

wad·dle (wod′°l), *v.,* **wad·dled, wad·dling.** 1. to walk with short, clumsy steps while swaying or rocking from side to side, as a duck does. —*n.* 2. a manner of moving in such a way: *to walk with a waddle.*

wade (wād), *v.,* **wad·ed, wad·ing.** 1. to walk through water, snow, mud, or anything that covers the lower part of the legs and slows one down. 2. to make slow, difficult progress: *to wade through a dull book.* 3. to pass through or across by wading: *to wade a stream.* 4. **wade in** (or **into**), to begin with energy or enthusiasm: *He waded into his work.*

wad·er (wā′dər), *n.* 1. a person or thing that wades. 2. Also, **wad′ing bird′.** any of various long-legged birds that wade in water to feed, such as the crane or heron. 3. a high, waterproof boot.

Wader (ibis)
(length 2½ ft.)

wa·fer (wā′fər), *n.* 1. a thin, crisp cake or biscuit, often sweetened and flavored. 2. a thin piece of candy. 3. a thin disk of bread used in Holy Communion. 4. a thin sheet of dried paste, gelatin, or the like, used for sealing letters, attaching papers, etc.

waf·fle (wof′əl), *n.* a crisp cake with a pattern of square hollows, made in a waffle iron.

waf′fle i′ron, a cooking utensil made of two metal plates marked with a deep, indented, gridlike pattern and hinged at one side, between which batter for waffles is cooked.

waft (waft, wäft), *v.* 1. to carry lightly and smoothly through the air or over water: *The wind wafted the curtains into the room.* 2. to float lightly through the air or over the water: *a scent of roses wafting from the garden.* —*n.* 3. a faint sound, odor, etc.: *a waft of music from a distant radio.* 4. a light current or gust: *a waft of air.*

wag (wag), *v.,* **wagged, wag·ging.** 1. to move from side to side, up and down, etc.: *a dog wagging its tail.* 2. to move in making gossip or in chattering: *Tongues were wagging over the scandal.* —*n.* 3. a person who likes to play jokes. 4. an act of wagging: *a wag of the tail.*

wage (wāj), *n.* 1. Often, **wages.** money paid for work or services: *a weekly wage.* 2. Usually, **wages.** *(used as sing. or pl.)* what comes or is given in return: *The wages of sin is death.* —*v.,* **waged, wag·ing.** 3. to carry on (a fight, quarrel, etc.): *to wage war.*

wa·ger (wā′jər), *n.* 1. a bet. —*v.* 2. to make a bet: *I wager that he won't come.* 3. to bet (something); gamble: *to wager a fortune.*

wag·gish (wag′ish), *adj.* like or characteristic of a wag: *a waggish comedian; waggish humor.*

wag·gle (wag′əl), *v.,* **wag·gled, wag·gling.** 1. to wobble or shake, esp. while in motion: *The old car waggled down the road.* 2. to wag (a finger), as in reproaching someone.

wag·on (wag′ən), *n.* 1. a horse-drawn vehicle used for hauling heavy loads. 2. any of various light trucks used for deliveries, transportation, etc.: *a milk wagon.* **3.** a small, open, four-wheeled vehicle with a handle, used as a toy by children. **4.** a patrol wagon.

waif (wāf), *n.* a person or animal without a home, esp. a small child.

wail (wāl), *v.* **1.** to make a mournful cry, as in grief or pain. **2.** to make a similar sound: *The wind wailed in the trees.* —*n.* **3.** a mournful cry: *the wail of a baby.*

wain·scot (wān′skət, wān′skot), *n.* **1.** a lining of wood paneling or the like for the walls of a room, esp. the lower part. —*v.*, **wain·scot·ed** *or* **wain·scot·ted; wain·scot·ing** *or* **wain·scot·ting. 2.** to line the walls of (a room) with woodwork.

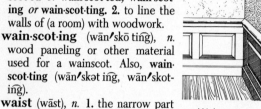
Wainscot

wain·scot·ing (wān′skō ting), *n.* wood paneling or other material used for a wainscot. Also, **wain·scot·ting** (wān′skət ing, wān′skot-ing).

waist (wāst), *n.* **1.** the narrow part of the human body between the ribs and the hips. **2.** the part of a garment covering this part of the body: *a dress belted at the waist.* **3.** the central or middle part of an object: *the waist of a violin; the waist of a ship.* [from the Middle English word *wast*, which comes from Old English *wæstm* "growth, form, figure"] —**waist′like′,** *adj.*

waist·band (wāst′band′), *n.* a band that encircles the waist, esp. as a part of a skirt, trousers, etc.

waist·coat (wes′kət, wāst′kōt′), *n. Chiefly British.* a man's vest.

waist·line (wāst′līn′), *n.* **1.** the narrowest part of the waist. **2.** the narrowest part of a woman's dress, at, above, or below the waist, according to fashion: *Waistlines will be low this fall.*

wait (wāt), *v.* **1.** to hold oneself ready for an event, arrival, etc.: *to wait for a train; to wait until night.* **2.** to await patiently: *Please wait your turn.* **3.** to await one's attention: *There is a parcel waiting for you.* **4.** to be postponed or left undone for a time: *That job can wait until next week.* **5.** to delay: *We'll wait supper for you.* **6.** to serve food at as a waiter or waitress: *to wait table.* —*n.* **7.** the act or an instance or period of waiting: *a long wait for the train.* **8. lie in wait,** to lie in ambush; be in hiding for an attack: *The robbers were lying in wait for the stagecoach.* **9. wait on, a.** to serve (the public) as a clerk, waiter, etc.: *to wait on customers in a store.* **b.** to make a formal call on (a person of rank): *The ambassador waited on Her Majesty.* **c.** *Informal.* to wait for: *We've been waiting on him for an hour.* **10. wait up,** *Informal.* **a.** to delay going to bed to await someone or something: *His mother waits up for him.* **b.** to halt and wait for someone to catch up: *The bigger boys waited up for the smaller ones.* [from the Old French word *waitier*, which comes from a Germanic word meaning "to watch"]

wait·er (wā′tər), *n.* **1.** a man who waits on diners, as in a restaurant. **2.** a tray for carrying dishes, a tea service, etc. **3.** a person who waits or awaits.

wait·ing (wā′ting), *n.* **1.** a period of waiting; pause;

interval; delay: *Long waiting made him impatient.* **2. in waiting,** in attendance, as upon a royal person: *She served the queen as lady in waiting.*

wait′ing room′, a room in a railroad station, doctor's office, etc., for those who wait.

wait·ress (wā′tris), *n.* a woman who waits on diners, as in a restaurant.

waive (wāv), *v.*, **waived, waiv·ing. 1.** to give up a claim to or refrain from insisting upon: *to waive a trial by jury; to waive a rule.* **2.** to postpone or put aside: *to waive action on a matter.*

waiv·er (wā′vər), *n.* **1.** a voluntary giving up of a right or a claim. **2.** a written statement of this.

wake¹ (wāk), *v.*, **waked** *or* **woke** (wōk); **waked** *or* **wok·en** (wō′kən); **wak·ing. 1.** to come or bring out of sleep; awaken; waken. **2.** to be or continue to be awake: *Waking or sleeping, I think of you.* **3.** to arouse or become aroused: *The story woke their interest. They woke to the danger they were in.* —*n.* **4.** a watch or vigil kept, esp. over a corpse before burial. [from the Old English word *wacian* "to wake"]

wake² (wāk), *n.* **1.** the track of waves left by a ship moving through the water. **2.** the path or course of anything that has passed: *the wake of a storm.* **3. in the wake of,** immediately after: *In the wake of the hurricane came the floods.* [from Scandinavian]

wake·ful (wāk′fəl), *adj.* **1.** unable or not wanting to sleep: *Worries made him wakeful.* **2.** characterized by absence of sleep: *a wakeful night.* **3.** watchful; alert: *a wakeful cat.* —**wake′ful·ly,** *adv.* —**wake′ful·ness,** *n.*

Wake′ Is′land, an island in the N Pacific, belonging to the U.S.: air base. 3 sq. mi.

wak·en (wā′kən), *v.* to wake. —**wak′en·ing,** *n.*

wale (wāl), *n.* **1.** a mark made on the skin by a stroke of a whip or rod; welt. **2.** one of the ridges that make up the texture of certain kinds of cloth, such as corduroy. **3.** any of certain very thick planks used on the outside of a wooden ship. —*v.*, **waled, wal·ing. 4.** to mark with wales. **5.** to weave with wales. [from the Old English word *walu* "ridge, rib"]

Wales (wālz), *n.* a division of the United Kingdom, in SW Great Britain. 8016 sq. mi.

walk (wôk), *v.* **1.** to move on foot at a moderate speed: *He walked and ran by turns.* **2.** to move about in this way for pleasure or exercise: *to walk in the woods.* **3.** to cause or help to walk: *to walk a dog; to walk a lame person.* **4.** to go along with on foot: *I'll walk you to the station.* **5.** to move or cause to move by rocking, shaking, etc.: *This typewriter walks when it vibrates.* **6.** to live one's life in a certain way: *He walked in truth and honor.* **7.** (in baseball) to move or allow (a batter) to move to first base by pitching four balls. —*n.* **8.** the act or an instance of walking. **9.** a distance walked or to be walked, often in terms

of time needed: *a ten-minute walk from town.* **10.** a way of walking. **11.** a particular job, career, etc.: *a new walk of life.* **12.** a place or path for walking: *winding, shaded walks.* **13.** (in baseball) the sending of a batter to first base by the pitching of four balls. **14. walk off with, a.** to steal; take without permission: *Who walked off with my pencil?* **b.** to win easily or be outstanding in: *to walk off with first prize.* **15. walk out, a.** to go on strike. **b.** to leave as a protest: *The delegate threatened to walk out of the meeting.* **16. walk out on,** to desert; abandon: *to walk out on one's family.* —**walk′er,** *n.*

walk·ie-talk·ie (wô′kē tô′kē), *n.* a combined radio transmitter and receiver light enough to be carried by hand.

walk-in (wôk′in′), *adj.* **1.** large enough to be walked into: *a walk-in closet.* —*n.* **2.** something large enough to be walked into, such as a closet. **3.** an easy victory in an election or other contest.

walk·ing (wô′kiṅg), *adj.* **1.** that walks or can walk. **2.** used in walking, esp. out of doors: *walking shoes.* **3.** suitable for or done by walking: *a walking tour of the city.* —*n.* **4.** the act or action of a person who walks. **5.** the conditions found in walking: *The hilly ground makes for hard walking.*

walk′ing stick′, **1.** a cane. **2.** any of several insects having a long, slender, twiglike body.

walk·out (wôk′out′), *n.* **1.** a strike by workers. **2.** the act of leaving or being absent from a meeting, esp. to show disagreement: *The angry delegates staged a walkout from the conference.*

Walking stick (length 2 to 3 in.)

walk-up (wôk′up′), *n.* **1.** an apartment above the ground floor of a building that has no elevator. **2.** the building itself.

wall (wôl), *n.* **1.** a solid, upright structure having a length and height much greater than its thickness, used to support, surround, etc., such as the side of a room from floor to ceiling, or a solid fence of brick or stone. **2.** anything that resembles a wall, as in protecting something, acting as a barrier, etc.: *the wall of the stomach; a wall of secrecy.* —*adj.* **3.** of, on, or concerning a wall: *wall space for books.* —*v.* **4.** to protect, confine, or divide with a wall: *to wall off a room.* —**wall′-like′,** *adj.*

Wallaby (height to 2½ ft.)

wal·la·by (wôl′ə bē), *n., pl.* **wal·la·bies** *or* **wal·la·by.** any of a number of small kangaroos, some of which are no larger than rabbits.

Wal·lace (wol′is, wô′lis), *n.* **Henry Agard,** 1888–1965, 33rd Vice President of the U.S. 1941–1945.

wall·board (wôl′bôrd′), *n.* a building material

manufactured in large sheets, used in making or covering walls, ceilings, etc.

wal·let (wol′it), *n.* a folding leather case for holding money, personal papers, etc.; billfold.

wall·eye (wôl′ī′), *n., pl.* **wall·eyes** *or* **wall·eye.** **1.** a large game fish found in the rivers and lakes of northeastern North America. **2.** any of a number of other fishes having large, staring eyes. **3.** the eye of a walleyed person or animal.

wall·eyed (wôl′īd′), *adj.* **1.** having eyes that stare off to the side, showing much white. **2.** having large, staring eyes: *walleyed fishes.*

wall·flow·er (wôl′flou′ər), *n.* **1.** a person, esp. a young woman, who sits apart at a dance or party because she is shy, unpopular, etc. **2.** a plant growing on the walls of buildings, cliffs, etc., and having yellow or orange flowers.

wal·lop (wol′əp), *v.* **1.** to hit hard; beat; thrash: *The bully walloped him.* **2.** to strike hard: *to wallop a baseball out of the field.* **3.** to defeat thoroughly: *Our team will wallop yours.*

wal·low (wol′ō), *v.* **1.** to roll around or lie in mud, water, etc.: *Pigs like to wallow.* **2.** to live or behave in a selfish or foolish way: *to wallow in wealth; to wallow in self-pity.* —*n.* **3.** the act of wallowing. **4.** a place where animals wallow.

wall·pa·per (wôl′pā′pər), *n.* **1.** paper, usually with a printed design in color, for covering the walls or ceilings of rooms, hallways, etc. —*v.* **2.** to decorate with wallpaper: *She wallpapered her bedroom.*

wal·nut (wôl′nut′), *n.* **1.** a round nut with a hard, wrinkled shell and a meaty, edible seed. **2.** the tree bearing this nut. **3.** the wood of this tree: *a table made of walnut.* [from the Old English word *wealh-hnutu,* literally "foreign nut"]

wal·rus (wôl′rəs, wol′rəs), *n., pl.* **wal·rus·es** *or* **wal·rus.** a sea mammal of the arctic regions, related to the seals, having flippers, a pair of large tusks, and a thick, tough skin.

waltz (wôltz), *n.* **1.** a whirling, gliding dance for couples, having three beats to a measure. **2.** a piece of music for such a dance: *The orchestra played a waltz.* —*v.* **3.** to dance a waltz. **4.** to lead (a partner) in a waltz: *He waltzed her around the room.* **5.** *Informal.* to move briskly or confidently: *She waltzed happily into the room.*

Walrus (length to 11 ft.)

wam·pum (wom′pəm), *n.* beads made from shells, pierced and strung, and formerly used by North American Indians for money and ornaments.

wan (won), *adj.,* **wan·ner, wan·nest. 1.** pale in a sickly way. **2.** showing or suggesting ill health, sadness, etc.: *a wan smile.* **3.** lacking in force: *wan efforts.* —**wan′ly,** *adv.* —**wan′ness,** *n.*

wand (wond), *n.* **1.** a slender stick or rod: *the wand of an orchestra conductor.* **2.** a rod that is carried as a sign of rank: *a wand of office.* **3.** a slender shoot or branch of a shrub or tree: *a willow wand.*

wan·der (won′dər), *v.* **1.** to move about aimlessly here and there; roam: *We wandered about the countryside.* **2.** to move or extend in a crooked or meandering course: *The river wanders over the plain.* **3.** to go astray; become lost: *The child wandered from home.* **4.** to stray from a subject because of lack of interest, inability to concentrate, etc.: *His attention wandered.* **5.** to travel about, on, or through: *to wander the streets.* **—wan′der·er,** *n.*

wan·der·lust (wän′dər lust′), *n.* a strong desire to travel: *His wanderlust led him to strange lands.*

wane (wān), *v.,* **waned, wan·ing. 1.** to become smaller, weaker, less bright, etc.: *The moon wanes after it is full.* See also **wax²** (def. 2). **2.** to come near to the end: *The day is waning.* **—n. 3.** the act of waning: *the wane of the moon; the wane of summer.* **4. on the wane,** becoming less; diminishing: *Her popularity is on the wane.*

wan·gle (waṅg′gəl), *v.,* **wan·gled, wan·gling.** *Informal.* to do, get, or bring about by scheming or tricks: *to wangle money from someone.* **—wan′gler,** *n.*

want (wont, wônt), *v.* **1.** to need or desire: *I want my dinner. I want to stay home.* **2.** to be lacking in: *to want confidence.* **3.** to require: *The house wants painting.* **4.** to seek or hunt: *The police want him for murder.* **5.** to be needy: *to want for money.* **—n. 6.** something wanted or needed: *My wants are few.* **7.** absence or lack: *plants dying for want of rain.* **8.** the state of being without the things necessary to life: *to live in want.* **9. want in** (or **out**), *Informal.* to desire to enter (or leave): *Open the door and see if the cat wants in.*

want·ing (won′tiṅg, wôn′tiṅg), *adj.* **1.** lacking; missing; absent: *The lid of the box is wanting.* **2.** not up to what is expected: *to be wanting in politeness.*

wan·ton (won′t'n), *adj.* **1.** without reason or justification: *a cruel, wanton attack.* **2.** loose in morals; lewd: *a wanton woman.* **—n. 3.** an immoral person, esp. a woman. **—wan′ton·ly,** *adv.* **—wan′ton·ness,** *n.*

war (wôr), *n.* **1.** armed conflict between nations or between groups within a nation: *a war between Germany and France; the war between the North and South.* **2.** any struggle or fight: *a war against vice.* **3.** the science or profession of military combat, tactics, etc.: *Napoleon and Caesar were skilled in war.* **—v.,** **warred, war·ring. 4.** to make or carry on war: *The two countries warred for years.* **5.** to struggle or fight in any way: *to war against vice.* [from the Old French word *werre,* which comes from Germanic]

War′ between′ the States′, the American Civil War.

war·ble (wôr′bəl), *v.,* **war·bled, war·bling. 1.** to sing with trills; trill: *birds warbling in the trees; to warble a song.* **—n. 2.** the act or sound of warbling.

war·bler (wôr′blər), *n.* a person or bird that warbles, esp. any of several small songbirds.

ward (wôrd), *n.* **1.** one of the districts into which some cities are divided for purposes of administration or voting. **2.** one of the sections of a hospital for a particular class or group of patients: *a maternity ward.* **3.** a section of a prison. **4.** a person who is under the legal guardianship of another. **5.** a ridge of metal in a lock to keep any key other than the proper one from turning. **—v. 6.** to turn away or aside (danger, harm, etc.) (usually fol. by *off*): *to ward off an attack.* [from the Old English word *weard* "guard, protector," or *weardian* "to guard, protect"]

-ward, a suffix used to form **1.** adjectives meaning at or toward the side or direction of: *leeward; backward.* **2.** adverbs meaning **a.** in the direction of: *sideward; skyward.* **b.** at or in the time of: *afterward.* Also, **-wards.**

war·den (wôr′d'n), *n.* **1.** a person appointed to watch over or take care of something: *a game warden.* **2.** the chief officer in charge of a prison.

ward·er (wôr′dər), *n.* a watchman or guard.

ward·robe (wôr′drōb), *n.* **1.** a collection or supply of clothes: *to buy a summer wardrobe.* **2.** a closet, cabinet, or room for keeping clothes.

-wards, another form of the suffix **-ward,** used in forming adverbs: *afterwards; backwards.*

ware (wâr), *n.* **1.** Usually, **wares.** articles for sale; goods: *The merchant displayed his wares.* **2.** a certain kind or class of manufactured article (usually used in combination): *silverware; glassware.* **3.** pottery; earthenware: *China is a hard, brittle ware.*

ware·house (wâr′hous′), *n.,* *pl.* **ware·hous·es** (wâr′hou′ziz). a building where goods are stored; storehouse: *to keep one's furniture in a warehouse.*

war·fare (wôr′fâr′), *n.* the act or process of waging a war: *warfare between two nations.*

war·head (wôr′hed′), *n.* the front part of a missile, torpedo, bomb, or the like, that contains the explosive charge: *atomic warheads.*

war·like (wôr′līk′), *adj.* **1.** fit or ready for war: *a strong, warlike people.* **2.** threatening war; hostile: *a warlike challenge.* **3.** of or referring to war: *warlike preparations.*

warm (wôrm), *adj.* **1.** having, giving out, or feeling moderate heat: *a warm summer; to feel warm.* **2.** keeping in the body's warmth: *warm clothing.* **3.** (of colors) suggesting warmth, as red or yellow tones. **4.** friendly or loving: *warm companionship.* **5.** having or showing strong or lively feelings: *a warm argument.* **6.** *Informal.* close to something sought, as in a child's game. **7. warm up, a.** to prepare for an athletic contest, ballet, musical performance, etc., by practicing or exercising. **b.** to become more friendly, interested, or agreeable: *to warm up to a plan; to warm up to one's new neighbors.* **—warm′ly,** *adv.*

warm-blood·ed (wôrm′blud′id), *adj.* **1.** having warm blood and a body temperature that changes little, regardless of the degree of heat or cold of the air, water, etc., surrounding the body: *Mammals and birds are warm-blooded, but reptiles are not.* See also **cold-blooded** (def. 1). **2.** having very strong or lively feelings; passionate. **—warm′-blood′ed·ness,** *n.*

warm·heart·ed (wôrm′här′tid), *adj.* having or showing kindness, sympathy, etc. —**warm′heart′ed·ly,** *adv.* —**warm′heart′ed·ness,** *n.*

warm′ing pan′, a long-handled, covered pan, usually of brass, filled with live coals, hot water, etc., formerly used for warming beds.

war·mong·er (wôr′muñg′gər, -moñg′gər), *n.* a person who wants or tries to bring about a war. —**war′mon·ger·ing,** *n.*

warmth (wôrmth), *n.* **1.** the quality or state of being warm: *the warmth of a summer day.* **2.** friendliness or lovingness: *the warmth of a happy family.* **3.** liveliness of feeling: *the warmth of an argument.*

warn (wôrn), *v.* **1.** to tell of a possible danger or trouble: *We were warned of bad weather.* **2.** to notify (someone) to go, keep at a distance, etc. (often fol. by *away, off,* etc.): *A sign warned us off the grounds.* **3.** to advise: *We were warned to go to the dentist.*

warn·ing (wôr′niñg), *n.* the act of a person or thing that warns. —**warn′ing·ly,** *adv.*

War of 1812, the war between the United States and Great Britain from 1812 to 1815.

War′ of Independ′ence, another name for **American Revolution.**

warp (wôrp), *v.* **1.** to bend or become bent out of shape: *The book cover was warped by the water.* **2.** to turn away from what is right, good, etc.: *Prejudice warped his thinking.* **3.** to move (a ship) by hauling on a rope that has been fastened to a buoy, anchor, etc. —*n.* **4.** a bend or twist from a straight or flat form: *a warp in a board.* **5.** a twist or quirk in one's thinking: *Loneliness gave his mind a strange warp.* **6.** the lengthwise threads of a woven fabric, crossed by and interlaced with the woof.

war·path (wôr′path′), *n., pl.* **war·paths** (wôr′pathz′, -paths′). **1.** the path or course taken by American Indians on the way to battle. **2. on the warpath,** angry; furious; indignant: *She's on the warpath because you left your room in a mess.*

war·rant (wôr′ənt, wor′ənt), *n.* **1.** a document that gives the right to do something: *The police cannot search a house without a warrant.* **2.** right; reason; justification: *You have no warrant to complain.* **3.** something that makes certain; guarantee: *His promise is a warrant that he will come.* —*v.* **4.** to be a good reason for; justify: *His exploits warrant a rousing welcome by the city.* **5.** to guarantee: *The product is warranted to give complete satisfaction.*

war′rant of′ficer, an officer in the U.S. armed forces ranking above enlisted men and below commissioned officers.

war·ran·ty (wôr′ən tē, wor′ən tē), *n., pl.* **war·ran·ties. 1.** a warrant. **2.** a written guarantee given to a purchaser.

war·ren (wôr′ən, wor′ən), *n.* **1.** a place in which small animals, esp. rabbits, breed or live. **2.** a building or area in which many persons live in crowded quarters: *the warrens of a slum.*

war·rior (wôr′yər), *n.* **1.** a man skilled in warfare;

soldier. **2.** any person of great courage who has a fighting spirit: *The president was an old warrior.*

War·saw (wôr′sô), *n.* the capital city of Poland, in the E part, on the Vistula River.

war·ship (wôr′ship′), *n.* a ship built or armed for combat.

wart (wôrt), *n.* **1.** a small, usually hard growth on the skin, caused by a virus infection. **2.** any small lump on the surface of certain plants, the skin of certain animals, etc. —**wart′like′,** *adj.* —**wart′y,** *adj.*

wart′ hog′, an African wild hog, having large tusks and warty growths on the face.

Wart hog
(2½ ft. high at shoulder)

war·time (wôr′tīm′), *n.* **1.** a time or period of war. —*adj.* **2.** caused by, characteristic of, or happening during such a period: *wartime rationing.*

war·y (wâr′ē), *adj.,* **war·i·er, war·i·est. 1.** watchful or on one's guard; cautious; careful: *A life of danger made him wary.* **2.** arising from or showing caution: *wary, carefully chosen words.* —**war′i·ly,** *adv.* —**war′i·ness,** *n.*

was (wuz, woz), *v.* first and third person singular, past tense of **be.**

wash (wosh, wôsh), *v.* **1.** to clean off dirt or other matter with a liquid, esp. water containing soap: *to wash one's face.* **2.** to remove (dirt or other matter) in this way: *to wash the grime out of clothes.* **3.** to clean oneself, clothes, etc., in this way: *to wash in the morning.* **4.** to undergo washing without damage: *a fabric that washes well.* **5.** to move by means of water: *The boat washed ashore during the storm.* **6.** to wear away by flowing: *The heavy rain washed gulleys in the sand.* **7.** to flow over, as water: *The breaking waves washed the beach.* **8.** to move in waves or with a rushing movement, as water: *The tide washed against the pier.* **9.** to be removed by the action of water: *This topsoil tends to wash away.* **10.** to cleanse from guilt; purify: *to be washed of one's sins.* **11.** to cover (a painting, drawing, etc.) with a thin layer of paint or ink. —*n.* **12.** the act or process of washing: *to give the car a wash.* **13.** a number of things washed together, such as clothing, sheets, etc.: *She hung out the wash to dry.* **14.** the flow, sweep, dash, or breaking of water: *the wash of the surf.* **15.** the rough or broken air or water left behind a moving ship, wing, propeller, etc. **16.** a liquid or lotion for treating the hair, skin, etc. (often used in combination): *a hair wash; an eyewash.* **17.** a thin layer of paint or ink. **18. wash down,** to clean completely by washing: *to wash down a car.* **19. wash out, a.** to get rid of by washing: *to wash out a stain.* **b.** to damage or destroy by the action of water: *The flood washed out the bridge.* **20. wash up, a.** to wash one's face and hands: *to wash up before dinner.* **b.** to be left on shore by the tide: *We found a shell that had washed up.*

Wash., Washington (State).

wash·a·ble (wosh′ə bəl, wô′shə bəl), *adj.* capable of being washed without shrinking, fading, or the like.

wash·board (wosh′bôrd′, wôsh′-), *n.* a frame having a ridged, metal surface on which clothes are rubbed while being washed.

wash·bowl (wosh′bōl′, wôsh′-), *n.* a large bowl or basin for washing one's hands and face, small pieces of clothing, etc. Also, **wash·ba·sin** (wosh′bā′sin, wôsh′-).

wash·cloth (wosh′klôth′, wôsh′-), *n.* a small cloth for washing one's face or body.

wash·er (wosh′ər, wô′shər), *n.* 1. a person who washes. 2. a washing machine. 3. a flat ring of metal, rubber, etc., used to hold a nut or bolt more tightly in place, prevent leakage, etc.

wash·er·wom·an (wosh′ər woom′ən, wô′shər-), *n.*, *pl.* **wash·er·wom·en.** a woman who washes clothes for a living; laundress. Also, **washwoman.**

wash·ing (wosh′ing, wô′shing), *n.* 1. the act of a person or thing that washes. 2. clothes, etc., washed at one time; wash. 3. a thin coat of paint or ink; wash.

wash′ing machine′, a household appliance for washing clothing, linens, etc.

Wash·ing·ton (wosh′ing tən, wô′shing tən), *n.* 1. Booker T., 1856–1915, U.S. black reformer, educator, author, and lecturer. 2. George, 1732–1799, U.S. general and statesman: 1st President of the U.S. 1789–1797. 3. Martha, 1732–1802, wife of George. 4. Also, **Washington, D.C.** the capital city of the United States, on the Potomac River between Maryland and Virginia. 5. Also, **Wash′ington State′.** a state in the NW United States, on the Pacific coast. 68,192 sq. mi. *Cap.:* Olympia. 6. **Mount,** a mountain in N New Hampshire: highest peak in the NE United States. 6293 ft.

BRITISH COLUMBIA / *Washington* / Seattle / Tacoma / Olympia / Spokane / Yakima / Columbia / Snake R. / River / IDAHO / OREGON / PACIFIC OCEAN / COAST RANGES / CASCADES / 0 50 100 150 MILES

Wash′ington's Birth′day, February 22, a legal holiday in most states of the U.S. in honor of the birth of George Washington: now officially observed on the third Monday in February.

wash·out (wosh′out′, wôsh′-), *n.* 1. a washing out of earth, gravel, etc. 2. *Informal.* an utter failure.

wash·room (wosh′room′, -room′, wôsh′-), *n.* a room having washbowls and other toilet facilities.

wash·stand (wosh′stand′, wôsh′-), *n.* a fixture or piece of furniture designed to hold water for use in washing one's hands or face.

wash·tub (wosh′tub′, wôsh′-), *n.* a tub for use in washing clothes, linens, etc.

wash·wom·an (wosh′woom′ən, wôsh′-), *n.*, *pl.* **wash·wom·en.** another word for **washerwoman.**

was·n't (wuz′ənt, woz′ənt), contraction of *was not.*

wasp (wosp), *n.* any of numerous flying insects resembling ants or bees, with a long, slender body, a narrow waist, and often a sharp sting.

Wasp
(length ½ in.)

wasp·ish (wos′pish), *adj.* quick to be angry or resentful. —**wasp′ish·ly,** *adv.* —**wasp′ish·ness,** *n.*

was·sail (wos′əl, wo sāl′), *n.* 1. a greeting to a person, used in England in early times when offering a cup of drink or when drinking to a person's health. 2. a revel or party with drinking of healths. —*v.* 3. to drink healths. —**was′sail·er,** *n.*

wast (wost, wəst), *v.* an old form of **was,** found now chiefly in Biblical and poetic writing (used with *thou*): *Thou wast beloved of the king.*

waste (wāst), *v.,* **wast·ed, wast·ing.** 1. to consume, spend, or employ uselessly or without good return: *to waste one's money on trifles.* 2. to fail or neglect to use: *to waste an opportunity.* 3. to wear away or dwindle bit by bit: *Illness wasted his body.* 4. to pass gradually, as time. 5. to destroy or ruin: *The cities were wasted by the enemy.* —*n.* 6. profitless expense or use: *a waste of time.* 7. neglect: *a waste of opportunity.* 8. gradual decay or destruction: *the waste of one's health.* 9. ruin, as by war, fire, etc. 10. a wild, barren, or desert place: *the cold wastes of the far north.* 11. anything left over from a manufacturing process: *scraps of metal waste.* 12. garbage or refuse. 13. **wastes,** excrement. —*adj.* 14. barren or useless: *waste places without rain.* 15. left over: *waste metal.* 16. thrown away as used or useless; discarded. 17. designed to hold or carry away waste: *a waste pipe.* 18. **go to waste,** to fail to be used. 19. **lay waste,** to destroy; ruin: *The forest was laid waste by fire.*

waste·bas·ket (wāst′bas′kit), *n.* a basket for small pieces of trash. Also, **waste′pa·per bas′ket.**

waste·ful (wāst′fəl), *adj.* tending to waste: *to be wasteful with one's time or money.* —**waste′ful·ly,** *adv.* —**waste′ful·ness,** *n.*

waste·land (wāst′land′), *n.* land that is barren or useless, as a desert: *a wasteland of rocks and sand.*

watch (woch), *v.* 1. to look closely to see what is done, happens, etc.: *If you watch, you will see the sun rise.* 2. to look at closely or with interest: *to watch animals in a zoo.* 3. to look or wait (usually fol. by *for*): *to watch for a signal.* 4. to keep oneself in readiness: *to watch for an opportunity.* 5. to be careful or cautious: *Watch when you cross the street.* 6. to keep one's eye on or stand guard over: *Please watch the kettle.* —*n.* 7. an act of looking or waiting for something. 8. close observation, as to guard or protect: *to keep a watch over a sick person.* 9. a period of time for watching or keeping guard. 10. a period of time, usually four hours, during which a part of a ship's crew is on duty, taking turns with another part. 11. a guard or guards. 12. a part of a ship's crew on duty. 13. a small, portable timepiece. 14. **on the watch,** alert; vigilant: *to be on the watch for shooting stars.* 15. **watch out,** to be cautious or alert: *Watch out for cars when you cross the street.* 16. **watch over,** to guard or care for protectively: *to watch over a sick child.* —**watch′er,** *n.*

watch·dog (woch′dôg′), *n.* a dog kept as a guard.

watch·ful (woch′fəl), *adj.* alert; observant. —**watch′ful·ly,** *adv.* —**watch′ful·ness,** *n.*

watch·mak·er (woch′mā′kər), *n.* a person who

makes or repairs watches.

watch·man (woch/mən), *n., pl.* **watch·men.** 1. a person who keeps guard over a building at night. 2. a person who guards or patrols the streets at night.

watch·tow·er (woch/tou/ər), *n.* a tower on which a sentinel keeps watch.

watch·word (woch/wûrd/), *n.* 1. a word or phrase that must be spoken to a guard or sentinel to obtain permission to pass; password. 2. a motto or slogan.

wa·ter (wô/tər, wot/ər), *n.* 1. a transparent, odorless, tasteless liquid, a compound of hydrogen and oxygen, H_2O, freezing at 32°F or 0°C and boiling at 212°F or 100°C. 2. a lake, river, ocean, or other body of this liquid: *We crossed the water in a canoe.* 3. a special kind or form of this liquid: *soda water; mineral water.* 4. **waters,** the water of a spring, lake, etc., or an area of an ocean: *blue waters; American waters.* 5. a level or stage of water: *Low water will be at 6:12 a.m.* 6. a wavy, bright pattern or marking on silk and other fabrics. —*v.* 7. to moisten, or drench with water: *to water the lawn.* 8. to supply with water: *to water horses.* 9. to drink water: *The animals watered at the stream.* 10. to dilute with water: *to water soup.* 11. to give off a watery liquid: *His eyes watered in the smoke.* 12. to cover with a bright, wavy pattern: *to water silk.* —*adj.* 13. of or referring to water: *a water supply.* 14. holding or capable of holding water: *a water jug.* 15. worked by water: *a water wheel.* 16. used in or on water: *water skis.* 17. **above water,** out of difficulty or trouble: *He had to borrow money to keep above water.* 18. **hold water,** to be true, logical, or reasonable: *His alibi doesn't hold water.*

Wa·ter Bear/er, the, another name for **Aquarius.**

wa/ter bee/tle, any of various black or dark-colored beetles that live in water.

wa/ter bird/, a swimming or wading bird, as a duck, crane, etc.

wa·ter·borne (wô/tər bôrn/, wot/ər-), *adj.* 1. floating or moving on water. 2. carried by ship or boat.

wa·ter·buck (wô/tər buk/, wot/ər-), *n.* any of several large African antelopes living in marshy or reedy places.

wa/ter buf/falo, a large, strong buffalo having flattened, curved horns, found in Africa, Asia, and the Philippines.

Water buffalo
(5 ½ ft. high at shoulder)

Wa·ter·bur·y (wô/tər ber/ē, wot/ər-), *n.* a city in W Connecticut.

wa/ter chest/nut, 1. a water plant bearing an edible, nutlike fruit. 2. the fruit itself.

wa/ter clock/, a device for measuring time by the flow of water.

wa/ter clos/et, a toilet.

wa·ter·col·or (wô/tər kul/ər, wot/ər-), *n.* 1. paint that is mixed with water. 2. a painting done with this paint. 3. the art of painting with this paint.

wa·ter·course (wô/tər kôrs/, wot/ər-), *n.* 1. a stream of water, as a river or brook. 2. the bed of a stream. 3. a channel or canal.

wa·ter·cress (wô/tər kres/, wot/ər-), *n.* 1. a cress that usually grows in clear, running water, having crisp, tasty leaves. 2. the leaves, used esp. in salads.

wa·ter·fall (wô/tər fôl/, wot/ər-), *n.* a steep flow or fall of water from a high place, such as a cliff.

wa·ter·fowl (wô/tər foul/, wot/ər-), *n.* a water bird, esp. a swan, goose, or duck.

wa·ter·front (wô/tər frunt/, wot/ər-), *n.* 1. land on the edge of a body of water: *They own a house on the waterfront.* 2. the part of a city or town on such land: *The Boston waterfront has many large piers.*

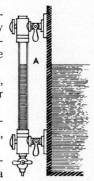

Water gauge
for tank
A, Water level

Wa·ter·gate (wô/tər gāt/, wot/ər-), *n.* a political scandal involving illegal activities during and after the re-election campaign in 1972 of President Nixon and which resulted in his resignation in 1974. [from the name of the building in Washington, D.C., that housed Democratic Committee headquarters and that was broken into by men connected with Republican campaign]

wa/ter gauge/, any device for indicating the height of water in a reservoir, tank, boiler, etc.

wa/tering place/, 1. a place where drinking water may be found by men or animals, such as a spring. 2. *Chiefly British.* a seaside resort or a spa.

wa/ter lil/y, any of various water plants having large, disklike, floating leaves and fragrant, beautiful flowers.

wa/ter line/, the line around the hull of a ship or boat that marks the surface of the water.

wa·ter·logged (wô/tər lôgd/, -logd/, wot/ər-), *adj.* flooded or soaked with water: *waterlogged shoes.*

Water lily

Wa·ter·loo (wô/tər lōō/, wot/ər-), *n.* 1. a village in central Belgium: Napoleon defeated here 1815. 2. any great defeat.

wa·ter·mark (wô/tər märk/, wot/ər-), *n.* 1. a mark showing the height to which water rises in a river, etc. 2. a light design or marking pressed on paper.

wa·ter·mel·on (wô/tər mel/ən, wot/ər-), *n.* 1. a large, roundish or long fruit of a trailing vine, having pink, sweet, edible flesh and a green rind. 2. the plant or vine.

wa/ter moc/casin, another name for **cottonmouth.**

wa/ter po/lo, a game played in the water by two teams of swimmers that try to pass a large, inflated ball across each other's goal line.

wa/ter pow/er, the power of falling or flowing water, used to drive machinery, turbines, etc. Also, **wa′-ter·pow′er.**

wa·ter·proof (wô′tər proof′, wot′ər-), *adj.* **1.** capable of keeping out water as a result of being treated with rubber, plastic, etc.: *a waterproof raincoat.* —*v.* **2.** to make waterproof: *to waterproof cloth.*

wa′ter rat′, any of various rodents that live near water, such as the muskrat.

wa·ter·shed (wô′tər shed′, wot′ər-), *n.* **1.** the ridge that divides two drainage areas; divide. **2.** the area drained by a river, stream, etc.: *the watershed of the Mississippi.*

wa′ter ski′, a short, broad ski used in water-skiing.

wa·ter-ski (wô′tər skē′, wot′ər-), *v.,* **wa·ter-skied, wa·ter-ski·ing.** to glide over the surface of water on water skis by grasping a towing rope pulled by a speedboat. —**wa′ter-ski′er,** *n.*

wa′ter span′iel, a large, heavy-coated spaniel used to retrieve waterfowl.

wa·ter·spout (wô′tər spout′, wot′ər-), *n.* **1.** a spout or pipe from which water runs. **2.** a funnel-shaped part of a cloud that touches and draws upon the surface of the water, mixing spray and mist.

Irish water spaniel (2 ft. high at shoulder)

wa·ter·tight (wô′tər tīt′, wot′-ər-), *adj.* **1.** built so tightly that water is unable to enter; without a leak. **2.** so soundly planned or made that no fault can be found: *a watertight alibi.*

wa′ter tow′er, a large, upright pipe or a tank raised high above the ground, used to store a supply of water and to provide steady water pressure for a town, area, etc.

wa·ter·way (wô′tər wā′, wot′ər-), *n.* a river, canal, or other channel used as a route for ships and boats.

wa′ter wheel′, a wheel turned by the action of moving water.

wa·ter·works (wô′tər wûrks′, wot′ər-), *n.pl.* a complete system for supplying water to a town or area, including reservoirs, pipes, pumps, etc.

wa·ter·y (wô′tə rē, wot′ə rē), *adj.* **1.** of, like, or concerning water: *the watery deeps.* **2.** containing much or too much water: *watery soup; watery soil.* **3.** giving forth water or a liquid like water: *watery eyes.*

watt (wot), *n.* a unit for measuring electrical power. [named after James *Watt*]

Watt (wot), *n.* **James,** 1736–1819, Scottish engineer and inventor.

wat·tle (wot′ʼl), *n.* **1.** Often, **wattles.** a number of rods or stakes interwoven with twigs or tree branches for making fences, walls, etc. **2.** a loose fold of flesh hanging from the beak or chin of certain birds and reptiles. —*v.,* **wat·tled, wat·tling. 3.** to frame, wall, bind, etc., with wattles. —*adj.* **4.** built with or made of wattles.

wave (wāv), *n.* **1.** a curving swell that moves across the surface of a body of water. **2.** a strong rise or increase of something: *a heat wave.* **3.** a curve or series of curves: *hair with a natural wave.* **4.** an act or instance of waving: *a wave of the hand.* **5.** a movement of energy from point to point in a medium or space in the form of pulses or vibrations. —*v.,* **waved, wav·ing. 6.** to move or cause to move to and fro: *to wave a flag.* **7.** to move the hand to and fro, esp. as a greeting: *She waved when she saw us.* **8.** to signal by waving the hand: *to wave good-by.* **9.** to direct or order by waving: *to wave a car to a stop.* —**wave′like′,** *adj.*

Wave (wāv), *n.* a member of the women's corps of the U.S. Navy.

wave·length (wāv′length′), *n.* (in physics) the distance between two successive peaks in a wave, measured in the direction of the movement of the wave.

wa·ver (wā′vər), *v.* **1.** to sway to and fro; flutter: *reeds wavering in the wind.* **2.** to flicker or quiver, as light: *wavering flames.* **3.** to become unsteady; begin to fail: *His health wavered.* **4.** to change or vary in an unsteady way: *Prices wavered.* **5.** to hesitate or show doubt: *He never wavers in his belief.*

wav·y (wā′vē), *adj.,* **wav·i·er, wav·i·est. 1.** having waves: *wavy hair.* **2.** having lines that look like waves: *a wavy pattern.* —**wav′i·ness,** *n.*

wax¹ (waks), *n.* **1.** See **beeswax** (def. 1). **2.** any substance resembling beeswax, such as paraffin. **3.** any of various fatty substances produced by plants, animals, or human beings: *Wax is found in the ear.* **4.** a substance containing wax, used as a polish for floors, furniture, etc. —*v.* **5.** to cover or coat with wax: *to wax furniture.* [from the Old English word *weax*]

wax² (waks), *v.* **1.** to increase in size, amount, etc.: *His fortunes waxed.* **2.** (of the moon) to grow in brightness and roundness. See also **wane** (def. 1). **3.** to grow or become: *He waxed enthusiastic about his plans.* [from the Old English word *weaxan*]

wax·en (wak′sən), *adj.* **1.** made of or containing wax: *a waxen candle.* **2.** resembling wax: *waxen skin.*

wax′ pa′per, a kind of wrapping paper made waterproof by a coating of paraffin. Also, **waxed′ pa′per.**

wax·wing (waks′wing′), *n.* any of several birds having a showy crest and wings with red, waxy tips.

wax·work (waks′wûrk′), *n.* **1.** a work modeled in wax, esp. the figure of a human being. **2. waxworks,** a place where a group of such figures is on public display.

wax·y (wak′sē), *adj.,* **wax·i·er, wax·i·est. 1.** resembling wax in appearance, texture, etc.: *a soft, smooth, waxy substance.* **2.** abounding in, covered with, or made of wax: *the waxy cells of a honeycomb.* —**wax′i·ness,** *n.*

Cedar waxwing (length 7 in.)

way (wā), *n.* **1.** manner, mode, or fashion: *to reply in a polite way.* **2.** a manner of behaving or acting: *He has many strange ways.* **3.** a method, plan, or means for doing something or reaching a goal: *a new way of cooking chicken.* **4.** a feature or respect; particular: *This plan is poor in several ways.* **5.** a direction: *Look this way.* **6.** neighborhood or vicinity: *There's* *rain out our way.* **7.** movement or passage to a goal: *He found his way through the dark.* **8.** distance: *We've come a long way.* **9.** a path or course to a place: *What is the shortest way to town?* **10.** an ancient Roman road: *the Appian Way.* **11.** a lane, path, etc.: *beautiful country ways.* **12.** a means of passage or travel (usually used in combination): *a doorway; a highway.* **13.** the course of action that one chooses or wills: *She has always had her own way.* **14.** the course of action that a person takes: *He lets nothing stand in his way.* **15.** state of health, well-being, etc.: *to be in a bad way.* **16.** a course of life or action: *The way of the poor is hard.* —*adv.* **17.** Also, **'way.** away; from this or that place: *Go way!* **18.** to a great degree or at quite a distance: *way down the road.* **19. by the way,** incidentally (used to introduce a question or comment): *By the way, did you get the package I sent you?* **20. by way of,** passing through or stopping in: *We came east by way of Chicago.* **21. give way,** to collapse; break down: *The roof gave way under the weight of the snow.* **22. give way to,** to yield to (force, threats, emotions, etc.): *to give way to tears when tired.* **23. go out of one's way,** to make a special effort, esp. to be of help: *Please don't go out of your way on my account.* **24. in a way,** to some extent: *In a way, English is my hardest subject.* **25. in someone's way,** making an obstacle, hindrance, or the like: *Isn't that footstool in your way?* Also, **in the way. 26. lead the way,** to show others the way, esp. as a guide: *You lead the way, and we'll follow.* **27. make way for, a.** to allow to pass: *Make way for the king!* **b.** to prepare or allow for: *The houses were torn down to make way for a new road.* **28. out of the way, a.** so as not to obstruct or hinder: *Take that chair out of the way.* **b.** away from the normal or most convenient route: *Isn't it out of the way to go through New Orleans?* **29. under way, a.** in preparation, under construction, etc.: *The new house is under way.* **b.** (of a ship) in motion after weighing anchor: *We should be under way by 10 o'clock.*

way·far·er (wā′fâr′ər), *n.* a traveler, esp. on foot.

way·lay (wā lā′), *v.,* **way·laid, way·lay·ing.** to lie in wait for and attack: *They were waylaid by robbers.*

-ways, a suffix used to form adverbs meaning **1.** in or toward the direction of: *sideways.* **2.** in the position of: *edgeways.* **3.** in the manner of: *noways.*

way·side (wā′sīd′), *n.* **1.** the land along the sides of a road, highway, path, etc.; roadside. —*adj.* **2.** being or found at or along the wayside: *a wayside inn.*

way·ward (wā′wərd), *adj.* **1.** turning away from what is right or proper; disobedient: *a wayward child; wayward behavior.* **2.** not steady or fixed: *a quick but wayward mind.* —**way′ward·ly,** *adv.* —**way′ward·ness,** *n.*

we (wē), *pron.* **1.** the plural of **I. 2.** oneself and another or others: *the world we live in.* **3.** oneself speaking as an authority, esp. as an editor or a royal person: *"We are not amused," said the queen.*

weak (wēk), *adj.* **1.** easily broken or damaged under strain or pressure: *The legs of the chair are weak.* **2.** lacking in strength or vigor due to youth, age, illness, etc.: *He was weak after his operation.* **3.** lacking in courage, power, etc.: *a weak will; a weak king.* **4.** poor, faulty, or unsound, such as an argument, piece of writing, etc. **5.** lacking the needed knowledge or skill: *I am weak in history.* **6.** of little force, flavor, etc.: *a weak pulse; weak tea.* **7.** showing weakness of body or mind: *a weak smile; a weak spirit.*

weak·en (wē′kən), *v.* to make or become weak or weaker.

weak·fish (wēk′fish′), *n., pl.* **weak·fish** *or* **weak·fish·es.** a food fish found along the Atlantic and Gulf coasts of the U.S.

weak·ling (wēk′ling), *n.* **1.** a person who lacks strength of body, character, will, etc. —*adj.* **2.** lacking strength; weak: *a weakling child.*

weak·ly (wēk′lē), *adj.,* **weak·li·er, weak·li·est. 1.** in poor health; sickly; feeble. —*adv.* **2.** in a weak or feeble manner.

weak·ness (wēk′nis), *n.* **1.** the state or quality of being weak; feebleness. **2.** a weak point; fault; defect: *Your argument has one serious weakness.* **3.** a liking or special fondness for some person or thing: *He has a weakness for candy.* **4.** the object of such a liking or fondness: *Chocolate mints are my weakness.*

weak′ verb′, a verb that forms its past tense and past participle by the addition of regular endings, without any change in the vowel of the stem: *walk, walked; leap, leapt.* See also **strong verb.**

wealth (welth), *n.* **1.** a great quantity of money or property; riches. **2.** a plentiful amount; abundance: *The book contains a wealth of illustrations.* **3.** rich or valuable contents or produce: *the wealth of the soil.*

wealth·y (wel′thē), *adj.,* **wealth·i·er, wealth·i·est. 1.** having great wealth; rich: *a wealthy financier.* **2.** having a plentiful amount or abundance of anything: *The mountains are wealthy in minerals.* —**wealth′i·ness,** *n.*

wean (wēn), *v.* **1.** to accustom (a child or young animal) to food other than its mother's milk. **2.** to cause (a person) to give up a habit, attitude, interest, etc.

weap·on (wep′ən), *n.* **1.** any instrument or mechanism used for attack or defense in a fight. **2.** any organ or part of the body of a person or animal, such as teeth, claws, fangs, horns, etc., that may be used in fighting. **3.** any means used against an opponent in a dispute or contest: *Good laws are our best weapons for the safeguarding of our rights.*

wear (wâr), *v.,* **wore** (wôr), **worn** (wôrn), **wear·ing. 1.** to carry or have on one's person as a covering, support, or ornament: *to wear a suit.* **2.** to show or display: *to wear a smile.* **3.** to reduce or damage by strain or rubbing: *He wore his shoes through on the sharp rocks.* **4.** to make (a hole, tear, etc.) in something by strain or rubbing: *He wore a hole in his jacket.* **5.** to make tired; weary (often fol. by *out* or *down*): *Shopping wears me out.* **6.** (of time) to pass gradually or slowly: *The days got hotter as the sum-*

mer wore on. **7.** to endure use, friction, strain, etc.; last: *Rubber soles wear well.* **8.** to reach (a certain state) under the effects of strain or use: *My patience wore thin after I'd waited an hour.* —*n.* **9.** the act of wearing, or the state of being worn: *articles for winter wear.* **10.** clothes; clothing: *travel wear.* **11.** damage resulting from use: *to show wear.* **12. wear down,** to reduce or damage by wearing: *to wear down the heels of one's shoes.* **13. wear off,** to lessen gradually in effect; disappear: *Her jaw was numb until the drug wore off.* **14. wear out,** to become useless through wear; use up completely: *These gloves wore out in a month. He wears out three pairs of shoes a year.* —**wear′er,** *n.*

wea·ri·some (wēr′ē səm), *adj.* **1.** causing fatigue; tiring; wearying: *a wearisome job.* **2.** tiresome or tedious; boring: *wearisome talk.*

wea·ry (wēr′ē), *adj.,* **wea·ri·er, wea·ri·est. 1.** physically or mentally exhausted; tired; fatigued. **2.** causing fatigue; tiring: *a weary climb.* **3.** causing boredom; tiresome: *a weary lecture.* **4.** having lost patience or interest (usually fol. by *of*): *to be weary of excuses; to be weary of reading.* —*v.,* **wea·ried, wea·ry·ing. 5.** to make or become weary: *The long train trip wearied us.* —**wea′ri·ly,** *adv.* —**wea′ri·ness,** *n.*

wea·sel (wē′zəl), *n., pl.* **wea·sels** *or* **wea·sel.** any of various small animals having a long, slender body, and feeding chiefly on small rodents.

weath·er (weth′ər), *n.* **1.** the state of the atmosphere at a particular time and place, with respect to wind, temperature, cloudiness, moisture, pressure, etc. —*v.* **2.** to expose to the action of the weather: *to weather lumber before using it.* **3.** to make or become discolored, damaged, roughened, etc., by exposure to the weather: *Rain has weathered the roof.* **4.** to come safely through: *to weather a storm.* **5.** to pass or sail to the windward of: *to weather a cape.* —*adj.* **6.** facing the wind; windward: *the weather side of a ship.* **7. under the weather,** *Informal.* **a.** not feeling well; ill; ailing. **b.** suffering from a hangover.

Weasel
(total length 16 in.)

weath·er·beat·en (weth′ər bēt′°n), *adj.* showing wear, damage, or roughness as a result of exposure to the weather: *a weather-beaten sail.*

weath·er·cock (weth′ər kok′), *n.* a weather vane in the shape of a rooster.

weath·er·glass (weth′ər glas′), *n.* an instrument, such as a barometer, for predicting the weather.

weath′er vane′, a device that rotates freely and points in the direction from which the wind is blowing.

Weave

weave (wēv), *v.,* **wove** (wōv) *or* for def. **7 weaved; wo·ven** (wō′vən) *or* **wove; weav·ing. 1.** to interlace (threads, yarns, strips, etc.) so as to form a

fabric or material. **2.** to make or form by interlacing: *to weave a basket.* **3.** to form (a web, cocoon, etc.); spin. **4.** to form by combining various things or parts: *to weave a story.* **5.** to combine (various things or parts) into a connected whole: *He took scenes from several stories and wove them into a play.* **6.** to twist into, through, or about; entwine: *to weave a ribbon around a wreath.* **7.** to move or cause to move in a winding or zigzag course: *to weave through a crowd.* —*n.* **8.** a method or pattern of weaving: *a twill weave.* —**weav′er,** *n.*

web (web), *n.* **1.** a fabric or material formed by weaving or interlacing. **2.** a thin, netlike material spun by spiders and some other insects. **3.** a membrane that connects the fingers or toes of an animal, as on a frog. **4.** any complicated pattern of facts, ideas, happenings, etc.: *a web of lies.* —*v.,* **webbed, web·bing. 5.** to cover, connect, etc., with a web.

webbed (webd), *adj.* **1.** joined by a membrane, as the toes or fingers of certain animals. **2.** made of web: *a chair with a webbed seat.*

web-foot·ed (web′foot′id), *adj.* having the toes joined by a web.

Web·ster (web′stər), *n.* **1. Daniel,** 1782–1852, U.S. statesman and orator. **2. Noah,** 1758–1843, U.S. lexicographer.

wed (wed), *v.,* **wed·ded, wed·ding. 1.** to marry; take (another person) as one's husband or wife. **2.** to unite (a couple) in marriage: *The preacher will wed them in the small chapel.* **3.** to bind or attach firmly: *to wed oneself to an idea.* **4.** to blend or unite perfectly: *to wed various weaves and colors into a single fabric.*

Wed., Wednesday.

we'd (wēd), contraction of *we had, we should,* or *we would.*

wed·ded (wed′id), *adj.* **1.** united in marriage; married: *a wedded couple.* **2.** of or concerning marriage: *wedded happiness.* **3.** closely bound; united: *two nations wedded by ties of commerce.* **4.** deeply attached; devoted: *He is wedded to his profession.*

wed·ding (wed′ing), *n.* **1.** the act or ceremony of marrying; marriage. **2.** the celebration of a marriage: *There was music and feasting at the wedding.* **3.** the anniversary of a marriage: *They celebrated their silver wedding.*

wedge (wej), *n.* **1.** a piece of wood, metal, or other hard material, having two of its faces meeting at a sharp angle, the narrow end of which may be driven into or between objects to split or separate them, or placed between or under objects to hold them apart or lift them. **2.** anything in the form of a wedge: *a wedge of pie.* **3.** anything that acts or serves as a wedge, in opening the way toward a goal, or in separating or disuniting: *His success in business was a wedge for entering politics.* —*v.,* **wedged, wedg·ing. 4.** to split or hold open or apart with a wedge: *to wedge apart two layers of rock.* **5.** to fasten tightly by driving in a wedge or wedges: *He wedged the picture to the frame with small wooden pegs.* **6.** to pack or thrust into or through a narrow space: *I wedged my way through the crowd.* —**wedge′like′,** *adj.*

wed·lock (wed'lok), *n.* the state of being married; matrimony: *to be joined in wedlock.*

Wednes·day (wenz'dē, wenz'dā), *n.* the fourth day of the week, following Tuesday.

wee (wē), *adj.*, **we·er, we·est.** very small; little; tiny.

weed (wēd), *n.* **1.** a valueless, troublesome plant growing wild, esp. one that crowds or damages the desired crop. —*v.* **2.** to remove weeds or troublesome plants from: *to weed a lawn.* **3. weed out,** to remove (useless or harmful persons or things): *to weed out the inexperienced players.* [from the Old English word *wēod* "a weed"] —**weed'like',** *adj.*

weeds (wēdz), *n.pl.* mourning clothes: *widow's weeds.* [from the Old English word *wǣd* "garment, clothing"]

weed·y (wē'dē), *adj.*, **weed·i·er, weed·i·est. 1.** full of weeds. **2.** of or like a weed. **3.** thin, scrawny, or awkward: *a weedy calf.* —**weed'i·ness,** *n.*

week (wēk), *n.* **1.** a period of seven days, esp. one beginning with Sunday and ending with Saturday. **2.** the portion of this period during which a person usually works or attends school: *a five-day week.*

week·day (wēk'dā'), *n.* any day of the week except Sunday or, often, Saturday and Sunday.

week·end (wēk'end'), *n.* **1.** the end of a week, esp. the period of time between Friday evening and Monday morning. —*adj.* **2.** of, for, or on a weekend.

week·ly (wēk'lē), *adj.* **1.** happening or appearing once every week: *a weekly visit; a weekly magazine.* **2.** computed or based on a period of a week: *a weekly wage.* **3.** of, for, or lasting a week: *a weekly supply of food.* —*n., pl.* **week·lies. 4.** a newspaper or magazine that is published once a week. —*adv.* **5.** once a week; by the week: *The help is paid weekly.*

wee·nie (wē'nē), *n. Informal.* another form of **wiener.**

weep (wēp), *v.*, **wept** (wept), **weep·ing. 1.** to express grief or any strong feeling by shedding tears: *to weep for joy.* **2.** to let fall or flow; shed: *to weep bitter tears.* **3.** to let flow or drip slowly; ooze; leak: *The pine trees were weeping sap.* **4.** to grieve; mourn: *They wept for their lost son.* —**weep'er,** *n.*

weep·ing (wē'ping), *adj.* **1.** shedding tears; tearful: *weeping mourners at a funeral.* **2.** dripping or oozing liquid: *the weeping clouds.* **3.** having slender, drooping branches: *a weeping willow.* —*n.* **4.** the act of a person or thing that weeps.

wee·vil (wē'vəl), *n.* any of numerous beetles that have the head prolonged into a snout and are destructive to grain, fruit, cotton, etc.

weft (weft), *n.* See **woof** (def. 1).

weigh (wā), *v.* **1.** to measure the weight of (a person or thing) by use of a scale, balance, or other mechanical device: *to weigh oneself.* **2.** to have a certain weight: *The baby weighs eight pounds.* **3.** to measure or deal out by weight or amount (often fol. by *out*): *Weigh out five pounds of sugar.* **4.** to make heavy; burden (often fol. by *down*): *Snow weighed down the branches.* **5.** to bear down; be a burden (often fol. by *on* or *upon*): *Financial worries weighed on his mind.* **6.** to have importance, influence, or effect: *Such excuses do not weigh with me.* **7.** to consider carefully; ponder: *Weigh all the possibilities before deciding.* **8. weigh anchor,** to raise a ship's anchor before getting under way. **9. weigh in,** (in sports) to be weighed before or immediately after a fight, race, or other contest: *to weigh in at 170 pounds.*

weight (wāt), *n.* **1.** the property that a material object has as a result of the pull of the earth's gravity upon it. **2.** the amount of this property, measured in units such as pounds, tons, etc.: *a weight of 20 tons.* **3.** a system of units for expressing weight: *avoirdupois weight.* **4.** a unit of weight: *The pound is a common weight.* **5.** a piece of metal of a definite weight, placed on one arm or dish of a scale to balance the object or material being weighed on the other. **6.** any heavy load, mass, or object: *Put down that weight and rest awhile.* **7.** any solid object that is useful because of its heaviness: *Get a weight to hold these papers down.* **8.** any load or burden: *the weight of responsibility.* **9.** importance or influence: *His opinions have weight with me.* **10.** any of various heavy metal objects, usually in the shape of a disk, used for lifting in competition or for exercise: *to work out with the weights.* —*v.* **11.** to add weight to; make heavy or heavier: *to weight a truck with cement blocks.* **12.** to burden; oppress: *to weight someone with responsibilities.* **13. pull one's weight,** to do one's share of a task: *to pull one's weight on a job.* **14. throw one's weight around,** to use one's wealth, position, or the like, to obtain special favors.

weight·less (wāt'lis), *adj.* having no weight; not subject to the pull of gravity: *A body orbiting freely in space is weightless.* —**weight'less·ness,** *n.*

weight·y (wā'tē), *adj.*, **weight·i·er, weight·i·est. 1.** having great weight; heavy: *a weighty cargo of stone.* **2.** burdensome or oppressive: *the weighty cares of public office.* **3.** important; significant: *a weighty question.* —**weight'i·ly,** *adv.* —**weight'i·ness,** *n.*

weir (wēr), *n.* **1.** a small dam in a river or stream. **2.** a fence or barrier made of stakes, brush, etc., placed across a stream or channel for catching fish.

weird (wērd), *adj.* **1.** mysterious in an unnatural way; unearthly; eerie: *Weird sounds came out of the cave.* **2.** very unusual, odd, or queer: *That's a weird hat.* —**weird'ly,** *adv.* —**weird'ness,** *n.*

wel·come (wel'kəm), *interj.* **1.** (used as a word of greeting): *Welcome, stranger!* —*n.* **2.** a kindly greeting or reception: *to give someone a warm welcome.* —*v.*, **wel·comed, wel·com·ing. 3.** to greet with pleasure or courtesy: *We welcomed them to our city.* **4.** to accept with pleasure: *After working so hard, we'd welcome a vacation.* **5.** to meet or greet in an unfriendly or defiant way: *They welcomed him with angry shouts.* —*adj.* **6.** gladly received: *a welcome guest.* **7.** gladly permitted to do, have, or use something: *He's welcome to wait here.* **8.** under no obligation for a favor: *You're very welcome, I'll be glad to*

act, āble, dâre, ärt; ebb, ēqual; if, īce; hot, ōver, ôrder; oil; bŏŏk; ōoze; out; up, ûrge; ə = a as in *alone*; ᵊ as in *button* (but'ᵊn), *fire* (fīᵊr); chief; shoe; thin; ᵺat; zh as in *measure* (mezh'ər). See full key inside cover.

help any time. **9. wear out one's welcome,** to behave in such a way that one is no longer welcome: *It's so late, we'd better go before we wear out our welcome.*

weld (weld), *v.* **1.** to join two pieces of metal or other material by melting or hammering together. **2.** to unite closely: *They were welded by a common interest.* **3.** to be welded or capable of being welded: *This is a metal that welds easily.* —*n.* **4.** the act of welding. **5.** a joint made by welding. —**weld′er,** *n.*

wel·fare (wel′fâr), *n.* **1.** the state of being healthy, happy, prosperous, etc.; well-being. **2.** Also, **wel′fare work′.** the efforts of a public agency, community, or business organization to provide benefits of various kinds, esp. to persons in need.

well¹ (wel), *adv.,* **bet·ter** (bet′ər), **best** (best). **1.** in a satisfactory manner: *Things are going well.* **2.** in a careful or thorough manner: *Study the rules well.* **3.** properly, rightly, or fairly: *I could not well refuse his plea.* **4.** with favor or approval; favorably: *The plan was well received.* **5.** to a considerable degree: *We sold the house at a price well above what we paid for it.* **6.** intimately or closely: *Do you know him well?* **7.** fortunately or advantageously: *The store is well located in the downtown business district.* **8.** easily or readily: *I can well understand why he is upset.* —*adj.,* **bet·ter** (bet′ər), **best** (best). **9.** in good health; healthy: *He is not a well man.* **10.** satisfactory, pleasing, or good: *All is well with us.* **11.** right, proper, or fortunate: *It is well that you decided to go.* —*interj.* **12.** (used to express surprise, approval or disapproval, impatience, etc.): *Well! What are you doing here?* **13.** (used to bridge a pause or hesitation in speaking, or to start a new train of expression): *Well, let's go.* **14. as well,** in addition; too: *He wore a sweater and a jacket as well.* **15. as well as,** in addition to being, doing, etc.: *She was smart as well as beautiful.* **16. leave well enough alone,** to avoid changing something that is satisfactory or cannot be improved: *You've done your best, so leave well enough alone.* [from the Old English word *wel*]
—**Usage.** See **good.**

well² (wel), *n.* **1.** a hole drilled or dug into the earth to obtain water, gas, oil, etc. **2.** a spring or natural source of water. **3.** a shaft or opening extending through the floors of a building or other structure, for admitting air or light or housing a stairway, elevator, etc. **4.** a hollow compartment or recess: *When the airplane is in flight, the landing gear is drawn up into its well.* **5.** a source of supply: *Nature is a well of inspiration.* —*v.* **6.** to rise, spring, or gush (often fol. by *up, out,* or *forth*): *Tears welled up in her eyes.* [the noun is from the Old English word *well* "a well," and the verb is from *wellan* "to boil"]

we'll (wēl), contraction of *we will* or *we shall.*

well-be·ing (wel′bē′ing), *n.* a state of health, happiness, prosperity, etc.; welfare.

well·born (wel′bôrn′), *adj.* born of a good or noble family.

well-bred (wel′bred′), *adj.* having or showing good breeding; refined; polite.

well-fed (wel′fed′), *adj.* properly nourished.

well-groomed (wel′grōōmd′), *adj.* properly cared for; clean; neat: *a well-groomed dog.*

Wel·ling·ton (wel′ing tən), *n.* **1. Duke of,** 1769–1852, British general and statesman, born in Ireland: defeated Napoleon at Waterloo. **2.** a seaport and the capital city of New Zealand, on S North Island.

well-known (wel′nōn′), *adj.* **1.** clearly or fully known: *You cannot deny the well-known evidence.* **2.** intimately known; familiar: *a well-known face.* **3.** widely known; famous: *a well-known novelist.*

well-mean·ing (wel′mē′ning), *adj.* **1.** having good intentions: *well-meaning but indulgent parents.* **2.** springing from good intentions: *well-meaning words.*

well-nigh (wel′nī′), *adv.* very nearly; almost: *I have well-nigh finished this book on hunting and fishing.*

well-off (wel′ôf′), *adj.* **1.** in a satisfactory or favorable condition: *We're just as well-off spending the day at home.* **2.** prosperous; well-to-do: *He can go away to college because his family is well-off.*

well·spring (wel′spring′), *n.* **1.** the source of a stream or spring; fountainhead. **2.** a plentiful source or supply of anything: *a wellspring of affection.*

well-to-do (wel′tə dōō′), *adj.* well supplied with money and the comforts of life; prosperous.

Welsh (welsh), *adj.* **1.** of or referring to Wales, its people, or their language. —*n.* **2.** the Welsh people. **3.** a Celtic language spoken in Wales.

Welsh·man (welsh′mən), *n., pl.* **Welsh·men.** a native or inhabitant of Wales.

Welsh′ rab′bit, a dish made of melted cheese, usually mixed with ale or beer, milk, and spices, served on toast or crackers. Also, **Welsh′ rare′bit.**

Welsh′ ter′rier, one of a Welsh breed of terriers having a wiry, black-and-tan coat.

welt (welt), *n.* **1.** a ridge or strip raised on the skin by a blow from a stick or whip. **2.** a strip of leather, set in between the sole and the upper part of a shoe, to reinforce the seam along which these parts are joined. —*v.* **3.** to beat or thrash, esp. with a stick or whip. **4.** to provide with a welt or welts.

Welsh terrier
(15 in. high
at shoulder)

wel·ter (wel′tər), *v.* **1.** to roll, toss, or heave, as waves, the sea, etc. **2.** to roll or writhe; wallow: *The pigs weltered in the mud.* **3.** to lie bathed in something, esp. blood. —*n.* **4.** a confused mass or heap; jumble. **5.** a commotion or turmoil. **6.** a rolling, tossing, or heaving motion.

wel·ter·weight (wel′tər wāt′), *n.* a boxer or wrestler who weighs between 136 and 147 pounds.

wen (wen), *n.* a harmless tumor on the skin, esp. on the scalp.

wench (wench), *n.* **1.** a girl or young woman. **2.** *Archaic.* a female servant; maid.

wend (wend), *v.* to direct (one's course); go: *They slowly wended their way home.*

went (went), *v.* the past tense of **go.**

wept (wept), *v.* the past tense and past participle of **weep.**

were (wûr), *v.* **1.** the past tense of **be,** used with *you,* *we*, and *they.* **2.** a form of **be** used with any subject, in clauses expressing a wish, doubt, supposition, etc.: *If I were rich, I would buy a yacht.*

we're (wēr), contraction of *we are.*

were·n't (wûrnt, wûr'ənt), contraction of *were not.*

were·wolf (wēr'wŏolf'), *n., pl.* **were·wolves** (wēr'-wŏolvz'). a person in folklore who is supposed to be able to change into a wolf or who has changed into a wolf. [from the Old English word *werwulf,* which comes from *wer* "man" + *wulf* "wolf"]

wert (wûrt), *v.* an old form of **were,** found now chiefly in Biblical and poetic writing (usually used with *thou*): *Thou wert my trusted friend.*

Wes·ley (wes'lē, wez'lē), *n.* **1. Charles,** 1707–1788, English evangelist and writer of hymns. **2.** his brother **John,** 1703–1791, English theologian: founder of Methodism.

west (west), *n.* **1.** one of the four principal compass points, the direction of the setting sun. *Abbr.:* W, W. **2.** the western part of a region or country. **3. the West, a.** the western part of the U.S. **b.** Europe and the Americas; the Occident. **c.** the noncommunist countries of Europe and the Americas. —*adj.* **4.** Also, **western.** situated in the west: *the west part of the state.* **5.** coming from the west: *a west wind.* —*adv.* **6.** toward the west: *to sail west.*

West' Berlin'. See under **Berlin.**

west·bound (west'bound'), *adj.* going toward the west: *westbound traffic.*

west·er·ly (wes'tər lē), *adj.* **1.** directed toward the west: *in a westerly course.* **2.** coming from the west: *The wind is westerly.* —*adv.* **3.** toward the west: *sailing westerly.* **4.** from this point, as a wind.

west·ern (wes'tərn), *adj.* **1.** See **west** (def. 4). **2.** *(often cap.)* of or referring to the western U.S. **3.** *(usually cap.)* of or referring to the Occident: *Western dress.* **4.** *(usually cap.)* of or referring to the noncommunist countries of Europe and the Americas.

West'ern Austral'ia, a state in W Australia. 975,-920 sq. mi. *Cap.:* Perth.

West·ern·er (wes'tər nər), *n.* a native or inhabitant of a western area, esp. of the western U.S.

West'ern Hem'isphere, the W part of the globe, including North and South America.

west·ern·most (wes'tərn mōst'), *adj.* farthest west.

West'ern Samo'a, an independent state in the W part of Samoa, formerly governed by New Zealand. 1133 sq. mi. See also **American Samoa.** —**West'ern Samo'an.**

West' Ger'many, a republic in central Europe: created in 1949 from the French, British, and American zones of occupied Germany. 94,905 sq. mi. *Cap.:* Bonn. —**West' Ger'man.**

West' In'dies, an archipelago in the N Atlantic Ocean between North and South America. —**West' In'dian.**

West' I'ri·an (ēr'ē än'), the W part of the island of New Guinea, a province of Indonesia since 1963: formerly a Dutch territory.

West'min·ster Ab'bey (west'min/stər), a Gothic church in London, England: burial place of English kings, statesmen, poets, etc.

west-north·west (west'nôrth'west'), *n.* **1.** the point on the compass halfway between west and northwest. *Abbr.:* WNW —*adj.* **2.** directed toward this point. **3.** coming from this point, as a wind. —*adv.* **4.** toward this point. **5.** from this point, as a wind: *The wind is blowing west-northwest.*

West' Pak'istan, the western part of Pakistan, separated from East Pakistan by India. 310,236 sq. mi.

West' Point', a United States military academy in SE New York on the Hudson River.

west-south·west (west'south'west'), *n.* **1.** the point on the compass halfway between west and southwest. *Abbr.:* WSW —*adj.* **2.** directed toward this point. **3.** coming from this point, as a wind. —*adv.* **4.** toward this point. **5.** from this point, as a wind: *The wind is blowing west-southwest.*

West' Virgin'ia, a state in the E United States. 24,181 sq. mi. *Cap.:* Charleston. —**West' Virgin'ian.**

west·ward (west'wərd), *adj.* **1.** moving toward or facing the west. **2.** situated in the west. —*adv.* **3.** Also, **west'wards.** toward the west: *to sail westward.* —*n.* **4.** a westward direction or point: *to sail to the westward.*

wet (wet), *adj.,* **wet·ter, wet·test. 1.** moistened, covered, or soaked with water or some other liquid. **2.** in a liquid form or state: *wet paint.* **3.** rainy; misty: *a wet climate.* **4.** permitting the sale of alcoholic beverages: *a wet county.* —*n.* **5.** wetness; moisture. **6.** rainy or damp weather: *Come in out of the wet and change into dry clothes.* —*v.,* **wet** *or* **wet·ted; wet·ting. 7.** to make wet. **8.** to become wet (often fol. by *through*): *My jacket wet through.* **9.** to urinate on or in (used esp. of children and animals). **10. all wet,** *Slang.* completely wrong or mistaken: *You're all wet about the facts.* **11. wet behind the ears,** *Informal.* not mature or experienced; green: *a good ballplayer, but still wet behind the ears.* —**wet'ness,** *n.* —**wet'ly,** *adv.*

we've (wēv), contraction of *we have.*

whack (hwak, wak), *Informal.* —*v.* **1.** to strike with a sharp, resounding blow. —*n.* **2.** a sharp, resounding blow. **3.** the sound of such a blow. **4.** a try; attempt: *to take a whack at a job.*

Sperm whale (length 60 ft.)

whale¹ (hwāl, wāl), *n., pl.* **whales** *or* **whale. 1.** any of the larger mammals that live in the ocean, having a fishlike body, forelimbs modified into flippers, and a flattened head. Some are hunted for their oil and also their flesh, which is used as a food and for fertilizer. —*v.*, **whaled, whal·ing. 2.** to hunt whales. [from the Old English word *hwæl*]

whale² (hwāl, wāl), *v.*, **whaled, whal·ing.** *Informal.* to whip or thrash soundly. [another form of the word *wale*]

whale·bone (hwāl**′**bōn**′**, wāl**′**-), *n.* **1.** an elastic, horny substance growing in place of teeth in the upper jaw of certain kinds of whales, forming a series of long, thin plates on each side of the palate, for straining out from the water the tiny sea animals on which such whales feed. **2.** a thin strip of this substance, formerly used for stiffening a corset, dress, etc.

whal·er (hwā**′**lər, wā**′**lər), *n.* **1.** a person engaged in whaling. **2.** a ship or boat used in whaling.

whal·ing (hwā**′**ling, wā**′**ling), *n.* the occupation or business of hunting, capturing, and processing whales for their oil, blubber, whalebone, etc.

wharf (hwôrf, wôrf), *n., pl.* **wharves** (hwôrvz, wôrvz) *or* **wharfs.** a structure, usually a long platform, sometimes roofed, built along a shore or out over the water, alongside of which ships and boats may be moored, loaded and unloaded, etc.; pier; dock.

what (hwot, wot), *pron.* **1.** which thing or things, action, event, condition, kind, etc.: *What happened?* **2.** that or those which: *Tell me what you want for lunch.* **3.** whatever; anything that: *come what may.* **4.** how much: *What did that hat cost?* —*adj.* **5.** which or which kind of: *What clothes shall I pack?* **6.** whatever or whichever: *You can borrow what books you need from the library.* **7.** how much: *What difference does it make?* **8.** so much; so great: *What trouble I'm having with mathematics!* —*adv.* **9.** to what extent or degree; how much: *What does it matter?* —*interj.* **10.** (used to express surprise, doubt, annoyance, etc.): *What, aren't you ready yet?* **11. what for,** *Informal.* **a.** for what reason; why: *What did you say that for?* **b.** severe punishment, scolding, or the like: *He really gave me what for when I was late again this morning.* **12. what have you,** *Informal.* and other things of the same kind; and so forth: *pie, cake, ice cream, and what have you.* **13. what if,** suppose that: *What if it rains at the picnic?* **14. what it takes,** that which is needed for success, such as intelligence, talent, good looks, etc.: *That boy sure has what it takes!* **15. what's what,** *Informal.* the true situation; all the facts: *Find out what's what, and let me know.* **16. what with,** with the addition or complication of: *What with the flu and two colds, I'm a month behind in my work.*

what'd (hwot**′**id, wot**′**id), contraction of *what did: What'd he do then?*

what·ev·er (hwot ev**′**ər, wot-), *pron.* **1.** anything that: *Eat whatever you like.* **2.** as much as; all that: *Take whatever you need from that money.* **3.** no matter what: *Whatever happens, don't get upset.* **4.** what (often used in questions, for greater emphasis): *Whatever are you thinking about?* —*adj.* **5.** in any amount: *We can use whatever help you give us.* **6.** no matter what or which: *Whatever job you accept, do it*

well. **7.** of any kind: *He eats no sweets whatever.*

what'll (hwot**′**əl, wot**′**əl), contraction of *what shall* or *what will.*

what·not (hwot**′**not**′**, wot**′**-), *n.* a stand with shelves for holding books, knickknacks, etc.

what's (hwots, wots), **1.** contraction of *what is: What's wrong?* **2.** contraction of *what has: What's he done now?* **3.** *Informal.* contraction of *what does: What's it matter where I've been?*

what·so·ev·er (hwot**′**sō ev**′**ər, wot**′**-), *pron., adj.* an emphatic form of **whatever:** *I couldn't find him in any place whatsoever.*

wheat (hwēt, wēt), *n.* **1.** the grain of any of various cereal grasses, used in the form of flour for making bread, cake, etc. **2.** a plant that bears such a grain.

wheat·en (hwēt**′**ʼn, wēt**′**ʼn), *adj.* of, referring to, or made of wheat.

whee·dle (hwēd**′**əl, wēd**′**əl), *v.*, **whee·dled, whee·dling. 1.** to persuade or influence (a person or persons) by flattery or slyness: *I wheedled him into joining the group.* **2.** to gain or get by flattery or slyness: *Try to wheedle the money out of your father.*

wheel (hwēl, wēl), *n.* **1.** a round frame or disk mounted on an axle around which it revolves. **2.** any machine, device, etc., shaped like a wheel or having a wheel as its main part: *a potter's wheel; a steering wheel.* **3.** *Informal.* a bicycle. **4. wheels,** the forces that move or control an elaborate system or activity: *the wheels of industry.* **5.** *Slang.* an important person. —*v.* **6.** to turn, revolve, rotate, or pivot on an axis or about a center: *I wheeled about to face him.* **7.** to move or carry on wheels: *She wheeled the baby carriage down the street.*

wheel·bar·row (hwēl**′**bar**′**ō, wēl**′**-), *n.* a frame or box for carrying small loads, mounted on a wheel or wheels at one end, the other end having two handles by which it is lifted and pushed.

wheel·chair (hwēl**′**chârʼ, wēl**′**-), *n.* a chair mounted on wheels, pushed by hand or electrically driven, used for moving sick or disabled persons.

Wheel·er (hwē**′**lər, wē**′**lər), *n.* **William A.,** 1819–1887, 19th Vice President of the U.S. 1877–1881.

wheel·wright (hwēl**′**rītʼ, wēl**′**-), *n.* a person whose occupation is making and repairing wheels, carriages, wagons, etc.

wheeze (hwēz, wēz), *v.*, **wheezed, wheez·ing. 1.** to breathe with difficulty and with a hissing or whistling sound: *His asthma caused him to wheeze.* **2.** to make a hissing or whistling sound: *The old engine wheezed and shook.* —*n.* **3.** the act or sound of wheezing. **4.** an old, familiar joke or saying.

wheez·y (hwē**′**zē, wē**′**zē), *adj.*, **wheez·i·er, wheez·i·est. 1.** breathing with difficulty: *He is wheezy from a chest cold.* **2.** making a hissing or whistling sound: *a wheezy motor.* —**wheez′i·ness,** *n.*

Whelk (length 3 in.)

whelk (hwelk, welk), *n.* any of several large, edible mollusks having a spiral-shaped shell.

whelp (hwelp, welp), *n.* **1.** the young of a dog, or of a wolf, bear, lion, tiger, seal, etc.; pup or cub. **2.** a mischievous or worthless boy or young man. *—v.* **3.** to give birth to (young).

when (hwen, wen), *adv.* **1.** at or during what time or period: *When will they leave?* *—conj.* **2.** at what or which time: *I'll tell you when to begin.* **3.** at or during the time that: *Call me when dinner is ready.* **4.** upon or after which; and then: *I had just come in when the telephone rang.* **5.** while on the contrary; whereas: *Why are you here when you should be in school?* **6.** in view of the fact that; if: *How can I study when you're making so much noise?* **7.** at any time that; whenever: *He always gets home late when he goes to the movies.* *—pron.* **8.** what or which time: *Till when is the store open?*

whence (hwens, wens), *adv.* **1.** from where: *Whence comes this stranger?* **2.** from what source or cause: *Whence comes this money?* *—conj.* **3.** from what or which place or source: *He told whence he had come.* **4.** from which: *We found the place whence the strange sounds were coming.* **5.** to the place or source from which: *Return whence you came.* *—Usage.* Because "from" is contained in the meaning of *whence,* the two words should not be used together: *Whence came he?* (not *from whence*).

when·ev·er (hwen ev′ər, wen-), *conj.* **1.** at or during whatever time: *We'll go whenever you're ready.* *—adv.* **2.** when (often used in questions, for greater emphasis): *Whenever have you seen such a sight?*

when's (hwenz, wenz), contraction of *when is* or *when has.*

when·so·ev·er (hwen′sō ev′ər, wen′-), *adv., conj.* at whatsoever time.

where (hwâr, wâr), *adv.* **1.** in or at what place or position: *Where is my pen?* **2.** in what respect or way; how: *Where does this affect us?* **3.** to or toward what place, position, or goal: *Where did you go?* **4.** from what place or source: *Where did you get that idea?* *—conj.* **5.** to, in, or at what place or position: *Tell me where it is.* **6.** to, in, or at the same place or position that: *The book is where you left it.* **7.** to, in, or at whatever place; wherever: *My dog goes where I go.* **8.** in or at which place: *The bus stopped at Salem, where we had lunch.* *—pron.* **9.** what place: *Where do you come from?* **10.** the place at or in which: *This is where the boat docks.* **11.** the point or moment at which: *That was where the phone rang.* *—Usage.* Careful writers and speakers avoid the unnecessary use of *at* or *to* with *where: Where is she?* (not *Where is she at?*) *Where did he go?* (not *Where did he go to?*).

where·a·bouts (hwâr′ə bouts′, wâr′-), *adv.* **1.** about where; at, in, or near what place: *Whereabouts is there a hotel?* *—n.pl.* **2.** the place where a person or thing is: *I know nothing regarding his whereabouts.*

where·as (hwâr az′, wâr-), *conj.* **1.** while on the contrary; but: *I was there early, whereas they arrived late.* **2.** considering that; since: *Whereas he has served faithfully, he deserves a reward.*

where·at (hwâr at′, wâr-), *conj.* **1.** at which: *It was a masked ball whereat many were present.* **2.** upon or because of which; whereupon: *I ordered him to leave, whereat he flew into a rage.*

where·by (hwâr bī′, wâr-), *conj.* by means of which: *He has a car whereby he drives to work.*

where·fore (hwâr′fôr, wâr′-), *adv.* **1.** for what reason; why: *Wherefore do they weep?* *—conj.* **2.** for which cause or reason: *We have liberty, wherefore let us be grateful.* *—n.* **3.** the cause or reason: *Consider the whys and wherefores of the situation.*

where·in (hwâr in′, wâr-), *conj.* **1.** in which: *That is the tomb wherein the king is buried.* *—adv.* **2.** in what respect or way: *Wherein have we been at fault?*

where·of (hwâr uv′, -ov′, wâr-), *conj.* of what, which, or whom: *I know whereof I speak.*

where·on (hwâr on′, -ôn′, wâr-), *conj.* on which: *That is the evidence whereon the case was judged.*

where's (hwârz, wârz), **1.** contraction of *where is: Where's my hat?* **2.** contraction of *where has: Where's he gone?*

where·so·ev·er (hwâr′sō ev′ər, wâr′-), *conj.* in, at, or to whatsoever place.

where·to (hwâr tōō′, wâr-), *adv.* **1.** to what, or to what place or purpose: *Whereto does evil lead us?* *—conj.* **2.** to which: *He made a fortune, whereto was added his inheritance.*

where·up·on (hwâr′ə pon′, wâr′-), *conj.* **1.** upon which: *Early in life we form habits whereupon we build our character.* **2.** at which; following which: *I said I had no money, whereupon he offered me some.* *—adv.* **3.** upon what: *Whereupon does our future depend?*

wher·ev·er (hwâr ev′ər, wâr-), *conj.* **1.** in, at, or to whatever place: *We live wherever we can find work.* *—adv.* **2.** where; in what place (often used in questions for greater emphasis): *Wherever did you find that ridiculous hat?*

where·with (hwâr with′, -with′, wâr-), *adv.* **1.** with what; by means of what: *Wherewith can we earn our living?* *—conj.* **2.** with which; by means of which: *They had no tools wherewith to build a house.*

where·with·al (hwâr′with ôl′, wâr′-), *n.* the means of supplying a particular purpose or need; what is necessary, esp. money: *Do you have the wherewithal to pay your rent?*

whet (hwet, wet), *v.,* **whet·ted, whet·ting. 1.** to sharpen (a knife, tool, etc.) by rubbing or grinding on a stone. **2.** to make keen or eager; arouse; stimulate: *to whet the appetite.* *—whet′ter, n.*

wheth·er (hweth′ər, weth′ər), *conj.* **1.** (used before the first of two or more choices or possibilities, with *or* being used before the others): *It doesn't matter whether we go or stay.* **2.** (used for stating a single choice or possibility, the other being understood): *Ask your mother whether you can go.* (In the preceding sentence, *or not* is understood.)

whet·stone (hwet′stōn′, wet′-), *n.* a stone for sharpening knives or tools by rubbing or grinding.

whew (hwyoo͞), *interj.* (a whistling exclamation or sound expressing astonishment, relief, disgust, discomfort, etc.): *Whew! It's hot in here!*

whey (hwā, wā), *n.* a watery liquid that separates from milk after it curdles, as in the making of cheese.

which (hwich, wich), *pron.* **1.** what one or ones: *Which of these do you want?* **2.** any one or ones that; whichever: *Choose which you like.* **3.** the one or ones that: *Tell me which you think will be most useful.* **4.** (used in relative clauses to refer to that or those mentioned earlier in the sentence): *The goods which we ordered have been delivered.* **5.** (used after a preposition to represent a thing or things previously mentioned): *This is the book about which I spoke to you.* —*adj.* **6.** what one or ones of (a certain number or group): *Which book do you prefer?* **7.** any; whatever: *Take which seat you like.* **8.** being previously mentioned or indicated: *It rained all day, during which time we played cards.*

which·ev·er (hwich ev′ər, wich-), *pron.* **1.** any one or ones (of a certain number or group): *Take whichever you like.* **2.** any one or ones that; no matter which: *Whichever you give him will make him content.* —*adj.* **3.** any; whatever; no matter which: *I'll go on whichever day you choose.*

whiff (hwif, wif), *n.* **1.** a slight gust or puff of wind, air, smoke, or the like. **2.** a slight trace of odor or smell. **3.** a single breath; sniff: *Take a whiff of this perfume.* —*v.* **4.** to blow or move in puffs. **5.** to breathe; sniff: *to whiff the salt air.*

Whig (hwig, wig), *n.* **1.** (in American history) a colonist who supported the Revolutionary War against England. **2.** a member of a political party of the U.S. from about 1834 to 1855, formed in opposition to the Democratic party. **3.** a member of one of the major political parties of Great Britain, opposed to the Tories. Since 1832 it has been known as the Liberal party.

while (hwīl, wīl), *n.* **1.** a period or interval of time of indefinite length: *He'll be here in a while.* —*conj.* **2.** during or in the time that: *We studied while Mother prepared dinner.* **3.** although; even though: *While I don't agree with you, I admit your right to speak.* **4.** and besides; and furthermore: *The floor was littered with crumbs, while papers strewed the tables.* **5.** *Informal.* on the other hand; whereas: *He is a senior at college, while his younger sister is a junior.* —*v.*, **whiled, whil·ing. 6.** to pass or spend (time), esp. in an idle or pleasant manner (usually fol. by *away*): *We whiled away the time singing.* **7. worth one's while,** worth one's time, trouble, or expense: *It would be worth your while to see the art exhibit.*

whilst (hwīlst, wīlst), *conj.* a British form of **while.**

whim (hwim, wim), *n.* a sudden or unusual notion or wish: *You must cater to all his whims when he's sick.*

whim·per (hwim′pər, wim′pər), *v.* **1.** to cry with low, broken sounds, as in fear or complaint: *The children whimpered because they were not allowed to go out.* —*n.* **2.** a whimpering cry or sound.

whim·sey (hwim′zē, wim′zē), *n.*, *pl.* **whim·seys.** another spelling of **whimsy.**

whim·si·cal (hwim′zi kəl, wim′zi kəl), *adj.* **1.** full of whimsy or fanciful notions; odd: *a whimsical writer of adventures.* **2.** amusing; droll: *a whimsical story.* —**whim′si·cal·ly,** *adv.*

whim·sy (hwim′zē, wim′zē), *n.*, *pl.* **whim·sies. 1.** odd or fanciful humor: *a play enlivened by whimsy.* **2.** an odd or fanciful notion; whim. Also, **whimsey.**

whine (hwīn, wīn), *v.*, **whined, whin·ing. 1.** to make a low, complaining cry or sound. **2.** to complain in a persistent, objectionable manner: *The students whine about long homework assignments.* —*n.* **3.** a whining sound or cry. —**whin′er,** *n.* —**whin′ing·ly,** *adv.*

whin·ny (hwin′ē, win′ē), *v.*, **whin·nied, whin·ny·ing. 1.** to utter the cry of a horse; neigh. —*n.* **2.** the cry a horse makes; neigh.

whip (hwip, wip), *n.* **1.** an instrument for striking or beating a person or an animal, usually made of a long flexible lash attached to a rod or handle. **2.** a stroke or blow made with a whip or anything resembling a whip. **3.** a dessert made of whipped cream or whipped egg whites, often with flavoring, fruits, etc.: *prune whip.* —*v.*, **whipped** *or* **whipt** (hwipt, wipt); **whip·ping. 4.** to beat or strike with a whip. **5.** to drive (animals) with a whip. **6.** to subject to hard training: *to whip a team into shape.* **7.** *Informal.* to defeat decisively; trounce: *Our team was whipped by a score of 10 to 0.* **8.** to pull, remove, throw, etc., with a quick jerking motion (usually fol. by *out, off,* etc.): *He whipped out his pistol and fired.* **9.** to toss or flap about, as with the wind, waves, etc. **10.** to beat (eggs, cream, etc.) to a froth. **11. whip up,** *Informal.* **a.** to put together hurriedly: *to whip up a meal out of a few leftovers.* **b.** to arouse; stir up; agitate: *The crowd was whipped up to a frenzy.*

whip·lash (hwip′lash′, wip′-), *n.* **1.** the lash of a whip. **2.** an injury to the neck caused by a sudden jerking of the head forward or backward.

whip·pet (hwip′it, wip′it), *n.* any of a breed of dogs resembling the greyhound, but much smaller, used for racing.

whip·poor·will (hwip′ər wil′, wip′ər wil′), *n.* a North American bird having plumage of gray, black, white, and tawny, that is active at night and has a call that sounds like its name.

Whippet
(22 in. high
at shoulder)

whir (hwûr, wûr), *v.*, **whirred, whir·ring. 1.** to move or turn rapidly with a humming or buzzing sound. —*n.* **2.** the act or sound of whirring.

whirl (hwûrl, wûrl), *v.* **1.** to move, turn, or spin rapidly: *The midget racers whirled around the track.* **2.** to cause to turn or spin rapidly: *He whirled his partner about the dance floor.* **3.** to have a feeling of spinning; be giddy or dizzy: *The hustle and bustle made my head whirl.* —*n.* **4.** the act of whirling. **5.** a rapid turning or spinning motion: *the whirl of propellers.* **6.** a short drive, walk, etc. **7.** a whirling mass of persons or things; bustle: *He was lost in the whirl of the crowd.* **8.** a rapid series of events or activities: *Our vacation was a whirl of parties.* **9.** a state of excitement or confusion. **10.** an attempt or trial; try: *Why not give the job a whirl?*

whirl·i·gig (hwûr′lə gig, wûr′lə gig), *n.* **1.** something that whirls or changes rapidly. **2.** a whirling motion or course. **3.** a merry-go-round. **4.** a toy for whirling or spinning, such as a pinwheel or a top.

whirl·pool (hwûrl′pool′, wûrl′-), *n.* a rapidly spinning mass of water, that exerts a downward sucking force at its center.

whirl·wind (hwûrl′wind′, wûrl′-), *n.* a rapidly spinning mass of air, bringing storms in its path.

whisk (hwisk, wisk), *v.* **1.** to sweep or brush with light strokes: *to whisk crumbs off the table.* **2.** to move or carry swiftly: *We were whisked away in a car.* **3.** to whip (eggs, cream, etc.) to a froth. —*n.* **4.** the act or motion of whisking. **5.** a whisk broom. **6.** a kitchen utensil made of wire loops held together in a handle, for beating or whipping eggs, cream, etc.

whisk′ broom′, a small broom with a short handle, used for brushing clothes, upholstery, etc.

whisk·er (hwis′kər, wis′kər), *n.* **1.** Usually, **whiskers. a.** the long hairs that grow on the sides of a man's face. **b.** the whiskers together with the hairs on the chin, or the beard. **2.** one of the hairs growing on a man's face. **3.** one of the long, stiff hairs growing about the mouth of certain animals, such as the cat, rat, etc. —**whisk′ered,** *adj.*

whis·key (hwis′kē, wis′kē), *n., pl.* **whis·keys.** an alcoholic liquor made by distilling a fermented mixture of certain grains, such as corn, barley, rye, etc. Also, **whisky.**

whis·ky (hwis′kē, wis′kē), *n., pl.* **whis·kies.** another spelling of **whiskey.**

whis·per (hwis′pər, wis′pər), *v.* **1.** to speak or say softly, using the breath, but without vibration of the vocal cords. **2.** to speak or say privately or secretly: *I know people have whispered about him, but I believe he is honest.* **3.** to make a soft, rustling sound: *The leaves whispered in the breeze.* —*n.* **4.** the tone or manner of speaking by whispering: *to say something in a whisper.* **5.** something whispered. **6.** a hint or rumor. **7.** a soft, rustling sound. —**whis′per·er,** *n.*

whist (hwist, wist), *n.* a card game resembling bridge, played usually by two pairs of players.

whis·tle (hwis′əl, wis′əl), *v.,* **whis·tled, whis·tling. 1.** to make a high-pitched musical sound by forcing the breath through a tight opening formed by the lips or teeth. **2.** to make a similar sound by blowing through an instrument or device in the form of a tube or pipe. **3.** to produce by whistling: *to whistle a tune.* **4.** to move, go, pass, etc., with a whistling sound: *The wind whistled through the caves.* —*n.* **5.** an instrument for producing sharp, shrill sounds by forcing the breath or a stream of air, steam, etc., through a narrow pipe or tube with one or more small openings. **6.** a sound made by whistling: *a whistle of astonishment.* —**whis′tler,** *n.*

whit (hwit, wit), *n.* the least amount; bit: *He's not feeling a whit better today.*

white (hwīt, wīt), *adj.,* **whit·er, whit·est. 1.** of the color of fresh snow or the margins of this page; reflecting nearly all the rays of sunlight. **2.** of or belonging to a people having light skin; Caucasian: *the white races of the world.* **3.** of a light or pale color: *the white meat of chicken.* **4.** pale or wan: *She turned white with fear.* **5.** silvery, as hair. **6.** pure; spotless; innocent: *a white spirit.* **7.** without malice; harmless: *white magic.* **8.** blank; not covered with writing or printing. —*n.* **9.** the color opposite to black that reflects nearly all the rays of sunlight; the color of fresh snow. **10.** a member of a light-skinned people; Caucasian. **11.** something that is white or of a light or pale color: *the white of the eye.* **12.** Often, **whites.** white clothing: *The sailors were in summer whites.* —*v.,* **whit·ed, whit·ing. 13.** to make white; whiten. —**white′ness,** *n.*

white′ ant′, another name for **termite.**

white·cap (hwīt′kap′, wīt′-), *n.* a wave that forms a foamy white crest as it breaks.

white′ cell′, a white corpuscle. Also, **white′ blood′ cell′.**

white-col·lar (hwīt′kol′ər, wīt′-), *adj.* of or belonging to the classes of business or professional workers whose jobs do not usually require manual labor.

white′ cor′puscle, one of the white or colorless cells of the blood that destroy germs in the bloodstream.

white′ feath′er, a symbol of cowardice.

white·fish (hwīt′fish′, wīt′-), *n., pl.* **white·fish** *or* **white·fish·es.** any of various silvery fishes found in lakes and used as food.

white′ flag′, a white flag or piece of white cloth, used as a symbol of surrender or truce.

White·horse (hwīt′hôrs′, wīt′-), *n.* the capital city of the Yukon Territory, in NW Canada.

White′ House′, the, 1. the official residence of the President of the United States, in Washington, D.C. **2.** the executive branch of the federal government: *Is the White House in favor of the new bill?*

white′ lie′, a lie told to spare someone embarrassment or to cover up a minor offense, etc.: *It was a white lie to say he would be well very soon.*

White′ Moun′tains, a mountain range in N New Hampshire, part of the Appalachian Mountains. Highest peak, Mt. Washington, 6293 ft.

whit·en (hwīt′′n, wīt′′n), *v.* to make or become white.

White′ Rus′sia, another name for **Byelorussia.** —**White′ Rus′sian.**

white·wash (hwīt′wosh′, -wôsh′, wīt′-), *n.* **1.** a white liquid, usually made of lime and water, for whitening walls, fences, etc. **2.** the act or means of covering up mistakes or offenses by deception, so as to protect a person or group from blame: *The committee's report was a whitewash of the chairman.* **3.** *Informal.* (in sports) a defeat in which the loser fails to score. —*v.* **4.** to whiten by coating with whitewash: *to whitewash the fence.* **5.** to protect from blame by means of a whitewash: *to whitewash a friend's mistake.* **6.** *Informal.* (in sports) to defeat (an opponent) without allowing him to score.

whith·er (hwiŧħ′ər, wiŧħ′ər), *adj., conj.* to what or which place; where: *Whither are we going?*

whit·ing[1] (hwī′tiṅg, wī′tiṅg), *n., pl.* **whit·ing** *or* **whit·ings.** any of various food fishes found along the Atlantic coast of North America. [perhaps from the Old English word *hwītling,* a kind of fish]

whit·ing[2] (hwī′tiṅg, wī′tiṅg), *n.* a white powdered chalk, used in making whitewash, putty, silver polish, etc. [from Old English]

whit·ish (hwī′tish, wī′tish), *adj.* tending toward white; of a color resembling white.

Whit·man (hwit′mən, wit′mən), *n.* **Walt,** 1819–1892, U.S. poet.

Whit·ney (hwit′nē, wit′nē), *n.* **1. Eli,** 1765–1825, U.S. inventor of the cotton gin. **2. Mount,** a mountain in E California. 14,495 ft.

Whit·sun·day (hwit′sun′dē, -dā, wit′-), *n.* the seventh Sunday after Easter; Pentecost.

Whit·sun·tide (hwit′sən tīd′, wit′-), *n.* the week beginning with Whitsunday, esp. the first three days of this week.

whit·tle (hwit′əl, wit′əl), *v.,* **whit·tled, whit·tling. 1.** to cut or shape (a stick, piece of wood, or the like) by carving off bits with a knife. **2.** to make (something) in this way: *to whittle a whistle out of a twig.* **3.** to reduce the amount of bit by bit (usually fol. by *down, away,* etc.): *to whittle down expenses.* —**whit′tler,** *n.*

whiz (hwiz, wiz), *v.,* **whizzed, whiz·zing. 1.** to make a humming or buzzing sound, as of something moving swiftly through the air: *The arrow whizzed over our heads.* **2.** to move or rush with such a sound. —*n.* **3.** a whizzing sound or movement. **4.** *Informal.* a person who has an extraordinary ability of a particular kind: *He's a whiz at skiing.*

who (hōō), *pron.* **1.** what person or persons: *Who told you that?* **2.** which person or persons: *I know who took it.* **3.** (used in relative clauses to represent someone mentioned previously): *The man who called this morning is here.* **4.** any person or persons that; whoever: *Let who will, take the blame.*

whoa (hwō, wō), *interj.* Stop! (used esp. to horses).

who·ev·er (hōō ev′ər), *pron.* **1.** whatever person; any person that: *Whoever borrowed the book should return it.* **2.** no matter who: *Whoever tells you that, don't believe it.* **3.** who (often used in questions, for greater emphasis): *Whoever said such a thing?*

whole (hōl), *adj.* **1.** making up the full amount, number, extent, etc.; entire, full, or total: *the whole ten days.* **2.** having no part or piece missing; complete: *a whole set of Shakespeare's works.* **3.** not cut up or divided; in one piece: *to swallow a biscuit whole.* **4.** unharmed or unbroken; sound. —*n.* **5.** an entire amount, or a sum of all the parts of something: *We*

have used up the whole of our supply of food. **6.** a number of things or parts forming a unit or system: *The sun and planets make up a whole.* **7. on the whole,** considering all the facts or circumstances; in general: *On the whole I'm pleased with your work this year.* —**whole′ness,** *n.*

whole·heart·ed (hōl′här′tid), *adj.* completely sincere, enthusiastic, etc.; earnest: *wholehearted approval.* —**whole′heart′ed·ly,** *adv.*

whole′ note′, (in music) a note having the time value of four quarter notes or two half notes. See illus. at **note.**

whole′ num′ber, a number that is not a fraction and does not contain a fraction; integer. 1, 21, 138, 1402 are whole numbers. See also **mixed number.**

whole·sale (hōl′sāl′), *n.* **1.** the sale of goods in large amounts, usually to merchants rather than directly to consumers (distinguished from *retail*). —*adj.* **2.** of or concerned with sale of goods by wholesale: *a wholesale price.* **3.** extensive; widespread; general: *wholesale destruction of forests by fire.* —*adv.* **4.** on wholesale terms, usually in large quantity at reduced prices. —*v.,* **whole·saled, whole·sal·ing. 5.** to sell or be sold by wholesale: *These combs wholesale at two dollars a gross.* —**whole′sal′er,** *n.*

whole·some (hōl′səm), *adj.* **1.** promoting health or well-being: *wholesome food.* **2.** having or showing physical, mental, or moral health: *a wholesome glow in the cheeks; a wholesome respect for the rights of others.* —**whole′some·ly,** *adv.* —**whole′some·ness,** *n.*

whole-wheat (hōl′hwēt′, -wēt′), *adj.* made from the complete grain of wheat, including the husk or bran: *whole-wheat bread.*

whol·ly (hō′lē, hōl′lē), *adv.* including or comprising the full amount, degree, etc.; completely; entirely: *He is wholly unfit for military service.*

whom (hōōm), *pron.* the objective case of **who,** used as the object of a verb or preposition: *Whom did you see? That is the boy with whom I went to school.*

whom·ev·er (hōōm ev′ər), *pron.* the objective case of **whoever,** used as the object of a verb or preposition: *He greeted whomever he met.*

whoop (hōōp, hwōōp, wōōp), *n.* **1.** a loud shout or cry of excitement, surprise, joy, etc.: *a war whoop.* **2.** the sound made by a person suffering from whooping cough. —*v.* **3.** to utter a loud shout or cry: *The children whooped with joy.* **4.** to make the sound accompanying a whooping cough.

whoop′ing cough′ (hōō′piṅg, hōōp′iṅg), a contagious disease, esp. of children, marked by a series of short, gasping coughs followed by a whooping sound.

whoop′ing crane′, a large, white, nearly extinct, North American crane, having a loud, whooping call.

whop·per (hwop′ər, wop′ər), *n. Informal.* **1.** something very large of its kind: *I caught a bluefish that was a whopper.* **2.** a big lie; a tall story: *He told a whopper about being lost in the desert.*

whore (hôr), *n.* a prostitute; harlot.

whorl (hwûrl, wûrl, hwôrl, wôrl), *n.* a circular or spiral arrangement of similar things, such as leaves or petals.

whose (hōōz), *pron.* **1.** the possessive case of **who,** used as an adjective: *Whose pen did you borrow? Whose are these galoshes?* **2.** the possessive case of **which,** used as an adjective: *That's a word whose meaning I don't know.* **3.** the one or ones belonging to what person or persons: *Whose did you pick up instead of your own?*

who·so·ev·er (hōō'sō ev'ər), *pron.* an emphatic form of **whoever:** *Whosoever does good will be rewarded.*

why (hwī, wī), *adv.* **1.** for what; for what reason, cause, or purpose: *Why did you leave so early?* *—conj.* **2.** for which reason, cause, or purpose: *I don't know why he was absent.* **3.** for which; on account of which: *I've told you the reason why I could not go.* **4.** the reason for which: *That is why I bought the smaller car.* *—n., pl.* **whys. 5.** the cause or reason: *It's useless to look for the whys and wherefores of his actions.* *—interj.* **6.** (used to express surprise, embarrassment, etc.): *Why, it's gone!*

Wich·i·ta (wich'i tô'), *n.* a city in S Kansas.

Wich'ita Falls', a city in N Texas.

wick (wik), *n.* a loosely woven or twisted braid or cord, used in a candle, lamp, or the like, for drawing up liquid fuel which is burned at its tip or edge.

wick·ed (wik'id), *adj.* **1.** morally bad or depraved; evil; sinful: *a wicked deed.* **2.** mischievous; naughty: *He's a wicked little rascal.* **3.** causing or capable of causing great harm or trouble: *a wicked headache.* *—wick'ed·ly, adv. —wick'ed·ness, n.*

wick·er (wik'ər), *n.* **1.** one or a number of slender, flexible twigs, used for weaving baskets, chairs, etc. **2.** things made of wicker; wicker work. *—adj.* **3.** made of wicker: *a wicker basket.*

wick·et (wik'it), *n.* **1.** a small door or gate, esp. one in or alongside a larger one. **2.** a small window, often set with a grille or grating, as in a ticket office, a teller's cage in a bank, etc. **3.** (in croquet) any of the wire hoops through which the ball must be hit.

wide (wīd), *adj.,* **wid·er, wid·est. 1.** being large when measured from side to side; broad: *a wide street.* **2.** having a certain extent from side to side: *The hall is eight feet wide.* **3.** of great area or extent; vast: *the wide prairie.* **4.** including a great number or variety of things, subjects, cases, etc.: *a wide selection of men's wear.* **5.** fully opened or extended: *eyes wide with excitement.* **6.** far from an intended point or goal (often fol. by *of*): *The shot was wide of the mark.* *—adv.* **7.** over a large area or space; in many scattered places: *We have searched far and wide for a good cook.* **8.** so as to be fully opened or extended: *Open your mouth wide.* **9.** so as to pass or strike far from an intended point or goal: *The second pitch went wide. —wide'ness, n.*

wide-a·wake (wīd'ə wāk'), *adj.* **1.** fully awake. **2.** keen or alert: *A busy store needs a wide-awake staff.*

wide-eyed (wīd'īd'), *adj.* having the eyes open wide, as in amazement, surprise, sleeplessness, etc.

wide·ly (wīd'lē), *adv.* **1.** to a wide extent: *arms widely spread.* **2.** over a vast space or area: *to wan-*

der widely. **3.** by or among many persons or groups: *a widely known author.* **4.** so as to include a large number or variety of things, subjects, cases, etc.: *to be widely informed.* **5.** by a great extent or amount: *The witnesses told widely differing stories.*

wid·en (wīd'ʳn), *v.* to make or become wide or wider; broaden; expand: *to widen a street.*

wide·spread (wīd'spred'), *adj.* **1.** covering or affecting a large area: *a widespread illness.* **2.** fully opened or extended: *widespread arms.*

wid·ow (wid'ō), *n.* **1.** a woman whose husband has died and who has not remarried. *—v.* **2.** to make a widow of: *The war widowed thousands of women.* *—wid'ow·hood', n.*

wid·ow·er (wid'ō ər), *n.* a man whose wife has died and who has not remarried.

width (width), *n.* **1.** extent or measurement from side to side; breadth; wideness: *The house is 30 feet in width.* **2.** a piece of something, esp. of cloth, cut across its full width.

wield (wēld), *v.* **1.** to have and use; exercise (power, influence, etc.). **2.** to handle or manage (a weapon, tool, etc.).

wie·ner (wē'nər), *n.* another word for **frankfurter.**

wife (wīf), *n., pl.* **wives** (wīvz). a woman who is married to a certain man; married woman.

wife·ly (wīf'lē), *adj.,* **wife·li·er, wife·li·est.** of, like, or proper for a wife: *wifely devotion.*

wig (wig), *n.* an artificial covering of hair for the head, used for concealing baldness or as part of a costume.

wig·gle (wig'əl), *v.,* **wig·gled, wig·gling. 1.** to move or go with twisting or jerking movements from side to side: *The dog wiggled his ears at the sound.* *—n.* **2.** a wiggling motion.

wig·gly (wig'lē), *adj.,* **wig·gli·er, wig·gli·est. 1.** wiggling or tending to wiggle: *a wiggly child.* **2.** twisting or wavy: *a wiggly line.*

wig·wag (wig'wag'), *v.,* **wig·wagged, wig·wag·ging. 1.** to move to and fro: *to wigwag a stick.* **2.** to signal by waving two flags, lights, or the like, to and fro according to a code. *—n.* **3.** the act or process of signaling in this way. **4.** a message sent in this way.

wig·wam (wig'wom), *n.* a hut or lodge used by some American Indian tribes, usually of rounded or oval shape, made of poles with bark, mats, or skins laid across them and tied together.

Wigwam

wild (wīld), *adj.* **1.** living in a state of nature; not tamed or domesticated: *a wild animal.* **2.** growing or produced without cultivation: *wild honey.* **3.** untilled or uninhabited by civilized people: *wild country.* **4.** uncivilized; savage: *wild Indians.* **5.** furious; violent: *a wild storm.* **6.** uncontrolled; unruly; disorderly: *a gang of wild boys.* **7.** greatly excited or enthusiastic: *We were wild with delight.* **8.** reckless; fantastic; crazy: *He's full of wild schemes for getting rich.*

9. wide of the mark: *a wild guess.* —*adv.* 10. in a wild manner; without control: *He fired wild and missed.* —*n.* 11. Often, **wilds.** wilderness; wasteland: *The expedition sailed for the wilds of Africa.* —**wild′ly,** *adv.* —**wild′ness,** *n.*

wild′ boar′, a wild swine from which most of the domestic hogs are believed to be derived.

wild·cat (wīld′kat′), *n.,* *pl.* **wild·cats** *or* for def. 1 **wild·cat.** **1.** any of various wild animals that are closely related to the domestic cat, esp. the lynx. **2.** a fierce, quick-tempered person. **3.** an oil well drilled in a field where no oil has yet been found. **4.** any risky business venture. —*adj.* **5.** risky or unsound: *a wildcat bank.* **6.** lawless or irresponsible: *a wildcat strike.*

Wild boar
(3 ft. high at shoulder)

wil·de·beest (wil′də bēst′), *n.* another name for gnu.

wil·der·ness (wil′dər nis), *n.* an uninhabited and uncultivated region; wasteland; desolate place: *They built a road through the wilderness.*

wild·fire (wīld′fīər′), *n.* **1.** a substance, formerly used in warfare, that burned rapidly and was hard to put out. **2.** anything that spreads quickly over a wide area: *The news spread like wildfire.*

wild′ flow′er, **1.** the flower of any plant that grows in fields, forests, etc., without cultivation. **2.** any such plant itself. Also, **wild′flow′er.**

wild·fowl (wīld′foul′), *n.* a game bird, esp. a wild duck, goose, pheasant, etc.

wild·life (wīld′līf′), *n.* animals living in nature; wild animals: *to study the wildlife of a region.*

wile (wīl), *n.* **1.** a sly trick intended to deceive or trap a person. —*v.,* **wiled, wil·ing. 2.** to lure by wiles: *Spring fever wiled him away from his studies.*

will[1] (wil), *auxiliary verb, past tense* **would** (wo͝od). **1.** (used with subjects of the second and third persons, and often also of the first person, to indicate simple future time) plan to or expect to; am (is, are, etc.) about to or going to: *I will come right over. It will rain tomorrow.* **2.** (used with any subject to express willingness or inclination): *I will help anyone who is in need.* **3.** (used esp. with subjects of the first person to indicate determination): *We will win, no matter what the odds are against us.* **4.** (used with any subject to indicate a command): *You will release the prisoners at once.* **5.** (used with any subject to indicate probability): *They will be asleep by this time.* **6.** (used with any subject to indicate customary or habitual action): *He will sit by the fire and read for hours.* **7.** (used with any subject to indicate capability or capacity): *A camel will go for days without water.* —*v.* **8.** to wish; desire; like: *Go where you will. Show me the way, if you will.* [from the Old English word *wyllan*]

—**Usage.** See **shall.**

will[2] (wil), *n.* **1.** the power of the mind to choose and control one's own actions: *a strong will.* **2.** something chosen or decided by the will; a wish, desire, or order: *The animal obeys your will.* **3.** a strong purpose or determination: *the will to win.* **4.** the way a person feels toward another; disposition: *ill will.* **5.** a legal document in which a person declares to whom and in what way his money and property are to be given after his death. —*v.,* **willed, will·ing. 6.** to decide upon or bring about by an act of the will: *If he wills success, he can achieve it.* **7.** to compel (a person) to do or be something by the power of one's will: *He willed himself to endure the pain.* **8.** to give by means of a legal will or testament; bequeath: *He willed his fortune to his wife.* **9.** to choose or decide: *The king did as he willed.* [the noun is from the Old English word *will* "will, wish, desire," and the verb is from *willian* "to will, wish"]

will·ful (wil′fəl), *adj.* **1.** done on purpose; deliberate; intentional: *willful destruction of property.* **2.** insisting on one's own way; unreasonably stubborn: *I didn't dare refuse such a willful man.* Also, **wil′ful.** —**will′ful·ly,** *adv.* —**will′ful·ness,** *n.*

Wil·liam I (wil′yəm), *("the Conqueror")* 1027–1087, king of England 1066–1087.

Wil·liams (wil′yəmz), *n.* **Roger,** 1603?–1683, English colonist: founder of Rhode Island colony 1636.

Wil·liams·burg (wil′yəmz bûrg′), *n.* a city in SE Virginia: colonial capital of Virginia.

will·ing (wil′ing), *adj.* **1.** agreeing or consenting; favorably inclined or disposed: *We'll leave now, if you're willing.* **2.** doing one's job or one's part cheerfully: *a willing worker.* **3.** done or offered cheerfully: *to give willing assistance.* —**will′ing·ly,** *adv.* —**will′ing·ness,** *n.*

will-o'-the-wisp (wil′ə ᵺə wisp′), *n.* **1.** a light that is seen flitting about at night over marshy ground, believed to be caused by the burning of gases released by decaying vegetable matter. **2.** anything, such as an impossible hope or aim, that deceives a person by luring him on.

wil·low (wil′ō), *n.* **1.** a tree or shrub having tough, flexible twigs or branches used for wicker work. **2.** the wood of this tree.

wil·low·y (wil′ō ē), *adj.* **1.** slender and graceful: *a willowy girl.* **2.** full of willows: *a willowy shore.*

wil·ly-nil·ly (wil′ē nil′ē), *adv.* willingly or unwillingly; whether one agrees or not: *You will leave tomorrow willy-nilly.*

Wil·son (wil′sən), *n.* **1. Henry,** 1812–1875, 18th Vice President of the U.S. 1873–1875. **2. Wood·row** (wo͝od′rō), 1856–1924, 28th President of the U.S. 1913–1921. **3. Mount,** a mountain in SW California, near Pasadena: observatory. 5710 ft.

wilt[1] (wilt), *v.* **1.** to make or become limp and drooping; wither: *The flowers wilted for lack of water.* **2.** to lose or cause to lose strength or confidence: *His self-assurance wilted when he got up to speak.* [from the Middle English word *welken*]

wilt[2] (wilt), *v.* an old form of **will**[1], found now chiefly in Biblical and poetic writing and used with *thou*: *Thou wilt go hence into the land of Canaan.*

wil·y (wī′lē), *adj.*, **wil·i·er**, **wil·i·est.** full of wiles; sly; crafty; cunning: *Wily Ulysses outwitted the Cyclops.* —**wil′i·ness**, *n.*

wim·ple (wim′pəl), *n.* a cloth for covering the head and neck, leaving only the face exposed, worn chiefly by nuns.

Wimple

win (win), *v.*, **won** (wun), **win·ning.**
1. to finish first in a race, contest, or the like: *Who won the game? The home team won.* **2.** to gain a victory in a war, battle, or the like: *Our troops won the battle.* **3.** to get by effort or skill: *the satisfaction of winning a college diploma.* **4.** to succeed in reaching, esp. by great effort: *The boat finally won the opposite shore.* **5.** to gain the consent or support of; persuade (often fol. by *over*): *He refused at first, but we finally won him over.* **6.** to be successful; prevail (often fol. by *out*): *I objected strongly to removing him from the team, but his opponents won out.* —*n.* **7.** an act of winning: *We've had five wins and two losses.*

wince (wins), *v.*, **winced**, **winc·ing.** **1.** to draw back or tense the body, as from pain, fear, or a blow; flinch: *I winced when the doctor poured iodine on the cut.* —*n.* **2.** the act of wincing.

winch (winch), *n.* a machine having a drum turned by a crank, used for hoisting or hauling by means of a rope, cable, or chain.

wind¹ (wind), *n.* **1.** air that is moving, usually rather rapidly, along the earth's surface. **2.** a swift current of air; gale, storm, or hurricane. **3.** any stream of air, as produced by the breath, a fan, bellows, etc. **4.** **winds,** the wind instruments of a band or orchestra: *a beautiful melody played by the winds.* **5.** breath, or the ability to breathe: *The blow knocked the wind out of me.* **6.** a hint or suggestion: *The president got wind of the plot against him.* **7.** air carrying a scent or smell: *The deer caught the wind of the hunters, and fled.* **8.** empty or boastful talk: *His threats are just so much wind.* —*v.* **9.** to make short of breath: *The long climb winded us.* [from an Old English word, which is related to Latin *ventus*]

wind² (wīnd), *v.*, **wound** (wound), **wind·ing.** **1.** to move in a bending or curving course: *The river winds through the forest.* **2.** to coil or twine about something: *Wind the thread on the spool.* **3.** to encircle or cover about with thread, wire, or the like: *to wind a bobbin with thread.* **4.** to form (something) into a ball, cylinder, etc., by coiling or twisting it about itself: *He wound the newspaper into a tight roll.* **5.** to give power to (a clock, mechanism, etc.) by turning a key or crank (often fol. by *up*): *to wind a watch.* **6.** to make (one's way) by twisting or turning: *The troops wound their way through the jungle.* —*n.* **7.** a twisting or bending shape, course, or movement: *the many winds of the river.* **8.** a single twist or turn in winding something: *Give the crank two more winds.* **9. wind up, a.** to end or conclude: *to wind up a vaca-*

tion. **b.** (of a baseball pitcher) to make movements with the arms, legs, etc., just before throwing the ball. **c.** to make tense or excited: *We were all wound up before the game.* [from the Old English word *windan*] —**wind′er**, *n.*

wind·break (wind′brāk′), *n.* a row of trees, a fence, or the like, for providing shelter from the wind: *We planted a windbreak of poplars.*

wind′ chill′, an estimate of the actual degree of coldness felt on exposed human flesh when air temperature is combined with wind speed.

wind·fall (wind′fôl′), *n.* **1.** something blown down by the wind, such as fruit. **2.** an unexpected profit.

wind·flow·er (wind′flou′ər), *n.* See **anemone** (def. 1).

wind·ing (wīn′ding), *n.* **1.** the act of a person or thing that winds. **2.** a bending or turning: *the winding of the forest trail.* **3.** something wound or coiled about something else: *the winding of an electromagnet.* —*adj.* **4.** bending or turning: *a winding stream.*

wind′ in′strument (wind), a musical instrument sounded by the breath or the force of air, such as the clarinet, flute, or trumpet.

wind·jam·mer (wind′jam′ər), *n. Informal.* any large sailing ship.

wind·lass (wind′ləs), *n.* a device for hauling or hoisting, usually having a horizontal drum or bar on which a rope attached to the load is wound; winch.

wind·mill (wind′mil′), *n.* any of various machines for grinding grain, pumping water, etc., driven by the force of the wind blowing against a number of sails or vanes attached to a shaft mounted at or near the top of a tower.

Windmill

win·dow (win′dō), *n.* **1.** an opening in a wall or other surface, such as the side of a car, train, etc., for letting in light or air, or for looking through. **2.** a frame with one or more panes of glass, set in such an opening. **3.** anything that provides a view of something: *The eyes are the windows of the soul.* [from the Middle English word *windowe*, which comes from a Scandinavian word meaning literally "wind eye"] —**win′dow·like′**, *adj.*

win·dow·pane (win′dō pān′), *n.* a plate of glass set in the frame of a window.

win·dow-shop (win′dō shop′), *v.*, **win·dow-shopped, win·dow-shop·ping.** to look at articles displayed in shop windows, usually without intending to buy anything. —**win′dow-shop′per**, *n.*

wind·pipe (wind′pīp′), *n.* the tube connecting the throat to the lungs, through which the air passes in breathing. See illus. at **lung**.

wind·row (wind′rō′), *n.* a row or line of hay,

sheaves of grain, etc., left to dry before being raked into heaps.

wind·shield (wind′shēld′), *n.* a sheet of glass, plastic, etc., set in the front of an automobile, motorcycle, or the like, allowing a view of the way ahead while giving protection from the wind.

Wind·sor (win′zər), *n.* **1.** a member of the present British royal family. **2.** a city in S Ontario, in SE Canada, opposite Detroit, Michigan.

Wind′sor chair′, *(sometimes l.c.)* a wooden chair having a spindle back and legs slanting outward: used esp. in 18th-century England and in the American colonies.

wind·storm (wind′stôrm′), *n.* a storm with heavy wind, but little or no rain.

wind·up (wīnd′up′), *n.* **1.** the conclusion of any activity; end or close: *the windup of business at the end of the season.* **2.** (in baseball) the movements of the body, arms, and legs of a pitcher in preparing to throw the ball.

wind·ward (wind′wərd), *adj.* **1.** located or moving in the direction from which the wind is blowing (opposite of *leeward*): *a cabin on the windward side of the ship.* —*n.* **2.** the point or direction from which the wind blows. **3.** the side toward the wind. —*adv.* **4.** toward the wind.

Wind′ward Is′lands, a group of islands in the SE West Indies.

wind·y (win′dē), *adj.,* **wind·i·er, wind·i·est. 1.** having or marked by wind: *a windy day.* **2.** exposed to the wind: *a windy hilltop.* **3.** talking a great deal, esp. in an empty, boastful, or boring manner: *a windy speaker; a windy speech.* —**wind′i·ness,** *n.*

wine (wīn), *n.* **1.** any of various alcoholic beverages made from the fermented juice of grapes. **2.** any of various similar beverages made from the fermented or unfermented juice of other fruits or plants: *blackberry wine.* **3.** a dark, purplish red. —*adj.* **4.** of a dark reddish color. —*v.,* **wined, win·ing. 5.** to serve wine to; entertain with wine. **6.** to drink wine. [from the Old English word *win,* which comes from Latin *vinum*]

wing (wing), *n.* **1.** either of the two appendages or parts of most birds and insects and of bats, etc., that are used for flying. **2.** anything resembling a wing in shape or use. **3.** one of the main supporting surfaces of an airplane. **4.** a part of a building projecting on one side of a central or main part: *to enlarge a house by adding a wing.* **5.** either of the two side portions of an army or fleet in battle formation. **6.** either of the spaces that extend out from the right and left sides of a stage: *The actors wait in the wings for their cues.* **7.** a political group holding leftist or rightist views. —*v.* **8.** to travel on wings; fly: *Birds winged across the sky.* **9.** to give wings to; enable to fly or move rapidly: *The sight of home winged their weary feet.* **10.** to wound or disable slightly, esp. in the wing or arm. **11. on the wing,** in flight; flying: *a bird on the wing.* **12. under one's wing,** under one's protection or care: *to take a stray cat under one's wing.* —**wing′like′,** *adj.*

wing′ chair′, a large upholstered chair having a short part that projects forward at each side of the back.

winged (wingd), *adj.* **1.** having wings. **2.** having a winglike part or parts: *a winged seed.* **3.** moving swiftly, as if on wings.

wing·less (wing′lis), *adj.* having no wings or wings that are too small to be of use.

Wing chair

wing·spread (wing′spred′), *n.* the distance from tip to tip of the outspread wings of a bird or other winged animal or object.

wink (wingk), *v.* **1.** to close and open one or both eyes quickly; blink. **2.** to close and open one eye quickly, as a hint or signal. **3.** to flash or twinkle: *The lights winked in the shop windows.* —*n.* **4.** the act of winking. **5.** a winking movement of the eye, in giving a hint or signal. **6.** a very brief time; an instant.

win·ner (win′ər), *n.* a person or thing that wins.

win·ning (win′ing), *n.* **1.** the act of a person or thing that wins. **2.** Usually, **winnings.** something won, esp. money. —*adj.* **3.** that wins; victorious: *the winning team in a game.* **4.** charming; pleasing: *a winning smile.* —**win′ning·ly,** *adv.*

Win·ni·peg (win′ə peg′), *n.* **1.** the capital city of Manitoba, in S Canada. **2. Lake,** a lake in S Canada, in Manitoba. 9300 sq. mi.

win·now (win′ō), *v.* **1.** to separate (grain) from chaff, esp. by throwing it into the air and allowing the wind to carry away the lighter particles. **2.** to drive (chaff) away from grain by such methods. **3.** to sort or sift out carefully: *to winnow the truth from the lies.* —**win′now·er,** *n.*

win·some (win′səm), *adj.* charming; attractive: *a winsome girl; a winsome manner.* [from the Old English word *wynsum,* which comes from *wyn* "joy" + the suffix *-sum* "full of." See *-some*] —**win′some·ly,** *adv.* —**win′some·ness,** *n.*

Win·ston-Sa·lem (win′stən sā′ləm), *n.* a city in N North Carolina.

win·ter (win′tər), *n.* **1.** the cold season between autumn and spring, usually between December 21st and March 21st. —*adj.* **2.** characteristic of or suitable for winter: *winter storms; winter clothing.* —*v.* **3.** to spend the winter: *Animals winter in the lowlands.*

win·ter·green (win′tər grēn′), *n.* a small, creeping evergreen shrub, having white, bell-shaped flowers, a red, berrylike fruit, and sweet-smelling leaves that yield an oil used as a flavoring.

win·ter·time (win′tər tīm′), *n.* the season of winter.

win·try (win′trē), *adj.* of, referring to, or resembling winter or winter weather: *wintry winds; a wintry expression.* —**win′tri·ness,** *n.*

wipe (wīp), *v.,* **wiped, wip·ing. 1.** to rub lightly with a cloth, paper, the hand, etc., in order to clean or dry: *to wipe the floor with a dry mop.* **2.** to remove by rubbing with or on something (usually fol. by *away, off,* etc.): *Wipe the mud off your shoes.* **3.** to drive out or away; banish; erase: *Wipe that smile off* *your face!* **4.** to put on or apply by rubbing with a cloth or the like: *to wipe polish on one's shoes.* —*n.* **5.** the act of wiping; a stroke or rub, as in wiping: *She gave the furniture a few quick wipes.* **6. wipe out, a.** to destroy; demolish: *An entire city was wiped out by the earthquake.* **b.** *Informal.* to murder; kill. —**wip′er,** *n.*

wire (wīᵊr), *n.* **1.** a long, slender thread of metal. **2.** a sheet or sheets of material woven from such threads, used for screens, fences, cages, etc. **3.** one or more threads of metal twisted or laid together and covered with an insulating material, used for carrying electric current. **4.** a long wire or cable used in telegraph or telephone systems. **5.** *Informal.* the telegraphic system: *to send a message by wire.* **6.** a telegram or cablegram. —*v.,* **wired, wir·ing. 7.** to furnish with wires: *to wire a fence.* **8.** to install wires or wiring in: *to wire a house for electricity.* **9.** to fasten or bind with wire: *to wire a broken jaw.* **10.** *Informal.* to send (a message, money, flowers, etc.) by telegraph. **11. hold the wire,** to wait at the telephone for some action to be completed by the person one is talking to: *Hold the wire and I'll see if he's here yet.* **12. under the wire,** just before a deadline, limit, or the like: *He got his application in under the wire.* —**wire′like′,** *adj.*

wire·hair (wīᵊr′hâr′), *n.* a fox terrier having a wiry coat. Also, **wire′-haired ter′rier.**

wire-haired (wīᵊr′hârd′), *adj.* having coarse, stiff, wirelike hair.

wire·less (wīᵊr′lis), *adj.* **1.** having no wire. **2.** of or referring to means of communication by radio waves, without the use of wires: *wireless telegraphy.* —*n.* **3.** a wireless telephone or telegraph system of communication. **4.** a wireless transmitting or receiving apparatus. **5.** *Chiefly British.* **a.** a radio. **b.** a wireless message. —*v.* **6.** to send (a message) by wireless.

Wirehair
(15½ in. high at shoulder)

wir·ing (wīᵊr′ing), *n.* **1.** the act or process of installing electrical or other kinds of wires. **2.** a system of wires for carrying electric current in a building, apparatus, etc.

wir·y (wīᵊr′ē), *adj.,* **wir·i·er, wir·i·est. 1.** made of or resembling wire: *wiry hair.* **2.** strong and lean: *a wiry acrobat.* —**wir′i·ness,** *n.*

Wis., Wisc., Wisconsin. Also, **Wisc.**

Wis·con·sin (wis kon′sən), *n.* a state in the N central United States. 56,154 sq. mi. *Cap.:* Madison. —**Wis·con′sin·ite′,** *n.*

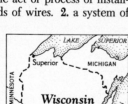

Wisconsin

wis·dom (wiz′dəm), *n.* **1.** the quality or state of being wise. **2.** the ability to judge what is true or right,

based on knowledge and experience. **3.** wise sayings or teachings: *the wisdom of Confucius.*

wis′dom tooth′, the last molar on each side of the upper and lower jaws. Wisdom teeth are the last teeth to break through the gums, usually appearing between the ages of 17 and 22.

wise¹ (wīz), *adj.,* **wis·er, wis·est. 1.** having wide knowledge and experience; able to judge properly what is true or right: *a wise old statesman.* **2.** showing or based on good judgment: *a wise decision.* **3.** having much learning; well-informed: *The hunter is wise in the ways of jungle beasts.* **4.** *Slang.* aware; in the know; informed: *He's wise to your tricks.* **5.** *Slang.* too bold and disrespectful: *Don't be so wise!* [from the Old English word *wīs*] —**wise′ly,** *adv.*

wise² (wīz), *n.* way or manner: *He is in no wise sorry.* [from an Old English word meaning "way, manner"]

-wise, a suffix used to form adverbs meaning **1.** in the direction of: *sidewise.* **2.** in the position of: *edgewise.* **3.** in the manner of: *clockwise; likewise.* **4.** with regard to: *moneywise.*

wise·crack (wīz′krak′), *Informal.* —*n.* **1.** a joke or witty remark, often one showing disrespect or contempt. —*v.* **2.** to make wisecracks.

wish (wish), *v.* **1.** to feel a longing or craving for; want; desire: *I wish peace and rest. I wish to travel.* **2.** to desire a person or thing to be, have, or do something: *I wish you good luck.* **3.** to request or command: *I wish you to be more respectful.* —*n.* **4.** a want, desire, longing, or craving: *My wish is for you to be happy.* **5.** a request or command: *It is the king's wish that you set sail at once.* **6.** an expression of a wish or hope: *to send best wishes.* **7.** something wished or desired: *Did you get your wish?* **8. wish on, a.** to force or impose: *I wouldn't wish that job on my worst enemy.* **b.** Also, **wish upon.** to make a wish using (an object) as a charm: *to wish on a star.*

wish·bone (wish′bōn′), *n.* a V-shaped bone located in front of the breastbone of most birds: often used in a game in which two persons each grasp a tip of the bone and snap it in two, the one holding the longer piece supposedly getting his wish.

wish·ful (wish′fəl), *adj.* **1.** having or expressing a wish; hopeful; desirous: *to be wishful of success.* **2.** based on wish or fancy, rather than facts: *wishful thinking.* —**wish′ful·ly,** *adv.* —**wish′ful·ness,** *n.*

wish·y-wash·y (wish′ē wosh′ē, -wô′shē), *adj.* **1.** (of liquids) thin and weak; watery: *wishy-washy coffee.* **2.** lacking in vigor or definiteness; weak or feeble: *a wishy-washy attempt to clean house.*

wisp (wisp), *n.* **1.** a small bunch or handful of straw, hay, or the like. **2.** a small tuft, as of hair, thread, or the like. **3.** a thin puff, as of smoke. **4.** a person or thing that is small or delicate: *a mere wisp of a girl.*

wis·te·ri·a (wi stēr′ē ə), *n.* a climbing shrub, related to the bean, having clusters of blue-violet, white, purple, or pink flowers. Also, **wis·tar′i·a.** [named in honor of C. *Wistar* (1761–1818), American anatomist]

wist·ful (wist′fəl), *adj.* 1. feeling or showing longing; wishful; yearning: *a wistful look.* 2. sadly thoughtful; pensive: *wistful eyes.* —wist′ful·ly, *adv.* —wist′ful·ness, *n.*

wit[1] (wit), *n.* 1. cleverness in using words or expressing ideas. 2. speech or writing that shows such ability. 3. a person having such an ability. 4. understanding, intelligence, or judgment. 5. Usually, **wits.** mental balance or sanity: *to be scared out of one's wits.* 6. **keep one's wits about one,** to remain calm and alert; be prepared for or equal to anything: *When driving in the rain, you'd best keep your wits about you.* [from Old English; related to *wit*[2]]

wit[2] (wit), *v.* 1. *Archaic.* to know. 2. **to wit,** that is to say; namely: *It was the time of the vernal equinox, to wit, the beginning of spring.* [from the Old English word *witan* "to know"]

witch (wich), *n.* 1. a woman who professes or is supposed to practice magic, esp. black magic; sorceress. 2. an ugly old woman; hag.

witch·craft (wich′kraft′), *n.* the art or practices of a witch; sorcery; magic.

witch′ doc′tor, (in some primitive societies) a man who attempts to cure sickness and to drive away evil spirits by the use of magic.

witch·er·y (wich′ə rē), *n., pl.* **witch·er·ies.** 1. witchcraft or magic. 2. fascination or charm: *the witchery of her beauty.*

witch′ ha′zel, 1. a shrub of eastern North America, having small, yellow flowers. 2. a liquid extracted from the leaves or bark of this plant, mixed with water and alcohol and used as a soothing lotion for the skin. [*witch* is another spelling of Middle English *wyche,* the name of a kind of elm]

with (wiᵬ, wiᵬ), *prep.* 1. accompanied by; accompanying: *I will go with you.* 2. in relation to (used esp. to suggest an association, connection, etc.): *to deal with a problem; to talk with someone.* 3. having or showing: *a man with ambition.* 4. by means of; by use of: *to cut with a knife; a coat lined with silk.* 5. containing or having: *tea with lemon.* 6. using or showing: *to work with diligence.* 7. in comparison or proportion to: *Their power increased with their numbers.* 8. in regard to: *to be pleased with a gift.* 9. because of: *to turn white with fear.* 10. in the region or sphere of; among: *It's day with us while it's night with the Chinese.* 11. from: *to part with something.* 12. against: *He fought with his brother over the money.* 13. in the keeping or service of: *to leave something with a friend.* 14. in the opinion or judgment of: *Her argument carried weight with the judges.* 15. at the same time as: *He went home with the coming of dark.* 16. immediately after; upon: *And with that last remark, she turned and left.* 17. of the same opinion as: *Are you with me or against me?* 18. as well as: *He can play football with the best of them.* 19. having been given: *With his parents' consent, he took a long trip.* 20. in spite of: *With all his wealth, he leads a simple life.* 21. in the same direction as: *We were driving with the traffic.* 22. **with child,** expecting a child; pregnant.

with·al (wiᵬ ôl′, wiᵬ-), *adv. Archaic.* 1. with it all; as well; besides. 2. with that; nevertheless.

with·draw (wiᵬ drô′, wiᵬ-), *v.,* **with·drew** (wiᵬ-drōō′, wiᵬ-), **with·drawn** (wiᵬ drôn′, wiᵬ-), **with·draw·ing.** 1. to draw back or away; remove: *He withdrew his savings from the bank.* 2. to go or move back or away; retire; retreat: *to withdraw from a contest.* 3. to retract or recall: *to withdraw a remark.* —with·draw′al, *n.*

with·drawn (wiᵬ drôn′, wiᵬ-), *v.* 1. the past participle of **withdraw.** —adj. 2. shy or quiet; retiring.

with·er (wiᵬ′ər), *v.* 1. to become or cause to become shrunken, faded, dry, or lifeless: *The grapes withered on the vine. The drought withered the buds.* 2. to cause a feeling of shame; affect harmfully: *a withering look; to wither one's hopes.*

with·ers (wiᵬ′ərz), *n. (used as pl.)* the highest part of the back, at the base of the neck, of a horse, cow, sheep, etc.

with·hold (wiᵬ hōld′, wiᵬ-), *v.,* **with·held** (wiᵬ-held′, wiᵬ-), **with·hold·ing.** 1. to hold back; restrain or check. 2. to refrain from giving or granting: *to withhold payment.*

with·in (wiᵬ in′, wiᵬ-), *adv.* 1. in or into the inner part; inside: *The main office is within.* 2. in or into a house, building, etc.; indoors: *A fire burned on the hearth within.* 3. in the mind, heart, or soul; inwardly. —prep. 4. inside of; in: *within a city; within a room.* 5. in the limits of; not beyond: *to live within one's income; within the law.* 6. at or to some point not beyond: *within a radius of a mile.*

with·out (wiᵬ out′, wiᵬ-), *prep.* 1. with the absence, omission, or avoidance of; lacking: *without help; without shoes.* 2. free from: *a world without hunger.* 3. at, on, or to the outside of: *both within and without the city.* 4. beyond the limits, range, or scope of: *to operate without the law.* —adv. 5. in or into an outer place; outside. 6. outside a house, building, etc.; out of doors: *The car is waiting without.*

with·stand (wiᵬ stand′, wiᵬ-), *v.,* **with·stood** (wiᵬ-stōōd′, wiᵬ-), **with·stand·ing.** to stand or hold out against; resist or oppose, esp. successfully: *to withstand invaders; to withstand rust.*

wit·less (wit′lis), *adj.* lacking wit or intelligence; stupid; foolish.

wit·ness (wit′nis), *v.* 1. to see or have knowledge of by being present: *to witness an accident.* 2. to be present at (an event) as a formal witness, spectator, etc.: *to witness a wedding.* 3. to testify to or give evidence of: *Her blush witnessed her embarrassment.* 4. to testify to the genuineness of (a document) by signing it: *to witness a person's will.* —n. 5. a person who, being present, sees or personally knows a thing; beholder; spectator. 6. a person or thing that gives or can give evidence. 7. a person who gives testimony, as in a court of law. 8. a person who signs a document as testimony that it is genuine. 9. proof or evidence: *His behavior bears witness to his good intentions.* 10. testimony: *to give false witness in a trial.*

wit·ted (wit′id), *adj.* having wit or wits (usually used in combination): *quick-witted; slow-witted.*

wit·ti·cism (wit′i siz′əm), *n.* a witty remark or sentence.

wit·ty (wit′ē), *adj.,* **wit·ti·er, wit·ti·est.** having or characterized by wit; amusingly clever: *a witty writer; a witty remark.* **—wit′ti·ness,** *n.*

wives (wīvz), *n.* the plural of **wife.**

wiz·ard (wiz′ərd), *n.* **1.** a man who professes to practice magic; magician or sorcerer. **2.** *Informal.* a very skilled or clever person: *a wizard at chemistry.*

wiz·ened (wiz′ənd), *adj.* shriveled and dried up as from age; withered: *a wizened face.*

wk., **1.** week. **2.** work.

WNW, west-northwest. Also, **W.N.W.**

wob·ble (wob′əl), *v.,* **wob·bled, wob·bling. 1.** to move or cause to move unsteadily from side to side: *The table wobbled on its uneven legs.* **2.** to hesitate or waver; be undecided. **—n. 3.** a wobbling motion. Also, **wabble.**

wob′bly (wob′lē), *adj.,* **wob·bli·er, wob·bli·est.** shaky or insteady: *a wobbly chair that almost collapsed.* **—wob′bli·ness,** *n.*

woe (wō), *n.* great sorrow, distress, affliction, or trouble: *She suffered a fall, among her other woes.*

woe·be·gone (wō′bi gôn′, -gon′), *adj.* overcome with or expressing woe: *a woebegone look.*

woe·ful (wō′fəl), *adj.* **1.** full of woe; wretched; unhappy: *a woeful farewell speech.* **2.** causing woe or wretchedness: *woeful news.* **3.** of very poor quality: *a woeful selection of dress goods.* **—woe′ful·ly,** *adv.*

woke (wōk), *v.* a past tense of **wake.**

wok·en (wō′kən), *v.* a past participle of **wake.**

wolf (woŏlf), *n., pl.* **wolves** (woŏlvz). any of several large animals, related to the dog, usually hunting in packs.

wolf·hound (woŏlf′hound′), *n.* any of several large dogs originally used in hunting wolves.

wol·ver·ine (woŏl′və rēn′), *n.* a strong, stocky animal of North America, related to the weasel, having blackish, shaggy hair with white markings.

Wolverine
(14 in. high at shoulder)

wom·an (woŏm′ən), *n., pl.* **wom·en** (wim′in). **1.** an adult female person. **2.** a female attendant, housekeeper, or servant. **3.** women considered as a group. [from the Old English word *wīfman,* which comes from *wīf* "female, wife" + *man* "human being"]

wom·an·hood (woŏm′ən hoŏd′), *n.* **1.** the state of being a woman; womanly character or qualities. **2.** women considered as a group.

wom·an·ish (woŏm′ə nish), *adj.* **1.** womanlike or feminine. **2.** (of a man) effeminate.

wo·man·kind (woŏm′ən kīnd′), *n.* women, as distinguished from men; the female sex.

wom·an·ly (woŏm′ən lē), *adj.* like, befitting, or be-

coming a woman; having feminine qualities; not masculine or girlish: *womanly grace.*

womb (woŏm), *n.* the part of the body of female mammals in which the young develop before birth; uterus.

wom·bat (wom′bat), *n.* any of several burrowing animals of Australia. The female wombat carries her young in a pouch.

wom·en (wim′in), *n.* the plural of **woman.**

wom·en·folk (wim′in fōk′), *n.* *(used as pl.)* **1.** women in general; all women. **2.** the women of a particular group or family.

wom′en's libera′tion, a social movement concerned with gaining rights and opportunities for women equal to those of men.

won (wun), *v.* the past tense and past participle of **win.**

won·der (wun′dər), *v.* **1.** to think curiously about; be curious to know: *to wonder about the origin of the earth; to wonder what happened.* **2.** to be filled with surprise, amazement, or awe; marvel (usually fol. by *at*): *He wondered at her self-control in such a crisis.* **— n. 3.** something that is strange and surprising: *the seven wonders of the world.* **4.** a feeling, as of curiosity, amazement, awe, or the like, aroused by what is strange and surprising.

won·der·ful (wun′dər fəl), *adj.* **1.** causing or arousing wonder: *The Grand Canyon is a wonderful sight.* **2.** excellent; extremely good: *a wonderful party.* **—won′der·ful·ly,** *adv.*

won·der·land (wun′dər land′), *n.* a land of wonders or marvels.

won·der·ment (wun′dər mənt), *n.* wonder or surprise.

won·drous (wun′drəs), *adj.* **1.** wonderful or remarkable. **—adv. 2.** *Archaic.* remarkably: *wondrous wise.*

wont (wônt, wōnt), *adj.* **1.** accustomed; used: *He was wont to wake up early.* **—n. 2.** custom, habit, or practice: *It was his wont to eat an early lunch.*

won't (wōnt, wunt), contraction of *will not.*

wont·ed (wôn′tid, wōn′tid, wun′tid), *adj.* customary, habitual, or usual: *He sat in his wonted place.*

woo (woŏ), *v.* **1.** to seek the favor, affection, or love of, esp. with a view to marriage; court. **2.** to seek to win: *to woo fame.* **3.** to seek to persuade (a person, group, etc.); try to gain the favor or approval of: *The candidate knew how to woo the crowd.*

wood (woŏd), *n.* **1.** the hard, fibrous substance that composes most of the stem and branches of a tree or shrub. **2.** this substance when made suitable for building or other purposes; timber or lumber. **3.** (in music) a woodwind. **4.** Usually, **woods.** a grove or forest. **—adj. 5.** made of wood; wooden. **6.** dwelling or growing in woods: *a wood bird.*

wood′ al′cohol, a colorless, poisonous, flammable liquid, used as a solvent, antifreeze, and fuel.

wood·bine (woŏd′bīn′), *n.* any of various climbing or trailing plants, such as the European honeysuckle or the Virginia creeper.

wood·chuck (wŏŏd′chuk′), *n.* a stocky, burrowing, North American marmot that hibernates in the winter; ground hog. [from the Algonquian word *wuchak* "fisher, marten, weasel"]

wood·cock (wŏŏd′kok′), *n.* a game bird having a long bill, short legs, and large eyes placed far back on the head.

wood·craft (wŏŏd′kraft′), *n.* 1. skill in anything concerning the woods or forest, such as hunting, trapping, etc. 2. the art of making or carving wooden objects.

Woodchuck
(total length 2 ft.)

wood·cut (wŏŏd′kut′), *n.* 1. a carved block of wood for making prints. 2. a print from such a block.

wood·cut·ter (wŏŏd′kut′ər), *n.* a person who cuts down trees or chops wood.

wood·ed (wŏŏd′id), *adj.* covered with or abounding in trees: *a wooded acre.*

wood·en (wŏŏd′ən), *adj.* 1. made of wood; wood: *a wooden ship.* 2. stiff or awkward: *a wooden piece of writing.* 3. dull or stupid: *a wooden stare.*

wood′ i′bis, any of several storks having white feathers on the body, a featherless head, and a curved bill.

wood·land (wŏŏd′land′, -lənd), *n.* 1. land covered with woods or trees. —*adj.* (wŏŏd′lənd). 2. of, concerning, or living in the woods.

wood·man (wŏŏd′mən), *n., pl.* **wood·men.** 1. a person who cuts down timber, esp. for fuel. 2. a person in charge of caring for a forest. 3. a woodsman.

wood·peck·er (wŏŏd′pek′ər), *n.* any of numerous birds having stiff tail feathers that help it to climb trees, and a hard, sharp bill that it hammers into the wood of trees in search of insects.

wood·pile (wŏŏd′pīl′), *n.* a pile or stack of firewood.

wood·shed (wŏŏd′shed′), *n.* a shed for keeping wood for fuel.

woods·man (wŏŏdz′mən), *n., pl.* **woods·men.** a man accustomed to life in the woods and skilled in woodcraft.

Redcrested
woodpecker
(length 17
to 19 in.)

wood′ thrush′, a large thrush common in the woodlands of eastern North America, noted for its loud, clear song.

wood·wind (wŏŏd′wind′), *n.* 1. any of the group of wind instruments that includes the flutes, clarinets, oboes, bassoons, and occasionally the saxophones. 2. **woodwinds,** the woodwind section of an orchestra or band. —*adj.* 3. of, concerning, or composed for woodwinds.

wood·work (wŏŏd′wûrk′), *n.* objects or parts made of wood, such as doors, stairways, moldings, etc.

wood·work·ing (wŏŏd′wûr′kiṅg), *n.* the act or art of making things of wood.

wood·y (wŏŏd′ē), *adj.,* **wood·i·er, wood·i·est.** 1. cov-

ered with woods; wooded. 2. consisting of or containing wood. 3. resembling wood, as in appearance, toughness, etc. —**wood′i·ness,** *n.*

woof (wŏŏf, wŏŏf), *n.* 1. Also, **weft.** (in woven fabrics) the yarn or threads carried by the shuttle of a loom from side to side across the threads of the warp. 2. fabric or the texture of fabric.

wool (wŏŏl), *n.* 1. the fine, soft, curly hair that forms the fleece of sheep and certain other animals. 2. yarn, fabric, or garments made of sheep's wool. 3. something having fine fibers resembling sheep's wool: *steel wool.* 4. *Informal.* human hair, esp. when short, thick, and curly. —*adj.* 5. made or consisting of wool: *a wool sweater.* 6. **pull the wool over someone's eyes,** to deceive or trick someone: *He thinks he's clever, but he can't pull the wool over my eyes.*

wool·en (wŏŏl′ən), *adj.* 1. made or consisting of wool: *woolen cloth.* 2. of or concerning wool or fabric made of wool: *a woolen mill.* —*n.* 3. **woolens,** wool cloth or clothing. Also, *British,* **wool′len.**

wool·gath·er·ing (wŏŏl′gath′ər iṅg), *n.* daydreaming or absentmindedness.

wool·ly (wŏŏl′ē), *adj.,* **wool·li·er, wool·li·est.** 1. consisting or made of wool: *woolly fleece.* 2. resembling wool: *woolly hair.* 3. clothed or covered in wool or something resembling wool: *a woolly caterpillar.* 4. *Informal.* rough and vigorous: *a wild and woolly frontier town.* 5. fuzzy or unclear: *woolly thinking.* —*n., pl.* **wool·lies.** 6. Usually, **woollies.** heavy, knitted underwear of wool.

Worces·ter (wŏŏs′tər), *n.* a city in central Massachusetts.

word (wûrd), *n.* 1. (in grammar) one or a sequence of speech sounds that makes up one of the smallest complete and independent units of meaning. 2. the written or printed letters or characters that stand for such a unit: *The telegram has 10 words.* 3. a brief statement or remark: *a word of praise.* 4. a short talk or conversation: *I'd like a word with you.* 5. **words,** angry speech; a quarrel: *They are fond of each other, but sometimes they have words.* 6. news or information. 7. assurance or promise: *to give one's word.* 8. a signal or command: *The teacher gave the word to begin the test.* 9. **the Word, a.** the Bible. **b.** the message of the gospel of Christ. —*v.* 10. to express in words; put into words: *He words his thoughts poorly.* 11. **eat one's words,** to take back something one has said: *I said he'd never make the team, but I had to eat my words.* 12. **take one at one's word,** to accept what one has said as true: *How could you take him at his word after the lies he's told?*

word·ing (wûr′diṅg), *n.* the manner in which something is expressed; choice of words; phrasing.

Words·worth (wûrdz′wûrth′), *n.* **William,** 1770–1850, English poet: poet laureate 1843–1850.

word·y (wûr′dē), *adj.,* **word·i·er, word·i·est.** using or having many, or too many, words: *a wordy explanation.* —**word′i·ness,** *n.*

wore (wôr), *v.* the past tense of **wear.**

work (wûrk), *n.* 1. effort made in order to produce or accomplish something; labor; toil. 2. something to be made or done; something that requires effort or labor; job or task: *The students finished their work in class.* **3.** employment as a means of earning one's living; occupation or profession: *to look for work.* **4.** the result of labor or effort; deed or achievement: *He is known for his good works.* **5.** a product of labor or activity: *a work of art.* **6.** place of employment: *to ride a bus to work.* **7. works, a.** a place for carrying on some labor or industry (usually used in combination): *ironworks.* **b.** the internal, moving parts or machinery of something: *the works of a watch.* **8.** (in physics) the effect produced by the use of energy. **9. the works,** *Slang.* the entirety of something; everything: *two hotdogs with ketchup, mustard, and the works.* —*v.* **10.** to do or cause to do work: *Does she work for a living? The company works its employees hard.* **11.** to be employed, esp. as a means of earning a living: *He hasn't worked for six weeks.* **12.** to act or operate properly; cause to operate: *The plan worked. Can you work this machine?* **13.** to bring about (a result) by or as if by work; cause: *to work a change.* **14.** to reach or cause to reach a specified condition, as if by continuous effort: *The nails have worked loose.* **15.** to achieve or win by effort: *He expects to work his way through college.* **16.** to make, fashion, shape, or prepare by work: *to work clay into a vase.* **17.** to make way with effort or under stress: *The ship works to windward.* **18.** to ferment, as a liquid. **19.** to solve: *to work an arithmetic problem.* **20.** to carry on operations in (a city, district, etc.): *The company has a dozen salesmen to work the South.* **21. at work, a.** at one's job or place of business: *Can't I phone him at work?* **b.** in operation, or performing one's job: *to watch a printing press at work.* **22. out of work,** without a job; unemployed. **23. work out, a.** to end satisfactorily: *Did that difficulty at school work out?* **b.** to find the solution of: *Help me work out this problem.* **c.** to become loose or separated: *The bolt worked out of the lock.* **d.** to amount to a total: *The whole thing works out to $19.* **e.** to exercise or train, esp. for athletic competition: *He works out every morning before breakfast.*

work·a·ble (wûr′kə bəl), *adj.* capable of being worked or carried out.

work·a·day (wûr′kə dā′), *adj.* **1.** of or suitable for working days. **2.** ordinary or commonplace.

work·bench (wûrk′bench′), *n.* a sturdy table at which an artisan works.

work·book (wûrk′book′), *n.* **1.** a book of instructions for operating a machine. **2.** a book containing questions, exercises, etc., intended to guide the work of a student in studying a certain subject.

work·day (wûrk′dā′), *n.* **1.** a day on which work is done; working day. **2.** the part of a day during which a person works: *a workday of seven hours.*

work·er (wûr′kər), *n.* **1.** a person who works. **2.** any of a class of ants, bees, wasps, or termites that cannot reproduce and that do most of the work in a colony or hive. See illus. at **bee.**

work·ing (wûr′king), *n.* **1.** the act of a person or thing that works. **2.** operation or action: *the working of a machine.* —*adj.* **3.** doing some form of work or labor, as for a living: *a working mother.* **4.** of, for, or concerning work: *working clothes; a working day.* **5.** good enough to be useful or effective: *a working knowledge of a foreign language.*

work·ing·man (wûr′king man′), *n., pl.* **work·ing·men.** a man who earns his living at some manual or industrial work.

work·man (wûrk′mən), *n., pl.* **work·men. 1.** a man employed or skilled in some craft. **2.** a workingman.

work·man·ship (wûrk′mən ship′), *n.* **1.** the art or skill of a workman. **2.** the quality or manner of work done: *The furniture was of fine workmanship.* **3.** the product or result of the labor or skill of a workman.

work·out (wûrk′out′), *n.* **1.** an athletic practice or trial session. **2.** physical exercise: *a workout in the gym.*

work·room (wûrk′room′, -room′), *n.* a room in which work is done.

work·shop (wûrk′shop′), *n.* **1.** a room or building in which work, esp. mechanical work, is carried on. **2.** a group of people who discuss, study, or work together on a project: *a theater workshop; an opera workshop.*

world (wûrld), *n.* **1.** the earth, considered as a planet. **2.** a particular division of the earth: *the New World.* **3.** a particular time or era in human history: *the ancient world.* **4.** mankind; the human race: *The world must try to eliminate war.* **5.** the public generally: *The whole world knows it.* **6.** the whole system of created things; the universe. **7.** a particular class of mankind, with common interests, aims, etc.: *the fashionable world.* **8.** society; secular or social life: *He withdrew from the world to practice his religion.* **9.** a general grouping of natural things: *the animal world.* **10.** any heavenly body. **11.** any sphere or state of existence: *the world to come.* **12.** a very great quantity or extent: *The rain will do the crops a world of good.* **13. come into the world,** to be born: *He came into the world in 1958.* **14. think the world of,** to be very fond of; admire greatly: *We think the world of that family.*

world·ly (wûrld′lē), *adj.,* **world·li·er, world·li·est. 1.** of or concerning this world as contrasted with heaven, spiritual life, etc. **2.** devoted to or concerned with the affairs, interests, or pleasures of this world: *a worldly man.* —**world′li·ness,** *n.*

World War I, the war, fought mainly in Europe and the Middle East, from 1914 to 1918 between France, Great Britain, Russia, the U.S., and their allies on one side and Germany, Austria-Hungary, Turkey, and their allies on the other.

World War II, the war, fought in Europe, N Africa, and the Pacific, from 1939 to 1945 between the Allies (Great Britain, France, the U.S., and Russia) and the Axis (Germany, Italy, and Japan).

world-wide (wûrld′wīd′), *adj.* extending throughout the world. Also, **world′wide′.**

worm (wûrm), *n.* **1.** any of numerous long, slender, legless creeping animals, such as earthworms, tapeworms, or the like. **2.** something resembling a worm in appearance, such as the thread of a screw. **3.** a contemptible person. **4. worms,** *(used as sing.)* a disease caused by parasitic worms in the intestines or in various tissues. —*v.* **5.** to move or act like a worm; creep or crawl slowly. **6.** to get by persistent and stealthy efforts (usually fol. by *out* or *from*): *to worm a secret out of a person.* **7.** to free from worms: *He wormed the puppies.* [from the Old English word *wyrm,* which is related to Latin *vermis*]

worm' gear', a gear wheel driven by a rotating cylinder.

worm·wood (wûrm'wŏŏd'), *n.* **1.** any of a number of herbs or plants of the Old World, having an aromatic smell and bitter taste. **2.** something very disappointing or unpleasant.

Worm gear

worm·y (wûr'mē), *adj.,* **worm·i·er, worm·i·est. 1.** containing worms. **2.** damaged by worms. —**worm'i·ness,** *n.*

worn (wôrn), *v.* **1.** the past participle of **wear.** —*adj.* **2.** damaged or lessened in value through use: *worn tires; a worn cuff.* **3.** wearied or exhausted.

worn-out (wôrn'out'), *adj.* **1.** worn or used until no longer fit for use. **2.** very tired; fatigued.

wor·ri·some (wûr'ē səm, wur'ē-), *adj.* **1.** causing worry: *a worrisome problem.* **2.** inclined to worry.

wor·ry (wûr'ē, wur'ē), *v.,* **wor·ried, wor·ry·ing. 1.** to feel uneasy or anxious; suffer from disturbing thoughts: *to worry about being late.* **2.** to make uneasy or anxious; trouble: *His debts worried him.* **3.** to seize with the teeth and shake or mangle, as an animal does: *a dog worrying a bone.* —*n., pl.* **wor·ries. 4.** a feeling of uneasiness and anxiety. **5.** a cause of such a feeling: *Rain is our only worry.*

worse (wûrs), *adj., comparative of* **bad** *and* **ill. 1.** bad or ill in a greater or higher degree; more evil, harmful, injurious, etc. **2.** in poorer health or condition: *The patient is worse today.* —*adv.* **3.** in a worse manner or degree: *Though he had practiced his speech, he was speaking worse than ever.* —*n.* **4.** that which is worse: *They received the bad news calmly, but there was worse to come.*

wors·en (wûr'sən), *v.* to make or become worse.

wor·ship (wûr'ship), *n.* **1.** reverent honor and devotion given to God or to some personage or object regarded as sacred. **2.** the expression of such honor and devotion by prayers, ceremonies, etc.; a religious service. **3.** great admiration or regard for some person or thing: *the worship of success.* **4.** (in Great Britain) a title of honor used in addressing certain magistrates or others of high rank (usually preceded by *his* or *your*). —*v.,* **wor·shiped** *or* **wor·shipped; wor·ship·ing** *or* **wor·ship·ping. 5.** to express reverent honor and devotion to: *to worship God.* **6.** to feel admiration or regard for (any person or thing). **7.** to take part in a religious service. [from the Old English

word *worthscipe* "worthiness"] —**wor'ship·er,** *n.*

wor·ship·ful (wûr'ship fəl), *adj.* **1.** worthy of honor. **2.** giving or expressing worship of something.

worst (wûrst), *adj., superlative of* **bad** *and* **ill. 1.** bad or ill in the highest or greatest degree; most evil, harmful, injurious, etc.: *His attendance record is the worst in the class.* **2.** in poorest health or condition: *the worst house on the block.* —*adv.* **3.** in the worst manner or degree: *He spells the worst of all.* —*n.* **4.** that which is worst: *He always expects the worst.* —*v.* **5.** to defeat or beat: *He worsted the amateur player easily.* **6. at worst,** if the worst happens; under the worst conditions: *At worst I'd miss the first inning.* **7. if worst comes to worst,** if the very worst should happen: *If worst comes to worst, she'll have to quit school and go to work.*

wor·sted (wŏŏs'tid, wûr'stid), *n.* **1.** a firmly twisted yarn or thread spun from wool. **2.** wool cloth woven from such yarns, having a hard, smooth surface. —*adj.* **3.** made of worsted: *a worsted suit.*

worth (wûrth), *prep.* **1.** good or important enough to justify (what is specified); deserving of: *advice worth taking; a place worth a trip.* **2.** having a value of, as in money: *The vase is worth $20.* **3.** having property or income equal to: *He is worth millions.* —*n.* **4.** excellence of character or quality; importance; usefulness: *men of worth.* **5.** value, as in money; wealth or possessions. **6.** a quantity of something of a specified value: *a dollar's worth of gasoline.* **7. for all one is worth,** with one's best effort; to the utmost: *He raked leaves for all he was worth.*

worth·less (wûrth'lis), *adj.* of no use, importance, or value; good-for-nothing; without worth: *All those stocks and bonds proved worthless.*

worth·while (wûrth'hwīl', -wīl'), *adj.* such as to repay one's time, effort, attention, or interest: *a worthwhile book.*

wor·thy (wûr'thē), *adj.,* **wor·thi·er, wor·thi·est. 1.** having merit, character, or excellence: *a worthy deed; a worthy man.* **2.** deserving (often fol. by *of* or an infinitive): *a book worthy of praise.* —*n., pl.* **wor·thies. 3.** a person of great worth or position: *The lawyer was one of the town's worthies.* —**wor'thi·ness,** *n.*

Wo·tan (vō'tän), *n.* (in Germanic mythology) a god identified with the Scandinavian god Odin.

would (wŏŏd, wəd), *v.* **1.** the past tense of **will**[1]. **2.** (used to express a wish): *I would it were true.* **3.** (used in place of *will,* to soften a statement or a question): *That would hardly be fair. Would you be so kind as to help me?*
—**Usage.** See **should.**

would-be (wŏŏd'bē'), *adj.* **1.** wishing to be: *a would-be hero.* **2.** intended to be: *a would-be joke.*

would·n't (wŏŏd'ʳnt), contraction of *would not.*

wouldst (wŏŏdst), *v.* an old form of **would,** found now chiefly in Biblical and poetic writing (used with *thou*): *Wouldst thou sup with us?*

wound[1] (wŏŏnd), *n.* **1.** an injury involving the cutting or tearing of the flesh. **2.** an injury or hurt to the feelings. —*v.* **3.** to inflict a wound upon; injure. **4.** to hurt the feelings, pride, etc., of (someone). [from the Old English word *wund*] —**wound·ed** (wōōn′did), *adj.* —**wound′ing·ly,** *adv.*

wound² (wound), *v.* the past tense and past participle of **wind².**

wove (wōv), *v.* a past tense of **weave.**

wo·ven (wō′vən), *v.* a past participle of **weave.**

wrack (rak), *n.* **1.** ruin or destruction: *gone to wrack and ruin.* **2.** seaweed or other vegetation cast on the shore.

wraith (rāth), *n.* **1.** a supernatural appearance of a living person supposed to be seen by others just before his death. **2.** a visible spirit or ghost.

wran·gle (raṅg′gəl), *v.,* **wran·gled, wran·gling. 1.** to argue or dispute, esp. in a noisy or angry way. —*n.* **2.** a noisy or angry argument or quarrel.

wrap (rap), *v.,* **wrapped** *or* **wrapt; wrap·ping. 1.** to enclose or cover in something folded about: *He wrapped his hand with the bandage.* **2.** to wind or fold (something) around as a covering: *She wrapped the scarf around her neck.* **3.** to enclose and make fast (an article, bundle, etc.) with a covering: *He wrapped the package in brown paper.* **4.** to surround, envelop, or hide: *The castle was wrapped in mist.* —*n.* **5.** something to be wrapped about the body in addition to the usual indoor clothing, such as a shawl, scarf, etc. **6. wrapped up in,** absorbed or engrossed in: *He was so wrapped up in his work he didn't hear the bell.* **7. wrap up, a.** *Informal.* to finish (an activity): *Wrap up this assignment before you start on another.* **b.** *Slang.* to wreck; demolish: *He wrapped up his car a week after he got it.*

wrap·per (rap′ər), *n.* **1.** a person or thing that wraps. **2.** a covering, as paper wrapped around magazines for mailing. **3.** a woman's loose bathrobe.

wrap·ping (rap′iṅg), *n.* a covering, such as paper, wrapped around a package, gift, etc.

wrath (rath), *n.* strong, fierce anger; fury or rage.

wrath·ful (rath′fəl), *adj.* very angry; full of or showing wrath. —**wrath′ful·ly,** *adv.*

wreak (rēk), *v.* **1.** to inflict (punishment, vengeance, etc.): *They wreaked havoc on the enemy.* **2.** to give full expression to (one's rage, ill humor, etc.).

wreath (rēth), *n., pl.* **wreaths** (rēthz). **1.** a circular band of flowers or leaves twisted together for decoration: *a Christmas wreath.* **2.** anything circular, curving, or spiral that resembles a wreath: *a wreath of clouds.* [from the Old English word *wræth,* which is related to *writhan* "to twist, wind"]

wreathe (rēth), *v.,* **wreathed, wreath·ing. 1.** to encircle or adorn with or as if with wreaths: *The table was wreathed with holly.* **2.** to shape (flowers, leaves, etc.) into a wreath. **3.** to envelop or cover: *a face wreathed in smiles.*

wreck (rek), *v.* **1.** to cause the ruin or destruction of; destroy: *Did he wreck his car?* **2.** to cause (a vessel) to undergo shipwreck. —*n.* **3.** any building, structure, etc., in a state of ruin. **4.** the ruin or destruction of a ship; shipwreck: *The wreck occurred near Cape*

Hatteras. **5.** the remains of anything, such as a vessel, that has been heavily damaged or ruined: *The wreck was found on the beach.* **6.** the serious damage or destruction of anything: *the wreck of one's hopes.* **7.** a person in poor condition physically or mentally.

wreck·age (rek′ij), *n.* **1.** the act of wrecking, or the state of being wrecked. **2.** the remains of something that has been wrecked.

wreck·er (rek′ər), *n.* **1.** a person or thing that wrecks. **2.** a truck equipped for towing away wrecked or disabled automobiles. **3.** a person whose business is the tearing down and removal of houses, buildings, etc.

wren (ren), *n.* any of numerous small songbirds having brown plumage and short tails.

wrench (rench), *v.* **1.** to twist suddenly with force; pull or force by a violent twist: *to wrench a gun from an attacker.* **2.** to injure or sprain by a sudden, violent twist: *She fell and wrenched her ankle.* **3.** to pull away or distort, as from the right use or meaning: *He wrenched the facts from their true meaning to suit his own scheme.* —*n.* **4.** a sudden, violent twist. **5.** a painful twist, as of the ankle. **6.** a tool for gripping and turning the head of a bolt, a nut, or the like. **7.** a sharp, distressing strain, as to the feelings. —**wrench′ing·ly,** *adv.*

Wrenches

wrest (rest), *v.* **1.** to take away by force; twist or pull: *to wrest a knife from a child.* **2.** to get by great effort: *to wrest a living from the soil.* **3.** to twist or turn (words) from the proper meaning or use.

wres·tle (res′əl), *v.,* **wres·tled, wres·tling. 1.** to engage in wrestling. **2.** to oppose (someone) in a wrestling contest. **3.** to struggle, as for mastery: *to wrestle with a problem.* —*n.* **4.** the act or a bout of wrestling. **5.** any struggle.

wres·tling (res′liṅg), *n.* a sport in which each of two opponents struggles hand to hand in an attempt to force or throw the other down.

wretch (rech), *n.* **1.** an unhappy or very unfortunate person. **2.** a contemptible or wicked person.

wretch·ed (rech′id), *adj.* **1.** very unfortunate; miserable. **2.** causing dissatisfaction, misery, or sorrow: *a wretched winter.* **3.** contemptible or mean: *He was a wretched old miser.* **4.** very poor or worthless: *That was a wretched concert.*

wrig·gle (rig′əl), *v.,* **wrig·gled, wrig·gling. 1.** to twist to and fro; squirm. **2.** to move along by twisting and turning, as a worm or snake does. **3.** to make one's way by tricks and dodges (often fol. by *out*): *to wriggle out of a difficulty.* —*n.* **4.** the act of wriggling; a wriggling movement.

wright (rīt), *n.* a person who makes or creates something (used in combination): *a wheelwright; a playwright.*

Wright (rīt), *n.* **1. Frank Lloyd,** 1869–1959, U.S. architect. **2. Orville,** 1871–1948, and his brother **Wilbur,** 1867–1912, U.S. inventors of first airplane.

act, āble, dâre, ärt; ebb, ēqual; if, īce; hot, ōver, ôrder; oil; bŏŏk; ōōze; out; up, ûrge; ə = a as in *alone*; ′ as in *button* (but′ən), *fire* (fīər); *chief*; *shoe*; *thin*; *ŧħat*; *zh* as in *measure* (mezh′ər). See full key inside cover.

wring (riṅg), *v.*, **wrung** (ruṅg), **wring·ing.** 1. to twist with force: *to wring the neck of a chicken.* 2. to twist and press, in order to force out water or other liquid: *to wring clothes.* 3. to force out by twisting and pressing: *to wring water from clothes.* 4. to force out or get as if by twisting: *to wring a secret from someone.* 5. to clasp tightly with or without twisting: *to wring one's hands in pain.* 6. to affect painfully; distress or torment: *The bad news wrung our hearts.*

wring·er (riṅg'ər), *n.* 1. a person or thing that wrings. 2. a device or machine that forces water or the like from anything wet: *a clothes wringer.*

wrin·kle¹ (riṅg'kəl), *n.* 1. a ridge or furrow on a surface; a small fold or crease: *The wrinkles on her face revealed her age.* —*v.*, **wrin·kled, wrin·kling.** 2. to form a wrinkle in; crease: *Don't wrinkle your dress.* 3. to become wrinkled. [from the Old English word *(ge)wrinclian* "to wind round"]

wrin·kle² (riṅg'kəl), *n. Informal.* a clever trick or device; a useful notion. [from the Middle English word *wrinc* "a trick"]

wrist (rist), *n.* the joint between the arm and the hand.

wrist·band (rist'band'), *n.* the band of a sleeve that covers the wrist.

wrist′ watch′, a watch attached to a strap or band worn around the wrist.

writ (rit), *n.* 1. (in law) an order issued by a court requiring the person to whom it is issued to do or refrain from doing something specified. 2. something written; a piece of writing: *sacred writ.*

write (rīt), *v.*, **wrote** (rōt), **writ·ten** (rit′ⁿn), **writ·ing.** 1. to trace or form letters, words, etc., with a pen, pencil, or the like: *to write with a pen.* 2. to trace or form (letters, words, etc.) on a surface: *Write your name on the blackboard.* 3. to produce by setting down words, figures, etc.: *to write two copies of a letter.* 4. to express in writing; give a written account: *He wrote that he was well.* 5. to produce as author or composer: *to write a poem; to write a symphony.* 6. to write as a profession: *He writes for the theater.* 7. to write a letter to: *She writes her family once a month.* 8. to draw up in written form; complete (a printed form) with writing: *to write a will; to write a check.* 9. to show clearly: *Honesty was written on his face.* 10. **write off,** to regard as lost, worthless, obsolete, etc.; decide to forget: *The plane was forced down over enemy territory and was written off.* 11. **write out,** to put into writing, esp. fully and completely: *Write out the agreement, and I'll sign it.* 12. **write up,** to write about, esp. in full detail: *Write up a report. The story was written up in the newspaper.*

writ·er (rī'tər), *n.* a person who writes, esp. one whose occupation or profession is writing.

writhe (rīth), *v.*, **writhed, writh·ing.** 1. to twist about; twist the body about, as in pain. 2. to suffer mentally, as from shame, grief, embarrassment, etc.

writ·ing (rī'tiṅg), *n.* 1. the act of a person or thing that writes. 2. written form: *to put down one's*

thoughts *in writing.* 3. style of writing; handwriting: *Can you read my writing?* 4. something written, such as a paper, document, letter, or the like. 5. a literary composition or production: *the writings of William Wordsworth.*

writ·ten (rit′ⁿn), *v.* 1. the past participle of **write.** —*adj.* 2. expressed in writing: *the written word.*

wrong (rôṅg), *adj.* 1. not in accordance with what is morally right: *a wrong way to behave.* 2. untrue or incorrect: *a wrong answer.* 3. not proper or usual; not suitable or appropriate: *the wrong way to hold a golf club; to say the wrong thing.* 4. out of order: *Something is wrong with this machine.* 5. not desired: *to catch the wrong bus.* 6. intended to be worn or kept inward or under: *You are wearing the sweater wrong side out.* —*n.* 7. an act that is wrong; an evil: *He committed many wrongs.* 8. the state or condition of being wrong. —*adv.* 9. in a wrong manner; not rightly: *You have guessed wrong again.* —*v.* 10. to do wrong to; treat unfairly or unjustly: *to wrong a friend.* 11. **go wrong, a.** to fail to function properly; go amiss: *Everything is going wrong today.* **b.** to begin to lead an immoral life: *No one could understand why he went wrong.* 12. **in the wrong,** deserving blame; in error: *It's important to admit when you're in the wrong.*

wrong·do·ing (rôṅg'dōo'iṅg), *n.* behavior or action that is wrong.

wrong·ful (rôṅg'fəl), *adj.* 1. full of wrong; unjust. 2. not legal; unlawful. —**wrong′ful·ly,** *adv.*

wrong·head·ed (rôṅg'hed'id), *adj.* wrong in judgment or opinion; misguided and stubborn. —**wrong′head′ed·ness,** *n.*

wrote (rōt), *v.* the past tense of **write.**

wroth (rôth), *adj.* angry or wrathful.

wrought (rôt), *v.* 1. a past tense and past participle of **work.** —*adj.* 2. worked or made: *a skillfully wrought antique table.* 3. produced or shaped by beating with a hammer, such as iron or silver articles.

wrought′ i′ron, a form of iron that contains little carbon and is easily forged or welded.

wrung (ruṅg), *v.* the past tense and past participle of **wring.**

wry (rī), *adj.*, **wri·er, wri·est.** 1. made by twisting the features: *a wry grin.* 2. unusually bent or twisted. 3. ironic or amusing: *wry remarks.* —**wry′ly,** *adv.* —**wry′ness,** *n.*

WSW, west-southwest. Also, **W.S.W.**

wt., weight.

W. Va., West Virginia.

Wy·eth (wī'əth), *n.* Andrew New·ell (nōo′əl), born 1917, U.S. painter.

Wyo., Wyoming.

Wy·o·ming (wī ō'miṅg), *n.* a state in the NW United States. 97,914 sq. mi. *Cap.:* Cheyenne. —**Wy·o·ming·ite** (wī ō'miṅg īt′), *n.*

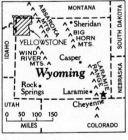

	Greek	Latin	Gothic	Modern Roman	
DEVELOPMENT OF UPPER-CASE LETTERS	×	X	𝔛	X	
DEVELOPMENT OF LOWER-CASE LETTERS	x	X	✕	𝔵	X
		Medieval		Gothic	Modern Roman

X, x (eks), *n., pl.* **X's** *or* **Xs, x's** *or* **xs. 1.** the 24th letter of the English alphabet. **2.** something having the shape of an X.

X, 1. the Roman numeral for 10. **2.** a person or thing whose identity is not known. **3.** the mark used as a signature by a person who cannot write. **4.** any unknown quantity or variable. **5.** a designation of a motion picture that no one under 17 may attend.

x, 1. any unknown quantity or variable. **2.** a sign that indicates multiplication: 8×10 *is 80.*

x (eks), *v.,* **x-ed** *or* **x'd** (ekst); **x-ing** *or* **x'ing** (ek′sing). to cross or mark out with or as if with an *x* (usually fol. by *out*): *to x out a mistake.*

Xa·vi·er (zā′vē ər), *n.* **Saint Francis,** 1506–1552, Spanish Jesuit missionary, esp. in India and Japan.

x-ax·is (eks′ak′sis), *n., pl.* **x-ax·es** (eks′ak′sēz). the horizontal axis on a graph along which the abscissa is measured. See also **y-axis.**

X chromosome, one of the two chromosomes that determine sex in man and animals, occurring in pairs in females and singly with a Y chromosome in males.

Xe, *Chem.* the symbol for **xenon.**

xe·bec (zē′bek), *n.* a small three-masted vessel, formerly used in the Mediterranean Sea by pirates from the Barbary Coast.

Xebec

xe·non (zē′non, zen′on), *n.* a rare, nearly inert gas, used esp. in radio, television, and light tubes: a chemical element. *Symbol:* Xe

xen·o·pho·bi·a (zen′ə fō′bē ə), *n.* a fear or dislike of foreigners or of anything that is foreign or strange. [from the Greek word *xénos* "stranger" + *phobia* "fear"] —**xen′o·pho′bic,** *adj.*

Xerx·es I (zûrk′sēz), 519?–465 B.C., king of Persia 486?–465.

Xer·ox (zēr′oks), *n. Trademark.* a process for making instant copies of written or printed matter.

Xmas, Christmas: a shortened form used only in informal writing. [*X* is from the first letter in the Greek name of *Christ*]

x-ray (eks′rā′), *n.* **1.** radiation similar to light but with a shorter wavelength and able to penetrate solids, to show the interior parts of an object, human body, etc. **2.** a picture made with x-rays, useful in diagnosing an illness, inspecting machinery, etc. —*v.* **3.** to examine, photograph, or treat (something) with x-rays. —*adj.* **4.** of, concerning, or using x-rays.

Xylophone

xy·lo·phone (zī′lə fōn′), *n.* a musical instrument consisting of wooden bars arranged in a row, according to size, and which are sounded by striking them with small wooden hammers.

Y

Semitic	Greek	Latin	Gothic	Modern Roman	
See the letters F and I		Y	𝔜	Y	DEVELOPMENT OF UPPER-CASE LETTERS

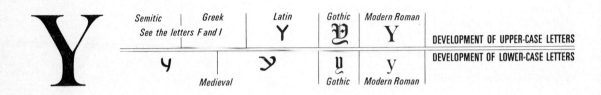

			Gothic	Modern Roman	DEVELOPMENT OF LOWER-CASE LETTERS
ч	ᵞ	Medieval	u	y	

Y, y (wī), *n., pl.* **Y's** *or* **Ys, y's** *or* **ys. 1.** the 25th letter of the English alphabet. **2.** something having the shape of a Y, esp. an intersection: *Turn left at the Y.*

Y, 1. *Chem.* the symbol for **yttrium. 2.** a symbol for an unknown quantity.

y, a symbol for an unknown quantity.

y., 1. yard. **2.** year.

-y, a suffix used to form **1.** adjectives meaning **a.** of or like: *woody.* **b.** having a tendency to: *grouchy.* **c.** full of or containing: *juicy.* **2.** nouns expressing **a.** the action of a verb: *inquiry.* **b.** a quality or condition: *honesty.* **3.** diminutive nouns: *Billy.*

yacht (yot), *n.* **1.** a vessel used for private cruising or racing. —*v.* **2.** to sail, cruise in, or race a yacht. —**yacht'ing,** *n.*

yachts·man (yots'mən), *n., pl.* **yachts·men.** a person who owns or sails a yacht.

yak (yak), *n.* a stocky, long-haired ox, wild or domesticated, found in Tibet and in central Asia.

yam (yam), *n.* **1.** the starchy, edible root of any of various climbing vines growing in warm regions. **2.** any of the vines having such a root. **3.** a kind of sweet potato. [from the Spanish word *ñame,* which comes from West African]

Yang·tze (yang'sē), *n.* a river in E Asia, flowing E to the East China Sea. about 3200 mi. long.

Yak
(6 ft. high at shoulder)

yank (yangk), *v.* **1.** to pull suddenly and sharply; jerk. —*n.* **2.** a sudden, sharp pull; jerk.

Yan·kee (yang'kē), *n.* **1.** a person born or living in New England. **2.** a person born or living in the northern U.S., esp. in a northeastern state that was part of the Union in the Civil War. **3.** any person born or living in the United States. —*adj.* **4.** of or concerning a Yankee or Yankees: *a demonstration of Yankee cleverness.*

yap (yap), *v.*, **yapped, yap·ping. 1.** to bark shrilly; yelp. —*n.* **2.** a shrill bark or yelp.

yard¹ (yärd), *n.* **1.** a unit of linear measurement equal to 3 feet, or 36 inches (0.9144 meter). **2.** a horizontal spar set on a mast, from which a sail is hung. [from the Old English word *gerd*]

yard² (yärd), *n.* **1.** an area of ground partially or completely surrounding a house, school, or other building. **2.** an enclosed area for a specific activity or purpose (often used in combination): *shipyard.* **3.** (in railroading) an area with a system of tracks where cars are switched, made into trains, stored, etc. [from the Old English word *geard* "enclosure"]

yard·age (yär'dij), *n.* the length or amount of something measured in yards.

yard·arm (yärd'ärm'), *n.* either end of a yard supporting a square sail.

yard·stick (yärd'stik'), *n.* **1.** a measuring stick one yard long. **2.** anything used as a standard for comparison.

yarn (yärn), *n.* **1.** any thread spun from natural or synthetic fibers to be used for weaving or knitting. **2.** any story or adventure, esp. an imaginary one.

yar·row (yar'ō), *n.* any of various strong-smelling plants with finely divided leaves and small, white flowers, used in some medicines.

yaw (yô), *v.* **1.** to be temporarily turned from a course; swerve: *Our ship yawed often in the heavy seas.* —*n.* **2.** a turning or swerving from a course.

yawl (yôl), *n.* **1.** a sailboat with a mainmast forward and a smaller mast close to the stern. **2.** a ship's small boat, with four or six oars.

Yawl

yawn (yôn), *v.* **1.** to open the mouth wide, esp. involuntarily, with a long inhalation of air, as from sleepiness or boredom. **2.** to be wide open or loom very wide or deep: *Outer space yawns before its explorers.* —*n.* **3.** the act of yawning.

y-ax·is (wī′ak′sis), *n.*, *pl.* **y-ax·es** (wī′ak′sēz). the vertical axis on a graph along which the ordinate is measured. See also **x-axis.**

Yb, *Chem.* the symbol for **ytterbium.**

Y chromosome, one of the two chromosomes that determine sex in man and animals, occurring only in the male: paired with an X chromosome.

yd., yard; yards.

ye[1] (yē), *pron., pl.* **ye.** an old word for **you.** [from the Old English word *gē*]

ye[2] (t͟hē), *definite article.* an old word for **the:** *ye olde tea shoppe.* [this spelling comes from a substitution of the letter *y* for an earlier letter representing the sound *th*]

yea (yā), *adv. Archaic.* **1.** yes. **2.** indeed; moreover. —*n.* **3.** a vote of yes, or the person who casts it.

year (yēr), *n.* **1.** the period of time, 365¼ days, in which the earth makes one complete revolution around the sun. **2.** the period of 365 days, or in leap year 366 days, divided into 12 months, that begins January 1 and ends December 31. **3.** any twelve-month period: *The company's fiscal year ends September 30.* **4.** a period of about 12 months measured from the beginning to the end of a project of work, study, or the like: *The school year is often two semesters.* **5.** the period from winter through fall, or the four seasons counted from any one of them. **6.** the time any planet takes to complete one revolution around the sun. **7. years, a.** age: *He's smart for his years.* **b.** old age: *a man of years who was respected by the townspeople.* **c.** a period of time marked by some event, condition, etc.: *years of famine and want.* **8. year in, year out,** every year without change; regularly or continuously: *Year in, year out they go to Miami in January.*

year·book (yēr′book′), *n.* a book published annually containing information about the past year.

year·ling (yēr′ling), *n.* **1.** an animal between one and two years of age. —*adj.* **2.** a year old.

year·ly (yēr′lē), *adj.* **1.** concerning a year or each year: *the yearly cycle of seasons.* **2.** occurring, seen, done, or made once each year: *the yearly family reunion.* **3.** lasting a year: *a yearly supply of paper.* —*adv.* **4.** once a year; each year: *We used to visit them yearly.*

yearn (yûrn), *v.* to long; have a strong desire: *She yearned for a new home.*

yearn·ing (yûr′ning), *n.* a powerful longing; deep desire: *a yearning to return to his childhood home.*

yeast (yēst), *n.* **1.** a yellowish, semifluid froth composed of certain very small fungi, used in making bread rise and in brewing. **2.** a small cake in which this substance is mixed with flour or meal.

yell (yel), *v.* **1.** to shoot or cry out loudly; scream, as with pain, fear, etc. **2.** to call loudly or tell by yelling: *to yell somebody's name.* **3.** to cheer as encouragement or from excitement. —*n.* **4.** a shout or loud cry, as from pain, fear, etc. **5.** a shout or cheer to encourage a team.

yel·low (yel′ō), *n.* **1.** the color of ripe lemons, butter, or gold. **2.** any paint or dye having this color. **3.** the yolk of an egg. —*adj.* **4.** of or having the color yellow. **5.** of a complexion suggesting or resembling yellow. **6.** *Informal.* cowardly. —*v.* **7.** to make or become yellow: *Paper yellows with age.*

yel′low fe′ver, a serious, often fatal, infectious disease in warm climates, caused by a virus transmitted to man by the bite of a certain mosquito, and having such symptoms as high fever, vomiting, and yellowing of the skin.

yel·low·ish (yel′ō ish), *adj.* resembling, becoming, or tinged with yellow: *That new diet has made his skin yellowish.*

yel′low jack′et, any of various wasps having bright yellow markings on a black body.

Yel′low Riv′er, another name for Hwang Ho.

Yel′low Sea′, an arm of the Pacific Ocean N of the East China Sea. It is located between China and Korea.

Yellow jacket (length ¾ in.)

Yel·low·stone Na′tional Park′ (yel′ō stōn′), a national park in NW Wyoming and nearby parts of Idaho and Montana: geysers, hot springs, etc.

yelp (yelp), *n.* **1.** a sharp, shrill cry. —*v.* **2.** to give such a cry.

Yem·en (yem′ən), *n.* People's Democratic Republic of. Formerly, Southern Yemen. a republic in S Arabia. about 112,000 sq. mi. **2.** Also, **Yemen Arab Republic.** a republic in SW Arabia. about 75,000 sq. mi. —**Yem′en·ite′,** *n., adj.*

yen[1] (yen), *n., pl.* **yen.** a money unit of Japan. [from a Japanese word, which comes from Chinese *yüan* "a round thing, a dollar"]

yen[2] (yen), *Informal.* —*n.* **1.** a craving or desire: *to have a yen for apple pie.* —*v.*, **yenned, yen·ning. 2.** to have a yen. [from Cantonese *yan* "a craving"]

yeo·man (yō′mən), *n., pl.* **yeo·men. 1.** (in the U.S. Navy) a petty officer having clerical duties. **2.** (in Great Britain) a farmer who cultivates his own land.

-yer, another form of the suffix **-er,** used to form nouns meaning one who is employed in or connected with something: *lawyer; sawyer.*

yes (yes), *adv.* **1.** (used to express agreement, consent, or approval): *Is he at home? Yes, he is.* **2.** (used to express emphasis or to introduce a more definite statement): *The play was good, yes, very good indeed.* **3.** (used to express polite interest or attention): *Yes, may I help you?* —*n., pl.* **yes·es. 4.** an affirmative reply: *to say yes to an offer.*

yes·ter·day (yes′tər dē, yes′tər dā′), *adv.* **1.** on the day before today. —*n.* **2.** the day before today. **3.** time in the recent past: *the cars of yesterday.*

yes·ter·year (yes′tər yēr′), *n.* last year; time not long past.

yet (yet), *adv.* **1.** at the present time; now: *Please don't go yet.* **2.** up to a particular time; thus far: *He hasn't yet spoken to me.* **3.** in the time still remaining; eventually: *He may yet change his mind.* **4.** as previously; still: *He came 20 years ago and is here yet.* **5.** in addition: *There was yet another letter in the mail today.* **6.** even; still (used to emphasize a comparative): *He acquired yet greater power.* **7.** still or nevertheless: *strange and yet true.* —*conj.* **8.** though; nevertheless: *It's good, yet it could be better.*

yew (yōō), *n.* **1.** any of several cone-bearing, evergreen trees of Europe, Asia, and Central America. **2.** the fine-grained wood of any such trees.

Yid·dish (yid′ish), *n.* **1.** a language developed from German, containing also some Hebrew and Slavic words, written in Hebrew letters. —*adj.* **2.** of, referring to, or expressed in Yiddish.

yield (yēld), *v.* **1.** to give forth by natural process; produce: *The farm yields enough food for the whole family.* **2.** to produce or furnish (payment, interest, or profit): *The investment yielded a good return.* **3.** to give up or surrender: *They yielded the fort to the enemy.* **4.** to give oneself up: *He yielded to temptation.* **5.** to give as required; concede: *to yield the right of way.* **6.** to give way to influence, argument, etc.: *Don't yield to his unfair demands.* **7.** to give way to force, pressure, etc.: *The table yielded under the heavy weight.* **8.** to give place: *to yield the floor to the Senator from Ohio.* —*n.* **9.** the quantity or amount yielded: *a yield of 40 bushels to the acre.*

yo·del (yōd′l), *v.,* **yo·deled** *or* **yo·delled; yo·del·ing** *or* **yo·del·ling. 1.** to sing with frequent changes from the ordinary voice to a high pitch and back again, in the manner of the Swiss mountaineers. **2.** to call or shout in this way. —*n.* **3.** a song, refrain, etc., sung in this way. **4.** a call or shout that is yodeled.

yoke (yōk), *n., pl.* for defs. 1, 2, 4-6 **yokes;** for def. 3 **yoke. 1.** a bar with two bow-shaped pieces, used for joining together animals, esp. oxen, at the neck. **2.** something resembling a yoke; a frame fitting the neck and shoulders of a person, for carrying a pair of buckets or the like. **3.** a pair of draft animals fastened together by a yoke.

Y, Yoke

4. something that binds together; bond or tie: *the yoke of marriage.* **5.** something that oppresses, enslaves, etc.; bondage: *the yoke of dictatorship.* **6.** a shaped piece of a garment fitted about the neck and shoulders or about the hips. —*v.,* **yoked, yok·ing. 7.** to put a yoke on (an animal); attach an animal to (a plow, wagon, etc.). **8.** to join, couple, or unite.

yo·kel (yō′kəl), *n.* a country bumpkin.

Yo·ko·ha·ma (yō′kə hä′mə) *n.* a port city in central Japan.

yolk (yōk, yōlk), *n.* the yellow substance of an egg.

Yom Kip·pur (yom kip′ər), a Jewish holy day that is observed by fasting and the recitation of prayers.

yon (yon), *Archaic.* —*adj., adv.* yonder.

yon·der (yon′dər), *adj.* **1.** being the more distant: *Yonder stream is deeper than this one.* —*adv.* **2.** at or in that place; over there.

Yon·kers (yoñ′kərz), *n.* a city in SE New York, near New York City.

yore (yôr), *n.* time past (used esp. in literature): *knights of yore.*

York (yôrk), *n.* a member of the royal house that ruled England from 1461 to 1485.

York·shire (yôrk′shēr, yôrk′shər), *n.* a county in N England.

York′shire pud′ding, an unsweetened cake made of batter, often served with roasts.

York′shire ter′rier, one of an English breed of toy terriers having a long, silky, straight coat that is dark steel-blue from the back of the skull to the tail and is tan on the head, chest, and legs.

York·town (yôrk′toun′), *n.* a village in SE Virginia: surrender in 1781 of Cornwallis to Washington.

Yorkshire terrier (8 in. high at shoulder)

Yo·sem′i·te Na′tional Park′ (yō sem′i tē), a national park in E California: waterfalls.

you (yōō), *pron.* **1.** (used of the person or persons being addressed): *I'm sure he called you, not me.* **2.** one or anyone; people in general: *a tiny animal you can't even see.*

you'd (yōōd), **1.** contraction of *you had: I wish you'd been there.* **2.** contraction of *you would: Tell us what you'd like.*

you'll (yōōl), contraction of *you will* or *you shall.*

young (yuñg), *adj.,* **young·er** (yuñg′gər), **young·est** (yuñg′gist). **1.** being in the first or early stage of life or growth: *a young child.* **2.** of or concerning youth: *in one's young days.* **3.** inexperienced: *too young for the job.* **4.** having the appearance or qualities of youth: *She is young for her age.* **5.** junior, as applied to the younger of two persons having the same name: *Young Mr. Smith looks like his father.* —*n.* **6.** young persons as a whole: *a game for young and old.* **7.** young offspring, esp. of animals.

Young (yuñg), *n.* Brigham, 1801–1877, U.S. Mormon leader.

young·ish (yuñg′ish), *adj.* rather young; not old.

young·ster (yuñg′stər), *n.* **1.** a young person. **2.** a child.

Youngs·town (yuñgz′toun′), *n.* a city in NE Ohio.

your (yŏŏr, yôr), *pron.* **1.** (a form of the possessive case of **you,** used as an adjective before the word or words modified): *your house.* **2.** (used as part of a title in addressing certain persons): *Your Honor.* **3.** (used to indicate that which concerns people in general): *If you add 2 and 2, your answer will be 4.*

you're (yŏŏr), contraction of *you are: You're quite right.*

yours (yŏŏrz, yôrz), *pron.* **1.** (a form of the possessive case of **you,** used as a predicate adjective): *Is this book yours?* **2.** the one or ones belonging to you: *Yours is the first seat in the row.*

your·self (yŏŏr self′, yôr-), *pron., pl.* **your·selves** (yŏŏr selvz′, yôr-). **1.** (used as emphasis or to refer back to the subject *you*): *Did you hurt yourself?* **2.** your normal self: *You'll soon be yourself again.* —Usage. See myself.

youth (yōōth), *n., pl.* **youths** (yōōths, yōōᵺz). **1.** the condition of being young: *She has certainly preserved her youth.* **2.** the time of being young; early life: *His youth was spent on a farm.* **3.** the first or early period of anything. **4.** a young man. **5.** young persons as a group: *the youth of America.*

youth·ful (yōōth′fəl), *adj.* **1.** having youth; young. **2.** of, concerning, or appropriate to youth. **3.** having the appearance and qualities of youth. —**youth′ful·ness,** *n.*

you've (yōōv), contraction of *you have: You've been very good today.*

yowl (youl), *v.* **1.** to utter a long, distressful cry, such as that of an animal; howl. —*n.* **2.** a yowling cry.

yr., **1.** year; years. **2.** your; yours.

yt·ter·bi·um (i tûr′bē əm), *n. Chem.* a metallic element of the rare-earth group. *Symbol:* Yb

yt·tri·um (i′trē əm), *n. Chem.* a rare, metallic element. *Symbol:* Y

Yu·ca·tán (yōō′kə tän′), *n.* a peninsula in SE Mexico and N Central America.

yuc·ca (yuk′ə), *n.* a plant of the warmer regions of America, having pointed, stiff leaves and white, waxy flowers.

Yu·go·slav (yōō′gō släv′), *n.* **1.** a native or inhabitant of Yugoslavia. —*adj.* **2.** of or concerning Yugoslavia or its inhabitants.

Yu·go·sla·vi·a (yōō′gō slä′vē ə), *n.* a republic in S Europe. 98,725 sq. mi. *Cap.:* Belgrade. —**Yu′go·sla′vi·an,** *n., adj.*

Yu·kon (yōō′kon), *n.* **1.** a territory in NW Canada. 207,076 sq. mi. *Cap.:* Whitehorse. **2.** a river of NW Canada, flowing through central Alaska to the Bering Sea. about 2000 mi. long. —**Yu′kon·er,** *n.*

Yucca (height about 8 ft.)

yule (yōōl), *n. (often cap.)* Christmas, or the Christmas season.

yule′ log′, a large log traditionally burned at Christmas.

yule·tide (yōōl′tīd′), *n.* **1.** *(often cap.)* the Christmas season. —*adj.* **2.** of, referring to, or characteristic of the Christmas season: *We sent yuletide greetings to all our friends.*

---

act, āble, dâre, ärt; ebb, ēqual; if, īce; hot, ōver, ôrder; oil; bŏŏk; ōōze; out; up, ûrge; ə = *a* as in *alone*; ᵊ as in *button* (but′ᵊn), *fire* (fiᵊr); ch̥ief; sh̥oe; th̥in; ᵵhat; zh as in *measure* (mezh̥′ər). See full key inside cover.

Z

	Semitic	Greek	Latin	Gothic	Modern Roman	
	𐤆	Ι	Ζ	Z	𝔷 Z	**DEVELOPMENT OF UPPER-CASE LETTERS**

DEVELOPMENT OF UPPER-CASE LETTERS

DEVELOPMENT OF LOWER-CASE LETTERS

Greek — *Medieval* — *Gothic* | *Modern Roman*

Z, z (zē), *n., pl.* **Z's** *or* **Zs, z's** *or* **zs.** the 26th letter of the English alphabet.

z, 1. a symbol for an unknown quantity. 2. zone.

z., 1. zero. 2. zinc.

Za·ïre (zä ēr′), *n.* 1. Former names, **Belgian Congo, Democratic Republic of the Congo.** an independent republic in central Africa. 905,328 sq. mi. *Cap.:* Kinshasa. See map at **Congo.** 2. a river in central Africa, flowing from SE Zaïre to the Atlantic Ocean. 3000 mi. long. Formerly called the Congo River.

Zam·be·zi (zam bē′zē), *n.* a river in S Africa, flowing S and E to the Indian Ocean: Victoria Falls. 1650 mi. long.

Zam·bi·a (zam′bē ə, zäm′bē ə), *n.* a republic in S Africa, formerly British. 288,130 sq. mi. Former name, **Northern Rhodesia.** —**Zam′bi·an,** *n., adj.*

za·ny (zā′nē), *adj.,* **za·ni·er, za·ni·est.** 1. comical or foolish; clownishly crazy. —*n., pl.* **za·nies.** 2. a silly person; simpleton. 3. a clown. [from *Zanni,* the name of a character in Italian puppet shows] —**za′ni·ness,** *n.*

Zan·zi·bar (zan′zə bär′), *n.* 1. an island off the E coast of Africa, formerly British: now part of Tanzania. 640 sq. mi. 2. a port city on this island.

zeal (zēl), *n.* enthusiastic interest in or devotion to a person, cause, or object; eager desire or endeavor: *to attack one's work with zeal.*

Zea·land (zē′lənd), *n.* the largest island of Denmark, in the Baltic Sea. 2709 sq. mi. —**Zea′land·er,** *n.*

zeal·ot (zel′ət), *n.* 1. a person who shows zeal. 2. a person who shows too much zeal; fanatic.

zeal·ous (zel′əs), *adj.* full of or due to zeal; eager: *He always had a zealous regard for the truth.* —**zeal′ous·ly,** *adv.* —**zeal′ous·ness,** *n.*

Zeb·e·dee (zeb′i dē′), *n.* (in the Bible) the father of the apostles James and John.

ze·bra (zē′brə), *n.* any of several horselike wild animals of Africa, having white bodies covered by dark stripes. [from a Portuguese word meaning literally "wild ass," which comes from Latin *equiferus* "wild horse," from *equus* "horse" + *ferus* "wild"] —**ze′bra·like′,** *adj.*

Zebra
(4 ft. high at shoulder)

ze·bra·fish (zē′brə fish′), *n., pl.* **ze·bra·fish·es** *or* **ze·bra·fish.** an egg-laying fish with zebralike stripes, often kept in aquariums.

ze·bra-plant (zē′brə plant′), *n.* a house plant having leaves striped with yellow-green and olive-green.

ze·bu (zē′byoo), *n.* a domesticated ox of Asia and Africa, having a large hump over the shoulders and loose, hanging skin under the throat. [from the French word *zébu,* which comes from Tibetan]

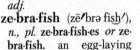

Zebu
(6 ft. high at shoulder)

Zech·a·ri·ah (zek′ə rī′ə), *n.* 1. (in the Bible) a Hebrew prophet of the 6th century B.C. 2. a book of the Old Testament bearing his name.

ze·nith (zē′nith), *n.* 1. the point in the sky that is directly overhead. 2. the highest point or state.

Zeph·a·ni·ah (zef′ə nī′ə), *n.* 1. (in the Bible) a Hebrew prophet of the 7th century B.C. 2. a book of the Old Testament bearing his name.

zeph·yr (zef′ər), *n.* 1. a wind blowing from the west. 2. any gentle, mild breeze.

zep·pe·lin (zep′ə lin), *n. (sometimes cap.)* a large,

gas-filled balloon having a long, cylindrical shape and propelled by engines.

ze·ro (zēr′ō), *n., pl.* **ze·ros** *or* **ze·roes. 1.** the numerical symbol 0, which stands for the absence of quantity. **2.** the lowest point or degree on a scale, as on the scale of a thermometer. **3.** naught; nothing: *Their efforts added up to zero.* **4.** the lowest point. —*adj.* **5.** amounting to zero: *zero degrees.*

ze′ro hour′, *Informal.* a decisive or critical hour.

zest (zest), *n.* keen relish; hearty enjoyment: *to play a game with zest.* —**zest′y,** *adj.*

Zeus (zōōs), *n.* (in Greek mythology) the supreme god, ruler of gods and men and husband of Hera: identified with the Roman god Jupiter.

zig·zag (zig′zag′), *n.* **1.** a line, course, or pattern consisting of a series of sharp turns or angles. **2.** one of such turns or angles, as in a line or path. —*adj.* **3.** of or formed in a zigzag: *a zigzag country road.* —*adv.* **4.** with frequent sharp turns from side to side: *The child ran zigzag down the beach.* —*v.,* **zig·zagged, zig·zag·ging. 5.** to go in a zigzag manner.

zil·lion (zil′yən), *n., pl.* **zil·lions** *or* (after a numeral) **zil·lion.** a humorous word for any very large number or amount: *He must owe about a zillion dollars.*

zinc (zingk), *n.* a silvery metal used in making galvanized iron and in alloys: a chemical element. *Symbol:* Zn

zin·ni·a (zin′ē ə), *n.* any of several North American plants grown for their colorful flowers.

Zi·on (zī′ən), *n.* (in the Bible) the hill in Jerusalem on which the Temple was built.

Zi·on·ism (zī′ə niz′əm), *n.* a world-wide movement for the establishment in Palestine of a national homeland for the Jews. —**Zi′on·ist,** *n., adj.*

zip¹ (zip), *Informal.* —*n.* **1.** a sudden, brief hissing sound, as of a bullet. **2.** energy, vim, or vigor. —*v.,* **zipped, zip·ping. 3.** to move with a zipping sound. **4.** to act or move with speed or energy: *I'll just zip upstairs.* [imitative of the sound]

zip² (zip), *v.,* **zipped, zip·ping.** to fasten or close with a zipper. [formed from *zipper*]

zip′ code′, (in the U.S. postal system) a numerical code that is written after the address on the envelope of a letter to help in the delivery of mail.

zip·per (zip′ər), *n.* a fastening device for clothing, valises, etc., made up of two parallel tracks of interlocking teeth and a sliding part that joins or separates them. [formerly a trademark]

zir·con (zûr′kon), *n.* a common mineral sometimes used in jewelry.

zir·co·ni·um (zər kō′nē əm), *n.* a rare metal used in making steel and in nuclear reactors: a chemical element. *Symbol:* Zr

zith·er (zith′ər), *n.* a musical instrument with numerous strings that are plucked with a pick and the fingertips.

Zither

Zn, *Chem.* the symbol for zinc.

zo·di·ac (zō′dē ak′), *n.* **1.** an imaginary belt of the heavens within which is the apparent annual path of the sun. It contains twelve divisions called signs of the zodiac, each of which is named after a constellation. **2.** a diagram representing this belt and these signs, usually containing pictures of the animals, human figures, etc., associated with the signs.

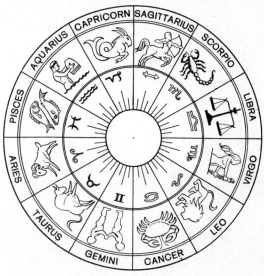

Zodiac

zom·bie (zom′bē), *n.* (according to the superstitious belief of some natives of the West Indies) a corpse that has been given life by a supernatural force.

zone (zōn), *n.* **1.** any of five divisions of the earth's surface, bounded by lines parallel to the equator, named according to the prevailing temperature. **2.** any area that differs in some respect, or is distinguished for some purpose, from adjoining areas: *a school zone; a war zone.* **3.** (in the U.S. postal system) any of the numbered districts into which a city is divided to speed the delivery of mail. **4.** an area in a city restricted by law to certain types of buildings and activities: *a residential zone.*

zoo (zōō), *n., pl.* **zoos.** a park or enclosure in which live animals are kept for public exhibition.

zo·o·log·i·cal (zō′ə loj′i kəl), *adj.* **1.** of or concerning zoology. **2.** relating to or concerned with animals.

zo′olog′ical gar′den, a zoo.

zo·ol·o·gy (zō ol′ə jē), *n.* the science dealing with animals. —**zo·ol′o·gist,** *n.*

zoom (zōōm), *v.* **1.** to move rapidly with a loud humming or buzzing sound. **2.** to fly suddenly and sharply upward at great speed for a short distance. —*n.* **3.** the act of zooming. **4.** a zooming sound.

Zo·ro·as·ter (zôr′ō as′tər), *n.* flourished 6th century B.C., Persian religious teacher.

zounds (zoundz), *interj. Archaic.* (used as a mild oath).

Zr, *Chem.* the symbol for zirconium.

act, āble, dâre, ärt; ebb, ēqual; if, īce; hot, ōver, ôrder; oil; bŏŏk; ōōze; out; up, ûrge; ə = *a* as in *alone;* ʔ as in *button* (but′ʔn), *fire* (fīʔr); chief; shoe; thin; ᵺat; zh as in *measure* (mezh′ər). See full key inside cover.

Zui·der Zee (zī′dər zē′), a former shallow inlet of the North Sea in the central Netherlands, now a lake. Also, **Zuy′der Zee′.**

Zu·lu (zōō′lōō), *n., pl.* **Zu·lus** *or* **Zu·lu. 1.** a member of a people inhabiting the coastal region of SE Africa. **2.** the language of the Zulus, belonging to the Bantu family. —*adj.* **3.** of or referring to the Zulus or their language.

Zu·rich (zōōr′ik), *n.* **1.** a city in N Switzerland, on Lake Zurich. **2. Lake of,** a lake in N Switzerland. 25 miles long.

zwie·back (zwī′bak′, zwē′bak′), *n.* a special bread made with eggs that is baked in a loaf, then sliced and toasted in an oven.

zy·gote (zī′gōt), *n.* the cell produced by the uniting of a sperm cell and an egg cell.

WORLD ATLAS

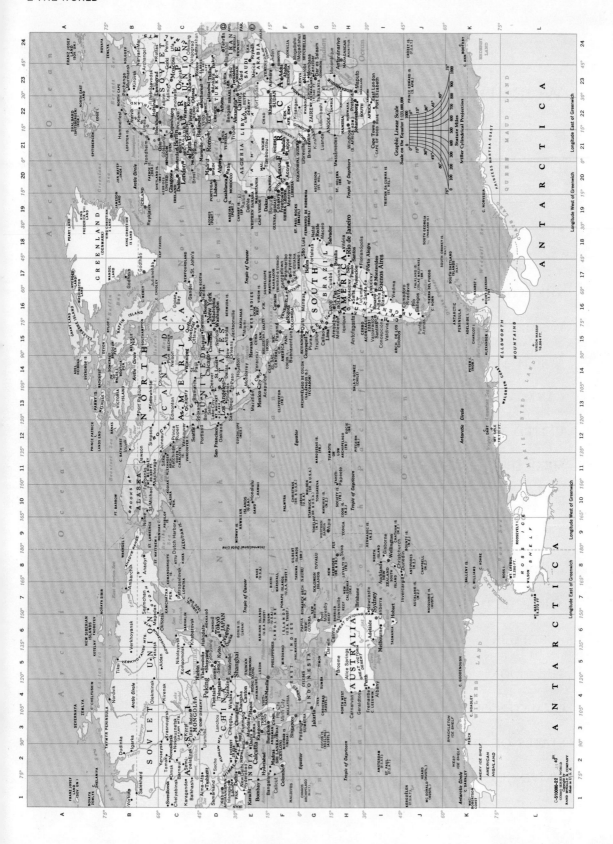

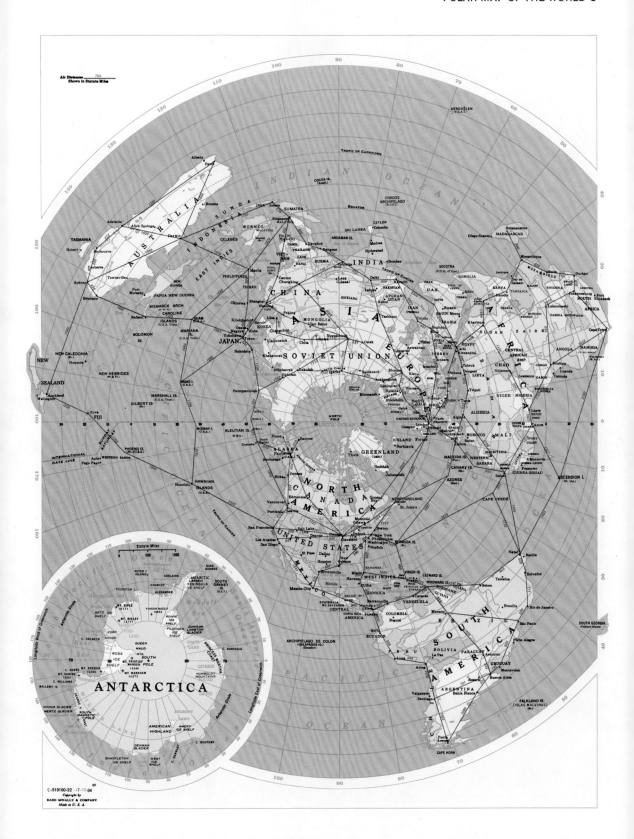

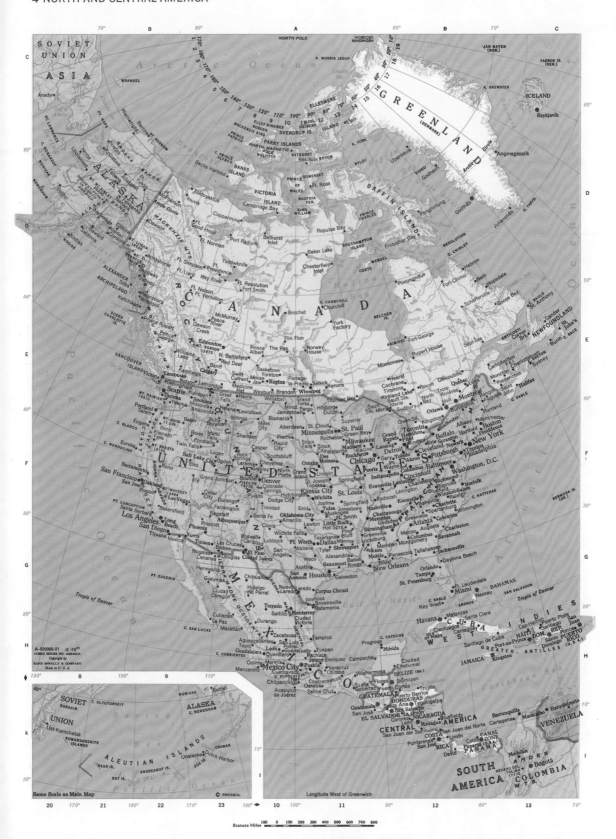

Statute Miles 100 0 100 200 300

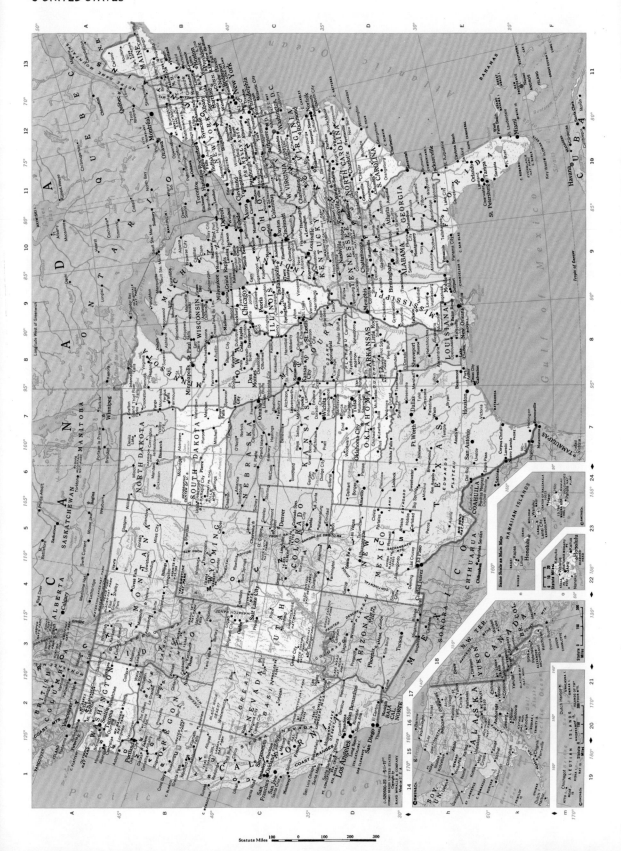

Statute Miles 100 0 100 200 300

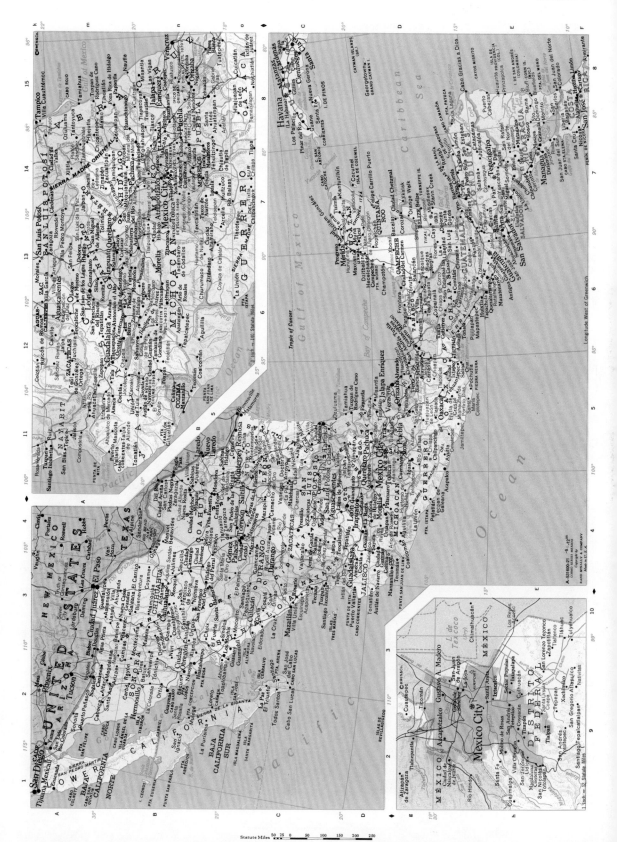

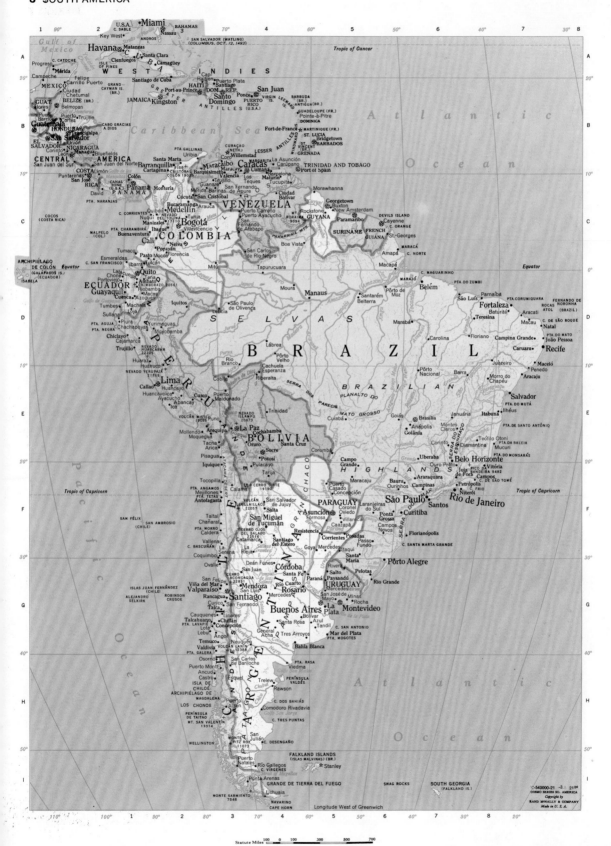

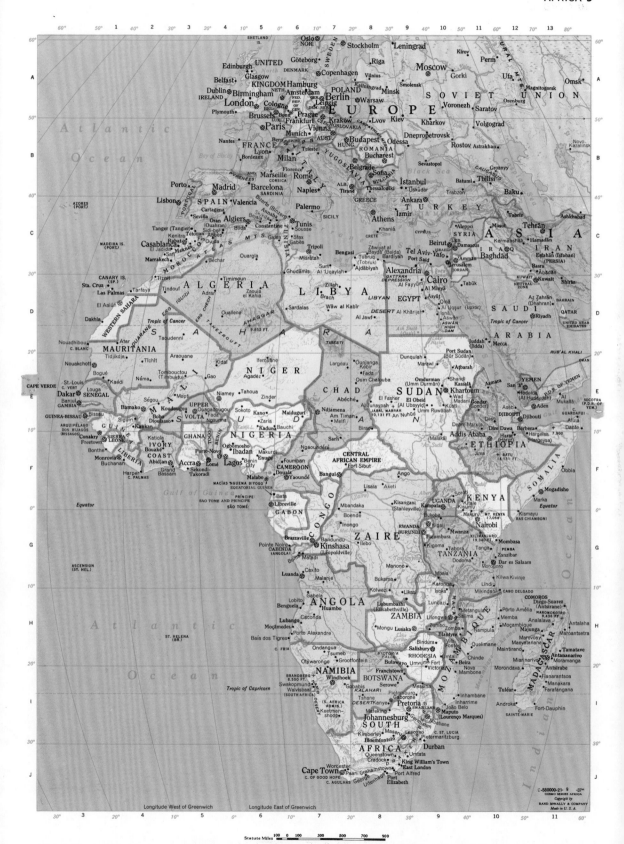

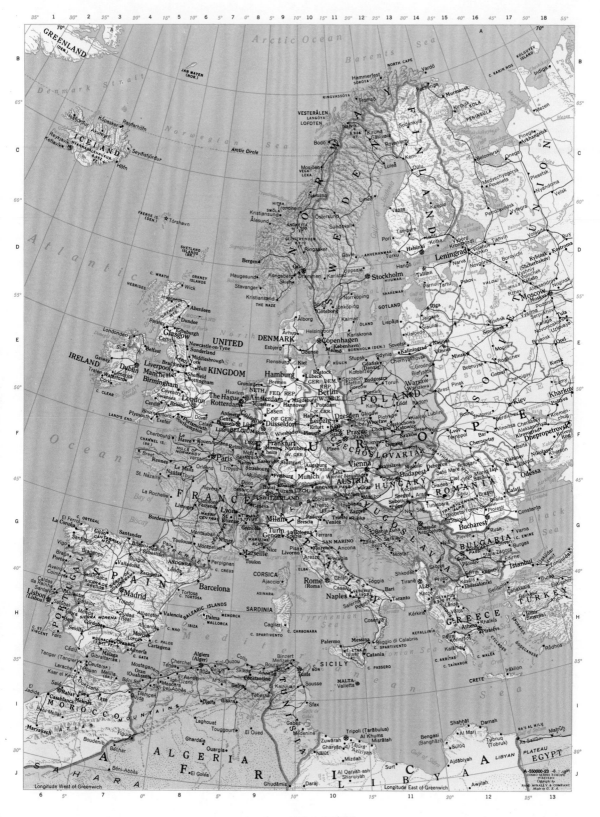

Statute Miles

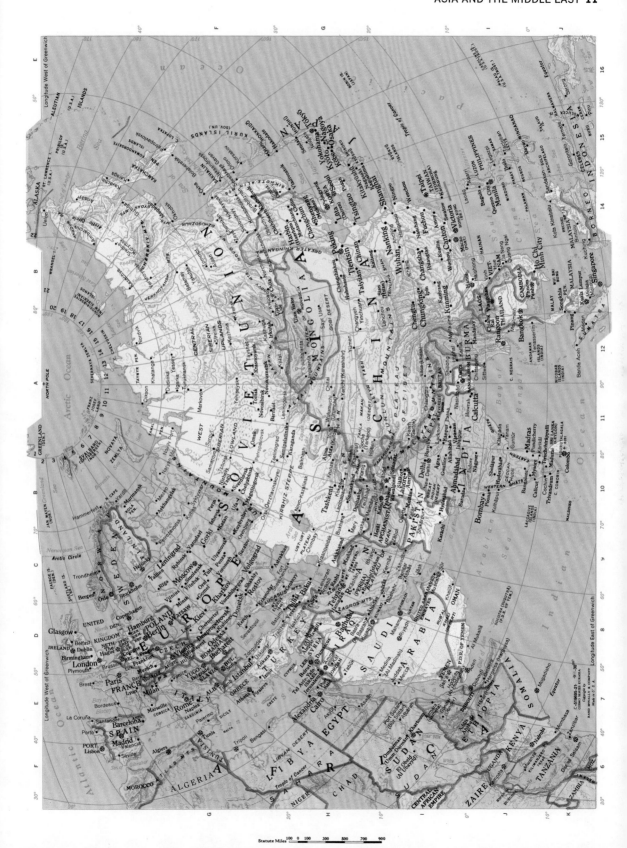

Statute Miles 100 0 100 300 500 700 900

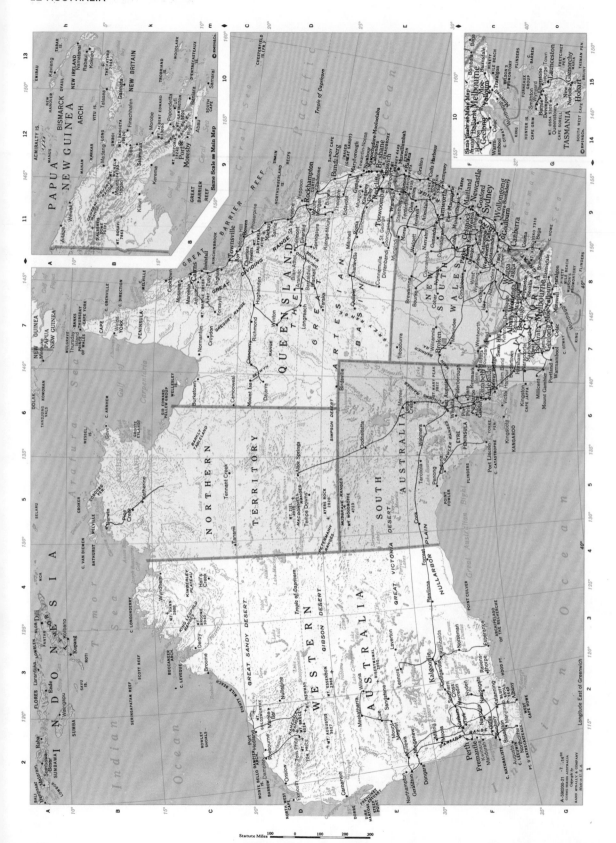

Statute Miles

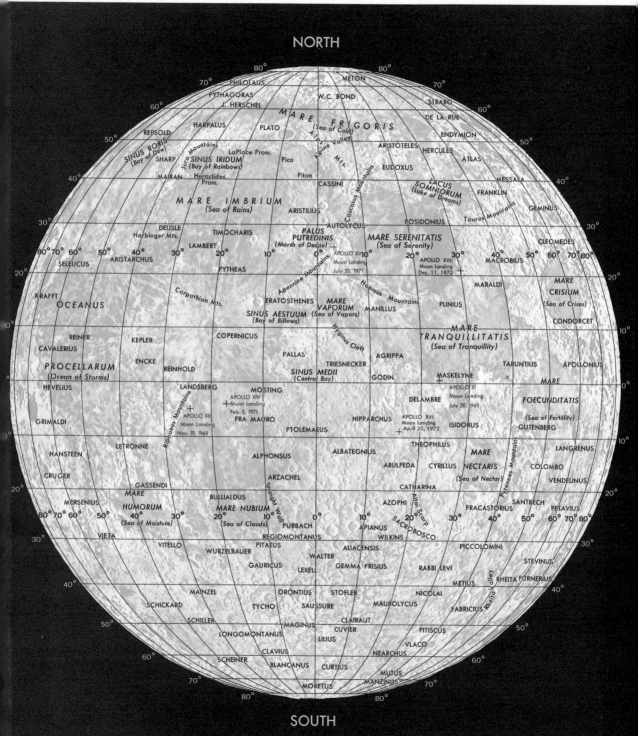

NORTH

PHILOLAUS
METON
80°
70°
PYTHAGORAS
W.C. BOND
STRABO
70°
60°
J. HERSCHEL
DE LA RUE
60°
MARE FRIGORIS
REPSOLD
HARPALUS
PLATO
(Sea of Cold)
ENDYMION
50°
50°
Jura Mountains
LaPlace Prom.
ARISTOTELES
HERCULES
SINUS RORIS
Alps
(Bay of Dew)
SHARP
SINUS IRIDUM
Pico
ATLAS
Alpine Valley
(Bay of Rainbows)
EUDOXUS
40°
MAIRAN
Heraclides
Piton
MESSALA
40°
Prom.
CASSINI
LACUS
FRANKLIN
SOMNIORUM
MARE IMBRIUM
(Lake of Dreams)
GEMINUS
30°
(Sea of Rains)
ARISTILLUS
Taurus Mountains
30°
AUTOLYCUS
POSIDONIUS
DELISLE
PALUS
CLEOMEDES
Harbinger Mts.
TIMOCHARIS
PUTREDINIS
MARE SERENITATIS
80°70° 60°
50°
LAMBERT
(Marsh of Decay)
(Sea of Serenity)
MACROBIUS
40°
30°
20°
10°
APOLLO XV
20°
30°
40°
50° 60° 70° 80°
SELEUCUS
ARISTARCHUS
Moon Landing
APOLLO XVII
July 30, 1971
Moon Landing
20°
PYTHEAS
Dec. 11, 1972
20°
KRAFFT
MARALDI
MARE
Carpathian Mts.
Apennine Mountains
Haemus Mountains
CRISIUM
OCEANUS
ERATOSTHENES
MARE
(Sea of Crises)
VAPORUM
PLINIUS
SINUS AESTUUM
MANILLUS
(Bay of Billows)
(Sea of Vapors)
CONDORCET
0°
10°
REINER
MARE
Hyginus Cleft
TARUNTIUS
CAVALERIUS
KEPLER
COPERNICUS
TRANQUILLITATIS
APOLLONIUS
(Sea of Tranquillity)
ENCKE
PALLAS
AGRIPPA
PROCELLARUM
REINHOLD
TRIESNECKER
GODIN
MARE
(Ocean of Storms)
SINUS MEDII
MASKELYNE
HEVELIUS
LANDSBERG
(Central Bay)
MOSTING
APOLLO XI
FOECUNDITATIS
APOLLO XIV
DELAMBRE
Moon Landing
July 20, 1969
Moon Landing
(Sea of Fertility)
GRIMALDI
Feb. 5, 1971
APOLLO XVI
10°
APOLLO XII
FRA MAURO
HIPPARCHUS
Moon Landing
ISIDORUS
GUTENBERG
Moon Landing
April 20, 1972
10°
Nov. 19, 1969
PTOLEMAEUS
THEOPHILUS
LETRONNE
ALBATEGNIUS
MARE
LANGRENUS
HANSTEEN
ALPHONSUS
ABULFEDA
NECTARIS
COLOMBO
CYRILLUS
CRUGER
ARZACHEL
(Sea of Nectar)
VENDELINUS
CATHARINA
20°
GASSENDI
20°
MERSENIUS
MARE
BULLIALDUS
AZOPHI
SANTBECH
PETAVIUS
80°70° 60°
50°
HUMORUM
FRACASTORIUS
40°
30°
(Sea of Moisture)
20°
10°
0°
10°
20°
30°
40°
50° 60° 70° 80°
VIETA
MARE NUBIUM
PURBACH
APIANUS
30°
REGIOMONTANUS
WILKINS
PICCOLOMINI
30°
VITELLO
(Sea of Clouds)
PITATUS
WURZELBAUER
ALIACENSIS
STEVINUS
WALTER
GAURICUS
GEMMA FRISIUS
RABBI LEVI
LEXELL
RHEITA
FURNERIUS
SCHICKARD
MAINZEL
ORONTIUS
STOFLER
NICOLAI
METIUS
40°
TYCHO
SAUSSURE
MAUROLYCUS
FABRICIUS
40°
SCHILLER
MAGINUS
CUVIER
PITISCUS
50°
LONGOMONTANUS
LILIUS
VLACO
50°
SCHEINER
CLAVIUS
NEARCHUS
BLANCANUS
CURTIUS
MUTUS
60°
CLAIRAUT
MANZINUS
60°
70°
MORETUS
70°
80°
80°

SOUTH

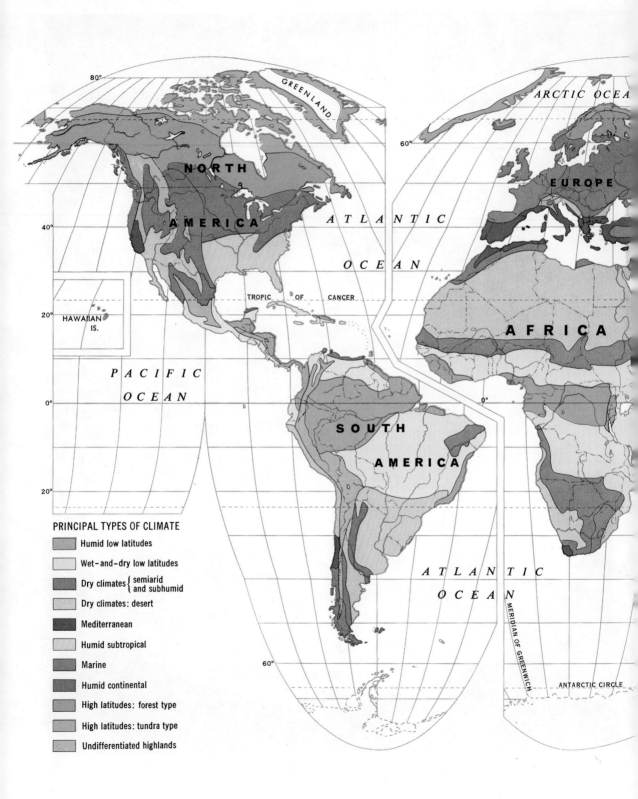

PRINCIPAL TYPES OF CLIMATE

Humid low latitudes

Wet–and–dry low latitudes

Dry climates { semiarid and subhumid

Dry climates: desert

Mediterranean

Humid subtropical

Marine

Humid continental

High latitudes: forest type

High latitudes: tundra type

Undifferentiated highlands